The Norton Anthology
of English Literature
THIRD EDITION

M. H. Abrams, *General Editor*
Professor of English, Cornell University

E. Talbot Donaldson
Professor of English, Indiana University

Hallett Smith
Professor of English, California Institute of Technology

Robert M. Adams
Professor of English, University of California at Los Angeles

Samuel Holt Monk
Professor Emeritus, University of Minnesota

Lawrence Lipking
Professor of English, Princeton University

George H. Ford
Professor of English, University of Rochester

David Daiches
Professor of English, University of Sussex

VOLUME 2

W · W · NORTON & COMPANY · INC · New York

Copyright © 1974, 1968, 1962 by
W. W. Norton & Company, Inc.

Since this page cannot legibly accommodate all
the copyright notices, the three pages following
constitute an extension of the copyright page.

Library of Congress Cataloging in Publication Data
Abrams, Meyer Howard, ed.
   The Norton anthology of English literature.
   1. English literature (Collections) I. Title.
PR1109.A22   1974   820'.8   73–19982

ISBN 0 393 09307 7 (Cloth Edition)
ISBN 0 393 09306 9 (Paper Edition)

All Rights Reserved

Published simultaneously in Canada
by George J. McLeod Limited, Toronto

Book design by John Woodlock

PRINTED IN THE UNITED STATES OF AMERICA

7 8 9 0

Contents

WILLIAM WORDSWORTH (1770–1850)   111

xii · *Contents*

The Victorian Age (1832–1901)   875

xx · *Contents*

The Twentieth Century
(1890 to the Present)

The Table of Contents for Volume 1 will be found on p. 2485

Preface
to the Third Edition

The Norton Anthology was invented for use in the indispensable course designed to introduce students to the greatness, continuity, and variety of British literature. Its strength is that it is grounded, not on a priori views of what might be taught in such a course, but on long experience in actually teaching it. The first edition of the anthology in 1962 was the product of more than a decade of experimentation with the introductory course by several of the editors, who then proceeded to test the book in their continued teaching. Ever since its publication, we have received a steady stream of suggestions—some of them solicited, but most volunteered—from hundreds of users, who view the anthology with a loyal but critical eye. This third edition is thus the product of a sustained collaboration between editors, teachers, and their students.

The changes in this edition are in line with recent scholarly discoveries and important shifts in critical interests. All of the changes, however, are guided by the principles that were established for the original edition. These are: (1) that the selection make possible a study in depth of the major British writers in verse and prose (now including novelists), in the context of the chief literary modes and traditions of their age; (2) that the representation be copious enough to allow each instructor to select the works that he prefers to teach; (3) that the student be given the most accurate possible texts, edited so as to make them immediately accessible and printed in a format that is easy to the hand and inviting to the eye; (4) that the editorial introductions and glosses be adequate to make an understanding of the texts independent of dictionaries and reference books, so that the book can be read anywhere—in the student's room, in a coffee lounge, or under a tree; and (5) that it be light and comfortably portable, on the ground that if students won't carry their anthology to class, lectures and discussions lose a major part of their value.

A scattering of selections, which a canvass of teachers revealed to be assigned infrequently or not at all, have been omitted; a very much greater number have been added. Among the medieval additions are Chaucer's early *Parliament of Fowls* and two more of his *Canterbury Tales*, as well as a third drama (*Abraham and Isaac*) and a second medieval romance, *Sir Orfeo*, shorter and less sophisticated than *Sir Gawain and the Green Knight*, which we retain. There are important additions to Spenser and to a number of 16th- and 17th-century poets. We have added a number of new prose writers for the same periods, and reviewed those that we have retained; more importantly, we have organized them according to their major concerns, so that for the first time a student is enabled to see a development both in style and in content for writers who are generally given short shrift in anthologies. Four Books of *Paradise Lost* (I, II, III, and IX) are reprinted in their totality, together with an increased representation of the other Books; while *Gulliver's Travels*, with the addition to Parts II and IV of Part I and the central passages of Part III, is now virtually complete. Other additions in the 18th century are Pope's *Eloisa to Abelard* and the Fourth Book of his *Dunciad*, as well as selections from John Gay, from Anne Finch (Countess of Winchilsea), from the Earl of Rochester, from the long poems of Christopher Smart, and from the prose writings of Johnson and Burke. There are several new poems (including parts of *Jerusalem*) and two important letters by William Blake. In accordance with our policy to include newly discovered masterpieces (our second edition made available Wordsworth's hitherto unpublished *Ruined Cottage*), we introduce, from manuscript, the whole of Wordsworth's earliest version of *The Prelude*, which he wrote in two parts in 1798–99—a work that can be read either as a very great independent poem or in comparison with our expanded selections from *The Prelude* of 1850, to which the passages in the *Two-Part Prelude* are keyed by footnote references. The anthology now includes substantial selections from Dorothy Wordsworth's great *Journals* and from De Quincey's *Confessions of an English Opium-Eater*, and new items from the prose writings of Hazlitt, Mill, Ruskin, and Carlyle, as well as a number of additional poems by Coleridge (including *This Lime-Tree Bower*, *The Pains of Sleep*, *Limbo*), Shelley (including the complete *Alastor*), Byron (the whole of an English Canto of *Don Juan*, the last that Byron wrote), Keats (all five of his great *Odes* are now reprinted), Tennyson (two complete *Idylls of the King*), Browning (an added dramatic monologue), Swinburne, and D. H. Lawrence. The representation of contemporary poetry has also been expanded; it now contains substantial selections from two poets who have attained a major status—Hugh MacDiarmid and David Jones—and a new section of ten poets who have done their most important work since the mid-20th century.

The addition of a number of new plays provides a comprehensive overview of English drama, from *Everyman* to *Endgame*. There are now three medieval plays (*Everyman*, *The Second Shepherds' Play*, and *Abraham and Isaac*) and four Elizabethan and Jacobean plays; in addition to Marlowe's *Doctor Faustus* and Shakespeare's *Henry IV, Part 1*, which we have offered since the first edition, we now have Shakespeare's *King Lear* and Webster's *Duchess of Malfi* (to the best of our knowledge, no other anthology of this nature provides a choice between two Shakespeare plays or the opportunity to study a masterpiece of the Jacobean period). There are also two masques (Johnson's *Pleasure Reconciled to Virtue* and Milton's *Comus*), a Restoration comedy (*The Way of the World*), selections from two Romantic closet dramas (Shelley's *Prometheus Unbound* and Byron's *Manfred*), Shaw's *Major Barbara*, and the concluding scene of Beckett's *Endgame*.

Another notable innovation in this edition stems from our conviction that it is not possible to represent justly the literature of the Victorian age without exemplifying its major and most distinctive genre, the novel. Consequently, Dickens and George Eliot are now given their due status as major writers by self-sufficient excerpts, chosen in a way adapted to the characteristic procedure of each novelist: Dickens is represented by selections that display his creative abundance and variety in self-contained dramatic scenes, and George Eliot is represented by coherent selections from *The Mill on the Floss* that show, from within the character's own mind, Maggie Tulliver in the process of growing up from childhood through adolescence to young womanhood. Other additions, long and short, now make it possible to study, from materials in the anthology, the development of prose fiction, from Bunyan's *Pilgrim's Progress* through Defoe's *Mrs. Veal*, Swift's *Gulliver's Travels*, the narrative *Spectator Papers*, Johnson's *Rasselas*, and the novels of Dickens and George Eliot, to a variety of novelists in our own century. In this last category, two complete short novels have been added, Conrad's *Heart of Darkness* and Lawrence's *The Fox* (supplementing two of Lawrence's short stories and a chapter from *The Rainbow*); there are short stories by E. M. Forster and Virginia Woolf; a second story, *Clay*, has been included from Joyce's *Dubliners*, in addition to the previous excerpts from all three of Joyce's novels; while new selections from two novels by Samuel Beckett, together with the scene from *Endgame*, acknowledge Beckett's importance as the most influential of living writers. And by a triumph of the papermaker's and bookmaker's art, these and other additions have been achieved without materially affecting the essential feature of a Norton anthology—its comfortable size and easy portability.

It should be noted that the new materials greatly enhance the possibilities for using the anthology to study topical, as well as historical and generic, developments in English literature. To cite only a few examples: The visionary mode in literature is now represented by Chaucer's dream-vision, *The Parliament of Fowls;* a new selection from Passus XXI (the "Harrowing of Hell") of *Piers Plowman;* Spenser's "Mutabilitie Cantos"; visionary poems by Crashaw, Vaughan, and Traherne; a new "Topic" on 18th-century theories of genius and the creative imagination; the poetry of Christopher Smart; William Blake's discussions of imaginative vision in prose and his exemplification of such vision in two new poems (*The Mental Traveller* and the opening and apocalyptic conclusion of his greatest "prophecy," *Jerusalem*); Coleridge's *Kubla Khan, The Pains of Sleep,* and *Limbo;* De Quincey's dream visions and dream fugues; Shelley's *Alastor;* Browning's *Childe Roland;* and the poems of Swinburne, Francis Thompson, and Yeats. A central literary form, the spiritual autobiography of crisis and the quest for identity, can now be studied in its major instances, religious and secular, such as Bunyan's *Grace Abounding,* Wordsworth's *Prelude,* Blake's *Jerusalem* (in one dimension of its reference), De Quincey's *Confessions,* Shelley's *Alastor,* Carlyle's *Sartor Resartus,* Mill's *Autobiography,* Tennyson's *In Memoriam,* and T. S. Eliot's *Little Gidding.* And the literature by and about women has been substantially supplemented so that it now includes, among other items, three of "the marriage group" of *The Canterbury Tales,* the Countess of Winchelsea, Anne Radcliffe, Dorothy Wordsworth, George Eliot (an essay on feminist writers of her time, as well as the chapters about Maggie Tulliver growing up in a man's world), selections from John Stuart Mill's *The Subjection of Women* and Tennyson's *Princess,* Elizabeth Barrett Browning, Emily Brontë, Christina Rossetti, Virginia Woolf, Elizabeth Jennings, and Doris Lessing.

Other features of the earlier editions have been retained, and in many instances improved. The Topics in the literary, critical, or intellectual ambience of a period have proved their usefulness as added reading, as illustrations in a lecture, or as starting places for assigned essays. In response to a canvass of teachers, some of the Topics have been dropped, others altered or supplemented, and a new one added. In accordance with our principle that texts for undergraduates should be no less scrupulously accurate than those for scholars, all of the Shelley texts, notoriously unreliable in all the inclusive editions of that poet, have been newly edited from manuscripts and earlier editions by Dr. Donald H. Reiman, and Jonathan

Wordsworth and Stephen Gill have prepared the text of Wordsworth's *Two-Part Prelude* of 1799 from a manuscript that, except
for fragments, has never before been published.

All texts are printed in the form which makes them most immediately available to their particular audience. In accordance with
this principle, we have normalized spelling and capitalization (and,
very sparingly, punctuation) according to modern American usage,
but only in cases where the change does not alter semantic, phonol-
ogical, or metric qualities, nor affect distinctive features of the
author's original publication. Thus the verse of Spenser, Burns,
Shelley, Hopkins, MacDiarmid, and David Jones, as well as the
prose of Dorothy Wordsworth's *Journals*, of Keats's letters, and of
the writings of Carlyle, Joyce, and Shaw have been reproduced
exactly; and only minor changes necessary for ready intelligibility
(mainly in punctuation) have been made in the poems etched by
William Blake. The works of Chaucer, as well as other writings in
Middle English that are not too difficult for the novice, have also
been left in the original language; each word, however is consistently spelled in that variant of its scribal forms which is closest to
modern English.

Each editor has reconsidered and rewritten his introductory essays
and has revised his footnotes to take advantage of recent scholarship
and also to make them as simple and lucid as possible. In selected
instances, editorial headnotes or footnotes briefly indicate possible
interpretations of a difficult work or passage. The reason for this
procedure is a practical one. The anthology includes some of the
most complex and problematic writings in the language, and the
normal procedure in teaching the course is to assign a number of
texts which there is no time to discuss adequately—or, often, to discuss at all—in the classroom. Our endeavor is to provide a necessary
modicum of guidance to the student, but in a fashion that simply
opens out possibilities for his independent judgment and that provides, not definitive readings, but points of departure for dialogue in
the classroom.

We continue other editorial procedures which have proved their
usefulness in the earlier editions. The historical and biographical
introductions, although succinct, are sufficiently informative to
eliminate the need for supplementary books on the lives of authors
and on the literary, social, and cultural history of England. In each
introduction we identify at the beginning a few dates which are of
crucial importance for orienting the student. After each text, we
cite (when known) the date of composition on the left and the
date of first publication in book form on the right; in some
instances, the latter is preceded by the date of first printing in a
periodical. Writings which include a large proportion of unfamiliar
words are glossed in the margin, in order that the reader may assim-

ilate the translation without interrupting the flow of his reading. In the limited instances when part of a text has been omitted, that fact is indicated by the word *From* before the title, and the place of the omission in the text is indicated by three asterisks.

The bibliographical guides at the end of each volume, keyed to periods and to the individual authors, are designed to encourage students to read further on their own, and also to serve as points of departure for assigned essays. All the bibliographies have been brought up to date for this third edition. As a convenience to the student who wants to build his own library of literary biography, history, and criticism, the symbol of a dagger indicates all titles currently available in paperback. The glossary of terms has now been considerably expanded under the title "Poetic Forms and Literary Terminology."

To the hundreds of teachers throughout the United States and Canada who have helped us to design and improve these volumes, the editors express their deep gratitude; they are too numerous to list here, but each will recognize the changes that he has suggested. We wish especially to acknowledge the advice of Scott Elledge (Cornell University); Jerome Beaty and J. Paul Hunter (Emory University); Marilyn Gaull (Temple University); Ronald Gottesman (University of Wisconsin at Parkside); Donald Gray (Indiana University); David Kalstone (Rutgers, The State University); Juliet McGrath (University of Rochester); and Hugh Maclean (The State University of New York at Albany). Our greatest debt is to George P. Brockway and John Benedict of W. W. Norton & Company, Inc., as well as to John Francis and Carol Schwab; to Norton's copyediting staff, especially Emily Garlin and Calvin K. Towle; and to James L. Mairs and Roy Tedoff of Norton's production department. All have helped greatly to mitigate the chronic dilemmas in the attempt to represent, justly and accurately, the immense scope of English literature within a single text.

M. H. Abrams

The Norton Anthology
of English Literature
THIRD EDITION

VOLUME 2

The Romantic Period

(1798-1832)

1789–1815: Revolutionary and Napoleonic period in France. 1789: The Revolution begins with the assembly of the States-General in May and the storming of the Bastille on July 14.—1793: King Louis XVI executed; England joins the alliance against France.—1793–94: The Reign of Terror under Robespierre.—1804: Napoleon crowned emperor. 1815: Napoleon defeated at Waterloo.

1798: *Lyrical Ballads* published anonymously by William Wordsworth and Samuel Taylor Coleridge.

1811–20: The Regency—George, Prince of Wales, acts as regent for George III, who was declared incurably insane.

1820: Accession of George IV.

1832: The Reform Bill carried in Parliament.

THE POLITICAL BACKGROUND: REVOLUTION AND REACTION

Following the common usage of historians of English literature, we will denote by the "Romantic period" the span between the year 1798, in which Wordsworth and Coleridge published their *Lyrical Ballads,* and 1832, when Sir Walter Scott died, when other major writers of the earlier century were either dead or no longer productive, and when the passage of the first Reform Bill inaugurated the Victorian era of cautious readjustment of political power to the economic and social realities of a new industrial age. This was a turbulent period in political and economic history, during which England was experiencing the ordeal of the change from a primarily agricultural society, where wealth and power had been largely concentrated in the landholding aristocracy, to a modern industrial nation, in which the balance of economic power was shifted to large-scale employers, who found themselves ranged against an immensely enlarging and increasingly restive working class. And this change occurred in a context first of the American and then of the much more radical French Revolution, of wars, of economic cycles of inflation and depression, and of the constant threat to the social structure from imported revolutionary ideologies to which the ruling classes responded by heresy-hunts and the repression of traditional liberties.

1

The early period of the French Revolution, marked by the Declaration of the Rights of Man and the storming of the Bastille to release the imprisoned political offenders, evoked enthusiastic support from English liberals and radicals alike. Two influential books indicate the radical social thinking stimulated by the Revolution. Tom Paine's *Rights of Man* (1791–92) justified the French Revolution against Edmund Burke's attack in his *Reflections on the Revolution in France* (1790), and advocated for England a democratic republic which was to be achieved, if lesser pressures failed, by popular revolution. More important for its influence on Wordsworth, Shelley, and other poets was William Godwin's *Inquiry Concerning Political Justice* (1793), which foretold an inevitable but peaceful evolution of society to a final stage in which all property would be equally distributed and all government would wither away. Later, however, English sympathizers dropped off as the Revolution followed its increasingly grim and violent course: the accession to power by the Jacobin extremists; the "September Massacres" of the imprisoned and helpless nobility in 1792, followed by the execution of the royal family; the invasion by the French Republic of the Rhineland and Netherlands, and its offer of armed assistance to all countries desiring to overthrow their governments, which brought England into the war against France; the guillotining of thousands in the Reign of Terror under Robespierre; and after the execution in their turn of the men who had directed the Terror, the emergence of Napoleon first as dictator and then as emperor of France. As Wordsworth wrote in *The Prelude* (XI.206–9),

> become oppressors in their turn,
> Frenchmen had changed a war of self-defense
> For one of conquest, losing sight of all
> Which they had struggled for * * *

For Wordsworth and all the English of liberal inclinations, these events posed a dilemma which has become familiar since the 1920's, in our parallel era of wars, revolutions, and the struggle by competing social ideologies —liberals had no side they could wholeheartedly espouse. Napoleon, the child and champion of the French Revolution, had become an arch-aggressor, a despot, and the founder of a new dynasty; yet almost all those who opposed him did so for the wrong reasons, so that his final defeat at Waterloo in 1815 proved to be the triumph, not of progress and reform, but of reactionary despotisms throughout continental Europe.

In England this period was one of harsh repressive measures. Public meetings were prohibited, habeas corpus suspended for the first time in over a hundred years, and advocates of even moderate measures of political change were charged with high treason in time of war. The Napoleonic wars put an end to reform, and to almost all genuine political life in England, for more than three decades.

Yet this was the very time when profound economic and social changes were creating a desperate need for corresponding changes in political arrangements and politics, and new classes—manufacturing, rather than agricultural—were beginning to demand a power in goverment proportionate to their wealth. The "Industrial Revolution"—the shift in methods of manufacturing which resulted from the invention of power-driven machinery to replace hand labor—had begun in the mid-18th century with improvements in machines for processing textiles, and was given immense impetus when James Watt perfected the steam engine in 1765. In the succeeding decades steam replaced wind and water as the primary source of power in one after another type of manufacturing; and at once, after centuries of almost imperceptibly slow change, there began that constantly accelerating and still continuing alteration in economic and social conditions which shows no signs of slowing down in the foreseeable future. A new laboring population massed in the sprawling mill towns which burgeoned in central and northern England. In rural communities the destruction of home industry was accompanied by a rapid growth of the process—lamented by Oliver Goldsmith in *The Deserted Village* as early as 1770—of enclosing the old open-field and communally worked farms into privately owned agricultural holdings. This process was necessary for the more efficient methods of agriculture and animal breeding required to supply a growing population (although some of the land thus acquired was turned into vast private parks); in any case, it created a new landless class which either migrated to the industrial towns or remained as farm laborers, subsisting on starvation wages eked out by an inadequate dole. The landscape of England began to take on its modern appearance: the hitherto open rural areas subdivided into a checkerboard of fields enclosed by hedges and stone walls, and the factories of the industrial and trading cities casting a pall of smoke over vast areas of jerry-built houses and slum tenements. Meanwhile, the population was becoming increasingly polarized into what Disraeli later called the "Two Nations"—the two classes of capital and labor, the large owner or trader and the possessionless wageworker, the rich and the poor.

No attempt was made to regulate this movement from the old economic world to the new, not only because of inertia and the power of vested interests, but because even the liberal reformers were dominated by the social philosophy of laissez faire. This theory of "let alone" holds that the general welfare can be ensured only by the free operation of economic laws; the government must maintain a policy of strict noninterference and leave each man to pursue his own private interests. For the great majority of the laboring class the results of this policy were inadequate wages, long hours of work under harsh discipline in sordid conditions, and the large-scale employment of women and children for tasks which destroyed both the body and the spirit. Reports by investigating committees on the coal mines, with male and female children of ten or even five years of age harnessed to heavy coal-sledges which they dragged by crawling on their hands and knees read like scenes from Dante's *Inferno*. In 1815 the conclusion of the French war, when the enlargement of the working force by demobilized troops coincided with the fall in the wartime demand for goods, brought on the first modern industrial depression. Since the workers had no vote and were prevented from unionizing by law, their sole recourse was to petitions, protest meetings, agitation, and hunger riots, which only frightened the ruling class into more repressive measures. In addition the introduction of new machines caused technological unemployment, and this provoked sporadic attempts by dispossessed workers to destroy the machines. After one such outbreak the House of Lords—despite Lord Byron's eloquent protest—passed a bill (1812) making death the penalty for destroying the frames used for weaving in the stocking industry. In 1819 meetings of workers were organized to demand Parliamentary reform. In August of that year, a huge but orderly assembly at St. Peter's Fields, Manchester, was wantonly charged by troops, who killed nine and severely injured hundreds more; this was the notorious "Peterloo Massacre," so named as a parody on the Battle of Waterloo. This event incited Shelley to write his great poems for the working class, *England in 1819, Song: "Men of England,"* and *To Sidmouth and Castlereagh.*

Suffering was largely confined to the poor, however, for all the while the landed classes, the industrialists, and many of the merchants prospered. In London the Regency period (1811–20) was for the leisure class a time of lavish display and moral laxity. In the provinces, the gentry in their great country houses carried on their familial and social concerns—reflected in the novels of Jane Austen—almost untouched by great national and international events.

But the pressures for reform could not be eliminated, especially since political disabilities were not limited to the working class. Gradually the working-class reformers acquired the support of the middle classes and the liberal Whigs. Finally, at a time of acute economic distress, and after unprecedented agitation and disorders that threatened to break out into revolution, the first Reform Bill was carried in 1832, amid widespread rejoicing. It eliminated the rotten boroughs (depopulated areas whose seat in Commons was at the disposal of a nobleman), redistributed parliamentary representation to include the new industrial cities, and extended the vote. Although about half the middle class and almost all the working class remained still without a franchise, the principle of peaceful adjustment of conflicting interests by Parliamentary majority had been firmly established; and reform was to go on until, by stages, England acquired universal adult suffrage.

"THE SPIRIT OF THE AGE"

All attempts at a single definition of Romanticism fall far short of matching the variegated facts of a time which exceeds almost all ages of English literature in the range and diversity of its achievements. No writer in Wordsworth's lifetime thought of himself as a "Romantic"; the word was not applied until half a century later, by English historians. Contemporary critics and reviewers treated them as independent individuals, or else grouped them (often invidiously, but with some basis in fact) into a number of separate schools: "the Lake School" of Wordsworth, Coleridge, and Robert Southey; "the Cockney School" of Leigh Hunt, Hazlitt, and associated writers, including John Keats; and "the Satanic School" of Byron, Shelley, and their followers.

Many of the major writers, however, did feel that there was something distinctive about their time—not a shared doctrine or literary quality, but a pervasive intellectual climate, which some of them called "the spirit of the age." They had the sense that (as Keats said in one of his sonnets) "Great spirits now on earth are sojourning," and that there was evidence all about of that release of energy, experimental boldness, and creative power which marks a literary renaissance. In his *Defense of Poetry* Shelley claimed that the literature of the age "has arisen as it were from a new birth," and that "an electric life burns" within the words of its best writers, which is "less their spirit than the spirit of the age." Shelley explained this literary spirit as the accompaniment of political and social revolution; and other writers agreed. Francis Jeffrey, foremost conservative reviewer of the day, connected "the revolution in our literature" with "the agitations of the French Revolution, and the discussions as well as the hopes and terrors to which it gave occasion." William Hazlitt, who published a book of essays called *The Spirit of the Age*, described how, in his early youth, the French Revolution seemed "the dawn of a new era, a new impulse had been given to men's minds." The new poetry of the school of Wordsworth, he maintained, "had its origin in the French Revolution. * * * It was a time of promise, a renewal of the world—and of letters."

The imagination of Romantic writers was, indeed, preoccupied with the fact and idea of revolution. In the early period of the French Revolution all the leading English writers except Edmund Burke were in sympathy with it, and Robert Burns, William Blake, Wordsworth, Coleridge, and Southey were among its fervent adherents. Later, even after the first boundless expectations had been disappointed by the events in France, the younger writers, including Hazlitt, Hunt, Shelley, and Byron, felt that its example, when purged of its errors, still comprised man's best hope. The Revolution generated a pervasive feeling that this was a great age of new beginnings, when, by discarding inherited procedures and outworn customs, everything was possible; and not only in political and social arrangements, but in intellectual and literary enterprises as well. In his *Prelude* Wordsworth wrote the classic description of the intoxicating spirit of the early 1790's, with "France standing on the top of golden hours, / And human nature seeming born again," so that "the whole Earth, / The beauty wore of promise." Something of this sense of suddenly expanding horizons and of limitless possibilities survived the shock of first disappointment at events in France and carried over to the year 1797, when Wordsworth and Coleridge, in excited daily communion, set out to revolutionize the theory and practice of poetry. The product of these discussions was the *Lyrical Ballads* of 1798.

POETIC THEORY AND POETIC PRACTICE

Wordsworth undertook to justify the new poetry by a critical manifesto or statement of poetic principles, in the form of an extended Preface to the second edition of *Lyrical Ballads* in 1800. In it he set himself in opposition to the literary *ancien régime*, those writers of the preceding century who, to his view, had imposed on poetry artificial conventions which distorted its free and natural development. Many of Wordsworth's later critical writings were attempts to clarify, buttress, or qualify points made in his first declaration. Coleridge declared that the Preface was "half a child of my own brain"; and although he soon developed doubts about certain of Words-worth's unguarded statements, and undertook to correct them in *Biographia Literaria* (1817), he did not question the necessity of Wordsworth's attempt to overturn the reigning tradition. In the course of the 18th century there had been increasing opposition to the neoclassic tradition of Dryden, Pope, and Dr. Johnson, and especially in the 1740's and later, there had emerged many of the critical concepts, as well as a number of the poetic subjects and forms, which were later exploited by Wordsworth and his contemporaries. Wordsworth's Preface nevertheless deserves its reputation as a turning point in English literature, for Wordsworth gathered up

isolated ideas, organized them into a coherent theory based on explicit critical principles, and made them the rationale for his own massive achievements as a poet. We can conveniently use the concepts in this extremely
influential essay as points of departure for a survey of distinctive elements in
the theory and poetry of the Romantic period.

1. *The Concept of Poetry and of the Poet.*

In neoclassic theory, poetry had been regarded as primarily an imitation
of human life—in a favorite figure, "a mirror held up to nature"—in a
form designed to instruct and give artistic pleasure to the reader. Wordsworth, in a reiterated statement, defined all good poetry as "the spontaneous overflow of powerful feelings." In a reversal of earlier aesthetic
theory, he thus located the source of poetry not in the outer world, but in
the individual poet, and identified as its essential material not men and
their actions, but the fluid feelings of the writer himself. Other Romantic
theories, however various, concurred in this crucial point by referring to the
mind and feelings of the individual writer, instead of to the outer world,
for the source and substance of a poem. Many writers identified poetry (in
metaphors parallel to Wordsworth's "overflow") as the "expression" or
"utterance" or "exhibition" of emotion. Blake and Shelley described a
poem as the poet's imaginative vision, which they opposed to the ordinary
world of public experience. Coleridge regarded poetry as the product of the
poet's imagination which—by a process that Coleridge called "a dim ana-
logue" of God's own creative activity—assimilates the materials of sense
into an organic entity that does not imitate the created world, but constitutes an equivalent creation of its own.

In accordance with the view that poetry expresses the poet's own mind,
imagination, and feelings, Romantic poems take as their subject matter, not
the actions of other men, but the experiences, thoughts, and feelings of the
poets who wrote them. The lyric poem written in the first person, which
had earlier been regarded as a minor poetic kind, became a major Romantic
form and was usually described as the most essentially poetic of all the
genres. And in the Romantic lyric the "I" is often not a mere *dramatis persona*, a typical lyric speaker such as the Petrarchan lover or Cavalier gallant
of Elizabethan and 17th-century love poems, but is recognizably the poet in
his private person. In the poems of Coleridge and Keats, for example, the
experiences and states of mind expressed by the lyric speaker often accord
closely with the personal confessions in the poets' letters and journals. Even
in his ostensibly fictional writings, narrative and dramatic, Byron usually
invites his readers to identify the hero with the author, whether the hero is
presented romantically (as in *Childe Harold*, *Manfred*, or the Oriental
tales) or in an ironic perspective (as in *Don Juan*). An extreme instance of
this tendency is Wordsworth's *Prelude*, which is a poem of epic length and
epic seriousness about the growth of the poet's own mind.

The Prelude exemplifies two other dominant tendencies in the period.
Like Blake, Coleridge in his early poems, Shelley, and Keats, Wordsworth
conceived himself as continuing the visionary tradition which goes back
through Milton and Spenser to the poet-prophets of the Bible. Also, *The
Prelude* represents a central form of English, as of European Romanticism
—a long work about the formation of the self, often centering on a crisis,

and presented in the radical metaphor of the poet's interior journey in quest of his true identity and destined spiritual home. Major examples of this form are Blake's *Milton*, the crucial episode of Asia's underground journey in Shelley's *Prometheus Unbound*, and Keats' *Endymion* and the *Fall of Hyperion*. In contemporary prose, we find equivalent developments: the subjectivity of the personal essays of Lamb, Hazlitt, and Leigh Hunt, and the currency of spiritual autobiography, whether fictionalized (Thomas Carlyle's *Sartor Resartus*) or presented as fact (Coleridge's *Biographia Literaria*, Thomas De Quincey's *Confessions of an English Opium Eater* and *Autobiographic Sketches*).

2. *Poetic Spontaneity and Freedom*.

Wordsworth defined good poetry not merely as the overflow but as "the *spontaneous* overflow" of feelings. In traditional aesthetic theory, poetry had been regarded as supremely an art; an art which in modern times could be practiced successfully only by a craftsman who had assimilated classical precedents, was aware of the "rules" governing the kind of poem he was writing, and (except for the felicities which, as Pope said, are "beyond the reach of art") deliberately employed tested means to achieve foreknown effects upon his audience. But to Wordsworth, although the writing of a poem may be preceded by reflection and followed by second thoughts, the immediate act of composition must be spontaneous—that is, arising from impulse, and free from all rules and the artful manipulation of means to foreseen ends—if the product is to be a genuine poem. Other important Romantic critics also voiced declarations of artistic independence. Keats listed as an "axiom" that "if poetry comes not as naturally as the leaves to a tree it had better not come at all." Blake insisted that he wrote from "Inspiration and Vision," and that his long "prophetic" poem, *Milton*, was given to him by an agency not himself, and "produced without Labor or Study." Shelley also maintained that it is "an error to assert that the finest passages of poetry are produced by labor and study," and suggested instead that they are the products of an unconscious creativity: "A great statue or picture grows under the power of the artist as a child in the mother's womb." "The definition of genius," Hazlitt remarked, "is that it acts unconsciously." The surviving work-sheets of the Romantic poets, however, as well as the testimony of observers, show that they worked and reworked their texts no less arduously—if perhaps more immediately under the impetus of first conception—than the craftsmen of earlier ages. Coleridge, who believed that truth lies in a union of opposites, came closer to the facts of Romantic practice when he claimed that the act of composing poetry involves the psychological contraries "of passion and of will, of *spontaneous* impulse and of *voluntary* purpose."

The emphasis in this period on the free activity of the imagination is related to an insistence on the essential role of instinct, intuition, and the feelings of "the heart" to supplement the judgments of the purely logical faculty, "the head," whether in the province of artistic beauty, philosophical and religious truth, or moral goodness. "Deep thinking," Coleridge wrote, "is attainable only by a man of deep feeling, and all truth is a species of revelation"; hence, "a metaphysical solution that does not tell you something in the heart is grievously to be suspected as apocryphal."

3. Romantic "Nature Poetry."

In his Preface Wordsworth wrote that "I have at all times endeavored to look steadily at my subject"; and in a supplementary Essay he complained that, from Dryden through Pope, there is scarcely an image from external nature "from which it can be inferred that the eye of the poet had been steadily fixed on his object." A glance at the table of contents of any collection of Romantic poems will indicate the degree to which the natural scene has become a primary poetic subject, while Wordsworth, Shelley, and even more Coleridge and Keats, described natural phenomena with an accuracy of observation which had no earlier match in its ability to capture the sensuous nuance.

Because of the prominence of landscape in this period, "Romantic poetry" has to the popular mind become almost synonymous with "nature poetry." Neither Romantic theory nor practice, however, justifies the opinion that the aim of this poetry was description for its own sake. Wordsworth in fact insisted that the ability to observe and describe objects accurately, although a necessary, is not at all a sufficient condition for poetry, "as its exercise supposes all the higher qualities of the mind to be passive, and in a state of subjection to external objects." And while most of the great Romantic lyrics—Wordsworth's *Tintern Abbey* and *Ode: Intimations of Immortality*, Coleridge's *Frost at Midnight* and *Dejection*, Shelley's *Ode to the West Wind*, Keats's *Nightingale*—begin with an aspect or change of aspect in the natural scene, this serves only as stimulus to the most characteristic human activity, that of thinking. Romantic "nature poems" are in fact meditative poems, in which the presented scene usually serves to raise an emotional problem or personal crisis whose development and resolution constitute the organizing principle of the poem. As Wordsworth said in his Prospectus to *The Recluse*, not nature, but "the Mind of Man" is "my haunt, and the main region of my song."

In addition, Romantic poems habitually imbue the landscape with human life, passion, and expressiveness. In part such descriptions represent the poetic equivalent of the metaphysical concept of nature, which had developed in deliberate revolt against the world views of the scientific philosophers of the 17th and 18th centuries, who had posited as the ultimate reality a mechanical world consisting of physical particles in motion. What is needed in philosophy, Coleridge wrote, is "the substitution of life and intelligence * * * for the philosophy of mechanism, which, in everything that is most worthy of the human intellect, strikes *Death*. * * *" But for many Romantic poets it was clearly also a matter of immediate experience to respond to the outer universe as a living entity which shares the feelings of the observer. James Thomson and other descriptive poets had described the created universe as giving direct access to God, and even as itself possessing the attributes of divinity; in *Tintern Abbey* and other poems Wordsworth exhibits toward the landscape attitudes and sentiments which men had earlier felt not only for God, but also for a father, a mother, or a beloved woman. Elsewhere, as in the great passage on crossing Simplon Pass (see *The Prelude* VI.624 ff.), Wordsworth also revives the ancient theological concept that God's creation constitutes a symbol system, a physical revelation parallel to the Revelation in the Scriptures—

> Characters of the great Apocalypse,
> The types and symbols of Eternity,
> Of first, and last, and midst, and without end.

This view of natural objects as corresponding to the spiritual world, served also as the understructure for a tendency, especially by Blake and Shelley, to write a symbolist poetry in which a rose, a sunflower, a mountain, a cave, or a cloud are presented as objects instinct with a significance beyond themselves. "I always seek in what I see," Shelley said, "the likeness of something beyond the present and tangible object." And for Blake mere nature, as perceived by the physical eye and un-humanized by the imagination, was spurned "as the dirt upon my feet, no part of me."

4. *The Glorification of the Commonplace.*

In two lectures on Wordsworth, Hazlitt declared that the school of poetry founded by Wordsworth was the literary equivalent of the French Revolution, translating political changes into poetical experiments. "Kings and queens were dethroned from their rank and station in legitimate tragedy or epic poetry, as they were decapitated elsewhere. * * * The paradox [these poets] set out with was that all things are by nature equally fit subjects for poetry; or that if there is any preference to be given, those that are the meanest and most unpromising are the best."

Hazlitt had in mind Wordsworth's statement that the aim of *Lyrical Ballads* was "to choose incidents and situations from common life," and to use a "selection of language really spoken by men," for which the source and model is "humble and rustic life." As Hazlitt shrewdly saw, this was more a social than a distinctively literary definition of the proper materials and language for poetry. Versifiers of the later decades of the 18th century had experimented in the simple treatment of simple subjects, and Robert Burns —like Wordsworth, a sympathizer with the French Revolution—had achieved great poetic success in the serious representation of humble life in a language really spoken by rustics. But Wordsworth buttressed his poetic practice by a theory which inverted the traditional hierarchy of poetic genres, subjects, and style by elevating humble and rustic life and the plain style, earlier appropriate to the lowly pastoral, into the principal subject and medium for poetry in general. And in his own practice, as Hazlitt also noted, Wordsworth went even further, and turned for the subjects of his serious poems not only to humble people but to the ignominious, but the outcast, the delinquent—to "convicts, female vagrants, gypsies * * * idiot boys and mad mothers," as well as to "peasants, peddlers, and village barbers." Hence the outrage of Lord Byron, who alone among his great contemporaries insisted that Dryden and Pope had laid out the proper road for poetry, and who—in spite of his liberalism in politics—maintained allegiance both to aristocratic proprieties and traditional poetic decorum:

> "Peddlers," and "Boats," and "Wagons"! Oh! ye shades
> Of Pope and Dryden, are we come to this?

But in his democratization of poetry, Hazlitt insisted, Wordsworth was "the most original poet now living." And certainly Wordsworth in *Lyrical Ballads* was in this respect, more radical than any of his contemporaries. He effected an immense enlargement of our imaginative sympathies and brought into the province of serious literature a range of materials and interests which are still being explored by writers of the present day.

It should be noted, however, that Wordsworth's aim in *Lyrical Ballads* was not a mere reproductive realism, but as he announced in his Preface, to throw over "situations from common life * * * a certain coloring of imagination, whereby ordinary things should be presented to the mind in an unusual aspect." As this passage indicates, Wordsworth's concern in his poetry was not only with "common life" but with "ordinary *things*"; no one can read his poems without noticing the extraordinary reverence which he attaches to words which in earlier writers had been derogatory—words like "common," "ordinary," "everyday," "humble," whether applied to people, to events, or to the visible scene. His aim throughout is to shake us out of the lethargy of custom so as to refresh our sense of wonder—indeed, of divinity—in the everyday, the trivial, and the familiar. In one of the events Wordsworth called "a spot of time," when he entered London for the first time, he describes how the "vulgar men about me, trivial forms * * * mean shapes" suddenly assumed a "weight and power" that lasted only a moment, "yet with Time it dwells, / And grateful memory, as a thing divine" (*The Prelude* VIII.543-59).

Dr. Johnson had said that "wonder is a pause of reason," and that "all wonder is the effect of novelty upon ignorance." But for many Romantic critics, to arouse in the sophisticated mind that sense of wonder felt by the ignorant and the innocent was a primary power of imagination and a major function of poetry. Commenting on the special imaginative quality of Wordsworth's early poetry (*Biographia*, Chapter VI), Coleridge commented: "To combine the child's sense of wonder and novelty with the appearances, which every day for perhaps forty years had rendered familiar * * * this is the character and privilege of genius," and its prime service is to awaken in the reader "freshness of sensation" in the representation of "familiar objects." Poetry, said Shelley in his *Defense of Poetry*, "reproduces the common universe" but "purges from our inward sight the film of familiarity which obscures from us the wonder of our being," and "creates anew the universe, after it has been blunted by reiteration." And in Carlyle's *Sartor Resartus* (1833–34), the chief—indeed the only—effect of the conversion of the protagonist from despairing unbelief is that he is able to sustain a sense of the "Natural Supernaturalism" in ordinary experience and so overcome the "custom" which "blinds us to the miraculousness of daily-recurring miracles." The great power of the imagination is that it makes the old world new again.

5. *The Supernatural and "Strangeness in Beauty."*

In most of his poems Coleridge, like Wordsworth, dealt with the everyday things of this world, and in *Frost at Midnight* he showed how well he too could achieve the effect of wonder in the familiar. But according to the agreed division of labor in *Lyrical Ballads*, Coleridge's function, he tells us, was to achieve wonder by a frank violation of natural laws and the ordinary course of events, in poems of which "the incidents and agents were to be, in part at least, supernatural." And in *The Ancient Mariner, Christabel,* and *Kubla Khan*, Coleridge opened up the realm of mystery and magic, in which ancient folklore, superstition, and demonology are used to impress upon the reader the sense of occult powers and unknown modes of being. Such poems are usually set in the distant past or in faraway places, or both; the milieu of *Kubla Khan*, for example, exploits the exoticism both of the Middle Ages and of the Orient. Next to Coleridge, the greatest master of this Romantic mode—in which supernatural events have a profound psychological import—was John Keats. In *La Belle Dame sans Merci* and *The Eve of St. Agnes* he adapted the old forms of ballad and romance to modern sophisticated use and, like Coleridge, established a medieval setting for events that violate the natural order. Hence the term "the medieval revival," frequently attached to the Romantic period, which comprehends also the ballad imitations and some of the verse tales and historical novels of Sir Walter Scott.

Another side of the tendency which Walter Pater later called "the addition of strangeness to beauty" was the Romantic interest in unusual modes of experience, of a kind which earlier writers had largely ignored as either too trivial or too aberrant for serious literary concern. Blake, Wordsworth, and Coleridge in their poetry explored visionary states of consciousness which are common among children but violate the standard categories of adult judgment. Coleridge was interested in mesmerism (what we now call hypnotism), and like Blake, Shelley, and Byron, studied the literature of the occult and the esoteric. Coleridge also shared with De Quincey a concern with dreams and nightmares; both authors exploited in their writings the heightened consciousness and distorted perceptions they experienced under their addiction to opium. Byron exploited the fascination of the forbidden and the appeal of the terrifying Satanic hero. And Keats was extraordinarily sensitive to the ambivalences of human experience—to the mingling, at their highest intensity, of pleasure and pain, to the destructiveness of love, and to the erotic quality of the longing for death. These phenomena had already been crudely explored by 18th-century writers of terror tales and Gothic fiction, and later in the 19th century all of them, sometimes exaggerated to blatant perversity, became the special literary province of Charles Baudelaire, Algernon Charles Swinburne, and writers of the European "Decadence."

INDIVIDUALISM, NONCONFORMITY, AND APOCALYPTIC EXPECTATION

Through the greater part of the 18th century, man had for the most part been viewed as a limited being in a strictly ordered and essentially unchanging world. A variety of philosophical and religious systems in this century coincided in a distrust of radical innovation, a respect for the precedents established through the ages by the common sense of mankind, and the recommendation to set accessible goals and avoid extremes, whether in politics, intellect, morality, or art. Many of the great literary works of the period joined in attacking "pride," or man's aspirations beyond the limits natural to his species. "The bliss of man," Pope wrote in *An Essay on Man*, "(could pride that blessing find) / Is not to act or think beyond mankind."

> This kind, this due degree
> Of blindness, weakness, Heaven bestows on thee.
> Submit.

The Romantic period, the age of burgeoning free enterprise and revolutionary hope, was also an age of radical individualism, in which both the philosophers and poets put an immensely higher estimate on man's potentialities and on his proper aims. In German post-Kantian philosophy, which generated many of the characteristic ideas of European Romanticism, the mind of man—what was called the "Subject" or "Ego"—took over various functions which had hitherto been the sole prerogative of Divinity. Most prominent was the rejection of a central 18th-century concept of the mind as a mirrorlike recipient of a universe already created and its replacement by the new concept of the mind as itself the creator of the universe it perceives. The English founders of the new poetry also described the mind as creating its own experience. In Blake, the mind creates its proper milieu only if it rejects the material world; in Coleridge and Wordsworth, the mind creates in collaboration with something given to it from without. Mind, wrote Coleridge in 1801, is "not passive" but "made in God's Image, and that too in the sublimest sense—the Image of the *Creator*." And Wordsworth declared in *The Prelude* (II.257–60) that the individual mind

> Doth, like an agent of the one great Mind
> Create, creator and receiver both,
> Working but in alliance with the works
> Which it beholds. * * *

Many Romantic writers also agreed that man's mind has access beyond sense to the infinite, through a special faculty they called either Reason or Imagination. In *The Prelude* (VI.592 ff.) Wordsworth describes a flash of imagination "that has revealed / The invisible world," and affirms:

> Our destiny, one being's heart and home,
> Is with infinitude, and only there;
> With hope it is, hope that can never die,
> Effort, and expectation, and desire,
> And something evermore about to be.

The aspect of man which, to the moralists of the preceding age, had been his essential sin, or his tragic error, now becomes his glory and his triumph: he refuses to submit to his limitations and, though finite, persists in setting infinite, hence inaccessible goals. Wordsworth characteristically goes on to declare that "under such banners militant, the soul / Seeks for no trophies, struggles for no spoils"; for him, the militant striving ends in physical quietism and moral fortitude. But for other writers, especially in Germany, man's proper destiny is ceaseless activity—a "*Streben nach dem Unendlichen*," a striving for the infinite. This view is epitomized by Goethe's Faust, who in his quest for the unattainable. violates ordinary moral limits, yet wins salvation by his very insatiability, which never stoops to contentment with any possibilities offered by this finite world. Man's infinite longing—in Shelley's phrase, "the desire of the moth for a star"—was a recurrent theme also in the English literature of the day. "Less than everything," Blake announced, "cannot satisfy man." Shelley's *Alastor* and Keat's *Endymion* both represent the quest for an indefinable and inaccessible goal, and Byron's *Manfred* has for its hero a man whose "powers and will" reach beyond the limits of that human clay "which clogs the ethereal essence," so that "his aspirations / Have been beyond the dwellers of the earth."

In the contemporary theory of art, we find critics rejecting the neoclassic ideal of a limited intention, perfectly accomplished, in favor of "the glory of the imperfect," in which the artist's very failure attests the largeness of his aim. And in their own work, Romantic writers deliberately put themselves in competition with their greatest predecessors, and experimented boldly in poetic language, versification, and design. Especially in their longer poems, they struck out in new directions, and in the space of a few decades produced an astonishing variety of forms constructed on novel principles of organization and style. Blake's symbolic lyrics and visionary "prophetic" poems; Coleridge's haunting ballad-narrative of sin and retribution, *The Ancient Mariner*; Wordsworth's epiclike spiritual autobiography, *The Prelude*; Shelley's cosmic symbolic drama, *Prometheus Unbound*; Keats's great sequence of *Odes* on the irreconcilable conflict in basic human desires; Byron's ironic survey of all European civilization, *Don Juan*—one can say of each of them, as Shelley said of *Don Juan*, that it was "something wholly new and relative to the age."

The great neoclassic writers had typically dealt with men as members of an organized, and usually an urban, society; of this society the author regarded himself as an integral part, its highest standards were those he spoke for, and to it as his audience he addressed himself. Some Romantic writers, on the other hand, deliberately isolated themselves from society in order to give scope to their individual vision. Wordsworth's projected masterwork he entitled *The Recluse*, and he described himself as "musing in solitude" on its subject, "the individual Mind that keeps her own / Inviolate retirement." And in almost all Wordsworth's poems, long or short, the words "single," "solitary," "by oneself," "alone" constitute a leitmotif; his imagination is released by the sudden apparition of a single figure or object, stark against an undifferentiated background. Coleridge also, and still more strikingly, Byron and Shelley, represented a solitary protagonist who is separated from society because he has rejected it, or because it has rejected him; these poets introduced what became a persistent theme in many Victorian and modern writers—the theme of exile, of the disinherited mind which cannot find a spiritual home in its native land and society or anywhere in the modern world. The solitary Romantic nonconformist was sometimes also a great sinner. Writers of that time were fascinated by the outlaws of myth, legend, or history—Cain, Satan, Faust, the Wandering Jew or the great, flawed figure of Napoleon—about whom they wrote and on whom they modeled a number of their villains or their heroes. In Coleridge's *Ancient Mariner* (as in Wordsworth's *Guilt and Sorrow* and *Peter Bell*) the guilty outcast—"alone, alone, all, all alone"—is made to realize and expiate his sin against the community of living things, so that he may reassume his place in the social order. But in Byron the violator of conventional laws and limits remains proudly unrepentant. His hero Manfred, a compound of guilt and superhuman greatness, cannot be defeated by death, successfully defying the demons who, in the tradition of Marlowe's *Dr. Faustus*, have come to drag his soul to hell: I "was my own destroyer, and will be / My own hereafter * * * / Back, ye baffled fiends!" A more reputable Romantic hero, who turns up frequently in Byron and other writers and is made the protagonist of Shelley's greatest poem, is the Prometheus of Greek mythology. He shares with Satan the status of superlative nonconformity, since he sets himself in opposition to deity itself; unlike Satan, however, he is the champion rather than the enemy of the human race.

Nowhere is the Romantic combination of boundless aspiration and the reliance on the power of the individual mind better exhibited than in the literary treatment of the ultimate hope of mankind. The French Revolution had aroused in many sympathizers the millennial expectations which are profoundly rooted in Hebrew and Christian tradition. "Few persons but those who have lived in it," Robert Southey reminisced in 1824, "can conceive or comprehend what the memory of the French Revolution was, nor what a visionary world seemed to open upon those who were just entering it. Old things seemed passing away, and nothing was dreamt of but the regeneration of the human race." Southey's language—like that of Wordsworth, Coleridge, Hazlitt, and other writers when they described their early Revolutionary fervor—is Biblical; and it reflects the extent to which, in England, the Revolution was championed especially by members of radical Protestant sects, who envisioned it on the model of Biblical prophecy.

The Bible ends with the book of Apocalypse (literally, "Revelation"), prophesying a return of man to his lost Edenic felicity, first in the millennium ("a thousand years") of an earthly kingdom, then in the eternity of "a new heaven and a new earth"; this consummation of history is symbolized as a marriage between the New Jerusalem and Christ the Lamb. At the outbreak of the French Revolution, Joseph Priestley and other Unitarian leaders hailed that event as the stage preceding the millennium prophesied in Revelation. Coleridge and Wordsworth, in their early poems, also interpreted the Revolution as the violent preliminary to the new earth and heaven of apocalyptic prophecy. And Blake's *The French Revolution* (1791) and *America, a Prophecy* (1793) represented both these revolutions as apocalyptic portents of the last days of the fallen world.

When the later events in France dashed their faith in political revolution as a means to the millennium, a number of Romantic writers salvaged their apocalyptic hope by giving it a new interpretation. They transferred the agency of apocalypse from mass action to the individual mind—from a political to a spiritual revolution—and proposed that "the new earth and new heaven" of Revelation is available here, now, to each man, if only he can make his visionary imagination triumph over his senses and his sense-bound understanding. Hence the extraordinary Romantic emphasis on a new way of *seeing* (which is the restoration of a lost earlier way of seeing) as man's chief aim in life. Blake's "Prophetic Books," for example, all deal with some aspects of the Fall and Redemption, and represent apocalypse as the recovery of the imaginative vision of things as they really are, seen "through and not with the eye." "The Nature of my Work is Visionary or Imaginative; it is an Endeavor to Restore what the Ancients called the Golden Age." This concept of the imaginative recreation of the old earth is still expressed in the original Biblical metaphor of a marriage—although now it is not a marriage of the New Jerusalem with the Lamb, but a reintegration of man's inner faculties into spiritual unity, or else a marriage between man's mind and the external world. Coleridge put this latter version succinctly, in *Dejection: An Ode*; it is the inner condition of "Joy," at life's highest moments, "Which, wedding nature to us, gives in dower / A new earth and new heaven." Wordsworth announced as the "high argument" for *The Recluse* (the same theme serves as underpattern for *The Prelude*) that "Paradise, and groves Elysian" are not "a history only of departed things"—

> For the discerning intellect of Man
> When wedded to this goodly universe
> In love and holy passion, shall find these
> A simple produce of the common day.

In Shelley's *Prometheus Unbound*, Prometheus represents archetypal man, whose total change of heart frees his imaginative capacity to envision, and to achieve, a regenerate world; the fourth act symbolizes this event in the mode of a marriage celebration in which the whole cosmos participates. Carlyle's *Sartor Resartus*, to mention one other example, is the history of an individual's savage spiritual crisis and conversion, which turns out to be the achievement of an individual apocalypse: "And I awoke to a new Heaven and a new Earth." But, as Carlyle goes on to indicate, this new earth is the old earth, but seen by his protagonist as though miraculously recreated, because he has learned to substitute the "Imaginative" faculty for what Carlyle represents as the chief faculty of the 18th-century Enlightenment, the "Logical, Mensurative faculty," or "Understanding." Writing in 1830–31, at the close of the period historians have labeled "Romantic," Carlyle thus summed up the tendency of a generation of writers to retain the ancient faith in apocalypse, but to interpret it not as a change in the world, but as a change in man's world view.

THE FAMILIAR ESSAY

At the close of the 18th century the reviews and magazines were written largely by hacks who acceded to the political bias and financial interests of the publisher and advertisers. The essays they included were weak imitations of the type established nearly a century earlier by the single-essay periodicals, the *Tatler* and the *Spectator*. In 1802, however, the *Edinburgh Review* inaugurated the modern type of periodical publication. It allowed considerable latitude to its writers, set its literary standards high, and was able to meet these standards by paying for contributions at rates good enough to command the best talents of the day.

The great and immediate success of this new enterprise stimulated the founding of rival reviews and magazines. (A "review," usually issued four times yearly, consisted primarily of essays on important books and discussions of contemporary issues; a "magazine" was a monthly publication which printed more miscellaneous materials, including a high proportion of original essays, poems, and stories.) In 1820 appeared the *London Magazine*, liberal in politics and contemporary in literary interests; in its short but notable career until 1829, it printed the work of a group of brilliant writers, including the three men who soon established themselves as the greatest essayists of the age—Lamb, Hazlitt, and De Quincey. These magazines, and others like them, elevated the essay in literary dignity and quality and revolutionized its form and substance. They competed strenuously for talent, paying well enough so that an author (at least if he were as prolific as Hazlitt) could earn a living as a free-lance essayist. Since allotment of space was flexible, each topic could find its appropriate length, instead of being held to the Procrustean brevity of the earlier essays modeled on Addison and Steele; in consequence, the new essays tended to be from two to four times as long as the 18th-century form. And writers were treated as serious craftsmen who were competent, within broad limits, to write as they pleased.

Under these new conditions the familiar essay—a commentary on a nontechnical subject written in a relaxed and intimate manner—flourished, and in a fashion that to some degree paralleled the course of Romantic poetry. Each of the major essayists was in fact closely associated with important poets and supported at least some of the new poetic developments in critical commentaries whose perceptiveness and discrimination render them permanently valuable. Like the poets, these essayists were personal and subjective; their essays are often candidly autobiographical, reminiscent, self-analytic; and when the writers treated other matters than themselves, they did so impressionistically, so that the material is seen reflected in the temperament of the essayist. The subject matter of the essays, like that of the poetry, exhibits an extension of range and sympathy far beyond the earlier limits of the leisure class and its fashionable concerns, to comprehend clerks, chimney sweeps, poor relations, handball players, prizefighters, and murderers. Most strikingly, the essayists resemble the poets in rebelling against 18th-century conventions to revive prose forms long disused and to develop new prose styles and structural principles. The result was a notable variety of achievement, ranging from Hazlitt's hard-hitting plain style and seemingly casual order of topics, through Lamb's delicately contrived rhetoric and meticulously controlled organization, to De Quincey's elaborate experiments in applying to prose the rhythms, harmonies, and thematic structure of music.

DRAMA

Although favorable to the essay, literary conditions in the early 19th century were unfavorable in the extreme to writing for the stage. By a licensing act which was not repealed until 1843, only the Drury Lane and Covent Garden theaters had the right to produce "legitimate"—that is to say, spoken—drama; the other theaters were restricted by law to entertainments in which there could be no dialogue except to music, and so put on mainly dancing, pantomime, and various types of musical plays. The two monopoly theaters were vast and ill-lighted, and their audiences were noisy and unruly; as a result, actors played in a grandiose and orotund style. To succeed under such conditions, plays had also to be blatant and magniloquent, so that the drama of that period (fettered also by rigid moral and political censorship) tended to the extremes of either farce or melodrama. None of the plays written by the professional playwrights of the time have survived, except in the limbo of scholarly monographs on the history of the theater.

Nonetheless, attracted irresistibly by the example of their idolized Shakespeare, all the major Romantic poets, and many minor ones, tried their hand at poetic plays. Some of these were deliberate closet dramas—Byron's *Manfred* and Shelley's *Prometheus Unbound*, for example, can hardly be visualized, much less produced—but others were expressly written for the stage. The poets, however, lacked experience with the hard necessities of the practical theater, and they were unable to throw off the artifice of an archaic style dominated by Elizabethan and Jacobean models.

Above all, the genius of an age which excelled in subjective or visionary literary forms was ill adapted to the theater, which is a peculiarly social genre and must represent a variety of men other than the author himself. Even Byron, the only important poet of his generation to produce major work in a literary kind—satire—which requires a highly developed social sensibility, did not succeed as a practical dramatist. His stage plays, while readable, mainly exhibit various aspects of the Byronic hero; they lack theatrical vigor and variety, and their thin-skinned author wisely refused to let them be put on before the merciless and demonstrative audiences of his day. Coleridge achieved a minor hit with his tragedy *Remorse*, which ran for twenty nights at the Drury Lane in 1813. The most successful Romantic dramatist was, surprisingly, Shelley. In *The Cenci* (1820) Shelley, with extraordinary tact and genuine theatrical acumen, converts a true story of the Italian Renaissance—of a monstrous father who violates his daughter and is in turn murdered by her—into a powerful version of his own central fable of the instinctive desire of evil to destroy, by degrading, the defiant individual, and of the moral triumph of the unconquerable single spirit, even in death. The play was not acted, however, until long after Shelley had died.

THE NOVEL

Two new types of fiction were prominent in the late 18th century. One was the "Gothic novel," which had been inaugurated in 1764 by Horace Walpole's *Castle of Otranto, A Gothic Story*. The term derives from the frequent setting of these tales in a gloomy castle of the Middle Ages, but it has been extended to a larger group of novels, set somewhere in the past, which exploit the possibilities of mystery and terror in sullen, craggy landscapes; decaying mansions with dank dungeons, secret passages, and stealthy ghosts; chilling supernatural phenomena; and often, persecution of a beautiful maiden by an obsessed and haggard villain. In her *Mysteries of Udolpho* (1794), and better still in *The Italian* (1797), Ann Radcliffe developed the figure of the mysterious and solitary *homme fatal*, torturing others because himself tortured by unspeakable guilt, who, though a villain, usurps the place of the hero in the reader's interest. Matthew Gregory Lewis, in *The Monk* (1797), which he wrote at the age of 20, has a similar protagonist, and brings to the fore the elements of diabolism, sensuality, and sadistic perversion which were pungent but discreetly submerged components in Mrs. Radcliffe's Gothic formula. The effects of Gothicism are apparent also in Romantic poetry: in Coleridge's medieval terror poem *Christabel*, in Byron's recurrent hero-villain, and in Shelley's inclinations (fostered by his early love for Gothic tales and his own youthful trials in that form) toward the fantastic and the macabre.

The second fictional mode popular at the turn of the century was the novel of purpose, often written to propagate the new social and political theories current in the period of the French Revolution. The best examples combine didactic intention with elements of Gothic terror. William Godwin, the political philosopher, wrote *Caleb Williams* (1794) to illustrate the thesis that the lower classes are helplessly subject to the power and privilege of the ruling class, but he did so in the form of a chilling story concerning the relentless pursuit and persecution by a wealthy squire of the young secretary who has come upon evidence that his employer has committed murder. Shelley's wife, Mary Godwin—the daughter of Mary Wollstonecraft, who in 1792 had written the first classic of feminist litera-ture, *A Vindication of the Rights of Woman*—achieved the most impres-sive instance of the thematic novel of terror. Her *Frankenstein* (1817) con-verts a story about a fabricated monster into a powerful representation of the moral distortion imposed on an individual who, because he diverges from the norm, is rejected by society.

The Romantic period produced two great novelists, Jane Austen and Sir Walter Scott. There were accomplished women poets in this period—Anna Letitia Barbauld, Letitia Elizabeth Landon, and Mary Tighe (who had some influence on Keats)—but the one woman of literary genius was Jane Austen (1775–1817). She was also the only major author who, untouched by the political, intellectual, and artistic revolutions of the age, stayed serenely within the culture and literary traditions of the neoclassic past. Charlotte Brontë, speaking for the Romantic sensibility, complained that Jane Austen's novels lack warmth, enthusiasm, energy; "she ruffles her reader by nothing vehement, disturbs him by nothing profound. The pas-sions are perfectly unknown to her. * * * " But Jane Austen deliberately elected to stay within the circumference of her own experience—the life of provincial English gentlefolk—and to maintain the decorum of the aloof and ironic novel of manners, based on such 18th-century antecedents as the comedy of manners of William Congreve and Richard Brinsley Sheridan and the works of earlier women novelists, Fanny Burney and Maria Edge-worth. Within these limits of both subject and form, Jane Austen achieved a fully particularized setting within which to examine the values men and women live by in their everyday social lives.

Sense and Sensibility and *Northanger Abbey* poke fun at two latter 18th-century deviations from the humanistic norm, the cult of sensibility and the taste for Gothic terrors. Austen's other novels, published between 1813 and 1818—*Mansfield Park, Persuasion*, and best of all, *Pride and Prejudice* and *Emma*—all deal with the subject of getting married. Not only was this in fact the central preoccupation and problem for the young leisure-class lady of that age; it also afforded Jane Austen her best opportun-ities for testing her heroines' practical sense and moral integrity, their degree of knowledge of the world and of themselves, and their capacity to demonstrate grace under pressure.

Sir Walter Scott (1771–1832) was contemporary with Jane Austen, and admired her greatly, but his work in fiction was at the opposite extreme from hers. In 1814, with the anonymous *Waverly*, he turned from narrative verse (in which Byron had displaced him in popularity) to narrative prose, and managed to write almost thirty long works of fiction in the eighteen years before he died. They are in the mode which he himself defined as romance, "the interest of which turns upon marvelous and uncommon inci-dents," in contrast to the novel such as Jane Austen wrote, in which "the events are accommodated to the ordinary train of human events, and the modern state of society." Scott's great originality lay in opening up to fiction the realm of history; he sometimes alters the order of events for novelistic purposes, yet he maintains fidelity to the spirit of the past and a meticulous accuracy in antiquarian detail. His great series of Scottish novels, including *Guy Mannering, The Antiquary, Old Mortality, Rob Roy* and (best of all) *The Heart of Midlothian*, are rooted in historical events from the 17th century up to his own time; *Ivanhoe* is set in 13th-century England and *Kenilworth* in the age of Elizabeth; and *Quentin Durward*, the best of his Continental romances, has for background the French Court of the 15th century.

Like his friend Byron, Scott wrote with dash and grandiosity in a kind of sustained improvisation; his plotting is often loose, his romantic lovers pallid, and his kings and chieftains large-scale puppets. But in his great scenes of action there is a scope and sweep that was not to be exceeded in fiction until the appearance of Leo Tolstoy's *War and Peace* in the 1860's. And although, unlike his liberal Romantic contemporaries, Scott's political sympathies were aristocratic and feudal, his most vivid and convincing characters are members of the middle and lower classes. His tradesmen, servants, peasantry, social outcasts, and demented old women, speaking a rich Scottish vernacular (Scott's language, like Robert Burns's in verse, tended to become stilted and conventional when he wrote in standard English), compose a populous world in which each person is an individual, rooted in the circumstances of his time and place and class and occupation. Scott had an immense international vogue, equaling that of Byron and Goethe, and became the acknowledged master of some of the greatest 19th-century novelists, including Balzac and Tolstoy. Jane Austen, on the other hand, during her lifetime was admired only by a limited group of English readers. But her novels have demonstrated greater staying power. Scott's combination of casualness in design and prodigality in detail puts off many readers who have formed their sensibilities on the well-made novel of the present century. But even after the achievements of such craftsmen in the form as Henry James, Jane Austen remains the sovereign of the intricate, spare, and graceful art of the novel of manners.

ROBERT BURNS
(1759–1796)

1786: *Poems, Chiefly in the Scottish Dialect* (Kilmarnock edition).
1787: Begins collecting, editing, and writing songs for *The Scots Musical Museum.*

A favorite myth of later 18th-century primitivists was that there existed natural poets who warbled their native woodnotes wild, independent of art or literary tradition. These artless poets were sought among peasants and proletarians, whose caste or rural habitation, it was thought, protected them from contamination by the artificialities of civilized life and culture. When Robert Burns published his first volume of *Poems,* in 1786, he was at once hailed by the literati of Edinburgh as an instance of the natural genius, a "Heaven-taught plowman" whose poems were the spontaneous overflow of his native feelings. Burns himself sometimes fostered this belief, and rather enjoyed playing the role of the poet by instinct. But in fact he was a well-read (although largely self-educated) man, whose quick intelligence and sensibility enabled him to make the most of limited opportunities. And although he broke clear of the contemporary conventions of decayed English neoclassicism, he did so not by instinct but as a deliberate craftsman who turned to two earlier traditions for his models —the Scottish oral tradition of folklore and folk song, and the highly developed Scottish literary tradition, which goes back to the late Middle Ages.

His father—William Burnes, as he spelled his name—was a God-fearing and hard-working farmer of Ayrshire, a county in southwestern Scotland, who could not make a go of it in a period of hard times and high rents, and died in 1784, broken in body and spirit. Robert, with his brother Gilbert, was forced to do the toil of a man while still a boy, and began to develop the heart trouble of which he was to die when only 37. Although his father had the Scotsman's esteem for education and saw to it that his sons attended school whenever they could, Burns's education in literature, theology, politics, and philosophy came mainly from his own reading. At the age of 15 he fell in love, and was immediately inspired by that event to write his first song. "Thus," Burns said, "with me began Love and Poesy." After he reached maturity, Burns cultivated assiduously both these propensities. He began a series of amorous affairs, producing in 1785 the first of a number of illegitimate children; he also extended greatly the range and quantity of his attempts at poetry. So rapid was his development as a poet that by the time he published the Kilmarnock edition, at the age of 27, he had written all but a few of his greatest long poems.

The Kilmarnock volume (so named from the town in which it was published) was one of the most extraordinary first volumes by any British poet, and it had a great and immediate success. Burns was at once acclaimed "Caledonia's Bard" and was lionized by the intellectuals and gentlefolk when he visited Edinburgh soon after his book came out. In this milieu the peasant-poet soon demonstrated that he could more than hold his own as a brilliant conversationalist and debater. But he was also wise enough to realize that once the novelty wore off, his eminence in this society would not endure. He had a fierce pride which was quick to resent any hint of contempt or condescension toward himself as a man of low degree. His sympathies were democratic, and he was an outspoken admirer of the American Revolution and of the republican experiment in France. In religion, too, he was a radical, professing "the Religion of Sentiment and Reason" in opposition to the strict Calvinism in which he had been raised, and he offended many pious Presbyterians by his devastating satires against the rigid tenets and the moral authoritarianism of the Scottish kirk. Furthermore, his sexual irregularities were notorious, less because they were out of the common order at that time than because of his bravado in flaunting them before the "unco guid"—as his biographer, DeLancey Ferguson, has said, "it was not so much that he was conspicuously sinful as that he sinned conspicuously." Most of Burns's friends in high station quickly fell away, and his later visits to Edinburgh did not repeat the social success of the first.

In 1788 Burns was given a commission as Excise officer, or tax inspector, and he settled down with Jean Armour, his former mistress—now his wife—at Ellisland, near Dumfries, combining his official duties with farming. This was the fourth farm on which Burns had worked; and when it, like the others, failed, he moved his family to the lively country town of Dumfries. Here he was fairly happy, despite recurrent illness and a chronic shortage of money. He performed his official duties efficiently and was respected by his fellow townspeople and esteemed by his superiors; he was a devoted family man and father; and he accumulated a circle of intimates to whom he could repair for conversation and conviviality. In 1787 James Johnson, an engraver, had enlisted Burns's aid in collecting Scottish folk songs for an anthology called *The Scots Musical Museum.* Burns soon became the real editor for several volumes of this work, devoting all of his free time to collecting, editing, restoring, and imitating traditional songs, or writing verses of his own to traditional dance tunes. Almost all of his creative work, during the last twelve years of his life, went into the writing of songs for the *Musical Museum* and for George Thomson's *Select Collection of Original Scottish Airs.* This was for Burns a devoted labor of love and patriotism, done anonymously, for which he refused to accept any pay, although badly in need of money; and he continued the work when he was literally on his deathbed.

Burns's best work was written in Scots, a northern dialect of English spoken by Scottish peasants and (on other than formal occasions) by most 18th-century Scottish gentlemen as well. When Burns attempted to write in standard English the result—except in an occasional lyric such as the lucid and graceful *Afton Water*—was stilted and conventional, with all the stock phrasing, sententiousness, and sentimentality of the genteel poetic tradition of his day. He is often considered a "pre-Romantic" who, anticipating Wordsworth, revived the English lyric, exploited the literary forms and legends of folk culture, and wrote in the language really spoken by the common man. But this reputation is based primarily on his songs. By far the major portion of the poems Burns published under his own name are concerned with men and manners and fall, technically, in the favorite genres of 18th-century poets; they include brilliant satire in a variety of forms, a number of fine verse epistles to friends and fellow poets, and one masterpiece of mock-heroic (or at least, seriocomic) narrative, *Tam o' Shanter*. The claim could be supported that, next to Pope, Burns is the greatest 18th-century master of these literary types. Yet Burns's writings in satire, epistle, and mock-heroic are very remote from Pope's, in their heartiness and verve, no less than in their dialect and intricate stanza forms. The reason for the difference is that Burns turned for his models not to Horace and the English neoclassic tradition, but to the native tradition which had been established in the golden age of Scottish poetry by Robert Henryson, William Dunbar, Gavin Douglas, and other Scottish Chaucerians of the 15th and 16th centuries. He knew this literature through his 18th-century Scottish predecessors, especially Allan Ramsay and Robert Fergusson, who had collected some of the ancient poems and written new ones based on the ancient models. Burns improved on these predecessors, but he derived from them much that is characteristic in his literary forms, subjects, diction, and stanzas.

Burns's songs, however, are more widely known than his longer poems, and have in themselves been adequate to sustain his reputation as a major poet. He wrote over 300 of them, in unequaled abundance and variety. In them he surrenders himself wholeheartedly to the emotion of the moment, evoked by all the great lyric subjects: love, drink, work, friendship, patriotism, and bawdry. His poetic character is hearty, generous, rollicking, tender, with a sympathy that encompasses men of all types, from national heroes to tavern roarers; like all the great poets of humanity, Burns had that poetical character which Keats described: "It lives in gusto, be it foul or fair, high or low, rich or poor, mean or elevated. It has as much delight in conceiving an Iago as an Imogen." Burns is not only the national poet of Scotland but also a song writer for all English-speaking people. Everywhere in the world on New Year's Eve when, helped by drink and the reminder of their bondage to time, men indulge their instinct of a common humanity, they join hands and sing a song of Burns.

Corn Rigs[1] an' Barley Rigs

It was upon a Lammas night,[2]
　　When corn rigs are bonnie,
　Beneath the moon's unclouded light
　　I held awa to Annie:
5　The time flew by wi' tentless° heed,　　　　　　*careless*
　　Till 'tween the late and early,

---

1. "Ridges," the space between plowed furrows.　2. I.e., early in August.

Wi' sma' persuasion she agreed
  To see me through the barley.

Chorus

Corn rigs, an' barley rigs,
10   An' corn rigs are bonnie:
I'll ne'er forget that happy night
  Amang the rigs wi' Annie.

The sky was blue, the wind was still,
  The moon was shining clearly;
15 I set her down wi' right good will,
  Amang the rigs o' barley;
I kent° her heart was a' my ain;   *knew*
  I loved her most sincerely;
I kissed her owre and owre again
20   Amang the rigs o' barley.
                    (*Chorus*)

I locked her in my fond embrace;
  Her heart was beating rarely;
My blessings on that happy place,
  Amang the rigs o' barley!
25 But by the moon and stars so bright,
  That shone that hour so clearly,
She ay° shall bless that happy night   *always*
  Amang the rigs o' barley.
                    (*Chorus*)

I hae been blythe wi' comrades dear;
30   I hae been merry drinking;
I hae been joyfu' gath'rin gear;°   *possessions*
  I hae been happy thinking:
But a' the pleasures e'er I saw,
  Though three times doubled fairly,
35 That happy night was worth them a',
  Amang the rigs o' barley.
                    (*Chorus*)

1783   1786

To a Mouse

ON TURNING HER UP IN HER NEST WITH
THE PLOW, NOVEMBER, 1785[1]

Wee, sleekit,° cow'rin', tim'rous beastie,   *sleek*
O, what a panic's in thy breastie!
Thou need na start awa sae hasty,
            Wi' bickering brattle![2]

1. Burns's brother said that this poem   scribes.
was composed on the occasion it de-   2. With headlong scamper.

5 I wad be laith° to rin an' chase thee   *loath*
       Wi' murd'ring pattle!°   *plowstaff*

I'm truly sorry man's dominion
Has broken Nature's social union,
An' justifies that ill opinion
10   Which makes thee startle
At me, thy poor, earth-born companion,
       An' fellow mortal!

I doubt na, whiles,° but thou may thieve;   *sometimes*
What then? poor beastie, thou maun° live!   *must*
15 A daimen-icker in a thrave[3]
      'S a sma' request:
I'll get a blessin' wi' the lave,°   *remainder*
       And never miss 't!

Thy wee-bit housie, too, in ruin!
20 Its silly° wa's the win's are strewin'!   *feeble*
An' naething, now, to big° a new ane,   *build*
      O' foggage° green!   *moss*
An' bleak December's winds ensuin',
      Baith snell° an' keen!   *bitter*

25 Thou saw the fields laid bare and waste,
An' weary winter comin' fast,
An' cozie here, beneath the blast,
      Thou thought to dwell,
Till crash! the cruel coulter° passed   *cutter-blade*
30   Out-through thy cell.

That wee-bit heap o' leaves an' stibble°   *stubble*
Has cost thee mony a weary nibble!
Now thou's turned out, for a' thy trouble,
      But° house or hald,[4]   *without*
35 To thole° the winter's sleety dribble,   *endure*
      An' cranreuch° cauld!   *hoarfrost*

But Mousie, thou art no thy lane,[5]
In proving foresight may be vain:
The best-laid schemes o' mice an' men
40   Gang aft a-gley,[6]
An' lea'e us nought but grief an' pain,
      For promised joy.

Still thou art blest compared wi' me!
The present only toucheth thee:
45 But och! I backward cast my e'e
      On prospects drear!
An' forward though I canna see,
      I guess an' fear!

1785   1786

3. An occasional ear in 24 sheaves.   5. Not alone.
4. Hold, holding (i.e., land).   6. Go oft **awry**.

Green Grow the Rashes[7]

Chorus
Green grow the rashes, O;
    Green grow the rashes, O;
The sweetest hours that e'er I spend,
Are spent amang the lasses, O!

5   There's nought but care on ev'ry han',
    In ev'ry hour that passes, O:
What signifies the life o' man,
An' 'twere na for the lasses, O.
                    (*Chorus*)

The warly° race may riches chase,   worldly
10   An' riches still may fly them, O;
An' though at last they catch them fast,
    Their hearts can ne'er enjoy them, O.
                    (*Chorus*)

But gie me a canny° hour at e'en,   quiet
My arms about my dearie, O;
15   An' warly cares, an' warly men,
    May a' gae tapsalteerie,° O!   topsy-turvy
                    (*Chorus*)

For you sae douce,° ye sneer at this,   sober
    Ye're nought but senseless asses, O:
The wisest man[8] the warl' saw,
20   He dearly loved the lasses, O.
                    (*Chorus*)

Auld nature swears, the lovely dears
    Her noblest work she classes, O:
Her prentice han' she tried on man,
    An' then she made the lasses, O.
                    (*Chorus*)

1784   1787

Holy Willie's Prayer[1]

O thou, wha in the Heavens dost dwell,
    Wha, as it pleases best thysel',

7. Burns's revision of a song long current in a number of versions, most of
them bawdy. "Rashes": rushes.
8. King Solomon.

1. This satire, in the form of a dramatic
monologue, was inspired by one William
Fisher, a self-righteous elder in the
parish of Mauchline, and is directed

Sends ane to heaven and ten to hell,
    A' for thy glory,
5 And no for ony guid or ill
    They've done afore thee!

I bless and praise thy matchless might,
Whan thousands thou hast left in night,
That I am here afore thy sight,
10   For gifts an' grace
A burnin' an' a shinin' light,
    To a' this place.

What was I, or my generation,
That I should get sic exaltation?
15 I, wha deserve most just damnation,
    For broken laws,
Sax° thousand years 'fore my creation,   *six*
    Through Adam's cause.

When frae my mither's womb I fell,
20 Thou might hae plungéd me in hell,
To gnash my gums, to weep and wail,
    In burnin' lakes,
Where damnéd devils roar and yell,
    Chained to their stakes;

25 Yet I am here a chosen sample,
To show thy grace is great and ample;
I'm here a pillar in thy temple,
    Strong as a rock,
A guide, a buckler, an example
30   To a' thy flock.

O Lord, thou kens what zeal I bear,
When drinkers drink, and swearers swear,
And singin' there and dancin' here,
    Wi' great an' sma':
35 For I am keepit by thy fear
    Free frae them a'.

But yet, O Lord! confess I must
At times I'm fashed° wi' fleshly lust;   *troubled*
An' sometimes too, in warldly trust,
40   Vile self gets in;
But thou remembers we are dust,
    Defiled in sin.

O Lord! yestreen, thou kens, wi' Meg—
Thy pardon I sincerely beg;
45 O! may't ne'er be a livin' plague

against a basic Calvinist tenet of the
old Scottish kirk. Holy Willie assumes
that he is one of the small minority,
God's "elect"; in other words, that he
has been predestined for grace, no matter what he does in this vale of tears.

To my dishonor,
An' I'll ne'er lift a lawless leg
　　　Again upon her.

Besides I farther maun° allow,　　　　　　　　　　*must*
50 Wi' Lizzie's lass, three times I trow—
But, Lord, that Friday I was fou,°　　　　　　　　*drunk*
　　　When I cam near her,
Or else thou kens thy servant true
　　　Wad never steer°her.　　　　　　　　　　　*molest*

55 May be thou lets this fleshly thorn
Beset thy servant e'en and morn
Lest he owre high and proud should turn,
　　　　　That he's sae gifted;
If sae, thy hand maun e'en be borne,
60 　　　　　Until thou lift it.

Lord, bless thy chosen in this place,
For here thou hast a chosen race;
But God confound their stubborn face,
　　　　　And blast their name,
65 Wha bring thy elders to disgrace
　　　An' public shame.

Lord, mind Gawn Hamilton's² deserts,
He drinks, an' swears, an' plays at cartes,°　　　　*cards*
Yet has sae mony takin' arts
70 　　　　　Wi' grit° an' sma',　　　　　　　　*great*
Frae God's ain priest the people's hearts
　　　He steals awa'.

An' when we chastened him therefor,
Thou kens how he bred sic a splore°　　　　　　*disturbance*
75 As set the warld in a roar
　　　　　O' laughin' at us;
Curse thou his basket and his store,
　　　　　Kail° and potatoes.　　　　　　　　*broth*

Lord, hear my earnest cry an' pray'r,
80 Against that presbyt'ry o' Ayr;
Thy strong right hand, Lord, make it bare
　　　　　Upo' their heads;
Lord, weigh it down, and dinna spare,
　　　For their misdeeds.

85 O Lord my God, that glib-tongued Aiken,
My very heart and soul are quakin',
To think how we stood sweatin', shakin',
　　　　　An' pissed wi' dread,
While he, wi' hingin'° lips and snakin',°　　　*hanging / sneering*
90 　　　　　Held up his head.

2. Burns's friend Gavin Hamilton, whom "Holy Willie" had brought up on moral charges before the Kirk Session of the Presbytery of Ayr; Hamilton was successfully defended by his counsel, Robert Aiken (referred to in line 85).

Lord, in the day of vengeance try him;
Lord, visit them wha did employ him,
And pass not in thy mercy by them,
      No hear their pray'r:
95 But, for thy people's sake, destroy them,
      And dinna spare.

But, Lord, remember me and mine
Wi' mercies temp'ral and divine,
That I for gear° and grace may shine   *goods, wealth*
100   Excelled by nane,
And a' the glory shall be thine,
      Amen, Amen!

1785   1789, 1799

Willie Brewed a Peck o' Maut[1]

O Willie brewed a peck o' maut,
    And Rob and Allan cam to see:
Three blither hearts, that lee-lang° night,   *livelong*
    Ye wad na found in Christendie.

Chorus

5 We are na fou,° we're no that fou,   *drunk*
    But just a drappie° in our e'e;   *drop*
The cock may craw, the day may daw,
    And ay we'll taste the barley bree.°   *brew*

Here are we met, three merry boys,
10   Three merry boys, I trow, are we;
And mony a night we've merry been,
    And mony mae° we hope to be!   *more*
      (*Chorus*)

It is the moon, I ken her horn,
    That's blinkin' in the lift° sae hie;°   *air / high*
15 She shines sae bright to wyle° us hame,   *entice*
    But, by my sooth she'll wait a wee.
      (*Chorus*)

Wha first shall rise to gang awa,
    A cuckold, coward loun° is he!   *scoundrel*
Wha first beside his chair shall fa',
20   He is the king amang us three!
      (*Chorus*)

1790

1. This best-known of Burns's many efforts in the ancient tradition of the drinking song was written on the occasion of a "joyous meeting" of Burns and Allan Masterton "with Mr. Wm. Nicol, of the High School, Edinburgh." "Maut" is malt—i.e., barley allowed to germinate in water, a basic ingredient both in beer and in Scotch whisky.

Tam o' Shanter[1]

Of Brownyis and of Bogillis full is this Buke.
—Gavin Douglas

When chapman billies[2] leave the street,
And drouthy° neebors neebors meet,   *thirsty*
As market days are wearing late,
An' folk begin to tak the gate;°   *road*
5 While we sit bousing at the nappy,°   *strong ale*
An' getting fou° and unco° happy,   *drunk / very*
We think na on the lang Scots miles,
The mosses, waters, slaps,° and stiles,   *gaps (in walls)*
That lie between us and our hame,
10 Where sits our sulky sullen dame,
Gathering her brows like gathering storm,
Nursing her wrath to keep it warm.
 This truth fand° honest Tam o' Shanter,   *found*
As he frae Ayr ae night did canter
15 (Auld Ayr, wham ne'er a town surpasses
For honest men and bonnie lasses).
 O Tam! hadst thou but been sae wise
As ta'en thy ain wife Kate's advice!
She tauld thee weel thou was a skellum,[3]
20 A bletherin', blusterin', drunken blellum;°   *babbler*
That frae November till October,
Ae market day thou was na sober;
That ilka melder[4] wi' the miller
Thou sat as lang as thou had siller;°   *silver, money*
25 That every naig° was ca'd° a shoe on,   *nag / driven*
The smith and thee gat roarin' fou on;
That at the Lord's house, even on Sunday,
Thou drank wi' Kirkton Jean till Monday.
She prophesied that, late or soon,
30 Thou would be found deep drowned in Doon;

1. This poem was written to order for a book on Scottish antiquities, and was based on a witch story told about Alloway Kirk, an old ruin near Burns's house in Ayr. As a mock-heroic rendering of folk material, *Tam o' Shanter* is comparable to the Nun's Priest's Tale of Chaucer, in excellence as well as genre. Burns recognized that the poem was his most sustained and finished artistic performance; it discovers "a spice of roguish waggery," but also shows "a force of genius and a finishing polish that I despair of ever excelling." The verve and seriocomic sympathy with which Burns manages this misadventure of a confirmed tippler won Wordsworth, a water-drinker, to passionate advocacy against the moralists who objected to Burns's ribaldry: "Who but some impenetrable dunce or narrow-minded puritan in works of art ever read without delight the picture which he has drawn of the convivial exaltation of the rustic adventurer, Tam o' Shanter? * * * I pity him who cannot perceive that, in all this, though there was no moral purpose, there is a moral effect" (letter to a friend of Burns, 1816).
2. Peddler fellows.
3. Good-for-nothing; "bletherin' ": chattering.
4. A "melder" is the amount of corn processed at a single grinding. "Ilka": every.

Or catched wi' warlocks° in the mirk°　　　　　*wizards / night*
By Alloway's auld haunted kirk.
　　Ah, gentle dames! it gars° me greet°　　　　　*makes / weep*
To think how mony counsels sweet,
35　How mony lengthened sage advices,
The husband frae the wife despises!
　　But to our tale: Ae market night,
Tam had got planted unco right,
Fast by an ingle,° bleezing° finely,　　　　　*fireplace / blazing*
40　Wi' reaming swats,⁵ that drank divinely;
And at his elbow, Souter° Johnny,　　　　　*Cobbler*
His ancient, trusty, drouthy crony;
Tam lo'ed him like a very brither;
They had been fou for weeks thegither.
45　The night drave on wi' sangs and clatter,
And ay the ale was growing better:
The landlady and Tam grew gracious,
Wi' favors secret, sweet, and precious;
The souter tauld his queerest stories;
50　The landlord's laugh was ready chorus:
The storm without might rair° and rustle,　　　　　*roar*
Tam did na mind the storm a whistle.
　　Care, mad to see a man sae happy,
E'en drowned himsel amang the nappy.
55　As bees flee hame wi' lades o' treasure,
The minutes winged their way wi' pleasure;
Kings may be blest, but Tam was glorious,
O'er a' the ills o' life victorious!
　　But pleasures are like poppies spread—
60　You seize the flow'r, its bloom is shed;
Or like the snow falls in the river—
A moment white, then melts forever;
Or like the borealis race,
That flit ere you can point their place;
65　Or like the rainbow's lovely form
Evanishing amid the storm.
Nae man can tether time nor tide;
The hour approaches Tam maun° ride;　　　　　*must*
That hour, o' night's black arch the keystane,
70　That dreary hour, he mounts his beast in;
And sic a night he taks the road in,
As ne'er poor sinner was abroad in.
　　The wind blew as 'twad blawn its last;
The rattling show'rs rose on the blast;
75　The speedy gleams the darkness swallowed;
Loud, deep, and lang, the thunder bellowed:
That night, a child might understand,
The Deil had business on his hand.
　　Weel mounted on his gray mare, Meg,

5. Foaming new ale.

80 A better never lifted leg,
Tam skelpit° on through dub° and mire,   *slapped / puddle*
Despising wind, and rain, and fire;
Whiles holding fast his gude blue bonnet;
Whiles crooning o'er some auld Scots sonnet;
85 Whiles glowring° round wi' prudent cares,   *staring*
Lest bogles° catch him unawares.   *hobgoblins*
Kirk-Alloway was drawing nigh,
Whare ghaists° and houlets° nightly cry.   *ghosts / owls*
 By this time he was cross the ford,
90 Where in the snaw the chapman smoored;[6]
And past the birks° and meikle stane,[7]   *birches*
Where drunken Charlie brak 's neck bane;
And through the whins,[8] and by the cairn,[8a]
Where hunters fand the murdered bairn;
95 And near the thorn, aboon the well,
Where Mungo's mither hanged hersel.
Before him Doon pours all his floods;
The doubling storm roars through the woods;
The lightnings flash from pole to pole;
100 Near and more near the thunders roll:
When, glimmering through the groaning trees,
Kirk-Alloway seemed in a bleeze;
Through ilka bore° the beams were glancing;   *hole*
And loud resounded mirth and dancing.
105 Inspiring bold John Barleycorn!
What dangers thou canst make us scorn!
Wi' tippenny,[9] we fear nae evil;
Wi' usquebae,° we'll face the devil!   *whisky*
The swats sae reamed in Tammie's noddle,
110 Fair play, he cared na deils a boddle![1]
But Maggie stood right sair astonished,
Till, by the heel and hand admonished,
She ventured forward on the light;
And, vow! Tam saw an unco° sight!   *strange*
115 Warlocks and witches in a dance!
Nae cotillon brent° new frae France,   *brand*
But hornpipes, jigs, strathspeys,[2] and reels,
Put life and mettle in their heels.
A winnock-bunker° in the east,   **window seat**
120 There sat auld Nick, in shape o' beast—
A touzie tyke,[3] black, grim, and large!
To gie them music was his charge:
He screwed the pipes and gart° them skirl.°   **made / screech**
Till roof and rafters a' did dirl.°   **rattle**
125 Coffins stood round like open presses,

---

6. The peddler smothered.
7. Big stone.
8. Furze (an evergreen shrub).
8a. Stones heaped up as a memorial.
9. Twopenny (of drink).

1. I.e., he didn't care a farthing about devils (a "boddle" is a very small copper coin).
2. Slow Highland dance.
3. Shaggy dog.

That shawed the dead in their last dresses;
And by some devilish cantraip° sleight   *charm, trick*
Each in its cauld hand held a light,
By which heroic Tam was able
To note upon the haly° table   *holy*
A murderer's banes in gibbet airns;°   *irons*
Twa span-lang,⁴ wee, unchristened bairns;
A thief new-cutted frae the rape°—   *rope*
Wi' his last gasp his gab° did gape;   *mouth*
Five tomahawks, wi' blude red rusted;
Five scimitars, wi' murder crusted;
A garter, which a babe had strangled;
A knife, a father's throat had mangled,
Whom his ain son o' life bereft—
The gray hairs yet stack to the heft;
Wi' mair of horrible and awfu',
Which even to name wad be unlawfu'.
    As Tammie glowred, amazed, and curious,
The mirth and fun grew fast and furious:
The piper loud and louder blew;
The dancers quick and quicker flew;
They reeled, they set, they crossed, they cleekit,°   *joined hands*
Till ilka carlin° swat and reekit,   *old woman*
And coost her duddies to the wark,⁵
And linkit° at it in her sark!°   *tripped lightly / shirt*
    Now Tam, O Tam! had thae been queans,°   *girls*
A' plump and strapping in their teens;
Their sarks, instead o' creeshie flannen,⁶
Been snaw-white seventeen hunder ⁷ linen!
Thir° breeks o' mine, my only pair,   *these*
That ance were plush, o' gude blue hair,
I wad hae gi'en them off my hurdies,°   *buttocks*
For ae blink o' the bonnie burdies!°   *maidens*
    But withered beldams, auld and droll,
Rigwoodie° hags wad spean° a foal,   *bony / wean*
Louping° and flinging on a crummock,°   *leaping / staff*
I wonder didna turn thy stomach.
    But Tam kent what was what fu' brawlie°   *finely*
There was ae winsome wench and walie°   *strapping*
That night enlisted in the core,°   *corps*
Lang after kent on Carrick shore!
(For mony a beast to dead she shot,
And perished mony a bonnie boat,
And shook baith meikle corn and bear,°   *barley*
And kept the countryside in fear.)
Her cutty° sark, o' Paisley harn,°   *short / yarn*
That while a lassie she had worn,
In longitude though sorely scanty,

4. Span-long (i.e., the distance from outstretched thumb to little finger).
5. Cast off her clothes for the work.
6. Greasy flannel.
7. Very fine linen, woven on a loom with 1700 strips.

It was her best, and she was vauntie.°   *proud*
175 Ah! little kent thy reverend grannie
That sark she coft° for her wee Nannie   *bought*
Wi' twa pund Scots ('twas a' her riches)
Wad ever graced a dance of witches!
But here my muse her wing maun cour;°   *lower*
180 Sic flights are far beyond her pow'r—
To sing how Nannie lap and flang
(A souple jade she was, and strang);
And how Tam stood, like ane bewitched,
And thought his very een enriched;
185 Even Satan glowred, and fidged fu' fain,[8]
And hotched° and blew wi' might and main: *jerked*
Till first ae caper, syne° anither,   *then*
Tam tint° his reason a' thegither,   *lost*
And roars out, "Weel done, Cutty-sark!"
190 And in an instant all was dark!
And scarcely had he Maggie rallied,
When out the hellish legion sallied.
As bees bizz out wi' angry fyke°   *fuss*
When plundering herds° assail their byke,°   *herdsmen / hive*
195 As open° pussie's mortal foes   *begin to bark*
When pop! she starts before their nose,
As eager runs the market crowd,
When "Catch the thief!" resounds aloud.
So Maggie runs; the witches follow,
200 Wi' mony an eldritch° skriech and hollow.   *unearthly*
Ah, Tam! ah, Tam! thou'll get thy fairin'!°   *deserts*
In hell they'll roast thee like a herrin'!
In vain thy Kate awaits thy comin'!
Kate soon will be a woefu' woman!
205 Now do thy speedy utmost, Meg,
And win the keystane o' the brig:°   *bridge*
There at them thou thy tail may toss,
A running stream they darena cross.
But ere the keystane she could make,
210 The fient a tail she had to shake![9]
For Nannie, far before the rest,
Hard upon noble Maggie pressed,
And flew at Tam wi' furious ettle;°   *intent*
But little wist she Maggie's mettle!
215 Ae spring brought off her master hale,°   *whole*
But left behind her ain gray tail:
The carlin claught° her by the rump,   *clutched*
And left poor Maggie scarce a stump.
Now, wha this tale o' truth shall read,
220 Each man and mother's son, take heed;
Whene'er to drink you are inclined,
Or cutty-sarks rin in your mind,

8. Fidgeted with pleasure.   9. I.e., she had no tail left at all.

Think! ye may buy the joys o'er dear;
Remember Tam o' Shanter's mare.

1790   1791

Afton Water[1]

Flow gently, sweet Afton, among thy green braes,
Flow gently, I'll sing thee a song in thy praise;
My Mary's asleep by thy murmuring stream,
Flow gently, sweet Afton, disturb not her dream.

Thou stock-dove whose echo resounds through the glen,   5
Ye wild whistling blackbirds in yon thorny den,
Thou green-crested lapwing, thy screaming forbear,
I charge you disturb not my slumbering fair.

How lofty, sweet Afton, thy neighboring hills,
Far marked with the courses of clear winding rills;   10
There daily I wander as noon rises high,
My flocks and my Mary's sweet cot[2] in my eye.

How pleasant thy banks and green valleys below,
Where wild in the woodlands the primroses blow;
There oft as mild evening weeps over the lea,   15
The sweet-scented birk[3] shades my Mary and me.

Thy crystal stream, Afton, how lovely it glides,
And winds by the cot where my Mary resides;
How wanton thy waters her snowy feet lave,
As gathering sweet flowerets she stems thy clear wave.   20

Flow gently, sweet Afton, among thy green braes,
Flow gently, sweet river, the theme of my lays;
My Mary's asleep by thy murmuring stream,
Flow gently, sweet Afton, disturb not her dream.

1789   1792

Ae Fond Kiss[4]

Ae fond kiss, and then we sever!
Ae fareweel, and then forever!
Deep in heart-wrung tears I'll pledge thee,
Warring sighs and groans I'll wage thee.
Who shall say that fortune grieves him   5

1. The Afton is a small river in Ayrshire. "Braes": slopes, hillsides.
2. Cottage.
3. Birch.
4. Written to Mrs. M'Lehose, with whom Burns had been engaged in a sentimental correspondence, on the occasion of her departure to rejoin her husband in the West Indies.

While the star of hope she leaves him?
Me, nae cheerfu' twinkle lights me,
Dark despair around benights me.

I'll ne'er blame my partial fancy,
Naething could resist my Nancy;   10
But to see her was to love her,
Love but her, and love forever.
Had we never loved sae kindly,
Had we never loved sae blindly,
Never met—or never parted,   15
We had ne'er been broken-hearted.

Fare thee weel, thou first and fairest!
Fare thee weel, thou best and dearest!
Thine be ilka joy and treasure,
Peace, enjoyment, love, and pleasure!   20
Ae fond kiss, and then we sever;
Ae fareweel, alas, forever!
Deep in heart-wrung tears I'll pledge thee,
Warring sighs and groans I'll wage thee.

1791   1792

Ye Flowery Banks[1]

Ye flowery banks o' bonnie Doon,
   How can ye blume sae fair?
How can ye chant, ye little birds,
   And I sae fu' o' care?

5 Thou'll break my heart, thou bonnie bird,
   That sings upon the bough;
Thou minds me o' the happy days,
   When my fause° luve was true.   *false*

Thou'll break my heart, thou bonnie bird,
10   That sings beside thy mate;
For sae I sat, and sae I sang,
   And wist na o' my fate.

Aft hae I roved by bonnie Doon,
   To see the woodbine twine,
15 And ilka° bird sang o' its luve,   *every*
   And sae did I o' mine.

Wi' lightsome heart I pu'd° a rose   *pulled*
   Frae aff its thorny tree;
But my fause luver staw° my rose,   *stole*
20   And left the thorn wi'me.

1. Burns wrote several versions of this song; the present one is the simplest and the best.

Wi' lightsome heart I pu'd a rose
    Upon a morn in June;
And sae I flourished on the morn,
    And sae was pu'd ere noon.

1792, 1808

Scots, Wha Hae[2]

Scots, wha hae wi' Wallace[3] bled,
Scots, wham Bruce has aften led,
Welcome to your gory bed,
        Or to victorie.

Now's the day, and now's the hour;   5
See the front o' battle lour;
See approach proud Edward's power—
        Chains and slaverie!

Wha will be a traitor-knave?
Wha can fill a coward's grave?   10
Wha sae base as be a slave?
        Let him turn and flee!

Wha for Scotland's King and law
Freedom's sword will strongly draw,
Freeman stand, or freeman fa',   15
        Let him follow me!

By oppression's woes and pains!
By your sons in servile chains!
We will drain our dearest veins,
        But they shall be free!   20

Lay the proud usurpers low!
Tyrants fall in every foe!
Liberty's in every blow!
        Let us do, or die!

1793   1794, 1815

For A' That and A' That[1]

Is there, for honest poverty,
    That hangs his head, and a' that?

2. In this best-known of Burns's patriotic songs, Robert Bruce is addressing his army before the great victory at Bannockburn (1314), at which the English were driven from Scotland.
3. Sir William Wallace (ca. 1272–1305), the great Scottish warrior in the wars against the English.
1. Burns's vigorous affirmation of the radical ideas of liberty, equality, and fraternity may have been based on Tom Paine's *Rights of Man*.

The coward slave, we pass him by,
　We dare be poor for a' that!
5　　For a' that, and a' that,
　　　Our toils obscure, and a' that;
　The rank is but the guinea's stamp,
　　The man's the gowd° for a' that.　　　　　　　*gold*

What though on hamely fare we dine,
10　Wear hodden-gray,[2] and a' that;
Gie fools their silks, and knaves their wine,
　A man's a man for a' that:
　　For a' that, and a' that,
　　　Their tinsel show, and a' that;
15　　The honest man, though e'er sae poor,
　　Is king o' men for a' that.

Ye see yon birkie,° ca'd a lord,　　　　*brisk young fellow*
　Wha struts, and stares, and a' that;
Though hundreds worship at his word,
20　He's but a coof° for a' that:　　　　　　　*dolt*
　　For a' that, and a' that,
　　　His riband, star, and a' that,
　　The man of independent mind,
　　He looks and laughs at a' that.

25 A prince can mak a belted knight,
　A marquis, duke, and a' that;
But an honest man's aboon° his might,　　　*above*
　Guid faith he mauna fa' that![3]
　　For a' that, and a' that,
30　　　Their dignities, and a' that,
　　The pith o' sense, and pride o' worth,
　　Are higher rank than a' that.

Then let us pray that come it may,
　As come it will for a' that,
35 That sense and worth, o'er a' the earth,
　May bear the gree,[4] and a' that.
　　For a' that, and a' that,
　　　It's coming yet, for a' that,
　　That man to man the warld o'er
40　　Shall brothers be for a' that.

1794　　　　　　　　　　　　　　　　　1795, 1799

A Red, Red Rose[1]

O My Luve's like a red, red rose,
　That's newly sprung in June;

---

2. A coarse cloth of undyed wool.
3. Must not claim that.
4. Win the prize.

1. Like many of Burns's songs, this one incorporates elements from several current folk songs.

O My Luve's like the melodie
　　That's sweetly played in tune.

As fair art thou, my bonnie lass,　　　　　　　5
　　So deep in luve am I;
And I will luve thee still, my dear,
　　Till a' the seas gang dry.

Till a' the seas gang dry, my dear,
　　And the rocks melt wi' the sun:　　　　　10
O I will love thee still, my dear,
　　While the sands o' life shall run.

And fare thee weel, my only luve,
　　And fare thee weel awhile!
And I will come again, my luve,　　　　　　15
　　Though it were ten thousand mile.

　　　　　　　　　　　　　　　　　　1796

Auld Lang Syne[1]

Should auld acquaintance be forgot,
　　And never brought to min'?
Should auld acquaintance be forgot,
　　And days o' lang syne?

　　　　　Chorus
5　　For auld lang syne, my dear,
　　　　For auld lang syne,
　　　　We'll tak a cup o' kindness yet,
　　　　For auld lang syne.

We twa hae run about the braes,°　　　　　　*slopes*
10　　And pu'd the gowans° fine,　　　　　　　*daisies*
But we've wandered mony a weary foot,
　　Sin' auld lang syne.
　　　　　　(*Chorus*)

We twa hae paidled i' the burn,°　　　　　　*stream*
　　From morning sun till dine;°　　　*dinner, noon*
15 But seas between us braid° hae roared,　　　*broad*
　　Sin' auld lang syne.
　　　　　　(*Chorus*)

And there's a hand, my trusty fiere,°　　　　*friend*
　　And gie's a hand o' thine;
And we'll tak a right gude-willie waught,[2]
20　　For auld lang syne.
　　　　　　(*Chorus*)

And surely ye'll be° your pint-stowp,°　　*pay for / pint-cup*
　　And surely I'll be mine;

1. Long ago.　　　　　　2. A very hearty swig.

And we'll tak a cup o' kindness yet,
For auld lang syne.

(*Chorus*)

1788

1796

WILLIAM BLAKE

(1757–1827)

1783:   *Poetical Sketches,* his first book of poems.
1794:   *Songs of Innocence and of Experience.*
1804–20: The two last and greatest "prophetic" poems,
Milton and *Jerusalem.*

What Blake called his "Spiritual Life" was as varied, free, and dramatic as his "Corporeal Life" was simple, limited, and unadventurous. His father was a London haberdasher. His only formal education was in art: at the age of 10 he entered a drawing school and later studied for a time at the school of the Royal Academy of Arts. At 14 he apprenticed for seven years to a well-known engraver, James Basire, read widely in his free time, and began to try his hand at poetry. At 24 he married Catherine Boucher, daughter of a market gardener. She was then illiterate, but Blake taught her to read and to help him in his engraving and printing. In the early and somewhat sentimentalized biographies, Catherine is represented as an ideal wife for an unorthodox and impecunious genius. Blake, however, must have been a trying domestic partner, and his vehement attacks on the torment caused by a possessive, jealous female will, which reached a climax in 1793 and remained prominent in his writings for another decade, probably reflect a troubled period at home. The couple were childless.

The Blakes for a time enjoyed a moderate prosperity while Blake gave drawing lessons, illustrated books, and engraved designs made by other artists. When the demand for his work slackened, Blake in 1800 moved to a cottage at Felpham, on the Sussex seacoast, under the patronage of the wealthy poetaster, biographer, and amateur of the arts, William Hayley, who with the best of narrow intentions tried to transform Blake into a conventional artist and breadwinner. But the caged eagle soon rebelled. Hayley, Blake wrote, "is the Enemy of my Spiritual Life while he pretends to be the Friend of my Corporeal."

At Felpham in 1803 occurred an event that left a permanent mark on Blake's mind and art. He had an altercation with one John Schofield, a private in the Royal Dragoons. Blake ordered the soldier out of his garden and, when the soldier replied with threats and curses against Blake and his wife, pushed him the fifty yards to the inn where he was quartered. Schofield brought charges that Blake had uttered seditious statements about King and country. Since England was at war with France, sedition was a hanging offense. Blake was acquitted; an event, according to a newspaper account, "which so gratified the auditory that the court was * * * thrown into an uproar by their noisy exultations." Nevertheless Schofield, his fellow-soldier Cock, and other participants in the trial haunted Blake's imagination and were enlarged to demonic characters who play a sinister role in *Jerusalem*. The event exacerbated Blake's sense that ominous forces were at work in the contemporary world and led him to complicate the symbolic obliquities by which he veiled the unorthodoxy of his religious and moral opinions, and the radicalism of the many allusions to contemporary affairs that he worked into his poems.

After three years at Felpham Blake moved back to London, determined to follow his "Divine Vision" though it meant a life of isolation, misunderstanding, and poverty. When his one great bid for public recognition, a one-man show put on in 1809, proved a total failure, Blake passed into almost complete obscurity. Only when he was in his 60's did he finally attract a small but devoted group of young painters who served as an audience for his work and his talk. Blake's old age was serene, self-confident, and joyous, largely free from the bursts of irascibility with which he had earlier responded to the shallowness and blindness of the English public. He died in his seventieth year.

Blake's first book of poems, *Poetical Sketches*, which he had printed when he was 26 years old, showed his dissatisfaction with the reigning poetic tradition and his restless quest for new forms and techniques. For lyric models he turned back to the Elizabethan and early 17th-century poets, to the Ossianic poems, Collins, Thomas Chatterton, and other 18th-century writers outside the tradition of Pope; he also experimented with partial rhymes and novel rhythms and employed bold figures of speech that at times approximate symbols. In *Songs of Innocence* (1789) Blake inaugurated the method of publication he used for his later original works, a procedure he had partly invented. He covered a copper plate with acid-proof wax, engraved away the wax from a design that incorporated both text and pictorial illustration, then applied acid so that the design was left in relief. With this plate he printed a page, which he later colored with water colors by hand and bound with the other pages to make up a volume. The procedure of making the plates was laborious and time-consuming, and Blake struck off very few copies of his works; for example, of *Songs of Innocence and Experience* 27 copies (both complete and incomplete) are known to exist; of *The Book of Thel*, 15; of *The Marriage of Heaven and Hell*, 9; and of *Jerusalem*, 5. It must be remembered that to read Blake's poem in a printed text is to see only an abstraction from an integral and mutually illuminating combination of words and design.

In the *Songs of Innocence* Blake assumes the stance that he is writing "happy songs / Every child may joy to hear." They show the fallen world, however, as it appears to the limited view of a naïve and acquiescent innocence. The "contrary" vision is expressed in *Songs of Experience* (1794), which reveal an ugly and terrifying world of poverty, disease, prostitution, war, exploitation, and social, institutional, and sexual repression. In the best of these Songs, such as *The Tyger* and *London*, Blake achieved his mature lyric technique of compressed metaphor and symbol which explode into a multiplicity of reference.

Gradually Blake's symbolic thinking about human history and his personal experience of life and suffering articulated themselves in the "Giant Forms" and their actions, which constitute a complete mythology. As Los said, speaking for all imaginative artists, "I must Create a System or be enslaved by another Man's." This coherent but constantly altering and enlarging system composed the subject matter, first of Blake's "minor prophecies," completed by 1795, and then of the major prophetic books on which he continued working until about 1820: *The Four Zoas, Milton,* and *Jerusalem.*

In his 60's Blake gave up poetry to devote himself to pictorial art. In the course of his life he produced hundreds of paintings and engravings, many of them illustrations for the work of other poets, including a representation of Chaucer's Canterbury pilgrims, a superb set of designs for the Book of Job, and a series of illustrations of Dante, on which he was still hard at work when he died. At the time of his death Blake was little known as an artist and almost entirely unknown as a poet. In the mid-19th century he acquired a group of admirers among the Pre-Raphaelites, who regarded him as a precursor. Since the mid 1920's, Blake has finally come into his own, both in poetry and painting, as one of the most dedicated, intellectually challenging, and astonishingly original of artists.

The explication of Blake's cryptic and complex prophetic books has been the preoccupation of many scholars. Blake wrote them in the persona, or "voice," of "the Bard / Who Present, Past, & Future sees"—that is, as a British poet who follows Spenser, and especially Milton, in a lineage going back to the prophets of the Bible. "The Nature of my Work," he said, "is Visionary or Imaginative." What Blake meant by the key terms "vision" and "imagination," however is often misrepresented by taking literally what he, speaking the traditional language of his great predecessors, intended in a figurative sense. "That which can be made Explicit to the Idiot," Blake declared, "is not worth my care." Blake was a born ironist who enjoyed mystifying his well-meaning but literal-minded friends and who took a defiant pleasure in shocking the dull and complacent "angels" of his day by being deliberately outrageous in representing his work and opinions.

Blake declared that "all he knew was in the Bible," and that "The Old & New Testaments are the Great Code of Art." This is an exaggeration of the truth that all his prophetic writings deal, in various formulations, with some aspects of the over-all Biblical plot of the creation and fall of man, the history of the generations of man in the fallen world, redemption, and the promise of a recovery of Eden and of a New Jerusalem. These events, however, Blake interprets in what he calls "the spiritual sense." For such a procedure he had considerable precedent, not in the Neoplatonic and occult thinkers with which some modern commentators align him, but in the "spiritual" interpreters of the Bible among the radical Protestant sects in 17th- and 18th-century England. In *The French Revolution, America: A Prophecy, Europe: A Prophecy,* and the trenchant prophetic satire, *A Marriage of Heaven and Hell*—all of which Blake wrote in the early 1790's while he was an ardent supporter of the French Revolution—he, like Wordsworth,

Coleridge, Southey, and a number of radical English theologians, represented the contemporary Revolution as the purifying violence that, according to Biblical prophecy, was the portent of the imminent redemption of man and the world. In Blake's later writings, however, Orc, the fiery spirit of revolution, gives way as central personage to Los, the type of the visionary imagination in the fallen world—an index of Blake's shift of emphasis from apocalypse by revolution to apocalypse by imagination.

BLAKE'S MATURE MYTH

Blake's first attempt to articulate his full myth of mankind's present, past, and future was *The Four Zoas*, begun in 1796 or 1797. A passage from the opening statement of its theme exemplifies the long verse line (what Blake called "the march of long resounding strong heroic verse") in which he wrote all his Prophetic Books and will serve also to outline the myth, or visualizable imaginative form, in which Blake's thought embodied itself:

> Four Mighty Ones are in every man: a Perfect Unity
> Cannot Exist, but from the Universal Brotherhood of Eden,
> The Universal Man. To Whom be Glory Evermore, Amen.* * *
> Los was the fourth immortal starry one, & in the Earth
> Of a bright Universe Empery attended day & night
> Days & nights of revolving joy, Urthona was his name
> In Eden: in the Auricular Nerves of Human life
> Which is the Earth of Eden, he his Emanations propagated.* * *
>   Daughter of Beulah, Sing
> His fall into Division & his Resurrection to Unity.

Blake's mythical premise, or starting point, is not a transcendent God but "The Universal Man" who is himself God and who incorporates the cosmos as well. (Blake elsewhere describes this founding image as "the Human Form Divine" and names him "Albion.") The fall, in this myth, is not the fall of man away from God but a falling apart of primal man, a "fall into Division." In this event the original sin is what Blake calls "Selfhood," the attempt of an isolated part to be self-sufficient. The break-up of the all-inclusive Universal Man in Eden into exiled parts, it is evident, identifies the fall of man with the creation—both of man and of nature, as we ordinarily know them. Universal Man divides first into the "Four Mighty Ones" who are the Zoas, or chief powers and component aspects of man, and these in turn divide sexually into male Spectres and female Emanations. (Thus in the quoted passage the Zoa known in the unfallen state of Eden as Urthona, the imaginative power, separates into the form of Los in the fallen world.) In addition to Eden there are three successively lower "states" of being in the fallen world, which Blake calls Beulah (a pastoral condition of easy and relaxed innocence, without clash of "contraries"), Generation (the realm of common human experience, suffering, and conflicting contraries), and Ulro (Blake's hell, the lowest state, or limit, of bleak rationality, tyranny, static negation, and isolated Selfhood). The fallen world moves through the cycles of its history, successively approaching and falling away from redemption, until, by the agency of the Redeemer (who is equated with the human imagination and is most potently operative in the prophetic poet), it will culminate in an apocalypse. In terms of his controlling image of the Universal Man, Blake describes this apocalypse as a return to the original, undivided condition, "his Resurrection to Unity."

Blake, although he did not know it, shared with a number of contemporary German philosophers the point of view—it has in our own time become the prevailing point of view—that man's fall (or the malaise of modern culture) is essentially a mode of psychic disintegration and of resultant alienation from oneself, one's world, and one's fellow-men, and that man's hope of recovery lies in a process of reintegration. As an imaginative poet, however, Blake does not present this view in abstract conceptual terms, but embodies it in picturable agents acting out an epic plot. What is confusing to many readers is that Blake uses different ways of representing the same vision of man in the world. For example, Blake alternates with his image of the division of Primal Man, the representation of the fall as a catastrophic alteration, in individual human beings, from imaginative vision to physical eyesight. The result of this alteration was that the cosmos, which in the original mode of unified imaginative perception, had been beheld as human and one, came to be seen as a multitude of isolated individuals in a de-humanized and alien nature. Conversely, the apocalypse toward which Blake—the imaginative artist who as an individual represents the mythical type-figure Los—is always working, is to enable all men to break through to a restored unity of vision. To such a vision all beings, together with the world they inhabit, will again be perceived as sharing the one life and the one humanity of that "Universal Brotherhood," the Human Form Divine, who is imaged as creating such a universe by the very act of so envisioning it.

Blake decries, as the mythical being "Vala," what we ordinarily mean by "nature," the universe perceived by the senses. It is, however, a mistake to equate his views with ascetic other worldiness. Blake does not look forward to a consummation that will wipe out the fleshly and the natural world and replace it by a transcendental substitute. Blake maintained, on the contrary, that we achieve redemption by liberating and intensifying the bodily senses —as he said, by "an improvement of sensual enjoyment"—and by attaining and sustaining that mode of vision that does not cancel the fallen world, but transfigures it, by revealing the lineaments of its eternal imaginative form. That is what Blake means when, in *A Vision of the Last Judgment* (included below), he says that "The Nature of my Work is Visionary or Imaginative," and that in the moment of apocalyptic redemption "Error or Creation will be Burnt Up & then & not till then Truth or Eternity will appear. It is Burnt up the Moment Men cease to behold it." Accordingly, in the apocalypse that concludes *Jerusalem*, the reunion of Albion the Universal Man with Jerusalem, his emanation, is accompanied by a freeing of man's senses and results in the recovery of a lost mode of vision that sees a nature which, because it is humanized, is a place where individual men, united as One Man, can feel at home.

The text for all of Blake's writings is that of *The Poetry and Prose of William Blake*, edited by David V. Erdman and Harold Bloom (New York, 1965). Blake's erratic spelling and punctuation have been altered when the original form might mislead the reader.

From POETICAL SKETCHES[1]

Song

How sweet I roam'd from field to field,
    And tasted all the summer's pride,
'Till I the prince of love[2] beheld,
    Who in the sunny beams did glide!

He shew'd me lilies for my hair,   5
    And blushing roses for my brow;
He led me through his gardens fair,
    Where all his golden pleasures grow.

With sweet May dews my wings were wet,
    And Phoebus fir'd my vocal rage;[3]   10
He caught me in his silken net,
    And shut me in his golden cage.

He loves to sit and hear me sing,
    Then, laughing, sports and plays with me;
Then stretches out my golden wing,   15
    And mocks my loss of liberty.

                         1783

To the Evening Star

Thou fair-hair'd angel of the evening,
Now, while the sun rests on the mountains, light
Thy bright torch of love;[4] thy radiant crown
Put on, and smile upon our evening bed!
Smile on our loves; and, while thou drawest the   5
Blue curtains of the sky, scatter thy silver dew
On every flower that shuts its sweet eyes
In timely sleep. Let thy west wind sleep on

1. *Poetical Sketches*, Blake's only volume of poems to be set in type, went to press in 1783, but was never put on sale. A preface written by an anonymous friend apologized for the poems on the ground that they had been composed between the ages of 12 and 20. Although, like the work of other youthful poets, they echo earlier writers (especially Spenser, Shakespeare, and Milton), many of them show remarkable originality. Some are radical experiments in meter and rhyme; *To the Evening Star* is a sonnet without rhyme, and shows great boldness in its use of metaphor (lines 8–10); while in this same sonnet (lines 11–14) and in the *Song* ("How sweet I roam'd") and *Mad Song*, the images begin to assume the added reach of meaning that characterizes Blake's mature symbolism.
2. In Greek myth, Eros or Cupid.
3. Fervor.
4. The evening star is Venus, goddess of love.

The lake; speak silence with thy glimmering eyes,
And wash the dusk with silver. Soon, full soon,   10
Dost thou withdraw; then the wolf rages wide,
And the lion glares thro' the dun forest:
The fleeces of our flocks are cover'd with
Thy sacred dew: protect them with thine influence.[5]

1783

Song[6]

Memory, hither come,
    And tune your merry notes;
And, while upon the wind,
    Your music floats,
I'll pore upon the stream,   5
Where sighing lovers dream,
And fish for fancies as they pass
Within the watery glass.

I'll drink of the clear stream,
    And hear the linnet's song;   10
And there I'll lie and dream
    The day along:
And, when night comes, I'll go
    To places fit for woe;
Walking along the darken'd valley,   15
    With silent Melancholy.

1783

Mad Song[7]

The wild winds weep,
    And the night is a-cold;
Come hither, Sleep,
    And my griefs infold:
But lo! the morning peeps   5
    Over the eastern steeps,
And the rustling birds of dawn
    The earth do scorn.

---

5. In astrology, the technical term for the occult power of stars over men.
6. Cf. *Under the Greenwood Tree* in *As You Like It* II.v.
7. Cf. the songs of the Fool in Shakespeare's great scene of madness and incipient madness in *King Lear*, Act. III. In a marginal comment on Spurzheim's *Observations on Insanity* (1817), Blake wrote: "Cowper came to me & said, 'O that I were insane always; I will never rest. * * * You retain health & yet are as mad as any of us all—over us all—mad as a refuge from unbelief—from Bacon Newton & Locke.'" (Cowper, like the other 18th-century poets, Christopher Smart and William Collins, went genuinely insane.)

Lo! to the vault
  Of pavéd heaven,   10
With sorrow fraught
  My notes are driven:
They strike the ear of night,
  Make weep the eyes of day;
They make mad the roaring winds,   15
  And the tempests play.

Like a fiend in a cloud
  With howling woe,
After night I do croud,
  And with night will go;   20
I turn my back to the east,
From whence comforts have increas'd;
For light doth seize my brain
With frantic pain.

                            1783

To the Muses

Whether on Ida's[8] shady brow,
  Or in the chambers of the East,
The chambers of the sun, that now
  From antient melody have ceas'd;

Whether in Heav'n ye wander fair,   5
  Or the green corners of the earth,
Or the blue regions of the air,
  Where the melodious winds have birth;

Whether on chrystal rocks ye rove,
  Beneath the bosom of the sea   10
Wand'ring in many a coral grove,
  Fair Nine,[9] forsaking Poetry!

How have you left the antient love
  That bards of old enjoy'd in you![10]
The languid strings do scarcely move!   15
  The sound is forc'd, the notes are few!

                            1783

8. Ida is a mountain in southern Phrygia, celebrated in classical mythology.
9. The nine Muses.
10. The poem is Blake's lament, in the diction of latter 18-century poetry, over the failure of the inspiration of the "bards," the older British poet-prophets.

From Songs of Innocence and of Experience

SHEWING THE TWO CONTRARY STATES OF THE HUMAN SOUL

From Songs of Innocence[1]

1789

The Author & Printer   W Blake

Introduction

Piping down the valleys wild
Piping songs of pleasant glee
On a cloud I saw a child,
And he laughing said to me,

"Pipe a song about a Lamb";   5
So I piped with merry chear;
"Piper pipe that song again"—
So I piped, he wept to hear.

"Drop thy pipe thy happy pipe
Sing thy songs of happy chear";   10
So I sung the same again
While he wept with joy to hear.

"Piper sit thee down and write
In a book that all may read"—
So he vanish'd from my sight.   15
And I pluck'd a hollow reed,

And I made a rural pen,
And I stain'd the water clear,
And I wrote my happy songs
Every child may joy to hear.   20

1789

1. *Songs of Innocence* was etched in 1789 and in 1794 was combined with other poems under the title above. Innocence is the state of the soul which, in these poems, is represented by the naïve outlook of the child who believes what he is told by his elders, and takes appearance for the reality and the best aspect of things for the whole truth. A number of the Songs represent this state in the mode of a pastoral or protected world. In other Songs, however, such as *The Chimney Sweeper* and *Holy Thursday,* a contrary possibility intrudes its ironic perspective, to reveal how precarious is the ignorantly innocent outlook upon the world.

But children need to grow up, and the state of innocence needs to yield to that of experience, which sees as real the world of materialism, poverty, oppression, prostitution, disease, and war, epitomized in the ghastly city of modern London. Some of the individual songs of innocence have a matched counterpart, or "contrary," in a terrifying song of experience; thus the meek lamb is replaced by the flaming, wrathful tiger. In Blake's later writings the "contrary states" become a dialectic of contraries, according to which naïve innocence must necessarily pass through and assimilate the opposing state of experience if it is to move on, by an act of imagination, to the third state, comprehending but transcending both the others, which he called "organized innocence."

❙ The Lamb ✓

Little Lamb, who made thee?
Dost thou know who made thee?
Gave thee life & bid thee feed,
By the stream & o'er the mead;
Gave thee clothing of delight,   5
Softest clothing wooly bright;
Gave thee such a tender voice,
Making all the vales rejoice!
Little Lamb who made thee?
Dost thou know who made thee?   10

Little Lamb I'll tell thee,
Little Lamb I'll tell thee!
He is calléd by thy name,
For he calls himself a Lamb:
He is meek & he is mild,   15
He became a little child:
I a child & thou a lamb,
We are calléd by his name.
Little Lamb God bless thee.
Little Lamb God bless thee.   20
1789

2 The Divine Image ✓

To Mercy, Pity, Peace, and Love,
All pray in their distress:
And to these virtues of delight
Return their thankfulness.

For Mercy, Pity, Peace, and Love,   5
Is God, our father dear:
And Mercy, Pity, Peace, and Love,
Is Man, his child and care.

For Mercy has a human heart,
Pity, a human face: 10
And Love, the human form divine,
And Peace, the human dress.

Then every man of every clime,
That prays in his distress,
Prays to the human form divine,   15
Love, Mercy, Pity, Peace.

And all must love the human form,
In heathen, Turk, or Jew.
Where Mercy, Love, & Pity dwell,
There God is dwelling too.   20
1789

The Chimney Sweeper

When my mother died I was very young,
And my father sold me while yet my tongue
Could scarcely cry " 'weep! 'weep! 'weep! 'weep!" [2]
So your chimneys I sweep & in soot I sleep.

There's little Tom Dacre, who cried when his head   5
That curl'd like a lambs back, was shav'd, so I said,
"Hush, Tom! never mind it, for when your head's bare,
You know that the soot cannot spoil your white hair."

And so he was quiet, & that very night,
As Tom was a-sleeping he had such a sight!   10
That thousands of sweepers, Dick, Joe, Ned, & Jack,
Were all of them lock'd up in coffins of black;

And by came an Angel who had a bright key,
And he open'd the coffins & set them all free;
Then down a green plain, leaping, laughing they run,   15
And wash in a river and shine in the Sun;

Then naked & white, all their bags left behind,
They rise upon clouds, and sport in the wind.
And the Angel told Tom, if he'd be a good boy,
He'd have God for his father & never want joy.   20

And so Tom awoke; and we rose in the dark
And got with our bags & our brushes to work.
Tho' the morning was cold, Tom was happy & warm;
So if all do their duty, they need not fear harm.

1789

Nurse's Song

When the voices of children are heard on the green
And laughing is heard on the hill,
My heart is at rest within my breast
And everything else is still.

"Then come home my children, the sun is gone down   5
And the dews of night arise;
Come, come, leave off play, and let us away
Till the morning appears in the skies."

2. The child's lisping attempt at the chimney sweeper's street cry, "Sweep! Sweep!"

"No, no, let us play, for it is yet day
And we cannot go to sleep;   10
Besides, in the sky, the little birds fly
And the hills are all coverd with sheep."

"Well, well, go & play till the light fades away
And then go home to bed."
The little ones leapéd & shouted & laugh'd   15
And all the hills ecchoéd.

ca. 1784   1789

3 Holy Thursday[3]

'Twas on a Holy Thursday, their innocent faces clean,
The children walking two & two, in red & blue & green,
Grey headed beadles [4] walkd before with wands as white as snow,
Till into the high dome of Paul's they like Thames' waters flow.

O what a multitude they seemd, these flowers of London town!   5
Seated in companies they sit with radiance all their own.
The hum of multitudes was there, but multitudes of lambs,
Thousands of little boys & girls raising their innocent hands.

Now like a mighty wind they raise to heaven the voice of song,
Or like harmonious thunderings the seats of heaven among.   10
Beneath them sit the aged men, wise guardians of the poor;
Then cherish pity, lest you drive an angel from your door.[5]

ca. 1784   1789

4 The Little Black Boy

My mother bore me in the southern wild,
And I am black, but O! my soul is white;
White as an angel is the English child:
But I am black as if bereav'd of light.

My mother taught me underneath a tree,   5
And sitting down before the heat of day,
She took me on her lap and kisséd me,
And pointing to the east, began to say:

"Look on the rising sun: there God does live,
And gives his light, and gives his heat away;   10

3. In the English church, the Thursday celebrating the ascension of Jesus (forty days after Easter). It was the custom on this day to march the children from the charity schools of London to a service at St. Paul's Cathedral.

4. Lower church officers, one of whose duties is to keep order.
5. Hebrews xiii.2: "Be not forgetful to entertain strangers: for thereby some have entertained angels unawares."

And flowers and trees and beasts and men receive
Comfort in morning, joy in the noon day.

"And we are put on earth a little space,
That we may learn to bear the beams of love,
And these black bodies and this sun-burnt face   15
Is but a cloud, and like a shady grove.

"For when our souls have learn'd the heat to bear,
The cloud will vanish; we shall hear his voice,
Saying: 'Come out from the grove, my love & care,
And round my golden tent like lambs rejoice.' "   20

Thus did my mother say, and kisséd me;
And thus I say to little English boy:
When I from black and he from white cloud free,
And round the tent of God like lambs we joy,

I'll shade him from the heat till he can bear   25
To lean in joy upon our father's knee;
And then I'll stand and stroke his silver hair,
And be like him, and he will then love me.

1789

From Songs of Experience

1794
The Author & Printer   W Blake

Introduction

Hear the voice of the Bard!
Who Present, Past, & Future sees;
Whose ears have heard
The Holy Word
That walk'd among the ancient trees;[6]   5

Calling the lapséd Soul
And weeping in the evening dew;
That might controll
The starry pole,
And fallen, fallen light renew!   10

6. Genesis iii.8: "And [Adam and Eve] heard the voice of the Lord God walking in the garden in the cool of the day." The Bard, whose imagination is not bound by time, has heard the voice of the Lord in Eden and calls to the fallen ("lapsed") soul and to the fallen Earth to turn full to the light and stop its endless cycle of alternating light and darkness. In Blake's symbolism the starry sky ("floor") and the margin of the sea ("watery shore")—see the final stanza—are symbols of the rigid rational order and the temporal and spatial bondage imposed on the free imagination by the material world known through the "corporeal eye."

"O Earth, O Earth, return!
Arise from out the dewy grass;
Night is worn,
And the morn
Rises from the slumberous mass.   15

"Turn away no more;
Why wilt thou turn away?
The starry floor
The watry shore
Is giv'n thee till the break of day."   20

1794

Earth's Answer

Earth rais'd up her head,
From the darkness dread & drear.
Her light fled:
Stony dread!
And her locks cover'd with grey despair.   5

"Prison'd on watry shore
Starry Jealousy does keep my den,
Cold and hoar
Weeping o'er
I hear the Father of the ancient men.[7]   10

"Selfish father of men,
Cruel, jealous, selfish fear!
Can delight
Chain'd in night
The virgins of youth and morning bear?   15

"Does spring hide its joy
When buds and blossoms grow?
Does the sower
Sow by night,
Or the plowman in darkness plow?   20

"Break this heavy chain
That does freeze my bones around;
Selfish! vain!
Eternal bane!
That free Love with bondage bound."   25

1794

7. The character Blake called "Urizen" in his later prophetic works. He represents perceptual, rational, and moral tyranny that binds the mind to the sensible order of time and space and imposes upon sexual desire (as upon all forms of creative human energy) the stultifying and distorting bondage of selfishness, fear, secrecy, shame, and jealousy.

The Clod & the Pebble

"Love seeketh not Itself to please,
Nor for itself hath any care;
But for another gives its ease,
And builds a Heaven in Hell's despair."

 So sang a little Clod of Clay,   5
 Trodden with the cattle's feet;
 But a Pebble of the brook,
 Warbled out these metres meet:

"Love seeketh only Self to please,
To bind another to its delight;   10
Joys in another's loss of ease,
And builds a Hell in Heaven's despite."

            1794

3 Holy Thursday ✔

Is this a holy thing to see,
In a rich and fruitful land,
Babes reducd to misery,
Fed with cold and usurous hand?

Is that trembling cry a song?   5
Can it be a song of joy?
And so many children poor?
It is a land of poverty!

And their sun does never shine,
And their fields are bleak & bare,   10
And their ways are fill'd with thorns;
It is eternal winter there.

For where-e'er the sun does shine,
And where-e'er the rain does fall,
Babe can never hunger there,   15
Nor poverty the mind appall.

            1794

The Chimney Sweeper

A little black thing among the snow
Crying "'weep, 'weep," in notes of woe!
"Where are thy father & mother? say?"
"They are both gone up to the church to pray.

"Because I was happy upon the heath, 5
And smil'd among the winter's snow;
They clothéd me in the clothes of death,
And taught me to sing the notes of woe.

"And because I am happy, & dance & sing,
They think they have done me no injury, 10
And are gone to praise God & his Priest & King,
Who make up a heaven of our misery."

1790–92   1794

Nurse's Song

When the voices of children, are heard on the green
And whisprings are in the dale,
The days of my youth rise fresh in my mind,
My face turns green and pale.

Then come home my children, the sun is gone down 5
And the dews of night arise;
Your spring & your day are wasted in play,
And your winter and night in disguise.

1794

The Sick Rose

O Rose, thou art sick.
The invisible worm
That flies in the night
In the howling storm

Has found out thy bed 5
Of crimson joy,
And his dark secret love
Does thy life destroy.

1794

The Tyger

Tyger! Tyger! burning bright
In the forests of the night,
What immortal hand or eye
Could frame thy fearful symmetry?

In what distant deeps or skies 5
Burnt the fire of thine eyes?
On what wings dare he aspire?
What the hand, dare seize the fire?

And what shoulder, & what art,
Could twist the sinews of thy heart? 10

And when thy heart began to beat,
What dread hand? & what dread feet?

What the hammer? what the chain?
In what furnace was thy brain?
What the anvil? what dread grasp   15
Dare its deadly terrors clasp?

When the stars threw down their spears,
And water'd heaven with their tears,
Did he smile his work to see?
Did he who made the Lamb make thee?   20

Tyger! Tyger! burning bright
In the forests of the night,
What immortal hand or eye
Dare frame thy fearful symmetry?

1790–92   1794

Ah Sun-Flower

Ah Sun-flower! weary of time,
Who countest the steps of the Sun,
Seeking after that sweet golden clime
Where the traveller's journey is done;

Where the Youth pined away with desire,   5
And the pale Virgin shrouded in snow,
Arise from their graves and aspire,
Where my Sun-flower wishes to go.

1794

The Garden of Love

I went to the Garden of Love,
And saw what I never had seen:
A Chapel was built in the midst,
Where I used to play on the green.

And the gates of this Chapel were shut,   5
And "Thou shalt not" writ over the door;
So I turn'd to the Garden of Love,
That so many sweet flowers bore,

And I saw it was filled with graves,
And tomb-stones where flowers should be: 10
And Priests in black gowns were walking their rounds,
And binding with briars my joys & desires.

1794

⁴ London ✓

I wander thro' each charter'd [1] street,
Near where the charter'd Thames does flow,
And mark in every face I meet
Marks of weakness, marks of woe.

In every cry of every Man,   5
In every Infant's cry of fear,
In every voice, in every ban,[2]
The mind-forg'd manacles I hear.

How the Chimney-sweeper's cry
Every blackning Church appalls;   10
And the hapless Soldier's sigh
Runs in blood down Palace walls.

But most thro' midnight streets I hear
How the youthful Harlot's curse
Blasts the new-born Infant's tear,[3]   15
And blights with plagues the Marriage hearse.[4]

1794

² The Human Abstract[5] ✓

Pity would be no more,
If we did not make somebody Poor;
And Mercy no more could be,
If all were as happy as we;

And mutual fear brings peace,   5
Till the selfish loves increase;
Then Cruelty knits a snare,
And spreads his baits with care.

He sits down with holy fears,
And waters the ground with tears;   10
Then Humility takes its root
Underneath his foot.

1. "Given liberty," but also, ironically, "pre-empted as private property, and rented out."
2. The various meanings of "ban" are relevant (political and legal prohibition, curse, public condemnation) as well as "banns" (marriage proclamation).
3. Implying prenatal blindness, resulting from a parent's venereal disease (the "plagues" of line 16) by earlier infection from the harlot.
4. In the older sense of "hearse": converts the marriage bed into a bier. Or possibly, since the current sense of the word had also come into use in Blake's day, "converts the marriage coach into a funeral hearse."
5. The matched contrary to *The Divine Image* in *Songs of Innocence*. The virtues of the earlier poem, "Mercy, Pity, Peace, and Love," are now seen as exploitation, cruelty, conflict, and hypocritical humility—the seed in the human brain of the Tree of Mystery, which darkens the natural world.

Soon spreads the dismal shade
Of Mystery over his head;
And the Catterpiller and Fly
Feed on the Mystery.   15

And it bears the fruit of Deceit,
Ruddy and sweet to eat;
And the Raven his nest has made
In its thickest shade.   20

The Gods of the earth and sea,
Sought thro' Nature to find this Tree,
But their search was all in vain:
There grows one in the Human Brain.

1790–92   1794

Infant Sorrow

My mother groand! my father wept.
Into the dangerous world I leapt:
Helpless, naked, piping loud;
Like a fiend hid in a cloud.

Struggling in my father's hands,   5
Striving against my swadling bands,
Bound and weary I thought best
To sulk upon my mother's breast.

1794

A Poison Tree

I was angry with my friend:
I told my wrath, my wrath did end.
I was angry with my foe:
I told it not, my wrath did grow.

And I waterd it in fears,   5
Night & morning with my tears;
And I sunnéd it with smiles,
And with soft deceitful wiles.

And it grew both day and night,
Till it bore an apple bright.
And my foe beheld it shine,   10
And he knew that it was mine,

And into my garden stole,
When the night had veild the pole;
In the morning glad I see   15
My foe outstretchd beneath the tree.

1794

To Tirzah [6]

Whate'er is Born of Mortal Birth
Must be consuméd with the Earth
To rise from Generation free;
Then what have I to do with thee? [7]

The Sexes sprung from Shame & Pride,   5
Blow'd [8] in the morn: in evening died;
But Mercy changd Death into Sleep;
The Sexes rose to work & weep.

Thou, Mother of my Mortal part,
With cruelty didst mould my Heart,   10
And with false self-deceiving tears
Didst bind my Nostrils, Eyes, & Ears.

Didst close my Tongue in senseless clay
And me to Mortal Life betray.
The Death of Jesus set me free,   15
Then what have I to do with thee?

ca. 1805

A Divine Image [9]

Cruelty has a Human Heart
And Jealousy a Human Face,
Terror, the Human Form Divine,
And Secrecy, the Human Dress.

The Human Dress is forgéd Iron,   5
The Human Form, a fiery Forge,
The Human Face, a Furnace seal'd,
The Human Heart, its hungry Gorge. [10]

1790–91

6. Tirzah was the capital of the Northern Kingdom of Israel and is conceived by Blake in opposition to Jerusalem, capital of the Southern Kingdom of Judah, whose tribes had been redeemed from captivity. In this poem, which was added to late versions of *Songs of Experience*, Tirzah represents that necessity inherent in nature, the realm of "generation," from which the "mortal part" of man derives, and which enslaves his heart and senses. Blake anticipates his emancipation from this bondage to the cycle of generation by the triumph of the imaginative over the natural body.

7. Echoing the words of Christ to his mother at the marriage in Cana, John ii.4.

8. Blossomed.

9. After etching this poem Blake omitted it from *Songs of Experience*, probably because *The Human Abstract* served as a more comprehensive and subtle contrary to *The Divine Image*, in *Songs of Innocence*.

10. Throat.

The Book of Thel [1]

The Author & Printer Willm Blake, 1789

PLATE i [2]

THEL'S MOTTO

Does the Eagle know what is in the pit?
Or wilt thou go ask the Mole?
Can Wisdom be put in a silver rod?
Or Love in a golden bowl? [3]

PLATE 1

I

The daughters of Mne [4] Seraphim led round their sunny flocks,
All but the youngest; she in paleness sought the secret air,

1. Although Blake dated the engraved poem 1789, its composition probably extended to 1791, so that he was working on it at the time he was writing the *Songs of Innocence* and some of the *Songs of Experience. The Book of Thel* treats the same two "states" and implies the need to pass from primitive innocence through experience in order to achieve a higher, organized innocence; now, however, Blake employs the narrative instead of the lyrical mode and embodies aspects of the developing myth which was fully enacted in his later prophetic books. And like the major prophecies, this poem is written in the fourteener, a long line of seven stresses.

Thel—her name probably derives from a Greek word for "wish" or "will" and suggests the timid failure of a desire to fulfil itself—is a virgin dwelling in the Vales of Har, which is equivalent to the sheltered condition of pastoral peace and naïve innocence in Blake's *Songs of Innocence* and will develop into the "Beulah" of his prophetic books. In the fragile beauty of this realm of unrealized potentiality, Thel lives a two-dimensional mirror image of existence (line 9). The Lily of the Valley and the Cloud try to comfort her by describing their content with their roles in the cycle of innocent existence. Thel, however, since she is a human potentiality, finds such comfort inapplicable to her condition of unfulfillment and uselessness, as a virgin without a male contrary and as a shepherdess whose sheep run no risks and need no care. The Clod of Clay then speaks for her child, the voiceless Worm, an emblem of phallic generation and a devourer of the mortal body in the fallen world; but the maternal Clay sees the role of the Worm, as well as her own, only from the perspective of

essential ignorance: "But how this is, sweet maid, I know not, and I cannot know." In her capacity, however, as the substance from which is formed the mortal body of man, the Clay invites Thel to try the experiment of dying into embodied life. With an abrupt and brutal shift in language and tone, Part IV expresses the shock of the revelation to Thel of the world of Generation and Experience —a revelation from which she flees in terror back to her sheltered, if inadequate, paradise.

The reader does not need to be an adept in Blakean mythology to recognize the symbolic reach of this poem in ordinary human experience—the elemental failure of nerve to meet the challenge of life as it is, the timid incapacity to risk the conflict, physicality, pain, and loss without which there is no possibility either of growth or of any kind of creativity.

2. The plate numbers identify the page, each with its own pictorial design, as originally printed by Blake. They are reproduced here because they are frequently used for reference to Blake's writings.

3. Ecclesiastes xii.5–6 describes a time when "fears shall be in the way * * * and desire shall fail: because man goeth to his long home, and the mourners go about the streets: Or ever the silver cord be loosed, or the golden bowl be broken." Blake presumably changed the silver cord to a rod in order to make it, with the golden bowl, a sexual symbol.

4. In his earlier poem *Tiriel*, Blake adopted the name "Mnetha" for the goddess of the vales of Har. Thel, the abbreviated form of this name indicates, is one of the daughters of the angelic Mnetha. In the Bible, Seraphim are the highest order of angels.

To fade away like morning beauty from her mortal day;
Down by the river of Adona [5] her soft voice is heard,
And thus her gentle lamentation falls like morning dew: 5

"O life of this our spring! why fades the lotus of the water?
Why fade these children of the spring? born but to smile & fall.
Ah! Thel is like a watry bow, and like a parting cloud,
Like a reflection in a glass, like shadows in the water,
Like dreams of infants, like a smile upon an infant's face, 10
Like the dove's voice, like transient day, like music in the air.
Ah! gentle may I lay me down, and gentle rest my head,
And gentle sleep the sleep of death and gentle hear the voice
Of him that walketh in the garden in the evening time."[6]

The Lilly of the valley, breathing in the humble grass, 15
Answer'd the lovely maid and said: "I am a watry weed,
And I am very small, and love to dwell in lowly vales;
So weak, the gilded butterfly scarce perches on my head;
Yet I am visited from heaven, and he that smiles on all
Walks in the valley and each morn over me spreads his hand, 20
Saying: 'Rejoice, thou humble grass, thou new-born lilly flower,
Thou gentle maid of silent valleys and of modest brooks;
For thou shalt be clothed in light, and fed with morning manna,
Till summer's heat melts thee beside the fountains and the springs
To flourish in eternal vales.' Then why should Thel complain? 25

PLATE 2
Why should the mistress of the vales of Har utter a sigh?"

She ceasd & smild in tears, then sat down in her silver shrine.

Thel answer'd: "O thou little virgin of the peaceful valley,
Giving to those that cannot crave, the voiceless, the o'ertired;
Thy breath doth nourish the innocent lamb, he smells thy milky
  garments, 5
He crops thy flowers, while thou sittest smiling in his face,
Wiping his mild and meekin [7] mouth from all contagious taints.
Thy wine doth purify the golden honey; thy perfume,
Which thou dost scatter on every little blade of grass that springs,
Revives the milkéd cow, & tames the fire-breathing steed. 10
But Thel is like a faint cloud kindled at the rising sun:
I vanish from my pearly throne, and who shall find my place?"

"Queen of the vales," the Lilly answered, "ask the tender cloud,
And it shall tell thee why it glitters in the morning sky,

---

5. Possibly suggesting an equation of
the Vales of Har to Spenser's Garden of
Adonis in *The Faerie Queene* III.vi, as
well as to the paradisal garden in

Genesis (in line 14).
6. Genesis iii.8.
7. Humble.

And why it scatters its bright beauty thro' the humid air.   15
Descend, O little cloud, & hover before the eyes of Thel."

The Cloud descended, and the Lilly bowd her modest head,
And went to mind her numerous charge among the verdant grass.

PLATE 3

II

"O little Cloud," the virgin said, "I charge thee tell to me,
Why thou complainest not when in one hour thou fade away:
Then we shall seek thee but not find; ah, Thel is like to Thee.
I pass away, yet I complain, and no one hears my voice."

The Cloud then shew'd his golden head & his bright form emerg'd,   5
Hovering and glittering on the air before the face of Thel.

"O virgin, know'st thou not our steeds drink of the golden springs
Where Luvah[8] doth renew his horses? Look'st thou on my youth,
And fearest thou, because I vanish and am seen no more,
Nothing remains? O maid, I tell thee, when I pass away,   10
It is to tenfold life, to love, to peace, and raptures holy:
Unseen descending, weigh my light wings upon balmy flowers,
And court the fair eyed dew, to take me to her shining tent;
The weeping virgin trembling kneels before the risen sun,
Till we arise link'd in a golden band, and never part,   15
But walk united, bearing food to all our tender flowers."

"Dost thou O little Cloud? I fear that I am not like thee;
For I walk through the vales of Har and smell the sweetest flowers,
But I feed not the little flowers; I hear the warbling birds,
But I feed not the warbling birds; they fly and seek their food;   20
But Thel delights in these no more, because I fade away,
And all shall say, 'Without a use this shining woman liv'd,
Or did she only live to be at death the food of worms?' "

The Cloud reclind upon his airy throne and answer'd thus:

"Then if thou art the food of worms, O virgin of the skies,   25
How great thy use, how great thy blessing! Every thing that lives
Lives not alone, nor for itself; fear not, and I will call
The weak worm from its lowly bed, and thou shalt hear its voice.
Come forth, worm of the silent valley, to thy pensive queen."

The helpless worm arose, and sat upon the Lilly's leaf,   30
And the bright Cloud saild on, to find his partner in the vale.

---

8. The earliest mention in Blake's work
of one of his "Giant Forms," the Zoas.
Luvah, the mythical embodiment of the
passional and sexual aspect of man, repairs to the Vales of Har simply in
order to rest and water his horses. The
cloud in this passage describes the cycle
of water, from cloud to rain and (by the
vaporizing action of the sun on the dew
and other forms of water) back to the
cloud.

PLATE 4

III

Then Thel astonish'd view'd the Worm upon its dewy bed.

"Art thou a Worm? Image of weakness, art thou but a Worm?
I see thee like an infant wrapped in the Lilly's leaf;
Ah, weep not, little voice, thou can'st not speak, but thou can'st weep.
Is this a Worm? I see thee lay helpless & naked, weeping,   5
And none to answer, none to cherish thee with mother's smiles."

The Clod of Clay heard the Worm's voice, & raisd her pitying head;
She bow'd over the weeping infant, and her life exhal'd
In milky fondness; then on Thel she fix'd her humble eyes.

"O beauty of the vales of Har! we live not for ourselves;   10
Thou seest me the meanest thing, and so I am indeed.
My bosom of itself is cold, and of itself is dark;

PLATE 5

But he that loves the lowly, pours his oil upon my head,
And kisses me, and binds his nuptial bands around my breast,
And says: 'Thou mother of my children, I have lovéd thee,
And I have given thee a crown that none can take away.'
But how this is, sweet maid, I know not, and I cannot know;   5
I ponder, and I cannot ponder; yet I live and love."

The daughter of beauty wip'd her pitying tears with her white veil,
And said: "Alas! I knew not this, and therefore did I weep.
That God would love a Worm, I knew, and punish the evil foot
That, wilful, bruis'd its helpless form; but that he cherish'd it   10
With milk and oil I never knew; and therefore did I weep,
And I complaind in the mild air, because I fade away,
And lay me down in thy cold bed, and leave my shining lot."

"Queen of the vales," the matron Clay answerd, "I heard thy sighs,
And all thy moans flew o'er my roof, but I have call'd them down. 15
Wilt thou, O Queen, enter my house? 'Tis given thee to enter
And to return; fear nothing, enter with thy virgin feet."

PLATE 6

IV

The eternal gates' terrific porter lifted the northern bar: [9]
Thel enter'd in & saw the secrets of the land unknown.
She saw the couches of the dead, & where the fibrous roots

9. Homer, in *Odyssey* XIII, described the Cave of the Naiades, of which the northern gate is for men and the southern gate for gods. The Neoplatonist Porphyro had allegorized it as an account of the descent of the soul into matter. Blake has Thel use the northern gate to pass from the state before birth into incarnate life.

Of every heart on earth infixes deep its restless twists:
A land of sorrows & of tears where never smile was seen.   5

She wanderd in the land of clouds thro' valleys dark, listning
Dolours & lamentations; waiting oft beside a dewy grave,
She stood in silence, listning to the voices of the ground,
Till to her own grave plot she came, & there she sat down,
And heard this voice of sorrow breathéd from the hollow pit: 10

"Why cannot the Ear be closed to its own destruction?
Or the glistning Eye to the poison of a smile?
Why are Eyelids stord with arrows ready drawn,
Where a thousand fighting men in ambush lie?
Or an Eye of gifts & graces, show'ring fruits & coinéd gold?   15
Why a Tongue impress'd with honey from every wind?
Why an Ear, a whirlpool fierce to draw creations in?
Why a Nostril wide inhaling terror, trembling, & affright?
Why a tender curb upon the youthful burning boy?
Why a little curtain of flesh on the bed of our desire?" [1]   20

The Virgin started from her seat, & with a shriek
Fled back unhinderd till she came into the vales of Har.

THE END

1789–91

1. From Thel's grave issues, apparently, the voice of Thel herself, expressing how experience would seem to her timid and shrinking temperament, should she elect to live out her life in the human world. The catalogue of experience runs through the various senses to end with touch, the primary sexual sense.

The Marriage of Heaven and Hell   This, the most immedi-
ately accessible of Blake's longer works, is a vigorous, deliberately outrageous, and at times comic, onslaught against the timidly conventional and
self-righteous members of society, as well as against many of the stock
opinions of orthodox Christian piety and morality. The seeming simplicity
of Blake's satiric attitude, however, is deceptive.

Initially, Blake accepts the terminology of middle-class Christian morality
("what the religious call Good & Evil") but reverses its values. In this conventional use Evil, which is manifested by the class of beings called Devils
and which consigns a man to the orthodox Hell, is everything associated
with the body and its desires and consists essentially of energy, abundance,
act, freedom. And conventional Good, which is manifested by Angels and
guarantees its adherents a place in the orthodox Heaven, is associated with
the Soul (regarded as entirely separate from the body) and consists of the
contrary qualities of reason, restraint, passivity, and prohibition. Blandly
adopting this current nomenclature, Blake elects to assume the diabolic
persona—what he calls "the voice of the Devil"—and to utter "Proverbs
of Hell." This ironic stance produces a vein of satire which is in the great
18th-century tradition of sustained ironic reversal, represented by works such
as Jonathan Swift's *Modest Proposal*.

But the transvaluation of standard criteria is only a first stage in Blake's complex irony, designed to startle the reader into recognizing the inadequacy of standard moral categories and stock responses. As he also says in the opening summary of his total argument, "Without Contraries is no progression," and "Reason and Energy" are both "necessary to Human existence." It turns out that Blake subordinates his satiric reversal of conventional values under a more inclusive point of view, according to which the real Good, as distinguished from the merely ironic Good, is not simply freedom from restraint, but a "marriage" of the contrary extremes of desire and restraint, energy and reason, the promptings of Hell and the limitations of Heaven—or as Blake calls these contraries, in the comprehensive terms he introduces in Plate 16, "the Prolific" and "the Devouring." These two classes, he adds, "should be enemies," and "whoever tries to reconcile them seeks to destroy existence." When Blake speaks not as moral satirist but as serious moralist, the good life is that abundant and strenuous life he describes as the sustained conflict, without victory or suppression, of simultaneous opposites.

Blake was stimulated to write this unique work in response to the books of the visionary Swedish theologian, Emanuel Swedenborg, whom he had at first admired but then had come to recognize as a conventional Angel in the disguise of a radical Devil. In Plate 3, the writings of Swedenborg are described as the winding clothes Blake discards as he is resurrected from the tomb of his past self, as a poet-prophet who heralds the apocalyptic promise of his age. For Blake wrote *The Marriage of Heaven and Hell* during the bright early years of the French Revolution, when he shared the expectations of a number of radical Englishmen, including the young poets Wordsworth, Coleridge, and Southey, that the Revolution was the universal violence which had been predicted by the Biblical prophets as a stage immediately preceding the millennium. The double role of *The Marriage* as both satire and revolutionary prophecy is made explicit in *A Song of Liberty*, which Blake engraved in 1792 and added as a coda.

The Marriage of Heaven and Hell

PLATE 2

The Argument

Rintrah [1] roars & shakes his fires in the burden'd air;
Hungry clouds swag[2] on the deep.

Once meek, and in a perilous path,
The just man kept his course along
The vale of death.   5

1. Rintrah plays the role of the angry Old Testament prophet Elijah as well as of John the Baptist, the voice "crying in the wilderness" (Matthew iii), preparing the way for Christ the Messiah. It has been plausibly suggested that stanzas 2–5 summarize the course of biblical history to the present time. "Once" (line 3) refers to Old Testament history after the fall of man; "Then" (line 9) is the time of the birth of Christ; "Till" (line 14) identifies the era when Christianity was perverted into an institutional religion; and "Now" (line 17) is the time of the wrathful portent of the French Revolution. In this final era, the hypocritical serpent represents the priest of the "angels" in the poem, while "the just man" is embodied in Blake himself, a raging poet and prophet in the guise of a Devil. 2. Sag or sway (or both).

66 · *William Blake*

Roses are planted where thorns grow,
And on the barren heath
Sing the honey bees.

Then the perilous path was planted,
And a river, and a spring,
On every cliff and tomb;
And on the bleached bones
Red clay[3] brought forth;   10

Till the villain left the paths of ease,
To walk in perilous paths, and drive
The just man into barren climes.   15

Now the sneaking serpent walks
In mild humility,
And the just man rages in the wilds
Where lions roam.   20

Rintrah roars & shakes his fires in the burdend air;
Hungry clouds swag on the deep.

PLATE 3

As a new heaven is begun, and it is now thirty-three years since
its advent, the Eternal Hell revives.[4] And lo! Swedenborg is the
Angel sitting at the tomb; his writings are the linen clothes folded
up. Now is the dominion of Edom, & the return of Adam into
Paradise; see Isaiah xxxiv & XXXV Chap.[5]

Without Contraries is no progression. Attraction and Repulsion,
Reason and Energy, Love and Hate, are necessary to Human existence.

3. In Hebrew, the literal meaning of "Adam," or created man. There is a probable reference to the birth of the Redeemer, the new Adam.
4. The Swedish scientist and religious philosopher, Emanuel Swedenborg (1688–1772) had predicted, on the basis of his visions, that the Last Judgment and the coming of the Kingdom of Heaven would occur in 1757. This was precisely the year of Blake's birth. Now, in 1790, Blake is thirty-three, the age at which Christ had been resurrected from the tomb; appropriately, Blake rises from the tomb of his past life in his new role as imaginative artist who will redeem his age. But, Blake ironically comments, the works he will engrave in his resurrection will constitute the Eternal Hell, the contrary inevitably brought into simultaneous being by Swedenborg's limited New Heaven.
5. Isaiah xxxiv prophesies "the day of the Lord's vengeance," a time of violent destruction and bloodshed; Isaiah xxxv

prophesies the redemption to follow, in which "the desert shall * * * blossom as the rose," "in the wilderness shall waters break out, and streams in the desert," and "no lion shall be there," but "an highway shall be there * * * and it shall be called the way of holiness." (Cf. "The Argument," lines 3–11, 20.) Blake combines with these chapters Isaiah lxiii, in which "Edom" is the place from which comes the man whose garments are red with the blood he has spilled; for as he says, "the day of vengeance is in mine heart, and the year of my redeemed is come." Blake interprets this last phrase as predicting the time when Adam would regain his lost Paradise.

With reference to affairs in 1790, Edom represents France, and the red man coming from Edom (to England) is the spirit of the French Revolution, which Blake represents as a portent of apocalyptic redemption and of the recovery of Paradise.

From these contraries spring what the religious call Good & Evil. Good is the passive that obeys Reason. Evil is the active springing from Energy.

Good is Heaven. Evil is Hell.

PLATE 4   The voice of the Devil

Devil is hero or spokesman

All Bibles or sacred codes have been the causes of the following Errors:

1. That Man has two real existing principles; Viz: a Body & a Soul.

body is only of s

2. That Energy, calld Evil, is alone from the Body, & that Reason, calld Good, is alone from the Soul.

3. That God will torment Man in Eternity for following his Energies. But the following Contraries to these are True:

1. Man has no Body distinct from his Soul; for that calld Body is a portion of Soul discernd by the five Senses, the chief inlets of Soul in this age.

2. Energy is the only life, and is from the Body; and Reason is the bound or outward circumference of Energy.

3. Energy is Eternal Delight

rmation

PLATE 5

Devil say energies are Repressed

Those who restrain desire, do so because theirs is weak enough to be restrained; and the restrainer or reason usurps its place & governs the unwilling.

And being restraind, it by degrees becomes passive, till it is only the shadow of desire.

The history of this is written in *Paradise Lost*,[6] & the Governor or Reason is call'd Messiah.

And the original Archangel, or possessor of the command of the heavenly host, is calld the Devil or Satan, and his children are call'd Sin & Death.[7]

But in the Book of Job, Milton's Messiah is call'd Satan.[8]

For this history has been adopted by both parties.

It indeed appear'd to Reason as if Desire was cast out; but the Devil's account is, that the Messi[PL 6]ah fell, & formed a heaven of what he stole from the Abyss.

This is shewn in the Gospel, where he prays to the Father to send the comforter or Desire that Reason may have Ideas to build

6. What follows, to the end of this section, is Blake's "diabolical" reading of Milton's *Paradise Lost*.
7. Satan's giving birth to Sin and then incestuously begetting Death upon her is described in II.745 ff.; the war in heaven, referred to three lines below, in which the Messiah defeated Satan and drove him out of heaven, is described in VI.824 ff.
8. Satan plays the role of the moral accuser and physical tormentor of Job.

Reason becomes a dictator

on; [9] the Jehovah of the Bible being no other than he who dwells in flaming fire. Know that after Christ's death, he became Jehovah.

But in Milton, the Father is Destiny, the Son, a Ratio of the five senses,[1] & the Holy-ghost, Vacuum!

Note. The reason Milton wrote in fetters when he wrote of Angels & God, and at liberty when of Devils & Hell, is because he was a true Poet and of the Devil's party without knowing it.

A Memorable Fancy [2]

As I was walking among the fires of hell, delighted with the enjoyments of Genius, which to Angels look like torment and insanity, I collected some of their Proverbs; thinking that as the sayings used in a nation mark its character, so the Proverbs of Hell shew the nature of Infernal wisdom better than any description of buildings or garments.

When I came home, on the abyss of the five senses, where a flat sided steep frowns over the present world, I saw a mighty Devil folded in black clouds, hovering on the sides of the rock; with cor- [PL 7]roding fires he wrote the following sentence [3] now perceived by the minds of men, & read by them on earth:

> How do you know but ev'ry Bird that cuts the airy way,
> Is an immense world of delight, clos'd by your senses five?

Proverbs of Hell [4]

In seed time learn, in harvest teach, in winter enjoy.
Drive your cart and your plow over the bones of the dead.
The road of excess leads to the palace of wisdom.
Prudence is a rich ugly old maid courted by Incapacity.
He who desires but acts not, breeds pestilence.
The cut worm forgives the plow.
Dip him in the river who loves water.
A fool sees not the same tree that a wise man sees.
He whose face gives no light, shall never become a star.
Eternity is in love with the productions of time.
The busy bee has no time for sorrow.
The hours of folly are measur'd by the clock; but of wisdom, no

9. Possibly John xiv.16–17, where Christ says he "will pray the Father, and he shall give you another Comforter * * * even the Spirit of truth."
1. The Latin *ratio* means both "reason" and "sum." Blake applies the term to the 18th-century view, following the empirical philosophy of John Locke, that the content of the mind is limited to the sum of the experience acquired by the five senses.

2. A parody of what Swedenborg called "memorable relations" of his literal-minded visions of the eternal world.
3. The "mighty Devil" is Blake, as he sees himself reflected in the shiny plate on which he is etching this very passage with "corroding fires"—i.e., acid. See also the third from last sentence in Plate 14.
4. A "diabolic" version of the Book of Proverbs in the Old Testament.

clock can measure.
All wholsom food is caught without a net or a trap.
Bring out number, weight, & measure in a year of dearth.
No bird soars too high, if he soars with his own wings.
A dead body revenges not injuries.
The most sublime act is to set another before you.
If the fool would persist in his folly he would become wise.
Folly is the cloke of knavery.
Shame is Pride's cloke.

PLATE 8

Prisons are built with stones of Law, Brothels with bricks of Religion.
The pride of the peacock is the glory of God.
The lust of the goat is the bounty of God.
The wrath of the lion is the wisdom of God.
The nakedness of woman is the work of God.
Excess of sorrow laughs. Excess of joy weeps.
The roaring of lions, the howling of wolves, the raging of the stormy
    sea, and the destructive sword, are portions of eternity too great
    for the eye of man.
The fox condemns the trap, not himself.
Joys impregnate. Sorrows bring forth.
Let man wear the fell of the lion, woman the fleece of the sheep.
The bird a nest, the spider a web, man friendship.
The selfish, smiling fool & the sullen, frowning fool shall be both
    thought wise, that they may be a rod.
What is now proved was once only imagin'd.
The rat, the mouse, the fox, the rabbit watch the roots; the lion, the
    tyger, the horse, the elephant, watch the fruits.
The cistern contains: the fountain overflows.
One thought fills immensity.
Always be ready to speak your mind, and a base man will avoid you.
Every thing possible to be believ'd is an image of truth.
The eagle never lost so much time as when he submitted to learn of
    the crow.

PLATE 9

The fox provides for himself, but God provides for the lion.
Think in the morning, Act in the noon, Eat in the evening, Sleep in
    the night.
He who has sufferd you to impose on him knows you.
As the plow follows words, so God rewards prayers.
The tygers of wrath are wiser than the horses of instruction.
Expect poison from the standing water.
You never know what is enough unless you know what is more than
    enough.
Listen to the fools reproach! it is a kingly title!
The eyes of fire, the nostrils of air, the mouth of water, the beard of
    earth.
The weak in courage is strong in cunning.

The apple tree never asks the beech how he shall grow, nor the lion the horse, how he shall take his prey.

The thankful reciever bears a plentiful harvest.

If others had not been foolish, we should be so.

The soul of sweet delight can never be defil'd.

When thou seest an Eagle, thou seest a portion of Genius; lift up thy head!

As the catterpiller chooses the fairest leaves to lay her eggs on, so the priest lays his curse on the fairest joys.

To create a little flower is the labour of ages.

Damn braces: Bless relaxes.

The best wine is the oldest, the best water the newest.

Prayers plow not! Praises reap not!

Joys laugh not! Sorrows weep not!

PLATE 10

The head Sublime, the heart Pathos, the genitals Beauty, the hands & feet Proportion.

As the air to a bird or the sea to a fish, so is contempt to the contemptible.

The crow wish'd every thing was black, the owl that every thing was white.

Exuberance is Beauty.

If the lion was advised by the fox, he would be cunning.

Improvement makes strait roads, but the crooked roads without Improvement are roads of Genius.

Sooner murder an infant in its cradle than nurse unacted desires.

Where man is not, nature is barren.

Truth can never be told so as to be understood, and not be believ'd.

> Enough! or Too much.

perception

assault on the priesthood

PLATE 11

The ancient Poets animated all sensible objects with Gods or Geniuses, calling them by the names and adorning them with the properties of woods, rivers, mountains, lakes, cities, nations, and whatever their enlarged & numerous senses could percieve.

And particularly they studied the genius of each city & country, placing it under its mental deity.

Till a system was formed, which some took advantage of & enslav'd the vulgar by attempting to realize or abstract the mental deities from their objects; thus began Priesthood,

Choosing forms of worship from poetic tales.

And at length they pronounced that the Gods had ordered such things.

Thus men forgot that All deities reside in the human breast.

PLATE 12 [13] Blake Allies himself with priesthood

A Memorable Fancy

The Prophets Isaiah and Ezekiel dined with me, and I asked them how they dared so roundly to assert that God spake to them; and whether they did not think at the time that they would be misunderstood, & so be the cause of imposition.

Isaiah answer'd: "I saw no God, nor heard any, in a finite organical perception; but my senses discover'd the infinite in every thing, and as I was then perswaded, & remain confirm'd, that the voice of honest indignation is the voice of God, I cared not for consequences, but wrote."

Then I asked: "Does a firm perswasion that a thing is so, make it so?"

He replied: "All poets believe that it does, & in ages of imagination this firm perswasion removed mountains; but many are not capable of a firm perswasion of any thing."

Then Ezekiel said: "The philosophy of the East taught the first principles of human perception. Some nations held one principle for the origin & some another; we of Israel taught that the Poetic Genius (as you now call it) was the first principle and all the others merely derivative, which was the cause of our despising the Priests & Philosophers of other countries, and prophecying that all Gods [PL 13] would at last be proved to originate in ours & to be the tributaries of the Poetic Genius; it was this that our great poet, King David, desired so fervently & invokes so patheticly, saying by this he conquers enemies & governs kingdoms; and we so loved our God, that we cursed in his name all the deities of surrounding nations, and asserted that they had rebelled; from these opinions the vulgar came to think that all nations would at last be subject to the Jews."

"This," said he, "like all firm perswasions, is come to pass, for all nations believe the Jews' code and worship the Jews' god, and what greater subjection can be?"

I heard this with some wonder, & must confess my own conviction. After dinner I ask'd Isaiah to favour the world with his lost works; he said none of equal value was lost. Ezekiel said the same of his.

I also asked Isaiah what made him go naked and barefoot three years? He answerd, "the same that made our friend Diogenes, the Grecian." [5]

I then asked Ezekiel why he eat dung, & lay so long on his right & left side? [6] He answered, "the desire of raising other men into a

5. In Isaiah xx.2–3, the Lord commanded Isaiah to go "naked and barefoot" for three years. Diogenes was the 4th-century Greek Cynic, whose extreme repudiation of civilized customs gave rise to anecdotes that he had renounced clothing.

6. The Lord gave these instructions to the prophet Ezekiel, iv.4–6.

perception of the infinite; this the North American tribes practise, & is he honest who resists his genius or conscience only for the sake of present ease or gratification?"

PLATE 14 & 15   *Blake describes creative process that produced poem*

The ancient tradition that the world will be consumed in fire at the end of six thousand years is true, as I have heard from Hell.

For the cherub with his flaming sword is hereby commanded to leave his guard at tree of life; [7] and when he does, the whole creation will be consumed, and appear infinite and holy, whereas it now appears finite & corrupt.

New perception

This will come to pass by an improvement of sensual enjoyment.

But first the notion that man has a body distinct from his soul is to be expunged; this I shall do, by printing in the infernal method, by corrosives, which in Hell are salutary and medicinal, melting apparent surfaces away, and displaying the infinite which was hid. [8]

If the doors of perception were cleansed every thing would appear to man as it is, infinite.

For man has closed himself up, till he sees all things thro' narrow chinks of his cavern.

PLATE 15

A Memorable Fancy

I was in a Printing house in Hell & saw the method in which knowledge is transmitted from generation to generation.

In the first chamber was a Dragon-Man, clearing away the rubbish from a cave's mouth; within, a number of Dragons were hollowing the cave.

In the second chamber was a Viper folding round the rock & the cave, and others adorning it with gold, silver, and precious stones.

unconscious

In the third chamber was an Eagle with wings and feathers of air; he caused the inside of the cave to be infinite; around were numbers of Eagle-like men, who built palaces in the immense cliffs.

In the fourth chamber were Lions of flaming fire, raging around & melting the metals into living fluids.

In the fifth chamber were Unnam'd forms, which cast the metals into the expanse.

There they were receiv'd by Men who occupied the sixth chamber, and took the forms of books & were arranged in libraries. [9]

---

7. In **Genesis iii.24,** when the Lord drove Adam and Eve from the Garden of Eden, he had placed Cherubims and a flaming sword at the eastern end "to keep the way of the tree of life."
8. See "A Memorable Fancy," Plates 6–7 above, footnote 3.
9. In this Memorable Fancy Blake allegorizes the procedure in designing, printing, and binding works of imaginative genius.

PLATE 16   *defines psychic terrain*

The Giants who formed this world into its sensual existence, and now seem to live in it in chains, are in truth the causes of its life & the sources of all activity; but the chains are the cunning of weak and tame minds which have power to resist energy; according to the proverb, the weak in courage is strong in cunning.

Thus one portion of being is the Prolific, the other, the Devouring: to the Devourer it seems as if the producer was in his chains; but it is not so, he only takes portions of existence and fancies that the whole.

But the Prolific would cease to be Prolific unless the Devourer as a sea received the excess of his delights.[1]

Some will say, "Is not God alone the Prolific?" I answer, "God only Acts & Is, in existing beings or Men."

These two classes of men are always upon earth, & they should be enemies; whoever tries [PL 17] to reconcile them seeks to destroy existence.

Religion is an endeavour to reconcile the two.

Note. Jesus Christ did not wish to unite but to separate them, as in the Parable of sheep and goats! & he says, "I came not to send Peace but a Sword."[2]

Messiah or Satan or Tempter was formerly thought to be one of the Antediluvians[3] who are our Energies.

show each eternal other their lot

A Memorable Fancy

17–20 – satirical drama between Angel and Blake

An Angel came to me and said: "O pitiable foolish young man! O horrible! O dreadful state! consider the hot burning dungeon thou art preparing for thyself to all eternity, to which thou art going in such career."

I said: "Perhaps you will be willing to shew me my eternal lot, & we will contemplate together upon it and see whether your lot or mine is most desirable."

So he took me thro' a stable & thro' a church & down into the church vault at the end of which was a mill; thro' the mill we went, and came to a cave; down the winding cavern we groped our tedious way till a void boundless as a nether sky appeard beneath us, & we held by the roots of trees and hung over this immensity, but I said: "If you please, we will commit ourselves to this void, and see whether Providence is here also, if you will not I will." But he answerd: "Do not presume, O young man, but as we here remain, behold thy lot which will soon appear when the darkness passes

---

1. The "Giants" in this section are man's creative energies, called "the Prolific," which are necessarily limited by their contrary, "the Devourer."

2. The parable of the sheep and the goats is in Matthew xxv.32–33; the saying of Christ, in Matthew x.34.
3. Men who lived before Noah's flood.

away." [4]

So I remaind with him sitting in the twisted [PL 18] root of an oak; he was suspended in a fungus which hung with the head downward into the deep.

By degrees we beheld the infinite Abyss, fiery as the smoke of a burning city; beneath us at an immense distance was the sun, black but shining; round it were fiery tracks on which revolv'd vast spiders, crawling after their prey, which flew, or rather swum in the infinite deep, in the most terrific shapes of animals sprung from corruption; & the air was full of them, & seemd composed of them; these are Devils, and are called Powers of the air. I now asked my companion which was my eternal lot? he said, "Between the black & white spiders."

But now, from between the black & white spiders a cloud and fire burst and rolled thro the deep, blackning all beneath, so that the nether deep grew black as a sea & rolled with a terrible noise; beneath us was nothing now to be seen but a black tempest, till looking east between the clouds & the waves, we saw a cataract of blood mixed with fire, and not many stones throw from us appeard and sunk again the scaly fold of a monstrous serpent. At last to the east, distant about three degrees, appeard a fiery crest above the waves. Slowly it reared like a ridge of golden rocks till we discovered two globes of crimson fire, from which the sea fled away in clouds of smoke; and now we saw it was the head of Leviathan; his forehead was divided into streaks of green & purple like those on a tyger's forehead: soon we saw his mouth & red gills hang just above the raging foam, tinging the black deep with beams of blood, advancing toward [PL 19] us with all the fury of a spiritual existence.

My friend the Angel climb'd up from his station into the mill; I remain'd alone, & then this appearance was no more, but I found myself sitting on a pleasant bank beside a river by moon light, hearing a harper who sung to the harp, & his theme was: "The man who never alters his opinion is like standing water, & breeds reptiles of the mind."

But I arose, and sought for the mill, & there I found my Angel, who surprised asked me how I escaped?

I answerd: "All that we saw was owing to your metaphysics: for when you ran away, I found myself on a bank by moonlight hearing a harper. But now we have seen my eternal lot, shall I shew you yours? He laughd at my proposal; but I by force suddenly caught

4. The "stable" is that where Jesus was born, which, allegorically, leads to the "church" founded in his name and to the "vault" where this institution effectually buried him. The "mill" in Blake is a symbol of mechanical and analytic philosophy; through this the pilgrims pass into the twisting cave of rationalistic theology and descend to an underworld which is an empty abyss. The point of this Blakean equivalent of a carnival fun house is that only after you have thoroughly confused yourself by this tortuous approach, and only if you then (as in the next two paragraphs) stare at this topsy-turvy emptiness long enough, will the void gradually assume the semblance of the comic horrors of the fantasied hell of angelic orthodoxy.

him in my arms, & flew westerly thro' the night, till we were elevated above the earth's shadow; then I flung myself with him directly into the body of the sun; here I clothed myself in white, & taking in my hand Swedenborg's volumes, sunk from the glorious clime, and passed all the planets till we came to Saturn; here I staid to rest & then leap'd into the void between Saturn & the fixed stars.

"Here," said I, "is your lot, in this space, if space it may be calld." Soon we saw the stable and the church, & I took him to the altar and open'd the Bible, and lo! it was a deep pit, into which I descended, driving the Angel before me; soon we saw seven houses of brick;[5] one we enterd; in it were a [PL 20] number of monkeys, baboons, & all of that species, chaind by the middle, grinning and snatching at one another, but withheld by the shortness of their chains: however, I saw that they sometimes grew numerous, and then the weak were caught by the strong, and with a grinning aspect, first coupled with & then devourd, by plucking off first one limb and then another till the body was left a helpless trunk. This, after grinning & kissing it with seeming fondness, they devourd too; and here & there I saw one savourily picking the flesh off of his own tail; as the stench terribly annoyd us both, we went into the mill, & I in my hand brought the skeleton of a body, which in the mill was Aristotle's Analytics.[6]

So the Angel said: "Thy phantasy has imposed upon me, & thou oughtest to be ashamed."

I answered: "We impose on one another, & it is but lost time to converse with you whose works are only Analytics."

Opposition is true Friendship.

PLATE 21

I have always found that Angels have the vanity to speak of themselves as the only wise; this they do with a confident insolence sprouting from systematic reasoning.

Thus Swedenborg boasts that what he writes is new; tho' it is only the Contents or Index of already publish'd books.

A man carried a monkey about for a shew, & because he was a little wiser than the monkey, grew vain, and conciev'd himself as much wiser than seven men. It is so with Swedenborg; he shews the folly of churches & exposes hypocrites, till he imagines that all are religious, & himself the single [PL 22] one on earth that ever broke a net.

Now hear a plain fact: Swedenborg has not written one new truth. Now hear another: he has written all the old falshoods.

5. The "seven churches which are in Asia," to which John addresses the Book of Revelation i.4. Blake now forces upon the angel his own diabolic view of angelic Biblical exegesis, theological speculation and disputation, and Hell—a view, Harold Bloom has remarked, which "makes monkeys out of the theologians."
6. Aristotle's treatises on logic.

And now hear the reason: He conversed with Angels who are all religious, & conversed not with Devils, who all hate religion, for he was incapable thro' his conceited notions.

Thus Swedenborg's writings are a recapitulation of all superficial opinions, and an analysis of the more sublime, but no further.

Have now another plain fact: Any man of mechanical talents may from the writings of Paracelsus or Jacob Behmen [7] produce ten thousand volumes of equal value with Swedenborg's, and from those of Dante or Shakespear, an infinite number.

But when he has done this, let him not say that he knows better than his master, for he only holds a candle in sunshine.

A Memorable Fancy

Once I saw a Devil in a flame of fire, who arose before an Angel that sat on a cloud, and the Devil utterd these words:

"The worship of God is, Honouring his gifts in other men, each according to his genius, and loving the [PL 23] greatest men best; those who envy or calumniate great men hate God, for there is no other God."

The Angel hearing this became almost blue; but mastering himself, he grew yellow, & at last white, pink, & smiling, and then replied:

"Thou Idolater, is not God One? & is not he visible in Jesus Christ? and has not Jesus Christ given his sanction to the law of ten commandments, and are not all other men fools, sinners, & nothings?"

The Devil answer'd; "Bray [8] a fool in a mortar with wheat, yet shall not his folly be beaten out of him; if Jesus Christ is the greatest man, you ought to love him in the greatest degree; now hear how he has given his sanction to the law of ten commandments: did he not mock at the sabbath, and so mock the sabbath's God? murder those who were murderd because of him? turn away the law from the woman taken in adultery? steal the labor of others to support him? bear false witness when he omitted making a defence before Pilate? covet when he pray'd for his disciples, and when he bid them shake off the dust of their feet against such as refused to lodge them? I tell you, no virtue can exist without breaking these ten commandments.·. Jesus was all virtue, and acted from im[PL 24]pulse, not from rules."

When he had so spoken, I beheld the Angel, who stretched out

---

7. Paracelsus (1493–1541), a Swiss physician and a pioneer in empirical medicine, was also a prominent theorist of the occult. Behmen is Jakob Boehme (1575–1624), a German shoemaker who developed a theosophical system which has had great and persisting influence both on theological and metaphysical speculation.
8. Pound into small pieces.

marriage

his arms, embracing the flame of fire, & he was consumed and arose as Elijah.[9]

Note. This Angel, who is now become a Devil, is my particular friend; we often read the Bible together in its infernal or diabolical sense, which the world shall have if they behave well.

I have also The Bible of Hell,[1] which the world shall have whether they will or no.

One Law for the Lion & Ox is Oppression.

1790–93   1790–93

PLATE 25

A Song of Liberty[2]

1. The Eternal Female groand! it was heard over all the Earth.
2. Albion's[3] coast is sick, silent; the American meadows faint!
3. Shadows of Prophecy shiver along by the lakes and the rivers and mutter across the ocean: France, rend down thy dungeon!
4. Golden Spain, burst the barriers of old Rome!
5. Cast thy keys, O Rome, into the deep down falling, even to eternity down falling,
6. And weep.
7. In her trembling hands she took the new born terror, howling.
8. On those infinite mountains of light now barr'd out by the Atlantic sea,[4] the new born fire stood before the starry king!
9. Flag'd with grey brow'd snows and thunderous visages, the jealous wings wav'd over the deep.
10. The speary hand burned aloft, unbuckled was the shield, forth went the hand of jealousy among the flaming hair, and [PL. 26] hurl'd the new born wonder thro' the starry night.
11. The fire, the fire, is falling!
12. Look up! look up! O citizen of London, enlarge thy countenance! O Jew, leave counting gold! return to thy oil and wine. O African! black African! (Go, wingéd thought, widen his forehead.)
13. The fiery limbs, the flaming hair, shot like the sinking sun into the western sea.

9. The angry Old Testament prophet; see the opening "Argument," footnote.
1. I.e., the poems and designs that Blake is working on.
2. Blake etched this poem in 1792 and sometimes bound it as an appendix to *The Marriage of Heaven and Hell*. It recounts the birth, manifested in the contemporary events in France, of the flaming Spirit of Revolution (whom Blake later called Orc), and describes his conflict with the tyrannical sky-god (whom Blake later called Urizen). The poem ends with the portent of the Spirit of Revolution shattering the ten commandments, or prohibitions against political, religious, and moral liberty, and bringing in a free and joyous new world.
3. England's.
4. The legendary continent of Atlantis, sunk beneath the sea; Blake uses it to represent the condition before the fall.

14. Wak'd from his eternal sleep, the hoary element roaring fled away:

15. Down rushd, beating his wings in vain, the jealous king; his grey brow'd councellors, thunderous warriors, curl'd veterans, among helms, and shields, and chariots, horses, elephants; banners, castles, slings and rocks,

16. Falling, rushing, ruining! buried in the ruins, on Urthona's ⁵ dens;

17. All night beneath the ruins; then, their sullen flames, faded, emerge round the gloomy king,

18. With thunder and fire, leading his starry hosts thro' the waste wilderness [PL 27] he promulgates his ten commands, glancing his beamy eyelids over the deep in dark dismay,

19. Where the son of fire in his eastern cloud, while the morning plumes her golden breast,

20. Spurning the clouds written with curses, stamps the stony law to dust, loosing the eternal horses from the dens of night, crying:

Empire is no more! and now the lion & wolf shall cease.⁶

CHORUS

Let the Priests of the Raven of dawn, no longer in deadly black, with hoarse note curse the sons of joy. Nor his accepted brethren, whom, tyrant, he calls free, lay the bound or build the roof. Nor pale religious letchery call that virginity, that wishes but acts not!

For every thing that lives is Holy.

1792   1792

For the Sexes: The Gates of Paradise¹

[*Prologue*]
Mutual Forgiveness of each Vice,
Such are the Gates of Paradise.
Against the Accuser's chief desire
Who walkd among the Stones of Fire
Jehovah's Finger Wrote the Law,   5
Then Wept! then rose in Zeal & Awe
And the Dead Corpse from Sinai's heat
Buried beneath his Mercy Seat.
O Christians, Christians! tell me Why
You rear it on your Altars high.   10

5. In the later Prophetic Books, Urthona is the unfallen form of Los, who in the fallen world represents the poetic imagination, the agent working for the regeneration of humanity.
6. Cf. Isaiah's prophecy, lxv.17–25, of "new heavens and a new earth," when "the wolf and the lamb shall feed together, and the lion shall eat straw like the bullock."
1. The two poems reprinted here introduce and conclude a series of emblems (drawings with explanatory captions) that Blake issued first under the title *For Children: The Gates of Paradise* and later amplified and reissued under the present title.

[*Epilogue*]
To The Accuser who is
The God of This World[2]

Truly My Satan thou art but a Dunce,
And dost not know the Garment from the Man;
Every Harlot was a Virgin once,
Nor canst thou ever change Kate into Nan.[3]

Tho thou art Worshipd by the Names Divine   5
Of Jesus & Jehovah: thou art still
The Son of Morn in weary Night's decline,
The lost Traveller's Dream under the Hill.

1818?   1818?

Poems from BLAKE'S NOTEBOOK[1]

Never Pain to Tell Thy Love

Never pain to tell thy love
Love that never told can be,
For the gentle wind does move
Silently, invisibly.

I told my love, I told my love,   5
I told her all my heart,
Trembling, cold, in ghastly fears—
Ah, she doth depart.

Soon as she was gone from me
A traveller came by   10
Silently, invisibly—
O, was no deny.

I Askéd a Thief

I askéd a thief to steal me a peach,
He turned up his eyes;
I ask'd a lithe lady to lie her down,
Holy & meek she cries.

2. Satan appears as the Accuser in the Book of Job. Blake's point is that orthodox Christians really worship Satan, although they call him Jesus and Jehovah.
3. "Kate" (the name of Blake's own wife) connotes virtue; "Nan" is a name often applied to prostitutes.
1. A commonplace book in which Blake drew sketches and jotted down verses and memoranda between the late 1780's and 1810. It is known as the "Rossetti Manuscript" because it later came into the possession of the poet and painter Dante Gabriel Rossetti. These poems were first published in imperfect form in 1863, then transcribed from the manuscript by Geoffrey Keynes in 1935.

As soon as I went   5
An angel came.
He wink'd at the thief
And smild at the dame—

And without one word said
Had a peach from the tree   10
And still as a maid
Enjoy'd the lady.

1796

Mock on, Mock on, Voltaire, Rousseau

Mock on, Mock on, Voltaire, Rousseau;[2]
Mock on, Mock on, 'tis all in vain.
You throw the sand against the wind,
And the wind blows it back again.

And every sand becomes a Gem   5
Reflected in the beams divine;
Blown back, they blind the mocking Eye,
But still in Israel's paths they shine.

The Atoms of Democritus
And Newton's Particles of light[3]   10
Are sands upon the Red sea shore,
Where Israel's tents do shine so bright.

Morning

To find the Western path
Right thro the Gates of Wrath
I urge my way;
Sweet Mercy leads me on,
With soft repentant moan   5
I see the break of day.

The war of swords & spears
Melted by dewy tears
Exhales on high;
The Sun is freed from fears   10
And with soft grateful tears
Ascends the sky.

2. Blake regards both Voltaire and Rousseau as representing rationalism and Deism.
3. Democritus (460–362 B.C.) proposed that atoms were ultimate components of the universe; Newton in his *Opticks* hypothesized that light consisted of minute material particles.

The Mental Traveller[1]

I traveld thro' a Land of Men
A Land of Men & Women too
And heard & saw such dreadful things
As cold Earth wanderers never knew

For there the Babe is born in joy   5
That was begotten in dire woe
Just as we Reap in joy the fruit
Which we in bitter tears did sow

And if the Babe is born a Boy
He's given to a Woman Old   10
Who nails him down upon a rock
Catches his shrieks in cups of gold

She binds iron thorns around his head
She pierces both his hands & feet
She cuts his heart out at his side   15
To make it feel both cold & heat

---

1. A useful clue to this cryptic narrative is Blake's assertion in *A Vision of the Last Judgment*: "Man passes on but States remain for ever. He passes thro them like a traveller who may . . . suppose that the places he has passed thro exist no more. . . . Every thing is Eternal." In the poem, the Mental Traveller is a visitor from another country—the "eternal" realm of imagination—to our fallen, temporal world. His travelogue describes the temporal sequence of States that he discovers, but which "cold Earth wanderers never knew" (line 4) because their knowledge of their lot is that of delusory sense-experience, not of imaginative vision. These States are the persisting forms through which all earthly existence passes; in Blake's prophetic poems they are named Beulah, Generation, and Ulro (see the headnote to Blake, above). The Traveller describes man's passage through the States as a revolving cycle in time; in the prophetic poems, this circling constitutes what scholars call the Orc cycle, in which the spontaneous, all-demanding, rebellious infant Orc matures inevitably into the rigid, materialistic, and isolated old man, Urizen, who then reverts to infancy and so begins the cycle anew. This temporal world is "A Land of Men & Women too" (line 2). That is, the sexes have fallen into separation and Selfhood, and the female character in the poem represents both human women and the alien-

ated human environment, which Blake elsewhere calls the delusory "Nature, Mother of all." The female principle is represented in the predominant guise in which she appears to the male perspective, at each stage of his development. The female cycle is thus complementary and opposite to that of the male, moving from an old, cruel, oppressive mother-figure (or wicked stepmother), through the form of mistress and prolific wife, to that of female infant, and on to oppressive crone again. The only way to break out of blind bondage to time is by a triumph of imagination that will provide the vision of the Mental Traveller—and of Blake the Bard.

The cycle in time is the form of each individual life, as well as of each historical culture. Blake's description of the cycle also involves pagan myth (especially the myth of Prometheus, lines 11 ff.), fairy-tales, and the Gospel story of Christ, as read in its literal and historical instead of in what Blake calls its "spiritual sense" (e.g., lines 13 ff., 93 ff.). But the full significance of this travelogue, like that of Blake's other myths, is open-ended rather than explicit. As Blake said in his letter to Dr. Trusler (below), "What is not too explicit is the fittest for instruction, because it rouzes the faculties to act."

This poem was not engraved by Blake, but it survived in what is known as the Pickering manuscript.

Her fingers number every Nerve
Just as a Miser counts his gold
She lives upon his shrieks & cries
And she grows young as he grows old   20

Till he becomes a bleeding youth
And she becomes a Virgin bright
Then he rends up his Manacles
And binds her down for his delight

He plants himself in all her Nerves   25
Just as a Husbandman his mould
And she becomes his dwelling place
And Garden fruitful seventy fold

An aged Shadow soon he fades
Wandring round an Earthly Cot[2]   30
Full filled all with gems & gold
Which he by industry had got

And these are the gems of the Human Soul
The rubies & pearls of a lovesick eye
The countless gold of the akeing heart   35
The martyrs groan & the lovers sigh

They are his meat they are his drink
He feeds the Beggar & the Poor
And the wayfaring Traveller
For ever open is his door   40

His grief is their eternal joy
They make the roofs & walls to ring
Till from the fire on the hearth
A little Female Babe does spring

And she is all of solid fire   45
And gems & gold that none his hand
Dares stretch to touch her Baby form
Or wrap her in his swaddling-band

But She comes to the Man she loves
If young or old or rich or poor   50
They soon drive out the aged Host
A Beggar at anothers door

He wanders weeping far away
Untill some other take him in
Oft blind & age-bent sore distrest   55
Untill he can a Maiden win

2. Cottage.

And to allay his freezing Age
The Poor Man takes her in his arms
The Cottage fades before his sight
The Garden & its lovely Charms   60

The Guests are scattered thro' the land
For the Eye altering alters all
The Senses roll themselves in fear
And the flat Earth becomes a Ball[3]

The Stars Sun Moon all shrink away   65
A desart vast without a bound
And nothing left to eat or drink
And a dark desert all around

The honey of her Infant lips
The bread & wine of her sweet smile   70
The wild game of her roving Eye
Does him to Infancy beguile

For as he eats & drinks[4] he grows
Younger & younger every day
And on the desart wild they both   75
Wander in terror & dismay

Like the wild Stag she flees away
Her fear plants many a thicket wild
While he pursues her night & day
By various arts of Love beguild   80

By various arts of Love & Hate
Till the wide desert planted oer
With Labyrinths of wayward Love
Where roams the Lion Wolf & Boar

Till he becomes a wayward Babe   85
And she a weeping Woman Old
Then many a Lover wanders here
The Sun & Stars are nearer rolld

The trees bring forth sweet Extacy
To all who in the desert roam   90
Till many a City there is Built
And many a pleasant Shepherds home

But when they find the frowning Babe
Terror strikes thro the region wide

3. Blake claimed that the post-Coperni-
can and Newtonian conception of the
earth "as of a Globe rolling thro Void-
ness . . . is a delusion of Ulro" (*Milton*,
Plate 29).
4. Man eats and drinks "the bread and
wine" of line 70—the delusive communion of the female as seductive harlot.

They cry the Babe the Babe is Born 95
And flee away on Every side

For who dare touch the frowning form
His arm is withered to its root
Lions Boars Wolves all howling flee
And every Tree does shed its fruit 100

And none can touch that frowning form
Except it be a Woman Old
She nails him down upon the Rock
And all is done as I have told

ca. 1803 1863

And Did Those Feet[1]

And did those feet in ancient time
Walk upon England's mountains green?
And was the holy Lamb of God
On England's pleasant pastures seen?

And did the Countenance Divine 5
Shine forth upon our clouded hills?
And was Jerusalem builded here,
Among these dark Satanic Mills?[2]

Bring me my Bow of burning gold:
Bring me my Arrows of desire:
Bring me my Spear: O clouds unfold! 10
Bring me my Chariot of fire!

I will not cease from Mental Fight,
Nor shall my Sword sleep in my hand,
Till we have built Jerusalem 15
In England's green & pleasant Land.

ca. 1804–10 ca. 1804–10

1. These quatrains occur in the Preface to Blake's prophetic poem *Milton*. There is an ancient belief, still current in parts of England, that Jesus came to England with Joseph of Arimathea. Blake adapts the legend to his own conception of a spiritual Israel, in which the significance of Biblical events are as relevant to England as to Palestine. By a particularly Blakean irony, this poem of mental war in the service of apocalyptic desire is widely used as a hymn by those of us whom Blake called "angels."
2. There may be an allusion here to industrial England; but the mill is primarily Blake's symbol for a mechanistic and utilitarian world view, according to which, as he said elsewhere, "the same dull round, even of a universe" becomes "a mill with complicated wheels."

Jerusalem   Jerusalem is the last, the longest, and the most carefully wrought of Blake's prophetic books. He probably composed the poem and etched the text and designs between 1804 and 1815 and printed its 100 plates during the next five years. Of the printings during Blake's lifetime, five complete copies survive; one of these, fully colored, has been reproduced in facsimile by the Blake Trust.

Blake's epic encompasses the violent era of the last days and the apocalyptic Second Coming of Jesus. Its primary source is thus the Bible, and especially two visionary books, Ezekiel in the Old Testament and Revelation in the New Testament. Blake translates the Biblical narratives and prophecies into his own basic myth (described above, in the introduction to Blake), in which the fall is the disintegration of Universal Man, when he succumbs to Selfhood, into four separated Zoas, their divided female Emanations, a remote and tyrannical God, and an alien material world. The end of the fallen world of space and time occurs when the Universal Man overcomes his Selfhood and thereby regains his undivided condition. Since Man's fall substitutes a nightmare for eternal reality, his re-integration is also represented as his awakening from the delusive dream of his "Sleep of Ulro" into "Eternal Life" (4.1–2, below). And by a second and simultaneous alternative, this same apocalyptic event is set forth as a triumph of the imagination over the senses, whereby man regains the "fourfold" vision that enables him once more to experience a humanized and civilized world, which is the Eden he has left and now regains.

In *Jerusalem*, as in all of Blake's prophetic works, we find not only these unannounced shifts in the radical metaphors of narrative representation, but also bizarre collocations of diverse matters, a fusion of mental and outer events, abrupt leaps in time and location, and incessant changes and interchanges in the agents, places, and actions. Blake did not simply invent this remarkable narrative strategy, but adapted to his own original purposes a thoroughly traditional mode of "typological" narration. The procedure had evolved during the composition of the sequential books of the Bible, had been elaborated over centuries of Biblical exegesis, and had been demonstrated by numberless preachers, pamphleteers, and writers of spiritual autobiographies; it had also been exploited by earlier poets such as William Langland in *Piers Plowman* and Edmund Spenser in *The Faerie Queene*. This way of sustaining multiplex references by a single narrative line largely dropped out of literature after the Renaissance; a recognizable version of the typological method, however, was revived by James Joyce in *Finnegans Wake* (1939), and has influenced the narrative method of a number of novelists in the present era.

Jerusalem requires a flexible way of reading that does not fix on a single meaning, or even on a determinate allegorical translation, for the chief persons, places, and events of the story are eternal "types" whose instances are not tied to a particular time and location, and whose significance radiates out in diverse dimensions: Biblical, autobiographical, historical, and mental. For example, Los, the mythical agent of imagination in the fallen world, is a type of Christ, and of every man, and especially of Blake himself; Los is beset, among other enemies, by various individuals who had figured in Blake's traumatic trial for treasonable utterances (see the Introduction), but these function as "Accusers" whose analogues exist in every individual consciousness; Los's troubles with his Emanation, Enitharmon, reflect Blake's occasional marital problems, but also represent general manifestations of distorted sexuality; Los's central conflict with his separated Spectre typifies the temptations of Christ in the wilderness, the worldly temptations besetting all artists, and specifically, Blake's own struggle against inner doubts about the efficacy of his imaginative labors and against the temptation to accommodate his work to the fashionable tastes of his age. Los, laboring at his furnaces and anvil to build Golgonooza the City of Art out of the materials of the fallen world, is a type of Blake, a poet without an audience and a prophet without honor, working with his engraving tools and acids in the stubborn attempt to effectuate his saving vision. Since Blake, however, is an English embodiment of the type of the poet-prophet, he names his Universal Man "Albion," which is an archaic name for England. Albion is not only a protagonist in the mythical plot but also constitutes the English nation and embodies the mountains, plains, rivers, and cities of geographical England; while his children—"the Sons and Daughters of Albion"—are the individual English men and women of Blake's day. But Albion-England is a type of the spiritual Israel, so that Blake freely parallels and interchanges English places and people with the places and people of the Biblical Israel, and retains for Albion's Emanation the name "Jerusalem"—the Bride of Israel in the Old Testament and of the Lamb in the New Testament—though he substitutes for "Jerusalem," at a critical moment in the plot, the feminine name for England, "Brittannia." The doings of Albion, Los, and the other Giant Forms typify the recurrent vicissitudes of fallen mankind. Accordingly, Blake's narrative of the last episode in the history of Israel involves the history of Albion-England during the era in which Blake composed the poem—the era of the protracted wars against France, the decline and defeat of Napoleon, and the post-war time of hardship and of political repression. In this latter dimension of reference, Blake's prophetic theme, announced in his Preface "To the Public," that "the Spirit of Jesus is continual forgiveness of Sin" involves an appeal to England to conclude with conquered France what David Erdman calls "a peace without vengeance" (*Blake, Prophet Against Empire*, Chap. 27). In a central episode Los takes a "globe of fire" and searches in detail "the interiors of Albion's Bosom"—that is, both the places and moral climate of contemporary England. In near-despair at the horrors he discovers there, he cries out:

> O Albion, if thou takest vengeance, if thou revengest thy wrongs,
> Thou art for ever lost! What can I do to hinder the Sons
> Of Albion from taking vengeance? or how shall I them perswade?
>
> (45.36–38)

As in all the major prophecies, the meter of *Jerusalem* is the "long resounding line" of seven stresses which Blake adapted from the early English measure called "fourteeners." In his Preface Blake said that he had considered writing in blank verse, but had rejected that meter as subject to "bondage" and chosen instead to allow "a variety in every line, both of cadences and number of syllables. Every word and every letter is studied and put in its fit place: the terrific numbers are reserved for the terrific parts— the mild and gentle, for the mild and gentle parts, and the prosaic, for inferior parts: all are necessary to each other. Poetry Fetter'd, Fetters the Human Race!"

The following selections are the beginning and end of the poem—the opening statement, in which Blake announces his epic argument and invokes his sacred Muse, and the conclusion, in which the artist and prophet Los, by his self-conquest and discovered imaginative truth, precipitates the denouement of the history of mankind.

From Jerusalem

The Emanation of The Giant Albion

Chapter 1

[INVOCATION]

PLATE 4

Of the Sleep of Ulro![1] and of the passage through
Eternal Death! and of the awaking to Eternal Life.

This theme calls me in sleep night after night, & ev'ry morn
Awakes me at sun-rise, then I see the Saviour over me
Spreading his beams of love, & dictating the words of this mild
    song.   5

"Awake! awake O sleeper of the land of shadows, wake! expand!
I am in you and you in me, mutual in love divine:
Fibres of love from man to man thro Albions pleasant land.
In all the dark Atlantic vale down from the hills of Surrey
A black water accumulates,[2] return Albion! return!   10
Thy brethren call thee, and thy fathers, and thy sons,
Thy nurses and thy mothers, thy sisters and thy daughters
Weep at thy souls disease, and the Divine Vision is darkend:
Thy Emanation that was wont to play before thy face,[3]
Beaming forth with her daughters into the Divine bosom—   15
Where hast thou hidden thy Emanation lovely Jerusalem
From the vision and fruition of the Holy-one?
I am not a God afar off, I am a brother and friend;
Within your bosoms I reside, and you reside in me:
Lo! we are One; forgiving all Evil; Not seeking recompense!   20
Ye are my members O ye sleepers of Beulah,[4] land of shades!"

1. Ulro is the lowest of the four states of existence, the extreme of Selfhood and bleak rationality. From this spiritual "Sleep" Albion at the end of the poem awakens into the "Eternal Life" of the highest state, Eden.
2. The waters of the Atlantic are a Blakean symbol of formless chaos.
3. An echo of Proverbs viii.22 ff., in which Wisdom, a female figure, says: "The Lord possessed me in the beginning of his way, before his works of old.

... And I was daily his delight, rejoicing always before him." Albion's Emanation, Jerusalem, is the feminine antitype of the male principle; in her unfallen state, she existed with Albion in a union of contraries which is the condition of "fruition" (line 17)—i.e., of all creative achievements in art and culture.
4. Beulah, the state just below Eden, is the realm of dreams, visions, and creative inspiration.

But the perturbed Man[5] away turns down the valleys dark,
Saying: "We are not One: we are Many, thou most simulative
Phantom of the over heated brain! shadow of immortality!
Seeking to keep my soul a victim to thy Love! which binds   25
Man the enemy of man into deceitful friendships:
Jerusalem is not! her daughters are indefinite:
By demonstration, man alone can live, and not by faith.
My mountains are my own, and I will keep them to myself:
The Malvern and the Cheviot, the Wolds[6] Plinlimmon &
     Snowdon   30
Are mine; here will I build my Laws of Moral Virtue!
Humanity shall be no more: but war & princedom & victory!"

So spoke Albion in jealous fears, hiding his Emanation
Upon the Thames and Medway, rivers of Beulah: dissembling
His jealousy before the throne divine, darkening, cold!   35

PLATE 5

The banks of the Thames are clouded! the ancient porches of
     Albion are
Darken'd! they are drawn thro' unbounded space, scatter'd upon
The Void in incoherent despair! Cambridge & Oxford & London,
Are driven among the starry Wheels,[7] rent away and dissipated,
In Chasms & Abysses of sorrow, enlarg'd without dimension, terri-
     ble.   5
Albions mountains run with blood, the cries of war & of tumult
Resound into the unbounded night, every Human perfection
Of mountain & river & city, are small & wither'd & darken'd
Cam is a little stream! Ely is almost swallowed up!
Lincoln & Norwich stand trembling on the brink of Udan-Adan![8] 10
Wales and Scotland shrink themselves to the west and to the north!
Mourning for fear of the warriors in the Vale of Entuthon-Beny-
     thon;
Jerusalem is scattered abroad like a cloud of smoke thro' non-entity:
Moab & Ammon & Amalek & Canaan & Egypt & Aram
Receive her little-ones for sacrifices and the delights of cruelty. 15

Trembling I sit day and night, my friends are astonish'd at me.
Yet they forgive my wanderings, I rest not from my great task!
To open the Eternal Worlds, to open the immortal Eyes
Of Man inwards into the Worlds of Thought: into Eternity
Ever expanding in the Bosom of God, the Human Imagination.   20
O Saviour pour upon me thy Spirit of meekness & love:

5. I.e., Albion, who in his jealous self-absorption denies the Saviour and contradicts his proclamations.
6. Albion is listing various British mountains and highlands.
7. The revolving, material stars represent the mechanical universe of Newtonian science.
8. A lake in the wilderness of Entuthon-Benython (line 12). The lake of Udan-Adan signifies formlessness and indefiniteness.

Annihilate the Selfhood[9] in me, be thou all my life!
Guide thou my hand which trembles exceedingly upon the rock of
    ages,[1]
While I write of the building of Golgonooza, & of the terrors of
    Entuthon:
Of Hand & Hyle & Coban, of Kwantok, Peachey, Brereton, Slayd &
    Hutton:[2]   25
Of the terrible sons & daughters of Albion, and their Generations.

Scofield! Kox, Kotope and Bowen, rovolve most mightily upon
The Furnace of Los: before the eastern gate[3] bending their fury.
They war, to destroy the Furnaces, to desolate Golgonooza:
And to devour the Sleeping Humanity of Albion in rage &
    hunger.   30
They revolve into the Furnaces Southward & are driven forth
    Northward
Divided into Male and Female forms time after time.
From these Twelve[4] all the Families of England spread abroad.

* * *

Chapter 4

[THE WAKING OF ALBION]

PLATE 90

For Los said:[5] "When the Individual appropriates Universality
He divides into Male & Female: & when the Male & Female,
Appropriate Individuality, they become an Eternal Death,
Hermaphroditic worshippers of a God of cruelty & law![6]   55
Your Slaves & Captives you compell to worship a God of Mercy.

---

9. Selfhood, making the private self the center of all reference, is the ultimate principle of separation, and it must be overcome if mankind is to be reunited.
1. This is the rock on which the sleeping Albion lies (Plate 94, line 1, below).
2. The twelve sons of Albion, whom Blake names in lines 25 and 27, and who play a recurrent and evil role in the epic action, include a number of men who were involved in Blake's trial for sedition in 1804. Schofield and Cock were the troopers who had filed the false charges of treasonable utterances; Quantock, Peachey, and Brereton were the judges in the trial; Kotope, Bowen, Hutton, and Slayd, it is supposed, also played a role in the court proceedings. Hand, Hyle, and Coban are invented names whose significance is conjectural.
3. Of Golgonooza; the east is associated with the Zoa Luvah, who in this poem signifies revolutionary France.
4. Blake makes the twelve Sons of Albion the English equivalent to the twelve sons who founded the twelve Tribes of Israel.
5. At the nadir of Albion's fortunes, Los grows stronger and more self-assured—that is, he gains in imaginative insight, and (in Plate 82, not included here) recognizes for the first time that he is the Zoa "Urthona, keeper of the Gates of Heaven." Here Los expresses his imaginative insights in a series of pronouncements about the present human condition and the means of its redemption. This testament is engraved by Los-Blake in the plates of the poem (line 57).
6. Blake applies the term hermaphrodite (a double-sexed creature) not to the unified state of sexuality before the fall, but to the condition of the divided and warring sexes in the fallen world.

These are the Demonstrations of Los, & the blows of my mighty
    Hammer."

So Los spoke. And the Giants of Albion, terrified & ashamed
With Los's thunderous Words, began to build trembling rocking
    Stones,[7]
For his Words roll in thunders & lightnings among the Temples,   60
Terrified, rocking to & fro upon the earth, & sometimes
Resting in a Circle in Malden or in Strathness or Dura,
Plotting to devour Albion & Los the friend of Albion,
Denying in private, mocking God & Eternal Life, & in Public
Collusion, calling themselves Deists, Worshipping the Maternal   65
Humanity; calling it Nature, and Natural Religion.[8]

But still the thunder of Los peals loud & thus the thunder's cry—

"These beautiful Witchcrafts of Albion are gratifyd by Cruelty:

PLATE 91

It is easier to forgive an Enemy than to forgive a Friend:
The man who permits you to injure him, deserves your vengeance:
He also will recieve it; go Spectre![9] obey my most secret desire,
Which thou knowest without my speaking: Go to these Fiends of
    Righteousness,
Tell them to obey their Humanities, & not pretend Holiness   5
When they are murderers: as far as my Hammer & Anvil permit
Go, tell them that the Worship of God is honouring his gifts
In other men, & loving the greatest men best, each according
To his Genius, which is the Holy Ghost in Man; there is no other
God, than that God who is the intellectual fountain of
    Humanity;   10
He who envies or calumniates, which is murder & cruelty,
Murders the Holy-one: Go tell them this & overthrow their cup,
Their bread, their altar-table, their incense & their oath,
Their marriage & their baptism, their burial & consecration:
I have tried to make friends by corporeal gifts but have only   15
Made enemies: I never made friends but by spiritual gifts,
By severe contentions of friendship & the burning fire of thought.

---

7. "Rocking stones" are huge boulders
delicately poised on a narrow base. They
were deposited in various parts of England during the Ice Age, but Blake supposes them to have been placed by
Giants (line 58), to form circular sanctuaries for Druidic worship in ancient
Celtic Britain.
8. For Blake, all false religions are
one. Accordingly, he here classifies together ancient British Druidism, 18th-cen-
tury Deism (which in Blake's use includes the views of the contemporary
Church of England), and Natural Religion (which sets out to demonstrate the
existence and nature of God independently of revelation, by arguing from the
evidences of design in nature).
9. Los himself, as the fallen Urthona
who has been separated from his Emanation, is the Spectre of Urthona (as in
95.19, below). In the narrative, however,
the fearful and worldly aspect of Los,
which tempts him to betray his vision
and be like other men, is given a separate identity as the Spectre of Los—a
dramatis persona against whom the imaginative part of Los must struggle, but
whom (as in lines 3–4) Los must involve
in his own artistic purposes, if his work
is to be the product of the integral man.

He who would see the Divinity must see him in his Children,
One first, in friendship & love, then a Divine Family, & in the midst
Jesus will appear; so he who wishes to see a Vision, a perfect
   Whole,   20
Must see it in its Minute Particulars, Organized, & not as thou,
O Fiend of Righteousness, pretendest; thine is a Disorganized
And snowy cloud, brooder of tempests & destructive War.[1]
You smile with pomp & rigor: you talk of benevolence & virtue!
I act with benevolence & Virtue & get murdered time after time: 25
You accumulate Particulars, & murder by analyzing, that you
May take the aggregate; & you call the aggregate Moral Law:
And you call that Swelld & bloated Form a Minute Particular.
But General Forms have their vitality in Particulars, & every
Particular is a Man, a Divine Member of the Divine Jesus."   30

So Los cried at his Anvil in the horrible darkness weeping!

The Spectre builded stupendous Works, taking the Starry Heavens
Like to a curtain & folding them according to his will,
Repeating the Smaragdine Table of Hermes[2] to draw Los down
Into the Indefinite, refusing to believe without demonstration.   35
Los reads the Stars of Albion! the Spectre reads the Voids
Between the Stars; among the arches of Albions Tomb sublime
Rolling the Sea in rocky paths: forming Leviathan
And Behemoth,[3] the War by Sea enormous & the War
By Land astounding: erecting pillars in the deepest Hell,   40
To reach the heavenly arches. Los beheld undaunted; furious
His heavd Hammer; he swung it round & at one blow,
In unpitying ruin driving down the pyramids of pride,[4]
Smiting the Spectre on his Anvil & the integuments of his Eye
And Ear unbinding in dire pain,[5] with many blows,   45
Of strict severity self-subduing, & with many tears labouring.

Then he sent forth the Spectre; all his pyramids were grains
Of sand, & his pillars dust on the flys wing: & his starry
Heavens a moth of gold & silver mocking his anxious grasp.

1. In Blake's view, only definite things and individual human identities ("Minute Particulars") are capable of being "Organized" into "a perfect Whole" corresponding to imaginative vision, in morality and politics no less than in art. The indefinite and the general (lines 22–30) can only make up an "aggregate" such as the "Moral Law," whose uniformity of application is achieved only by destroying all individual differences.
2. The Smaragdine ("emerald green") Book ascribed to the legendary Hermes Trismegistus ("thrice-great Hermes") was a basic text in hermeticism—the philosophical foundations of alchemy—and in the occult tradition generally. Blake rejects this tradition as simply another temptation by his rational Spectre.
3. In Job 40–41, the Lord overwhelms Job with the mystery and magnitude of his power in Nature by describing Behemoth, the great land-beast, and Leviathan, the great sea-beast. The Spectre tries to intimidate Los in the same way.
4. Lines 39–40 equate the two beasts with the naval and land wars against the French, and the hammer of Los's art is an allusion to two paintings which Blake had exhibited in 1809, showing Admiral Nelson guiding Leviathan and William Pitt, the wartime prime minister, guiding Behemoth.
5. Los destroys with his art the fetters of the senses which had constricted his Spectre's perceptions. Cf. below, 98.29–32.

Thus Los altered his Spectre, & every Ratio of his Reason[6]   50
He alterd time after time, with dire pain & many tears,
Till he had completely divided him into a separate space.[7]

Terrified Los sat to behold, trembling & weeping & howling:
"I care not whether a Man is Good or Evil; all that I care
Is whether he is a Wise Man or a Fool. Go! put off Holiness   55
And put on Intellect: or my thundrous Hammer shall drive thee
To wrath, which thou condemnest: till thou obey my voice."

So Los terrified cries, trembling & weeping & howling! "Beholding,

PLATE 92

What do I see? The Briton, Saxon, Roman, Norman amalgamating
In my Furnaces into One Nation, the English, & taking refuge
In the Loins of Albion.[8] The Canaanite united with the fugitive
Hebrew, whom she divided into Twelve,[9] & sold into Egypt,
Then scattered the Egyptian & Hebrew to the four Winds!   5
This sinful Nation Created in our Furnaces & Looms is Albion."

So Los spoke. Enitharmon answerd in great terror in Lambeths
    Vale:[1]

"The Poets Song draws to its period & Enitharmon is no more.
For if he be that Albion I can never weave him in my Looms,[2]
But when he touches the first fibrous thread, like filmy dew   10
My Looms will be no more & I, annihilate, vanish for ever.
Then thou wilt Create another Female according to thy Will."[3]

Los answerd swift as the shuttle of gold: "Sexes must vanish &
    cease
To be, when Albion arises from his dread repose, O lovely Enithar-
    mon,
When all their Crimes, their Punishments, their Accusations of
    Sin,   15

6. "Ratio" is Blake's term for the sum
of knowledge derived entirely from
sense-experience; the "Ratio of his Reason" signifies a systematic empirical philosophy such as John Locke's, which
Blake elsewhere called "a Philosophy of
Five Senses."
7. Los is now able—both in his conception and in his etched designs—to isolate
and locate, hence to master, the negating
aspect of his temperament.
8. The process of integration effected by
art begins with the amalgamation of all
English ethnic groups into a single nation.
9. I.e., into the twelve Tribes of Israel.
1. Los's Emanation jealously fears that

the end of her separate existence will
lead Los to replace her with another
woman. Lambeth, the district in London
where Blake had lived 1791–1800, indicates an allusion to Blake's wife, Catherine.
2. Enitharmon's looms weave the bodies
of men clothed in the time and space of
Generation.
3. An echo of *Paradise Lost*, IX. 827
ff.: ". . . then I shall be no more, / And
Adam wedded to another Eve, / Shall
live with her enjoying, I extinct; / A
death to think." Her jealousy determines
Eve to persuade Adam to share the forbidden apple, and so to complete the
fall.

All their Jealousies, Revenges, Murders, hidings of Cruelty in
    Deceit
Appear only in the Outward Spheres of Visionary Space and Time,
In the shadows of Possibility by Mutual Forgiveness forevermore,
And in the Vision & in the Prophecy, that we may Foresee & Avoid
The terrors of Creation & Redemption & Judgment, Beholding
    them   20
Displayd in the Emanative Visions of Canaan, in Jerusalem & in
    Shiloh
And in the Shadows of Remembrance, & in the Chaos of the
    Spectre,
Amalek, Edom, Egypt, Moab, Ammon, Ashur, Philistea, around
    Jerusalem,
Where the Druids reard their Rocky Circles[4] to make permanent
    Remembrance
Of Sin, & the Tree of Good & Evil sprang from the Rocky Circle &
    Snake   25
Of the Druid, along the Valley of Rephaim from Camberwell to
    Golgotha,
And framed the Mundane Shell[5] Cavernous in Length, Bredth &
    Highth."

PLATE 93

Enitharmon heard. She raisd her head like the mild Moon:

"O Rintrah! O Palamabron![6] What are your dire & awful purposes?
Enitharmons name is nothing before you: you forget all my Love!
The Mothers love of obedience is forgotten, & you seek a Love
Of the pride of dominion, that will Divorce Ocalythron &
    Elynittria[7]   5
Upon East Moor in Derbyshire & along the Valleys of Cheviot.
Could you Love me, Rintrah, if you Pride not in my Love,
As Reuben found Mandrakes in the field & gave them to his
    Mother?[8]
Pride meets with Pride upon the Mountains in the stormy day,

4. Sanctuaries made of rocks placed in a circle.
5. The visible sky with its planets and constellations. It is the shell of what Blake calls "the Mundane Egg"—the illusory natural world of three-dimensional space.
6. The first two sons of Los and Enitharmon. Rintrah embodies the wrath of the prophet at the oppression of man and Palamabron his pity for the victims; Rintrah is sometimes represented (as in line 10) guiding a plow, while Palamabron follows with a harrow.
7. The first and second daughters of Los and Enitharmon, and the Emanations (hence wives) of Rintrah and Palama-

bron. Enitharmon appeals to her sons not to emulate what she takes to be her husband's cruel rejection.
8. Genesis 29–30 tells the story of Leah, Jacob's unloved first wife, who bore him sons, and Rachel, his second and favorite wife, who was barren. Reuben, Leah's first-born son, finds mandrakes in the field which he gives to his mother. (The mandrake, whose roots are shaped like a man's legs, is supposed to be an aphrodisiac and to promote conception.) Rachel begs the mandrakes from her, and receives them on condition that Leah shall lie that night with Jacob. She does so, and conceives another son.

In that terrible Day of Rintrahs Plow & of Satans driving the
    Team.   10
Ah! then I heard my little ones weeping along the Valley!
Ah! then I saw my beloved ones fleeing from my Tent!
Merlin[9] was like thee, Rintrah, among the Giants of Albion;
Judah was like Palamabron: O Simeon! O Levi![1] ye fled away.
How can I hear my little ones weeping along the Valley,   15
Or how upon the distant Hills see my beloveds Tents?"

Then Los again took up his speech as Enitharmon ceast:

"Fear not, my Sons, this Waking Death.[2] He is become One with
    me.
Behold him here! We shall not Die! we shall be united in Jesus.
Will you suffer this Satan, this Body of Doubt that Seems but Is
    Not,   20
To occupy the very threshold of Eternal Life? If Bacon, Newton,
    Locke,[3]
Deny a Conscience in Man & The Communion of Saints & Angels,
Contemning the Divine Vision & Fruition, Worshiping the Deus
Of the Heathen,[4] The God of This World, & the Goddess Nature
Mystery, Babylon the Great, The Druid Dragon & hidden Harlot, 25
Is it not that Signal of the morning which was told us in the
    Beginning?"[5]

Thus they converse upon Mam-Tor.[6] The Graves thunder under
    their feet.

PLATE 94

Albion cold lays on his Rock: storms & snows beat round him
Beneath the Furnaces & the starry Wheels & the Immortal Tomb.
Howling winds cover him, roaring seas dash furious against him,
In the deep darkness broad lightnings glare, long thunders roll.

The weeds of Death inwrap his hands & feet, blown incessant   5
And washd incessant by the for-ever restless sea-waves foaming
    abroad
Upon the white Rock. England, a Female Shadow,[7] as deadly
    damps

9. The seer and wizard at King Arthur's court, who figures in the poem as an English instance of the imaginative man.
1. Judah, Simeon, and Levi were among the twelve sons of Jacob (later renamed Israel) who founded the twelve Tribes of Israel.
2. I.e., Los's Spectre.
3. Blake's unholy trinity, who represent, respectively, the natural morality, natural science, and natural philosophy of the contemporary English world-view.
4. I.e., the god of the heathen; Blake here classifies paganism with the other false religions (above, 90.66, note).
5. The seeming triumph of the views of Bacon, Newton, Locke, is the "Signal" of apocalypse in the sense that it is the deepest darkness just before the dawn. Los represents the morning of the first created day "in the Beginning" (Genesis i.5) as prefiguring the dawning of "the Eternal Day" of apocalypse (97.3).
6. Mam-Tor and Mam-Win are a double peak in Derbyshire, named for the female breasts that they resemble.
7. Vala, illusory and separated Nature, who is the "Shadow" of Albion's Emanation, Jerusalem. A Shadow is to the female principle what the Spectre is to the male.

Of the Mines of Cornwall & Derbyshire lays upon his bosom,
   heavy,
Moved by the wind in volumes of thick cloud, returning, folding
   round
His loins & bosom, unremovable by swelling storms & loud
   rending   10
Of enraged thunders. Around them the Starry Wheels of their
   Giant Sons
Revolve: & over them the Furnaces of Los, & the Immortal Tomb
   around,
Erin[8] sitting in the Tomb, to watch them unceasing night and day;
And the Body of Albion was closed apart from all Nations.[9]

Over them the famished Eagle screams on boney Wings, and
   around   15
Them howls the Wolf of famine; deep heaves the Ocean black,
   thundering
Around the wormy Garments of Albion: then pausing in deathlike
   silence.

Time was Finished![1] The Breath Divine Breathed over Albion
Beneath the Furnaces & starry Wheels and in the Immortal Tomb,
And England, who is Brittannia, awoke from Death on Albions
   bosom.[2]   20
She awoke pale & cold, she fainted seven times on the Body of
   Albion.

"O pitious Sleep, O pitious Dream! O God, O God, awake! I have
   slain
In Dreams of Chastity & Moral Law, I have Murdered Albion! Ah!
In Stone-henge & on London Stone & in the Oak Groves of Malden
I have Slain him in my Sleep with the Knife of the Druid. O Eng-
   land!   25
O all ye Nations of the Earth! behold ye the Jealous Wife.
The Eagle & the Wolf & Monkey & Owl & the King & Priest were
   there."[3]

8. Erin (Ireland) watches at the tomb of Albion, like the Marys at the tomb of Christ. Ireland serves as a protector of Imagination because, geographically, it is a buffer between England and the Atlantic chaos; it serves also as a symbol of hope for resurrection because, at the time the poem was composed, it was renewing its struggle for independence from England.

9. In *Jerusalem* 79.22 Blake wrote that England had once (as a type of the spiritual Israel) "encompassed the Nations." Now, however, Albion-England has shrunk into a separate little island.

1. The moment of apocalypse, equivalent to Revelation 21.1: "And I saw a new heaven and a new earth: for the first heaven and the first earth were passed away."

2. The "Female Shadow" Vala (line 7) has reunited with Jerusalem to constitute Brittannia—an alternate name for Jerusalem—when she has become a fit consort for Albion-England.

3. Now Brittannia realizes that, as a divided and jealous "Female Will" (the prideful desire for dominion within the human psyche), she has spiritually murdered Albion by her claims to "Chastity & Moral Law" (line 22). Throughout the poem Blake represents sadistic and murderous actions, including wars, as a manifestation of sexuality that has been perverted by religious and moral prohibitions.

PLATE 95

Her voice pierc'd Albions clay cold ear. He moved upon the Rock.
The Breath Divine went forth upon the morning hills, Albion
    mov'd
Upon the Rock, he opened his eyelids in pain; in pain he mov'd
His stony members, he saw England. Ah! shall the Dead live again?

The Breath Divine went forth over the morning hills. Albion rose   5
In anger, the wrath of God breaking bright, flaming on all sides
    around
His awful limbs: into the Heavens he walked, clothed in flames,
Loud thundering, with broad flashes of flaming lightning & pillars
Of fire, speaking the Words of Eternity in Human Forms, in dire-
    ful
Revolutions of Action & Passion, thro the Four Elements on all
    sides   10
Surrounding his awful Members. Thou seest the Sun in heavy
    clouds
Struggling to rise above the Mountains. In his burning hand
He takes his Bow, then chooses out his arrows of flaming gold;[4]
Murmuring, the Bowstring breathes with ardor! Clouds roll round
    the
Horns of the wide Bow, loud sounding winds sport on the moun-
    tain brows,   15
Compelling Urizen to his Furrow, & Tharmas to his Sheepfold,
And Luvah to his Loom. Urthona he beheld, mighty, labouring at
His Anvil, in the Great Spectre Los, unwearied labouring & weep-
    ing.
Therefore the Sons of Eden praise Urthonas Spectre in songs,
Because he kept the Divine Vision in time of trouble.[5]   20

As the Sun & Moon lead forward the Visions of Heaven & Earth,
England, who is Brittannia, enterd Albions bosom rejoicing,
Rejoicing in his indignation! adoring his wrathful rebuke.
She who adores not your frowns will only loathe your smiles.

PLATE 96

As the Sun & Moon lead forward the Visions of Heaven & Earth,
England, who is Brittannia, entered Albions bosom rejoicing.

Then Jesus appeared, standing by Albion as the Good Shepherd
By the lost Sheep that he hath found, & Albion knew that it

4. Cf. Blake's poem "And Did Those
Feet," above: these are the bows of
"Mental Fight" and the "Arrows of desire" in the struggles of intellect and art
which build the New Jerusalem in England's green and pleasant land.
5. The Zoas Urizen, Tharmas, and

Luvah, are restored to their proper
places and functions as "Sons of Eden."
They now recognize that Los was the
fallen form of the fourth Zoa, Urthona,
and praise him as the agent of imaginative deliverance.

Was the Lord, the Universal Humanity, & Albion saw his Form,　　5
A Man, & they conversed as Man with Man, in Ages of Eternity,
And the Divine Appearance was the likeness & similitude of Los.[6]

Albion said: O Lord, what can I do? my Selfhood cruel
Marches against thee deceitful from Sinai & from Edom
Into the Wilderness of Judah to meet thee in his pride.　　10
I behold the Visions of my deadly Sleep of Six Thousand Years[7]
Dazling around thy skirts like a Serpent of precious stones & gold;
I know it is my Self, O my Divine Creator & Redeemer."

Jesus replied: "Fear not, Albion, unless I die thou canst not live,
But if I die I shall arise again, & thou with me.　　15
This is Friendship & Brotherhood; without it Man Is Not."

So Jesus spoke. The Covering Cherub,[8] coming on in darkness,
Overshadowed them, & Jesus said: Thus do Men in Eternity
One for another to put off by forgiveness every sin."

Albion replyd: "Cannot Man exist without Mysterious　　20
Offering of Self for Another? Is this Friendship & Brotherhood?
I see thee in the likeness & similitude of Los my Friend."

Jesus said: "Wouldest thou love one who never died
For thee, or ever die for one who had not died for thee?
And if God dieth not for Man & giveth not himself　　25
Eternally for Man, Man could not exist! for Man is Love,
As God is Love: every kindness to another is a little Death
In the Divine Image, nor can Man exist but by Brotherhood."

So saying, the Cloud, overshadowing, divided them asunder.
Albion stood in terror: not for himself but for his Friend　　30
Divine, & Self was lost in the contemplation of faith,
And wonder at the Divine Mercy & at Los's sublime honour.

"Do I sleep amidst danger to Friends? O my Cities & Counties,
Do you sleep? Rouze up, Rouze up. Eternal Death is abroad."

---

6. At his Second Coming, Jesus stands revealed as a Man among Men. He resembles Los because the Redeemer embodies the Human Imagination (5.20, above) which Los enacts in his labors as artist and prophet.
7. Blake echoes the tradition that the time between the creation and apocalyptic end of the world is six thousand years, proportionate to the six days of the act of creation.
8. The term "Covering Cherub" is applied by Ezekiel, xxviii.16, to the evil King of Tyre. The allusion is to the Cherubim that God placed to guard the way to the Garden of Eden after the expulsion of Adam (Genesis iii.24), and Blake identifies it with the Antichrist—i.e., the ultimate error to be overcome if man is to regain access to Eden. At this final moment, the Covering Cherub manifests itself in order to cut Albion off from his Saviour.

So Albion spoke, & threw himself into the Furnaces of affliction.[9] 35
All was a Vision, all a Dream: the Furnaces became
Fountains of Living Waters flowing from the Humanity Divine,
And all the Cities of Albion rose from their Slumbers, and All
The Sons & Daughters of Albion on soft clouds Waking from
  Sleep.
Soon all around, remote, the Heavens burnt with flaming fires, 40
And Urizen & Luvah & Tharmas & Urthona arose into
Albions Bosom. Then Albion stood before Jesus in the Clouds
Of Heaven, Fourfold among the Visions of God in Eternity.

PLATE 97

"Awake! Awake, Jerusalem! O lovely Emanation of Albion,
Awake and overspread all Nations as in Ancient Time.
For lo! the Night of Death is past and the Eternal Day
Appears upon our Hills: Awake Jerusalem, and come away."

So spake the Vision of Albion, & in him so spake in my hearing 5
The Universal Father. Then Albion stretched his hand into Infini-
  tude
And took his Bow. Fourfold the Vision;[1] for bright beaming Urizen
Layd his hand on the South & took a breathing Bow of carved
  Gold,
Luvah his hand stretch'd to the East & bore a Silver Bow, bright
  shining,
Tharmas Westward a Bow of Brass, pure flaming, richly wrought, 10
Urthona Northward in thick storms a Bow of Iron, terrible thunder-
  ing.

And the Bow is a Male & Female[2] & the Quiver of the Arrows of
  Love
Are the Children of this Bow: a Bow of Mercy & Loving-kindness,
  laying
Open the hidden Heart in Wars of mutual Benevolence, Wars of
  Love.
And the Hand of Man grasps firm between the Male & Female
  Loves, 15

9. The ironic result of the Cherub's intervention is that Albion overcomes his
self-concern in his fear for another's
safety (lines 30–31), sacrifices himself
(line 35) for the Saviour who has sacrificed himself for him, and so reveals the
Covering Cherub to have been the Selfhood which he has by that very act annihilated, thereby removing the barrier
to Eden.
1. The four Zoas have been reunited in
Albion (96.41–43); therefore, the form
of Albion in Eden, together with all his
instruments, actions, and perceptions, are
described as fourfold—i.e., as a consonance of all the human attributes and
powers.
  A prime source of Blake's preoccupa-

tion with the number four was the vision
of the Divine Chariot in the first chapter
of Ezekiel: "Also out of the midst
thereof came the likeness of four living
creatures. [Blake's term "Zoas" derives
from the Greek word for "living creatures"; see, e.g., 98.24.] They had the
likeness of a man. And every one had
four faces, and every one had four
wings." In Blake's vision of the Human
Fourfold, each Zoa has four faces and is
associated with one of the four cardinal
points of the compass and with one of
the four senses of sight, smell, taste, and
hearing (lines 97.7–11, 98.16–18).
2. In the bows of the intellectual wars
of Eden, as in Albion himself, the sexes
are once again undivided.

And he Clothed himself in Bow & Arrows in awful state Fourfold
In the midst of his Twenty-eight Cities, each with his Bow breath-
    ing.

PLATE 98

Then each an Arrow flaming from his Quiver fitted carefully;
They drew fourfold the unreprovable String, bending thro the wide
    Heavens
The horned Bow Fourfold; loud sounding flew the flaming Arrow
    fourfold.

Murmuring, the Bow-string breathes with ardor. Clouds roll round
    the horns
Of the wide Bow, loud sounding Winds sport on the Mountains
    brows: 5
The Druid Spectre was Annihilate, loud thundring, rejoicing ter-
    rific, vanishing,
Fourfold Annihilation; & at the clangor of the Arrows of Intellect
The innumerable Chariots of the Almighty appeard in Heaven,
And Bacon & Newton & Locke, & Milton & Shakspear & Chaucer,[3]
A Sun of blood red wrath surrounding heaven on all sides
    around,   10
Glorious, incomprehensible by Mortal Man, & each Chariot was
    Sexual Threefold,

And every Man stood Fourfold. Each Four Faces had, One to the
    West,
One toward the East. One to the South, One to the North, the
    Horses Fourfold.
And the dim Chaos brightend beneath, above, around, eyed as the
    Peacock,[4]
According to the Human Nerves of Sensation, the Four Rivers of
    the Water of Life.[5]   15
South stood the Nerves of the Eye; East in Rivers of bliss the
    Nerves of the
Expansive Nostrils; West flowd the Parent Sense, the Tongue;
    North stood
The labyrinthine Ear; Circumscribing & Circumcising the excre-
    mentitious
Husk & Covering, into Vacuum evaporating, revealing the linea-
    ments of Man,
Driving outward the Body of Death in an Eternal Death & Resur-
    rection,   20

3. The three great English enemies of Imagination are restored to a state in which they can engage in productive intellectual war with their contraries, the three great English exponents of imaginative poetry.
4. In Ezekiel i.18, the rings formed by the moving wheels of the visionary char-iot "were full of eyes round about them four."
5. Genesis ii.10–14 describes a river which flows through the Garden of Eden and then divides into four streams. Blake calls the mainstream the River of Life and equates its four branches with the four Zoas.

Awaking it to Life among the Flowers of Beulah,[6] rejoicing in
    Unity
In the Four Senses, in the Outline, the Circumference, & Form, for
    ever
In Forgiveness of Sins which is Self Annihilation. It is the Cove-
    nant of Jehovah.[7]

The Four Living Creatures, Chariots of Humanity, Divine, Incom-
    prehensible,
In beautiful Paradises expand. These are the Four Rivers of Para-
    dise   25
And the Four Faces of Humanity, fronting the Four Cardinal Points
Of Heaven, going forward, forward irresistible from Eternity to
    Eternity.

And they conversed together in Visionary forms dramatic,[8] which
    bright
Redounded from their Tongues in thunderous majesty, in Visions,
In new Expanses, creating exemplars of Memory and of Intellect,   30
Creating Space, Creating Time, according to the wonders Divine
Of Human Imagination, throughout all the Three Regions
    immense
Of Childhood, Manhood & Old Age; & the all tremendous unfath-
    omable Non Ens[9]
Of Death was seen in regenerations terrific or complacent, varying
According to the subject of discourse, & every Word & Every
    Character   35
Was Human, according to the Expansion or Contraction, the
    Translucence or
Opakeness of Nervous fibres; such was the variation of Time &
    Space,
Which vary according as the Organs of Perception vary & they
    walked
To & fro in Eternity as One Man, reflecting each in each & clearly
    seen
And seeing, according to fitness & order.[1] And I heard Jehovah
    speak   40

6. To the Sons of Eden, the lower state
of Beulah serves as an occasional resort
for rest and recuperation from the strenuous creative life of the Intellect.
7. Blake represents "Forgiveness of
Sins" to be the true meaning of the Old
Testament Covenant of Jehovah with
Abraham (Genesis xv.18–21) and with
Moses, when He gave Moses the Ten
Commandments on Sinai (Exodus xix–
xx).
8. Since all conversation in Eden is imaginative, words and "Visions" are one
—the very form, that is, of the dramatic
poem, consisting of unified text and illu-
minations, that Blake engraved in the
fallen world.
9. Latin: Non-Being.
1. In the fallen state, the senses became
fixed and narrowed, incapable of perceiving reality as other than isolated individuals in a dehumanized nature of time
and space. In the regenerate state, mankind's senses are once again capable of
the "Expansion or Contraction" (line
36) which can distinguish without dividing, alternately contracting to perceive
individuals as a many-in-one and expanding to perceive Universal Man as a
one-in-many. Also, this flexible vision
once again perceives the spatio-temporal
objects of what had seemed an inanimate nature as in fact "All Human
Forms identified" (99.1–2)—that is, as a
world whose categories are informed by
the creative human imagination (88.30–
32), and therefore as a human place fit
for men to live in.

Terrific from his Holy Place & saw the Words of the Mutual Covenant Divine
On Chariots of gold & jewels, with Living Creatures starry & flaming,
With every Colour, Lion, Tyger, Horse, Elephant, Eagle, Dove, Fly, Worm,
And the all wondrous Serpent clothed in gems & rich array, Humanize
In the Forgiveness of Sins according to the Covenant of Jehovah.[2] They Cry: 45
"Where is the Covenant of Priam, the Moral Virtues of the Heathen?[3]
Where is the Tree of Good & Evil that rooted beneath the cruel heel
Of Albions Spectre, the Patriarch Druid? Where are all his Human Sacrifices
For Sin in War & in the Druid Temples of the Accuser of Sin, beneath
The Oak Groves of Albion that coverd the whole Earth beneath his Spectre?   50
Where are the Kingdoms of the World & all their glory that grew on Desolation,
The Fruit of Albions Poverty Tree, when the Triple Headed Gog-Magog Giant
Of Albion Taxed the Nations into Desolation & then gave the Spectrous Oath?"[4]

Such is the Cry from all the Earth, from the living Creatures of the Earth
And from the great City of Golgonooza in the Shadowy Generation,[5]   55
And from the Thirty-two Nations of the Earth among the Living Creatures,

2. Even the jeweled Serpent of Albion's Selfhood (see 96.11–13), the ultimate Adversary, is rendered human in this apocalypse of the imagination. Behind this passage lies the heterodox tradition that at the end of time God's grace, the "Forgiveness of Sins," will include even the serpent that tempted Eve.
3. In Homer's *Iliad*, Priam was the king of Troy; his "Covenant" consists of "the Moral Virtues of the Heathen" that are exemplified in classical epic poems. This system of values is annihilated, together with all other forms of Natural Religion, including (line 47) the morality and creed of institutional Christianity.
4. In Revelations xx.7–9, when Satan is released at the close of the millennium, he enlists Gog and Magog to besiege the Saints who had reigned with Christ; the destruction of these two beings is immediately followed by the Last Judgment. Blake's historical allusions—expedited by the fact that some hills near Cambridge, England, are called the Gog-Magog Hills—are to the heavy taxes imposed by the "Triple Headed" English legislature (the Lords Spiritual, Lords Temporal, and Commons) to support the Napoleonic wars, and to the requirement of an oath of allegiance. There is a suggested parallel also to the "decree from Caesar Augustus, that all the world should be taxed" (Mark ii.1 ff.), which brought Joseph and Mary to Bethlehem, where she gave birth to the Redeemer.
5. The City of Art and Civilization at which Los had labored in the fallen state of Generation; its triumphant realization in Eden is New Jerusalem, the perfected human community.

PLATE 99

All Human Forms identified, even Tree, Metal, Earth & Stone; all
Human Forms identified, living, going forth, & returning wearied
Into the Planetary lives of Years, Months, Days & Hours, reposing
And then Awaking into his Bosom in the Life of Immortality.   60

And I heard the Name of their Emanations; they are named
Jerusalem.[6]

The End of The Song
of Jerusalem

ca. 1804–15   ca. 1815–20

A Vision of The Last Judgment[1]

For the Year 1810
Additions to Blake's Catalogue of Pictures &c

    The Last Judgment [will be] when all those are Cast away who
trouble Religion with Questions concerning Good & Evil or Eating
of the Tree of those Knowledges or Reasonings which hinder the
Vision of God turning all into a Consuming fire. When Imaginative Art & Science & all Intellectual Gifts, all the Gifts of the Holy
Ghost, are lookd upon as of no use & only Contention remains to
Man then the Last Judgment begins & its Vision is seen by the
Imaginative Eye of Every one according to the situation he holds.
    [PAGE 68] The Last Judgment is not Fable or Allegory but Vi-
sion. Fable or Allegory are a totally distinct & inferior kind of
Poetry. Vision or Imagination is a Representation of what Eter-
nally Exists, Really & Unchangeably. Fable or Allegory is Formd by

---

6. All female Emanations are reunited in
Albion's Emanation, Jerusalem, as all
the Spectre-Zoas are reunited in Albion.
The reunified or New Jerusalem, as
Blake wrote in *The Four Zoas*, is "a
City, yet a Woman"; it is where imaginative man lives, and everything that he
loves.
1. In this essay Blake describes and
comments on his painting of the Last
Judgment, now lost, which is said to
have measured seven by five feet and
to have included a thousand figures.
The text has been transcribed and rearranged, as the sequence of the pages
indicate, from the scattered fragments
in Blake's Notebook. The opening and

closing parts are reprinted here as
Blake's fullest, although cryptic, statements of what he means by vision.
These sections deal with the relations
of imaginative vision to allegory, Greek
fable, and the Biblical story; to uncurbed human passion and intellectual
power; to conventional and coercive
virtue; to what is seen by the "corporeal" eye; to the arts; and to the Last
Judgment and the apocalyptic redemption of man and the created world
—an apocalypse which is to be achieved
by the triumph over the bodily eye of
human imagination, as manifested in
the creative artist.

the daughters of Memory. Imagination is Surrounded by the daughters of Inspiration who in the aggregate are calld Jerusalem. [P 69] Fable is Allegory but what Critics call The Fable is Vision itself. [P 68] The Hebrew Bible & the Gospel of Jesus are not Allegory but Eternal Vision or Imagination of All that Exists. Note here that Fable or Allegory is Seldom without some Vision. Pilgrim's Progress is full of it, the Greek Poets the same; but Allegory & Vision ought to be known as Two Distinct Things & so calld for the Sake of Eternal Life. Plato has made Socrates say that Poets & Prophets do not know or Understand what they write or Utter; this is a most Pernicious Falshood. If they do not, pray is an inferior Kind to be calld Knowing? Plato confutes himself.[2]

The Last Judgment is one of these Stupendous Visions. I have represented it as I saw it. To different People it appears differently as [P 69] every thing else does for tho on Earth things seem Permanent they are less permanent than a Shadow as we all know too well.

The Nature of Visionary Fancy or Imagination is very little Known & the Eternal nature & permanence of its ever Existent Images is considered as less permanent than the things of Vegetative & Generative Nature; yet the Oak dies as well as the Lettuce, but Its Eternal ·Image & Individuality never dies, but renews by its seed. Just so the Imaginative Image returns by the seed of Contemplative Thought. The Writings of the Prophets illustrate these conceptions of the Visionary Fancy by their various sublime & Divine Images as seen in the Worlds of Vision. * * *

Let it here be Noted that the Greek Fables originated in Spiritual Mystery [P 72] and Real Visions Which are lost & clouded in Fable & Allegory while the Hebrew Bible & the Greek Gospel are Genuine, Preservd by the Saviour's Mercy. The Nature of my Work is Visionary or Imaginative. It is an Endeavour to Restore what the Ancients calld the Golden Age.

[PAGE 69] This world of Imagination is the World of Eternity; it is the Divine bosom into which we shall all go after the death of the Vegetated body. This World of Imagination is Infinite & Eternal whereas the world of Generation or Vegetation is Finite & for a small moment Temporal. There Exist in that Eternal World the Permanent Realities of Every Thing which we see reflected in this Vegetable Glass of Nature.

All Things are comprehended in their Eternal Forms in the Divine [P 70] body of the Saviour, the True Vine of Eternity, The Human Imagination, who appeard to Me as Coming to Judgment among his Saints & throwing off the Temporal that the Eternal

---

2. In Plato's diologue *Ion*, in which Socrates traps Ion into admitting that, since poets compose by inspiration, they do so without knowing what they are doing.

might be Establishd. Around him were seen the Images of Existences according to a certain order suited to my Imaginative Eye.
* * *

[PAGE 87] Men are admitted into Heaven not because they have curbed & governd their Passions or have No Passions but because they have Cultivated their Understandings. The Treasures of Heaven are not Negations of Passion but Realities of Intellect from which All the Passions Emanate Uncurbed in their Eternal Glory. The Fool shall not enter into Heaven let him be ever so Holy. Holiness is not The Price of Enterance into Heaven. Those who are cast out Are All Those who, having no Passions of their own because No Intellect, Have spent their lives in Curbing & Governing other People's by the Various arts of Poverty & Cruelty of all kinds. Wo Wo Wo to you Hypocrites. Even Murder the Courts of Justice, more merciful than the Church, are compelld to allow is not done in Passion but in Cool Blooded Design & Intention.

The Modern Church Crucifies Christ with the Head Downwards.

[PAGE 92] Many Persons such as Paine & Voltaire with some of the Ancient Greeks say we will not converse concerning Good & Evil we will live in Paradise & Liberty. You may do so in Spirit but not in the Mortal Body as you pretend, till after the Last Judgment; for in Paradise they have no Corporeal & Mortal Body; that originated with the Fall & was calld Death & cannot be removed but by a Last Judgment; while we are in the world of Mortality we Must Suffer. The Whole Creation Groans to be deliverd; there will always be as many Hypocrites born as Honest Men & they will always have superior Power in Mortal Things. You cannot have Liberty in this World without what you call Moral Virtue & you cannot have Moral Virtue without the Slavery of that half of the Human Race who hate what you call Moral Virtue.

The Nature of Hatred & Envy & of All the Mischiefs in the World are here depicted. No one Envies or Hates one of his Own Party; even the devils love one another in their Way; they torment one another for other reasons than Hate or Envy; these are only employd against the Just. Neither can Seth Envy Noah, or Elijah Envy Abraham, but they may both of them Envy the Success [P 93] of Satan or of Og or Molech. The Horse never Envies the Peacock nor the Sheep the Goat but they Envy a Rival in Life & Existence whose ways & means exceed their own, let him be of what Class of Animals he will; a Dog will envy a Cat who is pamperd at the expense of his comfort, as I have often seen. The Bible never tells us that Devils torment one another thro Envy; it is thro this that they torment the Just; but for what do they torment one another? I answer, For the Coercive Laws of Hell, Moral Hypocrisy. They torment a Hypocrite when he is discovered; they Punish a Failure in the tormentor who has suffered the Subject of his torture to Escape. In Hell all is Self Righteousness; there is no such thing there as Forgiveness of Sin; he who does Forgive Sin is Crucified as an Abettor of Criminals, & he who performs Works of Mercy in Any shape whatever is punishd & if possible destroyd, not thro Envy or Hatred or Malice but thro Self Righteousness that thinks it does God service, which God is Satan. They do not Envy one another; they contemn & despise one another.

Forgiveness of Sin is only at the Judgment Seat of Jesus the Saviour, where the Accuser is cast out, not because he Sins but because he torments the Just & makes them do what he condemns as Sin & what he knows is opposite to their own Identity.

It is not because Angels are Holier than Men or Devils that makes them Angels but because they do not Expect Holiness from one another but from God only.

The Player is a liar when he Says Angels are happier than [P 94] Men because they are better. Angels are happier than Men & Devils because they are not always Prying after Good & Evil in one Another & eating the Tree of Knowledge for Satan's Gratification.

Thinking as I do that the Creator of this World is a very Cruel Being, & being a Worshipper of Christ, I cannot help saying: "the Son O how unlike the Father!" First God Almighty comes with a Thump on the Head. Then Jesus Christ comes with a balm to heal it.

The Last Judgment is an Overwhelming of Bad Art & Science. Mental Things are alone Real; what is Calld Corporeal Nobody Knows of its dwelling Place; it is in Fallacy & its Existence an Imposture. Where is the Existence Out of Mind or Thought? Where is it but in the Mind of a Fool? Some People flatter themselves that there will be No Last Judgment & [P 95] that Bad Art will be adopted & mixed with Good Art, That Error or Experiment will make a Part of Truth, & they Boast that it is its Foundation. These People flatter themselves; I will not Flatter them. Error is Created. Truth is Eternal. Error or Creation will be Burned Up, & then & not till then Truth or Eternity will appear. It is Burnt up the Moment Men cease to behold it. I assert for My self that I do not behold the Outward Creation & that to me it is hindrance & not Action; it is as the Dirt upon my feet, No part of Me. "What," it will be Questiond, "When the Sun rises do you not see a round Disk of fire somewhat like a Guinea?" O no no, I see an Innumerable company of the Heavenly host crying "Holy Holy Holy is the Lord God Almighty." I question not my Corporeal or Vegetative Eye any more than I would Question a Window concerning a Sight. I look thro it & not with it.

1810   1810

[Two Letters on Sight and Vision[1]]

To Dr. John Trusler (August 23, 1799)

Revd Sir

I really am sorry that you are falln out with the Spiritual World Especially if I should have to answer for it. I feel very sorry that your Ideas & Mine on Moral Painting differ so much as to have made you angry with my method of Study. If I am wrong I am wrong in good company. I had hoped your plan comprehended All Species of this Art & Especially that you would not regret that Species which gives Existence to Every other, namely Visions of Eternity. You say that I want somebody to Elucidate my Ideas. But you ought to know that What is Grand is necessarily obscure to Weak men. That which can be made Explicit to the Idiot is not worth my care. The wisest of the Ancients considerd what is not too Explicit as the fittest for Instruction because it rouzes the faculties to act. I name Moses Solomon Esop Homer Plato.

But as you have favord me with your remarks on my Design permit me in return to defend it against a mistaken one, which is, That I have supposed Malevolence without a Cause.[2]—Is not Merit in one a Cause of Envy in another & Serenity & Happiness &

1. Blake wrote each of these pronouncements about the difference between "corporeal" sight and imaginative vision at a time when a patron was putting pressure on him to turn from his visionary art to more fashionable modes of representation. The first letter is a passionate response to John Trusler (1735–1820), clergyman, bookseller, and author, who had objected to Blake's illustrations for one of Trusler's books. The second letter was addressed to Thomas Butts (d. 1845), a staunch supporter who, though only a chief clerk in the Public Record Office, bought more of Blake's works than did any other contemporary. To this friend Blake expresses his anguish at the demands of William Hayley (1745–1820), a well-to-do writer and patron of the arts who, after having settled the Blakes at Felpham in Sussex, was trying to impose on the artist, for what he thought were Blake's best interests, his own conventional standards and tastes.

In the second letter Blake includes a poem, "With happiness stretch'd across the hills," which expresses his distress at the vexations of his mundane life, and the conflict he felt between the need to provide for the material wants of his family and the betrayal this seemed to involve of his own artistic genius, which manifests itself to him in outward form as the accusing figure of Los. The poem distinguishes four ways of viewing the natural world. Its last six lines indicate that these four modes, from single up to fourfold vision, are related to the four "States" of human consciousness—from Ulro (the world-view of Newtonian science), through Generation, and Beulah, to the ultimate imaginative vision, Eden, in which the objects of the world of nature, freed from the illusory categories of time and space, are revealed in their eternal and human forms. This highest "fourfold vision" is correlated also, in Blake's mythology, with the "expanded" and integral vision of the world as perceived by the "human fourfold"—that is, by the four Zoas when they have been re-integrated into the redeemed Albion. (See Jerusalem, Plate 98, above.)

2. Blake had made for Trusler a watercolor drawing (which has survived), illustrating Malevolence. As Blake described this design in an earlier letter: "A Father, taking leave of his Wife & Child, Is watch'd by two Fiends incarnate, with intention that when his back is turned they will murder the mother & her infant."

Beauty a Cause of Malevolence? But Want of Money & the Distress of A Thief can never be alledged as the Cause of his Thievery, for many honest people endure greater hard ships with Fortitude. We must therefore seek the Cause elsewhere than in want of Money for that is the Misers passion, not the Thiefs.

I have therefore proved your Reasonings Ill proportiond, which you can never prove my figures to be. They are those of Michael Angelo Rafael & the Antique & of the best living Models. I percieve that your Eye is perverted by Caricature Prints, which ought not to abound so much as they do. Fun I love but too much Fun is of all things the most loathsom. Mirth is better than Fun & Happiness is better than Mirth—I feel that a Man may be happy in This World. And I know that This World Is a World of Imagination & Vision. I see Every thing I paint In This World, but Every body does not see alike. To the Eyes of a Miser a Guinea is more beautiful than the Sun & a bag worn with the use of Money has more beautiful proportions than a Vine filled with Grapes. The tree which moves some to tears of joy is in the Eyes of others only a Green thing that stands in the way. Some See Nature all Ridicule & Deformity & by these I shall not regulate my proportions, & Some Scarce see Nature at all. But to the Eyes of the Man of Imagination Nature is Imagination itself. As a man is So he Sees. As the Eye is formed such are its Powers. You certainly Mistake when you say that the Visions of Fancy are not to be found in This World. To Me This World is all One continued Vision of Fancy or Imagination & I feel Flatterd when I am told So. What is it sets Homer Virgil & Milton in so high a rank of Art? Why is the Bible more Entertaining & Instructive than any other book? Is it not because they are addressed to the Imagination which is Spiritual Sensation & but mediately to the Understanding or Reason? Such is True Painting and such was alone valued by the Greeks & the best modern Artists. Consider what Lord Bacon says, "Sense sends over to Imagination before Reason have judged & Reason sends over to Imagination before the Decree can be acted." See Advancem[t] of Learning, Part 2, P. 47 of first Edition.

But I am happy to find a Great Majority of Fellow Mortals who can Elucidate My Visions & Particularly they have been Elucidated by Children, who have taken a greater delight in contemplating my Pictures than I even hoped. Neither Youth nor Childhood is Folly or Incapacity. Some Children are Fools & so are some Old Men. But There is a vast Majority on the side of Imagination or Spiritual Sensation.

To Engrave after another Painter is infinitely more laborious than to Engrave ones own Inventions. And of the Size you require my price has been Thirty Guineas & I cannot afford to do it for less. I had Twelve for the Head I sent you as a Specimen, but after my own designs I could do at least Six times the quantity of labour in the same time, which will account for the difference of price, as also that Chalk Engraving is at least six times as laborious as Aqua tinta. I have no objection to Engraving after another Artist. Engraving is the profession I was apprenticed to, & should never have attempted to live by any thing else, If orders had not come in for my Designs & Paintings, which I have the pleasure to tell you are Increasing Every Day. Thus If I am a Painter it is not to be attributed to Seeking after. But I am contented whether I live by Painting or Engraving.

I am Revᵈ Sir Your very obedient servant

William Blake

To Thomas Butts (November 22, 1802)

[With Happiness Stretchd Across the Hills]

Dear Sir

After I had finishd my Letter I found that I had not said half what I intended to say, & in particular I wish to ask you what subject you choose to be painted on the remaining Canvas which I brought down with me (for there were three) and to tell you that several of the Drawings were in great forwardness; you will see by the Inclosed Account that the remaining Number of Drawings which you gave me orders for is Eighteen. I will finish these with all possible Expedition, if indeed I have not tired you or, as it is politely calld, Bored you too much already; or if you would rather cry out Enough, Off Off! tell me in a Letter of forgiveness if you were offended, & of accustomd friendship if you were not. But I will bore you more with some Verses which My Wife desires me to Copy out & send you with her kind love & Respect they were Composed above a twelve-month ago while Walking from Felpham to Lavant to meet my Sister:

> With happiness stretchd across the hills
> In a cloud that dewy sweetness distills
> With a blue sky spread over with wings
> And a mild sun that mounts & sings
> With trees & fields full of Fairy elves   5
> And little devils who fight for themselves
> Remembring the Verses that Hayley sung
> When my heart knockd against the root of my tongue
> With Angels planted in Hawthorn bowers
> And God himself in the passing hours   10
> With Silver Angels across my way
> And Golden Demons that none can stay

With my Father hovering upon the wind
And my Brother Robert just behind
And my Brother John the evil one[3]   15
In a black cloud making his mone
Tho dead they appear upon my path
Notwithstanding my terrible wrath
They beg they intreat they drop their tears
Filld full of hopes filld full of fears   20
With a thousand Angels upon the Wind
Pouring disconsolate from behind
To drive them off & before my way
A frowning Thistle implores my stay
What to others a trifle appears   25
Fills me full of smiles or tears
For double the vision my Eyes do see
And a double vision is always with me
With my inward Eye 'tis an old Man grey
With my outward a Thistle across my way   30
"If thou goest back," the thistle said,
"Thou art to endless woe betrayd
For here does Theotormon lower
And here is Enitharmons bower
And Los the terrible[4] thus hath sworn   35
Because thou backward dost return
Poverty Envy old age & fear
Shall bring thy Wife upon a bier
And Butts shall give what Fuseli gave
A dark black Rock & a gloomy Cave."[5]   40

I struck the Thistle with my foot
And broke him up from his delving root
"Must the duties of life each other cross
Must every joy be dung & dross
Must my dear Butts feel cold neglect   45
Because I give Hayley his due respect
Must Flaxman[6] look upon me as wild
And all my friends be with doubts beguild
Must my Wife live in my Sisters bane

3. Blake's father, James, had died in 1784. Three years later his brother, Robert, died of consumption; Blake, who was devoted to him and attended him on his deathbed for two sleepless weeks, said that all his life thereafter Robert conversed with him "daily and hourly in the spirit." "Brother John" was the ne'er-do-well of the family; he had enlisted as a soldier and died soon after.
4. Theotormon was one of the four sons of Los and his Emanation, Enitharmon. These personages serve here as guardians of Blake's fidelity to the promptings of his poetic genius.
5. The rock and cave are among Blake's recurrent symbols for the fallen, or "unimaginative," world. Henry Fuseli was a fellow-artist, friend, and admirer of Blake, but the two had recently quarreled; the threat is that Butts will do likewise, and so destroy his imaginative state.
6. John Flaxman was a well-known sculptor of the time; like Fuseli, he admired Blake's work and helped him in his profession, but the relations between the two artists were sometimes strained.

Or my sister survive on my Loves pain[7] 50
The curses of Los the terrible shade
And his dismal terrors make me afraid"

So I spoke & struck in my wrath
The old man weltering upon my path
Then Los appeard in all his power 55
In the Sun he appeared descending before
My face in fierce flames in my double sight
Twas outward a Sun: inward Los in his might[8]

"My hands are labour'd day & night
And Ease comes never in my sight 60
My Wife has no indulgence given
Except what comes to her from heaven
We eat little we drink less
This Earth breeds not our happiness
Another Sun feeds our lifes streams 65
We are not warmed with thy beams
Thou measurest not the Time to me
Nor yet the Space that I do see
My Mind is not with thy light arrayd
Thy terrors shall not make me afraid" 70

When I had my Defiance given
The Sun stood trembling in heaven
The Moon that glowd remote below
Became leprous & white as snow
And every Soul of men on the Earth 75
Felt affliction & sorrow & sickness & dearth
Los flamd in my path & the Sun was hot
With the bows of my Mind & the Arrows of Thought
My bowstring fierce with Ardour breathes
My arrows glow in their golden sheaves[9] 80
My brothers & father march before
The heavens drop with human gore

Now I a fourfold vision see
And a fourfold vision is given to me
Tis fourfold in my supreme delight 85
And threefold in soft Beulahs night
And twofold Always. May God us keep
From Single vision & Newtons sleep

I also inclose you some Ballads by Mr Hayley with prints to them
by Your Hble. Servt.[1] I should have sent them before now but

---

7. Blake's sister, Catherine, lived with Blake and his wife at Felpham, and the two Catherines did not get along with each other.
8. To the poet's "twofold" vision, the material sun is recognized, in its spiritual form, as Los.

9. Compare the bow and arrows of "Mental Fight" in the poem, "And Did Those Feet," above.
1. *Designs to a Series of Ballads written by William Hayley*, with engravings by Blake, was published in 1802.

could not get any thing done for You to please myself, for I do assure you that I have truly studied the two little pictures I now send & do not repent of the time I have spent upon them.

God bless you.

Yours
W B

P.S. I have taken the liberty to trouble you with a letter to my Brother which you will be so kind as to send or give him & oblige yours, W B

WILLIAM WORDSWORTH
(1770–1850)

1791–92: In France during the early period of the Revolution.
1797:   With his sister Dorothy at Alfoxden, Somersetshire, near Coleridge at Nether Stowey.
1798:   First edition of *Lyrical Ballads*.
1799:   William and Dorothy settle at Grasmere, in the Lake District.
1800:   Second edition of *Lyrical Ballads* in two volumes, with the famous Preface.
1807:   *Poems in Two Volumes*; end of the great decade.

Wordsworth was born in Cockermouth in West Cumberland, just on the northern fringe of the English Lake District; when his mother died, the 8-year-old boy was sent to school at Hawkshead, near Esthwaite Lake, in the heart of that thinly settled region which he and Coleridge were to transform into the poetic center of England. William and his three brothers boarded in the cottage of Ann Tyson, who gave the boys simple comfort, ample affection, and freedom to roam the countryside at will. A vigorous, willful, and sometimes moody boy, William spent his free days and sometimes "half the night" in the sports and rambles described in the first two books of *The Prelude*, "drinking in" (to use one of his favorite metaphors) the natural sights and sounds, and getting to know the cottagers, shepherds, and solitary wanderers who moved through his imagination and dreams into his later poetry. He also found time to read voraciously in the books owned by his young headmaster, William Taylor, who encouraged him in his inclination to poetry.

John Wordsworth, the poet's father, died suddenly when William was 13, leaving to his five children mainly the substantial sum owed him by Lord Lonsdale, whom he had served as attorney and as steward of the huge Lonsdale estate. That harsh and litigious nobleman managed to keep from paying the debt until he died in 1802. Wordsworth was nevertheless able to go up to St. John's College, Cambridge, in 1787, where he found very little in the limited curriculum of that time to appeal to him; he took his A.B. degree in 1791 without distinction.

During the summer vacation of his third year at Cambridge (1790), Wordsworth and his closest college friend, the Welshman Robert Jones, made a walking tour through France and the Alps (described in *The Prelude* VI) at the time when Frenchmen were joyously celebrating the first anniversary of the fall of the Bastille. Upon completing his course at Cambridge, Wordsworth spent four months in London, set off on another walking tour with Robert Jones through Wales (the time of the memorable ascent of Mount Snowdon in *The Prelude* XIV), and then went back alone to France in order to master the language and qualify as a traveling tutor.

In that year (between November, 1791, and December, 1792) Wordsworth became a fervent "democrat" and proselyte of the French Revolution —which seemed to him, as to many other generous spirits, to promise a "glorious renovation"—and he had a passionate love affair with Annette Vallon, the impetuous and warm-hearted daughter of a French surgeon at Blois. It seems clear that Wordsworth and Annette planned to marry, despite their difference in religion and political inclinations (Annette belonged to an old Catholic family whose sympathies were Royalist). But almost immediately after a daughter, Caroline, was born, lack of funds forced Wordsworth back to England. The outbreak of war between England and France made it impossible for him to rejoin Annette until they had drifted so far apart in sympathies that a permanent union no longer seemed practicable. Wordsworth's agonies of guilt, his divided loyalties between England and France, his gradual disillusion with the course of the Revolution in France—as he describes them in *The Prelude* X and XI —brought him to the verge of an emotional breakdown, when "sick, wearied out with contrarieties," he "yielded up moral questions in despair." His suffering, his near-collapse, and the successful effort, after his sharp break with his own past, to re-establish "a saving intercourse with my true self" are the experiences which underlie many of Wordsworth's greatest poems.

At this critical point a young friend, Raisley Calvert, died and left Wordsworth a sum of money just sufficient to enable him to live solely by his poetry. He settled in a rent-free cottage at Racedown, Dorsetshire, with his beloved sister Dorothy, who now began her long career as confidante, inspirer, and secretary. At that same time Wordsworth met Samuel Taylor Coleridge; two years later he moved to Alfoxden to be near Coleridge, who lived four miles away at Nether Stowey. Here, his recovery complete, he entered at the age of 27 upon the delayed springtime of his poetic career.

Even while he had been an undergraduate at Cambridge, Coleridge had detected signs of genius in Wordsworth's rather conventional poem about his tour in the Alps, *Descriptive Sketches*, published in 1793. Now he hailed Wordsworth unreservedly as "the best poet of the age." The two men met almost daily, talked for hours about poetry, and composed prolifically. So close was their association that they lost almost all sense of individual proprietorship in a composition. We find the same phrases occurring in poems of Wordsworth and Coleridge, as well as in the remarkable journals that Dorothy kept at the time; the two poets collaborated in some writings and freely traded thoughts and passages for others; and Coleridge even undertook to complete a few poems that Wordsworth had left unfinished.

The result of their joint efforts was a small volume, published anonymously in 1798, *Lyrical Ballads, With a Few Other Poems*. It opened with Coleridge's *Ancient Mariner*, included three other poems by Coleridge, a number of Wordsworth's verse anecdotes and psychological studies of humble people, some lyrics in which Wordsworth celebrated impulses from a vernal wood, and closed with Wordsworth's great descriptive and meditative poem in blank verse (not a "lyrical ballad," but one of the "other poems" of the title), *Tintern Abbey*. No other book of poems in English so plainly announces a new literary departure. William Hazlitt wrote that when he heard Coleridge read some of these newly written poems aloud, "the sense of a new style and a new spirit in poetry came over me," with something of the effect "that arises from the turning up of the fresh soil, or of the first welcome breath of spring." The professional reviewers were less enthusiastic. Nevertheless *Lyrical Ballads* sold out in two years, and Wordsworth published over his own name a new edition, dated 1800, to which he added a second volume of poems, many of them written in homesickness during a long, cold, and friendless winter he and Dorothy had spent in Goslar, Germany, 1798–99. In his famous Preface to this edition, planned, like so many of the poems, in close consultation with Coleridge, Wordsworth enunciated the principles of the new criticism which served as rationale for the new poetry. Notable among the other works written in this prolific period is the austere and powerful tragic poem *The Ruined Cottage*.

Late in 1799 Wordsworth and Dorothy moved back permanently to their native lakes, settling at Grasmere in the little house later named Dove Cottage; Coleridge, following them, rented Greta Hall at Keswick, thirteen miles away. In 1802 Wordsworth finally came into his father's inheritance and, after an amicable settlement with Annette Vallon, married Mary Hutchinson, a Lake Country girl whom he had known since childhood. The course of his existence after that time was broken by various disasters: the drowning in 1805 of his favorite brother John, a sea captain whose ship was wrecked in a storm; the death of two of his five children in 1812; a gradual estrangement from Coleridge, culminating in an open quarrel (1810) from which they were not completely reconciled for almost two decades; and, from the 1830's on, the physical and mental decline of his sister Dorothy. The life of his middle age, however, was one of steadily increasing prosperity and reputation, as well as of political and religious conservatism. In 1813 an appointment as Stamp Distributor (that is, revenue collector) for Westmoreland was concrete evidence of his recognition as a national poet. Gradually Wordsworth's residences, as he moved into more and more commodious quarters, became standard places of resort for tourists; he was awarded honorary degrees and, in 1843, appointed poet laureate. He died in 1850 at the age of 80; only then did his executors publish his masterpiece, *The Prelude*, the autobiographical poem which he had written in two parts in 1799 and then expanded to its full length in 1805, but which he continued to revise almost to the last decade of his long life.

Most of Wordsworth's greatest poetry had been written by 1807, when he published *Poems in Two Volumes;* and after *The Excursion* (1814) and the first collected edition of his poems (1815), although he continued to write voluminously, there is a conspicuous decline in his powers as a poet. The causes of what is often called "Wordsworth's anti-climax" have been much debated; the principal cause seems to be inherent in the very nature of his most characteristic writing. Wordsworth is above all the poet of the remembrance of things past, or as he himself put it, of "emotion recollected in tranquility." Some object or event in the present triggers a sudden renewal of feelings he had experienced in youth; the result is a poem exhibiting the sharp discrepancy between what Wordsworth called "two consciousnesses": himself as he is now and as he once was. But one's early emotional experience is not an inexhaustible resource for poetry. As Basil Willey has said, Wordsworth as a poet "was living upon capital"; and he knew it. As he says in *The Prelude* XII, while describing the recurrence of "spots of time" from his memories of childhood:

> The days gone by
> Return upon me almost from the dawn
> Of life: the hiding places of man's power
> Open; I would approach them, but they close.
> I see by glimpses now; when age comes on,
> May scarcely see at all. * * *

The past which Wordsworth recollected was one of emotional turmoil which is ordered, in the calmer present, into a hard-won equilibrium. The result was a poetry of excitation in calm; genius, as Wordsworth said, is "born to thrive by interchange / Of peace and excitation" (*Prelude* XIII.1–10). As time went on, however, the precarious equilibrium of his great creative period became a habit, and Wordsworth finally gained what, in the *Ode to Duty* (composed in 1804), he longed for, "a repose which ever is the same"—but at the expense of the agony and excitation which, under the calm surface, empowers his best and most characteristic poems.

Occasionally in his middle and later life a jolting experience would revive the intensity of Wordsworth's remembered emotion, and also his earlier poetic strength. The moving sonnet *Surprised by Joy*, for example, was written in his forties at the abrupt realization that time was beginning to diminish his grief at the death some years earlier of his little daughter Catherine. And when Wordsworth was 65 years old, the sudden report of the death of James Hogg called up the memory of other and greater poets whom Wordsworth had loved and outlived; the result was an "Extempore Effusion," written in a return to the simple quatrains of the early *Lyrical Ballads* and with a recovery of the great elegiac voice which had uttered the dirges to Lucy, 35 years before.

From LYRICAL BALLADS
We Are Seven[1]

—A simple Child,
That lightly draws its breath,
And feels its life in every limb,
What should it know of death?

I met a little cottage Girl: 5
She was eight years old, she said;
Her hair was thick with many a curl
That clustered round her head.

1. "Written at Alfoxden in the spring of 1798. * * * The little girl who is the heroine I met within the area of Goodrich Castle in the year 1793" (Wordsworth). Wordsworth also tells us that he composed the last line of the last stanza first, and that Coleridge contributed the initial stanza.

She had a rustic, woodland air,
And she was wildly clad:
Her eyes were fair, and very fair; 10
—Her beauty made me glad.

"Sisters and brothers, little Maid,
How many may you be?"
"How many? Seven in all," she said, 15
And wondering looked at me.

"And where are they? I pray you tell."
She answered, "Seven are we;
And two of us at Conway dwell,
And two are gone to sea. 20

"Two of us in the churchyard lie,
My sister and my brother;
And, in the churchyard cottage, I
Dwell near them with my mother."

"You say that two at Conway dwell, 25
And two are gone to sea,
Yet ye are seven! I pray you tell,
Sweet Maid, how this may be."

Then did the little Maid reply,
"Seven boys and girls are we; 30
Two of us in the churchyard lie,
Beneath the churchyard tree."

"You run about, my little Maid,
Your limbs they are alive;
If two are in the churchyard laid, 35
Then ye are only five."

"Their graves are green, they may be seen,"
The little Maid replied,
"Twelve steps or more from my mother's door,
And they are side by side. 40

"My stockings there I often knit,
My kerchief there I hem;
And there upon the ground I sit,
And sing a song to them.

"And often after sunset, sir, 45
When it is light and fair,
I take my little porringer,[2]
And eat my supper there.

"The first that died was sister Jane;
In bed she moaning lay, 50
Till God released her of her pain;
And then she went away.

2. Bowl for porridge.

"So in the churchyard she was laid;
And, when the grass was dry,
Together round her grave we played,
My brother John and I.   55

"And when the ground was white with snow,
And I could run and slide,
My brother John was forced to go,
And he lies by her side."   60

"How many are you, then," said I,
"If they two are in heaven?"
Quick was the little Maid's reply,
"O master! we are seven."

"But they are dead; those two are dead!   65
Their spirits are in heaven!"
'Twas throwing words away; for still
The little Maid would have her will,
And said, "Nay, we are seven!"

1798   1798

Lines Written in Early Spring

I heard a thousand blended notes,
While in a grove I sate reclined,
In that sweet mood when pleasant thoughts
Bring sad thoughts to the mind.

To her fair works did Nature link   5
The human soul that through me ran;
And much it grieved my heart to think
What man has made of man.

Through primrose tufts, in that green bower,
The periwinkle[3] trailed its wreaths;   10
And 'tis my faith that every flower
Enjoys the air it breathes.

The birds around me hopped and played,
Their thoughts I cannot measure—
But the least motion which they made,   15
It seemed a thrill of pleasure.

The budding twigs spread out their fan,
To catch the breezy air;
And I must think, do all I can,
That there was pleasure there.   20

If this belief from heaven be sent,
If such be Nature's holy plan,[4]

3. A trailing evergreen plant with
small blue flowers (U.S. myrtle).
4. The version of these lines printed in
the *Lyrical Ballads* of 1798 mentioned
neither heaven nor holiness: "If I these
thoughts may not prevent, / If such
be of my creed the plan."

Have I not reason to lament
What man has made of man?   *how people treat each other*

1798   1798

Expostulation and Reply[1]

"Why, William, on that old gray stone,
Thus for the length of half a day,
Why, William, sit you thus alone,
And dream your time away?

"Where are your books?—that light bequeathed   5
To beings else forlorn and blind!
Up! up! and drink the spirit breathed
From dead men to their kind.

"You look round on your Mother Earth,
As if she for no purpose bore you;   10
As if you were her first-born birth,
And none had lived before you!"

One morning thus, by Esthwaite lake,
When life was sweet, I knew not why,
To me my good friend Matthew[2] spake,   15
And thus I made reply:

"The eye—it cannot choose but see;
We cannot bid the ear be still;
Our bodies feel, where'er they be,
Against or with our will.   20

"Nor less I deem that there are Powers
Which of themselves our minds impress;
That we can feed this mind of ours
In a wise passiveness.

"Think you, 'mid all this mighty sum   25
Of things forever speaking,
That nothing of itself will come,
But we must still be seeking?

"—Then ask not wherefore, here, alone,
Conversing[3] as I may,   30
I sit upon this old gray stone,
And dream my time away."

1798   1798

1. This and the following companion-poem have often been attacked—and defended—as Wordsworth's solemn deliverance on the comparative merits of nature and of books. But they are a dialogue between two friends who are intimate enough to rally one another by the usual device of overstating parts of a whole truth. Wordsworth said that the pieces originated in a conversation "with a friend who was somewhat unreasonably attached to modern books of moral philosophy," and also that the lore of "a wise passiveness" made the poem a favorite among Quakers.
2. A fictitious schoolmaster who plays a role in others of Wordsworth's early poems.
3. In the old sense of "communing" (with the "things forever speaking").

The Tables Turned

AN EVENING SCENE ON THE SAME SUBJECT

Up! up! my friend, and quit your books,
Or surely you'll grow double;
Up! up! my friend, and clear your looks;
Why all this toil and trouble?

The sun, above the mountain's head,   5
A freshening luster mellow
Through all the long green fields has spread,
His first sweet evening yellow.

Books! 'tis a dull and endless strife:
Come, hear the woodland linnet,[1]   10
How sweet his music! on my life,
There's more of wisdom in it.

And hark! how blithe the throstle[2] sings!
He, too, is no mean preacher;
Come forth into the light of things,   15
Let Nature be your teacher.

She has a world of ready wealth,
Our minds and hearts to bless—
Spontaneous wisdom breathed by health,
Truth breathed by cheerfulness.   20

One impulse from a vernal wood
May teach you more of man,
Of moral evil and of good,
Than all the sages can.

Sweet is the lore which Nature brings;   25
Our meddling intellect
Misshapes the beauteous forms of things—
We murder to dissect.

Enough of Science and of Art;
Close up those barren leaves;
Come forth, and bring with you a heart   30
That watches and receives.

1798   1798

To My Sister[1]

It is the first mild day of March:
Each minute sweeter than before,

1. A small finch, common in Europe.
2. The song thrush.
1. "Composed in front of Alfoxden House. * * * The larch mentioned in the first stanza was standing when I revisited the place in May, 1841, more than forty years after" (Wordsworth). The "Sister" is, of course, Dorothy, and "Edward" (named in line 13) is the boy Basil Montagu, then living with the Wordsworths.

The redbreast sings from the tall larch
That stands beside our door.

There is a blessing in the air,   5
Which seems a sense of joy to yield
To the bare trees, and mountains bare,
And grass in the green field.

My Sister! ('tis a wish of mine)
Now that our morning meal is done,   10
Make haste, your morning task resign;
Come forth and feel the sun.

Edward will come with you—and, pray,
Put on with speed your woodland dress,
And bring no book; for this one day   15
We'll give to idleness.

No joyless forms shall regulate
Our living calendar;
We from today, my Friend, will date
The opening of the year.   20

Love, now a universal birth,
From heart to heart is stealing;
From earth to man, from man to earth:
—It is the hour of feeling.

One moment now may give us more   25
Than years of toiling reason;
Our minds shall drink at every pore
The spirit of the season.

Some silent laws our hearts will make,
Which they shall long obey;   30
We for the year to come may take
Our temper from today.

And from the blessed power that rolls
About, below, above,
We'll frame the measure of our souls: 35
They shall be tuned to love.

Then come, my Sister! come, I pray,
With speed put on your woodland dress;
And bring no book: for this one day
We'll give to idleness.   40

1798   1798

Lines[1]

Composed a Few Miles Above Tintern Abbey On Revisiting the Banks of the Wye During a Tour. July 13, 1798

Five years have passed; five summers, with the length
Of five long winters! and again I hear
These waters, rolling from their mountain-springs
With a soft inland murmur. Once again
Do I behold these steep and lofty cliffs,   5
That on a wild secluded scene impress
Thoughts of more deep seclusion; and connect
The landscape with the quiet of the sky.
The day is come when I again repose
Here, under this dark sycamore, and view   10
These plots of cottage ground, these orchard tufts,
Which at this season, with their unripe fruits,
Are clad in one green hue, and lose themselves
'Mid groves and copses. Once again I see
These hedgerows, hardly hedgerows, little lines   15
Of sportive wood run wild; these pastoral farms,
Green to the very door; and wreaths of smoke
Sent up, in silence, from among the trees!
With some uncertain notice, as might seem
Of vagrant dwellers in the houseless woods,   20
Or of some Hermit's cave, where by his fire
The Hermit sits alone.

           These beauteous forms,
Through a long absence, have not been to me
As is a landscape to a blind man's eye;
But oft, in lonely rooms, and 'mid the din   25
Of towns and cities, I have owed to them,
In hours of weariness, sensations sweet,
Felt in the blood, and felt along the heart;
And passing even into my purer mind,
With tranquil restoration—feelings too   30
Of unremembered pleasure; such, perhaps,
As have no slight or trivial influence
On that best portion of a good man's life,

1. "No poem of mine was composed under circumstances more pleasant for me to remember than this. I began it upon leaving Tintern, after crossing the Wye, and concluded it just as I was entering Bristol in the evening, after a ramble of 4 or 5 days, with my sister. Not a line of it was altered, and not any part of it written down till I reached Bristol" (Wordsworth). The poem is printed as the last item in *Lyrical Ballads*.
Wordsworth had first visited the Wye valley and the ruins of Tintern Abbey, in Monmouthshire, while on a solitary walking tour in August of 1793, when he was 23 years old. The puzzling difference between the present landscape and the remembered "picture of the mind" (line 61) gives rise to an intricately organized meditation, in which the poet reviews his past, evaluates the present, and (through his sister as intermediary) anticipates the future, until he ends by rounding back quietly upon the scene which had been his point of departure.

His little, nameless, unremembered, acts
Of kindness and of love. Nor less, I trust,   35
To them I may have owed another gift,
Of aspect more sublime; that blessed mood,
In which the burthen of the mystery,
In which the heavy and the weary weight
Of all this unintelligible world,   40
Is lightened—that serene and blessed mood,
In which the affections gently lead us on—
Until, the breath of this corporeal frame
And even the motion of our human blood
Almost suspended, we are laid asleep   45
In body, and become a living soul;
While with an eye made quiet by the power
Of harmony, and the deep power of joy,
We see into the life of things.

                   If this
Be but a vain belief, yet, oh! how oft—   50
In darkness and amid the many shapes
Of joyless daylight; when the fretful stir
Unprofitable, and the fever of the world,
Have hung upon the beatings of my heart—
How oft, in spirit, have I turned to thee,   55
O sylvan Wye! thou wanderer through the woods,
How often, has my spirit turned to thee!

   And now, with gleams of half-extinguished thought
With many recognitions dim and faint,
And somewhat of a sad perplexity,   60
The picture of the mind revives again;
While here I stand, not only with the sense
Of present pleasure, but with pleasing thoughts
That in this moment there is life and food
For future years. And so I dare to hope,   65
Though changed, no doubt, from what I was when first
I came among these hills; when like a roe
I bounded o'er the mountains, by the sides
Of the deep rivers, and the lonely streams,
Wherever nature led—more like a man   70
Flying from something that he dreads than one
Who sought the thing he loved. For nature then
(The coarser pleasures of my boyish days,
And their glad animal movements all gone by)
To me was all in all.—I cannot paint   75
What then I was. The sounding cataract
Haunted me like a passion; the tall rock,
The mountain, and the deep and gloomy wood,
Their colors and their forms, were then to me
An appetite; a feeling and a love,   80

That had no need of a remoter charm,
By thought supplied, nor any interest
Unborrowed from the eye.—That time is past,
And all its aching joys are now no more,
And all its dizzy raptures.[2] Not for this   85
Faint[3] I, nor mourn nor murmur; other gifts
Have followed; for such loss, I would believe,
Abundant recompense. For I have learned
To look on nature, not as in the hour
Of thoughtless youth; but hearing oftentimes   90
The still, sad music of humanity,
Nor harsh nor grating, though of ample power
To chasten and subdue. And I have felt
A presence that disturbs me with the joy
Of elevated thoughts; a sense sublime   95
Of something far more deeply interfused,
Whose dwelling is the light of setting suns,
And the round ocean and the living air,
And the blue sky, and in the mind of man:
A motion and a spirit, that impels   100
All thinking things, all objects of all thought,
And rolls through all things. Therefore am I still
A lover of the meadows and the woods,
And mountains; and of all that we behold
From this green earth; of all the mighty world   105
Of eye, and ear—both what they half create,[4]
And what perceive; well pleased to recognize
In nature and the language of the sense
The anchor of my purest thoughts, the nurse,
The guide, the guardian of my heart, and soul   110
Of all my moral being.

              Nor perchance,
If I were not thus taught, should I the more
Suffer my genial spirits[5] to decay:

---

2. Lines 66 ff. contain Wordsworth's famous description of the three stages of his growing up, defined in terms of his evolving relations to the natural scene: the young boy's purely physical responsiveness (lines 73–74); the post-adolescent's aching, dizzy, and equivocal passions—a love which is more like dread (lines 67–72, 75–85: this was his state of mind on the occasion of his first visit); his present state (lines 85 ff.), in which for the first time he adds thought to sense. All his knowledge of human suffering, so painfully acquired in the interim, chastens him while it enriches the visible scene like a chord of music, and he has gained also awareness of an immanent "pres-ence" which links his mind and all the elements of the external world.

3. Lose heart.

4. The fact that apparent changes in the sensible world have turned out to be projected by the changing mind of the observer gives evidence that the faculties "half create" the world; the part that is "perceived" (line 107) is what has remained unchanged between the two visits. This view that the "creative sensibility" contributes to its own perceptions is often reiterated in the early books of *The Prelude*.

5. "Genial" is here the adjectival form of the noun "genius" ("native powers").

For thou art with me here upon the banks
Of this fair river; thou my dearest Friend,[6]   115
My dear, dear Friend; and in thy voice I catch
The language of my former heart, and read
My former pleasures in the shooting lights
Of thy wild eyes. Oh! yet a little while
May I behold in thee what I was once,   120
My dear, dear Sister! and this prayer I make,
Knowing that Nature never did betray
The heart that loved her; 'tis her privilege,
Through all the years of this our life, to lead
From joy to joy: for she can so inform   125
The mind that is within us, so impress
With quietness and beauty, and so feed
With lofty thoughts, that neither evil tongues,
Rash judgments, nor the sneers of selfish men,
Nor greetings where no kindness is, nor all   130
The dreary intercourse of daily life,
Shall e'er prevail against us, or disturb
Our cheerful faith, that all which we behold
Is full of blessings. Therefore let the moon
Shine on thee in thy solitary walk;   135
And let the misty mountain winds be free
To blow against thee: and, in after years,
When these wild ecstasies shall be matured
Into a sober pleasure; when thy mind
Shall be a mansion for all lovely forms,   140
Thy memory be as a dwelling place
For all sweet sounds and harmonies; oh! then,
If solitude, or fear, or pain, or grief
Should be thy portion, with what healing thoughts
Of tender joy wilt thou remember me,   145
And these my exhortations! Nor, perchance—
If I should be where I no more can hear
Thy voice, nor catch from thy wild eyes these gleams
Of past existence[7]—wilt thou then forget
That on the banks of this delightful stream   150
We stood together; and that I, so long
A worshiper of Nature, hither came
Unwearied in that service; rather say
With warmer love—oh! with far deeper zeal
Of holier love. Nor wilt thou then forget,   155
That after many wanderings, many years
Of absence, these steep woods and lofty cliffs,
And this green pastoral landscape, were to me
More dear, both for themselves and for thy sake!

1798   1798

6. His sister Dorothy.
7. I.e., his own "past experience" five years before; see lines 116–19.

Preface to *Lyrical Ballads* (1802)   To the first edition of *Lyrical Ballads*, published jointly with Coleridge in 1798, Wordsworth prefixed an "Advertisement" which asserted that the majority of the poems were "to be considered as experiments" to determine "how far the language of conversation in the middle and lower classes of society is adapted to the purposes of poetic pleasure." In the second, two-volume edition of 1800 Wordsworth, relying on frequent conversations with Coleridge, expanded the Advertisement into a Preface which justified the new poetry not as experiments, but by reference to the principles of all good poetry. The Preface was enlarged for the third edition of *Lyrical Ballads*, published two years later; this version of 1802 is the one that is reprinted here.

The Preface deserves its reputation as a revolutionary manifesto in the theory of poetry. Like most radical statements, however, it claims to go back to the implicit principles which informed the great poetry of the past but have been perverted in recent practice. Most discussions of the Preface, following the lead of Coleridge in his *Biographia Literaria*, have focused on Wordsworth's assertions about the valid language of poetry, on which he bases his attack on the "poetic diction" of 18th-century poets. As Coleridge pointed out, Wordsworth's argument about this issue is far from clear. It is apparent, however, that Wordsworth undertook to overthrow the basic theory, as well as the reigning practice, of neoclassic poetry. That is, his Preface implicitly denies the assumption that the poetic genres constitute a hierarchy, from epic and tragedy at the top down through comedy, satire, pastoral, and the short lyric at the lower reaches of the poetic scale, and he rejects the traditional principle of "decorum," according to which the subject-matter (especially the social class of the protagonists) and the level of diction of a poem must conform to the status of the literary kind on the poetic scale.

When Wordsworth asserted in the Preface that he deliberately chose to represent "incidents and situations from common life," he translated his democratic sympathies into critical terms, justifying his use of peasants, children, outcasts, criminals, and idiot boys as serious subjects of poetic and even tragic concern. He also undertook to write in "a selection of language really used by men," on the grounds that there can be no "essential difference between the language of prose and metrical composition." In making this claim, Wordsworth subverted the neoclassic principle that the language of a poem must be elevated over standard speech by a special diction and by artful figures of speech, in order to match the language to the height and dignity of a particular genre. Wordsworth's own views about the valid language of poetry are based on the new and radical premise that "all good poetry is the spontaneous overflow of powerful feelings"—spontaneous, that is, at the moment of composition, even though the process is influenced by prior thought and acquired poetic skill. The equivalence which Wordsworth claims, therefore, between the valid language of poems and the prose language "really spoken by men" is not one of vocabulary nor of syntax, but an equivalence in emotional genesis—both, according to Wordsworth, are not contrived and artful constructions, but originate spontaneously, as the words and figures which, as Keats later put it, are "the true voice of feeling."

Wordsworth's assertions about the materials and diction of poetry have been immensely influential in expanding the range of serious literature to include the common man and ordinary things and events, as well as in justifying a poetry of sincerity rather than of artifice, expressed in the ordinary language of its time. But in the long view, other aspects of his Preface have been no less significant in establishing its importance, not only as a turning point in English criticism but also as a central document in modern culture. Wordsworth attributed to imaginative literature the primary role in keeping man emotionally alive and morally sensitive—that is, keeping him essentially human—in the face of the pressures of a technological and increasingly urban society, with its mass media and mass culture that threaten, as he presciently foresaw, to blunt the mind's "discriminatory powers" and to "reduce it to a state of almost savage torpor." However radical their literary application by Wordsworth, the values which permeate his Preface are the central humanistic values of the 18th-century Enlightenment—that is, the normative reference to that which is essential, simple, universal, and permanent in human nature. The great subjects of poetry, Wordsworth claims, are "the essential passions of the heart" and "the great and simple affections," as these qualities interact with "the beautiful and permanent forms of nature" and are expressed in a "naked and simple" language that is "adapted to interest mankind permanently." The great poet is not the practitioner of an artistic craft designed to satisfy the refined "taste" of a literary connoisseur. He is instead, Wordsworth says in a memorable phrase, "a man speaking to men," who is actuated by and affirms the primal human values—the joy of life, reverence for all manifestations of life, and the grandeur of the pleasure-principle which is the expression of the life-force and the natural sign of any activity that enhances life. The poet, he says, "rejoices more than other men in the spirit of life," and pays homage to "the naked dignity of man" and (in a phrase Wordsworth deliberately echoes from St. Paul) "to the grand elementary principle of pleasure, by which he knows and feels, and lives, and moves." In opposition to all the modern forces that tend to divide—or, as we now say, to "alienate" —man from his own essential nature, from outer nature, and from his fellow men, Wordsworth places the burden of sustaining human connections primarily on the poet: "He is the rock of defense of human nature; an upholder and preserver, carrying everywhere with him relationship and love."

From Preface to *Lyrical Ballads, with Pastoral and Other Poems* (1802)

The first volume of these poems has already been submitted to general perusal. It was published, as an experiment, which, I hoped, might be of some use to ascertain, how far, by fitting to metrical arrangement a selection of the real language of men in a state of vivid sensation, that sort of pleasure and that quantity of pleasure may be imparted, which a poet may rationally endeavor to impart. I had formed no very inaccurate estimate of the probable effect of those poems: I flattered myself that they who should be pleased with them would read them with more than common pleasure: and, on the other hand, I was well aware, that by those who should dislike them they would be read with more than common dislike. The result has differed from my expectation in this only, that I have pleased a greater number, than I ventured to hope I should please.

For the sake of variety, and from a consciousness of my own weakness, I was induced to request the assistance of a friend, who furnished me with the poems of the *Ancient Mariner,* the *Foster-Mother's Tale,* the *Nightingale,* and the poem entitled *Love.* I should not, however, have requested this assistance, had I not believed that the poems of my friend would in a great measure have the same tendency as my own, and that, though there would be found a difference, there would be found no discordance in the colors of our style; as our opinions on the subject of poetry do almost entirely coincide.[1]

Several of my friends are anxious for the success of these poems from a belief, that, if the views with which they were composed were indeed realized, a class of poetry would be produced, well adapted to interest mankind permanently, and not unimportant in the multiplicity, and in the quality of its moral relations: and on this account they have advised me to prefix a systematic defense of the theory upon which the poems were written. But I was unwilling to undertake the task, because I knew that on this occasion the reader would look coldly upon my arguments, since I might be suspected of having been principally influenced by the selfish and foolish hope of *reasoning* him into an approbation of these particular poems: and I was still more unwilling to undertake the task, because, adequately to display my opinions, and fully to enforce my arguments, would require a space wholly disproportionate to the nature of a preface. For to treat the subject with the clearness and coherence, of which I believe it susceptible, it would be necessary to give a full account of the present state of the public taste in this country, and to determine how far this taste is healthy or depraved; which, again, could not be determined, without pointing out, in what manner language and the human mind act and re-act on each other, and without retracing the revolutions, not of literature alone, but likewise of society itself. I have therefore altogether declined to enter regularly upon this defense; yet I am sensible, that there would be some impropriety in abruptly obtruding upon the public,

1. "The friend" of course is Coleridge. When he read this preface and the new poems included in this 1802 edition of *Lyrical Ballads,* Coleridge wrote to Robert Southey that although Wordsworth's Preface of 1800 had been "half a child of my own brain," he now suspects that "there is a radical difference in our theoretical opinions respecting poetry—this I shall endeavor to go to the bottom of." The results of this endeavor are Coleridge's discussions of Wordsworth's Preface in *Biographia Literaria,* chapters XIV and XVII.

without a few words of introduction, poems so materially different from those, upon which general approbation is at present bestowed.

It is supposed, that by the act of writing in verse an author makes a formal engagement that he will gratify certain known habits of association; that he not only thus apprises the reader that certain classes of ideas and expressions will be found in his book, but that others will be carefully excluded. This exponent or symbol held forth by metrical language must in different eras of literature have excited very different expectations: for example, in the age of Catullus, Terence and Lucretius, and that of Statius or Claudian;[2] and in our own country, in the age of Shakespeare and Beaumont and Fletcher, and that of Donne and Cowley, or Dryden, or Pope. I will not take upon me to determine the exact import of the promise which by the act of writing in verse an author, in the present day, makes to his reader; but I am certain, it will appear to many persons that I have not fulfilled the terms of an engagement thus voluntarily contracted. They who have been accustomed to the gaudiness and inane phraseology of many modern writers, if they persist in reading this book to its conclusion, will, no doubt, frequently have to struggle with feelings of strangeness and awkwardness: they will look round for poetry, and will be induced to inquire by what species of courtesy these attempts can be permitted to assume that title. I hope therefore the reader will not censure me, if I attempt to state what I have proposed to myself to perform; and also, (as far as the limits of a preface will permit) to explain some of the chief reasons which have determined me in the choice of my purpose: that at least he may be spared any unpleasant feeling of disappointment, and that I myself may be protected from the most dishonorable accusation which can be brought against an author, namely, that of an indolence which prevents him from endeavoring to ascertain what is his duty, or, when his duty is ascertained, prevents him from performing it.

The principal object, then, which I proposed to myself in these poems was to choose incidents and situations from common life, and to relate or describe them, throughout, as far as was possible, in a selection of language really used by men; and, at the same time, to throw over them a certain coloring of imagination, whereby ordinary things should be presented to the mind in an unusual way; and, further, and above all, to make these incidents and situations interesting by tracing in them, truly though not ostentatiously, the primary laws of our nature: chiefly, as far as regards the manner in which we associate ideas in a state of excitement.[3] Low and rustic

2. Wordsworth's implied contrast is between the naturalness and simplicity of the first three Roman poets (who wrote in the last two centuries B.C.) and the elaborate artifice of the last two Roman poets (Statius wrote in the 1st and Claudian in the 4th century A.D.).

3. Cf. Coleridge's account of their plan in *Biographia Literaria*, the beginning of Chapter XIV.

life was generally chosen, because in that condition, the essential passions of the heart find a better soil in which they can attain their maturity, are less under restraint, and speak a plainer and more emphatic language; because in that condition of life our elementary feelings coexist in a state of greater simplicity, and, consequently, may be more accurately contemplated, and more forcibly communicated; because the manners of rural life germinate from those elementary feelings; and, from the necessary character of rural occupations, are more easily comprehended; and are more durable; and lastly, because in that condition the passions of men are incorporated with the beautiful and permanent forms of nature. The language, too, of these men is adopted (purified indeed from what appear to be its real defects, from all lasting and rational causes of dislike or disgust) because such men hourly communicate with the best objects from which the best part of language is originally derived; and because, from their rank in society and the sameness and narrow circle of their intercourse, being less under the influence of social vanity they convey their feelings and notions in simple and unelaborated expressions. Accordingly, such a language, arising out of repeated experience and regular feelings, is a more permanent, and a far more philosophical language, than that which is frequently substituted for it by poets, who think that they are conferring honor upon themselves and their art, in proportion as they separate themselves from the sympathies of men, and indulge in arbitrary and capricious habits of expression, in order to furnish food for fickle tastes, and fickle appetites, of their own creation.[4]

I cannot, however, be insensible of the present outcry against the triviality and meanness both of thought and language, which some of my contemporaries have occasionally introduced into their metrical compositions; and I acknowledge that this defect, where it exists, is more dishonorable to the writer's own character than false refinement or arbitrary innovation, though I should contend at the same time that it is far less pernicious in the sum of its consequences. From such verses the poems in these volumes will be found distinguished at least by one mark of difference, that each of them has a worthy *purpose*. Not that I mean to say, that I always began to write with a distinct purpose formally conceived; but I believe that my habits of meditation have so formed my feelings, as that my descriptions of such objects as strongly excite those feelings, will be found to carry along with them a *purpose*. If in this opinion I am mistaken, I can have little right to the name of a poet. For all good poetry is the spontaneous overflow of powerful

4. "It is worthwhile here to observe that the affecting parts of Chaucer are almost always expressed in language pure and universally intelligible even to this day" [Wordsworth's note].

feelings: but though this be true, poems to which any value can be attached, were never produced on any variety of subjects but by a man, who being possessed of more than usual organic sensibility, had also thought long and deeply. For our continued influxes of feeling are modified and directed by our thoughts, which are indeed the representatives of all our past feelings; and, as by contemplating the relation of these general representatives to each other we discover what is really important to men, so, by the repetition and continuance of this act, our feelings will be connected with important subjects, till at length, if we be originally possessed of much sensibility, such habits of mind will be produced, that, by obeying blindly and mechanically the impulses of those habits, we shall describe objects, and utter sentiments, of such a nature and in such connection with each other, that the understanding of the being to whom we address ourselves, if he be in a healthful state of association, must necessarily be in some degree enlightened, and his affections ameliorated.

I have said that each of these poems has a purpose. I have also informed my reader what this purpose will be found principally to be: namely, to illustrate the manner in which our feelings and ideas are associated in a state of excitement. But, speaking in language somewhat more appropriate, it is to follow the fluxes and refluxes of the mind when agitated by the great and simple affections of our nature. This object I have endeavored in these short essays to attain by various means; by tracing the maternal passion through many of its more subtile windings, as in the poems of the *Idiot Boy* and the *Mad Mother*; by accompanying the last struggles of a human being, at the approach of death, cleaving in solitude to life and society, as in the poem of the *Forsaken Indian*; by showing, as in the stanzas entitled *We Are Seven*, the perplexity and obscurity which in childhood attend our notion of death, or rather our utter inability to admit that notion; or by displaying the strength of fraternal, or to speak more philosophically, of moral attachment when early associated with the great and beautiful objects of nature, as in *The Brothers*; or, as in the Incident of *Simon Lee*, by placing my reader in the way of receiving from ordinary moral sensations another and more salutary impression than we are accustomed to receive from them. It has also been part of my general purpose to attempt to sketch characters under the influence of less impassioned feelings, as in the *Two April Mornings, The Fountain, The Old Man Traveling, The Two Thieves*, &c. characters of which the elements are simple, belonging rather to nature than to manners, such as exist now, and will probably always exist, and which from their constitution may be distinctly and profitably contemplated. I will not abuse the indulgence of my reader by dwelling longer upon this subject;

but it is proper that I should mention one other circumstance which distinguishes these poems from the popular poetry of the day; it is this, that the feeling therein developed gives importance to the action and situation, and not the action and situation to the feeling. My meaning will be rendered perfectly intelligible by referring my reader to the poems entitled *Poor Susan* and the *Childless Father*, particularly to the last stanza of the latter poem.

I will not suffer a sense of false modesty to prevent me from asserting, that I point my reader's attention to this mark of distinction, far less for the sake of these particular poems than from the general importance of the subject. The subject is indeed important! For the human mind is capable of being excited without the application of gross and violent stimulants; and he must have a very faint perception of its beauty and dignity who does not know this, and who does not further know, that one being is elevated above another, in proportion as he possesses this capability. It has therefore appeared to me, that to endeavor to produce or enlarge this capability is one of the best services in which, at any period, a writer can be engaged; but this service, excellent at all times, is especially so at the present day. For a multitude of causes, unknown to former times, are now acting with a combined force to blunt the discriminating powers of the mind, and unfitting it for all voluntary exertion to reduce it to a state of almost savage torpor. The most effective of these causes are the great national events which are daily taking place, and the increasing accumulation of men in cities, where the uniformity of their occupations produces a craving for extraordinary incident, which the rapid communication of intelligence hourly gratifies.[5] To this tendency of life and manners the literature and theatrical exhibitions of the country have conformed themselves. The invaluable works of our elder writers, I had almost said the works of Shakespeare and Milton, are driven into neglect by frantic novels, sickly and stupid German tragedies,[6] and deluges of idle and extravagant stories in verse.—When I think upon this degrading thirst after outrageous stimulation, I am almost ashamed to have spoken of the feeble effort with which I have endeavored to counteract it; and, reflecting upon the magnitude of the general evil, I should be oppressed with no dishonorable melancholy, had I not a deep impression of certain inherent and indestructible qualities of the human mind, and likewise of certain powers in the great and permanent objects that act upon it, which are equally inherent

5. This was the period of the wars against France, of industrial urbanization, and of the rapid proliferation in England of daily newspapers.
6. Wordsworth had in mind the "Gothic" terror novels by writers such as Ann Radcliffe and Mathew Gregory Lewis, and the sentimental melodrama, then immensely popular in England, of August von Kotzebue and his German contemporaries.

and indestructible; and did I not further add to this impression a belief, that the time is approaching when the evil will be systematically opposed, by men of greater powers, and with far more distinguished success.

Having dwelt thus long on the subjects and aim of these poems, I shall request the reader's permission to apprise him of a few circumstances relating to their *style*, in order, among other reasons, that I may not be censured for not having performed what I never attempted. The reader will find that personifications of abstract ideas rarely occur in these volumes; and, I hope, are utterly rejected as an ordinary device to elevate the style, and raise it above prose. I have proposed to myself to imitate, and, as far as is possible, to adopt the very language of men; and assuredly such personifications do not make any natural or regular part of that language. They are, indeed, a figure of speech occasionally prompted by passion, and I have made use of them as such; but I have endeavored utterly to reject them as a mechanical device of style, or as a family language which writers in meter seem to lay claim to be prescription. I have wished to keep my reader in the company of flesh and blood, persuaded that by so doing I shall interest him. I am, however, well aware that others who pursue a different track may interest him likewise; I do not interfere with their claim, I only wish to prefer a different claim of my own. There will also be found in these volumes little of what is usually called poetic diction[7]; I have taken as much pains to avoid it as others ordinarily take to produce it; this I have done for the reason already alleged, to bring my language near to the language of men, and further, because the pleasure which I have proposed to myself to impart is of a kind very different from that which is supposed by many persons to be the proper object of poetry. I do not know how, without being culpably particular, I can give my reader a more exact notion of the style in which I wished these poems to be written, than by informing him that I have at all times endeavored to look steadily at my subject, consequently, I hope that there is in these poems little falsehood of description, and that my ideas are expressed in language fitted to their respective importance. Something I must have gained by this practice, as it is friendly to one property of all good poetry, namely good sense; but it has necessarily cut me off from a large portion of phrases and figures of speech which from father to son have long been regarded as the common inheritance of poets. I have also thought it expedient to restrict myself still further, having abstained from the use of many expressions, in themselves proper and beautiful, but which

7. In the sense of words, phrases, and figures of speech, not commonly used in conversation or prose, which are re-garded as especially appropriate to po-etry.

have been foolishly repeated by bad poets, till such feelings of disgust are connected with them as it is scarcely possible by any art of association to overpower.

If in a poem there should be found a series of lines, or even a single line, in which the language, though naturally arranged, and according to the strict laws of meter, does not differ from that of prose, there is a numerous class of critics, who, when they stumble upon these prosaisms, as they call them, imagine that they have made a notable discovery, and exult over the poet as over a man ignorant of his own profession. Now these men would establish a canon of criticism which the reader will conclude he must utterly reject, if he wishes to be pleased with these volumes. And it would be a most easy task to prove to him, that not only the language of a large portion of every good poem, even of the most elevated character, must necessarily, except with reference to the meter, in no respect differ from that of good prose, but likewise that some of the most interesting parts of the best poems will be found to be strictly the language of prose, when prose is well written. The truth of this assertion might be demonstrated by innumerable passages from almost all the poetical writings, even of Milton himself. I have not space for much quotation; but, to illustrate the subject in a general manner, I will here adduce a short composition of Gray, who was at the head of those who, by their reasonings, have attempted to widen the space of separation betwixt prose and metrical composition, and was more than any other man curiously elaborate in the structure of his own poetic diction.[8]

In vain to me the smiling mornings shine,
And reddening Phoebus lifts his golden fire:
The birds in vain their amorous descant join,
Or cheerful fields resume their green attire.
These ears, alas! for other notes repine;
A different object do these eyes require;
My lonely anguish melts no heart but mine;
And in my breast the imperfect joys expire;
Yet morning smiles the busy race to cheer,
And new-born pleasure brings to happier men;
The fields to all their wonted tribute bear;
To warm their little loves the birds complain.
I fruitless mourn to him that cannot hear,
And weep the more because I weep in vain.

It will easily be perceived that the only part of this sonnet which is of any value is the lines printed in italics: it is equally obvious, that,

8. Thomas Gray had written, in a letter to Richard West, that "the language of the age is never the language of poetry." The poem that follows is Gray's *Sonnet on the Death of Richard West*.

except in the rhyme, and in the use of the single word "fruitless" for fruitlessly, which is so far a defect, the language of these lines does in no respect differ from that of prose.

By the foregoing quotation I have shown that the language of prose may yet be well adapted to poetry; and I have previously asserted that a large portion of the language of every good poem can in no respect differ from that of good prose. I will go further. I do not doubt that it may be safely affirmed, that there neither is, nor can be, any essential difference between the language of prose and metrical composition. We are fond of tracing the resemblance between poetry and painting, and, accordingly, we call them sisters: but where shall we find bonds of connection sufficiently strict to typify the affinity betwixt metrical and prose composition? They both speak by and to the same organs; the bodies in which both of them are clothed may be said to be of the same substance, their affections are kindred, and almost identical, not necessarily differing even in degree; poetry[9] sheds no tears "such as Angels weep,"[1] but natural and human tears; she can boast of no celestial Ichor[2] that distinguishes her vital juices from those of prose; the same human blood circulates through the veins of them both.

* * *

Taking up the subject, then, upon general grounds, I ask what is meant by the word "poet"? What is a poet? To whom does he address himself? And what language is to be expected from him? He is a man speaking to men: a man, it is true, endued with more lively sensibility, more enthusiasm and tenderness, who has a greater knowledge of human nature, and a more comprehensive soul, than are supposed to be common among mankind; a man pleased with his own passions and volitions, and who rejoices more than other men in the spirit of life that is in him; delighting to contemplate similar volitions and passions as manifested in the goings-on of the universe, and habitually impelled to create them where he does not find them. To these qualities he has added a disposition to be affected more than other men by absent things as if they were present; an ability of conjuring up in himself passions, which are indeed far from being the same as those produced by real events, yet (especially in those parts of the general sympathy which are

9. "I here use the word 'Poetry' (though against my own judgment) as opposed to the word prose, and synonymous with metrical composition. But much confusion has been introduced into criticism by this contradistinction of poetry and prose, instead of the more philosophical one of poetry and matter of fact, or science. The only strict antithesis to prose is meter; nor is this, in truth, a *strict* antithesis; because lines and passages of meter so naturally occur in writing prose that it would be scarcely possible to avoid them, even were it desirable" [Wordsworth's note].
1. *Paradise Lost* I. 620.
2. In Greek mythology, the fluid in the veins of the gods.

pleasing and delightful) do more nearly resemble the passions produced by real events, than anything which, from the motions of
their own minds merely, other men are accustomed to feel in themselves; whence, and from practice, he has acquired a greater readiness and power in expressing what he thinks and feels, and especially those thoughts and feelings which, by his own choice, or from
the structure of his own mind, arise in him without immediate
external excitement.

But, whatever portion of this faculty we may suppose even the
greatest poet to possess, there cannot be a doubt but that the language which it will suggest to him, must, in liveliness and truth, fall
far short of that which is uttered by men in real life, under the
actual pressure of those passions, certain shadows of which the poet
thus produces, or feels to be produced, in himself. However exalted
a notion we would wish to cherish of the character of a poet, it is
obvious, that, while he describes and imitates passions, his situation
is altogether slavish and mechanical, compared with the freedom
and power of real and substantial action and suffering. So that it
will be the wish of the poet to bring his feelings near to those of
the persons whose feelings he describes, nay, for short spaces of
time perhaps, to let himself slip into an entire delusion, and even
confound and identify his own feelings with theirs; modifying only
the language which is thus suggested to him, by a consideration
that he describes for a particular purpose, that of giving pleasure.
Here, then, he will apply the principle on which I have so much
insisted, namely, that of selection; on this he will depend for removing what would otherwise be painful or disgusting in the passion; he
will feel that there is no necessity to trick out or to elevate nature:
and, the more industriously he applies this principle, the deeper will
be his faith that no words, which his fancy or imagination can suggest, will be to be compared with those which are the emanations
of reality and truth.

But it may be said by those who do not object to the general
spirit of these remarks, that, as it is impossible for the poet to produce upon all occasions language as exquisitely fitted for the passion
as that which the real passion itself suggests, it is proper that he
should consider himself as in the situation of a translator, who
deems himself justified when he substitutes excellences of another
kind for those which are unattainable by him; and endeavor occasionally to surpass his original, in order to make some amends for
the general inferiority to which he feels that he must submit. But
this would be to encourage idleness and unmanly despair. Further,
it is the language of men who speak of what they do not understand; who talk of poetry as a matter of amusement and idle pleasure; who will converse with us as gravely about a *taste* for poetry, as
they express it, as if it were a thing as indifferent as a taste for

rope-dancing, or Frontiniac[3] or sherry. Aristotle, I have been told, hath said, that poetry is the most philosophic of all writing:[4] it is so: its object is truth, not individual and local, but general, and operative; not standing upon external testimony, but carried alive into the heart by passion; truth which is its own testimony, which gives strength and divinity to the tribunal to which it appeals, and receives them from the same tribunal. Poetry is the image of man and nature. The obstacles which stand in the way of the fidelity of the biographer and historian, and of their consequent utility, are incalculably greater than those which are to be encountered by the poet who has an adequate notion of the dignity of his art. The poet writes under one restriction only, namely, that of the necessity of giving immediate pleasure to a human being possessed of that information which may be expected from him, not as a lawyer, a physician, a mariner, an astronomer or a natural philosopher, but as a man. Except this one restriction, there is no object standing between the poet and the image of things; between this, and the biographer and historian there are a thousand.

Nor let this necessity of producing immediate pleasure be considered as a degradation of the poet's art. It is far otherwise. It is an acknowledgment of the beauty of the universe, an acknowledgment the more sincere, because it is not formal, but indirect; it is a task light and easy to him who looks at the world in the spirit of love: further, it is a homage paid to the native and naked dignity of man, to the grand elementary principle of pleasure, by which he knows, and feels, and lives, and moves.[5] We have no sympathy but what is propagated by pleasure: I would not be misunderstood; but wherever we sympathize with pain it will be found that the sympathy is produced and carried on by subtle combinations with pleasure. We have no knowledge, that is, no general principles drawn from the contemplation of particular facts, but what has been built up by pleasure, and exists in us by pleasure alone. The man of science, the chemist and mathematician, whatever difficulties and disgusts they may have had to struggle with, know and feel this. However painful may be the objects with which the anatomist's knowledge is connected, he feels that his knowledge is pleasure; and where he has no pleasure he has no knowledge. What then does the poet? He considers man and the objects that surround him as acting and re-acting upon each other, so as to produce an infinite complexity of pain and pleasure; he considers man in his own nature and in his ordinary life as contemplating this with a certain quantity of immediate knowledge, with certain convictions, intuitions, and deductions

3. A sweet wine made from muscat grapes.
4. Aristotle in fact said that "poetry is more philosophic than history, since its statements are of the nature of univer-sals, whereas those of history are singulars" (*Poetics* 1451b).
5. A bold echo of the words of St. Paul, that in God "we live, and move, and have our being" (Acts xvii.28).

which by habit become of the nature of intuitions; he considers him as looking upon this complex scene of ideas and sensations, and finding everywhere objects that immediately excite in him sympathies which, from the necessities of his nature, are accompanied by an overbalance of enjoyment.

To this knowledge which all men carry about with them, and to these sympathies in which without any other discipline than that of our daily life we are fitted to take delight, the poet principally directs his attention. He considers man and nature as essentially adapted to each other,[6] and the mind of man as naturally the mirror of the fairest and most interesting qualities of nature. And thus the poet, prompted by this feeling of pleasure which accompanies him through the whole course of his studies, converses with general nature with affections akin to those, which, through labor and length of time, the man of science has raised up in himself, by conversing with those particular parts of nature which are the objects of his studies. The knowledge both of the poet and the man of science is pleasure; but the knowledge of the one cleaves to us as a necessary part of our existence, our natural and unalienable inheritance; the other is a personal and individual acquisition, slow to come to us, and by no habitual and direct sympathy connecting us with our fellow-beings. The man of science seeks truth as a remote and unknown benefactor; he cherishes and loves it in his solitude: the poet, singing a song in which all human beings join with him, rejoices in the presence of truth as our visible friend and hourly companion. Poetry is the breath and finer spirit of all knowledge; it is the impassioned expression which is in the countenance of all science. Emphatically may it be said of the poet, as Shakespeare hath said of man, "that he looks before and after."[7] He is the rock of defense of human nature; an upholder and preserver, carrying everywhere with him relationship and love. In spite of difference of soil and climate, of language and manners, of laws and customs, in spite of things silently gone out of mind and things violently destroyed, the poet binds together by passion and knowledge the vast empire of human society, as it is spread over the whole earth, and over all time. The objects of the poet's thoughts are everywhere; though the eyes and senses of man are, it is true, his favorite guides, yet he will follow wheresoever he can find an atmosphere of sensation in which to move his wings. Poetry is the first and last of all knowledge—it is as immortal as the heart of man. If the labors of men and science should ever create any material revolution, direct or indirect, in our condition, and in the impressions which we habitually receive, the poet will sleep then no more than at present, but he will be ready

6. On the mutual adaptation of man's mind and nature, see Wordsworth's

Prospectus to *The Recluse*, lines 63–71.
7. *Hamlet* IV.iv.37.

to follow the steps of the man of science, not only in those general indirect effects, but he will be at his side, carrying sensation into the midst of the objects of the science itself. The remotest discoveries of the chemist, the botanist, or mineralogist, will be as proper objects of the poet's art as any upon which it can be employed, if the time should ever come when these things shall be familiar to us, and the relations under which they are contemplated by the followers of these respective sciences shall be manifestly and palpably material to us as enjoying and suffering beings.[8] If the time should ever come when what is now called science, thus familiarized to men, shall be ready to put on, as it were, a form of flesh and blood, the poet will lend his divine spirit to aid the transfiguration, and will welcome the being thus produced, as a dear and genuine inmate of the household of man.—It is not, then, to be supposed that anyone, who holds that sublime notion of poetry which I have attempted to convey, will break in upon the sanctity and truth of his pictures by transitory and accidental ornaments, and endeavor to excite admiration of himself by arts, the necessity of which must manifestly depend upon the assumed meanness of his subject.

What I have thus far said applies to poetry in general; but especially to those parts of composition where the poet speaks through the mouths of his characters; and upon this point it appears to have such weight that I will conclude, there are few persons of good sense, who would not allow that the dramatic parts of composition are defective, in proportion as they deviate from the real language of nature, and are colored by a diction of the poet's own, either peculiar to him as an individual poet, or belonging simply to poets in general, to a body of men who, from the circumstance of their compositions being in meter, it is expected will employ a particular language.

It is not, then, in the dramatic parts of composition that we look for this distinction of language; but still it may be proper and necessary where the poet speaks to us in his own person and character. To this I answer by referring my reader to the description which I have before given of a poet. Among the qualities which I have enumerated as principally conducing to form a poet, is implied nothing differing in kind from other men, but only in degree. The sum of what I have there said is, that the poet is chiefly distinguished from other men by a greater promptness to think and feel without immediate external excitement, and a greater power in expressing such thoughts and feelings as are produced in him in that manner. But these passions and thoughts and feelings are the general passions and thoughts and feelings of men. And with what are they con-

8. Wordsworth is at least right in anticipating the poetry of the machine; he himself wrote an early instance, the sonnet *Steamboats, Viaducts, and Railways.*

nected? Undoubtedly with our moral sentiments and animal sensations, and with the causes which excite these; with the operations of the elements and the appearances of the visible universe; with storm and sunshine, with the revolutions of the seasons, with cold and heat, with loss of friends and kindred, with injuries and resentments, gratitude and hope, with fear and sorrow. These, and the like, are the sensations and objects which the poet describes, as they are the sensations of other men, and the objects which interest them. The poet thinks and feels in the spirit of the passions of men. How, then, can his language differ in any material degree from that of all other men who feel vividly and see clearly? It might be *proved* that it is impossible. But supposing that this were not the case, the poet might then be allowed to use a peculiar language when expressing his feelings for his own gratification, or that of men like himself. But poets do not write for poets alone, but for men. Unless therefore we are advocates for that admiration which depends upon ignorance, and that pleasure which arises from hearing what we do not understand, the poet must descend from this supposed height, and, in order to excite rational sympathy, he must express himself as other men express themselves. * * *

I have said that poetry is the spontaneous overflow of powerful feelings: it takes its origin from emotion recollected in tranquility: the emotion is contemplated till by a species of reaction the tranquility gradually disappears, and an emotion, kindred to that which was before the subject of contemplation, is gradually produced, and does itself actually exist in the mind. In this mood successful composition generally begins, and in a mood similar to this it is carried on; but the emotion, of whatever kind and in whatever degree, from various causes is qualified by various pleasures, so that in describing any passions whatsoever, which are voluntarily described, the mind will upon the whole be in a state of enjoyment. Now, if nature be thus cautious in preserving in a state of enjoyment a being thus employed, the poet ought to profit by the lesson thus held forth to him, and ought especially to take care, that whatever passions he communicates to his reader, those passions, if his reader's mind be sound and vigorous, should always be accompanied with an overbalance of pleasure. Now the music of harmonious metrical language, the sense of difficulty overcome, and the blind association of pleasure which has been previously received from works of rhyme or meter of the same or similar construction, an indistinct perception perpetually renewed of language closely resembling that of real life, and yet, in the circumstance of meter, differing from it so widely, all these imperceptibly make up a complex feeling of delight, which is of the most important use in tempering the painful feeling which will always be found intermingled with powerful descriptions of the deeper passions. This effect is always produced in pathetic and impassioned poetry; while, in lighter compositions, the ease and gracefulness with which the poet manages his numbers are themselves confessedly a principal source of the gratification of the reader. I might perhaps include all which it is *necessary* to say upon this subject by affirming, what few persons will deny, that, of two descriptions, either of passions, manners, or characters, each of them equally well executed, the one in prose and the other in verse, the verse will be read a hundred times where the prose is read once.

* * *

I know that nothing would have so effectually contributed to further the end which I have in view, as to have shown of what kind the pleasure is, and how the pleasure is produced, which is confessedly produced by metrical composition essentially different from that which I have here endeavored to recommend: for the reader will say that he has been pleased by such composition; and what can I do more for him? The power of any art is limited; and he will suspect, that, if I propose to furnish him with new friends, it is only upon condition of his abandoning his old friends. Besides, as I have said, the reader is himself conscious of the pleasure which he has received from such composition, composition to which he has peculiarly attached the endearing name of poetry; and all men feel an habitual gratitude, and something of an honorable bigotry for the objects which have long continued to please them; we not only wish to be pleased, but to be pleased in that particular way in which we have been accustomed to be pleased. There is a host of arguments in these feelings; and I should be the less able to combat them successfully, as I am willing to allow, that, in order entirely to enjoy the poetry which I am recommending, it would be necessary to give up much of what is ordinarily enjoyed. But, would my limits have permitted me to point out how this pleasure is produced, I might have removed many obstacles, and assisted my reader in perceiving that the powers of language are not so limited as he may suppose; and that it is possible that poetry may give other enjoyments, of a purer, more lasting, and more exquisite nature. This part of my subject I have not altogether neglected; but it has been less my present aim to prove, that the interest excited by some other kinds of poetry is less vivid, and less worthy of the nobler powers of the mind, than to offer reasons for presuming, that, if the object which I have proposed to myself were adequately attained, a species of poetry would be produced, which is genuine poetry; in its nature well adapted to interest mankind permanently, and likewise important in the multiplicity and quality of its moral relations.

From what has been said, and from a perusal of the poems, the reader will be able clearly to perceive the object which I have pro-

posed to myself: he will determine how far I have attained this
object; and, what is a much more important question, whether it be
worth attaining: and upon the decision of these two questions will
rest my claim to the approbation of the public.

1802

Strange Fits of Passion Have I Known[1]

Strange fits of passion have I known:
And I will dare to tell,
But in the Lover's ear alone,
What once to me befell.

When she I loved looked every day   5
Fresh as a rose in June,
I to her cottage bent my way,
Beneath an evening moon.

Upon the moon I fixed my eye,
All over the wide lea;   10
With quickening pace my horse drew nigh
Those paths so dear to me.

And now we reached the orchard plot;
And, as we climbed the hill,
The sinking moon to Lucy's cot   15
Came near, and nearer still.

In one of those sweet dreams I slept,
Kind Nature's gentlest boon!
And all the while my eyes I kept
On the descending moon.   20

My horse moved on; hoof after hoof
He raised, and never stopped:
When down behind the cottage roof,
At once, the bright moon dropped.

What fond and wayward thoughts will slide   25
Into a Lover's head!
"O mercy!" to myself I cried,
"If Lucy should be dead!"[2]

1799   1800

1. This and the four following pieces are
often grouped by editors as the "Lucy
poems," even though *A Slumber Did My
Spirit Steal* does not identify the "she"
who is the subject of that poem. All but
the last were written in 1799, while
Wordsworth and Dorothy were in Germany, and homesick. There has been diligent speculation about the identity of
Lucy, but it remains speculation; the one
certainty is that she is not the girl of

Wordsworth's *Lucy Gray*, below. "Fits
of passion": in an archaic sense, "sudden moods of intense grief."
2. An additional stanza in an earlier
MS. version demonstrates how a poem
may profit by omitting a passage which
is, in itself, excellent poetry: "I told
her this: her laughter light / Is ringing
in my ears; / And when I think upon
that night / My eyes are dim with
tears."

She Dwelt Among the Untrodden Ways

She dwelt among the untrodden ways
  Beside the springs of Dove,[3]
A Maid whom there were none to praise
  And very few to love;

A violet by a mossy stone   5
  Half hidden from the eye!
—Fair as a star, when only one
  Is shining in the sky.

She lived unknown, and few could know
  When Lucy ceased to be;   10
But she is in her grave, and, oh,
  The difference to me!

1799   1800

Three Years She Grew

Three years she grew in sun and shower,
Then Nature said, "A lovelier flower
On earth was never sown;
This Child I to myself will take;
She shall be mine, and I will make   5
A Lady of my own.[4]

"Myself will to my darling be
Both law and impulse: and with me
The Girl, in rock and plain,
In earth and heaven, in glade and bower,   10
Shall feel an overseeing power
To kindle or restrain.

"She shall be sportive as the fawn
That wild with glee across the lawn
Or up the mountain springs;   15
And hers shall be the breathing balm,
And hers the silence and the calm
Of mute insensate things.

"The floating clouds their state shall lend
To her; for her the willow bend;   20
Nor shall she fail to see
Even in the motions of the Storm
Grace that shall mold the Maiden's form
By silent sympathy.

---

3. There are several rivers by this name in England, including one in the Lake Country.

4. I.e., Lucy was three years old when Nature made this promise; line 37 makes clear that Lucy had reached the maturity foretold in the sixth stanza when she died.

"The stars of midnight shall be dear   25
To her; and she shall lean her ear
In many a secret place
Where rivulets dance their wayward round,
And beauty born of murmuring sound
Shall pass into her face.   30

"And vital feelings of delight
Shall rear her form to stately height,
Her virgin bosom swell;
Such thoughts to Lucy I will give
While she and I together live
Here in this happy dell."   35

Thus Nature spake—the work was done—
How soon my Lucy's race was run!
She died, and left to me
This heath, this calm, and quiet scene;   40
The memory of what has been,
And never more will be.

1799   1800

A Slumber Did My Spirit Seal

A slumber did my spirit seal;
    I had no human fears:
She seemed a thing that could not feel
    The touch of earthly years.

No motion has she now, no force;   5
    She neither hears nor sees;
Rolled round in earth's diurnal[1] course,
    With rocks, and stones, and trees.

1799   1800

I Traveled Among Unknown Men

I traveled among unknown men,
    In lands beyond the sea;
Nor, England! did I know till then
    What love I bore to thee.

'Tis past, that melancholy dream!   5
    Nor will I quit thy shore
A second time; for still I seem
    To love thee more and more.

Among thy mountains did I feel
    The joy of my desire;   10
And she I cherished turned her wheel
    Beside an English fire.

1. Daily.

Thy mornings showed, thy nights concealed,
    The bowers where Lucy played;
And thine too is the last green field   15
    That Lucy's eyes surveyed.

ca. 1801   1807

Lucy Gray[1]

OR SOLITUDE

Oft I had heard of Lucy Gray:
And, when I crossed the wild,
I chanced to see at break of day
The solitary child.

No mate, no comrade Lucy knew;   5
She dwelt on a wide moor,
  —The sweetest thing that ever grew
Beside a human door!

You yet may spy the fawn at play,
The hare upon the green;   10
But the sweet face of Lucy Gray
Will never more be seen.

"Tonight will be a stormy night—
You to the town must go;
And take a lantern, Child, to light   15
Your mother through the snow."

"That, Father! will I gladly do:
'Tis scarcely afternoon—
The minster[2] clock has just struck two,
And yonder is the moon!"   20

At this the Father raised his hook,
And snapped a faggot band;[3]
He plied his work—and Lucy took
The lantern in her hand.

Not blither is the mountain roe;   25
With many a wanton stroke
Her feet disperse the powdery snow,
That rises up like smoke.

The storm came on before its time;
She wandered up and down;   30

1. Written in 1799 while Wordsworth was in Germany, and founded on a true account of a young girl who drowned when she lost her way in a snowstorm. "The body however was found in the canal. The way in which the incident was treated and the spiritualizing of the character might furnish hints for contrasting the imaginative influences which I have endeavored to throw over common life with Crabbe's matter-of-fact style of treating subjects of the same kind" (Wordsworth). Compare Wordsworth's statement (in the Preface to *Lyrical Ballads*) of his undertaking to throw over ordinary things "a certain coloring of imagination."
2. Church.
3. Cord binding a bundle of sticks to be used for fuel.

And many a hill did Lucy climb,
But never reached the town.

The wretched parents all that night
Went shouting far and wide;
But there was neither sound nor sight   35
To serve them for a guide.

At daybreak on a hill they stood
That overlooked the moor;
And thence they saw the bridge of wood,
A furlong[4] from their door.   40

They wept—and, turning homeward, cried,
"In heaven we all shall meet";
—When in the snow the mother spied
The print of Lucy's feet.

Then downwards from the steep hill's edge   45
They tracked the footmarks small;
And through the broken hawthorn hedge,
And by the long stone wall;

And then an open field they crossed:
The marks were still the same;   50
They tracked them on, nor ever lost;
And to the bridge they came.

They followed from the snowy bank
Those footmarks, one by one,
Into the middle of the plank;   55
And further there were none!

—Yet some maintain that to this day
She is a living child;
That you may see sweet Lucy Gray
Upon the lonesome wild.   60

O'er rough and smooth she trips along,
And never looks behind;
And sings a solitary song
That whistles in the wind.

1799   1800

The Ruined Cottage   Wordsworth wrote *The Ruined Cottage* in
1797–98, but revised it several times before he finally published an expanded rendering of the story as Book I of *The Excursion*, in 1814. Not
until 1949 was *The Ruined Cottage*, as an independent poem, made available in the fifth volume of *The Poetical Works of William Wordsworth*,
edited by Ernest de Selincourt and Helen Darbishire, who printed a version
known as "MS. B." The version reprinted here is, however, from "MS. D,"

4. One eighth of a mile.

dating 1799 or 1800, as transcribed by Jonathan Wordsworth in *The Music of Humanity: A Critical Study of Wordsworth's "Ruined Cottage"* (1969).

This is a shorter and better poem than the one reprinted in *The Poetical Works*. The latter lacks the great concluding passage, lines 493–538, and includes in Part I more than 250 lines describing the youthful development of the peddler that are extraneous to the narrative proper and soften the hard naturalism of the story by introducing into it, at considerable length, the peddler's faith that nature teaches "deeply the lesson deep of love." The version in the first book of *The Excursion* is longer still, and attempts to mitigate the impact of Margaret's sufferings even more by attributing to her a Christian piety which is conventional rather than deeply realized. In the version reprinted here, however, we confront the blank facts of "a tale of silent suffering"—suffering which is undeserved, unrationalized, and irremissive. Like the narrating poet, we attend in "the impotence of grief" as the peddler describes how Margaret's fierce hope for the return of her husband slowly bends and then breaks her spirit, before destroying her life. Her deterioration under this relentless pressure is a moral one, measured by the bleak details of the correlative deterioration of her untended garden and cottage. The event is "a common tale," and it poses the implicit question, What are we to make of human life, in which such things happen?

The peddler's recovery of heart turns, unexpectedly, on his recognition that this human tragedy takes place within the unceasing and neutral operation—as the narrator says, "the calm oblivious tendencies"—of nature, which silently goes about the process of assimilating the human artifacts that have been wrought from it back into its own independent and continuing life. In a reversal as extreme as Wordsworth could make it, the peddler declares: "I turned away, / And walked along my road in happiness." By his artistry Wordsworth carries us along in imagination so that we too, whatever our own beliefs, feel what it is to be able to look upon and master the fact of human suffering, unsupported by any consoling creed of a beneficent power, whether in or out of nature.

Beyond any of Wordsworth's writings, even *Michael*, *The Ruined Cottage* demonstrates that distinctive quality which Walter Raleigh identified more than a half century ago as Wordsworth's "calm and almost terrible strength."

The Ruined Cottage

First Part

'Twas Summer and the sun was mounted high.
Along the south the uplands feebly glared
Through a pale steam, and all the northern downs,
In clearer air ascending, shewed far off
Their surfaces with shadows dappled o'er   5
Of deep embattled clouds. Far as the sight
Could reach those many shadows lay in spots
Determined and unmoved, with steady beams
Of clear and pleasant sunshine interposed—

Pleasant to him who on the soft cool grass   10
Extends his careless limbs beside the root
Of some huge oak whose aged branches make
A twilight of their own, a dewy shade
Where the wren warbles while the dreaming man,
Half conscious of that soothing melody,   15
With sidelong eye looks out upon the scene,
By those impending branches made more soft,
More soft and distant.

                Other lot was mine.
Across a bare wide Common I had toiled
With languid feet which by the slipp'ry ground   20
Were baffled still, and when I stretched myself
On the brown earth my limbs from very heat
Could find no rest, nor my weak arm disperse
The insect host which gathered round my face
And joined their murmurs to the tedious noise   25
Of seeds of bursting gorse that crackled round.
I rose and turned towards a group of trees
Which midway in that level stood alone;
And thither come at length, beneath a shade
Of clustering elms that sprang from the same root   30
I found a ruined house, four naked walls
That stared upon each other. I looked round
And near the door I saw an aged Man,
Alone and stretched upon the cottage bench,
An iron-pointed staff lay at his side.   35
With instantaneous joy I recognized
That pride of nature and of lowly life,
The venerable Armytage, a friend
As dear to me as is the setting sun.

                Two days before   40
We had been fellow travelers. I knew
That he was in this neighborhood, and now
Delighted found him here in the cool shade.
He lay, his pack of rustic merchandise
Pillowing his head. I guess he had no thought   45
Of his way-wandering life. His eyes were shut,
The shadows of the breezy elms above
Dappled his face. With thirsty heat oppressed
At length I hailed him, glad to see his hat
Bedewed with waterdrops, as if the brim   50
Had newly scooped a running stream. He rose
And pointing to a sunflower, bade me climb
The [   ] wall where that same gaudy flower
Looked out upon the road.

                It was a plot
Of garden ground now wild, its matted weeds   55
Marked with the steps of those whom as they passed,
The gooseberry trees that shot in long lank slips,

Or currants hanging from their leafless stems
In scanty strings, had tempted to o'erleap
The broken wall. Within that cheerless spot,   60
Where two tall hedgerows of thick alder boughs
Joined in a damp cold nook, I found a well
Half covered up with willow flowers and grass.
I slaked my thirst and to the shady bench
Returned, and while I stood unbonneted   65
To catch the motion of the cooler air,
The old Man said, "I see around me here
Things which you cannot see. We die, my Friend,
Nor we alone, but that which each man loved
And prized in his peculiar nook of earth   70
Dies with him, or is changed, and very soon
Even of the good is no memorial left.
The Poets, in their elegies and songs
Lamenting the departed, call the groves,
They call upon the hills and streams to mourn,   75
And senseless rocks—nor idly, for they speak
In these their invocations with a voice
Obedient to the strong creative power
Of human passion. Sympathies there are
More tranquil, yet perhaps of kindred birth,   80
That steal upon the meditative mind
And grow with thought. Beside yon spring I stood,
And eyed its waters till we seemed to feel
One sadness, they and I. For them a bond
Of brotherhood is broken; time has been   85
When every day the touch of human hand
Disturbed their stillness, and they ministered
To human comfort. When I stooped to drink
A spider's web hung to the water's edge,
And on the wet and slimy footstone lay   90
The useless fragment of a wooden bowl.
It moved my very heart.

                          The day has been
When I could never pass this road but she
Who lived within these walls, when I appeared,
A daughter's welcome gave me, and I loved her   95
As my own child. Oh Sir, the good die first,
And they whose hearts are dry as summer dust
Burn to the socket. Many a passenger
Has blessed poor Margaret for her gentle looks
When she upheld the cool refreshment drawn   100
From that forsaken spring, and no one came
But he was welcome, no one went away
But that it seemed she loved him. She is dead,
The worm is on her cheek, and this poor hut,
Stripped of its outward garb of household flowers,   105
Of rose and sweetbriar, offers to the wind
A cold bare wall whose earthy top is tricked

With weeds and the rank spear grass. She is dead,
And nettles rot and adders sun themselves
Where we have sate together while she nursed   110
Her infant at her breast. The unshod colt,
The wandring heifer and the Potter's ass,
Find shelter now within the chimney wall
Where I have seen her evening hearthstone blaze
And through the window spread upon the road   115
Its cheerful light. You will forgive me, sir,
But often on this cottage do I muse
As on a picture, till my wiser mind
Sinks, yielding to the foolishness of grief.

She had a husband, an industrious man,   120
Sober and steady. I have heard her say
That he was up and busy at his loom
In summer ere the mower's scythe had swept
The dewy grass, and in the early spring
Ere the last star had vanished. They who passed   125
At evening, from behind the garden fence
Might hear his busy spade, which he would ply
After his daily work till the daylight
Was gone, and every leaf and flower were lost
In the dark hedges. So they passed their days   130
In peace and comfort, and two pretty babes
Were their best hope next to the God in Heaven.

You may remember, now some ten years gone,
Two blighting seasons when the fields were left
With half a harvest. It pleased heaven to add   135
A worse affliction in the plague of war,
A happy land was stricken to the heart,
'Twas a sad time of sorrow and distress.
A wanderer among the cottages,
I with my pack of winter raiment saw   140
The hardships of that season. Many rich
Sunk down as in a dream among the poor,
And of the poor did many cease to be,
And their place knew them not. Meanwhile, abridged
Of daily comforts, gladly reconciled   145
To numerous self-denials, Margaret
Went struggling on through those calamitous years
With cheerful hope. But ere the second autumn
A fever seized her husband. In disease
He lingered long, and when his strength returned   150
He found the little he had stored to meet
The hour of accident, or crippling age,
Was all consumed. As I have said, 'twas now
A time of trouble: shoals of artisans
Were from their daily labor turned away   155
To hang for bread on parish charity,
They and their wives and children, happier far

Could they have lived as do the little birds
That peck along the hedges, or the kite
That makes her dwelling in the mountain rocks.   160

Ill fared it now with Robert, he who dwelt
In this poor cottage. At his door he stood
And whistled many a snatch of merry tunes
That had no mirth in them, or with his knife
Carved uncouth figures on the heads of sticks,   165
Then idly sought about through every nook
Of house or garden any casual task
Of use or ornament, and with a strange
Amusing but uneasy novelty
He blended where he might the various tasks   170
Of summer, autumn, winter, and of spring.
But this endured not, his good humor soon
Became a weight in which no pleasure was,
And poverty brought on a petted mood
And a sore temper. Day by day he drooped,   175
And he would leave his home, and to the town
Without an errand would he turn his steps,
Or wander here and there among the fields.
One while he would speak lightly of his babes
And with a cruel tongue, at other times   180
He played with them wild freaks of merriment,
And 'twas a piteous thing to see the looks
Of the poor innocent children. 'Every smile,'
Said Margaret to me here beneath these trees,
'Made my heart bleed.' ''   185

                    At this the old Man paused,
And looking up to those enormous elms
He said, " 'Tis now the hour of deepest noon.
At this still season of repose and peace,
This hour when all things which are not at rest
Are cheerful, while this multitude of flies   190
Fills all the air with happy melody,
Why should a tear be in an old man's eye?
Why should we thus with an untoward mind,
And in the weakness of humanity,
From natural wisdom turn our hearts away,   195
To natural comfort shut our eyes and ears,
And, feeding on disquiet, thus disturb
The calm of Nature with our restless thoughts?''

END OF THE FIRST PART

Second Part

He spake with somewhat of a solemn tone,
But when he ended there was in his face   200
Such easy cheerfulness, a look so mild,
That for a little time it stole away
All recollection, and that simple tale

Passed from my mind like a forgotten sound.
A while on trivial things we held discourse,   205
To me soon tasteless. In my own despite
I thought of that poor woman as of one
Whom I had known and loved. He had rehearsed
Her homely tale with such familiar power,
With such an active countenance, an eye   210
So busy, that the things of which he spake
Seemed present, and, attention now relaxed,
There was a heartfelt chillness in my veins.
I rose, and turning from that breezy shade
Went out into the open air, and stood   215
To drink the comfort of the warmer sun.
Long time I had not stayed ere, looking round
Upon that tranquil ruin, I returned
And begged of the old man that for my sake
He would resume his story.   220

                              He replied,
"It were a wantonness, and would demand
Severe reproof, if we were men whose hearts
Could hold vain dalliance with the misery
Even of the dead, contented thence to draw
A momentary pleasure, never marked   225
By reason, barren of all future good.
But we have known that there is often found
In mournful thoughts, and always might be found,
A power to virtue friendly; were't not so
I am a dreamer among men, indeed   230
An idle dreamer. 'Tis a common tale
By moving accidents uncharactered,
A tale of silent suffering, hardly clothed
In bodily form, and to the grosser sense
But ill adapted, scarcely palpable   235
To him who does not think. But at your bidding
I will proceed.

                        While thus it fared with them
To whom this cottage till that hapless year
Had been a blessed home, it was my chance
To travel in a country far remote;   240
And glad I was when, halting by yon gate
That leads from the green lane, again I saw
These lofty elm trees. Long I did not rest:
With many pleasant thoughts I cheered my way
O'er the flat common. At the door arrived,   245
I knocked, and when I entered, with the hope
Of usual greeting, Margaret looked at me
A little while, then turned her head away
Speechless, and sitting down upon a chair
Wept bitterly. I wist not what to do,   250
Or how to speak to her. Poor wretch, at last

She rose from off her seat, and then, oh Sir,
I cannot tell how she pronounced my name.
With fervent love, and with a face of grief
Unutterably helpless, and a look   255
That seemed to cling upon me, she enquired
If I had seen her husband. As she spake
A strange surprise and fear came to my heart,
Nor had I power to answer ere she told
That he had disappeared—just two months gone.   260
He left his house: two wretched days had passed,
And on the third by the first break of light,
Within her casement full in view she saw
A purse of gold.[1] 'I trembled at the sight,'
Said Margaret, 'for I knew it was his hand   265
That placed it there. And on that very day
By one, a stranger, from my husband sent,
The tidings came that he had joined a troop
Of soldiers going to a distant land.
He left me thus. Poor Man, he had not heart   270
To take farewell of me, and he feared
That I should follow with my babes, and sink
Beneath the misery of a soldier's life.'

This tale did Margaret tell with many tears,
And when she ended I had little power   275
To give her comfort, and was glad to take
Such words of hope from her own mouth as served
To cheer us both. But long we had not talked
Ere we built up a pile of better thoughts,
And with a brighter eye she looked around,   280
As if she had been shedding tears of joy.
We parted. It was then the early spring:
I left her busy with her garden tools,
And well remember, o'er that fence she looked,
And, while I paced along the footway path,   285
Called out and sent a blessing after me,
With tender cheerfulness, and with a voice
That seemed the very sound of happy thoughts.

I roved o'er many a hill and many a dale
With this my weary load, in heat and cold,   290
Through many a wood and many an open ground,
In sunshine or in shade, in wet or fair,
Now blithe, now drooping, as it might befall;
My best companions now the driving winds
And now the 'trotting brooks' and whispering trees,   295
And now the music of my own sad steps,
With many a short-lived thought that passed between
And disappeared.

1. The "bounty" that her husband had been paid for enlisting in the militia. The shortage of volunteers and England's sharply rising military needs had in some counties forced the bounty up from about £1 in 1757 to more than £16 in 1796 (J. R. Western, *English Militia in the Eighteenth Century*, 1965, p. 276).

I came this way again
Towards the wane of summer, when the wheat
Was yellow, and the soft and bladed grass   300
Sprang up afresh and o'er the hay field spread
Its tender green. When I had reached the door
I found that she was absent. In the shade,
Where we now sit, I waited her return.
Her cottage in its outward look appeared   305
As cheerful as before, in any shew
Of neatness little changed, but that I thought
The honeysuckle crowded round the door,
And from the wall hung down in heavier tufts,
And knots of worthless stonecrop started out   310
Along the window's edge, and grew like weeds
Against the lower panes. I turned aside
And strolled into her garden. It was changed.
The unprofitable bindweed spread his bells
From side to side, and with unwieldy wreaths   315
Had dragged the rose from its sustaining wall
And bent it down to earth. The border tufts,
Daisy, and thrift, and lowly camomile,
And thyme, had straggled out into the paths
Which they were used to deck.   320

Ere this an hour
Was wasted. Back I turned my restless steps,
And as I walked before the door it chanced
A stranger passed, and guessing whom I sought,
He said that she was used to ramble far.
The sun was sinking in the west, and now   325
I sate with sad impatience. From within
Her solitary infant cried aloud.
The spot though fair seemed very desolate,
The longer I remained more desolate;
And looking round I saw the cornerstones,   330
Till then unmarked, on either side the door
With dull red stains discolored, and stuck o'er
With tufts and hairs of wool, as if the sheep
That feed upon the commons thither came
Familiarly, and found a couching place   335
Even at her threshold.

The house clock struck eight:
I turned and saw her distant a few steps.
Her face was pale and thin, her figure too
Was changed. As she unlocked the door she said,
'It grieves me you have waited here so long,   340
But in good truth I've wandered much of late,
And sometimes, to my shame I speak, have need
Of my best prayers to bring me back again.'

While on the board she spread our evening meal,
She told me she had lost her elder child, 345
That he for months had been a serving boy,
Apprenticed by the parish. 'I perceive
You look at me, and you have cause. Today
I have been traveling far, and many days
About the fields I wander, knowing this 350
Only, that what I seek I cannot find.
And so I waste my time: for I am changed,
And to myself,' she said, 'have done much wrong,
And to this helpless infant. I have slept
Weeping, and weeping I have waked. My tears 355
Have flowed as if my body were not such
As others are, and I could never die.
But I am now in mind and in my heart
More easy, and I hope,' she said, 'that heaven
Will give me patience to endure the things 360
Which I behold at home.'

                              It would have grieved
Your very soul to see her. Sir, I feel
The story linger in my heart. I fear
'Tis long and tedious, but my spirit clings
To that poor woman. So familiarly 365
Do I perceive her manner and her look
And presence, and so deeply do I feel
Her goodness, that not seldom in my walks
A momentary trance comes over me,
And to myself I seem to muse on one 370
By sorrow laid asleep or borne away,
A human being destined to awake
To human life, or something very near
To human life, when he shall come again
For whom she suffered. Sir, it would have grieved 375
Your very soul to see her: evermore
Her eyelids drooped, her eyes were downward cast,
And when she at her table gave me food
She did not look at me. Her voice was low,
Her body was subdued. In every act 380
Pertaining to her house affairs appeared
The careless stillness which a thinking mind
Gives to an idle matter. Still she sighed,
But yet no motion of the breast was seen,
No heaving of the heart. While by the fire 385
We sate together, sighs came on my ear,
I knew not how, and hardly whence they came.
I took my staff, and when I kissed her babe
The tears stood in her eyes. I left her then
With the best hope and comfort I could give: 390
She thanked me for my will, but for my hope
It seemed she did not thank me.

                                        I returned
And took my rounds along this road again
Ere on its sunny bank the primrose flower
Had chronicled the earliest day of spring.   395
I found her sad and drooping. She had learned
No tidings of her husband; if he lived,
She knew not that he lived; if he were dead,
She knew not he was dead. She seemed the same
In person or appearance, but her house   400
Bespoke a sleepy hand of negligence.
The floor was neither dry nor neat, the hearth
Was comfortless,
The windows too were dim, and her few books,
Which one upon the other heretofore   405
Had been piled up against the corner panes
In seemly order, now with straggling leaves
Lay scattered here and there, open or shut,
As they had chanced to fall. Her infant babe
Had from its mother caught the trick of grief,   410
And sighed among its playthings. Once again
I turned towards the garden gate, and saw
More plainly still that poverty and grief
Were now come nearer to her. The earth was hard,
With weeds defaced and knots of withered grass;   415
No ridges there appeared of clear black mould,
No winter greenness. Of her herbs and flowers
It seemed the better part were gnawed away
Or trampled on the earth. A chain of straw,
Which had been twisted round the tender stem   420
Of a young apple tree, lay at its root;
The bark was nibbled round by truant sheep.
Margaret stood near, her infant in her arms,
And, seeing that my eye was on the tree,
She said, 'I fear it will be dead and gone   425
Ere Robert come again.'

                                Towards the house
Together we returned, and she inquired
If I had any hope. But for her Babe,
And for her little friendless Boy, she said,
She had no wish to live—that she must die   430
Of sorrow. Yet I saw the idle loom
Still in its place. His Sunday garments hung
Upon the selfsame nail, his very staff
Stood undisturbed behind the door. And when
I passed this way beaten by Autumn winds,   435
She told me that her little babe was dead,
And she was left alone. That very time,
I yet remember, through the miry lane
She walked with me a mile, when the bare trees

Trickled with foggy damps, and in such sort   440
That any heart had ached to hear her, begged
That wheresoe'r I went I still would ask
For him whom she had lost. We parted then,
Our final parting; for from that time forth
Did many seasons pass ere I returned   445
Into this tract again.

         Five tedious years
She lingered in unquiet widowhood,
A wife and widow. Needs must it have been
A sore heart-wasting. I have heard, my friend,
That in that broken arbor she would sit   450
The idle length of half a sabbath day;
There, where you see the toadstool's lazy head;
And when a dog passed by she still would quit
The shade and look abroad. On this old Bench
For hours she sate, and evermore her eye   455
Was busy in the distance, shaping things
Which made her heart beat quick. Seest thou that path?—
The green sward now has broken its gray line—
There to and fro she paced through many a day
Of the warm summer, from a belt of flax   460
That girt her waist, spinning the long-drawn thread
With backward steps. Yet ever as there passed
A man whose garments shewed the Soldier's red,
Or crippled Mendicant in Sailor's garb,
The little child who sate to turn the wheel   465
Ceased from his toil, and she, with faltering voice,
Expecting still to hear her husband's fate,
Made many a fond inquiry; and when they
Whose presence gave no comfort, were gone by,
Her heart was still more sad. And by yon gate,   470
Which bars the traveler's road, she often stood,
And when a stranger horseman came, the latch
Would lift, and in his face look wistfully,
Most happy if from aught discovered there
Of tender feeling she might dare repeat   475
The same sad question.

         Meanwhile her poor hut
Sunk to decay; for he was gone, whose hand
At the first nippings of October frost
Closed up each chink, and with fresh bands of straw
Chequered the green-grown thatch. And so she lived   480
Through the long winter, reckless and alone,
Till this reft house, by frost, and thaw, and rain,
Was sapped; and when she slept, the nightly damps
Did chill her breast, and in the stormy day
Her tattered clothes were ruffled by the wind   485
Even at the side of her own fire. Yet still

She loved this wretched spot, nor would for worlds
Have parted hence; and still that length of road,
And this rude bench, one torturing hope endeared,
Fast rooted at her heart. And here, my friend,   490
In sickness she remained; and here she died,
Last human tenant of these ruined walls."

The old Man ceased: he saw that I was moved.
From that low bench rising instinctively,
I turned aside in weakness, nor had power   495
To thank him for the tale which he had told.
I stood, and leaning o'er the garden gate
Reviewed that Woman's sufferings; and it seemed
To comfort me while with a brother's love
I blessed her in the impotence of grief.   500
At length towards the cottage I returned
Fondly, and traced with milder interest,
That secret spirit of humanity
Which, 'mid the calm oblivious tendencies
Of nature, 'mid her plants, her weeds and flowers,   505
And silent overgrowings, still survived.
The old man seeing this resumed, and said,
"My friend, enough to sorrow have you given,
The purposes of Wisdom ask no more:
Be wise and cheerful, and no longer read   510
The forms of things with an unworthy eye.
She sleeps in the calm earth, and peace is here.
I well remember that those very plumes,
Those weeds, and the high spear grass on that wall,
By mist and silent raindrops silvered o'er,   515
As once I passed, did to my mind convey
So still an image of tranquillity,
So calm and still, and looked so beautiful
Amid the uneasy thoughts which filled my mind,
That what we feel of sorrow and despair   520
From ruin and from change, and all the grief
The passing shews of being leave behind,
Appeared an idle dream that could not live
Where meditation was. I turned away,
And walked along my road in happiness."   525

He ceased. By this the sun declining shot
A slant and mellow radiance, which began
To fall upon us where beneath the trees
We sate on that low bench. And now we felt,
Admonished thus, the sweet hour coming on: 530
A linnet warbled from those lofty elms,
A thrush sang loud, and other melodies
At distance heard, peopled the milder air.
The old man rose and hoisted up his load.
Together casting then a farewell look   535

Upon those silent walls, we left the shade;
And, ere the stars were visible, attained
A rustic inn, our evening resting place.

THE END

1797–ca. 1799   1968

Michael[1]

A PASTORAL POEM

    If from the public way you turn your steps
Up the tumultuous brook of Greenhead Ghyll,[2]
You will suppose that with an upright path
Your feet must struggle; in such bold ascent
The pastoral mountains front you, face to face.   5
But, courage! for around that boisterous brook
The mountains have all opened out themselves,
And made a hidden valley of their own.
No habitation can be seen; but they
Who journey thither find themselves alone   10
With a few sheep, with rocks and stones, and kites[3]
That overhead are sailing in the sky.
It is in truth an utter solitude;
Nor should I have made mention of this dell
But for one object which you might pass by,   15
Might see and notice not. Beside the brook
Appears a straggling heap of unhewn stones!
And to that simple object appertains
A story—unenriched with strange events,
Yet not unfit, I deem, for the fireside,   20
Or for the summer shade. It was the first
Of those domestic tales that spake to me
Of Shepherds, dwellers in the valleys, men
Whom I already loved—not verily
For their own sakes, but for the fields and hills   25
Where was their occupation and abode.
And hence this Tale, while I was yet a Boy
Careless of books, yet having felt the power
Of Nature, by the gentle agency
Of natural objects, led me on to feel   30

1. This poem is founded on the actual misfortunes of a family at Grasmere. For the account of the sheepfold, see Dorothy Wordsworth's *Grasmere Journals*, Oct. 11, 1800. Wordsworth wrote to Thomas Poole, on April 9, 1801, that he had attempted to picture a man "agitated by two of the most powerful affections of the human heart; the parental affection, and the love of property, *landed* property, including the feelings of inheritance, home, and personal and family independence." The subtitle shows Wordsworth's shift of the term "pastoral" from aristocratic make-believe to the tragic suffering of people in what he called "humble and rustic life."
2. Greenhead Ghyll (a ghyll is a ravine forming the bed of a stream) is not far from Wordsworth's cottage at Grasmere. The other places named in the poem are also in that vicinity.
3. Hawks.

For passions that were not my own, and think
(At random and imperfectly indeed)
On man, the heart of man, and human life.
Therefore, although it be a history
Homely and rude, I will relate the same   35
For the delight of a few natural hearts;
And, with yet fonder feeling, for the sake
Of youthful Poets, who among these hills
Will be my second self when I am gone.

    Upon the forest side in Grasmere Vale   40
There dwelt a Shepherd, Michael was his name;
An old man, stout of heart, and strong of limb.
His bodily frame had been from youth to age
Of an unusual strength: his mind was keen,
Intense, and frugal, apt for all affairs,   45
And in his shepherd's calling he was prompt
And watchful more than ordinary men.
Hence had he learned the meaning of all winds,
Of blasts of every tone; and oftentimes,
When others heeded not, he heard the South   50
Make subterraneous music, like the noise
Of bagpipers on distant Highland hills.
The Shepherd, at such warning, of his flock
Bethought him, and he to himself would say,
"The winds are now devising work for me!"   55
And, truly, at all times, the storm, that drives
The traveler to a shelter, summoned him
Up to the mountains: he had been alone
Amid the heart of many thousand mists,
That came to him, and left him, on the heights.   60
So lived he till his eightieth year was past.
And grossly that man errs, who should suppose
That the green valleys, and the streams and rocks,
Were things indifferent to the Shepherd's thoughts.
Fields, where with cheerful spirits he had breathed   65
The common air; hills, which with vigorous step
He had so often climbed; which had impressed
So many incidents upon his mind
Of hardship, skill or courage, joy or fear;
Which, like a book, preserved the memory   70
Of the dumb animals, whom he had saved,
Had fed or sheltered, linking to such acts
The certainty of honorable gain;
Those fields, those hills—what could they less? had laid
Strong hold on his affections, were to him   75
A pleasurable feeling of blind love,
The pleasure which there is in life itself.

His days had not been passed in singleness.
His Helpmate was a comely matron, old—
Though younger than himself full twenty years.   80
She was a woman of a stirring life,
Whose heart was in her house; two wheels she had
Of antique form: this large, for spinning wool;
That small, for flax; and, if one wheel had rest,
It was because the other was at work.   85
The Pair had but one inmate in their house,
An only Child, who had been born to them
When Michael, telling o'er his years, began
To deem that he was old—in shepherd's phrase,
With one foot in the grave. This only Son,   90
With two brave sheep dogs tried in many a storm,
The one of an inestimable worth,
Made all their household. I may truly say,
That they were as a proverb in the vale
For endless industry. When day was gone,   95
And from their occupations out of doors
The Son and Father were come home, even then,
Their labor did not cease; unless when all
Turned to the cleanly supper board, and there,
Each with a mess of pottage and skimmed milk,   100
Sat round the basket piled with oaten cakes,
And their plain homemade cheese. Yet when the meal
Was ended, Luke (for so the Son was named)
And his old Father both betook themselves
To such convenient work as might employ   105
Their hands by the fireside; perhaps to card
Wool for the Housewife's spindle, or repair
Some injury done to sickle, flail, or scythe,
Or other implement of house or field.

  Down from the ceiling, by the chimney's edge,   110
That in our ancient uncouth country style
With huge and black projection overbrowed
Large space beneath, as duly as the light
Of day grew dim the Housewife hung a lamp;
An aged utensil, which had performed   115
Service beyond all others of its kind.
Early at evening did it burn—and late,
Surviving comrade of uncounted hours,
Which, going by from year to year, had found,
And left, the couple neither gay perhaps   120
Nor cheerful, yet with objects and with hopes,
Living a life of eager industry.
And now, when Luke had reached his eighteenth year,
There by the light of this old lamp they sate,
Father and Son, while far into the night   125

The Housewife plied her own peculiar work,
Making the cottage through the silent hours
Murmur as with the sound of summer flies.
This light was famous in its neighborhood,
And was a public symbol of the life   130
That thrifty Pair had lived. For, as it chanced,
Their cottage on a plot of rising ground
Stood single, with large prospect, north and south,
High into Easedale, up to Dunmail Raise,
And westward to the village near the lake;   135
And from this constant light, so regular,
And so far seen, the House itself, by all
Who dwelt within the limits of the vale,
Both old and young, was named The Evening Star.

    Thus living on through such a length of years,   140
The Shepherd, if he loved himself, must needs
Have loved his Helpmate; but to Michael's heart
This son of his old age was yet more dear—
Less from instinctive tenderness, the same
Fond spirit that blindly works in the blood of all—   145
Than that a child, more than all other gifts
That earth can offer to declining man,
Brings hope with it, and forward-looking thoughts,
And stirrings of inquietude, when they
By tendency of nature needs must fail.   150
Exceeding was the love he bare to him,
His heart and his heart's joy! For oftentimes
Old Michael, while he was a babe in arms,
Had done him female service, not alone
For pastime and delight, as is the use   155
Of fathers, but with patient mind enforced
To acts of tenderness; and he had rocked
His cradle, as with a woman's gentle hand.

    And in a later time, ere yet the Boy
Had put on boy's attire, did Michael love,   160
Albeit of a stern unbending mind,
To have the Young-one in his sight, when he
Wrought in the field, or on his shepherd's stool
Sate with a fettered sheep before him stretched
Under the large old oak, that near his door   165
Stood single, and, from matchless depth of shade,
Chosen for the Shearer's covert from the sun,
Thence in our rustic dialect was called
The Clipping Tree, a name which yet it bears.
There, while they two were sitting in the shade,   170
With others round them, earnest all and blithe,
Would Michael exercise his heart with looks
Of fond correction and reproof bestowed

Upon the Child, if he disturbed the sheep
By catching at their legs, or with his shouts   175
Scared them, while they lay still beneath the shears.

    And when by Heaven's good grace the boy grew up
A healthy Lad, and carried in his cheek
Two steady roses that were five years old;
Then Michael from a winter coppice[4] cut   180
With his own hand a sapling, which he hooped
With iron, making it throughout in all
Due requisites a perfect shepherd's staff,
And gave it to the Boy; wherewith equipped
He as a watchman oftentimes was placed   185
At gate or gap, to stem or turn the flock;
And, to his office prematurely called,
There stood the urchin, as you will divine,
Something between a hindrance and a help;
And for this cause not always, I believe,   190
Receiving from his Father hire of praise;
Though nought was left undone which staff, or voice,
Or looks, or threatening gestures, could perform.

    But soon as Luke, full ten years old, could stand
Against the mountain blasts, and to the heights,   195
Not fearing toil, nor length of weary ways,
He with his Father daily went, and they
Were as companions, why should I relate
That objects which the Shepherd loved before
Were dearer now? that from the Boy there came   200
Feelings and emanations—things which were
Light to the sun and music to the wind;
And that the old Man's heart seemed born again?

    Thus in his Father's sight the Boy grew up:
And now, when he had reached his eighteenth year,   205
He was his comfort and his daily hope.

    While in this sort the simple household lived
From day to day, to Michael's ear there came
Distressful tidings. Long before the time
Of which I speak, the Shepherd had been bound   210
In surety for his brother's son, a man
Of an industrious life, and ample means;
But unforeseen misfortunes suddenly
Had pressed upon him; and old Michael now
Was summoned to discharge the forfeiture,   215
A grievous penalty, but little less
Than half his substance. This unlooked-for claim,
At the first hearing, for a moment took

4. Grove of small trees.

More hope out of his life than he supposed
That any old man ever could have lost. 220
As soon as he had armed himself with strength
To look his trouble in the face, it seemed
The Shepherd's sole resource to sell at once
A portion of his patrimonial fields.
Such was his first resolve; he thought again, 225
And his heart failed him. "Isabel," said he,
Two evenings after he had heard the news,
"I have been toiling more than seventy years,
And in the open sunshine of God's love
Have we all lived; yet, if these fields of ours 230
Should pass into a stranger's hand, I think
That I could not lie quiet in my grave.
Our lot is a hard lot; the sun himself
Has scarcely been more diligent than I;
And I have lived to be a fool at last 235
To my own family. An evil man
That was, and made an evil choice, if he
Were false to us; and, if he were not false,
There are ten thousand to whom loss like this
Had been no sorrow. I forgive him—but 240
'Twere better to be dumb than to talk thus.

"When I began, my purpose was to speak
Of remedies and of a cheerful hope.
Our Luke shall leave us, Isabel; the land
Shall not go from us, and it shall be free; 245
He shall possess it, free as is the wind
That passes over it. We have, thou know'st,
Another kinsman—he will be our friend
In this distress. He is a prosperous man,
Thriving in trade—and Luke to him shall go, 250
And with his kinsman's help and his own thrift
He quickly will repair this loss, and then
He may return to us. If here he stay,
What can be done? Where everyone is poor,
What can be gained?"   At this the old Man paused, 255
And Isabel sat silent, for her mind
Was busy, looking back into past times.
There's Richard Bateman,[5] thought she to herself,
He was a parish boy—at the church door
They made a gathering for him, shillings, pence, 260
And halfpennies, wherewith the neighbors bought
A basket, which they filled with peddler's wares;

5. "The story alluded to here is well
known in the country. The chapel is
called Ings Chapel and is on the road
leading from Kendal to Ambleside"
[Wordsworth's note].

And, with this basket on his arm, the lad
Went up to London, found a master there,
Who, out of many, chose the trusty boy   265
To go and overlook his merchandise
Beyond the seas; where he grew wondrous rich,
And left estates and monies to the poor,
And, at his birthplace, built a chapel floored
With marble, which he sent from foreign lands.   270
These thoughts, and many others of like sort,
Passed quickly through the mind of Isabel,
And her face brightened. The old Man was glad,
And thus resumed: "Well, Isabel! this scheme
These two days has been meat and drink to me.   275
Far more than we have lost is left us yet.
We have enough—I wish indeed that I
Were younger—but this hope is a good hope.
Make ready Luke's best garments, of the best
Buy for him more, and let us send him forth   280
Tomorrow, or the next day, or tonight:
If he *could* go, the Boy should go tonight."

   Here Michael ceased, and to the fields went forth
With a light heart. The Housewife for five days
Was restless morn and night, and all day long   285
Wrought on with her best fingers to prepare
Things needful for the journey of her son.
But Isabel was glad when Sunday came
To stop her in her work; for, when she lay
By Michael's side, she through the last two nights   290
Heard him, how he was troubled in his sleep;
And when they rose at morning she could see
That all his hopes were gone. That day at noon
She said to Luke, while they two by themselves
Were sitting at the door, "Thou must not go;   295
We have no other Child but thee to lose,
None to remember—do not go away,
For if thou leave thy Father he will die."
The Youth made answer with a jocund voice;
And Isabel, when she had told her fears,   300
Recovered heart. That evening her best fare
Did she bring forth, and all together sat
Like happy people round a Christmas fire.

   With daylight Isabel resumed her work;
And all the ensuing week the house appeared   305
As cheerful as a grove in spring; at length
The expected letter from their kinsman came,
With kind assurances that he would do
His utmost for the welfare of the Boy;

To which requests were added that forthwith   310
He might be sent to him. Ten times or more
The letter was read over; Isabel
Went forth to show it to the neighbors round;
Nor was there at that time on English land
A prouder heart than Luke's. When Isabel   315
Had to her house returned, the old Man said,
"He shall depart tomorrow." To this word
The Housewife answered, talking much of things
Which, if at such short notice he should go,
Would surely be forgotten. But at length   320
She gave consent, and Michael was at ease.

   Near the tumultuous brook of Greenhead Ghyll,
In that deep valley, Michael had designed
To build a Sheepfold;[6] and, before he heard
The tidings of his melancholy loss,   325
For this same purpose he had gathered up
A heap of stones, which by the streamlet's edge
Lay thrown together, ready for the work.
With Luke that evening thitherward he walked;
And soon as they had reached the place he stopped,   330
And thus the old Man spake to him: "My son,
Tomorrow thou wilt leave me: with full heart
I look upon thee, for thou art the same
That wert a promise to me ere thy birth,
And all thy life hast been my daily joy.   335
I will relate to thee some little part
Of our two histories; 'twill do thee good
When thou art from me, even if I should touch
On things thou canst not know of. After thou
First cam'st into the world—as oft befalls   340
To newborn infants—thou didst sleep away
Two days, and blessings from thy Father's tongue
Then fell upon thee. Day by day passed on,
And still I loved thee with increasing love.
Never to living ear came sweeter sounds   345
Than when I heard thee by our own fireside
First uttering, without words, a natural tune;
While thou, a feeding babe, didst in thy joy
Sing at thy Mother's breast. Month followed month,
And in the open fields my life was passed   350
And on the mountains; else I think that thou
Hadst been brought up upon thy Father's knees.
But we were playmates, Luke; among these hills,
As well thou knowest, in us the old and young
Have played together, nor with me didst thou   355
Lack any pleasure which a boy can know."

---

6. Pen for sheep. "A sheepfold in these mountains is an unroofed building of stone walls, with different divisions" [Wordsworth's note].

Luke had a manly heart; but at these words
He sobbed aloud. The old Man grasped his hand,
And said, "Nay, do not take it so—I see
That these are things of which I need not speak.   360
Even to the utmost I have been to thee
A kind and a good Father: and herein
I but repay a gift which I myself
Received at others' hands; for, though now old
Beyond the common life of man, I still   365
Remember them who loved me in my youth.
Both of them sleep together; here they lived,
As all their Forefathers had done; and, when
At length their time was come, they were not loath
To give their bodies to the family mold.   370
I wished that thou shouldst live the life they lived,
But 'tis a long time to look back, my Son,
And see so little gain from threescore years.
These fields were burthened[7] when they came to me;
Till I was forty years of age, not more   375
Than half of my inheritance was mine.
I toiled and toiled; God blessed me in my work,
And till these three weeks past the land was free.
It looks as if it never could endure
Another master. Heaven forgive me, Luke,   380
If I judge ill for thee, but it seems good
That thou shouldst go."
                At this the old Man paused;
Then, pointing to the stones near which they stood,
Thus, after a short silence, he resumed:
"This was a work for us; and now, my Son,   385
It is a work for me. But, lay one stone—
Here, lay it for me, Luke, with thine own hands.
Nay, Boy, be of good hope—we both may live
To see a better day. At eighty-four
I still am strong and hale; do thou thy part;   390
I will do mine. I will begin again
With many tasks that were resigned to thee:
Up to the heights, and in among the storms,
Will I without thee go again, and do
All works which I was wont to do alone,   395
Before I knew thy face. Heaven bless thee, Boy!
Thy heart these two weeks has been beating fast
With many hopes; it should be so—yes—yes—
I knew that thou couldst never have a wish
To leave me, Luke; thou hast been bound to me   400
Only by links of love; when thou art gone,
What will be left to us!—But I forget
My purposes. Lay now the cornerstone,
As I requested; and hereafter, Luke,

7. I.e., mortgaged.

When thou art gone away, should evil men   405
Be thy companions, think of me, my Son,
And of this moment; hither turn thy thoughts,
And God will strengthen thee; amid all fear
And all temptation, Luke, I pray that thou
May'st bear in mind the life thy Fathers lived,   410
Who, being innocent, did for that cause
Bestir them in good deeds. Now, fare thee well—
When thou return'st, thou in this place wilt see
A work which is not here: a covenant
'Twill be between us; but, whatever fate   415
Befall thee, I shall love thee to the last,
And bear thy memory with me to the grave."

   The Shepherd ended here; and Luke stooped down,
And, as his Father had requested, laid
The first stone of the Sheepfold. At the sight   420
The old Man's grief broke from him; to his heart
He pressed his Son, he kisséd him and wept;
And to the house together they returned.
Hushed was that House in peace, or seeming peace
Ere the night fell; with morrow's dawn the Boy   425
Began his journey, and, when he had reached
The public way, he put on a bold face;
And all the neighbors, as he passed their doors,
Came forth with wishes and with farewell prayers,
That followed him till he was out of sight.   430

   A good report did from their kinsman come,
Of Luke and his well-doing; and the Boy
Wrote loving letters, full of wondrous news,
Which, as the Housewife phrased it, were throughout
"The prettiest letters that were ever seen."   435
Both parents read them with rejoicing hearts.
So, many months passed on; and once again
The Shepherd went about his daily work
With confident and cheerful thoughts; and now
Sometimes when he could find a leisure hour   440
He to that valley took his way, and there
Wrought at the Sheepfold. Meantime Luke began
To slacken in his duty; and, at length,
He in the dissolute city gave himself
To evil courses; ignominy and shame   445
Fell on him, so that he was driven at last
To seek a hiding place beyond the seas.

   There is a comfort in the strength of love;
'Twill make a thing endurable, which else
Would overset the brain, or break the heart;   450
I have conversed with more than one who well
Remember the old Man, and what he was

Years after he had heard this heavy news.
His bodily frame had been from youth to age
Of an unusual strength. Among the rocks   455
He went, and still looked up to sun and cloud,
And listened to the wind; and, as before,
Performed all kinds of labor for his sheep,
And for the land, his small inheritance.
And to that hollow dell from time to time   460
Did he repair, to build the Fold of which
His flock had need. 'Tis not forgotten yet
The pity which was then in every heart
For the old Man—and 'tis believed by all
That many and many a day he thither went,   465
And never lifted up a single stone.

    There, by the Sheepfold, sometimes was he seen
Sitting alone, or with his faithful Dog,
Then old, beside him, lying at his feet.
The length of full seven years, from time to time,   470
He at the building of this Sheepfold wrought,
And left the work unfinished when he died.
Three years, or little more, did Isabel
Survive her Husband: at her death the estate
Was sold, and went into a stranger's hand.   475
The Cottage which was named The Evening Star
Is gone—the plowshare has been through the ground
On which it stood; great changes have been wrought
In all the neighborhood; yet the oak is left
That grew beside their door; and the remains   480
Of the unfinished Sheepfold may be seen
Beside the boisterous brook of Greenhead Ghyll.

Oct. 11–Dec. 9, 1800   1800

Written in March[1]

WHILE RESTING ON THE BRIDGE AT THE FOOT
OF BROTHER'S WATER

    The cock is crowing,
    The stream is flowing,
    The small birds twitter,
    The lake doth glitter,
The green field sleeps in the sun;   5
    The oldest and youngest
    Are at work with the strongest;
    The cattle are grazing,
    Their heads never raising;
There are forty feeding like one!   10

1. For the composition of this poem, see Dorothy Wordsworth's *Grasmere Journals*, Apr. 16, 1802.

Like an army defeated
The snow hath retreated,
And now doth fare ill
On the top of the bare hill;
The plowboy is whooping—anon—**anon**:   15
There's joy in the mountains;
There's life in the fountains;
Small clouds are sailing,
Blue sky prevailing;
The rain is over and gone!   20

1802   1807

Resolution and Independence[1]

1

There was a roaring in the wind all night;
The rain came heavily and fell in floods;
But now the sun is rising calm and bright;
The birds are singing in the distant woods;
Over his own sweet voice the stock dove broods;   5
The jay makes answer as the magpie chatters;
And all the air is filled with pleasant noise of waters.

2

All things that love the sun are out of doors;
The sky rejoices in the morning's birth;
The grass is bright with raindrops; on the moors   10
The hare is running races in her mirth;
And with her feet she from the plashy earth
Raises a mist; that, glittering in the sun,
Runs with her all the way, wherever she doth run.

3

I was a Traveler then upon the moor;   15
I saw the hare that raced about with joy;
I heard the woods and distant waters roar;
Or heard them not, as happy as a boy:
The pleasant season did my heart employ:
My old remembrances went from me wholly;   20
And all the ways of men, so vain and melancholy.

1. For the meeting with the old leech-gatherer, see Dorothy Wordsworth's *Grasmere Journals*, Oct. 3, 1800. Wordsworth himself tells us that "I was in the state of feeling described in the beginning of the poem, while crossing over Barton Fell from Mr. Clarkson's, at the foot of Ullswater, towards Askam. The image of the hare I then observed on the ridge of the Fell." Eighteen months later (see *Grasmere Journals,* May 4 and 7, 1802), these events, recollected in tranquility, were transformed into this poem of personal crisis, mastered by an imaginative process of spontaneous mythmaking. The metamorphosis of the still old man (stanzas 8 ff.) ends when he modulates into the archetypal figure of the eternal and haunted wanderer, of whom Coleridge's Ancient Mariner had been the most recent embodiment. Unlike Coleridge's, however, Wordsworth's is a natural supernaturalism, for the old leech-gatherer remains stubbornly matter-of-fact.

4

But, as it sometimes chanceth, from the might
Of joy in minds that can no further go,
As high as we have mounted in delight
In our dejection do we sink as low;   25
To me that morning did it happen so;
And fears and fancies thick upon me came;
Dim sadness—and blind thoughts, I knew not, nor could name.

5

I heard the skylark warbling in the sky;
And I bethought me of the playful hare: 30
Even such a happy Child of earth am I;
Even as these blissful creatures do I fare;
Far from the world I walk, and from all care;
But there may come another day to me—
Solitude, pain of heart, distress, and poverty.   35

6

My whole life I have lived in pleasant thought,
As if life's business were a summer mood;
As if all needful things would come unsought
To genial faith, still rich in genial good;
But how can he expect that others should   40
Build for him, sow for him, and at his call
Love him, who for himself will take no heed at all?

7

I thought of Chatterton,[2] the marvelous Boy,
The sleepless Soul that perished in his pride;
Of him who walked in glory and in joy   45
Following his plow, along the mountainside;[3]
By our own spirits are we deified:
We Poets in our youth begin in gladness,
But thereof come in the end despondency and madness.

8

Now, whether it were by peculiar grace,   50
A leading from above, a something given,
Yet it befell that, in this lonely place,
When I with these untoward thoughts had striven,
Beside a pool bare to the eye of heaven
I saw a Man before me unawares: 55
The oldest man he seemed that ever wore gray hairs.

9

As a huge stone is sometimes seen to lie
Couched on the bald top of an eminence;

2. Thomas Chatterton (1752–70), a
poet of great talent who, in his loneliness and dire poverty, poisoned himself at the age of 17 and so became the
prime Romantic symbol of neglected
young genius.
3. Robert Burns, also considered at
that time as a natural poet who died
young and poor, without adequate recognition.

Wonder to all who do the same espy,
By what means it could thither come, and whence;   60
So that it seems a thing endued with sense:
Like a sea beast crawled forth, that on a shelf
Of rock or sand reposeth, there to sun itself;

10

Such seemed this Man,[4] not all alive nor dead,
Nor all asleep—in his extreme old age;   65
His body was bent double, feet and head
Coming together in life's pilgrimage;
As if some dire constraint of pain, or rage
Of sickness felt by him in times long past,
A more than human weight upon his frame had cast.   70

11

Himself he propped, limbs, body, and pale face,
Upon a long gray staff of shaven wood;
And, still as I drew near with gentle pace,
Upon the margin of that moorish flood
Motionless as a cloud that old Man stood,   75
That heareth not the loud winds when they call,
And moveth all together, if it move at all.

12

At length, himself unsettling, he the pond
Stirred with his staff, and fixedly did look
Upon the muddy water, which he conned,   80
As if he had been reading in a book;
And now a stranger's privilege I took,
And, drawing to his side, to him did say,
"This morning gives us promise of a glorious day."

13

A gentle answer did the old Man make,   85
In courteous speech which forth he slowly drew;
And him with further words I thus bespake,
"What occupation do you there pursue?
This is a lonesome place for one like you."
Ere he replied, a flash of mild surprise   90
Broke from the sable orbs of his yet-vivid eyes.

14

His words came feebly, from a feeble chest,
But each in solemn order followed each,
With something of a lofty utterance dressed—
Choice word and measured phrase, above the reach   95

---

4. In Wordsworth's own analysis of this passage, he says that the stone is endowed with something of life, the sea beast is stripped of some of its life to assimilate it to the stone, and the old man divested of enough life and motion to make "the two objects unite and coalesce in just comparison"; he used the passage to demonstrate his theory of how the "conferring, the abstracting, and the modifying powers of the Imagination * * * are all brought into conjunction" (Preface to the *Poems* of 1815). Compare Coleridge's analysis of the imagination in *Biographia Literaria*, Chapter XIII.

Of ordinary men; a stately speech;
Such as grave livers[5] do in Scotland use,
Religious men, who give to God and man their dues.

15

He told, that to these waters he had come
To gather leeches,[6] being old and poor: 100
Employment hazardous and wearisome!
And he had many hardships to endure:
From pond to pond he roamed, from moor to moor;
Housing, with God's good help, by choice or chance;
And in this way he gained an honest maintenance.   105

16

The old Man still stood talking by my side;
But now his voice to me was like a stream
Scarce heard; nor word from word could I divide;
And the whole body of the Man did seem
Like one whom I had met with in a dream;   110
Or like a man from some far region sent,
To give me human strength, by apt admonishment.

17

My former thoughts returned: the fear that kills;
And hope that is unwilling to be fed;
Cold, pain, and labor, and all fleshly ills;   115
And mighty Poets in their misery dead.
—Perplexed, and longing to be comforted,
My question eagerly did I renew,
"How is it that you live, and what is it you do?"

18

He with a smile did then his words repeat;   120
And said that, gathering leeches, far and wide
He traveled, stirring thus about his feet
The waters of the pools where they abide.
"Once I could meet with them on every side,
But they have dwindled long by slow decay;   125
Yet still I persevere, and find them where I may."

19

While he was talking thus, the lonely place,
The old Man's shape, and speech—all troubled me:
In my mind's eye I seemed to see him pace   130
About the weary moors continually,
Wandering about alone and silently.
While I these thoughts within myself pursued,
He, having made a pause, the same discourse renewed.

20

And soon with this he other matter blended,   135
Cheerfully uttered, with demeanor kind,

---

5. Those who live gravely.
6. Leeches were used to draw blood for curative purposes. A leech-gatherer, barelegged in shallow water, stirred the water to rouse them, and then picked them off his skin.

But stately in the main; and, when he ended,
I could have laughed myself to scorn to find
In that decrepit Man so firm a mind.
"God," said I, "be my help and stay[7] secure;
I'll think of the Leech Gatherer on the lonely moor!"   140

May 3–July 4, 1802   1807

The Green Linnet[1]

Beneath these fruit-tree boughs that shed
Their snow-white blossoms on my head,
With brightest sunshine round me spread
   Of spring's unclouded weather,
In this sequestered nook how sweet   5
To sit upon my orchard seat!
And birds and flowers once more to greet,
   My last year's friends together.

One have I marked, the happiest guest
In all this covert of the blest:
Hail to thee, far above the rest   10
   In joy of voice and pinion!
Thou, Linnet! in thy green array,
Presiding Spirit here today,
Dost lead the revels of the May;   15
   And this is thy dominion.

While birds, and butterflies, and flowers,
Make all one band of paramours,
Thou, ranging up and down the bowers,
   Art sole in thy employment: 20
A Life, a Presence like the Air,
Scattering thy gladness without care,
Too blest with any one to pair;
   Thyself thy own enjoyment.

Amid yon tuft of hazel trees,   25
That twinkle to the gusty breeze,
Behold him perched in ecstasies,
   Yet seeming still to hover;
There! where the flutter of his wings
Upon his back and body flings   30
Shadows and sunny glimmerings,
   That cover him all over.

My dazzled sight he oft deceives,
A brother of the dancing leaves;
Then flits, and from the cottage eaves   35

---

7. Support (a noun).

1. Coleridge used the last two stanzas to demonstrate Wordsworth's "perfect truth of nature in his images and de- scriptions." The extent and particularity of this description, however, are rare in Wordsworth, despite his reputation as a "nature poet."

Pours forth his song in gushes;
As if by that exulting strain
He mocked and treated with disdain
The voiceless Form he chose to feign,
While fluttering in the bushes.   40

1803   1807

Yew Trees[1]

There is a Yew Tree, pride of Lorton Vale,
Which to this day stands single, in the midst
Of its own darkness, as it stood of yore:
Not loath to furnish weapons for the bands
Of Umfraville or Percy ere they marched   5
To Scotland's heaths; or those that crossed the sea
And drew their sounding bows at Azincour,
Perhaps at earlier Crecy, or Poictiers.
Of vast circumference and gloom profound
This solitary Tree! a living thing   10
Produced too slowly ever to decay;
Of form and aspect too magnificent
To be destroyed. But worthier still of note
Are those fraternal Four of Borrowdale,
Joined in one solemn and capacious grove;   15
Huge trunks! and each particular trunk a growth
Of intertwisted fibers serpentine
Up-coiling, and inveterately convolved;
Nor uninformed with Phantasy, and looks
That threaten the profane—a pillared shade,   20
Upon whose grassless floor of red-brown hue,
By sheddings from the pining umbrage[2] tinged
Perennially—beneath whose sable roof
Of boughs, as if for festal purpose decked
With unrejoicing berries—ghostly Shapes   25
May meet at noontide; Fear and trembling Hope,
Silence and Foresight; Death the Skeleton
And Time the Shadow—there to celebrate,
As in a natural temple scattered o'er
With altars undisturbed of mossy stone,   30
United worship; or in mute repose
To lie, and listen to the mountain flood
Murmuring from Glaramara's[3] inmost caves.

ca. 1803   1815

1. An evergreen tree; its wood was used for the bows which won the English victories mentioned in the poem, in the late medieval wars against Scotland and France. In the *Biographia Literaria*, Chapter XXII, Coleridge cited lines 13 ff. as a prime example of the faculty of imagination, in which Wordsworth "stands nearest of all modern writers to Shakespeare and Milton; and yet in a kind perfectly unborrowed and his own."
2. Foliage that casts a shade.
3. Mountain rising from Borrowdale valley, in the Lake Country.

I Wandered Lonely as a Cloud[4]

I wandered lonely as a cloud
That floats on high o'er vales and hills,
When all at once I saw a crowd,
A host, of golden daffodils;
Beside the lake, beneath the trees,   5
Fluttering and dancing in the breeze.

Continuous as the stars that shine
And twinkle on the milky way,
They stretched in never-ending line
Along the margin of a bay: 10
Ten thousand saw I at a glance,
Tossing their heads in sprightly dance.

The waves beside them danced; but they
Outdid the sparkling waves in glee;
A poet could not but be gay,   15
In such a jocund company;
I gazed—and gazed—but little thought
What wealth the show to me had brought:

For oft, when on my couch I lie
In vacant or in pensive mood,   20
They flash upon that inward eye
Which is the bliss of solitude;
And then my heart with pleasure fills,
And dances with the daffodils.

1804   1807

My Heart Leaps Up

My heart leaps up when I behold
   A rainbow in the sky:
So was it when my life began;
So is it now I am a man;
So be it when I shall grow old,   5
   Or let me die!
The Child is father of the Man;
And I could wish my days to be
Bound each to each by natural piety.[1]

March 26, 1802   1807

4. The last stanza describes the kind of recollection in tranquillity from which this poem arose, two years after the original experience, which Dorothy Wordsworth described in her *Grasmere Journals* for Apr. 15, 1802.
1. As distinguished from piety based on the Scriptures, in which God makes the rainbow the token of his covenant with Noah and all his descendants. The religious sentiment that binds Wordsworth's mature self to that of his childhood is a continuing responsiveness to the miracle of ordinary things.

Ode: Intimations of Immortality

"This was composed during my residence at Town End, Grasmere; two years at least passed between the writing of the four first stanzas and the remaining part. To the attentive and competent reader the whole sufficiently explains itself; but there may be no harm in adverting here to particular feelings or *experiences* of my own mind on which the structure of the poem partly rests. Nothing was more difficult for me in childhood than to admit the notion of death as a state applicable to my own being. I have said elsewhere

> —A simple child,
> That lightly draws its breath,
> And feels its life in every limb,
> What should it know of death!—

But it was not so much from [feelings] of animal vivacity that *my* difficulty came as from a sense of the indomitableness of the spirit within me. I used to brood over the stories of Enoch and Elijah, and almost to persuade myself that, whatever might become of others, I should be translated, in something of the same way, to heaven. With a feeling congenial to this, I was often unable to think of external things as having external existence, and I communed with all that I saw as something not apart from, but inherent in, my own immaterial nature. Many times while going to school have I grasped at a wall or tree to recall myself from this abyss of idealism to the reality. At that time I was afraid of such processes. In later periods of life I have deplored, as we have all reason to do, a subjugation of an opposite character, and have rejoiced over the remembrances, as is expressed in the lines—

> Obstinate questionings
> Of sense and outward things,
> Fallings from us, vanishings; etc.

To that dreamlike vividness and splendor which invest objects of sight in childhood, everyone, I believe, if he would look back, could bear testimony, and I need not dwell upon it here: but having in the Poem regarded it as presumptive evidence of a prior state of existence, I think it right to protest against a conclusion, which has given pain to some good and pious persons, that I meant to inculcate such a belief. It is far too shadowy a notion to be recommended to faith, as more than an element in our instincts of immortality. But let us bear in mind that, though the idea is not advanced in revelation, there is nothing there to contradict it, and the fall of Man presents an analogy in its favor. Accordingly, a pre-existent state has entered into the popular creeds of many nations; and, among all persons acquainted with classic literature, is known as an ingredient in Platonic philosophy. Archimedes said that he could move the world if he had a point whereon to rest his machine. Who has not felt the same aspirations as regards the world of his own mind? Having to wield some of its elements when I was impelled to write this Poem on the 'Immortality of the Soul,' I took hold of the notion of pre-existence as having sufficient foundation in humanity for authorizing me to make for my purpose the best use of it I could as a Poet" (Wordsworth).

As Wordsworth says, Plato held the doctrine that the soul is immortal and exists separately from the body both before birth and after death. But while the *Ode* proposes that the soul only gradually loses "the vision splendid" after birth, Plato maintained the contrary: that the knowledge of the eternal Ideas, which the soul had acquired by direct acquaintance, is totally lost at the instant of birth, and must be gradually "recollected" by philosophical discipline in the course of this life (*Phaedo* 73–77). Wordsworth's concept resembles more closely the view of some Neo-Platonists that the glory of the unborn soul is gradually quenched by its descent into the darkness of matter.

Wordsworth was troubled by objections to the Christian heterodoxy of this apparent claim for the pre-existence, as against the orthodox belief in the survival, of the soul. He insisted that he did not intend to assert this as doctrine, but only to use it as a poetic postulate, enabling him to deal "as a poet" with an experience to which everyone, as he says, "if he would look back, could bear testimony." This experience is a universal human one: that the loss of youth involves the loss of a freshness and radiance investing all experience. Coleridge's *Dejection: An Ode,* which he wrote after he had heard the first four stanzas of Wordsworth's poem, employs a similar figurative technique for a comparable, though more devastating, experience of loss. As with all poems so large and rich as this one, there are divergent interpretations of its purport, emphases, and organization. But most commentators agree that the poem offers two different perspectives on the fact that growing up is also a stage on the way to death, and almost all agree that it is one of the greatest instances of the very difficult form of the irregular Pindaric ode. The Catholic poet G. M. Hopkins remarked: "For my part I should think St. George and St. Thomas of Canterbury wore roses in heaven for England's sake on the day that *Ode,* not without their intercession, was penned."

The original version of this poem had as its title only "Ode," and then as epigraph "*Paulo maiora canamus*" ("Let us sing of somewhat higher things") from Virgil's *Eclogue IV.*

Ode

INTIMATIONS OF IMMORTALITY FROM RECOLLECTIONS OF EARLY CHILDHOOD

> The Child is father of the Man;
> And I could wish my days to be
> Bound each to each by natural piety.[1]

1

There was a time when meadow, grove, and stream,
The earth, and every common sight,
  To me did seem
  Appareled in celestial light,
The glory and the freshness of a dream.   5
It is not now as it hath been of yore—
  Turn whereso'er I may,
   By night or day,
The things which I have seen I now can see no more.

1. The concluding lines of Wordsworth's *My Heart Leaps Up.*

2

The Rainbow comes and goes,   10
And lovely is the Rose,
The Moon doth with delight
Look round her when the heavens are bare,
Waters on a starry night
Are beautiful and fair;   15
The sunshine is a glorious birth;
But yet I know, where'er I go,
That there hath passed away a glory from the earth.

3

Now while the birds thus sing a joyous song,
And while the young lambs bound   20
As to the tabor's sound,[2]
To me alone there came a thought of grief:
A timely utterance[3] gave that thought relief,
And I again am strong:
The cataracts blow their trumpets from the steep; 25
No more shall grief of mine the season wrong;
I hear the Echoes through the mountains throng,
The Winds come to me from the fields of sleep,[4]
And all the earth is gay;
Land and sea   30
Give themselves up to jollity,
And with the heart of May
Doth every Beast keep holiday—
Thou Child of Joy,
Shout round me, let me hear thy shouts, thou happy 35
Shepherd-boy!

4

Ye blessed Creatures, I have heard the call
Ye to each other make; I see
The heavens laugh with you in your jubilee;
My heart is at your festival,
My head hath its coronal,[5]   40
The fullness of your bliss, I feel—I feel it all.
Oh, evil day! if I were sullen
While Earth herself is adorning,
This sweet May morning,
And the Children are culling   45
On every side,
In a thousand valleys far and wide,
Fresh flowers; while the sun shines warm,

2. A tabor is a small drum often used to beat time for dancing.
3. Perhaps *My Heart Leaps Up*, perhaps *Resolution and Independence*, perhaps not a poem at all.
4. Of the many suggested interpretations, the simplest is "from the fields where they were sleeping." Wordsworth often associated a rising wind with the revival of spirit and poetic inspiration; see, e.g., the opening passage of *The Prelude*.
5. Circlet of wild flowers, with which the shepherd boys trimmed their hats in May.

And the Babe leaps up on his Mother's arm—
    I hear, I hear, with joy I hear!   50
—But there's a Tree, of many, one,
A single Field which I have looked upon,
Both of them speak of something that is gone:
    The Pansy at my feet
    Doth the same tale repeat: 55
Whither is fled the visionary gleam?
Where is it now, the glory and the dream?

change

5

Our birth is but a sleep and a forgetting:
The Soul that rises with us, our life's Star,[6]
    Hath had elsewhere its setting,   60
    And cometh from afar:
    Not in entire forgetfulness,
    And not in utter nakedness,

The Soul is immortal

But trailing clouds of glory do we come
    From God, who is our home: 65
Heaven lies about us in our infancy!
Shades of the prison-house begin to close
    Upon the growing Boy
    But he
Beholds the light, and whence it flows,   70
    He sees it in his joy;
The Youth, who daily farther from the east
    Must travel, still is Nature's Priest,
    And by the vision splendid
    Is on his way attended;   75
At length the Man perceives it die away,
And fade into the light of common day.

6

Earth fills her lap with pleasures of her own;
Yearnings she hath in her own natural kind,
And, even with something of a Mother's mind,   80
    And no unworthy aim,
    The homely[7] Nurse doth all she can
To make her foster child, her Inmate Man,
    Forget the glories he hath known,
And that imperial palace whence he came.   85

human development

7

Behold the Child among his newborn blisses,
A six-years' Darling of a pygmy size!
See, where 'mid work of his own hand he lies,
Fretted[8] by sallies of his mother's kisses,
With light upon him from his father's eyes!   90
See, at his feet, some little plan or chart,
Some fragment from his dream of human life,

---

6. The sun, as metaphor for the soul.
7. In the old sense, "simple and friendly."

8. "Irritated," or possibly in the old sense, "checkered over."

Shaped by himself with newly-learned art;
  A wedding or a festival,
  A mourning or a funeral;   95
   And this hath now his heart,
  And unto this he frames his song;
   Then will he fit his tongue
To dialogues of business, love, or strife;
  But it will not be long   100
  Ere this be thrown aside,
  And with new joy and pride
The little Actor cons another part;
Filling from time to time his "humorous stage"[9]
With all the Persons, down to palsied Age, 105
That Life brings with her in her equipage;
  As if his whole vocation
  Were endless imitation.

      8

Thou, whose exterior semblance doth belie
  Thy Soul's immensity;   110
Thou best Philosopher, who yet dost keep
Thy heritage, thou Eye among the blind,
That, deaf and silent, read'st the eternal deep,
Haunted forever by the eternal mind—
  Mighty Prophet! Seer blest!   115
  On whom those truths do rest, .
Which we are toiling all our lives to find,
In darkness lost, the darkness of the grave;
Thou, over whom thy Immortality
Broods like the Day, a Master o'er a Slave, 120
A Presence which is not to be put by;
Thou little Child, yet glorious in the might
Of heaven-born freedom on thy being's height,
Why with such earnest pains dost thou provoke
The years to bring the inevitable yoke, 125
Thus blindly with thy blessedness at strife?
Full soon thy Soul shall have her earthly freight,
And custom lie upon thee with a weight,
Heavy as frost, and deep almost as life!

      9

  O joy! that in our embers   130
  Is something that doth live,
  That nature yet remembers
  What was so fugitive!
The thought of our past years in me doth breed
Perpetual benediction: not indeed   135
For that which is most worthy to be blest;
Delight and liberty, the simple creed

---

9. From a sonnet by Samuel Daniel, Elizabethan poet. In Daniel's age, "humerous" meant "capricious," and also referred to the various characters and temperaments ("humors") represented in drama.

Of Childhood, whether busy or at rest,
With new-fledged hope still fluttering in his breast—
          Not for these I raise   140
          The song of thanks and praise;
        But for those obstinate questionings
        Of sense and outward things,
        Fallings from us, vanishings;
        Blank misgivings of a Creature   145
Moving about in worlds not realized,[1]
High instincts before which our mortal **Nature**
Did tremble like a guilty Thing surprised;
          But for those first affections,
          Those shadowy recollections,
        Which, be they what they may,   150
Are yet the fountain light of all our day,
Are yet a master light of all our seeing;
        Uphold us, cherish, and have power to make
Our noisy years seem moments in the being   155
Of the eternal Silence: truths that wake,
            To perish never;
Which neither listlessness, nor mad endeavor,
            Nor Man nor Boy,
Nor all that is at enmity with joy,   160
Can utterly abolish or destroy!
          Hence in a season of calm weather
          Though inland far we be,
Our Souls have sight of that immortal sea
          Which brought us hither,   165
          Can in a moment travel thither,
And see the Children sport upon the shore,
And hear the mighty waters rolling evermore.

                              10
Then sing, ye Birds, sing, sing a joyous song!
          And let the young Lambs bound
          As to the tabor's sound!   170
We in thought will join your throng,
          Ye that pipe and ye that play,
          Ye that through your hearts today
          Feel the gladness of the May!
What though the radiance which was once so bright   175
Be now forever taken from my sight,
          Though nothing can bring back the hour
Of splendor in the grass, of glory in the flower;
          We will grieve not, rather find   180
          Strength in what remains behind;
          In the primal sympathy
          Which having been must ever be;
          In the soothing thoughts that spring
          Out of human suffering;   185

---

1. Not seeming real; see Wordsworth's comment in the headnote to the *Ode*.

In the faith that looks through death,
In years that bring the philosophic mind.

11

And O, ye Fountains, Meadows, Hills, and Groves,
Forebode not any severing of our loves!
Yet in my heart of hearts I feel your might;   190
I only have relinquished one delight
To live beneath your more habitual sway.
I love the Brooks which down their channels fret,
Even more than when I tripped lightly as they;
The innocent brightness of a newborn Day   195
    Is lovely yet;
The clouds that gather round the setting sun
Do take a sober coloring from an eye
That hath kept watch o'er man's mortality;
Another race hath been, and other palms are won[2].   200
Thanks to the human heart by which we live,
Thanks to its tenderness, its joys, and fears,
To me the meanest flower that blows can give
Thoughts that do often lie too deep for tears.

1802–4   1807

Ode to Duty[1]

Jam non consilio bonus, sed more eo perductus, ut non tantum recte facere possim, sed nisi recte facere non possim.

Stern Daughter of the Voice of God![2]
O Duty! if that name thou love

2. In Greece, foot races were often run for the prize of a branch or wreath of palm. Wordsworth's line echoes Paul, I Corinthians ix.24, who uses such races as a metaphor for life: "Know ye not that they which run in a race run all, but one receiveth the prize?"

1. "This Ode * * * is on the model of Gray's *Ode to Adversity* which is copied from Horace's *Ode to Fortune*. Many and many a time have I been twitted by my wife and sister for having forgotten this dedication of myself to the stern lawgiver" (Wordsworth).
This poem merits its reputation as a departure from Wordsworth's earlier poems and ideas. In it he abandons the descriptive-meditative pattern of his *Tintern Abbey* and *Ode: Intimations of Immortality* and reverts to the standard 18th-century form of an ode addressed to a personified abstraction. The moral idea of this poem also represents Wordsworth's reversion from his youthful reliance on natural impulse to a more orthodox ethical tradition. The poem makes no reference to that "Nature" which earlier had constituted for Wordsworth "both law and impulse," and, in *Tintern Abbey*, had been called "The guide, the guard-ian of my heart, and soul / Of all my moral being." The Duty, "Stern Daughter of the Voice of God," to which Wordsworth now commends himself, is the same concept as Milton's "right reason," God's representative in man, which Christian humanists had developed by combining the stern morality of the pagan Stoics with the concept of the inner voice of the Christian "conscience." (In one MS. variant Wordsworth described Duty as "sent from God" to keep us to the road "which conscience hath pronounced the best.")
The epigraph is translated, "Now I am not good by taking thought, but have been brought by habit to such a point that it is not so much that I am able to act rightly, but that I am unable to act other than rightly." Added in 1837, it is an adaptation from *Moral Epistles* CXX.10 by Seneca (4 B.C.–A.D. 65), Stoic philosopher and writer of tragedies.

2. Cf. *Paradise Lost* IX.652–54: "God so commanded, and left that Command / Sole Daughter of his voice; the rest, we live / Law to ourselves, our Reason is our Law."

Who are a light to guide, a rod
To check the erring, and reprove;
Thou, who art victory and law
When empty terrors overawe;   5
From vain temptations dost set free;
And calm'st the weary strife of frail humanity!

There are who ask not if thine eye
Be on them; who, in love and truth,   10
Where no misgiving is, rely
Upon the genial sense³ of youth:
Glad Hearts! without reproach or blot;
Who do thy work, and know it not:
Oh! if through confidence misplaced   15
They fail, thy saving arms, dread Power! around them cast.

Serene will be our days and bright,
And happy will our nature be,
When love is an unerring light,
And joy its own security.   20
And they a blissful course may hold
Even now, who, not unwisely bold,
Live in the spirit of this creed;
Yet seek thy firm support, according to their need.

I, loving freedom, and untried,   25
No sport of every random gust,
Yet being to myself a guide,
Too blindly have reposed my trust;
And oft, when in my heart was heard
Thy timely mandate, I deferred   30
The task, in smoother walks to stray;
But thee I now would serve more strictly, if I may.

Through no disturbance of my soul,
Or strong compunction⁴ in me wrought,
I supplicate for thy control;   35
But in the quietness of thought:
Me this unchartered freedom tires;
I feel the weight of chance desires:
My hopes no more must change their name,
I long for a repose that ever is the same.   40

Stern Lawgiver! yet thou dost wear
The Godhead's most benignant grace;
Nor know we anything so fair
As is the smile upon thy face:
Flowers laugh before thee on their beds   45
And fragrance in thy footing treads;

---

3. Innate vitality.
4. In the older sense, "sting of conscience," "remorse."

Thou dost preserve the stars from wrong;[5]
And the most ancient heavens, through thee, are fresh and strong.

To humbler functions, awful Power!
I call thee: I myself commend   50
Unto thy guidance from this hour;
Oh, let my weakness have an end!
Give unto me, made lowly wise,[6]
The spirit of self-sacrifice;
The confidence of reason give;   55
And in the light of truth thy Bondman let me live!
1804   1807

The Solitary Reaper[1]

Behold her, single in the field,
Yon solitary Highland Lass!
Reaping and singing by herself;
Stop here, or gently pass!
Alone she cuts and binds the grain,   5
And sings a melancholy strain;
O listen! for the Vale profound
Is overflowing with the sound.

No Nightingale did ever chaunt
More welcome notes to weary bands   10
Of travelers in some shady haunt,
Among Arabian sands;
A voice so thrilling ne'er was heard
In springtime from the Cuckoo bird,
Breaking the silence of the seas   15
Among the farthest Hebrides.

Will no one tell me what she sings?[2]—
Perhaps the plaintive numbers flow
For old, unhappy, far-off things,
And battles long ago;   20
Or is it some more humble lay,

5. Wordsworth's parallel between the moral law and the laws governing the motion of the stars is illuminated by Kant's famous statement: "Two things fill the mind with ever new and increasing admiration and awe * * * the starry heavens above and the moral law within."
6. Another echo from Milton, whose Christian-humanist ethic pervades this ode. The angel Raphael had advised Adam (*Paradise Lost* VIII.173–74), "Be lowly wise: / Think only what concerns thee and thy being."
1. One of the rare poems not based on Wordsworth's own experience. Wordsworth tells us that it was suggested by a passage in Thomas Wilkinson's *Tour of Scotland* (1824), which he had seen in MS.: "Passed by a female who was reaping alone, she sung in Erse [the Gaelic language of Scotland] as she bended over her sickle, the sweetest human voice I ever heard. Her strains were tenderly melancholy, and felt delicious long after they were heard no more."
2. Wordsworth did not understand Erse, the language in which she sings.

Familiar matter of today?
Some natural sorrow, loss, or pain,
That has been, and may be again?

Whate'er the theme, the Maiden sang   25
As if her song could have no ending;
I saw her singing at her work,
And o'er the sickle bending—
I listened, motionless and still;
And, as I mounted up the hill,   30
The music in my heart I bore,
Long after it was heard no more.

November 5, 1805   1807

Elegiac Stanzas

SUGGESTED BY A PICTURE OF PEELE CASTLE, IN A STORM,
PAINTED BY SIR GEORGE BEAUMONT[1]

I was thy neighbor once, thou rugged Pile!
Four summer weeks I dwelt in sight of thee:
I saw thee every day; and all the while
Thy Form was sleeping on a glassy sea.

So pure the sky, so quiet was the air!   5
So like, so very like, was day to day!
Whene'er I looked, thy Image still was there;
It trembled, but it never passed away.

How perfect was the calm! it seemed no sleep;
No mood, which season takes away, or brings: 10
I could have fancied that the mighty Deep
Was even the gentlest of all gentle Things.

Ah! then, if mine had been the Painter's hand,
To express what then I saw; and add the gleam,
The light that never was, on sea or land,   15
The consecration, and the Poet's dream;

I would have planted thee, thou hoary Pile
Amid a world how different from this!

1. Sir George Beaumont, a wealthy landscape painter, was Wordsworth's patron and close friend. Peele Castle is on a promontory opposite Rampside, Lancashire, where Wordsworth had spent a month in 1794, eleven years before he saw Beaumont's painting. A current tendency is to interpret this poem as an expression of Wordsworth's loss of faith in nature. It should be noted, however, that the focus of the poem is not on an altered view of nature, but on an altered knowledge of life and on the moral values necessary to manage the certainty of loss and suffering.

Beside a sea that could not cease to smile;
On tranquil land, beneath a sky of bliss.   20

Thou shouldst have seemed a treasure house divine
Of peaceful years; a chronicle of heaven—
Of all the sunbeams that did ever shine
The very sweetest had to thee been given.

A Picture had it been of lasting ease,   25
Elysian[2] quiet, without toil or strife;
No motion but the moving tide, a breeze,
Or merely silent Nature's breathing life.

Such, in the fond illusion of my heart,
Such Picture would I at that time have made,   30
And seen the soul of truth in every part,
A steadfast peace that might not be betrayed.

So once it would have been—'tis so no more;
I have submitted to a new control:
A power is gone, which nothing can restore;   35
A deep distress hath humanized my Soul.[3]

Not for a moment could I now behold
A smiling sea, and be what I have been:
The feeling of my loss will ne'er be old;
This, which I know, I speak with mind serene.   40

Then, Beaumont, Friend! who would have been the Friend,
If he had lived, of him whom I deplore,[4]
This work of thine I blame not, but commend;
This sea in anger, and that dismal shore.

O 'tis a passionate Work!—yet wise and well,   45
Well chosen is the spirit that is here;
That Hulk which labors in the deadly swell,
This rueful sky, this pageantry of fear!

And this huge Castle, standing here sublime,
I love to see the look with which it braves,   50
Cased in the unfeeling armor of old time,
The lightning, the fierce wind, and trampling waves.

Farewell, farewell the heart that lives alone,
Housed in a dream, at distance from the Kind![5]
Such happiness, wherever it be known,   55
Is to be pitied; for 'tis surely blind.

---

2. Elysium, in classical mythology, was the peaceful place where those favored by the gods dwelled after death.
3. Captain John Wordsworth, Wil-
liam's brother, had been drowned in a shipwreck on February 5, 1805. He is referred to in lines 41–42.
4. Mourn.
5. Mankind.

But welcome fortitude, and patient cheer,
And frequent sights of what is to be borne!
Such sights, or worse, as are before me here.—
Not without hope we suffer and we mourn.   60
1805   1807

SONNETS

Composed upon Westminster Bridge,
September 3, 1802[1]

Earth has not anything to show more fair:
Dull would he be of soul who could pass by
A sight so touching in its majesty;
This City now doth, like a garment, wear
The beauty of the morning; silent, bare,   5
Ships, towers, domes, theaters, and temples lie
Open unto the fields, and to the sky;
All bright and glittering in the smokeless air.
Never did sun more beautifully steep
In his first splendor, valley, rock, or hill;   10
Ne'er saw I, never felt, a calm so deep!
The river glideth at his own sweet will:
Dear God! the very houses seem asleep;
And all that mighty heart is lying still!
1802   1807

It Is a Beauteous Evening[2]

It is a beauteous evening, calm and free,
The holy time is quiet as a Nun
Breathless with adoration; the broad sun
Is sinking down in its tranquility;
The gentleness of heaven broods o'er the Sea: 5
Listen! the mighty Being is awake,
And doth with his eternal motion make
A sound like thunder—everlastingly.
Dear Child! dear Girl! that walkest with me here,
If thou appear untouched by solemn thought,   10
Thy nature is not therefore less divine:

1. The date of this experience was not
Sept. 3, but July 31, 1802; its occasion
was a trip to France. See Dorothy
Wordsworth's *Grasmere Journals* for
July, 1802. The conflict of feelings attending Wordsworth's brief return to
France, where he had once been a revolutionist and the lover of Annette Vallon, evoked a number of personal and
political sonnets, among them the three
which follow.
2. The girl walking with Wordsworth is
Caroline, his natural daughter by Annette Vallon. For the event described,
see *Grasmere Journals* for July, 1802.

Thou liest in Abraham's bosom[3] all the year,
And worship'st at the Temple's inner shrine,
God being with thee when we know it not.

1802   1807

Composed in the Valley near Dover,
On the Day of Landing

Here, on our native soil, we breathe once more.
The cock that crows, the smoke that curls, that sound
Of bells—those boys who in yon meadow ground
In white-sleeved shirts are playing; and the roar
Of the waves breaking on the chalky shore—   5
All, all are English. Oft have I looked round
With joy in Kent's green vales; but never found
Myself so satisfied in heart before.
Europe is yet in bonds; but let that pass,
Thought for another moment. Thou art free,   10
My Country! and 'tis joy enough and pride
For one hour's perfect bliss, to tread the grass
Of England once again, and hear and see,
With such a dear Companion[4] at my side.

August 30, 1802   1807

London, 1802[5]

Milton! thou shouldst be living at this hour:
England hath need of thee: she is a fen
Of stagnant waters: altar, sword, and pen,
Fireside, the heroic wealth of hall and bower,
Have forefeited their ancient English dower   5
Of inward happiness. We are selfish men;
Oh! raise us up, return to us again;
And give us manners, virtue, freedom, power.
Thy soul was like a Star, and dwelt apart;
Thou hadst a voice whose sound was like the sea: 10
Pure as the naked heavens, majestic, free,
So didst thou travel on life's common way,
In cheerful godliness; and yet thy heart
The lowliest duties on herself did lay.

September, 1802   1807

3. Where the souls destined for heaven rest after death. Luke xvi.22: "And it came to pass, that the beggar died, and was carried by the angels into Abraham's bosom."
4. Dorothy Wordsworth.
5. One of a series "written immediately after my return from France to London, when I could not but be **struck**, as here described, with the vanity and parade of our own country * * * as contrasted with the quiet, and I may say the desolation, that the revolution had produced in France" (Wordsworth).

The World Is Too Much with Us

The world is too much with us; late and soon,
Getting and spending, we lay waste our powers;
Little we see in Nature that is ours;
We have given our hearts away, a sordid boon![6]
This Sea that bares her bosom to the moon,   5
The winds that will be howling at all hours,
And are up-gathered now like sleeping flowers,
For this, for everything, we are out of tune;
It moves us not.—Great God! I'd rather be
A Pagan suckled in a creed outworn;   10
So might I, standing on this pleasant lea,
Have glimpses that would make me less forlorn;
Have sight of Proteus rising from the sea;
Or hear old Triton blow his wreathéd horn.[7]

1807

Surprised by Joy[8]

Surprised by joy—impatient as the Wind
I turned to share the transport—Oh! with whom
But thee, deep buried in the silent tomb,
That spot which no vicissitude can find?
Love, faithful love, recalled thee to my mind—   5
But how could I forget thee? Through what power,
Even for the least division of an hour,
Have I been so beguiled as to be blind
To my most grievous loss!—That thought's return
Was the worst pang that sorrow ever bore,   10
Save one, one only, when I stood forlorn,
Knowing my heart's best treasure was no more;
That neither present time, nor years unborn
Could to my sight that heavenly face restore.

1815

Composed by the Side of Grasmere Lake

Clouds, lingering yet, extend in solid bars
Through the gray west; and lo! these waters, steeled
By breezeless air to smoothest polish, yield
A vivid repetition of the stars;

6. Gift; it is the act of giving the heart away that is sordid.
7. Proteus: an old man of the sea who (in the *Odyssey*) can assume a variety of shapes. Triton: a sea deity, usually represented as blowing on a conch shell. The description of Proteus echoes *Paradise Lost* III.603–604, and that of Triton echoes Spenser's *Colin Clout's Come Home Again*, lines 244–45. Spenser and Milton are the two English poets to whom Wordsworth specifically allied himself.
8. "This was in fact suggested by my daughter Catherine, long after her death" (Wordsworth). Catherine Wordsworth died June 4, 1812, at the age of 4.

Jove, Venus, and the ruddy crest of Mars[9]   5
Amid his fellows beauteously revealed
At happy distance from earth's groaning field,
Where ruthless mortals wage incessant wars.
Is it a mirror?—or the nether Sphere[1]
Opening to view the abyss in which she feeds
Her own calm fires?—But list! a voice is near;
Great Pan himself low-whispering through the reeds,
"Be thankful, thou; for, if unholy deeds
Ravage the world, tranquillity is here!"

1807   1819

Afterthought[2]

I thought of thee,[3] my partner and my guide,
As being passed away.—Vain sympathies!
For, backward, Duddon! as I cast my eyes,
I see what was, and is, and will abide;
Still glides the Stream, and shall forever glide;   5
The Form remains, the Function never dies;
While we, the brave, the mighty, and the wise,
We Men, who in our morn of youth defied
The elements, must vanish—be it so!
Enough, if something from our hands have power   10
To live, and act, and serve the future hour;
And if, as toward the silent tomb we go,
Through love, through hope, and faith's transcendant dower,[4]
We feel that we are greater than we know.

1820

Mutability[5]

From low to high doth dissolution climb,
And sink from high to low, along a scale
Of awful notes, whose concord shall not fail;
A musical but melancholy chime,
Which they can hear who meddle not with crime,   5

9. Roman god of war.
1. The earth, region below the sphere of the moon.
2. The last in the sonnet sequence *The River Duddon*, which traces the course of the river from its source in the Lake Country to its terminus in the Irish Sea. The description of the course of a river, combined with the incidental meditations which the changing scene evokes, had been a common poetic formula in the "local poems"
of the 18th century, but Wordsworth employs it here for a memorable statement of one of his reiterated topics: the flow of water as an emblem of permanence in change.
3. I.e., the river.
4. Endowment, gift.
5. This great sonnet interrupts a rather pedestrian sequence, *Ecclesiastical Sonnets*, dealing with the history and ceremonies of the church in England.

Nor avarice, nor over-anxious care.
Truth fails not; but her outward forms that bear
The longest date do melt like frosty rime,
That in the morning whitened hill and plain
And is no more; drop like the tower sublime   10
Of yesterday, which royally did wear
His crown of weeds, but could not even sustain
Some casual shout that broke the silent air,
Or the unimaginable touch of Time.

1821   1822

Steamboats, Viaducts, and Railways[6]

Motions and Means, on land and sea at war
With old poetic feeling, not for this,
Shall ye, by Poets even, be judged amiss!
Nor shall your presence, howsoe'er it mar
The loveliness of Nature, prove a bar   5
To the Mind's gaining that prophetic sense
Of future change, that point of vision, whence
May be discovered what in soul ye are.
In spite of all that beauty may disown
In your harsh features, Nature doth embrace   10
Her lawful offspring in Man's art; and Time,
Pleased with your triumphs o'er his brother Space,
Accepts from your bold hands the proffered crown
Of hope, and smiles on you with cheer sublime.

1833   1835

Extempore Effusion upon the Death of James Hogg[1]

When first, descending from the moorlands,
I saw the Stream of Yarrow[2] glide
Along a bare and open valley,
The Ettrick Shepherd[3] was my guide.

---

6. In late middle age Wordsworth demonstrates, as he had predicted in the Preface to *Lyrical Ballads,* that the poet will assimilate to his subject matter the "material revolution" produced by science. Unlike most poets, furthermore, he boldly accepts as evidences of man's progress even the unlovely encroachments of technology upon his beloved natural scene.

1. Wordsworth's niece relates how Wordsworth was deeply moved by finding unexpectedly in a newspaper the account of the death of the poet James Hogg. "Half an hour afterwards he came into the room where the ladies were sitting and asked Miss Hutchinson [his sister-in-law] to write down some lines which he had just composed." All the poets named here, several of Wordsworth's closest friends among them, had died between 1832 and 1835.

2. A river in the southeast of Scotland.

3. James Hogg, the "Ettrick Shepherd" (he was born in Ettrick Forest, and was for a time a shepherd), was discovered as a writer by Sir Walter Scott, and became well known as a poet, essayist, and editor.

When last along its banks I wandered,   5
Through groves that had begun to shed
Their golden leaves upon the pathways,
My steps the Border-minstrel[4] led.

The mighty Minstrel breathes no longer,
'Mid moldering ruins low he lies;   10
And death upon the braes[5] of Yarrow,
Has closed the Shepherd-poet's eyes:

Nor has the rolling year twice measured,
From sign to sign, its steadfast course,
Since every mortal power of Coleridge   15
Was frozen at its marvelous source;

The rapt One, of the godlike forehead,
The heaven-eyed creature sleeps in earth:
And Lamb, the frolic and the gentle,
Has vanished from his lonely hearth.   20

Like clouds that rake the mountain summits,
Or waves that own no curbing hand,
How fast has brother followed brother,
From sunshine to the sunless land!

Yet I, whose lids from infant slumber   25
Were earlier raised, remain to hear
A timid voice, that asks in whispers,
"Who next will drop and disappear?"

Our haughty life is crowned with darkness,
Like London with its own black wreath,   30
On which with thee, O Crabbe![6] forth-looking,
I gazed from Hampstead's breezy heath.

As if but yesterday departed,
Thou too art gone before; but why,
O'er ripe fruit, seasonably gathered,   35
Should frail survivors heave a sigh?

Mourn rather for that holy Spirit,
Sweet as the spring, as ocean deep;
For her[7] who, ere her summer faded,
Has sunk into a breathless sleep.   40

No more of old romantic sorrows,
For slaughtered Youth or lovelorn Maid!
With sharper grief is Yarrow smitten,
And Ettrick mourns with her their Poet dead.

November 21, 1835   1835

4. Sir Walter Scott.
5. The sloping banks of a stream.
6. George Crabbe, the poet of rural and village life.
7. Felicia Hemans, a minor but prolific poetess, who died when only 42. She is best known in America for *The Landing of the Pilgrim Fathers* and "The Boy Stood on the Burning Deck."

Prospectus
to *The Recluse*[1]

On Man, on Nature, and on Human Life,
Musing in solitude, I oft perceive
Fair trains of imagery before me rise,
Accompanied by feelings of delight
Pure, or with no unpleasing sadness mixed;   5
And I am conscious of affecting thoughts
And dear remembrances, whose presence soothes
Or elevates the Mind, intent to weigh
The good and evil of our mortal state.
—To these emotions, whencesoe'er they come,   10
Whether from breath of outward circumstance,
Or from the Soul—an impulse to herself—
I would give utterance in numerous verse.[2]
Of Truth, of Grandeur, Beauty, Love, and Hope,
And melancholy Fear subdued by Faith;   15
Of blessed consolations in distress;
Of moral strength, and intellectual Power;
Of joy in widest commonalty spread;
Of the individual Mind that keeps her own
Inviolate retirement, subject there   20
To Conscience only, and the law supreme
Of that Intelligence which governs all,
I sing—"fit audience let me find though few!"[3]

1. Through most of his poetic life Wordsworth labored intermittently at a long philosophic poem called *The Recluse,* which he intended to be his masterwork. As Wordsworth described this project in the Preface to *The Excursion* (1814), it was to consist of an autobiographical introduction (the poem now called *The Prelude*) and three long parts; of these three he completed only Book I of Part I ("Home at Grasmere") and the whole of Part II, called *The Excursion.* In the Preface to *The Excursion,* Wordsworth printed this long extract (the concluding section of "Home at Grasmere") to serve "as a kind of *Prospectus* of the design and scope of the whole Poem"—i.e., of the entire *Recluse.*

The first version of this "Prospectus" may have been drafted as early as 1798 or 1800. In language thronged with echoes from *Paradise Lost,* Wordsworth announces an undertaking which he conceives to be no less inspired and sublime than Milton's. In it he will move higher than Milton's heaven and deeper than Milton's hell, past scenes evoking greater fear than Erebus and greater awe than Jehovah; but without ever leaving "the Mind of Man— / My haunt, and the main region of my song" (lines 40–41). And his "high argument" is that Paradise can be regained; not, however, as in Revelation xxi, and in Milton, by the marriage between the New Jerusalem and Christ the Lamb, but by a marriage between the "intellect of Man" and "this goodly universe," and the resulting new "creation * * * which they with blended might / Accomplish" (lines 47–71). In no other passage does Wordsworth reveal so clearly the extent to which he assimilates to his poetry the Biblical scheme of Milton's epic—assigning, however, the active role, from creation to redemption, to the human faculties, in their vital interaction with the external universe.

2. Harmonious verse; an echo of *Paradise Lost* V.150. The inspiring "breath of outward circumstance" parallels the "correspondent breeze" in the opening passage of *The Prelude,* just below.

3. *Paradise Lost* VII.31.

So prayed, more gaining than he asked, the Bard—
In holiest mood. Urania,[4] I shall need   25
Thy guidance, or a greater Muse, if such
Descend to earth or dwell in highest heaven!
For I must tread on shadowy ground, must sink
Deep—and, aloft ascending, breathe in worlds
To which the heaven of heavens[5] is but a veil.   30
All strength—all terror, single or in bands,
That ever was put forth in personal form—
Jehovah—with his thunder, and the choir
Of shouting Angels, and the empyreal thrones—
I pass them unalarmed. Not Chaos, not   35
The darkest pit of lowest Erebus,[6]
Nor aught of blinder vacancy, scooped out
By help of dreams—can breed such fear and awe
As fall upon us often when we look
Into our Minds, into the Mind of Man—   40
My haunt, and the main region of my song.
—Beauty—a living Presence of the earth,
Surpassing the most fair ideal Forms
Which craft of delicate Spirits hath composed
From earth's materials—waits upon my steps;   45
Pitches her tents before me as I move,
An hourly neighbor. Paradise, and groves
Elysian,[7] Fortunate Fields—like those of old
Sought in the Atlantic Main—why should they be
A history only of departed things,   50
Or a mere fiction of what never was?
For the discerning intellect of Man,
When wedded to this goodly universe
In love and holy passion, shall find these
A simple produce of the common day.   55
—I, long before the blissful hour arrives,
Would chant, in lonely peace, the spousal[8] verse
Of this great consummation—and, by words
Which speak of nothing more than what we are,
Would I arouse the sensual from their sleep   60
Of Death, and win the vacant and the vain
To noble raptures; while my voice proclaims
How exquisitely the individual Mind
(And the progressive powers perhaps no less
Of the whole species) to the external World   65

4. The Muse whom Milton had invoked in *Paradise Lost* vii.1–39.
5. In *Paradise Lost* the dwelling place beyond the visible heaven, of God and his angels. For line 34, see *Paradise Lost* II.430.
6. In classical myth, a dark region of the underworld; often used as a name for hell by Christian writers.
7. Elysium, in Greek myth, was the place where men favored by the gods live a happy life after death. It was sometimes identified with the "Islands of the Blessed," reputed to be located far out in the western sea—hence "sought in the Atlantic Main." See Horace, *Epodes* XVI.
8. Marital; hence a "spousal verse" is an epithalamion.

Is fitted—and how exquisitely, too—
Theme this but little heard of among men—
The external World is fitted to the Mind;
And the creation (by no lower name
Can it be called) which they with blended might   70
Accomplish—this is our high argument.[9]
—Such grateful haunts foregoing, if I oft
Must turn elsewhere—to travel near the tribes
And fellowships of men, and see ill sights
Of madding passions mutually inflamed;   75
Must hear Humanity in fields and groves
Pipe solitary anguish; or must hang
Brooding above the fierce confederate storm
Of sorrow, barricadoed[1] evermore
Within the walls of cities—may these sounds   80
Have their authentic comment; that even these
Hearing, I be not downcast or forlorn!—
Descend, prophetic Spirit! that inspir'st
The human Soul of universal earth,
Dreaming on things to come;[2] and dost possess   85
A metropolitan[3] temple in the hearts
Of mighty Poets: upon me bestow
A gift of genuine insight; that my Song
With starlike virtue in its place may shine,
Shedding benignant influence, and secure,   90
Itself, from all malevolent effect
Of those mutations that extend their sway
Throughout the nether sphere![4]—And if with this
I mix more lowly matter; with the thing
Contemplated, describe the Mind and Man   95
Contemplating; and who, and what he was—
The transitory Being that beheld
The Vision; when and where, and how he lived[5]—
Be not this labor useless. If such theme
May sort with highest objects, then—dread Power!   100
Whose gracious favor is the primal source
Of all illumination—may my Life
Express the image of a better time,
More wise desires, and simpler manners—nurse
My Heart in genuine freedom—all pure thoughts   105
Be with me—so shall thy unfailing love
Guide, and support, and cheer me to the end!

ca. 1798–1814   1814

---

9. Theme, as in *Paradise Lost* I.24: "the height of this great Argument."
1. Barricaded, as in *Paradise Lost* VIII.241.
2. Cf. "the prophetic soul / Of the wide world dreaming on things to come" (Shakespeare, *Sonnet* CVII).
3. Designating the principal seat of a religion.
4. In the Ptolemaic world picture, the spheres of the heavenly bodies were immutable, and only the earth (the "nether sphere," or region below the sphere of the moon) was subject to change. Compare *Paradise Lost* VII.375 and X.656–64.
5. Wordsworth thus justifies *The Prelude* and the autobiographical sections of *The Recluse*.

The Prelude *The Prelude* is Wordsworth's crowning achievement, the greatest and most original long poem since Milton's *Paradise Lost*. Its existence, however, was unknown to the public until after Wordsworth's death in 1850. When, three months later, *The Prelude* was published from manuscript, its title was given to it by the poet's wife; Wordsworth himself had referred to it variously as "the poem to Coleridge," "the poem on the growth of my own mind," and "the poem on my own poetical education."

For some 75 years this posthumous publication of 1850 was the only known text of *The Prelude*. Then in 1926 Ernest de Selincourt, working from manuscripts, printed an earlier version of the poem that Wordsworth had completed in 1805. Since that time other scholars have established the existence of a still earlier and much shorter version of *The Prelude*, in two parts, which Wordsworth had composed in 1798–99. The following seems to have been the process of composition that produced the three extant versions of the poem:

1. The two-part *Prelude* of 1799. Wordsworth originally planned, early in 1798, to include an account of his own development as a poet in his projected but never-completed philosophical poem *The Recluse* (see the title-footnote to the "Prospectus" for *The Recluse*, above). While living in Germany during the autumn and winter of 1798–99, he composed a number of passages about his early experiences with nature. What had been intended to be part of *The Recluse*, however, quickly evolved into an independent autobiographical poem, and by late 1799, when Wordsworth settled with his sister, Dorothy, at Grasmere, he had written a poem in two parts, 976 lines in length, which takes his life from infancy, through his years at Hawkshead School, to the age of 17. This poem survives in two fair copies (MS. U and MS. V), and its two parts correspond, by and large, to the contents of Books I and II of the later versions of *The Prelude*. We print in this anthology, for the first time, the earliest, two-part form of *The Prelude* in its entirety.

2. The 1805 *Prelude*. Late in 1801 Wordsworth began to expand the poem on his poetic life, and in 1804 he set to work intensively on the project. His initial plan was to write it in five books. Before he completed the five-book poem, however, he decided to enlarge it still further, to incorporate an account of his experiences in France and of his mental crisis after the failure of his hopes in the French Revolution, and to end the poem with his settlement at Grasmere and his taking up the great task of *The Recluse*. He completed this poem, in 13 books, in May of 1805. This is the version that Wordsworth read to Coleridge after his return from Malta (see "To William Wordsworth," below).

3. The 1850 *Prelude*. For the next 35 years Wordsworth tinkered with the text, polishing the style and qualifying some of its radical statements about the divine sufficiency of the human mind in its communion with nature; he did not, however, in any essential way alter its subject-matter or overall design. *The Prelude* that was published in July, 1850, is in 14 books and was printed from a fair copy, incorporating Wordsworth's latest revisions, which had been made in 1839. (Note that in the conventional

short references "the 1805 *Prelude*" specifies the date of completion, and "the 1850 *Prelude*" specifies the date of publication.) Selections from each of the books of this final version of *The Prelude* are reprinted below; they were chosen to show the overall design of the poem, as well as to include its main operative concepts and its most distinctive passages of poetry.

The Two-Part Prelude (1799) This work was composed 1798–99, soon after Wordsworth had discovered in *Tintern Abbey* (July, 1798) his distinctive voice and subject: the blank-verse poem of the remembrance of things past, in which the forming of an identity is presented as a continuing interaction between the solitary mind and the natural world. It is not certain whether Wordsworth considered this text to be a finished poem. At the opening the narrator plunges into the middle of things with a rhetorical question—"Was it for this . . . ?"—twice repeated, in which "this" lacks an antecedent reference. Wordsworth very likely had in mind to add an introductory section that would correspond in function to the opening of the 1805 and 1850 *Preludes*; in these later poems the "this" refers back to his frustration in his attempts to write a great work that would fulfill his obligation as an elected poet-prophet. (See the 1850 *Prelude*, below, I.1–274.) The ending of Part II, on the other hand, in which the narrator sums up the circumstances which have given him his assured stance and function in a time of troubles, has both the content and cadence of a valediction intended to conclude the poem.

Whether or not, however, Wordsworth thought to end his work at this point, *The Prelude* of 1799 is thematically an entity, narrating the key episodes, from the poet's infancy to the threshold of his maturity, by which nature has provided him with the "gift" of contentment with his life, a "visionary" capacity, and a confidence in human nature which he bespeaks "in these times of fear" and "of dereliction and dismay" (II.478–92). This text, unlike the later versions (which, for altered structural purposes, relocate some of the episodes in later books), allows us to read the unbroken sequence of his "spots of time"; that is, revelatory moments of early experience which turn out, in retrospect, to mark crucial stages in the growth of the poet's mind. And in this version much of the poetry, especially in Part I (recounting his solitary communings with the external world up to the age of 10), has a terse power which was weakened by Wordsworth's later attempts to smooth out the syntax and heighten the style, and to elaborate the detail of passages which had originally been simple and direct. The footnotes below make it easy to compare Wordsworth's first and last versions of *The Prelude*, by identifying the passages of 1799 which correspond to the selections of 1850.

This text of *The Two-Part Prelude* was edited by Jonathan Wordsworth and Stephen Gill, using MS. V as the basic text; MS. U was used mainly to supply the opening lines of the Second Part, which had been torn out of MS. V. It is printed here with the generous permission of the Trustees of the Wordsworth Library at Dove Cottage. A discussion of the manuscripts and the text will be published by these editors in the Norton Critical Edition of all three versions of *The Prelude*, now being prepared in collaboration with M. H. Abrams. The editors have reproduced the manuscripts exactly, except for one alteration. Wordsworth capitalized many common nouns, but without consistency; in the printed text, all these capitals have been altered to lower case, with the single exception of the word "Nature."

The Two-Part Prelude (1799)

Was it for this
That one, the fairest of all rivers,[1] loved
To blend his murmurs with my nurse's song,
And from his alder shades and rocky falls,
And from his fords and shallows, sent a voice   5
That flowed along my dreams? For this didst thou,
O Derwent, travelling over the green plains
Near my 'sweet birth-place',[2] didst thou, beauteous stream,
Make ceaseless music through the night and day
Which with its steady cadence tempering   10
Our human waywardness, composed my thoughts
To more than infant softness, giving me
Among the fretful dwellings of mankind
A knowledge, a dim earnest, of the calm
Which Nature breathes among the fields and groves?   15
Beloved Derwent, fairest of all streams,
Was it for this that I, a four years' child,
A naked boy, among thy silent pools
Made one long bathing of a summer's day,
Basked in the sun, or plunged into thy streams,   20
Alternate, all a summer's day, or coursed
Over the sandy fields, and dashed the flowers
Of yellow grunsel;[3] or, when crag and hill,
The woods, and distant Skiddaw's[4] lofty height,
Were bronzed with a deep radiance, stood alone   25
A naked savage in the thunder shower?

And afterwards, 'twas in a later day
Though early, when upon the mountain slope
The frost and breath of frosty wind had snapped
The last autumnal crocus, 'twas my joy   30
To wander half the night among the cliffs
And the smooth hollows where the woodcocks ran
Along the moonlight turf. In thought and wish
That time, my shoulder all with springes[5] hung,
I was a fell destroyer. Gentle powers,   35
Who give us happiness and call it peace,
When scudding on from snare to snare I plied

1. The river Derwent, which flowed past the garden of his father's house at Cockermouth, Cumberland, on the northern border of the Lake District. Lines 1–198 correspond to the passage from the 1850 *Prelude*, below, I.269–475.

2. Echoing Coleridge's *Frost at Midnight*, below, line 28.
3. A plant, also known as ragwort.
4. A mountain in Cumberland.
5. Bird snares.

My anxious visitation, hurrying on,
Still hurrying, hurrying onward, how my heart
Panted among the scattered yew-trees and the crags   40
That looked upon me, how my bosom beat
With expectation! Sometimes strong desire
Resistless overpowered me, and the bird
Which was the captive of another's toils
Became my prey; and when the deed was done   45
I heard among the solitary hills
Low breathings coming after me, and sounds
Of undistinguishable motion, steps
Almost as silent as the turf they trod.

   Nor less in springtime, when on southern banks   50
The shining sun had from his knot of leaves
Decoyed the primrose flower, and when the vales
And woods were warm, was I a rover then
In the high places, on the lonesome peaks,
Among the mountains and the winds. Though mean   55
And though inglorious were my views,[6] the end
Was not ignoble. Oh, when I have hung
Above the raven's nest, by knots of grass
Or half-inch fissures in the slippery rock
But ill sustained, and almost, as it seemed,   60
Suspended by the blast which blew amain,
Shouldering the naked crag, oh, at that time,
While on the perilous ridge I hung alone,
With what strange utterance did the loud dry wind
Blow through my ears; the sky seemed not a sky   65
Of earth, and with what motion moved the clouds!

   The mind of man is fashioned and built up
Even as a strain of music. I believe
That there are spirits which, when they would form
A favored being, from his very dawn   70
Of infancy do open out the clouds
As at the touch of lightning, seeking him
With gentle visitation—quiet powers,
Retired, and seldom recognized, yet kind,
And to the very meanest not unknown—   75
With me, though, rarely in my boyish days
They communed. Others too there are, who use,
Yet haply aiming at the self-same end,
Severer interventions,[7] ministry
More palpable—and of their school was I.   80

   They guided me: one evening led by them
I went alone into a shepherd's boat,

6. His intention was to steal ravens' eggs.
7. Wordsworth here introduces the distinction between the two antithetic "powers" of nature—the "gentle visitation" (line 73), as opposed to "severer interventions"—which cooperate in forming the poet's mind and imagination; see, e.g., I.194–98, 430–35; II.371–76. The incident that follows is an example of a severer intervention.

A skiff, that to a willow tree was tied
Within a rocky cave, its usual home.
The moon was up, the lake was shining clear   85
Among the hoary mountains; from the shore
I pushed, and struck the oars, and struck again
In cadence, and my little boat moved on,
Just like a man who walks with stately step
Though bent on speed. It was an act of stealth   90
And troubled pleasure. Not without the voice
Of mountain-echoes did my boat move on,
Leaving behind her still on either side
Small circles glittering idly in the moon,
Until they melted all into one track   95
Of sparkling light. A rocky steep uprose
Above the cavern of the willow tree,
And now, as suited one who proudly rowed
With his best skill, I fixed a steady view
Upon the top of that same craggy ridge,   100
The bound of the horizon—for behind
Was nothing but the stars and the grey sky.
She was an elfin pinnace;[8] twenty times
I dipped my oars into the silent lake,
And as I rose upon the stroke my boat   105
Went heaving through the water like a swan—
When from behind that rocky steep, till then
The bound of the horizon, a huge cliff,
As if with voluntary power instinct,
Upreared its head. I struck, and struck again,   110
And, growing still in stature, the huge cliff
Rose up between me and the stars, and still
With measured motion, like a living thing
Strode after me. With trembling hands I turned
And through the silent water stole my way   115
Back to the cavern of the willow tree.
There, in her mooring-place, I left my bark
And through the meadows homeward went with grave
And serious thoughts; and after I had seen
That spectacle, for many days my brain   120
Worked with a dim and undetermined sense
Of unknown modes of being. In my thoughts
There was a darkness—call it solitude
Or blank desertion—no familiar shapes
Of hourly objects, images of trees,   125
Of sea or sky, no colours of green fields,
But huge and mighty forms that do not live
Like living men moved slowly through my mind
By day, and were the trouble of my dreams.

Ah, not in vain ye beings of the hills,   130
And ye that walk the woods and open heaths

8. I.e., a small boat.

By moon or star-light, thus, from my first dawn
Of childhood, did ye love to intertwine
The passions that build up our human soul
Not with the mean and vulgar works of man,   135
But with high objects, with eternal things,
With life and Nature, purifying thus
The elements of feeling and of thought,
And sanctifying by such discipline
Both pain and fear, until we recognize   140
A grandeur in the beatings of the heart.
Nor was this fellowship vouchsafed to me
With stinted kindness. In November days,
When vapours rolling down the valleys made
A lonely scene more lonesome, among woods   145
At noon, and 'mid the calm of summer nights
When by the margin of the trembling lake
Beneath the gloomy hills I homeward went
In solitude, such intercourse was mine.

  And in the frosty season, when the sun   150
Was set, and visible for many a mile
The cottage windows through the twilight blazed,
I heeded not the summons. Clear and loud
The village clock tolled six; I wheeled about
Proud and exulting, like an untired horse   155
That cares not for its home. All shod with steel
We hissed along the polished ice in games
Confederate, imitative of the chace
And woodland pleasures, the resounding horn,
The pack loud bellowing, and the hunted hare.   160
So through the darkness and the cold we flew,
And not a voice was idle. With the din,
Meanwhile, the precipices rang aloud;
The leafless trees and every icy crag
Tinkled like iron; while the distant hills   165
Into the tumult sent an alien sound
Of melancholy, not unnoticed; while the stars,
Eastward, were sparkling clear, and in the west
The orange sky of evening died away.

  Not seldom from the uproar I retired   170
Into a silent bay, or sportively
Glanced sideway,[9] leaving the tumultuous throng,
To cut across the shadow of a star
That gleamed upon the ice. And oftentimes
When we had given our bodies to the wind,   175
And all the shadowy banks on either side
Came sweeping through the darkness, spinning still
The rapid line of motion, then at once
Have I, reclining back upon my heels,

9. Moved off at an angle.

Stopped short—yet still the solitary cliffs 180
Wheeled by me, even as if the earth had rolled
With visible motion her diurnal round.
Behind me did they stretch in solemn train,
Feebler and feebler, and I stood and watched
Till all was tranquil as a summer sea. 185

    Ye powers of earth, ye genii[1] of the springs
And ye that have your voices in the clouds,
And ye that are familiars of the lakes
And of the standing pools, I may not think
A vulgar hope was yours when ye employed 190
Such ministry—when ye through many a year
Thus, by the agency of boyish sports,
On caves and trees, upon the woods and hills,
Impressed upon all forms the characters
Of danger or desire, and thus did make 195
The surface of the universal earth
With meanings of delight, of hope and fear,
Work like a sea.

           Not uselessly employed,
I might pursue this theme through every change
Of exercise and sport to which the year 200
Did summon us in its delightful round.
We were a noisy crew; the sun in heaven
Beheld not vales more beautiful than ours,
Nor saw a race in happiness and joy
More worthy of the fields where they were sown. 205
I would record with no reluctant voice
Our home amusements by the warm peat fire
At evening, when with pencil and with slate,
In square divisions parcelled out, and all
With crosses and with cyphers scribbled o'er, 210
We schemed and puzzled, head opposed to head,
In strife too humble to be named in verse;[2]
Or round the naked table, snow-white deal,[3]
Cherry, or maple, sate in close array,
And to the combat—lu or whist[4]—led on 215
A thick-ribbed army, not as in the world
Discarded and ungratefully thrown by
Even for the very service they had wrought,
But husbanded through many a long campaign.
Oh, with what echoes on the board they fell— 220
Ironic diamonds, hearts of sable hue,[5]

1. Guardian spirits of a particular place. "Familiars" (line 188): attendant spirits.
2. Ticktacktoe; Wordsworth parodies neoclassic decorum by dignifying with high-flown phrases things too lowly to be named in poetry.
3. Boards cut from fir or pine.
4. Loo and whist are card games.

Wordsworth's description of these games, as played by boys with bedraggled cards, is a take-off on Pope's mock-heroic description of the game of ombre in *The Rape of the Lock*, III.25 ff.
5. I.e., the red hearts are black with dirt.

Queens gleaming through their splendour's last decay,
Knaves wrapt in one assimilating gloom,
And kings indignant at the shame incurred
By royal visages. Meanwhile abroad   225
The heavy rain was falling, or the frost
Raged bitterly with keen and silent tooth,
And, interrupting the impassioned game,
Oft from the neighbouring lake the splitting ice,
While it sank down towards the water, sent   230
Among the meadows and the hills its long
And frequent yellings, imitative some
Of wolves that howl along the Bothnic main.[6]

　　Nor with less willing heart would I rehearse
The woods of autumn, and their hidden bowers   235
With milk-white clusters hung; the rod and line—
True symbol of the foolishness of hope—
Which with its strong enchantment led me on
By rocks and pools, where never summer star
Impressed its shadow, to forlorn cascades   240
Among the windings of the mountain-brooks;
The kite in sultry calms from some high hill
Sent up, ascending thence till it was lost
Among the fleecy clouds—in gusty days
Launched from the lower grounds, and suddenly   245
Dashed headlong and rejected by the storm.
All these, and more, with rival claims demand
Grateful acknowledgement. It were a song
Venial,[7] and such as—if I rightly judge—
I might protract unblamed, but I perceive   250
That much is overlooked, and we should ill
Attain our object if, from delicate fears
Of breaking in upon the unity
Of this my argument, I should omit
To speak of such effects as cannot here   255
Be regularly classed, yet tend no less
To the same point, the growth of mental power
And love of Nature's works.

　　　　　　　　　　　　Ere I had seen
Eight summers—and 'twas in the very week
When I was first transplanted to thy vale,   260
Beloved Hawkshead;[8] when thy paths, thy shores
And brooks were like a dream of novelty
To my half infant mind—I chanced to cross
One of those open fields which, shaped like ears,
Make green peninsulas on Esthwaite's lake.   265
Twilight was coming on, yet through the gloom
I saw distinctly on the opposite shore,

6. The Gulf of Bothnia is a northern arm of the Baltic Sea.
7. Trivial, readily forgivable.
8. Where Wordsworth boarded and attended school.

Beneath a tree and close by the lake side,
A heap of garments, as if left by one
Who there was bathing. Half an hour I watched 270
And no one owned them; meanwhile the calm lake
Grew dark with all the shadows on its breast,
And now and then a leaping fish disturbed
The breathless stillness. The succeeding day
There came a company, and in their boat 275
Sounded with iron hooks and with long poles.
At length the dead man, 'mid that beauteous scene
Of trees and hills and water, bolt upright
Rose with his ghastly face.[9] I might advert
To numerous accidents in flood or field,[1] 280
Quarry or moor, or 'mid the winter snows,
Distresses and disasters, tragic facts
Of rural history, that impressed my mind
With images, to which in following years
Far other feelings were attached—with forms 285
That yet exist with independent life,
And, like their archetypes,[2] know no decay.

    There are in our existence spots of time
Which with distinct preeminence retain
A fructifying virtue,[3] whence, depressed 290
By trivial occupations and the round
Of ordinary intercourse, our minds—
Especially the imaginative power—
Are nourished and invisibly repaired;
Such moments chiefly seem to have their date 295
In our first childhood. I remember well,
While I was yet an urchin—one who scarce
Could hold a bridle—with ambitious hopes
I mounted, and we rode towards the hills.
We were a pair of horsemen: honest James[4] 300
Was with me, my encourager and guide.
We had not travelled long ere some mischance
Disjoined me from my comrade, and, through fear
Dismounting, down the rough and stony moor
I led my horse, and stumbling on, at length 305
Came to a bottom where in former times
A man, the murderer of his wife, was hung
In irons. Mouldered was the gibbet mast;
The bones were gone, the iron and the wood;
Only a long green ridge of turf remained 310
Whose shape was like a grave. I left the spot,
And reascending the bare slope I saw

---

9. Wordsworth later transferred the passage on the drowned man in Esthwaite (lines 258–79) to Book V of *The Prelude* of 1805 and 1850.
1. *Othello* I.iii.134–35: "Wherein I spake of most disastrous chances, / Of moving accidents by flood and field."
2. Apparently, the original objects in nature whose "forms" survive in Wordsworth's memory.
3. A power to make fruitful, productive.
4. His father's servant.

A naked pool that lay beneath the hills,
The beacon on the summit, and more near
A girl who bore a pitcher on her head   315
And seemed with difficult steps to force her way
Against the blowing wind. It was in truth
An ordinary sight, but I should need
Colours and words that are unknown to man
To paint the visionary dreariness   320
Which, while I looked all round for my lost guide,
Did at that time invest the naked pool,
The beacon on the lonely eminence,
The woman and her garments vexed and tossed
By the strong wind.

                    Nor less I recollect—   325
Long after, though my childhood had not ceased—
Another scene which left a kindred power
Implanted in my mind. One Christmas-time,
The day before the holidays began,[5]
Feverish, and tired, and restless, I went forth   330
Into the fields, impatient for the sight
Of those three horses which should bear us home,
My brothers and myself. There was a crag,
An eminence, which from the meeting-point
Of two highways ascending overlooked   335
At least a long half-mile of those two roads,
By each of which the expected steeds might come—
The choice uncertain. Thither I repaired
Up to the highest summit. 'Twas a day
Stormy and rough and wild, and on the grass   340
I sate half-sheltered by a naked wall.
Upon my right hand was a single sheep,
A whistling hawthorn on my left, and there,
Those two companions at my side, I watched
With eyes intensely straining, as the mist   345
Gave intermitting prospects of the wood
And plain beneath. Ere I to school returned
That dreary time, ere I had been ten days
A dweller in my father's house, he died,
And I and my two brothers, orphans then,   350
Followed his body to the grave. The event,
With all the sorrow which it brought, appeared
A chastisement; and when I called to mind
That day so lately passed, when from the crag
I looked in such anxiety of hope,   355
With trite reflexions of morality,
Yet with the deepest passion, I bowed low
To God who thus corrected my desires.

5. In December, 1783; Wordsworth, thirteen, was at Hawkshead school with two of
his brothers.

And afterwards the wind and sleety rain,
And all the business of the elements,   360
The single sheep, and the one blasted tree,
And the bleak music of that old stone wall,
The noise of wood and water, and the mist
Which on the line of each of those two roads
Advanced in such indisputable shapes[6]—   365
All these were spectacles and sounds to which
I often would repair, and thence would drink
As at a fountain. And I do not doubt
That in this later time, when storm and rain
Beat on my roof at midnight, or by day   370
When I am in the woods, unknown to me
The workings of my spirit thence are brought.[7]

    Nor, sedulous[8] as I have been to trace
How Nature by collateral interest
And by extrinsic passion, peopled first   375
My mind with forms or beautiful or grand
And made me love them, may I well forget
How other pleasures have been mine, and joys
Of subtler origin—how I have felt
Not seldom, even in that tempestuous time,   380
Those hallowed and pure motions of the sense
Which seem in their simplicity to own
An intellectual charm, that calm delight
Which, if I err not, surely must belong
To those first-born affinities that fit   385
Our new existence to existing things,
And, in our dawn of being, constitute
The bond of union betwixt life and joy.

    Yes, I remember when the changeful earth
And twice five seasons on my mind had stamped   390
The faces of the moving year, even then,
A child, I held unconscious intercourse
With the eternal beauty, drinking in
A pure organic pleasure from the lines
Of curling mist, or from the level plain   395
Of waters coloured by the steady clouds.
The sands of Westmoreland, the creeks and bays
Of Cumbria's[9] rocky limits, they can tell
How when the sea threw off his evening shade
And to the shepherd's hut beneath the crags   400

---

6. I.e., a shape one didn't dare to question.
7. Wordsworth transferred these two "spots of time" (lines 288–372) to Book XII of the 1850 *Prelude* (below, XII.208–335). This drastic relocation was impelled by the new design of *The Prelude* as a crisis-autobiography: having related how his Imagination was "im-paired," Wordsworth now describes how it was "restored" by the "renovating virtue" of such remembered moments of early experience.
8. Careful; "collateral": subordinate. Lines 373–440 correspond to the 1850 *Prelude*, II.544–612 (below).
9. Cumberland's.

Did send sweet notice of the rising moon,
How I have stood, to images like these
A stranger, linking with the spectacle
No body of associated forms,
And bringing with me no peculiar sense   405
Of quietness or peace—yet I have stood
Even while my eye has moved o'er three long leagues[1]
Of shining water, gathering, as it seemed,
Through the wide surface of that field of light
New pleasure, like a bee among the flowers.   410

    Thus often in those fits of vulgar[2] joy
Which through all seasons on a child's pursuits
Are prompt attendants, 'mid that giddy bliss
Which like a tempest works along the blood
And is forgotten, even then I felt   415
Gleams like the flashing of a shield. The earth
And common face of Nature spake to me
Rememberable things—sometimes, 'tis true,
By quaint associations, yet not vain
Nor profitless, if haply they impressed   420
Collateral objects and appearances,
Albeit lifeless then, and doomed to sleep
Until maturer seasons called them forth
To impregnate and to elevate the mind.
And if the vulgar joy by its own weight   425
Wearied itself out of the memory,
The scenes which were a witness of that joy
Remained, in their substantial lineaments
Depicted on the brain, and to the eye
Were visible, a daily sight. And thus   430
By the impressive agency of fear,
By pleasure and repeated happiness—
So frequently repeated—and by force
Of obscure feelings representative
Of joys that were forgotten, these same scenes, 435
So beauteous and majestic in themselves,
Though yet the day was distant, did at length
Become habitually dear, and all
Their hues and forms were by invisible links
Allied to the affections.

              I began   440
My story early, feeling, as I fear,
The weakness of a human love for days
Disowned by memory—ere the birth of spring
Planting my snowdrops among winter snows.
Nor will it seem to thee, my friend,[3] so prompt   445
In sympathy, that I have lengthened out

---

1. A league is approximately three miles.
2. Ordinary.
3. Coleridge, to whom this, like the later versions of the poem, is addressed.

With fond and feeble tongue a tedious tale.
Meanwhile my hope has been that I might fetch
Reproaches from my former years, whose power
May spur me on, in manhood now mature,   450
To honorable toil.[4] Yet should it be
That this is but an impotent desire—
That I by such inquiry am not taught
To understand myself, nor thou to know
With better knowledge how the heart was framed   455
Of him thou lovest—need I dread from thee
Harsh judgements if I am so loth to quit
Those recollected hours that have the charm
Of visionary things, and lovely forms
And sweet sensations, that throw back our life   460
And make our infancy a visible scene
On which the sun is shining?

End of the First Part

Second Part

Thus far, my friend, have we retraced the way
Through which I travelled when I first began
To love the woods and fields; the passion yet
Was in its birth, sustained, as might befal,
By nourishment that came unsought—for still   5
From week to week, from month to month, we lived
A round of tumult. Duly were our games
Prolonged in summer till the daylight failed:
No chair remained before the doors, the bench
And threshold steps were empty, fast asleep   10
The labourer and the old man who had sate
A later lingerer, yet the revelry
Continued and the loud uproar. At last,
When all the ground was dark and the huge clouds
Were edged with twinkling stars, to bed we went   15
With weary joints and with a beating mind.
Ah, is there one who ever has been young
And needs a monitory voice to tame
The pride of virtue and of intellect?
And is there one, the wisest and the best   20
Of all mankind, who does not sometimes wish
For things which cannot be, who would not give,
If so he might, to duty and to truth
The eagerness of infantine desire?
A tranquillizing spirit presses now   25

---

4. An indication that the opening ques- lays in undertaking his major poetic en-
tion, "Was it for this?" referred to de- terprise.

On my corporeal frame, so wide appears
The vacancy between me and those days,
Which yet have such self-presence in my heart
That sometimes when I think of them I seem
Two consciousnesses—conscious of myself,   30
And of some other being.[5]

                   A grey stone
Of native rock, left midway in the square
Of our small market village, was the home
And centre of these joys; and when, returned
After long absence thither I repaired,   35
I found that it was split and gone to build
A smart assembly-room[6] that perked and flared
With wash and rough-cast,[7] elbowing the ground
Which had been ours. But let the fiddle scream,
And be ye happy! Yet I know, my friends,   40
That more than one of you will think with me
Of those soft starry nights, and that old dame
From whom the stone was named,[8] who there had sate
And watched her table with its huckster's wares,
Assiduous, for the length of sixty years.   45

    We ran a boisterous race, the year span round
With giddy motion; but the time approached
That brought with it a regular desire
For calmer pleasures—when the beauteous scenes
Of Nature were collaterally attached   50
To every scheme of holiday delight,
And every boyish sport, less grateful else
And languidly pursued. When summer came
It was the pastime of our afternoons
To beat along the plain of Windermere[9]   55
With rival oars; and the selected bourn[1]
Was now an island musical with birds
That sang for ever, now a sister isle
Beneath an oak's umbrageous covert, sown
With lilies of the valley like a field,   60
And now a third small island where remained
An old stone table—and one mouldered cave—
A hermit's history. In such a race,
So ended, disappointment could be none,
Uneasiness, or pain, or jealousy;   65
We rested in the shade, all pleased alike,
Conquered and conqueror. Thus our selfishness
Was mellowed down, and thus the pride of strength
And the vainglory of superior skill
Were interfused with objects which subdued   70

5. The "two consciousnesses" are his present self and, co-present with it, the past self of his memory.
6. The Town Hall, built in 1790 on the Hawkshead Market Square.
7. "Wash": a wall-paint with a water base; "rough-cast": a coarse plaster.
8. It was called "the Stone of Rowe."
9. The surface of Lake Windermere.
1. Terminus of a journey.

And tempered them, and gradually produced
A quiet independence of the heart.
And to my friend who knows me I may add,
Unapprehensive of reproof, that hence
Ensued a diffidence and modesty,   75
And I was taught to feel—perhaps too much—
The self-sufficing power of solitude.

   No delicate viands sapped our bodily strength:
More than we wished we knew the blessing then
Of vigorous hunger, for our daily meals   80
Were frugal, Sabine fare[2]—and then, exclude[3]
A little weekly stipend, and we lived
Through three divisions of the quartered year
In pennyless poverty. But now, to school
Returned from the half-yearly holidays,   85
We came with purses more profusely filled,
Allowance which abundantly sufficed
To gratify the palate with repasts
More costly than the dame of whom I spake,
That ancient woman, and her board, supplied.   90
Hence inroads into distant vales, and long
Excursions far away among the hills,
Hence rustic dinners on the cool green ground—
Or in the woods, or by a riverside
Or fountain—festive banquets, that provoked   95
The languid action of a natural scene
By pleasure of corporeal appetite.

   Nor is my aim neglected if I tell
How twice in the long length of those half-years
We from our funds perhaps with bolder hand   100
Drew largely, anxious for one day at least
To feel the motion of the galloping steed;
And with the good old innkeeper, in truth
I needs must say that sometimes we have used
Sly subterfuge, for the intended bound   105
Of the day's journey was too distant far
For any cautious man: a structure famed
Beyond its neighbourhood, the antique walls
Of a large abbey,[4] with its fractured arch,
Belfry, and images, and living trees—   110
A holy scene. Along the smooth green turf
Our horses grazed. In more than inland peace
Left by the winds that overpass the vale
In that sequestered ruin, trees and towers—
Both silent and both motionless alike—   115
Hear all day long the murmuring sea that beats
Incessantly upon a craggy shore.

2. Modest meals, like those served at   4. Furness Abbey, 21 miles from Hawks-
Horace's Sabine Farm.   head.
3. Leave out of account.

Our steeds remounted, and the summons given,
With whip and spur we by the chantry[5] flew
In uncouth race, and left the cross-legged knight   120
And the stone abbot, and that single wren
Which one day sang so sweetly in the nave
Of the old church that, though from recent showers
The earth was comfortless, and, touched by faint
Internal breezes, from the roofless walls   125
The shuddering ivy dripped large drops, yet still
So sweetly 'mid the gloom the invisible bird
Sang to itself that there I could have made
My dwelling place, and lived for ever there,
To hear such music. Through the walls we flew   130
And down the valley, and, a circuit made
In wantonness of heart, through rough and smooth
We scampered homeward. O, ye rocks and streams,
And that still spirit of the evening air,
Even in this joyous time I sometimes felt   135
Your presence, when, with slackened step, we breathed
Along the sides of the steep hills, or when,
Lightened by gleams of moonlight from the sea,
We beat with thundering hoofs the level sand.

There was a row of ancient trees, since fallen,   140
That on the margin of a jutting land
Stood near the lake of Coniston, and made,
With its long boughs above the water stretched,
A gloom through which a boat might sail along
As in a cloister. An old hall[6] was near,   145
Grotesque and beautiful, its gavel[7] end
And huge round chimney to the top o'ergrown
With fields of ivy. Thither we repaired—
'Twas even a custom with us—to the shore,
And to that cool piazza. They who dwelt   150
In the neglected mansion-house supplied
Fresh butter, tea-kettle and earthern-ware,
And chafing-dish with smoking coals; and so
Beneath the trees we sate in our small boat,
And in the covert eat our delicate meal   155
Upon the calm smooth lake. It was a joy
Worthy the heart of one who is full grown
To rest beneath those horizontal boughs
And mark the radiance of the setting sun,
Himself unseen, reposing on the top   160
Of the high eastern hills. And there I said,
That beauteous sight before me—there I said
(Then first beginning in my thoughts to mark
That sense of dim similitude which links

5. A chapel endowed so that masses would be sung for the donor.
6. The Hall of Coniston, ancient seat of the Le Fleming family.
7. Gable.

Our moral feelings with external forms)   165
That in whatever region I should close
My mortal life I would remember you,
Fair scenes—that dying I would think on you,
My soul would send a longing look to you,
Even as that setting sun, while all the vale   170
Could nowhere catch one faint memorial gleam,
Yet with the last remains of his last light
Still lingered, and a farewell lustre threw
On the dear mountain-tops where first he rose.
'Twas then my fourteenth summer, and these words   175
Were uttered in a casual access
Of sentiment, a momentary trance
That far outran the habit of my mind.[8]

   Upon the eastern shore of Windermere
Above the crescent of a pleasant bay   180
There was an inn,[9] no homely-featured shed,
Brother of the surrounding cottages,
But 'twas a splendid place, the door beset
With chaises, grooms, and liveries, and within
Decanters, glasses and the blood-red wine.   185
In antient times, or ere the hall was built
On the large island, had the dwelling been
More worthy of a poet's love, a hut
Proud of its one bright fire and sycamore shade;
But though the rhymes were gone which once inscribed 190
The threshold, and large golden characters
On the blue-frosted signboard had usurped
The place of the old lion, in contempt
And mockery of the rustic painter's hand,
Yet to this hour the spot to me is dear   195
With all its foolish pomp. The garden lay
Upon a slope surmounted by the plain
Of a small bowling-green; beneath us stood
A grove, with gleams of water through the trees
And over the tree tops—nor did we want   200
Refreshment, strawberries and mellow cream—
And there through half an afternoon we played
On the smooth platform, and the shouts we sent
Made all the mountains ring. But ere the fall
Of night, when in our pinnace we returned   205
Over the dusky lake, and to the beach
Of some small island steered our course, with one—
The minstrel of our troop—and left him there,
And rowed off gently, while he blew his flute
Alone upon the rock, oh, then the calm   210

8. Wordsworth transferred a shortened
version of lines 140–178 to the 1850
Prelude, Book VIII: "Retrospect—Love
of Nature Leading to Love of Man."
9. The White Lion Inn at Bowness.

And dead still water lay upon my mind
Even with a weight of pleasure, and the sky,
Never before so beautiful, sank down
Into my heart and held me like a dream.

    Thus day by day my sympathies increased,   215
And thus the common range of visible things
Grew dear to me: already I began
To love the sun, a boy I loved the sun
Not as I since have loved him—as a pledge
And surety of my earthly life, a light   220
Which while I view I feel I am alive—
But for this cause, that I had seen him lay
His beauty on the morning hills, had seen
The western mountain touch his setting orb
In many a thoughtless hour, when, from excess   225
Of happiness, my blood appeared to flow
With its own pleasure, and I breathed with joy.
And from like feelings, humble though intense,
To patriotic and domestic love
Analagous, the moon to me was dear;   230
For I would dream away my purposes
Standing to look upon her, while she hung
Midway between the hills, as if she knew
No other region, but belonged to thee,
Yea, appertained by a peculiar right   235
To thee and thy grey huts, my native vale!

    Those incidental charms which first attached
My heart to rural objects, day by day
Grew weaker, and I hasten on to tell
How Nature, intervenient till this time   240
And secondary, now at length was sought
For her own sake. But who shall parcel out
His intellect by geometric rules,
Split like a province into round and square?
Who knows the individual hour in which   245
His habits were first sown even as a seed?
Who that shall point as with a wand, and say
'This portion of the river of my mind
Came from yon fountain'? Thou, my friend, art one
More deeply read in thy own thoughts, no slave   250
Of that false secondary power[1] by which
In weakness we create distinctions, then
Believe our puny boundaries are things
Which we perceive, and not which we have made.
To thee, unblinded by these outward shews,   255
The unity of all has been revealed;
And thou wilt doubt with me, less aptly skilled
Than many are to class the cabinet[2]

---

1. The analytic faculty, as opposed to the power to apprehend "the unity of all" (line 256).
2. Storage place.

Of their sensations, and in voluble phrase
Run through the history and birth of each   260
As of a single independent thing.
Hard task to analyze a soul, in which
Not only general habits and desires,
But each most obvious and particular thought—
Not in a mystical and idle sense,   265
But in the words of reason deeply weighed—
Hath no beginning.

                 Blessed the infant babe—
For with my best conjectures I would trace
The progress of our being—blessed the babe
Nursed in his mother's arms, the babe who sleeps   270
Upon his mother's breast, who, when his soul
Claims manifest kindred with an earthly soul,
Doth gather passion from his mother's eye.
Such feelings pass into his torpid life
Like an awakening breeze, and hence his mind,   275
Even in the first trial of its powers,
Is prompt and watchful, eager to combine
In one appearance all the elements
And parts of the same object, else detached
And loth to coalesce. Thus day by day   280
Subjected to the discipline of love,
His organs and recipient faculties
Are quickened, are more vigorous; his mind spreads,
Tenacious of the forms which it receives.
In one beloved presence—nay and more,   285
In that most apprehensive habitude[3]
And those sensations which have been derived
From this beloved presence—there exists
A virtue which irradiates and exalts
All objects through all intercourse of sense.   290
No outcast he, bewildered and depressed;
Along his infant veins are interfused
The gravitation and the filial bond
Of Nature that connect him with the world.
Emphatically such a being lives,   295
An inmate of this *active* universe.
From Nature largely he receives, nor so
Is satisfied, but largely gives again;
For feeling has to him imparted strength,
And—powerful in all sentiments of grief,   300
Of exultation, fear and joy—his mind,
Even as an agent of the one great mind,
Creates, creator and receiver both,
Working but in alliance with the works
Which it beholds. Such, verily, is the first   305
Poetic spirit of our human life—

---

3. I.e., in that customary mode of most sensitive perception.

By uniform controul of after years
In most abated and suppressed, in some
Through every change of growth or of decay
Preeminent till death.[4]

           From early days,   310
Beginning not long after that first time
In which, a babe, by intercourse of touch
I held mute dialogues with my mother's heart,[5]
I have endeavoured to display the means
Whereby this infant sensibility,   315
Great birthright of our being, was in me
Augmented and sustained. Yet is a path
More difficult before me, and I fear
That in its broken windings we shall need
The chamois'[6] sinews and the eagle's wing.   320
For now a trouble came into my mind
From obscure causes: I was left alone
Seeking this visible world, nor knowing why.
The props of my affections were removed,[7]
And yet the building stood, as if sustained   325
By its own spirit. All that I beheld
Was dear to me, and from this cause it came
That now to Nature's finer influxes
My mind lay open—to that more exact
And intimate communion which our hearts   330
Maintain with the minuter properties
Of objects which already are beloved,
And of those only.

           Many are the joys
Of youth, but oh, what happiness to live
When every hour brings palpable access   335
Of knowledge, when all knowledge is delight,
And sorrow is not there. The seasons came,
And every season brought a countless store
Of modes and temporary qualities
Which but for this most watchful power of love   340
Had been neglected, left a register
Of permanent relations else unknown.
Hence life, and change, and beauty, solitude
More active even than 'best society',[8]

4. Compare the 1850 version (II.232–65, below). The infant, secure in his mother's arms, experiences objects of sense which are irradiated by his assurance of maternal love, and so comes to feel at home in a world to which his mind has contributed, and which his own perceptions, therefore, in part create.
5. I.e., both the infant and the mother who clasps him feel the pulse of the other's heart.
6. A nimble, antelope-like animal inhabiting mountainous regions of Europe.
7. Wordsworth's mother had died the

month before his eighth birthday. The reference to "a trouble . . . / From obscure causes" (lines 321–22) makes it unclear whether he is referring to the loss of his mother (in whose arms he had come to feel secure in the world) or to an indefinite sense of being cut off from outer reality, such as he describes in lines 399–401, and later in the *Intimations* ode (above, lines 143–47).
8. In *Paradise Lost* IX.249, Adam says to Eve that "solitude sometimes is best society."

Society made sweet as solitude   345
By silent inobtrusive sympathies,
And gentle agitations of the mind
From manifold distinctions, difference
Perceived in things where to the common eye
No difference is, and hence, from the same source,   350
Sublimer joy. For I would walk alone
In storm and tempest, or in starlight nights
Beneath the quiet heavens, and at that time
Would feel whate'er there is of power in sound
To breathe an elevated mood, by form   355
Or image unprofaned; and I would stand
Beneath some rock, listening to sounds that are
The ghostly language of the ancient earth,
Or make their dim abode in distant winds.
Thence did I drink the visionary power.   360
I deem not profitless these fleeting moods
Of shadowy exaltation; not for this,
That they are kindred to our purer mind
And intellectual life,[9] but that the soul—
Remembering how she felt, but what she felt   365
Remembering not—retains an obscure sense
Of possible sublimity, to which
With growing faculties she doth aspire,
With faculties still growing, feeling still
That whatsoever point they gain they still   370
Have something to pursue.[1]

                          And not alone
In grandeur and in tumult, but no less
In tranquil scenes, that universal power
And fitness in the latent qualities
And essences of things, by which the mind   375
Is moved with feelings of delight, to me
Came strengthened with a superadded soul,
A virtue not its own. My morning walks
Were early: oft before the hours of school
I travelled round our little lake, five miles   380
Of pleasant wandering—happy time, more dear
For this, that one was by my side, a friend
Then passionately loved.[2] With heart how full
Will he peruse these lines, this page—perhaps
A blank to other men—for many years   385
Have since flowed in between us, and, our minds
Both silent to each other, at this time

---

9. I.e., not because they are related to
the purer (the non-sensuous, or "intellectual") part of our mind.
1. Compare the revelation that our destiny is with "something evermore about

to be" in Wordsworth's later passage
about crossing Simplon Pass (1850 *Prelude*, below, VI.604–8).
2. A note in the 1850 *Prelude* identifies
this friend as John Fleming.

We live as if those hours had never been.[3]
Nor seldom did I lift our cottage latch
Far earlier, and before the vernal thrush
Was audible,[4] among the hills I sate   390
Alone upon some jutting eminence
At the first hour of morning, when the vale
Lay quiet in an utter solitude.
How shall I trace the history, where seek   395
The origin of what I then have felt?
Oft in those moments such a holy calm
Did overspread my soul that I forgot
The agency of sight, and what I saw
Appeared like something in myself, a dream,   400
A prospect in my mind.

             'Twere long to tell
What spring and autumn, what the winter snows,
And what the summer shade, what day and night,
The evening and the morning, what my dreams
And what my waking thoughts, supplied to nurse   405
That spirit of religious love in which
I walked with Nature. But let this, at least,
Be not forgotten, that I still retained
My first creative sensibility,[5]
That by the regular action of the world   410
My soul was unsubdued. A plastic[6] power
Abode with me, a forming hand, at times
Rebellious, acting in a devious mood,
A local spirit of its own, at war
With general tendency, but for the most   415
Subservient strictly to the external things
With which it communed. An auxiliar light
Came from my mind, which on the setting sun
Bestowed new splendour; the melodious birds,
The gentle breezes, fountains that ran on   420
Murmuring so sweetly in themselves, obeyed
A like dominion, and the midnight storm
Grew darker in the presence of my eye.
Hence my obeisance, my devotion hence,
And *hence* my transport.   425

                    Nor should this, perchance,
Pass unrecorded, that I still had loved
The exercise and produce of a toil
Than analytic industry to me
More pleasing, and whose character I deem
Is more poetic, as resembling more   430
Creative agency—I mean to speak
Of that interminable building reared

---

3. I.e., in our separation we now live as
if we had never shared those morning
walks.
4. So early in the morning that the
thrush had not begun his spring song.
5. As described in lines 301–6.
6. Shaping, formative.

By observation of affinities
In objects where no brotherhood exists
To common minds. My seventeenth year was come,   435
And, whether from this habit rooted now
So deeply in my mind, or from excess
Of the great social principle of life
Coercing all things into sympathy,
To unorganic natures I transferred   440
My own enjoyments, or, the power of truth
Coming in revelation, I conversed
With things that really are, I at this time
Saw blessings spread around me like a sea.
Thus did my days pass on, and now at length   445
From Nature and her overflowing soul
I had received so much that all my thoughts
Were steeped in feeling. I was only then
Contented when with bliss ineffable
I felt the sentiment of being spread   450
O'er all that moves, and all that seemeth still,
O'er all that, lost beyond the reach of thought
And human knowledge, to the human eye
Invisible, yet liveth to the heart,
O'er all that leaps, and runs, and shouts, and sings,   455
Or beats the gladsome air, o'er all that glides
Beneath the wave, yea, in the wave itself
And mighty depth of waters. Wonder not
If such my transports were, for in all things
I saw one life, and felt that it was joy;   460
One song they sang and it was audible—
Most audible then when the fleshly ear,
O'ercome by grosser prelude of that strain,
Forgot its functions and slept undisturbed.[7]

    If this be error, and another faith   465
Find easier access to the pious mind,[8]
Yet were I grossly destitute of all
Those human sentiments which make this earth
So dear if I should fail with grateful voice
To speak of you, ye mountains, and ye lakes   470
And sounding cataracts, ye mists and winds
That dwell among the hills where I was born.
If, in my youth, I have been pure in heart,
If, mingling with the world, I am content
With my own modest pleasures, and have lived   475
With God and Nature communing, removed
From little enmities and low desires,
The gift is yours; if in these times of fear,
This melancholy waste of hopes o'erthrown,
If, 'mid indifference and apathy   480
And wicked exultation, when good men

---

7. For the later version of lines 401–64, see the 1850 *Prelude*, below, II.352–418.   8. Cf. lines 458–66 to *Tintern Abbey* (above), lines 43–50.

On every side fall off we know not how
To selfishness, disguised in gentle names
Of peace and quiet and domestic love—
Yet mingled, not unwillingly, with sneers   485
On visionary minds—if, in this time
Of dereliction and dismay, I yet
Despair not of our nature, but retain
A more than Roman confidence, a faith
That fails not, in all sorrow my support,   490
The blessing of my life, the gift is yours
Ye mountains, thine O Nature. Thou hast fed
My lofty speculations; and in thee
For this uneasy heart of ours I find
A never-failing principle of joy   495
And purest passion.

         Thou, my friend, wast reared
In the great city, 'mid far other scenes,[9]
But we by different roads at length have gained
The self-same bourne. And from this cause to thee
I speak unapprehensive of contempt,   500
The insinuated scoff of coward tongues,
And all that silent language which so oft
In conversation betwixt man and man
Blots from the human countenance all trace
Of beauty and of love. For thou hast sought   505
The truth in solitude, and thou art one
The most intense of Nature's worshippers,
In many things my brother, chiefly here
In this my deep devotion. Fare thee well.
Health and the quiet of a healthful mind   510
Attend thee, seeking oft the haunts of men—
But yet more often living with thyself,
And for thyself—so haply shall thy days
Be many, and a blessing to mankind.
         End of the Second Part

1798–99   1974

9. A reminiscence of Coleridge's *Frost at Midnight* (below), lines 51–52: "For I was reared / In the great city, pent 'mid cloisters dim."

The Prelude (1850)

When Wordsworth enlarged the two-part *Prelude* of 1799 into thirteen books (1805) and then into fourteen books (1850), he not only made it a poem of epic length but also heightened the style and introduced various thematic parallels with earlier epics, especially *Paradise Lost*. (For a central example, see Wordsworth's version of Milton's enterprise to "justify the ways of God to men," in the 1850 *Prelude*, below, XIV.157–70, 382–87). The expanded poem, however, is a personal history which turns on a mental crisis and recovery, and for such a narrative design the chief prototype is not the classical or Christian epic, but the spiritual autobiography of crisis. St. Augustine's *Confessions* established this great Christian form late in the 4th century, and it has had an uninterrupted history in European literature ever since. Among the scores of prose versions of the spiritual autobiography are the Catholic Dante's *Vita Nuova* (*The New Life*) and the Puritan Bunyan's *Grace Abounding to the Chief of Sinners*. Its greatest poetic instance is Dante's *Divine Comedy*, an allegorical account of the narrator's spiritual journey from earth through hell, purgatory, and paradise, back to earth.

As in *The Divine Comedy*, and in Augustine's *Confessions* itself, Wordsworth's recurrent metaphor is that of a journey, whose end—as T. S. Eliot put it in *Four Quartets*, his adaptation of the same form—is in its beginning, and in which it turns out that the end of the journey is "to arrive where we started / And know the place for the first time" (see the Quartet *Little Gidding*, below, lines 241–44). Wordsworth's *Prelude* opens with a literal journey whose chosen goal (I.70–71, 106–7) is "a known Vale, whither my feet should turn"—that is, the Vale of Grasmere. There are a number of later journeys, of which the most important are the crossing of the Alps in Book VI and, at the beginning of the final book, the ascent of Mount Snowdon which culminates in a definitive vision. In the course of the poem, however, such literal journeys become the metaphoric vehicle for an interior journey in a quest, both within the poet's memory and in his poetic enterprise itself, for his lost early self and his proper spiritual home. The poem ends by adverting to its own beginning, and leaves the poet settled in the Vale of Grasmere, ready finally to begin his great enterprise, *The Recluse* (XIV.302–11, 372–83).

In reading *The Prelude* as autobiography, we readily forget how traditional it is in both voice and form; and in our understandable preoccupation with its great poetic moments we are apt to overlook the elaborate artistry of its overall structure. Although the narrator is the actual Wordsworth, addressing himself to the English people of his own troubled age, he adopts a personal and a prophetic stance that goes back through Milton and Spenser to the poets and prophets of the Bible. And although the separate episodes are events from Wordsworth's own life, he does not describe these events as they had seemed to him at the time, but as they are interpreted in distant retrospect, re-ordered in sequence, and shaped into the inherited design of crisis and recovery, from which the author emerges as a different self in a transformed world.

Wordsworth, however, changes the traditional spiritual history in a radical way: he converts what had earlier been the supernatural Christian agencies of its providential plot into secular and humanistic terms. The true protagonist in Wordsworth's poem turns out, in fact, to be a power of his own mind which is capable of transforming the natural world with which it interacts; he calls this power "Imagination." "This faculty," he reveals in the last book (XIV.193 ff.), "hath been the feeding source of our long labor," and he goes on to say that the account of its appearance, development, loss, and restoration has constituted the submerged plot of the poem in its entirety. *The Prelude* has been called the greatest religious poem of the 19th century. Its religion, however, despite some pious phrases that Wordsworth cautiously inserted into the 1850 text, is not an inherited creed, nor even a religion of Nature, but rather a faith in the redeeming power of "the mind of man" which, the closing lines declare, compared with the unchanging earth, is "In beauty exalted, as it is itself / Of quality and fabric more divine."

From The Prelude
or
Growth of a Poet's Mind

AN AUTOBIOGRAPHICAL POEM

(1850)

From *Book I. Introduction—Childhood and Schooltime*

Oh there is blessing in this gentle breeze,[1]
A visitant that while it fans my cheek
Doth seem half-conscious of the joy it brings
From the green fields, and from yon azure sky.
Whate'er its mission, the soft breeze can come   5
To none more grateful than to me; escaped
From the vast city,[2] where I long had pined
A discontented sojourner: now free,
Free as a bird to settle where I will.
What dwelling shall receive me? in what vale   10
Shall be my harbor? underneath what grove
Shall I take up my home? and what clear stream
Shall with its murmur lull me into rest?
The earth is all before me.[3] With a heart
Joyous, nor scared at its own liberty,   15
I look about; and should the chosen guide
Be nothing better than a wandering cloud,
I cannot miss my way. I breathe again!
Trances of thought and mountings of the mind
Come fast upon me: it is shaken off,   20
That burthen of my own unnatural self,
The heavy weight of many a weary day
Not mine, and such as were not made for me.
Long months of peace (if such bold word accord

1. Wordsworth says, lines 46–50, that the preceding lines were uttered in the circumstances they describe. Until recently it was the standard opinion that the occasion was September of 1795 when Wordsworth, released from financial worries by a legacy, was on his way to find a home in Racedown, Dorset. It is much more likely, however, that the lines refer primarily to his walk to what was to be his home at Grasmere, deliberately fused with details from an earlier trip to Racedown, in order to make the walk the symbol of a new stage in the journey of his life. In 1804 this passage was adopted as the preamble for *The Prelude*, where it replaces the epic device (as in *Paradise Lost*) of the opening prayer to the Muse for inspiration. To be "inspired" is, in its literal sense, to be blown into by a divinity: Wordsworth begins his poem with a literal wind, the "breath of heaven," which (lines 33–42) becomes the stimulus for a correspondent inner breeze, marking both a springlike revival of the spirit after a wintry season and a burst of poetic power which Wordsworth equates with the inspiration of the Biblical prophets when touched by the Holy Spirit (lines 50–54). The revivifying breeze, material and spiritual, recurs as a kind of leitmotif in *The Prelude*, and also serves as the radical metaphor of Coleridge's *Dejection: An Ode* and Shelley's *Ode to the West Wind*.

2. Primarily London; but like the journey, the city serves as a type, symbolizing a release from spiritual bondage.

3. One of many echoes from *Paradise Lost*, where the line describes Adam and Eve beginning their new life after the expulsion from Eden: "The world was all before them" (XII.646).

With any promises of human life),   25
Long months of ease and undisturbed delight
Are mine in prospect; whither shall I turn,
By road or pathway, or through trackless field,
Uphill or down, or shall some floating thing
Upon the river point me out my course?   30

    Dear Liberty! Yet what would it avail
But for a gift that consecrates the joy?
For I, methought, while the sweet breath of heaven
Was blowing on my body, felt within
A correspondent breeze, that gently moved   35
With quickening virtue,[4] but is now become
A tempest, a redundant energy,
Vexing its own creation. Thanks to both,
And their congenial[5] powers, that, while they join
In breaking up a long-continued frost,   40
Bring with them vernal promises, the hope
Of active days urged on by flying hours—
Days of sweet leisure, taxed with patient thought
Abstruse, nor wanting punctual service high,
Matins and vespers of harmonious verse!   45

    Thus far, O Friend![6] did I, not used to make
A present joy the matter of a song,[7]
Pour forth that day my soul in measured strains
That would not be forgotten, and are here
Recorded: to the open fields I told   50
A prophecy: poetic numbers came
Spontaneously to clothe in priestly robe
A renovated spirit singled out,
Such hope was mine, for holy services.
My own voice cheered me, and, far more, the mind's   55
Internal echo of the imperfect sound;
To both I listened, drawing from them both
A cheerful confidence in things to come.

    Content and not unwilling now to give
A respite to this passion, I paced on   60
With brisk and eager steps; and came, at length,
To a green shady place, where down I sate
Beneath a tree, slackening my thoughts by choice,
And settling into gentler happiness.
'Twas autumn, and a clear and placid day,   65
With warmth, as much as needed, from a sun
Two hours declined towards the west; a day
With silver clouds, and sunshine on the grass,

---

4. Reviving power.
5. Kindred.
6. Samuel Taylor Coleridge, to whom the entire poem is addressed as a kind of immense verse letter. For Coleridge's reply, see *To William Wordsworth*.

7. His poetry, Wordsworth said in the Preface to *Lyrical Ballads*, usually originates as "emotion recollected in tranquility," not, as in the preamble just preceding, during the experience it describes.

And in the sheltered and the sheltering grove
A perfect stillness. Many were the thoughts
Encouraged and dismissed, till choice was made   70
Of a known Vale, whither my feet should turn,
Nor rest till they had reached the very door
Of the one cottage which methought I saw.
No picture of mere memory ever looked   75
So fair; and while upon the fancied scene
I gazed with growing love, a higher power
Than Fancy gave assurance of some work
Of glory there·forthwith to be begun,
Perhaps too there performed. Thus long I mused,   80
Nor e'er lost sight of what I mused upon,
Save when, amid the stately grove of oaks,
Now here, now there, an acorn, from its cup
Dislodged, through sere leaves rustled, or at once
To the bare earth dropped with a startling sound.   85
From that soft couch I rose not, till the sun
Had almost touched the horizon; casting then
A backward glance upon the curling cloud
Of city smoke, by distance ruralised;
Keen as a Truant or a Fugitive,   90
But as a Pilgrim resolute, I took,
Even with the chance equipment of that hour,
The road that pointed toward the chosen Vale.
It was a splendid evening, and my soul
Once more made trial of her strength, nor lacked   95
Eolian visitations;[8] but the harp
Was soon defrauded, and the banded host
Of harmony dispersed in straggling sounds,
And lastly utter silence! "Be it so;
Why think of anything but present good?"   100
So, like a home-bound laborer I pursued
My way beneath the mellowing sun, that shed
Mild influence;[9] nor left in me one wish
Again to bend the Sabbath of that time[1]
To a servile yoke. What need of many words?   105
A pleasant loitering journey, through three days
Continued, brought me to my hermitage.
I spare to tell of what ensued, the life
In common things—the endless store of things,
Rare, or at least so seeming, every day   110
Found all about me in one neighborhood—
The self-congratulation, and, from morn
To night, unbroken cheerfulness serene.
But speedily an earnest longing rose
To brace myself to some determined aim,   115

8. I.e., influences to which his soul responded like an Eolian harp (as in lines
33–38).
9. *Paradise Lost* VII.374–75: "the

Pleiades before him danced / Shedding
sweet influence."
1. That time of rest.

Reading or thinking; either to lay up
New stores, or rescue from decay the old
By timely interference: and therewith
Came hopes still higher, that with outward life
I might endue some airy phantasies   120
That had been floating loose about for years,
And to such beings temperately deal forth
The many feelings that oppressed my heart.
That hope hath been discouraged; welcome light
Dawns from the east, but dawns to disappear   125
And mock me with a sky that ripens not
Into a steady morning: if my mind,
Remembering the bold promise of the past,
Would gladly grapple with some noble theme,
Vain is her wish; where'er she turns she finds   130
Impediments from day to day renewed.

                         * * *

Far better never to have heard the name   255
Of zeal and just ambition, than to live
Baffled and plagued by a mind that every hour
Turns recreant to her task; takes heart again,
Then feels immediately some hollow thought
Hang like an interdict upon her hopes.   260
This is my lot; for either still I find
Some imperfection in the chosen theme,
Or see of absolute accomplishment
Much wanting, so much wanting, in myself,
That I recoil and droop, and seek repose   265
In listlessness from vain perplexity,
Unprofitably traveling toward the grave,
Like a false steward who hath much received
And renders nothing back.
                          Was it for this[2]
That one, the fairest of all rivers, loved   270
To blend his murmurs with my nurse's song,
And, from his alder shades and rocky falls,
And from his fords and shallows, sent a voice
That flowed along my dreams? For this, didst thou,
O Derwent! winding among grassy holms[3]   275
Where I was looking on, a babe in arms,
Make ceaseless music that composed my thoughts
To more than infant softness, giving me
Amid the fretful dwellings of mankind
A foretaste, a dim earnest, of the calm   280
That Nature breathes among the hills and groves.
When he had left the mountains and received

---

2. Lines 269–475 correspond to the   3. Flat ground next to a river.
Two-Part Prelude, above, I.1–198.

On his smooth breast the shadow of those towers
That yet survive, a shattered monument
Of feudal sway, the bright blue river passed   285
Along the margin of our terrace walk;[4]
A tempting playmate whom we dearly loved.
Oh, many a time have I, a five years' child,
In a small mill-race severed from his stream,
Made one long bathing of a summer's day;   290
Basked in the sun, and plunged and basked again
Alternate, all a summer's day, or scoured[5]
The sandy fields, leaping through flowery groves
Of yellow ragwort; or when rock and hill,
The woods, and distant Skiddaw's[6] lofty height,   295
Were bronzed with deepest radiance, stood alone
Beneath the sky, as if I had been born
On Indian plains, and from my mother's hut
Had run abroad in wantonness, to sport
A naked savage, in the thunder shower.   300

                              * * *

    Fair seedtime had my soul, and I grew up
Fostered alike by beauty and by fear:[7]
Much favored in my birthplace; and no less
In that belovéd Vale[8] to which erelong
We were transplanted—there were we let loose   305
For sports of wider range. Ere I had told
Ten birthdays, when among the mountain slopes
Frost, and the breath of frosty wind, had snapped
The last autumnal crocus, 'twas my joy
With store of springes[9] over my shoulder hung   310
To range the open heights where woodcocks run
Along the smooth green turf. Through half the night,
Scudding away from snare to snare, I plied
That anxious visitation—moon and stars
Were shining o'er my head. I was alone,   315
And seemed to be a trouble to the peace
That dwelt among them. Sometimes it befell
In these night wanderings, that a strong desire
O'erpowered my better reason, and the bird
Which was the captive of another's toil   320
Became my prey; and when the deed was done

---

4. The Derwent River flows by Cocker-mouth Castle and then past the garden terrace behind Wordsworth's father's house in Cockermouth, Cumberland.
5. Ran swiftly over.
6. A mountain in Cumberland.
7. Wordsworth introduces here a dialectic that plays a central role in the evolution of *The Prelude*. He represents his mind, confronting nature, as fostered in its growth by two antithetic principles, one associated with love and the other with fear. These principles correspond to the two main categories, "the beautiful" (or "the fair") and "the sublime," into which theorists of the landscape during the preceding century had classified the antithetic aspects of the natural scene. See, e.g., I.351–56, 466–75, 545. In the concluding Book, this antithesis is finally resolved; see below, XIV.162–70 and note.
8. The valley of Esthwaite, the location of Hawkshead, where Wordsworth attended school.
9. Bird snares.

I heard among the solitary hills
Low breathings coming after me, and sounds
Of undistinguishable motion, steps
Almost as silent as the turf they trod.   325

   Nor less, when spring had warmed the cultured[1] Vale,
Moved we as plunderers where the mother bird
Had in high places built her lodge; though mean
Our object and inglorious, yet the end
Was not ignoble. Oh! when I have hung   330
Above the raven's nest, by knots of grass
And half-inch fissures in the slippery rock
But ill sustained, and almost (so it seemed)
Suspended by the blast that blew amain,
Shouldering the naked crag, oh, at that time   335
While on the perilous ridge I hung alone,
With what strange utterance did the loud dry wind
Blow through my ear! the sky seemed not a sky
Of earth—and with what motion moved the clouds!

   Dust as we are, the immortal spirit grows   340
Like harmony in music; there is a dark
Inscrutable workmanship that reconciles
Discordant elements, makes them cling together
In one society. How strange that all
The terrors, pains, and early miseries,   345
Regrets, vexations, lassitudes interfused
Within my mind, should e'er have borne a part,
And that a needful part, in making up
The calm existence that is mine when I
Am worthy of myself! Praise to the end!   350
Thanks to the means which Nature deigned to employ;
Whether her fearless visitings, or those
That came with soft alarm, like hurtless light
Opening the peaceful clouds; or she may use
Severer interventions, ministry   355
More palpable, as best might suit her aim.[2]

   One summer evening (led by her) I found
A little boat tied to a willow tree
Within a rocky cave, its usual home.
Straight I unloosed her chain, and stepping in   360
Pushed from the shore. It was an act of stealth
And troubled pleasure, nor without the voice
Of mountain echoes did my boat move on;
Leaving behind her still, on either side,
Small circles glittering idly in the moon,   365
Until they melted all into one track

---

1. Cultivated.
2. A restatement of the double ministry of nature described in line 302; what follows is a second example of discipline by fear.

Of sparkling light. But now, like one who rows,
Proud of his skill, to reach a chosen point
With an unswerving line, I fixed my view
Upon the summit of a craggy ridge,
The horizon's utmost boundary; for above   370
Was nothing but the stars and the gray sky.
She was an elfin pinnace;[3] lustily
I dipped my oars into the silent lake,
And, as I rose upon the stroke, my boat
Went heaving through the water like a swan;   375
When, from behind that craggy steep till then
The horizon's bound, a huge peak, black and huge,
As if with voluntary power instinct,
Upreared its head.[4] I struck and struck again,   380
And growing still in stature the grim shape
Towered up between me and the stars, and still,
For so it seemed, with purpose of its own
And measured motion like a living thing,
Strode after me. With trembling oars I turned,   385
And through the silent water stole my way
Back to the covert of the willow tree;
There in her mooring place I left my bark,
And through the meadows homeward went, in grave
And serious mood; but after I had seen   390
That spectacle, for many days, my brain
Worked with a dim and undetermined sense
Of unknown modes of being; o'er my thoughts
There hung a darkness, call it solitude
Or blank desertion. No familiar shapes   395
Remained, no pleasant images of trees,
Of sea or sky, no colors of green fields;
But huge and mighty forms, that do not live
Like living men, moved slowly through the mind
By day, and were a trouble to my dreams.   400

    Wisdom and Spirit of the universe!
Thou Soul that art the eternity of thought,
That givest to forms and images a breath
And everlasting motion, not in vain
By day or starlight thus from my first dawn   405
Of childhood didst thou intertwine for me
The passions that build up our human soul;
Not with the mean and vulgar works of man,
But with high objects, with enduring things—
With life and nature—purifying thus   410
The elements of feeling and of thought,

---

3. Small boat.
4. In order to direct his boat in a straight line, the rower has fixed his eye on a point in the ridge of the nearby shore, which blocks out the landscape behind. As he moves farther out, the black peak suddenly rears into his altering angle of vision and seems to stride closer with each stroke of the oars.

And sanctifying, by such discipline,
Both pain and fear, until we recognize
A grandeur in the beatings of the heart.
Nor was this fellowship vouchsafed to me   415
With stinted kindness. In November days,
When vapors rolling down the valley made
A lonely scene more lonesome, among woods,
At noon and 'mid the calm of summer nights,
When, by the margin of the trembling lake,   420
Beneath the gloomy hills homeward I went
In solitude, such intercourse was mine;
Mine was it in the fields both day and night,
And by the waters, all the summer long.

    And in the frosty season, when the sun   425
Was set, and visible for many a mile
The cottage windows blazed through twilight gloom,
I heeded not their summons: happy time
It was indeed for all of us—for me
It was a time of rapture! Clear and loud   430
The village clock tolled six—I wheeled about,
Proud and exulting like an untired horse
That cares not for his home. All shod with steel,
We hissed along the polished ice in games
Confederate, imitative of the chase   435
And woodland pleasures—the resounding horn,
The pack loud chiming, and the hunted hare.
So through the darkness and the cold we flew,
And not a voice was idle; with the din
Smitten, the precipices rang aloud;   440
The leafless trees and every icy crag
Tinkled like iron; while far distant hills
Into the tumult sent an alien sound
Of melancholy not unnoticed, while the stars
Eastward were sparkling clear, and in the west   445
The orange sky of evening died away.
Not seldom from the uproar I retired
Into a silent bay, or sportively
Glanced sideway,[5] leaving the tumultuous throng,
To cut across the reflex[6] of a star   450
That fled, and, flying still before me, gleamed
Upon the glassy plain; and oftentimes,
When we had given our bodies to the wind,
And all the shadowy banks on either side
Came sweeping through the darkness, spinning still   455
The rapid line of motion, then at once
Have I, reclining back upon my heels,
Stopped short; yet still the solitary cliffs

5. Moved off obliquely.   6. Reflection.

Wheeled by me—even as if the earth had rolled
With visible motion her diurnal round!   460
Behind me did they stretch in solemn train,
Feebler and feebler, and I stood and watched
Till all was tranquil as a dreamless sleep.

    Ye Presences of Nature in the sky
And on the earth! Ye Visions of the hills!   465
And Souls of lonely places![7] can I think
A vulgar hope was yours when ye employed
Such ministry, when ye, through many a year
Haunting me thus among my boyish sports,
On caves and trees, upon the woods and hills,   470
Impressed upon all forms the characters
Of danger or desire; and thus did make
The surface of the universal earth
With triumph and delight, with hope and fear,
Work like a sea? * * *   475

    Nor, sedulous as I have been to trace
How Nature by extrinsic passion first   545
Peopled the mind with forms sublime or fair,[8]
And made me love them, may I here omit
How other pleasures have been mine, and joys
Of subtler origin; how I have felt,
Not seldom even in that tempestuous time,   550
Those hallowed and pure motions of the sense
Which seem, in their simplicity, to own
An intellectual[9] charm; that calm delight
Which, if I err not, surely must belong
To those first-born affinities that fit   555
Our new existence to existing things,
And, in our dawn of being, constitute
The bond of union between life and joy.

    Yes, I remember when the changeful earth,
And twice five summers on my mind had stamped   560
The faces of the moving year, even then
I held unconscious intercourse with beauty
Old as creation, drinking in a pure
Organic pleasure from the silver wreaths
Of curling mist, or from the level plain   565
Of waters colored by impending[1] clouds.

---

7. Wordsworth referred both to a single "Spirit" or "Soul" of the universe as a whole (e.g., lines 401–2, above) and to plural "Presences" and "Souls" inanimating the various parts of the universe. See the earlier version of this passage in *The Prelude* of 1799 (above), I.186 ff.
8. The passion at first was "extrinsic" because felt not for nature itself, but for nature as associated with the outdoor activities he loved. He now goes on to distinguish other "subtler" pleasures, felt in the very process of sensing the natural objects themselves.
9. As though they were abstract concepts rather than sensations.
1. Overhanging.

The sands of Westmoreland, the creeks and bays
Of Cumbria's[2] rocky limits, they can tell
How, when the Sea threw off his evening shade,
And to the shepherd's hut on distant hills   570
Sent welcome notice of the rising moon,
How I have stood, to fancies such as these
A stranger, linking with the spectacle
No conscious memory of a kindred sight,
And bringing with me no peculiar sense   575
Of quietness or peace; yet have I stood,
Even while mine eye hath moved o'er many a league[3]
Of shining water, gathering as it seemed,
Through every hairbreadth in that field of light,
New pleasure like a bee among the flowers.   580

　　Thus oft amid those fits of vulgar[4] joy
Which, through all seasons, on a child's pursuits
Are prompt attendants, 'mid that giddy bliss
Which, like a tempest, works along the blood
And is forgotten; even then I felt   585
Gleams like the flashing of a shield—the earth
And common face of Nature spake to me
Rememberable things; sometimes, 'tis true,
By chance collisions and quaint accidents
(Like those ill-sorted unions, work supposed   590
Of evil-minded fairies), yet not vain
Nor profitless, if haply they impressed
Collateral[5] objects and appearances,
Albeit lifeless then, and doomed to sleep
Until maturer seasons called them forth   595
To impregnate and to elevate the mind.
—And if the vulgar joy by its own weight
Wearied itself out of the memory,
The scenes which were a witness of that joy
Remained in their substantial lineaments   600
Depicted on the brain, and to the eye
Were visible, a daily sight; and thus
By the impressive discipline of fear,
By pleasure and repeated happiness,
So frequently repeated, and by force   605
Of obscure feelings representative
Of things forgotten, these same scenes so bright,
So beautiful, so majestic in themselves,
Though yet the day was distant, did become
Habitually dear, and all their forms   610
And changeful colors by invisible links
Were fastened to the affections. * * *

---

2. Cumberland's.
3. Approximately three miles.
4. Ordinary.
5. Accompanying but subordinate.

From *Book II. Schooltime* (*continued*)

Blest the infant Babe
(For with my best conjecture I would trace
Our Being's earthly progress),[1] blest the Babe,
Nursed in his Mother's arms, who sinks to sleep   235
Rocked on his Mother's breast; who with his soul
Drinks in the feelings of his Mother's eye!
For him, in one dear Presence, there exists
A virtue which irradiates and exalts
Objects through widest intercourse of sense.   240
No outcast he, bewildered and depressed:
Along his infant veins are interfused
The gravitation and the filial bond
Of nature that connect him with the world.
Is there a flower, to which he points with hand   245
Too weak to gather it, already love
Drawn from love's purest earthly fount for him
Hath beautified that flower; already shades
Of pity cast from inward tenderness
Do fall around him upon aught that bears   250
Unsightly marks of violence or harm.
Emphatically such a Being lives,
Frail creature as he is, helpless as frail,
An inmate of this active universe.
For feeling has to him imparted power   255
That through the growing faculties of sense
Doth like an agent of the one great Mind
Create, creator and receiver both,
Working but in alliance with the works
Which it beholds.[2]—Such, verily, is the first   260
Poetic spirit of our human life,
By uniform control of after years,
In most, abated or suppressed; in some,
Through every change of growth and of decay,
Pre-eminent till death. * * *   265

'Twere long to tell
What spring and autumn, what the winter snows,
And what the summer shade, what day and night,

---

1. Like the modern psychologist, Wordsworth recognized the importance of earliest infancy in the development of the individual mind, although he had then to invent the terms with which to analyze infant psychology. See the early version of this passage, *The Two-Part Prelude* (above), II.267 ff.
2. The infant, in the sense of security and love shed by his mother's presence on outer things, perceives what would otherwise be an alien world as a place to which he has a relationship like that of a son to a mother (lines 238–44). On such grounds Wordsworth asserts that the mind partially creates, by altering, the world it seems simply to perceive. In the succeeding passage (lines 360–74) Wordsworth repeats this concept in various metaphors signifying the give-and-take of outer world and inner mind and emotion.

Evening and morning, sleep and waking, thought 355
From sources inexhaustible, poured forth
To feed the spirit of religious love
In which I walked with Nature. But let this
Be not forgotten, that I still retained
My first creative sensibility;[3] 360
That by the regular action of the world
My soul was unsubdued. A plastic[4] power
Abode with me; a forming hand, at times
Rebellious, acting in a devious mood;
A local spirit of his own, at war 365
With general tendency, but, for the most,
Subservient strictly to external things
With which it communed. An auxiliar light
Came from my mind, which on the setting sun
Bestowed new splendor; the melodious birds, 370
The fluttering breezes, fountains that run on
Murmuring so sweetly in themselves, obeyed
A like dominion, and the midnight storm
Grew darker in the presence of my eye:
Hence my obeisance, my devotion hence, 375
And hence my transport.
               Nor should this, perchance,
Pass unrecorded, that I still had loved
The exercise and produce of a toil,
Than analytic industry to me
More pleasing, and whose character I deem 380
Is more poetic as resembling more
Creative agency. The song would speak
Of that interminable building reared
By observation of affinities
In objects where no brotherhood exists 385
To passive minds. My seventeenth year was come;
And, whether from this habit rooted now
So deeply in my mind, or from excess
In the great social principle of life
Coercing all things into sympathy, 390
To unorganic natures were transferred
My own enjoyments; or the power of truth
Coming in revelation, did converse
With things that really are;[5] I, at this time,
Saw blessings spread around me like a sea. 395
Thus while the days flew by, and years passed on,
From Nature and her overflowing soul,

3. I.e., the creative perception manifested by the babe in his mother's arms, above.
4. Shaping, formative.
5. Wordsworth is careful to indicate that there are alternative explanations for his sense that life pervades the inorganic as well as organic world: it may be the result either of a way of perceiving habitual since infancy, or of a projection of his own inner life, or it may be the perception of an objective truth.

I had received so much, that all my thoughts
Were steeped in feeling; I was only then
Contented, when with bliss ineffable   400
I felt the sentiment of Being spread
O'er all that moves and all that seemeth still;
O'er all that, lost beyond the reach of thought
And human knowledge, to the human eye
Invisible, yet liveth to the heart;   405
O'er all that leaps and runs, and shouts and sings,
Or beats the gladsome air; o'er all that glides
Beneath the wave, yea, in the wave itself,
And mighty depth of waters. Wonder not
If high the transport, great the joy I felt,   410
Communing in this sort through earth and heaven
With every form of creature, as it looked
Towards the Uncreated with a countenance
Of adoration, with an eye of love.[6]
One song they sang, and it was audible,   415
Most audible, then, when the fleshly ear,
O'ercome by humblest prelude of that strain,
Forgot her functions, and slept undisturbed.[7]

    If this be error, and another faith
Find easier access to the pious mind,   420
Yet were I grossly destitute of all
Those human sentiments that make this earth
So dear, if I should fail with grateful voice
To speak of you, ye mountains, and ye lakes
And sounding cataracts, ye mists and winds   425
That dwell among the hills where I was born.
If in my youth I have been pure in heart,
If, mingling with the world, I am content
With my own modest pleasures, and have lived
With God and Nature communing, removed   430
From little enmities and low desires,
The gift is yours; if in these times of fear,
This melancholy waste of hopes o'erthrown,
If, 'mid indifference and apathy,
And wicked exultation when good men   435
On every side fall off, we know not how,
To selfishness, disguised in gentle names
Of peace and quiet and domestic love,
Yet mingled not unwillingly with sneers
On visionary minds; if, in this time   440
Of dereliction and dismay, I yet
Despair not of our nature, but retain

6. Wordsworth did not add lines 412–14,   early version of this passage, see *The
giving a Christian frame to his experi-   Two-Part Prelude,* above, II.445 ff.
ence of the "one life," until the last re- 7. Cf. *Tintern Abbey,* lines 41–49.
vision of *The Prelude,* 1839. For the

A more than Roman confidence, a faith
That fails not, in all sorrow my support,
The blessing of my life; the gift is yours,   445
Ye winds and sounding cataracts! 'tis yours,
Ye mountains! thine, O Nature! Thou hast fed
My lofty speculations; and in thee,
For this uneasy heart of ours, I find
A never-failing principle of joy   450
And purest passion.

* * *

From *Book III. Residence at Cambridge*

The Evangelist St. John my patron was:[1]
Three Gothic courts are his, and in the first
Was my abiding place, a nook obscure;
Right underneath, the College kitchens made
A humming sound, less tunable than bees,   50
But hardly less industrious; with shrill notes
Of sharp command and scolding intermixed.
Near me hung Trinity's[2] loquacious clock,
Who never let the quarters, night or day,
Slip by him unproclaimed, and told the hours   55
Twice over with a male and female voice.
Her pealing organ was my neighbor too;
And from my pillow, looking forth by light
Of moon or favoring stars, I could behold
The antechapel where the statue stood   60
Of Newton with his prism and silent face,
The marble index of a mind forever
Voyaging through strange seas of Thought, alone.

Of College labors, of the Lecturer's room
All studded round, as thick as chairs could stand,   65
With loyal students faithful to their books,
Half-and-half idlers, hardy recusants,
And honest dunces—of important days,
Examinations, when the man was weighed
As in a balance! of excessive hopes,   70
Tremblings withal and commendable fears,
Small jealousies, and triumphs good or bad,
Let others that know more speak as they know.
Such glory was but little sought by me,
And little won. Yet from the first crude days   75
Of settling time in this untried abode,
I was disturbed at times by prudent thoughts,

1. Wordsworth was a student at St. John's College, Cambridge University, from 1787 to 1791.
2. Trinity College adjoins St. John's.

Roubiliac's statue of Newton, holding the prism with which he had conducted the experiments described in his *Optics*, stands in the west end of Trinity chapel.

Wishing to hope without a hope, some fears
About my future worldly maintenance,
And, more than all, a strangeness in the mind,   80
A feeling that I was not for that hour,
Nor for that place. * * *

    It hath been told that when the first delight
That flashed upon me from this novel show
Had failed, the mind returned into herself;
Yet true it is that I had made a change
In climate, and my nature's outward coat   205
Changed also slowly and insensibly.
Full oft the quiet and exalted thoughts
Of loneliness gave way to empty noise
And superficial pastimes; now and then
Forced labor, and more frequently forced hopes;   210
And, worst of all, a treasonable growth
Of indecisive judgments, that impaired
And shook the mind's simplicity.—And yet
This was a gladsome time. Could I behold—
Who, less insensible than sodden clay   215
In a sea river's bed at ebb of tide,
Could have beheld—with undelighted heart,
So many happy youths, so wide and fair
A congregation in its budding time
Of health, and hope, and beauty, all at once   220
So many divers samples from the growth
Of life's sweet season—could have seen unmoved
That miscellaneous garland of wild flowers
Decking the matron temples of a place
So famous through the world? To me, at least,   225
It was a goodly prospect: for, in sooth,
Though I had learnt betimes to stand unpropped,
And independent musings pleased me so
That spells seemed on me when I was alone,
Yet could I only cleave to solitude   230
In lonely places; if a throng was near
That way I leaned by nature; for my heart
Was social, and loved idleness and joy.

* * *

             Companionships,
Friendships, acquaintances, were welcome all.
We sauntered, played, or rioted;[3] we talked
Unprofitable talk at morning hours;
Drifted about along the streets and walks,
Read lazily in trivial books, went forth   250

---

3. This was a period of low ebb in the intellectual vigor and discipline of Cambridge, so that Wordsworth was able to indulge generously in the fringe activities of university life.

To gallop through the country in blind zeal
Of senseless horsemanship, or on the breast
Of Cam[4] sailed boisterously, and let the stars
Come forth, perhaps without one quiet thought.   255

* * *

Thus in submissive idleness, my Friend!
The laboring time of autumn, winter, spring,   630
Eight months! rolled pleasingly away; the ninth
Came and returned me to my native hills.

From *Book IV. Summer Vacation*[1]

Yes, that heartless chase
Of trivial pleasures was a poor exchange
For books and nature at that early age.
'Tis true some casual knowledge might be gained   300
Of character or life; but at that time,
Of manners put to school I took small note,
And all my deeper passions lay elsewhere.
Far better had it been to exalt the mind
By solitary study, to uphold   305
Intense desire through meditative peace;
And yet, for chastisement of these regrets,
The memory of one particular hour
Doth here rise up against me. 'Mid a throng
Of maids and youths, old men, and matrons staid,   310
A medley of all tempers, I had passed
The night in dancing, gaiety, and mirth,
With din of instruments and shuffling feet,
And glancing forms, and tapers glittering,
And unaimed prattle flying up and down;   315
Spirits upon the stretch, and here and there
Slight shocks of young love-liking interspersed,
Whose transient pleasure mounted to the head,
And tingled through the veins. Ere we retired,
The cock had crowed, and now the eastern sky   320
Was kindling, not unseen, from humble copse
And open field, through which the pathway wound,
And homeward led my steps. Magnificent
The morning rose, in memorable pomp,
Glorious as e'er I had beheld—in front,   325
The sea lay laughing at a distance; near,
The solid mountains shone, bright as the clouds,
Grain-tinctured,[2] drenched in empyrean light;
And in the meadows and the lower grounds
Was all the sweetness of a common dawn—   330

4. The river Cam, which flows through
Cambridge.
1. Wordsworth spent his first summer
vacation from the university at Hawkshead. In this passage he describes an
experience during the walk home after
an all-night dance.
2. Crimson. The "empyrean" was, in
ancient thought, the outer sphere of the
universe, composed of pure fire.

Dews, vapors, and the melody of birds,
And laborers going forth to till the fields.
Ah! need I say, dear Friend! that to the brim
My heart was full; I made no vows, but vows
Were then made for me; bond unknown to me   335
Was given, that I should be, else sinning greatly,
A dedicated Spirit. On I walked
In thankful blessedness, which yet survives.

* * *

From *Book V. Books*

          Oh! why hath not the Mind   45
Some element to stamp her image on
In nature somewhat nearer to her own?
Why, gifted with such powers to send abroad
Her spirit, must it lodge in shrines so frail?[1]

   One day, when from my lips a like complaint   50
Had fallen in presence of a studious friend,
He with a smile made answer, that in truth
'Twas going far to seek disquietude;
But on the front of his reproof confessed
That he himself had oftentimes given way   55
To kindred hauntings. Whereupon I told,
That once in the stillness of a summer's noon,
While I was seated in a rocky cave
By the seaside, perusing, so it chanced,
The famous history of the errant knight   60
Recorded by Cervantes,[2] these same thoughts
Beset me, and to height unusual rose,
While listlessly I sate, and, having closed
The book, had turned my eyes toward the wide sea.
On poetry and geometric truth,   65
And their high privilege of lasting life,
From all internal injury exempt,
I mused upon these chiefly; and at length,
My senses yielding to the sultry air,
Sleep seized me, and I passed into a dream.   70
I saw before me stretched a boundless plain
Of sandy wilderness, all black and void,
And as I looked around, distress and fear
Came creeping over me, when at my side,
Close at my side, an uncouth shape appeared   75
Upon a dromedary, mounted high.
He seemed an Arab of the Bedouin tribes:

1. Wordsworth is describing his recurrent fear that some holocaust might wipe out all books, the frail and perishable repositories of all man's wisdom and poetry.

2. I.e., Don Quixote. Wordsworth's nightmare involves all the elements of the poet's last waking experience. Mathematics had flourished among the Arabs —hence the Arabian rider (lines 75 ff.).

A lance he bore, and underneath one arm
A stone, and in the opposite hand a shell
Of a surpassing brightness. At the sight 80
Much I rejoiced, not doubting but a guide
Was present, one who with unerring skill
Would through the desert lead me; and while yet
I looked and looked, self-questioned what this freight
Which the newcomer carried through the waste 85
Could mean, the Arab told me that the stone
(To give it in the language of the dream)
Was "Euclid's Elements";[3] and "This," said he,
"Is something of more worth"; and at the word
Stretched forth the shell, so beautiful in shape, 90
In color so resplendent, with command
That I should hold it to my ear. I did so,
And heard that instant in an unknown tongue,
Which yet I understood, articulate sounds,
A loud prophetic blast of harmony; 95
An Ode, in passion uttered, which foretold
Destruction to the children of the earth
By deluge, now at hand. No sooner ceased
The song, than the Arab with calm look declared
That all would come to pass of which the voice 100
Had given forewarning, and that he himself
Was going then to bury those two books:
The one that held acquaintance with the stars,
And wedded soul to soul in purest bond
Of reason, undisturbed by space or time; 105
The other that was a god, yea, many gods,
Had voices more than all the winds, with power
To exhilarate the spirit, and to soothe,
Through every clime, the heart of human kind.
While this was uttering, strange as it may seem, 110
I wondered not, although I plainly saw
The one to be a stone, the other a shell;
Nor doubted once but that they both were books,
Having a perfect faith in all that passed.
Far stronger, now, grew the desire I felt 115
To cleave unto this man; but when I prayed
To share his enterprise, he hurried on
Reckless[4] of me: I followed, not unseen,
For oftentimes he cast a backward look,
Grasping his twofold treasure.—Lance in rest, 120
He rode, I keeping pace with him; and now
He, to my fancy, had become the knight
Whose tale Cervantes tells; yet not the knight,

---

3. Euclid was a Greek mathematician; his celebrated book on plane geometry and the theory of numbers continued to be used as a textbook into the 19th century.
4. Neglectful.

But was an Arab of the desert too;
Of these was neither, and was both at once.   125
His countenance, meanwhile, grew more disturbed;
And, looking backwards when he looked, mine eyes
Saw, over half the wilderness diffused,
A bed of glittering light: I asked the cause:
"It is," said he, "the waters of the deep   130
Gathering upon us"; quickening then the pace
Of the unwieldy creature he bestrode,
He left me: I called after him aloud;
He heeded not; but, with his twofold charge
Still in his grasp, before me, full in view,   135
Went hurrying o'er the illimitable waste,
With the fleet waters of a drowning world
In chase of him; whereat I waked in terror,
And saw the sea before me, and the book,
In which I had been reading, at my side.   140

* * *

There was a Boy:[5] ye knew him well, ye cliffs
And islands of Winander!—many a time   365
At evening, when the earliest stars began
To move along the edges of the hills,
Rising or setting, would he stand alone
Beneath the trees or by the glimmering lake,
And there, with fingers interwoven, both hands   370
Pressed closely palm to palm, and to his mouth
Uplifted, he, as through an instrument,
Blew mimic hootings to the silent owls,
That they might answer him; and they would shout
Across the watery vale, and shout again,   375
Responsive to his call, with quivering peals,
And long halloos and screams, and echoes loud,
Redoubled and redoubled, concourse wild
Of jocund din; and, when a lengthened pause
Of silence came and baffled his best skill,   380
Then sometimes, in that silence while he hung
Listening, a gentle shock of mild surprise
Has carried far into his heart the voice
Of mountain torrents; or the visible scene
Would enter unawares into his mind,   385
With all its solemn imagery, its rocks,
Its woods, and that uncertain heaven, received
Into the bosom of the steady lake.[6]

5. In an early MS version of this passage, Wordsworth slips from the third into the first-person pronoun; the experience he describes was thus apparently his own.
6. Coleridge wrote of the last line and a half ("that uncertain heaven * * * lake"): "Had I met these lines running wild in the deserts of Arabia, I should instantly have screamed out. 'Wordsworth.' "

This Boy was taken from his mates, and died
In childhood, ere he was full twelve years old.   390
Fair is the spot, most beautiful the vale
Where he was born; the grassy churchyard hangs
Upon a slope above the village school,
And through that churchyard when my way has led
On summer evenings, I believe that there   395
A long half hour together I have stood
Mute, looking at the grave in which he lies!

* * *

Here must we pause: this only let me add,
From heart experience, and in humblest sense   585
Of modesty, that he, who in his youth
A daily wanderer among woods and fields
With living Nature hath been intimate,
Not only in that raw unpracticed time
Is stirred to ecstasy, as others are,   590
By glittering verse; but further, doth receive,
In measure only dealt out to himself,
Knowledge and increase of enduring joy
From the great Nature that exists in works
Of mighty Poets.[7] Visionary power   595
Attends the motions of the viewless winds,
Embodied in the mystery of words:
There, darkness makes abode, and all the host
Of shadowy things work endless changes—there,
As in a mansion like their proper home,   600
Even forms and substances are circumfused
By that transparent veil with light divine,
And, through the turnings intricate of verse,
Present themselves as objects recognized,
In flashes, and with glory not their own.   605

From *Book VI. Cambridge and the Alps*

When the third summer freed us from restraint,[1]
A youthful friend, he too a mountaineer,
Not slow to share my wishes, took his staff,
And sallying forth, we journeyed side by side,   325
Bound to the distant Alps. A hardy slight
Did this unprecedented course imply
Of college studies and their set rewards;[2]

---

7. Having found a set of symbols in nature, Wordsworth now finds nature in the symbol systems of "mighty poets."
1. After reviewing briefly his second and third years at Cambridge, Wordsworth here describes his trip through France and Switzerland with a college friend, Robert Jones, in the succeeding summer vacation, 1790. France was then in the "golden hours" of the early period of the Revolution; the fall of the Bastille had occurred on July 14 of the preceding year.
2. English universities allow much longer vacations than those in America, on the optimistic assumption that they will be used primarily for intensive study. Wordsworth is facing his final examinations in the next college year.

Nor had, in truth, the scheme been formed by me
Without uneasy forethought of the pain,   330
The censures, and ill-omening, of those
To whom my worldly interests were dear.
But Nature then was sovereign in my mind,
And mighty forms, seizing a youthful fancy,
Had given a charter to irregular hopes.   335
In any age of uneventful calm
Among the nations, surely would my heart
Have been possessed by similar desire;
But Europe at that time was thrilled with joy,
France standing on the top of golden hours,   340
And human nature seeming born again.

* * *

When from the Vallais we had turned, and clomb
Along the Simplon's steep and rugged road,[3]
Following a band of muleteers, we reached
A halting place, where all together took
Their noontide meal. Hastily rose our guide,   565
Leaving us at the board; awhile we lingered,
Then paced the beaten downward way that led
Right to a rough stream's edge, and there broke off;
The only track now visible was one   570
That from the torrent's further brink held forth
Conspicuous invitation to ascend
A lofty mountain. After brief delay
Crossing the unbridged stream, that road we took,
And clomb with eagerness, till anxious fears   575
Intruded, for we failed to overtake
Our comrades gone before. By fortunate chance,
While every moment added doubt to doubt,
A peasant met us, from whose mouth we learned
That to the spot which had perplexed us first   580
We must descend, and there should find the road,
Which in the stony channel of the stream
Lay a few steps, and then along its banks;
And, that our future course, all plain to sight,
Was downwards, with the current of that stream.   585
Loath to believe what we so grieved to hear,
For still we had hopes that pointed to the clouds,
We questioned him again, and yet again;
But every word that from the peasant's lips
Came in reply, translated by our feelings,
Ended in this—*that we had crossed the Alps*.[4]   590

3. The Simplon Pass through the Alps.
4. As Dorothy Wordsworth baldly put
it later on, "The ambition of youth
was disappointed at these tidings." The
visionary experience that follows (lines
592–616) occurred not in the Alps but at
the time of writing the passage, as the
1805 text explicitly says: "Imagination!
lifting up itself / Before the eye and
progress of my Song."

Imagination —here the Power so called
Through sad incompetence of human speech,
That awful Power rose from the mind's abyss
Like an unfathered vapor[5] that enwraps,   595
At once, some lonely traveler. I was lost;
Halted without an effort to break through;
But to my conscious soul I now can say—
"I recognize thy glory": in such strength
Of usurpation, when the light of sense   600
Goes out, but with a flash that has revealed
The invisible world, doth greatness make abode,
There harbors; whether we be young or old,
Our destiny, our being's heart and home,
Is with infinitude, and only there;   605
With hope it is, hope that can never die,
Effort, and expectation, and desire,
And something evermore about to be.[6]
Under such banners militant, the soul
Seeks for no trophies, struggles for no spoils   610
That may attest her prowess, blest in thoughts
That are their own perfection and reward,
Strong in herself and in beatitude[7]
That hides her, like the mighty flood of Nile
Poured from his fount of Abyssinian clouds   615
To fertilize the whole Egyptian plain.

　　The melancholy slackening that ensued
Upon those tidings by the peasant given
Was soon dislodged. Downwards we hurried fast,
And, with the half-shaped road which we had missed,   620
Entered a narrow chasm. The brook and road
Were fellow travelers in this gloomy strait,
And with them did we journey several hours
At a slow pace. The immeasurable height
Of woods decaying, never to be decayed,   625
The stationary blasts of waterfalls,
And in the narrow rent at every turn
Winds thwarting winds, bewildered and forlorn,
The torrents shooting from the clear blue sky,
The rocks that muttered close upon our ears,   630
Black drizzling crags that spake by the wayside
As if a voice were in them, the sick sight
And giddy prospect of the raving stream,

5. Sudden vapor from no apparent source.
6. I.e., the imaginative vision reveals that his hitherto inexplicable disappointment—in that his hopes continued to point upward, although the trail led downward—signifies that man's glory and tragic dignity consist in sustaining the infinite striving of his insatiable spirit, against the inescapable limits of his mortal and finite possibilities.
7. The ultimate blessedness or happiness.

The unfettered clouds and region of the Heavens,
Tumult and peace, the darkness and the light—   635
Were all like workings of one mind, the features
Of the same face, blossoms upon one tree;
Characters of the great Apocalypse,[8]
The types and symbols of Eternity,
Of first, and last, and midst, and without end.[9]   640

* * *

From *Book VII. Residence in London*

Rise up, thou monstrous anthill on the plain
Of a too busy world![1] Before me flow,
Thou endless stream of men and moving things!   150
Thy everyday appearance, as it strikes—
With wonder heightened, or sublimed by awe—
On strangers, of all ages; the quick dance
Of colors, lights, and forms; the deafening din;
The comers and the goers face to face,   155
Face after face; the string of dazzling wares,
Shop after shop, with symbols, blazoned names,[2]
And all the tradesman's honors overhead:
Here, fronts of houses, like a title page,
With letters huge inscribed from top to toe,   160
Stationed above the door, like guardian saints;
There, allegoric shapes, female or male,
Or physiognomies of real men,
Land warriors, kings, or admirals of the sea,   165
Boyle,[3] Shakespeare, Newton, or the attractive head
Of some quack doctor, famous in his day.

* * *

As the black storm upon the mountaintop
Sets off the sunbeam in the valley, so   620
That huge fermenting mass of humankind
Serves as a solemn background, or relief,
To single forms and objects, whence they draw,
For feeling and contemplative regard,
More than inherent liveliness and power.   625
How oft, amid those overflowing streets,

8. The objects in this natural scene, exhibiting a coincidence of all opposites, are like the written words of the Apocalypse—i.e., of the Book of Revelation, the last book of the New Testament.
9. Cf. Revelation i.8: "I am Alpha and Omega, the beginning and the ending, saith the Lord"; the phrase is repeated in xxi.6, after the fulfillment of the last things. In *Paradise Lost* V.153–165 Milton says that the things created declare their Creator, and calls on all to extol

"him first, him last, him midst, and without end."
1. This is how London struck the young man from the country in the three and a half months he spent there in 1791.
2. The names ostentatiously inscribed on the shop signs.
3. Robert Boyle, the great 17th-century physicist and chemist. "Attractive": i.e., drawing people to him.

Have I gone forward with the crowd, and said
Unto myself, "The face of every one
That passes by me is a mystery!"
Thus have I looked, nor ceased to look, oppressed   630
By thoughts of what and whither, when and how,
Until the shapes before my eyes became
A second-sight procession, such as glides
Over still mountains, or appears in dreams;
And once, far-traveled in such mood, beyond   635
The reach of common indication, lost
Amid the moving pageant, I was smitten
Abruptly, with the view (a sight not rare)
Of a blind beggar, who, with upright face,
Stood, propped against a wall, upon his chest   640
Wearing a written paper, to explain
His story, whence he came, and who he was.
Caught by the spectacle my mind turned round
As with the might of waters; an apt type
This label seemed of the utmost we can know,   645
Both of ourselves and of the universe;
And, on the shape of that unmoving man,
His steadfast face and sightless eyes, I gazed,
As if admonished from another world.

* * *

           From these sights   675
Take one—that ancient festival, the Fair,
Holden where martyrs suffered in past time,
And named of St. Bartholomew;[4] there, see
A work completed to our hands, that lays,
If any spectacle on earth can do,   680
The whole creative powers of man asleep!—
For once, the Muse's help will we implore,
And she shall lodge us, wafted on her wings,
Above the press and danger of the crowd,
Upon some showman's platform. What a shock   685
For eyes and ears! what anarchy and din,
Barbarian and infernal—a phantasma,[5]
Monstrous in color, motion, shape, sight, sound!
Below, the open space, through every nook
Of the wide area, twinkles, is alive   690
With heads; the midway region, and above,

---

4. This huge fair was long held in Smithfield, the place where, on St. Bartholomew's Day, August 24, Protestants had been executed in Queen Mary's reign. The scene, which for Wordsworth laid "the whole creative powers of man asleep" (line 681), is exactly the kind that most stimulates those writers (including Chaucer, Shakespeare, and Dickens) who take inspiration from the vigor and bustle of variegated humanity. But "before it could touch [Wordsworth] near," as Walter Raleigh said, "an experience had to be simple and isolated."
5. Fantasy of a disordered mind.

Is thronged with staring pictures and huge scrolls,
Dumb proclamations of the Prodigies;
With chattering monkeys dangling from their poles,
And children whirling in their roundabouts;[6] 695
With those that stretch the neck and strain the eyes,
And crack the voice in rivalship, the crowd
Inviting; with buffoons against buffoons
Grimacing, writhing, screaming—him who grinds
The hurdy-gurdy, at the fiddle weaves, 700
Rattles the salt box, thumps the kettledrum,
And him who at the trumpet puffs his cheeks,
The silver-collared Negro with his timbrel,
Equestrians, tumblers, women, girls, and boys,
Blue-breeched, pink-vested, with high-towering plumes. 705
All movables of wonder, from all parts,
Are here—Albinos, painted Indians, Dwarfs,
The Horse of knowledge,[7] and the learned Pig,
The Stone-eater, the man that swallows fire,
Giants, Ventriloquists, the Invisible Girl, 710
The Bust that speaks and moves its goggling eyes,
The Waxwork, Clockwork, all the marvelous craft
Of modern Merlins,[8] Wild Beasts, Puppet-shows,
All out-o'-the-way, farfetched, perverted things,
All freaks of nature, all Promethean[9] thoughts 715
Of man, his dullness, madness, and their feats
All jumbled up together, to compose
A Parliament of Monsters. Tents and Booths
Meanwhile, as if the whole were one vast mill,
Are vomiting, receiving on all sides, 720
Men, Women, three-years' Children, Babes in arms.

Oh, blank confusion! true epitome
Of what the mighty City is herself
To thousands upon thousands of her sons,
Living amid the same perpetual whirl 725
Of trivial objects, melted and reduced
To one identity, by differences
That have no law, no meaning, and no end—
Oppression, under which even highest minds
Must labor, whence the strongest are not free. 730
But though the picture weary out the eye,
By nature an unmanageable sight,
It is not wholly so to him who looks
In steadiness, who hath among least things

6. Merry-go-rounds.
7. A horse trained to tap out answers
to numerical questions, etc.
8. Magicians. Merlin was the magician
in the Arthurian romances.

9. Creative, or highly inventive. Prometheus, in Greek mythology, made
man out of clay and taught him the
arts.

An under-sense of greatest; sees the parts 735
As parts, but with a feeling of the whole.

* * *

From *Book VIII. Retrospect—Love of Nature Leading to Love of Man*[1]

For me, when my affections first were led
From kindred, friends, and playmates, to partake
Love for the human creature's absolute self,
That noticeable kindliness of heart
Sprang out of fountains, there abounding most, 125
Where sovereign Nature dictated the tasks
And occupations which her beauty adorned,
And Shepherds were the men that pleased me first.

* * *

A rambling schoolboy, thus
I felt his presence in his own domain,
As of a lord and master, or a power,
Or genius, under Nature, under God,
Presiding; and severest solitude 260
Had more commanding looks when he was there.
When up the lonely brooks on rainy days
Angling I went, or trod the trackless hills
By mists bewildered, suddenly mine eyes
Have glanced upon him distant a few steps, 265
In size a giant, stalking through thick fog,
His sheep like Greenland bears; [1a] or, as he stepped
Beyond the boundary line of some hill-shadow,
His form hath flashed upon me, glorified
By the deep radiance of the setting sun;[2] 270
Or him have I descried in distant sky,
A solitary object and sublime,
Above all height! like an aerial cross
Stationed alone upon a spiry rock
Of the Chartreuse, for worship.[3] Thus was man 275

1. In this book Wordsworth reviews the first 21 years of his life in order to trace the transfer of his earlier feelings for nature to shepherds and other humble people who carry on their lonely duties almost as though they were moving parts of the landscape (cf. *Michael*, lines 1–39). Wordsworth's central concern is to describe the early development in his relatively inexperienced mind of an Image, or conceptual model, of the largeness, worth, and almost sacred dignity of generic Man (lines 256–81); an Image which proved invulnerable to the acid bath of his later experience of the vulgarity, meanness, and evil of which individual men are capable (lines 317–22).
1a. Polar bears.
2. A "glory" is a mountain phenomenon in which the enlarged figure of a man is seen projected by the sun upon the mist, with a radiance about its head. Cf. Coleridge's *Dejection,* line 54.
3. In his tour of the Alps Wordsworth had been deeply impressed by the Chartreuse, a Carthusian monastery in

Ennobled outwardly before my sight,
And thus my heart was early introduced
To an unconscious love and reverence
Of human nature; hence the human form
To me became an index of delight,   280
Of grace and honor, power and worthiness.
Meanwhile this creature—spiritual almost
As those of books, but more exalted far;
Far more of an imaginative form
Than the gay Corin[4] of the groves, who lives   285
For his own fancies, or to dance by the hour,
In coronal, with Phyllis in the midst—
Was, for the purposes of kind,[5] a man
With the most common; husband, father; learned,
Could teach, admonish; suffered with the rest   290
From vice and folly, wretchedness and fear;
Of this I little saw, cared less for it,
But something must have felt.

                    Call ye these appearances—
Which I beheld of shepherds in my youth,
This sanctity of Nature given to man—   295
A shadow, a delusion, ye who pore
On the dead letter, miss the spirit of things;
Whose truth is not a motion or a shape
Instinct with vital functions, but a block
Or waxen image which yourselves have made,   300
And ye adore! But blessed be the God
Of Nature and of Man that this was so;
That men before my inexperienced eyes
Did first present themselves thus purified,
Removed, and to a distance that was fit: 305
And so we all of us in some degree
Are led to knowledge, whencesoever led,
And howsoever; were it otherwise,
And we found evil fast as we find good
In our first years, or think that it is found,   310
How could the innocent heart bear up and live!
But doubly fortunate my lot; not here
Alone, that something of a better life
Perhaps was round me than it is the privilege
Of most to move in, but that first I looked   315
At Man through objects that were great or fair;
First communed with him by their help. And thus
Was founded a sure safeguard and defense
Against the weight of meanness, selfish cares,

the French Alps, with its soaring cross
visible against the sky. There is an
overtone here of the Christlike divinity
investing the "common" man (line
289).
4. "Corin" and "Phyllis," dancing in
their "coronals," or wreaths of flowers,
were stock characters in earlier pastoral literature.
5. I.e., in carrying out the tasks of
humankind.

Coarse manners, vulgar passions, that beat in   320
On all sides from the ordinary world
In which we traffic. * * *

    Yet deem not, Friend! that human kind with me   340
Thus early took a place pre-eminent;
Nature herself was, at this unripe time,
But secondary to my own pursuits
And animals activities, and all
Their trivial pleasures;[6] and when these had drooped   345
And gradually expired, and Nature, prized
For her own sake, became my joy, even then—
And upwards through late youth, until not less
Than two-and-twenty summers had been told—
Was Man in my affections and regards   350
Subordinate to her, her visible forms
And viewless agencies: a passion, she,
A rapture often, and immediate love
Ever at hand; he, only a delight
Occasional, an accidental grace,   355
His hour being not yet come. * * *

From *Book IX. Residence in France*[1]

    France lured me forth; the realm that I had crossed
So lately, journeying toward the snow-clad Alps.
But now, relinquishing the scrip and staff,[2]   35
And all enjoyment which the summer sun
Sheds round the steps of those who meet the day
With motion constant as his own, I went
Prepared to sojourn in a pleasant town,   40
Washed by the current of the stately Loire.[3]

    Through Paris lay my readiest course, and there
Sojourning a few days, I visited,
In haste, each spot of old or recent fame,
The latter chiefly; from the field of Mars   45
Down to the suburbs of St. Antony,
And from Mont Martyr southward to the Dome
Of Geneviève.[4] In both her clamorous Halls,

6. Cf, Wordsworth's account of the stages of his development in *Tintern Abbey*, lines 65–92 and note.
1. Wordsworth's second visit to France, while he was 21 and 22 years of age (1791–92), came during a crucial period of the French Revolution. This book deals with Wordsworth's stay at Paris, Orléans, and Blois, when he developed his passionate partisanship for the French people and the revolutionary cause.
2. The "scrip" (the bag or knapsack) and the "staff" are the traditional emblems of the foot pilgrim.
3. Orléans, on the Loire river, where Wordsworth stayed from late November, 1791, until he moved to Blois early the next year.
4. The "field of Mars" (the Champ de Mars), where Louis XVI swore fidelity to the new constitution. "The suburbs of St. Anthony": Faubourg St. Antoine, near the Bastille, a working-class quarter and center of revolutionary violence. "Mont Martyr": Montmartre, a hill on which revolutionary meetings were held. The "dome of Geneviève" became the Panthéon, a burial place for notable Frenchmen.

The National Synod[5] and the Jacobins,
I saw the Revolutionary Power   50
Toss like a ship at anchor, rocked by storms;
The Arcades I traversed, in the Palace huge
Of Orléans;[6] coasted round and round the line
Of Tavern, Brothel, Gaming-house, and Shop,
Great rendezvous of worst and best, the walk   55
Of all who had a purpose, or had not;
I stared and listened, with a stranger's ears,
To Hawkers and Haranguers, hubbub wild!
And hissing Factionists with ardent eyes,
In knots, or pairs, or single. Not a look   60
Hope takes, or Doubt or Fear is forced to wear,
But seemed there present; and I scanned them all,
Watched every gesture uncontrollable,
Of anger, and vexation, and despite,
All side by side, and struggling face to face,   65
With gaiety and dissolute idleness.

   Where silent zephyrs sported with the dust
Of the Bastille, I sate in the open sun,
And from the rubbish gathered up a stone,
And pocketed the relic, in the guise   70
Of an enthusiast: yet, in honest truth,
I looked for something that I could not find,
Affecting more emotion than I felt;
For 'tis most certain that these various sights,
However potent their first shock, with me   75
Appeared to recompense the traveler's pains
Less than the painted Magdalene of Le Brun,[7]
A beauty exquisitely wrought, with hair
Disheveled, gleaming eyes, and rueful cheek
Pale and bedropped with overflowing tears.   80

                    * * *

                    For myself, I fear   110
Now in connection with so great a theme
To speak (as I must be compelled to do)
Of one so unimportant; night by night
Did I frequent the formal haunts of men,
Whom, in the city, privilege of birth   115
Sequestered from the rest, societies
Polished in arts, and in punctilio[8] versed;
Whence, and from deeper causes, all discourse
Of good and evil of the time was shunned

5. The newly formed National Assembly. "Jacobins": the club of radical democratic revolutionists, named for the ancient convent of St. Jacques, their meeting place.
6. The arcades in the courtyard of the Palais Royal, a shopping center and Parisian rendezvous.
7. A theatrical painting of the weeping Mary Magdalene by Charles Le Brun (1619–90), then regarded as a religious masterpiece.
8. The niceties of social manners.

With scrupulous care; but these restrictions soon   120
Proved tedious, and I gradually withdrew
Into a noisier world, and thus ere long
Became a patriot;[9] and my heart was all
Given to the people, and my love was theirs.

* * *

Among that band of Officers was one,
Already hinted at, of other mold—
A patriot, thence rejected by the rest,   290
And with an oriental loathing spurned,
As of a different caste.[1] A meeker man
Than this lived never, nor a more benign,
Meek though enthusiastic. Injuries
Made *him* more gracious, and his nature then   295
Did breathe its sweetness out most sensibly,
As aromatic flowers on Alpine turf,
When foot hath crushed them. He through the events
Of that great change wandered in perfect faith,
As through a book, an old romance, or tale   300
Of Fairy, or some dream of actions wrought
Behind the summer clouds. By birth he ranked
With the most noble, but unto the poor
Among mankind he was in service bound,
As by some tie invisible, oaths professed   305
To a religious order. Man he loved
As man; and, to the mean and the obscure,
And all the homely[2] in their homely works,
Transferred a courtesy which had no air
Of condescension; but did rather seem   310
A passion and a gallantry, like that
Which he, a soldier, in his idler day
Had paid to woman: somewhat vain he was,
Or seemed so, yet it was not vanity,
But fondness, and a kind of radiant joy   315
Diffused around him, while he was intent
On works of love or freedom, or revolved
Complacently[3] the progress of a cause,
Whereof he was a part: yet this was meek
And placid, and took nothing from the man   320
That was delightful. Oft in solitude
With him did I discourse about the end
Of civil government, and its wisest forms;
Of ancient loyalty, and chartered rights,
Custom and habit, novelty and change;   325
Of self-respect, and virtue in the few

9. A republican in politics.
1. This memorable character sketch is of Michel Beaupuy, fifteen years older than Wordsworth, and one of the rare republicans among the officer corps of the regular army. By doctrine and force of character he did much to shape Wordsworth's radical sympathies.
2. Lowly.
3. With quiet satisfaction.

For patrimonial honor set apart,
And ignorance in the laboring multitude.
For he, to all intolerance indisposed,
Balanced these contemplations in his mind;   330
And I, who at that time was scarcely dipped
Into the turmoil, bore a sounder judgment
Than later days allowed; carried about me,
With less alloy to its integrity,
The experience of past ages, as, through help   335
Of books and common life, it makes sure way
To youthful minds, by objects over near
Not pressed upon, nor dazzled or misled
By struggling with the crowd for present ends.

* * *

Yet not the less,
Hatred of absolute rule, where will of one
Is law for all, and of that barren pride
In them who, by immunities unjust,
Between the sovereign and the people stand,   505
His helper and not theirs, laid stronger hold
Daily upon me, mixed with pity too
And love; for where hope is, there love will be
For the abject multitude. And when we chanced
One day to meet a hunger-bitten girl,   510
Who crept along fitting her languid gait
Unto a heifer's motion, by a cord
Tied to her arm, and picking thus from the lane
Its sustenance, while the girl with pallid hands
Was busy knitting in a heartless mood   515
Of solitude, and at the sight my friend
In agitation said, " 'Tis against *that*
That we are fighting," I with him believed
That a benignant spirit was abroad
Which might not be withstood, that poverty   520
Abject as this would in a little time
Be found no more, that we should see the earth
Unthwarted in her wish to recompense
The meek, the lowly, patient child of toil,
All institutes forever blotted out   525
That legalized exclusion, empty pomp
Abolished, sensual state and cruel power
Whether by edict of the one or few;
And finally, as sum and crown of all,
Should see the people having a strong hand   530
In framing their own laws; whence better days
To all mankind.[4] * * *

4. The following political aims constituted the radicalism of Wordsworth and Beaupuy: elimination of the extreme of poverty; the rewards of tillage to go to the tiller of the land; all careers opened to talents; abolition of absolute power, whether by a monarch or an oligarchy; and a greatly extended franchise.

From *Book X. Residence in France (continued)*[1]

Cheered with this hope,[2] to Paris I returned,
And ranged, with ardor heretofore unfelt,
The spacious city, and in progress passed   50
The prison[3] where the unhappy Monarch lay,
Associate with his children and his wife
In bondage; and the palace, lately stormed
With roar of cannon by a furious host.
I crossed the square (an empty area then!)   55
Of the Carrousel, where so late had lain
The dead, upon the dying heaped, and gazed
On this and other spots, as doth a man
Upon a volume whose contents he knows
Are memorable, but from him locked up,   60
Being written in a tongue he cannot read,
So that he questions the mute leaves with pain,
And half upbraids their silence. But that night
I felt most deeply in what world I was,
What ground I trod on, and what air I breathed.   65
High was my room and lonely, near the roof
Of a large mansion or hotel, a lodge
That would have pleased me in more quiet times;
Nor was it wholly without pleasure then.
With unextinguished taper I kept watch,   70
Reading at intervals; the fear gone by
Pressed on me almost like a fear to come.
I thought of those September massacres,
Divided from me by one little month,
Saw them and touched:[4] the rest was conjured up   75
From tragic fictions or true history,
Remembrances and dim admonishments.
The horse is taught his manage,[5] and no star
Of wildest course but treads back his own steps;
For the spent hurricane the air provides   80
As fierce a successor; the tide retreats
But to return out of its hiding place
In the great deep; all things have second birth;
The earthquake is not satisfied at once;
And in this way I wrought upon myself,   85
Until I seemed to hear a voice that cried,

1. At this period, October, 1792–August, 1794, Wordsworth's revolutionary enthusiasm was at its height.
2. The Parisian mob had stormed the Tuileries; the king had been deposed and imprisoned; and the Commune had organized the "September Massacres," in which 3,000 Royalist suspects were murdered. Wordsworth's "hope" was that the moderates were now taking over and would eliminate further violence.

3. I.e., the "Temple," where Louis XVI was held prisoner. "The palace" is the Tuileries; in front of this is the great square of "the Carrousel," where a number of the mob storming the palace had been killed.
4. I.e., his imagination of the September Massacres was so vivid as to be palpable.
5. The French *manège*, the prescribed action and paces of a trained horse.

To the whole city, "Sleep no more." The trance
Fled with the voice to which it had given birth;
But vainly comments of a calmer mind
Promised soft peace and sweet forgetfulness.
The place, all hushed and silent as it was,   90
Appeared unfit for the repose of night,
Defenseless as a wood where tigers roam.

* * *

           In this frame of mind,
Dragged by a chain of harsh necessity,
So seemed it—now I thankfully acknowledge,
Forced by the gracious providence of Heaven—
To England I returned,[6] else (though assured   225
That I both was and must be of small weight,
No better than a landsman on the deck
Of a ship struggling with a hideous storm)
Doubtless, I should have then made common cause
With some who perished; haply perished too,   230
A poor mistaken and bewildered offering—
Should to the breast of Nature have gone back,
With all my resolutions, all my hopes,
A Poet only to myself, to men
Useless, and even, belovéd Friend! a soul   235
To thee unknown![7] * * *

What, then, were my emotions, when in arms
Britain put forth her freeborn strength in league,
Oh, pity and shame! with those confederate Powers![8]   265
Not in my single self alone I found,
But in the minds of all ingenuous youth,
Change and subversion from that hour. No shock
Given to my moral nature had I known
Down to that very moment; neither lapse   270
Nor turn of sentiment that might be named
A revolution, save at this one time;
All else was progress on the selfsame path
On which, with a diversity of pace,
I had been traveling: this a stride at once   275
Into another region. As a light
And pliant harebell, swinging in the breeze
On some gray rock—its birthplace—so had I

6. Forced by the "harsh necessity" of
a lack of money, Wordsworth returned
to England late in 1792.
7. Wordsworth did not meet Coleridge,
the "belovéd Friend," until 1795.
8. England joined the war against
France in February, 1793. The great
moral crisis which almost wrecked
Wordsworth's life began with this sudden split between his profound attachments to the English land (the development of which he had described in

the early books of *The Prelude*) and
his later but heartfelt identification
with the cause of the French Revolution. What had seemed a single and
coherent development suddenly became
split into conflicting parts. The moral
turmoil he goes on to describe is remarkably parallel to that of many
young radicals of the 1930's and later,
who had staked their hopes for mankind on the Russian Revolution.

Wantoned, fast rooted on the ancient tower
Of my belovéd country, wishing not   280
A happier fortune than to wither there:
Now was I from that pleasant station torn
And tossed about in whirlwind. I rejoiced,
Yea, afterwards—truth most painful to record!—
Exulted, in the triumph of my soul,   285
When Englishmen by thousands were o'erthrown,
Left without glory on the field, or driven,
Brave hearts! to shameful flight.⁹ It was a grief—
Grief call it not, 'twas anything but that—
A conflict of sensations without name,   290
Of which *he* only, who may love the sight
Of a village steeple, as I do, can judge,
When, in the congregation bending all
To their great Father, prayers were offered up,
Or praises for our country's victories;   295
And, 'mid the simple worshipers, perchance
I only, like an uninvited guest
Whom no one owned, sate silent, shall I add,
Fed on the day of vengeance yet to come.

* * *

Most melancholy at that time, O Friend!
Were my day thoughts—my nights were miserable;¹⁰
Through months, through years, long after the last beat
Of those atrocities, the hour of sleep   400
To me came rarely charged with natural gifts,
Such ghastly visions had I of despair
And tyranny, and implements of death;
And innocent victims sinking under fear,
And momentary hope, and worn-out prayer,   405
Each in his separate cell, or penned in crowds
For sacrifice, and struggling with fond mirth
And levity in dungeons, where the dust
Was laid with tears. Then suddenly the scene
Changed, and the unbroken dream entangled me   410
In long orations, which I strove to plead
Before unjust tribunals—with a voice
Laboring, a brain confounded, and a sense,
Deathlike, of treacherous desertion, felt
In the last place of refuge—my own soul.   415

* * *

From *Book XI. France (concluded)*¹

O pleasant exercise of hope and joy!   105
For mighty were the auxiliars which then stood

9. The French defeated the English in the battle of Hondschoote, September 6, 1793.
10. The Reign of Terror, under Robes-pierre, had begun with the execution of the moderate Girondist leaders in October and November, 1793.
1. Book XI deals with the year from

Upon our side, us who were strong in love!
Bliss was it in that dawn to be alive,
But to be young was very Heaven! O times,
In which the meager, stale, forbidding ways   110
Of custom, law, and statute, took at once
The attraction of a country in romance!
When Reason seemed the most to assert her rights
When most intent on making of herself
A prime enchantress—to assist the work,   115
Which then was going forward in her name!
Not favored spots alone, but the whole Earth,
The beauty wore of promise—that which sets
(As at some moments might not be unfelt
Among the bowers of Paradise itself)   120
The budding rose above the rose full blown.[2]
What temper at the prospect did not wake
To happiness unthought of? The inert
Were roused, and lively natures rapt away!
They who had fed their childhood upon dreams,   125
The playfellows of fancy, who had made
All powers of swiftness, subtlety, and strength
Their ministers—who in lordly wise had stirred
Among the grandest objects of the sense,
And dealt with whatsoever they found there   130
As if they had within some lurking right
To wield it—they, too, who of gentle mood
Had watched all gentle motions, and to these
Had fitted their own thoughts, schemers more mild,
And in the region of their peaceful selves—   135
Now was it that *both* found, the meek and lofty
Did both find helpers to their hearts' desire,
And stuff at hand, plastic as they could wish—
Were called upon to exercise their skill,
Not in Utopia, subterranean fields,   140
Or some secreted island, Heaven knows where!
But in the very world, which is the world
Of all of us—the place where, in the end,
We find our happiness, or not at all!

Why should I not confess that Earth was then   145
To me, what an inheritance, new-fallen,
Seems, when the first time visited, to one
Who thither comes to find in it his home?
He walks about and looks upon the spot

August, 1794, through September, 1795: Wordsworth's growing disillusionment with the French Revolution, his recourse to abstract theories of man and politics, his despair and nervous breakdown, and the beginning of his recovery when he moved from London to Racedown.
2. A statement of the Romantic theme of the glory of the imperfect, which sets a higher value on promise than on achievement.

Bu. .ort, molds it and remolds,
Frenchm. .th things that are amiss,
For one of .o. them disappear.

* * *

But in the ey... . in their turn,
Of a false liberty. .. f self-defense
Striving to hide no. take. .ounted up,
Of mortified presum. .nought c. .. . While resen.
More firmly to old tenets; .dhered. ..
Their temper, strained them .ore; and thus, in .. .nds
Of contest, did opinions every day .. .cat.
Grow into consequence, till round my mind
They clung, as if they .ere its life, nay more,
The very being of the immortal soul.

210

215

220

* *

I summoned my best skill, and .. .led, intent
To anatomize the frame of socia. .fe,
Yea, the whole body of society
Searched to its heart.[5] Share with me, h. .d! the wish
That some dramatic tale, endued with shap.
Livelier, and flinging out less guarded words
Than suit the work we fashion, might set forth
What then I learned, or think I learned, of truth,
And the errors into which I fell, betrayed
By present objects, and by reasonings false
From their beginnings, inasmuch as drawn
Out of a heart that had been turned aside
From Nature's way by outward accidents,
And which was thus confounded, more and more
Misguided, and misguiding. So I fared,
Dragging all precepts, judgments, maxims, creeds,
Like culprits to the bar; calling the mind,
Suspiciously, to establish in plain day
Her titles and her honors; now believing,
Now disbelieving; endlessly perplexed

280

285

290

295

3. In late 1794 and early 1795 French troops had successes in Spain, Italy, Holland, and Germany.
4. I.e., the desire for power now outweighed the love of liberty.
5. Disappointed in the course of the actual Revolution, Wordsworth turned to the theories of William Godwin and other philosophers of the Enlighten-

ment. These theorists attempted to deduce the laws of ethics and government from rational premises; they fatally omitted, as Wordsworth later maintained, to take account of the moral promptings and loyalties of man's "heart"—i.e., of his instinctual and feelingful nature (see lines 353–56).

With impulse, motive, right and ...
Of obligation, what the rule a...
The sanction; till, demanding ...
And seeking it in everything, ...
All feeling of conviction, ... despair.
Sick, wearied out with ... strong disea...
Yielded up moral q... west ebb; I d...

This was the ... reason of leas...
This the soul's ...
Deeming our ...
Where wan...   305

Thank ... he bounteous spea...
The day ... here
T... admonition—like a book   335
That did b... cross a lonely road, and now
Is seen, heard, felt, and caught at every turn,
Companion never lost through many a league—   340
Maintained for me a saving intercourse
With my true self;[8] for, though ... dimmed and changed
Much, as it seemed, I was ... further changed
Than as a clouded and ... ing moon;
She whispered still ... l, preserved me still   345
She, in the midst ... seek beneath that name,
A Poet, made ... my office upon earth;
And that al... as hereafter will be shown,
And, last, as hereafter will be shown,
If willing audience fail not, Nature's self,   350
B... all varieties of human love
Assisted, led me back through opening day
To those sweet counsels between head and heart
Whence grew that genuine knowledge, fraught with peace,
Which, through the later sinkings of this cause,   355
Hath still upheld me, and upholds me now
In the catastrophe (for so they dream,
And nothing less), when, finally to close
And seal up all the gains of France, a Pope
Is summoned in, to crown an Emperor[9] * * *   360

6. At last.
7. After a long separation, from 1791 to 1794. Dorothy Wordsworth came to live with her brother at Racedown in 1795, and continued a member of his household until her death.
8. Dorothy and the renewed influence of nature (line 350) healed the inner fracture between his earlier and later self, which Wordsworth had described in Book X, lines 268 ff.
9. The ultimate blow to liberal hopes for France when, on December 2, 1804, Napoleon summoned Pope Pius VII to officiate at the ceremony elevating him to Emperor. At the last moment, Napoleon took the crown and donned it himself.

With cordial transport, molds it and remolds,   150
And is half-pleased with things that are amiss,
'Twill be such joy to see them disappear.

* * *

But now, become oppressors in their turn,
Frenchmen had changed a war of self-defense
For one of conquest,[3] losing sight of all
Which they had struggled for: now mounted up,
Openly in the eye of earth and heaven,   210
The scale of liberty.[4] I read her doom.
With anger vexed, with disappointment sore,
But not dismayed, nor taking to the shame
Of a false prophet. While resentment rose,
Striving to hide, what nought could heal, the wounds   215
Of mortified presumption, I adhered
More firmly to old tenets, and, to prove
Their temper, strained them more; and thus, in heat
Of contest, did opinions every day
Grow into consequence, till round my mind   220
They clung, as if they were its life, nay more,
The very being of the immortal soul.

* * *

I summoned my best skill, and toiled, intent
To anatomize the frame of social life,   280
Yea, the whole body of society
Searched to its heart.[5] Share with me, Friend! the wish
That some dramatic tale, endued with shapes
Livelier, and flinging out less guarded words
Than suit the work we fashion, might set forth   285
What then I learned, or think I learned, of truth,
And the errors into which I fell, betrayed
By present objects, and by reasonings false
From their beginnings, inasmuch as drawn
Out of a heart that had been turned aside   290
From Nature's way by outward accidents,
And which was thus confounded, more and more
Misguided, and misguiding. So I fared,
Dragging all precepts, judgments, maxims, creeds,
Like culprits to the bar; calling the mind,   295
Suspiciously, to establish in plain day
Her titles and her honors; now believing,
Now disbelieving; endlessly perplexed

3. In late 1794 and early 1795 French troops had successes in Spain, Italy, Holland, and Germany.
4. I.e., the desire for power now outweighed the love of liberty.
5. Disappointed in the course of the actual Revolution, Wordsworth turned to the theories of William Godwin and other philosophers of the Enlighten-ment. These theorists attempted to deduce the laws of ethics and government from rational premises; they fatally omitted, as Wordsworth later maintained, to take account of the moral promptings and loyalties of man's "heart"—i.e., of his instinctual and feelingful nature (see lines 353–56).

With impulse, motive, right and wrong, the ground
Of obligation, what the rule and whence
The sanction; till, demanding formal *proof*,   300
And seeking it in everything, I lost
All feeling of conviction, and, in fine,[6]
Sick, wearied out with contrarieties,
Yielded up moral questions in despair.   305

This was the crisis of that strong disease,
This the soul's last and lowest ebb; I drooped,
Deeming our blessed reason of least use
Where wanted most * * *

Then it was—
Thanks to the bounteous Giver of all good!—
That the belovéd Sister[7] in whose sight   335
Those days were passed, now speaking in a voice
Of sudden admonition—like a brook
That did but *cross* a lonely road, and now
Is seen, heard, felt, and caught at every turn,
Companion never lost through many a league—   340
Maintained for me a saving intercourse
With my true self;[8] for, though bedimmed and changed
Much, as it seemed, I was no further changed
Than as a clouded and a waning moon;
She whispered still that brightness would return;   345
She, in the midst of all, preserved me still
A Poet, made me seek beneath that name,
And that alone, my office upon earth;
And, lastly, as hereafter will be shown,
If willing audience fail not, Nature's self,   350
By all varieties of human love
Assisted, led me back through opening day
To those sweet counsels between head and heart
Whence grew that genuine knowledge, fraught with peace,
Which, through the later sinkings of this cause,   355
Hath still upheld me, and upholds me now
In the catastrophe (for so they dream,
And nothing less), when, finally to close
And seal up all the gains of France, a Pope
Is summoned in, to crown an Emperor[9] * * *   360

---

6. At last.
7. After a long separation, from 1791 to 1794, Dorothy Wordsworth came to live with her brother at Racedown in 1795, and continued a member of his household until her death.
8. Dorothy and the renewed influence of nature (line 350) healed the inner fracture between his earlier and later self, which Wordsworth had described in Book X, lines 268 ff.
9. The ultimate blow to liberal hopes for France when, on December 2, 1804, Napoleon summoned Pope Pius VII to officiate at the ceremony elevating him to Emperor. At the last moment, Napoleon took the crown and donned it himself.

From *Book XII. Imagination and Taste,*
How Impaired and Restored[1]

There are in our existence spots of time,
That with distinct pre-eminence retain
A renovating virtue, whence—depressed   210
By false opinion and contentious thought,
Or aught of heavier or more deadly weight,
In trivial occupations, and the round
Of ordinary intercourse—our minds
Are nourished and invisibly repaired;   215
A virtue, by which pleasure is enhanced,
That penetrates, enables us to mount,
When high, more high, and lifts us up when fallen.
This efficacious spirit chiefly lurks
Among those passages of life that give   220
Profoundest knowledge to what point, and how,
The mind is lord and master—outward sense
The obedient servant of her will. Such moments
Are scattered everywhere, taking their date
From our first childhood. I remember well,   225
That once, while yet my inexperienced hand
Could scarcely hold a bridle, with proud hopes
I mounted, and we journeyed towards the hills:
An ancient servant of my father's house
Was with me, my encourager and guide;   230
We had not traveled long, ere some mischance
Disjoined me from my comrade; and, through fear
Dismounting, down the rough and stony moor
I led my horse, and, stumbling on, at length
Came to a bottom, where in former times   235
A murderer had been hung in iron chains.
The gibbet-mast had moldered down, the bones
And iron case were gone; but on the turf,
Hard by, soon after that fell deed was wrought,
Some unknown hand had carved the murderer's name.   240
The monumental letters were inscribed
In times long past; but still, from year to year

1. Book XII reviews the "impairment" and gradual recovery of Wordsworth's creative sensibility in response to the natural world; its climax is the famed description of the "spots of time." These are moments of experience of what is in itself ordinary (line 254), but becomes luminous with a profound significance that, since it is bestowed by the perceiver, evidences the freedom and creative power of the imaginative mind (lines 220–23, 275–77). The recollection of such scenes nourishes and repairs the mind in those periods of depression or distraction when the imagination flags (lines 210–215). Wordsworth also recognizes (lines 277–86) that the recollection of such spots of time from his own early experience is the source of his greatest poetry, and that this source is not inexhaustible.

For Wordsworth's terse early description of these two spots of time, see *The Two-Part Prelude*, I.288–372 and the note to line 288.

By superstition of the neighborhood,
The grass is cleared away, and to this hour
The characters are fresh and visible: 245
A casual glance had shown them, and I fled,
Faltering and faint, and ignorant of the road;
Then, reascending the bare common, saw
A naked pool that lay beneath the hills,
The beacon on the summit, and more near,   250
A girl, who bore a pitcher on her head,
And seemed with difficult steps to force her way
Against the blowing wind. It was, in truth,
An ordinary sight; but I should need
Colors and words that are unknown to man,   255
To paint the visionary dreariness
Which, while I looked all round for my lost guide,
Invested moorland waste and naked pool,
The beacon crowning the lone eminence,
The female and her garments vexed and tossed   260
By the strong wind. When, in the blessed hours
Of early love, the loved one at my side,
I roamed, in daily presence of this scene,
Upon the naked pool and dreary crags,
And on the melancholy beacon, fell   265
A spirit of pleasure and youth's golden gleam;
And think ye not with radiance more sublime
For these remembrances, and for the power
They had left behind? So feeling comes in aid
Of feeling, and diversity of strength   270
Attends us, if but once we have been strong.
Oh! mystery of man, from what a depth
Proceed thy honors. I am lost, but see
In simple childhood something of the base
On which thy greatness stands; but this I feel,   275
That from thyself it comes, that thou must give,
Else never canst receive. The days gone by
Return upon me almost from the dawn
Of life: the hiding places of man's power
Open; I would approach them, but they close.   280
I see by glimpses now; when age comes on,
May scarcely see at all; and I would give,
While yet we may, as far as words can give,
Substance and life to what I feel, enshrining,
Such is my hope, the spirit of the Past   285
For future restoration.—Yet another
Of these memorials:
                          One Christmas time,[2]
On the glad eve of its dear holidays,

---

2. In 1813; Wordsworth was thirteen, and at Hawkshead School with two of his brothers.

Feverish, and tired, and restless, I went forth   290
Into the fields, impatient for the sight
Of those led palfreys[3] that should bear us home;
My brothers and myself. There rose a crag,
from the meeting point of two highways   295
Rising, overlooked them both, far stretched;
Tempt uncertain on which road to fix
I sate half-shelter'd the summit; 'twas a day
Upon my right hand wild, and on the grass   300
Upon my left a blasted naked wall;
With those companions shed a single sheep,
Straining my eyes intensely, side, I watched,
Gave intermitting prospect of the mist
And plain beneath. Ere we to school returned—   305
That dreary time—ere we had been ten days
Sojourners in my father's house, he died;
And I and my three brothers, orphans then,
Followed his body to the grave. The event,
With all the sorrow that it brought, appeared   310
A chastisement; and when I called to mind
That day so lately passed, when from the crag
I looked in such anxiety of hope,
With trite reflections of morality,
Yet in the deepest passion, I bowed low   315
To God, who thus corrected my desires;
And, afterwards, the wind and sleety rain,
And all the business of the elements,
The single sheep, and the one blasted tree,
And the bleak music from that old stone wall,   320
The noise of wood and water, and the mist
That on the line of each of those two roads
Advanced in such indisputable shapes;[4]
All these were kindred spectacles and sounds
To which I oft repaired, and thence would drink,   325
As at a fountain; and on winter nights,
Down to this very time, when storm and rain
Beat on my roof, or, haply, at noonday,
While in a grove I walk, whose lofty trees,
Laden with summer's thickest foliage, rock   330
In a strong wind, some working of the spirit,
Some inward agitations thence are brought,
Whate'er their office, whether to beguile
Thoughts over busy in the course they took,
Or animate an hour of vacant ease.   335

3. Small saddle horses.   4. I.e., shapes one didn't dare question.

From Book XIII. Imagination and Taste,
How Impaired and Restored (concluded)[1]

Here, calling up to mind what then I saw,
A youthful traveler, and see daily now
In the familiar circuit of my home,
Here might I pause, and bend in reverence   225
To Nature, and the power of human
To men as they are men within themselves—
How oft high service is performed within,
When all the external man is rude in gold,
Not like a temple rich with pomp protects   230
But a mere mountain chapel, and shower.
Its simple worshipers from song; of these,
Of these, said I, shall be for the task,
If future years mature me for the task,
Will I record the praises, making verse   235
Deal boldly with substantial things; in truth
And sanctity of passion, speak of these,
That justice may be done, obeisance paid
Where it *is* due: thus haply shall I teach,
Inspire; through unadulterated ears
Pour rapture, tenderness, and hope—my theme   240
No other than the very heart of man,
As found among the best of those who live,
Not unexalted by religious faith,
Nor uninformed by books, good books, though few,
In Nature's presence; thence may I select   245
Sorrow, that is not sorrow, but delight;
And miserable love, that is not pain
To hear of, for the glory that redounds
Therefrom to human kind, and what we are.
Be mine to follow with no timid step   250
Where knowledge leads me: it shall be my pride
That I have dared to tread this holy ground,
Speaking no dream, but things oracular;
Matter not lightly to be heard by those
Who to the letter of the outward promise   255
Do read the invisible soul;[2] by men adroit
In speech, and for communion with the world
Accomplished; minds whose faculties are then

1. Wordsworth has described, as part of his imaginative recovery, his learning to look again with sympathy upon "the unassuming things that hold / A silent station in this beauteous world," and his finding again "in Man an object of delight." Now he shows how, in reaction against his concern with great actions detached from moral purpose which constituted the French Revolution, he came to embrace the poetic doctrines of the Preface to *Lyrical Ballads*. He will write of simple, lowly men, whose patient endurance of suffering redounds to the glory of human kind, and who speak a language which is the spontaneous overflow of powerful feeling (lines 263–64).
2. I.e., this doctrine will not be lightly accepted by those who judge a man's inner worth by his exterior seeming.

Most active when they are most eloquent,
And elevated most when most admired.   260
Men may be found of other mold than these,
Who are their own upholders, to themselves
Encouragement, and energy, and will,
Expressing liveliest thoughts in lively words
As native passion dictates. * * *   265

From *Book XIV. Conclusion*

In one of those excursions (may they ne'er
Fade from remembrance!) through the northern tracts
Of Cambria ranging with a youthful friend,[1]
I left Bethgelert's huts at couching time,
And westward took my way, to see the sun   5
Rise, from the top of Snowdon. To the door
Of a rude cottage at the mountain's base
We came, and roused the shepherd who attends
The adventurous stranger's steps, a trusty guide;
Then, cheered by short refreshment, sallied forth.   10

It was a close, warm, breezeless summer night,
Wan, dull, and glaring, with a dripping fog
Low-hung and thick that covered all the sky;
But, undiscouraged, we began to climb
The mountainside. The mist soon girt us round,   15
And, after ordinary travelers' talk
With our conductor, pensively we sank
Each into commerce with his private thoughts;
Thus did we breast the ascent, and by myself
Was nothing either seen or heard that checked   20
Those musings or diverted, save that once
The shepherd's lurcher,[2] who, among the crags,
Had to his joy unearthed a hedgehog, teased
His coiled-up prey with barkings turbulent.
This small adventure, for even such it seemed   25
In that wild place and at the dead of night,
Being over and forgotten, on we wound
In silence as before. With forehead bent
Earthward, as if in opposition set
Against an enemy, I panted up   30
With eager pace, and no less eager thoughts.
Thus might we wear a midnight hour away,
Ascending at loose distance each from each,

1. Wordsworth climbed Mt. Snowdon, the highest peak in Wales ("Cambria"), with Robert Jones, the friend with whom he had also tramped through the Alps (Book VI). The climb started from the village of Bethgelert at "couching time," the time of night when the sheep lie down to sleep. This event had taken place in 1791 (or possibly 1793); Wordsworth presents it out of its chronological order to introduce at this point a great natural "type" or "emblem" (lines 66, 70) for the mind, and especially for the activity of the imagination, whose "restoration" he has described in the two preceding books.
2. A crossbred dog, used to hunt hares.

And I, as chanced, the foremost of the band;
When at my feet the ground appeared to brighten,   35
And with a step or two seemed brighter still;
Nor was time given to ask or learn the cause,
For instantly a light upon the turf
Fell like a flash, and lo! as I looked up,
The Moon hung naked in a firmament   40
Of azure without cloud, and at my feet
Rested a silent sea of hoary mist.
A hundred hills their dusky backs upheaved
All over this still ocean; and beyond,
Far, far beyond, the solid vapors stretched,   45
In headlands, tongues, and promontory shapes,
Into the main Atlantic, that appeared
To dwindle, and give up his majesty,
Usurped upon far as the sight could reach.
Not so the ethereal vault; encroachment none   50
Was there, nor loss;[3] only the inferior stars
Had disappeared, or shed a fainter light
In the clear presence of the full-orbed Moon,
Who, from her sovereign elevation, gazed
Upon the billowy ocean, as it lay   55
All meek and silent, save that through a rift—
Not distant from the shore whereon we stood,
A fixed, abysmal, gloomy, breathing-place—
Mounted the roar of waters, torrents, streams
Innumerable, roaring with one voice!   60
Heard over earth and sea, and, in that hour,
For so it seemed, felt by the starry heavens.

    When into air had partially dissolved
That vision, given to spirits of the night
And three chance human wanderers, in calm thought   65
Reflected, it appeared to me the type
Of a majestic intellect, its acts
And its possessions, what it has and craves,
What in itself it is, and would become.
There I beheld the emblem of a mind   70
That feeds upon infinity, that broods
Over the dark abyss, intent to hear
Its voices issuing forth to silent light
In one continuous stream; a mind sustained
By recognitions of transcendent power,   75
In sense conducting to ideal form,
In soul of more than mortal privilege.[4]
One function, above all, of such a mind
Had Nature shadowed there, by putting forth,

3. The mist projected in various shapes over the Atlantic Ocean, but did not "encroach" upon the heavens overhead.
4. The sense of lines 74–77 seems to be that the mind of a man who is gifted beyond the ordinary lot of mortals recognizes its power to transcend the senses by converting sensory objects into ideal forms.

'Mid circumstances awful and sublime,   80
That mutual domination which she loves
To exert upon the face of outward things,
So molded, joined, abstracted, so endowed
With interchangeable supremacy,
That men, least sensitive, see, hear, perceive,   85
And cannot choose but feel. The power, which all
Acknowledge when thus moved, which Nature thus
To bodily sense exhibits, is the express
Resemblance of that glorious faculty
That higher minds bear with them as their own.[5]   90
This is the very spirit in which they deal
With the whole compass of the universe:
They from their native selves can send abroad
Kindred mutations; for themselves create
A like existence; and, whene'er it dawns   95
Created for them, catch it, or are caught
By its inevitable mastery,
Like angels stopped upon the wing by sound
Of harmony from Heaven's remotest spheres.
Them the enduring and the transient both   100
Serve to exalt; they build up greatest things
From least suggestions; ever on the watch,
Willing to work and to be wrought upon,
They need not extraordinary calls
To rouse them; in a world of life they live,   105
By sensible impressions not enthralled,
But by their quickening impulse made more prompt
To hold fit converse with the spiritual world,
And with the generations of mankind
Spread over time, past, present, and to come,   110
Age after age, till Time shall be no more.
Such minds are truly from the Deity,
For they are Powers; and hence the highest bliss
That flesh can know is theirs—the consciousness
Of Whom they are, habitually infused   115
Through every image and through every thought,
And all affections[6] by communion raised
From earth to heaven, from human to divine;
Hence endless occupation for the Soul,
Whether discursive or intuitive;[7]   120
Hence cheerfulness for acts of daily life,
Emotions which best foresight need not fear,
Most worthy then of trust when most intense.

5. The "glorious faculty" is the imagination, which in its exhibition of mastery over sense—through its power to alter and re-create what is given to it in perception (lines 93–106)—is analogous to that aspect of the outer scene, in which the ordinary landscape is transfigured by the moonlit mist. Compare the mind as "lord and master" of outward sense in Book XII, lines 221–23.
6. Feelings, emotions.
7. An echo of *Paradise Lost* V.488. The "discursive" reason undertakes to reach truths through a logical sequence of premises, observations, and conclusions; the "intuitive" reason comprehends truths immediately.

Hence, amid ills that vex and wrongs that crush
Our hearts—if here the words of Holy Writ   125
May with fit reverence be applied—that peace
Which passeth understanding,[8] that repose
**In moral judgments which from this pure source
Must come, or will by man be sought in vain.**

Oh! who is he that hath his whole life long
Preserved, enlarged, this freedom in himself?
For this alone is genuine liberty:
Where is the favored being who hath held
That course unchecked, unerring, and untired,
In one perpetual progress smooth and bright?—   135
A humbler destiny have we retraced,
And told of lapse and hesitating choice,
And backward wanderings along thorny ways:
Yet—compassed round by mountain solitudes,
Within whose solemn temple I received   140
My earliest visitations, careless then
Of what was given me; and which now I range,
A meditative, oft a suffering man—
Do I declare—in accents which, from truth
Deriving cheerful confidence, shall blend   145
Their modulation with these vocal streams—
That, whatsoever falls my better mind,
Revolving with the accidents of life,
May have sustained, that, howsoe'er misled,
**Never did I, in quest of right and wrong,
Tamper with conscience from a private aim;
Nor was in any public hope the dupe
Of selfish passions; nor did ever yield
Willfully to mean cares or low pursuits,
But shrunk with apprehensive jealousy   155
From every combination which might aid
The tendency, too potent in itself,
Of use and custom to bow down the soul
Under a growing weight of vulgar sense,
And substitute a universe of death   160
For that which moves with light and life informed,
Actual, divine, and true.** To fear and love,
To love as prime and chief, for there fear ends,
Be this ascribed;[9] to early intercourse,

8. Philippians iv.7: "the peace of God, which passeth all understanding." This passage of Christian piety was added by Wordsworth in a late revision.
9. Wordsworth's mind, he had said early in *The Prelude*, had been "fostered alike by beauty and by fear" (I.302 and footnote); that is, by the opposing but equally necessary principles of the beautiful and terrifying, or "sublime," aspects of nature. Now, in his conclusion, the principles of fear and pain are said to be mistakenly equated with "evil," and to be ultimately transcended by their "adverse principles" of love and joy. This passage is equivalent to the theodicy of *Paradise Lost*—Milton's justification of evil and pain ("the ways of God to men," I.26) by reference to the fall and redemption—but is translated by Wordsworth into a natural theodicy of the interaction of man's mind with the external world. Cf. the Prospectus to *The Recluse*, above, lines 8–9, and the title footnote.

In presence of sublime or beautiful forms,   165
With the adverse principles of pain and joy—
Evil as one is rashly named by men
Who know not what they speak. By love subsists
All lasting grandeur, by pervading love;
That gone, we are as dust. * * *   170

    This spiritual Love acts not nor can exist
Without Imagination,[1] which, in truth,
Is but another name for absolute power   190
And clearest insight, amplitude of mind,
And Reason in her most exalted mood.
This faculty hath been the feeding source
Of our long labor: we have traced the stream
From the blind cavern whence is faintly heard   195
Its natal murmur; followed it to light
And open day; accompanied its course
Among the ways of Nature, for a time
Lost sight of it bewildered and engulfed;
Then given it greeting as it rose once more   200
In strength, reflecting from its placid breast
The works of man and face of human life;
And lastly, from its progress have we drawn
Faith in life endless, the sustaining thought
Of human Being, Eternity, and God.[2]   205

    Imagination having been our theme,
So also hath that intellectual Love,
For they are each in each, and cannot stand
Dividually.[3]—Here must thou be, O Man!
Power to thyself; no Helper hast thou here;   210
Here keepest thou in singleness thy state:
No other can divide with thee this work:
No secondary hand can intervene
To fashion this ability; 'tis thine,
The prime and vital principle is thine   215
In the recesses of thy nature, far
From any reach of outward fellowship,
Else is not thine at all. * * *

    And now, O Friend![4] this history is brought
To its appointed close: the discipline
And consummation of a Poet's mind,
In everything that stood most prominent,   305
Have faithfully been pictured; we have reached
The time (our guiding object from the first)

---

1. Cf. Shelley's *Defense of Poetry*: "The great secret of morals is love; or a going out of our own nature. * * * The great instrument of moral good is the imagination."
2. In the 1805 version, this read: "The feeling of life endless, the great thought / By which we live, Infinity and God."
3. Separately.
4. Coleridge, to whom the "thy" in lines 431–32 also refers.

When we may, not presumptuously, I hope,
Suppose my powers so far confirmed, and such
My knowledge, as to make me capable   310
Of building up a work that shall endure.

* * *

Having now
Told what best merits mention, further pains   370
Our present purpose seems not to require,
And I have other tasks. Recall to mind
The mood in which this labor was begun,
O Friend! The termination of my course
Is nearer now, much nearer; yet even then,   375
In that distraction and intense desire,
I said unto the life which I had lived,
Where art thou? Hear I not a voice from thee
Which 'tis reproach to hear?[5] Anon I rose
As if on wings, and saw beneath me stretched   380
Vast prospect of the world which I had been
And was; and hence this Song, which like a lark
I have protracted, in the unwearied heavens
Singing, and often with more plaintive voice
To earth attempered and her deep-drawn sighs,   385
Yet centering all in love, and in the end
All gratulant, if rightly understood.[6]

* * *

Oh! yet a few short years of useful life,   430
And all will be complete, thy race be run,
Thy monument of glory will be raised;
Then, though (too weak to tread the ways of truth)
This age fall back to old idolatry,
Though men return to servitude as fast   435
As the tide ebbs, to ignominy and shame,
By nations sink together,[7] we shall still
Find solace—knowing what we have learnt to know,
Rich in true happiness if allowed to be
Faithful alike in forwarding a day   440
Of firmer trust, joint laborers in the work
(Should Providence such grace to us vouchsafe)
Of their deliverance, surely yet to come.

5. As he approaches the end, Wordsworth recalls the beginning of *The Prelude*. The reproachful voice is that which
asked the question, "Was it for this?" in
I.269 ff. This query called forth a vision
of his remembered life, which he proceeded to explore in search both of the
sources of his poetic powers and the impediments to their fulfillment. The
"song" describing this quest, which he
then began, is the poem he is now completing.

6. Gratulant: expressive of joy. The poet
finds that suffering and frustration are
justified, when seen as part of the over-
all design of the life he has just reviewed. The passage echoes the conclusion of Pope's theodicy (the justification
of evil) in *An Essay on Man*, I.291–92:
"All discord, harmony not understood; /
All partial evil, universal good."
7. I.e., though men—whole nations of
them together—sink to ignominy and
shame.

Prophets of Nature, we to them will speak
A lasting inspiration, sanctified   **445**
By reason, blest by faith: what we have loved,
Others will love, and we will teach them how;
Instruct them how the mind of man becomes
A thousand times more beautiful than the earth
On which he dwells, above this frame of things
(Which, 'mid all revolution in the hopes
And fears of men, doth still remain unchanged)
In beauty exalted, as it is itself
Of quality and fabric more divine.[8]

1798–1839   1850

---

8. Cf. Wordsworth's assertion that "the Mind of Man" is "My haunt, and the main region of my song" in the Prospectus to *The Recluse*, lines 40–41.

DOROTHY WORDSWORTH

(1771–1855)

Dorothy Wordsworth has an enduring place in English literature even though she wrote not a single word for publication. Not until long after her death did scholars gradually retrieve and print her letters, a few poems (one written for children in her brother's household), and above all a series of journals that she kept sporadically between 1798 and 1828 because, she wrote, "I shall give William Pleasure by it." It has always been known, from tributes to her by Wordsworth and Coleridge, that she exerted an important influence on the lives and writings of both these men. It is now apparent that she also possessed a power exceeding that of the two poets for precise observation of people and the natural world, together with a genius for terse, luminous, and delicately nuanced description in prose. Her hastily scribbled journals are an incomparable record of what Coleridge, in *Frost at Midnight* called "all the numberless goings on of life" in "sea, hill, and wood" as well as in the "populous village," as noted by one who lived her life among rural folk, and as reflected in her own ardent and compassionate spirit.

Dorothy was born on Christmas day, 1771, 21 months after William; she was the only girl of five Wordsworth children. From her seventh year, when her mother died, she lived with various relatives—some of them tolerant and affectionate, others rigid and tyrannical—and saw William and her other brothers only occasionally, during the boys' summer vacations from school. In 1795, when she was 24, the bequest to William by Raisely Calvert enabled her to carry out a long-held plan to join her brother in a cottage at Racedown, and the two spent the rest of their long lives together, first in Dorsetshire, then in their beloved Lake Country.

Suddenly, after a severe illness in 1835, Dorothy suffered a physical and mental collapse, which is now diagnosed as the result of a hardening of arteries in the brain. She spent the rest of her existence in bed or in a wheelchair, huddled over a blazing fire even in the hottest weather. Hardest for her family to endure was the drastic change in her temperament: from a high-spirited and uncomplaining woman she became (save for brief intervals of lucidity) torpid, querulous, demanding. In this half-life she lingered for 20 years, attended devotedly by William until his death five years before her own in 1855.

Our selections are from the journal Dorothy kept in 1798 at Alfoxden, Somersetshire, where the Wordsworths had moved from Racedown in order to be near Coleridge at Nether Stowey, as well as from her journals while at Grasmere, (1800–1803), with Coleridge residing some 13 miles away at Greta Hall, Keswick. This is the period when both men emerged as major poets, and in their achievements Dorothy played an indispensable role. In Book XI of *The Prelude* Wordsworth says that, in the time of his spiritual crisis, Dorothy "maintained for me a saving intercourse / With my true self" and "preserved me still a Poet"; and, in a letter of 1797, Coleridge stressed the delicacy and tact in the response of Wordsworth's "exquisite sister" to the world of sense: "Her manners are simple, ardent, impressive. . . . Her information various—her eye watchful in minutest observation of nature—and her taste a perfect electrometer—it bends, protrudes, and draws in, at subtlest beauties & most recondite faults.

The passages from the journals reprinted below include many verbal sketches of natural appearances which turn up also in Wordsworth's and Coleridge's poems. Of at least equal importance for Wordsworth was their chronicling of the busy wayfaring life of rural England in the early 19th century. These were exceedingly hard times for country people, when the remorseless displacement of small farms and of household crafts by large-scale farms and mass industries was accelerated by the economic distress caused by protracted Continental wars. (See Wordsworth's comment in *The Ruined Cottage*, above, lines 133 ff.) Peddlers, maimed war veterans, leech-gatherers, adult and infant beggars, ousted farm families, fugitives, women abandoned by husbands or lovers streamed endlessly along the rural roads and into Wordsworth's brooding poetic imagination—often by way of Dorothy's prose records.

The excerpts from the journals also show the intensity of Dorothy's love for her brother. Inevitably, in our era, the mutual devotion of the orphaned brother and sister has evoked psychoanalytic speculation. It is important to note, however, that Mary Hutchinson, a gentle and open-hearted girl, had been Dorothy's closest friend ever since childhood, and that Dorothy encouraged Wordsworth's courtship and marriage, even though she realized that it entailed her own displacement as the focus of her brother's life. All the evidence indicates that their life in a single household never strained the affectionate relationship between the two women; indeed, Dorothy, until she became an invalid, added to her former functions as Wordsworth's chief support, adviser, and amanuensis a loving ministration to her brother's children.

Since the manuscript of the Alfoxden journal has disappeared, the text below is from the transcript published by William Knight in 1897. The selections from the Grasmere journals reproduce Mary Moorman's exact reprint of the manuscripts in the Wordsworth Library at Dove Cottage (Oxford University Press, 1971).

From The Alfoxden Journal

Jan. 31, 1798. Set forward to Stowey[1] at half-past five. A violent storm in the wood; sheltered under the hollies. When we left home the moon immensely large, the sky scattered over with clouds. These soon closed in, contracting the dimensions of the moon without concealing her.[2] The sound of the pattering shower, and the gusts of wind, very grand. Left the wood when nothing remained of the storm but the driving wind, and a few scattering drops of rain. Presently all clear, Venus first showing herself between the struggling clouds; afterwards Jupiter appeared. The hawthorn hedges, black and pointed, glittering with millions of diamond drops; the hollies shining with broader patches of light. The road to the village of Holford glittered like another stream. On our return, the wind high—a violent storm of hail and rain at the Castle of Comfort.[3] All the Heavens seemed in one perpetual motion when the rain ceased; the moon appearing, now half veiled, and now retired behind heavy clouds, the stars still moving, the roads very dirty.

* * *

Feb. 3. A mild morning, the windows open at breakfast, the redbreasts singing in the garden. Walked with Coleridge over the hills. The sea at first obscured by vapour; that vapour afterwards slid in one mighty mass along the sea-shore; the islands and one point of land clear beyond it. The distant country (which was purple in the clear dull air), overhung by straggling clouds that sailed over it, appeared like the darker clouds, which are often seen at a great distance apparently motionless, while the nearer ones pass quickly over them, driven by the lower winds. I never saw such a union of earth, sky, and sea. The clouds beneath our feet spread themselves to the water, and the clouds of the sky almost joined them. Gathered sticks in the wood; a perfect stillness. The redbreasts sang upon the leafless boughs. Of a great number of sheep in the field, only one standing. Returned to dinner at five o'clock. The moonlight still and warm as a summer's night at nine o'clock.

Feb. 4. Walked a great part of the way to Stowey with Coleridge. The morning warm and sunny. The young lasses seen on the hill-tops, in the villages and roads, in their summer holiday clothes—pink petticoats and blue. Mothers with their children in arms, and the little ones that could just walk, tottering by their side. Midges or small flies spinning in the sunshine; the songs of the lark and redbreast; daisies upon the turf; the hazels in blossom; honeysuckles budding. I saw one solitary strawberry flower under a hedge.

---

1. Coleridge's cottage at Nether Stowey, three miles from Alfoxden.
2. See Coleridge's *Christabel*, lines 16–19.

3. A tavern, halfway between Holford and Nether Stowey.

The furze gay with blossom. The moss rubbed from the pailings by the sheep, that leave locks of wool, and the red marks with which they are spotted, upon the wood.[4]

* * *

Feb. 8. Went up the Park, and over the tops of the hills, till we came to a new and very delicious pathway, which conducted us to the Coombe.[5] Sat a considerable time upon the heath. Its surface restless and glittering with the motion of the scattered piles of withered grass, and the waving of the spiders' threads.[6] On our return the mist still hanging over the sea, but the opposite coast clear, and the rocky cliffs distinguishable. In the deep Coombe, as we stood upon the sunless hill, we saw miles of grass, light and glittering, and the insects passing.

Feb. 9. William gathered sticks.

Feb. 10. Walked to Woodlands, and to the waterfall. The adder's-tongue and the ferns green in the low damp dell. These plants now in perpetual motion from the current of the air; in summer only moved by the drippings of the rocks.[7] A cloudy day.

* * *

Mar. 7. William and I drank tea at Coleridge's. A cloudy sky. Observed nothing particularly interesting—the distant prospect obscured. One only leaf upon the top of a tree—the sole remaining leaf—danced round and round like a rag blown by the wind.[8]

Mar. 8. Walked in the Park in the morning. I sate under the fir trees. Coleridge came after dinner, so we did not walk again. A foggy morning, but a clear sunny day.

Mar. 9. A clear sunny morning, went to meet Mr and Mrs Coleridge. The day very warm.

Mar. 10. Coleridge, Wm, and I walked in the evening to the top of the hill. We all passed the morning in sauntering about the park and gardens, the children playing about, the old man at the top of the hill gathering furze; interesting groups of human creatures, the young frisking and dancing in the sun, the elder quietly drinking in the life and soul of the sun and air.

Mar. 11. A cold day. The children went down towards the sea. William and I walked to the top of the hills above Holford. Met the blacksmith. Pleasant to see the labourer on Sunday jump with the friskiness of a cow upon a sunny day.

* * *

1798   1897

4. See Wordsworth's *The Ruined Cottage*, lines 330–336.
5. Hodder's Combe in the Quantock Hills, near Alfoxden; a "combe" (pronounced "koom") is a deep valley on the flank of a hill.
6. Cf. Coleridge's *The Ancient Mariner*, line 184: "Like restless gossameres."
7. See the description of the dell in Coleridge's *This Lime-Tree Bower*, lines 13–20.
8. Cf. *Christabel*, lines 49 ff.: "The one red leaf, the last of its clan. . . ."

From The Grasmere Journals

1800

May. 14. Wm and John set off into Yorkshire[1] after dinner at
½ past 2 o'clock, cold pork in their pockets. I left them at the turning of the Low-wood bay under the trees. My heart was so full that
I could hardly speak to W. when I gave him a farewell kiss. I sate a
long time upon a stone at the margin of the lake, and after a flood
of tears my heart was easier. The lake looked to me I knew not why
dull and melancholy, and the weltering on the shores seemed a
heavy sound. I walked as long as I could amongst the stones of the
shore. The wood rich in flowers. A beautiful yellow, palish yellow
flower, that looked thick round and double, and smelt very sweet—I
supposed it was a ranunculus—Crowfoot, the grassy-leaved Rabbit-
toothed white flower, strawberries, geranium—scentless violet, anemones two kinds, orchises, primroses. The heckberry very beautiful,
the crab coming out as a low shrub. Met a blind man, driving a
very large beautiful Bull and a cow—he walked with two sticks.
Came home by Clappersgate. The valley very green, many sweet
views up to Rydale head when I could juggle away the fine houses,
but they disturbed me even more than when I have been happier.
One beautiful view of the Bridge, without Sir Michael's.[2] Sate
down very often, though it was cold. I resolved to write a journal of
the time till W. and J. return, and I set about keeping my resolve
because I will not quarrel with myself, and because I shall give Wm
Pleasure by it when he comes home again. At Rydale a woman of
the village, stout and well dressed, begged a halfpenny—she had
never she said done it before, but these hard times— —Arrived at
home with a bad head-ach, set some slips of privett. The evening
cold, had a fire—my face now flame-coloured. It is nine o'clock. I
shall soon go to bed. A young woman begged at the door—she had
come from Manchester on Sunday morn with two shillings and a
slip of paper which she supposed a Bank note—it was a cheat. She
had buried her husband and three children within a year and a half
—all in one grave—burying very dear—paupers all put in one place
—20 shillings paid for as much ground as will bury a man—a stone
to be put over it or the right will be lost—11/6 each time the
ground is opened. Oh! that I had a letter from William!

* * *

Oct. 3. Very rainy all the morning. Little Sally learning to mark.
Wm walked to Ambleside after dinner. I went with him part of the
way—he talked much about the object of his Essay for the 2nd

1. William and his younger brother,
John Wordsworth, on the way to visit
Mary Hutchinson, whom William was to
marry two years later.
2. Sir Michael le Fleming's estate, Rydal
Hall.

volume of LB.[3] I returned expecting the Simpsons—they did not come. I should have met Wm but my teeth ached and it was showery and late—he returned after 10. Amos Cottle's[4] death in the Morning Post. Wrote to S. Lowthian.[5]

N.B. When Wm and I returned from accompanying Jones we met an old man almost double,[6] he had on a coat thrown over his shoulders above his waistcoat and coat. Under this he carried a bundle and had an apron on and a night cap. His face was interesting. He had dark eyes and a long nose. John who afterwards met him at Wythburn took him for a Jew. He was of Scotch parents but had been born in the army. He had had a wife 'and a good woman and it pleased God to bless us with ten children'. All these were dead but one of whom he had not heard for many years, a sailor. His trade was to gather leeches, but now leeches are scarce and he had not strength for it. He lived by begging and was making his way to Carlisle where he should buy a few godly books to sell. He said leeches were very scarce partly owing to this dry season, but many years they have been scarce—he supposed it owing to their being much sought after, that they did not breed fast, and were of slow growth. Leeches were formerly 2/6 [per] 100; they are now 30/. He had been hurt in driving a cart, his leg broke his body driven over his skull fractured. He felt no pain till he recovered from his first insensibility. 'It was then late in the evening, when the light was just going away.'

* * *

Oct. 11. A fine October morning. Sat in the house working all the morning. Wm composing—Sally Ashburner learning to mark. After Dinner we walked up Greenhead Gill in search of a sheepfold.[7] We went by Mr Oliff's and through his woods. It was a delightful day and the views looked excessively chearful and beautiful chiefly that from Mr Oliff's field where our house is to be built. The colours of the mountains soft and rich, with orange fern—the Cattle pasturing upon the hill-tops Kites sailing as in the sky above our heads—Sheep bleating and in lines and chains and patterns scattered over the mountains. They come down and feed on the little green islands in the beds of the torrents and so may be swept away. The Sheepfold is falling away it is built nearly in the form of a heart unequally divided. Look down the brook and see the drops

---

3. The Preface to the second edition of *Lyrical Ballads*, 1800.
4. The brother of Joseph Cottle, Bristol publisher of the first edition of *Lyrical Ballads*.
5. Sally Lowthian, who had been a servant in the house of Wordsworths' father.
6. Wordsworth's *Resolution and Independence*, composed one and a half

years later, incorporated various details of Dorothy's description of the leech-gatherer. See below, May 4 and 7, 1802, for Wordsworth working on the poem he originally called *The Leech Gatherer*.
7. The sheepfold, in Wordsworth's *Michael*; lines 1–17 of the poem describe the walk up Greenhead Ghyll.

rise upwards and sparkle in the air, at the little falls the higher sparkles the tallest. We walked along the turf of the mountain till we
came to a Cattle track—made by the cattle which come upon the
hills. We drank tea at Mr Simpson's returned at about nine—a fine
mild night.

Oct. 12. Beautiful day. Sate in the house writing in the morning
while Wm went into the Wood to compose. Wrote to John in the
morning—copied poems for the LB,[8] in the evening wrote to Mrs
Rawson. Mary Jameson and Sally Ashburner dined. We pulled
apples after dinner, a large basket full. We walked before tea by
Bainriggs to observe the many coloured foliage the oaks dark green
with yellow leaves, the birches generally still green, some near the
water yellowish. The Sycamore crimson and crimson-tufted, the
mountain ash a deep orange, the common ash Lemon colour but
many ashes still fresh in their summer green. Those that were discoloured chiefly near the water. William composing in the Evening.
Went to bed at 12 o'clock.

* * *

1801

Nov. 24, 1801. A rainy morning. We all were well except that
my head ached a little and I took my Breakfast in bed. I read a
little of Chaucer, prepared the goose for dinner, and then we all
walked out. I was obliged to return for my fur tippet and Spenser[9]
it was so cold. We had intended going to Easedale but we shaped
our course to Mr Gell's cottage. It was very windy and we heard the
wind everywhere about us as we went along the Lane but the walls
sheltered us. John Green's house looked pretty under Silver How.
As we were going along we were stopped at once, at the distance
perhaps of 50 yards from our favorite Birch tree. It was yielding to
the gusty wind with all its tender twigs, the sun shone upon it and
it glanced in the wind like a flying sunshiny shower. It was a tree in
shape with stem and branches but it was like a Spirit of water. The
sun went in and it resumed its purplish appearance the twigs still
yielding to the wind but not so visibly to us. The other Birch trees
that were near it looked bright and chearful, but it was a creature
by its own self among them. We could not get into Mr Gell's
grounds—the old tree fallen from its undue exaltation above the
Gate. A shower came on when we were at Benson's. We went
through the wood—it became fair—there was a rainbow which
spanned the lake from the Island house to the foot of Bainriggs.
The village looked populous and beautiful. Catkins are coming out

8. *Lyrical Ballads.*
9. A "Spencer" was a close-fitting jacket worn by women and children.

palm trees budding—the alder with its plumb coloured buds. We came home over the stepping stones. The Lake was foamy with white waves. I saw a solitary butter flower in the wood. *I* found it not easy to get over the stepping stones. Reached home at dinner time. Sent Peggy Ashburner some goose. She sent me some honey —with a thousand thanks. 'Alas! the gratitude of men has etc.'[1] I went in to set her right about this and sate a while with her. She talked about Thomas's having sold his land. 'Ay,' says she I said many a time 'He's not come fra London to buy our Land however.' Then she told me with what pains and industry they had made up their taxes interest etc. etc.—how they all got up at 5 o'clock in the morning to spin and Thomas carded, and that they had paid off a hundred pound of the interest. She said she used to take such pleasure in the cattle and sheep. 'O how pleased I used to be when they fetched them down, and when I had been a bit poorly I would gang out upon a hill and look over t' fields and see them and it used to do me so much good you cannot think.' Molly said to me when I came in 'poor Body.' She's very ill but one does not know how long she may last. Many a fair face may gang before her. We sate by the fire without work for some time then Mary read a poem of Daniell[2] upon Learning. After tea Wm read Spenser now and then a little aloud to us. We were making his waistcoat. We had a note from Mrs C., with bad news from poor C. very ill. William walked to John's Grove. I went to meet him—moonlight but it rained. I met him before I had got as far as John Baty's—he had been surprized and terrified by a sudden rushing of winds which seemed to bring earth sky and lake together, as if the whole were going to enclose him in—he was glad he was in a high Road.

In speaking of our walk on Sunday Evening the 22nd November I forgot to notice one most impressive sight. It was the moon and the moonlight seen through hurrying driving clouds immediately behind the Stone man upon the top of the hill on the Forest side. Every tooth and every edge of Rock was visible, and the Man stood like a Giant watching from the Roof of a lofty castle. The hill seemed perpendicular from the darkness below it. It was a sight that I could call to mind at any time it was so distinct.

* * *

1802

Mar. 4. Before we had quite finished Breakfast Calvert's man brought the horses for Wm.[3] We had a deal to do to shave—pens to make—poems to put in order for writing, to settle the dress pack

---

1. A quotation from Wordsworth's *Simon Lee*: "Alas! the gratitude of men / Hath oftener left me mourning."
2. Samuel Daniel's long poem *Musophi-* lus: *Containing a General Defense of Learning* (1599).
3. For a journey to Keswick, to visit Coleridge.

up etc. The man came before the pens were made and he was obliged to leave me with only two. Since he has left me (at ½ past 11) it is now 2 I have been putting the Drawers into order, laid by his clothes which we had thrown here and there and everywhere, filed two months' newspapers and got my dinner 2 boiled eggs and 2 apple tarts. I have set Molly on to clear the garden a little, and I myself have helped. I transplanted some snowdrops—The Bees are busy—Wm has a nice bright day. It was hard frost in the night. The Robins are singing sweetly. Now for my walk. I *will* be busy, I *will* look well and be well when he comes back to me. O the Darling! Here is one of his bitten apples! I can hardly find in my heart to throw it into the fire. I must wash myself, then off—I walked round the two Lakes crossed the stepping stones at Rydale Foot. Sate down where we always sit. I was full of thoughts about my darling. Blessings on him. I came home at the foot of our own hill under Loughrigg. They are making sad ravages in the woods. Benson's Wood is going and the wood above the River. The wind has blown down a [?small] fir tree on the Rock that terminates John's path—I suppose the wind of Wednesday night. I read German after my return till tea time. After tea I worked and read the LB, enchanted with the Idiot Boy. Wrote to Wm then went to Bed. It snowed when I went to Bed.

* * *

Mar. 22. A rainy day. William very poorly. Mr Luff came in after dinner and brought us 2 letters from Sara H. and one from poor Annette. I read Sara's letters while he was here. I finished my letters to M. and S. and wrote to my Br Richard. We talked a good deal about C. and other interesting things. We resolved to see Annette, and that Wm should go to Mary.[4] We wrote to Coleridge not to expect us till Thursday or Friday.

Mar. 23. A mild morning. William worked at the Cuckow poem.[5] I sewed beside him. After dinner he slept I read German, and at the closing in of day went to sit in the orchard. He came to me, and walked backwards and forwards. We talked about C. Wm repeated the poem to me. I left him there and in 20 minutes he came in, rather tired with attempting to write. He is now reading Ben Jonson I am going to read German it is about 10 o'clock, a quiet night. The fire flutters and the watch ticks I hear nothing else save the Breathing of my Beloved and he now and then pushes his book forward and turns over a leaf. Fletcher is not come home. No letter from C.

4. It had been arranged several months earlier that William was to marry Mary Hutchinson ("Sara H." in this entry is Mary's sister, with whom Coleridge had fallen in love). Now the Wordsworths resolve to go to France to settle affairs with Annette Vallon, mother of William's natural daughter, Caroline. William did not conceal the facts of his early love affair from his family, nor from Mary Hutchinson.
5. *To the Cuckoo.*

Apr. 15. It was a threatening misty morning—but mild. We set off after dinner from Eusemere. Mrs Clarkson went a short way with us but turned back. The wind was furious and we thought we must have returned. We first rested in the large Boat-house, then under a furze Bush opposite Mr Clarkson's. Saw the plough going in the field. The wind seized our breath the Lake was rough. There was a Boat by itself floating in the middle of the Bay below Water Millock. We rested again in the Water Millock Lane. The haw-thorns are black and green, the birches here and there greenish but there is yet more of purple to be seen on the Twigs. We got over into a field to avoid some cows—people working, a few primroses by the roadside, wood-sorrel flower, the anemone, scentless violets. strawberries, and that starry yellow flower which Mrs C. calls pile wort. When we were in the woods beyond Gowbarrow park we saw a few daffodils[6] close to the water side. We fancied that the lake had floated the seeds ashore and that the little colony had so sprung up. But as we went along there were more and yet more and at last under the boughs of the trees, we saw that there was a long belt of them along the shore, about the breadth of a country turnpike road. I never saw daffodils so beautiful they grew among the mossy stones about and about them, some rested their heads upon these stones as on a pillow for weariness and the rest tossed and reeled and danced and seemed as if they verily laughed and the wind that blew upon them over the lake, they looked so gay ever glancing ever changing. This wind blew directly over the lake to them. There was here and there a little knot and a few stragglers a few yards higher up but they were so few as not to disturb the simplicity and unity and life of that one busy highway. We rested again and again. The Bays were stormy, and we heard the waves at different distances and in the middle of the water like the sea. Rain came on—we were wet when we reached Luffs but we called in. Luckily all was chearless and gloomy so we faced the storm—we *must* have been wet if we had waited—put on dry clothes at Dobson's. I was very kindly treated by a young woman, the Landlady looked sour but it is her way. She gave us a goodish supper. Excellent ham and potatoes. We paid 7/ when we came away. William was sitting by a bright fire when I came downstairs. He soon made his way to the Library piled up in a corner of the window. He brought out a volume of Enfield's Speaker,[7] another miscellany, and an odd volume of Con-greve's plays. We had a glass of warm rum and water. We enjoyed ourselves and wished for Mary. It rained and blew when we went to bed. N.B. Deer in Gowbarrow park like skeletons.

---

6. Wordsworth did not compose his poem on the daffodils, *I Wandered Lonely as a Cloud*, until two years later; comparison with the poem will show how extensive was his use of Dorothy's prose description.
7. William Enfield's *The Speaker* (1774), a volume of selections suitable for elocution.

Apr. 16 (Good Friday). When I undrew my curtains in the morning, I was much affected by the beauty of the prospect and the change. The sun shone, the wind has passed away, the hills looked chearful, the river was very bright as it flowed into the lake. The Church rises up behind a little knot of Rocks, the steeple not so high as an ordinary 3 story house. Trees, in a row in the garden under the wall. After Wm had shaved we set forward. The valley is at first broken by little rocky woody knolls that make retiring places, fairy valleys in the vale, the river winds along under these hills travelling not in a bustle but not slowly to the lake. We saw a fisherman in the flat meadow on the other side of the water. He came towards us and threw his line over the two arched Bridge. It is a Bridge of a heavy construction, almost bending inwards in the middle, but it is grey and there is a look of anciently in the architecture of it that pleased me. As we go on the vale opens out more into one vale with somewhat of a cradle Bed. Cottages with groups of trees on the side of the hills. We passed a pair of twin Children 2 years old—Sate on the next bridge which we crossed a single arch. We rested again upon the Turf and looked at the same Bridge. We observed arches in the water occasioned by the large stones sending it down in two streams. A Sheep came plunging through the river, stumbled up the Bank and passed close to us, it had been frightened by an insignificant little Dog on the other side, its fleece dropped a glittering shower under its belly. Primroses by the roadside, pile wort that shone like stars of gold in the Sun, violets, strawberries, retired and half buried among the grass. When we came to the foot of Brothers water I left William sitting on the Bridge and went along the path on the right side of the Lake through the wood. I was delighted with what I saw. The water under the boughs of the bare old trees, the simplicity of the mountains and the exquisite beauty of the path. There was one grey cottage. I repeated the Glowworm[8] as I walked along. I hung over the gate, and thought I could have stayed for ever. When I returned I found William writing a poem descriptive of the sights and sounds we saw and heard. There was the gentle flowing of the stream, the glittering lively lake, green fields without a living creature to be seen on them, behind us, a flat pasture with 42 cattle feeding to our left the road leading to the hamlet, no smoke there, the sun shone on the bare roofs. The people were at work ploughing, harrowing and sowing—lasses spreading dung, a dog's barking now and then, cocks crowing, birds twittering, the snow in patches at the top of the highest hills, yellow palms, purple and green twigs on the Birches, ashes with their glittering spikes quite bare. The hawthorn a bright green with black stems under the oak. The moss of the oak glossy.

8. Wordsworth's poem beginning "Among all lovely things my Love had been," composed four days earlier; "my Love" in this line is Dorothy.

We then went on, passed two sisters at work, *they first passed us*, one with two pitch forks in her hand. The other had a spade. We had some talk with them. They laughed aloud after we were gone perhaps half in wantonness, half boldness. William finished his poem before we got to the foot of Kirkstone.[9] * * *

* * *

Apr. 29. A beautiful morning. The sun shone and all was pleasant. We sent off our parcel to Coleridge by the waggon. Mr Simpson heard the Cuckow today. Before we went out after I had written down the Tinker (which William finished this morning)[1] Luff called. He was very lame, limped into the kitchen—he came on a little Pony. We then went to John's Grove, sate a while at first. Afterwards William lay, and I lay in the trench under the fence— he with his eyes shut and listening to the waterfalls and the Birds. There was no one waterfall above another[2]—it was a sound of waters in the air—the voice of the air. William heard me breathing and rustling now and then but we both lay still, and unseen by one another. He thought that it would be as sweet thus to lie so in the grave, to hear the *peaceful* sounds of the earth and just to know that our dear friends were near. The Lake was still. There was a Boat out. Silver How reflected with delicate purple and yellowish hues as I have seen Spar. Lambs on the island and running races together by the half dozen in the round field near us. The copses green*ish*, hawthorn green.—Came home to dinner then went to Mr Simpson. We rested a long time under a wall. Sheep and lambs were in the field—cottages smoking. As I lay down on the grass, I observed the glittering silver line on the ridges of the Backs of the sheep, owing to their situation respecting the Sun—which made them look beautiful but with something of strangeness, like animals of another kind—as if belonging to a more splendid world. Met old Mr S. at the door—Mrs S. poorly. I got mullens and pansies. I was sick and ill and obliged to come home soon. We went to bed immediately—I slept up stairs. The air coldish where it was felt somewhat frosty.

* * *

May 4. William had slept pretty well and though he went to bed nervous and jaded in the extreme he rose refreshed. I wrote the Leech Gatherer[3] for him which he had begun the night before and of which he wrote several stanzas in bed this Monday morning. It was very hot, we called at Mr Simpson's door as we passed but did not go in. We rested several times by the way, read and repeated the Leech Gatherer. We were almost melted before we were at the

9. See the joyous lyric *Written in March*, above.

1. Wordsworth never published his comic poem *The Tinker*; it was first printed in 1897.

2. I.e., no waterfull could be heard individually.

3. The poem that was published as *Resolution and Independence*; for its origin, see the entry for October 3, 1800.

top of the hill. We saw Coleridge on the Wytheburn side of the water. He crossed the Beck to us. Mr Simpson was fishing there. William and I ate a Luncheon, then went on towards the waterfall. It is a glorious wild solitude under that lofty purple crag. It stood upright by itself. Its own self and its shadow below, one mass—all else was sunshine. We went on further. A Bird at the top of the crags was flying round and round and looked in thinness and transparency, shape and motion like a moth. We climbed the hill but looked in vain for a shade except at the foot of the great waterfall, and there we did not like to stay on account of the loose stones above our heads. We came down and rested upon a moss covered Rock, rising out of the bed of the River. There we lay ate our dinner and stayed there till about 4 o'clock or later. Wm and C. repeated and read verses. I drank a little Brandy and water and was in Heaven. The Stags horn is very beautiful and fresh springing upon the fells. Mountain ashes, green. We drank tea at a farm house. The woman had not a pleasant countenance, but was civil enough. She had a pretty Boy a year old whom she suckled. We parted from Coleridge at Sara's Crag after having looked at the Letters which C. carved in the morning. I kissed them all. Wm deepened the T with C.'s penknife.[4] We sate afterwards on the wall, seeing the sun go down and the reflections in the still water. C. looked well and parted from us chearfully, hopping up upon the side stones. On the Rays we met a woman with 2 little girls one in her arms the other about 4 years old walking by her side, a pretty little thing, but half starved. She had on a pair of slippers that had belonged to some gentleman's child, down at the heels—it was not easy to keep them on but, poor thing! young as she was, she walked carefully with them. Alas too young for such cares and such travels. The Mother when we accosted her told us that her husband had left her and gone off with another woman and how she '*pursued*' them. Then her fury kindled and her eyes rolled about. She changed again to tears. She was a Cockermouth woman 30 years of age—a child at Cockermouth when I was. I was moved and gave her a shilling—I believe 6[d] more than I ought to have given. We had the crescent moon with the 'auld moon in her arms'.[5] We rested often always upon the Bridges. Reached home at about 10 o'clock. The Lloyds had been here in our absence. We went soon to bed. I repeated verses to William while he was in bed—he was soothed and I left him. 'This is the spot'[6] over and over again.

* * *

4. The rock, which has since been blasted away for a new road, contained the carved letters: W.W., M.H., D.W., S.T.C., J.W., S.H. (M.H. and S.H. are Mary and Sara Hutchinson; J.W. is John Wordsworth.)

5. From the *Ballad of Sir Patrick Spens;* Coleridge cited the stanza of which this phrase is part as epigraph to *Dejection: An Ode.*

6. Wordsworth never completed this poem.

May 6. A sweet morning. We have put the finishing stroke to our Bower and here we are sitting in the orchard. It is one o'clock. We are sitting upon a seat under the wall which I found my Brother building up when I came to him with his apple—he had intended that it should have been done before I came. It is a nice cool shady spot. The small Birds are singing, Lambs bleating, Cuckow calling. The Thrush sings by Fits. Thomas Ashburner's axe is going quietly (without passion) in the orchard. Hens are cackling, Flies humming, the women talking together at their doors: Plumb and pear trees are in Blossom—apple trees greenish the opposite woods green, the crows are cawing. We have heard Ravens. The ash trees are in blossom, Birds flying all about us. The stitchwort is coming out, there is one budding Lychnis, the primroses are passing their prime. Celandine violets and wood sorrel for ever more little geraniums and pansies on the wall. We walked in the evening to Tail End to enquire about hurdles for the orchard shed and about Mr Luff's flower. The flower dead—no hurdles. I went to look at the falling wood—Wm also when he had been at Benson's went with me. They have left a good many small oak trees but we dare not hope that they are all to remain. The Ladies are come to Mr Gell's cottage. We saw them as we went and their light when we returned. When we came in we found a Magazine and Review and a letter from Coleridge with verses to Hartley and Sara H. We read the Review,[7] etc. The moon was a perfect Boat a silver Boat when we were out in the evening. The Birch Tree is all over green in *small* leaf more light and elegant than when it is full out. It bent to the breezes as if for the love of its own delightful motions. Sloethorns and Hawthorns in the hedges.

May 7. William had slept uncommonly well so, feeling himself strong, he fell to work at the Leech gatherer. He wrote hard at it till dinner time, then he gave over tired to death—he had finished the poem.[8] * * *

* * *

[*July.*] On Thursday morning, 29th, we arrived in London.[9] Wm left me at the Inn—I went to bed. Etc. etc. After various troubles and disasters we left London on Saturday morning at ½ past 5 or 6, the 31st of July (I have forgot which). We mounted the Dover Coach at Charing Cross. It was a beautiful morning. The City, St Paul's, with the River and a multitude of little Boats, made a most beautiful sight as we crossed Westminster Bridge. The houses were not overhung by their cloud of smoke and they were spread out endlessly, yet the sun shone so brightly with such a pure

7. Probably the journal *Monthly Review*.
8. Later entries show, however, that Wordsworth kept working on the manuscript until July 4.

9. On the way to France to visit Annette Vallon and Caroline; see the entry for March 22, 1802.

light that there was even something like the purity of one of
nature's own grand spectacles.[1] We rode on chearfully now with
the Paris Diligence before us, now behind. We walked up the steep
hills, beautiful prospects everywhere, till we even reached
Dover. * * *

* * * We arrived at Calais at 4 o'clock on Sunday morning, the
31st of July.[2] We stayed in the vessel till ½-past 7, then Wm went
for Letters, at about ½ past 8 or 9 we found out Annette and C.
chez Madame Avril dans la Rue de la Tête d'or. We lodged opposite two Ladies in tolerably decent-sized rooms but badly furnished,
and with large store of bad smells and dirt in the yard, and all
about. The weather was very hot. We walked by the sea-shore
almost every evening with Annette and Caroline or Wm and I
alone. I had a bad cold and could not bathe at first but William
did. It was a pretty sight to see as we walked upon the sands when
the tide was low perhaps a hundred people bathing about ¼ of a
mile distant from us, and we had delightful walks after the heat of
the day was passed away—seeing far off in the west the Coast of
England like a cloud crested with Dover Castle, which was but like
the summit of the cloud. The Evening star and the glory of the sky.
The Reflections in the water were more beautiful than the sky
itself, purple waves brighter than precious stones for ever melting
away upon the sands. * * *

* * *

[*Sept. 24.*] Mary first met us in the avenue. She looked so fat
and well that we were made very happy by the sight of her. Then
came Sara, and last of all Joanna.[3] Tom was forking corn standing
upon the corn cart. We dressed ourselves immediately and got tea
—the garden looked gay with asters and sweet peas. I looked at
everything with tranquillity and happiness—was ill on Saturday and
on Sunday and continued to be during most of the time of our stay.
Jack and George came on Friday Evening 1st October. On Saturday
2nd we rode to Hackness, William Jack George and Sara single, I
behind Tom. On Sunday 3rd Mary and Sara were busy packing. On
Monday 4th October 1802, my Brother William was married to
Mary Hutchinson. I slept a good deal of the night and rose fresh
and well in the morning. At a little after 8 o'clock I saw them go
down the avenue towards the Church. William had parted from me
upstairs. I gave him the wedding ring—with how deep a blessing! I
took it from my forefinger where I had worn it the whole of the

1. See Wordsworth's sonnet *Composed
upon Westminster Bridge.*
2. The actual date was August 1. One of
the walks by the sea that Dorothy goes
on to describe was the occasion for the
sonnet *It Is a Beauteous Evening.*
3. The Wordsworths have come to Gal-
low Hill, Yorkshire, for the marriage of
William and Mary. The people mentioned are Mary's sisters and brothers
(Sara, Joanna, Tom, Jack, and George
Hutchinson). Out of consideration for
Dorothy's overwrought feelings, only
Joanna, Jack, and Tom attended the ceremony at Brampton Church.

night before—he slipped it again onto my finger and blessed me fervently. When they were absent my dear little Sara prepared the breakfast. I kept myself as quiet as I could, but when I saw the two men running up the walk, coming to tell us it was over, I could stand it no longer and threw myself on the bed where I lay in stillness, neither hearing or seeing anything, till Sara came upstairs to me and said 'They are coming'. This forced me from the bed where I lay and I moved I knew not how straight forward, faster than my strength could carry me till I met my beloved William and fell upon his bosom. He and John Hutchinson led me to the house and there I stayed to welcome my dear Mary. As soon as we had breakfasted we departed.[4] It rained when we set off. Poor Mary was much agitated when she parted from her Brothers and Sisters and her home. Nothing particular occurred till we reached Kirby. We had sunshine and showers, pleasant talk, love and chearfulness. * * * It rained very hard when we reached Windermere. We sate in the rain at Wilcock's to change horses, and arrived at Grasmere at about 6 o'clock on Wednesday Evening, the 6th of October 1802. Molly was overjoyed to see us, for my part I cannot describe what I felt, and our dear Mary's feelings would I dare say not be easy to speak of. We went by candle light into the garden and were astonished at the growth of the Brooms, Portugal Laurels, etc. etc. etc. The next day, Thursday, we unpacked the Boxes. On Friday 8th we baked Bread, and Mary and I walked, first upon the Hill side, and then in John's Grove, then in view of Rydale, the first walk that I had taken with my Sister.

* * *

Dec. 24 1802, *Christmas Eve.* William is now sitting by me at ½ past 10 o'clock. I have been beside him ever since tea running the heel of a stocking, repeating some of his sonnets to him, listening to his own repeating, reading some of Milton's and the Allegro and Penseroso. It is a quiet keen frost. Mary is in the parlour below attending to the baking of cakes and Jenny Fletcher's pies. Sara is in bed in the toothache, and so we are—beloved William is turning over the leaves of Charlotte Smith's sonnets, but he keeps his hand to his poor chest pushing aside his breastplate. Mary is well and I am well, and Molly is as blithe as last year at this time. Coleridge came this morning with Wedgwood.[5] We all turned out of Wm's bedroom one by one to meet him. He looked well. We had to tell him of the Birth of his little Girl, born yesterday morning at 6 o'clock.[6] W. went with them to Wytheburn in the Chaise, and M.

---

4. Dorothy accompanied William and Mary on the three-day journey back to their cottage at Grasmere.

5. Tom Wedgwood, whose father had founded the famous pottery works, was a friend and generous patron of Coleridge.

6. Coleridge's daughter, Sara (1802–52).

and I met Wm on the Rays. It was not an unpleasant morning to
the feelings—far from it. The sun shone now and then, and there
was no wind, but all things looked chearless and distinct, no melt-
ings of sky into mountains—the mountains like stonework wrought
up with huge hammers.—Last Sunday was as mild a day as I ever
remember. We all set off together to walk. I went to Rydale and
Wm returned with me. M. and S.[7] went round the Lakes. There
were flowers of various kinds the topmost bell of a fox-glove, geraniums, daisies—a buttercup in the water (but this I saw two or three
days before) small yellow flowers (I do not know their name) in
the turf a large bunch of strawberry blossoms. Wm sate a while
with me, then went to meet M. and S.—Last Saturday I dined at
Mr Simpson's also a beautiful mild day. Monday was a frosty day,
and it has been frost ever since. On Saturday I dined with Mrs
Simpson. It is today Christmas-day Saturday 25th December 1802.
I am 31 years of age.—It is a dull frosty day.

* * *

1800–1803

7. Mary and her sister Sara Hutchinson.

SAMUEL TAYLOR COLERIDGE
(1772–1834)

1797: At Nether Stowey, Somersetshire; the Wordsworths
      settle nearby, at Alfoxden.
1798: *Lyrical Ballads*, which included *The Ancient Mariner*
      and several other poems by Coleridge.
1800: Moves to Greta Hall, Keswick, thirteen miles from the
      Wordsworths at Grasmere.
1816: Final residence at Highgate, near London, under the
      care of Dr. James Gillman.
1817: *Biographia Literaria*.

In *The Prelude* Wordsworth, recording his gratitude to the mountains,
lakes, and winds "that dwell among the hills where I was born," com-
miserates with Coleridge because "thou, my Friend! wert reared / In the
great city, 'mid far other scenes." Coleridge had in fact been born in the
small town of Ottery St. Mary, in rural Devonshire; but upon the death
of his father he had been sent to school at Christ's Hospital, in London.
He was a dreamy, enthusiastic, and extraordinarily precocious schoolboy;
Charles Lamb, his schoolmate and lifelong friend, in his essay on Christ's
Hospital has given us a vivid sketch of Coleridge's loneliness, his learning,
and his eloquence. When in 1791 Coleridge went up to Jesus College,
Cambridge, he was an accomplished scholar; but he found little intel-

lectual stimulation at the university, fell into idleness, dissoluteness, and debt, and in despair fled to London and enlisted in the Light Dragoons under the alias of Silas Tomkyn Comberbacke—probably the most inept cavalryman in the long history of the British army. Although rescued by his brothers and sent back to Cambridge, he left in 1794 without a degree.

In June, 1794, Coleridge met Robert Southey, then a student at Oxford who, like himself, had poetic aspirations, was a radical in religion and politics, and sympathized with the republican experiment in France. Together the two young men planned to establish an ideal democratic community in America for which Coleridge coined the name "Pantisocracy," signifying an equal rule by all. A plausible American real-estate agent persuaded them that the ideal location would be on the banks of the Susquehanna, in Pennsylvania. Twelve men undertook to go; and since perpetuation of the scheme required offspring, hence wives, Coleridge dutifully became engaged to Sara Fricker, conveniently at hand as the sister of Southey's fiancée. The Pantisocracy scheme collapsed, but at Southey's insistence Coleridge went through with the marriage, "resolved," as he said, "but wretched." Later Coleridge's radicalism waned, and he became a conservative—a highly philosophical one—in politics, and a staunch Anglican in religion.

Despite this inauspicious beginning, Coleridge was at first happy in his marriage. When Wordsworth (whom Coleridge met in 1795, and almost immediately judged "the best poet of the age") brought his sister Dorothy to settle at Alfoxden, only three miles from the Coleridges at Nether Stowey, the period of intimate communication and poetic collaboration began which was the golden time of Coleridge's life. An annuity of £150, granted to Coleridge by Thomas and Josiah Wedgwood, sons of the founder of the famous pottery firm, came just in time to deflect him from assuming a post as a Unitarian minister. After their momentous joint publication of *Lyrical Ballads* in 1798, Coleridge and the Wordsworths spent a winter in Germany, where Coleridge attended the University of Göttingen and began the lifelong study of Kant and the post-Kantian German philosophers and critics which helped to alter profoundly his thinking about philosophy, religion, and aesthetics.

Back in England, Coleridge in 1800 followed the Wordsworths to the Lake District, settling at Greta Hall, Keswick. He had become gradually disaffected from his wife, and in 1799 he fell helplessly and hopelessly in love with Sara Hutchinson, whose sister, Mary, Wordsworth married three years later. All his life Coleridge had suffered from numerous painful physical ailments; Wordsworth has described how sometimes, in a sudden spasm of agony, Coleridge would "throw himself down and writhe like a worm upon the ground." According to the standard medical prescription of the time, Coleridge had long been taking laudanum (opium dissolved in alcohol). In 1800–1801 heavy dosages taken for attacks of rheumatism made opium a necessity to him, and Coleridge soon recognized that the drug was a worse evil than the diseases it did not cure. *Dejection: An Ode*, published in 1802, was Coleridge's despairing farewell to health, happiness, and poetic creativity. A two-year sojourn on the Mediterranean island of Malta, intended to restore his health, instead completed his decline. When he returned to England in the late summer of 1806 he was a broken man, an inveterate drug addict, estranged from his wife, suffering from agonies of remorse, and subject to terrifying nightmares of guilt and despair from which his own shrieks awakened him. A bitter quarrel with Wordsworth in 1810 marked the nadir of his life and expectations.

Under these conditions Coleridge's literary efforts, however sporadic and fragmentary, were little short of heroic. In 1808 he gave his first course of public lectures in London, and in the next eleven years followed these with other series on both literary and philosophical topics. He wrote for newspapers and singlehandedly undertook to write, publish, and distribute a periodical, *The Friend*, which lasted for some fourteen months after January, 1809. A tragedy, *Remorse*, had in 1813 a very successful run of twenty performances at the Drury Lane Theatre. In 1816 he took up residence at Highgate, a northern suburb of London, under the supervision of the excellent and endlessly patient physician James Gillman, who managed to control, although not to eliminate, Coleridge's consumption of opium. The next three years were Coleridge's most sustained period of literary activity: while continuing to lecture and to write for the newspapers on a variety of subjects, he published the *Biographia Literaria*, *Zapolya* (a drama), a book consisting of the essays in *The Friend* (revised and greatly enlarged), two collections of poems, and several important treatises on philosophical and religious subjects; in these he undertook to establish a metaphysical basis for the Trinitarian theology to which he had turned after his youthful period of Unitarianism.

The remaining years of his life, which he spent with Dr. and Mrs. Gillman, were quieter and happier than any he had known since the turn of the century. He came to a peaceful understanding with his wife and was reconciled to Wordsworth, with whom he toured the Rhineland in 1828. His rooms at Highgate became a center for friends, for the London literati, and for a steady stream of pilgrims from England and America. They came to hear one of the wonders of the age, the Sage of Highgate's conversation—or monologue—for even in his decline, Coleridge's talk never entirely lost the almost incantatory power which Hazlitt has immortalized in *My First Acquaintance with Poets*. When he died, Coleridge left his friends with the sense that an incomparable intellect had vanished from the world. "The most *wonderful* man that I have ever known," Wordsworth declared, his voice breaking; and Charles Lamb: "His great and dear spirit haunts me. * * * Never saw I his likeness, nor probably the world can see again."

Coleridge's friends, however, abetted by Coleridge's own merciless self-judgments, set current the opinion, still common, that Coleridge was great in promise but not in performance. Even in his buoyant youth, before opium had drained his strength and weakened his will, Coleridge described his own character as "indolence capable of energies"; and it is true that while his mind was incessantly active and fertile, he lacked application and staying power, and he manifested early in life a powerful sense of guilt and a need for public expiation. After drug addiction sapped Coleridge's strength and will, even while it reinforced his emotional problems, Coleridge often adapted (or simply adopted) passages from other writers, with little or no acknowledgment, and sometimes in a context that seems designed at once to obfuscate his literary obligations and to reveal the subterfuge. Whatever the tangled motives for his procedure, Coleridge has repeatedly been charged with plagiarism, from his day to our own. After *The Ancient Mariner*, most of the poems he completed were written, like the first version of *Dejection: An Ode*, in a spasm of intense effort. Writings which required sustained planning and application were either left unfinished or, like the *Biographia Literaria*, made up of brilliant sections eked out with filler, in a desperate effort to meet a deadline. Many of his best speculations Coleridge merely confided to his notebooks and the ears of his friends, incorporated in letters, and poured out upon the margins of his own and other people's books.

Even so, it is only when measured against his own immense potentialities that Coleridge's achievements appear limited. In opposition to the prevailing British philosophy of empiricism and associationism, Coleridge for most of his mature life expounded his views of the mind as creative in perception, intuitive in its discovery of the first premises of metaphysics and religion, and capable of a poetic re-creation of the world of sense by the fusing and formative power of the "secondary imagination." Within the decade after Coleridge died, John Stuart Mill, the most acute student of contemporary thought, announced that Coleridge was one of "the two great seminal minds of England," the most important instigator and representative of the conservative intellectual movement of the day. Time has proved Mill's estimate of Coleridge to be just, for his influence is strongly evident in 19th-century English and American traditions of philosophical idealism, enlightened political conservatism, and liberal interpretations of Trinitarian theology. By present consensus, Coleridge is also one of the greatest and most influential of literary theorists; his ideas have become central points of reference even in many of the new critics who depreciate the Romantic poetry for which Coleridge, in his criticism, attempted to provide a rationale. And Coleridge's writings in verse, though small in bulk, are the work of a major and notably original poet.

Here, too, we tend to underestimate Coleridge's versatility—this time because of our preoccupation with his three poems of mystery and demonism, *The Ancient Mariner*, *Christabel*, and *Kubla Khan*. These are indeed great and unprecedented achievements, but Coleridge wrote them all within a few years, and then dropped the mode. No less impressive in their own way are the blank-verse poems of the lonely and meditative mind which, by an extension of his term for one of them, are called "Conversation Poems"; in the best of these, *Frost at Midnight*, Coleridge perfected that characteristic pattern of integrally related description and meditation which Wordsworth immediately adopted in *Tintern Abbey*. Coleridge himself adapted this pattern to the larger requirements of *Dejection*, a high achievement in a genre in which few poets have been successful, the irregular Pindaric ode. The verse epistle *To William Wordsworth* is at once the most insightful comment ever made about *The Prelude*, a superb tribute to a friend whom Coleridge thought the greatest poet since Milton, and a moving elegy on the death of his own poetic power. But even when he had mainly given up poetry, after 1805, Coleridge continued to write occasional short lyrics (represented below) which are remarkable equally for their quality, their diversity, and the extent to which they have been neglected by anthologists.

Sonnet to the River Otter[1]

Dear native Brook! wild Streamlet of the West!
 How many various-fated years have past,
 What happy and what mournful hours, since last
I skimmed the smooth thin stone along thy breast,
Numbering its light leaps! yet so deep impressed   5
Sink the sweet scenes of childhood, that mine eyes
 I never shut amid the sunny ray,
But straight with all their tints thy waters rise,
 Thy crossing plank, thy marge with willows grey,
And bedded sand that veined with various dyes   10
Gleamed through thy bright transparence! On my way,
 Visions of Childhood! oft have ye beguiled
Lone manhood's cares, yet waking fondest sighs:
 Ah! that once more I were a careless Child!

1793?   1796

The Eolian Harp[2]

COMPOSED AT CLEVEDON, SOMERSETSHIRE

My pensive Sara! thy soft cheek reclined
Thus on mine arm, most soothing sweet it is
To sit beside our Cot, our Cot o'ergrown
With white-flowered Jasmin, and the broad-leaved Myrtle,
(Meet emblems they of Innocence and Love!)   5
And watch the clouds, that late were rich with light,

1. Coleridge's model was W. L. Bowles's *To the River Itchin*. For the great impact of Bowles's sonnets on Coleridge's poetic theory and practice, see his *Biographia Lietraria*, Chapter 1. Coleridge expanded this poetic mode of natural description interwoven with memory and meditation into his "conversation poems," such as *The Eolian Harp, This Lime-Tree Bower*, and *Frost at Midnight*.
2. Named for Aeolus, god of the winds, the harp has strings stretched over a rectangular sounding box. The strings are tuned in unison. When placed in an opened window, the harp (also called "Eolian lute," "Eolian lyre," "wind harp") responds to the altering wind by sequences of musical chords. This instrument, which seems to voice nature's own music, was a favorite household furnishing in the period, and was repeatedly alluded to in Romantic poetry; see Geoffrey Grigson, *The Harp of Aeolus and Other Essays* (1947). It served also as one of the recurrent Romantic images for the mind—either the mind in poetic inspiration, as in the last stanza of Shelley's *Ode to the West Wind*, or else the mind in perception, responding to an intellectual breeze by trembling into consciousness, as in this poem. Coleridge, however, no sooner puts forward this concept than he retracts it, for it comes too close to the heresy of pantheism, which identifies God with the nature that, in the orthodox view, is His creation.

Coleridge wrote this poem to Sara Fricker, whom he married on October 4, 1795, and took to a cottage at Clevedon, overlooking the Bristol Channel. He later several times expanded and altered his original version; the famous lines 26–33, for example, were not incorporated until 1817. The poem was Coleridge's first achievement in the important Romantic form of the sustained blank-verse lyric of description and meditation, in the mode of conversation addressed to a silent auditor, which he perfected in *Frost at Midnight*, and which Wordsworth adopted for *Tintern Abbey*.

Slow saddening round, and mark the star of eve
Serenely brilliant (such should Wisdom be)
Shine opposite! How exquisite the scents
Snatched from yon bean-field! and the world *so* hushed!　10
The stilly murmur of the distant Sea
Tells us of silence.
　　　　　　　And that simplest Lute,
Placed length-ways in the clasping casement, hark!
How by the desultory breeze caressed,
Like some coy maid half yielding to her lover,　15
It pours such sweet upbraiding, as must needs
Tempt to repeat the wrong! And now, its strings
Boldlier swept, the long sequacious[3] notes
Over delicious surges sink and rise,
Such a soft floating witchery of sound　20
As twilight Elfins make, when they at eve
Voyage on gentle gales from Fairy-Land,
Where Melodies round honey-dropping flowers,
Footless and wild, like birds of Paradise,[4]
Nor pause, nor perch, hovering on untamed wing!　25
O! the one Life within us and abroad,
Which meets all motion and becomes its soul,
A light in sound, a sound-like power in light,
Rhythm in all thought, and joyance everywhere—
Methinks, it should have been impossible　30
Not to love all things in a world so filled;
Where the breeze warbles, and the mute still air
Is Music slumbering on her instrument.

　　And thus, my Love! as on the midway slope
Of yonder hill I stretch my limbs at noon,　35
Whilst through my half-closed eyelids I behold
The sunbeams dance, like diamonds, on the main,
And tranquil muse upon tranquillity:
Full many a thought uncalled and undetained,
And many idle flitting phantasies,　40
Traverse my indolent and passive brain,
As wild and various as the random gales
That swell and flutter on this subject Lute!

　　And what if all of animated nature
Be but organic Harps diversely framed,　45
That tremble into thought, as o'er them sweeps
Plastic and vast, one intellectual breeze,
At once the Soul of each, and God of all?

　　But thy more serious eye a mild reproof
Darts, O belovéd Woman! nor such thoughts　50
Dim and unhallowed dost thou not reject,

---

3. Successive
4. Brilliantly colored birds, found in New Guinea and adjacent islands. The native practice of removing the legs when preparing the skin led Europeans to believe that the birds were footless and spent their lives hovering in the air and feeding on nectar.

And biddest me walk humbly with my God.
Meek Daughter in the family of Christ!
Well hast thou said and holily dispraised
These shapings of the unregenerate mind;   55
Bubbles that glitter as they rise and break
On vain Philosophy's aye-babbling spring.
For never guiltless may I speak of him,
The Incomprehensible! save when with awe
I praise him, and with Faith that inly *feels*;   60
Who with his saving mercies heáled me,
A sinful and most miserable man,
Wildered and dark, and gave me to possess
Peace, and this Cot, and thee, heart-honored Maid!

1795–1817   1796, 1817

This Lime-Tree Bower My Prison

ADDRESSED TO CHARLES LAMB, OF THE INDIA HOUSE, LONDON

In the June of 1797 some long-expected friends paid a visit to the
author's cottage; and on the morning of their arrival, he met with an
accident, which disabled him from walking during the whole time of
their stay. One evening, when they had left him for a few hours, he
composed the following lines in the garden-bower.[1]

Well, they are gone, and here must I remain,
This lime-tree bower my prison! I have lost
Beauties and feelings, such as would have been
Most sweet to my remembrance even when age
Had dimmed mine eyes to blindness! They, meanwhile,   5
Friends, whom I never more may meet again,
On springy[2] heath, along the hill-top edge,
Wander in gladness, and wind down, perchance,
To that still roaring dell, of which I told;
The roaring dell, o'erwooded, narrow, deep,   10
And only speckled by the mid-day sun;
Where its slim trunk the ash from rock to rock
Flings arching like a bridge;—that branchless ash,
Unsunned and damp, whose few poor yellow leaves
Ne'er tremble in the gale, yet tremble still,   15
Fanned by the waterfall! and there my friends
Behold the dark green file of long lank weeds,
That all at once (a most fantastic sight!)
Still nod and drip beneath the dripping edge
Of the blue clay-stone.[3]

1. The time was in fact July 1797; the
visiting friends were William and Dorothy Wordsworth and Charles Lamb; the
accident was the fault of Mrs. Coleridge
—"dear Sara," Coleridge wrote, "accidentally emptied a skillet of boiling milk
on my foot"; and the bower consisted of
lime (i.e., linden) trees in the garden of
Thomas Poole, next door to Coleridge's

cottage at Nether Stowey. Coleridge related these facts in a letter to Robert
Southey, July 17, 1797, in which he transcribed the first version of this fine "conversation poem."
2. "*Elastic*, I mean" [Coleridge's note].
3. Compare Dorothy Wordsworth's description of the "low damp dell" in her
Alfoxden Journal for February 10, 1798.

Now, my friends emerge   20
Beneath the wide wide Heaven—and view again
The many-steepled tract magnificent
Of hilly fields and meadows, and the sea,
With some fair bark, perhaps, whose sails light up
The slip of smooth clear blue betwixt two Isles   25
Of purple shadow! Yes! they wander on
In gladness all; but thou, methinks, most glad,
My gentle-hearted Charles! for thou hast pined
And hungered after Nature, many a year,
In the great City pent,[4] winning thy way   30
With sad yet patient soul, through evil and pain
And strange calamity![5] Ah! slowly sink
Behind the western ridge, thou glorious Sun!
Shine in the slant beams of the sinking orb,
Ye purple heath-flowers! richlier burn, ye clouds!   35
Live in the yellow light, ye distant groves!
And kindle, thou blue Ocean! So my friend
Struck with deep joy may stand, as I have stood,
Silent with swimming sense; yea, gazing round
On the wide landscape, gaze till doth seem   40
Less gross than bodily; and of such hues
As veil the Almighty Spirit, when yet he makes
Spirits perceive his presence.

A delight
Comes sudden on my heart, and I am glad
As I myself were there! Nor in this bower,   45
This little lime-tree bower, have I not marked
Much that has soothed me. Pale beneath the blaze
Hung the transparent foliage; and I watched
Some broad and sunny leaf, and loved to see
The shadow of the leaf and stem above   50
Dappling its sunshine! And that walnut-tree
Was richly tinged, and a deep radiance lay
Full on the ancient ivy, which usurps
Those fronting elms, and now, with blackest mass
Makes their dark branches gleam a lighter hue   55
Through the late twilight: and though now the bat
Wheels silent by, and not a swallow twitters,
Yet still the solitary humblebee
Sings in the bean-flower! Henceforth I shall know
That Nature ne'er deserts the wise and pure;   60
No plot so narrow, be but Nature there,
No waste so vacant, but may well employ
Each faculty of sense, and keep the heart
Awake to Love and Beauty! and sometimes
'Tis well to be bereft of promised good,   65

4. Despite Coleridge's claim, Lamb eminently preferred London over what he
called "dead Nature"; see his Letter to
Wordsworth, January 30, 1801.

5. Some ten months earlier Charles
Lamb's sister, Mary, had stabbed her
mother to death in a fit of insanity.

That we may lift the soul, and contemplate
With lively joy the joys we cannot share.
My gentle-hearted Charles! when the last rook
Beat its straight path along the dusky air
Homewards, I blessed it! deeming its black wing   70
(Now a dim speck, now vanishing in light)
Had crossed the mighty Orb's dilated glory,
While thou stood'st gazing; or, when all was still,
Flew creeking o'er thy head, and had a charm
For thee, my gentle-hearted Charles, to whom   75
No sound is dissonant which tells of Life.

1797   1800

The Rime of the Ancient Mariner[1] ✓

IN SEVEN PARTS

Facile credo, plures esse Naturas invisibiles quam visibiles in rerum universitate. Sed horum [sic] *omnium familiam quis nobis enarrabit? et gradus et cognationes et discrimina et singulorum munera? Quid agunt? quae loca habitant? Harum rerum notitiam semper ambivit ingenium humanum, nunquam attigit. Juvat, interea, non diffiteor, quandoque in animo, tanquam in tabulâ, majoris et melioris mundi imaginem contemplari: ne mens assuefacta hodiernae vitae minutiis se contrahat nimis, et tota subsidat in pusillas cogitationes. Sed veritati interea invigilandum est, modusque servandus, ut certa ab incertis, diem a nocte, distinguamus.*

T. Burnet, *Archaeol. Phil.* p. 68.[2]

Argument

How a Ship, having first sailed to the Equator, was driven by storms to the cold Country towards the South Pole; how the Ancient Mariner cruelly and in contempt of the laws of hospitality killed a Seabird and how he was followed by many and strange Judgments: and in what manner he came back to his own Country.

1. Coleridge describes the origin of this poem in the opening section of Chapter XIV of *Biographia Literaria.* In a note on his *We Are Seven,* dictated to Isabella Fenwick in 1843, Wordsworth added some details. The poem, based on a dream of Coleridge's friend Cruikshank, was originally planned as a collaboration between the two friends, to pay the expense of a walking tour they took with Dorothy Wordsworth in November of 1797. Before he dropped out of the enterprise, Wordsworth suggested the shooting of the albatross and the navigation of the ship by the dead men; he also contributed lines 13–16 and 226–27.

The version of *The Ancient Mariner* printed in *Lyrical Ballads* (1798) contained many archaic words and spellings. In later editions Coleridge greatly improved the poem by pruning the archaisms, and by other revisions; he also added the Latin epigraph and the marginal glosses.

2. Latin epigraph: "I readily believe that there are more invisible than visible Natures in the universe. But who will explain for us the family of all these beings, and the ranks and relations and distinguishing features and functions of each? What do they do? What places do they inhabit? The human mind has always sought the knowledge of these things, but never attained it. Meanwhile I do not deny that it is helpful sometimes to contemplate in the mind, as on a tablet, the image of a greater and better world, lest the intellect, habituated to the petty things of daily life, narrow itself and sink wholly into trivial thoughts. But at the same time we must be watchful for the truth and keep a sense of proportion, so that we may distinguish the certain from the uncertain, day from night." Adapted by Coleridge from Thomas Burnet, *Archaeologiae philosophicae* (1692).

Part I

It is an ancient Mariner
And he stoppeth one of three.
—"By thy long gray beard and glittering eye,
Now wherefore stopp'st thou me?

The Bridegroom's doors are opened wide,   5
And I am next of kin;
The guests are met, the feast is set:
May'st hear the merry din."

He holds him with his skinny hand,
"There was a ship," quoth he.   10
"Hold off! unhand me, graybeard loon!"
Eftsoons[3] his hand dropped he.

He holds him with his glittering eye—
The Wedding Guest stood still,
And listens like a three years' child: 15
The Mariner hath his will.[4]

The Wedding Guest sat on a stone:
He cannot choose but hear;
And thus spake on that ancient man,
The bright-eyed Mariner.   20

"The ship was cheered, the harbor cleared,
Merrily did we drop
Below the kirk,[5] below the hill,
Below the lighthouse top.

The Sun came up upon the left,   25
Out of the sea came he!
And he shone bright, and on the right
Went down into the sea.

Higher and higher every day,
Till over the mast at noon[6]—"   30
The Wedding Guest here beat his breast,
For he heard the loud bassoon.

The bride hath paced into the hall,
Red as a rose is she;
Nodding their heads before her goes   35
The merry minstrelsy.

---

3. At once.
4. I.e., the Mariner has gained control of the will of the Wedding Guest by hypnosis—or, as it was called in Coleridge's time—by "mesmerism."
5. Church.
6. I.e., the ship had reached the equator (the "Line").

The Wedding Guest he beat his breast,
Yet he cannot choose but hear;
And thus spake on that ancient man,
The bright-eyed Mariner.   40

The ship driven
by a storm to-
ward the South
Pole.

"And now the STORM-BLAST came, and he
Was tyrannous and strong;
He struck with his o'ertaking wings,
And chased us south along.

With sloping masts and dipping prow,   45
As who pursued with yell and blow
Still treads the shadow of his foe,
And forward bends his head,
The ship drove fast, loud roared the blast,
And southward aye we fled.   50

And now there came both mist and snow,
And it grew wondrous cold:
And ice, mast-high, came floating by,
As green as emerald.

The land of ice,
and of fearful
sounds where no
living thing was
to be seen.

And through the drifts the snowy clifts   55
Did send a dismal sheen:
Nor shapes of men nor beasts we ken—
The ice was all between.

The ice was here, the ice was there,
The ice was all around: 60
It cracked and growled, and roared and howled,
Like noises in a swound![7]

Till a great sea
bird, called the
Albatross, came
through the
snow-fog, and
was received
with great joy
and hospitality.

At length did cross an Albatross,
Thorough the fog it came;
As if it had been a Christian soul,   65
We hailed it in God's name.

It ate the food it ne'er had eat,
And round and round it flew.
The ice did split with a thunder-fit;
The helmsman steered us through!   70

And lo! the Al-
batross proveth
a bird of good
omen, and fol-
loweth the ship
as it returned
northward
through fog and
floating ice.

And a good south wind sprung up behind;
The Albatross did follow,
And every day, for food or play,
Came to the mariners' hollo!

In mist or cloud, on mast or shroud,[8]   75
It perched for vespers nine;
Whiles all the night, through fog-smoke white,
Glimmered the white Moon-shine."

7. Swoon.   8. Rope supporting the mast.

"God save thee, ancient Mariner!
From the fiends, that plague thee thus!—   80
Why look'st thou so?"—With my crossbow
I shot the ALBATROSS.

Part II

The Sun now rose upon the right:[9]
Out of the sea came he,
Still hid in mist, and on the left   85
Went down into the sea.

And the good south wind still blew behind,
But no sweet bird did follow,
Nor any day for food or play
Came to the mariners' hollo!   90

And I had done a hellish thing,
And it would work 'em woe:
For all averred, I had killed the bird
That made the breeze to blow.
Ah wretch! said they, the bird to slay,   95
That made the breeze to blow!

Nor dim nor red, like God's own head,
The glorious Sun uprist:
Then all averred, I had killed the bird
That brought the fog and mist.   100
'Twas right, said they, such birds to slay,
That bring the fog and mist.

The fair breeze blew, the white foam flew,
The furrow followed free;
We were the first that ever burst   105
Into that silent sea.

Down dropped the breeze, the sails dropped down,
'Twas sad as sad could be;
And we did speak only to break
The silence of the sea!   110

All in a hot and copper sky,
The bloody Sun, at noon,
Right up above the mast did stand,
No bigger than the Moon.

Day after day, day after day,   115
We stuck, nor breath nor motion;
As idle as a painted ship
Upon a painted ocean.

9. I.e., having rounded Cape Horn, the ship heads north into the Pacific.

*And the Alba-
tross begins to
be avenged.*

Water, water, everywhere,
And all the boards did shrink;
Water, water, everywhere,
Nor any drop to drink.

120

The very deep did rot: O Christ!
That ever this should be!
Yea, slimy things did crawl with legs
Upon the slimy sea.

125

About, about, in reel and rout
The death-fires[1] danced at night;
The water, like a witch's oils,
Burnt green, and blue and white.

130

And some in dreams assuréd were
Of the Spirit that plagued us so;
Nine fathom deep he had followed us
From the land of mist and snow.

*A Spirit had
followed them;
one of the invis-
ible inhabitants
of this planet,
neither departed souls nor angels; concerning whom the learned Jew, Josephus, and
the Platonic Constantinopolitan, Michael Psellus, may be consulted. They are very
numerous, and there is no climate or element without one or more.*

And every tongue, through utter drought,
Was withered at the root;
We could not speak, no more than if
We had been choked with soot.

135

Ah! well-a-day! what evil looks
Had I from old and young!
Instead of the cross, the Albatross
About my neck was hung.

140

*The shipmates,
in their sore dis-
tress, would fain
throw the whole
guilt on the an-
cient Mariner: in
sign whereof they hang the dead sea bird round his neck.*

Part III

There passed a weary time. Each throat
Was parched, and glazed each eye.
A weary time! a weary time!
How glazed each weary eye,
When looking westward, I beheld
A something in the sky.

145

*The ancient Mar-
iner beholdeth a
sign in the ele-
ment afar off.*

At first it seemed a little speck,
And then it seemed a mist;
It moved and moved, and took at last
A certain shape, I wist.[2]

150

A speck, a mist, a shape, I wist!
And still it neared and neared:

1. The corposant, or St. Elmo's fire,
an atmospheric electricity on a ship's
mast or rigging, believed by the superstitious sailor to portend disaster.
2. Knew.

As if it dodged a water sprite,
It plunged and tacked and veered.   155

At its nearer approach, it seemeth him to be a ship; and at a dear ransom he freeth his speech from the bonds of thirst.

With throats unslaked, with black lips baked,
We could nor laugh nor wail;
Through utter drought all dumb we stood!
I bit my arm, I sucked the blood,   160
And cried, A sail! a sail!

With throats unslaked, with black lips baked,
Agape they heard me call:
A flash of joy;
Gramercy![3] they for joy did grin,
And all at once their breath drew in,   165
As they were drinking all.

And horror follows. For can it be a ship that comes onward without wind or tide?
See! see! (I cried) she tacks no more!
Hither to work us weal;[4]
Without a breeze, without a tide,
She steadies with upright keel!   170

The western wave was all aflame.
The day was well nigh done!
Almost upon the western wave
Rested the broad bright Sun;
When that strange shape drove suddenly   175
Betwixt us and the Sun.

It seemeth him but the skeleton of a ship.
And straight the Sun was flecked with bars,
(Heaven's Mother send us grace!)
As if through a dungeon grate he peered
With broad and burning face.   180

And its ribs are seen as bars on the face of the setting Sun.
Alas! (thought I, and my heart beat loud)
How fast she nears and nears!
Are those *her* sails that glance in the Sun,
Like restless gossameres?[5]

The Specter-Woman and her Deathmate, and no other on board the skeleton ship.
Are those *her* ribs through which the Sun   185
Did peer, as through a grate?
And is that Woman all her crew?
Is that a DEATH? and are there two?
Is DEATH that woman's mate?

Like vessel, like crew!
Her lips were red, *her* looks were free,   190
Her locks were yellow as gold:
Her skin was as white as leprosy,
The Nightmare LIFE-IN-DEATH was she,
Who thicks man's blood with cold.

Death and Life-in-Death have diced for the ship's crew, and she (the latter) winneth the ancient Mariner.
The naked hulk alongside came,   195
And the twain were casting dice;
"The game is done! I've won! I've won!"
Quoth she, and whistles thrice.

---

3. From the French *grand-merci*, "great thanks." 4. Benefit. 5. Filmy cobwebs floating in the air.

No twilight within the courts of the Sun.

The Sun's rim dips; the stars rush out:
At one stride comes the dark;
With far-heard whisper, o'er the sea,
Off shot the specter bark.   200

At the rising of the Moon,

We listened and looked sideways up!
Fear at my heart, as at a cup,
My lifeblood seemed to sip!   205
The stars were dim, and thick the night,
The steersman's face by his lamp gleamed white;
From the sails the dew did drip—
Till clomb above the eastern bar
The hornéd Moon, with one bright star   210
Within the nether tip.5a

One after another,

One after one, by the star-dogged Moon,
Too quick for groan or sigh,
Each turned his face with ghastly pang,
And cursed me with his eye.   215

His shipmates drop down dead.

Four times fifty living men,
(And I heard nor sigh nor groan)
With heavy thump, a lifeless lump,
They dropped down one by one.

But Life-in-Death begins her work on the ancient Mariner.

The souls did from their bodies fly—   220
They fled to bliss or woe!
And every soul, it passed me by,
Like the whizz of my crossbow!

Part IV

The Wedding Guest feareth that a Spirit is talking to him;

"I fear thee, ancient Mariner!
I fear thy skinny hand!   225
And thou art long, and lank, and brown,
As is the ribbed sea-sand.

I fear thee and thy glittering eye,
And thy skinny hand, so brown."—

But the ancient Mariner assureth him of his bodily life, and proceedeth to relate his horrible penance.

Fear not, fear not, thou Wedding Guest!   230
This body dropped not down.

Alone, alone, all, all alone,
Alone on a wide wide sea!
And never a saint took pity on
My soul in agony.   235

He despiseth the creatures of the calm,

The many men, so beautiful!
And they all dead did lie:
And a thousand thousand slimy things
Lived on; and so did I.

5a. An omen of impending evil.

And envieth that they should live, and so many lie dead.

I looked upon the rotting sea,
And drew my eyes away;
I looked upon the rotting deck,
And there the dead men lay.

I looked to heaven, and tried to pray;
But or ever a prayer had gushed,
A wicked whisper came, and made
My heart as dry as dust.

I closed my lids, and kept them close,
And the balls like pulses beat;
For the sky and the sea, and the sea and the sky
Lay like a load on my weary eye,
And the dead were at my feet.

But the curse liveth for him in the eye of the dead men.

The cold sweat melted from their limbs,
Nor rot nor reek did they:
The look with which they looked on me
Had never passed away.

An orphan's curse would drag to hell
A spirit from on high;
But oh! more horrible than that
Is the curse in a dead man's eye!
Seven days, seven nights, I saw that curse,
And yet I could not die.

The moving Moon went up the sky,
And nowhere did abide:
Softly she was going up,
And a star or two beside—

In his loneliness and fixedness he yearneth towards the journeying Moon, and the stars that still sojourn, yet still move onward; and everywhere the blue sky belongs to them, and is their appointed rest, and their native country and their own natural homes, which they enter unannounced, as lords that are certainly expected and yet there is a silent joy at their arrival.

Her beams bemocked the sultry main,
Like April hoar-frost spread;
But where the ship's huge shadow lay,
The charméd water burnt alway
A still and awful red.

By the light of the Moon he beholdeth God's creatures of the great calm.

Beyond the shadow of the ship,
I watched the water snakes:
They moved in tracks of shining white,
And when they reared, the elfish light
Fell off in hoary flakes.

Within the shadow of the ship
I watched their rich attire:
Blue, glossy green, and velvet black,
They coiled and swam; and every track
Was a flash of golden fire.

Their beauty and their happiness.

O happy living things! no tongue
Their beauty might declare:

240
245
250
255
260
265
270
275
280

He blesseth them
in his heart.

A spring of love gushed from my heart,
And I blessed them unaware: 285
Sure my kind saint took pity on me,
And I blessed them unaware.

The spell begins
to break.

The selfsame moment I could pray;
And from my neck so free
The Albatross fell off, and sank   290
Like lead into the sea.

Part V

Oh sleep! it is a gentle thing,
Beloved from pole to pole!
To Mary Queen the praise be given!
She sent the gentle sleep from Heaven,   295
That slid into my soul.

By grace of the
holy Mother, the
ancient Mariner
is refreshed with
rain.

The silly[6] buckets on the deck,
That had so long remained,
I dreamt that they were filled with dew;
And when I awoke, it rained.   300

My lips were wet, my throat was cold,
My garments all were dank;
Sure I had drunken in my dreams,
And still my body drank.

I moved, and could not feel my limbs: 305
I was so light—almost
I thought that I had died in sleep,
And was a blessed ghost.

He heareth
sounds and seeth
strange sights
and commotions
in the sky and
the element.

And soon I heard a roaring wind:
It did not come anear;   310
But with its sound it shook the sails,
That were so thin and sere.

The upper air burst into life!
And a hundred fire-flags sheen,[7]
To and fro they were hurried about!   315
And to and fro, and in and out,
The wan stars danced between.

And the coming wind did roar more loud,
And the sails did sigh like sedge;[8]
And the rain poured down from one black cloud;   320
The Moon was at its edge.

The thick black cloud was cleft, and still
The Moon was at its side:
Like waters shot from some high crag,
The lightning fell with never a jag,   325
A river steep and wide.

6. In the archaic sense: blessed, happy.
7. Shone. These are the Aurora Aus-
tralis, or Southern Lights.
8. A rushlike plant growing in wet soil.

*The bodies of
the ship's crew
are inspirited,
and the ship
moves on;*

The loud wind never reached the ship,
Yet now the ship moved on!
Beneath the lightning and the Moon
The dead men gave a groan.   330

They groaned, they stirred, they all uprose,
Nor spake, nor moved their eyes;
It had been strange, even in a dream,
To have seen those dead men rise.

The helmsman steered, the ship moved on;   335
Yet never a breeze up-blew;
The mariners all 'gan work the ropes,
Where they were wont to do;
They raised their limbs like lifeless tools—
We were a ghastly crew.   340

The body of my brother's son
Stood by me, knee to knee:
The body and I pulled at one rope,
But he said nought to me.

"I fear thee, ancient Mariner!"   345
Be calm, thou Wedding Guest!
'Twas not those souls that fled in pain,
Which to their corses[9] came again,
But a troop of spirits blest:

*But not by the
souls of the men,
nor by demons
of earth or mid-
dle air, but by a
blessed troop of
angelic spirits,
sent down by
the invocation of
the guardian
saint.*

For when it dawned—they dropped their arms, 350
And clustered round the mast;
Sweet sounds rose slowly through their mouths,
And from their bodies passed.

Around, around, flew each sweet sound,
Then darted to the Sun;   355
Slowly the sounds came back again,
Now mixed, now one by one.

Sometimes a-dropping from the sky
I heard the skylark sing;
Sometimes all little birds that are,   360
How they seemed to fill the sea and air
With their sweet jargoning![1]

And now 'twas like all instruments,
Now like a lonely flute;
And now it is an angel's song,   365
That makes the heavens be mute.

It ceased; yet still the sails made on
A pleasant noise till noon,
A noise like of a hidden brook

---

9. Corpses.

1. In Middle English, "warbling."

In the leafy month of June,   370
That to the sleeping woods all night
Singeth a quiet tune.

Till noon we quietly sailed on,
Yet never a breeze did breathe:
Slowly and smoothly went the ship,   375
Moved onward from beneath.

The lonesome Spirit from the South Pole carries on the ship as far as the Line, in obedience to the angelic troop, but still requireth vengeance.

Under the keel nine fathom deep,
From the land of mist and snow,
The spirit slid: and it was he
That made the ship to go.   380
The sails at noon left off their tune,
And the ship stood still also.

The Sun, right up above the mast,
Had fixed her to the ocean:
But in a minute she 'gan stir,   385
With a short uneasy motion—
Backwards and forwards half her length
With a short uneasy motion.

Then like a pawing horse let go,
She made a sudden bound: 390
It flung the blood into my head,
And I fell down in a swound.

The Polar Spirit's fellow demons, the invisible inhabitants of the element, take part in his wrong; and two of them relate, one to the other, that penance long and heavy for the ancient Mariner hath been accorded to the Polar Spirit, who returneth southward.

How long in that same fit I lay,
I have not[2] to declare;
But ere my living life returned,   395
I heard and in my soul discerned
Two voices in the air.

"Is it he?" quoth one, "Is this the man?
By him who died on cross,
With his cruel bow he laid full low   400
The harmless Albatross.

The spirit who bideth by himself
In the land of mist and snow,
He loved the bird that loved the man
Who shot him with his bow."   405

The other was a softer voice,
As soft as honeydew:
Quoth he, "The man hath penance done,
And penance more will do."

Part VI

FIRST VOICE

"But tell me, tell me! speak again,   410
Thy soft response renewing—

2. I.e., have not the knowledge.

What makes that ship drive on so fast?
What is the ocean doing?"

SECOND VOICE

"Still as a slave before his lord,
The ocean hath no blast;
His great bright eye most silently   415
Up to the Moon is cast—

If he may know which way to go;
For she guides him smooth or grim.
See, brother, see! how graciously   420
She looketh down on him."

FIRST VOICE

The Mariner hath been cast into a trance; for the angelic power causeth the vessel to drive northward faster than human life could endure.

"But why drives on that ship so fast,
Without or wave or wind?"

SECOND VOICE

"The air is cut away before,
And closes from behind.   425

Fly, brother, fly! more high, more high!
Or we shall be belated:
For slow and slow that ship will go,
When the Mariner's trance is abated."

The supernatural motion is retarded; the Mariner awakes, and his penance begins anew.

I woke, and we were sailing on   430
As in a gentle weather:
'Twas night, calm night, the moon was high;
The dead men stood together.

All stood together on the deck,
For a charnel-dungeon fitter:
All fixed on me their stony eyes,   435
That in the Moon did glitter.

The pang, the curse, with which they died,
Had never passed away:
I could not draw my eyes from theirs,
Nor turn them up to pray.   440

The curse is finally expiated.

And now this spell was snapped: once more
I viewed the ocean green,
And looked far forth, yet little saw
Of what had else been seen—   445

Like one, that on a lonesome road
Doth walk in fear and dread,
And having once turned round walks on,
And turns no more his head;
Because he knows, a frightful fiend   450
Doth close behind him tread.

But soon there breathed a wind on me,
Nor sound nor motion made:
Its path was not upon the sea,
In ripple or in shade.   455

It raised my hair, it fanned my cheek
Like a meadow-gale of spring—
It mingled strangely with my fears,
Yet it felt like a welcoming.

Swiftly, swiftly flew the ship,   460
Yet she sailed softly too:
Sweetly, sweetly blew the breeze—
On me alone it blew.

And the ancient Mariner beholdeth his native country.

Oh! dream of joy! is this indeed
The lighthouse top I see?   465
Is this the hill? is this the kirk?
Is this mine own countree?

We drifted o'er the harbor bar,
And I with sobs did pray—
O let me be awake, my God!   470
Or let me sleep alway.

The harbor bay was clear as glass,
So smoothly it was strewn!
And on the bay the moonlight lay,
And the shadow of the Moon.   475

The rock shone bright, the kirk no less,
That stands above the rock:
The moonlight steeped in silentness
The steady weathercock.

And the bay was white with silent light,   480
Till rising from the same,

The angelic spirits leave the dead bodies,

Full many shapes, that shadows were,
In crimson colors came.

And appear in their own forms of light.

A little distance from the prow
Those crimson shadows were: 485
I turned my eyes upon the deck—
Oh, Christ! what saw I there!

Each corse lay flat, lifeless and flat,
And, by the holy rood![3]
A man all light, a seraph man,   490
On every corse there stood.

This seraph band, each waved his hand:
It was a heavenly sight!

3. Cross. "Seraph": a shining celestial being, highest in the ranks of the angels.

They stood as signals to the land,
Each one a lovely light; 495

This seraph band, each waved his hand,
No voice did they impart—
No voice; but oh! the silence sank
Like music on my heart.

But soon I heard the dash of oars, 500
I heard the Pilot's cheer;
My head was turned perforce away
And I saw a boat appear.

The Pilot and the Pilot's boy,
I heard them coming fast: 505
Dear Lord in Heaven! it was a joy
The dead men could not blast.

I saw a third—I heard his voice:
It is the Hermit good!
He singeth loud his godly hymns 510
That he makes in the wood.
He'll shrieve my soul, he'll wash away
The Albatross's blood.

Part VII

*The Hermit of
the Wood*

This Hermit good lives in that wood
Which slopes down to the sea. 515
How loudly his sweet voice he rears!
He loves to talk with marineres
That come from a far countree.

He kneels at morn, and noon, and eve—
He hath a cushion plump: 520
It is the moss that wholly hides
The rotted old oak stump.

The skiff boat neared: I heard them talk,
"Why, this is strange, I trow!
Where are those lights so many and fair, 525
That signal made but now?"

*Approacheth the
ship with won-
der.*

"Strange, by my faith!" the Hermit said—
"And they answered not our cheer!
The planks looked warped! and see those sails,
How thin they are and sere! 530
I never saw aught like to them,
Unless perchance it were

Brown skeletons of leaves that lag
My forest-brook along;
When the ivy tod[4] is heavy with snow, 535

4. Clump of ivy.

And the owlet whoops to the wolf below,
That eats the she-wolf's young."

"Dear Lord! it hath a fiendish look,"
The Pilot made reply,
"I am a-feared"—"Push on, push on!"   540
Said the Hermit cheerily.

The boat came closer to the ship,
But I nor spake nor stirred;
The boat came close beneath the ship,
And straight a sound was heard.   545

Under the water it rumbled on,
Still louder and more dread:
It reached the ship, it split the bay;
The ship went down like lead.

Stunned by that loud and dreadful sound,   550
Which sky and ocean smote,
Like one that hath been seven days drowned
My body lay afloat;
But swift as dreams, myself I found
Within the Pilot's boat.   555

Upon the whirl, where sank the ship,
The boat spun round and round;
And all was still, save that the hill
Was telling of the sound.

I moved my lips—the Pilot shrieked   560
And fell down in a fit;
The holy Hermit raised his eyes,
And prayed where he did sit.

I took the oars: the Pilot's boy,
Who now doth crazy go,   565
Laughed loud and long, and all the while
His eyes went to and fro.
"Ha! ha!" quoth he, "full plain I see,
The Devil knows how to row."

And now, all in my own countree,   570
I stood on the firm land!
The Hermit stepped forth from the boat,
And scarcely he could stand.

"O shrieve me, shrieve me, holy man!"
The Hermit crossed his brow.[5]   575
"Say quick," quoth he, "I bid thee say—
What manner of man art thou?"

5. Made the sign of the cross on his forehead; "shrieve me": hear my confession and
grant me absolution.

Forthwith this frame of mine was wrenched
With a woeful agony,
Which forced me to begin my tale;   580
And then it left me free.

And ever and
anon throughout
his future life an   Since then, at an uncertain hour,
agony constrain-   That agony returns:
eth him to travel   And till my ghastly tale is told,
from land to
land;   This heart within me burns.   585

I pass, like night, from land to land;
I have strange power of speech;
That moment that his face I see,
I know the man that must hear me:
To him my tale I teach.   590

What loud uproar bursts from that door!
The wedding guests are there:
But in the garden-bower the bride
And bridemaids singing are:
And hark the little vesper bell,   595
Which biddeth me to prayer!

O Wedding Guest! this soul hath been
Alone on a wide wide sea:
So lonely 'twas, that God himself
Scarce seeméd there to be.   600

O sweeter than the marriage feast,
'Tis sweeter far to me,
To walk together to the kirk
With a goodly company!—

To walk together to the kirk,   605
And all together pray,
While each to his great Father bends,
Old men, and babes, and loving friends
And youths and maidens gay!

And to teach, by
his own exam-   Farewell, farewell! but this I tell   610
ple, love and rev-   To thee, thou Wedding Guest!
erence to all
things that God   He prayeth well, who loveth well
made and loveth.   Both man and bird and beast.

He prayeth best, who loveth best
All things both great and small;   615
For the dear God who loveth us,
He made and loveth all.[6]

---

6. Coleridge said in 1830, answering the objection of the poet, Mrs. Barbauld, that the poem "lacked a moral": "I told her that in my own judgment the poem had too much; and that the only, or chief fault, if I might say so, was the obtrusion of the moral sentiment so openly on the reader as a principle or cause of action in a work of pure imagination. It ought to have had no more moral than the *Arabian Nights'* tale of the merchant's sitting down to eat dates by the side of a well and throwing the shells aside, and lo! a genie starts up and says he *must* kill the aforesaid merchant *because* one of the date shells had, it seems, put out the eye of the genie's son."

The Mariner, whose eye is bright,
Whose beard with age is hoar,
Is gone: and now the Wedding Guest   620
Turned from the bridegroom's door.

He went like one that hath been stunned,
And is of sense forlorn:[7]
A sadder and a wiser man,
He rose the morrow morn.   625

1797–1816   1798, 1817

Kubla Khan

OR A VISION IN A DREAM. A FRAGMENT

The following fragment is here published at the request of a poet
of great and deserved celebrity,[1] and, as far as the author's own
opinions are concerned, rather as a psychological curiosity, than on
the ground of any supposed *poetic* merits.

In the summer of the year 1797, the author, then in ill health,
had retired to a lonely farmhouse between Porlock and Linton, on
the Exmoor confines of Somerset and Devonshire. In consequence
of a slight indisposition, an anodyne had been prescribed, from the
effects of which he fell asleep in his chair at the moment that he
was reading the following sentence, or words of the same substance,
in *Purchas's Pilgrimage*: "Here the Khan Kubla commanded a palace to be built, and a stately garden thereunto. And thus ten miles
of fertile ground were inclosed with a wall."[2] The author continued
for about three hours in a profound sleep, at least of the external
senses,[3] during which time he has the most vivid confidence that
he could not have composed less than from two to three hundred
lines; if that indeed can be called composition in which all the images rose up before him as *things*, with a parallel production of the
correspondent expressions, without any sensation or consciousness
of effort. On awaking he appeared to himself to have a distinct
recollection of the whole, and taking his pen, ink, and paper, instantly and eagerly wrote down the lines that are here preserved.

7. Forsaken.
1. Lord Byron.
2. "In Xamdu did Cublai Can build a
stately Palace, encompassing sixteene
miles of plaine ground with a wall,
wherein are fertile Meddowes, pleasant
springs, delightfull Streames, and all
sorts of beasts of chase and game, and
in the middest thereof a sumptuous
house of pleasure, which may be removed from place to place." From
Samuel Purchas, *Purchas his Pilgrimage* (1613). The historical Kublai

Khan founded the Mongol dynasty in
China in the 13th century.
3. In a note on a manuscript copy of
Kubla Khan, Coleridge gave a more
precise account of the nature of this
"sleep": "This fragment with a good
deal more, not recoverable, composed,
in a sort of reverie brought on by two
grains of opium, taken to check a dys-
entery, at a farmhouse between Porlock and Linton, a quarter of a mile
from Culbone Church, in the fall of
the year, 1797."

At this moment he was unfortunately called out by a person on business from Porlock, and detained by him above an hour, and on his return to his room, found, to his no small surprise and mortification, that though he still retained some vague and dim recollection of the general purport of the vision, yet, with the exception of some eight or ten scattered lines and images, all the rest had passed away like the images on the surface of a stream into which a stone has been cast, but, alas! without the after restoration of the latter!

> Then all the charm
> Is broken—all that phantom world so fair
> Vanishes, and a thousand circlets spread,
> And each misshape[s] the other. Stay awhile,
> Poor youth! who scarcely dar'st lift up thine eyes—
> The stream will soon renew its smoothness, soon
> The visions will return! And lo, he stays,
> And soon the fragments dim of lovely forms
> Come trembling back, unite, and now once more
> The pool becomes a mirror.
>
> [From Coleridge's *The Picture; or, the Lover's Resolution*,
> lines 91–100]

Yet from the still surviving recollections in his mind, the author has frequently purposed to finish for himself what had been originally, as it were, given to him. Σαμερον αδιον ασω:[4] but the to-morrow is yet to come.

> In Xanadu did Kubla Khan
> A stately pleasure dome decree:
> Where Alph,[5] the sacred river, ran
> Through caverns measureless to man
>   Down to a sunless sea.   5
> So twice five miles of fertile ground
> With walls and towers were girdled round:
> And there were gardens bright with sinuous rills,
> Where blossomed many an incense-bearing tree;
> And here were forests ancient as the hills,   10
> Enfolding sunny spots of greenery.
>
> But oh! that deep romantic chasm which slanted
> Down the green hill athwart a cedarn cover!

---

4. "I shall sing a sweeter song today." In the edition of 1834, Σαμερον ("today") was changed to αὑριον ("tomorrow"). Coleridge had in mind Theocritus, *Idyls* I.145: ἐς ὕστερον ἅδιον ᾁσῶ ("I shall sing a sweeter song on a later day").

5. Derived probably from the Greek river Alpheus, which flows into the Ionian Sea. Its waters were fabled to rise again in Sicily as the fountain of Arethusa; see Milton's *Lycidas*, lines 85 and 132.

A savage place! as holy and enchanted
As e'er beneath a waning moon was haunted   15
By woman wailing for her demon lover!
And from this chasm, with ceaseless turmoil seething,
As if this earth in fast thick pants were breathing,
A mighty fountain momently was forced:
Amid whose swift half-intermitted burst   20
Huge fragments vaulted like rebounding hail,
Or chaffy grain beneath the thresher's flail:
And 'mid these dancing rocks at once and ever
It flung up momently the sacred river.
Five miles meandering with a mazy motion   25
Through wood and dale the sacred river ran,
Then reached the caverns measureless to man,
And sank in tumult to a lifeless ocean:
And 'mid this tumult Kubla heard from far
Ancestral voices prophesying war!   30
        The shadow of the dome of pleasure
        Floated midway on the waves;
        Where was heard the mingled measure
        From the fountain and the caves.
It was a miracle of rare device,   35
A sunny pleasure dome with caves of ice!

        A damsel with a dulcimer
        In a vision once I saw:
        It was an Abyssinian maid,
        And on her dulcimer she played,   40
        Singing of Mount Abora.[6]
Could I revive within me
Her symphony and song,
To such a deep delight 'twould win me,
That with music loud and long,   45
I would build that dome in air,
That sunny dome! those caves of ice!
And all who heard should see them there,
And all should cry, Beware! Beware!
His flashing eyes, his floating hair!   50
Weave a circle round him thrice,[7]
And close your eyes with holy dread,
For he on honeydew hath fed,
And drunk the milk of Paradise.[8]

ca. 1797–98   1816

---

6. Apparently a reminiscence of *Paradise Lost* IV.280–82: "where Abassin Kings their issue guard, / Mount Amara, though this by some supposed / True Paradise under the Ethiop Line."
7. A magic ritual, to protect the inspired poet from intrusion.

8. Lines 50 ff. echo in part the description, in Plato's *Ion* 533–4, of inspired poets, who are "like Bacchic maidens who draw milk and honey from the rivers when they are under the influence of Dionysus but not when they are in their right mind."

Christabel[1]
Preface

The first part of the following poem was written in the year 1797, at Stowey, in the county of Somerset. The second part, after my return from Germany, in the year 1800, at Keswick, Cumberland. It is probable that if the poem had been finished at either of the former periods, or if even the first and second part had been published in the year 1800, the impression of its originality would have been much greater than I dare at present expect. But for this I have only my own indolence to blame. The dates are mentioned for the exclusive purpose of precluding charges of plagiarism or servile imitation from myself. For there is amongst us a set of critics, who seem to hold that every possible thought and image is traditional; who have no notion that there are such things as fountains in the world, small as well as great; and who would therefore charitably derive every rill they behold flowing from a perforation made in some other man's tank. I am confident, however, that as far as the present poem is concerned, the celebrated poets[2] whose writings I might be suspected of having imitated, either in particular passages, or in the tone and the spirit of the whole, would be among the first to vindicate me from the charge, and who, on any striking coincidence, would permit me to address them in this doggerel version of two monkish Latin hexameters.

> 'Tis mine and it is likewise yours;
> But an if this will not do;
> Let it be mine, good friend! for I
> Am the poorer of the two.

I have only to add that the meter of Christabel is not, properly speaking, irregular, though it may seem so from its being founded on a new principle: namely, that of counting in each line the accents, not the syllables.[3] Though the latter may vary from seven

---

1. Coleridge had planned to publish *Christabel* in the second edition of *Lyrical Ballads* (1800), but had not been able to complete the poem. When *Christabel* was finally published in 1816 in its present fragmentary state, Coleridge still had hopes of finishing it, for the Preface contained this sentence (deleted in the edition of 1834): "But as, in my very first conception of the tale, I had the whole present to my mind, with the wholeness, no less than the liveliness of a vision, I trust that I shall be able to embody in verse the three parts yet to come, in the course of the present year."
2. Sir Walter Scott and Lord Byron, who had read and admired *Christabel*

while it circulated in manuscript. Coleridge has in mind Scott's *Lay of the Last Minstrel* (1805) and Byron's *Siege of Corinth* (1816), which showed the influence of *Christabel*, especially in their meter.
3. Much of the older English versification, following the example of Anglo-Saxon poetry, had been based on stress, or "accent," and some of it shows as much freedom in varying the number of syllables as does *Christabel*. The poem, however, is a radical departure from the theory and practice of versification in the 18th century, which had been based on a recurrent number of syllables in each line.

to twelve, yet in each line the accents will be found to be only four. Nevertheless, this occasional variation in number of syllables is not introduced wantonly, or for the mere ends of convenience, but in correspondence with some transition in the nature of the imagery or passion.

Part I

'Tis the middle of night by the castle clock,
And the owls have awakened the crowing cock;
Tu—whit!——Tu—whoo!
And hark, again! the crowing cock,
How drowsily it crew.   5

Sir Leoline, the Baron rich,
Hath a toothless mastiff bitch;
From her kennel beneath the rock
She maketh answer to the clock,
Four for the quarters, and twelve for the hour;   10
Ever and aye, by shine and shower,
Sixteen short howls, not over loud;
Some say she sees my lady's shroud.

Is the night chilly and dark?
The night is chilly, but not dark.   15
The thin gray cloud is spread on high,
It covers but not hides the sky.
The moon is behind, and at the full;
And yet she looks both small and dull.
The night is chill, the cloud is gray: 20
'Tis a month before the month of May,
And the spring comes slowly up this way.

The lovely lady, Christabel,
Whom her father loves so well,
What makes her in the wood so late,   25
A furlong from the castle gate?
She had dreams all yesternight
Of her own betrothéd knight;
And she in the midnight wood will pray
For the weal[4] of her lover that's far away.   30

She stole along, she nothing spoke.
The sighs she heaved were soft and low,
And naught was green upon the oak
But moss and rarest mistletoe:
She kneels beneath the huge oak tree,   35
And in silence prayeth she.

The lady sprang up suddenly,
The lovely lady, Christabel!

---

4. Well-being.

It moaned as near, as near can be,
But what it is she cannot tell.—
On the other side it seems to be,   40
Of the huge, broad-breasted, old oak tree.

The night is chill; the forest bare;
Is it the wind that moaneth bleak?
There is not wind enough in the air   45
To move away the ringlet curl
From the lovely lady's cheek—
There is not wind enough to twirl
The one red leaf, the last of its clan,
That dances as often as dance it can,   50
Hanging so light, and hanging so high,
On the topmost twig that looks up at the sky.

Hush, beating heart of Christabel!
Jesu, Maria, shield her well!
She folded her arms beneath her cloak,   55
And stole to the other side of the oak.
        What sees she there?

There she sees a damsel bright,
Dressed in a silken robe of white,
That shadowy in the moonlight shone: 60
The neck that made that white robe wan,
Her stately neck, and arms were bare;
Her blue-veined feet unsandaled were,
And wildly glittered here and there
The gems entangled in her hair.   65
I guess, 'twas frightful there to see
A lady so richly clad as she—
Beautiful exceedingly!

Mary mother, save me now!
(Said Christabel), And who art thou?   70

The lady strange made answer meet,[5]
And her voice was faint and sweet—
Have pity on my sore distress,
I scarce can speak for weariness:
Stretch forth thy hand, and have no fear!   75
Said Christabel, How camest thou here?
And the lady, whose voice was faint and sweet,
Did thus pursue her answer meet—

My sire is of a noble line,
And my name is Geraldine: 80
Five warriors seized me yestermorn,
Me, even me, a maid forlorn:
They choked my cries with force and fright,

5. Appropriate.

And tied me on a palfrey white.
The palfrey was as fleet as wind, 85
And they rode furiously behind.
They spurred amain,[6] their steeds were white:
And once we crossed the shade of night.
As sure as Heaven shall rescue me,
I have no thought what men they be; 90
Nor do I know how long it is
(For I have lain entranced, I wis[7])
Since one, the tallest of the five,
Took me from the palfrey's back,
A weary woman, scarce alive. 95

Some muttered words his comrades spoke:
He placed me underneath this oak;
He swore they would return with haste;
Whither they went I cannot tell—
I thought I heard, some minutes past, 100
Sounds as of a castle bell.
Stretch forth thy hand (thus ended she),
And help a wretched maid to flee.

Then Christabel stretched forth her hand,
And comforted fair Geraldine: 105
O well, bright dame! may you command
The service of Sir Leoline;
And gladly our stout chivalry
Will he send forth and friends withal
To guide and guard you safe and free 110
Home to your noble father's hall.

She rose: and forth with steps they passed
That strove to be, and were not, fast.
Her gracious stars the lady blessed,
And thus spake on sweet Christabel: 115
All our household are at rest,
The hall as silent as the cell;
Sir Leoline is weak in health,
And may not well awakened be,
But we will move as if in stealth, 120
And I beseech your courtesy,
This night, to share your couch with me.

They crossed the moat, and Christabel
Took the key that fitted well;
A little door she opened straight, 125
All in the middle of the gate;
The gate that was ironed within and without,
Where an army in battle array had marched out.
The lady sank, belike through pain,

---

6. At top speed.
7. I believe; Coleridge's misinterpre-
tation of the Middle English adverb
"ywis," meaning "certainly."

And Christabel with might and main   130
Lifted her up, a weary weight,
Over the threshold of the gate:[8]
Then the lady rose again,
And moved, as she were not in pain.

So free from danger, free from fear,   135
They crossed the court: right glad they were.
And Christabel devoutly cried
To the lady by her side,
Praise we the Virgin all divine
Who hath rescued thee from thy distress!   140
Alas, alas! said **Geraldine**,
I cannot speak for weariness.
So free from danger, free from fear,
They crossed the court: right glad they were.

Outside her kennel, the mastiff old   145
Lay fast asleep, in moonshine cold.
The mastiff old did not awake,
Yet she an angry moan did make!
And what can ail the mastiff bitch?
Never till now she uttered yell   150
Beneath the eye of Christabel.
Perhaps it is the owlet's scritch:
For what can ail the mastiff bitch?

They passed the hall, that echoes still,
Pass as lightly as you will!   155
The brands were flat, the brands were dying,
Amid their own white ashes lying;
But when the lady passed, there came
A tongue of light, a fit of flame;
And Christabel saw the lady's eye,   160
And nothing else saw she thereby,
Save the boss of the shield of Sir Leoline tall,
Which hung in a murky old niche in the wall.
O softly tread, said Christabel,
My father seldom sleepeth well.   165

Sweet Christabel her feet doth bare,
And jealous of the listening air
They steal their way from stair to stair,
Now in glimmer, and now in gloom,
And now they pass the Baron's room,   170
As still as death, with stifled breath!
And now have reached her chamber door;
And now doth Geraldine press down
The rushes[9] of the chamber floor.

8. She cannot cross the threshold by her own power because it has been blessed against evil spirits; this is the first of several indications that Geraldine is a malign being.
9. Often used as a floor-covering in the Middle Ages.

The moon shines dim in the open air, 175
And not a moonbeam enters here.
But they without its light can see
The chamber carved so curiously,
Carved with figures strange and sweet,
All made out of the carver's brain, 180
For a lady's chamber meet:
The lamp with twofold silver chain
Is fastened to an angel's feet.

The silver lamp burns dead and dim;
But Christabel the lamp will trim. 185
She trimmed the lamp, and made it bright,
And left it swinging to and fro,
While Geraldine, in wretched plight,
Sank down upon the floor below.

O weary lady, Geraldine, 190
I pray you, drink this cordial wine!
It is a wine of virtuous powers;
My mother made it of wild flowers.

And will your mother pity me,
Who am a maiden most forlorn? 195
Christabel answered—Woe is me!
She died the hour that I was born.
I have heard the gray-haired friar tell
How on her deathbed she did say,
That she should hear the castle bell 200
Strike twelve upon my wedding day.
O mother dear! that thou wert here!
I would, said Geraldine, she were!
But soon with altered voice, said she—
"Off, wandering mother! Peak and pine! 205
I have power to bid thee flee."
Alas! what ails poor Geraldine?
Why stares she with unsettled eye?
Can she the bodiless dead espy?
And why with hollow voice cries she, 210
"Off, woman, off! this hour is mine—
Though thou her guardian spirit be,
Off, woman, off! 'tis given to me."

Then Christabel knelt by the lady's side,
And raised to heaven her eyes so blue— 215
Alas! said she, this ghastly ride—
Dear lady! it hath 'wildered you!
The lady wiped her moist cold brow,
And faintly said, " 'tis over now!"

Again the wild-flower wine she drank: 220
Her fair large eyes 'gan glitter bright,

And from the floor whereon she sank,
The lofty lady stood upright:
She was most beautiful to see,
Like a lady of a far countree.

And thus the lofty lady spake—
"All they who live in the upper sky,
Do love you, holy Christabel!
And you love them, and for their sake
And for the good which me befell.
Even I in my degree will try,
Fair maiden, to requite you well.
But now unrobe yourself; for I
Must pray, ere yet in bed I lie."
Quoth Christabel, So let it be!
And as the lady bade, did she.
Her gentle limbs did she undress,
And lay down in her loveliness.

But through her brain of weal and woe
So many thoughts moved to and fro,
That vain it were her lids to close;
So halfway from the bed she rose,
And on her elbow did recline
To look at the lady Geraldine.

Beneath the lamp the lady bowed,
And slowly rolled her eyes around;
Then drawing in her breath aloud,
Like one that shuddered, she unbound
The cincture[1] from beneath her breast:
Her silken robe, and inner vest,
Dropped to her feet, and full in view,
Behold! her bosom and half her side——
A sight to dream of, not to tell!
O shield her! shield sweet Christabel!

Yet Geraldine nor speaks nor stirs;
Ah! what a stricken look was hers!
Deep from within she seems halfway
To lift some weight with sick assay,[2]
And eyes the maid and seeks delay;
Then suddenly, as one defied,
Collects herself in scorn and pride,
And lay down by the maiden's side!—
And in her arms the maid she took,
            Ah well-a-day!
And with low voice and doleful look
These words did say:
"In the touch of this bosom there worketh a spell,
Which is lord of thy utterance, Christabel!

225

230

235

240

245

250

255

260

265

1. Belt.   2. Attempt.

Thou knowest tonight, and wilt know tomorrow,
This mark of my shame, this seal of my sorrow;   270
    But vainly thou warrest,
      For this is alone in
    Thy power to declare,
      That in the dim forest
    Thou heard'st a low moaning,   275
And found'st a bright lady, surpassingly fair;
And didst bring her home with thee in love and in charity,
To shield her and shelter her from the damp air."

The Conclusion to Part I

It was a lovely sight to see
The lady Christabel, when she   280
Was praying at the old oak tree.
    Amid the jagged shadows
    Of mossy leafless boughs,
    Kneeling in the moonlight,
    To make her gentle vows;   285
Her slender palms together pressed,
Heaving sometimes on her breast;
Her face resigned to bliss or bale[1]—
Her face, oh call it fair not pale,
And both blue eyes more bright than **clear**,   290
Each about to have a tear.

With open eyes (ah woe is me!)
Asleep, and dreaming fearfully,
Fearfully dreaming, yet I wis,
Dreaming that alone, which is—   295
O sorrow and shame! Can this be she,
The lady, who knelt at the old oak tree?
And lo! the worker of these harms,
That holds the maiden in her arms,
Seems to slumber still and mild,   300
As a mother with her child.

A star hath set, a star hath risen,
O Geraldine! since arms of thine
Have been the lovely lady's prison.
O Geraldine! one hour was thine—   305
Thou'st had thy will! By tairn[2] and rill,
The night birds all that hour were still.
But now they are jubilant anew,
From cliff and tower, tu—whoo! tu—whoo!
Tu—whoo! tu—whoo! from wood and fell![3]   310

And see! the lady Christabel
Gathers herself from out her trance;
Her limbs relax, her countenance

1. Evil, sorrow.   3. Elevated **moor, or hill.**
2. Tarn, a mountain pool.

Grows sad and soft; the smooth thin lids
Close o'er her eyes; and tears she sheds—
Large tears that leave the lashes bright! 315
And oft the while she seems to smile
As infants at a sudden light!

Yea, she doth smile, and she doth weep,
Like a youthful hermitess,
Beauteous in a wilderness, 320
Who, praying always, prays in sleep.
And, if she move unquietly,
Perchance, 'tis but the blood so free
Comes back and tingles in her feet.
No doubt, she hath a vision sweet. 325
What if her guardian spirit 'twere,
What if she knew her mother near?
But this she knows, in joys and woes,
That saints will aid if men will call:
For the blue sky bends over all! 330

Part II

Each matin bell, the Baron saith,
Knells us back to a world of death.
These words Sir Leoline first said,
When he rose and found his lady dead: 335
These words Sir Leoline will say
Many a morn to his dying day!

And hence the custom and law began
That still at dawn the sacristan,
Who duly pulls the heavy bell, 340
Five and forty beads must tell[4]
Between each stroke—a warning knell,
Which not a soul can choose but hear
From Bratha Head to Wyndermere.[5]

Saith Bracy the bard, So let it knell! 345
And let the drowsy sacristan
Still count as slowly as he can!
There is no lack of such, I ween,
As well fill up the space between.
In Langdale Pike[6] and Witch's Lair, 350
And Dungeon Ghyll[7] so foully rent,
With ropes of rock and bells of air
Three sinful sextons' ghosts are pent,
Who all give back, one after t'other,
The death note to their living brother; 355
And oft too, by the knell offended,

---

4. Pray while "telling" (keeping count on) the beads of a rosary. "Sacristan": sexton.
5. These and the following names are of localities in the English Lake Country.
6. Peak.
7. Ravine forming the bed of a stream.

Just as their one! two! three! is ended,
The devil mocks the doleful tale
With a merry peal from Borodale.

The air is still! through mist and cloud   360
That merry peal comes ringing loud;
And Geraldine shakes off her dread,
And rises lightly from the bed;
Puts on her silken vestments white,
And tricks her hair in lovely plight,[8]   365
And nothing doubting of her spell
Awakens the lady Christabel.
"Sleep you, sweet lady Christabel?
I trust that you have rested well."

And Christabel awoke and spied   370
The same who lay down by her side—
O rather say, the same whom she
Raised up beneath the old oak tree!
Nay, fairer yet! and yet more fair!
For she belike hath drunken deep   375
Of all the blessedness of sleep!
And while she spake, her looks, her air
Such gentle thankfulness declare,
That (so it seemed) her girded vests
Grew tight beneath her heaving breasts.   380
"Sure I have sinned!" said Christabel,
"Now heaven be praised if all be well!"
And in low faltering tones, yet sweet,
Did she the lofty lady greet
With such perplexity of mind   385
As dreams too lively leave behind.

So quickly she rose, and quickly arrayed
Her maiden limbs, and having prayed
That He, who on the cross did groan,
Might wash away her sins unknown,   390
She forthwith led fair Geraldine
To meet her sire, Sir Leoline.

The lovely maid and the lady tall
Are pacing both into the hall,
And pacing on through page and groom,   395
Enter the Baron's presence-room.

The Baron rose, and while he pressed
His gentle daughter to his breast,
With cheerful wonder in his eyes
The lady Geraldine espies,   400
And gave such welcome to the same,
As might beseem so bright a dame!

8. Plait.

But when he heard the lady's tale,
And when she told her father's name,
Why waxed Sir Leoline so pale,   405
Murmuring o'er the name again,
Lord Roland de Vaux of Tryermaine?

Alas! they had been friends in youth;
But whispering tongues can poison truth;
And constancy lives in realms above;   410
And life is thorny; and youth is vain;
And to be wroth with one we love
Doth work like madness in the brain.
And thus it chanced, as I divine,
With Roland and Sir Leoline.   415
Each spake words of high disdain
And insult to his heart's best brother:
They parted—ne'er to meet again!
But never either found another
To free the hollow heart from paining—   420
They stood aloof, the scars remaining,
Like cliffs which had been rent asunder;
A dreary sea now flows between—
But neither heat, nor frost, nor thunder,
Shall wholly do away, I ween,   425
The marks of that which once hath been.

Sir Leoline, a moment's space,
Stood gazing on the damsel's face:
And the youthful Lord of Tryermaine
Came back upon his heart again.   430

O then the Baron forgot his age,
His noble heart swelled high with rage;
He swore by the wounds in Jesu's side
He would proclaim it far and wide,
With trump and solemn heraldry,   435
That they, who thus had wronged the dame,
Were base as spotted infamy!
"And if they dare deny the same,
My herald shall appoint a week,
And let the recreant traitors seek   440
My tourney court—that there and then
I may dislodge their reptile souls
From the bodies and forms of men!"
He spake: his eye in lightning rolls!
For the lady was ruthlessly seized; and he kenned   445
In the beautiful lady the child of his friend!

And now the tears were on his face,
And fondly in his arms he took
Fair Geraldine, who met the embrace,
Prolonging it with joyous look.   450

Which when she viewed, a vision fell
Upon the soul of Christabel,
The vision of fear, the touch and pain!
She shrunk and shuddered, and saw again—
(Ah, woe is me! Was it for thee,   455
Thou gentle maid! such sights to see?)

Again she saw that bosom old,
Again she felt that bosom cold,
And drew in her breath with a hissing sound:
Whereat the Knight turned wildly round,   460
And nothing saw, but his own sweet maid
With eyes upraised, as one that prayed.
The touch, the sight, had passed away,
And in its stead that vision blest,
Which comforted her after-rest   465
While in the lady's arms she lay,
Had put a rapture in her breast,
And on her lips and o'er her eyes
Spread smiles like light!
                              With new surprise,
"What ails then my belovéd child?"   470
The Baron said—His daughter mild
Made answer, "All will yet be well!"
I ween, she had no power to tell
Aught else: so mighty was the spell.

Yet he, who saw this Geraldine,   475
Had deemed her sure a thing divine:
Such sorrow with such grace she blended,
As if she feared she had offended
Sweet Christabel, that gentle maid!
And with such lowly tones she prayed   480
She might be sent without delay
Home to her father's mansion.
                              "Nay!
Nay, by my soul!" said Leoline.
"Ho! Bracy the bard, the charge be thine!
Go thou, with music sweet and loud,   485
And take two steeds with trappings proud,
And take the youth whom thou lov'st best
To bear thy harp, and learn thy song,
And clothe you both in solemn vest,
And over the mountains haste along,   490
Lest wandering folk, that are abroad,
Detain you on the valley road.

"And when he has crossed the Irthing flood,
My merry bard! he hastes, he hastes
Up Knorren Moor, through Halegarth Wood,   495
And reaches soon that castle good
Which stands and threatens Scotland's wastes.

"Bard Bracy! bard Bracy! your horses are fleet,
Ye must ride up the hall, your music so sweet,
More loud than your horses' echoing feet! 500
And loud and loud to Lord Roland call,
Thy daughter is safe in Langdale hall!
Thy beautiful daughter is safe and free—
Sir Leoline greets thee thus through me!
He bids thee come without delay 505
With all thy numerous array
And take thy lovely daughter home:
And he will meet thee on the way
With all his numerous array
White with their panting palfreys' foam: 510
And, by mine honor! I will say,
That I repent me of the day
When I spake words of fierce disdain
To Roland de Vaux of Tryermaine!—
For since that evil hour hath flown, 515
Many a summer's sun hath shone;
Yet ne'er found I a friend again
Like Roland de Vaux of Tryermaine."

The lady fell, and clasped his knees,
Her face upraised, her eyes o'erflowing; 520
And Bracy replied, with faltering voice,
His gracious Hail on all bestowing!—
"Thy words, thou sire of Christabel,
Are sweeter than my harp can tell;
Yet might I gain a boon of thee, 525
This day my journey should not be,
So strange a dream hath come to me,
That I had vowed with music loud
To clear yon wood from thing unblest,
Warned by a vision in my rest! 530
For in my sleep I saw that dove,
That gentle bird, whom thou dost love,
And call'st by thy own daughter's name—
Sir Leoline! I saw the same
Fluttering, and uttering fearful moan, 535
Among the green herbs in the forest alone.
Which when I saw and when I heard,
I wondered what might ail the bird;
For nothing near it could I see,
Save the grass and green herbs underneath the old tree. 540

"And in my dream methought I went
To search out what might there be found;
And what the sweet bird's trouble meant,
That thus lay fluttering on the ground.
I went and peered, and could descry 545

No cause for her distressful cry;
But yet for her dear lady's sake
I stooped, methought, the dove to take,
When lo! I saw a bright green snake
Coiled around its wings and neck.   550
Green as the herbs on which it couched,
Close by the dove's its head it crouched;
And with the dove it heaves and stirs,
Swelling its neck as she swelled hers!
I woke; it was the midnight hour,   555
The clock was echoing in the tower;
But though my slumber was gone by,
This dream it would not pass away—
It seems to live upon my eye!
And thence I vowed this selfsame day   560
With music strong and saintly song
To wander through the forest bare,
Lest aught unholy loiter there."

Thus Bracy said: the Baron, the while,
Half-listening heard him with a smile;   565
Then turned to Lady Geraldine,
His eyes made up of wonder and love;
And said in courtly accents fine,
"Sweet maid, Lord Roland's beauteous dove,
With arms more strong than harp or song,   570
Thy sire and I will crush the snake!"
He kissed her forehead as he spake,
And Geraldine in maiden wise
Casting down her large bright eyes,
With blushing cheek and courtesy fine   575
She turned her from Sir Leoline;
Softly gathering up her train,
That o'er her right arm fell again;
And folded her arms across her chest,
And couched her head upon her breast,   580
And looked askance at Christabel——
Jesu, Maria, shield her well!

A snake's small eye blinks dull and shy;
And the lady's eyes they shrunk in her head,
Each shrunk up to a serpent's eye,   585
And with somewhat of malice, and more of dread,
At Christabel she looked askance!—
One moment—and the sight was fled!
But Christabel in dizzy trance
Stumbling on the unsteady ground   590
Shuddered aloud, with a hissing sound;
And Geraldine again turned round,
And like a thing, that sought relief,

Full of wonder and full of grief,
She rolled her large bright eyes divine   595
Wildly on Sir Leoline.

The maid, alas! her thoughts are gone,
She nothing sees—no sight but one!
The maid, devoid of guile and sin,
I know not how, in fearful wise,   600
So deeply had she drunken in
That look, those shrunken serpent eyes,
That all her features were resigned
To this sole image in her mind:
And passively did imitate   605
That look of dull and treacherous hate!
And thus she stood, in dizzy trance,
Still picturing that look askance
With forced unconscious sympathy
Full before her father's view—   610
As far as such a look could be
In eyes so innocent and blue!

And whence the trance was o'er, the maid
Paused awhile, and inly prayed:
Then falling at the Baron's feet,   615
"By my mother's soul do I entreat
That thou this woman send away!"
She said: and more she could not say:
For what she knew she could not tell,
O'ermastered by the mighty spell.   620

Why is thy cheek so wan and wild,
Sir Leoline? Thy only child
Lies at thy feet, thy joy, thy pride,
So fair, so innocent, so mild;
The same, for whom thy lady died!   625
O by the pangs of her dear mother
Think thou no evil of thy child!
For her, and thee, and for no other,
She prayed the moment ere she died:
Prayed that the babe for whom she died,   630
Might prove her dear lord's joy and pride!
    That prayer her deadly pangs beguiled,
        Sir Leoline!
    And wouldst thou wrong thy only child,
        Her child and thine?   635

Within the Baron's heart and brain
If thoughts, like these, had any share,
They only swelled his rage and pain,
And did but work confusion there.
His heart was cleft with pain and rage,   640
His cheeks they quivered, his eyes were wild,

Dishonored thus in his old age;
Dishonored by his only child,
And all his hospitality
To the wronged daughter of his friend   645
By more than woman's jealousy
Brought thus to a disgraceful end—
He rolled his eye with stern regard
Upon the gentle minstrel bard,
And said in tones abrupt, austere—   650
"Why, Bracy! dost thou loiter here?
I bade thee hence!" The bard obeyed;
And turning from his own sweet maid,
The aged knight, Sir Leoline,
Led forth the lady Geraldine!   655

The Conclusion to Part II

A little child, a limber elf,
Singing, dancing to itself,
A fairy thing with red round cheeks,
That always finds, and never seeks,
Makes such a vision to the sight   660
As fills a father's eyes with light;
And pleasures flow in so thick and fast
Upon his heart, that he at last
Must needs express his love's excess
With words of unmeant bitterness.   665
Perhaps 'tis pretty to force together
Thoughts so all unlike each other;
To mutter and mock a broken charm,
To dally with wrong that does no harm.
Perhaps 'tis tender too and pretty   670
At each wild word to feel within
A sweet recoil of love and pity.
And what, if in a world of sin
(O sorrow and shame should this be true!)
Such giddiness of heart and brain   675
Comes seldom save from rage and pain,
So talks as it's most used to do.

1797–1801   1816

Frost at Midnight[1]

The Frost performs its secret ministry,
Unhelped by any wind. The owlet's cry
Came loud—and hark, again! loud as before.
The inmates of my cottage, all at rest,
Have left me to that solitude, which suits   5

1. The scene is Coleridge's cottage at   his son Hartley.
Nether Stowey; the infant in line 7 is

Abstruser musings: save that at my side
My cradled infant slumbers peacefully.
'Tis calm indeed! so calm, that it disturbs
And vexes meditation with its strange
And extreme silentness. Sea, hill, and wood,   10
This populous village! Sea, and hill, and wood,
With all the numberless goings-on of life,
Inaudible as dreams! the thin blue flame
Lies on my low-burnt fire, and quivers not;
Only that film,[2] which fluttered on the grate,   15
Still flutters there, the sole unquiet thing.
Methinks its motion in this hush of nature
Gives it dim sympathies with me who live,
Making it a companionable form,
Whose puny flaps and freaks the idling Spirit   20
By its own moods interprets, everywhere
Echo or mirror seeking of itself,
And makes a toy of Thought.

                              But O! how oft,
How oft, at school, with most believing mind,
Presageful, have I gazed upon the bars,   25
To watch that fluttering *stranger!* and as oft
With unclosed lids, already had I dreamt
Of my sweet birthplace,[3] and the old church tower,
Whose bells, the poor man's only music, rang
From morn to evening, all the hot fair-day,   30
So sweetly, that they stirred and haunted me
With a wild pleasure, falling on mine ear
Most like articulate sounds of things to come!
So gazed I, till the soothing things, I dreamt,
Lulled me to sleep, and sleep prolonged my dreams!   35
And so I brooded all the following morn,
Awed by the stern preceptor's face,[4] mine eye
Fixed with mock study on my swimming book:
Save if the door half opened, and I snatched
A hasty glance, and still my heart leaped up,   40
For still I hoped to see the *stranger's* face,
Townsman, or aunt, or sister more beloved,
My playmate when we both were clothed alike![5]

    Dear Babe, that sleepest cradled by my side,
Whose gentle breathings, heard in this deep calm,   45
Fill up the interspersèd vacancies
And momentary pauses of the thought!
My babe so beautiful! it thrills my heart

---

2. "In all parts of the kingdom these films are called *strangers* and supposed to portend the arrival of some absent friend" [Coleridge's note]. The "film" is a piece of soot fluttering on the bar of the grate.
3. Coleridge was born at Ottery St. Mary, Devonshire, but went to school in London, beginning at the age of 9.
4. The "stern preceptor" at Coleridge's school, Christ's Hospital, was the Rev. James Boyer, whom Coleridge describes in *Biographia Literaria*, Chapter I.
5. I.e., when both Coleridge and his sister Ann still wore infant clothes.

With tender gladness, thus to look at thee,
And think that thou shalt learn far other lore,   50
And in far other scenes! For I was reared
In the great city, pent 'mid cloisters dim,
And saw nought lovely but the sky and stars.
But *thou*, my babe! shalt wander like a breeze
By lakes and sandy shores, beneath the crags   55
Of ancient mountain, and beneath the clouds,
Which image in their bulk both lakes and shores
And mountain crags: so shalt thou see and hear
The lovely shapes and sounds intelligible
Of that eternal language, which thy God   60
Utters, who from eternity doth teach
Himself in all, and all things in himself.
Great universal Teacher! he shall mold
Thy spirit, and by giving make it ask.

Therefore all seasons shall be sweet to thee,   65
Whether the summer clothe the general earth
With greenness, or the redbreast sit and sing
Betwixt the tufts of snow on the bare branch
Of mossy apple tree, while the nigh thatch
Smokes in the sun-thaw; whether the eave-drops fall   70
Heard only in the trances of the blast,
Or if the secret ministry of frost
Shall hang them up in silent icicles,
Quietly shining to the quiet Moon.

February, 1798   1798

Dejection: An Ode[1]

Late, late yestreen I saw the new Moon,
With the old Moon in her arms;
And I fear, I fear, my master dear!
We shall have a deadly storm.
Ballad of Sir Patrick Spence

1

Well! If the bard was weather-wise, who made
The grand old ballad of Sir Patrick Spence,
This night, so tranquil now, will not go hence

1. This poem originated in a verse letter of 340 lines, called *A Letter to* ———, which Coleridge wrote on the night of April 4, 1802, after hearing the opening stanzas of *Ode: Intimations of Immortality*, which Wordsworth had just composed. The *Letter* was addressed to Sara Hutchinson (whom Coleridge sometimes called "Asra"), the sister of Wordsworth's fiancée Mary. It picked up the theme of a loss in the quality of perceptual experience which Wordsworth had presented at the beginning of his *Ode*. In his original poem, Coleridge lamented at length his unhappy marriage and the hopelessness of his love for Sara Hutchinson. In the next six months Coleridge deleted more than half the original lines, revised and reordered the remaining passages, and so transformed a long verse confession into the compact and dignified *Dejection: An Ode*. He published the *Ode*, in substantially its present form, on October 4, 1802, Wordsworth's wedding day—and also the seventh anniversary of Coleridge's own disastrous marriage to Sara Fricker. Coleridge's implicit concern with the marital relation emerges in the marriage metaphors of lines 49 and 67–70.

Unroused by winds, that ply a busier trade
Than those which mold yon cloud in lazy flakes,   5
Or the dull sobbing draft, that moans and rakes
Upon the strings of this Aeolian lute,[2]
    Which better far were mute.
    For lo! the New-moon winter-bright!
    And overspread with phantom light,   10
    (With swimming phantom light o'erspread
    But rimmed and circled by a silver thread)
I see the old Moon in her lap, foretelling
    The coming-on of rain and squally blast.
And oh! that even now the gust were swelling,   15
    And the slant night shower driving loud and fast!
Those sounds which oft have raised me, whilst they awed,
    And sent my soul abroad,
Might now perhaps their wonted[3] impulse give,
Might startle this dull pain, and make it move and live!   20

hurry up (handwritten note in left margin)

2

A grief without a pang, void, dark, and drear,
    A stifled, drowsy, unimpassioned grief,
    Which finds no natural outlet, no relief,
    In word, or sigh, or tear—
O Lady![4] in this wan and heartless mood,   25
To other thoughts by yonder throstle wooed,
    All this long eve, so balmy and serene,
Have I been gazing on the western sky,
    And its peculiar tint of yellow green:
And still I gaze—and with how blank an eye!   30
And those thin clouds above, in flakes and bars,
That give away their motion to the stars;
Those stars, that glide behind them or between,
Now sparkling, now bedimmed, but always seen:
Yon crescent Moon, as fixed as if it grew   35
In its own cloudless, starless lake of blue;
I see them all so excellently fair,
I see, not feel, how beautiful they are!

3

    My genial[5] spirits fail;
    And what can these avail   40
To lift the smothering weight from off my breast?
    It were a vain endeavor,
    Though I should gaze forever
On that green light that lingers in the west:
I may not hope from outward forms to win   45
The passion and the life, whose fountains are within.

2. A stringed instrument played upon by the wind; see Coleridge's *The Eolian Harp*, note 1.
3. Customary.
4. In the original version "Sara"—i.e., Sara Hutchinson. After intervening ver-sions, in which the poem was addressed first to "William" (Wordsworth) and then to "Edmund," Coleridge introduced the noncommittal "Lady" in 1817.
5. In its old use as the adjective form of "genius": "My innate powers fail."

4

O Lady! we receive but what we give,
    And in our life alone does Nature live:
Ours is her wedding garment, ours her shroud![6]
    And would we aught behold, of higher worth,   50
Than that inanimate cold world allowed
To the poor loveless ever-anxious crowd,
    Ah! from the soul itself must issue forth
A light, a glory,[7] a fair luminous cloud
        Enveloping the Earth—   55
And from the soul itself must there be sent
    A sweet and potent voice, of its own birth,
Of all sweet sounds the life and element!

5

O pure of heart! thou need'st not ask of me
What this strong music in the soul may be!   60
What, and wherein it doth exist,
This light, this glory, this fair luminous mist,
This beautiful and beauty-making power.
    Joy,[8] virtuous Lady! Joy that ne'er was given,
Save to the pure, and in their purest hour,   65
Life, and Life's effluence, cloud at once and shower,
Joy, Lady! is the spirit and the power,
Which wedding Nature to us gives in dower
    A new Earth and new Heaven,[9]
Undreamt of by the sensual and the proud—   70
Joy is the sweet voice, Joy the luminous cloud—
    We in ourselves rejoice!
And thence flows all that charms or ear or sight,
    All melodies the echoes of that voice,
All colors a suffusion from that light.   75

6

There was a time when, though my path was rough,
    This joy within me dallied with distress,
And all misfortunes were but as the stuff
    Whence Fancy made me dreams of happiness:
For hope grew round me, like the twining vine,   80
And fruits, and foliage, not my own, seemed mine.
But now afflictions bow me down to earth:

6. I.e., whether nature is experienced as "inanimate" (line 51) or in living interchange with the observer depends on the apathy or joyous vitality of the observer's own spirit.
7. Coleridge commonly used "glory" not in the sense of a halo, merely, but as a term for a mountain phenomenon in which a walker sees his own figure projected by the sun in the mist, enlarged, and with a circle of light around its head. See Coleridge's *Constancy to an Ideal Object*, line 30.
8. Coleridge often uses "Joy" for a sense of abounding vitality and of harmony between one's inner life and the life of nature. He sometimes calls the contrary "exsiccation," or spiritual dryness.
9. The sense becomes clearer if line 68 is punctuated in the way that Coleridge himself punctuated it when quoting the passage in one of his essays: "Which, wedding Nature to us, gives in dower." I.e., "Joy" is the condition which (overcoming the alienation between mind and its milieu) marries us to "Nature," and gives by way of wedding portion ("dower") the experience of a renovated world.

Nor care I that they rob me of my mirth;
    But oh! each visitation
Suspends what nature gave me at my birth,   85
    My shaping spirit of Imagination.
For not to think of what I needs must feel,
    But to be still and patient, all I can;
And happly by abstruse research to steal
    From my own nature all the natural man—   90
    This was my sole resource, my only plan:
Till that which suits a part infects the whole,
And now is almost grown the habit of my soul.

                    7
Hence, viper thoughts, that coil around my mind,
    Reality's dark dream!   95
I turn from you, and listen to the wind,
    Which long has raved unnoticed. What a scream
Of agony by torture lengthened out
That lute sent forth! Thou Wind, that rav'st without,
    Bare crag, or mountain tairn,[1] or blasted tree,   100
Or pine grove whither woodman never clomb,
Or lonely house, long held the witches' home,
    Methinks were fitter instruments for thee,
Mad lutanist! who in this month of showers,
Of dark-brown gardens, and of peeping flowers,   105
Mak'st devils' yule,[2] with worse than wintry song,
The blossoms, buds, and timorous leaves among.
    Thou actor, perfect in all tragic sounds!
Thou mighty poet, e'en to frenzy bold!
    What tell'st thou now about?   110
    'Tis of the rushing of an host in rout,
    With groans, of trampled men, with smarting wounds—
At once they groan with pain, and shudder with the cold!
But hush! there is a pause of deepest silence!
    And all that noise, as of a rushing crowd,   115
With groans, and tremulous shudderings—all is over—
    It tells another tale, with sounds less deep and loud!
    A tale of less affright,
    And tempered with delight,
As Otway's[3] self had framed the tender lay—   120
    'Tis of a little child
    Upon a lonesome wild,
Not far from home, but she hath lost her way:
And now moans low in bitter grief and fear,
And now screams loud, and hopes to make her mother hear. 125
                    8
'Tis midnight, but small thoughts have I of sleep:
Full seldom may my friend such vigils keep!

---

1. Tarn, or mountain pool.
2. Christmas, in the perverted form in which it is celebrated by devils.
3. Thomas Otway (1652–85), a dram-atist noted for the pathos of his tragic passages. The poet originally named was "William," and the allusion was probably to Wordsworth's *Lucy Gray*.

Visit her, gentle Sleep! with wings of healing,
  And may this storm be but a mountain birth,[4]
May all the stars hang bright above her dwelling,   130
  Silent as though they watched the sleeping Earth!
    With light heart may she rise,
    Gay fancy, cheerful eyes,
  Joy lift her spirit, joy attune her voice;
To her may all things live, from pole to pole,   135
Their life the eddying of her living soul!
    O simple spirit, guided from above,
  Dear Lady! friend devoutest of my choice,
  Thus mayest thou ever, evermore rejoice.

April 4, 1802   1802, 1817

The Pains of Sleep[1]

Ere on my bed my limbs I lay,
It hath not been my use to pray
With moving lips or bended knees;
But silently, by slow degrees,
My spirit I to Love compose,   5
In humble trust mine eye-lids close,
With reverential resignation,
No wish conceived, no thought exprest,
Only a sense of supplication;
A sense o'er all my soul imprest   10
That I am weak, yet not unblest,
Since in me, round me, every where
Eternal Strength and Wisdom are.

But yester-night I prayed aloud
In anguish and in agony,   15
Up-starting from the fiendish crowd
Of shapes and thoughts that tortured me:
A lurid light, a trampling throng,
Sense of intolerable wrong,
And whom I scorned, those only strong!   20

Thirst of revenge, the powerless will
Still baffled, and yet burning still!

4. Probably, "May this be a typical mountain storm, short though violent," although it is possible that Coleridge intended an allusion to Horace's phrase, "the mountain labored and brought forth a mouse."

1. Coleridge included a draft of this poem in a letter to Robert Southey, September 11, 1803, in which he wrote that "my spirits are dreadful, owing entirely to the Horrors of every night—I truly dread to sleep. It is no shadow with me, but substantial Misery foot-thick, that makes me sit by my bedside of a morning, & cry—. I have abandoned all opiates except Ether be one; & that only in fits. . . ." The last sentence indicates what Coleridge did not know—that his guilty nightmares were probably what we now call "withdrawal symptoms" from opium. The dreams he describes are very similar to those that De Quincey represents as "The Pains of Opium" in his *Confessions*.

Desire with loathing strangely mixed
On wild or hateful objects fixed.
Fantastic passions! maddening brawl!   25
And shame and terror over all!
Deeds to be hid which were not hid,
Which all confused I could not know
Whether I suffered, or I did:
For all seemed guilt, remorse or woe,   30
My own or others still the same
Life-stifling fear, soul-stifling shame.

So two nights passed: the night's dismay
Saddened and stunned the coming day.
Sleep, the wide blessing, seemed to me   35
Distemper's worst calamity.
The third night, when my own loud scream
Had waked me from the fiendish dream,
O'ercome with sufferings strange and wild,
I wept as I had been a child;   40
And having thus by tears subdued
My anguish to a milder mood,
Such punishments, I said, were due
To natures deepliest stained with sin,—
For aye entempesting anew   45
The unfathomable hell within,
The horror of their deeds to view,
To know and loathe, yet wish and do!
Such griefs with such men well agree,
But wherefore, wherefore fall on me?   50
To be beloved is all I need,
And whom I love, I love indeed.
1803   1816

What Is Life?[2]

Resembles life, what once was held of light,
   Too simple in itself for human sight?
An absolute self? an element ungrounded?
All, that we see, all colors of all shade
      By encroach of darkness made?   5
Is life itself by consciousness unbounded?
And all the thoughts, pains, joys of mortal breath,
A war-embrace of wrestling life and death?

1804   1829

2. Written by Coleridge in a notebook kept at Malta in 1804, in order, he said, "to try a meter." It expresses a conception of life as a sustained opposition between the life principle and the death principle, in which the latter is the inevitable victor.

Phantom[3]

All look and likeness caught from earth
All accident of kin and birth,
Had passed away. There was no trace
Of aught on that illumined face,
Upraised beneath the rifted stone   5
But of one spirit all her own—
She, she herself, and only she,
Shone through her body visibly.

1805   1834

To William Wordsworth

COMPOSED ON THE NIGHT AFTER HIS RECITATION OF A POEM
ON THE GROWTH OF AN INDIVIDUAL MIND[1]

Friend of the wise! and teacher of the good!
Into my heart have I received that lay
More than historic, that prophetic lay
Wherein (high theme by thee first sung aright)
Of the foundations and the building up   5
Of a Human Spirit thou hast dared to tell
What may be told, to the understanding mind
Revealable; and what within the mind
By vital breathings secret as the soul
Of vernal growth, oft quickens in the heart   10
Thoughts all too deep for words![2]—

                  Theme hard as high!
Of smiles spontaneous, and mysterious fears
(The first-born they of Reason and twin birth),
Of tides obedient to external force,
And currents self-determined, as might seem,   15
Or by some inner Power; of moments awful,
Now in thy inner life, and now abroad,
When power streamed from thee, and thy soul received
The light reflected, as a light bestowed—
Of fancies fair, and milder hours of youth,   20
Hyblean[3] murmurs of poetic thought

3. A notebook Coleridge kept at Malta in 1804 makes it clear that the poem describes the appearance of Sara Hutchinson in a dream.
1. This was the poem (later called *The Prelude*) addressed to Coleridge, which Wordsworth had completed in 1805. After Coleridge returned from Malta, very low in health and spirits, Wordsworth read the poem aloud to him on the evenings of almost two weeks. Coleridge wrote most of his poem im-

mediately the reading was completed, on January 7, 1807.
2. Wordsworth had described the effect on his mind of the animating breeze ("vital breathings") in *The Prelude*, I.1-44 "Thoughts * * * words" echoes the last line of his *Intimations* ode. Coleridge then summarizes the major themes and events of *The Prelude*.
3. Sweet; Hybla, in ancient Sicily, was famous for its honey.

Industrious in its joy, in vales and glens
Native or outland, lakes and famous hills!
Or on the lonely highroad, when the stars
Were rising; or by secret mountain streams,   25
The guides and the companions of thy way!

Of more than Fancy, of the Social Sense
Distending wide, and man beloved as man,
Where France in all her towns lay vibrating
Like some becalméd bark beneath the burst   30
Of Heaven's immediate thunder, when no cloud
Is visible, or shadow on the main.
For thou wert there, thine own brows garlanded,
Amid the tremor of a realm aglow,
Amid a mighty nation jubilant,   35
When from the general heart of human kind
Hope sprang forth like a full-born deity!
——Of that dear Hope afflicted and struck down,
So summoned homeward, thenceforth calm and sure
From the dread watchtower of man's absolute self,   40
With light unwaning on her eyes, to look
Far on—herself a glory to behold,
The Angel of the vision! Then (last strain)
Of Duty, chosen Laws controlling choice,
Action and joy!—An Orphic song[4] indeed,   45
A song divine of high and passionate thoughts
To their own music chaunted!

                              O great bard!
Ere that last strain dying awed the air,
With steadfast eye I viewed thee in the choir
Of ever-enduring men. The truly great   50
Have all one age, and from one visible space
Shed influence! They, both in power and act,
Are permanent, and Time is not with them,
Save as it worketh for them, they in it.
Nor less a sacred roll, than those of old,   55
And to be placed, as they, with gradual fame
Among the archives of mankind, thy work
Makes audible a linkéd lay of Truth,
Of Truth profound a sweet continuous lay,
Not learnt, but native, her own natural notes!   60
Ah! as I listened with a heart forlorn,
The pulses of my being beat anew:
And even as Life returns upon the drowned,[5]
Life's joy rekindling roused a throng of pains—

---

4. As enchanting and oracular as the song of the legendary Orpheus. There may also be an allusion to the Orphic mysteries, involving spiritual death and rebirth; see lines 61–66. "The Angel of the Vision" probably alludes to "the great vision of the guarded mount" in Milton's *Lycidas*, line 161.
5. A death-in-life is also described in, e.g., *Dejection* and *Epitaph*.

Keen pangs of Love, awakening as a babe   65
Turbulent, with an outcry in the heart;
And fears self-willed, that shunned the eye of Hope;
And Hope that scarce would know itself from Fear;
Sense of past Youth, and Manhood come in vain,
And Genius given, and Knowledge won in vain;   70
And all which I had culled in wood-walks wild,
And all which patient toil had reared, and all,
Commune with thee had opened out—but flowers
Strewed on my corse, and borne upon my bier
In the same coffin, for the selfsame grave!   75

That way no more! and ill beseems it me,
Who came a welcomer in herald's guise,
Singing of Glory, and Futurity,
To wander back on such unhealthful road,
Plucking the poisons of self-harm! And ill   80
Such intertwine beseems triumphal wreaths
Strewed before thy advancing!

Nor do thou,
Sage bard! impair the memory of that hour
Of thy communion with my nobler mind[6]
By pity or grief, already felt too long!   85
Nor let my words import more blame than needs.
The tumult rose and ceased: for Peace is nigh
Where Wisdom's voice has found a listening heart.
Amid the howl of more than wintry storms,
The Halcyon[7] hears the voice of vernal hours   90
Already on the wing.

Eve following eve,[8]
Dear tranquil time, when the sweet sense of Home
Is sweetest! moments for their own sake hailed
And more desired, more precious, for thy song,
In silence listening, like a devout child,   95
My soul lay passive, by thy various strain
Driven as in surges now beneath the stars,
With momentary stars of my own birth,
Fair constellated foam, still darting off
Into the darkness; now a tranquil sea,   100
Outspread and bright, yet swelling to the moon.

And when—O friend! my comforter and guide!
Strong in thyself, and powerful to give strength!—
Thy long sustainéd song finally closed,
And thy deep voice had ceased—yet thou thyself   105
Wert still before my eyes, and round us both
That happy vision of belovéd faces—

6. I.e., during the early association between the two poets (1797-98).
7. A fabled bird, able to calm the sea,
where it nested in winter.
8. The evenings during which Wordsworth read his poem aloud.

Scarce conscious, and yet conscious of its close
I sate, my being blended in one thought
(Thought was it? or aspiration? or resolve?)   110
Absorbed, yet hanging still upon the sound—
And when I rose, I found myself in prayer.

1807   1817

Recollections of Love

1

How warm this woodland wild recess!
  Love surely hath been breathing here;
  And this sweet bed of heath, my dear!
Swells up, then sinks with faint caress,
  As if to have you yet more near.   5

2

Eight springs have flown since last I lay
  On seaward Quantock's heathy hills,[9]
  Where quiet sounds from hidden rills
Float here and there, like things astray,
  And high o'erhead the skylark shrills.   10

3

No voice as yet had made the air
  Be music with your name; yet why
  That asking look? that yearning sigh?
That sense of promise every where?
  Belovéd! flew your spirit by?   15

4

As when a mother doth explore
  The rose mark on her long-lost child,
  I met, I loved you, maiden mild!
As whom I long had loved before—
  So deeply had I been beguiled.   20

5

You stood before me like a thought,
  A dream remembered in a dream.
  But when those meek eyes first did seem
To tell me, Love within you wrought—
  O Greta,[10] dear domestic stream!   25

6

Has not, since then, Love's prompture deep,
  Has not Love's whisper evermore
  Been ceaseless, as thy gentle roar?
Sole voice, when other voices sleep,
  Dear under-song in clamor's hour.   30

ca. 1807   1817

9. Near Nether Stowey, Somerset, where
Coleridge had lived 1796–98.
10. The river Greta, which flowed past

Coleridge's home in Keswick, in the
Lake Country.

Limbo[1]

The sole true Something—This! In Limbo's Den
It frightens Ghosts, as here Ghosts frighten men.
Thence crossed unseized—and shall some fated hour
Be pulverised by Demogorgon's[2] power,
And given as poison to annihilate souls—   5
Even now it shrinks them—they shrink in as Moles
(Nature's mute monks, live mandrakes[3] of the ground)
Creep back from Light—then listen for its sound;—
See but to dread, and dread they know not why—
The natural alien of their negative eye.   10

'Tis a strange place, this Limbo!—not a Place,
Yet name it so;—where Time and weary Space
Fettered from flight, with night-mare sense of fleeing,
Strive for their last crepuscular half-being;—
Lank Space, and scytheless Time with branny[4] hands   15
Barren and soundless as the measuring sands,
Not marked by flit of Shades,—unmeaning they
As moonlight on the dial of the day!
But that is lovely—looks like Human Time,—
An Old Man with a steady look sublime,   20
That stops his earthly task to watch the skies;
But he is blind—a Statue hath such eyes;—
Yet having moonward turned his face by chance,
Gazes the orb with moon-like countenance,
With scant white hairs, with foretop bald and high,   25
He gazes still,—his eyeless face all eye;—
As 'twere an organ full of silent sight,
His whole face seemeth to rejoice in light!
Lip touching lip, all moveless, bust and limb—
He seems to gaze at that which seems to gaze on him!   30
    No such sweet sights doth Limbo den immure,
Walled round, and made a spirit-jail secure,
By the mere horror of blank Naught-at-all,

---

1. In traditional Catholic theology, "Limbo" designated the abode of those souls—virtuous pagans, the saints of the Old Testament, and infants who died before baptism—who, through no fault of their own, are excluded from access to God. In 1818, Coleridge cited lines 6–10 to characterize the views of "the partizans of a crass and sensual materialism." And in a letter of October 13, 1806, he had said that to advocates of "Atheism or Spinosism—God becomes a mere power in darkness, even as Gravitation . . . no Sun, no Light with vivifying Warmth, but a cold and dull moonshine, or rather star-light, which shews itself but shews nothing else" (compare lines 16 ff.). Coleridge, then, probably intended Limbo to represent the nightmarish world-view which, he thinks, is the consequence of a purely materialist metaphysics. The poem remained in manuscript in one of Coleridge's notebooks until it was published in 1893.
2. Demogorgon was described by Boccaccio and by Renaissance writers as the primeval father of all pagan gods, ruler of the nether world. For Shelley's Demogorgon see *Prometheus Unbound*, III.iv.
3. Plants with a forked root; according to legend, the root, similar in shape to the human body, shrieks when pulled from the ground.
4. Similar to bran, the husks of grain; thus, withered and brown.

Whose circumambience doth these ghosts enthral.
A lurid thought is growthless, dull Privation,   35
Yet that is but a Purgatory curse;
Hell knows a fear far worse,
A fear—a future state;—'tis positive Negation![5]

1817   1893

On Donne's Poetry[6]

With Donne, whose muse on dromedary[7] trots,
Wreathe iron pokers into truelove knots;
Rhyme's sturdy cripple, fancy's maze and clue,
Wit's forge and fire-blast, meaning's press and screw.

ca. 1818   1836

Work Without Hope

LINES COMPOSED 21ST FEBRUARY 1825

All Nature seems at work. Slugs leave their lair—
The bees are stirring—birds are on the wing—
And Winter slumbering in the open air
Wears on his smiling face a dream of Spring!
And I the while, the sole unbusy thing,   5
Nor honey make, nor pair, nor build, nor sing.

  Yet well I ken the banks where amaranths[8] blow,
Have traced the fount whence streams of nectar flow.
Bloom, O ye amaranths! bloom for whom ye may,
For me ye bloom not! Glide, rich streams, away!   10
With lips unbrightened, wreathless brow, I stroll:
And would you learn the spells that drowse my soul?
Work without Hope draws nectar in a sieve,
And Hope without an object cannot live.

1825   1828

Constancy to an Ideal Object

Since all that beat about in Nature's range
Or veer or vanish, why should'st thou remain
The only constant in a world of change,
O yearning Thought! that liv'st but in the brain?
Call to the Hours, that in the distance play,   5
The faery people of the future day——
Fond[9] Thought! not one of all that shining swarm

---

5. "The sole true Something" (line 1) which is "positive Negation" is like *le néant*—the existent nothingness—posited by some present-day Existentialist philosophers.
6. Donne as a poet had been in eclipse for most of the 18th century. This terse and penetrating comment shows the Ro- mantic poet's great, though ironically qualified, respect for the master of the metaphysical style.
7. The one-humped Arabian camel, trained for riding.
8. Mythical flowers that bloom perpetually.
9. Foolish.

Will breathe on thee with life-enkindling breath,
Till when, like strangers shelt'ring from a storm,
Hope and Despair meet in the porch of Death!   10
Yet still thou haunt'st me; and though well I see,
She[1] is not thou, and only thou art she,
Still, still as though some dear embodied Good,
Some living Love before my eyes there stood
With answering look a ready ear to lend,   15
I mourn to thee and say—"Ah! loveliest friend!
That this the meed[2] of all my toils might be,
To have a home, an English home, and thee!"
Vain repetition! Home and thou are one.
The peaceful'st cot the moon shall shine upon,   20
Lulled by the thrush and wakened by the lark,
Without thee were but a becalmèd bark,
Whose Helmsman on an ocean waste and wide
Sits mute and pale his moldering helm beside.

And art thou nothing? Such thou art, as when   25
The woodman winding westward up the glen
At wintry dawn, where o'er the sheep-track's maze
The viewless snow-mist weaves a glist'ning haze,
Sees full before him, gliding without tread,
An image with a glory round its head;[3]   30
The enamored rustic worships its fair hues,
Nor knows he makes the shadow he pursues!

         1828

Phantom or Fact

A DIALOGUE IN VERSE

AUTHOR

A lovely form there sate beside my bed,
And such a feeding calm its presence shed,
A tender love so pure from earthly leaven,
That I unnethe[4] the fancy might control,
'Twas my own spirit newly come from heaven,   5
Wooing its gentle way into my soul!
But ah! the change—It had not stirred, and yet—
Alas! that change how fain would I forget!
That shrinking back, like one that had mistook!
That weary, wandering, disavowing look!   10
'Twas all another, feature, look, and frame,
And still, methought, I knew, it was the same!

FRIEND

This riddling tale, to what does it belong?
Is't history? vision? or an idle song?
Or rather say at once, within what space   15
Of time this wild disastrous change took place?

---

1. Sara Hutchinson.
2. Reward.
3. A projected image of oneself in the mist. See Coleridge's *Dejection: An Ode,* line 54.
4. With difficulty.

AUTHOR

Call it a moment's work (and such it seems)
This tale's a fragment from the life of dreams;
But say that years matured the silent strife,
And 'tis a record from the dream of life.   20

ca. 1830   1834

Epitaph[1]

Stop, Christian passer-by!—Stop, child of God,
And read with gentle breast. Beneath this sod
A poet lies, or that which once seemed he.
O lift one thought in prayer for S. T. C.;
That he who many a year with toil of breath   5
Found death in life, may here find life in death!
Mercy for praise—to be forgiven for[2] fame
He asked, and hoped, through Christ. Do thou the same!

1833   1834

From Biographia Literaria[1]

From *Chapter I*

The discipline of his taste at school—Bowles's sonnets—Comparison between the poets before and since Mr. Pope.

* * * At school I enjoyed the inestimable advantage of a very

1. Written by Coleridge the year before he died. One version that he sent in a letter had as title: "Epitaph on a Poet little known, yet better known by the Initials of his name than by the Name Itself."
2. "'For' in the sense of 'instead of'" [Coleridge's note].
1. In March, 1815, Coleridge was preparing a collected edition of his poems, and planned to include "a general preface * * * on the principles of philosophic and genial criticism." Characteristically, the materials developed as Coleridge worked on them, until, on July 29, he declared that the preface had been extended into a complete work, "an Autobiographia Literaria"; it was to consist of two main parts, "my literary life and opinions, as far as poetry and *poetical* criticism [are] concerned," and a critique of Wordsworth's theory of poetic diction. This work was ready by 17 September 1815, but the *Biographia Literaria*, in two volumes, was not published until July, 1817. The delay was caused by a series of miscalculations by his printer, which forced Coleridge to add miscellaneous materials needed to eke out the length of his original manuscript.
The critique of Wordsworth's theory of diction, which Coleridge had been planning ever since 1802, when he had detected "a radical difference in our

theoretical opinions respecting poetry," is long, detailed, and subtly reasoned. In the selection from Chapter XVII, below, Coleridge agrees with Wordsworth's general aim of reforming the artifices of modern poetic diction, but he sharply denies Wordsworth's claim that there is no essential difference between the language of poetry and the language really spoken by men. The other selections printed here are devoted mainly to the central principle of Coleridge's own critical theory, the distinction between the mechanical "fancy" and the organic "imagination." Thus the biographical section of the *Biographia* (Chapters I and IV), dealing with the development of his poetic taste and theory, describes his gradual realization, climaxed by his first exposure to Wordsworth's poetry, "that fancy and imagination were two distinct and widely different faculties." The conclusion to Chapter XIII tersely summarizes this distinction, and the definition of poetry, at the end of Chapter XIV, develops at somewhat greater length the nature of the process and products of the "synthetic and magical power * * * of imagination." These cryptic paragraphs have proved to be the most widely discussed and influential passages ever written by an English critic.

sensible, though at the same time a very severe master. He[2] early molded my taste to the preference of Demosthenes to Cicero, of Homer and Theocritus to Virgil, and again of Virgil to Ovid. He habituated me to compare Lucretius (in such extracts as I then read), Terence, and, above all, the chaster poems of Catullus not only with the Roman poets of the so-called silver and brazen ages but with even those of the Augustan era; and, on grounds of plain sense and universal logic, to see and assert the superiority of the former in the truth and nativeness both of their thoughts and diction. At the same time that we were studying the Greek tragic poets, he made us read Shakespeare and Milton as lessons; and they were the lessons, too, which required most time and trouble to *bring up*, so as to escape his censure. I learnt from him that poetry, even that of the loftiest and, seemingly, that of the wildest odes, had a logic of its own as severe as that of science; and more difficult, because more subtle, more complex, and dependent on more, and more fugitive, causes. In the truly great poets, he would say, there is a reason assignable, not only for every word, but for the position of every word; and I well remember that, availing himself of the synonyms to the Homer of Didymus,[3] he made us attempt to show, with regard to each, *why* it would not have answered the same purpose, and *wherein* consisted the peculiar fitness of the word in the original text.

In our own English compositions (at least for the last three years of our school education) he showed no mercy to phrase, metaphor, or image unsupported by a sound sense, or where the same sense might have been conveyed with equal force and dignity in plainer words. Lute, harp, and lyre, muse, muses, and inspirations, Pegasus, Parnassus, and Hippocrene were all an abomination to him. In fancy I can almost hear him now, exclaiming, "Harp? Harp? Lyre? Pen and ink, boy, you mean! Muse, boy, muse? Your nurse's daughter, you mean! Pierian spring? Oh, aye! the cloister pump, I suppose!" Nay, certain introductions, similes, and examples were placed by name on a list of interdiction. Among the similes there was, I remember, that of the manchineel fruit,[4] as suiting equally well with too many subjects, in which, however, it yielded the palm at once to the example of Alexander and Clytus,[5] which was equally good and apt whatever might be the theme. Was it ambition? Alexander and Clytus! Flattery? Alexander and Clytus! Anger? Drunkenness? Pride? Friendship? Ingratitude? Late repentance? Still, still Alexander and Clytus! At length the praises of agriculture having been exemplified in the sagacious observation

---

2. "The Rev. James Boyer, many years Head Master of the Grammar School, Christ's Hospital" [Coleridge's note]. See also Charles Lamb's essay, *Christ's Hospital Five-and-Thirty Years Ago.*
3. Didymus of Alexandria (ca. 65 B.C.–A.D. 10) was the author of a commentary on the text of Homer.

4. Poisonous, though attractive in appearance.
5. Plutarch's *Life* of Alexander the Great relates that the king killed his friend Clytus in a drunken quarrel.

that, had Alexander been holding the plow, he would not have run his friend Clytus through with a spear, this tried and serviceable old friend was banished by public edict *in secula seculorum*.[6] I have sometimes ventured to think that a list of this kind or an *index expurgatorius* of certain well-known and ever returning phrases, both introductory and transitional, including the large assortment of modest egotisms and flattering illeisms,[7] etc., etc., might be hung up in our law courts and both Houses of Parliament with great advantage to the public as an important saving of national time, an incalculable relief to his Majesty's ministers; but, above all, as insuring the thanks of country attorneys and their clients, who have private bills to carry through the House.

Be this as it may, there was one custom of our master's which I cannot pass over in silence, because I think it imitable and worthy of imitation. He would often permit our theme exercises, under some pretext of want of time, to accumulate till each lad had four or five to be looked over. Then placing the whole number *abreast* on his desk, he would ask the writer why this or that sentence might not have found as appropriate a place under this or that other thesis; and if no satisfying answer could be returned and two faults of the same kind were found in one exercise, the irrevocable verdict followed, the exercise was torn up, and another on the same subject to be produced, in addition to the tasks of the day. The reader will, I trust, excuse this tribute of recollection to a man whose severities, even now, not seldom furnish the dreams by which the blind fancy would fain interpret to the mind the painful sensations of distempered sleep; but neither lessen nor dim the deep sense of my moral and intellectual obligations. He sent us to the university excellent Latin and Greek scholars and tolerable Hebraists. Yet our classical knowledge was the least of the good gifts which we derived from his zealous and conscientious tutorage. He is now gone to his final reward, full of years and full of honors, even of those honors which were dearest to his heart as gratefully bestowed by that school, and still binding him to the interests of that school in which he had been himself educated and to which during his whole life he was a dedicated thing. * * *

I had just entered on my seventeenth year when the sonnets of Mr. Bowles,[8] twenty in number, and just then published in a quarto pamphlet, were first made known and presented to me by a schoolfellow who had quitted us for the university and who, during the whole time that he was in our first form (or in our school

6. Forever ("for centuries of centuries").
7. Excessive use of the pronoun "he" (in Latin, *ille*).
8. William Lisle Bowles (1762–1850) published in 1789 two editions of a collection of sonnet setting forth the meditations evoked from a traveler by the changing scene.

language, a Grecian[9]), had been my patron and protector. I refer to Dr. Middleton, the truly learned and every way excellent Bishop of Calcutta. * * *

It was a double pleasure to me, and still remains a tender recollection, that I should have received from a friend so revered the first knowledge of a poet by whose works, year after year, I was so enthusiastically delighted and inspired. My earliest acquaintances will not have forgotten the undisciplined eagerness and impetuous zeal with which I laboured to make proselytes, not only of my companions, but of all with whom I conversed, of whatever rank and in whatever place. As my school finances did not permit me to purchase copies I made, within less than a year and a half, more than forty transcriptions, as the best presents I could offer to those who had in any way won my regard. And with almost equal delight did I receive the three or four following publications of the same author.

Though I have seen and known enough of mankind to be well aware that I shall perhaps stand alone in my creed, and that it will be well if I subject myself to no worse charge than that of singularity, I am not therefore deterred from avowing that I regard and ever have regarded the obligations of intellect among the most sacred of the claims of gratitude. A valuable thought, or a particular train of thoughts, gives me additional pleasure when I can safely refer and attribute it to the conversation or correspondence of another. My obligations to Mr. Bowles were indeed important and for radical good. At a very premature age, even before my fifteenth year, I had bewildered myself in metaphysics and in theological controversy. Nothing else pleased me. History and particular facts lost all interest in my mind. Poetry (though for a schoolboy of that age I was above par in English versification and had already produced two or three compositions which, I may venture to say without reference to my age, were somewhat above mediocrity, and which had gained me more credit than the sound good sense of my old master was at all pleased with), poetry itself, yea novels and romances, became insipid to me. In my friendless wanderings on our leave-days (for I was an orphan, and had scarce any connections in London), highly was I delighted if any passenger, especially if he were dressed in black,[10] would enter into conversation with me. For I soon found the means of directing it to my favorite subjects

> Of providence, foreknowledge, will, and fate,
> Fixed fate, free will, foreknowledge absolute,
> And found no end, in wandering mazes lost.[1]

9. Gifted students in the final class at Christ's Hospital who were being prepared for a university.

10. I.e., if he were a clergyman.
1. *Paradise Lost* II.559–61.

This preposterous pursuit was, beyond doubt, injurious both to my natural powers and to the progress of my education. It would perhaps have been destructive had it been continued; but from this I was auspiciously withdrawn, partly indeed by an accidental introduction to an amiable family,[2] chiefly however by the genial influence of a style of poetry so tender and yet so manly, so natural and real, and yet so dignified and harmonious, as the sonnets, etc., of Mr. Bowles! Well were it for me, perhaps, had I never relapsed into the same mental disease; if I had continued to pluck the flower and reap the harvest from the cultivated surface, instead of delving in the unwholesome quicksilver mines of metaphysic depths. But if in after time I have sought a refuge from bodily pain and mismanaged sensibility in abstruse researches, which exercised the strength and subtlety of the understanding without awakening the feelings of the heart; still there was a long and blessed interval, during which my natural faculties were allowed to expand and my original tendencies to develop themselves; my fancy, and the love of nature, and the sense of beauty in forms and sounds.

The second advantage which I owe to my early perusal and admiration of these poems (to which let me add, though known to me at a somewhat later period, the *Lewesdon Hill* of Mr. Crow)[3] bears more immediately on my present subject. Among those with whom I conversed there were, of course, very many who had formed their taste and their notions of poetry from the writings of Mr. Pope and his followers: or to speak more generally, in that school of French poetry condensed and invigorated by English understanding which had predominated from the last century. I was not blind to the merits of this school, yet as from inexperience of the world and consequent want of sympathy with the general subjects of these poems they gave me little pleasure, I doubtless undervalued the *kind*, and with the presumption of youth withheld from its masters the legitimate name of poets. I saw that the excellence of this kind consisted in just and acute observations on men and manners in an artificial state of society as its matter and substance, and in the logic of wit conveyed in smooth and strong epigrammatic couplets as its *form*. Even when the subject was addressed to the fancy or the intellect, as in the *Rape of the Lock* or the *Essay on Man*; nay, when it was a consecutive narration, as in that astonishing product of matchless talent and ingenuity, Pope's translation of the *Iliad*; still a *point* was looked for at the end of each second line, and the whole was as it were a sorites or, if I may exchange a logical for a

<hr>

2. The family of Mary Evans, with whom Coleridge fell deeply in love in 1788.
3. William Crow(e) (1745–1829) published in 1788 *Lewesdon Hill,* a long poem in blank verse which, like Bowles's sonnets, combined descriptions of the natural scene with associated moral and personal reflections.

grammatical metaphor, a *conjunction disjunctive*,[4] of epigrams. Meantime the matter and diction seemed to me characterized not so much by poetic thoughts as by thoughts *translated* into the language of poetry. On this last point I had occasion to render my own thoughts gradually more and more plain to myself by frequent amicable disputes concerning Darwin's *Botanic Garden*,[5] which for some years was greatly extolled, not only by the *reading* public in general, but even by those whose genius and natural robustness of understanding enabled them afterwards to act foremost in dissipating these "painted mists" that occasionally rise from the marshes at the foot of Parnassus. During my first Cambridge vacation I assisted a friend in a contribution for a literary society in Devonshire, and in this I remember to have compared Darwin's work to the Russian palace of ice, glittering, cold, and transitory. In the same essay too I assigned sundry reasons, chiefly drawn from a comparison of passages in the Latin poets with the original Greek from which they were borrowed, for the preference of Collins's odes to those of Gray, and of the simile in Shakespeare:

> How like a younker or a prodigal
> The scarfed bark puts from her native bay,
> Hugged and embraced by the strumpet wind!
> How like the prodigal doth she return,
> With over-weathered ribs and ragged sails,
> Lean, rent and beggared by the strumpet wind![6]

to the imitation in the *Bard*:

> Fair laughs the morn, and soft the zephyr blows
> While proudly riding o'er the azure realm
> In gallant trim the gilded vessel goes;
> YOUTH on the prow, and PLEASURE at the helm;
> Regardless of the sweeping whirlwind's sway,
> That, hushed in grim repose, expects its evening prey.[7]

(In which, by the bye, the words "realm" and "sway" are rhymes dearly purchased.) I preferred the original, on the ground that in the imitation it depended wholly in the compositor's putting, or not putting, a small capital both in this and in many other passages of the same poet whether the words should be personifications or mere abstracts. I mention this because, in referring various lines in Gray to their original in Shakespeare and Milton, and in the clear perception how completely all the propriety was lost in the transfer, I was at that early period led to a conjecture which, many

4. "Sorites": a sequence of interconnected syllogisms; "*conjunction disjunctive*": a word which connects the parts of a sentence but expresses an alternative or opposition: "or," "but," "lest," etc.

5. Published in 1789–91 by Erasmus Darwin (1731–1802); a long poem in closed couplets, presenting the science of botany in elaborate allegories.
6. *Merchant of Venice* II.vi.14–19.
7. Thomas Gray, *The Bard* (1757).

years afterwards, was recalled to me from the same thought having been started in conversation, but far more ably, and developed more fully, by Mr. Wordsworth; namely, that this style of poetry which I have characterized above as translations of prose thoughts into poetic language had been kept up by, if it did not wholly arise from, the custom of writing Latin verses and the great importance attached to these exercises in our public schools. Whatever might have been the case in the fifteenth century, when the use of the Latin tongue was so general among learned men that Erasmus is said to have forgotten his native language; yet in the present day it is not to be supposed that a youth can think in Latin, or that he can have any other reliance on the force or fitness of his phrases but the authority of the author from whence he had adopted them. Consequently he must first prepare his thoughts and then pick out from Virgil, Horace, Ovid, or perhaps more compendiously, from his *Gradus*,[8] halves and quarters of lines in which to embody them.

I never object to a certain degree of disputatiousness in a young man from the age of seventeen to that of four or five and twenty, provided I find him always arguing on one side of the question. The controversies occasioned by my unfeigned zeal for the honor of a favorite contemporary, then known to me only by his works, were of great advantage in the formation and establishment of my taste and critical opinions. In my defense of the lines running into each other instead of closing at each couplet, and of natural language, neither bookish nor vulgar, neither redolent of the lamp nor of the kennel, such as *I will remember thee*; instead of the same thought tricked up in the rag-fair finery of

> ——Thy image on her wing
> Before my Fancy's eye shall Memory bring,

I had continually to adduce the meter and diction of the Greek poets from Homer to Theocritus inclusive; and still more of our elder English poets from Chaucer to Milton. Nor was this all. But as it was my constant reply to authorities brought against me from later poets of great name that no authority could avail in opposition to Truth, Nature, Logic, and the Laws of Universal Grammar; actuated too by my former passion for metaphysical investigations, I labored at a solid foundation on which permanently to ground my opinions in the component faculties of the human mind itself and their comparative dignity and importance. According to the faculty or source from which the pleasure given by any poem or passage was derived I estimated the merit of such poem or passage. As the result of all my reading and meditation, I abstracted two

8. *Gradus ad Parnassum* ("Stairway to Parnassus"), a dictionary of Latin words, synonyms, and descriptive epithets, illustrated from the Latin poets. It was long used as a school text in Latin composition.

critical aphorisms, deeming them to comprise the conditions and criteria of poetic style: first, that not the poem which we have *read*, but that to which we *return* with the greatest pleasure, possesses the genuine power and claims the name of *essential* poetry. Second, that whatever lines can be translated into other words of the same language without diminution of their significance, either in sense of association or in any worthy feeling, are so far vicious in their diction. Be it however observed that I excluded from the list of worthy feelings the pleasure derived from mere novelty in the reader, and the desire of exciting wonderment at his powers in the author. Oftentimes since then, in perusing French tragedies, I have fancied two marks of admiration at the end of each line, as hieroglyphics of the author's own admiration at his own cleverness. Our genuine admiration of a great poet is a continuous undercurrent of feeling; it is everywhere present, but seldom anywhere as a separate excitement. I was wont boldly to affirm that it would be scarcely more difficult to push a stone out from the pyramids with the bare hand than to alter a word, or the position of a word, in Milton or Shakespeare (in their most important works at least), without making the author say something else, or something worse, than he does say. One great distinction I appeared to myself to see plainly, between even the characteristic faults of our elder poets and the false beauties of the moderns. In the former, from Donne to Cowley, we find the most fantastic out-of-the-way thoughts, but in the most pure and genuine mother English; in the latter, the most obvious thoughts, in language the most fantastic and arbitrary. Our faulty elder poets sacrificed the passion and passionate flow of poetry to the subtleties of intellect and to the starts of wit; the moderns to the glare and glitter of a perpetual yet broken and heterogeneous imagery, or rather to an amphibious something, made up half of image and half of abstract[9] meaning. The one sacrificed the heart to the head, the other both heart and head to point and drapery. * * *

From *Chapter IV*

Mr. Wordsworth's earlier poems—On fancy and imagination— The investigation of the distinction important to the fine arts.

 * * * During the last year of my residence at Cambridge I became acquainted with Mr. Wordsworth's first publication, entitled *Descriptive Sketches*;[1] and seldom, if ever, was the emergence of

9. "I remember a ludicrous instance in the poem of a young tradesman: 'No more will I endure Love's pleasing pain, / Or round my *heart's leg* tie his galling chain'" [Coleridge's note].

1. Published 1793, the year before Coleridge left Cambridge; a long descriptive-meditative poem in closed couplets, describing Wordsworth's walking tour in the Alps in 1790. See also *The Prelude* VI.

an original poetic genius above the literary horizon more evidently announced. In the form, style, and manner of the whole poem, and in the structure of the particular lines and periods, there is a harshness and acerbity connected and combined with words and images all aglow which might recall those products of the vegetable world, where gorgeous blossoms rise out of the hard and thorny rind and shell within which the rich fruit was elaborating. The language was not only peculiar and strong, but at times knotty and contorted, as by its own impatient strength; while the novelty and struggling crowd of images acting in conjunction with the difficulties of the style demanded always a greater closeness of attention than poetry (at all events than descriptive poetry) has a right to claim. It not seldom therefore justified the complaint of obscurity. In the following extract I have sometimes fancied that I saw an emblem of the poem itself and of the author's genius as it was then displayed:

> 'Tis storm; and hid in mist from hour to hour,
> All day the floods a deepening murmur pour,
> The sky is veiled, and every cheerful sight;
> Dark is the region as with coming night;
> And yet what frequent bursts of overpowering light!
> Triumphant on the bosom of the storm,
> Glances the fire-clad eagle's wheeling form;
> Eastward, in long perspective glittering, shine
> The wood-crowned cliffs that o'er the lake recline;
> Wide o'er the Alps a hundred streams unfold,
> At once to pillars turned that flame with gold;
> Behind his sail the peasant strives to shun
> The West, that burns like one dilated sun,
> Where in a mighty crucible expire
> The mountains, glowing hot, like coals of fire.[2]

The poetic Psyche, in its process to full development, undergoes as many changes as its Greek namesake, the butterfly.[3] And it is remarkable how soon genius clears and purifies itself from the faults and errors of its earliest products; faults which, in its earliest compositions, are the more obtrusive and confluent because, as heterogeneous elements which had only a temporary use, they constitute the very *ferment* by which themselves are carried off. Or we may compare them to some diseases, which must work on the humors and be thrown out on the surface in order to secure the patient from their future recurrence. I was in my twenty-fourth year when I had the happiness of knowing Mr. Wordsworth personally;[4] and, while memory lasts, I shall hardly forget the sudden effect pro-

2. *Descriptive Sketches* (1815 version), lines 332 ff.
3. "In Greek, Psyche is the common name for the soul and the butterfly"
[Coleridge's note].
4. The meeting occurred in September, 1795.

duced on my mind by his recitation of a manuscript poem which still remains unpublished, but of which the stanza and tone of style were the same as those of *The Female Vagrant* as originally printed in the first volume of the *Lyrical Ballads*.[5] There was here no mark of strained thought or forced diction, no crowd or turbulence of imagery, and, as the poet hath himself well described in his lines on revisiting the Wye, manly reflection and human associations had given both variety and an additional interest to natural objects which in the passion and appetite of the first love they had seemed to him neither to need or permit.[6] The occasional obscurities which had risen from an imperfect control over the resources of his native language had almost wholly disappeared, together with that worse defect of arbitrary and illogical phrases, at once hackneyed and fantastic, which hold so distinguished a place in the *technique* of ordinary poetry and will, more or less, alloy the earlier poems of the truest genius, unless the attention has been specifically directed to their worthlessness and incongruity. I did not perceive anything particular in the mere style of the poem alluded to during its recitation, except indeed such difference as was not separable from the thought and manner; and the Spenserian stanza which always, more or less, recalls to the reader's mind Spenser's own style, would doubtless have authorized in my then opinion a more frequent descent to the phrases of ordinary life than could, without an ill effect, have been hazarded in the heroic couplet. It was not however the freedom from false taste, whether as to common defects or to those more properly his own, which made so unusual an impression on my feelings immediately, and subsequently on my judgment. It was the union of deep feeling with profound thought; the fine balance of truth in observing with the imaginative faculty in modifying the objects observed; and above all the original gift of spreading the tone, the *atmosphere*, and with it the depth and height of the ideal world, around forms, incidents, and situations of which, for the common view, custom had bedimmed all the luster, had dried up the sparkle and the dewdrops. "To find no contradiction in the union of old and new, to contemplate the Ancient of Days and all his works with feelings as fresh as if all had then sprang forth at the first creative fiat, characterizes the mind that feels the riddle of the world and may help to unravel it. To carry on the feelings of childhood into the powers of manhood; to combine the child's sense of wonder and novelty with the appearances which every day for perhaps forty years had rendered familiar:

5. *Salisbury Plain* (1793–4), which was left in manuscript until Wordsworth published a revised version in 1842 under the title *Guilt and Sorrow*. An excerpt from *Salisbury Plain* was printed as *The Female Vagrant*, in *Lyrical Ballads* (1798).
6. Wordsworth's *Tintern Abbey*, lines 76 ff.

> With sun and moon and stars throughout the year
> And man and woman;[7]

this is the character and privilege of genius, and one of the marks which distinguish genius from talents. And therefore it is the prime merit of genius, and its most unequivocal mode of manifestation, so to represent familiar objects as to awaken in the minds of others a kindred feeling concerning them, and that freshness of sensation which is the constant accompaniment of mental no less than of bodily convalescence. Who has not a thousand times seen snow fall on water? Who has not watched it with a new feeling from the time that he has read Burns' comparison of sensual pleasure:

> To snow that falls upon a river
> A moment white—then gone forever![8]

In poems, equally as in philosophic disquisitions, genius produces the strongest impressions of novelty while it rescues the most admitted truths from the impotence caused by the very circumstance of their universal admission. Truths of all others the most awful and mysterious, yet being at the same time of universal interest, are too often considered as *so* true, that they lose all the life and efficiency of truth and lie bedridden in the dormitory of the soul side by side with the most despised and exploded errors." *The Friend*, p. 76, No. 5.[9]

This excellence, which in all Mr. Wordsworth's writings is more or less predominant and which constitutes the character of his mind, I no sooner felt than I sought to understand. Repeated meditations led me first to suspect (and a more intimate analysis of the human faculties, their appropriate marks, functions, and effects, matured my conjecture into full conviction) that fancy and imagination were two distinct and widely different faculties, instead of being, according to the general belief, either two names with one meaning, or at furthest the lower and higher degree of one and the same power. It is not, I own, easy to conceive a more apposite translation of the Greek *phantasia* than the Latin *imaginatio*; but it is equally true that in all societies there exists an instinct of growth, a certain collective unconscious good sense working progressively to desynonymize those words originally of the same meaning which the conflux of dialects had supplied to the more homogeneous languages, as the Greek and German, and which the same cause, joined with accidents of translation from original works of different countries, occasion in mixed languages like our own. The first and most important point to be proved is that two

---

7. Altered from Milton's sonnet *To Mr. Cyriack Skinner upon his Blindness.*
8. Altered from Burns, *Tam o' Shanter*, lines 61–62.
9. *The Friend* was a periodical published by Coleridge (1809–10).

conceptions perfectly distinct are confused under one and the same word, and (this done) to appropriate that word exclusively to one meaning, and the synonym (should there be one) to the other. But if (as will be often the case in the arts and sciences) no synonym exists, we must either invent or borrow a word. In the present instance the appropriation had already begun and been legitimated in the derivative adjective: Milton had a highly *imaginative*, Cowley a very *fanciful*, mind. If therefore I should succeed in establishing the actual existence of two faculties generally different, the nomenclature would be at once determined. To the faculty by which I had characterized Milton we should confine the term *imagination*; while the other would be contra-distinguished as *fancy*. Now were it once fully ascertained that this division is no less grounded in nature than that of delirium from mania, or Otway's

> Lutes, lobsters, seas of milk, and ships of amber,[1]

from Shakespeare's

> What! have his daughters brought him to this pass?[2]

or from the preceding apostrophe to the elements, the theory of the fine arts and of poetry in particular could not, I thought, but derive some additional and important light. It would in its immediate effects furnish a torch of guidance to the philosophical critic, and ultimately to the poet himself. In energetic minds truth soon changes by domestication into power; and from directing in the discrimination and appraisal of the product becomes influencive in the production. To admire on principle is the only way to imitate without loss of originality. * * *

From *Chapter XIII*

On the imagination, or esemplastic[3] power.

* * * The IMAGINATION, then, I consider either as primary, or secondary. The primary IMAGINATION I hold to be the living power and prime agent of all human perception, and as a repetition in the finite mind of the eternal act of creation in the infinite I AM. The secondary I consider as an echo of the former, coexisting with the conscious will, yet still as identical with the primary in the *kind* of its agency, and differing only in *degree*, and in the *mode* of its operation. It dissolves, diffuses, dissipates, in order to recreate; or where this process is rendered impossible, yet still, at all events, it struggles to idealize and to unify. It is essentially *vital*, even as all objects (*as* objects) are essentially fixed and dead.

---

1. Thomas Otway, in *Venice Preserved* (1682), wrote "laurels" in place of "lobsters" (V.ii.151).

2. *King Lear* III.iv.63.
3. Coleridge coined this word and used it to mean "molding into unity."

FANCY, on the contrary, has no other counters to play with but fixities and definites. The fancy is indeed no other than a mode of memory emancipated from the order of time and space; and blended with, and modified by that empirical phenomenon of the will which we express by the word CHOICE. But equally with the ordinary memory it must receive all its materials ready made from the law of association.[4] * * *

Chapter XIV

Occasion of the Lyrical Ballads, *and the objects originally proposed—Preface to the second edition—The ensuing controversy, its causes and acrimony—Philosophic definitions of a poem and poetry with scholia.*[5]

During the first year that Mr. Wordsworth and I were neighbors[6] our conversations turned frequently on the two cardinal points of poetry, the power of exciting the sympathy of the reader by a faithful adherence to the truth of nature, and the power of giving the interest of novelty by the modifying colors of imagination.[7] The sudden charm which accidents of light and shade, which moonlight or sunset diffused over a known and familiar landscape, appeared to represent the practicability of combining both. These are the poetry of nature. The thought suggested itself (to which of us I do not recollect) that a series of poems might be composed of two sorts. In the one, the incidents and agents were to be, in part at least, supernatural; and the excellence aimed at was to consist in the interesting of the affections by the dramatic truth of such emotions as would naturally accompany such situations, supposing them real. And real in *this* sense they have been to every human being who, from whatever source of delusion, has at any time believed himself under supernatural agency. For the second class, subjects were to be chosen from ordinary life; the characters and incidents were to be such as will be found in every village and its vicinity where there is a meditative and feeling mind to seek after them, or to notice them when they present themselves.

In this idea originated the plan of the *Lyrical Ballads*; in which

4. Coleridge conceives God's creation to be a continuous process, which has an analogy in the creative perception ("primary imagination") of all human minds. The creative process is repeated, or "echoed," on still a third level, by the "secondary imagination" of the poet, which dissolves the products of primary perception in order to shape them into a new and unified creation—the imaginative passage or poem. The "fancy," on the other hand, can only manipulate "fixities and definites" which, linked by association, come to it ready-made from perception. Its products, therefore, are not re-creations (echoes of God's original creative process), but mosaic-like reassemblies of existing bits and pieces.
5. Additional remarks, after a philosophic demonstration.
6. At **Nether Stowey and Alfoxden,** Somerset, in 1797.
7. Cf. Wordsworth's account in his Preface to *Lyrical Ballads*.

it was agreed that my endeavors should be directed to persons and characters supernatural, or at least romantic; yet so as to transfer from our inward nature a human interest and a semblance of truth sufficient to procure for these shadows of imagination that willing suspension of disbelief for the moment, which constitutes poetic faith. Mr. Wordsworth, on the other hand, was to propose to himself as his object to give the charm of novelty to things of every day, and to excite a feeling analogous to the supernatural, by awakening the mind's attention from the lethargy of custom and directing it to the loveliness and the wonders of the world before us; an inexhaustible treasure, but for which, in consequence of the film of familiarity and selfish solicitude, we have eyes yet see not, ears that hear not, and hearts that neither feel nor understand.[8]

With this view I wrote the *Ancient Mariner*, and was preparing, among other poems, the *Dark Ladie*, and the *Christabel*, in which I should have more nearly realized my ideal than I had done in my first attempt. But Mr. Wordsworth's industry had proved so much more successful and the number of his poems so much greater, that my compositions, instead of forming a balance, appeared rather an interpolation of heterogeneous matter.[9] Mr. Wordsworth added two or three poems written in his own character, in the impassioned, lofty, and sustained diction which is characteristic of his genius. In this form the *Lyrical Ballads* were published; and were presented by him, as an *experiment*,[1] whether subjects which from their nature rejected the usual ornaments and extra-colloquial style of poems in general might not be so managed in the language of ordinary life as to produce the pleasurable interest which it is the peculiar business of poetry to impart. To the second edition[2] he added a preface of considerable length; in which, notwithstanding some passages of apparently a contrary import, he was understood to contend for the extension of this style to poetry of all kinds, and to reject as vicious and indefensible all phrases and forms of style that were not included in what he (unfortunately, I think, adopting an equivocal expression) called the language of *real* life. From this preface, prefixed to poems in which it was impossible to deny the presence of original genius, however mistaken its direction might be deemed, arose the whole long continued controversy.[3] For from the conjunction of perceived power with supposed heresy I explain the inveteracy and in some instances, I grieve to say, the acri-

8. Cf. Isaiah vi.9–10.
9. The first edition of *Lyrical Ballads*, published anonymously in 1798, contained nineteen poems by Wordsworth, four by Coleridge.
1. "Experiments" was also the word used by Wordsworth in his "Advertisement" to the first edition.
2. Of 1800.
3. The controversy over Wordsworth's theory and poetical practice in the literary journals of the day.

monious passions with which the controversy has been conducted by the assailants.

Had Mr. Wordsworth's poems been the silly, the childish things which they were for a long time described as being; had they been really distinguished from the compositions of other poets merely by meanness of language and inanity of thought; had they indeed contained nothing more than what is found in the parodies and pretended imitations of them; they must have sunk at once, a dead weight, into the slough of oblivion, and have dragged the preface along with them. But year after year increased the number of Mr. Wordsworth's admirers. They were found too not in the lower classes of the reading public, but chiefly among young men of strong sensibility and meditative minds; and their admiration (inflamed perhaps in some degree by opposition) was distinguished by its intensity, I might almost say, by its *religious* fervor. These facts, and the intellectual energy of the author, which was more or less consciously felt where it was outwardly and even boisterously denied, meeting with sentiments of aversion to his opinions and of alarm at their consequences, produced an eddy of criticism which would of itself have borne up the poems by the violence with which it whirled them round and round. With many parts of this preface, in the sense attributed to them and which the words undoubtedly seem to authorize, I never concurred; but, on the contrary objected to them as erroneous in principle, and as contradictory (in appearance at least) both to other parts of the same preface and to the author's own practice in the greater number of the poems themselves. Mr. Wordsworth in his recent collection[4] has, I find, degraded this prefatory disquisition to the end of his second volume, to be read or not at the reader's choice. But he has not, as far as I can discover, announced any change in his poetic creed. At all events, considering it as the source of a controversy in which I have been honored more than I deserve by the frequent conjunction of my name with his, I think it expedient to declare once for all in what points I coincide with his opinions, and in what points I altogether differ. But in order to render myself intelligible I must previously, in as few words as possible, explain my ideas, first, of a POEM; and secondly, of POETRY itself, in *kind* and in *essence*.

The office of philosophical *disquisition* consists in just *distinction;* while it is the privilege of the philosopher to preserve himself constantly aware that distinction is not division. In order to obtain adequate notions of any truth, we must intellectually separate its distinguishable parts; and this is the technical *process* of philosophy. But having so done, we must then restore them in our conceptions to the unity in which they actually coexist; and this

4. Wordsworth's *Poems*, two volumes, 1815.

is the *result* of philosophy. A poem contains the same elements as a prose composition; the difference therefore must consist in a different combination of them, in consequence of a different object proposed. According to the difference of the object will be the difference of the combination. It is possible that the object may be merely to facilitate the recollection of any given facts or observations by artificial arrangement; and the composition will be a poem, merely because it is distinguished from prose by meter, or by rhyme, or by both conjointly. In this, the lowest sense, a man might attribute the name of a poem to the well-known enumeration of the days in the several months:

> Thirty days hath September
> April, June, and November, etc.

and others of the same class and purpose. And as a particular pleasure is found in anticipating the recurrence of sounds and quantities, all compositions that have this charm superadded, whatever be their contents, *may* be entitled poems.

So much for the superficial *form*. A difference of object and contents supplies an additional ground of distinction. The immediate purpose may be the communication of truths; either of truth absolute and demonstrable, as in works of science; or of facts experienced and recorded, as in history. Pleasure, and that of the highest and most permanent kind, may *result* from the *attainment* of the end; but it is not itself the immediate end. In other works the communication of pleasure may be the immediate purpose; and though truth, either moral or intellectual, ought to be the *ultimate* end, yet this will distinguish the character of the author, not the class to which the work belongs. Blessed indeed is that state of society in which the immediate purpose would be baffled by the perversion of the proper ultimate end; in which no charm of diction or imagery could exempt the Bathyllus even of an Anacreon, or the Alexis of Virgil,[5] from disgust and aversion!

But the communication of pleasure may be the immediate object of a work not metrically composed; and that object may have been in a high degree attained, as in novels and romances. Would then the mere superaddition of meter, with or without rhyme, entitle *these* to the name of poems? The answer is that nothing can permanently please which does not contain in itself the reason why it is so, and not otherwise. If meter be superadded, all other parts must be made consonant with it. They must be such as to justify the perpetual and distinct attention to each part which an exact correspondent recurrence of accent and sound are calculated to excite. The final definition then, so deduced, may be thus

---

5. The reference is to poems of homosexual love. "Bathyllus" was a beautiful boy praised by Anacreon, a Greek lyric poet (ca. 560–475 B.C.); "Alexis" was a young man loved by the shepherd Corydon in Virgil's *Eclogues* II.

worded. A poem is that species of composition which is opposed to works of science by proposing for its *immediate* object pleasure, not truth; and from all other species (having *this* object in common with it) it is discriminated by proposing to itself such delight from the *whole* as is compatible with a distinct gratification from each component *part*.

Controversy is not seldom excited in consequence of the disputants attaching each a different meaning to the same word; and in few instances has this been more striking than in disputes concerning the present subject. If a man chooses to call every composition a poem which is rhyme, or measure, or both, I must leave his opinion uncontroverted. The distinction is at least competent to characterize the writer's intention. If it were subjoined that the whole is likewise entertaining or affecting as a tale or as a series of interesting reflections, I of course admit this as another fit ingredient of a poem and an additional merit. But if the definition sought for be that of a *legitimate* poem, I answer it must be one the parts of which mutually support and explain each other; all in their proportion harmonizing with, and supporting the purpose and known influences of metrical arrangement. The philosophic critics of all ages coincide with the ultimate judgment of all countries in equally denying the praises of a just poem on the one hand to a series of striking lines or distichs,[6] each of which absorbing the whole attention of the reader to itself disjoins it from its context and makes it a separate whole, instead of a harmonizing part; and on the other hand, to an unsustained composition, from which the reader collects rapidly the general result unattracted by the component parts. The reader should be carried forward, not merely or chiefly by the mechanical impulse of curiosity, or by a restless desire to arrive at the final solution; but by the pleasurable activity of mind excited by the attractions of the journey itself. Like the motion of a serpent, which the Egyptians made the emblem of intellectual power; or like the·path of sound through the air; at every step he pauses and half recedes, and from the retrogressive movement collects the force which again carries him onward. "*Praecipitandus est liber spiritus*," says Petronius Arbiter most happily.[7] The epithet *liber* here balances the preceding verb; and it is not easy to conceive more meaning condensed in fewer words.

But if this should be admitted as a satisfactory character of a poem, we have still to seek for a definition of poetry. The writings of Plato, and Bishop Taylor, and the *Theoria Sacra* of Burnet,[8]

---

6. Pairs of lines.
7. "The free spirit [of the poet] must be hurled onward." From the *Satyricon*, by the lively Roman satirist, Petronius Arbiter (1st century A.D.).
8. Bishop Jeremy Taylor (1613–67), author of *Holy Living* and *Holy Dying*;

Thomas Burnet, author of *The Sacred Theory of the Earth* (1681–89). Coleridge greatly admired the elaborate and sonorous prose of both these writers; he took from a work by Burnet the Latin motto for *The Ancient Mariner*.

furnish undeniable proofs that poetry of the highest kind may exist without meter, and even without the contradistinguishing objects of a poem. The first chapter of Isaiah (indeed a very large proportion of the whole book) is poetry in the most emphatic sense; yet it would be not less irrational than strange to assert that pleasure, and not truth, was the immediate object of the prophet. In short, whatever *specific* import we attach to the word poetry, there will be found involved in it, as a necessary consequence, that a poem of any length neither can be, nor ought to be, all poetry.[9] Yet if a harmonious whole is to be produced, the remaining parts must be preserved *in keeping* with the poetry; and this can be no otherwise effected than by such a studied selection and artificial arrangement as will partake of *one*, though not a *peculiar*, property of poetry. And this again can be no other than the property of exciting a more continuous and equal attention than the language of prose aims at, whether colloquial or written.

My own conclusions on the nature of poetry, in the strictest use of the word, have been in part anticipated in the preceding disquisition on the fancy and imagination. What is poetry? is so nearly the same question with, what is a poet? that the answer to the one is involved in the solution of the other. For it is a distinction resulting from the poetic genius itself, which sustains and modifies the images, thoughts, and emotions of the poet's own mind. The poet, described in *ideal* perfection, brings the whole soul of man into activity, with the subordination of its faculties to each other, according to their relative worth and dignity. He diffuses a tone and spirit of unity that blends and (as it were) *fuses*, each into each, by that synthetic and magical power to which we have exclusively appropriated the name of imagination. This power, first put in action by the will and understanding and retained under their irremissive, though gentle and unnoticed, control (*laxis effertur habenis*[1]) reveals itself in the balance or reconciliation of opposite or discordant qualities:[2] of sameness, with difference; of the general, with the concrete; the idea, with the image; the individual, with the representative; the sense of novelty and freshness, with old and familiar objects; a more than usual state of emotion, with more than usual order; judgment ever awake and steady self-possession, with enthusiasm and feeling profound or vehement; and while it blends and harmonizes the natural and the artificial, still

9. Coleridge does not use the word "poetry" in the usual way, as a term for the class of all metrical compositions, but to designate those passages, whether in verse or prose, produced by the mind of genius in its supreme moments of imaginative activity.
1. I.e., driven with loosened reins.
2. Here Coleridge introduces into English criticism the concept that the high-est poetry incorporates and reconciles opposite or discordant elements; under the names of "irony" and "paradox," this concept has become a primary criterion of the "new criticism" of recent decades. Although admittedly derived from Coleridge, the concept, by a further irony, has usually been employed to derogate Romantic poetry.

subordinates art to nature; the manner to the matter; and our admiration of the poet to our sympathy with the poetry. "Doubtless,"
as Sir John Davies observes of the soul (and his words may with
slight alteration be applied, and even more appropriately, to the
poetic IMAGINATION):

> Doubtless this could not be, but that she turns
> Bodies to spirit by sublimation strange,
> As fire converts to fire the things it burns,
> As we our food into our nature change.
>
> From their gross matter she abstracts their forms,
> And draws a kind of quintessence from things;
> Which to her proper nature she transforms
> To bear them light on her celestial wings.
>
> Thus does she, when from individual states
> She doth abstract the universal kinds;
> Which then reclothed in divers names and fates
> Steal access through our senses to our minds.[3]

Finally, GOOD SENSE is the BODY of poetic genius, FANCY its
DRAPERY, MOTION its LIFE, and IMAGINATION the SOUL that is everywhere, and in each; and forms all into one graceful and intelligent
whole.

From *Chapter XVII*

*Examination of the tenets peculiar to Mr. Wordsworth—Rustic
life (above all, low and rustic life) especially unfavorable to the
formation of a human diction—The best parts of language the
products of philosophers, not clowns or shepherds—Poetry essentially ideal and generic—The language of Milton as much the
language of real life, yea, incomparably more so than that of the
cottager.*

As far then as Mr. Wordsworth in his preface contended, and
most ably contended, for a reformation in our poetic diction, as
far as he has evinced the truth of passion, and the *dramatic* propriety of those figures and metaphors in the original poets which,
stripped of their justifying reasons and converted into mere artifices
of connection or ornament, constitute the characteristic falsity in
the poetic style of the moderns; and as far as he has, with equal
acuteness and clearness, pointed out the process by which this
change was effected and the resemblances between that state into
which the reader's mind is thrown by the pleasurable confusion of
thought from an unaccustomed train of words and images and that
state which is induced by the natural language of impassioned feel-

3. Adapted from John Davies' *Nosce Teipsum* ("Know Thyself"), a philosophical
poem (1599).

ing, he undertook a useful task and deserves all praise, both for the attempt and for the execution. The provocations to this remonstrance in behalf of truth and nature were still of perpetual recurrence before and after the publication of this preface. I cannot likewise but add that the comparison of such poems of merit as have been given to the public within the last ten or twelve years with the majority of those produced previously to the appearance of that preface leave no doubt on my mind that Mr. Wordsworth is fully justified in believing his efforts to have been by no means ineffectual. Not only in the verses of those who have professed their admiration of his genius, but even of those who have distinguished themselves by hostility to his theory and depreciation of his writings, are the impressions of his principles plainly visible. It is possible that with these principles others may have been blended, which are not equally evident, and some which are unsteady and subvertible from the narrowness or imperfection of their basis. But it is more than possible that these errors of defect or exaggeration, by kindling and feeding the controversy, may have conduced not only to the wider propagation of the accompanying truths, but that, by their frequent presentation to the mind in an excited state they may have won for them a more permanent and practical result. A man will borrow a part from his opponent the more easily, if he feels himself justified in continuing to reject a part. While there remain important points in which he can still feel himself in the right, in which he still finds firm footing for continued resistance, he will gradually adopt those opinions which were the least remote from his own convictions as not less congruous with his own theory than with that which he reprobates. In like manner, with a kind of instinctive prudence, he will abandon by little and little his weakest posts, till at length he seems to forget that they had ever belonged to him, or affects to consider them at most as accidental and "petty annexments," the removal of which leaves the citadel unhurt and unendangered.

My own differences from certain supposed parts of Mr. Wordsworth's theory ground themselves on the assumption that his words had been rightly interpreted, as purporting that the proper diction for poetry in general consists altogether in a language taken, with due exceptions, from the mouths of men in real life, a language which actually constitutes the natural conversation of men under the influence of natural feelings.[4] My objection is, first, that in *any* sense this rule is applicable only to *certain* classes of poetry; secondly, that even to these classes it is not applicable, except in

---

4. Wordsworth, Preface to *Lyrical Ballads* (1800): "A selection of the real language of men in a state of vivid sensation. * * * Low and rustic life was generally chosen. * * * The language too of these men is adopted. * * *"

such a sense as hath never by anyone (as far as I know or have read) been denied or doubted; and, lastly, that as far as, and in that degree in which it is *practicable*, yet as a *rule* it is useless, if not injurious, and therefore either need not or ought not to be practiced. * * *

Here let me be permitted to remind the reader that the positions which I controvert are contained in the sentences—"a selection of the REAL language of men"; "the language of these men (i.e., men in low and rustic life) I propose to myself to imitate, and as far as possible to adopt the very language of men." "Between the language of prose and that of metrical composition there neither is, nor can be any essential difference." It is against these exclusively that my opposition is directed.

I object, in the very first instance, to an equivocation in the use of the word "real." Every man's language varies according to the extent of his knowledge, the activity of his faculties and the depth or quickness of his feelings. Every man's language has, first, its *individualities*; secondly, the common properties of the *class* to which he belongs; and thirdly, words and phrases of *universal* use. The language of Hooker, Bacon, Bishop Taylor, and Burke differs from the common language of the learned class only by the superior number and novelty of the thoughts and relations which they had to convey. The language of Algernon Sidney[5] differs not at all from that which every well-educated gentleman would wish to write, and (with due allowances for the undeliberateness and less connected train of thinking natural and proper to conversation) such as he would wish to talk. Neither one or the other differ half as much from the general language of cultivated society as the language of Mr. Wordsworth's homeliest composition differs from that of a common peasant. For "real" therefore we must substitute *ordinary*, or *lingua communis*.[6] And this, we have proved, is no more to be found in the phraseology of low and rustic life than in that of any other class. Omit the peculiarities of each, and the result of course must be common to all. And assuredly the omissions and changes to be made in the language of rustics before it could be transferred to any species of poem, except the drama or other professed imitation, are at least as numerous and weighty as would be required in adapting to the same purpose the ordinary language of tradesmen and manufacturers. Not to mention that the language so highly extolled by Mr. Wordsworth varies in every county, nay, in every village, according to the accidental character of the clergyman, the existence or nonexistence of schools; or even, perhaps, as the exciseman, publican, or barber happen to be, or not to be, zealous politicians and readers of the weekly newspaper *pro*

5. Algernon Sidney (1622-83), republican soldier and statesmen, author of *Discourses Concerning Government*.
6. "The common language."

bono publico.[7] Anterior to cultivation the *lingua communis* of every country, as Dante has well observed, exists everywhere in parts and nowhere as a whole.[8]

Neither is the case rendered at all more tenable by the addition of the words "in a state of excitement."[9] For the nature of a man's words, when he is strongly affected by joy, grief, or anger, must necessarily depend on the number and quality of the general truths, conceptions, and images, and of the words expressing them, with which his mind had been previously stored. For the property of passion is not to *create*, but to set in increased activity. At least, whatever new connections of thoughts or images, or (which is equally, if not more than equally, the appropriate effect of strong excitement) whatever generalizations of truth or experience the heat of passion may produce, yet the terms of their conveyance must have pre-existed in his former conversations, and are only collected and crowded together by the unusual stimulation. It is indeed very possible to adopt in a poem the unmeaning repetitions, habitual phrases, and other blank counters which an unfurnished or confused understanding interposes at short intervals in order to keep hold of his subject which is still slipping from him, and to give him time for recollection; or in mere aid of vacancy, as in the scanty companies of a country stage the same player pops backwards and forwards, in order to prevent the appearance of empty spaces, in the procession of *Macbeth* or *Henry VIIIth*. But what assistance to the poet or ornament to the poem these can supply, I am at a loss to conjecture. Nothing assuredly can differ either in origin or in mode more widely from the apparent tautologies of intense and turbulent feeling in which the passion is greater and of longer endurance than to be exhausted or satisfied by a single representation of the image or incident exciting it. Such repetitions I admit to be a beauty of the highest kind; as illustrated by Mr. Wordsworth himself from the song of Deborah. "At her feet he bowed, he fell, he lay down: at her feet he bowed, he fell: where he bowed, there he fell down dead."[10]

1815   1817

From Lectures on Shakespeare[1]
[*Fancy and Imagination in Shakespeare's Poetry*]

In the preceding lecture we have examined with what armor clothed and with what titles authorized Shakespeare came forward

---

7. "For the public welfare."
8. In *De vulgari eloquentia* ("On the Speech of the People") Dante discusses —and affirms—the fitness for poetry of the unlocalized Italian vernacular.
9. Wordsworth: "the manner in which we associate ideas in a state of excite-

ment."
10. Judges v.27. Cited by Wordsworth in a note to *The Thorn* as an example of the natural tautology of "impassioned feelings."
1. Although Coleridge's series of public lectures on Shakespeare and other

as a poet to demand the throne of fame as the dramatic poet of England; we have now to observe and retrace the excellencies which compelled even his contemporaries to seat him on that throne, although there were giants in those days contending for the same honor. Hereafter we shall endeavor to make out the title of the English drama, as created by and existing in Shakespeare, and its right to the supremacy of dramatic excellence in general. I have endeavored to prove that he had shown himself a *poet*, previously to his appearance [as] a dramatic poet—and that had no *Lear*, no *Othello*, no *Henry the Fourth*, no *Twelfth Night* appeared, we must have admitted that Shakespeare possessed the chief if not all the requisites of a poet—namely, deep feeling and exquisite sense of beauty, both as exhibited to the eye in combinations of form, and to the ear in sweet and appropriate melody (with the exception of Spenser he is [the sweetest of English poets]); that these feelings were under the command of *his own will*—that in his very first productions he projected his mind out of his own particular being, and felt and made others feel, on subjects [in] no way connected with himself, except by force of contemplation, and that sublime faculty, by which a great mind becomes that which it meditates on. To this we are to add the affectionate love of nature and natural objects, without which no man could have observed so steadily, or painted so truly and passionately the very minutest beauties of the external world. Next, we have shown that he possessed fancy, considered as the faculty of bringing together images dissimilar in the main by some one point or more of likeness distinguished.[2]

> Full gently now she takes him by the hand,
> A lily prisoned in a jail of snow,
> Or ivory in an alabaster band—
> So white a friend engirts so white a foe.

Still mounting, we find undoubted proof in his mind of imagination, or the power by which one image or feeling is made to modify many others and by a sort of *fusion to force many into one*—that which after showed itself in such might and energy in *Lear*, where the deep anguish of a father spreads the feeling of ingratitude and cruelty over the very elements of heaven. Various are the workings

---

poets contained much of his best criticism, he published none of this material, leaving only fragmentary remains of his lectures in notebooks, scraps of manuscript, and notes written in the margins of books. The following selections, which develop some of the basic ideas presented in *Biographia Literaria*, are taken from T. M. Raysor's edition, based on Coleridge's manuscripts and on contemporary reports, of *Coleridge's Shakespearean Criticism* (1930).

2. Coleridge here applies the distinction between fancy and imagination presented in *Biographia Literaria*, Chapter XIII. This passage from the narrative poem *Venus and Adonis* (lines 361–64) is an instance of fancy because the elements brought together remain an assemblage of recognizable and independent "fixities and definites," despite the isolated points of likeness which form the grounds of the comparison.

of this greatest faculty of the human mind—both passionate and tranquil. In its tranquil and purely pleasurable operation, it acts chiefly by producing out of many things, as they would have appeared in the description of an ordinary mind, described slowly and in unimpassioned succession, a oneness, even as nature, the greatest of poets, acts upon us when we open our eyes upon an extended prospect. Thus the flight of Adonis from the enamored goddess in the dusk of evening—

> Look how a bright star shooteth from the sky—
> So glides he in the night from Venus' eye.[3]

How many images and feelings are here brought together without effort and without discord—the beauty of Adonis—the rapidity of his flight—the yearning yet hopelessness of the enamored gazer—and a shadowy ideal character thrown over the whole.[4]—Or it acts by impressing the stamp of humanity, of human feeling, over inanimate objects * * *

> Lo, here the gentle lark, weary of rest,
> From his moist cabinet mounts up on high
> And wakes the morning, from whose silver breast
> The sun ariseth in his majesty;
> Who doth the world so gloriously behold
> That cedar tops and hills seem burnished gold.

And lastly, which belongs only to a great poet, the power of so carrying on the eye of the reader as to make him almost lose the consciousness of words—to make him *see* everything—and this without exciting any painful or laborious attention, without any *anatomy* of description (a fault not uncommon in descriptive poetry) but with the sweetness and easy movement of nature.

Lastly, he previously to his dramas, gave proof of a most profound, energetic, and philosophical mind, without which he might have been a very delightful poet, but not the great dramatic poet * * * But chance and his powerful instinct combined to lead him to his proper province—in the conquest of which we are to consider both the difficulties that opposed him, and the advantages. ca. 1808

[Mechanic vs. Organic Form][5]

The subject of the present lecture is no less than a question submitted to your understandings, emancipated from national prej-

3. *Venus and Adonis*, lines 815–16.
4. An instance of imagination, Coleridge claims, because the component parts—the shooting star and the flight of Adonis, together with the feelings with which both are perceived—dissolve into a new and seamless unity, different in character from the sum of its parts. In the following instance (lines 853–58), the imagination is said to fuse the neutral and inanimate objects with the human nature and feelings of the observer.
5. Coleridge is opposing the earlier view that, because he violates the critical "rules" based on classical drama,

udice: Are the plays of Shakespeare works of rude uncultivated genius, in which the splendor of the parts compensates, if aught can compensate, for the barbarous shapelessness and irregularity of the whole? To which not only the French critics, but even his own English admirers, say [yes]. Or is the form equally admirable with the matter, the judgment of the great poet not less deserving of our wonder than his genius? Or to repeat the question in other words, is Shakespeare a great dramatic poet on account only of these beauties and excellencies which he possesses in common with the ancients, but with diminished claims to our love and honor to the full extent of his difference from them? Or are these very differences additional proofs of poetic wisdom, at once results and symbols of living power as contrasted with lifeless mechanism, of free and rival originality as contradistinguished from servile imitation, or more accurately, [from] a blind copying of effects instead of a true imitation of the essential principles? Imagine not I am about to oppose genius to rules. No! the comparative value of these rules is the very cause to be tried. The spirit of poetry, like all other living powers, must of necessity circumscribe itself by rules, were it only to unite power with beauty. It must embody in order to reveal itself; but a living body is of necessity an organized one— and what is organization but the connection of parts to a whole, so that each part is at once end and means! This is no discovery of criticism; it is a necessity of the human mind—and all nations have felt and obeyed it, in the invention of meter and measured sounds as the vehicle and involucrum[6] of poetry, itself a fellow growth from the same life, even as the bark is to the tree.

No work of true genius dare want its appropriate form; neither indeed is there any danger of this. As it must not, so neither can it, be lawless! For it is even this that constitutes its genius—the power of acting creatively under laws of its own origination. How then comes it that not only single Zoili,[7] but whole nations have combined in unhesitating condemnation of our great dramatist, as a sort of African nature, fertile in beautiful monsters, as a wild heath where islands of fertility look greener from the surrounding waste, where the loveliest plants now shine out among unsightly weeds and now are choked by their parasitic growth, so intertwined

Shakespeare is a highly irregular dramatist whose occasional successes are the result of innate and untutored genius, operating without artistry or judgment. Coleridge's refutation is based on his distinction between the "mechanical form" conceived by neoclassical criticism, and "organic form." Mechanical form results from imposing a pattern of pre-existing rules on the literary material. Shakespeare's organic form, on the other hand, evolves like a plant by an inner principle, according not to rules but to the laws of its own growth, until it achieves an organic unity—a living interdependence of parts and whole in which, as Coleridge says, "each part is at once end and means." The concept of "organic form," in one or another interpretation, has become a cardinal principle in much modern criticism.

6. Outer covering of part of a plant.

7. Plural of "Zoilus," who in classical times was the standard example of a bad critic.

that we cannot disentangle the weed without snapping the flower. In this statement I have had no reference to the vulgar abuse of Voltaire,[8] save as far as his charges are coincident with the decisions of his commentators and (so they tell you) his almost idolatrous admirers. The true ground of the mistake, as has been well remarked by a continental critic,[9] lies in the confounding mechanical regularity with organic form. The form is mechanic when on any given material we impress a predetermined form, not necessarily arising out of the properties of the material, as when to a mass of wet clay we give whatever shape we wish it to retain when hardened. The organic form, on the other hand, is innate; it shapes as it develops itself from within, and the fulness of its development is one and the same with the perfection of its outward form. Such is the life, such the form. Nature, the prime genial artist, inexhaustible in diverse powers, is equally inexhaustible in forms. Each exterior is the physiognomy of the being within, its true image reflected and thrown out from the concave mirror. And even such is the appropriate excellence of her chosen poet, of our own Shakespeare, himself a nature humanized, a genial[1] understanding directing self-consciously a power and an implicit wisdom deeper than consciousness.[2]   1930

8. Voltaire (1694–1778) wrote critiques treating Shakespeare as a barbarous, irregular, and sometimes indecent natural genius.
9. August Wilhelm Schlegel, German critic and literary historian, whose *Lec-*

tures on Dramatic Art and Literature (1808–9) present many of the ideas Coleridge develops in this lecture.
1. The adjectival form of "genius."
2. I.e., the organic process of the imagination is in part unconscious.

GEORGE GORDON, LORD BYRON
(1788–1824)

1812:   *Childe Harold*, Cantos I and II.
1813–14: The Oriental tales, including *The Giaour, The Corsair, Lara.*
1816:   Separation from Lady Byron; leaves England, never to return.
1818:   Begins *Don Juan.*
1823:   Joins the Greek war for liberation from the Turks.

In his *History of English Literature*, written in the late 1850's, the French critic Hippolyte Taine gave only a few condescending pages to Wordsworth, Coleridge, Shelley, and Keats, and then devoted a long enthusiastic chapter to Lord Byron, "the greatest and most English of these artists; he is so great and so English that from him alone we shall learn more truths of his country and of his age than from all the rest together." Byron had achieved an immense European reputation during his own lifetime, while his great English contemporaries were admired only by small coteries in England and America, and through much of the 19th century he continued to be rated as one of the greatest of English poets and the very prototype of literary Romanticism. His influence was felt everywhere, not only among minor writers—in the two or three decades after his death, most European poets struck Byronic attitudes—but among the greatest poets and novelists (including Goethe in Germany, Balzac and Stendhal in France, Pushkin and Dostoevsky in Russia, and Melville in America), painters (especially Delacroix), and composers (especially Beethoven and Berlioz).

These facts may surprise the student who is aware of the modern estimate of Byron as the least consequential of the five great poets of his day, whose poems have little in common with the distinctive innovations of Wordsworth, Coleridge, Keats, or Shelley. Only Shelley, among these writers, thought highly of either Byron or his work; while Byron spoke slightingly of all of them except Shelley, and in fact insisted that, measured against the poetic practice of Pope, he and his contemporaries were "all in the wrong, one as much as another * * * we are upon a wrong revolutionary poetical system, or systems, not worth a damn in itself." Byron's masterpiece, *Don Juan*, is an instance of that favorite neoclassic type, a satire against modern civilization, which has much more in common with the methods and aims of Pope, Swift, Voltaire, or Sterne than with those of his own contemporaries. Even Byron's lyrics are old-fashioned: many are in the 18th-century gentlemanly mode of witty extemporization and epigram (*Written after Swimming from Sestos to Abydos*) or continue the Cavalier tradition of poetic gallantry and the elaborate development of a compliment to a lady (*She Walks in Beauty* or *There Be None of Beauty's Daughters*).

Byron's chief claim to be called an arch-Romantic is that he provided his age with what Taine called its "ruling personage; that is, the model that contemporaries invest with their admiration and sympathy." This personage is the "Byronic hero." He occurs in many guises in Byron's romances and dramas, but his central attribute is that of a saturnine, passionate, moody, and remorse-torn but unrepentant sinner, who, in proud moral isolation, relies on his absolute self against all institutional and moral trammels. This figure, infusing the archrebel in a nonpolitical form with a strong erotic interest, gathered together and embodied the implicit yearnings of Byron's time, was imitated in life as well as in art, and helped shape the intellectual as well as the cultural history of the later 19th century. Bertrand Russell, in his *History of Western Philosophy*, gives a chapter to Byron—not because he was a systematic thinker, but because "Byronism," the attitude of "Titanic cosmic self-assertion," established an outlook and way of feeling that entered 19th-century philosophy and eventually helped to form Nietzsche's concept of the Superman, the great hero who stands outside the jurisdiction of the ordinary criteria of good and evil.

Byron's contemporaries insisted on identifying the author with his fictional characters. But Byron's letters and the testimony of his friends show that, except for recurrent moods of black depression, his own temperament was in many respects the antithesis to that of his heroes. He was passionate and willful, but when in good humor he could be very much a man of the world in the 18th-century style—gregarious, lively, tolerant, and a witty conversationalist capable of taking an ironic attitude toward his own activities as well as those of other men. The aloof hauteur he exhibited in public was largely a mask to hide his painful diffidence when in a strange company; he possessed devoted friends, both men and women, and among them he was usually unassuming, companionable, sometimes even exuberant, and tactful; to his household dependents he was unfailingly generous and tenaciously loyal. But if Byronism was largely a fiction, produced by a collaboration between Byron's imagination and that of his public, then the fiction was historically more important than the poet in his actual person.

Byron was descended from two aristocratic families, both of them colorful, violent, and dissolute. His grandfather was an admiral known as "Foulweather Jack"; his great-uncle was the fifth Baron Byron, known to his rural neighbors as the "Wicked Lord," who was tried by his peers for killing his kinsman, William Chaworth, in a drunken duel; his father, Captain John Byron, was a rake and fortune-hunter who rapidly dissipated the patrimony of two wealthy wives. Byron's mother was a Scotswoman, Catherine Gordon of Gight, the last descendant of a line of lawless Scottish lairds. After her husband died (Byron was then 3), she brought up her son in near poverty in Aberdeen, where he was indoctrinated with the Calvinistic morality of Scottish Presbyterianism. Mrs. Byron was an ill-educated and almost pathologically irascible woman, who nevertheless had an abiding love for her son; they fought violently when together, but corresponded affectionately enough when apart, until her death in 1811.

When Byron was 10, the death of his great-uncle, preceded by that of more immediate heirs to the title, made him the sixth Lord Byron. In a fashion suitable to his new eminence he was sent to Harrow School, then to Trinity College, Cambridge. Byron had been born with a clubfoot, which was made worse by inept medical treatment, and this defect all his life caused him physical suffering and agonized embarrassment. His lameness increased his avidity for athletic prowess, and he played cricket and made himself an expert boxer, fencer, and horseman, and a powerful swimmer. He was also sexually precocious; when only 7, he fell in love with a little cousin, Mary Duff, and so violently that ten years later news of her marriage threw him into convulsions. Both at Cambridge and at his ancestral estate of Newstead, he engaged with more than ordinary vigor in the expensive pursuits and fashionable dissipations of a young Regency lord. As a result, despite a sizeable and increasing income, Byron got into financial difficulties from which he did not entirely extricate himself until late in his life. In the course of his schooling he formed many close friendships, the most important with John Cam Hobhouse, a sturdy political liberal and commonsense moralist who exerted a steadying influence throughout Byron's turbulent life.

Despite his distractions at the university, Byron found time to try his hand at lyric verse, which was published in 1807 in a slim and conventional volume entitled *Hours of Idleness*. This was treated with unmerited harshness by the pontifical *Edinburgh Review*, and Byron was provoked to write in reply his first important poem, *English Bards and Scotch Reviewers*, a vigorous satire in the couplet style of the late 18th-century followers of Pope, in which he incorporated skillful but tactless ridicule of all his major poetic contemporaries, including Scott, Wordsworth, and Coleridge.

After attaining his M.A. degree and his majority, Byron set out with Hobhouse in 1809 on a tour through Portugal and Spain to Malta, and then to little-known Albania, Greece, and Asia Minor. In this adventurous two-year excursion, Byron accumulated materials which he wove into most of his important poems, including his last work, *Don Juan*. The first literary product was *Childe Harold*; he wrote the opening two cantos while on the tour which the poem describes, published them in 1812 soon after his return to England, and, in his own oft-quoted phrase, "awoke one morning and found myself famous." He became the literary and social celebrity of fashionable London, enjoying an unprecedented success, which he at once increased by his series of highly readable Near-Eastern verse tales; in these the Byronic hero, in various embodiments, flaunts his misanthropy and undergoes a variety of violent and romantic adventures which current gossip attributed to the author himself. In his chronic shortage of money, Byron could well have used the huge income from these publications, but instead maintained his status as an aristocratic amateur by giving the royalties away. Occupying his inherited seat in the House of Lords, Byron also became briefly active on the extreme liberal side of the Whig party and spoke courageously in defense of the Nottingham weavers who, made desperate by technological unemployment, had resorted to destroying the new textile machines; he also supported other liberal measures, including that of Catholic Emancipation.

In the meantime Byron found himself besieged by women. He was extraordinarily handsome—"so beautiful a countenance," Coleridge wrote, "I scarcely ever saw. * * * his eyes the open portals of the sun—things of light, and for light"; because of a constitutional tendency to obesity, however, Byron was able to maintain his beauty only by recurring again and again to a starvation diet of biscuits, soda water, and strong cathartics. Often as a result of female initiative rather than his own, Byron incurred a sequence of liaisons with ladies of fashion. One of these, the flamboyant, eccentric, and hysterical young Lady Caroline Lamb, caused him so much distress by her frenzied pursuit and public tantrums that Byron turned for relief to marriage with Annabella Milbanke, who was in every way Lady Caroline's opposite, for she was naïve, unworldly, intellectual (with a special passion for mathematics), and not a little priggish; she persuaded herself that she could make Byron over in her own image. This ill-starred marriage produced a daughter (Augusta Ada) and many scenes in which Byron, goaded by financial difficulties, behaved so frantically that his wife suspected his sanity; after only one year, the union ended in a legal separation. The final blow came when Lady Byron discovered her husband's incestuous relations with his half sister, Augusta Leigh. The two had been raised apart, so that they were almost strangers when they met as adults; also, Byron seems to have had one attribute in common with the Byronic hero—a compulsion to try forbidden experience (including, as we now know, homosexual love affairs), joined with a tendency to court his own destruction. Byron's affection for his sister, however guilty, was genuine, and endured all through his life. This affair proved a delicious morsel even to the jaded palate of the dissolute Regency society; Byron was ostracized by all but a few friends, and finally forced to leave England forever on April 25, 1816.

Byron now resumed the travels incorporated in the third and fourth cantos of *Childe Harold*. At Geneva he lived for several months in close and intellectually fruitful relation to Shelley, who was accompanied by his wife, Mary Godwin, and by his wife's stepsister, Claire Clairmont—a misguided girl of 17 who had forced herself upon Byron while he was still in England and who in January, 1817, bore him a daughter, Allegra. In the fall of 1817 Byron established himself in Venice, where he inaugurated various affairs that culminated in a period of frenzied debauchery which, Byron estimated, involved more than 200 women, mainly of the lower classes. This period was nevertheless one of great literary creativity: often working through the later hours of the night, he finished his tragedy *Manfred*, wrote the fourth canto of *Childe Harold*, and after turning out *Beppo*, a short rehearsal in the narrative style and stanza of *Don Juan*, began the composition of *Don Juan* itself. In the colloquial ottava rima, Byron finally learned to write poetry as well as he had written prose.

Exhausted and bored by promiscuity, Byron in 1819 settled into a placid and relatively faithful relationship with Teresa Guiccioli, the young wife of the elderly Count Alessandro Guiccioli; according to the Italian upper-class mores of the times, having contracted a marriage of convenience, she could now with propriety attach Byron to herself as a *cavalier servente*. Through Teresa's nationalistic family, the Gambas, Byron became involved in the Carbonari plot against Austrian control over northern Italy. When the Gambas were forced by the authorities to move to Pisa, Byron followed them there, and for the second time joined Shelley. There grew up about the two friends the "Pisan Circle," which in addition to the Gambas included Shelley's friends Thomas Medwin and Edward and Jane Williams, as well as the Greek nationalist leader Prince Mavrocordatos, the picturesque Irish Count Taaffe, and the flamboyant and mendacious adventurer Edward Trelawny, who seems to have stepped out of one of Byron's romances. The circle was gradually broken up, first by Shelley's anger over Byron's treatment of his daughter Allegra (Byron had sent the child to be brought up as a Catholic in an Italian convent, where she died of a fever in 1822); then by the expulsion of the Gambas, whom Byron followed to Genoa; and finally by the drowning of Shelley and Williams in July, 1822.

Byron meanwhile had been steadily at work on a series of closet tragedies (including *Cain*, *Sardanapalus*, and *Marino Faliero*) and on his superb satire, *The Vision of Judgment*. He also continued writing his incomparable series of vivid, informative, and witty letters to his friends in England. But increasingly Byron devoted himself to the continuation of *Don Juan*. He had always been diffident in his self-judgments and easily swayed by literary advice. But now, confident that he had at last found his métier and was accomplishing a masterpiece, Byron kept on, in spite of persistent objections against the supposed immorality of the poem by the English public, by his publisher, John Murray, by his friends and well-wishers, and by his extremely decorous mistress, the Countess Guiccioli—by almost everyone, in fact, except the idealist, Shelley, who thought *Juan* incomparably better than anything he himself could write, and insisted "that every word of it is pregnant with immortality."

Byron finally broke off literature for action: he organized an expedition to assist in the Greek war for independence from the Turks. He knew too well the conditions in Greece, and had too skeptical an estimate of human nature, to entertain hope of success; but he was bored with love, with the domesticity of his relations to Teresa, and in some moods, with life itself. He had, in addition, by his own writings helped to kindle European enthusiasm for the Greek cause, and now felt honor-bound to try what could be done. In the dismal, marshy town of Missolonghi he lived a Spartan existence, undertaking to train troops whom he had himself subsidized and exhibiting great practical grasp and power of leadership amid an incredible confusion of factionalism, intrigue, and military ineptitude, and despite an unhappy passion for his Greek page boy, Loukas. Worn out, he succumbed to a series of feverish attacks and died just after he had reached his 36th birthday. To this day Byron is revered by the Greek people as a national hero.

Students of Byron still feel, as his friends had felt, the magnetic attraction of his antithetic and variable temperament. As Mary Shelley wrote six years after his death, when she read Thomas Moore's edition of his *Letters and Journals:* "The Lord Byron I find there is our Lord Byron— the fascinating—faulty—childish—philosophical being—daring the world —docile to a private circle—impetuous and indolent—gloomy and yet more gay than any other. * * * [I become] reconciled (as I used to in his lifetime) to those waywardnesses which annoyed me when he was away, through the delightful and buoyant tone of his conversation and manners." Of his inner discordances, Byron himself was well aware; he told his friend Lady Blessington: "I am so changeable, being everything by turns and nothing long—I am such a strange *mélange* of good and evil, that it would be difficult to describe me." Yet he remained faithful to his own code: a determination always to tell the truth as he saw it about the world and about himself—his refusal, unlike most of us, to suppress or conceal any of his moods is what made him seem so contradictory—and a dedication to the freedom of nations and individuals. As he went on to say to Lady Blessington: "There are but two sentiments to which I am constant—a strong love of liberty, and a detestation of cant."

Written after Swimming from Sestos to Abydos[1]

1

If, in the month of dark December,
    Leander, who was nightly wont
(What maid will not the tale remember?)
    To cross thy stream, broad Hellespont!

1. The Hellespont (now called the Dardanelles) is the narrow strait between Europe and Asia. In the ancient story, retold in Christopher Marlowe's *Hero and Leander,* young Leander of Abydos, on the Asian side, swam nightly to visit Hero, a priestess of the goddess Venus at Sestos, until he was drowned when he made the attempt in a storm. Byron and a young Lt. Ekenhead swam the Hellespont in the reverse direction on May 3, 1810. Byron alternated between complacency and humor in his many references to the event. In a note to the poem, Byron mentions that the distance was "upwards of four English miles, though the actual breadth is barely one. The rapidity of the current is such that no boat can row directly across. * * * The water was extremely cold, from the melting of the mountain snows."

2

If, when the wintry tempest roared,   5
  He sped to Hero, nothing loath,
And thus of old thy current poured,
  Fair Venus! how I pity both!

3

For *me*, degenerate modern wretch,
  Though in the genial month of May,   10
My dripping limbs I faintly stretch,
  And think I've done a feat today.

4

But since he crossed the rapid tide,
  According to the doubtful story,
To woo—and—Lord knows what beside,   15
  And swam for Love, as I for Glory;

5

'Twere hard to say who fared the best:
  Sad mortals! thus the gods still plague you!
He lost his labor, I my jest;
  For he was drowned, and I've the ague.   20

1810   1812

When We Two Parted

When we two parted
  In silence and tears,
Half broken-hearted
  To sever for years,
Pale grew thy cheek and cold,   5
  Colder thy kiss;
Truly that hour foretold
  Sorrow to this.

The dew of the morning
  Sunk chill on my brow—   10
It felt like the warning
  Of what I feel now.
Thy vows are all broken,
  And light is thy fame;
I hear thy name spoken,   15
  And share in its shame.

They name thee before me,
  A knell to mine ear;
A shudder comes o'er me—
  Why wert thou so dear?   20
They know not I knew thee,
  Who knew thee too well—
Long, long shall I rue thee,
  Too deeply to tell.

In secret we met—   25
    In silence I grieve,
That thy heart could forget,
    Thy spirit deceive.
If I should meet thee
    After long years,
How should I greet thee?—   30
    With silence and tears.

1813   1816

She Walks in Beauty[1]

1

She walks in beauty, like the night
    Of cloudless climes and starry skies;
And all that's best of dark and bright
    Meet in her aspect and her eyes:
Thus mellowed to that tender light   5
    Which heaven to gaudy day denies.

2

One shade the more, one ray the less,
    Had half impaired the nameless grace
Which waves in every raven tress,
    Or softly lightens o'er her face;   10
Where thoughts serenely sweet express
    How pure, how dear their dwelling place.

3

And on that cheek, and o'er that brow,
    So soft, so calm, yet eloquent,
The smiles that win, the tints that glow,   15
    But tell of days in goodness spent,
A mind at peace with all below,
    A heart whose love is innocent!

June 12, 1814   1815

Stanzas for Music

There Be None of Beauty's Daughters

1

There be none of Beauty's daughters
    With a magic like thee;
And like music on the waters
    Is thy sweet voice to me:
When, as if its sound were causing   5
    The charmèd ocean's pausing,
The waves lie still and gleaming,
    And the lulled winds seem dreaming;

1. One of the lyrics in *Hebrew Melodies* (1815), written to be set to adaptations of traditional Jewish tunes by the young musician Isaac Nathan. Byron wrote the lines the morning after he had met his beautiful young cousin by marriage, Mrs. Robert John Wilmot, who wore a black mourning gown brightened with spangles.

2

And the midnight moon is weaving
  Her bright chain o'er the deep;   10
Whose breast is gently heaving,
  As an infant's asleep:
So the spirit bows before thee,
To listen and adore thee;
With a full but soft emotion,   15
Like the swell of summer's ocean.

1816   1816

They Say That Hope Is Happiness

1

They say that Hope is happiness;
  But genuine Love must prize the past,
And Memory wakes the thoughts that bless:
  They rose the first—they set the last;

2

And all that Memory loves the most   5
  Was once our only Hope to be,
And all that Hope adored and lost
  Hath melted into Memory.

3

Alas! it is delusion all;
  The future cheats us from afar,   10
Nor can we be what we recall,
  Nor dare we think on what we are.

1816   1829

Darkness[1]

I had a dream, which was not all a dream.
The bright sun was extinguished, and the stars
Did wander darkling[2] in the eternal space,
Rayless, and pathless, and the icy earth
Swung blind and blackening in the moonless air;   5
Morn came and went—and came, and brought no day,
And men forgot their passions in the dread
Of this their desolation; and all hearts
Were chilled into a selfish prayer for light:
And they did live by watchfires—and the thrones,   10
The palaces of crownéd kings—the huts,
The habitations of all things which dwell,
Were burnt for beacons; cities were consumed,
And men were gathered round their blazing homes
To look once more into each other's face;   15
Happy were those who dwelt within the eye
Of the volcanoes, and their mountain torch:

---

1. A powerfully imagined blank-verse description of the end of life on earth— a speculation hardly less common in Byron's time than in ours. 2. In the dark.

A fearful hope was all the world contained;
Forests were set on fire—but hour by hour
They fell and faded—and the crackling trunks   20
Extinguished with a crash—and all was black.
The brows of men by the despairing light
Wore an unearthly aspect, as by fits
The flashes fell upon them; some lay down
And hid their eyes and wept; and some did rest   25
Their chins upon their clenchéd hands, and smiled;
And others hurried to and fro, and fed
Their funeral piles with fuel, and looked up
With mad disquietude on the dull sky,
The pall of a past world; and then again   30
With curses cast them down upon the dust,
And gnashed their teeth and howled: the wild birds shrieked
And, terrified, did flutter on the ground,
And flap their useless wings; the wildest brutes
Came tame and tremulous; and vipers crawled   35
And twined themselves among the multitude,
Hissing, but stingless—they were slain for food;
And War, which for a moment was no more,
Did glut himself again—a meal was bought
With blood, and each sate sullenly apart   40
Gorging himself in gloom: no love was left;
All earth was but one thought—and that was death
Immediate and inglorious; and the pang
Of famine fed upon all entrails—men
Died, and their bones were tombless as their flesh;   45
The meager by the meager were devoured,
Even dogs assailed their masters, all save one,
And he was faithful to a corse, and kept
The birds and beasts and famished men at bay,
Till hunger clung them, or the dropping dead   50
Lured their lank jaws; himself sought out no food,
But with a piteous and perpetual moan,
And a quick desolate cry, licking the hand
Which answered not with a caress—he died.
The crowd was famished by degrees; but two   55
Of an enormous city did survive,
And they were enemies: they met beside
The dying embers of an altar place,
Where had been heaped a mass of holy things
For an unholy usage; they raked up,   60
And shivering scraped with their cold skeleton hands
The feeble ashes, and their feeble breath
Blew for a little life, and made a flame
Which was a mockery; then they lifted up
Their eyes as it grew lighter, and beheld   65
Each other's aspects—saw, and shrieked, and died—
Even of their mutual hideousness they died,
Unknowing who he was upon whose brow

Famine had written Fiend. The world was void,
The populous and the powerful was a lump   70
Seasonless, herbless, treeless, manless, lifeless—
A lump of death—a chaos of hard clay.
The rivers, lakes, and ocean all stood still,
And nothing stirred within their silent depths;
Ships sailorless lay rotting on the sea,   75
And their masts fell down piecemeal: as they dropped
They slept on the abyss without a surge—
The waves were dead; the tides were in their grave,
The Moon, their mistress, had expired before;
The winds were withered in the stagnant air,   80
And the clouds perished; Darkness had no need
Of aid from them—She was the Universe.

1816   1816

From Childe Harold's Pilgrimage[1]

A ROMAUNT[2]

From *Canto I*

1

Oh, thou! in Hellas deemed of heavenly birth,
Muse! formed or fabled at the minstrel's will!
Since shamed full oft by later lyres on earth,
Mine dares not call thee from thy sacred hill:
Yet there I've wandered by thy vaunted rill;   5

1. *Childe Harold* is a travelogue, narrated by a melancholy, passionate, well-read, and very eloquent tourist. Byron wrote most of the first two cantos while on the tour through Spain, Portugal, Albania, and Greece which these cantos describe; when he published them, in 1812, they made him at one stroke the best known and most talked about living English poet. Byron took up *Childe Harold* again in 1816, during the European tour he made after the breakup of his marriage. Canto III, published in 1816, moves through Belgium, up the Rhine, then to Switzerland and the Alps. Canto IV, published in 1818, describes the great cities and monuments of Italy.

Byron chose for his poem the Spenserian stanza, and like James Thomson (in the *Castle of Indolence*) and other 18th-century predecessors, he attempted in the first canto to imitate, in a serio-comic fashion, the archaic language of his Elizabethan model. (The word "Childe" itself is the ancient term for a young noble awaiting knighthood.) But Byron soon dropped the archaisms; and in the last two cantos, he adapts Spenser's mellifluous stanza to his own assured and brassy magniloquence.

In the Preface to his first two cantos, Byron had insisted that the narrator,

Childe Harold, was "a fictitious character," merely "the child of imagination." But in the manuscript version of these cantos, he had himself called his hero "Childe Burun," the early form of his own family name; the world insisted on identifying the character as well as the travels of the protagonist with those of the author; and in the fourth canto Byron, abandoning the third-person *dramatis persona,* spoke out frankly in the first person.

In its shock tactics of apostrophes, imperatives, exclamations, hyperbole, and abrupt changes in subject, pace, and mood, the style of *Childe Harold* is without close parallel in English; to it Goethe applied the terms *Keckheit, Kühnheit, und Grandiosität:* "daring, dash, and grandiosity." It is no small feat in the author to have converted a meticulously accurate tourist's record of scenes, memorials, and museums into a dramatic and passionate experience. The result is like seeing Europe by flashes of lightning, for everything is presented, not as it is in itself, but as it affects the violent sensibility of that new cultural phenomenon, the Romantic Man of Feeling.

2. A romance, or narrative of adventure.

Yes! sighed o'er Delphi's long-deserted shrine,
Where, save that feeble fountain, all is still;
Nor mote my shell awake the weary Nine[3]
To grace so plain a tale—this lowly lay of mine.

2

Whilome[4] in Albion's isle there dwelt a youth,   10
Who ne in virtue's ways did take delight;
But spent his days in riot most uncouth,
And vexed with mirth the drowsy ear of Night.
Ah, me! in sooth he was a shameless wight,
Sore given to revel and ungodly glee;   15
Few earthly things found favor in his sight
Save concubines and carnal companie,
And flaunting wassailers[5] of high and low degree.

3

Childe Harold was he hight—but whence his name
And lineage long, it suits me not to say;   20
Suffice it that perchance they were of fame,
And had been glorious in another day:
But one sad losel[6] soils a name for aye,
However mighty in the olden time;
Nor all that heralds rake from coffined clay,   25
Nor florid prose, nor honeyed lies of rhyme,
Can blazon evil deeds, or consecrate a crime.

4

Childe Harold basked him in the noontide sun,
Disporting there like any other fly;
Nor deemed before his little day was done   30
One blast might chill him into misery.
But long ere scarce a third of his passed by,
Worse than adversity the Childe befell;
He felt the fullness of satiety:
Then loathed he in his native land to dwell,   35
Which seemed to him more lone than eremite's[7] sad cell.

5

For he through Sin's long labyrinth had run,
Nor made atonement when he did amiss;
Had sighed to many though he loved but one,
And that loved one, alas! could ne'er be his.   40
Ah, happy she! to 'scape from him whose kiss
Had been pollution unto aught so chaste;
Who soon had left her charms for vulgar bliss,
And spoiled her goodly lands to gild his waste,
Nor calm domestic peace had ever deigned to taste.   45

3. The "shell" is a lyre (Hermes is fabled to have invented the lyre by stretching strings over the hollow of a tortoise shell); the "Nine" are the Muses, whose "vaunted rill," (line 5) was the Castalian spring. "Mote": may.

4. Once upon a time.
5. Brazen topers.
6. Rascal. Byron's great-uncle, the 5th Lord Byron, had killed a kinsman in a drunken duel.
7. A religious hermit.

6

And now Childe Harold was sore sick at heart,
And from his fellow bacchanals would flee;
'Tis said, at times the sullen tear would start,
But Pride congealed the drop within his ee:[8]
Apart he stalked in joyless reverie,   50
And from his native land resolved to go,
And visit scorching climes beyond the sea;
With pleasure drugged, he almost longed for woe,
And e'en for change of scene would seek the shades below.

* * *

From *Canto III*

1

Is thy face like thy mother's, my fair child!
Ada![1] sole daughter of my house and heart?
When last I saw thy young blue eyes they smiled,
And then we parted—not as now we part,
But with a hope.——
　　　　　Awaking with a start,   5
The waters heave around me; and on high
The winds lift up their voices: I depart,
Whither I know not; but the hour's gone by,
When Albion's[2] lessening shores could grieve or glad mine eye.

2

Once more upon the waters! yet once more!   10
And the waves bound beneath me as a steed
That knows his rider. Welcome to their roar!
Swift be their guidance, wheresoe'er it lead!
Though the strained mast should quiver as a reed,
And the rent canvas fluttering strew the gale,   15
Still must I on; for I am as a weed,
Flung from the rock on Ocean's foam, to sail
Where'er the surge may sweep, the tempest's breath prevail.

3

In my youth's summer[3] I did sing of One,
The wandering outlaw of his own dark mind;   20
Again I seize the theme, then but begun,
And bear it with me, as the rushing wind
Bears the cloud onwards: in that tale I find
The furrows of long thought, and dried-up tears,
Which, ebbing, leave a sterile track behind,   25
O'er which all heavily the journeying years
Plod the last sands of life—where not a flower appears.

8. Eye.
1. Byron's daughter, Augusta Ada, born
December, 1816, a month before her
parents separated. Byron's "hope" (line
5) had been for a reconciliation, but
he was never to see Ada again.
2. England's.
3. Byron wrote Canto I at 21; he is
now 28.

4

Since my young days of passion—joy, or pain—
Perchance my heart and harp have lost a string,
And both may jar:[4] it may be that in vain   30
I would essay as I have sung to sing.
Yet, though a dreary strain, to this I cling,
So that it wean me from the weary dream
Of selfish grief or gladness—so it fling
Forgetfulness around me—it shall seem   35
To me, though to none else, a not ungrateful theme.

5

He, who grown aged in this world of woe,
In deeds, not years, piercing the depths of life,
So that no wonder waits him—nor below
Can love, or sorrow, fame, ambition, strife,   40
Cut to his heart again with the keen knife
Of silent, sharp endurance—he can tell
Why thought seeks refuge in lone caves, yet rife
With airy images, and shapes which dwell
Still unimpaired, though old, in the soul's haunted cell.   45

6

'Tis to create, and in creating live
A being more intense, that we endow
With form our fancy, gaining as we give
The life we image, even as I do now.
What am I? Nothing: but not so art thou,   50
Soul of my thought![5] with whom I traverse earth,
Invisible but gazing, as I glow
Mixed with thy spirit, blended with thy birth,
And feeling still with thee in my crushed feelings' dearth.

7

Yet must I think less wildly—I *have* thought   55
Too long and darkly, till my brain became,
In its own eddy boiling and o'erwrought,
A whirling gulf of phantasy and flame:
And thus, untaught in youth my heart to tame,
My springs of life were poisoned. 'Tis too late!   60
Yet am I changed; though still enough the same
In strength to bear what time can not abate,
And feed on bitter fruits without accusing Fate.

8

Something too much of this—but now 'tis past,
And the spell closes with its silent seal.[6]   65
Long absent HAROLD reappears at last;
He of the breast which fain no more would feel,
Wrung with the wounds which kill not but ne'er heal;
Yet Time, who changes all, had altered him
In soul and aspect as in age: years steal   70

4. Sound discordant.
5. I.e., Childe Harold, his literary creation.

6. I.e., he sets the seal of silence on his
personal tale ("spell").

Fire from the mind as vigor from the limb,
And life's enchanted cup but sparkles near the brim.

9

His had been quaffed too quickly, and he found
The dregs were wormwood; but he filled again,
And from a purer fount, on holier ground,   75
And deemed its spring perpetual; but in vain!
Still round him clung invisibly a chain
Which galled forever, fettering though unseen,
And heavy though it clanked not; worn with pain,
Which pined although it spoke not, and grew keen,   80
Entering with every step he took through many a scene.

10

Secure in guarded coldness, he had mixed
Again in fancied safety with his kind,
And deemed his spirit now so firmly fixed
And sheathed with an invulnerable mind,   85
That, if no joy, no sorrow lurked behind;
And he, as one, might 'midst the many stand
Unheeded, searching through the crowd to find
Fit speculation—such as in strange land
He found in wonderworks of God and Nature's hand.   90

11

But who can view the ripened rose, nor seek
To wear it? who can curiously behold
The smoothness and the sheen of beauty's cheek,
Nor feel the heart can never all grow old?
Who can contemplate Fame through clouds unfold   95
The star which rises o'er her steep, nor climb?
Harold, once more within the vortex, rolled
On with the giddy circle, chasing Time,
Yet with a nobler aim than in his youth's fond[7] prime.

12

But soon he knew himself the most unfit   100
Of men to herd with Man, with whom he held
Little in common; untaught to submit
His thoughts to others, though his soul was quelled
In youth by his own thoughts; still uncompelled,
He would not yield dominion of his mind   105
To spirits against whom his own rebelled,
Proud though in desolation; which could find
A life within itself, to breathe without mankind.

13

Where rose the mountains, there to him were friends;
Where rolled the ocean, thereon was his home;   110
Where a blue sky, and glowing clime, extends,
He had the passion and the power to roam;
The desert, forest, cavern, breaker's foam,
Were unto him companionship; they spake
A mutual language, clearer than the tome   115

7. Foolish.

Of his land's tongue, which he would oft forsake
For Nature's pages glassed[8] by sunbeams on the lake.

14

Like the Chaldean,[9] he could watch the stars,
Till he had peopled them with beings bright
As their own beams; and earth, and earth-born jars,   120
And human frailties, were forgotten quite:
Could he have kept his spirit to that flight
He had been happy; but this clay will sink
Its spark immortal, envying it the light
To which it mounts, as if to break the link   125
That keeps us from yon heaven which woos us to its brink.

15

But in Man's dwellings he became a thing
Restless and worn, and stern and wearisome,
Drooped as a wild-born falcon with clipped wing,
To whom the boundless air alone were home: 130
Then came his fit again, which to o'ercome,
As eagerly the barred-up bird will beat
His breast and beak against his wiry dome
Till the blood tinge his plumage, so the heat
Of his impeded soul would through his bosom eat.   135

16

Self-exiled Harold wanders forth again,
With nought of hope left—but with less of gloom;
The very knowledge that he lived in vain,
That all was over on this side the tomb,
Had made Despair a smilingness assume,   140
Which, though 'twere wild—as on the plundered wreck
When mariners would madly meet their doom
With draughts intemperate on the sinking deck—
Did yet inspire a cheer which he forebore to check.

17

Stop!—for thy tread is on an Empire's dust!   145
An Earthquake's spoil is sepulchered below!
Is the spot marked with no colossal bust,
Nor column trophied for triumphal show?
None;[1] but the moral's truth tells simpler so,
As the ground was before, thus let it be—   150
How that red rain hath made the harvest grow!
And is this all the world has gained by thee,
Thou first and last of fields, king-making Victory?

18

And Harold stands upon this place of skulls,
The grave of France, the deadly Waterloo!   155
How in an hour the power which gave annuls
Its gifts, transferring fame as fleeting too!

---

8. Made glassy.
9. A people of ancient Babylonia, expert in astronomy.

1. Napoleon's defeat at Waterloo, near Brussels, had occurred only the year before, on June 18, 1815.

In "pride of place" here last the eagle flew,[2]
Then tore with bloody talon the rent plain,
Pierced by the shaft of banded nations through;
Ambition's life and labors all were vain;   160
He wears the shattered links of the world's broken chain.[3]

19

Fit retribution! Gaul[4] may champ the bit
And foam in fetters—but is Earth more free?
Did nations combat to make *One* submit;   165
Or league to teach all kings true sovereignty?
What! shall reviving Thralldom again be
The patched-up idol of enlightened days?
Shall we, who struck the Lion down, shall we
Pay the Wolf homage? proffering lowly gaze   170
And servile knees to thrones? No; *prove*[5] before ye praise!

20

If not, o'er one fallen despot boast no more!
In vain fair cheeks were furrowed with hot tears
For Europe's flowers long rooted up before
The trampler of her vineyards; in vain years   175
Of death, depopulation, bondage, fears,
Have all been borne, and broken by the accord
Of roused-up millions: all that most endears
Glory is when the myrtle wreathes a sword
Such as Harmodius drew on Athens' tyrant lord.[6]   180

21

There was a sound of revelry by night,
And Belgium's capital had gathered then
Her Beauty and her Chivalry, and bright
The lamps shone o'er fair women and brave men;[7]
A thousand hearts beat happily; and when   185
Music arose with its voluptuous swell,
Soft eyes looked love to eyes which spake again,
And all went merry as a marriage bell—
But hush! hark! a deep sound strikes like a rising knell!

22

Did ye not hear it?—No; 'twas but the wind,   190
Or the car rattling o'er the stony street;
On with the dance! let joy be unconfined;
No sleep till morn, when Youth and Pleasure meet
To chase the glowing Hours with flying feet—
But hark!—that heavy sound breaks in once more,   195

2. The eagle was the standard of Napoleon. "Pride of place" is a term from
falconry, meaning the highest point of
flight (cf. *Macbeth* II.iv.12).
3. Napoleon was then a prisoner at St.
Helena.
4. France. Byron, like Shelley and other
liberals, saw the defeat of the Napoleonic tyranny as at the same time a victory for tyrannous kings and the forces
of extreme reaction throughout Europe.

5. Await the test (proof) of experience.
6. In 514 B.C. Harmodius and Aristogei-
ton, hiding their daggers in myrtle
(symbol of love), killed Hipparchus,
tyrant of Athens.
7. This famous ball, given by the
Duchess of Richmond on the eve of the
battle of Quatre Bras, which opened the
conflict at Waterloo, is also described
in Thackeray's *Vanity Fair*, Chapters
29–30.

As if the clouds its echo would repeat;
And nearer, clearer, deadlier than before!
Arm! Arm! it is—it is—the cannon's opening roar!

23

Within a windowed niche of that high hall
Sate Brunswick's fated chieftain;[8] he did hear   200
That sound the first amidst the festival,
And caught its tone with Death's prophetic ear;
And when they smiled because he deemed it near,
His heart more truly knew that peal too well
Which stretched his father on a bloody bier,   205
And roused the vengeance blood alone could quell:
He rushed into the field, and, foremost fighting, fell.

24

Ah! then and there was hurrying to and fro,
And gathering tears, and tremblings of distress,
And cheeks all pale, which but an hour ago   210
Blushed at the praise of their own loveliness;
And there were sudden partings, such as press
The life from out young hearts, and choking sighs
Which ne'er might be repeated; who could guess
If ever more should meet those mutual eyes,   215
Since upon night so sweet such awful morn could rise!

25

And there was mounting in hot haste: the steed,
The mustering squadron, and the clattering car,
Went pouring forward with impetuous speed,
And swiftly forming in the ranks of war;   220
And the deep thunder peal on peal afar;
And near, the beat of the alarming drum
Roused up the soldier ere the morning star;
While thronged the citizens with terror dumb,
Or whispering, with white lips—"The foe! They come! they come!"

26

And wild and high the "Cameron's gathering"[9] rose!   226
The war-note of Lochiel, which Albyn's hills
Have heard, and heard, too, have her Saxon foes—
How in the noon of night that pibroch[1] thrills,
Savage and shrill! But with the breath which fills   230
Their mountain pipe, so fill the mountaineers
With the fierce native daring which instills
The stirring memory of a thousand years,
And Evan's, Donald's fame[2] rings in each clansman's ears!

---

8. The Duke of Brunswick, nephew of George III of England, was killed in the battle of Quatre Bras, just as his father, commanding the Prussian army against Napoleon, had been killed at Auerstedt in 1806 (line 205).
9. The clan song of the Camerons, whose chief was called "Lochiel," after his estate. "Albyn's": Scotland's.
1. Bagpipe music, usually warlike in character.
2. Sir Evan and Donald Cameron, famous warriors in the Stuart cause in the 17th and 18th centuries.

27

And Ardennes[3] waves above them her green leaves,   235
Dewy with nature's teardrops, as they pass,
Grieving, if aught inanimate e'er grieves,
Over the unreturning brave—alas!
Ere evening to be trodden like the grass
Which now beneath them, but above shall grow   240
In its next verdure, when this fiery mass
Of living valor, rolling on the foe
And burning with high hope, shall molder cold and low.

28

Last noon beheld them full of lusty life,
Last eve in Beauty's circle proudly gay,   245
The midnight brought the signal-sound of strife,
The morn the marshaling in arms—the day
Battle's magnificently-stern array!
The thunderclouds close o'er it, which when rent
The earth is covered thick with other clay,   250
Which her own clay shall cover, heaped and pent,
Rider and horse—friend, foe—in one red burial blent!

* * *

36

There sunk the greatest, nor the worst of men,[4]
Whose spirit antithetically mixed
One moment of the mightiest, and again
On little objects with like firmness fixed,
Extreme in all things! hadst thou been betwixt,   320
Thy throne had still been thine, or never been;
For daring made thy rise as fall: thou seek'st
Even now to reassume the imperial mien,
And shake again the world, the Thunderer of the scene!

37

Conqueror and captive of the earth art thou!   325
She trembles at thee still, and thy wild name
Was ne'er more bruited in men's minds than now
That thou are nothing, save the jest of Fame,
Who wooed thee once, thy vassal, and became
The flatterer of thy fierceness, till thou wert   330
A god unto thyself; nor less the same
To the astounded kingdoms all inert,
Who deemed thee for a time whate'er thou didst assert.

38

Oh, more or less than man—in high or low,
Battling with nations, flying from the field;   335
Now making monarchs' necks thy footstool, now
More than thy meanest soldier taught to yield;
An empire thou couldst crush, command, rebuild,

3. A forested region covering parts of Belgium, France, and Luxembourg, which became a battlefield again in both World Wars.
4. I.e., Napoleon.

But govern not thy pettiest passion, nor,
However deeply in men's spirits skilled,
Look through thine own, nor curb the lust of war,   340
Nor learn that tempted Fate will leave the loftiest star.

39
Yet well thy soul hath brooked the turning tide
With that untaught innate philosophy,
Which, be it wisdom, coldness, or deep pride,   345
Is gall and wormwood to an enemy.
When the whole host of hatred stood hard by,
To watch and mock thee shrinking, thou hast smiled
With a sedate and all-enduring eye—
When Fortune fled her spoiled and favorite child,   350
He stood unbowed beneath the ills upon him piled.

40
Sager than in thy fortunes; for in them
Ambition steeled thee on too far to show
That just habitual scorn, which could contemn
Men and their thoughts; 'twas wise to feel, not so   355
To wear it ever on thy lip and brow,
And spurn the instruments thou wert to use
Till they were turned unto thine overthrow:
'Tis but a worthless world to win or lose;
So hath it proved to thee and all such lot[5] who choose.   360

41
If, like a tower upon a headlong rock,
Thou hadst been made to stand or fall alone,
Such scorn of man had helped to brave the shock;
But men's thoughts were the steps which paved thy throne,
Their admiration thy best weapon shone;   365
The part of Philip's son[6] was thine, not then
(Unless aside thy purple had been thrown)
Like stern Diogenes[7] to mock at men;
For sceptered cynics earth were far too wide a den.

42
But quiet to quick bosoms is a hell,   370
And *there* hath been thy bane; there is a fire
And motion of the soul which will not dwell
In its own narrow being, but aspire
Beyond the fitting medium of desire;
And, but once kindled, quenchless evermore,   375
Preys upon high adventure, nor can tire
Of aught but rest; a fever at the core,
Fatal to him who bears, to all who ever bore.

43
This makes the madmen who have made men mad
By their contagion; Conquerors and Kings,   380

5. Hazard.
6. Alexander the Great, son of Philip of Macedon.
7. The Greek philosopher of Cynicism, contemporary of Alexander. It is related that Alexander was so struck by his independence of mind that he said, "If I were not Alexander, I should wish to be Diogenes"; hence the allusion in line 369.

Founders of sects and systems, to whom add
Sophists, Bards, Statesmen, all unquiet things
Which stir too strongly the soul's secret springs,
And are themselves the fools to those they fool;
Envied, yet how unenviable! what stings   385
Are theirs! One breast laid open were a school
Which would unteach mankind the lust to shine or rule.

44

Their breath is agitation, and their life
A storm whereon they ride, to sink at last;
And yet so nursed and bigoted to strife,   390
That should their days, surviving perils past,
Melt to calm twilight, they feel overcast
With sorrow and supineness, and so die;
Even as a flame unfed which runs to waste
With its own flickering, or a sword laid by,   395
Which eats into itself and rusts ingloriously.

45

He who ascends to mountain tops, shall find
The loftiest peaks most wrapped in clouds and snow;
He who surpasses or subdues mankind,
Must look down on the hate of those below.   400
Though high *above* the sun of glory glow,
And far *beneath* the earth and ocean spread,
Round him are icy rocks, and loudly blow
Contending tempests on his naked head,
And thus reward the toils which to those summits led.[8]   405

* * *

52

Thus Harold inly said, and passed along,   460
Yet not insensibly to all which here
Awoke the jocund birds to early song
In glens which might have made even exile dear:
Though on his brow were graven lines austere,
And tranquil sternness which had ta'en the place   465
Of feelings fiercer far but less severe,
Joy was not always absent from his face,
But o'er it in such scenes would steal with transient trace.

53

Nor was all love shut from him, though his days
Of passion had consumed themselves to dust.   470
It is in vain that we would coldly gaze
On such as smile upon us; the heart must
Leap kindly back to kindness, though disgust
Hath weaned it from all wordlings: thus he felt,
For there was soft remembrance, and sweet trust   475
In one fond breast,[3] to which his own would melt,
And in its tenderer hour on that his bosom dwelt.

8. In the stanzas here omitted, Harold is abruptly sent sailing up the Rhine, meditating on the "thousand battles" that "have assailed thy banks."

3. Commentators agree that the reference is to Byron's half sister, Augusta Leigh.

54

And he had learned to love—I know not why,
For this in such as him seems strange of mood—
The helpless looks of blooming infancy,   480
Even in its earliest nurture; what subdued,
To change like this, a mind so far imbued
With scorn of man, it little boots to know;
But thus it was; and though in solitude
Small power the nipped affections have to grow,   485
In him this glowed when all beside had ceased to glow.

55

And there was one soft breast, as hath been said,
Which unto his was bound by stronger ties
Than the church links withal; and, though unwed,
That love was pure, and, far above disguise,   490
Had stood the test of mortal enmities
Still undivided, and cemented more
By peril, dreaded most in female eyes;
But this was firm, and from a foreign shore
Well to that heart might his these absent greetings pour! 495

* * *

68

Lake Leman[4] woos me with its crystal face,
The mirror where the stars and mountains view   645
The stillness of their aspect in each trace
Its clear depth yields of their far height and hue:
There is too much of man here, to look through
With a fit mind the might which I behold;
But soon in me shall Loneliness renew   650
Thoughts hid, but not less cherished than of old,
Ere mingling with the herd had penned me in their fold.

69

To fly from, need not be to hate, mankind:
All are not fit with them to stir and toil,
Nor is it discontent to keep the mind   655
Deep in its fountain, lest it overboil
In the hot throng, where we become the spoil
Of our infection, till too late and long
We may deplore and struggle with the coil,[5]
In wretched interchange of wrong for wrong   660
Midst a contentious world, striving where none are strong.

70

There, in a moment, we may plunge our years
In fatal penitence, and in the blight
Of our own soul turn all our blood to tears,
And color things to come with hues of night;   665
The race of life becomes a hopeless flight
To those that walk in darkness: on the sea,
The boldest steer but where their ports invite,

4. The Lake of Geneva, Switzerland.   5. Tumult.

But there are wanderers o'er Eternity
Whose bark drives on and on, and anchored ne'er shall be. 670

71

Is it not better, then, to be alone,
And love earth only for its earthly sake?
By the blue rushing of the arrowy Rhone,
Or the pure bosom of its nursing lake,
Which feeds it as a mother who doth make 675
A fair but froward infant her own care,
Kissing its cries away as these awake—
Is it not better thus our lives to wear,
Than join the crushing crowd, doomed to inflict or bear?

72

I live not in myself, but I become 680
Portion of that around me; and to me
High mountains are a feeling, but the hum
Of human cities torture: I can see
Nothing to loathe in nature, save to be
A link reluctant in a fleshly chain, 685
Classed among creatures, when the soul can flee,
And with the sky, the peak, the heaving plain
Of ocean, or the stars, mingle, and not in vain.[6]

73

And thus I am absorbed, and this is life:
I look upon the peopled desert past, 690
As on a place of agony and strife,
Where, for some sin, to sorrow I was cast,
To act and suffer, but remount at last
With a fresh pinion; which I feel to spring,
Though young, yet waxing vigorous, as the blast 695
Which it would cope with, on delighted wing,
Spurning the clay-cold bonds which round our being cling.

74

And when, at length, the mind shall be all free
From what it hates in this degraded form,
Reft of its carnal life, save what shall be 700
Existent happier in the fly and worm—
When elements to elements conform,
And dust is as it should be, shall I not
Feel all I see, less dazzling, but more warm?
The bodiless thought? the Spirit of each spot? 705
Of which, even now, I share at times the immortal lot?

75

Are not the mountains, waves, and skies a part
Of me and of my soul, as I of them?

6. Byron had lived in close contact with Shelley at Geneva and had toured the lake with him. At the time, he was introduced to concepts of nature in the poetry of Wordsworth, whom Shelley had pressed on Byron's attention; these ideas are reflected in Canto III, but the voice is Byron's. Byron said of this canto: "I was half mad during the time of its composition, between metaphysics, mountains, lakes, love unextinguishable, thoughts unutterable, and the nightmare of my own delinquencies."

Is not the love of these deep in my heart
With a pure passion? should I not contemn   710
All objects, if compared with these? and stem
A tide of suffering, rather than forego
Such feelings for the hard and worldly phlegm
Of those whose eyes are only turned below,
Gazing upon the ground, with thoughts which dare not glow?   715

* * *

85

Clear, placid Leman! thy contrasted lake,
With the wild world I dwelt in, is a thing
Which warns me with its stillness to forsake
Earth's troubled waters for a purer spring.   800
This quiet sail is as a noiseless wing
To waft me from distraction; once I loved
Torn ocean's roar, but thy soft murmuring
Sounds sweet as if a sister's voice reproved,
That I with stern delights should e'er have been so moved.   805

86

It is the hush of night, and all between
Thy margin and the mountains, dusk, yet clear,
Mellowed and mingling, yet distinctly seen,
Save darkened Jura,[7] whose capped heights appear
Precipitously steep; and drawing near,   810
There breathes a living fragrance from the shore,
Of flowers yet fresh with childhood; on the ear
Drops the light drip of the suspended oar,
Or chirps the grasshopper one good-night carol more.

87

He is an evening reveler, who makes   815
His life an infancy, and sings his fill;
At intervals, some bird from out the brakes[8]
Starts into voice a moment, then is still.
There seems a floating whisper on the hill,
But that is fancy, for the starlight dews   820
All silently their tears of love instill,
Weeping themselves away, till they infuse
Deep into Nature's breast the spirit of her hues.

88

Ye stars! which are the poetry of heaven!
If in your bright leaves we would read the fate   825
Of men and empires—'tis to be forgiven,
That in our aspirations to be great,
Our destinies o'erleap their mortal state,
And claim a kindred with you; for ye are
A beauty and a mystery, and create   830
In us such love and reverence from afar
That fortune—fame—power—life have named themselves a Star.

---

7. The mountain range between Switzerland and France, visible from the Lake of Geneva.
8. Thickets.

89

All heaven and earth are still—though not in sleep,
But breathless, as we grow when feeling most;
And silent, as we stand in thoughts too deep—
All heaven and earth are still. From the high host   835
Of stars to the lulled lake and mountain coast,
All is concentered in a life intense,
Where not a beam, nor air, nor leaf is lost,
But hath a part of being, and a sense   840
Of that which is of all Creator and defense.

90

Then stirs the feeling infinite, so felt
In solitude, where we are *least* alone;
A truth, which through our being then doth melt
And purifies from self: it is a tone,   845
The soul and source of music, which makes known
Eternal harmony, and sheds a charm,
Like to the fabled Cytherea's zone,[9]
Binding all things with beauty—'twould disarm
The specter Death, had he substantial power to harm. 850

91

Not vainly did the early Persian make
His altar the high places and the peak
Of earth-o'ergazing mountains, and thus take
A fit and unwalled temple, there to seek
The Spirit, in whose honor shrines are weak   855
Upreared of human hands. Come, and compare
Columns and idol-dwellings, Goth or Greek,
With Nature's realms of worship, earth and air,
Nor fix on fond abodes to circumscribe thy prayer!

92

The sky is changed!—and such a change! Oh night,   860
And storm, and darkness, ye are wondrous strong,
Yet lovely in your strength, as is the light
Of a dark eye in woman! Far along,
From peak to peak, the rattling crags among,
Leaps the live thunder! Not from one lone cloud,   865
But every mountain now hath found a tongue,
And Jura answers, through her misty shroud,
Back to the joyous Alps, who call to her aloud!

93

And this is in the night—Most glorious night!
Thou wert not sent for slumber! let me be   870
A sharer in thy fierce and far delight—
A portion of the tempest and of thee!
How the lit lake shines, a phosphoric sea,
And the big rain comes dancing to the earth!
And now again 'tis black—and now, the glee   875
Of the loud hills shakes with its mountain mirth,
As if they did rejoice o'er a young earthquake's birth.

9. The sash of Venus, which conferred the power to attract love.

94

Now, where the swift Rhone cleaves his way between
Heights which appear as lovers who have parted
In hate, whose mining depths so intervene   880
That they can meet no more, though brokenhearted!
Though in their souls, which thus each other thwarted,
Love was the very root of the fond rage
Which blighted their life's bloom, and then departed—
Itself expired, but leaving them an age   885
Of years all winters—war within themselves to wage:

95

Now, where the quick Rhone thus hath cleft his way,
The mightiest of the storms hath ta'en his stand:
For here, not one, but many, make their play,
And fling their thunderbolts from hand to hand,   890
Flashing and cast around: of all the band,
The brightest through these parted hills hath forked
His lightnings—as if he did understand,
That in such gaps as desolation worked,
There the hot shaft should blast whatever therein lurked.   895

96

Sky—mountains—river—winds—lake—lightnings! ye,
With night, and clouds, and thunder, and a soul
To make these felt and feeling, well may be
Things that have made me watchful; the far roll
Of your departing voices, is the knoll[1]   900
Of what in me is sleepless—if I rest.
But where of ye, oh tempests! is the goal?
Are ye like those within the human breast?
Or do ye find at length, like eagles, some high nest?

97

Could I embody and unbosom now   905
That which is most within me—could I wreak
My thoughts upon expression, and thus throw
Soul, heart, mind, passions, feelings, strong or weak,
All that I would have sought, and all I seek,
Bear, know, feel—and yet breathe—into *one* word,   910
And that one word were lightning, I would speak;
But as it is, I live and die unheard,
With a most voiceless thought, sheathing it as a sword.

98

The morn is up again, the dewy morn,
With breath all incense and with cheek all bloom,   915
Laughing the clouds away with playful scorn,
And living as if earth contained no tomb—
And glowing into day; we may resume
The march of our existence; and thus I,
Still on thy shores, fair Leman! may find room   920
And food for meditation, nor pass by
Much, that may give us pause, if pondered fittingly.

* * *

1. Knell (old form).

113

I have not loved the world, nor the world me;
I have not flattered its rank breath, nor bowed   1050
To its idolatries a patient knee—
Nor coined my cheek to smiles—nor cried aloud
In worship of an echo; in the crowd
They could not deem me one of such; I stood
Among them, but not of them; in a shroud   1055
Of thoughts which were not their thoughts, and still could,
Had I not filed[2] my mind, which thus itself subdued.

114

I have not loved the world, nor the world me—
But let us part fair foes; I do believe,
Though I have found them not, that there may be   1060
Words which are things, hopes which will not deceive,
And virtues which are merciful nor weave
Snares for the failing: I would also deem
O'er others' griefs that some sincerely grieve;
That two, or one, are almost what they seem—   1065
That goodness is no name, and happiness no dream.

115

My daughter! with thy name this song begun—
My daughter! with thy name thus much shall end!—
I see thee not—I hear thee not—but none
Can be so wrapped in thee; thou art the friend   1070
To whom the shadows of far years extend:
Albeit my brow thou never shouldst behold,
My voice shall with thy future visions blend,
And reach into thy heart—when mine is cold—
A token and a tone even from thy father's mold.   1075

116

To aid thy mind's development—to watch
Thy dawn of little joys—to sit and see
Almost thy very growth—to view thee catch
Knowledge of objects—wonders yet to thee!
To hold thee lightly on a gentle knee,   1080
And print on thy soft cheek a parent's kiss—
This, it should seem, was not reserved for me;
Yet this was in my nature—as it is,
I know not what is there, yet something like to this.

117

Yet, though dull Hate as duty should be taught,   1085
I know that thou wilt love me; though my name
Should be shut from thee, as a spell still fraught
With desolation, and a broken claim;
Though the grave closed between us—'twere the same;
I know that thou wilt love me; though to drain   1090
My blood from out thy being were an aim
And an attainment—all would be in vain—
Still thou wouldst love me, still that more than life retain.

---

2. Defiled. In a note Byron refers to *Macbeth* III.i.65 ("For Banquo's issue have I filed my mind").

118

The child of love—though born in bitterness
And nurtured in convulsion! Of thy sire   1095
These were the elements, and thine no less.
As yet such are around thee, but thy fire
Shall be more tempered and thy hope far higher.
Sweet be thy cradled slumbers! O'er the sea,
And from the mountains where I now respire,   1100
Fain would I waft such blessing upon thee,
As, with a sigh, I deem thou mightst have been to me!

From *Canto IV*

1

I stood in Venice, on the Bridge of Sighs,[1]
A palace and a prison on each hand:
I saw from out the wave her structures rise
As from the stroke of the enchanter's wand:
A thousand years their cloudy wings expand   5
Around me, and a dying Glory smiles
O'er the far times, when many a subject land
Looked to the wingéd Lion's[2] marble piles,
Where Venice sate in state, throned on her hundred isles!

2

She looks a sea Cybele,[3] fresh from ocean,   10
Rising with her tiara of proud towers
At airy distance, with majestic motion,
A ruler of the waters and their powers:
And such she was—her daughters had their dowers
From spoils of nations, and the exhaustless East   15
Poured in her lap all gems in sparkling showers:
In purple was she robed, and of her feast
Monarchs partook, and deemed their dignity increased.

3

In Venice Tasso's echoes are no more,
And silent rows the songless gondolier;[4]   20
Her palaces are crumbling to the shore,
And music meets not always now the ear:
Those days are gone—but Beauty still is here;
States fall, arts fade—but Nature doth not die,
Nor yet forget how Venice once was dear,   25
The pleasant place of all festivity,
The revel of the earth, the masque of Italy![5]

4

But unto us she hath a spell beyond
Her name in story, and her long array

1. A covered bridge between the Doge's Palace and the prison of San Marco.
2. The emblem of St. Mark, patron saint of Venice.
3. A nature goddess, sometimes represented wearing a crown ("tiara") of towers.
4. The gondoliers once had the custom of chanting stanzas of Tasso's *Jerusalem Delivered*.
5. "Masques" were lavish dramatic entertainments popular in the courts of the Renaissance, involving songs, dances, and elaborate costumes and staging.

Of mighty shadows, whose dim forms despond 30
Above the dogeless city's[6] vanished sway:
Ours is a trophy which will not decay
With the Rialto;[7] Shylock and the Moor
And Pierre cannot be swept or worn away—
The keystones of the arch! though all were o'er, 35
For us repeopled were[8] the solitary shore.

* * *

178

There is a pleasure in the pathless woods,
There is a rapture on the lonely shore, 1595
There is society where none intrudes,
By the deep sea, and music in its roar:
I love not Man the less, but Nature more,
From these our interviews, in which I steal
From all I may be, or have been before, 1600
To mingle with the Universe, and feel
What I can ne'er express, yet can not all conceal.

179

Roll on, thou deep and dark blue Ocean—roll!
Ten thousand fleets sweep over thee in vain;
Man marks the earth with ruin—his control 1605
Stops with the shore; upon the watery plain
The wrecks are all thy deed, nor doth remain
A shadow of man's ravage, save his own,
When, for a moment, like a drop of rain,
He sinks into thy depths with bubbling groan, 1610
Without a grave, unknelled, uncoffined, and unknown.

180

His steps are not upon thy paths—thy fields
Are not a spoil for him—thou dost arise
And shake him from thee; the vile strength he wields
For earth's destruction thou dost all despise, 1615
Spurning him from thy bosom to the skies,
And send'st him, shivering in thy playful spray
And howling, to his Gods, where haply lies
His petty hope in some near port or bay,
And dashest him again to earth—there let him lay.[9] 1620

181

The armaments which thunderstrike the walls
Of rock-built cities, bidding nations quake
And monarchs tremble in their capitals,
The oak leviathans,[1] whose huge ribs make
Their clay creator the vain title take 1625
Of lord of thee, and arbiter of war—

6. The last duke ("doge") of Venice was deposed by Napoleon in 1797.
7. The business district in Venice, a setting in *The Merchant of Venice* and *Othello* ("the Moor"), and also in Thomas Otway's tragedy, *Venice Preserved* (1682), in which Pierre (line 34) is a leading character.

8. Would be.
9. For "lie." Denounced by many critics, this has been called the most notorious solecism in English poetry. But Byron, like other English aristocrats of the time, deliberately affected a cavalier indifference to commonplace grammar.
1. Warships.

These are thy toys, and, as the snowy flake,
They melt into thy yeast of waves, which mar
Alike the Armada's pride or spoils of Trafalgar.[2]

182

Thy shores are empires, changed in all save thee— 1630
Assyria, Greece, Rome, Carthage, what are they?
Thy waters washed them power while they were free,
And many a tyrant since; their shores obey
The stranger, slave, or savage; their decay
Has dried up realms to deserts—not so thou, 1635
Unchangeable save to thy wild waves' play;
Time writes no wrinkle on thine azure brow—
Such as creation's dawn beheld, thou rollest now.

183

Thou glorious mirror, where the Almighty's form
Glasses[3] itself in tempests; in all time, 1640
Calm or convulsed—in breeze, or gale, or storm,
Icing the pole, or in the torrid clime
Dark-heaving—boundless, endless, and sublime—
The image of Eternity—the throne
Of the Invisible; even from out thy slime 1645
The monsters of the deep are made; each zone
Obeys thee; thou goest forth, dread, fathomless, alone.

184

And I have loved thee, Ocean! and my joy
Of youthful sports was on thy breast to be
Borne, like thy bubbles, onward: from a boy 1650
I wantoned with thy breakers—they to me
Were a delight; and if the freshening sea
Made them a terror—'twas a pleasing fear,
For I was as it were a child of thee,
And trusted to thy billows far and near, 1655
And laid my hand upon thy mane—as I do here.

185

My task is done—my song hath ceased—my theme
Has died into an echo; it is fit
The spell should break of this protracted dream.
The torch shall be extinguished which hath lit 1660
My midnight lamp—and what is writ, is writ—
Would it were worthier! but I am not now
That which I have been—and my visions flit
Less palpably before me—and the glow
Which in my spirit dwelt is fluttering, faint, and low. 1665

186

Farewell! a word that must be, and hath been—
A sound which makes us linger—yet—farewell!
Ye! who have traced the Pilgrim to the scene

2. The Spanish Armada, defeated by
the English in 1588, lost many ships in
a storm; another storm was responsible
for the loss of a number of French ships
that Nelson had captured at Trafalgar
(1805).
3. Mirrors.

Which is his last, if in your memories dwell
A thought which once was his, if on ye swell   1670
A single recollection, not in vain
He wore his sandal shoon and scallop shell;[4]
Farewell! with *him* alone may rest the pain,
If such there were—with *you*, the moral of his strain!

                                    1812, 1816, 1818

So We'll Go No More A-Roving[1]

1

So we'll go no more a-roving
   So late into the night,
Though the heart be still as loving,
   And the moon be still as bright.

2

For the sword outwears its sheath,   5
   And the soul wears out the breast,
And the heart must pause to breathe,
   And Love itself have rest.

3

Though the night was made for loving,
   And the day returns too soon,   10
Yet we'll go no more a-roving
   By the light of the moon.

1817   1836

4. Sandals and a scallop shell (worn on the hat) were traditional emblems of pilgrims to holy shrines.
1. Included in a letter to Thomas Moore, February 28, 1817, and written in the Lenten aftermath of a spell of feverish dissipation in the Carnival season at Venice. Byron wrote, "I find 'the sword wearing out the scabbard,' though I have but just turned the corner of twenty-nine." The poem is based on the refrain of a Scottish song, *The Jolly Beggar:* "And we'll gang nae mair a roving / Sae late into the nicht * * * "

Don Juan   Byron began his masterpiece (pronounced in the English fashion, *Don Joó-un*) in July of 1818, published it in installments, beginning with Cantos I and II in 1819, and continued working on it almost until his death. He extemporized the poem from episode to episode; "I *have* no plan," he said, "I *had* no plan; but I had or have materials." The work was composed with remarkable speed (the 888 lines of Canto XIII, for example, were accomplished within a week), and it seeks to give the effect of improvisation and comprehensiveness rather than of compression; it ought to be read rapidly, at a conversational pace.

   The poem breaks off in the sixteenth canto, but even in its unfinished state *Don Juan* is the longest satire, and one of the longest of all poems, written in English. Its hero, the Spanish libertine, had in the original legend been superhuman in his sexual energy and wickedness. Throughout

Byron's version the unspoken but persistent joke is that this violent and archetypal *homme fatal* of European legend is in fact more acted upon than active. Unfailingly amiable and well-intentioned, he is guilty largely of youth, charm, and a courteous and compliant spirit. The ladies do all the rest.

The chief models for the poem were the Italian seriocomic versions of medieval chivalric romances; the genre had been introduced by Pulci in the 15th century and achieved its greatest success in Ariosto's *Orlando Furioso* (1516). From these writers Byron caught the mixed moods and violent oscillations between the sublime and the ridiculous, as well as the easy, colloquial management of the complex ottava rima—an eight-line stanza in which the initial interlaced rhymes (*ababab*) build up to the comic turn in the final pat couplet (*cc*). Byron was influenced in the English use of this Italian form by a mildly amusing poem published in 1817, under the pseudonym of "Whistlecraft," by his friend John Hookham Frere. Other recognizable antecedents of *Don Juan* are Swift's *Gulliver's Travels* and Johnson's *Rasselas*, which also employed the naïve traveler as a satiric device, and Laurence Sterne's novel, *Tristram Shandy*, with its comic exploitation of a narrative medium blatantly subject to the whimsy of the author. But even the most original literary works play variations upon inherited conventions. Shelley at once recognized his friend's poem for what it was, "something wholly new and relative to the age."

Byron's most trusted literary advisers thought the poem disgracefully immoral, and John Murray took the precaution of printing the first two installments without identifying either Byron as the author or himself as the publisher. In our own day, however, the most common complaint is not that *Don Juan* is immoral, but that it is morally nihilistic—that the poem is destructive without limit, since it proposes no positive values as a base for the satire, but sees life, in the words of one critic, as "a strange meaningless pageant." Yet Byron insisted that *Don Juan* is "a *satire* on *abuses* of the present state of society," and "the most moral of poems." Though the final phrase exaggerates, it has a foundation of truth. What the poem most frequently attacks, in love, religion, and social relations, are very considerable vices—sham, hypocrisy, complacency, oppression, greed, and lust. Furthermore, the satire constantly, though silently, assumes as moral positives the qualities of courage, loyalty, generosity, and, above all, total candor; it merely implies that these virtues are excessively rare, and that the modern world is not constituted to reward, to encourage, or even to recognize them when they make their appearance. And *Don Juan* is zestfully on the side of life, in its abundant variety. "As to *Don Juan*," Byron wrote elatedly to a friend, "confess—confess, you dog and be candid. * * * It may be profligate, but is it not *life*, is it not *the thing*?"

It is a mistake to look to *Don Juan* primarily for the story. The controlling element is not the narrative but the narrator, and his temperament gives the work its unity. The poem is really an incessant monologue, in the course of which a story manages to be told. It opens with the first-person pronoun and immediately lets us into the story-teller's predicament: "I want a hero * * * " The voice then goes on, for almost two thousand stanzas, with effortless volubility and bewildering shifts of mood and perspective, using the occasion of Juan's misadventures to confide to us the speaker's thoughts and devastating judgments upon all the major institutions, activities, and values of Western society.

What Byron discovered in *Don Juan* was how to give literary expression to that aspect of his temperament which, in real life, his self-consciousness and reserve permitted him to display only in the security of a circle of intimate friends or in his wonderfully vivacious letters to people he trusted. The poet who in his brilliantly successful youth created the gloomy and misanthropic Byronic hero, in his later and sadder life created a character (not the hero, but the narrator of *Don Juan*) who is one of the great, and one of the most complex, comic inventions in literature.

From Don Juan

Fragment[1]

I would to heaven that I were so much clay,
　As I am blood, bone, marrow, passion, feeling—
Because at least the past were passed away—
　And for the future—(but I write this reeling,
Having got drunk exceedingly today,　　　　　　　　　　5
　So that I seem to stand upon the ceiling)
I say—the future is a serious matter—
And so—for God's sake—hock[2] and soda water!

From *Canto I*

1

I want a hero: an uncommon want,
　When every year and month sends forth a new one,
Till, after cloying the gazettes with cant,
　The age discovers he is not the true one;
Of such as these I should not care to vaunt,　　　　　5
　I'll therefore take our ancient friend Don Juan—
We all have seen him, in the pantomime,[1]
Sent to the devil somewhat ere his time.

* * *

5

Brave men were living before Agamemnon[2]
　And since, exceeding valorous and sage,
A good deal like him too, though quite the same none;　　　35

1. This stanza was written on the back of part of the MS. of Canto I.
2. A white Rhine wine, from the German *Hochheimer*.
1. The Juan legend was a popular subject in English pantomime.
2. In Homer's *Iliad*, the king commanding the Greeks in the siege of Troy. This line is translated from an ode by Horace.

But then they shone not on the poet's page,
And so have been forgotten—I condemn none,
　But can't find any in the present age
Fit for my poem (that is, for my new one);
So, as I said, I'll take my friend Don Juan.　　　　40

6

Most epic poets plunge *"in medias res"*[3]
　(Horace makes this the heroic turnpike road),
And then your hero tells, whene'er you please,
　What went before—by way of episode,
While seated after dinner at his ease,　　　　45
　Beside his mistress in some soft abode,
Palace, or garden, paradise, or cavern,
Which serves the happy couple for a tavern.

7

That is the usual method, but not mine—
　My way is to begin with the beginning;　　　　50
The regularity of my design
　Forbids all wandering as the worst of sinning,
And therefore I shall open with a line
　(Although it cost me half an hour in spinning)
Narrating somewhat of Don Juan's father,　　　　55
And also of his mother, if you'd rather.

8

In Seville was he born, a pleasant city,
　Famous for oranges and women—he
Who has not seen it will be much to pity,
　So says the proverb—and I quite agree;　　　　60
Of all the Spanish towns is none more pretty,
　Cadiz perhaps—but that you soon may see—
Don Juan's parents lived beside the river,
A noble stream, and called the Guadalquivir.

9

His father's name was Jóse[4]—*Don*, of course,　　　　65
　A true Hidalgo, free from every stain
Of Moor or Hebrew blood, he traced his source
　Through the most Gothic gentlemen of Spain;
A better cavalier ne'er mounted horse,
　Or, being mounted, e'er got down again,　　　　70
Than Jóse, who begot our hero, who
Begot—but that's to come—Well, to renew:

10

His mother was a learned lady, famed
　For every branch of every science known—
In every Christian language ever named,　　　　75
　With virtues equaled by her wit alone:
She made the cleverest people quite ashamed,
　And even the good with inward envy groan,

3. "Into the middle of things" (Horace, *Ars Poetica* 148).

4. Normally "José," of course; Byron transferred the accent for his meter.

Finding themselves so very much exceeded
In their own way by all the things that she did. 80

11

Her memory was a mine: she knew by heart
   All Calderon and greater part of Lopé,[5]
So that if any actor missed his part
   She could have served him for the prompter's copy;
For her Feinagle's[6] were an useless art, 85
   And he himself obliged to shut up shop—he
Could never make a memory so fine as
That which adorned the brain of Donna Inez.

12

Her favorite science was the mathematical,
   Her noblest virtue was her magnanimity, 90
Her wit (she sometimes tried at wit) was Attic[7] all,
   Her serious sayings darkened to sublimity;
In short, in all things she was fairly what I call
   A prodigy—her morning dress was dimity,
Her evening silk, or, in the summer, muslin, 95
And other stuffs, with which I won't stay puzzling.

13

She knew the Latin—that is, "the Lord's prayer,"
   And Greek—the alphabet—I'm nearly sure;
She read some French romances here and there,
   Although her mode of speaking was not pure; 100
For native Spanish she had no great care,
   At least her conversation was obscure;
Her thoughts were theorems, her words a problem,
As if she deemed that mystery would ennoble 'em.

* * *

22

'Tis pity learned virgins ever wed
   With persons of no sort of education,
Or gentlemen, who, though well born and bred, 170
   Grow tired of scientific conversation:
I don't choose to say much upon this head,
   I'm a plain man, and in a single station,
But—Oh! ye lords of ladies intellectual. 175
Inform us truly, have they not henpecked you all?

23

Don Jóse and his lady quarrelled—*why*,
   Not any of the many could divine,
Though several thousand people chose to try,
   'Twas surely no concern of theirs nor mine; 180
I loathe that low vice, curiosity;
   But if there's anything in which I shine,

5. Lope de Vega and Calderón de la Barca, the great Spanish dramatists of the early 17th century.
6. Gregor von Feinagle, a German expert on mnemonics, who had lectured in England in 1811.
7. Athenian. The common phrase "Attic salt" signifies the famed wit of the Athenians.

'Tis in arranging all my friends' affairs,
Not having, of my own, domestic cares.

24

And so I interfered, and with the best   185
  Intentions, but their treatment was not kind;
I think the foolish people were possessed,
  For neither of them could I ever find,
Although their porter afterwards confessed—
  But that's no matter, and the worst's behind,   190
For little Juan o'er me threw, downstairs,
A pail of housemaid's water unawares.

25

A little curly-headed, good-for-nothing,
  And mischief-making monkey from his birth;
His parents ne'er agreed except in doting   195
  Upon the most unquiet imp on earth;
Instead of quarreling, had they been but both in
  Their senses, they'd have sent young master forth
To school, or had him soundly whipped at home,
To teach him manners for the time to come.   200

26

Don Jóse and the Donna Inez led
  For some time an unhappy sort of life,
Wishing each other, not divorced, but dead;
  They lived respectably as man and wife,
Their conduct was exceedingly well-bred,   205
  And gave no outward signs of inward strife,
Until at length the smothered fire broke out,
And put the business past all kind of doubt.

27

For Inez called some druggists and physicians,
  And tried to prove her loving lord was *mad*,[8]   210
But as he had some lucid intermissions,
  She next decided he was only *bad*;
Yet when they asked her for her depositions,
  No sort of explanation could be had,
Save that her duty both to man and God   215
Required this conduct—which seemed very odd.

28

She kept a journal, where his faults were noted,
  And opened certain trunks of books and letters,
All which might, if occasion served, be quoted;
  And then she had all Seville for abettors,   220
Besides her good old grandmother (who doted);
  The hearers of her case became repeaters,
Then advocates, inquisitors, and judges,
Some for amusement, others for old grudges.

---

8. Lady Byron had thought her husband might be insane, and sought medical advice on the matter. This and other passages obviously allude to his wife, although Byron insisted that Donna Inez was not intended to be a caricature of Lady Byron.

29

And then this best and meekest woman bore   225
   With such serenity her husband's woes,
Just as the Spartan ladies did of yore,
   Who saw their spouses killed, and nobly chose
Never to say a word about them more—
   Calmly she heard each calumny that rose,   230
And saw *his* agonies with such sublimity,
That all the world exclaimed, "What magnanimity!"

* * *

32

Their friends had tried at reconciliation,
   Then their relations, who made matters worse   250
('Twere hard to tell upon a like occasion
   To whom it may be best to have recourse—
I can't say much for friend or yet relation);
   The lawyers did their utmost for divorce,
But scarce a fee was paid on either side   255
Before, unluckily, Don Jóse died.

33

He died: and most unluckily, because
   According to all hints I could collect
From counsel learned in those kinds of laws
   (Although their talk's obscure and circumspect),   260
His death contrived to spoil a charming cause;
   A thousand pities also with respect
To public feeling, which on this occasion
Was manifested in a great sensation.

* * *

37

Dying intestate, Juan was sole heir
   To a chancery suit,[9] and messuages, and lands,   290
Which, with a long minority and care,
   Promised to turn out well in proper hands:
Inez became sole guardian, which was fair,
   And answered but to nature's just demands;
An only son left with an only mother   295
Is brought up much more wisely than another.

38

Sagest of women, even of widows, she
   Resolved that Juan should be quite a paragon,
And worthy of the noblest pedigree
   (His sire was of Castile, his dam from Aragon).   300
Then for accomplishments of chivalry,
   In case our lord the king should go to war again,
He learned the arts of riding, fencing, gunnery,
And how to scale a fortress—or a nunnery.

9. A suit in what was then the highest English court, notorious for its delays.   "Messuages": houses and the adjoining lands.

39

But that which Donna Inez most desired,   305
    And saw into herself each day before all
The learned tutors whom for him she hired,
    Was that his breeding should be strictly moral:
Much into all his studies she inquired,
    And so they were submitted first to her, all,   310
Arts, sciences, no branch was made a mystery
To Juan's eyes, excepting natural history.[1]

40

The languages, especially the dead,
    The sciences, and most of all the abstruse,
The arts, at least all such as could be said   315
    To be the most remote from common use,
In all these he was much and deeply read;
    But not a page of anything that's loose,
Or hints continuation of the species,
Was ever suffered, lest he should grow vicious.   320

41

His classic studies made a little puzzle,
    Because of filthy loves of gods and goddesses,
Who in the earlier ages raised a bustle,
    But never put on pantaloons or bodices;
His reverend tutors had at times a tussle,   325
    And for their *Aeneids, Iliads,* and *Odysseys,*
Were forced to make an odd sort of apology,
For Donna Inez dreaded the mythology.

42

Ovid's a rake, as half his verses show him,
    Anacreon's morals are a still worse sample,   330
Catullus scarcely has a decent poem,
    I don't think Sappho's *Ode* a good example,
Although Longinus tells us there is no hymn
    Where the sublime soars forth on wings more ample;[2]
But Virgil's songs are pure, except that horrid one   335
Beginning with *"Formosum Pastor Corydon."*[3]

43

Lucretius' irreligion[4] is too strong
    For early stomachs, to prove wholesome food;
I can't help thinking Juvenal[5] was wrong,
    Although no doubt his real intent was good,   340
For speaking out so plainly in his song,
    So much indeed as to be downright rude;

1. Which includes biology and physiology.
2. The Greek rhetorician Longinus praises a passage from Sappho in *On the Sublime* X.
3. Virgil's *Eclogue II* begins: "The shepherd, Corydon, burned with love for the handsome Alexis."
4. In *De rerum natura* ("On the Nature of Things") Lucretius sets out to show that the universe can be explained without reference to any god.
5. The Latin satires of Juvenal attacked the corruption of Roman society in the first century A.D.

And then what proper person can be partial
To all those nauseous epigrams of Martial?

44

Juan was taught from out the best edition, 345
   Expurgated by learned men, who place,
Judiciously, from out the schoolboy's vision,
   The grosser parts; but fearful to deface
Too much their modest bard by this omission,
   And pitying sore his mutilated case, 350
They only add them all in an appendix,[6]
Which saves, in fact, the trouble of an index.

* * *

52

For my part I say nothing—nothing—but
   This I will say—my reasons are my own— 410
That if I had an only son to put
   To school (as God be praised that I have none)
'Tis not with Donna Inez I would shut
   Him up to learn his catechism alone,
No—no—I'd send him out betimes to college, 415
For there it was I picked up my own knowledge.

53

For there one learns—'tis not for me to boast,
   Though I acquired—but I pass over *that*,
As well as all the Greek I since have lost:
   I say that there's the place—but *"Verbum sat,"*[7] 420
I think I picked up too, as well as most,
   Knowledge of matters—but no matter *what*—
I never married—but, I think, I know
That sons should not be educated so.

54

Young Juan now was sixteen years of age, 425
   Tall, handsome, slender, but well knit: he seemed
Active, though not so sprightly, as a page;
   And everybody but his mother deemed
Him almost man; but she flew in a rage
   And bit her lips (for else she might have screamed) 430
If any said so, for to be precocious
Was in her eyes a thing the most atrocious.

55

Amongst her numerous acquaintance, all
   Selected for discretion and devotion,
There was the Donna Julia, whom to call 435
   Pretty were but to give a feeble notion
Of many charms in her as natural
   As sweetness to the flower, or salt to ocean,
Her zone[8] to Venus, or his bow to Cupid
(But this last simile is trite and stupid). 440

6. "Fact! There is, or was, such an edition, with all the obnoxious epigrams of Martial placed by themselves at the end" [Byron's note].
7. A word [to the wise] is sufficient.
8. Girdle.

56

The darkness of her Oriental eye
  Accorded with her Moorish origin
(Her blood was not all Spanish, by the by;
  In Spain, you know, this is a sort of sin).
When proud Granada fell, and, forced to fly,   445
  Boabdil wept,[9] of Donna Julia's kin
Some went to Africa, some stayed in Spain,
Her great-great-grandmamma chose to remain.

57

She married (I forget the pedigree)
  With an hidalgo,[1] who transmitted down   450
His blood less noble than such blood should be;
  At such alliances his sires would frown,
In that point so precise in each degree
  That they bred *in and in*, as might be shown,
Marrying their cousins—nay, their aunts, and nieces,   455
Which always spoils the breed, if it increases.

58

This heathenish cross restored the breed again,
  Ruined its blood, but much improved its flesh;
For from a root the ugliest in old Spain
  Sprung up a branch as beautiful as fresh;   460
The sons no more were short, the daughters plain:
  But there's a rumor which I fain would hush,
'Tis said that Donna Julia's grandmamma
Produced her Don more heirs at love than law.

59

However this might be, the race went on   465
  Improving still through every generation,
Until it centered in an only son,
  Who left an only daughter; my narration
May have suggested that this single one
  Could be but Julia (whom on this occasion   470
I shall have much to speak about), and she
Was married, charming, chaste, and twenty-three.

60

Her eye (I'm very fond of handsome eyes)
  Was large and dark, suppressing half its fire
Until she spoke, then through its soft disguise   475
  Flashed an expression more of pride than ire,
And love than either; and there would arise
  A something in them which was not desire,
But would have been, perhaps, but for the soul
Which struggled through and chastened down the whole.   480

61

Her glossy hair was clustered o'er a brow
  Bright with intelligence, and fair, and smooth;

9. The last Moorish king of Granada (then a province in Spain) wept when his capital fell to the Spaniards (1492).   1. A Spanish nobleman of the lower class.

Her eyebrow's shape was like the aërial bow,
   Her cheek all purple with the beam of youth,
Mounting, at times, to a transparent glow,   485
   As if her veins ran lightning; she, in sooth,
Possessed an air and grace by no means common:
   Her stature tall—I hate a dumpy woman.

62

Wedded she was some years, and to a man
   Of fifty, and such husbands are in plenty;   490
And yet, I think, instead of such a ONE
   'Twere better to have TWO of five-and-twenty,
Especially in countries near the sun:
   And now I think on't, *"mi vien in mente,"*[2]
Ladies even of the most uneasy virtue   495
Prefer a spouse whose age is short of thirty.

63

'Tis a sad thing, I cannot choose but say,
   And all the fault of that indecent sun,
Who cannot leave alone our helpless clay,
   But will keep baking, broiling, burning on,   500
That howsoever people fast and pray,
   The flesh is frail, and so the soul undone:
What men call gallantry, and gods adultery,
Is much more common where the climate's sultry.

64

Happy the nations of the moral North!   505
   Where all is virtue, and the winter season
Sends sin, without a rag on, shivering forth
   ('Twas snow that brought St. Anthony to reason);[3]
Where juries cast up what a wife is worth
   By laying whate'er sum, in mulct,[4] they please on   510
The lover, who must pay a handsome price,
Because it is a marketable vice.

65

Alfonso was the name of Julia's lord,
   A man well looking for his years, and who
Was neither much beloved nor yet abhorred: 515
   They lived together as most people do,
Suffering each other's foibles by accord,
   And not exactly either *one* or *two*;
Yet he was jealous, though he did not show it,
For jealousy dislikes the world to know it.

* * *

69

Juan she saw, and, as a pretty child,   545
   Caressed him often—such a thing might be
Quite innocently done, and harmless styled,

---

2. "It comes to my mind."
3. "For the particulars of St. Anthony's recipe for hot blood in cold weather, see Mr. Alban Butler's *Lives of the Saints*" [Byron's note].
4. By way of a fine or legal penalty.

When she had twenty years, and thirteen he;
But I am not so sure I should have smiled
    When he was sixteen, Julia twenty-three;   550
These few short years make wondrous alterations,
Particularly amongst sunburnt nations.

70

Whate'er the cause might be, they had become
    Changed; for the dame grew distant, the youth shy,
Their looks cast down, their greetings almost dumb,   555
    And much embarrassment in cither eye;
There surely will be little doubt with some
    That Donna Julia knew the reason why,
But as for Juan, he had no more notion
Than he who never saw the sea, of ocean.   560

71

Yet Julia's very coldness still was kind,
    And tremulously gentle her small hand
Withdrew itself from his, but left behind
    A little pressure, thrilling, and so bland
And slight, so very slight, that to the mind   565
    'Twas but a doubt; but ne'er magician's wand
Wrought change with all Armida's[5] fairy art
Like what this light touch left on Juan's heart.

72

And if she met him, though she smiled no more,
    She looked a sadness sweeter than her smile,   570
As if her heart had deeper thoughts in store
    She must not own, but cherished more the while,
For that compression in its burning core;
    Even innocence itself has many a wile,
And will not dare to trust itself with truth,   575
And love is taught hypocrisy from youth.

* * *

76

She vowed she never would see Juan more,
    And next day paid a visit to his mother,
And looked extremely at the opening door,
    Which, by the Virgin's grace, let in another;
Grateful she was, and yet a little sore—   605
    Again it opens, it can be no other,
'Tis surely Juan now—No! I'm afraid
That night the Virgin was no further prayed.

77

She now determined that a virtuous woman
    Should rather face and overcome temptation,   610
That flight was base and dastardly, and no man
    Should ever give her heart the least sensation;
That is to say, a thought beyond the common

---

5. The sorceress who seduces Rinaldo in Tasso's *Jerusalem Delivered*.

Preference, that we must feel upon occasion,
For people who are pleasanter than others,   615
But then they only seem so many brothers.

78

And even if by chance—and who can tell?
    The devil's so very sly—she should discover
That all within was not so very well,
    And, if still free, that such or such a lover   620
Might please perhaps, a virtuous wife can quell
    Such thoughts, and be the better when they're over;
And if the man should ask, 'tis but denial:
I recommend young ladies to make trial.

79

And then there are such things as love divine,   625
    Bright and immaculate, unmixed and pure,
Such as the angels think so very fine,
    And matrons, who would be no less secure,
Platonic, perfect, "just such love as mine":
    Thus Julia said—and thought so, to be sure,   630
And so I'd have her think, were I the man
On whom her reveries celestial ran.

* * *

86

So much for Julia. Now we'll turn to Juan.
    Poor little fellow! he had no idea
Of his own case, and never hit the true one;
    In feelings quick as Ovid's Miss Medea,[6]
He puzzled over what he found a new one,   685
    But not as yet imagined it could be a
Thing quite in course, and not at all alarming,
Which, with a little patience, might grow charming.

* * *

90

Young Juan wandered by the glassy brooks,
    Thinking unutterable things; he threw
Himself at length within the leafy nooks   715
    Where the wild branch of the cork forest grew;
There poets find materials for their books,
    And every now and then we read them through,
So that their plan and prosody are eligible,
Unless, like Wordsworth, they prove unintelligible.   720

91

He, Juan (and not Wordsworth), so pursued
    His self-communion with his own high soul,
Until his mighty heart, in its great mood,
    Had mitigated part, though not the whole
Of its disease; he did the best he could   725

6. In *Metamorphoses* VII, Ovid tells the story of Medea's mad infatuation for
Jason.

With things not very subject to control,
And turned, without perceiving his condition,
Like Coleridge, into a metaphysician.

92

He thought about himself, and the whole earth,
Of man the wonderful, and of the stars,
And how the deuce they ever could have birth;
And then he thought of earthquakes, and of wars,
How many miles the moon might have in girth,
Of air-balloons, and of the many bars
To perfect knowledge of the boundless skies—
And then he thought of Donna Julia's eyes.

93

In thoughts like these true wisdom may discern
Longings sublime, and aspirations high,
Which some are born with, but the most part learn
To plague themselves withal, they know not why:
'Twas strange that one so young should thus concern
His brain about the action of the sky;
If *you* think 'twas philosophy that this did,
I can't help thinking puberty assisted.

94

He pored upon the leaves, and on the flowers,
And heard a voice in all the winds; and then
He thought of wood nymphs and immortal bowers,
And how the goddesses came down to men:
He missed the pathway, he forgot the hours,
And when he looked upon his watch again,
He found how much old Time had been a winner—
He also found that he had lost his dinner.

* * *

103

'Twas on a summer's day—the sixth of June—
I like to be particular in dates,
Not only of the age, and year, but moon;
They are a sort of post house, where the Fates
Change horses, making history change its tune,
Then spur away o'er empires and o'er states,
Leaving at last not much besides chronology,
Excepting the post-obits[7] of theology.

104

'Twas on the sixth of June, about the hour
Of half-past six—perhaps still nearer seven—
When Julia sate within as pretty a bower
As e'er held houri in that heathenish heaven
Described by Mahomet, and Anacreon Moore,[8]

730
735
740
745
750
820
825

7. I.e., post-obit bonds (*post obitum*, "after death"): loans to an heir which fall due after the death of the person whose estate he is to inherit. Byron's meaning is probably that only theology purports to tell us what rewards are due in heaven.
8. Byron's friend, the poet Thomas Moore, who had translated the *Odes* of Anacreon; Byron is alluding to the

To whom the lyre and laurels have been given,   830
With all the trophies of triumphant song—
He won them well, and may he wear them long!

105

She sate, but not alone; I know not well
    How this same interview had taken place,
And even if I knew, I should not tell—   835
    People should hold their tongues in any case;
No matter how or why the thing befell,
    But there she and Juan, face to face—
When two such faces are so, 'twould be wise,
But very difficult, to shut their eyes.   840

106

How beautiful she looked! her conscious[9] heart
    Glowed in her cheek, and yet she felt no wrong.
Oh Love! how perfect is thy mystic art,
    Strengthening the weak, and trampling on the strong,
How self-deceitful is the sagest part   845
    Of mortals whom thy lure hath led along—
The precipice she stood on was immense,
So was her creed[1] in her own innocence.

107

She thought of her own strength, and Juan's youth,
    And of the folly of all prudish fears,   850
Victorious virtue, and domestic truth,
    And then of Don Alfonso's fifty years:
I wish these last had not occurred, in sooth,
    Because that number rarely much endears,
And through all climes, the snowy and the sunny,   855
Sounds ill in love, whate'er it may in money.

* * *

113

The sun set, and up rose the yellow moon:
    The devil's in the moon for mischief; they
Who called her CHASTE, methinks, began too soon
    Their nomenclature; there is not a day,   900
The longest, not the twenty-first of June,
    Sees half the business in a wicked way
On which three single hours of moonshine smile—
And then she looks so modest all the while.

114

There is a dangerous silence in that hour,   905
    A stillness, which leaves room for the full soul
To open all itself, without the power
    Of calling wholly back its self-control;
The silver light which, hallowing tree and tower,
    Sheds beauty and deep softness o'er the whole,   910

tale of *Paradise and the Peri* in   9. Feelingful.
Moore's Oriental poem *Lalla Rookh*.   1. Belief.

Breathes also to the heart, and o'er it throws
A loving languor, which is not repose.

115

And Julia sate with Juan, half embraced
   And half retiring from the glowing arm,
Which trembled like the bosom where 'twas placed;   915
   Yet still she must have thought there was no harm,
Or else 'twere easy to withdraw her waist;
   But then the situation had its charm,
And then——God knows what next—I can't go on;
I'm almost sorry that I e'er begun.   920

116

Oh Plato! Plato! you have paved the way,
   With your confounded fantasies, to more
Immoral conduct by the fancied sway
   Your system feigns o'er the controlless core
Of human hearts, than all the long array   925
   Of poets and romancers: You're a bore,
A charlatan, a coxcomb—and have been,
At best, no better than a go-between.

117

And Julia's voice was lost, except in sighs,
   Until too late for useful conversation;   930
The tears were gushing from her gentle eyes,
   I wish, indeed, they had not had occasion,
But who, alas! can love, and then be wise?
   Not that remorse did not oppose temptation;
A little still she strove, and much repented,   935
And whispering "I will ne'er consent"—consented.

* * *

126

'Tis sweet to win, no matter how, one's laurels
   By blood or ink; 'tis sweet to put an end
To strife; 'tis sometimes sweet to have our quarrels,
   Particularly with a tiresome friend:
Sweet is old wine in bottles, ale in barrels;   1005
   Dear is the helpless creature we defend
Against the world; and dear the schoolboy spot
We ne'er forget, though there we are forgot.

127

But sweeter still than this, than these, than all,
   Is first and passionate love—it stands alone,   1010
Like Adam's recollection of his fall;
   The tree of knowledge has been plucked—all's known—
And life yields nothing further to recall
   Worthy of this ambrosial sin, so shown,
No doubt in fable, as the unforgiven   1015
Fire which Prometheus[2] filched for us from heaven.

* * *

2. The Titan Prometheus incurred the wrath of Jupiter by stealing fire for mankind from heaven.

133

Man's a phenomenon, one knows not what,
   And wonderful beyond all wondrous measure;
'Tis pity though, in this sublime world, that
   Pleasure's a sin, and sometimes sin's a pleasure;   1060
Few mortals know what end they would be at,
   But whether glory, power, or love, or treasure,
The path is through perplexing ways, and when
The goal is gained, we die, you know—and then——

134

What then?—I do not know, no more do you—   1065
   And so good night.—Return we to our story:
'Twas in November, when fine days are few,
   And the far mountains wax a little hoary,
And clap a white cape on their mantles blue;
   And the sea dashes round the promontory,   1070
And the loud breaker boils against the rock,
And sober suns must set at five o'clock.

135

'Twas, as the watchmen say, a cloudy night;
   No moon, no stars, the wind was low or loud
By gusts, and many a sparkling hearth was bright   1075
   With the piled wood, round which the family crowd;
There's something cheerful in that sort of light,
   Even as a summer sky's without a cloud:
I'm fond of fire, and crickets, and all that,
A lobster salad, and champagne, and chat.   1080

136

'Twas midnight—Donna Julia was in bed,
   Sleeping, most probably—when at her door
Arose a clatter might awake the dead,
   If they had never been awoke before,
And that they have been so we all have read,   1085
   And are to be so, at the least, once more;
The door was fastened, but with voice and fist
First knocks were heard, then "Madam—Madam—hist!

137

"For God's sake, Madam—Madam—here's my master,
   With more than half the city at his back—   1090
Was ever heard of such a cursed disaster!
   'Tis not my fault—I kept good watch—Alack!
Do, pray, undo the bolt a little faster—
   They're on the stair just now, and in a crack
Will all be here; perhaps he yet may fly—   1095
Surely the window's not so *very* high!"

138

By this time Don Alfonso was arrived,
   With torches, friends, and servants in great number;
The major part of them had long been wived,
   And therefore paused not to disturb the slumber   1100
Of any wicked woman, who contrived

By stealth her husband's temples to encumber:[3]
Examples of this kind are so contagious,
Were *one* not punished, *all* would be outrageous.

139

I can't tell how, or why, or what suspicion   1105
    Could enter into Don Alfonso's head;
But for a cavalier of his condition[4]
    It surely was exceedingly ill-bred,
Without a word of previous admonition,
    To hold a levee[5] round his lady's bed,   1110
And summon lackeys, armed with fire and sword,
To prove himself the thing he most abhorred.

140

Poor Donna Julia! starting as from sleep
    (Mind that I do not say she had not slept),
Began at once to scream, and yawn, and weep;   1115
    Her maid, Antonia, who was an adept,
Contrived to fling the bedclothes in a heap,
    As if she had just now from out them crept:
I can't tell why she should take all this trouble
To prove her mistress had been sleeping double.   1120

141

But Julia mistress, and Antonia maid,
    Appeared like two poor harmless women, who
Of goblins, but still more of men, afraid,
    Had thought one man might be deterred by two,
And therefore side by side were gently laid,   1125
    Until the hours of absence should run through,
And truant husband should return, and say,
"My dear, I was the first who came away."

142

Now Julia found at length a voice, and cried,
    "In heaven's name, Don Alfonso, what d'ye mean?   1130
Has madness seized you? would that I had died
    Ere such a monster's victim I had been!
What may this midnight violence betide,
    A sudden fit of drunkenness or spleen?
Dare you suspect me, whom the thought would kill?   1135
Search, then, the room!"—Alfonso said, "I will."

143

He searched, *they* searched, and rummaged everywhere,
    Closet and clothes-press, chest and window seat,
And found much linen, lace, and several pair
    Of stockings, slippers, brushes, combs, complete,   1140
With other articles of ladies fair,
    To keep them beautiful, or leave them neat:
Arrass they pricked and curtains with their swords,
And wounded several shutters, and some boards.

3. Horns growing on the forehead were   4. Rank.
the traditional emblem of the cuckolded   5. Morning reception.
husband.

144

Under the bed they searched, and there they found— ₁₁₄₅
 No matter what—it was not that they sought;
They opened windows, gazing if the ground
 Had signs or footmarks, but the earth said nought;
And then they stared each other's faces round:
 'Tis odd, not one of all these seekers thought, ₁₁₅₀
And seems to me almost a sort of blunder,
Of looking *in* the bed as well as under.

145

During this inquisition Julia's tongue
 Was not asleep—"Yes, search and search," she cried,
"Insult on insult heap, and wrong on wrong! ₁₁₅₅
 It was for this that I became a bride!
For this in silence I have suffered long
 A husband like Alfonso at my side;
But now I'll bear no more, nor here remain,
If there be law or lawyers in all Spain. ₁₁₆₀

146

"Yes, Don Alfonso! husband now no more,
 If ever you indeed deserved the name,
Is't worthy of your years?—you have threescore—
 Fifty, or sixty, it is all the same—
Is't wise or fitting, causeless to explore ₁₁₆₅
 For facts against a virtuous woman's fame?
Ungrateful, perjured, barbarous Don Alfonso,
How dare you think your lady would go on so?"

* * *

159

The Senhor Don Alfonso stood confused; ₁₂₆₅
 Antonia bustled round the ransacked room,
And, turning up her nose, with looks abused
 Her master, and his myrmidons, of whom
Not one, except the attorney, was amused;
 He, like Achates,[6] faithful to the tomb, ₁₂₇₀
So there were quarrels, cared not for the cause,
Knowing they must be settled by the laws.

160

With prying snub nose, and small eyes, he stood,
 Following Antonia's motions here and there,
With much suspicion in his attitude; ₁₂₇₅
 For reputations he had little care;
So that a suit or action were made good,
 Small pity had he for the young and fair,
And ne'er believed in negatives, till these
Were proved by competent false witnesses. ₁₂₈₀

---

6. The *fidus Achates* ("faithful Achates") of Virgil's *Aeneid*, whose loyalty to Aeneas has become proverbial.

161

But Don Alfonso stood with downcast looks,
    And, truth to say, he made a foolish figure;
When, after searching in five hundred nooks,
    And treating a young wife with so much rigor,
He gained no point, except some self-rebukes,   1285
    Added to those his lady with such vigor
Had poured upon him for the last half hour,
Quick, thick, and heavy—as a thundershower.

162

At first he tried to hammer an excuse,
    To which the sole reply was tears, and sobs,   1290
And indications of hysterics, whose
    Prologue is always certain throes, and throbs,
Gasps, and whatever else the owners choose—
    Alfonso saw his wife, and thought of Job's;[7]
He saw too, in perspective, her relations,   1295
And then he tried to muster all his patience.

163

He stood in act to speak, or rather stammer,
    But sage Antonia cut him short before
The anvil of his speech received the hammer,
    With "Pray, sir, leave the room, and say no more,   1300
Or madam dies."—Alfonso muttered, "D—n her."
    But nothing else, the time of words was o'er;
He cast a rueful look or two, and did,
He knew not wherefore, that which he was bid.

164

With him retired his "*posse comitatus*,"[8]   1305
    The attorney last, who lingered near the door
Reluctantly, still tarrying there as late as
    Antonia let him—not a little sore
At this most strange and unexplained "*hiatus*"
    In Don Alfonso's facts, which just now wore   1310
An awkward look; as he revolved the case,
The door was fastened in his legal face.

165

No sooner was it bolted, than—Oh shame!
    Oh sin! Oh sorrow! and Oh womankind!
How can you do such things and keep your fame,   1315
    Unless this world, and t'other too, be blind?
Nothing so dear as an unfilched good name!
    But to proceed—for there is more behind:
With much heartfelt reluctance be it said,
Young Juan slipped, half-smothered, from the bed.   1320

7. Job's wife had advised her afflicted husband to "curse God, and die" (Job ii.9).
8. The complete form of the modern word "posse" (*posse comitatus* means literally "power of the county," i.e., the body of citizens summoned by a sheriff to preserve order in the county).

166

He had been hid—I don't pretend to say
   How, nor can I indeed describe the where—
Young, slender, and packed easily, he lay,
   No doubt, in little compass, round or square;
But pity him I neither must nor may
   His suffocation by that pretty pair;   1325
'Twere better, sure, to die so, than be shut
With maudlin Clarence in his malmsey butt.[9]

* * *

169

What's to be done? Alfonso will be back   1345
   The moment he has sent his fools away.
Antonia's skill was put upon the rack,
   But no device could be brought into play—
And how to parry the renewed attack?
   Besides, it wanted but few hours of day: 1350
Antonia puzzled; Julia did not speak,
But pressed her bloodless lip to Juan's cheek.

170

He turned his lip to hers, and with his hand
   Called back the tangles of her wandering hair;
Even then their love they could not all command,
   And half forgot their danger and despair: 1355
Antonia's patience now was at a stand—
   "Come, come, 'tis no time now for fooling there,"
She whispered, in great wrath—"I must deposit
This pretty gentleman within the closet."   1360

* * *

173

Now, Don Alfonso entering, but alone,
   Closed the oration of the trusty maid:
She loitered, and he told her to be gone,
   An order somewhat sullenly obeyed;   1380
However, present remedy was none,
   And no great good seemed answered if she stayed:
Regarding both with slow and sidelong view,
She snuffed the candle, curtsied, and withdrew.

174

Alfonso paused a minute—then begun   1385
   Some strange excuses for his late proceeding;
He would not justify what he had done,
   To say the best, it was extreme ill-breeding;
But there were ample reasons for it, none
   Of which he specified in this his pleading: 1390

9. The Duke of Clarence, brother of Richard III, was reputed to have been assassinated by being drowned in a cask ("butt") of malmsey, a sweet and aromatic wine.

His speech was a fine sample, on the whole,
Of rhetoric, which the learned call "*rigmarole.*"[1]

* * *

180

Alfonso closed his speech, and begged her pardon,
    Which Julia half withheld, and then half granted,
And laid conditions, he thought very hard on,   1435
    Denying several little things he wanted:
He stood like Adam lingering near his garden,
    With useless penitence perplexed and haunted,
Beseeching she no further would refuse,
When, lo! he stumbled o'er a pair of shoes.   1440

181

A pair of shoes!—what then? not much, if they
    Are such as fit with ladies' feet, but these
(No one can tell how much I grieve to say)
    Were masculine; to see them, and to seize,
Was but a moment's act.—Ah! well-a-day!   1445
    My teeth begin to chatter, my veins freeze—
Alfonso first examined well their fashion,
And then flew out into another passion.

182

He left the room for his relinquished sword,
    And Julia instant to the closet flew.   1450
"Fly, Juan, fly! for heaven's sake—not a word—
    The door is open—you may yet slip through
The passage you so often have explored—
    Here is the garden key—Fly—fly—Adieu!
Haste—haste! I hear Alfonso's hurrying feet—   1455
Day has not broke—there's no one in the street."

183

None can say that this was not good advice,
    The only mischief was, it came too late;
Of all experience 'tis the usual price,
    A sort of income tax laid on by fate: 1460
Juan had reached the room door in a trice,
    And might have done so by the garden gate,
But met Alfonso in his dressing gown,
Who threatened death—so Juan knocked him down.

184

Dire was the scuffle, and out went the light;   1465
    Antonia cried out "Rape!" and Julia "Fire!"
But not a servant stirred to aid the fight.
    Alfonso, pommeled to his heart's desire,
Swore lustily he'd be revenged this night;
    And Juan, too, blasphemed an octave higher;   1470
His blood was up: though young, he was a Tartar,[2]
And not at all disposed to prove a martyr.

1. Illogical sequence of vague statements.

2. "To catch a Tartar" is to tackle someone too strong for his assailant.

185

Alfonso's sword had dropped ere he could draw it,
    And they continued battling hand to hand,
For Juan very luckily ne'er saw it;
    His temper not being under great command,
If at that moment he had chanced to claw it,
    Alfonso's days had not been in the land
Much longer.—Think of husbands', lover's lives!
And how ye may be doubly widows—wives!

186

Alfonso grappled to detain the foe,
    And Juan throttled him to get away,
And blood ('twas from the nose) began to flow;
    At last, as they more faintly wrestling lay,
Juan contrived to give an awkward blow,
    And then his only garment quite gave way;
He fled, like Joseph,[3] leaving it; but there,
I doubt, all likeness ends between the pair.

187

Lights came at length, and men, and maids, who found
    An awkward spectacle their eyes before;
Antonia in hysterics, Julia swooned,
    Alfonso leaning, breathless, by the door;
Some half-torn drapery scattered on the ground,
    Some blood, and several footsteps, but no more:
Juan the gate gained, turned the key about,
And liking not the inside, locked the out.

188

Here ends this canto.—Need I sing, or say,
    How Juan, naked, favored by the night,
Who favors what she should not, found his way,
    And reached his home in an unseemly plight?
The pleasant scandal which arose next day,
    The nine days' wonder which was brought to light,
And how Alfonso sued for a divorce,
Were in the English newspapers, of course.

189

If you would like to see the whole proceedings,
    The depositions, and the cause at full,
The names of all the witnesses, the pleadings
    Of counsel to nonsuit,[4] or to annul,
There's more than one edition, and the readings
    Are various, but they none of them are dull;
The best is that in shorthand ta'en by Gurney,[5]
Who to Madrid on purpose made a journey.

---

3. In Genesis xxxix.7 ff. the chaste Joseph flees from the advances of Potiphar's wife, leaving "his garment in her hand."
4. Judgment against the plaintiff for failure to establish his case.
5. William B. Gurney, official shorthand writer for the Houses of Parliament and a famous court reporter.

190

But Donna Inez, to divert the train
    Of one of the most circulating scandals
That had for centuries been known in Spain,
    At least since the retirement of the Vandals,[6]   1515
First vowed (and never had she vowed in vain)
    To Virgin Mary several pounds of candles;
And then, by the advice of some old ladies,
She sent her son to be shipped off from Cadiz.   1520

191

She had resolved that he should travel through
    All European climes, by land or sea,
To mend his former morals, and get new,
    Especially in France and Italy
(At least this is the thing most people do).   1525
    Julia was sent into a convent; she
Grieved, but, perhaps, her feelings may be better
Shown in the following copy of her letter:

192

"They tell me 'tis decided; you depart:
    'Tis wise—'tis well, but not the less a pain;   1530
I have no further claim on your young heart,
    Mine is the victim, and would be again;
To love too much has been the only art
    I used—I write in haste, and if a stain
Be on this sheet, 'tis not what it appears;   1535
My eyeballs burn and throb, but have no tears.

193

"I loved, I love you, for this love have lost
    State, station, heaven, mankind's, my own esteem,
And yet cannot regret what it hath cost,
    So dear is still the memory of that dream;   1540
Yet, if I name my guilt, 'tis not to boast,
    None can deem harshlier of me than I deem:
I trace this scrawl because I cannot rest—
I've nothing to reproach, or to request.

194

"Man's love is of man's life a thing apart,   1545
    'Tis woman's whole existence; man may range
The court, camp, church, the vessel, and the mart;
    Sword, gown, gain, glory, offer in exchange
Pride, fame, ambition, to fill up his heart,
    And few there are whom these cannot estrange;   1550
Men have all these resources, we but one,
To love again, and be again undone."

* * *

6. The Germanic tribe which overran Spain and other parts of southern Europe in the 4th and 5th centuries; notorious for rape and violence.

198

This note was written upon gilt-edged paper
    With a neat little crow-quill, slight and new;
Her small white hand could hardly reach the taper,[7]
    It trembled as magnetic needles do,   1580
And yet she did not let one tear escape her;
    The seal a sunflower; *"Elle vous suit partout,"*[8]
The motto, cut upon a white cornelian;
The wax was superfine, its hue vermilion.

199

This was Don Juan's earliest scrape; but whether   1585
    I shall proceed with his adventures is
Dependent on the public altogether;
    We'll see, however, what they say to this,
Their favor in an author's cap's a feather,
    And no great mischief's done by their caprice;   1590
And if their approbation we experience,
Perhaps they'll have some more about a year hence.

200

My poem's epic, and is meant to be
    Divided in twelve books; each book containing,
With love, and war, a heavy gale at sea,   1595
    A list of ships, and captains, and kings reigning,
New characters; the episodes are three;
    A panoramic view of hell's in training,
After the style of Virgil and of Homer,
So that my name of Epic's no misnomer.   1600

201

All these things will be specified in time,
    With strict regard to Aristotle's rules,
The *Vade Mecum*[9] of the true sublime,
    Which makes so many poets, and some fools:
Prose poets like blank verse, I'm fond of rhyme,   1605
    Good workmen never quarrel with their tools;
I've got new mythological machinery,
And very handsome supernatural scenery.

202

There's only one slight difference between
    Me and my epic brethren gone before,
And here the advantage is my own, I ween   1610
    (Not that I have not several merits more,
But this will more peculiarly be seen):
    They so embellish that 'tis quite a bore
Their labyrinth of fables to thread through,   1615
Whereas this story's actually true.

---

7. The candle (in order to melt wax to seal the letter).
8. "She follows you everywhere."
9. Handbook (Latin, "go with me");

Byron is deriding the interpretation of Aristotle's *Poetics* ("rules") as a guide for writing epic and tragedy.

203

If any person doubt it, I appeal
   To history, tradition, and to facts,
To newspapers, whose truth all know and feel,
   To plays in five, and operas in three acts;   1620
All these confirm my statement a good deal,
   But that which more completely faith exacts
Is that myself, and several now in Seville,
Saw Juan's last elopement with the devil.[1]

204

If ever I should condescend to prose,   1625
   I'll write poetical commandments, which
Shall supersede beyond all doubt all those
   That went before; in these I shall enrich
My text with many things that no one knows,
   And carry precept to the highest pitch: 1630
I'll call the work "Longinus o'er a Bottle,
Or Every Poet his *own* Aristotle."

205

Thou shalt believe in Milton, Dryden, Pope;[2]
   Thou shalt not set up Wordsworth, Coleridge, Southey;
Because the first is crazed beyond all hope,   1635
   The second drunk, the third so quaint and mouthy:
With Crabbe it may be difficult to cope,
   And Campbell's Hippocrene[3] is somewhat drouthy:
Thou shalt not steal from Samuel Rogers, nor
Commit—flirtation with the muse of Moore.[4]   1640

206

Thou shalt not covet Mr. Sotheby's Muse,[5]
   His Pegasus, nor anything that's his;
Thou shalt not bear false witness like "the Blues"[6]
   (There's one, at least, is very fond of this);
Thou shalt not write, in short, but what I choose: 1645
   This is true criticism, and you may kiss—
Exactly as you please, or not,—the rod;
But if you don't, I'll lay it on, by G—d!

207

If any person should presume to assert
   This story is not moral, first I pray   1650
That they will not cry out before they're hurt,
   Then that they'll read it o'er again, and say

1. The usual plays on the Juan legend ended with Juan in hell; a recent version is George Bernard Shaw's *Man and Superman*.
2. This is one of many passages, in prose and verse, in which Byron vigorously defended Dryden and Pope against his Romantic contemporaries.
3. Fountain on Mt. Helicon whose waters supposedly gave inspiration.
4. George Crabbe, whom Byron admired, was the author of *The Village* (1783) and other realistic poems of rural life. Thomas Campbell, Samuel Rogers, and Thomas Moore were minor poets of the Romantic period; the last two were close friends of Byron's (cf. line 829 and note).
5. William Sotheby, contemporary poet and translator, was a wealthy man (see line 1642). Pegasus was the winged horse, symbolizing poetic inspiration.
6. I.e., "bluestockings," a contemporary term for pedantic lady intellectuals, among whom Byron numbered his wife (line 1644).

(But, doubtless, nobody will be so pert)
   That this is not a moral tale, though gay;
Besides, in Canto Twelfth, I mean to show
The very place where wicked people go.   1655

* * *

213

But now at thirty years my hair is gray
   (I wonder what it will be like at forty?
I thought of a peruke[7] the other day)—
   My heart is not much greener; and, in short, I   1700
Have squandered my whole summer while 'twas May,
   And feel no more the spirit to retort; I
Have spent my life, both interest and principal,
And deem not, what I deemed, my soul invincible.

214

No more—no more—Oh! never more on me   1705
   The freshness of the heart can fall like dew,
Which out of all the lovely things we see
   Extracts emotions beautiful and new,
Hived in our bosoms like the bag o' the bee:
   Think'st thou the honey with those objects grew?   1710
Alas! 'twas not in them, but in thy power
To double even the sweetness of a flower.

215

No more—no more—Oh! never more, my heart,
   Canst thou be my sole world, my universe!
Once all in all, but now a thing apart,   1715
   Thou canst not be my blessing or my curse:
The illusion's gone forever, and thou art
   Insensible, I trust, but none the worse,
And in thy stead I've got a deal of judgment,
Though heaven knows how it ever found a lodgment.   1720

216

My days of love are over; me no more
   The charms of maid, wife, and still less of widow
Can make the fool of which they made before—
   In short, I must not lead the life I did do;
The credulous hope of mutual minds is o'er,   1725
   The copious use of claret is forbid too,
So for a good old-gentlemanly vice,
I think I must take up with avarice.

* * *

219

What are the hopes of man? Old Egypt's King   1745
   Cheops erected the first pyramid
And largest, thinking it was just the thing
   To keep his memory whole, and mummy hid:
But somebody or other rummaging

7. Wig.

Burglariously broke his coffin's lid: 1750
Let not a monument give you or me hopes,
Since not a pinch of dust remains of Cheops.

220

But I, being fond of true philosophy,
  Say very often to myself, "Alas!
All things that have been born were born to die,   1755
  And flesh (which Death mows down to hay) is grass;
You've passed your youth not so unpleasantly,
  And if you had it o'er again—'twould pass—
So thank your stars that matters are no worse,
And read your Bible, sir, and mind your purse."   1760

221

But for the present, gentle reader! and
  Still gentler purchaser! the bard—that's I—
Must, with permission, shake you by the hand,
  And so your humble servant, and good-by!
We meet again, if we should understand   1765
  Each other; and if not, I shall not try
Your patience further than by this short sample—
'Twere well if others followed my example.

222

"Go, little book, from this my solitude!
  I cast thee on the waters—go thy ways!   1770
And if, as I believe, thy vein be good,
  The world will find thee after many days."
When Southey's read, and Wordsworth understood,
  I can't help putting in my claim to praise—
The four first rhymes are Southey's, every line:[8]   1775
For God's sake, reader! take them not for mine!

From *Canto II*

8

But to our tale: the Donna Inez sent
  Her son to Cadiz only to embark;
To stay there had not answered her intent,
  But why?—we leave the reader in the dark—   60
'Twas for a voyage the young man was meant,
  As if a Spanish ship were Noah's ark,
To wean him from the wickedness of earth,
And send him like a dove of promise forth.

9

Don Juan bade his valet pack his things   65
  According to direction, then received
A lecture and some money: for four springs
  He was to travel; and though Inez grieved
(As every kind of parting has its stings),
  She hoped he would improve—perhaps believed: 70

8. The lines occur in the last stanza of Southey's *Epilogue to the Lay of the Laureate.*

A letter, too, she gave (he never read it)
Of good advice—and two or three of credit.

* * *

11

Juan embarked—the ship got under way,
    The wind was fair, the water passing rough;
A devil of a sea rolls in that bay,
    As I, who've crossed it oft, know well enough;
And, standing upon deck, the dashing spray   85
    Flies in one's face, and makes it weather-tough:
And there he stood to take, and take again,
His first—perhaps his last—farewell of Spain.

12

I can't but say it is an awkward sight
    To see one's native land receding through   90
The growing waters; it unmans one quite,
    Especially when life is rather new:
I recollect Great Britain's coast looks white,
    But almost every other country's blue,
When gazing on them, mystified by distance,   95
We enter on our nautical existence.

* * *

17

And Juan wept, and much he sighed and thought,
    While his salt tears dropped into the salt sea,   130
"Sweets to the sweet" (I like so much to quote;
    You must excuse this extract—'tis where she,
The Queen of Denmark, for Ophelia brought
    Flowers to the grave);[1] and, sobbing often, he
Reflected on his present situation,   135
And seriously resolved on reformation.

18

"Farewell, my Spain! a long farewell!" he cried,
    "Perhaps I may revisit thee no more,
But die, as many an exiled heart hath died,
    Of its own thirst to see again thy shore: 140
Farewell, where Guadalquiver's waters glide!
    Farewell, my mother! and, since all is o'er,
Farewell, too, dearest Julia!—(here he drew
Her letter out again, and read it through).

19

"And oh! if e'er I should forget, I swear—   145
    But that's impossible, and cannot be—
Sooner shall this blue ocean melt to air,
    Sooner shall earth resolve itself to sea,
Than I resign thine image, oh, my fair!
    Or think of anything, excepting thee;   150

1. Hamlet V.i.266.

A mind diseased no remedy can physic—
(Here the ship gave a lurch, and he grew seasick.)

20

"Sooner shall heaven kiss earth—(here he fell sicker)
    Oh, Julia! what is every other woe?—
(For God's sake let me have a glass of liquor;   155
    Pedro, Battista, help me down below.)
Julia, my love—(you rascal, Pedro, quicker)—
    Oh, Julia!—(this cursed vessel pitches so)—
Beloved Julia, hear me still beseeching!"
(Here he grew inarticulate with retching.)   160

21

He felt that chilling heaviness of heart,
    Or rather stomach, which, alas! attends,
Beyond the best apothecary's art,
    The loss of love, the treachery of friends,
Or death of those we dote on, when a part   165
    Of us dies with them as each fond hope ends:
No doubt he would have been much more pathetic,
But the sea acted as a strong emetic.[2]

* * *

49

'Twas twilight, and the sunless day went down   385
    Over the waste of waters; like a veil,
Which, if withdrawn, would but disclose the frown
    Of one whose hate is masked but to assail.
Thus to their hopeless eyes the night was shown,
    And grimly darkled o'er the faces pale,   390
And the dim desolate deep: twelve days had Fear
Been their familiar, and now Death was here.

50

Some trial had been making at a raft,
    With little hope in such a rolling sea,
A sort of thing at which one would have laughed,   395
    If any laughter at such times could be,
Unless with people who too much have quaffed,
    And have a kind of wild and horrid glee,
Half epileptical, and half hysterical—
    Their preservation would have been a miracle.   400

51

At half-past eight o'clock, booms, hencoops, spars,
    And all things, for a chance, had been cast loose
That still could keep afloat the struggling tars,
    For yet they strove, although of no great use:
There was no light in heaven but a few stars,   405
    The boats put off o'ercrowded with their crews;
She gave a heel, and then a lurch to port,
And, going down head foremost—sunk, in short.

2. In stanzas 22–48 (here omitted) the   violent storm, which leaves her a help-
ship, bound for Leghorn, runs into a   less, sinking wreck.

52

Then rose from sea to sky the wild farewell—
 Then shrieked the timid, and stood still the brave—   410
Then some leaped overboard with dreadful yell,
 As eager to anticipate their grave;
And the sea yawned around her like a hell,
 And down she sucked with her the whirling wave,
Like one who grapples with his enemy,   415
And strives to strangle him before he die.

53

And first one universal shriek there rushed,
 Louder than the loud ocean, like a crash
Of echoing thunder; and then all was hushed,
 Save the wild wind and the remorseless dash   420
Of billows; but at intervals there gushed,
 Accompanied with a convulsive splash,
A solitary shriek, the bubbling cry
Of some strong swimmer in his agony.

* * *

56

Juan got into the longboat, and there
 Contrived to help Pedrillo[3] to a place;
It seemed as if they had exchanged their care,
 For Juan wore the magisterial face
Which courage gives, while poor Pedrillo's pair   445
 Of eyes were crying for their owner's case:
Battista, though (a name called shortly Tita),
Was lost by getting at some aqua-vita.[4]

57

Pedro, his valet, too, he tried to save,
 But the same cause, conducive to his loss,
Left him so drunk, he jumped into the wave   450
 As o'er the cutter's edge he tried to cross,
And so he found a wine-and-watery grave;
 They could not rescue him although so close,
Because the sea ran higher every minute,
And for the boat—the crew kept crowding in it.   455

* * *

103

As they drew nigh the land, which now was seen
 Unequal in its aspect here and there,
They felt the freshness of its growing green,
 That waved in forest tops, and smoothed the air,   820
And fell upon their glazed eyes like a screen
 From glistening waves, and skies so hot and bare—
Lovely seemed any object that should sweep
Away the vast, salt, dread, eternal deep.

3. Juan's tutor.   4. Brandy.

104

The shore looked wild, without a trace of man,   825
  And girt by formidable waves; but they
Were mad for land, and thus their course they ran,
  Though right ahead the roaring breakers lay:
A reef between them also now began
  To show its boiling surf and bounding spray,   830
But finding no place for their landing better,
They ran the boat for shore—and overset her.

105

But in his native stream, the Guadalquiver,
  Juan to lave his youthful limbs was wont;
And having learnt to swim in that sweet river,   835
  Had often turned the art to some account:
A better swimmer you could scarce see ever,
  He could, perhaps, have passed the Hellespont,
As once (a feat on which ourselves we prided)
Leander, Mr. Ekenhead, and I did.[5]   840

106

So, here, though faint, emaciated, and stark,
  He buoyed his boyish limbs, and strove to ply
With the quick wave, and gain, ere it was dark,
  The beach which lay before him, high and dry:
The greatest danger here was from a shark,   845
  That carried off his neighbor by the thigh;
As for the other two, they could not swim,
So nobody arrived on shore but him.

107

Nor yet had he arrived but for the oar,
  Which, providentially for him, was washed   850
Just as his feeble arms could strike no more,
  And the hard wave o'erwhelmed him as 'twas dashed
Within his grasp; he clung to it, and sore
  The waters beat while he thereto was lashed;
At last, with swimming, wading, scrambling, he   855
Rolled on the beach, half senseless, from the sea:

108

There, breathless, with his digging nails he clung
  Fast to the sand, lest the returning wave,
From whose reluctant roar his life he wrung,
  Should suck him back to her insatiate grave: 860
And there he lay, full length, where he was flung,
  Before the entrance of a cliff-worn cave,
With just enough of life to feel its pain,
And deem that it was saved, perhaps, in vain.

109

With slow and staggering effort he arose,   865
  But sunk again upon his bleeding knee

---

5. Like Leander in the myth, Byron
and Lt. Ekenhead had swum the Hellespont on May 3, 1810. See *Written
After Swimming from Sestos to Abydos.*

And quivering hand; and then he looked for those
   Who long had been his mates upon the sea;
But none of them appeared to share his woes,
   Save one, a corpse, from out the famished three,   870
Who died two days before, and now had found
An unknown barren beach for burial ground.

110

And as he gazed, his dizzy brain spun fast,
   And down he sunk; and as he sunk, the sand
Swam round and round, and all his senses passed: 875
   He fell upon his side, and his stretched hand
Drooped dripping on the oar (their jurymast),
   And, like a withered lily, on the land
His slender frame and pallid aspect lay,
As fair a thing as e'er was formed of clay.   880

111

How long in his damp trance young Juan lay
   He knew not, for the earth was gone for him,
And time had nothing more of night nor day
   For his congealing blood, and senses dim;
And how this heavy faintness passed away   885
   He knew not, till each painful pulse and limb,
And tingling vein seemed throbbing back to life,
For Death, though vanquished, still retired with strife.

112

His eyes he opened, shut, again unclosed,
   For all was doubt and dizziness; he thought   890
He still was in the boat, and had but dozed,
   And felt again with his despair o'erwrought,
And wished it death in which he had reposed,
   And then once more his feelings back were brought,
And slowly by his swimming eyes was seen   895
A lovely female face of seventeen.

113

'Twas bending close o'er his, and the small mouth
   Seemed almost prying into his for breath;
And chafing him, the soft warm hand of youth
   Recalled his answering spirits back from death;   900
And, bathing his chill temples, tried to soothe
   Each pulse to animation, till beneath
Its gentle touch and trembling care, a sigh
To these kind efforts made a low reply.

114

Then was the cordial poured, and mantle flung   905
   Around his scarce-clad limbs; and the fair arm
Raised higher the faint head which o'er it hung;
   And her transparent cheek, all pure and warm,
Pillowed his deathlike forehead; then she wrung
   His dewy curls, long drenched by every storm;   910

And watched with eagerness each throb that drew
A sigh from his heaved bosom—and hers, too.
115
And lifting him with care into the cave,
    The gentle girl, and her attendant—one
Young, yet her elder, and of brow less grave,
    And more robust of figure—then begun
To kindle fire, and as the new flames gave
    Light to the rocks that roofed them, which the sun
Had never seen, the maid, or whatsoe'er
She was, appeared distinct, and tall, and fair.
116
Her brow was overhung with coins of gold,
    That sparkled o'er the auburn of her hair,
Her clustering hair, whose longer locks were rolled
    In braids behind; and though her stature were
Even of the highest for a female mold,
    They nearly reached her heel; and in her air
There was a something which bespoke command,
As one who was a lady in the land.
117
Her hair, I said, was auburn; but her eyes
    Were black as death, their lashes the same hue,
Of downcast length, in whose silk shadow lies
    Deepest attraction; for when to the view
Forth from its raven fringe the full glance flies,
    Ne'er with such force the swiftest arrow flew;
'Tis as the snake late coiled, who pours his length,
And hurls at once his venom and his strength.

* * *

123
And these two tended him, and cheered him both
    With food and raiment, and those soft attentions,
Which are (as I must own) of female growth,
    And have ten thousand delicate inventions:
They made a most superior mess of broth,
    A thing which poesy but seldom mentions,
But the best dish that e'er was cooked since Homer's
Achilles ordered dinner for newcomers.[6]
124
I'll tell you who they were, this female pair,
    Lest they should seem princesses in disguise;
Besides, I hate all mystery, and that air
    Of claptrap, which your recent poets prize;
And so, in short, the girls they really were
    They shall appear before your curious eyes,
Mistress and maid; the first was only daughter
Of an old man, who lived upon the water.

6. A reference to the lavish feast with which Achilles entertained Ajax, Phoenix, and Ulysses (*Iliad* IX.193 ff.).

125

A fisherman he had been in his youth,
  And still a sort of fisherman was he;
But other speculations were, in sooth,   995
  Added to his connection with the sea,
Perhaps not so respectable, in truth:
  A little smuggling, and some piracy,
Left him, at last, the sole of many masters
Of an ill-gotten million of piasters.[7]   1000

126

A fisher, therefore, was he—though of men,
  Like Peter the Apostle[8]—and he fished
For wandering merchant vessels, now and then,
  And sometimes caught as many as he wished;
The cargoes he confiscated, and gain   1005
  He sought in the slave market too, and dished
Full many a morsel for that Turkish trade,
By which, no doubt, a good deal may be made.

127

He was a Greek, and on his isle had built
  (One of the wild and smaller Cyclades[9])   1010
A very handsome house from out his guilt,
  And there he lived exceedingly at ease;
Heaven knows what cash he got or blood he spilt,
  A sad[1] old fellow was he, if you please;
But this I know, it was a spacious building,   1015
Full of barbaric carving, paint, and gilding.

128

He had an only daughter, called Haidée,
  The greatest heiress of the Eastern Isles;
Besides, so very beautiful was she,
  Her dowry was as nothing to her smiles:
Still in her teens, and like a lovely tree   1020
  She grew to womanhood, and between whiles
Rejected several suitors, just to learn
How to accept a better in his turn.

129

And walking out upon the beach, below   1025
  The cliff, towards sunset, on that day she found,
Insensible—not dead, but nearly so—
  Don Juan, almost famished, and half drowned;
But being naked, she was shocked, you know,
  Yet deemed herself in common pity bound,   1030
As far as in her lay, "to take him in,
A stranger"[2] dying, with so white a skin.

---

7. Near Eastern coins.
8. Christ's words to Peter and Andrew, both fishermen: "Follow me, and I will make you fishers of men" (Matthew iv.19).
9. A group of islands in the Aegean Sea.
1. In the playful sense: "wicked."
2. Cf. Matthew xxv.35: "I was a stranger, and ye took me in."

130

But taking him into her father's house
   Was not exactly the best way to save,
But like conveying to the cat the mouse,
   Or people in a trance into their grave;   1035
Because the good old man had so much "*νους*,"[3]
   Unlike the honest Arab thieves so brave,
He would have hospitably cured the stranger
And sold him instantly when out of danger.   1040

131

And therefore, with her maid, she thought it best
   (A virgin always on her maid relies)
To place him in the cave for present rest:
   And when, at last, he opened his black eyes,
Their charity increased about their guest;   1045
   And their compassion grew to such a size,
It opened half the turnpike gates to heaven
(St. Paul says 'tis the toll which must be given).[4]

* * *

141

And Haidée met the morning face to face;
   Her own was freshest, though a feverish flush
Had dyed it with the headlong blood, whose race
   From heart to cheek is curbed into a blush,
Like to a torrent which a mountain's base,   1125
   That overpowers some Alpine river's rush,
Checks to a lake, whose waves in circles spread;
Or the Red Sea—but the sea is not red.

142

And down the cliff the island virgin came,
   And near the cave her quick light footsteps drew,   1130
While the sun smiled on her with his first flame,
   And young Aurora[5] kissed her lips with dew,
Taking her for a sister; just the same
   Mistake you would have made on seeing the two,
Although the mortal, quite as fresh and fair,   1135
Had all the advantage, too, of not being air.

143

And when into the cavern Haidée stepped
   All timidly, yet rapidly, she saw
That like an infant Juan sweetly slept;
   And then she stopped, and stood as if in awe   1140
(For sleep is awful), and on tiptoe crept
   And wrapped him closer, lest the air, too raw,
Should reach his blood, then o'er him still as death
Bent, with hushed lips, that drank his scarce-drawn breath.

* * *

3. Nous, "intelligence"; in England, pronounced so as to rhyme with "mouse."   4. I Corinthians xiii.13.
5. The dawn.

148

And she bent o'er him, and he lay beneath,
   Hushed as the babe upon its mother's breast,
Drooped as the willow when no winds can breathe,
   Lulled like the depth of ocean when at rest,   1180
Fair as the crowning rose of the whole wreath,
   Soft as the callow cygnet[6] in its nest;
In short, he was a very pretty fellow,
Although his woes had turned him rather yellow.

149

He woke and gazed, and would have slept again,   1185
   But the fair face which met his eyes forbade
Those eyes to close, though weariness and pain
   Had further sleep a further pleasure made;
For woman's face was never formed in vain
   For Juan, so that even when he prayed   1190
He turned from grisly saints, and martyrs hairy,
To the sweet portraits of the Virgin Mary.

150

And thus upon his elbow he arose,
   And looked upon the lady, in whose cheek
The pale contended with the purple rose,   1195
   As with an effort she began to speak;
Her eyes were eloquent, her words would pose,
   Although she told him, in good modern Greek,
With an Ionian accent, low and sweet,
That he was faint, and must not talk, but eat.   1200

* * *

168

And every day by daybreak—rather early
   For Juan, who was somewhat fond of rest—
She came into the cave, but it was merely
   To see her bird reposing in his nest;   1340
And she would softly stir his locks so curly,
   Without disturbing her yet slumbering guest,
Breathing all gently o'er his cheek and mouth,
As o'er a bed of roses the sweet South.[7]

169

And every morn his color freshlier came,   1345
   And every day helped on his convalescence;
'Twas well, because health in the human frame
   Is pleasant, besides being true love's essence,
For health and idleness to passion's flame
   Are oil and gunpowder; and some good lessons   1350
Are also learnt from Ceres[8] and from Bacchus,
Without whom Venus will not long attack us.

6. Young swan.   8. Goddess of the grain.
7. The south wind.

170

While Venus fills the heart (without heart really
    Love, though good always, is not quite so good),
Ceres presents a plate of vermicelli—   1355
    For love must be sustained like flesh and blood—
While Bacchus pours out wine, or hands a jelly:
    Eggs, oysters, too, are amatory food;
But who is their purveyor from above
Heaven knows—it may be Neptune, Pan, or Jove.   1360

171

When Juan woke he found some good things ready,
    A bath, a breakfast, and the finest eyes
That ever made a youthful heart less steady,
    Besides her maid's, as pretty for their size;
But I have spoken of all this already—   1365
    And repetition's tiresome and unwise—
Well—Juan, after bathing in the sea,
Came always back to coffee and Haidée.

172

Both were so young, and one so innocent,
    That bathing passed for nothing; Juan seemed   1370
To her, as 'twere, the kind of being sent,
    Of whom these two years she had nightly dreamed,
A something to be loved, a creature meant
    To be her happiness, and whom she deemed
To render happy; all who joy would win   1375
Must share it—Happiness was born a twin.

173

It was such pleasure to behold him, such
    Enlargement of existence to partake
Nature with him, to thrill beneath his touch,
    To watch him slumbering, and to see him wake: 1380
To live with him forever were too much;
    But then the thought of parting made her quake:
He was her own, her ocean-treasure, cast
Like a rich wreck—her first love, and her last.

174

And thus a moon rolled on, and fair Haidée   1385
    Paid daily visits to her boy, and took
Such plentiful precautions, that still he
    Remained unknown within his craggy nook;
At last her father's prows put out to sea,
    For certain merchantmen upon the look,   1390
Not as of yore to carry off an Io,[9]
But three Ragusan vessels, bound for Scio.[1]

175

Then came her freedom, for she had no mother,
    So that, her father being at sea, she was

9. Io, a mistress of Zeus persecuted by his jealous wife Hera, was kidnaped by Phoenician merchants.

1. Ragusa (or Dubrovnik), is an Adriatic port; Scio is the Italian name for Chios, an island near Turkey.

Free as a married woman, or such other   1395
  Female, as where she likes may freely pass,
Without even the encumbrance of a brother,
  The freest she that ever gazed on glass:
I speak of Christian lands in this comparison,
Where wives, at least, are seldom kept in garrison.   1400

176

Now she prolonged her visits and her talk
  (For they must talk), and he had learnt to say
So much as to propose to take a walk—
  For little had he wandered since the day
On which, like a young flower snapped from the stalk,   1405
  Drooping and dewy on the beach he lay—
And thus they walked out in the afternoon,
And saw the sun set opposite the moon.

177

It was a wild and breaker-beaten coast,
  With cliffs above, and a broad sandy shore,   1410
Guarded by shoals and rocks as by an host,
  With here and there a creek, whose aspect wore
A better welcome to the tempest-tossed;
  And rarely ceased the haughty billow's roar,
Save on the dead long summer days, which make   1415
The outstretched ocean glitter like a lake.

178

And the small ripple split upon the beach
  Scarcely o'erpass'd the cream of your champagne,
When o'er the brim the sparkling bumpers reach,
  That spring dew of the spirit! the heart's rain!   1420
Few things surpass old wine; and they may preach
  Who please—the more because they preach in vain—
Let us have wine and woman, mirth and laughter,
Sermons and soda water the day after.

179

Man, being reasonable, must get drunk;   1425
  The best of life is but intoxication:
Glory, the grape, love, gold, in these are sunk
  The hopes of all men, and of every nation;
Without their sap, how branchless were the trunk
  Of life's strange tree, so fruitful on occasion: 1430
But to return—Get very drunk; and when
You wake with headache, you shall see what then.

180

Ring for your valet—bid him quickly bring
  Some hock and soda water, then you'll know
A pleasure worthy Xerxes the great king;[2]   1435
  For not the blest sherbet, sublimed with snow,
Nor the first sparkle of the desert spring,

---

2. Xerxes, 5th-century Persian king, was said to have offered a reward to anyone who could discover a new kind of pleasure.

Nor Burgundy in all its sunset glow,
After long travel, ennui, love, or slaughter,
Vie with that draught of hock and soda water.   1440

181

The coast—I think it was the coast that I
   Was just describing—Yes, it *was* the coast—
Lay at this period quiet as the sky,
   The sands untumbled, the blue waves untossed,
And all was stillness, save the sea bird's cry,   1445
   And dolphin's leap, and little billow crossed
By some low rock or shelve, that made it fret
Against the boundary it scarcely wet.

182

And forth they wandered, her sire being gone,
   As I have said, upon an expedition;   1450
And mother, brother, guardian, she had none,
   Save Zoë, who, although with due precision
She waited on her lady with the sun,
   Thought daily service was her only mission,
Bringing warm water, wreathing her long tresses,   1455
And asking now and then for cast-off dresses.

183

It was the cooling hour, just when the rounded
   Red sun sinks down behind the azure hill,
Which then seems as if the whole earth it bounded,
   Circling all nature, hushed, and dim, and still,   1460
With the far mountain crescent half surrounded
   On one side, and the deep sea calm and chill
Upon the other, and the rosy sky,
With one star sparkling through it like an eye.

184

And thus they wandered forth, and hand in hand,   1465
   Over the shining pebbles and the shells,
Glided along the smooth and hardened sand,
   And in the worn and wild receptacles
Worked by the storms, yet worked as it were planned,
   In hollow halls, with sparry roofs and cells,   1470
They turned to rest; and, each clasped by an arm,
Yielded to the deep twilight's purple charm.

185

They looked up to the sky, whose floating glow
   Spread like a rosy ocean, vast and bright;
They gazed upon the glittering sea below,   1475
   Whence the broad moon rose circling into sight;
They heard the waves splash, and the wind so low,
   And saw each other's dark eyes darting light
Into each other—and, beholding this,
Their lips drew near, and clung into a kiss;   1480

186

A long, long kiss, a kiss of youth, and love,
  And beauty, all concéntrating like rays
Into one focus, kindled from above;
  Such kisses as belong to early days,
Where heart, and soul, and sense, in concert move,   1485
  And the blood's lava, and the pulse a blaze,
Each kiss a heart-quake—for a kiss's strength,
I think, it must be reckoned by its length.

187

By length I mean duration; theirs endured
  Heaven knows how long—no doubt they never reckoned;   1490
And if they had, they could not have secured
  The sum of their sensations to a second:
They had not spoken; but they felt allured,
  As if their souls and lips each other beckoned,
Which, being joined, like swarming bees they clung—   1495
Their hearts the flowers from whence the honey sprung.

188

They were alone, but not alone as they
  Who shut in chambers think it loneliness;
The silent ocean, and the starlight bay,
  The twilight glow, which momently grew less,   1500
The voiceless sands, and dropping caves, that lay
  Around them, made them to each other press,
As if there were no life beneath the sky
Save theirs, and that their life could never die.

189

They feared no eyes nor ears on that lone beach,   1505
  They felt no terrors from the night, they were
All in all to each other: though their speech
  Was broken words, they *thought* a language there—
And all the burning tongues the passions teach
  Found in one sigh the best interpreter   1510
Of nature's oracle—first love—that all
Which Eve has left her daughters since her fall.

190

Haidée spoke not of scruples, asked no vows,
  Nor offered any; she had never heard
Of plight and promises to be a spouse,   1515
  Or perils by a loving maid incurred;
She was all which pure ignorance allows,
  And flew to her young mate like a young bird;
And never having dreamt of falsehood, she
Had not one word to say of constancy.[3]   1520

191

She loved, and was belovéd—she adored,
  And she was worshiped; after nature's fashion,

---

3. Byron said, with reference to Haidée: "I was, and am, penetrated with the conviction that women only know evil from men, whereas men have no criterion to judge of purity or goodness but woman."

Their intense souls, into each other poured,
　If souls could die, had perished in that passion—
But by degrees their senses were restored,　　　　　　　1525
　Again to be o'ercome, again to dash on;
And, beating 'gainst *his* bosom, Haidée's heart
Felt as if never more to beat apart.

192

Alas! they were so young, so beautiful,
　So lonely, loving, helpless, and the hour　　　　　　1530
Was that in which the heart is always full,
　And, having o'er itself no further power,
Prompts deeds eternity cannot annul,
　But pays off moments in an endless shower
Of hell-fire—all prepared for people giving　　　　　　1535
Pleasure or pain to one another living.

193

Alas! for Juan and Haidée! they were
　So loving and so lovely—till then never,
Excepting our first parents, such a pair
　Had run the risk of being damned forever;　　　　　　1540
And Haidée, being devout as well as fair,
　Had, doubtless, heard about the Stygian river,[4]
And hell and purgatory—but forgot
Just in the very crisis she should not.

194

They look upon each other, and their eyes　　　　　　1545
　Gleam in the moonlight; and her white arm clasps
Round Juan's head, and his around hers lies
　Half buried in the tresses which it grasps;
She sits upon his knee, and drinks his sighs,
　He hers, until they end in broken gasps;　　　　　　1550
And thus they form a group that's quite antique,
Half naked, loving, natural, and Greek.

195

And when those deep and burning moments passed,
　And Juan sunk to sleep within her arms,
She slept not, but all tenderly, though fast,　　　　　　1555
　Sustained his head upon her bosom's charms;
And now and then her eye to heaven is cast,
　And then on the pale cheek her breast now warms,
Pillowed on her o'erflowing heart, which pants
With all it granted, and with all it grants.　　　　　　1560

196

An infant when it gazes on a light,
　A child the moment when it drains the breast,
A devotee when soars the Host[5] in sight,
　An Arab with a stranger for a guest,
A sailor when the prize has struck[6] in fight,　　　　　1565

4. The Styx, which flows through Hades.
5. The Eucharistic wafer.
6. Has lowered its flag in token of surrender.

A miser filling his most hoarded chest,
Feel rapture; but not such true joy are reaping
As they who watch o'er what they love while sleeping.

197

For there it lies so tranquil, so beloved,
  All that it hath of life with us is living;   1570
So gentle, stirless, helpless, and unmoved,
  And all unconscious of the joy 'tis giving;
All it hath felt, inflicted, passed, and proved,
  Hushed into depths beyond the watcher's diving;
There lies the thing we love with all its errors   1575
And all its charms, like death without its terrors.

198

The lady watched her lover—and that hour
  Of Love's, and Night's, and Ocean's solitude,
O'erflowed her soul with their united power;
  Amidst the barren sand and rocks so rude   1580
She and her wave-worn love had made their bower,
  Where nought upon their passion could intrude,
And all the stars that crowded the blue space
Saw nothing happier than her glowing face.

199

Alas! the love of women! it is known   1585
  To be a lovely and a fearful thing;
For all of theirs upon that die is thrown,
  And if 'tis lost, life hath no more to bring
To them but mockeries of the past alone,
  And their revenge is as the tiger's spring,   1590
Deadly, and quick, and crushing; yet, as real
Torture is theirs, what they inflict they feel.

200

They are right; for man, to man so oft unjust,
  Is always so to women; one sole bond
Awaits them, treachery is all their trust;   1595
  Taught to conceal, their bursting hearts despond
Over their idol, till some wealthier lust
  Buys them in marriage—and what rests beyond?
A thankless husband, next a faithless lover,
Then dressing, nursing, praying, and all's over.   1600

201

Some take a lover, some take drams or prayers,
  Some mind their household, others dissipation,
Some run away, and but exchange their cares,
  Losing the advantage of a virtuous station;
Few changes e'er can better their affairs,   1605
  Theirs being an unnatural situation,
From the dull palace to the dirty hovel:
Some play the devil, and then write a novel.[7]

7. The impetuous and hysterical Lady Caroline Lamb, having thrown herself at Byron and been after a time rejected, incorporated incidents from the affair in her novel, *Glenarvon* (1816).

202

Haidée was Nature's bride, and knew not this;
　　Haidée was Passion's child, born where the sun　　　　1610
Showers triple light, and scorches even the kiss
　　Of his gazelle-eyed daughters; she was one
Made but to love, to feel that she was his
　　Who was her chosen: what was said or done
Elsewhere was nothing. She had nought to fear,　　　　1615
Hope, care, nor love beyond, her heart beat *here*.

203

And oh! that quickening of the heart, that beat!
　　How much it costs us! yet each rising throb
Is in its cause as its effect so sweet,
　　That Wisdom, ever on the watch to rob　　　　1620
Joy of its alchemy, and to repeat
　　Fine truths; even Conscience, too, has a tough job
To make us understand each good old maxim,
So good—I wonder Castlereagh[8] don't tax 'em.

204

And now 'twas done—on the lone shore were plighted　　1625
　　Their hearts; the stars, their nuptial torches, shed
Beauty upon the beautiful they lighted:
　　Ocean their witness, and the cave their bed,
By their own feelings hallowed and united,
　　Their priest was Solitude, and they were wed:　　　　1630
And they were happy, for to their young eyes
Each was an angel, and earth paradise.

* * *

208

But Juan! had he quite forgotten Julia?
　　And should he have forgotten her so soon?
I can't but say it seems to me mostly truly a
　　Perplexing question; but, no doubt, the moon　　　　1660
Does these things for us, and whenever newly a
　　Strong palpitation rises, 'tis her boon,
Else how the devil is it that fresh features
Have such a charm for us poor human creatures?

209

I hate inconstancy—I loathe, detest,　　　　1665
　　Abhor, condemn, abjure the mortal made
Of such quicksilver clay that in his breast
　　No permanent foundation can be laid;
Love, constant love, has been my constant guest—
　　And yet last night, being at a masquerade,　　　　1670
I saw the prettiest creature, fresh from Milan,
Which gave me some sensations like a villain.

8. Robert Stewart, Viscount Castlereagh. British Foreign Secretary from 1812 to
1822.

210

But soon Philosophy came to my aid,
  And whispered, "Think of every sacred tie!"
"I will, my dear Philosophy!" I said,   1675
  "But then her teeth, and then, oh, Heaven! her eye!
I'll just inquire if she be wife or maid,
  Or neither—out of curiosity."
"Stop!" cried Philosophy, with air so Grecian
(Though she was masked then as a fair Venetian);   1680

211

"Stop!" so I stopped.—But to return: that which
  Men call inconstancy is nothing more
Than admiration due where nature's rich
  Profusion with young beauty covers o'er
Some favored object; and as in the niche   1685
  A lovely statue we almost adore,
This sort of adoration of the real
Is but a heightening of the "beau ideal."[9]

212

'Tis the perception of the beautiful,
  A fine extension of the faculties,   1690
Platonic, universal, wonderful,
  Drawn from the stars, and filtered through the skies,
Without which life would be extremely dull;
  In short, it is the use of our own eyes,
With one or two small senses added, just   1695
To hint that flesh is formed of fiery dust.

213

Yet 'tis a painful feeling, and unwilling,
  For surely if we always could perceive
In the same object graces quite as killing
  As when she rose upon us like an Eve,   1700
'Twould save us many a heartache, many a shilling
  (For we must get them anyhow, or grieve),
Whereas, if one sole lady pleased forever,
How pleasant for the heart, as well as liver!

* * *

216

In the meantime, without proceeding more
  In this anatomy, I've finished now
Two hundred and odd stanzas as before,
  That being about the number I'll allow
Each canto of the twelve, or twenty-four;   1725
  And, laying down my pen, I make my bow,
Leaving Don Juan and Haidée to plead
For them and theirs with all who deign to read.

9. Ideal beauty.

From *Canto III*

1

Hail, Muse! et cetera.—We left Juan sleeping,
    Pillowed upon a fair and happy breast,
And watched by eyes that never yet knew weeping,
    And loved by a young heart, too deeply blest
To feel the poison through her spirit creeping,   5
    Or know who rested there, a foe to rest,
Had soiled the current of her sinless years,
And turned her pure heart's purest blood to tears!

2

Oh, Love! what is it in this world of ours
    Which makes it fatal to be loved? Ah why   10
With cypress branches[1] hast thou wreathed thy bowers,
    And made thy best interpreter a sigh?
As those who dote on odors pluck the flowers,
    And place them on their breast—but place to die—
Thus the frail beings we would fondly cherish   15
Are laid within our bosoms but to perish.

3

In her first passion woman loves her lover,
    In all the others all she loves is love,
Which grows a habit she can ne'er get over,
    And fits her loosely—like an easy glove,   20
As you may find, whene'er you like to prove her:
    One man alone at first her heart can move;
She then prefers him in the plural number,
Not finding that the additions much encumber.

4

I know not if the fault be men's or theirs;   25
    But one thing's pretty sure; a woman planted[2]
(Unless at once she plunge for life in prayers)
    After a decent time must be gallánted;
Although, no doubt, her first of love affairs
    Is that to which her heart is wholly granted;   30
Yet there are some, they say, who have had *none*,
But those who have ne'er end with only *one*.

5

'Tis melancholy, and a fearful sign
    Of human frailty, folly, also crime,
That love and marriage rarely can combine,   35
    Although they both are born in the same clime;
Marriage from love, like vinegar from wine—
    A sad, sour, sober beverage—by time
Is sharpened from its high celestial flavor,
Down to a very homely household savor.   40

---

1. Signifying sorrow.

2. Abandoned (from the French *planter là*, to leave in the lurch).

6

There's something of antipathy, as 'twere,
    Between their present and their future state;
A kind of flattery that's hardly fair
    Is used until the truth arrives too late—
Yet what can people do, except despair?   45
    The same things change their names at such a rate;
For instance—passion in a lover's glorious,
But in a husband is pronounced uxorious.

7

Men grow ashamed of being so very fond;
    They sometimes also get a little tired   50
(But that, of course, is rare), and then despond:
    The same things cannot always be admired,
Yet 'tis "so nominated in the bond,"[3]
    That both are tied till one shall have expired.
Sad thought! to lose the spouse that was adorning   55
Our days, and put one's servants into mourning.

8

There's doubtless something in domestic doings
    Which forms, in fact, true love's antithesis;
Romances paint at full length people's wooings,
    But only give a bust of marriages;   60
For no one cares for matrimonial cooings,
    There's nothing wrong in a connubial kiss:
Think you, if Laura had been Petrarch's wife,
He would have written sonnets all his life?

9

All tragedies are finished by a death,   65
    All comedies are ended by a marriage;
The future states of both are left to faith,
    For authors fear description might disparage
The worlds to come of both, or fall beneath,
    And then both worlds would punish their miscarriage;   70
So leaving each their priest and prayer book ready,
They say no more of Death or of the Lady.[4]

10

The only two that in my recollection
    Have sung of heaven and hell, or marriage, are
Dante and Milton, and of both the affection   75
    Was hapless in their nuptials, for some bar
Of fault or temper ruined the connection
    (Such things, in fact, it don't ask much to mar);
But Dante's Beatrice and Milton's Eve
Were not drawn from their spouses, you conceive.   80

11

Some persons say that Dante meant theology
    By Beatrice, and not a mistress—I,

3. Shylock: "Is it so nominated in the   4. Alluding to a popular ballad, *Death*
bond?"   *The   Merchant   of   Venice*   *and the Lady.*
IV.i.254.

Although my opinion may require apology,
　　Deem this a commentator's phantasy,
Unless indeed it was from his own knowledge he　　　　　85
　　Decided thus, and showed good reason why;
I think that Dante's more abstruse ecstatics
Meant to personify the mathematics.

12

Haidée and Juan were not married, but
　　The fault was theirs, not mine: it is not fair,　　　　90
Chaste reader, then, in any way to put
　　The blame on me, unless you wish they were;
Then if you'd have them wedded, please to shut
　　The book which treats of this erroneous pair,
Before the consequences grow too awful;　　　　　　95
'Tis dangerous to read of loves unlawful.

13

Yet they were happy—happy in the illicit
　　Indulgence of their innocent desires;
But more imprudent grown with every visit,
　　Haidée forgot the island was her sire's;　　　　　100
When we have what we like, 'tis hard to miss it,
　　At least in the beginning, ere one tires;
Thus she came often, not a moment losing,
Whilst her piratical papa was cruising.

14

Let not his mode of raising cash seem strange,　　　　105
　　Although he fleeced the flags of every nation,
For into a prime minister but change
　　His title, and 'tis nothing but taxation;
But he, more modest, took an humbler range
　　Of life, and in an honester vocation　　　　　　110
Pursued o'er the high seas his watery journey,
And merely practiced as a sea attorney.

15

The good old gentleman had been detained
　　By winds and waves, and some important captures;
And, in the hope of more, at sea remained,　　　　　115
　　Although a squall or two had damped his raptures,
By swamping one of the prizes; he had chained
　　His prisoners, dividing them like chapters
In numbered lots; they all had cuffs and collars,
And averaged each from ten to a hundred dollars.　　　120

* * *

19

Then having settled his marine affairs,　　　　　　145
　　Despatching single cruisers here and there,
His vessel having need of some repairs,
　　He shaped his course to where his daughter fair
Continued still her hospitable cares;
　　But that part of the coast being shoal and bare,　　　150

And rough with reefs which ran out many a mile,
His port lay on the other side o' the isle.

20

And there he went ashore without delay,
  Having no customhouse nor quarantine
To ask him awkward questions on the way   155
  About the time and place where he had been:
He left his ship to be hove down next day,
  With orders to the people to careen;[5]
So that all hands were busy beyond measure,
In getting out goods, ballast, guns, and treasure.   160

* * *

27

He saw his white walls shining in the sun,
  His garden trees all shadowy and green;   210
He heard his rivulet's light bubbling run,
  The distant dog-bark; and perceived between
The umbrage of the wood so cool and dun,
  The moving figures, and the sparkling sheen
Of arms (in the East all arm)—and various dyes   215
Of colored garbs, as bright as butterflies.

28

And as the spot where they appear he nears,
  Surprised at these unwonted signs of idling,
He hears—alas! no music of the spheres,
  But an unhallowed, earthly sound of fiddling!   220
A melody which made him doubt his ears,
  The cause being past his guessing or unriddling;
A pipe, too, and a drum, and shortly after,
A most unoriental roar of laughter.

* * *

38

He did not know (alas! how men will lie)
  That a report (especially the Greeks)
Avouched his death (such people never die),
  And put his house in mourning several weeks—   300
But now their eyes and also lips were dry;
  The bloom, too, had returned to Haidée's cheeks.
Her tears, too, being returned into their fount,
She now kept house upon her own account.

39

Hence all this rice, meat, dancing, wine, and fiddling,   305
  Which turned the isle into a place of pleasure;
The servants all were getting drunk or idling,
  A life which made them happy beyond measure.
Her father's hospitality seemed middling,
  Compared with what Haidée did with his treasure;   310
'Twas wonderful how things went on improving,
While she had not one hour to spare from loving.

5. To tip a vessel on its side in order to clean and repair its hull.

40

Perhaps you think in stumbling on this feast,
    He flew into a passion, and in fact
There was no mighty reason to be pleased;   315
    Perhaps you prophesy some sudden act,
The whip, the rack, or dungeon at the least,
    To teach his people to be more exact,
And that, proceeding at a very high rate,
He showed the royal penchants of a pirate.   320

41

You're wrong.—He was the mildest mannered man
    That ever scuttled ship or cut a throat;
With such true breeding of a gentleman,
    You never could divine his real thought,
No courtier could, and scarcely woman can   325
    Gird more deceit within a petticoat;
Pity he loved adventurous life's variety,
He was so great a loss to good society.

* * *

48

Not that he was not sometimes rash or so,
    But never in his real and serious mood;
Then calm, concéntrated, and still, and slow,
    He lay coiled like the boa in the wood;   380
With him it never was a word and blow,
    His angry word once o'er, he shed no blood,
But in his silence there was much to rue,
And his *one* blow left little work for *two*.

49

He asked no further questions, and proceeded   385
    On to the house, but by a private way,
So that the few who met him hardly heeded,
    So little they expected him that day;
If love paternal in his bosom pleaded
    For Haidée's sake is more than I can say,   390
But certainly to one deemed dead returning,
This revel seemed a curious mode of mourning.

50

If all the dead could now return to life
    (Which God forbid!), or some, or a great many,
For instance, if a husband or his wife   395
    (Nuptial examples are as good as any),
No doubt whate'er might be their former strife,
    The present weather would be much more rainy—
Tears shed into the grave of the connection
Would share most probably its resurrection.   400

51

He entered in the house no more his home,
    A thing to human feelings the most trying,

And harder for the heart to overcome,
　　Perhaps, than even the mental pangs of dying;
To find our hearthstone turned into a tomb,　　　　405
　　And round its once warm precincts palely lying
The ashes of our hopes, is a deep grief,
Beyond a single gentleman's belief.

52

He entered in the house—his home no more,
　　For without hearts there is no home—and felt　　410
The solitude of passing his own door
　　Without a welcome: *there* he long had dwelt,
There his few peaceful days Time had swept o'er,
　　There his warm bosom and keen eye would melt
Over the innocence of that sweet child,　　　　415
His only shrine of feelings undefiled.

53

He was a man of a strange temperament,
　　Of mild demeanor though of savage mood,
Moderate in all his habits, and content
　　With temperance in pleasure, as in food,　　420
Quick to perceive, and strong to bear, and meant
　　For something better, if not wholly good;
His country's wrongs and his despair to save her
Had stung him from a slave to an enslaver.

* * *

96

But let me to my story: I must own,
　　If I have any fault, it is digression—
Leaving my people to proceed alone,
　　While I soliloquize beyond expression;　　　860
But these are my addresses from the throne,
　　Which put off business to the ensuing session:
Forgetting each omission is a loss to
The world, not quite so great as Ariosto.[6]

* * *

101

T' our tale.—The feast was over, the slaves gone,
　　The dwarfs and dancing girls had all retired;
The Arab lore and poet's song were done,
　　And every sound of revelry expired;　　　900
The lady and her lover, left alone,
　　The rosy flood of twilight's sky admired—
Ave Maria![7] o'er the earth and sea,
That heavenliest hour of Heaven is worthiest thee!

6. Byron warmly admired this poet, author of *Orlando Furioso* (1532), the greatest of the Italian chivalric romances.

7. "Hail, Mary": these words open a Roman Catholic prayer. *Ave Maria* is sometimes used to refer to evening (or morning), since the prayer is part of the service at these times.

102

Ave Maria! blessed be the hour!   905
   The time, the clime, the spot, where I so oft
Have felt that moment in its fullest power
   Sink o'er the earth so beautiful and soft,
While swung the deep bell in the distant tower,
   Or the faint dying day-hymn stole aloft,   910
And not a breath crept through the rosy air,
And yet the forest leaves seemed stirred with prayer.

103

Ave Maria! 'tis the hour of prayer!
   Ave Maria! 'tis the hour of love!
Ave Maria! may our spirits dare   915
   Look up to thine and to thy Son's above!
Ave Maria! oh that face so fair!
   Those downcast eyes beneath the Almighty dove—
What though 'tis but a pictured image strike—
That painting is no idol—'tis too like.   920

104

Some kinder casuists are pleased to say,
   In nameless print—that I have no devotion;
But set those persons down with me to pray,
   And you shall see who has the properest notion
Of getting into heaven the shortest way;   925
   My altars are the mountains and the ocean,
Earth, air, stars—all that springs from the great **Whole**,
Who hath produced, and will receive the soul.

* * *

From *Canto IV*

3

As boy, I thought myself a clever fellow,
   And wished that others held the same opinion;
They took it up when my days grew more mellow,
   And other minds acknowledged my dominion: 20
Now my sere fancy "falls into the yellow
   Leaf,"[1] and Imagination droops her pinion,
And the sad truth which hovers o'er my desk
Turns what was once romantic to burlesque.

4

And if I laugh at any mortal thing,   25
   'Tis that I may not weep; and if I weep,
'Tis that our nature cannot always bring
   Itself to apathy, for we must steep
Our hearts first in the depths of Lethe's spring,
   Ere what we least wish to behold will sleep: 30
Thetis baptized her mortal son in Styx;[2]
A mortal mother would on Lethe fix.

1. Cf. *Macbeth* V.iii.22–23: "My way   yellow leaf."
of life / Is fallen into the sere, the   2. The river in Hades into which the

5

Some have accused me of a strange design
   Against the creed and morals of the land,
And trace it in this poem every line:
   I don't pretend that I quite understand
My own meaning when I would be *very* fine;
   But the fact is that I have nothing planned,
Unless it were to be a moment merry,
A novel word in my vocabulary.

6

To the kind reader of our sober clime
   This way of writing will appear exotic;
Pulci[3] was sire of the half-serious rhyme,
   Who sang when chivalry was more Quixotic,
And reveled in the fancies of the time,
   True knights, chaste dames, huge giants, kings despotic;
But all these, save the last, being obsolete,
I chose a modern subject as more meet.

7

How I have treated it, I do not know;
   Perhaps no better than they have treated me
Who have imputed such designs as show
   Not what they saw, but what they wished to see:
But if it gives them pleasure, be it so;
   This is a liberal age, and thoughts are free:
Meantime Apollo plucks me by the ear,
And tells me to resume my story here.

* * *

26

Juan and Haidée gazed upon each other
   With swimming looks of speechless tenderness,
Which mixed all feelings, friend, child, lover, brother,
   All that the best can mingle and express
When two pure hearts are poured in one another,
   And love too much, and yet cannot love less;
But almost sanctify the sweet excess
By the immortal wish and power to bless.

27

Mixed in each other's arms, and heart in heart,
   Why did they not then die?—they had lived too long
Should an hour come to bid them breathe apart;
   Years could but bring them cruel things or wrong;
The world was not for them, nor the world's art
   For beings passionate as Sappho's song;
Love was born *with* them, *in* them, so intense,
It was their very spirit—not a sense.

nymph Thetis dipped Achilles, to make
him invulnerable. Lethe, another river
in Hades, brings oblivion of life.
3. Author of the *Morgante Maggiore*,
prototype of the Italian seriocomic romance from which Byron derived the
stanza and manner of *Don Juan*. See the
introduction to *Don Juan*.

28

They should have lived together deep in woods,
  Unseen as sings the nightingale; they were
Unfit to mix in these thick solitudes
  Called social, haunts of Hate, and Vice, and Care: 220
How lonely every freeborn creature broods!
  The sweetest songbirds nestle in a pair;
The eagle soars alone; the gull and crow
Flock o'er their carrion, just like men below.

29

Now pillowed cheek to cheek, in loving sleep,   225
  Haidée and Juan their siesta took,
A gentle slumber, but it was not deep,
  Forever and anon a something shook
Juan, and shuddering o'er his frame would creep;
  And Haidée's sweet lips murmured like a brook   230
A wordless music, and her face so fair
Stirred with her dream, as rose-leaves with the air;

30

Or as the stirring of a deep clear stream
  Within an Alpine hollow, when the wind
Walks o'er it, was she shaken by the dream,   235
  The mystical usurper of the mind—
O'erpowering us to be whate'er may seem
  Good to the soul which we no more can bind;
Strange state of being! (for 'tis still to be)
Senseless to feel, and with sealed eyes to see.   240

31

She dreamed of being alone on the seashore,
  Chained to a rock; she knew not how, but stir
She could not from the spot, and the loud roar
  Grew, and each wave rose roughly, threatening her;
And o'er her upper lip they seemed to pour,   245
  Until she sobbed for breath, and soon they were
Foaming o'er her lone head, so fierce and high—
Each broke to drown her, yet she could not die.

32

Anon—she was released, and then she strayed
  O'er the sharp shingles[4] with her bleeding feet,   250
And stumbled almost every step she made;
  And something rolled before her in a sheet,
Which she must still pursue howe'er afraid;
  'Twas white and indistinct, nor stopped to meet
Her glance nor grasp, for still she gazed and grasped,   255
And ran, but it escaped her as she clasped.

33

The dream changed—in a cave she stood, its walls
  Were hung with marble icicles; the work
Of ages on its water-fretted halls,

4. Loose pebbles.

Where waves might wash, and seals might breed and lurk;
Her hair was dripping, and the very balls   261
   Of her black eyes seemed turned to tears, and murk
The sharp rocks looked below each drop they caught,
Which froze to marble as it fell, she thought.

34

And wet, and cold, and lifeless at her feet,   265
   Pale as the foam that frothed on his dead brow,
Which she essayed in vain to clear (how sweet
   Were once her cares, how idle seemed they now!),
Lay Juan, nor could aught renew the beat
   Of his quenched heart; and the sea dirges low   270
Rang in her sad ears like a mermaid's song,
And that brief dream appeared a life too long.

35

And gazing on the dead, she thought his face
   Faded, or altered into something new—
Like to her father's features, till each trace   275
   More like and like to Lambro's aspect grew—
With all his keen worn look and Grecian grace;
   And starting, she awoke, and what to view?
Oh! Powers of Heaven! what dark eye meets she there?
'Tis—'tis her father's—fixed upon the pair!   280

36

Then shrieking, she arose, and shrieking fell,
   With joy and sorrow, hope and fear, to see
Him whom she deemed a habitant where dwell
   The ocean-buried, risen from death, to be
Perchance the death of one she loved too well: 285
   Dear as her father had been to Haidée,
It was a moment of that awful kind—
I have seen such—but must not call to mind.

37

Up Juan sprung to Haidée's bitter shriek,
   And caught her falling, and from off the wall   290
Snatched down his saber, in hot haste to wreak
   Vengeance on him who was the cause of all:
Then Lambro, who till now forebore to speak,
   Smiled scornfully, and said, "Within my call,
A thousand scimitars await the word;   295
Put up, young man, put up your silly sword."

38

And Haidée clung around him; "Juan, 'tis—
   'Tis Lambro—'tis my father! Kneel with me—
He will forgive us—yes—it must be—yes.
   Oh! dearest father, in this agony   300
Of pleasure and of pain—even while I kiss
   Thy garment's hem with transport, can it be
That doubt should mingle with my filial joy?
Deal with me as thou wilt, but spare this boy."

39

High and inscrutable the old man stood,   305
  Calm in his voice, and calm within his eye—
Not always signs with him of calmest mood:
  He looked upon her, but gave no reply;
Then turned to Juan, in whose cheek the blood
  Oft came and went, as there resolved to die;   310
In arms, at least, he stood, in act to spring
On the first foe whom Lambro's call might bring.

40

"Young man, your sword"; so Lambro once more said:
  Juan replied, "Not while this arm is free."
The old man's cheek grew pale, but not with dread,   315
  And drawing from his belt a pistol, he
Replied, "Your blood be then on your own head."
  Then looked close at the flint, as if to see
'Twas fresh—for he had lately used the lock[5]—
And next proceeded quietly to cock.   320

41

It has a strange quick jar upon the ear,
  That cocking of a pistol, when you know
A moment more will bring the sight to bear
  Upon your person, twelve yards off, or so;
A gentlemanly distance,[6] not too near,   325
  If you have got a former friend for foe;
But after being fired at once or twice,
The ear becomes more Irish, and less nice.[7]

42

Lambro presented, and one instant more
  Had stopped this Canto, and Don Juan's breath,   330
When Haidée threw herself her boy before;
  Stern as her sire: "On me," she cried, "let death
Descend—the fault is mine; this fatal shore
  He found—but sought not. I have pledged my faith;
I love him—I will die with him: I knew   335
Your nature's firmness—know your daughter's too."

43

A minute past, and she had been all tears,
  And tenderness, and infancy; but now
She stood as one who championed human fears—
  Pale, statue-like, and stern, she wooed the blow;   340
And tall beyond her sex, and their compeers,[8]
  She drew up to her height, as if to show
A fairer mark; and with a fixed eye scanned
Her father's face—but never stopped his hand.

---

5. That part of the gun which explodes
the charge.
6. I.e., dueling distance.
7. Finicky. Byron alludes to the propensity of hotheaded young Irishmen
to fight duels.
8. I.e., she was the match in height of
Lambro and Juan.

44

He gazed on her, and she on him; 'twas strange   345
    How like they looked! the expression was the same;
Serenely savage, with a little change
    In the large dark eye's mutual-darted flame;
For she, too, was as one who could avenge,
    If cause should be—a lioness, though tame;   350
Her father's blood before her father's face
Boiled up, and proved her truly of his race.

45

I said they were alike, their features and
    Their stature differing but in sex and years;
Even to the delicacy of their hand   355
    There was resemblance, such as true blood wears;
And now to see them, thus divided, stand
    In fixed ferocity, when joyous tears,
And sweet sensations, should have welcomed both,
Show what the passions are in their full growth.   360

46

The father paused a moment, then withdrew
    His weapon, and replaced it; but stood still,
And looking on her, as to look her through,
    "Not I," he said, "have sought this stranger's ill;
Not I have made this desolation: few   365
    Would bear such outrage, and forbear to kill;
But I must do my duty—how thou hast
Done thine, the present vouches for the past.

47

"Let him disarm; or, by my father's head,
    His own shall roll before you like a ball!"   370
He raised his whistle as the word he said,
    And blew; another answered to the call,
And rushing in disorderly, though led,
    And armed from boot to turban, one and all,
Some twenty of his train came, rank on rank;   375
He gave the word, "Arrest or slay the Frank."[9]

48

Then, with a sudden movement, he withdrew
    His daughter; while compressed within his clasp,
'Twixt her and Juan interposed the crew;
    In vain she struggled in her father's grasp—   380
His arms were like a serpent's coil: then flew
    Upon their prey, as darts an angry asp,
The file of pirates; save the foremost, who
Had fallen, with his right shoulder half cut through.

49

The second had his cheek laid open; but   385
    The third, a wary, cool old sworder, took
The blows upon his cutlass, and then put

9. Term used in the Near East to designate a western European.

His own well in; so well, ere you could look,
His man was floored, and helpless at his foot,
    With the blood running like a little brook   390
From two smart saber gashes, deep and red—
One on the arm, the other on the head.

50

And then they bound him where he fell, and bore
    Juan from the apartment: with a sign
Old Lambro bade them take him to the shore,   395
    Where lay some ships which were to sail at nine.
They laid him in a boat, and plied the oar
    Until they reached some galliots,[1] placed in line;
On board of one of these, and under hatches,
They stowed him, with strict orders to the watches.   400

51

The world is full of strange vicissitudes,
    And here was one exceedingly unpleasant:
A gentleman so rich in the world's goods,
    Handsome and young, enjoying all the present,
Just at the very time when he least broods   405
    On such a thing is suddenly to sea sent,
Wounded and chained, so that he cannot move,
And all because a lady fell in love.

* * *

56

Afric is all the sun's, and as her earth
    Her human clay is kindled; full of power
For good or evil, burning from its birth,
    The Moorish blood partakes the planet's hour,
And like the soil beneath it will bring forth: 445
    Beauty and love were Haidée's mother's dower;
But her large dark eye showed deep Passion's force,
Though sleeping like a lion near a source.

57

Her daughter, tempered with a milder ray,
    Like summer clouds all silvery, smooth, and fair,   450
Till slowly charged with thunder they display
    Terror to earth, and tempest to the air,
Had held till now her soft and milky way;
    But overwrought with passion and despair,
The fire burst forth from her Numidian[2] veins,   455
Even as the simoom[3] sweeps the blasted plains.

58

The last sight which she saw was Juan's gore,
    And he himself o'ermastered and cut down;
His blood was running on the very floor
    Where late he trod, her beautiful, her own;   460

1. A small, fast galley, propelled both by oars and sails.
2. North African.
3. A violent, hot, dust-laden desert wind.

Thus much she viewed an instant and no more—
   Her struggles ceased with one convulsive groan;
On her sire's arm, which until now scarce held
Her writhing, fell she like a cedar felled.

59

A vein had burst, and her sweet lips' pure dyes   465
   Were dabbled with the deep blood which ran o'er;
And her head drooped, as when the lily lies
   O'ercharged with rain: her summoned handmaids bore
Their lady to her couch with gushing eyes;
   Of herbs and cordials they produced their store,   470
But she defied all means they could employ,
Like one life could not hold, nor death destroy.

60

Days lay she in that state unchanged, though chill—
   With nothing livid,[4] still her lips were red;
She had no pulse, but death seemed absent still;   475
   No hideous sign proclaimed her surely dead;
Corruption came not in each mind to kill
   All hope; to look upon her sweet face bred
New thoughts of life, for it seemed full of soul—
She had so much, earth could not claim the whole.   480

* * *

69

Twelve days and nights she withered thus; at last,   545
   Without a groan, or sigh, or glance, to show
A parting pang, the spirit from her passed:
   And they who watched her nearest could not know
The very instant, till the change that cast
   Her sweet face into shadow, dull and slow,   550
Glazed o'er her eyes—the beautiful, the black—
Oh! to possess such luster—and then lack!

70

She died, but not alone; she held within
   A second principle of life, which might
Have dawned a fair and sinless child of sin;   555
   But closed its little being without light,
And went down to the grave unborn, wherein
   Blossom and bough lie withered with one blight;
In vain the dews of Heaven descend above
The bleeding flower and blasted fruit of love.   560

71

Thus lived—thus died she; never more on her
   Shall sorrow light, or shame. She was not made
Through years or moons the inner weight to bear,
   Which colder hearts endure till they are laid
By age in earth; her days and pleasures were   565
   Brief, but delightful—such as had not stayed

---

4. I.e., she was ashen pale.

Long with her destiny; but she sleeps well
By the seashore, whereon she loved to dwell.

72

That isle is now all desolate and bare,
   Its dwellings down, its tenants passed away;   570
None but her own and father's grave is there,
   And nothing outward tells of human clay;
Ye could not know where lies a thing so fair,
   No stone is there to show, no tongue to say
What was; no dirge, except the hollow sea's,   575
Mourns o'er the beauty of the Cyclades.

73

But many a Greek maid in a loving song
   Sighs o'er her name; and many an islander
With her sire's story makes the night less long;
   Valor was his, and beauty dwelt with her: 580
If she loved rashly, her life paid for wrong—
   A heavy price must all pay who thus err,
In some shape; let none think to fly the danger,
For soon or late Love is his own avenger.[5]

* * *

Canto XVI[5]

1

The antique Persians taught three useful things,
   To draw the bow, to ride, and speak the truth.
This was the mode of Cyrus, best of kings[6]—
   A mode adopted since by modern youth.
Bows have they, generally with two strings;   5
   Horses they ride without remorse or ruth;
At speaking truth perhaps they are less clever,
But draw the long bow[7] better now than ever.

2

The cause of this effect, or this defect,—
   "For this effect defective comes by cause,"[8]—   10

---

5. Juan's adventures continue. He is sold as a slave in Constantinople to an enamored Sultana; she disguises him as a girl and adds him to her husband's harem for convenience of access. Juan escapes, joins the Russian army which is besieging Ismail, and so distinguishes himself in the capture of the town that he is sent with despatches to St. Petersburg. There he becomes "man-mistress" to the insatiable Catherine the Great; as the result of her assiduous attentions, he falls into a physical decline and, for a salutary change of scene and climate, is sent on a diplomatic mission to England. Canto XVI was the last that Byron finished.
   When the Canto opens, Juan is one of many guests at the medieval country mansion of Lord Henry and Lady Adeline Amundeville, which is furnished, legend has it, with the ghost of a long-deceased monk. Three ladies have shown some interest in Juan: Lady Adeline, tall, fair, and statuesque; the dark, aloof, and mysterious Aurora Raby; and the buxom and flirtatious Duchess of Fitz-Fulke.

6. Cyrus, who by his conquests founded the great Persian empire in the 6th century B.C., was regarded by the Greeks as a model ruler. The Persians were reputed to have taught their boys only riding, archery, and veracity.

7. Colloquial: exaggerate the facts.

8. Said by Polonius in *Hamlet* II.ii.103.

Is what I have not leisure to inspect;
   But this I must say in my own applause,
Of all the Muses that I recollect,
   Whate'er may be her follies or her flaws
In some things, mine's beyond all contradiction   15
The most sincere that ever dealt in fiction.

3

And as she treats all things, and ne'er retreats
   From any thing, this Epic will contain
A wilderness of the most rare conceits,
   Which you might elsewhere hope to find in vain.   20
'Tis true there be some bitters with the sweets,
   Yet mixed so slightly that you can't complain,
But wonder they so few are, since my tale is
"De rebus cunctis et quibûsdam aliis."[9]

4

But of all truths which she has told, the most   25
   True is that which she is about to tell.
I said it was a story of a ghost—
   What then? I only knew it so befell.
Have you explored the limits of the coast,
   Where all the dwellers of the earth must dwell?   30
'Tis time to strike such puny doubters dumb as
The sceptics who would not believe Columbus.

5

Some people would impose now with authority,
   Turpin's or Monmouth Geoffry's Chronicle;[1]
Men whose historical superiority   35
   Is always greatest at a miracle.
But Saint Augustine has the great priority,
   Who bids all men believe the impossible,
Because 'tis so. Who nibble, scribble, quibble, he
Quiets at once with "*quia* impossibile."[2]   40

6

And therefore, mortals, cavil not at all;
   Believe:—if 'tis improbable, you *must*;
And if it is impossible, you *shall*:
   'Tis always best to take things upon trust.
I do not speak profanely, to recall   45
   Those holier mysteries, which the wise and just
Receive as gospel, and which grow more rooted,
As all truths must, the more they are disputed.

---

9. "Concerning all things and also some others." Thomas Aquinas is reported to have written a treatise, *De omnibus rebus* (*Concerning All Things*), followed by a second work, *De quibusdamque aliis* (*Concerning Some Other Things*).
1. Turpin, Archbishop of Rheims in the 8th century, was mistakenly thought to have been the author of a history of Charlemagne's reign; Geoffrey of Monmouth wrote the *History of the Kings of Britain* in the 12th century.
2. Tertullian, not Augustine, wrote (with reference to Christ's resurrection), "certum est quia impossibile est"—"it is certain because it is impossible."

7

I merely mean to say what Johnson said,[3]
    That in the course of some six thousand years,   50
All nations have believed that from the dead
    A visitant at intervals appears;
And what is strangest upon this strange head,
    Is, that whatever bar the reason rears
'Gainst such belief, there's something stronger still   55
In its behalf, let those deny who will.

8

The dinner and the soirée[4] too were done,
    The supper too discussed, the dames admired,
The banqueteers had dropped off one by one—
    The song was silent, and the dance expired: 60
The last thin petticoats were vanished, gone
    Like fleecy clouds into the sky retired,
And nothing brighter gleamed through the saloon
Than dying tapers—and the peeping moon.

9

The evaporation of a joyous day   65
    Is like the last glass of champagne, without
The foam which made its virgin bumper gay;
    Or like a system coupled with a doubt;
Or like a soda bottle when its spray
    Has sparkled and let half its spirit out;   70
Or like a billow left by storms behind,
Without the animation of the wind;

10

Or like an opiate which brings troubled rest,
    Or none; or like—like nothing that I know
Except itself—such is the human breast;   75
    A thing, of which similitudes can show
No real likeness—like the old Tyrian vest
    Dyed purple, none at present can tell how,
If from a shellfish or from cochineal.[5]
So perish every tyrant's robe piecemeal!   80

11

But next to dressing for a rout[6] or ball,
    Undressing is a woe; our robe de chambre
May sit like that of Nessus[7] and recall

---

3. Dr. Johnson wrote, in *Rasselas*, Chap. 31, that "there is no people . . . among whom apparitions of the dead are not related and believed," and that "some who deny it with their tongue, confess it by their fears."
4. Evening reception.
5. "The composition of the old Tyrian purple, whether from a shellfish or from cochineal, or from kermes, is still an article of dispute; and even its color— some say purple, others scarlet: I say nothing" [Byron's note]. The very ex-

pensive purple dye of the ancient Tyrians was made from the murex, a Mediterranean shellfish. The cochineal kermes was a dried insect used to make a scarlet dye.
6. A large evening party.
7. Deianira, the wife of Hercules, smeared her husband's robe with the poisoned blood of the centaur Nessus, which she mistakenly thought would serve as a love potion. When Hercules donned the robe, it killed him by consuming his flesh.

Thoughts quite as yellow, but less clear than amber.
Titus exclaimed, "I've lost a day!"[8] Of all   85
    The nights and days most people can remember,
(I have had of both, some not to be disdained)
I wish they'd state how many they have gained.

12

And Juan, on retiring for the night,
    Felt restless, and perplexed, and compromised;   90
He thought Aurora Raby's eyes more bright
    Than Adeline (such is advice) advised;
If he had known exactly his own plight,
    He probably would have philosophized;
A great resource to all, and ne'er denied   95
Till wanted; therefore Juan only sighed.

13

He sighed—the next resource is the full moon,
    Where all sighs are deposited; and now
It happened luckily, the chaste orb shone
    As clear as such a climate will allow;   100
And Juan's mind was in the proper tone
    To hail her with the apostrophe—"Oh, Thou!"
Of amatory egotism the *Tuism*,[9]
Which further to explain would be a truism.

14

But lover, poet, or astronomer,   105
    Shepherd, or swain, whoever may behold,
Feel some abstraction when they gaze on her:
    Great thoughts we catch from thence (besides a cold
Sometimes, unless my feelings rather err);
    Deep secrets to her rolling light are told;   110
The ocean's tides and mortal's brains she sways,
And also hearts, if there be truth in lays.

15

Juan felt somewhat pensive, and disposed
    For contemplation rather than his pillow:
The Gothic chamber, where he was enclosed,   115
    Let in the rippling sound of the lake's billow,
With all the mystery by midnight caused;
    Below his window waved (of course) a willow;
And he stood gazing out on the cascade
That flashed and after darkened in the shade.   120

16

Upon his table or his toilet,[1]—*which*
    Of these is not exactly ascertained—
(I state this, for I am cautious to a pitch

---

8. The Roman emperor Titus made this remark when he noted that the day had passed without his having done anyone a service.
9. The opposite of "egoism"; from the Latin *ego* (I) and *tu* (you).
1. Byron's irony is directed at the fashionable use of the French term "toilet" for the plain English dressing table.

Of nicety, where a fact is to be gained)
A lamp burned high, while he leant from a niche,   125
   Where many a gothic ornament remained,
In chiseled stone and painted glass, and all
That time has left our fathers of their Hall.

17

Then, as the night was clear though cold, he threw
   His chamber door wide open—and went forth   130
Into a gallery, of a somber hue,
   Long, furnished with old pictures of great worth,
Of knights and dames heroic and chaste too,
   As doubtless should be people of high birth.
But by dim lights the portraits of the dead   135
Have something ghastly, desolate, and dread.

18

The forms of the grim knight and pictured saint
   Look living in the moon; and as you turn
Backward and forward to the echoes faint
   Of your own footsteps—voices from the urn   140
Appear to wake, and shadows wild and quaint
   Start from the frames which fence their aspects stern,
As if to ask how you can dare to keep
A vigil there, where all but death should sleep.

19

And the pale smile of Beauties in the grave,   145
   The charms of other days, in starlight gleams
Glimmer on high; their buried locks still wave
   Along the canvas; their eyes glance like dreams
On ours, or spars[2] within some dusky cave,
   But death is imaged in their shadowy beams.   150
A picture is the past; even ere its frame
Be gilt, who sate hath ceased to be the same.

20

As Juan mused on mutability,
   Or on his mistress—terms synonymous—
No sound except the echo of his sigh   155
   Or step ran sadly through that antique house,
When suddenly he heard, or thought so, nigh,
   A supernatural agent—or a mouse,
Whose little nibbling rustle will embarrass
Most people as it plays along the arras.   160

21

It was no mouse, but lo! a monk, arrayed
   In cowl and beads and dusky garb,[3] appeared,
Now in the moonlight, and now lapsed in shade,
   With steps that trod as heavy, yet unheard;
His garments only a slight murmur made;   165

---

2. Stalactites.
3. According to legend, Byron's own ancestral estate, Newstead Abbey, was
haunted by the ghost of a Black Monk.

He moved as shadowy as the sisters weird,[4]
But slowly; and as he passed Juan by,
Glanced, without pausing, on him a bright eye.

22

Juan was petrified; he had heard a hint
  Of such a spirit in these halls of old,   170
But thought, like most men, there was nothing in't
  Beyond the rumor which such spots unfold,
Coined from surviving superstition's mint,
  Which passes ghosts in currency like gold,
But rarely seen, like gold compared with paper.   175
And *did* he see this? or was it a vapor?

23

Once, twice, thrice passed, repassed—the thing of air,
  Or earth beneath, or heaven, or t'other place;
And Juan gazed upon it with a stare,
  Yet could not speak or move; but, on its base   180
As stands a statue, stood: he felt his hair
  Twine like a knot of snakes around his face;
He taxed his tongue for words, which were not granted,
To ask the reverend person what he wanted.

24

The third time, after a still longer pause,   185
  The shadow passed away—but where? the hall
Was long, and thus far there was no great cause
  To think his vanishing unnatural:
Doors there were many, through which, by the laws
  Of physics, bodies whether short or tall   190
Might come or go; but Juan could not state
Through which the specter seemed to evaporate.

25

He stood—how long he knew not, but it seemed
  An age—expectant, powerless, with his eyes
Strained on the spot where first the figure gleamed;   195
  Then by degrees recalled his energies,
And would have passed the whole off as a dream,
  But could not wake; he was, he did surmise,
Waking already, and returned at length
Back to his chamber, shorn of half his strength.   200

26

All there was as he left it: still his taper
  Burnt, and not *blue*, as modest tapers use,
Receiving sprites with sympathetic vapor;[5]
  He rubbed his eyes, and they did not refuse
Their office; he took up an old newspaper;   205
  The paper was right easy to peruse;

---

4. An allusion to the three witches in *Macbeth*.
5. Candles burning with a blue flame were supposed to signify the presence of an evil spirit; see Coleridge's *Christabel*, lines 157–58.

He read an article the king attacking,
And a long eulogy of "Patent Blacking."[6]

27

This savored of this world; but his hand shook—
   He shut his door, and after having read
A paragraph, I think about Horne Tooke,[7]
   Undrest, and rather slowly went to bed.
There couched all snugly on his pillow's nook,
   With what he had seen his fantasy he fed,
And though it was no opiate, slumber crept
Upon him by degrees, and so he slept.

28

He woke betimes; and, as may be supposed,
   Pondered upon his visitant or vision,
And whether it ought not to be disclosed,
   At risk of being quizzed for superstition.
The more he thought, the more his mind was posed;
   In the meantime, his valet, whose precision
Was great, because his master brooked no less,
Knocked to inform him it was time to dress.

29

He dressed; and like young people, he was wont
   To take some trouble with his toilet, but
This morning rather spent less time upon't;
   Aside his very mirror soon was put;
His curls fell negligently o'er his front,
   His clothes were not curbed to their usual cut,
His very neckcloth's Gordian knot[8] was tied
Almost an hair's breadth too much on one side.

30

And when he walked down into the saloon,
   He sat him pensive o'er a dish of tea,
Which he perhaps had not discovered soon,
   Had it not happened scalding hot to be,
Which made him have recourse unto his spoon;
   So much distrait he was, that all could see
That something *was* the matter—Adeline
The first—but *what* she could not well divine.

31

She looked, and saw him pale, and turned as pale
   Herself; then hastily looked down, and muttered
Something, but what's not stated in my tale.
   Lord Henry said, his muffin was ill buttered;
The Duchess of Fitz-Fulke played with her veil,
   And looked at Juan hard, but nothing uttered.

210

215

220

225

230

235

240

245

---

6. An advertisement for shoe-polish.
7. A philologist (1736–1812) whom Byron admired as a supporter of political reform.

8. Intricate knot; Alexander the Great had undone the knot tied by King Gordius by cutting it with his sword.

Aurora Raby, with her large dark eyes,
Surveyed him with a kind of calm surprise.

32

But seeing him all cold and silent still,
 And every body wondering more or less,   250
Fair Adeline enquired, "If he were ill?"
 He started, and said, "Yes—no—rather—yes."
The family physician had great skill,
 And being present, now began to express
His readiness to feel his pulse and tell   255
The cause, but Juan said, "He was quite well."

33

"Quite well; yes; no."—These answers were mysterious,
 And yet his looks appeared to sanction both,
However they might savor of delirious;
 Something like illness of a sudden growth   260
Weighed on his spirit, though by no means serious.
 But for the rest, as he himself seemed loath
To state the case, it might be ta'en for granted
It was not the physician that he wanted.

34

Lord Henry, who had now discussed his chocolate,   265
 Also the muffin whereof he complained,
Said, Juan had not got his usual look elate,
 At which he marveled, since it had not rained;
Then asked her Grace[9] what news were of the Duke of late?
 Her Grace replied, *his* Grace was rather pained   270
With some slight, light, hereditary twinges
Of gout, which rusts aristocratic hinges.

35

Then Henry turned to Juan and addressed
 A few words of condolence on his state:
"You look," quoth he, "as if you had had your rest   275
 Broke in upon by the Black Friar of late."
"What Friar?" said Juan: and he did his best
 To put the question with an air sedate,
Or careless; but the effort was not valid
To hinder him from growing still more pallid.   280

36

"Oh! have you never heard of the Black Friar?
 The spirit of these walls?"—"In truth not I."
"Why Fame—but Fame you know's sometimes a liar—
 Tells an odd story, of which by the bye:
Whether with time the specter has grown shyer,   285
 Or that our sires had a more gifted eye
For such sights, though the tale is half believed,
The Friar of late has not been oft perceived.

9. I.e., the Duchess of Fitz-Fulke.

37

"The last time was—" "I pray," said Adeline—
  (Who watched the changes of Don Juan's brow,   290
And from its context thought she could divine
    Connections stronger than he chose to avow
With this same legend)—"if you but design
    To jest, you'll choose some other theme just now,
Because the present tale has oft been told,   295
And is not much improved by growing old."

38

"Jest!" quoth Milor,[1] "Why, Adeline, you know
    That we ourselves—'twas in the honeymoon—
Saw—" "Well, no matter, 'twas so long ago;
    But, come, I'll set your story to a tune."   300
Graceful as Dian when she draws her bow,
    She seized her harp, whose strings were kindled soon
As touched, and plaintively began to play
The air of " 'Twas a Friar of Orders Gray."

39

"But add the words," cried Henry, "which you made;   305
    For Adeline is half a poetess,"
Turning round to the rest, he smiling said.
    Of course the others could not but express
In courtesy their wish to see displayed
    By one *three* talents, for there were no less—   310
The voice, the words, the harper's skill, at once
Could hardly be united by a dunce.

40

After some fascinating hesitation—
    The charming of these charmers, who seem bound,
I can't tell why, to this dissimulation—   315
    Fair Adeline, with eyes fixed on the ground
At first, then kindling into animation,
    Added her sweet voice to the lyric sound,
And sang with much simplicity—a merit
Not the less precious, that we seldom hear it.   320

I

Beware! beware! of the Black Friar,
    Who sitteth by Norman stone,[2]
For he mutters his prayer in the midnight air,
    And his mass of the days that are gone.
When the Lord of the Hill, Amundeville,   325
    Made Norman Church his prey,
And expelled the friars, one friar still
    Would not be driven away.

---

1. My lord (Henry); a "milor" was the
humorous French term for an English
aristocrat.

2. A building in the Norman style of
Romanesque architecture.

II

Though he came in his might, with King Henry's right,
    To turn church lands to lay,[3]   330
With sword in hand, and torch to light
    Their walls, if they said nay,
A monk remained, unchased, unchained,
    And he did not seem formed of clay,
For he's seen in the porch, and he's seen in the church,   335
    Though he is not seen by day.

III

And whether for good, or whether for ill,
    It is not mine to say;
But still to the house of Amundeville
    He abideth night and day.   340
By the marriage bed of their lords, 'tis said,
    He flits on the bridal eve;
And 'tis held as faith, to their bed of death,
    He comes—but not to grieve.

IV

When an heir is born, he is hard to mourn,   345
    And when aught is to befall
That ancient line, in the pale moonshine
    He walks from hall to hall.
His form you may trace, but not his face,
    'Tis shadowed by his cowl;   350
But his eyes may be seen from the folds between,
    And they seem of a parted soul.

V

But beware! beware! of the Black Friar,
    He still retains his sway,
For he is yet the church's heir   355
    Who ever may be the lay.
Amundeville is lord by day,
    But the monk is lord by night.
Nor wine nor wassail could raise a vassal
    To question that frair's right.   360

VI

Say nought to him as he walks the hall,
    And he'll say nought to you;
He sweeps along in his dusky pall,
    As o'er the grass the dew.
Then Grammercy! for the Black Friar;   365
    Heaven sain[4] him! fair or foul,
And whatsoe'er may be his prayer,
    Let ours be for his soul.

---

3. The reference is to Henry VIII, who dissolved the Catholic monasteries and distributed the church property to laymen.
4. Bless.

41

The lady's voice ceased, and the thrilling wires
    Died from the touch that kindled them to sound;   370
And the pause followed, which when song expires,
    Pervades a moment those who listen round;
And then of course the circle much admires,
    Nor less applauds as in politeness bound,
The tones, the feeling, and the execution,   375
To the performer's diffident confusion.

42

Fair Adeline, though in a careless way,
    As if she rated such accomplishment
As the mere pastime of an idle day,
    Pursued an instant for her own content,   380
Would now and then as 'twere *without* display,
    Yet *with* display in fact, at times relent
To such performances with haughty smile,
To show she *could*, if it were worth her while.

43

Now this (but we will whisper it aside)   385
    Was—pardon the pedantic illustration—
Trampling on Plato's pride with greater pride,
    As did the Cynic on some like occasion;
Deeming the sage would be much mortified,
    Or thrown into a philosophic passion,   390
For a spoilt carpet—but the "Attic Bee"
Was much consoled by his own repartee.[5]

44

Thus Adeline would throw into the shade,
    (By doing easily whene'er she chose,
What dilettanti do with vast parade)   395
    Their sort of *half profession:* for it grows
To something like this when too oft displayed,
    And that it is so, every body knows,
Who have heard Miss That or This, or Lady T'other,
Show off—to please their company or mother.   400

45

Oh! the long evenings of duets and trios!
    The admirations and the speculations;
The "Mamma Mia's!" and the "Amor Mio's!"
    The "Tanti palpiti's" on such occasions:
The "Lasciami's," and quavering "Addio's!"[6]   405
    Amongst our own most musical of nations;

---

5. The "Attic Bee" is Plato, of whom it was said that bees settled on his lips when he was an infant as an omen that his language would be sweet as honey. The reference in the preceding lines is to the story that the Cynic philosopher Diogenes, coming to visit Plato, said as he stepped on the carpets, "I trample on the pride of Plato." Plato retorted, "Yes, Diogenes, with pride of another sort."
6. Clichés in the Italian songs then popular with English performers: the "so many heart-throbs," "allow me's," "farewells."

With "Tu mi chamas's" from Portingale,[7]
To soothe our ears, lest Italy should fail.

46

In Babylon's bravuras—as the home-
    Heart-ballads of Green Erin or Grey Highlands,   410
That brings Lochaber[8] back to eyes that roam
    O'er far Atlantic continents or islands,
The calentures of music which o'ercome
    All mountaineers with dreams that they are nigh lands,[9]
No more to be beheld but in such visions—   415
Was Adeline well versed, as compositions.[1]

47

She also had a twilight tinge of *"Blue,"*[2]
    Could write rhymes, and compose more than she wrote;
Made epigrams occasionally too
    Upon her friends, as every body ought.   420
But still from that sublimer azure hue,
    So much the present dye, she was remote,
Was weak enough to deem Pope a great poet,[3]
And what was worse, was not ashamed to show it.

48

Aurora—since we are touching upon taste,   425
    Which nowadays is the thermometer
By whose degrees all characters are classed—
    Was more Shakespearian, if I do not err.
The worlds beyond this world's perplexing waste
    Had more of her existence, for in her   430
There was a depth of feeling to embrace
Thoughts, boundless, deep, but silent too as Space.

49

Not so her gracious, graceful, graceless Grace,
    The full grown Hebe[4] of Fitz-Fulke, whose mind,
If she had any, was upon her face,
    And that was of a fascinating kind.   435
A little turn for mischief you might trace

---

7. Byron himself had twice translated into English this Portuguese song, "You Call Me"; thus his satiric comment on the fashionable songs of the time includes his own efforts.

8. A mountainous district in Scotland, the subject of "Farewell to Lochaber" by the 18th-century Scottish poet Allan Ramsay.

9. A "calenture" was a fever especially incident among sailors in tropical water; in his delirium, the victim supposed the sea to be green fields.

1. I.e., "Adeline was well versed in Babylon's bravuras—[such] as the home-heart-ballads of Green Erin . . ."; "calentures" is in apposition with "ballads." Byron is gently mocking both the subjects and distorted syntax of sentimental

("home-heart") ballads about Erin (Ireland) and the Highlands (Scotland), including those written by his good friends Thomas Moore and Sir Walter Scott.

2. A reference to the "bluestockings"—ladies with pedantic intellectual and scholarly pretensions.

3. As did Byron himself, who had written essays defending Pope's poetry against derogatory comments by William Lisle Bowles in his edition of Pope. The mocking reference to "that sublimer azure hue" (line 421) is directed against ladies who preferred the Wordsworthian "sublime" over the civilized poetry of Pope.

4. Pronounced Hee-bee: the goddess of youth, cupbearer of the gods, and bride of Hercules.

Also thereon—but that's not much; we find
Few females without some such gentle leaven,
For fear we should suppose us quite in heaven.   440

50

I have not heard she was at all poetic,
   Though once she was seen reading the "Bath Guide,"
And "Hayley's Triumphs,"[5] which she deemed pathetic,
   Because, she said, *her temper* had been tried
So much, the bard had really been prophetic   445
   Of what she had gone through with—since a bride.
But of all verse, what most insured her praise
Were sonnets to herself, or "Bouts rimés."[6]

51

'Twere difficult to say what was the object
   Of Adeline, in bringing this same lay   450
To bear on what appeared to her the subject
   Of Juan's nervous feelings on that day.
Perhaps she merely had the simple project
   To laugh him out of his supposed dismay;
Perhaps she might wish to confirm him in it,   455
Though why I cannot say—at least this minute.

52

But so far the immediate effect
   Was to restore him to his self propriety,
A thing quite necessary to the elect,
   Who wish to take the tone of their society: 460
In which you cannot be too circumspect,
   Whether the mode be persiflage or piety,
But wear the newest mantle of hypocrisy,
On pain of much displeasing the Gynocracy.[7]

53

And therefore Juan now began to rally   465
   His spirits, and without more explanation,
To jest upon such themes in many a sally.
   Her Grace too also seized the same occasion,
With various similar remarks to tally,
   But wished for a still more detailed narration   470
Of this same mystic Friar's curious doings,
About the present family's deaths and wooings.

54

Of these few could say more than has been said;
   They passed as such things do, for superstition
With some, while others, who had more in dread   475
   The theme, half credited the strange tradition;

---

5. Christopher Anstey's *The New Bath Guide* (1766) was a verse satire on life at Bath, the fashionable English watering place. William Hayley's *The Triumphs of Temper* (1781) was a sentimental piece of versifying.

6. "Rhymed endings"—a versifying game originating in 17th-century Paris; the aim was to incorporate given rhyme-words and a pre-established rhyme-scheme.

7. A government by women.

And much was talked on all sides on that head;
   But Juan, when cross-questioned on the vision,
Which some supposed (though he had not avowed it)
Had stirred him, answered in a way to cloud it.   480

55

And then, the midday having worn to one,
   The company prepared to separate;
Some to their several pastimes, or to none,
   Some wondering 'twas so early, some so late.
There was a goodly match too, to be run   485
   Between some greyhounds on my Lord's estate,
And a young race-horse of old pedigree,
Matched for the spring,[8] whom several went to see.

56

There was a picture dealer who had brought
   A special Titian, warranted original,
So precious that it was not to be bought,   490
   Though princes the possessor were besieging all.
The king himself had cheapened it,[9] but thought
   The Civil List[1] (he deigns to accept, obliging all
His subjects by his gracious acceptation)
Too scanty, in these times of low taxation.   495

57

But as Lord Henry was a connoisseur—
   The friend of artists, if not arts—the owner,
With motives the most classical and pure,
   So that he would have been the very donor,   500
Rather than seller, had his wants been fewer,
   So much he deemed his patronage an honor,
Had brought the Capo d'opera,[2] not for sale,
But for his judgment—never known to fail.

58

There was a modern Goth, I mean a Gothic   505
   Bricklayer of Babel, called an architect,
Brought to survey these gray walls,[3] which though so thick,
   Might have from time acquired some slight defect;
Who, after rummaging the Abbey through thick
   And thin, produced a plan whereby to erect   510
New buildings of correctest conformation,
And throw down old, which he called *restoration*.

59

The cost would be a trifle—an "old song"[4]
   Set to some thousands ('tis the usual burthen

---

8. Entered in a "match book" for the spring races.
9. Bargained for it.
1. The "Civil List" catalogued the sums voted by Parliament for the personal and household expenses of the king, and for the pensions granted by the king.
2. "Chief work"–i.e., masterpiece.

3. Byron's comment on contemporary architects who specialized in "restoring" medieval ("Gothic") mansions. Colonel Wildman, who had purchased Newstead Abbey from Byron, had undertaken extensive restoration of the estate.
4. "To buy for an old song" was then the idiom for buying cheaply.

Of that same tune, when people hum it long)— 515
   The price would speedily repay its worth in
An edifice no less sublime than strong,
   By which Lord Henry's good taste would go forth in
Its glory, through all ages shining sunny,
For Gothic daring shown in English money.[5] 520

60

There were two lawyers busy on a mortgage
   Lord Henry wished to raise for a new purchase;
Also a lawsuit upon tenures burgage,
   And one on tithes,[6] which sure are Discord's torches,
Kindling Religion till she throws down *her* gage, 525
   "Untying" squires "to fight against the churches";[7]
There was a prize ox, a prize pig, and ploughman,
For Henry was a sort of Sabine[8] showman.

61

There were two poachers caught in a steel trap
   Ready for jail, their place of convalescence; 530
There was a country girl in a close cap[9]
   And scarlet cloak (I hate the sight to see, since—
Since—since—in youth, I had the sad mishap—
   But luckily I have paid few parish fees since)
That scarlet cloak, alas! unclosed with Rigor, 535
Presents the problem of a double figure.

62

A reel within a bottle is a mystery,
   One can't tell how it e'er got in or out,
Therefore the present piece of natural history,
   I leave to those who are fond of solving doubt, 540
And merely state, though not for the consistory,[1]
   Lord Henry was a justice, and that Scout
The constable, beneath a warrant's banner,
Had bagged this poacher upon Nature's manor.

63

Now Justices of Peace must judge all pieces 545
   Of mischief of all kinds, and keep the game
And morals of the country from caprices
   Of those who have not a license for the same;
And of all things, excepting tithes and leases,

---

5. In a note Byron points out that he is echoing a Latin inscription on the sea walls of Venice: "Built by Roman daring with Venetian money."
6. "Tenure in burgage" was the legal phrase for property held by an overlord to whom the tenants paid yearly rent. "Tithes" were one-tenth of an annual income, levied to support the church.
7. " 'Though ye *untie* the winds and bid them fight / Against the churches.'— *Macbeth* [IV.i.52–53]" [Byron's note; he misquotes slightly].
8. The reference is to Horace's Sabine farm; i.e., Henry, like the Roman poet, is a gentleman-farmer.
9. A tight-fitting cap.
1. A diocesan court in the Church of England.

Perhaps these are most difficult to tame: 550
Preserving partridges and pretty wenches
Are puzzles to the most precautious benches.

64

The present culprit was extremely pale,
    Pale as if painted so; her cheek being red
By nature, as in higher dames less hale   555
    'Tis white, at least when they just rise from bed.
Perhaps she was ashamed of seeming frail,
    Poor soul! for she was country born and bred,
And knew no better in her immorality
Than to wax white—for blushes are for quality.   560

65

Her black, bright, downcast, yet espiegle[2] eye,
    Had gathered a large tear into its corner,
Which the poor thing at times essayed to dry,
    For she was not a sentimental mourner,
Parading all her sensibility,   565
    Nor insolent enough to scorn the scorner,
But stood in trembling, patient tribulation,
To be called up for her examination.

66

Of course these groups were scattered here and there,
    Not nigh the gay saloon of ladies gent.[3]   570
The lawyers in the study; and in air
    The prize pig, ploughman, poachers; the men sent
From town, viz. architect and dealer, were
    Both busy (as a general in his tent
Writing dispatches) in their several stations,   575
Exulting in their brilliant lucubrations.

67

But this poor girl was left in the great hall,
    While Scout, the parish guardian of the frail,
Discussed (he hated beer yclept the "small")[4]
    A mighty mug of *moral* double ale.   580
She waited until Justice could recall
    Its kind attentions to their proper pale,
To name a thing in nomenclature rather
Perplexing for most virgins—a child's father.

68

You see here was enough of occupation   585
    For the Lord Henry, linked with dogs and horses.
There was much bustle too and preparation
    Below stairs on the score of second courses,
Because, as suits their rank and situation,

2. French for "roguish," "mischievous." women."
3. A phrase used by Spenser: "gentle-   4. "Small beer" is weak beer.

Those who in counties have great land resources,   590
Have "public days," when all men may carouse,
Though not exactly what's called "open house."

69

But once a week or fortnight, *un*invited
   (Thus we translate a *general invitation*)
All country gentlemen, esquired[5] or knighted,   595
   May drop in without cards, and take their station
At the full board, and sit alike delighted
   With fashionable wines and conversation;
And as the Isthmus of the grand connection,
Talk o'er themselves, the past and next election.   600

70

Lord Henry was a great electioneerer,
   Burrowing for boroughs like a rat or rabbit.
But county contests cost him rather dearer,
   Because the neighboring Scotch Earl of Giftgabbit
Had English influence, in the self-same sphere here;   605
   His son, the Honorable Dick Dicedrabbit,
Was member for the "other Interest" (meaning
The same self-interest, with a different leaning).

71

Courteous and cautious therefore in his county,
   He was all things to all men, and dispensed   610
To some civility, to others bounty,
   And promises to all—which last commenced
To gather to a somewhat large amount, he
   Not calculating how much they condensed;
But what with keeping some, and breaking others,   615
His word had the same value as another's.

72

A friend to freedom and freeholders—yet
   No less a friend to government—he held,
That he exactly the just medium hit
   'Twixt place and patriotism—albeit compelled,   620
Such was his Sovereign's pleasure (though unfit,
   He added modestly, when rebels railed)
To hold some sinecures he wished abolished,
But that with them all law would be demolished.

73

He was "free to confess"—(whence comes this phrase?   625
   Is't English? No—'tis only parliamentary)
That innovation's spirit nowadays
   Had made more progress than for the last century.
He would not tread a factious path to praise,
   Though for the public weal disposed to venture high;   630
As for his place, he could but say this of it,
That the fatigue was greater than the profit.

5. Possessing the title "esquire"—signifying a gentleman by birth or position.

74

Heaven, and his friends, knew that a private life
　　Had ever been his sole and whole ambition;
But could he quit his king in times of strife　　　635
　　Which threatened the whole country with perdition?
When demagogues would with a butcher's knife
　　Cut through and through (oh! damnable incision!)
The Gordian or the Geordi-an knot, whose strings
Have tied together Commons, Lords, and Kings.　　640

75

Sooner "come place into the civil list
　　And champion him to be utmost"[6]—he would keep it,
Till duly disappointed or dismissed:
　　Profit he cared not for, let others reap it;
But should the day come when place ceased to exist,　　645
　　The country would have far more cause to weep it;
For how could it go on? Explain who can!
He gloried in the name of Englishman.

76

He was as independent—aye, much more—
　　Than those who were not paid for independence,　　650
As common soldiers, or a common—Shore,
　　Have in their several arts or parts ascendence
O'er the irregulars in lust or gore,
　　Who do not give professional attendance.
Thus on the mob all statesmen are as eager　　655
To prove their pride, as footmen to a beggar.

77

All this (save the last stanza) Henry said,
　　And thought. I say no more—I've said too much;
For all of us have either heard or read—
　　Off—or *upon* the hustings[7]—some slight such　　660
Hints from the independent heart or head
　　Of the official candidate. I'll touch
No more on this—the dinner bell hath rung,
And grace is said; the grace I *should* have *sung*—

78

But I'm too late, and therefore must make play.[8]　　665
　　'Twas a great banquet, such as Albion old
Was wont to boast—as if a glutton's tray
　　Were something very glorious to behold.
But 'twas a public feast and public day—
　　Quite full, right dull, guests hot, and dishes cold,　　670
Great plenty, much formality, small cheer,
And everybody out of their own sphere.

6. *Macbeth* III.i.70–71: "Rather than so, come, Fate, into the list / And champion me to th' utterance." Byron converts "list" (an arena for tournaments) into "Civil List" (of pensions granted by the king).

7. Platform on which candidates for Parliament addressed the voters.

8. I.e., the author should have quoted the grace said at the banquet, but he got there too late, and must make shift without it.

79

The squires familiarly formal, and
   My lords and ladies proudly condescending;
The very servants puzzling how to hand   675
   Their plates—without it might be too much bending
From their high places by the sideboard's stand—
   Yet like their masters fearful of offending.
For any deviation from the graces
Might cost both men and master too—their *places*.   680

80

There were some hunters bold, and coursers keen,
   Whose hounds ne'er erred, nor greyhounds deigned to lurch;
Some deadly shots too, Septembrizers,[9] seen
   Earliest to rise, and last to quit the search
Of the poor partridge through his stubble screen.   685
   There were some massy members of the church,
Takers of tithes, and makers of good matches,
And several who sung fewer psalms than catches.[1]

81

There were some country wags too—and, alas!
   Some exiles from the town, who had been driven   690
To gaze, instead of pavement, upon grass,
   And rise at nine in lieu of long eleven.
And lo! upon that day it came to pass,
   I sat next that o'erwhelming son of heaven,
The very powerful Parson, Peter Pith,[2]   695
The loudest wit I e'er was deafened with.

82

I knew him in his livelier London days,
   A brilliant diner out, though but a curate;
And not a joke he cut but earned its praise,
   Until preferment, coming at a sure rate,   700
(Oh, Providence! how wondrous are thy ways,
   Who would suppose thy gifts sometimes obdurate?)
Gave him, to lay the devil who looks o'er Lincoln,[3]
A fat fen vicarage, and nought to think on.

83

His jokes were sermons, and his sermons jokes;   705
   But both were thrown away amongst the fens;
For wit hath no great friend in aguish folks.
   No longer ready ears and short-hand pens
Imbibed the gay bon mot, or happy hoax:
   The poor priest was reduced to common sense,   710

9. Byron contemptuously compares hunters to the *septembriseurs*—those French revolutionaries who massacred helpless political prisoners in Paris, September 2–5, 1792.
1. A catch was a type of round contrived to effect a comic, and often indecent, combination of words.
2. The reference is to the Rev. Sydney Smith (1771–1845), renowned for his wit and exuberant humor on social occasions. In 1808 Smith left London to live at a rural vicarage in Yorkshire that had been bestowed upon him.
3. A gargoyle on St. Hugh's Chapel of Lincoln Cathedral is known as the "Devil looking over Lincoln."

Or to coarse efforts very loud and long,
To hammer a hoarse laugh from the thick throng.

84

There *is* a difference, says the song, "between
    A beggar and a queen,"[4] or *was* (of late
The latter worse used of the two we've seen—   715
    But we'll say nothing of affairs of state)
A difference "'twixt a bishop and a dean,"
    A difference between crockery ware and plate,
As between English beef and Spartan broth—
And yet great heroes have been bred by both.   720

85

But of all nature's discrepancies, none
    Upon the whole is greater than the difference
Beheld between the country and the town,
    Of which the latter merits every preference
From those who have few resources of their own,   725
    And only think, or act, or feel with reference
To some small plan of interest or ambition—
Both which are limited to no condition.

86

But "en avant!" The light loves languish o'er
    Long banquets and too many guests, although   730
A slight repast makes people love much more,
    Bacchus and Ceres being, as we know,
Even from our grammar upwards, friends of yore
    With vivifying Venus,[5] who doth owe
To these the invention of champagne and truffles: 735
Temperance delights her, but long fasting ruffles.

87

Dully passed o'er the dinner of the day;
    And Juan took his place, he knew not where,
Confused, in the confusion, and distrait,
    And sitting as if nailed upon his chair;   740
Though knives and forks clanged round as in a fray,
    He seemed unconscious of all passing there,
Till someone, with a groan, expressed a wish
(Unheeded twice) to have a fin of fish.

88

On which, at the *third* asking of the banns,[6]   745
    He started; and perceiving smiles around
Broadening to grins, he colored more than once,
    And hastily—as nothing can confound
A wise man more than laughter from a dunce—
    Inflicted on the dish a deadly wound,   750

4. An 18th-century song begins "There's a difference between a beggar and a queen." A later stanza begins "There's a difference to be seen, twixt a Bishop and a Dean"; this difference is that "A Dean cannot dish up a dinner like a Bishop."

5. An allusion to the Latin tag *Sine Cerere et Baccho friget Venus*—"without Ceres and Bacchus [food and wine] love grows cold."

6. A notice in church of an intended marriage, read aloud three times.

And with such hurry, that ere he could curb it,
He had paid his neighbor's prayer with half a turbot.[7]

89

This was no bad mistake, as it occurred,
    The supplicator being an amateur;
But others, who were left with scarce a third,   755
    Were angry—as they well might, to be sure.
They wondered how a young man so absurd
    Lord Henry at his table should endure;
And this, and his not knowing how much oats
Had fallen last market, cost his host three votes.   760

90

They little knew, or might have sympathized,
    That he the night before had seen a ghost;
A prologue which but slightly harmonized
    With the substantial company engrossed
By Matter, and so much materialized,   765
    That one scarce knew at what to marvel most
Of two things—how (the question rather odd is)
Such bodies could have souls, or souls such bodies.

91

But what confused him more than smile or stare
    From all the 'squires and 'squiresses around,   770
Who wondered at the abstraction of his air,
    Especially as he had been renowned
For some vivacity among the fair,
    Even in the country circle's narrow bound—
(For little things upon my Lord's estate   775
Were good small-talk for others still less great)—

92

Was, that he caught Aurora's eye on his,
    And something like a smile upon her cheek.
Now this he really rather took amiss:
    In those who rarely smile, their smiles bespeak   780
A strong external motive; and in this
    Smile of Aurora's there was nought to pique
Or hope, or love, with any of the wiles
Which some pretend to trace in ladies' smiles.

93

'Twas a mere quiet smile of contemplation,   785
    Indicative of some surprise and pity;
And Juan grew carnation with vexation,
    Which was not very wise and still less witty,
Since he had gained at least her observation.
    A most important outwork of the city—   790
As Juan should have known, had not his senses
By last night's ghost been driven from their defenses.

---

7. A European flatfish.

94

But what was bad, she did not blush in turn,
  Nor seem embarrassed—quite the contrary;
Her aspect was as usual, still—*not* stern—   795
  And she withdrew, but cast not down, her eye,
Yet grew a little pale—with what? concern?
  I know not; but her color ne'er was high—
Though sometimes faintly flushed—and always clear,
As deep seas in a Sunny Atmosphere.   800

95

But Adeline was occupied by fame
  This day; and watching, witching, condescending
To the consumers of fish, fowl and game,
  And dignity with courtesy so blending,
As all must blend whose part it is to aim   805
  (Especially as the sixth year is ending)[8]
At their lord's, son's, or similar connection's
Safe conduct through the rocks of re-elections.

96

Though this was most expedient on the whole,
  And usual—Juan, when he cast a glance   810
On Adeline while playing her grand role,
  Which she went through as though it were a dance,
(Betraying only now and then her soul
  By a look scarce perceptibly askance
Of weariness or scorn) began to feel   815
Some doubt how much of Adeline was *real*;

97

So well she acted, all and every part
  By turns—with that vivacious versatility,
Which many people take for want of heart.
  They err—'tis merely what is called mobility,[9]   820
A thing of temperament and not of art,
  Though seeming so, from its supposed facility;
And false—though true; for surely they're sincerest,
Who are strongly acted on by what is nearest.

98

This makes your actors, artists, and romancers,   825
  Heroes sometimes, though seldom—sages never;
But speakers, bards, diplomatists, and dancers,
  Little that's great, but much of what is clever;
Most orators, but very few financiers,
  Though all Exchequer Chancellors endeavor,   830

8. The maximum life of a Parliament was then seven years; the Amundevilles are beginning to electioneer a year ahead.
9. "In French, *mobilité*. . . . It may be defined as an excessive susceptibility of immediate impressions—at the same time without *losing* the past; and is, though sometimes apparently useful to the possessor, a most painful and unhappy attribute" [Byron's note; as the last clause shows, he has in mind his own volatile temperament].

Of late years, to dispense with Cocker's rigors,[1]
And grow quite figurative with their figures.

99

The poets of arithmetic are they
    Who, though they prove not two and two to be
Five, as they might do in a modest way,   835
    Have plainly made it out that four are three,
Judging by what they take, and what they pay.
    The Sinking Fund's unfathomable sea,[2]
That most unliquidating liquid, leaves
The debt unsunk, yet sinks all it receives.   840

100

While Adeline dispensed her airs and graces,
    The fair Fitz-Fulke seemed very much at ease;
Though too well bred to quiz men to their faces,
    Her laughing blue eyes with a glance would seize
The ridicules of people in all places—   845
    That honey of your fashionable bees—
And store it up for mischievous enjoyment;
And this at present was her kind employment.

101

However, the day closed, as days must close;
    The evening also waned—and coffee came.   850
Each carriage was announced, and ladies rose,
    And curtseying off, as curtsies country dame,[3]
Retired: with most unfashionable bows
    Their docile esquires also did the same,
Delighted with the dinner and their host,   855
But with the Lady Adeline the most.

102

Some praised her beauty; others her great grace;
    The warmth of her politeness, whose sincerity
Was obvious in each feature of her face,
    Whose traits were radiant with the rays of verity.   860
Yes; *she* was truly worthy *her* high place!
    No one could envy her deserved prosperity;
And then her dress—what beautiful simplicity
Draperied her form with curious felicity!

103

Meanwhile sweet Adeline deserved their praises,   865
    By an impartial indemnification
For all her past exertion and soft phrases,
    In a most edifying conversation,

1. Cocker's *Arithmetic* (1677); a later edition of that popular manual was still in use.
2. The Sinking Fund was devised by Walpole in 1717–18 as a scheme to reduce the national debt. Instead, it turned out to be a heavy loser; when it was abolished in 1823 (the year this canto was written), it was estimated to have cost the nation about 20 million pounds.
3. I.e., in the way a country dame curtsies.

Which turned upon their late guests' miens and faces,
  And families, even to the last relation; 870
Their hideous wives, their horrid selves and dresses,
And truculent distortion of their tresses.

104

True, *she* said little—'twas the rest that broke
  Forth into universal epigram;
But then 'twas to the purpose what she spoke: 875
  Like Addison's "faint praise," so wont to damn,[4]
Her own but served to set off every joke,
  As music chimes in with a melodrame.
How sweet the task to shield an absent friend!
I ask but this of mine, to—*not* defend. 880

105

There were but two exceptions to this keen
  Skirmish of wits o'er the departed; one,
Aurora, with her pure and placid mien;
  And Juan too, in general behind none
In gay remark on what he had heard or seen, 885
  Sat silent now, his usual spirits gone:
In vain he heard the others rail or rally,
He would not join them in a single sally.

106

'Tis true he saw Aurora look as though
  She approved his silence; she perhaps mistook 890
Its motive for that charity we owe
  But seldom pay the absent, nor would look
Further; it might or it might not be so.
  But Juan, sitting silent in his nook,
Observing little in his reverie, 895
Yet saw this much, which he was glad to see.

107

The ghost at least had done him this much good,
  In making him as silent as a ghost,
If in the circumstances which ensued
  He gained esteem where it was worth the most. 900
And certainly Aurora had renewed
  In him some feelings he had lately lost
Or hardened; feelings which, perhaps ideal,
Are so divine, that I must deem them real—

108

The love of higher things and better days; 905
  The unbounded hope, and heavenly ignorance
Of what is called the world, and the world's ways;
  The moment when we gather from a glance
More joy than from all future pride or praise,

---

4. From Pope's portrait of Atticus (i.e., Joseph Addison) in *Epistle to Dr. Arbuthnot*, line 201: "Damn with faint praise, assent with civil leer."

Which kindle manhood, but can ne'er entrance   910
The heart in an existence of its own,
Of which another's bosom is the zone.

109

Who would not sigh Αι αι ταν Κυθερειαν![5]
That *hath* a memory, or that *had* a heart?
Alas! *her* star must wane like that of Dian;[6]   915
Ray fades on ray, as years on years depart.
Anacreon only had the soul to tie an
Unwithering myrtle round the unblunted dart
Of Eros; but though thou hast played us many tricks,
Still we respect thee, "Alma Venus Genetrix"![7]   920

110

And full of sentiments, sublime as billows
Heaving between this world and worlds beyond,
Don Juan, when the midnight hour of pillows
Arrived, retired to his; but to despond
Rather than rest. Instead of poppies, willows   925
Waved o'er his couch; he meditated, fond
Of those sweet bitter thoughts which banish sleep,
And make the worldling sneer, the youngling weep.

111

The night was as before: he was undressed,
Saving his nightgown, which is an undress;   930
Completely "sans culotte,"[8] and without vest;
In short, he hardly could be clothed with less;
But apprehensive of his spectral guest,
He sat, with feelings awkward to express,
(By those who have not had such visitations)   935
Expectant of the ghost's fresh operations.

112

And not in vain he listened—Hush! what's that?
I see—I see—Ah, no!—'tis not—yet 'tis—
Ye powers! it is the—the—the—Pooh! the cat!
The devil may take that stealthy pace of his!   940
So like a spiritual pit-a-pat,
Or tiptoe of an amatory Miss,
Gliding the first time to a rendezvous,
And dreading the chaste echoes of her shoe.

113

Again—what is't? The wind? No, no—this time   945
It is the sable Friar as before,
With awful footsteps regular as rhyme,

---

5. From Bion's pastoral elegy, *Lament for Adonis:* "Alas, alas for Cytherea."
6. Cytherea's (i.e., Venus', or Love's) star must wane, as does Diana's (the moon).
7. A condensed excerpt from the two opening lines of Lucretius' *On the Nature of Things:* "O nurturing mother Venus."
8. "Without trousers"; the term was applied to ultra-violent republicans during the French Revolution, who wore pantaloons instead of the knee-breeches of the upper classes.

Or (as rhymes may be in these days) much more.
Again, through shadows of the night sublime,
    When deep sleep fell on men,[9] and the world wore   950
The starry darkness round her like a girdle
Spangled with gems—the monk made his blood curdle.

114

A noise like to wet fingers drawn on glass,
    Which sets the teeth on edge; and a slight clatter
Like showers which on the midnight gusts will pass,   955
    Sounding like very supernatural water,
Came over Juan's ear, which throbbed, alas!
    For immaterialism's a serious matter;
So that even those whose faith is the most great
In souls immortal, shun them tête-à-tête.   960

115

Were his eyes open?—Yes! and his mouth too.[1]
    Surprise has this effect—to make one dumb,
Yet leave the gate which Eloquence slips through
    As wide as if a long speech were to come.
Nigh and more nigh the awful echoes drew,   965
    Tremendous to a mortal tympanum:
His eyes were open, and (as was before
Stated) his mouth. What opened next?—the door.

116

It opened with a most infernal creak,
    Like that of Hell. "Lasciate ogni speranza   970
Voi che entrate!"[2] The hinge seemed to speak,
    Dreadful as Dante's rhima, or this stanza;
Or—but all words upon such themes are weak;
    A single shade's sufficient to entrance a
Hero—for what is substance to a Spirit?   975
Or how is't *matter* trembles to come near it?

117

The door flew wide, not swiftly—but, as fly
    The seagulls, with a steady, sober flight—
And then swung back; nor close—but stood awry,
    Half letting in long shadows on the light,   980
Which still in Juan's candlesticks burned high,
    For he had two, both tolerably bright,
And in the doorway, darkening Darkness, stood
The sable Friar in his solemn hood.

9. Job 4:13–14: "In thoughts from the visions of the night, when deep sleep falleth on men, / Fear came upon me, and trembling, which made all my bones to shake."
1. An echo of the question-and-answer devices in Coleridge's *Christabel*, e.g., lines 14–15: "Is the night chilly and dark? / The night is chilly, but not dark." Byron had greatly admired the poem in manuscript, and imitated its meter in *The Siege of Corinth* (1816).
2. Part of the inscription on the gate of hell in Dante's *Inferno* III.9: "Abandon all hope, ye who enter."

118

Don Juan shook, as erst he had been shaken   985
    The night before; but being sick of shaking,
He first inclined to think he had been mistaken,
    And then to be ashamed of such mistaking;
His own internal ghost began to awaken
    Within him, and to quell his corporal quaking—   990
Hinting that soul and body on the whole
Were odds against a disembodied soul.

119

And then his dread grew wrath, and his wrath fierce;
    And he arose, advanced—the shade retreated;
But Juan, eager now the truth to pierce,   995
    Followed, his veins no longer cold, but heated,
Resolved to thrust the mystery carte and tierce,[3]
    At whatsoever risk of being defeated:
The ghost stopped, menaced, then retired, until
He reached the ancient wall, then stood stone still.   1000

120

Juan put forth one arm—Eternal Powers!
    It touched no soul, nor body, but the wall,
On which the moonbeams fell in silvery showers
    Checkered with all the tracery of the hall;
He shuddered, as no doubt the bravest cowers   1005
    When he can't tell what 'tis that doth appall.
How odd, a single hobgoblin's non-entity
Should cause more fear than a whole host's identity![4]

121

But still the shade remained; the blue eyes glared,
    And rather variably for stony death;   1010
Yet one thing rather good the grave had spared,
    The ghost had a remarkably sweet breath.
A straggling curl showed he had been fair-haired;
    A red lip, with two rows of pearls beneath,
Gleamed forth, as through the casement's ivy shroud   1015
The moon peeped, just escaped from a gray cloud.

122

And Juan, puzzled, but still curious, thrust
    His other arm forth—Wonder upon wonder!
It pressed upon a hard but glowing bust,
    Which beat as if there was a warm heart under.   1020
He found, as people on most trials must,
    That he had made at first a silly blunder,
And that in his confusion he had caught
Only the wall, instead of what he sought.

---

3. Positions ("fourth" and "third") for thrust and parry in fencing.

4. I.e., "than the actuality of a whole host of men."

123

The ghost, if ghost it were, seemed a sweet soul   1025
  As ever lurked beneath a holy hood:
A dimpled chin, a neck of ivory, stole
  Forth into something much like flesh and blood;
Back fell the sable frock and dreary cowl,
  And they revealed—alas! that ere they should!   1030
In full, voluptuous, but *not o'ergrown* bulk,
The phantom of her frolic Grace—Fitz-Fulke!⁵

1818–23   1819–24

The Vision of Judgment¹

*By Quevedo Redivivus*²

SUGGESTED BY THE COMPOSITION SO ENTITLED BY THE AUTHOR OF
Wat Tyler

"A Daniel come to judgment! yea, a Daniel!
I thank thee, Jew, for teaching me that word."³

1

Saint Peter sat by the celestial gate:
  His keys were rusty, and the lock was dull,
So little trouble had been given of late;
  Not that the place by any means was full,
But since the Gallic era "eighty-eight"⁴   5

---

5. On this unresolved narrative chord the published *Don Juan* aptly concludes. After Byron's death, fourteen opening stanzas of Canto XVII were found; these were first published in 1903.

1. Although originally an ardent supporter of the French Revolution, Robert Southey soon turned a Tory and in 1813 was appointed poet laureate. Four years after the appointment he was dismayed by the unauthorized publication of his radical poetical drama *Wat Tyler*, which he had written in 1794 but had prudently left in manuscript. Byron reminds him of it in the subtitle. When King George III died in 1820—Shelley in his *Sonnet: England in 1819* had called him, accurately enough, "an old, mad, blind, despised, and dying king"— Southey did his official duty by writing *A Vision of Judgment* (1821). In this fulsome eulogy George III goes to heaven, confounds such detractors as John Wilkes and Junius, and obtains a testimonial of noble character from his old enemy, George Washington. The vision ends with the King, beatified, ceremoniously admitted to heaven.

Byron, responding to reports that Southey was vilifying him, had ridiculed the poet in his "Dedication" to Canto I of *Don Juan*. In the Preface to his *Vision of Judgment,* Southey then exhibited his bad judgment by denouncing Byron as head of the "Satanic School" of poetry, combining "lascivious" passages with "a satanic spirit of pride and audacious impiety." Byron immediately responded with *The Vision of Judgment,* in which he purports to tell the true story of how, with the unwitting help of Southey, King George managed to get into heaven. The poem is in the genre of the satiric attack on literary "dunces" by Dryden and Pope, but is written in the ottava rima stanza and the easy colloquial manner of Byron's *Don Juan*. In its quick, sure characterization, the pace and economy of its narrative, its inventiveness in detail, above all in the high spirits and unfailing good humor with which the author demolishes his opponent, this poem represents Byron at his masterful best.

2. "Quevedo Revived." Quevedo was a 17th-century Spanish author of *Sueños,* "Visions," written in prose and predominantly satirical in tone.

3. Quoted, not quite accurately, from *The Merchant of Venice,* IV.i.340–41.

4. The last year of the old régime in France, before the outbreak of the Revolution in 1789.

The devils had ta'en a longer, stronger pull,
And "a pull altogether," as they say
At sea—which drew most souls another way.

2

The angels all were singing out of tune,
    And hoarse with having little else to do,
Excepting to wind up the sun and moon,
    Or curb a runaway young star or two,
Or wild colt of a comet, which too soon
    Broke out of bounds o'er th' ethereal blue,
Splitting some planet with its playful tail,
As boats are sometimes by a wanton whale.

3

The guardian seraphs had retired on high,
    Finding their charges past all care below;
Terrestrial business filled nought in the sky
    Save the recording angel's black bureau;
Who found, indeed, the facts to multiply
    With such rapidity of vice and woe,
That he had stripped off both his wings in quills,
And yet was in arrear of human ills.

4

His business so augmented of late years,
    That he was forced, against his will no doubt
(Just like those cherubs, earthly ministers),
    For some resource to turn himself about,
And claim the help of his celestial peers,
    To aid him ere he should be quite worn out
By the increased demand for his remarks;
Six angels and twelve saints were named his clerks.

5

This was a handsome board—at least for heaven;
    And yet they had even then enough to do,
So many conquerors' cars were daily driven,
    So many kingdoms fitted up anew;
Each day too slew its thousands six or seven,
    Till at the crowning carnage, Waterloo,
They threw their pens down in divine disgust—
The page was so besmeared with blood and dust.

6

This by the way; 'tis not mine to record
    What angels shrink from: even the very devil
On this occasion his own work abhorred,
    So surfeited with the infernal revel:
Though he himself had sharpened every sword,
    It almost quenched his innate thirst of evil.
(Here Satan's sole good work deserves insertion—
'Tis, that he has both generals in reversion.[5])

---

5. Satan has the legal right to the future possession of both Napoleon and Wellington, the commanding officers at the Battle of Waterloo.

7

Let's skip a few short years of hollow peace,
    Which peopled earth no better, hell as wont,   50
And heaven none—they form the tyrant's lease,
    With nothing but new names subscribed upon 't;
'Twill one day finish: meantime they increase,
    "With seven heads and ten horns," and all in front,
Like Saint John's foretold beast;[6] but ours are born   55
Less formidable in the head than horn.

8

In the first year of freedom's second dawn[7]
    Died George the Third; although no tyrant, one
Who shielded tyrants, till each sense withdrawn
    Left him nor mental nor external sun: 60
A better farmer ne'er brushed dew from lawn,
    A worse king never left a realm undone!
He died—but left his subjects still behind,
One half as mad—and t'other no less blind.

9

He died! his death made no great stir on earth;   65
    His burial made some pomp; there was profusion
Of velvet, gilding, brass, and no great dearth
    Of aught but tears—save those shed by collusion.
For these things may be bought at their true worth;
    Of elegy there was the due infusion—   70
Bought also; and the torches, cloaks, and banners,
Heralds, and relics of old Gothic manners,

10

Formed a sepulchral melodrame. Of all
    The fools who flocked to swell or see the show,
Who cared about the corpse? The funeral   75
    Made the attraction, and the black the woe.
There throbbed not there a thought which pierced the pall;
    And when the gorgeous coffin was laid low,
It seemed the mockery of hell to fold
The rottenness of eighty years in gold.   80

11

So mix his body with the dust! It might
    Return to what it *must* far sooner, were
The natural compound left alone to fight
    Its way back into earth, and fire, and air;
But the unnatural balsams[8] merely blight   85
    What nature made him at his birth, as bare
As the mere million's base unmummied clay—
Yet all his spices but prolong decay.

12

He's dead—and upper earth with him has done;
    He's buried; save the undertaker's bill,   90

6. The Book of Revelation describes such a beast, xiii.1.

7. 1820 was a year of new revolutionary movements in Italy and other countries of southern Europe.

8. I.e., embalming fluids.

Or lapidary scrawl,[9] the world is gone
   For him, unless he left a German will;
But where's the proctor who will ask his son?[1]
   In whom his qualities are reigning still,
Except that household virtue, most uncommon,   95
Of constancy to a bad, ugly woman.

       13
"God save the king!" It is a large economy
   In God to save the like; but if he will
Be saving, all the better; for not one am I
   Of those who think damnation better still: 100
I hardly know too if not quite alone am I
   In this small hope of bettering future ill
By circumscribing, with some slight restriction,
The eternity of hell's hot jurisdiction.

       14
I know this is unpopular; I know   105
   'Tis blasphemous; I know one may be damned
For hoping no one else may e'er be so;
   I know my catechism; I know we're crammed
With the best doctrines till we quite o'erflow;
   I know that all save England's church have shammed,   110
And that the other twice two hundred churches
And synagogues have made a *damned* bad purchase.

       15
God help us all! God help me too! I am,
   God knows, as helpless as the devil can wish,
And not a whit more difficult to damn,   115
   Than is to bring to land a late-hooked fish,
Or to the butcher to purvey the lamb;
   Not that I'm fit for such a noble dish,
As one day will be that immortal fry
Of almost everybody born to die.   120

       16
Saint Peter sat by the celestial gate,
   And nodded o'er his keys; when, lo! there came
A wondrous noise he had not heard of late—
   A rushing sound of wind, and stream, and flame;
In short, a roar of things extremely great,   125
   Which would have made aught save a saint exclaim;
But he, with first a start and then a wink,
Said, "There's another star gone out, I think!"

       17
But ere he could return to his repose,
   A cherub flapped his right wing o'er his eyes—   130
At which St. Peter yawned, and rubbed his nose:
   "Saint porter," said the angel, "prithee rise!"
Waving a goodly wing, which glowed, as glows

9. Inscription cut into a stone monument.
1. A King's Proctor is an official who intervenes in the probate of a will, when chicanery is suspected. Byron alludes to the scandal that the will of George I, of the German House of Hanover, had been hidden by his son, George II, who was the grandfather of the late George III.

An earthly peacock's tail, with heavenly dyes:
To which the saint replied, "Well, what's the matter?   135
"Is Lucifer come back with all this clatter?"

18

"No," quoth the cherub; "George the Third is dead."
    "And who *is* George the Third?" replied the apostle:
"*What George? what Third?*" "The king of England," said
    The angel. "Well! he won't find kings to jostle   140
Him on his way; but does he wear his head;
    Because the last we saw here had a tustle,
And ne'er would have got into heaven's good graces,
Had he not flung his head in all our faces.[2]

19

"He was, if I remember, king of France;   145
    That head of his, which could not keep a crown
On earth, yet ventured in my face to advance
    A claim to those of martyrs—like my own:
If I had had my sword, as I had once
    When I cut ears off, I had cut him down;[3]   150
But having but my *keys*, and not my brand,
I only knocked his head from out his hand.

20

"And then he set up such a headless howl,
    That all the saints came out and took him in;
And there he sits by St. Paul, cheek by jowl;   155
    That fellow Paul—the parvenu! The skin
Of St. Bartholomew,[4] which makes his cowl
    In heaven, and upon earth redeemed his sin
So as to make a martyr, never sped
Better than did this weak and wooden head.   160

21

"But had it come up here upon its shoulders,
    There would have been a different tale to tell:
The fellow-feeling in the saint's beholders
    Seems to have acted on them like a spell;
And so this very foolish head heaven solders   165
    Back on its trunk: it may be very well,
And seems the custom here to overthrow
Whatever has been wisely done below."

22

The angel answered, "Peter! do not pout:
    The king who comes has head and all entire,   170
And never knew much what it was about—
    He did as doth the puppet—by its wire,
And will be judged like all the rest, no doubt:
    My business and your own is not to inquire
Into such matters, but to mind our cue—   175
Which is to act as we are bid to do."

2. Louis XVI, who had been guillotined in January, 1793.
3. When the officers came to take Jesus, "Simon Peter having a sword drew it, and smote the high priest's servant, and cut off his right ear" (John xviii.10). "Brand," line 151, is archaic for "sword."
4. According to tradition, the martyred St. Bartholomew was flayed alive.

23

While thus they spake, the angelic caravan,
    Arriving like a rush of mighty wind,
Cleaving the fields of space, as doth the swan
    Some silver stream (say Ganges, Nile, or Inde,   180
Or Thames, or Tweed), and 'midst them an old man
    With an old soul, and both extremely blind,
Halted before the gate, and in his shroud
Seated their fellow traveler on a cloud.

24

But bringing up the rear of this bright host   185
    A Spirit of a different aspect waved
His wings, like thunder clouds above some coast
    Whose barren beach with frequent wrecks is paved;
His brow was like the deep when tempest-tossed;
    Fierce and unfathomable thoughts engraved   190
Eternal wrath on his immortal face,
And *where* he gazed a gloom pervaded space.

25

As he drew near, he gazed upon the gate
    Ne'er to be entered more by him or Sin,
With such a glance of supernatural hate,   195
    As made Saint Peter wish himself within;
He pattered with his keys at a great rate,
    And sweated through his apostolic skin:
Of course his perspiration was but ichor,[5]
Or some such other spiritual liquor.   200

26

The very cherubs huddled all together,
    Like birds when soars the falcon; and they felt
A tingling to the tip of every feather,
    And formed a circle like Orion's belt
Around their poor old charge; who scarce knew whither   205
    His guards had led him, though they gently dealt
With royal manes[6] (for by many stories,
And true, we learn the angels all are Tories).

27

As things were in this posture, the gate flew
    Asunder, and the flashing of its hinges   210
Flung over space an universal hue
    Of many-colored flame, until its tinges
Reached even our speck of earth, and made a new
    Aurora borealis spread its fringes
O'er the North Pole; the same seen, when ice-bound,   215
By Captain Parry's[7] crew, in "Melville's Sound."

28

And from the gate thrown open issued beaming
    A beautiful and mighty Thing of Light,

---

5. The fluid in the veins of the gods.
6. In Roman religion, spirits of the dead (pronounced *mā'nēz*).

7. Captain William Edward Parry, in his account of his *Voyage in 1819–20,* in search of a northwest passage.

Radiant with glory, like a banner streaming
    Victorious from some world-o'erthrowing fight: 220
My poor comparisons must needs be teeming
    With earthly likenesses, for here the night
Of clay obscures our best conceptions, saving
Johanna Southcote,[8] or Bob Southey raving.

29

'Twas the archangel Michael: all men know   225
    The make of angels and archangels, since
There's scarce a scribbler has not one to show,
    From the fiends' leader to the angels' prince.
There also are some altarpieces, though
    I really can't say that they much evince   230
One's inner notions of immortal spirits;
But let the connoisseurs explain *their* merits.

30

Michael flew forth in glory and in good;
    A goodly work of him from whom all glory
And good arise; the portal past—he stood;   235
    Before him the young cherubs and saints hoary—
(I say *young*, begging to be understood
    By looks, not years; and should be very sorry
To state, they were not older than St. Peter,
But merely that they seemed a little sweeter).   240

31

The cherubs and the saints bowed down before
    That arch-angelic hierarch, the first
Of essences angelical, who wore
    The aspect of a god; but this ne'er nursed
Pride in his heavenly bosom, in whose core   245
    No thought, save for his Master's service, durst
Intrude, however glorified and high;
He knew him but the viceroy of the sky.

32

He and the somber silent Spirit met—
    They knew each other both for good and ill;   250
Such was their power, that neither could forget
    His former friend and future foe; but still
There was a high, immortal, proud regret
    In either's eye, as if 'twere less their will
Than destiny to make the eternal years   255
Their date of war, and their "champ clos"[9] the spheres.

33

But here they were in neutral space: we know
    From Job, that Satan hath the power to pay
A heavenly visit thrice a year or so;

8. Joanna Southcott (1750–1814) was a servant girl who, claiming direct communications from the Almighty, became head of a religious sect. In 1813 she proclaimed that she was about to give birth to a son, Shiloh, who would redeem the world. The pregnancy turned out to be a tumor, of which she died the following year.
9. "Enclosed field," the arena for knightly tournaments.

And that the "sons of God," like those of clay,   260
  Must keep him company;[1] and we might show
    From the same book, in how polite a way
The dialogue is held between the Powers
Of Good and Evil—but 'twould take up hours.

34

And this is not a theologic tract,   265
  To prove with Hebrew and with Arabic
If Job be allegory or a fact,
  But a true narrative; and thus I pick
From out the whole but such and such an act
  As sets aside the slightest thought of trick.   270
'Tis every tittle true, beyond suspicion,
And accurate as any other vision.

35

The spirits were in neutral space, before
  The gate of heaven; like eastern thresholds is
The place where Death's grand cause is argued o'er,[2]   275
  And souls despatched to that world or to this;
And therefore Michael and the other wore
  A civil aspect: though they did not kiss,
Yet still between his Darkness and his Brightness
There passed a mutual glance of great politeness.   280

36

The Archangel bowed, not like a modern beau,
  But with a graceful oriental bend,
Pressing one radiant arm just where below
  The heart in good men is supposed to tend.
He turned as to an equal, not too low,   285
  But kindly; Satan met his ancient friend
With more hauteur, as might an old Castilian
Poor noble meet a mushroom rich civilian.[3]

37

He merely bent his diabolic brow
  An instant; and then raising it, he stood   290
In act to assert his right or wrong, and show
  Cause why King George by no means could or should
Make out a case to be exempt from woe
  Eternal, more than other kings, endued
With better sense and hearts, whom history mentions,   295
Who long have "paved hell with their good intentions."[4]

38

Michael began: "What wouldst thou with this man,
  Now dead, and brought before the Lord? What ill
Hath he wrought since his mortal race began,
  That thou canst claim him? Speak! and do thy will,   300

---

1. Job 1.6. "There was a day when the sons of God came to present themselves before the Lord, and Satan came also among them."
2. The gateways of walled cities in the Middle East were sometimes used for public debates and to administer justice.
3. Byron contrasts ancient Spanish noblemen with *nouveaux riches* who spring up as rapidly as mushrooms.
4. An old English proverb.

If it be just: if in this earthly span
   He hath been greatly failing to fulfil
His duties as a king and mortal, say,
   And he is thine; if not, let him have way."

39

"Michael!" replied the Prince of Air, "even here,   305
   Before the Gate of him thou servest, must
I claim my subject: and will make appear
   That as he was my worshiper in dust,
So shall he be in spirit, although dear
   To thee and thine, because nor wine nor lust   310
Were of his weaknesses; yet on the throne
He reigned o'er millions to serve me alone.

40

"Look to *our* earth, or rather *mine*; it was,
   Once, more thy master's: but I triumph not
In this poor planet's conquest; nor, alas!   315
   Need he thou servest envy me my lot:
With all the myriads of bright worlds which pass
   In worship round him, he may have forgot
Yon weak creation of such paltry things:
I think few worth damnation save their kings—   320

41

"And these but as a kind of quitrent,[5] to
   Assert my right as lord: and even had
I such an inclination, 'twere (as you
   Well know) superfluous; they are grown so bad,
That hell has nothing better left to do   325
   Than leave them to themselves: so much more mad
And evil by their own internal curse,
Heaven cannot make them better, nor I worse.

42

"Look to the earth, I said, and say again:
   When this old, blind, mad, helpless, weak, poor worm   330
Began in youth's first bloom and flush to reign,
   The world and he both wore a different form,
And much of earth and all the watery plain
   Of ocean called him king: through many a storm
His isles had floated on the abyss of time;   335
For the rough virtues chose them for their clime.

43

"He came to his scepter young; he leaves it old:
   Look to the state in which he found his realm,
And left it; and his annals too behold,
   How to a minion first he gave the helm,[6]   340
How grew upon his heart a thirst for gold,
   The beggar's vice, which can but overwhelm
The meanest hearts; and for the rest, but glance
Thine eye along America and France.

5. A fixed rent, paid in place of services
to a feudal lord.
6. The unpopular Earl of Bute, whom

George III made Prime Minister in
1802.

44

" 'Tis true, he was a tool from first to last   345
    (I have the workmen safe); but as a tool
So let him be consumed. From out the past
    Of ages, since mankind have known the rule
Of monarchs—from the bloody rolls amassed
    Of sin and slaughter—from the Caesar's school,   350
Take the worst pupil; and produce a reign
More drenched with gore, more cumbered with the slain.

45

"He ever warred with freedom and the free:
    Nations as men, home subjects, foreign foes,
So that[7] they uttered the word 'Liberty!'
    Found George the Third their first opponent. Whose   355
History was ever stained as his will be
    With national and individual woes?
I grant his household abstinence; I grant
His neutral virtues, which most monarchs want;   360

46

"I know he was a constant consort; own
    He was a decent sire, and middling lord.
All this is much, and most upon a throne;
    As temperance, if at Apicius' board,[8]
Is more than at an anchorite's[9] supper shown.   365
    I grant him all the kindest can accord;
And this was well for him, but not for those
Millions who found him what oppression chose.

47

"The New World shook him off; the Old yet groans
    Beneath what he and his prepared, if not   370
Completed: he leaves heirs on many thrones
    To all his vices, without what begot
Compassion for him—his tame virtues; drones
    Who sleep, or despots who have now forgot
A lesson which shall be re-taught them, wake   375
Upon the thrones of earth; but let them quake!

48

"Five millions of the primitive,[1] who hold
    The faith which makes ye great on earth, implored
A *part* of that vast *all* they held of old—
    Freedom to worship—not alone your Lord,   380
Michael, but you, and you, Saint Peter! Cold
    Must be your souls, if you have not abhorred
The foe to Catholic participation
In all the license of a Christian nation.

49

"True! he allowed them to pray God; but as   385
    A consequence of prayer, refused the law

---

7. "Provided that."
8. I.e., At the table of Apicius (a famed Roman gourmet in the time of Augustus).
9. A religious hermit's.

1. The Irish Catholics. In 1795 George had opposed the Catholic Emancipation Bill, which gave Roman Catholics the right to hold public offices (line 383).

Which would have placed them upon the same base
   With those who did not hold the saints in awe."
But here Saint Peter started from his place,
   And cried, "You may the prisoner withdraw: 390
Ere heaven shall ope her portals to this Guelph,[2]
While I am guard, may I be damned myself!

50

"Sooner will I with Cerberus[3] exchange
   My office (and *his* is no sinecure)
Than see this royal Bedlam bigot range   395
   The azure fields of heaven, of that be sure!"
"Saint!" replied Satan, "you do well to avenge
   The wrongs he made your satellites endure;
And if to this exchange you should be given,
I'll try to coax *our* Cerberus up to heaven."   400

51

Here Michael interposed: "Good saint! and devil!
   Pray, not so fast; you both outrun discretion.
Saint Peter! you were wont to be more civil!
   Satan! excuse this warmth of his expression,
And condescension to the vulgar's level: 405
   Even saints sometimes forget themselves in session.
Have you got more to say?"—"No."—"If you please,
I'll trouble you to call your witnesses."

52

Then Satan turned and waved his swarthy hand,
   Which stirred with its electric qualities   410
Clouds farther off than we can understand,
   Although we find him sometimes in our skies;
Infernal thunder shook both sea and land
   In all the planets, and hell's batteries
Let off the artillery, which Milton mentions   415
As one of Satan's most sublime inventions.[4]

53

This was a signal unto such damned souls
   As have the privilege of their damnation
Extended far beyond the mere controls
   Of worlds past, present, or to come; no station   420
Is theirs particularly in the rolls
   Of hell assigned; but where their inclination
Or business carries them in search of game,
They may range freely—being damned the same.

54

They're proud of this—as very well they may,   425
   It being a sort of knighthood, or gilt key
Stuck in their loins;[5] or like an "entré"
   Up the back stairs, or such freemasonry.

---

2. The House of Hanover was descended from the German Guelphs.
3. The three-headed dog guarding the entrance to Hades.
4. In *Paradise Lost* VI. 469 ff., Satan announced his invention of the cannon for use in the war in heaven.
5. A gold key hung from the belt betokens certain official positions at the English court.

I borrow my comparisons from clay,
  Being clay myself. Let not those spirits be   430
Offended with such base low likenesses;
We know their posts are nobler far than these.

55

When the great signal ran from heaven to hell—
  About ten million times the distance reckoned
From our sun to its earth, as we can tell   435
  How much time it takes up, even to a second,
For every ray that travels to dispel
  The fogs of London, through which, dimly beaconed,
The weathercocks are gilt some thrice a year,
If that the *summer* is not too severe—   440

56

I say that I can tell—'twas half a minute:
  I know the solar beams take up more time
Ere, packed up for their journey, they begin it;
  But then their telegraph[6] is less sublime,
And if they ran a race, they would not win it   445
  'Gainst Satan's couriers bound for their own clime.
The sun takes up some years for every ray
To reach its goal—the devil not half a day.

57

Upon the verge of space, about the size
  Of half-a-crown, a little speck appeared   450
(I've seen a something like it in the skies
  In the Aegean, ere a squall); it neared,
And, growing bigger, took another guise;
  Like an aërial ship it tacked, and steered,
Or *was* steered (I am doubtful of the grammar   455
Of the last phrase, which makes the stanza stammer—

58

But take your choice); and then it grew a cloud;
  And so it was—a cloud of witnesses.
But such a cloud! No land e'er saw a crowd
  Of locusts numerous as the heavens saw these;   460
They shadowed with their myriads space; their loud
  And varied cries were like those of wild geese
(If nations may be likened to a goose),
And realized the phrase of "hell broke loose."[7]

59

Here crashed a sturdy oath of stout John Bull,   465
  Who damned away his eyes as heretofore:
There Paddy brogued "By Jasus!"—"What's your wull?"
  The temperate Scot exclaimed: the French ghost swore
In certain terms I shan't translate in full,
  As the first coachman will; and 'midst the war,   470

---

6. In its original sense, any apparatus   7. *Paradise Lost* IV. 918.
for transmitting signals at a distance.

The voice of Jonathan was heard to express,
    "*Our* president is going to war, I guess."[8]

60

Besides there were the Spaniard, Dutch, and Dane;
    In short, an universal shoal of shades,
From Otaheite's isle[9] to Salisbury Plain,   475
    Of all climes and professions, years and trades,
Ready to swear against the good king's reign,
    Bitter as clubs in cards are against spades;
All summoned by this grand "subpoena," to
Try if kings mayn't be damned like me or you.   480

61

When Michael saw this host, he first grew pale,
    As angels can; next, like Italian twilight,
He turned all colors—as a peacock's tail,
    Or sunset streaming through a Gothic skylight
In some old abbey, or a trout not stale,   485
    Or distant lightning on the horizon *by* night,
Or a fresh rainbow, or a grand review
Of thirty regiments in red, green, and blue.

62

Then he addressed himself to Satan: "Why—
    My good old friend, for such I deem you, though   490
Our different parties make us fight so shy,
    I ne'er mistake you for a *personal* foe;
Our difference is *political*, and I
    Trust that, whatever may occur below,
You know my great respect for you: and this   495
Makes me regret whate'er you do amiss—

63

"Why, my dear Lucifer, would you abuse
    My call for witnesses? I did not mean
That you should half of earth and hell produce;
    'Tis even superfluous, since two honest, clean,   500
True testimonies are enough: we lose
    Our time, nay, our eternity, between
The accusation and defense: if we
Hear both, 'twill stretch our immortality."

64

Satan replied, "To me the matter is   505
    Indifferent, in a personal point of view:
I can have fifty better souls than this
    With far less trouble than we have gone through
Already; and I merely argued his
    Late majesty of Britain's case with you   510
Upon a point of form: you may dispose
Of him; I've kings enough below, God knows!"

8. "Brother Jonathan" was the name applied to America and Americans, now replaced by "Uncle Sam"; the "I guess" was used by Byron as an obvious Americanism. This was written during the troubled Anglo-American relations after the War of 1812.
9. The old name for Tahiti.

65

Thus spoke the Demon (late called "multifaced"
   By multo-scribbling Southey[1]). "Then we'll call
One or two persons of the myriads placed   515
   Around our congress, and dispense with all
The rest," quoth Michael: "Who may be so graced
   As to speak first? there's choice enough—who shall
It be?" Then Satan answered, "There are many;
But you may choose Jack Wilkes[2] as well as any."   520

66

A merry, cock-eyed, curious-looking sprite
   Upon the instant started from the throng,
Dressed in a fashion now forgotten quite;
   For all the fashions of the flesh stick long
By people in the next world; where unite   525
   All the costumes since Adam's, right or wrong,
From Eve's fig leaf down to the petticoat,
Almost as scanty, of days less remote.

67

The spirit looked around upon the crowds
   Assembled, and exclaimed, "My friends of all   530
The spheres, we shall catch cold amongst these clouds;
   So let's to business: why this general call?
If those are freeholders I see in shrouds,
   And 'tis for an election that they bawl,
Behold a candidate with unturned coat!   535
Saint Peter, may I count upon your vote?"

68

"Sir," replied Michael, "you mistake; these things
   Are of a former life, and what we do
Above is more august; to judge of kings
   Is the tribunal met: so now you know."   540
"Then I presume those gentlemen with wings,"
   Said Wilkes, "are cherubs; and that soul below
Looks much like George the Third, but to my mind
A good deal older—Bless me! is he blind?"

69

"He is what you behold him, and his doom   545
   Depends upon his deeds," the Angel said.
"If you have aught to arraign in him, the tomb
   Gives license to the humblest beggar's head
To lift itself against the loftiest."—"Some,"
   Said Wilkes, "don't wait to see them laid in lead,   550
For such a liberty—and I, for one,
Have told them what I thought beneath the sun."

1. In *A Vision of Judgment* V. 70.
2. John Wilkes (1727–97), notorious libertine, wit, and courageous political radical, who in 1764 was expelled from the House of Commons and driven into exile for his libelous attack on George III in his weekly periodical, *The North Briton*. He later came back to England, became Lord Mayor of London, and was triumphantly returned to Parliament. For a supreme example of the wit and aplomb for which Byron admired Wilkes, see Boswell's account of Dr. Johnson's dinner with him in Volume 1.

70

"*Above* the sun repeat, then, what thou hast
    To urge against him," said the Archangel. "Why,"
Replied the spirit, "since old scores are past,   555
    Must I turn evidence? In faith, not I.
Besides, I beat him hollow at the last,
    With all his Lords and Commons:[3] in the sky
I don't like ripping up old stories, since
His conduct was but natural in a prince.   560

71

"Foolish, no doubt, and wicked, to oppress
    A poor unlucky devil without a shilling;
But then I blame the man himself much less
    Than Bute and Grafton,[4] and shall be unwilling
To see him punished here for their excess,   565
    Since they were both damned long ago, and still in
Their place below: for me, I have forgiven,
And vote his 'habeas corpus' into heaven."

72

"Wilkes," said the Devil, "I understand all this;
    You turned to half a courtier ere you died,[5]
And seem to think it would not be amiss   570
    To grow a whole one on the other side
Of Charon's ferry;[6] you forget that *his*
    Reign is concluded; whatsoe'er betide,
He won't be sovereign more: you've lost your labor   575
For at the best he will but be your neighbor.

73

"However, I knew what to think of it,
    When I beheld you in your jesting way
Flitting and whispering round about the spit
    Where Belial, upon duty for the day,   580
With Fox's lard was basting William Pitt,[7]
    His pupil; I knew what to think, I say:
That fellow even in hell breeds farther ills;
I'll have him *gagged*—'twas one of his own bills.[8]

74

"Call Junius!"[9] From the crowd a shadow stalked,   585

---

3. In 1782 Wilkes succeeded in getting the House of Commons to expunge the record of his expulsion.
4. The Duke of Grafton, like the Earl of Bute, was a minister subservient to George III.
5. Wilkes in his latter years softened his opposition and moved in higher social circles.
6. In Greek mythology, Charon ferried the dead to the underworld across the river Styx.
7. Charles James Fox, statesman and political opponent of William Pitt, prime minister under George III, was notably corpulent.
8. The Alien and Sedition Bills of 1795 severely restricted freedom of speech and of the press.
9. Pseudonym of the writer of a brilliant series of letters (1769–71), attacking supporters of George III and the King himself. His identity is an unsolved political mystery; among more than fifty possibilities proposed are Edmund Burke, John Horne Tooke, and Sir Philip Francis, mentioned in lines 631–32. When the letters were published as a book, the title-page read: *Letters of Junius, Stat Nominis Umbra* ("he stands, the shadow of a name"); hence the allusions, lines 593 ff., 667. The Latin phrase is from Lucan's *Pharsalia* I.135.

And at the name there was a general squeeze,
So that the very ghosts no longer walked
   In comfort, at their own aërial ease,
But were all rammed, and jammed (but to be balked,
   As we shall see), and jostled hands and knees,   590
Like wind compressed and pent within a bladder,
Or like a human colic, which is sadder.

75

The shadow came—a tall, thin, gray-haired figure,
   That looked as it had been a shade on earth;
Quick in its motions, with an air of vigor,
   But nought to mark its breeding or its birth: 595
Now it waxed little, then again grew bigger,
   With now an air of gloom, or savage mirth;
But as you gazed upon its features, they
Changed every instant—to *what*, none could say.   600

76

The more intently the ghosts gazed, the less
   Could they distinguish whose the features were;
The Devil himself seemed puzzled even to guess;
   They varied like a dream—now here, now there;
And several people swore from out the press,   605
   They knew him perfectly; and one could swear
He was his father: upon which another
Was sure he was his mother's cousin's brother:

77

Another, that he was a duke, or knight,
   An orator, a lawyer, or a priest,   610
A nabob,[1] a man-midwife; but the wight
   Mysterious changed his countenance at least
As oft as they their minds: though in full sight
   He stood, the puzzle only was increased;
The man was a phantasmagoria in   615
Himself—he was so volatile and thin.

78

The moment that you had pronounced him *one*,
   Presto! his face changed, and he was another;
And when that change was hardly well put on,
   It varied, till I don't think his own mother   620
(If that he had a mother) would her son
   Have known, he shifted so from one to t'other;
Till guessing from a pleasure grew a task,
At this epistolary "Iron Mask."[2]

79

For sometimes he like Cerberus would seem—   625
   "Three gentlemen at once" (as sagely says
Good Mrs. Malaprop[3]); then you might deem

---

1. A man of great wealth, especially one who has returned to England with a fortune acquired in India.
2. "The Man in the Iron Mask" was a state prisoner in the reign of Louis XIV, whose identity was thus concealed.
3. A character in R. B. Sheridan's *The Rivals*, who comically misused words; the word "malapropism" derives from her name.

That he was not even *one*; now many rays
Were flashing round him; and now a thick steam
   Hid him from sight—like fogs on London days: 630
Now Burke, now Tooke, he grew to people's fancies,
And certes often like Sir Philip Francis.

80

I've an hypothesis—'tis quite my own;
   I never let it out till now, for fear
Of doing people harm about the throne,   635
   And injuring some minister or peer,
On whom the stigma might perhaps be blown;
   It is—my gentle public, lend thine ear!
'Tis, that what Junius we are wont to call
Was *really*, *truly*, nobody at all.   640

81

I don't see wherefore letters should not be
   Written without hands, since we daily view
Them written without heads; and books, we see,
   Are filled as well without the latter too:
And really till we fix on somebody   645
   For certain sure to claim them as his due,
Their author, like the Niger's mouth,[4] will bother
The world to say if *there* be mouth or author.

82

"And who and what art thou?" the Archangel said.
   "For *that* you may consult my title page,"   650
Replied this mighty shadow of a shade:
   "If I have kept my secret half an age,
I scarce shall tell it now."—"Canst thou upbraid,"
   Continued Michael, "George Rex, or allege
Aught further?" Junius answered, "You had better   655
First ask him for *his* answer to my letter:

83

"My charges upon record will outlast
   The brass of both his epitaph and tomb."
"Repent'st thou not," said Michael, "of some past
   Exaggeration? something which may doom   660
Thyself if false, as him if true? Thou wast
   Too bitter—is it not so?—in thy gloom
Of passion?"—"Passion!" cried the phantom dim,
"I loved my country, and I hated him.

84

"What I have written, I have written:[5] let   665
   The rest be on his head or mine!" So spoke
Old "Nominis Umbra"; and while speaking yet,
   Away he melted in celestial smoke.
Then Satan said to Michael, "Don't forget
   To call George Washington, and John Horne Tooke,[6]   670

---

4. Several recent British expeditions to explore the course of the river Niger, in western Africa, had ended in failure.
5. Said by Pilate, John xix.22.

6. A prominent English opponent of the war against the American colonies; see note to line 585.

And Franklin"—but at this time there was heard
A cry for room, though not a phantom stirred.

85

At length with jostling, elbowing, and the aid
   Of cherubim appointed to that post,
The devil Asmodeus[7] to the circle made   675
   His way, and looked as if his journey cost
Some trouble. When his burden down he laid,
   "What's this?" cried Michael; "why, 'tis not a ghost?"
"I know it," quoth the incubus; "but he
Shall be one, if you leave the affair to me.   680

86

"Confound the renegado! I have sprained
   My left wing, he's so heavy; one would think
Some of his works about his neck were chained.
   But to the point; while hovering o'er the brink
Of Skiddaw (where as usual it still rained),[8]   685
   I saw a taper, far below me, wink,
And stooping, caught this fellow at a libel—
No less on history than the Holy Bible.

87

"The former is the devil's scripture, and
   The latter yours, good Michael: so the affair   690
Belongs to all of us, you understand.
   I snatched him up just as you see him there,
And brought him off for sentence out of hand:
   I've scarcely been ten minutes in the air—
At least a quarter it can hardly be: 695
I dare say that his wife is still at tea."

88

Here Satan said, "I know this man of old,
   And have expected him for some time here;
A sillier fellow you will scarce behold,
   Or more conceited in his petty sphere: 700
But surely it was not worth while to fold
   Such trash below your wing, Asmodeus dear:
We had the poor wretch safe (without being bored
With carriage) coming of his own accord.

89

"But since he's here, let's see what he has done."   705
   "Done!" cried Asmodeus, "he anticipates
The very business you are now upon,
   And scribbles as if head clerk to the Fates.
Who knows to what his ribaldry may run,
   When such an ass as this, like Balaam's,[9] prates?"   710
"Let's hear," quoth Michael, "what he has to say:
You know we're bound to that in every way."

7. The devil in Le Sage's *Le Diable Boiteux* ("The Lame Devil"), published 1707, who carries Don Cleofas to the summit of San Salvador.

8. Mount Skiddaw, near Southey's home in the Lake Country.

9. Balaam's ass was granted speech in Numbers xxii.28 ff.

90

Now the bard, glad to get an audience, which
   By no means often was his case below,
Began to cough, and hawk, and hem, and pitch   715
   His voice into that awful note of woe
To all unhappy hearers within reach
   Of poets when the tide of rhyme's in flow;
But stuck fast with his first hexameter,
Not one of all whose gouty feet would stir.   720

91

But ere the spavined dactyls[1] could be spurred
   Into recitative, in great dismay
Both cherubim and seraphim were heard
   To murmur loudly through their long array;
And Michael rose ere he could get a word   725
   Of all his foundered verses under way,
And cried, "For God's sake stop, my friend! 'twere best—
Non Di, non homines[2]—you know the rest."

92

A general bustle spread throughout the throng,
   Which seemed to hold all verse in detestation;   730
The angels had of course enough of song
   When upon service; and the generation
Of ghosts had heard too much in life, not long
   Before, to profit by a new occasion:
The monarch, mute till then, exclaimed, "What! what!   735
Pye[3] come again? No more—no more of that!"

93

The tumult grew; an universal cough
   Convulsed the skies, as during a debate,
When Castlereagh[4] has been up long enough
   (Before he was first minister of state,   740
I mean—the *slaves hear now*); some cried "Off, off!"
   As at a farce; till, grown quite desperate,
The bard Saint Peter prayed to interpose
(Himself an author)[5] only for his prose.

94

The varlet was not an ill-favored knave;   745
   A good deal like a vulture in the face,
With a hook nose and a hawk's eye, which gave
   A smart and sharper-looking sort of grace
To his whole aspect, which, though rather grave,

1. Southey's *A Vision of Judgment* was written in dactylic hexameters, a very awkward measure in English. A "spavined" horse is a lame one.
2. Horace, *Art of Poetry*, 372–73: "mediocribus esse poetis / Non homines, non di, non concessere columnae" ("mediocrity in poets has never been tolerated by either men, or gods, or booksellers").
3. Henry James Pye, a bad and much ridiculed poet, Southey's predecessor as poet laureate.
4. Viscount Castlereagh was foreign secretary when Byron wrote his poem. "The slaves hear now": i.e., now that he is Prime Minister members of the House of Commons listen obsequiously.
5. The reference is to the first and second epistles of Peter, very short books in the New Testament.

Was by no means so ugly as his case;
But that, indeed, was hopeless as can be,
Quite a poetic felony "*de se*."[6]   750

95

Then Michael blew his trump, and stilled the noise
    With one still greater, as is yet the mode
On earth besides; except some grumbling voice,   755
    Which now and then will make a slight inroad
Upon decorous silence, few will twice
    Lift up their lungs when fairly overcrowed;
And now the bard could plead his own bad cause,
With all the attitudes of self-applause.   760

96

He said—(I only give the heads)—he said,
    He meant no harm in scribbling; 'twas his way
Upon all topics; 'twas, besides, his bread,
    Of which he buttered both sides; 'twould delay
Too long the assembly (he was pleased to dread),   765
    And take up rather more time than a day,
To name his works—he would but cite a few—
"Wat Tyler"—"Rhymes on Blenheim"—"Waterloo."

97

He had written praises of a regicide;[7]
    He had written praises of all kings what ever;   770
He had written for republics far and wide,
    And then against them bitterer than ever:
For pantisocracy[8] he once had cried
    Aloud, a scheme less moral than 'twas clever;
Then grew a hearty anti-jacobin—   775
Had turned his coat—and would have turned his skin.

98

He had sung against all battles, and again
    In their high praise and glory; he had called
Reviewing "the ungentle craft,"[9] and then
    Become as base a critic as e'er crawled—   780
Fed, paid, and pampered by the very men
    By whom his muse and morals had been mauled:
He had written much blank verse, and blanker prose,
And more of both than anybody knows.

99

He had written Wesley's life—here turning round   785
    To Satan, "Sir, I'm ready to write yours,
In two octavo volumes, nicely bound,
    With notes and preface, all that most allures
The pious purchaser; and there's no ground
    For fear, for I can choose my own reviewers: 790

6. A felony "upon himself"; that is, suicide.
7. In an early poem on Henry Martin, one of the judges who had condemned Charles I to be beheaded.
8. An ideal community that Southey and Coleridge, in 1794–95, had planned to set up in America on the banks of the Susquehanna. The scheme was utopian, but in no way immoral.
9. In Southey's *The Remains of Henry Kirke White*, Vol. I (1808).

So let me have the proper documents,
That I may add you to my other saints."

100

Satan bowed, and was silent. "Well, if you,
    With amiable modesty, decline
My offer, what says Michael? There are few   795
    Whose memoirs could be rendered more divine.
Mine is a pen of all work; not so new
    As it was once, but I would make you shine
Like your own trumpet. By the way, my own
Has more of brass in it, and is as well blown.   800

101

"But talking about trumpets, here's my Vision!
    Now you shall judge, all people; yes, you shall
Judge with my judgment, and by my decision
    Be guided who shall enter heaven or fall.
I settle all these things by intuition,   805
    Times present, past, to come, heaven, hell, and all,
Like King Alfonso.[1] When I thus see double,
I save the Deity some worlds of trouble."

102

He ceased, and drew forth an MS.; and no
    Persuasion on the part of devils, saints,   810
Or angels, now could stop the torrent; so
    He read the first three lines of the contents;
But at the fourth, the whole spiritual show
    Had vanished, with variety of scents,
Ambrosial and sulphureous, as they sprang,   815
Like lightning, off from his "melodious twang."[2]

103

Those grand heroics acted as a spell:
    The angels stopped their ears and plied their pinions;
The devils ran howling, deafened, down to hell;
    The ghosts fled, gibbering, for their own dominions—   820
(For 'tis not yet decided where they dwell,
    And I leave every man to his opinions);
Michael took refuge in his trump—but, lo!
His teeth were set on edge, he could not blow!

104

Saint Peter, who has hitherto been known   825
    For an impetuous saint, upraised his keys,
And at the fifth line knocked the poet down;
    Who fell like Phaëton,[3] but more at ease,
Into his lake, for there he did not drown;
    A different web being by the Destinies   830

1. "King Alphonso [of Castile, in the 13th century] speaking of the Ptolemean system, said that had he been consulted at the creation of the world, he would have spared the Maker some absurdities" [Byron's note].
2. John Aubrey in his *Miscellanies upon Various Subjects* (1696) had described a ghost that vanished "with a curious perfume, and most melodious twang."
3. Phaethon, son of Apollo, tried to drive his father's chariot, the sun. He could not control the horses and was struck down into the sea by a thunderbolt of Zeus. The satiric point is that Apollo is the god of poetry as well as of the sun.

Woven for the Laureate's final wreath, whene'er
Reform shall happen either here or there.

105

He first sank to the bottom—like his works,
  But soon rose to the surface—like himself;
For all corrupted things are buoyed like corks,   835
  By their own rottenness, light as an elf,
Or wisp that flits o'er a morass: he lurks,
  It may be, still, like dull books on a shelf,
In his own den, to scrawl some "Life" or "Vision,"
As Welborn says—"the devil turned precisian."[4]   840

106

As for the rest, to come to the conclusion
  Of this true dream, the telescope is gone
Which kept my optics free from all delusion,
  And showed me what I in my turn have shown;
All I saw farther, in the last confusion,   845
  Was, that King George slipped into heaven for one;
And when the tumult dwindled to a calm,
I left him practising the hundredth psalm.[5]

1821   1822

Stanzas to the Po[1]

River, that rollest by the ancient walls,
  Where dwells the Lady of my love, when she
Walks by thy brink, and there perchance recalls
  A faint and fleeting memory of me;

What if thy deep and ample stream should be   5
  A mirror of my heart, where she may read
The thousand thoughts I now betray to thee,
  Wild as thy wave, and headlong as thy speed!

What do I say—a mirror of my heart?
  Are not thy waters sweeping, dark, and strong?   10
Such as my feelings were and are, thou art;
  And such as thou art were my passions long.

Time may have somewhat tamed them—not forever;
  Thou overflow'st thy banks, and not for aye
Thy bosom overboils, congenial river!   15
  Thy floods subside, and mine have sunk away—

But left long wrecks behind: and now again,
  Borne in our old unchanged career, we move:
Thou tendest wildly onwards to the main.
  And I—to loving *one* I should not love.   20

4. A "precisian" is a Puritan. Spoken by Welborn in Massinger's play, *A New Way to Pay Old Debts* (1626), I.i.6.
5. Which contains the relevant line, "Enter into his gates with thanksgiving."

1. This powerful lyric was written a month or two after Byron had fallen in love with the 19-year-old Italian Teresa Guiccioli. The Po is a river in northern Italy that flows into the Adriatic.

The current I behold will sweep beneath
    Her native walls, and murmur at her feet;
Her eyes will look on thee, when she shall breathe
    The twilight air, unharmed by summer's heat.

She will look on thee—I have looked on thee,   25
    Full of that thought; and, from that moment, ne'er
Thy waters could I dream of, name, or see,
    Without the inseparable sigh for her!

Her bright eyes will be imaged in thy stream—
    Yes! they will meet the wave I gaze on now: 30
Mine cannot witness, even in a dream,
    That happy wave repass me in its flow!

The wave that bears my tears returns no more:
    Will she return by whom that wave shall sweep?
Both tread thy banks, both wander on thy shore,   35
    I by thy source, she by the dark-blue deep.

But that which keepeth us apart is not
    Distance, nor depth of wave, nor space of earth,
But the distraction of a various lot,
    As various as the climates of our birth.   40

A stranger loves the Lady of the land,
    Born far beyond the mountains, but his blood
Is all meridian,[2] as if never fanned
    By the black wind that chills the polar flood.

My blood is all meridian; were it not,   45
    I had not left my clime, nor should I be,
In spite of tortures, ne'er to be forgot,
    A slave again of love—at least of thee.

'Tis vain to struggle—let me perish young—
    Live as I lived, and love as I have loved;   50
To dust if I return, from dust I sprung,
    And then, at least, my heart can ne'er be moved.

1819   1824

When a Man Hath No Freedom
to Fight for at Home[1]

When a man hath no freedom to fight for at home,
    Let him combat for that of his neighbors;
Let him think of the glories of Greece and of Rome,
    And get knocked on his head for his labors.

To do good to mankind is the chivalrous plan,   5
    And is always as nobly requited;

2. Southern.
1. The ironist's attitude toward gratuitous enlistment in a foreign war for national freedom—a cause to which Byron gave his own life less than four years later.

Then battle for freedom wherever you can,
And, if not shot or hanged, you'll get knighted.

November 5, 1820   1824

Stanzas Written on the Road Between Florence and Pisa

Oh, talk not to me of a name great in story—
The days of our youth are the days of our glory;
And the myrtle and ivy of sweet two-and-twenty
Are worth all your laurels,[1] though ever so plenty.

What are garlands and crowns to the brow that is wrinkled?   5
'Tis but as a dead-flower with May-dew besprinkled:
Then away with all such from the head that is hoary!
What care I for the wreaths that can *only* give glory?

Oh FAME!—if I e'er took delight in thy praises,
'Twas less for the sake of thy high-sounding phrases,   10
Than to see the bright eyes of the dear one discover
She thought that I was not unworthy to love her.

There chiefly I sought thee, *there* only I found thee;
Her glance was the best of the rays that surround thee;
When it sparkled o'er aught that was bright in my story,   15
I knew it was love, and I felt it was glory.

November, 1821   1830

1. Myrtle was sacred to Venus, goddess of love, and ivy to Bacchus, god of wine and revelry; a laurel crown was awarded by the Greeks as a mark of high honor.

PERCY BYSSHE SHELLEY

(1792–1822)

1811: Is expelled from Oxford and elopes with Harriet West-brook.

1818: Leaves England for Italy, never to return.

1819: The great year: *Prometheus Unbound, The Cenci, Ode to the West Wind,* and some of his best lyrics.

1820: Settles in Pisa and its vicinity; the "Pisan Circle."

Although he was an extreme heretic and nonconformist in all his life and thought, Shelley emerged from a solidly conservative background. His ancestors had been Sussex aristocrats since early in the 17th century; his grandfather, Sir Bysshe Shelley, made himself the richest man in Horsham, Sussex; his father, Timothy Shelley, was a hardheaded and conventional member of Parliament; Percy Shelley himself was in line for a baronetcy, and as befitted his station, was sent to be educated at Eton and at Oxford. He was slight of build, eccentric in manner, and unskilled in sports or fighting, and as a consequence, was mercilessly baited by older and stronger boys. Even then he saw the petty tyranny of schoolmasters and schoolmates as representative of man's general inhumanity to man, and dedicated his life to a war against all injustice and oppression. He describes the experience in the Dedication to *The Revolt of Islam*:

> So without shame, I spoke: "I will be wise,
> And just, and free, and mild, if in me lies
> Such power, for I grow weary to behold
> The selfish and the strong still tyrannize
> Without reproach or check." I then controlled
> My tears, my heart grew calm, and I was meek and bold.

At Oxford in the autumn of 1810 Shelley's closest friend was Thomas Jefferson Hogg, a self-centered and self-confident young man who shared Shelley's love of philosophy and scorn of orthodoxy. The two collaborated on a pamphlet, *The Necessity of Atheism*, which claimed that God's existence cannot be proved on empirical grounds. Shelley refused to repudiate the document before the authorities and, to his great shock and grief, was peremptorily expelled, terminating a university career that had lasted only six months. This event opened a breach between Shelley and his father that widened over the years.

Shelley went to London where, eager for a test of his zeal for social justice, he took up the cause of Harriet Westbrook, the pretty and warm-hearted daughter of a well-to-do tavern keeper, whose father, Shelley wrote to Hogg, "has persecuted her in a most horrible way by endeavoring to compel her to go to school." Harriet threw herself on Shelley's protection, and "gratitude and admiration," he wrote, "all demand that I shall love her *forever*." He eloped with Harriet to Edinburgh and married her, though against his firm conviction that marriage was a tyrannical and degrading social institution. He was then 18 years of age, and his bride 16. The young couple moved restlessly from place to place, living on a small allowance granted reluctantly by their families. In February of 1812, accompanied by Harriet's sister Eliza, they traveled to Dublin to distribute Shelley's *Address to the Irish People* and otherwise take part in the movement for Catholic emancipation and for the amelioration of the oppressed and poverty-stricken people.

Back in London, Shelley became a disciple of the radical social philosopher William Godwin, author of the *Inquiry Concerning Political Justice*. In 1813 he printed privately his first important work, *Queen Mab*, a long prophetic poem set in the fantastic frame of the journey of a disembodied soul through space, to whom the fairy Mab reveals in visions the woeful past, the dreadful present, and the utopian future. Announcing that "there is no God!" Mab decries institutional religion and codified morality as the causes of social evil. She predicts, by the action of the all-ruling goddess Necessity, the withering away of all institutions, and the return of man to his natural state of goodness and felicity.

In the following spring Shelley, who had drifted apart from Harriet, fell in love with the beautiful Mary Wollstonecraft Godwin. Acting according to his conviction that cohabitation without love is immoral, he abandoned Harriet, fled to France with Mary (taking along her half sister, Claire Clairmont), and—still acting in accordance with his belief in nonexclusive love—invited Harriet to come live with them in the relationship of a sister. Shelley's elopement with Mary outraged even her father, though his theoretical views of marriage had been no less liberal than

Shelley's, and despite the fact that Shelley, himself in financial difficulties, had earlier taken over Godwin's very substantial debts. When he returned to London, Shelley found that the general public, his family, and most of his friends regarded him not only as an atheist and revolutionary, but also as a gross immoralist. When, two years later, Harriet drowned herself in a fit of despair, the courts denied Shelley the custody of their two children. Shelley married Mary Godwin and, in 1818, moved to Italy; thereafter he saw himself in the role of an alien and outcast, scorned and rejected by the mankind to whose welfare he had dedicated his powers and his life.

In Italy he resumed his restless existence, moving from town to town and house to house. His health was usually bad. Although the death of his grandfather in 1815 had provided a substantial income, he dissipated so much of it by his warmhearted but improvident support of William Godwin, Leigh Hunt, and other indigent pensioners that he was constantly short of money and harried by creditors. Within nine months, in 1818–19, Clara and William, the beloved children of Percy and Mary Shelley, both died. This tragedy threw Mary into a state of apathy and self-absorption which destroyed the earlier harmony of her relationship with her husband, and from which even the birth of another son, Percy Florence, could not entirely rescue her.

In these desperate circumstances, in a state sometimes verging on despair, and knowing that he almost entirely lacked an audience, Shelley wrote his greatest works. In 1819 he completed his masterpiece, *Prometheus Unbound*, and wrote a fine tragedy, *The Cenci*, as well as numerous lyric poems; a visionary call for a proletarian revolution, *The Mask of Anarchy*; a discerning and witty satire on Wordsworth, *Peter Bell the Third*; and a penetrating political essay, *A Philosophical View of Reform*. His works of the next two years include *A Defence of Poetry*; *Epipsychidion*, a rhapsodic vision of love as a union, beyond earthly limits, with what the title identifies as "the soul out of my soul"; *Adonais*, his noble elegy on the death of Keats; and *Hellas*, a lyrical drama evoked by the Greek war for liberation from the Turks in which he again projected his vision of a new golden age. These writings, unlike the early *Queen Mab*, are the products of a mind enlarged and chastened by tragic experience, deepened by incessant philosophical speculation, and richly stored with the harvest of his reading—which Shelley carried on, as his friend Hogg said, "in season and out of season, at table, in bed, and especially during a walk," until he became one of the most erudite of poets. His delight in scientific discoveries and speculations continued, but his earlier zest for Gothic terrors and the social theories of the radical 18th-century optimists had given way to an absorption in Greek tragedy, Milton's *Paradise Lost*, and the Bible. While he did not give up his hopes for a millennial future (he wore a ring with the motto *Il buon tempo verrà*—"the good time will come"), he now attributed the evils of present society to man's own moral failures, and grounded the possibility of radical social reform upon a prior reform of man's moral nature through the redeeming power of love. Though often thought of as a simple-minded doctrinaire, Shelley in fact possessed a complex and energetically inquisitive intelligence which never halted at a fixed mental position; all his writings represent, not final solutions, but stages in a ceaseless exploration.

The poems of Shelley's maturity also show the influence of his study of

Plato and the Neo-Platonists. Shelley found congenial the Platonic division of the cosmos into two worlds—the ordinary world of change, mortality, evil, and suffering, and the criterion world of perfect and eternal Forms, of which the world of sense-experience is only a distant and illusory reflection. The earlier interpretations of Shelley as a downright Platonic idealist, however, have been drastically modified by recent investigations of his reading and writings. Shelley was a close student of English empirical philosophy, which limits knowledge to valid reasoning upon what is given in sense-experience, and within this tradition he felt a special affinity to the radical skepticism of David Hume. Shelley was indeed an idealist, but as C. E. Pulos has shown in *The Deep Truth: A Study of Shelley's Scepticism*, his was "a qualified idealism," holding provisionally to the ideas envisioned by an imagination which transcends experience, but refusing to assert that these ideas are anything more than high possibilities. As Shelley wrote, we quickly reach "the verge where words abandon us, and what wonder if we grow dizzy to look down the dark abyss of how little we know." Many of his major poems express the limits of certain knowledge, and the refusal to let his intuitions and his hopes harden into a philosophical or religious creed. To the skeptical idealism of the mature Shelley (see, e.g., the notes to his great lyrics from *Hellas*), the hope in the ultimate redemption of life by love and imagination is not a certainty, but a moral obligation. We must cling to hope because its contrary, despair about human possibility, is self-fulfilling, by ensuring the permanence of the conditions before which the mind has surrendered its aspirations. Hope does not guarantee achievement, but it keeps open the possibility of achievement, and so releases man's imaginative and creative powers, which are its only available means.

When in 1820 the Shelleys settled finally at Pisa, he came closer to finding contentment than at any time in his adult life. A group of friends, Shelley's "Pisan Circle," gathered around them, including for a while Lord Byron and the swashbuckling young Cornishman, Edward Trelawny. Chief in Shelley's affections, however, were Edward Williams, a retired lieutenant of a dragoon regiment serving in India, and his charming common-law wife, Jane, with whom Shelley carried on a flirtation and to whom he addressed some of his best lyrics and verse letters. The end came suddenly, and in a fashion pre-visioned in the ecstatic last stanza of *Adonais*, where Shelley had described his spirit as a ship driven by a violent storm out into the dark unknown. On July 8, 1822, Shelley and Edward Williams were sailing their open boat, the *Don Juan*, from Leghorn to their summer house near Lerici, on the Gulf of Spezia. A violent squall blew up and swamped the boat. When several days later the bodies were washed ashore they were cremated, and Shelley's ashes were buried in the Protestant Cemetery at Rome, near the graves of John Keats and of William Shelley, the poet's young son. He left unfinished *The Triumph of Life*, which was a new departure for Shelley and, in the estimation of many readers, promised to be his greatest poem. Byron, who did not pay moral compliments lightly, wrote to John Murray at the time of Shelley's death: "You were all brutally mistaken about Shelley, who was, without exception, the *best* and least selfish man I ever knew. I never knew one who was not a beast in comparison."

To many of the new critics (and despite the reverence toward him of W. B. Yeats, an admitted master of the poetry they most admire), Shelley was a favorite resort for supposed examples of intellectual and emotional immaturity, shoddy workmanship, and incoherent imagery. In recent years, however, Shelley has been the subject of many sympathetic critics, whose studies have clarified the complex and coherent structure of his symbolism and have increasingly confirmed Wordsworth's recognition that "Shelley is one of the best *artists* of us all: I mean in workmanship of style." Shelley's expansion of the metrical and sonantal resources of verse is without recent parallel in the history of English literature. Furthermore, his successful poems show an astonishing range of voice, from the sovereign order in rage of *Ode to the West Wind*, through the calm and heroic dignity of the utterances of Prometheus, and the near approximation to the inexpressible in the description of Asia's transfiguration and in the visionary conclusion of *Adonais*. Most surprising, in a poet who almost entirely lacked an audience, is the assured urbanity, the effortless command of the tone and language of a cultivated man of the world which is exemplified in passages that Shelley wrote all through his mature career, and most sustainedly in the great lyrics and verse letters that he composed during the last year of his life.

TEXTUAL NOTE

The printing of Shelley's writings has had a tangled history. Shelley had no chance to correct proofs for many of the poems published during his lifetime, especially those that appeared in periodicals, while a number of his poems were not printed until after his death. We know by reference to Shelley's manuscripts that his various editors and printers made many errors and introduced many changes. As a result all the standard editions of Shelley's collected poems—and the selections and anthologies that have been based on these editions—include important deviations from the poet's probable intention.

The texts of all the poems and prose reprinted here have been newly prepared by Dr. Donald H. Reiman of The Carl H. Pforzheimer Library in New York, and this selection of Shelley is the first broadly representative one which meets modern standards for textual validity. These texts are based on Shelley's extant holograph manuscripts and transcripts (many of which have only recently become available), on first editions of the poems, and on any later editions that may incorporate the author's own changes. The results of the collation were compared with the various earlier editions of Shelley, as well as with specialized editions and textual studies by his recent editors, especially G. M. Matthews; Lawrence John Zillman; Charles H. Taylor, Jr.; Irving Massey; John E. Jordan; and Judith V. Chernaik. The detailed rationale for these texts will be given by Dr. Reiman and Dr. Sharon P. Thompson in their Norton Critical Edition of *Shelley's Poetry and Prose*. It should be noted that:

1. The spelling has, in part, been regularized according to Shelley's preferred forms (e.g., "grey" rather than "gray"). Shelley's distinctions between "sat" and "sate" (which were pronounced differently) and between "desert" (usually an adjective) and "desart" (usually a noun) have been maintained. Obvious misspellings ("thier" for "their," "recieve" for "receive") have been corrected and some abbreviations ("&" for "and," "wᶜʰ" for "which") have been filled out. But such spellings as "antient," "gulph," and "knarled" (for "ancient," "gulf," and "gnarled"), which were perfectly correct in Shelley's day, have been retained.

2. Shelley's typical punctuation, as it occurs in those texts that he carefully prepared for printing, has been kept, and some of the rougher manuscripts and printed texts have been repunctuated according to the typical procedure manifested in his prepared texts. This punctuation will aid rather than hinder the modern reader, provided he remembers that Shelley's pointing, in the common fashion of his time, was primarily rhetorical rather than syntactical. That is, a punctuation mark indicates a phrasal pause in the reading, and the type of mark indicates, approximately, the length of the pause after each phrase; there is an increasingly longer pause in the sequence: comma, semicolon, colon, period, and dash. In addition, Shelley often relied on the natural pause at the end of a line of verse, where modern usage would call for a comma or other mark of punctuation.

3. Shelley's capitalizations have been followed, insofar as his final choices can be determined, because capitalizing nouns was one conventional means (along with printing in italics) used in Shelley's day to indicate rhetorical emphasis.

4. Inconsistencies in spelling, punctuation, and capitalization that occur in these texts either are Shelley's own (and may possess significance that editors and critics have not yet fathomed) or else they result from differences between Shelley's manuscripts and texts that were transcribed or printed by others. Presenting such ambiguous evidence should enable students and teachers both to avoid false generalizations and to explore possible critical reasons for such discrepancies.

Mutability

We are as clouds that veil the midnight moon;
　　How restlessly they speed, and gleam, and quiver,
Streaking the darkness radiantly!—yet soon
　　Night closes round, and they are lost for ever:

Or like forgotten lyres,[1] whose dissonant strings　　　　　5
　　Give various response to each varying blast,
To whose frail frame no second motion brings
　　One mood or modulation like the last.

We rest.—A dream has power to poison sleep;
　　We rise.—One wandering thought pollutes the day;　　10
We feel, conceive or reason, laugh or weep;
　　Embrace fond woe, or cast our cares away:

It is the same!—For, be it joy or sorrow,
　　The path of its departure still is free:
Man's yesterday may ne'er be like his morrow;　　　　15
　　Nought may endure but Mutability.

1816

1. Wind harps.

To Wordsworth[2]

Poet of Nature, thou hast wept to know
That things depart which never may return:
Childhood and youth, friendship and love's first glow,
Have fled like sweet dreams, leaving thee to mourn.
These common woes I feel. One loss is mine   5
Which thou too feel'st, yet I alone deplore.
Thou wert as a lone star, whose light did shine
On some frail bark in winter's midnight roar:
Thou hast like to a rock-built refuge stood
Above the blind and battling multitude: 10
In honoured poverty thy voice did weave
Songs consecrate to truth and liberty,—
Deserting these, thou leavest me to grieve,
Thus having been, that thou shouldst cease to be.

1816

2. Shelley's grieved comment on the poet of nature and of social radicalism after his views had become conservative.

Alastor; or, The Spirit of Solitude

According to Shelley's friend Thomas Love Peacock, the poet was "at a loss for a title, and I proposed that which he adopted: Alastor, or the Spirit of Solitude. The Greek word *Alastor* is an evil genius. . . . I mention the true meaning of the word because many have supposed *Alastor* to be the name of the hero" (*Memoirs of Shelley*). Peacock's definition of an *alastor* as "an *evil* genius" has compounded the problems that many readers have found in interpreting this work: the term "evil" does not seem to fit the attitude to the poet's solitary quest expressed within the poem; the poem seems to clash with some statements in Shelley's Preface; and the first and second paragraphs within the Preface seem inconsistent with each other. These problems, however, are largely resolved if we recognize that, in his first major achievement (he was only 23 when he wrote *Alastor*), Shelley established his characteristic procedure of working with multiple perspectives. Both Preface and poem explore alternative and conflicting possibilities in what Shelley calls "doubtful knowledge"—matters which are humanly essential, but in which no certainty is humanly possible.

The first paragraph of the Preface explains the "allegorical" plot. By "allegorical" Shelley means that the poem, like Medieval and Renaissance allegories such as Dante's *Divine Comedy* and Spenser's *Faerie Queene*, represents a spiritual need and aspiration in the vehicle of a journey and quest in the physical world. At the time of his full sexual awakening, Shelley's protagonist ceases to be "self-possessed"; that is, the natural objects within the world "cease to suffice," for he envisions a "Being," a female Other, who will answer to all that is best in his own self and will fulfill not only the requirements of his "intellectual faculties" and "imagination," but also his sexual needs, "the functions of sense." He commits himself to the search for "a prototype" of this vision in the real world, but since his desires are infinite and the world's possibilities are limited, his quest is doomed to end in his early death.

The second paragraph proceeds to pass judgment upon such a Poet in terms of the values of "actual men"—the requirements of human and social life in this world. Since the visionary Poet turned away from both human and natural community in search of the projected demands of his own psyche, his lot can be said to have been "avenged" by the *alastor*, the spirit of solitude, in the sense of "solitude" as alienation from both nature and humanity. The Preface goes on, however, to passionately elevate the moral status of such a visionary over the status of a second class of "meaner spirits" who also "keep aloof from sympathies with their kind," but only because they ignobly lack any capacity to project their imagination beyond their own narrow selves, and so are "morally dead." The Preface leaves open a possibility which Shelley proceeded to explore in *Prometheus Unbound* and other poems—the possibility that there exists a third class of men who sustain an imaginative vision, but undertake to realize it, not in self-centered solitude, but by effecting a transformation in human nature, society, and milieu.

Diverse attitudes expressed within the poem itself are clarified, once we realize that the story is narrated—as the many echoes from Wordsworth in the opening invocation suggest—in the persona of a Wordsworthian poet for whom nature suffices both to the demands of his imagination and to his need for community. This narrator-poet proceeds to tell, with insight and compassion, but from his own perspective, the history of a nameless visionary Poet who, having himself passed through a Wordsworthian phase, then gives up everything for a goal beyond possibility.

In this early poem Shelley established a form, conceptual frame, and imagery for the Romantic quest which not only shaped his own later poems, but also served as a paradigm for the writings of many other poets, from Byron's *Manfred* and Keats's *Endymion* and Invocation to *The Fall of Hyperion* to the quest-poems of Shelley's later admirer William Butler Yeats.

Alastor; or, The Spirit of Solitude

Preface

The poem entitled "Alastor," may be considered as allegorical of one of the most interesting situations of the human mind. It represents a youth of uncorrupted feelings and adventurous genius led forth by an imagination inflamed and purified through familiarity with all that is excellent and majestic, to the contemplation of the universe. He drinks deep of the fountains of knowledge, and is still insatiate. The magnificence and beauty of the external world sinks profoundly into the frame of his conceptions, and affords to their modifications a variety not to be exhausted. So long as it is possible for his desires to point towards objects thus infinite and unmeasured, he is joyous, and tranquil, and self-possessed. But the period arrives when these objects cease to suffice. His mind is at length suddenly awakened and thirsts for intercourse with an intelligence similar to itself. He images to himself the Being whom he loves. Conversant with speculations of the sublimest and most perfect natures, the vision in which he embodies his own imaginations unites all of wonderful, or wise, or beautiful, which the poet, the philosopher, or the lover could depicture. The intellectual faculties, the imagination, the functions of sense, have their respective requisitions on the sympathy of corresponding powers in other human beings. The Poet is represented as uniting these requisitions, and attaching them to a single image.[1] He seeks in vain for a prototype of his conception. Blasted by his disappointment, he descends to an untimely grave.

The picture is not barren of instruction to actual men. The Poet's self-centred seclusion was avenged by the furies of an irresistible passion pursuing him to speedy ruin. But that Power which strikes the luminaries of the world with sudden darkness and extinction, by awakening them to too exquisite a perception of its influences, dooms to a slow and poisonous decay those meaner spirits that dare to abjure its dominion. Their destiny is more abject and inglorious as their delinquency is more contemptible and pernicious. They who, deluded by no generous error, instigated by no sacred thirst of doubtful knowledge, duped by no illustrious superstition, loving nothing on this earth, and cherishing no hopes beyond, yet keep aloof from sympathies with their kind, rejoicing neither in human joy nor mourning with human grief; these, and such as they, have their apportioned curse. They languish, because none feel with them their common nature. They are morally dead. They are neither friends, nor lovers, nor fathers, nor citizens of the world, nor benefactors of their country. Among those who attempt to exist without human sympathy, the pure and tender-hearted perish through the intensity and passion of their search after its communities, when the vacancy of their spirit suddenly makes itself felt. All else, selfish, blind, and torpid, are those unforeseeing multitudes who constitute, together with their own, the lasting misery and loneliness of the world. Those who love not their fellow-beings live unfruitful lives, and prepare for their old age a miserable grave.

> "The good die first,
> And those whose hearts are dry as summer dust,
> Burn to the socket!"[2]

December 14, 1815.

---

1. Shelley's view that the object of love is an idealized antitype to all that is best within the self is clarified by a passage in his *Essay on Love*, which may well have been written at about the time of *Alastor*: "We dimly see within our intellectual nature . . . the ideal prototype of every thing excellent or lovely that we are capable of conceiving as belonging to the nature of men * * * [This is] a soul within our soul * * * The discovery of its anti-type * * * in such proportion as the type within demands; this is the invisible and unattainable point to which Love tends; and * * * without the possession of which there is no rest nor respite to the heart over which it rules."
2. Quoted from Wordsworth's *The Excursion* I.519–21; the passage occurs in *The Ruined Cottage* (above, lines 96–98), which Wordsworth reworked into the first Book of *The Excursion* (1814).

Alastor; or, The Spirit of Solitude

Nondum amabam, et amare amabam, quærebam quid amarem, amans amare.—*Confess. St. August.*[3]

Earth, ocean, air, beloved brotherhood!
If our great Mother[4] has imbued my soul
With aught of natural piety[5] to feel
Your love, and recompense the boon with mine;
If dewy morn, and odorous noon, and even,   5
With sunset and its gorgeous ministers,
And solemn midnight's tingling silentness;
If autumn's hollow sighs in the sere wood,
And winter robing with pure snow and crowns
Of starry ice the grey grass and bare boughs;   10
If spring's voluptuous pantings when she breathes
Her first sweet kisses, have been dear to me;
If no bright bird, insect, or gentle beast
I consciously have injured, but still loved
And cherished these my kindred; then forgive   15
This boast, beloved brethren, and withdraw
No portion of your wonted favour now!

Mother of this unfathomable world!
Favour my solemn song, for I have loved
Thee ever, and thee only; I have watched   20
Thy shadow, and the darkness of thy steps,
And my heart ever gazes on the depth
Of thy deep mysteries. I have made my bed
In charnels and on coffins, where black death
Keeps record of the trophies won from thee,   25
Hoping to still these obstinate questionings[6]
Of thee and thine, by forcing some lone ghost,
Thy messenger, to render up the tale
Of what we are. In lone and silent hours,
When night makes a weird sound of its own stillness,   30
Like an inspired and desperate alchymist

3. Condensed from a passage in St. Augustine, *Confessions* III.i: "Not yet did I love, though I loved to love, seeking what I might love, loving to love." Augustine thus describes his state of mind when he was addicted to illicit sexual love; the true object of his desire, which compels the tortuous spiritual journey of his life, he later discovered to be the infinite and transcendant God.
4. Nature, invoked as the common mother of the elements and of the poet.
5. Wordsworth, *My Heart Leaps Up* (above, lines 9–10): "And I could wish my days to be / Bound each to each by natural piety." Wordsworth also used these lines as the epigraph to his *Ode: Intimations of Immortality*.
6. *Ode: Intimations of Immortality*, line 143: ". . . those obstinate questionings / Of sense and outward things. . . ."

Staking his very life on some dark hope,
Have I mixed awful talk and asking looks
With my most innocent love, until strange tears
Uniting with those breathless kisses, made   35
Such magic as compels the charmed night
To render up thy charge: . . . and, though ne'er yet
Thou hast unveil'd thy inmost sanctuary,
Enough from incommunicable dream,
And twilight phantasms, and deep noonday thought,   40
Has shone within me, that serenely now
And moveless, as a long-forgotten lyre
Suspended in the solitary dome
Of some mysterious and deserted fane,[7]
I wait thy breath, Great Parent, that my strain   45
May modulate with murmurs of the air,
And motions of the forests and the sea,
And voice of living beings, and woven hymns
Of night and day, and the deep heart of man.[8]

There was a Poet whose untimely tomb   50
No human hands with pious reverence reared,
But the charmed eddies of autumnal winds
Built o'er his mouldering bones a pyramid
Of mouldering leaves in the waste wilderness:—
A lovely youth,—no mourning maiden decked   55
With weeping flowers, or votive cypress wreath,
The lone couch of his everlasting sleep:—
Gentle, and brave, and generous,—no lorn bard
Breathed o'er his dark fate one melodious sigh:
He lived, he died, he sung, in solitude.   60
Strangers have wept to hear his passionate notes,
And virgins, as unknown he past, have pined
And wasted for fond love of his wild eyes.
The fire of those soft orbs has ceased to burn,
And Silence, too enamoured of that voice,   65
Locks its mute music in her rugged cell.

By solemn vision, and bright silver dream,
His infancy was nutured. Every sight
And sound from the vast earth and ambient air,
Sent to his heart its choicest impulses.   70
The fountains of divine philosophy
Fled not his thirsting lips, and all of great
Or good, or lovely, which the sacred past
In truth or fable consecrates, he felt

7. Temple. The narrator calls on the
Mother, his natural muse, to make him
her wind-harp. Cf. the opening passage
of Wordsworth's *Prelude*, Coleridge's
Dejection: An Ode, and the conclusion
of Shelley's *Ode to the West Wind* and
of *Adonais*.

8. Cf. Wordsworth, *Tintern Abbey*, lines
95 ff.: "A presence . . . / Whose dwelling is . . . / the round ocean and the living air / And the blue sky, and in the
mind of man; / A motion and a spirit.
. . ."

And knew. When early youth had past, he left   75
His cold fireside and alienated home
To seek strange truths in undiscovered lands.
Many a wide waste and tangled wilderness
Has lured his fearless steps; and he has bought
With his sweet voice and eyes, from savage men,   80
His rest and food. Nature's most secret steps
He like her shadow has pursued, where'er
The red volcano overcanopies
Its fields of snow and pinnacles of ice
With burning smoke, or where bitumen lakes[9]   85
On black bare pointed islets ever beat
With sluggish surge, or where the secret caves
Rugged and dark, winding among the springs
Of fire and poison, inaccessible
To avarice or pride, their starry domes   90
Of diamond and of gold expand above
Numberless and immeasurable halls,
Frequent[1] with crystal column, and clear shrines
Of pearl, and thrones radiant with chrysolite.[2]
Nor had that scene of ampler majesty   95
Than gems or gold, the varying roof of heaven
And the green earth lost in his heart its claims
To love and wonder; he would linger long
In lonesome vales, making the wild his home,
Until the doves and squirrels would partake   100
From his innocuous hand his bloodless food,[3]
Lured by the gentle meaning of his looks,
And the wild antelope, that starts whene'er
The dry leaf rustles in the brake,[4] suspend
Her timid steps to gaze upon a form   105
More graceful than her own.

                                        His wandering step
Obedient to high thoughts, has visited
The awful ruins of the days of old:
Athens, and Tyre, and Balbec,[5] and the waste
Where stood Jerusalem, the fallen towers   110
Of Babylon, the eternal pyramids,
Memphis and Thebes,[6] and whatsoe'er of strange
Sculptured on alabaster obelisk,
Or jasper tomb, or mutilated sphynx,
Dark Æthiopia in her desert hills   115
Conceals. Among the ruined temples there,
Stupendous columns, and wild images

9. Lakes of pitch.
1. Crowded.
2. An olive-green stone.
3. Shelley was himself a vegetarian.
4. Thicket.
5. Tyre: once an important commercial city on the Phoenician coast; Balbec: an ancient city in Syria.
6. Memphis: the ruined capital of Lower Egypt; Thebes: the ancient capital of Upper Egypt.

Of more than man, where marble dæmons watch
The Zodiac's brazen mystery,[7] and dead men
Hang their mute thoughts on the mute walls around,[8]   120
He lingered, poring on memorials
Of the world's youth, through the long burning day
Gazed on those speechless shapes, nor, when the moon
Filled the mysterious halls with floating shades
Suspended he that task, but ever gazed   125
And gazed, till meaning on his vacant mind
Flashed like strong inspiration, and he saw
The thrilling secrets of the birth of time.

Meanwhile an Arab maiden brought his food,
Her daily portion, from her father's tent,   130
And spread her matting for his couch, and stole
From duties and repose to tend his steps:—
Enamoured, yet not daring for deep awe
To speak her love:—and watched his nightly sleep,
Sleepless herself, to gaze upon his lips   135
Parted in slumber, whence the regular breath
Of innocent dreams arose: then, when red morn
Made paler the pale moon, to her cold home
Wildered, and wan, and panting, she returned.

The Poet wandering on, through Arabie   140
And Persia, and the wild Carmanian waste,[9]
And o'er the aërial mountains which pour down
Indus and Oxus[1] from their icy caves,
In joy and exultation held his way;
Till in the vale of Cashmire, far within   145
Its loneliest dell, where odorous plants entwine
Beneath the hollow rocks a natural bower,
Beside a sparkling rivulet he stretched
His languid limbs. A vision on his sleep
There came, a dream of hopes that never yet   150
Had flushed his cheek. He dreamed a veiled maid
Sate near him, talking in low solemn tones.
Her voice was like the voice of his own soul
Heard in the calm of thought; its music long,
Like woven sounds of streams and breezes, held   155
His inmost sense suspended in its web
Of many-coloured woof and shifting hues.
Knowledge and truth and virtue were her theme,
And lofty hopes of divine liberty,
Thoughts the most dear to him, and poesy,   160

7. In the temple of Isis at Denderah,
Egypt, the Zodiac is represented on the
ceiling. Dæmons: in Greek mythology
demons were not evil spirits but minor
deities, or attendant spirits.

8. I.e., by quotations inscribed in the
stone.
9. A desert in southern Persia.
1. Rivers in Asia.

Herself a poet.[2] Soon the solemn mood
Of her pure mind kindled through all her frame
A permeating fire: wild numbers then
She raised, with voice stifled in tremulous sobs
Subdued by its own pathos: her fair hands   165
Were bare alone, sweeping from some strange harp
Strange symphony, and in their branching veins
The eloquent blood told an ineffable tale.
The beating of her heart was heard to fill
The pauses of her music, and her breath   170
Tumultuously accorded with those fits
Of intermitted song. Sudden she rose,
As if her heart impatiently endured
Its bursting burthen: at the sound he turned,
And saw by the warm light of their own life   175
Her glowing limbs beneath the sinuous veil
Of woven wind, her outspread arms now bare,
Her dark locks floating in the breath of night,
Her beamy bending eyes, her parted lips
Outstretched, and pale, and quivering eagerly.   180
His strong heart sunk and sickened with excess
Of love. He reared his shuddering limbs and quelled
His gasping breath, and spread his arms to meet
Her panting bosom: . . . she drew back a while,
Then, yielding to the irresistible joy,   185
With frantic gesture and short breathless cry
Folded his frame in her dissolving arms.
Now blackness veiled his dizzy eyes, and night
Involved and swallowed up the vision; sleep,
Like a dark flood suspended in its course,   190
Rolled back its impulse on his vacant brain.

  Roused by the shock he started from his trance—
The cold white light of morning, the blue moon
Low in the west, the clear and garish hills,
The distinct valley and the vacant woods,   195
Spread round him where he stood. Whither have fled
The hues of heaven that canopied his bower
Of yesternight? The sounds that soothed his sleep,
The mystery and the majesty of Earth,
The joy, the exultation? His wan eyes   200
Gaze on the empty scene as vacantly
As ocean's moon looks on the moon in heaven.
The spirit of sweet human love has sent
A vision to the sleep of him who spurned
Her choicest gifts. He eagerly pursues   205
Beyond the realms of dream that fleeting shade;
He overleaps the bounds. Alas! alas!

2. The envisioned maiden embodies all three qualities specified in the Preface: intellect (line 158), imagination (lines 160–61), and sexuality (lines 176 ff.).

Were limbs, and breath, and being intertwined
Thus treacherously? Lost, lost, for ever lost,
In the wide pathless desart of dim sleep,   210
That beautiful shape! Does the dark gate of death
Conduct to thy mysterious paradise,
O Sleep?[3] Does the bright arch of rainbow clouds,
And pendent mountains seen in the calm lake,
Lead only to a black and watery depth,   215
While death's blue vault, with loathliest vapours hung,
Where every shade which the foul grave exhales
Hides its dead eye from the detested day,
Conduct[4], O Sleep, to thy delightful realms?
This doubt with sudden tide flowed on his heart,   220
The insatiate hope which it awakened, stung
His brain even like despair.
                While day-light held
The sky, the Poet kept mute conference
With his still soul. At night the passion came,
Like the fierce fiend of a distempered dream,   225
And shook him from his rest, and led him forth
Into the darkness.—As an eagle grasped
In folds of the green serpent, feels her breast
Burn with the poison, and precipitates
Through night and day, tempest, and calm, and cloud,   230
Frantic with dizzying anguish, her blind flight
O'er the wide aëry wilderness:[5] thus driven
By the bright shadow of that lovely dream,
Beneath the cold glare of the desolate night,
Through tangled swamps and deep precipitous dells,   235
Startling with careless step the moon-light snake,
He fled. Red morning dawned upon his flight,
Shedding the mockery of its vital hues
Upon his cheek of death. He wandered on
Till vast Aornos seen from Petra's steep[6]   240
Hung o'er the low horizon like a cloud;
Through Balk,[7] and where the desolated tombs
Of Parthian kings scatter to every wind
Their wasting dust, wildly he wandered on,
Day after day, a weary waste of hours,   245
Bearing within his life the brooding care
That ever fed on its decaying flame.
And now his limbs were lean; his scattered hair
Sered by the autumn of strange suffering
Sung dirges in the wind; his listless hand   250
Hung like dead bone within its withered skin;

---

3. I.e., is death the only access to this maiden of his dream?
4. "Conduct" is a singular subjunctive verb; its subject is "vault" (line 216).
5. The eagle and serpent locked in mortal combat is a recurrent image in Shelley's poems.

6. Aornos is a high mountain and Petra ("the rock") a mountain stronghold in the northern part of Ancient Arabia.
7. Balk is the ancient Bactria; it is now part of Afghanistan, but in ancient times was Persian. The Parthians (line 243) inhabited northern Persia.

Life, and the lustre that consumed it, shone
As in a furnace burning secretly
From his dark eyes alone. The cottagers,
Who ministered with human charity   255
His human wants, beheld with wondering awe
Their fleeting visitant. The mountaineer,
Encountering on some dizzy precipice
That spectral form, deemed that the Spirit of wind
With lightning eyes, and eager breath, and feet   260
Disturbing not the drifted snow, had paused
In its career: the infant would conceal
His troubled visage in his mother's robe
In terror at the glare of those wild eyes,
To remember their strange light in many a dream   265
Of after-times; but youthful maidens, taught
By nature, would interpret half the woe
That wasted him, would call him with false names
Brother, and friend,[8] would press his pallid hand
At parting, and watch, dim through tears, the path   270
Of his departure from their father's door.

        At length upon the lone Chorasmian shore[9]
He paused, a wide and melancholy waste
Of putrid marshes. A strong impulse urged
His steps to the sea-shore. A swan was there,   275
Beside a sluggish stream among the reeds.
It rose as he approached, and with strong wings
Scaling the upward sky, bent its bright course
High over the immeasurable main.
His eyes pursued its flight.—"Thou hast a home,   280
Beautiful bird; thou voyagest to thine home,
Where thy sweet mate will twine her downy neck
With thine, and welcome thy return with eyes
Bright in the lustre of their own fond joy.
And what am I that I should linger here,   285
With voice far sweeter than thy dying notes,
Spirit more vast than thine, frame more attuned
To beauty, wasting these surpassing powers
In the deaf air, to the blind earth, and heaven
That echoes not my thoughts?" A gloomy smile   290
Of desperate hope wrinkled his quivering lips.
For sleep, he knew, kept most relentlessly
Its precious charge,[1] and silent death exposed,
Faithless perhaps as sleep, a shadowy lure,
With doubtful smile mocking its own strange charms.   295

---

8. The maidens call him "false" (i.e., mistaken) names signifying a shared human affection instead of his unearthly love.
9. The shore of Lake Aral in modern Russia, about 175 miles east of the Caspian Sea.
1. I.e., the maiden in the sleeper's dream. The passage goes on to express the skeptical fear that neither sleep nor death may yield the Poet his desire.

Startled by his own thoughts he looked around.
There was no fair fiend[2] near him, not a sight
Or sound of awe but in his own deep mind.
A little shallop[3] floating near the shore
Caught the impatient wandering of his gaze.   300
It had been long abandoned, for its sides
Gaped wide with many a rift, and its frail joints
Swayed with the undulations of the tide.
A restless impulse urged him to embark
And meet lone Death on the drear ocean's waste;   305
For well he knew that mighty Shadow loves
The slimy caverns of the populous deep.

   The day was fair and sunny, sea and sky
Drank its inspiring radiance, and the wind
Swept strongly from the shore, blackening the waves.   310
Following his eager soul, the wanderer
Leaped in the boat, he spread his cloak aloft
On the bare mast, and took his lonely seat,
And felt the boat speed o'er the tranquil sea
Like a torn cloud before the hurricane.   315

   As one that in a silver vision floats
Obedient to the sweep of odorous winds
Upon resplendent clouds, so rapidly
Along the dark and ruffled waters fled
The straining boat.—A whirlwind swept it on,   320
With fierce gusts and precipitating force,
Through the white ridges of the chafed sea.
The waves arose. Higher and higher still
Their fierce necks writhed beneath the tempest's scourge
Like serpents struggling in a vulture's grasp.   325
Calm and rejoicing in the fearful war
Of wave ruining on wave, and blast on blast
Descending, and black flood on whirlpool driven
With dark obliterating course, he sate:
As if their genii were the ministers   330
Appointed to conduct him to the light
Of those beloved eyes, the Poet sate
Holding the steady helm. Evening came on,
The beams of sunset hung their rainbow hues
High 'mid the shifting domes of sheeted spray   335
That canopied his path o'er the waste deep;
Twilight, ascending slowly from the east,
Entwin'd in duskier wreaths her braided locks
O'er the fair front and radiant eyes of day;
Night followed, clad with stars. On every side   340
More horribly the multitudinous streams

2. Apparently, an embodiment of the al-   lines.
luring, mocking death in the preceding   3. A light, open boat.

Of ocean's mountainous waste to mutual war
Rushed in dark tumult thundering, as to mock
The calm and spangled sky. The little boat
Still fled before the storm; still fled, like foam   345
Down the steep cataract of a wintry river;
Now pausing on the edge of the riven wave;
Now leaving far behind the bursting mass
That fell, convulsing ocean. Safely fled—
As if that frail and wasted human form,   350
Had been an elemental god.[4]
                          At midnight
The moon arose: and lo! the etherial cliffs
Of Caucasus, whose icy summits shone
Among the stars like sunlight, and around
Whose cavern'd base the whirlpools and the waves   355
Bursting and eddying irresistibly
Rage and resound for ever.—Who shall save?—
The boat fled on,—the boiling torrent drove,—
The crags closed round with black and jagged arms,
The shattered mountain overhung the sea,   360
And faster still, beyond all human speed,
Suspended on the sweep of the smooth wave,
The little boat was driven. A cavern there
Yawned, and amid its slant and winding depths
Ingulphed the rushing sea. The boat fled on   365
With unrelaxing speed.—"Vision and Love!"
The Poet cried aloud, "I have beheld
The path of thy departure. Sleep and death
Shall not divide us long!"

                         The boat pursued
The windings of the cavern.[5] Day-light shone   370
At length upon that gloomy river's flow;
Now, where the fiercest war among the waves
Is calm, on the unfathomable stream
The boat moved slowly. Where the mountain, riven,
Exposed those black depths to the azure sky,   375
Ere yet the flood's enormous volume fell
Even to the base of Caucasus, with sound
That shook the everlasting rocks, the mass
Filled with one whirlpool all that ample chasm;
Stair above stair the eddying waters rose,   380
Circling immeasurably fast, and laved
With alternating dash the knarled roots
Of mighty trees, that stretched their giant arms
In darkness over it. I' the midst was left,
Reflecting, yet distorting every cloud,   385

4. A god of one of the natural elements;
cf. line 1.
5. A boat beating upstream within a

cave, like the eagle and serpent, is a recurrent Shelleyan image.

A pool of treacherous and tremendous calm.
Seized by the sway of the ascending stream,
With dizzy swiftness, round, and round, and round,
Ridge after ridge the straining boat arose,
Till on the verge of the extremest curve,   390
Where, through an opening of the rocky bank,
The waters overflow, and a smooth spot
Of glassy quiet mid those battling tides
Is left, the boat paused shuddering.—Shall it sink
Down the abyss? Shall the reverting stress   395
Of that resistless gulph embosom it?
Now shall it fall?—A wandering stream of wind,
Breathed from the west, has caught the expanded sail,
And, lo! with gentle motion, between banks
Of mossy slope, and on a placid stream,   400
Beneath a woven grove it sails, and, hark!
The ghastly torrent mingles its far roar,
With the breeze murmuring in the musical woods.
Where the embowering trees recede, and leave
A little space of green expanse, the cove   405
Is closed by meeting banks, whose yellow flowers
For ever gaze on their own drooping eyes,
Reflected in the crystal calm.[6] The wave
Of the boat's motion marred their pensive task,
Which nought but vagrant bird, or wanton wind,   410
Or falling spear-grass, or their own decay
Had e'er disturbed before. The Poet longed
To deck with their bright hues his withered hair,
But on his heart its solitude returned,
And he forbore. Not the strong impulse hid   415
In those flushed cheeks, bent eyes, and shadowy frame,
Had yet performed its ministry: it hung
Upon his life, as lightning in a cloud
Gleams, hovering ere it vanish, ere the floods
Of night close over it.
                                 The noonday sun   420
Now shone upon the forest, one vast mass
Of mingling shade, whose brown magnificence
A narrow vale embosoms. There, huge caves,
Scooped in the dark base of their aëry rocks
Mocking its moans, respond and roar for ever.   425
The meeting boughs and implicated[7] leaves
Wove twilight o'er the Poet's path, as led
By love, or dream, or god, or mightier Death,
He sought in Nature's dearest haunt, some bank,

6. Another recurrent image: flowers overhanging their own reflection. It signifies here that, within the limits of the natural world, the correspondent Other satisfies the need of the Self for community. The Poet (lines 412 ff.) is momentarily tempted to let this realm of experience suffice, but his unsatisfiable need revives, and he is once more driven on in solitude by "the strong impulse," his *alastor*.
7. Intertwined.

Her cradle, and his sepulchre. More dark 430
And dark the shades accumulate. The oak,
Expanding its immense and knotty arms,
Embraces the light beech. The pyramids
Of the tall cedar overarching, frame
Most solemn domes within, and far below, 435
Like clouds suspended in an emerald sky,
The ash and the acacia floating hang
Tremulous and pale. Like restless serpents, clothed
In rainbow and in fire, the parasites,
Starred with ten thousand blossoms, flow around 440
The grey trunks, and, as gamesome infants' eyes,
With gentle meanings, and most innocent wiles,
Fold their beams round the hearts of those that love,
These twine their tendrils with the wedded boughs
Uniting their close union;[8] the woven leaves 445
Make net-work of the dark blue light of day,
And the night's noontide clearness, mutable
As shapes in the weird clouds. Soft mossy lawns
Beneath these canopies extend their swells,
Fragrant with perfumed herbs, and eyed with blooms 450
Minute yet beautiful. One darkest glen
Sends from its woods of musk-rose, twined with jasmine,
A soul-dissolving odour, to invite
To some more lovely mystery. Through the dell,
Silence and Twilight here, twin-sisters, keep 455
Their noonday watch, and sail among the shades,
Like vaporous shapes half seen; beyond, a well,
Dark, gleaming, and of most translucent wave,
Images all the woven boughs above,
And each depending leaf, and every speck 460
Of azure sky, darting between their chasms;
Nor aught else in the liquid mirror laves
Its portraiture, but some inconstant star
Between one foliaged lattice twinkling fair,
Or, painted bird, sleeping beneath the moon, 465
Or gorgeous insect floating motionless,
Unconscious of the day, ere yet his wings
Have spread their glories to the gaze of noon.

   Hither the Poet came. His eyes beheld
Their own wan light through the reflected lines 470
Of his thin hair, distinct in the dark depth
Of that still fountain; as the human heart,
Gazing in dreams over the gloomy grave,
Sees its own treacherous likeness there. He heard
The motion of the leaves, the grass that sprung 475
Startled and glanced and trembled even to feel

8. All these embracements and diverse modes of "union" exemplify the communion of things within the natural world.

An unaccustomed presence, and the sound
Of the sweet brook that from the secret springs
Of that dark fountain rose. A Spirit seemed
To stand beside him[9]—clothed in no bright robes   480
Of shadowy silver or enshrining light,
Borrowed from aught the visible world affords
Of grace, or majesty, or mystery;—
But, undulating woods, and silent well,
And leaping rivulet, and evening gloom   485
Now deepening the dark shades, for speech assuming
Held commune with him, as if he and it
Were all that was,—only . . . when his regard
Was raised by intense pensiveness, . . . two eyes,
Two starry eyes, hung in the gloom of thought,   490
And seemed with their serene and azure smiles
To beckon him.

        Obedient to the light
That shone within his soul, he went, pursuing
The windings of the dell.—The rivulet
Wanton and wild, through many a green ravine   495
Beneath the forest flowed. Sometimes it fell
Among the moss with hollow harmony
Dark and profound. Now on the polished stones
It danced; like childhood laughing as it went:
Then, through the plain in tranquil wanderings crept,   500
Reflecting every herb and drooping bud
That overhung its quietness.—"O stream!
Whose source is inaccessibly profound,
Whither do thy mysterious waters tend?
Thou imagest my life. Thy darksome stillness,   505
Thy dazzling waves, thy loud and hollow gulphs,
Thy searchless fountain, and invisible course
Have each their type in me: and the wide sky,
And measureless ocean may declare as soon
What oozy cavern or what wandering cloud   510
Contains thy waters, as the universe
Tell where these living thoughts reside, when stretched
Upon thy flowers my bloodless limbs shall waste
I' the passing wind!"

        Beside the grassy shore
Of the small stream he went; he did impress   515
On the green moss his tremulous step, that caught

9. This difficult passage describes another temptation to let Nature suffice,
parallel to that in lines 412 ff. The
"Spirit" is Nature, which assumes a
form—clothed in natural things and attributes, but lacking "light" (line 481)
—that seems to allow communication
(and communion) with the poet, and
gives him the momentary impression that
there is no ideal beyond itself (lines
486–88). But when (lines 488 ff.) the
Poet raises his eyes above the natural
scene, he sees the beckoning eyes of the
maiden of his vision and moves on
(lines 491–92), obedient to an inner light
which has no counterpart in Nature.

Strong shuddering from his burning limbs. As one
Roused by some joyous madness from the couch
Of fever, he did move; yet, not like him,
Forgetful of the grave, where, when the flame   520
Of his frail exultation shall be spent,
He must descend. With rapid steps he went
Beneath the shade of trees, beside the flow
Of the wild babbling rivulet; and now
The forest's solemn canopies were changed   525
For the uniform and lightsome evening sky.
Grey rocks did peep from the spare moss, and stemmed
The struggling brook: tall spires of windlestrae[1]
Threw their thin shadows down the rugged slope,
And nought but knarled roots[2] of antient pines   530
Branchless and blasted, clenched with grasping roots
The unwilling soil. A gradual change was here,
Yet ghastly. For, as fast years flow away,
The smooth brow gathers, and the hair grows thin
And white, and where irradiate[3] dewy eyes   535
Had shone, gleam stony orbs:—so from his steps
Bright flowers departed, and the beautiful shade
Of the green groves, with all their odorous winds
And musical motions. Calm, he still pursued
The stream, that with a larger volume now   540
Rolled through the labyrinthine dell; and there
Fretted a path through its descending curves
With its wintry speed. On every side now rose
Rocks, which, in unimaginable forms,
Lifted their black and barren pinnacles   545
In the light of evening, and its precipice
Obscuring the ravine, disclosed above,
Mid toppling stones, black gulphs and yawning caves,
Whose windings gave ten thousand various tongues
To the loud stream. Lo! where the pass expands   550
Its stony jaws, the abrupt mountain breaks,
And seems, with its accumulated crags,
To overhang the world: for wide expand
Beneath the wan stars and descending moon
Islanded seas, blue mountains, mighty streams,   555
Dim tracts and vast, robed in the lustrous gloom
Of leaden-coloured even, and fiery hills
Mingling their flames with twilight, on the verge
Of the remote horizon. The near scene,
In naked and severe simplicity,   560
Made contrast with the universe. A pine,
Rock-rooted, stretched athwart the vacancy
Its swinging boughs, to each inconstant blast
Yielding one only response, at each pause

---

1. Scottish dialect for "windlestraw"—   2. Apparently an error for "trunks."
tall, dried stalks of grass.   3. Used adjectivally: illumined, brilliant.

In most familiar cadence, with the howl   565
The thunder and the hiss of homeless streams
Mingling its solemn song, whilst the broad river,
Foaming and hurrying o'er its rugged path,
Fell into that immeasurable void
Scattering its waters to the passing winds.   570

    Yet the grey precipice and solemn pine
And torrent, were not all;—one silent nook
Was there. Even on the edge of that vast mountain,
Upheld by knotty roots and fallen rocks,
It overlooked in its serenity   575
The dark earth, and the bending vault of stars.
It was a tranquil spot, that seemed to smile
Even in the lap of horror. Ivy clasped
The fissured stones with its entwining arms,
And did embower with leaves for ever green,   580
And berries dark, the smooth and even space
Of its inviolated floor, and here
The children of the autumnal whirlwind bore,
In wanton sport, those bright leaves, whose decay,
Red, yellow, or etherially pale,   585
Rivals the pride of summer. 'Tis the haunt
Of every gentle wind, whose breath can teach
The wilds to love tranquillity. One step,
One human step alone, has ever broken
The stillness of its solitude:—one voice   590
Alone inspired its echoes,—even that voice
Which hither came, floating among the winds,
And led the loveliest among human forms
To make their wild haunts the depository
Of all the grace and beauty that endued   595
Its motions, render up its majesty,
Scatter its music on the unfeeling storm,
And to the damp leaves and blue cavern mould,
Nurses of rainbow flowers and branching moss,
Commit the colours of that varying cheek,   600
That snowy breast, those dark and drooping eyes.

    The dim and horned moon hung low, and poured
A sea of lustre on the horizon's verge
That overflowed its mountains. Yellow mist
Filled the unbounded atmosphere, and drank   605
Wan moonlight even to fulness: not a star
Shone, not a sound was heard; the very winds,
Danger's grim playmates, on that precipice
Slept, clasped in his embrace.—O, storm of death!
Whose sightless speed divides this sullen night: 610
And thou, colossal Skeleton, that, still
Guiding its irresistible career

In thy devastating omnipotence,
Art king of this frail world, from the red field
Of slaughter, from the reeking hospital, 615
The patriot's sacred couch, the snowy bed
Of innocence, the scaffold and the throne,
A mighty voice invokes thee. Ruin calls
His brother Death. A rare and regal prey
He hath prepared, prowling around the world; 620
Glutted with which thou mayst repose, and men
Go to their graves like flowers or creeping worms,
Nor ever more offer at thy dark shrine
The unheeded tribute of a broken heart.

When on the threshold of the green recess 625
The wanderer's footsteps fell, he knew that death
Was on him. Yet a little, ere it fled,
Did he resign his high and holy soul
To images of the majestic past,
That paused within his passive being now, 630
Like winds that bear sweet music, when they breathe
Through some dim latticed chamber. He did place
His pale lean hand upon the rugged trunk
Of the old pine. Upon an ivied stone
Reclined his languid head, his limbs did rest, 635
Diffused and motionless, on the smooth brink
Of that obscurest chasm;—and thus he lay,
Surrendering to their final impulses
The hovering powers of life. Hope and despair,
The torturers, slept; no mortal pain or fear 640
Marred his repose, the influxes of sense,
And his own being unalloyed by pain,
Yet feebler and more feeble, calmly fed
The stream of thought, till he lay breathing there
At peace, and faintly smiling:—his last sight 645
Was the great moon, which o'er the western line
Of the wide world her mighty horn suspended,
With whose dun[4] beams inwoven darkness seemed
To mingle. Now upon the jagged hills
It rests, and still as the divided frame 650
Of the vast meteor sunk, the Poet's blood,
That ever beat in mystic sympathy
With nature's ebb and flow, grew feebler still:
And when two lessening points of light alone
Gleamed through the darkness, the alternate gasp 655
Of his faint respiration scarce did stir
The stagnate night:[5]—till the minutest ray
Was quenched, the pulse yet lingered in his heart.

4. Dull, dim.
5. The Poet's life ebbs in consonance with the descent of the "hornéd moon," to the moment when only the two "points of light"—its horns—show above the hills.

It paused—it fluttered. But when heaven remained
Utterly black, the murky shades involved   660
An image, silent, cold, and motionless,
As their own voiceless earth and vacant air.
Even as a vapour fed with golden beams
That ministered on sunlight, ere the west
Eclipses it, was now that wonderous frame—   665
No sense, no motion, no divinity—
A fragile lute, on whose harmonious strings
The breath of heaven did wander—a bright stream
Once fed with many-voiced waves—a dream
Of youth, which night and time have quenched for ever,   670
Still, dark, and dry, and unremembered now.

O, for Medea's wondrous alchemy,[6]
Which wheresoe'er it fell made the earth gleam
With bright flowers, and the wintry boughs exhale
From vernal blooms fresh fragrance! O, that God,   675
Profuse of poisons, would concede the chalice
Which but one living man has drained,[7] who now,
Vessel of deathless wrath, a slave that feels
No proud exemption in the blighting curse
He bears, over the world wanders for ever,   680
Lone as incarnate death! O, that the dream
Of dark magician in his visioned cave,[8]
Raking the cinders of a crucible
For life and power, even when his feeble hand
Shakes in its last decay, were the true law   685
Of this so lovely world! But thou art fled
Like some frail exhalation; which the dawn
Robes in its golden beams,—ah! thou hast fled!
The brave, the gentle, and the beautiful,
The child of grace and genius. Heartless things   690
Are done and said i' the world, and many worms
And beasts and men live on, and mighty Earth
From sea and mountain, city and wilderness,
In vesper low or joyous orison,[9]
Lifts still its solemn voice:—but thou art fled—   695
Thou canst no longer know or love the shapes
Of this phantasmal scene, who have to thee
Been purest ministers, who are, alas!
Now thou art not. Upon those pallid lips
So sweet even in their silence, on those eyes   700
That image sleep in death, upon that form
Yet safe from the worm's outrage, let no tear
Be shed—not even in thought. Nor, when those hues

---

6. Medea brewed a magic potion to rejuvenate the dying Aeson; where some of the potion spilled on the ground, flowers sprang up (Ovid, *Metamorphoses* vii.275 ff.).
7. The Wandering Jew; according to a medieval legend, he had taunted Christ on the way to His crucifixion and was condemned to wander the world, deathless, until Christ's second coming.
8. Cave in which he has visions. The "dark magician" is an alchemist attempting to produce the elixir of enduring life.
9. Prayer; vesper: evening prayer.

Are gone, and those divinest lineaments,
Worn by the senseless wind, shall live alone   705
In the frail pauses of this simple strain,
Let not high verse, mourning the memory
Of that which is no more, or painting's woe
Or sculpture, speak in feeble imagery
Their own cold powers. Art and eloquence,   710
And all the shews o' the world are frail and vain
To weep a loss that turns their lights to shade.
It is a woe too "deep for tears,"[10] when all
Is reft at once, when some surpassing Spirit,
Whose light adorned the world around it, leaves   715
Those who remain behind, not sobs or groans,
The passionate tumult of a clinging hope;
But pale despair and cold tranquillity,
Nature's vast frame, the web of human things,
Birth and the grave, that are not as they were.   720

1815   1816

Mont Blanc[1]

LINES WRITTEN IN THE VALE OF CHAMOUNI

I

The everlasting universe of things
Flows through the mind, and rolls its rapid waves,

10. From the last line of Wordsworth's *Ode: Intimations of Immortality*: "Thoughts that do often lie too deep for tears."

1. Shelley wrote of this poem: "It was composed under the immediate impression of the deep and powerful feelings excited by the objects which it attempts to describe; and, as an indisciplined overflowing of the soul, rests its claim to approbation on an attempt to imitate the untamable wildness and inaccessible solemnity from which those feelings sprang."

Shelley's comment points to two important attributes of *Mont Blanc*. First, he attempts, as in other poems (supremely in *Ode to the West Wind*), to make the poem iconic, or directly imitative of the alternating "wildness" and "solemnity" of the scene and the consonant thought and feelings it evokes. Second, this work belongs to the genre of the "local" poem, a descriptive-meditative presentation of a precisely identified landscape. In this respect it resembles Wordsworth's *Tintern Abbey*, the major influence on *Mont Blanc*. Shelley's poem, like Wordsworth's, poses the question of the significance of the interchange between nature and the human mind; he proposes, however, a very different answer to that question.

The poem raises the central problem about the nature of "Power," the ultimate principle behind all natural and mental process. The symbol of this Power is the river Arve (lines 16–17), which has its "secret throne" at the summit of Mont Blanc, the highest peak in Europe, and beyond human access. The process of the Arve begins with the unseen fall of snow and the unheard play of winds at the far height of the mountain, becomes the Mer de Glace glacier, moves down the mountain, and melts into the river which runs through its ravine into the valley of Chamonix in southeastern France. Shelley's answer is austerely skeptical. He postulates only that "the power is there," at the inaccessible peak of Mont Blanc, but refuses to invest it with anthropomorphic intentions or values.

What we do know is that this Power, as it descends from its secret throne into the human ken, remorselessly destroys all things, animal and human (lines 100–20); yet in its simultaneous form as a river (lines 120–26), it with equal moral indifference is the "breath and blood of distant lands," and the source of life-giving rain. It is the enlightened human will alone which can convert this purposeless destroyer and preserver to its own human ends, even to the revolutionary end of total reform (lines 80–83). The poem ends like *Ode to the West Wind*, with a rhetorical question; the implication is that phenomenal nature is in itself but a universal blank, except as it is invested with significance by the imagination of man.

Now dark—now glittering—now reflecting gloom—
Now lending splendour, where from secret springs
The source of human thought its tribute brings   5
Of waters,—with a sound but half its own,
Such as a feeble brook will oft assume
In the wild woods, among the mountains lone,
Where waterfalls around it leap forever,
Where woods and winds contend, and a vast river   10
Over its rocks ceaselessly bursts and raves.

II

Thus thou, Ravine of Arve—dark, deep Ravine—
Thou many-coloured, many-voiced vale,
Over whose pines, and crags, and caverns sail
Fast cloud shadows and sunbeams: awful scene,   15
Where Power in likeness of the Arve comes down
From the ice gulphs that gird his secret throne,
Bursting through these dark mountains like the flame
Of lightning through the tempest;—thou dost lie,
Thy giant brood of pines around thee clinging,   20
Children of elder time, in whose devotion
The chainless winds still come and ever came
To drink their odours, and their mighty swinging
To hear—an old and solemn harmony;
Thine earthly rainbows stretched across the sweep   25
Of the etherial waterfall, whose veil
Robes some unsculptured image; the strange sleep
Which when the voices of the desart fail
Wraps all in its own deep eternity;—
Thy caverns echoing to the Arve's commotion,   30
A loud, lone sound no other sound can tame;
Thou art pervaded with that ceaseless motion,
Thou art the path of that unresting sound—
Dizzy Ravine! and when I gaze on thee
I seem as in a trance sublime and strange   35
To muse on my own separate phantasy,
My own, my human mind, which passively
Now renders and receives fast influencings,
Holding an unremitting interchange
With the clear universe of things around;[2]   40
One legion of wild thoughts, whose wandering wings
Now float above thy darkness, and now rest
Where that or thou art no unbidden guest,
In the still cave of the witch Poesy,
Seeking among the shadows that pass by   45
Ghosts of all things that are, some shade of thee,
Some phantom, some faint image; till the breast
From which they fled recalls them, thou art there![3]

2. This passage is remarkably parallel to a passage Shelley could not have read in *The Prelude*, published in 1850, in which Wordsworth discovers, in the landscape viewed from Mount Snowdon, the "type" or "emblem" of the human mind in its interchanges with nature. See *The Prelude*, above, XIV.63 ff.

3. The distinction is between an abstract concept, or image, of the Power and its concrete embodiment in the Arve.

III

Some say that gleams of a remoter world
Visit the soul in sleep,—that death is slumber,　　50
And that its shapes the busy thoughts outnumber
Of those who wake and live.—I look on high;
Has some unknown omnipotence unfurled
The veil of life and death? or do I lie
In dream, and does the mightier world of sleep　　55
Spread far around and inaccessibly
Its circles? For the very spirit fails,
Driven like a homeless cloud from steep to steep
That vanishes among the viewless[4] gales!
Far, far above, piercing the infinite sky,　　60
Mont Blanc appears,—still, snowy, and serene—
Its subject mountains their unearthly forms
Pile around it, ice and rock; broad vales between
Of frozen floods, unfathomable deeps,
Blue as the overhanging heaven, that spread　　65
And wind among the accumulated steeps;
A desart peopled by the storms alone,
Save when the eagle brings some hunter's bone,
And the wolf tracts her there—how hideously
Its shapes are heaped around! rude, bare, and high,　　70
Ghastly, and scarred, and riven.—Is this the scene
Where the old Earthquake-dæmon taught her young
Ruin? Were these their toys? or did a sea
Of fire, envelope once this silent snow?
None can reply—all seems eternal now.　　75
The wilderness has a mysterious tongue
Which teaches awful doubt, or faith so mild,
So solemn, so serene, that man may be
But for such faith with nature reconciled;[5]
Thou hast a voice, great Mountain, to repeal　　80
Large codes of fraud and woe; not understood
By all, but which[6] the wise, and great, and good
Interpret, or make felt, or deeply feel.

IV

The fields, the lakes, the forests, and the streams,
Ocean, and all the living things that dwell　　85
Within the dædal[7] earth; lightning, and rain,
Earthquake, and fiery flood, and hurricane,
The torpor of the year when feeble dreams
Visit the hidden buds, or dreamless sleep
Holds every future leaf and flower;—the bound　　90
With which from that detested trance they leap;

---

4. Invisible.
5. "Simply by holding such a faith"—such as Wordsworth's "cheerful faith" (lines 133–34) in *Tintern Abbey* "that all which we behold / Is full of blessings." In Shelley's balance of possibilities, the landscape is equally capable of teaching this faith and the "awful doubt" that nature is indifferent to human ends and values.
6. The reference is to "voice," line 80.
7. Intricately formed; derived from Dædalus, builder of the labyrinth in Crete.

The works and ways of man, their death and birth,
And that of him and all that his may be;
All things that move and breathe with toil and sound
Are born and die; revolve, subside and swell. 95
Power dwells apart in its tranquillity
Remote, serene, and inaccessible:
And *this*, the naked countenance of earth,
On which I gaze, even these primæval mountains
Teach the adverting mind. The glaciers creep 100
Like snakes that watch their prey, from their far fountains,
Slow rolling on; there, many a precipice,
Frost and the Sun in scorn of mortal power
Have piled: dome, pyramid, and pinnacle,
A city of death, distinct with many a tower 105
And wall impregnable of beaming ice.
Yet not a city, but a flood of ruin
Is there, that from the boundaries of the sky
Rolls its perpetual stream; vast pines are strewing
Its destined path, or in the mangled soil 110
Branchless and shattered stand; the rocks, drawn down
From yon remotest waste, have overthrown
The limits of the dead and living world,
Never to be reclaimed. The dwelling-place
Of insects, beasts, and birds, becomes its spoil; 115
Their food and their retreat forever gone,
So much of life and joy is lost. The race
Of man, flies far in dread; his work and dwelling
Vanish, like smoke before the tempest's stream,
And their place is not known. Below, vast caves 120
Shine in the rushing torrents' restless gleam,
Which from those secret chasms in tumult welling[8]
Meet in the vale, and one majestic River,
The breath and blood of distant lands, for ever
Rolls its loud waters to the ocean waves, 125
Breathes its swift vapours to the circling air.

v

Mont Blanc yet gleams on high:—the power is there,
The still and solemn power of many sights,
And many sounds, and much of life and death.
In the calm darkness of the moonless nights, 130
In the lone glare of day, the snows descend
Upon that Mountain; none beholds them there,
Nor when the flakes burn in the sinking sun,
Or the star-beams dart through them:—Winds contend
Silently there, and heap the snow with breath 135
Rapid and strong, but silently! Its home
The voiceless lightning in these solitudes
Keeps innocently, and like vapour broods

---

8. Like lines 9–11, an echo of Coleridge's description of the chasm and sacred
river in *Kubla Khan*, lines 12–24.

Over the snow. The secret strength of things
Which governs thought, and to the infinite dome   140
Of heaven is as a law, inhabits thee!
And what were thou,[9] and earth, and stars, and sea,
If to the human mind's imaginings
Silence and solitude were vacancy?

1816   1817

Hymn to Intellectual Beauty[1]

1

The awful shadow of some unseen Power
  Floats though unseen amongst us,—visiting
  This various world with as inconstant wing
As summer winds that creep from flower to flower.—
Like moonbeams that behind some piny mountain shower,   5
    It visits with inconstant glance
    Each human heart and countenance;
Like hues and harmonies of evening,—
    Like clouds in starlight widely spread,—
    Like memory of music fled,—   10
    Like aught that for its grace may be
Dear, and yet dearer for its mystery.

2

Spirit of BEAUTY, that dost consecrate
  With thine own hues all thou dost shine upon
  Of human thought or form,—where art thou gone?   15
Why dost thou pass away and leave our state,
This dim vast vale of tears, vacant and desolate?
    Ask why the sunlight not forever
    Weaves rainbows o'er yon mountain river,
Why aught should fail and fade that once is shewn,   20
    Why fear and dream and death and birth
    Cast on the daylight of this earth
    Such gloom,—why man has such a scope
For love and hate, despondency and hope?

3

No voice from some sublimer world hath ever   25
  To sage or poet these responses given—
  Therefore the name of God and ghosts and Heaven,
Remain the records of their vain endeavour,[2]
Frail spells—whose uttered charm might not avail to sever,
    From all we hear and all we see,   30
    Doubt, chance, and mutability.

---

9. Mont Blanc.
1. "Intellectual" means "non-sensible." "Intellectual Beauty" is beyond access by sense experience; it is postulated to account for occasional states of awareness which lend splendor, grace, and truth both to the natural world and to man's moral consciousness. To this mystery (stanzas 5–7) Shelley had, at its early visitation, dedicated his powers, and to it he now prays as he passes the noon of life (stanza 7).
2. The names (line 28) are groundless guesses at identifying the mystery by religious philosophers and poets (line 26).

Thy light alone—like mist o'er mountains driven,
    Or music by the night wind sent
    Through strings of some still instrument,[3]
    Or moonlight on a midnight stream,   35
Gives grace and truth to life's unquiet dream.

4

Love, Hope, and Self-esteem, like clouds depart
    And come, for some uncertain moments lent.
    Man were immortal, and omnipotent,
Didst thou, unknown and awful as thou art,   40
Keep with thy glorious train firm state within his heart.
        Thou messenger of sympathies,
        That wax and wane in lovers' eyes—
Thou—that to human thought art nourishment,
        Like darkness to a dying flame!   45
        Depart not as thy shadow came,
        Depart not—lest the grave should be,
Like life and fear, a dark reality.

5

While yet a boy I sought for ghosts, and sped
    Through many a listening chamber, cave and ruin,   50
    And starlight wood, with fearful steps pursuing
Hopes of high talk with the departed dead.
I called on poisonous names with which our youth is fed;[4]
        I was not heard—I saw them not—
        When musing deeply on the lot   55
Of life, at that sweet time when winds are wooing
        All vital things that wake to bring
        News of buds and blossoming,—
        Sudden, thy shadow fell on me;
I shrieked, and clasped my hands in extacy!   60

6

I vowed that I would dedicate my powers
    To thee and thine—have I not kept the vow?
    With beating heart and streaming eyes, even now
I call the phantoms of a thousand hours
Each from his voiceless grave: they have in visioned bowers   65
        Of studious zeal or love's delight
        Outwatched with me the envious night[5]—
They know that never joy illumed my brow
        Unlinked with hope that thou wouldst free
        This world from its dark slavery,   70
        That thou—O awful LOVELINESS,
Wouldst give whate'er these words cannot express.

---

3. A wind harp.
4. Lines 49–52 refer to Shelley's youthful experiments with magic. The "poisonous names" in line 53 are those in the prayers he had been taught as a child.
5. I.e., watched until the night, envious of their delight, had reluctantly departed.

7

The day becomes more solemn and serene
  When noon is past—there is a harmony
  In autumn, and a lustre in its sky,   75
Which through the summer is not heard or seen,
As if it could not be, as if it had not been!
    Thus let thy power, which like the truth
    Of nature on my passive youth
Descended, to my onward life supply   80
    Its calm—to one who worships thee,
    And every form containing thee,
    Whom, SPIRIT fair, thy spells did bind
To fear himself, and love all human kind.

1816   1817

Ozymandias[6]

I met a traveller from an antique land,
Who said—"Two vast and trunkless legs of stone
Stand in the desert. . . . Near them, on the sand,
Half sunk a shattered visage lies, whose frown,
And wrinkled lip, and sneer of cold command,   5
Tell that its sculptor well those passions read
Which yet survive, stamped on these lifeless things,
The hand that mocked them, and the heart that fed;[7]
And on the pedestal, these words appear:
My name is Ozymandias, King of Kings,   10
Look on my Works, ye Mighty, and despair!
Nothing beside remains. Round the decay
Of that colossal Wreck, boundless and bare
The lone and level sands stretch far away."

1817   1818

Sonnet

Lift not the painted veil which those who live
Call Life; though unreal shapes be pictured there
And it but mimic all we would believe
With colours idly spread,—behind, lurk Fear
And Hope, twin Destinies, who ever weave   5
Their shadows o'er the chasm, sightless and drear.

---

6. According to Diodorus Siculus, the Greek historian of the 1st century B.C., the largest statue in Egypt had the inscription: "I am Ozymandias, king of kings; if anyone wishes to know what I am and where I lie, let him surpass me in some of my exploits." Ozymandias was the Greek name for Ramses II of Egypt, 13th century B.C.

7. "The hand" is the sculptor's, who had "mocked" (both imitated and derided) the sculptured passions; "the heart" is the king's.

I knew one who had lifted it . . . . he sought,
For his lost heart was tender, things to love,
But found them not, alas; nor was there aught
The world contains, the which he could approve.   10
Through the unheeding many he did move,
A splendour among shadows—a bright blot
Upon this gloomy scene, a Spirit that strove
For truth, and like the Preacher[8] found it not.—

1818   1824

Stanzas Written in Dejection— December 1818, Near Naples[9]

The Sun is warm, the sky is clear,
The waves are dancing fast and bright,
Blue isles and snowy mountains wear
The purple noon's transparent might,
The breath of the moist earth is light   5
Around its unexpanded buds;
Like many a voice of one delight
The winds, the birds, the Ocean-floods;
The City's voice itself is soft, like Solitude's.

I see the Deep's untrampled floor   10
With green and purple seaweeds strown;
I see the waves upon the shore
Like light dissolved in star-showers, thrown;
I sit upon the sands alone;
The lightning of the noontide Ocean   15
Is flashing round me, and a tone
Arises from its measured motion,
How sweet! did any heart now share in my emotion.

Alas, I have nor hope nor health
Nor peace within nor calm around,   20
Nor that content surpassing wealth
The sage[1] in meditation found,
And walked with inward glory crowned;
Nor fame nor power nor love nor leisure—
Others I see whom these surround,   25
Smiling they live and call life pleasure:
To me that cup has been dealt in another measure.

Yet now despair itself is mild,
Even as the winds and waters are;

8. Author of the skeptical and pessimistic Book of Ecclesiastes in the Old Testament.
9. Shelley's first wife, Harriet, had drowned herself; Clara, his baby daughter by Mary Shelley, had just died; and Shelley himself was plagued by ill health, pain, financial worries, and the sense that he had failed as a poet.
1. Probably the Roman emperor Marcus Aurelius (2nd century A.D.), Stoic philosopher who wrote twelve books of *Meditations*.

I could lie down like a tired child   30
And weep away the life of care
Which I have borne and yet must bear
Till Death like Sleep might steal on me,
And I might feel in the warm air
My cheek grow cold, and hear the Sea   35
Breathe o'er my dying brain its last monotony.

Some might lament that I were cold,
As I, when this sweet day is gone
Which my lost heart, too soon grown old,
Insults with this untimely moan—   40
They might lament,—for I am one
Whom men love not, and yet regret;
Unlike this day, which, when the Sun
Shall on its stainless glory set,
Will linger though enjoyed, like joy in Memory yet.   45

1818   1824

A Song: "Men of England"[2]

Men of England, wherefore plough
For the lords who lay ye low?
Wherefore weave with toil and care
The rich robes your tyrants wear?

Wherefore feed and clothe and save   5
From the cradle to the grave
Those ungrateful drones who would
Drain your sweat—nay, drink your blood?

Wherefore, Bees of England, forge
Many a weapon, chain, and scourge,   10
That these stingless drones may spoil
The forced produce of your toil?

Have ye leisure, comfort, calm,
Shelter, food, love's gentle balm?
Or what is it ye buy so dear   15
With your pain and with your fear?

The seed ye sow, another reaps;
The wealth ye find, another keeps;
The robes ye weave, another wears;
The arms ye forge, another bears.   20

2. This and the two following poems were written at a time of turbulent unrest, after the return of troops from the Napoleonic Wars had precipitated a great economic depression. The *Song*, expressing Shelley's hope for a proletarian revolution, was originally planned as one of a series for workingmen; it has become, as the poet wished, a hymn of the British labor movement.

Sow seed—but let no tyrant reap:
Find wealth—let no impostor heap:
Weave robes—let not the idle wear:
Forge arms—in your defence to bear.

Shrink to your cellars, holes, and cells—   25
In halls ye deck another dwells.
Why shake the chains ye wrought? when see
The steel ye tempered glance on ye.

With plough and spade and hoe and loom
Trace your grave and build your tomb   30
And weave your winding-sheet—till fair
England be your Sepulchre.

1819   1839

England in 1819

An old, mad, blind, despised, and dying King;[3]
Princes, the dregs of their dull race, who flow
Through public scorn,—mud from a muddy spring;
Rulers who neither see nor feel nor know,
But leechlike to their fainting country cling   5
Till they drop, blind in blood, without a blow.
A people starved and stabbed in th'untilled field;
An army, whom liberticide and prey
Makes as a two-edged sword to all who wield;
Golden and sanguine laws[4] which tempt and slay;   10
Religion Christless, Godless—a book sealed;
A senate, Time's worst statute, unrepealed[5]—
Are graves from which a glorious Phantom[6] may
Burst, to illumine our tempestuous day.

1819   1839

To Sidmouth and Castlereagh[7]

As from their ancestral oak
    Two empty ravens wind their clarion,
Yell by yell, and croak by croak,

3. George III, who died in the next year, 1820.
4. Laws bought with gold, and leading to bloodshed.
5. The law imposing disabilities upon Dissenters and Roman Catholics.
6. I.e., a revolution.
7. Shelley's powerful satire is directed against Viscount Castlereagh, foreign secretary 1812–22, who took a leading part in the European settlement after the Battle of Waterloo, and Viscount Sidmouth (1757–1844), the home secretary, whose cruelly coercive measures (sup-ported by Castlereagh) against unrest in the laboring classes were in large part responsible for the "Peterloo massacre." Cavalry charged a huge but peaceable outdoor reform meeting in St. Peter's Field, with the result that some nine people were killed and 600 injured. ("Peterloo" is an ironic combination of "Waterloo" and "St. Peter's.")

When this poem was printed by Mrs. Shelley in 1839, it was given the title *Similes for Two Political Characters of 1819.*

When they scent the noonday smoke
Of fresh human carrion:—   5

As two gibbering night-birds flit
    From their bowers of deadly yew
Through the night to frighten it—
When the moon is in a fit,
    And the stars are none, or few:—   10

As a shark and dogfish wait
    Under an Atlantic isle
For the Negro-ship, whose freight
Is the theme of their debate,
    Wrinkling their red gills the while—   15

Are ye—two vultures sick for battle,
    Two scorpions under one wet stone,
Two bloodless wolves whose dry throats rattle,
Two crows perched on the murrained[8] cattle,
    Two vipers tangled into one.   20

1819   1832; 1839

The Indian Girl's Song[9]

I arise from dreams of thee
In the first sleep of night—
The winds are breathing low
And the stars are burning bright.
I arise from dreams of thee—   5
And a spirit in my feet
Has borne me—Who knows how?
To thy chamber window, sweet!—

The wandering airs they faint
On the dark silent stream—   10
The champak[1] odours fail
Like sweet thoughts in a dream;
The nightingale's complaint—
It dies upon her heart—
As I must die on thine   15
O beloved as thou art!

O lift me from the grass!
I die, I faint, I fail!
Let thy love in kisses rain
On my lips and eyelids pale.   20

8. A "murrain" is a malignant disease of domestic animals.
9. Usually entitled *The Indian Serenade*. As the title shows, it is not a personal utterance but a dramatic lyric, sung by an imagined East Indian girl and manifesting the conventional extravagance of an Oriental love poem.
1. An Indian species of magnolia.

My cheek is cold and white, alas!
My heart beats loud and fast.
Oh press it close to thine again
Where it will break at last.

1819   1822

Ode to the West Wind[2]

I

O wild West Wind, thou breath of Autumn's being,
Thou, from whose unseen presence the leaves dead
Are driven, like ghosts from an enchanter fleeing,

Yellow, and black, and pale, and hectic red,
Pestilence-stricken multitudes: O Thou,   5
Who chariotest to their dark wintry bed

The winged seeds, where they lie cold and low,
Each like a corpse within its grave, until
Thine azure sister of the Spring[3] shall blow

Her clarion[4] o'er the dreaming earth, and fill   10
(Driving sweet buds like flocks to feed in air)
With living hues and odours plain and hill:

Wild Spirit, which art moving everywhere;
Destroyer and Preserver; hear, O hear!

II

Thou on whose stream, 'mid the steep sky's commotion,   15
Loose clouds like Earth's decaying leaves are shed,
Shook from the tangled boughs of Heaven and Ocean,[5]

2. "This poem was conceived and chiefly written in a wood that skirts the Arno, near Florence, and on a day when that tempestuous wind, whose temperature is at once mild and animating, was collecting the vapors which pour down the autumnal rains" [Shelley's note]. As in other major Romantic poems—for example, the opening of Wordsworth's *Prelude*, Coleridge's *Dejection*, and the conclusion to Shelley's *Adonais*—the rising wind, linked with the cycle of the seasons, is presented as the outer correspondent to an inner change from apathy to spiritual vitality, and from imaginative sterility to a burst of creative power which is paralleled to the inspiration of the Biblical prophets. In Hebrew, Latin, Greek, and many other languages, the words for wind, breath, soul, and inspiration are all identical or related. Thus Shelley's west wind is a "spirit" (the Latin *spiritus*: wind, breath, soul, and the root word in "inspiration"), the "breath of Autumn's being," which on earth, sky, and sea destroys in the autumn in order to revive in the spring. Around this central image the poem weaves various cycles of death and regeneration—vegetational, human, and divine.

The stanza used in this ode was developed by Shelley from the interlaced three-line units of the Italian *terza rima*: *aba bcb cdc*, etc. Shelley's stanza consists of a set of four such tercets, closed by a couplet rhyming with the middle line of the preceding tercet: *aba bcb cdc ded ee.*
3. The west wind that will blow in the spring.
4. A high, shrill trumpet.
5. I.e., the fragmentary clouds ("leaves") are torn by the wind from the larger and higher clouds ("boughs"), which are formed by a union of air with vapor drawn up by the sun from the ocean. "Angels" (line 18) suggests the old sense: messengers, harbingers.

Angels of rain and lightning: there are spread
On the blue surface of thine aery surge,
Like the bright hair uplifted from the head   20

Of some fierce Mænad,[6] even from the dim verge
Of the horizon to the zenith's height,
The locks of the approaching storm. Thou Dirge

Of the dying year, to which this closing night
Will be the dome of a vast sepulchre,   25
Vaulted with all thy congregated might

Of vapours, from whose solid atmosphere
Black rain and fire and hail will burst: O hear!

III

Thou who didst waken from his summer dreams
The blue Mediterranean, where he lay,   30
Lulled by the coil of his chrystalline streams,[7]

Beside a pumice isle in Baiæ's bay,[8]
And saw in sleep old palaces and towers
Quivering within the wave's intenser day,[9]

All overgrown with azure moss and flowers   35
So sweet, the sense faints picturing them! Thou
For whose path the Atlantic's level powers

Cleave themselves into chasms, while far below
The sea-blooms and the oozy woods which wear
The sapless foliage of the ocean, know   40

Thy voice, and suddenly grow grey with fear,
And tremble and despoil themselves:[1] O hear!

IV

If I were a dead leaf thou mightest bear;
If I were a swift cloud to fly with thee;
A wave to pant beneath thy power, and share   45

The impulse of thy strength, only less free
Than thou, O Uncontrollable! If even
I were as in my boyhood, and could be

6. A female votary who danced frenziedly in the worship of Dionysus (Bacchus), the Greek god of wine and vegetation. As vegetation god, he was fabled to die in the fall and to be resurrected in the spring.
7. The currents that flow in the Mediterranean Sea, sometimes with a visible difference in color.
8. "Pumice": a porous volcanic stone.

"Baiæ's bay," west of Naples was the locale of imposing villas erected by Roman emperors.
9. Shelley once observed that, when reflected in water, colors are "more vivid yet blended with more harmony."
1. "The vegetation at the bottom of the sea * * * sympathizes with that of the land in the change of seasons" [Shelley's note].

The comrade of thy wanderings over Heaven,
As then, when to outstrip thy skiey speed   50
Scarce seemed a vision; I would ne'er have striven

As thus with thee in prayer in my sore need.
Oh! lift me as a wave, a leaf, a cloud!
I fall upon the thorns of life! I bleed!

A heavy weight of hours has chained and bowed   55
One too like thee: tameless, and swift, and proud.

V

Make me thy lyre,[2] even as the forest is:
What if my leaves are falling like its own!
The tumult of thy mighty harmonies

Will take from both a deep, autumnal tone,   60
Sweet though in sadness. Be thou, Spirit fierce,
My spirit! Be thou me, impetuous one!

Drive my dead thoughts over the universe
Like withered leaves to quicken a new birth!
And, by the incantation of this verse,   65

Scatter, as from an unextinguished hearth
Ashes and sparks, my words among mankind!
Be through my lips to unawakened Earth

The trumpet of a prophecy![3] O Wind,
If Winter comes, can Spring be far behind?   70

1819   1820

2. The Eolian lyre, which responds to the wind with alternating musical chords.
3. A reference to the "clarion" of line 10, as well as an allusion to the last trump of the apocalypse in Revelation xi.15.

Prometheus Unbound

Shelley composed this work in Italy between the autumn of 1818 and the close of 1819 and published it the following summer. Upon its completion he wrote in a letter, "It is a drama, with characters and mechanism of a kind yet unattempted; and I think the execution is better than any of my former attempts." It is based upon the *Prometheus Bound* of Aeschylus, which dramatizes the sufferings of Prometheus, unrepentant champion of mankind, who, because he had stolen fire from heaven, was condemned by Zeus to be chained to Mt. Caucasus and to be tortured by a vulture feeding upon his liver; in a lost sequel, Aeschylus reconciled Prometheus with his oppressor. Shelley continued Aeschylus' story, but transformed it into a symbolic drama about the origin of evil and its elimination. In such earlier writings as *Queen Mab* Shelley had expressed his belief that injustice and suffering can be eliminated by an external revolution which will wipe out or radically reform the sole causes of evil, existing social, political, and religious institutions. Implicit in *Prometheus*

Unbound, on the other hand, is the view that both the origin of evil and the possibility of reform are the moral responsibility of man himself. Social chaos and wars are a gigantic projection of man's moral disorder and inner division and conflict; tyrants are the outer representatives of the tyranny of man's baser over his better elements; hatred for others is an expression of self-contempt; and successful political reform is impossible unless man has first reformed his own nature at its roots, by substituting selfless love for divisive hate. Shelley thus incorporates into his secular myth of universal regeneration by an apocalypse of man's moral imagination, the ethical teaching of Christ on the Mount, as well as the highest classical morality represented in the *Prometheus* of Aeschylus. And Shelley warns (IV.562 ff.) that even should such a victory take place—the reintegration of splintered man, with a consequent restoration of moral and political order and a release of all man's creative powers in art and science—the price of its continuation is an unremitting vigilance lest the serpent deep in human nature should break loose and start the cycle all over again.

Shelley wrote in his Preface that Prometheus is, "as it were, the type of the highest perfection of moral and intellectual nature." But he also warned that it is a mistake to suppose that the poem contains "a reasoned system on the theory of human life. Didactic poetry is my abhorrence." *Prometheus Unbound* is not a dramatized philosophical essay, nor a moral allegory, but a large and intricate imaginative construction which involves premises about the nature of man and the springs of morality and creativity. The non-Christian poet, Yeats, called it one of "the sacred books of the world," and the Christian critic, C. S. Lewis, found in it many of the powers of Dante.

From Prometheus Unbound

A LYRICAL DRAMA

Dramatis Personae

PROMETHEUS	HERCULES
DEMOGORGON	THE PHANTASM OF JUPITER
JUPITER	THE SPIRIT OF THE EARTH
THE EARTH	THE SPIRIT OF THE MOON
OCEAN	SPIRITS OF THE HOURS
APOLLO	SPIRITS
MERCURY	ECHOES
ASIA	FAUNS
PANTHEA *Oceanides*	FURIES
IONE	

From *Act I*

SCENE—A *Ravine of Icy Rocks in the Indian Caucasus.* PROMETHEUS *is discovered bound to the Precipice.* PANTHEA *and* IONE *are seated at his feet. Time, night. During the Scene, morning slowly breaks.*

PROMETHEUS. Monarch of Gods and Dæmons,[1] and all Spirits
   But One, who throng those bright and rolling Worlds
   Which Thou and I alone of living things
   Behold with sleepless eyes! regard this Earth
   Made multitudinous with thy slaves, whom thou   5
   Requitest for knee-worship, prayer and praise,
   And toil, and hecatombs[2] of broken hearts,
   With fear and self-contempt and barren hope;
   Whilst me, who am thy foe, eyeless in hate,[3]
   Hast thou made reign and triumph, to thy scorn,   10
   O'er mine own misery and thy vain revenge.—
   Three thousand years of sleep-unsheltered hours
   And moments—aye divided by keen pangs
   Till they seemed years, torture and solitude,
   Scorn and despair,—these are mine empire:—   15
   More glorious far than that which thou surveyest
   From thine unenvied throne, O Mighty God!
   Almighty, had I deigned[4] to share the shame
   Of thine ill tyranny, and hung not here
   Nailed to this wall of eagle-baffling mountain,   20
   Black, wintry, dead, unmeasured; without herb,
   Insect, or beast, or shape or sound of life.
   Ah me, alas, pain, pain ever, forever!

   No change, no pause, no hope!—Yet I endure.
   I ask the Earth, have not the mountains felt?   25
   I ask yon Heaven—the all-beholding Sun,
   Has it not seen? The Sea, in storm or calm,
   Heaven's ever-changing Shadow, spread below—
   Have its deaf waves not heard my agony?
   Ah me, alas, pain, pain ever, forever!   30

   The crawling glaciers pierce me with the spears
   Of their moon-freezing chrystals, the bright chains
   Eat with their burning cold into my bones.
   Heaven's winged hound, polluting from thy lips
   His beak in poison not his own, tears up   35
   My heart;[5] and shapeless sights come wandering by,
   The ghastly people of the realm of dream,
   Mocking me: and the Earthquake-fiends are charged
   To wrench the rivets from my quivering wounds
   When the rocks split and close again behind;   40
   While from their loud abysses howling throng
   The genii of the storm, urging the rage
   Of whirlwind, and afflict me with keen hail.
   And yet to me welcome is Day and Night,

1. Prometheus is addressing Jupiter. The "One" in the next line is Demogorgon; see II.iv., below.
2. Large sacrificial offerings.
3. Blinded by hate.
4. I.e., you would have been all-powerful, if I had deigned.
5. The vulture, tearing daily at Prometheus' heart, was kissed by Jupiter by way of reward.

Whether one breaks the hoar frost of the morn, 45
Or starry, dim, and slow, the other climbs
The leaden-coloured East; for then they lead
The wingless, crawling Hours, one among whom
—As some dark Priest hales the reluctant victim—
Shall drag thee, cruel King, to kiss the blood 50
From these pale feet,[6] which then might trample thee
If they disdained not such a prostrate slave.
Disdain? Ah no! I pity thee.[7]—What Ruin
Will hunt thee undefended through wide Heaven!
How will thy soul, cloven to its depth with terror, 55
Gape like a Hell within! I speak in grief,
Not exultation, for I hate no more,
As then, ere misery made me wise.—The Curse
Once breathed on thee I would recall. Ye Mountains,
Whose many-voiced Echoes, through the mist 60
Of cataracts, flung the thunder of that spell!
Ye icy Springs, stagnant with wrinkling frost,
Which vibrated to hear me, and then crept
Shuddering through India! Thou serenest Air,
Through which the Sun walks burning without beams! 65
And ye swift Whirlwinds, who on poised wings
Hung mute and moveless o'er yon hushed abyss,
As thunder louder than your own made rock
The orbed world! If then my words had power—
Though I am changed so that aught evil wish 70
Is dead within, although no memory be
Of what is hate—let them not lose it now![8]
What was that curse? for ye all heard me speak.[9]

* * *

PHANTASM

Fiend, I defy thee! with a calm, fixed mind,
    All that thou canst inflict I bid thee do;
Foul Tyrant both of Gods and Humankind,
    One only being shalt thou not subdue. 265
Rain then thy plagues upon me here,
Ghastly disease, and frenzying fear;
And let alternate frost and fire
Eat into me, and be thine ire
Lightning and cutting hail and legioned forms 270
Of furies, driving by upon the wounding storms.

6. One of a number of implied parallels between the agony of Prometheus and the passion of Christ.

7. At this early point occurs the crisis of the action: the beginning of Prometheus' change of heart from hate to compassion, which is consummated in lines 303–5. The rest of the symbolic drama gradually unfolds the consequences of this moral triumph—of which Prometheus himself is unaware.

8. I.e., let my words not lose their power now.

9. In the passage here omitted, none dares to repeat the curse Prometheus had proclaimed against Jupiter for fear of that god's vengeance. Prometheus is finally forced to call up the Phantasm of Jupiter himself who, in the next excerpt, repeats the words of Prometheus' curse.

Aye, do thy worst. Thou art Omnipotent.
  O'er all things but thyself I gave thee power,
And my own will. Be thy swift mischiefs sent
    To blast mankind, from yon etherial tower.   275
Let thy malignant spirit move
In darkness over those I love:
On me and mine I imprecate
The utmost torture of thy hate
And thus devote to sleepless agony   280
This undeclining head while thou must reign on high.

But thou, who art the God and Lord—O thou
  Who fillest with thy soul this world of woe,
To whom all things of Earth and Heaven do bow
    In fear and worship—all-prevailing foe!   285
I curse thee! let a sufferer's curse
Clasp thee, his torturer, like remorse,
Till thine Infinity shall be
A robe of envenomed agony;[1]
And thine Omnipotence a crown of pain   290
To cling like burning gold round thy dissolving brain.

Heap on thy soul by virtue of this Curse
  Ill deeds, then be thou damned, beholding good;
Both infinite as is the Universe,
    And thou, and thy self-torturing solitude.   295
An awful Image of calm power
Though now thou sittest, let the hour
Come, when thou must appear to be
That which thou art internally.
And after many a false and fruitless crime   300
Scorn track thy lagging fall through boundless space and time.
    [*The* PHANTOM *vanishes.*]
PROMETHEUS. Were these my words, O Parent?
THE EARTH.   They were thine.
PROMETHEUS. It doth repent me: words are quick and vain;
  Grief for awhile is blind, and so was mine.
I wish no living thing to suffer pain.   305

THE EARTH

Misery, O misery to me,
That Jove at length should vanquish thee.[2]
Wail, howl aloud, Land and Sea,
The Earth's rent heart shall answer ye.
Howl, Spirits of the living and the dead,   310
Your refuge, your defence lies fallen and vanquished.

---

1. Like the poisoned shirt of the centaur
Nessus, which consumed Hercules' flesh
when he put it on.

2. Earth mistakes mercy for submission,
and therefore interprets Prometheus' victory as his defeat.

FIRST ECHO
Lies fallen and vanquished!

SECOND ECHO
Fallen and vanquished!

IONE[3]
Fear not—'tis but some passing spasm,
The Titan is unvanquished still.   315

* * *

From *Act II*[1]

SCENE IV—*The Cave of* DEMOGORGON, ASIA *and* PANTHEA.
PANTHEA. What veiled form sits on that ebon throne?
ASIA. The veil has fallen!
PANTHEA.   I see a mighty Darkness
Filling the seat of power; and rays of gloom
Dart round, as light from the meridian Sun,
Ungazed upon and shapeless—neither limb   5
Nor form nor outline; yet we feel it is
A living Spirit.
DEMOGORGON. Ask what thou wouldst know.
ASIA. What canst thou tell?
DEMOGORGON.   All things thou dar'st demand.
ASIA. Who made the living world?
DEMOGORGON.   God.
ASIA.   Who made all
That it contains—thought, passion, reason, will,   10
Imagination?
DEMOGORGON. God, Almighty God.
ASIA. Who made that sense[2] which, when the winds of Spring

---

3. Ione, Panthea, and Asia (in the following scene) are sisters and Oceanids —i.e., daughters of Oceanus.
1. Act II has opened with Asia—the feminine principle and embodiment of love, who was separated from Prometheus at the moment of his fall into divisive hate—in a lovely Indian valley at the first hour of the dawn of the spring season of redemption. Asia and her sister Panthea have been led, by a sweet and irresistible compulsion, first to the portal and then down into the depths of the cave of Demogorgon—the central enigma of Shelley's poem.
Commentators have usually equated Demogorgon with *necessity*, but the interpretation, though pertinent, is too neat and confining. More flexibly, he can be thought of as *process*, the inexorable way in which things evolve. But the ultimate mover of that process—the ultimate reason for things—must remain, Shelley skeptically insists, a mystery beyond the limits of accessible knowledge. Demogorgon, like the inaccessible Power represented by the Arve in *Mont Blanc* (above), is implacable, neutral, and the more terrifying because he himself is ignorant of the principle that controls him. He serves merely to stimulate Asia to ask once more the ultimate and persistent questions about the "why" of creation, good, and evil. But "the deep truth is imageless" (line 116). Demogorgon can give merely riddling answers, which in fact tell Asia only what she herself has thought already (lines 121–23). The one question he can answer unequivocally is not "why," but "when": the hour in the process when Prometheus shall arise. That hour (line 128) is now.
2. Presumably the sense by which one is aware of the "unseen Power" which Shelley calls "Intellectual Beauty"; see *Hymn to Intellectual Beauty*, stanza 2.

In rarest visitation, or the voice
Of one beloved heard in youth alone,
Fills the faint eyes with falling tears, which dim   15
The radiant looks of unbewailing flowers,
And leaves this peopled earth a solitude
When it returns no more?
DEMOGORGON.   Merciful God.
ASIA. And who made terror, madness, crime, remorse,
Which from the links of the great chain of things   20
To every thought within the mind of man
Sway and drag heavily—and each one reels
Under the load towards the pit of death;
Abandoned hope, and love that turns to hate;
And self-contempt, bitterer to drink than blood;   25
Pain, whose unheeded and familiar speech
Is howling and keen shrieks, day after day;
And Hell, or the sharp fear of Hell?[3]
DEMOGORGON.   He reigns.
ASIA. Utter his name—a world pining in pain
Asks but his name; curses shall drag him down.   30
DEMOGORGON. He reigns.
ASIA.   I feel, I know it—who?
DEMOGORGON.   He reigns.
ASIA. Who reigns? There was the Heaven and Earth at first
And Light and Love;—then Saturn,[4] from whose throne
Time fell, an envious shadow; such the state
Of the earth's primal spirits beneath his sway   35
As the calm joy of flowers and living leaves
Before the wind or sun has withered them
And semivital worms; but he refused
The birthright of their being, knowledge, power,
The skill which wields the elements, the thought   40
Which pierces this dim Universe like light,
Self-empire and the majesty of love,
For thirst of which they fainted. Then Prometheus
Gave wisdom, which is strength, to Jupiter
And with this law alone "Let man be free,"   45
Clothed him with the dominion of wide Heaven.
To know nor faith nor love nor law, to be
Omnipotent but friendless, is to reign;
And Jove now reigned; for on the race of man
First famine, and then toil, and then disease,   50
Strife, wounds, and ghastly death unseen before,
Fell; and the unseasonable seasons drove
With alternating shafts of frost and fire,
Their shelterless, pale tribes to mountain caves:

3. The nouns "hope," "love," etc. (lines 24–28), are all objects of the verb "made" (line 19).
4. In Greek myth, Saturn's reign was the golden age. In Shelley's version, Saturn refused to grant men knowledge and science, so that it was an age of ignorant innocence in which man's deepest needs were unfulfilled.

And in their desart hearts fierce wants he sent 55
And mad disquietudes, and shadows idle
Of unreal good, which levied mutual war,
So ruining the lair wherein they raged.
Prometheus saw, and waked the legioned hopes
Which sleep within folded Elysian flowers, 60
Nepenthe, Moly, Amaranth,[5] fadeless blooms,
That they might hide with thin and rainbow wings
The shape of Death; and Love he sent to bind
The disunited tendrils of that vine
Which bears the wine of life, the human heart; 65
And he tamed fire which, like some beast of prey,
Most terrible, but lovely, played beneath
The frown of man, and tortured to his will
Iron and gold, the slaves and signs of power,
And gems and poisons, and all subtlest forms 70
Hidden beneath the mountains and the waves.
He gave man speech, and speech created thought,
Which is the measure of the Universe;
And Science struck the thrones of Earth and Heaven
Which shook, but fell not; and the harmonious mind 75
Poured itself forth in all-prophetic song,
And music lifted up the listening spirit
Until it walked, exempt from mortal care,
Godlike, o'er the clear billows of sweet sound;
And human hands first mimicked and then mocked[6] 80
With moulded limbs more lovely than its own
The human form, till marble grew divine,
And mothers, gazing, drank the love men see
Reflected in their race, behold, and perish.[7]—
He told the hidden power of herbs and springs, 85
And Disease drank and slept. Death grew like sleep.
He taught the implicated orbits woven
Of the wide-wandering stars; and how the Sun
Changes his lair, and by what secret spell
The pale moon is transformed, when her broad eye 90
Gazes not on the interlunar[8] sea;
He taught to rule, as life directs the limbs,
The tempest-winged chariots of the Ocean,
And the Celt knew the Indian.[9] Cities then
Were built, and through their snow-like columns flowed 95
The warm winds, and the azure æther shone,
And the blue sea and shadowy hills were seen.

5. These are medicinal drugs and flowers in Greek myth. Asia (lines 59–97) is describing the various sciences and arts given to man by Prometheus, the culture-bringer.
6. I.e., sculptors first merely reproduced, but later improved upon ("mocked"), the beauty of the human form.
7. Expectant mothers looked at the beautiful statues so that their children might, by prenatal influence, be born with that beauty which makes beholders die of love.
8. The phase between old and new moon, when the moon is invisible.
9. The reference is to the ships in which the Celtic (here, British) races of Europe were able to sail to India.

Such the alleviations of his state
Prometheus gave to man—for which he hangs
Withering in destined pain—but who rains down   100
Evil, the immedicable plague, which while
Man looks on his creation like a God
And sees that it is glorious, drives him on,
The wreck of his own will, the scorn of Earth,
The outcast, the abandoned, the alone?—   105
Not Jove: while yet his frown shook Heaven, aye, when
His adversary from adamantine chains
Cursed him, he trembled like a slave. Declare
Who is his master? Is he too a slave?
DEMOGORGON. All spirits are enslaved which serve things evil: 110
  Thou knowest if Jupiter be such or no.
ASIA. Whom calledst thou God?
DEMOGORGON.   I spoke but as ye speak—
  For Jove is the supreme of living things.
ASIA. Who is the master of the slave?
DEMOGORGON.   —If the Abysm
  Could vomit forth its secrets:—but a voice   115
  Is wanting, the deep truth is imageless;[1]
  For what would it avail to bid thee gaze
  On the revolving world? what to bid speak
  Fate, Time, Occasion, Chance and Change? To these
  All things are subject but eternal Love.   120
ASIA. So much I asked before, and my heart gave
  The response thou hast given; and of such truths
  Each to itself must be the oracle.—
  One more demand . . . and do thou answer me
  As my own soul would answer, did it know   125
  That which I ask. Prometheus shall arise
  Henceforth the Sun of this rejoicing world:
  When shall the destined hour arrive?
DEMOGORGON.   Behold![2]
ASIA. The rocks are cloven, and through the purple night
  I see Cars drawn by rainbow-winged steeds   130
  Which trample the dim winds—in each there stands
  A wild-eyed charioteer, urging their flight.
  Some look behind, as fiends pursued them there,
  And yet I see no shapes but the keen stars:
  Others with burning eyes lean forth, and drink   135
  With eager lips the wind of their own speed,
  As if the thing they loved fled on before,
  And now—even now they clasped it; their bright locks
  Stream like a comet's flashing hair: they all
  Sweep onward.—
DEMOGORGON. These are the immortal Hours   140
  Of whom thou didst demand.—One waits for thee.

1. I.e., ultimate truths can be neither
known nor expressed.
2. Demogorgon's answer is a gesture: he
points to the approaching chariots
("cars").

ASIA. A Spirit with a dreadful countenance
   Checks its dark chariot by the craggy gulph.
   Unlike thy brethren, ghastly charioteer,
   Who art thou? whither wouldst thou bear me? Speak!   145
SPIRIT. I am the shadow of a destiny
   More dread than is my aspect: ere yon planet
   Has set, the Darkness[3] which ascends with me
   Shall wrap in lasting night Heaven's kingless throne.
ASIA. What meanest thou?
PANTHEA.   That terrible shadow floats   150
   Up from its throne, as may the lurid smoke
   Of earthquake-ruined cities o'er the sea.—
   Lo! it ascends the Car . . . the coursers fly
   Terrified; watch its path among the stars
   Blackening the night!
ASIA.   Thus I am answered—strange!   155
PANTHEA. See, near the verge another chariot stays;
   An ivory shell inlaid with crimson fire
   Which comes and goes within its sculptured rim
   Of delicate strange tracery—the young Spirit
   That guides it, has the dove-like eyes of hope.   160
   How its soft smiles attract the soul!—as light[4]
   Lures winged insects through the lampless air.

SPIRIT

My coursers are fed with the lightning,
   They drink of the whirlwind's stream
And when the red morning is brightening   165
   They bathe in the fresh sunbeam;
   They have strength for their swiftness I deem:
Then ascend with me, daughter of Ocean.

I desire—and their speed makes night kindle;
   I fear—they outstrip the Typhoon;   170
Ere the cloud piled on Atlas can dwindle
   We encircle the earth and the moon:
   We shall rest from long labours at noon:
Then ascend with me, daughter of Ocean.

SCENE v—*The Car pauses within a Cloud on the top of a snowy
Mountain.* ASIA, PANTHEA, *and the* SPIRIT OF THE HOUR.

SPIRIT

On the brink of the night and the morning
   My coursers are wont to respire,
But the Earth has just whispered a warning
   That their flight must be swifter than fire:
   They shall drink the hot speed of desire!   5

3. I.e., Demogorgon, who is ascending
(lines 150–55) to effect the dethronement
of Jupiter.
4. The ancient image of the soul, "psyche," was a moth. The chariot described
here will carry Asia to a reunion with
Prometheus.

ASIA. Thou breathest on their nostrils—but my breath
  Would give them swifter speed.
SPIRIT.   Alas, it could not.
PANTHEA. Oh Spirit! pause and tell whence is the light
  Which fills the cloud? the sun is yet unrisen.
SPIRIT. The sun will rise not until noon.[5]—Apollo   10
  Is held in Heaven by wonder—and the light
  Which fills this vapour, as the aerial hue
  Of fountain-gazing roses fills the water,
  Flows from thy mighty sister.
PANTHEA.   Yes, I feel . . .
ASIA. What is it with thee, sister? Thou art pale.   15
PANTHEA. How thou art changed! I dare not look on thee;
  I feel, but see thee not. I scarce endure
  The radiance of thy beauty.[6] Some good change
  Is working in the elements which suffer
  Thy presence thus unveiled.—The Nereids tell   20
  That on the day when the clear hyaline
  Was cloven at thy uprise, and thou didst stand
  Within a veined shell,[7] which floated on
  Over the calm floor of the chrystal sea,
  Among the Ægean isles, and by the shores   25
  Which bear thy name, love, like the atmosphere
  Of the sun's fire filling the living world,
  Burst from thee, and illumined Earth and Heaven
  And the deep ocean and the sunless caves
  And all that dwells within them; till grief cast   30
  Eclipse upon the soul from which it came:
  Such art thou now, nor is it I alone,
  Thy sister, thy companion, thine own chosen one,
  But the whole world which seeks thy sympathy.
  Hearest thou not sounds i' the air which speak the love   35
  Of all articulate beings? Feelest thou not
  The inanimate winds enamoured of thee?—List!   [*Music.*]
ASIA. Thy words are sweeter than aught else but his
  Whose echoes they are—yet all love is sweet,
  Given or returned; common as light is love   40
  And its familiar voice wearies not ever.
  Like the wide Heaven, the all-sustaining air,
  It makes the reptile equal to the God . . .
  They who inspire it most, are fortunate
  As I am now; but those who feel it most   45

5. Noon will be the time of the reunion between Prometheus and Asia.
6. In an earlier scene, Panthea had envisioned in a dream the radiant and eternal inner form of Prometheus emerging through his "wound-worn limbs." The corresponding transfiguration of Asia, prepared for by her descent to the underworld, now takes place.
7. The story told by the Nereids (sea nymphs) serves to associate Asia with Aphrodite, goddess of love, emerging (as in Botticelli's painting) from the Mediterranean on a seashell. "Hyaline": the glassy sea.

Are happier still, after long sufferings,
As I shall soon become.
PANTHEA.   List! Spirits speak.

VOICE IN THE AIR [*singing*]8
Life of Life! thy lips enkindle
  With their love the breath between them
And thy smiles before they dwindle   50
  Make the cold air fire; then screen them
In those looks where whoso gazes
Faints, entangled in their mazes.

Child of Light! thy limbs are burning
  Through the vest which seems to hide them   55
As the radiant lines of morning
  Through the clouds ere they divide them,
And this atmosphere divinest
Shrouds thee wheresoe'er thou shinest.

Fair are others;—none beholds thee   60
  But thy voice sounds low and tender
Like the fairest, for it folds thee
  From the sight, that liquid splendour,
And all feel, yet see thee never
As I feel now, lost forever!   65

Lamp of Earth! where'er thou movest
  Its dim shapes are clad with brightness
And the souls of whom thou lovest
  Walk upon the winds with lightness
Till they fail, as I am failing,   70
Dizzy, lost yet unbewailing!

ASIA
My soul is an enchanted Boat
  Which, like a sleeping swan, doth float
Upon the silver waves of thy sweet singing,
  And thine doth like an Angel sit   75
  Beside the helm conducting it
Whilst all the winds with melody are ringing.
  It seems to float ever, forever,
  Upon that many winding River
Between mountains, woods, abysses,   80
  A Paradise of wildernesses,
Till like one in slumber bound
Borne to the Ocean, I float down, around,
Into a Sea profound, of ever-spreading sound:

8. The voice attempts to describe, in a dizzying whirl of optical paradoxes, what it feels like to look upon the naked essence of love and beauty.

Meanwhile thy Spirit lifts its pinions   85
In Music's most serene dominions,
Catching the winds that fan that happy Heaven.
And we sail on, away, afar,
Without a course—without a star—
But by the instinct of sweet Music driven   90
Till through Elysian garden islets
By thee, most beautiful of pilots,
Where never mortal pinnace glided,
The boat of my desire is guided—
Realms where the air we breathe is Love   95
Which in the winds and on the waves doth move,
Harmonizing this Earth with what we feel above.

We have past Age's icy caves,
And Manhood's dark and tossing waves
And Youth's smooth ocean, smiling to betray;   100
Beyond the glassy gulphs we flee
Of shadow-peopled Infancy,
Through Death and Birth to a diviner day,[9]
A Paradise of vaulted bowers,
Lit by downward-gazing flowers   105
And watery paths that wind between
Wildernesses calm and green,
Peopled by shapes too bright to see,
And rest, having beheld; somewhat like thee,
Which walk upon the sea, and chaunt melodiously!   110

From *Act III*

SCENE I—*Heaven.* JUPITER *on his Throne;* THETIS *and the other Deities assembled.*

JUPITER. Ye congregated Powers of Heaven who share
The glory and the strength of him ye serve,
Rejoice! henceforth I am omnipotent.
All else had been subdued to me—alone
The soul of man, like unextinguished fire,   5
Yet burns towards Heaven with fierce reproach and doubt
And lamentation and reluctant prayer,
Hurling up insurrection, which might make
Our antique empire insecure, though built
On eldest faith, and Hell's coeval,[1] fear;   10
And though my curses through the pendulous air
Like snow on herbless peaks, fall flake by flake,
And cling to it[2]—though under my wrath's night

9. Asia is describing what it feels like to be transfigured—in the image of moving backward down the stream of time, through youth and infancy and birth itself, in order to die to this life and be born again to a "diviner" existence.
1. Of the same age.
2. "It" is "the soul of man," line 5 (as also in lines 14 and 16).

It climb the crags of life, step after step,
Which wound it, as ice wounds unsandalled feet, 15
It yet remains supreme o'er misery,
Aspiring . . . unrepressed; yet soon to fall:
Even now have I begotten a strange wonder,
That fatal Child,[3] the terror of the Earth,
Who waits but till the destined Hour arrive, 20
Bearing from Demogorgon's vacant throne
The dreadful might of ever living limbs
Which clothed that awful spirit unbeheld—
To redescend, and trample out the spark.[4]

Pour forth Heaven's wine, Idæan Ganymede,[5] 25
And let it fill the dædal cups like fire,
And from the flower-inwoven soil divine
Ye all triumphant harmonies arise
As dew from Earth under the twilight stars;
Drink! be the nectar circling through your veins 30
The soul of joy, ye ever-living Gods,
Till exultation burst in one wide voice
Like music from Elysian winds.
                        And thou
Ascend beside me, veiled in the light
Of the desire which makes thee one with me, 35
Thetis, bright Image of Eternity!—
When thou didst cry, "Insufferable might![6]
God! spare me! I sustain not the quick flames,
The penetrating presence; all my being,
Like him whom the Numidian seps[7] did thaw 40
Into a dew with poison, is dissolved,
Sinking through its foundations:"—even then
Two mighty spirits, mingling, made a third
Mightier than either—which unbodied now
Between us, floats, felt, although unbeheld, 45
Waiting the incarnation, which ascends—
Hear ye the thunder of the fiery wheels
Griding[8] the winds?—from Demogorgon's throne.—
Victory! victory! Feel'st thou not, O World,
The Earthquake of his chariot thundering up 50
Olympus?
      [*The Car of the* HOUR *arrives.* DEMOGORGON *descends, and*
     moves towards the Throne of JUPITER.]
         Awful Shape, what art thou? Speak!
DEMOGORGON. Eternity—demand no direr name.

3. The son of Jupiter and Thetis; Jupiter believes that he has begotten a child who will assume the bodily form of the conquered Demogorgon and then return to announce his victory and to trample out the resistance of Prometheus.
4. The "spark" of Prometheus' defiance.
5. Ganymede had been seized on Mt. Ida by an eagle and carried to heaven to be Jupiter's cupbearer. "dædal": skill-

fully wrought (from the name of the Greek craftsman, Dædalus).
6. This description of the union of Jupiter and Thetis is a grotesque parody of the reunion of Prometheus and Asia.
7. A serpent of Numidia (North Africa) whose bite was thought to cause putrefaction.
8. Cutting with a rasping sound.

Descend, and follow me down the abyss.
I am thy child,[9] as thou wert Saturn's child,
Mightier than thee: and we must dwell together   55
Henceforth in darkness.—Lift thy lightnings not.
The tyranny of Heaven none may retain,
Or reassume, or hold succeeding thee . . .
Yet if thou wilt—as 'tis the destiny
Of trodden worms to writhe till they are dead—   60
Put forth thy might.
JUPITER.   Detested prodigy!
Even thus beneath the deep Titanian prisons
I trample thee! . . . thou lingerest?

                                        Mercy! mercy!
No pity—no release, no respite! . . . Oh,
That thou wouldst make mine enemy my judge.   65
Even where he hangs, seared by my long revenge
On Caucasus—he would not doom me thus.—
Gentle and just and dreadless, is he not
The monarch of the world?[1] what then art thou? . . .
No refuge! no appeal— . . .
                              Sink with me then—   70
We two will sink on the wide waves of ruin
Even as a vulture and a snake outspent
Drop, twisted in inextricable fight,[2]
Into a shoreless sea.—Let hell unlock
Its mounded Oceans of tempestuous fire,   75
And whelm on them into the bottomless void
This desolated world and thee and me,
The conqueror and the conquered, and the wreck
Of that for which they combated.
                              Ai! Ai!
The elements obey me not. . . . I sink . . .   80
Dizzily down—ever, forever, down.
And, like a cloud, mine enemy above
Darkens my fall with victory! Ai, Ai![3]

From SCENE IV—*A Forest. In the Background a Cave.*
PROMETHEUS, ASIA, PANTHEA, IONE, *and the* SPIRIT OF THE EARTH.[4]

* * *

9. Ironically, and in a figurative sense:
Demogorgon's function follows from Jupiter's actions.
1. The ultimate irony: Jupiter appeals to
those very qualities of Prometheus for
which he has hitherto persecuted him,
begging for a mercy which Prometheus
has already granted him; but Prometheus' change from vengefulness to
mercy is in fact the cause of Jupiter's
present downfall.
2. The eagle (or vulture) and the snake
locked in equal combat—a favorite Shel-

leyan image.
3. Jupiter's scream is to be imagined
diminishing to silence.
4. After Jupiter's annihilation (described
in Scene ii), Hercules unbinds Prometheus, who is reunited with Asia and retires to a cave "where we will sit and
talk of time and change / * * * ourselves unchanged." In the speech which
concludes the act (reprinted here) the
Spirit of the Hour describes what happened when he sounded the apocalyptic
trumpet.

[*The* SPIRIT OF THE HOUR *enters.*]
PROMETHEUS. We feel what thou hast heard and seen—yet speak.
SPIRIT OF THE HOUR. Soon as the sound had ceased whose thunder
  filled
  The abysses of the sky, and the wide earth,
  There was a change . . . the impalpable thin air   100
  And the all-circling sunlight were transformed
  As if the sense of love dissolved in them
  Had folded itself round the sphered world.
  My vision then grew clear and I could see
  Into the mysteries of the Universe.   105
  Dizzy as with delight I floated down,
  Winnowing the lightsome air with languid plumes,
  My coursers sought their birthplace in the sun
  Where they henceforth will live exempt from toil,
  Pasturing flowers of vegetable fire—   110
  And where my moonlike car will stand within
  A temple, gazed upon by Phidian forms,[5]
  Of thee, and Asia and the Earth, and me
  And you fair nymphs, looking the love we feel,
  In memory of the tidings it has borne,   115
  Beneath a dome fretted with graven flowers,
  Poised on twelve columns of resplendent stone
  And open to the bright and liquid sky.
  Yoked to it by an amphisbænic snake[6]
  The likeness of those winged steeds will mock[7]   120
  The flight from which they find repose—Alas,
  Whither has wandered now my partial[8] tongue
  When all remains untold which ye would hear!—
  As I have said, I floated to the Earth:
  It was, as it is still, the pain of bliss   125
  To move, to breathe, to be; I wandering went
  Among the haunts and dwellings of mankind
  And first was disappointed not to see
  Such mighty change as I had felt within
  Expressed in outward things; but soon I looked,   130
  And behold! thrones were kingless, and men walked
  One with the other even as spirits do,
  None fawned, none trampled; hate, disdain or fear,
  Self-love or self-contempt on human brows
  No more inscribed, as o'er the gate of hell,   135
  "All hope abandon, ye who enter here";[9]
  None frowned, none trembled, none with eager fear

5. The crescent-shaped ("moonlike") chariot, its apocalytpic mission accomplished, will be frozen to stone, and will be surrounded by the sculptured forms of other agents in the drama. Phidias (5th century B.C.) was the noblest of Greek sculptors.
6. A mythical snake with a head at either end; it serves here as a symbolic warning that a reversal of the process is always possible. Cf. IV.561–69.
7. "Imitate" and also, in their immobility, "mock at" the flight they represent.
8. "Biased," or, possibly, "telling only part of the story."
9. The inscription over the gate of hell in Dante's *Inferno* III.9.

Gazed on another's eye of cold command
Until the subject of a tyrant's will
Became, worse fate, the abject of his own[1]   140
Which spurred him, like an outspent horse, to death.
None wrought his lips in truth-entangling lines
Which smiled the lie his tongue disdained to speak;
None with firm sneer trod out in his own heart
The sparks of love and hope, till there remained   145
Those bitter ashes, a soul self-consumed,
And the wretch crept, a vampire among men,
Infecting all with his own hideous ill.
None talked that common, false, cold, hollow talk
Which makes the heart deny the *yes* it breathes   150
Yet question that unmeant hypocrisy
With such a self-mistrust as has no name.
And women, too, frank, beautiful and kind
As the free Heaven which rains fresh light and dew
On the wide earth, past; gentle radiant forms,   155
From custom's evil taint exempt and pure;
Speaking the wisdom once they could not think,
Looking emotions once they feared to feel
And changed to all which once they dared not be,
Yet being now, made Earth like Heaven—nor pride   160
Nor jealousy nor envy nor ill shame,
The bitterest of those drops of treasured gall,
Spoilt the sweet taste of the nepenthe,[2] love.

Thrones, altars, judgement-seats and prisons; wherein
And beside which, by wretched men were borne   165
Sceptres, tiaras, swords and chains, and tomes
Of reasoned wrong, glozed on[3] by ignorance,
Were like those monstrous and barbaric shapes,
The ghosts of a no more remembered fame,
Which from their unworn obelisks look forth   170
In triumph o'er the palaces and tombs
Of those who were their conquerors, mouldering round.
Those imaged to the pride of Kings and Priests
A dark yet mighty faith, a power as wide
As is the world it wasted, and are now   175
But an astonishment; even so the tools
And emblems of its last captivity
Amid the dwellings of the peopled Earth,
Stand, not o'erthrown, but unregarded now.
And those foul shapes, abhorred by God and man—   180
Which under many a name and many a form
Strange, savage, ghastly, dark and execrable

---

1. I.e., he was so abjectly enslaved that
his own will accorded with the tyrants's
will.

2. A drug (probably opium) that brings
forgetfulness of pain and sorrow.
3. Annotated.

Were Jupiter,[4] the tyrant of the world;
And which the nations panic-stricken served
With blood, and hearts broken by long hope, and love   185
Dragged to his altars soiled and garlandless
And slain amid men's unreclaiming tears,
Flattering the thing they feared, which fear was hate—
Frown, mouldering fast, o'er their abandoned shrines.
The painted veil, by those who were, called life,[5]   190
Which mimicked, as with colours idly spread,
All men believed and hoped, is torn aside;
The loathsome mask has fallen, the man remains
Sceptreless, free, uncircumscribed—but man:
Equal, unclassed, tribeless, and nationless,   195
Exempt from awe, worship, degree, the King
Over himself; just, gentle, wise—but man:
Passionless? no—yet free from guilt or pain
Which were, for his will made, or suffered them,
Nor yet exempt, though ruling them like slaves,   200
From chance and death and mutability,
The clogs of that which else might oversoar
The loftiest star of unascended Heaven
Pinnacled dim in the intense inane.[6]

From *Act IV*[1]

SCENE—*A Part of the Forest near the Cave of* PROMETHEUS.

* * *

IONE.   Even whilst we speak
New notes arise. . . . What is that awful sound?   185

4. I.e., the gods, whatever their diverse names, were all really manifestations of Jupiter.
5. I.e., which was thought to be life by men as they were before their regeneration.
6. I.e., a dim point in the extreme of empty space. The sense of lines 198–204 is: if regenerate man were to be released from all earthly and biological conditions, he would become what even the stars are not—a pure ideal.
1. The original drama, completed in the spring of 1819, consisted of three acts. Later that year Shelley added a jubilant fourth act. In Revelation xxi, the apocalyptic replacement of the old world by "a new heaven and new earth" had been symbolized by the marriage of the Lamb with the New Jerusalem. Shelley's fourth act, somewhat like the conclusion of Blake's *Jerusalem* (above), expands this figure into a cosmic epithalamion, representing a union of divided elements which enacts everywhere the reunion of Prometheus and Asia that is taking place off-stage.

Shelley's model is the Renaissance masque, which combines song and dance with spectacular displays. Panthea and Ione serve as commentators on the action, which is divided into three episodes. In the first episode, omitted here, the purified "Spirits of the human mind" united in a ritual dance with the Hours of the glad new day. In the second episode (below, lines 194–318), there appear emblematic representations of the moon and the earth, each bearing an infant whose hour has come round at last; Shelley based this description in part on Chapter 1 of Ezekiel, the vision of the chariot of divine glory, which had traditionally been interpreted as a portent of apocalypse. The third episode (lines 319–502) is the bacchanalian dance of the love-intoxicated moon around her brother and paramour, the rejuvenescent earth. By way of coda (lines 549 to the end), Demogorgon calls upon all beings to hear his proclamation of the moral significance of this the great drama of man's self-betrayal and self-redemption.

PANTHEA. 'Tis the deep music of the rolling world
   Kindling within the strings of the waved air
   Æolian modulations.[2]
IONE.   Listen too,
   How every pause is filled with under-notes,
   Clear, silver, icy, keen, awakening tones   190
   Which pierce the sense and live within the soul
   As the sharp stars pierce Winter's chrystal air
   And gaze upon themselves within the sea.
PANTHEA. But see, where through two openings in the forest
   Which hanging branches overcanopy,   195
   And where two runnels of a rivulet
   Between the close moss violet-inwoven
   Have made their path of melody, like sisters
   Who part with sighs that they may meet in smiles,
   Turning their dear disunion to an isle   200
   Of lovely grief, a wood of sweet sad thoughts;
   Two visions of strange radiance float upon
   The Ocean-like inchantment of strong sound
   Which flows intenser, keener, deeper yet
   Under the ground and through the windless air.   205
IONE. I see a chariot like that thinnest boat
   In which the Mother of the Months is borne
   By ebbing light into her western cave
   When she upsprings from interlunar dreams,[3]
   O'er which is curved an orblike canopy   210
   Of gentle darkness, and the hills and woods
   Distinctly seen through that dusk aery veil
   Regard[4] like shapes in an enchanter's glass;
   Its wheels are solid clouds, azure and gold,
   Such as the genii of the thunderstorm   215
   Pile on the floor of the illumined sea
   When the Sun rushes under it; they roll
   And move and grow as with an inward wind.
   Within it sits a winged Infant, white
   Its countenance like the whiteness of bright snow,   220
   Its plumes are as feathers of sunny frost,
   Its limbs gleam white, through the wind-flowing folds
   Of its white robe, woof of ætherial pearl.
   Its hair is white,—the brightness of white light
   Scattered in strings,[5] yet its two eyes are Heavens   225
   Of liquid darkness, which the Deity

---

2. I.e., evoking music like that of the Eolian harp.
3. I.e., the chariot is a thin crescent-shape, like the new moon, when it carries the moon-goddess ("Mother of the Months") to the cave where she is reborn during the "interlunar" period—i.e., when the moon is entirely invisible.
4. Appear.
5. The infant resembles "one like unto the Son of man" in Revelation i.13–14: "His head and his hairs were white like wool, as white as snow." The description that follows, of the light radiated from the infant's eyes, echoes the description in Ezekiel's vision, i.27–8, of the "brightness round about" that "was the appearance of the likeness of the glory of the Lord."

Within, seems pouring, as a storm is poured
From jagged clouds, out of their arrowy lashes,
Tempering the cold and radiant air around
With fire that is not brightness; in its hand   230
It sways a quivering moonbeam, from whose point
A guiding power directs the chariot's prow
Over its wheeled clouds which as they roll
Over the grass and flowers and waves, wake sounds
Sweet as a singing rain of silver dew.   235
PANTHEA. And from the other opening in the wood
    Rushes with loud and whirlwind harmony
    A sphere, which is as many thousand spheres,
    Solid as chrystal, yet through all its mass
    Flow, as through empty space, music and light: 240
    Ten thousand orbs involving and involved,[6]
    Purple and azure, white and green and golden,
    Sphere within sphere, and every space between
    Peopled with unimaginable shapes
    Such as ghosts dream dwell in the lampless deep,   245
    Yet each intertranspicuous,[7] and they whirl
    Over each other with a thousand motions
    Upon a thousand sightless axles spinning
    And with the force of self-destroying swiftness,
    Intensely, slowly, solemnly roll on—   250
    Kindling with mingled sounds, and many tones.
    Intelligible words and music wild.—
    With mighty whirl the multitudinous Orb
    Grinds the bright brook into an azure mist
    Of elemental subtlety, like light,   255
    And the wild odour of the forest flowers,
    The music of the living grass and air,
    The emerald light of leaf-entangled beams
    Round its intense, yet self-conflicting[8] speed,
    Seem kneaded into one aerial mass   260
    Which drowns the sense. . . . Within the Orb itself,
    Pillowed upon its alabaster arms
    Like to a child o'erwearied with sweet toil,
    On its own folded wings and wavy hair,
    The Spirit of the Earth is laid asleep,   265
    And you can see its little lips are moving
    Amid the changing light of their own smiles
    Like one who talks of what he loves in dream—
IONE. 'Tis only mocking[9] the Orb's harmony. . .

6. The transparent sphere is an emblem of earth. The description of its spinning and that of its interior orbs echoes both Ezekiel i.15–17–"the appearance of the wheels and their work . . . was as it were a wheel in the middle of a wheel" —and *Paradise Lost* V.620–24, which describes the "mystical dance" of the angels in heaven, whose movements resemble the revolving spheres of the planets: "mazes intricate, / Eccentric, intervolved, yet regular / Then most, when most irregular they seem."
7. I.e., transparent, so that each can be seen through the others.
8. Because its component spheres are spinning in opposed directions.
9. Imitating.

PANTHEA. And from a star upon its forehead, shoot,   270
　Like swords of azure fire, or golden spears
　With tyrant-quelling myrtle[1] overtwined,
　Embleming Heaven and Earth united now,
　Vast beams like spokes of some invisible wheel
　Which whirl as the Orb whirls, swifter than thought,   275
　Filling the abyss with sunlike lightenings,
　And perpendicular now, and now transverse,
　Pierce the dark soil, and as they pierce and pass
　Make bare the secrets of the Earth's deep heart,[2]
　Infinite mine of adamant and gold,   280
　Valueless[3] stones, and unimagined gems,
　And caverns on chrystalline columns poised
　With vegetable silver overspread,
　Wells of unfathomed fire, and watersprings
　Whence the great Sea, even as a child, is fed   285
　Whose vapours clothe Earth's monarch mountain-tops
　With kingly, ermine snow; the beams flash on
　And make appear the melancholy ruins
　Of cancelled cycles;[4] anchors, beaks of ships,
　Planks turned to marble, quivers, helms and spears   290
　And gorgon-headed targes,[5] and the wheels
　Of scythed chariots,[6] and the emblazonry
　Of trophies, standards and armorial beasts[7]
　Round which Death laughed, sepulchred emblems
　Of dead Destruction, ruin within ruin!   295
　The wrecks beside of many a city vast,
　Whose population which the Earth grew over
　Was mortal but not human;[8] see, they lie,
　Their monstrous works and uncouth skeletons,
　Their statues, homes, and fanes;[9] prodigious shapes   300
　Huddled in grey annihilation, split,
　Jammed in the hard black deep; and over these
　The anatomies of unknown winged things,
　And fishes which were isles of living scale,
　And serpents, bony chains, twisted around   305
　The iron crags, or within heaps of dust
　To which the tortuous strength of their last pangs
　Had crushed the iron crags;—and over these
　The jagged alligator and the might
　Of earth-convulsing behemoth,[1] which once   310
　Were monarch beasts, and on the slimy shores

1. The myrtle, sacred to Venus, symbolizes love.
2. I.e., the star on the infant's forehead
radiates penetrating beams which (like
modern x-rays) reveal what lies beneath
the surface of the earth.
3. Priceless.
4. I.e., of civilizations that flourished,
then disappeared.
5. Shields embossed with a gorgon's
head.

6. Ancient war-chariots sometimes had
steel blades fastened to the revolving
wheels.
7. Animals in heraldic insignia.
8. I.e., a pre-human race of beings which
once overspread the earth.
9. Temples.
1. The huge land-animal described in
Job xl.15–24. Shelley apparently identifies
the Leviathan, the sea-beast in Job, as a
huge, extinct alligator (line 309).

And weed-overgrown continents of Earth
Increased and multiplied like summer worms
On an abandoned corpse, till the blue globe
Wrapt Deluge round it like a cloak, and they   315
Yelled, gaspt and were abolished; or some God
Whose throne was in a Comet, past, and cried—
"Be not!"—And like my words they were no more.[2]

THE EARTH

The joy, the triumph, the delight, the madness,
The boundless, overflowing, bursting gladness,   320
The vaporous exultation not to be confined![3]
Ha! ha! the animation of delight
Which wraps me, like an atmosphere of light,
And bears me as a cloud is borne by its own wind!

THE MOON

Brother mine, calm wanderer,   325
Happy globe of land and air,
Some Spirit[4] is darted like a beam from thee,
Which penetrates my frozen frame
And passes with the warmth of flame
With love and odour and deep melody   330
Through me, through me!—

THE EARTH

Ha! ha! the caverns of my hollow mountains,
My cloven fire-crags, sound-exulting fountains
Laugh with a vast and inextinguishable laughter.
The Oceans and the Desarts and the Abysses   335
And the deep air's unmeasured wildernesses
Answer from all their clouds and billows, echoing after.

They cry aloud as I do—"Sceptred Curse,[5]
Who all our green and azure Universe
Threatenedst to muffle round with black destruction, sending   340
A solid cloud to rain hot thunderstones,
And splinter and knead down my children's bones,
All I bring forth, to one void mass battering and blending,

"Until each craglike tower and storied column,
Palace and Obelisk and Temple solemn,   345

2. According to the theory of "Catastrophism" proposed by G. F. Cuvier, *Researches on Fossil Bones* (1812), successive geologic layers of fossils are evidence of a sequence of catastrophes—volcanic upheavals and gigantic floods—each of which wiped out the forms of life that then existed. Shelley proposes two hypotheses (lines 314–18): either the floods originated from some cataclysm on earth, or else they were prodigious tides caused by the gravitational pull of a passing comet.

In writing this passage, Shelley recalled Keats's *Endymion* III.123–36, which described the remains on the ocean floor of extinct cultures and animal species.
3. Literally, the earth's gases are bursting out through its volcanoes.
4. Physically, the gravitational force exerted by the earth on the satellite moon.
5. Jupiter.

My imperial mountains crowned with cloud and snow and fire,
  My sea-like forests, every blade and blossom
  Which finds a grave or cradle in my bosom,
Were stamped by thy strong hate into a lifeless mire,

"How art thou sunk, withdrawn, covered, drunk up   350
  By thirsty nothing, as the brackish cup
Drained by a desart-troop, a little drop for all;
  And from beneath, around, within, above,
  Filling thy void annihilation, Love
Bursts in like light on caves cloven by thunderball."   355

THE MOON

The snow upon my lifeless mountains
  Is loosened into living fountains,
My solid Oceans flow and sing and shine:
  A spirit from my heart bursts forth,
  It clothes with unexpected birth   360
My cold bare bosom: Oh! it must be thine
    On mine, on mine!

Gazing on thee I feel, I know,
  Green stalks burst forth, and bright flowers grow
And living shapes upon my bosom move: 365
  Music is in the sea and air,
  Winged clouds soar here and there,
Dark with the rain new buds are dreaming of:
    'Tis Love, all Love!

THE EARTH

It interpenetrates my granite mass,   370
  Through tangled roots and trodden clay doth pass
Into the utmost leaves and delicatest flowers;
  Upon the winds, among the clouds 'tis spread,
  It wakes a life in the forgotten dead,
They breathe a spirit up from their obscurest bowers,   375

And like a storm, bursting its cloudy prison
  With thunder and with whirlwind, has arisen
Out of the lampless caves of unimagined being,
  With earthquake shock and swiftness making shiver
  Thought's stagnant chaos, unremoved forever,   380
Till Hate and Fear and Pain, light-vanquished shadows, fleeing,

Leave Man, who was a many-sided mirror
  Which could distort to many a shape of error
This true fair world of things—a Sea reflecting Love;
  Which over all his kind, as the Sun's Heaven   385
  Gliding o'er Ocean, smooth, serene and even,
Darting from starry depths radiance and light, doth move:

Leave Man, even as a leprous child is left
Who follows a sick beast to some warm cleft
Of rocks, through which the might of healing springs is poured:
  Then when it wanders home with rosy smile   391
  Unconscious, and its mother fears awhile
It is a Spirit—then, weeps on her child restored.

Man, oh, not men[6]! a chain of linked thought,
  Of love and might to be divided not,   395
Compelling the elements with adamantine stress—
  As the Sun rules,[7] even with a tyrant's gaze,
  The unquiet Republic of the maze
Of Planets, struggling fierce towards Heaven's free wilderness.

Man, one harmonious Soul of many a soul   400
  Whose nature is its own divine controul
Where all things flow to all, as rivers to the sea;
  Familiar acts are beautiful through love;
  Labour and Pain and Grief in life's green grove
Sport like tame beasts—none knew how gentle they could be! 405

His Will, with all mean passions, bad delights,
  And selfish cares, its trembling satellites,
A spirit ill to guide, but mighty to obey,
  Is as a tempest-winged ship, whose helm
  Love rules, through waves which dare not overwhelm,   410
Forcing Life's wildest shores to own its sovereign sway.

All things confess his strength.—Through the cold mass
  Of marble and of colour his dreams pass;
Bright threads, whence mothers weave the robes their children
    wear;
  Language is a perpetual Orphic song,[8]   415
  Which rules with Dædal harmony a throng
Of thoughts and forms, which else senseless and shapeless were.

The lightning is his slave;[9] Heaven's utmost deep
  Gives up her stars, and like a flock of sheep
They pass before his eye, are numbered, and roll on!   420
  The tempest is his steed,—he strides the air;
  And the abyss shouts from her depth laid bare,
Heaven, hast thou secrets? Man unveils me; I have none.

THE MOON

The shadow of white Death has past

---

6. Human society, once splintered by hate, is now united by love into a single macrocosmic Man.
7. By gravitational force.
8. Like the music of Orpheus, which at-tracted and controlled beasts, rocks, and trees. "dædal": skillful, intricate.
9. The Earth describes regenerate man's scientific and technological triumphs.

From my path in Heaven at last,   425
A clinging shroud of solid frost and sleep;
And through my newly-woven bowers
Wander happy paramours
Less mighty, but as mild as those who keep
    Thy vales more deep.   430

THE EARTH

As the dissolving warmth of Dawn may fold
A half-unfrozen dew-globe, green and gold
And chrystalline, till it becomes a winged mist
    And wanders up the vault of the blue Day,
    Outlives the noon, and on the Sun's last ray   435
Hang o'er the Sea—a fleece of fire and amethyst.—

THE MOON

Thou art folded, thou art lying
In the light which is undying
Of thine own joy and Heaven's smile divine;
    All suns and constellations shower   440
    On thee a light, a life, a power
Which doth array thy sphere—thou pourest thine
    On mine, on mine!

THE EARTH

I spin beneath my pyramid of night[1]
Which points into the Heavens, dreaming delight,   445
Murmuring victorious joy in my enchanted sleep;
    As a youth lulled in love-dreams, faintly sighing,
    Under the shadow of his beauty lying
Which round his rest a watch of light and warmth doth keep.

THE MOON

As in the soft and sweet eclipse   450
When soul meets soul on lovers' lips,
High hearts are calm and brightest eyes are dull;
    So when thy shadow falls on me[2]
    Then am I mute and still,—by thee
Covered; of thy love, Orb most beautiful,   455
    Full, oh, too full!—

Thou art speeding round the Sun
Brightest World of many a one;
Green and azure sphere, which shinest
    With a light which is divinest   460
    Among all the lamps of Heaven
To whom life and light is given;
    I, thy chrystal paramour,

1. The conical shadow cast by the earth as it intercepts the sun's light.

2. In the eclipse of the moon, when it enters the earth's shadow.

Borne beside thee by a power
Like the polar Paradise,   465
Magnet-like, of lovers' eyes;[3]
I, a most enamoured maiden
Whose weak brain is overladen
With the pleasure of her love—
Maniac-like around thee move,   470
Gazing, an insatiate bride,
On thy form from every side
Like a Mænad, round the cup
Which Agave lifted up
In the weird Cadmæan forest.—[4]   475
Brother, wheresoe'er thou soarest
I must hurry, whirl and follow
Through the Heavens wide and hollow,
Sheltered by the warm embrace
Of thy soul, from hungry space,   480
Drinking, from thy sense and sight
Beauty, majesty, and might,
As a lover or a chameleon
Grows like what it looks upon,
As a violet's gentle eye   485
Gazes on the azure sky
Until its hue grows like what it beholds,
As a grey and watery mist
Glows like solid amethyst
Athwart the western mountain it enfolds,   490
When the sunset sleeps
    Upon its snow—

THE EARTH

And the weak day weeps[5]
    That it should be so.
O gentle Moon, the voice of thy delight   495
Falls on me like thy clear and tender light
Soothing the seaman, borne the summer night
    Through isles forever calm;
O gentle Moon, thy chrystal accents pierce
The caverns of my Pride's deep Universe,   500
Charming the tyger Joy, whose tramplings fierce
    Made wounds, which need thy balm.

* * *

DEMOGORGON

Man, who wert once a despot and a slave,—
    A dupe and a deceiver,—a Decay,—   550

---

3. As it circles the earth, the moon spins so as to keep her face constantly towards it.
4. The Mænads were female participants in the ecstatic worship of Dionysus (Bacchus). Agave, daughter of King Cadmus, in a blind frenzy tore her own son Pentheus to bits when he was caught spying on the Dionysiac rites.
5. I.e., with the dew at nightfall.

A Traveller from the cradle to the grave
   Through the dim night of this immortal Day:

ALL

Speak—thy strong words may never pass away.

DEMOGORGON

This is the Day which down the void Abysm
At the Earth-born's spell[6] yawns for Heaven's Despotism,   555
   And Conquest is dragged Captive through the deep;[7]
Love from its awful throne of patient power
In the wise heart, from the last giddy hour
   Of dread endurance, from the slippery, steep,
And narrow verge of crag-like Agony, springs   560
And folds over the world its healing wings.

Gentleness, Virtue, Wisdom and Endurance,—
These are the seals of that most firm assurance
   Which bars the pit over Destruction's strength;
And if, with infirm hand, Eternity,   565
Mother of many acts and hours, should free
   The serpent that would clasp her with his length—[8]
These are the spells by which to reassume
An empire o'er the disentangled Doom.[9]

To suffer woes which Hope thinks infinite;   570
To forgive wrongs darker than Death or Night;
   To defy Power, which seems Omnipotent;
To love, and bear; to hope till Hope creates
From its own wreck the thing it contemplates;
   Neither to change nor falter nor repent;   575
This, like thy glory, Titan! is to be
Good, great and joyous, beautiful and free;
This is alone Life, Joy, Empire and Victory.

1818–19   1820

The Cloud

I bring fresh showers for the thirsting flowers,
   From the seas and the streams;
I bear light shade for the leaves when laid

---

6. Prometheus' spell—i.e., his magical words of pity, in place of vengefulness.
7. Ephesians iv.8: "When [Christ] ascended up on high, he led captivity captive."
8. A final reminder that the serpent incessantly struggles to break loose and start the cycle all over again. Felicity must continue to be earned.
9. Shelley's four cardinal virtues (line 562), which seal the serpent in the pit, also constitute the formulas ("spells") by which to remaster him, should he again break loose. These virtues are expanded upon in the concluding lines (570–75).

In their noon-day dreams.
From my wings are shaken the dews that waken   5
   The sweet buds every one,
When rocked to rest on their mother's breast,
   As she dances about the Sun.
I wield the flail of the lashing hail,
   And whiten the green plains under,   10
And then again I dissolve it in rain,
   And laugh as I pass in thunder.

I sift the snow on the mountains below,
   And their great pines groan aghast;
And all the night 'tis my pillow white,   15
   While I sleep in the arms of the blast.
Sublime on the towers of my skiey bowers,
   Lightning my pilot sits;
In a cavern under is fettered the thunder,
   It struggles and howls at fits;[1]   20
Over Earth and Ocean, with gentle motion,
   This pilot is guiding me,
Lured by the love of the genii that move
   In the depths of the purple sea;[2]
Over the rills, and the crags, and the hills,   25
   Over the lakes and the plains,
Wherever he dream, under mountain or stream,
   The Spirit he loves remains;
And I all the while bask in Heaven's blue smile,[3]
   Whilst he is dissolving in rains.   30

The sanguine Sunrise, with his meteor eyes,
   And his burning plumes outspread,
Leaps on the back of my sailing rack,[4]
   When the morning star shines dead;
As on the jag of a mountain crag,   35
   Which an earthquake rocks and swings,
An eagle alit one moment may sit
   In the light of its golden wings.
And when Sunset may breathe, from the lit Sea beneath,
   Its ardours of rest and of love,   40
And the crimson pall of eve may fall
   From the depth of Heaven above,
With wings folded I rest, on mine aëry nest,
   As still as a brooding dove.

1. Fitfully.
2. I.e., atmospheric electricity, guiding the cloud (line 17), discharges as lightning when "lured" by the attraction of an opposite charge.
3. The upper part of the cloud remains exposed to the sun.
4. High, broken clouds, driven by the wind.

That orbed maiden with white fire laden 45
  Whom mortals call the Moon,
Glides glimmering o'er my fleece-like floor,
  By the midnight breezes strewn;
And wherever the beat of her unseen feet,
  Which only the angels hear, 50
May have broken the woof,[5] of my tent's thin roof,
  The stars peep behind her, and peer;
And I laugh to see them whirl and flee,
  Like a swarm of golden bees,
When I widen the rent in my wind-built tent, 55
  Till the calm rivers, lakes, and seas,
Like strips of the sky fallen through me on high,
  Are each paved with the moon and these.[6]

I bind the Sun's throne with a burning zone[7]
  And the Moon's with a girdle of pearl; 60
The volcanos are dim and the stars reel and swim
  When the whirlwinds my banner unfurl.
From cape to cape, with a bridge-like shape,
  Over a torrent sea,
Sunbeam-proof, I hang like a roof— 65
  The mountains its columns be!
The triumphal arch, through which I march
  With hurricane, fire, and snow,
When the Powers of the Air, are chained to my chair,
  Is the million-coloured Bow; 70
The sphere-fire[8] above its soft colours wove
  While the moist Earth was laughing below.

I am the daughter of Earth and Water,
  And the nursling of the Sky;
I pass through the pores, of the ocean and shores; 75
  I change, but I cannot die—
For after the rain, when with never a stain
  The pavilion of Heaven is bare,
And the winds and sunbeams, with their convex gleams,
  Build up the blue dome of Air[9]— 80
I silently laugh at my own cenotaph,[1]
  And out of the caverns of rain,
Like a child from the womb, like a ghost from the tomb,
  I arise, and unbuild it again.—

1820   1820

---

5. Texture.
6. I.e., the stars.
7. Girdle, belt.
8. The sunlight.
9. The blue color of the sky; the phenomenon, as Shelley indicates, results

from the way "sunbeams" are filtered by the earth's atmosphere.
1. The memorial monument ("cenotaph") of the dead cloud is the cloudless blue dome of the sky.

To a Sky-Lark[2]

Hail to thee, blithe Spirit!
    Bird thou never wert—
That from Heaven, or near it,
    Pourest thy full heart
In profuse strains of unpremeditated art.   5

Higher still and higher
    From the earth thou springest
Like a cloud of fire;
    The blue deep thou wingest,
And singing still dost soar, and soaring ever singest.   10

In the golden lightning
    Of the sunken Sun—
O'er which clouds are brightning,
    Thou dost float and run;
Like an unbodied joy whose race is just begun.   15

The pale purple even
    Melts around thy flight,
Like a star of Heaven
    In the broad day-light
Thou art unseen,—but yet I hear thy shrill delight,   20

Keen as are the arrows
    Of that silver sphere,[3]
Whose intense lamp narrows
    In the white dawn clear
Until we hardly see—we feel that it is there.   25

All the earth and air
    With thy voice is loud,
As when Night is bare
    From one lonely cloud
The moon rains out her beams—and Heaven is overflowed.   30

What thou art we know not;
    What is most like thee?
From rainbow clouds there flow not
    Drops so bright to see
As from thy presence showers a rain of melody.   35

2. The bird, freed from the bonds of earth and soaring beyond the reach of all the physical senses except hearing, is made the emblem of a non-material spirit of pure joy, beyond the possibility of empirical knowledge; see lines 15, 31.
3. The morning star.

Like a Poet hidden
    In the light of thought,
Singing hymns unbidden,
    Till the world is wrought
To sympathy with hopes and fears it heeded not: 40

Like a high-born maiden
    In a palace-tower,
Soothing her love-laden
    Soul in secret hour,
With music sweet as love—which overflows her bower: 45

Like a glow-worm golden
    In a dell of dew,
Scattering unbeholden
    Its aerial hue
Among the flowers and grass which screen it from the view: 50

Like a rose embowered
    In its own green leaves—
By warm winds deflowered—
    Till the scent it gives
Makes faint with too much sweet heavy-winged thieves:[4]   55

Sound of vernal showers
    On the twinkling grass,
Rain-awakened flowers,
    All that ever was
Joyous, and clear and fresh, thy music doth surpass.   60

Teach us, Sprite[5] or Bird,
    What sweet thoughts are thine;
I have never heard
    Praise of love or wine
That panted forth a flood of rapture so divine: 65

Chorus Hymeneal[6]
    Or triumphal chaunt
Matched with thine would be all
    But an empty vaunt,
A thing wherein we feel there is some hidden want.   70

What objects are the fountains
    Of thy happy strain?
What fields or waves or mountains?
    What shapes of sky or plain?
What love of thine own kind? what ignorance of pain?   75

---

4. I.e., the "warm winds," line 53.
5. Spirit.

6. Marital (from Hymen, Greek god of marriage).

With thy clear keen joyance
    Languor cannot be—
Shadow of annoyance
    Never came near thee;
Thou lovest—but ne'er knew love's sad satiety.   80

Waking or asleep,
    Thou of death must deem
Things more true and deep
    Than we mortals dream,
Or how could thy notes flow in such a chrystal stream?   85

We look before and after,
    And pine for what is not—
Our sincerest laughter
    With some pain is fraught—
Our sweetest songs are those that tell of saddest thought.   90

Yet if we could scorn
    Hate and pride and fear;
If we were things born
    Not to shed a tear,
I know not how thy joy we ever should come near.   95

Better than all measures
    Of delightful sound—
Better than all treasures
    That in books are found—
Thy skill to poet were, thou Scorner of the ground!   100

Teach me half the gladness
    That thy brain must know,
Such harmonious madness
    From my lips would flow
The world should listen then—as I am listening now.   105

1820   1820

Song of Apollo[7]

The sleepless Hours who watch me as I lie
    Curtained with star-enwoven tapestries
From the broad moonlight of the open sky;
    Fanning the busy dreams from my dim eyes,

7. Written, with the companion piece that follows, for the opening scene in Mary Shelley's verse drama *Midas*. Apollo, god of the sun, of healing, and of poetry and the other arts, sings this serenely Olympian hymn in a contest with Pan, the goatlike deity of flocks, forests, and wild life. In the play, old Tmolus, a mountain god who judges the contest, awards the prize to Apollo; when Midas, a mortal, objects, preferring Pan's song of earthly desire, passions, and suffering, Apollo affixes on him asses' ears.

Waken me when their mother, the grey Dawn,   5
Tells them that Dreams and that the moon is gone.

Then I arise; and climbing Heaven's blue dome,
    I walk over the mountains and the waves,
Leaving my robe upon the Ocean foam.
    My footsteps pave the clouds with fire; the caves   10
Are filled with my bright presence, and the air
Leaves the green Earth to my embraces bare.

The sunbeams are my shafts with which I kill
    Deceit, that loves the night and fears the day;
All men who do, or even imagine ill   15
    Fly me; and from the glory of my ray
Good minds, and open actions take new might
Until diminished, by the reign of night.

I feed the clouds, the rainbows and the flowers
    With their ætherial colours; the moon's globe   20
And the pure stars in their eternal bowers
    Are cinctured[8] with my power as with a robe;
Whatever lamps on Earth or Heaven may shine
Are portions of one spirit; which is mine.

I stand at noon upon the peak of Heaven;   25
    Then with unwilling steps, I linger down
Into the clouds of the Atlantic even;
    For grief that I depart they weep and frown—
What look is more delightful, than the smile
With which I soothe them from the Western isle?   30

I am the eye with which the Universe
    Beholds itself, and knows it is divine;
All harmony of instrument and verse,
    All prophecy and medicine are mine;
All light of art or nature—to my song   35
Victory and praise, in its own right, belong.

1820   1824

Song of Pan[9]

From the forests and highlands
    We come, we come,
From the river-girt islands
Where loud waves were dumb
Listening my sweet pipings.   5
    The wind in the reeds and the rushes,
    The bees on the bells of thyme,
    The birds in the myrtle bushes,
    The cicadæ[1] above in the lime,
        And the lizards below in the grass,   10

8. Girdled.   contest.
9. Pan's reply to Apollo in his singing   1. Locusts.

Were silent as even old Tmolus was,
   Listening my sweet pipings.

Liquid Peneus[2] was flowing—
   And all dark Tempe lay
In Olympus' shadow, outgrowing   15
   The light of the dying day,
   Speeded with my sweet pipings.
     The sileni and sylvans and fauns[3]
   And the nymphs of the woods and the waves,
To the edge of the moist river-lawns   20
   And the brink of the dewy caves,
     And all that did then attend and follow
Were as silent for love, as you now, Apollo,
   For envy of my sweet pipings.

I sang of the dancing stars,   25
   I sang of the dædal[4] Earth,
And of Heaven, and the giant wars,[5]
   And Love and Death and Birth;
     And then I changed my pipings,
   Singing how, down the vales of Mænalus   30
   I pursued a maiden and clasped a reed.[6]
   Gods and men, we are all deluded thus!—
   It breaks in our bosom and then we bleed;
   They wept as, I think, both ye now would,
If envy or age had not frozen your blood,   35
   At the sorrow of my sweet pipings.

1820   1824

The Two Spirits—An Allegory[7]

FIRST SPIRIT

O Thou who plumed with strong desire
Would float above the Earth—beware!
A shadow tracks thy flight of fire—
   Night is coming!
Bright are the regions of the air   5
And when winds and beams [   ]
It were delight to wander there—
   Night is coming!

2. The river Peneus flows through the lovely valley of Tempe, in northeastern Greece.
3. The male sileni, sylvans, and fauns, and the female nymphs, are all minor rural or woodland deities.
4. Intricately formed.
5. The wars of the Titans, sons of Earth, against the gods of Olympus.
6. Pan pursued the nymph, Syrinx, but as he caught her, she turned into a reed. From it he made Pan's pipe, the "syrinx."
7. The Second Spirit speaks for the poet's boundless desire, daring to soar above the limits of earth. The First Spirit expresses the timidity that binds it, safe but somnolent, to the "dull earth." The commentator who speaks the last two stanzas poses, without resolving, two alternate possibilities about the outcome of the flight of the aspiring Second Spirit.

SECOND SPIRIT

The deathless stars are bright above;
If I should cross the shade of night   10
Within my heart is the torch of love
    And that is day—
And the moon will smile with gentle light
On my golden plumes where'er they move;
The meteors will linger around my flight   15
    And make night day.

FIRST SPIRIT

But if the whirlwinds of darkness waken
Hail and Lightning and stormy rain—
See, the bounds of the air are shaken,
    Night is coming.   20
The red swift clouds of the hurricane
Yon declining sun have overtaken,
The clash of the hail sweeps o'er the plain—
    Night is coming.

SECOND SPIRIT

I see the glare and I hear the sound—   25
I'll sail on the flood of the tempest dark
With the calm within and light around
    Which make night day;
And thou when the gloom is deep and stark,
Look from thy dull earth slumberbound—   30
My moonlike flight thou then mayst mark
    On high, far away.

———

Some say there is a precipice
Where one vast pine hangs frozen to ruin
O'er piles of snow and chasms of ice   35
    Mid Alpine mountains;
And that the languid storm pursuing
That winged shape forever flies
Round those hoar branches, aye renewing
    Its aery fountains.   40

Some say when the nights are dry [and] clear
And the death dews sleep on the morass,
Sweet whispers are heard by the traveller
    Which make night day—
And a shape like his early love doth pass   45
Upborne by her wild and glittering hair,
And when he awakes on the fragrant grass
    He finds night day.

1819   1824

When Passion's Trance Is Overpast

When passion's trance is overpast,
If tenderness and truth could last
Or live—whilst all wild feelings keep
Some mortal slumber, dark and deep—
I should not weep, I should not weep!   5

It were enough to feel, to see
Thy soft eyes gazing tenderly . . .
And dream the rest—and burn and be
The secret food of fires unseen,
Could thou but be what thou hast been!   10

After the slumber of the year
The woodland violets reappear;
All things revive in field or grove
And sky and sea, but two, which move
And form all others—life and love.—   15

1819   1824

To Night[8]

Swiftly walk o'er the western wave,
          Spirit of Night!
Out of the misty eastern cave
Where, all the long and lone daylight
Thou wovest dreams of joy and fear,
Which make thee terrible and dear,   5
          Swift be thy flight!

Wrap thy form in a mantle grey,
          Star-inwrought!
Blind with thine hair the eyes of day,   10
Kiss her until she be wearied out—
Then wander o'er City and sea and land,
Touching all with thine opiate wand—
          Come, long-sought!

When I arose and saw the dawn   15
          I sighed for thee;
When Light rode high, and the dew was gone,
And noon lay heavy on flower and tree,
And the weary Day turned to his rest,[9]
Lingering like an unloved guest,   20
          I sighed for thee.

8. Night and darkness, as opposed to daylight, are often for Shelley symbols of the primordial powers and revelations of the poetic imagination. See, e.g., the opening of *The Triumph of Life*, below. 9. Here the "Day" is the male sun, not

Thy brother Death came, and cried,
 Wouldst thou me?
Thy sweet child Sleep, the filmy-eyed,
Murmured like a noontide bee,   25
Shall I nestle near thy side?
Wouldst thou me? and I replied,
 No, not thee!

Death will come when thou art dead,
 Soon, too soon—   30
Sleep will come when thou art fled;
Of neither would I ask the boon
I ask of thee, beloved Night—
Swift be thine approaching flight,
 Come soon, soon!   35

1820   1824

To ———

Music, when soft voices die,
Vibrates in the memory.—
Odours, when sweet violets sicken,
Live within the sense they quicken.—

Rose leaves, when the rose is dead,   5
Are heaped for the beloved's bed[10]—
And so thy thoughts,[1] when thou art gone,
Love itself shall slumber on. . . .

1821   1824

Memory[2]

Rose leaves, when the rose is dead,
Are heaped for the beloved's bed,
And so thy thoughts, when thou art gone,
Love itself shall slumber on. . . .

Music, when soft voices die,   5
Vibrates in the memory.—
Odours, when sweet violets sicken,
Live within the sense they quicken.—

1801

O World, O Life, O Time

O World, O Life, O Time,
On whose last steps I climb,

---

the female "day" with whom the Spirit
of Night dallies in stanza 2.
10. I.e., the fallen petals form a bed for
the dead rose.
1. I.e., my thoughts of thee.
2. *To* ——— is reproduced above as it

was printed by Mary Shelley in *Posthumous Poems* (1824). We reprint here the
(possibly incomplete) version in the
order, and with the title, found in Shelley's draft notebooks. Some scholars believe this to be the correct version.

Trembling at that where I had stood before,
When will return the glory of your prime?
No more, O never more!   5

Out of the day and night
A joy has taken flight—
Fresh spring and summer [   ] and winter hoar
Move my faint heart with grief, but with delight
No more, O never more!   10

1824

Choruses from Hellas[3]

Worlds on Worlds[4]

Worlds on worlds are rolling ever
From creation to decay,
Like the bubbles on a river
Sparkling, bursting, borne away.
But they[5] are still immortal   5
Who through Birth's orient[6] portal
And Death's dark chasm hurrying to and fro,
Clothe their unceasing flight
In the brief dust and light
Gathered around their chariots as they go;   10
New shapes they still may weave,
New Gods, new Laws receive,
Bright or dim are they as the robes they last
On Death's bare ribs had cast.

A Power from the unknown God,   15
A Promethean Conqueror[7] came;
Like a triumphal path he trod
The thorns of death and shame.
A mortal shape to him

3. *Hellas*, a closet drama written in the autumn of 1821, was inspired by the Greek war for independence against the Turks. In his Preface Shelley declared that he viewed this revolution as auguring the final overthrow of all tyranny. The choruses below are sung by Greek captive women. The first chorus describes the emergence of Christ into the revolving cycle of history; the second chorus concludes the drama.
4. "The popular notions of Christianity are represented in this chorus as true in their relation to the worship they superseded ... without considering their merits in a relation more universal. ... The concluding verses indicate a progressive state of more or less exalted existence. ... Let it not be supposed that I mean to dogmatise upon a subject [i.e., the problem of evil, and the possibility of its future elimination] upon which all men are equally ignorant. ... That there is a true solution to the riddle, and that in our present state that solution is unattainable by us, are propositions that may be regarded as equally certain: meanwhile, as it is the province of the poet to attach himself to those ideas which exalt and ennoble humanity, let him be permitted to have conjectured the condition of that futurity towards which we are all impelled by an inextinguishable thirst for immortality ..." [Shelley's note].
5. The immortal "beings which inhabit the planets and... clothe themselves in matter" [Shelley's note].
6. Eastern.
7. Christ, whom Shelley compares to Prometheus, who brought fire and the arts of civilization to mankind.

Was like the vapour dim   20
Which the orient planet animates with light;
    Hell, Sin and Slavery came,
    Like bloodhounds mild and tame,
Nor preyed until their Lord had taken flight;
    The moon of Mahomet[8]   25
    Arose, and it shall set:
While blazoned as on Heaven's immortal noon
    The cross leads generations on.

    Swift as the radiant shapes of sleep
        From one whose dreams are Paradise   30
    Fly, when the fond wretch wakes to weep,
        And Day peers forth with her blank eyes;
    So fleet, so faint, so fair,
    The Powers of earth and air
Fled from the folding-star[9] of Bethlehem: 35
    Apollo, Pan, and Love
    And even Olympian Jove
Grew weak, for killing Truth had glared on them;
    Our hills and seas and streams,
    Dispeopled of their dreams,   40
Their waters turned to blood, their dew to tears,
    Wailed for the golden years.

The World's Great Age[1]

The world's great age begins anew,
    The golden years return,[2]
The earth doth like a snake renew
    Her winter weeds[3] outworn;
Heaven smiles, and faiths and empires gleam,   5
Like wrecks of a dissolving dream.

    A brighter Hellas rears its mountains
        From waves serener far;

---

8. The crescent, emblem of Mohammedanism, which was founded six centuries
after the birth of Christ.
9. The star of evening, the time when
sheep are driven into the sheepfold.
Shelley goes on to describe the pagan
gods of earth and Olympus fleeing before the star of Bethlehem.
1. "Prophecies of wars, and rumours of
wars, etc., may safely be made by poet
or prophet in any age, but to anticipate
however darkly a period of regeneration
and happiness is a more hazardous exercise of the faculty which bards possess
or fain. It will remind the reader . . . of
Isaiah and Virgil, whose ardent spirits
. . . saw the possible and perhaps approaching state of society in which the

'lion shall lie down with the lamb,' and
omnis feret omnia tellus.' Let these great
names be my authority and excuse"
[Shelley's note]. The quotations are
from Isaiah's millennial prophecy (e.g.,
Chapters xxv, lxv), and Vergil's prediction, in Eclogue IV, of a return of the
golden age, when "all the earth will produce all things." Shelley's comments
here, and in the title-footnote to *Worlds
on Worlds*, are cogent expressions of the
skeptical idealism of his maturity.
2. In Greek myth, the first period of history, when Saturn reigned, was the
golden age.
3. Clothes (especially mourning garments) as well as dead vegetation.

A new Peneus[4] rolls his fountains
 Against the morning-star;   10
Where fairer Tempes bloom, there sleep
Young Cyclads[5] on a sunnier deep.

A loftier Argo[6] cleaves the main,
 Fraught with a later prize;
Another Orpheus[7] sings again,   15
 And loves, and weeps, and dies;
A new Ulysses leaves once more
Calypso[8] for his native shore.

O, write no more the tale of Troy,
 If earth Death's scroll must be!   20
Nor mix with Laian[9] rage the joy
 Which dawns upon the free:
Although a subtler Sphinx renew
Riddles of death Thebes never knew.

Another Athens shall arise   25
 And to remoter time
Bequeath, like sunset to the skies,
 The splendour of its prime;
And leave, if nought so bright may live,
All earth can take or Heaven can give.   30

Saturn and Love their long repose
 Shall burst, more bright and good
Than all who fell, than One who rose,
 Than many unsubdued:[1]
Not gold, not blood, their altar dowers,   35
But votive tears and symbol flowers.

O, cease! must hate and death return?
 Cease! must men kill and die?
Cease! drain not to its dregs the urn
 Of bitter prophecy.   40
The world is weary of the past,
O, might it die or rest at last!

1821   1822

4. The river that flows through the beautiful vale of Tempe (line 11).
5. The Cyclades, islands in the Aegean Sea.
6. On which Jason sailed in his quest for the Golden Fleece.
7. The legendary player on the lyre who was torn to pieces by the frenzied Thracian women while he was mourning the death of his wife, Eurydice.
8. The nymph deserted by Ulysses on his voyage back from the Trojan War to his native Ithaca.
9. King Laius of Thebes was killed in a quarrel by his son Oedipus, who did not recognize his father. Shortly thereafter, Oedipus delivered Thebes from the ravages of the Sphinx by answering its riddle (lines 23–24):
1. "Saturn and Love were among the deities of a real or imaginary state of innocence and happiness. 'All' those 'who fell' [are] the Gods of Greece, Asia, and Egypt; the 'One who rose' [is] Jesus Christ . . . and the 'many unsubdued' [are] the monstrous objects of the idolatry of China, India, the Antarctic islands, and the native tribes of America" [Shelley's note].

Adonais: An Elegy on the Death of John Keats[1]

[Thou wert the morning star among the living,
  Ere thy fair light had fled—
Now, having died, thou art as Hesperus, giving
  New splendour to the dead.][2]

1

I weep for Adonais—he is dead!
O, weep for Adonais! though our tears
Thaw not the frost which binds so dear a head!
And thou, sad Hour, selected from all years
To mourn our loss, rouse thy obscure compeers,   5
And teach them thine own sorrow, say: with me
Died Adonais; till the Future dares
Forget the Past, his fate and fame shall be
An echo and a light unto eternity!

2

Where wert thou mighty Mother,[3] when he lay,   10
When thy Son lay, pierced by the shaft which flies
In darkness?[4] where was lorn Urania

---

1. John Keats died in Rome February 23, 1821, and was buried there in the Protestant Cemetery. Shelley had met Keats, had invited him to be his guest at Pisa, and had gradually come to recognize him as "among the writers of the highest genius who have adorned our age" (Preface to *Adonais*). The name "Adonais" is derived from Adonis, the handsome youth who had been loved by the goddess Venus and slain by a wild boar; the function of the beast in this poem is attributed to the anonymous author of a vituperative review of Keats's *Endymion* in the *Quarterly Review*, April, 1818 (now known to be John Wilson Croker), whom Shelley mistakenly believed to be responsible for Keats's illness and death.

Shelley described *Adonais* in a letter as a "highly wrought piece of art." Its artistry consists in part in the care with which it follows the conventions of the pastoral elegy, established more than two thousand years earlier by the Greek Sicilian poets Theocritus, Bion, and Moschus—Shelley had himself translated into English Bion's *Lament for Adonis* and Moschus' *Lament for Bion*. We recognize the centuries-old poetic ritual in many verbal echoes, and in such devices as the mournful and accusing invocation to a muse (stanzas 2–4), the sympathetic participation of nature in the death of the poet (stanzas 14–17), the procession

of appropriate mourners (stanzas 30–35), the denunciation of unworthy practitioners of the pastoral or literary art (stanzas 17, 27–29, 36–37); and above all in the shift from despair at the finality of human death (lines 64, 190: "*He* will awake no more, oh, never more!") to consolation in the sudden and contradictory discovery that the grave is a gate to a higher existence (line 343: "Peace, peace! he is not dead, he doth not sleep"). These familiar elements Shelley transforms into a densely symbolic poetic construction; *Adonais* ranks with Milton's *Lycidas* among the supreme examples of the exacting form of the pastoral elegy.

2. Shelley prefixed to *Adonais* a Greek epigram, attributed to Plato; this is Shelley's own translation of the Greek. (See also *The Triumph of Life*, below, line 256 and footnote.) The planet Venus appears both as the morning star, Lucifer, and the evening star, Hesperus or Vesper. Shelley makes of this phenomenon a key symbol for Adonais' triumph over death, in stanzas 44–46.

3. Urania. She had originally been the Muse of astronomy, but the name was also an epithet for Venus. Shelley converts Venus Urania, who in Greek myth had been the lover of Adonis, into the mother of Adonais.

4. The allusion is to the anonymity of the review of *Endymion*.

When Adonais died? With veiled eyes,
'Mid listening Echoes, in her Paradise
She sate, while one,[5] with soft enamoured breath,   15
Rekindled all the fading melodies,
With which, like flowers that mock the corse[6] beneath,
He had adorned and hid the coming bulk of death.

3

O, weep for Adonais—he is dead!
Wake, melancholy Mother, wake and weep!   20
Yet wherefore? Quench within their burning bed
Thy fiery tears, and let thy loud heart keep
Like his, a mute and uncomplaining sleep;
For he is gone, where all things wise and fair
Descend;—oh, dream not that the amorous Deep   25
Will yet restore him to the vital air;
Death feeds on his mute voice, and laughs at our despair.

4

Most musical of mourners, weep again!
Lament anew, Urania!—He[7] died,
Who was the Sire of an immortal strain,   30
Blind, old, and lonely, when his country's pride,
The priest, the slave, and the liberticide,
Trampled and mocked with many a loathed rite
Of lust and blood; he went, unterrified,
Into the gulph of death; but his clear Sprite[8]   35
Yet reigns o'er earth; the third among the sons of light.[9]

5

Most musical of mourners, weep anew!
Not all to that bright station dared to climb;
And happier they their happiness who knew,
Whose tapers yet burn through that night of time   40
In which suns perished; others more sublime,
Struck by the envious wrath of man or God,
Have sunk, extinct in their refulgent prime;
And some yet live, treading the thorny road,
Which leads, through toil and hate, to Fame's serene abode.   45

---

5. I.e., the echo of Keats's voice in his poems.
6. Corpse.
7. Milton, regarded as precursor of the great poetic tradition in which Keats wrote: he had adopted Urania as the muse of *Paradise Lost*.
8. Spirit.
9. The three are Milton and his great predecessors in epic poetry, Homer and Dante.

6

But now, thy youngest, dearest one, has perished
The nursling of thy widowhood, who grew,
Like a pale flower by some sad maiden cherished,
And fed with true love tears, instead of dew;[1]
Most musical of mourners, weep anew!   50
Thy extreme[2] hope, the loveliest and the last,
The bloom, whose petals nipt before they blew
Died on the promise of the fruit, is waste;
The broken lily lies—the storm is overpast.

7

To that high Capital,[3] where kingly Death   55
Keeps his pale court in beauty and decay,
He came; and bought, with price of purest breath,
A grave among the eternal.—Come away!
Haste, while the vault of blue Italian day
Is yet his fitting charnel-roof! while still   60
He lies, as if in dewy sleep he lay;
Awake him not! surely he takes his fill
Of deep and liquid rest, forgetful of all ill.

8

He will awake no more, oh, never more!—
Within the twilight chamber spreads apace,   65
The shadow of white Death, and at the door
Invisible Corruption waits to trace
His extreme way to her dim dwelling-place;
The eternal Hunger sits, but pity and awe
Soothe her pale rage, nor dares she to deface   70
So fair a prey, till darkness, and the law
Of change, shall o'er his sleep the mortal curtain draw.

9

O, weep for Adonais!—The quick Dreams,
The passion-winged Ministers of thought,
Who were his flocks,[4] whom near the living streams   75
Of his young spirit he fed, and whom he taught
The love which was its music, wander not,—
Wander no more, from kindling brain to brain,
But droop there, whence they sprung; and mourn their lot
Round the cold heart, where, after their sweet pain,   80
They ne'er will gather strength, or find a home again.

---

1. An allusion to an incident in Keats's   3. I.e., Rome.
Isabella.   4. The products of Keats's imagination.
2. Last, as well as highest.

10

And one with trembling hands clasps his cold head,
And fans him with her moonlight wings, and cries;
"Our love, our hope, our sorrow, is not dead;
See, on the silken fringe of his faint eyes,   85
Like dew upon a sleeping flower, there lies
A tear some Dream has loosened from his brain."
Lost Angel of a ruined Paradise!
She knew not 'twas her own; as with no stain
She faded, like a cloud which had outwept its rain.   90

11

One from a lucid urn of starry dew
Washed his light limbs as if embalming them;
Another clipt her profuse locks, and threw
The wreath upon him, like an anadem,[5]
Which frozen tears instead of pearls begem;   95
Another in her wilful grief would break
Her bow and winged reeds, as if to stem
A greater loss with one which was more weak;
And dull the barbed fire against his frozen cheek.

12

Another Splendour on his mouth alit,   100
That mouth, whence it was wont to draw the breath
Which gave it strength to pierce the guarded wit,[6]
And pass into the panting heart beneath
With lightning and with music: the damp death
Quenched its caress upon his icy lips;   105
And, as a dying meteor stains a wreath
Of moonlight vapour, which the cold night clips,[7]
It flushed through his pale limbs, and past to its eclipse.

13

And others came . . . Desires and Adorations,
Winged Persuasions and veiled Destinies,   110
Splendours, and Glooms, and glimmering Incarnations
Of hopes and fears, and twilight Phantasies;
And Sorrow, with her family of Sighs,
And Pleasure, blind with tears, led by the gleam
Of her own dying smile instead of eyes,   115
Came in slow pomp;—the moving pomp might seem
Like pageantry of mist on an autumnal stream.

---

5. A rich garland.   7. Embraces.
6. The cautious intellect of the listener.

14

All he had loved, and moulded into thought,
From shape, and hue, and odour, and sweet sound,
Lamented Adonais. Morning sought   120
Her eastern watchtower, and her hair unbound,
Wet with the tears which should adorn the ground,
Dimmed the aerial eyes that kindle day;
Afar the melancholy thunder moaned,
Pale Ocean in unquiet slumber lay,   125
And the wild winds flew round, sobbing in their dismay.

15

Lost Echo sits amid the voiceless mountains,
And feeds her grief with his remembered lay,
And will no more reply to winds or fountains,
Or amorous birds perched on the young green spray, 130
Or herdsman's horn, or bell at closing day;
Since she can mimic not his lips, more dear
Than those for whose disdain she pined away
Into a shadow of all sounds:⁸—a drear
Murmur, between their songs, is all the woodmen hear.   135

16

Grief made the young Spring wild, and she threw down
Her kindling buds, as if she Autumn were,
Or they dead leaves; since her delight is flown
For whom should she have waked the sullen year?
To Phœbus was not Hyacinth so dear⁹   140
Nor to himself Narcissus, as to both
Thou Adonais: wan they stand and sere
Amid the faint companions of their youth,
With dew all turned to tears; odour, to sighing ruth.¹

17

Thy spirit's sister, the lorn nightingale²   145
Mourns not her mate with such melodious pain;
Not so the eagle, who like thee could scale
Heaven, and could nourish in the sun's domain
Her mighty youth with morning,³ doth complain,

8. Because of her unrequited love for Narcissus, who was enamored of his own reflection (line 141), the nymph Echo pined away until she was only a reflected sound.
9. Young Hyacinthus was loved by Phoebus Apollo, who accidentally killed him in a game of quoits. Apollo made the hyacinth flower spring from his blood.
1. Pity.
2. To whom Keats had written *Ode to a Nightingale*.
3. In the legend, the aged eagle, to renew his youth, flies toward the sun until his old plumage is burned off and the film cleared from his eyes.

Soaring and screaming round her empty nest,   150
As Albion[4] wails for thee: the curse of Cain
Light on his[5] head who pierced thy innocent breast,
And scared the angel soul that was its earthly guest!

18

Ah woe is me! Winter is come and gone,
But grief returns with the revolving year;   155
The airs and streams renew their joyous tone;
The ants, the bees, the swallows reappear;
Fresh leaves and flowers deck the dead Seasons' bier;
The amorous birds now pair in every brake,
And build their mossy homes in field and brere;[6]   160
And the green lizard, and the golden snake,
Like unimprisoned flames, out of their trance awake.

19

Through wood and stream and field and hill and Ocean
A quickening life from the Earth's heart has burst
As it has ever done, with change and motion,   165
From the great morning of the world when first
God dawned on Chaos; in its stream immersed
The lamps of Heaven flash with a softer light;
All baser things pant with life's sacred thirst;
Diffuse themselves; and spend in love's delight,   170
The beauty and the joy of their renewed might.

20

The leprous corpse touched by this spirit tender
Exhales itself in flowers of gentle breath;
Like incarnations of the stars, when splendour
Is changed to fragrance, they illumine death   175
And mock the merry worm that wakes beneath;
Nought we know, dies. Shall that alone which knows
Be as a sword consumed before the sheath
By sightless lightning?[7]—th'intense atom glows
A moment, then is quenched in a most cold repose.   180

21

Alas! that all we loved of him should be,
But for our grief, as if it had not been,
And grief itself be mortal! Woe is me!

4. England.
5. I.e., of the reviewer of *Endymion*.
6. Briar. "Brake": thicket.

7. The sword is the mind which knows;
the sheath is its vehicle, the material
body. "Sightless": invisible.

Whence are we, and why are we? of what scene
The actors or spectators? Great and mean   185
Meet massed in death, who lends what life must borrow.
As long as skies are blue, and fields are green,
Evening must usher night, night urge the morrow,
Month follow month with woe, and year wake year to sorrow.

22

He will awake no more, oh, never more!   190
"Wake thou," cried Misery, "childless Mother, rise
Out of thy sleep, and slake, in thy heart's core,
A wound more fierce than his with tears and sighs."
And all the Dreams that watched Urania's eyes,
And all the Echoes whom their sister's song   195
Had held in holy silence, cried: "Arise!"
Swift as a Thought by the snake Memory stung,
From her ambrosial rest the fading Splendour⁸ sprung.

23

She rose like an autumnal Night, that springs
Out of the East, and follows wild and drear   200
The golden Day, which, on eternal wings,
Even as a ghost abandoning a bier,
Had left the Earth a corpse. Sorrow and fear
So struck, so roused, so rapt Urania;
So saddened round her like an atmosphere   205
Of stormy mist; so swept her on her way
Even to the mournful place where Adonais lay.

24

Out of her secret Paradise she sped,
Through camps and cities rough with stone, and steel,
And human hearts, which to her aery tread   210
Yielding not, wounded the invisible
Palms of her tender feet where'er they fell:
And barbed tongues, and thoughts more sharp than they
Rent the soft Form they never could repel,
Whose sacred blood, like the young tears of May,   215
Paved with eternal flowers that undeserving way.

25

In the death chamber for a moment Death
Shamed by the presence of that living Might
Blushed to annihilation, and the breath

8. Urania.

Revisited those lips, and life's pale light   220
Flashed through those limbs, so late her dear delight.
"Leave me not wild and drear and comfortless,
As silent lightning leaves the starless night!
Leave me not!" cried Urania: her distress
Roused Death: Death rose and smiled, and met her vain caress. 225

26

"Stay yet awhile! speak to me once again;
Kiss me, so long but as a kiss may live;
And in my heartless[9] breast and burning brain
That word, that kiss shall all thoughts else survive
With food of saddest memory kept alive,   230
Now thou art dead, as if it were a part
Of thee, my Adonais! I would give
All that I am to be as thou now art!
But I am chained to Time, and cannot thence depart!

27

"Oh gentle child, beautiful as thou wert,   235
Why didst thou leave the trodden paths of men
Too soon, and with weak hands though mighty heart
Dare the unpastured dragon in his den?
Defenceless as thou wert, oh where was then
Wisdom the mirrored shield, or scorn the spear?[1]   240
Or hadst thou waited the full cycle, when
Thy spirit should have filled its crescent sphere,[2]
The monsters of life's waste had fled from thee like deer.

28

"The herded wolves, bold only to pursue;
The obscene ravens, clamorous o'er the dead;   245
The vultures to the conqueror's banner true
Who feed where Desolation first has fed,
And whose wings rain contagion;—how they fled,
When like Apollo, from his golden bow,
The Pythian of the age[3] one arrow sped   250
And smiled!—The spoilers tempt no second blow,
They fawn on the proud feet that spurn them lying low.

9. Because her heart had been given to Adonais.
1. The allusion is to Perseus, who had cut off Medusa's head while avoiding the direct sight of her (which would have turned him to stone) by looking only at her reflection in his shield.
2. I.e., when thy spirit, like the full moon, should have reached its maturity.
3. Byron, who had directed against critics of the age his satiric poem, *English Bards and Scotch Reviewers* (1809). The allusion is to Apollo, called "the Pythian" because he had slain the dragon Python.

29

"The sun comes forth, and many reptiles spawn;
He sets, and each ephemeral insect then
Is gathered into death without a dawn,   255
And the immortal stars awake again;
So is it in the world of living men:
A godlike mind soars forth, in its delight
Making earth bare and veiling heaven,[4] and when
It sinks, the swarms that dimmed or shared its light   260
Leave to its kindred lamps[5] the spirit's awful night."

30

Thus ceased she: and the mountain shepherds came
Their garlands sere, their magic mantles rent;
The Pilgrim of Eternity,[6] whose fame
Over his living head like Heaven is bent,   265
An early but enduring monument,
Came, veiling all the lightnings of his song
In sorrow; from her wilds Ierne sent
The sweetest lyrist of her saddest wrong,[7]
And love taught grief to fall like music from his tongue.   270

31

Midst others of less note, came one frail Form,[8]
A phantom among men; companionless
As the last cloud of an expiring storm
Whose thunder is its knell; he, as I guess,
Had gazed on Nature's naked loveliness,   275
Actæon-like, and now he fled astray
With feeble steps o'er the world's wilderness,
And his own thoughts, along that rugged way,
Pursued, like raging hounds, their father and their prey.[9]

32

A pardlike[1] Spirit beautiful and swift—   280
A Love in desolation masked;—a Power
Girt round with weakness;—it can scarce uplift
The weight of the superincumbent hour;
It is a dying lamp, a falling shower,

4. As the sun reveals the earth but veils the other stars.
5. The other stars (i.e., creative minds), of lesser brilliance than the sun.
6. Byron, who had referred to his Childe Harold as one of the "wanderers o'er eternity" (III.669).
7. Thomas Moore (1779–1852) from Ireland ("Ierne"), who had written poems about the oppression of his native land.
8. Shelley himself, represented in one of his aspects—like the Poet in *Alastor*, rather than the author of *Prometheus Unbound*.
9. Actaeon, while hunting, came upon the naked Diana bathing, and in punishment was turned into a stag and torn to pieces by his own hounds.
1. Leopard-like.

A breaking billow;—even whilst we speak   285
Is it not broken? On the withering flower
The killing sun smiles brightly: on a cheek
The life can burn in blood, even while the heart may break.

33

His head was bound with pansies overblown,
And faded violets, white, and pied, and blue;   290
And a light spear topped with a cypress cone,
Round whose rude shaft dark ivy tresses grew[2]
Yet dripping with the forest's noonday dew,
Vibrated, as the ever-beating heart
Shook the weak hand that grasped it; of that crew   295
He came the last, neglected and apart;
A herd-abandoned deer struck by the hunter's dart.

34

All stood aloof, and at his partial[3] moan
Smiled through their tears; well knew that gentle band
Who in another's fate now wept his own;   300
As in the accents of an unknown land,
He sung new sorrow; sad Urania scanned
The Stranger's mien, and murmured: "who art thou?"
He answered not, but with a sudden hand
Made bare his branded and ensanguined brow,   305
Which was like Cain's or Christ's[4]—Oh! that it should be so!

35

What softer voice is hushed over the dead?
Athwart what brow is that dark mantle thrown?
What form leans sadly o'er the white death-bed,
In mockery[5] of monumental stone,   310
The heavy heart heaving without a moan?
If it be He,[6] who, gentlest of the wise,
Taught, soothed, loved, honoured the departed one;
Let me not vex, with inharmonious sighs
The silence of that heart's accepted sacrifice.   315

36

Our Adonais has drunk poison—oh!
What deaf and viperous murderer could crown

2. Like the thyrsus, the leaf-entwined and cone-topped staff carried by Dionysus. The pansies are emblems of sorrowful thought; the cypress is an emblem of mourning.
3. I.e., with reference to himself.
4. His bloody ("ensanguined") brow bore a mark like that with which God had branded Cain for murdering Abel—or like that left by Christ's crown of thorns.
5. Imitation.
6. Leigh Hunt, close friend both of Keats and Shelley.

Life's early cup with such a draught of woe?
The nameless worm[7] would now itself disown:
It felt, yet could escape the magic tone   320
Whose prelude held all envy, hate, and wrong,
But what was howling in one breast alone,
Silent with expectation of the song,[8]
Whose master's hand is cold, whose silver lyre unstrung.

37

Live thou, whose infamy is not thy fame!   325
Live! fear no heavier chastisement from me,
Thou noteless blot on a remembered name!
But be thyself, and know thyself to be!
And ever at thy season be thou free
To spill the venom when thy fangs o'erflow: 330
Remorse and Self-contempt shall cling to thee;
Hot Shame shall burn upon thy secret brow,
And like a beaten hound tremble thou shalt—as now.

38

Nor let us weep that our delight is fled
Far from these carrion kites that scream below;   335
He wakes or sleeps with the enduring dead;
Thou canst not soar where he is sitting now.—
Dust to the dust! but the pure spirit shall flow
Back to the burning fountain whence it came,
A portion of the Eternal,[9] which must glow   340
Through time and change, unquenchably the same,
Whilst thy cold embers choke the sordid hearth of shame.

39

Peace, peace! he is not dead, he doth not sleep—
He hath awakened from the dream of life—
'Tis we, who lost in stormy visions, keep   345
With phantoms an unprofitable strife,
And in mad trance, strike with our spirit's knife
Invulnerable nothings.—*We* decay
Like corpses in a charnel; fear and grief
Convulse us and consume us day by day,   350
And cold hopes swarm like worms within our living clay.

7. The anonymous reviewer.
8. I.e., the promise of later greatness in Keats's early poems "held . . . silent" the expression of all malignant feelings except the reviewer's.
9. Shelley adopts for this poem the Neo-Platonic view that all life and all forms emanate from the Absolute, the eternal One. The Absolute is imaged as a radiant light-source and an overflowing fountain, which circulates continuously through the dross of matter (stanza 43) and back to its source.

40

He has outsoared the shadow of our night;[1]
Envy and calumny and hate and pain,
And that unrest which men miscall delight,
Can touch him not and torture not again;   355
From the contagion of the world's slow stain
He is secure, and now can never mourn
A heart grown cold, a head grown grey in vain;
Nor, when the spirit's self has ceased to burn,
With sparkless ashes load an unlamented urn.   360

41

He lives, he wakes—'tis Death is dead, not he;
Mourn not for Adonais.—Thou young Dawn
Turn all thy dew to splendour, for from thee
The spirit thou lamentest is not gone;
Ye caverns and ye forests, cease to moan!   365
Cease ye faint flowers and fountains, and thou Air
Which like a mourning veil thy scarf hadst thrown
O'er the abandoned Earth, now leave it bare
Even to the joyous stars which smile on its despair![2]

42

He is made one with Nature: there is heard   370
His voice in all her music, from the moan
Of thunder, to the song of night's sweet bird;[3]
He is a presence to be felt and known
In darkness and in light, from herb and stone,
Spreading itself where'er that Power may move   375
Which has withdrawn his being to its own;
Which wields the world with never wearied love,
Sustains it from beneath, and kindles it above.

43

He is a portion of the loveliness
Which once he made more lovely: he doth bear   380
His part, while the one Spirit's plastic[4] stress
Sweeps through the dull dense world, compelling there,
All new successions to the forms they wear;
Torturing th'unwilling dross that checks its flight

1. He has soared beyond the shadow cast by the earth as it intercepts the sun's light.
2. Shelley's science is as usual, accurate: it is the envelope of air around the earth which, by diffusing and reflecting sunlight, veils the stars.
3. The nightingale, in allusion to Keats's *Ode to a Nightingale*.
4. Formative, shaping.

To its own likeness, as each mass may bear;[5]   385
And bursting in its beauty and its might
From trees and beasts and men into the Heaven's light.

44

The splendours of the firmament of time
May be eclipsed, but are extinguished not;
Like stars to their appointed height they climb   390
And death is a low mist which cannot blot
The brightness it may veil.[6] When lofty thought
Lifts a young heart above its mortal lair,
And love and life contend in it, for what
Shall be its earthly doom, the dead live there[7]   395
And move like winds of light on dark and stormy air.

45

The inheritors of unfulfilled renown[8]
Rose from their thrones, built beyond mortal thought,
Far in the Unapparent. Chatterton
Rose pale, his solemn agony had not   400
Yet faded from him; Sidney, as he fought
And as he fell and as he lived and loved
Sublimely mild, a Spirit without spot,
Arose; and Lucan, by his death approved:[9]
Oblivion as they rose shrank like a thing reproved.   405

46

And many more, whose names on Earth are dark
But whose transmitted effluence cannot die
So long as fire outlives the parent spark,
Rose, robed in dazzling immortality.
"Thou art become as one of us," they cry,   410
"It was for thee yon kingless sphere has long
Swung blind in unascended majesty,
Silent alone amid an Heaven of song.
Assume thy winged throne, thou Vesper of our throng!"[1]

---

5. I.e., to the degree that a particular substance will permit. Different kinds of matter offer variable resistance to the attempts of the "one Spirit" to realize itself. The stars (line 387) are of such a refined matter that they permit an approximation to the radiance of the spirit itself.

6. The radiance of stars (i.e., of poets) persists, even when they are temporarily "eclipsed" by another heavenly body, or obscured by the veil of the earth's atmosphere.

7. I.e., in the thought of the "young heart" (line 393).

8. Poets who (like Keats) died young, before achieving their full measure of fame. Thomas Chatterton (1752–70) committed suicide at 17; Sir Philip Sidney (1554–86) died in battle at 32; and the Roman poet Lucan (A.D. 39–65) killed himself at 26 to escape a sentence of death for having plotted against Nero.

9. Justified, proved worthy.

1. Adonais assumes his place in the sphere of Vesper, the evening star, hitherto unoccupied ("kingless"), hence also "silent" amid the music of the other spheres.

47

Who mourns for Adonais? oh come forth   415
Fond wretch! and know thyself and him aright.
Clasp with thy panting soul the pendulous[2] Earth;
As from a centre, dart thy spirit's light
Beyond all worlds, until its spacious might
Satiate the void circumference: then shrink   420
Even to a point within our day and night;[3]
And keep thy heart light lest it make thee sink
When hope has kindled hope, and lured thee to the brink.

48

Or go to Rome, which is the sepulchre
O, not of him, but of our joy: 'tis nought   425
That ages, empires, and religions there
Lie buried in the ravage they have wrought;
For such as he can lend,—they borrow not
Glory from those who made the world their prey;
And he is gathered to the kings of thought   430
Who waged contention with their time's decay,
And of the past are all that cannot pass away.

49

Go thou to Rome,—at once the Paradise,
The grave, the city, and the wilderness;
And where it wrecks like shattered mountains rise,   435
And flowering weeds, and fragrant copses dress
The bones of Desolation's nakedness
Pass, till the Spirit of the spot shall lead
Thy footsteps to a slope of green access[4]
Where, like an infant's smile, over the dead,   440
A light of laughing flowers along the grass is spread.

50

And grey walls moulder round, on which dull Time
Feeds, like slow fire upon a hoary brand;
And one keen pyramid with wedge sublime,[5]
Pavilioning the dust of him who planned   445
This refuge for his memory, doth stand
Like flame transformed to marble; and beneath,
A field is spread, on which a newer band

---

2. Suspended.
3. The poet bids the wretch so foolish ("fond") as to mourn Adonais to stretch his imagination so as to reach the poet's own cosmic viewpoint, and then allow it to contract ("shrink") back to its ordinary vantage-point on earth—where, unlike Adonais in his heavenly place, we have an alternation of day and night (line 421).
4. The Protestant Cemetery, Keats's burial place.
5. The tomb of Gaius Cestius, a Roman tribune, just outside the cemetery.

Have pitched in Heaven's smile their camp of death
Welcoming him we lose with scarce extinguished breath.   450

51

Here pause: these graves are all too young as yet
To have outgrown the sorrow which consigned
Its charge to each; and if the seal is set,
Here, on one fountain of a mourning mind,[6]
Break it not thou! too surely shalt thou find   455
Thine own well full, if thou returnest home,
Of tears and gall. From the world's bitter wind
Seek shelter in the shadow of the tomb.
What Adonais is, why fear we to become?

52

The One remains, the many change and pass;   460
Heaven's light forever shines, Earth's shadows fly;
Life, like a dome of many-coloured glass,
Stains the white radiance of Eternity,
Until Death tramples it to fragments.[7]—Die,
If thou wouldst be with that which thou dost seek!   465
Follow where all is fled!—Rome's azure sky,
Flowers, ruins, statues, music, words, are weak
The glory they transfuse with fitting truth to speak.

53

Why linger, why turn back, why shrink, my Heart?
Thy hopes are gone before; from all things here   470
They have departed; thou shouldst now depart!
A light is past from the revolving year,
And man, and woman; and what still is dear
Attracts to crush, repels to make thee wither.
The soft sky smiles,—the low wind whispers near: 475
'Tis Adonais calls! oh, hasten thither,
No more let Life divide what Death can join together.

54

That Light whose smile kindles the Universe,
That Beauty in which all things work and move,
That Benediction which the eclipsing Curse   480

---

6. Shelley's three-year-old son, William, had recently been buried in the same cemetery.
7. Earthly life colors ("stains") the pure white light of the One, which is the source of all light (see lines 339–40 and note). The azure sky, flowers, etc., of lines 466–68 exemplify earthly colors which, however beautiful, fall far short of the "glory" of the pure Light which they transmit, but refract ("transfuse").

Of birth can quench not, that sustaining Love
Which through the web of being blindly wove
By man and beast and earth and air and sea,
Burns bright or dim, as each are mirrors of[8]
The fire for which all thirst;[9] now beams on me,   485
Consuming the last clouds of cold mortality.

55

The breath whose might I have invoked in song[1]
Descends on me; my spirit's bark is driven,
Far from the shore, far from the trembling throng
Whose sails were never to the tempest given;   490
The massy earth and sphered skies are riven!
I am borne darkly, fearfully, afar;
Whilst burning through the inmost veil of Heaven,
The soul of Adonais, like a star,
Beacons from the abode where the Eternal are.   495

1821   1821

A Dirge

Rough wind, that moanest loud
  Grief too sad for song;
Wild wind, when sullen cloud
  Knells all the night long;
Sad storm, whose tears are vain,   5
Bare woods, whose branches strain,
Deep caves and dreary main,—
  Wail, for the world's wrong!

1821   1824

When the Lamp Is Shattered

When the lamp is shattered
The light in the dust lies dead—
When the cloud is scattered
The rainbow's glory is shed—
When the lute is broken   5
Sweet tones are remembered not—
When the lips have spoken
Loved accents are soon forgot.

As music and splendour
Survive not the lamp and the lute,   10

8. I.e., according to the degree that each reflects.
9. The "thirst" of the human spirit is to return to the fountain and fire (the "burning fountain," line 339) which is its source.
1. Two years earlier, Shelley had "invoked" (prayed to, and also asked for) "the breath of Autumn's being" in his *Ode to the West Wind*.

The heart's echoes render
No song when the spirit is mute—
    No song—but sad dirges
Like the wind through a ruined cell
    Or the mournful surges   15
That ring the dead seaman's knell.

    When hearts have once mingled
Love first leaves the well-built nest[1]—
    The weak one is singled
To endure what it once possest.   20
    O Love! who bewailest
The frailty of all things here,
    Why choose you the frailest[2]
For your cradle, your home and your bier?

    Its passions will rock thee   25
As the storms rock the ravens on high—
    Bright Reason will mock thee
Like the Sun from a wintry sky—
    From thy nest every rafter
Will rot, and thine eagle home[3]   30
    Leave thee naked to laughter
When leaves fall and cold winds come.

1822   1824

To Jane. The Invitation[4]

Best and brightest, come away—
Fairer far than this fair day
Which like thee to those in sorrow
Comes to bid a sweet good-morrow
To the rough year just awake   5
In its cradle on the brake.—
The brightest hour of unborn spring
Through the winter wandering
Found, it seems, this halcyon morn
To hoar February born;   10
Bending from Heaven in azure mirth
It kissed the forehead of the earth
And smiled upon the silent sea,
And bade the frozen streams be free
And waked to music all their fountains,   15
And breathed upon the frozen mountains,
And like a prophetess of May

1. Love first flies off from the sturdier
heart.
2. I.e., the heart.
3. Like the lofty, and therefore exposed,
nest of the eagle.
4. "Jane" is Jane Williams, the common-law wife of Edward Williams, Shelley's close friend. This invitation to an
outdoor excursion exemplifies Shelley's
grace and urbanity, writing in the ancient tradition of the verse letter.

Strewed flowers upon the barren way,
Making the wintry world appear
Like one on whom thou smilest, dear.   20

Away, away from men and towns
To the wild wood and the downs,
To the silent wilderness
Where the soul need not repress
Its music lest it should not find   25
An echo in another's mind,
While the touch of Nature's art
Harmonizes heart to heart.—
I leave this notice on my door
For each accustomed visitor—   30
"I am gone into the fields
To take what this sweet hour yields.
Reflexion, you may come tomorrow,
Sit by the fireside with Sorrow—
You, with the unpaid bill, Despair,   35
You, tiresome verse-reciter Care,
I will pay you in the grave,
Death will listen to your stave[5]—
Expectation too, be off!
To-day is for itself enough—   40
Hope, in pity mock not woe
With smiles, nor follow where I go;
Long having lived on thy sweet food,
At length I find one moment's good
After long pain—with all your love   45
This you never told me of."

Radiant Sister of the day,
Awake, arise and come away
To the wild woods and the plains
And the pools where winter-rains   50
Image all their roof of leaves,
Where the pine its garland weaves
Of sapless green and ivy dun
Round stems that never kiss the Sun—
Where the lawns and pastures be   55
And the sandhills of the sea—
Where the melting hoar-frost wets
The daisy-star that never sets,
And wind-flowers, and violets
Which yet join not scent to hue   60
Crown the pale year weak and new,
When the night is left behind
In the deep east dun and blind
And the blue noon is over us,

5. Stanza, set of verses.

And the multitudinous   65
Billows murmur at our feet
Where the earth and ocean meet,
And all things seem only one
In the universal Sun.—

1822   1824; 1833

To Jane (The Keen Stars Were Twinkling)

The keen stars were twinkling
And the fair moon was rising among them,
    Dear Jane.
The guitar was tinkling
But the notes were not sweet 'till you sung them   5
    Again.—
As the moon's soft splendour
O'er the faint cold starlight of Heaven
    Is thrown—
So your voice most tender   10
To the strings without soul had then given
    Its own.

The stars will awaken,
Though the moon sleep a full hour later,
    Tonight;   15
No leaf will be shaken
While the dews of your melody scatter
    Delight.
Though the sound overpowers
Sing again, with your dear voice revealing   20
    A tone
Of some world far from ours,
Where music and moonlight and feeling
    Are one.

1822   1832; 1839

Lines Written in the Bay of Lerici[6]

Bright wanderer, fair coquette of Heaven,
To whom alone it has been given
To change and be adored for ever. . . .
Envy not this dim world, for never
But once within its shadow grew   5
One fair as [thou], but far more true.
She left me at the silent time
When the moon had ceased to climb
The azure dome of Heaven's steep,
And like an albatross asleep,   10
Balanced on her wings of light,

6. Another of Shelley's last lyrics, inspired by Jane Williams.

Hovered in the purple night,
Ere she sought her Ocean nest
In the chambers of the west.—
She left me, and I staid alone   15
Thinking over every tone,
Which though now silent to the ear
The enchanted heart could hear
Like notes which die when born, but still
Haunt the echoes of the hill: 20
And feeling ever—O too much—
The soft vibrations of her touch
As if her gentle hand even now
Lightly trembled on my brow;
And thus although she absent were   25
Memory gave me all of her
That even fancy dares to claim.—
Her presence had made weak and tame
All passions, and I lived alone,
In the time which is our own;   30
The past and future were forgot
As they had been, and would be, not.—
But soon, the guardian angel gone,
The demon⁷ reassumed his throne
In my faint heart . . . I dare not speak   35
My thoughts; but thus disturbed and weak
I sate and watched the vessels glide
Along the ocean bright and wide,
Like spirit-winged chariots sent
O'er some serenest element   40
To ministrations strange and far;
As if to some Elysian star
They sailed for drink to medicine
Such sweet and bitter pain as mine.
And the wind that winged their flight   45
From the land came fresh and light,
And the scent of sleeping flowers
And the coolness of the hours
Of dew, and the sweet warmth of day
Was scattered o'er the twinkling bay;   50
And the fisher with his lamp
And spear, about the low rocks damp
Crept, and struck the fish who came
To worship the delusive flame:
Too happy, they whose pleasure sought   55
Extinguishes all sense and thought
Of the regret that pleasure [leaves]⁸
Destroying life alone not peace.

1822   1862

7. I.e., the passions, with their compulsion to look before and after (lines 29–32).

8. This word has been suggested by earlier editors; Shelley left a blank space.

The Triumph of Life

Shelley left this poem in process when he died in early July, 1822. He took its central event from Petrarch's six *Trionfi*, "triumph" having the meaning of the Latin *triumphus*, the ceremonial entrance of a victorious general into ancient Rome in a procession which included his prisoners of war. The poem is strongly influenced by Dante's *Divine Comedy*, not only in its *terza rima* (the verse form also of Petrarch's *Trionfi*) but also in over-all conception, in a number of narrative details, and in style. It is notable that Shelley, like Keats in *The Fall of Hyperion*, left unfinished at his death a long poem in the form of a Dantean dream-vision, in which the poet faces up to the discovery that human history has been a continuous process of human suffering and defeat—and in Shelley's version, an almost unrelieved narrative of human weakness and evil-doing.

We ought to be cautious, however, of a tendency to dramatize Shelley's career by imposing on it the form of a tragic plot, moving inexorably to *The Triumph of Life*, from which there was no exit except the poet's own death. The vision in the poem of the frantic, quiescent, or despairing captives in the procession of Life—including all who have in the least degree compromised in spirit or aspiration with the passions, temptations, or values of fleshly life and the material world—is a desolate one, but its darkness is not unrelieved. There are the "sacred few" among humanity who have not compromised at all. The band of "mighty captives" chained to Life's car represent a full spectrum of relative worth, from mighty villains to mighty heroes. And although we lack Shelley's answer to the question posed at the end of the fragment—"then, what is Life?"—there is no determinative evidence that he planned to depart from the precedent of all his other long poems, in which he allowed some scope of possibility for redeeming life by the cardinal Shelleyan virtues; and above all by that love which, as he says near the close of *The Triumph of Life* (lines 472–76), led Dante safely "from the lowest depths of Hell" through Purgatory to Heaven and back to earth.

But any statement of how Shelley would have ended this fragment is speculative. What is certain is the vitality and the timbre of the poetic voice in the portion before us. No other narrative poem quite matches in its opening the assurance of Shelley's forty-line induction, as the sun springs forth like a bridegroom coming out of his chamber, to be greeted with the quiet ceremonies of natural worship by the revolving world, to whom it brings light, heat, and joyous reawakening—to all except the poet who composes himself to sleep as the world awakes, to undergo, in the transparent darkness of a trance, the crisis of his vision. And the promise of this extraordinary opening is fulfilled in the unflagging narrative drive, and in the ease and precision of language, of the rest of the poem, which expresses an *élan* even in its grimmest passages.

The Triumph of Life does not sound like the voice of a defeated poet at the end of his tether, but of a poet who, just attaining the height of his powers, was making a masterful new beginning.

The Triumph of Life[1]

Swift as a spirit hastening to his task
　　Of glory and of good, the Sun sprang forth
Rejoicing in his splendour, and the mask

Of darkness fell from the awakened Earth.
　　The smokeless altars of the mountain snows　　　　　5
　　　　Flamed above crimson clouds, and at the birth

Of light, the Ocean's orison[2] arose
　　To which the birds tempered their matin lay.
All flowers in field or forest which unclose

　　Their trembling eyelids to the kiss of day,　　　　　10
Swinging their censers in the element,
　　　　With orient[3] incense lit by the new ray

Burned slow and inconsumably, and sent
　　Their odorous sighs up to the smiling air,
And in succession due, did Continent,　　　　　15

　　Isle, Ocean, and all things that in them wear
The form and character of mortal mould
　　Rise as the Sun their father rose, to bear

Their portion of the toil which he of old
　　Took as his own and then imposed on them;　　　　　20
But I, whom thoughts which must remain untold

　　Had kept as wakeful as the stars that gem
The cone of night,[4] now they were laid asleep,
　　　　Stretched my faint limbs beneath the hoary stem

Which an old chestnut flung athwart the steep　　　　　25
　　Of a green Apennine:[5] before me fled
The night; behind me rose the day; the Deep

　　Was at my feet, and Heaven above my head
When a strange trance over my fancy grew
　　Which was not slumber, for the shade it spread　　　　　30

1. The text of Shelley's unfinished poem was prepared for this edition by Donald H. Reiman; it is a revised form of the text that Dr. Reiman transcribed from Shelley's manuscript draft in *Shelley's "The Triumph of Life": A Critical Study* (Urbana, Ill. 1965).
2. Prayer: to which (in the next line) the birds tuned their chanted morning prayer ("matin lay").
3. Eastern, morning.
4. The conical shadow cast by the earth.
5. The Apennines are a chain of mountains extending down the peninsula of Italy.

Was so transparent that the scene came through
   As clear as when a veil of light is drawn
O'er evening hills they glimmer;[6] and I knew

   That I had felt the freshness of that dawn,
Bathed in the same cold dew my brow and hair   35
   And sate as thus upon that slope of lawn

Under the self same bough, and heard as there
   The birds, the fountains and the Ocean hold
Sweet talk in music through the enamoured air.
   And then a Vision on my brain was rolled. . . .   40

As in that trance of wondrous thought I lay
   This was the tenour of my waking dream.
Methought I sate beside a public way

   Thick strewn with summer dust, and a great stream
Of people there was hurrying to and fro   45
   Numerous as gnats upon the evening gleam,

All hastening onward, yet none seemed to know
   Whither he went, or whence he came, or why
He made one of the multitude, yet so

   Was borne amid the crowd as through the sky   50
One of the million leaves of summer's bier.—
   Old age and youth, manhood and infancy,

Mixed in one mighty torrent did appear,
   Some flying from the thing they feared and some
Seeking the object of another's fear,   55

   And others as with steps towards the tomb
Pored on the trodden worms that crawled beneath,
   And others mournfully within the gloom

Of their own shadow walked, and called it death . . .
   And some fled from it[7] as it were a ghost,   60
Half fainting in the affliction of vain breath.

   But more with motions which each other crost
Pursued or shunned the shadows the clouds threw
   Or birds within the noonday ether lost,

---

6. Apparently, "[so that] they glimmer."   7. I.e., from their own shadow, death (line 59).

Upon that path where flowers never grew;   65
  And weary with vain toil and faint for thirst
Heard not the fountains whose melodious dew

Out of their mossy cells forever burst
Nor felt the breeze which from the forest told
  Of grassy paths, and wood lawns interspersed   70

With overarching elms and caverns cold,
  And violet banks where sweet dreams brood, but they
Pursued their serious folly as of old. . . .

And as I gazed methought that in the way
The throng grew wilder, as the woods of June   75
  When the South wind shakes the extinguished day.—

And a cold glare, intenser than the noon
  But icy cold, obscured with [   ] light
The Sun as he the stars. Like the young Moon

  When on the sunlit limits of the night   80
Her white shell trembles amid crimson air
  And whilst the sleeping tempest gathers might

Doth, as a herald of its coming, bear
  The ghost of her dead Mother, whose dim form
Bends in dark ether from her infant's chair,[8]   85

  So came a chariot on the silent storm
Of its own rushing splendour, and a Shape
  So sate within as one whom years deform

Beneath a dusky hood and double cape
  Crouching within the shadow of a tomb,   90
And o'er what seemed the head a cloud-like crape

  Was bent, a dun and faint etherial gloom
Tempering the light; upon the chariot's beam
  A Janus-visaged[9] Shadow did assume

8. The crescent new moon bearing the faint outline of the full moon in its arms —the omen of a coming storm, as in Coleridge's *Dejection: An Ode*, epigraph, and lines 9–14. The parallel is to the crescent-formed chariot bearing the dark Shape of Life.
9. The Roman god Janus was represented with two faces, looking before and after. The shadowy charioteer guiding his team (which is invisible in the glare), however, has four faces, all of them blindfolded ("banded," line 100). Harold Bloom points out that this description of the chariot of Life is a parodic version of Ezekiel's vision of a divine chariot in the likeness of four living creatures, each having four faces, and in their progress forming rings which "were full of eyes" (Ezekiel i.4–28); echoed in *Paradise Lost* VI. 749–72.

The guidance of that wonder-winged team.   95
  The Shapes which drew it in thick lightnings
Were lost: I heard alone on the air's soft stream

    The music of their ever moving wings.
All the four faces of that charioteer
  Had their eyes banded . . . little profit brings   100

Speed in the van and blindness in the rear,
  Nor then avail the beams that quench the Sun
Or that these banded eyes could pierce the sphere

    Of all that is, has been, or will be done.—
So ill was the car guided, but it past   105
  With solemn speed majestically on . . .

The crowd gave way, and I arose aghast,
  Or seemed to rise, so mighty was the trance,
And saw like clouds upon the thunder blast

    The million with fierce song and maniac dance   110
Raging around; such seemed the jubilee
  As when to greet some conqueror's advance

Imperial Rome poured forth her living sea
  From senatehouse and prison and theatre
When Freedom left those who upon the free   115

    Had bound a yoke which soon they stooped to bear.[1]
Nor wanted here the just similitude
  Of a triumphal pageant, for where'er

The chariot rolled a captive multitude
  Was driven; all those who had grown old in power   120
Or misery,—all who have their age subdued,

    By action or by suffering, and whose hour
Was drained to its last sand in weal or woe,
  So that the trunk survived both fruit and flower;

All those whose fame or infamy must grow   125
  Till the great winter lay the form and name
Of their own earth with them forever low[2]—

    All but the sacred few who could not tame
Their spirits to the Conqueror, but as soon
  As they had touched the world with living flame   130

---

1. I.e., free men, when they are en-   2. Until the world shall end in ice.
slaved, become subservient in spirit.

Fled back like eagles to their native noon,[3]
  Or those who put aside the diadem
Of earthly thrones or gems, till the last one

Were there; for they of Athens and Jerusalem[4]
Were neither mid the mighty captives seen   135
  Nor mid the ribald crowd that followed them

Or fled before. . . . Swift, fierce and obscene
  The wild dance maddens in the van, and those
Who lead it, fleet as shadows on the green,

Outspeed the chariot and without repose   140
Mix with each other in tempestuous measure
  To savage music. . . . Wilder as it grows,

They, tortured by the agonizing pleasure,
  Convulsed and on the rapid whirlwinds spun
Of that fierce spirit, whose unholy leisure   145

Was soothed by mischief since the world begun,
Throw back their heads and loose their streaming hair,
  And in their dance round her who dims the Sun

Maidens and youths fling their wild arms in air
  As their feet twinkle; now recede and now   150
Bending within each other's atmosphere

Kindle invisibly; and as they glow
Like moths by light attracted and repelled,
  Oft to new bright destruction come and go,

Till like two clouds into one vale impelled   155
  That shake the mountains when their lightnings mingle
And die in rain,—the fiery band which held

Their natures, snaps . . . ere the shock cease to tingle
One falls and then another in the path
  Senseless, nor is the desolation single,   160

Yet ere I can say *where* the chariot hath
  Past over them; nor other trace I find
But as of foam after the Ocean's wrath

3. Alluding to the legend that aged eagles renew their youth by flying toward the sun.
4. In the Roman triumphs, the conquered chieftains were chained to the conqueror's chariot, in order to heighten their dishonor. In Shelley's version, this "captive multitude" bound to the chariot (lines 118–20) includes all the men whose exceptional power or talent had made them famous or infamous (line 125), except the "sacred few." The latter are divided into two classes: those who had died young, and those who, having lived into older age, had resisted the corrupting influence of "earthly thrones or gems" (line 133). These few included, doubtless, Socrates and Jesus ("of Athens and Jerusalem," line 134).

Is spent upon the desert shore.—Behind,
Old men, and women foully disarrayed 165
  Shake their grey hair in the insulting wind,

Limp in the dance and strain with limbs decayed
  To reach the car of light which leaves them still
Farther behind and deeper in the shade.

But not the less with impotence of will 170
They wheel, though ghastly shadows interpose
  Round them and round each other, and fulfill

Their work and to the dust whence they arose
  Sink and corruption veils them as they lie—
And frost in these performs what fire in those.[5] 175

Struck to the heart by this sad pageantry,
Half to myself I said, "And what is this?
  Whose shape is that within the car? & why"—

I would have added—"is all here amiss?"
  But a voice answered . . "Life" . . . I turned and knew 180
(O Heaven have mercy on such wretchedness!)

That what I thought was an old root which grew
To strange distortion out of the hill side
  Was indeed one of that deluded crew,

And that the grass which methought hung so wide 185
  And white, was but his thin discoloured hair,
And that the holes it vainly sought to hide

Were or had been eyes.—"If thou canst forbear
To join the dance, which I had well forborne,"[6]
  Said the grim Feature, of my thought aware, 190

"I will tell all that which to this deep scorn
  Led me and my companions, and relate
The progress of the pageant since the morn;

"If thirst of knowledge doth not thus abate,
Follow it even to the night, but I 195
  Am weary" . . . Then like one who with the weight

5. In addition to the "mighty captives" described in lines 118–27, there are two other groups: (1) the young men and women in front of the chariot who, in an erotic frenzy, dance, couple, fall senseless, and are crushed, leaving as their only trace a sexual foam (lines 137–64); and (2) the old men and women at the rear of the procession, attempting impotently to catch up with the chariot and to imitate the young in their bacchanalian dance (lines 164–75).
6. I.e., "which I would have done well to avoid." "Feature": in the old sense, form, shape.

Of his own words is staggered, wearily
   He paused, and ere he could resume, I cried,
"First who art thou?" . . . "Before thy memory

   "I feared, loved, hated, suffered, did, and died,[7]   200
And if the spark with which Heaven lit my spirit
   Earth had with purer nutriment supplied

"Corruption would not now thus much inherit
   Of what was once Rousseau—nor this disguise
Stained that within which still disdains to wear it.—   205

   "If I have been extinguished, yet there rise
A thousand beacons from the spark I bore."[8]—
   "And who are those chained to the car?" "The Wise,

"The great, the unforgotten: they who wore
   Mitres and helms and crowns, or wreathes of light,[9]   210
Signs of thought's empire over thought; their lore

   "Taught them not this—to know themselves; their might
Could not repress the mutiny within,
   And for the morn of truth they feigned, deep night

"Caught them ere evening." "Who is he with chin   215
   Upon his breast and hands crost on his chain?"
"The Child of a fierce hour; he sought to win

   "The world, and lost all it did contain
Of greatness, in its hope destroyed; and more
   Of fame and peace than Virtue's self can gain   220

"Without the opportunity which bore
   Him on its eagle's pinion to the peak
From which a thousand climbers have before

   "Fall'n as Napoleon fell."—I felt my cheek
Alter to see the great form pass away   225
   Whose grasp had left the giant world so weak

That every pigmy kicked it as it lay—
   And much I grieved to think how power and will
In opposition rule our mortal day—

---

7. I.e., Rousseau had lived and died before Shelley was born.

8. The sparks of Rousseau's writings had kindled a thousand signal fires—including that of the French Revolution, of which one child was Napoleon, who is described in lines 215–27.

9. I.e., mitred churchmen, helmeted soldiers, crowned kings, and haloed philosopher-poets. With line 208 Rousseau begins to identify some of the "mighty captives" whom the narrator had noted earlier (lines 118 ff.).

And why God made irreconcilable
Good and the means of good;[1] and for despair
  I half disdained mine eye's desire to fill 230

With the spent vision of the times that were
  And scarce have ceased to be . . . "Dost thou behold,"
Said then my guide, "those spoilers spoiled, Voltaire, 235

  "Frederic, and Kant, Catherine, and Leopold,[2]
Chained hoary anarchs,[3] demagogue and sage
  Whose name the fresh world thinks already old—

"For in the battle Life and they did wage
  She remained conqueror—I was overcome 240
By my own heart alone, which neither age

  "Nor tears nor infamy nor now the tomb
Could temper to its object."[4]—"Let them pass"—
  I cried—"the world and its mysterious doom

"Is not so much more glorious than it was 245
  That I desire to worship those who drew
New figures on its false and fragile glass

  "As the old faded."—"Figures ever new
Rise on the bubble, paint them how you may;
  We have but thrown, as those before us threw, 250

"Our shadows on it as it past away.
  But mark, how chained to the triumphal chair
The mighty phantoms of an elder day—

  "All that is mortal of great Plato there
Expiates the joy and woe his master knew not; 255
  That star that ruled his doom was far too fair—

"And Life, where long that flower of Heaven grew not,
  Conquered the heart by love which gold or pain
Or age or sloth or slavery could subdue not[5]—

1. I.e., the desire as against the means
to do good.
2. Presumably Voltaire (the immensely
influential thinker of the 18th-century
Enlightenment) is the "demagogue";
Frederick the Great of Prussia, Catherine the Great of Russia, and Leopold II
of the Holy Roman Empire, all influenced by Voltaire's ideas, are the "anarchs"; and Immanuel Kant (the great
philosopher of the German Enlightenment) is the "sage."
3. Leaders who bring about anarchy.
4. While the nationalists of the Enlightenment were conquered by Life, Rousseau was self-conquered by his own
heart's limitless desires, which no experience could moderate ("temper") to be
content with an achievable object.
5. I.e., all of Plato except his immortal
philosophy is expiating the passions of
life which Socrates, "his master," escaped, but to which Plato succumbed because of his love for the boy Aster, who
died young (line 257). The name
"Aster" designates a flower, but also
means "star" in Greek (line 256). Aster
is the subject of the epigram attributed
to Plato, which Shelley used as the
motto for *Adonais*, above.

"And near [   ] walk the [   ] twain,   260
The tutor and his pupil,[6] whom Dominion
  Followed as tame as vulture in a chain.—

"The world was darkened beneath either pinion
  Of him whom from the flock of conquerors
Fame singled as her thunderbearing minion;   265

"The other long outlived both woes and wars,
Throned in new thoughts of men, and still had kept
  The jealous keys of truth's eternal doors

"If Bacon's spirit [   ] had not leapt
  Like lightning out of darkness; he compelled   270
The Proteus shape of Nature's as it slept

"To wake and to unbar the caves that held
The treasure of the secrets of its reign[7]—
  See the great bards of old who inly quelled

"The passions which they sung, as by their strain   275
  May well be known: their living melody
Tempers its own contagion to the vein

"Of those who are infected with it—I
Have suffered what I wrote, or viler pain![8]—

"And so my words were seeds of misery—   280
Even as the deeds of others."—"Not as theirs,"[9]
  I said—he pointed to a company

In which I recognized amid the heirs
  Of Cæsar's crime from him to Constantine.[1]
The Anarchs old whose force and murderous snares   285

  Had founded many a sceptre bearing line
And spread the plague of blood and gold abroad,
  And Gregory and John[2] and men divine

---

6. Aristotle and his pupil, Alexander the Great.

7. Shelley represents Aristotle, because of the authority long exerted by his philosophy on the minds of men, to have been no less a tyrant than Alexander; he would even now bar us from truth, had not Francis Bacon, the Renaissance thinker, reopened the way by his new method of scientific inquiry.

8. I.e., Rousseau, unlike the classical poets (lines 274–75), had himself suffered the passions he expresses in his writings.

9. I.e., "not the seeds of such misery as were the deeds of those men." "Theirs" refers to the evil "company," to whom Rousseau has pointed (line 282), just before the narrator speaks.

1. Caesar's "crime" had been to destroy the Roman Republic and to become the first of a line of emperors, his "heirs" extending to Constantine, who established Christianity as the religion of Rome early in the 4th century.

2. Pope Gregory the Great established the independent political power of the papacy; "John" is a name frequently assumed by Popes.

Who rose like shadows between Man and god
  Till that eclipse, still hanging under Heaven,   290
Was worshipped by the world o'er which they strode

  For the true Sun it quenched.[3]—"Their power was given
But to destroy," replied the leader—"I
  Am one of those who have created, even

"If it be but a world of agony."—   295
  "Whence camest thou and whither goest thou?
How did thy course begin," I said, "and why?

"Mine eyes are sick of this perpetual flow
Of people, and my heart of one sad thought.—
  Speak."[4] "Whence I came, partly I seem to know,   300

"And how and by what paths I have been brought
  To this dread pass, methinks even thou mayst guess;
Why this should be my mind can compass not;

"Whither the conqueror hurries me still less.
But follow thou, and from spectator turn   305
  Actor or victim in this wretchedness,

"And what thou wouldst be taught I then may learn
  From thee.—Now listen . . . In the April prime[5]
When all the forest tops began to burn

"With kindling green, touched by the azure clime   310
Of the young year, I found myself asleep
  Under a mountain, which from unknown time

"Had yawned into a cavern high and deep,
  And from it came a gentle rivulet
Whose water like clear air in its calm sweep   315

"Bent the soft grass and kept for ever wet
The stems of the sweet flowers, and filled the grove
  With sound which all who hear must needs forget

"All pleasure and all pain, all hate and love,
  Which they had known before that hour of rest: 320
A sleeping mother then would dream not of

"The only child who died upon her breast
At eventide, a king would mourn no more
  The crown of which his brow was dispossest

3. I.e., institutional Christianity has eclipsed the true God.
4. The rest of the fragment consists of Rousseau's allegorical account of his own life, in response to the only two of the narrator's four questions (lines 296–97) which, he says, the limitations of his knowledge permit him partially to answer.
5. Spring, the first season of the year.

"When the sun lingered o'er the Ocean floor   325
    To gild his rival's new prosperity.—
Thou wouldst forget thus vainly to deplore

"Ills, which if ills, can find no cure from thee,
The thought of which no other sleep will quell
    Nor other music blot from memory—   330

"So sweet and deep is the oblivious[6] spell.—
    Whether my life had been before that sleep
The Heaven which I imagine, or a Hell

"Like this harsh world in which I wake to weep,
I know not. I arose and for a space   335
    The scene of woods and waters seemed to keep,

"Though it was now broad day, a gentle trace
    Of light diviner than the common Sun
Sheds on the common Earth, but all the place

"Was filled with many sounds woven into one   340
Oblivious melody, confusing sense
    Amid the gliding waves and shadows dun;

"And as I looked the bright omnipresence
    Of morning through the orient[7] cavern flowed,
And the Sun's image radiantly intense   345

"Burned on the waters of the well that glowed
Like gold, and threaded all the forest maze
    With winding paths of emerald fire—there stood

"Amid the sun, as he amid the blaze
    Of his own glory, on the vibrating   350
Floor of the fountain, paved with flashing rays,

"A shape all light,[8] which with one hand did fling
Dew on the earth, as if she were the Dawn
    Whose invisible rain forever seemed to sing

---

6. Causing forgetfulness. Shelley models Rousseau's account of his life in part on Rousseau's own confessional writings and in part (as numerous verbal echoes indicate) on Wordsworth's *Ode: Intimations of Immortality* and its account of the westward course of man's life. Shelley, however, substitutes his own interpretations and evaluations for those expressed by Wordsworth.
7. Facing the east. The cavern runs from east to west through the mountain, and as Rousseau grows older, he follows the course of its rivulet westward.
8. "The shape all light," whose significance has been much disputed, seems to represent the Rousseauistic and Wordsworthean ideal of nature and of trust in the natural human instincts. The description of the shape echoes Wordsworth's description, in the *Intimations Ode*, of the celestial light, glory, and splendor which in his youth had invested the common earth. In Shelley's poem the enchanting feminine shape, formed by a reflection of the sun's light from the material medium of water, apparently leads Rousseau on only to betray him (382 ff., 400 ff.)

"A silver music on the mossy lawn,   355
    And still before her on the dusky grass
Iris[9] her many coloured scarf had drawn.—

"In her right hand she bore a chrystal glass
Mantling with bright Nepenthe;[1]—the fierce splendour
    Fell from her as she moved under the mass   360

"Of the deep cavern, and with palms so tender
    Their tread broke not the mirror of its billow,
Glided along the river, and did bend her

"Head under the dark boughs, till like a willow
Her fair hair swept the bosom of the stream   365
    That whispered with delight to be their pillow.—

"As one enamoured is upborne in dream
    O'er lily-paven lakes mid silver mist
To wondrous music, so this shape might seem

"Partly to tread the waves with feet which kist   370
The dancing foam, partly to glide along
    The airs that roughened the moist amethyst,

"Or the slant morning beams that fell among
    The trees, or the soft shadows of the trees;
And her feet ever to the ceaseless song   375

"Of leaves and winds and waves and birds and bees
And falling drops moved in a measure new
    Yet sweet, as on the summer evening breeze

"Up from the lake a shape of golden dew
    Between two rocks, athwart the rising moon,   380
Dances i' the wind where eagle never flew.—

"And still her feet, no less than the sweet tune
To which they moved, seemed as they moved, to blot
    The thoughts of him who gazed on them, and soon

"All that was seemed as if it had been not,   385
    As if the gazer's mind was strewn beneath
Her feet like embers, and she, thought by thought,

"Trampled its fires into the dust of death,
As Day upon the threshold of the east
    Treads out the lamps of night, until the breath   390

---

9. The rainbow.
1. A drug causing total forgetfulness. The sinister suggestion subtly introduced in the description of the shape ("the fierce splendor," line 359) is heightened by echoes from Milton's *Comus*, lines 671 ff., in which the enchanter Comus (born of Circe, "daughter of the Sun") tries to seduce the Lady by a beverage which Milton compared to Nepenthe.

"Of darkness reillumines even the least
   Of heaven's living eyes[2]—like day she came,
Making the night a dream; and ere she ceased

"To move, as one between desire and shame
Suspended, I said—'If, as it doth seem,   395
   Thou comest from the realm without a name,

" 'Into this valley of perpetual dream,
   Shew whence I came, and where I am, and why—
Pass not away upon the passing stream.'

" 'Arise and quench thy thirst,' was her reply.   400
And as a shut lily, stricken by the wand
   Of dewy morning's vital alchemy,

"I rose; and, bending at her sweet command,
   Touched with faint lips the cup she raised,
And suddenly my brain became as sand   405

"Where the first wave had more than half erased
The track of deer on desert Labrador,
   Whilst the fierce wolf from which they fled amazed

"Leaves his stamp visibly upon the shore
   Until the second bursts—so on my sight   410
Burst a new Vision never seen before.—

"And the fair shape waned in the coming light
As veil by veil the silent splendour drops
   From Lucifer, amid the chrysolite[3]

"Of sunrise ere it strike the mountain tops—   415
   And as the presence of that fairest planet
Although unseen is felt by one who hopes

"That his day's path may end as he began it
In that star's smile,[4] whose light is like the scent
   Of a jonquil when evening breezes fan it,   420

"Or the soft notes in which his dear lament
   The Brescian shepherd breathes,[5] or the caress
That turned his weary slumber to content.—

"So knew I in that light's severe excess
The presence of that shape which on the stream   425
   Moved, as I moved along the wilderness,

2. The stars.
3. A greenish gem.
4. I.e., of the star which is both the morning star, Lucifer (line 414) and the evening star, Venus.
5. "The favorite song, *Stanco di pascolar le pecorelle*, is a Brescian national air" [Mary Shelley's note]. The title translates, "I am tired of pasturing the sheep." Brescia is a region in northern Italy.

"More dimly than a day appearing dream,
  The ghost of a forgotten form of sleep,
A light from Heaven whose half extinguished beam

"Through the sick day in which we wake to weep   430
Glimmers, forever sought, forever lost.—
  So did that shape its obscure tenour keep

"Beside my path, as silent as a ghost;[6]
  But the new Vision, and its cold bright car,
With savage music, stunning music, crost   435

"The forest, and as if from some dread war
Triumphantly returning, the loud million
  Fiercely extolled the fortune of her star.—

"A moving arch of victory the vermilion
  And green and azure plumes of Iris had   440
Built high over her wind-winged pavilion,

"And underneath ætherial glory clad
The wilderness, and far before her flew
  The tempest of the splendour which forbade

"Shadow to fall from leaf or stone;—the crew   445
  Seemed in that light like atomies[7] that dance
Within a sunbeam.—Some upon the new

"Embroidery of flowers that did enhance
The grassy vesture of the desart, played,
  Forgetful of the chariot's swift advance;   450

"Others stood gazing till within the shade
  Of the great mountain its light left them dim.—
Others outspeeded it, and others made

"Circles around it like the clouds that swim
Round the high moon in a bright sea of air,   455
  And more did follow, with exulting hymn,

"The chariot and the captives fettered there,
  But all like bubbles on an eddying flood
Fell into the same track at last and were

"Borne onward.—I among the multitude   460
Was swept; me sweetest flowers delayed not long,
  Me not the shadow nor the solitude,

---

6. In lines 410–33 the brilliance of the chariot of Life makes the fair shape fade until, like the morning star, Lucifer (line 414) in the daytime, its presence is felt, although no longer seen.
7. Particles of dust.

"Me not the falling stream's Lethean song,
  Me, not the phantom of that early form
Which moved upon its motion,—but among   465

"The thickest billows of the living storm
I plunged, and bared my bosom to the clime
  Of that cold light, whose airs too soon deform.—

"Before the chariot had begun to climb
  The opposing steep of that mysterious dell,   470
Behold a wonder worthy of the rhyme

"Of him[8] whom from the lowest depths of Hell
Through every Paradise and through all glory
  Love led serene, and who returned to tell

"In words of hate and awe the wondrous story   475
  How all things are transfigured, except Love;
For deaf as is a sea which wrath makes hoary

"The world can hear not the sweet notes that move
The sphere whose light is melody to lovers[9]—
  A wonder worthy of his rhyme—the grove   480

"Grew dense with shadows to its inmost covers,
  The earth was grey with phantoms, and the air
Was peopled with dim forms, as when there hovers

"A flock of vampire-bats before the glare
Of the tropic sun, bringing ere evening   485
  Strange night upon some Indian isle,—thus were

"Phantoms diffused around, and some did fling
  Shadows of shadows, yet unlike themselves,
Behind them, some like eaglets on the wing

"Were lost in white blaze, others like elves   490
Danced in a thousand unimagined shapes
  Upon the sunny streams and grassy shelves;

"And others sate chattering like restless apes
  On vulgar paws and voluble like fire.
Some made a cradle of the ermined capes   495

"Of kingly mantles, some upon the tiar
Of pontiffs[1] sate like vultures, others played
  Within the crown which girt with empire

---

8. Dante, who describes this pilgrimage in *The Divine Comedy*; "Love" is embodied in that poem by Beatrice.
9. The third sphere of the planet Venus (Love), in Dante's Ptolemaic universe.
1. The tiara, or triple crown of the popes.

"A baby's or an idiot's brow, and made
　　Their nests in it; the old anatomies[2]　　　　　　500
Sate hatching their bare brood under the shade

"Of demon wings, and laughed from their dead eyes
　　To reassume the delegated power
　　Arrayed in which these worms did monarchize

"Who make this earth their charnel.[3]—Others more　　505
　　Humble, like falcons sate upon the fist
Of common men, and round their heads did soar,

"Or like small gnats and flies, as thick as mist
On evening marshes, thronged about the brow
　　Of lawyer, statesman, priest and theorist,　　　　510

"And others like discoloured flakes of snow
　　On fairest bosoms and the sunniest hair
Fell, and were melted by the youthful glow

"Which they extinguished; for like tears, they were
A veil to those from whose faint lids they rained　　515
　　In drops of sorrow.—I became aware

"Of whence those forms proceeded which thus stained
　　The track in which we moved; after brief space
From every form the beauty slowly waned,

"From every firmest limb and fairest face　　　　　520
The strength and freshness fell like dust, and left
　　The action and the shape without the grace

"Of life; the marble brow of youth was cleft
　　With care, and in the eyes where once hope shone
Desire like a lioness bereft　　　　　　　　　　525

"Of its last cub, glared ere it died; each one
Of that great crowd sent forth incessantly
　　These shadows, numerous as the dead leaves blown

"In Autumn evening from a poplar tree—
　　Each, like himself and like each other were,　　530
At first, but soon distorted, seemed to be　　．

"Obscure clouds moulded by the casual air;
And of this stuff the car's creative ray
　　Wrought all the busy phantoms that were there

---

2. Skeletonlike monsters.
3. The monarchs who had made the
earth one great cemetery ("charnel")
were like grave-worms, for they fed upon
the corpses they had slaughtered.

"As the sun shapes the clouds⁴—thus, on the way　　　535
　　Mask after mask fell from the countenance
And form of all, and long before the day

　　"Was old, the joy which waked like Heaven's glance
The sleepers in the oblivious valley, died,
　　And some grew weary of the ghastly dance　　　540

"And fell, as I have fallen by the way side,
　　Those soonest from whose forms most shadows past
And least of strength and beauty did abide."—

　　"Then, what is Life?" I said . . . the cripple cast
His eye upon the car which now had rolled　　　545
　　Onward, as if that look must be the last,

And answered . . . . "Happy those for whom the fold
　　Of

1822　　　　　　　　　　　　　　　　　　　　1824

4. The shadows and phantoms of lines 480 ff. originate (lines 516 ff.) in the qualities of beauty, strength, and freshness, which fall like masks away from the men and women in the procession, as their hope degenerates into mere desire. These shadows of lost physical qualities are soon distorted by the currents of the air and miscreated into phantoms by the light from the car of Life (lines 531–35).

From A Defence of Poetry

In 1820 Shelley's good friend Thomas Love Peacock published an ironic essay, *The Four Ages of Poetry*, implicitly directed against the towering claims for poetry and the poetic imagination by his Romantic contemporaries. Peacock adopted the premise of Wordsworth and other Romantic critics—that poetry in its origin was a primitive use of language and mind—but from this premise, Peacock proceeded to draw the conclusion that it has become a useless anachronism in this age of science and technology. Peacock was himself a poet, as well as the best contemporary prose satirist, and Shelley saw the joke; but he also recognized that the position which Peacock had ironically assumed was very close to that actually held in his day by Utilitarian philosophers and material-minded laymen who either attacked or contemptuously ignored the imaginative faculty and its achievements. He therefore undertook, as he good-humoredly wrote to Peacock, "to break a lance with you * * * in honor of my mistress Urania," even though he was only "the knight of the shield of shadow and the lance of gossamere." The result was *The Defence of Poetry*, planned to consist of three parts. The last two parts were never written, and even the existing section, written in 1821, remained unpublished until 1840, eighteen years after Shelley's death.

For many decades Shelley's *Defence* was regarded as one of the very few classic essays in literary criticism. Its reputation, however, diminished in the recent era of the new criticism. The chief interest after the 1920's was in applied commentary and the kind of critical theory that will provide useful distinctions for the close analysis of particular literary texts. But Shelley's main enterprise, although different, is no less valid and a rarer achievement in the history of critical writings. His emphasis is on the universal and permanent forms, qualities, and values that all great poems, as products of imagination, possess in common—on those aspects, as he puts it, in which time, person, and place "are convertible with respect to the highest poetry without injuring it as poetry." Shelley's position thus parallels that of William Blake, and has analogues to that of "archetypal" criticism in our own time. More than this: Shelley extends the term "poet" to comprehend all the creative minds that break out of the limitations of their age and place to approximate the enduring and general forms of value—including not only writers in verse and prose, but artists, legislators, and prophets, as well as the founders of a new organization of society, morality, or religion.

The very range of the *Defence* gives it unequaled importance as a ringing claim for the validity and indispensability of the visionary and creative imagination in all the great human concerns. Nor has any later writer exceeded the cogency of the attack, which Shelley includes, on our acquisitive society and its narrowly material concept of utility and progress. This bias has permitted man to make enormous progress in science and in his material well-being without a proportionate development of his "poetical faculty," the moral imagination; with the grotesque result, as Shelley says, that "man, having enslaved the elements, remains himself a slave."

From A Defence of Poetry

Part I

According to one mode of regarding those two classes of mental action, which are called reason and imagination, the former may be considered as mind contemplating the relations borne by one thought to another, however produced; and the latter, as mind acting upon those thoughts so as to colour them with its own light, and composing from them, as from elements, other thoughts, each containing within itself the principle of its own integrity. The one[1] is the τὸ ποιεῖν,[2] or the principle of synthesis, and has for its objects those forms which are common to universal nature and existence itself; the other is the τὸ λογιζειν,[3] or principle of analysis, and its action regards the relations of things, simply as relations; considering thoughts, not in their integral unity, but as the algebrai-

---

1. "The one" is the imagination; "the other" (in the same sentence) is the reason.
2. "Making." The Greek word from which "poet" derives means "maker," and the term "maker" had been adopted as a name for poets by Renaissance critics such as Sir Philip Sidney, in his *Apology for Poetry* (1505), which Shelley had carefully studied.
3. "Calculating," "reasoning."

cal representations which conduct to certain general results. Reason is the enumeration of quantities already known; Imagination is the perception of the value of those quantities, both separately and as a whole. Reason respects the differences, and imagination the similitudes of things. Reason is to Imagination as the instrument to the agent, as the body to the spirit, as the shadow to the substance.[4]

* * *

In the youth of the world, men dance and sing and imitate natural objects, observing[5] in these actions, as in all others, a certain rhythm or order. And, although all men observe a similar, they observe not the same order, in the motions of the dance, in the melody of the song, in the combinations of language, in the series of their imitations of natural objects. For there is a certain order or rhythm belonging to each of these classes of mimetic representation, from which the hearer and the spectator receive an intenser and purer pleasure than from any other: the sense of an approximation to this order has been called taste by modern writers. Every man in the infancy of art, observes an order which approximates more or less closely to that from which this highest delight results: but the diversity is not sufficiently marked, as that its gradations should be sensible, except in those instances where the predominance of this faculty of approximation to the beautiful (for so we may be permitted to name the relation between this highest pleasure and its cause) is very great. Those in whom it exists in excess are poets, in the most universal sense of the word; and the pleasure resulting from the manner in which they express the influence of society or nature upon their own minds, communicates itself to others, and gathers a sort of reduplication from that community. Their language is vitally metaphorical; that is, it marks the before unapprehended relations of things and perpetuates their apprehension, until the words which represent them, become, through time, signs for portions or classes of thoughts[6] instead of pictures of integral thoughts; and then if no new poets should arise to create afresh the associations which have been thus disorganised, language will be dead to all the nobler purposes of human intercourse. These similitudes or relations are finely said by Lord Bacon to be "the same footsteps of nature impressed upon the various subjects of the world"[7]—and he considers the faculty which perceives them as the storehouse of axioms common to all knowledge. In the infancy of society every author is necessarily a poet, because language itself is poetry; and to be a poet is to apprehend the true and the beautiful,

---

4. In the paragraph here omitted, Shelley defines poetry as "the expression of the imagination" and asserts that it is "connate with the origin of man."
5. Following.

6. I.e., abstract concepts.
7. In Bacon's *De Augmentis Scientiarum* (On the Enlargement of the Sciences). I.iii.

in a word, the good which exists in the relation, subsisting, first between existence and perception, and secondly between perception and expression. Every original language near to its source is in itself the chaos of a cyclic poem:[8] the copiousness of lexicography[9] and the distinctions of grammar are the works of a later age, and are merely the catalogue and the form of the creations of Poetry.

But Poets, or those who imagine and express this indestructible order, are not only the authors of language and of music, of the dance and architecture, and statuary, and painting; they are the institutors of laws, and the founders of civil society, and the inventors of the arts of life, and the teachers, who draw into a certain propinquity with the beautiful and the true, that partial apprehension of the agencies of the invisible world which is called religion.[1] Hence all original religions are allegorical, or susceptible of allegory, and, like Janus,[2] have a double face of false and true. Poets, according to the circumstances of the age and nation in which they appeared, were called, in the earlier epochs of the world, legislators, or prophets:[3] a poet essentially comprises and unites both these characters. For he not only beholds intensely the present as it is, and discovers those laws according to which present things ought to be ordered, but he beholds the future in the present, and his thoughts are the germs of the flower and the fruit of latest time. Not that I assert poets to be prophets in the gross sense of the word, or that they can foretell the form as surely as they foreknow the spirit of events: such is the pretence of superstition, which would make poetry an attribute of prophecy, rather than prophecy an attribute of poetry. A Poet participates in the eternal, the infinite, and the one; as far as relates to his conceptions, time and place and number are not. The grammatical forms which express the moods of time, and the difference of persons, and the distinction of place, are convertible with respect to the highest poetry without injuring it as poetry; and the choruses of Æschylus, and the book of Job, and Dante's Paradise, would afford, more than any other writings, examples of this fact, if the limits of this essay did not forbid citation. The creations of sculpture, painting, and music, are illustrations still more decisive.

* * *

A poem is the image of life expressed in its eternal truth. There is this difference between a story and a poem, that a story is a catalogue of detached facts, which have no other bond of connexion

---

8. A set of poems (e.g., "the Arthurian cycle") which deal with the same subject.
9. The making of a dictionary.
1. Shelley thus enlarges the discussion to include all creative insights, or imaginative break-throughs, of mankind in whatever area they may occur, including non-institutional religion.
2. Roman god of doorways, with two heads which face in opposite directions.
3. The Roman *vates* signified both prophet and poet.

than time, place, circumstance, cause and effect; the other is the creation of actions according to the unchangeable forms of human nature, as existing in the mind of the creator, which is itself the image of all other minds. The one is partial, and applies only to a definite period of time, and a certain combination of events which can never again recur; the other is universal, and contains within itself the germ of a relation to whatever motives or actions have place in the possible varieties of human nature. Time, which destroys the beauty and the use of the story of particular facts, stript of the poetry which should invest them, augments that of Poetry, and for ever develops new and wonderful applications of the eternal truth which it contains. Hence epitomes have been called the moths of just history;[4] they eat out the poetry of it. The story of particular facts is as a mirror which obscures and distorts that which should be beautiful: Poetry is a mirror which makes beautiful that which is distorted.

The parts of a composition may be poetical, without the composition as a whole being a poem. A single sentence may be considered as a whole, though it be found in a series of unassimilated portions; a single word even may be a spark of inextinguishable thought. And thus all the great historians, Herodotus, Plutarch, Livy, were poets; and although the plan of these writers, especially that of Livy, restrained them from developing this faculty in its highest degree, they make copious and ample amends for their subjection, by filling all the interstices of their subjects with living images.

Having determined what is poetry, and who are poets, let us proceed to estimate its effects upon society.

Poetry is ever accompanied with pleasure: all spirits on which it falls open themselves to receive the wisdom which is mingled with its delight. In the infancy of the world, neither poets themselves nor their auditors are fully aware of the excellence of poetry: for it acts in a divine and unapprehended manner, beyond and above consciousness; and it is reserved for future generations to contemplate and measure the mighty cause and effect in all the strength and splendour of their union. Even in modern times, no living poet ever arrived at the fulness of his fame; the jury which sits in judgment upon a poet, belonging as he does to all time, must be composed of his peers: it must be impanneled by Time from the selectest of the wise of many generations. A Poet is a nightingale, who sits in darkness and sings to cheer its own solitude with sweet sounds; his auditors are as men entranced by the melody of an unseen musician, who feel that they are moved and softened, yet know not whence or

---

4. By Bacon in *The Advancement of Learning* II.ii.4. "Epitomes": abstracts, summaries.

why. The poems of Homer and his contemporaries were the delight of infant Greece; they were the elements of that social system which is the column upon which all succeeding civilization has reposed. Homer embodied the ideal perfection of his age in human character; nor can we doubt that those who read his verses were awakened to an ambition of becoming like to Achilles, Hector, and Ulysses: the truth and beauty of friendship, patriotism, and persevering devotion to an object, were unveiled to the depths in these immortal creations: the sentiments of the auditors must have been refined and enlarged by a sympathy with such great and lovely impersonations, until from admiring they imitated, and from imitation they identified themselves with the objects of their admiration. Nor let it be objected, that these characters are remote from moral perfection, and that they can by no means be considered as edifying patterns for general imitation. Every epoch, under names more or less specious, has deified its peculiar errors; Revenge is the naked Idol of the worship of a semi-barbarous age; and Self-deceit is the veiled Image of unknown evil, before which luxury and satiety lie prostrate. But a poet considers the vices of his contemporaries as the temporary dress in which his creations must be arrayed, and which cover without concealing the eternal proportions of their beauty. An epic or dramatic personage is understood to wear them around his soul, as he may the antient armour or the modern uniform around his body; whilst it is easy to conceive a dress more graceful than either. The beauty of the internal nature cannot be so far concealed by its accidental vesture, but that the spirit of its form shall communicate itself to the very disguise, and indicate the shape it hides from the manner in which it is worn. A majestic form and graceful motions will express themselves through the most barbarous and tasteless costume. Few poets of the highest class have chosen to exhibit the beauty of their conceptions in its naked truth and splendour; and it is doubtful whether the alloy of costume, habit, &c., be not necessary to temper this planetary music[5] for mortal ears.

The whole objection, however, of the immorality of poetry[6] rests upon a misconception of the manner in which poetry acts to produce the moral improvement of man. Ethical science[7] arranges the elements which poetry has created, and propounds schemes and proposes examples of civil and domestic life: nor is it for want of admirable doctrines that men hate, and despise, and censure, and deceive, and subjugate one another. But Poetry acts in another and diviner manner. It awakens and enlarges the mind itself by render-

---

5. The music made by the revolving crystalline spheres of the planets, inaudible to human ears.
6. In the preceding paragraph Shelley has been implicitly dealing with the charge, voiced by Plato in his *Republic*, that poetry is immoral because it represents evil characters acting evilly.
7. Moral philosophy.

ing the receptacle of a thousand unapprehended combinations of thought. Poetry lifts the veil from the hidden beauty of the world, and makes familiar objects be as if they were not familiar; it reproduces[8] all that it represents, and the impersonations clothed in its Elysian light stand thenceforward in the minds of those who have once contemplated them, as memorials of that gentle and exalted content[9] which extends itself over all thoughts and actions with which it coexists. The great secret of morals is Love; or a going out of our own nature, and an identification of ourselves with the beautiful which exists in thought, action, or person, not our own. A man, to be greatly good, must imagine intensely and comprehensively; he must put himself in the place of another and of many others; the pains and pleasures of his species must become his own. The great instrument of moral good is the imagination;[1] and poetry administers to the effect by acting upon the cause. Poetry enlarges the circumference of the imagination by replenishing it with thoughts of ever new delight, which have the power of attracting and assimilating to their own nature all other thoughts, and which form new intervals and interstices whose void for ever craves fresh food. Poetry strengthens that faculty which is the organ of the moral nature of man, in the same manner as exercise strengthens a limb. A Poet therefore would do ill to embody his own conceptions of right and wrong, which are usually those of his place and time, in his poetical creations, which participate in neither. By this assumption of the inferior office of interpreting the effect, in which perhaps after all he might acquit himself but imperfectly, he would resign the glory in a participation in the cause.[2] There was little danger that Homer, or any of the eternal Poets, should have so far misunderstood themselves as to have abdicated this throne of their widest dominion. Those in whom the poetical faculty, though great, is less intense, as Euripides, Lucan, Tasso, Spenser, have frequently affected[3] a moral aim, and the effect of their poetry is diminished in exact proportion to the degree in which they compel us to advert to this purpose.[4]

* * *

It is difficult to define pleasure in its highest sense; the definition

---

8. Produces anew, recreates.
9. Contentment (pronounced con-tént).
1. Central to Shelley's theory is the concept (developed by 18th-century philosophers) of the sympathetic imagination—the faculty by which an individual is enabled to identify himself with the thoughts and feelings of other men. Shelley claims that the faculty which in poetry enables us to share the joys and sufferings of invented characters is also the basis of all morality, for it compels us to feel for others as we feel for ourselves.
2. The "effect," or the explicit moral

standards into which imaginative insights are translated at a particular time or place, is contrasted to the "cause" of all morality, the imagination itself.
3. Assumed, adopted.
4. In the omitted passage Shelley reviews the history of drama and poetry in relation to civilization and morality, and proceeds to refute the charge that poets are less useful than "reasoners and merchants." He begins by defining utility in terms of pleasure, and then distinguishes between the lower (physical and material) and the higher (imaginative) pleasures.

involving a number of apparent paradoxes. For, from an inexplicable defect of harmony in the constitution of human nature, the pain of the inferior is frequently connected with the pleasures of the superior portions of our being. Sorrow, terror, anguish, despair itself, are often the chosen expressions of an approximation to the highest good. Our sympathy in tragic fiction depends on this principle; tragedy delights by affording a shadow of the pleasure which exists in pain. This is the source also of the melancholy which is inseparable from the sweetest melody. The pleasure that is in sorrow is sweeter than the pleasure of pleasure itself. And hence the saying, "It is better to go to the house of mourning, than to the house of mirth."[5] Not that this highest species of pleasure is necessarily linked with pain. The delight of love and friendship, the ecstasy of the admiration of nature, the joy of the perception and still more of the creation of poetry, is often wholly unalloyed.

The production and assurance of pleasure in this highest sense is true utility. Those who produce and preserve this pleasure are Poets or poetical philosophers.

The exertions of Locke, Hume, Gibbon, Voltaire, Rousseau,[6] and their disciples, in favour of oppressed and deluded humanity, are entitled to the gratitude of mankind. Yet it is easy to calculate the degree of moral and intellectual improvement which the world would have exhibited, had they never lived. A little more nonsense would have been talked for a century or two; and perhaps a few more men, women, and children, burnt as heretics. We might not at this moment have been congratulating each other on the abolition of the Inquisition in Spain.[7] But it exceeds all imagination to conceive what would have been the moral condition of the world if neither Dante, Petrarch, Boccaccio, Chaucer, Shakespeare, Calderon, Lord Bacon, nor Milton, had ever existed; if Raphael and Michael Angelo had never been born; if the Hebrew poetry had never been translated; if a revival of the study of Greek literature had never taken place; if no monuments of antient sculpture had been handed down to us; and if the poetry of the religion of the antient world had been extinguished together with its belief. The human mind could never, except by the intervention of these excitements, have been awakened to the invention of the grosser sciences, and that application of analytical reasoning to the aberrations of society, which it is now attempted to exalt over the direct expression of the inventive and creative faculty itself.

We have more moral, political and historical wisdom, than we know how to reduce into practice; we have more scientific and eco-

---

5. Ecclesiastes vii.2.
6. In a note Shelley says that although Peacock had classified Rousseau with these other thinkers, "he was essentially a poet. The others, even Voltaire, were mere reasoners."
7. The Inquisition had been suspended in 1820, the year before Shelley wrote this essay; it was not abolished permanently until 1834.

nomical knowledge than can be accommodated to the just distribution of the produce which it multiplies. The poetry in these systems of thought, is concealed by the accumulation of facts and calculating processes. There is no want of knowledge respecting what is wisest and best in morals, government, and political economy, or at least, what is wiser and better than what men now practise and endure. But we let "*I dare not* wait upon *I would,* like the poor cat i' the adage."[8] We want the creative faculty to imagine that which we know; we want the generous impulse to act that which we imagine; we want the poetry of life: our calculations have outrun conception; we have eaten more than we can digest. The cultivation of those sciences which have enlarged the limits of the empire of man over the external world, has, for want of the poetical faculty, proportionally circumscribed those of the internal world; and man, having enslaved the elements, remains himself a slave. To what but a cultivation of the mechanical arts in a degree disproportioned to the presence of the creative faculty, which is the basis of all knowledge, is to be attributed the abuse of all invention for abridging and combining labour, to the exasperation of the inequality of mankind? From what other cause has it arisen that these inventions which should have lightened, have added a weight to the curse imposed on Adam? Thus Poetry, and the principle of Self, of which Money is the visible incarnation, are the God and Mammon of the world.

The functions of the poetical faculty are two-fold; by one it creates new materials for knowledge, and power and pleasure; by the other it engenders in the mind a desire to reproduce and arrange them according to a certain rhythm and order which may be called the beautiful and the good. The cultivation of poetry is never more to be desired than at periods when, from an excess of the selfish and calculating principle, the accumulation of the materials of external life exceed the quantity of the power of assimilating them to the internal laws of human nature. The body has then become too unwieldy for that which animates it.

Poetry is indeed something divine. It is at once the centre and circumference of knowledge; it is that which comprehends all science, and that to which all science must be referred. It is at the same time the root and blossom of all other systems of thought; it is that from which all spring, and that which adorns all; and that which, if blighted, denies the fruit and the seed, and withholds from the barren world the nourishment and the succession of the scions of the tree of life. It is the perfect and consummate surface and bloom of things; it is as the odour and the colour of the rose to the texture of the elements which compose it, as the form and the splendour of unfaded beauty to the secrets of anatomy and corrup-

8. *Macbeth* I.vii.44–45.

tion. What were Virtue, Love, Patriotism, Friendship—what were the scenery of this beautiful Universe which we inhabit; what were our consolations on this side of the grave, and what were our aspirations beyond it, if Poetry did not ascend to bring light and fire from those eternal regions where the owl-winged faculty of calculation dare not ever soar? Poetry is not like reasoning, a power to be exerted according to the determination of the will. A man cannot say, "I will compose poetry." The greatest poet even cannot say it: for the mind in creation is as a fading coal, which some invisible influence, like an inconstant wind, awakens to transitory brightness: this power arises from within, like the colour of a flower which fades and changes as it is developed, and the conscious portions of our natures are unprophetic either of its approach or its departure.[9] Could this influence be durable in its original purity and force, it is impossible to predict the greatness of the results; but when composition begins, inspiration is already on the decline, and the most glorious poetry that has ever been communicated to the world is probably a feeble shadow of the original conception of the Poet. I appeal to the great poets of the present day, whether it be not an error to assert that the finest passages of poetry are produced by labour and study. The toil and the delay recommended by critics, can be justly interpreted to mean no more than a careful observation of the inspired moments, and an artificial connexion of the spaces between their suggestions by the intertexture of conventional expressions; a necessity only imposed by the limitedness of the poetical faculty itself. For Milton conceived the Paradise Lost as a whole before he executed it in portions. We have his own authority also for the Muse having "dictated" to him the "unpremeditated song,"[1] and let this be an answer to those who would allege the fifty-six various readings of the first line of the Orlando Furioso.[2] Compositions so produced are to poetry what mosaic is to painting. This instinct and intuition of the poetical faculty is still more observable in the plastic and pictorial arts; a great statue or picture grows under the power of the artist as a child in the mother's womb; and the very mind which directs the hands in formation, is incapable of accounting to itself for the origin, the gradations, or the media of the process.

Poetry is the record of the best and happiest[3] moments of the happiest and best minds. We are aware of evanescent visitations of thought and feeling sometimes associated with place or person, sometimes regarding our own mind alone, and always arising unfore-

9. This passage reiterates the ancient belief that the highest poetry is "inspired," and therefore occurs independently of the intention, effort, or consciousness of the poet. Unlike earlier critics, however, Shelley attributes such poetry not to a god or muse but to the unconscious depths within the poet's own mind.

1. *Paradise Lost* IX.21–24.
2. The epic poem by the 16th-century Italian poet Ariosto, noted for his care in composition.
3. In the double sense of "most joyous" and "most apt or felicitous in invention."

seen and departing unbidden, but elevating and delightful beyond all expression: so that even in the desire and the regret they leave, there cannot but be pleasure, participating as it does in the nature of its object. It is as it were the interpenetration of a diviner nature through our own; but its footsteps are like those of a wind over a sea, which the coming calm erases, and whose traces remain only, as on the wrinkled sand which paves it. These and corresponding conditions of being are experienced principally by those of the most delicate sensibility and the most enlarged imagination; and the state of mind produced by them is at war with every base desire. The enthusiasm of virtue, love, patriotism, and friendship, is essentially linked with these emotions; and whilst they last, self appears as what it is, an atom to a Universe. Poets are not only subject to these experiences as spirits of the most refined organization, but they can colour all that they combine with the evanescent hues of this etherial world; a word, or a trait in the representation of a scene or a passion, will touch the enchanted chord, and reanimate, in those who have ever experienced these emotions, the sleeping, the cold, the buried image of the past. Poetry thus makes immortal all that is best and most beautiful in the world; it arrests the vanishing apparitions which haunt the interlunations[4] of life, and veiling them, or in language or in form, sends them forth among mankind, bearing sweet news of kindred joy to those with whom their sisters abide—abide, because there is no portal of expression from the caverns of the spirit which they inhabit into the universe of things. Poetry redeems from decay the visitations of the divinity in man.

Poetry turns all things to loveliness; it exalts the beauty of that which is most beautiful, and it adds beauty to that which is most deformed; it marries exultation and horror, grief and pleasure, eternity and change; it subdues to union under its light yoke, all irreconcilable things. It transmutes all that it touches, and every form moving within the radiance of its presence is changed by wondrous sympathy to an incarnation of the spirit which it breathes; its secret alchemy turns to potable gold[5] the poisonous waters which flow from death through life; it strips the veil of familiarity from the world, and lays bare the naked and sleeping beauty which is the spirit of its forms.

All things exist as they are perceived; at least in relation to the percipient. "The mind is its own place, and of itself can make a Heaven of Hell, a Hell of Heaven."[6] But poetry defeats the curse which binds us to be subjected to the accident of surrounding impressions. And whether it spreads its own figured curtain, or withdraws life's dark veil from before the scene of things, it equally cre-

---

4. The dark intervals between the old and new moon.
5. Alchemists aimed to produce a drinkable form of gold that would be an
elixir of life, curing all diseases.
6. Satan's speech, *Paradise Lost* I.254–55.

ates for us a being within our being. It makes us the inhabitants of a world to which the familiar world is a chaos. It reproduces the common universe of which we are portions and percipients, and it purges from our inward sight the film of familiarity which obscures from us the wonder of our being. It compels us to feel that which we perceive, and to imagine that which we know. It creates anew the universe, after it has been annihilated in our minds by the recurrence of impressions blunted by reiteration.[7] It justifies that bold and true word of Tasso: *Non merita nome di creatore, se non Iddio ed il Poeta.*[8]

A Poet, as he is the author to others of the highest wisdom, pleasure, virtue and glory, so he ought personally to be the happiest, the best, the wisest, and the most illustrious of men. As to his glory, let Time be challenged to declare whether the fame of any other institutor of human life be comparable to that of a poet. That he is the wisest, the happiest, and the best, inasmuch as he is a poet, is equally incontrovertible: the greatest Poets have been men of the most spotless virtue, of the most consummate prudence, and, if we could look into the interior of their lives, the most fortunate of men: and the exceptions, as they regard those who possessed the imaginative faculty in a high yet inferior degree, will be found on consideration to confirm rather than destroy the rule. Let us for a moment stoop to the arbitration of popular breath, and usurping and uniting in our own persons the incompatible characters of accuser, witness, judge and executioner, let us without trial, testimony, or form, determine that certain motives of those who are "there sitting where we dare not soar,"[9] are reprehensible. Let us assume that Homer was a drunkard, that Virgil was a flatterer, that Horace was a coward, that Tasso was a madman, that Lord Bacon was a peculator, that Raphael was a libertine, that Spenser was a poet laureate.[1] It is inconsistent with this division of our subject to cite living poets, but Posterity has done ample justice to the great names now referred to. Their errors have been weighed and found to have been dust in the balance; if their sins were as scarlet, they are now white as snow:[2] they have been washed in the blood of the mediator and the redeemer, Time. Observe in what a ludicrous chaos the imputations of real or fictitious crime have been confused in the contemporary calumnies against poetry and poets;[3] consider how

7. Shelley's version of a widespread Romantic doctrine that the poetic imagination transforms the familiar into the miraculous and recreates the old world into a new world. See, e.g., Coleridge's *Biographia Literaria*, above, Chap. IV, on "freshness of sensation"; and Carlyle's *Sartor Resartus*, below, Bk. III, Chap. 8, "Natural Supernaturalism."
8. "No one merits the name of Creator except God and the Poet." The sense, though not the exact wording, is to be found in Tasso, the 16th-century Italian poet.

9. *Paradise Lost* IV.829.
1. Charges, some of them valid, which had in fact been made against these authors.
2. Isaiah i.18.
3. Shelley alludes especially to the charges of immorality by contemporary reviewers against Lord Byron and himself.

little is, as it appears—or appears, as it is; look to your own motives, and judge not, lest ye be judged.

Poetry, as has been said, in this respect differs from logic, that it is not subject to the controul of the active powers of the mind, and that its birth and recurrence has no necessary connexion with consciousness or will. It is presumptuous to determine that these[4] are the necessary conditions of all mental causation, when mental effects are experienced insusceptible of being referred to them. The frequent recurrence of the poetical power, it is obvious to suppose, may produce in the mind an habit of order and harmony correlative with its own nature and with its effects upon other minds. But in the intervals of inspiration, and they may be frequent without being durable, a Poet becomes a man, and is abandoned to the sudden reflux of the influences under which others habitually live. But as he is more delicately organized than other men, and sensible to pain and pleasure, both his own and that of others, in a degree unknown to them, he will avoid the one and pursue the other with an ardour proportioned to this difference. And he renders himself obnoxious to calumny,[5] when he neglects to observe the circumstances under which these objects of universal pursuit and flight have disguised themselves in one another's garments.

But there is nothing necessarily evil in this error, and thus cruelty, envy, revenge, avarice, and the passions purely evil, have never formed any portion of the popular imputations on the lives of poets.

I have thought it most favourable to the cause of truth to set down these remarks according to the order in which they were suggested to my mind, by a consideration of the subject itself, instead of following that of the treatise that excited me to make them public.[6] Thus although devoid of the formality of a polemical reply; if the view they contain be just, they will be found to involve a refutation of the doctrines of the Four Ages of Poetry, so far at least as regards the first division of the subject. I can readily conjecture what should have moved the gall of the learned and intelligent author of that paper; I confess myself, like him, unwilling to be stunned by the Theseids[7] of the hoarse Codri of the day. Bavius and Mævius undoubtedly are, as they ever were, insufferable persons. But it belongs to a philosophical critic to distinguish rather than confound.

The first part of these remarks has related to Poetry in its elements and principles; and it has been shewn, as well as the narrow limits assigned them would permit, that what is called poetry, in a

4. I.e., consciousness or will. Shelley again proposes that some mental processes are unconscious—outside our control or awareness.
5. Exposed to slander.
6. Peacock's *Four Ages of Poetry*.

7. Epic poems about Theseus. Codrus (plural "Codri") was the Roman author of a long, dull *Theseid*, attacked by Juvenal and others; "Bavius and Maevius" were would-be poets satirized by Vergil in his third *Eclogue*.

restricted sense, has a common source with all other forms of order and of beauty, according to which the materials of human life are susceptible of being arranged, and which is Poetry in an universal sense.

The second part[8] will have for its object an application of these principles to the present state of the cultivation of Poetry, and a defence of the attempt to idealize the modern forms of manners and opinions, and compel them into a subordination to the imaginative and creative faculty. For the literature of England, an energetic development of which has ever preceded or accompanied a great and free development of the national will, has arisen as it were from a new birth. In spite of the low-thoughted envy which would undervalue contemporary merit, our own will be a memorable age in intellectual achievements, and we live among such philosophers and poets as surpass beyond comparison any who have appeared since the last national struggle for civil and religious liberty.[9] The most unfailing herald, companion, and follower of the awakening of a great people to work a beneficial change in opinion or institution, is Poetry. At such periods there is an accumulation of the power of communicating and receiving intense and impassioned conceptions respecting man and nature. The persons in whom this power resides, may often as far as regards many portions of their nature, have little apparent correspondence with that spirit of good of which they are the ministers. But even whilst they deny and abjure, they are yet compelled to serve, the Power which is seated upon the throne of their own soul. It is impossible to read the compositions of the most celebrated writers of the present day without being startled with the electric life which burns within their words. They measure the circumference and sound the depths of human nature with a comprehensive and all-penetrating spirit, and they are themselves perhaps the most sincerely astonished at its manifestations; for it is less their spirit than the spirit of the age.[1] Poets are the hierophants[2] of an unapprehended inspiration; the mirrors of the gigantic shadows which futurity casts upon the present; the words which express what they understand not; the trumpets which sing to battle, and feel not what they inspire; the influence which is moved not, but moves.[3] Poets are the unacknowledged legislators of the world.

1821   1840

8. Shelley, however, completed only the first part of his *Defence*.
9. In the age of Milton and the English Civil War.
1. By "the spirit of the age" Shelley identifies what was later to be called "the Romantic movement" in contemporary literature and philosophy; he recognized its greatness, as well as its relation to the ferment of ideas and aspirations effected by the French Revolution. See also below, Hazlitt's *Mr. Wordsworth*, from his book *The Spirit of the Age*.
2. Priests who are expositors of sacred mysteries.
3. Aristotle had said that God is the "Unmoved Mover" of the universe.

JOHN KEATS

(1795–1821)

1817: *Poems*, Keats's first book.
1818: *Endymion*.
1819: Keats's *annus mirabilis*, in which he writes almost all his greatest poems.
1820: Publishes the volume *Lamia, Isabella, The Eve of St. Agnes, and Other Poems.*

No major poet has had a less propitious origin. Keats's father was head ostler at a London livery stable; he married his employer's daughter and inherited the business. Mrs. Keats, by all reports, was a strongly sensuous woman, and a rather casual but affectionate mother to her four children —John (the first-born), his two brothers, and a sister. Keats was sent to the Reverend John Clarke's private school at Enfield, where he was a noisy, high-spirited boy; despite his small physique (when full-grown, he was barely over five feet in height), he distinguished himself in skylarking and fist-fights. Here Keats had the good fortune to have as a teacher Charles Cowden Clarke, son of the headmaster, who later became himself a man of letters; he encouraged Keats's passion for reading and, both at school and in the course of their later friendship, introduced him to Spenser and other poets, to music, and to the theater.

When Keats was 8 his father was killed by a fall from a horse, and when he was 14, his mother died of tuberculosis. Although the livery stable had prospered, and £8,000 had been left in trust to the children by Keats's grandmother, the estate remained tied up in a Chancery suit for all of Keats's lifetime. The children's guardian, Richard Abbey, was an unimaginative and practical-minded businessman; he took Keats out of school at the age of 15 and bound him apprentice to Thomas Hammond, a surgeon and apothecary at Edmonton. In 1815 Keats carried on his medical studies at Guy's Hospital, London, and the next year qualified to practice as an apothecary—but almost immediately, over his guardian's protests, he abandoned medicine for poetry.

This decision was influenced by Keats's friendship with Leigh Hunt, then editor of the *Examiner* and a leading political radical, a minor poet, and a prolific writer of criticism and periodical essays. Hunt, the first successful author of Keats's acquaintance, added his enthusiastic encouragement of Keat's poetic efforts to that of Clarke. More important, Hunt introduced him to writers greater than himself, Hazlitt, Lamb, and Shelley, as well as to Benjamin Robert Haydon, painter of grandiose historical and religious canvases. Through Hunt Keats also met John Hamilton Reynolds, and then Charles Wentworth Dilke and Charles Brown, men who became his intimate friends and provided him with an essential circumstance for a fledgling poet, a sympathetic and appreciative audience.

The rapidity and sureness of Keats's development has no match. He did not even undertake poetry until his 18th year, and for the next few years produced album verse which was at best merely competent and at times exhibited a labored vulgarity of sentiment and phrasing. Suddenly, in 1816, he spoke out loud and bold in *On First Looking into Chapman's Homer*, a major sonnet in the grand style. Later that same year he wrote *Sleep and Poetry*, in which he laid out for himself a poetic program deliberately modeled on the careers of the greatest poets, asking only

> for ten years, that I may overwhelm
> Myself in poesy; so I may do the deed
> That my own soul has to itself decreed.

For even while his health was good, Keats felt a foreboding of early death, and applied himself to his art with a desperate urgency. In 1817 Keats went on to compose *Endymion*, an ambitious undertaking of more than 4,000 lines. It is a profuse and often obscure allegory of the poet's quest for an ideal feminine counterpart and a flawless happiness beyond earthly possibility; in a number of passages, however, it already exhibits the sure movement and phrasing of his mature poetic style. But Keats's critical judgment and aspiration exceeded his achievement: long before he completed it, he declared impatiently that he carried on with the "slipshod" *Endymion* only as a poetic exercise and "trial of invention" and began to block out the more ambitious *Hyperion*, conceived on the model of Milton's *Paradise Lost* in that most demanding of forms, the epic poem. The extent of his success in achieving the Miltonic manner is what made Keats leave off before *Hyperion* was finished, for he recognized that he was uncommonly susceptible to poetic influences, and regarded this as a threat to his poetic individuality. "I will write independently," he insisted. "The Genius of Poetry must work out its own salvation in a man." He had refused the chance of intimacy with Shelley "that I might have my own unfettered scope"; he had broken away from Leigh Hunt's influence lest he get "the reputation of Hunt's *élève*"; now he shied away from domination by Milton's idiosyncratic and powerfully infectious style.

With the year 1818 began a series of disappointments and disasters which culminated in Keats's mortal illness. Sentimental legend used to fix the blame upon two anonymous articles: a scurrilous attack on Keats as a member of the "Cockney School" (that is, Leigh Hunt's radical literary circle) which appeared in the heavily Tory *Blackwood's Magazine*, and a savage mauling of *Endymion* in the *Quarterly Review*. Shelley gave impetus to this myth by his description of Keats as "a pale flower" in *Adonais*, and Byron, who knew even less about Keats, asserted that he was "snuffed out by an article." But in fact, Keats had the good sense to recognize that the attacks were motivated by Tory bias and class snobbery, and he had already passed his own severe judgment on *Endymion*: "My own domestic criticism," he said, "has given me pain without comparison beyond what *Blackwood* or the *Quarterly* could possibly inflict." More important was the financial distress of his brother George and his young bride, who had just emigrated to Kentucky and lost their money in an ill-advised investment; Keats, himself always short of funds, had now to turn to literary journey-work to eke out the family income. His younger brother Tom contracted tuberculosis, and the poet, in constant attendance upon him through the later months of 1818, helplessly watched him waste away until his death that December. In the spring and summer of that year Keats had taken a strenuous walking tour in the English Lake Country, Scotland, and Ireland; it was a glorious adventure, but a totally exhausting one in wet, cold weather, and Keats returned in August with a chronically ulcerated throat made increasingly ominous by the shadow of the tuberculosis which had killed his mother and brother. And in the late fall of 1818 Keats fell desperately, unwillingly, helplessly in love with Fanny Brawne. This pretty, vivacious, and mildly flirtatious girl of 18 had little interest in poetry, but she possessed an alert and sensible mind and loved Keats sincerely, and might well have made him an excellent wife. They became engaged, but Keats's dedication to poetry, his poverty, and his growing illness made marriage impossible and love a torment.

In this period of acute distress and emotional turmoil, within five years of his first trying his hand at poetry, Keats achieved the culmination of his brief poetic career. Between January and September of 1819, masterpiece followed masterpiece in astonishing succession: *The Eve of St. Agnes, La Belle Dame sans Merci*, all six of the great *Odes, Lamia*, and a sufficient number of fine sonnets to make him, with Wordsworth, the major Romantic craftsman in that form. All of these poems possess the distinctive qualities of the work of Keats's maturity: a slow-paced, gracious movement; a concreteness of description in which all the senses—tactile, gustatory, kinetic, organic, as well as visual and auditory—combine to give the total apprehension of an experience; an intense delight at the sheer existence of things outside himself, the poet seeming to lose his own identity in the fullness of identification with the object he contemplates; and a concentrated felicity of phrasing which reminded Keats's friends, as it has so many critics since, of the language of Shakespeare. And under the rich sensuous surface we find Keats's characteristic presentation of all experience as a tangle of inseparable but irreconcilable opposites. He finds melancholy in delight, and pleasure in pain; he feels the highest intensity of love as an approximation to death; he inclines equally toward a life of indolence and "sensation" and toward a life of thought; he is aware both of the attraction of an imaginative dream world without "disagreeables" and the remorseless pressure of the actual; he aspires at the same time for aesthetic detachment (what in his letters he called "negative capability") and for social responsibility.

His letters, no less remarkable than his poetry, show that Keats felt on his pulses the conflicts he dramatized in his major poems. Above all, they reveal him wrestling with the problem of evil and suffering in the world—what to make of our lives in the discovery that "the world is full of misery and heartbreak, pain, sickness and oppression." To the end of his life Keats, with stubborn courage, refused to seek comfort by substituting for the complexity and contradictions of experience, and of a life which must find its justification in this natural world, either the simplicity of inherited philosophical doctrines or the absolutes of a religious creed. At the close of his poetic career, in the latter part of 1819, Keats began to rework the epic *Hyperion* into the form of a dream vision which he called

The Fall of Hyperion. In the introductory section of this fragment the poet is told by the prophetess Moneta that he has hitherto been merely a dreamer; he must know that

> The poet and the dreamer are distinct,
> Diverse, sheer opposite, antipodes,

and that the height of poetry can only be reached by

> those to whom the miseries of the world
> Are misery, and will not let them rest.

Keats was seemingly planning to undertake a new direction and subject matter, when death intervened.

On the night of February 3, 1820, he coughed up some blood. He refused to evade the truth: "I cannot be deceived in that color; that drop of blood is my death warrant. I must die." That spring and summer a series of hemorrhages rapidly weakened him. In the autumn he allowed himself to be persuaded to seek a milder climate in Italy in the company of Joseph Severn, a young painter; but these last months were only what he called "a posthumous existence." He died in Rome on February 23, 1821, and was buried in the Protestant Cemetery. At times the agony of his disease, the apparent frustration of his hopes for great poetic achievement, and the despair of his passion for Fanny Brawne combined to compel even Keats's brave spirit to bitterness, resentment, and jealousy, but he always recovered his gallantry. His last letter, written to Charles Brown, concludes: "I can scarcely bid you good-bye, even in a letter. I always made an awkward bow. God bless you! John Keats."

No one can read Keats's poems and letters without an undersense of the immense waste of so extraordinary an intellect and genius cut off so early. What he might have accomplished is beyond conjecture; what we do know is that his achievement, when he stopped writing at the age of 24, greatly exceeds that at the corresponding age of Chaucer, Shakespeare, or Milton.

On First Looking into Chapman's Homer[1]

> Much have I traveled in the realms of gold,
>   And many goodly states and kingdoms seen;
>   Round many western islands have I been
> Which bards in fealty to Apollo hold.
> Oft of one wide expanse had I been told   5
>   That deep-browed Homer ruled as his demesne;[2]
>   Yet did I never breathe its pure serene[3]

1. Keats's former schoolteacher, Charles Cowden Clarke, introduced him to Homer in the vigorous translation of the Elizabethan poet George Chapman. They read through the night, and Keats walked home at dawn; this sonnet, his first great poem, reached Clarke by the ten o'clock mail that same morning. That it was Balboa, not Cortez, who caught his first sight of the Pacific from the heights of Darien, in Panama, matters to history but not to poetry.
2. Realm, feudal possession.
3. Clear expanse of air.

Till I heard Chapman speak out loud and bold:
Then felt I like some watcher of the skies
   When a new planet swims into his ken;   10
Or like stout Cortez when with eagle eyes
   He stared at the Pacific—and all his men
Looked at each other with a wild surmise—
   Silent, upon a peak in Darien.

October, 1816   1816

From Sleep and Poetry[1]

* * *

O for ten years, that I may overwhelm
Myself in poesy; so I may do the deed
That my own soul has to itself decreed.
Then will I pass the countries that I see
In long perspective, and continually   100
Taste their pure fountains. First the realm I'll pass
Of Flora, and old Pan:[2] sleep in the grass,
Feed upon apples red, and strawberries,
And choose each pleasure that my fancy sees;
Catch the white-handed nymphs in shady places,   105
To woo sweet kisses from averted faces—
Play with their fingers, touch their shoulders white
Into a pretty shrinking with a bite
As hard as lips can make it: till agreed,
A lovely tale of human life we'll read.   110
And one will teach a tame dove how it best
May fan the cool air gently o'er my rest;
Another, bending o'er her nimble tread,
Will set a green robe floating round her head,
And still will dance with ever varied ease,   115
Smiling upon the flowers and the trees:
Another will entice me on, and on
Through almond blossoms and rich cinnamon;
Till in the bosom of a leafy world

1. At the early age of 21, Keats set himself a rigorous regimen of poetic training modeled on the course followed by the greatest poets. Virgil had established the pattern of beginning with pastoral writing and proceeding gradually to the point at which he was ready to undertake the epic, and this pattern had been deliberately followed by Spenser and Milton. Keats's version of this program, as he describes it here, is to begin with the realm of "Flora, and old Pan" (line 102) and, within ten years, to climb up to the level of poetry dealing with "the agonies, the strife / Of human hearts" (lines 124–25). The latter achievement Keats found best represented among his contemporaries by Wordsworth and, less successfully, by Shelley—Keats's vision of the chariot of poesy (lines 125–154) echoes Shelley's allegorical visions. The program Keats set himself is illuminated by his analysis of Wordsworth's progress in his letter to J. H. Reynolds of May 3, 1818.
2. I.e., the carefree pastoral world. Flora was the Roman goddess of flowers, and Pan the Greek god of pastures, woods, and animal life.

We rest in silence, like two gems upcurled   120
In the recesses of a pearly shell.

And can I ever bid these joys farewell?
Yes, I must pass them for a nobler life,
Where I may find the agonies, the strife
Of human hearts: for lo! I see afar   125
O'ersailing the blue cragginess, a car[3]
And steeds with streamy manes—the charioteer
Looks out upon the winds with glorious fear:
And now the numerous tramplings quiver lightly
Along a huge cloud's ridge; and now with sprightly   130
Wheel downward come they into fresher skies,
Tipped round with silver from the sun's bright eyes.
Still downward with capacious whirl they glide;
And now I see them on the green-hill's side
In breezy rest among the nodding stalks.   135
The charioteer with wond'rous gesture talks
To the trees and mountains; and there soon appear
Shapes of delight, of mystery, and fear,
Passing along before a dusky space
Made by some mighty oaks: as they would chase   140
Some ever-fleeting music on they sweep.
Lo! how they murmur, laugh, and smile, and weep:
Some with upholden hand and mouth severe;
Some with their faces muffled to the ear
Between their arms; some, clear in youthful bloom,   145
Go glad and smilingly athwart the gloom;
Some looking back, and some with upward gaze;
Yes, thousands in a thousand different ways
Flit onward—now a lovely wreath of girls
Dancing their sleek hair into tangled curls;   150
And now broad wings. Most awfully intent
The driver of those steeds is forward bent,
And seems to listen: O that I might know
All that he writes with such a hurrying glow.

The visions all are fled—the car is fled   155
Into the light of heaven, and in their stead
A sense of real things comes doubly strong,
And, like a muddy stream, would bear along
My soul to nothingness: but I will strive
Against all doubtings, and will keep alive   160
The thought of that same chariot, and the strange
Journey it went * * *

Nov.–Dec., 1816   1817

---

3. This chariot, with its "charioteer" (line 127), represents the higher poetic imagination, which bodies forth (line 138), the matters "of delight, of mystery, and fear" that characterize the grander poetic forms.

On Seeing the Elgin Marbles for the First Time[4]

My spirit is too weak; mortality
  Weighs heavily on me like unwilling sleep,
  And each imagined pinnacle and steep
Of godlike hardship tells me I must die
Like a sick eagle looking at the sky.   5
  Yet 'tis a gentle luxury to weep,
  That I have not the cloudy winds to keep
Fresh for the opening of the morning's eye.
Such dim-conceivéd glories of the brain
  Bring round the heart an indescribable feud;   10
So do these wonders a most dizzy pain,
  That mingles Grecian grandeur with the rude
Wasting of old Time—with a billowy main,
  A sun, a shadow of a magnitude.

1817

On the Sea

It keeps eternal whisperings around
  Desolate shores, and with its mighty swell
  Gluts twice ten thousand Caverns, till the spell
Of Hecate leaves them their old shadowy sound.
Often 'tis in such gentle temper found,   5
  That scarcely will the very smallest shell
  Be moved for days from where it sometime fell,
When last the winds of Heaven were unbound.
Oh ye! who have your eyeballs vexed and tired,
  Feast them upon the wideness of the Sea;   10
  Oh ye! whose ears are dinned with uproar rude,
Or fed too much with cloying melody—
  Sit ye near some old Cavern's Mouth and brood,
Until ye start, as if the sea nymphs quired!

1817   1817

From Endymion[1]

A POETIC ROMANCE

Preface

    Knowing within myself the manner in which this Poem has been produced, it is not without a feeling of regret that I make it

---

4. Lord Elgin had brought to England in 1806 the marble statues and friezes which adorned the Parthenon at Athens; in 1816 they were purchased by the government for the British Museum. Keats's response to his first sight of these time-worn memorials of Grecian artistry is characteristically intense, mixed, and subtly analyzed.

1. This poem of more than 4,000 lines (based on the classical myth of a mortal beloved by the goddess of the moon)

public.

What manner I mean, will be quite clear to the reader, who must soon perceive great inexperience, immaturity, and every error denoting a feverish attempt, rather than a deed accomplished. The two first books, and indeed the two last, I feel sensible are not of such completion as to warrant their passing the press; nor should they if I thought a year's castigation would do them any good—it will not: the foundations are too sandy. It is just that this young ster should die away: a sad thought for me, if I had not some hope that while it is dwindling I may be plotting, and fitting myself for verses fit to live.

This may be speaking too presumptuously, and may deserve a punishment: but no feeling man will be forward to inflict it: he will leave me alone, with the conviction that there is not a fiercer hell than the failure in a great object. This is not written with the least atom of purpose to forestall criticisms of course, but from the desire I have to conciliate men who are competent to look, and who do look with a zealous eye, to the honor of English literature.

The imagination of a boy is healthy, and the mature imagination of a man is healthy; but there is a space of life between, in which the soul is in a ferment, the character undecided, the way of life uncertain, the ambition thick-sighted: thence proceeds mawkishness, and all the thousand bitters which those men I speak of must necessarily taste in going over the following pages.

I hope I have not in too late a day touched the beautiful mythology of Greece, and dulled its brightness: for I wish to try once more,[2] before I bid it farewell.

TEIGNMOUTH, April 10, 1818.

From *Book I*
[A THING OF BEAUTY]

A thing of beauty is a joy forever:
 Its loveliness increases; it will never
Pass into nothingness; but still will keep
A bower quiet for us, and a sleep

tells of Endymion's long and agonized search for an immortal goddess whom he had seen in several visions. In the course of his wanderings he comes upon an Indian maid who had been abandoned by the followers of Bacchus, and to his utter despair succumbs to a sensual passion for her, in apparent betrayal of his love for his heavenly ideal. In the resolution, the Indian maid reveals that she is herself Cynthia (Diana), goddess of the moon, and also the celestial goddess of his earlier visions.

Keats set himself to writing a long poem before he was entirely ready in range of knowledge, clarity of thought, or stylistic assurance; the poem reaches a high level only in single passages. The interpretation which seems best to fit the text is that ideal love and imaginative beauty are to be found only by way of instinctual impulses and earthly sexuality, which the ideal repeats, in one of Keats's phrases, "in a finer tone." The poem's constitution is so cloudy, however, that its purport is disputed. But Keats has disarmed all external criticism by his self-criticism in the candid and insightful Preface, which has become a classic statement of the characteristics of unripe genius.

2. In *Hyperion*, which Keats was already planning.

Full of sweet dreams, and health, and quiet breathing.   5
Therefore, on every morrow, are we wreathing
A flowery band to bind us to the earth,
Spite of despondence, of the inhuman dearth
Of noble natures, of the gloomy days,
Of all the unhealthy and o'er-darkened ways   10
Made for our searching: yes, in spite of all,
Some shape of beauty moves away the pall
From our dark spirits. Such the sun, the moon,
Trees old, and young, sprouting a shady boon
For simple sheep; and such are daffodils   15
With the green world they live in; and clear rills
That for themselves a cooling covert make
'Gainst the hot season; the mid-forest brake,[3]
Rich with a sprinkling of fair musk-rose blooms:
And such too is the grandeur of the dooms[4]   20
We have imagined for the mighty dead;
All lovely tales that we have heard or read:
An endless fountain of immortal drink,
Pouring unto us from the heaven's brink.[5]

Nor do we merely feel these essences   25
For one short hour; no, even as the trees
That whisper round a temple become soon
Dear as the temple's self, so does the moon,
The passion poesy, glories infinite,
Haunt us till they become a cheering light   30
Unto our souls, and bound to us so fast,
That, whether there be shine, or gloom o'ercast,
They always must be with us, or we die.

Therefore, 'tis with full happiness that I
Will trace the story of Endymion.   35
The very music of the name has gone
Into my being, and each pleasant scene
Is growing fresh before me as the green
Of our own valleys * * *

[THE "PLEASURE THERMOMETER"]

"Peona![6] ever have I longed to slake
My thirst for the world's praises: nothing base,   770
No merely slumberous phantasm, could unlace
The stubborn canvas for my voyage prepared—
Though now 'tis tattered; leaving my bark bared
And sullenly drifting: yet my higher hope

3. Thicket.
4. Judgments.
5. The poet sets up, and searches to resolve, the basic opposition between the inevitably "mortal" pleasures in this life and the conceived possibility of "immortal" delight. Thus "essences" (line 25) seem to be the things of beauty in this world, purged of the alloy of sadness and mutability that spoils ordinary experience. The central passage dealing with this theme is below, Book I, lines 777 ff.
6. The sister to whom Endymion confides his troubles.

Is of too wide, too rainbow-large a scope,   775
To fret at myriads of earthly wrecks.
Wherein lies happiness?[7] In that which becks
Our ready minds to fellowship divine,
A fellowship with essence; till we shine,
Full alchemized,[8] and free of space. Behold   780
The clear religion of heaven! Fold
A rose leaf round thy finger's taperness,
And soothe thy lips: hist, when the airy stress
Of music's kiss impregnates the free winds,
And with a sympathetic touch unbinds   785
Aeolian[9] magic from their lucid wombs:
Then old songs waken from enclouded tombs;
Old ditties sigh above their father's grave;
Ghosts of melodious prophesyings rave
Round every spot where trod Apollo's foot;   790
Bronze clarions awake, and faintly bruit,[1]
Where long ago a giant battle was;
And, from the turf, a lullaby doth pass
In every place where infant Orpheus slept.
Feel we these things?—that moment have we stepped   795
Into a sort of oneness, and our state
Is like a floating spirit's. But there are
Richer entanglements, enthrallments far
More self-destroying, leading, by degrees,
To the chief intensity: the crown of these   800
Is made of love and friendship, and sits high
Upon the forehead of humanity.
All its more ponderous and bulky worth
Is friendship, whence there ever issues forth
A steady splendor; but at the tiptop,   805
There hangs by unseen film, an orbèd drop
Of light, and that is love: its influence,
Thrown in our eyes, genders a novel sense,
At which we start and fret; till in the end,
Melting into its radiance, we blend,   810
Mingle, and so become a part of it—

7. Of lines 777–857, Keats wrote to his publisher, John Taylor: "When I wrote it, it was the regular stepping of the Imagination towards a Truth. My having written that Argument will perhaps be of the greatest Service to me of anything I ever did—It set before me at once the gradations of Happiness even like a kind of Pleasure Thermometer, and is my first step towards the chief attempt in the Drama—the playing of different Natures with Joy and Sorrow." The gradations on this "Pleasure Thermometer" mark the stages on the way to what Keats calls "happiness" (line 777)—his secular version of the religious concept of "felicity" which, in the orthodox view, is to be achieved by a surrender of oneself to God. For Keats the way to happiness lies through a fusion of ourselves, first sensuously, with the lovely objects of nature and art (lines 781–97), then on a higher level, with other human beings through "love and friendship" (line 801) but in the final degree, only through sexual love. By this "self-destroying," or total loss of personal identity through our imaginative identification with a beloved person outside ourselves, we escape from the material and spatial limits, and from the self-centered condition, of ordinary experience, to achieve a "fellowship with essence," which is a kind of immortality within our mortal existence (line 844).
8. Transformed by alchemy from a base to a precious metal.
9. From Aeolus, god of winds.
1. Make a sound.

Nor with aught else can our souls interknit
So wingedly: when we combine therewith,
Life's self is nourished by its proper pith,[2]
And we are nurtured like a pelican brood.[3]   815
Aye, so delicious is the unsating food,
That men, who might have towered in the van
Of all the congregated world, to fan
And winnow from the coming step of time
All chaff of custom, wipe away all slime   820
Left by men-slugs and human serpentry,
Have been content to let occasion die,
Whilst they did sleep in love's elysium.
And, truly, I would rather be struck dumb,
Than speak against this ardent listlessness: 825
For I have ever thought that it might bless
The world with benefits unknowingly;
As does the nightingale, upperchéd high,
And cloistered among cool and bunchéd leaves—
She sings but to her love, nor e'er conceives   830
How tiptoe Night holds back her dark gray hood.[4]
Just so may love, although 'tis understood
The mere commingling of passionate breath,
Produce more than our searching witnesseth:
What I know not: but who, of men, can tell   835
That flowers would bloom, or that green fruit would swell
To melting pulp, that fish would have bright mail,
The earth its dower of river, wood, and vale,
The meadows runnels, runnels pebble-stones,
The seed its harvest, or the lute its tones,   840
Tones ravishment, or ravishment its sweet
If human souls did never kiss and greet?

   "Now, if this earthly love has power to make
Men's being mortal, immortal; to shake
Ambition from their memories, and brim   845
Their measure of content: what merest whim,
Seems all this poor endeavor after fame,
To one, who keeps within his steadfast aim
A love immortal, an immortal too.
Look not so 'wildered; for these things are true,   850
And never can be born of atomies[5]
That buzz about our slumbers, like brain-flies,
Leaving us fancy-sick. No, no, I'm sure,
My restless spirit never could endure
To brood so long upon one luxury,   855
Unless it did, though fearfully, espy
A hope beyond the shadow of a dream."

---

2. Its own elemental substance.
3. Young pelicans were once thought to feed on their mother's flesh; so our life is nourished by another's life, with which it fuses in love.
4. I.e., in order better to hear.
5. Mites, tiny flying insects.

From *Book IV*

[THE CAVE OF QUIETUDE[1]]

There lies a den,
Beyond the seeming confines of the space
Made for the soul to wander in and trace
Its own existence, of remotest glooms.   515
Dark regions are around it, where the tombs
Of buried griefs the spirit sees, but scarce
One hour doth linger weeping, for the pierce
Of new-born woe it feels more inly smart:
And in these regions many a venomed dart   520
At random flies; they are the proper home
Of every ill: the man is yet to come
Who hath not journeyed in this native hell.
But few have ever felt how calm and well
Sleep may be had in that deep den of all.   525
There anguish does not sting; nor pleasure pall:
Woe-hurricanes beat ever at the gate,
Yet all is still within and desolate.
Beset with painful gusts, within ye hear
No sound so loud as when on curtained bier   530
The death-watch tick[2] is stifled. Enter none
Who strive therefore: on the sudden it is won.
Just when the sufferer begins to burn,
Then it is free to him; and from an urn,
Still fed by melting ice, he takes a draught—   535
Young Semele[3] such richness never quaffed
In her maternal longing! Happy gloom!
Dark Paradise! where pale becomes the bloom
Of health by due; where silence dreariest
Is most articulate; where hopes infest;   540
Where those eyes are the brightest far that keep
Their lids shut longest in a dreamless sleep.
O happy spirit-home! O wondrous soul!
Pregnant with such a den to save the whole

1. Endymion, although divided between his heavenly and earthly loves, has surrendered to his passion for the human Indian maiden. A pair of winged horses have carried the couple aloft, but as Endymion turns to his bride, she dissolves in the cold moonlight, leaving him alone. He plunges into the "Cave of Quietude"—a mental state (a "native hell," line 523) of total desolation, a "Dark Paradise" of pain and despair so extreme that they become indistinguishable from their own opposites of pleasure and happiness. Compare this description to the lesson of the nature of "high tragedy"—the aesthetic contemplation of human suffering which has passed beyond the bounds of both pain and pleasure—which the poet reads in the "wan" but "bright-blanched" face of Moneta; below, *The Fall of Hyperion*, I.256–82.

2. The death-watch beetle makes a sound like the ticking of a watch, supposed to portend death.

3. Semele presumptuously prayed that Jove unite with her not as man but as a god. When he did so, she was consumed by flames, but conceived Bacchus, who was rescued by Jove from the maternal ashes.

In thine own depth.[4] Hail, gentle Carian![5]   545
For, never since thy griefs and woes began,
Hast thou felt so content: a grievous feud
Hath led thee to this Cave of Quietude.
Aye, his lulled soul was there, although upborne
With dangerous speed: and so he did not mourn   550
Because he knew not whither he was going.
So happy was he, not the aërial blowing
Of trumpets at clear parley[6] from the east
Could rouse from that fine relish, that high feast.
They stung the feathered horse:[7] with fierce alarm   555
He flapped towards the sound. Alas, no charm
Could lift Endymion's head, or he had viewed
A skyey masque,[8] a pinioned multitude—
And silvery was its passing: voices sweet
Warbling the while as if to lull and greet   560
The wanderer in his path. Thus warbled they,
While past the vision went in bright array.[9]

Apr.–Nov., 1817   1818

In Drear-Nighted December

1

In drear-nighted December,
   Too happy, happy tree,
Thy branches ne'er remember
   Their green felicity:
   The north cannot undo them   5
   With a sleety whistle through them;
   Nor frozen thawings glue them
     From budding at the prime.[1]

2

In drear-nighted December,
   Too happy, happy brook,   10
Thy bubblings ne'er remember
   Apollo's[2] summer look;
   But with a sweet forgetting,
   They stay their crystal fretting,
   Never, never petting[3]   15
     About the frozen time.

4. The apparent meaning is that the soul, in the utter depth of its suffering, can produce a cave ("den") of quietude in which to heal itself.
5. Endymion was a native of Caria, in Asia Minor.
6. A trumpet call to assembly.
7. The winged horse on whose back Endymion lay.
8. A dramatic entertainment, involving dialogue, song, and dance by masked actors. "Pinioned": winged.
9. The flying chorus in this masque go on to sing a celebration of Diana's coming marriage—to Endymion himself, although he, listening, does not know it.
1. The earliest period; hence, spring.
2. I.e., the sun's.
3. Complaining.

3

Ah! would 'twere so with many
    A gentle girl and boy!
But were there ever any
    Writhed not of passéd joy?
The feel of *not* to feel it,[4]   20
When there is none to heal it
Nor numbéd sense to steel it,
    Was never said in rhyme.

December, 1817   1829

On Sitting Down to Read *King Lear* Once Again[1]

O golden-tongued Romance with serene lute!
    Fair pluméd Siren! Queen of far away!
    Leave melodizing on this wintry day,
Shut up thine olden pages, and be mute:
Adieu! for once again the fierce dispute   5
    Betwixt damnation and impassioned clay
    Must I burn through; once more humbly essay
The bitter-sweet of this Shakespearean fruit.
Chief Poet! and ye clouds of Albion,[2]
    Begetters of our deep eternal theme,   10
When through the old oak forest I am gone,
    Let me not wander in a barren dream,
But when I am consuméd in the fire,
Give me new Phoenix[3] wings to fly at my desire.

January, 1818   1838, 1848

When I Have Fears[4]

When I have fears that I may cease to be
    Before my pen has gleaned my teeming brain,
Before high-piléd books, in charact'ry,[5]
    Hold like rich garners the full-ripened grain;
When I behold, upon the night's starred face,   5
    Huge cloudy symbols of a high romance,

---

4. This version of line 21, from a recently discovered autograph copy, is adopted in preference to the earlier version in the printed form of the poem: "To know the change and feel it."
1. Keats pauses in revising *Endymion: A Poetic Romance* to read again Shakespeare's great tragedy. The word "Siren" (line 2) indicates Keats's feeling that Romance was enticing him from the poet's prime duty, to deal with "the agonies, the strife / Of human hearts" (*Sleep and Poetry*, lines 124–125).

2. Albion is the old Celtic name for England; *King Lear* is set in Celtic Britain. The "oak forest" of line 11 refers either to *King Lear* or (more likely) to the romance, *Endymion*.
3. The fabulous bird which periodically burns itself to death in order to rise anew from the ashes.
4. The first, and one of the most successful, of Keats's attempts at the sonnet in the Shakespearean rhyme scheme.
5. Characters; written or printed letters of the alphabet.

And think that I may never live to trace
    Their shadows, with the magic hand of chance;
And when I feel, fair creature of an hour,
    That I shall never look upon thee more,   10
Never have relish in the faery power
    Of unreflecting love!—then on the shore
Of the wide world I stand alone, and think
Till Love and Fame to nothingness do sink.

January, 1818   1848

To Homer

Standing aloof in giant ignorance,
    Of thee I hear and of the Cyclades,[6]
As one who sits ashore and longs perchance
    To visit dolphin-coral in deep seas.
So thou wast blind!—but then the veil was rent;   5
    For Jove uncurtained Heaven to let thee live,
And Neptune made for thee a spumy tent,
    And Pan made sing for thee his forest-hive;
Aye, on the shores of darkness there is light,
    And precipices show untrodden green;   10
There is a budding morrow in midnight,
    There is a triple sight in blindness keen;
Such seeing hadst thou, as it once befell
To Dian, Queen of Earth, and Heaven, and Hell.[7]

1818   1848

The Eve of St. Agnes[1]

1

St. Agnes' Eve—Ah, bitter chill it was!
The owl, for all his feathers, was a-cold;
The hare limped trembling through the frozen grass,

6. A group of islands in the Aegean Sea, off Greece; Keats's allusion is to his ignorance of the Greek language.

7. In later cults Diana was worshiped as a three-figured goddess, the deity of nature and of the moon, as well as queen of hell. The "triple sight" which blind Homer paradoxically commands is of these three regions, and also of heaven, sea, and earth (the realms of Jove, Neptune, and Pan, lines 6–8).

1. St. Agnes, martyred ca. 303 at the age of 13, is the patron saint of virgins. Legend has it that if a virtuous young girl performs the proper ritual, she will dream of her future husband on the evening before St. Agnes' Day, which falls on January 21. Keats combined this superstition with the Romeo and Juliet theme of young love thwarted by feuding families and told the story in a sequence of sensuously evolving Spenserian stanzas. The luxurious product has been called "a colored dream," but it is a complexly meaningful dream, in which the strong contrasts of heat and cold, crimson and silver, youth and age, revelry and austere penance, sensuality and chastity, life and death, hell and heaven, assume symbolic values. They are used to figure forth the extremes of spirituality and of grossness that are involved in sexuality, the difference between the dream and the reality of passion, and the ambivalences at the center of human love. The poem is Keats's first complete success in sustained narrative.

And silent was the flock in woolly fold:
Numb were the Beadsman's[2] fingers, while he told   5
His rosary, and while his frosted breath,
Like pious incense from a censer old,
Seemed taking flight for heaven, without a death,
Past the sweet Virgin's picture, while his prayer he saith.

2

His prayer he saith, this patient, holy man;   10
Then takes his lamp, and riseth from his knees,
And back returneth, meager, barefoot, wan,
Along the chapel aisle by slow degrees:
The sculptured dead, on each side, seem to freeze,
Imprisoned in black, purgatorial rails: 15
Knights, ladies, praying in dumb orat'ries,[3]
He passeth by; and his weak spirit fails
To think[4] how they may ache in icy hoods and mails.

3

Northward he turneth through a little door,
And scarce three steps, ere Music's golden tongue   20
Flattered[5] to tears this aged man and poor;
But no—already had his deathbell rung:
The joys of all his life were said and sung:
His was harsh penance on St. Agnes' Eve:
Another way he went, and soon among   25
Rough ashes sat he for his soul's reprieve,
And all night kept awake, for sinner's sake to grieve.

4

That ancient Beadsman heard the prelude soft;
And so it chanced, for many a door was wide,
From hurry to and fro. Soon, up aloft,   30
The silver, snarling trumpets 'gan to chide:
The level chambers, ready with their pride,[6]
Were glowing to receive a thousand guests:
The carvéd angels, ever eager-eyed,
Stared, where upon their heads the cornice rests,   35
With hair blown back, and wings put cross-wise on their breasts.

5

At length burst in the argent revelry,[7]
With plume, tiara, and all rich array,
Numerous as shadows haunting fairily
The brain, new stuffed, in youth, with triumphs gay   40
Of old romance. These let us wish away,
And turn, sole-thoughted, to one Lady there,
Whose heart had brooded, all that wintry day,
On love, and winged St. Agnes' saintly care,
As she had heard old dames full many times declare.   45

2. A "beadsman" is paid to pray for his benefactor. He "tells" (counts) the beads of his rosary, to keep track of his prayers.
3. Silent chapels.
4. I.e., when he thinks.
5. Beguiled, charmed.
6. Ostentation.
7. Silver-clad revelers.

6

They told her how, upon St. Agnes' Eve,
Young virgins might have visions of delight,
And soft adorings from their loves receive
Upon the honeyed middle of the night,
If ceremonies due they did aright;   50
As, supperless to bed they must retire,
And couch supine their beauties, lily white;
Nor look behind, nor sideways, but require
Of Heaven with upward eyes for all that they desire.

7

Full of this whim was thoughtful Madeline: 55
The music, yearning like a God in pain,
She scarcely heard: her maiden eyes divine,
Fixed on the floor, saw many a sweeping train
Pass by—she heeded not at all: in vain
Came many a tiptoe, amorous cavalier,   60
And back retired; not cooled by high disdain;
But she saw not: her heart was otherwhere:
She sighed for Agnes' dreams, the sweetest of the year.

8

She danced along with vague, regardless eyes,
Anxious her lips, her breathing quick and short: 65
The hallowed hour was near at hand: she sighs
Amid the timbrels,[8] and the thronged resort
Of whisperers in anger, or in sport;
'Mid looks of love, defiance, hate, and scorn,
Hoodwinked with faery fancy;[9] all amort,   70
Save to St. Agnes and her lambs unshorn,[1]
And all the bliss to be before tomorrow morn.

9

So, purposing each moment to retire,
She lingered still. Meantime, across the moors,
Had come young Porphyro, with heart on fire   75
For Madeline. Beside the portal doors,
Buttressed from moonlight,[2] stands he, and implores
All saints to give him sight of Madeline,
But for one moment in the tedious hours,
That he might gaze and worship all unseen;   80
Perchance speak, kneel, touch, kiss—in sooth such things have been.

10

He ventures in: let no buzzed whisper tell:
All eyes be muffled, or a hundred swords
Will storm his heart, Love's fev'rous citadel:
For him, those chambers held barbarian hordes,   85
Hyena foemen, and hot-blooded lords,

---

8. Small drums.
9. She was blinded ("hoodwinked"—as though the eyes were covered by a hood) by her charmed imagination; "all amort": as though dead.
1. On St. Agnes' Day it was the custom to offer lambs' wool at the altar, to be made into cloth by nuns.
2. Sheltered from the moonlight by the buttresses (the supports projecting from the wall).

Whose very dogs would execrations howl
Against his lineage: not one breast affords
Him any mercy, in that mansion foul,
Save one old beldame,[3] weak in body and in soul.   90

11

Ah, happy chance! the aged creature came,
Shuffling along with ivory-headed wand,[4]
To where he stood, hid from the torch's flame,
Behind a broad hall-pillar, far beyond
The sound of merriment and chorus bland:[5]   95
He startled her; but soon she knew his face,
And grasped his fingers in her palsied hand,
Saying, "Mercy, Porphyro! hie thee from this place;
They are all here tonight, the whole bloodthirsty race!

12

"Get hence! get hence! there's dwarfish Hildebrand;   100
He had a fever late, and in the fit
He curséd thee and thine, both house and land:
Then there's that old Lord Maurice, not a whit
More tame for his gray hairs—Alas me! flit!
Flit like a ghost away."—"Ah, Gossip[6] dear,   105
We're safe enough; here in this armchair sit,
And tell me how"—"Good Saints! not here, not here;
Follow me, child, or else these stones will be thy bier."

13

He followed through a lowly archéd way,
Brushing the cobwebs with his lofty plume,   110
And as she muttered "Well-a—well-a-day!"
He found him in a little moonlight room,
Pale, latticed, chill, and silent as a tomb.
"Now tell me where is Madeline," said he,
"O tell me, Angela, by the holy loom   115
Which none but secret sisterhood may see,
When they St. Agnes' wool are weaving piously."

14

"St. Agnes! Ah! it is St. Agnes' Eve—
Yet men will murder upon holy days:
Thou must hold water in a witch's sieve,[7]   120
And be liege lord of all the Elves and Fays,
To venture so: it fills me with amaze
To see thee, Porphyro!—St. Agnes' Eve!
God's help! my lady fair the conjuror plays[8]
This very night: good angels her deceive!   125
But let me laugh awhile, I've mickle[9] time to grieve."

15

Feebly she laugheth in the languid moon,

3. Old (and usually, homely) woman; an ironic development in English from the French meaning, "lovely lady."
4. Staff.
5. Soft.
6. In the old sense: godmother, or old friend.
7. A sieve made to hold water by witchcraft.
8. I.e., in her attempt to evoke the vision of her lover.
9. Much.

While Porphyro upon her face doth look,
Like puzzled urchin on an aged crone
Who keepeth closed a wondrous riddle-book,
As spectacled she sits in chimney nook.   130
But soon his eyes grew brilliant, when she told
His lady's purpose; and he scarce could brook[1]
Tears, at the thought of those enchantments cold,
And Madeline asleep in lap of legends old.   135

16

Sudden a thought came like a full-blown rose,
Flushing his brow, and in his painéd heart
Made purple riot: then doth he propose
A stratagem, that makes the beldame start:
"A cruel man and impious thou art: 140
Sweet lady, let her pray, and sleep, and dream
Alone with her good angels, far apart
From wicked men like thee. Go, go!—I deem
Thou canst not surely be the same that thou didst seem."

17

"I will not harm her, by all saints I swear,"   145
Quoth Porphyro: "O may I ne'er find grace
When my weak voice shall whisper its last prayer,
If one of her soft ringlets I displace,
Or look with ruffian passion in her face:
Good Angela, believe me by these tears;   150
Or I will, even in a moment's space,
Awake, with horrid shout, my foemen's ears,
And beard them, though they be more fanged than wolves and
    bears."

18

"Ah! why wilt thou affright a feeble soul?
A poor, weak, palsy-stricken, churchyard thing,   155
Whose passing bell[2] may ere the midnight toll;
Whose prayers for thee, each morn and evening,
Were never missed."—Thus plaining,[3] doth she bring
A gentler speech from burning Porphyro;
So woeful and of such deep sorrowing,   160
That Angela gives promise she will do
Whatever he shall wish, betide her weal or woe.

19

Which was, to lead him, in close secrecy,
Even to Madeline's chamber, and there hide
Him in a closet, of such privacy   165
That he might see her beauty unespied,
And win perhaps that night a peerless bride,
While legioned faeries paced the coverlet,
And pale enchantment held her sleepy-eyed.

---

1. "Brook" ordinarily means "endure," although Keats apparently uses it for "restrain."
2. Death knell.
3. Complaining.

Never on such a night have lovers met,   170
Since Merlin paid his Demon all the monstrous debt.[4]

20

"It shall be as thou wishest," said the Dame:
"All cates[5] and dainties shall be storéd there
Quickly on this feast night: by the tambour frame[6]
Her own lute thou wilt see: no time to spare,   175
For I am slow and feeble, and scarce dare
On such a catering trust my dizzy head.
Wait here, my child, with patience; kneel in prayer
The while: Ah! thou must needs the lady wed,
Or may I never leave my grave among the dead."   180

21

So saying, she hobbled off with busy fear.
The lover's endless minutes slowly passed:
The dame returned, and whispered in his ear
To follow her; with aged eyes aghast
From fright of dim espial. Safe at last,   185
Through many a dusky gallery, they gain
The maiden's chamber, silken, hushed, and chaste;
Where Porphyro took covert, pleased amain.[7]
His poor guide hurried back with agues in her brain.

22

Her falt'ring hand upon the balustrade,   190
Old Angela was feeling for the stair,
When Madeline, St. Agnes' charméd maid,
Rose, like a missioned spirit,[8] unaware:
With silver taper's light, and pious care,
She turned, and down the aged gossip led   195
To a safe level matting. Now prepare,
Young Porphyro, for gazing on that bed;
She comes, she comes again, like ringdove frayed[9] and fled.

23

Out went the taper as she hurried in;
Its little smoke, in pallid moonshine, died: 200
She closed the door, she panted, all akin
To spirits of the air, and visions wide:
No uttered syllable, or, woe betide!
But to her heart, her heart was voluble,
Paining with eloquence her balmy side;   205
As though a tongueless nightingale should swell
Her throat in vain, and die, heart-stifled, in her dell.

24

A casement high and triple-arched there was,
All garlanded with carven imag'ries
Of fruits, and flowers, and bunches of knot-grass,   210

4. Probably the episode in the Arthurian
legends in which Merlin, the magician,
lost his life when the wily Vivien turned
one of his spells against him.
5. Delicacies.

6. A drum-shaped embroidery frame.
7. Mightily.
8. Like an angel sent on a mission.
9. Frightened.

And diamonded with panes of quaint device,
Innumerable of stains and splendid dyes,
As are the tiger moth's deep-damasked wings;
And in the midst, 'mong thousand heraldries,
And twilight saints, and dim emblazonings,   215
A shielded scutcheon blushed with blood of queens and kings.[1]

25

Full on this casement shone the wintry moon,
And threw warm gules[2] on Madeline's fair breast,
As down she knelt for heaven's grace and boon;[3]
Rose-bloom fell on her hands, together pressed,   220
And on her silver cross soft amethyst,
And on her hair a glory, like a saint:
She seemed a splendid angel, newly dressed,
Save wings, for heaven—Porphyro grew faint:
She knelt, so pure a thing, so free from mortal taint.   225

26

Anon his heart revives: her vespers done,
Of all its wreathéd pearls her hair she frees;
Unclasps her warméd jewels one by one;
Loosens her fragrant bodice; by degrees
Her rich attire creeps rustling to her knees: 230
Half-hidden, like a mermaid in sea-weed,
Pensive awhile she dreams awake, and sees,
In fancy, fair St. Agnes in her bed,
But dares not look behind, or all the charm is fled.

27

Soon, trembling in her soft and chilly nest,   235
In sort of wakeful swoon, perplexed[4] she lay,
Until the poppied warmth of sleep oppressed
Her soothéd limbs, and soul fatigued away;
Flown, like a thought, until the morrow-day;
Blissfully havened both from joy and pain;   240
Clasped like a missal where swart Paynims pray;[5]
Blinded alike from sunshine and from rain,
As though a rose should shut, and be a bud again.

28

Stol'n to this paradise, and so entranced,
Porphyro gazed upon her empty dress,   245
And listened to her breathing, if it chanced
To wake into a slumberous tenderness;
Which when he heard, that minute did he bless,
And breathed himself: then from the closet crept,
Noiseless as fear in a wide wilderness,   250

---

1. I.e., among the genealogical emblems ("heraldries") and other devices ("emblazonings"), a heraldic shield signified by its colors that the family was of royal blood.
2. In heraldry, the color red.
3. Gift, blessing.
4. In a confused state between waking and sleeping.
5. Variously interpreted; perhaps: held tightly, cherished, like a Christian prayer book ("missal") in a land where the religion is that of dark-skinned pagans ("swart Paynims").

And over the hushed carpet, silent, stepped,
And 'tween the curtains peeped, where, lo!—how fast she slept.

29

Then by the bedside, where the faded moon
Made a dim, silver twilight, soft he set
A table, and, half anguished, threw thereon   255
A cloth of woven crimson, gold, and jet—
O for some drowsy Morphean amulet![6]
The boisterous, midnight, festive clarion,[7]
The kettledrum, and far-heard clarinet,
Affray his ears, though but in dying tone—   260
The hall door shuts again, and all the noise is gone.

30

And still she slept an azure-lidded sleep,
In blanchéd linen, smooth, and lavendered,
While he from forth the closet brought a heap
Of candied apple, quince, and plum, and gourd;[8]   265
With jellies soother than the creamy curd,
And lucent syrups, tinct with cinnamon;
Manna and dates, in argosy transferred
From Fez;[9] and spicéd dainties, every one,
From silken Samarcand to cedared Lebanon.   270

31

These delicates he heaped with glowing hand
On golden dishes and in baskets bright
Of wreathéd silver: sumptuous they stand
In the retired quiet of the night,
Filling the chilly room with perfume light.—   275
"And now, my love, my seraph[1] fair, awake!
Thou art my heaven, and I thine eremite:[2]
Open thine eyes, for meek St. Agnes' sake,
Or I shall drowse beside thee, so my soul doth ache."

32

Thus whispering, his warm, unnervéd arm   280
Sank in her pillow. Shaded was her dream
By the dusk curtains: 'twas a midnight charm
Impossible to melt as icéd stream:
The lustrous salvers in the moonlight gleam;
Broad golden fringe upon the carpet lies: 285
It seemed he never, never could redeem
From such a steadfast spell his lady's eyes;
So mused awhile, entoiled in wooféd fantasies.[3]

33

Awakening up, he took her hollow lute—
Tumultuous—and, in chords that tenderest be,   290

6. Sleep-producing charm.
7. High-pitched trumpet.
8. Melon. According to the legend, the dream lover would bring the virgin a feast of delicacies.
9. I.e., jellies softer ("soother") than the curds of cream, clear ("lucent") syrups tinged with cinnamon, and sweet gums ("manna") and dates transported in a great merchant ship ("argosy") from Fez.
1. One of the highest order of angels.
2. A religious hermit.
3. Entangled in a weave of fantasies.

He played an ancient ditty, long since mute,
In Provence called "*La belle dame sans merci*":[4]
Close to her ear touching the melody;
Wherewith disturbed, she uttered a soft moan:
He ceased—she panted quick—and suddenly   295
Her blue affrayéd eyes wide open shone:
Upon his knees he sank, pale as smooth-sculptured stone.

34

Her eyes were open, but she still beheld,
Now wide awake, the vision of her sleep:
There was a painful change, that nigh expelled   300
The blisses of her dream so pure and deep,
At which fair Madeline began to weep,
And moan forth witless words with many a sigh;
While still her gaze on Porphyro would keep,
Who knelt, with joinéd hands and piteous eye,   305
Fearing to move or speak, she looked so dreamingly.

35

"Ah, Porphyro!" said she, "but even now
Thy voice was at sweet tremble in mine ear,
Made tunable with every sweetest vow;
And those sad eyes were spiritual and clear:
How changed thou art! how pallid, chill, and drear!   310
Give me that voice again, my Porphyro,
Those looks immortal, those complainings dear!
Oh leave me not in this eternal woe,
For if thou diest, my Love, I know not where to go."   315

36

Beyond a mortal man impassioned far
At these voluptuous accents, he arose,
Ethereal, flushed, and like a throbbing star
Seen mid the sapphire heaven's deep repose;
Into her dream he melted, as the rose   320
Blendeth its odor with the violet—
Solution sweet: meantime the frost-wind blows
Like Love's alarum pattering the sharp sleet
Against the windowpanes; St. Agnes' moon hath set.

37

'Tis dark: quick pattereth the flaw-blown[5] sleet: 325
"This is no dream, my bride, my Madeline!"
'Tis dark: the icéd gusts still rave and beat:
"No dream, alas! alas! and woe is mine!
Porphyro will leave me here to fade and pine.—
Cruel! what traitor could thee hither bring?   330
I curse not, for my heart is lost in thine,
Though thou forsakest a deceivéd thing—
A dove forlorn and lost with sick unprunéd wing."

---

4. "The Lovely Lady Without Pity,"   ballad.
by the medieval poet, Alain Chartier.   5. Gust-blown.
Keats later used the title for his own

38

"My Madeline! sweet dreamer! lovely bride!
Say, may I be for aye thy vassal blest? 335
Thy beauty's shield, heart-shaped and vermeil[6] dyed?
Ah, silver shrine, here will I take my rest
After so many hours of toil and quest,
A famished pilgrim—saved by miracle.
Though I have found, I will not rob thy nest 340
Saving of thy sweet self; if thou think'st well
To trust, fair Madeline, to no rude infidel.

39

"Hark! 'tis an elfin-storm from faery land,
Of haggard[7] seeming, but a boon indeed:
Arise—arise! the morning is at hand— 345
The bloated wassaillers[8] will never heed—
Let us away, my love, with happy speed;
There are no ears to hear, or eyes to see—
Drowned all in Rhenish and the sleepy mead:[9]
Awake! arise! my love, and fearless be, 350
For o'er the southern moors I have a home for thee."

40

She hurried at his words, beset with fears,
For there were sleeping dragons all around,
At glaring watch, perhaps, with ready spears—
Down the wide stairs a darkling[1] way they found.— 355
In all the house was heard no human sound.
A chain-drooped lamp was flickering by each door;
The arras, rich with horseman, hawk, and hound,
Fluttered in the besieging wind's uproar;
And the long carpets rose along the gusty floor. 360

41

They glide, like phantoms, into the wide hall;
Like phantoms, to the iron porch, they glide;
Where lay the Porter, in uneasy sprawl,
With a huge empty flagon by his side:
The wakeful bloodhound rose, and shook his hide, 365
But his sagacious eye an inmate owns:[2]
By one, and one, the bolts full easy slide:
The chains lie silent on the footworn stones;
The key turns, and the door upon its hinges groans.

42

And they are gone: aye, ages long ago 370
These lovers fled away into the storm.
That night the Baron dreamt of many a woe,
And all his warrior-guests, with shade and form
Of witch, and demon, and large coffin-worm,
Were long be-nightmared. Angela the old 375

6. Vermilion.
7. Wild, untamed (originally, a wild hawk).
8. Drunken carousers.
9. Rhine wine and the sleep-producing mead (a heavy fermented drink made with honey).
1. In the dark.
2. Acknowledges a member of the household.

Died palsy-twitched, with meager face deform;
  The Beadsman, after thousand aves[3] told,
For aye unsought for slept among his ashes cold.
Jan.–Feb., 1819   1820

Bright Star[4]

Bright star, would I were steadfast as thou art—
  Not in lone splendor hung aloft the night
And watching, with eternal lids apart,
  Like nature's patient, sleepless Eremite,[5]
The moving waters at their priestlike task   5
  Of pure ablution[6] round earth's human shores,
Or gazing on the new soft fallen mask
  Of snow upon the mountains and the moors—
No—yet still steadfast, still unchangeable,
  Pillowed upon my fair love's ripening breast,   10
To feel forever its soft fall and swell,
  Awake forever in a sweet unrest,
Still, still to hear her tender-taken breath,
And so live ever—or else swoon to death.[7]
1819-20   1838

Why Did I Laugh Tonight?[8]

Why did I laugh tonight? No voice will tell:
  No God, no Demon of severe response,
Deigns to reply from Heaven or from Hell.
  Then to my human heart I turn at once.
Heart! Thou and I are here sad and alone;   5
  I say, why did I laugh? O mortal pain!
O Darkness! Darkness! ever must I moan,
  To question Heaven and Hell and Heart in vain.
Why did I laugh? I know this Being's lease,
  My fancy to its utmost blisses spreads;   10
Yet would I on this very midnight cease,
  And the world's gaudy ensigns[9] see in shreds;

---

3. The prayers beginning *Ave Maria* ("Hail Mary").
4. While on a tour of the Lake Country in 1818, Keats had said that the austere scenes "refine one's sensual vision into a sort of north star which can never cease to be open lidded and steadfast over the wonders of the great Power"; the thought developed into this sonnet. Keats drafted this poem in 1819, then copied it into his volume of Shakespeare's poems, while on the way to his death in Italy in September, 1820.
5. Hermit, religious solitary.
6. Washing, as part of a religious rite.

7. In the earlier version: "Half passionless, and so swoon on to death."
8. In the letter to his brother and sister-in-law, George and Georgiana Keats, into which he copied this sonnet, March 19, 1819, Keats wrote: "Though the first steps to it were through my human passions, they went away, and I wrote with my Mind—and perhaps I must confess a little bit of my heart. * * * I went to bed, and enjoyed an uninterrupted sleep. Sane I went to bed and sane I arose."
9. Banners.

Verse, Fame, and Beauty are intense indeed,
But Death intenser—Death is Life's high meed.

March, 1819   1848

La Belle Dame sans Merci[1]

O what can ail thee, Knight at arms,
    Alone and palely loitering?
The sedge has withered from the Lake
    And no birds sing!

O what can ail thee, Knight at arms,   5
    So haggard, and so woebegone?
The squirrel's granary is full
    And the harvest's done.

I see a lily on thy brow
    With anguish moist and fever dew,   10
And on thy cheeks a fading rose
    Fast withereth too.

I met a Lady in the Meads,
    Full beautiful, a faery's child,
Her hair was long, her foot was light   15
    And her eyes were wild.

I made a Garland for her head,
    And bracelets too, and fragrant Zone;[2]
She looked at me as she did love
    And made sweet moan.   20

I set her on my pacing steed
    And nothing else saw all day long,
For sidelong would she bend and sing
    A faery's song.

She found me roots of relish sweet,   25
    And honey wild, and manna dew,
And sure in language strange she said
    "I love thee true."

She took me to her elfin grot
    And there she wept and sighed full sore,   30
And there I shut her wild wild eyes
    With kisses four.

---

1. The title, though not the subject matter, was taken from a medieval poem by Alain Chartier and means "The Lovely Lady Without Pity." The story of a mortal destroyed by his love for a supernatural *femme fatale* has been told repeatedly in myth, fairy tale, and ballad, but never so hauntingly. The metrical key to its effect is the poignant and richly suggestive suspension achieved by shortening to two stresses the final line of each stanza. We print here Keats's first version, written in a letter to his brother and sister-in-law. The version published in 1820, "Ah, what can ail thee, wretched wight," is a rare instance in which Keats weakened a poem by revision.

Keats imitates a frequent procedure of folk ballads by casting the poem into the dialogue form. The first three stanzas are addressed to the Knight, and the rest of the poem is his reply.

2. Girdle.

And there she lulléd me asleep,
   And there I dreamed, Ah Woe betide!
The latest[3] dream I ever dreamt   35
   On the cold hill side.

I saw pale Kings, and Princes too,
   Pale warriors, death-pale were they all;
They cried, "La belle dame sans merci
   Thee hath in thrall!"   40

I saw their starved lips in the gloam
   With horrid warning gapéd wide,
And I awoke, and found me here
   On the cold hill's side.

And this is why I sojourn here,   45
   Alone and palely loitering;
Though the sedge is withered from the Lake
   And no birds sing.

April, 1819   1820

On the Sonnet[1]

If by dull rhymes our English must be chained,
   And, like Andromeda,[2] the Sonnet sweet
Fettered, in spite of painéd loveliness;
Let us find out, if we must be constrained,
   Sandals more interwoven and complete   5
To fit the naked foot of poesy;
Let us inspect the lyre, and weigh the stress
Of every chord,[3] and see what may be gained
   By ear industrious, and attention meet;
Misers of sound and syllable, no less
Than Midas[4] of his coinage, let us be   10
   Jealous of dead leaves in the bay-wreath crown;
So, if we may not let the Muse be free,
   She will be bound with garlands of her own.

April, 1819   1848

To Sleep

O soft embalmer of the still midnight,
   Shutting, with careful fingers and benign,

---

3. Last.
1. In a letter including this sonnet, Keats wrote that "I have been endeavoring to discover a better sonnet stanza than we have," objecting especially to the "pouncing rhymes" of the Petrarchan form and the inevitable tick of the closing couplet in the Shakespearean stanza. This and the two following poems exemplify Keats's experiments with variations upon these conventional sonnet patterns.
2. Andromeda was chained to a rock in order to placate a sea monster, but was rescued by Perseus.
3. Lyre-string.
4. King Midas was granted his wish that all he touched should turn to gold.

Our gloom-pleased eyes, embowered from the light,
    Enshaded in forgetfulness divine;
O soothest[1] Sleep! if so it please thee, close   5
    In midst of this thine hymn my willing eyes,
Or wait the amen, ere thy poppy[2] throws
    Around my bed its lulling charities;
Then save me, or the passéd day will shine
Upon my pillow, breeding many woes;   10
    Save me from curious[3] conscience, that still lords
Its strength for darkness, burrowing like a mole;
    Turn the key deftly in the oiléd wards,[4]
And seal the hushéd casket of my soul.

April, 1819   1838, 1848

On Fame

"You cannot eat your cake and have it too."
        —*Proverb*

How fevered is the man, who cannot look
    Upon his mortal days with temperate blood,
Who vexes all the leaves of his life's book,
    And robs his fair name of its maidenhood;
It is as if the rose should pluck herself,   5
    Or the ripe plum finger its misty bloom,
As if a Naiad,[5] like a meddling elf,
    Should darken her pure grot with muddy gloom;
But the rose leaves herself upon the briar,
    For winds to kiss and grateful bees to feed,   10
And the ripe plum still wears its dim attire;
    The undisturbéd lake has crystal space;
    Why then should man, teasing the world for grace,
Spoil his salvation for a fierce miscreed?[6]

April, 1819   1848

Ode to Psyche[1]

O Goddess! hear these tuneless numbers, wrung
    By sweet enforcement and remembrance dear,

---

1. Softest.
2. Opium is made from the dried juice of the opium poppy.
3. Scrupulous. "Lords": marshals, sets in order.
4. The ridges in a lock which determine the pattern of the key.
5. Water nymph.
6. I.e., the false doctrine ("miscreed") that the award of salvation can be won by achieving fame in this world. Cf. Milton's *Lycidas*, lines 78 ff.: "Fame is no plant that grows on mortal soil. * * * "
1. This poem initiated the sequence of five great odes that Keats wrote in late April and in May, 1819. Since it is copied into the same journal-letter which included *On the Sonnet*, it is likely that Keats's experiments with sonnet schemes led to the development of the intricate and varied stanzas of his odes, and also that Keats abandoned the sonnet upon discovering the richer possibilities of the more spacious form. In a letter of April 30, 1819, Keats said that of all his poems up to that time, *Psyche* "is the first and the only one with which I have taken even moderate pains. I have for the most part dashed off my lines in a hurry. This I have done lei-

And pardon that thy secrets should be sung
    Even into thine own soft-conchéd[2] ear:
Surely I dreamt today, or did I see   5
    The wingéd Psyche with awakened eyes?[2a]
I wandered in a forest thoughtlessly,
    And, on the sudden, fainting with surprise,
Saw two fair creatures, couchéd side by side
    In deepest grass, beneath the whisp'ring roof   10
Of leaves and trembled blossoms, where there ran
    A brooklet, scarce espied:

'Mid hushed, cool-rooted flowers, fragrant-eyed,
    Blue, silver-white, and budded Tyrian,[3]
They lay calm-breathing on the bedded grass;   15
    Their arms embracéd, and their pinions[4] too;
    Their lips touched not, but had not bade adieu,
As if disjoinéd by soft-handed slumber,
And ready still past kisses to outnumber
    At tender eye-dawn of aurorean love:[5]   20
    The wingéd boy I knew;
But who wast thou, O happy, happy dove?
    His Psyche true!

O latest born and loveliest vision far
    Of all Olympus' faded hierarchy![6]   25
Fairer than Phoebe's sapphire-regioned star,[7]
    Or Vesper, amorous glowworm of the sky;
Fairer than these, though temple thou hast none,
    Nor altar heaped with flowers;
Nor virgin choir to make delicious moan   30
    Upon the midnight hours;
No voice, no lute, no pipe, no incense sweet
    From chain-swung censer teeming;

surely—I think it reads the more richly for it and will I hope encourage me to write other things in even a more peaceable and healthy spirit." In the story told by the Roman author Apuleius in the 2nd century A.D., Psyche was a lovely mortal beloved by Cupid, "the winged boy," son of Venus. After various tribulations, imposed by Venus because she was jealous of Psyche's beauty, Psyche was wedded to Cupid and translated to heaven as an immortal.

The tendency in recent criticism of Keats is to read the *Ode* as a quasi-allegory, in which Psyche (in Greek: soul, or mind) represents "the human-soul-in-love" (Harold Bloom) or else the modern inward-oriented poetry of the mind (W. J. Bate). To this latter-day goddess, Keats in the last two stanzas promises to establish a place of worship within "some untrodden region" of his own mind, with himself as poet-priest and prophet.

2. Soft and shaped like a seashell.
2a. Another of Keats's inquiries into the relation of dreams to poetic vision; see, e.g., *Sleep and Poetry*, the concluding line of *Ode to a Nightingale*, the opening section of *The Fall of Hyperion: A Dream*.
3. The purple dye anciently made in Tyre.
4. Wings.
5. Aurora was the goddess of the dawn.
6. The ranks of the classic gods of Mt. Olympus. "You must recollect that Psyche was not embodied as a goddess before the time of Apuleius the Platonist who lived after the Augustan age, and consequently the goddess was never worshiped or sacrificed to with any of the ancient fervor—and perhaps never thought of in the old religion" (Keats, letter of April 30, 1819).
7. The moon, supervised by the goddess Phoebe (Diana). "Vesper": the evening star.

No shrine, no grove, no oracle, no heat
    Of pale-mouthed prophet dreaming.   35

O brightest! though too late for antique vows,
    Too, too late for the fond believing lyre,
When holy were the haunted forest boughs,
    Holy the air, the water, and the fire;
Yet even in these days so far retired   40
    From happy pieties, thy lucent fans,[8]
    Fluttering among the faint Olympians,
I see, and sing, by my own eyes inspired.
So let me be thy choir, and make a moan
      Upon the midnight hours;   45
Thy voice, thy lute, thy pipe, thy incense sweet
    From swingéd censer teeming;
Thy shrine, thy grove, thy oracle, thy heat
    Of pale-mouthed prophet dreaming.
Yes, I will be thy priest, and build a fane[9]   50
    In some untrodden region of my mind,
Where branchéd thoughts, new grown with pleasant pain,
    Instead of pines shall murmur in the wind:
Far, far around shall those dark-clustered trees
    Fledge[1] the wild-ridged mountains steep by steep;   55
And there by zephyrs, streams, and birds, and bees,
    The moss-lain Dryads[2] shall be lulled to sleep;
And in the midst of this wide quietness
A rosy sanctuary will I dress
With the wreathed trellis of a working brain,   60
    With buds, and bells, and stars without a name,
With all the gardener Fancy e'er could feign,
    Who breeding flowers, will never breed the same:
And there shall be for thee all soft delight
    That shadowy thought can win,   65
A bright torch, and a casement ope at night,
    To let the warm Love[3] in!

April, 1819   1820

Ode on a Grecian Urn[1]

1

Thou still unravished bride of quietness,
    Thou foster child of silence and slow time,

8. Shining wings.
9. Temple.
1. I.e., the trees shall stand, rank against rank, like layers of feathers.
2. Wood nymphs.
3. I.e., Cupid, god of love.
1. This urn, with its sculptured reliefs of Dionysian ecstasies, panting young lovers in flight and pursuit, a pastoral piper under spring foliage, and the quiet celebration of communal pieties, resembles parts of various vases, sculptures, and paintings; but it existed in all its particulars only in Keats's imagination. In the urn—which captures moments of intense experience in attitudes of grace and freezes them into marble immobility—Keats found the perfect correlative for his persistent concern with the longing for permanence in a world of change. The interpretation of the details with which Keats devel-

Sylvan[2] historian, who canst thus express
    A flowery tale more sweetly than our rhyme:
What leaf-fringed legend haunts about thy shape   5
    Of deities or mortals, or of both,
        In Tempe or the dales of Arcady?[3]
    What men or gods are these? What maidens loath?
What mad pursuit? What struggle to escape?
      What pipes and timbrels? What wild ecstasy?   10

2

Heard melodies are sweet, but those unheard
    Are sweeter; therefore, ye soft pipes, play on;
Not to the sensual ear,[4] but, more endeared,
    Pipe to the spirit ditties of no tone:
Fair youth, beneath the trees, thou canst not leave   15
    Thy song, nor ever can those trees be bare;
      Bold Lover, never, never canst thou kiss,
Though winning near the goal—yet, do not grieve;
    She cannot fade, though thou hast not thy bliss,
    Forever wilt thou love, and she be fair!   20

3

Ah, happy, happy boughs! that cannot shed
    Your leaves, nor ever bid the Spring adieu;
And, happy melodist, unwearied,
    Forever piping songs forever new;
More happy love! more happy, happy love!   25
    Forever warm and still to be enjoyed,
      Forever panting, and forever young;
All breathing human passion far above,
    That leaves a heart high-sorrowful and cloyed,
    A burning forehead, and a parching tongue.   30

4

Who are these coming to the sacrifice?
    To what green altar, O mysterious priest,
Lead'st thou that heifer lowing at the skies,
    And all her silken flanks with garlands dressed?
What little town by river or sea shore,   35
    Or mountain-built with peaceful citadel,
      Is emptied of this folk, this pious morn?
And, little town, thy streets forevermore
    Will silent be; and not a soul to tell
      Why thou art desolate, can e'er return.   40

ops this concept, however, is hotly disputed, all the way from the opening phrase—is "still" an adverb ("as yet") or an adjective ("motionless")?—to the two concluding lines, an ending which has already accumulated as much critical discussion as the "two-handed engine" in Milton's *Lycidas* or the cruxes in Shakespeare's plays. But these disputes testify to the enigmatic richness of meaning in the five short stanzas, and show that the ode has become a central point of reference in the criticism of the English lyric.

2. Rustic, representing a woodland scene.

3. Tempe is a beautiful valley in Greece, which has come to represent supreme rural beauty. The "dales of Arcady" are the valleys of Arcadia, a state in ancient Greece often used as a symbol of the pastoral ideal.

4. The ear of sense (as opposed to that of the "spirit," or imagination).

5

O Attic[5] shape! Fair attitude! with brede
  Of marble men and maidens overwrought,[6]
With forest branches and the trodden weed;
  Thou, silent form, dost tease us out of thought
As doth eternity: Cold Pastoral!   45
    When old age shall this generation waste,
      Thou shalt remain, in midst of other woe
  Than ours, a friend to man, to whom thou say'st,
  "Beauty is truth, truth beauty,"[7]—that is all
    Ye know on earth, and all ye need to know.   50
May, 1819   1820

Ode to a Nightingale[1]

1

My heart aches, and a drowsy numbness pains
  My sense, as though of hemlock[2] I had drunk,
Or emptied some dull opiate to the drains
  One minute past, and Lethe-wards[3] had sunk:
'Tis not through envy of thy happy lot,   5
  But being too happy in thine happiness—
    That thou, light-wingéd Dryad of the trees,
      In some melodious plot
  Of beechen green, and shadows numberless,
    Singest of summer in full-throated ease.   10

2

O, for a draught of vintage! that hath been
  Cooled a long age in the deep-delvéd earth,
Tasting of Flora[4] and the country green,
  Dance, and Provençal song,[5] and sunburnt mirth!
O for a beaker full of the warm South,   15

5. Greek. Attica was the region of Greece in which Athens was located.
6. Ornamented all over ("over-wrought") with an interwoven pattern ("brede").
7. The quotation marks around this phrase are found in the volume of poems Keats published in 1820; but there are no quotation marks in the version printed in *Annals of the Fine Arts* that same year, or in the four transcripts of the poem made by Keats's friends. This discrepancy has encouraged the diversity of critical interpretations of the last two lines. Leading critics disagree whether the whole of these lines is said by the urn, or "Beauty is truth, truth beauty" by the urn and the rest by Keats or else by an invented lyric speaker; whether the "ye" in the last line is addressed to the lyric speaker, to the readers, to the urn, or to the figures on the urn; whether "all ye know" is that beauty is truth, or this plus the statement in lines 46–48; and whether "beauty is truth" is a universal and profound metaphysical proposition, or an overstatement uttered in the course of a dramatic dialogue, or simply nonsense. (The various commentaries are collected in *Keats's Well-Read Urn*, ed. H. T. Lyon, 1958).
1. Charles Brown, with whom Keats was then living in Hampstead, wrote: "In the spring of 1819 a nightingale had built her nest near my house. Keats felt a tranquil and continual joy in her song; and one morning he took his chair from the breakfast table to the grass plot under a plum tree, where he sat for two or three hours. When he came into the house, I perceived he had some scraps of paper in his hand, and these he was quietly thrusting behind the books. On inquiry, I found those scraps, four or five in number, contained his poetic feeling on the song of our nightingale."
2. A poisonous herb, not the North American evergreen tree.
3. Toward Lethe, the river in Hades whose waters cause forgetfulness.
4. Roman goddess of flowers, or the flowers themselves.
5. Provence, in southern France, was in

Full of the true, the blushful Hippocrene,[6]
  With beaded bubbles winking at the brim,
    And purple-stainèd mouth;
That I might drink, and leave the world unseen,
  And with thee fade away into the forest dim: 20

3

Fade far away, dissolve, and quite forget
  What thou among the leaves hast never known,
    The weariness, the fever, and the fret
Here, where men sit and hear each other groan;
  Where palsy shakes a few, sad, last gray hairs,   25
    Where youth grows pale, and specter-thin, and dies;[7]
      Where but to think is to be full of sorrow
        And leaden-eyed despairs,
    Where Beauty cannot keep her lustrous eyes,
      Or new Love pine at them beyond tomorrow.   30

4

Away! away! for I will fly to thee,
  Not charioted by Bacchus and his pards,
But on the viewless wings of Poesy,[8]
  Though the dull brain perplexes and retards:
Already with thee! tender is the night,   35
  And haply the Queen-Moon is on her throne,
    Clustered around by all her starry Fays;[9]
      But here there is no light,
  Save what from heaven is with the breezes blown
    Through verdurous[1] glooms and winding mossy ways.   40

5

I cannot see what flowers are at my feet,
  Nor what soft incense hangs upon the boughs,
But, in embalmèd[2] darkness, guess each sweet
  Wherewith the seasonable month endows
The grass, the thicket, and the fruit tree wild;   45
  White hawthorn, and the pastoral eglantine;[3]
    Fast fading violets covered up in leaves;
      And mid-May's eldest child,
The coming musk-rose, full of dewy wine,
    The murmurous haunt of flies on summer eves.   50

6

Darkling[4] I listen; and for many a time
  I have been half in love with easeful Death,
Called him soft names in many a musèd[5] rhyme,

---

the late Middle Ages renowned for its troubadours, the writers and singers of love songs.
6. Pronounced *Hip'-ocreen:* fountain of the Muses on Mt. Helicon; hence, the waters of inspiration, here applied metaphorically to a beaker of wine.
7. Keats's brother, Tom, wasted by tuberculosis, had died the previous winter.
8. I.e., not by getting drunk on wine (the "vintage" of stanza two), but on the invisible ("viewless") wings of the

poetic fancy. (Bacchus, god of wine, was sometimes represented in a chariot drawn by "pards"—leopards.)
9. Fairies.
1. Green-foliaged.
2. Perfumed.
3. Sweetbrier, or honeysuckle.
4. In the dark.
5. Meditated. Two earlier poems ("rhymes") by Keats which called on "easeful Death" are the sonnets *Why Did I Laugh?* and *Bright Star.*

To take into the air my quiet breath;
Now more than ever seems it rich to die, 55
To cease upon the midnight with no pain,
    While thou art pouring forth thy soul abroad
      In such an ecstasy!
Still wouldst thou sing, and I have ears in vain—
    To thy high requiem become a sod. 60

7

Thou wast not born for death, immortal Bird!
    No hungry generations tread thee down;
The voice I hear this passing night was heard
    In ancient days by emperor and clown:
Perhaps the selfsame song that found a path 65
    Through the sad heart of Ruth[6] when, sick for home,
      She stood in tears amid the alien corn;[7]
        The same that ofttimes hath
Charmed magic casements, opening on the foam
    Of perilous seas, in faery lands forlorn. 70

8

Forlorn![8] the very word is like a bell
    To toll me back from thee to my sole self!
Adieu! the fancy[9] cannot cheat so well
    As she is famed to do, deceiving elf.
Adieu! adieu! thy plaintive anthem[10] fades 75
    Past the near meadows, over the still stream,
      Up the hill side; and now 'tis buried deep
        In the next valley-glades:
Was it a vision, or a waking dream?
    Fled is that music:—Do I wake or sleep?[11] 80

May, 1819   1819, 1820

Ode on Indolence[1]

"They toil not, neither do they spin."[2]

1

One morn before me were three figures seen,
    With bowed necks, and joined hands, side-faced;

6. The young widow in the Biblical Book of Ruth.
7. I.e., wheat.
8. One critic has said that "forlorn"—which means "long past" as well as "sorrowful"—"has its feet in two worlds," the faeryland of imagination and the woe of reality to which the word reawakens the lyric speaker.
9. I.e., "the viewless wings of Poesy" of line 33.
10. Hymn.
11. See *Ode to Psyche*, note to line 6.
1. On March 19, 1819, Keats wrote to George and Georgiana Keats: "This morning I am in a sort of temper indolent and supremely careless. . . . Neither Poetry, nor Ambition, nor Love have any alertness of countenance as they pass by me: they seem rather like three figures on a greek vase—a Man and two women—whom no one but myself could distinguish in their disguisement. This is the only happiness; and is a rare instance of advantage in the body overpowering the Mind." The Ode was probably written soon after this time, but was not published until long after the poet's death, in 1848.
2. Matthew vi.28.

And one behind the other stepped serene,
  In placid sandals, and in white robes graced;
They passed, like figures on a marble urn,
  When shifted round to see the other side;
    They came again; as when the urn once more
Is shifted round, the first seen shades return;
  And they were strange to me, as may betide
    With vases, to one deep in Phidian[3] lore.   10

    5

2

How is it, Shadows! that I knew ye not?
  How came ye muffled in so hush a masque?
Was it a silent deep-disguiséd plot
  To steal away, and leave without a task
My idle days? Ripe was the drowsy hour;   15
  The blissful cloud of summer-indolence
    Benumbed my eyes; my pulse grew less and less;
Pain had no sting, and pleasure's wreath no flower:
  O, why did ye not melt, and leave my sense
    Unhaunted quite of all but—nothingness?   20

3

A third time came they by;—alas! wherefore?
  My sleep had been embroidered with dim dreams;
My soul had been a lawn besprinkled o'er
  With flowers, and stirring shades, and baffled beams:
The morn was clouded, but no shower fell,   25
  Though in her lids hung the sweet tears of May;
    The open casement pressed a new-leaved vine,
Let in the budding warmth and throstle's lay;
  O Shadows! 'twas a time to bid farewell!
    Upon your skirts had fallen no tears of mine.   30

4

A third time passed they by, and, passing, turned
  Each one the face a moment whiles to me;
Then faded, and to follow them I burned
  And ached for wings because I knew the three;
The first was a fair Maid, and Love her name;   35
  The second was Ambition, pale of cheek,
    And ever watchful with fatiguéd eye;
The last, whom I love more, the more of blame
  Is heaped upon her, maiden most unmeek,—
    I knew to be my demon Poesy.   40

---

3. Phidias was the great Athenian sculptor of the 5th century B.C. who designed the marble sculptures for the Parthenon.

5

They faded, and, forsooth! I wanted wings:
    O folly! What is Love! and where is it?
And for that poor Ambition—it springs
    From a man's little heart's short fever-fit;
For Poesy!—no,—she has not a joy,—   45
    At least for me,—so sweet as drowsy noons,
        And evenings steep'd in honied indolence;
O, for an age so shelter'd from annoy,
    That I may never know how change the moons,
        Or hear the voice of busy common-sense!   50

6

So, ye three Ghosts, adieu! Ye cannot raise
    My head cool-bedded in the flowery grass;
For I would not be dieted with praise,
    A pet-lamb in a sentimental farce![4]
Fade softly from my eyes, and be once more   55
    In masque-like figures on the dreamy urn;
        Farewell! I yet have visions for the night,
And for the day faint visions there is store;
    Vanish, ye Phantoms! from my idle spright,[5]
        Into the clouds, and never more return!   60

1819   1848

4. In a letter of June 9, 1819, Keats wrote: "I have been very idle lately, very averse to writing; both from the overpowering idea of our dead poets and from abatement of my love of fame. I hope I am a little more of a Philosopher than I was, consequently a little less of a versifying Pet-lamb. . . . You will judge of my 1819 temper when I tell you that the thing I have most enjoyed this year has been writing an ode to Indolence."
5. Spirit.

Ode on Melancholy

Ode on Melancholy This is Keats's best-known statement of his recurrent theme of the inextricable contrarieties of life. The remarkable last stanza, in which Melancholy becomes a veiled goddess in a mystery religion, implies that it is the tragic human destiny that beauty, joy, and life itself take their quality and value from the very fact that they are transitory, and turn into their opposites.

    The poem originally included the following stanza, which Keats canceled in MS:

Though you should build a bark of dead men's bones,
    And rear a phantom gibbet for a mast,
Stitch creeds together for a sail, with groans
    To fill it out, blood-stained and aghast;
Although your rudder be a dragon's tail

Long severed, yet still hard with agony,
Your cordage large uprootings from the skull
Of bald Medusa, certes you would fail
To find the Melancholy—whether she
Dreameth in any isle of Lethe dull.

Ode on Melancholy

1

No, no, go not to Lethe,[1] neither twist
Wolfsbane, tight-rooted, for its poisonous wine;
Nor suffer thy pale forehead to be kissed
By nightshade,[2] ruby grape of Proserpine;
Make not your rosary of yew-berries,[3]   5
Nor let the beetle, nor the death-moth be
Your mournful Psyche,[4] nor the downy owl
A partner in your sorrow's mysteries;[5]
For shade to shade will come too drowsily,
And drown the wakeful anguish of the soul.[6]   10

2

But when the melancholy fit shall fall
Sudden from heaven like a weeping cloud,
That fosters the droop-headed flowers all,
And hides the green hill in an April shroud;
Then glut thy sorrow on a morning rose,   15
Or on the rainbow of the salt sand-wave,
Or on the wealth of globéd peonies;
Or if thy mistress some rich anger shows,
Imprison her soft hand, and let her rave,
And feed deep, deep upon her peerless eyes.   20

3

She[7] dwells with Beauty—Beauty that must die;
And Joy, whose hand is ever at his lips
Bidding adieu; and aching Pleasure nigh,
Turning to Poison while the bee-mouth sips:
Aye, in the very temple of Delight   25
Veiled Melancholy has her sov'reign shrine,

1. The waters of forgetfulness in Hades.
2. "Nightshade" and "wolfsbane" (line 2) are poisonous plants. Proserpine is the wife of Pluto and queen of the infernal regions.
3. A symbol of death.
4. In ancient times Psyche (the soul) was sometimes represented as a butterfly or moth, fluttering out of the mouth of a dying man. The allusion may also be to the death's-head moth, which has skull-like markings on its back. The "beetle" of line 6 refers to replicas of the large black beetle, the scarab, which were often placed by Egyptians in their tombs as a symbol of resurrection.
5. Secret religious rites.
6. I.e., sorrow needs contrast to sustain its intensity.
7. I.e., Melancholy, personified as a goddess whose chief place of worship ("shrine," line 26) is located "in the very temple of Delight" (line 25).

Though seen of none save him whose strenuous tongue
  Can burst Joy's grape against his palate fine;[8]
His soul shall taste the sadness of her might,
  And be among her cloudy trophies hung.[9]   30
May, 1819   1820

8. Sensitive, subtly discriminative.
9. A reference to the Greek and Roman practice of hanging trophies in the temples of the gods.

Lamia

Keats himself cited, as the source of his plot, a story in Robert Burton's *Anatomy of Melancholy* (1621): "One Menippus Lycius, a young man twenty-five years of age, that going betwixt Cenchreas and Corinth, met such a phantasm in the habit of a fair gentlewoman, which, taking him by the hand, carried him home to her house, in the suburbs of Corinth. * * * The young man, a philosopher, otherwise staid and discreet, able to moderate his passions, though not this of love, tarried with her a while to his great content, and at last married her, to whose wedding, amongst other guests, came Apollonius; who, by some probable conjectures, found her out to be a serpent, a lamia; and that all her furniture was, like Tantalus' gold, described by Homer, no substance but mere illusions. When she saw herself descried, she wept, and desired Apollonius to be silent, but he would not be moved, and thereupon she, plate, house, and all that was in it, vanished in an instant: many thousands took notice of this fact, for it was done in the midst of Greece."

In ancient demonology, a "lamia"—pronounced *lā'-mĭ-a*—was a monster in woman's form who preyed on human beings. There are various clues (see especially Part II, 229–38) that Keats invested the ancient legend with allegorical significance. Its interpretation, however, and even the inclination of Keats's own sympathies in the contest between Lamia and Apollonius, have been disputed. It is possible that Keats failed to make up his mind, or wavered in the course of composition. What seems to be Keats's indecision, however, may in fact indicate that he intended to present an inevitably fatal situation, in which no one is entirely blameless or blameworthy, and no character is meant to monopolize either our sympathy or antipathy. Lamia is an enchantress, a liar, and a calculating expert in *amour*; but she apparently intends no harm, is genuinely in love, and is very beautiful. And both male protagonists exhibit culpable extremes which alienate our sympathy. Lycius, though an attractive young lover, is gullible, a slave to his passions, and capable of gratuitous cruelty; while Apollonius, though realistically clear-sighted, is rigid, puritanical, and inhumane.

The poem, written between late June and early September, 1819, is a return, after the Spenserian stanzas of *The Eve of St. Agnes*, to the pentameter couplets Keats had used in *Endymion* and other early narrative poems. But Keats had in the meantime been studying Dryden's closed and strong-paced couplets. The initial lines of Dryden's version of Boccaccio's story *Cymon and Iphigenia* will show the kind of narrative model which helped Keats make the technical transition from the fluent but sprawling gracefulness of the opening of *Endymion* to the vigor and economy of the opening of *Lamia:*

In that sweet isle where Venus keeps her court,
And every grace, and all the loves, resort;
Where either sex is formed of softer earth,
And takes the bent of pleasure from their birth;
There lived a Cyprian lord, above the rest
Wise, wealthy, with a numerous issue blest; * * *

Lamia

Part I

Upon a time, before the faery broods
Drove Nymph and Satyr from the prosperous woods,[1]
Before King Oberon's bright diadem,
Scepter, and mantle, clasped with dewy gem,
Frighted away the Dryads and the Fauns   5
From rushes green, and brakes,[2] and cowslipped lawns,
The ever-smitten Hermes empty left
His golden throne, bent warm on amorous theft:[3]
From high Olympus had he stolen light,
On this side of Jove's clouds, to escape the sight   10
Of his great summoner, and made retreat
Into a forest on the shores of Crete.
For somewhere in that sacred island dwelt
A nymph, to whom all hoofèd Satyrs knelt;
At whose white feet the languid Tritons[4] poured   15
Pearls, while on land they withered and adored.
Fast by the springs where she to bathe was wont,
And in those meads where sometimes she might haunt,
Were strewn rich gifts, unknown to any Muse,
Though Fancy's casket were unlocked to choose.   20
Ah, what a world of love was at her feet!
So Hermes thought, and a celestial heat
Burnt from his wingèd heels to either ear,
That from a whiteness, as the lily clear,
Blushed into roses 'mid his golden hair,   25
Fallen in jealous curls about his shoulders bare.[5]
From vale to vale, from wood to wood, he flew,
Breathing upon the flowers his passion new,
And wound with many a river to its head,
To find where this sweet nymph prepared her secret bed: 30
In vain; the sweet nymph might nowhere be found,
And so he rested, on the lonely ground,
Pensive, and full of painful jealousies

1. Nymphs and satyrs—like the dryads and fauns in line 5—were all minor classical deities of the woods and fields, said here to have been driven off by Oberon, king of the fairies, who were supernatural beings of the postclassical era.
2. Thickets.
3. Hermes (or Mercury), wing-footed messenger at the summons of Jove (line 11), was notoriously amorous.
4. Minor sea gods.
5. The curls clung jealously to his bare shoulders. This line is the first of a number of Alexandrines, a device for introducing variety of movement that Keats learned from Dryden. Another such device is the triplet in lines 61–63.

Of the Wood-Gods, and even the very trees.
There as he stood, he heard a mournful voice,   35
Such as once heard, in gentle heart, destroys
All pain but pity: thus the lone voice spake:
"When from this wreathéd tomb shall I awake!
When move in a sweet body fit for life,
And love, and pleasure, and the ruddy strife   40
Of hearts and lips! Ah, miserable me!"
The God, dove-footed,[6] glided silently
Round bush and tree, soft-brushing, in his speed,
The taller grasses and full-flowering weed,
Until he found a palpitating snake,   45
Bright, and cirque-couchant[7] in a dusky brake.

      She was a gordian[8] shape of dazzling hue,
Vermilion-spotted, golden, green, and blue;
Striped like a zebra, freckled like a pard,
Eyed like a peacock,[9] and all crimson barred;   50
And full of silver moons, that, as she breathed,
Dissolved, or brighter shone, or interwreathed
Their lusters with the gloomier tapestries—
So rainbow-sided, touched with miseries,
She seemed, at once, some penanced lady elf,   55
Some demon's mistress, or the demon's self.
Upon her crest she wore a wannish[1] fire
Sprinkled with stars, like Ariadne's tiar:[2]
Her head was serpent, but ah, bitter-sweet!
She had a woman's mouth with all its pearls[3] complete: 60
And for her eyes: what could such eyes do there
But weep, and weep, that they were born so fair?
As Proserpine still weeps for her Sicilian air.[4]
Her throat was serpent, but the words she spake
Came, as through bubbling honey, for Love's sake,   65
And thus; while Hermes on his pinions lay,
Like a stooped falcon[5] ere he takes his prey.

      "Fair Hermes, crowned with feathers, fluttering light,
I had a splendid dream of thee last night:
I saw thee sitting, on a throne of gold,   70
Among the Gods, upon Olympus old,
The only sad•one; for thou didst not hear
The soft, lute-fingered Muses chaunting clear,
Nor even Apollo when he sang alone,
Deaf to his throbbing throat's long, long melodious moan. 75
I dreamt I saw thee, robed in purple flakes,
Break amorous through the clouds, as morning breaks,

6. Quietly as a dove.
7. Lying in a circular coil.
8. Intricately twisted, like the knot tied by King Gordius, which no one could undo.
9. Having multicolored spots, like the "eyes" in a peacock's tail. "Pard": leopard.
1. Rather dark.
2. Ariadne, who was transformed into a constellation, had been represented in a painting by Titian wearing a symbolic crown, or tiara ("tiar"), of stars.
3. "Pearls" had become almost a synonym for teeth in Elizabethan poetry.
4. Proserpine had been carried off to Hades by Pluto from the field of Enna, in Sicily.
5. "Stoop" is the term for the plunge of a falcon upon his prey.

And, swiftly as bright Phoebean dart,[6]
Strike for the Cretan isle; and here thou art!
Too gentle Hermes, hast thou found the maid?"   80
Whereat the star of Lethe[7] not delayed
His rosy eloquence and thus inquired:
"Thou smooth-lipped serpent, surely high inspired!
Thou beauteous wreath, with melancholy eyes,
Possess whatever bliss thou canst devise,   85
Telling me only where my nymph is fled—
Where she doth breathe!" "Bright planet, thou hast said,"
Returned the snake, "but seal with oaths, fair God!"
"I swear," said Hermes, "by my serpent rod,
And by thine eyes, and by thy starry crown!"   90
Light flew his earnest words, among the blossoms blown.
Then thus again the brilliance feminine:
"Too frail of heart! for this lost nymph of thine,
Free as the air, invisibly, she strays
About these thornless wilds; her pleasant days   95
She tastes unseen; unseen her nimble feet
Leave traces in the grass and flowers sweet;
From weary tendrils, and bowed branches green,
She plucks the fruit unseen, she bathes unseen:
And by my power is her beauty veiled   100
To keep it unaffronted, unassailed
By the love-glances of unlovely eyes,
Of Satyrs, Fauns, and bleared Silenus'[8] sighs.
Pale grew her immortality, for woe
Of all these lovers, and she grievéd so   105
I took compassion on her, bade her steep
Her hair in weïrd[9] syrups, that would keep
Her loveliness invisible, yet free
To wander as she loves, in liberty.
Thou shalt behold her, Hermes, thou alone,   110
If thou wilt, as thou swearest, grant my boon!"
Then, once again, the charméd God began
An oath, and through the serpent's ears it ran
Warm, tremulous, devout, psalterian.[1]
Ravished, she lifted her Circean[2] head,   115
Blushed a live damask, and swift-lisping said,
"I was a woman, let me have once more
A woman's shape, and charming as before.
I love a youth of Corinth—O the bliss!
Give me my woman's form, and place me where he is.   120
Stoop, Hermes, let me breathe upon thy brow,
And thou shalt see thy sweet nymph even now."
The God on half-shut feathers sank serene,

6. A ray of Phoebus Apollo, god of the sun.
7. Hermes, when he appeared like a star on the banks of Lethe, in the darkness of Hades. (One of Hermes' offices was to guide the souls of the dead to the lower regions.)
8. Silenus was a satyr, tutor of Bacchus, and always drunk.

9. Magical; Keats makes the word a dissyllable.
1. Either "like a psalm" or "like the sound of the psaltery" (an ancient stringed instrument).
2. Like that of Circe, the enchantress in the *Odyssey*. "Live damask": a living damask rose (large and fragrant pink rose).

She breathed upon his eyes, and swift was seen
Of both the guarded nymph near-smiling on the green.   125
It was no dream; or say a dream it was,
Real are the dreams of Gods, and smoothly pass
Their pleasures in a long immortal dream.
One warm, flushed moment, hovering, it might seem
Dashed by the wood-nymph's beauty, so he burned;   130
Then, lighting on the printless verdure, turned
To the swooned serpent, and with languid arm,
Delicate, put to proof the lithe Caducean charm.[3]
So done, upon the nymph his eyes he bent
Full of adoring tears and blandishment,   135
And towards her stepped: she, like a moon in wane,
Faded before him, cowered, nor could restrain
Her fearful sobs, self-folding like a flower
That faints into itself at evening hour:
But the God fostering her chilléd hand,   140
She felt the warmth, her eyelids opened bland,[4]
And, like new flowers at morning song of bees,
Bloomed, and gave up her honey to the lees.[5]
Into the green-recesséd woods they flew;
Nor grew they pale, as mortal lovers do.   145

   Left to herself, the serpent now began
To change; her elfin blood in madness ran,
Her mouth foamed, and the grass, therewith besprent,[6]
Withered at dew so sweet and virulent;
Her eyes in torture fixed, and anguish drear,   150
Hot, glazed, and wide, with lid-lashes all sear,
Flashed phosphor and sharp sparks, without one cooling tear.
The colors all inflamed throughout her train,
She writhed about, convulsed with scarlet pain:
A deep volcanian[7] yellow took the place   155
Of all her milder-mooonéd body's grace;
And, as the lava ravishes the mead,
Spoilt all her silver mail, and golden brede;[8]
Made gloom of all her frecklings, streaks and bars,
Eclipsed her crescents, and licked up her stars: 160
So that, in moments few, she was undressed
Of all her sapphires, greens, and amethyst,
And rubious-argent:[9] of all these bereft,
Nothing but pain and ugliness were left.
Still shone her crown; that vanished, also she   165
Melted and disappeared as suddenly;
And in the air, her new voice luting soft,
Cried, "Lycius! gentle Lycius!"—Borne aloft
With the bright mists about the mountains hoar
These words dissolved: Crete's forests heard no more.   170

3. I.e., put to the test the magic of the flexible Caduceus (Hermes' official staff).
4. Softly.
5. Dregs.
6. Sprinkled.
7. The color of sulphur (thrown up by a volcano), in contrast to her former silvery moon color.
8. "Mail": interlinked rings, as in a coat of armor; "brede": embroidery, interwoven pattern.
9. Silvery red.

Whither fled Lamia, now a lady bright,
A full-born beauty new and exquisite?
She fled into that valley they pass o'er
Who go to Corinth from Cenchreas' shore;[1]
And rested at the foot of those wild hills,   175
The rugged founts of the Peraean rills,
And of that other ridge whose barren back
Stretches, with all its mist and cloudy rack,
Southwestward to Cleone. There she stood
About a young bird's flutter from a wood,   180
Fair, on a sloping green of mossy tread,
By a clear pool, wherein she passionéd[2]
To see herself escaped from so sore ills,
While her robes flaunted with the daffodils.

Ah, happy Lycius!—for she was a maid   185
More beautiful than ever twisted braid,
Or sighed, or blushed, or on spring-flowered lea[3]
Spread a green kirtle to the minstrelsy:
A virgin purest lipped, yet in the lore
Of love deep learnéd to the red heart's core: 190
Not one hour old, yet of sciential brain
To unperplex bliss from its neighbor pain;[4]
Define their pettish limits, and estrange
Their points of contact, and swift counterchange;
Intrigue with the specious chaos,[5] and dispart   195
Its most ambiguous atoms with sure art;
As though in Cupid's college she had spent
Sweet days a lovely graduate, still unshent,[6]
And kept his rosy terms in idle languishment.

Why this fair creature chose so faerily   200
By the wayside to linger, we shall see;
But first 'tis fit to tell how she could muse
And dream, when in the serpent prison-house,
Of all she list[7] strange or magnificent:
How, ever, where she willed, her spirit went;   205
Whether to faint Elysium, or where
Down through tress-lifting waves the Nereids[8] fair
Wind into Thetis' bower by many a pearly stair;
Or where God Bacchus drains his cups divine,
Stretched out, at ease, beneath a glutinous pine;   210
Or where in Pluto's gardens palatine
Mulciber's columns gleam in far piazzian line.[9]

1. Cenchrea (Keats's "Cenchreas") was a harbor of Corinth, in southern Greece.
2. Felt intense excitement.
3. Meadow; "kirtle": gown.
4. I.e., of knowledgeable ("sciential") brain to disentangle ("unperplex") bliss from its closely-related pain, to define their quarreled-over ("pettish") limits, and to separate out ("estrange") their points of contact and the swift changes of each condition into its opposite. Cf. Keats's *Ode on Melancholy*, lines 25–26.
5. I.e., turn to her own artful purpose the seeming ("specious") chaos.
6. Unspoiled. "Rosy terms": the terms spent studying in "Cupid's college."
7. Wished.
8. Sea nymphs, of whom Thetis (the mother of Achilles) was one.
9. I.e., columns made by Mulciber

And sometimes into cities she would send
Her dream, with feast and rioting to blend;
And once, while among mortals dreaming thus,   215
She saw the young Corinthian Lycius
Charioting foremost in the envious race,
Like a young Jove with calm uneager face,
And fell into a swooning love of him.
Now on the moth-time of that evening dim   220
He would return that way, as well she knew,
To Corinth from the shore; for freshly blew
The eastern soft wind, and his galley now
Grated the quaystones with her brazen prow
In port Cenchreas, from Egina isle   225
Fresh anchored; whither he had been awhile
To sacrifice to Jove, whose temple there
Waits with high marble doors for blood and incense rare.
Jove heard his vows, and bettered his desire;
For by some freakful chance he made retire   230
From his companions, and set forth to walk,
Perhaps grown wearied of their Corinth talk:
Over the solitary hills he fared,
Thoughtless at first, but ere eve's star appeared
His phantasy was lost, where reason fades,   235
In the calmed twilight of Platonic shades.[1]
Lamia beheld him coming, near, more near—
Close to her passing, in indifference drear,
His silent sandals swept the mossy green;
So neighbored to him, and yet so unseen   240
She stood: he passed, shut up in mysteries,
His mind wrapped like his mantle, while her eyes
Followed his steps, and her neck regal white
Turned—syllabling thus, "Ah, Lycius bright,
And will you leave me on the hills alone?   245
Lycius, look back! and be some pity shown."
He did; not with cold wonder fearingly,
But Orpheus-like at an Eurydice;[2]
For so delicious were the words she sung,
It seemed he had loved them a whole summer long: 250
And soon his eyes had drunk her beauty up,
Leaving no drop in the bewildering cup,
And still the cup was full—while he, afraid
Lest she should vanish ere his lip had paid
Due adoration, thus began to adore;   255
Her soft look growing coy, she saw his chain so sure:
"Leave thee alone! Look back! Ah, Goddess, see
Whether my eyes can ever turn from thee!
For pity do not this sad heart belie[3]—

(Vulcan, god of fire and metalworking)
gleam in long lines around open courts
(piazzas). "Palatine": palatial.
1. I.e., he was absorbed in musing
about the obscurities of Plato's philosophy.
2. As Orpheus looked at Eurydice in

Hades. Orpheus was allowed by Pluto
to lead Eurydice back to earth on condition that he not look back at her, but
he could not resist doing so, and lost
her once more.
3. Be false to.

Even as thou vanishest so shall I die. 260
Stay! though a Naiad of the rivers, stay!
To thy far wishes will thy streams obey:
Stay! though the greenest woods be thy domain,
Alone they can drink up the morning rain:
Though a descended Pleiad,[4] will not one 265
Of thine harmonious sisters keep in tune
Thy spheres, and as thy silver proxy shine?
So sweetly to these ravished ears of mine
Came thy sweet greeting, that if thou shouldst fade
Thy memory will waste me to a shade— 270
For pity do not melt!"—"If I should stay,"
Said Lamia, "here, upon this floor of clay,
And pain my steps upon these flowers too rough,
What canst thou say or do of charm enough
To dull the nice[5] remembrance of my home? 275
Thou canst not ask me with thee here to roam
Over these hills and vales, where no joy is—
Empty of immortality and bliss!
Thou art a scholar, Lycius, and must know
That finer spirits cannot breathe below 280
In human climes, and live: Alas! poor youth,
What taste of purer air hast thou to soothe
My essence? What serener palaces,
Where I may all my many senses please,
And by mysterious sleights a hundred thirsts appease? 285
It cannot be—Adieu!" So said, she rose
Tiptoe with white arms spread. He, sick to lose
The amorous promise of her lone complain,
Swooned, murmuring of love, and pale with pain.
The cruel lady, without any show 290
Of sorrow for her tender favorite's woe,
But rather, if her eyes could brighter be,
With brighter eyes and slow amenity,
Put her new lips to his, and gave afresh
The life she had so tangled in her mesh: 295
And as he from one trance was wakening
Into another, she began to sing,
Happy in beauty, life, and love, and everything,
A song of love, too sweet for earthly lyres,
While, like held breath, the stars drew in their panting fires. 300
And then she whispered in such trembling tone,
As those who, safe together met alone
For the first time through many anguished days,
Use other speech than looks; bidding him raise
His drooping head, and clear his soul of doubt, 305
For that she was a woman, and without
Any more subtle fluid in her veins
Than throbbing blood, and that the selfsame pains
Inhabited her frail-strung heart as his.

4. One of the seven sisters composing   5. Detailed, minutely accurate.
the constellation Pleiades.

And next she wondered how his eyes could miss   310
Her face so long in Corinth, where, she said,
She dwelt but half retired, and there had led
Days happy as the gold coin could invent
Without the aid of love; yet in content
Till she saw him, as once she passed him by,   315
Where 'gainst a column he leant thoughtfully
At Venus' temple porch, 'mid baskets heaped
Of amorous herbs and flowers, newly reaped
Late on that eve, as 'twas the night before
The Adonian feast;[6] whereof she saw no more,   320
But wept alone those days, for why should she adore?
Lycius from death awoke into amaze,
To see her still, and singing so sweet lays;
Then from amaze into delight he fell
To hear her whisper woman's lore so well;   325
And every word she spake enticed him on
To unperplexed delight[7] and pleasure known.
Let the mad poets say whate'er they please
Of the sweets of Faeries, Peris,[8] Goddesses,
There is not such a treat among them all,   330
Haunters of cavern, lake, and waterfall,
As a real woman, lineal indeed
From Pyrrha's pebbles[9] or old Adam's seed.
Thus gentle Lamia judged, and judged aright,
That Lycius could not love in half a fright,   335
So threw the goddess off, and won his heart
More pleasantly by playing woman's part,
With no more awe than what her beauty gave,
That, while it smote, still guaranteed to save.
Lycius to all made eloquent reply,   340
Marrying to every word a twinborn sigh;
And last, pointing to Corinth, asked her sweet,
If 'twas too far that night for her soft feet.
The way was short, for Lamia's eagerness
Made, by a spell, the triple league decrease   345
To a few paces; not at all surmised
By blinded Lycius, so in her comprised.[1]
They passed the city gates, he knew not how,
So noiseless, and he never thought to know.

        As men talk in a dream, so Corinth all,   350
Throughout her palaces imperial,
And all her populous streets and temples lewd,[2]
Muttered, like tempest in the distance brewed,
To the wide-spreaded night above her towers.
Men, women, rich and poor, in the cool hours,   355

6. The feast of Adonis, beloved by Venus.
7. I.e., delight not mixed with its neighbor, pain; see line 192.
8. Fairylike creatures in Persian mythology.
9. Descended from the pebbles with which, in Greek myth, Pyrrha and Deucalion repeopled the earth after the flood.
1. Bound up.
2. Temples of Venus, whose worship sometimes involved ritual prostitution.

Shuffled their sandals o'er the pavement white,
Companioned or alone; while many a light
Flared, here and there, from wealthy festivals,
And threw their moving shadows on the walls,
Or found them clustered in the corniced shade   360
Of some arched temple door, or dusky colonnade.

    Muffling his face, of greeting friends in fear,
Her fingers he pressed hard, as one came near
With curled gray beard, sharp eyes, and smooth bald crown,
Slow-stepped, and robed in philosophic gown: 365
Lycius shrank closer, as they met and passed,
Into his mantle, adding wings to haste,
While hurried Lamia trembled: "Ah," said he,
"Why do you shudder, love, so ruefully?
Why does your tender palm dissolve in dew?"—   370
"I'm wearied," said fair Lamia: "tell me who
Is that old man? I cannot bring to mind
His features—Lycius! wherefore did you blind
Yourself from his quick eyes?" Lycius replied,
" 'Tis Apollonius sage, my trusty guide   375
And good instructor; but tonight he seems
The ghost of folly haunting my sweet dreams."

    While yet he spake they had arrived before
A pillared porch, with lofty portal door,
Where hung a silver lamp, whose phosphor glow   380
Reflected in the slabbéd steps below,
Mild as a star in water; for so new,
And so unsullied was the marble hue,
So through the crystal polish, liquid fine,
Ran the dark veins, that none but feet divine   385
Could e'er have touched there. Sounds Aeolian[3]
Breathed from the hinges, as the ample span
Of the wide doors disclosed a place unknown
Some time to any, but those two alone,
And a few Persian mutes, who that same year   390
Were seen about the markets: none knew where
They could inhabit; the most curious
Were foiled, who watched to trace them to their house:
And but the flitter-wingéd verse must tell,
For truth's sake, what woe afterwards befell,   395
'Twould humor many a heart to leave them thus,
Shut from the busy world of more incredulous.

Part II

    Love in a hut, with water and a crust,
Is—Love, forgive us!—cinders, ashes, dust;
Love in a palace is perhaps at last
More grievous torment than a hermit's fast:

3. Like sounds from the wind harp (Aeolus is god of winds), which responds
musically to a current of air.

That is a doubtful tale from faery land,   5
Hard for the non-elect to understand.
Had Lycius lived to hand his story down,
He might have given the moral a fresh frown,
Or clenched it quite: but too short was their bliss
To breed distrust and hate, that make the soft voice hiss.   10
Beside, there, nightly, with terrific glare,
Love, jealous grown of so complete a pair,
Hovered and buzzed his wings, with fearful roar,
Above the lintel of their chamber door,
And down the passage cast a glow upon the floor.   15

    For all this came a ruin: side by side
They were enthronéd, in the eventide,
Upon a couch, near to a curtaining
Whose airy texture, from a golden string,
Floated into the room, and let appear   20
Unveiled the summer heaven, blue and clear,
Betwixt two marble shafts: there they reposed,
Where use had made it sweet, with eyelids closed,
Saving a tithe which love still open kept,
That they might see each other while they almost slept;   25
When from the slope side of a suburb hill,
Deafening the swallow's twitter, came a thrill
Of trumpets—Lycius started—the sounds fled,
But left a thought, a buzzing in his head.
For the first time, since first he harbored in   30
That purple-linéd palace of sweet sin,
His spirit passed beyond its golden bourn
Into the noisy world almost forsworn.
The lady, ever watchful, penetrant,
Saw this with pain, so arguing a want   35
Of something more, more than her empery[4]
Of joys; and she began to moan and sigh
Because he mused beyond her, knowing well
That but a moment's thought is passion's passing bell.[5]
"Why do you sigh, fair creature?" whispered he: 40
"Why do you think?" returned she tenderly:
"You have deserted me—where am I now?
Not in your heart while care weighs on your brow:
No, no, you have dismissed me; and I go
From your breast houseless: aye, it must be so."   45
He answered, bending to her open eyes,
Where he was mirrored small in paradise,
"My silver planet, both of eve and morn![6]
Why will you plead yourself so sad forlorn,
While I am striving how to fill my heart   50
With deeper crimson, and a double smart?
How to entangle, trammel up, and snare
Your soul in mine, and labyrinth you there

4. Empire.
5. Death knell.
6. The planet Venus, which is both the morning and the evening star.

Like the hid scent in an unbudded rose?
Aye, a sweet kiss—you see your mighty woes.[7]   55
My thoughts! shall I unveil them? Listen then!
What mortal hath a prize, that other men
May be confounded and abashed withal,
But lets it sometimes pace abroad majestical,
And triumph, as in thee I should rejoice   60
Amid the hoarse alarm of Corinth's voice.
Let my foes choke, and my friends shout afar,
While through the throngéd streets your bridal car
Wheels round its dazzling spokes."—The lady's cheek
Trembled; she nothing said, but, pale and meek,   65
Arose and knelt before him, wept a rain
Of sorrows at his words; at last with pain
Beseeching him, the while his hand she wrung,
To change his purpose. He thereat was stung,
Perverse, with stronger fancy to reclaim   70
Her wild and timid nature to his aim:
Besides, for all his love, in self-despite,
Against his better self, he took delight
Luxurious in her sorrows, soft and new.
His passion, cruel grown, took on a hue   75
Fierce and sanguineous as 'twas possible
In one whose brow had no dark veins to swell.
Fine was the mitigated fury, like
Apollo's presence when in act to strike
The serpent—Ha, the serpent! certes, she   80
Was none. She burnt, she loved the tyranny,
And, all subdued, consented to the hour
When to the bridal he should lead his paramour.
Whispering in midnight silence, said the youth,
"Sure some sweet name thou hast, though, by my truth,   85
I have not asked it, ever thinking thee
Not mortal, but of heavenly progeny,
As still I do. Hast any mortal name,
Fit appellation for this dazzling frame?
Or friends or kinsfolk on the cited earth,   90
To share our marriage feast and nuptial mirth?"
"I have no friends," said Lamia, "no, not one;
My presence in wide Corinth hardly known:
My parents' bones are in their dusty urns
Sepulchered, where no kindled incense burns,   95
Seeing all their luckless race are dead, save me,
And I neglect the holy rite for thee.
Even as you list invite your many guests;
But if, as now it seems, your vision rests
With any pleasure on me, do not bid   100
Old Apollonius—from him keep me hid."
Lycius, perplexed at words so blind and blank,

---

7. Playfully: "You see how great your troubles were!"

Made close inquiry; from whose touch she shrank,
Feigning a sleep; and he to the dull shade
Of deep sleep in a moment was betrayed.   105

    It was the custom then to bring away
The bride from home at blushing shut of day,
Veiled, in a chariot, heralded along
By strewn flowers, torches, and a marriage song,
With other pageants: but this fair unknown   110
Had not a friend. So being left alone
(Lycius was gone to summon all his kin),
And knowing surely she could never win
His foolish heart from its mad pompousness,
She set herself, high-thoughted, how to dress   115
The misery in fit magnificence.
She did so, but 'tis doubtful how and whence
Came, and who were her subtle servitors.
About the halls, and to and from the doors,
There was a noise of wings, till in short space   120
The glowing banquet room shone with wide-archéd grace.
A haunting music, sole perhaps and lone
Supportress of the faery roof, made moan
Throughout, as fearful the whole charm might fade.
Fresh carvéd cedar, mimicking a glade   125
Of palm and plantain, met from either side,
High in the midst, in honor of the bride:
Two palms and then two plaintains, and so on,
From either side their stems branched one to one
All down the aisléd place; and beneath all   130
There ran a stream of lamps straight on from wall to wall.
So canopied, lay an untasted feast
Teeming with odors. Lamia, regal dressed,
Silently paced about, and as she went,
In pale contented sort of discontent,   135
Missioned her viewless servants to enrich
The fretted[8] splendor of each nook and niche.
Between the tree stems, marbled plain at first,
Came jasper panels; then, anon, there burst
Forth creeping imagery of slighter trees,   140
And with the larger wove in small intricacies.
Approving all, she faded at self-will,
And shut the chamber up, close, hushed and still,
Complete and ready for the revels rude,
When dreadful[9] guests would come to spoil her solitude.   145

    The day appeared, and all the gossip rout.
O senseless Lycius! Madman! wherefore flout
The silent-blessing fate, warm cloistered hours,
And show to common eyes these secret bowers?

---

8. Adorned with fretwork (interlaced   9. Terrifying.
patterns).

The herd approached; each guest, with busy brain,   150
Arriving at the portal, gazed amain,[1]
And entered marveling: for they knew the street,
Remembered it from childhood all complete
Without a gap, yet ne'er before had seen
That royal porch, that high-built fair demesne;[2]   155
So in they hurried all, 'mazed, curious and keen:
Save one, who looked thereon with eye severe,
And with calm-planted steps walked in austere;
'Twas Apollonius: something too he laughed,
As though some knotty problem, that had daft[3]   160
His patient thought, had now begun to thaw,
And solve and melt—'twas just as he foresaw.

He met within the murmurous vestibule
His young disciple. " 'Tis no common rule,
Lycius," said he, "for uninvited guest   165
To force himself upon you, and infest
With an unbidden presence the bright throng
Of younger friends; yet must I do this wrong,
And you forgive me." Lycius blushed, and led
The old man through the inner doors broad-spread;   170
With reconciling words and courteous mien
Turning into sweet milk the sophist's spleen.

Of wealthy luster was the banquet room,
Filled with pervading brilliance and perfume:
Before each lucid panel fuming stood   175
A censer fed with myrrh and spicéd wood,
Each by a sacred tripod held aloft,
Whose slender feet wide-swerved upon the soft
Wool-wooféd[4] carpets: fifty wreaths of smoke
From fifty censers their light voyage took   180
To the high roof, still mimicked as they rose
Along the mirrored walls by twin-clouds odorous.
Twelve spheréd tables, by silk seats ensphered,
High as the level of a man's breast reared
On libbard's[5] paws, upheld the heavy gold   185
Of cups and goblets, and the store thrice told
Of Ceres' horn[6] and, in huge vessels, wine
Come from the gloomy tun with merry shine.
Thus loaded with a feast the tables stood,
Each shrining in the midst the image of a God.   190

When in an antechamber every guest
Had felt the cold full sponge to pleasure pressed,
By minist'ring slaves, upon his hands and feet,
And fragrant oils with ceremony meet

---

1. Intently.
2. Estate.
3. Baffled, bewildered.
4. Woven.

5. Leopard's.
6. The horn of plenty, overflowing with the products of Ceres, goddess of vegetation.

Poured on his hair, they all moved to the feast   195
In white robes, and themselves in order placed
Around the silken couches, wondering
Whence all this mighty cost and blaze of wealth could spring.

    Soft went the music the soft air along,
While fluent Greek a voweled undersong   200
Kept up among the guests, discoursing low
At first, for scarcely was the wine at flow;
But when the happy vintage touched their brains,
Louder they talk, and louder come the strains
Of powerful instruments—the gorgeous dyes,   205
The space, the splendor of the draperies,
The roof of awful richness, nectarous cheer,
Beautiful slaves, and Lamia's self, appear,
Now, when the wine has done its rosy deed,
And every soul from human trammels freed,   210
No more so strange; for merry wine, sweet wine,
Will make Elysian shades not too fair, too divine.
Soon was God Bacchus at meridian height;
Flushed were their cheeks, and bright eyes double bright:
Garlands of every green, and every scent   215
From vales deflowered, or forest trees branch-rent,
In baskets of bright osiered[7] gold were brought
High as the handles heaped, to suit the thought
Of every guest; that each, as he did please,
Might fancy-fit his brows, silk-pillowed at his ease.   220

    What wreath for Lamia? What for Lycius?
What for the sage, old Apollonius?
Upon her aching forehead be there hung
The leaves of willow and of adder's tongue;[8]
And for the youth, quick, let us strip for him   225
The thyrsus,[9] that his watching eyes may swim
Into forgetfulness; and, for the sage,
Let spear-grass and the spiteful thistle wage
War on his temples. Do not all charms fly
At the mere touch of cold philosophy?[1]   230
There was an awful[2] rainbow once in heaven:
We know her woof, her texture; she is given
In the dull catalogue of common things.
Philosophy will clip an Angel's wings,
Conquer all mysteries by rule and line,   235
Empty the haunted air, and gnoméd mine[3]—

7. Plaited. An "osier" is a willow rod used in weaving baskets.
8. A fern whose spikes resemble a serpent's tongue.
9. The vine-covered staff of Bacchus, used to signify drunkenness.
1. "Philosophy" in the sense of "natural philosophy," or science. Benjamin Haydon tells in his *Autobiography* how, at a hard-drinking and high-spirited dinner party, Keats had agreed with Charles Lamb (to what extent jokingly, is not clear) that Newton's *Optics* "had destroyed all the poetry of the rainbow by reducing it to the prismatic colors."
2. Awe-inspiring.
3. Gnomes were guardians of mines.

Unweave a rainbow, as it erewhile made
The tender-personed Lamia melt into a shade.

By her glad Lycius sitting, in chief place,
Scarce saw in all the room another face,   240
Till, checking his love trance, a cup he took
Full brimmed, and opposite sent forth a look
'Cross the broad table, to beseech a glance
From his old teacher's wrinkled countenance,
And pledge him.[4] The bald-head philosopher   245
Had fixed his eye, without a twinkle or stir
Full on the alarmèd beauty of the bride,
Brow-beating her fair form, and troubling her sweet pride.
Lycius then pressed her hand, with devout touch,
As pale it lay upon the rosy couch: 250
'Twas icy, and the cold ran through his veins;
Then sudden it grew hot, and all the pains
Of an unnatural heat shot to his heart.
"Lamia, what means this? Wherefore dost thou start?
Know'st thou that man?" Poor Lamia answered not.   255
He gazed into her eyes, and not a jot
Owned[5] they the lovelorn piteous appeal:
More, more he gazed: his human senses reel:
Some hungry spell that loveliness absorbs;
There was no recognition in those orbs.   260
"Lamia!" he cried—and no soft-toned reply.
The many heard, and the loud revelry
Grew hush; the stately music no more breathes;
The myrtle[5a] sickened in a thousand wreaths.
By faint degrees, voice, lute, and pleasure ceased;   265
A deadly silence step by step increased,
Until it seemed a horrid presence there,
And not a man but felt the terror in his hair.
"Lamia!" he shrieked; and nothing but the shriek
With its sad echo did the silence break.   270
"Begone, foul dream!" he cried, gazing again
In the bride's face, where now no azure vein
Wandered on fair-spaced temples; no soft bloom
Misted the cheek; no passion to illume
The deep-recessèd vision—all was blight;   275
Lamia, no longer fair, there sat a deadly white.
"Shut, shut those juggling[6] eyes, thou ruthless man!
Turn them aside, wretch! or the righteous ban
Of all the Gods, whose dreadful images
Here represent their shadowy presences,   280
May pierce them on the sudden with the thorn
Of painful blindness; leaving thee forlorn,
In trembling dotage to the feeblest fright
Of conscience, for their long offended might,

4. Drink a toast to him.   of love.
5. Acknowledged.   6. Deceiving, full of trickery.
5a. Sacred to Venus, hence an emblem

For all thine impious proud-heart sophistries, 285
Unlawful magic, and enticing lies.
Corinthians! look upon that gray-beard wretch!
Mark how, possessed, his lashless eyelids stretch
Around his demon eyes! Corinthians, see!
My sweet bride withers at their potency." 290
"Fool!" said the sophist, in an undertone
Gruff with contempt; which a death-nighing moan
From Lycius answered, as heart-struck and lost,
He sank supine beside the aching ghost.
"Fool! Fool!" repeated he, while his eyes still 295
Relented not, nor moved; "from every ill
Of life have I preserved thee to this day,
And shall I see thee made a serpent's prey?"
Then Lamia breathed death breath; the sophist's eye,
Like a sharp spear, went through her utterly, 300
Keen, cruel, perceant,[7] stinging: she, as well
As her weak hand could any meaning tell,
Motioned him to be silent; vainly so,
He looked and looked again a level—No!
"A serpent!" echoed he; no sooner said, 305
Than with a frightful scream she vanishéd:
And Lycius' arms were empty of delight,
As were his limbs of life, from that same night.
On the high couch he lay!—his friends came round—
Supported him—no pulse, or breath they found, 310
And, in its marriage robe, the heavy body wound.
July–Aug., 1819 1820

7. Piercing.

The Fall of Hyperion
In September of 1818, at the close of his twenty-third year and while he was serving as nurse to his dying brother Tom, Keats undertook an epic poem, modeled on *Paradise Lost*, which he called *Hyperion*. Its subject, the displacement of Saturn and his fellow Titans by Zeus and the other Olympians, was taken from Greek mythology, but the primary epic question, like that in *Paradise Lost*, was *unde malum?*—whence and why evil? Keats set out to represent an answer, not in terms of the Christian or any other religious creed, but in humanistic terms, delimited to man and his natural milieu. The Titans had been equable and benign gods, ruling in the Saturnian, or golden, age of general felicity. Yet at the beginning of the poem all the Titans except Hyperion, god of the sun, have been dethroned; and the uncomprehending Saturn again and again raises the question, Who? Why? How? Is there blank unreason and injustice at the heart of the universe? Oceanus, god of the sea, offers a valid but incomplete solution: the gods, though themselves blameless, have fallen in the natural progression of things, according to which each stage of development is fated to give place to a higher excellence, "for 'tis the eternal law / That first in beauty should be first in might." And it is the part of wisdom and virtue among the Titans to accept this truth uncomplainingly,

> for to bear all naked truths,
> And to envisage circumstance, all calm,
> That is the top of sovereignty.

In Book III of the original *Hyperion* this is supplemented by the experience of Apollo, still a youth on earth but destined to displace Hyperion among the heavenly powers. He lives in "aching ignorance" of the universe and its processes, but he is aware of his ignorance and avid for knowledge. To him appears Mnemosyne, herself a Titan, but one who has deserted her fellow gods "For prophecies of thee, and for the sake / Of loveliness new born." Suddenly Apollo reads in the face of Mnemosyne—goddess of memory, who will be mother of the muses, and so of all the arts—the silent record of the defeat of the Titans and at once soars to the knowledge that he seeks: the deep understanding, at once intoxicating and agonizing, that life involves process, and process entails change and suffering, and that there can be no creative progress except by the defeat and destruction of the preceding stage. Apollo cries out:

> Knowledge enormous makes a god of me.
> Names, deeds, gray legends, dire events, rebellions,
> Majesties, sovran voices, agonies,
> Creations and destroyings, all at once
> Pour into the wide hollows of my brain
> And deify me, as if of some blithe wine
> Or elixir peerless I had drunk,
> And so become immortal.

This is an enlargement of Apollo's awareness to encompass the sense of the tragic nature of life which it has been the Titans' deficiency to lack. As the fragment breaks off Apollo is transfigured, like one who should "with fierce convulse / Die into life," not only into the god of the sun, who has earned the right to displace Hyperion, but also into the god of the highest poetry.

This extraordinary fragment Keats wrote mainly in the two months between late September and December, 1818, and he abandoned it entirely by April of 1819. Late that summer, however, he took up the theme again, under the title *The Fall of Hyperion: A Dream*. This time his primary model is Dante, especially the *Purgatorio*, which he had been carefully studying in Cary's translation. In *The Divine Comedy* all the narrated events had been represented as a vision granted to Dante at the beginning of the poem. In similar fashion Keats begins his new poem with a long induction in which the poet, in a dream, earns the right to a vision finally granted him by Moneta (her Latin name suggests "the Admonisher"), who replaces Mnemosyne; this vision incorporates the epic events narrated in the first *Hyperion*. The induction, in effect, shifts the center of poetic concern from the epic action to the evolving consciousness of the narrative poet himself, as he seeks his identity and status; it serves also to displace the earlier ordeal through which Apollo had become god of poetry by the ordeal of this particular poet.

As early as *Sleep and Poetry* (1816), Keats had begun to explore the baffling relation of dreams to insight, of wishful fantasies and illusions to imaginative truth, of the life of actuality and of humane action to the contemplative vision of the poet; and he had worked these matters into his poetic program to move from the realm of "Flora, and old Pan" to the "nobler life" of "the agonies, the strife / Of human hearts." He continued to widen these speculations in *Endymion* and a number of his shorter poems; and his letters show his ceaseless effort to assimilate his ever-enlarging experience, his sharpening sense of suffering humanity, and his awareness of the need for some equivalent of the "salvation" offered by a religious creed he could not accept, into his theory and program of poetry. (See especially the letters, included here, on "The Chambers of Human Life" and on "The Vale of Soul-Making.") Into the induction to the long "Dream" which constitutes *The Fall of Hyperion*, Keats works the results of his sustained attempts to differentiate escapist dreams, as well as the creeds of the religious "fanatic," from the imaginative vision of the poet; he presents these results as progressive discoveries which he had made at the various stages of his own development as a poet. The induction, therefore, is Keats's equivalent of a poem he never saw, Wordsworth's *Prelude*, the account of "the Growth of a Poet's Mind." But whereas Wordsworth had represented his evolution of mind, up to and through the crisis in which he discovered his poetic identity, in the mode of literal autobiography, Keats instead employs the pattern of a ritual initiation. In the course of this agonizing rite of passage the poet progresses, in quantum leaps of expanding awareness of what it is to be human, and a poet of humanity, to the stage at which, having passed through and beyond the sufferings of ordinary experience to achieve aesthetic insight and distance—the power (line 304) "To see as a god sees"—he has defined the kind of poet he is and earned the right to essay his epic poem of tragic suffering.

A number of reasons impelled Keats to abandon *The Fall of Hyperion* at the sixty-first line of the second Canto. Keats wrote to Reynolds on September 21, 1819:

I have given up Hyperion . . . Miltonic verse cannot be written but in an artful or rather artist's humour. I wish to give myself up to other sensations. English ought to be kept up. It may be interesting to you to pick out some lines from Hyperion and put a mark X to the false beauty proceeding from art, and one ‖ to the true voice of feeling.

The two *Hyperions* are astonishing achievements; but they are achievements, as Keats, with his matchless acumen in self-criticism recognized, which have the air of artistic *tours de force*, written in an age in which the high artifice of the epic matter and style had ceased to be the natural voice of the poet. In the same letter Keats mentions having composed two days earlier the ode *To Autumn*; in this, his last and most flawless major poem, the poet had envisaged the circumstance of the cycle of life and death, all calm, and had uttered his experience in the true voice of feeling.

The Fall of Hyperion

A DREAM

Canto I

Fanatics have their dreams, wherewith they weave
A paradise for a sect; the savage too
From forth the loftiest fashion of his sleep

Guesses at Heaven; pity these have not
Traced upon vellum or wild Indian leaf   5
The shadows of melodious utterance.
But bare of laurel they live, dream, and die;
For Poesy alone can tell her dreams,
With the fine spell of words alone can save
Imagination from the sable chain   10
And dumb enchantment. Who alive can say,
"Thou art no Poet—may'st not tell thy dreams"?
Since every man whose soul is not a clod
Hath visions, and would speak, if he had loved,
And been well nurtured in his mother tongue.   15
Whether the dream now purposed to rehearse
Be poet's or fanatic's will be known
When this warm scribe, my hand, is in the grave.

    Methought I stood where trees of every clime,
Palm, myrtle, oak, and sycamore, and beech,   20
With plantain, and spice-blossoms, made a screen;
In neighborhood of fountains (by the noise
Soft-showering in my ears), and (by the touch
Of scent) not far from roses. Turning round
I saw an arbor with a drooping roof   25
Of trellis vines, and bells, and larger blooms,
Like floral censers, swinging light in air;
Before its wreathéd doorway, on a mound
Of moss, was spread a feast of summer fruits,
Which, nearer seen, seemed refuse of a meal   30
By angel tasted or our Mother Eve;[1]
For empty shells were scattered on the grass,
And grape-stalks but half bare, and remnants more,
Sweet smelling, whose pure kinds I could not know.
Still was more plenty than the fabled horn[2]   35
Thrice emptied could pour forth, at banqueting
For Proserpine returned to her own fields,[3]
Where the white heifers low. And appetite
More yearning than on Earth I ever felt
Growing within, I ate deliciously;   40
And, after not long, thirsted, for thereby
Stood a cool vessel of transparent juice,
Sipped by the wandered bee, the which I took,
And, pledging all the mortals of the world,
And all the dead whose names are in our lips,   45
Drank. That full draught is parent of my theme.[4]
No Asian poppy nor elixir fine

1. In *Paradise Lost* V.321 ff., Eve serves the visiting angel, Raphael, with a meal of fruits and fruit juices. Keats thus adapts Milton's Eden to represent the early stage of his own experience and poetry.
2. The cornucopia, or horn of plenty.
3. When Proserpine each year is released by her husband, Pluto, god of the underworld, for a sojourn on earth, it is the beginning of spring.
4. The drink puts the poet to sleep and effects the dream within a dream which constitutes the rest of his poem.

Of the soon-fading jealous Caliphat;[5]
No poison gendered in close monkish cell,
To thin the scarlet conclave of old men,[6]   50
Could so have rapt unwilling life away.
Among the fragrant husks and berries crushed,
Upon the grass I struggled hard against
The domineering potion; but in vain:
The cloudy swoon came on, and down I sunk,   55
Like a Silenus[7] on an antique vase.
How long I slumbered 'tis a chance to guess.
When sense of life returned, I started up
As if with wings; but the fair trees were gone,
The mossy mound and arbor were no more: 60
I looked around upon the carvéd sides
Of an old sanctuary with roof august,
Builded so high, it seemed that filméd clouds
Might spread beneath, as o'er the stars of heaven;
So old the place was, I remembered none   65
The like upon the Earth: what I had seen
Of gray cathedrals, buttressed walls, rent towers,
The superannuations of sunk realms,
Or Nature's rocks toiled hard in waves and winds,
Seemed but the faulture of decrepit things   70
To that eternal doméd Monument.—
Upon the marble at my feet there lay
Store of strange vessels and large draperies,
Which needs had been of dyed asbestos wove,
Or in that place the moth could not corrupt,[8]   75
So white the linen, so, in some, distinct
Ran imageries from a somber loom.
All in a mingled heap confused there lay
Robes, golden tongs, censer and chafing dish,
Girdles, and chains, and holy jewelries.[9]   80

Turning from these with awe, once more I raised
My eyes to fathom the space every way;
The embosséd roof, the silent massy range
Of columns north and south, ending in mist
Of nothing; then to eastward, where black gates   85
Were shut against the sunrise evermore.[1]
Then to the west I looked, and saw far off
An image, huge of feature as a cloud,
At level of whose feet an altar slept,
To be approached on either side by steps,   90

---

5. A council of Caliphs, Mohammedan rulers, who plot to kill each other with a poisonous draft ("elixir").
6. The College of Cardinals.
7. An elderly satyr, usually represented as dead drunk.
8. Matthew vi.20. "Lay up for yourselves treasures in heaven, where neither moth nor rust doth corrupt."

9. Offerings to the gods were spread on the floor of Greek temples.
1. The poet cannot turn back to his origin in the east, and the ways north and south lead nowhere; he must travel the way of mortal life toward the sunset. Cf. the westering course of the sun in Wordsworth's *Ode: Intimations of Immortality*.

And marble balustrade, and patient travail
To count with toil the innumerable degrees.
Towards the altar sober-paced I went,
Repressing haste, as too unholy there;
And, coming nearer, saw beside the shrine   95
One minist'ring;[2] and there arose a flame.
When in mid-May the sickening East wind
Shifts sudden to the south, the small warm rain
Melts out the frozen incense from all flowers,
And fills the air with so much pleasant health   100
That even the dying man forgets his shroud;
Even so that lofty sacrificial fire,
Sending forth Maian[3] incense, spread around
Forgetfulness of everything but bliss,
And clouded all the altar with soft smoke;   105
From whose white fragrant curtains thus I heard
Language pronounced: "If thou canst not ascend
These steps,[4] die on that marble where thou art.
Thy flesh, near cousin to the common dust,
Will parch for lack of nutriment—thy bones   110
Will wither in few years, and vanish so
That not the quickest eye could find a grain
Of what thou now art on that pavement cold.
The sands of thy short life are spent this hour,
And no hand in the universe can turn   115
Thy hourglass, if these gummed leaves be burnt
Ere thou canst mount up these immortal steps."
I heard, I looked: two senses both at once,
So fine, so subtle, felt the tyranny
Of that fierce threat and the hard task proposed.   120
Prodigious seemed the toil; the leaves were yet
Burning—when suddenly a palsied chill
Struck from the paved level up my limbs,
And was ascending quick to put cold grasp
Upon those streams that pulse beside the throat: 125
I shrieked, and the sharp anguish of my shriek
Stung my own ears—I strove hard to escape
The numbness; strove to gain the lowest step.
Slow, heavy, deadly was my pace: the cold
Grew stifling, suffocating, at the heart;   130
And when I clasped my hands I felt them not.
One minute before death, my iced foot touched
The lowest stair; and as it touched, life seemed
To pour in at the toes: I mounted up,
As once fair angels on a ladder flew   135
From the green turf to Heaven.[5] "Holy Power,"

2. Who identifies herself, line 226, as
Moneta.
3. Maia was one of the Pleiades, a
daughter of Atlas and (by Zeus) the
mother of Hermes.
4. These steps which the poet must ascend to knowledge were probably sug-

gested by the stairs going up the steep
side of the Purgatorial Mount, in Dante's
Purgatorio.
5. The ladder by which, in a dream,
Jacob saw angels passing between heaven
and earth; Genesis xxviii.12 and *Paradise Lost* III.510–15.

Cried I, approaching near the hornéd shrine,[6]
"What am I that should so be saved from death?
What am I that another death come not
To choke my utterance sacrilegious, here?"   140
Then said the veiléd shadow: "Thou hast felt
What 'tis to die and live again before
Thy fated hour, that thou hadst power to do so
Is thy own safety; thou hast dated on
Thy doom."[7] "High Prophetess," said I, "purge off,   145
Benign, if so it please thee, my mind's film."
"None can usurp this height," returned that shade,
"But those to whom the miseries of the world
Are misery, and will not let them rest.
All else who find a haven in the world,   150
Where they may thoughtless sleep away their days,
If by a chance into this fane[8] they come,
Rot on the pavement where thou rottedst half."[9]
"Are there not thousands in the world," said I,
Encouraged by the sooth voice of the shade,   155
"Who love their fellows even to the death,
Who feel the giant agony of the world,
And more, like slaves to poor humanity,
Labor for mortal good? I sure should see
Other men here; but I am here alone."   160
"Those whom thou spak'st of are no vision'ries,"
Rejoined that voice. "They are no dreamers weak,
They seek no wonder but the human face;
No music but a happy-noted voice—
They come not here, they have no thought to come—   165
And thou art here, for thou art less than they.
What benefit canst thou, or all thy tribe,
To the great world? Thou art a dreaming thing,
A fever of thyself—think of the earth;
What bliss even in hope is there for thee?   170
What haven? every creature hath its home;
Every sole man hath days of joy and pain,
Whether his labors be sublime or low—
The pain alone, the joy alone, distinct.
Only the dreamer venoms all his days,   175
Bearing more woe than all his sins deserve.
Therefore, that happiness be somewhat shared,
Such things as thou art are admitted oft
Into like gardens thou didst pass erewhile,
And suffered in these temples: for that cause   180
Thou standest safe beneath this statue's knees."
"That I am favored for unworthiness,

6. As e.g., in Exodus xxvii.2, "And
thou shalt make the horns of [the altar]
upon the four corners thereof." In his
description of the temple and its accoutrements. Keats deliberately mingles
Hebrew, Christian, and pagan elements,
to represent the poet's passage through
the stage represented by all religions,
which are "dreams" made into the creed
for "a sect" (lines 1–18).
7. I.e., you have postponed the time
when you will be judged.
8. Temple.
9. I.e., "where you halfway rotted."

By such propitious parley medicined
In sickness not ignoble, I rejoice,
Aye, and could weep for love of such award." 185
So answered I, continuing, "If it please,
[1][Majestic shadow, tell me: sure not all
Those melodies sung into the World's ear
Are useless: sure a poet is a sage;
A humanist, physician to all men. 190
That I am none I feel, as vultures feel
They are no birds when eagles are abroad.
What am I then: Thou spakest of my tribe:
What tribe?" The tall shade veiled in drooping white
Then spake, so much more earnest, that the breath 195
Moved the thin linen folds that drooping hung
About a golden censer from the hand
Pendent—"Art thou not of the dreamer tribe?
The poet and the dreamer are distinct,
Diverse, sheer opposite, antipodes. 200
The one pours out a balm upon the World,
The other vexes it." Then shouted I
Spite of myself, and with a Pythia's spleen,[2]
"Apollo! faded! O far flown Apollo!
Where is thy misty pestilence[3] to creep 205
Into the dwellings, through the door crannies
Of all mock lyrists, large self worshipers
And careless Hectorers in proud bad verse?[4]
Though I breathe death with them it will be life
To see them sprawl before me into graves.][5] 210

1. Keats's friend, Richard Woodhouse, crossed out lines 187–210 in a manuscript of the poem, with the marginal comment next to lines 197–99: "K. seems to have intended to erase this & the next 21 lines." Perhaps his ground for this opinion is the repetition between lines 187 and 211, and between lines 194–98 and 216–20. Since there is no good evidence, however, that Keats planned to do more than merely revise this crucial passage, it is usually reprinted (as here) in brackets.
2. With the anger ("spleen") of the Pythia, the priestess who served at Delphi as the oracle of Apollo, the god of poetry.
3. Apollo was a sender of plagues, as well as the inspirer of prophecy and poetry.
4. This has been conjectured as referring to Byron, or else to several contemporaries, including Shelley and Wordsworth. But the poetic types, not individuals, are all that matter to Keats's argument.
5. In lines 147–210, we find a series of progressive distinctions: (1) between humanitarians who feel for "the miseries of the world" and those men who are "thoughtless" sleepers (lines 147–53);

(2) within the class of humanitarians, between those who actively "benefit * * * the great world" and the poets who are "visionaries" and "dreamers" (lines 161–69); (3) and within the class of poets, between those who are merely dreamers and those who are sages and healers (lines 187–202). As in the colloquy between Asia and Demogorgon (see above, Shelley's *Prometheus Unbound*, II.1–128), the interchange here represents, in dramatized form, a process of inner analysis and self-discovery on the part of the questing poet. Moneta's charges should not be read as final judgments but as tests to determine the "tribe" to which he belongs—tests he passes by the nature of the responses he makes. The fact that Moneta continuously alters the categories by which she judges him signifies that, in the very course of his self-investigation, he changes and grows into what he is at the end of the process. At this point, the fact that the narrator himself proceeds to bring charges against self-indulgent and irresponsible poets distinguishes him from the class of poets he denounces and thus shows that he is ready for the final stage of his ordeal, his initiation into the realm of the highest poetry,

Majestic shadow, tell me where I am,
Whose altar this; for whom this incense curls;
What image this whose face I cannot see,
For the broad marble knees; and who thou art,
Of accent feminine so courteous?"   215

    Then the tall shade, in drooping linens veiled,
Spoke out, so much more earnest, that her breath
Stirred the thin folds of gauze that drooping hung
About a golden censer from her hand
Pendent; and by her voice I knew she shed   220
Long-treasured tears. "This temple, sad and lone,
Is all spared from the thunder of a war
Foughten long since by giant hierarchy
Against rebellion: this old image here,
Whose carvéd features wrinkled as he fell,   225
Is Saturn's; I Moneta, left supreme,
Sole Priestess of his desolation."
I had no words to answer, for my tongue,
Useless, could find about its rooféd home
No syllable of a fit majesty   230
To make rejoinder to Moneta's mourn.
There was a silence, while the altar's blaze
Was fainting for sweet food. I looked thereon,
And on the pavéd floor, where nigh were piled
Faggots of cinnamon, and many heaps   235
Of other crispéd spice-wood; then again
I looked upon the altar, and its horns
Whitened with ashes, and its lang'rous flame,
And then upon the offerings again;
And so by turns—till sad Moneta cried,   240
"The sacrifice is done, but not the less
Will I be kind to thee for thy good will.
My power, which to me is still a curse,
Shall be to thee a wonder; for the scenes
Still swooning vivid through my globéd brain,   245
With an electral changing misery,
Thou shalt with those dull mortal eyes behold,
Free from all pain, if wonder pain thee not."
As near as an immortal's spheréd words
Could to a mother's soften, were these last: 250
And yet I had a terror of her robes,
And chiefly of the veils, that from her brow
Hung pale, and curtained her in mysteries,
That made my heart too small to hold its blood.
This saw that Goddess, and with sacred hand   255
Parted the veils. Then saw I a wan face,
Not pined by human sorrows, but bright-blanched

through the revelation of the "high
tragedy" (line 277) of what it means
to be human. This ultimate enlightenment, which begins with line 291 and
which was intended to constitute the
remainder of the poem, is a vision in a
dream within a dream (see line 46 and
footnote).

By an immortal sickness which kills not;
It works a constant change, which happy death
Can put no end to; deathwards progressing   260
To no death was that visage; it had passed
The lily and the snow; and beyond these
I must not think now, though I saw that face—
But for her eyes I should have fled away.
They held me back, with a benignant light,   265
Soft mitigated by divinest lids
Half-closed, and visionless entire they seemed
Of all external things; they saw me not,
But in blank splendor, beamed like the mild moon,
Who comforts those she sees not, who knows not   270
What eyes are upward cast. As I had found
A grain of gold upon a mountain's side,
And twinged with avarice strained out my eyes
To search its sullen entrails rich with ore,
So at the view of sad Moneta's brow,   275
I ached to see what things the hollow brain
Behind enwombéd: what high tragedy
In the dark secret chambers of her skull
Was acting, that could give so dread a stress
To her cold lips, and fill with such a light   280
Her planetary eyes; and touch her voice
With such a sorrow. "Shade of Memory!"
Cried I, with act adorant at her feet,
"By all the gloom hung round thy fallen house,
By this last temple, by the golden age,   285
By great Apollo, thy dear Foster Child,
And by thyself, forlorn divinity,
The pale Ómega[6] of a withered race,
Let me behold, according as thou saidst,
What in thy brain so ferments to and fro!"   290
No sooner had this conjuration passed
My devout lips, than side by side we stood
(Like a stunt bramble by a solemn pine)
Deep in the shady sadness of a vale,[7]
Far sunken from the healthy breath of morn,   295
Far from the fiery noon and eve's one star.
Onward I looked beneath the gloomy boughs,
And saw, what first I thought an image huge,
Like to the image pedestaled so high
In Saturn's temple. Then Moneta's voice   300
Came brief upon mine ear: "So Saturn sat
When he had lost his Realms—" whereon there grew
A power within me of enormous ken
To see as a god sees, and take the depth

6. The long *O*, final letter of the Greek alphabet; hence, "last member."
7. This was the opening line of the original *Hyperion*. The rest of the poem is a revised version of part of that first text, with the poet now represented as allowed to envision the course of events which Moneta remembers (lines 282, 289–90).

Of things as nimbly as the outward eye   305
Can size and shape pervade. The lofty theme
At those few words hung vast before my mind,
With half-unraveled web. I set myself
Upon an eagle's watch, that I might see,
And seeing ne'er forget. No stir of life   310
Was in this shrouded vale, not so much air
As in the zoning[8] of a summer's day
Robs not one light seed from the feathered grass,
But where the dead leaf fell there did it rest:
A stream went voiceless by, still deadened more   315
By reason of the fallen Divinity
Spreading more shade; the Naiad[9] 'mid her reeds
Pressed her cold finger closer to her lips.

    Along the margin-sand large footmarks went
No farther than to where old Saturn's feet   320
Had rested, and there slept, how long a sleep!
Degraded, cold, upon the sodden ground
His old right hand lay nerveless, listless, dead,
Unsceptred; and his realmless eyes[1] were closed,
While his bowed head seemed listening to the Earth,   325
His ancient mother,[2] for some comfort yet.

    It seemed no force could wake him from his place;
But there came one who, with a kindred hand
Touched his wide shoulders after bending low
With reverence, though to one who knew it not.   330
Then came the grievèd voice of Mnemosyne,[3]
And grieved I hearkened. "That divinity
Whom thou saw'st step from yon forlornest wood,
And with slow pace approach our fallen King,
Is Thea,[4] softest-natured of our Brood."   335
I marked the Goddess in fair statuary
Surpassing wan Moneta by the head,[5]
And in her sorrow nearer woman's tears.
There was a listening fear in her regard,
As if calamity had but begun;   340
As if the vanward clouds[6] of evil days
Had spent their malice, and the sullen rear
Was with its stored thunder laboring up.
One hand she pressed upon that aching spot
Where beats the human heart, as if just there,   345
Though an immortal, she felt cruel pain;
The other upon Saturn's bended neck
She laid, and to the level of his hollow ear

---

8. Course.
9. Water nymph.
1. Saturn's eyes, when open, express the fact that he has lost his realm.
2. Saturn and the other Titans were the children of Heaven and Earth.
3. As in II.50 below, Keats substitutes for "Moneta" the "Mnemosyne" of the first *Hyperion*. This may be a slip, but more likely indicates an alternative name for Moneta, in her role as participant in, and commentator on, the tragic action.
4. Sister and wife of Hyperion.
5. I.e., Thea was a head taller than Moneta.
6. The front line of clouds.

Leaning with parted lips, some words she spoke
In solemn tenor and deep organ tune;   350
Some mourning words, which in our feeble tongue
Would come in this-like accenting; how frail
To that large utterance of the early Gods!

    "Saturn! look up—and for what, poor lost King?[7]
I have no comfort for thee; no, not one;   355
I cannot cry, 'Wherefore thus sleepest thou?'
For Heaven is parted from thee, and the Earth
Knows thee not, so afflicted, for a God;
And Ocean too, with all its solemn noise,
Has from thy scepter passed, and all the air   360
Is emptied of thine hoary majesty:
Thy thunder, captious at the new command,
Rumbles reluctant o'er our fallen house;
And thy sharp lightning, in unpracticed hands,
Scorches and burns our once serene domain.   365
With such remorseless speed still come new woes,
That unbelief has not a space to breathe.[8]
Saturn! sleep on—me thoughtless,[1] why should I
Thus violate thy slumbrous solitude?
Why should I ope thy melancholy eyes?   370
Saturn! sleep on, while at thy feet I weep."

    As when upon a trancéd summer-night
Forests, branch-charméd by the earnest stars,[2]
Dream, and so dream all night without a noise,
Save from one gradual solitary gust,   375
Swelling upon the silence; dying off;
As if the ebbing air had but one wave;
So came these words, and went; the while in tears
She pressed her fair large forehead to the earth,
Just where her fallen hair might spread in curls,   380
A soft and silken mat for Saturn's feet.
Long, long those two were postured motionless,
Like sculpture builded up upon the grave
Of their own power. A long awful time
I looked upon them: still they were the same;   385
The frozen God still bending to the earth,
And the sad Goddess weeping at his feet,
Moneta silent. Without stay or prop,
But my own weak mortality, I bore
The load of this eternal quietude,   390
The unchanging gloom, and the three fixéd shapes
Ponderous upon my senses, a whole moon.
For by my burning brain I measured sure

---

7. Keats several times recalls *King Lear*,
in representing the condition of Saturn.
8. I.e., that disbelief has not an instant
to catch its breath.
1. I.e., how thoughtless I am!
2. Keats here sacrifices to epic severity

a notable figure in the first *Hyperion*
I, 72 ff., "As when, upon a trancéd
summer-night / Those green-robed sena-
tors of mighty woods, / Tall oaks,
branch-charméd by the earnest stars, /
Dream * * *.

Her silver seasons shedded on the night,
And ever day by day methought I grew
More gaunt and ghostly. Oftentimes I prayed   395
Intense, that Death would take me from the Vale
And all its burdens—gasping with despair
Of change, hour after hour I cursed myself;
Until old Saturn raised his faded eyes,   400
And looked around and saw his kingdom gone,
And all the gloom and sorrow of the place,
And that fair kneeling Goddess at his feet.
As the moist scent of flowers, and grass, and leaves,
Fills forest dells with a pervading air,   405
Known to the woodland nostril, so the words
Of Saturn filled the mossy glooms around,
Even to the hollows of time-eaten oaks,
And to the windings of the foxes' holes,
With sad low tones, while thus he spake, and sent   410
Strange musings to the solitary Pan.
"Moan, brethren, moan; for we are swallowed up
And buried from all godlike exercise
Of influence benign on planets pale,
And peaceful sway above man's harvesting,   415
And all those acts which Deity supreme
Doth ease its heart of love in. Moan and wail,
Moan, brethren, moan; for lo, the rebel spheres
Spin round, the stars their ancient courses keep,
Clouds still with shadowy moisture haunt the earth,   420
Still suck their fill of light from sun and moon;
Still buds the tree, and still the sea-shores murmur;
There is no death in all the Universe,
No smell of death—there shall be death[3]—moan, moan;
Moan, Cybele,[4] moan; for thy pernicious Babes   425
Have changed a god into a shaking palsy.
Moan, brethren, moan, for I have no strength left;
Weak as the reed—weak—feeble as my voice—
Oh, oh, the pain, the pain of feebleness.
Moan, moan, for still I thaw—or give me help;   430
Throw down those Imps,[5] and give me victory.
Let me hear other groans, and trumpets blown
Of triumph calm, and hymns of festival,
From the gold peaks of heaven's high-piléd clouds;
Voices of soft proclaim,[6] and silver stir   435
Of strings in hollow shells; and let there be
Beautiful things made new for the surprise
Of the sky-children." So he feebly ceased,
With such a poor and sickly sounding pause,
Methought I heard some old man of the earth   440

3. The passing of the Saturnian golden age (paralleled by Keats with the fable of the loss of Eden) has introduced suffering, and will also introduce death.
4. Pronounced Sĭb'elē; the wife of Saturn and mother of the Olympian gods, who have overthrown their parents.
5. I.e., his rebellious children.
6. Used as a noun, "proclamation."

Bewailing earthly loss; nor could my eyes
And ears act with that pleasant unison of sense
Which marries sweet sound with the grace of form,
And dolorous accent from a tragic harp
With large-limbed visions.[7]—More I scrutinized: 445
Still fixed he sat beneath the sable trees,
Whose arms spread straggling in wild serpent forms,
With leaves all hushed; his awful presence there
(Now all was silent) gave a deadly lie
To what I erewhile heard—only his lips   450
Trembled amid the white curls of his beard.
They told the truth, though, round, the snowy locks
Hung nobly, as upon the face of heaven
A mid-day fleece of clouds. Thea arose,
And stretched her white arm through the hollow dark,   455
Pointing some whither: whereat he too rose
Like a vast giant, seen by men at sea
To grow pale from the waves at dull midnight.[8]
They melted from my sight into the woods;
Ere I could turn, Moneta cried, "These twain   460
Are speeding to the families of grief,
Where roofed in by black rocks they waste, in pain
And darkness, for no hope."—And she spake on,
As ye may read who can unwearied pass
Onward from the Antechamber of this dream,   465
Where even at the open doors awhile
I must delay, and glean my memory
Of her high phrase—perhaps no further dare.

Canto II

"Mortal, that thou may'st understand aright,
I humanize my sayings to thine ear,
Making comparisons of earthly things;
Or thou might'st better listen to the wind,
Whose language is to thee a barren noise,   5
Though it blows legend-laden through the trees.—
In melancholy realms big tears are shed,
More sorrow like to this, and suchlike woe,
Too huge for mortal tongue, or pen of scribe.
The Titans fierce, self hid or prison bound,   10
Groan for the old allegiance[9] once more,
Listening in their doom for Saturn's voice.
But one of our whole eagle-brood still keeps
His sov'reignty, and rule, and majesty;
Blazing Hyperion on his orbéd fire   15
Still sits, still snuffs the incense teeming up
From Man to the Sun's God—yet unsecure,
For as upon the earth dire prodigies[1]

---

7. I.e., he could not attach this speech, like that of a feebly complaining old mortal, to the visible form of the large-limbed god who uttered it.
8. I.e., like a giant who is seen by men at sea to emerge, pale, from the waves.
9. The meter requires four syllables: al-lé-gī-ánce.
1. Terrifying omens.

Fright and perplex, so also shudders he;
Nor at dog's howl or gloom-bird's even screech,   20
Or the familiar visitings of one
Upon the first toll of his passing bell:[2]
But horrors, portioned to a giant nerve,
Make great Hyperion ache. His palace bright,
Bastioned with pyramids of glowing gold,   25
And touched with shade of bronzéd obelisks,
Glares a blood-red through all the thousand courts,
Arches, and domes, and fiery galleries;
And all its curtains of Aurorian clouds
Flush angerly; when he would taste the wreaths   30
Of incense breathed aloft from sacred hills,
Instead of sweets, his ample palate takes
Savor of poisonous brass and metals sick.
Wherefore when harbored in the sleepy West,
After the full completion of fair day,   35
For rest divine upon exalted couch
And slumber in the arms of melody,
He paces through the pleasant hours of ease
With strides colossal, on from hall to hall,
While far within each aisle and deep recess   40
His wingéd minions in close clusters stand
Amazed, and full of fear; like anxious men,
Who on a wide plain gather in sad troops,
When earthquakes jar their battlements and towers.
Even now, while Saturn, roused from icy trance,   45
Goes, step for step, with Thea from yon woods,
Hyperion, leaving twilight in the rear,
Is sloping to the threshold of the West.—
Thither we tend."—Now in clear light I stood,
Relieved from the dusk vale. Mnemosyne[3]   50
Was sitting on a square-edged polished stone,
That in its lucid depth reflected pure
Her priestess-garments. My quick eyes ran on
From stately nave to nave, from vault to vault,
Through bow'rs of fragrant and enwreathéd light   55
And diamond-pavéd lustrous long arcades.
Anon rushed by the bright Hyperion;
His flaming robes streamed out beyond his heels,
And gave a roar, as if of earthly fire,
That scared away the meek ethereal hours,   60
And made their dove-wings tremble. On he flared

1819   1856

---

2. Lines 20–22 might be paraphrased: "Not, however, at such portents as a dog's howl or the evening screech of the owl, nor with the well-known feelings ["visitings"] of someone when he hears the first stroke of his own death knell * * *" It had been the English custom to ring the church bell when a person was close to death, to invite hearers to pray for his departing soul. See, e.g., Shakespeare, *Venus and Adonis*, lines 701–2; and for "visitings," *Macbeth* I.v. 46.

To Autumn[1]

1

Season of mists and mellow fruitfulness,
  Close bosom-friend of the maturing sun;
Conspiring with him how to load and bless
  With fruit the vines that round the thatch-eaves run;
To bend with apples the mossed cottage-trees,   5
  And fill all fruit with ripeness to the core;
    To swell the gourd, and plump the hazel shells
With a sweet kernel; to set budding more,
And still more, later flowers for the bees,
Until they think warm days will never cease,   10
    For Summer has o'er-brimmed their clammy cells.

2

Who hath not seen thee oft amid thy store?
  Sometimes whoever seeks abroad may find
Thee sitting careless on a granary floor,
  Thy hair soft-lifted by the winnowing[2] wind;   15
Or on a half-reaped furrow sound asleep,
  Drowsed with the fume of poppies, while thy hook[3]
    Spares the next swath and all its twinèd flowers:
And sometimes like a gleaner thou dost keep
  Steady thy laden head across a brook;   20
  Or by a cider-press, with patient look,
    Thou watchest the last oozings hours by hours.

3

Where are the songs of Spring? Aye, where are they?
  Think not of them, thou hast thy music too—
While barred clouds bloom the soft-dying day,   25
  And touch the stubble-plains with rosy hue;
Then in a wailful choir the small gnats mourn
  Among the river sallows,[4] borne aloft
    Or sinking as the light wind lives or dies;
And full-grown lambs loud bleat from hilly bourn;[4a]   30
  Hedge crickets sing; and now with treble soft
  The redbreast whistles from a garden croft;[5]
    And gathering swallows twitter in the skies.

September 19, 1819   1820

---

1. Two days after this serene and gracious ode was composed, Keats wrote to J. H. Reynolds: "I never liked stubble fields so much as now—Aye, better than the chilly green of the spring. Somehow a stubble plain looks warm—in the same way that some pictures look warm—this struck me so much in my Sunday's walk that I composed upon it."
2. To "winnow" is to fan the chaff from the grain.
3. Scythe.
4. Willows.
4a. Region.
5. A "croft" is an enclosed plot of farm land.

This Living Hand[1]

This living hand, now warm and capable
Of earnest grasping, would, if it were cold
And in the icy silence of the tomb,
So haunt thy days and chill thy dreaming nights
That thou wouldst wish thine own heart dry of blood   5
So in my veins red life might stream again,
And thou be conscience-calmed—see here it is—
I hold it towards you.

Late 1819?   1898

1. Found written in the margin of a page of Keats's unfinished satire, *The Cap and Bells*, and commonly assumed to have been addressed to Fanny Brawne.

Letters   Keats's letters constitute a running commentary on his life, reading, thinking, and writing. They demonstrate an extraordinary intelligence, whose very lack of academic or technical training gives its expression a freedom from jargon and standard categories that is equally challenging and rewarding to the reader. Keats's early reputation as a poet of pure luxury, sensation, and art for art's sake has been revolutionized since, early this century, critics began to pay close attention to his letters. For Keats thought hard and persistently about life and art, and any seed of an ethical or critical idea that he picked up from his intellectual contemporaries (Hazlitt, Coleridge, Wordsworth) instantly germinated and flourished in the rich soil of his imagination. What T. S. Eliot said about the metaphysical poets applies equally to Keats in his letters: his "mode of feeling was directly and freshly altered by [his] reading and thought." And like Donne, he looked not only into the heart, but literally, "into the cerebral cortex, the nervous system, and the digestive tract." A number of Keats's casual comments on the poet and on poetry included below—especially those dealing with what we now call empathy, and with "negative capability"— have become standard points of reference in aesthetic theory. But nothing that Keats said did he himself regard as ultimate; each statement constituted only a stage in his continuing exploration into what he called "the mystery."

The text below is that of the edition of the *Letters* by Hyder E. Rollins (1958), which reproduces the original MSS. precisely, so that the reader may follow Keats's pen as, throwing spelling and grammar to the winds, it strains to keep up with the rush of his thoughts.

To Benjamin Bailey[1]
[*The Authenticity of the Imagination*]

[November 22, 1817]

My dear Bailey,

     * * * O I wish I was as certain of the end of all your troubles as

1. Bailey was one of Keats's closest friends. Keats had stayed with him the month before at Oxford, where Bailey was an undergraduate.

that of your momentary start about the authenticity of the Imagination. I am certain of nothing but of the holiness of the Heart's affections and the truth of Imagination—What the imagination seizes as Beauty must be truth[2]—whether it existed before or not—for I have the same Idea of all our Passions as of Love they are all in their sublime, creative of essential Beauty—In a Word, you may know my favorite Speculation by my first Book and the little song I sent in my last[3]—which is a representation from the fancy of the probable mode of operating in these Matters—The Imagination may be compared to Adam's dream[4]—he awoke and found it truth. I am the more zealous in this affair, because I have never yet been able to perceive how any thing can be known for truth by consequitive reasoning[5]—and yet it must be—Can it be that even the greatest Philosopher ever ~~when~~ arrived at his goal without putting aside numerous objections—However it may be, O for a Life of Sensations[6] rather than of Thoughts! It is "a Vision in the form of Youth" a Shadow of reality to come—and this consideration has further conv[i]nced me for it has come as auxiliary to another favorite Speculation of mine, that we shall enjoy ourselves here after by having what we called happiness on Earth repeated in a finer tone and so repeated[7]—And yet such a fate can only befall those who delight in sensation rather than hunger as you do after Truth—Adam's dream will do here and seems to be a conviction that Imagination and its empyreal reflection is the same as human Life and its spiritual repetition. But as I was saying—the simple imaginative Mind may have its rewards in the repeti[ti]on of its own silent Working coming continually on the spirit with a fine suddenness—to compare great things with small—have you never by being surprised with an old Melody—in a delicious place—by a delicious voice, fe[l]t over again your very speculations and surmises at the time it first operated on your soul—do you not remember forming to yourself the singer's face more beautiful that[8] it was possible and yet with the elevation of the Moment you did not think so—even then you were mounted on the Wings of Imagination so high—that the Prototype must be here after—that delicious face you will see—What a time! I am continually running away from the subject—sure this cannot be exactly the case with a complex Mind—one that is imaginative and at the same time careful of its fruits—who would exist partly on sensation partly on thought—to whom it is necessary that years should bring the philosophic Mind[9]—such an one I con-

2. The phrase occurs in a poetic context at the close of *Ode on a Grecian Urn*. Try substituting "real," or "reality," where Keats uses the word "truth."
3. The song was "O Sorrow," from *Endymion*.
4. In *Paradise Lost* VIII.452–90, Adam dreams that Eve has been created, and awakes to find her real.
5. Consecutive   reasoning—reasoning which moves by logical steps.
6. Not only sense experiences, but also the intuitive perceptions of truths, as opposed to truth achieved by consecutive reasoning.
7. Cf. the "Pleasure Thermometer" in *Endymion*, Book I, lines 777 ff.
8. For "than."
9. An echo of Wordsworth, *Ode: Intimations of Immortality*, line 187.

sider your's and therefore it is necessary to your eternal Happiness that you not only ~~have~~ drink this old Wine of Heaven which I shall call the redigestion of our most ethereal Musings on Earth; but also increase in knowledge and know all things. I am glad to hear you are in a fair Way for Easter—you will soon get through your unpleasant reading and then!—but the world is full of troubles and I have not much reason to think myself pesterd with many—I think Jane or Marianne has a better opinion of me than I deserve—for really and truly I do not think my Brothers illness connected with mine—you know more of the real Cause than they do—nor have I any chance of being rack'd as you have been[1]—you perhaps at one time thought there was such a thing as Worldly Happiness to be arrived at, at certain periods of time marked out—you have of necessity from your disposition been thus led away—I scarcely remember counting upon any Happiness—I look not for it if it be not in the present hour—nothing startles me beyond the Moment. The setting sun will always set me to rights—or if a Sparrow come before my Window I take part in its existince and pick about the Gravel. The first thing that strikes me on hea[r]ing a Misfortune having befalled another is this. Well it cannot be helped.—he will have the pleasure of trying the resourses of his spirit, and I beg now my dear Bailey that hereafter should you observe any thing cold in me not to but[2] it to the account of heartlessness but abstraction—for I assure you I sometimes feel not the influence of a Passion or Affection during a whole week—and so long this sometimes continues I begin to suspect myself and the genuiness of my feelings at other times—thinking them a few barren Tragedy-tears * * *

Your affectionate friend
John Keats—

To George and Thomas Keats
[*Negative Capability*]

[December 21, 27 (?), 1817]

My dear Brothers

I must crave your pardon for not having written ere this * * * I spent Friday evening with Wells[1] & went the next morning to see *Death on the Pale horse*. It is a wonderful picture, when West's age is considered;[2] But there is nothing to be intense upon; no women one feels mad to kiss; no face swelling into reality. the excellence of every Art is its intensity, capable of making all disagreeables evapo-

1. Keats's friends Jane and Marianne Reynolds feared that Keats's ill health at this time threatened tuberculosis, from which his brother Tom was suffering. Bailey had recently suffered pain (been "racked") because of an unsuccessful love affair.
2. For "put."
1. Charles Wells, a former schoolmate

of Tom Keats and, for a time, a friend of John Keats.
2. Benjamin West (1738–1820), painter of historical pictures, was an American who moved to England and became president of the Royal Academy. The "Christ Rejected" mentioned a few sentences farther on is also by West.

rate, from their being in close relationship with Beauty & Truth[3]—
Examine King Lear & you will find this examplified throughout; but
in this picture we have unpleasantness without any momentous
depth of speculation excited, in which to bury its repulsiveness—
The picture is larger than Christ rejected—I dined with Haydon[4]
the sunday after you left, & had a very pleasant day, I dined too
(for I have been out too much lately) with Horace Smith & met his
two Brothers with Hill & Kingston & one Du Bois,[5] they only served
to convince me, how superior humour is to wit in respect to enjoyment—These men say things which make one start, without making
one feel, they are all alike; their manners are alike; they all know
fashionables; they have a mannerism in their very eating & drinking,
in their mere handling a Decanter—They talked of Kean[6] & his
low company—Would I were with that company instead of yours
said I to myself! I know such like acquaintance will never do for
me & yet I am going to Reynolds, on wednesday—Brown & Dilke[7]
walked with me & back from the Christmas pantomime.[8] I had not
a dispute but a disquisition with Dilke, on various subjects; several
things dovetailed in my mind, & at once it struck me, what quality
went to form a Man of Achievement especially in Literature &
which Shakespeare posessed so enormously—I mean *Negative Capability*,[9] that is when man is capable of being in uncertainties, Mysteries, doubts, without any irritable reaching after fact & reason—
Coleridge, for instance, would let go by a fine isolated verisimilitude
caught from the Penetralium[1] of mystery, from being incapable of
remaining content with half knowledge. This pursued through Volumes would perhaps take us no further than this, that with a great
poet the sense of Beauty overcomes every other consideration, or
rather obliterates all consideration.

3. Keats's solution to a problem at
least as old as Aristotle: why do we
enjoy the aesthetic representation of a
subject which in real life would be ugly
or painful?
4. Keats's close friend, Benjamin Haydon, painter of grandiose historical and
religious pictures.
5. Horace Smith was one of the best
known literary wits of the day; the
others mentioned were men of letters
or of literary interests.
6. Edmund Kean, the noted Shakespearean actor of the early 19th century.
7. John Hamilton Reynolds, Charles
Armitage Brown, and Charles Wentworth Dilke were all writers and friends
of Keats.
8. Christmas pantomimes were performed each year at Drury Lane and
Covent Garden.
9. This famous and elusive phrase has
accumulated a heavy body of commentary. Two points may here suffice: (1)
Keats is concerned with a central aesthetic question of his day: to distinguish between what was called the "objective" poet, who simply and imper-
sonally presents his material, and the
"subjective" or "sentimental" poet, who
presents his material as it appears when
viewed through his personal interests,
beliefs, and feelings. The poet of "negative capability" is the objective poet.
(See the letter to Reynolds, Feb. 3,
1818, below.) (2) Keats goes on to
propose that, within a poem, the presentation of matter in an artistic form
that appeals to our "sense of Beauty"
is enough, independently of its truth or
falsity when considered outside the
poem according to nonartistic logical
criteria. T. S. Eliot illuminated an
important aspect of Keats's meaning
when he observed that a theory "which
has entered into poetry is established,
for its truth or falsity in one sense
ceases to matter, and its truth in another sense is proved" (*The Metaphysical Poets*).
1. The Latin *penetralia* signified the
innermost and most secret parts of a
temple.

Shelley's poem[2] is out & there are words about its being objected
too, as much as Queen Mab was. Poor Shelley I think he has his
Quota of good qualities, in sooth la!! Write soon to your most sincere friend & affectionate Brother

John

To John Hamilton Reynolds[1]
[*Wordsworth's Poetry*]

[February 3, 1818]

My dear Reynolds,
 * * * It may be said that we ought to read our Contemporaries.
that Wordsworth &c should have their due from us. but for the sake
of a few fine imaginative or domestic passages, are we to be bullied
into a certain Philosophy engendered in the whims of an Egotist[2]—
Every man has his speculations, but every man does not brood and
peacock over them till he makes a false coinage and deceives himself—Many a man can travel to the very bourne[2a] of Heaven, and yet
want confidence to put down his halfseeing. Sancho[3] will invent a
Journey heavenward as well as any body. We hate poetry that has a
palpable design upon us—and if we do not agree, seems to put its
hand in its breeches pocket. Poetry should be great & unobtrusive, a
thing which enters into one's soul, and does not startle it or amaze
it with itself but with its subject.—How beautiful are the retired
flowers! how would they lose their beauty were they to throng into
the highway crying out, admire me I am a violet! dote upon me I
am a primrose! Modern poets differ from the Elizabethans in this.
Each of the moderns like an Elector of Hanover governs his petty
state, & knows how many straws are swept daily from the Causeways in all his dominions & has a continual itching that all the
Housewives should have their coppers well scoured: the antients
were ~~Emperors of large~~ Emperors of vast Provinces, they had only
heard of the remote ones and scarcely cared to visit them.—I will
cut all this—I will have no more of Wordsworth or Hunt[4] in particular—Why should we be of the tribe of Manasseh, when we can
wander with Esau?[5] why should we kick against the Pricks, when we

2. *Laon and Cythna* (1817), which dealt with incest, and had to be re-called by the author; it was revised and republished as *The Revolt of Islam* (1818). *Queen Mab* (1813) was a youthful poem in which Shelley presented his radical program for the achievement of the millennium by the elimination of "kings, priests, and statesmen," and the reform of human institutions.
1. Reynolds, a close friend, was at this time an insurance clerk and also an able, though minor, poet and man of letters.
2. Keats immensely admired Words-worth, as succeeding letters will show,

and learned more from him than from any poetic contemporary. He had reservations, however, about the subjective and didactic qualities of Wordsworth's poetry (see the letter to George and Thomas Keats, above)—reservations which, in some moods, he stated in un-flattering terms.
2a. Boundary.
3. Sancho Panza, the earthy squire in *Don Quixote*.
4. Leigh Hunt, a poet who earlier had strongly influenced Keats's style.
5. I.e., why should we remain in a conventional way of life (as did the tribe of Manasseh, which followed the

can walk on Roses? Why should we be owls, when we can be Eagles? Why be teased with "nice Eyed wagtails," when we have in sight "the Cherub Contemplation"?[6]—Why with Wordsworths "Matthew with a bough of wilding in his hand" when we can have Jacques "under an oak &c"[7]—The secret of the Bough of Wilding will run through your head faster than I can write it—Old Matthew spoke to him some years ago on some nothing, & because he happens in an Evening Walk to imagine the figure of the old man—he must stamp it down in black & white, and it is henceforth sacred—I don't mean to deny Wordsworth's grandeur & Hunt's merit, but I mean to say we need not be teazed with grandeur & merit—when we can have them uncontaminated & unobtrusive. Let us have the old Poets, & robin Hood[8] Your letter and its sonnets gave me more pleasure than will the 4th Book of Childe Harold[9] & the whole of any body's life & opinions. * * *

Y[r] sincere friend and Coscribbler
John Keats.

To John Taylor[1]

[Keats's Axioms in Poetry]

[February 27, 1818]

My dear Taylor,

Your alteration strikes me as being a great improvement—the page looks much better. * * * It is a sorry thing for me that any one should have to overcome Prejudices in reading my Verses—that affects me more than any hypercriticism on any particular Passage. In *Endymion* I have most likely but moved into the Go-cart from the leading strings. In Poetry I have a few Axioms, and you will see how far I am from their Centre. 1st I think Poetry should surprise by a fine excess and not by Singularity—it should strike the Reader as a wording of his own highest thoughts, and appear almost a Remembrance—2nd Its touches of Beauty should never be half way therby making the reader breathless instead of content: the rise, the progress, the setting of imagery should like the Sun come natural natural too him—shine over him and set soberly although in magnificence leaving him in the Luxury of twilight—but it is easier to think what Poetry should be than to write it—and this leads me on to another axiom. That if Poetry comes not as naturally

conventional paths of Old Testament history) when we can become adventurers (like Esau, who sold his birthright in Genesis xxv.29–34 and became a domestic outlaw).

6. The first phrase is from Hunt's *Nymphs,* the second from Milton's *Il Penseroso* (line 54).

7. The Wordsworth phrase is from his poem *The Two April Mornings* (a "wilding" is an uncultivated tree or plant, especially the wild apple tree).

For Jacques "under an oak," see *As You Like It,* II.i.31.

8. A reference to two sonnets on Robin Hood by Reynolds which he had sent to Keats.

9. Canto IV of Byron's *Childe Harold* was being eagerly awaited by English readers.

1. Member of the publishing firm of Taylor and Hessey, to whom Keats wrote this letter while *Endymion* was being put through the press.

as the Leaves to a tree it had better not come at all. However it may be with me I cannot help looking into new countries with "O for a Muse of fire to ascend!"[2]—If Endymion serves me as a Pioneer perhaps I ought to be content. I have great reason to be content, for thank God I can read and perhaps understand Shakspeare to his depths, and I have I am sure many friends, who, if I fail, will attribute any change in my Life and Temper to Humbleness rather than to Pride—to a cowering under the Wings of great Poets rather than to a Bitterness that I am not appreciated. I am anxious to get Endymion printed that I may forget it and proceed. * * *

Your sincere and oblig[d] friend
John Keats—

P.S. You shall have a sho[r]t *Preface* in good time—

To John Hamilton Reynolds
[*Milton, Wordsworth, and the Chambers of Human Life*]

[May 3, 1818]

My dear Reynolds.

   * * * Were I to study physic or rather Medicine again,—I feel it would not make the least difference in my Poetry; when the Mind is in its infancy a Bias in is in reality a Bias, but when we have acquired more strength, a Bias becomes no Bias. Every department of knowledge we see excellent and calculated towards a great whole. I am so convinced of this, that I am glad at not having given away my medical Books, which I shall again look over to keep alive the little I know thitherwards; and moreover intend through you and Rice to become a sort of Pip-civilian.[1] An extensive knowledge is needful to thinking people—it takes away the heat and fever; and helps, by widening speculation, to ease the Burden of the Mystery:[2] a thing I begin to understand a little, and which weighed upon you in the most gloomy and true sentence in your Letter. The difference of high Sensations with and without knowledge appears to me this —in the latter case we are falling continually ten thousand fathoms deep and being blown up again without wings and with all [the] horror of a ~~Case~~ bare shoulderd Creature—in the former case, our shoulders are fledged,[3] and we go thro' the same ~~Fir~~ air and space without fear. * * *

   You say "I fear there is little chance of any thing else in this life." You seem by that to have been going through with a more painful and acute ~~test~~ zest the same labyrinth that I have—I have

---

2. Altered from Shakespeare's *Henry V*, Prologue, line 1.
1. Apparently, "a small-scale layman." James Rice, a lawyer, was one of Keats's favorite friends.
2. *Tintern Abbey*, line 38. Here begins

Keats's wonderfully insightful expansion of the significance of this and other phrases and passages in Wordsworth.
3. Grow wings.

come to the same conclusion thus far. My Branchings out therefrom have been numerous: one of them is the consideration of Wordsworth's genius and as a help, in the manner of gold being the meridian Line of worldly wealth,—how he differs from Milton.[4]—And here I have nothing but surmises, from an uncertainty whether Miltons apparently less anxiety for Humanity proceeds from his seeing further or no than Wordsworth: And whether Wordsworth has in truth epic passions, and martyrs himself to the human heart, the main region of his song[5]—In regard to his genius alone—we find what he says true as far as we have experienced and we can judge no further but by larger experience—for axioms in philosophy are not axioms until they are proved upon our pulses: We read fine—— things but never feel them to thee[6] full until we have gone the same steps as the Author.—I know this is not plain; you will know exactly my meaning when I say, that now I shall relish Hamlet more than I ever have done—Or, better—You are sensible no man can set down Venery[7] as a bestial or joyless thing until he is sick of it and therefore all philosophizing on it would be mere wording. Until we are sick, we understand not;—in fine, as Byron says, "Knowledge is Sorrow";[8] and I go on to say that "Sorrow is Wisdom"—and further for aught we can know for certainty! "Wisdom is folly" * * *

I will return to Wordsworth—whether or no he has an extended vision or a circumscribed grandeur—whether he is an eagle in his nest, or on the wing—And to be more explicit and to show you how tall I stand by the giant, I will put down a simile of human life as far as I now perceive it; that is, to the point to which I say we both have arrived at—Well—I compare human life to a large Mansion of Many Apartments, two of which I can only describe, the doors of the rest being as yet shut upon me—The first we step into we call the infant or thoughtless Chamber, in which we remain as long as we do not think—We remain there a long while, and notwithstanding the doors of the second Chamber remain wide open, showing a bright appearance, we care not to hasten to it; but are at length imperceptibly impelled by the awakening of the thinking principle —within us—we no sooner get into the second Chamber, which I shall call the Chamber of Maiden-Thought,[9] than we become intoxicated with the light and the atmosphere, we see nothing but pleasant wonders, and think of delaying there for ever in delight: However among the effects this breathing is father of is that tremendous one of sharpening one's vision into the ~~head~~ heart and nature of Man—of convincing ones nerves that the World is full

---

4. I.e., as gold is the standard of material wealth (in the way that the meridian line of Greenwich Observatory, England, is the reference for measuring degrees of longitude), so Milton is the standard of poetic value, by which we may measure Wordsworth.
5. Cf. "Prospectus" to *The Recluse*, line 41.
6. For "the."
7. Sexual indulgence.
8. *Manfred* I.i.10: "Sorrow is knowledge."
9. I.e., innocent thought, with the implication (as in "maiden voyage") of a first undertaking.

of Misery and Heartbreak, Pain, Sickness and oppression—whereby This Chamber of Maiden Thought becomes gradually darken'd and at the same time on all sides of it many doors are set open—but all dark—all leading to dark passages—We see not the ballance of good and evil. We are in a Mist—We are now in that state—We feel the "burden of the Mystery," To this point was Wordsworth come, as far as I can conceive when he wrote "Tintern Abbey" and it seems to me that his Genius is explorative of those dark Passages. Now if we live, and go on thinking, we too shall explore them. he is a Genius and superior [to] us, in so far as he can, more than we, make discoveries, and shed a light in them—Here I must think Wordsworth is deeper than Milton—though I think it has depended more upon the general and gregarious advance of intellect, than individual greatness of Mind—From the Paradise Lost and the other Works of Milton, I hope it is not too presuming, even between ourselves to say, his Philosophy, human and divine, may be tolerably understood by one not much advanced in years, In his time englishmen were just emancipated from a great superstition—and Men had got hold of certain points and resting places in reasoning which were too newly born to be doubted, and too much ~~oppressed~~ opposed by the Mass of Europe not to be thought etherial and authentically divine—who could gainsay his ideas on virtue, vice, and Chastity in Comus, just at the time of the dismissal of Cod-pieces[1] and a hundred other disgraces? who would not rest satisfied with his hintings at good and evil in the Paradise Lost, when just free from the inquisition and burrning in Smithfield?[2] The Reformation produced such immediate and greats benefits, that Protestantism was considered under the immediate eye of heaven, and its own remaining Dogmas and superstitions, then, as it were, regenerated, constituted those resting places and seeming sure points of Reasoning—from that I have mentioned, Milton, whatever he may have thought in the sequel,[3] appears to have been content with these by his writings—He did not think into the human heart, as Wordsworth has done—Yet Milton as a Philosop[h]er, had sure as great powers as Wordsworth—What is then to be inferr'd? O many things—It proves there is really a grand march of intellect—, It proves that a mighty providence subdues the mightiest Minds to the service of the time being, whether it be in human Knowledge or Religion— * * *

Your affectionate friend
John Keats.

---

1. In the 15th and 16th centuries the codpiece was a flap, often ornamental, which covered an opening in the front of men's breeches.

2. An open place northwest of the walls of the City of London where, in the 16th century, heretics were burned.
3. I.e., later on.

To Richard Woodhouse[1]

[A *Poet Has No Identity*]

[October 27, 1818]

My dear Woodhouse,

Your Letter gave me a great satisfaction; more on account of its friendliness, than any relish of that matter in it which is accounted so acceptable in the "genus irritabile"[2] The best answer I can give you is in a clerklike manner to make some observations on two principle points, which seem to point like indices into the midst of the whole pro and con, about genius, and views and atchievements and ambition and cœtera. 1st As to the poetical Character itself, (I mean that sort of which, if I am any thing, I am a Member; that sort distinguished from the wordsworthian or egotistical sublime; which is a thing per se and stands alone) it is not itself— it has no self—it is every thing and nothing—It has no character— it enjoys light and shade; it lives in gusto, be it foul or fair, high or low, rich or poor, mean or elevated—It has as much delight in conceiving an Iago as an Imogen.[3] What shocks the virtuous philosop[h]er, delights the camelion[4] Poet. It does no harm from its relish of the dark side of things any more than from its taste for the bright one; because they both end in speculation.[5] A Poet is the most unpoetical of any thing in existence; because he has no Identity—he is continually in for[6]—and filling some other Body—The Sun, the Moon, the Sea and Men and Women who are creatures of impulse are poetical and have about them an unchangeable attribute—the poet has none; no identity—he is certainly the most unpoetical of all God's Creatures. If then he has no self, and if I am a Poet, where is the Wonder that I should say I would ~~right~~ write no more? Might I not at that very instant [have] been cogitating on the Characters of saturn and Ops?[7] It is a wretched thing to confess; but is a very fact that not one word I ever utter can be taken for granted as an opinion growing out of my identical nature—how can it, when I have no nature? When I am in a room with People if I ever am free from speculating on creations of my own brain, then not myself goes home to myself: but the identity of every one in the room

1. Woodhouse was a young lawyer with literary interests who recognized Keats's talents and prepared, or preserved, manuscript copies of many of his poems and letters.
2. "The irritable race," a phrase Horace had applied to poets (Epistles II.ii.102).
3. Iago is the villain in Shakespeare's *Othello* and Imogen the virtuous heroine of his *Cymbeline*.
4. The chameleon is a lizard which camouflages itself by matching its color to its surroundings.

5. "In speculation" here means "in contemplation"—i.e., without affecting our practical judgment or actions.
6. Instead of "in for," Keats may have intended to write "informing."
7. Characters in Keats's *Hyperion.* Woodhouse had written Keats a letter, expressing concern at a remark by Keats that, since former writers had preempted the best poetic materials and styles, there was nothing new left for the modern poet.

begins to to press upon me[8] that, I am in a very little time an[ni]-
hilated—not only among Men; it would be the same in a Nursery
of children: I know not whether I make myself wholly understood:
I hope enough so to let you see that no dependence is to be placed
on what I said that day.

In the second place I will speak of my views, and of the life I
purpose to myself—I am ambitious of doing the world some good:
if I should be spared that may be the work of maturer years—in the
interval I will assay to reach to as high a summit in Poetry as the
nerve[9] bestowed upon me will suffer. The faint conceptions I have
of Poems to come brings the blood frequently into my forehead—
All I hope is that I may not lose all interest in human affairs—that
the solitary indifference I feel for applause even from the finest
Spirits, will not blunt any acuteness of vision I may have. I do not
think it will—I feel assured I should write from the mere yearning
and fondness I have for the Beautiful even if my night's labours
should be burnt every morning and no eye ever shine upon them.
But even now I am perhaps not speaking from myself; but from
some character in whose soul I now live. I am sure however that
this next sentence is from myself. I feel your anxiety, good opinion
and friendliness in the highest degree, and am

> Your's most sincerely
> John Keats

To George and Georgiana Keats[1]
["*The Vale of Soul-Making*"]

[February 14–May 3, 1819]

My Dear Brother & Sister——

* * * I have this moment received a note from Haslam[2] in
which he expects the death of his Father who has been for some
time in a state of insensibility—his mother bears up he says very
well—I shall go to twon[3] tommorrow to see him. This is the world
—thus we cannot expect to give way many hours to pleasure—Circumstances are like Clouds continually gathering and bursting—
While we are laughing the seed of some trouble is put into ~~he~~ the
wide arable land of events—while we are laughing it sprouts is[4]
grows and suddenly bears a poison fruit which we must pluck—
Even so we have leisure to reason on the misfortunes of our friends;
our own touch us too nearly for words. Very few men have ever

---

8. Perhaps "*so* to press upon me."
9. Sinew.
1. Keats's younger brother and his
wife, who had emigrated to Louisville,
Kentucky, in 1818. This is part of a
long letter, which Keats wrote over a
period of several months.
2. William Haslam, a young businessman and intimate friend.
3. For "town."
4. For "it."

arrived at a complete disinterestedness of Mind: very few have been influenced by a pure desire of the benefit of others—in the greater part of the Benefactors of & to Humanity some meretricious motive has sullied their greatness—some melodramatic scenery has facinated them—From the manner in which I feel Haslam's misfortune I perceive how far I am from any humble standard of disinterestedness—Yet this feeling ought to be carried to its highest pitch, as there is no fear of its ever injuring society—which it would do I fear pushed to an extremity—For in wild nature the Hawk would loose his Breakfast of Robins and the Robin his of Worms The Lion must starve as well as the swallow—The greater part of Men make their way with the same instinctiveness, the same unwandering eye from their purposes, the same animal eagerness as the Hawk—The Hawk wants a Mate, so does the Man—look at them both they set about it and procure on[e] in the same manner —They want both a nest and they both set about one in the same manner—they get their food in the same manner—The noble animal Man for his amusement smokes his pipe—the Hawk balances about the Clouds—that is the only difference of their leisures. This it is that makes the Amusement of Life—to a speculative Mind. I go among the Feilds and catch a glimpse of a stoat[5] or a fieldmouse peeping out of the withered grass—the creature hath a purpose and its eyes are bright with it—I go amongst the buildings of a city and I see a Man hurrying along—to what? The Creature has a purpose and his eyes are bright with it. But then as Wordsworth says, "we have all one human heart"[6]—there is an ellectric fire in human nature tending to purify—so that among these human creature[s] there is continully some birth of new heroism—The pity is that we must wonder at it: as we should at finding a pearl in rubbish—I have no doubt that thousands of people never heard of have had hearts comp[l]etely disinterested: I can remember but two—Socrates and Jesus—their Histories evince it—What I heard a little time ago, Taylor observe with respect to Socrates, may be said of Jesus— That he was so great as man that though he transmitted no writing of his own to posterity, we have his Mind and his sayings and his greatness handed to us by others. It is to be lamented that the history of the latter was written and revised by Men interested in the pious frauds of Religion. Yet through all this I see his splendour. Even here though I myself am pursueing the same instinctive course as the veriest human animal you can think of—I am however young writing at random—straining at particles of light in the midst of a great darkness—without knowing the bearing of any one assertion of any one opinion. Yet may I not in this be free from sin?[7] May

5. A weasel.
6. *The Old Cumberland Beggar*, line 153.

7. Keats speculates that though his instinctive course is not, any more than an animal's, "disinterested" (free from

there not be superior beings amused with any graceful, though instinctive attitude my mind my[8] fall into, as I am entertained with the alertness of a Stoat or the anxiety of a Deer? Though a quarrel in the streets is a thing to be hated, the energies displayed in it are fine; the commonest Man shows a grace in his quarrel—By a superior being our reasoning[s] may take the same tone—though erroneous they may be fine—This is the very thing in which consists poetry; and if so it is not so fine a thing as philosophy—For the same reason that an eagle is not so fine a thing as a truth—Give me this credit—Do you not think I strive—to know myself? Give me this credit—and you will not think that on my own accou[n]t I repeat Milton's lines

> "How charming is divine Philosophy
> Not harsh and crabbed as dull fools suppose
> But musical as is Apollo's lute"—[9]

No—no for myself—feeling grateful as I do to have got into a state of mind to relish them properly—Nothing ever becomes real till it is experienced—Even a Proverb is no proverb to you till your Life has illustrated it— * * *

The common cognomen of this world among the misguided and superstitious is "a vale of tears" from which we are to be redeemed by a certain arbitary interposition of God and taken to Heaven— What a little circumscribe[d] straightened notion! Call the world if you Please "The vale of Soul-making" Then you will find out the use of the world (I am speaking now in the highest terms for human nature admitting it to be immortal which I will here take for granted for the purpose of showing a thought which has struck me concerning it) I say "*Soul making*" Soul as distinguished from an Intelligence—There may be intelligences or sparks of the divinity in millions—but they are not Souls ~~the~~ till they acquire identities, till each one is personally itself. I[n]telligences are atoms of perception —they know and they see and they are pure, in short they are God —how then are Souls to be made? How then are these sparks which are God to have identity given them—so as ever to possess a bliss peculiar to each ones individual existence? How, but by the medium of a world like this? This point I sincerely wish to consider because I think it a grander system of salvation than the chrysteain religion —or rather it is a system of Spirit-creation[1]—This is effected by

selfish interests), it may still be, like an animal's, natural, hence innocent and possessed of an innate grace and beauty. He further supposes that this may be the nature of poetry, also, as distinguished from the deliberate and self-conscious process of philosophical reasoning. Compare the letter on "Negative Capability," Dec. 21, 1817, above.
8. For "may."
9. *Comus*, lines 475–77.

1. Keats is struggling magnificently for an analogy which will embody his solution to the ancient riddle of evil, as an alternative to what he understands to be the Christian view: evil exists as a test of man's merit of salvation in heaven, and this world is only a proving ground for a later and better life. Keats proposes that the function of the human experience of sorrow and

three grand materials acting the one upon the other for a series of years—These three Materials are the *Intelligence*—the *human heart* (as distinguished from intelligence or Mind) and the *World* or *Elemental space* suited for the proper action of *Mind and Heart* on each other for the purpose of forming the *Soul* or *Intelligence destined to possess the sense of Identity.* I can scarcely express what I but dimly perceive—and yet I think I perceive it—that you may judge the more clearly I will put it in the most homely form possible— I will call the *world* a School instituted for the purpose of teaching little children to read—I will call the *human heart* the *horn Book*[2] used in that School—and I will call the *Child able to read, the Soul* made from that *school* and its *hornbook.* Do you not see how necessary a World of Pains and troubles is to school an Intelligence and make it a soul? A Place where the heart must feel and suffer in a thousand diverse ways! Not merely is the Heart a Hornbook, It is the Minds Bible, it is the Minds experience, it is the teat from which the Mind or intelligence sucks its identity—As various as the Lives of Men are—so various become their souls, and thus does God make individual beings, Souls, Identical Souls of the sparks of his own essence—This appears to me a faint sketch of a system of Salvation which does not affront our reason and humanity—I am convinced that many difficulties which christians labour under would vanish before it—There is one wh[i]ch even now Strikes me—the Salvation of Children—In them the Spark or intelligence returns to God without any identity—it having had no time to learn of, and be altered by, the heart—or seat of the human Passions—It is pretty generally suspected that the chr[i]stian scheme has been coppied from the ancient persian and greek Philosophers. Why may they not have made this simple thing even more simple for common apprehension by introducing Mediators and Personages in the same manner as in the hethen mythology abstractions are personified— Seriously I think it probable that this System of Soul-making—may have been the Parent of all the more palpable and personal Schemes of Redemption, among the Zoroastrians the Christians and the Hindoos. For as one part of the human species must have their carved Jupiter; so another part must have the palpable and named Mediatior and saviour, their Christ their Oromanes and their Vishnu[2a]—

pain is to feed and discipline the formless and unstocked "intelligence" that a man possesses at birth, and thus to shape it into a rich and coherent "identity," or "soul." This result provides a justification ("salvation") for our suffering life on its own terms; that is, experience is its own reward, and not in heaven, but on earth. The passage is Keats's version of what Wordsworth says in the last two stanzas of his *Ode: Intimations of Immortality.*

2. A child's primer, which used to consist of a sheet of paper mounted on thin wood, protected by a sheet of transparent horn.

2a. Oromanes (Ahriman) was the principle of evil, locked in a persisting struggle with Ormazd, the principle of good, in the Zoroastrian religion. Vishnu was the deity who creates and preserves the world, in Hindu belief.

If what I have said should not be plain enough, as I fear it may not be, I will but[3] you in the place where I began in this series of thoughts—I mean, I began by seeing how man was formed by circumstances—and what are circumstances?—but touchstones of his heart—? and what are touch stones?—but proovings of his hearrt? —and what are proovings of his heart but fortifiers or alterers of his nature? and what is his altered nature but his soul?—and what was his soul before it came into the world and had These provings and alterations and perfectionings?—An intelligences—without Identity —and how is this Identity to be made? Through the medium of the Heart? And how is the heart to become this Medium but in a world of Circumstances?—There now I think what with Poetry and Theology you may thank your Stars that my pen is not very long winded— * * *

This is the 3ᵈ of May & every thing is in delightful forwardness: the violets are not withered, before the peeping of the first rose; You must let me know every thing, how parcels go & come, what papers you have, & what Newspapers you want, & other things— God bless you my dear Brother & Sister

Your ever Affectionate Brother
John Keats—

To Percy Bysshe Shelley[1]
[*"Load Every Rift with Ore"*]

[August 16, 1820]

My dear Shelley,

I am very much gratified that you, in a foreign country, and with a mind almost over occupied, should write to me in the strain of the Letter beside me. If I do not take advantage of your invitation it will be prevented by a circumstance I have very much at heart to prophesy[2]—There is no doubt that an english winter would put an end to me, and do so in a lingering hateful manner, therefore I must either voyage or journey to Italy as a soldier marches up to a battery. My nerves at present are the worst part of me, yet they feel soothed when I think that come what extreme may, I shall not be destined to remain in one spot long enough to take a hatred of any four particular bed-posts. I am glad you take any pleasure in my poor Poem;[3]—which I would willingly take the trouble to unwrite, if possible, did I care so much as I have done about Reputation. I received a copy of the Cenci,[4] as from yourself from Hunt. There

---

3. For "put."
1. Written in reply to a letter urging Keats (who was ill) to spend the winter with the Shelleys in Pisa.
2. His own death.
3. Keats's *Endymion*, Shelley had written, contains treasures, "though treasures poured forth with indistinct profusion." Keats here responds with advice in kind.
4. Shelley's blank-verse tragedy, *The Cenci*, had been published in the spring of 1820.

is only one part of it I am judge of; the Poetry, and dramatic effect, which by many spirits now a days is considered the mammon. A modern work it is said must have a purpose,[5] which may be the God —*an artist* must serve Mammon—he must have "self concentration" selfishness perhaps. You I am sure will forgive me for sincerely remarking that you might curb your magnanimity and be more of an artist, and "load every rift"[6] of your subject with ore. The thought of such discipline must fall like cold chains upon you, who perhaps never sat with your wings furl'd for six Months together. And is not this extraordina[r]y talk for the writer of Endymion? whose mind was like a pack of scattered cards—I am pick'd up and sorted to a pip.[7] My Imagination is a Monastry and I am its Monk—you must explain my metap⁶ʸ[8] to yourself. I am in expectation of Prometheus[9] every day. Could I have my own wish for its interest effected you would have it still in manuscript—or be but now putting an end to the second act. I remember you advising me not to publish my first-blights, on Hampstead heath—I am returning advice upon your hands. Most of the Poems in the volume I send you[1] have been written above two years, and would never have been publish'd but from a hope of gain; so you see I am inclined enough to take your advice now. I must exp[r]ess once more my deep sense of your kindness, adding my sincere thanks and respects for Mⁱˢ Shelley. In the hope of soon seeing you I remain

> most sincerely yours,
> John Keats—

5. Wordsworth had said this in his Preface to *Lyrical Ballads*. For "Mammon" see Matthew vi.24, and Luke xvi.13: "Ye cannot serve God and mammon."
6. Spenser, *Faerie Queene* II.vii.28: "With rich metall loaded every rifte."
7. Perfectly ordered; all the suits in the deck matched up ("pips" are the conventional spots on playing cards).
8. I.e., "metaphysics."
9. *Prometheus Unbound*, of which Shelley had promised Keats a copy.
1. Keats's volume of 1820, including *Lamia, The Eve of St. Agnes*, and the *Odes*. When Shelley drowned, he had this small book open in his pocket.

Romantic Lyric Poets

In the variety and magnitude of the lyric achievement by its major poets, the Romantic period ranks with Elizabethan and Jacobean times as one of the two greatest ages of the English lyric. It cannot approach the earlier period, however, in the number of second-order poets, many of them anonymous, who wrote excellent songs. The late 16th and early 17th centuries had been a great age of English vocal music, when there had been a pressing demand for poetic texts to match to the many exquisite airs and madrigals. In the Romantic period, however, lyric poems were mainly "art lyrics," written not to be sung but to be read, and no doubt the decline in the number of gifted amateurs who turned their hand to this form is related to the decline of England, through the 18th and 19th centuries, as a great singing nation.

This section represents Romantic poets good enough to have kept their places in all representative anthologies of lyric poems. It will be noted that there is no single, identifiable type of "Romantic lyric." The scope of these writers is very wide, ranging from Thomas Moore's tinkling echoes of Cavalier gallantries, through W. S. Landor's revitalization of the tradition of classic epigram, John Clare's successful achievement of Wordsworth's early aim (poems on common or seemingly trivial things, written in language really spoken by the peasant class), Scott's brilliant imitations of the popular ballad and George Darley's of Elizabethan song, Thomas Love Peacock's parody of the contemporary verse romance, the grotesque fantasy of Leigh Hunt's *The Fish, the Man, and the Spirit*, and the crossing of the Jacobean macabre with Gothic horror in the extraordinary songs of Thomas Lovell Beddoes.

WILLIAM LISLE BOWLES

(1762–1850)

Bowles was a clergyman who is noted in literature less for what he wrote than for his effect on other writers. In 1789 he published *Fourteen Sonnets*, which did much to revive that important poetic form, and also influenced the longer Romantic poems of the meditative description of a natural scene. And in 1806 he brought out an edition of Pope which derogated Pope's merits, starting a literary controversy in which Byron eloquently supported the virtues of the neoclassic poet.

In the first chapter of *Biographia Literaria*, Coleridge testifies to the extraordinary impact on his poetic sensibility and practice of Bowles's *Sonnets* of 1789; his enthusiasm was in considerable part shared by Wordsworth and Southey. Like *Frost at Midnight* and *Tintern Abbey*, Bowles's sonnets present a determinate speaker in a particular place; his opening description of the natural scene evokes a process of memory, meditation, and feeling, expressed in ordinary language, correlative with details of the scene, and sustained to the end of the poem.

To the River Itchin, Near Winton[1]

Itchin, when I behold thy banks again,
  Thy crumbling margin, and thy silver breast,
  On which the self-same tints still seem'd to rest,
Why feels my heart the shivering sense of pain?
Is it—that many a summer's day has past   5
  Since, in life's morn, I carolled on thy side?
  Is it—that oft, since then, my heart has sighed,
As Youth, and Hope's delusive gleams, flew fast?
  Is it—that those, who circled on thy shore,
  Companions of my youth, now meet no more?   10
Whate'er the cause, upon thy banks I bend,
  Sorrowing, yet feel such solace at my heart,
As at the meeting of some long-lost friend,
  From whom, in happier hours, we wept to part.

1789

Languid, and Sad, and Slow

Languid, and sad, and slow, from day to day
  I journey on, yet pensive turn to view
  (Where the rich landscape gleams with softer hue)
The streams, and vales, and hills, that steal away.
So fares it with the children of the earth: 5
  For when life's goodly prospect opens round,
  Their spirits beat to tread that fairy ground,
Where every vale sounds to the pipe of mirth.
But them vain hope and easy youth beguiles,
  And soon a longing look, like me, they cast   10
  Back on the pleasing prospect of the past:
Yet Fancy points where still far onward smiles
Some sunny spot, and her fair coloring blends,
'Till cheerless on their path the night descends.

1789

---

1. Compare Coleridge's Sonnet *to the River Otter*.

SIR WALTER SCOTT
(1771–1832)

Sir Walter Scott (he was made a baronet in 1820) spent a great part of his childhood in the valley of the Tweed River, and at that time and in many later rides along the Border and in the Highlands he absorbed Scottish gossip, history, legend, song, and folklore. He was an inordinate reader with a capacious memory, and even while he was studying law in Edinburgh he spent a great deal of time reading medieval romances, history, travel books, and other documents, which provided him with the anti-quarian learning he later poured into his novels. In 1802–3 he published an important three-volume collection of popular ballads, *Minstrelsy of the Scottish Border*, sometimes piecing out the missing parts of the ballads from his own invention. Between 1805 and 1813 he wrote a series of metrical romances loosely modeled on medieval narrative forms—including *The Lay of the Last Minstrel, Marmion, The Lady of the Lake*—which made him for a time the most widely read of English poets. When his public was won over by Byron's more brilliant narrative romances, Scott turned to writing (until 1827, anonymously) his great series of historical novels. He made a large fortune, but went deeply into debt by building up the huge, pseudo-medieval estate of Abbotsford on the banks of the Tweed, where he attempted to live the antique life of a lord of the manor. In 1826 the failure of the printing firm of James Ballantyne (in which Scott was a silent partner) and of his publisher, Archibald Constable, plunged him into financial disaster, from which he struggled heroically all the rest of his life to extricate himself. Only after his death were his debts finally paid off, with money realized by the sale of his copyrights.

The Dreary Change is Scott's quiet and controlled version of the Romantic theme of an apparent loss of glory in the landscape which is in fact a change in the mind of the observer. And in some of his lyrics deriving from the popular ballad and folk song, Scott (like Keats in *La Belle Dame Sans Merci*) captured from his originals the artistic values of understatement and terse suggestiveness.

The Dreary Change

The sun upon the Weirdlaw Hill,
  In Ettrick's vale, is sinking sweet;
The westland wind is hush and still,
  The lake lies sleeping at my feet.
Yet not the landscape to mine eye   5
  Bears those bright hues that once it bore;
Though evening, with her richest dye,
  Flames o'er the hills of Ettrick's shore.

With listless look along the plain,
  I see Tweed's silver current glide,   10
And coldly mark the holy fane
  Of Melrose rise in ruined pride.
The quiet lake, the balmy air,
  The hill, the stream, the tower, the tree—
Are they still such as once they were?   15
  Or is the dreary change in me?

Alas, the warped and broken board,
  How can it bear the painter's dye!

The harp of strained and tuneless chord,
  How to the minstrel's skill reply!   20
To aching eyes each landscape lowers,
  To feverish pulse each gale blows chill:
  And Araby's or Eden's bowers
    Were barren as this moorland hill.

1817

Jock of Hazeldean[4]

"Why weep ye by the tide, ladie?
  Why weep ye by the tide?
I'll wed ye to my youngest son,
  And ye sall be his bride:
And ye sall be his bride, ladie,   5
  Sae comely to be seen"—
But ay she loot the tears down fa'
  For Jock of Hazeldean.

"Now let this willfu' grief be done,
  And dry that cheek so pale;   10
Young Frank is chief of Errington
  And lord of Langley Dale;
His step is first in peaceful ha',
  His sword in battle keen"—
But ay she loot the tears down fa'   15
  For Jock of Hazeldean.

"A chain of gold ye sall not lack,
  Nor braid to bind your hair;
Nor mettled hound, nor managed[5] hawk,
  Nor palfrey fresh and fair;
And you, the foremost o' them a',   20
  Shall ride our forest queen"—
But ay she loot the tears down fa'
  For Jock of Hazeldean.

The kirk was decked at morningtide,   25
  The tapers glimmered fair;
The priest and bridegroom wait the bride,
  And dame and knight are there.
They sought her baith by bower and ha';
  The ladie was not seen!   30
She's o'er the Border and awa'
  Wi' Jock of Hazeldean.

1816

4. The first stanza is from a traditional   5. Trained.
Scottish ballad.

Proud Maisie[6]

Proud Maisie is in the wood
 Walking so early;
Sweet Robin sits on the bush,
 Singing so rarely.

"Tell me, thou bonny bird,   5
 When shall I marry me?"—
"When six braw[7] gentlemen
 Kirkward shall carry ye."

"Who makes the bridal bed,
 Birdie, say truly?"—   10
"The gray-headed sexton
 That delves the grave duly.

"The glowworm o'er grave and stone
 Shall light thee steady,
The owl from the steeple sing,   15
 'Welcome, proud lady.' "

                                    1818

6. Sung by crazy Madge Wildfire on her   (Chapter 40).
deathbed in *The Heart of Midlothian*   7. Fine.

ROBERT SOUTHEY
(1774–1843)

Time has dealt harshly with Robert Southey, for he is remembered mainly for his close association with poets greater than himself and for Byron's brilliant lampoons in *Don Juan* and *The Vision of Judgment*. He attended Oxford, was for a short time a fervent supporter of the French Revolution, and wrote an epic and two dramas inspired by that event. With Coleridge (who became his brother-in-law) he planned the frustrated "Pantisocracy" on the banks of the Susquehanna and collaborated on several poems. In 1803 he settled at Keswick in the Lake Country, within long walking distance of his friend Wordsworth; with advancing age, he settled into a Tory viewpoint more conservative than either Wordsworth's or Coleridge's. All his life a learned and hard-working professional writer, he produced thousands of pages of epic and shorter poems, history, essays, biographies, and anything else for which there was a market; he was awarded the laureateship in 1813.

The only Southey writings still widely read are a few lyrics, a beautifully lucid short *Life of Nelson* (1813), and—a piece so widely loved and often retold that it has lost its connection with its author and acquired the status of an anonymous "fairy tale"—the story of *The Three Bears*.

My Days Among the Dead Are Passed

My days among the dead are passed;
    Around me I behold,
Where'er these casual eyes are cast,
    The mighty minds of old;
My never-failing friends are they,   5
With whom I converse day by day.

With them I take delight in weal,
    And seek relief in woe;
And while I understand and feel
    How much to them I owe,   10
My cheeks have often been bedewed
With tears of thoughtful gratitude.

My thoughts are with the dead, with them
    I live in long-past years,
Their virtues love, their faults condemn,   15
    Partake their hopes and fears,
And from their lessons seek and find
Instruction with an humble mind.

My hopes are with the dead, anon
    My place with them will be,   20
And I with them shall travel on
    Through all futurity;
Yet leaving here a name, I trust,
That will not perish in the dust.

1818   1823

WALTER SAVAGE LANDOR
(1775–1864)

Landor was born well-to-do, and with a violently independent and combative temper: he quarreled with the authorities at Rugby and at Oxford,
with his wife and family, with servants and officials, with the governments of Europe (he was a Revolutionary sympathizer, and unlike most
of his literary contemporaries never wavered in his republicanism), and
with his neighbors, first in Wales and then in Italy; he was constantly
embroiled in expensive litigation. But in the course of his long life the
generous-hearted and outspoken poet also acquired many friends and admirers, ranging from Southey and Hazlitt in the Romantic generation to
Robert Browning, Charles Dickens, and Algernon Charles Swinburne
among the Victorians. He lived in Italy from 1815 to 1835. When he

returned to England he was lionized for a time as an active Romantic poet when all the others were dead or silent, but a notorious outburst, which led to court action, forced him in 1857 to take up once more his exile in Italy, where he died in his 90th year.

Most of the writings of this greatly irascible man, whether in prose or verse, have characteristics to which critics apply the terms "serene" and "marmoreal." His best-known prose works are the numerous *Imaginary Conversations* (1824–53), mainly between historical figures, and on literary, philosophic, and political topics. These have their strong admirers, but they are written in a style which is so elevated and remote that they sometimes suggest dialogues between heroic-sized Greek statues. He wrote many long narrative and dramatic poems, of which the most durable is the epic *Gebir*, published in the same year as *Lyrical Ballads* (1798). But Landor's supreme achievement, in which he emulated Greek and Roman models, is in the short lyric, usually an elegy or a courtly compliment which is stripped down until it approximates an epigram. He is the master of a form of verse very rare in English—the spare, elegant, and severely formal utterance of lyric passion.

Mother, I Cannot Mind My Wheel

Mother, I cannot mind my wheel;
   My fingers ache, my lips are dry:
Oh! if you felt the pain I feel!
   But oh, who ever felt as I!

No longer could I doubt him true,   5
   All other men may use deceit;
He always said my eyes were blue,
   And often swore my lips were sweet.

1806

Rose Aylmer[1]

Ah, what avails the sceptered race,
   Ah, what the form divine!
What every virtue, every grace!
   Rose Aylmer, all were thine.

Rose Aylmer, whom these wakeful eyes   5
   May weep, but never see,
A night of memories and of sighs
   I consecrate to thee.

1806

1. Rose Aylmer was the daughter of the fourth Baron Aylmer (hence "the sceptered race," line 1). She became a friend of Landor's in 1794 at the age of 17, and died suddenly in Calcutta, six years later.

The Three Roses[2]

When the buds began to burst,
Long ago, with Rose the First
I was walking; joyous then
Far above all other men,
Till before us up there stood   5
Britonferry's[3] oaken wood,
Whispering, "*Happy as thou art,*
Happiness and thou must part."
Many summers have gone by
Since a Second Rose and I   10
(Rose from that same stem) have told
This and other tales of old.
She upon her wedding day
Carried home my tenderest lay:[4]
From her lap I now have heard   15
Gleeful, chirping, Rose the Third.
Not for *her* this hand of mine
Rhyme with nuptial wreath shall twine;
Cold and torpid it must lie,
Mute the tongue, and closed the eye.   20

1855

On Seeing a Hair of Lucretia Borgia[5]

Borgia, thou once wert almost too august
And high for adoration—now thou'rt dust;
All that remains of thee these plaits infold,
Calm hair, meandering with pellucid gold!

1825, 1846

Past Ruined Ilion

Past ruined Ilion Helen lives,
    Alcestis rises from the shades;[6]
Verse calls them forth; 'tis verse that gives
    Immortal youth to mortal maids.

2. The first Rose was Rose Aylmer, the second her niece, and the third her grandniece.
3. In Wales.
4. Landor's epithalamion, *To a Bride*.
5. 1480–1519; Duchess of Ferrara, whose court became a notable center for scholars, poets, and artists.
6. Helen of Troy ("Ilion"); Alcestis gave her life in exchange for that of her husband, but was rescued from Hades ("the shades") by Hercules.

Soon shall oblivion's deepening veil 5
    Hide all the peopled hills you see,
The gay, the proud, while lovers hail
    These many summers you and me.

The tear for fading beauty check,
    For passing glory cease to sigh; 10
One form shall rise above the wreck,
    One name, Ianthe, shall not die.

                      1831

Dirce

Stand close around, ye Stygian set,[7]
    With Dirce in one boat conveyed!
Or Charon, seeing, may forget
    That he is old and she a shade.

                      1831

Twenty Years Hence

Twenty years hence my eyes may grow
If not quite dim, yet rather so,
Still yours from others they shall know
    Twenty years hence.

Twenty years hence though it may hap 5
That I be called to take a nap
In a cool cell where thunderclap
    Was never heard,

There breathe but o'er my arch of grass
A not too sadly sighed *Alas*, 10
And I shall catch, ere you can pass,
    That wingéd word.

                      1846

On His Seventy-fifth Birthday

I strove with none; for none was worth my strife,
    Nature I loved, and next to Nature, Art;
I warmed both hands before the fire of life,
    It sinks, and I am ready to depart.

1849   1849

7. I.e., the shades of the dead, ferried by Charon over the river Styx to Hades.

Well I Remember How You Smiled

Well I remember how you smiled
　　To see me write your name upon
The soft sea-sand. . . "O! *what a child!*
　　You think you're writing upon stone!"
I have since written what no tide　　　　　　　　5
　　Shall ever wash away, what men
Unborn shall read o'er ocean wide
　　And find Ianthe's name again.

1863

THOMAS MOORE
(1779–1852)

Although he was the Irish Catholic son of a Dublin grocer, Tom Moore became the fashionable versifier of Regency England. His *Irish Melodies*, published between 1807 and 1834 with accompanying music (some of the tunes were by Moore himself), were an immense success, and for many years his Irish wit, charm, liberalism, and singing voice made him a brilliant figure in literary and social circles, especially among the aristocratic Whig reformers. The same qualities made him one of Byron's closest friends. He wrote numerous satires, lampoons, and prose pieces. He is chiefly remembered, however, for *Lalla Rookh* (1817), written during the vogue for Oriental verse romances, which achieved a great European success; his fine *Life of Byron* (1830); and a handful of songs—most of them in the tradition of amatory gallantry that goes back to the 17th-century Cavaliers—which transcend the triviality, prettiness, and easy pathos of his lyric standard, and have won their way into that repertory which is sung on a social evening around the piano.

Believe Me, If All Those Endearing Young Charms

Believe me, if all those endearing young charms,
　　Which I gaze on so fondly today,
Were to change by tomorrow, and fleet in my arms,
　　Like fairy-gifts fading away,
Thou wouldst still be adored, as this moment thou art,　　　　5
　　Let thy loveliness fade as it will,
And around the dear ruin each wish of my heart
　　Would entwine itself verdantly still.

It is not while beauty and youth are thine own,
   And thy cheeks unprofaned by a tear   10
That the fervor and faith of a soul can be known,
   To which time will but make thee more dear;
No, the heart that has truly loved never forgets,
   But as truly loves on to the close,
As the sunflower turns on her god, when he sets,   15
   The same look which she turned when he rose.

                                 1808

The Harp That Once Through Tara's Halls[1]

   The harp that once through Tara's halls
     The soul of music shed,
   Now hangs as mute on Tara's walls
     As if that soul were fled.—
   So sleeps the pride of former days,   5
     So glory's thrill is o'er,
   And hearts that once beat high for praise
     Now feel that pulse no more.

   No more to chiefs and ladies bright
     The harp of Tara swells;   10
   The chord alone that breaks at night
     Its tale of ruin tells.
   Thus Freedom now so seldom wakes,
     The only throb she gives,
   Is when some heart indignant breaks,   15
     To show that still she lives.

                                 1834

The Time I've Lost in Wooing

   The time I've lost in wooing,
   In watching and pursuing
     The light that lies
     In woman's eyes,
   Has been my heart's undoing.   5
   Though Wisdom oft has sought me,
   I scorned the lore she brought me,
     My only books
     Were woman's looks,
   And folly's all they've taught me.   10

1. Tara, northwest of Dublin, was capital of Ireland during the Middle Ages, when that country was a great center of European civilization and learning.

Her smile when Beauty granted,
I hung with gaze enchanted,
　　Like him, the sprite,[2]
　　Whom maids by night
Oft meet in glen that's haunted.
Like him, too, Beauty won me,　　　　　　　　　　15
But while her eyes were on me;
　　If once their ray
　　Was turned away,
Oh! winds could not outrun me.　　　　　　　　　20

And are those follies going?
And is my proud heart growing
　　Too cold or wise
　　For brilliant eyes
Again to set it glowing?　　　　　　　　　　　25
No, vain, alas! th' endeavor
From bonds so sweet to sever;
　　Poor Wisdom's chance
　　Against a glance
Is now as weak as ever.　　　　　　　　　　30

1834

2. The Irish fairy; he can be controlled by mortals only when their eyes are
fixed on him.

LEIGH HUNT

(1784–1859)

James Henry Leigh Hunt was an impulsive, warm-hearted, but improvident man, who begot a large family, was in constant financial difficulties, and often fell back on the charity of his friends. But however inept in managing his personal affairs, Hunt was a fighting liberal journalist. With his brother John he began the *Examiner*, a weekly periodical which ran for fourteen years as the most formidable opponent of the oppressive Tory government. In 1812 the brothers were fined and imprisoned for denouncing the Prince Regent (later George IV) as a liar and "a fat Adonis of fifty." Leigh Hunt spent two rather comfortable years in jail, living with his family and free to write and receive visits from his friends and political admirers. In 1822 he took his family to Pisa to join Shelley and Byron in establishing a quarterly, the *Liberal*, but the drowning of Shelley and Byron's impatience with his collaborator brought the periodical to a close after only four issues. Back in England, Hunt carried on a great variety of activities through a long literary career, and before he died gained the friendship and somewhat qualified esteem of Browning, Thomas Carlyle, and Dickens.

As an informal essayist Hunt is copious, relaxed, and often engaging; but he was overshadowed by his great prose contemporaries, Lamb, Hazlitt, and

De Quincey. He was a voluminous reviewer and critic. His theatrical criticism is the best surviving record of the day-to-day popular theater; his literary criticism, while admirable for the sensitive taste and generosity with which he recognized and championed unpopular new poets, especially Shelley and Keats, lacks the theoretical penetration, the originality, and the distinction which characterized the critical writings of Coleridge and Hazlitt. Hunt also undertook a variety of poems, many of them on Italian and classical themes; the most ambitious, *The Story of Rimini* (1816), is written in loose and freely running couplets, and treats a serious theme in an incongruously arch and familiar style. For a short time this poem strongly influenced Hunt's young disciple, John Keats, who caught from it the relaxed meter and lush sensuousness that mar his early poems and thus gave some grounds for John Gibson Lockhart's grouping of Keats with Hunt in his brutal attack on the lower-class vulgarity of the "Cockney School of Poetry" in *Blackwood's Magazine* (1817).

The Fish, the Man, and the Spirit

TO A FISH

You strange, astonished-looking, angle-faced,
Dreary-mouthed, gaping wretches of the sea,
Gulping salt-water everlastingly,
Cold-blooded, though with red your blood be graced,
And mute, though dwellers in the roaring waste;   5
And you, all shapes beside, that fishy be—
Some round, some flat, some long, all devilry,
Legless, unloving, infamously chaste—

O scaly, slippery, wet, swift, staring wights,
What is't ye do? what life lead? eh, dull goggles?   10
How do ye vary your vile days and nights?
How pass your Sundays? Are ye still but joggles
In ceaseless wash? Still nought but gapes, and bites,
And drinks, and stares, diversified with boggles?[1]

A FISH ANSWERS

Amazing monster! that, for aught I know,   15
With the first sight of thee didst make our race
Forever stare! Oh flat and shocking face,
Grimly divided from the breast below!
Thou that on dry land horribly dost go
With a split body and most ridiculous pace,   20
Prong after prong, disgracer of all grace,
Long-useless-finned, haired, upright, unwet, slow!

O breather of unbreathable, sword-sharp air,
How canst exist? How bear thyself, thou dry
And dreary sloth? What particle canst share   25

1. Sudden movements of alarm.

Of the only blessed life, the watery?
I sometimes see of ye an actual *pair*
Go by! linked fin by fin! most odiously.

THE FISH TURNS INTO A MAN, AND THEN INTO A
SPIRIT, AND AGAIN SPEAKS

Indulge thy smiling scorn, if smiling still,
O man! and loathe, but with a sort of love;
For difference must its use by difference prove,   30
And, in sweet clang, the spheres with music fill.
One of the spirits am I, that at his will
Live in whate'er has life—fish, eagle, dove—
No hate, no pride, beneath nought, nor above,   35
A visitor of the rounds of God's sweet skill.

Man's life is warm, glad, sad, 'twixt loves and graves,
Boundless in hope, honored with pangs austere,
Heaven-gazing; and his angel-wings he craves:
The fish is swift, small-needing, vague yet clear,   40
A cold, sweet, silver life, wrapped in round waves,
Quickened with touches of transporting fear.

                                                    1836

Rondeau[2]

Jenny kissed me when we met,
    Jumping from the chair she sat in;
Time, you thief, who love to get
    Sweets into your list, put that in:
Say I'm weary, say I'm sad,   5
    Say that health and wealth have missed me,
Say I'm growing old, but add,
    Jenny kissed me.

                                                    1838

2. Jenny is said to be Mrs. Jane Welsh   the rondeau, an elaborate French verse
Carlyle. This is a shortened form of   form which normally has fifteen lines.

THOMAS LOVE PEACOCK
(1785–1866)

Peacock, the son of a London businessman, had a position with the East
India Company which allowed him leisure to devote to his writing. Although he was himself a poet, his *Four Ages of Poetry* (1820) was a sly
comment on the excesses of his Romantic contemporaries in the ironic
guise of a history of the decline of poetry from its golden past; it evoked

from his close friend Shelley *The Defense of Poetry* by way of refutation. Peacock's finest achievements are his inimitable novels—including *Headlong Hall* (1816), *Melincourt* (1817), *Nightmare Abbey* (1818), and *Crotchet Castle* (1831)—in which he gathers a group of argumentative eccentrics in a country house and sets them to talking. His protagonists represent extreme or bigoted or visionary points of view on all sides of the important topics of the day; among them are caricatures of his great contemporaries, Wordsworth, Coleridge, Southey, Byron, as well as his friend Shelley—who took no offense. The novels also included satiric songs. The one reprinted here is taken from *The Misfortunes of Elphin* (1829); it explodes the Romantic vogue of the long, pseudohistorical metrical romance in forty devastating lines.

The War Song of Dinas Vawr

The mountain sheep are sweeter,
But the valley sheep are fatter;
We therefore deemed it meeter
To carry off the latter.
We made an expedition;   5
We met a host, and quelled it;
We forced a strong position,
And killed the men who held it.

On Dyfed's richest valley,
Where herds of kine were browsing,   10
We made a mighty sally,
To furnish our carousing.
Fierce warriors rushed to meet us;
We met them, and o'erthrew them:
They struggled hard to beat us;   15
But we conquered them, and slew them.

As we drove our prize at leisure,
The king marched forth to catch us:
His rage surpassed all measure,
But his people could not match us.   20
He fled to his hall pillars;
And, ere our force we led off,
Some sacked his house and cellars,
While others cut his head off.

We there, in strife bewild'ring,   25
Spilt blood enough to swim in:
We orphaned many children,
And widowed many women.
The eagles and the ravens

We glutted with our foemen;   30
The heroes and the cravens,
The spearmen and the bowmen.

We brought away from battle,
And much their land bemoaned them,
Two thousand head of cattle,   35
And the head of him who owned them:
Ednyfed, king of Dyfed,
His head was borne before us;
His wine and beasts supplied our feasts,
And his overthrow, our chorus.

                                                          40
                                                   1829

JOHN CLARE
(1793–1864)

John Clare was the nearest thing to the pure and artless "natural poet" for whom primitivists had been searching ever since the mid-18th century. An earlier and far greater peasant poet, Robert Burns, had managed to acquire a solid liberal education; Clare, however, was born at Helpston, a Northamptonshire village, of a field laborer who was barely literate and a mother who was entirely illiterate, and himself obtained only sufficient schooling to teach him to read and write. Although he was a sickly and fearful child, he had to work hard in the field, where he found himself composing verse "for downright pleasure in giving vent to my feelings." In 1820 publication of his *Poems Descriptive of Rural Life* attracted critical attention, and on a trip to London he was made much of by leading writers of the day. But his celebrity soon dimmed, and his three later books of verse were failures. Under these and other disappointments his mind gave way in 1837, and he spent almost all the rest of his life in an asylum. The place was for him a refuge as well as a confinement, for he was treated kindly, allowed to wander about the countryside, and encouraged to go on writing his verses; some of his best achievements are the poems composed in his madness.

Clare did not, of course, write independently of a poetic tradition, for he had studied the poetry of James Thomson, Milton, Wordsworth, and Coleridge. But he managed to stay true to his own experience of unspectacular country sights and customs and to capture in his verse the country idiom. Clare's homely mouse, in the poem below, is a bit of pure rustic impressionism in a way that even Robert Burns's moralized mouse is not. And a small proportion of Clare's introspective asylum-poems achieve so haunting a poignancy and are spoken in so quietly distinctive a voice that they have made the great mass of mainly humdrum manuscripts he left at his death an exciting place of discovery for recent editors.

Mouse's Nest

I found a ball of grass among the hay
And progged[1] it as I passed and went away;
And when I looked I fancied something stirred,
And turned again and hoped to catch the bird—
When out an old mouse bolted in the wheats   5
With all her young ones hanging at her teats;
She looked so odd and so grotesque to me,
I ran and wondered what the thing could be,
And pushed the knapweed[2] bunches where I stood;
Then the mouse hurried from the craking[3] brood.   10
The young ones squeaked, and as I went away
She found her nest again among the hay.
The water o'er the pebbles scarce could run
And broad old cesspools[4] glittered in the sun.

ca. 1835–37   1935

I Am

I am—yet what I am, none cares or knows;
    My friends forsake me like a memory lost:
I am the self-consumer of my woes—
    They rise and vanish in oblivions host,
Like shadows in love frenzied stifled throes   5
    And yet I am, and live—like vapours tossed

Into the nothingness of scorn and noise,
    Into the living sea of waking dreams,
Where there is neither sense of life or joys,
    But the vast shipwreck of my life's esteems;   10
Even the dearest that I love the best
    Are strange—nay, rather, stranger than the rest.

I long for scenes where man hath never trod
    A place where woman never smiled or wept
There to abide with my Creator God,   15
    And sleep as I in childhood sweetly slept,
Untroubling and untroubled where I lie
    The grass below, above, the vaulted sky.

1842–64   1848

1. Prodded.
2. A plant with knobs of purple flowers.
3. Squawking.
4. Low spots where water has collected.

Clock a Clay[1]

In the cowslip's peeps[2] I lie
Hidden from the buzzing fly
While green grass beneath me lies
Pearled wi' dew like fishes' eyes
Here I lie a Clock a clay   5
Waiting for the time o' day

While grassy forests quake surprise
And the wild wind sobs and sighs
My gold home rocks as like to fall
On its pillar green and tall   10
When the pattering rain drives by
Clock a Clay keeps warm and dry

Day by day and night by night
All the week I hide from sight
In the cowslips peeps I lie   15
In rain and dew still warm and dry
Day and night and night and day
Red black spotted clock a clay

My home it shakes in wind and showers
Pale green pillar topped wi' flowers   20
Bending at the wild wind's breath
Till I touch the grass beneath
Here still I live lone clock a clay
Watching for the time of day

ca. 1848   1873

Song

I peeled bits of straw and I got switches too
From the gray peeling willow as idlers do,
And I switched at the flies as I sat all alone
Till my flesh, blood, and marrow was turned to dry bone.
My illness was love, though I knew not the smart,   5
But the beauty of love was the blood of my heart.
Crowded places, I shunned them as noises too rude

---

1. The ladybird, or ladybug. The sixth and last lines allude to the children's game of telling the hour by the number of taps it takes to make the ladybird fly away home.
2. Cf. the opening lines of Ariel's song in Act V of Shakespeare's *Tempest*: "Where the bee sucks, there suck I: / In a cowslip's bell I lie." "Peeps": i.e., pips —single blossoms of flowers growing in a cluster. The cowslip is a yellow primrose.

And fled to the silence of sweet solitude,
Where the flower in green darkness buds, blossoms, and fades,
Unseen of all shepherds and flower-loving maids—   10
The hermit bees find them but once and away;
There I'll bury alive and in silence decay.

I looked on the eyes of fair woman too long,
Till silence and shame stole the use of my tongue:
When I tried to speak to her I'd nothing to say,   15
So I turned myself round and she wandered away.
When she got too far off, why, I'd something to tell,
So I sent sighs behind her and walked to my cell.
Willow switches I broke and peeled bits of straws,
Ever lonely in crowds, in nature's own laws—   20
My ballroom the pasture, my music the bees,
My drink was the fountain, my church the tall trees.
Who ever would love or be tied to a wife
When it makes a man mad all the days of his life?

1842–64   1920

Song [Secret Love]

I hid my love when young while I
Couldn't bear the buzzing of a fly
I hid my love to my despite
Till I could not bear to look at light
I dare not gaze upon her face   5
But left her memory in each place
Where ere I saw a wild flower lie
I kissed and bade my love goodbye

I met her in the greenest dells
Where dew drops pearl the wood bluebells   10
The lost breeze kissed her bright blue eye
The bee kissed and went singing by
A sunbeam found a passage there
A gold chain round her neck so fair
As secret as the wild bee's song   15
She lay there all the summer long

I hid my love in field and town
Till e'en the breeze would knock me down
The bees seemed singing ballads o'er
The fly's buss[1] turned a Lion's roar   20
And even silence found a tongue
To haunt me all the summer long
The riddle nature could not prove
Was nothing else but secret love

1842–64   1920

___

1. Buzz; it may also mean "kiss."

An Invite to Eternity

Wilt thou go with me sweet maid
Say maiden wilt thou go with me
Through the valley depths of shade
Of night and dark obscurity
Where the path hath lost its way   5
Where the sun forgets the day
Where there's nor life nor light to see
Sweet maiden wilt thou go with me

Where stones will turn to flooding streams
Where plains will rise like ocean waves   10
Where life will fade like visioned dreams
And mountains darken into caves
Say maiden wilt thou go with me
Through this sad non-identity
Where parents live and are forgot   15
And sisters live and know us not

Say maiden wilt thou go with me
In this strange death of life to be
To live in death and be the same
Without this life or home or name   20
At once to be and not to be
That was and is not—yet to see
Things pass like shadows—and the sky
Above, below, around us lie.

The land of shadows wilt thou trace   25
And look nor know each other's face
The present mixed with reasons gone
And past and present all as one
Say maiden can thy life be led
To join the living with the dead   30
Then trace thy footsteps on with me
We're wed to one eternity

1842–64   1920

A Vision

I lost the love of heaven above
I spurned the lust of earth below
I felt the sweets of fancied love
And hell itself my only foe

I lost earth's joys but felt the glow   5
Of heaven's flame abound in me

Till loveliness and I did grow
The bard of immortality

I loved but woman fell away
I hid me from her faded fame   10
I snatched the sun's eternal ray
And wrote till earth was but a name

In every language upon earth
On every shore, o'er every sea,
I gave my name immortal birth,   15
And kept my spirit with the free

1844   1924

GEORGE DARLEY
(1795–1846)

Darley, an Irish mathematician, was one of the poets who figured in the "Elizabethan revival" of the later Romantic period. He wrote prose tales, dramatic criticism, and various dramas in the style of Shakespeare's contemporaries. His long work, *Nepenthe* (1835), includes most of his best lyrics, from which the first of the following poems has been selected; the last poem is from *Syren Songs* (1837). The distinctive charm of Darley's lyrics is that they recall, without merely mimicking, their Elizabethan and 17th-century originals. The stately lyric *It Is Not Beauty I Demand* was for years printed in Palgrave's *Golden Treasury* as a poem of the Caroline period.

The Phoenix[1]

O blest unfabled Incense Tree,
That burns in glorious Araby,
With red scent chalicing the air,
Till earth-life grow Elysian there!

Half-buried to her flaming breast   5
In this bright tree, she makes her nest,
Hundred-sunned Phoenix! when she must
Crumble at length to hoary dust!

Her gorgeous deathbed! her rich pyre
Burnt up with aromatic fire!   10
Her urn, sight high from spoiler men!
Her birthplace when self-born again!

---

1. A legendary bird: only one exists at a time; it dies periodically, singing in aromatic flames, and is reborn from the ashes.

The mountainless green wilds among,
Here ends she her unechoing song!
With amber tears and odorous sighs
Mourned by the desert where she dies!   15

1835

It Is Not Beauty I Demand

It is not Beauty I demand,
   A crystal brow, the moon's despair,
Nor the snow's daughter, a white hand,
   Nor mermaid's yellow pride of hair.

Tell me not of your starry eyes,   5
   Your lips that seem on roses fed,
Your breasts where Cupid trembling lies,
   Nor sleeps for kissing of his bed.

A bloomy pair of vermeil cheeks,
   Like Hebe's in her ruddiest hours,   10
A breath that softer music speaks
   Than summer winds a-wooing flowers.

These are but gauds; nay, what are lips?
   Coral beneath the ocean-stream,
Whose brink when your adventurer sips   15
   Full oft he perisheth on them.

And what are cheeks but ensigns oft
   That wave hot youth to fields of blood?
Did Helen's breast though ne'er so soft,
   Do Greece or Ilium any good?   20

Eyes can with baleful ardor burn,
   Poison can breath that erst perfumed,
There's many a white hand holds an urn
   With lovers' hearts to dust consumed.

For crystal brows—there's naught within,   25
   They are but empty cells for pride;
He who the Syren's hair would win
   Is mostly strangled in the tide.

Give me, instead of beauty's bust,
   A tender heart, a loyal mind,
Which with temptation I could trust,   30
   Yet never linked with error find.

One in whose gentle bosom I
   Could pour my secret heart of woes,
Like the care-burdened honey-fly   35
   That hides his murmurs in the rose.

My earthly comforter! whose love
　　So indefeasible might be,
That when my spirit won above
　　Hers could not stay for sympathy.　　　　40

1828

The Mermaidens' Vesper Hymn

Troop home to silent grots and caves!
　　Troop home! and mimic as you go
The mournful winding of the waves
　　Which to their dark abysses flow.

At this sweet hour, all things beside　　　　5
　　In amorous pairs to covert creep;
The swans that brush the evening tide
　　Homeward in snowy couples keep.

In his green den the murmuring seal
　　Close by his sleek companion lies;　　　　10
While singly we to bedward steal,
　　And close in fruitless sleep our eyes.

In bowers of love men take their rest,
　　In loveless bowers we sigh alone,
With bosom friends are others blest—　　　　15
　　But we have none! but we have none!

1837

THOMAS LOVELL BEDDOES
(1803–1849)

Beddoes was the most gifted poet of the late Romantic "Elizabethan revival." By profession a physician and anatomist, he studied at Oxford and Göttingen, then spent most of his mature life as a solitary wanderer among the universities of Germany and Switzerland, involving himself in various radical movements. His letters contain shrewd and caustic criticism of his own and others' writings, but also reveal an eccentricity and a despondency that sometimes verge on madness. His only two published volumes, *The Improvisatore* (1821) and *The Bride's Tragedy* (1822), he wrote while still an undergraduate at Oxford. His later writings consist mainly of massive fragments of drama and romance. The major work was *Death's Jest-Book, or The Fool's Tragedy*, begun in the later 1820's, incessantly patched and revised for the next quarter century, and left still unfinished at his death. A nightmarish drama of murder, disguise, revenge, and ghosts, it reveals that his chief models were Jacobean tragedy, English and German terror tales of the "Gothic" vogue, and the more fantastic among

the writings of Shelley. Beddoes' lyrics, many of which were incorporated
in his dramas, specialize in the sinister and the grotesquely comic effect,
and at their best achieve an exquisite movement and a thrilling felicity
of unexpected phrasing. Beddoes, like his Jacobean masters, John Webster
and Cyril Tourneur—and his contemporary master, Shelley—was much
obsessed by death, as a thing at once terrible and dear. He ended his own
life, after several unsuccessful attempts, by taking poison.

Song

How many times do I love thee, dear?
  Tell me how many thoughts there be
    In the atmosphere
    Of a new-fall'n year,
Whose white and sable hours appear
  The latest flake of Eternity—   5
So many times do I love thee, dear.

How many times do I love again?
  Tell me how many beads there are
        In a silver chain   10
        Of evening rain,
Unraveled from the tumbling main,
  And threading the eye of a yellow star—
So many times do I love again.

1824   1851

Song

Old Adam, the carrion crow,
  The old crow of Cairo;
He sat in the shower, and let it flow
  Under his tail and over his crest;
    And through every feather
    Leaked the wet weather;   5
And the bough swung under his nest;
For his beak it was heavy with marrow.
  Is that the wind dying? O no;
    It's only two devils, that blow
    Through a murderer's bones, to and fro,   10
    In the ghosts' moonshine.

Ho! Eve, my gray carrion wife,
  When we have supped on kings' marrow,
Where shall we drink and make merry our life?   15
  Our nest it is queen Cleopatra's skull,

'Tis cloven and cracked,
And battered and hacked,
But with tears of blue eyes it is full:
Let us drink then, my raven of Cairo.   20
Is that the wind dying? O no;
It's only two devils, that blow
Through a murderer's bones, to and fro,
In the ghosts' moonshine.

1825–28   1849–50

The Phantom Wooer

A ghost, that loved a lady fair,
Ever in the starry air
    Of midnight at her pillow stood;
And, with a sweetness skies above
The luring words of human love,   5
    Her soul the phantom wooed.
Sweet and sweet is their poisoned note,
The little snakes of silver throat,
In mossy skulls that nest and lie,
Ever singing, "Die, oh! die."   10

Young soul put off your flesh, and come
With me into the quiet tomb,
    Our bed is lovely, dark, and sweet;
The earth will swing us, as she goes,
Beneath our coverlid of snows,   15
    And the warm leaden sheet.
Dear and dear is their poisoned note,
The little snakes of silver throat,
In mossy skulls that nest and lie,
Ever singing, "Die, oh! die."   20

1844–48   1849–50

Song of the Stygian Naiades[1]

"What do you think the mermaids of the Styx were singing as I
watched them bathing the other day"—

1

Proserpine may pull her flowers,
    Wet with dew or wet with tears,
    Red with anger, pale with fears;
Is it any fault of ours,

1. Water nymphs of the river Styx,
which encircles the classical underworld,
where Proserpine dwells as the captive
bride of Pluto, its amorous king. Beelzebub (line 16) is a devil (sometimes
identified with Satan himself) in the
Christian hell.

If Pluto be an amorous king
  And come home nightly, laden
Underneath his broad bat-wing
  With a gentle earthly maiden?
Is it so, Wind, is it so?
All that I and you do know
Is that we saw fly and fix
'Mongst the flowers and reeds of Styx,
        Yesterday,
Where the Furies made their hay
For a bed of tiger cubs,
A great fly of Beelzebub's,
The bee of hearts, which mortals name
Cupid, Love, and Fie for shame.

2

Proserpine may weep in rage,
  But ere I and you have done
  Kissing, bathing in the sun,
What I have in yonder cage,
  She shall guess and ask in vain,
Bird or serpent, wild or tame;
  But if Pluto does 't again,
It shall sing out loud his shame.
    What hast caught then? What hast caught?
Nothing but a poet's thought,
  Which so light did fall and fix
  'Mongst the flowers and reeds of Styx,
        Yesterday,
Where the Furies made their hay
For a bed of tiger cubs,
A great fly of Beelzebub's,
The bee of hearts, which mortals name
Cupid, Love, and Fie for shame.

1830–39

1935

Romantic Essayists

CHARLES LAMB
(1775–1834)

1782–89: At Christ's Hospital school; Coleridge a fellow student.
1820–25: Contributes "Essays of Elia" to the *London Magazine*.

Lamb was almost the exact contemporary of Wordsworth and Coleridge; he numbered these two poets, as well as Keats, among his close friends, published his own early poems in combination with those of Coleridge in 1796 and 1797, and supported the *Lyrical Ballads* and some of the other avant-garde poetry of his time. Yet Lamb lacks almost all the traits and convictions we think of as characteristically "Romantic." He happily lived all his life in the city and its environs, sharing Dr. Johnson's opinion that he who tires of London tires of life. He could not abide Shelley or his poetry and he distrusted Coleridge's supernaturalism and Wordsworth's oracular sublimities and religion of nature, preferring the elements in their poems which were human and realistic. In an age when many of the important writers were fervent radicals and some became equally fervent reactionaries, Lamb remained uncommitted in both politics and religion; and although on intimate terms with such dedicated reformers as Hazlitt, William Godwin, Thomas Holcroft, and Leigh Hunt, he chose them, as he said, not for their opinions, but "for some individuality of character which they manifested." In his own writings, the one attribute he shared with his great contemporaries was that of *l'étalage du moi*, "the display of one's own personality": many of his best familiar essays, like Wordsworth's poems, are made up of his early experiences and feelings, recollected in tranquility. But it must be remembered that, although personal poetry was a new and distinctive Romantic form, the personal essay was already a well-established genre which had been developed by Montaigne as early as the 16th century.

Lamb was born in the Inner Temple, an ancient section of London where his father was clerk and assistant to a lawyer. At the age of 7 he entered Christ's Hospital, the "Bluecoat School" of his essay *Christ's Hospital Five and Thirty Years Ago*. He left the school before he was 15 and soon thereafter became a clerk in the accounting department of the huge commercial house, The East India Company, where he remained for 33 years. His adult life was quiet and unadventurous, but under its calm surface, as Walter Pater said, lay "something of the fateful domestic horror, of the beautiful heroism and devotedness too, of old Greek tragedy." When he was 22 his beloved sister Mary, ten years his senior, broke under the strain of caring for her invalid parents and in an insane paroxysm stabbed her mother to the heart. Lamb wrote to Coleridge:

My dearest friend—

* * * My poor dear dearest sister in a fit of insanity has been the death of her own mother. I was at hand only time enough to snatch the knife out of her grasp. She is at present in a madhouse, from whence I fear she must be moved to an hospital. God has preserved to me my senses. * * * My poor father was slightly wounded, and I am left to take care of him and my aunt. * * * Write—as religious a letter as possible—but no mention of what is gone and done with—with me former things are passed away, and I have something more to do than to feel—

God Almighty have us all in his keeping.—

C. Lamb

Upon her recovery Mary was released to the care of her brother, who devoted to her and to their common household the rest of his life. Mary's attacks recurred, briefly but periodically, and when the terribly familiar symptoms began to manifest themselves, Lamb and Mary would walk arm in arm and weeping to the asylum, carrying a strait jacket with them.

Most of the time, however, Mary was her normally serene and gracious self, and she shared her brother's delight in old books, the theater, art galleries, and the inexhaustible variousness of the great city. She shared also his gregariousness and genius for friendship. The Wednesday (sometimes Thursday) night gatherings at the Lambs attracted a varied company which included many of the leading writers and artists of England. Among his guests Lamb moved with his peculiar shuffling gait, dressed invariably in old-fashioned black of clerical cut, his body fragile, but surmounted by a fine head; everyone remarked on the sad sweetness of his smile. He drew furiously upon a pipe of strong tobacco and drank copiously; as the alcohol eased his habitual stammer, his puns and practical jokes grew ever more outrageous. Occasionally an evening ended with Lamb drunk under the table. But his friends invariably applied to him the epithet "gentle"—to his great indignation. "For God's sake," he exploded to Coleridge, "don't make me ridiculous any more by terming me gentle-hearted in print, or do it in better verses." "Substitute drunken dog, ragged-head, seld-shaven, odd-eyed, stuttering, or any other epithet which truly and properly belongs to the gentleman in question." Lamb had, in fact, a complex temperament, in which the playfulness overlay a somber melancholy and the freakishness sometimes manifested a touch of malice. To requests from Wordsworth and Coleridge for criticism of their poems he replied with a caustic candor not entirely appreciated by its beneficiaries. This charming egotist cherished his prejudices and distastes—he called them his "imperfect sympathies"—no less than he did his sympathies and enjoyments, and he never encountered pretentiousness, complacency, or a solemnity too profound and sustained without puncturing it by a well-honed witticism. "What choice venom!" exclaimed his friend Hazlitt, an expert on the subject—but while Hazlitt managed to antagonize almost everyone by his outspokenness, few could take offense, and none could long sustain it, at Lamb's antic speech and behavior.

To supplement his salary at the East India House, Lamb had early turned to writing in a variety of forms. When in 1818, at the age of 43, he published his *Works*, he apparently thought his major writing had already been accomplished. He had produced a good deal of minor verse;

a sentimental novel, *Rosamund Gray*; a blank verse tragedy in the Elizabethan manner, *John Woodvil*; a farce, *Mr. H——*, which was hissed by many (including the honest author) when it was produced at Drury Lane; and, in collaboration with his sister Mary, the excellent children's book, *Tales from Shakespeare*. His most impressive achievements were the brilliant comments incorporated in his anthology, important in the Elizabethan revival of that period, *Specimens of English Dramatic Poets Who Lived About the Time of Shakespeare*, together with two fine critical essays, *The Tragedies of Shakespeare* and *On the Genius and Character of Hogarth*. But not until two years after the appearance of his *Works* did Lamb begin to contribute to the *London Magazine* the *Essays of Elia*, which have elevated him to the rank of a major author.

Lamb's earlier attempts in the fictional forms show that he lacked the power of inventing characters and events, but in the familiar essay (in which he had, in effect, served a long apprenticeship in his letters to his friends) he was able to exploit his one great subject: himself, his connoisseurship of literature and of people, and his strong local attachments—"old chairs, old tables, streets, squares, where I have sunned myself, my old school." Under the pseudonym of an Italian clerk named Elia, whom he had known while briefly employed in the South Sea House, Lamb projects in his essays the character of a man who is whimsical but strong-willed, self-deprecating yet self-absorbed, a specialist in nostalgia and in that humor which balances delicately on the verge of pathos. So engaging is the literary persona which pervades his work that it has attracted a host of devotees who have established what has been called "the Elia industry." But the critical preoccupation with Lamb's seemingly ingenuous self-revelation has obscured the actual cunning of a deliberate and dedicated artist in prose. Lamb's style was not in any contemporary tradition. He wrote, as he said, "for antiquity"; his prose style, like that of Edmund Spenser's in verse, is an invented style. Although its basis is plain modern English, it is colored throughout by archaic words, expressions, and turns of syntax. In the conduct of his essays Lamb is capricious, droll, and (in the manner of earlier literary eccentrics such as Robert Burton and Laurence Sterne) he delights in tricks of words and thought and in the elaborate exploration of a literary conceit. Close imitators of Lamb's style invariably fall into archness and sentimentality. Lamb's inimitable feat was to transform whimsy into a classic type of the personal essay, uttered in one of the distinctive voices in English prose.

Christ's Hospital Five-and-Thirty Years Ago[1]

In Mr. Lamb's *Works*, published a year or two since, I find a magnificent eulogy on my old school, such as it was, or now ap-

1. Christ's Hospital, London (founded in 1552 by Edward VI), was run as a free boarding school for the sons of middle-class parents in straitened financial circumstances. Its students were known as "Bluecoat Boys," from their uniforms of a long blue gown and yellow stockings. Lamb had in 1813 published a magazine article, *Recollections of Christ's Hospital*, which the present essay undertakes to supplement by presenting the less formal side of school life. The "I" or narrator of the essay is Elia—a device which allows Lamb to combine his own circumstances and experiences with those of Coleridge, his older contemporary at the school.

pears to him to have been, between the years 1782 and 1789. It happens very oddly that my own standing at Christ's was nearly corresponding with his; and, with all gratitude to him for his enthusiasm for the cloisters, I think he has contrived to bring together whatever can be said in praise of them, dropping all the other side of the argument most ingeniously.

I remember L. at school, and can well recollect that he had some peculiar advantages, which I and others of his schoolfellows had not. His friends lived in town, and were near at hand; and he had the privilege of going to see them almost as often as he wished, through some invidious distinction, which was denied to us. The present worthy subtreasurer to the Inner Temple[2] can explain how that happened. He had his tea and hot rolls in a morning, while we were battening upon our quarter of a penny loaf—our *crug*—moistened with attenuated small beer, in wooden piggins,[3] smacking of the pitched leathern jack it was poured from. Our Monday's milk porrich, blue and tasteless, and the pease soup of Saturday, coarse and choking, were enriched for him with a slice of "extraordinary bread and butter," from the hot loaf of the Temple. The Wednesday's mess of millet,[4] somewhat less repugnant—(we had three banyan to four meat days in the week [5])—was endeared to his palate with a lump of double-refined, and a smack of ginger (to make it go down the more glibly) or the fragrant cinnamon. In lieu of our *half-pickled* Sundays, or *quite fresh* boiled beef on Thursdays (strong as *caro equina*[6]), with detestable marigolds floating in the pail to poison the broth—our scanty mutton scrags[7] on Friday—and rather more savory, but grudging, portions of the same flesh, rotten-roasted[8] or rare, on the Tuesdays (the only dish which excited our appetites, and disappointed our stomachs, in almost equal proportion)—he had his hot plate of roast veal, or the more tempting griskin[9] (exotics unknown to our palates), cooked in the paternal kitchen (a great thing), and brought him daily by his maid or aunt! I remember the good old relative (in whom love forbade pride) squatting down upon some odd stone in a by-nook of the cloisters, disclosing the viands (of higher regale than those cates which the ravens ministered to the Tishbite[1]); and the contending passions of L. at the unfolding. There was love for the bringer; shame for the thing brought, and the manner of its bringing; sympathy for those who were too many to share in it; and, at top of all, hunger (eldest, strongest of the passions!)

---

2. Randal Norris, who had befriended young Charles Lamb. The Inner Temple is one of the four Inns of Court, the center of the English legal profession.
3. Small wooden pails. The "jack" is a leather vessel coated on the outside with pitch. "Small beer" is low in alcoholic content. "Crug": slang for bread.
4. Cereal.
5. "Banyan days" is a nautical term for days when no meat is served; it derives from "banian," a member of a Hindu caste to whom meat is forbidden.
6. Horsemeat.
7. Necks.
8. Overdone.
9. The lean part of a loin of pork.
1. The prophet Elijah, fed by the ravens in I Kings xvii. "Cates": delicacies.

predominant, breaking down the stony fences of shame, and awkwardness, and a troubling over-consciousness.

I was a poor friendless boy. My parents, and those who should care for me, were far away. Those few acquaintances of theirs, which they could reckon upon being kind to me in the great city, after a little forced notice, which they had the grace to take of me on my first arrival in town, soon grew tired of my holiday visits. They seemed to them to recur too often, though I thought them few enough; and, one after another, they all failed me, and I felt myself alone among six hundred playmates.

O the cruelty of separating a poor lad from his early homestead! The yearnings which I used to have towards it in those unfledged years! How, in my dreams, would my native town (far in the west) come back, with its church, and trees, and faces! How I would wake weeping, and in the anguish of my heart exclaim upon sweet Calne in Wiltshire![8]

To this late hour of my life, I trace impressions left by the recollections of those friendless holidays. The long warm days of summer never return but they bring with them a gloom from the haunting memory of those *whole-day leaves*, when, by some strange arrangement, we were turned out for the livelong day, upon our own hands, whether we had friends to go to or none. I remember those bathing excursions to the New River which L. recalls with such relish, better, I think, than he can—for he was a home-seeking lad, and did not much care for such water pastimes: How merrily we would sally forth into the fields; and strip under the first warmth of the sun; and wanton like young dace[9] in the streams; getting us appetites for noon, which those of us that were penniless (our scanty morning crust long since exhausted) had not the means of allaying—while the cattle, and the birds, and the fishes were at feed about us and we had nothing to satisfy our cravings—the very beauty of the day, and the exercise of the pastime, and the sense of liberty, setting a keener edge upon them! How faint and languid, finally, we would return, towards nightfall, to our desired morsel, half-rejoicing, half-reluctant that the hours of our uneasy liberty had expired!

It was worse in the days of winter, to go prowling about the streets objectless—shivering at cold windows of print shops, to extract a little amusement; or haply, as a last resort in the hopes of a little novelty, to pay a fifty-times repeated visit (where our individual faces should be as well known to the warden as those of his own charges) to the Lions in the Tower—to whose levee, by courtesy immemorial, we had a prescriptive title to admission.[1]

L.'s governor (so we called the patron who presented us to the

8. Coleridge had come to school from Ottery St. Mary, Devonshire, in the southwest of England.
9. A small quick-darting fish.
1. The Bluecoat Boys had the right of free admission to the royal menagerie, then housed in the Tower of London. A "levee" is a formal morning reception.

foundation[2]) lived in a manner under his paternal roof. Any complaint which he had to make was sure of being attended to. This was understood at Christ's, and was an effectual screen to him against the severity of masters, or worse tyranny of the monitors. The oppressions of these young brutes are heart-sickening to call to recollection. I have been called out of my bed, and *waked for the purpose*, in the coldest winter nights—and this not once, but night after night—in my shirt, to receive the discipline of a leathern thong with eleven other sufferers, because it pleased my callow overseer, when there has been any talking heard after we were gone to bed, to make the six last beds in the dormitory, where the youngest children of us slept, answerable for an offense they neither dared to commit nor had the power to hinder. The same execrable tyranny drove the younger part of us from the fires, when our feet were perishing with snow; and, under the cruelest penalties, forbade the indulgence of a drink of water when we lay in sleepless summer nights fevered with the season and the day's sports.

There was one H——, who, I learned, in after days was seen expiating some maturer offense in the hulks.[3] (Do I flatter myself in fancying that this might be the planter of that name, who suffered—at Nevis, I think, or St. Kitts—some few years since? My friend Tobin was the benevolent instrument of bringing him to the gallows.) This petty Nero actually branded a boy who had offended him with a red-hot iron; and nearly starved forty of us with exacting contributions, to the one-half of our bread, to pamper a young ass, which, incredible as it may seem, with the connivance of the nurse's daughter (a young flame of his) he had contrived to smuggle in, and keep upon the leads[4] of the *ward*, as they called our dormitories. This game went on for better than a week, till the foolish beast, not able to fare well but he must cry roast meat —happier than Caligula's minion,[5] could he have kept his own counsel—but foolisher, alas! than any of his species in the fables —waxing fat, and kicking, in the fullness of bread, one unlucky minute would needs proclaim his good fortune to the world below; and, laying out his simple throat, blew such a ram's-horn blast, as (toppling down the walls of his own Jericho[6]) set concealment any longer at defiance. The client was dismissed, with certain attentions, to Smithfield; but I never understood that the patron underwent any censure on the occasion. This was in the stewardship of L.'s admired Perry.[7]

2. I.e., who vouched for a candidate for entrance to Christ's Hospital. Lamb's patron was Samuel Salt, a lawyer and Member of Parliament, for whom Lamb's father served as clerk.
3. Prison ship. (In Lamb's time the plural "hulks" had come to be used for the singular.) Nevis and St. Kitts are islands in the West Indies.
4. A flat roof.

5. The favorite horse of the Emperor Caligula, who was fed gilded oats and appointed to the post of chief consul.
6. Joshua toppled the walls of Jericho by trumpet blasts (Joshua vi.16–20). "Smithfield": a market for horses and cattle.
7. John Perry, steward of the school, described in Lamb's earlier essay.

Under the same *facile* administration, can L. have forgotten the cool impunity with which the nurses used to carry away openly, in open platters, for their own tables, one out of two of every hot joint, which the careful matron had been seeing scrupulously weighed out for our dinners? These things were daily practiced in that magnificent apartment which L. (grown connoisseur since, we presume) praises so highly for the grand paintings "by Verrio,[8] and others," with which it is "hung round and adorned." But the sight of sleek, well-fed bluecoat boys in pictures was, at that time, I believe, little consolatory to him, or us, the living ones, who saw the better part of our provisions carried away before our faces by harpies; and ourselves reduced (with the Trojan in the hall of Dido)

To feed our mind with idle portraiture.[9]

L. has recorded the repugnance of the school to *gags*, or the fat of fresh beef boiled; and sets it down to some superstition. But these unctuous morsels are never grateful to young palates (children are universally fat-haters), and in strong, coarse, boiled meats, *unsalted*, are detestable. A *gag-eater* in our time was equivalent to a *ghoul*, and held in equal detestation.——— suffered under the imputation.

. . . . 'Twas said
He ate strange flesh.[1]

He was observed, after dinner, carefully to gather up the remnants left at his table (not many nor very choice fragments, you may credit me)—and, in an especial manner, these disreputable morsels, which he would convey away and secretly stow in the settle that stood at his bedside. None saw when he ate them. It was rumored that he privately devoured them in the night. He was watched, but no traces of such midnight practices were discoverable. Some reported that on leave-days he had been seen to carry out of the bounds a large blue check handkerchief, full of something. This then must be the accursed thing. Conjecture next was at work to imagine how he could dispose of it. Some said he sold it to the beggars. This belief generally prevailed. He went about moping. None spake to him. No one would play with him. He was excommunicated; put out of the pale of the school. He was too powerful a boy to be beaten, but he underwent every mode of that negative punishment which is more grievous than many stripes. Still he persevered. At length he was observed by two of his school-

---

8. Antonio Verrio, Italian painter of the 17th century. While living in England, he painted a large picture of the mathematics students of Christ's Hospital being received by James II.

9. In Virgil's *Aeneid* I.464; Aeneas is inspecting the paintings in Dido's temple to Juno.
1. Loosely quoted from Shakespeare's *Antony and Cleopatra* I.iv.67.

fellows, who were determined to get at the secret, and had traced him one leave-day for the purpose, to enter a large worn-out building, such as there exist specimens of in Chancery Lane, which are let out to various scales of pauperism, with open door and a common staircase. After him they silently slunk in, and followed by stealth up four flights, and saw him tap at a poor wicket, which was opened by an aged woman, meanly clad. Suspicion was now ripened into certainty. The informers had secured their victim. They had him in their toils. Accusation was formally preferred, and retribution most signal was looked for. Mr. Hathaway, the then steward (for this happened a little after my time), with that patient sagacity which tempered all his conduct, determined to investigate the matter before he proceeded to sentence. The result was that the supposed mendicants, the receivers or purchasers of the mysterious scraps, turned out to be the parents of ———, an honest couple come to decay—whom this seasonable supply had, in all probability, saved from mendicancy; and that this young stork, at the expense of his own good name, had all this while been only feeding the old birds!—The governors on this occasion, much to their honor, voted a present relief to the family of ———, and presented him with a silver medal. The lesson which the steward read upon RASH JUDGMENT, on the occasion of publicly delivering the medal to ———, I believe would not be lost upon his auditory.—I had left school then, but I well remember ———. He was a tall, shambling youth, with a cast in his eye, not at all calculated to conciliate hostile prejudices. I have since seen him carrying a baker's basket. I think I heard he did not do quite so well by himself as he had done by the old folks.

I was a hypochondriac lad;[2] and the sight of a boy in fetters, upon the day of my first putting on the blue clothes, was not exactly fitted to assuage the natural terrors of initiation. I was of tender years, barely turned of seven; and had only read of such things in books, or seen them but in dreams. I was told he had *run away*. This was the punishment for the first offense.—As a novice I was soon after taken to see the dungeons. These were little, square, Bedlam[3] cells, where a boy could just lie at his length upon straw and a blanket—a mattress, I think, was afterwards substituted —with a peep of light, let in askance, from a prison orifice at top, barely enough to read by. Here the poor boy was locked in by himself all day, without sight of any but the porter who brought him his bread and water—who *might not speak to him*—or of the beadle, who came twice a week to call him out to receive his periodical chastisement, which was almost welcome, because it separated him for a brief interval from solitude—and here he

---

2. From now on Elia speaks as Lamb, rather than as Coleridge.

3. St. Mary of Bethlehem, an insane asylum in London.

was shut up by himself *of nights* out of the reach of any sound, to suffer whatever horrors the weak nerves, and superstition incident to his time of life, might subject him to. This was the penalty for the second offense. Wouldst thou like, reader, to see what became of him in the next degree?

The culprit, who had been a third time an offender, and whose expulsion was at this time deemed irreversible, was brought forth, as at some solemn auto da fé,[4] arrayed in uncouth and most appalling attire—all trace of his late "watchet weeds"[5] carefully effaced, he was exposed in a jacket resembling those which London lamplighters formerly delighted in, with a cap of the same. The effect of this divestiture was such as the ingenious devisers of it could have anticipated. With his pale and frighted features, it was as if some of those disfigurements in Dante[6] had seized upon him. In this disguisement he was brought into the hall (*L.'s favorite state room*), where awaited him the whole number of his schoolfellows, whose joint lessons and sports he was thenceforth to share no more; the awful presence of the steward, to be seen for the last time; of the executioner beadle, clad in his state robe for the occasion; and of two faces more, of direr import, because never but in these extremities visible. These were governors; two of whom by choice, or charter, were always accustomed to officiate at these *Ultima Supplicia;*[7] not to mitigate (so at least we understood it), but to enforce the uttermost stripe. Old Bamber Gascoigne, and Peter Aubert, I remember, were colleagues on one occasion, when the beadle turning rather pale, a glass of brandy was ordered to prepare him for the mysteries. The scourging was, after the old Roman fashion, long and stately. The lictor[8] accompanied the criminal quite round the hall. We were generally too faint, with attending to the previous disgusting circumstances, to make accurate report with our eyes of the degree of corporal suffering inflicted. Report, of course, gave out the back knotty and livid. After scourging, he was made over, in his *San Benito,*[9] to his friends, if he had any (but commonly such poor runagates were friendless), or to his parish officer, who, to enhance the effect of the scene, had his station allotted to him on the outside of the hall gate.

These solemn pageantries were not played off so often as to spoil the general mirth of the community. We had plenty of exercise and recreation *after* school hours; and, for myself, I must confess that I was never happier than *in* them. The Upper and the Lower Grammar Schools were held in the same room; and an imaginary line only divided their bounds. Their character was as different as that of the inhabitants on the two sides of the Pyrenees. The Rev.

4. The ceremony prior to the execution of heretics under the Spanish Inquisition (literally, "act of faith").
5. Blue clothes.
6. I.e., of the sinners in Dante's *Inferno;* see Canto XX.

7. Extreme punishments.
8. A Roman officer who cleared the way for the chief magistrates.
9. The yellow robe worn by the condemned heretic at an auto da fé

James Boyer[1] was the Upper Master; but the Rev. Matthew Field presided over that portion of the apartment of which I had the good fortune to be a member. We lived a life as careless as birds. We talked and did just what we pleased, and nobody molested us. We carried an accidence,[2] or a grammar, for form; but, for any trouble it gave us, we might take two years in getting through the verbs deponent, and another two in forgetting all that we had learned about them. There was now and then the formality of saying a lesson, but if you had not learned it, a brush across the shoulders (just enough to disturb a fly) was the sole remonstrance. Field never used the rod; and in truth he wielded the cane with no great good will—holding it "like a dancer." It looked in his hands rather like an emblem than an instrument of authority; and an emblem, too, he was ashamed of. He was a good, easy man, that did not care to ruffle his own peace, nor perhaps set any great consideration upon the value of juvenile time. He came among us, now and then, but often stayed away whole days from us; and when he came it made no difference to us—he had his private room to retire to, the short time he stayed, to be out of the sound of our noise. Our mirth and uproar went on. We had classics of our own, without being beholden to "insolent Greece or haughty Rome,"[3] that passed current among us—*Peter Wilkins*—the *Adventures of the Hon. Captain Robert Boyle*—the *Fortunate Bluecoat Boy*[4]—and the like. Or we cultivated a turn for mechanic and scientific operations; making little sundials of paper; or weaving those ingenious parentheses called *cat cradles*; or making dry peas to dance upon the end of a tin pipe; or studying the art military over that laudable game "French and English,"[4a] and a hundred other such devices to pass away the time—mixing the useful with the agreeable—as would have made the souls of Rousseau and John Locke chuckle to have seen us.[5]

Matthew Field belonged to that class of modest divines who affect to mix in equal proportion the *gentleman*, the *scholar*, and the *Christian*; but, I know not how, the first ingredient is generally found to be the predominating dose in the composition. He was engaged in gay parties, or with his courtly bow at some episcopal levee, when he should have been attending upon us. He had for many years the classical charge of a hundred children, during the four or five first years of their education, and his very highest form seldom proceeded further than two or three of the introductory fables

1. This teacher is also described by Coleridge in *Biographia Literaria*, Chapter I.

2. A table of the declension of nouns and conjugation of verbs in Greek and Latin. "Verbs deponent": verbs with an active meaning but passive form.

3. Ben Jonson's *To the Memory of * * * William Shakespeare*, line 39.

4. All three were popular adventure stories or romances of the day.

4a. A page is covered with dots and the contestants, with eyes closed, try to draw a line which will cover the maximum number of the dots.

5. These two philosophers recommended systems of education which combined theory with practical experience.

of Phaedrus.[6] How things were suffered to go on thus, I cannot guess. Boyer, who was the proper person to have remedied these abuses, always affected, perhaps felt, a delicacy in interfering in a province not strictly his own. I have not been without my suspicions, that he was not altogether displeased at the contrast we presented to his end of the school. We were a sort of Helots to his young Spartans.[7] He would sometimes, with ironic deference, send to borrow a rod of the Under Master, and then, with sardonic grin, observe to one of his upper boys, "how neat and fresh the twigs looked." While his pale students were battering their brains over Xenophon and Plato, with a silence as deep as that enjoined by the Samite,[8] we were enjoying ourselves at our ease in our little Goshen.[9] We saw a little into the secrets of his discipline, and the prospect did but the more reconcile us to our lot. His thunders rolled innocuous for us: his storms came near, but never touched us; contrary to Gideon's miracle, while all around were drenched, our fleece was dry.[1] His boys turned out the better scholars; we, I suspect, have the advantage in temper. His pupils cannot speak of him without something of terror allaying their gratitude; the remembrance of Field comes back with all the soothing images of indolence, and summer slumbers, and work like play, and innocent idleness, and Elysian exemptions, and life itself a "playing holiday."

Though sufficiently removed from the jurisdiction of Boyer, we were near enough (as I have said) to understand a little of his system. We occasionally heard sounds of the *Ululantes*, and caught glances of Tartarus.[2] B. was a rabid pedant. His English style was cramped to barbarism. His Easter anthems (for his duty obliged him to those periodical flights) were grating as scrannel pipes.[3]— He would laugh, aye, and heartily, but then it must be at Flaccus's quibble about *Rex*[4]—or at the *tristis serveritas in vultu*, or *inspicere in patinas*, of Terence[5]—thin jests, which at their first broaching could hardly have had *vis*[6] enough to move a Roman muscle.—

6. A Roman author of the 1st century A.D., author of a collection of beast fables, including such children's favorites as "The Fox and the Sour Grapes" and "King Log and King Watersnake."
7. The Spartans exhibited drunken Helots (slaves) as a warning example to their children.
8. Pythogoras of Samos, Greek mathematician and philosopher of the 6th century B.C., forbade his pupils to speak until they had studied with him five years.
9. Where the Jews dwelt, protected from the swarms of flies with which the Lord plagued the Egyptians in Exodus viii.22.
1. Judges vi.37–38. As a sign to Gideon, the Lord soaked his sheepskin while leaving the earth around it dry.

2. In the *Aeneid* VI.557–58, Aeneas hears the groans and the sound of the lash from Tartarus, the infernal place of punishment for the wicked. "*Ululantes*" means "howling sufferers."
3. "Harsh pipes," an echo of Milton's *Lycidas*, line 124.
4. In *Satires* I.vii of Horace (Quintus Horatius Flaccus), there is a pun on *Rex* as both a surname and the word for "king."
5. In Terence's *Andrea* V.ii one character says of a notorious liar that he has "a sober severity in his countenance." In his *Adelphi* III.iii, after a father has advised his son to look into the lives of men as a mirror, the slave advises the kitchen scullions "to look into the stew pans" as a mirror.
6. Force; a term in rhetorical theory.

He had two wigs, both pedantic, but of different omen. The one serene, smiling, fresh powdered, betokening a mild day. The other, an old, discolored, unkempt, angry caxon,[7] denoting frequent and bloody execution. Woe to the school, when he made his morning appearance in his *passy*, or *passionate wig*. No comet expounded surer.[8]—J. B. had a heavy hand. I have known him double his knotty fist at a poor trembling child (the maternal milk hardly dry upon its lips) with a "Sirrah, do you presume to set your wits at me?"—Nothing was more common than to see him make a headlong entry into the schoolroom, from his inner recess, or library, and, with turbulent eye, singling out a lad, roar out, "Od's my life, sirrah" (his favorite adjuration), "I have a great mind to whip you"—then, with as sudden a retracting impulse, fling back into his lair—and, after a cooling lapse of some minutes (during which all but the culprit had totally forgotten the context) drive headlong out again, piecing out his imperfect sense, as if it had been some Devil's Litany, with the expletory yell—"*and I* WILL, *too*."—In his gentler moods, when the *rabidus furor*[9] was assuaged, he had resort to an ingenious method, peculiar, for what I have heard, to himself, of whipping the boy, and reading the Debates,[1] at the same time; a paragraph, and a lash between; which in those times, when parliamentary oratory was most at a height and flourishing in these realms, was not calculated to impress the patient with a veneration for the diffuser graces of rhetoric.

Once, and but once, the uplifted rod was known to fall ineffectual from his hand—when droll squinting W—— having been caught putting the inside of the master's desk to a use for which the architect had clearly not designed it, to justify himself, with great simplicity averred, that *he did not know that the thing had been forewarned*. This exquisite irrecognition of any law antecedent to the *oral* or *declaratory* struck so irresistibly upon the fancy of all who heard it (the pedagogue himself not excepted)—that remission was unavoidable.

L. has given credit to B.'s great merits as an instructor. Coleridge, in his literary life, has pronounced a more intelligible and ample encomium on them. The author of the *Country Spectator*[2] doubts not to compare him with the ablest teachers of antiquity. Perhaps we cannot dismiss him better than with the pious ejaculation of C.—when he heard that his old master was on his deathbed: "Poor J. B.!—may all his faults be forgiven; and may he be wafted to bliss by little cherub boys all head and wings, with no *bottoms* to reproach his sublunary infirmities."

---

7. A type of wig.
8. Comets were superstitiously regarded as omens of disaster.
9. Mad rage.
1. The record of debates in Parliament.

2. Thomas Middleton, who was at school with Lamb and Coleridge, edited the magazine *Country Spectator* (1792–93) and later became Bishop of Calcutta.

Under him were many good and sound scholars bred.—First Grecian[3] of my time was Lancelot Pepys Stevens, kindest of boys and men, since Co-grammar-master (and inseparable companion) with Dr. T——e. What an edifying spectacle did this brace of friends present to those who remembered the antisocialities of their predecessors!—You never met the one by chance in the street without a wonder, which was quickly dissipated by the almost immediate sub-appearance of the other. Generally arm-in-arm, these kindly coadjutors lightened for each other the toilsome duties of their profession, and when, in advanced age, one found it convenient to retire, the other was not long in discovering that it suited him to lay down the fasces[4] also. Oh, it is pleasant, as it is rare, to find the same arm linked in yours at forty, which at thirteen helped it to turn over the *Cicero De Amicitia*,[5] or some tale of Antique Friendship, which the young heart even then was burning to anticipate!—Co-Grecian with S. was Th——, who has since executed with ability various diplomatic functions at the Northern courts. Th—— was a tall, dark, saturnine youth, sparing of speech, with raven locks.—Thomas Fanshaw Middleton followed him (now Bishop of Calcutta), a scholar and a gentleman in his teens. He has the reputation of an excellent critic; and is author (besides the *Country Spectator*) of a *Treatise on the Greek Article*, against Sharpe. M. is said to bear his miter high in India, where the *regni novitas*[6] (I dare say) sufficiently justifies the bearing. A humility quite as primitive as that of Jewel or Hooker[7] might not be exactly fitted to impress the minds of those Anglo-Asiatic diocesans with a reverence for home institutions, and the church which those fathers watered. The manners of M. at school, though firm, were mild and unassuming.—Next to M. (if not senior to him) was Richards, author of the *Aboriginal Britons*, the most spirited of the Oxford Prize Poems; a pale, studious Grecian.—Then followed poor S——, ill-fated M——! of these the Muse is silent.[8]

> Finding some of Edward's race
> Unhappy, pass their annals by.[9]

Come back into memory, like as thou wert in the dayspring of thy fancies, with hope like a fiery column before thee—the dark pillar not yet turned—Samuel Taylor Coleridge—Logician, Metaphysician, Bard!—How have I seen the casual passer through the cloisters stand still, entranced with admiration (while he weighed

3. The Grecians were the small group of superior scholars selected to be sent to a university (usually Cambridge) on a Christ's Hospital scholarship.
4. The bundle of rods, serving as the handle of an ax, carried before the Roman magistrates as a symbol of office.
5. Cicero's essay "On Friendship."
6. Newness of the reign.
7. Famous divines in the 16th century.

during the early period of the Anglican Church
8. Lamb identified these students as Scott, who died insane, and Maunde, who was expelled from the school.
9. Altered from Matthew Prior's *Carmen Seculare* (1700). "Edward's race" is applied to the students of Christ's hospital, founded by Edward VI.

the disproportion between the *speech* and the *garb* of the young Mirandola[1]), to hear thee unfold, in thy deep and sweet intonations, the mysteries of Jamblichus, or Plotinus[2] (for even in those years thou waxedst not pale at such philosophic draughts), or reciting Homer in his Greek, or Pindar—while the walls of the old Grey Friars[3] re-echoed to the accents of the *inspired charity-boy!* —Many were the "wit combats" (to dally awhile with the words of old Fuller) between him and C. V. Le G——, "which two I behold like a Spanish great galleon, and an English man-of-war; Master Coleridge, like the former, was built far higher in learning, solid, but slow in his perfromances. C. V. L., with the English man-of-war, lesser in bulk, but lighter in sailing, could turn with all tides, tack about, and take advantage of all winds, by the quickness of his wit and invention."[4]

Nor shalt thou, their compeer, be quickly forgotten, Allen, with the cordial smile, and still more cordial laugh, with which thou wert the *Nireus formosus*[5] of the school), in the days of thy maturer poignant jest of theirs; or the anticipation of some more material, and, peradventure practical one, of thine own. Extinct are those smiles, with that beautiful countenance, with which (for thou wert the *Nireus formosus*[4] of the school), in the days of thy maturer waggery, thou didst disarm the wrath of infuriated town-damsel, who, incensed by provoking pinch, turning tigress-like round, suddenly converted by thy angel look, exchanged the half-formed terrible "*bl——*," for a gentler greeting—"*bless thy handsome face!*"

Next follow two, who ought to be now alive, and the friends of Elia—the junior Le G—— and F——;[6] who impelled, the former by a roving temper, the latter by too quick a sense of neglect—ill capable of enduring the slights poor Sizars[7] are sometimes subject to in our seats of learning—exchanged their Alma Mater for the camp; perishing, one by climate, and one on the plains of Salamanca: Le G——, sanguine, volatile, sweet-natured; F——, dogged, faithful, anticipative of insult, warmhearted, with something of the old Roman height about him.

Fine, frank-hearted Fr——, the present master of Hertford, with Marmaduke T——,[8] mildest of missionaries—and both my good friends still—close the catalogue of Grecians in my time.

1820

1. Pico della Mirandola, the brilliant and charming humanist and philosopher of the Italian Renaissance, who died in 1494 at the age of 31.
2. Neo-Platonic philosophers.
3. Christ's Hospital was located in buildings that had once belonged to the Grey Friars (i.e., Franciscans).
4. Lamb adapts to Coleridge and Charles Valentine Le Grice the famous description of the wit combats between Shakespeare (the "man-of-war") and Ben Jonson (the "great galleon") in Thomas Fuller's *Worthies of England* (1662).
5. "The handsome Nireus," a Greek warrior in Homer's *Iliad* II.
6. Samuel Le Grice became an army officer and died in the West Indies; "F——" was Joseph Favell.
7. An undergraduate at Cambridge University who receives an allowance toward his expenses.
8. Frederick William Franklin and Marmaduke Thompson.

The Two Races of Men[1]

The human species, according to the best theory I can form of it, is composed of two distinct races, *the men who borrow*, and *the men who lend*. To these two original diversities may be reduced all those impertinent classifications of Gothic and Celtic tribes, white men, black men, red men. All the dwellers upon earth, "Parthians, and Medes, and Elamites," [2] flock hither, and do naturally fall in with one or other of these primary distinctions. The infinite superiority of the former, which I choose to designate as the *great race*, is discernible in their figure, port, and a certain instinctive sovereignty. The latter are born degraded. "He shall serve his brethren." [3] There is something in the air of one of this cast, lean and suspicious; contrasting with the open, trusting, generous manners of the other.

Observe who have been the greatest borrowers of all ages—Alcibiades—Falstaff—Sir Richard Steele—our late incomparable Brinsley [4]—what a family likeness in all four!

·What a careless, even deportment hath your borrower! what rosy gills! what a beautiful reliance on Providence doth he manifest—taking no more thought than lilies! [5] What contempt for money—accounting it (yours and mine especially) no better than dross! What a liberal confounding of those pedantic distinctions of *meum* and *tuum*! [6] or rather, what a noble simplification of language (beyond Tooke [7]), resolving these supposed opposites into one clear, intelligible pronoun adjective! What near approaches doth he make to the primitive *community* [8]—to the extent of one half of the principle at least!

He is the true taxer who "calleth all the world up to be taxed"; [9] and the distance is as vast between him and *one of us*, as subsisted betwixt the Augustan Majesty and the poorest obolary [1] Jew that paid it tribute pittance at Jerusalem! His exactions, too, have such a cheerful, voluntary air! So far removed from your sour parochial or

---

1. A small masterpiece in the tradition of the mock encomium, or ironic praise of the unpraiseworthy, such as Erasmus's *The Praise of Folly*. Lamb's oldest and closest friend, Coleridge, figures twice in the essay. In the role of heroic borrower of books almost never returned, he is Comberbatch—a private joke, for the name was identifiable only by Coleridge and a few initiates; in his second role, in which he returns books with the lavish interest of his extraordinary marginalia, he is S. T. C.—initials by which he was already known to many readers.
2. Acts ii.9.
3. Noah's curse upon his youngest son,

Ham, in Genesis ix.25.
4. Richard Brinsley Sheridan (1751–1816), dramatist, producer, and statesman.
5. I.e., than "the lilies of the field," in Matthew vi.28 and Luke xii.26–7.
6. Mine and thine.
7. John Horne Tooke, author of *The Diversions of Purley* (1786–98), a book on philology.
8. The community of the Apostles, who held all their possessions in common, Acts ii.44–5.
9. See Luke ii.1; this is the call that brought Joseph and Mary to Bethlehem.
1. Possessing an obolus, a Greek penny.

state-gatherers—those ink-horn varlets, who carry their want of welcome in their faces! He cometh to you with a smile, and troubleth you with no receipt; confining himself to no set season. Every day is his Candlemas, or his Feast of Holy Michael.[2] He applieth the *lene tormentum*[3] of a pleasant look to your purse—which to that gentle warmth expands her silken leaves, as naturally as the cloak of the traveler, for which sun and wind contended! He is the true Propontic which never ebbeth![4] The sea which taketh handsomely at each man's hand. In vain the victim, whom he delighteth to honor, struggles with destiny; he is in the net. Lend therefore cheerfully, O man ordained to lend—that thou lose not in the end, with thy worldly penny, the reversion[5] promised. Combine not preposterously in thine own person the penalties of Lazarus and of Dives![6]—but, when thou seest the proper authority coming, meet it smilingly, as it were half-way. Come, a handsome sacrifice! See how light *he* makes of it! Strain not courtesies with a noble enemy.

Reflections like the foregoing were forced upon my mind by the death of my old friend, Ralph Bigod, Esq,[7] who departed this life on Wednesday evening; dying, as he had lived, without much trouble. He boasted himself a descendant from mighty ancestors of that name, who heretofore held ducal dignities in this realm. In his actions and sentiments he belied not the stock to which he pretended. Early in life he found himself invested with ample revenues; which, with that noble disinterestedness which I have noticed as inherent in men of the *great race*, he took almost immediate measures entirely to dissipate and bring to nothing: for there is something revolting in the idea of a king holding a private purse; and the thoughts of Bigod were all regal. Thus furnished, by the very act of disfurnishment; getting rid of the cumbersome luggage of riches, more apt (as one sings)

> To slacken virtue, and abate her edge,
> Than prompt her to do aught may merit praise,[8]

he set forth, like some Alexander, upon his great enterprise, "Borrowing and to borrow!"[9]

In his periegesis,[1] or triumphant progress throughout this island, it has been calculated that he laid a tithe[2] part of the inhabitants

---

2. Feb. 2 and Sept. 29—English quarter-days, when rents fall due.
3. "The gentle spur"; said by Horace about wine, *Odes* III.xxi.13.
4. See *Othello* III.iii.453–56.
5. The right of future possession—"promised," if you cast your bread upon the waters, Ecclesiastes xi.1, or lend to the poor, Proverbs xix.17.
6. Dives, the "rich man," finds when he dies that he is in hell, while Lazarus, who had been a beggar on earth, after death goes to dwell in "Abraham's bosom"; Luke xvi.19–26.
7. He has been identified as John Fenwick, editor of a newspaper, *Albion*.
8. Milton, *Paradise Regained* II.455–56.
9. Playing upon Revelation vi.2, "and he went forth conquering, and to conquer."
1. Tour.
2. One-tenth.

under contribution. I reject this estimate as greatly exaggerated—but having had the honor of accompanying my friend, divers times, in his perambulations about this vast city, I own I was greatly struck at first with the prodigious number of faces we met, who claimed a sort of respectful acquaintance with us. He was one day so obliging as to explain the phenomenon. It seems, these were his tributaries; feeders of his exchequer; gentlemen, his good friends (as he was pleased to express himself), to whom he had occasionally been beholden for a loan. Their multitudes did no way disconcert him. He rather took a pride in numbering them; and, with Comus, seemed pleased to be "stocked with so fair a herd." [3]

With such sources, it was a wonder how he contrived to keep his treasury always empty. He did it by force of an aphorism, which he had often in his mouth, that "money kept longer than three days stinks." So he made use of it while it was fresh. A good part he drank away (for he was an excellent tosspot), some he gave away, the rest he threw away, literally tossing and hurling it violently from him —as boys do burrs, or as if it had been infectious—into ponds, or ditches, or deep holes—inscrutable cavities of the earth; or he would bury it (where he would never seek it again) by a river's side under some bank, which (he would facetiously observe) paid no interest—but out away from him it must go peremptorily, as Hagar's offspring [4] into the wilderness, while it was sweet. He never missed it. The streams were perennial which fed his fisc. [5] When new supplies became necessary, the first person that had the felicity to fall in with him, friend or stranger, was sure to contribute to the deficiency. For Bigod had an *undeniable* way with him. He had a cheerful, open exterior, a quick jovial eye, a bald forehead, just touched with gray (*cana fides*). [6] He anticipated no excuse, and found none. And, waiving for a while my theory as to the *great race*, I would put it to the most untheorizing reader, who may at times have disposable coin in his pocket, whether it is not more repugnant to the kindliness of his nature to refuse such a one as I am describing, than to say *no* to a poor petitionary rogue (your bastard borrower), who, by his mumping visnomy [7] tells you, that he expects nothing better; and, therefore, whose preconceived notions and expectations you do in reality so much less shock in the refusal.

When I think of this man; his fiery glow of heart; his swell of feeling; how magnificent, how *ideal* he was; how great at the midnight hour; and when I compare with him the companions with whom I have associated since, I grudge the saving of a few idle ducats, and think that I am fallen into the society of *lenders*, and *little men*.

---

3. Adapted from Milton's *Comus* 152.
4. Ishmael, the son of Hagar, in Genesis xxi.9 ff.
5. Public treasury.
6. "Hoary trustworthiness," i.e., of his gray hair; the phrase is in Virgil's *Aeneid* I.292.
7. Dialect for "mumbling physiognomy."

To one like Elia, whose treasures are rather cased in leather covers than closed in iron coffers, there is a class of alienators [8] more formidable than that which I have touched upon; I mean your *borrowers of books*—those mutilators of collections, spoilers of the symmetry of shelves, and creators of odd volumes. There is Comberbatch,[9] matchless in his depredations!

That foul gap in the bottom shelf facing you, like a great eye-tooth knocked out—(you are now with me in my little back study in Bloomsbury, reader!)—with the huge Switzerlike [1] tomes on each side (like the Guildhall giants, in their reformed posture, guardant of nothing) once held the tallest of my folios, *Opera Bonaventurae*,[2] choice and massy divinity, to which its two supporters (school divinity also, but of a lesser caliber—Bellarmine, and Holy Thomas), showed but as dwarfs—itself an Ascapart! [3] *that* Comberbatch abstracted upon the faith of a theory he holds, which is more easy, I confess, for me to suffer by than to refute, namely, that "the title to property in a book (my Bonaventure, for instance), is in exact ratio to the claimant's powers of understanding and appreciating the same." Should he go on acting upon this theory, which of our shelves is safe?

The slight vacuum in the left-hand case—two shelves from the ceiling—scarcely distinguishable but by the quick eye of a loser—— was whilom the commodious resting place of Browne on Urn Burial. C. will hardly allege that he knows more about that treatise than I do, who introduced it to him, and was indeed the first (of the moderns) to discover its beauties—but so have I known a foolish lover to praise his mistress in the presence of a rival more qualified to carry her off than himself. Just below, Dodsley's dramas want their fourth volume, where Vittoria Corombona is! The remainder nine are as distasteful as Priam's refuse sons, when the Fates *borrowed* Hector. [4] Here stood the Anatomy of Melancholy, in sober state. There loitered the Complete Angler; quiet as in life, by some stream side. In yonder nook, John Buncle, a widower-volume, with "eyes closed," mourns his ravished mate.[5]

8. Those who alienate property—i.e., transfer it to another.
9. Coleridge had left college for a brief and disastrous career as a cavalryman in the Light Dragoons, under the alias of Silas Tomkyn Comberbacke.
1. "Switzers" are Swiss guardsmen, selected for their imposing stature.
2. The theological *Works* of St. Bonaventure (1221–74); the "supporters" are St. Robert Bellarmine (1542–1621) and St. Thomas Aquinas (ca. 1225–74).
3. A giant, in the 14th-century verse romance, *Bevis of Hampton*.
4. I.e., the remaining nine volumes of Dodsley's *Collection* are rated as low by the lender as (in Homer's *Iliad*) Priam's remaining sons were rated by the Trojan king, after his greatest son, Hector, had been killed in battle.
5. The books in this paragraph: Sir Thomas Browne, *Hydriotaphia, or Urn Burial* (1658); Robert Dodsley's *Select Collection of Old Plays* (1744); John Webster's tragedy, *The White Devil, or Vittoria Corombona* (ca. 1608); Robert Burton, *The Anatomy of Melancholy* (1621); Izaak Walton, *The Compleat Angler* (1653); Thomas Amory, *John Buncle, Esq.* (1756–66)—a novel about a man who successively married seven wives, each of whom died within a few years.

One justice I must do my friend, that if he sometimes, like the sea, sweeps away a treasure, at another time, sealike, he throws up as rich an equivalent to match it. I have a small under-collection of this nature (my friend's gatherings in his various calls), picked up, he has forgotten at what odd places, and deposited with as little memory as mine. I take in these orphans, the twice-deserted. These proselytes of the gate are welcome as the true Hebrews. There they stand in conjunction; natives, and naturalized. The latter seem as little disposed to inquire out their true lineage as I am. I charge no warehouse-room for these deodands,[6] nor shall ever put myself to the ungentlemanly trouble of advertising a sale of them to pay expenses.

To lose a volume to C. carries some sense and meaning in it. You are sure that he will make one hearty meal on your viands, if he can give no account of the platter after it. But what moved thee, wayward, spiteful K,[7] to be so importunate to carry off with thee, in spite of tears and adjurations to thee to forbear, the Letters of that princely woman, the thrice noble Margaret Newcastle?—knowing at the time, and knowing that I knew also, thou most assuredly wouldst never turn over one leaf of the illustrious folio—what but the mere spirit of contradiction, and childish love of getting the better of thy friend? Then, worst cut of all! to transport it with thee to the Gallican land—

> Unworthy land to harbor such a sweetness,
> A virtue in which all ennobling thoughts dwelt,
> Pure thoughts, kind thoughts, high thoughts, her sex's wonder![8]

——hadst thou not thy playbooks, and books of jests and fancies, about thee, to keep thee merry, even as thou keepest all companies with thy quips and mirthful tales? Child of the Greenroom,[9] it was unkindly done of thee. Thy wife, too, that part-French, better-part Englishwoman!—that *she* could fix upon no other treatise to bear away, in kindly token of remembering us, than the works of Fulke Greville, Lord Brook [10]—of which no Frenchman, nor woman of France, Italy, or England, was ever by nature constituted to comprehend a tittle! *Was there not Zimmerman on Solitude?*

Reader, if haply thou art blessed with a moderate collection, be shy of showing it; or if thy heart overfloweth to lend them, lend thy books; but let it be to such a one as S. T. C.—he will return them (generally anticipating the time appointed) with usury; enriched with annotations, tripling their value. I have had experience. Many

---

6. In English law, objects that are forfeited to the crown (because they have caused a human death).
7. James Kenney (1780–1849), an actor, who has borrowed and taken to France the *Sociable Letters* (1664) of Margaret Cavendish, Duchess of Newcastle.
8. Possibly composed by Lamb himself.
9. The room where actors await their cues.
10. Sir Fulke Greville, Baron Brooke (1554–1628). J. G. von Zimmerman's *Solitude* was translated into English about 1791.

are these precious MSS. of his (in *matter* oftentimes, and almost in *quantity* not unfrequently, vying with the originals) in no very clerkly hand—legible in my Daniel; [11] in old Burton; in Sir Thomas Browne; and those abstruser cogitations of the Greville, now, alas! wandering in Pagan lands. I counsel thee, shut not thy heart, nor thy library, against S. T. C.

1820, 1823

New Year's Eve

Every man hath two birthdays: two days, at least, in every year, which set him upon revolving the lapse of time, as it affects his mortal duration. The one is that which in an especial manner he termeth *his*. In the gradual desuetude of old observances, this custom of solemnizing our proper birthday hath nearly passed away, or is left to children, who reflect nothing at all about the matter, nor understand anything in it beyond cake and orange. But the birth of a New Year is of an interest too wide to be pretermitted by king or cobbler. No one ever regarded the first of January with indifference. It is that from which all date their time, and count upon what is left. It is the nativity of our common Adam.

Of all sound of all bells—bells, the music nighest bordering upon heaven—most solemn and touching is the peal which rings out the Old Year. I never hear it without a gathering-up of my mind to a concentration of all the images that have been diffused over the past twelvemonth; all I have done or suffered, performed or neglected—in that regretted time. I begin to know its worth, as when a person dies. It takes a personal color; nor was it a poetical flight in a contemporary, when he exclaimed,

I saw the skirts of the departing Year.[1]

It is no more than what in sober sadness every one of us seems to be conscious of, in that awful leave-taking. I am sure I felt it, and all felt it with me, last night; though some of my companions affected rather to manifest an exhilaration at the birth of the coming year, than any very tender regrets for the decease of its predecessor. But I am none of those who

Welcome the coming, speed the parting guest.[2]

I am naturally, beforehand, shy of novelties; new books, new faces, new years—from some mental twist which makes it difficult in me to face the prospective. I have almost ceased to hope; and am sanguine only in the prospects of other (former) years. I plunge

11. Samuel Daniel, the poet (1562–1619).
1. Coleridge, *Ode to the Departing Year*, line 8, in the version of 1797.

2. This line occurs in Alexander Pope's translation of the *Odyssey* XV.84, and again in his imitation of Horace's *Satires* (II.ii.160).

into foregone visions and conclusions. I encounter pell-mell with past disappointments. I am armor-proof against old discouragements. I forgive, or overcome in fancy, old adversaries. I play over again *for love*, as the gamesters phrase it, games, for which I once paid so dear. I would scarce now have any of those untoward accidents and events of my life reversed. I would no more alter them than the incidents of some well-contrived novel. Methinks it is better that I should have pined away seven of my goldenest years, when I was thrall to the fair hair and fairer eyes of Alice W——n,[3] than that so passionate a love adventure should be lost. It was better that our family should have missed that legacy, which old Dorrell cheated us of,[3a] than that I should have at this moment two thousand pounds *in banco*, and be without the idea of that specious old rogue.

In a degree beneath manhood, it is my infirmity to look back upon those early days. Do I advance a paradox, when I say that, skipping over the intervention of forty years, a man may have leave to love *himself*, without the imputation of self-love?

If I know aught of myself, no one whose mind is introspective—and mine is painfully so—can have a less respect for his present identity than I have for the man Elia. I know him to be light, and vain, and humorsome; a notorious ———; addicted to ———; averse from counsel, neither taking it nor offering it; ——— besides; a stammering buffoon; what you will; lay it on, and spare not; I subscribe to it all, and much more, than thou canst be willing to lay at his door—but for the child Elia, that "other me," there, in the background—I must take leave to cherish the remembrance of that young master—with as little reference, I protest, to this stupid changeling of five-and-forty, as if it had been a child of some other house, and not of my parents. I can cry over its patient smallpox at five, and rougher medicaments. I can lay its poor fevered head upon the sick pillow at Christ's,[4] and wake with it in surprise at the gentle posture of maternal tenderness hanging over it, that unknown had watched its sleep. I know how it shrank from any the least color of falsehood.—God help thee, Elia, how art thou changed! Thou art sophisticated.[4a]—I know how honest, how courageous (for a weakling) it was—how religious, how imaginative, how hopeful! From what have I not fallen, if the child I remember was indeed myself—and not some dissembling guardian, presenting a false identity, to give the rule to my unpracticed steps, and regulate the tone of my moral being!

That I am fond of indulging, beyond a hope of sympathy, in such retrospection may be the symptom of some sickly idiosyncrasy. Or

---

3. Elia's Alice Winterton; she may be the Anne Simmons with whom Lamb had been in love when a youth.
3a. William Dorell, who had witnessed the will of Lamb's father; Lamb believed he had helped cheat the children of their proper inheritance.
4. Christ's Hospital school, which Lamb had attended.
4a. In the old sense: adulterated, altered for the worse.

is it owing to another cause; simply, that being without wife or family, I have not learned to project myself enough out of myself; and having no offspring of my own to dally with, I turn back upon memory, and adopt my own early idea, as my heir and favorite? If these speculations seem fantastical to thee, reader (a busy man perchance), if I tread out of the way of thy sympathy, and am singularly-conceited only, I retire, impenetrable to ridicule, under the phantom cloud of Elia.

The elders, with whom I was brought up, were of a character not likely to let slip the sacred observance of any old institution; and the ringing out of the Old Year was kept by them with circumstances of peculiar ceremony.—In those days the sound of those midnight chimes, though it seemed to raise hilarity in all around me, never failed to bring a train of pensive imagery into my fancy. Yet I then scarce conceived what it meant, or thought of it as a reckoning that concerned me. Not childhood alone, but the young man till thirty, never feels practically that he is mortal. He knows it indeed, and, if need were, he could preach a homily on the fragility of life; but he brings it not home to himself, any more than in a hot June we can appropriate to our imagination the freezing days of December. But now, shall I confess a truth?—I feel these audits but too powerfully. I begin to count the probabilities of my duration, and to grudge at the expenditure of moments and shortest periods, like misers' farthings. In proportion as the years both lessen and shorten, I set more count upon their periods, and would fain lay my ineffectual finger upon the spoke of the great wheel. I am not content to pass away "like a weaver's shuttle."[5] Those metaphors solace me not, nor sweeten the unpalatable draught of mortality. I care not to be carried with the tide that smoothly bears human life to eternity; and reluct at the inevitable course of destiny. I am in love with this green earth; the face of town and country; the unspeakable rural solitudes, and the sweet security of streets. I would set up my tabernacle here. I am content to stand still at the age to which I am arrived; I, and my friends: to be no younger, no richer, no handsomer. I do not want to be weaned by age; or drop, like mellow fruit, as they say, into the grave.—Any alteration, on this earth of mine, in diet or in lodging, puzzles and discomposes me. My household gods plant a terrible fixed foot, and are not rooted up without blood. They do not willingly seek Lavinian shores.[6] A new state of being staggers me.

Sun, and sky, and breeze, and solitary walks, and summer holidays, and the greenness of fields, and the delicious juices of meats and fishes, and society, and the cheerful glass, and candlelight, and fireside conversations, and innocent vanities, and jests, and *irony*

5. Altered from Job vii.6.
6. Italy, so called in the *Aeneid* because Aeneas, after his wanderings, married Lavinia there and founded the Roman race. Since Aeneas transported his "household gods" with him from Troy to Italy, Lamb's allusion simply means that he is disinclined to wander.

itself—do these things go out with life?

Can a ghost laugh, or shake his gaunt sides, when you are pleasant with him?

And you, my midnight darlings, my Folios![7] must I part with the intense delight of having you (huge armfuls) in my embraces? Must knowledge come to me, if it come at all, by some awkward experiment of intuition, and no longer by this familiar process of reading?

Shall I enjoy friendships there, wanting the smiling indications which point me to them here—the recognizable face—the "sweet assurance of a look"?[8]

In winter this intolerable disinclination to dying—to give it its mildest name—does more especially haunt and beset me. In a genial August noon, beneath a sweltering sky, death is almost problematic. At those times do such poor snakes as myself enjoy an immortality. Then we expand and burgeon. Then are we as strong again, as valiant again, as wise again, and a great deal taller. The blast that nips and shrinks me, puts me in thoughts of death. All things allied to the insubstantial wait upon that master feeling: cold, numbness, dreams, perplexity; moonlight itself, with its shadowy and spectral appearances—that cold ghost of the sun, or Phoebus' sickly sister, like that innutritious one denounced in the Canticles.[9]—I am none of her minions—I hold with the Persian.[1]

Whatsoever thwarts, or puts me out of my way, brings death into my mind. All partial evils, like humors, run into that capital plague sore.—I have heard some profess an indifference to life. Such hail the end of their existence as a port of refuge; and speak of the grave as of some soft arms, in which they may slumber as on a pillow. Some have wooed death—but out upon thee, I say, thou foul, ugly phantom! I detest, abhor, execrate, and (with Friar John[2]) give thee to six-score thousand devils, as in no instance to be excused or tolerated, but shunned as an universal viper; to be branded, proscribed, and spoken evil of! In no way can I be brought to digest thee, thou thin, melancholy *Privation*, or more frightful and confounding *Positive!*[3]

Those antidotes, prescribed against the fear of thee, are altogether frigid and insulting, like thyself. For what satisfaction hath a man, that he shall "lie down with kings and emperors in death,"[4] who in his lifetime never greatly coveted the society of such bedfellows?—or, forsooth, that "so shall the fairest face appear"?[5]—

7. The large volumes in which the older English writers were often printed.
8. Altered from Matthew Roydon's elegy on Sir Philip Sidney.
9. The Song of Solomon viii.8: "We have a little sister, and she hath no breasts." Elia's allusion is to the moon, described as the weaker sister of Phoebus, the sun.
1. The ancient Persians were sun-worshipers.

2. A bellicose character in Rabelais's *Gargantua*.
3. I.e., death as the absence of existence or, more terrifying still, an actual being. Cf. Coleridge's *Limbo*, lines 30–33.
4. Job iii.13–14: "Then had I been at rest, with kings and counselors of the earth."
5. Line 9 of *William and Margaret*, a ballad-imitation written in 1724 by David Mallet.

why, to comfort me, must Alice W——n be a goblin? More than all, I conceive disgust at those impertinent and misbecoming familiarities inscribed upon your ordinary tombstones. Every dead man must take upon himself to be lecturing me with his odious truism that "such as he now is, I must shortly be." Not so shortly, friend, perhaps as thou imaginest. In the meantime I am alive. I move about. I am worth twenty of thee. Know thy betters! Thy New Years' days are past. I survive, a jolly candidate for 1821. Another cup of wine—and while that turncoat bell, that just now mournfully chanted the obsequies of 1820 departed, with changed notes lustily rings in a successor, let us attune to its peal the song made on a like occasion, by hearty, cheerful Mr. Cotton.[6]—

The New Year

Hark, the cock crows, and yon bright star
Tells us the day himself's not far;
And see where, breaking from the night,
He gilds the western hills with light.
With him old Janus doth appear,
Peeping into the future year,
With such a look as seems to say,
The prospect is not good that way.
Thus do we rise ill sights to see,
And 'gainst ourselves to prophesy;
When the prophetic fear of things
A more tormenting mischief brings,
More full of soul-tormenting gall,
Than direst mischiefs can befall.
But stay! but stay! methinks my sight,
Better informed by clearer light,
Discerns sereneness in that brow,
That all contracted seemed but now.
His reversed face may show distaste,
And frown upon the ills are past;
But that which this way looks is clear,
And smiles upon the Newborn Year.
He looks too from a place so high,
The year lies open to his eye;
And all the moments open are
To the exact discoverer.
Yet more and more he smiles upon
The happy revolution.
Why should we then suspect or fear
The influences of a year,
So smiles upon us the first morn,
And speaks us good so soon as born?
Plague on't! the last was ill enough,
This cannot but make better proof;
Or, at the worst, as we brushed through

6. Charles Cotton, a genial poet of the mid-17th century.

The last, why so we may this too;
And then the next in reason should
Be superexcellently good:
For the worst ills (we daily see)
Have no more perpetuity
Than the best fortunes that do fall;
Which also bring us wherewithal
Longer their being to support,
Than those do of the other sort:
And who has one good year in three,
And yet repines at destiny,
Appears ungrateful in the case,
And merits not the good he has.
Then let us welcome the New Guest
With lusty brimmers of the best;
Mirth always should Good Fortune meet,
And renders e'en Disaster sweet:
And though the Princess turn her back,
Let us but line ourselves with sack,[7]
We better shall by far hold out,
Till the next Year she face about.

How say you, reader—do not these verses smack of the rough magnanimity of the old English vein? Do they not fortify like a cordial; enlarging the heart, and productive of sweet blood, and generous spirits, in the concoction? Where be those puling fears of death, just now expressed or affected?—Passed like a cloud—absorbed in the purging sunlight of clear poetry—clean washed away by a wave of genuine Helicon,[8] your only spa for these hypochondries—And now another cup of the generous! and a merry New Year, and many of them to you all, my masters!

1821

From On the Artificial Comedy of the Last Century[1]

The Artificial Comedy, or Comedy of Manners, is quite extinct on our stage. Congreve and Farquhar[2] show their heads once in

7. A former name for sherry and other strong white wines from Spain and the Canary Islands.
8. A mountain on which flowed springs sacred to the Muses. A "spa" is a mineral spring, here thought of as curing morbid depression ("hypochondries").
1. This essay, a defense of the moral man's privilege to enjoy the gay immoralties of Restoration comedy, has been the occasion of much discussion and controversy. Thomas Babington Macaulay, for instance, said that Lamb was mistaken because comedy is (in the terms of neoclassic criticism) "an imitation, under whatever conventions, of real life," and therefore subject to ordinary moral criteria. Lamb overstated his case in implying that the profligate

society in Restoration plays had no counterpart in reality, but his central theoretical claim has become an important premise in modern criticism. He proposes that the "artificial comedies" are unlike realistic drama in that they do not imitate the real world, but create "a world of themselves"; the spectator, taking a kind of moral holiday, adapts himself to the conditions of this artificial world and enjoys its characters and events by a suspension of his ordinary sensibilities.
2. William Congreve, Restoration dramatist whose *The Way of the World* is the most brilliant comedy of the period. George Farquhar (1678–1707), author of a number of comedies; the best known is *The Beaux' Stratagem*.

seven years only; to be exploded and put down instantly. The times cannot bear them. Is it for a few wild speeches, an occasional license or dialogue? I think not altogether. The business of their dramatic characters will not stand the moral test. We screw everything up to that. Idle gallantry in a fiction, a dream, the passing pageant of an evening, startles us in the same way as the alarming indications of profligacy in a son or ward in real life should startle a parent or guardian. We have no such middle emotions as dramatic interests left. We see a stage libertine playing his loose pranks of two hours' duration, and of no after consequence, with the severe eyes which inspect real vices with their bearings upon two worlds. We are spectators to a plot or intrigue (not reducible in life to the point of strict morality), and take it all for truth. We substitute a real for a dramatic person, and judge him accordingly. We try him in our courts, from which there is no appeal to the *dramatis personae*, his peers. We have been spoiled with—not sentimental comedy—but a tyrant far more pernicious to our pleasures which has succeeded to it, the exclusive and all-devouring drama of common life; where the moral point is everything; where, instead of the fictitious half-believed personages of the stage (the phantoms of old comedy), we recognize ourselves, our brothers, aunts, kinsfolk, allies, patrons, enemies—the same as in life—with an interest in what is going on so hearty and substantial, that we cannot afford our moral judgment, in its deepest and most vital results, to compromise or slumber for a moment. What is *there* transacting by no modification is made to affect us in any other manner than the same events or characters would do in our relationships of life. We carry our fireside concerns to the theater with us. We do not go thither, like our ancestors, to escape from the pressure of reality, so much as to confirm our experience of it; to make assurance double, and take a bond of fate. We must live our toilsome lives twice over, as it was the mournful privilege of Ulysses to descend twice to the shades.[3] All that neutral ground of character, which stood between vice and virtue; or which in fact was indifferent to neither, where neither properly was called in question; that happy breathing-place from the burthen of a perpetual moral questioning—the sanctuary and quiet Alsatia of hunted casuistry[4]—is broken up and disfranchised, as injurious to the interests of society. The privileges of the place are taken away by law. We dare not dally with images, or names, of wrong. We bark like foolish dogs at shadows. We dread infection from the scenic representation of disorder, and fear a painted pustule. In our anxiety that our morality should not take cold, we wrap it up in a great

3. In Homer's *Odyssey*, Ulysses visited Hades to interview the shade of the blind soothsayer, Tiresias. He descended a second time, of course, at his death.
4. "Alsatia" was a district near White-friars which, until 1697, served as a legal sanctuary for debtors. Lamb's point is that the comedy of manners offers a sanctuary for man, eternally harried by "casuistry" (logical consideration of the problems of right and wrong).

blanket surtout[5] of precaution against the breeze and sunshine.

I confess for myself that (with no great delinquencies to answer for) I am glad for a season to take an airing beyond the diocese of the strict conscience—not to live always in the precincts of the law courts—but now and then, for a dream-while or so, to imagine a world with no meddling restrictions—to get into recesses, whither the hunter cannot follow me—

> secret shades
> Of woody Ida's inmost grove,
> While yet there was no fear of Jove.[6]

I come back to my cage and my restraint the fresher and more healthy for it. I wear my shackles more contentedly for having respired the breath of an imaginary freedom. I do not know how it is with others, but I feel the better always for the perusal of one of Congreve's—nay, why should I not add even of Wycherley's[7]—comedies. I am the gayer at least for it; and I could never connect those sports of a witty fancy in any shape with any result to be drawn from them to imitation in real life. They are a world of themselves almost as much as fairyland. Take one of their characters, male or female (with few exceptions they are alike), and place it in a modern play, and my virtuous indignation shall rise against the profligate wretch as warmly as the Catos of the pit[8] could desire; because in a modern play I am to judge of the right and the wrong. The standard of *police* is the measure of *political justice*. The atmosphere will blight it; it cannot live here. It has got into a moral world, where it has no business, from which it must needs fall headlong; as dizzy, and incapable of making a stand, as a Swedenborgian bad spirit that has wandered unawares into the sphere of one of his Good Men, or Angels.[9] But in its own world do we feel the creature is so very bad?—The Fainalls and the Mirabells, the Dorimants and the Lady Touchwoods,[1] in their own sphere, do not offend my moral sense; in fact they do not appeal to it at all. They seem engaged in their proper element. They break through no laws, or conscientious restraints. They know of none. They have got out of Christendom into the land—what shall I call it?—of cuckoldry—the Utopia of gallantry, where pleasure is duty, and the manners perfect freedom. It is altogether

---

5. Long and heavy overcoat.
6. Milton, *Il Penseroso*, lines 28–30. Ida is a mountain in Crete where Jove was said to have been born.
7. William Wycherley (1640–1716), whose comedies (e.g., *The Country Wife*) were considered profligate even by Restoration standards.
8. Cato (234–149 B.C.) was noted for his opposition to the luxury and decadence of Rome. The "pit," in an English theater, is that part of the audi-

torium which is on the main floor, below the stage.
9. Emanuel Swedenborg, the 18th-century Swedish scientist and mystic, held that there are several heavens and hells, peopled by corresponding good and evil spirits.
1. Characters in Restoration comedies: Fainall and Mirabell in Congreve's *Way of the World*, Dorimant in Etherege's *Man of Mode*, and Lady Touchwood in Congreve's *Double-Dealer*.

a speculative scene of things, which has no reference whatever to the world that is. No good person can be justly offended as a spectator, because no good person suffers on the stage. Judged morally, every character in these plays—the few exceptions only are *mistakes*—is alike essentially vain and worthless. The great art of Congreve is especially shown in this, that he has entirely excluded from his scenes—some little generosities in the part of Angelica[2] perhaps excepted—not only anything like a faultless character, but any pretensions to goodness or good feelings whatsoever. Whether he did this designedly, or instinctively, the effect is as happy, as the design (if design) was bold. I used to wonder at the strange power which his *Way of the World* in particular possesses of interesting you all along in the pursuits of characters, for whom you absolutely care nothing—for you neither hate nor love his personages—and I think it is owing to this very indifference for any that you endure the whole. He has spread a privation of moral light, I will call it, rather than by the ugly name of palpable darkness, over his creations; and his shadows flit before you without distinction or preference. Had he introduced a good character, a single gush of moral feeling, a revulsion of the judgment to actual life and actual duties, the impertinent Goshen[3] would have only lighted to the discovery of deformities, which now are none, because we think them none.

Translated into real life, the characters of his and his friend Wycherley's dramas are profligates and strumpets—the business of their brief existence, the undivided pursuit of lawless gallantry. No other spring of action, or possible motive of conduct, is recognized; principles which, universally acted upon, must reduce this frame of things to a chaos. But we do them wrong in so translating them. No such effects are produced, in *their* world. When we are among them, we are amongst a chaotic people. We are not to judge them by our usages. No reverend institutions are insulted by their proceedings—for they have none among them. No peace of families is violated—for no family ties exist among them. No purity of the marriage bed is stained—for none is supposed to have a being. No deep affections are disquieted, no holy wedlock bands are snapped asunder—for affection's depth and wedded faith are not of the growth of that soil. There is neither right nor wrong—gratitude or its opposite—claim or duty—paternity or sonship. Of what consequence is it to Virtue, or how is she at all concerned about it, whether Sir Simon or Dapperwit steal away Miss Martha; or who is the father of Lord Froth's or Sir Paul Pliant's children?[4]

The whole is a passing pageant, where we should sit as uncon-

---

2. In Congreve's *Love for Love.*
3. In Exodus viii.22, the place the Jews dwelt, immune from the swarms of flies with which the Lord plagued the Egyptians.

4. Sir Simon, Dapperwit, and Martha are in Wycherley's *Love in a Wood;* Lord Froth and Sir Paul in Congreve's *Double-Dealer.*

cerned at the issues, for life or death, as at a battle of the frogs and mice. But, like Don Quixote, we take part against the puppets, and quite as impertinently. We dare not contemplate an Atlantis,[5] a scheme out of which our coxcombical moral sense is for a little transitory ease excluded. We have not the courage to imagine a state of things for which there is neither reward nor punishment. We cling to the painful necessities of shame and blame. We would indict our very dreams.

Amidst the mortifying circumstances attendant upon growing old, it is something to have seen the *School for Scandal* in its glory. This comedy grew out of Congreve and Wycherley, but gathered some allays of the sentimental comedy which followed theirs. It is impossible that it should be now *acted*, though it continues, at long intervals, to be announced in the bills. Its hero, when Palmer[6] played it at least, was Joseph Surface. When I remember the gay boldness, the graceful solemn plausibility, the measured step, the insinuating voice—to express it in a word—the downright *acted* villainy of the part, so different from the pressure of conscious actual wickedness—the hypocritical assumption of hypocrisy—which made Jack so deservedly a favorite in that character, I must needs conclude the present generation of playgoers more virtuous than myself, or more dense. I freely confess that he divided the palm with me with his better brother; that, in fact, I liked him quite as well. Not but there are passages—like that, for instance, where Joseph is made to refuse a pittance to a poor relation—incongruities which Sheridan was forced upon by the attempt to join the artificial with the sentimental comedy, either of which must destroy the other—but over these obstructions Jack's manner floated him so lightly that a refusal from him no more shocked you than the easy compliance of Charles gave you in reality any pleasure; you got over the paltry question as quickly as you could, to get back into the regions of pure comedy, where no cold moral reigns. The highly artificial manner of Palmer in this character counteracted every disagreeable impression which you might have received from the contrast, supposing them real, between the two brothers. You did not believe in Joseph with the same faith with which you believed in Charles. The latter was a pleasant reality, the former a no less pleasant poetical foil to it. The comedy, I have said, is incongruous; a mixture of Congreve with sentimental incompatibilities; the gaiety upon the whole is buoyant; but it required the consummate art of Palmer to reconcile the discordant elements.[7] * * *

1822

---

5. A mythical island in the western ocean which is supposed to have sunk beneath the sea.
6. Jack Palmer, famous comic actor of the late 18th century, especially noted for his playing of Joseph Surface.
7. The remainder of the essay is a critique of some of the actors who had appeared in the old comedies of manners.

Old China

I have an almost feminine partiality for old china. When I go to see any great house, I inquire for the china closet, and next for the picture gallery. I cannot defend the order of preference, but by saying that we have all some taste or other, of too ancient a date to admit of our remembering distinctly that it was an acquired one. I can call to mind the first play, and the first exhibition, that I was taken to; but I am not conscious of a time when china jars and saucers were introduced into my imagination.

I had no repugnance then—why should I now have?—to those little, lawless, azure-tinctured grotesques, that under the notion of men and women float about, uncircumscribed by any element, in that world before perspective—a china teacup.

I like to see my old friends—whom distance cannot diminish—figuring up in the air (so they appear to our optics), yet on terra firma still—for so we must in courtesy interpret that speck of deeper blue, which the decorous artist, to present absurdity, had made to spring up beneath their sandals.

I love the men with women's faces, and the women, if possible, with still more womanish expressions.

Here is a young and courtly mandarin, handing tea to a lady from a salver—two miles off. See how distance seems to set off respect! And here the same lady, or another—for likeness is identity on teacups—is stepping into a little fairy boat, moored on the hither side of this calm garden river, with a dainty mincing foot, which in a right angle of incidence (as angles go in our world) must infallibly land her in the midst of a flowery mead—a furlong off on the other side of the same strange stream!

Farther on—if far or near can be predicated of their world—see horses, trees, pagodas, dancing the hays.[1]

Here—a cow and rabbit couchant,[2] and coextensive—so objects show, seen through the lucid atmosphere of fine Cathay.[3]

I was pointing out to my cousin last evening, over our Hyson[4] (which we are old-fashioned enough to drink unmixed still of an afternoon), some of these *speciosa miracula*[5] upon a set of extraordinary old blue china (a recent purchase) which we were now for the first time using; and could not help remarking how favorable circumstances had been to us of late years that we could afford to please the eye sometimes with trifles of this sort—when a passing

---

1. An English country dance with a serpentining movement.
2. Heraldic term: lying down with the head raised.

3. The old European name for China.
4. A Chinese green-tea.
5. "Shining wonders."

sentiment seemed to overshade the brows of my companion. I am quick at detecting these summer clouds in Bridget.[6]

"I wish the good old times would come again," she said, "when we were not quite so rich. I do not mean that I want to be poor; but there was a middle state"—so she was pleased to ramble on— "in which I am sure we were a great deal happier. A purchase is but a purchase, now that you have money enough and to spare. Formerly it used to be a triumph. When we coveted a cheap luxury (and, O! how much ado I had to get you to consent in those times!)—we were used to have a debate two or three days before, and to weigh the *for* and *against*, and think what we might spare it out of, and what saving we could hit upon, that should be an equivalent. A thing was worth buying then, when we felt the money that we paid for it.

"Do you remember the brown suit, which you made to hang upon you, till all your friends cried shame upon you, it grew so threadbare—and all because of that folio Beaumont and Fletcher,[7] which you dragged home late at night from Barker's in Covent Garden? Do you remember how we eyed it for weeks before we could make up our minds to the purchase, and had not come to a determination till it was near ten o'clock of the Saturday night, when you set off from Islington,[8] fearing you should be too late—and when the old bookseller with some grumbling opened his shop, and by the twinkling taper (for he was setting bedwards) lighted out the relic from his dusty treasures—and when you lugged it home, wishing it were twice as cumbersome—and when you presented it to me—and when we were exploring the perfectness of it (*collating,* you called it)—and while I was repairing some of the loose leaves with paste, which your impatience would not suffer to be left till daybreak—was there no pleasure in being a poor man? or can those neat black clothes which you wear now, and are so careful to keep brushed, since we have become rich and finical, give you half the honest vanity with which you flaunted it about in that overworn suit—your old corbeau[9]—for four or five weeks longer than you should have done, to pacify your conscience for the mighty sum of fifteen—or sixteen shillings was it?—a great affair we thought it then—which you had lavished on the old folio. Now you can afford to buy any book that pleases you, but I do not see that you ever bring me home any nice old purchases now.

"When you came home with twenty apologies for laying out a less number of shillings upon that print after Leonardo,[1] which we

---

6. In Lamb's essays, his name for his sister, Mary.
7. The Elizabethan dramatic collaborators, whose plays were first collected in a large folio volume in 1647.
8. In the north of London, where the Lambs had been living.

9. A dark green cloth, almost black (hence its name, the French for "raven").
1. Leonardo da Vinci (1452–1519), the great Italian painter. The painting is the one known as "Modesty and Vanity."

christened the 'Lady Blanch'; when you looked at the purchase, and thought of the money—and thought of the money, and looked again at the picture—was there no pleasure in being a poor man? Now, you have nothing to do but to walk into Colnaghi's, and buy a wilderness of Leonardos. Yet do you?

"Then, do you remember our pleasant walks to Enfield, and Potter's Bar, and Waltham,[2] when we had a holiday—holidays, and all other fun, are gone now we are rich—and the little hand-basket in which I used to deposit our day's fare of savory cold lamb and salad —and how you would pry about at noontide for some decent house, where we might go in and produce our store—only paying for the ale that you must call for—and speculate upon the looks of the landlady, and whether she was likely to allow us a tablecloth— and wish for such another honest hostess as Izaak Walton has described many a one on the pleasant banks of the Lea, when he went a-fishing—and sometimes they would prove obliging enough, and sometimes they would look grudgingly upon us—but we had cheerful looks still for one another, and would eat our plain food savorily, scarcely grudging Piscator[3] his Trout Hall? Now—when we go out a day's pleasuring, which is seldom, moreover, we *ride* part of the way—and go into a fine inn, and order the best of dinners, never debating the expense—which, after all, never has half the relish of those chance country snaps,[3a] when we were at the mercy of uncertain usage, and a precarious welcome.

"You are too proud to see a play anywhere now but in the pit. Do you remember where it was we used to sit, when we saw the *Battle of Hexham*, and the *Surrender of Calais*,[4] and Bannister and Mrs. Bland in the *Children in the Wood*[5]—when we squeezed out our shillings apiece to sit three or four times in a season in the one-shilling gallery—where you felt all the time that you ought not to have brought me—and more strongly I felt obligation to you for having brought me—and the pleasure was the better for a little shame—and when the curtain drew up, what cared we for our place in the house, or what mattered it where we were sitting, when our thoughts were with Rosalind in Arden, or with Viola at the Court of Illyria.[6] You used to say that the gallery was the best place of all for enjoying a play socially—that the relish of such exhibitions must be in proportion to the infrequency of going—that the company we met there, not being in general readers of plays, were obliged to attend the more, and did attend, to what was going on, on the stage—because a word lost would have been a chasm, which it was impossible for them to fill up. With such reflections we

2. All three are suburbs to the north of London.
3. The fisherman in Izaak Walton's *Complete Angler* (1653).
3a. Snacks.
4. Comedies by George Colman (1762–1836).
5. By Thomas Morton (1764–1838).
6. Rosalind in *As You Like It* and Viola in *Twelfth Night*.

consoled our pride then—and I appeal to you whether, as a woman, I met generally with less attention and accommodation than I have done since in more expensive situations in the house? The getting in indeed, and the crowding up those inconvenient stair-cases, was bad enough—but there was still a law of civility to woman recognized to quite as great an extent as we ever found in the other passages—and how a little difficulty overcome heightened the snug seat and the play, afterwards! Now we can only pay our money and walk in. You cannot see, you say, in the galleries now. I am sure we saw, and heard too, well enough then—but sight, and all, I think, is gone with our poverty.

"There was pleasure in eating strawberries, before they became quite common—in the first dish of peas, while they were yet dear—to have them for a nice supper, a treat. What treat can we have now? If we were to treat ourselves now—that is, to have dainties a little above our means, it would be selfish and wicked. It is the very little more that we allow ourselves beyond what the actual poor can get at that makes what I call a treat—when two people living to-gether, as we have done, now and then indulge themselves in a cheap luxury, which both like; while each apologizes, and is willing to take both halves of the blame to his single share. I see no harm in people making much of themselves, in that sense of the word. It may give them a hint how to make much of others. But now—what I mean by the word—we never do make much of ourselves. None but the poor can do it. I do not mean the veriest poor of all, but persons as we were, just above poverty.

"I know what you were going to say, that it is mighty pleasant at the end of the year to make all meet—and much ado we used to have every Thirty-first Night of December to account for our ex-ceedings—many a long face did you make over your puzzled ac-counts, and in contriving to make it out how we had spent so much—or that we had not spent so much—or that it was im-possible we should spend so much next year—and still we found our slender capital decreasing—but then, betwixt ways, and projects, and compromises of one sort or another, and talk of curtailing this charge, and doing without that for the future—and the hope that youth brings, and laughing spirits (in which you were never poor till now), we pocketed up our loss, and in conclusion, with 'lusty brimmers' (as you used to quote it out of *hearty cheerful Mr. Cotton*,[7] as you called him), we used to welcome in 'the coming guest.' Now we have no reckoning at all at the end of the old year—no flat-tering promises about the new year doing better for us."

Bridget is so sparing of her speech on most occasions that when she gets into a rhetorical vein, I am careful how I interrupt it. I

---

7. Charles Cotton, the 17th-century poet, a favorite of Lamb's; the quotations are from his poem *The New Year*.

could not help, however, smiling at the phantom of wealth which her dear imagination had conjured up out of a clear income of poor ———— hundred pounds a year. "It is true we were happier when we were poorer, but we were also younger, my cousin. I am afraid we must put up with the excess, for if we were to shake the superflux into the sea, we should not much mend ourselves. That we had much to struggle with, as we grew up together, we have reason to be most thankful. It strengthened and knit our compact closer. We could never have been what we have been to each other, if we had always had the sufficiency which you now complain of. The resisting power—those natural dilations of the youthful spirit, which circumstances cannot straiten—with us are long since passed away. Competence to age is supplementary youth, a sorry supplement indeed, but I fear the best that is to be had. We must ride where we formerly walked: live better and lie softer—and shall be wise to do so—than we had means to do in those good old days you speak of. Yet could those days return—could you and I once more walk our thirty miles a day—could Bannister and Mrs. Bland again be young, and you and I be young to see them—could the good old one-shilling gallery days return—they are dreams, my cousin, now—but could you and I at this moment, instead of this quiet argument, by our well-carpeted fireside, sitting on this luxurious sofa—be once more struggling up those inconvenient staircases, pushed about, and squeezed, and elbowed by the poorest rabble of poor gallery scramblers—could I once more hear those anxious shrieks of yours—and the delicious *Thank God, we are safe,* which always followed when the topmost stair, conquered, let in the first light of the whole cheerful theater down beneath us—I know not the fathom line that ever touched a descent so deep as I would be willing to bury more wealth in than Croesus had, or the great Jew R——[8] is supposed to have, to purchase it. And now do just look at that merry little Chinese waiter holding an umbrella, big enough for a bed-tester, over the head of that pretty insipid half Madonna-ish chit of a lady in that very blue summerhouse."

1823

8. Nathan Meyer Rothschild (1777–1836) founded the English branch of the great European banking house.

WILLIAM HAZLITT
(1778–1830)

1813–14: Begins writing dramatic criticism and general essays.
1815–22: The height of his powers as essayist and as lecturer
on English poetry and drama.

"I started in life," Hazlitt wrote, "with the French Revolution, and I have lived, alas! to see the end of it. * * * Since then, I confess, I have no longer felt myself young, for with that my hopes fell." He was born into a radical circle, for the elder William Hazlitt, his father, was a Unitarian minister who declared from the pulpit his advocacy both of American independence and of the French Revolution. When young William was 5 years old, his father took the family to America in search of liberty and founded the first Unitarian Church in Boston; but four years later he returned to settle at Wem, in Shropshire. Despite the persistent attacks of reviewers and the backsliding of his once-radical friends, Hazlitt himself never wavered in his loyalty to liberty, equality, and the principles behind the overthrow of the monarchy in France. His first literary production, at the age of 13, was a letter to a newspaper in indignant protest against the mob which sacked Joseph Priestley's house, when the scientist and preacher had celebrated publicly the second anniversary of the fall of the Bastille. His last book, published in the year he died, was a four-volume life of Napoleon, in whom Hazlitt stubbornly insisted on seeing a noble-intentioned champion of the emancipation of mankind.

Hazlitt was a long time finding his vocation. When he attended the Hackney College, London, between the age of 15 and 18, he plunged into philosophical studies with such zeal that he ruined his health. In 1799 he took up the study of painting, and did not give up the ambition to become a portraitist until 1812. Hazlitt's first books dealt with philosophy, economics, and politics, and his first job as a journalist was as Parliamentary reporter for the *Morning Chronicle*. It was not until 1813, at the age of 36, that he began contributing dramatic criticism and miscellaneous essays to various periodicals, and so discovered what he had been born to do. Years of wide reading and hard thinking had made him thoroughly ready: within the next decade Hazlitt demonstrated himself to be a highly popular lecturer on Shakespeare, Elizabethan drama, and English poetry; a superb connoisseur of the theater and of painting; one of the two most important literary critics of the day (Coleridge is the other); and a master of the familiar essay.

Unlike his contemporaries, Coleridge, Lamb, and De Quincey, whose writings look back to the elaborate prose stylists of the earlier 17th century, Hazlitt developed a fast-moving, hard-hitting prose in what has been aptly called a "literary-colloquial English": it gives the effect of good talk, but heightened. He wrote, indeed, almost as fast as he talked, turning out at a single sitting enough text to fill ten or fifteen printed pages, almost without correction and (despite the density of literary quotations) without reference to books or notes. This rapidity was possible only because his essays are relatively planless. Hazlitt characteristically lays down a topic and then expands upon it by piling up relevant observations and instances, expressed in a sequence of forthright and relatively uncomplicated sentences; the essay accumulates instead of developing, and it does not come to a conclusion, but simply stops. Hazlitt's prose is unfailingly energetic; but his most satisfying essays, considered as rounded and integral works of literary art, are those which, like *My First Acquaintance with Poets* and *The Fight*, have a narrative subject matter to give them a principle of organization.

In his demeanor Hazlitt was excessively bashful, suspicious, and gauche. Coleridge described him in 1803 as "brow-hanging, shoe-contemplative, strange. He is, I verily believe, kindly-natured * * * but he is jealous, gloomy, and of an irritable pride." Hazlitt's gracelessness and lack of talent for domesticity doomed him to be unlucky in love. At the age of 30 he married Sarah Stoddart, three years his senior, separated from her after ten inharmonious years, and several years later secured her consent to a Scottish divorce, in the hope he could marry Sarah Walker, the young daughter of his landlord in London. But the girl was a cold and faithless coquette, who (as Hazlitt himself relates in his confessional *Liber Amoris*) mercilessly teased and then jilted her infatuated lover. When in 1824 he married a widow with a substantial income, she too left him within three years, in part because of the antagonism of young William, Hazlitt's son by his first wife.

Hazlitt, it must be remembered, had grown up as a member of a highly unpopular minority, both in religion and politics; he found his friends deserting to the side of reaction; and his naturally combative disposition was exacerbated by the malignant abuse directed against him in the periodicals of that day. In the course of his life he managed to quarrel violently, in private and in print, with almost all the people he had once most admired and liked, including Coleridge, Wordsworth, and Leigh Hunt; even Charles Lamb, with whom his friendship was the most intimate and enduring, was not always safe from Hazlitt's rasping tongue. But we may let the tolerant Lamb speak for the rare and admirable qualities which emerged when Hazlitt relaxed in company he felt he could trust: "I think W.H. to be, in his natural state, one of the wisest and finest spirits breathing. * * * I think I shall go to my grave without finding, or expecting to find, such another companion."

What appealed to Hazlitt's personal admirers, as to the readers of his essays, was his courage and uncompromising honesty, and above all, his ardor, and his zest for life in all its variety—including even, as he announced in the title of a characteristic essay, *The Pleasure of Hating*. Hazlitt intensely relished, and could matchlessly communicate, the particular qualities of diverse things—whether a passage of poetry, a painting, a natural prospect, a person, or a well-directed blow in a prize fight. Despite the recurrent frustrations of his 52 years of existence, he was able, on looking back, to say with his last breath: "Well, I've had a happy life."

My First Acquaintance with Poets[1]

My father was a Dissenting Minister, at Wem, in Shropshire; and in the year 1798 (the figures that compose that date are to me like the "dreaded name of Demogorgon"[2]) Mr. Coleridge came to Shrewsbury, to succeed Mr. Rowe in the spiritual charge of a Unitarian congregation there. He did not come till late on the Saturday afternoon before he was to preach; and Mr. Rowe, who himself went down to the coach, in a state of anxiety and expectation, to look for the arrival of his successor, could find no one at all answering the description but a round-faced man, in a short black coat (like a shooting jacket) which hardly seemed to have been made for him, but who seemed to be talking at a great rate to his fellow passengers. Mr. Rowe had scarce returned to give an account of his disappointment, when the round-faced man in black entered, and dissipated all doubts on the subject, by beginning to talk. He did not cease while he stayed; nor has he since, that I know of. He held the good town of Shrewsbury in delightful suspense for three weeks that he remained there, "fluttering the *proud Salopians*, like an eagle in a dovecote";[3] and the Welsh mountains that skirt the horizon with their tempestuous confusion, agree to have heard no such mystic sounds since the days of

High-born Hoel's harp or soft Llewellyn's lay![4]

As we passed along between Wem and Shrewsbury, and I eyed their blue tops seen through the wintry branches, or the red rustling leaves of the sturdy oak trees by the roadside, a sound was in my ears as of a Siren's song; I was stunned, startled with it, as from deep sleep; but I had no notion then that I should ever be able to express my admiration to others in motley imagery or quaint allusion, till the light of his genius shone into my soul, like the

1. This essay was written a quarter century after the events it describes. Coleridge and Wordsworth had long given up their early radicalism, and both men had since quarreled violently with Hazlitt—hence the essay's elegiac note in dealing with the genius of the two poets. Nevertheless Hazlitt communicates the intense excitement he had felt when Coleridge awakened him to the sense of his own literary possibilities, and the essay remains an incomparable portrait of Wordsworth and Coleridge early in 1798, the period of their closest collaboration.

2. *Paradise Lost* II.964–65. To mythographers of the Renaissance, Demogorgon was a mysterious and terrifying demon, sometimes described as ancestor of all the gods. He plays a role in Shelley's *Prometheus Unbound*.

3. Adapted from Shakespeare's *Coriolanus* V.vi.114–15. "Salopians" are inhabitants of Shropshire.

4. Gray's *The Bard*, line 28.

sun's rays glittering in the puddles of the road. I was at that time dumb, inarticulate, helpless, like a worm by the wayside, crushed, bleeding, lifeless; but now, bursting from the deadly bands that bound them,

With Styx nine times round them,[5]

my ideas float on winged words, and as they expand their plumes, catch the golden light of other years. My soul has indeed remained in its original bondage, dark, obscure, with longings infinite and unsatisfied; my heart, shut up in the prison house of this rude clay, has never found, nor will it ever find, a heart to speak to; but that my understanding also did not remain dumb and brutish, or at length found a language to express itself, I owe to Coleridge. But this is not to my purpose.

My father lived ten miles from Shrewsbury, and was in the habit of exchanging visits with Mr. Rowe, and with Mr. Jenkins of Whitechurch (nine miles farther on) according to the custom of Dissenting Ministers in each other's neighborhood. A line of communication is thus established, by which the flame of civil and religious liberty is kept alive, and nourishes its smoldering fire unquenchable, like the fires in the *Agamemnon* of Aeschylus, placed at different stations, that waited for ten long years to announce with their blazing pyramids the destruction of Troy. Coleridge had agreed to come over to see my father, according to the courtesy of the country, as Mr. Rowe's probable successor; but in the meantime, I had gone to hear him preach the Sunday after his arrival. A poet and a philosopher getting up into a Unitarian pulpit to preach the Gospel was a romance in these degenerate days, a sort of revival of the primitive spirit of Christianity, which was not to be resisted.

It was in January of 1798, that I rose one morning before daylight, to walk ten miles in the mud, and went to hear this celebrated person preach. Never, the longest day I have to live, shall I have such another walk as this cold, raw, comfortless one, in the winter of the year 1798. *Il y a des impressions que ni le temps ni les circonstances peuvent effacer. Dusse-je vivre des siècles entiers, le doux temps de ma jeunesse ne peut renaître pour moi, ni s'effacer jamais dans ma mémoire.*[6] When I got there, the organ was playing the 100th psalm, and when it was done, Mr. Coleridge rose and gave out his text, "And he went up into the mountain to pray, *himself, alone.*"[7] As he gave out this text, his voice "rose like a steam of rich distilled perfume,"[8] and when he

---

5. Adapted from Pope's *Ode on St. Cecilia's Day,* lines 90–91.
6. "There are some impressions which neither time nor circumstances can efface. Might I live whole centuries, the sweet time of my youth could not be reborn for me, nor ever erased from my memory." Based on Rousseau's epistolary novel, *La Nouvelle Héloïse* (1761), Part VI, Letter 7.
7. Cf. Matthew xiv.23; John vi.15.
8. Milton's *Comus,* line 556.

came to the two last words, which he pronounced loud, deep, and distinct, it seemed to me, who was then young, as if the sounds had echoed from the bottom of the human heart, and as if that prayer might have floated in solemn silence through the universe. The idea of St. John came into my mind, "of one crying in the wilderness, who had his loins girt about, and whose food was locusts and wild honey."[9] The preacher then launched into his subject, like an eagle dallying with the wind. The sermon was upon peace and war; upon church and state—not their alliance but their separation—on the spirit of the world and the spirit of Christianity, not as the same, but as opposed to one another. He talked of those who had "inscribed the cross of Christ on banners dripping with human gore." He made a poetical and pastoral excursion—and to show the fatal effects of war, drew a striking contrast between the simple shepherd boy, driving his team afield, or sitting under the hawthorn, piping to his flock, "as though he should never be old,"[1] and the same poor country lad, crimped,[2] kidnapped, brought into town, made drunk, at an alehouse, turned into a wretched drummer boy, with his hair sticking on end with powder and pomatum, a long cue at his back, and tricked out in the loathsome finery of the profession of blood.

> Such were the notes our once-loved poet sung.[3]

And for myself, I could not have been more delighted if I had heard the music of the spheres. Poetry and Philosophy had met together. Truth and Genius had embraced, under the eye and with the sanction of Religion. This was even beyond my hopes. I returned home well satisfied. The sun that was still laboring pale and wan through the sky, obscured by thick mists, seemed an emblem of the *good cause;*[4] and the cold dank drops of dew, that hung half melted on the beard of the thistle, had something genial and refreshing in them; for there was a spirit of hope and youth in all nature, that turned everything into good. The face of nature had not then the brand of *Jus Divinum*[5] on it:

> Like to that sanguine flower inscribed with woe.[6]

On the Tuesday following, the half-inspired speaker came. I was called down into the room where he was, and went half-hoping, half-afraid. He received me very graciously, and I listened for a long time without uttering a word. I did not suffer in his opinion by my silence. "For those two hours," he afterwards was pleased to say, "he was conversing with W. H.'s forehead!" His appearance

9. See Matthew iii. 3–4 and Mark i.3–6.
1. Sir Philip Sidney's *Arcadia* I.ii.
2. Trapped into enlisting in military service.
3. The first line of Pope's *Epistle to Robert, Earl of Oxford.*

4. The cause of liberty, i.e., the French Revolution.
5. The divine right (of kings).
6. I.e., the hyacinth, believed to be marked with the Greek lament "AI AI"; the line is from Milton's *Lycidas* (106).

was different from what I had anticipated from seeing him before. At a distance, and in the dim light of the chapel, there was to me a strange wildness in his aspect, a dusky obscurity, and I thought him pitted with the smallpox. His complexion was at that time clear, and even bright—

As are the children of yon azure sheen.[7]

His forehead was broad and high, light as if built of ivory, with large projecting eyebrows, and his eyes rolling beneath them, like a sea with darkened luster. "A certain tender bloom his face o'erspread,"[8] a purple tinge as we see it in the pale thoughtful complexions of the Spanish portrait painters, Murillo and Velasquez. His mouth was gross, voluptuous, open, eloquent; his chin good-humored and round; but his nose, the rudder of the face, the index of the will, was small, feeble, nothing—like what he has done. It might seem that the genius of his face as from a height surveyed and projected him (with sufficient capacity and huge aspiration) into the world unknown of thought and imagination, with nothing to support or guide his veering purpose, as if Columbus had launched his adventurous course for the New World in a scallop,[9] without oars or compass. So at least I comment on it after the event. Coleridge in his person was rather above the common size, inclining to the corpulent, or like Lord Hamlet, "somewhat fat and pursy."[1] His hair (now, alas! gray) was then black and glossy as the raven's, and fell in smooth masses over his forehead. This long pendulous hair is peculiar to enthusiasts, to those whose minds tend heavenward; and is traditionally inseparable (though of a different color) from the pictures of Christ. It ought to belong, as a character, to all who preach *Christ crucified*, and Coleridge was at that time one of those!

It was curious to observe the contrast between him and my father, who was a veteran in the cause, and then declining into the vale of years. He had been a poor Irish lad, carefully brought up by his parents, and sent to the University of Glasgow (where he studied under Adam Smith[2]) to prepare him for his future destination. It was his mother's proudest wish to see her son a Dissenting Minister. So if we look back to past generations (as far as eye can reach) we see the same hopes, fears, wishes, followed by the same disappointments, throbbing in the human heart; and so we may see them (if we look forward) rising up forever, and disappearing, like vaporish bubbles, in the human breast! After being tossed about from congregation to congregation in the heats of the Unitarian

---

7. See James Thomson, *The Castle of Indolence* II.xxxiii.
8. See *ibid.* I.lvii.
9. Probably for "shallop," a small boat.

1. Cf. *Hamlet* V.ii.298.
2. Scottish philosopher and author of the great economic treatise, *The Wealth of Nations* (1776).

controversy, and squabbles about the American war,[3] he had been relegated to an obscure village, where he was to spend the last thirty years of his life, far from the only converse that he loved, the talk about disputed texts of Scripture and the cause of civil and religious liberty. Here he passed his days, repining but resigned, in the study of the Bible, and the perusal of the Commentators— huge folios, not easily got through, one of which would outlast a winter! Why did he pore on these from morn to night (with the exception of a walk in the fields or a turn in the garden to gather broccoli plants or kidney beans of his own rearing, with no small degree of pride and pleasure)? Here were "no figures nor no fantasies"[4]—neither poetry nor philosophy—nothing to dazzle, nothing to excite modern curiosity; but to his lackluster eyes there appeared, within the pages of the ponderous, unwieldy, neglected tomes, the sacred name of JEHOVAH in Hebrew capitals: pressed down by the weight of the style, worn to the last fading thinness of the understanding, there were glimpses, glimmering notions of the patriarchal wanderings, with palm trees hovering in the horizon, and processions of camels at the distance of three thousand years; there was Moses with the Burning Bush, the number of the Twelve Tribes, types, shadows,[5] glosses on the law and the prophets; there were discussions (dull enough) on the age of Methuselah, a mighty speculation! there were outlines, rude guesses at the shape of Noah's Ark and of the riches of Solomon's Temple; questions as to the date of the creation, predictions of the end of all things; the great lapses of time, the strange mutations of the globe were unfolded with the voluminous leaf, as it turned over; and though the soul might slumber with an hieroglyphic veil of inscrutable mysteries drawn over it, yet it was in a slumber ill-exchanged for all the sharpened realities of sense, wit, fancy, or reason. My father's life was comparatively a dream; but it was a dream of infinity and eternity, of death, the resurrection, and a judgment to come!

No two individuals were ever more unlike than were the host and his guest. A poet was to my father a sort of nondescript: yet whatever added grace to the Unitarian cause was to him welcome. He could hardly have been more surprised or pleased if our visitor had worn wings. Indeed, his thoughts had wings; and as the silken sounds rustled round our little wainscoted parlor, my father threw back his spectacles over his forehead, his white hairs mixing with its sanguine hue; and a smile of delight beamed across his rugged cordial face, to think that Truth had found a new ally in Fancy! Besides, Coleridge seemed to take considerable notice of me, and

3. The American Revolution, with which a number of radical Unitarian preachers were in sympathy.
4. *Julius Caesar* II.i.231.
5. "Types" were characters and events in the Old Testament believed to prefigure analogous matters in the New Testament. "Shadows" were Old Testament foreshadowings of later events, or symbols of moral and theological truths.

that of itself was enough. He talked very familiarly, but agreeably, and glanced over a variety of subjects. At dinner time he grew more animated, and dilated in a very edifying manner on Mary Wollstonecraft and Mackintosh.[6] The last, he said, he considered (on my father's speaking of his *Vindiciae Gallicae* as a capital performance) as a clever scholastic[7] man—a master of the topics—or as the ready warehouseman of letters, who knew exactly where to lay his hand on what he wanted, though the goods were not his own. He thought him no match for Burke, either in style or matter. Burke was a metaphysician, Mackintosh a mere logician. Burke was an orator (almost a poet) who reasoned in figures, because he had an eye for nature: Mackintosh, on the other hand, was a rhetorician, who had only an eye to commonplaces. On this I ventured to say that I had always entertained a great opinion of Burke, and that (as far as I could find) the speaking of him with contempt might be made the test of a vulgar democratical mind. This was the first observation I ever made to Coleridge, and he said it was a very just and striking one. I remember the leg of Welsh mutton and the turnips on the table that day had the finest flavor imaginable. Coleridge added that Mackintosh and Tom Wedgwood[8] (of whom, however, he spoke highly) had expressed a very indifferent opinion of his friend Mr. Wordsworth, on which he remarked to them— "He strides on so far before you that he dwindles in the distance!" Godwin[9] had once boasted to him of having carried on an argument with Mackintosh for three hours with dubious success; Coleridge told him—"If there had been a man of genius in the room, he would have settled the question in five minutes." He asked me if I had ever seen Mary Wollstonecraft, and I said I had once for a few moments, and that she seemed to me to turn off Godwin's objections to something she advanced with quite a playful, easy air. He replied, that "this was only one instance of the ascendancy which people of imagination exercised over those of mere intellect." He did not rate Godwin very high (this was caprice or prejudice, real or affected) but he had a great idea of Mrs. Wollstonecraft's powers of conversation, none at all of her talent for book-making. We talked a little about Holcroft.[1] He had been asked if he was not much struck *with* him, and he said, he thought himself in more danger of being struck *by* him. I complained that he would

6. Mary Wollstonecraft was a radical author, the wife of William Godwin and mother of Shelley's second wife. Sir James Mackintosh, Scottish philosopher, wrote *Vindiciae Gallicae* ("Defense of France," 1791), in opposition to Edmund Burke's *Reflections on the French Revolution*.

7. The Scholastics, medieval philosophers and theologians, organized their thought systematically, often under various "topics"—standard headings, or "commonplaces" (see the third sentence following).

8. Son of Josiah Wedgwood (1730–95), who founded the great pottery firm which still exists.

9. William Godwin (1756–1836), radical philosopher and didactic novelist, author of the influential *Inquiry Concerning Political Justice* (1793).

1. Thomas Holcroft, another radical contemporary, author of plays and novels.

not let me get on at all, for he required a definition of even the commonest word, exclaiming, "What do you mean by a *sensation*, sir? What do you mean by an *idea?*" This, Coleridge said, was barricadoing the road to truth: it was setting up a turnpike gate at every step we took. I forget a great number of things, many more than I remember; but the day passed off pleasantly, and the next morning Mr. Coleridge was to return to Shrewsbury. When I came down to breakfast, I found that he had just received a letter from his friend, T. Wedgwood, making him an offer of £150 a year if he chose to waive his present pursuit, and devote himself entirely to the study of poetry and philosophy. Coleridge seemed to make up his mind to close with this proposal in the act of tying on one of his shoes. It threw an additional damp on his departure. It took the wayward enthusiast quite from us to cast him into Deva's winding vales,[2] or by the shores of old romance. Instead of living at ten miles' distance, of being the pastor of a Dissenting congregation at Shrewsbury, he was henceforth to inhabit the Hill of Parnassus, to be a Shepherd on the Delectable Mountains.[3] Alas! I knew not the way thither, and felt very little gratitude for Mr. Wedgwood's bounty. I was presently relieved from this dilemma; for Mr. Coleridge, asking for a pen and ink, and going to a table to write something on a bit of card, advanced towards me with undulating step, and giving me the precious document, said that that was his address, *Mr. Coleridge, Nether Stowey, Somersetshire;* and that he should be glad to see me there in a few weeks' time, and, if I chose, would come half-way to meet me. I was not less surprised than the shepherd boy (this simile is to be found in *Cassandra*[4]) when he sees a thunderbolt fall close at his feet. I stammered out my acknowledgments and acceptance of this offer (I thought Mr. Wedgwood's annuity a trifle to it) as well as I could; and this mighty business being settled, the poet-preacher took leave, and I accompanied him six miles on the road. It was a fine morning in the middle of winter, and he talked the whole way. The scholar in Chaucer is described as going

——sounding on his way.[5]

So Coleridge went on his. In digressing, in dilating, in passing from subject to subject, he appeared to me to float in air, to slide on ice. He told me in confidence (going along) that he should have preached two sermons before he accepted the situation at Shrews-

2. Milton, *Lycidas*, line 55: "Nor yet where Deva spreads her wizard stream" ("Deva" is the river Dee, in Wales). Since Milton speaks in that passage of "Druid bards," Hazlitt means that Coleridge will devote himself to imaginative writing.
3. An allegorical locale in Bunyan's *Pilgrim's Progress*, here used as another periphrasis for the occupation of poetry.
4. A romance by the 17th-century French writer La Calprenède.
5. *The Canterbury Tales*, General Prologue, line 309: "Souning in moral vertu was his speeche" (in Chaucer, the meaning of "souning in" is either "resounding in" or "consonant with").

bury, one on Infant Baptism, the other on the Lord's Supper, showing that he could not administer either, which would have effectually disqualified him for the object in view. I observed that he
continually crossed me on the way by shifting from one side of
the footpath to the other. This struck me as an odd movement;
but I did not at that time connect it with any instability of purpose or involuntary change of principle, as I have done since. He
seemed unable to keep on in a straight line. He spoke slightingly
of Hume[6] (whose *Essay on Miracles* he said was stolen from an
objection started in one of South's[7] sermons—*Credat Judaeus Ap-
pella!*) I was not very much pleased at this account of Hume, for
I had just been reading, with infinite relish, that completest of all
metaphysical *choke-pears*,[8] his *Treatise on Human Nature*, to which
the *Essays*, in point of scholastic subtlety and close reasoning, are
mere elegant trifling, light summer reading. Coleridge even denied
the excellence of Hume's general style, which I think betrayed a
want of taste or candor. He however made me amends by the manner in which he spoke of Berkeley.[9] He dwelt particularly on his
Essay on Vision as a masterpiece of analytical reasoning. So it undoubtedly is. He was exceedingly angry with Dr. Johnson for striking the stone with his foot, in allusion to this author's theory of
matter and spirit, and saying, "Thus I confute him, sir."[1] Coleridge drew a parallel (I don't know how he brought about the
connection) between Bishop Berkeley and Tom Paine.[2] He said
the one was an instance of a subtle, the other of an acute mind,
than which no two things could be more distinct. The one was
a shop-boy's quality, the other the characteristic of a philosopher.
He considered Bishop Butler[3] as a true philosopher, a profound
and conscientious thinker, a genuine reader of nature and of his
own mind. He did not speak of his *Analogy*, but of his *Sermons
at the Rolls' Chapel*, of which I had never heard. Coleridge somehow always contrived to prefer the *unknown* to the *known*. In this
instance he was right. The *Analogy* is a tissue of sophistry, of wire-
drawn, theological special-pleading; the *Sermons* (with the Preface
to them) are in a fine vein of deep, matured reflection, a candid
appeal to our observation of human nature, without pedantry and
without bias. I told Coleridge I had written a few remarks, and
was sometimes foolish enough to believe that I had made a discovery on the same subject (the *Natural Disinterestedness of the*

6. David Hume, 18th-century Scottish philosopher.
7. Robert South (1634–1716), Angli-
can divine. The Latin phrase, from
Horace, *Satires* I.v.100, means, "Let
Apella the Jew believe it"—implying
that he himself does not.
8. A very sour variety of pear; hence,
anything hard to take in.
9. Bishop George Berkeley, 18th-cen-
tury idealist philosopher, and author of

an *Essay Toward a New Theory of
Vision* (1709).
1. See Boswell's *Life of Johnson* for
the year 1763.
2. Philosophical supporter of the American and French Revolutions and author of *Common Sense* and *The Rights
of Man*.
3. Joseph Butler. 18th-century theologian and moral philosopher, author of
the *Analogy of Religion* (1736).

Human Mind[4])—and I tried to explain my view of it to Coleridge, who listened with great willingness, but I did not succeed in making myself understood. I sat down to the task shortly afterwards for the twentieth time, got new pens and paper, determined to make clear work of it, wrote a few meager sentences in the skeleton-style of a mathematical demonstration, stopped halfway down the second page; and, after trying in vain to pump up any words, images, notions, apprehensions, facts, or observations, from that gulf of abstraction in which I had plunged myself for four or five years preceding, gave up the attempt as labor in vain, and shed tears of helpless despondency on the blank unfinished paper. I can write fast enough now. Am I better than I was then? Oh no! One truth discovered, one pang of regret at not being able to express it, is better than all the fluency and flippancy in the world. Would that I could go back to what I then was! Why can we not revive past times as we can revisit old places? If I had the quaint Muse of Sir Philip Sidney to assist me, I would write a *Sonnet to the Road between Wem and Shrewsbury*, and immortalize every step of it by some fond enigmatical conceit. I would swear that the very milestones had ears, and that Harmer Hill stooped with all its pines, to listen to a poet, as he passed! I remember but one other topic of discourse in this walk. He mentioned Paley,[5] praised the naturalness and clearness of his style, but condemned his sentiments, thought him a mere time-serving casuist, and said that "the fact of his work on Moral and Political Philosophy being made a textbook in our universities was a disgrace to the national character." We parted at the six-mile stone; and I returned homeward pensive but much pleased. I had met with unexpected notice from a person whom I believed to have been prejudiced against me. "Kind and affable to me had been his condescension, and should be honored ever with suitable regard."[6] He was the first poet I had known, and he certainly answered to that inspired name. I had heard a great deal of his powers of conversation, and was not disappointed. In fact, I never met with anything at all like them, either before or since. I could easily credit the accounts which were circulated of his holding forth to a large party of ladies and gentlemen, an evening or two before, on the Berkeleian Theory, when he made the whole material universe look like a transparency of fine words; and another story (which I believe he has somewhere told himself)[7] of his being asked to a party at Birmingham, of his smoking tobacco and going to sleep after dinner on a sofa, where the company found him, to their no small surprise, which was in-

---

4. Published as *An Essay on the Principles of Human Action* (1805).
5. William Paley, author of *Evidences of Christianity* (1794), and supporter of a utilitarian theology and morality.

6. Paraphrasing Adam's words about the angel Raphael in *Paradise Lost* VIII.648–50.
7. See *Biographia Literaria*, Chapter X.

creased to wonder when he started up of a sudden, and rubbing his eyes, looked about him, and launched into a three hours' description of the third heaven, of which he had had a dream, very different from Mr. Southey's *Vision of Judgment*,[8] and also from that other *Vision of Judgment*, which Mr. Murray, the secretary of the Bridge Street Junto, has taken into his especial keeping!

On my way back, I had a sound in my ears, it was the voice of Fancy: I had a light before me, it was the face of Poetry. The one still lingers there, the other has not quitted my side! Coleridge in truth met me half-way on the ground of philosophy, or I should not have been won over to his imaginative creed. I had an uneasy, pleasurable sensation all the time, till I was to visit him. During those months the chill breath of winter gave me a welcoming; the vernal air was balm and inspiration to me. The golden sunsets, the silver star of evening, lighted me on my way to new hopes and prospects. *I was to visit Coleridge in the spring*. This circumstance was never absent from my thoughts, and mingled with all my feelings. I wrote to him at the time proposed, and received an answer postponing my intended visit for a week or two, but very cordially urging me to complete my promise then. This delay did not damp, but rather increased my ardor. In the meantime, I went to Llangollen Vale,[9] by way of initiating myself in the mysteries of natural scenery; and I must say I was enchanted with it. I had been reading Coleridge's description of England in his fine *Ode on the Departing Year*, and I applied it, *con amore*,[1] to the objects before me. That valley was to me (in a manner) the cradle of a new existence: in the river that winds through it, my spirit was baptized in the waters of Helicon![2]

I returned home, and soon after set out on my journey with unworn heart and untired feet. My way lay through Worcester and Gloucester, and by Upton, where I thought of Tom Jones and the adventure of the muff.[3] I remember getting completely wet through one day, and stopping at an inn (I think it was at Tewkesbury) where I sat up all night to read *Paul and Virginia*.[4] Sweet were the showers in early youth that drenched my body, and sweet the drops of pity that fell upon the books I read! I recollect a remark of Coleridge's upon this very book that nothing could show the gross indelicacy of French manners and the entire corruption of their imagination more strongly than the behavior of the heroine in the

8. Robert Southey's sycophantic memorial poem describing the entrance into heaven of George III. "Mr. Murray" was Charles Murray, solicitor to an Association, located at New Bridge Street, for "Opposing Disloyal and Seditious Principles"; he prosecuted John Hunt for publishing Byron's *Vision of Judgment*, a brilliant parody of Southey's poem. Hazlitt derisively refers to the Association as a "junto"—

i.e., a group formed for political intrigue.
9. In north Wales (about 35 miles from Wem).
1. "With love," fervently.
2. A mountain sacred to Apollo and the Muses.
3. Henry Fielding's *Tom Jones* X.v. ff.
4. A sentimental love idyll (1788) by Bernardin de Saint-Pierre.

last fatal scene, who turns away from a person on board the sinking vessel, that offers to save her life, because he has thrown off his
clothes to assist him in swimming. Was this a time to think of
such a circumstance? I once hinted to Wordsworth, as we were
sailing in his boat on Grasmere lake, that I thought he had borrowed the idea of his *Poems on the Naming of Places* from the
local inscriptions of the same kind in *Paul and Virginia.* He did
not own the obligation, and stated some distinction without a difference in defense to his claim to originality. Any the slightest variation would be sufficient for this purpose in his mind; for whatever
he added or omitted would inevitably be worth all that any one
else had done, and contain the marrow of the sentiment. I was
still two days before the time fixed for my arrival, for I had taken
care to set out early enough. I stopped these two days at Bridgewater, and when I was tired of sauntering on the banks of its muddy
river, returned to the inn and read *Camilla.*[5] So have I loitered
my life away, reading books, looking at pictures, going to plays,
hearing, thinking, writing on what pleased me best. I have wanted
only one thing to make me happy; but wanting that, have wanted
everything![6]

I arrived, and was well received. The country about Nether
Stowey is beautiful, green and hilly, and near the seashore. I saw
it but the other day, after an interval of twenty years, from a hill
near Taunton. How was the map of my life spread out before me,
as the map of the country lay at my feet! In the afternoon, Coleridge took me over to Alfoxden, a romantic old family mansion
of the St. Aubins, where Wordsworth lived. It was then in the
possession of a friend of the poet's, who gave him the free use of
it.[7] Somehow, that period (the time just after the French Revolution) was not a time when *nothing was given for nothing.* The
mind opened and a softness might be perceived coming over the
heart of individuals, beneath "the scales that fence" our self-interest. Wordsworth himself was from home, but his sister kept house,
and set before us a frugal repast; and we had free access to her
brother's poems, the *Lyrical Ballads*, which were still in manuscript,
or in the form of *Sybilline Leaves.*[8] I dipped into a few of these
with great satisfaction, and with the faith of a novice. I slept that
night in an old room wth blue hangings, and covered with the
round-faced family portraits of the age of George I and II and from
the wooded declivity of the adjoining park that overlooked my window, at the dawn of day, could

——hear the loud stag speak.[9]

5. A novel by Fanny Burney, published
1796.
6. The love of Sarah Walker; see the
introduction to Hazlitt, above.
7. A mistake; Wordsworth paid rent.

8. I.e., "prophetic writings"; used by
Coleridge as the title for his published
poems in 1817.
9. From Ben Jonson's poem *To Sir
Robert Wroth*, line 22.

In the outset of life (and particularly at this time I felt it so) our imagination has a body to it. We are in a state between sleeping and waking, and have indistinct but glorious glimpses of strange shapes, and there is always something to come better than what we see. As in our dreams the fullness of the blood gives warmth and reality to the coinage of the brain, so in youth our ideas are clothed, and fed, and pampered with our good spirits; we breathe thick with thoughtless happiness, the weight of future years presses on the strong pulses of the heart, and we repose with undisturbed faith in truth and good. As we advance, we exhaust our fund of enjoyment and of hope. We are no longer wrapped in *lamb's wool*, lulled in Elysium. As we taste the pleasures of life, their spirit evaporates, the sense palls; and nothing is left but the phantoms, the lifeless shadows of what *has been!*

That morning, as soon as breakfast was over, we strolled out into the park, and seating ourselves on the trunk of an old ash tree that stretched along the ground, Coleridge read aloud with a sonorous and musical voice, the ballad of *Betty Foy*.[1] I was not critically or skeptically inclined. I saw touches of truth and nature, and took the rest for granted. But in the *Thorn*, the *Mad Mother*, and the *Complaint of a Poor Indian Woman*, I felt that deeper power and pathos which have been since acknowledged,

> In spite of pride, in erring reason's spite,[2]

as the characteristics of this author; and the sense of a new style and a new spirit in poetry came over me. It had to me something of the effect that arises from the turning up of the fresh soil, or of the first welcome breath of spring,

> While yet the trembling year is unconfirmed.[3]

Coleridge and myself walked back to Stowey that evening, and his voice sounded high

> Of Providence, foreknowledge, will, and fate,
> Fixed fate, free will, foreknowledge absolute,[4]

as we passed through echoing grove, by fairy stream or waterfall, gleaming in the summer moonlight! He lamented that Wordsworth was not prone enough to believe in the traditional superstitions of the place, and that there was a something corporeal, a *matter-of-fact-ness*, a clinging to the palpable, or often to the petty, in his poetry, in consequence. His genius was not a spirit that descended to him through the air; it sprung out of the ground like a flower, or unfolded itself from a green spray, on which the goldfinch sang.

1. Wordsworth's *Idiot Boy;* like the other poems mentioned, it was included in *Lyrical Ballads.*
2. Pope's *Essay on Man* I.293.
3. James Thomson, *The Seasons,* "Spring," line 18.
4. *Paradise Lost* II.559–60.

792 · *William Hazlitt*

He said, however (if I remember right) that this objection must be confined to his descriptive pieces, that his philosophic poetry had a grand and comprehensive spirit in it, so that his soul seemed to inhabit the universe like a palace, and to discover truth by intuition, rather than by deduction. The next day Wordsworth arrived from Bristol at Coleridge's cottage. I think I see him now. He answered in some degree to his friend's description of him, but was more gaunt and Don Quixote-like. He was quaintly dressed (according to the *costume* of that unconstrained period) in a brown fustian[5] jacket and striped pantaloons. There was something of a roll, a lounge in his gait, not unlike his own Peter Bell.[6] There was a severe, worn pressure of thought about his temples, a fire in his eye (as if he saw something in objects more than the outward appearance), an intense high narrow forehead, a Roman nose, cheeks furrowed by strong purpose and feeling, and a convulsive inclination to laughter about the mouth, a good deal at variance with the solemn, stately expression of the rest of his face. Chantry's bust wants the marking traits; but he was teased into making it regular and heavy; Haydon's head of him, introduced into the *Entrance of Christ into Jerusalem*, is the most like his drooping weight of thought and expression.[7] He sat down and talked very naturally and freely, with a mixture of clear gushing accents in his voice, a deep guttural intonation, and a strong tincture of the northern *burr*, like the crust on wine. He instantly began to make havoc of the half of a Cheshire cheese on the table, and said triumphantly that "his marriage with experience had not been so unproductive as Mr. Southey's in teaching him a knowledge of the good things of this life." He had been to see the *Castle Specter* by Monk Lewis,[8] while at Bristol, and described it very well. He said "it fitted the taste of the audience like a glove." This *ad captandum*[9] merit was, however, by no means a recommendation of it, according to the severe principles of the new school, which reject rather than court popular effect. Wordsworth, looking out of the low, latticed window, said, "How beautifully the sun sets on that yellow bank!" I thought within myself, "With what eyes these poets see nature!" and ever after, when I saw the sunset stream upon the objects facing it, conceived I had made a discovery, or thanked Mr. Wordsworth for having made one for me! We went over to Alfoxden again the day following, and Wordsworth read us the story of *Peter Bell* in the open air; and the comment made upon it by his face and voice was very different from that of

---

5. A coarse and heavy cotton cloth.
6. The protagonist in Wordsworth's *Peter Bell*.
7. Sir Francis Chantrey, a sculptor; Benjamin Robert Haydon, painter of grandiose historical and religious pictures.

8. Matthew Gregory Lewis (1775–1818), called "Monk" Lewis from his horror tale, *The Monk* (1795). *The Castle Specter* was a play, also in the Gothic terror-mode.
9. "For the sake of captivating" an audience.

some later critics! Whatever might be thought of the poem, "his face was as a book where men might read strange matters,"[1] and he announced the fate of his hero in prophetic tones. There is a *chaunt* in the recitation both of Coleridge and Wordsworth, which acts as a spell upon the hearer, and disarms the judgment. Perhaps they have deceived themselves by making habitual use of this ambiguous accompaniment. Coleridge's manner is more full, animated, and varied; Wordsworth's more equable, sustained, and internal. The one might be termed more *dramatic*, the other more *lyrical*. Coleridge has told me that he himself liked to compose in walking over uneven ground, or breaking through the straggling branches of a copse wood; whereas Wordsworth always wrote (if he could) walking up and down a straight gravel walk, or in some spot where the continuity of his verse met with no collateral interruption. Returning that same evening, I got into a metaphysical argument with Wordsworth, while Coleridge was explaining the different notes of the nightingale to his sister, in which we neither of us succeeded in making ourselves perfectly clear and intelligible. Thus I passed three weeks at Nether Stowey and in the neighborhood, generally devoting the afternoons to a delightful chat in an arbor made of bark by the poet's friend Tom Poole, sitting under two fine elm trees, and listening to the bees humming round us while we quaffed our flip.[2] It was agreed, among other things, that we should make a jaunt down the Bristol Channel, as far as Linton. We set off together on foot, Coleridge, John Chester, and I. This Chester was a native of Nether Stowey, one of those who were attracted to Coleridge's discourse as flies are to honey, or bees in swarming-time to the sound of a brass pan. He "followed in the chase like a dog who hunts, not like one that made up the cry."[3] He had on a brown cloth coat, boots, and corduroy breeches, was low in stature, bowlegged, had a drag in his walk like a drover, which he assisted by a hazel switch, and kept on a sort of trot by the side of Coleridge, like a running footman by a state coach, that he might not lose a syllable or sound that fell from Coleridge's lips. He told me his private opinion, that Coleridge was a wonderful man. He scarcely opened his lips, much less offered an opinion the whole way: yet of the three, had I to choose during that journey, I would be John Chester. He afterwards followed Coleridge into Germany, where the Kantean philosophers were puzzled how to bring him under any of their categories. When he sat down at table with his idol, John's felicity was complete; Sir Walter Scott's, or Mr. Blackwood's, when they sat down at the same table with the King,[4] was not more so. We passed Dunster on our right, a small town be-

1. See *Macbeth* I.v.63–64.
2. Spiced and sweetened ale.
3. Cf. *Othello* II.iii.369–70.
4. At a banquet given to George IV at Edinburgh, in 1822. William Blackwood, publisher of *Blackwood's Magazine*, was, like Scott, a Tory; hence the irony.

tween the brow of a hill and the sea. I remember eying it wistfully as it lay below us: contrasted with the woody scene around, it looked as clear, as pure, as *embrowned* and ideal as any landscape I have seen since, of Gaspar Poussin's or Domenichino's. We had a long day's march—(our feet kept time to the echoes of Coleridge's tongue)—through Minehead and by the Blue Anchor, and on to Linton, which we did not reach till near midnight, and where we had some difficulty in making a lodgment. We however knocked the people of the house up at last, and we were repaid for our apprehensions and fatigue by some excellent rashers of fried bacon and eggs. The view in coming along had been splendid. We walked for miles and miles on dark brown heaths overlooking the channel, with the Welsh hills beyond, and at times descended into little sheltered valleys close by the seaside, with a smuggler's face scowling by us, and then had to ascend conical hills with a path winding up through a coppice to a barren top, like a monk's shaven crown, from one of which I pointed out to Coleridge's notice the bare masts of a vessel on the very edge of the horizon and within the red-orbed disk of the setting sun, like his own specter-ship in the *Ancient Mariner*. At Linton the character of the seacoast becomes more marked and rugged. There is a place called the Valley of Rocks (I suspect this was only the poetical name for it) bedded among precipices overhanging the sea, with rocky caverns beneath, into which the waves dash, and where the seagull forever wheels its screaming flight. On the tops of these are huge stones thrown transverse, as if an earthquake had tossed them there, and behind these is a fretwork of perpendicular rocks, something like the Giant's Causeway.[5] A thunderstorm came on while we were at the inn, and Coleridge was running out bareheaded to enjoy the commotion of the elements in the Valley of Rocks, but as if in spite, the clouds only muttered a few angry sounds, and let fall a few refreshing drops. Coleridge told me that he and Wordsworth were to have made this place the scene of a prose tale,[6] which was to have been in the manner of, but far superior to, the *Death of Abel*, but they had relinquished the design. In the morning of the second day, we breakfasted luxuriously in an old-fashioned parlor, on tea, toast, eggs, and honey, in the very sight of the beehives from which it had been taken, and a garden full of thyme and wild flowers that had produced it. On this occasion Coleridge spoke of Virgil's *Georgics*, but not well. I do not think he had much feeling for the classical or elegant. It was in this room that we found a little worn-out copy of the *Seasons*,[7] lying in a window seat, on which Coleridge exclaimed, "*That* is true fame!" He said Thomson was

5. A mass of rocks on the northern Irish coast.
6. The "prose tale" exists as a fragment, *The Wanderings of Cain*. The

Death of Abel (1758) is by the once celebrated Swiss poet, Salomon Gessner.
7. By James Thomson, published 1726–30.

a great poet, rather than a good one; his style was as meretricious
as his thoughts were natural. He spoke of Cowper as the best modern poet. He said the *Lyrical Ballads* were an experiment about to
be tried by him and Wordsworth, to see how far the public taste
would endure poetry written in a more natural and simple style
than had hitherto been attempted; totally discarding the artifices
of poetical diction, and making use only of such words as had probably been common in the most ordinary language since the days
of Henry II. Some comparison was introduced between Shakespeare
and Milton. He said "he hardly knew which to prefer. Shakespeare
appeared to him a mere stripling in the art; he was as tall and as
strong, with infinitely more activity than Milton, but he never appeared to have come to man's estate; or if he had, he would not
have been a man, but a monster." He spoke with contempt of
Gray, and with intolerance of Pope. He did not like the versification
of the latter. He observed that "the ears of these couplet-writers
might be charged with having short memories, that could not retain
the harmony of whole passages." He thought little of Junius[8] as a
writer; he had a dislike of Dr. Johnson; and a much higher opinion
of Burke as an orator and politician, than of Fox or Pitt. He however thought him very inferior in richness of style and imagery to
some of our elder prose writers, particularly Jeremy Taylor.[9] He
liked Richardson, but not Fielding; nor could I get him to enter
into the merits of *Caleb Williams*.[1] In short, he was profound and
discriminating with respect to those authors whom he liked, and
where he gave his judgment fair play; capricious, perverse, and prejudiced in his antipathies and distastes. We loitered on the "ribbed
sea-sands,"[2] in such talk as this, a whole morning, and I recollect
met with a curious seaweed, of which John Chester told us the
country name! A fisherman gave Coleridge an account of a boy
that had been drowned the day before, and that they had tried
to save him at the risk of their own lives. He said "he did not know
how it was that they ventured, but, sir, we have a *nature* towards
one another." This expression, Coleridge remarked to me, was
a fine illustration of that theory of disinterestedness which I (in
common with Butler) had adopted. I broached to him an argument of mine to prove that *likeness* was not mere association of
ideas. I said that the mark in the sand put one in mind of a man's
foot, not because it was part of a former impression of a man's
foot (for it was quite new) but because it was like the shape of a
man's foot. He assented to the justness of this distinction (which

8. The pseudonym of an author (his
identity is still unknown) of a series
of attacks on George III and various
politicians, 1769–72.
9. The 17th-century divine, author of
Holy Living (1650) and *Holy Dying*
(1651).

1. Samuel Richardson and Henry Fielding, the great 18th-century novelists.
Caleb Williams (1794) was a novel
by William Godwin.
2. Echoing *The Ancient Mariner*, line
227.

I have explained at length elsewhere, for the benefit of the curious) and John Chester listened; not from any interest in the subject, but because he was astonished that I should be able to suggest anything to Coleridge that he did not already know. We returned on the third morning, and Coleridge remarked the silent cottage-smoke curling up the valleys where, a few evenings before, we had seen the lights gleaming through the dark.

In a day or two after we arrived at Stowey, we set out, I on my return home, and he for Germany. It was a Sunday morning, and he was to preach that day for Dr. Toulmin of Taunton. I asked him if he had prepared anything for the occasion? He said he had not even thought of the text, but should as soon as we parted. I did not go to hear him,—this was a fault—but we met in the evening at Bridgewater. The next day we had a long day's walk to Bristol, and sat down, I recollect, by a well-side on the road, to cool ourselves and satisfy our thirst, when Coleridge repeated to me some descriptive lines from his tragedy of *Remorse*; which I must say became his mouth and that occasion better than they, some years after, did Mr. Elliston's and the Drury Lane boards,[3]

> Oh memory! shield me from the world's poor strife,
> And give those scenes thine everlasting life.

I saw no more of him for a year or two, during which period he had been wandering in the Hartz Forest in Germany; and his return was cometary, meteorous, unlike his setting out. It was not till some time after that I knew his friends Lamb and Southey. The last always appears to me (as I first saw him) with a common-place-book under his arm, and the first with a bon mot in his mouth. It was at Godwin's that I met him with Holcroft and Coleridge, where they were disputing fiercely which was the best —*Man as he was, or man as he is to be.* "Give me," says Lamb, "man as he is *not* to be." This saying was the beginning of a friend-ship between us, which I believe still continues.—Enough of this for the present.

> But there is matter for another rhyme,
> And I to this may add a second tale.[4]

1823

3. Robert William Elliston, a well-known actor. Coleridge's *Remorse* was produced at Drury Lane Theatre in 1813.
4. Wordsworth, *Hart-Leap Well*, lines 95–96.

From Mr. Wordsworth[1]

Mr. Wordsworth's genius is a pure emanation of the Spirit of the Age. Had he lived in any other period of the world, he would never have been heard of. As it is, he has some difficulty to contend with the hebetude[2] of his intellect, and the meanness of his subject. With him "lowliness is young ambition's ladder":[3] but he finds it a toil to climb in this way the steep of Fame. His homely Muse can hardly raise her wing from the ground, nor spread her hidden glories to the sun. He has "no figures nor no fantasies, which busy *passion* draws in the brains of men":[4] neither the gorgeous machinery of mythologic lore, nor the splendid colors of poetic diction. His style is vernacular: he delivers household truths. He sees nothing loftier than human hopes; nothing deeper than the human heart. This he probes, this he tampers with, this he poises, with all its incalculable weight of thought and feeling, in his hands; and at the same time calms the throbbing pulses of his own heart, by keeping his eye ever fixed on the face of nature. If he can make the life-blood flow from the wounded breast, this is the living coloring with which he paints his verse: if he can assuage the pain or close up the wound with the balm of solitary musing, or the healing power of plants and herbs and "skyey influences,"[5] this is the sole triumph of his art. He takes the simplest elements of nature and of the human mind, the mere abstract conditions inseparable from our being, and tries to compound a new system of poetry from them; and has perhaps succeeded as well as any one could. "*Nihil humani a me alienum puto*"[6]—is the motto of his works. He thinks nothing low or indifferent of which this can be affirmed: every thing that professes to be more than this, that is not an absolute essence of truth and feeling, he holds to be vitiated, false, and spurious. In a word, his poetry is founded on setting up an opposition (and pushing it to the utmost length) between the natural and the artificial; between the spirit of humanity, and the spirit of fashion and of the world!

1. This was one of a series of essays on contemporary philosophers, poets, and statesmen which Hazlitt published in 1825 with the title *The Spirit of the Age: or Contemporary Portraits.* Like Shelley, Hazlitt attributed what was most distinctive in the intellectual and literary enterprise of his era to the impact on imagination of the French Revolution. See, e.g., the concluding page of Shelley's *Defence of Poetry.*

In this essay Hazlitt deals with Wordsworth's *Lyrical Ballads* and other early poems. With notable insight Hazlitt, alone among contemporary critics, writes a sociological study of Wordsworth's in-novations in poetry and criticism. He recognizes that the traditional hierarchy of poetic genres, subjects, and diction had reflected the class-structure of society, and that, by "leveling" this hierarchy, Wordsworth had effected a literary equivalent of the political and social revolution in France.
2. Dullness, lethargy.
3. Said by Brutus in *Julius Caesar* II.i.22.
4. *Ibid.,* II.i.231; Hazlitt substitutes "passion" for Brutus' word "care."
5. *Measure for Measure* III.i.9.
6. From the Roman writer of comedy, Terence: "Nothing that is human do I consider alien to me."

It is one of the innovations of the time. It partakes of, and is carried along with, the revolutionary movement of our age: the political changes of the day were the model on which he formed and conducted his poetical experiments. His Muse (it cannot be denied, and without this we cannot explain its character at all) is a leveling one. It proceeds on a principle of equality, and strives to reduce all things to the same standard. It is distinguished by a proud humility. It relies upon its own resources, and disdains external show and relief. It takes the commonest events and objects, as a test to prove that nature is always interesting from its inherent truth and beauty, without any of the ornaments of dress or pomp of circumstances to set it off. Hence the unaccountable mixture of seeming simplicity and real abstruseness in the *Lyrical Ballads*. Fools have laughed at, wise men scarcely understand them. He takes a subject or a story merely as pegs or loops to hang thought and feeling on; the incidents are trifling, in proportion to his contempt for imposing appearances; the reflections are profound, according to the gravity and the aspiring pretensions of his mind.

His popular, inartificial style gets rid (at a blow) of all the trappings of verse, of all the high places of poetry: "the cloud-capped towers, the solemn temples, the gorgeous palaces," are swept to the ground, and "like the baseless fabric of a vision, leave not a wreck behind."[7] All the traditions of learning, all the superstitions of age, are obliterated and effaced. We begin *de novo*, on a *tabula rasa*[8] of poetry. The purple pall, the nodding plume of tragedy are exploded as mere pantomime and trick, to return to the simplicity of truth and nature. Kings, queens, priests, nobles, the altar and the throne, the distinctions of rank, birth, wealth, power, "the judge's robe, the marshal's truncheon, the ceremony that to great ones 'longs,"[9] are not to be found here. The author tramples on the pride of art with greater pride. The Ode and Epode, the Strophe and the Antistrophe, he laughs to scorn. The harp of Homer, the trump of Pindar and of Alcaeus[1] are still. The decencies of costume, the decorations of vanity are stripped off without mercy as barbarous, idle, and Gothic.[2] The jewels in the crisped hair,[3] the diadem on the polished brow are thought meretricious, theatrical, vulgar; and nothing contents his fastidious taste beyond a simple garland of flowers. Neither does he avail himself of the advantages which nature or accident holds out to him. He chooses to have his subject a foil to his invention, to owe nothing but to himself. He gathers manna in the wilderness, he strikes the barren rock for the gushing moisture. He elevates the mean by the strength of his own aspirations; he

---

7. Altered from Prospero's speech in *The Tempest* IV.i.151–156.
8. "We begin anew, on a clean slate."
9. Altered from *Measure for Measure* II.ii.59–61.
1. Pindar and Alcaeus were Greek writers of odes.
2. I.e., uncouth; belonging to the Dark Ages.
3. From William Collins' ode, *The Manners*, line 55: "Whose jewels in his crisped ["curly"] hair."

clothes the naked with beauty and grandeur from the stores of his own recollections. No cypress grove loads his verse with funeral pomp: but his imagination lends "a sense of joy"

> To the bare trees and mountains bare,
> And grass in the green field.[4]

No storm, no shipwreck startles us by its horrors: but the rainbow lifts its head in the cloud, and the breeze sighs through the withered fern. No sad vicissitude of fate, no overwhelming catastrophe in nature deforms his page: but the dew-drop glitters on the bending flower, the tear collects in the glistening eye.

> Beneath the hills, along the flowery vales,
> The generations are prepared; the pangs,
> The internal pangs are ready; the dread strife
> Of poor humanity's afflicted will,
> Struggling in vain with ruthless destiny.[5]

As the lark ascends from its low bed on fluttering wing, and salutes the morning skies; so Mr. Wordsworth's unpretending Muse, in russet[6] guise, scales the summits of reflection, while it makes the round earth its footstool, and its home!

Possibly a good deal of this may be regarded as the effect of disappointed views and an inverted ambition. Prevented by native pride and indolence from climbing the ascent of learning or greatness, taught by political opinions to say to the vain pomp and glory of the world, "I hate ye,"[7] seeing the path of classical and artificial poetry blocked up by the cumbrous ornaments of style and turgid *commonplaces*, so that nothing more could be achieved in that direction but by the most ridiculous bombast or the tamest servility; he has turned back partly from the bias of his mind, partly perhaps from a judicious policy—has struck into the sequestered vale of humble life, sought out the Muse among sheep-cotes and hamlets and the peasant's mountain-haunts, has discarded all the tinsel pageantry of verse, and endeavored (not in vain) to aggrandize the trivial and add the charm of novelty to the familiar. No one has shown the same imagination in raising trifles into importance: no one has displayed the same pathos in treating of the simplest feelings of the heart. Reserved, yet haughty, having no unruly or violent passions, (or those passions having been early suppressed,) Mr. Wordsworth has passed his life in solitary musing, or in daily converse with the face of nature. He exemplifies in an eminent degree the power of *association*; for his poetry has no other source or character. He has dwelt among pastoral scenes, till each object has

---

4. Wordsworth, *To My Sister*, lines 6–9.
5. Wordsworth, *The Excursion* VI.53 ff. The first line is misquoted: "Amid the groves, under the shadowy hills. . . ."
6. A coarse homespun cloth, worn by country people.
7. Shakespeare and John Fletcher, *King Henry the Eighth* III.ii.365: "Vain pomp and glory of this world, I hate ye!"

become connected with a thousand feelings, a link in the chain of thought, a fiber of his own heart. Everyone is by habit and familiarity strongly attached to the place of his birth, or to objects that recall the most pleasing and eventful circumstances of his life. But to the author of the *Lyrical Ballads*, nature is a kind of home; and he may be said to take a personal interest in the universe. There is no image so insignificant that it has not in some mood or other found the way into his heart: no sound that does not awaken the memory of other years.—

> To him the meanest flower that blows can give
> Thoughts that do often lie too deep for tears.[8]

The daisy looks up to him with sparkling eye as an old acquaintance: the cuckoo haunts him with sounds of early youth not to be expressed: a linnet's nest startles him with boyish delight: an old withered thorn is weighed down with a heap of recollections: a grey cloak, seen on some wild moor, torn by the wind, or drenched in the rain, afterwards becomes an object of imagination to him: even the lichens on the rock have a life and being in his thoughts. He has described all these objects in a way and with an intensity of feeling that no one else had done before him, and has given a new view or aspect of nature. He is in this sense the most original poet now living, and the one whose writings could the least be spared: for they have no substitute elsewhere. The vulgar do not read them, the learned, who see all things through books, do not understand them, the great despise, the fashionable may ridicule them: but the author has created himself an interest in the heart of the retired and lonely student of nature, which can never die. Persons of this class will still continue to feel what he has felt: he has expressed what they might in vain wish to express, except with glistening eye and faltering tongue! There's a lofty philosophic tone, a thoughtful humanity, infused into his pastoral vein. Remote from the passions and events of the great world, he has communicated interest and dignity to the primal movements of the heart of man, and ingrafted his own conscious reflections on the casual thoughts of hinds and shepherds. Nursed amidst the grandeur of mountain scenery, he has stooped to have a nearer view of the daisy under his feet, or plucked a branch of white-thorn from the spray: but in describing it, his mind seems imbued with the majesty and solemnity of the objects around him—the tall rock lifts its head in the erectness of his spirit; the cataract roars in the sound of his verse; and in its dim and mysterious meaning, the mists seem to gather in the hollows of Helvellyn, and the forked Skiddaw[9] hovers in the distance. There is little mention of mountainous scenery in Mr.

8. Adapted from the conclusion of Wordsworth's *Ode: Intimations of Im-* *mortality.*
9. Mountains in the Lake District.

Wordsworth's poetry; but by internal evidence one might be almost sure that it was written in a mountainous country, from its bareness, its simplicity, its loftiness and its depth!

* * *

1825

From On Shakespeare and Milton[1]

* * * The striking peculiarity of Shakespeare's mind was its generic quality, its power of communication with all other minds —so that it contained a universe of thought and feeling within itself, and had no one peculiar bias, or exclusive excellence more than another. He was just like any other man, but that he was like all other men. He was the least of an egotist that it was possible to be. He was nothing in himself; but he was all that others were, or that they could become. He not only had in himself the germs of every faculty and feeling, but he could follow them by anticipation, intuitively, into all their conceivable ramifications, through every change of fortune or conflict of passion, or turn of thought. He had "a mind reflecting ages past,"[2] and present—all the people that ever lived are there. There was no respect of persons with him. His genius shone equally on the evil and on the good, on the wise and the foolish, the monarch and the beggar: "All corners of the earth, kings, queens, and states, maids, matrons, nay, the secrets of the grave,"[3] are hardly hid from his searching glance. He was like the genius of humanity, changing places with all of us at pleasure, and playing with our purposes as with his own. He turned the globe round for his amusement, and surveyed the generations of men, and the individuals as they passed, with their different concerns, passions, follies, vices, virtues, actions, and motives—as well those that they knew, as those which they did not know, or acknowledge to themselves. The dreams of childhood, the ravings

---

1. This essay constituted the third in a series of *Lectures on the English Poets* that Hazlitt delivered with great success in London during January and February, 1818. It exemplifies Hazlitt's typical procedure in criticism—the unsystematic piling of statement on statement; the emphasis on particular lines or passages; the relish for the brief, intense expression; the sudden flashes of critical insight. It also develops one of Hazlitt's major critical ideas, the distinction between Shakespeare's objectivity and the subjectivity of Wordsworth and the "modern school," who project their own egos and moods into everything they undertake to describe. Milton, according to Hazlitt, falls between. John Keats attended Hazlitt's lectures, and the trace of Hazlitt's ideas can be detected in Keats's own poetic "axioms" and in his opposition of what he called Wordsworth's "egotistical sublime" to the higher poetry exemplified by Shakespeare, who exists in his work only as he identifies himself, by sympathetic self-projection, with the characters that he imagines. See Keats's letters of February 3, February 27, and October 27, 1818.

2. From a poem on Shakespeare prefixed to the Second Folio of his plays (1632).

3. See Shakespeare's *Cymbeline* III.iv. 39–40.

of despair, were the toys of his fancy. Airy beings waited at his call, and came at his bidding. Harmless fairies "nodded to him, and did him curtesies":[4] and the night hag bestrode the blast at the command of "his so potent art."[5] The world of spirits lay open to him, like the world of real men and women: and there is the same truth in his delineations of the one as of the other; for if the preternatural characters he describes could be supposed to exist, they would speak, and feel, and act, as he makes them. He had only to think of any thing in order to become that thing, with all the circumstances belonging to it. When he conceived of a character, whether real or imaginary, he not only entered into all its thoughts and feelings, but seemed instantly, and as if by touching a secret spring, to be surrounded with all the same objects, "subject to the same skyey influences,"[6] the same local, outward, and unforeseen accidents which would occur in reality. Thus the character of Caliban not only stands before us with a language and manners of its own, but the scenery and situation of the enchanted island he inhabits, the traditions of the place, its strange noises, its hidden recesses, "his frequent haunts and ancient neighborhood,"[7] are given with a miraculous truth of nature, and with all the familiarity of an old recollection. The whole "coheres semblably together"[8] in time, place, and circumstance. In reading this author, you do not merely learn what his characters say—you see their persons. By something expressed or understood, you are at no loss to decipher their peculiar physiognomy, the meaning of a look, the grouping, the by-play, as we might see it on the stage. A word, an epithet, paints a whole scene, or throws us back whole years in the history of the person represented. So (as it has been ingeniously remarked)[9] when Prospero describes himself as left alone in the boat with his daughter, the epithet which he applies to her, "Me and thy *crying* self,"[1] flings the imagination instantly back from the grown woman to the helpless condition of infancy, and places the first and most trying scene of his misfortunes before us, with all that he must have suffered in the interval. How well the silent anguish of Macduff is conveyed to the reader, by the friendly expostulation of Malcolm—"What! man, ne'er pull your hat upon your brows!"[2] Again, Hamlet, in the scene with Rosencrantz and Guildenstern,[3] somewhat abruptly concludes his fine soliloquy on life by saying, "Man delights not me, nor woman neither, though by your smiling you seem to say so." Which is explained by their answer—"My lord, we had no such stuff in our thoughts. But we smiled to think, if you delight not in man, what lenten entertainment the players shall receive from you, whom we met on the way"

4. Cf. *A Midsummer Night's Dream* III.i.177.
5. See *The Tempest* V.i.50.
6. See *Measure for Measure* III.i.9.
7. Cf. Milton's *Comus*, line 314.
8. See Shakespeare, *2 Henry IV* V.i.73.

9. By Coleridge, in a lecture on Shakespeare given in December, 1811.
1. *The Tempest* I.ii.132.
2. *Macbeth* IV.iii.208.
3. *Hamlet* II.ii.

—as if while Hamlet was making this speech, his two old school-fellows from Wittenberg had been really standing by, and he had seen them smiling by stealth, at the idea of the players crossing their minds. It is not "a combination and a form"[4] of words, a set speech or two, a preconcerted theory of a character, that will do this: but all the persons concerned must have been present in the poet's imagination, as at a kind of rehearsal; and whatever would have passed through their minds on the occasion, and have been observed by others, passed through his, and is made known to the reader. * * *

The account of Ophelia's death begins thus:

> There is a willow hanging o'er a brook,
> That shows its hoary leaves in the glassy stream.[5]

Now this is an instance of the same unconscious power of mind which is as true to nature as itself. The leaves of the willow are, in fact, white underneath, and it is this part of them which would appear "hoary" in the reflection in the brook. The same sort of intuitive power, the same faculty of bringing every object in nature, whether present or absent, before the mind's eye, is observable in the speech of Cleopatra, when conjecturing what were the employments of Antony in his absence: "He's speaking now, or murmuring, where's my serpent of old Nile?"[6] How fine to make Cleopatra have this consciousness of her own character, and to make her feel that it is this for which Antony is in love with her! She says, after the battle of Actium, when Antony has resolved to risk another fight, "It is my birthday; I had thought to have held it poor: but since my lord is Antony again, I will be Cleopatra."[7] What other poet would have thought of such a casual resource of the imagination, or would have dared to avail himself of it? The thing happens in the play as it might have happened in fact.—That which, perhaps, more than any thing else distinguishes the dramatic productions of Shakespeare from all others is this wonderful truth and individuality of conception. Each of his characters is as much itself, and as absolutely independent of the rest, as well as of the author, as if they were living persons, not fictions of the mind. The poet may be said, for the time, to identify himself with the character he wishes to represent, and to pass from one to another, like the same soul successively animating different bodies. By an art like that of the ventriloquist, he throws his imagination out of himself, and makes every word appear to proceed from the mouth of the person in whose name it is given. His plays alone are properly expressions of the passions, not descriptions of them. His characters are real beings of flesh and blood; they speak like men, not like

---

4. *Ibid*. III.iv.60.
5. *Ibid*. IV.vii.168–69, somewhat mis-quoted.
6. *Antony and Cleopatra* I.v.24–25.
7. *Ibid*. III.xiii.185–87.

authors. One might suppose that he had stood by at the time, and overheard what passed. As in our dreams we hold conversations with ourselves, make remarks, or communicate intelligence, and have no idea of the answer which we shall receive, and which we ourselves make, till we hear it: so the dialogues in Shakespeare are carried on without any consciousness of what is to follow, without any appearance of preparation or premeditation. The gusts of passion come and go like sounds of music borne on the wind. Nothing is made out by formal inference and analogy, by climax and antithesis: all comes, or seems to come, immediately from nature. Each object and circumstance exists in his mind, as it would have existed in reality: each several train of thought and feeling goes on of itself, without confusion or effort. In the world of his imagination, everything has a life, a place, and being of its own! * * *

The great fault of a modern school of poetry[8] is that it is an experiment to reduce poetry to a mere effusion of natural sensibility; or what is worse, to divest it both of imaginary splendor and human passion, to surround the meanest objects with the morbid feelings and devouring egotism of the writers' own minds. Milton and Shakespeare did not so understand poetry. They gave a more liberal interpretation both to nature and art. They did not do all they could to get rid of the one and the other, to fill up the dreary void with the Moods of their own Minds.[9] They owe their power over the human mind to their having had a deeper sense than others of what was grand in the objects of nature, or affecting in the events of human life. But to the men I speak of there is nothing interesting, nothing heroical, but themselves. To them the fall of gods or of great men is the same. They do not enter into the feeling. They cannot understand the terms. They are even debarred from the last poor, paltry consolation of an unmanly triumph over fallen greatness; for their minds reject, with a convulsive effort and intolerable loathing, the very idea that there ever was, or was thought to be, anything superior to themselves. All that has ever excited the attention or admiration of the world, they look upon with the most perfect indifference; and they are surprised to find that the world repays their indifference with scorn. "With what measure they mete, it has been meted to them again."[1]

Shakespeare's imagination is of the same plastic kind as his conception of character or passion. "It glances from heaven to earth, from earth to heaven."[2] Its movement is rapid and devious. It unites the most opposite extremes: or, as Puck says, in boasting of his own feats, "puts a girdle round about the earth in forty min-

8. I.e., what Hazlitt elsewhere called "the Lake school of poetry," of which "Mr. Wordsworth is at the head." Hazlitt's phrase, the "effusion of natural sensibility," may echo Wordsworth's claim that poetry is "the spontaneous overflow of natural feelings."

9. Wordsworth had entitled one section of his *Poems* of 1807, "Moods of My Own Mind."
1. Cf. Mark iv.24; Luke vi.38.
2. Cf. *A Midsummer Night's Dream* V.i.13.

utes."[3] He seems always hurrying from his subject, even while describing it; but the stroke, like the lightning's, is sure as it is sudden. He takes the widest possible range, but from that very range he has his choice of the greatest variety and aptitude of materials. He brings together images the most alike, but placed at the greatest distance from each other; that is, found in circumstances of the greatest dissimilitude. From the remoteness of his combinations, and the celerity with which they are effected, they coalesce the more indissolubly together. The more the thoughts are strangers to each other, and the longer they have been kept asunder, the more intimate does their union seem to become. Their felicity is equal to their force. Their likeness is made more dazzling by their novelty. They startle, and take the fancy prisoner in the same instant. * * *

Shakespeare discovers in his writings little religious enthusiasm, and an indifference to personal reputation; he had none of the bigotry of his age, and his political prejudices were not very strong. In these respects, as well as in every other, he formed a direct contrast to Milton. Milton's works are a perpetual invocation to the Muses; a hymn to Fame. He had his thoughts constantly fixed on the contemplation of the Hebrew theocracy, and of a perfect commonwealth; and he seized the pen with a hand just warm from the touch of the ark of faith. His religious zeal infused its character into his imagination; so that he devotes himself with the same sense of duty to the cultivation of his genius, as he did to the exercise of virtue, or the good of his country. The spirit of the poet, the patriot, and the prophet vied with each other in his breast. His mind appears to have held equal communion with the inspired writers, and with the bards and sages of ancient Greece and Rome:

> Blind Thamyris, and blind Maeonides,
> And Tiresias, and Phineus, prophets old.[4]

He had a high standard, with which he was always comparing himself, nothing short of which could satisfy his jealous ambition. He thought of nobler forms and nobler things than those he found about him. He lived apart, in the solitude of his own thoughts, carefully excluding from his mind whatever might distract its purposes or alloy its purity, or damp its zeal. "With darkness and with dangers compassed round,"[5] he had the mighty models of antiquity always present to his thoughts, and determined to raise a monument of equal height and glory, "piling up every stone of luster from the brook,"[6] for the delight and wonder of posterity. He had girded himself up, and as it were, sanctified his genius to this service from his youth. * * *

3. Cf. *ibid.* II.i.175–76.
4. *Paradise Lost* III.35–36.
5. *Ibid.* VII.27.
6. *Ibid.* XI.324–25.

Milton has borrowed more than any other writer, and exhausted every source of imitation, sacred or profane; yet he is perfectly distinct from every other writer. He is a writer of centos,[7] and yet in originality scarcely inferior to Homer. The power of his mind is stamped on every line. The fervor of his imagination melts down and renders malleable, as in a furnace, the most contradictory materials. In reading his works, we feel ourselves under the influence of a mighty intellect, that the nearer it approaches to others becomes more distinct from them. The quantity of art in him shows the strength of his genius: the weight of his intellectual obligations would have oppressed any other writer. Milton's learning has the effect of intuition. He describes objects, of which he could only have read in books, with the vividness of actual observation. His imagination has the force of nature. He makes words tell as pictures.

> Him followed Rimmon, whose delightful seat
> Was fair Damascus, on the fertile banks
> Of Abbana and Pharphar, lucid streams.[8]

The word *lucid* here gives to the idea all the sparkling effect of the most perfect landscape.

And again:

> As when a vulture on Imaus bred,
> Whose snowy ridge the roving Tartar bounds,
> Dislodging from a region scarce of prey,
> To gorge the flesh of lambs and yeanling kids
> On hills where flocks are fed, flies towards the springs
> Of Ganges or Hydaspes, Indian streams;
> But in his way lights on the barren plains
> Of Sericana, where Chineses drive
> With sails and wind their cany wagons light.[9]

If Milton had taken a journey for the express purpose, he could not have described this scenery and mode of life better. Such passages are like demonstrations of natural history. Instances might be multiplied without end.

We might be tempted to suppose that the vividness with which he describes visible objects was owing to their having acquired an unusual degree of strength in his mind, after the privation of his sight; but we find the same palpableness and truth in the descriptions which occur in his early poems. In *Lycidas* he speaks of "the great vision of the guarded mount,"[1] with that preternatural weight of impression with which it would present itself suddenly to "the pilot of some small night-foundered skiff":[2] and the lines in the *Penseroso*, describing "the wandering moon,"

> Riding near her highest noon,
> Like one that had been led astray

---

7. Literary compositions made up of quotations from other works.
8. *Paradise Lost* I.467–69.
9. *Ibid* III.431–39.
1. Line 161.
2. *Paradise Lost* I.204.

Through the heaven's wide pathless way,[3]

are as if he had gazed himself blind in looking at her. There is also the same depth of impression in his descriptions of the objects of all the different senses, whether colors, or sounds, or smells—the same absorption of his mind in whatever engaged his attention at the time. It has been indeed objected to Milton, by a common perversity of criticism, that his ideas were musical rather than picturesque, as if because they were in the highest degree musical, they must be (to keep the sage critical balance even, and to allow no one man to possess two qualities at the same time) proportionably deficient in other respects. But Milton's poetry is not cast in any such narrow, commonplace mold; it is not so barren of resources. His worship of the Muse was not so simple or confined. A sound arises "like a steam of rich distilled perfumes";[4] we hear the pealing organ, but the incense on the altars is also there, and the statues of the gods are ranged around! The ear indeed predominates over the eye, because it is more immediately affected, and because the language of music blends more immediately with, and forms a more natural accompaniment to, the variable and indefinite associations of ideas conveyed by words. But where the associations of the imagination are not the principal thing, the individual object is given by Milton with equal force and beauty. The strongest and best proof of this, as a characteristic power of his mind, is that the persons of Adam and Eve, of Satan, etc., are always accompanied, in our imagination, with the grandeur of the naked figure; they convey to us the ideas of sculpture. * * *

Again, nothing can be more magnificent than the portrait of Beelzebub:

> With Atlantean shoulders fit to bear
> The weight of mightiest monarchies:[5]

Or the comparison of Satan, as he "lay floating many a rood," to "that sea beast,"

> Leviathan, which God of all his works
> Created hugest that swim the ocean-stream![6]

What a force of imagination is there in this last expression! What an idea it conveys of the size of that hugest of created beings, as if it shrunk up the ocean to a stream, and took up the sea in its nostrils as a very little thing! Force of style is one of Milton's greatest excellences. Hence, perhaps, he stimulates us more in the reading, and less afterwards. The way to defend Milton against all impugners is to take down the book and read it. * * *

To proceed to a consideration of the merits of *Paradise Lost*, in the most essential point of view, I mean as to the poetry of character

3. Lines 67–70.
4. *Comus*, line 556.
5. *Paradise Lost* II.306–7.
6. *Ibid.* I.196, 200–202.

and passion. I shall say nothing of the fable, or of other technical objections or excellences; but I shall try to explain at once the foundation of the interest belonging to the poem. I am ready to give up the dialogues in Heaven, where, as Pope justly observes, "God the Father turns a school-divine";[7] nor do I consider the battle of the angels as the climax of sublimity, or the most successful effort of Milton's pen. In a word, the interest of the poem arises from the daring ambition and fierce passions of Satan, and from the account of the paradisaical happiness, and the loss of it by our first parents. Three-fourths of the work are taken up with these characters, and nearly all that relates to them is unmixed sublimity and beauty. The two first books alone are like two massy pillars of solid gold.

Satan is the most heroic subject that ever was chosen for a poem; and the execution is as perfect as the design is lofty. He was the first of created beings, who, for endeavoring to be equal with the highest, and to divide the empire of heaven with the Almighty, was hurled down to hell. His aim was no less than the throne of the universe; his means, myriads of angelic armies bright, the third part of the heavens, whom he lured after him with his countenance, and who durst defy the Omnipotent in arms. His ambition was the greatest, and his punishment was the greatest; but not so his despair, for his fortitude was as great as his sufferings. His strength of mind was matchless as his strength of body; the vastness of his designs did not surpass the firm, inflexible determination with which he submitted to his irreversible doom, and final loss of all good. His power of action and of suffering was equal. He was the greatest power that was ever overthrown, with the strongest will left to resist or to endure. He was baffled, not confounded. He stood like a tower; or

> As when Heaven's fire
> Hath scathed the forest oaks or mountain pines.[8]

He was still surrounded with hosts of rebel angels, armed warriors, who own him as their sovereign leader, and with whose fate he sympathizes as he views them round, far as the eye can reach; though he keeps aloof from them in his own mind, and holds supreme counsel only with his own breast. An outcast from Heaven, Hell trembles beneath his feet, Sin and Death are at his heels, and mankind are his easy prey.

> All is not lost; th' unconquerable will,
> And study of revenge, immortal hate,
> And courage never to submit or yield,
> And what else is not to be overcome,[9]

7. Pope's Horatian *Epistle to Augustus*, lines 101–2.

8. *Paradise Lost* I.612–13.
9. *Ibid.* I.106–9.

are still his. The sense of his punishment seems lost in the magnitude of it; the fierceness of tormenting flames is qualified and made innoxious by the greater fierceness of his pride; the loss of infinite happiness to himself is compensated in thought, by the power of inflicting infinite misery on others. Yet Satan is not the principle of malignity, or of the abstract love of evil—but of the abstract love of power, of pride, of self-will personified, to which last principle all other good and evil, and even his own, are subordinate. From this principle he never once flinches. His love of power and contempt for suffering are never once relaxed from the highest pitch of intensity. His thoughts burn like a hell within him; but the power of thought holds dominion in his mind over every other consideration. The consciousness of a determined purpose, of "that intellectual being, those thoughts that wander through eternity," though accompanied with endless pain, he prefers to nonentity, to "being swallowed up and lost in the wide womb of uncreated night."[1] He expresses the sum and substance of all ambition in one line. "Fallen cherub, to be weak is miserable, doing or suffering!"[2] After such a conflict as his, and such a defeat, to retreat in order, to rally, to make terms, to exist at all, is something; but he does more than this—he founds a new empire in hell, and from it conquers this new world, whither he bends his undaunted flight, forcing his way through nether and surrounding fires. The poet has not in all this given us a mere shadowy outline; the strength is equal to the magnitude of the conception. The Achilles of Homer is not more distinct; the Titans were not more vast; Prometheus chained to his rock was not a more terrific example of suffering and of crime. Wherever the figure of Satan is introduced, whether he walks or flies, "rising aloft incumbent on the dusky air,"[3] it is illustrated with the most striking and appropriate images: so that we see it always before us, gigantic, irregular, portentous, uneasy, and disturbed—but dazzling in its faded splendor, the clouded ruins of a god. The deformity of Satan is only in the depravity of his will; he has no bodily deformity to excite our loathing or disgust. The horns and tail are not there, poor emblems of the unbending, unconquered spirit, of the writhing agonies within. Milton was too magnanimous and open an antagonist to support his argument by the by-tricks of a hump and cloven foot; to bring into the fair field of controversy the good old Catholic prejudices of which Tasso and Dante have availed themselves, and which the mystic German critics would restore. He relied on the justice of his cause, and did not scruple to give the devil his due. Some persons may think that he has carried his liberality too far, and injured the cause he pro-

---

1. See *ibid*. II.147–50. These words are spoken by Belial, not Satan.
2. *Ibid* I.157–58.
3. *Ibid*. I.225–26.

fessed to espouse by making him the chief person in his poem. Considering the nature of his subject, he would be equally in danger of running into this fault, from his faith in religion, and his love of rebellion; and perhaps each of these motives had its full share in determining the choice of his subject. * * *

1818

From The Fight[1]

* * * The morning dawns; that dim but yet clear light appears, which weighs like solid bars of metal on the sleepless eyelids; the guests drop down from their chambers one by one—but it was too late to think of going to bed now (the clock was on the stroke of seven), we had nothing for it but to find a barber's (the pole that glittered in the morning sun lighted us to his shop), and then a nine miles' march to Hungerford. The day was fine, the sky was blue, the mists were retiring from the marshy ground, the path was tolerably dry, the sitting up all night had not done us much harm—at least the cause was good; we talked of this and that with amicable difference, roving and sipping of many subjects, but still invariably we returned to the fight. At length, a mile to the left of Hungerford, on a gentle eminence, we saw the ring surrounded by covered carts, gigs, and carriages, of which hundreds had passed us on the road; Toms gave a youthful shout, and we hastened down a narrow lane to the scene of action.

Reader, have you ever seen a fight? If not, you have a pleasure to come, at least if it is a fight like that between the Gas-man and Bill Neate. The crowd was very great when we arrived on the spot; open carriages were coming up, with streamers flying and music playing, and the country people were pouring in over hedge and ditch in all directions, to see their hero beat or be beaten. The odds were still on Gas, but only about five to four. Gully[2] had been down to try Neate, and had backed him considerably, which was a damper to the sanguine confidence of the adverse party. About two hundred thousand pounds were pending. The Gas says he has lost £3000 which were promised him by different gentlemen if he had won. He had presumed too much on himself, which had made others presume on him. This spirited and formidable young fellow

---

1. The famous prize fight between Tom Hickman, "the Gas-man," and Bill Neate on December 11, 1821, which was fought in the early 19th-century style, with bare fists and no limit on the number of rounds. Hazlitt's report was published a few months later; it has set a standard of excellence, not only for sports reporting, but for all descriptions of violent human action, since that time. The first part of the essay, which is here omitted, describes how Hazlitt managed to make his way to the vicinity of the fight (its location had to be kept secret from the authorities) and sat up all night at an inn talking with fellow *aficionados* of the sport.

2. John Gully, a notable prizefighter, recently retired.

seems to have taken for his motto the old maxim that "there are three things necessary to success in life—*Impudence! Impudence! Impudence!*" It is so in matters of opinion, but not in the *Fancy*,[3] which is the most practical of all things, though even here confidence is half the battle, but only half. Our friend had vapored[4] and swaggered too much, as if he wanted to grin and bully his adversary out of the fight. "Alas! the Bristol man was not so tamed!"[5]—"This is *the grave-digger*," would Tom Hickman exclaim in the moments of intoxication from gin and success, showing his tremendous right hand, "this will send many of them to their long homes; I haven't done with them yet!" Why should he—though he had licked four of the best men within the hour, yet why should he threaten to inflict dishonorable chastisement on my old master Richmond,[6] a veteran going off the stage, and who has borne his sable honors meekly? Magnanimity, my dear Tom, and bravery, should be inseparable. Or why should he go up to his antagonist, the first time he ever saw him at the Fives Court,[7] and measuring him from head to foot with a glance of contempt, as Achilles surveyed Hector,[8] say to him, "What, are you Bill Neate? I'll knock more blood out of that great carcass of thine, this day fortnight, than you ever knocked out of a bullock's!" It was not manly, 'twas not fighter-like. If he was sure of the victory (as he was not), the less said about it the better. Modesty should accompany the *Fancy* as its shadow. The best men were always the best behaved. Jem Belcher, the Game Chicken[9] (before whom the Gas-man could not have lived) were civil, silent men. So is Cribb, so is Tom Belcher, the most elegant of sparrers, and not a man for every one to take by the nose. I enlarged on this topic in the mail[1] (while Turtle was asleep), and said very wisely (as I thought) that impertinence was a part of no profession. A boxer was bound to beat his man, but not to thrust his fist, either actually or by implication, in everyone's face. Even a highwayman, in the way of trade, may blow out your brains, but if he uses foul language at the same time, I should say he was no gentleman. A boxer, I would infer, need not be a blackguard or a coxcomb, more than another. Perhaps I press this point too much on a fallen man—Mr. Thomas Hickman has by this time learnt that first of all lessons, "That man was made to mourn."[2] He has lost nothing by the late fight but his presumption; and that every man may do as well without! By an over-display of this quality,

---

3. A slang term for the fighting game.
4. Blustered.
5. Altered from Cowper, *The Task* II.322.
6. Bill Richmond, a colored boxer, now an instructor; he had apparently given boxing lessons to Hazlitt.
7. A building near Leicester Square used for various sports, including boxing. "Fives" is a form of handball.

8. During the single combat of these champions before the walls of Troy (*Iliad* XXII).
9. Henry Pearce, who, like Jem Belcher, his teacher, was a famous fighter.
1. The Bath mail coach, on which Hazlitt had ridden to the fight with Tom Turtle, a trainer.
2. Title of a poem by Robert Burns.

however, the public had been prejudiced against him, and the *knowing-ones* were taken in. Few but those who had bet on him wished Gas to win. With my own prepossessions on the subject, the result of the 11th of December appeared to me as fine a piece of poetical justice as I had ever witnessed. The difference of weight between the two combatants (14 stone to 12)[3] was nothing to the sporting men. Great, heavy, clumsy, long-armed Bill Neate kicked the beam in the scale of the Gas-man's vanity. The amateurs were frightened at his big words, and thought that they would make up for the difference of six feet and five feet nine. Truly, the FANCY are not men of imagination. They judge of what has been, and cannot conceive of anything that is to be. The Gas-man had won hitherto; therefore he must beat a man half as big again as himself —and that to a certainty. Besides, there are as many feuds, factions, prejudices, pedantic notions in the FANCY as in the state or in the schools. Mr. Gully is almost the only cool, sensible man among them, who exercises an unbiased discretion, and is not a slave to his passions in these matters. But enough of reflections, and to our tale. The day, as I have said, was fine for a December morning. The grass was wet, and the ground miry, and plowed up with multitudinous feet, except that, within the ring itself, there was a spot of virgin green closed in and unprofaned by vulgar tread, that shone with dazzling brightness in the midday sun. For it was now noon, and we had an hour to wait. This is the trying time. It is then the heart sickens, as you think what the two champions are about, and how short a time will determine their fate. After the first blow is struck, there is no opportunity for nervous apprehensions; you are swallowed up in the immediate interest of the scene—but

> Between the acting of a dreadful thing
> And the first motion, all the interim is
> Like a phantasma or a hideous dream.[4]

I found it so as I felt the sun's rays clinging to my back, and saw the white wintry clouds sink below the verge of the horizon. "So," I thought, "my fairest hopes have faded from my sight!—so will the Gas-man's glory, or that of his adversary, vanish in an hour." The *swells*[5] were parading in their white box coats, the outer ring was cleared with some bruises on the heads and shins of the rustic assembly (for the *cockneys* had been distanced by the sixty-six miles[6]); the time drew near, I had got a good stand; a bustle, a buzz, ran through the crowd, and from the opposite side entered

---

3. A "stone" is fourteen pounds, so that in his heavyweight bout, Neate weighed 196 pounds and the Gas-man 168.
4. Shakespeare's *Julius Caesar* II.i.63–65.
5. Gentlemen of fashion, dressed in "box coats" (heavy overcoats for driv-

ing a carriage; the "box" is the driver's seat).
6. I.e., the Londoners ("cockneys"), having a long distance to come, found that the countrymen had taken the best posts.

Neate, between his second and bottle-holder. He rolled along, swathed in his loose great coat, his knock-knees bending under his huge bulk; and, with a modest cheerful air, threw his hat into the ring. He then just looked round, and began quietly to undress; when from the other side there was a similar rush and an opening made, and the Gas-man came forward with a conscious air of anticipated triumph, too much like the cock-of-the walk. He strutted about more than became a hero, sucked oranges with a supercilious air, and threw away the skin with a toss of his head, and went up and looked at Neate, which was an act of supererogation. The only sensible thing he did was, as he strode away from the modern Ajax, to fling out his arms, as if he wanted to try whether they would do their work that day. By this time they had stripped, and presented a strong contrast in appearance. If Neate was like Ajax, "with Atlantean shoulders, fit to bear"[7] the pugilistic reputation of all Bristol, Hickman might be compared to Diomed,[8] light, vigorous, elastic, and his back glistened in the sun, as he moved about, like a panther's hide. There was now a dead pause—attention was awestruck. Who at that moment, big with a great event, did not draw his breath short—did not feel his heart throb? All was ready. They tossed up for the sun,[9] and the Gas-man won. They were led up to the *scratch*[1]—shook hands, and went at it.

In the first round[2] everyone thought it was all over. After making play a short time, the Gas-man flew at his adversary like a tiger, struck five blows in as many seconds, three first, and then following him as he staggered back, two more, right and left, and down he fell, a mighty ruin. There was a shout, and I said, "There is no standing this." Neate seemed like a lifeless lump of flesh and bone, round which the Gas-man's blows played with the rapidity of electricity or lightning, and you imagined he would only be lifted up to be knocked down again. It was as if Hickman held a sword or a fire in that right hand of his, and directed it against an unarmed body. They met again, and Neate seemed, not cowed, but particularly cautious. I saw his teeth clenched together and his brows knit close against the sun. He held out both his arms at full length straight before him, like two sledge hammers, and raised his left an inch or two higher. The Gas-man could not get over this guard—they struck mutually and fell, but without advantage on either side. It was the same in the next round; but the balance of power was thus restored—the fate of the battle was suspended. No one could tell how it would end. This was the only moment in which opinion

7. *Paradise Lost* II.306; "Atlantean" is the adjectival form of Atlas, the Titan who supports the heavens.
8. A Greek warrior in the *Iliad*.
9. To determine which fighter should face into the sun.
1. The line drawn across the ring, at which boxers formerly joined battle.
2. By the old rules, each "round" was ended by a knockdown. In this match there was a half-minute interval between rounds, and the fight ended when one of the boxers failed to take his feet in time for the next round.

was divided; for, in the next, the Gas-man aiming a mortal blow at his adversary's neck with his right hand, and failing from the length he had to reach, the other returned it with his left at full swing, planted a tremendous blow on his cheek-bone and eyebrow, and made a red ruin of that side of his face. The Gas-man went down, and there was another shout—a roar of triumph as the waves of fortune rolled tumultuously from side to side. This was a settler. Hickman got up, and "grinned horrible a ghastly smile,"[3] yet he was evidently dashed in his opinion of himself; it was the first time he had ever been so punished; all one side of his face was perfect scarlet, and his right eye was closed in dingy blackness, as he advanced to the fight, less confident, but still determined. After one or two rounds, not receiving another such remembrancer, he rallied and went at it with his former impetuosity. But in vain. His strength had been weakened—his blows could not tell at such a distance—he was obliged to fling himself at his adversary, and could not strike from his feet; and almost as regularly as he flew at him with his right hand, Neate warded the blow, or drew back out of its reach, and felled him with the return of his left. There was little cautious sparring—no half-hits—no tapping and trifling, none of the *petit-maitreship*[4] of the art—they were almost all knock-down blows: the fight was a good stand-up fight. The wonder was the half-minute time. If there had been a minute or more allowed between each round, it would have been intelligible how they should by degrees recover strength and resolution; but to see two men smashed to the ground, smeared with gore, stunned, senseless, the breath beaten out of their bodies; and then, before you recover from the shock, to see them rise up with new strength and courage, stand ready to inflict or receive mortal offense, and rush upon each other "like two clouds over the Caspian"[5]—this is the most astonishing thing of all: this is the high and heroic state of man! From this time forward the event became more certain every round, and about the twelfth it seemed as if it must have been over. Hickman generally stood with his back to me; but in the scuffle, he had changed positions, and Neate just then made a tremendous lunge at him, and hit him full in the face. It was doubtful whether he would fall backwards or forwards; he hung suspended for a second or two, and then fell back, throwing his hands in the air, and with his face lifted up to the sky. I never saw anything more terrific than his aspect just before he fell. All traces of life, of natural expression, were gone from him. His face was like a human skull, a death's-head, spouting blood. The eyes were filled with blood, the nose streamed with blood, the mouth gaped blood. He was not like an actual man, but like a preternatural, spectral appearance, or like

3. A description of Death in *Paradise Lost* II.846.
4. *Petit-maitre* ("little master"), the

French term for a dandy or fop.
5. See *Paradise Lost* II.714–16.

one of the figures in Dante's *Inferno*. Yet he fought on after this for several rounds, still striking the first desperate blow, and Neate standing on the defensive, and using the same cautious guard to the last, as if he had still all his work to do; and it was not till the Gas-man was so stunned in the seventeenth or eighteenth round that his senses forsook him, and he could not come to time, that the battle was declared over. Ye who despise the Fancy, do something to show as much *pluck*, or as much self-possession as this, before you assume a superiority which you have never given a single proof of by any one action in the whole course of your lives! When the Gas-man came to himself, the first words he uttered were, "Where am I? What is the matter?" "Nothing is the matter, Tom —you have lost the battle, but you are the bravest man alive." And Jackson whispered to him, "I am collecting a purse for you, Tom." —Vain sounds, and unheard at that moment! Neate instantly went up and shook him cordially by the hand, and seeing some old acquaintance, began to flourish with his fists, calling out, "Ah, you always said I couldn't fight. What do you think now?" But all in good humor, and without any appearance of arrogance; only it was evident Bill Neate was pleased that he had won the fight. When it was over, I asked Cribb if he did not think it was a good one? He said, "*Pretty well!*" The carrier pigeons now mounted into the air, and one of them flew with the news of her husband's victory to the bosom of Mrs. Neate. Alas, for Mrs. Hickman!

Mais au revoir, as Sir Fopling Flutter[6] says. I went down with Toms; I returned with Jack Pigott, whom I met on the ground. Toms is a rattle brain; Pigott is a sentimentalist. Now, under favor, I am a sentimentalist too—therefore I say nothing, but that the interest of the excursion did not flag as I came back. Pigott and I marched along the causeway leading from Hungerford to Newbury, now observing the effect of a brilliant sun on the tawny meads or moss-colored cottages, now exulting in the fight, now digressing to some topic of general and elegant literature. My friend was dressed in character for the occasion, or like one of the FANCY; that is, with a double portion of greatcoats, clogs,[7] and overhauls: and just as we had agreed with a couple of country lads to carry his superfluous wearing apparel to the next town, we were overtaken by a return post-chaise, into which I got, Pigott preferring a seat on the bar. There were two strangers already in the chaise, and on their observing they supposed I had been to the fight, I said I had, and concluded they had done the same. They appeared, however, a little shy and sore on the subject, and it was not till after several hints dropped, and questions put, that it turned out that they had missed it. One of these friends had undertaken to drive the other there in

6. In *The Man of Mode*, by the Restoration dramatist Sir George Etherege.

7. Stout, thick-soled shoes; "overhauls" are overalls.

his gig: they had set out, to make sure work, the day before at three in the afternoon. The owner of the one-horse vehicle scorned to ask his way, and drove right on to Bagshot, instead of turning off at Hounslow: there they stopped all night, and set off the next day across the country to Reading, from whence they took coach, and got down within a mile or two of Hungerford, just half an hour after the fight was over. This might be safely set down as one of the miseries of human life. We parted with these two gentlemen who had been to see the fight, but had returned as they went, at Wolhampton, where we were promised beds (an irresistible temptation, for Pigott had passed the preceding night at Hungerford as we had done at Newbury), and we turned into an old bow-windowed parlor with a carpet and a snug fire; and after devouring a quantity of tea, toast, and eggs, sat down to consider, during an hour of philosophic leisure, what we should have for supper. In the midst of an Epicurean deliberation between a roasted fowl and mutton chops with mashed potatoes, we were interrupted by an inroad of Goths and Vandals[8]—*O procul este profani*—not real flashmen,[9] but interlopers, noisy pretenders, butchers from Tothill Fields, brokers from Whitechapel, who called immediately for pipes and tobacco, hoping it would not be disagreeable to the gentlemen, and began to insist that it was *a cross*.[1] Pigott withdrew from the smoke and noise into another room, and left me to dispute the point with them for a couple of hours *sans intermission* by the dial.[2] The next morning we rose refreshed; and on observing that Jack had a pocket volume in his hand, in which he read in the intervals of our discourse, I inquired what it was, and learned to my particular satisfaction that it was a volume of the *New Eloise*.[3] Ladies, after this, will you contend that a love for the FANCY is incompatible with the cultivation of sentiment? We jogged on as before, my friend setting me up in a genteel drab greatcoat and green silk handkerchief (which I must say became me exceedingly), and after stretching our legs for a few miles, and seeing Jack Randall, Ned Turner, and Scroggins, pass on the top of one of the Bath coaches, we engaged with the driver of the second to take us to London for the usual fee. I got inside, and found three other passengers. One of them was an old gentleman with an aquiline nose, powdered hair, and a pigtail, and who looked as if he had played many a rubber at the Bath rooms.[4] I said to myself, he is very like Mr. Windham; I wish he would enter into conversation, that I might hear what fine observations would come from those finely-turned features.

---

8. I.e., barbarian invaders. The Latin tag which follows means, "Away, unhallowed ones!" (*Aeneid* VI.258).
9. Patrons of boxing.
1. I.e., that the fight was fixed.
2. "Without intermission, according to the clock." See *As You Like It* II.vii. 32–33.
3. *La Nouvelle Héloise*, novel by Rousseau.
4. In the card rooms at Bath, a resort town.

However, nothing passed, till, stopping to dine at Reading, some inquiry was made by the company about the fight, and I gave (as the reader may believe) an eloquent and animated description of it. When we got into the coach again, the old gentleman, after a graceful exordium,[5] said, he had, when a boy, been to a fight between the famous Broughton and George Stevenson, who was called the *Fighting Coachman*, in the year 1770, with the late Mr. Windham. This beginning flattered the spirit of prophecy within me and riveted my attention. He went on—"George Stevenson was coachman to a friend of my father's. He was an old man when I saw him some years afterwards. He took hold of his own arm and said, 'there was muscle here once, but now it is no more than this young gentleman's.' He added, 'Well, no matter; I have been here long, I am willing to go hence, and I hope I have done no more harm than another man.' Once," said my unknown companion, "I asked him if he had ever beat Broughton? He said yes; that he had fought with him three times, and the last time he fairly beat him, though the world did not allow it. 'I'll tell you how it was, master. When the seconds lifted us up in the last round, we were so exhausted that neither of us could stand, and we fell upon one another, and as Master Broughton fell uppermost, the mob gave it in his favor, and he was said to have won the battle. But,' says he, 'the fact was, that as his second (John Cuthbert) lifted him up, he said to him, "I'll fight no more, I've had enough"; which,' says Stevenson, 'you know gave me the victory. And to prove to you that this was the case, when John Cuthbert was on his deathbed, and they asked him if there was anything on his mind which he wished to confess, he answered, "Yes, that there was one thing he wished to set right, for that certainly Master Stevenson won that last fight with Master Broughton; for he whispered him as he lifted him up in the last round of all, that he had had enough." ' " "This," said the Bath gentleman, "was a bit of human nature"; and I have written this account of the fight on purpose that it might not be lost to the world. He also stated as a proof of the candor of mind in this class of men, that Stevenson acknowledged that Broughton could have beat him in his best day; but that he (Broughton) was getting old in their last rencounter. When we stopped in Piccadilly, I wanted to ask the gentleman some questions about the late Mr. Windham, but had not courage. I got out, resigned my coat and green silk handkerchief to Pigott (loath to part with these ornaments of life), and walked home in high spirits.

P.S. Toms called upon me the next day, to ask me if I did not think the fight was a complete thing? I said I thought it was. I hope he will relish my account of it.

1822

5. The formal opening of an oration.

THOMAS DE QUINCEY
(1785–1859)

1821:   Begins literary career with *Confessions of an Eng-
         lish Opium-Eater.*
1853–60: "Collective Edition" of his writings.

De Quincey's father was a wealthy merchant, who died when Thomas was 7 years old. The boy was a precocious scholar, especially in Latin and Greek, and a gentle and bookish introvert; he found it difficult to adapt himself to discipline and routine, and was thrown into panic by any emergency that called for decisive action. He ran away from Manchester Grammar School and after a summer spent tramping through Wales, broke off completely from his family and guardians and went to London in the hope that he could obtain from moneylenders an advance on his prospective inheritance. There at the age of 17 he spent a terrible winter of loneliness and destitution, befriended only by some kindly streetwalkers. These early experiences with the sinister part of city life later became persistent elements in his dreams of terror.

After a reconciliation with his guardians he entered Worcester College, Oxford, on an inadequate allowance. He spent the years 1803–8 in sporadic attendance, isolated as usual, and devoting himself especially to two subjects not then part of the university curriculum: English literature and the German language. He left abruptly in the middle of his examination for the B.A. with honors because he could not face the ordeal of the oral part of the examination.

De Quincey had been an early and fervent admirer of Wordsworth and Coleridge. No sooner did he come of age and into his inheritance than, with his usual combination of generosity and improvidence, he made Coleridge an anonymous gift of £300. He visited with the Wordsworths at Grasmere, became an intimate friend, and when they left Dove Cottage for Allan Bank, took up his own residence at Dove Cottage in order to be near them. Here he built up a fine library and for a time lived the life of a rural scholar, trying to decide how to eke out his dwindling resources. In the meantime he fell in love with Margaret Simpson, the daughter of a small local landholder and farmer and, after she had borne him an illegitimate son, married her in February, 1817. This affair led to an estrangement from the Wordsworths and increased the drain on his resources. Worse still, De Quincey at this time became completely enslaved to opium. He had been taking the drug regularly since 1804, when, in accordance with the medical practice of the time, he had turned to it for relief from rheumatic pains in his face. A variety of physical ailments had led to increasingly large and frequent doses; now, driven by pain, poverty, and despair, he indulged in huge quantities of laudanum (opium dissolved in alcohol). From this time on, although he struggled intermittently to break the habit and often succeeded in reducing the dosage, he was never able to free himself from "the pleasures and pains of opium." It was during his periods of maximum addiction, and especially in the recurrent agonies of cutting down his opium allowance, that he had the grotesque and terrifying dreams which he wove into the pattern of his literary fantasies.

In desperation De Quincey at last, at the age of 36, turned to writing for a livelihood. The *Confessions of an English Opium-Eater*, which he contributed in two installments to the *London Magazine*, scored an immediate success and was at once reprinted as a book, but it earned De Quincey very little money. After frequent visits to London, and a number of varied contributions to the *London Magazine*, he moved his family to Edinburgh in 1828, in order to write for *Blackwood's Magazine*. For almost all the rest of his life De Quincey led a frantic existence, beset by rheumatism, toothache, stomach trouble, erysipelas, and finally gout, struggling with his native irresolution and melancholia and the horrors of the opium habit, dodging his creditors and the constant threat of imprisonment for debt. All the while he ground out articles on any salable subject in a ceaseless struggle to keep his eight children from starving to death. Only after his mother died and left him a small income was he able, in his 60's, to live in comparative ease and freedom under the care of his loyal and practical-minded daughters. The last decade of his life De Quincey spent mainly in gathering, revising, and expanding his essays for his "Collective Edition"; the final volume appeared in 1860, the year after his death.

Although De Quincey's life, in its externals, was disorderly, and his best-known writings were sensational in their matter, he was not a Bohemian dabbler in drugs and abnormality, but staunchly conventional and conservative—a rigid moralist, a sturdy Tory, and a faithful champion of the Church of England. Everybody who knew this shy and elusive little man has testified to his gentleness, his courteous and musical speech, and his elaborate and exquisite manners. Less obvious, under the surface timidity and irresolution, were the toughness and courage which sustained him through a long life of seemingly hopeless struggle.

Although more than 150 of De Quincey's anonymous essays have been identified, the great bulk of them were pieces of hasty journalism which are now read only by scholars. These range over history, political economy, and philosophy; while in his commentaries on recent and contemporary German writers and thinkers, together with his translations from the German, De Quincey served for a time as an important avenue of access for Englishmen to the great new literature of the late 18th-century German renaissance. As a literary critic De Quincey was capable of a fine essay in critical impressionism, *On the Knocking at the Gate in Macbeth*, but he was too whimsical and unsystematic to rank with his greater contemporaries, Coleridge and Hazlitt; his best theoretical contributions are essays on "Style" and "Rhetoric." He wrote a number of vivid and candid biographical sketches of writers he knew personally, especially Wordsworth, Coleridge, Southey, and Lamb. His most distinctive and impressive achievements, however, are the writings which start with fact and move into macabre fantasy (*On Murder Considered as One of the Fine Arts*), and especially those that begin as quiet autobiography and develop into an elaborate and lurid construction made up from the materials of his dreams (*Confessions of an English Opium-Eater, Autobiographic Sketches, Suspiria de Profundis,* and *The English Mail Coach*). In these last pieces De Quincey revived the ornate prose style of the 17th-century writers, Sir Thomas Browne, Jeremy Taylor, and John Milton. To the modern reader De Quincey's slowly evolving sentences and paragraphs often seem too contrived, in their elaborate patterning of phrases, clauses, and sound sequences, to sustain his earlier reputation as one of the supreme prose stylists. What interests us more today in these fantasies is their subject matter and the novel principles which govern their over-all structure. He opened up to English literature the night-side of human consciousness, with all its grotesque strangeness, its *Angst* (anxiety), and its pervasive sense of guilt and alienation. "In dreams," De Quincey wrote, long before Sigmund Freud, "perhaps under some secret conflict of the midnight sleeper, lighted up to the consciousness at the time, but darkened to the memory as soon as all is finished, each several child of our mysterious race completes for himself the treason of the aboriginal fall." And for these dream writings De Quincey developed a mode of organization which is not based on chronological narrative, or exposition, or argument, but on the statement, variation, development, and counterpoint of thematic imagery, in a pattern derived from the art of music, in which he had a deep and abiding interest. For although by temperament a conservative, De Quincey was in his writings a radical innovator, whose experiments look ahead to the materials and methods of such modern masters in prose and verse as James Joyce, Franz Kafka, and T. S. Eliot.

Confessions of an English Opium-Eater The *Confessions* were published anonymously in two issues of the *London Magazine,* September and October, 1821, and were reprinted as a book the following year. In 1856 De Quincey revised the book for a collected edition of his writings, expanding it to well over twice its original length. The author was over 70 years old at the time, and privately expressed the judgment—shared by all readers since—that the expanded edition lacks the immediacy and artistic economy of the original. The selections below are from the first version of the *Confessions,* as printed in 1822.

The book is divided into three parts. The first part, "Preliminary Confessions," deals with De Quincey's early experiences—at school, in Wales, and in London—prior to taking opium. Part Two, "The Pleasures of Opium" (omitted here), describes the effects of his early moderate and occasional indulgence in the drug on his perceptions and reveries. Part Three, "The Pains of Opium," is an elaborate reconstruction of his fantastic nightmares; these, in modern medical opinion, are in part withdrawal symptoms, during periods when he tried to cut down his use of opium.

In De Quincey's own lifetime, and ever since, the charge has been brought that the reports of these dreams were largely fabricated by the author. But De Quincey himself always insisted that they were substantially accurate; and both the fact and the content of such anguished nightmares are corroborated by the testimony of another laudanum addict, Samuel Taylor Coleridge, in his poem *The Pains of Sleep* (1803).

From Confessions of an English Opium-Eater

From *Preliminary Confessions*[1]

* * * Another person there was at that time, whom I have since sought to trace with far deeper earnestness, and with far deeper sorrow at my failure. This person was a young woman, and one of that unhappy class who subsist upon the wages of prostitution. I feel no shame, nor have any reason to feel it, in avowing, that I was then on familiar and friendly terms with many women in that unfortunate condition. The reader needs neither smile at this avowal, nor frown. For, not to remind my classical readers of the old Latin proverb—"*Sine Cerere*," &c.,[2] it may well be supposed that in the existing state of my purse, my connection with such women could not have been an impure one. But the truth is, that at no time of my life have I been a person to hold myself polluted by the touch or approach of any creature that wore a human shape: on the contrary, from my very earliest youth it has been my pride to converse familiarly, *more Socratico*,[3] with all human beings, man, woman, and child, that chance might fling in my way: a practice which is friendly to the knowledge of human nature, to good feelings, and to that frrankness of address which becomes a man who would be thought a philosopher. For a philosopher should not see with the eyes of the poor limitary[4] creature, calling himself a man of the world, and filled with narrow and self-regarding prejudices of birth and education, but should look upon himself as a Catholic[5] creature, and as standing in an equal relation to high and low—to educated and uneducated, to the guilty and the innocent. Being myself at that time of necessity a peripatetic, or a walker of the street, I naturally fell in more frequently with those female peripatetics who are technically called street-walkers. Many of these women had occasionally taken my part against watchmen who wished to drive me off the steps of houses where I was sitting. But one amongst them, the one on whose account I have at all introduced this subject—yet no! let me not class thee, oh noble-minded Ann——, with that order of women; let me find, if it be possible, some gentler name to designate the condition of her to whose

---

1. The 17-year-old De Quincey, unhappy at Manchester Grammar School, has run away and taken refuge in London, his whereabouts unknown to his mother and his guardians. He had slept outdoors for two months, but has now been permitted, by a disreputable and seedy lawyer, to sleep in an unoccupied, unfurnished, and rat-infested house. There he and a 10-year-old girl, nameless and of uncertain parentage, huddle together for warmth, eking out a famished existence on whatever scraps De Quincey can scavenge from his landlord's frugal breakfast. He goes on to describe his friendship with the young prostitute, Ann.
2. *Sine Cerere et Baccho friget Venus*— "without Ceres and Bacchus [food and wine], love grows cold."
3. "In the manner of Socrates"; i.e., by a dialogue of questions and answers.
4. Limited.
5. In the sense of "inclusive in tastes and understanding."

bounty and compassion, ministering to my necessities when all the world had forsaken me, I owe it that I am at this time alive.—For many weeks I had walked at nights with this poor friendless girl up and down Oxford Street, or had rested with her on steps and under the shelter of porticos. She could not be so old as myself: she told me, indeed, that she had not completed her sixteenth year. By such questions as my interest about her prompted, I had gradually drawn forth her simple history. Hers was a case of ordinary occurrence (as I have since had reason to think), and one in which, if London beneficence had better adapted its arrangements to meet it, the power of the law might oftener be interposed to protect, and to avenge. But the stream of London charity flows in a channel which, though deep and mighty, is yet noiseless and underground; not obvious or readily accessible to poor houseless wanderers: and it cannot be denied that the outside air and framework of London society is harsh, cruel, and repulsive. In any case, however, I saw that part of her injuries might easily have been redressed; and I urged her often and earnestly to lay her complaint before a magistrate: friendless as she was, I assured her that she would meet with immediate attention; and that English justice, which was no respecter of persons, would speedily and amply avenge her on the brutal ruffian who had plundered her little property. She promised me often that she would; but she delayed taking the steps I pointed out from time to time: for she was timid and dejected to a degree which showed how deeply sorrow had taken hold of her young heart: and perhaps she thought justly that the most upright judge, and the most righteous tribunals, could do nothing to repair her heaviest wrongs. Something, however, would perhaps have been done: for it had been settled between us at length, but unhappily on the very last time but one that I was ever to see her, that in a day or two we should go together before a magistrate, and that I should speak on her behalf. This little service it was destined, however, that I should never realize. Meantime, that which she rendered to me, and which was greater than I could ever have repaid her, was this:—One night, when we were pacing slowly along Oxford Street, and after a day when I had felt more than usually ill and faint, I requested her to turn off with me into Soho Square: thither we went; and we sat down on the steps of a house, which, to this hour, I never pass without a pang of grief, and an inner act of homage to the spirit of that unhappy girl, in memory of the noble action which she there performed. Suddenly, as we sat, I grew much worse: I had been leaning my head against her bosom; and all at once I sank from her arms and fell backwards on the steps. From the sensations I then had, I felt an inner conviction of the liveliest kind that without some powerful and reviving stimulus, I

should either have died on the spot—or should at least have sunk to
a point of exhaustion from which all re-ascent under my friendless
circumstances would soon have become hopeless. Then it was, at
this crisis of my fate, that my poor orphan companion—who had
herself met with little but injuries in this world—stretched out a
saving hand to me. Uttering a cry of terror, but without a moment's
delay, she ran off into Oxford Street, and in less time than could be
imagined, returned to me with a glass of port wine and spices, that
acted upon my empty stomach (which at that time would have
rejected all solid food) with an instantaneous power of restoration:
and for this glass the generous girl without a murmur paid out of
her own humble purse at a time—be it remembered!—when she
had scarcely wherewithal to purchase the bare necessaries of life,
and when she could have no reason to expect that I should ever be
able to reimburse her.——Oh! youthful benefactress! how often in
succeeding years, standing in solitary places, and thinking of thee
with grief of heart and perfect love, how often have I wished that,
as in ancient times the curse of a father was believed to have a
supernatural power, and to pursue its object with a fatal necessity of
self-fulfillment,—even so the benediction of a heart oppressed with
gratitude, might have a like prerogative; might have power given to
it from above to chase—to haunt—to waylay[6]—to overtake—to
pursue thee into the central darkness of a London brothel, or (if it
were possible) into the darkness of the grave—there to awaken thee
with an authentic message of peace and forgiveness, and of final reconciliation!

I do not often weep: for not only do my thoughts on subjects
connected with the chief interests of man daily, nay hourly, descend
a thousand fathoms "too deep for tears";[7] not only does the sternness of my habits of thought present an antagonism to the feelings
which prompt tears—wanting of necessity to those who, being protected usually by their levity from any tendency to meditative
sorrow, would by that same levity be made incapable of resisting it
on any casual access of such feelings:—but also, I believe that all
minds which have contemplated such objects as deeply as I have
done, must, for their own protection from utter despondency, have
early encouraged and cherished some tranquilizing belief as to the
future balances and the hieroglyphic meanings of human sufferings.
On these accounts, I am cheerful to this hour; and, as I have said, I
do not often weep. Yet some feelings, though not deeper or more
passionate, are more tender than others; and often, when I walk at

6. From Wordsworth's *She Was a Phantom of Delight*, line 10: "To haunt, to
startle, and way-lay." De Quincey was
an early and enthusiastic admirer of
Wordsworth's poetry.
7. From the last line of Wordsworth's
Ode: Intimations of Immortality.

this time in Oxford Street by dreamy lamplight, and hear those airs played on a barrel-organ which years ago solaced me and my dear companion (as I must always call her), I shed tears, and muse with myself at the mysterious dispensation which so suddenly and so critically separated us for ever.[8] * * *

From *Introduction to the Pains of Opium*[9]

* * * I remember, about this time, a little incident, which I mention, because, trifling as it was, the reader will soon meet it again in my dreams, which it influenced more fearfully than could be imagined. One day a Malay knocked at my door. What business a Malay could have to transact amongst English mountains, I cannot conjecture: but possibly he was on his road to a seaport about forty miles distant.

The servant who opened the door to him was a young girl born and bred amongst the mountains,[1] who had never seen an Asiatic dress of any sort: his turban, therefore, confounded her not a little: and, as it turned out, that his attainments in English were exactly of the same extent as hers in the Malay, there seemed to be an impassable gulf fixed between all communication of ideas, if either party had happened to possess any. In this dilemma, the girl, recollecting the reputed learning of her master (and, doubtless, giving me credit for a knowledge of all the languages of the earth, besides, perhaps, a few of the lunar ones), came and gave me to understand that there was a sort of demon below, whom she clearly imagined that my art could exorcise from the house. I did not immediately go down: but, when I did, the group which presented itself, arranged as it was by accident, though not very elaborate, took hold of my fancy and my eye in a way that none of the statuesque attitudes exhibited in the ballets at the Opera House, though so ostentatiously complex, had ever done. In a cottage kitchen, but paneled on the wall with dark wood that from age and rubbing resembled oak, and looking more like a rustic hall of entrance than a kitchen, stood the Malay—his turban and loose trousers of dingy white relieved upon the dark paneling: he had placed himself nearer to the girl than she seemed to relish; though her native spirit of mountain intrepidity contended with the feeling of simple awe which her countenance expressed as she gazed upon the tiger-cat

8. De Quincey goes on to narrate that, having been given some money by a family friend who recognized him in the street, he had traveled to Eton to ask a young nobleman whom he knew to stand security for a loan that De Quincey was soliciting from a money-lender. When he returned to London three days later, Ann had disappeared.
9. It is 1816; De Quincey is living at Dove Cottage, Grasmere, and for three years has been addicted to laudanum—i.e., opium dissolved in alcohol. At this time, he has succeeded in reducing his daily dosage from 8,000 to 1,000 drops, with a consequent improvement in health and energy.
1. The lovely Barbara Lewthwaite, whom Wordsworth had described as a "child of beauty rare" in his poem *The Pet Lamb*.

before her. And a more striking picture there could not be imagined, than the beautiful English face of the girl, and its exquisite fairness, together with her erect and independent attitude, contrasted with the sallow and bilious skin of the Malay, enameled or veneered with mahogany, by marine air, his small, fierce, restless eyes, thin lips, slavish gestures and adorations. Half-hidden by the ferocious looking Malay, was a little girl from a neighboring cottage who had crept in after him, and was now in the act of reverting its head, and gazing upwards at the turban and the fiery eyes beneath it, whilst with one hand he caught at the dress of the young woman for protection. My knowledge of the Oriental tongues is not remarkably extensive, being indeed confined to two words—the Arabic word for barley, and the Turkish for opium (madjoon), which I have learnt from Anastasius.[2] And, as I had neither a Malay dictionary, nor even Adelung's *Mithridates*,[3] which might have helped me to a few words, I addressed him in some lines from the Iliad; considering that, of such languages as I possessed, Greek, in point of longitude, came geographically nearest to an Oriental one. He worshiped[4] me in a most devout manner, and replied in what I suppose was Malay. In this way I saved my reputation with my neighbors: for the Malay had no means of betraying the secret. He lay down upon the floor for about an hour, and then pursued his journey. On his departure, I presented him with a piece of opium. To him, as an Orientalist, I concluded that opium must be familiar: and the expression of his face convinced me that it was. Nevertheless, I was struck with some little consternation when I saw him suddenly raise his hand to his mouth, and (in the schoolboy phrase) bolt the whole, divided into three pieces, at one mouthful. The quantity was enough to kill three dragoons and their horses: and I felt some alarm for the poor creature: but what could be done? I had given him the opium in compassion for his solitary life, on recollecting that if he had traveled on foot from London, it must be nearly three weeks since he could have exchanged a thought with any human being. I could not think of violating the laws of hospitality, by having him seized and drenched with an emetic, and thus frightening him into a notion that we were going to sacrifice him to some English idol. No: there was clearly no help for it:—he took his leave: and for some days I felt anxious: but as I never heard of any Malay being found dead, I became convinced that he was used[5] to opium: and that I must have done him the

2. *Anastasius, or Memoirs of a Greek*, was a novel published anonymously by Thomas Hope in 1819. It included a description of the physical effects of opium which De Quincey considered a "grievous misrepresentation."
3. *Mithridates* was a book on Oriental languages by the German philologist J. C. Adelung (1732–1806).
4. Bowed down to.
5. "This, however, is not a necessary conclusion: the varieties of effect produced by opium on different constitutions are infinite" [De Quincey's note].

service I designed, by giving him one night of respite from the pains
of wandering.

This incident I have digressed to mention, because this Malay
(partly from the picturesque exhibition he assisted to frame, partly
from the anxiety I connected with his image for some days) fastened afterwards upon my dreams, and brought other Malays with
him worse than himself, that ran "amuck" at me, and led me into a
world of troubles. * * *

From *The Pains of Opium*

* * *

I have thus described and illustrated my intellectual torpor, in
terms that apply, more or less, to every part of the four years during
which I was under the Circean[6] spells of opium. But for misery and
suffering, I might, indeed, be said to have existed in a dormant
state. I seldom could prevail on myself to write a letter; an answer
of a few words, to any that I received, was the utmost that I could
accomplish; and often *that* not until the letter had lain weeks, or
even months, on my writing table. Without the aid of M.[7] all
records of bills paid, or *to be* paid, must have perished: and my
whole domestic economy, whatever became of Political Economy,[8]
must have gone into irretrievable confusion.—I shall not afterwards
allude to this part of the case: it is one, however, which the opium-
eater will find, in the end, as oppressive and tormenting as any
other, from the sense of incapacity and feebleness, from the direct
embarrassments incident to the neglect or procrastination of each
day's appropriate duties, and from the remorse which must often
exasperate the stings of these evils to a reflective and conscientious
mind. The opium-eater loses none of his moral sensibilities, or aspirations: he wishes and longs, as earnestly as ever, to realize what he
believes possible, and feels to be exacted by duty; but his intellectual apprehension of what is possible infinitely outruns his power,
not of execution only, but even of power to attempt. He lies under
the weight of incubus and nightmare: he lies in sight of all that he
would fain perform, just as a man forcibly confined to his bed by
the mortal languor of a relaxing disease, who is compelled to witness injury or outrage offered to some object of his tenderest love:
—he curses the spells which chain him down from motion:—he
would lay down his life if he might get up and walk; but he is powerless as an infant, and cannot even attempt to rise.

I now pass to what is the main subject of these latter confessions,
to the history and journal of what took place in my dreams; for

6. Like those of Circe (the enchantress
in the *Odyssey* who turned Odysseus' men
into swine).
7. Margaret Simpson, whom De Quincey
had married in 1817.
8. Inspired by David Ricardo's *Princi-*

ples of Political Economy (1817), De
Quincey had begun to write, but never
completed, a work he called *Prolego-
mena to All Future Systems of Political
Economy.*

these were the immediate and proximate cause of my acutest suffering.

The first notice I had of any important change going on in this part of my physical economy, was from the re-awakening of a state of eye generally incident to childhood, or exalted states of irritability. I know not whether my reader is aware that many children, perhaps most, have a power of painting, as it were, upon the darkness, all sorts of phantoms; in some, that power is simply a mechanic affection of the eye; others have a voluntary, or a semi-voluntary power to dismiss or to summon them; or, as a child once said to me when I questioned him on this matter, "I can tell them to go, and they go; but sometimes they come, when I don't tell them to come." Whereupon I told him that he had almost as unlimited a command over apparitions, as a Roman centurion[9] over his soldiers. —In the middle of 1817, I think it was, that this faculty became positively distressing to me: at night, when I lay awake in bed, vast processions passed along in mournful pomp; friezes of never-ending stories, that to my feelings were as sad and solemn as if they were stories drawn from times before Oedipus or Priam—before Tyre— before Memphis.[1] And, at the same time, a corresponding change took place in my dreams; a theater seemed suddenly opened and lighted up within my brain, which presented nightly spectacles of more than earthly splendor. And the four following facts may be mentioned, as noticeable at this time:

1. That, as the creative state of the eye increased, a sympathy seemed to arise between the waking and the dreaming states of the brain in one point—that whatsoever I happened to call up and to trace by a voluntary act upon the darkness was very apt to transfer itself to my dreams; so that I feared to exercise this faculty; for, as Midas turned all things to gold, that yet baffled his hopes and defrauded his human desires,[2] so whatsoever things capable of being visually represented I did but think of in the darkness, immediately shaped themselves into phantoms of the eye; and, by a process apparently no less inevitable, when thus once traced in faint and visionary colors, like writings in sympathetic ink,[3] they were drawn out by the fierce chemistry of my dreams, into insufferable splendor that fretted my heart.

2. For this, and all other changes in my dreams, were accompanied by deep-seated anxiety and gloomy melancholy, such as are wholly incommunicable by words. I seemed every night to descend, not metaphorically, but literally to descend, into chasms and sunless

9. A Roman officer commanding a troop of 100 soldiers (a "century").
1. Oedipus, king of Thebes; Priam, king of Troy; Tyre, the chief city of Phoenicia; Memphis, the capital of ancient Egypt. De Quincey is calling the roll of great civilizations in the past.

2. When granted his rash wish that all he touched should turn to gold, King Midas was horrified to discover that his food, drink, and beloved daughter all became gold at his touch.
3. Invisible ink.

abysses, depths below depths, from which it seemed hopeless that I could ever reascend. Nor did I, by waking, feel that I *had* re-ascended. This I do not dwell upon; because the state of gloom which attended these gorgeous spectacles, amounting at least to utter darkness, as of some suicidal despondency, cannot be approached by words.

3. The sense of space, and in the end, the sense of time, were both powerfully affected. Buildings, landscapes, &c. were exhibited in proportions so vast as the bodily eye is not fitted to receive. Space swelled, and was amplified to an extent of unutterable infinity. This, however, did not disturb me so much as the vast expansion of time; I sometimes seemed to have lived for 70 or 100 years in one night; nay, sometimes had feelings representative of a millennium passed in that time, or, however, of a duration far beyond the limits of any human experience.

4. The minutest incidents of childhood, or forgotten scenes of later years, were often revived: I could not be said to recollect them; for if I had been told of them when waking, I should not have been able to acknowledge them as parts of my past experience. But placed as they were before me, in dreams like intuitions, and clothed in all their evanescent circumstances and accompanying feelings, I *recognized* them instantaneously. I was once told by a near relative of mine,[4] that having in her childhood fallen into a river, and being on the very verge of death but for the critical assistance which reached her, she saw in a moment her whole life, in its minutest incidents, arrayed before her simultaneously as in a mirror; and she had a faculty developed as suddenly for comprehending the whole and every part. This, from some opium experiences of mine, I can believe; I have, indeed, seen the same thing asserted twice in modern books, and accompanied by a remark which I am convinced is true; viz. that the dread book of account, which the Scriptures speak of,[5] is, in fact, the mind itself of each individual. Of this, at least, I feel assured, that there is no such thing as *forgetting* possible to the mind; a thousand accidents may, and will interpose a veil between our present consciousness and the secret inscriptions on the mind; accidents of the same sort will also rend away this veil; but alike, whether veiled or unveiled, the inscription remains forever; just as the stars seem to withdraw before the common light of day, whereas, in fact, we all know that it is the light which is drawn over them as a veil—and that they are waiting to be revealed, when the obscuring daylight shall have withdrawn.

Having noticed these four facts as memorably distinguishing my dreams from those of health, I shall now cite a case illustrative of the first fact; and shall then cite any others that I remember, either

---

4. According to family report, the "near relative" was De Quincey's mother.

5. The books listing everyone's name at the Last Judgment (Revelation xx.12).

in their chronological order, or any other that may give them more effect as pictures to the reader.

I had been in youth, and even since, for occasional amusement, a great reader of Livy,[6] whom, I confess, that I prefer, both for style and matter, to any other of the Roman historians; and I had often felt as most solemn and appalling sounds, and most emphatically representative of the majesty of the Roman people, the two words so often occurring in Livy—*Consul Romanus;*[7] especially when the consul is introduced in his military character. I mean to say, that the words king—sultan—regent, &c. or any other titles of those who embody in their own persons the collective majesty of a great people, had less power over my reverential feelings. I had also, though no great reader of history, made myself minutely and critically familiar with one period of English history, viz. the period of the Parliamentary War, having been attracted by the moral grandeur of some who figured in that day, and by the many interesting memoirs which survive those unquiet times. Both these parts of my lighter reading, having furnished me often with matter of reflection, now furnished me with matter for my dreams. Often I used to see, after painting upon the blank darkness a sort of rehearsal whilst waking, a crowd of ladies, and perhaps a festival, and dances. And I heard it said, or I said to myself, "These are English ladies from the unhappy times of Charles I. These are the wives and the daughters of those who met in peace, and sat at the same tables, and were allied by marriage or by blood; and yet, after a certain day in August, 1642,[8] never smiled upon each other again, nor met but in the field of battle; and at Marston Moor, at Newbury, or at Naseby,[9] cut asunder all ties of love by the cruel saber, and washed away in blood the memory of ancient friendship."—The ladies danced, and looked as lovely as the court of George IV.[1] Yet I knew, even in my dream, that they had been in the grave for nearly two centuries.—This pageant would suddenly dissolve: and, at a clapping of hands, would be heard the heart-quaking sound of *Consul Romanus;* and immediately came "sweeping by," in gorgeous paludaments, Paulus or Marius,[2] girt round by a company of centurions, with the crimson tunic hoisted on a spear,[3] and followed by the *alalagmos*[3] of the Roman legions.

---

6. Titus Livius (59 B.C.–A.D. 17), author of a huge history of Rome in 142 books.
7. "Roman consul," one of two officials, elected annually, who wielded the chief military and judicial authority in Republican Rome.
8. The raising of the king's banner on Castle Hill, Nottingham, on August 22, 1642, signaled the beginning of the English Civil War.
9. Scenes of the defeat of King Charles's forces in the Civil War.
1. The reigning monarch at the time the *Confessions* were written.
2. Lucius Paulus (d. 160 B.C.) and Caius Marius (d. 86 B.C.) were Roman generals who won famous victories. "Paludaments": the cloaks worn by Roman generals.
3. "The signal which announced a day of battle" [De Quincey's note to the revised edition]. "*Alalagmos*": "A word expressing collectively the gathering of the Roman war-cries" [De Quincey's note to the revised edition]. The word is Greek.

Many years ago, when I was looking over Piranesi's Antiquities of Rome, Mr. Coleridge, who was standing by, described to me a set of plates by that artist, called his *Dreams*,[4] and which record the scenery of his own visions during the delirium of a fever. Some of them (I describe only from memory of Mr. Coleridge's account) represented vast Gothic halls: on the floor of which stood all sorts of engines and machinery, wheels, cables, pulleys, levers, catapults, &c. &c. expressive of enormous power put forth, and resistance overcome. Creeping along the sides of the walls, you perceived a staircase; and upon it, groping his way upwards, was Piranesi himself: follow the stairs a little further, and you perceive it come to a sudden abrupt termination, without any balustrade, and allowing no step onwards to him who had reached the extremity, except into the depths below. Whatever is to become of poor Piranesi, you suppose, at least, that his labors must in some way terminate here. But raise your eyes, and behold a second flight of stairs still higher: on which again Piranesi is perceived, but this time standing on the very brink of the abyss. Again elevate your eye, and a still more aerial flight of stairs is beheld: and again is poor Piranesi busy on his aspiring labors: and so on, until the unfinished stairs and Piranesi both are lost in the upper gloom of the hall.—With the same power of endless growth and self-reproduction did my architecture proceed in dreams. In the early stage of my malady, the splendors of my dreams were indeed chiefly architectural: and I beheld such pomp of cities and palaces as was never yet beheld by the waking eye, unless in the clouds. From a great modern poet[5] I cite part of a passage which describes, as an appearance actually beheld in the clouds, what in many of its circumstances I saw frequently in sleep:

> The appearance, instantaneously disclosed,
> Was of a mighty city—boldly say
> A wilderness of building, sinking far
> And self-withdrawn into a wondrous depth,
> Far sinking into splendor—without end!
> Fabric it seem'd of diamond, and of gold,
> With alabaster domes, and silver spires,
> And blazing terrace upon terrace, high
> Uplifted; here, serene pavilions bright
> In avenues disposed; there towers begirt
> With battlements that on their restless fronts
> Bore stars—illumination of all gems!
> By earthly nature had the effect been wrought
> Upon the dark materials of the storm

4. Giovanni Piranesi (1720–78), a Venetian especially famed for his many etchings of ancient and modern Rome. He did not publish prints called *Dreams*; De Quincey doubtless refers to his series called *Carceri d'Invenzione*, "Imaginary Prisons." The description which De Quincey recalls from Coleridge's conversation is remarkably apt for these terrifying architectural fantasies.
5. The quotation is from Wordsworth's *The Excursion*, Book II, lines 834 ff.; they describe a cloud structure after a storm.

Now pacified: on them, and on the coves,
And mountain-steeps and summits, whereunto
The vapors had receded,—taking there
Their station under a cerulean sky, &c. &c.

The sublime circumstance—"battlements that on their *restless* fronts bore stars,"—might have been copied from my architectural dreams, for it often occurred.—We hear it reported of Dryden, and of Fuseli[6] in modern times, that they thought proper to eat raw meat for the sake of obtaining splendid dreams: how much better for such a purpose to have eaten opium, which yet I do not remember that any poet is recorded to have done, except the dramatist Shadwell:[7] and in ancient days, Homer is, I think, rightly reputed to have known the virtues of opium.[8]

To my architecture succeeded dreams of lakes—and silvery expanses of water:—these haunted me so much, that I feared (though possibly it will appear ludicrous to a medical man) that some dropsical[9] state or tendency of the brain might thus be making itself (to use a metaphysical word) *objective*; and the sentient organ *project* itself as its own object.—For two months I suffered greatly in my head—a part of my bodily structure which had hitherto been so clear from all touch or taint of weakness (physically, I mean), that I used to say of it, as the last Lord Orford[1] said of his stomach, that it seemed likely to survive the rest of my person.— Till now I had never felt a headache even, or any the slightest pain, except rheumatic pains caused by my own folly. However, I got over this attack, though it must have been verging on something very dangerous.

The waters now changed their character,—from translucent lakes, shining like mirrors, they now became seas and oceans. And now came a tremendous change, which, unfolding itself slowly like a scroll, through many months, promised an abiding torment; and, in fact, it never left me until the winding up of my case. Hitherto the human face had mixed often in my dreams, but not despotically, nor with any special power of tormenting. But now that which I have called the tyranny of the human face began to unfold itself. Perhaps some part of my London life might be answerable for this. Be that as it may, now it was that upon the rocking waters of the ocean the human face began to appear: the sea appeared paved with innumerable faces, upturned to the heavens: faces, imploring,

6. John Henry Fuseli (1741–1825) was born in Switzerland and painted in England. He was a friend of William Blake, and was noted for his paintings of nightmarish fantasies.
7. Thomas Shadwell was a Restoration dramatist and poet; he is now better known as caricatured by Dryden (in *Mac Flecknoe* and other satires) than for his own writings.
8. In the *Odyssey*, Book IV, Homer lauded nepenthe (which is probably opium) as a "drug to heal all pain and anger, and bring forgetfulness of every sorrow."
9. Afflicted with dropsy—an accumulation of fluid in the bodily tissues and cavities.
1. Horace Walpole, the 18th-century wit and letter-writer, author of the Gothic novel *The Castle of Otranto* (1764).

wrathful, despairing, surged upwards by thousands, by myriads, by generations, by centuries:—my agitation was infinite,—my mind tossed—and surged with the ocean.

May, 1818

The Malay has been a fearful enemy for months. I have been every night, through his means, transported into Asiatic scenes. I know not whether others share in my feelings on this point; but I have often thought that if I were compelled to forego England, and to live in China, and among Chinese manners and modes of life and scenery, I should go mad. The causes of my horror lie deep; and some of them must be common to others. Southern Asia, in general, is the seat of awful images and associations. As the cradle of the human race, it would alone have a dim and reverential feeling connected with it. But there are other reasons. No man can pretend that the wild, barbarous, and capricious superstitions of Africa, or of savage tribes elsewhere, affect him in the way that he is affected by the ancient, monumental, cruel, and elaborate religions of Indostan, &c. The mere antiquity of Asiatic things, of their institutions, histories, modes of faith, &c. is so impressive, that to me the vast age of the race and name overpowers the sense of youth in the individual. A young Chinese seems to me an antediluvian man renewed. Even Englishmen, though not bred in any knowledge of such institutions, cannot but shudder at the mystic sublimity of castes[2] that have flowed apart, and refused to mix, through such immemorial tracts of time; nor can any man fail to be awed by the names of the Ganges, or the Euphrates. It contributes much to these feelings, that southern Asia is, and has been for thousands of years, the part of the earth most swarming with human life; the great *officina gentium*.[3] Man is a weed in those regions. The vast empires also, into which the enormous population of Asia has always been cast, give a further sublimity to the feelings associated with all Oriental names or images. In China, over and above what it has in common with the rest of southern Asia, I am terrified by the modes of life, by the manners, and the barrier of utter abhorrence, and want of sympathy, placed between us by feelings deeper than I can analyze. I could sooner live with lunatics, or brute animals. All this, and much more than I can say, or have time to say, the reader must enter into before he can comprehend the unimaginable horror which these dreams of Oriental imagery, and mythological tortures, impressed upon me. Under the connecting feeling of tropical heat and vertical sunlights, I brought together all creatures, birds, beasts, reptiles, all trees and plants, usages and appearances, that are found in all tropical regions, and assembled them together in China or Indostan. From kindred feelings, I soon brought Egypt

2. The reference is to the Hindu caste system, with its sharp division between four hereditary social classes.
3. "Manufactory of populations."

and all her gods under the same law. I was stared at, hooted at, grinned at, chattered at, by monkeys, by paroquets, by cockatoos. I ran into pagodas: and was fixed, for centuries, at the summit, or in secret rooms; I was the idol; I was the priest; I was worshiped; I was sacrificed. I fled from the wrath of Brama through all the forests of Asia: Vishnu hated me: Seeva laid wait for me.[4] I came suddenly upon Isis and Osiris: I had done a deed, they said, which the ibis and the crocodile trembled at.[5] I was buried, for a thousand years, in stone coffins, with mummies and sphinxes, in narrow chambers at the heart of eternal pyramids. I was kissed, with cancerous kisses, by crocodiles; and laid, confounded with all unutterable slimy things, amongst reeds and Nilotic mud.

I thus give the reader some slight abstraction of my Oriental dreams, which always filled me with such amazement at the monstrous scenery, that horror seemed absorbed, for a while, in sheer astonishment. Sooner or later, came a reflux of feeling that swallowed up the astonishment, and left me, not so much in terror, as in hatred and abomination of what I saw. Over every form, and threat, and punishment, and dim sightless incarceration, brooded a sense of eternity and infinity that drove me into an oppression as of madness. Into these dreams only, it was, with one or two slight exceptions, that any circumstances of physical horror entered. All before had been moral and spiritual terrors. But here the main agents were ugly birds, or snakes, or crocodiles; especially the last. The cursed crocodile became to me the object of more horror than almost all the rest. I was compelled to live with him; and (as was always the case almost in my dreams) for centuries. I escaped sometimes, and found myself in Chinese houses, with cane tables, &c. All the feet of the tables, sofas, &c. soon became instinct with life: the abominable head of the crocodile, and his leering eyes, looked out at me, multiplied into a thousand repetitions: and I stood loathing and fascinated. And so often did this hideous reptile haunt my dreams, that many times the very same dream was broken up in the very same way: I heard gentle voices speaking to me (I hear every thing when I am sleeping); and instantly I awoke: it was broad noon; and my children were standing, hand in hand, at my bedside; come to show me their colored shoes, or new frocks, or to let me see them dressed for going out. I protest that so awful was the transition from the damned crocodile, and the other unutterable monsters and abortions of my dreams, to the sight of innocent *human* natures and of infancy, that, in the mighty and sudden revulsion of mind, I wept, and could not forbear it, as I kissed their faces.

---

4. In the Hindu triad, Brahma is the creative aspect of divine reality, Vishnu is its maintainer, and Shiva its destroyer.
5. Isis was the ancient Egyptian goddess of fertility; she was the sister and wife of Osiris, whose annual death and rebirth represented the seasonal cycle of nature. The ibis (a long-legged wading bird) and the crocodile were sacred animals in ancient Egypt.

June, 1819

I have had occasion to remark, at various periods of my life, that the deaths of those whom we love, and indeed the contemplation of death generally, is (*ceteris paribus*)[6] more affecting in summer than in any other season of the year. And the reasons are these three, I think: first, that the visible heavens in summer appear far higher, more distant, and (if such a solecism may be excused) more infinite; the clouds, by which chiefly the eye expounds the distance of the blue pavilion stretched over our heads, are in summer more voluminous, massed, and accumulated in far grander and more towering piles: secondly, the light and the appearances of the declining and the setting sun are much more fitted to be types and characters of the Infinite: and, thirdly, (which is the main reason) the exuberant and riotous prodigality of life naturally forces the mind more powerfully upon the antagonist thought of death, and the wintry sterility of the grave. For it may be observed, generally, that wherever two thoughts stand related to each other by a law of antagonism, and exist, as it were, by mutual repulsion, they are apt to suggest each other. On these accounts it is that I find it impossible to banish the thought of death when I am walking alone in the endless days of summer; and any particular death, if not more affecting, at least haunts my mind more obstinately and besiegingly in that season. Perhaps this cause, and a slight incident which I omit, might have been the immediate occasions of the following dream; to which, however, a predisposition must always have existed in my mind; but having been once roused, it never left me, and split into a thousand fantastic varieties, which often suddenly reunited, and composed again the original dream.

I thought that it was a Sunday morning in May, that it was Easter Sunday, and as yet very early in the morning. I was standing, as it seemed to me, at the door of my own cottage. Right before me lay the very scene which could really be commanded from that situation, but exalted, as was usual, and solemnized by the power of dreams. There were the same mountains, and the same lovely valley at their feet; but the mountains were raised to more than Alpine height, and there was interspace far larger between them of meadows and forest lawns; the hedges were rich with white roses; and no living creature was to be seen, excepting that in the green churchyard there were cattle tranquilly reposing upon the verdant graves, and particularly round about the grave of a child whom I had tenderly loved,[7] just as I had really beheld them, a little before sunrise in the same summer, when that child died. I gazed upon the well-known scene, and I said aloud (as I thought) to myself, "It yet wants much of sunrise; and it is Easter Sunday; and that is the day

6. "Other things being the same."
7. The child was Wordsworth's daughter, Catherine, to whom De Quincey had been devoted; she died at the age of four. She is the subject of Wordsworth's moving sonnet *Surprised by Joy*.

on which they celebrate the first-fruits of resurrection. I will walk abroad; old griefs shall be forgotten today; for the air is cool and still, and the hills are high, and stretch away to heaven; and the forest-glades are as quiet as the churchyard; and, with the dew, I can wash the fever from my forehead, and then I shall be unhappy no longer." And I turned, as if to open my garden gate; and immediately I saw upon the left a scene far different; but which yet the power of dreams had reconciled into harmony with the other. The scene was an Oriental one; and there also it was Easter Sunday, and very early in the morning. And at a vast distance were visible, as a stain upon the horizon, the domes and cupolas of a great city—an image or faint abstraction, caught perhaps in childhood from some picture of Jerusalem. And not a bow-shot from me, upon a stone, and shaded by Judean palms, there sat a woman; and I looked; and it was—Ann! She fixed her eyes upon me earnestly; and I said to her at length: "So then I have found you at last." I waited: but she answered me not a word. Her face was the same as when I saw it last, and yet again how different! Seventeen years ago, when the lamplight fell upon her face, as for the last time I kissed her lips (lips, Ann, that to me were not polluted), her eyes were streaming with tears: the tears were now wiped away; she seemed more beautiful than she was at that time, but in all other points the same, and not older. Her looks were tranquil, but with unusual solemnity of expression; and I now gazed upon her with some awe, but suddenly her countenance grew dim, and, turning to the mountains, I perceived vapors rolling between us; in a moment, all had vanished; thick darkness came on; and, in the twinkling of an eye, I was far away from mountains, and by lamplight in Oxford Street, walking again with Ann—just as we walked seventeen years before, when we were both children.

As a final specimen, I cite one of a different character, from 1820.

The dream commenced with a music which now I often heard in dreams—a music of preparation and of awakening suspense; a music like the opening of the Coronation Anthem,[8] and which, like *that*, gave the feeling of a vast march—of infinite cavalcades filing off—and the tread of innumerable armies. The morning was come of a mighty day—a day of crisis and of final hope for human nature, then suffering some mysterious eclipse, and laboring in some dread extremity. Somewhere, I knew not where—somehow, I knew not how—by some beings, I knew not whom—a battle, a strife, an agony, was conducting,—was evolving like a great drama, or piece of music; with which my sympathy was the more insupportable from my confusion as to its place, its cause, its nature, and its possible issue. I, as is usual in dreams (where, of necessity, we make our-

8. Composed by Handel for the coronation of George II, 1727.

selves central to every movement), had the power, and yet had not
the power, to decide it. I had the power, if I could raise myself, to
will it; and yet again had not the power, for the weight of twenty
Atlantics was upon me, or the oppression of inexpiable guilt.
"Deeper than ever plummet sounded,"[9] I lay inactive. Then, like a
chorus, the passion deepened. Some greater interest was at stake;
some mightier cause than ever yet the sword had pleaded, or trumpet had proclaimed. Then came sudden alarms: hurryings to and
fro: trepidations of innumerable fugitives, I knew not whether from
the good cause or the bad: darkness and lights: tempest and human
faces: and at last, with the sense that all was lost, female forms, and
the features that were worth all the world to me, and but a moment
allowed,—and clasped hands, and heart-breaking partings, and then
—everlasting farewells! and with a sigh, such as the caves of hell
sighed when the incestuous mother uttered the abhorred name of
death,[10] the sound was reverberated—everlasting farewells! and
again, and yet again reverberated—everlasting farewells!

And I awoke in struggles, and cried aloud—"I will sleep no
more!"[11]

* * *

1821   1821; 1822

On the Knocking at the Gate in *Macbeth*[1]

From my boyish days I had always felt a great perplexity on one
point in *Macbeth*. It was this: The knocking at the gate which
succeeds to the murder of Duncan produced to my feelings an effect for which I never could account. The effect was that it reflected back upon the murderer a peculiar awfulness and a depth of

9. From Shakespeare's *The Tempest*
III.iii.101.
10. The reference is to Milton's *Paradise
Lost*, Book II, lines 777 ff. The "incestuous mother" is Sin, who is doubly incestuous: she is the daughter of Satan,
who begot Death upon her, and she was
in turn raped by her son and gave birth
to a pack of "yelling Monsters."
11. Macbeth says (II.ii.35–36): "Methought I heard a voice cry 'Sleep no
more! / Macbeth does murder sleep.'"
1. This essay, one of the best-known
critiques of Shakespeare, deals with the
scene in *Macbeth* (II.ii–iii) in which,
just after they have murdered Duncan, Macbeth and his wife are startled by a loud knocking at the gate.

De Quincey exhibits the procedure
in Romantic criticism of making, as
he says, the "understanding" wait upon
the "feelings." Instead of judging
the success or failure of a passage
by its conformity to prior critical
theory, De Quincey brings in theory
only to explain his impression or immediate emotional response to the passage. The final paragraph demonstrates
a weakness of this Romantic position
when it is driven to an extreme, for it
converts the reasonable view that Shakespeare must be presumed right until
shown to be wrong into the untenable
view that Shakespeare is an artistic
deity who can do no wrong.

solemnity; yet, however obstinately I endeavored with my understanding to comprehend this, for many years I never could see *why*
it should produce such an effect.

Here I pause for one moment, to exhort the reader never to pay
any attention to his understanding when it stands in opposition
to any other faculty of his mind. The mere understanding, however
useful and indispensable, is the meanest faculty in the human mind,
and the most to be distrusted; and yet the great majority of people
trust to nothing else—which may do for ordinary life, but not for
philosophical purposes. Of this out of ten thousand instances that
I might produce I will cite one. Ask of any person whatsoever who
is not previously prepared for the demand by a knowledge of the
perspective to draw in the rudest way the commonest appearance
which depends upon the laws of that science—as, for instance, to
represent the effect of two walls standing at right angles to each
other, or the appearance of the houses on each side of a street as
seen by a person looking down the street from one extremity. Now,
in all cases, unless the person has happened to observe in pictures
how it is that artists produce these effects, he will be utterly unable to make the smallest approximation to it. Yet why? For he
has actually seen the effect every day of his life. The reason is that
he allows his understanding to overrule his eyes. His understanding,
which includes no intuitive knowledge of the laws of vision, can
furnish him with no reason why a line which is known and can
be proved to be a horizontal line should not *appear* a horizontal
line: a line that made any angle with the perpendicular less than a
right angle would seem to him to indicate that his houses were all
tumbling down together. Accordingly, he makes the line of his
houses a horizontal line, and fails, of course, to produce the effect
demanded. Here, then, is one instance out of many in which not
only the understanding is allowed to overrule the eyes, but where
the understanding is positively allowed to obliterate the eyes, as
it were; for not only does the man believe the evidence of his understanding in opposition to that of his eyes, but (what is monstrous)
the idiot is not aware that his eyes ever gave such evidence. He
does not know that he has seen (and therefore *quoad* his consciousness[2] has *not* seen) that which he *has* seen every day of his life.

But to return from this digression. My understanding could furnish no reason why the knocking at the gate in *Macbeth* should
produce any effect, direct or reflected. In fact, my understanding
said positively that it could *not* produce any effect. But I knew better; I felt that it did; and I waited and clung to the problem until
further knowledge should enable me to solve it. At length, in 1812,

2. I.e., so far as his consciousness is concerned.

Mr. Williams made his debut on the stage of Ratcliffe Highway, and executed those unparalleled murders which have procured for him such a brilliant and undying reputation.[3] On which murders, by the way, I must observe that in one respect they have had an ill effect, by making the connoisseur in murder very fastidious in his taste, and dissatisfied by anything that has been since done in that line. All other murders look pale by the deep crimson of his; and, as an amateur[4] once said to me in a querulous tone, "There has been absolutely nothing *doing* since his time, or nothing that's worth speaking of." But this is wrong; for it is unreasonable to expect all men to be great artists, and born with the genius of Mr. Williams. Now, it will be remembered that in the first of these murders (that of the Marrs) the same incident (of a knocking at the door[5] soon after the work of extermination was complete) did actually occur which the genius of Shakespeare has invented; and all good judges, and the most eminent dilettanti,[6] acknowledged the felicity of Shakespeare's suggestion as soon as it was actually realized. Here, then, was a fresh proof that I was right in relying on my own feeling, in opposition to my understanding; and I again set myself to study the problem. At length I solved it to my own satisfaction; and my solution is this: Murder, in ordinary cases, where the sympathy is wholly directed to the case of the murdered person, is an incident of coarse and vulgar horror; and for this reason—that it flings the interest exclusively upon the natural but ignoble instinct by which we cleave to life: an instinct which, as being indispensable to the primal law of self-preservation, is the same in kind (though different in degree) amongst all living creatures. This instinct, therefore, because it annihilates all distinctions, and degrades the greatest of men to the level of "the poor beetle that we tread on,"[7] exhibits human nature in its most abject and humiliating attitude. Such an attitude would little suit the purposes of the poet. What then must he do? He must throw the interest on the murderer. Our sympathy must be with *him* (of course I mean a sympathy of comprehension, a sympathy by which we enter into his feelings, and are made to understand them—not a sympathy of pity or approbation).[8] In the murdered person, all strife of thought,

3. John Williams, a sailor, had thrown London into a panic (the date was actually December, 1811) by murdering the Marr family and, twelve days later, the Williamson family. De Quincey described these murders at length in the Postscript to his two essays *On Murder Considered as One of the Fine Arts*.
4. Here, a fancier or follower of an art or sport.
5. By a maidservant of the Marrs, returning from the purchase of oysters for supper.
6. Lovers of the fine arts.
7. Shakespeare's *Measure for Measure* III.i.79.
8. In a note De Quincey decries "the unscholarlike use of the word sympathy, at present so general, by which, instead of taking it in its proper sense, as the act of reproducing in our minds the feelings of another, whether for hatred, indignation, love, pity, or approbation, it is made a mere synonym of the word *pity* * * *"

all flux and reflux of passion and of purpose, are crushed by one overwhelming panic; the fear of instant death smites him "with its petrific[9] mace." But in the murderer, such a murderer as a poet will condescend to, there must be raging some great storm of passion—jealousy, ambition, vengeance, hatred—which will create a hell within him; and into this hell we are to look.

In *Macbeth,* for the sake of gratifying his own enormous and teeming faculty of creation, Shakespeare has introduced two murderers: and, as usual in his hands, they are remarkably discriminated; but—though in Macbeth the strife of mind is greater than in his wife, the tiger spirit not so awake, and his feelings caught chiefly by contagion from her—yet, as both were finally involved in the guilt of murder, the murderous mind of necessity is finally to be presumed in both. This was to be expressed; and, on its own account, as well as to make it a more proportionable antagonist to the unoffending nature of their victim, "the gracious Duncan," and adequately to expound "the deep damnation of his taking off,"[1] this was to be expressed with peculiar energy. We were to be made to feel that the human nature—i.e., the divine nature of love and mercy, spread through the hearts of all creatures, and seldom utterly withdrawn from man—was gone, vanished, extinct, and that the fiendish nature had taken its place. And, as this effect is marvelously accomplished in the *dialogues* and *soliloquies* themselves, so it is finally consummated by the expedient under consideration; and it is to this that I now solicit the reader's attention. If the reader has ever witnessed a wife, daughter, or sister in a fainting fit, he may chance to have observed that the most affecting moment in such a spectacle is *that* in which a sigh and a stirring announce the recommencement of suspended life. Or, if the reader has ever been present in a vast metropolis on the day when some great national idol was carried in funeral pomp to his grave, and, chancing to walk near the course through which it passed, has felt powerfully, in the silence and desertion of the streets, and in the stagnation of ordinary business, the deep interest which at that moment was possessing the heart of man—if all at once he should hear the death-like stillness broken up by the sound of wheels rattling away from the scene, and making known that the transitory vision was dissolved, he will be aware that at no moment was his sense of the complete suspension and pause in ordinary human concerns so full and affecting as at that moment when the suspension ceases, and the goings-on of human life are suddenly resumed. All action in any direction is best expounded, measured, and made apprehensible, by reaction. Now, apply this to the case in *Macbeth.* Here, as I

9. Petrifying, turning to stone (from *Paradise Lost* X.294).   1. *Macbeth* III.i.66 and I.vii.20.

have said, the retiring of the human heart and the entrance of the
fiendish heart was to be expressed and made sensible. Another
world has stepped in; and the murderers are taken out of the region
of human things, human purposes, human desires. They are transfigured: Lady Macbeth is "unsexed";[2] Macbeth has forgot that he
was born of woman; both are conformed to the image of devils;
and the world of devils is suddenly revealed. But how shall this be
conveyed and made palpable? In order that a new world may step
in, this world must for a time disappear. The murderers and the
murder must be insulated—cut off by an immeasurable gulf from
the ordinary tide and succession of human affairs—locked up and
sequestered in some deep recess; we must be made sensible that
the world of ordinary life is suddenly arrested, laid asleep, tranced,
racked into a dread armistice; time must be annihilated, relation
to things without abolished; and all must pass self-withdrawn into
a deep syncope[3] and suspension of earthly passion. Hence it is that,
when the deed is done, when the work of darkness is perfect, then
the world of darkness passes away like a pageantry in the clouds: the
knocking at the gate is heard, and it makes known audibly that
the reaction has commenced; the human has made its reflux upon
the fiendish; the pulses of life are beginning to beat again; and the
re-establishment of the goings-on of the world in which we live first
makes us profoundly sensible of the awful parenthesis that had suspended them.

O mighty poet! Thy works are not as those of other men, simply
and merely great works of art, but are also like the phenomena of
nature, like the sun and the sea, the stars and the flowers, like frost
and snow, rain and dew, hailstorm and thunder, which are to be
studied with entire submission of our own faculties, and in the perfect faith that in them there can be no too much or too little,
nothing useless or inert, but that, the farther we press in our discoveries, the more we shall see proofs of design and self-supporting
arrangement where the careless eye had seen nothing but accident!

1823

---

2. Steeling herself to the murder, Lady
Macbeth calls on the spirits of hell to
"unsex me here" (I.v.42).
3. Fainting spell.

From The English Mail Coach[1]
From *II. The Vision of Sudden Death*[2]

* * * On this occasion the usual silence and solitude prevailed along the road. Not a hoof nor a wheel was to be heard. And, to strengthen this false luxurious confidence in the noiseless roads, it happened also that the night was one of peculiar solemnity and peace. For my own part, though slightly alive to the possibilities of peril, I had so far yielded to the influence of the mighty calm as to sink into a profound reverie. The month was August; in the middle of which lay my own birthday—a festival to every thoughtful man suggesting solemn and often sigh-born thoughts. The county was my own native county—upon which, in its southern section, more than upon any equal area known to man past or present, had descended the original curse of labor in its heaviest form, not mastering the bodies only of men, as of slaves, or criminals in mines, but working through the fiery will. Upon no equal space of earth was, or ever had been, the same energy of human power put forth daily. At this particular season also of the assizes,[3] that dreadful hurricane of flight and pursuit, as it might have seemed to a stranger, which swept to and from Lancaster all day long, hunting the county up and down, and regularly subsiding back into silence about sunset, could not fail (when united with this permanent distinction of Lancashire as the very metropolis and citadel of labor) to point the thoughts pathetically upon that counter-vision of rest, of saintly repose from strife and sorrow, towards which, as to their secret

1. The three essays joined under this title were first published anonymously in *Blackwood's Magazine* for 1849. *The Glory of Motion* gave an account of the fast English coaches which carried both passengers and mail; it emphasized their function in disseminating military news, especially that of the great victory over Napoleon at Waterloo. *The Vision of Sudden Death*, partly reproduced here, describes De Quincey's experience of a near accident. *Dream-Fugue*, reprinted in its entirety, treats this incident as it entered into De Quincey's dreams of terror.
    A fugue is a musical composition in which a theme, or "subject," is introduced successively by various voices and then developed in contrapuntal fashion. When he reprinted these essays in his "Collective Edition" (1854), De Quincey undertook to explain the "logic" of his composition for the perplexed critics of his day. He pointed out that the whole of the *Dream-Fugue* "radiates as a natural expansion" of *The Vision of Sudden Death:* "So far as I know, every element in the shifting movements of the Dream derived itself either primarily from the incidents of

the actual scene, or from secondary features associated with the mail."
    The structure of this essay, though its materials are no doubt derived, as De Quincey says, from his dreams, does not simply reproduce these dreams. Instead, the essay states a thematic subject and then enriches, varies, and develops it until it reaches a grand climax which incorporates the Christian pattern of death, grace, and resurrection. De Quincey was attempting in prose what T. S. Eliot, in *Four Quartets,* was to attempt a century later in verse —the adaptation of a musical form to a literary medium of expression.
2. In the first part of this essay, De Quincey has described his situation as a lone passenger on the top of the mail coach from Manchester to Glasgow on a summer night two or three years after the Battle of Waterloo. To relieve his fatigue he takes a dose of opium and sinks "into a profound reverie"; the one-eyed coachman drowses off; the great coach rushes on unguided through the extraordinarily peaceful night.
3. The sessions of the superior courts in each of the English counties.

haven, the profounder aspirations of man's heart are in solitude continually traveling. Obliquely upon our left we were nearing the sea; which also must, under the present circumstances, be repeating the general state of halcyon repose. The sea, the atmosphere, the light, bore each an orchestral part in this universal lull. Moonlight and the first timid tremblings of the dawn were by this time blending; and the blendings were brought into a still more exquisite state of unity by a slight silvery mist, motionless and dreamy, that covered the woods and fields, but with a veil of equable transparency. Except the feet of our own horses—which, running on a sandy margin of the road, made but little disturbance—there was no sound abroad. In the clouds and on the earth prevailed the same majestic peace; and, in spite of all that the villain of a schoolmaster has done for the ruin of our sublimer thoughts, which are the thoughts of our infancy, we still believe in no such nonsense as a limited atmosphere. Whatever we may swear with our false feigning lips, in our faithful hearts we still believe, and must forever believe, in fields of air traversing the total gulf between earth and the central heavens. Still, in the confidence of children that tread without fear *every* chamber in their father's house, and to whom no door is closed, we, in that Sabbatic vision which sometimes is revealed for an hour upon nights like this, ascend with easy steps from the sorrow-stricken fields of earth upwards to the sandals of God.

Suddenly, from thoughts like these I was awakened to a sullen sound, as of some motion on the distant road. It stole upon the air for a moment; I listened in awe; but then it died away. Once roused, however, I could not but observe with alarm the quickened motion of our horses. Ten years' experience had made my eye learned in the valuing of motion; and I saw that we were now running thirteen miles an hour. I pretend to no presence of mind. On the contrary, my fear is that I am miserably and shamefully deficient in that quality as regards action. The palsy of doubt and distraction hangs like some guilty weight of dark unfathomed remembrances upon my energies when the signal is flying for *action*. But, on the other hand, this accursed gift I have, as regards *thought*, that in the first step towards the possibility of a misfortune I see its total evolution; in the radix[4] of the series I see too certainly and too instantly its entire expansion; in the first syllable of the dreadful sentence I read already the last. It was not that I feared for ourselves. *Us* our bulk and impetus charmed against peril in any collision. And I had ridden through too many hundreds of perils that were frightful to approach, that were matter of laughter to look back upon, the first face of which was horror, the parting face a jest—for any anxiety to rest upon *our* interests. The mail was not built, I felt assured, nor bespoke, that could betray *me*

4. Root; here used in its mathematical sense, as the basic number of a numerical system.

who trusted to its protection. But any carriage that we could meet would be frail and light in comparison of ourselves. And I remarked this ominous accident of our situation—we were on the wrong side of the road. But then, it may be said, the other party, if other there was, might also be on the wrong side; and two wrongs might make a right. *That* was not likely. The same motive which had drawn *us* to the right-hand side of the road—viz., the luxury of the soft beaten sand as contrasted with the paved center—would prove attractive to others. The two adverse carriages would therefore, to a certainty, be traveling on the same side; and from this side, as not being ours in law, the crossing over to the other would, of course, be looked for from *us*. Our lamps, still lighted, would give the impression of vigilance on our part. And every creature that met us would rely upon *us* for quartering.[5] All this, and if the separate links of the anticipation had been a thousand times more, I saw, not discursively, or by effort, or by succession, but by one flash of horrid simultaneous intuition.

Under this steady though rapid anticipation of the evil which *might* be gathering ahead, ah! what a sullen mystery of fear, what a sigh of woe, was that which stole upon the air, as again the far-off sound of a wheel was heard! A whisper it was—a whisper from, perhaps, four miles off—secretly announcing a ruin that, being foreseen, was not the less inevitable; that, being known, was not therefore healed. What could be done—who was it that could do it—to check the storm-flight of these maniacal horses? Could I not seize the reins from the grasp of the slumbering coachman? You, reader, think that it would have been in *your* power to do so. And I quarrel not with your estimate of yourself. But, from the way in which the coachman's hand was vised between his upper and lower thigh, this was impossible. Easy was it? See, then, that bronze equestrian statue. The cruel rider has kept the bit in his horse's mouth for two centuries. Unbridle him for a minute, if you please, and wash his mouth with water. Easy was it? Unhorse me, then, that imperial rider; knock me those marble feet from those marble stirrups of Charlemagne.

The sounds ahead strengthened, and were now too clearly the sounds of wheels. Who and what could it be? Was it industry in a taxed cart? Was it youthful gaiety in a gig?[6] Was it sorrow that loitered, or joy that raced? For as yet the snatches of sound were too intermitting, from distance, to decipher the character of the motion. Whoever were the travelers, something must be done to warn them. Upon the other party rests the active responsibility, but upon *us*—and, woe is me! that *us* was reduced to my frail opium-shattered self—rests the responsibility of warning. Yet, how should this be accomplished? Might I not sound the guard's horn? Already,

5. I.e., pulling aside in order to yield the right of way.

6. A small two-wheeled carriage, drawn by one horse.

on the first thought, I was making my way over the roof to the guard's seat. But this, from the accident which I have mentioned, of the foreign mails being piled upon the roof, was a difficult and even dangerous attempt to one cramped by nearly three hundred miles of outside traveling. And, fortunately, before I had lost much time in the attempt, our frantic horses swept round an angle of the road which opened upon us that final stage where the collision must be accomplished and the catastrophe sealed. All was apparently finished. The court was sitting; the case was heard; the judge had finished; and only the verdict was yet in arrear.

Before us lay an avenue straight as an arrow, six hundred yards, perhaps, in length; and the umbrageous trees, which rose in a regular line from either side, meeting high overhead, gave to it the character of a cathedral aisle. These trees lent a deeper solemnity to the early light; but there was still light enough to perceive, at the farther end of this Gothic aisle, a frail reedy gig, in which were seated a young man, and by his side a young lady. Ah, young sir! what are you about? If it is requisite that you should whisper your communications to this young lady—though really I see nobody, at an hour and on a road so solitary, likely to overhear you—is it therefore requisite that you should carry your lips forward to hers? The little carriage is creeping on at one mile an hour; and the parties within it, being thus tenderly engaged, are naturally bending down their heads. Between them and eternity, to all human calculation, there is but a minute and a half. Oh heavens! what is it that I shall do? Speaking or acting, what help can I offer? Strange it is, and to a mere auditor of the tale might seem laughable, that I should need a suggestion from the *Iliad* to prompt the sole resource that remained. Yet so it was. Suddenly I remembered the shout of Achilles, and its effect.[7] But could I pretend to shout like the son of Peleus, aided by Pallas? No: but then I needed not the shout that should alarm all Asia militant; such a shout would suffice as might carry terror into the hearts of two thoughtless young people and one gig-horse. I shouted—and the young man heard me not. A second time I shouted—and now he heard me, for now he raised his head.

Here, then, all had been done that, by me, *could* be done; more on *my* part was not possible. Mine had been the first step; the second was for the young man; the third was for God. If, said I, this stranger is a brave man, and if indeed he loves the young girl at his side—or, loving her not, if he feels the obligation, pressing upon every man worthy to be called a man, of doing his utmost for a woman confided to his protection—he will at least make some effort to save her. If *that* fails, he will not perish the more, or by a death more cruel, for having made it; and he will die as a brave

7. In *Iliad* XVIII the unarmed Achilles, aided by the voice of Pallas Athena, shouts so loudly that he frightens the Trojans away from the corpse of his friend Patroclus.

man should, with his face to the danger, and with his arm about the woman that he sought in vain to save. But, if he makes no effort, shrinking without a struggle from his duty, he himself will not the less certainly perish for this baseness of poltroonery. He will die no less: and why not? Wherefore should we grieve that there is one craven less in the world? No; *let* him perish, without a pitying thought of ours wasted upon him; and, in that case, all our grief will be reserved for the fate of the helpless girl who now, upon the least shadow of failure in *him*, must by the fiercest of translations—must without time for a prayer—must within seventy seconds—stand before the judgment seat of God.

But craven he was not: sudden had been the call upon him, and sudden was his answer to the call. He saw, he heard, he comprehended, the ruin that was coming down: already its gloomy shadow darkened above him; and already he was measuring his strength to deal with it. Ah! what a vulgar thing does courage seem when we see nations buying it and selling it for a shilling a day:[8] ah! what a sublime thing does courage seem when some fearful summons on the great deeps of life carries a man, as if running before a hurricane, up to the giddy crest of some tumultuous crisis from which lie two courses, and a voice says to him audibly, "One way lies hope; take the other, and mourn forever!" How grand a triumph if, even then, amidst the raving of all around him, and the frenzy of the danger, the man is able to confront his situation—is able to retire for a moment into solitude with God, and to seek his counsel from *Him!*

For seven seconds, it might be, of his seventy, the stranger settled his countenance steadfastly upon us, as if to search and value every element in the conflict before him. For five seconds more of his seventy he sat immovably, like one that mused on some great purpose. For five more, perhaps, he sat with eyes upraised, like one that prayed in sorrow, under some extremity of doubt, for light that should guide him to the better choice. Then suddenly he rose; stood upright; and, by a powerful strain upon the reins, raising his horse's forefeet from the ground, he slewed him round on the pivot of his hind legs, so as to plant the little equipage in a position nearly at right angles to ours. Thus far his condition was not improved; except as a first step had been taken towards the possibility of a second. If no more were done, nothing was done; for the little carriage still occupied the very center of our path, though in an altered direction. Yet even now it may not be too late: fifteen of the seventy seconds may still be unexhausted; and one almighty bound may avail to clear the ground. Hurry, then, hurry! for the flying moments—*they* hurry. Oh, hurry, hurry, my brave young man! for the cruel hoofs of our horses—*they* also hurry! Fast are the flying moments, faster are the hoofs of our horses. But fear

8. **The daily pay of the English soldier.**

not for *him*, if human energy can suffice; faithful was he that drove to his terrific duty; faithful was the horse to *his* command. One blow, one impulse given with voice and hand, by the stranger, one rush from the horse, one bound as if in the act of rising to a fence, landed the docile creature's forefeet upon the crown or arching center of the road. The larger half of the little equipage had then cleared our over-towering shadow: *that* was evident even to my own agitated sight. But it mattered little that one wreck should float off in safety if upon the wreck that perished were embarked the human freightage. The rear part of the carriage—was *that* certainly beyond the line of absolute ruin? What power could answer the question? Glance of eye, thought of man, wing of angel, which of these had speed enough to sweep between the question and the answer, and divide the one from the other? Light does not tread upon the steps of light more indivisibly than did our all-conquering arrival upon the escaping efforts of the gig. *That* must the young man have felt too plainly. His back was now turned to us; not by sight could he any longer communicate with the peril; but, by the dreadful rattle of our hardness, too truly had his ear been instructed that all was finished as regarded any effort of *his*. Already in resignation he had rested from his struggle; and perhaps in his heart he was whispering, "Father, which art in heaven, do Thou finish above what I on earth have attempted." Faster than ever millrace we ran past them in our inexorable flight. Oh, raving of hurricanes that must have sounded in their young ears at the moment of our transit! Even in that moment the thunder of collision spoke aloud. Either with the swingle-bar,[9] or with the haunch of our near leader, we had struck the off wheel of the little gig; which stood rather obliquely, and not quite so far advanced as to be accurately parallel with the nearwheel. The blow, from the fury of our passage, resounded terrifically. I rose in horror, to gaze upon the ruins we might have caused. From my elevated station I looked down, and looked back upon the scene; which in a moment told its own tale, and wrote all its records on my heart forever.

Here was the map of the passion[10] that now had finished. The horse was planted immovably, with his forefeet upon the paved crest of the central road. He of the whole party might be supposed untouched by the passion of death. The little cany carriage—partly, perhaps, from the violent torsion of the wheels in its recent movement, partly from the thundering blow we had given to it—as if it sympathized with human horror, was all alive with tremblings and shiverings. The young man trembled not, nor shivered. He sat like a rock. But *his* was the steadiness of agitation frozen into rest by horror. As yet he dared not to look round; for he knew that, if anything remained to do, by him it could no longer be done. And

9. The swinging bar to which the traces of a harness are fastened.
10. In the old sense: suffering. De Quincey means to suggest Christ's passion on the cross, preparatory to the concluding section of the fugue.

as yet he knew not for certain if their safety were accomplished. But the lady——

But the lady——! Oh, heavens! will that spectacle ever depart from my dreams, as she rose and sank upon her seat, sank and rose, threw up her arms wildly to heaven, clutched at some visionary object in the air, fainting, praying, raving, despairing? Figure to yourself, reader, the elements of the case; suffer me to recall before your mind the circumstances of that unparalleled situation. From the silence and deep peace of this saintly summer night—from the pathetic blending of this sweet moonlight, dawnlight, dreamlight—from the manly tenderness of this flattering, whispering, murmuring love—suddenly as from the woods and fields—suddenly as from the chambers of the air opening in revelation—suddenly as from the ground yawning at her feet, leaped upon her, with the flashing of cataracts, Death the crowned phantom, with all the equipage of his terrors, and the tiger roar of his voice.

The moments were numbered; the strife was finished; the vision was closed. In the twinkling of an eye, our flying horses had carried us to the termination of the umbrageous aisle; at the right angles we wheeled into our former direction; the turn of the road carried the scene out of my eyes in an instant, and swept it into my dreams forever.

III. *Dream-Fugue Founded on the Preceding Theme of Sudden Death*

> *Whence the sound*
> *Of instruments, that made melodious chime,*
> *Was heard, of harp and organ; and who moved*
> *Their stops and chords was seen; his volant[11] touch*
> *Instinct through all proportions, low and high,*
> *Fled and pursued transverse the resonant fugue.*
> PARADISE LOST XI. 558–63.

TUMULTUOSISSIMAMENTE[1]

Passion of sudden death! that once in youth I read and interpreted by the shadows of thy averted signs![2]—rapture of panic taking the shape (which amongst tombs in churches I have seen) of woman bursting her sepulchral bonds—of woman's Ionic[3] form bending forward from the ruins of her grave with arching foot, with eyes upraised, with clasped adoring hands—waiting, watching, trembling, praying for the trumpet's call to rise from dust forever! Ah, vision too fearful of shuddering humanity on the brink of almighty abysses!—vision that didst start back, that didst reel away, like a shriveling scroll from before the wrath of fire racing on the wings of the wind! Epilepsy so brief of horror, wherefore is it that thou canst not die? Passing so suddenly into darkness, wherefore is it

11. Flying.
1. "Very tumultuously"—in imitation of a composer's instruction to the performer of a piece of music.
2. In a note De Quincey reminds us that he interpreted the lady's agony from her gestures alone, "never once catching the lady's full face, and even her profile imperfectly."
3. Graceful; from the Greek Ionic column, which is more graceful and feminine than the heavier Doric.

that still thou sheddest thy sad funeral blights upon the gorgeous mosaics of dreams? Fragment of music too passionate, heard once, and heard no more, what aileth thee, that thy deep rolling chords come up at intervals through all the worlds of sleep, and after forty years have lost no element of horror?

1

Lo, it is summer—almighty summer! The everlasting gates of life and summer are thrown open wide; and on the ocean, tranquil and verdant as a savannah, the unknown lady from the dreadful vision and I myself are floating—she upon a fairy pinnace,[4] and I upon an English three-decker. Both of us are wooing gales of festal happiness within the domain of our common country, within that ancient watery park, within the pathless chase of ocean, where England takes her pleasure as a huntress through winter and summer, from the rising to the setting sun. Ah, what a wilderness of floral beauty was hidden, or was suddenly revealed, upon the tropic islands through which the pinnace moved! And upon her deck what a bevy of human flowers: young women how lovely, young men how noble, that were dancing together, and slowly drifting towards *us* amidst music and incense, amidst blossoms from forests and gorgeous corymbi[5] from vintages, amidst natural caroling, and the echoes of sweet girlish laughter. Slowly the pinnace nears us, gaily she hails us, and silently she disappears beneath the shadow of our mighty bows. But then, as at some signal from heaven, the music, and the carols, and the sweet echoing of girlish laughter— all are hushed. What evil has smitten the pinnace, meeting or overtaking her? Did ruin to our friends couch within our own dreadful shadow? Was our shadow the shadow of death? I looked over the bow for an answer, and, behold! the pinnace was dismantled; the revel and the revelers were found no more; the glory of the vintage was dust; and the forests with their beauty were left without a witness upon the seas. "But where," and I turned to our crew— "where are the lovely women that danced beneath the awning of flowers and clustering corymbi? Whither have fled the noble young men that danced with *them?*" Answer there was none. But suddenly the man at the masthead, whose countenance darkened with alarm, cried out, "Sail on the weather beam![6] Down she comes upon us: in seventy seconds she also will founder."

2

I looked to the weather side, and the summer had departed. The sea was rocking, and shaken with gathering wrath. Upon its surface sat mighty mists, which grouped themselves into arches and long cathedral aisles. Down one of these, with the fiery pace of a quarrel[7] from a crossbow, ran a frigate right athwart our course. "Are they mad?" some voice exclaimed from our deck. "Do they woo their

---

4. A light sailing vessel.
5. Clusters of grapes or other fruits.
6. To windward, at right angles to the
ship.
7. The square-headed arrow for a crossbow.

ruin?" But in a moment, as she was close upon us, some impulse of a heady current[8] or local vortex gave a wheeling bias to her course, and off she forged without a shock. As she ran past us, high aloft amongst the shrouds[9] stood the lady of the pinnace. The deeps opened ahead in malice to receive her, towering surges of foam ran after her, the billows were fierce to catch her. But far away she was borne into desert spaces of the sea: whilst still by sight I followed her, as she ran before the howling gale, chased by angry sea birds and by maddening billows; still I saw her, as at the moment when she ran past us, standing amongst the shrouds, with her white draperies streaming before the wind. There she stood, with hair disheveled, one hand clutched amongst the tackling—rising, sinking, fluttering, trembling, praying; there for leagues I saw her as she stood, raising at intervals one hand to heaven, amidst the fiery crests of the pursuing waves and the raving of the storm; until at last, upon a sound from afar of malicious laughter and mockery, all was hidden forever in driving showers; and afterwards, but when I know not, nor how,

3

Sweet funeral bells from some incalculable distance, wailing over the dead that die before the dawn, awakened me as I slept in a boat moored to some familiar shore. The morning twilight even then was breaking; and, by the dusky revelations which it spread, I saw a girl, adorned with a garland of white roses about her head for some great festival, running along the solitary strand in extremity of haste. Her running was the running of panic; and often she looked back as to some dreadful enemy in the rear. But, when I leaped ashore, and followed on her steps to warn her of a peril in front, alas! from me she fled as from another peril, and vainly I shouted to her of quicksands that lay ahead. Faster and faster she ran; round a promontory of rocks she wheeled out of sight; in an instant I also wheeled round it, but only to see the treacherous sands gathering above her head. Already her person was buried; only the fair young head and the diadem of white roses around it were still visible to the pitying heavens; and, last of all, was visible one white marble arm. I saw by the early twilight this fair young head, as it was sinking down to darkness—saw this marble arm, as it rose above her head and her treacherous grave, tossing, faltering, rising, clutching, as at some false deceiving hand stretched out from the clouds—saw this marble arm uttering her dying hope, and then uttering her dying despair. The head, the diadem, the arm—these all had sunk; at last over these also the cruel quicksand had closed; and no memorial of the fair young girl remained on earth, except my own solitary tears, and the funeral bells from the desert seas, that, rising again more softly, sang a requiem over the grave

8. A current directly opposed to a ship's course. 9. The ropes attached to the top of a mast which help to support it.

of the buried child, and over her blighted dawn.

I sat, and wept in secret the tears that men have ever given to the memory of those that died before the dawn, and by the treachery of earth, our mother. But suddenly the tears and funeral bells were hushed by a shout as of many nations, and by a roar as from some great king's artillery, advancing rapidly along the valleys, and heard afar by echoes from the mountains. "Hush!" I said, as I bent my ear earthwards to listen—"hush!—this either is the very anarchy of strife, or else"—and then I listened more profoundly, and whispered as I raised my head—"or else, oh heavens! it is *victory* that is final, victory that swallows up all strife."

4

Immediately, in trance, I was carried over land and sea to some distant kingdom, and placed upon a triumphal car, amongst companions crowned with laurel. The darkness of gathering midnight, brooding over all the land, hid from us the mighty crowds that were weaving restlessly about ourselves as a center: we heard them, but saw them not. Tidings had arrived, within an hour, of a grandeur that measured itself against centuries; too full of pathos they were, too full of joy, to utter themselves by other language than by tears, by restless anthems, and *Te Deums*[1] reverberated from the choirs and orchestras of earth. These tidings we that sat upon the laureled car had it for our privilege to publish amongst all nations. And already, by signs audible through the darkness, by snortings and tramplings, our angry horses, that knew no fear of fleshly weariness, upbraided us with delay. Wherefore *was* it that we delayed? We waited for a secret word, that should bear witness to the hope of nations as now accomplished for ever. At midnight the secret word arrived; which word was—*Waterloo and Recovered Christendom!* The dreadful word shone by its own light; before us it went; high above our leaders' heads it rode, and spread a golden light over the paths which we traversed. Every city, at the presence of the secret word, threw open its gates. The rivers were conscious as we crossed. All the forests, as we ran along their margins, shivered in homage to the secret word. And the darkness comprehended it.[2]

Two hours after midnight we approached a mighty Minster.[3] Its gates, which rose to the clouds, were closed. But, when the dreadful word that rode before us reached them with its golden light, silently they moved back upon their hinges; and at a flying gallop our equipage entered the grand aisle of the cathedral. Headlong was our pace; and at every altar, in the little chapels and oratories to the right hand and left of our course, the lamps, dying or sickening, kindled anew in sympathy with the secret word that was flying past. Forty leagues we might have run in the cathedral, and as yet no strength of morning light had reached us, when before us we

1. From the hymn, *Te Deum laudamus,*
"We praise thee, O God."

2. An echo from John i.5.
3. A large church.

saw the aerial galleries of organ and choir. Every pinnacle of the fretwork, every station of advantage amongst the traceries, was crested by white-robed choristers that sang deliverance; that wept no more tears, as once their fathers had wept; but at intervals that sang together to the generations, saying,

> Chant the deliverer's praise in every tongue,

and receiving answers from afar,

> Such as once in heaven and earth were sung.

And of their chanting was no end; of our headlong pace was neither pause nor slackening.

Thus as we ran like torrents—thus as we swept with bridal rapture over the Campo Santo[4] of the cathedral graves—suddenly we became aware of a vast necropolis rising upon the far-off horizon— a city of sepulchers, built within the saintly cathedral for the warrior dead that rested from their feuds on earth. Of purple granite was the necropolis; yet, in the first minute, it lay like a purple stain upon the horizon, so mighty was the distance. In the second minute it trembled through many changes, growing into terraces and towers of wondrous altitude, so mighty was the pace. In the third minute already, with our dreadful gallop, we were entering its suburbs. Vast sarcophagi rose on every side, having towers and turrets that, upon the limits of the central aisle, strode forward with haughty intrusion, that ran back with mighty shadows into answering recesses. Every sarcophagus showed many bas-reliefs[5]—bas-reliefs of battles and of battlefields; battles from forgotten ages, battles from yesterday; battlefields that, long since, nature had healed and reconciled to herself with the sweet oblivion of flowers; battlefields that were yet angry and crimson with carnage. Where the terraces ran, there did *we* run; where the towers curved, there did *we* curve. With the flight of swallows our horses swept round every angle. Like rivers in flood wheeling round headlands, like hurricanes that ride into the secrets of forests, faster than ever light unwove the mazes of darkness, our flying equipage carried earthly passions, kindled warrior instincts, amongst the dust that lay around us—dust oftentimes of our noble fathers that had slept in God from Crécy to Trafalgar.[6] And now had we reached the last sarcophagus, now were we abreast of the last bas-relief, already had we recovered the arrow-like flight of the illimitable central aisle, when coming up this aisle to meet us we beheld afar off a female

---

4. "Holy Field"—i.e., the cemetery. In a note De Quincey points out that the graves within English cathedrals "often form a flat pavement over which carriages and horses *might* run."

5. "Low reliefs": sculptured figures projecting from a background.

6. Crécy, France, was in 1346 the scene of the victory over the French knights by the English archers under Edward III; at Trafalgar Cape, off the coast of Spain, Nelson in 1805 destroyed Napoleon's fleet.

child, that rode in a carriage as frail as flowers. The mists which went before her hid the fawns that drew her, but could not hide the shells and tropic flowers with which she played—but could not hide the lovely smiles by which she uttered her trust in the mighty cathedral, and in the cherubim that looked down upon her from the mighty shafts of its pillars. Face to face she was meeting us; face to face she rode, as if danger there were none. "Oh, baby!" I exclaimed, "shalt thou be the ransom for Waterloo? Must we, that carry tidings of great joy to every people, be messengers of ruin to thee!" In horror I rose at the thought; but then also, in horror at the thought, rose one that was sculptured on a bas-relief—a Dying Trumpeter. Solemnly from the field of battle he rose to his feet; and, unslinging his stony trumpet, carried it, in his dying anguish, to his stony lips—sounding once, and yet once again; proclamation that, in *thy* ears, oh baby! spoke from the battlements of death. Immediately deep shadows fell between us, and aboriginal silence. The choir had ceased to sing. The hoofs of our horses, the dreadful rattle of our harness, the groaning of our wheels, alarmed the graves no more. By horror the bas-relief had been unlocked unto life. By horror we, that were so full of life, we men and our horses, with their fiery forelegs rising in mid air to their everlasting gallop, were frozen to a bas-relief. Then a third time the trumpet sounded; the seals were taken off all pulses; life, and the frenzy of life, tore into their channels again; again the choir burst forth in sunny grandeur, as from the muffling of storms and darkness; again the thunderings of our horses carried temptation into the graves. One cry burst from our lips, as the clouds, drawing off from the aisle, showed it empty before us—"Whither has the infant fled?—is the young child caught up to God?" Lo! afar off, in a vast recess, rose three mighty windows to the clouds; and on a level with their summits, at height insuperable to man, rose an altar of purest alabaster. On its eastern face was trembling a crimson glory. A glory was it from the reddening dawn that now streamed *through* the windows? Was it from the crimson robes of the martyrs painted *on* the windows? Was it from the bloody bas-reliefs of earth? There, suddenly, within that crimson radiance, rose the apparition of a woman's head, and then of a woman's figure. The child it was—grown up to woman's height. Clinging to the horns of the altar, voiceless she stood—sinking, rising, raving, despairing; and behind the volume of incense that, night and day, streamed upwards from the altar, dimly was seen the fiery font, and the shadow of that dreadful being who should have baptized her with the baptism of death. But by her side was kneeling her better angel, that hid his face with wings; that wept and pleaded for *her*; that prayed when *she* could *not*; that fought with Heaven by tears for *her* deliverance; which also, as he raised his immortal countenance from his wings, I saw, by the glory in his eye, that from Heaven he had won at last.

5

Then was completed the passion of the mighty fugue. The golden tubes of the organ, which as yet had but muttered at intervals—gleaming amongst clouds and surges of incense—threw up, as from fountains unfathomable, columns of heart-shattering music. Choir and anti-choir were filling fast with unknown voices. Thou also, Dying Trumpeter, with thy love that was victorious, and thy anguish that was finishing, didst enter the tumult; trumpet and echo—farewell love, and farewell anguish—rang through the dreadful sanctus. [7] Oh, darkness of the grave! that from the crimson altar and from the fiery font wert visited and searched by the effulgence in the angel's eyes—were these indeed thy children? Pomps of life, that, from the burials of centuries, rose again to the voice of perfect joy, did ye indeed mingle with the festivals of Death? Lo! as I looked back for seventy leagues through the mighty cathedral, I saw the quick and the dead that sang together to God, together that sang to the generations of man. All the hosts of jubilation, like armies that ride in pursuit, moved with one step. Us, that, with laureled heads, were passing from the cathedral, they overtook, and, as with a garment, they wrapped us round with thunders greater than our own. As brothers we moved together; to the dawn that advanced, to the stars that fled; rendering thanks to God in the highest—that, having hid His face through one generation behind thick clouds of War, once again was ascending, from the Campo Santo of Waterloo was ascending, in the visions of Peace; rendering thanks for thee, young girl! whom having overshadowed with His ineffable passion of death, suddenly did God relent, suffered thy angel to turn aside His arm, and even in thee, sister unknown! shown to me for a moment only to be hidden forever, found an occasion to glorify His goodness. A thousand times, amongst the phantoms of sleep, have I seen thee entering the gates of the golden dawn, with the secret word riding before thee, with the armies of the grave behind thee, seen thee sinking, rising, raving, despairing; a thousand times in the worlds of sleep have seen thee followed by God's angel through storms, through desert seas, through the darkness of quicksands, through dreams and the dreadful revelations that are in dreams; only that at the last, with one sling of His victorious arm, He might snatch thee back from ruin, and might emblazon in thy deliverance the endless resurrections of His love!

1849

---

7. The last part of the Preface to the Mass (repeated thrice, "Holy, Holy, Holy").

Topics in Romantic Literature

THE SATANIC AND BYRONIC HERO

Not until the age of the American and French Revolutions, more than a century after Milton wrote *Paradise Lost*, did some readers begin to take the side of Satan in the war between Heaven and Hell, admiring him as the archrebel who had taken on no less an antagonist than Omnipotence itself. In his ironic *Marriage of Heaven and Hell* Blake claimed that Milton himself had unconsciously, but justly, taken the part of the Devil (representing rebellious energy) against Jehovah (representing oppressive limitation). Thirty years later, Shelley similarly maintained that Satan is the moral superior to Milton's tyrannical God, but he admitted that Satan's greatness of character is flawed by vengefulness and pride. It was precisely this aspect of flawed grandeur, however, that made Satan so attractive a model for Shelley's friend Byron. Byron's more immediate precedents were the protagonists of some of the Gothic terror novels of the later 18th century—especially Schedoni in Mrs. Radcliffe's *The Italian*, who embodied many of the sinister and terrifying aspects of Milton's Satan—in addition to the towering historical figure of Napoleon Bonaparte, who to the contemporary imagination also combined moral culpability with superhuman power and grandeur. Byron first sketched out his hero in 1812, in the opening stanzas of *Childe Harold's Pilgrimage*, Canto I (see above, p. 297); at this stage he is rather crudely depicted as a young man, prematurely sated by sin, who wanders about in the attempt to escape society and his own memories. Conrad, hero of *The Corsair*, has become more isolated, darker, more complex in his history and inner conflict, and therefore more frightening and compelling to the reader. The hero of *Lara* (1814) is a finished product; he reappears, with variations, in Canto III (1816) of *Childe Harold* (see above, stanzas 2–16, 52–55), and again as the hero of Byron's poetic drama, *Manfred* (1817).

In his developed form the Byronic hero is an alien, mysterious, and gloomy spirit, in all his passions and powers immensely greater than the common run of mankind, whom he regards with contempt as a lesser breed of being than himself. He harbors an inner demon, a torturing memory of an enormous though nameless guilt, which drives him restlessly toward an inevitable doom. He lives according to a simple and rigid code of his own: to the one he truly, though fatally, loves, he is faithful to death, and he will not betray a trust. He is absolutely self-reliant, inflexibly pursuing his own ends against any opposition, human or superhuman, and he exerts on men and women alike an attraction which is the more irresistible because it involves terror at his obliviousness to ordinary human concerns and values.

Coleridge early recognized the disquieting elements in the appeal of the Satanic-Napoleonic-Byronic figure, and in the brilliant passage reproduced below, he warned his age against it; but in vain. This personage immensely affected the life, the art, and even the philosophy of the 19th century. He became the model for the behavior of avant-garde young men and gave focus to the yearnings of emancipated young women. Pale ghosts of the Byronic hero wander through hundreds of second-rate European poems and novels. But among the descendants of this figure we also find the protagonists of masterpieces, including Heathcliff in *Wuthering Heights*, Ahab in *Moby Dick*, and the hero of Pushkin's great poem *Eugene Oniegin*.

JOHN MILTON: [Satan]

         * * * He, above the rest
In shape and gesture proudly eminent,
Stood like a tower. His form had yet not lost
All her original brightness, nor appeared
Less then Archangel ruined, and the excess
Of glory obscured: as when the sun new-risen
Looks through the horizontal misty air
Shorn of his beams, or from behind the moon,
In dim eclipse, disastrous twilight sheds
On half the nations, and with fear of change
Perplexes monarchs. Darkened so, yet shone
Above them all the archangel; but his face
Deep scars of thunder had intrenched, and care
Sat on his faded cheek, but under brows
Of dauntless courage, and considerate pride
Waiting revenge. Cruel his eye, but cast
Signs of remorse and passion, to behold
The fellows of his crime, the followers rather
(Far other once beheld in bliss), condemned
Forever now to have their lot in pain * * *
                     [*Paradise Lost* I.589–608]

ROMANTIC COMMENTS ON MILTON'S SATAN

WILLIAM BLAKE

Those who restrain desire do so because theirs is weak enough to be restrained; and the restrainer or reason usurps its place and governs the unwilling.

And being restrained, it by degrees becomes passive, till it is only the shadow of desire.

The history of this is written in *Paradise Lost*, and the Governor or Reason is called Messiah.

And the original Archangel, or possessor of the command of the heavenly host, is called the Devil or Satan, and his children are called Sin & Death. * * *

But in Milton, the Father is Destiny, the Son a Ratio of the five senses, and the Holy-ghost Vacuum!

Note: The reason Milton wrote in fetters when he wrote of Angels and God, and at liberty when of Devils and Hell, is because he was a true Poet and of the Devil's party without knowing it.

[From *The Marriage of Heaven and Hell*, ca. 1790–93]

PERCY BYSSHE SHELLEY

1

* * * Milton's poem contains within itself a philosophical refutation of that system, of which, by a strange and natural antithesis, it has been a chief popular support. Nothing can exceed the energy and magnificence of the character of Satan as expressed in *Paradise Lost*. It is a mistake to suppose that he could ever have been intended for the popular personification of evil. Implacable hate, patient cunning, and a sleepless refinement of device to inflict the extremest anguish on an enemy, these things are evil; and, although venial in a slave, are not to be forgiven in a tyrant; although redeemed by much that ennobles his defeat in one subdued, are marked by all that dishonors his conquest in the victor. Milton's Devil as a moral being is as far superior to his God, as one who perseveres in some purpose which he has conceived to be excellent in spite of adversity and torture is to one who in the cold security of undoubted triumph inflicts the most horrible revenge upon his enemy, not from any mistaken notion of inducing him to repent of a perseverance in enmity, but with the alleged design of exasperating him to deserve new torments. Milton has so far violated the popular creed (if this shall be judged to be a violation) as to have alleged no superiority of moral virtue to his God over his Devil.

[From *A Defense of Poetry*, 1821]

2

* * * The only imaginary being resembling in any degree Prometheus is Satan; and Prometheus is, in my judgement, a more poetical character than Satan, because, in addition to courage, and majesty, and firm and patient opposition to omnipotent force, he is susceptible of being described as exempt from the taints of ambition, envy, revenge, and a desire for personal aggrandizement, which, in the hero of *Paradise Lost*, interfere with the interest. The character of Satan engenders in the mind a pernicious casuistry which leads us to weigh his faults with his wrongs, and to excuse the former because the latter exceed all measure. In the minds of those who consider that magnificent fiction with a religious feeling it engenders something worse. But Prometheus is, as it were, the type of the highest perfection of moral and intellectual nature, impelled by the purest and the truest motives to the best and noblest ends.

[From Preface to *Prometheus Unbound*, 1820]

SAMUEL TAYLOR COLERIDGE

But in its utmost abstraction and consequent state of reprobation, the will becomes Satanic pride and rebellious self-idolatry in the relations of the spirit to itself, and remorseless despotism relatively to others; the more hopeless as the more obdurate by its subjugation of sensual impulses, by its superiority to toil and pain and pleasure; in short, by the fearful resolve to find in itself alone the one absolute motive of action, under which all other motives from within and from without must be either subordinated or crushed.

This is the character which Milton has so philosophically as well as sublimely embodied in the Satan of his *Paradise Lost*. Alas! too often has it been embodied in real life. Too often has it given a dark and savage grandeur to the historic page. And wherever it has appeared, under whatever circumstances of time and country, the same ingredients have gone to its composition; and it has been identified by the same attributes. Hope in which there is no cheerfulness; steadfastness within and immovable resolve, with outward restlessness and whirling activity; violence with guile; temerity with cunning; and, as the result of all, interminableness of object with perfect indifference of means; these are the qualities that have constituted the commanding genius; these are the marks that have characterized the masters of mischief, the liberticides, and mighty hunters of mankind, from Nimrod[1] to Bonaparte. And from inattention to the possibility of such a character as well as from ignorance of its elements, even men of honest intentions too frequently become fascinated. Nay, whole nations have been so far duped by this want of insight and reflection as to regard with palliative admiration, instead of wonder and abhorrence, the Molochs[2] of human nature, who are indebted for the larger portion of their meteoric success to their total want of principle, and who surpass the gen-

1. In Genesis x.9 Nimrod is described as "a mighty hunter before the Lord." This passage was traditionally interpreted to mean that Nimrod hunted down men, and so was the prototype for all tyrants and bloody conquerors.

2. I.e., monsters of evil (Moloch is an evil idol of the Old Testament to whom first-born children were sacrificed; he is also one of the fallen angels in *Paradise Lost*).

erality of their fellow creatures in one act of courage only, that of
daring to say with their whole heart, "Evil, be thou my good!"

[From *The Statesman's Manual*, 1816]

THE EVOLUTION OF THE BYRONIC HERO
ANN RADCLIFFE: [The Italian Villain]

There lived in the Dominican convent of the Santo Spirito, at
Naples, a man called Father Schedoni; an Italian, as his name imported, but whose family was unknown, and from some circumstances, it appeared that he wished to throw an impenetrable veil
over his origin. * * * Some few persons in the convent, who had
been interested by his appearance, believed that the peculiarities
of his manners, his severe reserve and unconquerable silence, his
solitary habits and frequent penances, were the effect of misfortune
preying upon a haughty and disordered spirit; while others conjectured them the consequence of some hideous crime gnawing
upon an awakened conscience. * * *

Among his associates no one loved him, many disliked him, and
more feared him. His figure was striking, but not so from grace;
it was tall, and, though extremely thin, his limbs were large and
uncouth, and as he stalked along, wrapped in the black garments
of his order, there was something terrible in its air; something almost superhuman. His cowl, too, as it threw a shade over the livid
paleness of his face, increased its severe character, and gave an effect to his large melancholy eye, which approached to horror. His
was not the melancholy of a sensible and wounded heart, but apparently that of a gloomy and ferocious disposition. There was
something in his physiognomy extremely singular, and that cannot easily be defined. It bore the traces of many passions, which
seemed to have fixed the features they no longer animated. An
habitual gloom and severity prevailed over the deep lines of his
countenance; and his eyes were so piercing that they seemed to
penetrate, at a single glance, into the hearts of men, and to read
their most secret thoughts; few persons could support their scrutiny,
or even endure to meet them twice.

[From *The Italian, or The Confessional of the
Black Penitents,* 1797]

LORD BYRON: *From* Lara[1]

17

In him inexplicably mixed appeared
Much to be loved and hated, sought and feared; 290
Opinion varying o'er his hidden lot,
In praise or railing ne'er his name forgot:
His silence formed a theme for others' prate—
They guessed—they gazed—they fain would know his fate.
What had he been? what was he, thus unknown, 295
Who walked their world, his lineage only known?
A hater of his kind? yet some would say,
With them he could seem gay amidst the gay;
But owned that smile, if oft observed and near,
Waned in its mirth, and withered to a sneer; 300
That smile might reach his lip but passed not by,
None e'er could trace its laughter to his eye:
Yet there was softness too in his regard,
At times, a heart as not by nature hard,
But once perceived, his spirit seemed to chide 305
Such weakness as unworthy of its pride,
And steeled itself, as scorning to redeem
One doubt from others' half-withheld esteem;
In self-inflicted penance of a breast
Which tenderness might once have wrung from rest; 310
In vigilance of grief that would compel
The soul to hate for having loved too well.

18

There was in him a vital scorn of all:
As if the worst had fallen which could befall,
He stood a stranger in this breathing world, 315
An erring spirit from another hurled;
A thing of dark imaginings, that shaped
By choice the perils he by chance escaped;
But 'scaped in vain, for in their memory yet
His mind would half exult and half regret. 320
With more capacity for love than earth
Bestows on most of mortal mold and birth,
His early dreams of good outstripped the truth,
And troubled manhood followed baffled youth;
With thought of years in phantom chase misspent, 325
And wasted powers for better purpose lent;
And fiery passions that had poured their wrath
In hurried desolation o'er his path,
And left the better feelings all at strife

---

1. "Lara" is the assumed name of *The Corsair*'s Conrad, who has given up piracy and retired to his ancestral home. Lady Byron related that Byron once said, with respect to Lara: "There's more [of me] in that than any of them." Saying this he shuddered, and avoided her eye.

In wild reflection o'er his stormy life;   330
But haughty still and loath himself to blame,
He called on Nature's self to share the shame,
And charged all faults upon the fleshly form
She gave to clog the soul, and feast the worm;
Till he at last confounded good and ill,   335
And half mistook for fate the acts of will.
Too high for common selfishness, he could
At times resign his own for others' good,
But not in pity, not because he ought,
But in some strange perversity of thought,   340
That swayed him onward with a secret pride
To do what few or none would do beside;
And this same impulse would, in tempting time,
Mislead his spirit equally to crime;
So much he soared beyond, or sunk beneath,   345
The men with whom he felt condemned to breathe,
And longed by good or ill to separate
Himself from all who shared his mortal state.
His mind abhorring this had fixed her throne
Far from the world, in regions of her own: 350
Thus coldly passing all that passed below,
His blood in temperate seeming now would flow:
Ah! happier if it ne'er with guilt had glowed,
But ever in that icy smoothness flowed!
'Tis true, with other men their path he walked,   355
And like the rest in seeming did and talked,
Nor outraged Reason's rules by flaw nor start,
His madness was not of the head, but heart;
And rarely wandered in his speech, or drew
His thoughts so forth as to offend the view.   360

19

With all that chilling mystery of mien,
And seeming gladness to remain unseen,
He had (if 'twere not nature's boon) an art
Of fixing memory on another's heart:
It was not love perchance, nor hate, nor aught   365
That words can image to express the thought;
But they who saw him did not see in vain,
And once beheld, would ask of him again:
And those to whom he spake remembered well,
And on the words, however light, would dwell: 370
None knew, nor how, nor why, but he entwined
Himself perforce around the hearer's mind;
There he was stamped, in liking, or in hate,
If greeted once; however brief the date
That friendship, pity, or aversion knew,   375
Still there within the inmost thought he grew.
You could not penetrate his soul, but found,
Despite your wonder, to your own he wound;

His presence haunted still; and from the breast
He forced an all unwilling interest: 380
Vain was the struggle in that mental net,
His spirit seemed to dare you to forget!

* * *

1814   1814

LORD BYRON: *From* Manfred: A Dramatic Poem[1]

* * *

MANFRED. Pronounce—what is thy mission?
SPIRIT.   Come!
ABBOT. What art thou, unknown being? answer!— speak!   80
SPIRIT. The genius of this mortal.—Come! 'tis time.
MANFRED. I am prepared for all things, but deny
   The power which summons me. Who sent thee here?
SPIRIT. Thou'lt know anon—Come! Come!
MANFRED.   I have commanded
   Things of an essence greater far than thine,   85
   And striven with thy masters. Get thee hence!
SPIRIT. Mortal! thine hour is come—Away! I say.
MANFRED. I knew, and know my hour is come, but not
   To render up my soul to such as thee:
   Away! I'll die as I have lived—alone.   90
SPIRIT. Then I must summon up my brethren.—Rise!
      [*Other Spirits rise up.*]
ABBOT. Avant! ye evil ones!—Avaunt! I say—
   Ye have no power where piety hath power,
   And I do charge ye in the name—
SPIRIT.   Old man!
   We know ourselves, our mission, and thine order;   95
   Waste not thy holy words on idle uses,
   It were in vain: this man is forfeited.
   Once more I summon him—Away! away!
MANFRED. I do defy ye—though I feel my soul
   Is ebbing from me, yet I do defy ye;   100
   Nor will I hence, while I have earthly breath
   To breathe my scorn upon ye—earthly strength
   To wrestle, though with spirits; what ye take
   Shall be ta'en limb by limb.

1. Byron wrote *Manfred* in 1816–17. The Faustian protagonist has exhausted the scope of experience, including (it is hinted) an incestuous relationship with his sister Astarte who, apparently, has in her remorse taken her own life. Manfred, in total despair of life's possibilities, invokes the dark supernatural being Arimanes, who grants him a vision of the dead Astarte; she tells him that "tomorrow ends thy earthly ills." In the following excerpt, the conclusion of the last scene of the play (III.iv), a Spirit appears to claim Manfred; the Abbot, after having unsuccessfully tried to convert Manfred, stands by him *in extremis*.

SPIRIT.   Reluctant mortal!
  Is this the Magian[2] who would so pervade   105
  The world invisible, and make himself
  Almost our equal?—Can it be that thou
  Art thus in love with life? the very life
  Which made thee wretched!
MANFRED.   Thou false fiend, thou liest!
  My life is in its last hour—*that* I know,   110
  Nor would redeem a moment of that hour.
  I do not combat against death, but thee
  And thy surrounding angels; my past power
  Was purchased by no compact with thy crew,
  But by superior science—penance—daring—   115
  And length of watching—strength of mind—and skill
  In knowledge of our fathers—when the earth
  Saw men and spirits walking side by side
  And gave ye no supremacy: I stand
  Upon my strength—I do defy—deny—   120
  Spurn back, and scorn ye!—
SPIRIT.   But thy many crimes
  Have made thee—
MANFRED.   What are they to such as thee?
  Must crimes be punished but by other crimes,
  And greater criminals?—Back to thy hell!
  Thou hast no power upon me, *that* I feel;   125
  Thou never shalt possess me, *that* I know:
  What I have done is done; I bear within
  A torture which could nothing gain from thine:
  The mind which is immortal makes itself
  Requital for its good or evil thoughts,   130
  Is its own origin of ill and end,
  And its own place and time[3]—its innate sense,
  When stripped of this mortality, derives
  No color from the fleeting things without,
  But is absorbed in sufferance or in joy,   135
  Born from the knowledge of its own desert.
  Thou didst not tempt me, and thou couldst not tempt me;
  I have not been thy dupe nor am thy prey—
  But was my own destroyer, and will be
  My own hereafter.—Back, ye baffled fiends!   140
  The hand of death is on me—but not yours!
     [*The Demons disappear.*]
ABBOT. Alas! how pale thou art—thy lips are white—
  And thy breast heaves—and in thy gasping throat
  The accents rattle. Give thy prayers to Heaven—
  Pray—albeit but in thought—but die not thus.   145

2. I.e., Magus—a wielder of occult
power.

3. An echo of Satan's claim in *Paradise
Lost* I.254 ff.

MANFRED. 'Tis over—my dull eyes can fix thee not;
    But all things swim around me, and the earth
    Heaves as it were beneath me. Fare thee well—
    Give me thy hand.
ABBOT.   Cold—cold—even to the heart—
    But yet one prayer—Alas! how fares it with thee?   150
MANFRED. Old man! 'tis not so difficult to die.
        [MANFRED *expires*.]
ABBOT. He's gone—his soul hath ta'en its earthless flight—
    Whither? I dread to think—but he is gone.
1816–17   1817

ROMANTIC POEMS IN PROCESS

In reaction against the neoclassic view that the composition of poetry was
primarily a deliberate act, controlled by the explicit rules and implicit
principles of "art," most Romantic poets insisted that composition was
primarily a matter of spontaneous impulse, or of inspiration, or of unconscious mental processes. But as Richard Aldington recently remarked about
poetry, "genius is not enough; one must also work." However much the
Romantic poem might be unforced or involuntary in its origin, poetic
vision did not obviate revision, nor did spontaneity seem to be incompatible with selecting, eliminating, and making second or third trials, in
the very process of composing. Wordsworth, in fact, corrected and recor-
rected his writings, both before and after first publication, as much as any
poet on record: he spent over half his life revising the first version of *The
Prelude*. Byron loved to display himself in the role of the noble amateur
who dashes off verses with unprofessional casualness and bravura. But
though Byron composed very fast, and after he had fixed a poem on paper
hated to go back and revise in cold blood, his drafts show that even the
easy colloquialism and seeming casualness of *Don Juan* was achieved only
after a great deal of trial and error at getting a stanza or passage to work
out.

These selections show the Romantic poets actually at work. The passages
from Wordsworth and Coleridge exemplify revisions which were made
some time after the earlier version had already been written out or printed.
The selections from Blake, Shelley, Byron, and Keats, on the other hand,
reproduce passages from the drafts of some of their best poems, scribbled in
the heat of first invention. Here we look on as the poet—whether or not he
believes himself inspired, and no matter how rapidly he achieves a result
that he is willing to let stand—carries on his inevitably tentative and groping efforts to meet the simultaneous requirements of meaning, syntax,
meter, sound pattern, and the limits imposed by the chosen stanza. And
because these are very good poets, the seeming conflict between the requirements of meaning and of form results not in the distortion but in the
perfection of the poetic statement.

WILLIAM BLAKE: The Tyger[1]

[*First Draft*]

The Tyger

1   Tyger Tyger burning bright
In the forests of the night
What immortal hand or eye
~~Dare~~ ~~Could~~ frame thy fearful symmetry

        Burnt in
2   ~~In what~~ distant deeps or skies
~~The cruel~~ ~~Burnt the~~ fire of thine eyes
On what wings dare he aspire
What the hand dare sieze the fire

3   And what shoulder & what art
Could twist the sinews of thy heart
And when thy heart began to beat
What dread hand & what dread feet

    ~~Could fetch it from the furnace deep~~
    ~~And in thy horrid ribs dare steep~~
    ~~In the well of sanguine woe~~
    ~~In what clay & in what mould~~
    ~~Were thy eyes of fury rolld~~

    Where   where
4   ~~What~~ the hammer ~~what~~ the chain
In what furnace was thy brain

                              dread grasp
    What the anvil what ~~the arm~~ ~~arm~~ ~~grasp~~ ~~clasp~~
Dare ~~Could~~ its deadly terrors ~~clasp~~ ~~grasp~~ clasp

6   Tyger Tyger burning bright
In the forests of the night
What immortal hand & eye
          frame
Dare ~~form~~ thy fearful symmetry

[*Trial Stanzas*]

Burnt in distant deeps or skies
The cruel fire of thine eye,
Could heart descend or wings aspire
What the hand dare sieze the fire

1. These drafts have been taken from a notebook used by William Blake, called "The Rossetti MS." because it was once owned by Dante Gabriel Rossetti, the Victorian poet and painter. The first draft appears on p. 109 of the MS., the trial stanzas and second full draft on p. 108 (Blake worked from back to front of the book). The stanza and line numbers are Blake's own. Geoffrey Keynes's *Notebook of William Blake* (1935) is a photographic facsimile of the MS.

5♂ And ~~did he laugh~~ his work to see

       dare he ~~smile laugh~~

       ~~ankle~~

~~What the shoulder what the knee~~

4 ~~Did~~ he who made the lamb make thee

   Dare

1 When the stars threw down their spears

2 And waterd heaven with their tears

[Second Full Draft]

Tyger Tyger burning bright
In the forests of the night
What Immortal hand & eye
Dare frame thy fearful symmetry

And what shoulder & what art
Could twist the sinews of thy heart
And when thy heart began to beat
What dread hand & what dread feet

When the stars threw down their spears
And waterd heaven with their tears
Did he smile his work to see
Did he who made the lamb make thee

Tyger Tyger burning bright
In the forests of the night
What immortal hand & eye
Dare frame thy fearful symmetry

[Final Version, 1794][2]

Tyger! Tyger! burning bright
In the forests of the night,
What immortal hand or eye
Could frame thy fearful symmetry?

In what distant deeps or skies
Burnt the fire of thine eyes?
On what wings dare he aspire?
What the hand dare sieze the fire?

And what shoulder, & what art,
Could twist the sinews of thy heart?
And when thy heart began to beat,
What dread hand? & what dread feet?

What the hammer? what the chain?
In what furnace was thy brain?
What the anvil? what dread grasp
Dare its deadly terrors clasp?

2. As published in *Songs of Experience*.

When the stars threw down their spears,
And water'd heaven with their tears,
Did he smile his work to see?
Did he who made the Lamb make thee?

Tyger! Tyger! burning bright
In the forests of the night,
What immortal hand or eye,
Dare frame thy fearful symmetry?

WILLIAM WORDSWORTH: She Dwelt Among the Untrodden Ways

[*Version in a Letter to Coleridge,
December, 1798, or January, 1799*][3]

My hope was one, from cities far
  Nursed on a lonesome heath:
Her lips were red as roses are,
  Her hair a woodbine wreath.

She lived among the untrodden ways   5
  Beside the springs of Dove,
A maid whom there were none to praise,
  And very few to love;

A violet by a mossy stone
  Half-hidden from the eye!   10
Fair as a star when only one
  Is shining in the sky!

And she was graceful as the broom[4]
  That flowers by Carron's side;
But slow distemper checked her bloom,   15
  And on the Heath she died.

Long time before her head lay low
  Dead to the world was she:
But now she's in her grave, and Oh!
  The difference to me!   20

[*Final Version, 1800*][5]

She dwelt among the untrodden ways
  Beside the springs of Dove
A Maid whom there were none to praise
  And very few to love:

---

3. Printed in Ernest de Selincourt's *Early Letters of William and Dorothy Wordsworth* (1935).
4. A shrub with long slender branches and yellow flowers; the Carron is a river in northwestern Scotland.
5. As published in the second edition of *Lyrical Ballads*.

A violet by a mossy stone   5
    Half hidden from the eye!
—Fair as a star, when only one
    Is shining in the sky.

She lived unknown, and few could know
    When Lucy ceased to be;   10
But she is in her grave, and, oh,
    The difference to me!

SAMUEL TAYLOR COLERIDGE: *From*
Dejection: An Ode[6]

[*From* A Letter to ————, *April 4, 1802*]

'Tis Midnight! and small Thoughts have I of Sleep.
Full seldom may my Friend such Vigils keep—
O breathe She softly in her gentle Sleep!
Cover her, gentle Sleep! with wings of Healing.
And be this Tempest but a Mountain Birth!   220
May all the Stars hang bright above her Dwelling,
Silent, as though they *watch'd* the sleeping Earth!
Healthful and light, my Darling! may'st thou rise
With clear and chearful Eyes—
And of the same good Tidings to me send!   225
For oh! beloved Friend!
I am not the buoyant Thing I was of yore
When like an own Child, I to Joy belong'd:
For others mourning oft, myself oft sorely wrong'd,
Yet bearing all things then, as if I nothing bore!   230

                    * * *

Sister and Friend of my devoutest Choice
Thou being innocent and full of love,
And nested with the Darlings of thy Love,   325
    And feeling in thy Soul, Heart, Lips, and Arms
Even what the conjugal and mother Dove,
That borrows genial Warmth from those, she warms,
Feels in the thrill'd wings, blessedly outspread—   330
Thou free'd awhile from Cares and human Dread

---

6. In 1937 Ernest de Selincourt printed from MS. the original version of *Dejection*, which was a confessional verse letter addressed to Sara Hutchinson, Wordsworth's sister-in-law, with whom Coleridge was secretly in love. On October 4, 1802, Coleridge published anonymously in the *Morning Post* a much shortened version, entitled *Dejection: An Ode*, which differs only in details from the final text that he printed in his collected poems, *Sybilline Leaves*, in 1817. The excerpts demonstrate how Coleridge pulled two passages out of the middle and the end of the original verse letter, purged them of embarrassingly candid personal details, and fused them into the impersonal concluding stanza of his great *Ode*.

By the Immenseness of the Good and Fair
   Which thou seest everywhere—
Thus, thus, should'st thou rejoice!
To thee would all things live from Pole to Pole;   335
Their life the Eddying of thy living Soul—
O dear! O Innocent! O full of Love!
A very Friend! A Sister of my Choice—
O dear, as Light and Impulse from above,
Thus may'st thou ever, evermore rejoice!   340

[*From* Dejection: An Ode, *version of* 1817]

8

'Tis midnight, but small thoughts have I of sleep:
Full seldom may my friend such vigils keep!
Visit her, gentle Sleep! with wings of healing,
   And may this storm be but a mountain-birth,
May all the stars hang bright above her dwelling,   130
   Silent as though they watched the sleeping Earth!
      With light heart may she rise,
      Gay fancy, cheerful eyes,
Joy lift her spirit, joy attune her voice;
To her may all things live, from pole to pole,   135
Their life the eddying of her living soul!
   O simple spirit, guided from above,
Dear Lady! friend devoutest of my choice,
Thus mayest thou ever, evermore rejoice.

LORD BYRON: *From* Don Juan[7]
[*First Draft: Canto III, Stanza 9*]

1   ~~Life is a play and men~~
      All tragedies are finished by a death,
2   All Comedies are ended by a marriage,
3   ~~For Life can go no further~~
      ~~These two form the last gasp of Passion's breath~~
4   ~~All further is a blank—I won't disparage~~
5   ~~That holy state—but certainly beneath~~
6   ~~The Sun—of human things~~
3   ~~These two are levellers, and human breath~~
      ~~So—These point the epigram of human breath;~~
      ~~Or any~~—The future states of both are left to faith,
4   ~~Though Life and love I like not to disparage~~
      ~~The~~ For authors ~~think~~ description might disparage
          fear
5   ~~'Tis strange that poets never try to wreathe~~ [*sic?*]
      ~~With cith~~ ~~'Tis strange that poets of the Catholic faith~~
6   ~~Ne'er go beyond—and~~ ~~but seem to dread miscarriage~~

7. Reproduced from transcripts made from Byron's manuscripts in T. G. Steffan and W. W. Pratt, *Byron's "Don Juan"* (1957); the line numbers were added by these editors. The stanzas were published by Byron in their amended form.

7 ~~So dramas close with death or settlement for life~~
 ~~Veiling Leaving the future states of Love and Life~~
 ~~The paradise beyond like that of life~~
8 ~~And neer describing either~~
 ~~To mere conjecture of a devil and or wife~~
 ~~And don't say much of paradise or wife~~
5 The worlds to come of both—~~&~~ or fall beneath,
6 And ~~all   both the worlds would blame them for miscarriage~~
 And then both worlds would punish their miscarriage—
7 ~~So leaving both with priest & prayerbook ready~~
 So leaving ~~Clerg both a~~ each their Priest and prayerbook ready,
8 They say no more of death or of the Lady.

[First Draft: Canto XIV, Stanza 95]

1 Alas! ~~I speak by~~ Experience— ~~never~~ yet
 ~~quote~~   seldom
2–4 ~~I had a paramour   and I've had many~~
 ~~To whom I did not cause a deep~~ regret—
 ~~some small~~
 ~~Whom I had not some reason to~~ regret
 ~~For Whom— I did not feel myself~~ a Zany—
1–4 Alas! by all experience, seldom yet
 (I merely quote what I have heard from many)
 Had lovers not some reason to regret
 The passion which made Solomon a Zany.
5 ~~I also had a wife not to forget—~~
 I've also seen some wives—not to forget—
6 The marriage state—the best or worst of any—
7 Who ~~was~~ the very ~~paragon~~ of wives,
 were   paragons
8 Yet made the misery of ~~both our~~ lives.
 ~~many~~
 ~~several~~
 ~~of~~ at least two

PERCY BYSSHE SHELLEY: O World, O Life, O Time[8]

[First Stage]

Ah time, oh night, oh day
~~Ni nal ni na, na ni~~
~~Ni na ni na, ni na~~
Oh life O death, O time
 Time a di
~~Never Time~~

8. The draft versions of this poem, one of Shelley's most concentrated lyrics, are scattered through one of Shelley's notebooks—although apparently in the reverse order from that in which Shelley composed them. These drafts have been transcribed by H. Buxton Forman in *Note Books of Percy Bysshe Shelley* (1911). They show Shelley working with fragmentary words and phrases, and simultaneously with a wordless pattern of pulses which marked out, roughly, the meter of the single lines and the shape of the lyric stanzas. Bennett Weaver has analyzed the evolution of this lyric in "Shelley Works out the Rhythms of *A Lament*," *PMLA* (1932), pp. 570–576. The first two stages appear on pp. 23 and 60 of the notebook, respectively.

Ah time, a time O-time
~~Time!~~

[*Second Stage*]

Oh time, oh night oh day
~~O day oh night, alas~~
O Death time night ~~oh~~
Oh, Time
Oh time o night oh day

[*Third Stage*]9

[1]

Na na, na na na' na
Nă nă na na na—nă nă
Nă nă nă nă nā nā
Na na nā nā nâ ă na

Na na na—nă nă—na na
Na na na na—na na na na na
Na na na na na.
          Na na
Na na na na na
          Na na
Na na na na na ˘ na!

[2]

Oh time, oh night, o day
          alas
O day ~~serenest,~~ o day
O day alas the day
That thou shouldst sleep when we awake to say

O time time—o death—o day
O day, o death for life is far from thee
O thou wert never free
For death is now with thee
~~And life is far from~~
O death, o day for life is far from thee

[*Published Version*, 1824]

O world! O life! O time!
On whose last steps I climb,.
     Trembling at that where I had stood before;
When will return the glory of your prime?
          No more—Oh, never more!   5

Out of the day and night
A joy has taken flight;
     Fresh spring, and summer, and winter hoar,

9. The two parts of this stage—Shelley's wordless metrical pattern and his third version of the poem—appear on facing pp. 61 and 62 of the notebook.

Move my faint heart with grief, but with delight
No more—Oh, never more!   10

JOHN KEATS: *From* The Eve of St. Agnes[1]

[Stanza 24]

1 A Casement ~~ach'd~~ tripple archd and diamonded
2 With many coloured glass fronted the Moon
3 In midst ~~of which~~ wereof a shilded soutcheon shed
4 · High blushing gules ~~upon she kneeled saintly~~ down
5 And inly prayed for grace and heavenly boon
6 The blood red gules fell on her silver cross
7 And ~~her~~ white(est) hands devout

There was
1 A Casement tripple archd and high
2 All garlanded with carven imageries
3 Of fruits & ~~trailing~~ flowers and sunny corn
   ears parchd

1 A Casement high and tripple archd there was
2 All gardneded with carven imageries
3 Of fruits and flowers and bunches of knot grass;
4 And diamonded with panes of quaint device
5 Innumerable of stains and splendid dies
6 As is the tger moths ~~rich~~ deep ~~damasked~~ sunset wjngs
   ~~As is the wing of evening tiger moths;~~
7 ~~And~~ in ~~the~~ whereft midst 'momg ~~man~~ thousand heraldries
8 And ~~dim twilight~~ twilight saints and dim emblasonings
9 A shielded scutcheon blushd with Blood of Queens & Kings

[Stanza 25]

1 Full on this Casement shone the wintry moon
2 And threw ~~red~~ warm rich gules on Madelines fair ~~face~~ breast
3 As down she kneel'd for heavens grace and boon
4 ~~And~~ rose ~~with red~~ bloom ^fell on her hang togeth
   ~~Tinging her pious~~ hands ~~together~~ prest
5 And ^on her silver cross soft Amethyst
6 And on her hair a glory like a Saint's
7 Shee seem'd ~~like an immortal agel drest~~
   silvery angel newly drest,

1. Transcribed from what is probably the best known of all manuscripts, that which contains Keats's first draft of all but the first seven stanzas of The Eve of St. Agnes; it is now in the Harvard University Library. The line numbers are not Keats's.

8   Save wings, for heaven—~~Porphyro~~ ^{Lionel} grew faint

9   She knelt too pure a thing, too free from motal taint

[*Stanza 26*]

1   But soon his heart revives—her prayers said

2   ~~She lays aside her veil~~ _{pearled}
      strips her hair of all its ∧wreathed ~~pearl~~

3   ~~Unclasps her bosom jewels~~
    ~~And twists it in one knot upon her head~~

1   But soon his heart revives—her prayers (ing) ^{soon} done,

2   Sh(Of)   all her (its) wreathed pearl she strips her hair

3   Unclasps her warmed jewels one by one

4   Loosens ~~her~~ ^{her bursting}∧ ~~boddice from her~~
      ~~her Boddice lace~~ string
      ~~her Boddice and her bosom bar~~
      her
    [HERE KEATS BEGINS A NEW SHEET]
    Loosens her fragrant ~~boddice~~ and doth bare

5   Her

1   ^{Anon} ~~But soon~~ his heart revives—her praying done

2   Of all its wreathéd pearl her hair she ~~strips~~ ^{frees}

3   Unclasps her warmed jewels one by one

4   Loosens her fragrant boddice: ~~and down slips~~ ^{by degrees} ~~to her knees~~

5   Her sweet attire ~~falls light creeps down by~~
      creeps rusteling to her knees

6   Half hidden like a ~~Syren of the Sea~~ ^{Mermaid} ^{in sea weed}

7   ‹ ~~And more melodious~~ ·   ^{dreaming}
      She stands awhile in∧thought, and sees

8   In fancy fair Saint Agnes in her bed

9   But dares not look behind or all the charm is ~~fled~~ dead

[*Stanza 30*]

1   ~~But~~
    ~~And still she slept:~~
    And still she slept an azure-lidded sleep

2   In blanched linen smooth and lavender'd;

3   While he from frorth the closet brought a heap

4   Of candied ~~sweets sweets with~~ ^{fruits} and plumb and gourd
      apple   Quince

5   With jellies soother than the ~~dairy~~ ^{creamed} curd

6   And lucent syrups ~~smooth~~ ^{tinct} with crannamon

7 ~~And sugar'd dates from that o'er Euphrates fard~~
           ~~in Brigantine transferred~~
                   ~~transferred~~
     Manna and daites in Bragine ~~wild transferrd~~
             ~~and Manna~~

7a ~~And Manna wild and~~
                 ~~Bragantine~~
                 ~~sugar'd~~ dates transferrd

     argosy [in left margin]
8 ~~In Brigantine from Fez~~
    From fez—and spiced danties every one
      ~~glutted~~
9 From ~~wealthy~~ Samarchand to cedard lebanon
    silken

The Victorian Age

(1832-1901)

1832:   The First Reform Bill.
1837:   Victoria becomes queen.
1846:   The Corn Laws repealed.
1851:   The Great Exhibition in London.
1859:   Charles Darwin's *Origin of Species* published.
1870–71:   Franco-Prussian War.
1901:   Death of Victoria.

AN AGE OF EXPANSION

During the long reign of Queen Victoria England reached her highest point of development as a world power. In the 18th century the pivotal city of Western civilization had been Paris; by the second half of the 19th century this center of influence had shifted to London, a city which expanded from about 2 million inhabitants when Victoria came to the throne to 6.5 million at the time of her death. The rapid growth of London is one of the many indications of the most important development of the age: the shift from a way of life based on the ownership of land to a modern urban economy based on trade and manufacturing. "We have been living, as it were, the life of three hundred years in thirty" was the impression formed by Dr. Thomas Arnold during the early stages of England's industrialization. By the end of the century—after the resources of steam power had been more fully exploited for fast railways and iron ships, for looms, printing presses, and farmers' combines, and after the introduction of the telegraph, intercontinental cable, anesthetics, and universal compulsory education—an observer might have felt that three thousand years rather than three hundred had been crammed into his lifetime.

Because England was the first country to become industrialized, her transformation was an especially painful one, but being first had a compensation: it was profitable. An early start enabled England to capture markets all over the globe. Her cotton and other manufactured products were exported in English ships, a merchant fleet whose size was without parallel in other countries. The profits gained from her trade led also to extensive capital investments in all continents (especially in the underdeveloped sections of her own Empire) so that after England had become the world's workshop, London became, from 1870 on, the world's banker.

The effect of these developments on Victorian character has been described by the historian David Thomson. The period, he says in *England and the Nineteenth Century*, "is one of strenuous activity and dynamic change, of ferment of ideas and recurrent social unrest, of great inventiveness and expansion." And he adds:

The whole meaning of Victorian England is lost if it is thought of as a country of stuffy complacency and black top-hatted moral priggery. Its frowsty crinolines and dingy hansom cabs, its gas-lit houses and over-ornate draperies, concealed a people engaged in a tremendously exciting adventure —the daring experiment of fitting industrial man into a democratic society. Their failures, faults, and ludicrous shortcomings are all too apparent: but the days when Mr. Lytton Strachey could afford to laugh at the foibles of the "Eminent Victorians" have passed, and we must ask ourselves the question of whether we *can* laugh at our great-grandfathers' attempts to solve problems to which we have so far failed to find an answer. At least the Victorians found greatness, stability, and peace: and the whole world, marveling, envied them for it.

The reactions of Victorian writers to the fast-paced expansion of England were various. Thomas Babington Macaulay (1800–59) relished the spectacle as wholly delightful. During the prosperous 1850's Macaulay's essays and histories, with their recitations of the statistics of industrial growth, constituted a Hymn to Progress as well as a celebration of the superior qualities of the English people—"the greatest and most highly civilized people that ever the world saw." And later in the century there were lesser jingoists whose writings confidently pointed out the reasons for further national self-congratulation. More representative, perhaps, was Tennyson, whose capacity to relish industrial change was only sporadic. Much of the time he felt instead that leadership in commerce and industry was being paid for at a terrible price in human happiness. In their experience a so-called "progress" had been gained only by abandoning the traditional rhythms of life and traditional patterns of human relationships which had sustained mankind for centuries. In the melancholy poetry of Matthew Arnold this note is often struck:

> For what wears out the life of mortal men?
> 'Tis that from change to change their being rolls;
> 'Tis that repeated shocks, again, again,
> Exhaust the energy of strongest souls.

An occasional ride on a roller coaster may be exhilarating, but to be chained aboard for a lifetime is a nightmare.

Despite the industrial and political pre-eminence of England during the period, it is evident that most perceptive Victorians suffered from an anxious sense of something lost, a sense too of being displaced persons in a world made alien by technological changes which had been exploited too quickly for the adaptive powers of the human psyche. In this respect, as in many others, the Victorians may remind us of their English-speaking counterparts in America during the second half of the 20th century who have taken over a leading position in the Western world with similar mixed feelings of satisfaction and anxiety.

DIFFERENT CRITICAL REACTIONS TO THE VICTORIAN AGE

To suggest a similarity between the Victorians and ourselves (a similarity, not an identity) seems a necessary preliminary for a reading of their writings. In the earlier decades of the 20th century such an understanding perspective was conspicuously absent. It was then the fashion for most literary critics to treat their Victorian predecessors as somewhat absurd creatures with whose way of life they had little in common. Lytton Strachey's skillful puncturing of over-inflated Victorian balloons is characteristic of the attitudes of the Georgian period (1911–36). A subtler example occurs in Virginia Woolf's *Orlando*, a delightful fictionalized survey of English literature from Elizabethan times to 1928, in which the Victorians are presented in terms of dampness, rain, and proliferating vegetation:

Ivy grew in unparalleled profusion. Houses that had been of bare stone were smothered in greenery. * * * And just as the ivy and the evergreen rioted in the damp earth outside, so did the same fertility show itself within. The life of the average woman was a succession of childbirths. * * * Giant cauliflowers towered deck above deck till they rivaled * * * the elm trees themselves. Hens laid incessantly eggs of no special tint. * * * The whole sky itself as it spread wide above the British Isles was nothing but a vast feather bed.

This witty description not only identifies a distinguishing quality of Victorian life and literature—creative energy—but it reveals that the author of the passage did not admire such creative energy. In fact she felt terrified by it as if it might smother her. Mrs. Woolf was the daughter of Sir Leslie Stephen (1832–1904), himself an eminent Victorian. Growing up under such towering shadows, she and her generation had to fight back. Yet the demolishing of these Victorian predecessors was achieved by a narrowing of sympathies. As Mrs. Woolf herself says of her heroine, Orlando: "The spirit of the nineteenth century was antipathetic to her in the extreme, and thus it took her and broke her, and she was aware of her defeat at its hands."

The Georgian reaction against the Victorians is now only a matter of the history of taste, but its aftereffects still sometimes crop up when the term "Victorian" is employed in an exclusively pejorative sense. Most of us would rather be called a thief than a prude, and if the connotation of "Victorian" is narrowed down to suggest "prude" and nothing else, we remain seriously hampered in enjoying to the full what the Victorian writers accomplished. Sympathy may not be essential, but condescension is fatal to understanding.

Happily, in most critical studies of more recent date, the Georgian note of condescension has disappeared. Indeed the pendulum has swung far to the other side. In *In Bluebeard's Castle* (1971) the critic George Steiner notes how most of us are affected by images of the past which are "often as highly structured and selective as myths," in particular an image of a lost garden of Eden. For Steiner, that lost Eden is now to be located in the golden age of Victoria, "that great summer" of human civilization. "Our sensibility locates that garden in England and western Europe between ca. the 1820's and 1915." Steiner's evaluation would have astounded earlier 20th-century critics to whom Victorian England seemed not Eden but Hell.

But to revert from image and myth to history leads to a second difficulty about the term "Victorian." For a period almost seventy years in length we can hardly expect our generalizations to be uniformly applicable. As a preliminary corrective it is helpful to subdivide the age into these phases: Early Victorian (1832–48); Mid-Victorian (1848–70); Late Victorian (1870–1901).

THE EARLY PERIOD (1832–48): A TIME OF TROUBLES

The early phase has been sometimes characterized as the Time of Troubles. In 1832 the passing of a Reform Bill had seemed to satisfy many of the demands of the middle classes, who were gradually taking over control of England's economy. The bill extended the right to vote to all men owning property worth ten pounds or more in annual rent. In effect the voting public hereafter included the lower middle classes but not the working classes (the latter had to wait their turn until 1867 when a second Reform Bill was passed). Even more important than the extension of the franchise was the abolition in 1832 of an archaic electoral system whereby some of the new industrial cities were unrepresented in Parliament while "rotten boroughs" (communities which had become depopulated) elected the nominees of the local squire. Because it broke up the monopoly of power that the conservative landowners had so long enjoyed (the Tory party had been in office almost continuously from 1783 until 1830), the Reform Bill represents the beginning of a new age. Yet this celebrated piece of legislation could hardly be expected to solve all of the economic, social, and political problems that had been building up while England was developing into a modern democratic and industrialized state. In the early 1840's a severe depression, with widespread unemployment, led to rioting. Even without the provocation of unemployment, conditions in the new industrial and coal-mining areas were sufficiently inflammatory to create fears of revolution. Workers and their families in the slums of such cities as Manchester lived like packs of rats in a sewer, and the conditions under which women and children toiled in mines and factories were unimaginably brutal. Elizabeth Barrett's poem *The Cry of the Children* (1843) may strike us as hysterical exaggeration, but it was based upon reliable evidence concerning children of five years of age who dragged heavy tubs of coal through low-ceilinged mine-passages for sixteen hours a day. Life in early Victorian mines and factories was much like Thomas Hobbes's "state of nature"—"poor, nasty, brutish, and short."

The owners of mines and factories regarded themselves as innocent of blame for such conditions, for they were wedded to an economic theory of laissez faire, which assumed that unregulated working conditions would ultimately benefit everyone. A sense of the seemingly hopeless complexity of the situation during the Hungry 1840's is provided by an entry for 1842 in the diary of the statesman Charles Greville, an entry written at the same time that Carlyle was making his contribution to the "Condition of England Question," *Past and Present*. Conditions in the north of England, Greville reports, were "appalling."

There is an immense and continually increasing population, no adequate demand for labor, * * * no confidence, but a universal alarm, disquietude, and discontent. Nobody can sell anything. * * * Certainly I have never seen * * * so serious a state of things as that which now stares us in the face; and this after thirty years of uninterrupted peace, and the most ample scope afforded for the development of all our resources. * * * One remarkable feature in the present condition of affairs is that nobody can account for it, and nobody pretends to be able to point out any remedy.

In reality many remedies were being pointed out. One of the most striking was put forward by the Chartists, a large organization of workingmen. In 1838 the organization drew up a "People's Charter" advocating the extension of the right to vote, the use of secret balloting, and other legislative reforms. For ten years the Chartist leaders engaged in agitation to have their program adopted by Parliament. Their fiery speeches, addressed to large mobs of discontented people, alarmed those who were not themselves suffering from hunger. In *Locksley Hall*, Tennyson seems to have had the Chartist mobs in mind when he pictured the threat posed by this time of troubles: "Slowly comes a hungry people, as a lion, creeping nigher, / Glares at one that nods and winks behind a slowly-dying fire." Although in the eyes of posterity the Chartist program seems an eminently reasonable one, it was premature in the 1840's. More immediately feasible was the agitation to abolish the high tariffs on imported grains, tariffs known as the Corn Laws (the word "corn" in England refers to wheat and other grains). These high tariffs had been established to protect English farm products from having to compete with low-priced products imported from abroad. Landowners and farmers fought to keep these tariffs in force so that high prices for their wheat would be assured, but the rest of the population suffered severely from the exorbitant price of bread or, in years of bad crops, from scarcity of food. In 1845 serious crop failures in England and the outbreak of potato blight in Ireland convinced Sir Robert Peel, the Tory Prime Minister, that traditional protectionism must be abandoned. In 1846 the Corn Laws were repealed by Parliament, and the way was paved for the introduction of a system of Free Trade whereby goods could be imported with the payment of only minimal tariff duties. Although Free Trade did not eradicate the slums of Manchester, it worked well for many years and helped to relieve the major crisis of the Victorian economy. In 1848, when armed revolutions were exploding violently in every country in Europe, England was relatively unaffected. A monster Chartist demonstration fizzled out harmlessly in London, and Englishmen settled down to enjoy two decades of prosperity.

This Time of Troubles left its mark on some early Victorian literature. "Insurrection is a most sad necessity," Carlyle writes in his *Past and Present*, "and governors who wait for that to instruct them are surely getting into the fatalest courses." A similar refrain runs through Carlyle's history *The French Revolution* (1837), with its warning that an irresponsible English government might suffer the same fate as the irresponsible government of Louis XVI had suffered. Memories of the French Reign of Terror lasted longer than memories of Trafalgar and Waterloo, memories freshened by later outbreaks of civil strife, "the red fool-fury of the Seine" as Tennyson described one of the violent overturnings of government in France. It is the novelists of the 1840's and early 1850's, however, who show the most marked response to the industrial and political scene. Vivid records of these conditions are to be found in the fiction of Charles Kingsley (1819–75), Elizabeth Gaskell (1810–65), and Benjamin Disraeli (1804–81), a novelist who became Prime Minister. For his novel *Sybil* (1845) Disraeli chose an appropriate subtitle, *The Two Nations*—a phrase that pointed up the line dividing the England of the rich from the other nation, the England of the poor.

THE MID-VICTORIAN PERIOD (1848–70): ECONOMIC PROSPERITY AND RELIGIOUS CONTROVERSY

In the decades following the Time of Troubles some Victorian writers, such as Dickens, continued to make critical attacks on the shortcomings of the Victorian social scene. Even more critical and indignant than Dickens was John Ruskin, who abandoned the criticism of art during this period in order to expose the faults of Victorian industry and commerce, as in his prophetic history of architecture, *The Stones of Venice* (1853) or in his attacks upon laissez-faire economics in *Unto This Last* (1862). Generally speaking, however, the comfortable and commonsensical novels of Anthony Trollope (1815–82) are a more characteristic reflection of the mid-Victorian attitude towards the social and political scene. This second phase of the Victorian age had many harassing problems, but it was a time of prosperity. On the whole its institutions worked well. Even the badly-bungled war against Russia in the Crimea (1854–56) did not seriously affect the growing sense of satisfaction that the challenging difficulties of the 1840's had been solved or would be solved by English wisdom and energy. The monarchy was proving its worth in a modern setting. The queen and her husband, Prince Albert, were themselves models of middle-class domesticity and devotion to duty. The aristocracy was discovering that Free Trade was enriching rather than impoverishing their estates; agriculture flourished together with trade and industry. And through a succession of Factory Acts in Parliament, which restricted child labor and limited hours of employment, the condition of the working classes was also being gradually improved. When we speak of Victorian complacency or stability or optimism, we are usually referring to this mid-Victorian phase—"The Age of Improvement," as the historian Asa Briggs has called it. "Of all the decades in our history," writes G. M. Young, "a wise man would choose the eighteen-fifties to be young in."

In 1851 Prince Albert opened the Great Exhibition in Hyde Park where a gigantic glass greenhouse, the Crystal Palace, had been erected to display the exhibits of modern industry and science. The Crystal Palace was one of the first buildings constructed according to modern architectural principles in which materials such as glass and iron are employed for purely functional ends (much late Victorian furniture, on the other hand, with its fantastic and irrelevant ornamentation, was constructed according to the opposite principle). The building itself, as well as the exhibits, symbolized the triumphant feats of Victorian technology. As Benjamin Disraeli wrote to a friend in 1862: "It is a privilege to live in this age of rapid and brilliant events. What an error to consider it a utilitarian age. It is one of infinite romance."

In the strenuous assertiveness of some of Robert Browning's poetry one might detect parallels to the confident mood inspired by the Great Exhibition. Generally, however, most mid-Victorian poetry and critical prose was less preoccupied with technology, economics, and politics than with the conflict between religion and science. This conflict was not, of course, altogether a new one. Tennyson's *In Memoriam* (1850), like much mid-Victorian literature, carries on the religious debates of earlier decades. These debates, in their earlier form, had been generally between the Utilitarians, the followers of Jeremy Bentham (1772–1832) and the philosophical conservatives, the followers of S. T. Coleridge. As John Stuart Mill demonstrates in his excellent essays on Bentham and Coleridge, these two writers divided between them the allegiance of all thoughtful men in England. Bentham and his disciples were reformers of a distinctive cast of mind. Their aim was to test all institutions, government or church or the law, in the light of human reason and common sense in order to determine whether such institutions were useful—that is, whether they contributed to the greatest happiness of the greatest numbers of men. This "Utilitarian" test was an extremely effective method of correcting inefficiencies in government administration: the drastic remodeling of the Civil Service in Victorian England was a tribute to Benthamite thinking. But such a test, if applied to a long-established institution like the Church of England, or to religious belief in general, could have, and did have, disruptive effects. Was religious belief useful for the needs of a reasonable man? To the Benthamites the answer was evident: religious belief was merely an outmoded superstition.

Opponents of Utilitarianism, including Coleridge, argued that Bentham's view of human nature was unrealistically narrow, that man had always needed a faith as profoundly as he had needed food, and that if reason seemed to demonstrate the irrelevance of religion then reason must be an inadequate mode of arriving at truth. These anti-Utilitarians were of two types. The first were those such as Carlyle, who abandoned institutional Christianity yet sought to retain some sort of substitute religious belief—a quest that is vividly described in his spiritual autobiography, *Sartor Resartus*. Others, led by John Henry Newman, argued that only a powerful, dogmatic, and traditional religious institution could withstand the attacks of irreverent thinkers of the Benthamite stamp. In the 1830's and 1840's (before he was converted to Roman Catholicism), Newman became the leader of an impressive crusade to strengthen the Church of England. The movement he headed is known under various names including "The Oxford Movement," because it originated at Oxford University, or as "Tractarianism," because Newman and his conservative followers developed their arguments in defense of a High Church in a series of pamphlets or tracts. Whatever name it went by, Newman's campaign produced a lively controversy. When Arthur Hugh Clough and Matthew Arnold were at Oxford in the early 1840's, the university was seething with religious debates, debates that were to have a marked effect on the poetry written by both men in the 1850's.

In mid-Victorian England these controversies continued, but with an added intensification. Leadership in the anticlerical position passed gradually from the Utilitarians to some of the leaders of science, in particular to Thomas Henry Huxley, who popularized the theories of Charles Darwin. Although many English scientists were themselves men of strong religious convictions, the impact of their scientific discoveries seemed consistently damaging to established faiths. Complaining about the "flimsiness" of his own religious faith in 1851, Ruskin exclaimed: "If only the Geologists would let me alone, I could do very well, but those dreadful hammers! I hear the clink of them at the end of every cadence of the Bible verses."

The damage lamented by Ruskin was effected in two ways. First the scientific attitude of mind was applied towards a study of the Bible itself. This kind of investigation, developed especially in Germany, was known as the "Higher Criticism." Instead of treating the Bible as a sacredly infallible document, scientifically-minded scholars examined it as a mere text of history and presented evidence about its composition that believers, especially in Protestant countries, found disconcerting, to say the least. The second kind of damage was effected by the view of man implicit in the discoveries of Geology and Astronomy, the new and "Terrible Muses" of literature, as Tennyson called them in a late poem. Geology, by extending the history of the earth backwards millions of years, reduced the stature of man in time. John Tyndall, an eminent physicist, said in an address at Belfast in 1874 that in the 18th century, men had an "unwavering trust" in the "chronology of the Old Testament," but in Victorian times men have had to become accustomed to "the idea that not for six thousand, nor for sixty thousand, nor for six thousand thousand, but for aeons embracing untold millions of years, this earth has been the theater of life and death. The riddle of the rocks has been read by the geologist and paleontologist, from sub-Cambrian depths to the deposits thickening over the sea bottoms of today. And upon the leaves of that stone book are * * * stamped the characters, plainer and surer than those formed by the ink of history, which carry the mind back into abysses of past time." The discoveries of astronomers, by extending a knowledge of stellar distances to dizzying expanses, were likewise disconcerting. Carlyle's friend, John Sterling, remarked in a letter of 1837 how geology "gives one the same sort of bewildering view of the abysmal extent of Time that Astronomy does of Space." To Tennyson's speaker in *Maud* (1855) the stars are "innumerable" tyrants of "iron skies." They are "Cold fires, yet with power to burn and brand/His nothingness into man."

In the mid-Victorian period Biology reduced mankind even further into "nothingness." Darwin's great treatise, *The Origin of Species* (1859), was interpreted by the nonscientific public in a variety of ways. Some chose to assume that evolution was synonymous with progress, but most readers recognized that Darwin's theory of natural selection conflicted not only with the concept of creation derived from the Bible but also with long-established assumptions of the values attached to man's special role in the world. Darwin's later treatise, *The Descent of Man* (1871), raised more explicitly the haunting question of man's identification with the animal kingdom. If the principle of survival of the fittest was accepted as the key to conduct, there remained the inquiry: fittest for what? As John Fowles noted in 1968, Darwin's theories made the Victorians feel "infinitely isolated." "By the 1860's the great iron structures of their philosophies, religions, and social stratifications were already beginning to look dangerously corroded to the more perspicacious."

Disputes about evolutionary science, like the disputes about the Oxford Movement, are a reminder that beneath the placidly prosperous surface of the mid-Victorian age there were serious conflicts and anxieties. In the same year as the Great Exhibition, with its celebration of the triumphs of trade and industry, Charles Kingsley wrote, "The young men and women of our day are fast parting from their parents and each other; the more thoughtful are wandering either towards Rome, towards sheer materialism, or towards an unchristian and unphilosophic spiritualism."

THE LATE PERIOD (1870–1901): DECAY OF VICTORIAN VALUES

The third phase of the Victorian age is more difficult to categorize. At first glance its point of view seems merely an extension of mid-Victorianism whose golden glow lingered on through the Jubilee years of 1887 and 1897 (years celebrating the fiftieth and sixtieth anniversaries of the queen's accession) down to 1914. For many Victorians, this final phase of the century was a time of serenity and security, the age of house parties and long weekends in the country. In the amber of Henry James's prose is immortalized a sense of the comfortable pace of these pleasant, well-fed gatherings. Life in London, too, was for many an exhilarating heyday. In *My Life and Loves*, the Irish-American Frank Harris, often a severe critic of the English scene, records his recollections of the gaiety of London in the 1880's: "London: who would give even an idea of its varied delights: London, the center of civilization, the queen city of the world without a peer in the multitude of its attractions, as superior to Paris as Paris is to New York." And English energies seemed undiminished. Gustave Doré reported after a visit to England that an alderman in London did more work in a day than his continental counterpart would do in a week. Yet as the leading social critic of the 1860's, Matthew Arnold, had tried to show, there were anomalies in the seemingly smooth-working institutions of mid-Victorian England, and after 1870 flaws became evident. The sudden emergence of Bismarck's Germany after the defeat of France in 1871 was progressively to confront England with powerful threats to her naval and military position and also to her exclusive pre-eminence in trade and industry. The recovery of the United States after the Civil War likewise provided new and serious competition. In 1873 and 1874 such severe economic depressions occurred that the rate of emigration rose to an alarming degree. Another threat to the domestic balance of power was the growth of labor as a political and economic force. In 1867, under Disraeli's guidance, a second Reform Bill had been passed which extended the right to vote to sections of the working classes, and this, together with the subsequent development of trade unions, made labor a political force to be reckoned with. The Labour Party represented a wide variety of shades of socialism. Some labor leaders were disciples of the Tory-Socialism of John Ruskin and shared his idealistic conviction that the middle-class economic and political system, with its distrust of state interference, was irresponsible and immoral. Other labor leaders had been infected instead by the revolutionary theories of Karl Marx and Friedrich Engels as expounded in their *Communist Manifesto* of 1847 and in Marx's *Capital* (1867, 1885, 1895). Perhaps the first English author of note to be connected with Marxism was the poet and painter William Morris. Morris, himself a man of some independent means, was too much of an individualist to follow consistently an orthodox Marxist line, but he did share with Marx a conviction that utopia could be achieved only after the working classes had, by revolution, taken control of government and industry.

In much of the literature of this final phase of Victorianism we can sense an over-all change of attitudes. Some of the late Victorian writers expressed the change openly by simply attacking the major mid-Victorian idols. Samuel Butler (1835–1902), for example, set about demolishing Darwin, Tennyson, and Prime Minister Gladstone, figures whose aura of authority reminded him of his own father. For the more worldly and casual-mannered Prime Minister Disraeli, on the other hand, Butler could express considerable admiration: "Earnestness was his greatest danger, but if he did not quite overcome it (as who indeed can? it is the last enemy that shall be subdued), he managed to veil it with a fair amount of success." In his novel, *The Way of All Flesh*, much of which was written in the 1870's, Butler satirized family life, in particular the tyrannical self-righteousness of a Victorian father, his own father (a clergyman) serving as his model. Butler's open revolt was perhaps premature. More typical were Walter Pater and his followers, writers who concluded that the striving of their predecessors was ultimately pointless, that the answers to man's problems are not to be found, and that our role is to enjoy the fleeting moments of beauty in "this short day of frost and sun." It is symptomatic of this shift in point of view that Edward FitzGerald's beautiful translation of the *Rubáiyát of Omar Khayyám* (1859), with its melancholy theme that life's problems are insoluble, went virtually unnoticed in the 1860's but became a popular favorite in subsequent decades. The most dramatic illustration of the shift is provided by the life and works of Pater's disciple, Oscar Wilde. In Dickens' *David Copperfield*, the hero affirms: "I have always been thoroughly in earnest." Forty-four years later, Wilde's comedy, *The Importance of Being Earnest* (1895), turns this typical mid-Victorian word, "earnest," into a pun, a key joke in this comic spectacle of earlier Victorian values being turned upside down.

EARNESTNESS, RESPECTABILITY, AND THE EVANGELICALS

Wilde's decades, the 1880's and 1890's, when being earnest was apparently not important, can be legitimately overlooked if we are trying to categorize the Victorian age as a whole instead of distinguishing the stages of its development. Why has the term "earnest" been so often applied to the typical Victorian writers? It should be noted that the quality of earnestness (or as some historians call it, more appropriately, "eagerness") was not strained. It did not exclude high spirits and humor. An age which relished the comic genius of Dickens and Thackeray, the grotesque humor of Browning and Carlyle, the nonsensical whimsy of Edward Lear and Lewis Carroll, was not exclusively dedicated to mere solemnity. Nevertheless the general Victorian preference for earnestness of spirit was firmly rooted and can best be accounted for by distinguishing it not from what came after but from what went before it.

The connections between literature in the Romantic and Victorian ages are close. Victorian poets as different as Browning and Swinburne both derive from Shelley. Tennyson is a follower of Keats, Arnold is a follower of Wordsworth, and many other instances of such continuity and influence may be cited. Most Victorian writers, both in poems and in essays, grappled with the same religious issues that had been a central concern for Wordsworth, Blake, and Shelley. As M. H. Abrams demonstrates in *Natural Supernaturalism*, the post-Romantics from Tennyson through Yeats continued the Romantic endeavor to salvage "the cardinal values of their religious heritage by reconstituting them in a way that would make them intellectually acceptable, as well as emotionally pertinent, for the time being."

A dividing point, however, may be observed in Carlyle's well-known advice to his contemporaries in 1834: "Close thy *Byron*; open thy *Goethe*." Carlyle's advice could be interpreted in two ways. The first is with reference to literary forms. A Victorian writer might avoid the wild excesses, the lack of controlled form of much Romantic writing. Byron himself foresaw that such a reformation was necessary. "We are all on a wrong tack ('Lakers' and all)," he wrote. "Our successors will have to go back to the riding school * * * and learn to ride the great horse." Some of Byron's Victorian successors ignored his prediction; they too rode Pegasus bareback as casually as he had done. Yet several Victorian poets, Tennyson in particular, do fulfill Byron's prediction. The energy of Romantic literature persists, but it is channeled into a stricter concern for disciplined forms. It is significant that the Romantic poet most influential in the Victorian age was Keats, the most form-conscious of the Romantics, rather than Byron.

Carlyle himself was not primarily concerned with a chastening of literary forms. He was saying, in effect: "Stop moping. There is work to be done, work that requires the earnest efforts of all of us." Byronism, in this context, meant the easygoing aristocratic code of the Regency, with its preference for a happy-go-lucky enjoyment of the physical pleasures of life, for hunting and hard drinking and lounging. Lord Melbourne, Victoria's first Prime Minister, embodied such a view of life and found himself out of place under the new dispensation—an "autumn rose" as Strachey called him. Carlyle's gospel, on the other hand, was soon to be extremely timely for the new generation. From 1830 on there developed what the historian Arnold Toynbee calls a "challenge." The earnest strivings of the Victorians provided the needed "response." A speech made by the heroine of *Jane Eyre* sums up these developments. After she refuses to accept a proposal by the Byronic-style Mr. Rochester to live with him and he is bewailing his lonely lot, Jane Eyre advises him sternly: "Mr. Rochester * * * we are born to strive and endure—you as well as I: do so."

A further indication of the timeliness of Carlyle's call to action in *Sartor Resartus* is its Evangelical tone. In its strictest sense "Evangelical" refers to part of a branch of the Church of England called the Low Church. In the 18th century many Anglicans had been profoundly affected by the teachings of John Wesley. Without setting up a separate church, they had sought to instill some of Wesley's ideals and religious enthusiasm into the phlegmatic and easygoing Established Church of which they were members. Zealously dedicated to good causes (they were responsible for the emancipation of all the slaves in the British Empire as early as 1833), advocates of a strict puritan code of morality, and righteously censorious of worldliness in others, the Evangelicals became a powerful and active minority in the early part of the 19th century. Much of their power depended on the fact that their view of life and religion was virtually identical with that of a much larger group, the Nonconformists—that is, the Baptists, Methodists, Congregationalists, and other Protestant sects outside the Church of England. When united for action with this large group of sects, whose membership included a generous proportion of successful businessmen, the Evangelicals were a formidable force. For this reason, the term "Evangelical" is often stretched to refer to the puritan code and spiritual zeal shared by this combination of the Protestant sects and the Evangelical wing of the church.

Finally, the term "Evangelical" has been loosely applied to cover any kind of enthusiastic concern for reform. It is thus used to describe anyone infected with the *spirit* of the Evangelical movement even though he does not subscribe to its ethical code or its beliefs. Victorian earnestness may therefore be explained partly as a response to a challenging situation and partly as rooted in an active religious movement that left its stamp on agnostics as well as on believers. Arnold's friend Arthur Clough, who became a skeptic, attributed his own persistent obsession with problems of conscience to the Evangelical revival. The movement "beginning with Wesleyanism, and culminating at last in Puseyism" was responsible, he said, for an "over-excitation of the religious sense, resulting in this irrational, almost animal irritability of conscience." George Eliot is another example of this Evangelical legacy. After having abandoned Christianity and having flouted convention by living for years with a married man, she devoted her novels to painstaking analyses of problems of conscience and moral choice. It would be difficult to name a Victorian writer of any consequence who remained an Evangelical in the true sense of the term; it would be equally difficult to name one who was not affected by what Evangelicalism had stood for.

If we also consider the puritan code of morality advocated by the Nonconformists and Evangelicals rather than their earnestness of spirit, it is once more apparent why Carlyle's recommendation to close the volumes of Byron was appropriate. During Byron's lifetime those advocating the puritan code had been a minority. After 1832 they gradually came to represent if not a numerical majority at least the most potent voice in Victorian England. And they were not reluctant to make that voice heard.

The code of puritanism and respectability is symbolized by the joyless Victorian Sunday. In 1837, a new Sunday Observance Bill was introduced into Parliament. Although the Bill did not quite pass, the Sober Sunday ritual became established by custom if not by law. To later generations, even more repressive was the puritans' standard of sexual behavior, with its intense concern for female innocence—or, as its opponents contended, for female ignorance. The history of Victorian asceticism is nevertheless much more complex than common supposition allows, as may be suggested by the fact that in 1850 8,000 prostitutes were known by the police to be operating in London. In the city of Leeds, a few years earlier, statistics indicate that there were two churches and 39 chapels or meeting houses to compete with 451 taverns and 98 brothels. For a striking corrective to the commonly accepted suppositions about Victorian asceticism, Steven Marcus' study of the sexual habits of different classes of mid-19th-century English society, *The Other Victorians* (1966), may be consulted.

The middle-class puritan code was largely derived from the Old Testament, but it also reflected commercial experience in which sobriety, hard work, and a joyless abstention from worldly pleasures paid off, paradoxically enough, in worldly success. Intermixed with this ascetic code was an insistence upon respectability—an insistence reflecting the insecurity of a newly powerful class in a fluid society, a class anxious to have a fixed set of manners by which to live and to measure themselves and the families of others.

Hence developed the phenomenon of "Mrs. Grundyism": conformity in its worst sense—that is, external conformity.

It is against this background that John Stuart Mill's essay *On Liberty* (1859) should be read. The status of liberty in Victorian England was actually one of the most outstanding achievements of the age. For continental agitators of Left, Right, or Center in politics, Victorian England was the land of freedom, an asylum where the policeman was a friendly protector instead of an instrument of tyranny. To this asylum flocked General Torrijos (whose plot against the Spanish monarchy involved Tennyson); Mazzini, the Italian nationalist; Louis Napoleon of France; Kossuth, the Hungarian patriot; Prince Metternich of Austria; and Karl Marx himself, whose major work, *Capital*, was conceived in the Reading Room of the British Museum. The Victorian achievement in religious as well as political freedom is also impressive. Atheist orators such as Charles Bradlaugh enjoyed the privilege of addressing large audiences. As Amy Cruse affirms, "no age has done more towards giving religious freedom in thought and speech and practice."

Under such circumstances, why did Mill consider liberty a problem? Mill was inspired by his experience that individuality is threatened not merely by political tyrannies or entrenched religions. It is threatened also by the less tangible pressures exerted by society itself, in particular by the middle-class conventions which weighed upon the nonconformist in society rather than upon the Nonconformist in religion. In Hardy's late-Victorian novel, *Jude the Obscure*, a novel which contributed to the breakdown of the puritan code in literature, it is revealing that when the heroine resolves to leave her husband she justifies her action by citing a passage from Mill's *On Liberty*.

THE ROLE OF WOMEN IN VICTORIAN LIFE AND LITERATURE

Hardy's heroine might also have cited a later treatise by Mill on a different aspect of liberty: *The Subjection of Women* (1869) in which he boldly challenged the long-established assumptions about women's roles in society. Although Mill's was a minority report at that date (he was subjected to a barrage of ridicule from such magazines as *Punch*), his treatise brought into focus a number of issues that had been under debate in earlier decades. The Women Question, as it was called, was concerned with issues of sexual inequality in politics, economic life, education, and social intercourse. In the political sphere it was abundantly evident that women continued to rank as second-class citizens. Like millions of working-class men, they could not vote or hold office except the highest office of queen (and Victoria was in general an anti-feminist). Petitions to Parliament advocating women's suffrage were introduced as early as the 1840's, but they did not become law until 1918. Less prolonged was the agitation to allow married women the right to own and handle their own property instead of being exclusively dependent upon the wishes of their husbands, agitation which culminated successfully in the passing of the Married Women's Property Acts (1870–1908). Previous legislation, the Factory Acts, corrected some of the worst aspects of women's employment in mines and factories, including the 16-hour day, although here the argument for reform was based not on women's equality but rather on the earlier chivalric view of their comparative frailty of physique.

To review these instances of gross inequality should not obscure how important a part women did play in shaping the life of the age. *De jure*, they seemed powerless dependents; *de facto* they often wielded a great deal of power. In Mill's view the drive for power derived from the very conditions of sexual inequality. "Where liberty cannot be hoped for, and power can, power becomes the grand object of human desire." On the domestic scene one of the ways such power could be manifested, as writers of Victorian comedy and farce often showed, was simple shrewishness. Thus when Dickens' Mr. Bumble, after being browbeaten by his formidable wife, learns that "the law supposes that your wife acts under your direction," he is astounded. " 'If the law supposes that,' said Mr. Bumble . . . 'the law is a ass—a idiot. If that's the eye of the law, the law is a bachelor.' " On a more serious level, as many a Victorian biography can show, women of character had other ways of making their wills prevail, a control extending beyond the household. Although a Victorian grandmother was unable to vote, she might exert a much more decisive influence on events than her husband did in exercising his ballot.

Issues of the legal status of women, issues that could be settled by legislation, are rarely featured in Victorian novels or poems. When novelists and poets dealt with feminist topics, they commonly portrayed women's domestic and social roles as educated companions of men or as doll-like subordinates. Tennyson's long poem *The Princess* (1847), with its fantasy of a college being established for women from whose precincts all males are excluded, was inspired by contemporary discussions of the need for women to obtain an education more advanced than what had been provided by the popular finishing schools such as Miss Pinkerton's Academy in Thackeray's *Vanity Fair*. Such discussions led, in the following year, to the establishment of the first college for women in London, an experiment later recommended by Thomas Henry Huxley, a strong advocate of advanced education for women.

But Huxley and Mill were in the minority against popularly accepted lore: "Average Weight of Man's Brain 3½ lbs.; Woman's 2 lbs. 11 ozs." In such quarters it would follow that a woman who tried to cultivate her intellect beyond drawing-room accomplishments was violating the order of Nature and of religious tradition. Woman was to be valued, instead, for other qualities considered to be especially characteristic of her sex: tenderness of understanding, unworldliness and innocence, domestic affection, and, in various degrees, submissiveness. An early Victorian guide book, *The Female Instructor*, in reminding wives of their dependent roles, recommended always wearing one's wedding ring so that whenever a wife felt "ruffled" she might "cast your eyes upon it, and call to mind who gave it you." Indeed, as George Eliot maintained in her essay on Mary Wollstonecraft, the exalted pedestal on which women had been placed by men was one of the principal obstacles to their achieving any change of status.

It is commonly said that, as a result, Victorian women, married or unmarried, suffered painfully from boredom. The experiences of Caroline Helstone in Charlotte Brontë's *Shirley* (1849) would illustrate. Living in the home of her uncle, a clergyman, she finds no outlet for her energies, and her boredom becomes so intense that she longs for death—a situation repeated, 70 years later, in D. H. Lawrence's story of a clergyman's daughter, *The Virgin and the Gipsy*. A reviewer of *Shirley* commented:

The author is very bitter against *men* . . . she speaks as one outraged and aggrieved by their contemptuous treatment of her sex. We discern symptoms of a bitterness . . . almost a fierceness—for which there is probably some good cause. But there are few women of strong powers of mind, such as the author of this book unquestionably is, who do not feel that the social position of women is not at all what it should be, and hence she speaks in her angry and indignant tone.

Yet generalizations about bored Victorian females need to be severely qualified. In the same year *Shirley* appeared, Harriet Martineau noted that "nineteen-twentieths of the women in England earn their bread." Although the millions of women employed as domestics, or as seamstresses, or factory workers, or farm laborers, had many problems, excessive leisure was not one of them. To be bored was the privilege of wives and daughters in upper- and middle-class families in which feminine idleness was treasured as a status symbol. It was this small and important segment of the population about which most Victorian novels were written, and, on the evidence of such writings, it would seem that even among this segment not all women were discontented. Some found the leisured role enjoyable, as, for example, Celia Brooke Chetham in George Eliot's *Middlemarch*. Her sister Dorothea, on the other hand, found the traditional womanly dispensation a painfully frustrating one. It was on behalf of such women that J. S. Mill's argument was developed, and it also applied to another group in which frustration was common, the governesses. Jane Eyre, reflecting that among both men and women, "millions are in silent revolt against their lot" adds:

Women are supposed to be very calm generally: but women feel just as men feel; they need exercise for their faculties and a field for their efforts as much as their brothers do; they suffer from too rigid a restraint, too absolute a stagnation, precisely as men would suffer; and it is narrow-minded in their more privileged fellow-creatures to say that they ought to confine themselves to making puddings and knitting stockings, to playing on the piano and embroidering bags. It is thoughtless to condemn them, or laugh at them, if they seek to do more or learn more than custom has pronounced necessary for their sex.

George Meredith, in his *Essay on Comedy* (1873), develops the same argument; the test of a civilization, he writes, is whether men "consent to talk on equal terms with their women, and to listen to them." Yet at least two reviewers of *Jane Eyre*, both women, regarded such proposals as virtually seditious. Margaret Oliphant called the novel "a wild declaration of the 'Rights of Women' in a new aspect." And Elizabeth Rigby attacked its "pervading tone of ungodly discontent."

Such discontent, whether godly or ungodly, sometimes found satisfying outlets in Victorian society, as the career of Florence Nightingale (1820–1910) illustrates. Many women became novelists, and by mid-century their output was prodigious. Inevitably some of these novelists were hacks, of whom George Eliot made fun in her essay "Silly Novels by Lady Novelists" (1855). Others were professionally competent and often prolific, such as Mrs. Frances Trollope (1780–1863), who published 40 books in the last 30 years of her life. A few were major artists such as the Brontë sisters and Mrs. Elizabeth Gaskell. And one, George Eliot, was one of the great novelists of the language.

THE DIVERSITY OF VICTORIAN LITERATURE

The weight of the puritan code on the literature of early and mid-Victorian England was, as we might expect, considerable. It was most evident in the novels, for novels were commonly read aloud in family gatherings, and the need to avoid topics which might cause embarrassment to young girls established taboos that the novelist could not dare ignore, although he might sometimes skillfully circumvent them. Thackeray and others offered protests, but it was not until near the end of the century or later that the novelists broke clear of those restrictions. The poets, and also the writers of that important Victorian form, the extended essay, fared better. When Browning was writing *The Ring and the Book* he was obviously unconcerned about whether his poem might raise blushes on prudish cheeks, and Swinburne's *Poems and Ballads* flouts the taboos in the manner of the French poets whom he admired. Both volumes appeared in the 1860's at the same time as the essays of Matthew Arnold with their attacks on the narrowness of the puritan middle-class mind.

Too much can be made of the importance of these taboos as literary conventions in the Victorian age. A much more significant kind of pressure from the Victorian audience on its writers, one that they were themselves inclined to comply with, was the desire on the part of readers to be guided and edified. The newly expanding reading public, despite its air of solid confidence, wanted help from its authors, and its authors were understandably flattered by the request. Only a few, such as D. G. Rossetti, ignored it; the others all exhibit, in varying degrees, an air of prophecy and mission. Carlyle in his lectures *On Heroes* identifies the writer or "Poet" such as Shakespeare with the great prophets such as Mahomet, and in his own writings it is evident that he sought to make his mark as a seer rather than as a mere man of letters. The very high status that even Matthew Arnold claimed for literature is evident in his statement that "most of what now passes with us for religion and philosophy will be replaced by poetry." Perhaps the most extreme example of a Victorian writer with a sense of mission is, however, John Ruskin, a writer who had opinions on every topic. Tennyson, here as in most instances, is more representative. To provide firm guidance in problems of science and religion, the destiny of nations and daily life, was a task that sometimes appealed to Tennyson and sometimes appalled him. As we might expect, several of his poems are concerned with the dilemma of a writer's divided duty towards his public and his art— a dilemma that has become even more acute in the 20th century as the reading public has further expanded.

The existence of this dilemma may help to explain another characteristic of Victorian literature: its variety both in style and in subject matter. Variety is in part a symptom of the Victorian writer's bold independence and his zest for literary experiment for its own sake, but it is also a symptom of an absence of any final general agreement concerning the function of literature and art in a democratic society. The writer and his audience might usually agree that instruction was a desirable attribute of a work of literature, but what was to constitute the instruction and what was the appropriate mode in which to convey it? Tennyson's poem *The Lotos-Eaters* (1842) and Browning's poem *The Bishop Orders his Tomb* (1845) were published within the space of three years. The one is in the grand manner of English poetry, the culmination of a poetic tradition emphasizing beautiful cadences and vowel sounds: "To watch the crisping ripples on the beach, / And tender curving lines of creamy spray." The colloquial speech of Browning's bishop, as he hisses his hatred of a rival, seems to belong to a different century: "Shrewd was that snatch from out the corner south / He graced his carrion with, God curse the same!" And if we ignore the stylistic differences here and concentrate upon a possible similarity—that both poems, like many Victorian writings, evoke the past of myth and history— what is to be done to align these works with other works of the same period? What resemblance is there to Dickens' *Oliver Twist* (1838) for example, with its realistic scenes of a sordid workhouse, or to Carlyle's *Past and Present* (1843) with its idiosyncratic manner of exposing the sufferings of the Victorian poor, or to John Ruskin's *Modern Painters* (1843) with its rhapsodic celebrations of alpine scenery and romantic sunsets? As a result, most candid literary historians admit that while we may confidently identify the distinguishing characteristics of individual Victorian writers, of a Browning, a Dickens, or a Newman, it is extremely difficult to devise satisfactory statements about Victorian literature that are generally applicable to most or all of these writers. This admission is distressing to tidy minds, but in itself it tells us something distinctive about Victorian literature as a whole.

What we can perhaps isolate is what Jerome Buckley calls the "temper" of Victorian literature, a state of mind and emotion already described in this introduction as an eager or earnest response to the expanding horizons of 19th-century life. We also encounter some frequently recurring subjects in Victorian literature, including a preoccupation with man's relationship to God. Also shared in common is an awareness of time, a strong sense of past and future times as well as of present time. As for quality, we have to confront another phase of Victorian variety in the very unevenness of the literary achievements of the age. Exaggerated conceptions about the writer's role as prophet may help to account for the more absurd lapses into which Victorian authors seem at times to fall. Moreover, as its interior decorating will illustrate, the Victorian age was not an age of delicate taste, although some of its poets, as we have seen, did succeed in subduing the excesses of Romanticism. In general, instead of taste and decorum, the Victorian age tended to value strenuous energy. Compared with later periods it was less afraid to risk a fall. If it seems in many respects a golden age in literature with a distracting admixture of tinsel, the roll call of some of its major authors of novels, essays, and poems remains an impressive summary of achievement. Only in drama is there a conspicuous blank, or, at least, only in the writing of plays. The theatre, throughout the period, was itself a flourishing and popular institution, but despite well-intentioned efforts, the Victorians were generally unsuccessful in creating for it plays of lasting interest (except for the remarkable comic operas of Gilbert and Sullivan). Even when major writers like Tennyson, Browning, and Henry James were lured by the popular impact of stage performances to try their hand at drama, the results were disappointing. Only as the century drew to its close did significant writing for the stage re-emerge after long absence, in the lively dramas of Oscar Wilde and George Bernard Shaw.

THE VICTORIAN NOVEL

One literary genre in particular throve luxuriantly in Victorian times: the novel. In the present edition, novels are represented by selections from Charles Dickens and George Eliot, two of the several major novelists of the age. Often the novelists confront the same issues and employ similar styles as their contemporaries among the poets and essayists (the stylistic affinities between Browning and Dickens, for example, are striking). One significant difference, however, is that the novelists for the most part do not share the preoccupation of the Victorian poets and essayists with man's relationship to God. Like their greatest predecessors—Fielding, Richardson, and Jane Austen—most of the Victorian novelists were primarily concerned with man in society and with those aspects of experience categorized by the title of Lionel Trilling's essay: "Manners, Morals and the Novel," to which we can add an additional topic—Money. Typically these stories center on the struggles of a protagonist, male or female, to find himself in relation to other men and women, in love or marriage, with family or neighbors, or with associates in his working career. Occasionally such a search may take on quasi-religious dimensions, as in the later novels of Thomas Hardy or in that unclassifiable sport among Victorian novels, *Wuthering Heights*, and more indirectly, in George Eliot's novels, with their persistent concern with the role of free will and fate in the lives of their characters. On the whole, however, the Victorian novelists were less occupied with man's relation to God than with his relation to other people.

And for the most part, the other people were the reader's contemporaries. The historical novel, as established by Sir Walter Scott, remained popular throughout the post-Romantic period, but it was a form especially congenial to the lesser novelists, such as Bulwer Lytton (*The Last Days of Pompeii*, 1834) or Charles Reade (*The Cloister and the Hearth*, 1861). While the major novelists occasionally tried their hand at historical fiction, their preference was for the contemporary. Whether the story was set in the rural landscapes of Eliot's Warwickshire, Trollope's cathedral towns, or Dickens' fogbound London, readers expected a representation of daily 19th-century life that would be recognizably familiar to them.

To satisfy such expectations they were provided with a rich fare. Dickens was praised by Walter Bagehot for having described London "like a special correspondent for posterity." His contemporaries and successors among the novelists were also skillful reporters, and most of them were more scrupulously concerned with detailed realism than he had been. Disputes about the degree of Dickens' realism have persisted among critical readers from his day to ours, but what is now generally recognized is that he was much more than a brilliant reporter, and that the heightening and stylization of his novels produce effects like poetic drama that are very different from straightforward realism. "Every writer of fiction," he said, "although he may not adopt the dramatic form, writes, in effect, for the stage." The attitude to this aspect of his writing by other novelists is of crucial importance in understanding how the Victorian novel developed. Among Dickens' rivals and successors there was a common agreement that the stagey aspect of his novels was his most glaring fault, and each novelist in turn set out to correct that fault by his own example of what he believed was a more realistic representation of life. Thackeray's masterpiece, *Vanity Fair* (1848), has to a modern reader many mannerisms of its own, but is much less blatantly mannered than a characteristic Dickens novel. "The Art of Novels," Thackeray affirmed in a letter, "*is* to represent Nature: to convey as strongly as possible the sentiment of reality." In Thackeray's disciple, Anthony Trollope, and later in the drab narratives of George Gissing, a lesser figure, there is a similar reduction of stagelike scenes and effects. In George Eliot this reaction against novelistic theatricalism took a more influential turn: she set out to explore what the theatrical writer rarely explores—the inner lives of her characters. Early in the 20th century, the young D. H. Lawrence, beginning his career as a novelist, remarked to a friend: "You see, it was really George Eliot who started it all, and how wild they all were with her for doing it. It was she who started putting all the action inside. Before, you know, with Fielding and the others, it had been outside. Now I wonder which is right?" Lawrence himself decided, as a practicing novelist, that Fielding and his Victorian followers could be as right as George Eliot, but most early 20th-century novelists preferred to follow Eliot's example and concentrate on the inner lives of their characters; and critical readers, adapting their tastes to the new mode, were disposed to undervalue Victorian novels which had portrayed man acting rather than man recollecting, or reflecting, or trying to come to a decision.

Contributing to this underevaluation of the Victorian achievement was the assumption that novels published in serial form (as Victorian novels had usually been published) must be slapdash productions altogether deficient in art, or as Henry James characterized them, "large loose baggy monsters." James's affectionate derogation is applicable to such a novel as Dickens' early *Pickwick Papers,* but it does not apply at all to some of Dickens' later novels such as *Bleak House* (a masterpiece of narrative construction), Eliot's *Middlemarch* (1872), Hardy's *Jude the Obscure* (1895), or the tight and intricate plotting of Wilkie Collins' detective novel, *The Moonstone* (1868). Serial publication, as later critics have come to recognize, did not necessarily preclude artful storytelling, and it had advantages to offset the possible disadvantages of fragmentation. Publication by installments challenged the novelist to sustain the interest of his readers; in every single number he had to entertain them or, to use the traditional critical term, to provide delight. Like an actor or public speaker, the Victorian novelist had a sense, during the very process of writing his book, of how his audience was responding to his performance. And it was an audience that offered a special challenge because of its exceptional diversity; Victorian readers ranged from the sophisticated and well-read lawyer to the semiliterate household servant. The present-day division of the novel-reading public into highbrow, middlebrow, and lowbrow existed only in embryonic form in the Victorian age, and did not become a significant controlling influence on the novelist until late in the century.

This popular genre is thus especially representative of all but the religious attitudes that have been emphasized in this account of the Victorian period: the earnest sense of responsibility, the occasional lapses of taste, and the overflowing creative energy of its writers. Near the end of his life Thackeray drew a comparison between himself and Dickens: "I am played out. All I can do now is to bring out my old puppets. * * * But, if he live to be ninety, Dickens will still be creating new characters. In his art that man is marvelous." Wrung from a novelist whose own writings occupy more than twenty thick volumes, this compliment is quintessentially Victorian.

THOMAS CARLYLE
(1795–1881)

1833: *Sartor Resartus* published in *Fraser's Magazine*.
1834: Moves to London from Craigenputtock in Scotland.
1837: *The French Revolution* published.
1843: *Past and Present* published.
1866: Death of Jane Carlyle.

W. B. Yeats once asked William Morris what writers had inspired the socialist movement of the 1880's, and Morris replied: "Oh, Ruskin and Carlyle, but somebody should have been beside Carlyle and punched his head every five minutes." Morris's mixed feelings of admiration and exasperation are typical of the response Carlyle evokes in many readers. Anyone approaching his prose for the first time should expect to be sometimes bewildered. Like George Bernard Shaw, Carlyle discovered, early in life, that exaggeration can be a highly effective way of gaining the attention of an audience. But it can also be a way of distracting an audience unfamiliar with the idiosyncrasies of his rhetoric and unprepared for the distinctive enjoyments his writings can provide.

One of the idiosyncrasies of his prose is that it is meant to be read aloud. As a talker Carlyle was as famous in his day as Dr. Johnson in his. Charles Darwin testified that he was "the best worth listening to of any man I know." No Boswell has adequately recorded this talk, but no Boswell was needed, for Carlyle has contrived to get the sound of his own spoken voice into his writings. It is a noisy and emphatic voice, startling upon first acquaintance. To become familiar with its unusual sounds and rhythms, one can best begin by reading aloud from some of Carlyle's portraits of his contemporaries which are included in the following selections. Many of these colorful portraits are from his letters, and it becomes evident that the mannerisms of the author were simply the mannerisms of the man and were congenial and appropriate for the author's purposes.

Carlyle was 41 years old when Victoria became queen of England. He had been born in the same year as Keats, yet he is rarely grouped with his contemporaries among the Romantic writers. Instead his name is linked with younger men such as Dickens, Browning, and Ruskin, the early generation of Victorian writers. The classification is fitting, for it was Carlyle's role to foresee the problems that were to preoccupy the Victorians and early to report upon his experiences in confronting these problems. After 1837 his loud voice began to attract an audience, and he soon became one of the most influential figures of the age, affecting the attitudes of scientists, statesmen, and especially of men of letters. His wife once complained that Ralph Waldo Emerson had no ideas (except mad ones) that he had not derived from Carlyle. "But pray, Mrs. Carlyle," replied a friend, "*who has?*"

Before attaining such prestige among the Victorians, however, Carlyle had a long wait. His early career is the dramatic story of struggles against narrowness of background, poverty, ill-health, and religious uncertainties.

Carlyle was born in Ecclefechan, a village in Scotland, the eldest child of a large family. His mother, at the time of her marriage, had been illiterate. His father, James Carlyle, a stonemason and later a farmer, was proudly characterized by his son as a peasant. The key to the character of James Carlyle was the Scottish Calvinism which he instilled into the members of his household. Frugality, hard work, a tender but undemonstrative family loyalty, and a peculiar blend of self-denial and self-righteousness were characteristic features of Carlyle's childhood home. The stamp of its discipline, imprinted upon him for life, can be detected even in Carlyle's sense of humor, which was highly developed yet limited. The trivial banter of London's bohemia did not merely bore him; it drove him to furious repudiations. His incapacity to enjoy the fun of Charles Lamb is comparable to his father's stern rejection of workmen who wasted time.

With his father's aid the young Carlyle was educated at Annan Academy and at Edinburgh University, the subject of his special interest being mathematics; he left without taking a degree. It was his parents' hope that their son would become a clergyman, but in this respect Thomas made a severe break with his ancestry. He was a prodigious reader, and his exposure to such skeptical writers as Hume, Voltaire, and Gibbon had undermined his faith. Gibbon's *Decline and Fall of the Roman Empire,* he told Emerson, was "the splendid bridge from the old world to the new." By the time he was 23, Carlyle had crossed the bridge and had abandoned his Christian faith and his proposed career as a clergyman. During the period in which he was thinking through his religious position, he supported himself by teaching school in Scotland, and later by tutoring private pupils, but from 1824 to the end of his life he relied exclusively upon his writings for his livelihood. His early writings consisted of translations, biographies, and critical studies of Goethe and other German authors, to whose view of life he was deeply attracted. The German Romantics (loosely grouped by Carlyle under the label "Mystics") were the second most important influence on his life and character, exceeded only by his early family experiences. Aided by the writings of these German poets and philosophers, he arrived finally at a faith in life that served as a substitute for the Christian faith he had lost.

His most significant early essay, *Characteristics,* appeared in *The Edinburgh Review* in 1831. A year earlier he had begun writing his full-length autobiographical novel, *Sartor Resartus,* a work which he had great difficulty in persuading anyone to publish. In book form *Sartor* first appeared in America in 1836, where Carlyle's follower, Emerson, had prepared an enthusiastic audience for this unusual work. His American following (which was later to become a vast one) did little at first, however, to relieve the poverty in which he still found himself after fifteen years of writing. In 1837 the tide at last turned when he published *The French Revolution.* "O it has been a great success, dear," his wife assured him, but her husband, embittered by the long struggle, was incredulous that the sought-for recognition had at last come to him.

It was in character for his wife, Jane Welsh Carlyle, to be less surprised by his success than he was. That Thomas Carlyle was a genius had been an article of faith to her from her first meeting with him in 1821. A clever girl, the daughter of a doctor of good family, Jane Welsh had many suitors. When in 1826 she finally accepted Carlyle, her family and friends were shocked. This peasant's son, of no fixed employment, seemed a fantastic choice. Subsequent events seemed to confirm her family's verdict. Not long after marriage, Carlyle insisted upon their retiring to a remote farm at Craigenputtock where for six years (1828–34) this sociable woman was obliged to live in isolation and loneliness. After they moved to London in 1834 and settled in a house on Cheyne Walk in Chelsea, Jane Carlyle was considerably happier and enjoyed her role as hostess. Her husband, however, remained a difficult man to live with. His stomach ailments, irascible nerves, and preoccupation with his writings, as well as the lionizing to which he was subjected, left him with little inclination for domestic amenities.

This marriage of the Carlyles has aroused almost as much interest as that of the Brownings. Their friend the Reverend W. H. Brookfield (whose marriage was an unhappy one) once said cynically that marrying is "dipping into a pitcher of snakes for the chance of an eel," and partisan biographers have argued that Jane Welsh drew a snake instead of an eel. Even without such partisanship, it is easy to be sorry for the wife. Yet if we study her letters, before and after her marriage, it is evident that she got what she asked for. She wanted a man of genius who would change the world. She paid for what she wanted by years of comparative poverty, ill health, and loneliness. Just before her death in 1866, she had the satisfaction of enjoying to the full a high point of her husband's triumph when the peasant's son she had chosen returned to Scotland to deliver his inaugural address as Lord Rector of Edinburgh University.

During the first thirty years of Carlyle's residence in London he wrote extensive historical works and many pamphlets concerning contemporary issues. After *The French Revolution* he edited, in 1845, the *Letters and Speeches of Oliver Cromwell,* a Puritan leader of heroic dimensions in Carlyle's eyes, and later wrote a full-length biography, *The History of Friedrich II of Prussia, Called Frederick the Great* (1858–65). Carlyle's pamphleteering is seen at its best in *Past and Present* (1843) and in its most violent phase in his *Latter-Day Pamphlets* (1850). Following the death of his wife, he wrote very little. For the remaining fifteen years of his life he confined himself to reading, or to talking to the stream of visitors who called at Cheyne Walk to listen to the "Sage of Chelsea," as he came to be called. In 1874 he accepted the Prussian Order of Merit from Bismarck but declined an English baronetcy offered by Disraeli. In 1881 he died and was buried near his family in Ecclefechan churchyard.

To understand Carlyle's role as historian, biographer, and social critic, it is essential to understand his attitude towards religion. The qualities of his prose style as well as his mature evaluation of past and present are ultimately attributable to religious experiences undergone in his earlier years. By the time he was 23, he had been shorn of his faith in Christianity. At this stage, as Carlyle observed with dismay, many men seemed content simply to stop. A Utilitarian such as James Mill or some of his common-sensical professors at the University of Edinburgh regarded society and the universe itself as machines. To such men the machines might sometimes seem complex, but they were not mysterious, for machines are subject to man's control and understanding through reason and observation. To Carlyle, and to many others, life without a sense of the divine was a mean-ingless nightmare. In the first part of "The Everlasting No," a chapter of *Sartor Resartus*, he gives a memorable picture of the horrors of such a soulless world that drove him in 1822 to thoughts of suicide. The 18th-century Enlightenment had left him not in light but in darkness. As William Barrett says of modern man, in his study of 20th-century Ex-istentialism: "The individual is thrust out of the sheltered nest that society has provided. He can no longer hide his nakedness by the old disguises."

Barrett's choice of terms here is identical with Carlyle's metaphor of the "Clothes Philosophy." The naked man seeks clothing for protection. One solution, represented by Coleridge and his followers, was to repudiate the skepticism of Voltaire and Hume and to return to the protective be-liefs and rituals of the Christian church. To Carlyle such a return was pointless. The traditional Christian coverings were worn out—"Hebrew Old Clothes" he called them. His own solution, described in "The Ever-lasting Yea," was to tailor a new suit of beliefs from German philosophy, shreds of Scottish Calvinism, and his own observations. The following sum-marizes his basic religious attitude: "Gods die with the men who have con-ceived them. But the god-stuff roars eternally, like the sea. * * * Even the gods must be born again. We must be born again." Although this passage is from *The Plumed Serpent*, by D. H. Lawrence (a writer who resembles Carlyle at almost every point), it might have come from any one of Car-lyle's own books—most especially from *Sartor Resartus*, in which he de-scribes his being born again—his "Fire-baptism"—into a new secular faith.

On what evidence was the new faith based? Carlyle and Lawrence might contend that the word "evidence" is irrelevant here. Or Carlyle might cite the religious experience itself, the moment of insight when he saw the realities behind the appearances. He might also cite his realization that all the sciences he had studied had failed to answer the important ques-tions confronting man, which remain what he called "mysteries." From this latter realization there derives what seems an anti-intellectual strain in Carlyle. He speaks often of the limitations of the conscious analytic intellect and praises instead the instinctive responses of the unconsciously healthy soul, responses which include a sense of religious awe.

The most appropriate term to describe Carlyle's central position is *vi-talism*. The presence of energy in the world was, in itself, for him, a sign of the godhead. Carlyle therefore judges everything in terms of the pres-ence or absence of some vital spark. The minds of men, books, societies, churches, or even landscapes, are rated as alive or dead, dynamic or merely mechanical. The government of Louis XVI, for example, was obviously moribund, doomed to be swept away by the dynamic forces of the French Revolution. The government of Victorian England seemed likewise to be doomed unless infused with vital energies of leadership and an awareness of the real needs of mankind. When an editor complained that his essay *Characteristics* was "inscrutable," Carlyle remarked: "My own fear was that it might be too *scrutable;* for it indicates decisively enough that Society (in my view) is utterly condemned to destruction, and even now beginning its long travail-throes of Newbirth."

This preoccupation with revolution and the destruction of the old orders suggests that Carlyle's politics were radical, but his position is bewilderingly difficult to classify. During the Hungry 1840's, he was one of the most outspoken critics of middle-class bunglings and of the economic theory of laissez faire which, in his opinion, was ultimately responsible for these bunglings. On behalf of the millions of people suffering from the miseries attendant upon a major breakdown of industry and agriculture he did strenuous work. At other times, because of his insistence upon strong and heroic leadership, Carlyle appears to be a violent conservative, or, as some have argued, virtually a fascist. That some aspects of his political position are similar to fascism is beyond dispute. The theory of democracy seemed to him to be based on an unrealistic premise about the basic needs of mankind, and he had no confidence that democratic institutions could work efficiently. A few men in every age are, in his view, leaders; the rest are followers and are happy only as followers. Society should be organized so that these gifted leaders can have scope to govern effectively. Such leaders are, for Carlyle, heroes. George Bernard Shaw, who learned much from Carlyle, would call them supermen. Liberals and democrats, however, might call them dictators. Although Carlyle was aware that the Western world was committed to a faith in a system of balloting and of legislative debate, he was confident that the system would eventually break down. The democratic assumption that all voters are equally capable of choice and the assumption that men value liberty more than they value order seemed to him nonsense. To all of us nurtured in presuppositions about the virtues of the democratic system of politics, it is instructive to confront this potent Victorian critic of democracy. But it is also instructive to observe how his political authoritarianism became intensified as he grew older. In his earlier writings Carlyle was arguing, in effect, that in politics, as well as in religion, men need the guiding hand of some kind of father. In his later writings, on the other hand, he seems to be arguing for the need of some kind of ruthless commander. His opinions about how governors should treat Negro workers on the Jamaica plantations make painful reading. As he himself said, these fierce *Latter-Day Pamphlets* had "divided me altogether from the mob of 'Progress-of-the-Species' and other vulgar." One distinction should, however, be noted. Concerning the English and Irish laborers thrown out of work by economic circumstances Carlyle writes with affectionate compassion. But toward anyone who does not *want* to work (as he had been informed was the case in Jamaica), he writes with the savage contempt of the hard-working northerner. Once more the test remains for Carlyle the presence or absence of energy.

The effect of vitalism on Carlyle's prose style will also be evident. At the time he began to write, the essayists of the 18th century, Samuel Johnson in particular, were the models of good prose. Carlyle recognized that their style, however admirable an instrument for reasoning, analysis, and generalized exposition, did not suit his purposes. Like a poet, he wanted to convey the sense of experience itself. Like a preacher or prophet, he wanted to exhort or inspire his readers rather than to develop a chain of logical argument. Like a psychoanalyst, he wanted to explore the unconscious and irrational levels of human life, the hidden nine tenths of the iceberg rather than the conscious and rational fraction above the surface. To this end he developed his highly individual manner of writing, with its vivid imagery of fire and barnyard and zoo, its mixture of Biblical rhythms and explosive talk, and its inverted and unorthodox syntax. Classicists may complain, as Landor did, that the result is not English. Carlyle would reply that it is not 18th-century English, but that his style was appropriate for a Victorian who reports of revolutions in society and in thought. In reply to a friend who had protested about his stylistic experiments Carlyle exclaimed: "Do you reckon this really a time for Purism of Style? I do not: with whole ragged battalions of Scott's Novel Scotch, with Irish, German, French, and even Newspaper Cockney * * * storming in on us, and the whole structure of our Johnsonian English breaking up from its foundations—revolution *there* as visible as anywhere else!" Carlyle's defense of his style can be tested by his history, *The French Revolution.* One may agree or disagree with the historian's explanations of how the fire started or how it was extinguished. But the fire itself is unquestionably there before us, roaring, palpable, giving off a heat of its own.

In 1847 Emerson made his second visit to Carlyle in England and recorded his impressions of his writings and talk: "In Carlyle, as in Byron, one is more struck with the rhetoric than with the matter. He has manly superiority rather than intellectuality, and so makes good hard hits all the time. There is more character than intellect in every sentence, herein strongly resembling Samuel Johnson." We should misunderstand Emerson if we took this verdict to be unkind. What he says has the virtue of putting Carlyle into the appropriate company of Byron and Dr. Johnson instead of Immanuel Kant and St. Thomas Aquinas. There are readers in the 20th century, of whom D. H. Lawrence was one, who find Carlyle's religious position, even his political position, worthy of imitation. But for most readers he survives rather as a man of letters, the inventor of a distinctive and extremely effective prose medium which can bring to life for us the very texture of events in scenes such as when a king confronts a guillotine, a young agnostic confronts the devil, or a talker such as Coleridge stupefies an audience of admiring disciples.

[Carlyle's Portraits of His Contemporaries][1]

[KING WILLIAM IV AT 69]

The old King came driving to the ground, near where I was standing: he was in regimentals [2] with a most copious plume of feathers, so that while he sat all shrunk together in the open carriage, you saw little else but a lock of feathers, and might have taken our Defender of the Faith for some singular species of *Clocker* [3] coming thither. On dismounting, he showed an innocent respectable old face; straddled out his legs greatly (which seemed weak), rested on his heels, *stiddering* [4] himself, and looked round with much simplicity what they wanted next with him. The Review itself was a wheeling and marching of foot and horse, several thousands; a flaring and a blaring from trumpet and drum, with artillery-vollies, sham-charges, and then a continued explosion of musketry and cannon from the whole posse of them, like a long explosion of Mount Ætna: all very grand.

[From a letter to his mother, July 19, 1835]

[QUEEN VICTORIA AT 18]

Yesterday, going through one of the Parks, I saw the poor little Queen. She was in an open carriage, preceded by three or four swift red-coated troopers; all off for Windsor just as I happened to pass. Another carriage or carriages followed with maids-of-honour, etc.: the whole drove very fast. It seemed to me the poor little Queen was a bit modest, nice sonsy [5] little lassie; blue eyes, light hair, fine white skin; of extremely small stature: she looked timid, anxious, almost frightened; for the people looked at her in perfect silence; one old liveryman alone touched his hat to her: I was heartily sorry for the poor bairn,—tho' perhaps she might have said as Parson Swan did, "*Greet* [6] not for me brethren; for verily, yea verily, I

---

1. Carlyle once said that "human Portraits, faithfully drawn, are of all pictures the welcomest on human walls." With his pen, rather than with brush, he himself has created a strikingly colorful gallery of his contemporaries.

A few of the following selections (all of them excerpted by the present editor) were written for publication, in particular the elaborate portrait of Coleridge; the majority of them, however, are from his letters. They are thus sketches rather than portraits—sometimes, in fact, caricatures. As Charles Sanders, a biographer, has shown, Carlyle has earned the title of the Victorian Rembrandt. But with his sharp eye for absurdities he is often the Victorian Daumier or Rowlandson. This element of caricature can be partly explained in terms of difference of age. It will be noted that most of the celebrities described were men older than Carlyle, and he had the customary determination of youth to make fun of the pretensions of an older and established generation. In Carlyle's case there was the additional urge to be irreverent in that he was a provincial in a great metropolis with the provincial's need to assert his independence of judgment.

The portraits are not presented chronologically. The first two are sketches of royalty; the others are of English writers. Titles for each portrait have been assigned by the editor.
2. I.e., in military uniform.
3. Clucking hen (Scottish).
4. Steadying (Scottish).
5. Sweet (Scottish).
6. Weep.

greet not for mysel'." It is a strange thing to look at the fashion of this world!

[From a letter to his mother, April 12, 1838]

[CHARLES LAMB AT 56]

Charles Lamb I sincerely believe to be in some considerable degree *insane*. A more pitiful, ricketty, gasping, staggering, stammering Tom fool I do not know. He is witty by denying truisms, and abjuring good manners. His speech wriggles hither and thither with an incessant painful fluctuation; not an opinion in it or a fact or even a phrase that you can thank him for: more like a convulsion fit than natural systole and diastole.—Besides he is now a confirmed shameless drunkard: *asks* vehemently for gin-and-water in strangers' houses; tipples until he is utterly mad, and is only not thrown out of doors because he is too much despised for taking such trouble with him. Poor Lamb! Poor England where such a despicable abortion is named genius!—He said: There are just two things I regret in English History; first that Guy Faux's plot did not take effect (there would have been so glorious an *explosion*); second that the Royalists did not hang Milton (then we might have laughed at them); etc., etc.

[From *Notebooks*, November 2, 1831]

[SAMUEL TAYLOR COLERIDGE AT 53] [7]

Coleridge sat on the brow of Highgate Hill, in those years, looking down on London and its smoke-tumult, like a sage escaped from the inanity of life's battle; attracting towards him the thoughts of innumerable brave souls still engaged there. His express contributions to poetry, philosophy, or any specific province of human literature or enlightenment, had been small and sadly intermittent; but he had, especially among young inquiring men, a higher than literary, a kind of prophetic or magician character. He was thought to hold, he alone in England, the key of German and other Transcendentalisms; knew the sublime secret of believing by "the reason" what "the understanding" had been obliged to fling out as incredible; and could still, after Hume and Voltaire had done their best and worst with him, profess himself an orthodox Christian, and say and print to the Church of England, with its singular old rubrics and surplices at Allhallowtide,[8] *Esto perpetua*. A sublime man; who, alone in those dark days, had saved his crown of spiritual

7. In 1816 Coleridge moved to a London suburb as a permanent guest in the home of James Gillman. Here he received visits from admirers of his philosophy such as Carlyle's friend, John Sterling, from whose biography, by Carlyle, this selection has been taken. Carlyle's visits were made during his first residence in London in 1824–25.

8. November 1, a festival in honor of all the saints, celebrated by the Roman Catholic and Angelican Churches. The Latin means, "Be thou everlasting"— the last words of Paolo Sarpi (1552–1623), theologian and historian, addressed to the city of Venice.

manhood; escaping from the black materialisms, and revolutionary deluges, with "God, Freedom, Immortality" still his: a king of men. The practical intellects of the world did not much heed him, or carelessly reckoned him a metaphysical dreamer: but to the rising spirits of the young generation he had this dusky sublime character; and sat there as a kind of *Magus*,[9] girt in mystery and enigma; his Dodona [1] oak-grove (Mr. Gillman's house at Highgate) whispering strange things, uncertain whether oracles or jargon.

The Gillmans did not encourage much company, or excitation of any sort, round their sage; nevertheless access to him, if a youth did reverently wish it, was not difficult. He would stroll about the pleasant garden with you, sit in the pleasant rooms of the place,— perhaps take you to his own peculiar room, high up, with a rearward view, which was the chief view of all. A really charming outlook, in fine weather. Close at hand, wide sweep of flowery leafy gardens, their few houses mostly hidden, the very chimney-pots veiled under blossomy umbrage, flowed gloriously down hill, gloriously issuing in wide-tufted undulating plain-country, rich in all charms of field and town. Waving blooming country of the brightest green; dotted all over with handsome villas, handsome groves; crossed by roads and human traffic, here inaudible or heard only as a musical hum: and behind all swam, under olive-tinted haze, the illimitable limitary ocean of London, with its domes and steeples definite in the sun, big Paul's and the many memories attached to it hanging high over all. Nowhere, of its kind, could you see a grander prospect on a bright summer day, with the set of the air going southward,—southward, and so draping with the city-smoke not *you* but the city. Here for hours would Coleridge talk, concerning all conceivable or inconceivable things; and liked nothing better than to have an intelligent, or failing that, even a silent and patient human listener. He distinguished himself to all that ever heard him as at least the most surprising talker extant in this world,— and to some small minority, by no means to all, as the most excellent.

The good man, he was now getting old, towards sixty perhaps; and gave you the idea of a life that had been full of sufferings; a life heavy-laden, half-vanquished, still swimming painfully in seas of manifold physical and other bewilderment. Brow and head were round, and of massive weight, but the face was flabby and irresolute. The deep eyes, of a light hazel, were as full of sorrow as of inspiration; confused pain looked mildly from them, as in a kind of mild astonishment. The whole figure and air, good and amiable otherwise, might be called flabby and irresolute; expressive of weakness

9. An oriental magician or sorcerer.
1. An oracle in Greece. Prophecies were voiced by priests who interpreted the rustling sounds made by oak leaves stirred by the wind.

under possibility of strength. He hung loosely on his limbs, with knees bent, and stooping attitude; in walking, he rather shuffled than decisively stept; and a lady once remarked, he never could fix which side of the garden walk would suit him best, but continually shifted, in corkscrew fashion, and kept trying both. A heavy-laden, high-aspiring and surely much-suffering man. His voice, naturally soft and good, had contracted itself into a plaintive snuffle and singsong; he spoke as if preaching,—you would have said, preaching earnestly and also hopelessly the weightiest things. I still recollect his "object" and "subject," terms of continual recurrence in the Kantean province; and how he sang and snuffled them into "om-m-mject" and "sum-m-mject," with a kind of solemn shake or quaver, as he rolled along. No talk, in his century or in any other, could be more surprising. * * *

Nothing could be more copious than his talk; and furthermore it was always, virtually or literally, of the nature of a monologue; suffering no interruption, however reverent; hastily putting aside all foreign additions, annotations, or most ingenuous desires for elucidation, as well-meant superfluities which would never do. Besides, it was talk not flowing anywhither like a river, but spreading everywhither in inextricable currents and regurgitations like a lake or sea; terribly deficient in definite goal or aim, nay often in logical intelligibility; *what* you were to believe or do, on any earthly or heavenly thing, obstinately refusing to appear from it. So that, most times, you felt logically lost; swamped near to drowning in this tide of ingenious vocables, spreading out boundless as if to submerge the world.

To sit as a passive bucket and be pumped into, whether you consent or not, can in the long-run be exhilarating to no creature; how eloquent soever the flood of utterance that is descending. But if it be withal a confused unintelligible flood of utterance, threatening to submerge all known landmarks of thought, and drown the world and you!—I have heard Coleridge talk, with eager musical energy, two stricken hours, his face radiant and moist, and communicate no meaning whatsoever to any individual of his hearers,—certain of whom, I for one, still kept eagerly listening in hope; the most had long before given up, and formed (if the room were large enough) secondary humming groups of their own. He began anywhere: you put some question to him, made some suggestive observation: instead of answering this, or decidedly setting out towards answer of it, he would accumulate formidable apparatus, logical swim-bladders, transcendental life-preservers and other precautionary and vehiculatory gear, for setting out; perhaps did at last get under way, —but was swiftly solicited, turned aside by the glance of some radiant new game on this hand or that, into new courses; and ever into new; and before long into all the Universe, where it was uncertain what game you would catch, or whether any.

His talk, alas, was distinguished, like himself, by irresolution: it disliked to be troubled with conditions, abstinences, definite fulfilments;—loved to wander at its own sweet will, and make its auditor and his claims and humble wishes a mere passive bucket for itself! He had knowledge about many things and topics, much curious reading; but generally all topics led him, after a pass or two, into the high seas of theosophic philosophy, the hazy infinitude of Kantean transcendentalism, with its "sum-m-mjects" and "om-m-mjects." Sad enough; for with such indolent impatience of the claims and ignorances of others, he had not the least talent for explaining this or anything unknown to them; and you swam and fluttered in the mistiest wide unintelligible deluge of things, for most part in a rather profitless uncomfortable manner.

Glorious islets, too, I have seen rise out of the haze; but they were few, and soon swallowed in the general element again. Balmy sunny islets, islets of the blest and the intelligible:—on which occasions those secondary humming groups would all cease humming, and hang breathless upon the eloquent words; till once your islet got wrapt in the mist again, and they could recommence humming. * * * Coleridge was not without what talkers call wit, and there were touches of prickly sarcasm in him, contemptuous enough of the world and its idols and popular dignitaries; he had traits even of poetic humour: but in general he seemed deficient in laughter; or indeed in sympathy for concrete human things either on the sunny or on the stormy side. One right peal of concrete laughter at some convicted flesh-and-blood absurdity, one burst of noble indignation at some injustice or depravity, rubbing elbows with us on this solid Earth, how strange would it have been in that Kantean haze-world, and how infinitely cheering amid its vacant air-castles and dim-melting ghosts and shadows! None such ever came. His life had been an abstract thinking and dreaming, idealistic, passed amid the ghosts of defunct bodies and of unborn ones. The meaning singsong of that theosophico-metaphysical monotony left on you, at last, a very dreary feeling. * * *

But indeed, to the young ardent mind, instinct with pious nobleness, yet driven to the grim deserts of Radicalism for a faith, his speculations had a charm much more than literary, a charm almost religious and prophetic. The constant gist of his discourse was lamentation over the sunk condition of the world; which he recognised to be given-up to Atheism and Materialism, full of mere sordid misbeliefs, mispursuits and misresults. All Science had become mechanical; the science not of men, but of a kind of human beavers. Churches themselves had died away into a godless mechanical condition; and stood there as mere Cases of Articles, mere Forms of Churches; like the dried carcasses of once-swift camels, which you find left withering in the thirst of the universal desert, —ghastly portents for the present, beneficent ships of the desert no more. Men's souls were blinded, hebetated,[2] and sunk under the influence of Atheism and Materialism, and Hume and Voltaire: the world for the present was as an extinct world, deserted of God, and incapable of welldoing till it changed its heart and spirit. This, expressed I think with less of indignation and with more of long-drawn querulousness, was always recognisable as the ground-tone: —in which truly a pious young heart, driven into Radicalism and the opposition party, could not but recognise a too sorrowful truth; and ask of the Oracle, with all earnestness, What remedy, then?

The remedy, though Coleridge himself professed to see it as in sunbeams, could not, except by processes unspeakably difficult, be described to you at all. On the whole, those dead Churches, this dead English Church especially, must be brought to life again. Why not? It was not dead; the soul of it, in this parched-up body, was tragically asleep only. Atheistic Philosophy was true on its side, and Hume and Voltaire could on their own ground speak irrefragably for themselves against any Church: but lift the Church and them into a higher sphere of argument, *they* died into inanition, the Church revivified itself into pristine florid vigour,—became once more a living ship of the desert, and invincibly bore you over stock and stone. But how, but how! By attending to the "reason" of man, said Coleridge, and duly chaining-up the "understanding" of man: the V*ernunft* (Reason) and V*erstand* (Understanding) of the Germans, it all turned upon these, if you could well understand them, —which you couldn't. For the rest, Mr. Coleridge had on the anvil various Books, especially was about to write one grand Book On *the Logos*, which would help to bridge the chasm for us. So much appeared, however: Churches, though proved false (as you had imagined), were still true (as you were to imagine): here was an Artist who could burn you up an old Church, root and branch; and then as the Alchymists professed to do with organic substances in general, distil you an "Astral Spirit" from the ashes, which was the very image of the old burnt article, its airdrawn counterpart,— this you still had, or might get, and draw uses from, if you could. Wait till the Book on the Logos were done;—alas, till your own terrene eyes, blind with conceit and the dust of logic, were purged, subtilised and spiritualised into the sharpness of vision requisite for discerning such an "om-m-mject."—The ingenuous young English head, of those days, stood strangely puzzled by such revelations; uncertain whether it were getting inspired, or getting infatuated

2. Dulled.

into flat imbecility; and strange effulgence, of new day or else of deeper meteoric night, coloured the horizon of the future for it.

[From *Life of John Sterling*, 1851]

[WILLIAM WORDSWORTH IN HIS SEVENTIES]

On a summer morning (let us call it 1840 then) I was apprised by Taylor[3] that Wordsworth had come to town, and would meet a small party of us at a certain tavern in St. James's Street, at breakfast, to which I was invited for the given day and hour. We had a pretty little room, quiet though looking street-ward (tavern's name is quite lost to me); the morning sun was pleasantly tinting the opposite houses, a balmy, calm and sunlight morning. Wordsworth, I think, arrived just along with me; we had still five minutes of sauntering and miscellaneous talking before the whole were assembled. I do not positively remember any of them, except that James Spedding[1] was there, and that the others, not above five or six in whole, were polite intelligent quiet persons, and, except Taylor and Wordsworth, not of any special distinction in the world. Breakfast was pleasant, fairly beyond the common of such things. Wordsworth seemed in good tone, and, much to Taylor's satisfaction, talked a great deal; about "poetic" correspondents of his own (i.e. correspondents for the sake of his poetry; especially one such who had sent him, from Canton, an excellent chest of tea; correspondent grinningly applauded by us all); then about ruralities and miscellanies. * * * These were the first topics. Then finally about literature, literary laws, practices, observances, at considerable length, and turning wholly on the mechanical part, including even a good deal of shallow enough etymology, from me and others, which was well received. On all this Wordsworth enlarged with evident satisfaction, and was joyfully reverent of the "wells of English undefiled";[2] though stone dumb as to the deeper rules and wells of Eternal Truth and Harmony, which you were to try and set forth by said undefiled wells of English or what other speech you had! To me a little disappointing, but not much; though it would have given me pleasure had the robust veteran man emerged a little out of vocables into things, now and then, as he never once chanced to do. For the rest, he talked well in his way; with veracity, easy brevity and force, as a wise tradesman would of his tools and workshop,—and as no unwise one could. His voice was good, frank and sonorous, though practically clear distinct and forcible rather than melodious; the tone of him businesslike, sedately confident; no discourtesy, yet no anxiety about being courteous. A fine whole-

3. Henry Taylor, contemporary playwright.
1. Editor of the works of Francis Bacon.
2. Spenser, *Faerie Queene* IV.ii.32—referring to Chaucer.

some rusticity, fresh as his mountain breezes, sat well on the stalwart veteran, and on all he said and did. You would have said he was a usually taciturn man; glad to unlock himself to audience sympathetic and intelligent, when such offered itself. His face bore marks of much, not always peaceful, meditation; the look of it not bland or benevolent so much as close impregnable and hard: a man *multa tacere loquive paratus,*[3] in a world where he had experienced no lack of contradictions as he strode along! The eyes were not very brilliant, but they had a quiet clearness; there was enough of brow and well shaped; rather too much of cheek ("horse face" I have heard satirists say); face of squarish shape and decidedly longish, as I think the head itself was (its "length" going horizontal); he was large-boned, lean, but still firm-knit tall and strong-looking when he stood, a right good old steel-grey figure, with rustic simplicity and dignity about him, and a vivacious strength looking through him which might have suited one of those old steel-grey markgrafs[4] whom Henry the Fowler set up to ward the "marches" and do battle with the intrusive heathen in a stalwart and judicious manner.

On this and other occasional visits of his, I saw Wordsworth a number of times, at dinner, in evening parties; and we grew a little more familiar, but without much increase of real intimacy or affection springing up between us. He was willing to talk with me in a corner, in noisy extensive circles, having weak eyes, and little loving the general babble current in such places. One evening, probably about this time, I got him upon the subject of great poets, who I thought might be admirable equally to us both; but was rather mistaken, as I gradually found. Pope's partial failure I was prepared for; less for the narrowish limits visible in Milton and others. I tried him with Burns, of whom he had sung tender recognition; but Burns also turned out to be a limited inferior creature, any genius he had a theme for one's pathos rather; even Shakespeare himself had his blind sides, his limitations; gradually it became apparent to me that of transcendent unlimited there was, to this critic, probably but one specimen known, Wordsworth himself! He by no means said so, or hinted so, in words; but on the whole it was all I gathered from him in this considerable *tête-à-tête* of ours; and it was not an agreeable conquest. New notion as to poetry or poet I had not in the smallest degree got; but my insight into the depths of Wordsworth's pride in himself had considerably augmented; and it did not increase my love of him; though I did not in the least hate it either, so quiet was it, so fixed, unappealing, like a dim old lichened crag on the wayside, the private meaning of which, in con-

3. "Prepared to speak out or to pass over much in silence."
4. Governors appointed by Henry I of Germany, "the Fowler" (876–936), to guard the borders ("marches") of his kingdom.

trast with any public meaning it had, you recognised with a kind
of not wholly melancholy grin. * * *

During the last seven or ten years of his life, Wordsworth felt
himself to be a recognised lion, in certain considerable London
circles, and was in the habit of coming up to town with his wife
for a month or two every season, to enjoy his quiet triumph and
collect his bits of tribute *tales quales*.[5] * * * Wordsworth took
his bit of lionism very quietly, with a smile sardonic rather than
triumphant, and certainly got no harm by it, if he got or expected
little good. His wife, a small, withered, puckered, winking lady,
who never spoke, seemed to be more in earnest about the affair,
and was visibly and sometimes ridiculously assiduous to secure her
proper place of precedence at table. * * * The light was always
afflictive to his eyes; he carried in his pocket something like a skeleton brass candlestick, in which, setting it on the dinner-table, between him and the most afflictive or nearest of the chief lights, he
touched a little spring, and there flirted out, at the top of his brass
implement, a small vertical green circle which prettily enough threw
his eyes into shade, and screened him from that sorrow. In proof
of his equanimity as lion I remember, in connection with this green
shade, one little glimpse. * * * Dinner was large, luminous, sumptuous; I sat a long way from Wordsworth; dessert I think had come
in, and certainly there reigned in all quarters a cackle as of Babel
(only politer perhaps), which far up in Wordsworth's quarter (who
was leftward on my side of the table) seemed to have taken a
sententious, rather louder, logical and quasi-scientific turn, heartily
unimportant to gods and men, so far as I could judge of it and
of the other babble reigning. I looked upwards, leftwards, the coast
being luckily for a moment clear; there, far off, beautifully screened
in the shadow of his vertical green circle, which was on the farther
side of him, sate Wordsworth, silent, slowly but steadily gnawing
some portion of what I judged to be raisins, with his eye and attention placidly fixed on these and these alone. The sight of whom,
and of his rock-like indifference to the babble, quasi-scientific and
other, with attention turned on the small practical alone, was comfortable and amusing to me, who felt like him but could not eat
raisins. This little glimpse I could still paint, so clear and bright
is it, and this shall be symbolical of all.

In a few years, I forget in how many and when, these Wordsworth appearances in London ceased; we heard, not of ill-health
perhaps, but of increasing love of rest; at length of the long sleep's
coming; and never saw Wordsworth more. One felt his death as the
extinction of a public light, but not otherwise.

[From *Reminiscences*, 1867, 1881]

5. Of such a sort.

[ALFRED TENNYSON AT 34]

Alfred is one of the few British or Foreign Figures (a not increasing number I think!) who are and remain beautiful to me;—a true human soul, or some authentic approximation thereto, to whom your own soul can say, Brother!—However, I doubt he will not come; he often skips me, in these brief visits to Town; skips everybody indeed; being a man solitary and sad, as certain men are, dwelling in an element of gloom,—carrying a bit of Chaos about him, in short, which he is manufacturing into Cosmos!

Alfred is the son of a Lincolnshire Gentleman Farmer, I think; indeed, you see in his verses that he is a native of "moated granges," and green, fat pastures, not of mountains and their torrents and storms. He had his breeding at Cambridge, as if for the Law or Church; being master of a small annuity on his Father's decease, he preferred clubbing with his Mother and some Sisters, to live unpromoted and write Poems. In this way he lives still, now here, now there; the family always within reach of London, never in it; he himself making rare and brief visits, lodging in some old comrade's rooms. I think he must be under forty, not much under it. One of the finest-looking men in the world. A great shock of rough dusty-dark hair; bright-laughing hazel eyes; massive aquiline face, most massive yet most delicate; of sallow-brown complexion, almost Indian-looking; clothes cynically loose, free-and-easy;—smokes infinite tobacco. His voice is musical metallic,—fit for loud laughter and piercing wail, and all that may lie between; speech and speculation free and plenteous: I do not meet, in these late decades, such company over a pipe!—We shall see what he will grow to. He is often unwell; very chaotic,—his way is through Chaos and the Bottomless and Pathless; not handy for making out many miles upon.

[From a letter to Emerson, August 5, 1844]

[WILLIAM MAKEPEACE THACKERAY AT 42]

Thackeray has very rarely come athwart me since his return: he is a big fellow, soul and body; of many gifts and qualities (particularly in the Hogarth[6] line, with a dash of Sterne[7] superadded), of enormous *appetite* withal, and very uncertain and chaotic in all points except his *outer breeding*, which is fixed enough, and *perfect* according to the modern English style. I rather dread explosions in his history. A *big*, fierce, weeping, hungry man; not a strong one.

[From a letter to Emerson, September 9, 1853]

---

6. William Hogarth (1697–1764), a realistic and satirical painter of English life.

7. Laurence Sterne (1713–68), whose novels are often sentimental.

From Characteristics[1]

The healthy know not of their health, but only the sick: this is the Physician's Aphorism; and applicable in a far wider sense than he gives it. We may say, it holds no less in moral, intellectual, political, poetical, than in merely corporeal therapeutics; that wherever, or in what shape soever, powers of the sort which can be named *vital* are at work, herein lies the test of their working right or working wrong.

In the Body, for example, as all doctors are agreed, the first condition of complete health is, that each organ perform its function unconsciously, unheeded; let but any organ announce its separate existence, were it even boastfully, and for pleasure, not for pain, then already has one of those unfortunate "false centres of sensibility" established itself, already is derangement there. The perfection of bodily well-being is, that the collective bodily activities seem one; and be manifested, moreover, not in themselves, but in the action they accomplish. * * *

However, without venturing into the abstruse, or too eagerly asking Why and How, in things where our answer must needs prove, in great part, an echo of the question, let us be content to remark farther, in the merely historical way, how that Aphorism of the bodily Physician holds good in quite other departments. Of the Soul, with her activities, we shall find it no less true than of the Body: nay, cry the Spiritualists, is not that very division of the unity, Man, into a dualism of Soul and Body, itself the symptom of disease; as, perhaps, your frightful theory of Materialism, of his being but a Body, and therefore, at least, once more a unity, may be the paroxysm which was critical, and the beginning of cure! But omitting this, we observe, with confidence enough, that the truly strong mind, view it as Intellect, as Morality, or under any other aspect, is nowise the mind acquainted with its strength; that here

1. First published in the *Edinburgh Review*, ostensibly as a review of two books of philosophy which had appeared in 1830 and 1831: *An Essay on the Origin and Prospects of Man* by Thomas Hope, and *Philosophical Lectures* by Friedrich von Schlegel. Hope was a Utilitarian writer, and his analytical treatise may have inspired the first half of the essay, in which Carlyle exposes what seems to him the most characteristic symptom of modern man's diseased state of mind and spirit: self-consciousness. Schlegel's book, an example of the German transcendental philosophy which Carlyle admired, may have inspired the second half of his essay, in which he points out the encouraging prospects for the future if mankind can find a new religious faith. Yet it is only near the end of *Characteristics* that Carlyle finally refers directly to these two books as such, for his real object, as his title suggests, is not to write a mere book review but to describe the state of mind and society characteristic of the age. This early essay, even in the necessarily abridged form adopted here, contains in embryo all the basic religious and political ideas that Carlyle was to develop in his later writings.

as before the sign of health is Unconsciousness. In our inward, as in our outward world, what is mechanical lies open to us; not what is dynamical and has vitality. Of our Thinking, we might say, it is but the mere upper surface that we shape into articulate Thoughts; —underneath the region of argument and conscious discourse, lies the region of meditation; here, in its quiet mysterious depths, dwells what vital force is in us; here, if aught is to be created, and not merely manufactured and communicated, must the work go on. Manufacture is intelligible, but trivial; Creation is great, and cannot be understood. Thus if the Debater and Demonstrator, whom we may rank as the lowest of true thinkers, knows what he has done, and how he did it, the Artist, whom we rank as the highest, knows not; must speak of Inspiration, and in one or the other dialect, call his work the gift of a divinity.

But on the whole "genius is ever a secret to itself";[2] of this old truth we have, on all sides, daily evidence. The Shakespeare takes no airs for writing *Hamlet* and the *Tempest*, understands not that it is anything surprising: Milton, again, is more conscious of his faculty, which accordingly is an inferior one. On the other hand, what cackling and strutting must we not often hear and see, when, in some shape of academical prolusion, maiden speech, review article, this or the other well-fledged goose has produced its goose-egg, of quite measurable value, were it the pink of its whole kind; and wonders why all mortals do not wonder!

Foolish enough, too, was the College Tutor's surprise at Walter Shandy:[3] how, though unread in Aristotle, he could nevertheless argue; and not knowing the name of any dialectic tool, handled them all to perfection. Is it the skilfulest anatomist that cuts the best figure[4] at Sadler's Wells? or does the boxer hit better for knowing that he has a *flexor longus* and a *flexor brevis*?[5] But indeed, as in the higher case of the Poet, so here in that of the Speaker and Inquirer, the true force is an unconscious one. The healthy Understanding, we should say, is not the Logical, argumentative, but the Intuitive; for the end of Understanding is not to prove and find reasons, but to know and believe. Of logic, and its limits, and uses and abuses, there were much to be said and examined; one fact, however, which chiefly concerns us here, has long been familiar: that the man of logic and the man of insight; the Reasoner and the Discoverer, or even Knower, are quite separable, —indeed, for most part, quite separate characters. In practical matters, for example, has it not become almost proverbial that the man of logic cannot prosper? This is he whom business-people call Sys-

---

2. From an essay by the German poet J. C. F. von Schiller (1759–1805).
3. Laurence Sterne, *Tristram Shandy* I.xix.

4. Makes the most striking appearance. "Sadler's Wells" refers to a London theater.
5. Technical terms for bodily muscles.

tematic and Theoriser and Word-monger; his *vital* intellectual force lies dormant or extinct, his whole force is mechanical, conscious: of such a one it is foreseen that, when once confronted with the infinite complexities of the real world, his little compact theorem of the world will be found wanting; that unless he can throw it overboard and become a new creature, he will necessarily founder. * * * Never since the beginning of Time was there, that we hear or read of, so intensely self-conscious a Society. Our whole relations to the Universe and to our fellow-man have become an Inquiry, a Doubt; nothing will go on of its own accord, and do its function quietly; but all things must be probed into, the whole working of man's world be anatomically studied. Alas, anatomically studied, that it may be medically aided! Till at length indeed, we have come to such a pass, that except in this same *medicine*, with its artifices and appliances, few can so much as imagine any strength or hope to remain for us. The whole Life of Society must now be carried on by drugs: doctor after doctor appears with his nostrum, of Co-operative Societies, Universal Suffrage, Cottage-and-Cow systems, Repression of Population, Vote by Ballot. To such height has the dyspepsia of Society reached; as indeed the constant grinding internal pain, or from time to time the mad spasmodic throes, of all Society do otherwise too mournfully indicate.

Far be it from us to attribute, as some unwise persons do, the disease itself to this unhappy sensation that there is a disease! The Encyclopedists[6] did not produce the troubles of France; but the troubles of France produced the Encyclopedists, and much else. The Self-consciousness is the symptom merely; nay, it is also the attempt towards cure. We record the fact, without special censure; not wondering that Society should feel itself, and in all ways complain of aches and twinges, for it has suffered enough. * * *

But leaving this, let us rather look within, into the Spiritual condition of Society, and see what aspects and prospects offer themselves there. * * * To begin with our highest Spiritual function, with Religion, we might ask, Whither has Religion now fled? Of Churches and their establishments we here say nothing; nor of the unhappy domains of Unbelief, and how innumerable men, blinded in their minds, have grown to "live without God in the world";[7] but, taking the fairest side of the matter, we ask, What is the nature of that same Religion, which still lingers in the hearts of the few who are called, and call themselves, specially the Religious? Is it a healthy religion, vital, unconscious of itself; that shines forth spontaneously in doing of the Work, or even in preaching of the Word? Unhappily, no. Instead of heroic martyr Conduct, and in-

---

6. Diderot, Voltaire, and other critics of the established order in France who were contributors to the *Encyclopédie*

(1751–52, 1776–80).
7. Cf. Ephesians ii.12.

spired and soul-inspiring Eloquence, whereby Religion itself were brought home to our living bosoms, to live and reign there, we have "Discourses on the Evidences,"[8] endeavouring, with smallest result, to make it probable that such a thing as Religion exists. The most enthusiastic Evangelicals do not preach a Gospel, but keep describing how it should and might be preached: to awaken the sacred fire of faith, as by a sacred contagion, is not their endeavour; but, at most, to describe how Faith shows and acts, and scientifically distinguish true Faith from false. Religion, like all else, is conscious of itself, listens to itself; it becomes less and less creative, vital; more and more mechanical. Considered as a whole, the Christian Religion of late ages has been continually dissipating itself into Metaphysics; and threatens now to disappear, as some rivers do, in deserts of barren sand.

Of Literature, and its deep-seated, wide-spread maladies, why speak? Literature is but a branch of Religion, and always participates in its character: however, in our time, it is the only branch that still shows any greenness; and, as some think, must one day become the main stem. * * * Nay, is not the diseased self-conscious state of Literature disclosed in this one fact, which lies so near us here, the prevalence of Reviewing! Sterne's wish for a reader "that would give-up the reins of his imagination into his author's hands, and be pleased he knew not why, and cared not wherefore,"[9] might lead him a long journey now. Indeed, for our best class of readers, the chief pleasure, a very stinted one, is this same knowing of the Why; which many a Kames and Bossu[1] has been, ineffectually enough, endeavouring to teach us: till at last these also have laid down their trade; and now your Reviewer is a mere *taster*; who tastes, and says, by the evidence of such palate, such tongue, as he has got, It is good, It is bad. Was it thus that the French carried out certain inferior creatures on their Algerine Expedition, to taste the wells for them, and try whether they were poisoned? Far be it from us to disparage our own craft, whereby we have our living! Only we must note these things: that Reviewing spreads with strange vigour; that such a man as Byron reckons the Reviewer and the Poet equal; that at the last Leipzig Fair, there was advertised a Review of Reviews. By and by it will be found that all Literature has become one boundless self-devouring Review; and, as in London routs,[2] we have to *do* nothing, but only to *see* others do nothing.—Thus does Literature also, like a sick thing, superabundantly "listen to itself."

No less is this unhealthy symptom manifest, if we cast a glance

8. *Evidences of Christianity* (1794) by William Paley, a Utilitarian theologian.
9. Sterne's *Tristram Shandy* (III.xii).
1. Henry Home, Lord Kames (1696–

1782), author of *Elements of Criticism;* René le Bossu (1631–89), French literary critic.
2. Fashionable gatherings.

on our Philosophy, on the character of our speculative Thinking. Nay already, as above hinted, the mere existence and necessity of a Philosophy is an evil. Man is sent hither not to question, but to work: "the end of man," it was long ago written, "is an Action, not a Thought."[3] In the perfect state, all Thought were but the picture and inspiring symbol of Action; Philosophy, except as Poetry and Religion, would have no being. And yet how, in this imperfect state, can it be avoided, can it be dispensed with? Man stands as in the centre of Nature; his fraction of Time encircled by Eternity, his handbreadth of Space encircled by Infinitude: how shall he forbear asking himself, What am I; and Whence; and Whither? How too, except in slight partial hints, in kind asseverations and assurances, such as a mother quiets her fretfully inquisitive child with, shall he get answer to such inquiries?

The disease of Metaphysics, accordingly, is a perennial one. In all ages, those questions of Death and Immortality, Origin of Evil, Freedom and Necessity, must, under new forms, anew make their appearance; ever, from time to time, must the attempt to shape for ourselves some Theorem of the Universe be repeated. And ever unsuccessfully: for what Theorem of the Infinite can the Finite render complete? We, the whole species of Mankind, and our whole existence and history, are but a floating speck in the illimitable ocean of the All; yet *in* that ocean; indissoluble portion thereof; partaking of its infinite tendencies: borne this way and that by its deep-swelling tides, and grand ocean currents;—of which what faintest chance is there that we should ever exhaust the significance, ascertain the goings and comings? A region of Doubt, therefore, hovers forever in the background; in Action alone can we have certainty. Nay properly Doubt is the indispensable inexhaustible material whereon Action works, which Action has to fashion into Certainty and Reality; only on a canvas of Darkness, such is man's way of being, could the many-coloured picture of our Life paint itself and shine. * * *

Now this is specially the misery which has fallen on man in our Era. Belief, Faith has well-nigh vanished from the world. The youth on awakening in this wondrous Universe no longer finds a competent theory of its wonders. Time was, when if he asked himself, What is man, What are the duties of man? the answer stood ready written for him. But now the ancient "ground-plan of the All" belies itself when brought into contact with reality; Mother Church has, to the most, become a superannuated Step-mother, whose lessons go disregarded; or are spurned at, and scornfully gainsaid. For young Valour and thirst of Action no ideal Chivalry invites to heroism, prescribes what is heroic: the old ideal of Man-

3. Aristotle, *Ethics* I.iii.

hood has grown obsolete, and the new is still invisible to us, and we grope after it in darkness, one clutching this phantom, another that; Werterism,[4] Byronism, even Brummelism, each has its day. For Contemplation and love of Wisdom, no Cloister now opens its religious shades; the Thinker must, in all senses, wander homeless, too often aimless, looking up to a Heaven which is dead for him, round to an Earth which is deaf. Action, in those old days, was easy, was voluntary, for the divine worth of human things lay acknowledged; Speculation was wholesome, for it ranged itself as the handmaid of Action; what could not so range itself died out by its natural death, by neglect. Loyalty still hallowed obedience, and made rule noble; there was still something to be loyal to: the Godlike stood embodied under many a symbol in men's interests and business; the Finite shadowed forth the Infinite; Eternity looked through Time. The Life of man was encompassed and overcanopied by a glory of Heaven, even as his dwelling-place by the azure vault.

How changed in these new days! Truly may it be said, the Divinity has withdrawn from the Earth; or veils himself in that widewasting Whirlwind of a departing Era, wherein the fewest can discern his goings. Not Godhead, but an iron, ignoble circle of Necessity embraces all things; binds the youth of these times into a sluggish thrall, or else exasperates him into a rebel. Heroic Action is paralysed; for what worth now remains unquestionable with him? At the fervid period when his whole nature cries aloud for Action, there is nothing sacred under whose banner he can act; the course and kind and conditions of free Action are all but undiscoverable. Doubt storms-in on him through every avenue; inquiries of the deepest, painfulest sort must be engaged with; and the invincible energy of young years waste itself in sceptical, suicidal cavillings; in passionate "questionings of Destiny," whereto no answer will be returned.

For men, in whom the old perennial principle of Hunger (be it Hunger of the poor Day-drudge who stills it with eighteenpence a-day, or of the ambitious Place-hunter who can nowise still it with so little) suffices to fill-up existence, the case is bad; but not the worst. These men have an aim, such as it is; and can steer towards it, with chagrin enough truly; yet, as their hands are kept full, without desperation. Unhappier are they to whom a higher instinct has been given; who struggle to be persons, not machines; to whom the Universe is not a warehouse, or at best a fancy-bazaar, but a mystic temple and hall of doom. For such men there lie properly two courses open. The lower, yet still an estimable class, take up with worn-out Symbols of the Godlike; keep trimming and trucking be-

---

4. The cultivation of melancholy based on the model of Goethe's novel, *The Sorrows of Young Werther*. "Brum- melism": a fad for wearing elegant clothes in the manner of Beau Brummel, a dandy of George IV's time.

tween these and Hypocrisy, purblindly enough, miserably enough. A numerous intermediate class end in Denial; and form a theory that there is no theory; that nothing is certain in the world, except this fact of Pleasure being pleasant; so they try to realise what trifling modicum of Pleasure they can come at, and to live contented therewith, winking hard. Of these we speak not here; but only of the second nobler class, who also have dared to say No and cannot yet say Yea; but feel that in the No they dwell as in a Golgotha, where life enters not, where peace is not appointed them.

Hard, for most part, is the fate of such men; the harder the nobler they are. In dim forecastings, wrestles within them the "Divine Idea of the World" yet will nowhere visibly reveal itself. They have to realise a Worship for themselves, or live unworshipping. The Godlike has vanished from the world; and they, by the strong cry of their soul's agony, like true wonder-workers, must again evoke its presence. This miracle is their appointed task; which they must accomplish, or die wretchedly: this miracle has been accomplished by such; but not in our land; our land yet knows not of it. Behold a Byron, in melodious tones, "cursing his day": he mistakes earthborn passionate Desire for heaven-inspired Freewill; without heavenly load-star, rushes madly into the dance of meteoric lights that hover on the mad Mahlstrom; and goes down among its eddies. Hear a Shelley filling the earth with inarticulate wail; like the infinite, inarticulate grief and weeping of forsaken infants. A noble Friedrich Schlegel,[5] stupefied in that fearful loneliness, as of a silenced battle-field, flies back to Catholicism; as a child might to its slain mother's bosom, and cling there. In lower regions, how many a poor Hazlitt must wander on God's verdant earth, like the Unblest on burning deserts; passionately dig wells, and draw up only the dry quicksand; believe that he is seeking Truth, yet only wrestle among endless Sophisms, doing desperate battle as with spectre-hosts; and die and make no sign!

To the better order of such minds any mad joy of Denial has long since ceased: the problem is not now to deny, but to ascertain and perform. Once in destroying the False, there was a certain inspiration; but now the genius of Destruction has done its work, there is now nothing more to destroy. The doom of the Old has long been pronounced, and irrevocable; the Old has passed away: but, alas, the New appears not in its stead; the Time is still in pangs of travail with the New. Man has walked by the light of conflagrations, and amid the sound of falling cities; and now there is darkness, and long watching till it be morning. The voice even of the faithful can but exclaim: "As yet struggles the twelfth hour of the Night: birds of darkness are on the wing, spectres uproar,

---

5. German literary critic and leader of the Romantic school (1772–1829). In 1808 he joined the Roman Catholic Church.

the dead walk, the living dream.—Thou, Eternal Providence, wilt cause the day to dawn!"[6]

Such being the condition, temporal and spiritual, of the world at our Epoch, can we wonder that the world "listens to itself," and struggles and writhes, everywhere externally and internally, like a thing in pain? Nay, is not even this unhealthy action of the world's Organisation, if the symptom of universal disease, yet also the symptom and sole means of restoration and cure? The effort of Nature, exerting her medicative force to cast-out foreign impediments, and once more become One, become whole? In Practice, still more in Opinion, which is the precursor and prototype of Practice, there must needs be collision, convulsion; much has to be ground away. Thought must needs be Doubt and Inquiry before it can again be Affirmation and Sacred Precept. Innumerable "Philosophies of Man," contending in boundless hubbub, must annihilate each other, before an inspired Poesy and Faith for Man can fashion itself together. * * *

For ourselves, the loud discord which jars in these two Works,[7] in innumerable works of the like import, and generally in all the Thought and Action of this period, does not any longer utterly confuse us. Unhappy who, in such a time, felt not, at all conjunctures, ineradicably in his heart the knowledge that a God made this Universe, and a Demon not! And shall Evil always prosper, then? Out of all Evil comes Good; and no Good that is possible but shall one day be real. Deep and sad as is our feeling that we stand yet in the bodeful Night; equally deep, indestructible is our assurance that the Morning also will not fail. Nay already, as we look round, streaks of a dayspring are in the east; it is dawning; when the time shall be fulfilled, it will be day. The progress of man towards higher and nobler developments of whatever is highest and noblest in him, lies not only prophesied to Faith, but now written to the eye of Observation, so that he who runs may read.

One great step of progress, for example, we should say, in actual circumstances, was this same; the clear ascertainment that we are in progress. About the grand Course of Providence, and his final Purposes with us, we can know nothing, or almost nothing: man begins in darkness, ends in darkness; mystery is everywhere around us and in us, under our feet, among our hands. Nevertheless so much has become evident to every one, that this wondrous Mankind is advancing somewhither; that at least all human things are, have been and forever will be, in Movement and Change;—as, indeed, for beings that exist in Time, by virtue of Time, and are made

6. "Jean Paul's *Hesperus*" [Carlyle's note]. Jean Paul Richter (1763–1825) was a German humorist.

7. Books by Hope and Schlegel. See the title note.

of Time, might have been long since understood. In some provinces, it is true, as in Experimental Science, this discovery is an old one; but in most others it belongs wholly to these latter days. How often, in former ages, by eternal Creeds, eternal Forms of Government and the like, has it been attempted, fiercely enough, and with destructive violence, to chain the Future under the Past; and say to the Providence, whose ways with man are mysterious, and through the great deep: Hitherto shalt thou come, but no farther! A wholly insane attempt; and for man himself, could it prosper, the frightfulest of all enchantments, a very Life-in-Death. Man's task here below, the destiny of every individual man, is to be in turns Apprentice and Workman; or say rather, Scholar, Teacher, Discoverer: by nature he has a strength for learning, for imitating; but also a strength for acting, for knowing on his own account. Are we not in a world seen to be Infinite; the relations lying closest together modified by those latest discovered and lying farthest asunder? Could you ever spell-bind man into a Scholar merely, so that he had nothing to discover, to correct; could you ever establish a Theory of the Universe that were entire, unimprovable, and which needed only to be got by heart; man then were spiritually defunct, the Species we now name Man had ceased to exist. But the gods, kinder to us than we are to ourselves, have forbidden such suicidal acts. As Phlogiston[8] is displaced by Oxygen, and the Epicycles of Ptolemy by the Ellipses of Kepler,[9] so does Paganism give place to Catholicism, Tyranny to Monarchy, and Feudalism to Representative Government,—where also the process does not stop. Perfection of Practice, like completeness of Opinion, is always approaching, never arrived; Truth, in the words of Schiller, *immer wird, nie ist*; never *is*, always *is a-being*.

Sad, truly, were our condition did we know but this, that Change is universal and inevitable. Launched into a dark shoreless sea of Pyrrhonism, what would remain for us but to sail aimless, hopeless; or make madly merry, while the devouring Death had not yet ingulfed us? As indeed, we have seen many, and still see many do. Nevertheless so stands it not. The venerator of the Past (and to what pure heart is the Past, in that "moonlight of memory," other than sad and holy?) sorrows not over its departure, as one utterly bereaved. The true Past departs not, nothing that was worthy in the Past departs; no Truth or Goodness realised by man ever dies, or can die; but is all still here, and, recognised or not, lives and works through endless changes. If all things, to speak in the German dialect, are discerned by us, and exist for us, in an element of

8. A hypothetical substance which, according to older theories of chemistry, was part of all combustible objects and was released in burning.
9. Ptolemy, an astronomer of Alexandria, 2nd century A.D. Johannes Kepler (1571–1630), German astronomer whose theories of planetary orbits (together with the earlier discoveries of Copernicus) supplanted the Ptolemaic theories.

Time, and therefore of Mortality and Mutability; yet Time itself reposes on Eternity: the truly Great and Transcendental has its basis and substance in Eternity; stands revealed to us as Eternity in a vesture of Time. Thus in all Poetry, Worship, Art, Society, as one form passes into another, nothing is lost: it is but the superficial, as it were the *body* only, that grows obsolete and dies; under the mortal body lies a *soul* which is immortal; which anew incarnates itself in fairer revelation; and the Present is the living sumtotal of the whole Past.

In Change, therefore, there is nothing terrible, nothing supernatural: on the contrary, it lies in the very essence of our lot and life in this world. To-day is not yesterday: we ourselves change; how can our Works and Thoughts, if they are always to be the fittest, continue always the same? Change, indeed, is painful; yet ever needful; and if Memory have its force and worth, so also has Hope. Nay, if we look well to it, what is all Derangement, and necessity of great Change, in itself such an evil, but the product simply of *increased resources* which the old *methods* can no longer administer; of new wealth which the old coffers will no longer contain? What is it, for example, that in our own day bursts asunder the bonds of ancient Political Systems, and perplexes all Europe with the fear of Change, but even this: the increase of social resources, which the old social methods will no longer sufficiently administer? The new omnipotence of the Steam-engine is hewing asunder quite other mountains than the physical. Have not our economical distresses, those barnyard Conflagrations[1] themselves, the frightfulest madness of our mad epoch, their rise also in what is a real increase: increase of Men; of human Force; properly, in such a Planet as ours, the most precious of all increases? It is true again, the ancient methods of administration will no longer suffice. Must the indomitable millions, full of old Saxon energy and fire, lie cooped-up in this Western Nook, choking one another, as in a Blackhole of Calcutta,[2] while a whole fertile untenanted Earth, desolate for want of the ploughshare, cries: Come and till me, come and reap me?[3] If the ancient Captains can no longer yield guidance, new must be sought after: for the difficulty lies not in nature, but in artifice; the European Calcutta-Blackhole has no walls but air ones and paper ones. —So too, Scepticism itself, with its innumerable mischiefs, what is it but the sour fruit of a most blessed increase, that of Knowledge; a fruit too that will not always continue *sour?*

In fact, much as we have said and mourned about the unproduc-

---

1. Rick-burning in the 1820's and 1830's by disgruntled farm laborers in England.
2. A small room in which 146 European men and women were imprisoned by the Indians in 1756. After one night,
only 23 remained alive.
3. Carlyle often urged emigration to America as a solution to the overcrowding of Europe. One of his brothers did emigrate, and became a farmer in Ontario, Canada.

tive prevalence of Metaphysics, it was not without some insight into the use that lies in them. Metaphysical Speculation, if a necessary evil, is the forerunner of much good. The fever of Scepticism must needs burn itself out, and burn out thereby the Impurities that caused it; then again will there be clearness, health. The principle of life, which now struggles painfully, in the outer, thin and barren domain of the Conscious or Mechanical, may then withdraw into its inner sanctuaries, its abysses of mystery and miracle; withdraw deeper than ever into that domain of the Unconscious, by nature infinite and inexhaustible; and creatively work there. From that mystic region, and from that alone, all wonders, all Poesies, and Religions, and Social Systems have proceeded: the like wonders, and greater and higher, lie slumbering there; and, brooded on by the spirit of the waters, will evolve themselves, and rise like exhalations from the Deep. * * *

Remarkable it is, truly, how everywhere the eternal fact begins again to be recognised, that there is a Godlike in human affairs; that God not only made us and beholds us, but is in us and around us; that the Age of Miracles, as it ever was, now is. Such recognition we discern on all hands and in all countries: in each country after its own fashion. In France, among the younger nobler minds, strangely enough; where, in their loud contention with the Actual and Conscious, the Ideal or Unconscious is, for the time, without exponent; where Religion means not the parent of Polity, as of all that is highest, but Polity itself; and this and the other earnest man has not been wanting, who could audibly whisper to himself: "Go to, I will make religion." In England still more strangely; as in all things, worthy England will have its way: by the shrieking of hysterical women,[4] casting out of devils, and other "gifts of the Holy Ghost." Well might Jean Paul say, in this his twelfth hour of the Night, "the living dream"; well might he say, "the dead walk."[5] Meanwhile let us rejoice rather that so much has been seen into, were it through never so diffracting media, and never so madly distorted; that in all dialects, though but half-articulately, this high Gospel begins to be preached: Man is still Man. The genius of Mechanism, as was once before predicted, will not always sit like a choking incubus on our soul; but at length, when by a new magic Word the old spell is broken, become our slave, and as familiar-spirit do all our bidding. "We are near awakening when we dream that we dream."[6]

He that has an eye and a heart can even now say: Why should I falter? Light has come into the world; to such as love Light, so

4. An allusion to followers of Carlyle's friend, the preacher Edward Irving. Women in Irving's congregation asserted that they had acquired the gift of tongues.

5. See note 6 above, Jean Paul's *Hesperus.*
6. Quoted from a work by the German poet Novalis (1772–1801).

as Light must be loved, with a boundless all-doing, all-enduring love. For the rest, let that vain struggle to read the mystery of the Infinite cease to harass us. It is a mystery which, through all ages, we shall only read here a line of, there another line of. Do we not already know that the name of the Infinite is GOOD, is GOD? Here on Earth we are as Soldiers, fighting in a foreign land; that understand not the plan of the campaign, and have no need to understand it; seeing well what is at our hand to be done. Let us do it like Soldiers; with submission, with courage, with a heroic joy. "Whatsoever thy hand findeth to do, do it with all thy might."[7] Behind us, behind each one of us, lie Six Thousand Years of human effort, human conquest: before us is the boundless Time, with its as yet uncreated and unconquered Continents and Eldorados, which we, even we, have to conquer, to create; and from the bosom of Eternity there shine for us celestial guiding stars.

> "My inheritance how wide and fair!
> Time is my fair seed-field, of Time I'm heir."[8]

1831   1831

From Sartor Resartus[1]
The Everlasting No

Under the strange nebulous envelopment, wherein our Professor has now shrouded himself, no doubt but his spiritual nature is nevertheless progressive, and growing: for how can the "Son of

---

7. Ecclesiastes ix:10.
8. From Goethe's romance, *Wilhelm Meisters Wanderjahre* (1821).
1. *Sartor Resartus* is a combination of novel, autobiography, and essay. To present some of his own experiences, Carlyle invented a hero, Professor Diogenes Teufelsdröckh of Germany, whose name itself (meaning "God-Begotten Devil's Dung") suggests the grotesque and fantastic humor which Carlyle used to expound a serious treatise. Teufelsdröckh tells the story of his unhappiness in love and of his difficulties in religion. He also airs his opinions on a variety of subjects. Interspersed between the Professor's words (which are in quotation marks) are the remarks of an editor, also imaginary, who has the task of putting together the story from assorted documents written by Teufelsdröckh. The title, meaning "The Tailor Re-Tailored," refers to the editor's role of patching the story together. The title also refers to Carlyle's so-called "Clothes Philosophy," which is expounded by the hero in many chapters of *Sartor*. In effect this Clothes Philosophy is an attempt to demonstrate the difference between the appearances of things and their reality. The appearance of a man depends upon the costume he wears; the reality of a man is the body underneath the costume. By analogy, Carlyle suggests that institutions, such as churches or governments, are like clothes. They may be useful "visible emblems" of the spiritual forces which they cover, but they wear out and have to be replaced by new clothes. The Christian church, for example, which once expressed man's permanent religious desires, is, in Carlyle's terms, worn out and must be discarded. But the underlying religious spirit must be recognized and kept alive at all costs. In this respect, the Clothes Philosophy has much in common with the theory of archetypal experiences developed in the 20th century by the psychiatrist Carl Jung. Carlyle extends his analogy, however, into many other areas. Clothes hide the body just as the world of nature cloaks

Time," in any case, stand still? We behold him, through those dim years, in a state of crisis, of transition: his mad Pilgrimings, and general solution into aimless Discontinuity, what is all this but a mad Fermentation; wherefrom, the fiercer it is, the clearer product will one day evolve itself?

Such transitions are ever full of pain: thus the Eagle when he moults is sickly; and, to attain his new beak, must harshly dash-off the old one upon rocks. What Stoicism soever our Wanderer, in his individual acts and motions, may affect, it is clear that there is a hot fever of anarchy and misery raging within; coruscations of which flash out: as, indeed, how could there be other? Have we not seen him disappointed, bemocked of Destiny, through long years? All that the young heart might desire and pray for has been denied; nay, as in the last worst instance, offered and then snatched away. Ever an "excellent Passivity"; but of useful, reasonable Activity, essential to the former as Food to Hunger, nothing granted: till at length, in this wild Pilgrimage, he must forcibly seize for himself an Activity, though useless, unreasonable. Alas, his cup of bitterness, which had been filling drop by drop, ever since that first "ruddy morning" in the Hinterschlag Gymnasium,[2] was at the very lip; and then with that poison-drop, of the Towgood-and-Blumine business,[3] it runs over, and even hisses over in a deluge of foam.

He himself says once, with more justice than originality: "Man is, properly speaking, based upon Hope, he has no other possession but Hope; this world of his is emphatically the Place of Hope." What, then, was our Professor's possession? We see him, for the present, quite shut-out from Hope; looking not into the golden orient, but vaguely all round into a dim copper firmament, pregnant with earthquake and tornado.

Alas, shut-out from Hope, in a deeper sense than we yet dream of! For, as he wanders wearisomely through this world, he has now lost all tidings of another and higher. Full of religion, or at least of religiosity, as our Friend has since exhibited himself, he hides not that, in those days, he was wholly irreligious: "Doubt had darkened into Unbelief," says he; "shade after shade goes grimly over your soul, till you have the fixed, starless, Tartarean black." To such readers as have reflected, what can be called reflecting, on man's life, and happily discovered, in contradiction to much Profit-

the reality of God and as the body itself cloaks the reality of man's soul. The discovery of these realities behind the appearances is, for Carlyle and for his hero, the initial stage of a solution to the dilemmas of life.

Teufelsdröckh's religious development, as described in the following chapters, may be contrasted with J. S. Mill's account of his own crisis of spirit in his *Autobiography*. Our first three selections are Chapters VII–IX of Book II.

2. "Smite-Behind Grammar School"; Teufelsdröckh's unhappiness had begun with his loneliness at this school.
3. Blumine, a girl loved by Teufelsdröckh, had married his friend Towgood. His distress is pictured in the preceding chapter, entitled "Sorrows of Teufelsdröckh."

and-loss Philosophy,[4] speculative and practical, that Soul is *not* synonymous with Stomach; who understand, therefore, in our Friend's words, "that, for man's well-being, Faith is properly the one thing needful; how, with it, Martyrs, otherwise weak, can cheerfully endure the shame and the cross; and without it, Worldlings puke-up their sick existence, by suicide, in the midst of luxury": to such it will be clear that, for a pure moral nature, the loss of his religious Belief was the loss of everything. Unhappy young man! All wounds, the crush of long-continued Destitution, the stab of false Friendship and of false Love, all wounds in thy so genial heart, would have healed again, had not its life-warmth been withdrawn. Well might he exclaim, in his wild way: "Is there no God, then; but at best an absentee God, sitting idle, ever since the first Sabbath, at the outside of his Universe, and *seeing* it go? Has the word Duty no meaning; is what we call Duty no divine Messenger and Guide, but a false earthly Fantasm, made-up of Desire and Fear, of emanations from the Gallows and from Dr. Graham's Celestial-Bed?[5] Happiness of an approving Conscience! Did not Paul of Tarsus, whom admiring men have since named Saint, feel that *he* was 'the chief of sinners';[6] and Nero of Rome, jocund in spirit (*wohlgemuth*), spend much of his time in fiddling? Foolish Word-monger and Motive-grinder, who in thy Logic-mill hast an earthly mechanism for the Godlike itself, and wouldst fain grind me out Virtue from the husks of Pleasure,—I tell thee, Nay! To the unregenerate Prometheus Vinctus[7] of a man, it is ever the bitterest aggravation of his wretchedness that he is conscious of Virtue, that he feels himself the victim not of suffering only, but of injustice. What then? Is the heroic inspiration we name Virtue but some Passion; some bubble of the blood, bubbling in the direction others *profit* by? I know not: only this I know, If what thou namest Happiness be our true aim, then are we all astray. With Stupidity and sound Digestion man may front much. But what, in these dull unimaginative days, are the terrors of Conscience to the diseases of the Liver! Not on Morality, but on Cookery, let us build our stronghold: there brandishing our frying-pan, as censer, let us offer sweet incense to the Devil, and live at ease on the fat things *he* has provided for his Elect!"

Thus has the bewildered Wanderer to stand, as so many have done, shouting question after question into the Sibyl-cave of Destiny,[8]

4. Utilitarian theory of ethics that our actions should be based on calculating the sum of pleasures and pains which would result from such actions. This "hedonistic calculus" horrified Carlyle because it left out of account man's religious instincts.
5. James Graham (1745–94), a quack doctor, had invented an elaborate bed which was supposed to cure sterility in couples using it. In this passage the bed is apparently a symbol of sexual desires.
6. See I Timothy i.15.
7. I.e., Prometheus Bound; this is also the title of a play by Aeschylus depicting the sufferings of a hero who defied Zeus.
8. An allusion to Virgil's *Aeneid* VI.

and receive no Answer but an Echo. It is all a grim Desert, this once-fair world of his; wherein is heard only the howling of wild-beasts, or the shrieks of despairing, hate-filled men; and no Pillar of Cloud by day, and no Pillar of Fire by night,[9] any longer guides the Pilgrim. To such length has the spirit of Inquiry carried him. "But what boots it (*was thut's*)?" cries he: "it is but the common lot in this era. Not having come to spiritual majority prior to the *Siècle de Louis Quinze*,[1] and not being born purely a Loghead (*Dummkopf*), thou hast no other outlook. The whole world is, like thee, sold to Unbelief, their old Temples of the Godhead, which for long have not been rainproof, crumble down; and men ask now: Where is the Godhead; our eyes never saw him?"

Pitiful enough were it, for all these wild utterances, to call our Diogenes wicked. Unprofitable servants as we all are, perhaps at no era of his life was he more decisively the Servant of Goodness, the Servant of God, than even now when doubting God's existence. "One circumstance I note," says he: "after all the nameless woe that Inquiry, which for me, what it is not always, was genuine Love of Truth, had wrought me, I nevertheless still loved Truth, and would bate no jot of my allegiance to her. 'Truth'! I cried, 'though the Heavens crush me for following her: no Falsehood! though a whole celestial Lubberland[2] were the price of Apostasy.' In conduct it was the same. Had a divine Messenger from the clouds, or miraculous Handwriting on the wall, convincingly proclaimed to me *This thou shalt do*, with what passionate readiness, as I often thought, would I have done it, had it been leaping into the infernal Fire. Thus, in spite of all Motive-grinders, and Mechanical Profit-and-Loss Philosophies, with the sick ophthalmia and hallucination they had brought on, was the Infinite nature of Duty still dimly present to me: living without God in the world, of God's light I was not utterly bereft; if my as yet sealed eyes, with their unspeakable longing, could nowhere see Him, nevertheless in my heart He was present, and His heaven-written Law still stood legible and sacred there."

Meanwhile, under all these tribulations, and temporal and spiritual destitutions, what must the Wanderer, in his silent soul, have endured! "The painfullest feeling," writes he, "is that of your own Feebleness (*Unkraft*); ever, as the English Milton says, to be weak is the true misery.[3] And yet of your Strength there is and can be no clear feeling, save by what you have prospered in, by what you have done. Between vague wavering Capability and fixed indubitable Performance, what a difference! A certain inarticulate Self-conscious-

36 ff., where Aeneas questions the Cumaean sibyl.
9. Exodus xiii.21.
1. "The Century of Louis XV," an allusion to Voltaire's history of the skeptical and enquiring spirit of 18th-century France during the reign of Louis XV (1710–74): *Précis du Siècle de Louis XV.*
2. Land of Plenty.
3. *Paradise Lost* I.157: "Fallen cherub, to be weak is miserable."

ness dwells dimly in us; which only our Works can render articulate and decisively discernible. Our Works are the mirror wherein the spirit first sees its natural lineaments. Hence, too, the folly of that impossible Precept, *Know thyself;*[4] till it be translated into this partially possible one, *Know what thou canst work-at.*

"But for me, so strangely unprosperous had I been, the net-result of my Workings amounted as yet simply to—Nothing. How then could I believe in my Strength, when there was as yet no mirror to see it in? Ever did this agitating, yet, as I now perceive, quite frivolous question, remain to me insoluble: Hast thou a certain Faculty, a certain Worth, such even as the most have not; or art thou the completest Dullard of these modern times? Alas! the fearful Unbelief is unbelief in yourself; and how could I believe? Had not my first, last Faith in myself, when even to me the Heavens seemed laid open, and I dared to love, been all-too cruelly belied? The speculative Mystery of Life grew ever more mysterious to me: neither in the practical Mystery[5] had I made the slightest progress, but been everywhere buffeted, foiled, and contemptuously cast-out. A feeble unit in the middle of a threatening Infinitude, I seemed to have nothing given me but eyes, whereby to discern my own wretchedness. Invisible yet impenetrable walls, as of Enchantment, divided me from all living: was there, in the wide world, any true bosom I could press trustfully to mine? O Heaven, No, there was none! I kept a lock upon my lips: why should I speak much with that shifting variety of so-called Friends, in whose withered, vain and too-hungry souls Friendship was but an incredible tradition? In such cases, your resource is to talk little, and that little mostly from the Newspapers. Now when I look back, it was a strange isolation I then lived in. The men and women around me, even speaking with me, were but Figures; I had, practically, forgotten that they were alive, that they were not merely automatic. In midst of their crowded streets and assemblages, I walked solitary; and (except as it was my own heart, not another's, that I kept devouring) savage also, as the tiger in his jungle. Some comfort it would have been, could I, like a Faust,[6] have fancied myself tempted and tormented of the Devil; for a Hell, as I imagine, without Life, though only diabolic Life, were more frightful: but in our age of Down-pulling and Disbelief, the very Devil has been pulled down, you cannot so much as believe in a Devil. To me the Universe was all void of Life, of Purpose, of Volition, even of Hostility: it was one huge, dead, immeasurable Steam-engine, rolling on, in its dead indifference, to grind me limb from limb. O, the vast, gloomy, solitary Golgotha,[7] and Mill of

---

4. This maxim was inscribed in gold letters over the portico of the temple at Delphi.
5. A profession or practical occupation.

6. Faust, the hero of a drama by Goethe, was tempted by the Devil.
7. Calvary, the place where Christ was crucified.

Death! Why was the Living banished thither companionless, conscious? Why, if there is no Devil; nay, unless the Devil is your God?"

A prey incessantly to such corrosions, might not, moreover, as the worst aggravation to them, the iron constitution even of a Teufelsdröckh threaten to fail? We conjecture that he has known sickness; and, in spite of his locomotive habits, perhaps sickness of the chronic sort. Hear this, for example: "How beautiful to die of broken-heart, on Paper! Quite another thing in practice; every window of your Feeling, even of your Intellect, as it were, begrimed and mud-bespattered, so that no pure ray can enter; a whole Drug-shop in your inwards; the fordone soul drowning slowly in quagmires of Disgust!"

Putting all which external and internal miseries together, may we not find in the following sentences, quite in our Professor's still vein, significance enough? "From Suicide a certain aftershine (*Nachschein*) of Christianity withheld me: perhaps also a certain indolence of character; for, was not that a remedy I had at any time within reach? Often, however, was there a question present to me: Should some one now, at the turning of that corner, blow thee suddenly out of Space, into the other World, or other No-World, by pistol-shot,—how were it? On which ground, too, I have often, in sea-storms and sieged cities and other death-scenes, exhibited an imperturbability, which passed, falsely enough, for courage."

"So had it lasted," concludes the Wanderer, "so had it lasted, as in bitter protracted Death-agony, through long years. The heart within me, unvisited by any heavenly dewdrop, was smouldering in sulphurous, slow-consuming fire. Almost since earliest memory I had shed no tear; or once only when I, murmuring half-audibly, recited Faust's Deathsong, that wild *Selig der den er im Siegesglanze findet* (Happy whom *he* finds in Battle's splendour),[8] and thought that of this last Friend[9] even I was not forsaken, that Destiny itself could not doom me not to die. Having no hope, neither had I any definite fear, were it of Man or of Devil: nay, I often felt as if it might be solacing, could the Arch-Devil himself, though in Tartarean terrors, but rise to me, that I might tell him a little of my mind. And yet, strangely enough, I lived in a continual, indefinite, pining fear; tremulous, pusillanimous, apprehensive of I knew not what: it seemed as if all things in the Heavens above and the Earth beneath would hurt me; as if the Heavens and the Earth were but boundless jaws of a devouring monster, wherein I, palpitating, waited to be devoured.

"Full of such humour, and perhaps the miserablest man in the

---

8. Adapted from Goethe's *Faust* I.iv.
1573–76.   9. Death.

whole French Capital or Suburbs, was I, one sultry Dogday,[1] after much perambulation, toiling along the dirty little *Rue Saint-Thomas de l'Enfer*,[2] among civic rubbish enough, in a close atmosphere, and over pavements hot as Nebuchadnezzar's Furnace; whereby doubtless my spirits were little cheered; when, all at once, there rose a Thought in me, and I asked myself: 'What *art* thou afraid of? Wherefore, like a coward, dost thou forever pip and whimper, and go cowering and trembling? Despicable biped! what is the sumtotal of the worst that lies before thee? Death? Well, Death; and say the pangs of Tophet[3] too, and all that the Devil and Man may, will or can do against thee! Hast thou not a heart; canst thou not suffer whatsoever it be; and, as a Child of Freedom, though outcast, trample Tophet itself under thy feet, while it consumes thee? Let it come, then; I will meet it and defy it!' And as I so thought, there rushed like a stream of fire over my whole soul; and I shook base Fear away from me forever. I was strong, of unknown strength; a spirit, almost a god. Ever from that time, the temper of my misery was changed: not Fear or whining Sorrow was it, but Indignation and grim fire-eyed Defiance.

"Thus had the EVERLASTING No[4] (*das ewige Nein*) pealed authoritatively through all the recesses of my Being, of my ME; and then was it that my whole ME stood up, in native God-created majesty, and with emphasis recorded its Protest. Such a Protest, the most important transaction in Life, may that same Indignation and Defiance, in a psychological point of view, be fitly called. The Everlasting No had said: 'Behold, thou art fatherless, outcast, and the Universe is mine (the Devil's)'; to which my whole Me now made answer: '*I* am not thine, but Free, and forever hate thee!'

"It is from this hour that I incline to date my Spiritual Newbirth, or Baphometic Fire-baptism;[5] perhaps I directly thereupon began to be a Man."

Centre of Indifference

Though, after this "Baphometic Fire-baptism" of his, our Wanderer signifies that his Unrest was but increased; as indeed, "Indignation and Defiance," especially against things in general, are not the most peaceable inmates; yet can the Psychologist surmise that it was no longer a quite hopeless Unrest; that henceforth it had at least a

---

1. A hot and unwholesome summer period, coinciding with the prominence of Sirius, the Dog Star, is called the season of the dog days.
2. "St. Thomas-of-Hell Street." In later life Carlyle admitted that this incident was based upon his own experience during a walk in Edinburgh (rather than in Paris) when he was 26 or 27 years of age. For a period of three weeks, he said, he had been suffering from "total sleeplessness."

3. Hell.
4. This phrase does not signify the hero's protest. It represents the sum of all the forces that had denied meaning to life. These negative forces, which had hitherto held the hero in bondage, are repudiated by his saying, "No!" to the "Everlasting No."
5. A transformation by a flash of spiritual illumination. The term may derive from Baphomet, an idol that inspired such spiritual experiences.

fixed centre to revolve round. For the fire-baptised soul, long so scathed and thunder-riven, here feels its own Freedom, which feeling is its Baphometic Baptism: the citadel of its whole kingdom it has thus gained by assault, and will keep inexpugnable; outwards from which the remaining dominions, not indeed without hard battling, will doubtless by degrees be conquered and pacificated. Under another figure, we might say, if in that great moment, in the *Rue Saint-Thomas de l'Enfer*, the old inward Satanic School[1] was not yet thrown out of doors, it received peremptory judicial notice to quit; —whereby, for the rest, its howl-chantings, Ernulphus-cursings,[2] and rebellious gnashings of teeth, might, in the meanwhile, become only the more tumultuous, and difficult to keep secret.

Accordingly, if we scrutinise these Pilgrimings well, there is perhaps discernible henceforth a certain incipient method in their madness. Not wholly as a Spectre does Teufelsdröckh now storm through the world; at worst as a spectre-fighting Man, nay who will one day be a Spectre-queller. If pilgriming restlessly to so many "Saints' Wells,"[3] and ever without quenching of his thirst, he nevertheless finds little secular wells, whereby from time to time some alleviation is ministered. In a word, he is now, if not ceasing, yet intermitting to "eat his own heart"; and clutches round him outwardly on the NOT-ME for wholesomer food. Does not the following glimpse exhibit him in a much more natural state?

"Towns also and Cities, especially the ancient, I failed not to look upon with interest. How beautiful to see thereby, as through a long vista, into the remote Time; to have as it were, an actual section of almost the earliest Past brought safe into the Present, and set before your eyes! There, in that old City, was a live ember of Culinary Fire put down, say only two-thousand years ago; and there, burning more or less triumphantly, with such fuel as the region yielded, it has burnt, and still burns, and thou thyself seest the very smoke thereof. Ah! and the far more mysterious live ember of Vital Fire was then also put down there; and still miraculously burns and spreads; and the smoke and ashes thereof (in these Judgment-Halls and Church-yards), and its bellows-engines (in these Churches), thou still seest; and its flame, looking out from every kind countenance, and every hateful one, still warms thee or scorches thee.

"Of Man's Activity and Attainment the chief results are aeriform, mystic, and preserved in Tradition only: such are his Forms of Government, with the Authority they rest on; his Customs, or Fashions both of Cloth-habits and of Soul-habits; much more his collec-

---

1. A term coined by Robert Southey to characterize the self-assertive and rebellious temper of the poetry of Byron and Shelley.
2. A curse devised by Ernulf (1040–1124), Bishop of Rochester, when sentencing persons to excommunication. See Sterne's *Tristram Shandy* III.xi.
3. Holy fountains or wells whose waters were reputed to restore health. Here a figurative allusion to Teufelsdröckh's unsuccessful search, at this time, for a religious solution to his problems.

tive stock of Handicrafts, the whole Faculty he has acquired of manipulating Nature: all these things, as indispensable and priceless as they are, cannot in any way be fixed under lock and key, but must flit, spirit-like, on impalpable vehicles, from Father to Son; if you demand sight of them, they are nowhere to be met with. Visible Plowmen and Hammermen there have been, ever from Cain and Tubalcain downwards: [4] but where does your accumulated Agricultural, Metallurgic, and other Manufacturing SKILL lie warehoused? It transmits itself on the atmospheric air, on the sun's rays (by Hearing and by Vision); it is a thing aeriform, impalpable, of quite spiritual sort. In like manner, ask me not. Where are the LAWS where is the GOVERNMENT? In vain wilt thou go to Schönbrunn, to Downing Street, to the Palais Bourbon: [5] thou findest nothing there but brick or stone houses, and some bundles of Papers tied with tape. Where, then, is that same cunningly-devised almighty GOVERNMENT of theirs to be laid hands on? Everywhere, yet nowhere: seen only in its works, this too is a thing aeriform, invisible; or if you will, mystic and miraculous. So spiritual (*geistig*) is our whole daily Life: all that we do springs out of Mystery, Spirit, invisible Force; only like a little Cloud-image, or Armida's Palace,[6] air-built, does the Actual body itself forth from the great mystic Deep.

"Visible and tangible products of the Past, again, I reckon-up to the extent of three. Cities, with their Cabinets and Arsenals; then tilled Fields, to either or to both of which divisions Roads with their Bridges, may belong; and thirdly—Books. In which third truly, the last invented, lies a worth far surpassing that of the two others. Wondrous indeed is the virtue of a true Book. Not like a dead city of stones, yearly crumbling, yearly needing repair; more like a tilled field, but then a spiritual field: like a spiritual tree, let me rather say, it stands from year to year, and from age to age (we have Books that already number some hundred-and-fifty human ages); and yearly comes its new produce of leaves (Commentaries, Deductions, Philosophical, Political Systems; or were it only Sermons, Pamphlets, Journalistic Essays), every one of which is talismanic and thaumaturgic,[7] for it can persuade men. O thou who art able to write a Book, which once in the two centuries or oftener there is a man gifted to do, envy not him whom they name City-builder, and inexpressibly pity him whom they name Conqueror or City-burner! Thou too art a Conqueror and Victor; but of the true sort, namely over the Devil: thou too hast built what will outlast all marble and metal, and be a wonder-bringing City of the Mind, a Temple and Seminary and Prophetic Mount, whereto all kindreds of the Earth will pilgrim. —Fool! why journeyest thou wearisomely, in thy antiquarian fervour, to gaze on the stone pyramids of Geeza, or the clay ones of

---

4. See Genesis, iv.1–22.
5. Headquarters of government in Vienna, London, and Paris, respectively.
6. The magic palace of a beautiful enchantress in Tasso's *Jerusalem Delivered*.
7. Miracle-working.

Sacchara?[8] These stand there, as I can tell thee, idle and inert, looking over the Desert, foolishly enough, for the last three-thousand years: but canst thou not open thy Hebrew BIBLE, then, or even Luther's Version thereof?"

No less satisfactory is his sudden appearance not in Battle, yet on some Battle-field; which, we soon gather, must be that of Wagram;[9] so that here, for once, is a certain approximation to distinctiveness of date. Omitting much, let us impart what follows:

"Horrible enough! A whole Marchfeld[1] strewed with shell-splinters, cannon-shot, ruined tumbrils, and dead men and horses; stragglers still remaining not so much as buried. And those red mould heaps: ay, there lie the Shells of Men, out of which all the Life and Virtue has been blown; and now are they swept together, and crammed-down out of sight, like blown Egg-shells!—Did Nature, when she bade the Donau bring down his mould-cargoes from the Carinthian and Carpathian Heights, and spread them out here into the softest, richest level,—intend thee, O Marchfeld, for a corn-bearing Nursery, whereon her children might be nursed; or for a Cockpit, wherein they might the more commodiously be throttled and tattered? Were thy three broad Highways, meeting here from the ends of Europe, made for Ammunition-wagons, then? Were thy Wagrams and Stillfrieds[2] but so many ready-built Casemates,[3] wherein the house of Hapsburg might batter with artillery, and with artillery be battered? König Ottokar, amid yonder hillocks, dies under Rodolf's truncheon; here Kaiser Franz falls a-swoon under Napoleon's: within which five centuries, to omit the others, how has thy breast, fair Plain, been defaced and defiled! The greensward is torn-up and trampled-down; man's fond care of it, his fruit-trees, hedge-rows, and pleasant dwellings, blown away with gunpowder; and the kind seedfield lies a desolate, hideous Place of Sculls.— Nevertheless, Nature is at work; neither shall these Powder-Devilkins with their utmost devilry gainsay her: but all that gore and carnage will be shrouded-in, absorbed into manure; and next year the Marchfeld will be green, nay greener. Thrifty unwearied Nature, ever out of our great waste educing some little profit of thy own,— how dost thou, from the very carcass of the Killer, bring Life for the Living![4]

"What, speaking in quite unofficial language, is the net-purport and upshot of war? To my own knowledge, for example, there dwell

---

8. Pyramids at Ghizeh and Sakkara near Cairo.
9. A village in Austria; site of Napoleon's victory over the Austrians, July, 1809.
1. A fertile plain in Austria whose soil (according to Teufelsdröckh) was brought down from the Carpathian mountains by the Danube (Donau) River.
2. Stillfried was the site of a battle in which Ottokar, King ("könig") of Bohemia, was killed by the forces of Rudolph of Hapsburg in 1278. In 1809 the Hapsburg armies, under Emperor Francis ("Franz") I, were in turn defeated by Napoleon at nearby Wagram.
3. Fortified chambers.
4. Cf. Byron's reflections on the battle-field at Waterloo: "How that red rain hath made the harvest grow!"—*Childe Harold's Pilgrimage*, III.xvii.150.

and toil, in the British village of Dumdrudge, usually some five-hundred souls. From these, by certain 'Natural Enemies'[5] of the French, there are successively selected, during the French war, say thirty able-bodied men: Dumdrudge, at her own expense, has suckled and nursed them: she has, not without difficulty and sorrow, fed them up to manhood, and even trained them to crafts, so that one can weave, another build, another hammer, and the weakest can stand under thirty stone avoirdupois. Nevertheless, amid much weeping and swearing, they are selected; all dressed in red; and shipped away, at the public charges, some two-thousand miles, or say only to the south of Spain;[6] and fed there till wanted. And now to that same spot, in the south of Spain, are thirty similar French artisans, from a French Dumdrudge, in like manner wending: till at length, after infinite effort, the two parties come into actual juxtaposition; and Thirty stands fronting Thirty, each with a gun in his hand. Straightway the word 'Fire!' is given: and they blow the souls out of one another; and in place of sixty brisk useful craftsmen, the world has sixty dead carcasses, which it must bury, and anew shed tears for. Had these men any quarrel? Busy as the Devil is, not the smallest! They lived far enough apart; were the entirest strangers; nay, in so wide a Universe, there was even, unconsciously, by Commerce, some mutual helpfulness between them. How then? Simpleton! their Governors had fallen-out; and, instead of shooting one another, had the cunning to make these poor blockheads shoot.— Alas, so is it in Deutschland, and hitherto in all other lands; still as of old, 'what devilry soever Kings do, the Greeks must pay the piper!'[7]—In that fiction of the English Smollet,[8] it is true, the final Cessation of War is perhaps prophetically shadowed forth; where the two Natural Enemies, in person, take each a Tobacco-pipe, filled with Brimstone; light the same, and smoke in one another's faces, till the weaker gives in: but from such predicted Peace-Era, what blood-filled trenches, and contentious centuries, may still divide us!"

Thus can the Professor, at least in lucid intervals, look away from his own sorrows, over the many-coloured world, and pertinently enough note what is passing there. We may remark, indeed, that for the matter of spiritual culture, if for nothing else, perhaps few periods of his life were richer than this. Internally, there is the most momentous instructive Course of Practical Philosophy, with Experiments, going on; towards the right comprehension of which his Peripatetic[9] habits, favourable to Meditation, might help him rather than hinder. Externally, again, as he wanders to and fro, there are, if for the longing heart little substance, yet for the seeing eye

5. Term often used in English newspapers to account for the frequency of wars between the English and French.
6. Where British armies fought against Napoleon, 1808–14.
7. Cf. Horace, *Epistles*, I.ii.14.
8. See Chapter XLI of *The Adventures of Ferdinand Count Fathom* by Tobias Smollett (1721–71).
9. Walking about, after the manner of Aristotle who delivered his lectures while walking in the Lyceum.

sights enough: in these so boundless Travels of his, granting that the Satanic School was even partially kept down, what an incredible knowledge of our Planet, and its Inhabitants and their Works, that is to say, of all knowable things, might not Teufelsdröckh acquire!

"I have read in most Public Libraries," says he, "including those of Constantinople and Samarcand: in most Colleges, except the Chinese Mandarin ones, I have studied, or seen that there was no studying. Unknown Languages have I oftenest gathered from their natural repertory, the Air, by my organ of Hearing; Statistics, Geographics, Topographics came, through the Eye, almost of their own accord. The ways of Man, how he seeks food, and warmth, and protection for himself, in most regions, are ocularly known to me. Like the great Hadrian,[1] I meted-out much of the terraqueous Globe with a pair of Compasses[2] that belonged to myself only.

"Of great Scenes why speak? Three summer days, I lingered reflecting, and even composing (*dichtete*), by the Pine-chasms of Vaucluse; and in that clear Lakelet [3] moistened my bread. I have sat under the Palm-trees of Tadmor; [4] smoked a pipe among the ruins of Babylon. The great Wall of China I have seen; and can testify that it is of gray brick, coped and covered with granite, and shows only second-rate masonry.—Great Events, also, have not I witnessed? Kings sweated-down (*ausgemergelt*) into Berlin-and-Milan Customhouse-Officers; [5] the World well won, and the World well lost; [6] oftener than once a hundred-thousand individuals shot (by each other) in one day. All kindreds and peoples and nations dashed together, and shifted and shovelled into heaps, that they might ferment there, and in time unite. The birth-pangs of Democracy,[7] wherewith convulsed Europe was groaning in cries that reached Heaven, could not escape me.

"For great Men I have ever had the warmest predilection; and can perhaps boast that few such in this era have wholly escaped me. Great Men are the inspired (speaking and acting) Texts of that divine BOOK OF REVELATION, whereof a Chapter is completed from epoch to epoch, and by some named HISTORY; to which inspired Texts your numerous talented men, and your innumerable untalented men, are the better or worse exegetic Commentaries, and wagonload of too-stupid, heretical or orthodox, weekly Sermons. For my study, the inspired Texts themselves! Thus did not I, in very early days, having disguised me as tavern-waiter, stand behind

1. Roman emperor (76–138) who traveled extensively throughout his empire.
2. I.e., legs.
3. A pool at the base of a mountain in Vaucluse in southern France. The adjacent "Pine-chasms" were one of Petrarch's favorite haunts. For Teufelsdröckh the area served as one of the "secular wells" that helped to restore him to spiritual health.

4. Palmyra in Syria.
5. Napoleon reduced some of Europe's kings to the status of mere tax collectors for his regime.
6. Cf. the title of Dryden's play *All for Love, or the World Well Lost.*
7. As manifested in the revolutionary outbreaks in France (1789 and 1830) and in the agitations in England preceding the Reform Bill of 1832.

the field-chairs, under that shady Tree at Treisnitz by the Jena High-way;[8] waiting upon the great Schiller and greater Goethe; and hearing what I have not forgotten. For—"

—But at this point the Editor recalls his principle of caution, some time ago laid down, and must suppress much. Let not the sacredness of Laurelled, still more, of Crowned Heads, be tampered with. Should we, at a future day, find circumstances altered, and the time come for Publication, then may these glimpses into the privacy of the Illustrious be conceded; which for the present were little better than treacherous, perhaps traitorous Eavesdroppings. Of Lord Byron, therefore, of Pope Pius, Emperor Tarakwang, and the "White Water-roses"[9] (Chinese Carbonari) with their mysteries, no notice here! Of Napoleon himself we shall only, glancing from afar, remark that Teufelsdröckh's relation to him seems to have been of very varied character. At first we find our poor Professor on the point of being shot as a spy; then taken into private conversation, even pinched on the ear, yet presented with no money; at last indignantly dismissed, almost thrown out of doors, as an "Ideologist." "He himself," says the Professor, "was among the completest Ideologists, at least Ideopraxists:[1] in the Idea (*in der Idee*) he lived, moved and fought. The man was a Divine Missionary, though unconscious of it; and preached, through the cannon's throat, that great doctrine, *La carrière ouverte aux talens* (The Tools to him that can handle them), which is our ultimate Political Evangel, wherein alone can liberty lie. Madly enough he preached, it is true, as Enthusiasts[2] and first Missionaries are wont, with imperfect utterance, amid much frothy rant; yet as articulately perhaps as the case admitted. Or call him, of you will, an American Backwoodsman, who had to fell un-penetrated forests, and battle with innumerable wolves, and did not entirely forbear strong liquor, rioting, and even theft; whom, notwithstanding, the peaceful Sower will follow, and, as he cuts the boundless harvest, bless."

More legitimate and decisively authentic is Teufelsdröckh's appearance and emergence (we know not well whence) in the solitude of the North Cape, on that June Midnight. He has a "light-blue Spanish cloak" hanging round him, as his "most commodious, principal, indeed sole upper-garment"; and stands there, on the World-promontory, looking over the infinite Brine, like a little blue Belfry (as we figure), now motionless indeed, yet ready, if stirred, to ring quaintest changes.

"Silence as of death," writes he; "for Midnight, even in the Arctic latitudes, has its character: nothing but the granite cliffs ruddy-tinged, the peaceable gurgle of that slow-heaving Polar Ocean, over

---

8. Where Goethe and Schiller met during the 1790's when they were collaborating on their writings.
9. Like the Carbonari in Italy, a secret revolutionary society in China during the regime of Emperor "Tarakwang" (Tao Kuang, 1821–50).
1. Those who put ideas into practice.
2. Religious fanatics.

which in the utmost North the great Sun hangs low and lazy, as if he too were slumbering. Yet is his cloud-couch wrought of crimson and cloth-of-gold; yet does his light stream over the mirror of waters, like a tremulous fire-pillar, shooting downwards to the abyss, and hide itself under my feet. In such moments, Solitude also is invaluable; for who would speak, or be looked on, when behind him lies all Europe and Africa, fast asleep, except the watchmen; and before him the silent Immensity, and Palace of the Eternal, whereof our Sun is but a porch-lamp?

"Nevertheless, in this solemn moment comes a man, or monster, scrambling from among the rock-hollows; and, shaggy, huge as the Hyperborean [3] Bear, hails me in Russian speech: most probably, therefore, a Russian Smuggler. With courteous brevity, I signify my indifference to contraband trade, my humane intentions, yet strong wish to be private. In vain: the monster, counting doubtless on his superior stature, and minded to make sport for himself, or perhaps profit, were it with murder, continues to advance; ever assailing me with his importunate train-oil[4] breath; and now has advanced, till we stand both on the verge of the rock, the deep Sea rippling greedily down below. What argument will avail? On the thick Hyperborean, cherubic reasoning, seraphic eloquence were lost. Prepared for such extremity, I, deftly enough, whisk aside one step; draw out, from my interior reservoirs, a sufficient Birmingham Horse-pistol, and say, 'Be so obliging as retire, Friend (*Er ziehe sich zurück, Freund*), and with promptitude!' This logic even the Hyperborean understands: fast enough, with apologetic, petitionary growl, he sidles off; and, except for suicidal as well as homicidal purposes, need not return.

"Such I hold to be the genuine use of Gunpowder: that it makes all men alike tall. Nay, if thou be cooler, cleverer than I, if thou have more *Mind*, though all but no *Body* whatever, then canst thou kill me first, and are the taller. Hereby, at last, is the Goliath powerless, and the David resistless; savage Animalism is nothing, inventive Spiritualism is all.

"With respect to Duels, indeed, I have my own ideas. Few things, in this so surprising world, strike me with more surprise. Two little visual Spectra of men, hovering with insecure enough cohesion in the midst of the UNFATHOMABLE, and to dissolve therein, at any rate, very soon,—make pause at the distance of twelve paces asunder; whirl round; and, simultaneously by the cunningest mechanism, explode one another into Dissolution; and off-hand become Air, and Nonextant! Deuce on it (*verdammt*), the little spitfires!—Nay, I think with old Hugo von Trimberg:[5] 'God must needs laugh outright, could such a thing be, to see his wondrous Manikins here below.' "

3. From the far North.   5. Medieval poet (1260–1309).
4. Whale oil.

But amid these specialties, let us not forget the great generality, which is our Chief guest here: How prospered the inner man of Teufelsdröckh under so much outward shifting? Does Legion [6] still lurk in him, though repressed; or has he exorcised that Devil's Brood? We can answer that the symptoms continue promising. Experience is the grand spiritual Doctor; and with him Teufelsdröckh has been long a patient, swallowing many a bitter bolus.[7] Unless our poor Friend belong to the numerous class of Incurables, which seems not likely, some cure will doubtless be effected. We should rather say that Legion, or the Satanic School, was now pretty well extirpated and cast out, but next to nothing introduced in its room; whereby the heart remains, for the while, in a quiet but no comfortable state.

"At length, after so much roasting," thus writes our Autobiographer, "I was what you might name calcined. Pray only that it be not rather, as is the more frequent issue, reduced to a *caput-mortuum!*[8] But in any case, by mere dint of practice, I had grown familiar with many things. Wretchedness was still wretched; but I could now partly see through it, and despise it. Which highest mortal, in this inane Existence, had I not found a Shadow-hunter, or Shadow-hunted; and, when I looked through his brave garnitures, miserable enough? Thy wishes have all been sniffed aside, thought I: but what, had they ever been all granted! Did not the Boy Alexander weep because he had not two Planets to conquer; or a whole Solar System; or after that, a whole Universe? *Ach Gott*, when I gazed into these Stars, have they not looked-down on me as if with pity, from their serene spaces; like Eyes glistening with heavenly tears over the little lot of man! Thousands of human generations, all as noisy as our own, have been swallowed-up of Time, and there remains no wreck of them any more; and Arcturus and Orion and Sirius and the Pleiades are still shining in their courses, clear and young, as when the Shepherd first noted them in the plain of Shinar.[9] Pshaw! what is this paltry little Dog-cage[1] of an Earth; what art thou that sittest whining there? Thou art still Nothing, Nobody: true; but who, then, is Something, Somebody? For thee the Family of Man has no use; it rejects thee; thou art wholly as a dissevered limb: so be it; perhaps it is better so!"

Too-heavy-laden Teufelsdröckh! Yet surely his bands are loosen-

6. Unclean spirits as described in Mark v.9.
7. Large pill.
8. Death's head.
9. The shepherd is probably Abraham, who was commanded by the Lord to "tell the stars, if thou be able to number them" (Genesis xv.5). Shinar was a plain in the Sumerian region (in mod-

ern times, Iraq). Abraham migrated from the Sumerian city of Ur (Genesis x.10; xi.31).
1. A drum-shaped cage that turns when a dog runs inside the cylinder. This dog-powered device, attached to a kitchen spit, was used for turning joints of meat during roasting.

ing; one day he will hurl the burden far from him, and bound forth free and with a second youth.

The Everlasting Yea

"Temptations in the Wilderness!"[2] exclaims Teufelsdröckh: "Have we not all to be tried with such? Not so easily can the old Adam, lodged in us by birth, be dispossessed. Our Life is compassed round with Necessity; yet is the meaning of Life itself no other than Freedom, than Voluntary Force: thus have we a warfare; in the beginning, especially, a hard-fought battle. For the God-given mandate, *Work thou in Welldoing*, lies mysteriously written, in Promethean[3] Prophetic Characters, in our hearts; and leaves us no rest, night or day, till it be deciphered and obeyed; till it burn forth, in our conduct, a visible, acted Gospel of Freedom. And as the clay-given mandate, *Eat thou and be filled,* at the same time persuasively proclaims itself through every nerve,—must not there be a confusion, a contest, before the better Influence can become the upper?

"To me nothing seems more natural than that the Son of Man, when such God-given mandate first prophetically stirs within him, and the Clay must now be vanquished, or vanquish,—should be carried of the spirit into grim Solitudes, and there fronting the Tempter do grimmest battle with him; defiantly setting him at naught, till he yield and fly. Name it as we choose: with or without visible Devil, whether in the natural Desert of rocks and sands, or in the populous moral Desert of selfishness and baseness,—to such Temptation are we all called. Unhappy if we are not! Unhappy if we are but Half-men, in whom that divine handwriting has never blazed forth, all-subduing, in true sun-splendour; but quivers dubiously amid meaner lights: or smoulders, in dull pain, in darkness, under earthly vapours!—Our Wilderness is the wide World in an Atheistic Century; our Forty Days are long years of suffering and fasting: nevertheless, to these also comes an end. Yes, to me also was given, if not Victory, yet the consciousness of Battle, and the resolve to persevere therein while life or faculty is left. To me also, entangled in the enchanted forests, demon-peopled, doleful of sight and of sound, it was given, after weariest wanderings, to work out my way into the higher sunlit slopes—of that Mountain which has no summit, or whose summit is in Heaven only!"

He says elsewhere, under a less ambitious figure; as figures are, once for all, natural to him: "Has not thy Life been that of most sufficient men (*tüchtigen Männer*) thou hast known in this generation? An outflush of foolish young Enthusiasm, like the first

2. Matthew iv.1.
3. Fiery or fiery-spirited, an allusion to Prometheus, the defiant Titan who brought the secret of fire-making to man.

938 · *Thomas Carlyle*

fallow-crop, wherein are as many weeds as valuable herbs: this all parched away, under the Droughts of practical and spiritual Unbelief, as Disappointment, in thought and act, often-repeated gave rise to Doubt, and Doubt gradually settled into Denial! If I have had a second-crop, and now see the perennial greensward, and sit under umbrageous[4] cedars, which defy all Drought (and Doubt); herein too, be the Heavens praised, I am not without examples, and even exemplars."

So that, for Teufelsdröckh also, there has been a "glorious revolution":[5] these mad shadow-hunting and shadow-hunted Pilgrimings of his were but some purifying "Temptation in the Wilderness," before his Apostolic work (such as it was) could begin; which Temptation is now happily over, and the Devil once more worsted! Was "that high moment in the *Rue de l'Enfer*," then, properly the turning-point of the battle; when the Fiend said, *Worship me or be torn in shreds*; and was answered valiantly with an *Apage Satana?*[6] —Singular Teufelsdröckh, would thou hadst told thy singular story in plain words! But it is fruitless to look there, in those Paper-bags,[7] for such. Nothing but innuendoes, figurative crotchets: a typical Shadow, fitfully wavering, prophetico-satiric; no clear logical Picture. "How paint to the sensual eye," asks he once, "what passes in the Holy-of-Holies of Man's Soul; in what words, known to these profane times, speak even afar-off of the unspeakable?" We ask in turn: Why perplex these times, profane as they are, with needless obscurity, by omission and by commission? Not mystical only is our Professor, but whimsical; and involves himself, now more than ever, in eye-bewildering *chiaroscuro*.[8] Successive glimpses, here faithfully imparted, our more gifted readers must endeavour to combine for their own behoof.

He says: "The hot Harmattan wind[9] had raged itself out; its howl went silent within me; and the long-deafened soul could now hear. I paused in my wild wanderings; and sat me down to wait, and consider; for it was as if the hour of change drew nigh. I seemed to surrender, to renounce utterly, and say: Fly, then, false shadows of Hope; I will chase you no more, I will believe you no more. And ye too, haggard spectres of Fear, I care not for you; ye too are all shadows and a lie. Let me rest here: for I am way-weary and life-weary; I will rest here, were it but to die: to die or to live is alike to me; alike insignificant."—And again: "Here, then, as I lay in that CENTRE OF INDIFFERENCE; cast, doubtless by benignant upper Influence, into a healing sleep, the heavy dreams rolled gradually away, and I awoke to a new Heaven and a new Earth.[1] The first

---

4. Shady.
5. The overthrow of James II of England in 1688.
6. "Get thee hence, Satan!" (Matthew iv.8–10).
7. Bags containing documents and writings by Teufelsdröckh.
8. Light and shade.
9. A hot dry wind in Africa.
1. Revelation xxi.1.

preliminary moral Act, Annihilation of Self (*Selbsttödtung*), had been happily accomplished; and my mind's eyes were now unsealed, and its hands ungyved."[2]

Might we not also conjecture that the following passage refers to his Locality, during this same "healing sleep"; that his Pilgrim-staff lies cast aside here, on "the high table-land"; and indeed that the repose is already taking wholesome effect on him? If it were not that the tone, in some parts, has more of riancy,[3] even of levity, than we could have expected! However, in Teufelsdröckh, there is always the strangest Dualism: light dancing, with guitar-music, will be going on in the fore-court, while by fits from within comes the faint whimpering of woe and wail. We transcribe the piece entire:

"Beautiful it was to sit there, as in my skyey Tent, musing and meditating; on the high table-land, in front of the Mountains; over me, as roof, the azure Dome, and around me, for walls, four azure-flowing curtains,—namely, of the Four azure winds, on whose bottom-fringes also I have seen gilding. And then to fancy the fair Castles that stood sheltered in these Mountain hollows; with their green flower-lawns, and white dames and damosels, lovely enough: or better still, the straw-roofed Cottages, wherein stood many a Mother baking bread, with her children round her:—all hidden and protectingly folded-up in the valley-folds; yet there and alive, as sure as if I beheld them. Or to see, as well as fancy, the nine Towns and Villages, that lay round my mountain-seat, which, in still weather, were wont to speak to me (by their steeple-bells) with metal tongue; and, in almost all weather, proclaimed their vitality by repeated Smoke-clouds; whereon, as on a culinary horologe,[4] I might read the hour of the day. For it was the smoke of cookery, as kind housewives at morning, midday, eventide, were boiling their husbands' kettles; and ever a blue pillar rose up into the air, successively or simultaneously, from each of the nine, saying, as plainly as smoke could say: Such and such a meal is getting ready here. Not uninteresting! For you have the whole Borough, with all its love-makings and scandal-mongeries, contentions and content-ments, as in miniature, and could cover it all with your hat.—If, in my wide Wayfarings, I had learned to look into the business of the World in its details, here perhaps was the place for combining it into general propositions, and deducing inferences therefrom.

"Often also could I see the black Tempest marching in anger through the Distance: round some Schreckhorn,[5] as yet grim-blue, would the eddying vapour gather, and there tumultuously eddy, and flow down like a mad witch's hair; till, after a space, it vanished, and, in the clear sunbeam, your Schreckhorn stood smiling grim-

2. Unfettered.
3. Gaiety.
4. Clock.

5. "Peak of Terror." A mountain in Switzerland.

white, for the vapour had held snow. How thou fermentest and elaboratest, in thy great fermenting-vat and laboratory of an Atmosphere, of a World, O Nature!—Or what is Nature? Ha! why do I not name thee GOD? Art not thou the 'Living Garment of God'? O Heavens, is it, in very deed, HE, then, that ever speaks through thee; that lives and loves in thee, that lives and loves in me?

"Fore-shadows, call them rather fore-splendours, of that Truth, and Beginning of Truths, fell mysteriously over my soul. Sweeter than Dayspring to the Shipwrecked in Nova Zembla;[6] ah, like the mother's voice to her little child that strays bewildered, weeping, in unknown tumults; like soft streamings of celestial music to my too-exasperated heart, came that Evangel. The Universe is not dead and demoniacal, a charnel-house with spectres; but godlike, and my Father's!

"With other eyes, too, could I now look upon my fellow man; with an infinite Love, an infinite Pity. Poor, wandering, wayward man! Art thou not tired, and beaten with stripes, even as I am? Ever, whether thou bear the royal mantle or the beggar's gabardine, art thou not so weary, so heavy-laden; and thy Bed of Rest is but a Grave. O my Brother, my Brother, why cannot I shelter thee in my bosom, and wipe away all tears from thy eyes! Truly, the din of many-voiced Life, which, in this solitude, with the mind's organ, I could hear, was no longer a maddening discord, but a melting one; like inarticulate cries, and sobbings of a dumb creature, which in the ear of Heaven are prayers. The poor Earth, with her poor joys, was now my needy Mother, not my cruel Stepdame; man, with his so mad Wants and so mean Endeavours, had become the dearer to me; and even for his sufferings and his sins, I now first named him Brother. Thus I was standing in the porch of that 'Sanctuary of Sorrow';[7] by strange, steep ways had I too been guided thither; and ere long its sacred gates would open, and the 'Divine Depth of Sorrow' lie disclosed to me."

The Professor says, he here first got eye on the Knot that had been strangling him, and straightway could unfasten it, and was free. "A vain interminable controversy," writes he, "touching what is at present called Origin of Evil, or some such thing, arises in every soul, since the beginning of the world; and in every soul, that would pass from idle Suffering into actual Endeavouring, must first be put an end to. The most, in our time, have to go content with a simple, incomplete enough Suppression of this controversy; to a few some Solution of it is indispensable. In every new era, too, such Solution comes-out in different terms; and ever the Solution

6. A Dutch sea captain, whose ship was wrecked off the island of Nova Zembla in the Arctic in 1596, recorded in his journal his thankfulness at the coming of daylight.
7. Adapted from Goethe's *Wilhelm Meister.*

of the last era has become obsolete, and is found unserviceable. For
it is man's nature to change his Dialect from century to century;
he cannot help it though he would. The authentic *Church-Cate-
chism* of our present century has not yet fallen into my hands:
meanwhile, for my own private behoof, I attempt to elucidate the
matter so. Man's Unhappiness, as I construe, comes of his Greatness; it is because there is an Infinite in him, which with all his
cunning he cannot quite bury under the Finite. Will the whole
Finance Ministers and Upholsterers and Confectioners of modern
Europe undertake, in joint-stock company, to make one Shoeblack
HAPPY? They cannot accomplish it, above an hour or two; for the
Shoeblack also has a Soul quite other than his Stomach; and would
require, if you consider it, for his permanent satisfaction and satura-
tion, simply this allotment, no more, and no less: *God's infinite
Universe altogether to himself*, therein to enjoy infinitely, and fill
every wish as fast as it rose. Oceans of Hochheimer,[8] a Throat like
that of Ophiuchus:[9] speak not of them; to the infinite Shoeblack
they are as nothing. No sooner is your ocean filled, than he grum-
bles that it might have been of better vintage. Try him with half
of a Universe, of an Omnipotence, he sets to quarrelling with the
proprietor of the other half, and declares himself the most mal-
treated of men.—Always there is a black spot in our sunshine: it is
even as I said, the *Shadow of Ourselves*.

"But the whim we have of Happiness is somewhat thus. By certain valuations, and averages, of our own striking, we come upon
some sort of average terrestrial lot; this we fancy belongs to us by
nature, and of indefeasible right. It is simple payment of our wages,
of our deserts; requires neither thanks nor complaint; only such
overplus as there may be do we account Happiness; any *deficit* again
is Misery. Now consider that we have the valuation of our own
deserts ourselves, and what a fund of Self-conceit there is in each
of us,—do you wonder that the balance should so often dip the
wrong way, and many a Blockhead cry: See there, what a payment;
was ever worthy gentleman so used!—I tell thee, Blockhead, it all
comes of thy Vanity; of what thou *fanciest* those same deserts of
thine to be. Fancy that thou deservest to be hanged (as is most
likely), thou wilt feel it happiness to be only shot: fancy that thou
deservest to be hanged in a hair-halter, it will be a luxury to die
in hemp.

"So true is it, what I then say, that *the Fraction of Life can be
increased in value not so much by increasing your Numerator as by
lessening your Denominator*. Nay, unless my Algebra deceive me,
Unity itself divided by *Zero* will give *Infinity*. Make thy claim of
wages a zero, then; thou hast the world under thy feet. Well did

8. Rhine wine or hock from Hochheim. 9. The serpent in the constellation
Serpentarius.

the Wisest of our time write: 'It is only with Renunciation (*Entsagen*) that Life, properly speaking, can be said to begin.'[1]

"I asked myself: What is this that, ever since earliest years, thou hast been fretting and fuming, and lamenting and self-tormenting, on account of? Say it in a word: is it not because thou art not HAPPY? Because the THOU (sweet gentleman) is not sufficiently honoured, nourished, soft-bedded, and lovingly cared for? Foolish soul! What Act of Legislature was there that *thou* shouldst be Happy? A little while ago thou hadst no right to *be* at all. What if thou wert born and predestined not to be Happy, but to be Unhappy! Art thou nothing other than a Vulture, then, that fliest through the Universe seeking after somewhat to *eat*; and shrieking dolefully because carrion enough is not given thee? Close thy *Byron*; open thy *Goethe*."

"*Es leuchtet mir ein*,[2] I see a glimpse of it!" cries he elsewhere: "there is in man a HIGHER than Love of Happiness: he can do without Happiness, and instead thereof find Blessedness! Was it not to preach-forth this same HIGHER that sages and martyrs, the Poet and the Priest, in all times, have spoken and suffered; bearing testimony, through life and through death, of the Godlike that is in Man, and how in the Godlike only has he Strength and Freedom? Which God-inspired Doctrine art thou also honoured to be taught; O Heavens! and broken with manifold merciful Afflictions, even till thou become contrite, and learn it! O, thank thy Destiny for these; thankfully bear what yet remain: thou hadst need of them; the Self in thee needed to be annihilated. By benignant fever-paroxysms is Life rooting out the deep-seated chronic Diseases, and triumphs over Death. On the roaring billows of Time, thou art not engulfed, but borne aloft into the azure of Eternity. Love not Pleasure; love God.[3] This is the EVERLASTING YEA, wherein all contradiction is solved: wherein whoso walks and works, it is well with him."

And again: "Small is it that thou canst trample the Earth with its injuries under thy feet, as old Greek Zeno[4] trained thee: thou canst love the Earth while it injures thee, and even because it injures thee; for this a Greater than Zeno was needed, and he too was sent. Knowest thou that '*Worship of Sorrow*'?[5] The Temple thereof, founded some eighteen centuries ago, now lies in ruins, overgrown with jungle, the habitation of doleful creatures: nevertheless, venture forward; in a low crypt, arched out of falling fragments, thou findest the Altar still there, and its sacred Lamp perennially burning."

1. Adapted from *Wilhelm Meister;* "the wisest of our time" is Goethe.
2. An exclamation of Wilhelm Meister's.
3. II Timothy iii.4.
4. Greek Stoic philosopher of the 3rd century B.C. After being injured in a fall Zeno is reputed to have struck the earth with his hand as if the earth were responsible for his injury. Afterwards he committed suicide. Hence is said to "trample the Earth."
5. Christianity.

Without pretending to comment on which strange utterances, the Editor will only remark, that there lies beside them much of a still more questionable character; unsuited to the general apprehension; nay wherein he himself does not see his way. Nebulous disquisitions on Religion, yet not without bursts of splendour; on the "perennial continuance of Inspiration"; on Prophecy; that there are "true Priests, as well as Baal-Priests,[6] in our own day": with more of the like sort. We select some fractions, by way of finish to this farrago.

"Cease, my much-respected Herr von Voltaire," thus apostrophises the Professor: "shut thy sweet voice; for the task appointed thee seems finished. Sufficiently hast thou demonstrated this proposition, considerable or otherwise: That the Mythus of the Christian Religion looks not in the eighteenth century as it did in the eighth. Alas, were thy six-and-thirty quartos, and the six-and-thirty thousand other quartos and folios, and flying sheets or reams, printed before and since on the same subject, all needed to convince us of so little! But what next? Wilt thou help us to embody the divine Spirit of that Religion in a new Mythus, in a new vehicle and vesture, that our Souls, otherwise too like perishing, may live? What! thou hast no faculty in that kind? Only a torch for burning, no hammer for building? Take our thanks, then, and —— thyself away.

"Meanwhile what are antiquated Mythuses to me? Or is the God present, felt in my own heart, a thing which Herr von Voltaire will dispute out of me; or dispute into me? To the '*Worship of Sorrow*' ascribe what origin and genesis thou pleasest, *has* not that Worship originated, and been generated; is it not *here?* Feel it in thy heart, and then say whether it is of God! This is Belief; all else is Opinion, —for which latter whoso will let him worry and be worried."

"Neither," observes he elsewhere, "shall ye tear-out one another's eyes, struggling over 'Plenary Inspiration,'[7] and suchlike: try rather to get a little even Partial Inspiration, each of you for himself. One BIBLE I know, of whose Plenary Inspiration doubt is not so much as possible; nay with my own eyes I saw the God's-Hand writing it: thereof all other Bibles are but leaves,—say, in Picture-Writing to assist the weaker faculty."

Or, to give the wearied reader relief, and bring it to an end, let him take the following perhaps more intelligible passage:

"To me, in this our life," says the Professor, "which is an internecine warfare with the Time-spirit, other warfare seems questionable. Hast thou in any way a Contention with thy brother, I advise thee, think well what the meaning thereof is. If thou gauge

6. False priests. See I Kings xviii.17–40.
7. Doctrine that all statements in the Bible are supernaturally inspired and authoritative. Voltaire had sought to demonstrate that this doctrine was absurd.

it to the bottom, it is simply this: 'Fellow, see! thou art taking more than thy share of Happiness in the world, something from *my* share: which, by the Heavens, thou shalt not; nay I will fight thee rather.'—Alas, and the whole lot to be divided is such a beggarly matter, truly a 'feast of shells,'[8] for the substance has been spilled out: not enough to quench one Appetite; and the collective human species clutching at them!—Can we not, in all such cases, rather say: 'Take it, thou too-ravenous individual; take that pitiful additional fraction of a share, which I reckoned mine, but which thou so wantest; take it with a blessing: would to Heaven I had enough for thee!'—If Fichte's *Wissenschaftslehre*[9] be, 'to a certain extent, Applied Christianity,' surely to a still greater extent, so is this. We have here not a Whole Duty of Man,[1] yet a Half Duty, namely the Passive half: could we but do it, as we can demonstrate it!

"But indeed Conviction, were it never so excellent, is worthless till it convert itself into Conduct. Nay properly Conviction is not possible till then; inasmuch as all Speculation is by nature endless, formless, a vortex amid vortices: only by a felt indubitable certainty of Experience does it find any centre to revolve round, and so fashion itself into a system. Most true is it, as a wise man teaches us, that 'Doubt of any sort cannot be removed except by Action.'[2] On which ground, too, let him who gropes painfully in darkness or uncertain light, and prays vehemently that the dawn may ripen into day, lay this other precept well to heart, which to me was of invaluable service: '*Do the Duty which lies nearest thee*,' which thou knowest to be a Duty! Thy second Duty will already have become clearer.

"May we not say, however, that the hour of Spiritual Enfranchisement is even this: When your Ideal World, wherein the whole man has been dimly struggling and inexpressibly languishing to work, becomes revealed, and thrown open; and you discover, with amazement enough, like the Lothario in *Wilhelm Meister*, that your 'America is here or nowhere'? The Situation that has not its Duty, its Ideal, was never yet occupied by man. Yes here, in this poor, miserable, hampered, despicable Actual, wherein thou even now standest, here or nowhere is thy Ideal: work it out therefrom; and working, believe, live, be free. Fool! the Ideal is in thyself, the impediment too is in thyself: thy Condition is but the stuff thou art to shape that same Ideal out of: what matters whether such stuff be of this sort or that, so the Form thou give it be heroic, be poetic? O thou that pinest in the imprisonment of the Actual, and criest bitterly to the gods for a kingdom wherein to rule and create, know

---

8. Empty eggshells.
9. "The Doctrine of Knowledge"; by the German philosopher Johann Gottlieb Fichte (1762–1814).
1. Title of an anonymous book of reli-

gious instruction first published in 1659.
2. This and the following quotation are from Goethe's *Wilhelm Meister*.

this of a truth: the thing thou seekest is already with thee, 'here or nowhere,' couldst thou only see!

"But it is with man's Soul as it was with Nature: the beginning of Creation is—Light.[3] Till the eye have vision, the whole members are in bonds.[4] Divine moment, when over the tempest-tost Soul, as once over the wild-weltering Chaos, it is spoken: Let there be Light! Ever to the greatest that has felt such moment, is it not miraculous and God-announcing; even as, under simpler figures, to the simplest and least. The mad primeval Discord is hushed; the rudely-jumbled conflicting elements bind themselves into separate Firmaments: deep silent rock-foundations are built beneath; and the skyey vault with its everlasting Luminaries above: instead of a dark wasteful Chaos, we have a blooming, fertile, heaven-encompassed World.

"I too could now say to myself: Be no longer a Chaos, but a World, or even Worldkin. Produce! Produce! Were it but the pitifullest infinitesimal fraction of a Product, produce it, in God's name! 'Tis the utmost thou hast in thee: out with it, then. Up, up! Whatsoever thy hand findeth to do, do it with thy whole might. Work while it is called Today; for the Night cometh, wherein no man can work."[5]

Natural Supernaturalism[1]

It is in his stupendous Section, headed *Natural Supernaturalism*, that the Professor first becomes a Seer; and, after long effort, such as we have witnessed, finally subdues under his feet this refractory Clothes-Philosophy, and takes victorious possession thereof. Phantasms enough he has had to struggle with; "Cloth-webs and Cobwebs," of Imperial Mantles, Superannuated Symbols, and what not:

---

3. Cf. Genesis i.3.
4. Cf. Matthew vi.22–23.
5. Adapted from Ecclesiastes ix.10 and John ix.4.
1. Book III, Chapter 8. The characteristically paradoxical title of this chapter can best be understood by reference to the chapter on miracles in David Hume's *An Enquiry Concerning Human Understanding* (1748), to which Carlyle makes several direct and indirect allusions in his own exposition of the nature of the miraculous. In his skeptical analysis of miracles (Christian miracles in particular), Hume asserts: "A miracle is a violation of the laws of nature. * * * It is no miracle that a man, seemingly in good health, should die on a sudden. * * * But it is a miracle that a dead man should come to life, because that

has never been observed in any age or country." The young Carlyle seems to have been impressed by Hume's arguments, as he had also been impressed (and depressed) by Gibbon's relentless exposure of traditional Christianity in *The Decline and Fall of the Roman Empire*. In his later resolution of his dilemma, he bypassed Hume's arguments. Instead of arguing whether miracles in the traditional sense (such as the resurrection of Christ) have occurred, he contends that *everything* in our experience is a miracle of a supernatural and inexplicable order, hence an appropriate cause for wonder and joy. The natural *is* supernatural. "To me," said Wordsworth, "the meanest flower that blows can give / Thoughts that do often lie too deep for tears."

yet still did he courageously pierce through. Nay, worst of all, two quite mysterious, world-embracing Phantasms, TIME and SPACE, have ever hovered round him, perplexing and bewildering: but with these also he now resolutely grapples, these also he victoriously rends asunder. In a word, he has looked fixedly on Existence, till one after the other, its earthly hulls and garnitures have all melted away; and now, to his rapt vision, the interior celestial Holy of Holies lies disclosed.

Here, therefore, properly it is that the Philosophy of Clothes attains to Transcendentalism;[2] this last leap, can we but clear it, takes us safe into the promised land, where *Palingenesia*,[3] in all senses, may be considered as beginning. "Courage, then!" may our Diogenes exclaim, with better right than Diogenes the First once did.[4] This stupendous Section we, after long painful meditation, have found not to be unintelligible; but, on the contrary, to grow clear, nay radiant, and all-illuminating. Let the reader, turning on it what utmost force of speculative intellect is in him, do his part; as we, by judicious selection and adjustment, shall study to do ours:

"Deep has been, and is, the significance of Miracles," thus quietly begins the Professor; "far deeper perhaps than we imagine. Meanwhile, the question of questions were: What specially. is a Miracle? To that Dutch King of Siam, an icicle had been a miracle; whoso had carried with him an air-pump, and vial of vitriolic ether, might have worked a miracle.[5] To my Horse, again, who unhappily is still more unscientific, do not I work a miracle, and magical '*Open sesame!*'[6] every time I please to pay twopence, and open for him an impassable *Schlagbaum*, or shut Turnpike?

"'But is not a real Miracle simply a violation of the Laws of Nature?' ask several. Whom I answer by this new question: What are the Laws of Nature? To me perhaps the rising of one from the dead were no violation of these Laws, but a confirmation; were some far deeper Law, now first penetrated into, and by Spiritual Force, even as the rest have all been, brought to bear on us with its Material Force.

"Here too may some inquire, not without astonishment: On what ground shall one, that can make Iron swim,[7] come and declare that therefore he can teach Religion? To us, truly, of the Nineteenth Century, such declaration were inept enough; which

---

2. A term loosely used here to refer to any philosophy which opposes materialism or empiricism, and which asserts the domination of the intuitive or spiritual over the material [C. F. Harrold].

3. Rebirth.

4. Near the end of a dull lecture, Diogenes ("the First"), a philosopher of the Cynic school, called out to his fellow listeners: "Courage, friends! I see land."

5. In his chapter on miracles, Hume cites an incident of an Indian prince refusing to believe that water can be turned into ice. Carlyle notes that anybody could do so by treating a flask of sulphuric ether with an air pump.

6. The magic password for opening a door in the cavern in the story *Ali Baba and the Forty Thieves*, in *The Arabian Nights*.

7. Elisha's miracle of causing an axehead to float in water (II Kings i.17).

nevertheless to our fathers, of the First Century, was full of meaning.

"'But is it not the deepest Law of Nature that she be constant?' cries an illuminated class: 'Is not the Machine of the Universe fixed to move by unalterable rules?' Probable enough, good friends: nay I, too, must believe that the God, whom ancient inspired men assert to be 'without variableness or shadow of turning,'[8] does indeed never change; that Nature, that the Universe, which no one whom it so pleases can be prevented from calling a Machine, does move by the most unalterable rules. And now of you, too, I make the old inquiry: What those same unalterable rules, forming the complete Statute-Book of Nature, may possibly be?

"They stand written in our Works of Science, say you; in the accumulated records of Man's Experience?—Was Man with his Experience present at the Creation, then, to see how it all went on? Have any deepest scientific individuals yet dived down to the foundations of the Universe, and gauged everything there? Did the Maker take them into His counsel; that they read His groundplan of the incomprehensible All; and can say, This stands marked therein, and no more than this? Alas, not in anywise! These scientific individuals have been nowhere but where we also are; have seen some handbreadths deeper than we see into the Deep that is infinite, without bottom as without shore.

"Laplace's Book on the Stars,[9] wherein he exhibits that certain Planets, with their Satellites, gyrate round our worthy Sun, at a rate and in a course, which, by greatest good fortune, he and the like of him have succeeded in detecting,—is to me as precious as to another. But is this what thou namest 'Mechanism of the Heavens,' and 'System of the World'; this, wherein Sirius and the Pleiades, and all Herschel's[1] Fifteen-thousand Suns per minute, being left out, some paltry handful of Moons, and inert Balls, had been—looked at, nicknamed, and marked in the Zodiacal Way-bill;[2] so that we can now prate of their Whereabout; their How, their Why, their What, being hid from us, as in the signless Inane?

"System of Nature! To the wisest man, wide as is his vision, Nature remains of quite *infinite* depth, of quite infinite expansion; and all Experience thereof limits itself to some few computed centuries and measured square-miles. The course of Nature's phases, on this our little fraction of a Planet, is partially known to us: but who knows what deeper courses these depend on; what infinitely larger

---

8. James i.17.
9. Pierre Laplace (1749–1827) wrote *A Treatise on Celestial Mechanics* (1799–1825) and other astronomical studies.
1. Sir William Herschel (1738–1832) was an astronomer credited with discovering

thousands of stars and other celestial bodies.
2. A way-bill was a document issued with freight shipments, providing complete information about contents and routes.

Cycle (of causes) our little Epicycle[3] revolves on? To the Minnow every cranny and pebble, and quality and accident, of its little native Creek may have become familiar: but does the Minnow understand the Ocean Tides and periodic Currents, the Trade-winds, and Monsoons, and Moon's Eclipses; by all which the condition of its little Creek is regulated, and may, from time to time (*un*miraculously enough), be quite overset and reversed? Such a minnow is Man; his Creek this Planet Earth; his Ocean the immeasurable All; his Monsoons and periodic Currents the mysterious Course of Providence through Æons of Æons.

"We speak of the Volume of Nature: and truly a Volume it is, —whose Author and Writer is God. To read it! Dost thou, does man, so much as well know the Alphabet thereof? With its Words, Sentences, and grand descriptive Pages, poetical and philosophical, spread out through Solar Systems, and Thousands of Years, we shall not try thee. It is a Volume written in celestial hieroglyphs, in the true Sacred-writing; of which even Prophets are happy that they can read here a line and there a line. As for your Institutes, and Academies of Science, they strive bravely; and, from amid the thick-crowded, inextricably intertwisted hieroglyphic writing, pick out, by dextrous combination, some Letters in the vulgar Character, and therefrom put together this and the other economic Recipe,[4] of high avail in Practice. That Nature is more than some boundless Volume of such Recipes, or huge, well-nigh inexhaustible Domestic-Cookery Book, of which the whole secret will in this manner one day evolve itself, the fewest dream.

"Custom," continues the Professor, "doth make dotards of us all.[5] Consider well, thou wilt find that Custom is the greatest of Weavers; and weaves air-raiment for all the Spirits of the Universe; whereby indeed these dwell with us visibly, as ministering servants, in our houses and workshops; but their spiritual nature becomes, to the most, forever hidden. Philosophy complains that Custom has hoodwinked us, from the first; that we do everything by Custom, even Believe by it; that our very Axioms, let us boast of Free-thinking as we may, are oftenest simply such Beliefs as we have never heard questioned. Nay, what is Philosophy throughout but a continual battle against Custom; an ever-renewed effort to *transcend* the sphere of blind Custom, and so become Transcendental?

"Innumerable are the illusions and legerdemain-tricks of Custom: but of all these, perhaps the cleverest is her knack of persuading us that the Miraculous, by simple repetition, ceases to be Miraculous. True, it is by this means we live; for man must work as well as

---

3. In Ptolemaic astronomy, a circle in which a planet moves, the center of this circle being carried round on the circumference of a larger circle (the "infinitely larger Cycle").

4. I.e., a law in Economics, such as the Law of Supply and Demand.
5. Cf. *Hamlet* I.iii.83: "Thus conscience does make cowards of us all."

wonder: and herein is Custom so far a kind nurse, guiding him to his true benefit. But she is a fond foolish nurse, or rather we are false foolish nurselings, when, in our resting and reflecting hours, we prolong the same deception. Am I to view the Stupendous with stupid indifference, because I have seen it twice, or two-hundred, or two-million times? There is no reason in Nature or in Art why I should: unless, indeed, I am a mere Work-Machine, for whom the divine gift of Thought were no other than the terrestrial gift of Steam is to the Steam-engine; a power whereby cotton might be spun, and money and money's worth realised.

"Notable enough too, here as elsewhere, wilt thou find the potency of Names; which indeed are but one kind of such custom-woven, wonder-hiding Garments. Witchcraft, and all manner of Spectre-work, and Demonology, we have now named Madness and Diseases of the Nerves. Seldom reflecting that still the new question comes upon us: What is Madness, what are Nerves? Ever, as before, does Madness remain a mysterious-terrific, altogether *infernal* boiling-up of the Nether Chaotic Deep, through this fair-painted Vision of Creation, which swims thereon, which we name the Real. Was Luther's Picture of the Devil[6] less a Reality, whether it were formed within the bodily eye, or without it? In every the wisest Soul lies a whole world of internal Madness, an authentic Demon-Empire; out of which, indeed, his world of Wisdom has been creatively built together, and now rests there, as on its dark foundations does a habitable flowery Earth-rind.

"But deepest of all illusory Appearances, for hiding Wonder, as for many other ends, are your two grand fundamental world-enveloping Appearances, SPACE and TIME. These, spun and woven for us from before Birth itself, to clothe our celestial ME for dwelling here, and yet to blind it,—lie all-embracing, as the universal canvas, or warp and woof, whereon all minor Illusions, in this Phantasm Existence, weave and paint themselves. In vain, while here on Earth, shall you endeavour to strip them off; you can, at best, but rend them asunder for moments, and look through.

. . . .

"Fortunatus had a wishing Hat, which when he put on, and wished himself Anywhere, behold he was There.7 By this means had Fortunatus triumphed over Space, he had annihilated Space; for him there was no Where, but all was Here. Were a Hatter to prosper in this sort for all mankind, what a world we should have of it! Still stranger, should, on the opposite side of the street, another

6. Martin Luther threw his inkstand at an apparition of the Devil which visited his study when he was translating the Psalms.

7. In the legend on which Thomas Dekker based his play *Old Fortunatus* (1600), a magic hat enabled the owner instantaneously to be anywhere he wished.

Hatter establish himself; and, as his fellow-craftsman made Space-annihilating Hats, make Time-annihilating! Of both would I purchase, were it with my last groschen;[8] but chiefly of this latter. To clap-on your felt, and, simply by wishing that you were Any*where*, straightway to be *There!* Next to clap-on your other felt, and, simply by wishing that you were Any*when*, straightway to be *Then!* This were indeed the grander: shooting at will from the Fire-Creation of the World to its Fire-Consummation; here historically present in the First Century, conversing face to face with Paul and Seneca;[9] there prophetically in the Thirty-first, conversing also face to face with other Pauls and Senecas, who as yet stand hidden in the depth of that late Time!

"Or thinkest thou it were impossible, unimaginable? Is the Past annihilated, then, or only past; is the Future non-extant, or only future? Those mystic faculties of thine, Memory and Hope, already answer: already through those mystic avenues, thou the Earth-blinded summonest both Past and Future, and communest with them, though as yet darkly, and with mute beckonings. The curtains of Yesterday drop down, the curtains of Tomorrow roll up; but Yesterday and Tomorrow both *are*. Pierce through the Time-element, glance into the Eternal. Believe what thou findest written in the sanctuaries of Man's Soul, even as all Thinkers, in all ages, have devoutly read it there: that Time and Space are not God, but creations of God; that with God as it is a universal HERE, so is it an everlasting NOW.

"And seest thou therein any glimpse of IMMORTALITY?—O Heaven! Is the white Tomb of our Loved One, who died from our arms, and had to be left behind us there, which rises in the distance, like a pale, mournfully receding Milestone, to tell how many toilsome uncheered miles we have journeyed on alone,—but a pale spectral Illusion! Is the Friend still mysteriously Here, even as we are Here mysteriously with God!—Know of a truth that only the Time-shadows have perished, or are perishable; that the real Being of whatever was, and whatever will be, *is* even now and forever. This, should it come, and whatever will be, *is* mayest ponder at thy leisure; for it is no idly seem new, thou twenty centuries: believe it thou mayest or the next not.

"That the Thought-forms, Space and Time, should come, thou canst we are sent into this Earth to live, should come our whole Practical reasonings, conceptions, and unavoidable inings, seems altogether fit, just, and unavoidable should, furthermore, usurp such sway over pure spirit all, tion, and blind us to the wonder everywhere lying close on us, seems nowise so. Admit Space and Time to their due rank as Forms of Thought;[1] nay even, if thou wilt, to their quite undue rank of Realities: and consider, then, with thyself how their thin disguises hide from us the brightest God-effulgences! Thus, were it not miraculous, could I stretch forth my hand and clutch the Sun? Yet thou seest me daily stretch forth my hand and therewith clutch many a thing, and swing it hither and thither. Art thou a grown baby, then, to fancy that the Miracle lies in miles of distance, or in pounds avoirdupois of weight; and not to see that the true inexplicable God-revealing Miracle lies in this, that I can stretch forth my hand at all; that I have free Force to clutch aught therewith? Innumerable other of this sort are the deceptions, and wonder-hiding stupefactions, which Space practices on us.

"Still worse is it with regard to Time. Your grand antimagician, and universal wonder-hider, is this same lying Time. Had we but the Time-annihilating Hat, to put on for once only, we should see ourselves in a World of Miracles, wherein all fabled or authentic Thaumaturgy,[2] and feats of Magic, were outdone. But unhappily we have not such a Hat; and man, poor fool that he is, can seldom and scantily help himself without one.

"Were it not wonderful, for instance, had Orpheus, or Amphion, built the walls of Thebes by the mere sound of his Lyre?[3] Yet tell me, Who built these walls of Weissnichtwo; summoning out all the sandstone rocks, to dance along from the *Steinbruch* (now a huge Troglodyte Chasm,[4] with frightful green-mantled pools), and shape themselves into Doric and Ionic pillars, squared ashlar houses[5] and noble streets? Was it not the still higher Orpheus, or Orpheuses, who, in past centuries, by the divine Music of Wisdom, succeeded in civilising Man? Our highest Orpheus walked in Judea, eighteen-hundred years ago: his sphere-melody, flowing in wild native tones, took captive the ravished souls of men; and, being of a true sphere-melody, still flows and sounds, though now with thousandfold accompaniments, and rich symphonies, through all our hearts; and modulates, and divinely leads them. Is that a wonder, which happens in two hours; and does it cease to be wonderful if happening in two million? Not only was Thebes built by the music of an Orpheus; but without the music of some inspired Orpheus was no city ever built, no work that man glories in ever done.

1. The idea that time and space are modes of perception rather than realities is derived from the philosophy of Immanuel Kant (1724–1804), author of *A Critique of Pure Reason* (1781).
2. The working of miracles and magical occurrences.
3. The musicians Orpheus and Amphion effected miracles: Orpheus, with his lyre, could spellbind wild beasts; Amphion's playing, during the building of Thebes, caused the stones for the walls to be drawn into place.
4. The emptied stone-quarry (*Steinbruch*) looks now like the site of primitive cave-dwellers (Troglodytes).
5. Houses made of squared blocks of hewn stone.

"Sweep away the Illusion of Time; glance, if thou have eyes, from the near moving-cause to its far-distant Mover: The stroke that came transmitted through a whole galaxy of elastic balls, was it less a stroke than if the last ball only had been struck, and sent flying? O, could I (with the Time-annihilating Hat) transport thee direct from the Beginnings to the Endings, how were thy eyesight unsealed, and thy heart set flaming in the Light-sea of celestial wonder! Then sawest thou that this fair Universe, were it in the meanest province thereof, is in very deed the star-domed City of God;[6] that through every star, through every grass-blade, and most through every Living Soul, the glory of a present God still beams. But Nature, which is the Time-vesture of God, and reveals Him to the wise, hides Him from the foolish.

"Again, could anything be more miraculous than an actual authentic Ghost? The English Johnson longed, all his life, to see one; but could not, though he went to Cock Lane, and thence to the church-vaults, and tapped on coffins.[7] Foolish Doctor! Did he never, with the mind's eye as well as with the body's, look round him into that full tide of human Life he so loved; did he never so much as look into Himself? The good Doctor was a Ghost, as actual and authentic as heart could wish; well-nigh a million of Ghosts were travelling the streets by his side. Once more I say, sweep away the illusion of Time; compress the threescore years into three minutes: what else was he, what else are we? Are we not Spirits, that are shaped into a body, into an Appearance; and that fade away again into air and Invisibility? This is no metaphor, it is a simple scientific *fact*; we start out of Nothingness, take figure, and are Apparitions; round us, as round the veriest spectre, is Eternity; and to Eternity minutes are as years and æons. Come there not tones of Love and Faith, as from celestial harp-strings, like the Song of beatified Souls? And again, do not we squeak and jibber (in our discordant, screech-owlish debatings and recriminatings); and glide bodeful, and feeble, and fearful; or uproar (*poltern*), and revel in our mad Dance of the Dead,—till the scent of the morning air[8] summons us to our still Home; and dreamy Night becomes awake and Day? Where now is Alexander of Macedon: does the steel Host, that yelled in fierce battle-shouts at Issus and Arbela,[9] remain behind him; or have they all vanished utterly, even as perturbed Goblins must? Napoleon too, and his Moscow Retreats and Austerlitz Campaigns! Was it all other than the veriest Spectre-hunt; which has now, with its howling tumult that made Night hideous, flitted away?—Ghosts! There are nigh a thousand-million walking

---

6. Title of St. Augustine's famous work.
7. The Cock Lane ghost in London, which proved to be a fraud, was investigated by Dr. Johnson. See Boswell for the year 1763.
8. Cf. *Hamlet* I.i.148–56 and v.58.
9. Sites of two victories won by the army of Alexander the Great against the Persians under Darius (333–31 B.C.).

the Earth openly at noon-tide; some half-hundred have vanished from it, some half-hundred have arisen in it, ere thy watch ticks once.

"O Heaven, it is mysterious, it is awful to consider that we not only carry each a future Ghost within Him; but are, in very deed, Ghosts! These Limbs, whence had we them; this stormy Force; this life-blood with its burning Passion? They are dust and shadow, a Shadow-system gathered round our ME; wherein, through some moments or years, the Divine Essence is to be revealed in the Flesh. That warrior on his strong war-horse, fire flashes through his eyes; force dwells in his arm and heart: but warrior and war-horse are a vision; a revealed Force, nothing more. Stately they tread the Earth, as if it were a firm substance: fool! the Earth is but a film; it cracks in twain, and warrior and war-horse sink beyond plummet's sounding.[1] Plummet's? Fantasy herself will not follow them. A little while ago, they were not; a little while, and they are not, their very ashes are not.

"So has it been from the beginning, so will it be to the end. Generation after generation takes to itself the Form of a Body; and forth-issuing from Cimmerian[2] Night, on Heaven's mission APPEARS. What Force and Fire is in each he expends: one grinding in the mill of Industry; one hunter-like climbing the giddy Alpine heights of Science; one madly dashed in pieces on the rocks of Strife, in war with his fellow:—and then the Heaven-sent is recalled; his earthly Vesture falls away, and soon even to sense becomes a vanished Shadow. Thus, like some wild-flaming, wild-thundering train of Heaven's Artillery, does this mysterious MANKIND thunder and flame, in long-drawn, quick-succeeding grandeur, through the unknown Deep. Thus, like a God-created, fire-breathing Spirit-host, we emerge from the Inane;[3] haste stormfully across the astonished Earth; then plunge again into the Inane. Earth's mountains are levelled, and her seas filled up, in our passage: can the Earth, which is but dead and a vision, resist Spirits which have reality and are alive? On the hardest adamant some footprint of us is stamped-in; the last Rear of the host will read traces of the earliest Van. But whence? —O Heaven, whither? Sense knows not; Faith knows not; only that it is through Mystery to Mystery, from God and to God.

> We *are such stuff*
> As dreams are made of, and our little Life
> Is rounded with a sleep![4]

1830–31   1833–34

---

1. *The Tempest* V.i.56. A plummet is a weight at the end of a line used to sound the depth of water under a ship.
2. I.e., a people living in perpetual darkness. See *Odyssey* XI.14.

3. The formless void of infinite space [NED].
4. *The Tempest* IV.i.156–58, a favorite passage for Carlyle, here slightly misquoted (Shakespeare wrote: "dreams are made on").

From Past and Present[1]
From *Democracy*

If the Serene Highnesses and Majesties do not take note of that,[2] then, as I perceive, *that* will take note of itself! The time for levity, insincerity, and idle babble and play-acting, in all kinds, is gone by; it is a serious, grave time. Old long-vexed questions, not yet solved in logical words or parliamentary laws, are fast solving themselves in facts, somewhat unblessed to behold! This largest of questions, this question of Work and Wages, which ought, had we heeded Heaven's voice, to have begun two generations ago or more, cannot be delayed longer without hearing Earth's voice. "Labour" will verily need to be somewhat "organized," as they say,—God knows with what difficulty. Man will actually need to have his debts and earnings a little better paid by man; which, let Parliaments speak of them, or be silent of them, are eternally his due from man, and cannot, without penalty and at length not without death-penalty,[3] be withheld. How much ought to cease among us straightway; how much ought to begin straightway, while the hours yet are!

Truly they are strange results to which this of leaving all to "Cash"; of quietly shutting up the God's Temple, and gradually opening wide-open the Mammon's Temple, with "Laissez-faire, and Every man for himself,"—have led us in these days! We have Upper, speaking Classes, who indeed do "speak" as never man spake before; the withered flimsiness, godless baseness and barrenness of whose Speech might of itself indicate what kind of Doing and practical Governing went on under it! For Speech is the gaseous element out of which most kinds of Practice and Performance,

1. In 1842 there were reputedly 1.5 million unemployed in England (out of a population of 18 million). The closing of factories and the reduction of wages led to severe rioting in the manufacturing districts. Bread-hungry mobs (as well as the Chartist mobs who demanded political reforms) caused many observers to dread that a large-scale revolution was imminent. Carlyle was himself so appalled by the plight of the industrial workers that he postponed his researches into the life and times of Cromwell in order to air his views on the contemporary crisis. *Past and Present*, a book written in seven weeks, was a call for heroic leadership. Cromwell and other historic leaders are cited, but the principal example from the past is Abbot Samson, a medieval monk who established order in the monasteries under his charge. Carlyle hoped that the "Captains of Industry" might provide a comparable leadership in 1843. He was aware that the spread of democracy was inevitable, but he had little confidence in it as a method of producing leaders. Nor did he have any confidence, at this time, in the landed aristocracy who seemed to him preoccupied with fox-hunting, preserving their game, and upholding the tariffs on grain (the Corn Laws). In place of a "Do nothing Aristocracy" there was need for a "Working Aristocracy." The first selection here printed is from Book III, Chapter 13.

2. The previous chapter, "Reward," had urged that English manufacturers needed the help of everyone, and that Parliament should remove the tariffs (Corn Laws) restricting the growth of trade and industry.

3. I.e., by the outbreak of a revolution, as in France.

especially all kinds of moral Performance, condense themselves, and take shape; as the one is, so will the other be. Descending, accordingly, into the Dumb Class in its Stockport Cellars[4] and Poor-Law Bastilles,[5] have we not to announce that they are hitherto unexampled in the History of Adam's Posterity?

Life was never a May-game for men: in all times the lot of the dumb millions born to toil was defaced with manifold sufferings, injustices, heavy burdens, avoidable and unavoidable; not play at all, but hard work that made the sinews sore and the heart sore. As bond-slaves, *villani, bordarii, sochemanni,* nay indeed as dukes, earls and kings, men were oftentimes made weary of their life; and had to say, in the sweat of their brow and of their soul, Behold, it is not sport, it is grim earnest, and our back can bear no more! Who knows not what massacrings and harryings there have been; grinding, long-continuing, unbearable injustices,—till the heart had to rise in madness, and some *"Eu Sachsen, nimith euer sachses,* You Saxons, out with your gully-knives, then!" You Saxons, some "arrestment," partial "arrestment of the Knaves and Dastards" has become indispensable!—The page of Dryasdust[6] is heavy with such details.

And yet I will venture to believe that in no time, since the beginnings of Society, was the lot of those same dumb millions of toilers so entirely unbearable as it is even in the days now passing over us. It is not to die, or even to die of hunger, that makes a man wretched; many men have died; all men must die,—the last exit of us all is in a Fire-Chariot of Pain.[7] But it is to live miserable we know not why; to work sore and yet gain nothing; to be heartworn, weary, yet isolated, unrelated, girt-in with a cold universal Laissez-faire: it is to die slowly all our life long, imprisoned in a deaf, dead, Infinite Injustice, as in the accursed iron belly of a Phalaris' Bull![8] This is and remains for ever intolerable to all men whom God has made. Do we wonder at French Revolutions, Chartisms, Revolts of Three Days? The times, if we will consider them, are really unexampled.

Never before did I hear of an Irish Widow reduced to "prove her sisterhood by dying of typhus-fever and infecting seventeen persons,"—saying in such undeniable way, "You *see,* I was your sister!"[9] Sisterhood, brotherhood, was often forgotten; but not till the rise of these ultimate Mammon and Shotbelt Gospels[1] did I ever

---

4. In a cellar in the slum district of Stockport, an industrial town near Manchester, three children were poisoned by their starving parents in order to collect insurance benefits from a burial society.
5. I.e. workhouse for the unemployed.
6. An imaginary author of dull histories.
7. Cf. II Kings ii.11–12.
8. Phalaris was a Sicilian tyrant whose victims were roasted alive by being confined inside the brass figure of a bull under which a fire was lit.
9. An incident referred to several times in *Past and Present.* Dickens in *Bleak House* also showed how indifference to the lack of sanitation in London slums led to the spread of disease to other parts of the city.
1. "Mammon Gospel" signifies the pursuit of wealth according to the eco-

see it so expressly denied. If no pious Lord or *Law-ward* would remember it, always some pious Lady ("*Hlaf dig*," Benefactress, "*Loaf-giveress*," they say she is,—blessings on her beautiful heart!) was there, with mild mother-voice and hand, to remember it; some pious thoughtful *Elder*, what we now call "Prester," *Presbyter* or "Priest," was there to put all men in mind of it, in the name of the God who had made all.

Not even in Black Dahomey[2] was it ever, I think, forgotten to the typhus-fever length. Mungo Park,[3] resourceless, had sunk down to die under the Negro Village-Tree, a horrible White object in the eyes of all. But in the poor Black Woman, and her daughter who stood aghast at him, whose earthly wealth and funded capital consisted of one small calabash of rice, there lived a heart richer than "*Laissez-faire*": they, with a royal munificence, boiled their rice for him; they sang all night to him, spinning assiduous on their cotton distaffs, as he lay to sleep: "Let us pity the poor white man; no mother has he to fetch him milk, no sister to grind him corn!" Thou poor black Noble One,—thou *Lady* too: did not a God make thee too; was there not in thee too something of a God!—

Gurth,[4] born thrall of Cedric the Saxon, has been greatly pitied by Dryasdust and others. Gurth, with the brass collar round his neck, tending Cedric's pigs in the glades of the wood, is not what I call an exemplar of human felicity: but Gurth, with the sky above him, with the free air and tinted boscage and umbrage round him, and in him at least the certainty of supper and social lodging when he came home; Gurth to me seems happy, in comparison with many a Lancashire and Buckinghamshire man, of these days, not born thrall of anybody! Gurth's brass collar did not gall him: Cedric *deserved* to be his Master. The pigs were Cedric's, but Gurth too would get his parings of them. Gurth had the inexpressible satisfaction of feeling himself related indissolubly, though in a rude brass-collar way, to his fellow-mortals in this Earth. He had superiors, inferiors, equals.—Gurth is now "emancipated" long since; has what we call "Liberty." Liberty, I am told, is a Divine thing. Liberty when it becomes the "Liberty to die by starvation" is not so divine!

Liberty? The true liberty of a man, you would say, consisted in his finding out, or being forced to find out, the right path, and to walk thereon. To learn, or to be taught, what work he actually was able for; and then by permission, persuasion, and even compulsion, to set about doing of the same! That is his true blessed-

---

nomic code of laissez faire, whereby no one took the responsibility of caring for the starving widow. "Shotbelt Gospel": the attitudes of land-owning aristocracy who were committed to preserving their exclusive right to shoot game birds and animals.

2. A state in west Africa where savage customs, such as human sacrifice and cannibalism, persisted.

3. Explorer and author of *Travels in the Interior of Africa* (1799). In 1806 he was killed by Africans.

4. A swineherd described in Scott's *Ivanhoe*.

ness, honour, "liberty" and maximum of wellbeing: if liberty be not that, I for one have small care about liberty. You do not allow a palpable madman to leap over precipices; you violate his liberty, you that are wise; and keep him, were it in strait-waistcoats, away from the precipices! Every stupid, every cowardly and foolish man is but a less palpable madman: his true liberty were that a wiser man, that any and every wiser man, could, by brass collars, or in whatever milder or sharper way, lay hold of him when he was going wrong, and order and compel him to go a little righter. O, if thou really art my *Senior*, Seigneur, my *Elder*, Presbyter or Priest, —if thou art in very deed my *Wiser*, may a beneficent instinct lead and impel thee to "conquer" me, to command me! If thou do know better than I what is good and right, I conjure thee in the name of God, force me to do it; were it by never such brass collars, whips and handcuffs, leave me not to walk over precipices! That I have been called, by all the Newspapers, a "free man" will avail me little, if my pilgrimage have ended in death and wreck. O that the Newspapers had called me slave, coward, fool, or what it pleased their sweet voices to name me, and I had attained not death, but life!—Liberty requires new definitions.

A conscious abhorrence and intolerance of Folly, of Baseness, Stupidity, Poltroonery and all that brood of things, dwells deep in some men: still deeper in others an *un*conscious abhorrence and intolerance, clothed moreover by the beneficent Supreme Powers in what stout appetites, energies, egoisms so-called, are suitable to it;—these latter are your Conquerors, Romans, Normans, Russians, Indo-English; Founders of what we call Aristocracies. Which indeed have they not the most "divine right" to found;—being themselves very truly Ἄριστοι, BRAVEST, BEST; and conquering generally a confused rabble of WORST, or at lowest, clearly enough, of WORSE? I think their divine right, tried, with affirmatory verdict, in the greatest Law-Court known to me, was good! A class of men who are dreadfully exclaimed against by Dryasdust; of whom nevertheless beneficent Nature has oftentimes had need; and may, alas, again have need.

When, across the hundredfold poor scepticisms, trivialisms, and constitutional cobwebberies of Dryasdust, you catch any glimpse of a William the Conqueror,[5] a Tancred of Hauteville[6] or such like,—do you not discern veritably some rude outline of a true God-made King; whom not the Champion of England[7] cased in

---

5. King William I of England (reigned 1066–87), surnamed the Conqueror after the Battle of Hastings in 1066. Being an illegitimate son, he also bore the surname of William the Bastard. Although some historians condemn William as a ruthless ruler, he is ranked by Carlyle as a hero because of his strong and efficient government. William fulfilled the requirements of the kingly hero described by Carlyle in his lectures *On Heroes:* a man fittest "to *command* over us * * * to tell us what we are to *do*."
6. Norman hero of the First Crusade.
7. An official who goes through a formality, at coronation ceremonies, of demanding whether anyone challenges

tin, but all Nature and the Universe were calling to the throne? It is absolutely necessary that he get thither. Nature does not mean her poor Saxon children to perish, of obesity, stupor or other malady, as yet: a stern Ruler and Line of Rulers therefore is called in, —a stern but most beneficent *perpetual House-Surgeon* is by Nature herself called in, and even the appropriate *fees* are provided for him! Dryasdust talks lamentably about Hereward[8] and the Fen Counties; fate of Earl Waltheof;[9] Yorkshire and the North reduced to ashes; all of which is undoubtedly lamentable. But even Dryasdust apprises me of one fact: "A child, in this William's reign, might have carried a purse of gold from end to end of England." My erudite friend, it is a fact which outweighs a thousand! Sweep away thy constitutional, sentimental, and other cobwebberies; look eye to eye, if thou still have any eye, in the face of this big burly William Bastard: thou wilt see a fellow of most flashing discernment, of most strong lion-heart;—in whom, as it were, within a frame of oak and iron, the gods have planted the soul of "a man of genius"! Dost thou call that nothing? I call it an immense thing! —Rage enough was in this Willelmus Conquaestor, rage enough for his occasions;—and yet the essential element of him, as of all such men, is not scorching *fire*, but shining illuminative *light*. Fire and light are strangely interchangeable; nay, at bottom, I have found them different forms of the same most godlike "elementary substance" in our world: a thing worth stating in these days. The essential element of this Conquaestor is, first of all, the most suneyed perception of what *is* really what on this God's-Earth;—which, thou wilt find, does mean at bottom "Justice," and "Virtues" not a few: *Conformity* to what the Maker has seen good to make; that, I suppose, will mean Justice and a Virtue or two?—

Dost thou think Willelmus Conquaestor would have tolerated ten years' jargon, one hour's jargon, on the propriety of killing Cotton-manufactures by partridge Corn-Laws?[1] I fancy, this was not the man to knock out of his night's-rest with nothing but a noisy bedlamism in your mouth! "Assist us still better to bush the partridges; strangle Plugson who spins the shirts?"[2]—*"Par la Splendeur de Dieu!"*[3]—Dost thou think Willelmus Conquaestor, in this new time, with Steam-engine Captains of Industry on one hand

the right of the monarch to ascend the throne. He wears full armor ("cased in tin"). A symbol for Carlyle of outworn feudal customs.

8. Hereward the Wake, an outlaw whose exploits against William the Conqueror made him seem a romantic figure like Robin Hood.

9. His execution in 1075, on a supposedly trumped-up charge, is cited as a blot on William's record as king.

1. See the title note.

2. This speech sums up the pleas of the High Tariff lobby in Parliament. "Keep the Corn Laws intact so that the aristocratic landlords may continue to enjoy shooting partridges on their estates; subdue the manufacturing leaders by preventing trade." ("Plugson of Undershot" was Carlyle's term to describe the new class of industrial leaders.)

3. "By the splendor of God!"—one of William's oaths.

of him, and Joe-Manton Captains of Idleness[4] on the other, would
have doubted which *was* really the BEST; which did deserve strangling, and which not?

I have a certain indestructible regard for Willelmus Conquaestor.
A resident House-Surgeon, provided by Nature for her beloved English People, and even furnished with the requisite fees, as I said;
for he by no means felt himself doing Nature's work, this Willelmus, but his own work exclusively! And his own work withal it
was; informed *"par la Splendeur de Dieu."*—I say, it is necessary
to get the work out of such a man, however harsh that be! When
a world, not yet doomed for death, is rushing down to ever-deeper
Baseness and Confusion, it is a dire necessity of Nature's to bring
in her ARISTOCRACIES, her BEST, even by forcible methods. When
their descendants or representatives cease entirely to *be* the Best,
Nature's poor world will very soon rush down again to Baseness;
and it becomes a dire necessity of Nature's to cast them out.
Hence French Revolutions, Five-point Charters, Democracies, and
a mournful list of *Etceteras*, in these our afflicted times. * * *

Democracy, the chase of Liberty in that direction, shall go its
full course; unrestrained by him of Pferdefuss-Quacksalber, or any
of *his* household. The Toiling Millions of Mankind, in most vital
need and passionate instinctive desire of Guidance, shall cast away
False-Guidance; and hope, for an hour, that No-Guidance will
suffice them: but it can be for an hour only. The smallest item of
human Slavery is the oppression of man by his Mock-Superiors;
the palpablest, but I say at bottom the smallest. Let him shake off
such oppression, trample it indignantly under his feet; I blame
him not, I pity and commend him. But oppression by your Mock-
Superiors well shaken off, the grand problem yet remains to solve:
That of finding government by your Real-Superiors! Alas, how shall
we ever learn the solution of that, benighted, bewildered, sniffing,
sneering, godforgetting unfortunates as we are? It is a work for
centuries; to be taught us by tribulations, confusions, insurrections,
obstructions; who knows if not by conflagration and despair! It is
a lesson inclusive of all other lessons; the hardest of all lessons
to learn. * * *

Captains of Industry[1]

If I believed that Mammonism with its adjuncts was to continue
henceforth the one serious principle of our existence, I should
reckon it idle to solicit remedial measures from any Government,
the disease being insusceptible of remedy. Government can do
much, but it can in no wise do all. Government, as the most conspicuous object in Society, is called upon to give signal of what

4. The idle aristocracy who wasted
time shooting partridges with guns
made by Joseph Manton, a London
gunsmith.

1. From Book IV, Chapter 4.

shall be done; and, in many ways, to preside over, further, and command the doing of it. But the Government cannot do, by all its signalling and commanding, what the Society is radically indisposed to do. In the long-run every Government is the exact symbol of its People, with their wisdom and unwisdom; we have to say, Like People like Government.—The main substance of this immense Problem of Organizing Labour, and first of all of Managing the Working Classes, will, it is very clear, have to be solved by those who stand practically in the middle of it; by those who themselves work and preside over work. Of all that can be enacted by any Parliament in regard to it, the germs must already lie potentially extant in those two Classes, who are to obey such enactment. A Human Chaos *in* which there is no light, you vainly attempt to irradiate by light shed *on* it: order never can arise there.

But it is my firm conviction that the "Hell of England" will *cease* to be that of "not making money"; that we shall get a nobler Hell and a nobler Heaven! I anticipate light *in* the Human Chaos, glimmering, shining more and more; under manifold true signals from without That light shall shine. Our deity no longer being Mammon,—O Heavens, each man will then say to himself: "Why such deadly haste to make money? I shall not go to Hell, even if I do not make money! There is another Hell, I am told!" Competition, at railway-speed, in all branches of commerce and work will then abate:—good felt-hats for the head, in every sense, instead of seven-feet lath-and-plaster hats on wheels,[2] will then be discoverable! Bubble-periods,[3] with their panics and commercial crises, will again become infrequent; steady modest industry will take the place of gambling speculation. To be a noble Master, among noble Workers, will again be the first ambition with some few; to be a rich Master only the second. How the Inventive Genius of England, with the whirr of its bobbins and billy-rollers[4] shoved somewhat into the backgrounds of the brain, will contrive and devise, not cheaper produce exclusively, but fairer distribution of the produce at its present cheapness! By degrees, we shall again have a Society with something of Heroism in it, something of Heaven's Blessing on it; we shall again have, as my German friend[5] asserts, "instead of Mammon-Feudalism with unsold cotton-shirts and Preservation of the Game, noble just Industrialism and Government by the Wisest!"

It is with the hope of awakening here and there a British man to know himself for a man and divine soul, that a few words of parting admonition, to all persons to whom the Heavenly Powers

2. A London hatter's mode of advertising. Carlyle considered most advertisements to be wasteful.
3. Periods of violent fluctuation in the stock market caused by unsound speculating.
4. Machines used to prepare cotton or wool for spinning.
5. Teufelsdröckh, the hero of *Sartor Resartus*.

have lent power of any kind in this land, may now be addressed. And first to those same Master-Workers, Leaders of Industry; who stand nearest, and in fact powerfullest, though not most prominent, being as yet in too many senses a Virtuality rather than an Actuality.

The Leaders of Industry, if Industry is ever to be led, are virtually the Captains of the World; if there be no nobleness in them, there will never be an Aristocracy more. But let the Captains of Industry consider: once again, are they born of other clay than the old Captains of Slaughter; doomed for ever to be not Chivalry, but a mere gold-plated *Doggery*,—what the French well name *Canaille*, "Doggery" with more or less gold carrion at its disposal? Captains of Industry are the true Fighters, henceforth recognizable as the only true ones: Fighters against Chaos, Necessity and the Devils and Jötuns;[6] and lead on Mankind in that great, and alone true, and universal warfare; the stars in their courses fighting for them, and all Heaven and all Earth saying audibly, Well done! Let the Captains of Industry retire into their own hearts, and ask solemnly, If there is nothing but vulturous hunger for fine wines, valet reputation and gilt carriages, discoverable there? Of hearts made by the Almighty God I will not believe such a thing. Deep-hidden under wretchedest god-forgetting Cants, Epicurisms, Dead-Sea Apisms;[7] forgotten as under foullest fat Lethe mud and weeds, there is yet, in all hearts born into this God's-World, a spark of the Godlike slumbering. Awake, O nightmare sleepers; awake, arise, or be for ever fallen! This is not playhouse poetry; it is sober fact. Our England, our world cannot live as it is. It will connect itself with a God again, or go down with nameless throes and fire-consummation to the Devils. Thou who feelest aught of such a Godlike stirring in thee, any faintest intimation of it as through heavy-laden dreams, follow *it*, I conjure thee. Arise, save thyself, be one of those that save thy country.

Bucaniers,[8] Chactaw Indians, whose supreme aim in fighting is that they may get the scalps, the money, that they may amass scalps and money; out of such came no Chivalry, and never will! Out of such came only gore and wreck, infernal rage and misery; desperation quenched in annihilation. Behold it, I bid thee, behold there, and consider! What is it that thou have a hundred thousand-pound bills laid up in thy strong-room, a hundred scalps hung up in thy wigwam? I value not them or thee. Thy scalps and thy thousand-pound bills are as yet nothing, if no nobleness from

6. Giants of Scandinavian mythology.
7. A tribe of men living near the Dead Sea were transformed into apes because they had ignored the prophecies of Moses. This story, of Mohammedan origin, is used by Carlyle to represent the possible fate of nations which are indifferent to their social problems.
8. Buccaneers.

within irradiate them; if no Chivalry, in action, or in embryo ever struggling towards birth and action, be there.

Love of men cannot be bought by cash-payment; and without love, men cannot endure to be together. You cannot lead a Fighting World without having it regimented, chivalried: the thing, in a day, becomes impossible; all men in it, the highest at first, the very lowest at last, discern consciously, or by a noble instinct, this necessity. And can you any more continue to lead a Working World unregimented, anarchic? I answer, and the Heavens and Earth are now answering, No! The thing becomes not "in a day" impossible; but in some two generations it does. Yes, when fathers and mothers, in Stockport hunger-cellars, begin to eat their children, and Irish widows have to prove their relationship by dying of typhus-fever; and amid Governing "Corporations of the Best and Bravest," busy to preserve their game by "bushing," dark millions of God's human creatures start up in mad Chartisms, impracticable Sacred-Months, and Manchester Insurrections;[9]—and there is a virtual Industrial Aristocracy as yet only half-alive, spell-bound amid money-bags and ledgers; and an actual Idle Aristocracy seemingly near dead in somnolent delusions, in trespasses and double-barrels;[1] "sliding," as on inclined-planes, which every new year they *soap* with new Hansard's-jargon[2] under God's sky, and so are "sliding" ever faster, towards a "scale" and balance-scale whereon is written *Thou art found Wanting*:—in such days, after a generation or two, I say, it does become, even to the low and simple, very palpably impossible! No Working World, any more than a Fighting World, can be led on without a noble Chivalry of Work, and laws and fixed rules which follow out of that,—far nobler than any Chivalry of Fighting was. As an anarchic multitude on mere Supply-and-demand, it is becoming inevitable that we dwindle in horrid suicidal convulsion, and self-abrasion, frightful to the imagination, into *Chactaw* Workers. With wigwams and scalps,—with palaces and thousand-pound bills; with savagery, depopulation, chaotic desolation! Good Heavens, will not one French Revolution and Reign of Terror suffice us, but must there be two? There will be two if needed; there will be twenty if needed; there will be precisely as many as are needed. The Laws of Nature will have themselves fulfilled. That is a thing certain to me.

Your gallant battle-hosts and work-hosts, as the others did, will need to be made loyally yours; they must and will be regulated, methodically secured in their just share of conquest under you;—

9. In 1819 a large open-air labor meeting in Manchester was broken up by charging cavalry. Thirteen men and women were massacred, and many others were wounded.
1. Carlyle is suggesting that the only concern of the landed aristocrats is to keep trespassers off their game preserves and reserve shooting rights to themselves.
2. Parliamentary oratory, as in Hansard's printed record of debates in the House of Commons.

joined with you in veritable brotherhood, sonhood, by quite other and deeper ties than those of temporary day's wages! How would mere redcoated regiments, to say nothing of chivalries, fight for you, if you could discharge them on the evening of the battle, on payment of the stipulated shillings,—and they discharge you on the morning of it! Chelsea Hospitals,[3] pensions, promotions, rigorous lasting covenant on the one side and on the other, are indispensable even for a hired fighter. The Feudal Baron, much more, —how could he subsist with mere temporary mercenaries round him, at sixpence a day; ready to go over to the other side, if sevenpence were offered? He could not have subsisted;—and his noble instinct saved him from the necessity of even trying! The Feudal Baron had a Man's Soul in him; to which anarchy, mutiny, and the other fruits of temporary mercenaries, were intolerable: he had never been a Baron otherwise, but had continued a Chactaw and Bucanier. He felt it precious, and at last it became habitual, and his fruitful enlarged existence included it as a necessity, to have men round him who in heart loved him; whose life he watched over with rigour yet with love; who were prepared to give their life for him, if need came. It was beautiful; it was human! Man lives not otherwise, nor can live contented, anywhere or anywhen. Isolation is the sum-total of wretchedness to man. To be cut off, to be left solitary: to have a world alien, not your world; all a hostile camp for you; not a home at all, of hearts and faces who are yours, whose you are! It is the frightfullest enchantment; too truly a work of the Evil One. To have neither superior, nor inferior, nor equal, united manlike to you. Without father, without child, without brother. Man knows no sadder destiny. "How is each of us," exclaims Jean Paul,[4] "so lonely in the wide bosom of the All!" Encased each as in his transparent "ice-palace"; our brother visible in his, making signals and gesticulations to us;—visible, but for ever unattainable: on his bosom we shall never rest, nor he on ours. It was not a God that did this; no!

Awake, ye noble Workers, warriors in the one true war: all this must be remedied. It is you who are already half-alive, whom I will welcome into life; whom I will conjure in God's name to shake off your enchanted sleep, and live wholly! Cease to count scalps, goldpurses; not in these lies your or our salvation. Even these, if you count only these, will not be left. Let bucaniering be put far from you; alter, speedily abrogate all laws of the bucaniers, if you would gain any victory that shall endure. Let God's justice, let pity, nobleness and manly valour, with more gold-purses or with fewer, testify themselves in this your brief Life-transit to all the Eternities, the Gods and Silences. It is to you I call; for ye are not dead, ye

---

3. Home for disabled veterans.

4. Jean Paul Richter (1763–1825), German humorist.

are already half-alive: there is in you a sleepless dauntless energy, the prime-matter of all nobleness in man. Honour to you in your kind. It is to you I call: ye know at least this, That the mandate of God to His creature man is: Work! The future Epic of the World rests not with those that are near dead, but with those that are alive, and those that are coming into life.

Look around you. Your world-hosts are all in mutiny, in confusion, destitution; on the eve of fiery wreck and madness! They will not march farther for you, on the sixpence a day and supply-and-demand principle: they will not; nor ought they, nor can they. Ye shall reduce them to order, begin reducing them. To order, to just subordination; noble loyalty in return for noble guidance. Their souls are driven nigh mad; let yours be sane and ever saner. Not as a bewildered bewildering mob; but as a firm regimented mass, with real captains over them, will these men march any more. All human interests, combined human endeavours, and social growths in this world, have, at a certain stage of their development, required organizing: and Work, the grandest of human interests, does now require it.

God knows, the task will be hard: but no noble task was ever easy. This task will wear away your lives, and the lives of your sons and grandsons: but for what purpose, if not for tasks like this, were lives given to men? Ye shall cease to count your thousand-pound scalps, the noble of you shall cease! Nay, the very scalps, as I say, will not long be left if you count on these. Ye shall cease wholly to be barbarous vulturous Chactaws, and become noble European Nineteenth-Century Men. Ye shall know that Mammon, in never such gigs[5] and flunkey "respectabilities," is not the alone God; that of himself he is but a Devil, and even a Brute-god.

Difficult? Yes, it will be difficult. The short-fibre cotton; that too was difficult. The waste cotton-shrub, long useless, disobedient, as the thistle by the wayside,—have ye not conquered it; made it into beautiful bandana webs; white woven shirts for men; bright-tinted air-garments wherein flit goddesses? Ye have shivered mountains asunder, made the hard iron pliant to you as soft putty: the Forest-giants, Marsh-jötuns bear sheaves of golden grain; Aegir the Sea-demon[6] himself stretches his back for a sleek highway to you, and on Firehorses and Windhorses ye career. Ye are most strong. Thor red-bearded, with his blue sun-eyes, with his cheery heart and strong thunder-hammer, he and you have prevailed. Ye are most strong, ye Sons of the icy North, of the far East,—far marching from your rugged Eastern Wildernesses, hitherward from the grey Dawn of Time! Ye are Sons of the Jötun-land; the land of Diffi-

5. To own a gig (a light carriage) was a sign of respectable status comparable to owning certain kinds of automobiles today. Carlyle ridiculed the passion for respectability as "gigmanity."
6. From Scandinavian mythology.

culties Conquered. Difficult? You must try this thing. Once try it with the understanding that it will and shall have to be done. Try it as ye try the paltrier thing, making of money! I will bet on you once more, against all Jötuns, Tailor-gods,[7] Double-barrelled Lawwards, and Denizens of Chaos whatsoever!

1843   1843

7. False gods.

JOHN STUART MILL
(1806–1873)

In many American colleges the writings of J. S. Mill are studied in courses in government or in philosophy, and it may therefore be asked why they should also have a place in the study of literature. It is evident that Mill is the least literary of the important Victorian prose writers. His analytic mind, preoccupied with abstractions rather than letters, his self-effacing that are the concern of the more typical one marks of a writer whose manner, and his relatively colorless style rather than in the rendering of particular experiences for own sake. Yet a knowledge of Mill's value lies in his generalizations from intellectual history of his century, a writings is essential to our understanding of Victorian literature. He is one of the leading figuring with the political and religious problems thinker whose honest profound influence on writers as diverse as Arnold, of his age was to b...

Swinburne, and at home in London under the direction of his father, Mill was a reader of the Utilitarian James Mill believed that ordinary James Mills to develop our intellectual capacities early enough, and schooling demonstrated his point by the extraordinary results he achieved in his son. A child read Greek and Latin, and as his intensive education enabled him to start his career *Autobiography* took advantage of a quarter of century" over his contemporaries. Mill worked in the office of the East India Company for many years and also served a term in Parliment in the 1860's, but his principal energies were devoted to his wrings on such subjects as logic and philosophy, political principles, and economics. He began as a disciple of the Utilitarian theories of his father and of Jeremy Bentham but became gradually dissatisfied with the narrowness of their conception of human motives. His honesty and open-mindedness enabled him to appreciate the values of such anti-Utilitarians as Coleridge and Carlyle, and, whenever possible, to incorporate some of these values into the Utilitarian system. His essay on Coleridge's enlightened conservatism in politics and religion is a striking example of Mill's capacity for sympathetic understanding. In part this sympathy was gained by the lesson he learned through experiencing a nervous breakdown during his early 20's. This painful event, described in the chapter of his *Autobiography* included below, taught him that the lack of concern for the affections and emotions of men, characteristic of the Utilitarian system of thought (and typified by his own education), was a fatal flaw in that system. His tribute to the therapeutic value of art (because of its effect on human emotions), both in his *Autobiography* and in his early essay *What Is Poetry*, would have astonished Mill's master, Bentham, who had equated poetry with pushpin, a trifling game.

Mill's emotional life was also broadened by his love for Harriet Taylor, a married woman who shared his intellectual interests and eventually became his wife, in 1851, after the death of her husband. Mill later described her as "the inspirer, and in part the author, of all that is best in my writings." Under her influence he became an advocate for the cause of female emancipation, one of several unpopular movements to which he was dedicated. Throughout human history, as Mill saw it, the role of a husband has always been legally that of a tyrant, and the object of his far-seeing essay *The Subjection of Women* (1869) was to change law and public opinion so that half the human race might be liberated from slavery into the status of individuals. The subjection of women was, however, only one aspect of the tyranny against which he fought. His fundamental concern was to prevent the subjection of man in a democracy. His classic treatise *On Liberty* (1859) is not a tradition in a democracy. His classic treatise *On Liberty* ...; it is an attack against tyrannical kings or dictators ... mocracies such as America, tyrannical majorities. Mill foresaw that in ... individualists (intellectual individuals ... sure toward conformity might crush ... he called a "collective mediocrits in particular) to the level of ... in his discussions of the advantages throughout all of his writings, ... demonstrating that the individual is more ... socialism, Mill is concerned ... as church or state. In *On Liberty* we find ... rtant than institutions ... he process of his reasoning, but here, where the theoretical example of ... central, his logic is charged with eloquence. ... individualism is

A similar eloquence is evident in a passage from his *Principles of Political Economy* (1848), a prophetic comment on the fate of the individual in an overpopulated world:

> There is room in the world, no doubt, and even in old ... arts of life ... increase of population, supposing ... I confess I ... kept per ... solitude ... capital to increase. But even if innocuous, ... It is not good for a man to be ... world from which solitude is ... for desiring it. * * * It is not good for a man ... the sense of being often alone, is times in the presence of his species. Solitude, ... of character: and solitude in the tirpated, is a very poor ideal. Solitude ... of meditation and grander, is the cradle of thoughts and essential to any depth of meditation ... is the cradle ... individual, but which society presence of natural beauty and grander ... good for he individual ... contemplating the aspirations which are not only good ... satisfaction ... of nature; with every could ill do without. Nor is there much ... spontaneous activity ... capable of growing food world with nothing left to the ... cultivation, which is ... pasture ploughed up, all rood of land brought into cultivation ... waste or natural ... man's use exterminated for human beings; every flowery ... domesticated for ... tree rooted out, and quadrupeds or birds for food, every hedgerow or superfluous ... could grow without being as his rivals for food, every ... wild shrub or flower ... agriculture. If the earth must scarcely a place left where a ... improved agriculture ... to things that the eradicated as a weed in the name ... pleasantness which it owes ... extirpate from it, for lose that great portion of its ... population would ... unlimited increase of wealth and population would

the mere purpose of enabling it to support a larger, but not a better or a happier population, I sincerely hope, for the sake of posterity, that they will be content to be stationary, long before necessity compels them to it.

What Is Poetry?

It has often been asked, What Is Poetry? And many and various are the answers which have been returned. The vulgarest of all— one with which no person possessed of the faculties to which poetry addresses itself can ever have been satisfied—is that which confounds poetry with metrical composition; yet to this wretched mockery of a definition many have been led back by the failure of all their attempts to find any other that would distinguish what they have been accustomed to call poetry from much which they have known only under other names.

That, however, the word "poetry" imports something quite peculiar in its nature; something which may exist in what is called prose as well as in verse; something which does not even require the instrument of words, but can speak through the other audible symbols called musical sounds, and even through the visible ones which are the language of sculpture, painting, and architecture— all this, we believe, is and must be felt, though perhaps indistinctly, by all upon whom poetry in any of its shapes produces any impression beyond that of tickling the ear. The distinction between poetry and what is not poetry, whether explained or not, is felt to be fundamental; and, where every one feels a difference, a difference there must be. All other appearances may be fallacious; but the appearance of a difference is a real difference. Appearances too, like other things, must have a cause; and that which can cause anything, even an illusion, must be a reality. And hence, while a half-philosophy disdains the classifications and distinctions indicated by popular language, philosophy carried to its highest point frames new ones, but rarely sets aside the old, content with correcting and regularizing them. It cuts fresh channels for thought, but does not fill up such as it finds ready-made: it traces, on the countrary, more deeply, broadly, and distinctly, those into which the current has spontaneously flowed.

Let us then attempt, in the way of modest inquiry, not to coerce and confine Nature within the bounds of an arbitrary definition, but rather to find the boundaries which she herself has set, and erect a barrier round them; not calling mankind to account for having misapplied the word "poetry," but attempting to clear up the conception which they already attach to it, and to bring forward as a distinct principle that which, as a vague feeling, has really guided them in their employment of the term.

The object of poetry is confessedly to act upon the emotions; and therein is poetry sufficiently distinguished from what Wordsworth affirms to be its logical opposite; namely, not prose. but matter of fact, or science.[1] The one addresses itself to the belief; the other, to the feelings. The one does its work by convincing or persuading; the other, by moving. The one acts by presenting a proposition to the understanding; the other, by offering interesting objects of contemplation to the sensibilities.

This, however, leaves us very far from a definition of poetry. This distinguishes it from one thing; but we are bound to distinguish it from everything. To bring thoughts or images before the mind, for the purpose of acting upon the emotions, does not belong to poetry alone. It is equally the province (for example) of the novelist: and yet the faculty of the poet and that of the novelist are as distinct as any other two faculties; as the faculties of the novelist and of the orator, or of the poet and the metaphysician. The two characters may be united, as characters the most disparate may; but they have no natural connection.

Many of the greatest poems are in the form of fictitious narratives; and, in almost all good serious fictions, there is true poetry. But there is a radical distinction between the interest felt in a story as such, and the interest excited by poetry; for the one is derived from incident, the other from the representation of feeling. In one, the source of the emotion excited is the exhibition of a state or states of human sensibility; in the other, of a series of states of mere outward circumstances. Now, all minds are capable of being affected more or less by representations of the latter kind, and all, or almost all, by those of the former; yet the two sources of interest correspond to two distinct and (as respects their greatest development) mutually exclusive characters of mind.

At what age is the passion for a story, for almost any kind of story, merely as a story, the most intense? In childhood. But that also is the age at which poetry, even of the simplest description, is least relished and least understood; because the feelings with which it is especially conversant are yet undeveloped, and, not having been even in the slightest degree experienced, cannot be sympathized with. In what stage of the progress of society, again, is storytelling most valued, and the storyteller in greatest request and honor? In a rude state like that of the Tartars and Arabs at this day, and of almost all nations in the earliest ages. But, in this state of society, there is little poetry except ballads, which are mostly narrative—that is, essentially stories—and derive their principal interest from the incidents. Considered as poetry, they are of the lowest and most elementary kind: the feelings depicted, or rather indicated, are the simplest our nature has; such joys and griefs as the immediate pressure of some outward event excites in rude minds, which live wholly immersed in outward things, and have never, either from choice or a force they could not resist,

1. See above, Wordsworth's Preface to *Lyrical Ballads*.

turned themselves to the contemplation of the world within. Passing now from childhood, and from the childhood of society, to the grown-up men and women of this most grown-up and unchildlike age, the minds and hearts of greatest depth and elevation are commonly those which take greatest delight in poetry: the shallowest and emptiest, on the contrary, are, at all events, not those least addicted to novel-reading. This accords, too, with all analogous experience of human nature. The sort of persons whom not merely in books, but in their lives, we find perpetually engaged in hunting for excitement from without, are invariably those who do not possess, either in the vigor of their intellectual powers or in the depth of their sensibilities, that which would enable them to find ample excitement nearer home. The most idle and frivolous persons take a natural delight in fictitious narrative: the excitement it affords is of the kind which comes from without. Such persons are rarely lovers of poetry, though they may fancy themselves so because they relish novels in verse. But poetry, which is the delineation of the deeper and more secret workings of human emotion, is interesting only to those to whom it recalls what they have felt, or whose imagination it stirs up to conceive what they could feel, or what they might have been able to feel, had their outward circumstances been different.

Poetry, when it is really such, is truth; and fiction also, if it is good for anything, is truth: but they are different truths. The truth of poetry is to paint the human soul truly: the truth of fiction is to give a true picture of life. The two kinds of knowledge are different, and come by different ways, come mostly to different persons. Great poets are often proverbially ignorant of life. What they know has come by observation of themselves: they have found within them one highly delicate and sensitive specimen of human nature, on which the laws of emotion are written in large characters, such as can be read off without much study. Other knowledge of mankind, such as comes to men of the world by outward experience, is not indispensable to them as poets: but, to the novelist, such knowledge is all in all; he has to describe outward things, not the inward man; actions and events, not feelings; and it will not do for him to be numbered among those, who, as Madame Roland said of Brissot, know man, but not *men.*[2]

All this is no bar to the possibility of combining both elements, poetry and narrative or incident, in the same work, and calling it either a novel or a poem; but so may red and white combine on the same human features or on the same canvas. There is one order of composition which requires the union of poetry and incident, each in its highest kind—the dramatic. Even there, the two elements are perfectly distinguishable, and may exist of un-

---

2. Jacques Pierre Brissot (1754–93), a leading reformer during the French Revolution, is characterized in the *Mém-* *oires* of Jeanne Manon Roland (1754–93).

equal quality and in the most various proportion. The incidents of a dramatic poem may be scanty and ineffective, though the delineation of passion and character may be of the highest order, as in Goethe's admirable "Torquato Tasso"; or, again, the story as a mere story may be well got up for effect, as is the case with some of the most trashy productions of the Minerva Press:[3] it may even be, what those are not, a coherent and probable series of events, though there be scarcely a feeling exhibited which is not represented falsely, or in a manner absolutely commonplace. The combination of the two excellences is what renders Shakespeare so generally acceptable, each sort of readers finding in him what is suitable to their faculties. To the many, he is great as a storyteller; to the few, as a poet.

In limiting poetry to the delineation of states of feeling, and denying the name where nothing is delineated but outward objects, we may be thought to have done what we promised to avoid— to have not found, but made, a definition in opposition to the usage of language, since it is established by common consent that there is a poetry called descriptive. We deny the charge. Description is not poetry because there is descriptive poetry, no more than science is poetry because there is such a thing as a didactic poem. But an object which admits of being described, or a truth which may fill a place in a scientific treatise, may also furnish an occasion for the generation of poetry, which we thereupon choose to call descriptive or didactic. The poetry is not in the object itself, nor in the scientific truth itself, but in the state of mind in which the one and the other may be contemplated. The mere delineation of the dimensions and colors of external objects is not poetry, no more than a geometrical ground-plan of St. Peter's or Westminster Abbey is painting. Descriptive poetry consists, no doubt, in description, but in description of things as they appear, not as they are; and it paints them, not in their bare and natural lineaments, but seen through the medium and arrayed in the colors of the imagination set in action by the feelings. If a poet describes a lion, he does not describe him as a naturalist would, nor even as a traveler would, who was intent upon stating the truth, the whole truth, and nothing but the truth. He describes him by imagery, that is, by suggesting the most striking likenesses and contrasts which might occur to a mind contemplating a lion, in the state of awe, wonder, or terror, which the spectacle naturally excites, or is, on the occasion, supposed to excite. Now, this is describing the lion professedly, but the state of excitement of the spectator really. The lion may be described falsely or with exaggeration and the poetry be all the better: but, if the human emotion be not painted with scrupulous truth, the poetry is bad poetry; i.e., is not poetry at all, but a failure.

Thus far, our progress towards a clear view of the essentials of

---

3. Early 19th-century publishing house that fostered the production of sentimental novels.

poetry has brought us very close to the last two attempts at a definition of poetry which we happen to have seen in print, both of them by poets, and men of genius. The one is by Ebenezer Elliott, the author of "Corn-law Rhymes," and other poems of still greater merit. "Poetry," says he, "is impassioned truth." [4] The other is by a writer in "Blackwood's Magazine," and comes, we think, still nearer the mark. He defines poetry, "man's thoughts tinged by his feelings." There is in either definition a near approximation to what we are in search of. Every truth which a human being can enunciate, every thought, even every outward impression, which can enter into his consciousness, may become poetry, when shown through any impassioned medium; when invested with the coloring of joy, or grief, or pity, or affection, or admiration, or reverence, or awe, or even hatred or terror; and, unless so colored, nothing, be it as interesting as it may, is poetry. But both these definitions fail to discriminate between poetry and eloquence. Eloquence, as well as poetry, is impassioned truth; eloquence, as well as poetry, is thoughts colored by the feelings. Yet common apprehension and philosophic criticism alike recognize a distinction between the two: there is much that everyone would call eloquence, which no one would think of classing as poetry. A question will sometimes arise, whether some particular author is a poet; and those who maintain the negative commonly allow, that, though not a poet, he is a highly eloquent writer. The distinction between poetry and eloquence appears to us to be equally fundamental with the distinction between poetry and narrative, or between poetry and description, while it is still farther from having been satisfactorily cleared up than either of the others.

Poetry and eloquence are both alike the expression or utterance of feeling: but, if we may be excused the antithesis, we should say that eloquence is *heard*; poetry is *over*heard. Eloquence supposes an audience. The peculiarity of poetry appears to us to lie in the poet's utter unconsciousness of a listener. Poetry is feeling confessing itself to itself in moments of solitude, and embodying itself in symbols which are the nearest possible representations of the feeling in the exact shape in which it exists in the poet's mind. Eloquence is feeling pouring itself out to other minds, courting their sympathy, or endeavoring to influence their belief, or move them to passion or to action.

All poetry is of the nature of soliloquy. It may be said that poetry which is printed on hot-pressed paper, and sold at a bookseller's shop, is a soliloquy in full dress and on the stage. It is so; but there is nothing absurd in the idea of such a mode of soliloquizing. What we have said to ourselves we may tell to others afterwards; what we have said or done in solitude we may voluntarily reproduce when we know that other eyes are upon us. But

4. Preface to *Corn-Law Rhymes* (1828) by Ebenezer Elliot (1781–1849).

no trace of consciousness that any eyes are upon us must be visible in the work itself. The actor knows that there is an audience present: but, if he act as though he knew it, he acts ill. A poet may write poetry, not only with the intention of printing it, but for the express purpose of being paid for it. That it should *be* poetry, being written under such influences, is less probable, not, however, impossible; but no otherwise possible than if he can succeed in excluding from his work every vestige of such lookings-forth into the outward and every-day world, and can express his emotions exactly as he has felt them in solitude, or as he is conscious that he should feel them, though they were to remain for ever unuttered, or (at the lowest) as he knows that others feel them in similar circumstances of solitude. But when he turns round, and addresses himself to another person; when the act of utterance is not itself the end, but a means to an end—viz., by the feelings he himself expresses, to work upon the feelings, or upon the belief or the will of another; when the expression of his emotions, or of his thoughts tinged by his emotions, is tinged also by that purpose, by that desire of making an impression upon another mind—then it ceases to be poetry, and becomes eloquence.

Poetry, accordingly, is the natural fruit of solitude and meditation; eloquence, of intercourse with the world. The persons who have most feeling of their own, if intellectual culture has given them a language in which to express it, have the highest faculty of poetry: those who best understand the feelings of others are the most eloquent. The persons and the nations who commonly excel in poetry are those whose character and tastes render them least dependent upon the applause or sympathy or concurrence of the world in general. Those to whom that applause, that sympathy, that concurrence, are most necessary, generally excel most in eloquence. And hence, perhaps, the French, who are the least poetical of all great and intellectual nations, are among the most eloquent; the French also being the most sociable, the vainest, and the least self-dependent.

If the above be, as we believe, the true theory of the distinction commonly admitted between eloquence and poetry, or even though it be not so, yet if, as we cannot doubt, the distinction above stated be a real bona fide distinction, it will be found to hold, not merely in the language of words, but in all other language, and to intersect the whole domain of art.

Take, for example, music. We shall find in that art, so peculiarly the expression of passion, two perfectly distinct styles—one of which may be called the poetry, the other the oratory, of music. This difference, being seized, would put an end to much musical sectarianism. There has been much contention whether the music of the modern Italian school, that of Rossini,[5] and his suc-

5. G. A. Rossini (1792–1868), composer of operas.

cessors, be impassioned or not. Without doubt, the passion it expresses is not the musing, meditative tenderness or pathos or grief of Mozart or Beethoven; yet it is passion, but garrulous passion, the passion which pours itself into other ears, and therein the better calculated for dramatic effect, having a natural adaptation for dialogue. Mozart also is great in musical oratory; but his most touching compositions are in the opposite style, that of soliloquy. Who can imagine "Dove sono" [6] *heard?* We imagine it *over*heard.

Purely pathetic music commonly partakes of soliloquy. The soul is absorbed in its distress and, though there may be bystanders, it is not thinking of them. When the mind is looking within, and not without, its state does not often or rapidly vary; and hence the even, uninterrupted flow, approaching almost to monotony, which a good reader or a good singer will give to words or music of a pensive or melancholy cast. But grief, taking the form of a prayer or of a complaint, becomes oratorical: no longer low and even and subdued, it assumes a more emphatic rhythm, a more rapidly returning accent; instead of a few slow, equal notes, following one after another at regular intervals, it crowds note upon note, and often assumes a hurry and bustle like joy. Those who are familiar with some of the best of Rossini's serious compositions, such as the air "Tu che i miseri conforti," [7] in the opera of "Tancredi," or the duet "Ebben per mia memoria," [8] in "La Gazza Ladra," will at once understand and feel our meaning. Both are highly tragic and passionate: the passion of both is that of oratory, not poetry. The like may be said of that most moving invocation in Beethoven's "Fidelio,"

> "Komm, Hoffnung, lass das letzte Stern
> Der Müde nicht erbleichen "—[9]

in which Madame Schröder Devrient exhibited such consummate powers of pathetic expression. How different from Winter's beautiful "Paga fui," [1] the very soul of melancholy exhaling itself in solitude! fuller of meaning, and therefore more profoundly poetical, than the words for which it was composed; for it seems to express, not simple melancholy, but the melancholy of remorse.

If from vocal music we now pass to instrumental, we may have a specimen of musical oratory in any fine military symphony or march; while the poetry of music seems to have attained its consummation in Beethoven's "Overture to Egmont," so wonderful in its mixed expression of grandeur and melancholy.

6. "Where are fled [the lovely moments?]"—soprano aria from Act III of Mozart's opera *The Marriage of Figaro*.
7. "You, who give comfort to the wretched," soprano aria from Rossini's *Tancredi* (1813).
8. "Indeed according to my memory," soprano aria from Rossini's *La Gazza Ladra* (1817).
9. "Come, Hope, let not the weary person's last star fade out." Aria from *Fidelio* (1805). Mill seems to be quoting from memory. The passage should read: "Komm, Hoffnung, lass den letzten Stern / Der Müden nicht erbleichen."
1. "I have been contented." Aria from the once-popular opera *Il Ratto di Proserpina* by Peter Winter (1775–1825), first performed in London in 1804.

In the arts which speak to the eye, the same distinctions will be found to hold, not only between poetry and oratory, but between poetry, oratory, narrative, and simple imitation or description.

Pure description is exemplified in a mere portrait or a mere landscape, productions of art, it is true, but of the mechanical rather than of the fine arts; being works of simple imitation, not creation. We say, a mere portrait or a mere landscape; because it is possible for a portrait or a landscape, without ceasing to be such, to be also a picture, like Turner's [2] landscapes, and the great portraits by Titian or Vandyke.

Whatever in painting or sculpture expresses human feeling— or character, which is only a certain state of feeling grown habitual —may be called, according to circumstances, the poetry or the eloquence of the painter's or the sculptor's art: the poetry, if the feeling declares itself by such signs as escape from us when we are unconscious of being seen; the oratory, if the signs are those we use for the purpose of voluntary communication.

The narrative style answers to what is called historical painting, which it is the fashion among connoisseurs to treat as the climax of the pictorial art. That it is the most difficult branch of the art, we do not doubt, because, in its perfection, it includes the perfection of all the other branches; as, in like manner, an epic poem, though, in so far as it is epic (i.e., narrative), it is not poetry at all, is yet esteemed the greatest effort of poetic genius, because there is no kind whatever of poetry which may not appropriately find a place in it. But an historical picture as such, that is, as the representation of an incident, must necessarily, as it seems to us, be poor and ineffective. The narrative powers of painting are extremely limited. Scarcely any picture, scarcely even any series of pictures, tells its own story without the aid of an interpreter. But it is the single figures, which, to us, are the great charm even of an historical picture. It is in these that the power of the art is really seen. In the attempt to narrate, visible and permanent signs are too far behind the fugitive audible ones, which follow so fast one after another; while the faces and figures in a narrative picture, even though they be Titian's, stand still. Who would not prefer one "Virgin and Child" of Raphael to all the pictures which Rubens, with his fat, frouzy Dutch Venuses, ever painted?—though Rubens, besides excelling almost everyone in his mastery over the mechanical parts of his art, often shows real genius in *grouping* his figures, the peculiar problem of historical painting. But then, who, except a mere student of drawing and coloring, ever cared to look twice at any of the figures themselves? The power of painting lies in poetry, of which Rubens had not the slightest tincture, not in narrative, wherein he might have excelled.

2. J. W. M. Turner (1775–1851), English landscape painter.

The single figures, however, in an historical picture, are rather the eloquence of painting than the poetry. They mostly (unless they are quite out of place in the picture) express the feelings of one person as modified by the presence of others. Accordingly, the minds whose bent leads them rather to eloquence than to poetry rush to historical painting. The French painters, for instance, seldom attempt, because they could make nothing of, single heads, like those glorious ones of the Italian masters with which they might feed themselves day after day in their own Louvre. They must all be historical; and they are, almost to a man, attitudinizers. If we wished to give any young artist the most impressive warning our imagination could devise against that kind of vice in the pictorial which corresponds to rant in the histrionic art, we would advise him to walk once up and once down the gallery of the Luxembourg.[3] Every figure in French painting or statuary seems to be showing itself off before spectators. They are not poetical, but in the worst style of corrupted eloquence.

1833, 1859

From Coleridge[1]

The name of Coleridge is one of the few English names of our time which are likely to be oftener pronounced, and to become symbolical of more important things, in proportion as the inward workings of the age manifest themselves more and more in outward facts. Bentham[2] excepted, no Englishman of recent date has left his impress so deeply in the opinions and mental tendencies of those among us who attempt to enlighten their practice by philosophical meditation. If it be true, as Lord Bacon affirms, that a knowledge of the speculative opinions of the men between twenty and thirty years of age is the great source of political prophecy, the existence of Coleridge will show itself by no slight or ambiguous traces in the coming history of our country; for no one has contributed more to shape the opinions of those among its younger men, who can be said to have opinions at all.

The influence of Coleridge, like that of Bentham, extends far beyond those who share in the peculiarities of his religious or philosophical creed. He has been the great awakener in this country of the spirit of philosophy, within the bounds of traditional opinions. He has been, almost as truly as Bentham, "the great questioner of things established"; for a questioner needs not necessarily

3. A palace in Paris, where paintings of scenes from French history were exhibited.
1. In his *Autobiography* Mill discusses Samuel Taylor Coleridge as a poet. In the present essay he discusses Coleridge as a political and religious phi-

losopher whose conversation and writings on conservatism had a profound influence on Mill's contemporaries in the 1820's and 1830's.
2. Jeremy Bentham (1748–1832), originator of Utilitarian theories of politics and ethics.

be an enemy. By Bentham, beyond all others, men have been led to ask themselves, in regard to any ancient or received opinion, Is it true? and by Coleridge, What is the meaning of it? The one took his stand *outside* the received opinion, and surveyed it as an entire stranger to it: the other looked at it from within, and endeavored to see it with the eyes of a believer in it; to discover by what apparent facts it was at first suggested, and by what appearances it has ever since been rendered continually credible—has seemed, to a succession of persons, to be a faithful interpretation of their experience. Bentham judged a proposition true or false as it accorded or not with the result of his own inquiries; and did not search very curiously into what might be meant by the proposition, when it obviously did not mean what he thought true. With Coleridge, on the contrary, the very fact that any doctrine had been believed by thoughtful men, and received by whole nations or generations of mankind, was part of the problem to be solved; was one of the phenomena to be accounted for. And, as Bentham's short and easy method of referring all to the selfish interests of aristocracies or priests or lawyers, or some other species of imposters, could not satisfy a man who saw so much farther into the complexities of the human intellect and feelings, he considered the long or extensive prevalence of any opinion as a presumption that it was not altogether a fallacy; that, to its first authors at least, it was the result of a struggle to express in words something which had a reality to them, though perhaps not to many of those who have since received the doctrine by mere tradition. The long duration of a belief, he thought, is at least proof of an adaptation in it to some portion or other of the human mind: and if, on digging down to the root, we do not find, as is generally the case, some truth, we shall find some natural want or requirement of human nature which the doctrine in question is fitted to satisfy; among which wants the instincts of selfishness and of credulity have a place, but by no means an exclusive one. From this difference in the points of view of the two philosophers, and from the too rigid adherence of each to his own, it was to be expected that Bentham should continually miss the truth which is in the traditional opinions, and Coleridge that which is out of them and at variance with them. But it was also likely that each would find, or show the way to finding, much of what the other missed.

It is hardly possible to speak of Coleridge, and his position among his contemporaries, without reverting to Bentham: they are connected by two of the closest bonds of association—resemblance and contrast. It would be difficult to find two persons of philosophic eminence more exactly the contrary of one another. Compare their modes of treatment of any subject, and you might fancy them inhabitants of different worlds. They seem to have scarcely a principle or a premise in common. Each of them sees scarcely any thing but what the other does not see. Bentham would have regarded Coleridge with a peculiar measure of the good-humored contempt with which he was accustomed to regard all modes of philosophizing different from his own. Coleridge would probably have made Bentham one of the exceptions to the enlarged and liberal appreciation which (to the credit of *his* mode of philosophizing) he extended to most thinkers of any eminence from whom he differed. But contraries, as logicians say, are but *quae in eodem genere maxime distant*—the things which are farthest from one another in the same kind. These two agreed in being the men, who, in their age and country, did most to enforce, by precept and example, the necessity of a philosophy. They agreed in making it their occupation to recall opinions to first principles; taking no proposition for granted without examining into the grounds of it, and ascertaining that it possessed the kind and degree of evidence suitable to its nature. They agreed in recognizing that sound theory is the only foundation for sound practice; and that whoever despises theory, let him give himself what airs of wisdom he may, is self-convicted of being a quack. If a book were to be compiled containing all the best things ever said on the rule-of-thumb school of political craftsmanship, and on the insufficiency for practical purposes of what the mere practical man calls experience, it is difficult to say whether the collection would be more indebted to the writings of Bentham or of Coleridge. They agreed, too, in perceiving that the groundwork of all other philosophy must be laid in the philosophy of the mind. To lay this foundation deeply and strongly, and to raise a superstructure in accordance with it, were the objects to which their lives were devoted. They employed, indeed, for the most part, different materials; but as the materials of both were real observations, the genuine product of experience, the results will, in the end, be found, not hostile, but supplementary, to one another. Of their methods of philosophizing, the same thing may be said: they were different, yet both were legitimate logical processes. In every respect, the two men are each other's "completing counterpart": the strong points of each correspond to the weak points of the other. Whoever could master the premises and combine the methods of both would possess the entire English philosophy of his age. Coleridge used to say that every one is born either a Platonist or an Aristotelian: it may be similarly affirmed that every Englishman of the present day is by implication either a Benthamite or a Coleridgian; holds views of human affairs which can only be proved true on the principles either of Bentham or of Coleridge. * * *

1840

From On Liberty

From Chapter III. Of Individuality as One of the Elements of Well-Being

* * * Few persons, out of Germany, even comprehend the meaning of the doctrine which Wilhelm von Humboldt, so eminent both as a savant and as a politician, made the text of a treatise— that "the end of man, or that which is prescribed by the eternal or immutable dictates of reason, and not suggested by vague and transient desires, is the highest and most harmonious development of his powers to a complete and consistent whole"; that, therefore, the object "towards which every human being must ceaselessly direct his efforts, and on which especially those who design to influence their fellow men must ever keep their eyes, is the individuality of power and development"; that for this there are two requisites, "freedom, and variety of situations"; and that from the union of these arise "individual vigor and manifold diversity," which combine themselves in "originality."[1]

Little, however, as people are accustomed to a doctrine like that of Von Humboldt, and surprising as it may be to them to find so high a value attached to individuality, the question, one must nevertheless think, can only be one of degree. No one's idea of excellence in conduct is that people should do absolutely nothing but copy one another. No one would assert that people ought not to put into their mode of life, and into the conduct of their concerns, any impress whatever of their own judgment, or of their own individual character. On the other hand, it would be absurd to pretend that people ought to live as if nothing whatever had been known in the world before they came into it; as if experience had as yet done nothing towards showing that one mode of existence, or conduct, is preferable to another. Nobody denies that people should be so taught and trained in youth, as to know and benefit by the ascertained results of human experience. But it is the privilege and proper condition of a human being, arrived at the maturity of his faculties, to use and interpret experience in his own way. It is for him to find out what part of recorded experience is properly applicable to his own circumstances and character. The traditions and customs of other people are, to a certain extent, evidence of what their experience has taught *them*; presumptive evidence, and as such, have a claim to his deference: but, in the first place, their experience may be too narrow; or they may not have interpreted it rightly. Secondly, their interpretation of experience may be

1. From *The Sphere and Duties of Government*, by Baron Wilhelm von Humboldt (1767–1835), Prussian statesman and man of letters. Originally written in 1791, this treatise was first published in Germany in 1852 and was translated into English in 1854.

correct, but unsuitable to him. Customs are made for customary circumstances, and customary characters; and his circumstances or his character may be uncustomary. Thirdly, though the customs be both good as customs, and suitable to him, yet to conform to custom, merely *as* custom, does not educate or develop in him any of the qualities which are the distinctive endowment of a human being. The human faculties of perception, judgment, discriminative feeling, mental activity, and even moral preference are exercised only in making a choice. He who does anything because it is the custom makes no choice. He gains no practice either in discerning or in desiring what is best. The mental and moral, like the muscular powers, are improved only by being used. The faculties are called into no exercise by doing a thing merely because others do it, no more than by believing a thing only because others believe it. If the grounds of an opinion are not conclusive to the person's own reason, his reason cannot be strengthened, but is likely to be weakened, by his adopting it: and if the inducements to an act are not such as are consentaneous[2] to his own feelings and character (where affection, or the rights of others, are not concerned) it is so much done towards rendering his feelings and character inert and torpid, instead of active and energetic.

He who lets the world, or his own portion of it, choose his plan of life for him has no need of any other faculty than the apelike one of imitation. He who chooses his plan for himself employs all his faculties. He must use observation to see, reasoning and judgment to foresee, activity to gather materials for decision, discrimination to decide, and when he has decided, firmness and self-control to hold to his deliberate decision. And these qualities he requires and exercises exactly in proportion as the part of his conduct which he determines according to his own judgment and feelings is a large one. It is possible that he might be guided in some good path, and kept out of harm's way, without any of these things. But what will be his comparative worth as a human being? It really is of importance, not only what men do, but also what manner of men they are that do it. Among the works of man, which human life is rightly employed in perfecting and beautifying, the first in importance surely is man himself. Supposing it were possible to get houses built, corn grown, battles fought, causes tried, and even churches erected and prayers said, by machinery—by automatons in human form—it would be a considerable loss to exchange for these automatons even the men and women who at present inhabit the more civilized parts of the world, and who assuredly are but starved specimens of what nature can and will produce. Human nature is not a machine to be built after a model, and set to do exactly the work prescribed for it, but a tree, which requires to grow and develop itself on all sides, according to the tendency of the inward forces

2. Agreeable.

which make it a living thing.

It will probably be conceded that it is desirable people should exercise their understandings, and that an intelligent following of custom, or even occasionally an intelligent deviation from custom, is better than a blind and simply mechanical adhesion to it. To a certain extent it is admitted that our understanding should be our own: but there is not the same willingness to admit that our desires and impulses should be our own likewise; or that to possess impulses of our own, and of any strength, is anything but a peril and a snare. Yet desires and impulses are as much a part of a perfect human being, as beliefs and restraints: and strong impulses are only perilous when not properly balanced; when one set of aims and inclinations is developed into strength, while others, which ought to coexist with them, remain weak and inactive. It is not because men's desires are strong that they act ill; it is because their consciences are weak. There is no natural connection between strong impulses and a weak conscience. The natural connection is the other way. To say that one person's desires and feelings are stronger and more various than those of another is merely to say that he has more of the raw material of human nature, and is therefore capable, perhaps of more evil, but certainly of more good. Strong impulses are but another name for energy. Energy may be turned to bad uses; but more good may always be made of an energetic nature than of an indolent and impassive one. Those who have most natural feeling are always those whose cultivated feelings may be made the strongest. The same strong susceptibilities which make the personal impulses vivid and powerful are also the source from whence are generated the most passionate love of virtue, and the sternest self-control. It is through the cultivation of these that society both does its duty and protects its interests: not by rejecting the stuff of which heroes are made, because it knows not how to make them. A person whose desires and impulses are his own—are the expression of his own nature, as it has been developed and modified by his own culture—is said to have a character. One whose desires and impulses are not his own, has no character, no more than a steam engine has a character. If, in addition to being his own, his impulses are strong, and are under the government of a strong will, he has an energetic character. Whoever thinks that individuality of desires and impulses should not be encouraged to unfold itself must maintain that society has no need of strong natures—is not the better for containing many persons who have much character—and that a high general average of energy is not desirable.

In some early states of society, these forces might be, and were, too much ahead of the power which society then possessed of disciplining and controlling them. There has been a time when the element of spontaneity and individuality was in excess, and the social principle had a hard struggle with it. The difficulty then was to induce men of strong bodies or minds to pay obedience to any rules which required them to control their impulses. To overcome this difficulty, law and discipline, like the Popes struggling against the Emperors, asserted a power over the whole man, claiming to control all his life in order to control his character—which society had not found any other sufficient means of binding. But society has now fairly got the better of individuality; and the danger which threatens human nature is not the excess, but the deficiency, of personal impulses and preferences. Things are vastly changed, since the passions of those who were strong by station or by personal endowment were in a state of habitual rebellion against laws and ordinances, and required to be rigorously chained up to enable the persons within their reach to enjoy any particle of security. In our times, from the highest class of society down to the lowest, everyone lives as under the eye of a hostile and dreaded censorship. Not only in what concerns others, but in what concerns only themselves, the individual or the family do not ask themselves—what do I prefer? or, what would suit my character and disposition? or, what would allow the best and highest in me to have fair play, and enable it to grow and thrive? They ask themselves, what is suitable to my position? what is usually done by persons of my station and pecuniary circumstances? or (worse still) what is usually done by persons of a station and circumstances superior to mine? I do not mean that they choose what is customary, in preference to what suits their own inclination. It does not occur to them to have any inclination, except for what is customary. Thus the mind itself is bowed to the yoke: even in what people do for pleasure, conformity is the first thing thought of; they like in crowds; they exercise choice only among things commonly done: peculiarity of taste, eccentricity of conduct, are shunned equally with crimes: until by dint of not following their own nature, they have no nature to follow: their human capacities are withered and starved: they become incapable of any strong wishes or native pleasures, and are generally without either opinions or feelings of home growth, or properly their own. Now is this, or is it not, the desirable condition of human nature?

It is so, on the Calvinistic theory. According to that, the one great offense of man is self-will. All the good of which humanity is capable is comprised in obedience. You have no choice; thus you must do, and no otherwise: "whatever is not a duty is a sin." Human nature being radically corrupt, there is no redemption for anyone until human nature is killed within him. To one holding this theory of life, crushing out any of the human faculties, capacities, and susceptibilities is no evil: man needs no capacity but that of surrendering himself to the will of God: and if he uses any of his faculties for any other purpose but to do that supposed will more effectually, he is better without them. This is the theory of Calvinism; and it is held, in a mitigated form, by many who do not consider themselves Calvinists; the mitigation consisting in giving a less ascetic interpretation to the alleged will of God; asserting it to be his will that mankind should gratify some of their inclinations; of course not in the manner they themselves prefer, but in the way of obedience, that is, in a way prescribed to them by authority; and, therefore, by the necessary conditions of the case, the same for all.

In some such insidious form there is at present a strong tendency to this narrow theory of life, and to the pinched and hidebound type of human character which it patronizes. Many persons, no doubt, sincerely think that human beings thus cramped and dwarfed are as their Maker designed them to be; just as many have thought that trees are a much finer thing when clipped into pollards,[3] or cut out into figures of animals, than as nature made them. But if it be any part of religion to believe that man was made by a good Being, it is more consistent with that faith to believe that this Being gave all human faculties that they might be cultivated and unfolded, not rooted out and consumed, and that he takes delight in every nearer approach made by his creatures to the ideal conception embodied in them, every increase in any of their capabilities of comprehension, of action, or of enjoyment. There is a different type of human excellence from the Calvinistic; a conception of humanity as having its nature bestowed on it for other purposes than merely to be abnegated. "Pagan self-assertion" is one of the elements of human worth, as well as "Christian self-denial."[4] There is a Greek ideal of self-development, which the Platonic and Christian ideal of self-government blends with, but does not supersede. It may be better to be a John Knox than an Alcibiades, but it is better to be a Pericles than either;[5] nor would a Pericles, if we had one in these days, be without anything good which belonged to John Knox.

It is not by wearing down into uniformity all that is individual in themselves, but by cultivating it and calling it forth, within the limits imposed by the rights and interests of others, that human beings become a noble and beautiful object of contemplation; and as the works partake the character of those who do them, by the same process human life also becomes rich, diversified, and animating, furnishing more abundant aliment to high thoughts and elevating feelings, and strengthening the tie which binds every individual to the race, by making the race infinitely better worth belonging to. In proportion to the development of his individuality, each person becomes more valuable to himself, and is therefore capable of being more valuable to others. There is a greater fullness

3. Trees that acquire an artificial shape by being cut back so as to produce a mass of dense foliage.
4. From the *Essays* (1848) of John Sterling, a minor writer and friend of Thomas Carlyle's.

5. John Knox (1505–72) was the stern Scottish Calvinist reformer; Alcibiades (450–404 B.C.) was a dissolute Athenian commander, and Pericles (500–429 B.C.) was a model statesman in Athens.

of life about his own existence, and when there is more life in the units there is more in the mass which is composed of them. As much compression as is necessary to prevent the stronger specimens of human nature from encroaching on the rights of others cannot be dispensed with; but for this there is ample compensation even in the point of view of human development. The means of development which the individual loses by being prevented from gratifying his inclinations to the injury of others are chiefly obtained at the expense of the development of other people. And even to himself there is a full equivalent in the better development of the social part of his nature, rendered possible by the restraint put upon the selfish part. To be held to rigid rules of justice for the sake of others develops the feelings and capacities which have the good of others for their object. But to be restrained in things not affecting their good, by their mere displeasure, develops nothing valuable, except such force of character as may unfold itself in resisting the restraint. If acquiesced in, it dulls and blunts the whole nature. To give any fair play to the nature of each, it is essential that different persons should be allowed to lead different lives. In proportion as this latitude has been exercised in any age, has that age been noteworthy to posterity. Even despotism does not produce its worst effects, so long as individuality exists under it; and whatever crushes individuality is despotism, by whatever name it may be called, and whether it professes to be enforcing the will of God or the injunctions of men.

Having said that Individuality is the same thing with development, and that it is only the cultivation of individuality which produces, or can produce, well-developed human beings, I might here close the argument: for what more or better can be said of any condition of human affairs than that it brings human beings themselves nearer to the best thing they can be? or what worse can be said of any obstruction to good than that it prevents this? Doubtless, however, these considerations will not suffice to convince those who most need convincing; and it is necessary further to show that these developed human beings are of some use to the undeveloped—to point out to those who do not desire liberty, and would not avail themselves of it, that they may be in some intelligible manner rewarded for allowing other people to make use of it without hindrance.

In the first place, then, I would suggest that they might possibly learn something from them. It will not be denied by anybody, that originality is a valuable element in human affairs. There is always need of persons not only to discover new truths, and point out when what were once truths are true no longer, but also to commence new practices, and set the example of more enlightened conduct, and better taste and sense in human life. This cannot well be gainsaid by anybody who does not believe that the world has already attained perfection in all its ways and practices. It is true that this benefit is not capable of being rendered by everybody alike: there are but few persons, in comparison with the whole of mankind, whose experiments, if adopted by others, would be likely to be any improvement on established practice. But these few are the salt of the earth; without them, human life would become a stagnant pool. Not only is it they who introduce good things which did not before exist; it is they who keep the life in those which already existed. If there were nothing new to be done, would human intellect cease to be necessary? Would it be a reason why those who do the old things should forget why they are done, and do them like cattle, not like human beings? There is only too great a tendency in the best beliefs and practices to degenerate into the mechanical; and unless there were a succession of persons whose ever-recurring originality prevents the grounds of those beliefs and practices from becoming merely traditional, such dead matter would not resist the smallest shock from anything really alive, and there would be no reason why civilization should not die out, as in the Byzantine Empire. Persons of genius, it is true, are, and are always likely to be, a small minority; but in order to have them, it is necessary to preserve the soil in which they grow. Genius can only breathe freely in an *atmosphere* of freedom. Persons of genius are, *ex vi termini*,[6] *more* individual than any other people—less capable, consequently, of fitting themselves, without hurtful compression, into any of the small number of molds which society provides in order to save its members the trouble of forming their own character. If from timidity they consent to be forced into one of these molds, and to let all that part of themselves which cannot expand under the pressure remain unexpanded, society will be little the better for their genius. If they are of a strong character, and break their fetters, they become a mark for the society which has not succeeded in reducing them to commonplace, to point at with solemn warning as "wild," "erratic," and the like; much as if one should complain of the Niagara River for not flowing smoothly between its banks like a Dutch canal.

I insist thus emphatically on the importance of genius, and the necessity of allowing it to unfold itself freely both in thought and in practice, being well aware that no one will deny the position in theory, but knowing also that almost everyone, in reality, is totally indifferent to it. People think genius a fine thing if it enables a man to write an exciting poem, or paint a picture. But in its true sense, that of originality in thought and action, though no one says that it is not a thing to be admired, nearly all, at heart, think that they can do very well without it. Unhappily this is too natural to be wondered at. Originality is the one thing which unoriginal minds cannot feel the use of. They cannot see what it is to do for

6. Latin for "by force of the term," i.e., by definition.

them: how should they? If they could see what it would do for them, it would not be originality. The first service which originality has to render them is that of opening their eyes: which being once fully done, they would have a chance of being themselves original. Meanwhile, recollecting that nothing was ever yet done which some-one was not the first to do, and that all good things which exist are the fruits of originality, let them be modest enough to believe that there is something still left for it to accomplish, and assure them-selves that they are more in need of originality, the less they are conscious of the want.

In sober truth, whatever homage may be professed, or even paid, to real or supposed mental superiority, the general tendency of things throughout the world is to render mediocrity the ascendant power among mankind. In ancient history, in the middle ages, and in a diminishing degree through the long transition from feudality to the present time, the individual was a power in himself; and if he had either great talents or a high social position, he was a con-siderable power. At present individuals are lost in the crowd. In politics it is almost a triviality to say that public opinion now rules the world. The only power deserving the name is that of masses, and of governments while they make themselves the organ of the tend-encies and instincts of masses. This is as true in the moral and social relations of private life as in public transactions. Those whose opinions go by the name of public opinion, are not always the same sort of public: in America they are the whole white population; in England, chiefly the middle class. But they are always a mass, that is to say, collective mediocrity. And what is a still greater novelty, the mass do not now take their opinions from dignitaries in Church or State, from ostensible leaders, or from books. Their thinking is done for them by men much like themselves, addressing them or speaking in their name, on the spur of the moment, through the newspapers. I am not complaining of all this. I do not assert that anything better is compatible, as a general rule, with the present low state of the human mind. But that does not hinder the govern-ment of mediocrity from being mediocre government. No govern-ment by a democracy or a numerous aristocracy, either in its political acts or in the opinions, qualities, and tone of mind which it fosters, ever did or could rise above mediocrity, except in so far as the sovereign Many have let themselves be guided (which in their best times they always have done) by the counsels and influence of a more highly gifted and instructed One or Few. The initiation of all wise or noble things, comes and must come from individuals; generally at first from some one individual. The honor and glory of the average man is that he is capable of following that initiative; that he can respond internally to wise and noble things, and be led to them with his eyes open. I am not countenancing the sort of "hero worship" which applauds the strong man of genius for forcibly seizing on the government of the world and making it do his bidding in spite of itself. All he can claim is freedom to point out the way. The power of compelling others into it is not only inconsistent with the freedom and development of all the rest, but corrupting to the strong man himself. It does seem, however, that when the opinions of masses of merely average men are everywhere become or becoming the dominant power, the counterpoise and corrective to that tendency would be the more and more pronounced individuality of those who stand on the higher eminences of thought. It is in these circumstances most especially that exceptional individuals, instead of being deterred, should be encouraged in acting differently from the mass. In other times there was no advantage in their doing so, unless they acted not only differently, but better. In this age, the mere example of nonconformity, the mere refusal to bend the knee to custom, is itself a service. Precisely because the tyranny of opinion is such as to make eccentricity a reproach, it is desirable, in order to break through that tyranny, that people should be eccentric. Eccentricity has always abounded when and where strength of character has abounded; and the amount of eccentricity in a society has generally been proportional to the amount of genius, mental vigor, and moral courage which it contained. That so few now dare to be eccentric marks the chief danger of the time. * * *

There is one characteristic of the present direction of public opinion, peculiarly calculated to make it intolerant of any marked demonstration of individuality. The general average of mankind are not only moderate in intellect, but also moderate in inclinations: they have no tastes or wishes strong enough to incline them to do anything unusual, and they consequently do not understand those who have, and class all such with the wild and intemperate whom they are accustomed to look down upon. Now, in addition to this fact which is general, we have only to suppose that a strong movement has set in towards the improvement of morals, and it is evident what we have to expect. In these days such a movement has set in; much has actually been effected in the way of increased regularity of conduct, and discouragement of excesses; and there is a philanthropic spirit abroad, for the exercise of which there is no more inviting field than the moral and prudential improvement of our fellow creatures. These tendencies of the times cause the public to be more disposed than at most former periods to prescribe general rules of conduct, and endeavor to make everyone conform to the approved standard. And that standard, express or tacit, is to desire nothing strongly. Its ideal of character is to be without any marked character; to maim by compression, like a Chinese lady's foot, every part of human nature which stands out prominently, and tends to make the person markedly dissimilar in outline to commonplace humanity.

As is usually the case with ideals which exclude one half of what is desirable, the present standard of approbation produces only an inferior imitation of the other half. Instead of great energies guided by vigorous reason, and strong feelings strongly controlled by a conscientious will, its result is weak feelings and weak energies, which therefore can be kept in outward conformity to rule without any strength either of will or reason. Already energetic characters on any large scale are becoming merely traditional. There is now scarcely any outlet for energy in this country except business. The energy expended in this may still be regarded as considerable. What little is left from that employment, is expended on some hobby; which may be a useful, even a philanthropic hobby, but is always some one thing, and generally a thing of small dimensions. The greatness of England is now all collective: individually small, we only appear capable of anything great by our habit of combining; and with this our moral and religious philanthropies are perfectly contented. But it was men of another stamp than this that made England what it has been; and men of another stamp will be needed to prevent its decline.

The despotism of custom is everywhere the standing hindrance to human advancement, being in unceasing antagonism to that disposition to aim at something better than customary, which is called, according to circumstances, the spirit of liberty, or that of progress or improvement. The spirit of improvement is not always a spirit of liberty, for it may aim at forcing improvements on an unwilling people; and the spirit of liberty, in so far as it resists such attempts, may ally itself locally and temporarily with the opponents of improvement; but the only unfailing and permanent source of improvement is liberty, since by it there are as many possible independent centers of improvement as there are individuals. The progressive principle, however, in either shape, whether as the love of liberty or of improvement, is antagonistic to the sway of Custom, involving at least emancipation from that yoke; and the contest between the two constitutes the chief interest of the history of mankind. The greater part of the world has, properly speaking, no history, because the depotism of Custom is complete. This is the case over the whole East. Custom is there, in all things, the final appeal; justice and right mean conformity to custom; the argument of custom no one, unless some tyrant intoxicated with power, thinks of resisting. And we see the result. Those nations must once have had originality; they did not start out of the ground populous, lettered, and versed in many of the arts of life; they made themselves all this, and were then the greatest and most powerful nations of the world. What are they now? The subjects or dependants of tribes whose forefathers wandered in the forests when theirs had magnificent palaces and gorgeous temples, but over whom custom exercised only a divided rule with liberty and progress. A people, it appears, may be progressive for a certain length of time, and then stop: when does it stop? When it ceases to possess individuality. If a similar change should befall the nations of Europe, it will not be in exactly the same shape: the despotism of custom with which these nations are threatened is not precisely stationariness. It proscribes singularity, but it does not preclude change, provided all change together. We have discarded the fixed costumes of our forefathers; everyone must still dress like other people, but the fashion may change once or twice a year. We thus take care that when there is change it shall be for change's sake, and not from any idea of beauty or convenience; for the same idea of beauty or convenience would not strike all the world at the same moment, and be simultaneously thrown aside by all at another moment. But we are progressive as well as changeable: we continually make new inventions in mechanical things, and keep them until they are again superseded by better; we are eager for improvement in politics, in education, even in morals, though in this last our idea of improvement chiefly consists in persuading or forcing other people to be as good as ourselves. It is not progress that we object to; on the contrary, we flatter ourselves that we are the most progressive people who ever lived. It is individuality that we war against: we should think we had done wonders if we had made ourselves all alike; forgetting that the unlikeness of one person to another is generally the first thing which draws the attention of either to the imperfection of his own type, and the superiority of another, or the possibility, by combining the advantages of both, of producing something better than either. We have a warning example in China—a nation of much talent, and, in some respects, even wisdom, owing to the rare good fortune of having been provided at an early period with a particularly good set of customs, the work, in some measure, of men to whom even the most enlightened European must accord, under certain limitations, the title of sages and philosophers. They are remarkable, too, in the excellence of their apparatus for impressing, as far as possible, the best wisdom they possess upon every mind in the community, and securing that those who have appropriated most of it shall occupy the posts of honor and power. Surely the people who did this have discovered the secret of human progressiveness, and must have kept themselves steadily at the head of the movement of the world. On the contrary, they have become stationary—have remained so for thousands of years; and if they are ever to be farther improved, it must be by foreigners. They have succeeded beyond all hope in what English philanthropists are so industriously working at—in making a people all alike, all governing their thoughts and conduct by the same maxims and rules; and these are the fruits. The modern regime of public opinion is, in an unorganized form, what the Chinese educational and political systems are in an organized; and unless individuality shall be able successfully to assert itself against this yoke, Europe, notwithstanding its noble antecedents and its professed Christianity, will tend to become another China. * * *

1859

From The Subjection of Women

The object of this Essay is to explain as clearly as I am able, the grounds of an opinion which I have held from the very earliest period when I had formed an opinion at all on social or political matters, and which, instead of being weakened or modified, has been constantly growing stronger by the progress of reflection and the experience of life: That the principle which regulates the existing social relations between the two sexes—the legal subordination of one sex to the other—is wrong in itself, and now one of the chief hindrances to human improvement; and that it ought to be replaced by a principle of perfect equality, admitting no power or privilege on the one side, nor disability on the other.

* * *

Some will object, that a comparison cannot fairly be made between the government of the male sex and the forms of unjust power[1] which I have adduced in illustration of it, since these are arbitrary, and the effect of mere usurpation, while it on the contrary is natural. But was there ever any domination which did not appear natural to those who possessed it? There was a time when the division of mankind into two classes, a small one of masters and a numerous one of slaves, appeared, even to the most cultivated minds, to be a natural, and the only natural, condition of the human race. No less an intellect, and one which contributed no less to the progress of human thought, than Aristotle, held this opinion without doubt or misgiving; and rested it on the same premises on which the same assertion in regard to the dominion of men over women is usually based, namely that there are different natures among mankind, free natures, and slave natures; that the Greeks were of a free nature, the barbarian races of Thracians and Asiatics of a slave nature. But why need I go back to Aristotle? Did not the slaveowners of the Southern United States maintain the same doctrine, with all the fanaticism with which men cling to the theories that justify their passions and legitimate their personal interests? Did they not call heaven and earth to witness that the dominion of the white man over the black is natural, that the black race is by nature incapable of freedom, and marked out for slavery? some even going so far as to say that the freedom of manual laborers is an

---

1. As examples of unjust power Mill had cited the forceful control of slaves by slave-owners or of nations by military despots.

unnatural order of things anywhere. Again, the theorists of absolute monarchy have always affirmed it to be the only natural form of government; issuing from the patriarchal, which was the primitive and spontaneous form of society, framed on the model of the paternal, which is anterior to society itself, and, as they contend, the most natural authority of all. * * * So true is it that unnatural generally means only uncustomary, and that everything which is usual appears natural. The subjection of women to men being a universal custom, any departure from it quite naturally appears unnatural. But how entirely, even in this case, the feeling is dependent on custom, appears by ample experience. Nothing so much astonishes the people of distant parts of the world, when they first learn anything about England, as to be told that it is under a queen: the thing seems to them so unnatural as to be almost incredible. To Englishmen this does not seem in the least degree unnatural, because they are used to it; but they do feel it unnatural that women should be soldiers or members of parliament. In the feudal ages, on the contrary, war and politics were not thought unnatural to women, because not unusual; it seemed natural that women of the privileged classes should be of manly character, inferior in nothing but bodily strength to their husbands and fathers. The independence of women seemed rather less unnatural to the Greeks than to other ancients, on account of the fabulous Amazons (whom they believed to be historical), and the partial example afforded by the Spartan women; who, though no less subordinate by law than in other Greek states, were more free in fact, and being trained to bodily exercises in the same manner with men, gave ample proof that they were not naturally disqualified for them. There can be little doubt that Spartan experience suggested to Plato, among many other of his doctrines, that of the social and political equality of the two sexes.[2]

But, it will be said, the rule of men over women differs from all these others in not being a rule of force: it is accepted voluntarily; women make no complaint, and are consenting parties to it. In the first place, a great number of women do not accept it. Ever since there have been women able to make their sentiments known by their writings (the only mode of publicity which society permits to them), an increasing number of them have recorded protests against their present social condition: and recently many thousands of them, headed by the most eminent women known to the public, have petitioned Parliament for their admission to the Parliamentary Suffrage. The claim of women to be educated as solidly, and in the same branches of knowledge, as men, is urged with growing intensity, and with a great prospect of success; while the demand for their admission into professions and occupations hitherto closed against

2. See Plato, *The Republic*, V.

them, becomes every year more urgent. Though there are not in this country, as there are in the United States, periodical Conventions and an organized party to agitate for the Rights of Women,[3] there is a numerous and active Society organized and managed by women, for the more limited object of obtaining the political franchise. Nor is it only in our own country and in America that women are beginning to protest, more or less collectively, against the disabilities under which they labor. France, and Italy, and Switzerland, and Russia now afford examples of the same thing. How many more women there are who silently cherish similar aspirations, no one can possibly know; but there are abundant tokens how many *would* cherish them, were they not so strenuously taught to repress them as contrary to the proprieties of their sex. * * *

All causes, social and natural, combine to make it unlikely that women should be collectively rebellious to the power of men. They are so far in a position different from all other subject classes, that their masters require something more from them than actual service. Men do not want solely the obedience of women, they want their sentiments. All men, except the most brutish, desire to have, in the woman most nearly connected with them, not a forced slave but a willing one, not a slave merely, but a favorite. They have therefore put everything in practice to enslave their minds. The masters of all other slaves rely, for maintaining obedience, on fear; either fear of themselves, or religious fears. The masters of women wanted more than simple obedience, and they turned the whole force of education to effect their purpose. All women are brought up from the very earliest years in the belief that their ideal of character is the very opposite to that of men; not self-will, and government by self-control, but submission, and yielding to the control of others. All the moralities tell them that it is the duty of women, and all the current sentimentalities that it is their nature, to live for others; to make complete abnegation of themselves, and to have no life but in their affections. And by their affections are meant the only ones they are allowed to have—those to the men with whom they are connected, or to the children who constitute an additional and indefeasible tie between them and a man. When we put together three things—first, the natural attraction between opposite sexes; secondly, the wife's entire dependence on the husband, every privilege or pleasure she has being either his gift, or depending entirely on his will; and lastly, that the principal object of human pursuit, consideration, and all objects of social ambition, can in general be sought or obtained by her only through him, it would be a miracle if the object of being attractive to men had not become the polar star of feminine education and formation of character. And,

3. Such as the Women's Rights Convention held at Worcester, Massachusetts in October, 1850, which had occasioned an essay by Mill's wife entitled *Enfranchisement of Women* (1851).

this great means of influence over the minds of women having been acquired, an instinct of selfishness made men avail themselves of it to the utmost as a means of holding women in subjection, by representing to them meekness, submissiveness, and resignation of all individual will into the hands of a man, as an essential part of sexual attractiveness. Can it be doubted that any of the other yokes which mankind have succeeded in breaking, would have subsisted till now if the same means had existed, and had been as sedulously used, to bow down their minds to it? If it had been made the object of the life of every young plebeian to find personal favor in the eyes of some patrician, of every young serf with some seigneur; if domestication with him, and a share of his personal affections, had been held out as the prize which they all should look out for, the most gifted and aspiring being able to reckon on the most desirable prizes; and if, when this prize had been obtained, they had been shut out by a wall of brass from all interests not centering in him, all feelings and desires but those which he shared or inculcated; would not serfs and seigneurs, plebeians and patricians, have been as broadly distinguished at this day as men and women are? and would not all but a thinker here and there, have believed the distinction to be a fundamental and unalterable fact in human nature?

The preceding considerations are amply sufficient to show that custom, however universal it may be, affords in this case no presumption, and ought not to create any prejudice, in favor of the arrangements which place women in social and political subjection to men. But I may go farther, and maintain that the course of history, and the tendencies of progressive human society, afford not only no presumption in favor of this system of inequality of rights, but a strong one against it; and that, so far as the whole course of human improvement up to this time, the whole stream of modern tendencies, warrants any inference on the subject, it is, that this relic of the past is discordant with the future, and must necessarily disappear.

For, what is the peculiar character of the modern world—the difference which chiefly distinguishes modern institutions, modern social ideas, modern life itself, from those of times long past? It is, that human beings are no longer born to their place in life, and chained down by an inexorable bond to the place they are born to, but are free to employ their faculties, and such favorable chances as offer, to achieve the lot which may appear to them most desirable. * * *

On the other point which is involved in the just equality of women, their admissibility to all the functions and occupations hitherto retained as the monopoly of the stronger sex, I should anticipate no difficulty in convincing anyone who has gone with me on the subject of the equality of women in the family. I believe that their disabilities elsewhere are only clung to in order to maintain their subordination in domestic life; because the generality of the male sex cannot yet tolerate the idea of living with an equal. Were it not for that, I think that almost everyone, in the existing state of opinion in politics and political economy, would admit the injustice of excluding half the human race from the greater number of lucrative occupations, and from almost all high social functions; ordaining from their birth either that they are not, and cannot by any possibility become, fit for employments which are legally open to the stupidest and basest of the other sex, or else that however fit they may be, those employments shall be interdicted to them, in order to be preserved for the exclusive benefit of males. In the last two centuries, when (which was seldom the case) any reason beyond the mere existence of the fact was thought to be required to justify the disabilities of women, people seldom assigned as a reason their inferior mental capacity; which, in times when there was a real trial of personal faculties (from which all women were not excluded) in the struggles of public life, no one really believed in. The reason given in those days was not women's unfitness, but the interest of society, by which was meant the interest of men: just as the *raison d'état*, meaning the convenience of the government, and the support of existing authority, was deemed a sufficient explanation and excuse for the most flagitious crimes. In the present day, power holds a smoother language, and whomsoever it oppresses, always pretends to do so for their own good: accordingly, when anything is forbidden to women, it is thought necessary to say, and desirable to believe, that they are incapable of doing it, and that they depart from their real path of success and happiness when they aspire to it. But to make this reason plausible (I do not say valid), those by whom it is urged must be prepared to carry it to a much greater length than anyone ventures to do in the face of present experience. It is not sufficient to maintain that women on the average are less gifted than men on the average, with certain of the higher mental faculties, or that a smaller number of women than of men are fit for occupations and functions of the highest intellectual character. It is necessary to maintain that no women at all are fit for them, and that the most eminent women are inferior in mental faculties to the most mediocre of the men on whom those functions at present devolve. For if the performance of the function is decided either by competition, or by any mode of choice which secures regard to the public interest, there needs to be no apprehension that any important employments will fall into the hands of women inferior to average men, or to the average of their male competitors. The only result would be that there would be fewer women than men in such employments; a result certain to happen in any case, if only from the preference always likely to be felt by the majority of women for the one vocation in which there is

nobody to compete with them. Now, the most determined deprecia-
tor of women will not venture to deny, that when we add the experience of recent times to that of ages past, women, and not a few
merely, but many women, have proved themselves capable of everything, perhaps without a single exception, which is done by men,
and of doing it successfully and creditably. The utmost that can be
said is, that there are many things which none of them have succeeded in doing as well as they have been done by some men—
many in which they have not reached the very highest rank. But
there are extremely few, dependent only on mental faculties, in
which they have not attained the rank next to the highest. Is not
this enough, and much more than enough, to make it a tyranny to
them, and a detriment to society, that they should not be allowed
to compete with men for the exercise of these functions? Is it not a
mere truism to say, that such functions are often filled by men far
less fit for them than numbers of women, and who would be beaten
by women in any fair field of competition? What difference does it
make that there may be men somewhere, fully employed about
other things, who may be still better qualified for the things in
question than these women? Does not this take place in all competitions? Is there so great a superfluity of men fit for high duties,
that society can afford to reject the service of any competent
person? Are we so certain of always finding a man made to our
hands for any duty or function of social importance which falls
vacant, that we lose nothing by putting a ban upon one-half of
mankind, and refusing beforehand to make their faculties available,
however distinguished they may be? And even if we could do without them, would it be consistent with justice to refuse to them their
fair share of honor and distinction, or to deny to them the equal
moral right of all human beings to choose their occupation (short
of injury to others) according to their own preferences, at their own
risk? Nor is the injustice confined to them: it is shared by those
who are in a position to benefit by their services. To ordain that any
kind of persons shall not be physicians, or shall not be advocates, or
shall not be members of parliament, is to injure not them only, but
all who employ physicians or advocates, or elect members of parliament, and who are deprived of the stimulating effect of greater
competition on the exertions of the competitors, as well as
restricted to a narrower range of individual choice.

* * *

There remains a question, not of less importance than those
already discussed, and which will be asked the most importunately
by those opponents whose conviction is somewhat shaken on the
main point. What good are we to expect from the changes proposed in our customs and institutions? Would mankind be at all
better off if women were free? If not, why disturb their minds, and

attempt to make a social revolution in the name of an abstract right?

* * *

To which let me first answer, the advantage of having the most universal and pervading of all human relations regulated by justice instead of injustice. The vast amount of this gain to human nature, it is hardly possible, by any explanation or illustration, to place in a stronger light than it is placed by the bare statement, to anyone who attaches a moral meaning to words. All the selfish propensities, the self-worship, the unjust self-preference, which exist among mankind, have their source and root in, and derive their principal nourishment from, the present constitution of the relation between men and women. Think what it is to a boy, to grow up to manhood in the belief that without any merit or any exertion of his own, though he may be the most frivolous and empty or the most ignorant and stolid of mankind, by the mere fact of being born a male he is by right the superior of all and every one of an entire half of the human race: including probably some whose real superiority to himself he has daily or hourly occasion to feel; but even if in his whole conduct he habitually follows a woman's guidance, still, if he is a fool, she thinks that of course she is not, and cannot be, equal in ability and judgment to himself; and if he is not a fool, he does worse—he sees that she is superior to him, and believes that, notwithstanding her superiority, he is entitled to command and she is bound to obey. What must be the effect on his character, of this lesson?[4] And men of the cultivated classes are often not aware how deeply it sinks into the immense majority of male minds. For, among right-feeling and well-bred people, the inequality is kept as much as possible out of sight; above all, out of sight of the children. As much obedience is required from boys to their mother as to their father: they are not permitted to domineer over their sisters, nor are they accustomed to see these postponed to them, but the contrary; the compensations of the chivalrous feeling being made prominent, while the servitude which requires them is kept in the background. Well brought-up youths in the higher classes thus often escape the bad influences of the situation in their early years, and only experience them when, arrived at manhood, they fall under the dominion of facts as they really exist. Such people are little aware, when a boy is differently brought up, how early the notion of his inherent superiority to a girl arises in his mind; how it grows with his growth and strengthens with his strength; how it is inoculated by one schoolboy upon another; how early the youth thinks himself superior to his mother, owing her perhaps forbearance, but no real respect; and

---

4. Cf. Thackeray on such marriages: "it is worse still, for the man himself perhaps, whenever in his dim comprehen- sion the idea dawns that his slave and drudge yonder is, in truth, his superior." —*Henry Esmond*, I.xi.

how sublime and sultan-like a sense of superiority he feels, above all, over the woman whom he honors by admitting her to a partnership of his life. Is it imagined that all this does not pervert the whole manner of existence of the man, both as an individual and as a social being? It is an exact parallel to the feeling of a hereditary king that he is excellent above others by being born a king, or a noble by being born a noble. The relation between husband and wife is very like that between lord and vassal, except that the wife is held to more unlimited obedience than the vassal was. However the vassal's character may have been affected, for better and for worse, by his subordination, who can help seeing that the lord's was affected greatly for the worse? whether he was led to believe that his vassals were really superior to himself, or to feel that he was placed in command over people as good as himself, for no merits of labors of his own, but merely for having, as Figaro says, taken the trouble to be born. The self-worship of the monarch, or of the feudal superior, is matched by the self-worship of the male. Human beings do not grow up from childhood in the possession of unearned distinctions, without pluming themselves upon them. Those whom privileges not acquired by their merit, and which they feel to be disproportioned to it, inspire with additional humility, are always the few, and the best few. The rest are only inspired with pride, and the worst sort of pride, that which values itself upon accidental advantages, not of its own achieving. Above all, when the feeling of being raised above the whole of the other sex is combined with personal authority over one individual among them; the situation, if a school of conscientious and affectionate forbearance to those whose strongest points of character are conscience and affection, is to men of another quality a regularly constituted Academy or Gymnasium for training them in arrogance and overbearingness; which vices, if curbed by the certainty of resistance in their intercourse with other men, their equals, break out towards all who are in a position to be obliged to tolerate them, and often revenge themselves upon the unfortunate wife for the involuntary restraint which they are obliged to submit to elsewhere.

The example afforded, and the education given to the sentiments, by laying the foundation of domestic existence upon a relation contradictory to the first principles of social justice, must, from the very nature of man, have a perverting influence of such magnitude, that it is hardly possible with our present experience to raise our imaginations to the conception of so great a change for the better as would be made by its removal. All that education and civilization are doing to efface the influences on character of the law of force, and replace them by those of justice, remains merely on the surface, as long as the citadel of the enemy is not attacked. The principle of the modern movement in morals and politics, is that conduct, and conduct alone, entitles to respect: that not what men are, but what they do, constitutes their claim to deference; that, above all, merit, and not birth, is the only rightful claim to power and authority. If no authority, not in its nature temporary, were allowed to one human being over another, society would not be employed in building up propensities with one hand which it has to curb with the other. The child would really, for the first time in man's existence on earth, be trained in the way he should go, and when he was old there would be a chance that he would not depart from it. But so long as the right of the strong to power over the weak rules in the very heart of society, the attempt to make the equal right of the weak the principle of its outward actions will always be an uphill struggle; for the law of justice, which is also that of Christianity, will never get possession of men's inmost sentiments; they will be working against it, even when bending to it.

The second benefit to be expected from giving to women the free use of their faculties, by leaving them the free choice of their employments, and opening to them the same field of occupation and the same prizes and encouragements as to other human beings, would be that of doubling the mass of mental faculties available for the higher service of humanity. Where there is now one person qualified to benefit mankind and promote the general improvement, as a public teacher, or an administrator of some branch of public or social affairs, there would then be a chance of two. Mental superiority of any kind is at present everywhere so much below the demand; there is such a deficiency of persons competent to do excellently anything which it requires any considerable amount of ability to do; that the loss to the world, by refusing to make use of one-half of the whole quantity of talent it possesses, is extremely serious. It is true that this amount of mental power is not totally lost. Much of it is employed, and would in any case be employed, in domestic management, and in the few other occupations open to women and from the remainder indirect benefit is in many individual cases obtained, through the personal influence of individual women over individual men. But these benefits are partial; their range is extremely circumscribed; and if they must be admitted, on the one hand, as a deduction from the amount of fresh social power that would be acquired by giving freedom to one-half of the whole sum of human intellect, there must be added, on the other, the benefit of the stimulus that would be given to the intellect of men by the competition; or (to use a more true expression) by the necessity that would be imposed on them of deserving precedency before they could expect to obtain it.

* * *

When we consider the positive evil caused to the disqualified half of the human race by their disqualification—first in the loss of the most inspiriting and elevating kind of personal enjoyment, and next in the weariness, disappointment, and profound dissatisfaction with life, which are so often the substitute for it; one feels that among all the lessons which men require for carrying on the struggle against the inevitable imperfections of their lot on earth, there is no lesson which they more need, than not to add to the evils which nature inflicts, by their jealous and prejudiced restrictions on one another. Their vain fears only substitute other and worse evils for those which they are idly apprehensive of: while every restraint on the freedom of conduct of any of their human fellow creatures, (otherwise than by making them responsible for any evil actually caused by it), dries up *pro tanto*[5] the principal fountain of human happiness, and leaves the species less rich, to an inappreciable degree, in all that makes life valuable to the individual human being.

From Autobiography

From *Chapter V. A Crisis in My Mental History.* *One Stage Onward*

For some years after this time[1] I wrote very little, and nothing regularly, for publication: and great were the advantages which I derived from the intermission. It was of no common importance to me, at this period, to be able to digest and mature my thoughts for my own mind only, without any immediate call for giving them out in print. Had I gone on writing, it would have much disturbed the important transformation in my opinions and character, which took place during those years. The origin of this transformation, or at least the process by which I was prepared for it, can only be explained by turning some distance back.

From the winter of 1821, when I first read Bentham, and especially from the commencement of the *Westminster Review*, I had what might truly be called an object in life; to be a reformer of the world. My conception of my own happiness was entirely identified with this object. The personal sympathies I wished for were those of fellow laborers in this enterprise. I endeavored to pick up as many flowers as I could by the way; but as a serious and permanent personal satisfaction to rest upon, my whole reliance was placed on this; and I was accustomed to felicitate myself on the certainty of a happy life which I enjoyed, through placing my happiness in something durable and distant, in which some progress might be always making, while it could never be exhausted by complete attainment. This did very well for several years, during which the general improvement going on in the world and the idea of myself as engaged with others in struggling to promote it, seemed enough to fill up an interesting and animated existence. But the time came

5. By so much.
1. 1828. Mill had been contributing articles to the *Westminster Review*.

when I awakened from this as from a dream. It was in the autumn of 1826. I was in a dull state of nerves, such as everybody is occasionally liable to; unsusceptible to enjoyment or pleasurable excitement; one of those moods when what is pleasure at other times becomes insipid or indifferent; the state, I should think, in which converts to Methodism usually are, when smitten by their first "conviction of sin." In this frame of mind it occurred to me to put the question directly to myself: "Suppose that all your objects in life were realized; that all the changes in institutions and opinions which you are looking forward to could be completely effected at this very instant: would this be a great joy and happiness to you?" And an irrepressible self-consciousness distinctly answered, "No!" At this my heart sank within me: the whole foundation on which my life was constructed fell down. All my happiness was to have been found in the continual pursuit of this end. The end had ceased to charm, and how could there ever again be any interest in the means? I seemed to have nothing left to live for.

At first I hoped that the cloud would pass away of itself; but it did not. A night's sleep, the sovereign remedy for the smaller vexations of life, had no effect on it. I awoke to a renewed consciousness of the woeful fact. I carried it with me into all companies, into all occupations. Hardly anything had power to cause me even a few minutes' oblivion of it. For some months the cloud seemed to grow thicker and thicker. The lines in Coleridge's *Dejection*—I was not then acquainted with them—exactly describe my case:

> A grief without a pang, void, dark and drear,
> A drowsy, stifled, unimpassioned grief,
> Which finds no natural outlet or relief
> In word, or sigh, or tear.[2]

In vain I sought relief from my favorite books; those memorials of past nobleness and greatness from which I had always hitherto drawn strength and animation. I read them now without feeling, or with the accustomed feeling minus all its charm; and I became persuaded that my love of mankind, and of excellence for its own sake, had worn itself out. I sought no comfort by speaking to others of what I felt. If I had loved anyone sufficiently to make confiding my griefs a necessity, I should not have been in the condition I was. I felt, too, that mine was not an interesting, or in any way respectable distress. There was nothing in it to attract sympathy. Advice, if I had known where to seek it, would have been most precious. The words of Macbeth to the physician[3] often occurred to my thoughts. But there was no one on whom I could build the faintest hope of such assistance. My father, to whom it would have been natural to me to have recourse in any practical difficulties, was the last person to whom, in such a case as this, I

---

2. *Dejection: An Ode*, lines 21–24.
3. "Canst thou not minister to a mind diseas'd * * * ?" (*Macbeth* V.iii.40–44).

looked for help. Everything convinced me that he had no knowledge of any such mental state as I was suffering from, and that even if he could be made to understand it, he was not the physician who could heal it. My education, which was wholly his work, had been conducted without any regard to the possibility of its ending in this result; and I saw no use in giving him the pain of thinking that his plans had failed, when the failure was probably irremediable, and, at all events, beyond the power of *his* remedies. Of other friends, I had at that time none to whom I had any hope of making my condition intelligible. It was however abundantly intelligible to myself; and the more I dwelt upon it, the more hopeless it appeared.

My course of study had led me to believe that all mental and moral feelings and qualities, whether of a good or of a bad kind, were the results of association; that we love one thing, and hate another, take pleasure in one sort of action or contemplation, and pain in another sort, through the clinging of pleasurable or painful ideas to those things, from the effect of education or of experience. As a corollary from this, I had always heard it maintained by my father, and was myself convinced, that the object of education should be to form the strongest possible associations of the salutary class; associations of pleasure with all things beneficial to the great whole, and of pain with all things hurtful to it. This doctrine appeared inexpugnable; but it now seemed to me, on retrospect, that my teachers had occupied themselves but superficially with the means of forming and keeping up these salutary associations. They seemed to have trusted altogether to the old familiar instruments, praise and blame, reward and punishment. Now, I did not doubt that by these means, begun early, and applied unremittingly, intense associations of pain and pleasure, especially of pain, might be created, and might produce desires and aversions capable of lasting undiminished to the end of life. But there must always be something artificial and casual in associations thus produced. The pains and pleasures thus forcibly associated with things are not connected with them by any natural tie; and it is therefore, I thought, essential to the durability of these associations that they should have beome so intense and inveterate as to be practically indissoluble, before the habitual exercise of the power of analysis had commenced. For I now saw, or thought I saw, what I had always before received with incredulity—that the habit of analysis has a tendency to wear away the feelings: as indeed it has, when no other mental habit is cultivated, and the analyzing spirit remains without its natural complements and correctives. The very excellence of analysis (I argued) is that it tends to weaken and undermine whatever is the result of prejudice; that it enables us mentally to separate ideas which have only casually clung together: and no associations whatever could ultimately resist this dissolving force, were it not that we owe to analysis our clearest knowledge of the permanent sequences in nature; the real connections between Things, not dependent on our will and feelings; natural laws, by virtue of which, in many cases, one thing is inseparable from another in fact; which laws, in proportion as they are clearly perceived and imaginatively realized, cause our ideas of things which are always joined together in Nature to cohere more and more closely in our thoughts. Analytic habits may thus even strengthen the associations between causes and effects, means and ends, but tend altogether to weaken those which are, to speak familiarly, a *mere* matter of feeling. They are therefore (I thought) favorable to prudence and clear-sightedness, but a perpetual worm at the root both of the passions and of the virtues; and, above all, fearfully undermine all desires, and all pleasures, which are the effects of association, that is, according to the theory I held, all except the purely physical and organic; of the entire insufficiency of which to make life desirable, no one had a stronger conviction than I had. These were the laws of human nature, by which, as it seemed to me, I had been brought to my present state. All those to whom I looked up were of opinion that the pleasure of sympathy with human beings, and the feelings which made the good of others, and especially of mankind on a large scale, the object of existence, were the greatest and surest sources of happiness. Of the truth of this I was convinced, but to know that a feeling would make me happy if I had it, did not give me the feeling. My education, I thought, had failed to create these feelings in sufficient strength to resist the dissolving influence of analysis, while the whole course of my intellectual cultivation had made precocious and premature analysis the inveterate habit of my mind. I was thus, as I said to myself, left stranded at the commencement of my voyage, with a well-equipped ship and a rudder, but no sail; without any real desire for the ends which I had been so carefully fitted out to work for: no delight in virtue, or the general good, but also just as little in anything else. The fountains of vanity and ambition seemed to have dried up within me, as completely as those of benevolence. I had had (as I reflected) some gratification of vanity at too early an age: I had obtained some distinction, and felt myself of some importance, before the desire of distinction and of importance had grown into a passion: and little as it was which I had attained, yet having been attained too early, like all pleasures enjoyed too soon, it had made me *blasé* and indifferent to the pursuit. Thus neither selfish nor unselfish pleasures were pleasures to me. And there seemed no power in nature sufficient to begin the formation of my character anew, and create in a mind now irretrievably analytic, fresh associations of pleasure with any of the objects of human desire.

These were the thoughts which mingled with the dry heavy dejection of the melancholy winter of 1826–7. During this time I was not incapable of my usual occupations. I went on with them mechanically, by the mere force of habit. I had been so drilled in a certain sort of mental exercise that I could still carry it on when all the spirit had gone out of it. I even composed and spoke several speeches at the debating society, how, or with what degree of success, I know not. Of four years continual speaking at that society, this is the only year of which I remember next to nothing. Two lines of Coleridge, in whom alone of all writers I have found a true description of what I felt, were often in my thoughts, not at this time (for I had never read them), but in a later period of the same mental malady:

> Work without hope draws nectar in a sieve,
> And hope without an object cannot live.[4]

In all probability my case was by no means so peculiar as I fancied it, and I doubt not that many others have passed through a similar state; but the idiosyncrasies of my education had given to the general phenomenon a special character, which made it seem the natural effect of causes that it was hardly possible for time to remove. I frequently asked myself if I could, or if I was bound to go on living, when life must be passed in this manner. I generally answered to myself, that I did not think I could possibly bear it beyond a year. When, however, not more than half that duration of time had elapsed, a small ray of light broke in upon my gloom. I was reading, accidentally, Marmontel's *Mémoires*,[5] and came to the passage which relates his father's death, the distressed position of the family, and the sudden inspiration by which he, then a mere boy, felt and made them feel that he would be everything to them—would supply the place of all that they had lost. A vivid conception of that scene and its feelings came over me, and I was moved to tears. From this moment my burden grew lighter. The oppression of the thought that all feeling was dead within me was gone. I was no longer hopeless: I was not a stock or a stone. I had still, it seemed, some of the material out of which all worth of character, and all capacity for happiness, are made. Relieved from my ever present sense of irremediable wretchedness, I gradually found that the ordinary incidents of life could again give me some pleasure; that I could again find enjoyment, not intense, but sufficient for cheerfulness, in sunshine and sky, in books, in conversation, in public affairs; and that there was, once more, excitement, though of a moderate kind, in exerting myself for my opinions, and for the public good. Thus the cloud gradually drew off, and I again enjoyed life: and though I had several relapses, some of which lasted many months, I never again was as miserable as I had been.

The experiences of this period had two very marked effects on

4. From Coleridge's short poem *Work Without Hope*.

5. J. F. Marmontel (1723–99), whose *Mémoires* were published in 1804.

my opinions and character. In the first place, they led me to adopt a theory of life, very unlike that on which I had before acted, and having much in common with what at that time I certainly had never heard of, the anti-self-consciousness theory of Carlyle.[6] I never, indeed, wavered in the conviction that happiness is the test of all rules of conduct, and the end of life. But I now thought that this end was only to be attained by not making it the direct end. Those only are happy (I thought) who have their minds fixed on some object other than their own happiness; on the happiness of others, on the improvement of mankind, even on some art or pursuit, followed not as a means, but as itself an ideal end. Aiming thus at something else, they find happiness by the way. The enjoyments of life (such was now my theory) are sufficient to make it a pleasant thing, when they are taken *en passant*, without being made a principal object. Once make them so, and they are immediately felt to be insufficient. They will not bear a scrutinizing examination. Ask yourself whether you are happy, and you cease to be so. The only chance is to treat, not happiness, but some end external to it, as the purpose of life. Let your self-consciousness, your scrutiny, your self-interrogation exhaust themselves on that; and if otherwise fortunately circumstanced you will inhale happiness with the air you breathe, without dwelling on it or thinking about it, without either forestalling it in imagination, or putting it to flight by fatal questioning. This theory now became the basis of my philosophy of life. And I still hold to it as the best theory for all those who have but a moderate degree of sensibility and of capacity for enjoyment, that is, for the great majority of mankind.

The other important change which my opinions at this time underwent was that I, for the first time, gave its proper place, among the prime necessities of human well-being, to the internal culture of the individual. I ceased to attach almost exclusive importance to the ordering of outward circumstances, and the training of the human being for speculation and for action.

I had now learnt by experience that the passive susceptibilities needed to be cultivated as well as the active capacities, and required to be nourished and enriched as well as guided. I did not, for an instant, lose sight of, or undervalue, that part of the truth which I had seen before; I never turned recreant to intellectual culture, or ceased to consider the power and practice of analysis as an essential condition both of individual and of social improvement. But I thought that it had consequences which required to be corrected, by joining other kinds of cultivation with it. The maintenance of a due balance among the faculties now seemed to me of primary importance. The cultivation of the feelings became one of the cardinal points in my ethical and philosophical creed. And my thoughts and inclinations turned in an increasing degree toward

6. See Carlyle's *Characteristics* and Chapter IX of *Sartor Resartus*, "The Everlasting Yea."

whatever seemed capable of being instrumental to that object.

I now began to find meaning in the things which I had read or heard about the importance of poetry and art as instruments of human culture. But it was some time longer before I began to know this by personal experience. The only one of the imaginative arts in which I had from childhood taken great pleasure was music; the best effect of which (and in this it surpasses perhaps every other art) consists in exciting enthusiasm; in winding up to a high pitch those feelings of an elevated kind which are already in the character, but to which this excitement gives a glow and a fervor, which, though transitory at its utmost height, is precious for sustaining them at other times. This effect of music I had often experienced; but like all my pleasurable susceptibilities it was suspended during the gloomy period. I had sought relief again and again from this quarter, but found none. After the tide had turned, and I was in process of recovery, I had been helped forward by music, but in a much less elevated manner. I at this time first became acquainted with Weber's *Oberon*,[7] and the extreme pleasure which I drew from its delicious melodies did me good, by showing me a source of pleasure to which I was as susceptible as ever. The good, however, was much impaired by the thought that the pleasure of music (as is quite true of such pleasure as this was, that of mere tune) fades with familiarity, and requires either to be revived by intermittence, or fed by continual novelty. And it is very characteristic both of my then state, and of the general tone of my mind at this period of my life, that I was seriously tormented by the thought of the exhaustibility of musical combinations. The octave consists only of five tones and two semitones, which can be put together in only a limited number of ways, of which but a small proportion are beautiful: most of these, it seemed to me, must have been already discovered, and there could not be room for a long succession of Mozarts and Webers, to strike out, as these had done, entirely new and surpassingly rich veins of musical beauty. This source of anxiety may, perhaps, be thought to resemble that of the philosophers of Laputa,[8] who feared lest the sun should be burnt out. It was, however, connected with the best feature in my character, and the only good point to be found in my very unromantic and in no way honorable distress. For though my dejection, honestly looked at, could not be called other than egotistical, produced by the ruin, as I thought, of my fabric of happiness, yet the destiny of mankind in general was ever in my thoughts, and could not be separated from my own. I felt that the flaw in my life must be a flaw in life itself; that the question was whether, if the reformers of society and government could succeed in their objects, and every person in the

7. A romantic opera composed by Carl Maria von Weber (1786–1826).   8. See *Gulliver's Travels*, Part III.

community were free and in a state of physical comfort, the pleasures of life, being no longer kept up by struggle and privation, would cease to be pleasures. And I felt that unless I could see my way to some better hope than this for human happiness in general, my dejection must continue; but that if I could see such an outlet, I should then look on the world with pleasure; content as far as I was myself concerned, with any fair share of the general lot.

This state of my thoughts and feelings made the fact of my reading Wordsworth for the first time (in the autumn of 1828), an important event in my life. I took up the collection of his poems from curiosity, with no expectation of mental relief from it, though I had before resorted to poetry with that hope. In the worst period of my depression, I had read through the whole of Byron (then new to me), to try whether a poet, whose peculiar department was supposed to be that of the intenser feelings, could rouse any feeling in me. As might be expected, I got no good from this reading, but the reverse. The poet's state of mind was too like my own. His was the lament of a man who had worn out all pleasures, and who seemed to think that life, to all who possess the good things of it, must necessarily be the vapid, uninteresting thing which I found it. His Harold and Manfred had the same burden on them which I had; and I was not in a frame of mind to desire any comfort from the vehement sensual passion of his Giaours,   ▪ the sullenness of his Laras.[9] But while Byron was exactly what did not suit my condition, Wordsworth was exactly what did. I had looked into *The Excursion*[1] two or three years before, and found little in it; and I should probably have found as little had I read it at this time. But the miscellaneous poems, in the two-volume edition of 1815 (to which little of value was added in the latter part of the author's life), proved to be the precise thing for my mental wants at that particular juncture.

In the first place, these poems addressed themselves powerfully to one of the strongest of my pleasurable susceptibilities, the love of rural objects and natural scenery; to which I had been indebted not only for much of the pleasure of my life, but quite recently for relief from one of my longest relapses into depression. In this power of rural beauty over me, there was a foundation laid for taking pleasure in Wordsworth's poetry; the more so, as his scenery lies mostly among mountains, which, owing to my early Pyrenean excursion,[2] were my ideal of natural beauty. But Wordsworth would never have had any great effect on me, if he had merely placed

9. The heroes of some of Byron's early poems were usually gloomy and self-preoccupied. Mill refers here to *Childe Harold's Pilgrimage* (1812–18), *Manfred* (1817), *The Giaour* (1813) and *Lara* (1814).
1. A long meditative poem by Words-

worth, published in 1814.
2. At 15 Mill had been deeply affected by the landscape of the Pyrenees in Spain, a mountainous region which also made a strong impression upon Tennyson.

before me beautiful pictures of natural scenery. Scott does this still better than Wordsworth, and a very second-rate landscape does it more effectually than any poet. What made Wordsworth's poems a medicine for my state of mind, was that they expressed, not mere outward beauty, but states of feeling, and of thought colored by feeling, under the excitement of beauty. They seemed to be the very culture of the feelings, which I was in quest of. In them I seemed to draw from a source of inward joy, of sympathetic and imaginative pleasure, which could be shared in by all human beings; which had no connection with struggle or imperfection, but would be made richer by every improvement in the physical or social condition of mankind. From them I seemed to learn what would be the perennial sources of happiness, when all the greater evils of life shall have been removed. And I felt myself at once better and happier as I came under their influence. There have certainly been, even in our own age, greater poets than Wordsworth; but poetry of deeper and loftier feeling could not have done for me at that time what his did. I needed to be made to feel that there was real, permanent happiness in tranquil contemplation. Wordsworth taught me this, not only without turning away from, but with a greatly increased interest in the common feelings and common destiny of human beings. And the delight which these poems gave me proved that with culture of this sort, there was nothing to dread from the most confirmed habit of analysis. At the conclusion of the Poems came the famous *Ode*, falsely called Platonic, *Intimations of Immortality*: in which, along with more than his usual sweetness of melody and rhythm, and along with the two passages of grand imagery but bad philosophy so often quoted, I found that he too had had similar experience to mine; that he also had felt that the first freshness of youthful enjoyment of life was not lasting; but that he had sought for compensation, and found it, in the way in which he was now teaching me to find it. The result was that I gradually, but completely, emerged from my habitual depression, and was never again subject to it. I long continued to value Wordsworth less according to his intrinsic merits than by the measure of what he had done for me. Compared with the greatest poets, he may be said to be the poet of unpoetical natures, possessed of quiet and contemplative tastes. But unpoetical natures are precisely those which require poetic cultivation. This cultivation Wordsworth is much more fitted to give than poets who are intrinsically far more poets than he. * * *

1873

ALFRED, LORD TENNYSON
(1809–1892)

1830: *Poems,Chiefly Lyrical.*
1833: Death of Arthur Hallam.
1842: *Poems.*
1850: *In Memoriam.* Tennyson appointed poet laureate.
1859: *Idylls of the King* (first four books).

Whether or not Alfred Tennyson was the greatest of the Victorian poets, as affirmed by many critics today, there is no doubt that in his own lifetime he was the most popular of poets. On the bookshelves of almost every family of readers in England and the United States, from 1850 onwards, were the works of a man who had incontestably gained the title that Walt Whitman longed for: "The Poet of the People." Popularity inevitably provided provocation for a reaction in the decades following his death. In the course of repudiating their Victorian predecessors, the Edwardians and Georgians established the fashion of making fun of Tennyson's great achievements. Samuel Butler (1835–1902), who anticipated early 20th-century tastes, has a characteristic entry in his *Notebooks*: "Talking it over, we agreed that Blake was no good because he learnt Italian at 60 in order to study Dante, and we knew Dante was no good because he was so fond of Virgil, and Virgil was no good because Tennyson ran him, and as for Tennyson—well, Tennyson goes without saying." In the second half of the 20th century, Butler's confident assumption that Tennyson's poetry was simply contemptible no longer "goes without saying." The delights to be found in this superb "lord of language"—as Tennyson himself addresses his favorite predecessor, Virgil—have been rediscovered, and Tennyson's stature as one of the major poets of any age has been re-established. In 1892, the year of his death, he himself had made an accurate prophecy of his changing status in his lines on *Poets and Critics*:

> What is true at last will tell:
> Few at first will place thee well;
> Some too low would have thee shine,
> Some too high—no fault of thine—
> Hold thine own, and work thy will!

Like his poetry, Tennyson's life and character have been reassessed in the 20th century. To many of his contemporaries he seemed a remote wizard, secure in his laureate's robes, a man whose life had been sheltered, marred only by the loss of his best friend in youth. During much of his career Tennyson may have been isolated, but his was not a sheltered life in the real sense of the word. Although he grew up in a parsonage, it was not the kind of parsonage one encounters in the novels of Jane Austen. It was a household dominated by frictions and loyalties and broodings over ancestral inheritances, in which the children showed marked strains of instability and eccentricity.

Alfred was the fourth son in a family of twelve children. One of his brothers had to be confined to an insane asylum for life; another was long a victim of the opium habit; another had violent quarrels with his father, who had become a drunkard. This father, the Reverend Dr. George Tennyson, was the eldest son of a wealthy landowner. He had been obliged to become a clergyman, a profession he disliked, because he had been disinherited in favor of his younger brother. George Tennyson therefore settled in a small rectory at Somersby in Lincolnshire where he tutored his sons in classical and modern languages to prepare them for entering the university.

Before leaving this strange household for Cambridge, Alfred had already demonstrated a flair for writing verse—precocious exercises in the manner of Milton or Byron or the Elizabethan dramatists. He had even published a volume in 1827, in collaboration with his brother Charles, *Poems by Two Brothers*. This feat drew him to the attention of a group of gifted undergraduates at Cambridge, the "Apostles," who encouraged him to devote his life to poetry. Up until this time, the young man had known scarcely anyone outside the circle of his own family. Despite his massive frame and powerful physique, he was painfully shy, and the friendships he found at Cambridge, as well as the intellectual and political discussions in which he participated, served to give him confidence and to widen his horizons as a poet. The most important of these friendships was with Arthur Hallam, a leader of the Apostles, who later became engaged to Tennyson's sister. Hallam's sudden death, in 1833, seemed an overwhelming calamity to his friend. Not only the long elegy *In Memoriam* but many of Tennyson's other poems are tributes to this early friendship.

Alfred's career at Cambridge was interrupted and finally broken off in 1831 by family dissensions and financial need, and he returned home to study and practice the craft of poetry. His early volumes (1830 and 1832) were attacked as "obscure" or "affected" by some of the reviewers. Tennyson suffered acutely under hostile criticism, but he also profited from it. His volume of 1842 demonstrated a remarkable advance in taste and technical excellence, and in 1850 he at last attained fame and full critical recognition with *In Memoriam*. In the same year he became poet laureate in succession to Wordsworth. The struggle during the previous twenty years had been made especially painful by the long postponement of his marriage to Emily Sellwood, with whom he had fallen in love in 1836 but could not marry, because of poverty, until 1850.

His life thereafter was a comfortable one. He was as popular as Byron had been, and his fame lasted for much longer. The earnings from his poetry (sometimes exceeding £10,000 a year) enabled him to purchase a house in the country and to enjoy the kind of seclusion he liked. His notoriety was enhanced, like that of G. B. Shaw and Walt Whitman, by his colorful appearance. Huge and shaggy, in cloak and broadbrimmed hat, gruff in manner as a farmer, he impressed everyone as what is called a "character." The pioneer photographer, Julia Cameron, who took magnificent portraits of him, called him "the most beautiful old man on earth." He also had a booming voice, when reading his poetry, that electrified listeners much as Dylan Thomas electrified audiences in the 20th century: "mouthing out his hollow o's and a's, / Deep-chested music." Moreover, for many Victorian readers, he seemed not only a great poetical phrasemaker and a striking individual but also a wise man whose occasional pronouncements on politics or world affairs represented the national voice itself. In 1884 he accepted a peerage. In 1892 he died and was buried in Westminster Abbey.

It is often said that success was bad for Tennyson, and that after *In Memoriam* his poetic power seriously declined. That in his last 42 years certain of his mannerisms became accentuated is true. One of the difficulties of his dignified blank verse was, as he said himself, that it is hard to describe commonplace objects and "at the same time to retain poetical elevation." The ornateness of his later style sometimes betrayed him into such blunders as describing a basketful of fish as "Enoch's ocean spoil / In ocean-smelling osier." In others of his later poems, those dealing with national affairs, there is also an increased shrillness of tone—a mannerism accentuated by Tennyson's realizing that like Dickens he had a vast public behind him to back up his pronouncements.

It is foolish, however, to try to shelve all of Tennyson's later productions. In 1855 he published his experimental monologue *Maud*, perhaps his finest long poem. In 1859 he published four books of his *Idylls of the King*, a large-scale epic which occupied most of his energies in the second half of his career. About this late poem, completed in twelve books, in 1888, there is less agreement. Some readers consider it to be complacent—mere "lollipops," as Carlyle called it. Yet *Idylls of the King* is not simply a hymn to progress. It records, instead, a cycle of change from a society that has emerged from a wasteland into civilization but which may revert to a wasteland once more. In any event, even if this ambitious epic does not always show Tennyson in his best vein, there is no sign of decline in his late lyrics. The 80-year-old poet who wrote *Crossing the Bar* had certainly not lost his touch.

The problem of Tennyson's development is really of more significance for the period before 1850 rather than afterwards. W. H. Auden has stated that Tennyson had "the finest ear, perhaps, of any English poet." The interesting point is that Tennyson did not "have" such an ear: he developed it. Studies of the original versions of his poems in the 1830 and 1832 volumes demonstrate that not only was his taste uncertain at the outset of his career but that his sense of meter was originally unreliable. The harmonics he was to achieve from 1842 onwards had to be learned just as a pianist with a weak left hand has to overcome his weakness by constant exercise. Like Chaucer or Keats or Pope, Tennyson studied his predecessors assiduously to perfect his technique. Anyone wanting to learn the traditional craft of English verse can study with profit the various stages of revision that such poems as *The Lotos-Eaters* were subjected to by this painstaking and artful poet.

If the early Tennyson was uncertain of meter, he had other skills that were immediately in evidence. One of these was a capacity for linking scenery to states of mind. As early as 1835, J. S. Mill identified the special kind of scene-painting to be found in early poems such as *Mariana*: "* * * not the power of producing that rather vapid species of composition usually termed descriptive poetry * * * but the power of *creating* scenery, in keeping with some state of human feeling so fitted to it as to be the embodied symbol of it, and to summon up the state of feeling itself, with a force not to be surpassed by anything but reality."

A second aspect of Tennyson's early development was his increased preoccupation with problems of his day. If Mill praised his capacity to render landscape, he also urged, in his review, Tennyson's further responsibilities—to "cultivate, and with no half devotion, philosophy as well as poetry." Advice of this kind Tennyson was already predisposed to heed. The death of Hallam, the religious uncertainties which he had himself experienced, together with his own extensive study of writings by geologists, astronomers, and biologists, led him to confront many of the religious issues that bewildered his generation and later generations. The result was *In Memoriam* (1850), a long elegy written over a period of seventeen years, embodying the poet's reflections on man's relation to God and to nature.

Was Tennyson intellectually equipped to deal with the great questions raised in *In Memoriam?* The answer may depend on a reader's religious and philosophical presuppositions. Some, such as T. H. Huxley, considered Tennyson an intellectual giant, a thinker who had mastered the scientific thought of his century and fully confronted the issues it raised. Others dismissed Tennyson, in this phase, as a lightweight. Auden went so far as to call him the "stupidest" of English poets. We might say more accurately that his mind was slow, ponderous, brooding, and we should add that for the composition of *In Memoriam* such qualities of mind were assets, not liabilities. In these terms we can understand when Tennyson's poetry really fails to measure up: it is when he writes of events of the moment over which his thoughts and feelings have had no time to brood. Several of his poems are essentially newspaper pieces. They are Letters to the Editor, in effect, with the ephemeral heat and simplicity we expect of such productions. *The Charge of the Light Brigade*, inspired by a report in *The Times* of a cavalry charge at Balaclava during the Crimean War, is one of the best of his productions in this category.

Tennyson's poems of contemporary events were inevitably popular in his own day. So too were those poems where, as in *Locksley Hall*, he dipped into the future. The technological changes wrought by Victorian inventors and engineers fascinated him. Sometimes they gave him an assurance of human progress as swaggeringly exultant as that of Macaulay. At other times the horrors of industrialism's by-products in the slums, the bloodshed of war, the greed of the newly rich, destroyed his hopes that man was evolving upwards. Such a late poem as *The Dawn* embodies an attitude which he found in Virgil: "Thou majestic in thy sadness at the doubtful doom of human kind."

For despite Tennyson's fascination with technological developments, he was essentially a poet of the countryside, a man whose whole being was conditioned by the recurring rhythms of rural rather than urban life. He had the countryman's awareness of traditional roots and his sense of the past. It is appropriate that most of his best poems are about the past, not about the present or future. The past is his great theme: his own past (as in *All Along the Valley*), his country's past (as in *The Revenge*), the past of mankind, the past of the world itself:

> There rolls the deep where grew the tree.
> O earth, what changes hast thou seen!
> There where the long street roars hath been
> The stillness of the central sea.

Tennyson is the first major writer to express this awareness of the vast extent of geological time that has haunted human consciousness since Victorian scientists exposed the history of the earth's crust. In his more usual vein, however, it is the recorded past of mankind that inspires him, the classical past in particular. Classical themes, as Douglas Bush has noted, "generally banished from his mind what was timid, parochial, sentimental * * * and evoked his special gifts and most authentic emotions, his rich and wistful sense of the past, his love of nature, and his power of style."

One returns, finally then, to the question of language. At the time of his death, a critic complained that Tennyson was merely "a discoverer of words rather than of ideas." The same complaint has been made by George Bernard Shaw and others—not about Tennyson but about Shakespeare.

The Kraken[1]

Below the thunders of the upper deep,
Far, far beneath in the abysmal sea,
His ancient, dreamless, uninvaded sleep
The Kraken sleepeth: faintest sunlights flee
About his shadowy sides; above him swell 5
Huge sponges of millennial growth and height;
And far away into the sickly light,
From many a wondrous grot and secret cell
Unnumbered and enormous polypi[2]
Winnow with giant arms the slumbering green. 10
There hath he lain for ages, and will lie
Battening upon huge sea worms in his sleep,
Until the latter fire[3] shall heat the deep;
Then once by man and angels to be seen,
In roaring he shall rise and on the surface die. 15

1830

---

1. A mythical sea beast of gigantic size.
2. Octopuses.
3. Fire which would finally consume the world. See Revelation xvi.3–9, and xiii.1.

Mariana[1]

"Mariana in the moated grange."
Measure for Measure

With blackest moss the flower plots
  Were thickly crusted, one and all;
The rusted nails fell from the knots
  That held the pear to the gable wall.
The broken sheds looked sad and strange: 5
  Unlifted was the clinking latch;
  Weeded and worn the ancient thatch
Upon the lonely moated grange.
     She only said, "My life is dreary,
       He cometh not," she said;   10
     She said, "I am aweary, aweary,
       I would that I were dead!"

Her tears fell with the dews at even;
  Her tears fell ere the dews were dried;
She could not look on the sweet heaven,   15
  Either at morn or eventide.
After the flitting of the bats,
  When thickest dark did trance[2] the sky,
  She drew her casement curtain by,
And glanced athwart the glooming flats.   20
     She only said, "The night is dreary,
       He cometh not," she said;
     She said, "I am aweary, aweary,
       I would that I were dead!"

Upon the middle of the night,   25
  Waking she heard the nightfowl crow;
The cock sung out an hour ere light;
  From the dark fen the oxen's low
Came to her; without hope of change,
  In sleep she seemed to walk forlorn,   30
  Till cold winds woke the gray-eyed morn
About the lonely moated grange.
     She only said, "The day is dreary,
       He cometh not," she said;
     She said, "I am aweary, aweary,   35
       I would that I were dead!"

1. Mariana, in Shakespeare's *Measure for Measure* (III.i.277), waits in a grange (an outlying farmhouse) for her lover who has deserted her.
2. Traverse (noted by R. W. Hill).

About a stonecast from the wall
   A sluice with blackened waters slept,
And o'er it many, round and small,
   The clustered marish-mosses[3] crept.   40
Hard by a poplar shook alway,
   All silver-green with gnarléd bark:
For leagues no other tree did mark
The level waste, the rounding gray.
     She only said, "My life is dreary,   45
       He cometh not," she said;
     She said, "I am aweary, aweary,
       I would that I were dead!"

And ever when the moon was low,
   And the shrill winds were up and away,   50
In the white curtain, to and fro,
   She saw the gusty shadow sway.
But when the moon was very low,
   And wild winds bound within their cell,[4]
The shadow of the poplar fell   55
Upon her bed, across her brow.
     She only said, "The night is dreary,
       He cometh not," she said;
     She said, "I am aweary, aweary,
       I would that I were dead!"   60

All day within the dreamy house,
   The doors upon their hinges creaked;
The blue fly sung in the pane; the mouse
   Behind the moldering wainscot shrieked,[5]
Or from the crevice peered about.   65
   Old faces glimmered through the doors,
   Old footsteps trod the upper floors,
Old voices called her from without.
     She only said, "My life is dreary,
       He cometh not," she said;   70
     She said, "I am aweary, aweary,
       I would that I were dead!"

The sparrow's chirrup on the roof,
   The slow clock ticking, and the sound
Which to the wooing wind aloof
   The poplar made, did all confound   75
Her sense; but most she loathed the hour

---

3. "The little marsh-moss lumps that float on the surface of water" [Tennyson's comment].

4. According to Virgil, Aeolus, god of winds, kept the winds imprisoned in a cave. See *Aeneid*, I, 50–59.

5. Cf. "And a time for the wind * * * to shake the wainscot where the field-mouse trots / And to shake the tattered arras. * * * " (T. S. Eliot, *Four Quartets: East Coker*, lines 11–13).

When the thick-moted sunbeam lay
Athwart the chambers, and the day
Was sloping toward his western bower.   80
Then, said she, "I am very dreary,
   He will not come," she said;
She wept, "I am aweary, aweary,
   Oh God, that I were dead!"

                                     1830

Sonnet

She took the dappled partridge flecked with blood,
   And in her hand the drooping pheasant bare,
   And by his feet she held the woolly hare,
And like a master painting where she stood,
Looked some new goddess of an English wood.   5
   Nor could I find an imperfection there,
   Nor blame the wanton act that showed so fair—
To me whatever freak[6] she plays is good.
Hers is the fairest Life that breathes with breath,
   And *their* still plumes and azure eyelids closed   10
      Made quiet Death so beautiful to see
That Death lent grace to Life and Life to Death
   And in one image Life and Death reposed,
      To make my love an Immortality.

ca. 1830   1931

The Lady of Shalott
Part I

On either side the river lie
Long fields of barley and of rye,
That clothe the wold[1] and meet the sky;
And through the field the road runs by
   To many-towered Camelot;[2]   5
And up and down the people go,
Gazing where the lilies blow[3]
Round an island there below,
   The island of Shalott.

Willows whiten, aspens quiver,   10
Little breezes dusk and shiver

6. Prank.
1. Rolling plains.
2. Legendary city in which King Arthur's palace was located.
3. Bloom.

Through the wave that runs forever
By the island in the river
    Flowing down to Camelot.
Four gray walls, and four gray towers,   15
Overlook a space of flowers,
And the silent isle imbowers
    The Lady of Shalott.

By the margin, willow-veiled,
Slide the heavy barges trailed   20
By slow horses; and unhailed
The shallop⁴ flitteth silken-sailed
    Skimming down to Camelot:
But who hath seen her wave her hand?
Or at the casement seen her stand?   25
Or is she known in all the land,
    The Lady of Shalott?

Only reapers, reaping early
In among the bearded barley,
Hear a song that echoes cheerly   30
From the river winding clearly,
    Down to towered Camelot;
And by the moon the reaper weary,
Piling sheaves in uplands airy,
Listening, whispers " 'Tis the fairy   35
    Lady of Shalott."

Part II

There she weaves by night and day
A magic web with colors gay.
She has heard a whisper say,
A curse is on her if she stay   40
    To look down to Camelot.
She knows not what the curse may be,
And so she weaveth steadily,
And little other care hath she,
    The Lady of Shalott.   45

And moving through a mirror clear⁵
That hangs before her all the year,
Shadows of the world appear.
There she sees the highway near
    Winding down to Camelot;   50
There the river eddy whirls,
And there the surly village churls,
And the red cloaks of market girls,
    Pass onward from Shalott.

4. A light open boat.
5. Weavers used mirrors, placed facing their looms, in order to see the progress of their work.

Sometimes a troop of damsels glad,   55
An abbot on an ambling pad,[6]
Sometimes a curly shepherd lad,
Or long-haired page in crimson clad,
      Goes by to towered Camelot;
And sometimes through the mirror blue   60
The knights come riding two and two:
She hath no loyal knight and true,
      The Lady of Shalott.

But in her web she still delights
To weave the mirror's magic sights,   65
For often through the silent nights
A funeral, with plumes and lights
      And music, went to Camelot;
Or when the moon was overhead,
Came two young lovers lately wed: 70
"I am half sick of shadows," said
      The Lady of Shalott.

Part III

A bowshot from her bower eaves,
He rode between the barley sheaves,
The sun came dazzling through the leaves,   75
And flamed upon the brazen greaves[7]
      Of bold Sir Lancelot.
A red-cross knight[8] forever kneeled
To a lady in his shield,
That sparkled on the yellow field,   80
      Beside remote Shalott.

The gemmy bridle glittered free,
Like to some branch of stars we see
Hung in the golden Galaxy.
The bridle bells rang merrily   85
      As he rode down to Camelot;
And from his blazoned baldric[9] slung
A mighty silver bugle hung,
And as he rode his armor rung,
      Beside remote Shalott.   90

All in the blue unclouded weather
Thick-jeweled shone the saddle leather,
The helmet and the helmet-feather
Burned like one burning flame together,
      As he rode down to Camelot;   95
As often through the purple night,
Below the starry clusters bright,

---

6. Easy-paced horse.
7. Armor protecting the leg below the knee.
8. Cf. Spenser's *Faerie Queen* I and

III.ii.17–25.
9. A richly decorated sash worn diagonally across the breast.

Some bearded meteor, trailing light,
    Moves over still Shalott.

His broad clear brow in sunlight glowed;   100
On burnished hooves his war horse trode;
From underneath his helmet flowed
His coal-black curls as on he rode,
    As he rode down to Camelot.
From the bank and from the river   105
He flashed into the crystal mirror,
"Tirra lirra," by the river
    Sang Sir Lancelot.

She left the web, she left the loom,
She made three paces through the room,   110
She saw the water lily bloom,
She saw the helmet and the plume,
    She looked down to Camelot.
Out flew the web and floated wide;
The mirror cracked from side to side;   115
"The curse is come upon me," cried
    The Lady of Shalott.

Part IV

In the stormy east wind straining,
The pale yellow woods were waning,
The broad stream in his banks complaining,   120
Heavily the low sky raining
    Over towered Camelot;
Down she came and found a boat
Beneath a willow left afloat,
And round about the prow she wrote   125
    The Lady of Shalott.

And down the river's dim expanse
Like some bold seër in a trance,
Seeing all his own mischance—
With a glassy countenance   130
    Did she look to Camelot.
And at the closing of the day
She loosed the chain, and down she lay;
The broad stream bore her far away,
    The Lady of Shalott.   135

Lying, robed in snowy white
That loosely flew to left and right—
The leaves upon her falling light—
Through the noises of the night
    She floated down to Camelot;   140
And as the boat-head wound along
The willowy hills and fields among,

They heard her singing her last song,
　　The Lady of Shalott.

Heard a carol, mournful, holy,　　　　　　　　145
Chanted loudly, chanted lowly,
Till her blood was frozen slowly,
And her eyes were darkened wholly,
　　Turned to towered Camelot.
For ere she reached upon the tide　　　　　　150
The first house by the waterside,
Singing in her song she died,
　　The Lady of Shalott.

Under tower and balcony,
By garden wall and gallery,　　　　　　　　　155
A gleaming shape she floated by,
Dead-pale between the houses high,
　　Silent into Camelot.
Out upon the wharfs they came,
Knight and burgher, lord and dame,　　　　　160
And round the prow they read her name,
　　The Lady of Shalott.

Who is this? and what is here?
And in the lighted palace near
Died the sound of royal cheer;　　　　　　　165
And they crossed themselves for fear,
　　All the knights at Camelot:
But Lancelot mused a little space;
He said, "She has a lovely face;
God in his mercy lend her grace,　　　　　　170
　　The Lady of Shalott."

1832　　　　　　　　　　　　　　　　　1832, 1842

The Lotos-Eaters[1]

"Courage!" he[2] said, and pointed toward the land,
"This mounting wave will roll us shoreward soon."
In the afternoon they came unto a land[3]

1. Based on a short episode from the *Odyssey* (IX.82–97) in which the weary Greek veterans of the Trojan War are tempted by a desire to abandon their long voyage homeward. As Odysseus later reported: "On the tenth day we set foot on the land of the lotos-eaters who eat a flowering food. * * * I sent forth certain of my company [who] * * * mixed with the men of the lotos-eaters who * * * gave them of the lotos to taste. Now whosoever of them did eat the honey-sweet fruit of the lotos had no more wish to bring tidings nor to come back, but there he chose to abide * * * forgetful of his homeward way."

　　Tennyson expands Homer's brief account into an elaborate picture of weariness and the desire for rest and death. The descriptions in the first stanzas are similar to Spenser's *Faerie Queene* (II.vi). The final section derives, in part, from Lucretius' conception of the gods in *De rerum natura*.
2. Odysseus (or Ulysses).
3. The repetition of "land" from line 1 was deliberate; Tennyson said that

In which it seeméd always afternoon.
All round the coast the languid air did swoon,
Breathing like one that hath a weary dream.
Full-faced above the valley stood the moon;
And, like a downward smoke, the slender stream
Along the cliff to fall and pause and fall did seem.

A land of streams! some, like a downward smoke,
Slow-dropping veils of thinnest lawn,[4] did go;
And some through wavering lights and shadows broke,
Rolling a slumbrous sheet of foam below.
They saw the gleaming river seaward flow
From the inner land; far off, three mountaintops
Three silent pinnacles of aged snow,
Stood sunset-flushed; and, dewed with showery drops,
Up-clomb the shadowy pine above the woven copse.

The charméd sunset lingered low adown
In the red West; through mountain clefts the dale
Was seen far inland, and the yellow down[5]
Bordered with palm, and many a winding vale
And meadow, set with slender galingale;[6]
A land where all things always seemed the same!
And round about the keel with faces pale,
Dark faces pale against that rosy flame,
The mild-eyed melancholy Lotos-eaters came.

Branches they bore of that enchanted stem,
Laden with flower and fruit, whereof they gave
To each, but whoso did receive of them
And taste, to him the gushing of the wave
Far far away did seem to mourn and rave
On alien shores; and if his fellow spake,
His voice was thin, as voices from the grave;
And deep-asleep he seemed, yet all awake,
And music in his ears his beating heart did make.

They sat them down upon the yellow sand,
Between the sun and moon upon the shore;
And sweet it was to dream of Fatherland,
Of child, and wife, and slave; but evermore
Most weary seemed the sea, weary the oar,
Weary the wandering fields of barren foam.
Then some one said, "We will return no more";
And all at once they sang, "Our island home[7]
Is far beyond the wave; we will no longer roam."

5

10

15

20

25

30

35

40

45

this "no rhyme" was "lazier" in its
effect. Compare "afternoon" (lines 3–4)
and the rhyming of "adown" and
"down" (lines 19, 21).

4. A fine, thin linen.
5. An open plain on high ground.
6. A plant resembling tall coarse grass.
7. Ithaca.

Choric Song[8]

1

There is sweet music here that softer falls
Than petals from blown roses on the grass,
Or night-dews on still waters between walls
Of shadowy granite, in a gleaming pass;
Music that gentlier on the spirit lies,   50
Than tired eyelids upon tired eyes;[9]
Music that brings sweet sleep down from the blissful skies.
Here are cool mosses deep,
And through the moss the ivies creep,
And in the stream the long-leaved flowers weep,   55
And from the craggy ledge the poppy hangs in sleep.

2

Why are we weighed upon with heaviness,
And utterly consumed with sharp distress,
While all things else have rest from weariness?
All things have rest: why should we toil alone,   60
We only toil, who are the first of things,
And make perpetual moan,
Still from one sorrow to another thrown;
Nor ever fold our wings,
And cease from wanderings,   65
Nor steep our brows in slumber's holy balm;
Nor harken what the inner spirit sings,
"There is no joy but calm!"—
Why should we only toil, the roof and crown of things?[1]

3

Lo! in the middle of the wood,   70
The folded leaf is wooed from out the bud
With winds upon the branch, and there
Grows green and broad, and takes no care,
Sun-steeped at noon, and in the moon
Nightly dew-fed; and turning yellow   75
Falls, and floats adown the air.
Lo! sweetened with the summer light,
The full-juiced apple, waxing over-mellow,
Drops in a silent autumn night.
All its allotted length of days   80
The flower ripens in its place,
Ripens and fades, and falls, and hath no toil,
Fast-rooted in the fruitful soil.

4

Hateful is the dark blue sky,
Vaulted o'er the dark blue sea.   85
Death is the end of life; ah, why

8. Sung by the mariners.
9. Tennyson wanted the word to be pronounced as *tie-yerd* rather than *tier'd* or *tire-èd*, thus "making the word neither monosyllabic or disyllabic, but a dreamy child of the two."

1. Cf.: "Why then dost thou, O man, that of them all / Art Lord, and eke of nature Soveraine, / Wilfully * * * wast thy joyous houres in needlesse paine * * * ?" (Spenser's *Faerie Queene*, II.vi.17).

Should life all labor be?
Let us alone. Time driveth onward fast,
And in a little while our lips are dumb.
Let us alone. What is it that will last?
All things are taken from us, and become   90
Portions and parcels of the dreadful past.
Let us alone. What pleasure can we have
To war with evil? Is there any peace
In ever climbing up the climbing wave?
All things have rest, and ripen toward the grave   95
In silence—ripen, fall, and cease:
Give us long rest or death, dark death, or dreamful ease.[2]

5

How sweet it were, hearing the downward stream,
With half-shut eyes ever to seem   100
Falling asleep in a half-dream!
To dream and dream, like yonder amber light,
Which will not leave the myrrh-bush on the height;
To hear each other's whispered speech;
Eating the Lotos day by day,   105
To watch the crisping[3] ripples on the beach,
And tender curving lines of creamy spray;
To lend our hearts and spirits wholly
To the influence of mild-minded melancholy;
To muse and brood and live again in memory,   110
With those old faces of our infancy
Heaped over with a mound of grass,
Two handfuls of white dust, shut in an urn of brass!

6

Dear is the memory of our wedded lives,
And dear the last embraces of our wives
And their warm tears; but all hath suffered change;   115
For surely now our household hearths are cold,
Our sons inherit us, our looks are strange,
And we should come like ghosts to trouble joy.
Or else the island princes[4] overbold
Have eat our substance, and the minstrel sings   120
Before them of the ten years' war in Troy,
And our great deeds, as half-forgotten things.
Is there confusion in the little isle?
Let what is broken so remain.
The Gods are hard to reconcile;   125
'Tis hard to settle order once again.
There *is* confusion worse than death,
Trouble on trouble, pain on pain,
Long labor unto aged breath,
Sore tasks to hearts worn out by many wars   130
And eyes grown dim with gazing on the pilot-stars.

2. Cf.: "Sleepe after toyle, port after stormie seas, / Ease after warre, death after life does greatly please." (*Faerie Queene*, I.ix.40).
3. Curling.
4. Penelope's suitors.

7

But, propped on beds of amaranth[5] and moly,
How sweet—while warm airs lull us, blowing lowly—
With half-dropped eyelid still,   135
Beneath a heaven dark and holy,
To watch the long bright river drawing slowly
His waters from the purple hill—
To hear the dewy echoes calling
From cave to cave through the thick-twined vine—   140
To watch the emerald-colored water falling
Through many a woven acanthus[6] wreath divine!
Only to hear and see the far-off sparkling brine,
Only to hear were sweet, stretched out beneath the pine.

8

The Lotos blooms below the barren peak,   145
The Lotos blows by every winding creek;
All day the wind breathes low with mellower tone;
Through every hollow cave and alley lone
Round and round the spicy downs the yellow Lotos dust is blown.
We have had enough of action, and of motion we,   150
Rolled to starboard, rolled to larboard, when the surge was seething
    free,
Where the wallowing monster spouted his foam-fountains in the sea.
Let us swear an oath, and keep it with an equal mind,
In the hollow Lotos land to live and lie reclined
On the hills like Gods together, careless of mankind.   155
For they lie beside their nectar, and the bolts[7] are hurled
Far below them in the valleys, and the clouds are lightly curled
Round their golden houses, girdled with the gleaming world;
Where they smile in secret, looking over wasted lands,
Blight and famine, plague and earthquake, roaring deeps and fiery
    sands,   160
Clanging fights, and flaming towns, and sinking ships, and praying
    hands.
But they smile, they find a music centered in a doleful song
Steaming up, a lamentation and an ancient tale of wrong,
Like a tale of little meaning though the words are strong;
Chanted from an ill-used race of men that cleave the soil,   165
Sow the seed, and reap the harvest with enduring toil,
Storing yearly little dues of wheat, and wine and oil;
Till they perish and they suffer—some, 'tis whispered—down in hell
Suffer endless anguish, others in Elysian valleys dwell,
Resting weary limbs at last on beds of asphodel.[8]   170
Surely, surely, slumber is more sweet than toil, the shore
Than labor in the deep mid-ocean, wind and wave and oar;
O, rest ye, brother mariners, we will not wander more.

1832, 1842

---

5. A legendary unfading flower; "moly": a flower with magical properties mentioned by Homer.
6. A plant resembling a thistle. Its leaves were the model for ornaments on Corinthian columns.
7. Thunderbolts.
8. A yellow lilylike flower supposed to grow in the Elysian valleys.

You Ask Me, Why, Though Ill at Ease[1]

You ask me, why, though ill at ease,
  Within this region I subsist,
  Whose spirits falter in the mist,
And languish for the purple seas.

It is the land that freemen till,   5
  That sober-suited Freedom chose,
  The land, where girt with friends or foes
A man may speak the thing he will;

A land of settled government,
  A land of just and old renown,   10
  Where Freedom slowly broadens down
From precedent to precedent;

Where faction seldom gathers head,
  But, by degrees to fullness wrought,
  The strength of some diffusive thought   15
Hath time and space to work and spread.

Should banded unions[2] persecute
  Opinion, and induce a time
  When single thought is civil crime,
And individual freedom mute;   20

Though power should make from land to land
  The name of Britain trebly great—
  Though every channel of the State
Should fill and choke with golden sand—

Yet waft me from the harbor-mouth,   25
  Wild wind! I seek a warmer sky,
  And I will see before I die
The palms and temples of the South.

1833   1842

Lines

Here[3] often, when a child I lay reclined,
  I took delight in this locality.
Here stood the infant Ilion of the mind,
  And here the Grecian ships did seem to be.

1. Written at the time of the disturbances during and after the passing of the Reform Bill of 1832.
2. Any organized political groups, not necessarily trade unions.
3. At Mablethorpe, on the Lincolnshire coast.

The drain-cut levels of the marshy lea—
Gray sea banks and pale sunsets—dreary wind,
Dim shores, dense rains, and heavy-clouded sea!

1833   1850

Ulysses[1]

It little profits that an idle king,
By this still hearth, among these barren crags,
Matched with an aged wife, I mete and dole
Unequal laws[2] unto a savage race,
That hoard, and sleep, and feed, and know not me.   5

   I cannot rest from travel; I will drink
Life to the lees. All times I have enjoyed
Greatly, have suffered greatly, both with those
That loved me, and alone; on shore, and when
Through scudding drifts[3] the rainy Hyades   10
Vexed the dim sea. I am become a name;
For always roaming with a hungry heart
Much have I seen and known—cities of men
And manners, climates, councils, governments,
Myself not least, but honored of them all—   15
And drunk delight of battle with my peers,
Far on the ringing plains of windy Troy.
I am a part of all that I have met;
Yet all experience is an arch wherethrough
Gleams that untraveled world whose margin fades   20
Forever and forever when I move.
How dull it is to pause, to make an end,
To rust unburnished, not to shine in use!
As though to breathe were life! Life piled on life
Were all too little, and of one to me   25
Little remains; but every hour is saved
From that eternal silence, something more,
A bringer of new things; and vile it were

---

1. According to Dante, after Ulysses had returned home to Ithaca and had settled down to rule his island kingdom, he became restless and desired to set out on another voyage of exploration to the west. In old age he persuaded a band of his followers to accompany him on such a voyage. "Consider your origin," he addressed them, "ye were not formed to live like brutes, but to follow virtue and knowledge" (*Inferno* XXVI).

   The contrast between the conscientious administrator, Telemachus, and the energetic quester, his father, has been variously interpreted. A few readers argue that Ulysses is not represented in the monologue as a great hero but as irresponsible. Tennyson himself stated that the poem expressed his own "need of going forward and braving the struggle of life" after the death of Hallam.

2. Measure out rewards and punishments.

3. Driving showers of spray and rain; the "Hyades" are a group of stars whose rising was assumed to be followed by rain.

For some three suns to store and hoard myself,
And this gray spirit yearning in desire   30
To follow knowledge like a sinking star,
Beyond the utmost bound of human thought.

    This is my son, mine own Telemachus,
To whom I leave the scepter and the isle—
Well-loved of me, discerning to fulfill   35
This labor, by slow prudence to make mild
A rugged people, and through soft degrees
Subdue them to the useful and the good.
Most blameless is he, centered in the sphere
Of common duties, decent not to fail   40
In offices of tenderness, and pay
Meet adoration to my household gods,
When I am gone. He works his work, I mine.

    There lies the port; the vessel puffs her sail;
There gloom the dark, broad seas. My mariners,   45
Souls that have toiled, and wrought, and thought with me—
That ever with a frolic welcome took
The thunder and the sunshine, and opposed
Free hearts, free foreheads—you and I are old;
Old age hath yet his honor and his toil.   50
Death closes all; but something ere the end,
Some work of noble note, may yet be done,
Not unbecoming men that strove with Gods.
The lights begin to twinkle from the rocks;
The long day wanes; the slow moon climbs; the deep   55
Moans round with many voices. Come, my friends,
'Tis not too late to seek a newer world.
Push off, and sitting well in order smite
The sounding furrows; for my purpose holds
To sail beyond the sunset, and the baths   60
Of all the western stars,[4] until I die.
It may be that the gulfs will wash us down;
It may be we shall touch the Happy Isles,[5]
And see the great Achilles, whom we knew.
Though much is taken, much abides; and though   65
We are not now that strength which in old days
Moved earth and heaven, that which we are, we are—
One equal temper of heroic hearts,
Made weak by time and fate, but strong in will
To strive, to seek, to find, and not to yield.   70

1833   1842

---

4. The outer ocean or river which, in Greek cosmology, surrounded the flat circle of the earth, and into which the stars descended.

5. Elysium, or the Islands of the Blessed, where heroes such as Achilles were supposed to enjoy life after death. These islands were thought to be in the far-western ocean.

Tithonus[1]

The woods decay, the woods decay and fall,
The vapors weep their burthen to the ground,
Man comes and tills the field and lies beneath,
And after many a summer dies the swan.[2]
Me only cruel immortality   5
Consumes; I wither slowly in thine arms,[3]
Here at the quiet limit of the world,
A white-haired shadow roaming like a dream
The ever-silent spaces of the East,
Far-folded mists, and gleaming halls of morn.   10
    Alas! for this gray shadow, once a man—
So glorious in his beauty and thy choice,
Who madest him thy chosen, that he seemed
To his great heart none other than a God!
I asked thee, "Give me immortality."   15
Then didst thou grant mine asking with a smile,
Like wealthy men who care not how they give.
But thy strong Hours indignant worked their wills,
And beat me down and marred and wasted me,
And though they could not end me, left me maimed   20
To dwell in presence of immortal youth,
Immortal age beside immortal youth,
And all I was in ashes. Can thy love,
Thy beauty, make amends, though even now,
Close over us, the silver star,[4] thy guide,   25
Shines in those tremulous eyes that fill with tears
To hear me? Let me go; take back thy gift.
Why should a man desire in any way
To vary from the kindly race of men,
Or pass beyond the goal of ordinance[5]   30
Where all should pause, as is most meet for all?
    A soft air fans the cloud apart; there comes
A glimpse of that dark world where I was born.
Once more the old mysterious glimmer steals
From thy pure brows, and from thy shoulders pure,   35
And bosom beating with a heart renewed.
Thy cheek begins to redden through the gloom,
Thy sweet eyes brighten slowly close to mine,
Ere yet they blind the stars, and the wild team[6]

1. Tithonus, a Trojan prince, was loved by the goddess of the dawn, Eos or Aurora, who obtained for him the gift of living forever but neglected to obtain for him the gift of everlasting youth. In the monologue, Tithonus appears as an aged man, dwelling still in the palace of the goddess, and cut off by his frustrating predicament from the normal cycle of human life which culminates in death. To him immortality, not death, is "cruel."
2. Some species of swans live for at least fifty years.
3. I.e., the arms of Eos.
4. The morning star that precedes the dawn.
5. What is decreed or ordained as human destiny.
6. The horses that draw Eos' chariot into the sky at daybreak.

Which love thee, yearning for thy yoke, arise,   40
And shake the darkness from their loosened manes,
And beat the twilight into flakes of fire.
    Lo! ever thus thou growest beautiful
In silence, then before thine answer given
Departest, and thy tears are on my cheek.   45
    Why wilt thou ever scare me with thy tears,
And make me tremble lest a saying learnt,
In days far-off, on that dark earth, be true?
"The Gods themselves cannot recall their gifts."
    Ay me! ay me! with what another heart   50
In days far-off, and with what other eyes
I used to watch—if I be he that watched—
The lucid outline forming round thee; saw
The dim curls kindle into sunny rings;
Changed with thy mystic change, and felt my blood   55
Glow with the glow that slowly crimsoned all
Thy presence and thy portals, while I lay,
Mouth, forehead, eyelids, growing dewy-warm
With kisses balmier than half-opening buds
Of April, and could hear the lips that kissed   60
Whispering I knew not what of wild and sweet,
Like that strange song I heard Apollo sing,
While Ilion like a mist rose into towers.[7]
    Yet hold me not forever in thine East;
How can my nature longer mix with thine?   65
Coldly thy rosy shadows bathe me, cold
Are all thy lights, and cold my wrinkled feet
Upon thy glimmering thresholds, when the steam
Floats up from those dim fields about the homes
Of happy men that have the power to die,   70
And grassy barrows of the happier dead.
Release me, and restore me to the ground.
Thou seest all things, thou wilt see my grave;
Thou wilt renew thy beauty morn by morn,
I earth in earth forget these empty courts,   75
And thee returning on thy silver wheels.

1833, 1859   1860

Break, Break, Break

Break, break, break,
    On thy cold gray stones, O Sea!
And I would that my tongue could utter
    The thoughts that arise in me.

O, well for the fisherman's boy,   5
    That he shouts with his sister at play!
O, well for the sailor lad,
    That he sings in his boat on the bay!

7. The walls of Troy (Ilion) were   strains of Apollo's music.
supposed to have been built to the

And the stately ships go on
    To their haven under the hill;   10
But O for the touch of a vanished hand,
    And the sound of a voice that is still!

Break, break, break,
    At the foot of thy crags, O Sea!
But the tender grace of a day that is dead   15
    Will never come back to me.

1834   1842

The Epic [Morte d'Arthur][1]

At Francis Allen's on the Christmas eve—
The game of forfeits done—the girls all kissed
Beneath the sacred bush[2] and passed away—
The parson Holmes, the poet Everard Hall,
The host, and I sat round the wassail-bowl,   5
Then halfway ebbed; and there we held a talk,
How all the old honor had from Christmas gone,
Or gone or dwindled down to some odd games
In some odd nooks like this; till I, tired out
With cutting eights that day upon the pond,   10
Where, three times slipping from the outer edge,
I bumped the ice into three several stars,
Fell in a doze; and half-awake I heard
The parson taking wide and wider sweeps,
Now harping on the church-commissioners,[3]   15
Now hawking at geology and schism;
Until I woke, and found him settled down
Upon the general decay of faith
Right through the world: "at home was little left,
And none abroad; there was no anchor, none,   20
To hold by." Francis, laughing, clapped his hand
On Everard's shoulder, with "I hold by him."
"And I," quoth Everard, "by the wassail-bowl."
"Why yes," I said, "we knew your gift that way
At college; but another which you had—   25
I mean of verse (for so we held it then),
What came of that?" "You know," said Frank, "he burnt
His epic, his King Arthur, some twelve books"—

1. At age 24, Tennyson proposed to write a long epic on King Arthur. Five years later he had completed one book of the twelve, the story of Arthur's death, which he published in 1842 under the title *Morte d'Arthur*. In this early version, the story is given a framework entitled *The Epic*, which consists of a short introductory section (51 lines) and an epilogue (30 lines), describing a party on Christmas Eve in modern times, at which the poet reads *Morte d'Arthur* to his friends. In 1869, Tennyson incorporated *Morte d'Arthur* into his long narrative poem, *Idylls of the King*; it appears there as the twelfth book, under the new title, *The Passing of Arthur*. At this time *The Epic* framework was discarded and some lines added. The 1842 version can be reconstructed (only two lines are modified) by reading *The Passing of Arthur*, lines 170–440.
2. Mistletoe.
3. Commissioners appointed by the government in 1835 to regulate finances of the Anglican Church.

And then to me demanding why: "O, sir,
He thought that nothing new was said, or else   30
Something so said 'twas nothing—that a truth
Looks freshest in the fashion of the day;
God knows; he has a mint of reasons; ask.
It pleased *me* well enough." "Nay, nay," said Hall,
"Why take the style of those heroic times?   35
For nature brings not back the mastodon,
Nor we those times; and why should any man
Remodel models? these twelve books of mine
Were faint Homeric echoes,[4] nothing-worth,
Mere chaff and draff, much better burnt." "But I,"   40
Said Francis, "picked the eleventh from this hearth,
And have it; keep a thing, its use will come.
I hoard it as a sugarplum for Holmes."
He laughed, and I, though sleepy, like a horse
That hears the corn-bin open, pricked my ears;   45
For I remembered Everard's college fame
When we were Freshmen. Then at my request
He brought it; and the poet, little urged,
But with some prelude of disparagement,
Read, mouthing out his hollow o's and a's,
Deep-chested music, and to this result.[5]   50

* * *

Here ended Hall, and our last light, that long
Had winked and threatened darkness, flared and fell;   325
At which the parson, sent to sleep with sound,
And waked with silence, grunted "Good!" but we
Sat rapt: it was the tone with which he read—
Perhaps some modern touches here and there
Redeemed it from the charge of nothingness—   330
Or else we loved the man, and prized his work;
I know not; but we sitting, as I said,
The cock crew loud, as at that time of year
The lusty bird takes every hour for dawn.[6]
Then Francis, muttering, like a man ill-used,   335
"There now—that's nothing!" drew a little back,
And drove his heel into the smoldered log,
That sent a blast of sparkles up the flue.
And so to bed, where yet in sleep I seemed
To sail with Arthur under looming shores,   340
Point after point; till on to dawn, when dreams
Begin to feel the truth and stir of day,
To me, methought, who waited with the crowd,
There came a bark that, blowing forward, bore
King Arthur, like a modern gentleman   345
Of stateliest port; and all the people cried,

---

4. Cf. Walter Savage Landor's comment after reading *Morte d'Arthur* in manuscript: "It is more Homeric than any poem of our time, and rivals some of the noblest parts of the *Odyssey*."
5. Here followed the 271 lines of *Morte d'Arthur* in 1842 (see below, *The Passing of Arthur*, lines 170–440). *The Epic* then continued as follows.
6. See *Hamlet* I.i.157–60 on the legend of the cock's crowing "all night long" on Christmas Eve.

"Arthur is come again: he cannot die."
Then those that stood upon the hills behind
Repeated—"Come again, and thrice as fair";
And, further inland, voices echoed—"Come   350
With all good things, and war shall be no more."
At this a hundred bells began to peal,
That with the sound I woke, and heard indeed
The clear church bells ring in the Christmas morn.

1833–38   1842

Sonnet[1]

How thought you that this thing could captivate?
    What are those graces that could make her dear,
    Who is not worth the notice of a sneer
To rouse the vapid devil of her hate?
A speech conventional, so void of weight   5
    That after it has buzzed about one's ear,
    'Twere rich refreshment for a week to hear
The dentist babble or the barber prate;

A hand displayed with many a little art;
    An eye that glances on her neighbor's dress;   10
        A foot too often shown for my regard;
An angel's form—a waiting-woman's[2] heart;
    A perfect-featured face, expressionless,
        Insipid, as the Queen upon a card.

1836   1931

Move Eastward, Happy Earth

Move eastward, happy earth, and leave
    Yon orange sunset waning slow;
From fringes of the faded eve,
    O happy planet, eastward go,
Till over thy dark shoulder glow   5
    Thy silver sister-world,[3] and rise
    To glass herself in dewy eyes
That watch me from the glen below.

Ah, bear me with thee, smoothly borne,
    Dip forward under starry light,   10

1. Perhaps inspired by Tennyson's disillusioned feelings toward Rosa Baring, a beautiful girl of high social station in Somersby, for whom he had a short-lived infatuation.

2. Female servant's.
3. The planet Venus, or perhaps the moon, which will be reflected in the eyes of the speaker's beloved.

And move me to my marriage morn,
    And round again to happy night.

ca. 1836   1842

The Eagle: A Fragment

He clasps the crag with crooked hands;
Close to the sun in lonely lands,
Ringed with the azure world, he stands.

The wrinkled sea beneath him crawls:
He watches from his mountain walls,   5
And like a thunderbolt he falls.

1851

Locksley Hall[1]

Comrades, leave me here a little, while as yet 'tis early morn;
Leave me here, and when you want me, sound upon the bugle horn.

'Tis the place, and all around it, as of old, the curlews call,
Dreary gleams[2] about the moorland flying over Locksley Hall;

Locksley Hall, that in the distance overlooks the sandy tracts,   5
And the hollow ocean-ridges roaring into cataracts.

Many a night from yonder ivied casement, ere I went to rest,
Did I look on great Orion sloping slowly to the west.

Many a night I saw the Pleiads,[3] rising through the mellow shade,
Glitter like a swarm of fireflies tangled in a silver braid.   10

Here about the beach I wandered, nourishing a youth sublime
With the fairy tales of science, and the long result of time;

When the centuries behind me like a fruitful land reposed;
When I clung to all the present for the promise that it closed;[4]

When I dipped into the future far as human eye could see,   15
Saw the vision of the world and all the wonder that would be.—

1. The situation in this poem—of a young man's being jilted by a girl who chose to marry a wealthy landowner—may have been suggested to Tennyson by the experience of his brother. Frederick Tennyson, a hot-tempered man, had fallen in love with his cousin, Julia Tennyson, and was similarly unsuccessful. It may also have been inspired by Tennyson's own frustrated courtship of Rosa Baring, who rejected the young poet in favor of a wealthy suitor. Concerning the ranting tone of the speaker (a tone accentuated by the heavily marked trochaic meter), Tennyson himself said: "The whole poem represents young life, its good side, its deficiencies, and its yearnings."
2. Tennyson stated that "gleams" does not refer to "curlews" flying but to streaks of light.
3. The Pleiades, a seven-starred constellation.
4. Enclosed.

In the spring a fuller crimson comes upon the robin's breast;
In the spring the wanton lapwing gets himself another crest;

In the spring a livelier iris changes on the burnished dove;[5]
In the spring a young man's fancy lightly turns to thoughts of love. 20

Then her cheek was pale and thinner than should be for one so young,
And her eyes on all my motions with a mute observance hung.

And I said, "My cousin Amy, speak, and speak the truth to me,
Trust me, cousin, all the current of my being sets to thee."

On her pallid cheek and forehead came a color and a light,   25
As I have seen the rosy red flushing in the northern night.

And she turned—her bosom shaken with a sudden storm of sighs—
All the spirit deeply dawning in the dark of hazel eyes—

Saying, "I have hid my feelings, fearing they should do me wrong";
Saying, "Dost thou love me, cousin?" weeping, "I have loved thee
     long."   30

Love took up the glass of Time, and turned it in his glowing hands;
Every moment, lightly shaken, ran itself in golden sands.

Love took up the harp of Life, and smote on all the chords with
     might;
Smote the chord of Self, that, trembling, passed in music out of
     sight.

Many a morning on the moorland did we hear the copses ring,   35
And her whisper thronged my pulses with the fullness of the spring.

Many an evening by the waters did we watch the stately ships,
And our spirits rushed together at the touching of the lips.

O my cousin, shallow-hearted! O my Amy, mine no more!
O the dreary, dreary moorland! O the barren, barren shore!   40

Falser than all fancy fathoms, falser than all songs have sung,
Puppet to a father's threat, and servile to a shrewish tongue!

Is it well to wish thee happy?—having known me—to decline
On a range of lower feelings and a narrower heart than mine!

Yet it shall be; thou shalt lower to his level day by day,   45
What is fine within thee growing coarse to sympathize with clay.

As the husband is, the wife is; thou art mated with a clown,[6]
And the grossness of his nature will have weight to drag thee down.

He will hold thee, when his passion shall have spent its novel force,
Something better than his dog, a little dearer than his horse.   50

What is this? his eyes are heavy; think not they are glazed with wine.
Go to him, it is thy duty; kiss him, take his hand in thine.

It may be my lord is weary, that his brain is overwrought;
Soothe him with thy finer fancies, touch him with thy lighter
    thought.

He will answer to the purpose, easy things to understand—   55
Better thou wert dead before me, though I slew thee with my hand!

Better thou and I were lying, hidden from the heart's disgrace,
Rolled in one another's arms, and silent in a last embrace.

Cursed be the social wants that sin against the strength of youth!
Cursed be the social lies that warp us from the living truth!   60

Cursed be the sickly forms that err from honest Nature's rule!
Cursed be the gold that gilds the straitened[7] forehead of the fool!

Well—'tis well that I should bluster!—Hadst thou less unworthy
    proved—
Would to God—for I had loved thee more than ever wife was loved.

Am I mad, that I should cherish that which bears but bitter fruit? 65
I will pluck it from my bosom, though my heart be at the root.

Never, though my mortal summers to such length of years should
    come
As the many-wintered crow[8] that leads the clanging rookery home.

Where is comfort? in division of the records of the mind?
Can I part her from herself, and love her, as I knew her, kind?   70

I remember one that perished; sweetly did she speak and move;
Such a one do I remember, whom to look at was to love.

Can I think of her as dead, and love her for the love she bore?
No—she never loved me truly; love is love for evermore.

Comfort? comfort scorned of devils! this is truth the poet[9] sings, 75
That a sorrow's crown of sorrow is remembering happier things.

Drug thy memories, lest thou learn it, lest thy heart be put to proof,
In the dead unhappy night, and when the rain is on the roof.

Like a dog, he hunts in dreams, and thou art staring at the wall,
Where the dying night-lamp flickers, and the shadows rise and
    fall.
                                                  80

Then a hand shall pass before thee, pointing to his drunken sleep,
To thy widowed[1] marriage-pillows, to the tears that thou wilt weep.

Thou shalt hear the "Never, never," whispered by the phantom years.
And a song from out the distance in the ringing of thine ears;

And an eye shall vex thee, looking ancient kindness on thy pain. 85
Turn thee, turn thee on thy pillow; get thee to thy rest again.

Nay, but Nature brings thee solace; for a tender voice will cry.
'Tis a purer life than thine, a lip to drain thy trouble dry.

---

7. Narrowed.
8. A rook, a long-lived bird.
9. Dante (*Inferno* V.121–23).

1. Presumably figurative. Her marriage
having become a mockery, she is widowed.

Baby lips will laugh me down; my latest rival brings thee rest.
Baby fingers, waxen touches, press me from the mother's breast. 90

O, the child too clothes the father with a dearness not his due.
Half is thine and half is his; it will be worthy of the two.

O, I see thee old and formal, fitted to thy petty part,
With a little hoard of maxims preaching down a daughter's heart.

"They were dangerous guides the feelings—she herself was not ex-
    empt— 95
Truly, she herself had suffered"—Perish in thy self-contempt!

Overlive it—lower yet—be happy! wherefore should I care?
I myself must mix with action, lest I wither by despair.

What is that which I should turn to, lighting upon days like these?
Every door is barred with gold, and opens but to golden keys. 100

Every gate is thronged with suitors, all the markets overflow.
I have but an angry fancy; what is that which I should do?

I had been content to perish, falling on the foeman's ground,
When the ranks are rolled in vapor, and the winds are laid with
    sound.[2]

But the jingling of the guinea helps the hurt that Honor feels, 105
And the nations do but murmur, snarling at each other's heels.

Can I but relive in sadness? I will turn that earlier page.
Hide me from my deep emotion, O thou wondrous Mother-Age![3]

Make me feel the wild pulsation that I felt before the strife,
When I heard my days before me, and the tumult of my life; 110

Yearning for the large excitement that the coming years would yield,
Eager-hearted as a boy when first he leaves his father's field,

And at night along the dusky highway near and nearer drawn,
Sees in heaven the light of London flaring like a dreary dawn;

And his spirit leaps within him to be gone before him then, 115
Underneath the light he looks at, in among the throngs of men;

Men, my brothers, men the workers, ever reaping something new;
That which they have done but earnest[4] of the things that they
    shall do.

For I dipped into the future, far as human eye could see,
Saw the Vision of the world, and all the wonder that would be; 120

Saw the heavens fill with commerce, argosies of magic sails,[5]
Pilots of the purple twilight, dropping down with costly bales;

2. It was once believed that the firing of
artillery stilled the winds.
3. Perhaps signifying the consolations of
a future age of progress. See also line
185.
4. A pledge.
5. Probably airships, such as balloons.

Heard the heavens fill with shouting, and there rained a ghastly dew
From the nations' airy navies grappling in the central blue;

Far along the world-wide whisper of the south wind rushing
    warm,   125
With the standards of the peoples plunging through the thunder-
    storm;

Till the war drum throbbed no longer, and the battle flags were
    furled
In the Parliament of man, the Federation of the world.

There the common sense of most shall hold a fretful realm in awe,
And the kindly earth shall slumber, lapped in universal law.   130

So I triumphed ere my passion sweeping through me left me dry,
Left me with the palsied heart, and left me with the jaundiced eye;

Eye, to which all order festers, all things here are out of joint.
Science moves, but slowly, slowly, creeping on from point to point;

Slowly comes a hungry people, as a lion, creeping nigher,   135
Glares at one that nods and winks behind a slowly-dying fire.

Yet I doubt not through the ages one increasing purpose runs,
And the thoughts of men are widened with the process of the suns.

What is that to him that reaps not harvest of his youthful joys,
Though the deep heart of existence beat forever like a boy's?   140

Knowledge comes, but wisdom lingers, and I linger on the shore,
And the individual withers, and the world is more and more.

Knowledge comes, but wisdom lingers, and he bears a laden breast,
Full of sad experience, moving toward the stillness of his rest.

Hark, my merry comrades call me, sounding on the bugle horn,   145
They to whom my foolish passion were a target for their scorn.

Shall it not be scorn to me to harp on such a moldered string?
I am shamed through all my nature to have loved so slight a thing.

Weakness to be wroth with weakness! woman's pleasure, woman's
    pain—
Nature made them blinder motions bounded in a shallower brain.   150

Woman is the lesser man, and all thy passions, matched with mine,
Are as moonlight unto sunlight, and as water unto wine—

Here at least, where nature sickens, nothing. Ah, for some retreat
Deep in yonder shining Orient, where my life began to beat,

Where in wild Mahratta-battle[6] fell my father evil-starred—   155
I was left a trampled orphan, and a selfish uncle's ward.

Or to burst all links of habit—there to wander far away,
On from island unto island at the gateways of the day.

6. A reference to wars waged by a   in India (1803 and 1817).
Hindu people against the British forces

Larger constellations burning, mellow moons and happy skies,
Breadths of tropic shade and palms in cluster, knots of Paradise. 160

Never comes the trader, never floats an European flag,
Slides the bird o'er lustrous woodland, swings the trailer[7] from the
    crag;

Droops the heavy-blossomed bower, hangs the heavy-fruited tree—
Summer isles of Eden lying in dark purple spheres of sea.

There methinks would be enjoyment more than in this march of
    mind, 165
In the steamship, in the railway, in the thoughts that shake man-
    kind.

There the passions cramped no longer shall have scope and breath-
    ing space;
I will take some savage woman, she shall rear my dusky race.

Iron-jointed, supple-sinewed, they shall dive, and they shall run,
Catch the wild goat by the hair, and hurl their lances in the sun; 170

Whistle back the parrot's call, and leap the rainbows of the brooks,
Not with blinded eyesight poring over miserable books—

Fool, again the dream, the fancy! but I *know* my words are wild,
But I count the gray barbarian lower than the Christian child.

I, to herd with narrow foreheads, vacant of our glorious gains. 175
Like a beast with lower pleasures, like a beast with lower pains!

Mated with a squalid savage—what to me were sun or clime?
I the heir of all the ages, in the foremost files of time—

I that rather held it better men should perish one by one,
Than that earth should stand at gaze like Joshua's moon in
    Ajalon![8] 180

Not in vain the distance beacons. Forward, forward let us range,
Let the great world spin forever down the ringing grooves[9] of change.

Through the shadow of the globe we sweep into the younger day;
Better fifty years of Europe than a cycle of Cathay.[1]

Mother-Age—for mine I knew not—help me as when life begun; 185
Rift the hills, and roll the waters, flash the lightnings, weigh the sun.

O, I see the crescent promise of my spirit hath not set.
Ancient founts of inspiration well through all my fancy yet.

Howsoever these things be, a long farewell to Locksley Hall!
Now for me the woods may wither, now for me the roof-tree fall. 190

---

7. A vine.
8. At the command of Joshua, the sun
and moon stood still while the Israelites
completed the slaughter of their enemies
in the valley of Ajalon (Joshua x.12–
13).

9. Railroad tracks. Tennyson at one
time had the impression that train
wheels ran in grooved rails.
1. China, regarded in the 19th century as a static, unprogressive country.

Comes a vapor from the margin, blackening over heath and holt,
Cramming all the blast before it, in its breast a thunderbolt.

Let it fall on Locksley Hall, with rain or hail, or fire or snow;
For the mighty wind arises, roaring seaward, and I go.

1837–38   1842

From THE PRINCESS[1]

Sweet and Low

Sweet and low, sweet and low,
  Wind of the western sea,
Low, low, breathe and blow,
  Wind of the western sea!
Over the rolling waters go,   5
Come from the dying moon, and blow,
  Blow him again to me;
While my little one, while my pretty one, sleeps.

Sleep and rest, sleep and rest,
  Father will come to thee soon;   10
Rest, rest, on mother's breast,
  Father will come to thee soon;
Father will come to his babe in the nest,
Silver sails all out of the west
  Under the silver moon;   15
Sleep, my little one, sleep, my pretty one, sleep.

1850

The Splendor Falls

The splendor falls on castle walls
  And snowy summits old in story;
The long light shakes across the lakes,
  And the wild cataract leaps in glory.
Blow, bugle, blow, set the wild echoes flying,   5
Blow, bugle; answer, echoes, dying, dying, dying.

O, hark, O, hear! how thin and clear,
  And thinner, clearer, farther going!
O, sweet and far from cliff and scar[2]
  The horns of Elfland faintly blowing!
Blow, let us hear the purple glens replying,   10
Blow, bugle; answer, echoes, dying, dying, dying.

1. *The Princess*, a long narrative poem, contains interludes in which occasional songs are sung. The six of these in our selection rank among the finest of Tennyson's lyrics, and various 19th- and 20th-century composers have set them to music.
2. Mountainside.

O love, they die in yon rich sky,
    They faint on hill or field or river;
Our echoes roll from soul to soul,   15
    And grow forever and forever.
Blow, bugle, blow, set the wild echoes flying,
And answer, echoes, answer, dying, dying, dying.

1850

Tears, Idle Tears[3]

    Tears, idle tears, I know not what they mean,
Tears from the depth of some divine despair
Rise in the heart, and gather to the eyes,
In looking on the happy autumn-fields,
And thinking of the days that are no more.   5

    Fresh as the first beam glittering on a sail,
That brings our friends up from the underworld,
Sad as the last which reddens over one
That sinks with all we love below the verge;
So sad, so fresh, the days that are no more.   10

    Ah, sad and strange as in dark summer dawns
The earliest pipe of half-awakened birds
To dying ears, when unto dying eyes
The casement slowly grows a glimmering square;
So sad, so strange, the days that are no more.   15

    Dear as remembered kisses after death,
And sweet as those by hopeless fancy feigned
On lips that are for others; deep as love,
Deep as first love, and wild with all regret;
O Death in Life, the days that are no more!   20

1847

Ask Me No More

Ask me no more: the moon may draw the sea;
    The cloud may stoop from heaven and take the shape,
    With fold to fold, of mountain or of cape;
But O too fond, when have I answered thee?
              Ask me no more.   5

Ask me no more: what answer should I give?
    I love not hollow cheek or faded eye:

3. Tennyson commented: "This song came to me on the yellowing autumn-tide at Tintern Abbey, full for me of its bygone memories." This locale would be for him associated both with Wordsworth's *Tintern Abbey* and with memories of Hallam, who was buried across the Bristol Channel in this area. "It is what I have always felt even from a boy, and what as a boy I called the 'passion of the past.' And it is so always with me now; it is the distance that charms me in the landscape, the picture and the past, and not the immediate today in which I move."

Yet, O my friend, I will not have thee die!
Ask me no more, lest I should bid thee live;
        Ask me no more.   **10**

Ask me no more: thy fate and mine are sealed;
  I strove against the stream and all in vain;
  Let the great river take me to the main.
No more, dear love, for at a touch I yield;
        Ask me no more.   **15**
                      1850

Now Sleeps the Crimson Petal

Now sleeps the crimson petal, now the white;
Nor waves the cypress in the palace walk;
Nor winks the gold fin in the porphyry font.
The firefly wakens; waken thou with me.

Now droops the milk-white peacock like a ghost,   **5**
And like a ghost she glimmers on to me.

Now lies the Earth all Danaë[4] to the stars,
And all thy heart lies open unto me.

Now slides the silent meteor on, and leaves
A shining furrow, as thy thoughts in me.   **10**

Now folds the lily all her sweetness up,
And slips into the bosom of the lake.
So fold thyself, my dearest, thou, and slip
Into my bosom and be lost in me.
                      1847

Come Down, O Maid

Come down, O maid, from yonder mountain height.
What pleasure lives in height (the shepherd sang),
In height and cold, the splendor of the hills?
But cease to move so near the heavens, and cease
To glide a sunbeam by the blasted pine,   **5**
To sit a star upon the sparkling spire;
And come, for Love is of the valley, come,
For Love is of the valley, come thou down
And find him; by the happy threshold, he,
Or hand in hand with Plenty in the maize,   **10**
Or red with spirted purple of the vats,
Or foxlike in the vine;[5] nor cares to walk

4. Danaë, a Greek princess, was confined in a metal tower by her father to prevent suitors from coming near her. Zeus, however, succeeded in visiting her in the form of a shower of gold. Their offspring was the hero Perseus.
5. This image comes from the Song of Solomon ii.15.

With Death and Morning on the Silver Horns,[6]
Nor wilt thou snare him in the white ravine,
Nor find him dropped upon the firths of ice,[7]   15
That huddling slant in furrow-cloven falls
To roll the torrent out of dusky doors.[8]
But follow; let the torrent dance thee down
To find him in the valley; let the wild
Lean-headed eagles yelp alone, and leave   20
The monstrous ledges there to slope, and spill
Their thousand wreaths of dangling water-smoke,
That like a broken purpose waste in air.
So waste not thou, but come; for all the vales
Await thee; azure pillars of the hearth[9]   25
Arise to thee; the children call, and I
Thy shepherd pipe, and sweet is every sound,
Sweeter thy voice, but every sound is sweet;
Myriads of rivulets hurrying through the lawn,
The moan of doves in immemorial elms,   30
And murmuring of innumerable bees.

1847

["The Woman's Cause Is Man's"][1]

"Blame not thyself too much," I said, "nor blame
Too much the sons of men and barbarous laws;   240
These were the rough ways of the world till now.
Henceforth thou hast a helper, me, that know
The woman's cause is man's: they rise or sink
Together, dwarfed or godlike, bond or free:
For she that out of Lethe scales with man   245
The shining steps of Nature, shares with man
His nights, his days, moves with him to one goal,
Stays all the fair young planet in her hands—
If she be small, slight-natured, miserable,
How shall men grow? but work no more alone!   250
Our place is much: as far as in us lies
We two will serve them both in aiding her—
Will clear away the parasitic forms
That seem to keep her up but drag her down—
Will leave her space to burgeon out of all   255
Within her—let her make herself her own
To give or keep, to live and learn and be
All that not harms distinctive womanhood.

6. Mountain peaks.
7. Glaciers.
8. Heaps of rock and refuse at the base of a glacier through which the mountain torrent forces its way down to the valley below.
9. Columns of smoke from the houses in the valley.
1. *The Princess* tells the story of a prince who courts the young and beautiful Princess Ida, who has established a university from which men are excluded; she has also vowed she will never marry. At the end she is persuaded that her feminist experiment was a failure, but the prince assures her that ideal relations between men and women may be achieved in the future. Our selection, covering the prince's key speech, is from book VII, lines 239–91.

For woman is not undevelopt man,
But diverse: could we make her as the man,   260
Sweet Love were slain: his dearest bond is this,
Not like to like, but like in difference.
Yet in the long years liker must they grow;
The man be more of woman, she of man;
He gain in sweetness and in moral height,   265
Nor lose the wrestling thews that throw the world;
She mental breadth, nor fail in childward care,
Nor lose the childlike in the larger mind;
Till at the last she set herself to man,
Like perfect music unto noble words;   270
And so these twain, upon the skirts of Time,
Sit side by side, full-summed in all their powers,
Dispensing harvest, sowing the To-be,
Self-reverent each and reverencing each,
Distinct in individualities,   275
But like each other even as those who love.
Then comes the statelier Eden back to men:
Then reign the world's great bridals, chaste and calm:
Then springs the crowning race of humankind.
May these things be!"
                   Sighing she spoke "I fear
They will not."   280
            "Dear, but let us type them now
In our own lives, and this proud watchword rest
Of equal; seeing either sex alone
Is half itself, and in true marriage lies
Nor equal, nor unequal: each fulfils   285
Defect in each, and always thought in thought,
Purpose in purpose, will in will, they grow,
The single pure and perfect animal,
The two-celled heart beating, with one full stroke,
Life."
     And again sighing she spoke: "A dream   290
That once was mine! what woman taught you this?"
1839–47   1847

In Memoriam A. H. H.

In Memoriam A. H. H. Like most of Tennyson's writings, *In Memoriam* shows his debt to earlier poetry. In its celebration of male friendship, as Christopher Ricks has shown, the poem has many affinities with Shakespeare's *Sonnets*, and as an elegy it is of course in the tradition of Milton's *Lycidas* and Shelley's *Adonais*. Its structure, however, is strikingly different. Resembling a song cycle more than a symphony, it is made up of individual lyric units, seemingly self-sustaining, that may be enjoyed by themselves even though the full pleasure to be derived from each component depends upon its relationship to the poem as a whole. The circumstances of the poem's composition help to explain how this new kind of elegy was evolved. The sudden death of Arthur Hallam at the age of 22 had a profound effect on Tennyson. The young poet had cherished Hallam not only as his closest friend and the fiancé of his sister but as an all-wise counselor upon whose judgment he depended for guidance. This fatherly prop having been pulled away, Tennyson was overwhelmed with doubts about the meaning of life and man's role in the universe, doubts reinforced by his own study of geology and other sciences. As a kind of poetic diary recording the variety of his feelings and reflections he began to compose a series of lyrics. These "short swallow-flights of song," as he calls them, written at intervals over a period of seventeen years, were later grouped into one long elegy in which a progressive development from despair to some sort of hope, as in section 95, is recorded.

Some of the early sections of the poem resemble traditional pastoral elegies, including those portraying the voyage during which Hallam's body was brought to England for burial (sections 9–11, 13–15, 19). Other early sections portraying the speaker's loneliness, in which even Christmas festivities seem joyless (section 28), are more distinctive. With the passage of time, indicated by anniversaries and by recurring changes of the seasons, the speaker comes to accept the loss and to assert his belief in life and in an afterlife. In particular the recurring Christmases (sections 28, 78, 104) indicate the stages of his development, yet the pattern of progress in the poem is not a simple unimpeded movement upwards. Dramatic conflicts recur throughout. Thus the most intense expression of doubt occurs not at the beginning of *In Memoriam* but as late as sections 54, 55, and 56.

The quatrain form in which the whole poem is written is usually called the "*In Memoriam* stanza," although it had been occasionally used by earlier poets. So rigid a form taxed Tennyson's ingenuity in achieving variety, but it is one of several means by which the diverse parts of the poem are knitted together.

The introductory section, consisting of eleven stanzas, is commonly referred to as the "Prologue," although Tennyson did not assign a title to it. It was written in 1849 after the rest of the poem was complete.

From In Memoriam A. H. H.

OBIIT MDCCCXXXIII

Strong Son of God, immortal Love,
    Whom we, that have not seen thy face,
    By faith, and faith alone, embrace,
Believing where we cannot prove;[1]

Thine are these orbs[2] of light and shade;   5
    Thou madest Life in man and brute;
    Thou madest Death; and lo, thy foot
Is on the skull which thou hast made.

Thou wilt not leave us in the dust:
    Thou madest man, he knows not why,   10

1. See John xx.24–29, in which Jesus rebukes Thomas for his doubts concerning the Resurrection: "Blessed are they that have not seen, and yet have believed." For first line of poem, cf. *Love*, by George Herbert: "Immortal Love, Author of this great frame, / Sprung from that beauty which can never fade, / How hath Man parceled out Thy glorious name, / And thrown it on the dust which Thou hast made?" [noted by R. W. Hill].
2. Planets.

He thinks he was not made to die;
And thou hast made him: thou art just.

Thou seemest human and divine,
  The highest, holiest manhood, thou.
  Our wills are ours, we know not how;   15
Our wills are ours, to make them thine.

Our little systems[3] have their day;
  They have their day and cease to be;
  They are but broken lights of thee,
And thou, O Lord, art more than they.   20

We have but faith: we cannot know,
  For knowledge is of things we see;
  And yet we trust it comes from thee,
A beam in darkness: let it grow.

Let knowledge grow from more to more,   25
  But more of reverence in us dwell;
  That mind and soul, according well,
May make one music as before,[4]

But vaster. We are fools and slight;
  We mock thee when we do not fear: 30
  But help thy foolish ones to bear;
Help thy vain worlds to bear thy light.

Forgive what seemed my sin in me,
  What seemed my worth since I began;
  For merit lives from man to man,   35
And not from man, O Lord, to thee.

Forgive my grief for one removed,
  Thy creature, whom I found so fair.
  I trust he lives in thee, and there
I find him worthier to be loved.   40

Forgive these wild and wandering cries,
  Confusions of a wasted[5] youth;
  Forgive them where they fail in truth,
And in thy wisdom make me wise.

1849

1

I held it truth, with him who sings
  To one clear harp in divers tones,[6]
  That men may rise on stepping stones
Of their dead selves to higher things.

---

3. Systems of religion and philosophy.   5. Desolated.
4. As in the days of fixed religious faith.   6. Identified by Tennyson as Goethe.

But who shall so forecast the years
   And find in loss a gain to match?
   Or reach a hand through time to catch
The far-off interest of tears?   5

Let Love clasp Grief lest both be drowned,
   Let darkness keep her raven gloss.   10
   Ah, sweeter to be drunk with loss,
To dance with Death, to beat the ground,

Than that the victor Hours should scorn
   The long result of love, and boast,
   "Behold the man that loved and lost,   15
But all he was is overworn."

2

Old yew, which graspest at the stones
   That name the underlying dead,
   Thy fibers net the dreamless head,
Thy roots are wrapped about the bones.

The seasons bring the flower again,   5
   And bring the firstling to the flock;
   And in the dusk of thee the clock
Beats out the little lives of men.

O, not for thee the glow, the bloom,
   Who changest not in any gale,   10
   Nor branding summer suns avail
To touch thy thousand years of gloom;[7]

And gazing on thee, sullen tree,
   Sick for[8] thy stubborn hardihood,
   I seem to fail from out my blood   15
And grow incorporate into thee.

3

O Sorrow, cruel fellowship,
   O Priestess in the vaults of Death,
   O sweet and bitter in a breath,
What whispers from thy lying lip?

"The stars," she whispers, "blindly run;   5
   A web is woven across the sky;
   From out waste places comes a cry,
And murmurs from the dying sun;

"And all the phantom, Nature, stands—
   With all the music in her tone,   10
   A hollow echo of my own—
A hollow form with empty hands."

---

7. The ancient yew tree, growing in the grounds near the clock tower and church where Hallam was to be buried, seems neither to blossom in spring nor change from its dark mournful color in summer.
8. Envying or longing to share.

And shall I take a thing so blind,
 Embrace her[9] as my natural good;
 Or crush her, like a vice of blood,
Upon the threshold of the mind?   15

4

To Sleep I give my powers away;
 My will is bondsman to the dark;
 I sit within a helmless bark,
And with my heart I muse and say:

O heart, how fares it with thee now,   5
 That thou should fail from thy desire,
 Who scarcely darest to inquire,
"What is it makes me beat so low?"

Something it is which thou hast lost,
 Some pleasure from thine early years.   10
 Break thou deep vase of chilling tears,
That grief hath shaken into frost![10]

Such clouds of nameless trouble cross
 All night below the darkened eyes;
 With morning wakes the will, and cries,
"Thou shalt not be the fool of loss."   15

5

I sometimes hold it half a sin
 To put in words the grief I feel;
 For words, like Nature, half reveal
And half conceal the Soul within.

But, for the unquiet heart and brain,   5
 A use in measured language lies;
 The sad mechanic exercise,
Like dull narcotics, numbing pain.

In words, like weeds,[1] I'll wrap me o'er,
 Like coarsest clothes against the cold;   10
 But that large grief which these enfold
Is given in outline and no more.

* * *

7

Dark house,[2] by which once more I stand
 Here in the long unlovely street,
 Doors, where my heart was used to beat
So quickly, waiting for a hand,

A hand that can be clasped no more—   5
 Behold me, for I cannot sleep,

---

9. I.e., sorrow.
10. Tennyson comments: "Water can be brought below freezing-point and not turn into ice—if it be kept still; but if it be moved suddenly it turns into ice and may break a vase."
1. Garments.
2. House on Wimpole Street, in London, where Hallam had lived.

And like a guilty thing I creep
At earliest morning to the door.

He is not here; but far away
   The noise of life begins again,   10
   And ghastly through the drizzling rain
On the bald street breaks the blank day.

* * *

9

Fair ship, that from the Italian shore
   Sailest the placid ocean-plains
   With my lost Arthur's loved remains,
Spread thy full wings, and waft him o'er.

So draw him home to those that mourn   5
   In vain; a favorable speed
   Ruffle thy mirrored mast, and lead
Through prosperous floods his holy urn.

All night no ruder air perplex
   Thy sliding keel, till Phosphor,[3] bright   10
   As our pure love, through early light
Shall glimmer on the dewey decks.

Sphere all your lights around, above;
   Sleep, gentle heavens, before the prow;
   Sleep, gentle winds, as he sleeps now,   15
My friend, the brother of my love;

My Arthur, whom I shall not see
   Till all my widowed race be run;
   Dear as the mother to the son,
More than my brothers are to me.   20

10

I hear the noise about thy keel;
   I hear the bell struck in the night;
   I see the cabin window bright;
I see the sailor at the wheel.

Thou bring'st the sailor to his wife,   5
   And traveled men from foreign lands;
   And letters unto trembling hands:
And, thy dark freight, a vanished life.

So bring him; we have idle dreams;
   This look of quiet flatters thus   10
   Our home-bred fancies. O, to us,
The fools of habit, sweeter seems

3. The morning star.

The forest cracked, the waters curled,   5
    The cattle huddled on the lea;
    And wildly dashed on tower and tree
The sunbeam strikes along the world:

And but for fancies, which aver
    That all thy motions gently pass   10
    Athwart a plane of molten glass,
I scarce could brook the strain and stir

That makes the barren branches loud;
    And but for fear it is not so,
    The wild unrest that lives in woe   15
Would dote and pore on yonder cloud

That rises upward always higher,
    And onward drags a laboring breast,
    And topples round the dreary west,
A looming bastion fringed with fire.   20

* * *

19

The Danube to the Severn[2] gave
    The darkened heart that beat no more;
    They laid him by the pleasant shore,
And in the hearing of the wave.

There twice a day the Severn fills;   5
    The salt sea water passes by,
    And hushes half the babbling Wye,[3]
And makes a silence in the hills.

The Wye is hushed nor moved along,
    And hushed my deepest grief of all,   10
    When filled with tears that cannot fall,
I brim with sorrow drowning song.

The tide flows down, the wave again
    Is vocal in its wooded walls;
    My deeper anguish also falls,   15
And I can speak a little then.

* * *

21

I sing to him that rests below,
    And, since the grasses round me wave,

2. Hallam died at Vienna on the Danube. His burial place is on the banks of the Severn, a tidal river in the southwest of England.
3. The water of the Wye River, a tributary of the Severn, is dammed up as the tide flows in, and its sound is silenced until, with the turn of the tide, its "wave" once more becomes "vocal" (lines 13–14); these stanzas were written at Tintern Abbey in the Wye River country.

I take the grasses of the grave,[4]
And make them pipes whereon to blow.

The traveler hears me now and then,   5
   And sometimes harshly will he speak:
   "This fellow would make weakness weak,
And melt the waxen hearts of men."

Another answers: "Let him be,
   He loves to make parade of pain,   10
   That with his piping he may gain
The praise that comes to constancy."

A third is wroth: "Is this an hour
   For private sorrow's barren song,
   When more and more the people throng   15
The chairs and thrones of civil power?

"A time to sicken and to swoon,
   When Science reaches forth her arms[5]
   To feel from world to world, and charms
Her secret from the latest moon?"[6]   20

Behold, ye speak an idle thing;
   Ye never knew the sacred dust.
   I do but sing because I must,
And pipe but as the linnets sing;

And one is glad; her note is gay,   25
   For now her little ones have ranged;
   And one is sad; her note is changed,
Because her brood is stolen away.

22

The path by which we twain did go,
   Which led by tracts that pleased us well,
   Through four sweet years arose and fell,
From flower to flower, from snow to snow;

And we with singing cheered the way,   5
   And, crowned with all the season lent,
   From April on to April went,
And glad at heart from May to May.

But where the path we walked began
   To slant the fifth autumnal slope,[7]   10
   As we descended following Hope,
There sat the Shadow feared of man;

4. The speaker assumes that the burial was in the churchyard; in fact, Hallam's body was interred in a vault inside St. Andrews church at Clevedon, Somersetshire, on January 3, 1834. See section 10, lines 11–16.
5. Astronomical instruments such as telescopes.
6. Probably alluding to the discovery, in 1846, of the planet Neptune and its moon.
7. Hallam died in early autumn (September 15, 1833) in the fifth year of the friendship.

Who broke our fair companionship,
   And spread his mantle dark and cold,
   And wrapped thee formless in the fold,
And dulled the murmur on thy lip,   15

And bore thee where I could not see
   Nor follow, though I walk in haste,
   And think that somewhere in the waste
The Shadow sits and waits for me.   20

23

Now, sometimes in my sorrow shut,
   Or breaking into song by fits,
   Alone, alone, to where he sits,
The Shadow cloaked from head to foot,

Who keeps the keys of all the creeds,   5
   I wander, often falling lame,
   And looking back to whence I came,
Or on to where the pathway leads;

And crying, How changed from where it ran
   Through lands where not a leaf was dumb,   10
   But all the lavish hills would hum
The murmur of a happy Pan;

When each by turns was guide to each,
   And Fancy light from Fancy caught,
   And Thought leapt out to wed with Thought   15
Ere Thought could wed itself with Speech;

And all we met was fair and good,
   And all was good that Time could bring,
   And all the secret of the Spring
Moved in the chambers of the blood;   20

And many an old philosophy
   On Argive heights divinely sang,[8]
   And round us all the thicket rang
To many a flute of Arcady.[9]

24

And was the day of my delight
   As pure and perfect as I say?
   The very source and fount of day
Is dashed with wandering isles of night.[1]

If all was good and fair we met,   5
   This earth had been the Paradise
   It never looked to human eyes
Since our first sun arose and set.

And is it that the haze of grief
   Makes former gladness loom so great?   10

8. In classical times the Greek city of Argos was renowned for its music.
9. Sheep-raising region in Greece associated with pastoral poetry.
1. Moving spots on the sun.

The lowness of the present state,
That sets the past in this relief?

Or that the past will always win
    A glory from its being far,
    And orb into the perfect star   15
We saw not when we moved therein? [2]

25

I know that this was Life—the track
    Whereon with equal feet we fared;
    And then, as now, the day prepared
The daily burden for the back.

But this it was that made me move   5
    As light as carrier birds in air;
    I loved the weight I had to bear,
Because it needed help of Love;

Nor could I weary, heart or limb,
    When mighty Love would cleave in twain   10
    The lading of a single pain,
And part it, giving half to him.

26

Still onward winds the dreary way;
    I with it, for I long to prove
    No lapse of moons can canker Love,
Whatever fickle tongues may say.

And if that eye which watches guilt   5
    And goodness, and hath power to see
    Within the green the mouldered tree,
And towers fallen as soon as built—

O, if indeed that eye foresee
    Or see—in Him is no before—   10
    In more of life true life no more
And Love the indifference to be,

Then might I find, ere yet the morn
    Breaks hither over Indian seas,
    That Shadow waiting with the keys,   15
To shroud me from my proper scorn. [3]

27

I envy not in any moods
    The captive void of noble rage,
    The linnet born within the cage,
That never knew the summer woods;

2. The speaker speculates whether past experiences seem so much more "pure and perfect" (line 2) than present ones because they are far distant from us in time just as our planet Earth would have the deceptive appearance of being a perfect orb if we viewed it from a great distance in space, as from another planet. See *Locksley Hall Sixty Years After*, lines 187–92.

3. The Deity, being outside time, sees (rather than foresees) whether or not the rest of life ("more of life," line 11) will be pointless. If pointless then the way for the speaker to deal with his self-scorn ("proper scorn") might be to seek death.

I envy not the beast that takes   5
    His license in the field of time,
    Unfettered by the sense of crime,
To whom a conscience never wakes;

Nor, what may count itself as blest,
    The heart that never plighted troth   10
    But stagnates in the weeds of sloth;
Nor any want-begotten rest.[4]

I hold it true, whate'er befall;
    I feel it, when I sorrow most;
    'Tis better to have loved and lost   15
Than never to have loved at all.

28

The time draws near the birth of Christ.[5]
    The moon is hid, the night is still;
    The Christmas bells from hill to hill
Answer each other in the mist.

Four voices of four hamlets round,   5
    From far and near, on mead and moor,
    Swell out and fail, as if a door
Were shut between me and the sound;

Each voice four changes [6] on the wind,
    That now dilate, and now decrease,   10
    Peace and goodwill, goodwill and peace,
Peace and goodwill, to all mankind.

This year I slept and woke with pain,
    I almost wished no more to wake,
    And that my hold on life would break   15
Before I heard those bells again;

But they my troubled spirit rule,
    For they controlled me when a boy;
    They bring me sorrow touched with joy,
The merry, merry bells of Yule.   20

* * *

30

With trembling fingers did we weave
    The holly round the Christmas hearth;
    A rainy cloud possessed the earth,
And sadly fell our Christmas eve.

At our old pastimes in the hall   5
    We gamboled, making vain pretense
    Of gladness, with an awful sense
Of one mute Shadow watching all.

4. Complacency resulting from some
deficiency or "want."
5. The first Christmas after Hallam's
death (1833); the setting is Tennyson's
family home in Lincolnshire.
6. Different sequences in which church
bells are pealed.

We paused: the winds were in the beech;
   We heard them sweep the winter land;   10
   And in a circle hand-in-hand
Sat silent, looking each at each.

Then echo-like our voices rang;
   We sung, though every eye was dim,
   A merry song we sang with him   15
Last year; impetuously we sang.

We ceased; a gentler feeling crept
   Upon us: surely rest is meet.[7]
   "They rest," we said, "their sleep is sweet,"
And silence followed, and we wept.   20

Our voices took a higher range;
   Once more we sang: "They do not die
   Nor lose their mortal sympathy,
Nor change to us, although they change;

"Rapt [8] from the fickle and the frail   25
   With gathered power, yet the same,
   Pierces the keen seraphic flame
From orb to orb,[9] from veil to veil."

Rise, happy morn, rise, holy morn,
   Draw forth the cheerful day from night: 30
   O Father, touch the east, and light
The light that shone when Hope was born.

* * *

34

My own dim life should teach me this,
   That life shall live forevermore,
   Else earth is darkness at the core,
And dust and ashes all that is;

This round of green, this orb of flame,   5
   Fantastic beauty; such as lurks
   In some wild poet, when he works
Without a conscience or an aim.[1]

What then were God to such as I?
   'Twere hardly worth my while to choose   10
   Of things all mortal, or to use
A little patience ere I die;

'Twere best at once to sink to peace,
   Like birds the charming serpent draws,[2]

---

7. Proper or appropriate.
8. Carried away from.
9. The angelic spirit ("flame") of the dead moves from star to star.
1. Perhaps Thomas Lovell Beddoes, a brilliantly promising but erratic poet, admired by Tennyson, who committed suicide in 1849.
2. Some snakes are reputed to capture their prey by casting a charm.

To drop head-foremost in the jaws   15
Of vacant darkness and to cease.

35

Yet if some voice that man could trust
  Should murmur from the narrow house,
  "The cheeks drop in, the body bows;
Man dies, nor is there hope in dust";

Might I not say? "Yet even here,   5
  But for one hour, O Love, I strive
  To keep so sweet a thing alive."
But I should turn mine ears and hear

The moanings of the homeless sea,
  The sound of streams that swift or slow   10
  Draw down Aeonian hills,[3] and sow
The dust of continents to be;

And Love would answer with a sigh,
  "The sound of that forgetful shore
  Will change my sweetness more and more,   15
Half-dead to know that I shall die."

O me, what profits it to put
  An idle case? If Death were seen
  At first as Death, Love had not been,
Or been in narrowest working shut,   20

Mere fellowship of sluggish moods,
  Or in his coarsest Satyr-shape
  Had bruised the herb and crushed the grape,
And basked and battened in the woods.[4]

* * *

39

Old warder of these buried bones,
  And answering now my random stroke
  With fruitful cloud and living smoke,
Dark yew, that graspest at the stones

And dippest toward the dreamless head,   5
  To thee too comes the golden hour
  When flower is feeling after flower;[5]
But Sorrow—fixed upon the dead,

And darkening the dark graves of men—
  What whispered from her lying lips?   10

3. Hills that are aeons old, seemingly everlasting.
4. Lines 18 ff. may be paraphrased: if we knew death to be final and that no afterlife were possible, love could not exist except on a primitive or bestial level.

5. The ancient yew tree in the graveyard was described in section 2 as never changing. Now the speaker discovers that in the flowering season, if the tree is struck ("my random stroke," line 2), it gives off a cloud of golden pollen.

Thy gloom is kindled at the tips,[6]
And passes into gloom again.

* * *

44

How fares it with the happy dead?
    For here the man is more and more;
    But he forgets the days before
God closed the doorways of his head.[7]

The days have vanished, tone and tint,   5
    And yet perhaps the hoarding sense [8]
    Gives out at times (he knows not whence)
A little flash, a mystic hint;

And in the long harmonious years
    (If Death so taste Lethean springs [9])   10
    May some dim touch of earthly things
Surprise thee ranging with thy peers.

If such a dreamy touch should fall,
    O turn thee round, resolve the doubt;
    My guardian angel will speak out   15
In that high place, and tell thee all.

* * *

47

That each, who seems a separate whole,
    Should move his rounds,[1] and fusing all
    The skirts [2] of self again, should fall
Remerging in the general Soul,

Is faith as vague as all unsweet.   5
    Eternal form shall still divide
    The eternal soul from all beside;
And I shall know him when we meet;

And we shall sit at endless feast,
    Enjoying each the other's good.   10
    What vaster dream can hit the mood
Of Love on earth? He seeks at least

Upon the last and sharpest height,
    Before the spirits fade away,
    Some landing place, to clasp and say,   15
"Farewell! We lose ourselves in light."

---

6. Only the tips of the yew-branches are in flower.
7. This difficult stanza has been variously interpreted. If "man" (line 2) refers to the dead, the passage means that in our living world the dead man is more and more remembered, but that he, in the afterworld, is shut off through death from remembering past experiences on earth. Alternatively if "man" refers to living mankind rather than to the "happy dead," the passage means that as man grows up (line 2) he forgets his earliest infancy, especially the two-year period before the sutures of his skull are closed.
8. Memory.
9. I.e., springs of forgetfulness.
1. I.e., go through the customary circuit of life.
2. Outer edges or fringes.

48

If these brief lays, of Sorrow born,
　　Were taken to be such as closed
　　Grave doubts and answers here proposed,
Then these were such as men might scorn.

Her [3] care is not to part and prove;　　　　　5
　　She takes, when harsher moods remit,
　　What slender shade of doubt may flit,
And makes it vassal unto love;

And hence, indeed, she sports with words,
　　But better serves a wholesome law,　　　　10
　　And holds it sin and shame to draw
The deepest measure from the chords;

Nor dare she trust a larger lay,
　　But rather loosens from the lip
　　Short swallow-flights of song, that dip　　15
Their wings in tears, and skim away.

* * *

50

Be near me when my light is low,
　　When the blood creeps, and the nerves prick
　　And tingle; and the heart is sick,
And all the wheels of being slow.

Be near me when the sensuous frame　　　　5
　　Is racked with pangs that conquer trust;
　　And Time, a maniac scattering dust,
And Life, a Fury slinging flame.

Be near me when my faith is dry,
　　And men the flies of latter spring,　　　　10
　　That lay their eggs, and sting and sing
And weave their petty cells and die.

Be near me when I fade away,
　　To point the term of human strife,
　　And on the low dark verge of life　　　　15
The twilight of eternal day.

* * *

54

O, yet we trust that somehow good
　　Will be the final goal of ill,
　　To pangs of nature, sins of will,
Defects of doubt, and taints of blood;

That nothing walks with aimless feet;　　　　5
　　That not one life shall be destroyed,

---

3. I.e., sorrow's.

Or cast as rubbish to the void,
When God hath made the pile complete;

That not a worm is cloven in vain;
    That not a moth with vain desire   10
    Is shriveled in a fruitless fire,
Or but subserves another's gain.

Behold, we know not anything;
    I can but trust that good shall fall
    At last—far off—at last, to all,   15
And every winter change to spring.

So runs my dream; but what am I?
    An infant crying in the night;
    An infant crying for the light,
And with no language but a cry.   20

55

The wish, that of the living whole
    No life may fail beyond the grave,
    Derives it not from what we have
The likest God within the soul?

Are God and Nature then at strife,   5
    That Nature lends such evil dreams?
    So careful of the type [4] she seems,
So careless of the single life,

That I, considering everywhere
    Her secret meaning in her deeds,   10
    And finding that of fifty seeds
She often brings but one to bear,

I falter where I firmly trod,
    And falling with my weight of cares
    Upon the great world's altar-stairs   15
That slope through darkness up to God,

I stretch lame hands of faith, and grope,
    And gather dust and chaff, and call
    To what I feel is Lord of all,
And faintly trust the larger hope.[5]   20

56

"So careful of the type?" but no.
    From scarpéd [6] cliff and quarried stone
    She [7] cries, "A thousand types are gone;
I care for nothing, all shall go.

"Thou makest thine appeal to me: 5
    I bring to life, I bring to death;
    The spirit does but mean the breath:
I know no more." And he, shall he,

4. Species.
5. As expressed in lines 1–2 of this section.
6. Cut away so that the strata are exposed.
7. Nature.

Man, her last work, who seemed so fair,
    Such splendid purpose in his eyes,   10
    Who rolled the psalm to wintry skies,
Who built him fanes [8] of fruitless prayer,

Who trusted God was love indeed
    And love Creation's final law—
    Though Nature, red in tooth and claw   15
With ravine, shrieked against his creed—

Who loved, who suffered countless ills,
    Who battled for the True, the Just,
    Be blown about the desert dust,
Or sealed within the iron hills? [9]   20

No more? A monster then, a dream,
    A discord. Dragons of the prime,
    That tare [1] each other in their slime,
Were mellow music matched with [2] him.

O life as futile, then, as frail!   25
    O for thy voice to soothe and bless!
    What hope of answer, or redress?
Behind the veil, behind the veil.

57

Peace; come away: [3] the song of woe
    Is after all an earthly song.
    Peace; come away: we do him wrong
To sing so wildly: let us go.

Come; let us go: your cheeks are pale;   5
    But half my life I leave behind.
    Methinks my friend is richly shrined;
But I shall pass, my work will fail.

Yet in these ears, till hearing dies,
    One set slow bell will seem to toll   10
    The passing of the sweetest soul
That ever looked with human eyes.

I hear it now, and o'er and o'er,
    Eternal greetings to the dead;
    And "Ave,[4] Ave, Ave," said,   15
"Adieu, adieu," forevermore.

58

In those sad words I took farewell.
    Like echoes in sepulchral halls,
    As drop by drop the water falls
In vaults and catacombs, they fell;

---

8. Temples.
9. Preserved like fossils in rock.
1. Tore (archaic).
2. In comparison with.

3. Perhaps addressed to Emily Tennyson, the poet's sister and Hallam's fiancée.
4. Hail.

And, falling, idly broke the peace   5
   Of hearts that beat from day to day,
   Half-conscious of their dying clay,
And those cold crypts where they shall cease.

The high Muse answered: "Wherefore grieve
   Thy brethren with a fruitless tear?   10
   Abide a little longer here,
And thou shalt take a nobler leave."

59

O Sorrow, wilt thou live with me
   No casual mistress, but a wife,[5]
   My bosom friend and half of life;
As I confess it needs must be?

O Sorrow, wilt thou rule my blood,   5
   Be sometimes lovely like a bride,
   And put thy harsher moods aside,
If thou wilt have me wise and good?

My centered passion cannot move,
   Nor will it lessen from today;   10
   But I'll have leave at times to play
As with the creature of my love;

And set thee forth, for thou art mine,
   With so much hope for years to come,
   That, howsoe'er I know thee, some   15
Could hardly tell what name were thine.

* * *

64

Dost thou[6] look back on what hath been,
   As some divinely gifted man,
   Whose life in low estate began
And on a simple village green;

Who breaks his birth's invidious bar,   5
   And grasps the skirts of happy chance,
   And breasts the blows of circumstance,
And grapples with his evil star;

Who makes by force his merit known
   And lives to clutch the golden keys,[7]   10
   To mold a mighty state's decrees,
And shape the whisper of the throne;

And moving up from high to higher,
   Becomes on Fortune's crowning slope

---

5. Cf. *Richard II*, V.i.93–94: "Come, come, in wooing sorrow let's be brief, / Since, wedding it, there is such length in grief" [noted by Christopher Ricks].
6. I.e., Hallam.
7. Badges of high public office.

The pillar of a people's hope,   15
The center of a world's desire;

Yet feels, as in a pensive dream,
    When all his active powers are still,
    A distant dearness in the hill,
A secret sweetness in the stream,   20

The limit of his narrower fate,
    While yet beside its vocal springs
    He played at counselors and kings,
With one that was his earliest mate;

Who plows with pain his native lea   25
    And reaps the labor of his hands,
    Or in the furrow musing stands:
"Does my old friend remember me?"
                        * * *
                        67
When on my bed the moonlight falls,
    I know that in thy place of rest
    By that broad water of the west[8]
There comes a glory on the walls:

Thy marble bright in dark appears,   5
    As slowly steals a silver flame
    Along the letters of thy name,
And o'er the number of thy years.

The mystic glory swims away,
    From off my bed the moonlight dies;   10
    And closing eaves of wearied eyes
I sleep till dusk is dipped in gray;

And then I know the mist is drawn
    A lucid veil from coast to coast,
    And in the dark church like a ghost   15
Thy tablet glimmers to the dawn.
                        * * *
                        70
I cannot see the features right,
    When on the gloom I strive to paint
    The face I know; the hues are faint
And mix with hollow masks of night;

Cloud-towers by ghostly masons wrought,   5
    A gulf that ever shuts and gapes,
    A hand that points, and palléd shapes
In shadowy thoroughfares of thought;

8. The Severn River.

And crowds that stream from yawning doors,
　　And shoals of puckered faces drive;　　　　　　　10
　　Dark bulks that tumble half alive,
And lazy lengths on boundless shores;

Till all at once beyond the will
　　I hear a wizard music roll,
　　And through a lattice on the soul　　　　　　　15
Looks thy fair face and makes it still.

71

Sleep, kinsman thou to death and trance
　　And madness, thou [9] has forged at last
　　A night-long present of the past
In which we went through summer France.[1]

Hadst thou such credit with the soul?　　　　　　5
　　Then bring an opiate trebly strong,
　　Drug down the blindfold sense of wrong,
That so my pleasure may be whole;

While now we talk as once we talked
　　Of men and minds, the dust of change,　　　　10
　　The days that grow to something strange,
In walking as of old we walked

Beside the river's wooded reach,
　　The fortress, and the mountain ridge,
　　The cataract flashing from the bridge,　　　　15
The breaker breaking on the beach.

72

Risest thou thus, dim dawn, again,[2]
　　And howlest, issuing out of night,
　　With blasts that blow the poplar white,
And lash with storm the streaming pane?

Day, when my crowned estate [3] begun　　　　　5
　　To pine in that reverse of doom,[4]
　　Which sickened every living bloom,
And blurred the splendor of the sun;

Who usherest in the dolorous hour
　　With thy quick tears that make the rose　　　10
　　Pull sideways, and the daisy close
Her crimson fringes to the shower;

Who mightst have heaved a windless flame
　　Up the deep East, or, whispering, played

---

9. I.e., sleep.
1. In the summer of 1830, Hallam and Tennyson went through southern France en route to Spain.
2. September 15, 1834, the first anniversary of Hallam's death.
3. State of happiness.
4. The reversal of disaster which doom brought upon him when Hallam died.

A checker-work of beam and shade   15
Along the hills, yet looked the same,

As wan, as chill, as wild as now;
    Day, marked as with some hideous crime,
    When the dark hand struck down through time,
And canceled nature's best: but thou,   20

Lift as thou mayst thy burthened brows
    Through clouds that drench the morning star,
    And whirl the ungarnered sheaf afar,
And sow the sky with flying boughs,

And up thy vault with roaring sound   25
    Climb thy thick noon, disastrous day;
    Touch thy dull goal of joyless gray,
And hide thy shame beneath the ground.

* * *

75

I leave thy praises unexpressed
    In verse that brings myself relief,
    And by the measure of my grief
I leave thy greatness to be guessed.

What practice howsoe'er expert   5
    In fitting aptest words to things,
    Or voice the richest-toned that sings,
Hath power to give thee as thou wert?

I care not in these fading days
    To raise a cry that lasts not long,   10
    And round thee with the breeze of song
To stir a little dust of praise.

Thy leaf has perished in the green,
    And, while we breathe beneath the sun,
    The world which credits what is done   15
Is cold to all that might have been.

So here shall silence guard thy fame;
    But somewhere, out of human view,
    Whate'er thy hands are set to do
Is wrought with tumult of acclaim.   20

* * *

78

Again at Christmas [5] did we weave
    The holly round the Christmas hearth;
    The silent snow possessed the earth,
And calmly fell our Christmas eve.

_____

5. The second Christmas (1834) after Hallam's death.

The yule clog [6] sparkled keen with frost,   5
   No wing of wind the region swept,
   But over all things brooding slept
The quiet sense of something lost.

As in the winters left behind,
   Again our ancient games had place,   10
   The mimic picture's [7] breathing grace,
And dance and song and hoodman-blind.

Who showed a token of distress?
   No single tear, no mark of pain—
   O sorrow, then can sorrow wane?   15
O grief, can grief be changed to less?

O last regret, regret can die!
   No—mixed with all this mystic frame,
   Her [8] deep relations are the same,
But with long use her tears are dry.   20

* * *

82

I wage not any feud with Death
   For changes wrought on form and face;
   No lower life that earth's embrace
May breed with him can fright my faith.

Eternal process moving on,   5
   From state to state the spirit walks;
   And these are but the shattered stalks,
Or ruined chrysalis of one.

Nor blame I Death, because he bare
   The use of virtue out of earth;   10
   I know transplanted human worth
Will bloom to profit, otherwhere.

For this alone on Death I wreak
   The wrath that garners in my heart:
   He put our lives so far apart   15
We cannot hear each other speak.

83

Dip down upon the northern shore,
   O sweet new-year [9] delaying long;
   Thou doest expectant Nature wrong;
Delaying long, delay no more.

What stays thee from the clouded noons,   5
   Thy sweetness from its proper place?
   Can trouble live with April days,
Or sadness in the summer moons?

6. Log.
7. A game in which the participants pose in the manner of some famous statue or painting and the spectators try to guess what work of art is being mimicked.
8. I.e., sorrow's.
9. Spring of 1835.

Bring orchis, bring the foxglove spire,
    The little speedwell's [1] darling blue,
    Deep tulips dashed with fiery dew,
Laburnums, dropping-wells of fire.   10

O thou, new-year, delaying long,
    Delayest the sorrow in my blood,
    That longs to burst a frozen bud   15
And flood a fresher throat with song.

84

When I contemplate all alone
    The life that had been thine below,
    And fix my thoughts on all the glow
To which thy crescent would have grown,

I see thee sitting crowned with good,   5
    A central warmth diffusing bliss
    In glance and smile, and clasp and kiss,
On all the branches of thy blood;

Thy blood, my friend, and partly mine;
    For now the day was drawing on,   10
    When thou shouldst link thy life with one
Of mine own house, and boys of thine

Had babbled "Uncle" on my knee;
    But that remorseless iron hour
    Made cypress of her orange flower,[2]   15
Despair of hope, and earth of thee.

I seem to meet their least desire,
    To clap their cheeks, to call them mine.
    I see their unborn faces shine
Beside the never-lighted fire.   20

I see myself an honored guest,
    Thy partner in the flowery walk
    Of letters, genial table talk,
Or deep dispute, and graceful jest;

While now thy prosperous labor fills   25
    The lips of men with honest praise,
    And sun by sun the happy days
Descend below the golden hills

With promise of a morn as fair;
    And all the train of bounteous hours
    Conduct, by paths of growing powers,   30
To reverence and the silver hair;

Till slowly worn her earthly robe,
    Her lavish mission richly wrought,

---

1. A blue spring flower.
2. Orange blossoms are associated with brides—here the poet's sister, Emily Tennyson, to whom Hallam had been engaged.

Leaving great legacies of thought,   35
Thy spirit should fail from off the globe;

What time mine own might also flee,
    As linked with thine in love and fate,
    And, hovering o'er the dolorous strait
To the other shore, involved in thee,   40

Arrive at last the blessed goal,
    And He that died in Holy Land
    Would reach us out the shining hand,
And take us as a single soul.

What reed was that on which I leant?   45
    Ah, backward fancy, wherefore wake
    The old bitterness again, and break
The low beginnings of content?
                    * * *
                      86
Sweet after showers, ambrosial air,
    That rollest from the gorgeous gloom
    Of evening over brake and bloom
And meadow, slowly breathing bare

The round of space,[3] and rapt below   5
    Through all the dewy-tasseled wood,
    And shadowing down the hornéd flood[4]
In ripples, fan my brows and blow

The fever from my cheek, and sigh
    The full new life that feeds thy breath   10
    Throughout my frame, till Doubt and Death,
Ill brethren, let the fancy fly

From belt to belt of crimson seas
    On leagues of odor streaming far,
    To where in yonder orient star   15
A hundred spirits whisper "Peace."
                      87
I passed beside the reverend walls[5]
    In which of old I wore the gown;
    I roved at random through the town,
And saw the tumult of the halls;

And heard once more in college fanes   5
    The storm their high-built organs make,
    And thunder-music, rolling, shake
The prophet blazoned on the panes;

3. Air that is slowly clearing the clouds
from the sky.
4. "Between two promontories." [Tenny-
son's comment].
5. Of Trinity College, Cambridge University.

And caught once more the distant shout,
  The measured pulse of racing oars   10
  Among the willows; paced the shores
And many a bridge, and all about

The same gray flats again, and felt
  The same, but not the same; and last
  Up that long walk of limes I passed   15
To see the rooms in which he dwelt.

Another name was on the door.
  I lingered; all within was noise
  Of songs, and clapping hands, and boys
That crashed the glass and beat the floor;   20

Where once we held debate, a band
  Of youthful friends,[6] on mind and art,
  And labor, and the changing mart,
And all the framework of the land;

When one would aim an arrow fair,   25
  But send it slackly from the string;
  And one would pierce an outer ring,
And one an inner, here and there;

And last the master bowman, he,
  Would cleave the mark. A willing ear   30
  We lent him. Who but hung to hear
The rapt oration flowing free

From point to point, with power and grace
  And music in the bounds of law,[7]
  To those conclusions when we saw   35
The God within him light his face,

And seem to lift the form, and glow
  In azure orbits heavenly-wise;
  And over those ethereal eyes
The bar of Michael Angelo?[8]   40

                88
Wild bird, whose warble, liquid sweet,
  Rings Eden through the budded quicks,[9]

6. The "Apostles," an undergraduate club to which Tennyson and Hallam had belonged.
7. An essay presented by Hallam at Cambridge in 1831 provides an example of his skill in theological argument (see *The Writings of Arthur Hallam,* edited by T. H. V. Motter, 1943, pp. 198–213). This essay, much admired by Tennyson, may have influenced the main argument of *In Memoriam.* In his essay Hallam develops an idea he had stated in a letter to Tennyson's sister: "It is by the heart, not by the head, that we must all be convinced of the two great fundamental truths, the reality of Love, and the reality of Evil." See also *In Memoriam,* section 109, lines 1–8 below.
8. Hallam, like Michelangelo, had a prominent ridge of bone above his eyes.
9. Hawthorn hedges. The "wild bird" is presumably a nightingale.

O tell me where the senses mix,
O tell me where the passions meet,

Whence radiate: fierce extremes employ 45
   Thy spirits in the darkening leaf,[1]
   And in the midmost heart of grief
Thy passion clasps a secret joy;

And I—my harp would prelude woe—
   I cannot all command the strings; 50
   The glory of the sum of things
Will flash along the chords and go.

89

Witch elms that counterchange the floor
Of this flat lawn with dusk and bright;[2]
   And thou, with all thy breadth and height
Of foliage, towering sycamore;

How often, hither wandering down, 5
   My Arthur found your shadows fair,
   And shook to all the liberal air
The dust and din and steam of town!

He brought an eye for all he saw;
   He mixed in all our simple sports; 10
   They pleased him, fresh from brawling courts
And dusty purlieus of the law.[3]

O joy to him in this retreat,
   Immantled in ambrosial dark,
   To drink the cooler air, and mark 15
The landscape winking through the heat!

O sound to rout the brood of cares,
   The sweep of scythe in morning dew,
   The gust that round the garden flew,
And tumbled half the mellowing pears! 20

O bliss, when all in circle drawn
   About him, heart and ear were fed
   To hear him, as he lay and read
The Tuscan poets[4] on the lawn!

Or in the all-golden afternoon 25
   A guest, or happy sister, sung,
   Or here she brought the harp and flung
A ballad to the brightening moon.

Nor less it pleased in livelier moods,
   Beyond the bounding hill to stray, 30

1. Cf. Keats' *Ode to a Nightingale* (lines 10 and 60) and his sonnet on *King Lear*, line 5.
2. Shadows of the elm tree checker the lawn at Somersby, the Tennysons' country home.
3. Hallam became a law student in London after leaving Cambridge.
4. Petrarch and Dante.

And break the livelong summer day
With banquet in the distant woods;

Whereat we glanced from theme to theme,
    Discussed the books to love or hate,
    Or touched the changes of the state,   35
Or threaded some Socratic dream;[5]

But if I praised the busy town,
    He loved to rail against it still,
    For "ground in yonder social mill
We rub each other's angles down,   40

"And merge," he said, "in form and gloss
    The picturesque of man and man."
    We talked: the stream beneath us ran,
The wine-flask lying couched in moss,

Or cooled within the glooming wave;   45
    And last, returning from afar,
    Before the crimson-circled star [6]
Had fallen into her father's grave,

And brushing ankle-deep in flowers,
    We heard behind the woodbine veil   50
    The milk that bubbled in [7] the pail,
And buzzings of the honeyed hours.

* * *

91

When rosy plumelets tuft the larch,
    And rarely [8] pipes the mounted thrush,
    Or underneath the barren bush
Flits by the sea-blue bird [9] of March;

Come, wear the form by which I know   5
    Thy spirit in time among thy peers;
    The hope of unaccomplished years
Be large and lucid round thy brow.

When summer's hourly-mellowing change
    May breathe, with many roses sweet,   10
    Upon the thousand waves of wheat
That ripple round the lowly grange,

Come; not in watches of the night,
    But where the sunbeam broodeth warm,
    Come, beauteous in thine after form,   15
And like a finer light in light.

* * *

5. I.e., worked our way through some discourse of Socrates (as recorded by Plato).
6. Venus, which will sink into the west as the sun has done. According to the nebular hypothesis, planets were flung from the sun into the outer spaces of our solar system; in this sense the sun is the "father" of planets.
7. Into.
8. Exquisitely.
9. Kingfisher.

93

I shall not see thee. Dare I say
   No spirit ever brake the band
   That stays him from the native land
Where first he walked when clasped in clay?[1]

No visual shade of someone lost,   5
   But he, the Spirit himself, may come
   Where all the nerve of sense is numb,
Spirit to Spirit, Ghost to Ghost.

Oh, therefore from thy sightless[2] range
   With gods in unconjectured bliss,   10
   Oh, from the distance of the abyss
Of tenfold-complicated change,

Descend, and touch, and enter; hear
   The wish too strong for words to name,
   That in this blindness of the frame[3]   15
My Ghost may feel that thine is near.

94

How pure at heart and sound in head,
   With what divine affections bold
   Should be the man whose thought would hold
An hour's communion with the dead.

In vain shalt thou, or any, call   5
   The spirits from their golden day,
   Except, like them, thou too canst say,
My spirit is at peace with all.

They haunt the silence of the breast,
   Imaginations calm and fair,   10
   The memory like a cloudless air,
The conscience as a sea at rest;

But when the heart is full of din,
   And doubt beside the portal waits,
   They can but listen at the gates,   15
And hear the household jar within.

95

By night we lingered on the lawn,
   For underfoot the herb was dry;
   And genial warmth; and o'er the sky
The silvery haze of summer drawn;

And calm that let the tapers burn   5
   Unwavering: not a cricket chirred;

---

1. I.e., when he was alive and clothed in
flesh.

2. Invisible.
3. The living body.

The brook alone far off was heard,
And on the board the fluttering urn.[4]

And bats went round in fragrant skies,
    And wheeled or lit the filmy shapes[5]   10
    That haunt the dusk, with ermine capes
And woolly breasts and beaded eyes;

While now we sang old songs that pealed
    From knoll to knoll, where, couched at ease,
    The white kine glimmered, and the trees   15
Laid their dark arms[6] about the field.

But when those others, one by one,
    Withdrew themselves from me and night,
    And in the house light after light
Went out, and I was all alone,   20

A hunger seized my heart; I read
    Of that glad year which once had been,
    In those fallen leaves which kept their green,
The noble letters of the dead.

And strangely on the silence broke   25
    The silent-speaking words, and strange
    Was love's dumb cry defying change
To test his worth; and strangely spoke

The faith, the vigor, bold to dwell
    On doubts that drive the coward back,   30
    And keen through wordy snares to track
Suggestion to her inmost cell.

So word by word, and line by line,
    The dead man touched me from the past,
    And all at once it seemed at last   35
The[7] living soul was flashed on mine,

And mine in this was wound, and whirled
    About empyreal heights of thought,
    And came on that which is, and caught
The deep pulsations of the world,   40

Aeonian music[8] measuring out
    The steps of Time—the shocks of Chance—
    The blows of Death. At length my trance
Was canceled, stricken through with doubt.[9]

4. Urn to boil water for tea or coffee, heated by a fluttering flame.
5. The white-winged night moths called ermine moths.
6. Cast the shadows of their branches.
7. Printed "His" in the first edition; and line 37 read, in the first edition, "And mine in his was wound."
8. The music of the universe which has pulsated for aeons of time.
9. In a letter of 1874 replying to an inquiry about his experience of mystical

Vague words! but ah, how hard to frame   45
  In matter-molded forms of speech,
  Or even for intellect to reach
Through memory that which I became.

Till now the doubtful dusk revealed
  The knolls once more where, couched at ease,   50
  The white kine glimmered, and the trees
Laid their dark arms about the field;

And sucked from out the distant gloom
  A breeze began to tremble o'er
  The large leaves of the sycamore,   55
And fluctuate all the still perfume,

And gathering freshlier overhead,
  Rocked the full-foliaged elms, and swung
  The heavy-folded rose, and flung
The lilies to and fro, and said,   60

"The dawn, the dawn," and died away;
  And East and West, without a breath,
  Mixed their dim lights, like life and death,
To broaden into boundless day.

96

You say, but with no touch of scorn,
  Sweet-hearted, you,[1] whose light blue eyes
  Are tender over drowning flies,
You tell me, doubt is Devil-born.

I know not: one[2] indeed I knew   5
  In many a subtle question versed,
  Who touched a jarring lyre at first,
But ever strove to make it true;

Perplexed in faith, but pure in deeds,
  At last he beat his music out.   10

---

trances, Tennyson wrote: "A kind of waking trance I have frequently had, quite up from boyhood, when I have been all alone. This has generally come upon me through repeating my own name two or three times to myself silently, till all at once, as if were out of the intensity of the consciousness of individuality, the individuality itself seemed to dissolve and fade away into boundless being, and this not a confused state, but the clearest of the clearest, the surest of the surest, the weirdest of the weirdest, utterly beyond words, where death was an almost laughable impossibility, the loss of personality (if so it

were) seeming no extinction but the only true life. * * * This might * * * be the state which St. Paul describes, 'Whether in the body I cannot tell, or whether out of the body I cannot tell.' * * * I am ashamed of my feeble description. Have I not said the state is utterly beyond words? But in a moment, when I come back to my normal state of 'sanity,' I am ready to fight for *mein liebes Ich* [my dear self], and hold that it will last for aeons of aeons."—*Alfred Lord Tennyson, A Memoir*, 1897, I, 320.
1. A woman of simple faith, perhaps Emily Sellwood.
2. Hallam.

There lives more faith in honest doubt,
Believe me, than in half the creeds.

He fought his doubts and gathered strength,
    He would not make his judgment blind,
    He faced the specters of the mind   15
And laid them; thus he came at length

To find a stronger faith his own,
    And Power was with him in the night,
    Which makes the darkness and the light,
And dwells not in the light alone,   20

But in the darkness and the cloud,[3]
    As over Sinaï's peaks of old,
    While Israel made their gods of gold,
Although the trumpet blew so loud.

* * *

99

Risest thou thus, dim dawn, again,[4]
    So loud with voices of the birds,
    So thick with lowings of the herds,
Day, when I lost the flower of men;

Who tremblest through thy darkling red   5
    On yon swollen brook that bubbles fast[5]
    By meadows breathing of the past,
And woodlands holy to the dead;

Who murmurest in the foliage eaves
    A song that slights the coming care,[6]   10
    And Autumn laying here and there
A fiery finger on the leaves;

Who wakenest with thy balmy breath
    To myriads on the genial earth,
    Memories of bridal, or of birth,[7]   15
And unto myriads more, of death.

Oh, wheresoever those[8] may be,
    Betwixt the slumber of the poles,
    Today they count as kindred souls;
They know me not, but mourn with me.   20

* * *

3. See Exodus xix.16–25. After veiling Mount Sinai in a "cloud" of smoke, God addressed Moses from the darkness.
4. September 15, 1835, the second anniversary of Hallam's death.
5. Reflections of the clouded red light of dawn quiver on the surface of the fast-moving water. Cf. Shakespeare's *Sonnets* (33): "Full many a glorious morning have I seen * * * Gilding pale streams with heavenly alchemy."
4. I.e., disregards future events such as death or the coming of autumn. Cf. Shelley's *Ode to the West Wind.*
7. Cf. *Epilogue*, below, lines 117–28.
8. I.e., the "myriads" who remember death.

103

On that last night before we went
　　From out the doors where I was bred,[9]
　　I dreamed a vision of the dead,
Which left my after-morn content.

Methought I dwelt within a hall,　　　　　　　　5
　　And maidens with me; distant hills
　　From hidden summits fed with rills
A river sliding by the wall.

The hall with harp and carol rang.
　　They sang of what is wise and good　　　10
　　And graceful. In the center stood
A statue veiled, to which they sang;

And which, though veiled, was known to me,
　　The shape of him I loved, and love
　　Forever. Then flew in a dove　　　　　　15
And brought a summons from the sea; [1]

And when they learnt that I must go,
　　They wept and wailed, but led the way
　　To where the little shallop [2] lay
At anchor in the flood below;　　　　　　　20

And on by many a level mead,
　　And shadowing bluff that made the banks,
　　We glided winding under ranks
Of iris and the golden reed;

And still as vaster grew the shore　　　　　25
　　And rolled the floods in grander space,
　　The maidens gathered strength and grace
And presence, lordlier than before;

And I myself, who sat apart
　　And watched them, waxed in every limb;　　30
　　I felt the thews of Anakim,[3]
The pulses of a Titan's heart;

As one would sing the death of war,
　　And one would chant the history
　　Of that great race which is to be,[4]　　35
And one the shaping of a star;

Until the forward-creeping tides
　　Began to foam, and we to draw

9. In 1837 Tennyson and his family moved away from their home in Lincolnshire, which had been closely associated with his friendship with Hallam. In section 104 the move seems to occur in 1835, the year of the third Christmas after Hallam's death.
1. Cf. *Crossing the Bar:* "And one clear call for me."
2. A light open boat.
3. Plural of *Anak;* i.e., a reference to the giant sons of Anak. See Numbers xiii.33. The Titans (line 32) were giants of Greek mythology.
4. See the account of the "crowning race" in *Epilogue,* below, lines 128–44.

From deep to deep, to where we saw
A great ship lift her shining sides.[5]   40

The man we loved was there on deck,
    But thrice as large as man he bent
    To greet us. Up the side I went,
And fell in silence on his neck;

Whereat those maidens with one mind   45
    Bewailed their lot; I did them wrong:
    "We served thee here," they said, "so long,
And wilt thou leave us now behind?"

So rapt [6] I was, they could not win
    An answer from my lips, but he   50
    Replying, "Enter likewise ye
And go with us:" they entered in.

And while the wind began to sweep
    A music out of sheet and shroud,
    We steered her toward a crimson cloud   55
That landlike slept along the deep.

104

The time draws near the birth of Christ; [7]
    The moon is hid, the night is still;
    A single church below the hill
Is pealing, folded in the mist.

A single peal of bells below,   5
    That wakens at this hour of rest
    A single murmur in the breast,
That these are not the bells I know.

Like strangers' voices here they sound,
    In lands where not a memory strays,   10
    Nor landmark breathes of other days,
But all is new unhallowed ground.

*   *   *

106

Ring out, wild bells, to the wild sky,
    The flying cloud, the frosty light:
    The year is dying in the night;
Ring out, wild bells, and let him die.

Ring out the old, ring in the new,   5
    Ring, happy bells, across the snow:
    The year is going, let him go;
Ring out the false, ring in the true.

---

5. Cf. *Morte d'Arthur*, lines 255–322, in which Bedivere is left behind as Arthur's barge, the ship of death, sails away. In the present dream vision, not only is the speaker taken aboard but also his companions, who represent the creative arts of this world—"all the human powers and talents that do not pass with life but go along with it," as Tennyson said of this passage.
6. Entranced.
7. See note 9 to section 103.

Ring out the grief that saps the mind,
 For those that here we see no more;   10
 Ring out the feud of rich and poor,
Ring in redress to all mankind.

Ring out a slowly dying cause,
 And ancient forms of party strife;
 Ring in the nobler modes of life,   15
With sweeter manners, purer laws.

Ring out the want, the care, the sin,
 The faithless coldness of the times;
 Ring out, ring out my mournful rhymes,
But ring the fuller minstrel in.   20

Ring out false pride in place and blood,
 The civic slander and the spite;
 Ring in the love of truth and right,
Ring in the common love of good.

Ring out old shapes of foul disease;   25
 Ring out the narrowing lust of gold;
 Ring out the thousand wars of old,
Ring in the thousand years of peace.

Ring in the valiant man and free,
 The larger heart, the kindlier hand;   30
 Ring out the darkness of the land,
Ring in the Christ that is to be.[8]

107

It is the day when he was born,[9]
 A bitter day that early sank
 Behind a purple-frosty bank
Of vapor, leaving night forlorn.

The time admits not flowers or leaves   5
 To deck the banquet. Fiercely flies
 The blast of North and East, and ice
Makes daggers at the sharpened eaves,

And bristles all the brakes and thorns
 To yon hard crescent, as she hangs   10
 Above the wood which grides [1] and clangs
Its leafless ribs and iron horns

Together, in the drifts [2] that pass
 To darken on the rolling brine

---

8. These allusions to the second coming of Christ and to the millennium are derived from Revelation xx, but Tennyson has interpreted the Biblical account in his own way. He once told his son of his conviction that "the forms of Christian religion would alter; but that the spirit of Christ would still grow from more to more."
9. February 1.
1. Clashes with a strident noise.
2. Either cloud-drifts or clouds of snow.

That breaks the coast. But fetch the wine,   15
Arrange the board and brim the glass;

Bring in great logs and let them lie,
    To make a solid core of heat;
    Be cheerful-minded, talk and treat
Of all things even as he were by;   20

We keep the day. With festal cheer,
    With books and music, surely we
    Will drink to him, whate'er he be,
And sing the songs he loved to hear.

* * *

109

Heart-affluence in discursive talk
    From household fountains never dry;
    The critic clearness of an eye
That saw through all the Muses' walk; [3]

Seraphic intellect and force   5
    To seize and throw the doubts of man;
    Impassioned logic, which outran
The hearer in its fiery course;

High nature amorous of the good,
    But touched with no ascetic gloom;
    And passion pure in snowy bloom   10
Through all the years of April blood;

A love of freedom rarely felt,
    Of freedom in her regal seat
    Of England; not the schoolboy heat,
The blind hysterics of the Celt; [4]   15

And manhood fused with female grace
    In such a sort, the child would twine
    A trustful hand, unasked, in thine,
And find his comfort in thy face;   20

All these have been, and thee mine eyes
    Have looked on: if they looked in vain,
    My shame is greater who remain,
Nor let thy wisdom make me wise.

* * *

115

Now fades the last long streak of snow,
    Now burgeons every maze of quick [5]
    About the flowering squares,[6] and thick
By ashen roots the violets blow.

---

3. The realm of art and literature.   section 127, lines 7–8.
4. In particular the French at the time   5. In hawthorn hedges.
of the Revolution of 1789. See also   6. Fields.

Now rings the woodland loud and long,   5
   The distance takes a lovelier hue,
   And drowned in yonder living blue
The lark becomes a sightless song.

Now dance the lights on lawn and lea,
   The flocks are whiter down the vale,   10
   And milkier every milky sail
On winding stream or distant sea;

Where now the seamew pipes, or dives
   In yonder greening gleam, and fly
   The happy birds, that change their sky   15
To build and brood, that live their lives

From land to land; and in my breast
   Spring wakens too, and my regret
   Becomes an April violet,
And buds and blossoms like the rest.   20

* * *

118

Contémplate all this work of Time,
   The giant laboring in his youth;
   Nor dream of human love and truth,
As dying Nature's earth and lime;

But trust that those we call the dead   5
   Are breathers of an ampler day
   For ever nobler ends. They[7] say,
The solid earth whereon we tread

In tracts of fluent heat began,
   And grew to seeming-random forms,   10
   The seeming prey of cyclic storms,
Till at the last arose the man;

Who throve and branched from clime to clime,
   The herald of a higher race,
   And of himself in higher place,   15
If so he type[8] this work of time

Within himself, from more to more;
   Or, crowned with attributes of woe
   Like glories, move his course, and show
That life is not as idle ore,   20

But iron dug from central gloom,
   And heated hot with burning fears,
   And dipped in baths of hissing tears,
And battered with the shocks of doom

---

7. Geologists and astronomers.   8. Emulate, prefigure as a type.

To shape and use. Arise and fly   25
   The reeling Faun, the sensual feast;
   Move upward, working out the beast,
And let the ape and tiger die.

119

Doors, where my heart was used to beat
   So quickly, not as one that weeps
   I come once more; the city sleeps;
I smell the meadow in the street;

I hear a chirp of birds; I see   5
   Betwixt the black fronts long-withdrawn
   A light blue lane of early dawn,
And think of early days and thee,

And bless thee, for thy lips are bland,
   And bright the friendship of thine eye;   10
   And in my thoughts with scarce a sigh
I take the pressure of thine hand.

120

I trust I have not wasted breath:
   I think we are not wholly brain,
   Magnetic mockeries;[9] not in vain,
Like Paul[1] with beasts, I fought with Death;

Not only cunning casts in clay: 5
   Let Science prove we are, and then
   What matters Science unto men,
At least to me? I would not stay.

Let him, the wiser man who springs
   Hereafter, up from childhood shape   10
   His action like the greater ape,
But I was *born* to other things.

121

Sad Hesper[2] o'er the buried sun
   And ready, thou, to die with him,
   Thou watchest all things ever dim
And dimmer, and a glory done.

The team is loosened from the wain,[3]   5
   The boat is drawn upon the shore;
   Thou listenest to the closing door,
And life is darkened in the brain.

Bright Phosphor,[4] fresher for the night,
   By thee the world's great work is heard   10

---

9. Mechanisms operated by responses to electrical forces.
1. I Corinthians xv.32.
2. Evening star.
3. Hay wagon.
4. Morning star.

Beginning, and the wakeful bird;
Behind thee comes the greater light.[5]

The market boat is on the stream,
    And voices hail it from the brink;
    Thou hear'st the village hammer clink,   15
And see'st the moving of the team.

Sweet Hesper-Phosphor, double name[6]
    For what is one, the first, the last,
    Thou, like my present and my past,
Thy place is changed; thou art the same.   20
         * * *

123

There rolls the deep where grew the tree.
    O earth, what changes hast thou seen!
    There where the long street roars hath been
The stillness of the central sea.[7]

The hills are shadows, and they flow   5
    From form to form, and nothing stands;
    They melt like mist, the solid lands,
Like clouds they shape themselves and go.

But in my spirit will I dwell,
    And dream my dream, and hold it true;   10
    For though my lips may breathe adieu,
I cannot think the thing farewell.

124

That which we dare invoke to bless;
    Our dearest faith; our ghastliest doubt;
    He, They, One, All; within, without;
The Power in darkness whom we guess—

I found Him not in world or sun,   5
    Or eagle's wing, or insect's eye,[8]
    Nor through the questions men may try,
The petty cobwebs we have spun.

If e'er when faith had fallen asleep,
    I heard a voice, "believe no more,"   10
    And heard an ever-breaking shore
That tumbled in the Godless deep,

---

5. Cf. Genesis i.16: "The greater light to rule the day."
6. The same planet, Venus, is both evening star and morning star.
7. Cf. a passage from Sir Charles Lyell's *The Principles of Geology* (1832), a book well-known to Tennyson. In discussing the "interchange of sea and land" that has occurred "on the surface of our globe" Lyell remarks: "In the Mediterranean alone, many flourishing inland towns and a still greater number of ports now stand where the sea rolled its waves since the era when civilized nations first grew in Europe."
8. He does not discover satisfactory proof of God's existence in the 18th-century argument that because objects in nature are designed there must exist a designer.

A warmth within the breast would melt
   The freezing reason's colder part,
   And like a man in wrath the heart
Stood up and answered, "I have felt."   15

No, like a child in doubt and fear:
   But that blind clamor made me wise;
   Then was I as a child that cries,
But, crying, knows his father near;   20

And what I am beheld again
   What is, and no man understands;
   And out of darkness came the hands
That reach through nature, molding men.

* * *

126

Love is and was my lord and king,
   And in his presence I attend
   To hear the tidings of my friend,
Which every hour his couriers bring.

Love is and was my king and lord,   5
   And will be, though as yet I keep
   Within the court on earth, and sleep
Encompassed by his faithful guard,

And hear at times a sentinel
   Who moves about from place to place,
   And whispers to the worlds of space,   10
In the deep night, that all is well.

127

And all is well, though faith and form[9]
   Be sundered in the night of fear;
   Well roars the storm to those that hear
A deeper voice across the storm,

Proclaiming social truth shall spread,
   And justice, even though thrice again   5
   The red fool-fury of the Seine
Should pile her barricades with dead.[1]

But ill for him that wears a crown,[2]
   And him, the lazar, in his rags!   10
   They tremble, the sustaining crags;
The spires of ice are toppled down,

9. Traditional institutions through which faith was formerly expressed, such as the Church. See Carlyle's essay, *Characteristics*, above.
1. Revolutionary uprisings in France, in each of which a king lost his throne (line 9): in 1789 against Louis XVI, in 1830 against Charles X, and in 1848 against Louis Philippe. The third (line 6) would have been a prophecy if, as Tennyson recollected, section 126 was finished at a date earlier than 1848.
2. See 2 *Henry IV*, III.i.31: "Uneasy lies the head that wears a crown." "Lazar": pauper suffering from disease.

And molten up, and roar in flood;
  The fortress crashes from on high,
  The brute earth lightens[3] to the sky,   15
And the great Aeon[4] sinks in blood,

And compassed by the fires of hell,
  While thou, dear spirit, happy star,
  O'erlook'st the tumult from afar,
And smilest, knowing all is well.   20
* * *

129

Dear friend, far off, my lost desire,
  So far, so near in woe and weal,
  O loved the most, when most I feel
There is a lower and a higher;

Known and unknown, human, divine;   5
  Sweet human hand and lips and eye;
  Dear heavenly friend that canst not die,
Mine, mine, forever, ever mine;

Strange friend, past, present, and to be;
  Loved deeplier, darklier understood;   10
  Behold, I dream a dream of good,
And mingle all the world with thee.

130

Thy voice is on the rolling air;[5]
  I hear thee where the waters run;
  Thou standest in the rising sun,[6]
And in the setting thou art fair.

What art thou then? I cannot guess;   5
  But though I seem in star and flower
  To feel thee some diffusive power,
I do not therefore love thee less.

My love involves the love before;
  My love is vaster passion now;   10
  Tho' mix'd with God and Nature thou,
I seem to love thee more and more.

Far off thou art, but ever nigh;
  I have thee still, and I rejoice;
  I prosper, circled with thy voice;   15
I shall not lose thee tho' I die.

---

3. Is lit up by fire.
4. A vast tract of time, here perhaps modern western civilization.
5. Cf. Shelley, *Adonais*, 370 ff.: "He is made one with Nature: there is heard /
His voice in all her music" [noted by Christopher Ricks].
6. "And I saw an angel standing in the sun." Revelation xix.17.

131

O living will[7] that shalt endure
   When all that seems shall suffer shock,
   Rise in the spiritual rock,[8]
Flow through our deeds and make them pure,

That we may lift from out of dust   5
   A voice as unto him that hears,
   A cry above the conquered years
To one that with us works, and trust,

With faith that comes of self-control,
   The truths that never can be proved   10
   Until we close with all we loved,
And all we flow from, soul in soul.

From *Epilogue*[9]
* * *

And rise, O moon, from yonder down,
   Till over down and over dale
   All night the shining vapor sail
And pass the silent-lighted town,

The white-faced halls, the glancing rills,   5
   And catch at every mountain head,
   And o'er the friths[1] that branch and spread
Their sleeping silver through the hills;

And touch with shade the bridal doors,
   With tender gloom the roof, the wall;   10
   And breaking let the splendor fall
To spangle all the happy shores

By which they rest, and ocean sounds,
   And, star and system rolling past,
   A soul shall draw from out the vast   15
And strike his being into bounds,

And, moved through life of lower phase,
   Result in man,[2] be born and think,
   And act and love, a closer link
Betwixt us and the crowning race   20

Of those that, eye to eye, shall look
   On knowledge; under whose command

7. Tennyson later commented that he meant here the moral will of mankind.
8. Christ (see I Corinthians x.4).
9. The *Epilogue* describes the wedding day of Tennyson's sister Cecilia to Edmund Lushington. At the conclusion (reprinted here) the speaker reflects upon their moonlit wedding night and the kind of offspring which will result from their union.
1. Inlets of the sea.
2. A child will be conceived and will develop in embryo through various stages. This development is similar to the evolution of man from the animal to the human level and perhaps to a future higher stage of development.

Is Earth and Earth's, and in their hand
Is Nature like an open book;

No longer half-akin to brute,   25
    For all we thought and loved and did,
    And hoped, and suffered, is but seed
Of what in them is flower and fruit;

Whereof the man that with me trod
    This planet was a noble type   30
    Appearing ere the times were ripe,
That friend of mine who lives in God,

That God, which ever lives and loves,
    One God, one law, one element,
    And one far-off divine event,   35
To which the whole creation moves.

1833–50   1850

The Charge of the Light Brigade[1]

1
Half a league, half a league,
Half a league onward,
All in the valley of Death
    Rode the six hundred.
"Forward, the Light Brigade!   5
Charge for the guns!" he said.
Into the valley of Death
    Rode the six hundred.

2
"Forward, the Light Brigade!"
Was there a man dismayed?   10
Not though the soldier knew
    Someone had blundered.
Theirs not to make reply,
Theirs not to reason why,
Theirs but to do and die.   15
Into the valley of Death
    Rode the six hundred.

3
Cannon to right of them,
Cannon to left of them,
Cannon in front of them   20
    Volleyed and thundered;
Stormed at with shot and shell,

1. During the Crimean War, owing to confusion of orders, a brigade of British cavalry charged some entrenched batteries of Russian artillery. This blunder cost the lives of three fourths of the 600 horsemen engaged (see Cecil Woodham-Smith, *The Reason Why*, 1954). Tennyson rapidly composed his "ballad" (as he called the poem) after reading an account of the battle in a newspaper.

Boldly they rode and well,
Into the jaws of Death,
Into the mouth of hell   25
  Rode the six hundred.

4

Flashed all their sabers bare,
Flashed as they turned in air
Sab'ring the gunners there,
Charging an army, while   30
  All the world wondered.
Plunged in the battery smoke
Right through the line they broke;
Cossack and Russian
Reeled from the saber stroke   35
  Shattered and sundered.
Then they rode back, but not,
  Not the six hundred.

5

Cannon to right of them,
Cannon to left of them,
Cannon behind them   40
  Volleyed and thundered;
Stormed at with shot and shell,
While horse and hero fell,
They that had fought so well
Came through the jaws of Death,   45
Back from the mouth of hell,
All that was left of them,
  Left of six hundred.

6

When can their glory fade?
O the wild charge they made!   50
  All the world wondered.
Honor the charge they made!
Honor the Light Brigade,
  Noble six hundred!

1854   55
                                                    1854

From Maud[1]

VIII

She came to the village church,
  And sat by a pillar alone;

1. The speaker is a young man, living alone in the country, whose disillusionment after his father's suicide has left him full of a bitterness that borders on madness. He is restored to sanity and intense happiness when he discovers that Maud, the beautiful daughter of a local landowner, accepts his love for her. The following selections tell of his proposal to her and her acceptance of him. Later in the poem he loses Maud after killing her brother in a duel.

  Maud was a poem that Tennyson especially enjoyed reading aloud. He called it "a little *Hamlet*," but it is closer to *Romeo and Juliet* in its picture of love in the midst of family feuds.

An angel watching an urn
Wept over her, carved in stone;
And once, but once, she lifted her eyes,   305
And suddenly, sweetly, strangely blushed
To find they were met by my own;
And suddenly, sweetly, my heart beat stronger
And thicker, until I heard no longer
The snowy-banded, dilettante,   310
Delicate-handed priest intone;
And thought, is it pride? and mused and sighed,
"No surely, now it cannot be pride."

* * *

XVI

Catch not my breath, O clamorous heart,
Let not my tongue be a thrall to my eye,
For I must tell her before we part,
I must tell her, or die.

* * *

XVIII

1

I have led her home, my love, my only friend.
There is none like her, none.   600
And never yet so warmly ran my blood
And sweetly, on and on
Calming itself to the long-wished-for end,
Full to the banks, close on the promised good.

2

None like her, none.   605
Just now the dry-tongued laurels' pattering talk
Seemed her light foot along the garden walk,
And shook my heart to think she comes once more.
But even then I heard her close the door;
The gates of heaven are closed, and she is gone.   610

3

There is none like her, none,
Nor will be when our summers have deceased.
O, art thou² sighing for Lebanon
In the long breeze that streams to thy delicious East,
Sighing for Lebanon,   615
Dark cedar, though thy limbs have here increased,
Upon a pastoral slope as fair,
And looking to the South and fed
With honeyed rain and delicate air,
And haunted by the starry head   620
Of her whose gentle will has changed my fate,
And made my life a perfumed altar-flame;
And over whom thy darkness must have spread

---

2. The cedar-of-Lebanon tree in Maud's garden.

With such delight as theirs of old, thy great
Forefathers of the thornless garden, there   625
Shadowing the snow-limbed Eve from whom she came?

4

Here will I lie, while these long branches sway,
And you fair stars that crown a happy day
Go in and out as if at merry play,
Who am no more so all forlorn   630
As when it seemed far better to be born
To labor and the mattock-hardened hand
Than nursed at ease and brought to understand
A sad astrology,[3] the boundless plan
That makes you tyrants in your iron skies,   635
Innumerable, pitiless, passionless eyes,
Cold fires, yet with power to burn and brand
His nothingness into man.

5

But now shine on, and what care I,
Who in this stormy gulf have found a pearl   640
The countercharm of space and hollow sky,[4]
And do accept my madness, and would die
To save from some slight shame one simple girl?—

6

Would die, for sullen-seeming Death may give
More life to Love than is or ever was   645
In our low world, where yet 'tis sweet to live.
Let no one ask me how it came to pass;
It seems that I am happy, that to me
A livelier emerald twinkles in the grass,
A purer sapphire melts into the sea.   650

7

Not die, but live a life of truest breath,
And teach true life to fight with mortal wrongs.
O, why should Love, like men in drinking songs,
Spice his fair banquet with the dust of death?
Make answer, Maud my bliss,   655
Maud made my Maud by that long loving kiss,
Life of my life, wilt thou not answer this?
"The dusky strand of Death inwoven here
With dear Love's tie, makes Love himself more dear."

8

Is that enchanted moan only the swell   660
Of the long waves that roll in yonder bay?
And hark the clock within, the silver knell
Of twelve sweet hours that passed in bridal white,
And died to live, long as my pulses play;
But now by this my love has closed her sight   665
And given false death[5] her hand, and stolen away

---

3. Astronomy.
4. Something that offsets his former fears of the vastness of space revealed by modern astronomy.
5. I.e., sleep.

To dreamful wastes where footless fancies dwell
Among the fragments of the golden day.
May nothing there her maiden grace affright!
Dear heart, I feel with thee the drowsy spell. 670
My bride to be, my evermore delight,
My own heart's heart, my ownest own, farewell;
It is but for a little space I go.
And ye[6] meanwhile far over moor and fell
Beat to the noiseless music of the night! 675
Has our whole earth gone nearer to the glow
Of your soft splendors that you look so bright?
I have climbed nearer out of lonely hell.
Beat, happy stars, timing with things below,
Beat with my heart more blest than heart can tell, 680
Blest, but for some dark undercurrent woe
That seems to draw—but it shall not be so;
Let all be well, be well.

* * *

1855

In the Valley of Cauteretz[7]

All along the valley, stream that flashest white,
Deepening thy voice with the deepening of the night,
All along the valley, where thy waters flow,
I walked with one I loved two and thirty years ago.
All along the valley, while I walked today, 5
The two and thirty years were a mist that rolls away;
For all along the valley, down thy rocky bed,
Thy living voice to me was as the voice of the dead,
And all along the valley, by rock and cave and tree,
The voice of the dead was a living voice to me. 10

1861   1864

Idylls of the King When John Milton was considering subjects suitable for an epic poem, one of those he entertained was the story of the Christian British king, Arthur, a semi-legendary leader of about 500 A.D. who fought off the heathen Saxon invaders who had swarmed into Britain after the withdrawal of the Roman legions. Tennyson likewise saw that the Arthurian story had epic potential and selected it for his life-work as "the greatest of all poetical subjects." At intervals, over a period of 50 years, he labored over the 12 books that make up his *Idylls of the King*, completing the work in 1888.

6. The stars.
7. A valley in the French Pyrenees visited by Tennyson and Hallam in
1830 and revisited by Tennyson in 1861.

The principal source of Tennyson's stories of Arthur and his knights was Sir Thomas Malory's *Morte Darthur*, a version which Malory translated into English prose from French sources in 1470. As Talbot Donaldson has suggested, one basis of the appeal of the Arthurian stories, like the legends of Robin Hood and stories of the American West, is that all three represent the struggle of individuals to restore order in situations of chaos and anarchy, a task performed in the face of "seemingly overwhelming odds." The individual stories in Tennyson's *Idylls* have the same basic appeal, but the overall design of the whole poem is more ambitious and impressive. The *Idylls of the King* represent the rise and fall of a civilization. They imply that after 2000 years of Christianity, Western civilization may be going through a cycle in which it must confront the possibilities of a renewal in the future or an apocalyptic extinction. The first book, *The Coming of Arthur*, introduces the basic myth of a springtime hero transforming a wasteland and inspiring faith and hope in the highest values of civilized life among his devoted followers. Succeeding books move through summer and autumn and culminate in the bleak wintry scene of Arthur's last battle in which his order perishes in a civil war; the leader of the enemy forces is his own nephew, Sir Modred.

Throughout the later books of the *Idylls* the forces of opposition grow in strength, and disaffections infect leading figures of the Round Table itself. The most glaring example is the adulterous relationship between Guinevere, Arthur's "sumptuous" queen (as Tennyson once described her), and the king's chief lieutenant and friend, Sir Launcelot. Many other fallings away subsequently come to light, such as the perfidious betrayal by Sir Gawain in *Pelleas and Ettarre*, and the cynical conduct of Sir Tristram, whose story is told in the bitter tenth book, *The Last Tournament*. Even Merlin, Arthur's trusted magician and counselor, becomes corrupted and can perform no further offices for the king (*Merlin and Vivien*). These accumulating signs of decline and fall figure prominently in the two late idylls that make up the following selections.

From Idylls of the King

Dedication[1]

These to His Memory—since he held them dear,
Perchance as finding there unconsciously
Some image of himself—I dedicate,
I dedicate, I consecrate with tears—
These Idylls.

      And indeed he seems to me   5
Scarce other than my king's ideal knight,
"Who reverenced his conscience as his king;
Whose glory was, redressing human wrong;

---

1. Tennyson's dedication of his *Idylls* to Prince Albert, Queen Victoria's husband, who had died in 1861, was more than a mere formality on the part of the Poet Laureate. Because of his earnest dedication to duty, his statesmanship, his work for peace, Albert seemed to Tennyson to have been almost a modern reincarnation of King Arthur.

Who spake no slander, no, nor listened to it;
Who loved one only and who clave to her—"[2]   10
Her—over all whose realms to their last isle,
Commingled with the gloom of imminent war,
The shadow of his loss drew like eclipse,
Darkening the world. We have lost him; he is gone.
We know him now; all narrow jealousies   15
Are silent, and we see him as he moved,
How modest, kindly, all-accomplished, wise,
With what sublime repression of himself,
And in what limits, and how tenderly;
Not swaying to this faction or to that;   20
Not making his high place the lawless perch
Of winged ambitions, nor a vantage-ground
For pleasure; but through all this tract of years
Wearing the white flower of a blameless life,
Before a thousand peering littlenesses,   25
In that fierce light which beats upon a throne,
And blackens every blot: for where is he,
Who dares foreshadow for an only son
A lovelier life, a more unstained, than his?
Or how should England dreaming of *his* sons   30
Hope more for these than some inheritance
Of such a life, a heart, a mind as thine,
Thou noble Father of her Kings to be,
Laborious for her people and her poor—
Voice in the rich dawn of an ampler day—   35
Far-sighted summoner of War and Waste
To fruitful strifes and rivalries of peace—
Sweet nature gilded by the gracious gleam
Of letters, dear to Science, dear to Art,
Dear to thy land[3] and ours, a Prince indeed,   40
Beyond all titles, and a household name,
Hereafter, through all times, Albert the Good.

Break not, O woman's-heart, but still endure;
Break not, for thou art Royal, but endure,
Remembering all the beauty of that star
Which shone so close beside Thee that ye made   45
One light together, but has passed and leaves
The Crown a lonely splendor.
                                   May all love,
His love, unseen but felt, o'ershadow thee,
The love of all thy sons encompass thee,   50
The love of all thy daughters cherish thee,
The love of all thy people comfort thee,
Till God's love set thee at his side again!

                                                  1862

---

2. A paraphrase of King Arthur's words
(*Idylls* XI.472) summarizing the ideals
of the knights of the Round Table.

3. Albert was a native of Saxe-Coburg
in Germany.

Pelleas and Ettarre[1]

King Arthur made new knights to fill the gap
Left by the Holy Quest;[2] and as he sat
In hall at old Caerleon,[3] the high doors
Were softly sundered, and through these a youth,
Pelleas, and the sweet smell of the fields   5
Passed, and the sunshine came along with him.

   "Make me thy knight, because I know, Sir King,
All that belongs to knighthood, and I love."
Such was his cry: for having heard the King
Had let proclaim a tournament—the prize   10
A golden circlet and a knightly sword,
Full fain had Pelleas for his lady won
The golden circlet, for himself the sword:
And there were those who knew him near the King,
And promised for him: and Arthur made him knight.   15

   And this new knight, Sir Pelleas of the isles—
But lately come to his inheritance,
And lord of many a barren isle was he—
Riding at noon, a day or twain before,
Across the forest called of Dean,[4] to find   20
Caerleon and the King, had felt the sun
Beat like a strong knight on his helm, and reeled
Almost to falling from his horse; but saw
Near him a mound of even-sloping side,
Whereon a hundred stately beeches grew,   25
And here and there great hollies under them;
But for a mile all round was open space,
And fern and heath: and slowly Pelleas drew
To that dim day, then binding his good horse
To a tree, cast himself down; and as he lay   30
At random looking over the brown earth
Through that green-glooming twilight of the grove,
It seemed to Pelleas that the fern without
Burned as a living fire of emeralds,
So that his eyes were dazzled looking at it.   35
Then o'er it crossed the dimness of a cloud
Floating, and once the shadow of a bird
Flying, and then a fawn; and his eyes closed.
And since he loved all maidens, but no maid
In special, half-awake he whispered, "Where?   40
O where? I love thee, though I know thee not.
For fair thou art and pure as Guinevere,

1. The ninth book of the *Idylls*. Most of the story, except the ending, is based on Malory's *Morte Darthur* (IV. 21–24). Tennyson said of it: "Almost the saddest of the Idylls. The breaking of the storm."
2. In the preceding idyll, *The Holy Grail*, many knights had misguidedly deserted the Round Table to seek the Holy Grail.
3. Ancient village in Monmouthshire, near Wales, where Arthur often held his court.
4. Extensive tract in the river Wye region adjacent to Monmouthshire.

And I will make thee with my spear and sword
As famous—O my Queen, my Guinevere,
For I will be thine Arthur when we meet." 45

    Suddenly wakened with a sound of talk
And laughter at the limit of the wood,
And glancing through the hoary boles, he saw,
Strange as to some old prophet might have seemed
A vision hovering on a sea of fire, 50
Damsels in divers colors like the cloud
Of sunset and sunrise, and all of them
On horses, and the horses richly trapped
Breast-high in that bright line of bracken stood:
And all the damsels talked confusedly, 55
And one was pointing this way, and one that,
Because the way was lost.

              And Pelleas rose,
And loosed his horse, and led him to the light,
There she that seemed the chief among them said,
"In happy time behold our pilot-star! 60
Youth, we are damsels-errant, and we ride,
Armed as ye see, to tilt against the knights
There at Caerleon, but have lost our way:
To right? to left? straight forward? back again?
Which? tell us quickly."

            Pelleas gazing thought, 65
"Is Guinevere herself so beautiful?"
For large her violet eyes looked, and her bloom
A rosy dawn kindled in stainless heavens,
And round her limbs, mature in womanhood;
And slender was her hand and small her shape; 70
And but for those large eyes, the haunts of scorn,
She might have seemed a toy to trifle with,
And pass and care no more. But while he gazed
The beauty of her flesh abashed the boy,
As though it were the beauty of her soul: 75
For as the base man, judging of the good,
Puts his own baseness in him by default
Of will and nature, so did Pelleas lend
All the young beauty of his own soul to hers,
Believing her; and when she spake to him, 80
Stammered, and could not make her a reply.
For out of the waste islands had he come,
Where saving his own sisters he had known
Scarce any but the women of his isles,
Rough wives, that laughed and screamed against the gulls, 85
Makers of nets, and living from the sea.

Then with a slow smile turned the lady round
And looked upon her people; and as when
A stone is flung into some sleeping tarn,
The circle widens till it lip the marge,   90
Spread the slow smile through all her company.
Three knights were thereamong; and they too smiled,
Scorning him; for the lady was Ettarre,
And she was a great lady in her land.

   Again she said, "O wild and of the woods,   95
Knowest thou not the fashion of our speech?
Or have the Heavens but given thee a fair face,
Lacking a tongue?"

                    "O damsel," answered he,
"I woke from dreams; and coming out of gloom
Was dazzled by the sudden light, and crave   100
Pardon: but will ye to Caerleon? I
Go likewise: shall I lead you to the King?"

   "Lead then," she said; and through the woods they went.
And while they rode, the meaning in his eyes,
His tenderness of manner, and chaste awe,   105
His broken utterances and bashfulness,
Were all a burthen to her, and in her heart
She muttered, "I have lighted on a fool,
Raw, yet so stale!" But since her mind was bent
On hearing, after trumpet blown, her name   110
And title, "Queen of Beauty," in the lists
Cried—and beholding him so strong, she thought
That peradventure he will fight for me,
And win the circlet: therefore flattered him,
Being so gracious, that he wellnigh deemed   115
His wish by hers was echoed; and her knights
And all her damsels too were gracious to him,
For she was a great lady.

                        And when they reached
Caerleon, ere they passed to lodging, she,
Taking his hand, "O the strong hand," she said,   120
"See! look at mine! but wilt thou fight for me,
And win me this fine circlet, Pelleas,
That I may love thee?"

                    Then his helpless heart
Leaped, and he cried, "Ay! wilt thou if I win?"
'Ay, that will I," she answered, and she laughed,   125
And straitly nipped the hand, and flung it from her;
Then glanced askew at those three knights of hers,
Till all her ladies laughed along with her.

"O happy world," thought Pelleas, "all, meseems,
Are happy; I the happiest of them all."   130
Nor slept that night for pleasure in his blood,
And green wood-ways, and eyes among the leaves;
Then being on the morrow knighted, sware
To love one only. And as he came away,
The men who met him rounded on their heels   135
And wondered after him, because his face
Shone like the countenance of a priest of old
Against the flame about a sacrifice
Kindled by fire from heaven: so glad was he.

Then Arthur made vast banquets, and strange knights   140
From the four winds came in: and each one sat,
Though served with choice from air, land, stream, and sea,
Oft in mid-banquet measuring with his eyes
His neighbor's make and might: and Pelleas looked
Noble among the noble, for he dreamed   145
His lady loved him, and he knew himself
Loved of the King: and him his new-made knight
Worshipped, whose lightest whisper moved him more
Than all the ranged reasons of the world.

Then blushed and brake the morning of the jousts,   150
And this was called "The Tournament of Youth":
For Arthur, loving his young knight, withheld
His older and his mightier from the lists,
That Pelleas might obtain his lady's love,
According to her promise. and remain   155
Lord of the tourney. And Arthur had the jousts
Down in the flat field by the shore of Usk[5]
Holden: the gilded parapets were crowned
With faces, and the great tower filled with eyes
Up to the summit, and the trumpets blew.   160
There all day long Sir Pelleas kept the field
With honor: so by that strong hand of his
The sword and golden circlet were achieved.

Then rang the shout his lady loved: the heat
Of pride and glory fired her face; her eye   165
Sparkled; she caught the circlet from his lance,
And there before the people crowned herself:
So for the last time she was gracious to him.

Then at Caerleon for a space—her look
Bright for all others, cloudier on her knight—   170
Lingered Ettarre: and seeing Pelleas droop,
Said Guinevere, "We marvel at thee much,
O damsel, wearing this unsunny face

5. River near Caerleon.

To him who won thee glory!" And she said,
"Had ye not held your Lancelot in your bower,
My Queen, he had not won." Whereat the Queen,   175
As one whose foot is bitten by an ant,
Glanced down upon her, turned and went her way.

But after, when her damsels, and herself,
And those three knights all set their faces home,
Sir Pelleas followed. She that saw him cried,   180
"Damsels—and yet I should be shamed to say it—
I cannot bide Sir Baby. Keep him back
Among yourselves. Would rather that we had
Some rough old knight who knew the worldly way,   185
Albeit grizzlier than a bear, to ride
And jest with: take him to you, keep him off,
And pamper him with papmeat, if ye will,
Old milky fables of the wolf and sheep,
Such as the wholesome mothers tell their boys.   190
Nay, should ye try him with a merry one
To find his mettle, good: and if he fly us,
Small matter! let him." This her damsels heard,
And mindful of her small and cruel hand,
They, closing round him through the journey home,   195
Acted her hest,[6] and always from her side
Restrained him with all manner of device,
So that he could not come to speech with her.
And when she gained her castle, upsprang the bridge,
Down rang the grate of iron through the groove,   200
And he was left alone in open field.
    "These be the ways of ladies," Pelleas thought,
"To those who love them, trials of our faith.
Yea, let her prove me to the uttermost,
For loyal to the uttermost am I."   205
So made his moan; and, darkness falling, sought
A priory not far off, there lodges, but rose
With morning every day, and, moist or dry,
Full-armed upon his charger all day long.
Sat by the walls, and no one opened to him.   210

And this persistence turned her scorn to wrath.
Then calling her three knights, she charged them, "Out!
And drive him from the walls." And out they came,
But Pelleas overthrew them as they dashed
Against him one by one; and these returned,
But still he kept his watch beneath the wall.   215

Thereon her wrath became a hate; and once,
A week beyond, while walking on the walls
With her three knights, she pointed downward, "Look,

6. Command.

He haunts me—I cannot breathe—besieges me;   220
Down! strike him! put my hate into your strokes,
And drive him from my walls." And down they went,
And Pelleas overthrew them one by one;
And from the tower above him cried Ettarre,
"Bind him, and bring him in."
                    He heard her voice;   225
Then let the strong hand, which had overthrown
Her minion-knights,[7] by those he overthrew
Be bounden straight, and so they brought him in.

    Then when he came before Ettarre, the sight
Of her rich beauty made him at once glance   230
More bondsman in his heart than in his bonds.
Yet with good cheer he spake, "Behold me, Lady,
A prisoner, and the vassal of thy will;
And if thou keep me in thy donjon here,
Content am I so that I see thy face   235
But once a day: for I have sworn my vows,
And thou hast given thy promise, and I know
That all these pains are trials of my faith,
And that thyself, when thou hast seen me strained
And sifted to the utmost, wilt at length   240
Yield me thy love and know me for thy knight."

    Then she began to rail so bitterly,
With all her damsels, he was stricken mute;
But when she mocked his vows and the great King,
Lighted on words: "For pity of thine own self,   245
Peace, Lady, peace: is he not thine and mine?"
"Thou fool," she said, "I never heard his voice
But longed to break away. Unbind him now,
And thrust him out of doors; for save he be
Fool to the midmost marrow of his bones,   250
He will return no more." And those, her three,
Laughed, and unbound, and thrust him from the gate.

    And after this, a week beyond, again
She called them, saying, "There he watches yet,
There like a dog before his master's door!   255
Kicked, he returns: do ye not hate him, ye?
Ye know yourselves: how can ye bide at peace,
Affronted with his fulsome innocence?
Are ye but creatures of the board and bed,
No men to strike? Fall on him all at once,   260
And if ye slay him I reck not: if ye fail,
Give ye the slave mine order to be bound,
Bind him as heretofore, and bring him in:
It may be ye shall slay him in his bonds."
        She spake; and at her will they couched their spears,   265

---

7. Minion: compliant and obsequious dependent of a ruler.

Three against one: and Gawain[8] passing by,
Bound upon solitary adventure, saw
Low down beneath the shadow of those towers
A villainy, three to one: and through his heart
The fire of honor and all noble deeds   270
Flashed, and he called, "I strike upon thy side—
The caitiffs!" "Nay," said Pelleas, "but forbear;
He needs no aid who doth his lady's will."

   So Gawain, looking at the villainy done,
Forbore, but in his heat and eagerness   275
Trembled and quivered, as the dog, withheld
A moment from the vermin that he sees
Before him, shivers, ere he springs and kills.

   And Pelleas overthrew them, one to three;
And they rose up, and bound, and brought him in.   280
Then first her anger, leaving Pelleas, burned
Full on her knights in many an evil name
Of craven, weakling, and thrice-beaten hound:
"Yet, take him, ye that scarce are fit to touch,
Far less to bind, your victor, and thrust him out,   285
And let who will release him from his bonds.
And if he comes again"—there she brake short;
And Pelleas answered, "Lady, for indeed
I loved you and I deemed you beautiful,
I cannot brook to see your beauty marred   290
Through evil spite: and if ye love me not,
I cannot bear to dream you so forsworn:
I had liefer ye were worthy of my love,
Than to be loved again of you—farewell;
And though ye kill my hope, not yet my love,   295
Vex not yourself: ye will not see me more."

   While thus he spake, she gazed upon the man
Of princely bearing, though in bonds, and thought,
"Why have I pushed him from me? this man loves,
If love there be: yet him I loved not. Why?   300
I deemed him fool? yea, so? or that in him
A something—was it nobler than myself?—
Seemed my reproach? He is not of my kind.
He could not love me, did he know me well.
Nay, let him go— and quickly." And her knights   305
Laughed not, but thrust him bounden out of door.

   Forth sprang Gawain, and loosed him from his bonds,
And flung them o'er the walls; and afterward,
Shaking his hands, as from a lazar's[9] rag,
"Faith of my body," he said, "and art thou not—   310

---

8. A nephew of King Arthur and one of   9. Leper's.
his chief knights.

Yea thou art he, whom late our Arthur made
Knight of his table; yea and he that won
The circlet? wherefore hast thou so defamed
Thy brotherhood in me and all the rest,
As let these caitiffs on thee work their will?"   315

    And Pelleas answered, "O, their wills are hers
For whom I won the circlet; and mine, hers,
Thus to be bounden, so to see her face,
Marred though it be with spite and mockery now,
Other than when I found her in the woods;   320
And though she hath me bounden but in spite,
And all to flout me, when they bring me in,
Let me be bounden, I shall see her face;
Else must I die through mine unhappiness."

    And Gawain answered kindly though in scorn,   325
"Why, let my lady bind me if she will,
And let my lady beat me if she will:
But an[1] she send her delegate to thrall
These fighting hands of mine—Christ kill me then
But I will slice him handless by the wrist,   330
And let my lady sear the stump for him,
Howl as he may. But hold me for your friend:
Come, ye know nothing: here I pledge my troth,
Yea, by the honor of the Table Round,
I will be leal[2] to thee and work thy work,   335
And tame thy jailing princess to thine hand.
Lend me thine horse and arms, and I will say
That I have slain thee. She will let me in
To hear the manner of thy fight and fall;
Then, when I come within her counsels, then   340
From prime to vespers will I chant thy praise
As prowest[3] knight and truest lover, more
Than any have sung thee living, till she long
To have thee back in lusty life again,
Not to be bound, save by white bonds and warm,   345
Dearer than freedom. Wherefore now thy horse
And armor: let me go: be comforted:
Give me three days to melt her fancy, and hope
The third night hence will bring thee news of gold."

    Then Pelleas lent his horse and all his arms,   350
Saving the goodly sword, his prize, and took
Gawain's, and said, "Betray me not, but help—
Art thou not he whom men call light-of-love?"

    "Ay," said Gawain, "for women be so light."
Then bounded forward to the castle walls,   355

---

1. If.
2. Loyal.

3. Bravest or noblest.

And raised a bugle hanging from his neck,
And winded it, and that so musically
That all the old echoes hidden in the wall
Rang out like hollow woods at hunting-tide.

    Up ran a score of damsels to the tower;   360
"Avaunt," they cried, "our lady loves thee not."
But Gawain lifting up his vizor said,
"Gawain am I, Gawain of Arthur's court,
And I have slain this Pelleas whom ye hate:
Behold his horse and armor. Open gates,   365
And I will make you merry."

                           And down they ran,
Her damsels, crying to their lady, "Lo!
Pelleas is dead—he told us—he that hath
His horse and armor: will ye let him in?
He slew him! Gawain, Gawain of the court,   370
Sir Gawain—there he waits below the wall,
Blowing his bugle as who should say him nay."

    And so, leave given, straight on through open door
Rode Gawain, whom she greeted courteously.
"Dead, is it so?" she asked. "Ay, ay," said he,   375
"And oft in dying cried upon your name."
"Pity on him," she answered, "a good knight,
But never let me bide one hour at peace."
"Ay," thought Gawain, "and you be fair enow:
But I to your dead man have given my troth,   380
That whom ye loathe, him will I make you love."

    So those three days, aimless about the land,
Lost in a doubt, Pelleas wandering
Waited, until the third night brought a moon
With promise of large light on woods and ways.   385

    Hot was the night and silent; but a sound
Of Gawain ever coming, and this lay—
Which Pelleas had heard sung before the Queen,
And seen her sadden listening—vexed his heart,
And marred his rest—"A worm within the rose."   390

    "A rose, but one, none other rose had I,
A rose, one rose, and this was wondrous fair,
One rose, a rose that gladdened earth and sky,
One rose, my rose, that sweetened all mine air—
I cared not for the thorns; the thorns were there.   395

    "One rose, a rose to gather by and by,
One rose, a rose, to gather and to wear,
No rose but one—what other rose had I?

One rose, my rose; a rose that will not die,— 400
He dies who loves it,—if the worm be there."

This tender rhyme, and evermore the doubt,
"Why lingers Gawain with his golden news?"
So shook him that he could not rest, but rode
Ere midnight to her walls, and bound his horse
Hard by the gates. Wide open were the gates, 405
And no watch kept; and in through these he passed,
And heard but his own steps, and his own heart
Beating, for nothing moved but his own self,
And his own shadow. Then he crossed the court,
And spied not any light in hall or bower, 410
But saw the postern portal also wide
Yawning; and up a slope of garden, all
Of roses white and red, and brambles mixed
And overgrowing them, went on, and found,
Here too, all hushed below the mellow moon, 415
Save that one rivulet from a tiny cave
Came lightening downward, and so spilled itself
Among the roses, and was lost again.

Then was he ware of three pavilions reared
Above the bushes, gilden-peaked: in one, 420
Red after revel, droned her lurdane[4] knights
Slumbering, and their three squires across their feet:
In one, their malice on the placid lip
Frozen by sweet sleep, four of her damsels lay:
And in the third, the circlet of the jousts 425
Bound on her brow, were Gawain and Ettarre.[5]

Back, as a hand that pushes through the leaf
To find a nest and feels a snake, he drew:
Back, as a coward slinks from what he fears
To cope with, or a traitor proven, or hound 430
Beaten, did Pelleas in an utter shame
Creep with his shadow through the court again,
Fingering at his sword-handle until he stood
There on the castle-bridge once more, and thought,
"I will go back, and slay them where they lie." 435

And so went back, and seeing them yet in sleep
Said, "Ye, that so dishallow the holy sleep,

4. Heavy and stupid.
5. Cf. Malory IV. 23: "And then it was in the month of May, that she and sir Gawaine went out of the castle and supped in a pavilion, and there was a bed made, and there sir Gawaine and the lady Ettarre went to bed together; and in another pavilion she laid her damsels; and in the third pavilion she laid part of her knights: for then she had no dread nor fear of sir Pelles. And there sir Gawaine lay with her, doing his pleasure in that pavilion, two days and two nights, against the faithful promise that he made to sir Pelles."

Your sleep is death," and drew the sword, and thought,
"What! slay a sleeping knight? the King hath bound
And sworn me to this brotherhood"; again,   440
"Alas that ever a knight should be so false."
Then turned, and so returned, and groaning laid
The naked sword athwart their naked throats,
There left it, and them sleeping; and she lay,
The circlet of the tourney round her brows,   445
And the sword of the tourney across her throat.

    And forth he passed, and mounting on his horse
Stared at her towers that, larger than themselves
In their own darkness, thronged into the moon.
Then crushed the saddle with his thighs, and clenched   450
His hands, and maddened with himself and moaned:

    "Would they have risen against me in their blood
At the last day? I might have answered them
Even before high God. O towers so strong,
Huge, solid, would that even while I gaze   455
The crack of earthquake shivering to your base
Split you, and Hell burst up your harlot roofs
Bellowing, and charred you through and through within,
Black as the harlot's heart—hollow as a skull!
Let the fierce east scream through your eyelet-holes,   460
And whirl the dust of harlots round and round
In dung and nettles! hiss, snake—I saw him there—
Let the fox bark, let the wolf yell. Who yells
Here in the still sweet summer night, but I—
I, the poor Pelleas whom she called her fool?   465
Fool, beast—he, she, or I? myself most fool;
Beast too, as lacking human wit—disgraced,
Dishonored all for trial of true love—
Love?—we be all alike: only the King
Hath made us fools and liars. O noble vows!   470
O great and sane and simple race of brutes
That own[6] no lust because they have no law!
For why should I have loved her to my shame?
I loathe her, as I loved her to my shame.
I never loved her, I but lusted for her—   475
Away—"
        He dashed the rowel into his horse,
And bounded forth and vanished through the night.

    Then she, that felt the cold touch on her throat,
Awaking knew the sword, and turned herself
To Gawain: "Liar, for thou hast not slain
This Pelleas! here he stood, and might have slain   480

6. Acknowledge.

Me and thyself." And he that tells the tale
Says that her ever-veering fancy turned
To Pelleas, as the one true knight on earth,
And only lover; and through her love her life   485
Wasted and pined, desiring him in vain.

But he by wild and way, for half the night,
And over hard and soft, striking the sod
From out the soft, the spark from off the hard,
Rode till the star above the wakening sun,   490
Beside that tower where Percivale was cowled,[7]
Glanced from the rosy forehead of the dawn.
For so the words were flashed into his heart
He knew not whence or wherefore: "O sweet star,
Pure on the virgin forehead of the dawn!"   495
And there he would have wept, but felt his eyes
Harder and drier than a fountain bed
In summer: thither came the village girls
And lingered talking, and they come no more
Till the sweet heavens have filled it from the heights 500
Again with living waters in the change
Of seasons: hard his eyes; harder his heart
Seemed; but so weary were his limbs, that he,
Gasping, "Of Arthur's hall am I, but here,
Here let me rest and die," cast himself down,   505
And gulfed his griefs in inmost sleep; so lay,
Till shaken by a dream, that Gawain fired
The hall of Merlin, and the morning star
Reeled in the smoke, brake into flame, and fell.

He woke, and being ware of someone nigh,   510
Sent hands upon him, as to tear him, crying,
"False! and I held thee pure as Guinevere."

But Percivale stood near him and replied,
"Am I but false as Guinevere is pure?
Or art thou mazed with dreams? or being one   515
Of our free-spoken Table hast not heard
That Lancelot"—there he checked himself and paused.

Then fared it with Sir Pelleas as with one
Who gets a wound in battle, and the sword
That made it plunges through the wound again,   520
And pricks it deeper: and he shrank and wailed,
"Is the Queen false?" and Percivale was mute.
"Have any of our Round Table held their vows?"
And Percivale made answer not a word.
"Is the King true?" "The King!" said Percivale.   525

7. Percivale, one of the most devout of   Table to become a monk in a priory.
Arthur's knights, had left the Round

"Why then let man couple at once with wolves.
What! art thou mad?"

                    But Pelleas, leaping up,
Ran through the doors and vaulted on his horse
And fled: small pity upon his horse had he,
Or on himself, or any, and when he met   530
A cripple, one that held a hand for alms—
Hunched as he was, and like an old dwarf-elm
That turns its back on the salt blast, the boy
Paused not, but overrode him, shouting, "False,
And false with Gawain!" and so left him bruised   535
And battered, and fled on, and hill and wood
Went ever streaming by him till the gloom,
That follows on the turning of the world,
Darkened the common path: he twitched the reins,
And made his beast that better knew it, swerve   540
Now off it and now on; but when he saw
High up in heaven the hall that Merlin built,
Blackening against the dead-green stripes of even,
"Black nest of rats," he groaned, "ye build too high."

    Not long thereafter from the city gates   545
Issued Sir Lancelot riding airily,
Warm with a gracious parting from the Queen,
Peace at his heart, and gazing at a star
And marveling what it was: on whom the boy,
Across the silent seeded meadow-grass   550
Borne, clashed: and Lancelot, saying, "What name hast thou
That ridest here so blindly and so hard?"
"No name, no name," he shouted, "a scourge am I
To lash the treasons of the Table Round."
"Yea, but thy name?" "I have many names," he cried: 555
"I am wrath and shame and hate and evil fame,
And like a poisonous wind I pass to blast
And blaze the crime of Lancelot and the Queen."
"First over me," said Lancelot, "shalt thou pass."
"Fight therefore," yelled the youth, and either knight   560
Drew back a space, and when they closed, at once
The weary steed of Pelleas floundering flung
His rider, who called out from the dark field,
"Thou art false as Hell: slay me: I have no sword."
Then Lancelot, "Yea, between thy lips—and sharp;   565
But here will I disedge[8] it by thy death."
"Slay then," he shrieked, "my will is to be slain,"
And Lancelot, with his heel upon the fallen,
Rolling his eyes, a moment stood, then spake:
"Rise, weakling; I am Lancelot; say thy say."   570

8. I.e., blunt your sharp tongue.

And Lancelot slowly rode his warhorse back
To Camelot, and Sir Pelleas in brief while
Caught his unbroken limbs from the dark field,
And followed to the city. It chanced that both
Brake into hall together, worn and pale.   575
There with her knights and dames was Guinevere.
Full wonderingly she gazed on Lancelot
So soon returned, and then on Pelleas, him
Who had not greeted her, but cast himself
Down on a bench, hard-breathing. "Have ye fought?"   580
She asked of Lancelot. "Ay, my Queen," he said.
"And thou hast overthrown him?" "Ay, my Queen."
Then she, turning to Pelleas, "O young knight,
Hath the great heart of knighthood in thee failed
So far thou canst not bide, unfrowardly,   585
A fall from *him*?" Then, for he answered not,
"Or hast thou other griefs? If I, the Queen,
May help them, loose thy tongue, and let me know."
But Pelleas lifted up an eye so fierce
She quailed; and he, hissing "I have no sword,"   590
Sprang from the door into the dark.[9] The Queen
Looked hard upon her lover, he on her;
And each foresaw the dolorous day to be:
And all talk died, as in a grove all song
Beneath the shadow of some bird of prey;   595
Then a long silence came upon the hall,
And Modred[10] thought, "The time is hard at hand."
1869   1869

The Passing of Arthur[1]

That story which the bold Sir Bedivere,[2]
First made and latest left of all the knights,
Told, when the man was no more than a voice

9. Malory's version ends differently. His
Pelleas is rescued from despair by a
damsel of the Lake who, by enchantment, contrives a punishment for the
haughty Ettarre. "So the lady Ettarre
died for sorrow, and the damsel of the
lake rejoiced sir Pelles, and loved together during their lives." Tennyson's
Pelleas, as we learn in *The Last Tournament* (the idyll following *Pelleas and Ettarre*) is so disillusioned by the corruptions he has discovered that he establishes a mock court of his own where
his followers indulge in drunken revelry.
Through a messenger he reports to Arthur: "Tell thou the King * * * / My
tower is full of harlots, like his court, /
But mine are worthier, seeing they profess / To be none other than themselves."
10. Arthur's nephew, who leads the
forces that revolt against the king.
1. On the composition of this final Idyll
and its relation to Tennyson's *Morte
d'Arthur* of 1842, see note to *The Epic*.
The principal source was Sir Thomas
Malory's *Morte Darthur* XXI.4–5. Preceding the action of this Idyll, Arthur
had been in France with his nephew Gawain fighting against the forces of Lancelot. Learning at that time of the gathering of an army against him in England, under the leadership of his nephew
Modred, Arthur returned there to engage
in his last battle. Upon landing at
Dover, Gawain was slain.
2. A knight who had long been close to
the king, described in *The Coming of
Arthur*: "Bedivere, the first of all his
knights / knighted by Arthur at his
crowning."

In the white winter of his age, to those
With whom he dwelt, new faces, other minds.   5

For on their march to westward, Bedivere,
Who slowly paced among the slumbering host,
Heard in his tent the moanings of the King:

"I found Him in the shining of the stars,
I marked Him in the flowering of His fields,   10
But in His ways with men I find Him not.
I waged His wars, and now I pass and die.
O me! for why is all around us here
As if some lesser god had made the world,
But had not force to shape it as he would,   15
Till the High God behold it from beyond,
And enter it, and make it beautiful?
Or else as if the world were wholly fair,
But that these eyes of men are dense and dim,
And have not power to see it as it is: 20
Perchance, because we see not to the close;—
For I, being simple, thought to work His will,
And have but stricken with the sword in vain;
And all whereon I learned in wife and friend
Is traitor to my peace, and all my realm   25
Reels back into the beast, and is no more.
My God, thou has forgotten me in my death:[3]
Nay—God my Christ—I pass but shall not die."

Then, ere that last weird battle in the west,
There came on Arthur sleeping, Gawain killed   30
In Lancelot's war, the ghost of Gawain blown
Along a wandering wind, and past his ear
Went shrilling, "Hollow, hollow all delight!
Hail, King! tomorrow thou shalt pass away.
Farewell! there is an isle of rest for thee.   35
And I am blown along a wandering wind,
And hollow, hollow, hollow all delight."
And fainter onward, like wild birds that change
Their season in the night and wail their way
From cloud to cloud, down the long wind the dream   40
Shrilled; but in going mingled with dim cries
Far in the moonlit haze among the hills,
As of some lonely city sacked by night,
When all is lost, and wife and child with wail
Pass to new lords; and Arthur woke and called,   45
"Who spake? A dream. O light upon the wind,
Thine, Gawain, was the voice—are these dim cries
Thine? or doth all that haunts the waste and wild
Mourn, knowing it will go along with me?"

3. Cf. "My God, my God, why hast thou forsaken me?" Matthew xxvii.46.

This heard the bold Sir Bedivere and spake: 50
"O me, my King, let pass whatever will,
Elves, and the harmless glamor of the field;[4]
But in their stead thy name and glory cling
To all high places like a golden cloud
Forever: but as yet thou shalt not pass.   55
Light was Gawain in life, and light in death
Is Gawain, for the ghost is as the man;
And care not thou for dreams from him, but rise—
I hear the steps of Modred in the west,
And with him many of thy people, and knights   60
Once thine, whom thou hast loved, but grosser grown
Than heathen, spitting at their vows and thee.
Right well in heart they know thee for the King.
Arise, go forth and conquer as of old."

Then spake King Arthur to Sir Bedivere: 65
"Far other is this battle in the west
Whereto we move, than when we strove in youth,
And brake the petty kings, and fought with Rome,
Or thrust the heathen from the Roman wall,
And shook him through the north. Ill doom is mine   70
To war against my people and my knights.
The king who fights his people fights himself.
And they thy knights, who loved me once, the stroke
That strikes them dead is as my death to me.
Yet let us hence, and find or feel a way   75
Through this blind haze, which ever since I saw
One lying in the dust at Almesbury,[5]
Hath folded in the passes of the world."

Then rose the King and moved his host by night,
And ever pushed Sir Modred, league by league,   80
Back to the sunset bound of Lyonnesse—[6]
A land of old upheaven from the abyss
By fire, to sink into the abyss again;
Where fragments of forgotten peoples dwelled,
And the long mountains ended in a coast   85
Of ever-shifting sand, and far away
The phantom circle of a moaning sea.
There the pursuer could pursue no more,
And he that fled no further fly the King;
And there, that day when the great light of heaven   90
Burned at his lowest in the rolling year,
On the waste sand by the waste sea they closed.
Nor ever yet had Arthur fought a fight

---

4. Tennyson said the reference is to "the legends which cluster round the King's name." One legend told of the elves' bestowing gifts on Arthur as a child.
5. The convent to which Guinevere had withdrawn; during the king's farewell visit to her there, she had lain in the dust at his feet.
6. Legendary land extending west from Cornwall which sank into the sea.

Like this last, dim, weird battle of the west.
A deathwhite mist slept over sand and sea:
Whereof the chill, to him who breathed it, drew   95
Down with his blood, till all his heart was cold
With formless fear; and even on Arthur fell
Confusion, since he saw not whom he fought.
For friend and foe were shadows in the mist,   100
And friend slew friend not knowing whom he slew;
And some had visions out of golden youth,
And some beheld the faces of old ghosts
Look in upon the battle; and in the mist
Was many a noble deed, many a base,   105
And chance and craft and strength in single fights,
And ever and anon with host to host
Shocks, and the splintering spear, the hard mail hewn,
Shield-breakings, and the clash of brands, the crash
Of battleaxes on shattered helms, and shrieks   110
After the Christ, of those who falling down
Looked up for heaven, and only saw the mist;
And shouts of heathen and the traitor knights,
Oaths, insult, filth, and monstrous blasphemies,
Sweat, writhings, anguish, laboring of the lungs   115
In that close mist, and cryings for the light,
Moans of the dying, and voices of the dead.

      Last, as by some one deathbed after wail
Of suffering, silence follows, or through death
Or deathlike swoon, thus over all that shore,   120
Save for some whisper of the seething seas,
A dead hush fell; but when the dolorous day
Grew drearier toward twilight falling, came
A bitter wind, clear from the North, and blew
The mist aside, and with that wind the tide   125
Rose, and the pale King glanced across the field
Of battle: but no man was moving there;
Nor any cry of Christian heard thereon,
Nor yet of heathen; only the wan wave
Brake in among dead faces, to and fro   130
Swaying the helpless hands, and up and down
Tumbling the hollow helmets of the fallen,
And shivered brands that once had fought with Rome,
And rolling far along the gloomy shores
The voice of days of old and days to be.   135

      Then spake King Arthur to Sir Bedivere,
And whiter than the mist that all day long
Had held the field of battle was the King:

      "Hearest thou this great voice that shakes the world,
And wastes the narrow realm whereon we move,   140
And beats upon the faces of the dead,

My dead, as though they had not died for me?—
O Bedivere, for on my heart hath fallen
Confusion, till I know not what I am,
Nor whence I am, nor whether I be King.   145
Behold, I seem but King among the dead."

    Then spake the bold Sir Bedivere: "My King,
King everywhere! and so the dead have kings,
There also will I worship thee as King.
Yet still thy life is whole, and still I live   150
Who love thee; but who hates thee, he that brought
The heathen back among us, yonder stands,
Modred, unharmed, the traitor of thine house."

    Then spake the King: "My house hath been my doom.
But call not thou this traitor of my house   155
Who hath but dwelled beneath one roof with me.
My house are rather they who sware my vows,
Yea, even while they brake them, owned me King.
And well for thee, saying in my dark hour,
When all the purport of my throne hath failed,   160
That quick or dead thou holdest me for King.
King am I, whatsoever be their cry;
And one last act of kinghood shalt thou see
Yet, ere I pass." And uttering this the King
Made at the man: then Modred smote his liege   165
Hard on that helm which many a heathen sword
Had beaten thin; while Arthur at one blow,
Striking the last stroke with Excalibur,
Slew him, and all but slain himself, he fell.

    So all day long the noise of battle rolled   170
Among the mountains by the winter sea;
Until King Arthur's Table, man by man,
Had fallen in Lyonnesse about their lord,
King Arthur. Then, because his wound was deep,
The bold Sir Bedivere uplifted him,   175
And bore him to a chapel nigh the field,
A broken chancel with a broken cross,
That stood on a dark strait of barren land:
On one side lay the Ocean, and on one
Lay a great water, and the moon was full.   180

    Then spake King Arthur to Sir Bedivere:
"The sequel of today unsolders all
The goodliest fellowship of famous knights
Whereof this world holds record. Such a sleep
They sleep—the men I loved. I think that we   185
Shall never more, at any future time,
Delight our souls with talk of knightly deeds,

Walking about the gardens and the halls
Of Camelot, as in the days that were.
I perish by this people which I made,— 190
Though Merlin sware that I should come again
To rule once more;[7] but, let what will be, be,
I am so deeply smitten through the helm
That without help I cannot last till morn.
Thou therefore take my brand[8] Excalibur, 195
Which was my pride: for thou rememberest how
In those old days, one summer noon, an arm
Rose up from out the bosom of the lake,
Clothed in white samite,[9] mystic, wonderful,
Holding the sword—and how I rowed across 200
And took it, and have worn it, like a king;
And, wheresoever I am sung or told
In aftertime, this also shall be known:
But now delay not: take Excalibur,
And fling him far into the middle mere:[1] 205
Watch what thou seëst, and lightly[2] bring me word."

To him replied the bold Sir Bedivere:
"It is not meet, Sir King, to leave thee thus,
Aidless, alone, and smitten through the helm—
A little thing may harm a wounded man; 210
Yet I thy hest will all perform at full,
Watch what I see, and lightly bring thee word."

So saying, from the ruined shrine he stepped,
And in the moon athwart the place of tombs,
Where lay the mighty bones of ancient men, 215
Old knights, and over them the sea-wind sang
Shrill, chill, with flakes of foam. He, stepping down
By zigzag paths, and juts of pointed rock,
Came on the shining levels of the lake.

There drew he forth the brand Excalibur, 220
And o'er him, drawing it, the winter moon,
Brightening the skirts of a long cloud, ran forth
And sparkled keen with frost against the hilt:
For all the haft twinkled with diamond sparks,
Myriads of topaz-lights, and jacinth-work[3] 225
Of subtlest jewelry. He gazed so long
That both his eyes were dazzled as he stood,
This way and that dividing the swift mind,
In act to throw: but at the last it seemed

7. Cf. Malory XXI.7: "Some men yet say in many parts of England that King Arthur is not dead, but by the will of our Lord in another place. And men say that he will come again."

8. Sword.
9. A rich, heavy silk.
1. Middle of the lake.
2. Quickly.
3. A "jacinth" is a red gem.

Better to leave Excalibur concealed 230
There in the many-knotted waterflags,
That whistled stiff and dry about the marge.
So strode he back slow to the wounded King.

Then spake King Arthur to Sir Bedivere:
"Hast thou performed my mission which I gave? 235
What is it thou hast seen? or what hast heard?"

And answer made the bold Sir Bedivere:
"I heard the ripple washing in the reeds,
And the wild water lapping on the crag."

To whom replied King Arthur, faint and pale: 240
"Thou hast betrayed thy nature and thy name,
Not rendering true answer, as beseemed
Thy fëalty, nor like a noble knight:
For surer sign had followed, either hand,
Or voice, or else a motion of the mere. 245
This is a shameful thing for men to lie.
Yet now, I charge thee, quickly go again,
As thou art lief[4] and dear, and do the thing
I bade thee, watch, and lightly bring me word."

Then went Sir Bedivere the second time 250
Across the ridge, and paced beside the mere,
Counting the dewy pebbles, fixed in thought;
But when he saw the wonder of the hilt,
How curiously[5] and strangely chased, he smote
His palms together, and he cried aloud: 255

"And if indeed I cast the brand away,
Surely a precious thing, one worthy note,
Should thus be lost forever from the earth,
Which might have pleased the eyes of many men.
What good should follow this, if this were done? 260
What harm, undone? Deep harm to disobey,
Seeing obedience is the bond of rule.
Were it well to obey then, if a king demand
An act unprofitable, against himself?
The King is sick, and knows not what he does. 265
What record, or what relic of my lord
Should be to aftertime, but empty breath
And rumors of a doubt? But were this kept,
Stored in some treasure-house of mighty kings,
Some one might show it at a joust of arms, 270
Saying, 'King Arthur's sword, Excalibur,
Wrought by the lonely maiden of the Lake.

---

4. Beloved.   5. Skillfully; "chased": adorned.

Nine years she wrought it, sitting in the deeps
Upon the hidden bases of the hills.'
So might some old man speak in the aftertime   275
To all the people, winning reverence.
But now much honor and much fame were lost."

     So spake he, clouded with his own conceit,[6]
And hid Excalibur the second time,
And so strode back slow to the wounded king.   280

     Then spoke King Arthur, breathing heavily:
"What is it thou hast seen? or what hast heard?"

     And answer made the bold Sir Bedivere:
"I heard the water lapping on the crag,
And the long ripple washing in the reeds."   285

     To whom replied King Arthur, much in wrath:
"Ah, miserable and unkind, untrue,
Unknightly, traitor-hearted! Woe is me!
Authority forgets a dying king,
Laid widowed of the power in his eye   290
That bowed the will. I see thee what thou art,
For thou, the latest-left of all my knights,
In whom should meet the offices of all,
Thou wouldst betray me for the precious hilt;
Either from lust of gold, or like a girl   295
Valuing the giddy pleasure of the eyes.
Yet, for a man may fail in duty twice,
And the third time may prosper, get thee hence:
But, if thou spare to fling Excalibur,
I will arise and slay thee with my hands."   300

     Then quickly rose Sir Bedivere, and ran,
And, leaping down the ridges lightly, plunged
Among the bullrush beds, and clutched the sword,
And strongly wheeled and threw it. The great brand
Made lightnings in the splendor of the moon,   305
And flashing round and round, and whirled in an arch,
Shot like a streamer of the northern morn,
Seen where the moving isles of winter shock[7]
By night, with noises of the Northern Sea.
So flashed and fell the brand Excalibur: 310
But ere he dipped the surface, rose an arm
Clothed in white samite, mystic, wonderful,
And caught him by the hilt, and brandished him
Three times, and drew him under in the mere.
And lightly went the other to the King.   315

---

6. Vain and foolish fancies.   "northern morn": the northern lights.
7. I.e., where the icebergs collide;

Then spoke King Arthur, drawing thicker breath:
"Now see I by thine eyes that this is done.
Speak out: what is it thou hast heard, or seen?"

And answer made the bold Sir Bedivere:
"Sir King, I closed mine eyelids, lest the gems   320
Should blind my purpose, for I never saw,
Nor shall see, here or elsewhere, till I die,
Not though I live three lives of mortal men,
So great a miracle as yonder hilt.
Then with both hands I flung him, wheeling him;   325
But when I looked again, behold an arm,
Clothed in white samite, mystic, wonderful,
That caught him by the hilt, and brandished him
Three times, and drew him under in the mere."

And answer made King Arthur, breathing hard: 330
"My end draws nigh; 'tis time that I were gone.
Make broad thy shoulders to receive my weight,
And bear me to the margin; yet I fear
My wound hath taken cold, and I shall die."

So saying, from the pavement he half rose,   335
Slowly, with pain, reclining on his arm,
And looking wistfully with wide blue eyes
As in a picture. Him Sir Bedivere
Remorsefully regarded through his tears,
And would have spoken, but he found not words;   340
Then took with care, and kneeling on one knee,
O'er both his shoulders drew the languid hands,
And rising bore him through the place of tombs.

But, as he walked, King Arthur panted hard,
Like one that feels a nightmare on his bed   345
When all the house is mute. So sighed the King,
Muttering and murmuring at his ear, "Quick, quick!
I fear it is too late, and I shall die."
But the other swiftly strode from ridge to ridge,
Clothed with his breath, and looking, as he walked,   350
Larger than human on the frozen hills.
He heard the deep behind him, and a cry
Before. His own thought drove him like a goad.
Dry clashed his harness in the icy caves
And barren chasms, and all to left and right   355
The bare black cliff clanged round him, as he based
His feet on juts of slippery crag that rang
Sharp-smitten with the dint of armèd heels—
And on a sudden, lo! the level lake,
And the long glories of the winter moon.   360

Then saw they how there hove a dusky barge,
Dark as a funeral scarf from stem to stern,
Beneath them; and descending they were ware
That all the decks were dense with stately forms,
Black-stoled, black-hooded, like a dream—by these   365
Three Queens with crowns of gold: and from them rose
A cry that shivered to the tingling stars,
And, as it were one voice, an agony
Of lamentation, like a wind that shrills
All night in a waste land, where no one comes,   370
Or hath come, since the making of the world.

Then murmured Arthur, "Place me in the barge."
So to the barge they came. There those three Queens
Put forth their hands, and took the King, and wept.
But she, that rose the tallest of them all   375
And fairest, laid his head upon her lap,
And loosed the shattered casque,[8] and chafed his hands,
And called him by his name, complaining loud,
And dropping bitter tears against a brow
Striped with dark blood: for all his face was white   380
And colorless, and like the withered moon
Smote by the fresh beam of the springing east;
And all his greaves and cuisses dashed with drops
Of onset;[9] and the light and lustrous curls—
That made his forehead like a rising sun   385
High from the daïs-throne—were parched with dust;
Or, clotted into points and hanging loose,
Mixed with the knightly growth that fringed his lips.
So like a shattered column lay the King;
Not like that Arthur who, with lance in rest,   390
From spur to plume a star of tournament,
Shot through the lists at Camelot, and charged
Before the eyes of ladies and of kings.

Then loudly cried the bold Sir Bedivere:
"Ah! my Lord Arthur, whither shall I go?   395
Where shall I hide my forehead and my eyes?
For now I see the true old times are dead,
When every morning brought a noble chance,
And every chance brought out a noble knight.
Such times have been not since the light that led   400
The holy Elders with the gift of myrrh.[1]
But now the whole Round Table is dissolved
Which was an image of the mighty world,

---

8. Helmet.
9. "Greaves": armor to protect the leg below the knee; "cuisses": armor to protect the front of the thighs; "onset": blood from battle.
1. I.e., the star that guided the three kings ("Elders") to the Christ Child at Bethlehem.

And I, the last, go forth companionless,
And the days darken round me, and the years,   405
Among new men, strange faces, other minds."

    And slowly answered Arthur from the barge:
"The old order changeth, yielding place to new,
And God fulfills himself in many ways,
Lest one good custom should corrupt the world.   410
Comfort thyself: what comfort is in me?
I have lived my life, and that which I have done
May He within himself make pure! but thou,
If thou shouldst never see my face again,
Pray for my soul. More things are wrought by prayer   415
Than this world dreams of. Wherefore, let thy voice
Rise like a fountain for me night and day.
For what are men better than sheep or goats
That nourish a blind life within the brain,
If, knowing God, they lift not hands of prayer   420
Both for themselves and those who call them friend?
For so the whole round earth is every way
Bound by gold chains about the feet of God.
But now farewell. I am going a long way
With these thou seëst—if indeed I go   425
(For all my mind is clouded with a doubt)—
To the island-valley of Avilion;[2]
Where falls not hail, or rain, or any snow,
Nor ever wind blows loudly; but it lies
Deep-meadowed, happy, fair with orchard lawns   430
And bowery hollows crowned with summer sea,
Where I will heal me of my grievous wound."

    So said he, and the barge with oar and sail
Moved from the brink, like some full-breasted swan
That, fluting a wild carol ere her death,   435
Ruffles her pure cold plume, and takes the flood
With swarthy webs. Long stood Sir Bedivere
Revolving many memories, till the hull
Looked one black dot against the verge of dawn,
And on the mere the wailing died away.   440

    But when that moan had passed for evermore,
The stillness of the dead world's winter dawn
Amazed him, and he groaned, "The King is gone."
And therewithal came on him the weird rhyme,
"From the great deep to the great deep he goes."   445

2. Avalon, in Celtic mythology and me-   where heroes enjoyed life after death.
dieval romance, the Vale of the Blessed

Whereat he slowly turned and slowly clomb
The last hard footstep of that iron crag;
Thence marked the black hull moving yet, and cried,
"He passes to be King among the dead,
And after healing of his grievous wound   450
He comes again; but—if he come no more—
O me, be yon dark Queens in yon black boat,
Who shrieked and wailed, the three whereat we gazed
On that high day, when, clothed with living light,
They stood before his throne in silence, friends   455
Of Arthur, who should help him at his need?"

    Then from the dawn it seemed there came, but faint
As from beyond the limit of the world,
Like the last echo born of a great cry,
Sounds, as if some fair city were one voice   460
Around a king returning from his wars.

    Thereat once more he moved about, and clomb
Even to the highest he could climb, and saw,
Straining his eyes beneath an arch of hand,
Or thought he saw, the speck that bare the King,   465
Down that long water opening on the deep
Somewhere far off, pass on and on, and go
From less to less and vanish into light.
And the new sun rose bringing the new year.

1833–69   1869

A Dedication[1]

Dear, near and true—no truer Time himself
Can prove you, though he make you evermore
Dearer and nearer, as the rapid of life
Shoots to the fall—take this and pray that he
Who wrote it, honoring your sweet faith in him,   5
May trust himself; and after praise and scorn,
As one who feels the immeasurable world,
Attain the wise indifference of the wise;
And after Autumn past—if left to pass
His autumn into seeming-leafless days—   10
Draw toward the long frost and longest night,
Wearing his wisdom lightly, like the fruit
Which in our winter woodland looks a flower.

                                                 1864

1. To the poet's wife, Emily.

I Stood on a Tower

I stood on a tower in the wet,
And New Year and Old Year met,
And winds were roaring and blowing;
And I said, "O years, that meet in tears,
Have ye aught that is worth the knowing?   5
Science enough and exploring,
Wanderers coming and going,
Matter enough for deploring,
But aught that is worth the knowing?"
Seas at my feet were flowing,   10
Waves on the shingle pouring,
Old Year roaring and blowing,
And New Year blowing and roaring.

1865   1868

Northern Farmer[1]

NEW STYLE

1

Dosn't thou 'ear my 'erse's[2] legs, as they canters awaäy?
Proputty,[3] proputty, proputty—that's what I 'ears 'em saäy.
Proputty, proputty, proputty—Sam, thou's an ass for thy paaïns;
Theer's moor sense i' one o' 'is legs, nor in all thy braaïns.

2

Whoä—theer's a craw[4] to pluck wi' tha, Sam: youn's Parson's
    'ouse—   5
Dosn't thou knaw that a man mun be eäther a man or a mouse?
Time to think on it then; for thou'll be twenty to weeäk.[5]
Proputty, proputty—woä then, woä—let ma 'ear mysén[6] speäk.

3

Me an' thy muther, Sammy, 'as beän a-talkin' o' thee;
Thou's beän talkin' to muther, an' she beän a-tellin' it me.   10

---

1. This monologue exemplifies the diversity of Tennyson's talents. A passionate attachment to land and property, which was portrayed sympathetically by Wordsworth in *Michael*, is here represented humorously. The harsh common sense of the farmer's attitude towards love and marriage is reinforced by his jaw-breaking north-English dialect.
    This is the second of a pair of monologues in dialect. In the first, *Northern Farmer: Old Style*, the speaker is a bailiff who has spent his life supervising the farmlands of a wealthy squire. In the second, the "new style" farmer is himself an independent landowner.
2. Horse's.
3. Property.
4. Crow.
5. This week.
6. Myself.

Thou'll not marry for munny—thou's sweet upo' Parson's lass—
Noä—thou'll marry for luvv—an' we boäth on us thinks tha an ass.

4

Seeäed her todaäy goä by—Saäint's-daäy—they was ringing the
    bells.
She's a beauty, thou thinks—an' soä is scoors o' gells,[7]
Them as 'as munny an' all—wot's a beauty!—the flower as blaws. 15
But proputty, proputty sticks, an' proputty, proputty graws.

5

Do'ant be stunt;[8] taäke time. I knaws what maäkes tha sa mad.
Warn't I craäzed fur the lasses mysén when I wur a lad?
But I knawed a Quaäker feller as often 'as towd[9] ma this:
"Doänt thou marry for munny, but goä wheer munny is!"   20

6

An' I went wheer munny war; an' thy muther coom to 'and,
Wi' lots o' munny laaïd by, an' a nicetish bit o' land.
Maäybe she warn't a beauty—I niver giv it a thowt—
But warn't she as good to cuddle an' kiss as a lass as 'ant nowt?[1]

7

Parson's lass 'ant nowt, an she weänt 'a nowt[2] when 'e's deäd,   25
Mun be a guvness, lad, or summut, and addle[3] her breäd.
Why? fur 'e's nobbut[4] a curate, an' weänt niver get hissén clear,
An' 'e maäde the bed as 'e ligs[5] on afoor 'e coomed to the shere.

8

An' thin 'e coomed to the parish wi' lots o' Varsity debt,
Stook to his taaïl they did, an' 'e 'ant got shut on 'em[6] yet.
An' 'e ligs on 'is back i' the grip,[7] wi' noän to lend 'im a shuvv,   30
Woorse nor a far-weltered yowe;[8] fur, Sammy, 'e married fur luvv.

9

Luvv? what's luvv? thou can luvv thy lass an' 'er munny too,
Mäukin' 'em goä togither, as they've good right to do.
Couldn' I luvv thy muther by cause o' 'er munny laaïd by?   35
Naäy—fur I luvved 'er a vast sight moor fur it; reäson why.

10

Aye, an' thy muther says thou wants to marry the lass,
Cooms of a gentleman burn;[9] an' we boäth on us thinks tha an ass.

---

7. Scores of girls.
8. Stubborn.
9. Told.
1. Has nothing.
2. Won't have anything.
3. Earn.

4. Only.
5. Lies; "shere": shire.
6. Rid of them.
7. Ditch.
8. Ewe lying on her back.
9. Born.

Woä then, proputty, wiltha?—an ass as near as mays nowt[1]—
Woä then, wiltha? dangtha!—the bees is as fell as owt.[2]   40

11

Breäk me a bit o' the esh[3] for his 'eäd, lad, out o' the fence!
Gentleman burn! what's gentleman burn? is it shillins an' pence?
Proputty, proputty's ivrything 'ere, an', Sammy, I'm blest
If it isn't the saäme oop younder, fur them as 'as it's the best.

12

Tis'n them as 'as munny as breäks into 'ouses an' steäls,   45
Them as 'as coäts to their backs an' taäkes their regular meäls.
Noä, but it's them as niver knaws wheer a meäl's to be 'ad.
Taäke my word for it, Sammy, the poor in a loomp is bad.

13

Them or thir feythers, tha sees, mun 'a beän a laäzy lot,
Fur work mun 'a gone to the gittin' whiniver munny was got.   50
Feyther 'ad ammost nowt; leästways 'is munny was 'id.
But 'e tued an' moiled[4] issén deäd, an' 'e died a good un, 'e did.

14

Looök thou theer wheer Wrigglesby beck[5] cooms out by the 'ill!
Feyther run oop[6] to the farm, an' I runs oop to the mill;
An' I'll run oop to the brig,[7] an' that thou'll live to see;   55
And if thou marries a good un I'll leäve the land to thee.

15

Thim's my noätions, Sammy, wheerby I meäns to stick;
But if thou marries a bad un, I'll leäve the land to Dick.—
Coom oop, proputty, proputty—that's what I 'ears 'im saäy—
Proputty, proputty, proputty—canter an' canter awaäy.   60

1869

Flower in the Crannied Wall

Flower in the crannied wall,
I pluck you out of the crannies,
I hold you here, root and all, in my hand,
Little flower—but if I could understand
What you are, root and all, and all in all,   5
I should know what God and man is.

1869

---

1. Makes nothing.
2. The flies are as mean as anything.
3. A branch of ash leaves (to keep the flies off the horse's head).
4. Toiled and drudged.
5. Brook.
6. I.e., father's property ran up.
7. Bridge.

The Revenge[1]

A BALLAD OF THE FLEET

1

At Flores in the Azores Sir Richard Grenville lay,
And a pinnace, like a fluttered bird, came flying from far away:
"Spanish ships of war at sea! we have sighted fifty-three!"
Then sware Lord Thomas Howard: " 'Fore God I am no coward;
But I cannot meet them here, for my ships are out of gear,   5
And the half my men are sick. I must fly, but follow quick.
We are six ships of the line; can we fight with fifty-three?"

2

Then spake Sir Richard Grenville: "I know you are no coward;
You fly them for a moment to fight with them again.
But I've ninety men and more that are lying sick ashore.   10
I should count myself the coward if I left them, my Lord Howard,
To these Inquisition dogs and the devildoms of Spain."

3

So Lord Howard passed away with five ships of war that day,
Till he melted like a cloud in the silent summer heaven;
But Sir Richard bore in hand all his sick men from the land   15
Very carefully and slow,
Men of Bideford in Devon,
And we laid them on the ballast down below;
For we brought them all aboard,
And they blessed him in their pain, that they were not left to
     Spain,   20
To the thumbscrew and the stake, for the glory of the Lord.

4

He had only a hundred seamen to work the ship and to fight,
And he sailed away from Flores till the Spaniard came in sight,
With his huge sea-castles heaving upon the weather bow.
"Shall we fight or shall we fly?
Good Sir Richard, tell us now,   25
For to fight is but to die!
There'll be little of us left by the time this sun be set."
And Sir Richard said again: "We be all good English men.
Let us bang these dogs of Seville, the children of the devil,   30
For I never turned my back upon Don or devil yet."

---

1. Based on Sir Walter Ralegh's account of an engagement in 1591 off the coast of Flores, one of the islands of the Azores, in which five Spanish ships were sunk by the *Revenge* during a fifteen-hour battle. See Volume 1 of this anthology, p. 755.

5

Sir Richard spoke and he laughed, and we roared a hurrah, and so
The little Revenge ran on sheer into the heart of the foe,
With her hundred fighters on deck, and her ninety sick below;
For half of their fleet to the right and half to the left were seen,   35
And the little Revenge ran on through the long sea lane between.

6

Thousands of their soldiers looked down from their decks and
      laughed,
Thousands of their seamen made mock at the mad little craft
Running on and on, till delayed
By their mountain-like San Philip that, of fifteen hundred tons,   40
And up-shadowing high above us with her yawning tiers of guns,
Took the breath from our sails, and we stayed.

7

And while now the great San Philip hung above us like a cloud
Whence the thunderbolt will fall
Long and loud,   45
Four galleons drew away
From the Spanish fleet that day,
And two upon the larboard and two upon the starboard lay,
And the battle thunder broke from them all.

8

But anon the great San Philip, she bethought herself and went,   50
Having that within her womb that had left her ill content;
For a dozen times they came with their piles and musqueteers,
And the rest they came aboard us, and they fought us hand to hand,
And a dozen times we shook 'em off as a dog that shakes his ears
When he leaps from the water to the land.   55

9

And the sun went down, and the stars came out far over the
      summer sea,
But never a moment ceased the fight of the one and the fifty-three.
Ship after ship, the whole night long, their high-built galleons came,
Ship after ship, the whole night long, with her battle thunder and
      flame;
Ship after ship, the whole night long, drew back with her dead and
      her shame.   60
For some were sunk and many were shattered, and so could fight us
      no more—
God of battles, was ever a battle like this in the world before?

10

For he said, "Fight on! fight on!"
Though his vessel was all but a wreck;
And it chanced that, when half of the short summer night was
      gone,   65

With a grisly wound to be dressed he had left the deck,
But a bullet struck him that was dressing it suddenly dead,
And himself he was wounded again in the side and the head,
And he said, "Fight on! fight on!"

11

And the night went down, and the sun smiled out far over the
    summer sea,   70
And the Spanish fleet with broken sides lay round us all in a ring;
But they dared not touch us again, for they feared that we still
    could sting,
So they watched what the end would be.
And we had not fought them in vain,
But in perilous plight were we,   75
Seeing forty of our poor hundred were slain,
And half of the rest of us maimed for life
In the crash of the cannonades and the desperate strife;
And the sick men down in the hold were most of them stark and
    cold,
And the pikes were all broken or bent, and the powder was all of
    it spent;   80
And the masts and the rigging were lying over the side;
But Sir Richard cried in his English pride:
"We have fought such a fight for a day and a night
As may never be fought again!
We have won great glory, my men!   85
And a day less or more
At sea or ashore,
We die—does it matter when?
Sink me the ship, Master Gunner—sink her, split her in twain!
Fall into the hands of God, not into the hands of Spain!"   90

12

And the gunner said, "Aye, aye," but the seamen made reply:
"We have children, we have wives,
And the Lord hath spared our lives.
We will make the Spaniard promise, if we yield, to let us go;
We shall live to fight again and to strike another blow."   95
And the lion there lay dying, and they yielded to the foe.

13

And the stately Spanish men to their flagship bore him then,
Where they laid him by the mast, old Sir Richard caught at last,
And they praised him to his face with their courtly foreign grace;
But he rose upon their decks, and he cried: 100
"I have fought for Queen and Faith like a valiant man and true;
I have only done my duty as a man is bound to do.
With a joyful spirit I Sir Richard Grenville die!"
And he fell upon their decks, and he died.

14

And they stared at the dead that had been so valiant and true,   105
And had holden the power and glory of Spain so cheap
That he dared her with one little ship and his English few;
Was he devil or man? He was devil for aught they knew,
But they sank his body with honor down into the deep,
And they manned the Revenge with a swarthier alien crew,   110
And away she sailed with her loss and longed for her own;
When a wind from the lands they had ruined awoke from sleep,
And the water began to heave and the weather to moan,
And or ever that evening ended a great gale blew,
And a wave like the wave that is raised by an earthquake grew,   115
Till it smote on their hulls and their sails and their masts and their
    flags,
And the whole sea plunged and fell on the shot-shattered navy of
    Spain,
And the little Revenge herself went down by the island crags
To be lost evermore in the main.

1878

To Virgil

WRITTEN AT THE REQUEST OF THE MANTUANS[1] FOR THE
NINETEENTH CENTENARY OF VIRGIL'S DEATH

1

Roman Virgil, thou that singest
    Ilion's lofty temples robed in fire,
Ilion falling, Rome arising,
    wars, and filial faith, and Dido's pyre;[2]

2

Landscape-lover, lord of language
    more than he that sang the "Works and Days,"[3]
All the chosen coin of fancy
    flashing out from many a golden phrase;

3

Thou that singest wheat and woodland,
    tilth and vineyard, hive and horse and herd;   5
All the charm of all the Muses
    often flowering in a lonely word;

4

Poet of the happy Tityrus[4]
    piping underneath his beechen bowers;

---

1. Inhabitants of Mantua, the city near
which Virgil was born.
2. The allusions in this stanza are to incidents in Virgil's *Aeneid*, especially the
fall of Troy (Ilion).

3. Hesiod, a Greek poet, whose *Works
and Days* anticipated Virgil's *Georgics* in
its pictures of farm life.
4. A shepherd in Virgil's *Eclogue* I.

Poet of the poet-satyr[5]
    whom the laughing shepherd bound with flowers;

5

Chanter of the Pollio,[6] glorying
    in the blissful years again to be,
Summers of the snakeless meadow,
    unlaborious earth and oarless sea;   10

6

Thou that seest Universal
    Nature moved by Universal Mind;
Thou majestic in thy sadness
    at the doubtful doom of human kind;

7

Light among the vanished ages;
    star that gildest yet this phantom shore;
Golden branch[7] amid the shadows,
    kings and realms that pass to rise no more;

8

Now thy Forum roars no longer,
    fallen every purple Caesar's dome—   15
Though thine ocean-roll of rhythm
    sound forever of Imperial Rome—

9

Now the Rome of slaves hath perished,
    and the Rome of freemen[8] holds her place,
I, from out the Northern Island
    sundered once from all the human race,

10

I salute thee, Mantovano,[9]
    I that loved thee since my day began,
Wielder of the stateliest measure
    ever molded by the lips of man.   20

1882   1882

"*Frater Ave atque Vale*"[1]

Row us out from Desenzano,[2] to your Sirmione row!
So they rowed, and there we landed—"O venusta Sirmio!"

5. Silenus, in *Eclogue* VI.
6. A friend of Virgil's who is celebrated in *Eclogue* IV.
7. A golden bough enabled Aeneas to enter the world of the shades. See *Aeneid* VI.208 ff.
8. Italy had only recently been liberated and unified.
9. Mantuan.
1. "Brother, hail and farewell," a line from an elegy by the Roman poet Catul-

lus on the death of his brother (CI.10). Tennyson himself had recently lost his brother Charles.
2. A town on Lake Garda in Italy, which Tennyson visited in 1880. Sirmione is a beautiful peninsula jutting into the lake, on which Catullus had his summer home. Catullus' poem in honor of the locality includes the phrase "*O venusta Sirmio!*" ("O lovely Sirmio!").

There to me through all the groves of olive in the summer glow,
There beneath the Roman ruin where the purple flowers grow,
Came that "Ave atque Vale" of the Poet's hopeless woe, 5
Tenderest of Roman poets nineteen hundred years ago,
"Frater Ave atque Vale"—as we wandered to and fro
Gazing at the Lydian[3] laughter of the Garda Lake below
Sweet Catullus's all-but-island, olive-silvery Sirmio!

18801883

The Dawn

"You are but children."
—EGYPTIAN PRIEST TO SOLON

Red of the Dawn!
Screams of a babe in the red-hot palms of a Moloch[1] of Tyre,
Man with his brotherless dinner on man in the tropical wood,
Priests in the name of the Lord passing souls through fire to the
fire,
Head-hunters and boats of Dahomey[2] that float upon human
blood!5

Red of the Dawn!
Godless fury of peoples, and Christless frolic of kings,
And the bolt of war dashing down upon cities and blazing farms,
For Babylon was a child newborn, and Rome was a babe in arms,
And London and Paris and all the rest are as yet but in leading
strings.10

Dawn not Day,
While scandal is mouthing a bloodless name at *her* cannibal feast,
And rake-ruined bodies and souls go down in a common wreck,
And the Press of a thousand cities is prized for it smells of the
beast,
Or easily violates virgin Truth for a coin or a check.15

Dawn not Day!
Is it Shame, so few should have climbed from the dens in the level
below,
Men, with a heart and a soul, no slaves of a four-footed will?
But if twenty million of summers are stored in the sunlight still,
We are far from the noon of man, there is time for the race to
grow.20

---

3. The Etruscans, who settled near Lake Garda, were thought to be descended from the Lydians of Asia Minor.
1. A god to whom children were sacrificed as burnt offerings.

2. West African country in which the custom of human sacrifice persisted in the 19th century. In 1892, after a war, Dahomey became a French colony.

Red of the Dawn!
Is it turning a fainter red? So be it, but when shall we lay
   The Ghost of the Brute that is walking and haunting us yet, and
      be free?
   In a hundred, a thousand winters? Ah, what will *our* children be?
The men of a hundred thousand, a million summers away?   25

                         1892

The Silent Voices

When the dumb Hour, clothed in black,
Brings the Dreams about my bed,
Call me not so often back,
Silent Voices of the dead,
Toward the lowland ways behind me,   5
And the sunlight that is gone!
Call me rather, silent voices,
Forward to the starry track
Glimmering up the heights beyond me
On, and always on!   10

                         1892

Crossing the Bar[1]

Sunset and evening star,
   And one clear call for me!
And may there be no moaning of the bar,[2]
   When I put out to sea,

But such a tide as moving seems asleep,   5
   Too full for sound and foam,
When that which drew from out the boundless deep
   Turns again home.

Twilight and evening bell,
   And after that the dark!
And may there be no sadness of farewell,   10
   When I embark;

For though from out our bourne[3] of Time and Place
   The flood may bear me far,
I hope to see my Pilot face to face
   When I have crossed the bar.   15

1889   1889

1. Although not the last poem written by Tennyson, *Crossing the Bar* appears, at his request, as the final poem in all collections of his work.   2. Mournful sound of the ocean beating on a sand bar at the mouth of a harbor.
3. Boundary.

ROBERT BROWNING

(1812–1889)

1846:   Marriage to Elizabeth Barrett and residence in Italy.
1855:   *Men and Women* published.
1861:   Death of Elizabeth Barrett Browning.
1868–69: *The Ring and the Book* published.

During the years of his marriage Robert Browning was sometimes referred to as "Mrs. Browning's husband." Elizabeth Barrett, who seems to us now a minor figure, was at that time a famous poet while her husband was a relatively unknown experimenter whose poems were greeted with misunderstanding or indifference. Not until the 1860's did he at last gain a public and become recognized as the rival or equal of Tennyson. In the 20th century his reputation has persisted, but in an unusual way: his poetry is admired by two groups of readers widely different in tastes. To one group his work is a moral tonic. Such readers appreciate him as a man who lived bravely and as a writer who showed life to be a joyful battle, the imperfections of this world being remedied, under the dispensations of an all-loving God, by the perfections of the next. Typical of this group are the Browning Societies which have flourished in England and America. Members of these societies usually regard their poet as a wise philosopher and religious teacher who resolved the doubts which had troubled Arnold and Tennyson and which have continued to trouble later generations of less confident writers.

A second group of readers enjoy Browning less for his attempt to solve problems of religious doubt than for his attempt to solve the problems of how poetry should be written. Such poets as Ezra Pound and Robert Lowell have valued him as a major artist; they have recognized that more than any other 19th-century poet (even including Hopkins), it was Browning who energetically hacked through a trail that has subsequently become the main road of 20th-century poetry. In *Poetry and the Age* (1953) Randall Jarrell remarked how "the dramatic monologue, which once had depended for its effect upon being a departure from the norm of poetry, now became in one form or another the norm." Later poets such as Edward Lucie-Smith in England and Richard Howard in America are especially close to Browning's mode. In 1969, Howard dedicated a volume of monologues to Browning: "to the great poet of otherness * * * who said, as I should like to say, 'I'll tell my state as though 'twere none of mine.' "

The dramatic monologue, as Browning uses it, enables the reader, speaker, and poet to be located at an appropriate distance from each other, aligned in such a way that the reader must work *through* the words of the speaker toward the meaning of the poet himself. For example, in the well-known early monologue *My Last Duchess*, we listen to the Duke as he speaks of his dead wife, and it is almost as if we were overhearing a man talking into the telephone of a booth adjacent to ours. From his one-sided conversation we piece together the situation, both past and present, and we infer what sort of woman the Duchess really was, and what sort of man is the Duke. Ultimately we may also infer what the poet himself thinks of the speaker he has created. In this instance, from evidence outside the poem we know that Browning had a special aversion for domestic tyrants. His own father-in-law was to provide him with a striking example of the breed, and it is revealing that in his longest poem, *The Ring and the Book*, he once more explored the story of another domestic tyrant who, like the Duke, was irritated by his wife's virtues. Yet from *My Last Duchess* itself, if we exclude external evidence, it is interesting to note how persuasive is the Duke's own side of the story:

> She had
> A heart—how shall I say?—too soon made glad,
> Too easily impressed; she liked whate'er
> She looked on, and her looks went everywhere.

Although Browning contrives that our verdict as jurymen will be a just one, he does allow us a considerable amount of latitude. And in some of his later monologues we are really obliged to grope toward a choice. In reading *A Grammarian's Funeral*, for example, can we be sure that the central character is a hero? Or is he merely a fool? Browning has not made the answer easy for us.

In addition to his experiments with the dramatic monologue Browning also made experiments with language and syntax. The grotesque rhymes and jaw-breaking diction which he often employs have been repugnant to some critics; George Santayana, for instance, dismissed him as a clumsy barbarian. But to those who understand Browning's aims, the incongruities of language are not literally incongruous but functional, a humorous and appropriate counterpart to an imperfect world. Ezra Pound's tribute to "Old Hippety-Hop o' the accents," as he addresses Browning, is both affectionate and memorable:

> Heart that was big as the bowels of Vesuvius
> Words that were winged as her sparks in eruption,
> Eagled and thundered as Jupiter Pluvius
> Sound in your wind past all signs o' corruption.

This capacity to attract the admiration of such a diversity of readers, sophisticated and unsophisticated, is one of several ways in which Browning's writings can be likened to those of Dickens and Shakespeare.

The personal life of Robert Browning falls into three phases: his years as a child and young bachelor, as a husband, and as a widower. Each of these phases is most appropriately considered in relation to his development as a poet.

He was born in Camberwell, a London suburb, within a few months of the births of Dickens and Thackeray. His father, a bank clerk, was a learned man with an extensive library. His mother was a kindly, religious-minded woman, interested in music, whose love for her brilliant son was warmly reciprocated. Until the time of his marriage at the age of 34 Browning was rarely absent from his parents' home. He attended a boarding school near

Camberwell, traveled a little, and was a student at the University of London for a short period, but he preferred to pursue his education at home where he was tutored in foreign languages, music, boxing, and horsemanship, and where he read omnivorously. From this unusual education he acquired a store of knowledge upon which to draw for the background of his poems.

The "obscurity" of which his contemporaries complained in his earlier poetry may be partly accounted for by the circumstances of Browning's education. He was inclined to assume that his out-of-the-ordinary learning was generally shared by educated readers. Often it was not. But the obscurity of such poems as *Sordello* is attributable not only to the nature of Browning's learning but to the poet's anxious desire to avoid exposing himself too explicitly before his readers. His first poem, *Pauline*, published when he was 21, had been modeled in the example of Shelley, the most personal of poets. When a review by John Stuart Mill pointed out that the young author was parading a "morbid state" of self-worship, Browning was overwhelmed with embarrassment. He resolved to avoid confessional writings thereafter.

One way of reducing the personal element in his poetry was to write plays instead of soul-searching narratives or lyrics. In 1836, encouraged by the actor W. C. Macready, Browning began work on his first play, *Strafford*, a historical tragedy that lasted only four nights when it was produced at a London theater in 1837. For ten years the young writer struggled to produce other plays that would better hold the attention of an audience, but as stage productions they all remained failures. Browning nevertheless profited from this otherwise disheartening experience. Writing dialogue for actors led him to explore another form more congenial to his genius, the dramatic monologue, a form that enabled him through imaginary speakers to avoid explicit autobiography and yet did not demand that these speakers act out their story with the speed or the simplifications that stage production demands.

Browning's resolution to avoid the subjective manner of Shelley did not preclude his being influenced by the earlier poet in other ways. At 14, when he first discovered Shelley's works, he became an atheist and liberal. Although he outgrew the atheism, after a struggle, and also the extreme phases of his liberalism, he retained from Shelley's influence something permanent and more difficult to define: an ardent dedication to ideals (often undefined ideals) and an energetic striving toward goals (often undefined goals). This quality of aspiration is much more mixed with earthiness—even worldliness—in Browning's character than in Shelley's. To soar upwards on a skylark's wing was not to Browning's taste. He is more like Robert Frost's swinger of birches who climbs a tree toward heaven but is anxious to swing down to earth again before getting too far away.

Yet the element of worldliness should not obscure from us Browning's ardent romanticism. His love affair with Elizabeth Barrett was romantic in several of the senses of that hard-worked adjective. It is easy to see why the well-known story of their courtship has been retold by novelists, dramatists, and movie-producers, for the situation had the dramatic ingredients of Browning's own favorite story of St. George rescuing the maiden from the dragon. Almost everything seemed unpropitious when Browning met Elizabeth Barrett in 1845. She was six years older than he was, a semi-invalid, jealously guarded by her possessively tyrannical father. But love, as the poet was to say later, is best, and love swept aside all obstacles. After their elopement to Italy, the former semi-invalid was soon enjoying good health and a full life. The husband likewise seemed to thrive during the years of this remarkable marriage. Like many English poets he was especially at ease in the warm lands of the Mediterranean. His most memorable volume of poems, *Men and Women* (1855), reflects his enjoyment of Italy: its picturesque landscapes and lively street scenes as well as its monuments from the past—its Renaissance past in particular, a period of expanding energies which was congenial to his own expansive temperament.

The happy fifteen-year sojourn in Italy ended in 1861 with Elizabeth's death. The widower returned to London with his son. During the 28 years remaining to him, the quantity of verse he produced did not diminish. Nor, during the first decade, did it decrease in quality. His greatest single work, *The Ring and the Book*, a poem on the vast scale of a long novel, was published in 1868. His later writings, however, suffer from a certain mechanical repetition of mannerism and an excess of argumentation—faults into which he may have been lead by the unqualified enthusiasm of his admirers, for it was during this period that he gained his great following. When he died, in 1889, he was buried in Westminster Abbey.

During these London years Browning became abundantly fond of social life. He dined at the homes of friends and at clubs, where he enjoyed port wine and conversation. He would talk loudly and emphatically about many topics—except his own poetry, about which he was usually reticent. His reticence bothered many of his admirers. American women visiting in London, after having looked forward to meeting the author whose poems had inspired them to higher things, were disappointed—almost appalled—when they met the man at a dinner party. He did not "look like a poet." His late poem *House* may show why he gave such an impression. Behind the façade of the hearty diner-out, Browning could live and think as he pleased, just as he had discovered in writing his monologues the advantage, for him, of indirect speaking. Each speaker of monologue provides a mask for the poet.

Despite his bursts of outspokenness, Browning's character is thus not so clearly known to us as that of Tennyson or Arnold or Carlyle. Hardy once said that Browning's character seemed to him "*the* literary puzzle of the 19th century." To solve the puzzle one biographer, Mrs. Betty Miller, has tried to show that Browning was not such a happy and confident person as he is usually represented to have been, an impression that can be reinforced by the note of desperation in such poems as *Childe Roland*. And although a later biography by Maisie Ward corrects the eccentricities of this interpretation, her study also demonstrates that Browning was a complex figure. Like Yeats, he was a poet preoccupied with masks.

Just as Browning's character is harder to identify than that of Tennyson, so also are his poems more difficult to relate to the age in which they were written than are the sometimes topical poems of Tennyson. Our first impression may be that there is no connection whatever. Bishops and painters of the Renaissance, physicians of the Roman Empire, musicians of 18th-century Germany—as we explore this gallery of talking portraits we seem to be in a world of time long past, remote from the world of steam engines and disputes about man's descent from the ape.

Yet our first impression is misleading. Many of these portraits explore problems that confronted Browning's contemporaries, especially problems of faith and doubt, good and evil, and problems of the function of the artist in modern life. *Caliban upon Setebos*, for example, is a highly topical critique of Darwinism and of natural (as opposed to supernatural) religions. Browning's own attitude towards these topics is partially concealed because of his use of speakers and of settings from earlier ages, yet we do encounter certain recurrent religious assumptions that we can safely assign to the poet himself. The most recurrent is that God has created an imperfect world as a kind of testing-ground, a "vale of soul-making," as Keats had said. It followed, for Browning's purposes, that man's soul must be immortal and that heaven itself be perfect. As Abt Vogler affirms: "On the earth the broken arcs; in the heaven, a perfect round." Armed with such a faith, Browning gives the impression that he was himself untroubled by the doubts that gnawed at the hearts of Arnold and Clough and Tennyson. The "evidence" presented by historical criticism of the Bible he could dismiss as simply irrelevant, just as D. H. Lawrence, a later romantic, disposed of evolution by contending that he did not feel the evidence for it in his solar plexus.

This kind of religious conviction attracts many readers who expect poetry to provide uplift and reassurances. Other readers find it an insurmountable obstacle, as fatuous as Macaulay's faith in progress. To what extent our capacity to enjoy the writings of an author is hindered if his religious position seems repellent to us is one of the most important problems in modern criticism. The problem is much too vast to explore here, but there is at least room to insert a qualifying clause to modify the indictment that Browning's critics too hastily draw up against his cheerful religious position. A blind optimist might be simply unreadable, but Browning's optimism was not blind. Few writers, in fact, seem to have been more aware of the existence of evil. His gallery of villains—murderers, sadistic husbands, mean and petty manipulators—is an extraordinary one. Nothing is more essential to a fair-minded study of his poetry than our recognition that his apparent optimism is consistently being tested by his bringing to light the evils of man's nature. Readers who prefer to dispose of his writings by pinning them down in a formulated phrase, instead of reading them with attention, invariably cite the following lines as summing up all of Browning:

> God's in his heaven—
> All's right with the world!

But if we turn to the poem in which these lines appear, we have to modify our formulation. *Pippa Passes* is a collection of sordid tales such as one encounters on the front page of the most lurid style of newspaper. The heroine, who works in a sweatshop 364 days a year, is about to be sent to Rome as a prostitute; a man and woman living in adultery have just murdered the woman's husband; a waspish set of Bohemians have tricked a youth into marriage. Because Pippa's innocence seems to counteract the sordidness of the other scenes, we may say afterwards that God is in his heaven. But that all's right with the world is merely affirmed by the girl; the poem does not show it.

A second aspect of Browning's poetry that separates it from the Victorian age is its style. The most representative Victorian poets such as Tennyson or Dante Gabriel Rossetti write in the manner of Keats, Milton, Spenser,

and of classical poets such as Virgil. Theirs is the central stylistic tradition
in English poetry, one which favors smoothly polished texture and pleasing
liquidity of sound. Browning draws from a different tradition, more colloquial and discordant, a tradition which includes the poetry of John
Donne, the soliloquies of Shakespeare, the comic verse of the early 19th-
century poet Thomas Hood, and certain features of the narrative style of
Chaucer. Of most significance are Browning's affinities with Donne. Both
poets sacrifice, on occasion, the pleasures of harmony and of a consistent
elevation of tone by using a harshly discordant style and unexpected juxta-
positions that startle us into an awareness of a world of everyday realities
and trivialities. Browning's late poem, *The Householder*, is an excellent
example of this Donne-like vein. Readers who dislike this kind of poetry in
Browning or in Donne argue that it suffers from prosiness. Oscar Wilde
once described the novelist George Meredith as "a prose Browning." And
so, he added, was Browning. Wilde's joke may help us to relate Browning
to his contemporaries. For if Browning seems out of step with his fellow
Victorian poets, he is by no means out of step with his contemporaries in
prose. The grotesque, which plays such a prominent role in the style and
subject matter of Carlyle and Dickens, and in the aesthetic theories of John
Ruskin, is equally prominent in Browning's verse:

> Fee, faw, fum! bubble and squeak!
> Blessedest Thursday's the fat of the week.
> Rumble and tumble, sleek and rough,
> Stinking and savory, smug and gruff.

These opening lines of *Holy-Cross Day* display a kind of noisy jocularity
in presenting a situation of grave seriousness similar to that used by Carlyle
in his *Sartor Resartus*.

The link between Browning and the Victorian prose writers is not limited to style. With the later generation of Victorian novelists, George Eliot,
George Meredith, and Henry James, Browning shares a central preoccupation. Like Eliot in particular, he was interested in exposing the devious
ways in which our minds work and the complexity of our motives. "My
stress lay on incidents in the development of a human soul," he wrote;
"little else is worth study." His psychological insights can be illustrated in
such poems as *The Bishop Orders His Tomb* or *Dîs Aliter Visum*.
Although these are spoken monologues, not inner monologues in the
manner of James Joyce, yet the insight into the workings of the minds of
men is similarly acute. As in reading Joyce, we must be on our guard to
follow the rapid shifts of the speaker's mental processes as jumps are made
from one cluster of associations to another.

But Browning's role as a forerunner of 20th-century literature should not
blind us to his essential Victorianism. Energy is the most characteristic
aspect of his writing, and energy is perhaps the most characteristic aspect of
Victorian literature in general. Often, of course, such energy was misdi-
rected. Gerard Manley Hopkins identified this failing precisely when he
complained of Browning's "Broad Church" way of talking, like "a man
bouncing up from table with his mouth full of bread and cheese and saying
that he meant to stand no blasted nonsense." At its best, however, such
buoyancy is a virtue imparting a creative vitality to all of Browning's writings.

Porphyria's Lover[1]

The rain set early in tonight,
    The sullen wind was soon awake,
It tore the elm-tops down for spite,
    And did its worst to vex the lake:
    I listened with heart fit to break.   5
When glided in Porphyria; straight
    She shut the cold out and the storm,
And kneeled and made the cheerless grate
    Blaze up, and all the cottage warm;
    Which done, she rose, and from her form   10
Withdrew the dripping cloak and shawl,
    And laid her soiled gloves by, untied
Her hat and let the damp hair fall,
    And, last, she sat down by my side
    And called me. When no voice replied,   15
She put my arm about her waist,
    And made her smooth white shoulder bare,
And all her yellow hair displaced,
    And, stooping, made my cheek lie there,
    And spread, o'er all, her yellow hair,   20
Murmuring how she loved me—she
    Too weak, for all her heart's endeavor,
To set its struggling passion free
    From pride, and vainer ties dissever,
    And give herself to me forever.   25
But passion sometimes would prevail,
    Nor could tonight's gay feast restrain
A sudden thought of one so pale
    For love of her, and all in vain:
    So, she was come through wind and rain.   30
Be sure I looked up at her eyes
    Happy and proud; at last I knew
Porphyria worshiped me: surprise
    Made my heart swell, and still it grew
    While I debated what to do.   35
That moment she was mine, mine, fair,
    Perfectly pure and good: I found
A thing to do, and all her hair
    In one long yellow string I wound
    Three times her little throat around,   40
And strangled her. No pain felt she;
    I am quite sure she felt no pain.
As a shut bud that holds a bee,

1. One of a pair of monologues originally published under the title *Mad-*
house Cells, a title that emphasized the
abnormal state of mind of the speaker.

I warily oped her lids: again
   Laughed the blue eyes without a stain.   45
And I untightened next the tress
   About her neck; her cheek once more
Blushed bright beneath my burning kiss:
   I propped her head up as before,
   Only, this time my shoulder bore   50
Her head, which droops upon it still:
   The smiling rosy little head,
So glad it has its utmost will,
   That all it scorned at once is fled,
   And I, its love, am gained instead!   55
Porphyria's love: she guessed not how
   Her darling one wish would be heard.
And thus we sit together now,
   And all night long we have not stirred,
   And yet God has not said a word!   60

1834   1836, 1842

Soliloquy of the Spanish Cloister[1]

1

Gr-r-r—there go, my heart's abhorrence!
   Water your damned flowerpots, do!
If hate killed men, Brother Lawrence,
   God's blood, would not mine kill you!
What? your myrtle bush wants trimming?   5
   Oh, that rose has prior claims—
Needs its leaden vase filled brimming?
   Hell dry you up with its flames!

2

At the meal we sit together:
   Salve tibi![2] I must hear   10
Wise talk of the kind of weather,
   Sort of season, time of year:
Not a plenteous cork crop: scarcely
   Dare we hope oak-galls,[3] *I doubt:*
What's the Latin name for "parsley"?   15
   What's the Greek name for Swine's Snout?

3

Whew! We'll have our platter burnished,
   Laid with care on our own shelf!
With a fire-new spoon we're furnished,
   And a goblet for ourself,   20

1. No period of history is specified in this poem. The monastery setting is timeless and serves to intensify the pressure of meanness and hatred that is boiling up in the speaker.

2. "Hail to thee!" This and other speeches in italics are supposed to be the words of Brother Lawrence.
3. Abnormal outgrowths on oak trees, used for tanning.

Rinsed like something sacrificial
    Ere 'tis fit to touch our chaps[4]—
Marked with L. for our initial!
    (He-he! There his lily snaps!)

4

Saint, forsooth! While brown Dolores   25
    Squats outside the Convent bank
With Sanchicha, telling stories,
    Steeping tresses in the tank,
Blue-black, lustrous, thick like horsehairs,
    —Can't I see his dead eye glow,   30
Bright as 'twere a Barbary corsair's?[5]
    (That is, if he'd let it show!)

5

When he finishes refection,[6]
    Knife and fork he never lays
Cross-wise, to my recollection,   35
    As do I, in Jesu's praise.
I the Trinity illustrate,
    Drinking watered orange pulp—
In three sips the Arian[7] frustrate;
    While he drains his at one gulp.   40

6

Oh, those melons? If he's able
    We're to have a feast! so nice!
One goes to the Abbot's table,
    All of us get each a slice.
How go on your flowers? None double?   45
    Not one fruit-sort can you spy?
Strange!—And I, too, at such trouble,
    Keep them close-nipped on the sly!

7

There's a great text in Galatians,[8]
    Once you trip on it, entails   50
Twenty-nine distinct damnations,
    One sure, if another fails:
If I trip him just a-dying,
    Sure of heaven as sure can be,
Spin him round and send him flying   55
    Off to hell, a Manichee?[9]

8

Or, my scrofulous French novel
    On gray paper with blunt type!

---

4. Jaws.
5. Pirate of the Barbary Coast of northern Africa, renowned for fierceness and lechery.
6. Dinner.
7. Heretical followers of Arius (256–336), who denied the doctrine of the Trinity.
8. The speaker hopes to obtain Lawrence's damnation by luring him into a heresy, this to be accomplished by exposing him to the difficult task of interpreting "Galatians" in an unswervingly orthodox way. In Galatians v.15–23, St. Paul specifies an assortment of "works of the flesh" that lead to damnation, which could make up a total of "twenty-nine."
9. A heretic, a follower of the Persian prophet of the 3rd century, Mani.

Simply glance at it, you grovel
    Hand and foot in Belial's gripe: 60
If I double down its pages
    At the woeful sixteenth print,
When he gathers his greengages,
    Ope a sieve and slip it in't?

        9
Or, there's Satan!—one might venture   65
    Pledge one's soul to him,[1] yet leave
Such a flaw in the indenture
    As he'd miss till, past retrieve,
Blasted lay that rose-acacia
    We're so proud of! *Hy, Zy, Hine . . .*[2]   70
'St, there's Vespers! *Plena gratiá*
    Ave, Virgo![3] Gr-r-r—you swine!

ca. 1839   1842

My Last Duchess[1]

FERRARA

That's my last Duchess painted on the wall,
Looking as if she were alive. I call
That piece a wonder, now: Fràu Pandolf's[2] hands
Worked busily a day, and there she stands.
Will't please you sit and look at her? I said   5
"Frà Pandolf" by design, for never read
Strangers like you that pictured countenance,
The depth and passion of its earnest glance,
But to myself they turned (since none puts by
The curtain I have drawn for you, but I)   10
And seemed as they would ask me, if they durst,
How such a glance came there; so, not the first
Are you to turn and ask thus Sir, 'twas not
Her husband's presence only, called that spot
Of joy into the Duchess' cheek: perhaps   15
Frà Pandolf chanced to say "Her mantle laps
Over my lady's wrist too much," or "Paint
Must never hope to reproduce the faint
Half-flush that dies along her throat": such stuff
Was courtesy, she thought, and cause enough   20

1. The speaker would pledge his own soul to Satan in return for blasting Lawrence and his "rose-acacia," but the pledge would be so cleverly worded that the speaker would not have to pay, himself, his debt to Satan. There would be an escape-clause, a "flaw in the indenture," for himself.
2. Perhaps the opening of a mysterious curse against Lawrence.
3. "Full of grace, Hail, Virgin!" The speaker's twisted state of mind may be reflected in his mixed-up version of the prayer to Mary: "Ave, Maria, gratia plena."

1. The poem is based on incidents in the life of Alfonso II, Duke of Ferrara in Italy, whose first wife, Lucrezia, a young girl, died in 1561 after three years of marriage. Following her death, the Duke negotiated through an agent to marry a niece of the Count of Tyrol. Browning represents the Duke as addressing this agent.
2. Brother Pandolf, an imaginary painter.

For calling up that spot of joy. She had
A heart—how shall I say?—too soon made glad,
Too easily impressed; she liked whate'er
She looked on, and her looks went everywhere.
Sir, 'twas all one! My favor at her breast,   25
The dropping of the daylight in the West,
The bough of cherries some officious fool
Broke in the orchard for her, the white mule
She rode with round the terrace—all and each
Would draw from her alike the approving speech,   30
Or blush, at least. She thanked men—good! but thanked
Somehow—I know not how—as if she ranked
My gift of a nine-hundred-years-old name
With anybody's gift. Who'd stoop to blame
This sort of trifling? Even had you skill   35
In speech—(which I have not)—to make your will
Quite clear to such an one, and say, "Just this
Or that in you disgusts me; here you miss,
Or there exceed the mark"—and if she let
Herself be lessoned so, nor plainly set   40
Her wits to yours, forsooth, and made excuse
—E'en then would be some stooping; and I choose
Never to stoop. Oh sir, she smiled, no doubt,
Whene'er I passed her; but who passed without
Much the same smile? This grew; I gave commands;   45
Then all smiles stopped together. There she stands
As if alive. Will't please you rise? We'll meet
The company below, then. I repeat,
The Count your master's known munificence
Is ample warrant that no just pretense   50
Of mine for dowry will be disallowed;
Though his fair daughter's self, as I avowed
At starting, is my object. Nay, we'll go
Together down, sir. Notice Neptune, though,
Taming a sea horse, thought a rarity,   55
Which Claus of Innsbruck[3] cast in bronze for me!

1842   1842

The Laboratory
Ancien Régime

1

Now that I, tying thy glass mask tightly,
May gaze thro' these faint smokes curling whitely,
As thou pliest thy trade in this devil's-smithy—
Which is the poison to poison her, prithee?

2

He is with her, and they know that I know   5
Where they are, what they do: they believe my tears flow
While they laugh, laugh at me, at me fled to the drear
Empty church, to pray God in, for them!—I am here.

3. An unidentified or imaginary sculptor. The Count of Tyrol had his capital at
Innsbruck.

3

Grind away, moisten and mash up thy paste,
Pound at thy powder—I am not in haste!   10
Better sit thus, and observe thy strange things,
Than go where men wait me and dance at the King's.

4

That in the mortar—you call it a gum?
Ah, the brave tree whence such gold oozings come!
And yonder soft phial, the exquisite blue,   15
Sure to taste sweetly, is that poison too?

5

Had I but all of them, thee and thy treasures,
What a wild crowd of invisible pleasures!
To carry pure death in an earring, a casket,
A signet, a fan-mount, a filigree basket!   20

6

Soon, at the King's,[1] a mere lozenge to give,
And Pauline should have just thirty minutes to live!
But to light a pastile, and Elise, with her head
And her breast and her arms and her hands, should drop dead!

7

Quick—is it finished? The color's too grim!   25
Why not soft like the phial's, enticing and dim?
Let it brighten her drink, let her turn it and stir,
And try it and taste, ere she fix and prefer!

8

What a drop! She's not little, no minion [2] like me!
That's why she ensnared him: this never will free   30
The soul from those masculine eyes—say, "no!"
To that pulse's magnificent come-and-go.

9

For only last night, as they whispered, I brought
My own eyes to bear on her so, that I thought
Could I keep them one half minute fixed, she would fall   35
Shriveled; she fell not; yet this does it all!

10

Not that I bid you spare her the pain;
Let death be felt and the proof remain:
Brand, burn up, bite into its grace—
He is sure to remember her dying face!   40

11

Is it done? Take my mask off! Nay, be not morose;
It kills her, and this prevents seeing it close:
The delicate droplet, my whole fortune's fee!
If it hurts her, beside, can it ever hurt me?

---

1. Probably King Louis XIV of France (1643–1715). In the 1670's a police investigation disclosed that an extraordinary number of women and men attached to the King's court had been disposing of rivals and enemies by poisonings. Some 36 of the accused courtiers and the dealers from whom they had purchased poisons were punished by torture and burnt to death.
2. A dainty and delicate person.

12

Now, take all my jewels, gorge gold to your fill,   45
    You may kiss me, old man, on my mouth if you will!
But brush this dust off me, lest horror it brings
    Ere I know it—next moment I dance at the King's!
ca. 1844   1844

The Lost Leader[1]

1

Just for a handful of silver he left us,
    Just for a riband to stick in his coat—
Found the one gift of which fortune bereft us,
    Lost all the others she lets us devote;
They, with the gold to give, doled him out silver,   5
    So much was theirs who so little allowed:
How all our copper had gone for his service!
    Rags—were they purple, his heart had been proud!
We that had loved him so, followed him, honored him,
    Lived in his mild and magnificent eye,   10
Learned his great language, caught his clear accents,
    Made him our pattern to live and to die!
Shakespeare was of us, Milton was for us,
    Burns, Shelley, were with us—they watch from their graves!
He alone breaks from the van[2] and the freemen   15
    —He alone sinks to the rear and the slaves!

2

We shall march prospering—not through his presence;
    Songs may inspirit us—not from his lyre;
Deeds will be done—while he boasts his quiescence,
    Still bidding crouch whom the rest bade aspire: 20
Blot out his name, then, record one lost soul more,
    One task more declined, one more footpath untrod,
One more devils'-triumph and sorrow for angels,
    One wrong more to man, one more insult to God!
Life's night begins: let him never come back to us!   25
    There would be doubt, hesitation and pain,
Forced praise on our part—the glimmer of twilight,
    Never glad confident morning again!
Best fight on well, for we taught him—strike gallantly,
    Menace our heart ere we master his own;   30
Then let him receive the new knowledge and wait us,
    Pardoned in heaven, the first by the throne!
1843   1845

1. William Wordsworth, who had been an ardent liberal in his youth, had become a political conservative in later years. In old age, when he accepted a grant of money from the government ("a handful of silver") and also the office of poet laureate ("a riband to stick in his coat"), he alienated some of his young admirers such as Browning, whose liberalism was then as ardent as Wordsworth's had once been.
    Cf. J. G. Whittier's poem *Ichabod*, which embodies a similar sense of sorrowful indignation over the apostasy of Daniel Webster, a great leader formerly admired by the poet.
2. Vanguard of the army of liberalism.

How They Brought the Good News from Ghent to Aix[1]

(16—)

1

I sprang to the stirrup, and Joris, and he;
I galloped, Dirck galloped, we galloped all three;
"Good speed!" cried the watch, as the gate-bolts undrew;
"Speed!" echoed the wall to us galloping through;
Behind shut the postern, the lights sank to rest,   5
And into the midnight we galloped abreast.

2

Not a word to each other; we kept the great pace
Neck by neck, stride by stride, never changing our place;
I turned in my saddle and made its girths tight,
Then shortened each stirrup, and set the pique[2] right,   10
Rebuckled the cheek-strap, chained slacker the bit,
Nor galloped less steadily Roland a whit.

3

'Twas moonset at starting; but while we drew near
Lokeren, the cocks crew and twilight dawned clear;
At Boom, a great yellow star came out to see;   15
At Düffeld, 'twas morning as plain as could be;
And from Mecheln church-steeple we heard the half-chime,
So, Joris broke silence with, "Yet there is time!"

4

At Aershot, up leaped of a sudden the sun,
And against him the cattle stood black every one,   20
To stare through the mist at us galloping past,
And I saw my stout galloper Roland at last,
With resolute shoulders, each butting away
The haze, as some bluff river headland its spray:

5

And his low head and crest, just one sharp ear bent back   25
For my voice, and the other pricked out on his track;
And one eye's black intelligence—ever that glance
O'er its white edge at me, his own master, askance!
And the thick heavy spume-flakes which ay and anon
His fierce lips shook upwards in galloping on.   30

6

By Hasselt, Dirck groaned; and cried Joris, "Stay spur!
Your Roos galloped bravely, the fault's not in her,
We'll remember at Aix"—for one heard the quick wheeze
Of her chest, saw the stretched neck and staggering knees,
And sunk tail, and horrible heave of the flank,   35
As down on her haunches she shuddered and sank.

---

1. The distance between Ghent, in Flanders, and Aix-la-Chapelle is about one hundred miles. Browning said that the incident, occurring during the wars between Flanders and Spain, was an imaginary one.
2. Spur or pommel.

7

So, we were left galloping, Joris and I,
Past Looz and past Tongres, no cloud in the sky;
The broad sun above laughed a pitiless laugh,
'Neath our feet broke the brittle bright stubble like chaff;   40
Till over by Dalhem a dome-spire sprang white,
And "Gallop," gasped Joris, "for Aix is in sight!"

8

"How they'll greet us!"—and all in a moment his roan
Rolled neck and croup over, lay dead as a stone;
And there was my Roland to bear the whole weight   45
Of the news which alone could save Aix from her fate,
With his nostrils like pits full of blood to the brim,
And with circles of red for his eye-sockets' rim.

9

Then I cast loose my buffcoat, each holster let fall,
Shook off both my jack boots, let go belt and all,   50
Stood up in the stirrup, leaned, patted his ear,
Called my Roland his pet name, my horse without peer;
Clapped my hands, laughed and sang, any noise, bad or good,
Till at length into Aix Roland galloped and stood.

10

And all I remember is—friends flocking round   55
As I sat with his head 'twixt my knees on the ground;
And no voice but was praising this Roland of mine,
As I poured down his throat our last measure of wine,
Which (the burgesses voted by common consent)
Was no more than his due who brought good news from Ghent.   60
ca. 1844   1845

Home-Thoughts, from Abroad

1

Oh, to be in England
Now that April's there,
And whoever wakes in England
Sees, some morning, unaware,
That the lowest boughs and the brushwood sheaf   5
Round the elm-tree bole are in tiny leaf,
While the chaffinch sings on the orchard bough
In England—now!

2

And after April, when May follows,
And the whitethroat builds, and all the swallows!   10
Hark, where my blossomed peartree in the hedge
Leans to the field and scatters on the clover
Blossoms and dewdrops—at the bent spray's edge—
That's the wise thrush; he sings each song twice over,

Lest you should think he never could recapture   15
The first fine careless rapture!
And though the fields look rough with hoary dew,
All will be gay when noontide wakes anew
The buttercups, the little children's dower
—Far brighter than this gaudy melon-flower!   20

ca. 1845   1845

Home-Thoughts, from the Sea

Nobly, nobly Cape Saint Vincent[1] to the northwest died away;
Sunset ran, one glorious blood-red, reeking into Cadiz Bay;
Bluish 'mid the burning water, full in face Trafalgar[2] lay;
In the dimmest northeast distance dawned Gibraltar grand and gray;
"Here and here did England help me: how can I help England?"—
        say,   5
Whoso turns as I, this evening, turn to God to praise and pray,
While Jove's planet[3] rises yonder, silent over Africa.
1844   1845

The Bishop Orders His Tomb at Saint Praxed's Church[1]

ROME, 15—

Vanity, saith the preacher, vanity![2]
Draw round my bed: is Anselm keeping back?
Nephews—sons mine . . . ah God, I know not! Well—
She, men would have to be your mother once,
Old Gandolf envied me, so fair she was!   5
What's done is done, and she is dead beside,
Dead long ago, and I am Bishop since,
And as she died so must we die ourselves,
And thence ye may perceive the world's a dream.
Life, how and what is it? As here I lie   10

1. Off the coast of Portugal, scene of British naval victory under Admiral Nelson (1797).
2. A cape in Spain, where Nelson won his great victory over Napoleon's fleets (1805).
3. Jupiter.

1. In *Fra Lippo Lippi* Browning represents the dawn of the Renaissance in Italy, with its fresh zest for "the beauty and the wonder and the power" of man's experiences in this world. In the present monologue he portrays a later stage of the Renaissance when such worldliness, full-blown, had infected even some of the leading churchmen of Italy. Browning's portrait of the dying bishop is, however, not primarily a satire against corruption in the church. It is a brilliant exposition of the workings of a mind, a mind that has been conditioned by special historical circumstances. The Victorian historian of art, John Ruskin, said of this poem: "I know of no other piece of modern English, prose or poetry, in which there is so much told, as in these lines, of the Renaissance spirit—its worldliness, inconsistency, pride, hypocrisy, ignorance of itself, love of art, of luxury, and of good Latin. It is nearly all that I have said of the central Renaissance in thirty pages of the *Stones of Venice*, put into as many lines, Browning's also being the antecedent work."

St. Praxed's Church was named in honor of St. Praxedes, a Roman virgin of the 2nd century who gave her riches to poor Christians. Both the bishop and his predecessor, Gandolf, are imaginary persons.
2. Cf. Ecclesiastes i.2.

In this state chamber, dying by degrees,
Hours and long hours in the dead night, I ask
"Do I live, am I dead?" Peace, peace seems all.
Saint Praxed's ever was the church for peace;
And so, about this tomb of mine. I fought   15
With tooth and nail to save my niche, ye know:
—Old Gandolf cozened[3] me, despite my care;
Shrewd was that snatch from out the corner south
He graced his carrion with, God curse the same!
Yet still my niche is not so cramped but thence   20
One sees the pulpit o' the epistle side,[4]
And somewhat of the choir, those silent seats,
And up into the aery dome where live
The angels, and a sunbeam's sure to lurk:
And I shall fill my slab of basalt[5] there,   25
And 'neath my tabernacle[6] take my rest,
With those nine columns round me, two and two,
The odd one at my feet where Anselm stands:
Peach-blossom marble all, the rare, the ripe
As fresh-poured red wine of a mighty pulse.[7]   30
—Old Gandolf with his paltry onion-stone,[8]
Put me where I may look at him! True peach,
Rosy and flawless: how I earned the prize!
Draw close: that conflagration of my church
—What then? So much was saved if aught were missed!   35
My sons, ye would not be my death? Go dig
The white-grape vineyard where the oil-press stood,
Drop water gently till the surface sink,
And if ye find . . . Ah God, I know not, I! . . .
Bedded in store of rotten fig leaves soft,   40
And corded up in a tight olive-frail,[9]
Some lump, ah God, of *lapis lazuli*,[1]
Big as a Jew's head cut off at the nape,
Blue as a vein o'er the Madonna's breast . . .
Sons, all have I bequeathed you, villas, all,   45
That brave Frascati[2] villa with its bath,
So, let the blue lump poise between my knees,
Like God the Father's globe on both his hands
Ye worship in the Jesu Church[3] so gay,
For Gandolf shall not choose but see and burst!   50
Swift as a weaver's shuttle fleet our years:[4]
Man goeth to the grave, and where is he?

---

3. Cheated.
4. The Epistles of the New Testament are read from the right-hand side of the altar (as one faces it).
5. Dark-colored igneous rock.
6. Stone canopy or tentlike roof, presumably supported by the "nine columns" under which the sculptured effigy of the Bishop would lie on the slab of basalt.
7. Browning uses "pulse" in the special sense of a pulpy mash of fermented grapes from which a strong wine might be poured off. In a later poem, the *Epilogue* to *Pacchiarotto*, he likens such wine to "viscous blood" that has been "squeezed gold" from the "pulp" of the grapes.
8. An inferior marble that peels in layers.
9. Basket for holding olives.
1. Valuable bright blue stone.
2. Suburb of Rome, used as a resort by wealthy Italians.
3. Il Gesù, a Jesuit church in Rome.
4. Cf. Job vii.6.

Did I say basalt for my slab, sons? Black[5]—
'Twas ever antique-black I meant! How else
Shall ye contrast my frieze[6] to come beneath?   55
The bas-relief in bronze ye promised me,
Those Pans and Nymphs ye wot of, and perchance
Some tripod, thyrsus, with a vase or so,
The Saviour at his sermon on the mount,
Saint Praxed in a glory, and one Pan   60
Ready to twitch the Nymph's last garment off,
And Moses with the tables[7] . . . but I know
Ye mark me not! What do they whisper thee,
Child of my bowels, Anselm? Ah, ye hope
To revel down my villas while I gasp   65
Bricked o'er with beggar's moldy travertine[8]
Which Gandolf from his tomb-top chuckles at!
Nay, boys, ye love me—all of jasper, then!
'Tis jasper ye stand pledged to, lest I grieve
My bath must needs be left behind, alas!   70
One block, pure green as a pistachio nut,
There's plenty jasper somewhere in the world—
And have I not Saint Praxed's ear to pray
Horses for ye, and brown Greek manuscripts,
And mistresses with great smooth marbly limbs?   75
—That's if ye carve my epitaph aright,
Choice Latin, picked phrase, Tully's[9] every word,
No gaudy ware like Gandolf's second line—
Tully, my masters? Ulpian[1] serves his need!
And then how I shall lie through centuries,   80
And hear the blessed mutter of the mass,
And see God made and eaten all day long,[2]
And feel the steady candle flame, and taste
Good strong thick stupefying incense-smoke!
For as I lie here, hours of the dead night,   85
Dying in state and by such slow degrees,
I fold my arms as if they clasped a crook,[3]
And stretch my feet forth straight as stone can point,
And let the bedclothes, for a mortcloth,[4] drop
Into great laps and folds of sculptor's-work: 90
And as yon tapers dwindle, and strange thoughts
Grow, with a certain humming in my ears,

5. Black marble.
6. Continuous band of sculpture.
7. The "bas-relief" (or sculpture in which the figures do not project far from the background surface) would consist of a mixture of pagan and religious scenes (lines 57–62). Among the former would be a "tripod," on which priestesses at the oracle of Delphi sat to make their prophecies, and a "thyrsus," a long staff carried in processions in honor of Bacchus, the god of wine. The religious scenes would include St. Praxed with her halo ("a glory") and Moses with the stone tablets ("tables") on which the Ten Commandments were written. Such intermingling of pagan and Christian traditions, characteristic of the Renaissance, had been attacked in 1841 in *Contrasts*, a book on architecture by A. W. Pugin, a Roman Catholic.
8. Italian limestone.
9. A familiar name for Marcus Tullius Cicero, whose writing was the model, during the Renaissance, of classical Latin prose.
1. Late Latin prose-writer, not considered a model of good style.
2. Reference to the doctrine of transubstantiation.
3. Bishop's staff or crozier.
4. Rich cloth spread over a dead body or coffin.

About the life before I lived this life,
And this life too, popes, cardinals, and priests,
Saint Praxed at his sermon on the mount,[5]   95
Your tall pale mother with her talking eyes,
And new-found agate urns as fresh as day,
And marble's language, Latin pure, discreet
—Aha, ELUCESCEBAT[6] quoth our friend?
No Tully, said I, Ulpian at the best!   100
Evil and brief hath been my pilgrimage.[7]
All *lapis*, all, sons! Else I give the Pope
My villas! Will ye ever eat my heart?
Ever your eyes were as a lizard's quick,
They glitter like your mother's for my soul,   105
Or ye would heighten my impoverished frieze,
Pierce out its starved design, and fill my vase
With grapes, and add a vizor and a Term,[8]
And to the tripod ye would tie a lynx
That in his struggle throws the thyrsus down,   110
To comfort me on my entablature[9]
Whereon I am to lie till I must ask
"Do I live, am I dead?" There, leave me, there!
For ye have stabbed me with ingratitude
To death—ye wish it—God, ye wish it! Stone—   115
Gritstone,[10] a-crumble! Clammy squares which sweat
As if the corpse they keep were oozing through—
And no more *lapis* to delight the world!
Well go! I bless ye. Fewer tapers there,
But in a row: and, going, turn your backs   120
—Aye, like departing altar-ministrants,
And leave me in my church, the church for peace,
That I may watch at leisure if he leers—
Old Gandolf, at me, from his onion-stone,
As still he envied me, so fair she was!   125
1844   1845

Meeting at Night[1]

1

The gray sea and the long black land;
And the yellow half-moon large and low;
And the startled little waves that leap

5. The bishop is confusing St. Praxed (a woman) with Christ—an indication that his mind is wandering.
6. Word from Gandolf's epitaph meaning "he was illustrious." The bishop considers the form of the verb to be in "gaudy" bad taste. If the epitaph had been copied from Cicero instead of from Ulpian, the word would have been *elucebat*.
7. Cf. Genesis xlvii.9.
8. "Vizor": part of a helmet, often represented in sculpture. "Term": statue of Terminus, the Roman god of boundaries, usually represented without arms.
9. Horizontal platform supporting a statue or effigy.
10. Coarse sandstone such as that used for grindstones.
1. This poem and the one which follows it appeared originally under the single title *Night and Morning*. The speaker in both is a man.

In fiery ringlets from their sleep,
As I gain the cove with pushing prow,   5
And quench its speed i' the slushy sand.

2

Then a mile of warm sea-scented beach;
Three fields to cross till a farm appears;
A tap at the pane, the quick sharp scratch
And blue spurt of a lighted match,   10
And a voice less loud, through its joys and fears,
Than the two hearts beating each to each!

1845

Parting at Morning

Round the cape of a sudden came the sea,
And the sun looked over the mountain's rim:
And straight was a path of gold for him,[2]
And the need of a world of men for me.

1845

A Toccata of Galuppi's[1]

1

Oh, Galuppi, Baldassaro, this is very sad to find!
I can hardly misconceive you; it would prove me deaf and blind;
But although I take your meaning, 'tis with such a heavy mind!

2

Here you come with your old music, and here's all the good it brings.
What, they lived once thus at Venice where the merchants were
  the kings,
Where Saint Mark's is, where the Doges used to wed the sea with   5
  rings?[2]

2. The sun.
1. There are three speakers in this short poem. The first is a 19th-century scientist in England who is listening to a musical composition by Baldassaro Galuppi (1706–85), a Venetian. The music evokes for this scientist the voice of the dead composer (the third speaker) who comments upon the pointless and butterfly-like frivolity of his 18th-century contemporaries. The second group of voices is made up of comments by members of Galuppi's audience as they respond to the different moods of his clavichord-playing during a party which the scientist imagines to have taken place in Venice.
  A "toccata" is defined in Grove's *Dictionary of Music* as a "touch-piece,

or a composition intended to exhibit the touch and execution of the performer." The same authority states that "no particular composition was taken as the basis of the poem," but Browning is known to have himself played on the organ some unpublished compositions by Galuppi, and one of these, not yet identified, may have occasioned the poem. Browning's interest in music was keen, and his knowledge of the art was more extensive than that of most English poets.
2. An annual ceremony in which the Doge, the Venetian chief magistrate, threw a ring into the water to symbolize the bond between his city, with its maritime empire, and the sea.

3

Aye, because the sea's the street there; and 'tis arched by . . . what
    you call
. . . Shylock's bridge[3] with houses on it, where they kept the carni-
    val:
I was never out of England—it's as if I saw it all.

4

Did young people take their pleasure when the sea was warm in
    May?   10
Balls and masks[4] begun at midnight, burning ever to midday,
When they made up fresh adventures for the morrow, do you say?

5

Was a lady such a lady, cheeks so round and lips so red—
On her neck the small face buoyant, like a bellflower on its bed,
O'er the breast's superb abundance where a man might base his
    head?   15

6

Well, and it was graceful of them—they'd break talk off and afford
—She, to bite her mask's black velvet—he, to finger on his sword,
While you sat and played toccatas, stately at the clavichord?[5]

7

What? Those lesser thirds so plaintive, sixths diminished, sigh on
    sigh,
Told them something? Those suspensions, those solutions—"Must
    we die?"   20
Those commiserating sevenths[6]—"Life might last! we can but
    try!"

8

"Were you happy?"—"Yes."—"And are you still as happy?"—
    "Yes. And you?"
—"Then, more kisses!"—"Did I stop them, when a million seemed
    so few?"
Hark, the dominant's persistence till it must be answered to!

9

So, an octave struck the answer. Oh, they praised you, I dare say! 25
"Brave Galuppi! that was music; good alike at grave and gay!
I can always leave off talking when I hear a master play!"

10

Then they left you for their pleasure: till in due time, one by one,
Some with lives that came to nothing, some with deeds as well un-
    done,   29
Death stepped tacitly and took them where they never see the sun.

3. The Rialto, a bridge over the Grand
Canal.
4. Masquerades.
5. A keyboard instrument in which the
strings are struck by metal hammers.
As a mechanism it resembles a piano,
but the sound is more like that of a
harpsichord.
6. This term and others in these lines
all refer to the technical devices used
by Galuppi to produce alternating moods
in his music, conflict in each instance
being resolved into harmony. Thus the
"dominant" (the fifth note of the
scale), after being persistently sounded,
is answered by a resolving chord (lines
24–25).

11

But when I sit down to reason, think to take my stand nor swerve,
While I triumph o'er a secret wrung from nature's close reserve,
In you come with your cold music till I creep through every nerve.

12

Yes, you, like a ghostly cricket, creaking where a house was burned:
"Dust and ashes, dead and done with, Venice spent what Venice
    earned.
The soul, doubtless, is immortal—where a soul can be discerned.   35

13

"Yours for instance: you know physics, something of geology,
Mathematics are your pastime; souls shall rise in their degree;
Butterflies may dread extinction—you'll not die, it cannot be!

14

"As for Venice and her people, merely born to bloom and drop,   40
Here on earth they bore their fruitage, mirth and folly were the
    crop:
What of soul was left, I wonder, when the kissing had to stop?

15

"Dust and ashes!" So you creak it, and I want the heart to scold.
Dear dead women, with such hair, too—what's become of all the
    gold
Used to hang and brush their bosoms? I feel chilly and grown old.   44
ca. 1847   1855

Memorabilia[1]

1

Ah, did you once see Shelley plain,
    And did he stop and speak to you
And did you speak to him again?
    How strange it seems and new!

2

But you were living before that,   5
    And also you are living after;
And the memory I started at—
    My starting moves your laughter.

3

I crossed a moor, with a name of its own
    And a certain use in the world no doubt,   10
Yet a hand's-breadth of it shines alone
    'Mid the blank miles round about:

1. The title means "things worth remembering." Browning reports that he once met a stranger in a bookstore who mentioned having talked with Shelley. "Suddenly the stranger paused, and burst into laughter as he observed me staring at him with blanched face. * * * I still vividly remember how strangely the presence of a man who had seen and spoken with Shelley affected me."

4

For there I picked up on the heather
  And there I put inside my breast
A molted feather, an eagle feather!   15
  Well, I forget the rest.

ca. 1851   1855

Love Among the Ruins[1]

1

Where the quiet-colored end of evening smiles,
  Miles and miles
On the solitary pastures where our sheep
  Half-asleep
Tinkle homeward through the twilight, stray or stop   5
  As they crop—
Was the site once of a city great and gay
  (So they say),
Of our country's very capital, its prince
  Ages since   10
Held his court in, gathered councils, wielding far
  Peace or war.

2

Now—the country does not even boast a tree,
  As you see,
To distinguish slopes of verdure, certain rills   15
  From the hills
Intersect and give a name to (else they run
  Into one),
Where the domed and daring palace shot its spires
  Up like fires   20
O'er the hundred-gated circuit of a wall
  Bounding all,
Made of marble, men might march on nor be pressed,
  Twelve abreast.

3

And such plenty and perfection, see, of grass   25
  Never was!
Such a carpet as, this summertime, o'erspreads
  And embeds
Every vestige of the city, guessed alone,
  Stock or stone—   30
Where a multitude of men breathed joy and woe
  Long ago;
Lust of glory pricked their hearts up, dread of shame
  Struck them tame;

1. The ruins may be those of such cities as Babylon or Nineveh or one of the Etruscan cities of Italy.

The unusual stanza used in this poem was invented by Browning. The contrast between past and present, which is the core of the poem, is reinforced by devoting one half of each stanza to the past and the other half to the present.

And that glory and that shame alike, the gold   35
    Bought and sold.

4

Now—the single little turret that remains
    On the plains,
By the caper overrooted, by the gourd
    Overscored,   40
While the patching houseleek's[2] head of blossom winks
    Through the chinks—
Marks the basement whence a tower in ancient time
    Sprang sublime,
And a burning ring, all round, the chariots traced   45
    As they raced,
And the monarch and his minions and his dames
    Viewed the games.

5

And I know, while thus the quiet-colored eve
    Smiles to leave
To their folding, all our many-tinkling fleece   50
    In such peace,
And the slopes and rills in undistinguished gray
    Melt away—
That a girl with eager eyes and yellow hair   55
    Waits me there
In the turret whence the charioteers caught soul
    For the goal,
When the king looked, where she locks now, breathless, dumb
    Till I come.   60

6

But he looked upon the city, every side,
    Far and wide,
All the mountains topped with temples, all the glades'
    Colonnades,
All the causeys,[3] bridges, aqueducts—and then,   65
    All the men!
When I do come, she will speak not, she will stand,
    Either hand
On my shoulder, give her eyes the first embrace
    Of my face,   70
Ere we rush, ere we extinguish sight and speech
    Each on each.

7

In one year they sent a million fighters forth
    South and north,
And they built their gods a brazen pillar high   75
    As the sky,
Yet reserved a thousand chariots in full force—
    Gold, of course,

2. Common European plant, with petals clustered in the shape of rosettes.

3. Causeways or roads raised above low ground.

Oh heart! oh blood that freezes, blood that burns!
  Earth's returns   80
For whole centuries of folly, noise, and sin!
  Shut them in,
With their triumphs and their glories and the rest!
  Love is best.

1852   1855

Women and Roses[1]

1

I dream of a red-rose tree.
And which of its roses three
Is the dearest rose to me?

2

Round and round, like a dance of snow
In a dazzling drift, as its guardians, go   5
Floating the women faded for ages,
Sculptured in stone, on the poet's pages.
Then follow women fresh and gay,
Living and loving and loved today.
Last, in the rear, flee the multitude of maidens, 10
Beauties yet unborn. And all, to one cadence,
They circle their rose on my rose tree.

3

Dear rose, thy term is reached,
Thy leaf hangs loose and bleached:
Bees pass it unimpeached.[2]   15

4

Stay then, stoop, since I cannot climb,
You, great shapes of the antique time!
How shall I fix you, fire you, freeze you,
Break my heart at your feet to please you?
Oh, to possess and be possessed!   20
Hearts that beat 'neath each pallid breast!
Once but of love, the poesy, the passion,
Drink but once and die!—In vain, the same fashion,
They circle their rose on my rose tree.

5

Dear rose, thy joy's undimmed,   25
Thy cup is ruby-rimmed,
Thy cup's heart nectar-brimmed.

6

Deep, as drops from a statue's plinth[3]
The bee sucked in by the hyacinth,

---

1. Like Chaucer in the *Romaunt of the Rose* and also like Tennyson in *Maud*, the speaker in the following dream lyric associates roses with fair women and a garden of roses with the garden of love. The beautiful women of the past are first evoked (stanzas 3, 4); then those of the present (stanzas 5, 6); and finally those of the future (stanzas 7, 8). All, however, elude him.
2. Unhindered.
3. Base.

So will I bury me while burning,   30
Quench like him at a plunge my yearning,
Eyes in your eyes, lips on your lips!
Fold me fast where the cincture[4] slips,
Prison all my soul in eternities of pleasure,
Girdle me for once! But no—the old measure,   35
They circle their rose on my rose tree.

7

Dear rose without a thorn,
Thy bud's the babe unborn:
First streak of a new morn.

8

Wings, lend wings for the cold, the clear!   40
What is far conquers what is near.
Roses will bloom nor want beholders,
Sprung from the dust where our flesh molders.
What shall arrive with the cycle's change?
A novel grace and a beauty strange.
I will make an Eve, be the artist that began her,   45
Shaped her to his mind!—Alas! in like manner
They circle their rose on my rose tree.

1852   1855

"Childe Roland to the Dark Tower Came"[1]

(SEE EDGAR'S SONG IN "LEAR")

1

My first thought was, he lied in every word,
That hoary cripple, with malicious eye
Askance[2] to watch the working of his lie
On mine, and mouth scarce able to afford

---

4. Ornamental belt worn by women, usually across the hips.
1. Browning stated that this poem "came upon me as a kind of dream," and that it was written in one day. Although the poem was among those of his own writings that pleased him most, he was reluctant to explain what the dream (or nightmare) signified. He once agreed with a friend's suggestion that the meaning might be expressed in the statement: "He that endureth to the end shall be saved." Most readers have responded to the poem in this way, finding in the story of Roland's quest an inspiring expression of defiance and courage. Other readers find the poem to be more expressive of despair than of enduring hope, and it is at least true that the landscape is as grim and nightmarelike as in such 20th-century writings as T. S. Eliot's *Hollow Men* or Franz Kafka's *Penal Colony*. It has been said of *Childe Roland* that every reader can be his own allegorist, and such a poem thus poses a further large question of whether or not total comprehension of a work is always essential for appreciation of literature.

The lines from Shakespeare's *King Lear* (III.iv.187–90), from which the title is taken, are spoken when Lear is about to enter a hovel on the heath, and Edgar, feigning madness, chants the fragment of a song reminiscent of quests and challenges in fairy tales: "Child Rowland to the dark tower came; / His word was still / 'Fie, foh, and fum! / I smell the blood of a British man.' " A "childe" is a youth of gentle birth, usually a candidate for knighthood.
2. Squinting sidewise.

Suppression of the glee, that pursed and scored   5
    Its edge, at one more victim gained thereby.

2

What else should he be set for, with his staff?
    What, save to waylay with his lies, ensnare
    All travelers who might find him posted there,
And ask the road? I guessed what skull-like laugh   10
Would break, what crutch 'gin write my epitaph
    For pastime in the dusty thoroughfare,

3

If at his counsel I should turn aside
    Into that ominous tract which, all agree,
    Hides the Dark Tower. Yet acquiescingly   15
I did turn as he pointed: neither pride
Nor hope rekindling at the end descried,
    So much as gladness that some end might be.

4

For, what with my whole world-wide wandering,
    What with my search drawn out through years, my hope   20
    Dwindled into a ghost not fit to cope
With that obstreperous joy success would bring,
I hardly tried now to rebuke the spring
    My heart made, finding failure in its scope.

5

As when a sick man very near to death[3]   25
    Seems dead indeed, and feels begin and end
    The tears and takes the farewell of each friend,
And hears one bid the other go, draw breath
Freelier outside ("since all is o'er," he saith,
    "And the blow fallen no grieving can amend"),   30

6

While some discuss if near the other graves
    Be room enough for this, and when a day
    Suits best for carrying the corpse away,
With care about the banners, scarves and staves:
And still the man hears all, and only craves   35
    He may not shame such tender love and stay.

7

Thus, I had so long suffered in this quest,
    Heard failure prophesied so oft, been writ
    So many times among "The Band"—to wit,
The knights who to the Dark Tower's search addressed   40
Their steps—that just to fail as they, seemed best,
    And all the doubt was now—should I be fit?

8

So, quiet as despair, I turned from him,
    That hateful cripple, out of his highway
    Into the path he pointed. All the day   45

---

3. Cf. *A Valediction: Forbidding Mourning*, lines 1–4, by John Donne, a poet much admired by Browning.

Had been a dreary one at best, and dim
  Was settling to its close, yet shot one grim
    Red leer to see the plain catch its estray.[4]

9

For mark! no sooner was I fairly found
  Pledged to the plain, after a pace or two,
    Than, pausing to throw backward a last view   50
O'er the safe road, 'twas gone; gray plain all round:
Nothing but plain to the horizon's bound.
  I might go on; naught else remained to do.

10

So, on I went. I think I never saw   55
  Such starved ignoble nature; nothing throve:
    For flowers—as well expect a cedar grove!
But cockle,[5] spurge, according to their law
Might propagate their kind, with none to awe,
  You'd think; a burr had been a treasure trove.   60

11

No! penury, inertness and grimace,
  In some strange sort, were the land's portion. "See
    Or shut your eyes," said Nature peevishly,
"It nothing skills: I cannot help my case;
'Tis the Last Judgment's fire must cure this place,   65
  Calcine[6] its clods and set my prisoners free."

12

If there pushed any ragged thistle stalk
  Above its mates, the head was chopped; the bents[7]
    Were jealous else. What made those holes and rents
In the dock's[8] harsh swarth leaves, bruised as to balk   70
All hope of greenness? 'tis a brute must walk
  Pashing their life out, with a brute's intents.

13

As for the grass, it grew as scant as hair
  In leprosy; thin dry blades pricked the mud
    Which underneath looked kneaded up with blood.   75
One stiff blind horse, his every bone a-stare,
Stood stupefied, however he came there:
  Thrust out past service from the devil's stud!

14

Alive? he might be dead for aught I know,
  With that red gaunt and colloped[9] neck a-strain,   80
    And shut eyes underneath the rusty mane;
Seldom went such grotesqueness with such woe;
I never saw a brute I hated so;
  He must be wicked to deserve such pain.

4. Literally, a domestic animal that has strayed away from its home.
5. A weed that bears burrs. "Spurge" is a bitter-juiced weed.
6. Turn to powder by heat.
7. Coarse, stiff grasses.
8. Coarse plant.
9. Ridged.

15

I shut my eyes and turned them on my heart.   85
     As a man calls for wine before he fights,
     I asked one draught of earlier, happier sights,
Ere fitly I could hope to play my part.
Think first, fight afterwards—the soldier's art:
     One taste of the old time sets all to rights.   90

16

Not it! I fancied Cuthbert's reddening face
     Beneath its garniture of curly gold,
     Dear fellow, till I almost felt him fold
An arm in mine to fix me to the place,
That way he used. Alas, one night's disgrace!   95
     Out went my heart's new fire and left it cold.

17

Giles then, the soul of honor—there he stands
     Frank as ten years ago when knighted first.
     What honest man should dare (he said) he durst.
Good—but the scene shifts—faugh! what hangman hands   100
Pin to his breast a parchment? His own bands
     Read it. Poor traitor, spit upon and cursed!

18

Better this present than a past like that;
     Back therefore to my darkening path again!
     No sound, no sight as far as eye could strain.   105
Will the night send a howlet[1] or a bat?
I asked: when something on the dismal flat
     Came to arrest my thoughts and change their train.

19

A sudden little river crossed my path
     As unexpected as a serpent comes.
     No sluggish tide congenial to the glooms;   110
This, as it frothed by, might have been a bath
For the fiend's glowing hoof—to see the wrath
     Of its black eddy bespate[2] with flakes and spumes.

20

So petty yet so spiteful! All along,   115
     Low scrubby alders kneeled down over it;
     Drenched willows flung them headlong in a fit
Of mute despair, a suicidal throng:
The river which had done them all the wrong,
     Whate'er that was, rolled by, deterred no whit.   120

21

Which, while I forded—good saints, how I feared
     To set my foot upon a dead man's cheek,
     Each step, or feel the spear I thrust to seek
For hollows, tangled in his hair or beard!
—It may have been a water rat I speared,   125
     But, ugh! it sounded like a baby's shriek.

1. Owl.   2. Bespattered.

22

Glad was I when I reached the other bank.
　　Now for a better country. Vain presage!
　　Who were the stragglers, what war did they wage,
Whose savage trample thus could pad the dank
Soil to a plash? Toads in a poisoned tank,　　　　　　　130
　　Or wild cats in a red-hot iron cage—

23

The fight must so have seemed in that fell cirque.[3]
　　What penned them there, with all the plain to choose?
　　No footprint leading to that horrid mews,[4]　　　　135
None out of it. Mad brewage set to work
Their brains, no doubt, like galley slaves the Turk
　　Pits for his pastime, Christians against Jews.

24

And more than that—a furlong on—why, there!
　　What bad use was that engine for, that wheel,　　　140
　　Or brake,[5] not wheel—that harrow fit to reel
Men's bodies out like silk? with all the air
Of Tophet's[6] tool, on earth left unaware,
　　Or brought to sharpen its rusty teeth of steel.

25

Then came a bit of stubbed ground, once a wood,　　145
　　Next a marsh, it would seem, and now mere earth
　　Desperate and done with; (so a fool finds mirth,
Makes a thing and then mars it, till his mood
Changes and off he goes!) within a rood[7]—
　　Bog, clay and rubble, sand and stark black dearth.　　150

26

Now blotches rankling, colored gay and grim,
　　Now patches where some leanness of the soil's
　　Broke into moss or substances like boils;
Then came some palsied oak, a cleft in him
Like a distorted mouth that splits its rim　　　　　155
　　Gaping at death, and dies while it recoils.

27

And just as far as ever from the end!
　　Naught in the distance but the evening, naught
　　To point my footstep further! At the thought,
A great black bird, Apollyon's[8] bosom friend,　　　160
Sailed past, nor beat his wide wing dragon-penned[9]
　　That brushed my cap—perchance the guide I sought.

---

3. Dreadful arena.
4. Enclosed stable yard.
5. A toothed machine used for separating the fibers of flax or hemp. Here an instrument of torture.
6. Hell's. See also Jeremiah xix.4–5.
7. Quarter acre of land.

8. In Revelation ix.11, Apollyon is "an angel of the bottomless pit." In Bunyan's *Pilgrim's Progress*, he is a hideous "monster"; "he had wings like a dragon."
9. With wings or pinions like those of a dragon.

28

For, looking up, aware I somehow grew,
   'Spite of the dusk, the plain had given place
   All round to mountains—with such name to grace   165
Mere ugly heights and heaps now stolen in view.
How thus they had surprised me—solve it, you!
   How to get from them was no clearer case.

29

Yet half I seemed to recognize some trick
   Of mischief happened to me, God knows when—   170
   In a bad dream perhaps. Here ended, then,
Progress this way. When, in the very nick
Of giving up, one time more, came a click
   As when a trap shuts—you're inside the den!

30

Burningly it came on me all at once,   175
   This was the place! those two hills on the right,
   Crouched like two bulls locked horn in horn in fight;
While to the left, a tall scalped mountain . . . Dunce,
Dotard, a-dozing at the very nonce,[1]
   After a life spent training for the sight!   180

31

What in the midst lay but the Tower itself?
   The round squat turret, blind as the fool's heart,[2]
   Built of brown stone, without a counterpart
In the whole world. The tempest's mocking elf
Points to the shipman thus the unseen shelf   185
   He strikes on, only when the timbers start.

32

Not see? because of night perhaps?—why, day
   Came back again for that! before it left,
   The dying sunset kindled through a cleft:
The hills, like giants at a hunting, lay,   190
Chin upon hand, to see the game at bay—
   "Now stab and end the creature—to the heft!"[3]

33

Not hear? when noise was everywhere! it tolled
   Increasing like a bell. Names in my ears
   Of all the lost adventurers my peers—   195
How such a one was strong, and such was bold,
And such was fortunate, yet each of old
   Lost, lost! one moment knelled the woe of years.

34

There they stood, ranged along the hillsides, met
   To view the last of me, a living frame   200

---

1. Moment.
2. Cf. "The fool hath said in his heart, There is no God" (Psalms xiv.1).
3. Handle of dagger or sword.

For one more picture! in a sheet of flame
I saw them and I knew them all. And yet
Dauntless the slug-horn[4] to my lips I set,
  And blew. *"Childe Roland to the Dark Tower came."*

1852   1855

Respectability

1

Dear, had the world in its caprice
  Deigned to proclaim "I know you both,
  Have recognized your plighted troth,
Am sponsor for you: live in peace!"—
How many precious months and years   5
  Of youth had passed, that speed so fast,
  Before we found it out at last,
The world, and what it fears?

2

How much of priceless life were spent
  With men that every virtue decks,   10
  And women models of their sex,
Society's true ornament—
Ere we dared wander, nights like this,
  Through wind and rain, and watch the Seine,
  And feel the Boulevard break again   15
To warmth and light and bliss?

3

I know! the world proscribes not love;
  Allows my fingers to caress
  Your lips' contour and downiness,
Provided it supply a glove.
The world's good word!—the Institute![1]   20
  Guizot receives Montalembert!
  Eh? Down the court three lampions[2] flare:
Put forward your best foot!

ca. 1852   1855

4. This Scottish word meant the war cry or slogan (*slug-horn*) of a clan about to engage in battle, but in 1770 the poet Chatterton was misled into using it to mean a kind of trumpet or horn. Browning followed Chatterton's example, although the original meaning would also be relevant here.

1. A building in Paris, which the lovers are approaching in their walk. The speaker is reminded that at a meeting of the French Academy, held in the Institute, occurred a glaring instance of the hypocrisy which he thinks is characteristic of all social relations. In 1852, François Guizot had delivered a flowery speech of welcome in honor of Charles Montalembert, an author whom Guizot at heart despised.

2. Ornamental lamps illuminating the courtyard of the Institute.

Fra Lippo Lippi[1]

I am poor brother Lippo, by your leave!
You need not clap your torches to my face.
Zooks,[2] what's to blame? you think you see a monk!
What, 'tis past midnight, and you go the rounds,
And here you catch me at an alley's end   5
Where sportive ladies leave their doors ajar?
The Carmine's[3] my cloister: hunt it up,
Do—harry out, if you must show your zeal,
Whatever rat, there, haps on his wrong hole,
And nip each softling of a wee white mouse,   10
Weke, weke, that's crept to keep him company!
Aha, you know your betters! Then, you'll take
Your hand away that's fiddling on my throat,
And please to know me likewise. Who am I?
Why, one, sir, who is lodging with a friend   15
Three streets off—he's a certain . . . how d'ye call?
Master—a . . . Cosimo of the Medici,[4]
I' the house that caps the corner. Boh! you were best!
Remember and tell me, the day you're hanged,
How you affected such a gullet's gripe![5]   20
But you,[6] sir, it concerns you that your knaves
Pick up a manner nor discredit you:
Zooks, are we pilchards,[7] that they sweep the streets
And count fair prize what comes into their net?
He's Judas to a tittle, that man is![8]   25
Just such a face! Why, sir, you make amends.
Lord, I'm not angry! Bid your hangdogs go
Drink out this quarter-florin to the health
Of the munificent House that harbors me
(And many more beside, lads! more beside!)   30
And all's come square again. I'd like his face—
His, elbowing on his comrade in the door

1. This monologue portrays the dawn of the Renaissance in Italy at a point when the medieval attitude towards life and art was about to be displaced by a fresh appreciation of earthly pleasures. It was from Giorgio Vasari's *Lives of the Painters* that Browning derived most of his information about the life of the Florentine painter and friar, Lippo Lippi (1406–69), but the theory of art propounded by Lippi in the poem was developed by the poet himself. Browning's own partiality for this poem may be attributed, in part, to his having identified himself with his hero, an artist whose aesthetic principles made him a misfit among his more pharisaical contemporaries.

2. A shortened version of "Gadzooks," a mild oath now obscure in meaning but perhaps resembling a phrase still in use: "God's truth."
3. Italian for "Carmelite," an order of mendicant friars to which Lippi belongs.
4. Lippi's patron, banker and virtual ruler of Florence.
5. I.e., how you had the arrogance to choke the gullet of someone with my connections.
6. The officer in charge of the patrol of policemen or watchmen.
7. Small fish.
8. I.e., one of the watchmen has a face that would serve as a model for a painting of Judas.

With the pike and lantern—for the slave that holds
John Baptist's head a-dangle by the hair
With one hand ("Look you, now," as who should say)   35
And his weapon in the other, yet unwiped!
It's not your chance to have a bit of chalk,
A wood-coal or the like? or you should see!
Yes, I'm the painter, since you style me so.
What, brother Lippo's doings, up and down,   40
You know them and they take you? like enough!
I saw the proper twinkle in your eye—
'Tell you, I liked your looks at very first.
Let's sit and set things straight now, hip to haunch.
Here's spring come, and the nights one makes up bands   45
To roam the town and sing out carnival,[9]
And I've been three weeks shut within my mew,[1]
A-painting for the great man, saints and saints
And saints again. I could not paint all night—
Ouf! I leaned out of window for fresh air.   50
There came a hurry of feet and little feet,
A sweep of lute-strings, laughs, and whifts of song—
Flower o' the broom,
Take away love, and our earth is a tomb!
Flower o' the quince,   55
I let Lisa go, and what good in life since?[2]
Flower o' the thyme—and so on. Round they went.
Scarce had they turned the corner when a titter
Like the skipping of rabbits by moonlight—three slim shapes,
And a face that looked up . . . zooks, sir, flesh and blood,   60
That's all I'm made of! Into shreds it went,
Curtain and counterpane and coverlet,
All the bed-furniture—a dozen knots,
There was a ladder! Down I let myself,
Hands and feet, scrambling somehow, and so dropped,   65
And after them. I came up with the fun
Hard by Saint Laurence,[3] hail fellow, well met—
Flower o' the rose,
If I've been merry, what matter who knows?
And so as I was stealing back again   70
To get to bed and have a bit of sleep
Ere I rise up tomorrow and go work
On Jerome knocking at his poor old breast
With his great round stone to subdue the flesh,[4]
You snap me of the sudden. Ah, I see!   75
Though your eye twinkles still, you shake your head—
Mine's shaved—a monk, you say—the sting's in that!
If Master Cosimo announced himself,

---

9. Season of revelry before the commencement of Lent.
1. Private den.
2. This and other interspersed flower-songs are called *stornelli* in Italy.

3. San Lorenzo, a church in Florence.
4. A picture of St. Jerome (ca. 340–420), whose ascetic observances were hardly a congenial subject for such a painter as Lippi.

Mum's the word naturally; but a monk!
Come, what am I a beast for? tell us, now!   80
I was a baby when my mother died
And father died and left me in the street.
I starved there, God knows how, a year or two
On fig skins, melon parings, rinds and shucks,
Refuse and rubbish. One fine frosty day,   85
My stomach being empty as your hat,
The wind doubled me up and down I went.
Old Aunt Lapaccia trussed me with one hand
(Its fellow was a stinger as I knew),
And so along the wall, over the bridge,   90
By the straight cut to the convent. Six words there,
While I stood munching my first bread that month:
"So, boy, you're minded," quoth the good fat father
Wiping his own mouth, 'twas refection time[5]—
"To quit this very miserable world?"   95
Will you renounce" . . . "the mouthful of bread?" thought I;
By no means! Brief, they made a monk of me;
I did renounce the world, its pride and greed,
Palace, farm, villa, shop, and banking house,
Trash, such as these poor devils of Medici   100
Have given their hearts to—all at eight years old.
Well, sir, I found in time, you may be sure,
'Twas not for nothing—the good bellyful,
The warm serge and the rope that goes all round,
And day-long blessed idleness beside!   105
"Let's see what the urchin's fit for"—that came next.
Not overmuch their way, I must confess.
Such a to-do! They tried me with their books:
Lord, they'd have taught me Latin in pure waste!
Flower o' the clove,   110
All the Latin I construe is "amo," I love!
But, mind you, when a boy starves in the streets
Eight years together, as my fortune was,
Watching folk's faces to know who will fling
The bit of half-stripped grape bunch he desires,   115
And who will curse or kick him for his pains—
Which gentleman processional and fine,
Holding a candle to the Sacrament,
Will wink and let him lift a plate and catch
The droppings of the wax to sell again,   120
Or holla for the Eight[6] and have him whipped—
How say I?—nay, which dog bites, which lets drop
His bone from the heap of offal in the street—
Why, soul and sense of him grow sharp alike,
He learns the look of things, and none the less   125
For admonition from the hunger-pinch.
I had a store of such remarks, be sure,

5. Mealtime.   6. **Florentine magistrates.**

Which, after I found leisure, turned to use.
I drew men's faces on my copybooks,
Scrawled them within the antiphonary's marge,[7]   130
Joined legs and arms to the long music-notes,
Found eyes and nose and chin for A's and B's,
And made a string of pictures of the world
Betwixt the ins and outs of verb and noun,
On the wall, the bench, the door. The monks looked black.   135
"Nay," quoth the Prior,[8] "turn him out, d' ye say?
In no wise. Lose a crow and catch a lark.
What if at last we get our man of parts,
We Carmelites, like those Camaldolese
And Preaching Friars,[9] to do our church up fine   140
And put the front on it that ought to be!"
And hereupon he bade me daub away.
Thank you! my head being crammed, the walls a blank,
Never was such prompt disemburdening.
First, every sort of monk, the black and white,   145
I drew them, fat and lean: then, folk at church,
From good old gossips waiting to confess
Their cribs of barrel droppings, candle ends—
To the breathless fellow at the altar-foot,
Fresh from his murder, safe and sitting there   150
With the little children round him in a row
Of admiration, half for his beard and half
For that white anger of his victim's son
Shaking a fist at him with one fierce arm,
Signing himself with the other because of Christ   155
(Whose sad face on the cross sees only this
After the passion[1] of a thousand years)
Till some poor girl, her apron o'er her head
(Which the intense eyes looked through), came at eve
On tiptoe, said a word, dropped in a loaf,   160
Her pair of earrings and a bunch of flowers
(The brute took growling), prayed, and so was gone.
I painted all, then cried " 'Tis ask and have;
Choose, for more's ready!"—laid the ladder flat,
And showed my covered bit of cloister wall.   165
The monks closed in a circle and praised loud
Till checked, taught what to see and not to see,
Being simple bodies—"That's the very man!
Look at the boy who stoops to pat the dog!
That woman's like the Prior's niece who comes   170
To care about his asthma: it's the life!"
But there my triumph's straw-fire flared and funked;[2]
Their betters took their turn to see and say:
The Prior and the learned pulled a face

7. Margin of music book used for
choral singing.
8. Head of a Carmelite convent.
9. Benedictine and Dominican religious orders, respectively.
1. Sufferings.
2. Went up in smoke.

And stopped all that in no time. "How? what's here?   175
Quite from the mark of painting, bless us all!
Faces, arms, legs and bodies like the true
As much as pea and pea! it's devil's game!
Your business is not to catch men with show,
With homage to the perishable clay,   180
But lift them over it, ignore it all,
Make them forget there's such a thing as flesh.
Your business is to paint the souls of men—
Man's soul, and it's a fire, smoke . . . no, it's not . . .
It's vapor done up like a newborn babe—   185
(In that shape when you die it leaves your mouth)
It's . . . well, what matters talking, it's the soul!
Give us no more of body than shows soul!
Here's Giotto,[3] with his Saint a-praising God,
That sets us praising—why not stop with him?   190
Why put all thoughts of praise out of our head
With wonder at lines, colors, and what not?
Paint the soul, never mind the legs and arms!
Rub all out, try at it a second time.
Oh, that white smallish female with the breasts,   195
She's just my niece . . . Herodias,[4] I would say—
Who went and danced and got men's heads cut off!
Have it all out!" Now, is this sense, I ask?
A fine way to paint soul, by painting body
So ill, the eye can't stop there, must go further   200
And can't fare worse! Thus, yellow does for white
When what you put for yellow's simply black,
And any sort of meaning looks intense
When all beside itself means and looks naught.
Why can't a painter lift each foot in turn,   205
Left foot and right foot, go a double step,
Make his flesh liker and his soul more like,
Both in their order? Take the prettiest face,
The Prior's niece . . . patron-saint—is it so pretty
You can't discover if it means hope, fear,   210
Sorrow or joy? won't beauty go with these?
Suppose I've made her eyes all right and blue,
Can't I take breath and try to add life's flash,
And then add soul and heighten them threefold?
Or say there's beauty with no soul at all—   215
(I never saw it—put the case the same—)
If you get simple beauty and naught else,
You get about the best thing God invents:
That's somewhat: and you'll find the soul you have missed,
Within yourself, when you return him thanks.   220

3. Great Florentine painter (1276–1337), whose stylized pictures of religious subjects were admired as models of pre-Renaissance art.
4. See Matthew, xiv.1–12, for an account of John the Baptist's execution after he had aroused the displeasure of Herodias, sister-in-law of King Herod. It was her daughter, Salome, who performed the dance.

"Rub all out!" Well, well, there's my life, in short,
And so the thing has gone on ever since.
I'm grown a man no doubt, I've broken bounds:
You should not take a fellow eight years old
And make him swear to never kiss the girls.   225
I'm my own master, paint now as I please—
Having a friend, you see, in the Corner-house![5]
Lord, it's fast holding by the rings in front—
Those great rings serve more purposes than just
To plant a flag in, or tie up a horse!   230
And yet the old schooling sticks, the old grave eyes
Are peeping o'er my shoulder as I work,
The heads shake still—"It's art's decline, my son!
You're not of the true painters, great and old;
Brother Angelico's the man, you'll find;   235
Brother Lorenzo stands his single peer:[6]
Fag on at flesh, you'll never make the third!"
Flower o' the pine,
You keep your mistr . . . manners, and I'll stick to mine!
I'm not the third, then: bless us, they must know!   240
Don't you think they're the likeliest to know,
They with their Latin? So, I swallow my rage,
Clench my teeth, suck my lips in tight, and paint
To please them—sometimes do and sometimes don't;
For, doing most, there's pretty sure to come   245
A turn, some warm eve finds me at my saints—
A laugh, a cry, the business of the world—
(*Flower o' the peach,*
Death for us all, and his own life for each!)
And my whole soul revolves, the cup runs over,   250
The world and life's too big to pass for a dream,
And I do these wild things in sheer despite,
And play the fooleries you catch me at,
In pure rage! The old mill-horse, out at grass
After hard years, throws up his stiff heels so,   255
Although the miller does not preach to him
The only good of grass is to make chaff.[7]
What would men have? Do they like grass or no—
May they or mayn't they? all I want's the thing
Settled forever one way. As it is,   260
You tell too many lies and hurt yourself:
You don't like what you only like too much,
You do like what, if given you at your word,
You find abundantly detestable.
For me, I think I speak as I was taught;   265
I always see the garden and God there
A-making man's wife: and, my lesson learned,

5. The Medici palace.
6. Fra Angelico (1387–1455) and Lorenzo Monaco (1370–1425), whose paintings were in the approved traditional manner.
7. Straw.

The value and significance of flesh,
I can't unlearn ten minutes afterwards.

    You understand me: I'm a beast, I know.   270
But see, now—why, I see as certainly
As that the morning star's about to shine,
What will hap some day. We've a youngster here
Comes to our convent, studies what I do,
Slouches and stares and lets no atom drop: 275
His name is Guidi[8]—he'll not mind the monks—
They call him Hulking Tom, he lets them talk—
He picks my practice up—he'll paint apace,
I hope so—though I never live so long,
I know what's sure to follow. You be judge!   280
You speak no Latin more than I, belike;
However, you're my man, you've seen the world
—The beauty and the wonder and the power,
The shapes of things, their colors, lights and shades,
Changes, surprises—and God made it all!   285
—For what? Do you feel thankful, aye or no,
For this fair town's face, yonder river's line,
The mountain round it and the sky above,
Much more the figures of man, woman, child,
These are the frame to? What's it all about?   290
To be passed over, despised? or dwelt upon,
Wondered at? oh, this last of course!—you say.
But why not do as well as say—paint these
Just as they are, careless what comes of it?
God's works—paint any one, and count it crime   295
To let a truth slip. Don't object, "His works
Are here already; nature is complete:
Suppose you reproduce her—(which you can't)
There's no advantage! You must beat her, then."
For, don't you mark? we're made so that we love   300
First when we see them painted, things we have passed
Perhaps a hundred times nor cared to see;
And so they are better, painted—better to us,
Which is the same thing. Art was given for that;
God uses us to help each other so,   305
Lending our minds out. Have you noticed, now,
Your cullion's[9] hanging face? A bit of chalk,
And trust me but you should, though! How much more,
If I drew higher things with the same truth!
That were to take the Prior's pulpit-place,   310
Interpret God to all of you! Oh, oh,
It makes me mad to see what men shall do
And we in our graves! This world's no blot for us,
Nor blank; it means intensely, and means good:
To find its meaning is my meat and drink.   315
"Aye, but you don't so instigate to prayer!"

8. Guidi or Masaccio (1401–28), a painter who may have been Lippi's master rather than his pupil. Like Lippi he was in revolt against the medieval theory of art.
9. Rascal's.

Strikes in the Prior: "when your meaning's plain
It does not say to folk—remember matins,
Or, mind you fast next Friday!" Why, for this
What need of art at all? A skull and bones,   320
Two bits of stick nailed crosswise, or, what's best,
A bell to chime the hour with, does as well.
I painted a Saint Laurence[1] six months since
At Prato, splashed the fresco in fine style:
"How looks my painting, now the scaffold's down?"   325
I ask a brother: "Hugely," he returns—
"Already not one phiz of your three slaves
Who turn the Deacon off his toasted side,
But it's scratched and prodded to our heart's content,
The pious people have so eased their own   330
With coming to say prayers there in a rage:
We get on fast to see the bricks beneath,
Expect another job this time next year,
For pity and religion grow i' the crowd—
Your painting serves its purpose!" Hang the fools!   335

    —That is—you'll not mistake an idle word
Spoke in a huff by a poor monk, God wot,
Tasting the air this spicy night which turns
The unaccustomed head like Chianti wine!
Oh, the church knows! don't misreport me, now!   340
It's natural a poor monk out of bounds
Should have his apt word to excuse himself:
And hearken how I plot to make amends.
I have bethought me: I shall paint a piece
. . . There's for you! Give me six months, then go, see   345
Something in Sant' Ambrogio's![2] Bless the nuns!
They want a cast o' my office.[3] I shall paint
God in the midst, Madonna and her babe,
Ringed by a bowery flowery angel brood,
Lilies and vestments and white faces, sweet   350
As puff on puff of grated orris-root[4]
When ladies crowd to Church at midsummer.
And then i' the front, of course a saint or two—
Saint John, because he saves the Florentines,
Saint Ambrose, who puts down in black and white   355
The convent's friends and gives them a long day,
And Job, I must have him there past mistake,
The man of Uz (and Us without the z,
Painters who need his patience). Well, all these
Secured at their devotion, up shall come   360
Out of a corner when you least expect,
As one by a dark stair into a great light,

1. A scene representing the fiery martyr-dom of Saint Laurence; a "fresco" is painted quickly on fresh plaster over a surface of bricks. Prato is a town near Florence.
2. A convent church in Florence.
3. Sample of my work. The completed painting, which Browning saw in Florence, is Lippi's "Coronation of the Virgin."
4. Powder (like talcum) made from sweet-smelling roots of a flower.

Music and talking, who but Lippo! I!—
Mazed, motionless and moonstruck—I'm the man!
Back I shrink—what is this I see and hear?   365
I, caught up with my monk's things by mistake,
My old serge gown and rope that goes all round,
I, in this presence, this pure company!
Where's a hole, where's a corner for escape?
Then steps a sweet angelic slip of a thing   370
Forward, puts out a soft palm—"Not so fast!"
—Addresses the celestial presence, "nay—
He made you and devised you, after all,
Though he's none of you! Could Saint John there draw—
His camel-hair[5] make up a painting-brush?   375
We come to brother Lippo for all that,
Iste perfecit opus!"[6] So, all smile—
I shuffle sideways with my blushing face
Under the cover of a hundred wings
Thrown like a spread of kirtles when you're gay   380
And play hot cockles,[7] all the doors being shut,
Till, wholly unexpected, in there pops
The hothead husband! Thus I scuttle off
To some safe bench behind, not letting go
The palm of her, the little lily thing   385
That spoke the good word for me in the nick,
Like the Prior's niece . . . Saint Lucy, I would say.
And so all's saved for me, and for the church
A pretty picture gained. Go, six months hence!
Your hand, sir, and good-by: no lights, no lights!   390
The street's hushed, and I know my own way back,
Don't fear me! There's the gray beginning. Zooks!

ca. 1853   1855

The Last Ride Together

1

I said—Then, dearest, since 'tis so,
Since now at length my fate I know,
Since nothing all my love avails,
Since all, my life seemed meant for, fails,
    Since this was written and needs must be—   5
My whole heart rises up to bless
Your name in pride and thankfulness!
Take back the hope you gave—I claim
Only a memory of the same,

---

5. "And John was clothed with camel's hair" (Mark i.6).
6. "This man made the work." In this painting, as later completed, these words

appear beside a figure which Browning took to be Lippi's self-portrait.
7. A game in which a player wears a blindfold. "Kirtles": skirts.

—And this beside, if you will not blame,
    Your leave for one more last ride with me.   10

2

My mistress bent that brow of hers;
Those deep dark eyes where pride demurs
When pity would be softening through,
Fixed me a breathing-while or two   15
    With life or death in the balance: right!
The blood replenished me again;
My last thought was at least not vain:
I and my mistress, side by side
Shall be together, breathe and ride,   20
So, one day more am I deified.
    Who knows but the world may end tonight?

3

Hush! if you saw some western cloud
All billowy-bosomed, over-bowed
By many benedictions—sun's   25
And moon's and evening star's at once—
    And so, you, looking and loving best,
Conscious grew, your passion drew
Cloud, sunset, moonrise, star-shine too,
Down on you, near and yet more near,   30
Till flesh must fade for heaven was here!—
Thus leant she and lingered[1]—joy and fear!
    Thus lay she a moment on my breast.

4

Then we began to ride. My soul
Smoothed itself out, a long-cramped scroll   35
Freshening and fluttering in the wind.
Past hopes already lay behind.
    What need to strive with a life awry?
Had I said that, had I done this,
So might I gain, so might I miss.
Might she have loved me? just as well   40
She might have hated, who can tell!
Where had I been now if the worst befell?
    And here we are riding, she and I.

5

Fail I alone, in words and deeds?
Why, all men strive and who succeeds?   45
We rode; it seemed my spirit flew,
Saw other regions, cities new,
    As the world rushed by on either side.
I thought—All labor, yet no less
Bear up beneath their unsuccess.   50
Look at the end of work, contrast
The petty done, the undone vast,
This present of theirs with the hopeful past!
    I hoped she would love me; here we ride.   55

---

1. Before she mounts her horse.

6

What hand and brain went ever paired?
What heart alike conceived and dared?
What act proved all its thought had been?
What will but felt the fleshly screen?
    We ride and I see her bosom heave.   60
There's many a crown for who can reach.
Ten lines, a statesman's life in each![2]
The flag stuck on a heap of bones,
A soldier's doing! what atones?
They scratch his name on the Abbey stones.   65
    My riding is better, by their leave.

7

What does it all mean, poet? Well,
Your brains beat into rhythm, you tell
What we felt only; you expressed
You hold things beautiful the best,   70
    And pace them in rhyme so, side by side.
'Tis something, nay 'tis much: but then,
Have you yourself what's best for men?
Are you—poor, sick, old ere your time—
Nearer one whit your own sublime   75
Than we who never have turned a rhyme?
    Sing, riding's a joy! For me, I ride.

8

And you, great sculptor—so, you gave
A score of years to Art, her slave,
And that's your Venus, whence we turn   80
To yonder girl that fords the burn![3]
    You acquiesce, and shall I repine?
What, man of music, you grown gray
With notes and nothing else to say,
Is this your sole praise from a friend,   85
"Greatly his opera's strains intend,
But in music we know how fashions end!"
    I gave my youth; but we ride, in fine.[4]

9

Who knows what's fit for us? Had fate
Proposed bliss here should sublimate   90
My being—had I signed the bond—
Still one must lead some life beyond,
    Have a bliss to die with, dim-descried.
This foot once planted on the goal,
This glory-garland round my soul,   95
Could I descry such? Try and test!
I sink back shuddering from the quest.

2. If a man tries hard enough, he may be crowned with what seems to be success. He might become, for example, an eminent "statesman." Yet his only memorial would be a short sketch of his career ("ten lines") in some history or biographical dictionary.
3. Crosses the brook.
4. In short.

Earth being so good, would Heaven seem best?[5]
Now, Heaven and she are beyond this ride.
                    10
And yet—she has not spoke so long!   100
What if heaven be that, fair and strong
At life's best, with our eyes upturned
Whither life's flower is first discerned,
        We, fixed so, ever should so abide?
What if we still ride on, we two   105
With life forever old yet new,
Changed not in kind but in degree,
The instant made eternity—
And heaven just prove that I and she
        Ride, ride together, forever ride?   110

                                                                1855

Andrea del Sarto[1]

(CALLED "THE FAULTLESS PAINTER")

But do not let us quarrel any more,
No, my Lucrezia; bear with me for once:
Sit down and all shall happen as you wish.
You turn your face, but does it bring your heart?
I'll work then for your friend's friend, never fear,   5
Treat his own subject after his own way,
Fix his own time, accept too his own price,
And shut the money into this small hand
When next it takes mine. Will it? tenderly?
Oh, I'll content him—but tomorrow, Love!   10
I often am much wearier than you think,

5. If fate had decreed that he could possess his mistress fully, life on earth would have been so blissful that heaven could offer nothing for him to look forward to after death. Hence (he argues) to preserve "a bliss to die with" (line 93), it is better that she never really became his on earth.

1. This portrait of Andrea del Sarto (1486–1531) was derived from a biography written by his pupil, Giorgio Vasari, author of *The Lives of the Painters*. Vasari's account seeks to explain why his Florentine master, one of the most skillful painters of the Renaissance, never altogether fulfilled the promise he had shown early in his career and why he had never arrived (in Vasari's opinion) at the level of such artists as Raphael. Vasari noted that Andrea suffered from "a certain timidity of mind * * * which rendered it impossible that those evidences of ardor and animation, which are proper to the more exalted character, should

ever appear in him."

Browning also follows Vasari's account of Andrea's marriage to a beautiful widow, Lucrezia, "an artful woman who made him do as she pleased in all things." Vasari reports that Andrea's "immoderate love for her soon caused him to neglect the studies demanded by his art," and that this infatuation had "more influence over him than the glory and honor towards which he had begun to make such hopeful advances."

Browning's poem has often been praised for its exposition of a paradoxical theory of success and failure, but it has other qualities as well. Its slow-paced, enervated blank-verse line, its setting of a quiet evening in autumn, its comparative lack of the movement and noise that we expect in Browning's energetic verse create a unity of impression that is unobtrusive yet effective.

This evening more than usual, and it seems
As if—forgive now—should you let me sit
Here by the window with your hand in mine
And look a half-hour forth on Fiesole,[2]   15
Both of one mind, as married people use,
Quietly, quietly the evening through,
I might get up tomorrow to my work
Cheerful and fresh as ever. Let us try.
Tomorrow, how you shall be glad for this!   20
Your soft hand is a woman of itself,
And mine the man's bared breast she curls inside.
Don't count the time lost, neither; you must serve
For each of the five pictures we require:
It saves a model. So! keep looking so—   25
My serpentining beauty, rounds on rounds![3]
—How could you ever prick those perfect ears,
Even to put the pearl there! oh, so sweet—
My face, my moon, my everybody's moon,
Which everybody looks on and calls his,   30
And, I suppose, is looked on by in turn,
While she looks—no one's: very dear, no less.[4]
You smile? why, there's my picture ready made,
There's what we painters call our harmony!
A common grayness silvers everything[5]—   35
All in a twilight, you and I alike
—You, at the point of your first pride in me
(That's gone you know)—but I, at every point;
My youth, my hope, my art, being all toned down
To yonder sober pleasant Fiesole.   40
There's the bell clinking from the chapel top;
That length of convent wall across the way
Holds the trees safer, huddled more inside;
The last monk leaves the garden; days decrease,
And autumn grows, autumn in everything.   45
Eh? the whole seems to fall into a shape
As if I saw alike my work and self
And all that I was born to be and do,
A twilight-piece. Love, we are in God's hand.
How strange now, looks the life he makes us lead;   50
So free we seem, so fettered fast we are!
I feel he laid the fetter: let it lie!
This chamber for example—turn your head—
All that's behind us! You don't understand
Nor care to understand about my art,   55
But you can hear at least when people speak:
And that cartoon,[6] the second from the door

2. A suburb on the hills overlooking Florence.
3. Coils of hair like the coils of a serpent.
4. Her affections are centered upon no one person, not even upon her husband, yet she is nevertheless dear to him. Cf. *My Last Duchess*, lines 23–24.
5. The predominant color in many of Andrea's paintings is silver gray.
6. Drawing.

—It is the thing, Love! so such things should be—
Behold Madonna!—I am bold to say.
I can do with my pencil what I know,
What I see, what at bottom of my heart   60
I wish for, if I ever wish so deep—
Do easily, too—when I say, perfectly,
I do not boast, perhaps: yourself are judge,
Who listened to the Legate's[7] talk last week,   65
And just as much they used to say in France.
At any rate 'tis easy, all of it!
No sketches first, no studies, that's long past:
I do what many dream of, all their lives,
—Dream? strive to do, and agonize to do,   70
And fail in doing. I could count twenty such
On twice your fingers, and not leave this town,
Who strive—you don't know how the others strive
To paint a little thing like that you smeared
Carelessly passing with your robes afloat—   75
Yet do much less, so much less, Someone[8] says
(I know his name, no matter)—so much less!
Well, less is more, Lucrezia: I am judged.
There burns a truer light of God in them,
In their vexed beating stuffed and stopped-up brain,   80
Heart, or whate'er else, than goes on to prompt
This low-pulsed forthright craftsman's hand of mine.
Their works drop groundward, but themselves, I know,
Reach many a time a heaven that's shut to me,
Enter and take their place there sure enough,   85
Though they come back and cannot tell the world.
My works are nearer heaven, but I sit here.
The sudden blood of these men! at a word—
Praise them, it boils, or blame them, it boils too.
I, painting from myself and to myself,   90
Know what I do, am unmoved by men's blame
Or their praise either. Somebody remarks
Morello's[9] outline there is wrongly traced,
His hue mistaken; what of that? or else,
Rightly traced and well ordered; what of that?   95
Speak as they please, what does the mountain care?
Ah, but a man's reach should exceed his grasp,
Or what's a heaven for? All is silver-gray
Placid and perfect with my art: the worse!
I know both what I want and what might gain,   100
And yet how profitless to know, to sigh
"Had I been two, another and myself,
Our head would have o'erlooked the world!"[1] No doubt.
Yonder's a work now, of that famous youth

7. A deputy of the Pope.
8. Probably Michelangelo (1475–1564).
9. A mountain peak outside Florence.
1. I.e., if I had been both an aspiring,

dedicated, and soul-conscious artist as
well as a faultless craftsman, the combination would have been unsurpassable.
See also line 140 ("we half-men").

The Urbinate[2] who died five years ago.   105
('Tis copied, George Vasari sent it me.)[3]
Well, I can fancy how he did it all,
Pouring his soul, with kings and popes to see,
Reaching, that heaven might so replenish him,
Above and through his art—for it gives way;   110
That arm is wrongly put—and there again—
A fault to pardon in the drawing's lines,
Its body, so to speak: its soul is right,
He means right—that, a child may understand.
Still, what an arm! and I could alter it: 115
But all the play, the insight and the stretch—
Out of me, out of me! And wherefore out?
Had you enjoined them on me, given me soul,
We might have risen to Rafael, I and you!
Nay, Love, you did give all I asked, I think—   120
More than I merit, yes, by many times.
But had you—oh, with the same perfect brow,
And perfect eyes, and more than perfect mouth,
And the low voice my soul hears, as a bird
The fowler's pipe,[4] and follows to the snare—   125
Had you, with these the same, but brought a mind!
Some women do so. Had the mouth there urged
"God and the glory! never care for gain.
The present by the future, what is that?
Live for fame, side by side with Agnolo![5]   130
Rafael is waiting: up to God, all three!"
I might have done it for you. So it seems:
Perhaps not. All is as God overrules.
Beside, incentives come from the soul's self;
The rest avail not. Why do I need you?   135
What wife had Rafael, or has Agnolo?
In this world, who can do a thing, will not;
And who would do it, cannot, I perceive:
Yet the will's somewhat—somewhat, too, the power—
And thus we half-men struggle. At the end,   140
God, I conclude, compensates, punishes.
'Tis safer for me, if the award be strict,
That I am something underrated here.
Poor this long while, despised, to speak the truth.
I dared not, do you know, leave home all day,   145
For fear of chancing on the Paris lords.
The best is when they pass and look aside;
But they speak sometimes; I must bear it all.
Well may they speak! That Francis,[6] that first time,

2. Raphael (1483–1520), born at Ur-bino.
3. In saying that the painting is a copy, Andrea may perhaps be concerned to prevent Lucrezia from selling it.
4. Whistle or call used by hunters to lure wildfowl into range.
5. Michelangelo.
6. King Francis I of France had invited Andrea to his court at Fontaine-bleau and warmly encouraged him in his painting. On returning to Florence, however, Andrea is reputed to have stolen some funds entrusted to him by

And that long festal year at Fontainebleau! 150
I surely then could sometimes leave the ground,
Put on the glory, Rafael's daily wear,
In that humane great monarch's golden look—
One finger in his beard or twisted curl
Over his mouth's good mark that made the smile, 155
One arm about my shoulder, round my neck,
The jingle of his gold chain in my ear,
I painting proudly with his breath on me,
All his court round him, seeing with his eyes,
Such frank French eyes, and such a fire of souls 160
Profuse, my hand kept plying by those hearts—
And, best of all, this, this, this face beyond,
This in the background, waiting on my work,
To crown the issue with a last reward!
A good time, was it not, my kingly days? 165
And had you not grown restless . . . but I know—
'Tis done and past; 'twas right, my instinct said;
Too live the life grew, golden and not gray,
And I'm the weak-eyed bat no sun should tempt
Out of the grange whose four walls make his world.[7] 170
How could it end in any other way?
You called me, and I came home to your heart.
The triumph was—to reach and stay there; since
I reached it ere the triumph, what is lost?
Let my hands frame your face in your hair's gold,
You beautiful Lucrezia that are mine! 175
"Rafael did this, Andrea painted that;
The Roman's is the better when you pray,
But still the other's Virgin was his wife—"
Men will excuse me. I am glad to judge
Both pictures in your presence; clearer grows 180
My better fortune, I resolve to think.
For, do you know, Lucrezia, as God lives,
Said one day Agnolo, his very self,
To Rafael . . . I have known it all these years . . . 185
(When the young man was flaming out his thoughts
Upon a palace wall for Rome to see,
Too lifted up in heart because of it)
"Friend, there's a certain sorry little scrub
Goes up and down our Florence, none cares how, 190
Who, were he set to plan and execute
As you are, pricked on by your popes and kings,
Would bring the sweat into that brow of yours!"
To Rafael's—And indeed the arm is wrong.
I hardly dare . . . yet, only you to see, 195

Francis, and to please Lucrezia he built
a house with the money. Now he is
afraid of being insulted by "Paris lords"
on the streets.
7. The bat, a creature of evening,
thrives best in the confines of the
"four walls" of a farm building
("grange"). See also line 261 in which
Andrea thinks of heaven as a place of
four walls.

Give the chalk here—quick, thus the line should go!
Aye, but the soul! he's Rafael! rub it out!
Still, all I care for, if he spoke the truth,
(What he? why, who but Michel Agnolo?
Do you forget already words like those?)   200
If really there was such a chance, so lost—
Is, whether you're—not grateful—but more pleased.
Well, let me think so. And you smile indeed!
This hour has been an hour! Another smile?
If you would sit thus by me every night   205
I should work better, do you comprehend?
I mean that I should earn more, give you more.
See, it is settled dusk now; there's a star;
Morello's gone, the watch-lights show the wall,
The cue-owls[8] speak the name we call them by.   210
Come from the window, love—come in, at last,
Inside the melancholy little house
We built to be so gay with. God is just.
King Francis may forgive me: oft at nights
When I look up from painting, eyes tired out,   215
The walls become illumined, brick from brick
Distinct, instead of mortar, fierce bright gold,
That gold of his I did cement them with!
Let us but love each other. Must you go?
That Cousin here again? he waits outside?   220
Must see you—you, and not with me? Those loans?
More gaming debts to pay?[9] you smiled for that?
Well, let smiles buy me! have you more to spend?
While hand and eye and something of a heart
Are left me, work's my ware, and what's it worth?   225
I'll pay my fancy. Only let me sit
The gray remainder of the evening out,
Idle, you call it, and muse perfectly
How I could paint, were I but back in France,
One picture, just one more—the Virgin's face,   230
Not yours this time! I want you at my side
To hear them—that is, Michel Agnolo—
Judge all I do and tell you of its worth.
Will you? Tomorrow, satisfy your friend.
I take the subjects for his corridor,   235
Finish the portrait out of hand—there, there,
And throw him in another thing or two
If he demurs; the whole should prove enough
To pay for this same Cousin's freak. Beside,
What's better and what's all I care about,   240
Get you the thirteen scudi[1] for the ruff!

8. An owl whose cry sounds like the Italian word *ciù*.
9. Lucrezia's "Cousin" (or lover or "friend") owes gambling debts to a creditor. Andrea has already contracted (lines 5–10) to pay off these debts by painting some pictures according to the creditor's specifications. Now he agrees to pay off further debts.
1. Italian coins.

Love, does that please you? Ah, but what does he,
The Cousin! What does he to please you more?

    I am grown peaceful as old age tonight.
I regret little, I would change still less.
Since there my past life lies, why alter it?   245
The very wrong to Francis!—it is true
I took his coin, was tempted and complied,
And built this house and sinned, and all is said.
My father and my mother died of want.[2]   250
Well, had I riches of my own? you see
How one gets rich! Let each one bear his lot.
They were born poor, lived poor, and poor they died:
And I have labored somewhat in my time
And not been paid profusely. Some good son   255
Paint my two hundred pictures—let him try!
No doubt, there's something strikes a balance. Yes,
You loved me quite enough, it seems tonight.
This must suffice me here. What would one have?
In heaven, perhaps, new chances, one more chance—   260
Four great walls in the New Jerusalem,
Meted on each side by the angel's reed,[3]
For Leonard,[4] Rafael, Agnolo and me
To cover—the three first without a wife,
While I have mine! So—still they overcome   265
Because there's still Lucrezia—as I choose.

    Again the Cousin's whistle! Go, my Love.

ca. 1853   1855

Two in the Campagna[1]

1

  I wonder do you feel today
    As I have felt since, hand in hand,
  We sat down on the grass, to stray
    In spirit better through the land,
  This morn of Rome and May?   5

2

  For me, I touched a thought, I know,
    Has tantalized me many times,
    (Like turns of thread the spiders throw
      Mocking across our path) for rhymes
  To catch at and let go.   10

2. According to Vasari, Andrea's infatuation for Lucrezia prompted him to stop supporting his poverty-stricken parents.
3. Measuring rod. For "New Jerusalem," see Revelation xxi.10–21.

4. Leonardo da Vinci (1452–1519).
1. The Campagna is the name for the level plains and pasture lands near Rome where the ruins of ancient cities are overrun with wild flowers.

3

Help me to hold it! First it left
 The yellowing fennel,[2] run to seed
There, branching from the brickwork's cleft,
 Some old tomb's ruin: yonder weed
Took up the floating weft,[3]   15

4

Where one small orange cup amassed
 Five beetles—blind and green they grope
Among the honey-meal: and last,
 Everywhere on the grassy slope
I traced it. Hold it fast!   20

5

The champaign[4] with its endless fleece
 Of feathery grasses everywhere!
Silence and passion, joy and peace,
 An everlasting wash of air—
Rome's ghost since her decease.   25

6

Such life here, through such lengths of hours,
 Such miracles performed in play,
Such primal naked forms of flowers,
 Such letting nature have her way
While heaven looks from its towers! 30

7

How say you? Let us, O my dove,
 Let us be unashamed of soul,
As earth lies bare to heaven above!
 How is it under our control
To love or not to love?   35

8

I would that you were all to me,
 You that are just so much, no more.
Nor yours nor mine, nor slave nor free!
 Where does the fault lie? What the core
O' the wound, since wound must be? 40

9

I would I could adopt your will,
 See with your eyes, and set my heart
Beating by yours, and drink my fill
 At your soul's springs—your part my part
In life, for good and ill.   45

10

No. I yearn upward, touch you close,
 Then stand away. I kiss your cheek,
Catch your soul's warmth—I pluck the rose
 And love it more than tongue can speak—
Then the good minute goes.   50

2. A yellow-flowered plant from which   of a web.
a pungent spice is derived.   4. Here, the Campagna.
3. Threads crossing from side to side

11

Already how am I so far
    Out of that minute? Must I go
Still like the thistle-ball, no bar,
    Onward, whenever light winds blow,
Fixed by no friendly star?   55

12

Just when I seemed about to learn!
    Where is the thread now? Off again!
The old trick! Only I discern—
    Infinite passion, and the pain
Of finite hearts that yearn.   60

1854   1855

A Grammarian's Funeral[1]

SHORTLY AFTER THE REVIVAL OF LEARNING IN EUROPE

Let us begin and carry up this corpse,
    Singing together.
Leave we the common crofts, the vulgar thorpes[2]
    Each in its tether[3]
Sleeping safe on the bosom of the plain,   5
    Cared for till cock-crow:
Look out if yonder be not day again
    Rimming the rock-row!
That's the appropriate country; there, man's thought,
    Rarer, intenser,
Self-gathered for an outbreak, as it ought,   10
    Chafes in the censer.
Leave we the unlettered plain its herd and crop;[4]
    Seek we sepulture
On a tall mountain, citied to the top,
    Crowded with culture!   15
All the peaks soar, but one the rest excels;
    Clouds overcome it;
No! yonder sparkle is the citadel's
    Circling its summit.   20

1. The speaker is one of the students who are bearing the body of their scholarly master to the mountaintop for burial. The student's defense of the dead grammarian's idealistic dedication to knowledge and faith in a future life is expressed in some of the harshest-sounding and most laborious verse ever written by Browning. It is this grotesque combination of opposites (soaring idealism in conjunction with harsh or petty realities) that gives *A Grammarian's Funeral* its distinctive tone.
No model for the grammarian has been specifically identified. Browning seems to have had in mind the kind of early Renaissance scholar whose devotion to the Greek language made it possible for others to enjoy the more recognizably significant aspects of the revival of learning.
2. "Crofts" are small tracts of land farmed by peasants; "thorpes" are villages.
3. Restricted to a narrow sphere like an animal tied to a stake.
4. Flatlands at the base of the mountain which are populated by illiterate shepherds and peasants. "Sepulture": burial place.

Thither our path lies; wind we up the heights:
    Wait ye the warning?
Our low life was the level's and the night's;
    He's for the morning.
Step to a tune, square chests, erect each head,   25
    'Ware[5] the beholders!
This is our master, famous, calm, and dead,
    Borne on our shoulders.

Sleep, crop and herd! sleep, darkling thorpe and croft,
    Safe from the weather!   30
He, whom we convoy to his grave aloft,
    Singing together,
He was a man born with thy face and throat,
    Lyric Apollo![6]
Long he lived nameless: how should spring take note   35
    Winter would follow?
Till lo, the little touch, and youth was gone!
    Cramped and diminished,
Moaned he, "New measures, other feet anon!
    My dance is finished?"   40
No, that's the world's way: (keep the mountain-side,
    Make for the city!)
He knew the signal, and stepped on with pride
    Over men's pity;
Left play for work, and grappled with the world   45
    Bent on escaping:
"What's in the scroll," quoth he, "thou keepest furled?
    Show me their shaping,
Theirs who most studied man, the bard and sage—
    Give!"—So, he gowned him,[7]   50
Straight got by heart that book to its last page:
    Learned, we found him.
Yea, but we found him bald too, eyes like lead,
    Accents uncertain:
"Time to taste life," another would have said,   55
    "Up with the curtain!"
This man said rather, "Actual life comes next?
    Patience a moment!
Grant I have mastered learning's crabbed text,
    Still there's the comment.[8]   60
Let me know all! Prate not of most or least,
    Painful or easy!
Even to the crumbs I'd fain eat up the feast,
    Aye, nor feel queasy."
Oh, such a life as he resolved to live,   65
    When he had learned it,

---

5. Look out for!
6. God of music and embodiment of male beauty.
7. Dressed in academic gown; became a scholar.
8. Commentaries or annotations upon a text.

When he had gathered all books had to give!
    Sooner, he spurned it.
Image the whole, then execute the parts—
    Fancy the fabric   70
Quite, ere you build, ere steel strike fire from quartz,
    Ere mortar dab brick!

(Here's the town gate reached: there's the market place
    Gaping before us.)
Yea, this in him was the peculiar grace   75
    (Hearten our chorus!)
That before living he'd learn how to live—
    No end to learning:
Earn the means first—God surely will contrive
    Use for our earning.   80
Others mistrust and say, "But time escapes:
    Live now or never!"
He said, "What's time? Leave Now for dogs and apes!
    Man has Forever."
Back to his book then: deeper drooped his head: 85
    Calculus[9] racked him:
Leaden before, his eyes grew dross of lead:
    Tussis[1] attacked him.
"Now, master, take a little rest!"—not he!
    (Caution redoubled,   90
Step two abreast, the way winds narrowly!)
    Not a whit troubled
Back to his studies, fresher than at first,
    Fierce as a dragon
He (soul-hydroptic[2] with a sacred thirst)   95
    Sucked at the flagon.
Oh, if we draw a circle premature,
    Heedless of far gain,
Greedy for quick returns of profit, sure
    Bad is our bargain!   100
Was it not great? did not he throw on God
    (He loves the burthen)—
God's task to make the heavenly period
    Perfect the earthen?
Did not he magnify the mind, show clear   105
    Just what it all meant?
He would not discount life, as fools do here,
    Paid by installment.
He ventured neck or nothing—heaven's success
    Found, or earth's failure:
"Wilt thou trust death or not?" He answered "Yes: 110
    Hence with life's pale lure!"
That low man seeks a little thing to do,
    Sees it and does it:

9. A stone such as a gallstone.   2. Insatiably soul-thirsty.
1. A cough.

This high man, with a great thing to pursue,   115
    Dies ere he knows it.
That low man goes on adding one to one,
    His hundred's soon hit:
This high man, aiming at a million,
    Misses an unit.[3]   120
That, has the world here—should he need the next,
    Let the world mind him!
This, throws himself on God, and unperplexed
    Seeking shall find him.
So, with the throttling hands of death at strife,   125
    Ground he at grammar;
Still, through the rattle, parts of speech were rife:
    While he could stammer
He settled *Hoti's* business—let it be!—
    Properly based *Oun*—   130
Gave us the doctrine of the enclitic *De*,[4]
    Dead from the waist down.
Well, here's the platform, here's the proper place:
    Hail to your purlieus,
All ye highfliers of the feathered race,   135
    Swallows and curlews!
Here's the top peak; the multitude below
    Live, for they can, there:
This man decided not to Live but Know—
    Bury this man there?   140
Here—here's his place, where meteors shoot, clouds form,
    Lightnings are loosened,
Stars come and go! Let joy break with the storm,
    Peace let the dew send!
Lofty designs must close in like effects: 145
    Loftily lying,
Leave him—still loftier than the world suspects,
    Living and dying.

ca. 1854   1855

Confessions

1

What is he buzzing in my ears?
    "Now that I come to die,
Do I view the world as a vale of tears?"
    Ah, reverend sir, not I!

2

What I viewed there once, what I view again   5
    Where the physic bottles stand

3. A small item such as some trifling worldly pleasure.
4. "*Hoti*," "*Oun*," and "*De*" are Greek particles meaning "that," "then," and "towards." An unaccented word such as *de* is "enclitic" when it affects the accentuation of a word adjacent to it.

On the table's edge—is a suburb lane,
    With a wall to my bedside hand.

3
That lane sloped, much as the bottles do,
    From a house you could descry   10
O'er the garden wall: is the curtain blue
    Or green to a healthy eye?

4
To mine, it serves for the old June weather
    Blue above lane and wall;
And that farthest bottle labeled "Ether"   15
    Is the house o'ertopping all.

5
At a terrace, somewhere near the stopper,
    There watched for me, one June,
A girl: I know, sir, it's improper,
    My poor mind's out of tune.   20

6
Only, there was a way . . . you crept
    Close by the side to dodge
Eyes in the house, two eyes except:
    They styled their house "The Lodge."

7
What right had a lounger up their lane?   25
    But, by creeping very close,
With the good wall's help—their eyes might strain
    And stretch themselves to O's,

8
Yet never catch her and me together,
    As she left the attic, there,
By the rim of the bottle labeled "Ether,"   30
    And stole from stair to stair,

9
And stood by the rose-wreathed gate. Alas,
    We loved, sir—used to meet:
How sad and bad and mad it was—
    But then, how it was sweet!   35

ca. 1859

1864

Youth and Art

1
It once might have been, once only:
    We lodged in a street together,
You, a sparrow on the housetop lonely,
    I, a lone she-bird of his feather.

2

Your trade was with sticks and clay,   5
    You thumbed, thrust, patted, and polished,
Then laughed, "They will see some day
    Smith made, and Gibson[1] demolished."

3

My business was song, song, song;
    I chirped, cheeped, trilled, and twittered,   10
"Kate Brown's on the boards ere long,
    And Grisi's[2] existence embittered!"

4

I earned no more by a warble
    Than you by a sketch in plaster;
You wanted a piece of marble,   15
    I needed a music master.

5

We studied hard in our styles,
    Chipped each at a crust like Hindoos,
For air looked out on the tiles,
    For fun watched each other's windows.   20

6

You lounged, like a boy of the South,
    Cap and blouse—nay, a bit of beard, too;
Or you got it, rubbing your mouth
    With fingers the clay adhered to.

7

And I—soon managed to find   25
    Weak points in the flower-fence facing,
Was forced to put up a blind
    And be safe in my corset lacing.

8

No harm! It was not my fault
    If you never turned your eye's tail up,   30
As I shook upon E *in alt*,[3]
    Or ran the chromatic scale up:

9

For spring bade the sparrows pair,
    And the boys and girls gave guesses,
And stalls in our street looked rare   35
    With bulrush and watercresses.

10

Why did not you pinch a flower
    In a pellet of clay and fling it?
Why did not I put a power
    Of thanks in a look, or sing it?   40

11

I did look, sharp as a lynx,
    (And yet the memory rankles)

1. John Gibson (1790–1866), English sculptor.
2. Giulia Grisi (1811–69), a famous Italian soprano.
3. High E.

When models arrived, some minx
    Tripped upstairs, she and her ankles.

12

But I think I gave you as good!   45
    "That foreign fellow—who can know
How she pays, in a playful mood,
    For his tuning her that piano?"

13

Could you say so, and never say
    "Suppose we join hands and fortunes,
And I fetch her from over the way,   50
    Her, piano, and long tunes and short tunes"?

14

No, no: you would not be rash,
    Nor I rasher and something over:
You've to settle yet Gibson's hash,   55
    And Grisi yet lives in clover.

15

But you meet the Prince[4] at the Board,
    I'm queen myself at *bals-paré*,[5]
I've married a rich old lord,
    And you're dubbed knight and an R. A.   60

16

Each life unfulfilled, you see;
    It hangs still, patchy and scrappy:
We have not sighed deep, laughed free,
    Starved, feasted, despaired—been happy.

17

And nobody calls you a dunce,   65
    And people suppose me clever:
This could but have happened once,
    And we missed it, lost it forever.

ca. 1860   1864

4. Perhaps Prince Albert, a patron of the arts. Now that the sculptor has acquired a title and is an "R. A." (a member of the respectable Royal Academy of Arts), he serves on committees or boards with the prince.   5. Fancy-dress balls.

Caliban upon Setebos

Two closely related controversies of the Victorian period led Browning to write this poem (whose title means "Caliban's thoughts about Setebos"). The first, stimulated by Darwin, was concerned with man's origins and his relation to other animals (the poem teems with animal life; in 295 lines, as Park Honan has shown, there are 63 references to animals). Caliban, the half-man and half-monster of Shakespeare's *Tempest*, provided the poet with a model of how the mind of a primitive creature may operate. The second controversy concerned the nature of God and God's responsibility for the existence of suffering in the world. Like many men, Caliban thinks of God's nature as similar to his own. His anthropomorphic conception of the deity, whom he calls Setebos, is confined to what he has observed of life on his island and to what he has observed of himself. From the former derives his "natural theology," that is, his identifying the character of God from evidences provided by nature rather than from the evidence of supernatural revelation. From the latter, his observation of his own character, derives Caliban's conception of God's willful power. Caliban himself admires power and thinks of God in Calvinistic terms as a being who selects at random some creatures who are to be saved and others who are to be condemned to suffer.

An obstacle for the reader is Caliban's use of the third person pronoun. He says that he "never speaks his mind save housed as now"—that is, he thinks if he is adequately hidden under the slush in his cave, the deity will not catch him thinking; he may remind us of the hero of George Orwell's 1984 trying to evade the Thought Police. But to make especially sure of not being caught, Caliban refers to himself in the third person. Thus " 'Will sprawl" means "Caliban will sprawl" (an apostrophe before the verb usually indicates that Caliban himself is the implied subject). When he feels that Setebos will not hear him, he then slips into the first person (e.g., line 56 or 68). The deity is also referred to in the third person but with an initial capital letter ("He").

Caliban upon Setebos

OR NATURAL THEOLOGY IN THE ISLAND

"Thou thoughtest that I was altogether such a one as thyself."[1]

['Will sprawl, now that the heat of day is best,
Flat on his belly in the pit's much mire,
With elbows wide, fists clenched to prop his chin.
And, while he kicks both feet in the cool slush,
And feels about his spine small eft-things[2] course,   5
Run in and out each arm, and make him laugh:
And while above his head a pompion plant,[3]
Coating the cave-top as a brow its eye,
Creeps down to touch and tickle hair and beard,
And now a flower drops with a bee inside,   10
And now a fruit to snap at, catch and crunch—
He looks out o'er yon sea which sunbeams cross
And recross till they weave a spider web
(Meshes of fire, some great fish breaks at times)
And talks to his own self, howe'er he please,   15
Touching that other, whom his dam[4] called God.
Because to talk about Him, vexes—ha,
Could He but know! and time to vex is now,
When talk is safer than in wintertime.
Moreover Prosper[5] and Miranda sleep   20

1. Psalms 50:21. The speaker is God.
2. Water lizards.
3. Pumpkin plant.
4. Caliban's mother, Sycorax.
5. Prospero the magician, who is Caliban's master in *The Tempest*. Miranda is Prospero's daughter.

In confidence he drudges at their task,
And it is good to cheat the pair, and gibe,
Letting the rank tongue blossom into speech.]

Setebos, Setebos, and Setebos!
'Thinketh, He dwelleth i' the cold o' the moon.   25

'Thinketh He made it, with the sun to match,
But not the stars; the stars came otherwise;
Only made clouds, winds, meteors, such as that:
Also this isle, what lives and grows thereon,
And snaky sea which rounds and ends the same.   30

'Thinketh, it came of being ill at ease:
He hated that He cannot change His cold,
Nor cure its ache. 'Hath spied an icy fish
That longed to 'scape the rock-stream where she lived,
And thaw herself within the lukewarm brine   35
O' the lazy sea her stream thrusts far amid,
A crystal spike 'twixt two warm walls of wave;[6]
Only, she ever sickened, found repulse
At the other kind of water, not her life,
(Green-dense and dim-delicious, bred o' the sun)   40
Flounced back from bliss she was not born to breathe,
And in her old bounds buried her despair,
Hating and loving warmth alike: so He.

'Thinketh, He made thereat the sun, this isle,
Trees and the fowls here, beast and creeping thing.   45
Yon otter, sleek-wet, black, lithe as a leech;
Yon auk,[7] one fire-eye in a ball of foam,
That floats and feeds; a certain badger brown
He hath watched hunt with that slant white-wedge eye
By moonlight; and the pie[8] with the long tongue   50
That pricks deep into oakwarts for a worm,
And says a plain word when she finds her prize,
But will not eat the ants; the ants themselves
That build a wall of seeds and settled stalks
About their hole—He made all these and more,   55
Made all we see, and us, in spite: how else?
He could not, Himself, make a second self
To be His mate; as well have made Himself:
He would not make what he mislikes or slights,
An eyesore to Him, or not worth His pains: 60
But did, in envy, listlessness, or sport,
Make what Himself would fain, in a manner, be—
Weaker in most points, stronger in a few,
Worthy, and yet mere playthings all the while,
Things He admires and mocks too—that is it.   65

6. I.e., the thin stream of cold water   7. Sea bird.
which is driven into the warm ocean   8. Magpie.
like a spike between walls.

Because, so brave, so better though they be,
It nothing skills if He begin to plague.[9]
Look now, I melt a gourd-fruit into mash,
Add honeycomb and pods, I have perceived,
Which bite like finches when they bill and kiss—   70
Then, when froth rises bladdery,[1] drink up all,
Quick, quick, till maggots scamper through my brain;
Last, throw me on my back i' the seeded thyme,
And wanton, wishing I were born a bird.
Put case, unable to be what I wish,   75
I yet could make a live bird out of clay:
Would not I take clay, pinch my Caliban
Able to fly?—for, there, see, he hath wings,
And great comb like the hoopoe's[2] to admire,
And there, a sting to do his foes offense,   80
There, and I will that he begin to live,
Fly to yon rock-top, nip me off the horns
Of grigs[3] high up that make the merry din,
Saucy through their veined wings, and mind me not.
In which feat, if his leg snapped, brittle clay,   85
And he lay stupid-like—why, I should laugh;
And if he, spying me, should fall to weep,
Beseech me to be good, repair his wrong,
Bid his poor leg smart less or grow again—
Well, as the chance were, this might take or else   90
Not take my fancy: I might hear his cry,
And give the mankin three sound legs for one,
Or pluck the other off, leave him like an egg,
And lessoned he was mine and merely clay.
Were this no pleasure, lying in the thyme,   95
Drinking the mash, with brain become alive,
Making and marring clay at will? So He.

'Thinketh, such shows nor right nor wrong in Him,
Nor kind, nor cruel: He is strong and Lord.
'Am strong myself compared to yonder crabs   100
That march now from the mountain to the sea;
'Let twenty pass, and stone the twenty-first,
Loving not, hating not, just choosing so.
'Say, the first straggler that boasts purple spots
Shall join the file, one pincer twisted off;   105
'Say, this bruised fellow shall receive a worm,
And two worms he whose nippers end in red;
As it likes me each time, I do: so He.

Well then, 'supposeth He is good i' the main,
Placable if His mind and ways were guessed,   110
But rougher than His handiwork, be sure!

9. I.e., our superior virtues are of no
help to us if God elects to inflict plagues
upon us.

1. Bubbly.
2. Bird with bright plumage.
3. Grasshoppers.

Oh, He hath made things worthier than Himself,
And envieth that, so helped, such things do more
Than He who made them! What consoles but this?
That they, unless through Him, do naught at all,   115
And must submit: what other use in things?
'Hath cut a pipe of pithless elder-joint
That, blown through, gives exact the scream o' the jay
When from her wing you twitch the feathers blue:
Sound this, and little birds that hate the jay   120
Flock within stone's throw, glad their foe is hurt:
Put case such pipe could prattle and boast forsooth,
"I catch the birds, I am the crafty thing,
I make the cry my maker cannot make
With his great round mouth; he must blow through mine!"   125
Would not I smash it with my foot? So He.

But wherefore rough, why cold and ill at ease?
Aha, that is a question! Ask, for that,
What knows—the something over Setebos
That made Him, or He, may be, found and fought,   130
Worsted, drove off and did to nothing,[4] perchance.
There may be something quiet o'er His head,
Out of His reach, that feels nor joy nor grief,
Since both derive from weakness in some way.
I joy because the quails come; would not joy   135
Could I bring quails here when I have a mind:
This Quiet, all it hath a mind to, doth.
'Esteemeth stars the outposts of its couch,
But never spends much thought nor care that way.
It may look up, work up—the worse for those   140
It works on! 'Careth but for Setebos[5]
The many-handed as a cuttlefish,
Who, making Himself feared through what He does,
Looks up, first, and perceives he cannot soar
To what is quiet and hath happy life;   145
Next looks down here, and out of very spite
Makes this a bauble-world to ape yon real,
These good things to match those as hips[6] do grapes.
'Tis solace making baubles, aye, and sport.
Himself peeped late, eyed Prosper at his books   150
Careless and lofty, lord now of the isle:
Vexed, 'stitched a book of broad leaves, arrow-shaped,
Wrote thereon, he knows what, prodigious words;
Has peeled a wand and called it by a name;
Weareth at whiles for an enchanter's robe   155
The eyed skin of a supple oncelot;[7]

4. Completely overcame.
5. Caliban is concerned to appease only Setebos, not the other deity—the Quiet.
6. Hard fruits produced by wild roses.

7. Browning may have invented this term from the Spanish *oncela* or from the French *ocelot*. Both words signify a leopard or spotted wildcat.

And hath an ounce[8] sleeker than youngling mole,
A four-legged serpent he makes cower and couch,
Now snarl, now hold its breath and mind his eye,
And saith she is Miranda and my wife: 160
'Keeps for his Ariel[9] a tall pouch-bill crane
He bids go wade for fish and straight disgorge;
Also a sea beast, lumpish, which he snared,
Blinded the eyes of, and brought somewhat tame,
And split its toe-webs, and now pens the drudge   165
In a hole o' the rock and calls him Caliban;
A bitter heart that bides its time and bites.
'Plays thus at being Prosper in a way,
Taketh his mirth with make-believes: so He.

His dam held that the Quiet made all things   170
Which Setebos vexed only: 'holds not so.
Who made them weak, meant weakness He might vex.
Had He meant other, while His hand was in,
Why not make horny eyes no thorn could prick,
Or plate my scalp with bone against the snow,   175
Or overscale my flesh 'neath joint and joint,
Like an orc's[1] armor? Aye—so spoil His sport!
He is the One now: only He doth all.

'Saith, He may like, perchance, what profits Him.
Aye, himself loves what does him good; but why?   180
'Gets good no otherwise. This blinded beast
Loves whoso places flesh-meat on his nose,
But, had he eyes, would want no help, but hate
Or love, just as it liked him: He hath eyes.
Also it pleaseth Setebos to work,   185
Use all His hands, and exercise much craft,
By no means for the love of what is worked.
'Tasteth, himself, no finer good i' the world
When all goes right, in this safe summertime,
And he wants little, hungers, aches not much,   190
Than trying what to do with wit and strength.
'Falls to make something: 'piled yon pile of turfs,
And squared and stuck there squares of soft white chalk,
And, with a fish-tooth, scratched a moon on each,
And set up endwise certain spikes of tree,   195
And crowned the whole with a sloth's skull a-top,
Found dead i' the woods, too hard for one to kill.
No use at all i' the work, for work's sole sake;
'Shall some day knock it down again: so He.

'Saith He is terrible: watch His feats in proof!   200
One hurricane will spoil six good months' hope.
He hath a spite against me, that I know,

8. A large, ferocious leopard, six or seven feet in length.
9. In *The Tempest*, a spirit who serves

Prospero.
1. Killer whale's.

Just as He favors Prosper, who knows why?
So it is, all the same, as well I find.
'Wove wattles half the winter, fenced them firm   205
With stone and stake to stop she-tortoises
Crawling to lay their eggs here: well, one wave,
Feeling the foot of Him upon its neck,
Gaped as a snake does, lolled out its large tongue,
And licked the whole labor flat; so much for spite.   210
'Saw a ball[2] flame down late (yonder it lies)
Where, half an hour before, I slept i' the shade:
Often they scatter sparkles: there is force!
'Dug up a newt He may have envied once
And turned to stone, shut up inside a stone.   215
Please Him and hinder this?—What Prosper does?[3]
Aha, if He would tell me how! Not He!
There is the sport: discover how or die!
All need not die, for of the things o' the isle
Some flee afar, some dive, some run up trees;   220
Those at His mercy—why, they please Him most
When . . . when . . . well, never try the same way twice!
Repeat what act has pleased, He may grow wroth.
You must not know His ways, and play Him off,
Sure of the issue. 'Doth the like himself: 225
'Spareth a squirrel that it nothing fears
But steals the nut from underneath my thumb,
And when I threat, bites stoutly in defense:
'Spareth an urchin[4] that contrariwise
Curls up into a ball, pretending death   230
For fright at my approach: the two ways please.
But what would move my choler more than this,
That either creature counted on its life
Tomorrow and next day and all days to come,
Saying, forsooth, in the inmost of its heart,   235
"Because he did so yesterday with me,
And otherwise with such another brute,
So must he do henceforth and always."—Aye?
Would teach the reasoning couple what "must" means!
'Doth as he likes, or wherefore Lord? So He.   240

'Conceiveth all things will continue thus,
And we shall have to live in fear of Him
So long as He lives, keeps His strength: no change,
If He have done His best, make no new world
To please Him more, so leave off watching this—   245
If He surprise not even the Quiet's self
Some strange day—or, suppose, grow into it
As grubs grow butterflies: else, here are we,
And there is He, and nowhere help at all.

2. Meteorite.
3. I.e., shall I please Setebos, as
Prospero does, and thus prevent my
being punished as the newt was punished?
4. Hedgehog.

'Believeth with the life, the pain shall stop. 250
His dam held different, that after death
He both plagued enemies and feasted friends:
Idly![5] He doth His worst in this our life,
Giving just respite lest we die through pain,
Saving last pain for worst—with which, an end. 255
Meanwhile, the best way to escape His ire
Is, not to seem too happy. 'Sees, himself,
Yonder two flies, with purple films and pink,
Bask on the pompion-bell above: kills both.
'Sees two black painful beetles roll their ball 260
On head and tail as if to save their lives:
Moves them the stick away they strive to clear.

Even so, 'would have Him misconceive, suppose
This Caliban strives hard and ails no less,
And always, above all else, envies Him; 265
Wherefore he mainly dances on dark nights,
Moans in the sun, gets under holes to laugh,
And never speaks his mind save housed as now:
Outside, 'groans, curses. If He caught me here,
O'erheard this speech, and asked "What chucklest at?" 270
'Would, to appease Him, cut a finger off,
Or of my three kid yearlings burn the best,
Or let the toothsome apples rot on tree,
Or push my tame beast for the orc to taste:
While myself lit a fire, and made a song 275
And sung it, "*What I hate, be consecrate
To celebrate Thee and Thy state, no mate
For Thee; what see for envy in poor me?*"
Hoping the while, since evils sometimes mend,
Warts rub away and sores are cured with slime, 280
That some strange day, will either the Quiet catch
And conquer Setebos, or likelier He
Decrepit may doze, doze, as good as die.

———————

[What, what? A curtain o'er the world at once!
Crickets stop hissing; not a bird—or, yes, 285
There scuds His raven that has told Him all!
It was fool's play this prattling! Ha! The wind
Shoulders the pillared dust, death's house o' the move,
And fast invading fires begin! White blaze—
A tree's head snaps—and there, there, there, there, there, 290
His thunder follows! Fool to gibe at Him!
Lo! 'Lieth flat and loveth Setebos!
'Maketh his teeth meet through his upper lip,

5. I.e., Caliban thinks his mother's opinion was wrong or idle. God's sport with man is confined to this world; there is no afterlife.

Will let those quails fly, will not eat this month
    One little mess of whelks,[6] so he may 'scape!]
ca. 1860   295
                                                          1864

Prospice[7]

Fear death?—to feel the fog in my throat,
    The mist in my face,
When the snows begin, and the blasts denote
    I am nearing the place,
The power of the night, the press of the storm,   5
    The post of the foe;
Where he stands, the Arch Fear in a visible form,
    Yet the strong man must go:
For the journey is done and the summit attained,
    And the barriers fall,   10
Though a battle's to fight ere the guerdon be gained,
    The reward of it all.
I was ever a fighter, so—one fight more,
    The best and the last!
I would hate that death bandaged my eyes, and forbore, 15
    And bade me creep past.
No! let me taste the whole of it, fare like my peers
    The heroes of old,
Bear the brunt, in a minute pay glad life's arrears
    Of pain, darkness, and cold.   20
For sudden the worst turns the best to the brave,
    The black minute's at end,
And the elements' rage, the fiend-voices that rave,
    Shall dwindle, shall blend,
Shall change, shall become first a peace out of pain,   25
    Then a light, then thy breast,
O thou soul of my soul![8] I shall clasp thee again,
    And with God be the rest!
ca. 1861   1864

Abt Vogler[1]

(AFTER HE HAS BEEN EXTEMPORIZING UPON THE MUSICAL
    INSTRUMENT OF HIS INVENTION)

1

Would that the structure brave, the manifold music I build,
    Bidding my organ obey, calling its keys to their work,

6. Shellfish.
7. The title means "Look forward."
8. Browning's wife.
1. Georg Joseph Vogler (1749–1814), a German priest and musician, held the honorary title of *Abbé* or *Abt*. As a composer, teacher, and designer of musical instruments he was well known

Claiming each slave of the sound, at a touch, as when Solomon
willed
Armies of angels that soar, legions of demons that lurk,
Man, brute, reptile, fly—alien of end and of aim, 5
Adverse, each from the other heaven-high, hell-deep removed—
Should rush into sight at once as he named the ineffable Name,[2]
And pile him a palace straight, to pleasure the princess he
loved!

2

Would it might tarry like his, the beautiful building of mine,
This which my keys in a crowd pressed and importuned to
raise! 10
Ah, one and all, how they helped, would dispart now and now com-
bine,
Zealous to hasten the work, heighten their master his praise!
And one would bury his brow with a blind plunge down to hell,
Burrow awhile and build, broad on the roots of things,
Then up again swim into sight, having based me my palace well, 15
Founded it, fearless of flame, flat on the nether springs.

3

And another would mount and march, like the excellent minion he
was,
Aye, another and yet another, one crowd but with many a crest,
Raising my rampired walls of gold as transparent as glass,
Eager to do and die, yield each his place to the rest: 20
For higher still and higher (as a runner tips with fire,
When a great illumination surprises a festal night—
Outlining round and round Rome's dome from space to spire)[3]
Up, the pinnacled glory reached, and the pride of my soul was
in sight.

4

In sight? Not half! for it seemed, it was certain, to match man's
birth, 25
Nature in turn conceived, obeying an impulse as I;
And the emulous heaven yearned down, made effort to reach the
earth,
As the earth had done her best, in my passion, to scale the sky:

in his own day, but he was most famous
as an extemporizer at the organ. Browning's soliloquy represents Vogler at
the organ joyfully improvising a piece
of music and then reflecting upon the
ephemeral existence of such a unique
work of art and of its possible relation
to God's purposes in heaven and on
earth. In this connection, a suggestive
comparison can be made between Browning's conception of a palace of music
inhabited by the "wonderful Dead" and
W. B. Yeats's conception of a heaven
of art in his Byzantium poems.
A characteristic feature of *Abt Vogler*
is the use of exceptionally long sentences, densely packed with details,
which may evoke for us the effects of
rolling organ music. The resulting movement is markedly different from the brisk
staccato rhythms of *A Toccata of
Galuppi's*.
The "musical instrument of his invention" is a compact organ called the
Orchestrion.
2. According to Jewish legend, King
Solomon (because he possessed a seal
inscribed with the "ineffable Name" of
God) had the power of compelling the
demons of earth and air to perform his
bidding.
3. On festival nights the dome of St.
Peter's in Rome is illuminated by a series
of lights ignited by a torchbearer.

Novel splendors burst forth, grew familiar and dwelt with mine,
   Not a point nor peak but found and fixed its wandering star;   30
Meteor-moons, balls of blaze: and they did not pale nor pine,
   For earth had attained to heaven, there was no more near nor
     far.

5

Nay more; for there wanted not who walked in the glare and glow,
   Presences plain in the place; or, fresh from the Protoplast,[4]
Furnished for ages to come, when a kindlier wind should blow,   35
   Lured now to begin and live, in a house to their liking at last;
Or else the wonderful Dead who have passed through the body and
     gone,
   But were back once more to breathe in an old world worth
     their new:
What never had been, was now; what was, as it shall be anon;
   And what is—shall I say, matched both? for I was made per-
     fect too.   40

6

All through my keys that gave their sounds to a wish of my soul,
   All through my soul that praised as its wish flowed visibly forth,
All through music and me! For think, had I painted the whole,
   Why, there it had stood, to see, nor the process so wonder-
     worth:
Had I written the same, made verse—still, effect proceeds from
     cause,
   Ye know why the forms are fair, ye hear how the tale is told;   45
It is all triumphant art, but art in obedience to laws,
   Painter and poet are proud in the artist-list enrolled—

7

But here is the finger of God, a flash of the will that can,
   Existent behind all laws, that made them and, lo, they are!   50
And I know not if, save in this, such gift be allowed to man,
   That out of three sounds he frame, not a fourth sound, but a
     star.[5]
Consider it well: each tone of our scale in itself is naught;
   It is everywhere in the world—loud, soft, and all is said:
Give it to me to use! I mix it with two in my thought: 55
   And, there! Ye have heard and seen: consider and bow the
     head!

8

Well, it is gone at last, the palace of music I reared;
   Gone! and the good tears start, the praises that come too slow;
For one is assured at first, one scarce can say that he feared,
   That he even gave it a thought, the gone thing was to go.   60
Never to be again! But many more of the kind
   As good, nay, better perchance: is this your comfort to me?

---

4. The original or archetypal form of
a species. The "presences" from this
source are beings of the future, not
yet existing, who are "lured" into life
by the music. Cf. *Women and Roses*,
stanzas 7 and 8.
5. I.e., the musician's combining of
three notes into a new harmonic unit
is a creative act as miraculous as the
creation of a star.

To me, who must be saved because I cling with my mind
    To the same, same self, same love, same God: aye, what was,
    shall be.

9

Therefore to whom turn I but to thee, the ineffable Name?   65
    Builder and maker, thou, of houses not made with hands![6]
What, have fear of change from thee who art ever the same?
    Doubt that thy power can fill the heart that thy power expands?
There shall never be one lost good! What was, shall live as before;
    The evil is null, is naught, is silence implying sound;   70
What was good shall be good, with, for evil, so much good more;
    On the earth the broken arcs; in the heaven, a perfect round.

10

All we have willed or hoped or dreamed of good shall exist;
    Not its semblance, but itself; no beauty, nor good, nor power
Whose voice has gone forth, but each survives for the melodist   75
    When eternity affirms the conception of an hour.
The high that proved too high, the heroic for earth too hard,
    The passion that left the ground to lose itself in the sky,
Are music sent up to God by the lover and the bard;
    Enough that he heard it once: we shall hear it by-and-by.   80

11

And what is our failure here but a triumph's evidence
    For the fullness of the days? Have we withered or agonized?
Why else was the pause prolonged but that singing might issue
    thence?
    Why rushed the discords in but that harmony should be
    prized?
Sorrow is hard to bear, and doubt is slow to clear,   85
    Each sufferer says his say, his scheme of the weal and woe:
But God has a few of us whom he whispers in the ear;
    The rest may reason and welcome: 'tis we musicians know.

12

Well, it is earth with me; silence resumes her reign:
    I will be patient and proud, and soberly acquiesce.   90
Give me the keys. I feel for the common chord again,
    Sliding by semitones, till I sink to the minor—yes,
And I blunt it into a ninth, and I stand on alien ground,
    Surveying awhile the heights I rolled from into the deep;
Which, hark, I have dared and done, for my resting place is
    found,   95
    The C Major of this life:[7] so, now I will try to sleep.

1864

6. See II Corinthians v.1, in which St. Paul speaks of "a building of God, an house not made with hands, eternal in the heavens."

7. Vogler's last moments of playing express first his sadness that he cannot remain forever among the "heights" of the music he has temporarily created, and afterwards his acceptance of this return to man's ordinary existence. Thus he plays in a "minor" key, pauses for a short space on the "alien ground" of a "ninth" (a discord which requires a resolution), and finally concludes in "C Major," a key without sharps or flats and representing the plane of ordinary life.

Dîs Aliter Visum; Or, Le Byron de Nos Jours[1]

I

Stop, let me have the truth of that!
  Is that all true? I say, the day
Ten years ago when both of us
  Met on a morning, friends—as thus
We meet this evening, friends or what?—   5

II

Did you—because I took your arm
  And sillily smiled, "A mass of brass
That sea looks, blazing underneath!"
  While up the cliff-road edged with heath,
We took the turns nor came to harm—   10

III

Did you consider "Now makes twice
  That I have seen her, walked and talked
With this poor pretty thoughtful thing,
  Whose worth I weigh: she tries to sing;
Draws, hopes in time the eye grows nice;[2]   15

IV

"Reads verse and thinks she understands;
  Loves all, at any rate, that's great,
Good, beautiful; but much as we
  Down at the bath-house love the sea,
Who breathe its salt and bruise its sands: 20

V

"While . . . do but follow the fishing-gull
  That flaps and floats from wave to cave!

---

1. The first half of the title, from Virgil's *Aeneid* II.428, is a comment on the slaying of a good man who seemingly deserved a better fate but "the gods willed it otherwise." The second half of the title presumably points up the difference between Byron's impetuous conduct as a lover and the timid behavior of the poet who is his latter-day successor, the Byron of *our* days. At least two 19th-century French poets had been called the French Byron (Alphonse Lamartine and Alfred de Musset), but Browning does not seem to have had a special model in mind.

This monologue is Browning's most complex treatment of a situation frequently recurrent in his poems: that of a person, late in life, who looks back on a lost opportunity of establishing a love-relationship. The speaker, a woman in her early thirties, encounters an elderly French poet with whom she had fallen in love ten years earlier. At the hotel on the coast of France where they meet, as the poem opens, the poet has been reminding her of their previous acquaintance. She stops his narrative to offer her own vehemently expressed version of why he had rejected the chance of loving her as a young girl. Her analysis of his motives involves her imagining what his thoughts had been ten years earlier, and these imagined thoughts include speeches that he supposes *she* might make. The woman not only recreates the situation but passes judgment on the poet's failure. Because her indictment of him is expressed in terms that echo ideas of love and heaven frequently expressed in other poems by Browning, we get the impression that she is the author's spokeswoman, but this impression is complicated by our judgment of the distortion imposed by the intensity of her hatred. Was she incipiently this shrewish ten years earlier, we wonder, or was her present character shaped by that disillusioning experience and by the incompatible marriage she has made in the interval?

2. Discriminating.

There's the sea-lover, fair my friend![3]
 What then? Be patient, mark and mend!
Had you the making of your skull?"   25

VI

And did you, when we faced the church
 With spire and sad slate roof, aloof
From human fellowship so far,
 Where a few graveyard crosses are,
And garlands for the swallows' perch,—   30

VII

Did you determine, as we stepped
 O'er the lone stone fence, "Let me get
Her for myself, and what's the earth
 With all its art, verse, music, worth—
Compared with love, found, gained, and kept?   35

VIII

"Schumann's our music-maker now;
 Has his march-movement youth and mouth?
Ingres's the modern man that paints;
 Which will lean on me, of his saints?
Heine[4] for songs; for kisses, how?"   40

IX

And did you, when we entered, reached
 The votive frigate,[5] soft aloft
Riding on air this hundred years,
 Safe-smiling at old hopes and fears,—
Did you draw profit while she preached?   45

X

Resolving, "Fools we wise men grow!
 Yes, I could easily blurt out curt
Some question that might find reply
 As prompt in her stopped lips, dropped eye,
And rush of red to cheek and brow: 50

XI

"Thus were a match made, sure and fast,
 'Mid the blue weed-flowers round the mound
Where, issuing, we shall stand and stay
 For one more look at baths and bay,
Sands, seagulls, and the old church last—   55

XII

"A match 'twixt me, bent, wigged and lamed,
 Famous, however, for verse and worse,

---

3. The poet thinks that the amateurish quality of the girl's involvement with art and literature is similar to the bathers' relative ignorance of the true nature of the sea. The bathers are acquainted only with the sea's fringes, as contrasted with the gull, who is fully immersed in his element.
4. Heinrich Heine (1800–1856), poet; Robert Schumann (1810–1856) composer; Jean August Ingres (1780–1867), painter. Cf. *The Last Ride Together*, stanzas 7 and 8.
5. Model of a ship hanging in the church as a thanksgiving offering for the safe return of sailors from a stormy voyage. The ship "preached" assurances to the man about the possible risks involved in a relationship with the girl.

Sure of the Fortieth spare Armchair[6]
   When gout and glory seat me there,
So, one whose love-freaks pass unblamed,—   60

XIII

"And this young beauty, round and sound
   As a mountain-apple, youth and truth
With loves and doves, at all events
   With money in the Three per Cents;[7]
Whose choice of me would seem profound:—   65

XIV

"She might take me as I take her.
   Perfect the hour would pass, alas!
Climb high, love high, what matter? Still,
   Feet, feelings, must descend the hill:
An hour's perfection can't recur.   70

XV

"Then follows Paris and full time
   For both to reason: 'Thus with us!'[8]
She'll sigh, 'Thus girls give body and soul
   At first word, think they gain the goal,
When 'tis the starting-place they climb!   75

XVI

" 'My friend makes verse and gets renown;
   Have they all fifty years, his peers?
He knows the world, firm, quiet and gay;
   Boys will become as much one day:
They're fools; he cheats, with beard less brown.   80

XVII

" 'For boys say, *Love me or I die!*
   He did not say, *The truth is, youth
I want, who am old and know too much;
   I'd catch youth: lend me sight and touch!*
Drop heart's blood where life's wheels grate dry!'   85

XVIII

"While I should make rejoinder"—(then
   It was, no doubt, you ceased that least
Light pressure of my arm in yours)
   " 'I can conceive of cheaper cures
For a yawning-fit o'er books and men.   90

XIX

" 'What? All I am, was, and might be,
   All, books taught, art brought, life's whole strife,

---

6. One of the 40 seats in the French Academy to which famous writers are elected when a vacancy occurs through death of a member.
7. Her private income is from safe investments in government bonds.
8. The man imagines what they would say or think of each other if, after their "hour's perfection," they descended to the everyday realities of living in Paris together. What she *might* have said (stanzas 15–18) leads to his resolution to break off the relationship.

Painful results since precious, just
  Were fitly exchanged, in wise disgust,
For two cheeks freshened by youth and sea?   95
                    XX
" 'All for a nosegay!—what came first;
  With fields on flower, untried each side;
I rally, need my books and men,
  And find a nosegay': drop it, then,
No match yet made for best or worst!"   100
                    XXI
That ended me. You judged the porch
  We left by, Norman; took our look
At sea and sky; wondered so few
  Find out the place for air and view;
Remarked the sun began to scorch;   105
                    XXII
Descended, soon regained the baths,
  And then, good-bye! Years ten since then:
Ten years! We meet: you tell me, now,
  By a window-seat for that cliff-brow,
On carpet-stripes for those sand-paths.   110
                    XXIII
Now I may speak: you fool, for all
  Your lore! WHO made things plain in vain?
What was the sea for? What, the gray
  Sad church, that solitary day,
Crosses and graves and swallows' call?   115
                    XXIV
Was there naught better than to enjoy?
  No feat which, done, would make time break,
And let us pent-up creatures through
  Into eternity, our due?
No forcing earth teach heaven's employ?   120
                    XXV
No wise beginning, here and now,
  What cannot grow complete (earth's feat)
And heaven must finish,[9] there and then?
  No tasting earth's true food for men,
Its sweet in sad, its sad in sweet?   125
                    XXVI
No grasping at love, gaining a share
  O' the sole spark from God's life at strife
With death, so, sure of range above
  The limits here? For us and love,
Failure; but, when God fails, despair.[1]   130

---

9. Cf. *Abt Vogler*, line 72: "On the earth the broken arcs; in the heaven, a perfect round."
1. To believe that love, because imper- fect, is not worth the risk is a denial of God's role, a blasphemy. Cf. *A Grammarian's Funeral*, line 10.

XXVII

This you call wisdom? Thus you add
　　Good unto good again, in vain?
You loved, with body worn and weak;
　　I loved, with faculties to seek:
Were both loves worthless since ill-clad? 　　　135

XXVIII

Let the mere starfish in his vault
　　Crawl in a wash of weed, indeed,
Rose-jacynth to the fingertips:
　　He, whole in body and soul, outstrips
Man, found with either in default.[2] 　　　140

XXIX

But what's whole, can increase no more,
　　Is dwarfed and dies, since here's its sphere.
The devil laughed at you in his sleeve!
　　You knew not? That I well believe;
Or you had saved two souls: nay, four. 　　　145

XXX

For Stephanie sprained last night her wrist,
　　Ankle or something. "Pooh," cry you?
At any rate she danced, all say,
　　Vilely; her vogue has had its day.
Here comes my husband from his whist. 　　　150

ca. 1862 　　　　　　　　　　　　　　　　　　　　　1864

Rabbi Ben Ezra[1]

1

　　Grow old along with me!
　　The best is yet to be,
The last of life, for which the first was made:
　　Our times are in His hand
　　Who saith, "A whole I planned,
Youth shows but half; trust God: see all nor be afraid!" 　　　5

2

　　Not that, amassing flowers,
　　Youth sighed, "Which rose make ours,
Which lily leave and then as best recall?"

2. In its perfect adaptation to a limited earthly environment the starfish "out-strips" man. Man's distinctive role, by contrast, is to aspire to the unobtainable.
1. The speaker, Abraham Ibn Ezra (ca. 1092–1167), was an eminent Biblical scholar of Spain, but Brown-ing makes little attempt to present him as a distinct individual or to relate him to the age in which he lived. Unlike the more characteristic monologues, *Rabbi Ben Ezra* is not dramatic but declamatory.

Not that, admiring stars,   10
It yearned, "Nor Jove, nor Mars;
Mine be some figured flame which blends, transcends them all!"

3
Not for such hopes and fears
Annulling youth's brief years,
Do I remonstrate: folly wide the mark!   15
Rather I prize the doubt
Low kinds exist without,
Finished and finite clods, untroubled by a spark.

4
Poor vaunt of life indeed,
Were man but formed to feed   20
On joy, to solely seek and find and feast:
Such feasting ended, then
As sure an end to men;
Irks care the crop-full bird? Frets doubt the maw-crammed beast?[2]

5
Rejoice we are allied   25
To That which doth provide
And not partake, effect and not receive!
A spark disturbs our clod;
Nearer we hold of God
Who gives, than of His tribes that take, I must believe.   30

6
Then, welcome each rebuff
That turns earth's smoothness rough,
Each sting that bids nor sit nor stand but go!
Be our joys three parts pain!
Strive, and hold cheap the strain;   35
Learn, nor account the pang; dare, never grudge the throe![3]

7
For thence—a paradox
Which comforts while it mocks—
Shall life succeed in that it seems to fail:
What I aspired to be,   40
And was not, comforts me:
A brute I might have been, but would not sink i' the scale.

8
What is he but a brute
Whose flesh has soul to suit,
Whose spirit works lest arms and legs want play?   45
To man, propose this test—
Thy body at its best,
How far can that project thy soul on its lone way?

2. I.e., does care disturb a bird whose ("maw") is full?
gullet ("crop") is full of food? does   3. Anguish.
doubt trouble an animal whose stomach

9

Yet gifts should prove their use:
I own the Past profuse   50
Of power each side, perfection every turn:
Eyes, ears took in their dole,
Brain treasured up the whole;
Should not the heart beat once, "How good to live and learn"?

10

Not once beat, "Praise be Thine!
I see the whole design,   55
I, who saw power, see now love perfect too:
Perfect I call Thy plan:
Thanks that I was a man!
Maker, remake, complete—I trust what Thou shalt do!"   60

11

For pleasant is this flesh;
Our soul, in its rose-mesh[4]
Pulled ever to the earth, still yearns for rest;
Would we some prize might hold
To match those manifold   65
Possessions of the brute—gain most, as we did best!

12

Let us not always say,
"Spite of this flesh today
I strove, made head, gained ground upon the whole!"
As the bird wings and sings,   70
Let us cry, "All good things
Are ours, nor soul helps flesh more, now, than flesh helps soul!"

13

Therefore I summon age
To grant youth's heritage,
Life's struggle having so far reached its term: 75
Thence shall I pass, approved
A man, for aye removed
From the developed brute; a god though in the germ.

14

And I shall thereupon
Take rest, ere I be gone   80
Once more on my adventure brave and new:[5]
Fearless and unperplexed,
When I wage battle next,
What weapons to select, what armor to indue.[6]

15

Youth ended, I shall try   85
My gain or loss thereby;

4. The body, which holds the soul in   5. In the next life.
its net.   6. Put on.

Leave the fire ashes,[7] what survives is gold:
     And I shall weigh the same,
     Give life its praise or blame:
Young, all lay in dispute; I shall know, being old.   90

16

     For note, when evening shuts,
     A certain moment cuts
The deed off, calls the glory from the gray:
     A whisper from the west
     Shoots—"Add this to the rest,   95
Take it and try its worth: here dies another day."

17

     So, still within this life,
     Though lifted o'er its strife,
Let me discern, compare, pronounce at last,
     "This rage was right i' the main,   100
     That acquiescence vain:
The Future I may face now I have proved the Past."

18

     For more is not reserved
     To man, with soul just nerved
To act tomorrow what he learns today: 105
     Here, work enough to watch
     The Master work, and catch
Hints of the proper craft, tricks of the tool's true play.

19

     As it was better, youth
     Should strive, through acts uncouth,   110
Toward making, than repose on aught f   d made:
     So, better, age, exempt
     From strife, should know, than tempt[8]
Further. Thou waitedst age: wait death nor be afraid!

20

     Enough now, if the Right   115
     And Good and Infinite
Be named here, as thou callest thy hand thine own,
     With knowledge absolute,
     Subject to no dispute
From fools that crowded youth, nor let thee feel alone.[9]   120

21

     Be there, for once and all,
     Severed great minds from small,
Announced to each his station in the Past!
     Was I, the world arraigned,[1]

---

7. If the fire leaves ashes.
8. Attempt.
9. Stanzas 20 and 21 affirm that in age we can more readily think independently than in youth. Maturity enables us to ignore the pressure of having to conform to the thinking of the crowd of small-minded people.
1. Was I, whom the world arraigned.

Were they, my soul disdained,   125
Right? Let age speak the truth and give us peace at last!

                22
Now, who shall arbitrate?
Ten men love what I hate,
Shun what I follow, slight what I receive;
Ten, who in ears and eyes   130
Match me: we all surmise,
They this thing, and I that: whom shall my soul believe?

                23
Not on the vulgar mass
Called "work," must sentence pass,
Things done, that took the eye and had the price;   135
O'er which, from level stand,
The low world laid its hand,
Found straightway to its mind, could value in a trice:

                24
But all, the world's coarse thumb
And finger failed to plumb,   140
So passed in making up the main account;
All instincts immature,
All purposes unsure,
That weighed not as his work, yet swelled the man's amount:

                25
Thoughts hardly to be packed   145
Into a narrow act,
Fancies that broke through language and escaped;
All I could never be,
All, men ignored in me,
This, I was worth to God, whose wheel[2] the pitcher shaped.   150

                26
Aye, note that Potter's wheel,
That metaphor! and feel
Why time spins fast, why passive lies our clay—
Thou, to whom fools propound,[3]
When the wine makes its round,   155
"Since life fleets, all is change; the Past gone, seize today!"

                27
Fool! All that is, at all,
Lasts ever, past recall;
Earth changes, but thy soul and God stand sure:
What entered into thee,   160
That was, is, and shall be:
Time's wheel runs back or stops: Potter and clay endure.

---

2. The potting-wheel on which the speaker's highest qualities of soul were shaped into an enduring "pitcher" by God. See Isaiah lxiv.8.
3. Perhaps addressed to Omar Khay-yám, whose poem, *The Rubáiyát*, urged men to eat, drink, and be merry. Edward FitzGerald's translation of Omar's poem had appeared in 1859.

28

He fixed thee 'mid this dance
Of plastic circumstance,
This Present, thou, forsooth, wouldst fain arrest:[4]   165
Machinery just meant
To give thy soul its bent,
Try thee and turn thee forth, sufficiently impressed.

29

What though the earlier grooves
Which ran the laughing loves   170
Around thy base,[5] no longer pause and press?
What though, about thy rim,
Skull-things in order grim
Grow out, in graver mood, obey the sterner stress?

30

Look not thou down but up!   175
To uses of a cup,
The festal board, lamp's flash, and trumpet's peal,
The new wine's foaming flow,
The Master's lips a-glow!
Thou, heaven's consummate cup, what need'st thou with earth's
wheel?   180

31

But I need, now as then,
Thee, God, who moldest men;
And since, not even while the whirl was worst,
Did I—to the wheel of life
With shapes and colors rife,   185
Bound dizzily—mistake my end, to slake Thy thirst:

32

So, take and use Thy work:
Amend what flaws may lurk,
What strain o' the stuff, what warpings past the aim!
My times be in Thy hand!   190
Perfect the cup as planned!
Let age approve of youth, and death complete the same!
ca. 1862   1864

Apparent Failure

"We shall soon lose a celebrated building."
PARIS NEWSPAPER

1

No, for I'll save it! Seven years since,
I passed through Paris, stopped a day
To see the baptism of your Prince;[1]

---

4. I.e., you would be glad to stop ("arrest") time at this present point of your life.
5. Base of the clay pitcher.

1. Prince Louis, son of Napoleon III, was baptized in June, 1856. Browning had witnessed the event.

Saw, made my bow, and went my way:
Walking the heat and headache off, 5
I took the Seine-side, you surmise,
Thought of the Congress, Gortschakoff,
Cavour's appeal and Buol's replies,[2]
So sauntered till—what met my eyes?

2

Only the Doric little Morgue! 10
The dead-house where you show your drowned:
Petrarch's Vaucluse makes proud the Sorgue,[3]
Your Morgue has made the Seine renowned.
One pays one's debt in such a case;
I plucked up heart and entered—stalked, 15
Keeping a tolerable face
Compared with some whose cheeks were chalked:
Let them! No Briton's to be balked!

3

First came the silent gazers; next,
A screen of glass, we're thankful for; 20
Last, the sight's self, the sermon's text,
The three men who did most abhor
Their life in Paris yesterday,
So killed themselves: and now, enthroned
Each on his copper couch, they lay 25
Fronting me, waiting to be owned.
I thought, and think, their sin's atoned.

4

Poor men, God made, and all for that!
The reverence struck me; o'er each head
Religiously was hung its hat, 30
Each coat dripped by the owner's bed,
Sacred from touch: each had his berth,
His bounds, his proper place of rest,
Who last night tenanted on earth
Some arch, where twelve such slept abreast— 35
Unless the plain asphalt seemed best.

5

How did it happen, my poor boy?
You wanted to be Buonaparte
And have the Tuileries[4] for toy,
And could not, so it broke your heart? 40
You, old one by his side, I judge,
Were, red as blood, a socialist,
A leveler! Does the Empire grudge
You've gained what no Republic missed?
Be quiet, and unclench your fist! 45

2. The Congress of Paris which met in 1856 to establish peace terms after the Crimean War. Russia was represented by Prince Alexander Gortschakoff, Piedmont by Count Cavour, and Austria by Count von Buol-Schauenstein.
3. The Sorgue River is renowned because the poet Petrarch lived in Vaucluse, a village on its banks.
4. The palace in Paris where the kings of France had resided.

6

And this—why, he was red in vain,
　　Or black[5]—poor fellow that is blue!
What fancy was it turned your brain?
　　Oh, women were the prize for you!
Money gets women, cards and dice　　　　　　　50
　　Get money, and ill luck gets just
The copper couch and one clear nice
　　Cool squirt of water o'er your bust,
The right thing to extinguish lust!

7

It's wiser being good than bad;　　　　　　　　55
　　It's safer being meek than fierce:
It's fitter being sane than mad.
　　My own hope is, a sun will pierce
The thickest cloud earth ever stretched;
　　That, after Last, returns the First,　　　　　60
Though a wide compass round be fetched;
　　That what began best, can't end worst,
Nor what God blessed once, prove accursed.

1863　　　　　　　　　　　　　　　　　　　　　　1864

O Lyric Love[1]

O lyric Love, half angel and half bird
And all a wonder and a wild desire—
Boldest of hearts that ever braved the sun,
Took sanctuary within the holier blue,
And sang a kindred soul out to his face—　　　　5
Yet human at the red-ripe of the heart—
When the first summons from the darkling earth
Reached thee amid thy chambers, blanched their blue,
And bared them of the glory—to drop down,
To toil for man, to suffer or to die—　　　　　10
This is the same voice: can thy soul know change?
Hail then, and hearken from the realms of help!
Never may I commence my song, my due
To God who best taught song by gift of thee,
Except with bent head and beseeching hand—　　15
That still, despite the distance and the dark,
What was, again may be; some interchange
Of grace, some splendor once thy very thought,
Some benediction anciently thy smile:

5. Reference to a gambling game, *rouge-et-noir*, in which red or black may win the stakes.
1. These lines, which conclude Book I of *The Ring and the Book*, are addressed to the poet's wife, who had died in 1861. Ten out of the twelve books of this long poem are dramatic monologues, each speaker commenting upon the murder of Pompilia Franceschini by her husband, Guido. In Books I and XII, however, Browning usually speaks, as in this dedicatory passage, in his own person.

—Never conclude, but raising hand and head   20
  Thither where eyes, that cannot reach, yet yearn
For all hope, all sustainment, all reward,
  Their utmost up and on—so blessing back
In those thy realms of help, that heaven thy home,
  Some whiteness which, I judge, thy face makes proud,   25
Some wanness where, I think, thy foot may fall!

                                    1868

The Householder
[*Epilogue to* Fifine at the Fair]

1

Savage I was sitting in my house, late, lone:
  Dreary, weary with the long day's work:
Head of me, heart of me, stupid as a stone:
  Tongue-tied now, now blaspheming like a Turk;
When, in a moment, just a knock, call, cry,   5
  Half a pang and all a rapture, there again were we!—
"What, and is it really you again?" quoth I:
  "I again, what else did you expect?" quoth She.

2

"Never mind, hie away from this old house—
  Every crumbling brick embrowned with sin and shame!   10
Quick, in its corners ere certain shapes arouse!
  Let them—every devil of the night—lay claim,
Make and mend, or rap and rend, for me! Good-by!
  God be their guard from disturbance at their glee,
Till, crash, comes down the carcass in a heap!" quoth I: 15
  "Nay, but there's a decency required!" quoth She.

3

"Ah, but if you knew how time has dragged, days, nights!
  All the neighbor-talk with man and maid—such men!
All the fuss and trouble of street sounds, window sights:
  All the worry of flapping door and echoing roof; and then,   20
All the fancies . . . Who were they had leave, dared try
  Darker arts that almost struck despair in me?
If you knew but how I dwelt down here!" quoth I:
  "And was I so better off up there?" quoth She.

4

"Help and get it over! *Reunited to his wife*   25
  (How draw up the paper lets the parish-people know?)
Lies M., or N., departed from this life,
  Day the this or that, month and year the so and so.
What i' the way of final flourish? Prose, verse? Try!
  Affliction sore long time he bore, or, what is it to be?   30
Till God did please to grant him ease. Do end!" quoth I:
  "I end with—Love is all and Death is naught!" quoth She.

1872   1872

House

1

Shall I sonnet-sing you about myself?
    Do I live in a house you would like to see?
Is it scant of gear, has it store of pelf?
    "Unlock my heart with a sonnet-key?"

2

Invite the world, as my betters have done?   5
    "Take notice: this building remains on view,
Its suites of reception every one,
    Its private apartment and bedroom too;

3

"For a ticket, apply to the Publisher."
    No: thanking the public, I must decline.   10
A peep through my window, if folk prefer;
    But, please you, not foot over threshold of mine!

4

I have mixed with a crowd and heard free talk
    In a foreign land where an earthquake chanced:
And a house stood gaping, naught to balk   15
    Man's eye wherever he gazed or glanced.

5

The whole of the frontage shaven sheer,
    The inside gaped: exposed to day,
Right and wrong and common and queer,
    Bare, as the palm of your hand, it lay.   20

6

The owner? Oh, he had been crushed, no doubt!
    "Odd tables and chairs for a man of wealth!
What a parcel of musty old books about!
    He smoked—no wonder he lost his health!

7

"I doubt if he bathed before he dressed.   25
    A brazier?—the pagan, he burned perfumes!
You see it is proved, what the neighbors guessed:
    His wife and himself had separate rooms."

8

Friends, the goodman of the house at least
    Kept house to himself till an earthquake came: 30
'Tis the fall of its frontage permits you feast
    On the inside arrangement you praise or blame.

9

Outside should suffice for evidence:
    And whoso desires to penetrate
Deeper, must dive by the spirit-sense—   35
    No optics like yours, at any rate!

10

"Hoity toity! A street to explore,
  Your house the exception! '*With this same key
Shakespeare unlocked his heart*,' once more!" [2]
  Did Shakespeare? If so, the less Shakespeare he!   40

1876

To Edward FitzGerald[1]

I chanced upon a new book yesterday;
I opened it, and, where my finger lay
  'Twixt page and uncut page, these words I read—
Some six or seven at most—and learned thereby
That you, FitzGerald, whom by ear and eye   5
  She never knew, "thanked God my wife was dead."
Aye, dead! and were yourself alive, good Fitz,
How to return you thanks would task my wits.
  Kicking you seems the common lot of curs—
While more appropriate greeting lends you grace,   10
Surely to spit there glorifies your face—
  Spitting from lips once sanctified by hers.

1889   1889

Epilogue to *Asolando*[2]

At the midnight in the silence of the sleep-time,
  When you[3] set your fancies free,
Will they pass to where—by death, fools think, imprisoned—

2. The quotation is from Wordsworth's *Scorn Not the Sonnet*, which praises the sonnet form as the one in which Shakespeare had revealed his true self. In theory, if not in practice, Browning strongly disapproved of a poet who "unlocked his heart" in public. A striking example of this failing was *The House of Life*, a sonnet sequence by D. G. Rossetti, published in 1870. It has been conjectured that the glimpses into the intimacies of domestic life and love relations, featured in Rossetti's sonnets, probably prompted Browning to present his case on behalf of an artist's right to privacy and need for reticence.
1. In 1861 FitzGerald wrote to a friend: "Mrs. Browning's death is rather a relief to me, I must say: no more *Aurora Leighs* [title of a popular poem by Mrs. Browning], thank God! * * * She and her sex had better mind the kitchen and the children." Browning discovered the passage among FitzGerald's posthumously published letters and in white heat wrote this rejoinder which was published in the *Athenaeum*. In defense of his poem, Browning wrote a long and eloquent letter to the Tennysons (who had been close friends of FitzGerald), which has been published in the *Times Literary Supplement* (June 3, 1965), 464.
2. The final poem in *Asolando*, a volume published on the day of Browning's death. Browning is said to have recognized that because the third stanza sounded "like bragging" he ought to consider canceling it. "But it's the simple truth," he added, "and as it's true, it shall stand."
3. Any loved person who survives the speaker.

Low he lies who once so loved you, whom you loved so,
—Pity me? 5
Oh to love so, be so loved, yet so mistaken!
  What had I on earth to do
With the slothful, with the mawkish, the unmanly?
Like the aimless, helpless, hopeless, did I drivel
—Being—who? 10

One who never turned his back but marched breast forward,
  Never doubted clouds would break,
Never dreamed, though right were worsted, wrong would triumph,
Held we fall to rise, are baffled to fight better,
  Sleep to wake. 15

No, at noonday in the bustle of man's work-time
  Greet the unseen[4] with a cheer!
Bid him forward, breast and back as either should be,
"Strive and thrive!" cry, "Speed—fight on, fare ever
  There as here!" 20
1889   1890

4. The speaker, after he is dead.

CHARLES DICKENS

(1812–70)

1836–37: *Pickwick Papers.*
1842:   First visit to America.
1849–50: *David Copperfield.*
1865–66: *Our Mutual Friend.*

In her biography of Charles Dickens, Una Pope-Hennessy makes an interesting comparison between the childhood experiences of three eminent Victorian writers. In 1824, living within a few miles of each other in London, were three boys approximately 12 years old. One was Robert Browning, who was enjoying his happy boyhood in a suburb, soaking up learning in his father's library. The second, William Makepeace Thackeray, the future author of *Vanity Fair*, was less happy but certainly secure enough as a student of classics at Charterhouse, one of the leading schools of England. The third, Charles Dickens, had recently been taken out of school and was menially employed pasting labels on bottles of shoe polish in a rat-infested warehouse on the Thames. Despite this seemingly crushing handicap, it was Dickens, less than 13 years later, who had become a famous writer, and the other two were to remain virtually unknown until mid-century. The phenomenal success of Dickens' first novel, *Pickwick Papers* (which appeared in the same year that Victoria became Queen), was repeated during the remainder of his lifetime with the publication of some 15 novels, as well as volumes of stories, travel books, and seemingly countless sketches and essays contributed to the two popular magazines of which he was editor, *Household Words* and *All the Year Round*. Even more remarkable is that more than a hundred years after the last of these novels was published, Dickens' writings continue to attract a vast public. In 1970, the occasion of the centenary of his death, a special issue of *The Dickensian* reported that in the United States alone more than a million copies of his novels are sold annually. And among discriminating critics of fiction, as well as among a vast public, Dickens' status, after suffering a temporary slump earlier in this century, is comparably impressive. In attempting to account for such long-standing popularity and high status among critics, one inevitably falls back upon the elusive term *genius*. Genius, itself, cannot be accounted for, yet it is possible to review aspects of a writer's experience that contributed to the particular slant his genius took. In the instance of Dickens, it was the early experiences that seem to have been especially relevant.

As the eldest son and second child in a family of eight children and himself to become the father of ten children, Charles Dickens had abundant insight into the role a family may play in the shaping of an individual, a role that he celebrated enthusiastically in some of his fiction. Especially celebrative are his accounts of family feasts, such as the Cratchit dinner in *A Christmas Carol*, as examples of the regenerative qualities of warmth and affection in human relationships. And if in his later novels he sometimes pictures travesties of such feasts (as in the gruesome Christmas dinner in *Great Expectations* or the birthday dinner at the Podsnaps in *Our Mutual Friend*) the travesty only reinforces, by inversion, an ideal family scene. Yet despite this recurring festive reference point, it is remarkable how often Dickens' novels bypass a normal family situation and focus, instead, on orphans who have been cut off from parental ties and support. The contrast between a world of secure affection and one involving a descent into a state of neglect and loneliness is a crucial and recurring pattern in Dickens' novels. It is a view of experience similar to what we encounter in melodrama. As Dickens himself described stage melodrama, in *Oliver Twist*, "the tragic and comic scenes" are presented in "regular alternation." And, he adds:

Such changes appear absurd; but they are not so unnatural as they would seem at first sight. The transitions in real life from well-spread boards to death-beds, and from mourning-weeds to holiday garments, are not a whit less startling.

In commenting on these rapid changes of fortune Dickens may have had his own early experiences in mind. The first 11 or 12 years of his childhood had been happy ones. His father, a clerk in the Navy Pay Office, was employed in Portsmouth (where Charles was born) and other ports in Kent on the south coast. This region, largely pre-industrial and past-oriented, remained an Eden-like pastoral setting that Dickens often evokes in his novels, and he was to return here for the last ten years of his life when he bought Gad's Hill, an estate near Rochester. As a boy he attended a good school, discovered his favorite 18th-century novelists and essayists, and generally enjoyed himself. This idyll was shattered after his family moved to London, where his father's casual mismanagement of his income finally led to his imprisonment for debt and to his 12-year-old son being sent to work in a blacking warehouse. The employment lasted only a few months, but to the boy, and to the man in retrospect, the time seemed endless. A sense of abandonment by his parents set up in his mind a specter of insecurity that was never to disappear. The experience also may have contributed to the zealous resolution to excel and an almost ruthless energy which Dickens brought to bear on all pursuits he took up, in particular his writing. As he noted in a letter of 1855: "Whoever is devoted to an Art must be content to deliver himself wholly up to it, and to find his recompense in it." Dickens has often been characterized as the great recorder of the Victorian age or as one of its major critics, but he was also, in his energetic pursuit of his goals, the embodiment of his age, the archetypal Victorian.

In the 11 years between the warehouse and the publication of his first novel, Dickens stored up a variety of experiences on which to draw for his writings. A small legacy enabled the father to be released from debtor's prison, and so his son was able to return to school and, at 15, to begin work as an office boy in a lawyer's firm. By considerable reading in the library of the British Museum and by studying shorthand, Dickens completed his own education and training and became a successful newpaper reporter of debates in Parliament and of other political events. The experiences as a reporter were to be variously useful. They helped to develop his ear. Listening to the speeches of parliamentarians and politicians increased his acutely developed awareness of the absurd pomposities of oratory not only of politicians but of lawyers and of Nonconformist clergymen such as Mr. Chadband, in *Bleak House*, one of the funniest of his vast gallery of orotund speechifiers. Reporting also sharpened Dickens' eye. It was said of him that he could walk through a street of shops and record afterwards every item on display in every shop window. Like Browning's Fra Lippo in his earlier excursions in the streets of Florence, Dickens learned "the look of things." Although his novels are never catalogues in the manner of the Naturalist school of fiction—to him the accumulation of fact without imaginative coloration represented a dreary "dark age" for literature—his novels have always appealed to a reader's sense of place. They seem reassuringly based on accurate and detailed observation, especially observation of the London scene of which he early made himself a master. And Dickens' vision has also a special quality: it is cinematographic. A pioneer filmmaker, D. W. Griffith, found Dickens' techniques a model for montage, and such scenes as the opening chapter of *Bleak House* seem to focus our attention, in the manner of cinema, upon a macrocosmic overview that leads us into the microcosmic heart of the scene.

Drawing on these and other resources, Dickens published a volume of stories and London street scenes, *Sketches by Boz*, in 1836, and the following year, his first novel, which appeared in 20 monthly installments, each consisting of 3 or 4 chapters (except the final double number consisting of 7 or 8 chapters). Publication thus stretched out over a period of more than a year and a half. Most of Dickens' novels were published in this way; a few, such as *Great Expectations* and *A Tale of Two Cities*, appeared instead as weekly serials in a magazine. Dickens preferred the monthly numbers form, and over the course of his career he gradually perfected his control of the mode by carefully planning the whole narrative so that the individual installment would retain the interest of his readers and yet the completed novel, when published, would be a unified whole. The early novels (*Pickwick Papers* in particular) were much more haphazardly constructed not only because of the method of publication but because of the kind of story being told. Dickens' early novels were in the vein of his 18th-century predecessors in whom he had reveled while reading as a boy, the picaresque novels of Smollett in particular, in which a group of characters move from place to place and engage in a series of adventures usually involving encounters with highly colorful individuals in varied walks of life. In *Pickwick Papers* such characters included Cockney coachmen, country gentry, vagabonds like Mr. Jingle, and amiable eccentrics like Mr. Pickwick himself. In *Oliver Twist* (1837–38) the cast shifted to London's underworld. In *Nicholas Nickleby* (1838–39) it took in the world of provincial actors and exploiting schoolmasters. And in *The Old Curiosity Shop* (1840) the journey centered on the pilgrimage of a favorite Victorian heroine, Little Nell, whose capacity for selfless renunciation, even unto death, reduced the most sophisticated critics to tears.

Dickens had thus early abundantly proven himself a master of humor, pathos, and suspense. On the crest of this established reputation, in 1842 he visited America, with his wife, Catherine, whom he had married six years earlier. The visit was generally disillusioning for the high expectations of the young liberal visitor. This experience provided him with materials for a travel book and also for one more venture into the picaresque form of novel. *Martin Chuzzlewit* (1843–44) includes several chapters involving the hero's visit to America and his meetings there with a new gallery of what has come to be called "Dickens characters," although the most vivid examples are those in the English sections of the novel rather than the American, especially the garrulous nurse, Mrs. Gamp.

For the remaining 24 years, beginning with *Dombey and Son* (1846), Dickens gradually modified the picaresque formula of his earlier novels and sought to organize each book around a less dispersive sequence of actions so as to stress some more or less topical issue, such as the law's delays in *Bleak House*, issues in which the fates of all his characters are involved. These later novels sold well in Dickens' lifetime, but most of them were less well received by reviewers than his earlier novels had been. Critics complained of the diminishment of the exuberant high spirits that had made *Pickwick Papers* an early Victorian landmark. As one critic noted, in 1864, "*Pickwick* has been to us very much what the *Rape of the Lock* was to poets of the last century." Such critics resented what seemed to them the pretentious criticisms of Victorian society in late novels like *Hard Times* (1853) or *Our Mutual Friend* (1864–65). And they pointed out that Dickens' social criticism is often contradictory, and in this, at least, they were right. Dickens' view of society was divided between his nostalgic sense of an old order, perhaps a mythical one, in which kindness makes social institutions run, and his contrasting faith in the possibilities of progress in an efficient industrial age. As a citizen, his thinking was generally in the second camp. As a novelist he was in both. His treatment of machines in his novels, especially the railways, reflects the ambivalence of a love-hate relationship. For a later generation of critics, the contradictions are not necessarily a demerit, for they can involve the reader in the very tensions out of which the novels grew. As Angus Wilson, a novelist close to Dickens in spirit, said of him in 1970: "Few themes in Dickens's fiction are without their inherent contradictions in this fragmented man who lived an integrated life only by an overwhelming act of will. What matters, of course, is the success with which he uses his many inherent conflicts to force from himself—painfully and gaily at the same time—artistic unities of a very high order."

Full appreciation of such "artistic unities" depends, of course, on a reading of the whole of such late masterpieces as *Bleak House*. Nevertheless these and all of Dickens' novels do lend themselves unusually well to representation by selections. Dickens' method of composition in installments that are, in part, self-contained, facilitates excerpting. It may also be noted that Dickens himself resorted to excerpting from his novels when he began appearing on public platforms to perform readings from his fiction, at first for charitable purposes in the 1850's and later for his own profit. His success in this role, including a second tour of America in 1867, was again prodigious. In his youth, Dickens had wanted to be an actor, and one of his happiest diversions, through his lifetime, was to direct and perform in companies of amateur actors. This theatrical flair certainly affects the quality of all his fiction, which was composed to be read aloud, if not acted. His daughter, Mary, once saw her father jump up from his writing desk and rush to a mirror "in which I could see the reflection of some extraordinary facial contortions which he was making. He returned rapidly to his desk, wrote furiously for a few moments . . . and then he began talking in a low voice."

In the last decade of his life, as his letters testify, Dickens' public readings gave him intense satisfactions. His marriage had become an unhappy one, and in 1858 he was formally separated from his wife. His infatuation with a young actress, reputedly his mistress, apparently did not materially reduce his sense that despite the façade of monumental successes, he had somehow missed out in life's feast. At his public reading-desk, in these last years, he found compensations for such frustration through a communication with his audiences even more direct than he had established so memorably from his writing-desk.

Three months after his farewell reading, Dickens died at Gad's Hill, following a morning at work on his uncompleted novel, *The Mystery of Edwin Drood*. He was buried in Westminister Abbey. It is noteworthy that in attendance at the funeral service was Alfred Tennyson, the only other Victorian writer to approach Dickens' eminence and his significance for his age. And it was appropriate, given the distinctive nature of his prose, that this novelist should be buried in Poets' Corner. As the poet Robert Buchanan said of him two years later: —

Dickens was beyond all parallel the greatest imaginative creator of his generation, and . . . his poetry, the best of it, although written in unrhymed speech, is worth more, and will probably last longer, than all the Verse-poetry of his age, splendid as some of that poetry has been.

Only recently have editors of Victorian novels begun applying modern methods of scholarship to provide reliably accurate texts. The texts for the following selections from Dickens are those that seem to be the most satisfactory available editions: for *Martin Chuzzlewit,* the edition prepared by P. N. Furbank; for *Our Mutual Friend,* that prepared by Stephen Gill; for *David Copperfield,* the text edited by George Ford; for *Hard Times* and *Bleak House,* the text prepared by George Ford and Sylvère Monod.

From Martin Chuzzlewit[1]

[*Mrs. Gamp and Mr. Mould*]

Mr. Mould was surrounded by his household gods. He was enjoying the sweets of domestic repose, and gazing on them with a calm delight. The day being sultry, and the window open, the legs of Mr. Mould were on the window-seat, and his back reclined against the shutter. Over his shining head a handkerchief was drawn, to guard his baldness from the flies. The room was fragrant with the smell of punch, a tumbler of which grateful compound stood upon a small round table, convenient to the hand of Mr. Mould; so deftly mixed, that as his eye looked down into the cool transparent drink, another eye, peering brightly from behind the crisp lemon-peel, looked up at him, and twinkled like a star.

Deep in the City, and within the ward of Cheap,[2] stood Mr. Mould's establishment. His Harem, or, in other words, the common sitting-room of Mrs. Mould and family, was at the back, over the little counting-house behind the shop; abutting on a churchyard small and shady. In this domestic chamber Mr. Mould now sat; gazing, a placid man, upon his punch and home. If, for a moment at a time, he sought a wider prospect, whence he might return with freshened zest to these enjoyments, his moist glance wandered like a

1. Of the 75 named characters in Dickens' sixth novel, *Martin Chuzzlewit* (1843), perhaps the most colorful is Mrs. Sarah Gamp, a fat red-faced widow who earns her livelihood as a nurse and midwife: "Like most persons who have attained to great eminence in their professions, she took to hers very kindly; insomuch, that setting aside her natural predelictions as a woman, she went to a lying-in or to a laying-out with equal zest and relish." In the novel Mrs. Gamp is called upon to prepare for burial the body of one of the Chuzzlewit family. To perform these offices she is highly recommended by an undertaker, Mr. Mould.
Mrs. Gamp's funeral employment leads afterwards to her getting an appointment as a home-nurse for an elderly man, Mr. Chuffey. On this occasion, as on all others, Mrs. Gamp's principal concern is not with her patient's welfare but with assuring that she herself will be amply supplied, on the job, with food

and drink (cucumbers, pickled salmon, and gin are special favorites of hers).
In colleges of nursing today, the expression "a Mrs. Gamp" is still in use to describe a nurse who is totally irresponsible or incompetent, and, in these terms, it could be solemnly argued that Dickens' portrait is a satire aimed at improving conditions in the nursing profession before the days of Florence Nightingale. While his portrait may have contributed to such an end, its primary effect is, like many of Dickens' early creations, pure comedy. In later life, when reading his own works to public audiences, Dickens particularly enjoyed doing Mrs. Gamp, and sometimes he had to interrupt his reading because he himself was as convulsed with laughter as the members of his audience. This selection is from Chapter 25.
2. One of the 26 wards within the City, i.e., the core section (once walled) of the metropolis of London.

sunbeam through a rural screen of scarlet runners, trained on strings before the window; and he looked down, with an artist's eye, upon the graves.

The partner of his life, and daughters twain, were Mr. Mould's companions. Plump as any partridge was each Miss Mould, and Mrs. M. was plumper than the two together. So round and chubby were their fair proportions, that they might have been the bodies once belonging to the angels' faces[3] in the shop below, grown up, with other heads attached to make them mortal. Even their peachy cheeks were puffed out and distended, as though they ought of right to be performing on celestial trumpets. The bodiless cherubs in the shop, who were depicted as constantly blowing those instruments for ever and ever without any lungs, played, it is to be presumed, entirely by ear.

Mr. Mould looked lovingly at Mrs. Mould, who sat hard by, and was a helpmate to him in his punch as in all other things. Each seraph daughter, too, enjoyed her share of his regards, and smiled upon him in return. So bountiful were Mr. Mould's possessions, and so large his stock in trade, that even there, within his household sanctuary, stood a cumbrous press, whose mahogany maw was filled with shrouds, and winding-sheets, and other furniture of funerals. But, though the Misses Mould had been brought up, as one may say, beneath his eye, it had cast no shadow on their timid infancy or blooming youth. Sporting behind the scenes of death and burial from cradlehood, the Misses Mould knew better. Hatbands, to them, were but so many yards of silk or crape; the final robe but such a quantity of linen. The Misses Mould could idealize a player's habit, or a court-lady's petticoat, or even an act of parliament. But they were not to be taken in by palls. They made them sometimes.

The premises of Mr. Mould were hard of hearing to the boisterous noises in the great main streets, and nestled in a quiet corner, where the City strife became a drowsy hum, that sometimes rose and sometimes fell and sometimes altogether ceased: suggesting to a thoughtful mind a stoppage in Cheapside.[4] The light came sparkling in among the scarlet runners, as if the churchyard winked at Mr. Mould, and said, "We understand each other"; and from the distant shop a pleasant sound arose of coffin-making with a low melodious hammer, rat, tat, tat, tat, alike promoting slumber and digestion.

"Quite the buzz of insects," said Mr. Mould, closing his eyes in a perfect luxury. "It puts one in mind of the sound of animated nature in the agricultural districts. It's exactly like the woodpecker tapping."

3. Print of a popular painting by Sir Joshua Reynolds, "Heads of Angels," exhibited in 1787, which portrays a girl's head in five different poses resembling "bodiless cherubs."
4. A busy street in the City.

"The woodpecker tapping the hollow *elm* tree," observed Mrs. Mould, adapting the words of the popular melody to the description of wood commonly used in the trade.[5]

"Ha, ha!" laughed Mr. Mould. "Not at all bad, my dear. We shall be glad to hear from you again, Mrs. M. Hollow elm tree, eh! Ha, ha! Very good indeed. I've seen worse than that in the Sunday papers, my love."

Mrs. Mould, thus encouraged, took a little more of the punch, and handed it to her daughters, who dutifully followed the example of their mother.

"Hollow *elm* tree, eh?" said Mr. Mould, making a slight motion with his legs in his enjoyment of the joke. "It's beech in the song. Elm, eh? Yes, to be sure. Ha, ha, ha! Upon my soul, that's one of the best things I know!" He was so excessively tickled by the jest that he couldn't forget it, but repeated twenty times, "Elm, eh? Yes, to be sure. Elm, of course. Ha, ha, ha! Upon my life, you know, that ought to be sent to somebody who could make use of it. It's one of the smartest things that ever was said. Hollow *elm* tree, eh? Of course. Very hollow. Ha, ha, ha!"

Here a knock was heard at the room door.

"That's Tacker, I know," said Mrs. Mould, "by the wheezing he makes. Who that hears him now, would suppose he'd ever had wind enough to carry the feathers on his head![6] Come in, Tacker."

"Beg your pardon, ma'am," said Tacker, looking in a little way. "I thought our Governor was here."

"Well! So he is," cried Mould.

"Oh! I didn't see you, I'm sure," said Tacker, looking in a little farther. "You wouldn't be inclined to take a walking one of two, with the plain wood and a tin plate,[7] I suppose?"

"Certainly not," replied Mr. Mould, "much too common. Nothing to say to it."

"I told 'em it was precious low," observed Mr. Tacker.

"Tell 'em to go somewhere else. We don't do that style of business here," said Mr. Mould. "Like their impudence to propose it. Who is it?"

"Why," returned Tacker, pausing, "that's where it is, you see. It's the beadle's son-in-law."

"The beadle's son-in-law, eh?" said Mould. "Well, I'll do it if the beadle follows in his cocked hat; not else. We carry it off that way, by looking official, but it'll be low enough then. His cocked hat, mind!"

---

5. A song written in America by Thomas Moore (1779–1852), "The Woodpecker," concludes: "Every leaf was at rest, and I heard not a sound, / But the woodpecker tapping the hollow beech tree."
6. An undertaker's assistant, a "featherman," walked ahead of the hearse in funeral processions. On his head he carried a tray loaded with ostrich plumes, dyed black.
7. For a "walking" funeral without a coach, the coffin would be of cheap wood and the fittings tin-plated instead of being silver or brass.

"I'll take care, sir," rejoined Tacker. "Oh! Mrs. Gamp's below, and wants to speak to you."

"Tell Mrs. Gamp to come upstairs," said Mould. "Now, Mrs. Gamp, what's *your* news?"

The lady in question was by this time in the doorway, curtseying to Mrs. Mould. At the same moment a peculiar fragrance was borne upon the breeze, as if a passing fairy had hiccoughed, and had previously been to a wine-vaults.

Mrs. Gamp made no response to Mr. Mould, but curtseyed to Mrs. Mould again, and held up her hands and eyes, as in a devout thanksgiving that she looked so well. She was neatly, but not gaudily attired, in the weeds she had worn when Mr. Pecksniff had the pleasure of making her acquaintance; and was perhaps the turning of a scale more snuffy.

"There are some happy creeturs," Mrs. Gamp observed, "as time runs back'ards with, and you are one, Mrs. Mould; not that he need do nothing except use you in his most owldacious way for years to come, I'm sure; for young you are and will be. I says to Mrs. Harris," Mrs. Gamp continued, "only t'other day; the last Monday evening fortnight as ever dawned upon this Piljian's Projiss of a mortal wale;[8] I says to Mrs. Harris when she says to me, 'Years and our trials, Mrs. Gamp, sets marks upon us all.'—'Say not the words Mrs. Harris, if you and me is to be continual friends, for sech is not the case. Mrs. Mould,' I says, making so free, I will confess, as use the name," (she curtseyed here), " 'is one of them that goes agen the observation straight: and never, Mrs. Harris, whilst I've a drop of breath to draw, will I set by, and not stand up, don't think it.'—'I ast your pardon, ma'am,' says Mrs. Harris, 'and I humbly grant your grace; for if ever a woman lived as would see her feller creeturs into fits to serve her friends, well do I know that woman's name is Sairey Gamp.' "

At this point she was fain to stop for breath; and advantage may be taken of the circumstance, to state that a fearful mystery surrounded this lady of the name of Harris, whom no one in the circle of Mrs. Gamp's acquaintance had ever seen; neither did any human being know her place of residence, though Mrs. Gamp appeared on her own showing to be in constant communication with her. There were conflicting rumors on the subject; but the prevalent opinion was that she was a phantom of Mrs. Gamp's brain—as Messrs. Doe and Roe[9] are fictions of the law—created for the express purpose of holding visionary dialogues with her on all manner of subjects, and invariably winding up with a compliment to the excellence of her nature.

8. Probably the Valley of Humiliation and the Valley of the Shadow of Death in Bunyan's *Pilgrim's Progress*.

9. John Doe and Richard Roe, fictitious names used by lawyers to refer to plaintiffs and defendants.

"And likeways what a pleasure," said Mrs. Gamp, turning with a tearful smile towards the daughters, "to see them two young ladies as I know'd afore a tooth in their pretty heads was cut, and have many a day seen—ah, the sweet creeturs!—playing at berryins down in the shop, and follerin' the orderbook to its long home in the iron safe! But that's all past and over, Mr. Mould"; as she thus got in a carefully regulated routine to that gentleman, she shook her head waggishly; "That's all past and over now, sir, an't it?"

"Changes, Mrs. Gamp, changes!" returned the undertaker.

"More changes too, to come, afore we've done with changes, sir," said Mrs. Gamp, nodding yet more waggishly than before. "Young ladies with such faces thinks of something else besides berryins, don't they, sir?"

"I am sure I don't know, Mrs. Gamp," said Mould, with a chuckle.—"Not bad in Mrs. Gamp, my dear?"

"Oh yes, you do know, sir!" said Mrs. Gamp, "and do does Mrs. Mould, your ansome pardner too, sir; and so do I, although the blessing of a daughter was denied me; which, if we had had one, Gamp would certainly have drunk its little shoes right off its feet, as with our precious boy he did, and arterwards send the child a errand to sell his wooden leg for any money it would fetch as matches in the rough, and bring it home in liquor: which was truly done beyond his years, for ev'ry individle penny that child lost at toss or buy[1] for kidney ones; and come home arterwards quite bold, to break the news, and offering to drown himself if that would be a satisfaction to his parents.—Oh yes, you do know, sir," said Mrs. Gamp, wiping her eye with her shawl, and resuming the thread of her discourse. "There's something besides births and berryins in the newspapers, an't there, Mr. Mould?"

Mr. Mould winked at Mrs. Mould, whom he had by this time taken on his knee, and said: "No doubt. A good deal more, Mrs. Gamp. Upon my life, Mrs. Gamp is very far from bad, my dear!"

"There's marryings, an't there, sir?" said Mrs. Gamp, while both the daughters blushed and tittered. "Bless their precious hearts, and well they knows it! Well you know'd it too, and well did Mrs. Mould, when you was at their time of life! But my opinion is, you're all of one age now. For as to you and Mrs. Mould, sir, ever having grandchildren—"

"Oh! Fie, fie! Nonsense, Mrs. Gamp," replied the undertaker. "Devilish smart, though. Ca-pi-tal!" This was in a whisper. "My dear"—aloud again—"Mrs. Gamp can drink a glass of rum, I dare say. Sit down, Mrs. Gamp, sit down."

Mrs. Gamp took the chair that was nearest the door, and casting

---

1. Gambling game played by street vendors selling meat pies. Tossing a coin would decide whether the customer paid or got his pies free (here kidney pies) [T. W. Hill's note].

up her eyes towards the ceiling, feigned to be wholly insensible to the fact of a glass of rum being in preparation, until it was placed in her hand by one of the young ladies, when she exhibited the greatest surprise.

"A thing," she said, "as hardly ever, Mrs. Mould, occurs with me unless it is when I am indispoged, and find my half a pint of porter settling heavy on the chest. Mrs. Harris often and often says to me, 'Sairey Gamp,' she says, 'you raly do amaze em!' 'Mrs. Harris,' I says to her, 'why so? Give it a name, I beg.' 'Telling the truth then, ma'am,' says Mrs. Harris, 'and shaming him as shall be nameless[2] betwixt you and me, never did I think till I know'd you, as any woman could sick-nurse and monthly[3] likeways, on the little that you takes to drink.' 'Mrs. Harris,' I says to her, 'none on us knows what we can do till we tries; and wunst, when me and Gamp kept ouse, I thought so too. But now,' I says, 'my half a pint of porter fully satisfies; perwisin', Mrs. Harris, that it is brought reg'lar, and draw'd mild. Whether I sicks or monthlies, ma'am, I hope I does my duty, but I am but a poor woman, and I earns my living hard; therefore I *do* require it, which I makes confession, to be brought reg'lar and draw'd mild.'"

The precise connection between these observations and the glass of rum, did not appear; for Mrs. Gamp proposing as a toast "The best of lucks to all!" took off the dram in quite a scientific manner, without any further remarks.

"And what's your news, Mrs. Gamp?" asked Mould again, as that lady wiped her lips upon her shawl, and nibbled a corner off a soft biscuit, which she appeared to carry in her pocket as a provision against contingent drams. "How's Mr. Chuffey?"

"Mr. Chuffey, sir," she replied, "is jest as usual; he an't no better and he an't no worse. I take it very kind in the gentleman to have wrote up to you and said, 'let Mrs. Gamp take care of him till I come home'; but ev'ry think he does is kind. There an't a many like him. If there was, we shouldn't want no churches."

"What do you want to speak to me about, Mrs. Gamp?" said Mould, coming up the point.

'Jest this, sir,' Mrs. Gamp returned, "with thanks to you for asking. There *is* a gent, sir, at the Bull in Holborn, as has been took ill there, and is bad abed. They have a day nurse as was recommended from Bartholomew's;[4] and well I knows her, Mr. Mould, her name bein' Mrs. Prig, the best of creeturs. But she is otherways engaged at night, and they are in wants of night-watching; consequent she says to them, having reposed the greatest friendliness in

---

2. Cf. "Tell truth, and shame the Devil." (*Henry IV*, First Part, III.i.58).
3. Perform ordinary nursing and mid-

wife-nursing.
4. St. Bartholomew's Hospital in London.

me for twenty year, 'The soberest person going, and the best of blessings in a sick room, is Mrs. Gamp. Send a boy to Kingsgate Street,' she says 'and snap her up at any price, for Mrs. Gamp is worth her weight and more in goldian guineas.' My landlord brings the message down to me and says, 'bein' in a light place where you are, and this job promising so well, why not unite the two?' 'No, sir,' I says, 'not unbeknown to Mr. Mould, and therefore do not think it. But I will go to Mr. Mould," I says, 'and ast him, if you like.'" Here she looked sideways at the undertaker, and came to a stop.

"Night-watching, eh?" said Mould, rubbing his chin.

"From eight o'clock till eight, sir. I will not deceive you," Mrs. Gamp rejoined.

"And then go back, eh?" said Mould.

"Quite free then, sir, to attend to Mr. Chuffey. His ways bein' quiet, and his hours early, he'd be abed sir, nearly all the time. I will not deny," said Mrs. Gamp with meekness, "that I am but a poor woman, and that the money is a object; but do not let that act upon you, Mr. Mould. Rich folks may ride on camels, but it ain't so easy for 'em to see out of a needle's eye.[5] That is my comfort, and I hope I knows it."

"Well, Mrs. Gamp," observed Mould, "I don't see any particular objection to your earning an honest penny under such circumstances. I should keep it quiet, I think, Mrs. Gamp. I wouldn't mention it to Mr. Chuzzlewit on his return, for instance, unless it were necessary, or he asked you point-blank."

"The very words was on my lips, sir," Mrs. Gamp rejoined. "Suppoging that the gent should die, I hope I might take the liberty of saying as I know'd someone in the undertaking line, and yet give no offense to you, sir?"

"Certainly, Mrs. Gamp," said Mould, with much condescension. "You may casually remark, in such a case, that we do the thing pleasantly and in a great variety of styles, and are generally considered to make it as agreeable as possible to the feelings of the survivors. But don't obtrude it, don't obtrude it. Easy, easy! My dear, you may as well give Mrs. Gamp a card or two, if you please."

Mrs. Gamp received them, and scenting no more rum in the wind (for the bottle was locked up again) rose to take her departure.

"Wishing ev'ry happiness to this happy family," said Mrs. Gamp, "with all my heart. Good arternoon, Mrs. Mould! If I was Mr. Mould, I should be jealous of you, ma'am; and I'm sure, if I was you, I should be jealous of Mr. Mould."

5. Cf. "It is easier for a camel to go through the eye of a needle, than for a rich man to enter into the kingdom of God" (Matthew xix.24).

"Tut, tut! Bah, bah! Go along, Mrs. Gamp!" cried the delighted undertaker.

"As to the young ladies," said Mrs. Gamp, dropping a curtsey, "bless their sweet looks—how they can never reconsize it with their duties to be so grown up with such young parents, it an't for sech as me to give a guess at."

"Nonsense, nonsense. Be off, Mrs. Gamp!" cried Mould. But in the height of his gratification he actually pinched Mrs. Mould as he said it.

"I'll tell you what, my dear," he observed, when Mrs. Gamp had at last withdrawn and shut the door, "that's a ve-ry shrewd woman. That's a woman whose intellect is immensely superior to her station in life. That's a woman who observes and reflects in an uncommon manner. She's the sort of woman now," said Mould, drawing his silk handkerchief over his head again, and composing himself for a nap, "one would almost feel disposed to bury for nothing: and do it neatly, too!"

Mrs. Mould and her daughters fully concurred in these remarks; the subject of which had by this time reached the street, where she experienced so much inconvenience from the air, that she was obliged to stand under an archway for a short time, to recover herself. Even after this precaution, she walked so unsteadily as to attract the compassionate regards of divers kind-hearted boys, who took the liveliest interest in her disorder; and in their simple language, bade her be of good cheer, for she was "only a little screwed."

Whatever she was, or whatever name the vocabulary of medical science would have bestowed upon her malady, Mrs. Gamp was perfectly acquainted with the way home again; and arriving at the house of Anthony Chuzzlewit & Son, lay down to rest. Remaining there until seven o'clock in the evening, and then persuading poor old Chuffey to betake himself to bed, she sallied forth upon her new engagement. First, she went to her private lodgings in Kingsgate Street, for a bundle of robes and wrappings comfortable in the night season; and then repaired to the Bull in Holborn, which she reached as the clocks were striking eight.

As she turned into the yard, she stopped; for the landlord, landlady, and head chambermaid, were all on the threshold together, talking earnestly with a young gentleman who seemed to have just come or to be just going away. * * *

* * * Mrs. Gamp felt the necessity of advancing, bundle in hand, and introducing herself.

"The night-nurse," she observed, "from Kingsgate Street, well beknown to Mrs. Prig the day-nurse, and the best of creeturs. How is the poor dear gentleman, tonight? If he an't no better yet, still that is what must be expected and prepared for. It an't the fust time by a many score, ma'am," dropping a curtsey to the landlady, "that Mrs. Prig and me has nussed together, turn and turn about, one off, one on. We knows each other's ways, and often gives relief when others failed. Our charges is but low, sir": Mrs. Gamp addressed herself to John[6] on this head: "considerin' the nater of our painful dooty. If they wos made accordin' to our wishes, they would be easy paid."

Regarding herself as having now delivered her inauguration address, Mrs. Gamp curtseyed all round, and signified her wish to be conducted to the scene of her official duties. The chambermaid led her, through a variety of intricate passages, to the top of the house; and pointing at length to a solitary door at the end of a gallery, informed her that yonder was the chamber where the patient lay. That done, she hurried off with all the speed she could make.

Mrs. Gamp traversed the gallery in a great heat from having carried her large bundle up so many stairs, and tapped at the door, which was immediately opened by Mrs. Prig, bonneted and shawled and all impatience to be gone. Mrs. Prig was of the Gamp build, but not so fat; and her voice was deeper and more like a man's. She had also a beard.

"I began to think you warn't a-coming!" Mrs. Prig observed, in some displeasure.

"It shall be made good tomorrow night," said Mrs. Gamp, "honorable. I had to go and fetch my things." She had begun to make signs of inquiry in reference to the position of the patient and his overhearing them—for there was a screen before the door—when Mrs. Prig settled that point easily.

"Oh!" she said aloud, "he's quiet, but his wits is gone. It an't no matter wot you say."

"Anythin' to tell afore you goes, my dear?" asked Mrs. Gamp, setting her bundle down inside the door, and looking affectionately at her partner.

"The pickled salmon," Mrs. Prig replied, "is quite delicious. I can partick'ler recommend it. Don't have nothink to say to the cold meat, for it tastes of the stable. The drinks is all good."

Mrs. Gamp expressed herself much gratified.

"The physic and them things is on the drawers and mankle-shelf," said Mrs. Prig, cursorily. "He took his last slime draught at seven. The easy-chair an't soft enough. You'll want his piller."

Mrs. Gamp thanked her for these hints, and giving her a friendly good night, held the door open until she had disappeared at the other end of the gallery. Having thus performed the hospitable duty of seeing her safely off, she shut it, locked it on the inside, took up

6. John Westlock, a former friend of the patient.

her bundle, walked round the screen, and entered on her occupation of the sick chamber.

"A little dull, but not so bad as might be," Mrs. Gamp remarked. "I'm glad to see a parapidge, in case of fire, and lots of roofs and chimley-pots to walk upon."

It will be seen from these remarks that Mrs. Gamp was looking out of window. When she had exhausted the prospect, she tried the easy-chair, which she indignantly declared was "harder than a brickbadge."[7] Next she pursued her researches among the physic-bottles, glasses, jugs, and teacups; and when she had entirely satisfied her curiosity on all these subjects of investigation, she untied her bonnet-strings and strolled up to the bedside to take a look at the patient.

A young man—dark and not ill-looking—with long black hair, that seemed the blacker for the whiteness of the bedclothes. His eyes were partly open, and he never ceased to roll his head from side to side upon the pillow, keeping his body almost quiet. He did not utter words; but every now and then gave vent to an expression of impatience or fatigue, sometimes of surprise; and still his restless head—oh, weary, weary hour!—went to and fro without a moment's intermission.

Mrs. Gamp solaced herself with a pinch of snuff, and stood looking at him with her head inclined a little sideways, as a connoisseur might gaze upon a doubtful work of art. By degrees, a horrible remembrance of one branch of her calling took possession of the woman; and stooping down, she pinned his wandering arms against his sides, to see how he would look if laid out as a dead man. Hideous as it may appear, her fingers itched to compose his limbs in that last marble attitude.

"Ah!" said Mrs. Gamp, walking away from the bed, "he'd make a lovely corpse."

She now proceeded to unpack her bundle; lighted a candle with the aid of a fire-box on the drawers; filled a small kettle as a preliminary to refreshing herself with a cup of tea in the course of the night; laid what she called "a little bit of fire," for the same philanthropic purpose; and also set forth a small teaboard, that nothing might be wanting for her comfortable enjoyment. These preparations occupied so long, that when they were brought to a conclusion it was high time to think about supper; so she rang the bell and ordered it.

"I think, young woman," said Mrs. Gamp to the assistant chambermaid, in a tone of expressive weakness, "that I could pick a little bit of pickled salmon, with a nice little sprig of fennel, and a sprin-

7. Brickbat (presumably) — a piece of brick commonly used as a missile in street fights.

kling of white pepper. I takes new bread, my dear, with jeest a little pat of fresh butter, and a mossel of cheese. In case there should be such a thing as a cowcumber in the 'ouse, will you be so kind as to bring it, for I'm rather partial to 'em, and they does a world of good in a sick room. If they draws the Brighton Old Tipper[8] here, I takes *that* ale at night, my love; it bein' considered wakeful by the doctors. And whatever you do, young woman, don't bring more than a shilling's-worth of gin and water-warm when I rings the bell a second time; for that is always my allowance, and I never takes a drop beyond!"

Having preferred these moderate requests, Mrs. Gamp observed that she would stand at the door until the order was executed, to the end that the patient might not be disturbed by her opening it a second time; and therefore she would thank the young woman to "look sharp."

A tray was brought with everything upon it, even to the cucumber; and Mrs. Gamp accordingly sat down to eat and drink in high good humor. The extent to which she availed herself of the vinegar, and supped up that refreshing fluid with the blade of her knife, can scarcely be expressed in narrative.

"Ah!" sighed Mrs. Gamp, as she meditated over the warm shilling's-worth, "what a blessed thing it is—living in a wale—to be contented! What a blessed thing it is to make sick people happy in their beds, and never mind one's self as long as one can do a service! I don't believe a finer cowcumber was ever grow'd. I'm sure I never seen one!"

She moralized in the same vein until her glass was empty, and then administered the patient's medicine, by the simple process of clutching his windpipe, to make him gasp, and immediately pouring it down his throat.

"I a'most forgot the piller, I declare!" said Mrs. Gamp, drawing it away. "There! Now he's comfortable as can be, I'm sure! I must try to make myself as much so as I can."

With this view, she went about the construction of an extemporaneous bed in the easy-chair, with the addition of the next easy one for her feet. Having formed the best couch that the circumstances admitted of, she took out of her bundle a yellow night-cap, of prodigious size, in shape resembling a cabbage; which article of dress she fixed and tied on with the utmost care, previously divesting herself of a row of bald old curls that could scarcely be called false, they were so very innocent of anything approaching to deception. From the same repository she brought forth a nightjacket, in which she also attired herself. Finally, she produced a watchman's

---

8. Extra strong ale named after a brewer in Brighton, Thomas Tipper, described in Chapter 19 as "the celebrated staggering ale, or Real Old Brighton Tipper."

coat, which she tied round her neck by the sleeves, so that she became two people; and looked, behind, as if she were in the act of being embraced by one of the old patrol.

All these arrangements made, she lighted the rushlight, coiled herself up on her couch, and went to sleep. Ghostly and dark the room became, and full of lowering shadows. The distant noises in the streets were gradually hushed; the house was quiet as a sepulchre; the dead of night was coffined in the silent city.

* * * * * *

1843–44

From David Copperfield[1]

[*The Journey to Salem House School*][2]

The coach was in the yard, shining very much all over, but without any horses to it as yet; and it looked in that state as if nothing was more unlikely than its ever going to London. I was thinking this, and wondering what would ultimately become of my box, which Mr. Barkis had put down on the yard-pavement by the pole (he having driven up the yard to turn his cart), and also what would ultimately become of me, when a lady looked out of a bow-window where some fowls and joints of meat were hanging up, and said:

"Is that the little gentleman from Blunderstone?"

"Yes, ma'am," I said.

"What name?" inquired the lady.

"Cooperfield, ma'am," I said.

"That won't do," returned the lady. "Nobody's dinner is paid for here, in that name."

"Is it Murdstone, ma'am?" I said.

---

1. Dickens' favorite novel was *David Copperfield* (1849–50). Like *Great Expectations* it is a novel of development, a *Bildungsroman*, recording, in first-person narrative, the painful and pleasurable experiences of growing up from childhood to maturity. Often these experiences center on a journey to new surroundings made by the central character, as the two following selections illustrate. The first journey, when David Copperfield is about 8 or 9 years old, is by coach from his home in Suffolk to a boarding-school near London, Salem House, to which he is sent by his step-father, Mr. Murdstone, after a violent incident in which the boy was goaded into biting Mr. Murdstone's hand.

David Copperfield's unhappy experiences at Salem House, both during the period before school term begins and afterwards, culminate in his encounters with the sadistic headmaster, Mr. Creakle, a former "small hop-dealer" in London who "had taken to the schooling business after being bankrupt in hops, and making away with Mrs. Creakle's money." The depth of David's unhappiness occurs, however, when he is a couple of years older. After the death of his mother he is removed from Salem House school and put to work in a blacking warehouse in London from which he finally resolves to run away and seek shelter with an aunt in Dover, whom he has never seen. The second selection features this desperate six-day journey on foot and its aftermath.

2. From Chapters V and VI.

"If you're Master Murdstone," said the lady, "why do you go and give another name, first?"

I explained to the lady how it was, who then rang a bell, and called out, "William! show the coffee-room!" upon which a waiter came running out of a kitchen on the opposite side of the yard to show it, and seemed a good deal surprised when he was only to show it to me.

It was a large long room with some large maps in it. I doubt if I could have felt much stranger if the maps had been real foreign countries, and I cast away in the middle of them. I felt it was taking a liberty to sit down, with my cap in my hand, on the corner of the chair nearest the door; and when the waiter laid a cloth on purpose for me, and put a set of casters on it, I think I must have turned red all over with modesty.

He brought me some chops, and vegetables, and took the covers off in such a bouncing manner that I was afraid I must have given him some offense. But he greatly relieved my mind by putting a chair for me at the table, and saying very affably, "Now, six-foot! come on!"

I thanked him, and took my seat at the board; but found it extremely difficult to handle my knife and fork with anything like dexterity, or to avoid splashing myself with the gravy, while he was standing opposite, staring so hard, and making me blush in the most dreadful manner every time I caught his eye. After watching me into the second chop, he said:

"There's half a pint of ale for you. Will you have it now?"

I thanked him and said "Yes." Upon which he poured it out of a jug into a large tumbler, and held it up against the light, and made it look beautiful.

"My eye!" he said. "It seems a good deal, don't it?"

"It does seem a good deal," I answered with a smile. For it was quite delightful to me to find him so pleasant. He was a twinkling-eyed, pimple-faced man, with his hair standing upright all over his head; and as he stood with one arm a-kimbo, holding up the glass to the light with the other hand, he looked quite friendly.

"There was a gentleman here yesterday," he said—"a stout gentleman, by the name of Topsawyer—perhaps you know him?"

"No," I said, "I don't think——"

"In breeches and gaiters, broad-brimmed hat, grey coat, speckled choker," said the waiter.

"No," I said bashfully, "I haven't the pleasure——"

"He came in here," said the waiter, looking at the light through the tumbler, "ordered a glass of this ale—*would* order it—I told him not—drank it, and fell dead. It was too old for him. It oughtn't to be drawn; that's the fact."

I was very much shocked to hear of this melancholy accident, and said I thought I had better have some water.

"Why, you see," said the waiter, still looking at the light through the tumbler, with one of his eyes shut up, "our people don't like things being ordered and left. It offends 'em. But I'll drink it, if you like. I'm used to it, and use is everything. I don't think it'll hurt me, if I throw my head back, and take it off quick. Shall I?"

I replied that he would much oblige me by drinking it, if he thought he could do it safely, but by no means otherwise. When he did throw his head back, and take it off quick, I had a horrible fear, I confess, of seeing him meet the fate of the lamented Mr. Topsawyer, and fall lifeless on the carpet. But it didn't hurt him. On the contrary, I thought he seemed the fresher for it.

"What have we got here?" he said, putting a fork into my dish. "Not chops?"

"Chops," I said.

"Lord bless my soul!" he exclaimed, "I didn't know they were chops. Why a chop's the very thing to take off the bad effects of that beer! Ain't it lucky?"

So he took a chop by the bone in one hand, and a potato in the other, and ate away with a very good appetite, to my extreme satisfaction. He afterwards took another chop, and another potato; and after that another chop and another potato. When he had done, he brought me a pudding, and having set it before me, seemed to ruminate, and to become absent in his mind for some moments.

"How's the pie?" he said, rousing himself.

"It's a pudding," I made answer.

"Pudding!" he exclaimed. "Why, bless me, so it is! What!" looking at it nearer. "You don't mean to say it's a batter-pudding?"

"Yes, it is indeed."

"Why, a batter-pudding," he said, taking up a table-spoon, "is my favourite pudding! Ain't that lucky? Come on, little 'un, and let's see who'll get most."

The waiter certainly got most. He entreated me more than once to come in and win, but what with his table-spoon to my tea-spoon, his dispatch to my dispatch, and his appetite to my appetite, I was left far behind at the first mouthful, and had no chance with him. I never saw anyone enjoy a pudding so much, I think; and he laughed, when it was all gone, as if his enjoyment of it lasted still.

Finding him so very friendly and companionable, it was then that I asked for the pen and ink and paper, to write to Peggotty.[3] He not only brought it immediately, but was good enough to look over me while I wrote the letter. When I had finished it, he asked me where I was going to school.

I said, "Near London," which was all I knew.

---

3. David's mother's maid.

"Oh! my eye!" he said, looking very low-spirited, "I am sorry for that."

"Why?" I asked him.

"Oh, Lord!" he said, shaking his head, "that's the school where they broke the boy's ribs—two ribs—a little boy he was. I should say he was—let me see—how old are you, about?"

I told him between eight and nine.

"That's just his age," he said. "He was eight years and six months old when they broke his first rib; eight years and eight months old when they broke his second, and did for him."

I could not disguise from myself, or from the waiter, that this was an uncomfortable coincidence, and inquired how it was done. His answer was not cheering to my spirits, for it consisted of two dismal words, "With whopping."

The blowing of the coach-horn in the yard was a seasonable diversion, which made me get up and hesitatingly inquire, in the mingled pride and diffidence of having a purse (which I took out of my pocket), if there were anything to pay.

"There's a sheet of letter-paper," he returned. "Did you ever buy a sheet of letter-paper?"

I could not remember that I ever had.

"It's dear," he said, "on account of the duty. Threepence. That's the way we're taxed in this country. There's nothing else, except the waiter. Never mind the ink. *I* lose by that."

"What should you—what should I—how much ought I to— what would it be right to pay the waiter, if you please?" I stammered, blushing.

"If I hadn't a family, and that family hadn't the cow-pock," said the waiter, "I wouldn't take a sixpence. If I didn't support a aged pairint, and a lovely sister,"—here the waiter was greatly agitated— "I wouldn't take a farthing. If I had a good place, and was treated well here, I should beg acceptance of a trifle, instead of taking of it. But I live on broken wittles—and I sleep on the coals"—here the waiter burst into tears.

I was very much concerned for his misfortunes, and felt that any recognition short of ninepence would be mere brutality and hardness of heart. Therefore I gave him one of my three bright shillings, which he received with much humility and veneration, and spun up with his thumb, directly afterwards, to try the goodness of.

It was a little disconcerting to me, to find, when I was being helped up behind the coach, that I was supposed to have eaten all the dinner without any assistance. I discovered this, from overhearing the lady in the bow-window say to the guard, "Take care of that child, George, or he'll burst!" and from observing that the women-servants who were about the place came out to look and giggle at me as a young phenomenon. My unfortunate friend the waiter, who had quite recovered his spirits, did not appear to be disturbed by this, but joined in the general admiration without being at all confused. If I had any doubt of him, I suppose this half awakened it; but I am inclined to believe that with the simple confidence of a child, and the natural reliance of a child upon superior years (qualities I am very sorry any children should prematurely change for worldly wisdom), I had no serious mistrust of him on the whole, even then.

I felt it rather hard, I must own, to be made, without deserving it, the subject of jokes between the coachman and guard as to the coach drawing heavy behind, on account of my sitting there, and as to the greater expediency of my traveling by wagon. The story of my supposed appetite getting wind among the outside passengers, they were merry upon it likewise; and asked me whether I was going to be paid for, at school, as two brothers or three, and whether I was contracted for, or went upon the regular terms; with other pleasant questions. But the worst of it was, that I knew I should be ashamed to eat anything, when an opportunity offered, and that, after a rather light dinner, I should remain hungry all night—for I had left my cakes behind, at the hotel, in my hurry. My apprehensions were realized. When we stopped for supper I couldn't muster courage to take any, though I should have liked it very much, but sat by the fire and said I didn't want anything. This did not save me from more jokes, either; for a husky-voiced gentleman with a rough face, who had been eating out of a sandwich-box nearly all the way, except when he had been drinking out of a bottle, said I was like a boa-constrictor, who took enough at one meal to last him a long time; after which he actually brought a rash out upon himself with boiled beef.

We had started from Yarmouth at three o'clock in the afternoon, and we were due in London about eight next morning. It was Midsummer weather, and the evening was very pleasant. When we passed through a village, I pictured to myself what the insides of the houses were like, and what the inhabitants were about; and when boys came running after us, and got up behind and swung there for a little way, I wondered whether their fathers were alive, and whether they were happy at home. I had plenty to think of, therefore, besides my mind running continually on the kind of place I was going to—which was an awful speculation. Sometimes, I remember, I resigned myself to thoughts of home and Peggotty; and to endeavoring, in a confused blind way, to recall how I had felt, and what sort of boy I used to be, before I bit Mr. Murdstone: which I couldn't satisfy myself about by any means, I seemed to have bitten him in such a remote antiquity.

The night was not so pleasant as the evening, for it got chilly; and being put between two gentlemen (the rough-faced one and another) to prevent my tumbling off the coach, I was nearly smothered by their falling asleep, and completely blocking me up. They squeezed me so hard sometimes, that I could not help crying out, "Oh, if you please!"—which they didn't like at all, because it woke them. Opposite me was an elderly lady in a great fur cloak, who looked in the dark more like a haystack than a lady, she was wrapped up to such a degree. This lady had a basket with her, and she hadn't known what to do with it, for a long time, until she found that, on account of my legs being short, it could go underneath me. It cramped and hurt me so, that it made me perfectly miserable; but if I moved in the least, and made a glass that was in the basket rattle against something else (as it was sure to do), she gave me the cruelest poke with her foot, and said, "Come, don't *you* fidget. *Your* bones are young enough, I'm sure!"

At last the sun rose, and then my companions seemed to sleep easier. The difficulties under which they had labored all night, and which had found utterance in the most terrific gasps and snorts, are not to be conceived. As the sun got higher, their sleep became lighter, and so they gradually one by one awoke. I recollect being very much surprised by the feint everybody made, then, of not having been to sleep at all, and by the uncommon indignation with which everyone repelled the charge. I labor under the same kind of astonishment to this day, having invariably observed that of all human weaknesses, the one to which our common nature is the least disposed to confess (I cannot imagine why) is the weakness of having gone to sleep in a coach.

What an amazing place London was to me when I saw it in the distance, and how I believed all the adventures of all my favorite heroes to be constantly enacting and re-enacting there, and how I vaguely made it out in my own mind to be fuller of wonders and wickedness than all the cities of the earth, I need not stop here to relate. We approached it by degrees, and got, in due time, to the inn in the Whitechapel district, for which we were bound. I forget whether it was the Blue Bull, or the Blue Boar; but I know it was the Blue Something, and that its likeness was painted up on the back of the coach.

The guard's eye lighted on me as he was getting down, and he said at the booking-office door:

"Is there anybody here for a yoongster booked in the name of Murdstone, from Bloonderstone, Sooffolk, to be left till called for?"

Nobody answered.

"Try Copperfield, if you please, sir," said I, looking helplessly down.

"Is there anybody here for a yoongster, booked in the name of Murdstone, from Bloonderstone, Sooffolk, but owning to the name of Copperfield, to be left till called for?" said the guard. "Come! *Is* there anybody?"

No. There was nobody. I looked anxiously around; but the inquiry made no impression on any of the bystanders, if I except a man in gaiters, with one eye, who suggested that they had better put a brass collar round my neck, and tie me up in the stable.

A ladder was brought, and I got down after the lady, who was like a haystack: not daring to stir, until her basket was removed. The coach was clear of passengers by that time, the luggage was very soon cleared out, the horses had been taken out before the luggage, and now the coach itself was wheeled and backed off by some hostlers, out of the way. Still, nobody appeared, to claim the dusty youngster from Blunderstone, Suffolk.

More solitary than Robinson Crusoe, who had nobody to look at him, and see that he was solitary, I went into the booking-office, and, by invitation of the clerk on duty, passed behind the counter, and sat down on the scale at which they weighed the luggage. Here, as I sat looking at the parcels, packages, and books, and inhaling the smell of stables (ever since associated with that morning), a procession of most tremendous considerations began to march through my mind. Supposing nobody should ever fetch me, how long would they consent to keep me there? Would they keep me long enough to spend seven shillings? Should I sleep at night in one of those wooden bins, with the other luggage, and wash myself at the pump in the yard in the morning; or should I be turned out every night, and expected to come again to be left till called for, when the office opened next day? Supposing there was no mistake in the case, and Mr. Murdstone had devised this plan to get rid of me, what should I do? If they allowed me to remain there until my seven shillings were spent, I couldn't hope to remain there when I began to starve. That would obviously be inconvenient and unpleasant to the customers, besides entailing on the Blue Whatever-it-was, the risk of funeral expenses. If I started off at once, and tried to walk back home, how could I ever find my way, how could I ever hope to walk so far, how could I make sure of anyone but Peggotty, even if I got back? If I found out the nearest proper authorities, and offered myself to go for a soldier, or a sailor, I was such a little fellow that it was most likely they wouldn't take me in. These thoughts, and a hundred other such thoughts, turned me burning hot, and made me giddy with apprehension and dismay. I was in the height of my fever when a man entered and whispered to the clerk, who presently slanted me off the scale, and pushed me over to him, as if I were weighted, bought, delivered, and paid for.

As I went out of the office, hand in hand with this new acquaintance, I stole a look at him. He was a gaunt, sallow young man, with
hollow cheeks, and a chin almost as black as Mr. Murdstone's; but
there the likeness ended, for his whiskers were shaved off, and his
hair, instead of being glossy, was rusty and dry. He was dressed in
a suit of black clothes which were rather rusty and dry too, and
rather short in the sleeves and legs; and he had a white neck-kerchief
on, that was not over-clean. I did not, and do not suppose that this
neck-kerchief was all the linen he wore, but it was all he showed or
gave any hint of.

"You're the new boy?" he said.

"Yes, sir," I said.

I suppose I was. I didn't know.

"I'm one of the masters at Salem House," *he* said.

I made him a bow and felt very much overawed. * * *

A short walk brought us—I mean the Master and me—to Salem
House, which was enclosed with a high brick wall, and looked very
dull. Over a door in this wall was a board with SALEM HOUSE upon it;
and through a grating in this door we were surveyed, when we rang
the bell, by a surly face, which I found, on the door being opened,
belonged to a stout man with a bull-neck, a wooden leg, overhanging
temples, and his hair cut close all round his head.

"The new boy," said the Master.

The man with the wooden leg eyed me all over—it didn't take
long, for there was not much of me—and locked the gate behind us,
and took out the key. We were going up to the house, among some
dark heavy trees, when he called after my conductor.

"Hallo!"

We looked back, and he was standing at the door of a little lodge,
where he lived, with a pair of boots in his hand.

"Here! The cobbler's been," he said, "since you've been out, Mr.
Mell, and he says he can't mend 'em any more. He says there ain't
a bit of the original boot left, and he wonders you expect it."

With these words he threw the boots towards Mr. Mell, who
went back a few paces to pick them up, and looked at them (very
disconsolately, I was afraid) as we went on together. I observed
then, for the first time, that the boots he had on were a good deal
the worse for wear, and that his stocking was just breaking out in
one place, like a bud.

Salem House was a square brick building with wings, of a bare
and unfurnished appearance. All about it was so very quiet, that I
said to Mr. Mell I supposed the boys were out; but he seemed surprised at my not knowing that it was holiday-time. That all the
boys were at their several homes. That Mr. Creakle, the proprietor,
was down by the sea-side with Mrs. and Miss Creakle. And that I

was sent in holiday-time as a punishment for my misdoing. All of which he explained to me as he went along.

I gazed upon the schoolroom into which he took me, as the most forlorn and desolate place I had ever seen. I see it now. A long room, with three long rows of desks, and six forms,[4] and bristling all round with pegs for hats and slates. Scraps of old copy-books and exercises litter the dirty floor. Some silkworms' houses, made of the same materials, are scattered over the desks. Two miserable little white mice, left behind by their owner, are running up and down in a fusty castle made of pasteboard and wire, looking in all the corners with their red eyes for anything to eat. A bird, in a cage very little bigger than himself, makes a mournful rattle now and then in hopping on his perch, two inches high, or dropping from it; but neither sings nor chirps. There is a strange unwholesome smell upon the room, like mildewed corduroys, sweet apples wanting air, and rotten books. There could not well be more ink splashed about it, if it had been roofless from its first construction, and the skies had rained, snowed, hailed, and blown ink through the varying seasons of the year.

Mr. Mell having left me while he took his irreparable boots upstairs, I went softly to the upper end of the room, observing all this as I crept along. Suddenly I came upon a pasteboard placard, beautifully written, which was lying on the desk, and bore these words: "*Take care of him. He bites.*"

I got upon the desk immediately, apprehensive of at least a great dog underneath. But, though I looked all round with anxious eyes, I could see nothing of him. I was still engaged in peering about, when Mr. Mell came back, and asked me what I did up there?

"I beg your pardon, sir," says I, "if you please, I'm looking for the dog."

"Dog?" says he. "What dog?"

"Isn't it a dog, sir?"

"Isn't what a dog?"

"That's to be taken care of, sir; that bites?"

"No, Copperfield," says he, gravely, "that's not a dog. That's a boy. My instructions are, Copperfield, to put this placard on your back. I am sorry to make such a beginning with you, but I must do it."

With that he took me down, and tied the placard, which was neatly constructed for the purpose, on my shoulders like a knapsack; and wherever I went, afterwards, I had the consolation of carrying it.

What I suffered from that placard nobody can imagine. Whether it was possible for people to see me or not, I always fancied that

4. Benches.

somebody was reading it. It was no relief to turn round and find nobody; for wherever my back was, there I imagined somebody always to be. That cruel man with the wooden leg, aggravated my sufferings. He was in authority, and if he ever saw me leaning against a tree, or a wall, or the house, he roared out from his lodge-door in a stupendous voice, "Hallo, you sir! You Copperfield! Show that badge conspicuous, or I'll report you!" The playground was a bare graveled yard, open to all the back of the house and the offices; and I knew that the servants read it, and the butcher read it, and the baker read it; that everybody, in a word, who came backwards and forwards to the house, of a morning when I was ordered to walk there, read that I was to be taken care of, for I bit. I recollect that I positively began to have a dread of myself, as a kind of wild boy who did bite.

There was an old door in this playground, on which the boys had a custom of carving their names. It was completely covered with such inscriptions. In my dread of the end of the vacation and their coming back, I could not read a boy's name, without inquiring in what tone and with what emphasis *he* would read, "Take care of him. He bites." There was one boy—a certain J. Steerforth—who cut his name very deep and very often, who I conceived, would read it in a rather strong voice, and afterwards pull my hair. There was another boy, one Tommy Traddles, who I dreaded would make game of it, and pretend to be dreadfully frightened of me. There was a third, George Demple, who I fancied would sing it. I have looked, a little shrinking creature, at that door, until the owners of all the names—there were five-and-forty of them in the school then, Mr. Mell said—seemed to send me to Coventry[5] by general acclamation, and to cry out, each in his own way, "Take care of him. He bites!"

It was the same with the places at the desks and forms. It was the same with the groves of deserted bedsteads I peeped at, on my way to, and when I was in, my own bed. I remember dreaming night after night, of being with my mother as she used to be, or of going to a party at Mr. Peggotty's, or traveling outside the stage-coach, or of dining again with my unfortunate friend the waiter, and in all these circumstances making people scream and stare, by the unhappy disclosure that I had nothing on but my little night-shirt, and that placard.

In the monotony of my life, and in my constant apprehension of the re-opening of the school, it was such an insupportable affliction! I had long tasks every day to do with Mr. Mell; but I did them, there being no Mr. and Miss Murdstone here, and got through them without disgrace. Before, and after them, I walked about—su-

5. To ostracize me.

pervised, as I have mentioned, by the man with the wooden leg. How vividly I call to mind the damp about the house, the green cracked flagstones in the court, an old leaky water-butt, and the discolored trunks of some of the grim trees, which seemed to have dripped more in the rain than other trees, and to have blown less in the sun! At one we dined, Mr. Mell and I, at the upper end of a long bare dining-room, full of deal tables, and smelling of fat. Then, we had more tasks until tea, which Mr. Mell drank out of a blue tea-cup, and I out of a tin pot. All day long, and until seven or eight in the evening, Mr. Mell, at his own detached desk in the school-room, worked hard with pen, ink, ruler, books, and writing-paper, making out the bills (as I found) for last half-year. When he had put up his things for the night, he took out his flute, and blew at it, until I almost thought he would gradually blow his whole being into the large hole at the top, and ooze away at the keys.

I picture my small self in the dimly-lighted rooms, sitting with my head upon my hand, listening to the doleful performance of Mr. Mell, and conning tomorrow's lessons. I picture myself with my books shut up, still listening to the doleful performance of Mr. Mell, and listening through it to what used to be at home, and to the blowing of the wind on Yarmouth flats, and feeling very sad and solitary. I picture myself going up to bed, among the unused rooms, and sitting on my bedside crying for a comfortable word from Peggotty. I picture myself coming downstairs in the morning, and looking through a long ghastly gash of a staircase window at the school-bell hanging on the top of an outhouse with a weather-cock above it; and dreading the time when it shall ring J. Steerforth and the rest to work. Such time is only second, in my foreboding apprehensions, to the time when the man with the wooden leg shall unlock the rusty gate to give admission to the awful Mr. Creakle. I cannot think I was a very dangerous character in any of these aspects, but in all of them I carried the same warning on my back.

Mr. Mell never said much to me, but he was never harsh to me. I suppose we were company to each other, without talking. I forgot to mention that he would talk to himself sometimes, and grin, and clench his fist, and grind his teeth, and pull his hair in an unaccountable manner. But he had these peculiarities. At first they frightened me, though I soon got used to them.

I had led this life about a month, when the man with the wooden leg began to stump about with a mop and a bucket of water, from which I inferred that preparations were making to receive Mr. Creakle and the boys. I was not mistaken; for the mop came into the school-room before long, and turned out Mr. Mell and me, who lived where we could, and got on how we could, for some days, during which we were always in the way of two or three young women, who had rarely shown themselves before, and were so continually in the midst of dust that I sneezed almost as much as if Salem House had been a great snuff-box.

One day I was informed by Mr. Mell that Mr. Creakle would be home that evening. In the evening, after tea, I heard that he was come. Before bed-time, I was fetched by the man with the wooden leg to appear before him.

Mr. Creakle's part of the house was a good deal more comfortable than ours, and he had a snug bit of garden that looked pleasant after the dusty playground, which was such a desert in miniature, that I thought no one but a camel, or a dromedary, could have felt at home in it. It seemed to me a bold thing even to take notice that the passage looked comfortable, as I went on my way, trembling, to Mr. Creakle's presence: which so abashed me, when I was ushered into it, that I hardly saw Mrs. Creakle or Miss Creakle (who were both there, in the parlor), or anything but Mr. Creakle, a stout gentleman with a bunch of watch-chain and seals, in an arm-chair, with a tumbler and bottle beside him.

"So!" said Mr. Creakle. "This is the young gentleman whose teeth are to be filed! Turn him round."

The wooden-legged man turned me about so as to exhibit the placard; and having afforded time for a full survey of it, turned me about again, with my face to Mr. Creakle, and posted himself at Mr. Creakle's side. Mr. Creakle's face was fiery, and his eyes were small, and deep in his head; he had thick veins in his forehead, a little nose, and a large chin. He was bald on top of his head; and had some thin wet-looking hair that was just turning grey, brushed across each temple, so that the two sides interlaced on his forehead. But the circumstance about him which impressed me most, was, that he had no voice, but spoke in a whisper. The exertion this cost him, or the consciousness of talking in that feeble way, made his angry face so much more angry, and his thick veins so much thicker, when he spoke, that I am not surprised, on looking back, at this peculiarity striking me as his chief one.

"Now," said Mr. Creakle. "What's the report of this boy?"

"There's nothing against him yet," returned the man with the wooden leg. "There has been no opportunity."

I thought Mr. Creakle was disappointed. I thought Mrs. and Miss Creakle (at whom I now glanced for the first time, and who were, both, thin and quiet) were not disappointed.

"Come here, sir!' said Mr. Creakle, beckoning to me.

"Come here!" said the man with the wooden leg, repeating the gesture.

"I have the happiness of knowing your father-in-law,"[6] whispered Mr. Creakle, taking me by the ear; "and a worthy man he is, and a

6. Stepfather.

man of a strong character. He knows me, and I know him. Do *you*
know me? Hey?" said Mr. Creakle, pinching my ear with ferocious
playfulness.

"Not yet, sir," I said, flinching with the pain.

"Not yet? Hey?" repeated Mr. Creakle. "But you will soon. Hey?"

"You will soon. Hey?" repeated the man with the wooden leg. I
afterwards found that he generally acted, with his strong voice, as
Mr. Creakle's interpreter to the boys.

I was very much frightened, and said I hoped so, if he pleased. I
felt, all this while, as if my ear were blazing; he pinched it so hard.

"I'll tell you what I am," whispered Mr. Creakle, letting it go at
last, with a screw at parting that brought the water into my eyes.
"I'm a Tartar."

"A Tartar," said the man with the wooden leg.

"When I say I'll do a thing, I do it," said Mr. Creakle; "and
when I say I will have a thing done, I will have it done."

"—Will have a thing done, I will have it done," repeated the
man with the wooden leg.

"I am a determined character," said Mr. Creakle. "That's what I
am. I do my duty. That's what I do. My flesh and blood," he
looked at Mrs. Creakle as he said this, "when it rises against me, is
not my flesh and blood. I discard it. Has that fellow," to the man
with the wooden leg, "been here again?"

"No," was the answer.

"No," said Mr. Creakle. "He knows better. He knows me. Let
him keep away. I say let him keep away," said Mr. Creakle, striking
his hand upon the table, and looking at Mrs. Creakle, "for he
knows me. Now you have begun to know me too, my young friend,
and you may go. Take him away."

I was very glad to be ordered away, for Mrs. and Miss Creakle
were both wiping their eyes, and I felt as uncomfortable for them as
I did for myself. But I had a petition on my mind which concerned
me so nearly, that I couldn't help saying, though I wondered at my
own courage:

"If you please, sir——"

Mr. Creakle whispered, "Hah! What's this?" and bent his eyes
upon me, as if he would have burnt me up with them.

"If you please, sir," I faltered, "if I might be allowed (I am very
sorry indeed, sir, for what I did) to take this writing off, before the
boys come back——"

Whether Mr. Creakle was in earnest, or whether he only did it to
frighten me, I don't know, but he made a burst out of his chair,
before which I precipitately retreated, without waiting for the escort
of the man with the wooden leg, and never once stopped until I
reached my own bedroom, where, finding I was not pursued, I went
to bed, as it was time, and lay quaking, for a couple of hours.

* * *

[The Journey from London to Dover]⁷

I had resolved to run away.—To go, by some means or other, down into the country, to the only relation I had in the world, and tell my story to my aunt, Miss Betsey.

I have already observed that I don't know how this desperate idea came into my brain. But, once there, it remained there; and hardened into a purpose than which I have never entertained a more determined purpose in my life. I am far from sure that I believed there was anything hopeful in it, but my mind was thoroughly made up that it must be carried into execution.

* * *

A plan had occurred to me for passing the night, which I was going to carry into execution. This was, to lie behind the wall at the back of my old school, in a corner where there used to be a haystack. I imagined it would be a kind of company to have the boys, and the bedroom where I used to tell the stories, so near me: although the boys would know nothing of my being there, and the bedroom would yield me no shelter.

I had had a hard day's work, and was pretty well jaded when I came climbing out, at last, upon the level of Blackheath. It cost me some trouble to find out Salem House; but I found it, and I found a haystack in the corner, and I lay down by it; having first walked round the wall, and looked up at the windows, and seen that all was dark and silent within. Never shall I forget the lonely sensation of first lying down, without a roof above my head!

Sleep came upon me as it came on many other outcasts, against whom house-doors were locked, and house-dogs barked, that night —and I dreamed of lying on my old schoolbed, talking to the boys in my room; and found myself sitting upright, with Steerforth's name upon my lips, looking wildly at the stars that were glistening and glimmering above me. When I remembered where I was at that untimely hour, a feeling stole upon me that made me get up, afraid of I don't know what, and walk about. But the fainter glimmering of the stars, and the pale light in the sky where the day was coming, reassured me: and my eyes being very heavy, I lay down again, and slept—though with a knowledge in my sleep that it was cold—until the warm beams of the sun, and the ringing of the getting-up bell at Salem House, awoke me. If I could have hoped that Steerforth was there, I would have lurked about until he came out alone; but I knew he must have left long since. Traddles still remained, perhaps, but it was very doubtful; and I had not sufficient confidence in his discretion or good luck, however strong my reliance on his good-nature, to wish to trust him with my situation. So I crept away from the wall as Mr. Creakle's boys were getting up, and struck into the long dusty track which I had first

7. From Chapters XII and XIII.

known to be the Dover Road when I was one of them, and when I little expected that any eyes would ever see me the wayfarer I was now, upon it.

What a different Sunday morning from the old Sunday morning at Yarmouth! In due 'ime I heard the church-bells ringing, as I plodded on; and I met people who were going to church; and I passed a church or two where the congregation were inside, and the sound of singing came out into the sunshine, while the beadle sat and cooled himself in the shade of the porch, or stood beneath the yew-tree, with his hand to his forehead, glowering at me going by. But the peace and rest of the old Sunday morning were on everything, except me. That was the difference. I felt quite wicked in my dirt and dust, with my tangled hair. But for the quiet picture I had conjured up, of my mother in her youth and beauty, weeping by the fire, and my aunt relenting to her, I hardly think I should have had the courage to go on until next day. But it always went before me, and I followed.

I got, that Sunday, through three-and-twenty miles on the straight road, though not very easily, for I was new to that kind of toil. I see myself, as evening closes in, coming over the bridge at Rochester, footsore and tired, and eating bread that I had bought for supper. One or two little houses, with the notice, "Lodgings for Travelers," hanging out, had tempted me; but I was afraid of spending the few pence I had, and was even more afraid of the vicious looks of the trampers I had met or overtaken. I sought no shelter, therefore, but the sky; and toiling into Chatham,—which, in that night's aspect, is a mere dream of chalk, and drawbridges, and mastless ships in a muddy river, roofed like Noah's arks,—crept, at last, upon a sort of grass-grown battery overhanging a lane, where a sentry was walking to and fro. Here I lay down, near a cannon; and, happy in the society of the sentry's footsteps, though he knew no more of my being above him than the boys at Salem House had known of my lying by the wall, slept soundly until morning.

Very stiff and sore of foot I was in the morning, and quite dazed by the beating of drums and marching of troops, which seemed to hem me in on every side when I went down towards the long narrow street. Feeling that I could go but a very little way that day, if I were to reserve any strength for getting to my journey's end, I resolved to make the sale of my jacket its principal business. Accordingly, I took the jacket off, that I might learn to do without it; and carrying it under my arm, began a tour of inspection of the various slop-shops.

It was a likely place to sell a jacket in; for the dealers in second-hand clothes were numerous, and were, generally speaking, on the look-out for customers at their shop-doors. But, as most of them

had, hanging up among their stock, an officer's coat or two, epau-
lettes and all, I was rendered timid by the costly nature of their
dealings, and walked about for a long time without offering my merchandise to anyone.

This modesty of mine directed my attention to the marine-store
shops, and such shops as Mr. Dolloby's,[8] in preference to the regular dealers. At last I found one that I thought looked promising, at
the corner of a dirty lane, ending in an inclosure full of stinging-
nettles, against the palings of which some second-hand sailors'
clothes, that seemed to have overflowed the shop, were fluttering
among some cots, and rusty guns, and oilskin hats, and certain trays
full of so many old rusty keys of so many sizes that they seemed
various enough to open all the doors in the world.

Into this shop, which was low and small, and which was darkened rather than lighted by a little window, overhung with clothes,
and was descended into by some steps, I went with a palpitating
heart; which was not relieved when an ugly old man, with the lower
part of his face all covered with a stubbly grey beard, rushed out of
a dirty den behind it, and seized me by the hair of my head. He
was a dreadful old man to look at, in a filthy flannel waistcoat, and
smelling terribly of rum. His bedstead, covered with a tumbled and
ragged piece of patchwork, was in the den he had come from, where
another little window showed a prospect of more stinging-nettles,
and a lame donkey.

"Oh, what do you want?" grinned this old man, in a fierce,
monotonous whine. "Oh, my eyes and limbs, what do you want?
Oh, my lungs and liver, what do you want? Oh, goroo, goroo!"

I was so much dismayed by these words, and particularly by the
repetition of the last unknown one, which was a kind of rattle in
his throat, that I could make no answer; hereupon the old man, still
holding me by the hair, repeated:

"Oh, what do you want? Oh, my eyes and limbs, what do you
want? Oh, my lungs and liver, what do you want? Oh, goroo!"—
which he screwed out of himself, with an energy that made his eyes
start in his head.

"I wanted to know," I said, trembling, "if you would buy a jacket."

"Oh, let's see the jacket!" cried the old man. "Oh, my heart on
fire, show the jacket to us; Oh, my eyes and limbs, bring the jacket
out!"

With that he took his trembling hands, which were like the
claws of a great bird, out of my hair; and put on a pair of spectacles, not at all ornamental to his inflamed eyes.

"Oh, how much for the jacket?" cried the old man, after examining it. "Oh—goroo!—how much for the jacket?"

"Half-a-crown," I answered, recovering myself.

8. Second-hand clothing dealer to whom David has sold his vest.

"Oh, my lungs and liver," cried the old man, "no! Oh, my eyes, no! Oh, my limbs, no! Eighteenpence. Goroo!"

Every time he uttered this ejaculation, his eyes seemed to be in danger of starting out; and every sentence he spoke, he delivered in a sort of tune, always exactly the same, and more like a gust of wind, which begins low, mounts up high, and falls again, than any other comparison I can find for it.

"Well," said I, glad to have closed the bargain, "I'll take eighteenpence."

"Oh, my liver!" cried the old man, throwing the jacket on a shelf. "Get out of the shop! Oh, my lungs, get out of the shop! Oh, my eyes and limbs—goroo!—don't ask for money; make it an exchange."

I never was so frightened in my life before or since; but I told him humbly that I wanted money, and that nothing else was of any use to me, but that I would wait for it, as he desired, outside, and had no wish to hurry him. So I went outside, and sat down in the shade in a corner. And I sat there so many hours, that the shade became sunlight, and the sunlight became shade again, and still I sat there waiting for the money.

There never was such another drunken madman in that line of business, I hope. That he was well known in the neighborhood, and enjoyed the reputation of having sold himself to the devil, I soon understood from the visits he received from the boys, who continually came skirmishing about the shop, shouting that legend, and calling to him to bring out his gold. "You ain't poor, you know, Charley, as you pretend. Bring out your gold. Bring out some of the gold you sold yourself to the devil for. Come! It's in the lining of the mattress, Charley. Rip it open and let's have some!" This, and many offers to lend him a knife for the purpose, exasperated him to such a degree, that the whole day was a succession of rushes on his part, and flights on the part of the boys. Sometimes in his rage he would take me for one of them, and come at me, mouthing as if he were going to tear me in pieces; then, remembering me, just in time, would dive into the shop, and lie upon his bed, as I thought from the sound of his voice, yelling in a frantic way, to his own windy tune, the Death of Nelson; with an Oh! before every line, and innumerable Goroos interspersed.[9] As if this were not bad enough for me, the boys, connecting me with the establishment, on account of the patience and perseverance with which I sat outside, half-dressed, pelted me, and used me very ill all day.

He made many attempts to induce me to consent to an exchange;

---

9. Popular song about the Battle of Trafalgar, from the opera *The Americans* (1811) by John Braham and S. J. Arnold. The "Oh!" was an embellishment not present in the text: "In honor's cause my life was pass'd / In honor's cause I fall at last, / For England, home, and beauty, / For England, home, and beauty."

at one time coming out with a fishing-rod, at another with a fiddle, at another with a cocked hat, at another with a flute. But I resisted all these overtures, and sat there in desperation; each time asking him, with tears in my eyes, for my money or my jacket. At last he began to pay me in halfpence at a time; and was full two hours getting by easy stages to a shilling.

"Oh, my eyes and limbs!" he then cried, peeping hideously out of the shop, after a long pause, "will you go for twopence more?"

"I can't," I said; "I shall be starved."

"Oh, my lungs and liver, will you go for threepence?"

"I would go for nothing, if I could," I said, "but I want the money badly."

"Oh, go—roo!" (it is really impossible to express how he twisted this ejaculation out of himself, as he peeped round the doorpost at me, showing nothing but his crafty old head;) "will you go for fourpence?"

I was so faint and weary that I closed with this offer; and taking the money out of his claw, not without trembling, went away more hungry and thirsty than I had ever been, a little before sunset. But at an expense of threepence I soon refreshed myself completely; and, being in better spirits then, limped seven miles upon my road.

My bed at night was under another haystack, where I rested comfortably, after having washed my blistered feet in a stream, and dressed them as well as I was able, with some cool leaves. When I took the road again next morning, I found that it lay through a succession of hop-grounds and orchards. It was sufficiently late in the year for the orchards to be ruddy with ripe apples; and in a few places the hop-pickers were already at work. I thought it all extremely beautiful, and made up my mind to sleep among the hops that night: imagining some cheerful companionship in the long perspectives of poles, with the graceful leaves twining round them.

The trampers were worse than ever that day, and inspired me with a dread that is yet quite fresh in my mind. Some of them were most ferocious-looking ruffians, who stared at me as I went by; and stopped, perhaps, and called after me to come back and speak to them, and when I took to my heels, stoned me. I recollect one young fellow—a tinker, I suppose, from his wallet and brazier—who had a woman with him, and who faced about and stared at me thus; and then roared to me in such a tremendous voice to come back, that I halted and looked round.

"Come here, when you're called," said the tinker, "or I'll rip your young body open."

I thought it best to go back. As I drew nearer to them, trying to propitiate the tinker by my looks, I observed that the woman had a black eye.

"Where are you going?" said the tinker, gripping the bosom of my shirt with his blackened hand.

"I am going to Dover," I said.

"Where do you come from?" asked the tinker, giving his hand another turn in my shirt, to hold me more securely.

"I come from London," I said.

"What lay are you upon?" asked the tinker. "Are you a prig?"[1]

"N—no," I said.

"Ain't you, by G—? If you make a brag of your honesty to me," said the tinker, "I'll knock your brains out."

With his disengaged hand he made a menace of striking me, and then looked at me from head to foot.

"Have you got the price of a pint of beer about you?" said the tinker. "If you have, out with it, afore I take it away!"

I should certainly have produced it, but that I met the woman's look, and saw her very slightly shake her head, and form "No!" with her lips.

"I am very poor," I said, attempting to smile, "and have got no money."

"Why, what do you mean?" said the tinker, looking so sternly at me, that I almost feared he saw the money in my pocket.

"Sir!" I stammered.

"What do you mean," said the tinker, "by wearing my brother's silk handkercher! Give it over here!" And he had mine off my neck in a moment, and tossed it to the woman.

The woman burst into a fit of laughter, as if she thought this a joke, and tossed it back to me, nodded once, as slightly as before, and made the word "Go!" with her lips. Before I could obey, however, the tinker seized the handkerchief out of my hand with a roughness that threw me away like a feather, and putting it loosely round his own neck, turned upon the woman with an oath, and knocked her down. I never shall forget seeing her fall backward on the hard road, and lie there with her bonnet tumbled off, and her hair all whitened in the dust; nor, when I looked back from a distance, seeing her sitting on the pathway, which was a bank by the roadside, wiping the blood from her face with a corner of her shawl, while he went on ahead.

This adventure frightened me so, that afterwards, when I saw any of these people coming, I turned back until I could find a hiding-place, where I remained until they had gone out of sight; which happened so often, that I was very seriously delayed. But under this difficulty, as under all the other difficulties of my journey, I seemed to be sustained and led on by my fanciful picture of my mother in her youth, before I came into the world. It always kept me com-

---

1. Thief.

pany. It was there, among the hops, when I lay down to sleep; it was with me on my waking in the morning; it went before me all day. I have associated it, ever since, with the sunny street of Canterbury, dozing as it were in the hot light; and with the sight of its old houses and gateways, and the stately, grey Cathedral, with the rooks sailing round the towers. When I came, at last, upon the bare, wide downs near Dover, it relieved the solitary aspect of the scene with hope; and not until I reached that first great aim of my journey, and actually set foot in the town itself, on the sixth day of my flight, did it desert me. But then, strange to say, when I stood with my ragged shoes, and my dusty, sunburnt, half-clothed figure, in the place so long desired, it seemed to vanish like a dream, and to leave me helpless and dispirited.

I inquired about my aunt among the boatmen first, and received various answers. One said she lived in the South Foreland Light, and had singed her whiskers by doing so; another, that she was made fast to the great buoy outside the harbor, and could only be visited at half-tide; a third, that she was locked up in Maidstone Jail for child-stealing; a fourth, that she was seen to mount a broom, in the last high wind, and make direct for Calais. The fly-drivers, among whom I inquired next, were equally jocose and equally disrespectful; and the shopkeepers, not liking my appearance, generally replied, without hearing what I had to say, that they had got nothing for me. I felt more miserable and destitute than I had done at any period of my running away. My money was all gone, I had nothing left to dispose of; I was hungry, thirsty, and worn out; and seemed as distant from my end as if I had remained in London.

The morning had worn away in these inquiries, and I was sitting on the step of an empty shop at a street corner, near the market-lace, deliberating upon wandering towards those other places which had been mentioned, when a fly-driver, coming by with his carriage, dropped a horsecloth. Something good-natured in the man's face, as I handed it up, encouraged me to ask him if he could tell me where Miss Trotwood lived; though I had asked the question so often, that it almost died upon my lips.

"Trotwood," said he. "Let me see. I know the name, too. Old lady?"

"Yes," I said, "rather."

"Pretty stiff in the back?" said he, making himself upright.

"Yes," I said. "I should think it very likely."

"Carries a bag?" said he: "bag with a good deal of room in it: is gruffish, and comes down upon you, sharp?"

My heart sank within me as I acknowledged the undoubted accuracy of this description.

"Why then, I tell you what," said he. "If you go up there," pointing with his whip towards the heights, "and keep right on till you come to some houses facing the sea, I think you'll hear of her. My opinion is, she won't stand anything, so here's a penny for you."

I accepted the gift thankfully, and bought a loaf with it. Dispatching this refreshment by the way, I went in the direction my friend had indicated, and walked on a good distance without coming to the houses he had mentioned. At length I saw some before me; and approaching them, went into a little shop (it was what we used to call a general shop, at home), and inquired if they could have the goodness to tell me where Miss Trotwood lived. I addressed myself to a man behind the counter, who was weighing some rice for a young woman; but the latter, taking the inquiry to herself, turned round quickly.

"My mistress?" she said. "What do you want with her, boy?"

"I want," I replied, "to speak to her, if you please."

"To beg of her, you mean," retorted the damsel.

"No," I said, "indeed." But suddenly remembering that in truth I came for no other purpose, I held my peace in confusion, and felt my face burn.

My aunt's handmaid, as I supposed she was from what she had said, put her rice in a little basket and walked out of the shop; telling me that I could follow her, if I wanted to know where Miss Trotwood lived. I needed no second permission; though I was by this time in such a state of consternation and agitation, that my legs shook under me. I followed the young woman, and we soon came to a very neat little cottage with cheerful bow-windows: in front of it, a small square graveled court or garden full of flowers, carefully tended, and smelling deliciously.

"This is Miss Trotwood's," said the young woman. "Now you know; and that's all I have got to say." With which words she hurried into the house, as if to shake off the responsibility of my appearance; and left me standing at the garden-gate, looking disconsolately over the top of it towards the parlor-window, where a muslin curtain partly undrawn in the middle, a large round green screen or fan fastened on to the window-sill, a small table, and a great chair, suggested to me that my aunt might be at that moment seated in awful state.

My shoes were by this time in a woeful condition. The soles had shed themselves bit by bit, and the upper leathers had broken and burst until the very shape and form of shoes had departed from them. My hat (which had served me for a night-cap, too) was so crushed and bent, that no old battered handleless saucepan on a dunghill need have been ashamed to vie with it. My shirt and trousers, stained with heat, dew, grass, and the Kentish soil on which I had slept—and torn besides—might have frightened the birds from my aunt's garden, as I stood at the gate. My hair had known no comb or brush since I left London. My face, neck, and hands, from unaccustomed exposure to the air and sun, were burnt to a berry-brown. From head to foot I was powdered almost as white with chalk and dust, as if I had come out of a lime-kiln. In this plight, and with a strong consciousness of it, I waited to introduce myself to, and make my first impression on, my formidable aunt.

The unbroken stillness of the parlor-window leading me to infer, after a while, that she was not there, I lifted up my eyes to the window above it, where I saw a florid, pleasant-looking gentleman, with a grey head, who shut up one eye in a grotesque manner, nodded his head at me several times, shook it at me as often, laughed, and went away.

I had been discomposed enough before; but I was so much the more discomposed by this unexpected behavior, that I was on the point of slinking off, to think how I had best proceed, when there came out of the house a lady with her handkerchief tied over her cap, and a pair of gardening gloves on her hands, wearing a gardening pocket like a toll-man's apron, and carrying a great knife. I knew her immediately to be Miss Betsey, for she came stalking out of the house exactly as my poor mother had so often described her stalking up our garden at Blunderstone Rookery.

"Go away!" said Miss Betsey, shaking her head, and making a distant chop in the air with her knife. "Go along! No boys here!"

I watched her, with my heart at my lips, as she marched to a corner of her garden, and stooped to dig up some little root there. Then, without a scrap of courage, but with a great deal of desperation, I went softly in and stood beside her, touching her with my finger.

"If you please, ma'am," I began.

She started and looked up.

"If you please, aunt."

"Eh?" exclaimed Miss Betsey, in a tone of amazement I have never heard approached.

"If you please, aunt, I am your nephew."

"Oh, Lord!" said my aunt. And sat flat down in the garden-path.

"I am David Copperfield, of Blunderstone, in Suffolk—where you came, on the night when I was born, and saw my dear mama. I have been very unhappy since she died. I have been slighted, and taught nothing, and thrown upon myself and put to work not fit for me. It made me run away to you. I was robbed at first setting out, and have walked all the way, and have never slept in a bed since I began the journey." Here my self-support gave way all at once; and with a movement of my hands, intended to show her my ragged state, and call it to witness that I had suffered something, I broke into a passion of crying, which I suppose had been pent up within me all the week.

My aunt, with every sort of expression but wonder discharged from her countenance, sat on the gravel, staring at me, until I began to cry; when she got up in a great hurry, collared me, and took me into the parlor. Her first proceeding there was to unlock a tall press; bring out several bottles, and pour some of the contents of each into my mouth. I think they must have been taken out at random, for I am sure I tasted aniseed water, anchovy sauce, and salad dressing. When she had administered these restoratives, as I was still quite hysterical, and unable to control my sobs, she put me on the sofa, with a shawl under my head, and the handkerchief from her own head under my feet, lest I should sully the cover; and then, sitting herself down behind the green fan or screen I have already mentioned, so that I could not see her face, ejaculated at intervals, "Mercy on us!" letting those exclamations off like minute guns.

After a time she rang the bell. "Janet," said my aunt, when her servant came in. "Go upstairs, give my compliments to Mr. Dick, and say I wish to speak to him."

Janet looked a little surprised to see me lying stiffly on the sofa (I was afraid to move lest it should be displeasing to my aunt), but went on her errand. My aunt, with her hands behind her, walked up and down the room, until the gentleman who had squinted at me from the upper window came in laughing.

"Mr. Dick," said my aunt, "don't be a fool, because nobody can be more discreet than you can, when you choose. We all know that. So don't be a fool, whatever you are."

The gentleman was serious immediately, and looked at me, I thought, as if he would entreat me to say nothing about the window.

"Mr. Dick," said my aunt, "you have heard me mention David Copperfield? Now don't pretend not to have a memory, because you and I know better."

"David Copperfield?" said Mr. Dick, who did not appear to me to remember much about it. "*David* Copperfield? Oh yes, to be sure. David, certainly."

"Well," said my aunt, "this is his boy, his son. He would be as like his father as it's possible to be, if he was not so like his mother, too."

"His son?" said Mr. Dick. "David's son? Indeed!"

"Yes," pursued my aunt, "and he has done a pretty piece of business. He has run away. Ah! His sister, Betsey Trotwood, never would have run away." My aunt shook her head firmly, confident in the character and behavior of the girl who never was born.

"Oh! you think she wouldn't have run away?" said Mr. Dick.

"Bless and save the man," exclaimed my aunt, sharply, "how he talks! Don't I know she wouldn't? She would have lived with her godmother, and we should have been devoted to one another. Where, in the name of wonder, should his sister, Betsey Trotwood, have run from, or to?"

"Nowhere," said Mr. Dick.

"Well then," returned my aunt, softened by the reply, "how can you pretend to be wool-gathering, Dick, when you are as sharp as a surgeon's lancet? Now, here you see young David Copperfield, and the question I put to you is, what shall I do with him?"

"What shall you do with him?" said Mr. Dick, feebly, scratching his head. "Oh! do with him?"

"Yes," said my aunt, with a grave look, and her forefinger held up. "Come! I want some very sound advice."

"Why, if I was you," said Mr. Dick, considering, and looking vacantly at me, "I should—" The contemplation of me seemed to inspire him with a sudden idea, and he added, briskly, "I should wash him!"

"Janet," said my aunt, turning round with a quiet triumph, which I did not then understand, "Mr. Dick sets us all right. Heat the bath!"[2]

* * *

Janet reporting it [the bed] to be quite ready, I was taken up to it; kindly, but in some sort like a prisoner; my aunt going in front, and Janet bringing up the rear. The only circumstance which gave me any new hope, was my aunt's stopping on the stairs to inquire about a smell of fire that was prevalent there; and Janet's replying that she had been making tinder down in the kitchen, of my old shirt. But there were no other clothes in my room than the odd heap of things I wore; and when I was left there, with a little taper which my aunt forewarned me would burn exactly five minutes, I heard them lock my door on the outside. Turning these things over in my mind, I deemed it possible that my aunt, who could know nothing of me, might suspect I had a habit of running away, and took precautions, on that account, to have me in safe keeping.

The room was a pleasant one, at the top of the house, overlooking the sea, on which the moon was shining brilliantly. After I had said my prayers, and the candle had burned out, I remember how I still sat looking at the moonlight on the water, as if I could hope to read my fortune in it, as in a bright book; or to see my mother with her child, coming from Heaven, along that shining path, to look upon me as she had looked when I last saw her sweet face. I remember how the solemn feeling with which at length I turned my eyes away, yielded to the sensation of gratitude and rest which the sight

2. The day passes with David being   taken to bed.
bathed, rested, and fed, and by nightfall

of the white-curtained bed—and how much more the lying softly down upon it, nestling in the snow-white sheets!—inspired. I remember how I thought of all the solitary places under the night sky where I had slept, and how I prayed that I never might be houseless any more, and never might forget the houseless. I remember how I seemed to float, then, down the melancholy glory of that track upon the sea, away into the world of dreams.

1849–50   1849–50

From Bleak House[1]

In Chancery

London. Michaelmas Term lately over, and the Lord Chancellor sitting in Lincoln's Inn Hall.[2] Implacable November weather. As much mud in the streets, as if the waters had but newly retired from the face of the earth, and it would not be wonderful to meet a Megalosaurus, forty feet long or so, waddling like an elephantine lizard up Holborn Hill. Smoke lowering down from chimney-pots, making a soft black drizzle, with flakes of soot in it as big as full-grown snowflakes—gone into mourning, one might imagine, for the death of the sun. Dogs, undistinguishable in mire. Horses, scarcely better; splashed to their very blinkers. Foot passengers, jostling one another's umbrellas, in a general infection of ill temper, and losing their foothold at street corners, where tens of thousands of other foot passengers have been slipping and sliding since the day broke (if the day ever broke), adding new deposits to the crust upon crust of mud, sticking at those points tenaciously to the pavement, and accumulating at compound interest.

Fog everywhere. Fog up the river, where it flows among green aits[3] and meadows; fog down the river, where it rolls defiled among the tiers of shipping, and the waterside pollutions of a great (and dirty) city. Fog on the Essex marshes, fog on the Kentish heights. Fog creeping into the cabooses of collier-brigs, fog lying out on the yards, and hovering in the rigging of great ships; fog drooping on the gunwales of barges and small boats. Fog in the eyes and throats

---

1. *Bleak House* (1852–53) is the first of Dickens' so-called "dark period" novels. In *Bleak House* the institution of law, as represented by the inept practices of the Court of Chancery, is shown to have withering effects on the lives of a galaxy of characters. The opening chapter, by its linking of the dirty fog of a modern city to the obfuscation of legal procedures embodied in the case of Jarndyce

and Jarndyce, provides a striking overture for the life-stories that follow it.
2. During regular terms (such as Michaelmas term, November 2–25) the Court of Chancery held its sessions in Westminster Hall. Between terms it moved to Lincoln's Inn Hall.
3. Small islands in the River Thames above London.

of ancient Greenwich pensioners,[4] wheezing by the firesides of their wards; fog in the stem and bowl of the afternoon pipe of the wrathful skipper, down in his close cabin; fog cruelly pinching the toes and fingers of his shivering little 'prentice boy on deck. Chance people on the bridges peeping over the parapets into a nether sky of fog, with fog all around them, as if they were up in a balloon, and hanging in the misty clouds.

Gas looming through the fog in divers places in the streets, much as the sun may, from the spongey fields, be seen to loom by husbandman and plowboy. Most of the shops lighted two hours before their time—as the gas seems to know, for it has a haggard and unwilling look.

The raw afternoon is rawest, and the dense fog is densest, and the muddy streets are muddiest, near that leaden-headed old obstruction, appropriate ornament for the threshold of a leaden-headed old corporation: Temple Bar.[5] And hard by Temple Bar, in Lincoln's Inn Hall, at the very heart of the fog, sits the Lord High Chancellor in his High Court of Chancery.

Never can there come fog too thick, never can there come mud and mire too deep, to assort with the groping and floundering condition which this High Court of Chancery, most pestilent of hoary sinners, holds, this day, in the sight of heaven and earth.

On such an afternoon, if ever, the Lord High Chancellor ought to be sitting here—as here he is—with a foggy glory round his head, softly fenced in with crimson cloth and curtains, addressed by a large advocate with great whiskers, a little voice, and an interminable brief, and outwardly directing his contemplation to the lantern[6] in the roof, where he can see nothing but fog. On such an afternoon, some score of members of the High Court of Chancery bar ought to be—as here they are—mistily engaged in one of ten thousand stages of an endless cause, tripping one another up on slippery precedents, groping knee-deep in technicalities, running their goat-hair and horse-hair warded[7] heads against walls of words, and making a pretense of equity with serious faces, as players might. On such an afternoon, the various solicitors in the cause, some two or three of whom have inherited it from their fathers, who made a fortune by it, ought to be—as are they not?—ranged in a line, in a long matted well[8] (but you might look in vain for Truth at the bottom of it), between the registrar's red table and the silk gowns,

4. Retired sailors in the Naval Hospital at Greenwich.
5. This barrier-archway, spanning a street that led to the old walled City of London, was adjacent to the Middle Temple, a "corporation" for the training of lawyers. Being an "obstruction" to traffic, the archway was removed in 1878.
6. Lantern-shaped structure surmounting the roof, designed to provide ventilation.
7. Protected by wigs of goat-hair (worn by judges) or horse-hair (worn by ordinary lawyers).
8. Courtroom floor covered with coconut matting.

with bills, cross-bills, answers, rejoinders, injunctions, affidavits, issues, references to masters[9], masters' reports, mountains of costly nonsense, piled before them. Well may the court be dim, with wasting candles here and there; well may the fog hang heavy in it, as if it would never get out; well may the stained glass windows lose their color, and admit no light of day into the place; well may the uninitiated from the streets, who peep in through the glass panes in the door, be deterred from entrance by its owlish aspect, and by the drawl languidly echoing to the roof from the padded dais where the Lord High Chancellor looks into the lantern that has no light in it, and where the attendant wigs are all stuck in a fog bank! This is the Court of Chancery; which has its decaying houses and its blighted lands in every shire; which has its worn-out lunatic in every madhouse,[1] and its dead in every churchyard; which has its ruined suitor, with his slipshod heels and threadbare dress, borrowing and begging through the round of every man's acquaintance; which gives to monied might, the means abundantly of wearying out the right; which so exhausts finances, patience, courage, hope; so overthrows the brain and breaks the heart; that there is not an honorable man among its practitioners who would not give—who does not often give—the warning, "Suffer any wrong that can be done you, rather than come here!"

Who happen to be in the Lord Chancellor's court this murky afternoon besides the Lord Chancellor, the counsel in the cause, two or three counsel who are never in any cause, and the well of solicitors before mentioned? There is the registrar below the Judge, in wig and gown; and there are two or three maces, or petty-bags, or privy purses,[2] or whatever they may be, in legal court suits. These are all yawning; for no crumb of amusement ever falls from JARNDYCE AND JARNDYCE (the cause in hand), which was squeezed dry years upon years ago. The shorthand writers, the reporters of the court, and the reporters of the newspapers, invariably decamp with the rest of the regulars when Jarndyce and Jarndyce comes on. Their places are a blank. Standing on a seat at the side of the hall, the better to peer into the curtained sanctuary, is a little mad old woman in a squeezed bonnet, who is always in court, from its sitting to its rising, and always expecting some incomprehensible judgment to be given in her favor. Some say she really is, or was, a party to a suit; but no one knows for certain, because no one cares. She carries some small litter in her reticule which she calls her documents; principally consisting of paper matches and dry lavender. A

9. Court officers who prepared reports for the Lord Chancellor on cases that might be brought before the court. Because all evidence in Chancery cases had to be gathered in written form as "bills, cross bills," etc., the quantity of documentation could reach staggering proportions, especially in long-standing cases involving some disputed point about a legacy, as in Jarndyce and Jarndyce.
1. Chancery jurisdiction included decisions about the sanity of contestants in law cases and also the assignment of insane persons to asylums.
2. Courtroom officials.

sallow prisoner has come up, in custody, for the half-dozenth time, to make a personal application "to purge himself of his contempt"; which, being a solitary surviving executor who has fallen into a state of conglomeration about accounts of which it is not pretended that he had ever any knowledge, he is not at all likely ever to do. In the meantime his prospects in life are ended. Another ruined suitor, who periodically appears from Shropshire, and breaks out into efforts to address the Chancellor at the close of the day's business, and who can by no means be made to understand that the Chancellor is legally ignorant of his existence after making it desolate for a quarter of a century, plants himself in a good place and keeps an eye on the Judge, ready to call out "My Lord!" in a voice of sonorous complaint, on the instant of his rising. A few lawyers' clerks and others who know this suitor by sight, linger, on the chance of his furnishing some fun, and enlivening the dismal weather a little.

Jarndyce and Jarndyce drones on. This scarecrow of a suit has, in course of time, become so complicated that no man alive knows what it means. The parties to it understand it least; but it has been observed that no two Chancery lawyers can talk about it for five minutes, without coming to a total disagreement as to all the premises. Innumerable children have been born into the cause; innumerable young people have married into it; innumerable old people have died out of it. Scores of persons have deliriously found themselves made parties in Jarndyce and Jarndyce, without knowing how or why; whole families have inherited legendary hatreds with the suit. The little plaintiff or defendant, who was promised a new rocking-horse when Jarndyce and Jarndyce should be settled, has grown up, possessed himself of a real horse, and trotted away into the other world. Fair wards of court[3] have faded into mothers and grandmothers; a long procession of Chancellors has come in and gone out; the legion of bills in the suit have been transformed into mere bills of mortality; there are not three Jarndyces left upon the earth perhaps, since old Tom Jarndyce in despair blew his brains out at a coffee-house in Chancery Lane; but Jarndyce and Jarndyce still drags its dreary length before the Court, perennially hopeless.

Jarndyce and Jarndyce has passed into a joke. That is the only good that has ever come of it. It has been death to many, but it is a joke in the profession. Every master in Chancery has had a reference out of it. Every Chancellor was "in it," for somebody or other, when he was counsel at the bar. Good things have been said about it by blue-nosed, bulbous-shoed old benchers,[4] in select port-wine committee after dinner in hall. Articled clerks[5] have been in the habit of fleshing their legal wit upon it. The last Lord Chancellor

---

3. Minors, for whom guardians were appointed by the Court of Chancery.
4. Senior officers in one of the colleges of law, the Inns of Court.

5. Trainees for the legal profession who have made contracts (articles) as apprentices with their employers.

1254 · *Charles Dickens*

handled it neatly when, correcting Mr. Blowers, the eminent silk
gown who said that such a thing might happen when the sky rained
potatoes, he observed, "or when we get through Jarndyce and Jarndyce, Mr. Blowers";—a pleasantry that particularly tickled the
maces, bags, and purses.

How many people out of the suit, Jarndyce and Jarndyce has
stretched forth its unwholesome hand to spoil and corrupt, would
be a very wide question. From the master, upon whose impaling
files reams of dusty warrants in Jarndyce and Jarndyce have grimly
writhed into many shapes; down to the copying-clerk in the Six
Clerks' Office,[6] who has copied his tens of thousands of Chancery
folio pages under that eternal heading; no man's nature has been
made better by it. In trickery, evasion, procrastination, spoliation,
botheration, under false pretenses of all sorts, there are influences
that can never come to good. The very solicitors' boys who have
kept the wretched suitors at bay, by protesting time out of mind
that Mr. Chizzle, Mizzle, or otherwise, was particularly engaged and
had appointments until dinner, may have got an extra moral twist
and shuffle into themselves out of Jarndyce and Jarndyce. The
receiver in the cause has acquired a goodly sum of money by it, but
has acquired too a distrust of his own mother, and a contempt for
his own kind. Chizzle, Mizzle, and otherwise, have lapsed into a
habit of vaguely promising themselves that they will look into that
outstanding little matter, and see what can be done for Drizzle—
who was not well used—when Jarndyce and Jarndyce shall be got
out of the office. Shirking and sharking,[7] in all their many varieties,
have been sown broadcast by the ill-fated cause; and even those who
have contemplated its history from the outermost circle of such evil
have been insensibly tempted into a loose way of letting bad things
alone to take their own bad course, and a loose belief that if the
world go wrong, it was, in some off-hand manner, never meant to
go right.

Thus, in the midst of the mud and at the heart of the fog, sits
the Lord High Chancellor in his High Court of Chancery.

"Mr. Tangle," says the Lord High Chancellor, latterly something
restless under the eloquence of that learned gentleman.

"Mlud," says Mr. Tangle. Mr. Tangle knows more of Jarndyce
and Jarndyce than anybody. He is famous for it—supposed never to
have read anything else since he left school.

"Have you nearly concluded your argument?"

"Mlud, no—variety of points—feel it my duty tsubmit—lud-
ship," is the reply that slides out of Mr. Tangle.

---

6. A Chancery office that charged special fees for copying documents. A
"Chancery folio page" consisted of
ninety words of copy.
7. Cheating and swindling.

"Several members of the bar are still to be heard, I believe?" says the Chancellor, with a slight smile.

Eighteen of Mr. Tangle's learned friends, each armed with a little summary of eighteen hundred sheets, bob up like eighteen hammers in a piano-forte, make eighteen bows, and drop into their eighteen places of obscurity.

"We will proceed with the hearing on Wednesday fortnight," says the Chancellor. For the question at issue is only a question of costs, a mere bud on the forest tree of the parent suit, and really will come to a settlement one of these days.

The Chancellor rises; the bar rises; the prisoner is brought forward in a hurry; the man from Shropshire cries, "My lord!" Maces, bags, and purses indignantly proclaim silence, and frown at the man from Shropshire.

"In reference," proceeds the Chancellor, still on Jarndyce and Jarndyce, "to the young girl——"

"Begludship's pardon—boy," says Mr. Tangle, prematurely.

"In reference," proceeds the Chancellor, with extra distinctness, "to the young girl and boy, the two young people,"

(Mr. Tangle crushed.)

"Whom I directed to be in attendance to-day, and who are now in my private room, I will see them and satisfy myself as to the expediency of making the order for their residing with their uncle."

Mr. Tangle on his legs again.

"Begludship's pardon—dead."

"With their," Chancellor looking through his double eyeglass at the papers on his desk, "grandfather."

"Begludship's pardon—victim of rash action—brains."

Suddenly a very little counsel, with a terrific bass voice, arises, fully inflated, in the back settlements of the fog, and says, "Will your lordship allow me? I appear for him. He is a cousin, several times removed. I am not at the moment prepared to inform the Court in what exact remove he *is* a cousin; but he *is* a cousin."

Leaving this address (delivered like a sepulchral message) ringing in the rafters of the roof, the very little counsel drops, and the fog knows him no more. Everybody looks for him. Nobody can see him.

"I will speak with both the young people," says the Chancellor anew, "and satisfy myself on the subject of their residing with their cousin. I will mention the matter tomorrow morning when I take my seat."

The Chancellor is about to bow to the bar, when the prisoner is presented. Nothing can possibly come of the prisoner's conglomeration, but his being sent back to prison; which is soon done. The man from Shropshire ventures another demonstrative "My lord!" but the Chancellor, being aware of him, has dexterously vanished.

Everybody else quickly vanishes too. A battery of blue bags is loaded with heavy charges of papers and carried off by clerks; the little mad old woman marches off with her documents; the empty court is locked up. If all the injustice it has committed, and all the misery it has caused, could only be locked up with it, and the whole burned away in a great funeral pyre—why so much the better for other parties than the parties in Jarndyce and Jarndyce!

****

1852–53

From Hard Times[1]

The One Thing Needful

"Now, what I want is, Facts. Teach these boys and girls nothing but Facts. Facts alone are wanted in life. Plant nothing else, and root out everything else. You can only form the minds of reasoning animals upon Facts; nothing else will ever be of any service to them. This is the principle on which I bring up my own children, and this is the principle on which I bring up these children. Stick to Facts, sir!"

The scene was a plain, bare, monotonous vault of a schoolroom, and the speaker's square forefinger emphasized his observations by underscoring every sentence with a line on the schoolmaster's sleeve. The emphasis was helped by the speaker's square wall of a forehead, which had his eyebrows for its base, while his eyes found commodious cellarage in two dark caves, overshadowed by the wall. The emphasis was helped by the speaker's mouth, which was wide, thin, and hard set. The emphasis was helped by the speaker's voice, which was inflexible, dry, and dictatorial. The emphasis was helped by the speaker's hair, which bristled on the skirts of his bald head, a plantation of firs to keep the wind from its shining surface, all covered with knobs, like the crust of a plum pie, as if the head had scarcely warehouse-room for the hard facts stored inside. The speaker's obstinate carriage, square coat, square legs, square shoulders—

1. *Hard Times* appeared as a serial in short weekly installments in 1854. The novel is set in a manufacturing town in the English midlands, Coketown, in which the leading citizens, Mr. Gradgrind and Mr. Bounderby, represent the philosophy of Utilitarianism, at least in one of its phases. Gradgrind, in particular, considers that imaginative pursuits such as poetry, or fanciful entertainments such as a circus, divert the mind from its proper concern with fact and analysis. According to these principles he has brought up his own family, and to inculcate them further he has established a school. The teacher, Mr. M'Choakumchild, is pictured as representative of the teachers being turned out by training colleges in the 1850's, whose training had stressed the acquisition of factual knowlege—as Philip Collins has shown in his *Dickens and Education*. Our selections are from Book I, Chapters One, Two, and Five.

nay, his very neckcloth, trained to take him by the throat with an unaccommodating grasp, like a stubborn fact, as it was—all helped the emphasis.

"In this life, we want nothing but Facts, sir; nothing but Facts!"

The speaker, and the schoolmaster, and the third grown person present, all backed a little, and swept with their eyes the inclined plane of little vessels then and there arranged in order, ready to have imperial gallons of facts poured into them until they were full to the brim.

Murdering the Innocents

Thomas Gradgrind, sir. A man of realities. A man of facts and calculations. A man who proceeds upon the principle that two and two are four, and nothing over, and who is not to be talked into allowing for anything over. Thomas Gradgrind, sir—peremptorily Thomas—Thomas Gradgrind. With a rule and a pair of scales, and the multiplication table always in his pocket, sir, ready to weigh and measure any parcel of human nature, and tell you exactly what it comes to. It is a mere question of figures, a case of simple arithmetic. You might hope to get some other nonsensical belief into the head of George Gradgrind, or Augustus Gradgrind, or John Gradgrind, or Joseph Gradgrind (all supposititious, nonexistent persons), but into the head of Thomas Gradgrind—no, sir!

In such terms Mr. Gradgrind always mentally introduced himself, whether to his private circle of acquaintance, or to the public in general. In such terms, no doubt, substituting the words "boys and girls" for "sir," Thomas Gradgrind now presented Thomas Gradgrind to the little pitchers before him, who were to be filled so full of facts.

Indeed, as he eagerly sparkled at them from the cellarage before mentioned, he seemed a kind of cannon loaded to the muzzle with facts, and prepared to blow them clean out of the regions of childhood at one discharge. He seemed a galvanizing apparatus, too, charged with a grim mechanical substitute for the tender young imaginations that were to be stormed away.

"Girl number twenty," said Mr. Gradgrind, squarely pointing with his square forefinger, "I don't know that girl. Who is that girl?"

"Sissy Jupe, sir," explained number twenty, blushing, standing up, and curtseying.

"Sissy is not a name," said Mr. Gradgrind. "Don't call yourself Sissy. Call yourself Cecilia."

"It's father as calls me Sissy, sir," returned the young girl in a trembling voice, and with another curtsey.

"Then he has no business to do it," said Mr. Gradgrind. "Tell him he mustn't. Cecilia Jupe. Let me see. What is your father?"

"He belongs to the horse-riding, if you please, sir."

Mr. Gradgrind frowned, and waved off the objectionable calling with his hand.

"We don't want to know anything about that, here. You mustn't tell us about that, here. Your father breaks horses, don't he?"

"If you please, sir, when they can get any to break, they do break horses in the ring, sir."

"You mustn't tell us about the ring here. Very well, then. Describe your father as a horsebreaker. He doctors sick horses, I dare say?"

"Oh, yes, sir."

"Very well, then. He is a veterinary surgeon, a farrier, and horse-breaker. Give me your definition of a horse."

(Sissy Jupe thrown into the greatest alarm by this demand.)

"Girl number twenty unable to define a horse!" said Mr. Grad-grind, for the general behoof of all the little pitchers. "Girl number twenty possessed of no facts in reference to one of the commonest of animals! Some boy's definition of a horse. Bitzer, yours."

The square finger, moving here and there, lighted suddenly on Bitzer, perhaps because he chanced to sit in the same ray of sun-light which, darting in at one of the bare windows of the intensely whitewashed room, irradiated Sissy. For, the boys and girls sat on the face of the inclined plane in two compact bodies, divided up the center by a narrow interval; and Sissy, being at the corner of a row on the sunny side, came in for the beginning of a sunbeam, of which Bitzer, being at the corner of a row on the other side, a few rows in advance, caught the end. But, whereas the girl was so dark-eyed and dark-haired that she seemed to receive a deeper and more lustrous color from the sun, when it shone upon her, the boy was so light-eyed and light-haired that the self-same rays appeared to draw out of him what little color he ever possessed. His cold eyes would hardly have been eyes, but for the short ends of lashes which, by bringing them into immediate contrast with something paler than themselves, expressed their form. His short-cropped hair might have been a mere continuation of the sandy freckles on his forehead and face. His skin was so unwholesomely deficient in the natural tinge, that he looked as though, if he were cut, he would bleed white.

"Bitzer," said Thomas Gradgrind. "Your definition of a horse."

"Quadruped. Graminivorous. Forty teeth, namely twenty-four grinders, four eye-teeth, and twelve incisive. Sheds coat in the spring; in marshy countries, sheds hoofs, too. Hoofs hard, but requir-ing to be shod with iron. Age known by marks in mouth." Thus (and much more) Bitzer.

"Now, girl number twenty," said Mr. Gradgrind, "you know what a horse is."

She curtseyed again, and would have blushed deeper, if she could have blushed deeper than she had blushed all this time. Bitzer, after rapidly blinking at Thomas Gradgrind with both eyes at once, and so catching the light upon his quivering ends of lashes that they looked like the antennae of busy insects, put his knuckles to his freckled forehead, and sat down again.

The third gentleman now stepped forth. A mighty man at cutting and drying, he was; a government officer; in his way (and in most other people's too), a professed pugilist; always in training, always with a system to force down the general throat like a bolus,[2] always to be heard of at the bar of his little Public-office, ready to fight all England. To continue in the fistic phraseology, he had a genius for coming up to the scratch,[3] wherever and whatever it was, and proving himself an ugly customer. He would go in and damage any subject whatever with his right, follow up with his left, stop, exchange, counter, bore his opponent (he always fought All England)[4] to the ropes, and fall upon him neatly. He was certain to knock the wind out of common sense, and render that unlucky adversary deaf to the call of time. And he had it in charge from high authority to bring about the great Public-office Millennium, when Commissioners[5] should reign upon earth.

"Very well," said this gentleman, briskly smiling, and folding his arms. "That's a horse. Now, let me ask you, girls and boys, Would you paper a room with representations of horses?"

After a pause, one half of the children cried in chorus, "Yes, sir!" Upon which the other half, seeing in the gentleman's face that Yes was wrong, cried out in chorus, "No, sir!"—as the custom is, in these examinations.

"Of course, No. Why wouldn't you?"

A pause. One corpulent slow boy, with a wheezy manner of breathing, ventured the answer, Because he wouldn't paper a room at all, but would paint it.

"You *must* paper it," said the gentleman, rather warmly.

"You must paper it," said Thomas Gradgrind, "whether you like it or not. Don't tell *us* you wouldn't paper it. What do you mean, boy?"

"I'll explain to you, then," said the gentleman, after another and a dismal pause, "why you wouldn't paper a room with representations of horses. Do you ever see horses walking up and down the sides of rooms in reality—in fact? Do you?"

2. A large pill.
3. A line drawn across the center of the ring in the early days of prize fighting. Contestants would begin a match by stepping up to opposite sides of this line, and the match would end when one of the two could no longer come up to the scratch line at the beginning of a new round.
4. Fighting according to a national code of rules for the prize ring—one of the codes superseded by the adoption of the Marquis of Queensbury's rules in 1866.
5. Administrative officials in various departments of government such as Customs or Income Taxes.

"Yes, sir!" from one half. "No, sir!" from the other.

"Of course, No," said the gentleman, with an indignant look at the wrong half. "Why, then, you are not to see anywhere what you don't see in fact; you are not to have anywhere what you don't have in fact. What is called Taste, is only another name for Fact."

Thomas Gradgrind nodded his approbation.

"This is a new principle, a discovery, a great discovery," said the gentleman. "Now I'll try you again. Suppose you were going to carpet a room. Would you use a carpet having a representation of flowers upon it?"

There being a general conviction by this time that "No, sir!" was always the right answer to this gentleman, the chorus of No was very strong. Only a few feeble stragglers said Yes; among them Sissy Jupe.

"Girl number twenty," said the gentleman, smiling in the calm strength of knowledge.

Sissy blushed, and stood up.

"So you would carpet your room—or your husband's room, if you were a grown woman, and had a husband—with representations of flowers, would you," said the gentleman. "Why would you?"

"If you please, sir, I am very fond of flowers," returned the girl.

"And is that why you would put tables and chairs upon them, and have people walking over them with heavy boots?"

"It wouldn't hurt them, sir. They wouldn't crush and wither if you please, sir. They would be the pictures of what was very pretty and pleasant, and I would fancy"—

"Ay, ay, ay! But you mustn't fancy," cried the gentleman, quite elated by coming so happily to his point. "That's it! You are never to fancy."

"You are not, Cecilia Jupe," Thomas Gradgrind solemnly repeated, "to do anything of that kind."

"Fact, fact, fact!" said the gentleman. And "Fact, fact, fact!" repeated Thomas Gradgrind.

"You are to be in all things regulated and governed," said the gentleman, "by fact. We hope to have before long, a board of fact, composed of commissioners of fact, who will force the people to be a people of fact, and of nothing but fact. You must discard the word Fancy altogether. You have nothing to do with it. You are not to have, in any object of use or ornament, what would be a contradiction in fact. You don't walk upon flowers in fact; you cannot be allowed to walk upon flowers in carpets. You don't find that foreign birds and butterflies come and perch upon your crockery; you cannot be permitted to paint foreign birds and butterflies upon your crockery. You never meet with quadrupeds going up and down walls; you must not have quadrupeds represented upon walls. You must use," said the gentleman, "for all these purposes, combinations and modifications (in primary colors) of mathematical figures which are susceptible of proof and demonstration. This is the new discovery. This is Fact. This is taste."

The girl curtseyed and sat down. She was very young, and she looked as if she were frightened by the matter of fact prospect the world afforded.

"Now, if Mr. M'Choakumchild," said the gentleman, "will proceed to give his first lesson here, Mr. Gradgrind, I shall be happy, at your request, to observe his mode of procedure."

Mr. Gradgrind was much obliged. "Mr. M'Choakumchild, we only wait for you."

So, Mr. M'Choakumchild began in his best manner. He and some one hundred and forty other schoolmasters had been lately turned at the same time, in the same factory, on the same principles, like so many piano-forte legs. He had been put through an immense variety of paces, and had answered volumes of head-breaking questions. Orthography, etymology, syntax, and prosody, biography, astronomy, geography, and general cosmography, the sciences of compound proportion, algebra, land-surveying and leveling, vocal music and drawing from models, were all at the ends of his ten chilled fingers. He had worked his stony way into Her Majesty's most Honourable Privy Council's Schedule B,[6] and had taken the bloom off the higher branches of mathematics and physical science, French, German, Latin, and Greek. He knew all about all the Water Sheds of all the world (whatever they are), and all the histories of all the peoples, and all the names of all the rivers and mountains, and all the productions, manners, and customs of all the countries, and all their boundaries and bearings on the two-and-thirty points of the compass. Ah, rather overdone, M'Choakumchild. If he had only learned a little less, how infinitely better he might have taught much more!

He went to work, in this preparatory lesson, not unlike Morgiana[7] in the Forty Thieves; looking into all the vessels ranged before him, one after another, to see what they contained. Say, good M'Choakumchild. When from thy boiling store thou shalt fill each jar brimful by-and-by, dost thou think that thou wilt always kill outright the robber Fancy lurking within—or sometimes only maim him and distort him?

* * *

[*Coketown*]

Coketown, to which Messrs. Bounderby and Gradgrind now walked, was a triumph of fact; it had no greater taint of fancy in it

---

6. A syllabus established in 1846 specifying what subjects were to be mastered by candidates training to become teachers. Schedule B was drawn up by a sub-committee of the Privy Council.

7. Ali Baba's slave in the *Arabian Nights' Entertainments* who killed forty thieves by pouring boiling oil into the jars in which they were hiding.

than Mrs. Gradgrind herself.[8] Let us strike the keynote, Coketown, before pursuing our tune.

It was a town of red brick, or of brick that would have been red if the smoke and ashes had allowed it; but as matters stood it was a town of unnatural red and black like the painted face of a savage. It was a town of machinery and tall chimneys, out of which interminable serpents of smoke trailed themselves forever and ever, and never got uncoiled. It had a black canal in it, and a river that ran purple with ill-smelling dye, and vast piles of buildings full of windows where there was a rattling and a trembling all day long, and where the piston of the steam-engine worked monotonously up and down like the head of an elephant in a state of melancholy madness. It contained several large streets all very like one another, and many small streets still more like one another, inhabited by people equally like one another, who all went in and out at the same hours, with the same sound upon the same pavements, to do the same work, and to whom every day was the same as yesterday and tomorrow, and every year the counterpart of the last and the next.

These attributes of Coketown were in the main inseparable from the work by which it was sustained; against them were to be set off, comforts of life which found their way all over the world, and elegancies of life which made, we will not ask how much of the fine lady, who could scarcely bear to hear the place mentioned. The rest of its features were voluntary, and they were these.

You saw nothing in Coketown but what was severely workful. If the members of a religious persuasion built a chapel there—as the members of eighteen religious persuasions had done—they made it a pious warehouse of red brick, with sometimes (but this is only in highly ornamented examples) a bell in a birdcage on the top of it. The solitary exception was the New Church; a stuccoed edifice with a square steeple over the door, terminating in four short pinnacles like florid wooden legs. All the public inscriptions in the town were painted alike, in severe characters of black and white. The jail might have been the infirmary, the infirmary might have been the jail, the town hall might have been either, or both, or anything else, for anything that appeared to the contrary in the graces of their construction. Fact, fact, fact, everywhere in the material aspect of the town; fact, fact, fact, everywhere in the immaterial. The M'Choakumchild school was all fact, and the school of design was all fact, and the relations between master and man were all fact, and everything was fact between the lying-in hospital and the cemetery, and what you couldn't state in figures, or show to be purchasa-

8. As Chapter 4 indicated, Mr. Gradgrind's choice of wife had been guided by seeking someone unimaginative. "She had 'no nonsense' about her. By nonsense he meant fancy."

ble in the cheapest market and salable in the dearest, was not, and never should be, world without end, Amen.

A town so sacred to fact, and so triumphant in its assertion, of course got on well? Why no, not quite well. No? Dear me!

No. Coketown did not come out of its own furnaces, in all respects like gold that had stood the fire. First, the perplexing mystery of the place was, Who belonged to the eighteen denominations? Because, whoever did, the laboring people did not. It was very strange to walk through the streets on a Sunday morning, and note how few of *them* the barbarous jangling of bells that was driving the sick and nervous mad, called away from their own quarter, from their own close rooms, from the corners of their own streets, where they lounged listlessly, gazing at all the church and chapel going, as at a thing with which they had no manner of concern. Nor was it merely the stranger who noticed this, because there was a native organization in Coketown itself, whose members were to be heard of in the House of Commons every session, indignantly petitioning for acts of parliament that should make these people religious by main force. Then came the Teetotal Society, who complained that these same people *would* get drunk, and showed in tabular statements that they did get drunk, and proved at tea parties that no inducement, human or Divine (except a medal), would induce them to forego their custom of getting drunk. Then came the chemist and druggist, with other tabular statements, showing that when they didn't get drunk, they took opium. Then came the experienced chaplain of the jail, with more tabular statements, outdoing all the previous tabular statements, and showing that the same people *would* resort to low haunts, hidden from the public eye, where they heard low singing and saw low dancing, and mayhap joined in it; where A. B., aged twenty-four next birthday, and committed for eighteen months' solitary, had himself said (not that he had ever shown himself particularly worthy of belief) his ruin began, as he was perfectly sure and confident that otherwise he would have been a tip-top moral specimen. Then came Mr. Gradgrind and Mr. Bounderby, the two gentlemen at this present moment walking through Coketown, and both eminently practical, who could, on occasion, furnish more tabular statements derived from their own personal experience, and illustrated by cases they had known and seen, from which it clearly appeared—in short, it was the only clear thing in the case—that these same people were a bad lot altogether, gentlemen; that do what you would for them they were never thankful for it, gentlemen; that they were restless, gentlemen; that they never knew what they wanted; that they lived upon the best, and bought fresh butter; and insisted on Mocha coffee, and rejected all but prime parts of meat, and yet were eter-

nally dissatisfied and unmanageable. In short, it was the moral of
the old nursery fable:

> There was an old woman, and what do you think?
> She lived upon nothing but victuals and drink;
> Victuals and drink were the whole of her diet,
> And yet this old woman would NEVER be quiet.

Is it possible, I wonder, that there was any analogy between the
case of the Coketown population and the case of the little Grad-
grinds? Surely, none of us in our sober senses and acquainted with
figures, are to be told at this time of day, that one of the foremost
elements in the existence of the Coketown working-people had been
for scores of years deliberately set at naught? That there was any
Fancy in them demanding to be brought into healthy existence
instead of struggling on in convulsions? That exactly in the ratio as
they worked long and monotonously, the craving grew within them
for some physical relief—some relaxation, encouraging good humor
and good spirits, and giving them a vent—some recognized holiday,
though it were but for an honest dance to a stirring band of music
—some occasional light pie in which even M'Choakumchild had no
finger—which craving must and would be satisfied aright, or must
and would inevitably go wrong, until the laws of the Creation were
repealed?

1854

From Our Mutual Friend[1]

Podsnappery

Mr. Podsnap was well to do, and stood very high in Mr. Podsnap's opinion. Beginning with a good inheritance, he had married
a good inheritance, and had thriven exceedingly in the Marine
Insurance way, and was quite satisfied. He never could make out
why everybody was not quite satisfied, and he felt conscious that he
set a brilliant social example in being particularly well satisfied with
most things, and, above all other things, with himself.

Thus happily acquainted with his own merit and importance,
Mr. Podsnap settled that whatever he put behind him he put out of
existence. There was a dignified conclusiveness—not to add a grand
convenience—in this way of getting rid of disagreeables which had

1. Dickens' last completed novel, published in 1864–65, portrays a large-scale
cross-section of Victorian society in
which the amassing and displaying of
wealth are obsessive preoccupations of
various classes of characters. These include the solidly established middle class
represented by Mr. and Mrs. Podsnap,
and the newly rich represented by Mr.
and Mrs. Veneering (who appear as
guests at the Podsnap dinner party). Our
selection is from Chapter 11.

done much towards establishing Mr. Podsnap in his lofty place in Mr. Podsnap's satisfaction. "I don't want to know about it; I don't choose to discuss it; I don't admit it!" Mr. Podsnap had even acquired a peculiar flourish of his right arm in often clearing the world of its most difficult problems, by sweeping them behind him (and consequently sheer away) with those words and a flushed face. For they affronted him.

Mr. Podsnap's world was not a very large world, morally; no, nor even geographically; seeing that although his business was sustained upon commerce with other countries, he considered other countries, with that important reservation, a mistake, and of their manners and customs would conclusively observe, "Not English!" when, PRESTO! with a flourish of the arm, and a flush of the face, they were swept away. Elsewhere, the world got up at eight, shaved close at a quarter-past, breakfasted at nine, went to the City at ten, came home at half-past five, and dined at seven. Mr. Podsnap's notions of the Arts in their integrity might have been stated thus. Literature; large print, respectfully descriptive of getting up at eight, shaving close at a quarter-past, breakfasting at nine, going to the City at ten, coming home at half-past five, and dining at seven. Painting and Sculpture; models and portraits representing Professors of getting up at eight, shaving close at a quarter-past, breakfasting at nine, going to the City at ten, coming home at half-past five, and dining at seven. Music; a respectable performance (without variations) on stringed and wind instruments, sedately expressive of getting up at eight, shaving close at a quarter-past, breakfasting at nine, going to the City at ten, coming home at half-past five, and dining at seven. Nothing else to be permitted to those same vagrants the Arts, on pain of excommunication. Nothing else To Be— anywhere!

As a so eminently respectable man, Mr. Podsnap was sensible of its being required of him to take Providence under his protection. Consequently he always knew exactly what Providence meant. Inferior and less respectable men might fall short of that mark, but Mr. Podsnap was always up to it. And it was very remarkable (and must have been very comfortable) that what Providence meant, was invariably what Mr. Podsnap meant.

These may be said to have been the articles of a faith and school which the present chapter takes the liberty of calling, after its representative man, Podsnappery. They were confined within close bounds, as Mr. Podsnap's own head was confined by his shirtcollar; and they were enunciated with a sounding pomp that smacked of the creaking of Mr. Podsnap's own boots.

There was a Miss Podsnap. And this young rocking-horse was being trained in her mother's art of prancing in a stately manner without ever getting on. But the high parental action was not yet imparted to her, and in truth she was but an undersized damsel, with high shoulders, low spirits, chilled elbows, and a rasped surface of nose, who seemed to take occasional frosty peeps out of child-hood into womanhood, and to shrink back again, overcome by her mother's head-dress and her father from head to foot—crushed by the mere dead weight of Podsnappery.

A certain institution in Mr. Podsnap's mind which he called "the young person" may be considered to have been embodied in Miss Podsnap, his daughter. It was an inconvenient and exacting institu-tion, as requiring everything in the universe to be filed down and fitted to it. The question about everything was, would it bring a blush into the cheek of the young person? And the inconvenience of the young person was, that, according to Mr. Podsnap, she seemed always liable to burst into blushes when there was no need at all. There appeared to be no line of demarcation between the young person's excessive innocence, and another person's guiltiest knowledge. Take Mr. Podsnap's word for it, and the soberest tints of drab, white, lilac, and gray were all flaming red to the trouble-some Bull of a young person.

The Podsnaps lived in a shady angle adjoining Portman Square. They were a kind of people certain to dwell in the shade, wherever they dwelled. Miss Podsnap's life had been, from her first appear-ance on this planet, altogether of a shady order; for, Mr. Podsnap's young person was likely to get little good out of association with other young persons, and had therefore been restricted to compan-ionship with not very congenial older persons, and with massive fur-niture. Miss Podsnap's early views of life being principally derived from the reflections of it in her father's boots, and in the walnut and rosewood tables of the dim drawing rooms, and in their swarthy giants of looking-glasses, were of a somber cast; and it was not won-derful that now, when she was on most days solemnly tooled[2] through the Park by the side of her mother in a great tall custard-colored phaeton, she showed above the apron of that vehicle like a dejected young person sitting up in bed to take a startled look at things in general, and very strongly desiring to get her head under the counterpane again.

Said Mr. Podsnap to Mrs. Podsnap, "Georgiana is almost eight-een."

Said Mrs. Podsnap to Mr. Podsnap, assenting, "Almost eighteen."

Said Mr. Podsnap then to Mrs. Podsnap, "Really I think we should have some people on Georgiana's birthday."

Said Mrs. Podsnap then to Mr. Podsnap, "Which will enable us to clear off all those people who are due."

So it came to pass that Mr. and Mrs. Podsnap requested the

2. Driven.

honor of the company of seventeen friends of their souls at dinner; and that they substituted other friends of their souls for such of the seventeen original friends of their souls as deeply regretted that a prior engagement prevented their having the honor of dining with Mr. and Mrs. Podsnap, in pursuance of their kind invitation; and that Mrs. Podsnap said of all these inconsolable personages, as she ꞏꞏ them off with a pencil in her list, "Asked, at any rate, and ꞏꞏꞏꞏꞏ, and that they successfully disposed of a good many to be asked to ꞏꞏls in this way, and felt their consciences much take a haunch of mutton ꞏꞏ of their souls who were not entitled clearing off of these worthies, Mrs. Podsnap ꞏꞏ om to be invited to come and evening to the dinner, and looked in at the music shop to ꞏꞏspeak a ꞏꞏꞏ half-past nine. For the ꞏꞏꞏ a small and early well-conducted automaton to come and play quadrilles for a carpet dance.

Mr. and Mrs. Veneering, and Mr. and Mrs. Veneering's brand new bride and bridegroom, were of the dinner company; but the Podsnap establishment had nothing else in common with the Veneerings. Mr. Podsnap could tolerate taste in a mushroom man[4] who stood in need of that sort of thing, but was far above it himself. Hideous solidity was the characteristic of the Podsnap plate. Everything was made to look as heavy as it could, and to take up as much room as possible. Everything said boastfully, "Here you have as much of me in my ugliness as if I were only lead; but I am so many ounces of precious metal worth so much an ounce;—wouldn't you like to melt me down?" A corpulent straddling epergne, blotched all over as if it had broken out in an eruption rather than been ornamented, delivered this address from an unsightly silver platform in the center of the table. Four silver wine-coolers, each furnished with four staring heads, each head obtrusively carrying a big silver ring in each of its ears, conveyed the sentiment up and down the table, and handed it on to the pot-bellied silver salt-cellars. All the big silver spoons and forks widened the mouths of the company expressly for the purpose of thrusting the sentiment down their throats with every morsel they ate.

The majority of the guests were like the plate, and included several heavy articles weighing ever so much. But there was a foreign gentleman among them: whom Mr. Podsnap had invited after much debate with himself—believing the whole European conti-

---

3. The second-class guests get no dinner at the reception. Instead they will be immersed in the pervading smells of the dinner that had been served earlier to the first-class guests, in particular the steamy smell of a dish of mutton, in which they will figuratively bathe.

4. A parvenu, one whose wealth and social position has suddenly and recently shot into prominence. Of the Veneerings it was said earlier: "All their furniture was new . . . their plate was new."

nent to be in mortal alliance against the young person—and there was a droll disposition, not only on the part of Mr. Podsnap but of everybody else, to treat him as if he were a child who was hard of hearing.

As a delicate concession to this unfortunately born foreigner, Mr. Podsnap, in receiving him, had presented his wife as "Madame Podsnap"; also his daughter as "Mademoiselle Podsnap," with some inclination to add "ma fille," in which bold venture, however, he checked himself. The Veneerings being at that time the only oth- arrivals, he had added (in a condescendingly explanator— "Monsieur Vey-nair-reeng," and had then subsi London, Londres, "How Do You Like London?" Mr. Podno his station of host, as if he . nature of a powder or London

The foreign gentleman admired it.

"You find it Very Large" said Mr. Podsnap, spaciously.

The foreign gentleman found it very large.

"And Very Rich?"

The foreign gentleman found it, without doubt, énormément riche.

"Enormously Rich, We say," returned Mr. Podsnap, in a condescending manner. "Our English adverbs do Not terminate in Mong, and We Pronounce the 'ch' as if there were a 't' before it. We say Ritch."

"Reetch," remarked the foreign gentleman.

"And Do You Find, Sir," pursued Mr. Podsnap, with dignity, "Many Evidences that Strike You, of our British Constitution in the Streets Of The World's Metropolis, London, Londres, London?"

The foreign gentleman begged to be pardoned, but did not altogether understand.

"The Constitution Britannique," Mr. Podsnap explained, as if he were teaching in an infant school. "We Say British, But You Say Britannique, You Know" (forgivingly, as if that were not his fault). "The Constitution, Sir."

The foreign gentleman said, "Mais, yees; I know eem."

A youngish sallowish gentleman in spectacles, with a lumpy forehead, seated in a supplementary chair at a corner of the table, here caused a profound sensation by saying in a raised voice "ESKER," and then stopping dead.

"Mais oui," said the foreign gentleman, turning towards him. "Est-ce que? Quoi donc?"[5]

But the gentleman with the lumpy forehead having for the time delivered himself of all that he found behind his lumps, spake for the time no more.

5. "Is it that . . . ? What, then?"

"I Was Inquiring," said Mr. Podsnap, resuming the thread of his discourse, "Whether You Have Observed in our Streets as We should say, Upon our Pavvy as You would say, any Tokens—"

The foreign gentleman, with patient courtesy entreated pardon; "But what was tokenz?"

"Marks," said Mr. Podsnap; "Signs, you know, Appearances—Traces."

"Ah! Of a Orse?" inquired the foreign gentleman.

"We call it Horse," said Mr. Podsnap, with forbearance. "In England, Angleterre, England, We Aspirate the 'H,' and We Say 'Horse.' Only our Lower Classes Say 'Orse!' "

"Pardon," said the foreign gentleman; "I am alwiz wrong!"

"Our Language," said Mr. Podsnap, with a gracious consciousness of being always right, "is Difficult. Ours is a Copious Language, and Trying to Strangers. I will not Pursue my Question."

But the lumpy gentleman, unwilling to give it up, again madly said, "Esker," and again spake no more.

"It merely referred," Mr. Podsnap explained, with a sense of meritorious proprietorship, "to Our Constitution, Sir. We Englishmen are Very Proud of our Constitution, Sir. It Was Bestowed Upon Us By Providence. No Other Country is so Favored as This Country."

"And ozer countries?—" the foreign gentleman was beginning, when Mr. Podsnap put him right again.

"We do not say Ozer; we say Other: the letters are 'T' and 'H'; You say Tay and Aish, You Know; (still with clemency). The sound is 'th'—'th!' "

"And *oth*er countries," said the foreign gentleman. "They do how?"

"They do, Sir," returned Mr. Podsnap, gravely shaking his head; "they do—I am sorry to be obliged to say it—*as* they do."

"It was a little particular of Providence," said the foreign gentleman, laughing; "for the frontier is not large."

* * *

1864–65

GEORGE ELIOT

(1819–1880)

1846:   *The Life of Jesus* (translation).
1859:   *Adam Bede.*
1860:   *The Mill on the Floss.*
1871–72: *Middlemarch.*

Like many English novelists (Dickens being an exception) George Eliot came to novel-writing relatively late in life. She was 40 when her first novel, *Adam Bede,* an outstandingly popular work, was published. The lives of her characters are therefore viewed from the vantage point of maturity and extensive experience, and this perspective is accentuated by her practice of setting her stories back in time to the period of her own childhood, or even earlier. In most of her novels she evokes a pre-industrial rural scene or the small-town life of the English Midlands, which she views with a combination of nostalgia and candid awareness of their limitations. This quality, admirably illustrated by the opening chapter of *The Mill on the Floss,* may have influenced the work of a later master of retrospective vision, Marcel Proust. *The Mill on the Floss* was, for Proust, the best loved of books: two pages of it, he said, "reduce me to tears."

The place Eliot looks back upon is usually the Warwickshire countryside, where, under her real name, Marian Evans, she spent her childhood at Arbury Farm, of which her father, Robert Evans, was supervisor and land agent. The time was the 1820's and 1830's (1819, the year of her birth, be it noted, was an *annus mirabilis* for the 19th century, for in the same year were born John Ruskin, Herman Melville, Walt Whitman, Arthur Hugh Clough, and Queen Victoria herself). During these decades Marian Evans read widely in and out of school and was also strongly affected by Evangelicalism; she even advocated, at one point in her girlhood, giving up novelists such as Scott (who was later to influence her own novel-writing) on the grounds that fiction was frivolous and time-wasting. Her mother's death led to her leaving school at 16, and in the next four or five years she seems to have experienced bouts of depression and self-doubt. In a letter of 1871, looking back to this period, she likened her state of mind to that of Mary Wollstonecraft at the time of her attempted suicide: "Hopelessness has been to me, all through my life, but especially in the painful years of my youth, the chief source of wasted energy with all the consequent bitterness of regret. Remember, it has happened to many to be glad they did not commit suicide, though they once ran for the final leap, or as Mary Wollstonecraft did, wetted their garments well in the rain hoping to sink the better when they plunged."

At the age of 21 Marian Evans moved with her father to the town of Coventry, and in this new setting her intellectual horizons were extensively widened. As the result of her association with a group of freethinking intellectuals, and her own studies of theology, she reluctantly decided that she could no longer believe in the Christian religion, although because of the intensity of her father's distress on this occasion she agreed to go through the formalities of attending church with him until the time of his death in 1849. These preoccupations with theological issues led to her first book, a translation of *The Life of Jesus,* by D. F. Strauss, one of the leading figures of the Higher Criticism in Germany. This criticism was the work of a group of scholars dedicated to testing the historical authenticity of Biblical narratives in the light of modern methods of research. For the rest of her life Marian Evans continued to read extensively in English and Continental philosophy, and when she moved to London in 1851, her impressive intellectual credentials led to her appointment as an assistant editor of the *Westminster Review,* a learned journal formerly edited by John Stuart Mill. Fortifying her intellectual credentials for such an appointment was her remarkable personal charm. Henry James, after meeting her for the first time, reported to his father that he had fallen in love "with this great horse-faced blue-stocking."

How much of this intellectual and religious background is carried over into Eliot's novels is difficult to determine precisely. Unlike the characters of such intellectual novelists as Aldous Huxley, her characters only rarely discuss issues directly, and, as W. J. Harvey notes, she never produced a "novel of ideas." Yet all her novels, as Harvey adds, are involved with "what ordinary men mean when they talk of having a 'philosophy of life.'"

Her treatment in her novels of what was called the Woman Question was similarly indirect. Her temperate essay on the early feminist Mary Wollstonecraft (included in the following selections) exemplifies her interest in feminist causes, but if we consider her novels, rather than her essays, it is evident that she did not believe in subverting her fiction to platform performances. The experiences of such of her heroines as Dorothea Brooke and Maggie Tulliver dramatize some of the frustrations of women in a male-dominated culture, but they remain dramatizations rather than tracts. "My function," she wrote, "is that of the *aesthetic* not the doctrinal teacher."

Aside from her rural upbringing and her intellectual development, a third important aspect of her experience was her falling in love, early in the 1850's, with George Henry Lewes, a brilliant critic of literature and philosophy. Lewes, a married man and father of three children, could not obtain a divorce. Marian Evans therefore elected to live with him as a common-law wife, and what they called their "marriage" lasted happily until his death in 1878. In the last year of her life she formally married an admirer and friend, J. W. Cross, who became her biographer. Her earlier decision to live with Lewes was painfully made: "Light and easily broken ties are what I neither desire theoretically nor could live for practically. Women who are satisfied with such ties do *not* act as I have done—they obtain what they desire and are still invited to dinner." Especially painful to her was the realization that her decision would cost her the love of her brother, Isaac Evans, to whom she had been deeply attached since childhood; Isaac never spoke to her again after the event. It is reasonable to conjecture that this experience affects the stress, in all of her novels, on incidents involving choice. All of her characters are tested by situations in which they must choose, and the choices, as in *The Mill on the Floss,* are often agonizingly painful.

Although she had occasionally tried her hand at fiction earlier in life, it was only after her relation with Lewes became established that she turned her full attention to this form. *Scenes from Clerical Life* appeared in magazine installments in 1857 under the pen name that misled most of her readers (Dickens excepted) into believing the author to be a man—a "university man," it was commonly said, to Eliot's amusement and satisfaction. This work was followed by six or seven full-length novels in the 1860's and 1870's, most of which repeated the success of *Adam Bede* with the Victorian reading public, and which, after a period of being out of favor earlier in our century, are now once more deeply admired by readers and critics. Virginia Woolf praised *Middlemarch* as "one of the few English novels written for grown-up people," and later readers find a similar maturity, combined with a powerful creative energy, in other novels by Eliot such as *The Mill on the Floss* and *Daniel Deronda*. One of her most impressive qualities is her special brand of realism. Like the novels of Flaubert and others of the realist school, her novels astonish us with their insights into human behavior and their almost relentless exposure of human motives. But unlike Flaubert, George Eliot performs her analyses with compassion. It is this distinctive compounding of realism with pity that makes her, according to the French critic Brunetière, a better realist, finally, than her famous contemporary, the author of *Madame Bovary*.

The Mill on the Floss The selections from Eliot's novels, unlike those from Dickens, are restricted to a single novel. The reason for this different mode of selection indicates a difference in the characteristic qualities of the two novelists. Dickens, as we have seen, was able to offer highly successful public readings by selecting episodes from an assortment of his novels, episodes that are largely self-contained units requiring minimal framing from the surrounding narratives. If Eliot had sought to put together an assortment of selections from her novels comparable to those chosen by Dickens, she would have found the task infinitely more difficult. With her, the microcosm of a scene usually requires the macrocosm of the novel to make it comprehensible to an audience. Her novels are much more exclusively preoccupied with the development of characters than are those of Dickens. Our selections, in consequence, are restricted to one novel, and, within that novel, to a sequence of scenes in the life and development of one character, the heroine.

The Mill on the Floss, Eliot's second novel, was published in 1860. Set in a provincial town near the east coast of England, in the 1820's and 1830's, it records the education and tempestuous development, over a span of ten years, of Maggie Tulliver, whose father owns a water mill near the town of St. Ogg's. A precocious child, Maggie at the age of nine has read every book she can get her hands on. Her bookish tastes are not shared by her 13-year-old brother, Tom, to whom she is intensely attached. Tom regards education as a painful chore that he has to put up with because of his father's wishes. At the expensive private boarding school (where he is visited by Maggie) he is not happy, and he is almost relieved when the bankruptcy and illness of his father bring his schooling to an end and enable him to enter business, at which he excels. Maggie also is sent to boarding school for a period and likewise has to return home, at the age of 13, because of the family's misfortunes. She later continues her education by reading on her own, and, during the span of a year, by discussing her reading with Philip Wakem, the crippled son of a lawyer and a man of considerable sophistication, five years her senior. Her meetings with Philip have to be secret because of her brother's aversion to him; they are terminated when she is 17, shortly after Philip's proposing marriage to her.

Two years later they meet again while Maggie is on vacation from the schoolteaching which she had taken up, after the death of her father, in order to establish her independence. During this vacation she is faced with a whole series of painful choices. At 19, Maggie has matured from the dark, shaggy misfit of her childhood into an extraordinarily beautiful young woman who attracts the love of a second man, Stephen Guest, who up to the time of meeting her had been mildly in love with her cousin and closest friend, Lucy Deane. Maggie's struggles to choose between renunciation (as recommended by her earlier readings of Thomas à Kempis) and participation in the world of music and passion, to which she is powerfully inclined, are finally terminated by an autumnal flood in which she and her brother, Tom, are accidentally drowned (an incident not included in the following selections).

The Mill on the Floss could have been subtitled, like Eliot's later great novel *Middlemarch*, "A Study of Provincial Life." The book teems with portraits of Maggie's aunts and uncles, whose stolid, unimaginative lives form a vast backdrop against which we watch Maggie's struggles towards an identity of a different order. The following selections omit this background, to record stages in a girl's intellectual and emotional development in home and at school up to the point at which relationships with men become the overriding problem of her life.

As noted in the selections for *Dickens*, only recently have editors of Victorian novels begun applying modern methods of scholarship to provide reliably accurate texts. The following text of *The Mill on the Floss* is that prepared by the distinguished Eliot scholar Gordon Haight.

From The Mill on the Floss

[The Childhood of Maggie Tulliver][1]

[Mill Revisited]

broadening Floss hurries on between its . . . and the loving tide, rushing to meet it, checks its . . . with an impetuous embrace. On this mighty tide the black . . . laden with the fresh-scented fir-planks, with the . . . oil-bearing seed, or with the dark glitter of coal— and . . . to the town of St. Ogg's, which shows its aged, fluted . . . roofs and the broad gables of its wharves between the low wooded . . . and the river brink, tinging the water with a soft purple hue . . . the transient glance of this February sun. Far away on

1. . . . I, "Boy and Girl." Chapter 1, "Outside Dorlcote Mill."

each hand stretch the rich pastures, and the patches of dark earth, made ready for the seed of broad-leaved green crops, or touched already with the tint of the tender-bladed autumn-sown corn. There is a remnant still of the last year's golden clusters of beehive ricks rising at intervals beyond the hedgerows; and everywhere the hedgerows are studded with trees: the distant ships seem to be lifting their masts and stretching their red-brown sails close among the branches of the spreading ash. Just by the red-roofed town the tributary Ripple flows with a lively current into the Floss. How lovely the little river is, with its dark, changing wavelets! It seems to me like a living companion while I wander along the bank and listen to its low placid voice, as to the voice of one who is deaf and loving. I remember those large dipping willows. I remember the stone bridge.

And this is Dorlcote Mill. I must stand a minute or two here on the bridge and look at it, though the clouds are threatening, and it is far on in the afternoon. Even in this leafless time of departing February it is pleasant to look at—perhaps the chill damp season adds a charm to the trimly-kept, comfortable dwelling-house, as old as the elms and chestnuts that shelter it from the northern blast. The stream is brimful now, and lies high in this little withy plantation, and half drowns the grassy fringe of the croft[2] in front of the house. As I look at the full stream, the vivid grass, the delicate bright-green powder softening the outline of the great trunks and branches that gleam from under the bare purple boughs, I am in love with moistness, and envy the white ducks that are dipping their heads far into the water here among the withes, unmindful of the awkward appearance they make in the drier world above.

The rush of the water, and the booming of the mill, bring a dreamy deafness, which seems to heighten the peacefulness of the scene. They are like a great curtain of sound, shutting one out from the world beyond. And now there is the thunder of the huge covered wagon coming home with sacks of grain. That honest wagoner is thinking of his dinner, getting sadly dry in the oven at this late hour; but he will not touch it in his heart till he has fed his horses, the strong, submissive, meek-eyed beasts, who, I fancy, are looking mild reproach at him from between their blinkers, that he should crack his whip at them in that awful manner as if they needed that hint! See how they stretch their shoulders up the slope towards the bridge, with all the more energy because they are so near home. Look at their grand shaggy feet that seem to grasp the firm earth, at the patient strength of their necks, bowed under the heavy collar, at the mighty muscles of their struggling haunches! I should like well to hear them neigh over their hardly-earned feed of corn, and see them, with their moist necks freed from the harness, dip their

2. Patch of farmland adjacent to a house or cottage.

eager nostrils into the muddy pond. Now they are on the bridge, and down they go again at a swifter pace, and the arch of the covered wagon disappears at the turning behind the trees.

Now I can turn my eyes towards the mill again, and watch the unresting wheel sending out its diamond jets of water. That little girl is watching it too: she has been standing on just the same spot at the edge of the water ever since I paused on the bridge. And that queer white cur with the brown ear seems to be leaping and barking in ineffectual remonstrance with the wheel; perhaps he is jealous, because his playfellow in the beaver bonnet is so rapt in its movement. It is time the little playfellow went in, I think; and there is a very bright fire to tempt her: the red light shines out under the deepening gray of the sky. It is time, too, for me to leave off resting my arms on the cold stone of this bridge. . . .

Ah, my arms are really benumbed. I have been pressing my elbows on the arms of my chair, and dreaming that I was standing on the bridge in front of Dorlcote Mill, as it looked one February afternoon many years ago. Before I dozed off, I was going to tell you what Mr. and Mrs. Tulliver were talking about, as they sat by the bright fire in the left-hand parlor, on that very afternoon I have been dreaming of.

[Maggie Anticipates Her Brother's Return. Age Nine][3]

It was a heavy disappointment to Maggie that she was not allowed to go with her father in the gig when he went to fetch Tom home from the academy; but the morning was too wet, Mrs. Tulliver said, for a little girl to go out in her best bonnet. Maggie took the opposite view very strongly, and it was a direct consequence of this difference of opinion that when her mother was in the act of brushing out the reluctant black crop, Maggie suddenly rushed from under her hands and dipped her head in a basin of water standing near—in the vindictive determination that there should be no more chance of curls that day.

"Maggie, Maggie," exclaimed Mrs. Tulliver, sitting stout and helpless with the brushes on her lap, "what is to become of you if you're so naughty? I'll tell your aunt Glegg and your aunt Pullet when they come next week, and they'll never love you any more. O dear, O dear! look at your clean pinafore, wet from top to bottom. Folks 'ull think it's a judgment on me as I've got such a child—they'll think I've done summat wicked."

Before this remonstrance was finished, Maggie was already out of hearing, making her way towards the great attic that ran under the old high-pitched roof, shaking the water from her black locks as she ran, like a Skye terrier escaped from his bath. This attic was Mag-

---

3. Book I, "Boy and Girl." Chapter 4, "Tom Is Expected."

gie's favorite retreat on a wet day, when the weather was not too cold; here she fretted out all her ill-humors, and talked aloud to the worm-eaten floors and the worm-eaten shelves, and the dark rafters festooned with cobwebs; and here she kept a Fetish which she punished for all her misfortunes. This was the trunk of a large wooden doll, which once stared with the roundest of eyes above the reddest of cheeks; but was now entirely defaced by a long career of vicarious suffering. Three nails driven into the head commemorated as many crises in Maggie's nine years of earthly struggle; that luxury of vengeance having been suggested to her by the picture of Jael destroying Sisera in the old Bible.[4] The last nail had been driven in with a fiercer stroke than usual, for the Fetish on that occasion represented aunt Glegg. But immediately afterwards Maggie had reflected that if she drove many nails in, she would not be so well able to fancy that the head was hurt when she knocked it against the wall, nor to comfort it, and make believe to poultice it, when her fury was abated; for even aunt Glegg would be pitiable when she had been hurt very much, and thoroughly humiliated, so as to beg her niece's pardon. Since then she had driven no more nails in, but had soothed herself by alternately grinding and beating the wooden head against the rough brick of the great chimneys that made two square pillars supporting the roof. That was what she did this morning on reaching the attic, sobbing all the while with a passion that expelled every other form of consciousness—even the memory of the grievance that had caused it. As at last the sobs were getting quieter, and the grinding less fierce, a sudden beam of sunshine, falling through the wire lattice across the worm-eaten shelves, made her throw away the Fetish and run to the window. The sun was really breaking out; the sound of the mill seemed cheerful again; the granary doors were open; and there was Yap, the queer white-and-brown terrier, with one ear turned back, trotting about and sniffing vaguely, as if he were in search of a companion. It was irresistible. Maggie tossed her hair back and ran downstairs, seized her bonnet without putting it on, peeped, and then dashed along the passage lest she should encounter her mother, and was quickly out in the yard, whirling round like a Pythoness, and singing as she whirled, "Yap, Yap, Tom's coming home!" while Yap danced and barked round her, as much as to say, if there was any noise wanted he was the dog for it.

* * *

[A Reunion with Tom. Age Nine][5]

Tom was to arrive early in the afternoon, and there was another fluttering heart besides Maggie's when it was late enough for the

4. See Judges v.24–31. Sisera, leader of an invasion against Israel, was slain by a woman, Jael, who hammered a nail into his head.
5. Book I, "Boy and Girl." From Chapter 5, "Tom Comes Home."

sound of the gig-wheels to be expected; for if Mrs. Tulliver had a strong feeling, it was fondness for her boy. At last the sound came —that quick light bowling of the gig-wheels—and in spite of the wind, which was blowing the clouds about, and was not likely to respect Mrs. Tulliver's curls and cap-strings, she came outside the door, and even held her hand on Maggie's offending head, forgetting all the griefs of the morning.

"There he is, my sweet lad! But, Lord ha' mercy! he's got never a collar on; it's been lost on the road, I'll be bound, and spoilt the set."

Mrs. Tulliver stood with her arms open; Maggie jumped first on one leg and then on the other; while Tom descended from the gig, and said, with masculine reticence as to the tender emotions, "Hallo! Yap—what! are you there?"

Nevertheless he submitted to be kissed willingly enough, though Maggie hung on his neck in rather a strangling fashion, while his blue-gray eyes wandered towards the croft and the lambs and the river, where he promised himself that he would begin to fish the first thing tomorrow morning. He was one of those lads that grow everywhere in England, and, at twelve or thirteen years of age, look as much alike as goslings:—a lad with light-brown hair, cheeks of cream and roses, full lips, indeterminate nose and eyebrows—a physiogonomy in which it seems impossible to discern anything but the generic character of boyhood; as different as possible from poor Maggie's phiz, which Nature seemed to have molded and colored with the most decided intention. But that same Nature has the deep cunning which hides itself under the appearance of openness, so that simple people think they can see through her quite well, and all the while she is secretly preparing a refutation of their confident prophecies. Under these average boyish physiognomies that she seems to turn off by the gross, she conceals some of her most rigid, inflexible purposes, some of her most unmodifiable characters; and the dark-eyed, demonstrative, rebellious girl may after all turn out to be a passive being compared with this pink-and-white bit of masculinity with the indeterminate features.

"Maggie," said Tom, confidentially, taking her into a corner, as soon as his mother was gone out to examine his box, and the warm parlor had taken off the chill he had felt from the long drive, "you don't know what I've got in *my* pockets," nodding his head up and down as a means of rousing her sense of mystery.

"No," said Maggie. "How stodgy they look, Tom! Is it marls (marbles) or cobnuts?" Maggie's heart sank a little, because Tom always said it was "no good" playing with *her* at those games—she played so badly.

"Marls! no; I've swopped all my marls with the little fellows, and cobnuts are no fun, you silly, only when the nuts are green. But see here!" He drew something half out of his right-hand pocket.

"What is it?" said Maggie, in a whisper. "I can see nothing but a bit of yellow."

"Why it's . . . a . . . new . . . guess, Maggie!"

"O, I *can't* guess, Tom," said Maggie, impatiently.

"Don't be a spitfire, else I won't tell you," said Tom, thrusting his hand back into his pocket, and looking determined.

"No, Tom," said Maggie, imploringly, laying hold of the arm that was held stiffly in the pocket. "I'm not cross, Tom; it was only because I can't bear guessing. *Please* be good to me."

Tom's arm slowly relaxed, and he said, "Well, then it's a new fishline—two new uns—one for you, Maggie, all to yourself. I wouldn't go halves in the toffee and gingerbread on purpose to save the money; and Gibson and Spouncer fought with me because I wouldn't. And here's hooks; see here! . . . I say, *won't* we go and fish tomorrow down by the Round Pool? And you shall catch your own fish, Maggie, and put the worms on, and everything—won't it be fun?"

Maggie's answer was to throw her arms round Tom's neck and hug him, and hold her cheek against his without speaking, while he slowly unwound some of the line, saying, after a pause,

"Wasn't I a good brother, now, to buy you a line all to yourself? You know, I needn't have bought it, if I hadn't liked."

"Yes, very, very good . . . I *do* love you, Tom."

Tom had put the line back in his pocket, and was looking at the hooks one by one, before he spoke again.

"And the fellows fought me, because I wouldn't give in about the toffee."

"O dear! I wish they wouldn't fight at your school, Tom. Didn't it hurt you?"

"Hurt me? no," said Tom, putting up the hooks again, taking out a large pocket-knife, and slowly opening the largest blade, which he looked at meditatively as he rubbed his finger along it. Then he added—

"I gave Spouncer a black eye, I know—that's what he got by wanting to leather *me*; I wasn't going to go halves because anybody leathered me."

"O how brave you are, Tom! I think you're like Samson. If there came a lion roaring at me, I think you'd fight him—wouldn't you, Tom?"

"How can a lion come roaring at you, you silly thing? There's no lions, only in the shows."

"No; but if we were in the lion countries—I mean Africa, where it's very hot—the lions eat people there. I can show it you in the book where I read it."

"Well, I should get a gun and shoot him."

"But if you hadn't got a gun—we might have gone out, you know, not thinking—just as we go fishing; and then a great lion might run towards us roaring, and we couldn't get away from him. What should you do, Tom?"

Tom paused, and at last turned away contemptuously, saying, "But the lion *isn't* coming. What's the use of talking?"

"But I like to fancy how it would be," said Maggie, following him. "Just think what you would do, Tom."

"O don't bother, Maggie! you're such a silly—I shall go and see my rabbits."

Maggie's heart began to flutter with fear. She dared not tell the sad truth at once, but she walked after Tom in trembling silence as he went out, thinking how she could tell him the news so as to soften at once his sorrow and his anger; for Maggie dreaded Tom's anger of all things—it was quite a different anger from her own.

"Tom," she said, timidly, when they were out of doors, "how much money did you give for your rabbits?"

"Two half-crowns and a sixpence," said Tom, promptly.

"I think I've got a deal more than that in my steel purse upstairs. I'll ask mother to give it you."

"What for?" said Tom. "I don't want *your* money, you silly thing. I've got a great deal more money than you, because I'm a boy. I always have half-sovereigns and sovereigns for my Christmas boxes, because I shall be a man, and you only have five-shilling pieces, because you're only a girl."

"Well, but, Tom—if mother would let me give you two half-crowns and a sixpence out of my purse to put into your pocket and spend, you know; and buy some more rabbits with it?"

"More rabbits? I don't want any more."

"O, but, Tom, they're all dead."

Tom stopped immediately in his walk and turned round towards Maggie. "You forgot to feed 'em, then, and Harry forgot?" he said, his color heightening for a moment, but soon subsiding. "I'll pitch into Harry—I'll have him turned away. And I don't love you, Maggie. You shan't go fishing with me tomorrow. I told you to go and see the rabbits every day." He walked on again.

"Yes, but I forgot—and I couldn't help it, indeed, Tom. I'm so very sorry," said Maggie, while the tears rushed fast.

"You're a naughty girl," said Tom, severely, "and I'm sorry I bought you the fish-line. I don't love you."

"O, Tom, it's very cruel," sobbed Maggie. "I'd forgive you, if *you* forgot anything—I wouldn't mind what you did—I'd forgive you and love you."

"Yes, you're a silly—but I never *do* forget things—I don't."

"O, please forgive me, Tom; my heart will break," said Maggie, shaking with sobs, clinging to Tom's arm, and laying her wet cheek on his shoulder.

Tom shook her off, and stopped again, saying in a peremptory tone, "Now, Maggie, you just listen. Aren't I a good brother to you?"

"Ye-ye-es," sobbbed Maggie, her chin rising and falling convulsedly.

"Didn't I think about your fish-line all this quarter, and mean to buy it, and saved my money o' purpose, and wouldn't go halves in the toffee, and Spouncer fought me because I wouldn't?"

"Ye-ye-es . . . and I . . . lo-lo-love you so, Tom."

"But you're a naughty girl. Last holidays you licked the paint off my lozenge box, and the holidays before that you let the boat drag my fish-line down when I'd set you to watch it, and you pushed your head through my kite, all for nothing."

"But I didn't mean," said Maggie; "I couldn't help it."

"Yes, you could," said Tom, "if you'd minded what you were doing. And you're a naughty girl, and you shan't go fishing with me tomorrow."

With this terrible conclusion, Tom ran away from Maggie towards the mill, meaning to greet Luke there, and complain to him of Harry.

Maggie stood motionless, except from her sobs, for a minute or two; then she turned round and ran into the house, and up to her attic, where she sat on the floor, and laid her head against the worm-eaten shelf, with a crushing sense of misery. Tom was come home, and she had thought how happy she should be—and now he was cruel to her. What use was anything, if Tom didn't love her? O, he was very cruel! Hadn't she wanted to give him the money, and said how very sorry she was? She knew she was naughty to her mother, but she had never been naughty to Tom—had never *meant* to be naughty to him.

"O, he is cruel!" Maggie sobbed aloud, finding a wretched pleasure in the hollow resonance that came through the empty space of the attic. She never thought of beating or grinding her Fetish; she was too miserable to be angry.

These bitter sorrows of childhood! when sorrow is all new and strange, when hope has not yet got wings to fly beyond the days and weeks, and the space from summer to summer seems measureless.

Maggie soon thought she had been hours in the attic, and it must be tea-time, and they were all having their tea, and not thinking of her. Well, then, she would stay up there and starve herself—hide herself behind the tub, and stay there all night; and then they would all be frightened, and Tom would be sorry. Thus Maggie thought in the pride of her heart, as she crept behind the tub; but presently she began to cry again at the idea that they didn't mind her being there. If she went down again to Tom now—would he forgive her?—perhaps her father would be there, and he would take her part. But, then, she wanted Tom to forgive her because he loved her, not because his father told him. No, she would never go down if Tom didn't come to fetch her. This resolution lasted in great intensity for five dark minutes behind the tub; but then the need of being loved, the strongest need in poor Maggie's nature, began to wrestle with her pride, and soon threw it. She crept from behind her tub into the twilight of the long attic, but just then she heard a quick footstep on the stairs.

Tom had been too much interested in his talk with Luke, in going the round of the premises, walking in and out where he pleased, and whittling sticks without any particular reason, except that he didn't whittle sticks at school, to think of Maggie and the effect his anger had produced on her. He meant to punish her, and that business having been performed, he occupied himself with other matters, like a practical person. But when he had been called in to tea, his father said, "Why, where's the little wench?" and Mrs. Tulliver, almost at the same moment said, "Where's your little sister?"—both of them having supposed that Maggie and Tom had been together all the afternoon.

"I don't know," said Tom. He didn't want to "tell" of Maggie, though he was angry with her; for Tom Tulliver was a lad of honor.

"What! hasn't she been playing with you all this while?" said the father. "She'd been thinking o' nothing but your coming home."

"I haven't seen her this two hours," says Tom, commencing on the plumcake.

"Goodness heart! she's got drownded," exclaimed Mrs. Tulliver, rising from her seat and running to the window. "How could you let her do so?" she added, as became a fearful woman, accusing she didn't know whom of she didn't know what.

"Nay, nay, she's none drownded," said Mr. Tulliver. "You've been naughty to her, I doubt, Tom?"

"I'm sure I haven't, father," said Tom, indignantly. "I think she's in the house."

"Perhaps up in that attic," said Mrs. Tulliver, "a-singing and talking to herself, and forgetting all about mealtimes."

"You go and fetch her down, Tom," said Mr. Tulliver, rather sharply, his perspicacity or his fatherly fondness for Maggie making him suspect that the lad had been hard upon "the little un," else she would never have left his side. "And be good to her, do you hear? Else I'll let you know better."

Tom never disobeyed his father, for Mr. Tulliver was a peremptory man, and, as he said, would never let anybody get hold of his whip-hand; but he went out rather sullenly, carrying his piece of plumcake, and not intending to reprieve Maggie's punishment, which was no more than she deserved. Tom was only thirteen, and had no decided views in grammar and arithmetic, regarding them for the most part as open questions, but he was particularly clear and positive on one point—namely, that he would punish everybody who deserved it: why, he wouldn't have minded being punished himself, if he deserved it; but, then, he never *did* deserve it.

It was Tom's step, then, that Maggie heard on the stairs, when her need of love had triumphed over her pride, and she was going down with her swollen eyes and dishevelled hair to beg for pity. At least her father would stroke her head and say, "Never mind, my wench." It is a wonderful subduer, this need of love—this hunger of the heart—as peremptory as that other hunger by which Nature forces us to submit to the yoke, and change the face of the world.

But she knew Tom's step, and her heart began to beat violently with the sudden shock of hope. He only stood still at the top of the stairs and said, "Maggie, you're to come down." But she rushed to him and clung round his neck, sobbing, "O Tom, please forgive me —I can't bear it—I will always be good—always remember things —do love me—please, dear Tom!"

We learn to restrain ourselves as we get older. We keep apart when we have quarrelled, express ourselves in well-bred phrases, and in this way preserve a dignified alienation, showing much firmness on one side, and swallowing much grief on the other. We no longer approximate in our behavior to the mere impulsiveness of the lower animals, but conduct ourselves in every respect like members of a highly civilized society. Maggie and Tom were still very much like young animals, and so she could rub her cheek against his, and kiss his ear in a random, sobbing way; and there were tender fibers in the lad that had been used to answer to Maggie's fondling; so that he behaved with a weakness quite inconsistent with his resolution to punish her as much as she deserved: he actually began to kiss her in return, and say—

"Don't cry, then, Magsie—here, eat a bit o' cake."

Maggie's sobs began to subside, and she put out her mouth for the cake and bit a piece: and then Tom bit a piece, just for company, and they ate together and rubbed each other's cheeks and brows and noses together, while they ate, with a humiliating resemblance to two friendly ponies.

"Come along, Magsie, and have tea," said Tom at last, when there was no more cake except what was downstairs.

So ended the sorrows of this day, and the next morning Maggie was trotting with her own fishing-rod in one hand and a handle of the basket in the other, stepping always, by a peculiar gift, in the muddiest places, and looking darkly radiant under her beaver-bonnet because Tom was good to her. She had told Tom, however, that she should like him to put the worms on the hook for her, although she accepted his word when he assured her that worms couldn't feel (it was Tom's private opinion that it didn't much matter if they did). He knew all about worms, and fish, and those things; and what birds were mischievous, and how padlocks opened, and which way the handles of the gates were to be lifted. Maggie thought this sort of knowledge was very wonderful—much more difficult than remembering what was in the books; and she was rather in awe of Tom's superiority, for he was the only person who called her knowledge "stuff," and did not feel surprised at her cleverness. Tom, indeed, was of opinion that Maggie was a silly little thing; all girls were silly—they couldn't throw a stone so as to hit anything, couldn't do anything with a pocket-knife, and were frightened at frogs. Still he was very fond of his sister, and meant always to take care of her, make her his housekeeper, and punish her when she did wrong.

They were on their way to the Round Pool—that wonderful pool, which the floods had made a long while ago: no one knew how deep it was; and it was mysterious, too, that it should be almost a perfect round, framed in with willows and tall reeds, so that the water was only to be seen when you got close to the brink. The sight of the old favorite spot always heightened Tom's good-humor, and he spoke to Maggie in the most amicable whispers, as he opened the precious basket, and prepared their tackle. He threw her line for her, and put the rod into her hand. Mgagie thought it probable that the small fish would come to her hook, and the large ones to Tom's. But she had forgotten all about the fish, and was looking dreamily at the glassy water, when Tom said, in a loud whisper, "Look, look, Maggie!" and came running to prevent her from snatching her line away.

Maggie was frightened lest she had been doing something wrong, as usual, but presently Tom drew out her line and brought a large tench bouncing on the grass.

Tom was excited.

"O Magsie! you little duck! Empty the basket."

Maggie was not conscious of unusual merit, but it was enough that Tom called her Magsie, and was pleased with her. There was nothing to mar her delight in the whispers and the dreamy silences, when she listened to the light dipping sounds of the rising fish, and the gentle rustling, as if the willows and the reeds and the water had their happy whisperings also. Maggie thought it would make a very nice heaven to sit by the pool in that way, and never be scolded. She never knew she had a bite till Tom told her; but she liked fishing very much.

It was one of their happy mornings. They trotted along and sat down together, with no thought that life would ever change much for them: they would only get bigger and not to go school, and it would always be like the holidays; they would always live together and be fond of each other. And the mill with its booming—the great chestnut-tree under which they played at houses—their own little river, the Ripple, where the banks seemed like home, and Tom was always seeing the water-rats, while Maggie gathered the purple plumy tops of the reeds, which she forgot and dropped afterwards—above all, the great Floss, along which they wandered with a sense of travel, to see the rushing spring-tide, the awful Eager, come up like a hungry monster, or to see the Great Ash which had once wailed and groaned like a man—these things would always be just the same to them. Tom thought people were at a disadvantage who lived on any other spot of the globe; and Maggie, when she read about Christiana passing "the river over which there is no bridge,"[6] always saw the Floss between the green pastures by the Great Ash.

Life did change for Tom and Maggie; and yet they were not wrong in believing that the thoughts and loves of these first years would always make part of their lives. We could never have loved the earth so well if we had had no childhood in it,—if it were not the earth where the same flowers come up again every spring that we used to gather with our tiny fingers as we sat lisping to ourselves on the grass—the same hips and haws on the autumn hedgerows—the same redbreasts that we used to call "God's birds," because they did no harm to the precious crops. What novelty is worth that sweet monotony where everything is known, and *loved* because it is known?

The wood I walk in on this mild May day, with the young yellow-brown foliage of the oaks between me and the blue sky, the white star-flowers and the blue-eyed speedwell and the ground ivy at my feet—what grove of tropic palms, what strange ferns or splendid broad-petaled blossoms, could ever thrill such deep and delicate fibres within me as this home-scene? These familiar flowers, these well-remembered bird-notes, this sky, with its fitful brightness, these furrowed and grassy fields, each with a sort of personality given to it by the capricious hedgerows—such things as these are the mother tongue of our imagination, the language that is laden with all the subtle inextricable associations the fleeting hours of our childhood left behind them. Our delight in the sunshine on the deep-bladed grass today, might be no more than the faint perception of wearied souls, if it were not for the sunshine and the grass in the far-off years which still live in us,[7] and transform our perception into love.

6. Christiana, in Bunyan's *Pilgrim's Progress*, ends her pilgrimage by crossing the river to the Celestial City, "the river where there is no bridge."
7. Cf. Wordsworth, e.g., *Ode: Intimations of Immortality*, sections 9–10.

[*Maggie Visits Tom's Boarding-School. Age 10*][8]

* * * And O how Tom longed for playfellows! In his secret heart he yearned to have Maggie with him, and was almost ready to dote on her exasperating acts of forgetfulness; though, when he was at home, he always represented it as a great favor on his part to let Maggie trot by his side on his pleasure excursions.

And before this dreary half-year was ended, Maggie actually came. Mrs. Stelling had given a general invitation for the little girl to come and stay with her brother: so when Mr. Tulliver drove over to King's Lorton late in October, Maggie came too, with the sense that she was taking a great journey, and beginning to see the world. It was Mr. Tulliver's first visit to see Tom, for the lad must learn not to think too much about home.

"Well, my lad," he said to Tom, when Mr. Stelling had left the room to announce the arrival to his wife, and Maggie had begun to kiss Tom freely, "you look rarely! School agrees with you."

Tom wished he had looked rather ill.

"I don't think I *am* well, father," said Tom; "I wish you'd ask Mr. Stelling not to let me do Euclid—it brings on the toothache, I think."

(The toothache was the only malady to which Tom had ever been subject.)

"Euclid, my lad—why, what's that?" said Mr. Tulliver.

"O, I don't know: it's definitions, and axioms, and triangles, and things. It's a book I've got to learn in—there's no sense in it."

"Go, go!" said Mr. Tulliver, reprovingly, "you mustn't say so. You must learn what your master tells you. He knows what it's right for you to learn."

"*I'll* help you now, Tom," said Maggie, with a little air of patronizing consolation. "I'm come to stay ever so long, if Mrs. Stelling asks me. I've brought my box and my pinafores, haven't I, father?"

"*You* help me, you silly little thing!" and Tom, in such high spirits at this announcement that he quite enjoyed the idea of confounding Maggie by showing her a page of Euclid. "I should like to see you doing one of *my* lessons! Why, I learn Latin too! Girls never learn such things. They're too silly."

'I know what Latin is very well," said Maggie, confidently. "Latin's a language. There are Latin words in the Dictionary. There's bonus, a gift."

"Now, you're just wrong there, Miss Maggie!" said Tom, secretly astonished. "You think you're very wise! But 'bonus' means 'good,' as it happens—bonus, bona, bonum."

8. Book II, "School Time." From Chapter 1, "Tom's First Half."

"Well, that's no reason why it shouldn't mean 'gift,' " said Maggie, stoutly. "It may mean several things—almost every word does. There's 'lawn,'—it means the grass-plot, as well as the stuff pocket-handkerchiefs are made of."

"Well done, little 'un," said Mr. Tulliver, laughing, while Tom felt rather disgusted with Maggie's knowingness, though beyond measure cheerful at the thought that she was going to stay with him. Her conceit would soon be overawed by the actual inspection of his books.

Mrs. Stelling, in her pressing invitation, did not mention a longer time than a week for Maggie's stay; but Mr. Stelling, who took her between his knees, and asked her where she stole her dark eyes from, insisted that she must stay a fortnight. Maggie thought Mr. Stelling was a charming man, and Mr. Tulliver was quite proud to leave his little wench where she would have an opportunity of showing her cleverness to appreciating strangers. So it was agreed that she should not be fetched home till the end of the fortnight.

"Now, then, come with me into the study, Maggie," said Tom, as their father drove away. "What do you shake and toss your head now for, you silly?" he continued; for though her hair was now under a new dispensation, and was brushed smoothly behind her ears, she seemed still in imagination to be tossing it out of her eyes. "It makes you look as if you were crazy."

"O, I can't help it," said Maggie, impatiently. "Don't tease me, Tom. O, what books!" she exclaimed, as she saw the bookcases in the study. "How I should like to have as many books as that!"

"Why, you couldn't read one of 'em," said Tom, triumphantly. "They're all Latin."

"No, they aren't," said Maggie. "I can read the back of this . . . History of the Decline and Fall of the Roman Empire."

"Well, what does that mean? *You* don't know," said Tom, wagging his head.

"But I could soon find out," said Maggie, scornfully.

"Why, how?"

"I should look inside, and see what it was about."

"You'd better not, Miss Maggie," said Tom, seeing her hand on the volume. "Mr. Stelling lets nobody touch his books without leave, and I shall catch it, if you take it out."

"O, very well! Let me see all *your* books, then," said Maggie, turning to throw her arms around Tom's neck, and rub his cheek with her small round nose.

Tom, in the gladness of his heart at having dear old Maggie to dispute with and crow over again, seized her round the waist, and began to jump with her round the large library table. Away they jumped with more and more vigor, till Maggie's hair flew from behind her ears, and twirled about like an animated mop. But the

revolutions round the table became more and more irregular in their
sweep, till at least reaching Mr. Stelling's reading-stand, they sent it
thundering down with its heavy lexicons to the floor. Happily it was
the ground-floor, and the study was a one-storied wing to the house,
so that the downfall made no alarming resonance, though Tom
stood dizzy and aghast for a few minutes, dreading the appearance
of Mr. and Mrs. Stelling.

"O, I say, Maggie," said Tom at last, lifting up the stand, "we
must keep quiet here, you know. If we break anything, Mrs. Stelling
'll make us cry peccavi."[9]

"What's that?" said Maggie.

"O, it's the Latin for a good scolding," said Tom, not without
some pride in his knowledge.

"Is she a cross woman?" said Maggie.

"I believe you!" said Tom, with an emphatic nod.

"I think all women are crosser than men," said Maggie. "Aunt
Glegg's a great deal crosser than Uncle Glegg, and mother scolds
me more than father does."

"Well, *you'll* be a woman some day," said Tom, "so *you* needn't
talk."

"But I shall be a *clever* woman," said Maggie, with a toss.

"O, I daresay, and a nasty conceited thing. Everybody 'll hate
you."

"But you oughtn't to hate me, Tom: it'll be very wicked of you,
for I shall be your sister."

"Yes, but if you're a nasty disagreeable thing, I *shall* hate you."

"O but, Tom, you won't! I shan't be disagreeable. I shall be very
good to you—and I shall be good to everybody. You won't hate me
really, will you, Tom?"

"O, bother! never mind! Come, it's time for me to learn my lessons. See here! what I've got to do," said Tom, drawing Maggie
towards him and showing her his theorem, while she pushed her
hair behind her ears, and prepared herself to prove her capability of
helping him in Euclid. She began to read with full confidence in
her own powers, but presently, becoming quite bewildered, her face
flushed with irritation. It was unavoidable—she must confess her
incompetency, and she was not fond of humiliation.

"It's nonsense!" she said, "and very ugly stuff—nobody need
want to make it out."

"Ah, there now, Miss Maggie!" said Tom, drawing the book
away, and wagging his head at her, "you see you're not so clever as
you thought you were."

"O," said Maggie, pouting, "I daresay I could make it out, if I'd
learned what goes before, as you have."

9. "I have sinned."

"But that's what you just couldn't, Miss Wisdom," said Tom. "For it's all the harder when you know what goes before: for then you've got to say what definition 3. is and what axiom V. is. But get along with you now: I must go on with this. Here's the Latin Grammar. See what you can make of that."

Maggie found the Latin Grammar quite soothing after her mathematical mortification; for she delighted in new words, and quickly found that there was an English Key at the end, which would make her very wise about Latin, at slight expense. She presently made up her mind to skip the rules in the Syntax—the examples became so absorbing. These mysterious sentences, snatched from an unknown context,—like strange horns of beasts, and leaves of unknown plants, brought from some far-off region,—gave boundless scope to her imagination, and were all the more fascinating because they were in a peculiar tongue of their own, which she could learn to interpret. It was really very interesting—the Latin Grammar that Tom had said no girls could learn: and she was proud because she found it interesting. The most fragmentary examples were her favorites. *Mors omnibus est communis*[1] would have been jejune, only she liked to know the Latin; but the fortunate gentleman whom every one congratulated because he had a son "endowed with *such* a disposition"[2] afforded her a great deal of pleasant conjecture, and she was quite lost in the "thick grove penetrable by no star," when Tom called out,

"Now, then, Magsie, give us the Grammar!"

"O, Tom, it's such a pretty book!" she said, as she jumped out of the large armchair to give it him; "it's much prettier than the Dictionary. I could learn Latin very soon. I don't think it's at all hard."

"O, I know what you've been doing," said Tom; "you've been reading the English at the end. Any donkey can do that."

Tom seized the book and opened it with a determined and businesslike air, as much as to say that he had a lesson to learn which no donkeys would find themselves equal to. Maggie, rather piqued, turned to the bookcases to amuse herself with puzzling out the titles.

Presently Tom called to her: "Here, Magsie, come and hear if I can say this. Stand at that end of the table, where Mr. Stelling sits when he hears me."

Maggie obeyed, and took the open book.

"Where do you begin, Tom?"

---

1. "Death is common to us all"—Cicero.
2. According to Gordon Haight's edition of *The Mill on the Floss*, this passage (translated from Terence) and all the following passages are from *The Eton Latin Grammar*, ed. T. W. C. Edwards, 24th ed., 1850. This popular textbook illustrated grammatical rules with quotations from classical authors. As Haight shows, the quotation about the "thick grove" is from Statius.

"O, I begin at '*Appellativa arborum*,'"[3] because I say all over again what I've been learning this week."

Tom sailed along pretty well for three lines; and Maggie was beginning to forget her office of prompter in speculating as to what *mas* could mean, which came twice over, when he stuck fast at *Sunt etiam volucrum*. . . .

"Don't tell me, Maggie; *Sunt etiam volucrum . . . Sunt etiam volucrum . . . ut ostrea, cetus*. . . ."

"No," said Maggie, opening her mouth and shaking her head.

"*Sunt etiam volucrum*," said Tom, very slowly, as if the next words might be expected to come sooner when he gave them this strong hint that they were waited for.

"C, e, u," said Maggie, getting impatient.

"O, I know—hold your tongue," said Tom. "*Ceu passer, hirundo; Ferarum . . . ferarum*. . . ." Tom took his pencil and made several hard dots with it on his book-cover . . . "*ferarum*. . . ."

"O dear, O dear, Tom," said Maggie, "what a time you are! *Ut*. . . ."

"*Ut, ostrea*. . . ."

"No, no," said Maggie, "*ut, tigris*. . . ."

"O yes, now I can do," said Tom; "it was *tigris, vulpes*, I'd forgotten: *ut tigris, vulpes; et Piscium*."[4]

With some further stammering and repetition, Tom got through the next few lines.

"Now, then," he said, "the next is what I've just learnt for tomorrow. Give me hold of the book a minute."

After some whispered gabbling, assisted by the beating of his fist on the table, Tom returned the book.

"*Mascula nomina in a*,[5] he began.

"No, Tom," said Maggie, "that doesn't come next. Its *Nomen non creskens genittivo*. . . ."

"*Creskens genittivo*," exclaimed Tom, with a derisive laugh, for Tom had learned this omitted passage for his yesterday's lesson, and a young gentleman does not require an intimate or extensive acquaintance with Latin before he can feel the pitiable absurdity of a false quantity. "*Creskens genittivo!* What a little silly you are, Maggie!"

"Well, you needn't laugh, Tom, for you didn't remember it at

---

3. "The names of trees." Tom has been memorizing rules for the masculine (*mas*) gender of nouns involving the Latin name for trees, birds, animals, and fishes, classifications which he mixes up. Thus *Sunt etiam volucrum* ("There are also birds") should be exemplified by *ceu passer, hirundo* ("such as a sparrow, a swallow"). Tom, instead, exemplifies as birds *ut ostrea, cetus* ("such as an oyster, a whale").
4. Under *Ferarum* ("of wild animals") Tom should have cited as examples the tiger and fox: (*ut, tigris, vulpes*). Instead he exemplifies animals by *ut, ostrea* ("for example, an oyster"). The fourth classification, *Piscium*, is for fish.
5. "Masculine nouns ending in *a*."

all. I'm sure it's spelt so; how was I to know?"

"Phee-e-e-h! I told you girls couldn't learn Latin. It's *Nomen non crescens genitivo.*"[6]

"Very well, then," said Maggie, pouting. "I can say that as well as you can. And you don't mind your stops. For you ought to stop twice as long at a semicolon as you do at a comma, and you make the longest stops where there ought to be no stop at all."

"O, well, don't chatter. Let me go on."

They were presently fetched to spend the rest of the evening in the drawing-room, and Maggie became so animated with Mr. Stelling, who, she felt sure, admired her cleverness, that Tom was rather amazed and alarmed at her audacity. But she was suddenly subdued by Mr. Stelling's alluding to a little girl of whom he had heard that she once ran away to the gypsies.

"What a very odd little girl that must be!" said Mrs. Stelling, meaning to be playful—but a playfulness that turned on her supposed oddity was not at all to Maggie's taste. She feared that Mr. Stelling, after all, did not think much of her, and went to bed in rather low spirits. Mrs. Stelling, she felt, looked at her as if she thought her hair was very ugly because it hung down straight behind.

Nevertheless it was a very happy fortnight to Maggie, this visit to Tom. She was allowed to be in the study while he had his lessons, and in her various readings got very deep into the examples in the Latin Grammar. The astronomer who hated women generally,[7] caused her so much puzzling speculation that she one day asked Mr. Stelling if all astronomers hated women, or whether it was only this particular astronomer. But, forestalling his answer, she said,

"I suppose it's all astronomers: because, you know, they live up in high towers, and if the women came there, they might talk and hinder them from looking at the stars."

Mr. Stelling liked her prattle immensely, and they were on the best terms. She told Tom she should like to go to school to Mr. Stelling, as he did, and learn just the same things. She knew she could do Euclid, for she had looked into it again, and she saw what A B C meant: they were the names of the lines.

"I'm sure you couldn't do it, now," said Tom; "and I'll just ask Mr. Stelling if you could."

"I don't mind," said the little conceited minx. "I'll ask him myself."

"Mr. Stelling," she said, that same evening when they were in

---

6. "Nouns not increasing [the number of syllables] for the genitive case"—the dispute about "false quantity" concerned which syllable of *genitivo* should be stressed. Also in dispute was whether the second *c* in *crescens* should be hard or soft.

7. The textbook, presumably to illustrate a nice point about the phrase *ad unam*, meaning "generally," had cited as an example: "Astronomus exosus ad unam mulieres" [Haight's note].

the drawing-room, "couldn't I do Euclid, and all Tom's lessons, if you were to teach me instead of him?"

"No; you couldn't," said Tom, indignantly. "Girls can't do Euclid: can they, sir?"

"They can pick up a little of everything, I daresay," said Mr. Stelling. "They've a great deal of superficial cleverness; but they couldn't go far into anything. They're quick and shallow."

Tom, delighted with this verdict, telegraphed his triumph by wagging his head at Maggie behind Mr. Stelling's chair. As for Maggie, she had hardly ever been so mortified. She had been so proud to be called "quick" all her little life, and now it appeared that this quickness was the brand of inferiority. It would have been better to be slow, like Tom.

"Ha, ha! Miss Maggie!" said Tom, when they were alone; "you see it's not such a fine thing to be quick. You'll never go far into anything, you know."

And Maggie was so oppressed by this dreadful destiny that she had no spirit for a retort.

But when this small apparatus of shallow quickness was fetched away in the gig by Luke, and the study was once more quite lonely for Tom, he missed her grievously. He had really been brighter, and had got through his lessons better, since she had been there; and she had asked Mr. Stelling so many questions about the Roman empire, and whether there really ever was a man who said, in Latin, "I would not buy it for a farthing or a rotten nut," or whether that had only been turned into Latin, that Tom had actually come to a dim understanding of the fact that there had once been people upon the earth who were so fortunate as to know Latin without learning it through the medium of the Eton Grammar. This luminous idea was a great addition to his historical acquirements during this half-year, which were otherwise confined to an epitomized history of the Jews.

But the dreary half-year *did* come to an end. How glad Tom was to see the last yellow leaves fluttering before the cold wind! The dark afternoons, and the first December snow, seemed to him far livelier than the August sunshine; and that he might make himself the surer about the flight of the days that were carrying him homeward, he stuck twenty-one sticks deep in a corner of the garden, when he was three weeks from the holidays, and pulled one up every day with a great wrench, throwing it to a distance with a vigor of will which would have carried it to limbo, if it had been in the nature of sticks to travel so far.

But it was worth purchasing, even at the heavy price of the Latin Grammar—the happiness of seeing the bright light in the parlor at home, as the gig passed noiselessly over the snow-covered bridge; the happiness of passing from the cold air to the warmth and the kisses and the smiles of that familiar hearth, where the pattern of the rug and the grate and the fire-irons were "first ideas" that it was no more possible to criticize than the solidity and extension of matter. There is no sense of ease like the ease we felt in those scenes where we were born, where objects became dear to us before we had known the labor of choice, and where the outer world seemed only an extension of our own personality: we accepted and loved it as we accepted our own sense of existence and our own limbs. Very commonplace, even ugly, that furniture of our early home might look if it were put up to auction; an improved taste in upholstery scorns it; and is not the striving after something better and better in our surroundings, the grand characteristic that distinguishes man from the brute—or, to satisfy a scrupulous accuracy of definition, that distinguishes the British man from the foreign brute? But heaven knows where that striving might lead us, if our affections had not a trick of twining round those old inferior things —if the loves and sanctities of our life had no deep immovable roots in memory. One's delight in an elderberry bush overhanging the confused leafage of a hedgerow bank, as a more gladdening sight than the finest cistus or fuchsia spreading itself on the softest undulating turf, is an entirely unjustifiable preference to a nursery-gardener, or to any of those severely regulated minds who are free from the weakness of any attachment that does not rest on a demonstrable superiority of qualities. And there is no better reason for preferring this elderberry bush than that it stirs an early memory —that it is no novelty in my life, speaking to me merely through my present sensibilities to form and color, but the long companion of my existence, that wove itself into my joys when joys were vivid.

[*Maggie's Discovery of Thomas à Kempis. Age 13*][8]
* * *

Maggie's sense of loneliness, and utter privation of joy, had deepened with the brightness of advancing spring. All the favorite outdoor nooks about home, which seemed to have done their part with her parents in nurturing and cherishing her, were now mixed up with the home-sadness, and gathered no smile from the sunshine. Every affection, every delight the poor child had had, was like an aching nerve to her. There was no music for her any more—no piano, no harmonized voices, no delicious stringed instruments, with their passionate cries of imprisoned spirits sending a strange vibration through her frame. And of all her school-life there was nothing left her now but her little collection of schoolbooks, which she turned over with a sickening sense that she knew them all, and they were all barren of comfort. Even at school she had often

8. Book IV, "The Valley of Humiliation." From Chapter 3, "A Voice from the Past."

wished for books with *more* in them: everything she learned there seemed like the ends of long threads that snapped immediately. And now—without the indirect charm of school-emulation—Télémaque[9] was mere bran; so were the hard dry questions on Christian Doctrine: there was no flavor in them—no strength. Sometimes Maggie thought she could have been contented with absorbing fancies; if she could have had all Scott's novels and all Byron's poems!—then, perhaps, she might have found happiness enough to dull her sensibility to her actual daily life. And yet . . . they were hardly what she wanted. She could make dream-worlds of her own—but no dream-world would satisfy her now. She wanted some explanation of this hard, real life: the unhappy-looking father, seated at the dull breakfast-table; the childish, bewildered mother; the little sordid tasks that filled the hours, or the more oppressive emptiness of weary, joyless leisure; the need of some tender, demonstrative love; the cruel sense that Tom didn't mind what she thought or felt, and that they were no longer playfellows together; the privation of all pleasant things that had come to *her* more than to others: she wanted some key that would enable her to understand, and, in understanding, endure, the heavy weight that had fallen on her young heart. If she had been taught "real learning and wisdom, such as great men knew," she thought she should have held the secrets of life; if she had only books, that she might learn for herself what wise men knew! Saints and martyrs had never interested Maggie so much as sages and poets. She knew little of saints and martyrs, and had gathered, as a general result of her teaching, that they were a temporary provision against the spread of Catholicism, and had all died at Smithfield.[1]

In one of these meditations it occurred to her that she had forgotten Tom's schoolbooks, which had been sent home in his trunk. But she found the stock unaccountably shrunk down to the few old ones which had been well thumbed—the Latin Dictionary and Grammar, a Delectus, a torn Eutropius, the well-worn Virgil, Aldrich's Logic,[2] and the exasperating Euclid. Still, Latin, Euclid, and Logic would surely be a considerable step in masculine wisdom—in that knowledge which made men contented, and even glad to live. Not that the yearning for effectual wisdom was quite unmixed: a certain mirage would now and then rise on the desert of the future, in which she seemed to see herself honored for her surprising attainments. And so the poor child, with her soul's hunger and her illusions of self-flattery, began to nibble at this thick-rinded fruit of the tree of knowledge, filling her vacant hours with Latin, geometry,

9. Didactic narrative (1699) by François Fénelon.
1. Marketplace in London where Protestant martyrs were executed during the reign of Queen Mary (1553–58).

2. *The Rudiments of the Art of Logic* by Henry Aldrich (1647–1710). Originally published in Latin, this textbook had a long-lasting popularity.

and the forms of the syllogism, and feeling a gleam of triumph now and then that her understanding was quite equal to these peculiarly masculine studies. For a week or two she went on resolutely enough, though with an occasional sinking of heart, as if she had set out toward the Promised Land alone, and found it a thirsty, trackless, uncertain journey. In the severity of her early resolution, she would take Aldrich out into the fields, and then look off her book towards the sky, where the lark was twinkling, or to the reeds and bushes by the river, from which the waterfowl rustled forth on its anxious, awkward flight—with a startled sense that the relation between Aldrich and this living world was extremely remote for her. The discouragement deepened as the days went on, and the eager heart gained faster and faster on the patient mind. Somehow, when she sat at the window with her book, her eyes *would* fix themselves blankly on the outdoor sunshine; then they would fill with tears, and sometimes, if her mother was not in the room, the studies would all end in sobbing. She rebelled against her lot, she fainted under its loneliness, and fits even of anger and hatred towards her father and mother, who were so unlike what she would have them to be—towards Tom, who checked her, and met her thought or feeling always by some thwarting difference—would flow out over her affections and conscience like a lava stream, and frighten her with a sense that it was not difficult for her to become a demon. Then her brain would be busy with wild romances of a flight from home in search of something less sordid and dreary: she would go to some great man—Walter Scott, perhaps—and tell him how wretched and how clever she was, and he would surely do something for her. But, in the middle of her vision, her father would perhaps enter the room for the evening, and, surprised that she sat still without noticing him, would say, complainingly, "Come, am I to fetch my slippers myself?" The voice pierced through Maggie like a sword: there was another sadness besides her own, and she had been thinking of turning her back on it and forsaking it.

This afternoon, the sight of Bob's[3] cheerful freckled face had given her discontent a new direction. She thought it was part of the hardship of her life that there was laid upon her the burthen of larger wants than others seemed to feel—that she had to endure this wide hopeless yearning for that something, whatever it was, that was greatest and best on this earth. She wished she could have been like Bob, with his easily satisfied ignorance, or like Tom, who had something to do on which he could fix his mind with a steady purpose, and disregard everything else. Poor child! as she leaned her head against the window-frame, with her hands clasped tighter and

3. Bob Jakin, an unsophisticated and cheerful-spirited neighbor who had given Maggie a present of some books.

tighter, and her foot beating the ground, she was as lonely in her trouble as if she had been the only girl in the civilized world of that day who had come out of her school-life with a soul untrained for inevitable struggles—with no other part of her inherited share in the hard-won treasures of thought, which generations of painful toil have laid up for the race of men, than shreds and patches of feeble literature and false history—with much futile information about Saxon and other kings of doubtful example—but unhappily quite without that knowledge of the irreversible laws within and without her, which, governing the habits, becomes morality, and, developing the feelings of submission and dependence, becomes religion:—as lonely in her trouble as if every other girl besides herself had been cherished and watched over by elder minds, not forgetful of their own early time, when need was keen and impulse strong.

At last Maggie's eyes glanced down on the books that lay on the window-shelf, and she half forsook her reverie to turn over listlessly the leaves of the "Portrait Gallery," but she soon pushed this aside to examine the little row of books tied together with string. "Beauties of the Spectator," "Rasselas," "Economy of Human Life," "Gregory's Letters"[4]—she knew the sort of matter that was inside all these: the "Christian Year"[5]—that seemed to be a hymn-book, and she laid it down again; but *Thomas à Kempis?*[6]—the name had come across her in her reading, and she felt the satisfaction, which every one knows, of getting some ideas to attach to a name that strays solitary in the memory. She took up the little, old, clumsy book[6] with some curiosity: it had the corners turned down in many places, and some hand, now for ever quiet, had made at certain passages strong pen-and-ink marks, long since browned by time. Maggie turned from leaf to leaf, and read where the quiet hand pointed. ... "Know that the love of thyself doth hurt thee more than anything in the world. ... If thou seekest this or that, and wouldst be here or there to enjoy thy own will and pleasure, thou shalt never be quiet nor free from care: for in everything somewhat will be wanting, and in every place there will be some that will cross thee. ... Both above and below, which way soever thou dost turn thee, everywhere thou shalt find the Cross: and everywhere of necessity thou must have patience, if thou wilt have inward peace, and enjoy an everlasting crown. ... If thou desire to mount unto this height, thou must set out courageously, and lay the axe to the root, that thou mayst pluck up and destroy that hidden inordinate inclination to thyself, and unto all private and earthly good. On this sin, that a

4. Four works of moral advice and wisdom: *The Spectator* (1711) by Joseph Addison; *Rasselas* (1759) by Samuel Johnson; *Economy of Human Life* (1750) reputedly by Lord Chesterfield; letters by Pope Gregory the Great (540–634).
5. Volume of religious verse (1827) by John Keble, leader of the Oxford Movement.
6. *The Imitation of Christ* by the monk Thomas à Kempis (1380–1471).

man inordinately loveth himself, almost all dependeth, whatsoever is thoroughly to be overcome; which evil being once overcome and subdued, there will presently ensue great peace and tranquility. . . . It is but little thou sufferest in comparison of them that have suffered so much, were so strongly tempted, so grievously afflicted, so many ways tried and exercised. Thou oughtest therefore to call to mind the more heavy sufferings of others, that thou mayest the easier bear thy little adversities. And if they seem not little unto thee, beware lest thy impatience be the cause thereof. . . . Blessed are those ears that receive the whispers of the divine voice, and listen not to the whisperings of the world. Blessed are those ears which hearken not unto the voice which soundeth outwardly, but unto the Truth, which teacheth inwardly. . . ."

A strange thrill of awe passed through Maggie while she read, as if she had been wakened in the night by a strain of solemn music, telling of beings whose souls had been astir while hers was in stupor. She went on from one brown mark to another, where the quiet hand seemed to point, hardly conscious that she was reading —seeming rather to listen while a low voice said—

"Why dost thou here gaze about, since this is not the place of thy rest? In heaven ought to be thy dwelling, and all earthly things are to be looked on as they forward thy journey thither. All things pass away, and thou together with them. Beware thou cleave not unto them, lest thou be entangled and perish. . . . If a man should give all his substance, yet it is as nothing. And if he should do great penances, yet are they but little. And if he should attain to all knowledge, he is yet far off. And if he should be of great virtue, and very fervent devotion, yet is there much wanting; to wit, one thing, which is most necessary for him. What is that? That having left all, he leave himself, and go wholly out of himself, and retain nothing of self-love. . . . I have often said unto thee, and now again I say the same, Forsake thyself, resign thyself, and thou shalt enjoy much inward peace. . . . Then shall all vain imaginations, evil perturbations, and superfluous cares fly away; then shall immoderate fear leave thee, and inordinate love shall die."

Maggie drew a long breath and pushed her heavy hair back, as if to see a sudden vision more clearly. Here, then, was a secret of life that would enable her to renounce all other secrets—here was a sublime height to be reached without the help of outward things—here was insight, and strength, and conquest, to be won by means entirely within her own soul, where a supreme Teacher was waiting to be heard. It flashed through her like the suddenly apprehended solution of a problem, that all the miseries of her young life had come from fixing her heart on her own pleasure, as if that were the central necessity of the universe; and for the first time she saw the possibility of shifting the position from which she looked at the gratification of her own desires—of taking her stand out of herself, and looking at her own life as an insignificant part of a divinely-guided whole. She read on and on in the old book, devouring eagerly the dialogues with the invisible Teacher, the pattern of sorrow, the source of all strength; returning to it after she had been called away, and reading till the sun went down behind the willows. With all the hurry of an imagination that could never rest in the present, she sat in the deepening twilight forming plans of self-humiliation and entire devotedness; and, in the ardor of first discovery, renunciation seemed to her the entrance into that satisfaction which she had so long been craving in vain. She had not perceived —how could she until she had lived longer?—the inmost truth of the old monk's outpourings, that renunciation remains sorrow, though a sorrow borne willingly. Maggie was still panting for happiness, and was in ecstasy because she had found the key to it. She knew nothing of doctrines and systems—of mysticism or quietism; but this voice out of the far-off middle ages was the direct communication of a human soul's belief and experience, and came to Maggie as an unquestioned message.

I suppose that is the reason why the small old-fashioned book, for which you need only pay sixpence at a book-stall, works miracles to this day, turning bitter waters into sweetness: while expensive sermons and treatises, newly issued, leave all things as they were before. It was written down by a hand that waited for the heart's prompting; it is the chronicle of a solitary, hidden anguish, struggle, trust and triumph—not written on velvet cushions to teach endurance to those who are treading with bleeding feet on the stones. And so it remains to all time a lasting record of human needs and human consolations: the voice of a brother who, ages ago, felt and suffered and renounced—in the cloister, perhaps, with serge gown and tonsured head, with much chanting and long fasts, and with a fashion of speech different from ours—but under the same silent far-off heavens, and with the same passionate desires, the same strivings, the same failures, the same weariness.

In writing the history of unfashionable families, one is apt to fall into a tone of emphasis which is very far from being the tone of good society, where principles and beliefs are not only of an extremely moderate kind, but are always presupposed, no subjects being eligible but such as can be touched with a light and graceful irony. But then, good society has its claret and its velvet-carpets, its dinner-engagements six weeks deep, its opera and its fairy ball-rooms; rides off its ennui on thoroughbred horses, lounges at the club, has to keep clear of crinoline vortices,[7] gets its science done by Faraday, and its religion by the superior clergy who are to be

---

7. I.e., of becoming involved with ladies who wear wide-hooped skirts.

met in the best houses: how should it have time or need for belief and emphasis? But good society, floated on gossamer wings of light irony, is of very expensive production; requiring nothing less than a wide and arduous national life condensed in unfragrant deafening factories, cramping itself in mines, sweating at furnaces, grinding, hammering, weaving under more or less oppression of carbonic acid[8]—or else, spread over sheep-walks, and scattered in lonely houses and huts on the clayey or chalky corn-lands, where the rainy days look dreary. This wide national life is based entirely on emphasis—the emphasis of want, which urges it into all the activities necessary for the maintenance of good society and light irony: it spends its heavy years often in a chill, uncarpeted fashion, amidst family discord unsoftened by long corridors. Under such circumstances, there are many among its myriads of souls who have absolutely needed an emphatic belief: life in this unpleasurable shape demanding some solution even to unspeculative minds; just as you inquire into the stuffing of your couch when anything galls you there, whereas eiderdown and perfect French springs excite no question. Some have an emphatic belief in alcohol, and seek their *ekstasis or* outside standing-ground in gin; but the rest require something that good society calls "enthusiasm," something that will present motives in an entire absence of high prizes, something that will give patience and feed human love when the limbs ache with weariness, and human looks are hard upon us—something, clearly, that lies outside personal desires, that includes resignation for ourselves and active love for what is not ourselves. Now and then, that sort of enthusiasm finds a far-echoing voice that comes from an experience springing out of the deepest need. And it was by being brought within the long lingering vibrations of such a voice that Maggie, with her girl's face and unnoted sorrows, found an effort and a hope that helped her through years of loneliness, making out a faith for herself without the aid of established authorities and appointed guides—for they were not at hand, and her need was pressing. From what you know of her, you will not be surprised that she threw some exaggeration and wilfulness, some pride and impetuosity, even into her self-renunciation: her own life was still a drama for her, in which she demanded of herself that her part should be played with intensity. And so it came to pass that she often lost the spirit of humility by being excessive in the outward act; she often strove after too high a flight, and came down with her poor little half-fledged wings dabbled in the mud. For example, she not only determined to work at plain sewing, that she might contribute something towards the fund in the tin box, but she went, in the first instance, in her zeal of self-mortification, to ask for it at a lin-

8. Concentrations of carbon dioxide gas present in the unventilated rooms of sweatshops.

en-shop in St. Ogg's, instead of getting it in a more quiet and indirect way; and could see nothing but what was entirely wrong and unkind, nay, persecuting, in Tom's reproof of her for this unnecessary act. "I don't like *my* sister to do such things," said Tom; "*I'll* take care that the debts are paid, without your lowering yourself in that way." Surely there was some tenderness and bravery mingled with the worldliness and self-assertion of that little speech; but Maggie held it as dross, overlooking the grains of gold, and took Tom's rebuke as one of her outward crosses. Tom was very hard to her, she used to think, in her long night-watchings—to her who had always loved him so; and then she strove to be contented with that hardness, and to require nothing. That is the path we all like when we set out on our abandonment of egoism—the path of martyrdom and endurance, where the palm-branches grow, rather then the steep highway of tolerance, just allowance, and self-blame, where there are no leafy honors to be gathered and worn.

The old books, Virgil, Euclid, and Aldrich—that wrinkled fruit of the tree of knowledge—had been all laid by; for Maggie had turned her back on the vain ambition to share the thoughts of the wise. In her first ardour she flung away the books with a sort of triumph that she had risen above the need of them; and if they had been her own, she would have burned them, believing that she would never repent. She read so eagerly and constantly in her three books, the Bible, Thomas-à-Kempis, and the "Christian Year" (no longer rejected as a "hymn-book"), that they filled her mind with a continual stream of rhythmic memories; and she was too ardently learning to see all nature and life in the light of her new faith, to need any other material for her mind to work on, as she sat with her well-plied needle, making shirts and other complicated stitchings, falsely called "plain"—by no means plain to Maggie, since wristband and sleeve and the like had a capability of being sewed in wrong side outwards in moments of mental wandering.

Hanging diligently over her sewing, Maggie was a sight any one might have been pleased to look at. That new inward life of hers, notwithstanding some volcanic upheavings of imprisoned passions, yet shone out in her face with a tender soft light that mingled itself as added loveliness with the gradually enriched color and outline of her blossoming youth. Her mother felt the change in her with a sort of puzzled wonder that Maggie should be "growing up so good;" it was amazing that this once "contrairy" child was become so submissive, so backward to assert her own will. Maggie used to look up from her work and find her mother's eyes fixed upon her: they were watching and waiting for the large young glance, as if her elder frame got some needful warmth from it. The mother was getting fond of her tall, brown girl, the only bit of furniture now on which she could bestow her anxiety and pride; and Maggie, in spite of her own ascetic wish to have no personal adornment, was obliged to give way to her mother about her hair, and submit to have the abundant black locks plaited into a coronet on the summit of her head, after the pitiable fashion of those antiquated times.

"Let your mother have that bit o' pleasure, my dear," said Mrs. Tulliver; "I'd trouble enough with your hair once."

So Maggie, glad of anything that would soothe her mother, and cheer their long day together, consented to the vain decoration, and showed a queenly head above her old frocks—steadily refusing, however, to look at herself in the glass. Mrs. Tulliver liked to call the father's attention to Maggie's hair and other unexpected virtues, but he had a brusque reply to give.

"I knew well enough what she'd be, before now—it's nothing new to me. But it's a pity she isn't made o' commoner stuff—she'll be thrown away, I doubt: there'll be nobody to marry her as is fit for her."

And Maggie's graces of mind and body fed his gloom. He sat patiently enough while she read him a chapter, or said something timidly when they were alone together about trouble being turned into a blessing. He took it all as part of his daughter's goodness, which made his misfortunes the sadder to him because they damaged her chance in life. In a mind charged with an eager purpose and an unsatisfied vindictiveness, there is no room for new feelings: Mr. Tulliver did not want spiritual consolation—he wanted to shake off the degradation of debt, and to have his revenge.

[A *Meeting with Philip Wakem. Age* 17][9]

Early in the following April, nearly a year after that dubious parting you have just witnessed, you may, if you like, again see Maggie entering the Red Deeps through the group of Scotch firs. But it is early afternoon and not evening, and the edge of sharpness in the spring air makes her draw her large shawl close about her and trip along rather quickly; though she looks round, as usual, that she may take in the sight of her beloved trees. There is a more eager, inquiring look in her eyes than there was last June, and a smile is hovering about her lips, as if some playful speech were awaiting the right hearer. The hearer was not long in appearing.

"Take back your *Corinne*,"[1] said Maggie, drawing a book from under her shawl. "You were right in telling me she would do me no good; but you were wrong in thinking I should wish to be like her."

"Wouldn't you really like to be a tenth Muse, then, Maggie?" said Philip, looking up in her face as we look at a first parting in the clouds that promises us a bright heaven once more.

9. Book V, "Wheat and Tares." Chapter 4, "Another Love Scene."

1. Love story by Madame de Staël, published 1807.

"Not at all," said Maggie, laughing. "The Muses were uncomfortable goddesses, I think—obliged always to carry rolls and musical instruments about with them. If I carried a harp in this climate, you know, I must have a green baize cover for it—and I should be sure to leave it behind me by mistake."

"You agree with me in not liking Corinne, then?"

"I didn't finish the book," said Maggie. "As soon as I came to the blond-haired young lady reading in the park, I shut it up, and determined to read no further. I foresaw that that light-complexioned girl would win away all the love from Corinne and make her miserable. I'm determined to read no more books where the blond-haired women carry away all the happiness. I should begin to have a prejudice against them. If you could give me some story, now, where the dark woman triumphs, it would restore the balance. I want to avenge Rebecca and Flora MacIvor, and Minna[2] and all the rest of the dark unhappy ones. Since you are my tutor, you ought to preserve my mind from prejudices—you are always arguing against prejudices."

"Well, perhaps you will avenge the dark women in your own person, and carry away all the love from your cousin Lucy. She is sure to have some handsome young man of St. Ogg's at her feet now: and you have only to shine upon him—your fair little cousin will be quite quenched in your beams."

"Philip, that is not pretty of you, to apply my nonsense to anything real," said Maggie, looking hurt. "As if I, with my old gowns and want of all accomplishments, could be a rival of dear little Lucy, who knows and does all sorts of charming things, and is ten times prettier than I am—even if I were odious and base enough to wish to be her rival. Besides, I never go to aunt Deane's when any one is there: it is only because dear Lucy is good, and loves me, that she comes to see me, and will have me go to see her sometimes."

"Maggie," said Philip, with surprise, "it is not like you to take playfulness literally. You must have been in St. Ogg's this morning, and brought away a slight infection of dullness."

"Well," said Maggie, smiling, "if you meant that for a joke, it was a poor one; but I thought it was a very good reproof. I thought you wanted to remind me that I am vain, and wish everyone to admire me most. But it isn't for that, that I'm jealous for the dark women—not because I'm dark myself. It's because I always care the most about the unhappy people: if the blond girl were forsaken, I should like *her* best. I always take the side of the rejected lover in the stories."

2. Brunettes in novels by Scott: *Ivanhoe* (1819); *Waverley* (1814); *The Pirate* (1822).

"Then you would never have the heart to reject one yourself—should you, Maggie?" said Philip, flushing a little.

"I don't know," said Maggie, hesitatingly. Then with a bright smile—"I think perhaps I could if he were very conceited; and yet, if he got extremely humiliated afterwards, I should relent."

"I've often wondered, Maggie," Philip said, with some effort, "whether you wouldn't really be more likely to love a man that other women were not likely to love."

"That would depend on what they didn't like him for," said Maggie, laughing. "He might be very disagreeable. He might look at me through an eyeglass stuck in his eye, making a hideous face, as young Torry does. I should think other women are not fond of that; but I never felt any pity for young Torry. I've never any pity for conceited people, because I think they carry their comfort about with them."

"But suppose, Maggie—suppose it was a man who was not conceited—who felt he had nothing to be conceited about—who had been marked from childhood for a peculiar kind of suffering—and to whom you were the day-star of his life—who loved you, worshiped you, so entirely that he felt it happiness enough for him if you would let him see you at rare moments. . . ."

Philip paused with a pang of dread lest his confession should cut short this very happiness—a pang of the same dread that had kept his love mute through long months. A rush of self-consciousness told him that he was besotted to have said all this. Maggie's manner this morning had been as unconstrained and indifferent as ever.

But she was not looking indifferent now. Struck with the unusual emotion in Philip's tone, she had turned quickly to look at him, and as he went on speaking, a great change came over her face—a flush and slight spasm of the features such as we see in people who hear some news that will require them to readjust their conceptions of the past. She was quite silent, and, walking on towards the trunk of a fallen tree, she sat down, as if she had no strength to spare for her muscles. She was trembling.

"Maggie," said Philip, getting more and more alarmed in every fresh moment of silence, "I was a fool to say it—forget that I've said it. I shall be contented if things can be as they were."

The distress with which he spoke urged Maggie to say something. "I am so surprised, Philip—I had not thought of it." And the effort to say this brought the tears down too.

"Has it made you hate me, Maggie?" said Philip, impetuously. "Do you think I'm a presumptuous fool?"

"O Philip!" said Maggie, "how can you think I have such feelings?—as if I were not grateful for *any* love. But . . . but I had never thought of your being my lover. It seemed so far off—like a

dream—only like one of the stories one imagines—that I should
ever have a lover."

"Then can you bear to think of me as your lover, Maggie?" said
Philip, seating himself by her, and taking her hand, in the elation
of a sudden hope. "*Do* you love me?"

Maggie turned rather pale: this direct question seemed not easy
to answer. But her eyes met Philip's, which were in this moment
liquid and beautiful with beseeching love. She spoke with hesitation, yet with sweet, simple, girlish tenderness.

"I think I could hardly love anyone better: there is nothing but
what I love you for." She paused a little while, and then added,
"But it will be better for us not to say any more about it—won't it,
dear Philip? You know we couldn't even be friends, if our friendship were discovered. I have never felt that I was right in giving way
about seeing you—though it has been so precious to me in some
ways; and now the fear comes upon me strongly again, that it will
lead to evil."

"But no evil has come, Maggie; and if you had been guided by
that fear before, you would only have lived through another dreary
benumbing year, instead of reviving into your real self."

Maggie shook her head. "It has been very sweet, I know—all the
talking together, and the books, and the feeling that I had the walk
to look forward to, when I could tell you the thoughts that had
come into my head while I was away from you. But it has made me
restless: it has made me think a great deal about the world; and I
have impatient thoughts again—I get weary of my home—and then
it cuts me to the heart afterwards, that I should ever have felt weary
of my father and mother. I think what you call being benumbed
was better—better for me—for then my selfish desires were
benumbed."

Philip had risen again, and was walking backwards and forwards
impatiently.

"No, Maggie, you have wrong ideas of self-conquest, as I've often
told you. What you call self-conquest—blinding and deafening
yourself to all but one train of impressions—is only the culture of
monomania in a nature like yours."

He had spoken with some irritation, but now he sat down by her
again, and took her hand.

"Don't think of the past now, Maggie; think only of our love. If
you can really cling to me with all your heart, every obstacle will be
overcome in time: we need only wait. I can live on hope. Look at
me, Maggie; tell me again, it is possible for you to love me. Don't
look away from me to that cloven tree; it is a bad omen."

She turned her large dark glance upon him with a sad smile.

"Come, Maggie, say one kind word, or else you were better to me
at Lorton. You asked me if I should like you to kiss me—don't you

remember?—and you promised to kiss me when you met me again. You never kept the promise."

The recollection of that childish time came as a sweet relief to Maggie. It made the present moment less strange to her. She kissed him almost as simply and quietly as she had done when she was twelve years old. Philip's eyes flashed with delight, but his next words were words of discontent.

"You don't seem happy enough, Maggie: you are forcing yourself to say you love me, out of pity."

"No, Philip," said Maggie, shaking her head, in her old childish way; "I'm telling you the truth. It is all new and strange to me; but I don't think I could love anyone better than I love you. I should like always to live with you—to make you happy. I have always been happy when I have been with you. There is only one thing I will not do for your sake: I will never do anything to wound my father. You must never ask that from me."

"No, Maggie: I will ask nothing—I will bear everything—I'll wait another year only for a kiss, if you will only give me the first place in your heart."

"No," said Maggie, smiling, "I won't make you wait so long as that." But then, looking serious again, she added, as she rose from her seat—

"But what would your own father say, Philip? O, it is quite impossible we can ever be more than friends—brother and sister in secret, as we have been. Let us give up thinking of everything else."

"No, Maggie, I can't give you up—unless you are deceiving me —unless you really only care for me as if I were your brother. Tell me the truth."

"Indeed, I do, Philip. What happiness have I ever had so great as being with you?—since I was a little girl—the days Tom was good to me. And your mind is a sort of world to me: you can tell me all I want to know. I think I should never be tired of being with you."

They were walking hand in hand, looking at each other; Maggie, indeed, was hurrying along, for she felt it time to be gone. But the sense that their parting was near, made her more anxious lest she should have unintentionally left some painful impression on Philip's mind. It was one of those dangerous moments when speech is at once sincere and deceptive—when feeling, rising high above its average depth, leaves flood-marks which are never reached again.

They stopped to part among the Scotch firs.

"Then my life will be filled with hope, Maggie—and I shall be happier than other men, in spite of all? We *do* belong to each other—for always—whether we are apart or together?"

"Yes, Philip: I should like never to part: I should like to make your life very happy."

"I am waiting for something else—I wonder whether it will come."

Maggie smiled, with glistening tears, and then stooped her tall head to kiss the pale face that was full of pleading, timid love—like a woman's.

She had a moment of real happiness then—a moment of belief that, if there were sacrifice in this love, it was all the richer and more satisfying.

She turned away and hurried home, feeling that in the hour since she had trodden this road before, a new era had begun for her. The tissue of vague dreams must now get narrower and narrower, and all the threads of thought and emotion be gradually absorbed in the woof of her actual daily life.

[Aftermath of an Evening with Stephen Guest. Age 19][3]

When Maggie went up to her bedroom that night, it appeared that she was not at all inclined to undress. She set down her candle on the first table that presented itself, and began to walk up and down her room, which was a large one, with a firm, regular, and rather rapid step, which showed that the exercise was the instinctive vent of strong excitement. Her eyes and cheeks had an almost feverish brilliancy; her head was thrown backward, and her hands were clasped with the palms outward, and with that tension of the arms which is apt to accompany mental absorption.

Had anything remarkable happened?

Nothing that you are not likely to consider in the highest degree unimportant. She had been hearing some fine music sung by a fine bass voice—but then it was sung in a provincial, amateur fashion, such as would have left a critical ear much to desire. And she was conscious of having been looked at a great deal, in rather a furtive manner, from beneath a pair of well-marked horizontal eyebrows, with a glance that seemed somehow to have caught the vibratory influence of the voice. Such things could have had no perceptible effect on a thoroughly well-educated young lady, with a perfectly balanced mind, who had had all the advantages of fortune, training, and refined society. But if Maggie had been that young lady, you would probably have known nothing about her: her life would have had so few vicissitudes that it could hardly have been written; for the happiest women, like the happiest nations, have no history.

In poor Maggie's highly-strung, hungry nature—just come away from a third-rate schoolroom, with all its jarring sounds and petty round of tasks—these apparently trivial causes had the effect of rousing and exalting her imagination in a way that was mysterious

3. Book VI, "The Great Temptation." Chapter 3, "Confidential Moments."

to herself. It was not that she thought distinctly of Mr. Stephen Guest, or dwelt on the indications that he looked at her with admiration; it was rather that she felt the half-remote presence of a world of love and beauty and delight, made up of vague, mingled images from all the poetry and romance she had ever read, or had ever woven in her dreamy reveries. Her mind glanced back once or twice to the time when she had courted privation, when she had thought all longing, all impatience was subdued; but that condition seemed irrecoverably gone, and she recoiled from the remembrance of it. No prayer, no striving now, would bring back that negative peace: the battle of her life, it seemed, was not to be decided in that short and easy way—by perfect renunciation at the very threshold of her youth. The music was vibrating in her still—Purcell's music, with its wild passion and fancy—and she could not stay in the recollection of that bare, lonely past. She was in her brighter airial world again, when a little tap came at the door: of course it was her cousin, who entered in ample white dressing-gown.

"Why, Maggie, you naughty child, haven't you begun to undress?" said Lucy, in astonishment. "I promised not to come and talk to you, because I thought you must be tired. But here you are, looking as if you were ready to dress for a ball. Come, come, get on your dressing-gown, and unplait your hair."

"Well, *you* are not very forward," retorted Maggie, hastily reaching her own pink cotton gown, and looking at Lucy's light-brown hair brushed back in curly disorder.

"O, I have not much to do. I shall sit down and talk to you till I see you are really on the way to bed."

While Maggie stood and unplaited her long black hair over her pink drapery, Lucy sat down near the toilette-table, watching her with affectionate eyes, and head a little aside, like a pretty spaniel. If it appears to you at all incredible that young ladies should be led on to talk confidentially in a situation of this kind, I will beg you to remember that human life furnishes many exceptional cases.

"You really *have* enjoyed the music tonight, haven't you, Maggie?"

"O yes, that is what prevents me from feeling sleepy. I think I should have no other mortal wants, if I could always have plenty of music. It seems to infuse strength into my limbs, and ideas into my brain. Life seems to go on without effort, when I am filled with music. At other times one is conscious of carrying a weight."

"And Stephen has a splendid voice, hasn't he?"

"Well, perhaps we are neither of us judges of that," said Maggie, laughing, as she seated herself and tossed her long hair back. "You are not impartial, and I think any barrel-organ splendid."

"But tell me what you think of him, now. Tell me exactly—good and bad too."

"O, I think you should humiliate him a little. A lover should not be so much at ease, and so self-confident. He ought to tremble more."

"Nonsense, Maggie! As if anyone could tremble at me! You think he is conceited—I see that. But you don't dislike him, do you?"

"Dislike him! No. Am I in the habit of seeing such charming people, that I should be very difficult to please? Besides, how could I dislike any one that promised to make you happy, you dear thing!" Maggie pinched Lucy's dimpled chin.

"We shall have more music tomorrow evening," said Lucy, looking happy already, "for Stephen will bring Philip Wakem with him."

"O Lucy, I can't see him," said Maggie, turning pale. "At least, I could not see him without Tom's leave."

"Is Tom such a tyrant as that?" said Lucy, surprised. "I'll take the responsibility, then—tell him it was my fault."

"But, dear," said Maggie, falteringly, "I promised Tom very solemnly—before my father's death—I promised him I would not speak to Philip without his knowledge and consent. And I have a great dread of opening the subject with Tom—of getting into a quarrel with him again."

"But I never heard of anything so strange and unreasonable. What harm can poor Philip have done? May I speak to Tom about it?"

"O no, pray don't, dear," said Maggie. "I'll go to him myself tomorrow, and tell him that you wish Philip to come. I've thought before of asking him to absolve me from my promise, but I've not had the courage to determine on it."

They were both silent for some moments, and then Lucy said—

"Maggie, you have secrets from me, and I have none from you."

Maggie looked meditatively away from Lucy. Then she turned to her and said, "I *should* like to tell you about Philip. But, Lucy, you must not betray that you know it to any one—least of all to Philip himself, or to Mr. Stephen Guest."

The narrative lasted long, for Maggie had never before known the relief of such an outpouring: she had never before told Lucy anything of her inmost life; and the sweet face bent towards her with sympathetic interest, and the little hand pressing hers, encouraged her to speak on. On two points only she was not expansive. She did not betray fully what still rankled in her mind as Tom's great offense—the insults he had heaped on Philip. Angry as the remembrance still made her, she could not bear that any one else should know it all—both for Tom's sake and Philip's. And she could not bear to tell Lucy of the last scene between her father and Wakem, though it was this scene which she had ever since felt to be a new barrier between herself and Philip. She merely said, she saw now that Tom was, on the whole, right in regarding any prospect of love and marriage between her and Philip as put out of the question by the relation of the two families. Of course Philip's father would never consent.

"There, Lucy, you have had my story," said Maggie, smiling, with the tears in her eyes. "You see I am like Sir Andrew Aguecheek—I was adored once."[4]

"Ah, now I see how it is you know Shakespeare and everything, and have learned so much since you left school; which always seemed to me witchcraft before—part of your general uncanniness," said Lucy.

She mused a little with her eyes downward, and then added, looking at Maggie, "It is very beautiful that you should love Philip: I never thought such a happiness would befall him. And in my opinion, you ought not to give him up. There are obstacles now; but they may be done away with in time."

Maggie shook her head.

"Yes, yes," persisted Lucy; "I can't help being hopeful about it. There is something romantic in it—out of the common way—just what everything that happens to you ought to be. And Philip will adore you like a husband in a fairy tale. O, I shall puzzle my small brain to contrive some plot that will bring everybody into the right mind, so that you may marry Philip, when I marry—somebody else. Wouldn't that be a pretty ending to all my poor, poor Maggie's troubles?"

Maggie tried to smile, but shivered, as if she felt a sudden chill.

"Ah, dear, you are cold," said Lucy. "You must go to bed; and so must I. I dare not think what time it is."

They kissed each other, and Lucy went away—possessed of a confidence which had a strong influence over her subsequent impressions. Maggie had been thoroughly sincere: her nature had never found it easy to be otherwise. But confidences are sometimes blinding, even when they are sincere.

[An After-Dinner Visit with Stephen Guest. Age 19][5]

It is evident to you now, that Maggie had arrived at a moment in her life which must be considered by all prudent persons as a great opportunity for a young woman. Launched into the higher society of St. Ogg's, with a striking person, which had the advantage of being quite unfamiliar to the majority of beholders, and with such moderate assistance of costume as you have seen foreshadowed in Lucy's anxious colloquy with aunt Pullet, Maggie was certainly at a new starting-point in life. At Lucy's first evening-party, young Torry fatigued his facial muscles more than usual in order that "the dark-

4. *Twelfth Night* III.iii.197.
5. Book VI, "The Great Temptation."

Chapter 6, "Illustrating the Laws of Attraction."

eyed girl there, in the corner," might see him in all the additional
style conferred by his eyeglass; and several young ladies went home
intending to have short sleeves with black lace, and to plait their
hair in a broad coronet at the back of their head—"That cousin of
Miss Deane's looked so very well." In fact, poor Maggie, with all
her inward consciousness of a painful past and her presentiment of
a troublous future, was on the way to become an object of some
envy—a topic of discussion in the newly-established billiard-room,
and between fair friends who had no secrets from each other on the
subject of trimmings. The Miss Guests, who associated chiefly on
terms of condescension with the families of St. Ogg's, and were the
glass of fashion there, took some exception to Maggie's manners.
She had a way of not assenting at once to the observations current
in good society, and of saying that she didn't know whether those
observations were true or not, which gave her an air of *gaucherie*,
and impeded the even flow of conversation; but it is a fact capable
of an amiable interpretation, that ladies are not the worst disposed
towards a new acquaintance of their own sex because she has points
of inferiority. And Maggie was so entirely without those pretty airs
of coquetry which had the traditional reputation of driving gentlemen to despair, that she won some feminine pity for being so ineffective in spite of her beauty. She had not had many advantages,
poor thing! and it must be admitted there was no pretension about
her: her abruptness and unevenness of manner were plainly the
result of her secluded and lowly circumstances. It was only a
wonder that there was no tinge of vulgarity about her, considering
what the rest of poor Lucy's relations were: an allusion which
always made the Miss Guests shudder a little. It was not agreeable
to think of any connection by marriage with such people as the
Gleggs and the Pullets; but it was of no use to contradict Stephen,
when once he had set his mind on anything, and certainly there
was no possible objection to Lucy in herself—no one could help
liking her. She would naturally desire that the Miss Guests should
behave kindly to this cousin of whom she was so fond, and Stephen
would make a great fuss if they were deficient in civility. Under
these circumstances the invitations to Park House were not wanting; and elsewhere, also, Miss Deane was too popular and too distinguished a member of society in St. Ogg's for any attention towards
her to be neglected.

Thus Maggie was introduced for the first time to the young lady's
life, and knew what it was to get up in the morning without any
imperative reason for doing one thing more than another. This new
sense of leisure and unchecked enjoyment amidst the soft-breathing
airs and garden-scents of advancing spring—amidst the new abundance of music, and lingering stolls in the sunshine, and the delicious dreaminess of gliding on the river—could hardly be without

some intoxicating effect on her, after her years of privation; and even in the first week Maggie began to be less haunted by her sad memories and anticipations. Life was certainly very pleasant just now: it was becoming very pleasant to dress in the evening, and to feel that she was one of the beautiful things of this springtime. And there were admiring eyes always awaiting her now; she was no longer an unheeded person, liable to be chid, from whom attention was continually claimed, and on whom no one felt bound to confer any. It was pleasant, too, when Stephen and Lucy were gone out riding, to sit down at the piano alone, and find that the old fitness between her fingers and the keys remained, and revived, like a sympathetic kinship not to be worn out by separation—to get the tunes she had heard the evening before, and repeat them again and again until she had found a way of producing them so as to make them a more pregnant, passionate language to her. The mere concord of octaves was a delight to Maggie, and she would often take up a book of studies rather than any melody, that she might taste more keenly by abstraction the more primitive sensation of intervals. Not that her enjoyment of music was of the kind that indicates a great specific talent; it was rather that her sensibility to the supreme excitement of music was only one form of that passionate sensibility which belonged to her whole nature, and made her faults and virtues all merge in each other—made her affections sometimes an impatient demand, but also prevented her vanity from taking the form of mere feminine coquetry and device, and gave it the poetry of ambition. But you have known Maggie a long while, and need to be told, not her characteristics, but her history, which is a thing hardly to be predicted even from the completest knowledge of characteristics. For the tragedy of our lives is not created entirely from within. "Character," says Novalis, in one of his questionable aphorisms—"character is destiny." But not the whole of our destiny. Hamlet, Prince of Denmark, was speculative and irresolute, and we have a great tragedy in consequence. But if his father had lived to a good old age, and his uncle had died an early death, we can conceive Hamlet's having married Ophelia, and got through life with a reputation of sanity, notwithstanding many soliloquies, and some moody sarcasms towards the fair daughter of Polonius, to say nothing of the frankest incivility to his father-in-law.

Maggie's destiny, then, is at present hidden, and we must wait for it to reveal itself like the course of an unmapped river: we only know that the river is full and rapid, and that for all rivers there is the same final home. Under the charm of her new pleasures, Maggie herself was ceasing to think, with her eager prefiguring imagination, of her future lot; and her anxiety about her first interview with Philip was losing its predominance: perhaps, unconsciously to herself, she was not sorry that the interview had been deferred.

For Philip had not come the evening he was expected, and Mr. Stephen Guest brought word that he was gone to the coast—probably, he thought, on a sketching expedition; but it was not certain when he would return. It was just like Philip—to go off in that way without telling anyone. It was not until the twelfth day that he returned, to find both Lucy's notes awaiting him: he had left before he knew of Maggie's arrival.

Perhaps one had need be nineteen again to be quite convinced of the feelings that were crowded for Maggie into those twelve days— of the length to which they were stretched for her by the novelty of her experience in them, and the varying attitudes of her mind. The early days of an acquaintance almost always have this importance for us, and fill up a larger space in our memory than longer subsequent periods, which have been less filled with discovery and new impressions. There were not many hours in those twelve days in which Mr. Stephen Guest was not seated by Lucy's side, or standing near her at the piano, or accompanying her on some outdoor excursion: his attentions were clearly becoming more assiduous; and that was what everyone had expected. Lucy was very happy: all the happier because Stephen's society seemed to have become much more interesting and amusing since Maggie had been there. Playful discussions—sometimes serious ones—were going forward, in which both Stephen and Maggie revealed themselves, to the admiration of the gentle unobtrusive Lucy; and it more than once crossed her mind what a charming quartet they should have through life when Maggie married Philip. Is it an inexplicable thing that a girl should enjoy her lover's society the more for the presence of a third person, and be without the slightest spasm of jealousy that the third person had the conversation habitually directed to her? Not when that girl is as tranquil-hearted as Lucy, thoroughly possessed with a belief that she knows the state of her companions' affections, and not prone to the feelings which shake such a belief in the absence of positive evidence against it. Besides, it was Lucy by whom Stephen sat, to whom he gave his arm, to whom he appealed as the person sure to agree with him; and every day there was the same tender politeness towards her, the same consciousness of her wants and care to supply them. Was there really the same?—it seemed to Lucy that there was more; and it was no wonder that the real significance of the change escaped her. It was a subtle act of conscience in Stephen that even he himself was not aware of. His personal attentions to Maggie were comparatively slight, and there had even sprung up an apparent distance between them, that prevented the renewal of that faint resemblance to gallantry into which he had fallen the first day in the boat. If Stephen came in when Lucy was out of the room—if Lucy left them together, they never spoke to each other: Stephen perhaps, seemed to be examining books on music, and Maggie bent her head assiduously over her work. Each was oppressively conscious of the other's presence, even to the finger-ends. Yet each looked and longed for the same thing to happen the next day. Neither of them had begun to reflect on the matter, or silently to ask, "To what does all this tend?" Maggie only felt that life was revealing something quite new to her; and she was absorbed in the direct, immediate experience, without any energy left for taking account of it and reasoning about it. Stephen wilfully abstained from self-questioning, and would not admit to himself that he felt an influence which was to have any determining effect on his conduct. And when Lucy came into the room again, they were once more unconstrained: Maggie could contradict Stephen and laugh at him, and he could recommend to her consideration the example of that most charming heroine, Miss Sophia Western, who had a great "respect for the understandings of men."[6] Maggie could look at Stephen—which, for some reason or other, she always avoided when they were alone; and he could even ask her to play his accompaniment for him, since Lucy's fingers were so busy with that bazaar-work; and lecture her on hurrying the *tempo*, which was certainly Maggie's weak point.

One day—it was the day of Philip's return—Lucy had formed a sudden engagement to spend the evening with Mrs. Kenn, whose delicate state of health, threatening to become confirmed illness through an attack of bronchitis, obliged her to resign her functions at the coming bazaar into the hands of other ladies, of whom she wished Lucy to be one. The engagement had been formed in Stephen's presence, and he had heard Lucy promise to dine early and call at six o'clock for Miss Torry, who brought Mrs. Kenn's request.

"Here is another of the moral results of this idiotic bazaar," Stephen burst forth, as soon as Miss Torry had left the room—"taking young ladies from the duties of the domestic hearth into scenes of dissipation among urn-rugs and embroidered reticules! I should like to know what is the proper function of women, if it is not to make reasons for husbands to stay at home, and still stronger reasons for bachelors to go out. If this goes on much longer, the bonds of society will be dissolved."

"Well, it will not go on much longer," said Lucy, laughing, "for the bazaar is to take place on Monday week."

"Thank heaven!" said Stephen. "Kenn himself said the other day, that he didn't like this plan of making vanity do the work of charity; but just as the British public is not reasonable enough to bear direct taxation, so St. Ogg's has not got force of motive

6. Henry Fielding's *Tom Jones* (1749) XVII.3.

enough to build and endow schools without calling in the force of folly."

"Did he say so?" said little Lucy, her hazel eyes opening wide with anxiety. "I never heard him say anything of that kind: I thought he approved of what we were doing.'

"I'm sure he approves *you*," said Stephen, smiling at her affectionately; "your conduct in going out tonight looks vicious, I own, but I know there is benevolence at the bottom of it."

"O, you think too well of me," said Lucy, shaking her head, with a pretty blush, and there the subject ended. But it was tacitly understood that Stephen would not come in the evening, and on the strength of that tacit understanding he made his morning visit the longer, not saying good-bye until after four.

Maggie was seated in the drawing-room alone, shortly after dinner, with Minny on her lap, having left her uncle to his wine and his nap, and her mother to the compromise between knitting and nodding, which, when there was no company, she always carried on in the dining-room till tea-time. Maggie was stooping to caress the tiny silken pet, and comforting him for his mistress's absence, when the sound of a footstep on the gravel made her look up, and she saw Mr. Stephen Guest walking up the garden, as if he had come straight from the river. It was very unusual to see him so soon after dinner! He often complained that their dinner-hour was late at Park House. Nevertheless, there he was, in his black dress: he had evidently been home, and must have come again by the river. Maggie felt her cheeks glowing and her heart beating: it was natural she should be nervous, for she was not accustomed to receive visitors alone. He had seen her look up through the open window, and raised his hat as he walked towards it, to enter that way instead of by the door. He blushed too, and certainly looked as foolish as a young man of some wit and self-possession can be expected to look, as he walked in with a roll of music in his hand, and said, with an air of hesitating improvisation—

"You are surprised to see me again, Miss Tulliver—I ought to apologize for coming upon you by surprise, but I wanted to come into the town, and I got our man to row me; so I thought I would bring these things from the Maid of Artois'[7] for your cousin: I forgot them this morning. Will you give them to her?"

"Yes," said Maggie, who had risen confusedly with Minny in her arms, and now, not quite knowing what else to do, sat down again.

Stephen laid down his hat, with the music, which rolled on the floor, and sat down in the chair close by her. He had never done so before, and both he and Maggie were quite aware that it was an entirely new position.

"Well, you pampered minion!" said Stephen, leaning to pull the

7. Opera by M. W. Balfe, produced in London in 1836.

long curly ears that drooped over Maggie's arm. It was not a suggestive remark, and as the speaker did not follow it up by further
development, it naturally left the conversation at a standstill. It
seemed to Stephen like some action in a dream, that he was obliged
to do, and wonder at himself all the while—to go on stroking
Minny's head. Yet it was very pleasant: he only wished he dared
look at Maggie, and that she would look at him—let him have one
long look into those deep strange eyes of hers, and then he would
be satisfied, and quite reasonable after that. He thought it was
becoming a sort of monomania with him, to want that long look
from Maggie; and he was racking his invention continually to find
out some means by which he could have it without its appearing
singular and entailing subsequent embarrassment. As for Maggie,
she had no distinct thought—only the sense of a presence like that
of a closely-hovering broad-winged bird in the darkness, for she was
unable to look up, and saw nothing but Minny's black wavy coat.

But this must end some time—perhaps it ended very soon, and
only *seemed* long, as a minute's dream does. Stephen at last sat
upright sideways in his chair, leaning one hand and arm over the
back and looking at Maggie. What should he say?

"We shall have a splendid sunset, I think; shan't you go out and
see it?"

"I don't know," said Maggie. Then, courageously raising her eyes
and looking out of the window, "If I'm not playing cribbage with
my uncle."

A pause: during which Minny is stroked again, but has sufficient
insight not to be grateful for it—to growl rather.

"Do you like sitting alone?"

A rather arch look came over Maggie's face, and, just glancing at
Stephen, she said, "Would it be quite civil to say 'yes'?"

"It *was* rather a dangerous question for an intruder to ask," said
Stephen, delighted with that glance, and getting determined to stay
for another. "But you will have more than half an hour to yourself
after I am gone," he added, taking out his watch. "I know Mr.
Deane never comes in till half-past seven."

Another pause, during which Maggie looked steadily out of the
window, till by a great effort she moved her head to look down at
Minny's back again, and said—

"I wish Lucy had not been obliged to go out. We lose our
music."

"We shall have a new voice tomorrow night," said Stephen.
"Will you tell your cousin that our friend Philip Wakem is come
back? I saw him as I went home."

Maggie gave a little start—it seemed hardly more than a vibration that passed from head to foot in an instant. But the new
images summoned by Philip's name, dispersed half the oppressive

spell she had been under. She rose from her chair with a sudden resolution, and, laying Minny on his cushion, went to reach Lucy's
large work-basket from its corner. Stephen was vexed and disappointed: he thought, perhaps Maggie didn't like the name of
Wakem to be mentioned to her in that abrupt way—for he now
recalled what Lucy had told him of the family quarrel. It was of no
use to stay any longer. Maggie was seating herself at the table with
her work, and looking chill and proud: and he—he looked like a
simpleton for having come. A gratuitous, entirely superfluous visit
of that sort was sure to make a man disagreeable and ridiculous. Of
course it was palpable to Maggie's thinking, that he had dined hastily in his own room for the sake of setting off again and finding her
alone.

A boyish state of mind for an accomplished young gentleman of
five-and-twenty, not without legal knowledge! But a reference to history, perhaps, may make it not incredible.

At this moment Maggie's ball of knitting-wool rolled along the
ground, and she started up to reach it. Stephen rose too, and, picking up the ball, met her with a vexed complaining look that gave
his eyes quite a new expression to Maggie, whose own eyes met
them as he presented the ball to her.

"Good-bye," said Stephen, in a tone that had the same beseeching discontent as his eyes. He dared not put out his hand—he
thrust both hands into his tail-pockets as he spoke. Maggie thought
she had perhaps been rude.

"Won't you stay?" she said timidly, not looking away, for that
would have seemed rude again.

"No, thank you," said Stephen, looking still into the half-unwill-
ing, half-fascinated eyes, as a thirsty man looks towards the track of
the distant brook. "The boat is waiting for me. . . . You'll tell your
cousin?"

"Yes."

"That I brought the music, I mean?"

"Yes."

' And that Philip is come back."

"Yes." (Maggie did not notice Philip's name this time.)

"Won't you come out a little way into the garden?" said Stephen, in a still gentler tone, but the next moment he was vexed
that she did not say "No," for she moved away now towards the
open window, and he was obliged to take his hat and walk by her
side. But he thought of something to make him amends.

"Do take my arm," he said, in a low tone, as if it were a secret.

There is something strangely winning to most women in that
offer of the firm arm: the help is not wanted physically at that
moment, but the sense of help—the presence of strength that is
outside them and yet theirs—meets a continual want of the imagi-

nation. Either on that ground or some other, Maggie took the arm. And they walked together round the grass plot and under the drooping green of the laburnums, in the same dim dreamy state as they had been in a quarter of an hour before; only that Stephen had had the look he longed for, without yet perceiving in himself the symptoms of returning reasonableness, and Maggie had darting thoughts across the dimness:—how came she to be there?—why had she come out? Not a word was spoken. If it had been, each would have been less intensely conscious of the other.

"Take care of this step," said Stephen, at last.

"O, I will go in now," said Maggie, feeling that the step had come like a rescue. "Good evening."

In an instant she had withdrawn her arm, and was running back to the house. She did not reflect that this sudden action would only add to the embarrassing recollections of the last half-hour. She had no thought left for that. She only threw herself into the low arm-chair, and burst into tears.

"O Philip, Philip, I wish we were together again—so quietly—in the Red Deeps."

Stephen looked after her a moment, then went on to the boat, and was soon landed at the wharf. He spent the evening in the bil-liard-room, smoking one cigar after another, and losing "lives" at pool. But he would not leave off. He was determined not to think —not to admit any more distinct remembrance than was urged upon him by the perpetual presence of Maggie. He was looking at her, and she was on his arm.

But there came the necessity of walking home in the cool star-light, and with it the necessity of cursing his own folly, and bitterly determining that he would never trust himself alone with Maggie again. It was all madness: he was in love, thoroughly attached to Lucy, and engaged—engaged as strongly as an honorable man need be. He wished he had never seen this Maggie Tulliver, to be thrown into a fever by her in this way: she would make a sweet, strange, troublesome, adorable wife to some man or other, but he would never have chosen her for himself. Did she feel as he did? He hoped she did—not. He ought not to have gone. He would master himself in future. He would make himself disagreeable to her— quarrel with her perhaps. Quarrel with her? Was it possible to quar-rel with a creature who had such eyes—defying and deprecating, contradicting and clinging, imperious and beseeching—full of deli-cious opposites. To see such a creature subdued by love for one would be a lot worth having—to another man.

There was a muttered exclamation which ended this inward solil-oquy, as Stephen threw away the end of his last cigar, and thrusting his hands into his pockets, stalked along at a quieter pace through the shrubbery. It was not of a benedictory kind.

[*An Afternoon Visit with Stephen Guest at the Farm. Age 19*][8]

Maggie had been four days at her aunt Moss's, giving the early June sunshine quite a new brightness in the care-dimmed eyes of that affectionate woman, and making an epoch for her cousins great and small, who were learning her words and actions by heart, as if she had been a transient avatar of perfect wisdom and beauty.

She was standing on the causeway with her aunt and a group of cousins feeding the chickens, at that quiet moment in the life of the farmyard before the afternoon milking-time. The great buildings round the hollow yard were as dreary and tumbledown as ever, but over the old garden-wall the straggling rose-bushes were beginning to toss their summer weight, and the gray wood and old bricks of the house, on its higher level, had a look of sleepy age in the broad afternoon sunlight, that suited the quiescent time. Maggie, with her bonnet over her arm, was smiling down at the hatch of small fluffy chickens, when her aunt exclaimed—

"Goodness me! who is that gentleman coming in at the gate?"

It was a gentleman on a tall bay horse; and the flanks and neck of the horse were streaked black with fast riding. Maggie felt a beating at head and heart—horrible as the sudden leaping to life of a savage enemy who had feigned death.

"Who is it, my dear?" said Mrs. Moss, seeing in Maggie's face the evidence that she knew.

"It is Mr. Stephen Guest," said Maggie, rather faintly. "My cousin Lucy's——a gentleman who is very intimate at my cousin's."

Stephen was already close to them, had jumped off his horse, and now raised his hat as he advanced.

"Hold the horse, Willy," said Mrs. Moss to the twelve-year-old boy.

"No, thank you," said Stephen, pulling at the horse's impatiently tossing head. "I must be going again immediately. I have a message to deliver to you, Miss Tulliver—on private business. May I take the liberty of asking you to walk a few yards with me?"

He had a half-jaded, half-irritated look, such as a man gets when he has been dogged by some care or annoyance that makes his bed and his dinner of little use to him. He spoke almost abruptly, as if his errand were too pressing for him to trouble himself about what would be thought by Mrs. Moss of his visit and request. Good Mrs. Moss, rather nervous in the presence of this apparently haughty gentleman, was inwardly wondering whether she would be doing right or wrong to invite him again to leave his horse and walk in, when Maggie, feeling all the embarrassment of the situation, and unable to say anything, put on her bonnet, and turned to walk towards the gate.

8. Book VI, "The Great Temptation." Chapter 11, "In the Lane."

Stephen turned too, and walked by her side, leading his horse.

Not a word was spoken till they were out in the lane, and had walked four or five yards, when Maggie, who had been looking straight before her all the while, turned again to walk back, saying, with haughty resentment—

"There is no need for me to go any farther. I don't know whether you consider it gentlemanly and delicate conduct to place me in a position that forced me to come out with you—or whether you wished to insult me still further by thrusting an interview upon me in this way."

"Of course you are angry with me for coming," said Stephen, bitterly. "Of course it is of no consequence what a man has to suffer—it is only your woman's dignity that you care about."

Maggie gave a slight start, such as might have come from the slightest possible electric shock.

"As if it were not enough that I'm entangled in this way—that I'm mad with love for you—that I resist the strongest passion a man can feel, because I try to be true to other claims—but you must treat me as if I were a coarse brute, who would willingly offend you. And when, if I had my own choice, I should ask you to take my hand, and my fortune, and my whole life, and do what you liked with them! I know I forgot myself. I took an unwarrantable liberty.[9] I hate myself for having done it. But I repented immediately—I've been repenting ever since. You ought not to think it unpardonable: a man who loves with his whole soul, as I do you, is liable to be mastered by his feelings for a moment; but you know—you must believe—that the worst pain I could have is to have pained you—that I would give the world to recall the error."

Maggie dared not speak—dared not turn her head. The strength that had come from resentment was all gone, and her lips were quivering visibly. She could not trust herself to utter the full forgiveness that rose in answer to that confession.

They were come nearly in front of the gate again, and she paused, trembling.

"You must not say these things—I must not hear them," she said, looking down in misery, as Stephen came in front of her, to prevent her from going farther towards the gate. "I'm very sorry for any pain you have to go through; but it is of no use to speak."

"Yes, it *is* of use," said Stephen, impetuously. "It would be of use if you would treat me with some sort of pity and consideration, instead of doing me vile injustice in your mind. I could bear everything more quietly if I knew you didn't hate me for an insolent coxcomb. Look at me—see what a hunted devil I am: I've been riding thirty miles every day to get away from the thought of you."

---

9. Alluding to a previous incident in which Stephen had impulsively embraced Maggie at a dance.

Maggie did not—dared not look. She had already seen the harassed face. But she said, gently—

"I don't think any evil of you."

"Then, dearest, look at me," said Stephen, in deepest, tenderest tones of entreaty. "Don't go away from me yet. Give me a moment's happiness—make me feel you've forgiven me."

"Yes, I do forgive you," said Maggie, shaken by those tones, and all the more frightened at herself. "But pray let me go in again. Pray go away."

A great tear fell from under her lowered eyelids.

"I can't go away from you—I can't leave you," said Stephen, with still more passionate pleading. "I shall come back again if you send me away with this coldness—I can't answer for myself. But if you will go with me only a little way, I can live on that. You see plainly enough that your anger has only made me ten times more unreasonable."

Maggie turned. But Tancred, the bay horse, began to make such spirited remonstrances against this frequent change of direction, that Stephen, catching sight of Willy Moss peeping through the gate, called out, "Here! just come and hold my horse for five minutes."

"O no," said Maggie, hurriedly, "my aunt will think it so strange."

"Never mind," Stephen answered, impatiently; "they don't know the people at St. Ogg's. Lead him up and down just here, for five minutes," he added to Willy, who was now close to them; and then he turned to Maggie's side, and they walked on. It was clear that she *must* go on now.

"Take my arm," said Stephen, entreatingly; and she took it, feeling all the while as if she were sliding downwards in a nightmare.

"There is no end to this misery," she began, struggling to repel the influence by speech. "It is wicked—base—ever allowing a word or look that Lucy—that others might not have seen. Think of Lucy."

"I do think of her—bless her. If I didn't—" Stephen had laid his hand on Maggie's that rested on his arm, and they both felt it difficult to speak.

"And I have other ties," Maggie went on, at last, with a desperate effort,—"even if Lucy did not exist."

"You are engaged to Philip Wakem?" said Stephen, hastily. "Is it so?"

"I consider myself engaged to him—I don't mean to marry anyone else."

Stephen was silent again until they had turned out of the sun into a side lane, all grassy and sheltered. Then he burst out impetuously—

cousins in, with kind thoughtfulness. It might be a joyful thing that Maggie had a rich and handsome lover, but she would naturally feel embarrassed at coming in again:—and it might *not* be joyful. In either case, Mrs. Moss waited anxiously to receive Maggie by herself. The speaking face told plainly enough that, if there was joy, it was of a very agitating, dubious sort.

"Sit down here a bit, my dear." She drew Maggie into the porch, and sat down on the bench by her:—there was no privacy in the house.

"O Aunt Gritty, I'm very wretched. I wish I could have died when I was fifteen. It seemed so easy to give things up then—it is so hard now."

The poor child threw her arms round her aunt's neck, and fell into long, deep sobs.

1860

Margaret Fuller and Mary Wollstonecraft[1]

The dearth of new books just now gives us time to recur to less recent ones which we have hitherto noticed but slightly; and among these we choose the late edition of Margaret Fuller's *Woman in the Nineteenth Century*, because we think it has been unduly thrust into the background by less comprehensive and candid productions on the same subject. Notwithstanding certain defects of taste and a sort of vague spiritualism and grandiloquence which belong to all but the very best American writers, the book is a valuable one: it has the enthusiasm of a noble and sympathetic nature, with the moderation and breadth and large allowance of a vigorous and cultivated understanding. There is no exaggeration of woman's moral excellence or intellectual capabilities; no injudicious insistence on

---

1. In October 1855, George Eliot contributed a book-review essay to *The Leader* on two important feminist publications: *A Vindication of the Rights of Woman* (1792) by Mary Wollstonecraft, and *Woman in the Nineteenth Century* (1843–55) by the American writer Margaret Fuller. *The Rights of Woman* is noteworthy as a pioneering discussion that, for reasons indicated by Eliot, had been overlooked by many Victorians. At that date Mary Wollstonecraft (1759–1797) was more likely to be remembered as the wife of William Godwin and the mother of Shelley's wife, Mary, than as the author of this remarkable work. Much better known at this date was the essayist Margaret Fuller (1810–1850), editor of *The Dial* in America, a writer whom George Eliot had warmly esteemed.

As Barbara Hardy notes, despite "her generous sympathy with Victorian feminism" George Eliot "played no active part in the movement." Eliot seems to have shared the view of women's relation to men expressed by the Prince in Tennyson's *Princess*, whose speeches she cites in this essay. As she herself wrote in 1854, in another essay, *Women in France*:

Women became superior in France by being admitted to a common fund of ideas, to common objects of interest with men; and this must ever be the essential condition at once of true womanly culture and of true social well-being. . . . Let the whole field of reality be laid open to woman as well as to man, and then that which is peculiar in the mental modification, instead of being, as it is now, a source of discord and repulsion between the sexes, will be found to be a necessary complement to the truth and beauty of life.

her fitness for this or that function hitherto engrossed by men; but a calm plea for the removal of unjust laws and artificial restrictions, so that the possibilities of her nature may have room for full development, a wisely stated demand to disencumber her of the

> Parasitic forms
> That seem to keep her up, but drag her down—
> And leave her field to burgeon and to bloom
> From all within her, make herself her own
> To give or keep, to live and learn and be
> All that not harms distinctive womanhood.[2]

It is interesting to compare this essay of Margaret Fuller's published in its earliest form in 1843,[3] with a work on the position of woman, written between sixty and seventy years ago—we mean Mary Wollstonecraft's *Rights of Woman*. The latter work was not continued beyond the first volume; but so far as this carries the subject, the comparison, at least in relation to strong sense and loftiness of moral tone, is not at all disadvantageous to the woman of the last century. There is in some quarters a vague prejudice against the *Rights of Woman* as in some way or other a reprehensible book, but readers who go to it with this impression will be surprised to find it eminently serious, severely moral, and withal rather heavy—the true reason, perhaps, that no edition has been published since 1796, and that it is now rather scarce. There are several points of resemblance, as well as of striking difference, between the two books. A strong understanding is present in both; but Margaret Fuller's mind was like some regions of her own American continent, where you are constantly stepping from the sunny 'clearings' into the mysterious twilight of the tangled forest—she often passes in one breath from forcible reasoning to dreamy vagueness; moreover, her unusually varied culture gives her great command of illustration. Mary Wollstonecraft, on the other hand, is nothing if not rational; she has no erudition, and her grave pages are lit up by no ray of fancy. In both writers we discern, under the brave bearing of a strong and truthful nature, the beating of a loving woman's heart, which teaches them not to undervalue the smallest offices of domestic care or kindliness. But Margaret Fuller, with all her passionate sensibility, is more of the literary woman, who would not have been satisfied without intellectual production; Mary Wollstonecraft, we imagine, wrote not at all for writing's sake, but from the pressure of other motives. So far as the difference of date allows, there is a striking coincidence in their trains of thought; indeed, every important idea in the *Rights of Woman*, except the combination of home education with a common day-school for boys and girls, reappears in Margaret Fuller's essay.

---

2. Tennyson, *The Princess* VII.253–58. As noted by Thomas Pinney, the quotation, slightly inaccurate, is from the un- revised 1847 text of the poem.
3. Original version published in *The Dial*; revised and expanded in 1855.

One point on which they both write forcibly is the fact that, while men have a horror of such faculty or culture in the other sex as tends to place it on a level with their own, they are really in a state of subjection to ignorant and feeble-minded women. Margaret Fuller says:

> Wherever man is sufficiently raised above extreme poverty or brutal stupidity, to care for the comforts of the fireside, or the bloom and ornament of life, woman has always power enough, if she chooses to exert it, and is usually disposed to do so, in proportion to her ignorance and childish vanity. Unacquainted with the importance of life and its purposes, trained to a selfish coquetry and love of petty power, she does not look beyond the pleasure of making herself felt at the moment, and governments are shaken and commerce broken up to gratify the pique of a female favorite. The English shopkeeper's wife does not vote, but it is for her interest that the politician canvasses by the coarsest flattery.

Again:

> All wives, bad or good, loved or unloved, inevitably influence their husbands from the power their position not merely gives, but necessitates of coloring evidence and infusing feelings in hours when the—patient, shall I call him?—is off his guard.

Hear now what Mary Wollstonecraft says on the same subject:

> Women have been allowed to remain in ignorance and slavish dependence many, very many years, and still we hear of nothing but their fondness of pleasure and sway, their preference of rakes and soldiers, their childish attachment to toys, and the vanity that makes them value accomplishments more than virtues. History brings forward a fearful catalogue of the crimes which their cunning has produced, when the weak slaves have had sufficient address to overreach their masters. . . . When, therefore, I call women slaves, I mean in a political and civil sense; for indirectly they obtain too much power, and are debased by their exertions to obtain illicit sway. . . . The libertinism, and even the virtues of superior men, will always give women of some description great power over them; and these weak women, under the influence of childish passions and selfish vanity, *will throw a false light over the objects which the very men view with their eyes who ought to enlighten their judgment.* Men of fancy, and those sanguine characters who mostly hold the helm of human affairs in general, relax in the society of women; and surely I need not cite to the most superficial reader of history the numerous examples of vice and oppression which the private intrigues of female favorites have produced; not to dwell on the mischief that naturally arises from the blundering interposition of well-meaning folly. *For in the transactions of business it is much better to have to deal with a knave than a fool, because a knave adheres to some plan, and any plan of reason may be seen through sooner than a sudden*

flight of folly. The power which vile and foolish women have had over wise men who possessed sensibility is notorious.

There is a notion commonly entertained among men that an instructed woman, capable of having opinions, is likely to prove an unpracticable yoke-fellow, always pulling one way when her husband wants to go the other, oracular in tone, and prone to give curtain lectures[4] on metaphysics. But surely, so far as obstinacy is concerned, your unreasoning animal is the most unmanageable of creatures, where you are not allowed to settle the question by a cudgel, a whip and bridle, or even a string to the leg. For our own parts, we see no consistent or commodious medium between the old plan of corporal discipline and that thorough education of women which will make them rational beings in the highest sense of the word. Wherever weakness is not harshly controlled it must *govern*, as you may see when a strong man holds a little child by the hand, how he is pulled hither and thither, and wearied in his walk by his submission to the whims and feeble movements of his companion. A really cultured woman, like a really cultured man, will be ready to yield in trifles. So far as we see, there is no indissoluble connection between infirmity of logic and infirmity of will, and a woman quite innocent of an opinion in philosophy, is as likely as not to have an indomitable opinion about the kitchen. As to airs of superiority, no woman ever had them in consequence of true culture, but only because her culture was shallow or unreal, only as a result of what Mrs. Malaprop well calls "the ineffectual qualities in a woman"[5]—mere acquisitions carried about, and not knowledge thoroughly assimilated so as to enter into the growth of the character.

To return to Margaret Fuller, some of the best things she says are on the folly of absolute definitions of woman's nature and absolute demarcations of woman's mission. "Nature," she says, "seems to delight in varying the arrangements, as if to show that she will be fettered by no rule; and we must admit the same varieties that she admits." Again: "If nature is never bound down, nor the voice of inspiration stifled, that is enough. We are pleased that women should write and speak, if they feel need of it, from having something to tell; but silence for ages would be no misfortune, if that silence be from divine command, and not from man's tradition." And here is a passage, the beginning of which has been often quoted:

> If you ask me what offices they [women] may fill, I reply— any. I do not care what case you put; let them be sea-captains if

---

4. See Douglas Jerrold's comic sketches of a wife who delivers nightly lectures to her husband from behind their bed-curtains, *Mrs. Caudle's Curtain Lectures* (1846).
5. In response to compliments about her "intellectual accomplishments," Mrs. Malaprop exclaims: "Ah! few gentlemen, nowadays, know how to value the ineffectual qualities in a woman!" See *The Rivals* III.ii (1775), by Richard Brinsley Sheridan.

you will. I do not doubt there are women well fitted for such an office, and, if so, I should be as glad as to welcome the Maid of Saragossa, or the Maid of Missolonghi, or the Suliote heroine, or Emily Plater.[6] I think women need, especially at this juncture, a much greater range of occupation than they have, to rouse their latent powers. ... In families that I know, some little girls like to saw wood, others to use carpenter's tools. Where these tastes are indulged, cheerfulness and good-humor are promoted. Where they are forbidden, because "such things are not proper for girls," they grow sullen and mischievous. Fourier had observed these wants of women, as no one can fail to do who watches the desires of. little girls, or knows the *ennui* that haunts grown women, except where they make to themselves a serene little world by art of some kind. He, therefore, in proposing a great variety of employments, in manufactures or the care of plants and animals, allows for one-third of women as likely to have a taste for masculine pursuits, one-third of men for feminine.[7] ... I have no doubt, however, that a large proportion of women would give themselves to the same employments as now, because there are circumstances that must lead them. Mothers will delight to make the nest soft and warm. Nature would take care of that; no need to clip the wings of any bird that wants to soar and sing, or finds in itself the strength of pinion for a migratory flight unusual to its kind. The difference would be that *all* need not be constrained to employments for which *some* are unfit.

Apropos of the same subject, we find Mary Wollstonecraft offering a suggestion which the women of the United States have already begun to carry out. She says:

Women, in particular, all want to be ladies, which is simply to have nothing to do, but listlessly to go they scarcely care where, for they cannot tell what. But what have women to do in society? I may be asked, but to loiter with easy grace; surely you would not condemn them all to suckle fools and chronicle small beer.[8] No. *Women might certainly study the art of healing, and be physicians as well as nurses.* ... Business of various kinds they might likewise pursue, if they were educated in a more orderly manner. ... Women would not then marry for a support, as men accept of places under government, and neglect the implied duties.

Men pay a heavy price for their reluctance to encourage self-help and independent resources in women. The precious meridian years

6. The Maid of Saragossa was Maria Agustin, who fought against the French at the seige of Saragossa, in Spain, in 1808 (see Byron's *Childe Harold's Pilgrimage* I.liv–lvi); the Maid of Missolonghi, an unidentified Greek, must have made some heroic exploit during the Turkish seiges of that town in 1822 or 1826; the Suliote heroine was probably Moscha, who led a band of 300 women to rout the Turks during the seige of Souli, in Albania, in 1803; Emily Plater, a Polish patriot, became a captain in command of a company in the insurgent army fighting the Russians in 1831.

7. Charles Fourier (1772–1837), in his utopian treatise *The New Industrial World* (1829–30), develops these theories in his discussion of "The Little Hordes."

8. Iago on the role of women (*Othello* II.i.160).

of many a man of genius have to be spent in the toil of routine, that an "establishment" may be kept up for a woman who can understand none of his secret yearnings,[9] who is fit for nothing but to sit in her drawing-room like a doll-Madonna in her shrine. No matter. Anything is more endurable than to change our established formulae about women, or to run the risk of looking up to our wives instead of looking down on them. *Sit divus, dummodo non sit vivus* (let him be a god, provided he be not living), said the Roman magnates of Romulus;[1] and so men say of women, let them be idols, useless absorbents of previous things, provided we are not obliged to admit them to be strictly fellow-beings, to be treated, one and all, with justice and sober reverence.

On one side we hear that woman's position can never be improved until women themselves are better; and, on the other, that women can never become better until their position is improved—until the laws are made more just, and a wider field opened to feminine activity. But we constantly hear the same difficulty stated about the human race in general. There is a perpetual action and reaction between individuals and institutions; we must try and mend both by little and little—the only way in which human things can be mended. Unfortunately, many over-zealous champions of women assert their actual equality with men—nay, even their moral superiority to men—as a ground for their release from oppressive laws and restrictions. They lose strength immensely by this false position. If it were true, then there would be a case in which slavery and ignorance nourished virtue, and so far we should have an argument for the continuance of bondage. But we want freedom and culture for woman, because subjection and ignorance have debased her, and with her, Man; for—

> If she be small, slight-natured, miserable,
> How shall men grow?[2]

Both Margaret Fuller and Mary Wollstonecraft have too much sagacity to fall into this sentimental exaggeration. Their ardent hopes of what women may become do not prevent them from seeing and painting women as they are. On the relative moral excellence of men and women Mary Wollstonecraft speaks with the most decision:

> Women are supposed to possess more sensibility, and even humanity, than men, and their strong attachments and instantaneous emotions of compassion are given as proofs; but the clinging affection of ignorance has seldom anything noble in it, and may mostly be resolved into selfishness, as well as the affection of chil-

---

9. Cf. Eliot's fictional representation of such a situation in her account of Dr. Lydgate's married life in *Middlemarch*.
1. Cf. *Historia Augusta*, "Geta" II, in which the same cynical comment is made on a proposal to have a man deified.
2. Tennyson, *The Princess* VII.249–50.

dren and brutes. I have known many weak women whose sensibility was entirely engrossed by their husbands; and as for their humanity, it was very faint indeed, or rather it was only a transient emotion of compassion. Humanity does not consist "in a squeamish ear," says an eminent orator.[3] "It belongs to the mind as well as to the nerves." But this kind of exclusive affection, though it degrades the individual, should not be brought forward as a proof of the inferiority of the sex, because it is the natural consequence of confined views; for even women of superior sense, having their attention turned to little employments and private plans, rarely rise to heroism, unless when spurred on by love! and love, as an heroic passion, like genius, appears but once in an age. I therefore agree with the moralist who asserts "that women have seldom so much generosity as men"; and that their narrow affections, to which justice and humanity are often sacrificed, render the sex apparently inferior, especially as they are commonly inspired by men; but I contend that the heart would expand as the understanding gained strength, if women were not depressed from their cradles.

We had marked several other passages of Margaret Fuller's for extract, but as we do not aim at an exhaustive treatment of our subject, and are only touching a few of its points, we have, perhaps, already claimed as much of the reader's attention as he will be willing to give to such desultory material.

1855

3. Unidentified, perhaps Edmund Burke (1729–97).

MATTHEW ARNOLD
(1822–1888)

1853: *Poems* (with Preface) published.
1857: Elected Professor of Poetry at Oxford.
1869: *Culture and Anarchy* published.

How is a full and enjoyable life to be lived in a modern industrial society? This was the recurrent topic in the poetry and prose of Matthew Arnold. In his poetry the question itself is raised; in his prose some answers are attempted. Arnold's mode of posing such questions may not always satisfy us, and his answers may sometimes be simply wrong. What is less excusable, as he himself said of Ruskin, is that he could be not only wrong but dogmatic when he was wrong. On the whole, however, his writings have fared well with posterity. "The misapprehensiveness of his age is exactly what a poet is sent to remedy," wrote Browning. Oddly enough it is to Arnold's work rather than to Browning's that the statement seems more appropriate. And its applicability to Arnold has persisted from Victorian times to ours, in part because the "misapprehensiveness" has also persisted. Of all the major Victorian writers, as F. R. Leavis has said, it is Arnold who, "because of the peculiar quality of his intelligence and the peculiar nature of his relation to his time, will repay special study in a way no others will."

Matthew Arnold was born in Laleham, a village in the valley of the Thames. That his childhood was spent in the vicinity of a river seems appropriate, for clear-flowing streams were later to appear in his poems as symbols of serenity. At 6, Arnold was moved to Rugby School, where his father, Dr. Thomas Arnold, had become headmaster. As a clergyman Dr. Arnold was a leader of the liberal or Broad Church and hence one of the principal opponents of John Henry Newman. As a headmaster he became famous as an educational reformer, a teacher who instilled into his pupils an earnest preoccupation with moral and social issues and also an awareness of the connection between liberal studies and modern life. At Rugby his eldest son, Matthew, was directly exposed to the powerful force of the father's mind and character. The son's attitude towards this force was a mixture of attraction and repulsion. That he was permanently influenced by his father is evident in his poems and in his writings on religion and politics, but like many sons of clergymen, he made a determined effort in his youth to be different. At Oxford he behaved like a character from one of Evelyn Waugh's early novels. Elegantly and colorfully dressed, alternately languid or merry in manner, he attracted attention as a dandy whose irreverent jokes irritated his more solemn undergraduate friends and acquaintances. With Rugby standards he appeared to have no connection. Even his studies did not seem to occupy him seriously. By a session of cramming, he managed to earn second-class honors in his final examinations, a near disaster that was redeemed by his election to a fellowship at Oriel College.

Arnold's biographers usually dismiss his youthful frivolity of spirit as a temporary pose or mask, but it was more. It remained to color his prose style, brightening his most serious criticism with geniality and wit. For most readers the jauntiness of his prose is a virtue, although for others it is offensive. Anyone suspicious of urbanity and irony would applaud Whitman's sour comment that Arnold is "one of the dudes of literature." A more appropriate estimate of his manner is provided by Arnold's own description of Sainte-Beuve as a critic: "a critic of measure, not exuberant; of the center, not provincial * * * with gay and amiable temper, his manner as good as his matter—the '*critique souriant*' [smiling critic]."

Unlike Tennyson or Carlyle, Arnold had to confine his writing and reading to his spare time. In 1847 he took the post of private secretary to Lord Lansdowne, and in 1851, the year of his marriage, he became an inspector of schools, a position which he held for 35 years. Although his work as an inspector may have reduced his output as a writer, it had several advantages. His extensive traveling in England took him to the homes of the more ardently Protestant middle classes, and when he criticized the dullness of middle-class life (as he often did), Arnold knew his subject intimately. His position also led to travel on the Continent to study the schools of Europe. As a critic of English education he was thus able to make helpful comparisons and to draw on a stock of fresh ideas in the same way as in his literary criticism he used his knowledge of French, German, Italian, and classical literatures to measure the achievements of English writers. Despite the monotony of much of his work as an inspector, Arnold became convinced of its importance. It was work that contributed to what he regarded as the most important need of his century: the development of a satisfactory system of education for the middle classes.

In 1849 Arnold published *The Strayed Reveler*, the first of his volumes of poetry. Eight years later, as a tribute to his poetic achievement, he was elected to the Professorship of Poetry at Oxford, a part-time position which he held for ten years. Later, like Dickens and Thackeray before him, Arnold toured America in order to make money by lecturing. For his two visits (1883 and 1886) there was the further inducement of seeing his daughter Lucy, who had married an American. Two years after his second visit to the United States, Arnold died of a sudden heart attack.

Arnold's career as a writer can be divided roughly into four periods. In the 1850's appeared most of his poems; in the 1860's, his literary criticism and social criticism; in the 1870's, his religious and educational writings, and in the 1880's, his second set of essays in literary criticism.

About his career as a poet, two questions are repeatedly asked. The first is whether his poetry is as effective or better than his prose; the second is why he virtually stopped writing poetry after 1860. The first has, of course, been variously answered. Many would endorse Tennyson's request in a letter: "Tell Mat not to write any more of those prose things like *Literature and Dogma*, but to give us something like his *Thyrsis, Scholar Gypsy*, or *Forsaken Merman*." At the opposite extreme is a recent critic, J. D. Jump, who has a high regard for Arnold's prose but considers only one of the poems to have merit: *Dover Beach*. Such readers complain, and with good cause, of Arnold's bad habits as a poet: for example, his excessive reliance upon italics instead of upon meter as a method of emphasizing the meaning of a line. Or they cite the prosy flatness with which he opens his fine sonnet *To a Friend*: "Who prop, thou ask'st, in these bad days, my mind?" Contrariwise, when Arnold leaves the flat plane of versified reflections and attempts to scale the heights of what he called "the grand style," there is a different kind of uncertainty which becomes evident, as in *Sohrab and Rustum*, in the over-elaborated similes. Yet the success of such lovely poems as *Thyrsis* is more than enough to overcome the indictments of the critics. Often, as in *Thyrsis*, he is at his best as a poet of nature. Settings of seashore or river or mountaintop provide something more than picturesque backdrops for these poems; they function to draw the meaning together. A concern for rendering outdoor nature may seem a curious accomplishment for so sophisticated a writer, but as his contemporaries noted, Arnold is in this respect, as in several others, similar to Thomas Gray.

Arnold's own verdict on the qualities of his poetry is a reasonable one. In a letter to his mother, in 1869, he writes: "My poems represent, on the whole, the main movement of mind of the last quarter of a century, and thus they will probably have their day as people become conscious to themselves of what that movement of mind is, and interested in the literary productions which reflect it. It might be fairly urged that I have less poetical sentiment than Tennyson, and less intellectual vigor and abundance that Browning; yet, because I have perhaps more of a fusion of the two than either of them, and have more regularly applied that fusion to the main line of modern development, I am likely enough to have my turn, as they have had theirs."

The emphasis in the letter upon "movement of mind" suggests that Arnold's poetry and prose should be studied together. Such an approach can be fruitful provided that it does not obscure the important difference between Arnold the poet and Arnold the critic. T. S. Eliot once said of his own writings that "in one's prose reflections one may be legitimately occupied with ideals, whereas in the writing of verse, one can deal only with actuality." Arnold's writings provide a nice verification of Eliot's seeming paradox. As a poet he usually records his own experiences, his own feelings of loneliness and isolation as a lover, his longing for a serenity that he cannot find, his melancholy sense of the passing of youth (more than for many men, Arnold's thirtieth birthday was an awesome landmark after which he felt, he said, "three parts iced over"). Above all he records his despair in a universe in which man's role seemed as incongruous as it was later to seem to Thomas Hardy. In a memorable passage of his *Stanzas from the Grande Chartreuse* he describes himself as "wandering between two worlds, one dead, / The other powerless to be born." And addressing the representatives of a faith which seems to him dead, he cries: "Take me, cowled forms, and fence me round, / Till I possess my soul again."

As a poet, then, like T. S. Eliot and W. H. Auden, Arnold provides a record of a sick individual in a sick society. This was "actuality" as he experienced it. As a prose-writer, a formulator of "ideals," he seeks a different role. It is the role of what Auden calls the "healer" of a sick society, or as he himself called Goethe, the "Physician of the iron age." And in this difference we have a clue to the question previously raised: why did Arnold virtually abandon the writing of poetry and shift into criticism? Among other reasons he abandoned it because he was dissatisfied with the kind of poetry he himself was writing.

In one of his excellent letters to his friend Arthur Hugh Clough in the 1850's (letters which provide the best insight we have into Arnold's mind and tastes) this note of dissatisfaction is struck: "I am glad you like the *Gypsy Scholar*—but what does it *do* for you? Homer *animates*—Shakespeare *animates*—in its poor way I think *Sohrab and Rustum animates*— the *Gypsy Scholar* at best awakens a pleasing melancholy. But this is not what we want." It is evident that early in his career Arnold had evolved a theory of what poetry should do for its readers, a theory based, in part, on his impression of what classical poetry had achieved. To help make life bearable, poetry, in Arnold's view, must bring joy. As he says in the Preface to his *Poems* in 1853, it must "inspirit and rejoice the reader"; it must "convey a charm, and infuse delight." Such a demand does not exclude tragic poetry but does exclude works "in which suffering finds no vent in action; in which a continual state of mental distress is prolonged." Of Charlotte Brontë's novel *Villette* he says witheringly: "The writer's mind contains nothing but hunger, rebellion, and rage. * * * No fine writing can hide this thoroughly, and it will be fatal to her in the long run." Judged by such a standard, most 19th-century poems, including *Empedocles on Etna* and others by Arnold, were unsatisfactory. And when Arnold tried himself to write poems which would meet his own requirements—*Sohrab* *and Rustum* or *Balder Dead*—he was not at his best. By the late 1850's he thus found himself at a dead end. By turning aside to literary criticism he was able partially to escape the dilemma. In his prose his melancholy and "morbid" personality was subordinated to the resolutely cheerful and purposeful character he had created for himself by an effort of will.

Arnold's two volumes of *Essays in Criticism* (1865 and 1888) repeatedly shows how authors as different as Marcus Aurelius, Tolstoy, Homer, and Wordsworth provide the virtues he sought in his reading. Among these virtues was plainness of style. Although he could on occasion recommend the richness of language of such poets as Keats or Tennyson—their "natural magic" as he himself called it—Arnold's usual preference was for literature that was unadorned. And beyond stylistic excellences the principal virtue he admired as a critic was what he called the quality of "high seriousness." Given a world in which formal religion appeared to be of subordinate importance, it became increasingly important to Arnold that the poet must be a serious thinker who could offer guidance for his readers. Arnold's attitude towards religion helps to account for his finally asking perhaps too much from literature. Excessive expectations underlie his most glaring blunder as a critic: his solemnly inadequate discussion of Chaucer's lack of high seriousness in *The Study of Poetry*.

In *The Function of Criticism* it is apparent that Arnold regarded good literary criticism, as he regarded literature itself, as a potent force in producing a civilized society. From a close study of this basic essay one could forecast the third stage of his career: his excursion into the criticism of society which was to culminate in *Culture and Anarchy* (1869) and *Friendship's Garland* (1871).

Arnold's starting point as a critic of society is different from that of Carlyle and John Ruskin. The older prophets attacked the Victorian middle classes on the grounds of their materialism, their selfish indifference to the sufferings of the poor—their immorality, in effect. Arnold argued instead that the "Philistines," as he called them, were not so much wicked as ignorant, narrow-minded, and suffering from the dullness of their private lives. This novel analysis was reinforced by Arnold's conviction that the world of the future would be a middle-class world, a world dominated therefore by a class inadequately equipped for leadership and inadequately equipped to enjoy civilized living.

To establish this point, Arnold employed cajolery, satire, and even quotations from the newspapers with considerable effect. He also employed catchwords (such as "sweetness and light") which have remained useful slogans even though they are an obstacle to understanding the complexities of his position. His view of civilization, for example, was pared down to a four-point formula of the four "powers": conduct, intellect and knowledge, beauty, social life and manners. The formula was simple and workable. Applying it to French or American civilizations, he had a scale by which to show up the virtues of different countries as well as their inadequacies. Applying the formula to his own country, Arnold usually awarded the Victorian middle classes an "A" in the first category (of conduct) but a failing grade in the other three categories.

Arnold's relentless exposure of middle-class narrow-mindedness eventually led him into the arena of religious controversy. As a critic of religious institutions he was arguing, in effect, that just as the middle classes did not know how to lead full lives, so also did they not know how to read the Bible intelligently or attend church intelligently. His three full-length studies of the Bible, including *Literature and Dogma* (1873), are best considered in this way as a postscript to his social criticism. The Bible, to Arnold, was a great work of literature like the *Odyssey*, and the Church of England was a great national institution like Parliament. Both Bible and church must be preserved not because historical Christianity was credible but because both, when properly understood, were agents of what he called "culture"—they contributed to making mankind more civilized.

The term *culture* is perhaps Arnold's most familiar catchword, although what he meant by it has sometimes been misunderstood. For him the term connotes the qualities of an open-minded intelligence (as described in *The Function of Criticism*)—a refusal to take things on authority. In this respect, Arnold appears close to T. H. Huxley and J. S. Mill. But the word also connotes a full awareness of man's past and a capacity to enjoy the best works of art, literature, history, and philosophy that have come down to us from that past. As a way of viewing life in all its aspects, including the social, political, and religious, culture represents for Arnold the most effective way of curing the ills of a sick society. It is his principal prescription.

To attempt to define culture brings one to a final aspect of Arnold's career as a critic: his writings on education, in which he sought to make cultural values, as he said, "prevail." Most obviously these writings comprise his reply to Huxley in his admirably reasoned essay, *Literature and Science*, as well as his volumes of official reports written as an inspector of schools. Less obviously they comprise all of his prose. At the core of these writings is his belief that good education is the crucial need for modern man. Arnold was essentially a great teacher raised to the nth degree. He has the faults of a teacher: a tendency to repeat himself, to lean too hard on formulated phrases, and he displays something of the lectern manner at times. He also has the great teacher's virtues, in particular the virtue of skillfully conveying to us the conviction on which all his arguments are based. This conviction is that the humanist tradition of which he is the expositor can enable the individual man or woman to live life more fully as well as to change the course of society. For these values Arnold fought. He boxed with the gloves on—kid gloves, his opponents used to say—and he provided a lively exhibition of footwork that is a pleasure in itself for us to witness. Yet the gracefulness of the display should not obscure the fact that he is landing hard blows squarely on what Carlyle called the vast blockheadism.

Although his lifelong attacks against the inadequacies of puritanism make Arnold one of the most anti-Victorian figures of the Victorian age, there is an assumption behind his attacks that is itself characteristically Victorian. This assumption is that the puritan middle classes *can* be changed, that they are, as we would more clumsily say, educable. In 1852, writing to Clough on the subject of equality (a political objective in which he believed by conviction if not by instinct), he observed: "I am more and more convinced that the world tends to become more comfortable for the mass, and more uncomfortable for those of any natural gift or distinction—and it is as well perhaps that it should be so—for hitherto the gifted have astonished and delighted the world, but not trained or inspired or in any real way changed it." Arnold's gifts as a poet and critic enabled him to do both: to delight the world and also to change it.

Shakespeare

Others abide our question. Thou art free.
We ask and ask—Thou smilest and art still,
Out-topping knowledge. For the loftiest hill,
Who to the stars uncrowns his majesty,

Planting his steadfast footsteps in the sea,[1]   5
Making the heaven of heavens his dwelling place,
Spares but the cloudy border of his base
To the foiled searching of mortality;

And thou, who didst the stars and sunbeams know,
Self-schooled, self-scanned, self-honored, self-secure,   10
Didst tread on earth unguessed at.—Better so!

All pains the immortal spirit must endure,
All weakness which impairs, all griefs which bow,
Find their sole speech in that victorious brow.

1844   1849

In Harmony with Nature[2]

TO A PREACHER

"In harmony with Nature?" Restless fool,
Who with such heat dost preach what were to thee,
When true, the last impossibility—
To be like Nature strong, like Nature cool!

Know, man hath all which Nature hath, but more,   5
And in that *more* lie all his hopes of good.
Nature is cruel, man is sick of blood;
Nature is stubborn, man would fain adore;

Nature is fickle, man hath need of rest;
Nature forgives no debt, and fears no grave;   10
Man would be mild, and with safe conscience blest.

Man must begin, know this, where Nature ends;
Nature and man can never be fast friends.
Fool, if thou canst not pass her, rest her slave!

1844(?)   1849

1. Cf. William Cowper's Olney Hymn 35: "God moves in a mysterious way / His wonders to perform; / He plants his footsteps in the sea, / And rides upon the storm."
2. Originally entitled: "To an Independent Preacher, who preached that we should be 'In Harmony with Nature.'"

To a Friend

Who prop, thou ask'st, in these bad days, my mind?—
He much, the old man,[3] who, clearest-souled of men,
Saw The Wide Prospect, and the Asian Fen,
And Tmolus hill, and Smyrna bay, though blind.

Much he, whose friendship I not long since won,   5
That halting slave, who in Nicopolis [4]
Taught Arrian, when Vespasian's brutal son [5]
Cleared Rome of what most shamed him. But be his

My special thanks, whose even-balanced soul,
From first youth tested up to extreme old age,   10
Business could not make dull, nor passion wild;

Who saw life steadily, and saw it whole;
The mellow glory of the Attic stage,
Singer of sweet Colonus,[4] and its child.

                                                    1849

The Forsaken Merman[1]

Come, dear children, let us away;
Down and away below!
Now my brothers call from the bay,
Now the great winds shoreward blow,
Now the salt tides seaward flow;
Now the wild white horses play,   5
Champ and chafe and toss in the spray.
Children dear, let us away!
This way, this way!

Call her once before you go—   10
Call once yet!
In a voice that she will know:
"Margaret! Margaret!"
Children's voices should be dear
(Call once more) to a mother's ear;   15

---

3. Homer, who was reputed to have been born in Smyrna, a seaport of what is now Turkey. From Smyrna he saw across the sea to Europe ("The Wide Prospect") as well as to the nearby marshes ("Fen") and mountain ranges ("Tmolus hill") of Asia Minor.
4. Epictetus, a lame philosopher who was exiled to Nicopolis where he taught Stoicism to Arrian, a Greek historian.
5. I.e., the Emperor Domitian (81–96). Because the philosophers had "shamed" him, he had ordered their expulsion from Rome.
4. Sophocles (496–406 B.C.), a native of Colonus, sang of his town in his *Oedipus at Colonus*.
1. For a comparison of Arnold's skillful telling of this story with the Danish version from which he derived it, see C. B. Tinker and H. F. Lowry: *The Poetry of Arnold: A Commentary* (1940), pp. 129–132.

Children's voices, wild with pain—
Surely she will come again!
Call her once and come away;
This way, this way!
"Mother dear, we cannot stay!   20
The wild white horses foam and fret."
Margaret! Margaret!

Come, dear children, come away down;
Call no more!
One last look at the white-walled town,   25
And the little gray church on the windy shore,
Then come down!
She will not come though you call all day;
Come away, come away!

Children dear, was it yesterday   30
We heard the sweet bells over the bay?
In the caverns where we lay,
Through the surf and through the swell,
The far-off sound of a silver bell?
Sand-strewn caverns, cool and deep,   35
Where the winds are all asleep;
Where the spent lights quiver and gleam,
Where the salt weed sways in the stream,
Where the sea beasts, ranged all round,
Feed in the ooze of their pasture ground;   40
Where the sea snakes coil and twine,
Dry their mail and bask in the brine;
Where great whales come sailing by,
Sail and sail, with unshut eye,
Round the world for ever and aye?   45
When did music come this way?
Children dear, was it yesterday?

Children dear, was it yesterday
(Call yet once) that she went away?
Once she sate with you and me,   50
On a red gold throne in the heart of the sea,
And the youngest sate on her knee.
She combed its bright hair, and she tended it well,
When down swung the sound of a far-off bell.
She sighed, she looked up through the clear green sea;   55
She said: "I must go, for my kinsfolk pray
In the little gray church on the shore today.
'Twill be Easter time in the world—ah me!
And I lose my poor soul, Merman! here with thee."
I said: "Go up, dear heart, through the waves;   60
Say thy prayer, and come back to the kind sea caves!"
She smiled, she went up through the surf in the bay.
Children dear, was it yesterday?

Children dear, were we long alone?
"The sea grows stormy, the little ones moan;   65
Long prayers," I said, "in the world they say;
Come!" I said; and we rose through the surf in the bay.
We went up the beach, by the sandy down
Where the sea stocks bloom, to the white-walled town;
Through the narrow paved streets, where all was still,   70
To the little gray church on the windy hill.
From the church came a murmur of folk at their prayers,
But we stood without in the cold blowing airs.
We climbed on the graves, on the stones worn with rains,
And we gazed up the aisle through the small leaded panes.   75
She sate by the pillar; we saw her clear:
"Margaret, hist! come quick, we are here!
Dear heart," I said, "we are long alone;
The sea grows stormy, the little ones moan."
But, ah, she gave me never a look,   80
For her eyes were sealed to the holy book!
Loud prays the priest; shut stands the door.
Come away, children, call no more!
Come away, come down, call no more!

Down, down, down!   85
Down to the depths of the sea!
She sits at her wheel in the humming town,
Singing most joyfully.
Hark what she sings: "O joy, O joy,
For the humming street, and the child with its toy!   90
For the priest, and the bell, and the holy well;
For the wheel where I spun,
And the blessed light of the sun!"
And so she sings her fill,
Singing most joyfully,   95
Till the spindle drops from her hand,
And the whizzing wheel stands still.
She steals to the window, and looks at the sand,
And over the sand at the sea;
And her eyes are set in a stare;   100
And anon there breaks a sigh,
And anon there drops a tear,
From a sorrow-clouded eye,
And a heart sorrow-laden,
A long, long sigh;   105
For the cold strange eyes of a little Mermaiden
And the gleam of her golden hair.

Come away, away children;
Come children, come down!
The hoarse wind blows coldly;   110
Lights shine in the town.
She will start from her slumber

When gusts shake the door;
She will hear the winds howling,
Will hear the waves roar.   115
We shall see, while above us
The waves roar and whirl,
A ceiling of amber,
A pavement of pearl.
Singing: "Here came a mortal,   120
But faithless was she!
And alone dwell forever
The kings of the sea."

But, children, at midnight,
When soft the winds blow,   125
When clear falls the moonlight,
When spring tides are low;
When sweet airs come seaward
From heaths starred with broom,
And high rocks throw mildly ·   130
On the blanched sands a gloom;
Up the still, glistening beaches,
Up the creek we will hie,
Over the banks of bright seaweed
The ebb tide leaves dry.   135
We will gaze, from the sand hills,
At the white, sleeping town;
At the church on the hillside—
And then come back down.
Singing: "There dwells a loved one,   140
But cruel is she!
She left lonely forever
The kings of the sea."

                                                              1849

Isolation. To Marguerite[1]

We were apart; yet, day by day,
I bade my heart more constant be.
I bade it keep the world away,
And grow a home for only thee;

1. Addressed to a girl Arnold is reputed to have met in Switzerland in the 1840's. It has been commonly assumed that she was French or Swiss, but some recent biographies speculate she might have been Mary Claude, a girl Arnold knew in England at this same period, who, although English, had connections with Germany and had translated German prose and verse.

Nor feared but thy love likewise grew, 5
Like mine, each day, more tried, more true.

The fault was grave! I might have known,
What far too soon, alas! I learned—
The heart can bind itself alone,
And faith may oft be unreturned. 10
Self-swayed our feelings ebb and swell—
Thou lov'st no more—Farewell! Farewell!

Farewell!—and thou, thou lonely heart,[2]
Which never yet without remorse
Even for a moment didst depart 15
From thy remote and spheréd course
To haunt the place where passions reign—
Back to thy solitude again!

Back! with the conscious thrill of shame
Which Luna[3] felt, that summer night, 20
Flash through her pure immortal frame,
When she forsook the starry height
To hang over Endymion's sleep
Upon the pine-grown Latmian steep.

Yet she, chaste queen, had never proved 25
How vain a thing is mortal love,
Wandering in Heaven, far removed.
But thou hast long had place to prove
This truth—to prove, and make thine own:
"Thou hast been, shalt be, art, alone." 30

Or, if not quite alone, yet they
Which touch thee are unmating things—
Ocean and clouds and night and day;
Lorn autumns and triumphant springs;
And life, and others' joy and pain, 35
And love, if love, of happier men.

Of happier men—for they, at least,
Have *dreamed* two human hearts might blend
In one, and were through faith released
From isolation without end 40
Prolonged; nor knew, although not less
Alone than thou, their loneliness.

1857

---

2. Presumably the speaker's heart, not Marguerite's.
3. Luna (or Diana), the goddess of chastity and of the moon, fell in love with Endymion, a handsome shepherd, whom she discovered asleep on Mt. Latmos.

To Marguerite—Continued

Yes! in the sea of life enisled,
With echoing straits between us thrown,
Dotting the shoreless watery wild,
We mortal millions live *alone*.
The islands feel the enclasping flow,   5
And then their endless bounds they know.

But when the moon their hollows lights,
And they are swept by balms of spring,
And in their glens, on starry nights,
The nightingales divinely sing;   10
And lovely notes, from shore to shore,
Across the sounds and channels pour—

Oh! then a longing like despair
Is to their farthest caverns sent;
For surely once, they feel, we were   15
Parts of a single continent!
Now round us spreads the watery plain—
Oh might our marges meet again!

Who ordered that their longing's fire
Should be, as soon as kindled, cooled?   20
Who renders vain their deep desire?—
A God, a God their severance ruled!
And bade betwixt their shores to be
The unplumbed, salt, estranging sea.

ca. 1849   1852

The Buried Life

Light flows our war of mocking words, and yet,
Behold, with tears mine eyes are wet!
I feel a nameless sadness o'er me roll.
Yes, yes, we know that we can jest,
We know, we know that we can smile!   5
But there's a something in this breast,
To which thy light words bring no rest,
And thy gay smiles no anodyne.
Give me thy hand, and hush awhile,
And turn those limpid eyes on mine,   10
And let me read there, love! thy inmost soul.

Alas! is even love too weak
To unlock the heart, and let it speak?
Are even lovers powerless to reveal
To one another what indeed they feel?   15
I knew the mass of men concealed
Their thoughts, for fear that if revealed
They would by other men be met
With blank indifference, or with blame reproved;
I knew they lived and moved   20
Tricked in disguises, alien to the rest
Of men, and alien to themselves—and yet
The same heart beats in every human breast!
But we, my love!—doth a like spell benumb
Our hearts, our voices?—must we too be dumb?   25

Ah! well for us, if even we,
Even for a moment, can get free
Our heart, and have our lips unchained;
For that which seals them hath been deep-ordained!

Fate, which foresaw   30
How frivolous a baby man would be—
By what distractions he would be possessed,
How he would pour himself in every strife,
And well-nigh change his own identity—
That it might keep from his capricious play   35
His genuine self, and force him to obey
Even in his own despite his being's law,
Bade through the deep recesses of our breast
The unregarded river of our life
Pursue with indiscernible flow its way;   40
And that we should not see
The buried stream, and seem to be
Eddying at large in blind uncertainty,
Though driving on with it eternally.

But often, in the world's most crowded streets,[1]   45
But often, in the din of strife,
There rises an unspeakable desire
After the knowledge of our buried life;
A thirst to spend our fire and restless force
In tracking out our true, original course;   50
A longing to inquire
Into the mystery of this heart which beats
So wild, so deep in us—to know
Whence our lives come and where they go.
And many a man in his own breast then delves,   55

1. This passage, like many others in Arnold's poetry, illustrates the impact on his writings of Wordsworth. In this instance cf. Wordsworth's *Tintern Abbey*, lines 25–27: "But oft, in lonely rooms, and 'mid the din / Of towns and cities, I have owed to them, / In hours of weariness, sensations sweet."

But deep enough, alas! none ever mines.
And we have been on many thousand lines,
And we have shown, on each, spirit and power;
But hardly have we, for one little hour,
Been on our own line, have we been ourselves—   60
Hardly had skill to utter one of all
The nameless feelings that course through our breast,
But they course on forever unexpressed.
And long we try in vain to speak and act
Our hidden self, and what we say and do   65
Is eloquent, is well—but 'tis not true!
And then we will no more be racked
With inward striving, and demand
Of all the thousand nothings of the hour
Their stupefying power;   70
Ah yes, and they benumb us at our call!
Yet still, from time to time, vague and forlorn,
From the soul's subterranean depth upborne
As from an infinitely distant land,
Come airs, and floating echoes, and convey   75
A melancholy into all our day.[2]

Only—but this is rare—
When a beloved hand is laid in ours,
When, jaded with the rush and glare
Of the interminable hours,   80
Our eyes can in another's eyes read clear,
When our world-deafened ear
Is by the tones of a loved voice caressed—
A bolt is shot back somewhere in our breast,
And a lost pulse of feeling stirs again.   85
The eye sinks inward, and the heart lies plain,
And what we mean, we say, and what we would, we know.
A man becomes aware of his life's flow,
And hears its winding murmur; and he sees
The meadows where it glides, the sun, the breeze.   90

And there arrives a lull in the hot race
Wherein he doth forever chase
That flying and elusive shadow, rest.
An air of coolness plays upon his face,
And an unwonted calm pervades his breast.   95
And then he thinks he knows
The hills where his life rose,
And the sea where it goes.

1852

2. Cf. Wordsworth's *Ode: Intimations of Immortality*, lines 151–53: "Those shadowy recollections, / Which, be they what they may, / Are yet the fountain light of all our day."

Memorial Verses[1]

APRIL, 1850

Goethe in Weimar sleeps, and Greece,
Long since, saw Byron's struggle cease.
But one such death remained to come;
The last poetic voice is dumb—
We stand today by Wordsworth's tomb.   5

When Byron's eyes were shut in death,
We bowed our head and held our breath.
He taught us little; but our soul
Had *felt* him like the thunder's roll.
With shivering heart the strife we saw   10
Of passion with eternal law;
And yet with reverential awe
We watched the fount of fiery life
Which served for that Titanic strife.

When Goethe's death was told, we said: 15
Sunk, then, is Europe's sagest head.
Physician of the iron age,
Goethe has done his pilgrimage.
He took the suffering human race,
He read each wound, each weakness clear;   20
And struck his finger on the place,
And said: *Thou ailest here, and here!*
He looked on Europe's dying hour
Of fitful dream and feverish power;
His eye plunged down the weltering strife,   25
The turmoil of expiring life—
He said: *The end is everywhere,*
Art still has truth, take refuge there!
And he was happy, if to know
Causes of things, and far below   30
His feet to see the lurid flow
Of terror, and insane distress,
And headlong fate, be happiness.

1. This elegy was written shortly after Wordsworth had died in April, 1850, at the age of 80. Arnold had known the poet as a man and deeply admired his writings—as is evident not only in this poem but in his late essay, *Wordsworth*. Byron, who died in Greece in 1824, had affected Arnold profoundly in his youth, but later that strenuous "Titanic" po-etry seemed to him less satisfactory, its value limited by its lack of serenity. His final verdict on Byron can be encountered in his essay in *Essays in Criticism: Second Series*. Goethe, who died in 1832, was regarded by Arnold as a great philosophical poet and the most significant man of letters of the early 19th century.

And Wordsworth!—Ah, pale ghosts, rejoice!
For never has such soothing voice   35
Been to your shadowy world conveyed,
Since erst, a morn, some wandering shade
Heard the clear song of Orpheus[2] come
Through Hades, and the mournful gloom.
Wordsworth has gone from us—and ye,   40
Ah, may ye feel his voice as we!
He too upon a wintry clime
Had fallen—on this iron time
Of doubts, disputes, distractions, fears.
He found us when the age had bound   45
Our souls in its benumbing round;
He spoke, and loosed our heart in tears.
He laid us as we lay at birth
On the cool flowery lap of earth,
Smiles broke from us and we had ease;   50
The hills were round us, and the breeze
Went o'er the sunlit fields again;
Our foreheads felt the wind and rain.
Our youth returned; for there was shed
On spirits that had long been dead,   55
Spirits dried up and closely furled,
The freshness of the early world.

Ah! since dark days still bring to light
Man's prudence and man's fiery might,
Time may restore us in his course   60
Goethe's sage mind and Byron's force;
But where will Europe's latter hour
Again find Wordsworth's healing power?
Others will teach us how to dare,
And against fear our breast to steel;   65
Others will strengthen us to bear—
But who, ah! who, will make us feel?
The cloud of mortal destiny,
Others will front it fearlessly—
But who, like him, will put it by?   70

Keep fresh the grass upon his grave
O Rotha,[3] with thy living wave!
Sing him thy best! for few or none
Hears thy voice right, now he is gone.

1850   1850

2. By means of his beautiful music, Orpheus won his way through Hades in his search for the shade of his dead wife, Eurydice.
3. A river near Wordsworth's burial place.

Longing

Come to me in my dreams, and then
By day I shall be well again!
For then the night will more than pay
The hopeless longing of the day.

Come, as thou cam'st a thousand times,   5
A messenger from radiant climes,
And smile on thy new world, and be
As kind to others as to me!

Or, as thou never cam'st in sooth,
Come now, and let me dream it truth;   10
And part my hair, and kiss my brow,
And say: *My love! why sufferest thou?*

Come to me in my dreams, and then
By day I shall be well again!
For then the night will more than pay   15
The hopeless longing of the day.

                                    1852

Lines Written in Kensington Gardens[4]

In this lone, open glade I lie,
Screened by deep boughs on either hand;
And at its end, to stay the eye,
Those black-crowned, red-boled pine trees stand!

Birds here make song, each bird has his,   5
Across the girdling city's hum.
How green under the boughs it is!
How thick the tremulous sheep-cries come![5]
Sometimes a child will cross the glade
To take his nurse his broken toy;   10
Sometimes a thrush flit overhead
Deep in her unknown day's employ.

Here at my feet what wonders pass,
What endless, active life is here!
What blowing daisies, fragrant grass!   15
An air-stirred forest, fresh and clear.

4. A park in the heart of London.
5. Sheep are sometimes grazed in London parks.

Scarce fresher is the mountain sod
Where the tired angler lies, stretched out,
And, eased of basket and of rod,
Counts his day's spoil, the spotted trout.   20

In the huge world, which roars hard by,
Be others happy if they can!
But in my helpless cradle I
Was breathed on by the rural Pan.

I, on men's impious uproar hurled,   25
Think often, as I hear them rave,
That peace has left the upper world
And now keeps only in the grave.

Yet here is peace forever new!
When I who watch them am away,   30
Still all things in this glade go through
The changes of their quiet day.

Then to their happy rest they pass!
The flowers upclose, the birds are fed,
The night comes down upon the grass,   35
The child sleeps warmly in his bed.

Calm soul of all things! make it mine
To feel, amid the city's jar,
That there abides a peace of thine,
Man did not make, and cannot mar.   40

The will to neither strive nor cry,
The power to feel with others give!
Calm, calm me more! nor let me die
Before I have begun to live.

1852

Philomela[1]

Hark! ah, the nightingale—
The tawny-throated!
Hark, from that moonlit cedar what a burst!
What triumph! hark!—what pain!

O wanderer from a Grecian shore,   5
Still, after many years, in distant lands,
Still nourishing in thy bewildered brain

1. The Greek tale of violence evoked by the song of the nightingale concerned two sisters, Philomela and Procne. In Arnold's version, Philomela was married to a king of Thrace. After learning that her husband had raped

That wild, unquenched, deep-sunken, old-world pain—
Say, will it never heal?
And can this fragrant lawn   10
With its cool trees, and night,
And the sweet, tranquil Thames,
And moonshine, and the dew,
To thy racked heart and brain
Afford no balm?   15

Dost thou tonight behold,
Here, through the moonlight on this English grass,
The unfriendly palace in the Thracian wild?
Dost thou again peruse
With hot cheeks and seared eyes   20
The too clear web,[2] and thy dumb sister's shame?
Dost thou once more assay
Thy flight, and feel come over thee,
Poor fugitive, the feathery change
Once more, and once more seem to make resound   25
With love and hate, triumph and agony,
Lone Daulis, and the high Cephissian vale?[3]
Listen, Eugenia[4]—
How thick the bursts come crowding through the leaves!
Again—thou hearest?   30
Eternal passion!
Eternal pain!

1848   1853

Requiescat[5]

Strew on her roses, roses,
    And never a spray of yew!
In quiet she reposes;
    Ah, would that I did too!

Her mirth the world required;   5
    She bathed it in smiles of glee.
But her heart was tired, tired,
    And now they let her be.

Procne and cut out her tongue to prevent the outrage being discovered, Philomela was transformed into a nightingale.
2. A picture in needlework made by
Procne to tell what had happened to
her.

3. Daulis, a city in Phocis, where
Philomela's transformation took place;
the "Cephissian vale" was a river valley in Phocis.
4. Unidentified listener.
5. "May she rest."

Her life was turning, turning,
   In mazes of heat and sound.   10
But for peace her soul was yearning,
   And now peace laps her round.

Her cabined, ample spirit,
   It fluttered and failed for breath.
Tonight it doth inherit   15
   The vasty hall of death.

                     1853

The Scholar Gypsy   The story of a 17th-century student who left
Oxford and joined a band of gypsies had made a strong impression on
Arnold. In the poem he wistfully imagines that the spirit of this scholar
is still to be encountered in the Cumner countryside near Oxford, having achieved immortality by a serene pursuit of the secret of human existence. Like Keats's nightingale, the scholar has escaped "the weariness,
the fever, and the fret" of modern life.

   At the outset, the poet addresses a shepherd who has been helping him
in his search for traces of the scholar. The shepherd is addressed as "you."
After line 61, with the shift to "thou" and "thy," the person addressed
is the scholar himself, and the poet thereafter sometimes uses the pronoun "we" to indicate he is speaking for all mankind of later generations.

   About the setting Arnold wrote to his brother Tom on May 15, 1857:
"You alone of my brothers are associated with that life at Oxford, the
freest and most delightful part, perhaps, of my life, when with you and
Clough and Walrond I shook off all the bonds and formalities of the place,
and enjoyed the spring of life and that unforgotten Oxfordshire and
Berkshire country. Do you remember a poem of mine called 'The Scholar
Gipsy'? It was meant to fix the remembrance of those delightful wanderings
of ours in the Cumner Hills."

   The passage from Joseph Glanvill's *Vanity of Dogmatizing* (1661)
which inspired the poem was included by Arnold as a note:

There was very lately a lad in the University of Oxford, who was by his
poverty forced to leave his studies there; and at last to join himself to a
company of vagabond gypsies. Among these extravagant people, by the
insinuating subtilty of his carriage, he quickly got so much of their love and
esteem as that they discovered to him their mystery. After he had been
a pretty while exercised in the trade, there chanced to ride by a couple of
scholars, who had formerly been of his acquaintance. They quickly spied
out their old friend among the gypsies; and he gave them an account of
the necessity which drove him to that kind of life, and told them that
the people he went with were not such imposters as they were taken for,
but that they had a traditional kind of learning among them, and could
do wonders by the power of imagination, their fancy binding that of
others: that himself had learned much of their art, and when he had
compassed the whole secret, he intended, he said, to leave their company, and give the world an account of what he had learned.

The Scholar Gypsy

Go, for they call you, shepherd, from the hill;
  Go, shepherd, and untie the wattled cotes![1]
    No longer leave thy wistful flock unfed,
  Nor let thy bawling fellows rack their throats,
    Nor the cropped herbage shoot another head.   5
      But when the fields are still,
  And the tired men and dogs all gone to rest,
    And only the white sheep are sometimes seen
    Cross and recross the strips of moon-blanched green,
Come, shepherd, and again begin the quest!   10

Here, where the reaper was at work of late—
  In this high field's dark corner, where he leaves
    His coat, his basket, and his earthen cruse,[2]
  And in the sun all morning binds the sheaves,
    Then here, at noon, comes back his stores to use—   15
      Here will I sit and wait,
  While to my ear from uplands far away
    The bleating of the folded[3] flocks is borne,
    With distant cries of reapers in the corn[4]—
All the live murmur of a summer's day.   20

Screened is this nook o'er the high, half-reaped field,
  And here till sundown, shepherd! will I be.
    Through the thick corn the scarlet poppies peep,
  And round green roots and yellowing stalks I see
    Pale pink convolvulus in tendrils creep;   25
      And air-swept lindens yield
  Their scent, and rustle down their perfumed showers
    Of bloom on the bent grass[5] where I am laid,
    And bower me from the August sun with shade;
And the eye travels down to Oxford's towers.   30

And near me on the grass lies Glanvill's book—
  Come, let me read the oft-read tale again!
    The story of the Oxford scholar poor,
  Of pregnant parts[6] and quick inventive brain,
    Who, tired of knocking at preferment's door,   35
      One summer morn forsook
  His friends, and went to learn the gypsy lore,
    And roamed the world with that wild brotherhood,
    And came, as most men deemed, to little good,
But came to Oxford and his friends no more.   40

But once, years after, in the country lanes,
  Two scholars, whom at college erst he knew,

---

1. Sheepfolds woven from sticks.
2. Pot or jug for carrying his drink.
3. Penned up.
4. Grain or wheat.
5. A stiff kind of grass.
6. Teeming with ideas.

Met him, and of his way of life inquired;
Whereat he answered, that the gypsy crew,
   His mates, had arts to rule as they desired   45
      The workings of men's brains,
And they can bind them to what thoughts they will.
"And I," he said, "the secret of their art,
   When fully learned, will to the world impart;
But it needs heaven-sent moments for this skill."   50

This said, he left them, and returned no more.—
   But rumors hung about the countryside,
      That the lost Scholar long was seen to stray,
   Seen by rare glimpses, pensive and tongue-tied,
      In hat of antique shape, and cloak of gray,   55
      The same the gypsies wore.
Shepherds had met him on the Hurst [7] in spring;
   At some lone alehouse in the Berkshire moors,
   On the warm ingle-bench,[8] the smock-frocked boors
Had found him seated at their entering,   60

But, 'mid their drink and clatter, he would fly.
   And I myself seem half to know thy looks,
      And put the shepherds, wanderer! on thy trace;
And boys who in lone wheatfields scare the rooks[9]
      I ask if thou hast passed their quiet place;   65
      Or in my boat I lie
Moored to the cool bank in the summer heats,
   'Mid wide grass meadows which the sunshine fills,
   And watch the warm, green-muffled Cumner hills,
And wonder if thou haunt'st their shy retreats.   70

For most, I know, thou lov'st retired ground!
   Thee at the ferry Oxford riders blithe,
      Returning home on summer nights, have met
   Crossing the stripling Thames[1] at Bab-lock-hithe,
      Trailing in the cool stream thy fingers wet,   75
      As the punt's rope chops round;[2]
And leaning backward in a pensive dream,
   And fostering in thy lap a heap of flowers
   Plucked in shy fields and distant Wychwood bowers,
And thine eyes resting on the moonlit stream.   80

And then they land, and thou art seen no more!—

---

7. A hill near Oxford. All the place names in the poem (except those in the final two stanzas) refer to the countryside near Oxford.
8. Fireside bench. "Boors," here, are rustics.
9. Boys hired to frighten crows away from eating wheat grains. See Hardy's novel *Jude the Obscure*, I.ii.
1. I.e., the narrow upper reaches of the river before it broadens out to its full width.
2. The scholar's flat-bottomed boat ("punt") is tied up by a rope at the river bank near the ferry-crossing like the speaker's boat (in the previous stanza), which was "moored to the cool bank." The motion of the boat as it is stirred by the current of the river causes the chopping sound of the rope in the water.

Maidens, who from the distant hamlets come
  To dance around the Fyfield elm in May,
Oft through the darkening fields have seen thee roam,
  Or cross a stile into the public way.   85
    Oft thou hast given them store
Of flowers—the frail-leafed, white anemone,
  Dark bluebells drenched with dews of summer eves,
  And purple orchises with spotted leaves—
But none hath words she can report of thee.   90

And, above Godstow Bridge, when hay time's here
  In June, and many a scythe in sunshine flames,
  Men who through those wide fields of breezy grass
Where black-winged swallows haunt the glittering Thames,
  To bathe in the abandoned lasher pass,[3]   95
    Have often passed thee near
Sitting upon the river bank o'ergrown;
  Marked thine outlandish garb, thy figure spare,
  Thy dark vague eyes, and soft abstracted air—
But, when they came from bathing, thou wast gone!   100

At some lone homestead in the Cumner hills,
  Where at her open door the housewife darns,
  Thou hast been seen, or hanging on a gate
To watch the threshers in the mossy barns.
  Children, who early range these slopes and late   105
    For cresses from the rills,
Have known thee eying, all an April day,
  The springing pastures and the feeding kine;
  And marked thee, when the stars come out and shine,
Through the long dewy grass move slow away.   110

In autumn, on the skirts of Bagley Wood—
  Where most the gypsies by the turf-edged way
  Pitch their smoked tents, and every bush you see
With scarlet patches tagged and shreds of gray,
  Above the forest ground called Thessaly—   115
    The blackbird, picking food,
Sees thee, nor stops his meal, nor fears at all;
  So often has he known thee past him stray,
  Rapt, twirling in thy hand a withered spray,
And waiting for the spark from heaven to fall.   120

And once, in winter, on the causeway chill
  Where home through flooded fields foot-travelers go,
  Have I not passed thee on the wooden bridge,
Wrapped in thy cloak and battling with the snow,
  Thy face tow'rd Hinksey and its wintry ridge?   125
    And thou hast climbed the hill,
And gained the white brow of the Cumner range;

3. Water that spills over a dam or weir.

Turned once to watch, while thick the snowflakes fall,
The line of festal light in Christ Church hall[4]—
Then sought thy straw in some sequestered grange.   130

But what—I dream! Two hundred years are flown
Since first thy story ran through Oxford halls,
And the grave Glanvill did the tale inscribe
That thou wert wandered from the studious walls
To learn strange arts, and join a gypsy tribe;   135
And thou from earth art gone
Long since, and in some quiet churchyard laid—
Some country nook, where o'er thy unknown grave
Tall grasses and white flowering nettles wave,
Under a dark, red-fruited yew tree's shade.   140

—No, no, thou hast not felt the lapse of hours!
For what wears out the life of mortal men?
'Tis that from change to change their being rolls;
'Tis that repeated shocks, again, again,
Exhaust the energy of strongest souls   145
And numb the elastic powers.
Till having used our nerves with bliss and teen,[5]
And tired upon a thousand schemes our wit,
To the just-pausing Genius[6] we remit
Our worn-out life, and are—what we have been.   150

Thou hast not lived, why should'st thou perish, so?
Thou hadst *one* aim, *one* business, *one* desire;
Else wert thou long since numbered with the dead!
Else hadst thou spent, like other men, thy fire!
The generations of thy peers are fled,   155
And we ourselves shall go;
But thou possessest an immortal lot,
And we imagine thee exempt from age
And living as thou liv'st on Glanvill's page,
Because thou hadst—what we, alas! have not.   160

For early didst thou leave the world, with powers
Fresh, undiverted to the world without,
Firm to their mark, not spent on other things;
Free from the sick fatigue, the languid doubt,
Which much to have tried, in much been baffled, brings.   165
O life unlike to ours!
Who fluctuate idly without term or scope,
Of whom each strives, nor knows for what he strives,
And each half[7] lives a hundred different lives;
Who wait like thee, but not, like thee, in hope.   170

Thou waitest for the spark from heaven! and we,
Light half-believers of our casual creeds,
Who never deeply felt, nor clearly willed,

4. The dining hall of an Oxford college.
5. Vexation.
6. Perhaps the spirit of the universe,
which pauses briefly to receive back
the life given to us.
7. An adverb modifying "lives."

Whose insight never has borne fruit in deeds,
  Whose vague resolves never have been fulfilled;   175
    For whom each year we see
Breeds new beginnings, disappointments new;
  Who hesitate and falter life away,
  And lose tomorrow the ground won today—
Ah! do not we, wanderer! await it too?   180
Yes, we await it!—but it still delays,
  And then we suffer! and amongst us one,[8]
    Who most has suffered, takes dejectedly
His seat upon the intellectual throne;
  And all his store of sad experience he   185
    Lays bare of wretched days;
Tells us his misery's birth and growth and signs,
  And how the dying spark of hope was fed,
  And how the breast was soothed, and how the head,
And all his hourly varied anodynes.   190

This for our wisest! and we others pine,
  And wish the long unhappy dream would end,
    And waive all claim to bliss, and try to bear;
With close-lipped patience for our only friend,
  Sad patience, too near neighbor to despair—   195
    But none has hope like thine!
Thou through the fields and through the woods dost stray,
  Roaming the countryside, a truant boy,
  Nursing thy project in unclouded joy,
And every doubt long blown by time away.   200

O born in days when wits were fresh and clear,
  And life ran gaily as the sparkling Thames;
    Before this strange disease of modern life,
With its sick hurry, its divided aims,
  Its heads o'ertaxed, its palsied hearts, was rife—   205
    Fly hence, our contact fear!
Still fly, plunge deeper in the bowering wood!
  Averse, as Dido[9] did with gesture stern
  From her false friend's approach in Hades turn,
Wave us away, and keep thy solitude!   210

Still nursing the unconquerable hope,
  Still clutching the inviolable shade,
    With a free, onward impulse brushing through,
By night, the silvered branches of the glade—
  Far on the forest skirts, where none pursue.   215
    On some mild pastoral slope
Emerge, and resting on the moonlit pales
  Freshen thy flowers as in former years
  With dew, or listen with enchanted ears,

---

8. Probably Tennyson, whose *In Memoriam* had appeared in 1850, or perhaps Goethe.
9. Dido committed suicide after her lover, Aeneas, deserted her. When he later encountered her in Hades, she turned sternly away from him.

From the dark dingles,[10] to the nightingales!   220
But fly our paths, our feverish contact fly!
    For strong the infection of our mental strife,
        Which, though it gives no bliss, yet spoils for rest;
    And we should win thee from thy own fair life,
        Like us distracted, and like us unblest.   225
            Soon, soon thy cheer would die,
    Thy hopes grow timorous, and unfixed thy powers,
        And thy clear aims be cross and shifting made;
    And then thy glad perennial youth would fade,
        Fade, and grow old at last, and die like ours.   230

Then fly our greetings, fly our speech and smiles!
    —As some grave Tyrian trader, from the sea,
        Descried at sunrise an emerging prow
    Lifting the cool-haired creepers stealthily,
        The fringes of a southward-facing brow   235
            Among the Aegean isles;
    And saw the merry Grecian coaster come,
        Freighted with amber grapes, and Chian wine,
        Green, bursting figs, and tunnies[1] steeped in brine—
    And knew the intruders on his ancient home,   240

The young lighthearted masters of the waves—
    And snatched his rudder, and shook out more sail;
        And day and night held on indignantly
    O'er the blue Midland waters with the gale,
        Betwixt the Syrtes[2] and soft Sicily,   245
            To where the Atlantic raves
    Outside the western straits; and unbent sails
        There, where down cloudy cliffs, through sheets of foam,
        Shy traffickers, the dark Iberians[3] come;
    And on the beach undid his corded bales.[4]   250

                                                        1853

10. Small deep valleys.
1. Tuna fish.
2. Shoals off the coast of North Africa.
3. Dark inhabitants of Spain and Portugal—perhaps associated with gypsies.
4. The elaborate simile of the final two stanzas has been variously interpreted and misinterpreted. The trader from Tyre is disconcerted when, peering out through the foliage ("fringes") that screens his hiding place, he sees noisy intruders entering his harbor. Like the Scholar Gypsy, when similarly intruded upon by hearty extroverts, he resolves to flee and seek a new home.
    The reference (line 249) to the Iberians as "*shy* traffickers" (traders) is explained by Kenneth Allott as having been derived from Herodotus' *History* (IV.196). Herodotus describes a distinctive method of selling goods established by Carthaginian merchants who used to sail through the straits of Gibraltar to trade with the inhabitants of the coast of West Africa.

The Carthaginians would leave bales of their merchandise on display along the beaches and, without having seen their prospective customers, would return to their ships. The shy natives would then come down from their inland hiding places and set gold beside the bales they wished to buy. When the natives withdrew in their turn, the Carthaginians would return to the beach and decide whether payments were adequate, a process repeated until agreement was reached. On the Atlantic coasts this method of bargaining persisted into the 19th century. As William Beloe, a translator of Herodotus, noted in 1844: "In this manner they transact their exchange without seeing one another, or without the least instance of dishonesty * * * on either side." For the solitary Tyrian trader such a procedure, with its avoidance of *contact* (line 221), would have been especially appropriate.

Dover Beach

The sea is calm tonight.
The tide is full, the moon lies fair
Upon the straits—on the French coast the light
Gleams and is gone; the cliffs of England stand,
Glimmering and vast, out in the tranquil bay.   5
Come to the window, sweet is the night air!
Only, from the long line of spray
Where the sea meets the moon-blanched land,
Listen! you hear the grating roar[1]
Of pebbles which the waves draw back, and fling,   10
At their return, up the high strand,
Begin, and cease, and then again begin,
With tremulous cadence slow, and bring
The eternal note of sadness in.

Sophocles long ago   15
Heard it on the Aegean, and it brought
Into his mind the turbid ebb and flow
Of human misery;[2] we
Find also in the sound a thought,
Hearing it by this distant northern sea.   20

The Sea of Faith
Was once, too, at the full, and round earth's shore
Lay like the folds of a bright girdle furled.[3]
But now I only hear
Its melancholy, long, withdrawing roar,   25
Retreating, to the breath
Of the night wind, down the vast edges drear
And naked shingles[4] of the world.

Ah, love, let us be true
To one another! for the world, which seems   30
To lie before us like a land of dreams,
So various, so beautiful, so new,
Hath really neither joy, nor love, nor light,
Nor certitude, nor peace, nor help for pain;
And we are here as on a darkling plain   35

1. Cf. Wordsworth's *It Is a Beauteous Evening:* "Listen! the mighty Being is awake, / And doth with his eternal motion make / A sound like thunder—everlastingly."
2. See Sophocles' *Antigone,* lines 583 ff.
3. This difficult line means, in general, that at high tide the sea envelops the land closely. Its forces are "gathered" up (to use Wordsworth's term for it) like the "folds" of bright clothing ("girdle") which have been compressed ("furled"). At ebb tide, as the sea retreats, it is unfurled and spread out. It still surrounds the shoreline but not as an "enclasping flow" (as Arnold speaks of the sea in *To Marguerite, Continued*). See also *2 Henry IV*, III.i.49–51: "to see / The beachy girdle of the ocean / Too wide for Neptune's hips."
4. Beaches covered with pebbles.

Swept with confused alarms of struggle and flight,
Where ignorant armies [5] clash by night.

ca. 1851   1867

Stanzas from the Grande Chartreuse[1]

Through Alpine meadows soft-suffused
With rain, where thick the crocus blows,
Past the dark forges long disused,
The mule track from Saint Laurent goes.
The bridge is crossed, and slow we ride,   5
Through forest, up the mountainside.

The autumnal evening darkens round,
The wind is up, and drives the rain;
While, hark! far down, with strangled sound
Doth the Dead Guier's[2] stream complain,   10
Where that wet smoke, among the woods,
Over his boiling cauldron broods.

Swift rush the spectral vapors white
Past limestone scars[3] with ragged pines,
Showing—then blotting from our sight!—   15
Halt—through the cloud-drift something shines!
High in the valley, wet and drear,
The huts of Courrerie appear.

Strike leftward! cries our guide; and higher
Mounts up the stony forest way.   20
At last the encircling trees retire;
Look! through the showery twilight gray
What pointed roofs are these advance?—
A palace of the Kings of France?

Approach, for what we seek is here!   25
Alight, and sparely sup, and wait
For rest in this outbuilding near;
Then cross the sward and reach that gate.
Knock; pass the wicket! Thou art come
To the Carthusians' world-famed home.   30

5. Perhaps the revolutions of 1848 or a reference to the siege of Rome by the French in 1849. The date of composition of the poem is unknown, although generally assumed to be 1851.
1. A monastery situated high in the French Alps. It was established in 1084 by St. Bruno, founder of the Carthusians (line 30), whose austere regimen of solitary contemplation, fasting, and religious exercises (lines 37–44) had remained virtually unchanged for centuries.

Arnold visited the site September 7, 1851, accompanied by his bride. His account may be compared with that by Wordsworth (*Prelude* VI. 416–88) who had made a similar visit in 1790.
2. The Guiers Mort river flows down from the monastery and joins the Guiers Vif in the valley below. Wordsworth speaks of the two rivers as "the sister streams of Life and Death."
3. Precipices.

The silent courts, where night and day
Into their stone-carved basins cold
The splashing icy fountains play—
The humid corridors behold!
Where, ghostlike in the deepening night,   35
Cowled forms brush by in gleaming white.

The chapel, where no organ's peal
Invests the stern and naked prayer—
With penitential cries they kneel
And wrestle; rising then, with bare   40
And white uplifted faces stand,
Passing the Host from hand to hand;[4]

Each takes, and then his visage wan
Is buried in his cowl once more.
The cells!—the suffering Son of Man   45
Upon the wall—the knee-worn floor—
And where they sleep, that wooden bed,
Which shall their coffin be, when dead![5]

The library, where tract and tome
Not to feed priestly pride are there,   50
To hymn the conquering march of Rome,
Nor yet to amuse, as ours are!
They paint of souls the inner strife,
Their drops of blood, their death in life.

The garden, overgrown—yet mild,   55
See, fragrant herbs[6] are flowering there!
Strong children of the Alpine wild
Whose culture is the brethren's care;
Of human tasks their only one,
And cheerful works beneath the sun.   60

Those halls, too, destined to contain
Each its own pilgrim-host of old,
From England, Germany, or Spain—
All are before me! I behold
The House, the Brotherhood austere!   65
—And what am I, that I am here?

For rigorous teachers seized my youth,
And purged its faith, and trimmed its fire,
Showed me the high, white star of Truth,

4. Arnold, during his short visit, may not actually have witnessed the service of the Mass in the monastery. The consecrated wafer (the Host) is not passed from the hand of the officiating priest to the hands of the communicant (as is the practice in Arnold's own Anglican church) but placed, instead, on the tongue of the communicant (who kneels rather than stands). See Tinker and Lowry, *The Poetry of Matthew Arnold: A Commentary*, pp. 249–51.
5. A Carthusian is buried on a wooden plank but does not sleep in a coffin.
6. From which the liqueur, Chartreuse, is manufactured. Sales of this liqueur provide the principal revenues for upkeep of the monastery.

There bade me gaze, and there aspire.   70
Even now their whispers pierce the gloom:
What dost thou in this living tomb?

Forgive me, masters of the mind![7]
At whose behest I long ago
So much unlearnt, so much resigned—   75
I come not here to be your foe!
I seek these anchorites, not in ruth,[8]
To curse and to deny your truth;

Not as their friend, or child, I speak!
But as, on some far northern strand,   80
Thinking of his own Gods, a Greek
In pity and mournful awe might stand
Before some fallen Runic stone—[9]
For both were faiths, and both are gone.

Wandering between two worlds, one dead,   85
The other powerless to be born,
With nowhere yet to rest my head,
Like these, on earth I wait forlorn.
Their faith, my tears, the world deride—
I come to shed them at their side.   90

Oh, hide me in your gloom profound,
Ye solemn seats of holy pain!
Take me, cowled forms, and fence me round,
Till I possess my soul again;
Till free my thoughts before me roll,   95
Not chafed by hourly false control!

For the world cries your faith is now
But a dead time's exploded dream;
My melancholy, sciolists[1] say,
Is a passed mode, an outworn theme—   100
As if the world had ever had
A faith, or sciolists been sad!

Ah, if it *be* passed, take away,
At least, the restlessness, the pain;
Be man henceforth no more a prey   105
To these out-dated stings again!
The nobleness of grief is gone—
Ah, leave us not the fret alone!

---

7. Writers whose insistence upon testing religious beliefs in the light of fact and reason persuaded Arnold that faith in Christianity (especially in the Roman Catholic or Anglo Catholic forms) was no longer tenable in the modern world.
8. Remorse for having adopted the rationalist view of Christianity.
9. A monument inscribed in Teutonic letters (runes), emblematic of a Nordic religion that has become extinct. The relic reminds the Greek that his own religion is likewise dying and will soon be extinct. See Arnold's *Preface* of 1853, second paragraph.
1. Superficial-minded persons who pretend to know the answers to all questions.

But—if you[2] cannot give us ease—
Last of the race of them who grieve   110
Here leave us to die out with these
Last of the people who believe!
Silent, while years engrave the brow;
Silent—the best are silent now.

Achilles[3] ponders in his tent,   115
The kings of modern thought[4] are dumb;
Silent they are, though not content,
And wait to see the future come.
They have the grief men had of yore,
But they contend and cry no more.   120

Our fathers[5] watered with their tears
This sea of time whereon we sail,
Their voices were in all men's ears
Who passed within their puissant hail.
Still the same ocean round us raves,   125
But we stand mute, and watch the waves.

For what availed it, all the noise
And outcry of the former men?—
Say, have their sons achieved more joys,
Say, is life lighter now than then?   130
The sufferers died, they left their pain—
The pangs which tortured them remain.

What helps it now, that Byron bore,
With haughty scorn which mocked the smart,
Through Europe to the Aetolian shore[6]   135
The pageant of his bleeding heart?
That thousands counted every groan,
And Europe made his woe her own?

What boots it, Shelley! that the breeze
Carried thy lovely wail away,   140
Musical through Italian trees
Which fringe thy soft blue Spezzian bay?[7]
Inheritors of thy distress
Have restless hearts one throb the less?

---

2. It is not clear whether the speaker has resumed addressing his "rigorous teachers" (line 67) or (as would seem more likely) a combination of the sciolists, who scorn the speaker's melancholy and the worldly, who scorn the faith of the monks. See his address to the "sons of the world" (lines 160–68).
3. Achilles, after the death of Patroclus, refused to participate in the Trojan war; hence similar to modern intellectual leaders who refuse to speak out about

their frustrated sense of alienation.
4. Variously but never satisfactorily identified as Newman or Carlyle (the latter was said to have preached the gospel of silence in 40 volumes). Another advocate of stoical silence was the French poet, Alfred de Vigny (1797–1863).
5. Predecessors among the Romantic writers such as Byron.
6. Region in Greece where Byron died.
7. The Gulf of Spezzia in Italy, where Shelley was drowned.

Or are we easier, to have read, 145
O Obermann![8] the sad, stern page,
Which tells us how thou hidd'st thy head
From the fierce tempest of thine age
In the lone brakes of Fontainebleau,
Or chalets near the Alpine snow? 150

Ye slumber in your silent grave!—
The world, which for an idle day
Grace to your mood of sadness gave,
Long since hath flung her weeds[9] away.
The eternal trifler[1] breaks your spell; 155
But we—we learnt your lore too well!

Years hence, perhaps, may dawn an age,
More fortunate, alas! than we,
Which without hardness will be sage,
And gay without frivolity. 160
Sons of the world, oh, speed those years;
But, while we wait, allow our tears!

Allow them! We admire with awe
The exulting thunder of your race;
You give the universe your law, 165
You triumph over time and space!
Your pride of life, your tireless powers,
We laud them, but they are not ours.

We are like children reared in shade
Beneath some old-world abbey wall, 170
Forgotten in a forest glade,
And secret from the eyes of all.
Deep, deep the greenwood round them waves,
Their abbey, and its close[2] of graves!

But, where the road runs near the stream, 175
Oft through the trees they catch a glance
Of passing troops in the sun's beam—
Pennon, and plume, and flashing lance!
Forth to the world those soldiers fare,
To life, to cities, and to war! 180

And through the wood, another way,
Faint bugle notes from far are borne,
Where hunters gather, staghounds bay,[3]
Round some fair forest-lodge at morn.
Gay dames are there, in sylvan green; 185
Laughter and cries—those notes between!

8. Melancholy hero of *Obermann* (1804),
a novel by Senancour.
9. Mourning clothes.
1. The sciolist, as in line 99.

2. Enclosure.
3. Cf. the contrast between recluses and
hunters in *The Scholar Gypsy*, lines 71–
81.

The banners flashing through the trees
Make their blood dance and chain their eyes;
That bugle music on the breeze
Arrests them with a charmed surprise.   190
Banner by turns and bugle woo:
Ye shy recluses, follow too!

O children, what do ye reply?—
"Action and pleasure, will ye roam
Through these secluded dells to cry   195
And call us?—but too late ye come!
Too late for us your call ye blow,
Whose bent was taken long ago.

"Long since we pace this shadowed nave;
We watch those yellow tapers shine,   200
Emblems of hope over the grave,
In the high altar's depth divine;
The organ carries to our ear
Its accents of another sphere.

"Fenced early in this cloistral round   205
Of reverie, of shade, of prayer,
How should we grow in other ground?
How can we flower in foreign air?
—Pass, banners, pass, and bugles, cease;
And leave our desert to its peace!"   210

1852(?)   1855

Thyrsis[1]

A MONODY, TO COMMEMORATE THE AUTHOR'S FRIEND, ARTHUR HUGH CLOUGH, WHO DIED AT FLORENCE, 1861

How changed is here each spot man makes or fills!
  In the two Hinkseys[2] nothing keeps the same;

1. In the 1840's, at Oxford, Clough had been one of Arnold's closest friends. After the death of this fellow poet, twenty years later, Arnold revisited the Thames-valley countryside which they had explored together. The familiar scenes prompted him to review the changes wrought by time on the ideals shared in his Oxford days with Clough, ideals symbolized, in part, by a distant elm and by the story of the Scholar Gypsy. The survival of these ideals in the face of the difficulties of modern life is the subject of this elegy. Unlike Tennyson in such elegies as *In Memoriam*, Arnold rarely touches here upon other kinds of immortality.

As a framework for his elegy, Arnold draws on the same Greek and Latin pastoral tradition from which Milton's *Lycidas* and Shelley's *Adonais* were derived. Hence Clough is referred to by one of the traditional names for a shepherd-poet, Thyrsis, and Arnold himself as Corydon. The sense of distancing which results from this traditional elegiac mode is reduced considerably by the realism of the setting with its bleak wintry landscape at twilight, a landscape which is brightened, in turn, by evocations of the return of hopeful springtime.
2. The villages of North Hinksey and South Hinksey.

The village street its haunted mansion lacks,
And from the sign is gone Sibylla's name,[3]
   And from the roofs the twisted chimney stacks—   5
      Are ye too changed, ye hills?
See, 'tis no foot of unfamiliar men
   Tonight from Oxford up your pathway strays!
      Here came I often, often, in old days—
Thyrsis and I; we still had Thyrsis then.   10

Runs it not here, the track by Childsworth Farm,
   Past the high wood, to where the elm tree crowns
      The hill behind whose ridge the sunset flames?
The signal-elm, that looks on Ilsley Downs,
   The Vale, the three lone weirs, the youthful Thames?—   15
      This winter eve is warm,
Humid the air! leafless, yet soft as spring,
   The tender purple spray on copse and briers!
      And that sweet city with her dreaming spires,
She needs not June for beauty's heightening,   20

Lovely all times she lies, lovely tonight!—
   Only, methinks, some loss of habit's power
      Befalls me wandering through this upland dim.
Once passed I blindfold here, at any hour;
   Now seldom come I, since I came with him.   25
      That single elm tree bright
Against the west—I miss it! is it gone?
   We prized it dearly; while it stood, we said,
      Our friend, the Gypsy Scholar, was not dead;
While the tree lived, he in these fields lived on.   30

Too rare, too rare, grow now my visits here,
   But once I knew each field, each flower, each stick;
      And with the countryfolk acquaintance made
By barn in threshing time, by new-built rick.
   Here, too, our shepherd pipes we first assayed.   35
      Ah me! this many a year
My pipe is lost, my shepherd's holiday!
   Needs must I lose them, needs with heavy heart
      Into the world and wave of men depart;
But Thyrsis of his own will went away.[4]   40

It irked him to be here, he could not rest.
   He loved each simple joy the country yields,
      He loved his mates; but yet he could not keep,[5]
For that a shadow loured on the fields,
   Here with the shepherds and the silly[6] sheep.   45
      Some life of men unblest

3. Sibylla Kerr had been the proprietress of a tavern in South Hinksey.
4. Arnold left Oxford out of the necessity for earning a living; Clough left as a matter of principle when in 1848 he resigned a fellowship rather than subscribe to the creed of the Anglican Church.
5. Stay.
6. Innocent.

He knew, which made him droop, and filled his head.
    He went; his piping took a troubled sound
      Of storms[7] that rage outside our happy ground;
    He could not wait their passing, he is dead.   50

So, some tempestuous morn in early June,
    When the year's primal burst of bloom is o'er,
      Before the roses and the longest day—
    When garden walks and all the grassy floor
      With blossoms red and white of fallen May   55
        And chestnut flowers are strewn—
    So have I heard the cuckoo's parting cry,
      From the wet field, through the vexed garden trees,
      Come with the volleying rain and tossing breeze:
    The bloom is gone, and with the bloom go I!   60

Too quick despairer, wherefore wilt thou go?
    Soon will the high Midsummer pomps come on,
      Soon will the musk carnations break and swell,
    Soon shall we have gold-dusted snapdragon,
      Sweet-william with his homely cottage smell,   65
        And stocks in fragrant blow;
    Roses that down the alleys shine afar,
      And open, jasmine-muffled lattices,
      And groups under the dreaming garden trees,
    And the full moon, and the white evening star.   70

He hearkens not! light comer, he is flown!
    What matters it? next year he will return,
      And we shall have him in the sweet spring days,
    With whitening hedges, and uncrumpling fern,
      And bluebells trembling by the forest ways,   75
        And scent of hay new-mown.
    But Thyrsis never more we swains shall see;
      See him come back, and cut a smoother reed,
      And blow a strain the world at last shall heed—
    For Time, not Corydon, hath conquered thee!   80

Alack, for Corydon no rival now!—
    But when Sicilian shepherds lost a mate,
      Some good survivor with his flute would go,
    Piping a ditty sad for Bion's fate;[8]
      And cross the unpermitted ferry's flow,[9]   85
        And relax Pluto's brow,
    And make leap up with joy the beauteous head
      Of Proserpine, among whose crownéd hair
      Are flowers first opened on Sicilian air,
    And flute his friend, like Orpheus, from the dead.[1]   90

7. Religious and political controversies.
8. Moschus, a Greek poet, composed a pastoral elegy upon the death of the poet Bion in Sicily.
9. The river Styx across which the dead were ferried to the underworld where Pluto ruled with his queen, Proserpine. In spring, Proserpine's returning above ground in Sicily would cause the flowers to blossom.
1. Orpheus' music enabled him to enter the "unpermitted" realms of the dead and to bring his wife, Eurydice, back with him to the land of the living.

O easy access to the hearer's grace
   When Dorian shepherds[2] sang to Proserpine!
     For she herself had trod Sicilian fields,
  She knew the Dorian water's gush divine,
     She knew each lily white which Enna yields,[3]   95
       Each rose with blushing face;
  She loved the Dorian pipe, the Dorian strain.
     But ah, of our poor Thames she never heard!
     Her foot the Cummer cowslips never stirred;
  And we should tease her with our plaint in vain!   100

Well! wind-dispersed and vain the words will be,
   Yet, Thyrsis, let me give my grief its hour
     In the old haunt, and find our tree-topped hill!
  Who, if not I, for questing here hath power?
     I know the wood which hides the daffodil,   105
       I know the Fyfield tree,
  I know what white, what purple fritillaries[4]
     The grassy harvest of the river fields,
     Above by Ensham, down by Sandford, yields,
  And what sedged brooks are Thames's tributaries;   110

I know these slopes; who knows them if not I?—
   But many a dingle[5] on the loved hillside,
     With thorns once studded, old, white-blossomed trees,
  Where thick the cowslips grew, and far descried
     High towered the spikes of purple orchises,   115
       Hath since our day put by
  The coronals of that forgotten time;
     Down each green bank hath gone the plowboy's team,
     And only in the hidden brookside gleam
  Primroses, orphans of the flowery prime.   120

Where is the girl, who by the boatman's door,
   Above the locks, above the boating throng,
     Unmoored our skiff when through the Wytham flats,
  Red loosestrife[6] and blond meadowsweet among
     And darting swallows and light water-gnats,   125
       We tracked the shy Thames shore?
  Where are the mowers, who, as the tiny swell
     Of our boat passing heaved the river grass,
     Stood with suspended scythe to see us pass?—
  They all are gone, and thou art gone as well!   130

Yes, thou art gone! and round me too the night
   In ever-nearing circle weaves her shade.
     I see her veil draw soft across the day,

2. The Dorian Greeks had colonized Sicily, the home of pastoral poetry.
3. From a meadow near Enna, a Sicilian town, Proserpine had been carried off to the underworld by Pluto (or Dis). Cf. the touchstone lines admired by Arnold in *Paradise Lost* (IV.268–71): "that fair field / Of Enna, where Proserpine gathering flowers, / Herself a fairer flower, by gloomy Dis / Was gathered * * * "
4. Flowers commonly found in moist meadows.
5. Small deep valley.
6. Flowers which grow on banks of streams.

I feel her slowly chilling breath invade
    The cheek grown thin, the brown hair sprent[7] with gray; 135
      I feel her finger light
Laid pausefully upon life's headlong train;
    The foot less prompt to meet the morning dew,
    The heart less bounding at emotion new,
And hope, once crushed, less quick to spring again.   140

And long the way appears, which seemed so short
    To the less practiced eye of sanguine youth;
    And high the mountaintops, in cloudy air,
The mountaintops where is the throne of Truth,[8]
    Tops in life's morning sun so bright and bare!   145
      Unbreachable the fort
Of the long-battered world uplifts its wall;
    And strange and vain the earthly turmoil grows,
    And near and real the charm of thy repose,
And night as welcome as a friend would fall.   150

But hush! the upland hath a sudden loss
    Of quiet!—Look, adown the dusk hillside,
    A troop of Oxford hunters going home,
As in old days, jovial and talking, ride!
    From hunting with the Berkshire hounds they come.   155
      Quick! let me fly, and cross
Into yon farther field!—'Tis done; and see,
    Backed by the sunset, which doth glorify
    The orange and pale violet evening sky,
Bare on its lonely ridge, the Tree! the Tree!   160

I take the omen! Eve lets down her veil,
    The white fog creeps from bush to bush about,
    The west unflushes, the high stars grow bright,
And in the scattered farms the lights come out.
    I cannot reach the signal-tree tonight,   165
      Yet, happy omen, hail!
Hear it from thy broad lucent Arno vale[9]
    (For there thine earth-forgetting eyelids keep
    The morningless and unawakening sleep
Under the flowery oleanders pale),   170

Hear it, O Thyrsis, still our tree is there!—
    Ah, vain! These English fields, this upland dim,
    These brambles pale with mist engarlanded,
That lone, sky-pointing tree, are not for him;
    To a boon southern country he is fled,   175
      And now in happier air,
Wandering with the great Mother's[1] train divine

7. Sprinkled.
8. Cf. Pope's *Essay on Criticism*, II.220–32.
9. Clough was buried in Florence, which is situated in the valley of the Arno River.

1. Demeter (whose name may mean Earth Mother) was worshiped as the goddess of agriculture. The "immortal chants" (line 181) would be sung in her honor by her followers, members of the "train divine" (line 176).

(And purer or more subtle soul than thee,
I trow, the mighty Mother doth not see)
Within a folding of the Apennine,[2]   180

Thou hearest the immortal chants of old!—
Putting his sickle to the perilous grain
In the hot cornfield of the Phrygian king,[3]
For thee the Lityerses song again
Young Daphnis with his silver voice doth sing;   185
Sings his Sicilian fold,
His sheep, his hapless love, his blinded eyes—
And how a call celestial round him rang,
And heavenward from the fountain brink he sprang,
And all the marvel of the golden skies.   190

There thou art gone, and me thou leavest here
Sole in these fields! yet will I not despair.
Despair I will not, while I yet descry
'Neath the mild canopy of English air
That lonely tree against the western sky.   195
Still, still these slopes, 'tis clear,
Our Gypsy Scholar haunts, outliving thee!
Fields where soft sheep from cages pull the hay,
Woods with anemones in flower till May,
Know him a wanderer still; then why not me?   200

A fugitive and gracious light he seeks,
Shy to illumine; and I seek it too.
This does not come with houses or with gold,
With place, with honor, and a flattering crew;
'Tis not in the world's market bought and sold—   205
But the smooth-slipping weeks
Drop by, and leave its seeker still untired;
Out of the heed of mortals he is gone,
He wends unfollowed, he must house alone;
Yet on he fares, by his own heart inspired.   210

Thou too, O Thyrsis, on like quest wast bound;
Thou wanderedst with me for a little hour!
Men gave thee nothing; but this happy quest,
If men esteemed thee feeble, gave thee power,

2. Mountains near Florence.
3. Arnold includes a note from Servius'
commentary on Virgil's *Eclogues:*
"Daphnis, the ideal Sicilian shepherd
of Greek pastoral poetry, was said to
have followed into Phrygia his mistress Piplea, who had been carried off by
robbers, and to have found her in the
power of the king of Phrygia, Lityerses.
Lityerses used to make strangers try a
contest with him in reaping corn, and to
put them to death if he overcame them.
Hercules arrived in time to save Daphnis, took upon himself the reaping
contest with Lityerses, overcame him,
and slew him. The Lityerses song connected with this tradition was, like the
Linus song, one of the early plaintive
strains of Greek popular poetry, and
used to be sung by corn reapers. Other
traditions represented Daphnis as beloved by a nymph who exacted from
him an oath to love no one else. He fell
in love with a princess, and was struck
blind by the jealous nymph. Mercury,
who was his father, raised him to
heaven, and made a fountain spring up
in the place from which he ascended. At
this fountain the Sicilians offered yearly
sacrifices."

If men procured thee trouble, gave thee rest.   215
    And this rude Cumner ground,
Its fir-topped Hurst, its farms, its quiet fields,
    Here cam'st thou in thy jocund youthful time,
    Here was thine height of strength, thy golden prime!
And still the haunt beloved a virtue yields.   220

What though the music of thy rustic flute
    Kept not for long its happy, country tone;
      Lost it too soon, and learnt a stormy note[4]
Of men contention-tossed, of men who groan,
      Which tasked thy pipe too sore, and tired thy throat— 225
      It failed, and thou wast mute!
Yet hadst thou alway visions of our light,
    And long with men of care thou couldst not stay,
    And soon thy foot resumed its wandering way,
Left human haunt, and on alone till night.   230

Too rare, too rare, grow now my visits here!
    'Mid city noise, not, as with thee of yore,
    Thyrsis! in reach of sheep-bells is my home.
—Then through the great town's harsh, heart-wearying roar,
    Let in thy voice a whisper often come,   235
      To chase fatigue and fear:
Why faintest thou? I wandered till I died.
    Roam on! The light we sought is shining still.
    Dost thou ask proof? Our tree yet crowns the hill,
Our Scholar travels yet the loved hillside.   240

1866

Palladium

Set where the upper streams of Simois[5] flow
Was the Palladium,[6] high 'mid rock and wood;
And Hector was in Ilium, far below,
And fought, and saw it not—but there it stood!

It stood, and sun and moonshine rained their light   5
On the pure columns of its glen-built hall.
Backward and forward rolled the waves of fight
Round Troy—but while this stood, Troy could not fall.

So, in its lovely moonlight, lives the soul.
Mountains surround it, and sweet virgin air;   10
Cold plashing, past it, crystal waters roll;
We visit it by moments, ah, too rare!

4. Clough's poetry often dealt with contemporary religious problems
5. A river near Troy.
6. An ancient statue of the goddess Pallas Athena. The safety of Troy (Ilium) was thought to depend upon the statue's being retained in the city.

We shall renew the battle in the plain
Tomorrow—red with blood will Xanthus[7] be;
Hector and Ajax will be there again,   15
Helen will come upon the wall to see.

Then we shall rust in shade, or shine in strife,
And fluctuate 'twixt blind hopes and blind despairs,
And fancy that we put forth all our life,
And never know how with the soul it fares.   20

Still doth the soul, from its lone fastness high,
Upon our life a ruling effluence send.
And when it fails, fight as we will, we die;
And while it lasts, we cannot wholly end.

                                        1867

The Better Part

Long fed on boundless hopes, O race of man,
How angrily thou spurn'st all simpler fare!
"Christ," someone says, "was human as we are;
No judge eyes us from Heaven, our sin to scan;

"We live no more, when we have done our span."—   5
"Well, then, for Christ," thou answerest, "who can care?
From sin, which Heaven records not, why forbear?
Live we like brutes our life without a plan!"

So answerest thou; but why not rather say:
"Hath man no second life?—*Pitch this one high!*   10
Sits there no judge in Heaven, our sin to see?—

"*More strictly, then, the inward judge obey!
Was Christ a man like us? Ah! let us try
If we, then, too, can be such men as he!*"

                                        1867

Growing Old[1]

What is it to grow old?
Is it to lose the glory of the form,
The luster of the eye?
Is it for beauty to forego her wreath?
—Yes, but not this alone.   5

7. A river near Troy.
1. Arnold's poem may have been
prompted as a rejoinder to Browning's

enthusiastic picture of old age in
Rabbi Ben Ezra (1864).

Is it to feel our strength—
Not our bloom only, but our strength—decay?
Is it to feel each limb
Grow stiffer, every function less exact,
Each nerve more loosely strung?   10

Yes, this, and more; but not
Ah, 'tis not what in youth we dreamed 'twould be!
'Tis not to have our life
Mellowed and softened as with sunset glow,
A golden day's decline.   15

'Tis not to see the world
As from a height, with rapt prophetic eyes,
And heart profoundly stirred;
And weep, and feel the fullness of the past,[2]
The years that are no more.   20

It is to spend long days
And not once feel that we were ever young;
It is to add, immured
In the hot prison of the present, month
To month with weary pain.   25

It is to suffer this,
And feel but half, and feebly, what we feel.
Deep in our hidden heart
Festers the dull remembrance of a change,
But no emotion—none.   30

It is—last stage of all—
When we are frozen up within, and quite
The phantom of ourselves,
To hear the world applaud the hollow ghost
Which blamed the living man.   35

1867

The Last Word

Creep into thy narrow bed,
Creep, and let no more be said!
Vain thy onset! all stands fast.
Thou thyself must break at last.

Let the long contention cease!   5
Geese are swans, and swans are geese.
Let them have it how they will!
Thou art tired; best be still.

2. Cf. Tennyson's *Tears, Idle Tears.*

They out-talked thee, hissed thee, tore thee?
Better men fared thus before thee;   10
Fired their ringing shot and passed,
Hotly charged—and sank at last.

Charge once more, then, and be dumb!
Let the victors, when they come,
When the forts of folly fall,
Find thy body by the wall!

1867

Preface to *Poems* (1853)

In two small volumes of poems, published anonymously, one in
1849, the other in 1852, many of the poems which compose the
present volume have already appeared. The rest are now published
for the first time.

I have, in the present collection, omitted the poem from which
the volume published in 1852 took its title.[1] I have done so, not
because the subject of it was a Sicilian Greek born between two and
three thousand years ago, although many persons would think this a
sufficient reason. Neither have I done so because I had, in my own
opinion, failed in the delineation which I intended to effect. I intended to delineate the feelings of one of the last of the Greek religious philosophers, one of the family of Orpheus and Musaeus,[2]
having survived his fellows, living on into a time when the habits of
Greek thought and feeling had begun fast to change, character to
dwindle, the influence of the Sophists[3] to prevail. Into the feelings of
a man so situated there entered much that we are accustomed
to consider as exclusively modern; how much, the fragments[4] of
Empedocles himself which remain to us are sufficient at least to
indicate. What those who are familiar only with the great monuments of early Greek genius suppose to be its exclusive character-

1. *Empedocles on Etna,* the long poem
that supplied the title for Arnold's second collection of poems, portrays the
disillusioned reflections of the Greek
philosopher and scientist Empedocles and
culminates in the speaker's suicide on
Mount Etna in Sicily, in the 5th century
B.C. Because of his dissatisfaction with
what he calls the "morbid" tone of
Empedocles on Etna Arnold continued to
exclude it from his volumes of poetry
until 1867 when he reprinted it at the
request, he said, "of a man of genius,
whom it had the honor and good fortune
to interest—Mr. Robert Browning." It
should be noted that in the arguments
developed in the *Preface* against his own
poem (and against 19th-century poetry
in general) Arnold is exclusively concerned with narrative and dramatic poetry. The *Preface,* as he himself remarked
in 1854, "leaves * * * untouched the
question, how far, and in what manner,
the opinions there expressed respecting
the choice of subjects apply to lyric poetry; that region of the poetical field
which is chiefly cultivated at present."
2. Pupil of the poet and musician Orpheus. The latter was the legendary
founder of the Orphic religion that flourished in 6th-century Greece and later declined.
3. Greek rhetoricians, often criticized because of their reputed concern for niceties
of expression over substance of knowledge.
4. Empedocles' writings (medical and
scientific treatises in verse) have survived only in fragments.

istics, have disappeared; the calm, the cheerfulness, the disinterested objectivity have disappeared; the dialogue of the mind with itself has commenced; modern problems have presented themselves, we hear already the doubts, we witness the discouragement, of Hamlet and of Faust.

The representation of such a man's feelings must be interesting, if consistently drawn. We all naturally take pleasure, says Aristotle, in any imitation or representation whatever;[5] this is the basis of our love of poetry; and we take pleasure in them, he adds, because all knowledge is naturally agreeable to us; not to the philosopher only, but to mankind at large. Every representation therefore which is consistently drawn may be supposed to be interesting, inasmuch as it gratifies this natural interest in knowledge of all kinds. What is *not* interesting is that which does not add to our knowledge of any kind; that which is vaguely conceived and loosely drawn; a representation which is general, indeterminate, and faint, instead of being particular, precise, and firm.

Any accurate representation may therefore be expected to be interesting; but, if the representation be a poetical one, more than this is demanded. It is demanded, not only that it shall interest, but also that it shall inspirit and rejoice the reader; that it shall convey a charm, and infuse delight. For the Muses, as Hesiod says, were born that they might be "a forgetfulness of evils, and a truce from cares":[6] and it is not enough that the poet should add to the knowledge of men, it is required of him also that he should add to their happiness. "All art," says Schiller, "is dedicated to Joy, and there is no higher and no more serious problem, than how to make men happy. The right art is that alone, which creates the highest enjoyment."[7]

A poetical work, therefore, is not yet justified when it has been shown to be an accurate, and therefore interesting representation; it has to be shown also that it is a representation from which men can derive enjoyment. In presence of the most tragic circumstances, represented in a work of Art, the feeling of enjoyment, as is well known, may still subsist; the representation of the most utter calamity, of the liveliest anguish, is not sufficient to destroy it; the more tragic the situation, the deeper becomes the enjoyment; and the situation is more tragic in proportion as it becomes more terrible.

What then are the situations, from the representation of which, though accurate, no poetical enjoyment can be derived? They are those in which the suffering finds no vent in action; in which a continuous state of mental distress is prolonged, unrelieved by

---

5. See Aristotle, *Poetics,* especially 1, 2, 4, 7, 14.
6. From *Theogony* 52–56, by the early Greek poet Hesiod.
7. J. C. F. von Schiller, *On the Use of the Chorus in Tragedy,* prefatory essay to *The Bride of Messina* (1803). See *Friedrich Schiller's Works* (1903), VIII, 224.

incident, hope, or resistance; in which there is everything to be endured, nothing to be done. In such situations there is inevitably something morbid, in the description of them something monotonous. When they occur in actual life, they are painful, not tragic; the representation of them in poetry is painful also.

To this class of situations, poetically faulty as it appears to me, that of Empedocles, as I have endeavored to represent him, belongs; and I have therefore excluded the poem from the present collection.

And why, it may be asked, have I entered into this explanation respecting a matter so unimportant as the admission or exclusion of the poem in question? I have done so, because I was anxious to avow that the sole reason for its exclusion was that which has been stated above; and that it has not been excluded in deference to the opinion which many critics of the present day appear to entertain against subjects chosen from distant times and countries: against the choice, in short, of any subjects but modern ones.

"The poet," it is said, and by an intelligent critic, "the poet who would really fix the public attention must leave the exhausted past, and draw his subjects from matters of present import, and *therefore* both of interest and novelty."[8]

Now this view I believe to be completely false. It is worth examining, inasmuch as it is a fair sample of a class of critical dicta everywhere current at the present day, having a philosophical form and air, but no real basis in fact; and which are calculated to vitiate the judgment of readers of poetry, while they exert, so far as they are adopted, a misleading influence on the practice of those who write it.

What are the eternal objects of poetry, among all nations and at all times? They are actions; human actions; possessing an inherent interest in themselves, and which are to be communicated in an interesting manner by the art of the poet.[9] Vainly will the latter imagine that he has everything in his own power; that he can make an intrinsically inferior action equally delightful with a more excellent one by his treatment of it; he may indeed compel us to admire his skill, but his work will possess, within itself, an incurable defect.

The poet, then, has in the first place to select an excellent action; and what actions are the most excellent? Those, certainly, which most powerfully appeal to the great primary human affections: to those elementary feelings which subsist permanently in the race, and which are independent of time. These feelings are permanent and the same; that which interests them is permanent and the same also. The modernness or antiquity of an action, therefore, has nothing to do with its fitness for poetical representation; this de-

8. In the *Spectator* of April 2nd, 1853. The words quoted were not used with reference to poems of mine [Arnold's note]. According to Arnold the "intel- ligent critic" was R. S. Rintoul, editor of the *Spectator*.
9. Cf. Aristotle, *Poetics* 6.

pends upon its inherent qualities. To the elementary part of our nature, to our passions, that which is great and passionate is eternally interesting; and interesting solely in proportion to its greatness and to its passion. A great human action of a thousand years ago is more interesting to it than a smaller human action of today, even though upon the representation of this last the most consummate skill may have been expended, and though it has the advantage of appealing by its modern language, familiar manners, and contemporary allusions, to all our transient feelings and interests. These, however, have no right to demand of a poetical work that it shall satisfy them; their claims are to be directed elsewhere. Poetical works belong to the domain of our permanent passions; let them interest these, and the voice of all subordinate claims upon them is at once silenced.

Achilles, Prometheus, Clytemnestra, Dido—what modern poem presents personages as interesting, even to us moderns, as these personages of an "exhausted past"? We have the domestic epic dealing with the details of modern life which pass daily under our eyes;[1] we have poems representing modern personages in contact with the problems of modern life, morel, intellectual, and social; these works have been produced by poets the most distinguished of their nation and time; yet I fearlessly assert that *Hermann and Dorothea, Childe Harold, Jocelyn, The Excursion,*[2] leave the reader cold in comparison with the effect produced upon him by the latter books of the *Iliad,* by the *Oresteia,*[3] or by the episode of Dido.[4] And why is this? Simply because in the three last-named cases the action is greater, the personages nobler, the situations more intense: and this is the true basis of the interest in a poetical work, and this alone.

It may be urged, however, that past actions may be interesting in themselves, but that they are not to be adopted by the modern poet, because it is impossible for him to have them clearly present to his own mind, and he cannot therefore feel them deeply, nor represent them forcibly. But this is not necessarily the case. The externals of a past action, indeed, he cannot know with the precision of a contemporary; but his business is with its essentials. The outward man of Oedipus or of Macbeth, the houses in which they lived, the ceremonies of their courts, he cannot accurately figure to himself; but neither do they essentially concern him. His business is with their inward man; with their feelings and behavior in certain tragic situations, which engage their passions as men; these have in them nothing local and casual; they are as accessible to the modern poet as to a contemporary.

---

1. Perhaps alluding to such poems as Tennyson's *The Princess* (1847) and Alexander Smith's *Life Drama* (1853). 2. Long poems by Goethe (1797), Byron (1818), Lamartine (1836), and Wordsworth (1814), respectively. 3. A trilogy of plays by Aeschylus concerned with the stories of Agamemnon, Clytemnestra, and their son, Orestes. 4. See Virgil's *Aeneid* IV.

The date of an action, then, signifies nothing: the action itself, its selection and construction, this is what is all-important. This the Greeks understood far more clearly than we do. The radical difference between their poetical theory and ours consists, as it appears to me, in this: that, with them, the poetical character of the action in itself, and the conduct of it, was the first consideration; with us, attention is fixed mainly on the value of the separate thoughts and images which occur in the treatment of an action. They regarded the whole; we regard the parts. With them, the action predominated over the expression of it; with us, the expression predominates over the action. Not that they failed in expression, or were inattentive to it; on the contrary, they are the highest models of expression, the unapproached masters of the *grand style:* but their expression is so excellent because it is so admirably kept in its right degree of prominence; because it is so simple and so well subordinated; because it draws its force directly from the pregnancy of the matter which it conveys. For what reason was the Greek tragic poet confined to so limited a range of subjects? Because there are so few actions which unite in themselves, in the highest degree, the conditions of excellence: and it was not thought that on any but an excellent subject could an excellent poem be constructed. A few actions, therefore, eminently adapted for tragedy, maintained almost exclusive possession of the Greek tragic stage; their significance appeared inexhaustible; they were as permanent problems, perpetually offered to the genius of every fresh poet. This too is the reason of what appears to us moderns a certain baldness of expression in Greek tragedy; of the triviality with which we often reproach the remarks of the chorus, where it takes part in the dialogue: that the action itself, the situation of Orestes, or Merope, or Alcmaeon,[5] was to stand the central point of interest, unforgotten, absorbing, principal; that no accessories were for a moment to distract the spectator's attention from this; that the tone of the parts was to be perpetually kept down, in order not to impair the grandiose effect of the whole. The terrible old mythic story on which the drama was founded stood, before he entered the theater, traced in its bare outlines upon the spectator's mind; it stood in his memory, as a group of statuary, faintly seen, at the end of a long and dark vista: then came the poet, embodying outlines, developing situations, not a word wasted, not a sentiment capriciously thrown in: stroke upon stroke, the drama proceeded: the light deepened upon the group; more and more it revealed itself to the riveted gaze of the spectator: until at last, when the final words were spoken, it stood before him in broad sunlight, a model of immortal beauty.

5. Merope, queen of Messene in Greece, appears in plays by Euripides and in Arnold's own play *Merope* (1858). Alcmaeon was the son of a legendary Greek hero, who like Orestes, avenged his father's death by killing his mother. He was the subject of several Greek plays now lost.

This was what a Greek critic demanded; this was what a Greek poet endeavored to effect. It signified nothing to what time an action belonged; we do not find that the *Persae* occupied a particularly high rank among the dramas of Aeschylus, because it represented a matter of contemporary interest:[6] this was not what a cultivated Athenian required, he required that the permanent elements of his nature should be moved; and dramas of which the action, though taken from a long-distant mythic time, yet was calculated to accomplish this in a higher degree than that of the *Persae*, stood higher in his estimation accordingly. The Greeks felt, no doubt, with their exquisite sagacity of taste, that an action of present times was too near them, too much mixed up with what was accidental and passing, to form a sufficiently grand, detached, and self-subsistent object for a tragic poem: such objects belonged to the domain of the comic poet, and of the lighter kinds of poetry. For the more serious kinds, for *pragmatic* poetry, to use an excellent expression of Polybius,[7] they were more difficult and severe in the range of subjects which they permitted. Their theory and practice alike, the admirable treatise of Aristotle, and the unrivaled works of their poets, exclaim with a thousand tongues—"All depends upon the subject; choose a fitting action, penetrate yourself with the feeling of its situations; this done, everything else will follow."

But for all kinds of poetry alike there was one point on which they were rigidly exacting; the adaptability of the subject to the kind of poetry selected, and the careful construction of the poem.

How different a way of thinking from this is ours! We can hardly at the present day understand what Menander[8] meant when he told a man who inquired as to the progress of his comedy that he had finished it, not having yet written a single line, because he had constructed the action of it in his mind. A modern critic would have assured him that the merit of his piece depended on the brilliant things which arose under his pen as he went along. We have poems which seem to exist merely for the sake of single lines and passages; not for the sake of producing any total impression. We have critics who seem to direct their attention merely to detached expressions, to the language about the action, not to the action itself. I verily think that the majority of them do not in their hearts believe that there is such a thing as a total impression to be derived from a poem at all, or to be demanded from a poet; they think the term a commonplace of metaphysical criticism. They will permit the poet to select any action he pleases, and to suffer that action to go as it will, provided he gratifies them with occasional bursts of fine writing, and with a shower of isolated

---

6. Aeschylus' *Persians* (472 B.C.) portrays the Greek victory over the Persian invaders, which had occurred only a few years before the play was produced.

7. Greek historian (202–120 B.C.).
8. Greek writer of comedies (342–292 B.C.).

thoughts and images. That is, they permit him to leave their poetical sense ungratified, provided that he gratifies their rhetorical sense and their curiosity. Of his neglecting to gratify these, there is little danger. He needs rather to be warned against the danger of attempting to gratify these alone; he needs rather to be perpetually reminded to prefer his action to everything else; so to treat this, as to permit its inherent excellences to develop themselves, without interruption from the intrusion of his personal peculiarities; most fortunate, when he most entirely succeeds in effecting himself, and in enabling a noble action to subsist as it did in nature.

But the modern critic not only permits a false practice; he absolutely prescribes false aims.—"A true allegory of the state of one's own mind in a representative history," the poet is told, "is perhaps the highest thing that one can attempt in the way of poetry." [9] And accordingly he attempts it. An allegory of the state of one's own mind, the highest problem of an art which imitates actions! No assuredly, it is not, it never can be so: no great poetical work has ever been produced with such an aim. *Faust* itself, in which something of the kind is attempted, wonderful passages as it contains, and in spite of the unsurpassed beauty of the scenes which relate to Margaret, *Faust* itself, judged as a whole, and judged strictly as a poetical work, is defective: its illustrious author, the greatest poet of modern times, the greatest critic of all times, would have been the first to acknowledge it; he only defended his work, indeed, by asserting it to be "something incommensurable."[1]

The confusion of the present times is great, the multitude of voices counseling different things bewildering, the number of existing works capable of attracting a young writer's attention and of becoming his models, immense. What he wants is a hand to guide him through the confusion, a voice to prescribe to him the aim which he should keep in view, and to explain to him that the value of the literary works which offer themselves to his attention is relative to their power of helping him forward on his road towards this aim. Such a guide the English writer at the present day will nowhere find. Failing this, all that can be looked for, all indeed that can be desired is, that his attention should be fixed on excellent models; that he may reproduce, at any rate, something of their excellence, by penetrating himself with their works and by catching their spirit, if he cannot be taught to produce what is excellent independently.

Foremost among these models for the English writer stands Shakespeare: a name the greatest perhaps of all poetical names;

9. *North British Review,* **XIX** (August, 1853), 180 (U.S. edition). Arnold seems not to have noticed that Goethe (a critic he revered) had been cited earlier in the article as the authority for this critical generalization.
1. J. Eckermann, *Conversations with Goethe,* Jan. 3, 1830.

a name never to be mentioned without reverence. I will venture, however, to express a doubt, whether the influence of his works, excellent and fruitful for the readers of poetry, for the great majority, has been of unmixed advantage to the writers of it. Shakespeare indeed chose excellent subjects; the world could afford no better than Macbeth, or Romeo and Juliet, or Othello: he had no theory respecting the necessity of choosing subjects of present import, or the paramount interest attaching to allegories of the state of one's own mind; like all great poets, he knew well what constituted a poetical action; like them, wherever he found such an action, he took it; like them, too, he found his best in past times. But to these general characteristics of all great poets he added a special one of his own; a gift, namely, of happy, abundant, and ingenious expression, eminent and unrivaled: so eminent as irresistibly to strike the attention first in him, and even to throw into comparative shade his other excellences as a poet. Here has been the mischief. These other excellences were his fundamental excellences *as a poet*; what distinguishes the artist from the mere amateur, says Goethe, is *Architectonicè* in the highest sense;[2] that power of execution, which creates, forms, and constitutes: not the profoundness of single thoughts, not the richness of imagery, not the abundance of illustration. But these attractive accessories of a poetical work being more easily seized than the spirit of the whole, and these accessories being possessed by Shakespeare in an unequaled degree, a young writer having recourse to Shakespeare as his model runs great risk of being vanquished and absorbed by them, and, in consequence, of reproducing, according to the measure of his power, these, and these alone.[3] Of this preponderating quality of Shakespeare's genius, accordingly almost the whole of modern English poetry has, it appears to me, felt the influence. To the exclusive attention on the part of his imitators to this it is in a great degree owing, that of the majority of modern poetical works the details alone are valuable, the composition worthless. In reading them one is perpetually reminded of that terrible sentence on a modern French poet: *Il dit tout ce qu'il veut, mais malheureusement il n'a rien à dire.*[4]

Let me give an instance of what I mean. I will take it from the works of the very chief among those who seem to have been formed in the school of Shakespeare: of one whose exquisite

2. In Goethe's essay *Concerning the So-called Dilettantism* (1799) in his *Werke*, 1851, XXV, 322.

3. Cf. Arnold's letter to Clough (Oct. 28, 1852): "More and more I feel that the difference between a mature and a youthful age of the world compels the poetry of the former to use great plainness of speech * * * and that Keats and Shelley were on a false track when they

set themselves to reproduce the exuberance of expression, the charm, the richness of images, and the felicity, of the Elizabethan poets."

4. "He says everything he wishes to, but unfortunately he has nothing to say"— a comment on Théophile Gautier (1811–72) whose emphasis on style was severely criticized by Arnold in his late essay *Wordsworth* (see below).

genius and pathetic death render him forever interesting. I will take the poem of *Isabella, or the Pot of Basil*, by Keats. I choose this rather than the *Endymion*, because the latter work (which a modern critic has classed with the *Fairy Queen!* [5]) although undoubtedly there blows through it the breath of genius, is yet as a whole so utterly incoherent, as not strictly to merit the name of a poem at all. The poem of *Isabella*, then, is a perfect treasure-house of graceful and felicitous words and images: almost in every stanza there occurs one of those vivid and picturesque turns of expression, by which the object is made to flash upon the eye of the mind, and which thrill the reader with a sudden delight. This one short poem contains, perhaps, a greater number of happy single expressions which one could quote than all the extant tragedies of Sophocles. But the action, the story? The action in itself is an excellent one; but so feebly is it conceived by the poet, so loosely constructed, that the effect produced by it, in and for itself, is absolutely null. Let the reader, after he has finished the poem of Keats, turn to the same story in the *Decameron*:[6] he will then feel how pregnant and interesting the same action has become in the hands of a great artist, who above all things delineates his object; who subordinates expression to that which it is designed to express.

I have said that the imitators of Shakespeare, fixing their attention on his wonderful gift of expression, have directed their imitation to this, neglecting his other excellences. These excellences, the fundamental excellences of poetical art, Shakespeare no doubt possessed them—possessed many of them in a splendid degree; but it may perhaps be doubted whether even he himself did not sometimes give scope to his faculty of expression to the prejudice of a higher poetical duty. For we must never forget that Shakespeare is the great poet he is from his skill in discerning and firmly conceiving an excellent action, from his power of intensely feeling a situation, of intimately associating himself with a character; not from his gift of expression, which rather even leads him astray, degenerating sometimes into a fondness for curiosity of expression, into an irritability of fancy, which seems to make it impossible for him to say a thing plainly, even when the press of the action demands the very directest language, or its level character the very simplest. Mr. Hallam, than whom it is impossible to find a saner and more judicious critic, has had the courage (for at the present day it needs courage) to remark, how extremely and faultily difficult Shakespeare's language often is.[7] It is so: you may find main scenes in some of his greatest tragedies, *King Lear* for instance, where the language is so artificial, so curiously tortured,

---

5. In the *North British Review*, XIX (Aug., 1853), 172, 74, Keats' *Endymion* is twice linked with Spenser's *Faerie Queene* as "leisurely compositions of the sweet sensuous order."

6. Boccaccio's *Decameron*, 4th day, 5th novel.

7. Henry Hallam, historian (1779–1859), *Introduction to the Literature of Europe* (1838–39), Ch. 23.

and so difficult, that every speech has to be read two or three times before its meaning can be comprehended. This over-curiousness of expression is indeed but the excessive employment of a wonderful gift—of the power of saying a thing in a happier way than any other man; nevertheless, it is carried so far that one understands what M. Guizot meant, when he said that Shakespeare appears in his language to have tried all styles except that of simplicity.[8] He has not the severe and scrupulous self-restraint of the ancients, partly no doubt, because he had a far less cultivated and exacting audience. He has indeed a far wider range than they had, a far richer fertility of thought; in this respect he rises above them. In his strong conception of his subject, in the genuine way in which he is penetrated with it, he resembles them, and is unlike the moderns. But in the accurate limitation of it, the conscientious rejection of superfluities, the simple and rigorous development of it from the first line of his work to the last, he falls below them, and comes nearer to the moderns. In his chief works, besides what he has of his own, he has the elementary soundness of the ancients; he has their important action and their large and broad manner; but he has not their purity of method. He is therefore a less safe model; for what he has of his own is personal, and inseparable from his own rich nature; it may be imitated and exaggerated, it cannot be learned or applied as an art. He is above all suggestive; more valuable, therefore, to young writers as men than as artists. But clearness of arrangement, rigor of development, simplicity of style—these may to a certain extent be learned; and these may, I am convinced, be learned best from the ancients, who although infinitely less suggestive than Shakespeare, are thus, to the artist, more instructive.

What, then, it will be asked, are the ancients to be our sole models? the ancients with their comparatively narrow range of experience, and their widely different circumstances? Not, certainly, that which is narrow in the ancients, nor that in which we can no longer sympathize. An action like the action of the *Antigone* of Sophocles, which turns upon the conflict between the heroine's duty to her brother's corpse and that to the laws of her country, is no longer one in which it is possible that we should feel a deep interest. I am speaking too, it will be remembered, not of the best sources of intellectual stimulus for the general reader, but of the best models of instruction for the individual writer. This last may certainly learn of the ancients, better than anywhere else, three things which it is vitally important for him to know: the all-importance of the choice of a subject; the necessity of accurate construction; and the subordinate character of expression. He will learn from them how unspeakably superior

8. F. P. G. Guizot, French historian (1787–1874), discussing Shakespeare's sonnets in his *Shakespeare et son Temps* (1852), p. 114.

is the effect of the one moral impression left by a great action treated as a whole, to the effect produced by the most striking single thought or by the happiest image. As he penetrates into the spirit of the great classical works, as he becomes gradually aware of their intense significance, their noble simplicity, and their calm pathos, he will be convinced that it is this effect, unity and profoundness of moral impression, at which the ancient poets aimed; that it is this which constitutes the grandeur of their works, and which makes them immortal. He will desire to direct his own efforts towards producing the same effect. Above all, he will deliver himself from the jargon of modern criticism, and escape the danger of producing poetical works conceived in the spirit of the passing time, and which partake of its transitoriness.

The present age makes great claims upon us; we owe it service, it will not be satisfied without our admiration. I know not how it is, but their commerce with the ancients appears to me to produce, in those who constantly practice it, a steadying and composing effect upon their judgment, not of literary works only, but of men and events in general. They are like persons who have had a very weighty and impressive experience; they are more truly than others under the empire of facts, and more independent of the language current among those with whom they live. They wish neither to applaud nor to revile their age; they wish to know what it is, what it can give them, and whether this is what they want. What they want, they know very well; they want to educe and cultivate what is best and noblest in themselves; they know, too, that this is no easy task—χαλεπὸν, as Pittacus said, χαλεπὸν ἐσθλὸν ἔμμεναι [9]—and they ask themselves sincerely whether their age and its literature can assist them in the attempt. If they are endeavoring to practice any art, they remember the plain and simple proceedings of the old artists, who attained their grand results by penetrating themselves with some noble and significant action, not by inflating themselves with a belief in the pre-eminent importance and greatness of their own times. They do not talk of their mission, nor of interpreting their age, nor of the coming poet; all this, they know, is the mere delirium of vanity; their business is not to praise their age, but to afford to the men who live in it the highest pleasure which they are capable of feeling. If asked to afford this by means of subjects drawn from the age itself, they ask what special fitness the present age has for supplying them. They are told that it is an era of progress, an age commissioned to carry out the great ideas of industrial development and social amelioration. They reply that with all this they can do nothing; that the elements they need for the exercise of their art are great actions, calculated powerfully and delightfully to affect what is permanent in the human soul;

9. "It is hard to be good." An aphorism of Pittacus, a Greek sage, 7th century B.C.

that so far as the present age can supply such actions, they will gladly make use of them; but that an age wanting in moral grandeur can with difficulty supply such, and an age of spiritual discomfort with difficulty be powerfully and delightfully affected by them.

A host of voices will indignantly rejoin that the present age is inferior to the past neither in moral grandeur nor in spiritual health. He who possesses the discipline I speak of will content himself with remembering the judgments passed upon the present age, in this respect, by the two men, the one of strongest head, the other of widest culture, whom it has produced; by Goethe and by Niebuhr.[1] It will be sufficient for him that he knows the opinions held by these two great men respecting the present age and its literature; and that he feels assured in his own mind that their aims and demands upon life were such as he would wish, at any rate, his own to be; and their judgment as to what is impeding and disabling such as he may safely follow. He will not, however, maintain a hostile attitude towards the false pretensions of his age: he will content himself with not being overwhelmed by them. He will esteem himself fortunate if he can succeed in banishing from his mind all feelings of contradiction, and irritation, and impatience; in order to delight himself with the contemplation of some noble action of a heroic time, and to enable others, through his representation of it, to delight in it also.

I am far indeed from making any claim, for myself, that I possess this discipline; or for the following poems, that they breathe its spirit. But I say, that in the sincere endeavor to learn and practice, amid the bewildering confusion of our times, what is sound and true in poetical art, I seemed to myself to find the only sure guidance, the only solid footing, among the ancients. They, at any rate, knew what they wanted in art, and we do not. It is this uncertainty which is disheartening, and not hostile criticism. How often have I felt this when reading words of disparagement or of cavil: that it is the uncertainty as to what is really to be aimed at which makes our difficulty, not the dissatisfaction of the critic, who himself suffers from the same uncertainty. *Non me tua fervida terrent Dicta; . . . Dii me terrent, et Jupiter hostis.*[2]

Two kinds of *dilettanti*, says Goethe, there are in poetry: he who neglects the indispensable mechanical part, and thinks he has done enough if he shows spirituality and feeling; and he who seeks to arrive at poetry merely by mechanism, in which he can acquire an artisan's readiness, and is without soul and matter.[3] And he adds, that the first does most harm to art, and the last to

1. B. G. Niebuhr (1776–1831), German historian.
2. Virgil, *Aeneid* XII. 894–95: "Your fiery speeches do not frighten me; it is the gods and the enmity of Jupiter that frighten me" (Turnus, a warrior abandoned by the gods, is replying to Aeneas who has taunted him with being afraid).
3. See note 2, Goethe's essay, above.

himself. If we must be *dilettanti*; if it is impossible for us, under the circumstances amidst which we live, to think clearly, to feel nobly, and to delineate firmly; if we cannot attain to the mastery of the great artists; let us, at least, have so much respect for our art as to prefer it to ourselves. Let us not bewilder our successors; let us transmit to them the practice of poetry, with its boundaries and wholesome regulative laws, under which excellent works may again, perhaps, at some future time, be produced, not yet fallen into oblivion through our neglect, not yet condemned and canceled by the influence of their eternal enemy, caprice.

From The Function of Criticism at the Present Time[1]

Many objections have been made to a proposition which, in some remarks of mine on translating Homer,[2] I ventured to put forth; a proposition about criticism, and its importance at the present day. I said: "Of the literature of France and Germany, as of the intellect of Europe in general, the main effort, for now many years, has been a critical effort; the endeavor, in all branches of knowledge, theology, philosophy, history, art, science, to see the object as in itself it really is." I added, that owing to the operation in English literature of certain causes, "almost the last thing for which one would come to English literature is just that very thing which now Europe most desires—criticism"; and that the power and value of English literature was thereby impaired. More than one rejoinder declared that the importance I here assigned to criticism was excessive, and asserted the inherent superiority of the creative effort of the human spirit over its critical effort. And the other day, having been led by a Mr. Shairp's excellent notice of Wordsworth[3] to turn again to his biography, I found, in the words of this great man, whom I, for one, must always listen to with the profoundest respect,

1. This essay served as an introduction to Arnold's volume of *Essays in Criticism* (1865). As a declaration of intentions, it can serve as a standard for measuring his total accomplishment in criticism. The essay makes us aware that criticism, for Arnold, meant a great deal more than casual book-reviewing or mere censoriousness. He was not a Utilitarian, yet his object in this essay is to show that good criticism is useful. Creative writers, he argues, can profit in a special way from good criticism, but all of us can also derive from it benefits of the greatest value. In particular, we may develop a civilized attitude of mind in which to examine the social, political, aesthetic, and religious problems which confront us.
2. *On Translating Homer* (1861).
3. J. C. Shairp's essay *Wordsworth:*

The Man and the Poet was published in 1864. Arnold comments in a footnote: "I cannot help thinking that a practice, common in England during the last century, and still followed in France, of printing a notice of this kind—a notice by a competent critic—to serve as an introduction to an eminent author's works, might be revived among us with advantage. To introduce all succeeding editions of Wordsworth, Mr. Shairp's notice might, it seems to me, excellently serve; it is written from the point of view of an admirer, nay, of a disciple, and that is right; but then the disciple must be also, as in this case he is, a critic, a man of letters, not, as too often happens, some relation or friend with no qualification for his task except affection for his author."

a sentence passed on the critic's business, which seems to justify every possible disparagement of it. Wordsworth says in one of his letters:

"The writers in these publications (the Reviews), while they prosecute their inglorious employment, cannot be supposed to be in a state of mind very favorable for being affected by the finer influences of a thing so pure as genuine poetry."

And a trustworthy reporter of his conversation quotes a more elaborate judgment to the same effect:

"Wordsworth holds the critical power very low, infinitely lower than the inventive; and he said today that if the quantity of time consumed in writing critiques on the works of others were given to original composition, of whatever kind it might be, it would be much better employed; it would make a man find out sooner his own level, and it would do infinitely less mischief. A false or malicious criticism may do much injury to the minds of others; a stupid invention, either in prose or verse, is quite harmless."

It is almost too much to expect of poor human nature, that a man capable of producing some effect in one line of literature, should, for the greater good of society, voluntarily doom himself to impotence and obscurity in another. Still less is this to be expected from men addicted to the composition of the "false or malicious criticism" of which Wordsworth speaks. However, everybody would admit that a false or malicious criticism had better never have been written. Everybody, too, would be willing to admit, as a general proposition, that the critical faculty is lower than the inventive. But is it true that criticism is really, in itself, a baneful and injurious employment; is it true that all time given to writing critiques on the works of others would be much better employed if it were given to original composition, of whatever kind this may be? Is it true that Johnson had better have gone on producing more *Irenes*[4] instead of writing his *Lives of the Poets*; nay, is it certain that Wordsworth himself was better employed in making his Ecclesiastical Sonnets[5] than when he made his celebrated Preface so full of criticism, and criticism of the works of others? Wordsworth was himself a great critic, and it is to be sincerely regretted that he has not left us more criticism; Goethe was one of the greatest of critics, and we may sincerely congratulate ourselves that he has left us so much criticism. Without wasting time over the exaggeration which Wordsworth's judgment on criticism clearly contains, or over an attempt to trace the causes—not difficult, I think, to be traced— which may have led Wordsworth to this exaggeration, a critic may

---

4. *Irene* is the name of a clumsy play by Samuel Johnson.
5. A sonnet sequence by Wordsworth, usually regarded as minor verse. The Preface is to his *Lyrical Ballads* of 1800.

with advantage seize an occasion for trying his own conscience, and for asking himself of what real service, at any given moment, the practice of criticism either is or may be made to his own mind and spirit, and to the minds and spirits of others.

The critical power is of lower rank than the creative. True; but in assenting to this proposition, one or two things are to be kept in mind. It is undeniable that the exercise of a creative power, that a free creative activity, is the highest function of man; it is proved to be so by man's finding in it his true happiness. But it is undeniable, also, that men may have the sense of exercising this free creative activity in other ways than in producing great works of literature or art; if it were not so, all but a very few men would be shut out from the true happiness of all men. They may have it in well-doing, they may have it in learning, they may have it even in criticizing. This is one thing to be kept in mind. Another is, that the exercise of the creative power in the production of great works of literature or art, however high this exercise of it may rank, is not at all epochs and under all conditions possible; and that therefore labor may be vainly spent in attempting it, which might with more fruit be used in preparing for it, in rendering it possible. This creative power works with elements, with materials; what if it has not those materials, those elements, ready for its use? In that case it must surely wait till they are ready. Now, in literature—I will limit myself to literature, for it is about literature that the question arises—the elements with which the creative power works are ideas; the best ideas on every matter which literature touches, current at the time. At any rate we may lay it down as certain that in modern literature no manifestation of the creative power not working with these can be very important or fruitful. And I say *current* at the time, not merely accessible at the time; for creative literary genius does not principally show itself in discovering new ideas, that is rather the business of the philosopher. The grand work of literary genius is a work of synthesis and exposition, not of analysis and discovery; its gift lies in the faculty of being happily inspired by a certain intellectual and spiritual atmosphere, by a certain order of ideas, when it finds itself in them; of dealing divinely with these ideas, presenting them in the most effective and attractive combinations—making beautiful works with them, in short. But it must have the atmosphere, it must find itself amidst the order of ideas, in order to work freely; and these it is not so easy to command. This is why great creative epochs in literature are so rare, this is why there is so much that is unsatisfactory in the productions of many men of real genius; because, for the creation of a masterwork of literature two powers must concur, the power of the man and the power of the moment, and the man is not enough without the moment; the creative power has, for its happy exercise, appointed elements, and those elements are not in its own control.

Nay, they are more within the control of the critical power. It is the business of the critical power, as I said in the words already quoted, "in all branches of knowledge, theology, philosophy, history, art, science, to see the object as in itself it really is." Thus it tends, at last, to make an intellectual situation of which the creative power can profitably avail itself. It tends to establish an order of ideas, if not absolutely true, yet true by comparison with that which it displaces; to make the best ideas prevail. Presently these new ideas reach society, the touch of truth is the touch of life, and there is a stir and growth everywhere; out of this stir and growth come the creative epochs of literature.

Or, to narrow our range, and quit these considerations of the general march of genius and of society—considerations which are apt to become too abstract and impalpable—everyone can see that a poet, for instance, ought to know life and the world before dealing with them in poetry; and life and the world being in modern times very complex things, the creation of a modern poet, to be worth much, implies a great critical effort behind it; else it must be a comparatively poor, barren, and short-lived affair. This is why Byron's poetry had so little endurance in it, and Goethe's so much; both Byron and Goethe had a great productive power, but Goethe's was nourished by a great critical effort providing the true materials for it, and Byron's was not; Goethe knew life and the world, the poet's necessary subjects, much more comprehensively and thoroughly than Byron. He knew a great deal more of them, and he knew them much more as they really are.

It has long seemed to me that the burst of creative activity in our literature, through the first quarter of this century, had about it in fact something premature; and that from this cause its productions are doomed, most of them, in spite of the sanguine hopes which accompanied and do still accompany them, to prove hardly more lasting than the productions of far less splendid epochs. And this prematureness comes from its having proceeded without having its proper data, without sufficient materials to work with. In other words, the English poetry of the first quarter of this century, with plenty of energy, plenty of creative force, did not know enough. This makes Byron so empty of matter, Shelley so incoherent, Wordsworth even, profound as he is, yet so wanting in completeness and variety. Wordsworth cared little for books, and disparaged Goethe. I admire Wordsworth, as he is, so much that I cannot wish him different; and it is vain, no doubt, to imagine such a man different from what he is, to suppose that he *could* have been different. But surely the one thing wanting to make Wordsworth an even greater poet than he is—his thought richer, and his influence of wider application—was that he should have read more books, among them, no doubt, those of that Goethe whom he disparaged without reading him.

But to speak of books and reading may easily lead to a misunderstanding here. It was not really books and reading that lacked to our poetry at this epoch: Shelley had plenty of reading, Coleridge had immense reading. Pindar and Sophocles—as we all say so glibly, and often with so little discernment of the real import of what we are saying—had not many books; Shakespeare was no deep reader. True; but in the Greece of Pindar and Sophocles, in the England of Shakespeare, the poet lived in a current of ideas in the highest degree animating and nourishing to the creative power; society was, in the fullest measure, permeated by fresh thought, intelligent and alive. And this state of things is the true basis for the creative power's exercise, in this it finds its data, its materials, truly ready for its hand; all the books and reading in the world are only valuable as they are helps to this. Even when this does not actually exist, books and reading may enable a man to construct a kind of semblance of it in his own mind, a world of knowledge and intelligence in which he may live and work. This is by no means an equivalent to the artist for the nationally diffused life and thought of the epochs of Sophocles or Shakespeare; but, besides that it may be a means of preparation for such epochs, it does really constitute, if many share in it, a quickening and sustaining atmosphere of great value. Such an atmosphere the many-sided learning and the long and widely combined critical effort of Germany formed for Goethe, when he lived and worked. There was no national glow of life and thought there as in the Athens of Pericles[6] or the England of Elizabeth. That was the poet's weakness. But there was a sort of equivalent for it in the complete culture and unfettered thinking of a large body of Germans. That was his strength. In the England of the first quarter of this century there was neither a national glow of life and thought, such as we had in the age of Elizabeth, nor yet a culture and a force of learning and criticism such as were to be found in Germany. Therefore the creative power of poetry wanted, for success in the highest sense, materials and a basis; a thorough interpretation of the world was necessarily denied to it.

At first sight it seems strange that out of the immense stir of the French Revolution and its age should not have come a crop of works of genius equal to that which came out of the stir of the great productive time of Greece, or out of that of the Renascence, with its powerful episode the Reformation. But the truth is that the stir of the French Revolution took a character which essentially distinguished it from such movements as these. These were, in the main, disinterestedly intellectual and spiritual movements; movements in which the human spirit looked for its satisfaction in itself

6. Pericles (d. 429 B.C.), the leading statesman of Athens during a period of the city's most outstanding achievements in art, literature, and politics.

and in the increased play of its own activity. The French Revolution took a political, practical character. The movement, which went on in France under the old *régime*, from 1700 to 1789, was far more really akin than that of the Revolution itself to the movement of the Renascence; the France of Voltaire and Rousseau told far more powerfully upon the mind of Europe than the France of the Revolution. Goethe reproached this last expressly with having "thrown quiet culture back." Nay, and the true key to how much in our Byron, even in our Wordsworth, is this!—that they had their source in a great movement of feeling, not in a great movement of mind. The French Revolution, however—that object of so much blind love and so much blind hatred—found undoubtedly its motive power in the intelligence of men, and not in their practical sense; this is what distinguishes it from the English Revolution of Charles the First's time. This is what makes it a more spiritual event than our Revolution, an event of much more powerful and worldwide interest, though practically less successful; it appeals to an order of ideas which are universal, certain, permanent. 1789 asked of a thing, Is it rational? 1642 asked of a thing, Is it legal? or, when it went furthest, Is it according to conscience? This is the English fashion, a fashion to be treated, within its own sphere, with the highest respect; for its success, within its own sphere, has been prodigious. But what is law in one place is not law in another; what is law here today is not law even here tomorrow; and as for conscience, what is binding on one man's conscience is not binding on another's. The old woman who threw her stool at the head of the surpliced minister in St. Giles's Church at Edinburgh[7] obeyed an impulse to which millions of the human race may be permitted to remain strangers. But the prescriptions of reason are absolute, unchanging, of universal validity; *to count by tens is the easiest way of counting*—that is a proposition of which everyone, from here to the Antipodes, feels the force; at least I should say so if we did not live in a country where it is not impossible that any morning we may find a letter in the *Times* declaring that a decimal coinage is an absurdity.[7a] That a whole nation should have been penetrated with an enthusiasm for pure reason, and with an ardent zeal for making its prescriptions triumph, is a very remarkable thing, when we consider how little of mind, or anything so worthy and quickening as mind, comes into the motives which alone, in general, impel great masses of men. In spite of the extravagant direction given to this enthusiasm, in spite of the crimes and follies in which it lost itself, the French Revolution derives from the force, truth, and universality of the ideas which it took for its law, and from the passion

7. In 1637 rioting broke out in Scotland against a new kind of church service prescribed by Charles I. The riot was started by an old woman hurling a stool at a clergyman.

7a. In 1863 a proposal in Parliament to introduce the French decimal system for weights and measures had provoked articles in the *Times* defending the English system (of ounces and pounds or inches and feet) as more practical.

with which it could inspire a multitude for these ideas, a unique and still living power; it is—it will probably long remain—the greatest, the most animating event in history. And as no sincere passion for the things of the mind, even though it turn out in many respects an unfortunate passion, is ever quite thrown away and quite barren of good, France has reaped from hers one fruit—the natural and legitimate fruit though not precisely the grand fruit she expected: she is the country in Europe where *the people* is most alive.

But the mania for giving an immediate political and practical application to all these fine ideas of the reason was fatal. Here an Englishman is in his element: on this theme we can all go on for hours. And all we are in the habit of saying on it has undoubtedly a great deal of truth. Ideas cannot be too much prized in and for themselves, cannot be too much lived with; but to transport them abruptly into the world of politics and practice, violently to revolutionize this world to their bidding—that is quite another thing. There is the world of ideas and there is the world of practice; the French are often for suppressing the one and the English the other; but neither is to be suppressed. A member of the House of Commons said to me the other day: "That a thing is an anomaly, I consider to be no objection to it whatever." I venture to think he was wrong; that a thing is an anomaly *is* an objection to it, but absolutely and in the sphere of ideas: it is not necessarily, under such and such circumstances, or at such and such a moment, an objection to it in the sphere of politics and practice. Joubert[8] has said beautifully: "*C'est la force et le droit qui règlent toutes choses dans le monde; la force en attendant le droit.*"—"Force and right are the governors of this world; force till right is ready." *Force till right is ready*; and till right is ready, force, the existing order of things, is justified, is the legitimate ruler. But right is something moral, and implies inward recognition, free assent of the will; we are not ready for right—*right*, so far as we are concerned, *is not ready*—until we have attained this sense of seeing it and willing it. The way in which for us it may change and transform force, the existing order of things, and become, in its turn, the legitimate ruler of the world, should depend on the way in which, when our time comes, we see it and will it. Therefore for other people enamored of their own newly discerned right, to attempt to impose it upon us as ours, and violently to substitute their right for our force, is an act of tyranny, and to be resisted. It sets at nought the second great half of our maxim, *force till right is ready*. This was the grand error of the French Revolution; and its movement of ideas, by quitting the intellectual sphere and rushing furiously into the political sphere, ran, indeed, a prodigious and memorable course, but produced no such intellectual fruit as the movement of ideas of the Renascence,

8. Joseph Joubert (1754–1824), French moralist about whom Arnold wrote one of his *Essays in Criticism*.

and created, in opposition to itself, what I may call an *epoch of concentration*. The great force of that epoch of concentration was England; and the great voice of that epoch of concentration was Burke.[9] It is the fashion to treat Burke's writings on the French Revolution as superannuated and conquered by the event; as the eloquent but unphilosophical tirades of bigotry and prejudice. I will not deny that they are often disfigured by the violence and passion of the moment, and that in some directions Burke's view was bounded, and his observation therefore at fault. But on the whole, and for those who can make the needful corrections, what distinguishes these writings is their profound, permanent, fruitful, philosophical truth. They contain the true philosophy of an epoch of concentration, dissipate the heavy atmosphere which its own nature is apt to engender round it, and make its resistance rational instead of mechanical.

But Burke is so great because, almost alone in England, he brings thought to bear upon politics, he saturates politics with thought. It is his accident that his ideas were at the service of an epoch of concentration, not of an epoch of expansion; it is his characteristic that he so lived by ideas, and had such a source of them welling up within him, that he could float even an epoch of concentration and English Tory politics with them. It does not hurt him that Dr. Price[1] and the Liberals were enraged with him; it does not even hurt him that George the Third and the Tories were enchanted with him. His greatness is that he lived in a world which neither English Liberalism nor English Toryism is apt to enter—the world of ideas, not the world of catchwords and party habits. So far is it from being really true of him that he "to party gave up what was meant for mankind,"[2] that at the very end of his fierce struggle with the French Revolution, after all his invectives against its false pretensions, hollowness, and madness, with his sincere convictions of its michievousness, he can close a memorandum on the best means of combating it, some of the last pages [2a] he ever wrote—the *Thoughts on French Affairs*, in December 1791—with these striking words:

"The evil is stated, in my opinion, as it exists. The remedy must be where power, wisdom, and information, I hope, are more united with good intentions than they can be with me. I have done with this subject, I believe, forever. It has given me many anxious moments for the last two years. *If a great change is to be made in human affairs, the minds of men will be fitted to it; the general opinions and feelings will draw that way. Every fear, every hope will*

9. Edmund Burke (1729–97), prominent statesman and author of *Reflections on the French Revolution* (1790), which expressed the conservative opposition to revolutionary theories.
1. Richard Price (1723–91), a pro-revolutionary clergyman who was an opponent of Burke's.

2. See Oliver Goldsmith's poem, *Retaliation* (1774).
2a. Arnold was mistaken; Burke continued to write for another six years after 1791. According to Arnold's editor, R. H. Super, the mistake was caused by misunderstanding a passage in one of Burke's letters.

forward it; and then they who persist in opposing this mighty current in human affairs, will appear rather to resist the decrees of Providence itself, than the mere designs of men. They will not be resolute and firm, but perverse and obstinate."

That return of Burke upon himself has always seemed to me one of the finest things in English literature, or indeed in any literature. That is what I call living by ideas: when one side of a question has long had your earnest support, when all your feelings are engaged, when you hear all round you no language but one, when your party talks this language like a steam engine and can imagine no other— still to be able to think, still to be irresistibly carried, if so it be, by the current of thought to the opposite side of the question, and, like Balaam,[3] to be unable to speak anything *but what the Lord has put in your mouth.* I know nothing more striking, and I must add that I know nothing more un-English.

For the Englishman in general is like my friend the Member of Parliament, and believes, point-blank, that for a thing to be an anomaly is absolutely no objection to it whatever. He is like the Lord Auckland of Burke's day, who, in a memorandum on the French Revolution, talks of certain "miscreants, assuming the name of philosophers, who have presumed themselves capable of establishing a new system of society." The Englishman has been called a political animal, and he values what is political and practical so much that ideas easily become objects of dislike in his eyes, and thinkers, "miscreants," because ideas and thinkers have rashly meddled with politics and practice. This would be all very well if the dislike and neglect confined themselves to ideas transported out of their own sphere, and meddling rashly with practice; but they are inevitably extended to ideas as such, and to the whole life of intelligence; practice is everything, a free play of the mind is nothing. The notion of the free play of the mind upon all subjects being a pleasure in itself, being an object of desire, being an essential provider of elements without which a nation's spirit, whatever compensations it may have for them, must, in the long run, die of inanition, hardly enters into an Englishman's thoughts. It is noticeable that the word *curiosity,* which in other languages is used in a good sense, to mean, as a high and fine quality of man's nature, just this disinterested love of a free play of the mind on all subjects, for its own sake—it is noticeable, I say, that this word has in our language no sense of the kind, no sense but a rather bad and disparaging one. But criticism, real criticism, is essentially the exercise of this very quality. It obeys an instinct prompting it to try to know the best that is known and thought in the world, irrespectively of practice, politics, and everything of the kind; and to value knowledge and thought as they approach this best, without the intrusion

3. Cf. Numbers xxii.38.

of any other considerations whatever. This is an instinct for which there is, I think, little original sympathy in the practical English nature, and' what there was of it has undergone a long benumbing period of blight and suppression in the epoch of concentration which followed the French Revolution.

But epochs of concentration cannot well endure forever; epochs of expansion, in the due course of things, follow them. Such an epoch of expansion seems to be opening in this country. In the first place all danger of a hostile forcible pressure of foreign ideas upon our practice has long disappeared; like the traveler in the fable, therefore, we begin to wear our cloak a little more loosely.[4] Then, with a long peace, the ideas of Europe steal gradually and amicably in, and mingle, though in infinitesimally small quantities at a time, with our own notions. Then, too, in spite of all that is said about the absorbing and brutalizing influence of our passionate material progress, it seems to me indisputable that this progress is likely, though not certain, to lead in the end to an apparition of intellectual life; and that man, after he has made himself perfectly comfortable and has now to determine what to do with himself next, may begin to remember that he has a mind, and that the mind may be made the source of great pleasure. I grant it is mainly the privilege of faith, at present, to discern this end to our railways, our business, and our fortune-making; but we shall see if, here as elsewhere, faith is not in the end the true prophet. Our ease, our traveling, and our unbounded liberty to hold just as hard and securely as we please to the practice to which our notions have given birth, all tend to beget an inclination to deal a little more freely with these notions themselves, to canvass them a little, to penetrate a little into their real nature. Flutterings of curiosity, in the foreign sense of the word, appear amongst us, and it is in these that criticism must look to find its account. Criticism first; a time of true creative activity, perhaps—which, as I have said, must inevitably be preceded amongst us by a time of criticism—hereafter, when criticism has done its work.

It is of the last importance that English criticism should clearly discern what rule for its course, in order to avail itself of the field now opening to it, and to produce fruit for the future, it ought to take. The rule may be summed up in one word—*disinterestedness*.[5] And how is criticism to show disinterestedness? By keeping aloof from what is called "the practical view of things"; by resolutely following the law of its own nature, which is to be a free play of the mind on all subjects which it touches. By steadily refusing to lend itself to any of those ulterior, political, practical considerations about ideas, which plenty of people will be sure to attach to them,

4. See Aesop's fable of the wind and the sun.
5. This key word in Arnold's argument connotes independence and objectivity of mind. It should not be confused, as it often is, with mere lack of interest.

which perhaps ought often to be attached to them, which in this country at any rate are certain to be attached to them quite sufficiently, but which criticism has really nothing to do with. Its business is, as I have said, simply to know the best that is known and thought in the world, and by in its turn making this known, to create a current of true and fresh ideas. Its business is to do this with inflexible honesty, with due ability; but its business is to do no more, and to leave alone all questions of practical consequences and applications, questions which will never fail to have due prominence given to them. Else criticism, besides being really false to its own nature, merely continues in the old rut which it has hitherto followed in this country, and will certainly miss the chance now given to it. For what is at present the bane of criticism in this country? It is that practical considerations cling to it and stifle it. It subserves interests not its own. Our organs of criticism are organs of men and parties having practical ends to serve, and with them those practical ends are the first thing and the play of mind the second; so much play of mind as is compatible with the prosecution of those practical ends is all that is wanted. An organ like the *Revue des Deux Mondes*,[6] having for its main function to understand and utter the best that is known and thought in the world, existing, it may be said, as just an organ for a free play of the mind, we have not. But we have the *Edinburgh Review*, existing as an organ of the old Whigs, and for as much play of mind as may suit its being that; we have the *Quarterly Review*, existing as an organ of the Tories, and for as much play of mind as may suit its being that; we have the *British Quarterly Review*, existing as an organ of the political Dissenters, and for as much play of mind as may suit its being that; we have the *Times*, existing as an organ of the common, satisfied, well-to-do Englishman, and for as much play of mind as may suit its being that. And so on through all the various fractions, political and religious, of our society; every fraction has, as such, its organ of criticism, but the notion of combining all fractions in the common pleasure of a free disinterested play of mind meets with no favor. Directly this play of mind wants to have more scope, and to forget the pressure of practical considerations a little, it is checked, it is made to feel the chain. We saw this the other day in the extinction, so much to be regretted, of the *Home and Foreign Review*.[6a] Perhaps in no organ of criticism in this country was there so much knowledge, so much play of mind; but these could not save it. The *Dublin Review* subordinates play of mind to the practical business of English and Irish Catholicism, and lives. It must needs be that men should act in sects and parties, that each of these sects and parties should have its organ, and should make

6. An international magazine of exceptionally high quality, founded in Paris in 1829.

6a. A liberal Catholic periodical, founded in 1862, which ceased publication in 1864.

this organ subserve the interests of its action; but it would be well, too, that there should be a criticism, not the minister of these interests, not their enemy, but absolutely and entirely independent of them. No other criticism will ever attain any real authority or make any real way towards its end—the creating a current of true and fresh ideas.

It is because criticism has so little kept in the pure intellectual sphere, has so little detached itself from practice, has been so directly polemical and controversial, that it has so ill accomplished, in this country, its best spiritual work, which is to keep man from a self-satisfaction which is retarding and vulgarizing, to lead him towards perfection, by making his mind dwell upon what is excellent in itself, and the absolute beauty and fitness of things. A polemical practical criticism makes men blind even to the ideal imperfection of their practice, makes them willingly assert its ideal perfection, in order the better to secure it against attack; and clearly this is narrowing and baneful for them. If they were reassured on the practical side, speculative considerations of ideal perfection they might be brought to entertain, and their spiritual horizon would thus gradually widen. Sir Charles Adderley[7] says to the Warwickshire farmers:

"Talk of the improvement of breed! Why, the race we ourselves represent, the men and women, the old Anglo-Saxon race, are the best breed in the whole world. . . . The absence of a too enervating climate, too unclouded skies, and a too luxurious nature, has produced so vigorous a race of people, and has rendered us so superior to all the world."

Mr. Roebuck[8] says to the Sheffield cutlers:

"I look around me and ask what is the state of England? Is not property safe? Is not every man able to say what he likes? Can you not walk from one end of England to the other in perfect security? I ask you whether, the world over or in past history, there is anything like it? Nothing. I pray that our unrivaled happiness may last."

Now obviously there is a peril for poor human nature in words and thoughts of such exuberant self-satisfaction, until we find ourselves safe in the streets of the Celestial City.

> *Das wenige verschwindet leicht dem Blicke*
> *Der vorwärts sieht, wie viel noch übrig bleibt*—[9]

says Goethe; "the little that is done seems nothing when we look forward and see how much we have yet to do." Clearly this is a

---

7. 1814–1905; conservative politician and wealthy landowner.
8. John Arthur Roebuck (1801–79), radical politician and representative in Parliament for the industrial city of Sheffield.
9. Goethe's *Iphigenie auf Tauris* I.ii.91–92.

better line of reflection for weak humanity, so long as it remains on this earthly field of labor and trial.

But neither Sir Charles Adderley nor Mr. Roebuck is by nature inaccessible to considerations of this sort. They only lose sight of them owing to the controversial life we all lead, and the practical form which all speculation takes with us. They have in view opponents whose aim is not ideal, but practical; and in their zeal to uphold their own practice against these innovators, they go so far as even to attribute to this practice an ideal perfection. Somebody has been wanting to introduce a six-pound franchise,[1] or to abolish church-rates, or to collect agricultural statistics by force, or to diminish local self-government. How natural, in reply to such proposals, very likely improper or ill-timed, to go a little beyond the mark and to say stoutly, "Such a race of people as we stand, so superior to all the world! The old Anglo-Saxon race, the best breed in the whole world! I pray that our unrivaled happiness may last! I ask you whether, the world over or in past history, there is anything like it?" And so long as criticism answers this dithyramb by insisting that the old Anglo-Saxon race would be still more superior to all others if it had no church-rates, or that our unrivaled happiness would last yet longer with a six-pound franchise, so long will the strain, "The best breed in the whole world!" swell louder and louder, everything ideal and refining will be lost out of sight, and both the assailed and their critics will remain in a sphere, to say the truth, perfectly unvital, a sphere in which spiritual progression is impossible. But let criticism leave church-rates and the franchise alone, and in the most candid spirit, without a single lurking thought of practical innovation, confront with our dithyramb this paragraph on which I stumbled in a newspaper immediately after reading Mr. Roebuck:

"A shocking child murder has just been committed at Nottingham. A girl named Wragg left the workhouse there on Saturday morning with her young illegitimate child. The child was soon afterwards found dead on Mapperly Hills, having been strangled. Wragg is in custody."

Nothing but that; but, in juxtaposition with the absolute eulogies of Sir Charles Adderley and Mr. Roebuck, how eloquent, how suggestive are those few lines! "Our old Anglo-Saxon breed, the best in the whole world!"—how much that is harsh and ill-favored there is in this best! *Wragg!* If we are to talk of ideal perfection, of "the best in the whole world," has anyone reflected what a touch of grossness in our race, what an original shortcoming in the more delicate spiritual perceptions, is shown by the natural growth amongst us of such hideous names—Higginbottom, Stiggins, Bugg!

1. A radical proposal to extend the right to vote to anyone owning land worth £6 annual rent. "Church-rates": taxes supporting the Church of England.

In Ionia and Attica they were luckier in this respect than "the best race in the world"; by the Ilissus[2] there was no Wragg, poor thing! And "our unrivaled happiness"—what an element of grimness, bareness, and hideousness mixes with it and blurs it; the workhouse, the dismal Mapperly Hills[2a]—how dismal those who have seen them will remember—the gloom, the smoke, the cold, the strangled illegitimate child! "I ask you whether, the world over or in past history, there is anything like it?" Perhaps not, one is inclined to answer; but at any rate, in that case, the world is very much to be pitied. And the final touch—short, bleak and inhuman: *Wragg is in custody*. The sex lost in the confusion of our unrivaled happiness; or (shall I say?) the superfluous Christian name lopped off by the straightforward vigor of our old Anglo-Saxon breed! There is profit for the spirit in such contrasts as this; criticism serves the cause of perfection by establishing them. By eluding sterile conflict, by refusing to remain in the sphere where alone narrow and relative conceptions have any worth and validity, criticism may diminish its momentary importance, but only in this way has it a chance of gaining admittance for those wider and more perfect conceptions to which all its duty is really owed. Mr. Roebuck will have a poor opinion of an adversary who replies to his defiant songs of triumph only by murmuring under his breath, *Wragg is in custody*; but in no other way will these songs of triumph be induced gradually to moderate themselves, to get rid of what in them is excessive and offensive, and to fall into a softer and truer key.

It will be said that it is a very subtle and indirect action which I am thus prescribing for criticism, and that, by embracing in this manner the Indian virtue of detachment and abandoning the sphere of practical life, it condemns itself to a slow and obscure work. Slow and obscure it may be, but it is the only proper work of criticism. The mass of mankind will never have any ardent zeal for seeing things as they are; very inadequate ideas will always satisfy them. On these inadequate ideas reposes, and must repose, the general practice of the world. That is as much as saying that whoever sets himself to see things as they are will find himself one of a very small circle; but it is only by this small circle resolutely doing its own work that adequate ideas will ever get current at all. The rush and roar of practical life will always have a dizzying and attracting effect upon the most collected spectator, and tend to draw him into its vortex; most of all will this be the case where that life is so powerful as it is in England. But it is only by remaining collected, and refusing to lend himself to the point of view of the practical man, that the critic can do the practical man any service; and it is only by the greatest sincerity in pursuing his own course, and by at last convincing even the practical man of his sin-

2. A stream in Attica, Greece.
2a. Adjacent to the coal-mining and industrial area of Nottingham (later associated with the writings of D. H. Lawrence).

cerity, that he can escape misunderstandings which perpetually threaten him.

For the practical man is not apt for fine distinctions, and yet in these distinctions truth and the highest culture greatly find their account. But it is not easy to lead a practical man—unless you reassure him as to your practical intentions, you have no chance of leading him—to see that a thing which he has always been used to look at from one side only, which he greatly values, and which, looked at from that side, quite deserves, perhaps, all the prizing and admiring which he bestows upon it—that this thing, looked at from another side, may appear much less beneficent and beautiful, and yet retain all its claims to our practical allegiance. Where shall we find language innocent enough, how shall we make the spotless purity of our intentions evident enough, to enable us to say to the political Englishman that the British Constitution itself, which, seen from the practical side, looks such a magnificent organ of progress and virtue, seen from the speculative side—with its compromises, its love of facts, its horror of theory, its studied avoidance of clear thoughts—that, seen from this side, our august Constitution sometimes looks—forgive me, shade of Lord Somers![3]—a colossal machine for the manufacture of Philistines?[4] How is Cobbett[5] to say this and not be misunderstood, blackened as he is with the smoke of a lifelong conflict in the field of political practice? how is Mr. Carlyle to say it and not be misunderstood, after his furious raid into this field with his *Latter-day Pamphlets?* how is Mr. Ruskin, after his pugnacious political economy?[6] I say, the critic must keep out of the region of immediate practice in the political, social, humanitarian sphere if he wants to make a beginning for that more free speculative treatment of things, which may perhaps one day make its benefits felt even in this sphere, but in a natural and thence irresistible manner.

Do what he will, however, the critic will still remain exposed to frequent misunderstandings, and nowhere so much as in this country. For here people are particularly indisposed even to comprehend that without this free disinterested treatment of things, truth and the highest culture are out of the question. So immersed are they in practical life, so accustomed to take all their notions from this life and its processes, that they are apt to think that truth and culture themselves can be reached by the processes of this life, and that it is an impertinent singularity to think of reaching them in

3. John Somers (1651–1716), statesman responsible for formulating the Declaration of Rights.
4. The unenlightened middle classes whose opposition to the men of culture is parallel to the Biblical tribe which fought against the people of Israel, "the children of light." Arnold's repeated use of this parallel has established the term

in our language.
5. William Cobbett (1762–1835), vehement reformer whose political position anticipated that of Dickens.
6. Reference to *Unto this Last* (1862) in which Ruskin shifted from art criticism to an attack on traditional theories of economics.

any other. "We are all *terrae filii*,"[7] cries their eloquent advocate; "all Philistines together. Away with the notion of proceeding by any other course than the course dear to the Philistines; let us have a social movement, let us organize and combine a party to pursue truth and new thought, let us call it *the liberal party*, and let us all stick to each other, and back each other up. Let us have no nonsense about independent criticism, and intellectual delicacy, and the few and the many. Don't let us trouble ourselves about foreign thought; we shall invent the whole thing for ourselves as we go along. If one of us speaks well, applaud him; if one of us speaks ill, applaud him too; we are all in the same movement, we are all liberals, we are all in pursuit of truth." In this way the pursuit of truth becomes really a social, practical, pleasurable affair, almost requiring a chairman, a secretary, and advertisements; with the excitement of an occasional scandal, with a little resistance to give the happy sense of difficulty overcome; but, in general, plenty of bustle and very little thought. To act is so easy, as Goethe says; to think is so hard! It is true that the critic has many temptations to go with the stream, to make one of the party movement, one of these *terrae filii*; it seems ungracious to refuse to be a *terrae filius* when so many excellent people are; but the critic's duty is to refuse, or, if resistance is vain, at least to cry with Obermann: *Périssons en résistant.*[8] * * *

For criticism, these are elementary laws; but they never can be popular, and in this country they have been very little followed, and one meets with immense obstacles in following them. That is a reason for asserting them again and again. Criticism must maintain its independence of the practical spirit and its aims. Even with well-meant efforts of the practical spirit it must express dissatisfaction, if in the sphere of the ideal they seem impoverishing and limiting. It must not hurry on to the goal because of its practical importance. It must be patient, and know how to wait; and flexible, and know how to attach itself to things and how to withdraw from them. It must be apt to study and praise elements that for the fullness of spiritual perfection are wanted, even though they belong to a power which in the practical sphere may be maleficent. It must be apt to discern the spiritual shortcomings or illusions of powers that in the practical sphere may be beneficent. And this without any notion of favoring or injuring, in the practical sphere, one power or the other; without any notion of playing off, in this sphere, one power against the other. When one looks, for instance, at the English Divorce Court—an institution which perhaps has its practical conveniences, but which in the

---

7. "Sons of the earth."
8. "Let us die resisting." Three paragraphs are omitted here. They consist of a highly allusive account of a controversy concerning Biblical history. The discussion further illustrates the difficulties of a critic's remaining impartial.

ideal sphere is so hideous; an institution which neither makes divorce impossible nor makes it decent, which allows a man to get rid of his wife, or a wife of her husband, but makes them drag one another first, for the public edification, through a mire of unutterable infamy—when one looks at this charming institution, I say, with its crowded trials, its newspaper reports, and its money compensations, this institution in which the gross unregenerate British Philistine has indeed stamped an image of himself—one may be permitted to find the marriage theory of Catholicism refreshing and elevating. Or when Protestantism, in virtue of its supposed rational and intellectual origin, gives the law to criticism too magisterially, criticism may and must remind it that its pretensions, in this respect, are illusive and do it harm; that the Reformation was a moral rather than an intellectual event; that Luther's theory of grace no more exactly reflects the mind of the spirit than Bossuet's philosophy of history[9] reflects it; and that there is no more antecedent probability of the Bishop of Durham's[1] stock of ideas being agreeable to perfect reason than of Pope Pius the Ninth's. But criticism will not on that account forget the achievements of Protestantism in the practical and moral sphere; nor that, even in the intellectual sphere, Protestantism, though in a blind and stumbling manner, carried forward the Renascence, while Catholicism threw itself violently across its path.

I lately heard a man of thought and energy contrasting the want of ardor and movement which he now found amongst young men in this country with what he remembered in his own youth, twenty years ago. "What reformers we were then!" he exclaimed; "What a zeal we had! how we canvassed every institution in Church and State, and were prepared to remodel them all on first principles!" He was inclined to regret, as a spiritual flagging, the lull which he saw. I am disposed rather to regard it as a pause in which the turn to a new mode of spiritual progress is being accomplished. Everything was long seen, by the young and ardent amongst us, in inseparable connection with politics and practical life. We have pretty well exhausted the benefits of seeing things in this connection, we have got all that can be got by so seeing them. Let us try a more disinterested mode of seeing them; let us betake ourselves more to the serener life of the mind and spirit. This life, too, may have its excesses and dangers; but they are not for us at present. Let us think of quietly enlarging our stock of true and fresh ideas, and not, as soon as we get an idea or half an idea, be running out with it into the street, and trying to make it rule there. Our ideas will, in the end, shape the world all the better for matur-

9. Bishop Jacques Bossuet (1627–1704) whose theory of history is limited by its Roman Catholic bias (in Arnold's view), just as Martin Luther's exclusive view of grace reflects the bias of extreme Protestantism.
1. An Anglican bishop.

ing a little. Perhaps in fifty years' time it will in the English House of Commons be an objection to an institution that it is an anomaly, and my friend the Member of Parliament will shudder in his grave. But let us in the meanwhile rather endeavor that in twenty years' time it may, in English literature, be an objection to a proposition that it is absurd. That will be a change so vast, that the imagination almost fails to grasp it. *Ab integro saeclorum nascitur ordo*.[2]

If I have insisted so much on the course which criticism must take where politics and religion are concerned, it is because, where these burning matters are in question, it is most likely to go astray. I have wished, above all, to insist on the attitude which criticism should adopt towards things in general; on its right tone and temper of mind. But then comes another question as to the subject matter which literary criticism should most seek. Here, in general, its course is determined for it by the idea which is the law of its being; the idea of a disinterested endeavor to learn and propagate the best that is known and thought in the world, and thus to establish a current of fresh and true ideas. By the very nature of things, as England is not all the world, much of the best that is known and thought in the world cannot be of English growth, must be foreign; by the nature of things, again, it is just this that we are least likely to know, while English thought is streaming in upon us from all sides, and takes excellent care that we shall not be ignorant of its existence. The English critic of literature, therefore, must dwell much on foreign thought, and with particular heed on any part of it, which, while significant and fruitful in it- ~~self, is for any reason~~ specially likely to escape him. Again, judging is often spoken of as the critic's one business, and so in some sense it is; but the judgment which almost insensibly forms itself in a fair and clear mind, along with fresh knowledge, is the valuable one; and thus knowledge, and ever fresh knowledge, must be the critic's great concern for himself. And it is by communicating fresh knowledge, and letting his own judgment pass along with it—but insensibly, and in the second place, not the first, as a sort of companion and clue, not as an abstract lawgiver—that the critic will generally do most good to his readers. Sometimes, no doubt, for the sake of establishing an author's place in literature, and his relation to a central standard (and if this is not done, how are we to get at our *best in the world?*) criticism may have to deal with a subject matter so familiar that fresh knowledge is out of the question, and then it must be all judgment; an enunciation and detailed application of principles. Here the great safeguard is never to let oneself become abstract, always to retain an intimate and lively consciousness of the truth of what one is saying, and, the moment this fails us, to be sure that something is wrong. Still under all circumstances,

2. "Order is born from the renewal of the ages" (Virgil, *Eclogues* IV.5).

this mere judgment and application of principles is, in itself, not the most satisfactory work to the critic; like mathematics, it is tautological, and cannot well give us, like fresh learning, the sense of creative activity.

But stop, some one will say; all this talk is of no practical use to us whatever; this criticism of yours is not what we have in our minds when we speak of criticism; when we speak of critics and criticism, we mean critics and criticism of the current English literature of the day; when you offer to tell criticism its function, it is to this criticism that we expect you to address yourself. I am sorry for it, for I am afraid I must disappoint these expectations. I am bound by my own definition of criticism: *a disinterested endeavor to learn and propagate the best that is known and thought in the world.* How much of current English literature comes into this "best that is known and thought in the world"? Not very much I fear; certainly less, at this moment, than of the current literature of France or Germany. Well, then, am I to alter my definition of criticism, in order to meet the requirements of a number of practicing English critics, who, after all, are free in their choice of a business? That would be making criticism lend itself just to one of those alien practical considerations, which, I have said, are so fatal to it. One may say, indeed, to those who have to deal with the mass—so much better disregarded—of current English literature, that they may at all events endeavor, in dealing with this, to try it, so far as they can, by the standard of the best that is known and thought in the world; one may say, that to get anywhere near this standard, every critic should try and possess one great litera- ture, at least, besides his own; and the more unlike his own, the better. But, after all, the criticism I am really concerned with— the criticism which alone can much help us for the future, the criticism which, throughout Europe, is at the present day meant, when so much stress is laid on the importance of criticism and the critical spirit—is a criticism which regards Europe as being, for intellectual and spiritual purposes, one great confederation, bound to a joint action and working to a common result; and whose mem- bers have, for their proper outfit, a knowledge of Greek, Roman, and Eastern antiquity, and of one another. Special, local, and tem- porary advantages being put out of account, that modern nation will in the intellectual and spiritual sphere make most progress, which most thoroughly carries out this program. And what is that but saying that we too, all of us, as individuals, the more thor- oughly we carry it out, shall make the more progress?

There is so much inviting us!—what are we to take? what will nourish us in growth towards perfection? That is the question which, with the immense field of life and of literature lying before him, the critic has to answer; for himself first, and afterwards for others. In this idea of the critic's business the essays brought together in the following pages have had their origin; in this idea, widely different as are their subjects, they have, perhaps, their unity.

I conclude with what I said at the beginning: to have the sense of creative activity is the great happiness and the great proof of being alive, and it is not denied to criticism to have it; but then criticism must be sincere, simple, flexible, ardent, ever widening its knowledge. Then it may have, in no contemptible measure, a joyful sense of creative activity; a sense which a man of insight and conscience will prefer to what he might derive from a poor, starved, fragmentary, inadequate creation. And at some epochs no other creation is possible.

Still, in full measure, the sense of creative activity belongs only to genuine creation; in literature we must never forget that. But what true man of letters ever can forget it? It is no such common matter for a gifted nature to come into possession of a current of true and living ideas, and to produce amidst the inspiration of them, that we are likely to underrate it. The epochs of Aeschylus and Shakespeare make us feel their pre-eminence. In an epoch like those is, no doubt, the true life of literature; there is the promised land, towards which criticism can only beckon. That promised land it will not be ours to enter, and we shall die in the wilderness: but to have desired to enter it, to have saluted it from afar, is already, perhaps, the best distinction among contemporaries; it will certainly be the best title to esteem with posterity.

1864, 1865

From Maurice de Guérin[1]
[A Definition of Poetry]

The grand power of poetry is its interpretative power; by which I mean, not a power of drawing out in black and white an explanation of the mystery of the universe, but the power of so dealing with things as to awaken in us a wonderfully full, new, and intimate sense of them, and of our relations with them. When this sense is awakened in us, as to objects without us, we feel ourselves to be in contact with the essential nature of those objects, to be no longer bewildered and oppressed by them, but to have their secret, and to be in harmony with them; and this feeling calms and satisfies us as no other can. Poetry, indeed, interprets in another way besides this; but one of its two ways of interpreting, of exercising its highest power, is by awakening this sense in us. I will not now inquire whether this sense is illusive, whether it can be proved not to be

---

1. 1810–39; a minor French poet. The essay was included in *Essays in Criticism: First Series.*

illusive, whether it does absolutely make us possess the real nature of things; all I say is, that poetry can awaken it in us, and that to awaken it is one of the highest powers of poetry. The interpretations of science do not give us this intimate sense of objects as the interpretations of poetry give it; they appeal to a limited faculty, and not to the whole man. * * *

I have said that poetry interprets in two ways; it interprets by expressing, with magical felicity, the physiognomy and movement of the outward world, and it interprets by expressing, with inspired conviction, the ideas and laws of the inward world of man's moral and spiritual nature. In other words, poetry is interpretative both by having *natural magic* in it, and by having *moral profundity*. In both ways it illuminates man; it gives him a satisfying sense of reality; it reconciles him with himself and the universe. Thus Aeschylus's "δράσαντι παθεῖν"[2] and his "ἀνήριθμον γέλασμα"[3] are alike interpretative. Shakespeare interprets both when he says,

> Full many a glorious morning have I seen,
> Flatter the mountaintops with sovereign eye;[4]

and when he says,

> There's a divinity that shapes our ends,
> Rough-hew them as we will.[5]

These great poets unite in themselves the faculty of both kinds of interpretation, the naturalistic and the moral. But it is observable that in the poets who unite both kinds, the latter (the moral) usually ends by making itself the master. In Shakespeare the two kinds seem wonderfully to balance one another; but even in him the balance leans; his expression tends to become too little sensuous and simple, too much intellectualized. The same thing may be yet more strongly affirmed of Lucretius and of Wordsworth. In Shelley there is not a balance of the two gifts, nor even a coexistence of them, but there is a passionate straining after them both, and this is what makes Shelley, as a man, so interesting; I will not now inquire how much Shelley achieves as a poet, but whatever he achieves, he in general fails to achieve natural magic in his expression; in Mr. Palgrave's charming *Treasury*[6] may be seen a gallery of his failures.[7] But in Keats and Guérin, in whom the faculty of

---

2. "The doer must suffer." From Aeschylus' *Choephori* (line 313).
3. "Countless laughter." From Aeschylus' *Prometheus Bound* (line 90).
4. Shakespeare, *Sonnets* XXXIII.1–2.
5. *Hamlet* V.ii.10–11.
6. Francis Palgrave's anthology of poems, *The Golden Treasury*, was first published in 1861.
7. "Compare, for example, his *Lines Written in the Euganean Hills*, with Keats's *Ode to Autumn* . . . The latter piece *renders* Nature; the former *tries to render* her. I will not deny, however, that Shelley has natural magic in his rhythm; what I deny is, that he has it in his language. It always seems to me that the right sphere for Shelley's genius was the sphere of music, not of poetry; the medium of sounds he can master, but to master the more difficult medium of words he has neither intellectual force enough nor sanity enough" [Arnold's note].

naturalistic interpretation is overpoweringly predominant, the natural magic is perfect; when they speak of the world they speak like Adam naming by divine inspiration the creatures; their expression corresponds with the thing's essential reality.

1863, 1865

From Culture and Anarchy[1]

From *Chapter I. Sweetness and Light*

[PURITANISM AND CULTURE]

The impulse of the English race towards moral development and self-conquest has nowhere so powerfully manifested itself as in Puritanism. Nowhere has Puritanism found so adequate an expression as in the religious organization of the Independents.[2] The modern Independents have a newspaper, the *Nonconformist*, written with great sincerity and ability. The motto, the standard, the profession of faith which this organ of theirs carries aloft, is: "The Dissidence of Dissent and the Protestantism of the Protestant religion." There is sweetness and light, and an ideal of complete harmonious human perfection! One need not go to culture and poetry to find language to judge it. Religion, with its instinct for perfection, supplies language to judge it, language, too, which is in our mouths every day. "Finally, be of one mind, united in feeling," says St. Peter.[3] There is an ideal which judges the Puritan ideal: "The Dissidence of Dissent and the Protestantism of the Protestant religion!" And religious organizations like this are what people believe in, rest in, would give their lives for! Such, I say, is the wonderful virtue of even the beginnings of perfection, of having conquered even the plain faults of our animality, that the religious organization which has helped us to do it can seem to us some-

---

1. As a critic of social life, Arnold sought to test Victorian institutions according to whether they seemed to him civilized. A characteristic quality of the civilized state of mind is summed up, for his purposes, in his formula "sweetness and light," a phrase suggesting reasonableness of temper and intellectual insight. Arnold derived the phrase from a fable contrasting the spider with the bee in Swift's *Battle of the Books.* The spider (representing a narrow, self-centered, and uncultured mind) spins out of itself "nothing at all but flybane and cobweb." The bee (representing a cultured mind that has drawn nourishment from the humanist tradition) ranges far and wide and brings to its hive honey and also wax out of which candles may be made. Therefore the bee, Swift says, furnishes mankind "with the two noblest of things, which are sweetness and light."

The three following excerpts illustrate aspects of Arnold's indictment of the middle classes for their lack of sweetness and light. The first and third expose the narrowness and dullness of middle-class Puritan religious institutions in both the 17th and 19th centuries. The second, "Doing As One Likes," shows the limitations of the middle-class political bias and the irresponsibility of *laissez faire.* Here Arnold is most close to Carlyle and Ruskin. These three extracts indicate why it has been said that Matthew Arnold discovered the foibles of Main Street fifty years before Sinclair Lewis exposed them in his novels of American life.

2. A 17th-century Puritan group (of which Cromwell was an adherent), allied with the Congregationalists.

3. Cf. I Peter iii.8.

thing precious, salutary, and to be propagated, even when it wears such a brand of imperfection on its forehead as this. And men have got such a habit of giving to the language of religion a special application, of making it a mere jargon, that for the condemnation which religion itself passes on the shortcomings of their religious organizations they have no ear; they are sure to cheat themselves and to explain this condemnation away. They can only be reached by the criticism which culture, like poetry, speaking a language not to be sophisticated, and resolutely testing these organizations by the ideal of a human perfection complete on all sides, applies to them.

But men of culture and poetry, it will be said, are again and again failing, and failing conspicuously, in the necessary first stage to a harmonious perfection, in the subduing of the great obvious faults of our animality, which it is the glory of these religious organizations to have helped us to subdue. True, they do often so fail. They have often been without the virtues as well as the faults of the Puritan; it has been one of their dangers that they so felt the Puritan's faults that they too much neglected the practice of his virtues. I will not, however, exculpate them at the Puritan's expense. They have often failed in morality, and morality is indispensable. And they have been punished for their failure, as the Puritan has been rewarded for his performance. They have been punished wherein they erred; but their ideal of beauty, of sweetness and light, and a human nature complete on all its sides, remains the true ideal of perfection still; just as the Puritan's ideal of perfection remains narrow and inadequate, although for what he did well he has been richly rewarded. Notwithstanding the mighty results of the Pilgrim Fathers' voyage, they and their standard of perfection are rightly judged when we figure to ourselves Shakespeare or Virgil—souls in whom sweetness and light, and all that in human nature is most humane, were eminent—accompanying them on their voyage, and think what intolerable company Shakespeare and Virgil would have found them! In the same way let us judge the religious organizations which we see all around us. Do not let us deny the good and the happiness which they have accomplished; but do not let us fail to see clearly that their idea of human perfection is narrow and inadequate, and that the Dissidence of Dissent and the Protestantism of the Protestant religion will never bring humanity to its true goal. As I said with regard to wealth: Let us look at the life of those who live in and for it—so I say with regard to the religious organizations. Look at the life imaged in such a newspaper as the *Nonconformist*—a life of jealousy of the Establishment,[4] disputes, tea-meetings, openings of chapels, sermons; and then think of it as an ideal of a human life completing

4. The Church of England or the Established Church.

itself on all sides, and aspiring with all its organs after sweetness, light, and perfection!

From *Chapter II. Doing As One Likes*

* * * When I began to speak of culture, I insisted on our bondage to machinery, on our proneness to value machinery as an end in itself, without looking beyond it to the end for which alone, in truth, it is valuable. Freedom, I said, was one of those things which we thus worshiped in itself, without enough regarding the ends for which freedom is to be desired. In our common notions and talk about freedom, we eminently show our idolatry of machinery. Our prevalent notion is—and I quoted a number of instances to prove it—that it is a most happy and important thing for a man merely to be able to do as he likes. On what he is to do when he is thus free to do as he likes, we do not lay so much stress. Our familiar praise of the British Constitution under which we live, is that it is a system of checks—a system which stops and paralyzes any power in interfering with the free action of individuals. To this effect Mr. Bright,[1] who loves to walk in the old ways of the Constitution, said forcibly in one of his great speeches, what many other people are every day saying less forcibly, that the central idea of English life and politics is *the assertion of personal liberty*. Evidently this is so; but evidently, also, as feudalism, which with its ideas, and habits of subordination was for many centuries silently behind the British Constitution, dies out, and we are left with nothing but our system of checks, and our notion of its being the great right and happiness of an Englishman to do as far as possible what he likes, we are in danger of drifting towards anarchy. We have not the notion, so familiar on the Continent and to antiquity, of *the State*—the nation in its collective and corporate character, entrusted with stringent powers for the general advantage, and controlling individual wills in the name of an interest wider than that of individuals. We say, what is very true, that this notion is often made instrumental to tyranny; we say that a State is in reality made up of the individuals who compose it, and that every individual is the best judge of his own interests. Our leading class is an aristocracy, and no aristocracy likes the notion of a State-authority greater than itself, with a stringent administrative machinery superseding the decorative inutilities of lord-lieutenancy, deputy-lieutenancy, and the *posse comitatus*,[2] which are all in its own hands. Our middle class, the great representative of trade and Dissent, with its maxims of every man for himself in business, every man for himself in religion, dreads

1. John Bright, 19th-century orator and reformer.
2. I.e., "power of the county"—a feudal method of enforcing law by local authorities instead of by agencies of the central government.

a powerful administration which might somehow interfere with it; and besides, it has its own decorative inutilities of vestrymanship and guardianship, which are to this class what lord-lieutenancy and the county magistracy are to the aristocratic class, and a stringent administration might either take these functions out of its hands, or prevent its exercising them in its own comfortable, independent manner, as at present.

Then as to our working class. This class, pressed constantly by the hard daily compulsion of material wants, is naturally the very center and stronghold of our national idea, that it is man's ideal right and felicity to do as he likes. I think I have somewhere related how M. Michelet[3] said to me of the people of France, that it was "a nation of barbarians civilized by the conscription." He meant that through their military service the idea of public duty and of discipline was brought to the mind of these masses, in other respects so raw and uncultivated. Our masses are quite as raw and uncultivated as the French; and so far from their having the idea of public duty and of discipline, superior to the individual's self-will, brought to their mind by a universal obligation of military service, such as that of the conscription—so far from their having this, the very idea of a conscription is so at variance with our English notion of the prime right and blessedness of doing as one likes, that I remember the manager of the Clay Cross works in Derbyshire told me during the Crimean war, when our want of soldiers was much felt and some people were talking of a conscription, that sooner than submit to a conscription the population of that district would flee to the mines, and lead a sort of Robin Hood life underground.

For a long time, as I have said, the strong feudal habits of subordination and deference continued to tell upon the working class. The modern spirit has now almost entirely dissolved those habits, and the anarchical tendency of our worship of freedom in and for itself, of our superstitious faith, as I say, in machinery, is becoming very manifest. More and more, because of this our blind faith in machinery, because of our want of light to enable us to look beyond machinery to the end for which machinery is valuable, this and that man, and this and that body of men, all over the country, are beginning to assert and put in practice an Englishman's right to do what he likes; his right to march where he likes, meet where he likes, enter where he likes, hoot as he likes, threaten as he likes, smash as he likes.[4] All this, I say, tends to anarchy; and though a number of excellent people, and particularly my friends of the Liberal or progressive party, as they call themselves, are kind enough to reassure us by saying that these are trifles, that a few

3. Jules Michelet (1798–1874), French historian.
4. Reference to the riots of 1866 in which a London mob demolished the iron railings enclosing Hyde Park.

transient outbreaks of rowdyism signify nothing, that our system
of liberty is one which itself cures all the evils which it works, that
the educated and intelligent classes stand in overwhelming strength
and majestic repose, ready, like our military force in riots, to act
at a moment's notice—yet one finds that one's Liberal friends
generally say this because they have such faith in themselves and
their nostrums, when they shall return, as the public welfare requires, to place and power. But this faith of theirs one cannot
exactly share, when one has so long had them and their nostrums
at work, and see that they have not prevented our coming to our
present embarrassed condition. And one finds, also, that the outbreaks of rowdyism tend to become less and less of trifles, to become more frequent rather than less frequent; and that meanwhile
our educated and intelligent classes remain in their majestic repose,
and somehow or other, whatever happens, their overwhelming
strength, like our military force in riots, never does act.

How, indeed, *should* their overwhelming strength act, when the
man who gives an inflammatory lecture, or breaks down the park
railings, or invades a Secretary of State's office, is only following an
Englishman's impulse to do as he likes; and our own conscience tells
us that we ourselves have always regarded this impulse as something primary and sacred? Mr. Murphy[5] lectures at Birmingham,
and showers on the Catholic population of that town "words," says
the Home Secretary, "only fit to be addressed to thieves or murderers." What then? Mr. Murphy has his own reasons of several
kinds. He suspects the Roman Catholic Church of designs upon
Mrs. Murphy; and he says if mayors and magistrates do not care
for their wives and daughters, he does. But, above all, he is doing
as he likes; or, in worthier language, asserting his personal liberty.
"I will carry out my lectures if they walk over my body as a dead
corpse, and I say to the Mayor of Birmingham that he is my servant
while I am in Birmingham, and as my servant he must do his duty
and protect me." Touching and beautiful words, which find a
sympathetic chord in every British bosom! The moment it is plainly
put before us that a man is asserting his personal liberty, we are
half disarmed; because we are believers in freedom, and not in
some dream of a right reason to which the assertion of our freedom
is to be subordinated. Accordingly, the Secretary of State had to
say that although the lecturer's language was "only fit to be addressed to thieves or murderers," yet, "I do not think he is to be
deprived, I do not think that anything I have said could justify the
inference that he is to be deprived, of the right of protection in a
place built by him for the purpose of these lectures; because the
language was not language which afforded grounds for a criminal

5. An orator whose inflammatory anti-
Catholic public speech *The Errors of*
the Roman Church led to rioting in
Birmingham and other cities in 1867.

that the Puritans needed them more; or that Mr. Murphy, the Birmingham lecturer, and the Rev. W. Cattle[5] and his friends, need them more?

The Puritan's great danger is that he imagines himself in possession of a rule telling him the *unum necessarium*, or one thing needful, and that he then remains satisfied with a very crude conception of what this rule really is and what it tells him, thinks he has now knowledge and henceforth needs only to act, and, in this dangerous state of assurance and self-satisfaction, proceeds to give full swing to a number of the instincts of his ordinary self. Some of the instincts of his ordinary self he has, by the help of his rule of life, conquered; but others which he has not conquered by this help he is so far from perceiving to need subjugation, and to be instincts of an inferior self, that he even fancies it to be his right and duty, in virtue of having conquered a limited part of himself, to give unchecked swing to the remainder. He is, I say, a victim of Hebraism, of the tendency to cultivate strictness of conscience rather than spontaneity of consciousness. And what he wants is a larger conception of human nature, showing him the number of other points at which his nature must come to its best, besides the points which he himself knows and thinks of. There is no *unum necessarium*, or one thing needful, which can free human nature from the obligation of trying to come to its best at all these points. The real *unum necessarium* for us is to come to our best at all points. Instead of our "one thing needful," justifying in us vulgarity, hideousness, ignorance, violence— our vulgarity, hideousness, ignorance, violence, are really so many touchstones which try our one thing needful, and which prove that in the state, at any rate, in which we ourselves have it, it is not all we want. And as the force which encourages us to stand staunch and fast by the rule and ground we have is Hebraism, so the force which encourages us to go back upon this rule, and to try the very ground on which we appear to stand, is Hellenism —a turn for giving our consciousness free play and enlarging its range. And what I say is, not that Hellenism is always for everybody more wanted than Hebraism, but that for the Rev. W. Cattle at this particular moment, and for the great majority of us his fellow countrymen, it is more wanted.

* * *

The newspapers a short time ago contained an account of the suicide of a Mr. Smith, secretary to some insurance company, who, it was said, "labored under the apprehension that he would come

5. A Nonconformist clergyman who was chairman of the anti-Catholic meeting addressed by Murphy in 1867. See "Doing As One Likes," above.

to poverty, and that he was eternally lost." And when I read these words, it occurred to me that the poor man who came to such a mournful end was, in truth, a kind of type—by the selection of his two grand objects of concern, by their isolation from everything else, and their juxtaposition to one another—of all the strongest, most respectable, and most representative part of our nation. "He labored under the apprehension that he would come to poverty, and that he was eternally lost." The whole middle class have a conception of things—a conception which makes us call them Philistines—just like that of this poor man; though we are seldom, of course, shocked by seeing it take the distressing, violently morbid, and fatal turn, which it took with him. But how generally, with how many of us, are the main concerns of life limited to these two: the concern for making money, and the concern for saving our souls! And how entirely does the narrow and mechanical conception of our secular business proceed from a narrow and mechanical conception of our religious business! What havoc do the united conceptions make of our lives! It is because the second-named of these two master-concerns presents to us the one thing needful in so fixed, narrow, and mechanical a way, that so ignoble a fellow master-concern to it as the first-named becomes possible; and, having been once admitted, takes the same rigid and absolute character as the other.

Poor Mr. Smith had sincerely the nobler master-concern as well as the meaner—the concern for saving his soul (according to the narrow and mechanical conception which Puritanism has of what the salvation of the soul is), as well as the concern for making money. But let us remark how many people there are, especially outside the limits of the serious and conscientious middle class to which Mr. Smith belonged, who take up with a meaner master-concern—whether it be pleasure, or field sports, or bodily exercises, or business, or popular agitation—who take up with one of these exclusively, and neglect Mr. Smith's nobler master-concern, because of the mechanical form which Hebraism has given to this noble master-concern. Hebraism makes it stand, as we have said, as something talismanic, isolated, and all-sufficient, justifying our giving our ordinary selves free play in bodily exercises, or business, or popular agitation, if we have made our account square with this master-concern; and, if we have not, rendering other things indifferent, and our ordinary self all we have to follow, and to follow with all the energy that is in us, till we do. Whereas the idea of perfection at all points, the encouraging in ourselves spontaneity of consciousness, the letting a free play of thought live and flow around all our activity, the indisposition to allow one side of our activity to stand as so all-important and all-sufficing that it makes other sides indiffer-

ent—this bent of mind in us may not only check us in following
unreservedly a mean master-concern of any kind, but may even, also,
bring new life and movement into that side of us with which alone
Hebraism concerns itself, and awaken a healthier and less mechanical
activity there. Hellenism may thus actually serve to further the
designs of Hebraism.

* * *

1868, 1869

From Wordsworth[1]

* * * Wordsworth has been in his grave for some thirty years,
and certainly his lovers and admirers cannot flatter themselves that
this great and steady light of glory as yet shines over him. He is not
fully recognized at home; he is not recognized at all abroad. Yet I
firmly believe that the poetical performance of Wordsworth is, after
that of Shakespeare and Milton, of which all the world now recognizes the worth, undoubtedly the most considerable in our language from the Elizabethan age to the present time. Chaucer is
anterior; and on other grounds, too, he cannot well be brought
into the comparison. But taking the roll of our chief poetical names,
besides Shakespeare and Milton, from the age of Elizabeth downwards, and going through it—Spenser, Dryden, Pope, Gray, Goldsmith, Cowper, Burns, Coleridge, Scott, Campbell, Moore, Byron,
Shelley, Keats (I mention those only who are dead)—I think it
certain that Wordsworth's name deserves to stand, and will finally
stand, above them all. Several of the poets named have gifts and
excellences which Wordsworth has not. But taking the performance
of each as a whole, I say that Wordsworth seems to me to have left
a body of poetical work superior in power, in interest, in the qualities which give enduring freshness, to that which any one of the
others has left.

But this is not enough to say. I think it certain, further, that if
we take the chief poetical names of the Continent since the death
of Molière, and, omitting Goethe, confront the remaining names
with that of Wordsworth, the result is the same. Let us take Klop-
stock, Lessing, Schiller, Uhland, Rückert, and Heine for Germany;
Filicaia, Alfieri, Manzoni, and Leopardi for Italy; Racine, Boileau,
Voltaire, André Chénier, Béranger, Lamartine, Musset, M. Victor

1. In one of his letters to Clough, Arnold remarked that those who cannot
read Greek literature "should read nothing but Milton and parts of Wordsworth: the state should see to it." The
following essay, which served as the
introduction to a volume of Wordsworth's poems selected by Arnold, demonstrates the reasons for this admiration. A further tribute to Wordsworth
is expressed in Arnold's poem *Memorial
Verses*. The opening paragraphs of the
essay, which are omitted here, review
the history of Wordsworth's reputation.

Hugo (he has been so long celebrated that although he still lives I may be permitted to name him) for France. Several of these, again, have evidently gifts and excellences to which Wordsworth can make no pretension. But in real poetical achievement it seems to me indubitable that to Wordsworth, here again, belongs the palm. It seems to me that Wordsworth has left behind him a body of poetical work which wears, and will wear, better on the whole than the performance of any one of these personages, so far more brilliant and celebrated, most of them, than the homely poet of Rydal.[2] Wordsworth's performance in poetry is on the whole, in power, in interest, in the qualities which give enduring freshness, superior to theirs.

This is a high claim to make for Wordsworth. But if it is a just claim, if Wordsworth's place among the poets who have appeared in the last two or three centuries is after Shakespeare, Molière, Milton, Goethe, indeed, but before all the rest, then in time Wordsworth will have his due. We shall recognize him in his place, as we recognize Shakespeare and Milton; and not only we ourselves shall recognize him, but he will be recognized by Europe also. Meanwhile, those who recognize him already may do well, perhaps, to ask themselves whether there are not in the case of Wordsworth certain special obstacles which hinder or delay his due recognition by others, and whether these obstacles are not in some measure removable.

The *Excursion* and the *Prelude,* his poems of greatest bulk, are by no means Wordsworth's best work. His best work is in his shorter pieces, and many indeed are there of these which are of first-rate excellence. But in his seven volumes the pieces of high merit are mingled with a mass of pieces very inferior to them; so inferior to them that it seems wonderful how the same poet should have produced both. Shakespeare frequently has lines and passages in a strain quite false, and which are entirely unworthy of him. But one can imagine him smiling if one could meet him in the Elysian Fields and tell him so; smiling and replying that he knew it perfectly well himself, and what did it matter? But with Wordsworth the case is different. Work altogether inferior, work quite uninspired, flat, and dull, is produced by him with evident unconsciousness of its defects, and he presents it to us with the same faith and seriousness as his best work. Now a drama or an epic fill the mind, and one does not look beyond them; but in a collection of short pieces the impression made by one piece requires to be continued and sustained by the piece following. In reading Wordsworth the impression made by one of his fine pieces is too often dulled and

2. **Rydal Mount,** Wordsworth's home in the Lake District.

spoiled by a very inferior piece coming after it.

Wordsworth composed verses during a space of some sixty years; and it is no exaggeration to say that within one single decade of those years, between 1798 and 1808, almost all his really first-rate work was produced. A mass of inferior work remains, work done before and after this golden prime, imbedding the first-rate work and clogging it, obstructing our approach to it, chilling, not unfrequently, the high-wrought mood with which we leave it. To be recognized far and wide as a great poet, to be possible and receivable as a classic, Wordsworth needs to be relieved of a great deal of the poetical baggage which now encumbers him. To administer this relief is indispensable, unless he is to continue to be a poet for the few only—a poet valued far below his real worth by the world.[3] * * *

Disengaged from the quantity of inferior work which now obscures them, the best poems of Wordsworth, I hear many people say, would indeed stand out in great beauty, but they would prove to be very few in number, scarcely more than a half a dozen. I maintain, on the other hand, that what strikes me with admiration, what establishes in my opinion Wordsworth's superiority, is the great and ample body of powerful work which remains to him, even after all his inferior work has been cleared away. He gives us so much to rest upon, so much which communicates his spirit and engages ours!

This is of very great importance. If it were a comparison of single pieces, or of three or four pieces, by each poet, I do not say that Wordsworth would stand decisively above Gray, or Burns, or Coleridge, or Keats, or Manzoni, or Heine. It is in his ampler body of powerful work that I find his superiority. His good work itself, his work which counts, is not all of it, of course, of equal value. Some kinds of poetry are in themselves lower kinds than others. The ballad kind is a lower kind: the didactic kind, still more, is a lower kind. Poetry of this latter sort counts, too, sometimes, by its biographical interest partly, not by its poetical interest pure and simple; but then this can only be when the poet producing it has the power and importance of Wordsworth, a power and importance which he assuredly did not establish by such didactic poetry alone. Altogether, it is, I say, by the great body of powerful and significant work which remains to him, after every reduction and deduction has been made, that Wordsworth's superiority is proved.

To exhibit this body of Wordsworth's best work, to clear away obstructions from around it, and to let it speak for itself, is what every lover of Wordsworth should desire. Until this has been done,

---

3. Two paragraphs, here omitted, criticize Wordsworth's system of classifying his poems.

Wordsworth, whom we, to whom he is dear, all of us know and feel to be so great a poet, has not had a fair chance before the world. When once it has been done, he will make his way best, not by our advocacy of him, but by his own worth and power. We may safely leave him to make his way thus, we who believe that a superior worth and power in poetry finds in mankind a sense responsive to it and disposed at last to recognize it. Yet at the outset, before he has been duly known and recognized, we may do Wordsworth a service, perhaps, by indicating in what his superior power and worth will be found to consist, and in what it will not.

Long ago, in speaking of Homer, I said that the noble and profound application of ideas to life is the most essential part of poetic greatness. I said that a great poet receives his distinctive character of superiority from his application, under the conditions immutably fixed by the laws of poetic beauty and poetic truth, from his application, I say, to his subject, whatever it may be, of the ideas

On man, on nature, and on human life,[4]

which he has acquired for himself. The line quoted is Wordsworth's own; and his superiority arises from his powerful use, in his best pieces, his powerful application to his subject, of ideas "on man, on nature, and on human life."

Voltaire, with his signal acuteness, most truly remarked that "no nation has treated in poetry moral ideas with more energy and depth than the English nation." And he adds: "There, it seems to me, is the great merit of the English poets." Voltaire does not mean, by "treating in poetry moral ideas," the composing moral and didactic poems—that brings us but a very little way in poetry. He means just the same thing as was meant when I spoke above "of the noble and profound application of ideas to life"; and he means the application of these ideas under the conditions fixed for us by the laws of poetic beauty and poetic truth. If it is said that to call these ideas *moral* ideas is to introduce a strong and injurious limitation, I answer that it is to do nothing of the kind, because moral ideas are really so main a part of human life. The question, *how to live*, is itself a moral idea; and it is the question which most interests every man, and with which, in some way or other, he is perpetually occupied. A large sense is of course to be given to the term *moral*. Whatever bears upon the question, "how to live," comes under it.

> Nor love thy life, nor hate; but, what thou liv'st,
> Live well; how long or short, permit to heaven.[5]

---

4. *The Recluse*, line 754.   5. *Paradise Lost* XI.553–54.

In those fine lines Milton utters, as everyone at once perceives, a moral idea. Yes, but so too, when Keats consoles the forward-bending lover on the Grecian Urn, the lover arrested and presented in immortal relief by the sculptor's hand before he can kiss, with the line,

> Forever wilt thou love, and she be fair,[6]

he utters a moral idea. When Shakespeare says that

> We are such stuff
> As dreams are made on, and our little life
> Is rounded with a sleep,[7]

he utters a moral idea.

Voltaire was right in thinking that the energetic and profound treatment of moral ideas, in this large sense, is what distinguishes the English poetry. He sincerely meant praise, not dispraise or hint of limitation; and they err who suppose that poetic limitation is a necessary consequence of the fact, the fact being granted as Voltaire states it. If what distinguishes the greatest poets is their powerful and profound application of ideas to life, which surely no good critic will deny, then to prefix to the term ideas here the term moral makes hardly any difference, because human life itself is in so preponderating a degree moral.

It is important, therefore, to hold fast to this: that poetry is at bottom a criticism of life; that the greatness of a poet lies in his powerful and beautiful application of ideas to life—to the question: How to live. Morals are often treated in a narrow and false fashion; they are bound up with systems of thought and belief which have had their day; they are fallen into the hands of pedants and professional dealers; they grow tiresome to some of us. We find attraction, at times, even in a poetry of revolt against them; in a poetry which might take for its motto Omar Khayyám's words: "Let us make up in the tavern for the time which we have wasted in the mosque." Or we find attractions in a poetry indifferent to them: in a poetry where the contents may be what they will, but where the form is studied and exquisite. We delude ourselves in either case; and the best cure for our delusion is to let our minds rest upon that great and inexhaustible word *life*, until we learn to enter into its meaning. A poetry of revolt against moral ideas is a poetry of revolt against life; a poetry of indifference towards moral ideas is a poetry of indifference towards *life*.

Epictetus had a happy figure for things like the play of the senses, or literary form and finish, or argumentative ingenuity, in compari-

---

6. *Ode on a Grecian Urn,* line 20.   7. *The Tempest* IV.i.156–58.

son with "the best and master thing" for us, as he called it, the
concern, how to live. Some people were afraid of them, he said, or
they disliked and undervalued them. Such people were wrong; they
were unthankful or cowardly. But the things might also be over-
prized, and treated as final when they are not. They bear to life
the relation which inns bear to home. "As if a man, journeying
home, and finding a nice inn on the road, and liking it, were to
stay forever at the inn! Man, thou hast forgotten thine object; thy
journey was not *to* this, but *through* this. 'But this inn is taking.'
And how many other inns, too, are taking, and how many fields
and meadows! but as places of passage merely. You have an object,
which is this: to get home, to do your duty to your family, friends,
and fellow-countrymen, to attain inward freedom, serenity, happiness, contentment. Style takes your fancy, arguing takes your fancy,
and you forget your home and want to make your abode with them
and to stay with them, on the plea that they are taking. Who denies
that they are taking? but as places of passage, as inns. And when
I say this, you suppose me to be attacking the care for style, the
care for argument. I am not; I attack the resting in them, the not
looking to the end which is beyond them."

Now, when we come across a poet like Théophile Gautier[8] we
have a poet who has taken up his abode at an inn, and never got
farther. There may be inducements to this or that one of us, at this
or that moment, to find delight in him, to cleave to him; but after
all, we do not change the truth about him—we only stay ourselves
in his inn along with him. And when we come across a poet like
Wordsworth, who sings

> Of truth, of grandeur, beauty, love, and hope,
> And melancholy fear subdued by faith,
> Of blessed consolations in distress,
> Of moral strength and intellectual power,
> Of joy in widest commonalty spread—[9]

then we have a poet intent on "the best and master thing," and who
prosecutes his journey home. We say, for brevity's sake, that he
deals with *life*, because he deals with that in which life really consists. This is what Voltaire means to praise in the English poets—
this dealing with what is really life. But always it is the mark of
the greatest poets that they deal with it; and to say that the English

8. Théophile Gautier (1811–72), a poet
whose preoccupation with "literary form
and finish" and indifference towards
edification in literature made him an
important exponent of art for art's sake
in France, like D. G. Rossetti in England. Arnold often deplored his fellow
Victorians' fondness for the stunning
phrasemaking of such poets as Tennyson, Keats, and Rossetti.
9. *The Recluse*, lines 767–71.

poets are remarkable for dealing with it, is only another way of saying, what is true, that in poetry the English genius has especially shown its power.

Wordsworth deals with it, and his greatness lies in his dealing with it so powerfully. I have named a number of celebrated poets above all of whom he, in my opinion, deserves to be placed. He is to be placed above poets like Voltaire, Dryden, Pope, Lessing, Schiller, because these famous personages, with a thousand gifts and merits, never, or scarcely ever, attain the distinctive accent and utterance of the high and genuine poets—

> *Quique pii vates et Phoebo digna locuti,*[1]

at all. Burns, Keats, Heine, not to speak of others in our list, have this accent—who can doubt it? And at the same time they have treasures of humor, felicity, passion, for which in Wordsworth we shall look in vain. Where, then, is Wordsworth's superiority? It is here; he deals with more of *life* than they do; he deals with *life*, as a whole, more powerfully.

No Wordsworthian will doubt this. Nay, the fervent Wordsworthian will add, as Mr. Leslie Stephen does, that Wordsworth's poetry is precious because his philosophy is sound; that his "ethical system is as distinctive and capable of exposition as Bishop Butler's"; that his poetry is informed by ideas which "fall spontaneously into a scientific system of thought."[2] But we must be on our guard against the Wordsworthians, if we want to secure for Wordsworth his due rank as a poet. The Wordsworthians are apt to praise him for the wrong things, and to lay far too much stress upon what they call his philosophy. His poetry is the reality, his philosophy—so far, at least, as it may put on the form and habit of "a scientific system of thought," and the more that it puts them on—is the illusion. Perhaps we shall one day learn to make this proposition general, and to say: Poetry is the reality, philosophy the illusion. But in Wordsworth's case, at any rate, we cannot do him justice until we dismiss his formal philosophy.

The *Excursion* abounds with philosophy and therefore the *Excursion* is to the Wordsworthian what it never can be to the disinterested lover of poetry—a satisfactory work. "Duty exists," says Wordsworth, in the *Excursion*; and then he proceeds thus—

> . . . Immutably survive,
> For our support, the measures and the forms,
> Which an abstract Intelligence supplies,

---

1. "Those devout bards who utter things worthy of Phoebus" (Virgil, *Aeneid* VI.662).

2. From an essay on "Wordsworth's Ethics" in *Hours in a Library* by Leslie Stephen (1832–1904).

Whose kingdom is, where time and space are not.[3]

And the Wordsworthian is delighted, and thinks that here is a sweet union of philosophy and poetry. But the disinterested lover of poetry will feel that the lines carry us really not a step farther than the proposition which they would interpret; that they are a tissue of elevated but abstract verbiage, alien to the very nature of poetry.

Or let us come direct to the center of Wordsworth's philosophy, as "an ethical system, as distinctive and capable of systematical exposition as Bishop Butler's"—

> . . . One adequate support
> For the calamities of mortal life
> Exists, one only—an assured belief
> That the procession of our fate, howe'er
> Sad or disturbed, is ordered by a Being
> Of infinite benevolence and power;
> Whose everlasting purposes embrace
> All accidents, converting them to good.[4]

That is doctrine such as we hear in church too, religious and philosophic doctrine; and the attached Wordsworthian loves passages of such doctrine, and brings them forward in proof of his poet's excellence. But however true the doctrine may be, it has, as here presented, none of the characters of *poetic* truth, the kind of truth which we require from a poet, and in which Wordsworth is really strong.

Even the "intimations" of the famous *Ode*, those cornerstones of the supposed philosophic system of Wordsworth—the idea of the high instincts and affections coming out in childhood, testifying of a divine home recently left, and fading away as our life proceeds—this idea, of undeniable beauty as a play of fancy, has itself not the character of poetic truth of the best kind; it has no real solidity. The instinct of delight in Nature and her beauty had no doubt extraordinary strength in Wordsworth himself as a child. But to say that universally this instinct is mighty in childhood, and tends to die away afterwards, is to say what is extremely doubtful. In many people, perhaps with the majority of educated persons, the love of nature is nearly imperceptible at ten years old, but strong and operative at thirty. In general we may say of these high instincts of early childhood, the base of the alleged systematic philosophy of Wordsworth, what Thucydides says of the early achievements of the Greek race: "It is impossible to speak with certainty of what is so remote; but from all that we can really investigate, I should say

3. *The Excursion* IV.73–76.   4. *The Excursion* IV.10–17.

that they were no very great things."

Finally, the "scientific system of thought" in Wordsworth gives us at least such poetry as this, which the devout Wordsworthian accepts—

> O for the coming of that glorious time
> When, prizing knowledge as her noblest wealth
> And best protection, this Imperial Realm,
> While she exacts allegiance, shall admit
> An obligation, on her part, to *teach*
> Them who are born to serve her and obey;
> Binding herself by statute to secure,
> For all the children whom her soil maintains,
> The rudiments of letters, and inform
> The mind with moral and religious truth.[5]

Wordsworth calls Voltaire dull, and surely the production of these un-Voltairian lines must have been imposed on him as a judgment! One can hear them being quoted at a Social Science Congress; one can call up the whole scene. A great room in one of our dismal provincial towns; dusty air and jaded afternoon daylight; benches full of men with bald heads and women in spectacles; an orator lifting up his face from a manuscript written within and without to declaim these lines of Wordsworth; and in the soul of any poor child of nature who may have wandered in thither, an unutterable sense of lamentation, and mourning, and woe!

"But turn we," as Wordsworth says, "from these bold, bad men,"[6] the haunters of Social Science Congresses. And let us be on our guard, too, against the exhibitors and extollers of a "scientific system of thought" in Wordsworth's poetry. The poetry will never be seen aright while they thus exhibit it. The cause of its greatness is simple, and may be told quite simply. Wordsworth's poetry is great because of the extraordinary power with which Wordsworth feels the joy offered to us in nature, the joy offered to us in the simple primary affections and duties; and because of the extraordinary power with which, in case after case, he shows us this joy, and renders it so as to make us share it.

The source of joy from which he thus draws is the truest and most unfailing source of joy accessible to man. It is also accessible universally. Wordsworth brings us word, therefore, according to his own strong and characteristic line, he brings us word

> Of joy in widest commonalty spread.[7]

Here is an immense advantage for a poet. Wordsworth tells of what all seek, and tells of it at its truest and best source, and yet a

---

5. *The Excursion* IX.293–302.   *Fleming.*
6. In Wordsworth's poem *To the Lady*   7. *The Recluse,* line 771.

source where all may go and draw for it.

Nevertheless, we are not to suppose that everything is precious which Wordsworth, standing even at this perennial and beautiful source, may give us. Wordsworthians are apt to talk as if it must be. They will speak with the same reverence of *The Sailor's Mother*, for example, as of *Lucy Gray*. They do their master harm by such lack of discrimination. *Lucy Gray* is a beautiful success; *The Sailor's Mother* is a failure. To give aright what he wishes to give, to interpret and render successfully, is not always within Wordsworth's own command. It is within no poet's command; here is the part of the Muse, the inspiration, the God, the "not ourselves." In Wordsworth's case, the accident, for so it may almost be called, of inspiration, is of peculiar importance. No poet, perhaps, is so evidently filled with a new and sacred energy when the inspiration is upon him; no poet, when it fails him, is so left "weak as is a breaking wave."[8] I remember hearing him say that "Goethe's poetry was not inevitable enough." The remark is striking and true; no line in Goethe, as Goethe said himself, but its maker knew well how it came there. Wordsworth is right, Goethe's poetry is not inevitable; not inevitable enough. But Wordsworth's poetry, when he is at his best, is inevitable, as inevitable as Nature herself. It might seem that Nature not only gave him the matter for his poem, but wrote his poem for him. He has no style. He was too conversant with Milton not to catch at times his master's manner, and he has fine Miltonic lines; but he has no assured poetic style of his own, like Milton. When he seeks to have a style he falls into ponderosity and pomposity. In the *Excursion* we have his style, as an artistic product of his own creation; and although Jeffrey[9] completely failed to recognize Wordsworth's real greatness, he was yet not wrong in saying of the *Excursion*, as a work of poetic style: "This will never do." And yet magical as is that power, which Wordsworth has not, of assured and possessed poetic style, he has something which is an equivalent for it.

Everyone who has any sense for these things feels the subtle turn, the heightening, which is given to a poet's verse by his genius for style. We can feel it in the

> After life's fitful fever he sleeps well[1]—

of Shakespeare; in the

> . . . though fall'n on evil days,
> On evil days though fall'n, and evil tongues[2]—

---

8. Wordsworth, *A Poet's Epitaph*, line 58.
9. Francis Jeffrey (1773–1850), contributor to the *Edinburgh Review*.
1. *Macbeth* III.ii.23.
2. *Paradise Lost* VII.25–26.

spade, and even the *Thanksgiving Ode*—everything of Wordsworth, I think, except *Vaudracour and Julia*. It is not for nothing that one has been brought up in the veneration of a man so truly worthy of homage; that one has seen him and heard him, lived in his neighborhood, and been familiar with his country. No Wordsworthian has a tenderer affection for this pure and sage master than I, or is less really offended by his defects. But Wordsworth is something more than the pure and sage master of a small band of devoted followers, and we ought not to rest satisfied until he is seen to be what he is. He is one of the very chief glories of English Poetry; and by nothing is England so glorious as by her poetry. Let us lay aside every weight which hinders our getting him recognized as this, and let our one study be to bring to pass, as widely as possible and as truly as possible, his own word concerning his poems: "They will co-operate with the benign tendencies in human nature and society, and will, in their degree, be efficacious in making men wiser, better, and happier."[6]

1879

The Study of Poetry[1]

"The future of poetry is immense, because in poetry, where it is worthy of its high destinies, our race, as time goes on, will find an ever surer and surer stay. There is not a creed which is not shaken, not an accredited dogma which is not shown to be questionable, not a received tradition which does not threaten to dissolve. Our religion has materialized itself in the fact, in the supposed fact; it has attached its emotion to the fact, and now the fact is failing it. But for poetry the idea is everything; the rest is a world of illusion, of divine illusion. Poetry attaches its emotion to the idea; the idea *is* the fact. The strongest part of our religion today is its unconscious poetry."

Let me be permitted to quote these words of my own, as uttering the thought which should, in my opinion, go with us and govern

6. Wordsworth's letter to Lady Beaumont, May 21, 1807.
1. Aside from its vindication of the importance of literature, this essay is an interesting example of the variety of Arnold's own reading. To know literature in only one language seemed to him not to know literature. His personal *Notebooks* show that throughout his active life he continued to read books in French, German, Italian, Latin, and Greek. His favorite authors in these languages are used by him as a means of testing English poetry. The testing is sometimes a severe one. Readers may also protest that despite Arnold's own wit, his essay is limited by an incomplete recognition of the values of comic literature, a shortcoming abundantly evident in the discussion of Chaucer. Nevertheless, whether we agree or disagree with some of Arnold's verdicts, we can be attracted by the combination of traditionalism and impressionism on which these verdicts are based, and we can enjoy the memorable phrasemaking in which the verdicts are expressed. *The Study of Poetry* has been extraordinarily potent in shaping literary tastes in England and in America.

us in all our study of poetry. In the present work[2] it is the course of one great contributory stream to the world-river of poetry that we are invited to follow. We are here invited to trace the stream of English poetry. But whether we set ourselves, as here, to follow only one of the several streams that make the mighty river of poetry, or whether we seek to know them all, our governing thought should be the same. We should conceive of poetry worthily, and more highly than it has been the custom to conceive of it. We should conceive of it as capable of higher uses, and called to higher destinies, than those which in general men have assigned to it hitherto. More and more mankind will discover that we have to turn to poetry to interpret life for us, to console us, to sustain us. Without poetry, our science will appear incomplete; and most of what now passes with us for religion and philosophy will be replaced by poetry. Science, I say, will appear incomplete without it. For finely and truly does Wordsworth call poetry "the impassioned expression which is in the countenance of all science";[3] and what is a countenance without its expression? Again, Wordsworth finely and truly calls poetry "the breath and finer spirit of all knowledge": our religion, parading evidences such as those on which the popular mind relies now; our philosophy, pluming itself on its reasonings about causation and finite and infinite being; what are they but the shadows and dreams and false shows of knowledge? The day will come when we shall wonder at ourselves for having trusted to them, for having taken them seriously; and the more we perceive their hollowness, the more we shall prize "the breath and finer spirit of knowledge" offered to us by poetry.

But if we conceive thus highly of the destinies of poetry, we must also set our standard for poetry high, since poetry, to be capable of fulfilling such high destinies, must be poetry of a high order of excellence. We must accustom ourselves to a high standard and to a strict judgment. Sainte-Beuve[4] relates that Napoleon one day said, when somebody was spoken of in his presence as a charlatan: "Charlatan as much as you please; but where is there *not* charlatanism?"—"Yes," answers Sainte-Beuve, "in politics, in the art of governing mankind, that is perhaps true. But in the order of thought, in art, the glory, the eternal honor is that charlatanism shall find no entrance; herein lies the inviolableness of that noble portion of man's being." It is admirably said, and let us hold fast to it. In poetry, which is thought and art in one, it is the glory, the eternal honor, that charlatanism shall find no entrance; that this noble sphere be kept inviolate and inviolable. Charlatanism is for confusing or obliterating the distinctions between excellent and in-

---

2. An anthology of English poetry for which Arnold's essay served as the introduction.
3. See Wordsworth's Preface to *Lyrical* *Ballads.*
4. Charles Augustin Sainte-Beuve (1804–69), French critic who influenced Arnold.

ferior, sound and unsound or only half-sound, true and untrue or only half-true. It is charlatanism, conscious or unconscious, whenever we confuse or obliterate these. And in poetry, more than anywhere else, it is unpermissible to confuse or obliterate them. For in poetry the distinction between excellent and inferior, sound and unsound or only half-sound, true and untrue or only half-true, is of paramount importance. It is of paramount importance because of the high destinies of poetry. In poetry, as a criticism of life under the conditions fixed for such a criticism by the laws of poetic truth and poetic beauty, the spirit of our race will find, we have said, as time goes on and as other helps fail, its consolation and stay. But the consolation and stay will be of power in proportion to the power of the criticism of life. And the criticism of life will be of power in proportion as the poetry conveying it is excellent rather than inferior, sound rather than unsound or half-sound, true rather than untrue or half-true.

The best poetry is what we want; the best poetry will be found to have a power of forming, sustaining, and delighting us, as nothing else can. A clearer, deeper sense of the best in poetry, and of the strength and joy to be drawn from it, is the most precious benefit which we can gather from a poetical collection such as the present. And yet in the very nature and conduct of such a collection there is inevitably something which tends to obscure in us the consciousness of what our benefit should be, and to distract us from the pursuit of it. We should therefore steadily set it before our minds at the outset, and should compel ourselves to revert constantly to the thought of it as we proceed.

Yes; constantly in reading poetry, a sense for the best, the really excellent, and of the strength and joy to be drawn from it, should be present in our minds and should govern our estimate of what we read. But this real estimate, the only true one, is liable to be superseded, if we are not watchful, by two other kinds of estimate, the historic estimate and the personal estimate, both of which are fallacious. A poet or a poem may count to us historically, they may count to us on grounds personal to ourselves, and they may count to us really. They may count to us historically. The course of development of a nation's language, thought, and poetry, is profoundly interesting; and by regarding a poet's work as a stage in this course of development we may easily bring ourselves to make it of more importance as poetry than in itself it really is, we may come to use a language of quite exaggerated praise in criticizing it; in short, to overrate it. So arises in our poetic judgments the fallacy caused by the estimate which we may call historic. Then, again, a poet or a poem may count to us on grounds personal to ourselves. Our personal affinities, likings, and circumstances, have great power to sway our estimate of this or that poet's work, and to make us attach more importance to it as poetry than in itself it really possesses, because to us it is, or has been, of high importance. Here also we overrate the object of our interest, and apply to it a language of praise which is quite exaggerated. And thus we get the source of a second fallacy in our poetic judgments—the fallacy caused by an estimate which we may call personal.

Both fallacies are natural. It is evident how naturally the study of the history and development of a poetry may incline a man to pause over reputations and works once conspicuous but now obscure, and to quarrel with a careless public for skipping, in obedience to mere tradition and habit, from one famous name or work in its national poetry to another, ignorant of what it misses, and of the reason for keeping what it keeps, and of the whole process of growth in its poetry. The French have become diligent students of their own early poetry, which they long neglected; the study makes many of them dissatisfied with their so-called classical poetry, the court-tragedy of the seventeenth century, a poetry which Pellisson[5] long ago reproached with its want of the true poetic stamp, with its *politesse stérile et rampante*,[6] but which nevertheless has reigned in France as absolutely as if it had been the perfection of classical poetry indeed. The dissatisfaction is natural; yet a lively and accomplished critic, M. Charles d'Héricault, the editor of Clément Marot,[7] goes too far when he says that "the cloud of glory playing round a classic is a mist as dangerous to the future of a literature as it is intolerable for the purposes of history." "It hinders," he goes on, "it hinders us from seeing more than one single point, the culminating and exceptional point; the summary, fictitious and arbitrary, of a thought and of a work. It substitutes a halo for a physiognomy, it puts a statue where there was once a man, and hiding from us all trace of the labor, the attempts, the weaknesses, the failures, it claims not study but veneration; it does not show us how the thing is done, it imposes upon us a model. Above all, for the historian this creation of classic personages is inadmissible; for it withdraws the poet from his time, from his proper life, it breaks historical relationships, it blinds criticism by conventional admiration, and renders the investigation of literary origins unacceptable. It gives us a human personage no longer, but a God seated immovable amidst His perfect work, like Jupiter on Olympus; and hardly will it be possible for the young student, to whom such work is exhibited at such a distance from him, to believe that it did not issue ready made from that divine head."

All this is brilliantly and tellingly said, but we must plead for a

5. Paul Pellison, 17th-century French critic.
6. "Conventionality that is barren and bombastic."
7. D'Héricault's edition of Marot was published in 1868. The graceful poetry of Clément Marot (ca. 1495–1544) was admired and imitated in late 19th-century England, sometimes at the expense of overlooking the excellences of the more severely classical 17th-century French poets such as Racine.

distinction. Everything depends on the reality of a poet's classic character. If he is a dubious classic, let us sift him; if he is a false classic, let us explode him. But if he is a real classic, if his work belongs to the class of the very best (for this is the true and right meaning of the word *classic, classical*), then the great thing for us is to feel and enjoy his work as deeply as ever we can, and to appreciate the wide difference between it and all work which has not the same high character. This is what is salutary, this is what is formative; this is the great benefit to be got from the study of poetry. Everything which interferes with it, which hinders it, is injurious. True, we must read our classic with open eyes, and not with eyes blinded with superstition; we must perceive when his work comes short, when it drops out of the class of the very best, and we must rate it, in such cases, at its proper value. But the use of this negative criticism is not in itself, it is entirely in its enabling us to have a clearer sense and a deeper enjoyment of what is truly excellent. To trace the labor, the attempts, the weaknesses, the failures of a genuine classic, to acquaint oneself with his time and his life and his historical relationships, is mere literary dilettantism unless it has that clear sense and deeper enjoyment for its end. It may be said that the more we know about a classic the better we shall enjoy him; and, if we lived as long as Methuselah and had all of us heads of perfect clearness and wills of perfect steadfastness, this might be true in fact as it is plausible in theory. But the case here is much the same as the case with the Greek and Latin studies of our schoolboys. The elaborate philological groundwork which we require them to lay is in theory an admirable preparation for appreciating the Greek and Latin authors worthily. The more thoroughly we lay the groundwork, the better we shall be able, it may be said, to enjoy the authors. True, if time were not so short, and schoolboys' wits not so soon tired and their power of attention exhausted; only, as it is, the elaborate philological preparation goes on, but the authors are little known and less enjoyed. So with the investigator of "historic origins" in poetry. He ought to enjoy the true classic all the better for his investigations; he often is distracted from the enjoyment of the best, and with the less good he overbusies himself, and is prone to overrate it in proportion to the trouble which it has cost him.

The idea of tracing historic origins and historical relationships cannot be absent from a compilation like the present. And naturally the poets to be exhibited in it will be assigned to those persons for exhibition who are known to prize them highly, rather than to those who have no special inclination towards them. Moreover the very occupation with an author, and the business of exhibiting him, disposes us to affirm and amplify his importance. In the present work, therefore, we are sure of frequent temptation to adopt the historic estimate, or the personal estimate, and to forget the real estimate; which latter, nevertheless, we must employ if we are to make poetry yield us its full benefit. So high is that benefit, the benefit of clearly feeling and of deeply enjoying the really excellent, the truly classic in poetry, that we do well, I say, to set it fixedly before our minds as our object in studying poets and poetry, and to make the desire of attaining it the one principle to which, as the *Imitation* says, whatever we may read or come to know, we always return. *Cum multa legeris et cognoveris, ad unum semper oportet redire principium.*[8]

The historic estimate is likely in especial to affect our judgment and our language when we are dealing with ancient poets; the personal estimate when we are dealing with poets our contemporaries, or at any rate modern. The exaggerations due to the historic estimate are not in themselves, perhaps, of very much gravity. Their report hardly enters the general ear; probably they do not always impose even on the literary men who adopt them. But they lead to a dangerous abuse of language. So we hear Cædmon,[9] amongst our own poets, compared to Milton. I have already noticed the enthusiasm of one accomplished French critic for "historic origins." Another eminent French critic, M. Vitet, comments upon that famous document of the early poetry of his nation, the *Chanson de Roland.*[1] It is indeed a most interesting document. The *joculator* or *jongleur*[2] Taillefer, who was with William the Conqueror's army at Hastings, marched before the Norman troops, so said the tradition, singing "of Charlemagne and of Roland and of Oliver, and of the vassals who died at Roncevaux"; and it is suggested that in the *Chanson de Roland* by one Turoldus or *Théroulde,* a poem preserved in a manuscript of the twelfth century in the Bodleian Library at Oxford, we have certainly the matter, perhaps even some of the words, of the chant which Taillefer sang. The poem has vigor and freshness; it is not without pathos. But M. Vitet is not satisfied with seeing in it a document of some poetic value, and of very high historic and linguistic value; he sees in it a grand and beautiful work, a monument of epic genius. In its general design he finds the grandiose conception, in its details he finds the constant union of simplicity with greatness, which are the marks, he truly says, of the genuine epic, and distinguish it from the artificial epic of literary ages. One thinks of Homer; this is the sort of praise which is given to Homer, and justly given. Higher praise there cannot well be, and it is the praise due to epic poetry of the highest order only, and to no other. Let us try, then, the *Chanson de Ro-*

land at its best. Roland, mortally wounded, lays himself down under a pine tree, with his face turned towards Spain and the enemy—

> *De plusurs choses à remembrer li prist,*
> *De tantes teres cume li bers cunquist,*
> *De dulce France, des humes de sun lign,*
> *De Carlemagne sun seignor ki l'nurrit.*[3]

That is primitive work, I repeat, with an undeniable poetic quality of its own. It deserves such praise, and such praise is sufficient for it. But now turn to Homer—

> Ὥς φάτο τοὺς δ' ἤδη κάτεχεν φυσίζοος αἶα
> ἐν Λακεδαίμονι αὖθι, φίλῃ ἐν πατρίδι γαίῃ.[4]

We are here in another world, another order of poetry altogether; here is rightly due such supreme praise as that which M. Vitet gives to the *Chanson de Roland*. If our words are to have any meaning, if our judgments are to have any solidity, we must not heap that supreme praise upon poetry of an order immeasurably inferior.

Indeed there can be no more useful help for discovering what poetry belongs to the class of the truly excellent, and can therefore do us most good, than to have always in one's mind lines and expressions of the great masters, and to apply them as a touchstone to other poetry. Of course we are not to require this other poetry to resemble them; it may be very dissimilar. But if we have any tact we shall find them, when we have lodged them well in our minds, an infallible touchstone for detecting the presence or absence of high poetic quality, and also the degree of this quality, in all other poetry which we may place beside them. Short passages, even single lines, will serve our turn quite sufficiently. Take the two lines which I have just quoted from Homer, the poet's comment on Helen's mention of her brothers—or take his

> Ἆ δειλώ, τί σφῶϊ δόμεν Πηλῆϊ ἄνακτι
> θνητῷ; ὑμεῖς δ' ἐστὸν ἀγήρω τ' ἀθανάτω τε.
> ἦ ἵνα δυστήνοισι μετ' ἀνδράσιν ἄλγε' ἔχητον;[5]

the address of Zeus to the horses of Peleus—or take finally his

> Καὶ σέ, γέρον, τὸ πρὶν μὲν ἀκούομεν ὄλβιον εἶναι·[6]

3. "'Then began he to call many things to remembrance—all the lands which his valor conquered and pleasant France, and the men of his lineage, and Charlemagne his liege lord who nourished him.' *Chanson de Roland* III.939–42" [Arnold's note].
4. "'So said she; they long since in Earth's soft arms were reposing, / There, in their own dear land, their fatherland, Lacedaemon.' *Iliad* III.243–

44 (translated by Dr. Hawtrey)" [Arnold's note].
5. "'Ah, unhappy pair, why gave we you to King Peleus, to a mortal? but ye are without old age, and immortal. Was it that with men born to misery ye might have sorrow?' *Iliad* XVII.443–45" [Arnold's note].
6. "'Nay, and thou too, old man, in former days wast, as we hear, happy.' *Iliad* XXIV.543" [Arnold's note].

the words of Achilles to Priam, a suppliant before him. Take that incomparable line and a half of Dante, Ugolino's tremendous words—

> Io no piangeva; sì dentro impietrai.
> Piangevan elli . . .[7]

take the lovely words of Beatrice to Virgil—

> Io son fatta da Dio, sua mercè, tale,
> Che la vostra miseria non mi tange,
> Nè fiamma d'esto incendio non m'assale . . .[8]

take the simple, but perfect, single line—

> In la sua volontade è nostra pace.[9]

Take of Shakespeare a line or two of Henry the Fourth's expostulation with sleep—

> Wilt thou upon the high and giddy mast
> Seal up the shipboy's eyes, and rock his brains
> In cradle of the rude imperious surge . . .[1]

and take, as well, Hamlet's dying request to Horatio—

> If thou didst ever hold me in thy heart,
> Absent thee from felicity awhile,
> And in this harsh world draw thy breath in pain,
> To tell my story . . .[2]

Take of Milton that Miltonic passage—

> Darkened so, yet shone
> Above them all the archangel; but his face
> Deep scars of thunder had intrenched, and care
> Sat on his faded cheek . . .[3]

add two such lines as—

> And courage never to submit or yield
> And what is else not to be overcome . . .[4]

and finish with the exquisite close to the loss of Proserpine, the loss

> . . . which cost Ceres all that pain
> To seek her through the world.[5]

7. " 'I wailed not, so of stone I grew within; *they* wailed.' *Inferno* XXXIII. 49–50" [Arnold's note].
8. " 'Of such sort hath God, thanked be His mercy, made me, that your misery toucheth me not, neither doth the flame of this fire strike me.' *Inferno* II.91–93" [Arnold's note].

9. " 'In His will is our peace.' *Paradiso* III.85" [Arnold's note].
1. *2 Henry IV* III.i.18–20.
2. *Hamlet* V.ii.357–60.
3. *Paradise Lost* I.599–602.
4. *Ibid.* I.108–9.
5. *Ibid.* IV.271–72.

These few lines, if we have tact and can use them, are enough even of themselves to keep clear and sound our judgments about poetry, to save us from fallacious estimates of it, to conduct us to a real estimate.

The specimens I have quoted differ widely from one another, but they have in common this: the possession of the very highest poetical quality. If we are thoroughly penetrated by their power, we shall find that we have acquired a sense enabling us, whatever poetry may be laid before us, to feel the degree in which a high poetical quality is present or wanting there. Critics give themselves great labor to draw out what in the abstract constitutes the characters of a high quality of poetry. It is much better simply to have recourse to concrete examples—to take specimens of poetry of the high, the very highest quality, and to say: The characters of a high quality of poetry are what is expressed *there*. They are far better recognized by being felt in the verse of the master, than by being perused in the prose of the critic. Nevertheless if we are urgently pressed to give some critical account of them, we may safely, perhaps, venture on laying down, not indeed how and why the characters arise, but where and in what they arise. They are in the matter and substance of the poetry, and they are in its manner and style. Both of these, the substance and matter on the one hand, the style and manner on the other, have a mark, an accent, of high beauty, worth, and power. But if we are asked to define this mark and accent in the abstract, our answer must be: No, for we should thereby be darkening the question, not clearing it. The mark and accent are as given by the substance and matter of that poetry, by the style and manner of that poetry, and of all other poetry which is akin to it in quality.

Only one thing we may add as to the substance and matter of poetry, guiding ourselves by Aristotle's profound observation that the superiority of poetry over history consists in its possessing a higher truth and a higher seriousness (φιλοσοφώτερον καὶ σπουδαιότερον).[6] Let us add, therefore, to what we have said, this: that the substance and matter of the best poetry acquire their special character from possessing, in an eminent degree, truth and seriousness. We may add yet further, what is in itself evident, that to the style and manner of the best poetry their special character, their accent, is given by their diction, and, even yet more, by their movement. And though we distinguish between the two characters, the two accents, of superiority, yet they are nevertheless vitally connected one with the other. The superior character of truth and seriousness, in the matter and substance of the best poetry, is inseparable from the superiority of diction and movement marking its style and manner. The two superiorities are closely related, and

6. Aristotle, *Poetics* IX.

are in steadfast proportion one to the other. So far as high poetic truth and seriousness are wanting to a poet's matter and substance, so far also, we may be sure, will a high poetic stamp of diction and movement be wanting to his style and manner. In proportion as this high stamp of diction and movement, again, is absent from a poet's style and manner, we shall find, also, that high poetic truth and seriousness are absent from his substance and matter.

So stated, these are but dry generalities; their whole force lies in their application. And I could wish every student of poetry to make the application of them for himself. Made by himself, the application would impress itself upon his mind far more deeply than made by me. Neither will my limits allow me to make any full application of the generalities above propounded; but in the hope of bringing out, at any rate, some significance in them, and of establishing an important principle more firmly by their means, I will, in the space which remains to me, follow rapidly from the commencement the course of our English poetry with them in my view.

Once more I return to the early poetry of France, with which our own poetry, in its origins, is indissolubly connected. In the twelfth and thirteenth centuries, that seed time of all modern language and literature, the poetry of France had a clear predominance in Europe. Of the two divisions of that poetry, its productions in the *langue d'oïl* and its productions in the *langue d'oc*,[7] the poetry of the *langue d'oc*, of southern France, of the troubadours, is of importance because of its effect on Italian literature—the first literature of modern Europe to strike the true and grand note, and to bring forth, as in Dante and Petrarch it brought forth, classics. But the predominance of French poetry in Europe, during the twelfth and thirteenth centuries, is due to its poetry of the *langue d'oïl*, the poetry of northern France and of the tongue which is now the French language. In the twelfth century the bloom of this romance poetry was earlier and stronger in England, at the court of our Anglo-Norman kings, than in France itself. But it was a bloom of French poetry; and as our native poetry formed itself, it formed itself out of this. The romance poems which took possession of the heart and imagination of Europe in the twelfth and thirteenth centuries are French; "they are," as Southey justly says, "the pride of French literature, nor have we anything which can be placed in competition with them." Themes were supplied from all quarters: but the romance setting which was common to them all, and which gained the ear of Europe, was French. This constituted for the French poetry, literature, and language, at the height of the Middle Age, an unchallenged predominance. The

7. Medieval dialects of France; in the northern dialect, from which modern French derives, the word *oui* ("yes") was pronounced *oïl;* in the southern dialect it was pronounced *oc.*

Italian Brunetto Latini, the master of Dante, wrote his *Treasure* in French because, he says, *"la parleure en est plus délitable et plus commune à toutes gens."*[8] In the same century, the thirteenth, the French romance writer, Christian of Troyes, formulates the claims, in chivalry and letters, of France, his native country, as follows:

> *Or vous ert par ce livre apris,*
> *Que Gresse ot de chevalerie*
> *Le premier los et de clergie;*
> *Puis vint chevalerie à Rome,*
> *Et de la clergie la some,*
> *Qui ore est en France venue.*
> *Diex doinst qu'ele i soit retenue*
> *Et que li lius li abelisse*
> *Tant que de France n'isse*
> *L'onor qui s'i est arestée!*

"Now by this book you will learn that first Greece had the renown for chivalry and letters; then chivalry and the primacy in letters passed to Rome, and now it is come to France. God grant it may be kept there; and that the place may please it so well, that the honor which has come to make stay in France may never depart thence!"

Yet it is now all gone, this French romance poetry, of which the weight of substance and the power of style are not unfairly represented by this extract from Christian of Troyes. Only by means of the historic estimate can we persuade ourselves now to think that any of it is of poetical importance.

But in the fourteenth century there comes an Englishman nourished on this poetry; taught his trade by this poetry, getting words, rhyme, meter from this poetry; for even of that stanza which the Italians used, and which Chaucer derived immediately from the Italians, the basis and suggestion was probably given in France. Chaucer (I have already named him) fascinated his contemporaries, but so too did Christian of Troyes and Wolfram of Eschenbach.[9] Chaucer's power of fascination, however, is enduring; his poetical importance does not need the assistance of the historic estimate; it is real. He is a genuine source of joy and strength, which is flowing still for us and will flow always. He will be read, as time goes on, far more generally than he is read now. His language is a cause of difficulty for us; but so also, and I think in quite as great a degree, is the language of Burns. In Chaucer's case, as in that of Burns, it is a difficulty to be unhesitatingly accepted and overcome.

If we ask ourselves wherein consists the immense superiority of Chaucer's poetry over the romance poetry—why it is that in passing from this to Chaucer we suddenly feel ourselves to be in an-

---

8. "French speech is more delightful and more commonly known to all peo-   ples."
9. 12th-century German poet.

other world, we shall find that his superiority is both in the substance of his poetry and in the style of his poetry. His superiority in substance is given by his large, free, simple, clear yet kindly view of human life—so unlike the total want, in the romance poets, of all intelligent command of it. Chaucer has not their helplessness; he has gained the power to survey the world from a central, a truly human point of view. We have only to call to mind the Prologue to *The Canterbury Tales*. The right comment upon it is Dryden's: "It is sufficient to say, according to the proverb, that *here is God's plenty*." And again: "He is a perpetual fountain of good sense."[1] It is by a large, free, sound representation of things, that poetry, this high criticism of life, has truth of substance; and Chaucer's poetry has truth of substance.

Of his style and manner, if we think first of the romance poetry and then of Chaucer's divine liquidness of diction, his divine fluidity of movement, it is difficult to speak temperately. They are irresistible, and justify all the rapture with which his successors speak of his "gold dewdrops of speech."[2] Johnson misses the point entirely when he finds fault with Dryden for ascribing to Chaucer the first refinement of our numbers, and says that Gower[3] also can show smooth numbers and easy rhymes. The refinement of our numbers means something far more than this. A nation may have versifiers with smooth numbers and easy rhymes, and yet may have no real poetry at all. Chaucer is the father of our splendid English poetry; he is our "well of English undefiled,"[4] because by the lovely charm of his diction, the lovely charm of his movement, he makes an epoch and founds a tradition. In Spenser, Shakespeare, Milton, Keats, we can follow the tradition of the liquid diction, the fluid movement, of Chaucer; at one time it is his liquid diction of which in these poets we feel the virtue, and at another time it is his fluid movement. And the virtue is irresistible.

Bounded as is my space, I must yet find room for an example of Chaucer's virtue, as I have given examples to show the virtue of the great classics. I feel disposed to say that a single line is enough to show the charm of Chaucer's verse; that merely one line like this—

O martyr souded[5] in virginitee!

has a virtue of manner and movement such as we shall not find in all the verse of romance poetry—but this is saying nothing. The

---

1. Both quotations are from Dryden's Preface to his *Fables* (1700).
2. *The Life of Our Lady*, a poem by John Lydgate (ca. 1370–ca. 1451).
3. John Gower (ca. 1325–1408), friend of Chaucer and author of the *Confessio Amantis*, a long poem in octosyllabic couplets.

4. Said of Chaucer by Spenser (*Faerie Queene* IV.ii.32).
5. "The French *soudé*: soldered, fixed fast" [Arnold's note]. The line is from the Prioress's Tale (line 127): Chaucer wrote "souded to" rather than "souded in."

virtue is such as we shall not find, perhaps, in all English poetry, outside the poets whom I have named as the special inheritors of Chaucer's tradition. A single line, however, is too little if we have not the strain of Chaucer's verse well in our memory; let us take a stanza. It is from *The Prioress's Tale*, the story of the Christian child murdered in a Jewry—

> My throte is cut unto my nekke-bone
> Saidè this child, and as by way of kinde
> I should have deyd, yea, longè time agone;
> But Jesu Christ, as ye in bookès finde,
> Will that his glory last and be in minde,
> And for the worship of his mother dere
> Yet may I sing O *Alma* loud and clere.

Wordsworth has modernized this Tale, and to feel how delicate and evanescent is the charm of verse, we have only to read Wordsworth's first three lines of this stanza after Chaucer's—

> My throat is cut unto the bone, I trow,
> Said this young child, and by the law of kind
> I should have died, yea, many hours ago.

The charm is departed. It is often said that the power of liquidness and fluidity in Chaucer's verse was dependent upon a free, a licentious dealing with language, such as is now impossible; upon a liberty, such as Burns too enjoyed, of making words like *neck*, *bird*, into a dissyllable by adding to them, and words like *cause*, *rhyme*, into a dissyllable by sounding the *e* mute. It is true that Chaucer's fluidity is conjoined with this liberty, and is admirably served by it; but we ought not to say that it was dependent upon it. It was dependent upon his talent. Other poets with a like liberty do not attain to the fluidity of Chaucer; Burns himself does not attain to it. Poets, again, who have a talent akin to Chaucer's, such as Shakespeare or Keats, have known how to attain to his fluidity without the like liberty.

And yet Chaucer is not one of the great classics. His poetry transcends and effaces, easily and without effort, all the romance poetry of Catholic Christendom; it transcends and effaces all the English poetry contemporary with it, it transcends and effaces all the English poetry subsequent to it down to the age of Elizabeth. Of such avail is poetic truth of substance, in its natural and necessary union with poetic truth of style. And yet, I say, Chaucer is not one of the great classics. He has not their accent. What is wanting to him is suggested by the mere mention of the name of the first great classic of Christendom, the immortal poet who died eighty years before Chaucer—Dante. The accent of such verse as

In la sua volontade è nostra pace . . .

is altogether beyond Chaucer's reach; we praise him, but we feel that this accent is out of the question for him. It may be said that it was necessarily out of the reach of any poet in the England of that stage of growth. Possibly; but we are to adopt a real, not a historic, estimate of poetry. However we may account for its absence, something is wanting, then, to the poetry of Chaucer, which poetry must have before it can be placed in the glorious class of the best. And there is no doubt what that something is. It is the σπουδαιότης, the high and excellent seriousness, which Aristotle assigns as one of the grand virtues of poetry. The substance of Chaucer's poetry, his view of things and his criticism of life, has largeness, freedom, shrewdness, benignity; but it has not this high seriousness. Homer's criticism of life has it, Dante's has it, Shakespeare's has it. It is this chiefly which gives to our spirits what they can rest upon; and with the increasing demands of our modern ages upon poetry, this virtue of giving us what we can rest upon will be more and more highly esteemed. A voice from the slums of Paris, fifty or sixty years after Chaucer, the voice of poor Villon[6] out of his life of riot and crime, has at its happy moments (as, for instance, in the last stanza of *La Belle Heaulmière*[7]) more of this important poetic virtue of seriousness than all the productions of Chaucer. But its apparition in Villon, and in men like Villon, is fitful; the greatness of the great poets, the power of their criticism of life, is that their virtue is sustained.

To our praise, therefore, of Chaucer as a poet there must be this limitation: he lacks the high seriousness of the great classics, and therewith an important part of their virtue. Still, the main fact for us to bear in mind about Chaucer is his sterling value according to that real estimate which we firmly adopt for all poets. He has poetic truth of substance, though he has not high poetic seriousness, and corresponding to his truth of substance he has an exquisite virtue of style and manner. With him is born our real poetry.

For my present purpose I need not dwell on our Elizabethan poetry, or on the continuation and close of this poetry in Milton. We all of us profess to be agreed in the estimate of this poetry; we all of us recognize it as great poetry, our greatest, and Shake-

---

6. François Villon (1431–84), French poet and vagabond.
7. "The name *Heaulmière* is said to be derived from a headdress (helm) worn as a mask by courtesans. In Villon's ballad, a poor old creature of this class laments her days of youth and beauty. The last stanza of the ballad runs thus —'*Ainsi le bon temps regretons / Entre nous, pauvres vieilles sottes, / Assises bas, à croppetons, / Tout en ung tas comme pelottes; / A petit feu de chenevottes / Tost allumées, tost estainctes, / Et jadis fusmes si mignottes! / Ainsi en prend à maintz et maintes.*' [It may be translated:] 'Thus amongst ourselves we regret the good time, poor silly old things, low-seated on our heels, all in a heap like so many balls; by a little fire of hemp stalks, soon lighted, soon spent. And once we were such darlings! So fares it with many and many a one'" [Arnold's note].

speare and Milton as our poetical classics. The real estimate, here, has universal currency. With the next age of our poetry divergency and difficulty begin. An historic estimate of that poetry has established itself; and the question is, whether it will be found to coincide with the real estimate.

The age of Dryden, together with our whole eighteenth century which followed it, sincerely believed itself to have produced poetical classics of its own, and even to have made advance, in poetry, beyond all its predecessors. Dryden regards as not seriously disputable the opinion "that the sweetness of English verse was never understood or practiced by our fathers."[8] Cowley could see nothing at all in Chaucer's poetry. Dryden heartily admired it, and, as we have seen, praised its matter admirably; but of its exquisite manner and movement all he can find to say is that "there is the rude sweetness of a Scotch tune in it, which is natural and pleasing, though not perfect."[9] Addison, wishing to praise Chaucer's numbers, compares them with Dryden's own. And all through the eighteenth century, and down even into our own times, the stereotyped phrase of approbation for good verse found in our early poetry has been, that it even approached the verse of Dryden, Addison, Pope, and Johnson.

Are Dryden and Pope poetical classics? Is the historic estimate, which represents them as such, and which has been so long established that it cannot easily give way, the real estimate? Wordsworth and Coleridge, as is well known, denied it; but the authority of Wordsworth and Coleridge does not weigh much with the young generation, and there are many signs to show that the eighteenth century and its judgments are coming into favor again. Are the favorite poets of the eighteenth century classics?

It is impossible within my present limits to discuss the question fully. And what man of letters would not shrink from seeming to dispose dictatorially of the claims of two men who are, at any rate, such masters in letters as Dryden and Pope; two men of such admirable talent, both of them, and one of them, Dryden, a man, on all sides, of such energetic and genial power? And yet, if we are to gain the full benefit from poetry, we must have the real estimate of it. I cast about for some mode of arriving, in the present case, at such an estimate without offense. And perhaps the best way is to begin, as it is easy to begin, with cordial praise.

When we find Chapman, the Elizabethan translator of Homer, expressing himself in his preface thus: "Though truth in her very nakedness sits in so deep a pit, that from Gades to Aurora and Ganges few eyes can sound her, I hope yet those few here will so

8. Dryden's *Essay on Dramatic Poesy.* (1618–67).
Cowley is the poet. Abraham Cowley 9. Dryden's Preface to his *Fables.*

discover and confirm that, the date being out of her darkness in this morning of our poet, he shall now gird his temples with the sun," we pronounce that such a prose is intolerable. When we find Milton writing: "And long it was not after, when I was confirmed in this opinion, that he, who would not be frustrate of his hope to write well hereafter in laudable things, ought himself to be a true poem"[1]—we pronounce that such a prose has its own grandeur, but that it is obsolete and inconvenient. But when we find Dryden telling us: "What Virgil wrote in the vigor of his age, in plenty and at ease, I have undertaken to translate in my declining years; struggling with wants, oppressed with sickness, curbed in my genius, liable to be misconstrued in all I write"[2]—then we exclaim that here at last we have the true English prose, a prose such as we would all gladly use if we only knew how. Yet Dryden was Milton's contemporary.

But after the Restoration the time had come when our nation felt the imperious need of a fit prose. So, too, the time had likewise come when our nation felt the imperious need of freeing itself from the absorbing preoccupation which religion in the Puritan age had exercised. It was impossible that this freedom should be brought about without some negative excess, without some neglect and impairment of the religious life of the soul; and the spiritual history of the eighteenth century shows us that the freedom was not achieved without them. Still, the freedom was achieved; the preoccupation, an undoubtedly baneful and retarding one if it had continued, was got rid of. And as with religion amongst us at that period, so it was also with letters. A fit prose was a necessity; but it was impossible that a fit prose should establish itself amongst us without some touch of frost to the imaginative life of the soul. The needful qualities for a fit prose are regularity, uniformity, precision, balance. The men of letters, whose destiny it may be to bring their nation to the attainment of a fit prose, must of necessity, whether they work in prose or in verse, give a predominating, an almost exclusive attention to the qualities of regularity, uniformity, precision, balance. But an almost exclusive attention to these qualities involves some repression and silencing of poetry.

We are to regard Dryden as the puissant and glorious founder, Pope as the splendid high priest, of our age of prose and reason, of our excellent and indispensable eighteenth century. For the purposes of their mission and destiny their poetry, like their prose, is admirable. Do you ask me whether Dryden's verse, take it almost where you will, is not good?

> A milk-white Hind, immortal and unchanged,
> Fed on the lawns and in the forest ranged.[3]

---

1. Milton's *Apology for Smectymnuus.*
2. Dryden's *Postscript to the Reader* in his translation of Virgil.
3. *The Hind and the Panther* I.1–2.

I answer: Admirable for the purposes of the inaugurator of an age of prose and reason. Do you ask me whether Pope's verse, take it almost where you will, is not good?

> To Hounslow Heath I point, and Banstead Down;
> Thence comes your mutton, and these chicks my own.[4]

I answer: Admirable for the purposes of the high priest of an age of prose and reason. But do you ask me whether such verse proceeds from men with an adequate poetic criticism of life, from men whose criticism of life has a high seriousness, or even, without that high seriousness, has poetic largeness, freedom, insight, benignity? Do you ask me whether the application of ideas to life in the verse of these men, often a powerful application, no doubt, is a powerful *poetic* application? Do you ask me whether the poetry of these men has either the matter or the inseparable manner of such an adequate poetic criticism; whether it has the accent of

> Absent thee from felicity awhile . . .

or of

> And what is else not to be overcome . . .

or of

> O martyr souded in virginitee!

I answer: It has not and cannot have them; it is the poetry of the builders of an age of prose and reason. Though they may write in verse, though they may in a certain sense be masters of the art of versification, Dryden and Pope are not classics of our poetry, they are classics of our prose.

Gray is our poetical classic of that literature and age; the position of Gray is singular, and demands a word of notice here. He has not the volume or the power of poets who, coming in times more favorable, have attained to an independent criticism of life. But he lived with the great poets, he lived, above all, with the Greeks, through perpetually studying and enjoying them; and he caught their poetic point of view for regarding life, caught their poetic manner. The point of view and the manner are not self-sprung in him, he caught them of others; and he had not the free and abundant use of them. But whereas Addison and Pope never had the use of them, Gray had the use of them at times. He is the scantiest and frailest of classics in our poetry, but he is a classic.

And now, after Gray, we are met, as we draw towards the end of the eighteenth century, we are met by the great name of Burns. We enter now on times where the personal estimate of poets begins to be rife, and where the real estimate of them is not reached

4. *Imitations of Horace,* Satire II.ii. 143–44.

without difficulty. But in spite of the disturbing pressures of personal partiality, of national partiality, let us try to reach a real estimate of the poetry of Burns.

By his English poetry Burns in general belongs to the eighteenth century, and has little importance for us.

> Mark ruffian Violence, distained with crimes,
> Rousing elate in these degenerate times;
> View unsuspecting Innocence a prey,
> As guileful Fraud points out the erring way;
> While subtle Litigation's pliant tongue
> The life-blood equal sucks of Right and Wrong![5]

Evidently this is not the real Burns, or his name and fame would have disappeared long ago. Nor is Clarinda's love-poet, Sylvander,[6] the real Burns either. But he tells us himself: "These English songs gravel me to death. I have not the command of the language that I have of my native tongue. In fact, I think that my ideas are more barren in English than in Scotch. I have been at *Duncan Gray* to dress it in English, but all I can do is desperately stupid."[7] We English turn naturally, in Burns, to the poems in our own language, because we can read them easily; but in those poems we have not the real Burns.

The real Burns is of course in his Scotch poems. Let us boldly say that of much of this poetry, a poetry dealing perpetually with Scotch drink, Scotch religion, and Scotch manners, a Scotchman's estimate is apt to be personal. A Scotchman is used to this world of Scotch drink, Scotch religion, and Scotch manners; he has a tenderness for it; he meets its poet half way. In this tender mood he reads pieces like the *Holy Fair* or *Halloween*. But this world of Scotch drink, Scotch religion, and Scotch manners is against a poet, not for him, when it is not a partial countryman who reads him; for in itself it is not a beautiful world, and no one can deny that it is of advantage to a poet to deal with a beautiful world. Burns's world of Scotch drink, Scotch religion, and Scotch manners, is often a harsh, a sordid, a repulsive world; even the world of his *Cotter's Saturday Night* is not a beautiful world. No doubt a poet's criticism of life may have such truth and power that it triumphs over its world and delights us. Burns may triumph over his world, often he does triumph over his world, but let us observe how and where. Burns is the first case we have had where the bias of the personal estimate tends to mislead; let us look at him closely, he can bear it.

Many of his admirers will tell us that we have Burns, convivial, genuine, delightful, here—

---

5. *On the Death of Lord President Dundas*, lines 25–30.
6. Burns, styling himself Sylvander, carried on an idyllic correspondence with a Mrs. Maclehose, addressing her as Clarinda.
7. Letter to George Thomson, October 19, 1794.

> Leeze me on drink! it gies us mair
>   Than either school or college;
> It kindles wit, it waukens lair,
>   It pangs us fou o' knowledge.
> Be't whisky gill or penny wheep
>   Or ony stronger potion,
> It never fails, on drinking deep,
>   To kittle up our notion
>   By night or day.[8]

There is a great deal of that sort of thing in Burns, and it is unsatisfactory, not because it is bacchanalian poetry, but because it has not that accent of sincerity which bacchanalian poetry, to do it justice, very often has. There is something in it of bravado, something which makes us feel that we have not the man speaking to us with his real voice; something, therefore, poetically unsound.

With still more confidence will his admirers tell us that we have the genuine Burns, the great poet, when his strain asserts the independence, equality, dignity, of men, as in the famous song *For A' That and A' That*—

> A prince can mak' a belted knight,
>   A marquis, duke, and a' that;
> But an honest man's aboon his might,
>   Guid faith he mauna fa' that!
>   For a' that, and a' that,
>   Their dignities, and a' that,
>   The pith o' sense, and pride o' worth,
>   Are higher rank than a' that.

Here they find his grand, genuine touches; and still more, when this puissant genius, who so often set morality at defiance, falls moralizing—

> The sacred lowe o' weel-placed love
>   Luxuriantly indulge it;
> But never tempt th' illicit rove,
>   Though naething should divulge it.
> I waive the quantum o' the sin,
>   The hazard o' concealing,
> But och! it hardens a' within,
>   And petrifies the feeling.[9]

Or in a higher strain—

> Who made the heart, 'tis He alone
>   Decidedly can try us;
> He knows each chord, its various tone;
>   Each spring, its various bias.
> Then at the balance let's be mute,

---

8. *The Holy Fair*, lines 163–71.   9. *Epistle to a Young Friend*, lines 41–48.

> We never can adjust it;
> What's *done* we partly may compute,
> But know not what's resisted.[1]

Or in a better strain yet, a strain, his admirers will say, unsurpassable—

> To make a happy fireside clime
> To weans and wife,
> That's the true pathos and sublime
> Of human life.[2]

There is criticism of life for you, the admirers of Burns will say to us; there is the application of ideas to life! There is, undoubtedly. The doctrine of the last-quoted lines coincides almost exactly with what was the aim and end, Xenophon tells us, of all the teaching of Socrates. And the application is a powerful one; made by a man of vigorous understanding, and (need I say?) a master of language.

But for supreme poetical success more is required than the powerful application of ideas to life; it must be an application under the conditions fixed by the laws of poetic truth and poetic beauty. Those laws fix as an essential condition, in the poet's treatment of such matters as are here in question, high seriousness—the high seriousness which comes from absolute sincerity. The accent of high seriousness, born of absolute sincerity, is what gives to such verse as

> *In la sua volontade è nostra pace* . . .

to such criticism of life as Dante's, its power. Is this accent felt in the passages which I have been quoting from Burns? Surely not; surely, if our sense is quick, we must perceive that we have not in those passages a voice from the very inmost soul of the genuine Burns; he is not speaking to us from these depths, he is more or less preaching. And the compensation for admiring such passages less, for missing the perfect poetic accent in them, will be that we shall admire more the poetry where that accent is found.

No; Burns, like Chaucer, comes short of the high seriousness of the great classics, and the virtue of matter and manner which goes with that high seriousness is wanting to his work. At moments he touches it in a profound and passionate melancholy, as in those four immortal lines taken by Byron as a motto for *The Bride of Abydos*, but which have in them a depth of poetic quality such as resides in no verse of Byron's own—

> Had we never loved sae kindly,
> Had we never loved sae blindly,

1. *Address to the Unco Guid*, lines 57–64. 2. *Epistle to Dr. Blacklock*, lines 51–54.

Never met, or never parted,
We had ne'er been broken-hearted.[3]

But a whole poem of that quality Burns cannot make; the rest,
in the *Farewell to Nancy*, is verbiage.

We arrive best at the real estimate of Burns, I think, by conceiving his work as having truth of matter and truth of manner,
but not the accent or the poetic virtue of the highest masters. His
genuine criticism of life, when the sheer poet in him speaks, is
ironic; it is not—

Thou Power Supreme, whose mighty scheme
These woes of mine fulfill,
Here firm I rest, they must be best
Because they are Thy will![4]

It is far rather: "Whistle owre the lave o't!"[5] Yet we may say of
him as of Chaucer, that of life and the world, as they come before
him, his view is large, free, shrewd, benignant—truly poetic, therefore; and his manner of rendering what he sees is to match. But
we must note, at the same time, his great difference from Chaucer.
The freedom of Chaucer is heightened, in Burns, by a fiery, reckless energy; the benignity of Chaucer deepens, in Burns, into an
overwhelming sense of the pathos of things—of the pathos of human nature, the pathos, also, of nonhuman nature. Instead of the
fluidity of Chaucer's manner, the manner of Burns has spring,
bounding swiftness. Burns is by far the greater force, though he
has perhaps less charm. The world of Chaucer is fairer, richer, more
significant than that of Burns; but when the largeness and freedom of Burns get full sweep, as in *Tam o' Shanter*, or still more
in that puissant and splendid production, *The Jolly Beggars*, his
world may be what it will, his poetic genius triumphs over it. In
the world of *The Jolly Beggars* there is more than hideousness
and squalor, there is bestiality; yet the piece is a superb poetic success. It has a breadth, truth, and power which make the famous
scene in Auerbach's Cellar, of Goethe's *Faust*, seem artificial and
tame beside it, and which are only matched by Shakespeare and
Aristophanes.

Here, where his largeness and freedom serve him so admirably,
and also in those poems and songs where to shrewdness he adds
infinite archness and wit, and to benignity infinite pathos, where
his manner is flawless, and a perfect poetic whole is the result—
in things like the address to the mouse whose home he had ruined,
in things like *Duncan Gray, Tam Glen, Whistle and I'll Come to
You, My Lad, Auld Lang Syne* (this list might be made much
longer)—here we have the genuine Burns, of whom the real esti-

3. *Ae Fond Kiss* (also called *A Fare-*
well to Nancy), lines 13–16.
4. *Winter: A Dirge*, lines 17–20.

5. "Whistle over what's left of it." The
phrase is a refrain from one of Burns's
poems.

mate must be high indeed. Not a classic, nor with the excellent σπουδαιότης[6] of the great classics, nor with a verse rising to a criticism of life and a virtue like theirs; but a poet with thorough truth of substance and an answering truth of style, giving us a poetry sound to the core. We all of us have a leaning towards the pathetic, and may be inclined perhaps to prize Burns most for his touches of piercing, sometimes almost intolerable, pathos; for verse like—

> We twa hae paidl't i' the burn
> From mornin' sun till dine;
> But seas between us braid hae roared
> Sin auld lang syne . . .[7]

where he is as lovely as he is sound. But perhaps it is by the perfection of soundness of his lighter and archer masterpieces that he is poetically most wholesome for us. For the votary misled by a personal estimate of Shelley, as so many of us have been, are, and will be—of that beautiful spirit building his many-colored haze of words and images

> Pinnacled dim in the intense inane[8]—

no contact can be wholesomer than the contact with Burns at his archest and soundest. Side by side with the

> On the brink of the night and the morning
> My coursers are wont to respire,
> But the Earth has just whispered a warning
> That their flight must be swifter than fire . . .[9]

of *Prometheus Unbound*, how salutary, how very salutary, to place this from *Tam Glen*—

> My minnie does constantly deave me
> And bids me beware o' young men;
> They flatter, she says, to deceive me;
> But wha can think sae o' Tam Glen?

But we enter on burning ground as we approach the poetry of times so near to us—poetry like that of Byron, Shelley, and Wordsworth—of which the estimates are so often not only personal, but personal with passion. For my purpose, it is enough to have taken the single case of Burns, the first poet we come to of whose work the estimate formed is evidently apt to be personal, and to have suggested how we may proceed, using the poetry of the great classics as a sort of touchstone, to correct this estimate, as we had previously corrected by the same means the historic estimate where we met with it. A collection like the present, with its succession of cele-

6. "High seriousness."   iv.204.
7. *Auld Lang Syne*, lines 17–20.   9. *Ibid*. II.v.1–4.
8. Shelley, *Prometheus Unbound* III.

brated names and celebrated poems, offers a good opportunity to us for resolutely endeavoring to make our estimates of poetry real. I have sought to point out a method which will help us in making them so, and to exhibit it in use so far as to put anyone who likes in a way of applying it for himself.

At any rate the end to which the method and the estimate are designed to lead, and from leading to which, if they do lead to it, they get their whole value—the benefit of being able clearly to feel and deeply to enjoy the best, the truly classic, in poetry—is an end, let me say it once more at parting, of supreme importance. We are often told that an era is opening in which we are to see multitudes of a common sort of readers, and masses of a common sort of literature; that such readers do not want and could not relish anything better than such literature, and that to provide it is becoming a vast and profitable industry. Even if good literature entirely lost currency with the world, it would still be abundantly worth while to continue to enjoy it by oneself. But it never will lose currency with the world, in spite of momentary appearances; it never will lose supremacy. Currency and supremacy are insured to it, not indeed by the world's deliberate and conscious choice, but by something far deeper—by the instinct of self-preservation in humanity.

1880

Literature and Science[1]

Practical people talk with a smile of Plato and of his absolute ideas: and it is impossible to deny that Plato's ideas do often seem unpractical and unpracticable, and especially when one views them in connection with the life of a great work-a-day world like the United States. The necessary staple of the life of such a world Plato regards with disdain; handicraft and trade and the working professions he regards with disdain; but what becomes of the life of an industrial modern community if you take handicraft and trade and the working professions out of it? The base mechanic arts and handicrafts, says Plato, bring about a natural weakness in the principle of excellence in a man, so that he cannot govern the ignoble growths in him, but nurses them, and cannot understand fostering any other. Those who exercise such arts and trades, as they have their bodies, he says, marred by their vulgar businesses,

1. Delivered as a lecture during Arnold's tour of the United States in 1883, and published in *Discourses in America* (1885), this essay has become a classic contribution to a subject endlessly debated. Its main argument was summed up by Stuart P. Sherman: "If Arnold had said outright that the study of letters helps us to *bear* the grand results of science, he would not have been guilty of a superficial epigram; he would have spoken from the depths of his experience."

so they have their souls, too, bowed and broken by them. And if one of these uncomely people has a mind to seek self-culture and philosophy, Plato compares him to a bald little tinker, who has scraped together money, and has got his release from service, and has had a bath, and bought a new coat, and is rigged out like a bridegroom about to marry the daughter of his master who has fallen into poor and helpless estate.

Nor do the working professions fare any better than trade at the hands of Plato. He draws for us an inimitable picture of the working lawyer, and of his life of bondage; he shows how this bondage from his youth up has stunted and warped him, and made him small and crooked of soul, encompassing him with difficulties which he is not man enough to rely on justice and truth as means to encounter, but has recourse, for help out of them, to falsehood and wrong. And so, says Plato, this poor creature is bent and broken, and grows up from boy to man without a particle of soundness in him, although exceedingly smart and clever in his own esteem.

One cannot refuse to admire the artist who draws these pictures. But we say to ourselves that his ideas show the influence of a primitive and obsolete order of things, when the warrior caste and the priestly caste were alone in honor, and the humble work of the world was done by slaves. We have now changed all that; the modern majesty consists in work, as Emerson declares; and in work, we may add, principally of such plain and dusty kind as the work of cultivators of the ground, handicraftsmen, men of trade and business, men of the working professions. Above all is this true in a great industrious community such as that of the United States.

Now education, many people go on to say, is still mainly governed by the ideas of men like Plato, who lived when the warrior caste and the priestly or philosophical class were alone in honor, and the really useful part of the community were slaves. It is an education fitted for persons of leisure in such a community. This education passed from Greece and Rome to the feudal communities of Europe, where also the warrior caste and the priestly caste were alone held in honor, and where the really useful and working part of the community, though not nominally slaves as in the pagan world, were practically not much better off than slaves, and not more seriously regarded. And how absurd it is, people end by saying, to inflict this education upon an industrious modern community, where very few indeed are persons of leisure, and the mass to be considered has not leisure, but is bound, for its own great good, and for the great good of the world at large, to plain labor and to industrial pursuits, and the education in question tends necessarily to make men dissatisfied with these pursuits and unfitted for them!

That is what is said. So far I must defend Plato, as to plead that his view of education and studies is in the general, as it seems to me, sound enough, and fitted for all sorts and conditions of men, whatever their pursuits may be. "An intelligent man," says Plato, "will prize those studies which result in his soul getting soberness, righteousness, and wisdom, and will less value the others."[2] I cannot consider *that* a bad description of the aim of education, and of the motives which should govern us in the choice of studies, whether we are preparing ourselves for a hereditary seat in the English House of Lords or for the pork trade in Chicago.

Still I admit that Plato's world was not ours, that his scorn of trade and handicraft is fantastic, that he had no conception of a great industrial community such as that of the United States, and that such a community must and will shape its education to suit its own needs. If the usual education handed down to it from the past does not suit it, it will certainly before long drop this and try another. The usual education in the past has been mainly literary. The question is whether the studies which were long supposed to be the best for all of us are practically the best now; whether others are not better. The tyranny of the past, many think, weighs on us injuriously in the predominance given to letters in education. The question is raised whether, to meet the needs of our modern life, the predominance ought not now to pass from letters to science; and naturally the question is nowhere raised with more energy than here in the United States. The design of abasing what is called "mere literary instruction and education," and of exalting what is called "sound, extensive, and practical scientific knowledge," is, in this intensely modern world of the United States, even more perhaps than in Europe, a very popular design, and makes great and rapid progress.

I am going to ask whether the present movement for ousting letters from their old predominance in education, and for transferring the predominance in education to the natural sciences, whether this brisk and flourishing movement ought to prevail, and whether it is likely that in the end it really will prevail. An objection may be raised which I will anticipate. My own studies have been almost wholly in letters, and my visits to the field of the natural sciences have been very slight and inadequate, although those sciences have always strongly moved my curiosity. A man of letters, it will perhaps be said, is not competent to discuss the comparative merits of letters and natural science as means of education. To this objection I reply, first of all, that his incompetence, if he attempts the discussion but is really incompetent for it, will be abundantly visible; nobody will be taken in; he will have plenty of sharp observers and critics to save mankind from that danger. But the line I am going to follow is, as you will soon discover, so extremely

2. Plato, *Republic* IX.591.

simple, that perhaps it may be followed without failure even by one who for a more ambitious line of discussion would be quite incompetent.

Some of you may possibly remember a phrase of mine which has been the object of a good deal of comment; an observation to the effect that in our culture, the aim being *to know ourselves and the world*, we have, as the means to this end, *to know the best which has been thought and said in the world*.[3] A man of science, who is also an excellent writer and the very prince of debaters, Professor Huxley, in a discourse at the opening of Sir Josiah Mason's college at Birmingham,[4] laying hold of this phrase, expanded it by quoting some more words of mine, which are these: "The civilized world is to be regarded as now being, for intellectual and spiritual purposes, one great confederation, bound to a joint action and working to a common result; and whose members have for their proper outfit a knowledge of Greek, Roman, and Eastern antiquity, and of one another. Special local and temporary advantages being put out of account, that modern nation will in the intellectual and spiritual sphere make most progress, which most thoroughly carries out this program."

Now on my phrase, thus enlarged, Professor Huxley remarks that when I speak of the above-mentioned knowledge as enabling us to know ourselves and the world, I assert *literature* to contain the materials which suffice for thus making us know ourselves and the world. But it is not by any means clear, says he, that after having learnt all which ancient and modern literatures have to tell us, we have laid a sufficiently broad and deep foundation for that criticism of life, that knowledge of ourselves and the world, which constitutes culture. On the contrary, Professor Huxley declares that he finds himself "wholly unable to admit that either nations or individuals will really advance, if their oufit draws nothing from the stores of physical science. An army without weapons of precision, and with no particular base of operations, might more hopefully enter upon a campaign on the Rhine, than a man, devoid of a knowledge of what physical science has done in the last century, upon a criticism of life."

This shows how needful it is for those who are to discuss any matter together, to have a common understanding as to the sense of the terms they employ—how needful, and how difficult. What Professor Huxley says, implies just the reproach which is so often brought against the study of belles-lettres, as they are called: that the study is an elegant one, but slight and ineffectual; a smattering of Greek and Latin and other ornamental things, of little use for anyone whose object is to get at truth, and to be a practical man.

3. See *The Function of Criticism at the Present Time.*

4. See T. H. Huxley's lecture *Science and Culture.*

So, too, M. Renan[5] talks of the "superficial humanism" of a school course which treats us as if we were all going to be poets, writers, preachers, orators, and he opposes this humanism to positive science, or the critical search after truth. And there is always a tendency in those who are remonstrating against the predominance of letters in education, to understand by letters belles-lettres, and by belles-lettres a superficial humanism, the opposite of science or true knowledge.

But when we talk of knowing Greek and Roman antiquity, for instance, which is the knowledge people have called the humanities, I for my part mean a knowledge which is something more than a superficial humanism, mainly decorative. "I call all teaching *scientific*," says Wolf,[6] the critic of Homer, "which is systematically laid out and followed up to its original sources. For example: a knowledge of classical antiquity is scientific when the remains of classical antiquity are correctly studied in the original languages." There can be no doubt that Wolf is perfectly right; that all learning is scientific which is systematically laid out and followed up to its original sources, and that a genuine humanism is scientific.

When I speak of knowing Greek and Roman antiquity, therefore, as a help to knowing ourselves and the world, I mean more than a knowledge of so much vocabulary, so much grammar, so many portions of authors in the Greek and Latin languages, I mean knowing the Greeks and Romans, and their life and genius, and what they were and did in the world; what we get from them, and what is its value. That, at least, is the ideal; and when we talk of endeavoring to know Greek and Roman antiquity, as a help to knowing ourselves and the world, we mean endeavoring so to know them as to satisfy this ideal, however much we may still fall short of it.

The same also as to knowing our own and other modern nations, with the like aim of getting to understand ourselves and the world. To know the best that has been thought and said by the modern nations, is to know, says Professor Huxley, "only what modern *literatures* have to tell us; it is the criticism of life contained in modern literature." And yet "the distinctive character of our times," he urges, "lies in the vast and constantly increasing part which is played by natural knowledge." And how, therefore, can a man, devoid of knowledge of what physical science has done in the last century, enter hopefully upon a criticism of modern life?

Let us, I say, be agreed about the meaning of the terms we are using. I talk of knowing the best which has been thought and uttered in the world; Professor Huxley says this means knowing *literature*. Literature is a large word; it may mean everything writ-

5. Ernest Renan (1823–92), French religious philosopher and author of *The Life of Jesus*.
6. Friedrich August Wolf (1759–1824), German scholar.

ten with letters or printed in a book. Euclid's *Elements* and Newton's *Principia* are thus literature. All knowledge that reaches us through books is literature. But by literature Professor Huxley means belles-lettres. He means to make me say, that knowing the best which has been thought and said by the modern nations is knowing their belles-lettres and no more. And this is no sufficient equipment, he argues, for a criticism of modern life. But as I do not mean, by knowing ancient Rome, knowing merely more or less of Latin belles-lettres, and taking no account of Rome's military, and political, and legal, and administrative work in the world; and as, by knowing ancient Greece, I understand knowing her as the giver of Greek art, and the guide to a free and right use of reason and to scientific method, and the founder of our mathematics and physics and astronomy and biology—I understand knowing her as all this, and not merely knowing certain Greek poems, and histories, and treatises, and speeches—so as to the knowledge of modern nations also. By knowing modern nations, I mean not merely knowing their belles-lettres, but knowing also what has been done by such men as Copernicus, Galileo, Newton, Darwin. "Our ancestors learned," says Professor Huxley, "that the earth is the center of the visible universe, and that man is the cynosure of things terrestrial; and more especially was it inculcated that the course of nature had no fixed order, but that it could be, and constantly was, altered." "But for us now," continues Professor Huxley, "the notions of the beginning and the end of the world entertained by our forefathers are no longer credible. It is very certain that the earth is not the chief body in the material universe, and that the world is not subordinated to man's use. It is even more certain that nature is the expression of a definite order, with which nothing interferes." "And yet," he cries, "the purely classical education advocated by the representatives of the humanists in our day gives no inkling of all this."

In due place and time I will just touch upon that vexed question of classical education; but at present the question is as to what is meant by knowing the best which modern nations have thought and said. It is not knowing their belles-lettres merely which is meant. To know Italian belles-lettres is not to know Italy, and to know English belles-lettres is not to know England. Into knowing Italy and England there comes a great deal more, Galileo and Newton amongst it. The reproach of being a superficial humanism, a tincture of belles-lettres, may attach rightly enough to some other disciplines; but to the particular discipline recommended when I proposed knowing the best that has been thought and said in the world, it does not apply. In that best I certainly include what in modern times has been thought and said by the great observers and knowers of nature.

There is, therefore, really no question between Professor Huxley and me as to whether knowing the great results of the modern scientific study of nature is not required as a part of our culture, as well as knowing the products of literature and art. But to follow the processes by which those results are reached, ought, say the friends of physical science, to be made the staple of education for the bulk of mankind. And here there does arise a question between those whom Professor Huxley calls with playful sarcasm "the Levites of culture," and those whom the poor humanist is sometimes apt to regard as its Nebuchadnezzars.[7]

The great results of the scientific investigation of nature we are agreed upon knowing, but how much of our study are we bound to give to the processes by which those results are reached? The results have their visible bearing on human life. But all the processes, too, all the items of fact, by which those results are reached and established, are interesting. All knowledge is interesting to a wise man, and the knowledge of nature is interesting to all men. It is very interesting to know, that, from the albuminous white of the egg, the chick in the egg gets the materials for its flesh, bones, blood, and feathers; while, from the fatty yolk of the egg, it gets the heat and energy which enable it at length to break its shell and begin the world. It is less interesting, perhaps, but still it is interesting, to know that when a taper burns, the wax is converted into carbonic acid and water. Moreover, it is quite true that the habit of dealing with facts, which is given by the study of nature, is, as the friends of physical science praise it for being, an excellent discipline. The appeal, in the study of nature, is constantly to observation and experiment; not only is it said that the thing is so, but we can be made to see that it is so. Not only does a man tell us that when a taper burns the wax is converted into carbonic acid and water, as a man may tell us, if he likes, that Charon[8] is punting his ferry boat on the river Styx, or that Victor Hugo is a sublime poet, or Mr. Gladstone the most admirable of statesmen; but we are made to see that the conversion into carbonic acid and water does actually happen. This reality of natural knowledge it is, which makes the friends of physical science contrast it, as a knowledge of things, with the humanist's knowledge, which is, say they, a knowledge of words. And hence Professor Huxley is moved to lay it down that, "for the purpose of attaining real culture, an exclusively scientific education is at least as effectual as an exclusively literary education." And a certain President of the Section for Mechanical Science in the British Association is, in Scripture phrase, "very bold," and de-

---

7. Huxley implied that the humanists are hidebound conservatives like the Levites, priests who were preoccupied with traditional ritual observances. Arnold implies that the scientists may be like Nebuchadnezzar, a Babylonian king who destroyed the temple of Jerusalem.
8. Boatman in Greek mythology who conducted the souls of the dead across the river Styx.

clares that if a man, in his mental training, "has substituted literature and history for natural science, he has chosen the less useful alternative." But whether we go these lengths or not, we must all admit that in natural science the habit gained of dealing with facts is a most valuable discipline, and that everyone should have some experience of it.

More than this, however, is demanded by the reformers. It is proposed to make the training in natural science the main part of education, for the great majority of mankind at any rate. And here, I confess, I part company with the friends of physical science, with whom up to this point I have been agreeing. In differing from them, however, I wish to proceed with the utmost caution and diffidence. The smallness of my own acquaintance with the disciplines of natural science is ever before my mind, and I am fearful of doing these disciplines an injustice. The ability and pugnacity of the partisans of natural science make them formidable persons to contradict. The tone of tentative inquiry, which befits a being of dim faculties and bounded knowledge, is the tone I would wish to take and not to depart from. At present it seems to me, that those who are for giving to natural knowledge, as they call it, the chief place in the education of the majority of mankind, leave one important thing out of their account: the constitution of human nature. But I put this forward on the strength of some facts not at all recondite, very far from it; facts capable of being stated in the simplest possible fashion, and to which, if I so state them, the man of science will, I am sure, be willing to allow their due weight.

Deny the facts altogether, I think, he hardly can. He can hardly deny, that when we set ourselves to enumerate the powers which go to the building up of human life, and say that they are the power of conduct, the power of intellect and knowledge, the power of beauty, and the power of social life and manners—he can hardly deny that this scheme, though drawn in rough and plain lines enough, and not pretending to scientific exactness, does yet give a fairly true representation of the matter. Human nature is built up by these powers; we have the need for them all. When we have rightly met and adjusted the claims of them all, we shall then be in a fair way for getting soberness and righteousness, with wisdom. This is evident enough, and the friends of physical science would admit it.

But perhaps they may not have sufficiently observed another thing: namely, that the several powers just mentioned are not isolated, but there is, in the generality of mankind, a perpetual tendency to relate them one to another in divers ways. With one such way of relating them I am particularly concerned now. Following our instinct for intellect and knowledge, we acquire pieces of knowledge; and presently, in the generality of men, there arises the desire to relate these pieces of knowledge to our sense for conduct, to our sense for beauty—and there is weariness and dissatisfaction if the desire is balked. Now in this desire lies, I think, the strength of that hold which letters have upon us.

All knowledge is, as I said just now, interesting; and even items of knowledge which from the nature of the case cannot well be related, but must stand isolated in our thoughts, have their interest. Even lists of exceptions have their interest. If we are studying Greek accents, it is interesting to know that *pais* and *pas*, and some other monosyllables of the same form of declension, do not take the circumflex upon the last syllable of the genitive plural, but vary, in this respect, from the common rule. If we are studying physiology, it is interesting to know that the pulmonary artery carries dark blood and the pulmonary vein carries bright blood, departing in this respect from the common rule for the division of labor between the veins and the arteries. But everyone knows how we seek naturally to combine the pieces of our knowledge together, to bring them under general rules, to relate them to principles; and how unsatisfactory and tiresome it would be to go on forever learning lists of exceptions, or accumulating items of fact which must stand isolated.

Well, that same need of relating our knowledge, which operates here within the sphere of our knowledge itself, we shall find operating, also, outside that sphere. We experience, as we go on learning and knowing—the vast majority of us experience—the need of relating what we have learnt and known to the sense which we have in us for conduct, to the sense which we have in us for beauty.

A certain Greek prophetess of Mantineia in Arcadia, Diotima by name, once explained to the philosopher Socrates that love, and impulse, and bent of all kinds, is, in fact, nothing else but the desire in men that good should forever be present to them. This desire for good, Diotima assured Socrates, is our fundamental desire, of which fundamental desire every impulse in us is only some one particular form.[9] And therefore this fundamental desire it is, I suppose—this desire in men that good should be forever present to them—which acts in us when we feel the impulse for relating our knowledge to our sense for conduct and to our sense for beauty. At any rate, with men in general the instinct exists. Such is human nature. And the instinct, it will be admitted, is innocent, and human nature is preserved by our following the lead of its innocent instincts. Therefore, in seeking to gratify this instinct in question, we are following the instinct of self-preservation in humanity.

But, no doubt, some kinds of knowledge cannot be made to directly serve the instinct in question, cannot be directly related to the sense for beauty, to the sense for conduct. These are instrument

9. Plato, *Symposium* 201–7.

knowledges; they lead on to other knowledges, which can. A man who passes his life in instrument knowledges is a specialist. They may be invaluable as instruments to something beyond, for those who have the gift thus to employ them; and they may be disciplines in themselves wherein it is useful for everyone to have some schooling. But it is inconceivable that the generality of men should pass all their mental life with Greek accents or with formal logic. My friend Professor Sylvester,[1] who is one of the first mathematicians in the world, holds transcendental doctrines as to the virtue of mathematics, but those doctrines are not for common men. In the very Senate House and heart of our English Cambridge[2] I once ventured, though not without an apology for my profaneness, to hazard the opinion that for the majority of mankind a little of mathematics, even, goes a long way. Of course this is quite consistent with their being of immense importance as an instrument to something else; but it is the few who have the aptitude for thus using them, not the bulk of mankind.

The natural sciences do not, however, stand on the same footing with these instrument knowledges. Experience shows us that the generality of men will find more interest in learning that, when a taper burns, the wax is converted into carbonic acid and water, or in learning the explanation of the phenomenon of dew, or in learning how the circulation of the blood is carried on, than they find in learning that the genitive plural of *pais* and *pas* does not take the circumflex on the termination. And one piece of natural knowledge is added to another, and others are added to that, and at last we come to propositions so interesting as Mr. Darwin's famous proposition that "our ancestor was a hairy quadruped furnished with a tail and pointed ears, probably arboreal in his habits." Or we come to propositions of such reach and magnitude as those which Professor Huxley delivers, when he says that the notions of our forefathers about the beginning and the end of the world were all wrong, and that nature is the expression of a definite order with which nothing interferes.

Interesting, indeed, these results of science are, important they are, and we should all of us be acquainted with them. But what I now wish you to mark is, that we are still, when they are propounded to us and we receive them, we are still in the sphere of intellect and knowledge. And for the generality of men there will be found, I say, to arise, when they have duly taken in the proposition that their ancestor was "a hairy quadruped furnished with a tail and pointed ears, probably arboreal in his habits," there will be found to arise an invincible desire to relate this proposition to

1. James T. Sylvester, professor of mathematics at Johns Hopkins University.
2. At Cambridge University, mathematics have been traditionally emphasized. In its original form, *Literature and Science* had been delivered as a lecture at Cambridge.

the sense in us for conduct, and to the sense in us for beauty. But this the men of science will not do for us, and will hardly even profess to do. They will give us other pieces of knowledge, other facts, about other animals and their ancestors, or about plants, or about stones, or about stars; and they may finally bring us to those great "general conceptions of the universe, which are forced upon us all," says Professor Huxley, "by the progress of physical science." But still it will be *knowledge* only which they give us; knowledge not put for us into relation with our sense for conduct, our sense for beauty, and touched with emotion by being so put; not thus put for us, and therefore, to the majority of mankind, after a certain while, unsatisfying, wearying.

Not to the born naturalist, I admit. But what do we mean by a born naturalist? We mean a man in whom the zeal for observing nature is so uncommonly strong and eminent, that it marks him off from the bulk of mankind. Such a man will pass his life happily in collecting natural knowledge and reasoning upon it, and will ask for nothing, or hardly anything, more. I have heard it said that the sagacious and admirable naturalist whom we lost not very long ago, Mr. Darwin, once owned to a friend that for his part he did not experience the necessity for two things which most men find so necessary to them—religion and poetry; science and the domestic affections, he thought, were enough. To a born naturalist, I can well understand that this should seem so. So absorbing is his occupation with nature, so strong his love for his occupation, that he goes on acquiring natural knowledge and reasoning upon it, and has little time or inclination for thinking about getting it related to the desire in man for conduct, the desire in man for beauty. He relates it to them for himself as he goes along, so far as he feels the need; and he draws from the domestic affections all the additional solace necessary. But then Darwins are extremely rare. Another great and admirable master of natural knowledge, Faraday,[3] was a Sandemanian. That is to say, he related his knowledge to his instinct for conduct and to his instinct for beauty, by the aid of that respectable Scottish sectary,[4] Robert Sandeman. And so strong, in general, is the demand of religion and poetry to have their share in a man, to associate themselves with his knowing, and to relieve and rejoice it, that, probably, for one man amongst us with the disposition to do as Darwin did in this respect, there are at least fifty with the disposition to do as Faraday.

Education lays hold upon us, in fact, by satisfying this demand. Professor Huxley holds up to scorn medieval education, with its neglect of the knowledge of nature, its poverty even of literary studies, its formal logic devoted to "showing how and why that

3. Michael Faraday (1791–1867), famous chemist.
4. I.e., a zealous member of a sect.

Robert Sandeman (1718–71) was the founder of a Scottish sect bearing his name.

which the Church said was true must be true." But the great medieval Universities were not brought into being, we may be sure, by the zeal for giving a jejune and contemptible education. Kings have been their nursing fathers, and queens have been their nursing mothers, but not for this. The medieval Universities came into being, because the supposed knowledge, delivered by Scripture and the Church, so deeply engaged men's hearts, by so simply, easily, and powerfully relating itself to their desire for conduct, their desire for beauty. All other knowledge was dominated by this supposed knowledge and was subordinated to it, because of the surpassing strength of the hold which it gained upon the affections of men, by allying itself profoundly with their sense for conduct, their sense for beauty.

But now, says Professor Huxley, conceptions of the universe fatal to the notions held by our forefathers have been forced upon us by physical science. Grant to him that they are thus fatal, that the new conceptions must and will soon become current everywhere, and that everyone will finally perceive them to be fatal to the beliefs of our forefathers. The need of humane letters, as they are truly called, because they serve the paramount desire in men that good should be forever present to them—the need of humane letters, to establish a relation between the new conceptions, and our instinct for beauty, our instinct for conduct, is only the more visible. The Middle Age could do without humane letters, as it could do without the study of nature, because its supposed knowledge was made to engage its emotions so powerfully. Grant that the supposed knowledge disappears, its power of being made to engage the emotions will of course disappear along with it—but the emotions themselves, and their claim to be engaged and satisfied, will remain. Now if we find by experience that humane letters have an undeniable power of engaging the emotions, the importance of humane letters in a man's training becomes not less, but greater, in proportion to the success of modern science in extirpating what it calls "medieval thinking."

Have humane letters, then, have poetry and eloquence, the power here attributed to them of engaging the emotions, and do they exercise it? And if they have it and exercise it, *how* do they exercise it, so as to exert an influence upon man's sense for conduct, his sense for beauty? Finally, even if they both can and do exert an influence upon the senses in question, how are they to relate to them the results—the modern results—of natural science? All these questions may be asked. First, have poetry and eloquence the power of calling out the emotions? The appeal is to experience. Experience shows that for the vast majority of men, for mankind in general, they have the power. Next, do they exercise it? They do. But then, *how* do they exercise it so as to affect man's sense for

conduct, his sense for beauty? And this is perhaps a case for applying the Preacher's words: "Though a man labor to seek it out, yet
he shall not find it; yea, farther, though a wise man think to know
it, yet shall he not be able to find it."[5] Why should it be one thing,
in its effect upon the emotions, to say, "Patience is a virtue," and
quite another thing, in its effect upon the emotions, to say with
Homer,

$$\tau\lambda\eta\tau\grave{o}\nu \ \gamma\grave{a}\rho \ \text{Mo}\hat{\iota}\rho\alpha\iota \ \theta\upsilon\mu\grave{o}\nu \ \theta\acute{\epsilon}\sigma\alpha\nu \ \grave{\alpha}\nu\theta\rho\acute{\omega}\pi o\iota\sigma\iota\nu^6—$$

"for an enduring heart have the destinies appointed to the children
of men"? Why should it be one thing, in its effect upon the emotions, to say with the philosopher Spinoza, *Felicitas in eo consistit
quod homo suum esse conservare potest*—"Man's happiness consists in his being able to preserve his own essence,"[7] and quite another thing, in its effect upon the emotions, to say with the Gospel,
"What is a man advantaged, if he gain the whole world, and lose
himself, forfeit himself?"[8] How does this difference of effect arise?
I cannot tell, and I am not much concerned to know; the important
thing is that it does arise, and that we can profit by it. But how,
finally, are poetry and eloquence to exercise the power of relating
the modern results of natural science to man's instinct for conduct,
his instinct for beauty? And here again I answer that I do not
know *how* they will exercise it, but that they can and will exercise
it I am sure. I do not mean that modern philosophical poets and
modern philosophical moralists are to come and relate for us, in
express terms, the results of modern scientific research to our instinct for conduct, our instinct for beauty. But I mean that we shall
find, as a matter of experience, if we know the best that has been
thought and uttered in the world, we shall find that the art and
poetry and eloquence of men who lived, perhaps, long ago, who
had the most limited natural knowledge, who had the most erroneous conceptions about many important matters, we shall find
that this art, and poetry, and eloquence, have in fact not only the
power of refreshing and delighting us, they have also the power—
such is the strength and worth, in essentials, of their authors' criticism of life—they have a fortifying, and elevating, and quickening,
and suggestive power, capable of wonderfully helping us to relate
the results of modern science to our need for conduct, our need
for beauty. Homer's conceptions of the physical universe were, I
imagine, grotesque; but really, under the shock of hearing from
modern science that "the world is not subordinated to man's use,
and that man is not the cynosure of things terrestrial," I could, for
my own part, desire no better comfort than Homer's line which I
quoted just now,

5. "Ecclesiastes viii.17" [Arnold's note].   7. Spinoza, *Ethics* IV.xviii.
6. "*Iliad* XXIV.49" [Arnold's note].   8. Cf. Luke ix.25.

τλητὸν γὰρ Μοῖραι θυμὸν θέσαν ἀνθρώποισιν—

"for an enduring heart have the destinies appointed to the children of men"!

And the more that men's minds are cleared, the more that the results of science are frankly accepted, the more that poetry and eloquence come to be received and studied as what in truth they really are—the criticism of life by gifted men, alive and active with extraordinary power at an unusual number of points—so much the more will the value of humane letters, and of art also, which is an utterance having a like kind of power with theirs, be felt and acknowledged, and their place in education be secured.

Let us therefore, all of us, avoid indeed as much as possible any invidious comparison between the merits of humane letters, as means of education, and the merits of the natural sciences. But when some President of a Section for Mechanical Science insists on making the comparison, and tells us that "he who in his training has substituted literature and history for natural science has chosen the less useful alternative," let us make answer to him that the student of humane letters only, will, at least, know also the great general conceptions brought in by modern physical science; for science, as Professor Huxley says, forces them upon us all. But the student of the natural sciences only, will, by our very hypothesis, know nothing of humane letters; not to mention that in setting himself to be perpetually accumulating natural knowledge, he sets himself to do what only specialists have in general the gift for doing genially. And so he will probably be unsatisfied, or at any rate incomplete, and even more incomplete than the student of humane letters only.

I once mentioned in a school report, how a young man in one of our English training colleges having to paraphrase the passage in *Macbeth* beginning,

Can'st thou not minister to a mind diseased?[9]

turned this line into, "Can you not wait upon the lunatic?" And I remarked what a curious state of things it would be, if every pupil of our national schools knew, let us say, that the moon is two thousand one hundred and sixty miles in diameter, and thought at the same time that a good paraphrase for

Can'st thou not minister to a mind diseased?

was, "Can you not wait upon the lunatic?" If one is driven to choose, I think I would rather have a young person ignorant about the moon's diameter, but aware that "Can you not wait upon the lunatic?" is bad, than a young person whose education had been

9. *Macbeth* V.iii.40.

such as to manage things the other way.

Or to go higher than the pupils of our national schools. I have in my mind's eye a member of our British Parliament who comes to travel here in America, who afterwards relates his travels, and who shows a really masterly knowledge of the geology of this great country and of its mining capabilities, but who ends by gravely suggesting that the United States should borrow a prince from our Royal Family, and should make him their king, and should create a House of Lords of great landed proprietors after the pattern of ours; and then America, he thinks, would have her future happily and perfectly secured. Surely, in this case, the President of the Section for Mechanical Science would himself hardly say that our member of Parliament, by concentrating himself upon geology and mineralogy, and so on, and not attending to literature and history, had "chosen the more useful alternative."

If then there is to be separation and option between humane letters on the one hand, and the natural sciences on the other, the great majority of mankind, all who have not exceptional and overpowering aptitudes for the study of nature, would do well, I cannot but think, to chose to be educated in humane letters rather than in the natural sciences. Letters will call out their being at more points, will make them live more.

I said that before I ended I would just touch on the question of classical education, and I will keep my word. Even if literature is to retain a large place in our education, yet Latin and Greek, say the friends of progress, will certainly have to go. Greek is the grand offender in the eyes of these gentlemen. The attackers of the established course of study think that against Greek, at any rate, they have irresistible arguments. Literature may perhaps be needed in education, they say; but why on earth should it be Greek literature? Why not French or German? Nay, "has not an Englishman models in his own literature of every kind of excellence?"[1] As before, it is not on any weak pleadings of my own that I rely for convincing the gainsayers; it is on the constitution of human nature itself, and on the instinct of self-preservation in humanity. The instinct for beauty is set in human nature, as surely as the instinct for knowledge is set there, or the instinct for conduct. If the instinct for beauty is served by Greek literature and art as it is served by no other literature and art, we may trust to the instinct of self-preservation in humanity for keeping Greek as part of our culture. We may trust to it for even making the study of Greek more prevalent than it is now. Greek will come, I hope, some day to be studied more rationally than at present; but it will be increasingly studied as men increasingly feel the need in them for beauty, and how powerfully Greek art and Greek literature can serve this need.

1. Quoted from Huxley's *Science and Culture*.

Women will again study Greek, as Lady Jane Grey[2] did; I believe that in that chain of forts, with which the fair host of the Amazons are now engirdling our English universities,[3] I find that here in America, in colleges like Smith College in Massachusetts, and Vassar College in the State of New York, and in the happy families of the mixed universities out West, they are studying it already.

Defuit una mihi symmetria prisca—"The antique symmetry was the one thing wanting to me," said Leonardo da Vinci; and he was an Italian. I will not presume to speak for the Americans, but I am sure that, in the Englishman, the want of this admirable symmetry of the Greeks is a thousand times more great and crying than in any Italian. The results of the want show themselves most glaringly, perhaps, in our architecture, but they show themselves, also, in all our art. *Fit details strictly combined, in view of a large general result nobly conceived;* that is just the beautiful *symmetria prisca* of the Greeks, and it is just where we English fail, where all our art fails. Striking ideas we have, and well-executed details we have; but that high symmetry which, with satisfying and delightful effect, combines them, we seldom or never have. The glorious beauty of the Acropolis at Athens did not come from single fine things stuck about on that hill, a statue here, a gateway there—no, it arose from all things being perfectly combined for a supreme total effect. What must not an Englishman feel about our deficiencies in this respect, as the sense for beauty, whereof this symmetry is an essential element, awakens and strengthens within him! what will not one day be his respect and desire for Greece and its *symmetria prisca*, when the scales drop from his eyes as he walks the London streets, and he sees such a lesson in meanness as the Strand, for instance, in its true deformity! But here we are coming to our friend Mr. Ruskin's province,[4] and I will not intrude upon it, for he is its very sufficient guardian.

And so we at last find, it seems, we find flowing in favor of the humanities the natural and necessary stream of things, which seemed against them when we started. The "hairy quadruped furnished with a tail and pointed ears, probably arboreal in his habits," this good fellow carried hidden in his nature, apparently, something destined to develop into a necessity for humane letters. Nay, more; we seem finally to be even led to the further conclusion that our hairy ancestor carried in his nature, also, a necessity for Greek.

And therefore, to say the truth, I cannot really think that humane letters are in much actual danger of being thrust out from their leading place in education, in spite of the array of authorities against

2. Lady Jane Grey (1537–54) was reputed to be a learned scholar in Greek. She was proclaimed Queen of England in 1553, but was forced to abdicate the throne nine days afterwards. Later she was executed by order of Queen Mary.

3. Colleges for women at Oxford and Cambridge.
4. In such books as *The Stones of Venice* John Ruskin (1819–1900) had criticized the "meanness" of Victorian architecture.

them at this moment. So long as human nature is what it is, their attractions will remain irresistible. As with Greek, so with letters generally: they will some day come, we may hope, to be studied more rationally, but they will not lose their place. What will happen will rather be that there will be crowded into education other matters besides, far too many; there will be, perhaps, a period of unsettlement and confusion and false tendency; but letters will not in the end lose their leading place. If they lose it for a time, they will get it back again. We shall be brought back to them by our wants and aspirations. And a poor humanist may possess his soul in patience, neither strive nor cry, admit the energy and brilliancy of the partisans of physical science, and their present favor with the public, to be far greater than his own, and still have a happy faith that the nature of things works silently on behalf of the studies which he loves, and that, while we shall all have to acquaint ourselves with the great results reached by modern science, and to give ourselves as much training in its disciplines as we can conveniently carry, yet the majority of men will always require humane letters; and so much the more, as they have the more and the greater results of science to relate to the need in man for conduct, and to the need in him for beauty.

1882, 1885

Lyric and Narrative Poetry

For the early part of the 19th century, the Romantic period, it is relatively easy to decide which of the English poets were the major ones. For the later part of the century, the ranking is much less fixed. Tennyson and Browning and perhaps Arnold come first to mind, but after these three there remain a number of other interesting poets whose stature is still a matter of dispute. Algernon Charles Swinburne, for example, is regarded by some critics as the major Victorian poet, towering over Tennyson and Browning not only in bulk but in quality. Others have discovered the highest merits in the delicate art of Christina Rossetti or in the philosophical verses of George Meredith. Although such attempts to reclassify writers into major or minor categories can develop into a trifling game, they help to indicate the vitality of the ten poets represented below. To read this group of writers enhances our realization of the total achievement of the Victorian age in poetry. And this realization would be further enhanced if to this group were added the names of some of the late Victorian poets whose writings are included in the 20th-century section of the present anthology, in particular, Gerard Manley Hopkins, A. E. Housman, and Thomas Hardy.

Aside from their having published their poems between 1837 and 1901, what have these ten poets in common? Our first impression may be that it is impossible to yoke any of them together. In their marked differences of manner and subject, they illustrate the variety and individualism in Victorian literature already discussed in the introduction to this period. Certain recurrences and similarities can, nevertheless, be detected. One topic that is unexpectedly prominent (unexpected because of the reputed strain of puritanism in the age) is love. In Victorian poetry love is as recurrently written about as it had been in the age of Donne and his followers. Unlike their 17th-century predecessors, however, the Victorian poets rarely made witty proposals for gathering rosebuds; they explored other aspects of the love relationship. In Dante Gabriel Rossetti's poems, for example, the union of lovers is distinctively pictured as a state of timeless equilibrium, lushly sensual and yet beyond the senses. And in Meredith's poems we encounter a subtle analysis of states of mind of lovers who have become incompatible. The prominent role of love in the lyrics and narratives of these ten writers also provides a link with a major Victorian love poet, Robert Browning, analyst and celebrator of the relations between men and women. As a love poem *The Last Ride Together* was ranked by George Saintsbury (often a severe critic of Browning) as "perhaps the very best that we have produced for two hundred years."

Another recurring subject with which most of these ten poets were preoccupied is religious faith and doubt. Here the link with the major figures is with Tennyson and Arnold. After a reading of *In Memoriam* or of *Dover Beach*, it is instructive to turn to Edward FitzGerald's *Rubáiyát* or Swinburne's *Hymn to Proserpine* to discover how the dilemmas that concerned the major poets concerned the lesser-known poets as well. The range of religious positions exemplified by the ten writers is remarkable. The spectrum extends from the negative fatalism expressed in FitzGerald's translation, through Arthur Hugh Clough's jocular yet earnest skepticism, to the religious affirmations of Christina Rossetti or Francis Thompson.

The styles and forms employed by these poets may likewise impress us at first as being so diverse as to have nothing in common, but again certain unifying recurrences can be detected. In style it is evident that although several of the poets resolved to escape the magnetic attraction of Tennyson's manner, they were usually drawn into its powerful field. In versification, although making considerable use of traditional lyric forms such as the sonnet, most of the poets preferred experimenting with new or unusual metrical patterns. In line with their metrical experiments are their experiments in the art of narrative poetry. During an age which witnessed the emergence of the novel as one of the dominant forms of literature, the poets, like Tennyson in *Maud*, sought new ways of telling stories in verse. Some of them, such as Emily Brontë, George Meredith, and William Morris, were novelists as well as poets, and were therefore especially aware that poetry can offer unusual resources for the writer of narratives, as the compression and intensification achieved in Morris's early poems or in Meredith's *Modern Love* will illustrate. Others, in particular Clough, sought to write narrative poems as if they were novels, poems that are long, casual in tone, and usually prosaic in style. Once again the diversity of the Victorian effort in poetry is evident, yet also evident is that these two different kinds of narrative poems, each being a response to the same challenge offered by the prose fiction of the age, are in fact closely related to each other.

ELIZABETH BARRETT BROWNING
(1806–1861)

Elizabeth Barrett's poetry, much of it ardently concerned with liberal causes, was popular during the Victorian age. Today her name is remembered primarily for the sequence of sonnets in which she recorded the stages of her love for her husband, Robert Browning, a sequence she presented under the guise of a translation from the Portuguese language.

From Sonnets from the Portuguese

22

When our two souls stand up erect and strong,
Face to face, silent, drawing nigh and nigher,

Until the lengthening wings break into fire
At either curvéd point—what bitter wrong
Can the earth do to us, that we should not long   5
Be here contented? Think! In mounting higher,
The angels would press on us and aspire
To drop some golden orb of perfect song
Into our deep, dear silence. Let us stay
Rather on earth, Beloved—where the unfit,   10
Contrarious moods of men recoil away
And isolate pure spirits, and permit
A place to stand and love in for a day,
With darkness and the death-hour rounding it.

43

How do I love thee? Let me count the ways.
I love thee to the depth and breadth and height
My soul can reach, when feeling out of sight
For the ends of Being and ideal Grace.
I love thee to the level of everyday's   5
Most quiet need, by sun and candle light.
I love thee freely, as men strive for Right;
I love thee purely, as they turn from Praise.
I love thee with the passion put to use
In my old griefs, and with my childhood's faith.   10
I love thee with a love I seemed to lose
With my lost saints—I love thee with the breath,
Smiles, tears, of all my life!—and, if God choose,
I shall but love thee better after death.

1850

EMILY BRONTË
(1818–1848)

Before completing her famous novel, *Wuthering Heights*, Emily Brontë
wrote a number of poems recording experiences of love which often seem
similar to the strange passion of Heathcliff and Catherine Earnshaw in
her novel. Such lyrics were part of a long narrative concerning Gondal,
an imaginary kingdom the scenery of which resembled the locality in
Yorkshire where Emily had grown up with her two sisters, Charlotte and
Anne. Various pairs of lovers are the speakers in the poems. At the time
of their first publication in 1846 these unsual poems, with their hymnlike
stanzas, were ignored. In the 20th century, however, their haunting picture
of a love that defies death has aroused considerable interest.

Remembrance

Cold in the earth—and the deep snow piled above thee,
Far, far removed, cold in the dreary grave!
Have I forgot, my only Love, to love thee,
Severed at last by Time's all-severing wave?

Now, when alone, do my thoughts no longer hover   5
Over the mountains, on that northern shore,
Resting their wings where heath and fern leaves cover
Thy noble heart forever, ever more?

Cold in the earth—and fifteen wild Decembers,
From those brown hills, have melted into spring;   10
Faithful, indeed, is the spirit that remembers
After such years of change and suffering!

Sweet Love of youth, forgive, if I forget thee,
While the world's tide is bearing me along;
Other desires and other hopes beset me,   15
Hopes which obscure, but cannot do thee wrong!

No later light has lightened up my heaven,
No second morn has ever shone for me;
All my life's bliss from thy dear life was given,
All my life's bliss is in the grave with thee.   20

But, when the days of golden dreams had perished,
And even Despair was powerless to destroy,
Then did I learn how existence could be cherished,
Strengthened, and fed without the aid of joy.

Then did I check the tears of useless passion—   25
Weaned my young soul from yearning after thine;
Sternly denied its burning wish to hasten
Down to that tomb already more than mine.

And, even yet, I dare not let it languish,
Dare not indulge in memory's rapturous pain;   30
Once drinking deep of that divinest anguish,
How could I seek the empty world again?

1846

The Prisoner

A FRAGMENT

In the dungeon crypts idly did I stray,[1]
Reckless of the lives wasting there away;

---

1. The speaker, a man, is visiting a dungeon in his father's castle.

"Draw the ponderous bars! open, Warder stern!"
He dared not say me nay—the hinges harshly turn.

"Our guests are darkly lodged," I whispered, gazing through   5
The vault, whose grated eye showed heaven more gray than blue
(This was when glad Spring laughed in awaking pride);
"Aye, darkly lodged enough!" returned my sullen guide.

Then, God forgive my youth! forgive my careless tongue!
I scoffed, as the chill chains on the damp flagstones rung: 10
"Confined in triple walls, art thou so much to fear,
That we must bind thee down and clench thy fetters here?"

The captive raised her face; it was as soft and mild
As sculptured marble saint; or slumbering unweaned child;
It was so soft and mild, it was so sweet and fair,   15
Pain could not trace a line, or grief a shadow there!

The captive raised her hand and pressed it to her brow;
"I have been struck," she said, "and I am suffering now;
Yet these are little worth, your bolts and irons strong:
And, were they forged in steel, they could not hold me long."   20

Hoarse laughed the jailor grim: "Shall I be won to hear;
Dost think, fond,² dreaming wretch, that I shall grant thy prayer?
Or, better still, wilt melt my master's heart with groans?
Ah! sooner might the sun thaw down these granite stones.

"My master's voice is low, his aspect bland and kind,   25
But hard as hardest flint the soul that lurks behind;
And I am rough and rude, yet not more rough to see
Than is the hidden ghost that has its home in me."

About her lips there played a smile of almost scorn.
"My friend," she gently said, "you have not heard me mourn;   30
When you my kindred's lives, *my* lost life can restore,
Then may I weep and sue—but never, friend, before!

"Still, let my tyrants know, I am not doomed to wear
Year after year in gloom, and desolate despair;
A messenger of Hope comes every night to me,   35
And offers for short life, eternal liberty.

"He comes with western winds, with evening's wandering airs,
With that clear dusk of heaven that brings the thickest stars,
Winds take a pensive tone, and stars a tender fire,
And visions rise, and change, that kill me with desire.   40

2. Foolish.

"Desire for nothing known in my maturer years,
When Joy grew mad with awe, at counting future tears.
When, if my spirit's sky was full of flashes warm,
I knew not whence they came, from sun or thunderstorm.

"But, first, a hush of peace—a soundless calm descends;   45
The struggle of distress and fierce impatience ends;
Mute music soothes my breast—unuttered harmony,
That I could never dream, till Earth was lost to me.

"Then dawns the Invisible; the Unseen its truth reveals;
My outward sense is gone, my inward essence feels: 50
Its wings are almost free—its home, its harbor found,
Measuring the gulf, it stoops—and dares the final bound.

"Oh! dreadful is the check—intense the agony—
When the ear begins to hear, and the eye begins to see;
When the pulse begins to throb, the brain to think again;   55
The soul to feel the flesh, and the flesh to feel the chain.

"Yet I would lose no sting, would wish no torture less;
The more that anguish racks, the earlier it will bless;
And robed in fires of hell, or bright with heavenly shine,
If it but herald death, the vision is divine!"[3]   60

She ceased to speak, and we, unanswering, turned to go—
We had no further power to work the captive woe:
Her cheek, her gleaming eye, declared that man had given
A sentence, unapproved, and overruled by Heaven.

1846

No Coward Soul Is Mine[4]

No coward soul is mine,
No trembler in the world's storm-troubled sphere;
I see Heaven's glories shine,
And faith shines equal, arming me from fear.

3. Cf. the words of the dying Catherine in *Wuthering Heights*: "The thing that irks me most is this shattered prison [my body]. * * * I'm tired of being enclosed here. I'm wearying to escape into that glorious world, and to be always there. * * * I shall be incomparably beyond and above you all."
4. According to Charlotte Brontë, these are the last lines written by her sister.

> O God within my breast,   5
> Almighty, ever-present Deity!
>   Life—that in me has rest,
> As I—undying Life—have power in Thee!
>
>   Vain are the thousand creeds
> That move men's hearts—unutterably vain;   10
>   Worthless as withered weeds,
> Or idlest froth amid the boundless main,
>
>   To waken doubt in one
> Holding so fast by Thine infinity;
>   So surely anchored on   15
> The steadfast rock of immortality.
>
>   With wide-embracing love
> Thy spirit animates eternal years
>   Pervades and broods above,
> Changes, sustains, dissolves, creates, and rears.   20
>
>   Though earth and man were gone,
> And suns and universes ceased to be,
>   And Thou were left alone,
> Every existence would exist in Thee.
>
>   There is not room for Death,   25
> Nor atom that his might could render void;
>   Thou—Thou art Being and Breath,
> And what Thou art may never be destroyed.

1850

DANTE GABRIEL ROSSETTI
(1828–1882)

Rossetti was the son of an Italian patriot whose political activities had
led to his being exiled to England. The Rossetti household in London
was one in which liberal politics and other controversial topics were hotly
debated, but the son did not catch the infection. Displaying extraordinary
early promise both as a painter and as a poet, Dante Gabriel Rossetti confined his interest to art. The beauty of colors and textures, above all the
beauty of a woman's face and figure, made up for him a world isolated
from the Victorian scene. His view of life and art, derived in part from
his close study of Keats's poems and letters, anticipated by many years
the aesthetic movement later to be represented by such men as Walter
Pater, Oscar Wilde, and the painter James McNeill Whistler, who were
to insist that art must be exclusively concerned with the beautiful, not with
the useful or didactic.

The beauty that Rossetti admired in the faces of women was of a distinctive kind. In at least two of his models he found what he sought. The first was his wife, Elizabeth Siddal, whose suicide in 1862 haunted him with a sense of guilt for the rest of his life. The other was Jane Morris, the wife of his friend William Morris. In Rossetti's paintings both of these models are shown with dreamy stares, as if they were breathless from visions of heaven, but counteracting this impression is an emphasis on parted lips and fully rounded curves suggesting a more earthly kind of ecstasy. A similar combination is to be found in Rossetti's poems. *The Blessed Damozel*, first written when he was 18, portrays a heaven that is warm with physical bodies. And *The House of Life* (1870), his sonnet sequence, undertakes to explore the relationship of spirit to body in love. Some Victorian readers saw no Dante-like spirituality in *The House of Life*. Robert Buchanan saw in the poem nothing but lewd sensuality, and in 1871 he published a pamphlet, *The Fleshly School of Poetry*, which treated Rossetti's poetry to the most severe abuse. Buchanan's attack hurt the poet profoundly and contributed to the recurring seizures of nervous depression from which he suffered in the remaining years of his life.

Rossetti and his artist friends used to call such women as Jane Morris "stunners." The epithet can also be applied to Rossetti's own poetry, especially his later writings. In his maturity he used stunning polysyllabic diction to give an effect of opulence and density to his lines. His earlier poems such as *My Sister's Sleep* are usually much less elaborate in manner and can be related to the Pre-Raphaelite movement of which, in 1848, he became a founder and energetic leader.

This Pre-Raphaelite Brotherhood, as it was called, was a group of young artists and writers. The most prominent members were painters such as John Everett Millais, William Holman Hunt, and Rossetti himself. Their principal object was to reform English painting by repudiating the established academic style in favor of a revival of the simplicity and pure colors of pre-Renaissance art. Because each artist preferred to develop his own individual manner, the Brotherhood did not cohere for more than a few years. Rossetti himself grew away from the Pre-Raphaelite manner and cultivated a more richly ornate style of painting. In both the early and late phases of his writing and painting, however, it can be said that he remained a poet in his painting and a painter in his poetry. "Color and meter," he once said, "these are the true patents of nobility in painting and poetry, taking precedence of all intellectual claims."

The Blessed Damozel[1]

The blessed damozel leaned out
   From the gold bar of heaven;
   Her eyes were deeper than the depth

---

1. "Damozel," a poetic version of the word "damsel," signifying a young unmarried lady. Rossetti once explained that *The Blessed Damozel* is related to Poe's *Raven*, a poem which he admired. "I saw that Poe had done the utmost it was possible to do with the grief of the lover on earth, and so I determined to reverse the conditions, and give utterance to the yearning of the loved one in heaven."

Of waters stilled at even;
She had three lilies in her hand,
    And the stars in her hair were seven.   5

Her robe, ungirt from clasp to hem,
    No wrought flowers did adorn,
But a white rose of Mary's gift,
    For service meetly worn;   10
Her hair that lay along her back
    Was yellow like ripe corn.[2]

Herseemed[3] she scarce had been a day
    One of God's choristers;
The wonder was not yet quite gone   15
    From that still look of hers;
Albeit, to them she left, her day
    Had counted as ten years.

(To one it is ten years of years.
    . . . Yet now, and in this place,   20
Surely she leaned o'er me—her hair
    Fell all about my face. . . .
Nothing: the autumn-fall of leaves.
    The whole year sets apace.)

It was the rampart of God's house   25
    That she was standing on;
By God built over the sheer depth
    The which is Space begun;
So high, that looking downward thence
    She scarce could see the sun.   30

It lies in heaven, across the flood
    Of ether, as a bridge.
Beneath the tides of day and night
    With flame and darkness ridge
The void, as low as where this earth   35
    Spins like a fretful midge.

Around her, lovers, newly met
    'Mid deathless love's acclaims,
Spoke evermore among themselves
    Their heart-remembered names;   40
And the souls mounting up to God
    Went by her like thin flames.

And still she bowed herself and stooped
    Out of the circling charm;
Until her bosom must have made   45
    The bar she leaned on warm,
And the lilies lay as if asleep
    Along her bended arm.

2. Grain.   3. It seemed to her.

From the fixed place of heaven she saw
    Time like a pulse shake fierce   50
Through all the worlds. Her gaze still strove
    Within the gulf to pierce
Its path; and now she spoke as when
    The stars sang in their spheres.

The sun was gone now; the curled moon   55
    Was like a little feather
Fluttering far down the gulf; and now
    She spoke through the still weather.
Her voice was like the voice the stars
    Had when they sang together.   60

(Ah, sweet! Even now, in that bird's song,
    Strove not her accents there,
Fain to be harkened? When those bells
    Possessed the midday air,
Strove not her steps to reach my side   65
    Down all the echoing stair?)

"I wish that he were come to me,
    For he will come," she said.
"Have I not prayed in heaven?—on earth,
    Lord, Lord, has he not prayed?   70
Are not two prayers a perfect strength?
    And shall I feel afraid?

"When round his head the aureole clings,
    And he is clothed in white,
I'll take his hand and go with him   75
    To the deep wells of light;
As unto a stream we will step down,
    And bathe there in God's sight.

"We two will stand beside that shrine,
    Occult, withheld, untrod,   80
Whose lamps are stirred continually
    With prayer sent up to God;
And see our old prayers, granted, melt
    Each like a little cloud.

"We two will lie i' the shadow of   85
    That living mystic tree[4]
Within whose secret growth the Dove
    Is sometimes felt to be,
While every leaf that His plumes touch
    Saith His Name audibly.   90

"And I myself will teach to him,
    I myself, lying so,
The songs I sing here; which his voice

4. See Revelation xxii.2.

Shall pause in, hushed and slow,
And find some knowledge at each pause,   95
    Or some new thing to know."

(Alas! We two, we two, thou say'st!
    Yea, one wast thou with me
That once of old. But shall God lift
    To endless unity   100
The soul whose likeness with thy soul
    Was but its love for thee?)

"We two," she said, "will seek the groves
    Where the lady Mary is,
With her five handmaidens, whose names   105
    Are five sweet symphonies,
Cecily, Gertrude, Magdalen,
    Margaret, and Rosalys.

"Circlewise sit they, with bound locks
    And foreheads garlanded;   110
Into the fine cloth white like flame
    Weaving the golden thread,
To fashion the birth-robes for them
    Who are just born, being dead.

"He shall fear, haply, and be dumb;   115
    Then will I lay my cheek
To his, and tell about our love,
    Not once abashed or weak;
And the dear Mother will approve
    My pride, and let me speak.   120

"Herself shall bring us, hand in hand,
    To Him round whom all souls
Kneel, the clear-ranged unnumbered heads
    Bowed with their aureoles;
And angels meeting us shall sing   125
    To their citherns and citoles.[5]

"There will I ask of Christ the Lord
    Thus much for him and me—
Only to live as once on earth
    With Love—only to be,   130
As then awhile, forever now,
    Together, I and he."

She gazed and listened and then said,
    Less sad of speech than mild—
"All this is when he comes." She ceased.   135
    The light thrilled toward her, filled
With angels in strong, level flight.
    Her eyes prayed, and she smiled.

5. Guitar-like instruments.

(I saw her smile.) But soon their path
   Was vague in distant spheres;   140
And then she cast her arms along
   The golden barriers,
And laid her face between her hands,
   And wept. (I heard her tears.)

1846   1850

My Sister's Sleep[6]

She fell asleep on Christmas Eve.
   At length the long-ungranted shade
   Of weary eyelids overweighed
The pain nought else might yet relieve.

Our mother, who had leaned all day   5
   Over the bed from chime to chime,
   Then raised herself for the first time,
And as she sat her down, did pray.

Her little worktable was spread
   With work to finish. For the glare   10
   Made by her candle, she had care
To work some distance from the bed.

Without, there was a cold moon up,
   Of winter radiance sheer and thin;
   The hollow halo it was in   15
Was like an icy crystal cup.

Through the small room, with subtle sound
   Of flame, by vents the fireshine drove
   And reddened. In its dim alcove
The mirror shed a clearness round.   20

I had been sitting up some nights,
   And my tired mind felt weak and blank;
   Like a sharp strengthening wine it drank
The stillness and the broken lights.

Twelve struck. That sound, by dwindling years   25
   Heard in each hour, crept off; and then
   The ruffled silence spread again,
Like water that a pebble stirs.

Our mother rose from where she sat;
   Her needles, as she laid them down,   30
   Met lightly, and her silken gown
Settled—no other noise than that.

---

6. The incident in this poem is imaginary, not autobiographical.

"Glory unto the Newly Born!"
    So, as said angels, she did say,   35
    Because we were in Christmas Day,
Though it would still be long till morn:

Just then in the room over us
    There was a pushing back of chairs,
    As some who had sat unawares
So late, now heard the hour, and rose.   40

With anxious softly-stepping haste
    Our mother went where Margaret lay,
    Fearing the sounds o'erhead—should they
Have broken her long watched-for rest!

She stooped an instant, calm, and turned,   45
    But suddenly turned back again;
    And all her features seemed in pain
With woe, and her eyes gazed and yearned.

For my part, I but hid my face,
    And held my breath, and spoke no word.   50
    There was none spoken; but I heard
The silence for a little space.

Our mother bowed herself and wept;
    And both my arms fell, and I said,
    "God knows I knew that she was dead."   55
And there, all white, my sister slept.

Then kneeling, upon Christmas morn
    A little after twelve o'clock,
    We said, ere the first quarter struck,
"Christ's blessing on the newly born!"   60

1847   1850

The Woodspurge

The wind flapped loose, the wind was still,
Shaken out dead from tree and hill;
I had walked on at the wind's will—
I sat now, for the wind was still.

Between my knees my forehead was—   5
My lips, drawn in, said not Alas!
My hair was over in the grass,
My naked ears heard the day pass.

My eyes, wide open, had the run
Of some ten weeds to fix upon;   10
Among those few, out of the sun,
The woodspurge flowered, three cups in one.

From perfect grief there need not be
   Wisdom or even memory;
   One thing then learned remains to me—   15
The woodspurge has a cup of three.

1856   1870

From The House of Life

The Sonnet

A Sonnet is a moment's monument—
   Memorial from the Soul's eternity
   To one dead deathless hour. Look that it be,
Whether for lustral[7] rite or dire portent,
Of its own arduous fullness reverent;   5
   Carve it in ivory or in ebony,
   As Day or Night may rule; and let Time see
Its flowering crest impearled and orient.

A Sonnet is a coin; its face reveals
   The soul—its converse, to what Power 'tis due—   10
Whether for tribute to the august appeals
   Of Life, or dower in Love's high retinue,
It serve; or, 'mid the dark wharf's cavernous breath,
In Charon's[8] palm it pay the toll to Death.

4. Lovesight

When do I see thee most, belovéd one?
   When in the light the spirits of mine eyes
   Before thy face, their altar, solemnize
The worship of that Love through thee made known?
Or when in the dusk hours (we two alone)   5
   Close-kissed and eloquent of still replies
   Thy twilight-hidden glimmering visage lies,
And my soul only sees thy soul its own?

O love, my love! if I no more should see
Thyself, nor on the earth the shadow of thee,   10
   Nor image of thine eyes in any spring—
How then should sound upon Life's darkening slope
The ground-whirl of the perished leaves of Hope,
   The wind of Death's imperishable wing?

19. Silent Noon

Your hands lie open in the long fresh grass—
   The finger-points look through like rosy blooms;
   Your eyes smile peace. The pasture gleams and glooms

---

7. Purification.
8. The ferryman who, for a fee, rowed the souls of the dead across the river Styx.

'Neath billowing skies that scatter and amass.
All round our nest, far as the eye can pass, 5
   Are golden kingcup-fields with silver edge
   Where the cow-parsley skirts the hawthorn hedge.
'Tis visible silence, still as the hourglass.

Deep in the sun-searched growths the dragonfly
Hangs like a blue thread loosened from the sky— 10
   So this winged hour is dropped to us from above.
Oh! clasp we to our hearts, for deathless dower,
This close-companioned inarticulate hour
   When twofold silence was the song of love.

49. Willowwood—I

I sat with Love upon a woodside well,
   Leaning across the water, I and he;
   Nor ever did he speak nor looked at me,
But touched his lute wherein was audible
The certain secret thing he had to tell. 5
   Only our mirrored eyes met silently
   In the low wave; and that sound came to be
The passionate voice I knew; and my tears fell.

And at their fall, his eyes beneath grew hers;
And with his foot and with his wing feathers 10
   He swept the spring that watered my heart's drouth.
Then the dark ripples spread to waving hair,
And as I stooped, her own lips rising there
   Bubbled with brimming kisses at my mouth.

63. Inclusiveness

The changing guests, each in a different mood,
   Sit at the roadside table and arise;
   And every life among them in like wise
Is a soul's board set daily with new food.
What man has bent o'er his son's sleep, to brood 5
   How that face shall watch his when cold it lies?—
   Or thought, as his own mother kissed his eyes,
Of what her kiss was when his father wooed?

May not this ancient room thou sitt'st in dwell
   In separate living souls for joy or pain? 10
   Nay, all its corners may be painted plain
Where Heaven shows pictures of some life spent well;
   And may be stamped, a memory all in vain,
Upon the sight of lidless eyes in Hell.

71. The Choice—I

Eat thou and drink; tomorrow thou shalt die.
   Surely the earth, that's wise being very old,
   Needs not our help. Then loose me, love, and hold

Thy sultry hair up from my face; that I
May pour for thee this golden wine, brim-high,   5
   Till round the glass thy fingers glow like gold.
   We'll drown all hours: thy song, while hours are tolled,
Shall leap, as fountains veil the changing sky.

Now kiss, and think that there are really those,
  My own high-bosomed beauty, who increase   10
   Vain gold, vain lore, and yet might choose our way!
   Through many years they toil; then on a day
They die not—for their life was death—but cease;
And round their narrow lips the mold falls close.

72. *The Choice—II*

Watch thou and fear; tomorrow thou shalt die.
  Or art thou sure thou shalt have time for death?
  Is not the day which God's word promiseth
To come man knows not when? In yonder sky,
Now while we speak, the sun speeds forth; can I   5
  Or thou assure him of his goal? God's breath
  Even at this moment haply quickeneth
The air to a flame; till spirits, always nigh

Though screened and hid, shall walk the daylight here.
  And dost thou prate of all that man shall do?   10
   Canst thou, who hast but plagues, presume to be
   Glad in his gladness that comes after thee?
Will *his* strength slay *thy* worm in Hell? Go to:
Cover thy countenance, and watch, and fear.

73. *The Choice—III*

Think thou and act; tomorrow thou shalt die.
  Outstretched in the sun's warmth upon the shore,
  Thou say'st: "Man's measured path is all gone o'er:
Up all his years, steeply, with strain and sigh,
Man clomb until he touched the truth; and I,   5
  Even I, am he whom it was destined for."
  How should this be? Art thou then so much more
Than they who sowed, that thou shouldst reap thereby?

Nay, come up hither. From this wave-washed mound
  Unto the furthest flood-brim look with me;   10
Then reach on with thy thought till it be drowned.
  Miles and miles distant though the last line be,
And though thy soul sail leagues and leagues beyond—
  Still, leagues beyond those leagues, there is more sea.

97. *A Superscription*

Look in my face; my name is Might-have-been;
  I am also called No-more, Too-late, Farewell;

Unto thine ear I hold the dead-sea shell
Cast up thy Life's foam-fretted feet between;
Unto thine eyes the glass[9] where that is seen   5
    Which had Life's form and Love's, but by my spell
    Is now a shaken shadow intolerable,
Of ultimate things unuttered the frail screen.

Mark me, how still I am! But should there dart
    One moment through thy soul the soft surprise   10
    Of that winged Peace which lulls the breath of sighs—
Then shalt thou see me smile, and turn apart
Thy visage to mine ambush at thy heart
    Sleepless with cold commemorative eyes.

101. *The One Hope*

When vain desire at last and vain regret
    Go hand in hand to death, and all is vain,
    What shall assuage the unforgotten pain
And teach the unforgetful to forget?
Shall Peace be still a sunk stream long unmet—   5
    Or may the soul at once in a green plain
    Stoop through the spray of some sweet life-fountain
And cull the dew-drenched flowering amulet?[1]
Ah! when the wan soul in that golden air
    Between the scriptured petals softly blown   10
    Peers breathless for the gift of grace unknown,
Ah! let none other alien spell soe'er
But only the one Hope's one name be there—
    Not less nor more, but even that word alone.

1848–80   1870, 1881

She Bound Her Green Sleeve

A FRAGMENT

She bound her green sleeve on my helm,
    Sweet pledge of love's sweet meed;[2]
Warm was her bared arm round my neck
    As well she bade me speed;
And her kiss clings still between my lips,   5
    Heart's beat and strength at need.

1870   1886

9. Mirror.   harm.
1. A charm to protect the wearer from   2. Reward.

The Orchard-Pit

A FRAGMENT

Piled deep below the screening apple branch
   They lie with bitter[3] apples in their hands:
And some are only ancient bones that blanch,
And some had ships that last year's wind did launch,
   And some were yesterday the lords of lands.   5

In the soft dell, among the apple trees,
   High up above the hidden pit she stands,[4]
And there forever sings, who gave to these,
That lie below, her magic hour of ease,
   And those her apples holden in their hands.   10

This in my dreams is shown me; and her hair
   Crosses my lips and draws my burning breath;
Her song spreads golden wings upon the air,
Life's eyes are gleaming from her forehead fair,
   And from her breasts the ravishing eyes of Death.   15

Men say to me that sleep hath many dreams,
   Yet I knew never but this dream alone:
There, from a dried-up channel, once the stream's,
The glen slopes up; even such in sleep it seems
   As to my waking sight the place well known.   20

My love I call her, and she loves me well:
   But I love her as in the maelstrom's cup
The whirled stone loves the leaf inseparable
That clings to it round all the circling swell,
   And that the same last eddy swallows up.   25

1869   1886

3. There is some evidence that Rossetti wrote "bitten" rather than "bitter"—a misprint that would affect our interpretation of the poem. See Oswald Doughty's edition of the *Poems* (1957), p. 307.

4. Cf. Swinburne's *Garden of Proserpine*, lines 49–50: "Pale, beyond porch and portal, / Crowned with calm leaves, she stands."

CHRISTINA ROSSETTI

(1830–1894)

Christina, the sister of Dante Gabriel Rossetti, was a devout High Church Anglican whose quiet life was dedicated to the care of relatives and to good works for church and charity. On two occasions her religious principles were responsible for breaking off plans for marriage. Her first fiancé reverted to Roman Catholicism, and in the second case the lover seemed insufficiently concerned with religion. In both instances she suffered painfully, and, as might be expected, most of her love lyrics are records of frustration and parting. Only rarely does she write of the happiness of union.

Her volume of 1862, *Goblin Market and Other Poems,* was the first collection of poetry in the Pre-Raphaelite manner to gain recognition from the public. The long narrative poem providing the volume with its title became an early established favorite as a seemingly simple moral fable for children. Later readers have likened it to Coleridge's ballad *The Ancient Mariner* and detect in it a more complex representation of religious themes of temptation and sin redeemed by vicarious suffering, although the fruit that tempts Laura is clearly not from the Tree of Knowledge but from an orchard of sensual delights. In its deceptively simple style, *Goblin Market,* like most of her poems, demonstrates her affinity with the early aims of the Pre-Rephaelite group, but her lyric gift is distinctive enough to defy historical classification. England, the birthplace of poets, has produced few women poets of note, but of these few Christina Rossetti is perhaps the finest.

Song

When I am dead, my dearest,
   Sing no sad songs for me;
Plant thou no roses at my head,
   Nor shady cypress tree.
Be the green grass above me   5
   With showers and dewdrops wet;
And if thou wilt, remember,
   And if thou wilt, forget.

I shall not see the shadows,
   I shall not feel the rain;   10
I shall not hear the nightingale
   Sing on as if in pain.
And dreaming through the twilight
   That doth not rise nor set,
Haply I may remember,   15
   And haply may forget.

1848   1862

After Death

The curtains were half drawn; the floor was swept
   And strewn with rushes; rosemary and may
   Lay thick upon the bed on which I lay,
Where, through the lattice, ivy-shadows crept.
He leaned above me, thinking that I slept   5
   And could not hear him; but I heard him say,
   "Poor child, poor child"; and as he turned away
Came a deep silence, and I knew he wept.
He did not touch the shroud, or raise the fold
   That hid my face, or take my hand in his,   10
   Or ruffle the smooth pillows for my head.

He did not love me living; but once dead
He pitied me; and very sweet it is
To know he still is warm though I am cold.

1849   1862

A Birthday

My heart is like a singing bird
    Whose nest is in a watered shoot:
My heart is like an apple tree
    Whose boughs are bent with thickset fruit;
My heart is like a rainbow shell   5
    That paddles in a halcyon sea;
My heart is gladder than all these
    Because my love is come to me.

Raise me a dais of silk and down;
    Hang it with vair¹ and purple dyes;   10
Carve it in doves and pomegranates,
    And peacocks with a hundred eyes;
Work it in gold and silver grapes,
    In leaves and silver fleurs-de-lys;
Because the birthday of my life   15
    Is come, my love is come to me.

1857   1861

An Apple Gathering

I plucked pink blossoms from mine apple tree
    And wore them all that evening in my hair:
Then in due season when I went to see
    I found no apples there.

With dangling basket all along the grass   5
    As I had come I went the selfsame track:
My neighbors mocked me while they saw me pass
    So empty-handed back.

Lilian and Lilias smiled in trudging by,
    Their heaped-up basket teased me like a jeer;   10
Sweet-voiced they sang beneath the sunset sky,
    Their mother's home was near.

Plump Gertrude passed me with her basket full,
    A stronger hand than hers helped it along;
A voice talked with her through the shadows cool   15
    More sweet to me than song.

---

1. Squirrel fur.

Ah Willie, Willie, was my love less worth
    Than apples with their green leaves piled above?
I counted rosiest apples on the earth
    Of far less worth than love.   20

So once it was with me you stooped to talk
    Laughing and listening in this very lane;
To think that by this way we used to walk
    We shall not walk again!

I let my neighbors pass me, ones and twos   25
    And groups; the latest said the night grew chill,
And hastened: but I loitered; while the dews
    Fell fast I loitered still.

1857   1861

Uphill

Does the road wind uphill all the way?
    Yes, to the very end.
Will the day's journey take the whole long day?
    From morn to night, my friend.

But is there for the night a resting place?   5
    A roof for when the slow dark hours begin.
May not the darkness hide it from my face?
    You cannot miss that inn.

Shall I meet other wayfarers at night?
    Those who have gone before.
Then must I knock, or call when just in sight?   10
    They will not keep you standing at that door.

Shall I find comfort, travel-sore and weak?
    Of labor you shall find the sum.
Will there be beds for me and all who seek?   15
    Yea, beds for all who come.

1858   1861

Goblin Market

Morning and evening
Maids heard the goblins cry:
"Come buy our orchard fruits,
Come buy, come buy:
Apples and quinces,   5
Lemons and oranges,

Plump unpecked cherries,
Melons and raspberries,
Bloom-down-cheeked peaches,
Swart-headed mulberries,   10
Wild free-born cranberries,
Crabapples, dewberries,
Pineapples, blackberries,
Apricots, strawberries;—
All ripe together   15
In summer weather,—
Morns that pass by,
Fair eyes that fly;
Come buy, come buy:
Our grapes fresh from the vine,   20
Pomegranates full and fine,
Dates and sharp bullaces,
Rare pears and greengages,
Damsons[1] and bilberries,
Taste them and try: 25
Currants and gooseberries,
Bright-fire-like barberries,
Figs to fill your mouth,
Citrons from the South,
Sweet to tongue and sound to eye;   30
Come buy, come buy."
Evening by evening
Among the brookside rushes,
Laura bowed her head to hear,
Lizzie veiled her blushes: 35
Crouching close together
In the cooling weather,
With clasping arms and cautioning lips,
With tingling cheeks and finger tips.
"Lie close," Laura said,   40
Pricking up her golden head:
"We must not look at goblin men,
We must not buy their fruits:
Who knows upon what soil they fed
Their hungry thirsty roots?"   45
"Come buy," call the goblins
Hobbling down the glen.
"Oh," cried Lizzie, "Laura, Laura,
You should not peep at goblin men."
Lizzie covered up her eyes,   50
Covered close lest they should look;
Laura reared her glossy head,
And whispered like the restless brook:
'Look, Lizzie, look, Lizzie,

---

1. Bullaces, greengages, and damsons are varieties of plums.

Down the glen tramp little men.   55
One hauls a basket,
One bears a plate,
One lugs a golden dish
Of many pounds' weight.
How fair the vine must grow   60
Whose grapes are so luscious;
How warm the wind must blow
Through those fruit bushes."
"No," said Lizzie: "No, no, no;
Their offers should not charm us,   65
Their evil gifts would harm us."
She thrust a dimpled finger
In each ear, shut eyes and ran:
Curious Laura chose to linger
Wondering at each merchant man.   70
One had a cat's face,
One whisked a tail,
One tramped at a rat's pace,
One crawled like a snail,
One like a wombat prowled obtuse and furry,   75
One like a ratel[2] tumbled hurry skurry.
She heard a voice like voice of doves
Cooing all together:
They sounded kind and full of loves
In the pleasant weather.   80

Laura stretched her gleaming neck
Like a rush-imbedded swan,
Like a lily from the beck,[3]
Like a moonlit poplar branch,
Like a vessel at the launch   85
When its last restraint is gone.

Backwards up the mossy glen
Turned and trooped the goblin men,
With their shrill repeated cry,
"Come buy, come buy."   90
When they reached where Laura was
They stood stock still upon the moss,
Leering at each other,
Brother with queer brother;
Signaling each other,   95
Brother with sly brother.
One set his basket down,
One reared his plate;
One began to weave a crown

---

2. Ratel (pronounced ray-tell): South African mammal resembling a badger.   3. Small brook.

Of tendrils, leaves, and rough nuts brown   100
(Men sell not such in any town);
One heaved the golden weight
Of dish and fruit to offer her:
"Come buy, come buy," was still their cry.
Laura stared but did not stir,   105
Longed but had no money.
The whisk-tailed merchant bade her taste
In tones as smooth as honey,
The cat-faced purr'd,
The rat-paced spoke a word   110
Of welcome, and the snail-paced even was heard;
One parrot-voiced and jolly
Cried "Pretty Goblin" still for "Pretty Polly";
One whistled like a bird.

But sweet-tooth Laura spoke in haste: 115
"Good Folk, I have no coin;
To take were to purloin:
I have no copper in my purse,
I have no silver either,
And all my gold is on the furze   120
That shakes in windy weather
Above the rusty heather."
"You have much gold upon your head,"
They answered all together:
"Buy from us with a golden curl."   125
She clipped a precious golden lock,
She dropped a tear more rare than pearl,
Then sucked their fruit globes fair or red.
Sweeter than honey from the rock,
Stronger than man-rejoicing wine,   130
Clearer than water flowed that juice;
She never tasted such before,
How should it cloy with length of use?
She sucked and sucked and sucked the more
Fruits which that unknown orchard bore;   135
She sucked until her lips were sore;
Then flung the emptied rinds away
But gathered up one kernel stone,
And knew not was it night or day
As she turned home alone.   140

Lizzie met her at the gate
Full of wise upbraidings:
"Dear, you should not stay so late,
Twilight is not good for maidens;
Should not loiter in the glen   145
In the haunts of goblin men.
Do you not remember Jeanie,

How she met them in the moonlight,
Took their gifts both choice and many,
Ate their fruits and wore their flowers   150
Plucked from bowers
Where summer ripens at all hours?
But ever in the noonlight
She pined and pined away;
Sought them by night and day,   155
Found them no more, but dwindled and grew gray;
Then fell with the first snow,
While to this day no grass will grow
Where she lies low:
I planted daisies there a year ago   160
That never blow.
You should not loiter so."
"Nay, hush," said Laura:
"Nay, hush, my sister:
I ate and ate my fill,   165
Yet my mouth waters still:
Tomorrow night I will
Buy more"; and kissed her.
"Have done with sorrow;
I'll bring you plums tomorrow   170
Fresh on their mother twigs,
Cherries worth getting;
You cannot think what figs
My teeth have met in,
What melons icy-cold   175
Piled on a dish of gold
Too huge for me to hold,
What peaches with a velvet nap,
Pellucid grapes without one seed:
Odorous indeed must be the mead   180
Whereon they grow, and pure the wave they drink
With lilies at the brink,
And sugar-sweet their sap."

Golden head by golden head,
Like two pigeons in one nest   185
Folded in each other's wings,
They lay down in their curtained bed:
Like two blossoms on one stem,
Like two flakes of new-fallen snow,
Like two wands of ivory   190
Tipped with gold for awful[4] kings.
Moon and stars gazed in at them,
Wind sang to them lullaby,
Lumbering owls forebore to fly,

4. Awe-inspiring.

Not a bat flapped to and fro   195
Round their nest:
Cheek to cheek and breast to breast
Locked together in one nest.

Early in the morning
When the first cock crowed his warning,   200
Neat like bees, as sweet and busy,
Laura rose with Lizzie:
Fetched in honey, milked the cows,
Aired and set to rights the house,
Kneaded cakes of whitest wheat,   205
Cakes for dainty mouths to eat,
Next churned butter, whipped up cream,
Fed their poultry, sat and sewed;
Talked as modest maidens should:
Lizzie with an open heart,   210
Laura in an absent dream,
One content, one sick in part;
One warbling for the mere bright day's delight,
One longing for the night.

At length slow evening came: 215
They went with pitchers to the reedy brook;
Lizzie most placid in her look,
Laura most like a leaping flame,
They drew the gurgling water from its deep.
Lizzie plucked purple and rich golden flags,   220
Then turning homeward said: "The sunset flushes
Those furthest loftiest crags;
Come, Laura, not another maiden lags.
No willful squirrel wags,
The beasts and birds are fast asleep."   225
But Laura loitered still among the rushes.
And said the bank was steep.

And said the hour was early still,
The dew not fallen, the wind not chill;
Listening ever, but not catching   230
The customary cry,
"Come buy, come buy,"
With its iterated jingle
Of sugar-baited words:
Not for all her watching   235
Once discerning even one goblin
Racing, whisking, tumbling, hobbling—
Let alone the herds
That used to tramp along the glen,
In groups or single,   240
Of brisk fruit-merchant men.

Till Lizzie urged, "O Laura, come;
I hear the fruit-call, but I dare not look:
You should not loiter longer at this brook:
Come with me home.   245
The stars rise, the moon bends her arc,
Each glow-worm winks her spark,
Let us get home before the night grows dark:
For clouds may gather
Though this is summer weather,   250
Put out the lights and drench us through;
Then if we lost our way what should we do?

Laura turned cold as stone
To find her sister heard that cry alone,
That goblin cry,   255
"Come buy our fruits, come buy."
Must she then buy no more such dainty fruit?
Must she no more such succous pasture find,
Gone deaf and blind?
Her tree of life dropped from the root: 260
She said not one word in her heart's sore ache:
But peering through the dimness, nought discerning,
Trudged home, her pitcher dripping all the way;
So crept to bed, and lay
Silent till Lizzie slept;   265
Then sat up in a passionate yearning.
And gnashed her teeth for balked desire, and wept
As if her heart would break.

Day after day, night after night,
Laura kept watch in vain   270
In sullen silence of exceeding pain.
She never caught again the goblin cry,
"Come buy, come buy";—
She never spied the goblin men
Hawking their fruits along the glen: 275
But when the noon waxed bright
Her hair grew thin and gray;
She dwindled, as the fair full moon doth turn
To swift decay and burn
Her fire away.   280

One day remembering her kernelstone
She set it by a wall that faced the south;
Dewed it with tears, hoped for a root,
Watched for a waxing shoot,
But there came none.   285
It never saw the sun,
It never felt the trickling moisture run:
While with sunk eyes and faded mouth

She dreamed of melons, as a traveler sees
False waves in desert drouth   290
With shade of leaf-crowned trees,
And burns the thirstier in the sandful breeze.

She no more swept the house,
Tended the fowls or cows,
Fetched honey, kneaded cakes of wheat,   295
Brought water from the brook:
But sat down listless in the chimneynook
And would not eat.

Tender Lizzie could not bear
To watch her sister's cankerous care,   300
Yet not to share.
She night and morning
Caught the goblins' cry:
"Come buy our orchard fruits,
Come buy, come buy":—   305
Beside the brook, along the glen,
She heard the tramp of goblin men,
The voice and stir
Poor Laura could not hear;
Longed to buy fruit to comfort her,   310
But feared to pay too dear.
She thought of Jeanie in her grave,
Who should have been a bride;
But who for joys brides hope to have
Fell sick and died   315
In her gay prime,
In earliest winter time,
With the first glazing rime,
With the first snow-fall of crisp winter time.

Till Laura dwindling   320
Seemed knocking at Death's door.
Then Lizzie weighed no more
Better and worse;
But put a silver penny in her purse,
Kissed Laura, crossed the heath with clumps of furze   325
At twilight, halted by the brook:
And for the first time in her life
Began to listen and look.

Laughed every goblin
When they spied her peeping: 330
Came towards her hobbling,
Flying, running, leaping,
Puffing and blowing,
Chuckling, clapping, crowing,
Cluckling and gobbling,   335

Mopping and mowing,
Full of airs and graces,
Pulling wry faces,
Demure grimaces,
Cat-like and rat-like,   340
Ratel- and wombat-like,
Snail-paced in a hurry,
Parrot-voiced and whistler,
Helter skelter, hurry skurry,
Chattering like magpies,   345
Fluttering like pigeons,
Gliding like fishes,—
Hugged her and kissed her:
Squeezed and caressed her:
Stretched up their dishes,   350
Panniers, and plates:
"Look at our apples
Russet and dun,
Bob at our cherries,
Bite at our peaches,   355
Citrons and dates,
Grapes for the asking,
Pears red with basking
Out in the sun,
Plums on their twigs;   360
Pluck them and suck them,—
Pomegranates, figs."

"Good folk," said Lizzie,
Mindful of Jeanie:
"Give me much and many":   365
Held out her apron,
Tossed them her penny
"Nay, take a seat with us,
Honor and eat with us,"
They answered grinning: 370
"Our feast is but beginning.
Night yet is early,
Warm and dew-pearly,
Wakeful and starry:
Such fruits as these   375
No man can carry;
Half their bloom would fly,
Half their dew would dry,
Half their flavor would pass by.
Sit down and feast with us,   380
Be welcome guest with us,
Cheer you and rest with us."—
"Thank you, said Lizzie: "But one waits
At home alone for me:

So without further parleying,   385
If you will not sell me any
Of your fruits though much and many,
Give me back my silver penny
I tossed you for a fee."—
The began to scratch their pates,   390
No longer wagging, purring,
But visibly demurring,
Grunting and snarling.
One called her proud,
Cross-grained, uncivil;   395
Their tones waxed loud,
Their looks were evil.
Lashing their tails
They trod and hustled her,
Elbowed and jostled her,   400
Clawed with their nails,
Barking, mewing, hissing, mocking,
Tore her gown and soiled her stocking,
Twitched her hair out by the roots,
Stamped upon her tender feet,   405
Held her hands and squeezed their fruits
Against her mouth to make her eat.

White and golden Lizzie stood,
Like a lily in a flood,—
Like a rock of blue-veined stone   410
Lashed by tides obstreperously,—
Like a beacon left alone
In a hoary roaring sea,
Sending up a golden fire,—
Like a fruit-crowned orange-tree   415
White with blossoms honey-sweet
Sore beset by wasp and bee,—
Like a royal virgin town
Topped with gilded dome and spire
Close beleaguered by a fleet   420
Mad to tug her standard down.

One may lead a horse to water,
Twenty cannot make him drink.
Though the goblins cuffed and caught her,
Coaxed and fought her,   425
Bullied and besought her,
Scratched her, pinched her black as ink,
Kicked and knocked her,
Mauled and mocked her,
Lizzie uttered not a word;   430
Would not open lip from lip
Lest they should cram a mouthful in:

But laughed in heart to feel the drip
Of juice that syruped all her face,
And lodged in dimples of her chin,   435
And streaked her neck which quaked like curd.
At last the evil people,
Worn out by her resistance,
Flung back her penny, kicked their fruit
Along whichever road they took,   440
Not leaving root or stone or shoot;
Some writhed into the ground,
Some dived into the brook
With ring and ripple,
Some scudded on the gale without a sound,   445
Some vanished in the distance.

In a smart, ache, tingle,
Lizzie went her way;
Knew not was it night or day;
Sprang up the bank, tore through the furze,   450
Threaded copse and dingle,
And heard her penny jingle
Bouncing in her purse,—
Its bounce was music to her ear.
She ran and ran   455
As if she feared some goblin man
Dogged her with gibe or curse
Or something worse:
But not one goblin skurried after,
Nor was she pricked by fear;   460
The kind heart made her windy-paced
That urged her home quite out of breath with haste
And inward laughter.

She cried, "Laura," up the garden,
"Did you miss me?   465
Come and kiss me.
Never mind my bruises,
Hug me, kiss me, suck my juices
Squeezed from goblin fruits for you,
Goblin pulp and goblin dew.   470
Eat me, drink me, love me;
Laura, make much of me;
For your sake I have braved the glen
And had to do with goblin merchant men."

Laura started from her chair,   475
Flung her arms up in the air,
Clutched her hair:
"Lizzie, Lizzie, have you tasted
For my sake the fruit forbidden?

Must your light like mine be hidden,   480
Your young life like mine be wasted,
Undone in mine undoing,
And ruined in my ruin,
Thirsty, cankered, goblin-ridden?"—
She clung about her sister,   485
Kissed and kissed and kissed her:
Tears once again
Refreshed her shrunken eyes,
Dropping like rain
After long sultry drouth;   490
Shaking with anguish, fear, and pain,
She kissed and kissed her with a hungry mouth.

Her lips began to scorch,
That juice was wormwood to her tongue,
She loathed the feast: 495
Writhing as one possessed she leaped and sung,
Rent all her robe, and wrung
Her hands in lamentable haste,
And beat her breast,
Her locks streamed like the torch
Borne by a racer at full speed,   500
Or like the mane of horses in their flight,
Or like an eagle when she stems[5] the light
Straight toward the sun,
Or like a caged thing freed,
Or like a flying flag when armies run.   505

Swift fire spread through her veins, knocked at her heart,
Met the fire smoldering there
And overbore its lesser flame;
She gorged on bitterness without a name: 510
Ah fool, to choose such part
Of soul-consuming care!
Sense failed in the mortal strife:
Like the watch-tower of a town
Which an earthquake shatters down,   515
Like a lightning-stricken mast,
Like a wind-uprooted tree
Spun about,
Like a foam-topped waterspout
Cast down headlong in the sea,   520
She fell at last;
Pleasure past and anguish past,
Is it death or is it life?

Life out of death.
That night long Lizzie watched by her,   525
Counted her pulse's flagging stir,

5. Breasts or makes headway against.

Felt for her breath,
Held water to her lips, and cooled her face
With tears and fanning leaves.
But when the first birds chirped about their eaves,   530
And early reapers plodded to the place
Of golden sheaves,
And dew-wet grass
Bowed in the morning winds so brisk to pass,
And new buds with new day   535
Opened of cup-like lilies on the stream,
Laura awoke as from a dream,
Laughed in the innocent old way,
Hugged Lizzie but not twice or thrice;
Her gleaming locks showed not one thread of gray,   540
Her breath was sweet as May,
And light danced in her eyes.

Days, weeks, months, years
Afterwards, when both were wives
With children of their own;   545
Their mother-hearts beset with fears,
Their lives bound up in tender lives;
Laura would call the little ones
And tell them of her early prime,
Those pleasant days long gone   550
Of not-returning time:
Would talk about the haunted glen,
The wicked quaint fruit-merchant men,
Their fruits like honey to the throat
But poison in the blood   555
(Men sell not such in any town):
Would tell them how her sister stood
In deadly peril to do her good,
And win the fiery antidote:
Then joining hands to little hands   560
Would bid them cling together,—
"For there is no friend like a sister
In calm or stormy weather;
To cheer one on the tedious way,
To fetch one if one goes astray,   565
To lift one if one totters down,
To strengthen whilst one stands."

1859   1862

A Life's Parallels

Never on this side of the grave again,
    On this side of the river,
On this side of the garner of the grain,
    Never.

Ever while time flows on and on and on,   5
 That narrow noiseless river,
Ever while corn bows heavy-headed, wan,
 Ever.

Never despairing, often fainting, ruing,
 But looking back, ah never!   10
Faint yet pursuing, faint yet still pursuing
 Ever.

ca. 1881   1893

Cardinal Newman[1]

In the grave whither thou goest.

O weary Champion of the Cross, lie still:
 Sleep thou at length the all-embracing sleep;
 Long was thy sowing day, rest now and reap:
Thy fast was long, feast now thy spirit's fill.
Yea take thy fill of love, because thy will   5
 Chose love not in the shallows but the deep:
 Thy tides were spring tides, set against the neap[2]
Of calmer souls: thy flood rebuked their rill.
Now night has come to thee—please God, of rest:
 So some time must it come to every man;   10
 To first and last, where many last are first.
Now fixed and finished thine eternal plan,
 Thy best has done its best, thy worst its worst:
 Thy best its best, please God, thy best its best.

1890   1893

Sleeping at Last

Sleeping at last, the trouble and tumult over,
 Sleeping at last, the struggle and horror past,
Cold and white, out of sight of friend and of lover,
 Sleeping at last.

No more a tired heart downcast or overcast,   5
No more pangs that wring or shifting fears that hover,
 Sleeping at last in a dreamless sleep locked fast.

Fast asleep. Singing birds in their leafy cover
 Cannot wake her, nor shake her the gusty blast.
Under the purple thyme and the purple clover   10
 Sleeping at last.

1893   1896

---

1. Written on the occasion of the death of John Henry Newman. For an account of the theological controversies in which Newman had been involved, see the Critical and Controversial Prose section below. The epigraph is from Ecclesiastes ix.10.

2. Tides which do not rise to the high-water mark of the spring tides.

GEORGE MEREDITH
(1828–1909)

Like Thomas Hardy, George Meredith preferred writing poetry to writing novels, but it was as the author of *The Ordeal of Richard Feverel* (1859), *The Egoist* (1879), and other novels that he made his mark. His poems nevertheless deserve more attention than they have yet received, especially *Modern Love* (1862). This sequence of sixteen-line sonnets is a kind of novel in verse which analyzes the sufferings of a man and wife whose marriage is breaking up. *Modern Love* was probably derived, in part, from Meredith's own experiences. At 21, at the outset of his career as a writer in London, he married a daughter of the satirist Thomas Love Peacock. Nine years later, after a series of quarrels, his wife eloped to Europe with another artist. The Merediths were never reconciled, and in 1861 she died.

Meredith's second marriage was a happier one and reinforced his optimistic assumptions that the order of nature is good, assumptions that are sometimes developed in his poems.

From Modern Love

1

By this he knew she wept with waking eyes:
That, at his hand's light quiver by her head,
The strange low sobs that shook their common bed
Were called into her with a sharp surprise,
And strangled mute, like little gaping snakes,   5
Dreadfully venomous to him. She lay
Stone-still, and the long darkness flowed away
With muffled pulses. Then, as midnight makes
Her giant heart of Memory and Tears
Drink the pale drug of silence, and so beat   10
Sleep's heavy measure, they from head to feet
Were moveless, looking through their dead black years
By vain regret scrawled over the blank wall.
Like sculptured effigies they might be seen
Upon their marriage tomb, the sword between;[1]   15
Each wishing for the sword that severs all.

2

It ended, and the morrow brought the task.
Her eyes were guilty gates, that let him in
By shutting all too zealous for their sin:
Each sucked a secret, and each wore a mask.

1. The now silent couple are as motionless as recumbent stone statues on top of a tomb. In medieval legend, a naked sword between lovers ensured chastity.

But, oh, the bitter taste her beauty had!⁵
He sickened as at breath of poison-flowers:
A languid humor stole among the hours,
And if their smiles encountered, he went mad,
And raged deep inward, till the light was brown
Before his vision, and the world, forgot,⁚₀
Looked wicked as some old dull murder spot.
A star with lurid beams, she seemed to crown
The pit of infamy: and then again
He fainted on his vengefulness, and strove
To ape the magnanimity of love,⁚₅
And smote himself, a shuddering heap of pain.

3

This was the woman; what now of the man?²
But pass him. If he comes beneath a heel,
He shall be crushed until he cannot feel,
Or, being callous, haply till he can.
But he is nothing—nothing? Only mark⁵
The rich light striking out from her on him!
Ha! what a sense it is when her eyes swim
Across the man she singles, leaving dark
All else! Lord God, who mad'st the thing so fair,
See that I am drawn to her even now!⁚₀
It cannot be such harm on her cool brow
To put a kiss? Yet if I meet him there!
But she is mine! Ah, no! I know too well
I claim a star whose light is overcast:
I claim a phantom woman in the Past.⁚₅
The hour has struck, though I heard not the bell!

15

I think she sleeps: it must be sleep, when low
Hangs that abandoned arm toward the floor;
The face turned with it. Now make fast the door.
Sleep on: it is your husband, not your foe.
The Poet's black stage-lion³ of wronged love⁵
Frights not our modern dames—well if he did!
Now will I pour new light upon that lid,
Full-sloping like the breasts beneath. "Sweet dove,
Your sleep is pure. Nay, pardon: I disturb.
I do not? good!" Her waking infant-stare⁚₀
Grows woman to the burden⁴ my hands bear:
Her own handwriting to me when no curb
Was left on Passion's tongue. She trembles through;
A woman's tremble—the whole instrument—

---

2. I.e., a rival with whom the wife has fallen in love.
3. Probably a reference to Shakespeare's portrait of a jealous husband in *Othello*.
4. A letter once written by the wife to the husband.

I show another letter[5] lately sent. 15
The words are very like: the name is new.

16

In our old shipwrecked days there was an hour,
When in the firelight steadily aglow,
Joined slackly, we beheld the red chasm grow
Among the clicking coals. Our library bower
That eve was left to us: and hushed we sat 5
As lovers to whom Time is whispering.
From sudden-opened doors we heard them sing:
The nodding elders mixed good wine with chat.
Well knew we that Life's greatest treasure lay
With us, and of it was our talk. "Ah, yes! 10
Love dies!" I said: I never thought it less.
She yearned to me that sentence to unsay.
Then when the fire domed blackening, I found
Her cheek was salt against my kiss, and swift
Up the sharp scale of sobs her breast did lift— 15
Now am I haunted by that taste! that sound!

17

At dinner, she is hostess, I am host.
Went the feast ever cheerfuller? She keeps
The Topic over intellectual deeps
In buoyancy afloat. They see no ghost.
With sparkling surface-eyes we ply the ball: 5
It is in truth a most contagious game:
HIDING THE SKELETON, shall be its name.
Such play as this the devils might appall!
But here's the greater wonder: in that we,
Enamored of an acting naught can tire, 10
Each other, like true hypocrites, admire;
Warm-lighted looks, Love's ephemeridae,[6]
Shoot gayly o'er the dishes and the wine.
We waken envy of our happy lot.
Fast, sweet, and golden, shows the marriage knot. 15
Dear guests, you now have seen Love's corpse-light[7] shine.

50

Thus piteously Love closed[8] what he begat:
The union of this ever diverse pair!
These two were rapid falcons in a snare,
Condemned to do the flitting of the bat.
Lovers beneath the singing sky of May, 5
They wandered once; clear as the dew on flowers:

5. A letter she has recently written to the man she now loves.
6. Insects which live for one day only.
7. Phosphorescent light such as seen in marshes. When appearing in a cemetery it was believed to portend a funeral.
8. The wife has died.

But they fed not on the advancing hours:
Their hearts held cravings for the buried day.
Then each applied to each that fatal knife,
Deep questioning, which probes to endless dole.   10
Ah, what a dusty answer gets the soul
When hot for certainties in this our life!—
In tragic hints here see what evermore
Moves dark as yonder midnight ocean's force,
Thundering like ramping hosts of warrior horse,   15
To throw that faint thin line upon the shore!

                                                   1862

Dirge in Woods

A wind sways the pines,
          And below
Not a breath of wild air;
Still as the mosses that glow
On the flooring and over the lines   5
Of the roots here and there.
The pine tree drops its dead;
They are quiet, as under the sea.
Overhead, overhead
Rushes life in a race,   10
As the clouds the clouds chase;
          And we go,
And we drop like the fruits of the tree,
          Even we,
          Even so.   15

                                                   1870

Lucifer in Starlight

On a starred night Prince Lucifer uprose.
Tired of his dark dominion, swung the fiend
Above the rolling ball, in cloud part screened,
Where sinners hugged their specter of repose.
Poor prey to his hot fit of pride were those.   5
And now upon his western wing he leaned,
Now his huge bulk o'er Afric's sands careened,
Now the black planet shadowed Arctic snows.
Soaring through wider zones that pricked his scars[9]
With memory of the old revolt from Awe,   10
He reached a middle height, and at the stars,
Which are the brain of heaven, he looked, and sank.
Around the ancient track marched, rank on rank,
The army of unalterable law.

                                                   1883

9. The vast expanse of sky reminds
Satan of the wounds he suffered when
his revolt against God was crushed and
he was hurled from heaven to hell.

WILLIAM MORRIS
(1834–1896)

In his Apology to *The Earthly Paradise* Morris described himself as "the idle singer of an empty day," yet the word "idle," applied to him, seems incongruous or comic. Painter, businessman, poet, designer of furniture, printer, weaver, and political agitator, Morris was one of the most active men of his century.

Although anthologies usually feature his incidental lyrics, Morris was primarily, like Chaucer, a narrative poet. His early volume *The Defense of Guenevere* (1858) contains his most effective narratives: poems such as *The Haystack in the Floods* illustrate his flair for intense and concentrated storytelling. In his later volumes Morris abandons this promising vein and presents more diffuse and easily readable retellings of the sagas of Iceland as in *Sigurd the Volsung* (1876) or of classical legends as in *The Life and Death of Jason* (1867) and *The Earthly Paradise* (1868). The readability of these popular classical narratives is partly attributable to Morris's treatment of the rhymed couplet, a form he preferred to blank verse. In his hands the rhyming is so contrivedly unobtrusive that the narrative seems to flow without interruption. The following passage is representative (on a starlit night Medea first declares her love for Jason):

> "Upon the day thou weariest of me,
> I wish that thou mayst somewhat think of this,
> And 'twixt thy new-found kisses, and the bliss
> Of something sweeter than thine old delight,
> Remember thee a little of this night
> Of marvels, and this starlit, silent place,
> And these two lovers standing face to face."

Such poems had a marked influence on the early poetry of W. B. Yeats, who was honored when Morris said of his early volume of poems (*The Wanderings of Oisin*, 1889): "You write my kind of poetry."

Morris, in turn, was deeply attached to his own literary master, John Ruskin. Like Ruskin he became progressively dissatisfied with the drabness of the modern industrial world, and in later years became convinced that a political revolution was needed to restore mankind to a state in which work could once more be enjoyed, without the exploitation of workers that seemed to him prevalent in Victorian England. His prose narrative, *News from Nowhere* (1891), embodies his ideal of such a state, an ideal dependent partly on his study of Karl Marx but more upon his lifelong love for the color and vitality of medieval life.

Christ Keep the Hollow Land[1]

Christ keep the Hollow Land
All the summertide;

1. From a song sung by the heroine of a prose story, *The Hollow Land*, which was published in the *Oxford and Cambridge Magazine.*

Still we cannot understand
Where the waters glide:

Only dimly seeing them   5
Coldly slipping through
Many green-lipped cavern mouths
Where the hills are blue.

1856

The Haystack in the Floods[2]

Had she come all the way for this,
To part at last without a kiss?
Yea, had she borne the dirt and rain
That her own eyes might see him slain
Beside the haystack in the floods?   5

Along the dripping leafless woods,
The stirrup touching either shoe,
She rode astride as troopers do;
With kirtle kilted to her knee,
To which the mud splashed wretchedly;   10
And the wet dripped from every tree
Upon her head and heavy hair,
And on her eyelids broad and fair;
The tears and rain ran down her face.
By fits and starts they rode apace,   15
And very often was his place
Far off from her; he had to ride
Ahead, to see what might betide
When the roads crossed; and sometimes, when
There rose a murmuring from his men,   20
Had to turn back with promises.
Ah me! she had but little ease;
And often for pure doubt and dread
She sobbed, made giddy in the head
By the swift riding; while, for cold,   25
Her slender fingers scarce could hold
The wet reins; yea, and scarcely, too,
She felt the foot within her shoe
Against the stirrup: all for this,
To part at last without a kiss   30
Beside the haystack in the floods.

For when they neared that old soaked hay,
They saw across the only way
That Judas, Godmar, and the three

2. After the defeat of the French at
Poitiers in 1356, an English knight, Sir
Robert de Marny, is riding with Jehane, his mistress, to reach the frontier of
Gascony, which was in English hands.

Red running lions dismally   35
Grinned from his pennon, under which
In one straight line along the ditch,
They counted thirty heads.

              So then
While Robert turned round to his men,
She saw at once the wretched end,   40
And, stooping down, tried hard to rend
Her coif the wrong way from her head,
And hid her eyes; while Robert said:
"Nay, love, 'tis scarcely two to one;
At Poictiers where we made them run   45
So fast—why, sweet my love, good cheer,
The Gascon frontier is so near,
Nought after this."

             But: "O!" she said,
"My God! my God! I have to tread
The long way back without you; then   50
The court at Paris; those six men;[3]
The gratings of the Chatelet;
The swift Seine on some rainy day
Like this, and people standing by,
And laughing, while my weak hands try   55
To recollect how strong men swim.[4]
All this, or else a life with him,
For which I should be damned at last,
Would God that this next hour were past!"

He answered not, but cried his cry,   60
"St. George for Marny!" cheerily;
And laid his hand upon her rein.
Alas! no man of all his train
Gave back that cheery cry again;
And, while for rage his thumb beat fast   65
Upon his sword hilt, someone cast
About his neck a kerchief long,
And bound him.

             Then they went along
To Godmar; who said: "Now, Jehane,
Your lover's life is on the wane   70

---

3. The judges. The "Chatelet" is a prison in Paris.
4. In trial by water, a woman accused of witchcraft or other crimes was thrown into the river to determine her guilt or innocence. For this ordeal, the accused would customarily have her hands tied. If she sank she was deemed innocent and thereafter spared by being hauled from the water. If she floated she was guilty and thereafter burned. In Morris' version Jehane would have no chance of escaping death; if she swam she would be burned, and if she sank she would be drowned. See line 107.

So fast, that, if this very hour
You yield not as my paramour,
He will not see the rain leave off:
Nay, keep your tongue from gibe and scoff,
Sir Robert, or I slay you now."   75

She laid her hand upon her brow,
Then gazed upon the palm, as though
She thought her forehead bled, and: "No!"
She said, and turned her head away,
As there was nothing else to say,   80
And everything were settled: red
Grew Godmar's face from chin to head:
"Jehane, on yonder hill there stands
My castle, guarding well my lands;
What hinders me from taking you,   85
And doing that I list to do
To your fair willful body, while
Your knight lies dead?"

              A wicked smile
Wrinkled her face, her lips grew thin,
A long way out she thrust her chin: 90
"You know that I should strangle you
While you were sleeping; or bite through
Your throat, by God's help: ah!" she said,
"Lord Jesus, pity your poor maid!
For in such wise they hem me in,   95
I cannot choose but sin and sin,
Whatever happens: yet I think
They could not make me eat or drink,
And so should I just reach my rest."
"Nay, if you do not my behest,   100
O Jehane! though I love you well,"
Said Godmar, "would I fail to tell
All that I know?" "Foul lies," she said.
"Eh? lies, my Jehane? by God's head,
At Paris folks would deem them true!   105
Do you know, Jehane, they cry for you:
'Jehane the brown! Jehane the brown!
Give us Jehane to burn or drown!'
Eh!—gag me Robert!—sweet my friend,
This were indeed a piteous end   110
For those long fingers, and long feet,
And long neck, and smooth shoulders sweet;
An end that few men would forget
That saw it. So, an hour yet:
Consider, Jehane, which to take   115
Of life or death!"

            So, scarce awake,
Dismounting, did she leave that place,

And totter some yards: with her face
Turned upward to the sky she lay,
Her head on a wet heap of hay,   120
And fell asleep: and while she slept,
And did not dream, the minutes crept
Round to the twelve again; but she,
Being waked at last, sighed quietly,
And strangely childlike came, and said: 125
"I will not." Straightway Godmar's head,
As though it hung on strong wires, turned
Most sharply round, and his face burned.

For Robert, both his eyes were dry,
He could not weep, but gloomily   130
He seemed to watch the rain; yea, too,
His lips were firm; he tried once more
To touch her lips; she reached out, sore
And vain desire so tortured them,
The poor gray lips, and now the hem   135
Of his sleeve brushed them.

                                With a start
Up Godmar rose, thrust them apart;
From Robert's throat he loosed the bands
Of silk and mail; with empty hands
Held out, she stood and gazed, and saw,   140
The long bright blade without a flaw
Glide out from Godmar's sheath, his hand
In Robert's hair; she saw him bend
Back Robert's head; she saw him send
The thin steel down; the blow told well,   145
Right backward the knight Robert fell,
And moaned as dogs do, being half dead,
Unwitting, as I deem: so then
Godmar turned grinning to his men,
Who ran, some five or six, and beat   150
His head to pieces at their feet.

Then Godmar turned again and said:
"So, Jehane, the first fitte[5] is read!
Take note, my lady, that your way
Lies backward to the Chatelet!"   155
She shook her head and gazed awhile
At her cold hands with a rueful smile,
As though this thing had made her mad.

This was the parting that they had
Beside the haystack in the floods.   160

                                         1858

5. Section or canto of a poem.

From The Earthly Paradise

An Apology

Of Heaven or Hell I have no power to sing,
I cannot ease the burden of your fears,
Or make quick-coming death a little thing,
Or bring again the pleasure of past years,
Nor for my words shall ye forget your tears,   5
Or hope again for aught that I can say,
The idle singer of an empty day.

But rather, when, aweary of your mirth,
From full hearts still unsatisfied ye sigh,
And, feeling kindly unto all the earth,   10
Grudge every minute as it passes by,
Made the more mindful that the sweet days die—
Remember me a little then, I pray,
The idle singer of an empty day.

The heavy trouble, the bewildering care   15
That weighs us down who live and earn our bread,
These idle verses have no power to bear;
So let me sing of names remembéred,
Because they, living not, can ne'er be dead,
Or long time take their memory quite away   20
From us poor singers of an empty day.

Dreamer of dreams, born out of my due time,
Why should I strive to set the crooked straight?[6]
Let it suffice me that my murmuring rhyme
Beats with light wing against the ivory gate,[7]   25
Telling a tale not too importunate
To those who in the sleepy region stay,
Lulled by the singer of an empty day.

Folk say a wizard to a northern king
At Christmastide such wondrous things did show,   30
That through one window men beheld the spring,
And through another saw the summer glow,
And through a third the fruited vines a-row,
While still, unheard, but in its wonted way,
Piped the drear wind of that December day.   35

So with this Earthly Paradise it is,
If ye will read aright, and pardon me,
Who strive to build a shadowy isle of bliss
Midmost the beating of the steely sea,

---

6. In 1856, when Morris was an undergraduate, he wrote in a letter: "I can't enter into politico-social subjects with any interest, for on the whole I see that things are in a muddle, and I have no power or vocation to set them right in ever so little a degree. My work is the embodiment of dreams in one form or another."

7. At the cave of Morpheus, god of dreams, were two gates: through the gate of horn came prophetic dreams, and through the ivory gate came fictitious dreams.

Where tossed about all hearts of men must be;⁢   40
Whose ravening monsters mighty men shall slay,
Not the poor singer of an empty day.

                    1868–70

A Death Song[8]

What cometh here from west to east a-wending?
And who are these, the marchers stern and slow?
We bear the message that the rich are sending
Aback to those who bade them wake and know.
Not one, not one, nor thousands must they slay,   5
But one and all if they would dusk the day.

We asked them for a life of toilsome earning—
They bade us bide their leisure for our bread;
We craved to speak to tell our woeful learning—
We come back speechless, bearing back our dead.   10
Not one, not one, nor thousands must they slay,
But one and all if they would dusk the day.

They will not learn; they have no ears to hearken;
They turn their faces from the eyes of fate;
Their gay-lit halls shut out the skies that darken.   15
But, lo! this dead man knocking at the gate.
Not one, not one, nor thousands must they slay,
But one and all if they would dusk the day.

Here lies the sign that we shall break our prison;
Amidst the storm he won a prisoner's rest;   20
But in the cloudy dawn the sun arisen
Brings us our day of work to win the best.
Not one, not one, nor thousands must they slay,
But one and all if they would dusk the day.

                    1891

For the Bed at Kelmscott[9]

    The wind's on the wold
    And the night is a-cold,
    And Thames runs chill
    'Twixt mead and hill;
    But kind and dear   5
    Is the old house here,
    And my heart is warm
    'Midst winter's harm.

8. In a Socialist parade of 1887, in which Morris was one of the marchers, his friend Alfred Linnell was beaten by the police and died of injuries. Morris printed this poem as a penny pamphlet to raise money for Linnell's family.
9. Kelmscott Manor was owned by Morris. The bed itself is the speaker.

Rest, then, and rest,
And think of the best
'Twixt summer and spring,   10
When all birds sing
In the town of the tree,
And ye lie in me
And scarce dare move,
Lest the earth and its love   15
Should fade away
Ere the full of the day.
I am old and have seen
Many things that have been—   20
Both grief and peace
And wane and increase.
No tale I tell
Of ill or well,
But this I say,   25
Night treadeth on day.
And for worst and best
Right good is rest.

1893

EDWARD FITZGERALD
(1809–1883)

Omar Khayyám was a 12th-century mathematician, astronomer, and teacher, from Nishapur in Persia. He was also the author of numerous rhymed quatrains, a verse form called *rubā'i* in Persian. Omar's four-lined epigrams were subsequently brought together in collections called *Rubáiyát* and recorded in various manuscripts.

Over 700 years later, in 1857, one such Omar manuscript came into the hands of Edward FitzGerald, a Victorian man of letters, who made from it one of the most popular poems in the English language. FitzGerald was a scholar of comfortable means who lived in the country reading the classics and cultivating his garden. He also cultivated his friendships with writers like Tennyson, Thackeray, and Carlyle, to whom he wrote charming letters. His translations from Greek and Latin were largely ignored, and so too, at first, was his translation of Omar's Persian verses, which he published anonymously. In 1859, only two reviewers noticed the appearance of the *Rubáiyát*, and the edition was soon remaindered. Two years later the volume was discovered by D. G. Rossetti, and enthusiasm for it gradually spread, until edition after edition was called for. The demand for the poem led FitzGerald to revise his translation considerably by further polishing his already finely polished stanzas (the fifth version of these revisions appears below).

The Italians have a witty saying that translations are like spouses: a beautiful translation is apt to be unfaithful, and a faithful translation is apt to be ugly. Experts have argued at great length whether FitzGerald's adaptation of Omar's poem is a faithful translation, but no one argues its beauty.

One reader said of FitzGerald's witty and melancholy masterpiece: "It reads like the latest and freshest expression of the perplexity and of the doubt of the generation to which we ourselves belong." This comment was made by the American Charles Eliot Norton writing in 1869. Norton's favorable opinion has been endorsed by later generations as well. The *Rubáiyát* has much in common with another late Victorian volume, *The Shropshire Lad* by A. E. Housman, and the remarkable popularity of these two collections of nostalgic lyrics is a reminder that to be popular, especially among young readers, poetry does not have to offer optimistic edification. As George Moore said, "The sadness of life is the joy of art."

The Rubáiyát of Omar Khayyám

1

Wake! For the Sun, who scattered into flight
The Stars before him from the Field of Night,
   Drives Night along with them from Heav'n and strikes
The Sultán's Turret with a Shaft of Light.

2

Before the phantom of False morning[1] died,   5
Methought a Voice within the Tavern cried,
   "When all the Temple is prepared within,
Why nods the drowsy Worshiper outside?"

3

And, as the Cock crew, those who stood before
The Tavern shouted—"Open, then, the Door!   10
   You know how little while we have to stay,
And, once departed, may return no more."

4

Now the New Year[2] reviving old Desires,
The thoughtful Soul to Solitude retires,
   Where the WHITE HAND OF MOSES on the Bough
Puts out, and Jesus from the Ground suspires.[3]   15

5

Iram[4] indeed is gone with all his Rose,
And Jamshyd's[5] Sev'n-ringed Cup where no one knows;
   But still a Ruby kindles in the Vine,
And many a Garden by the Water blows.   20

6

And David's lips are locked; but in divine
High-piping Pehleví,[6] with "Wine! Wine! Wine!

1. "A transient Light on the Horizon about an hour before the * * * True Dawn" [FitzGerald's note].
2. In Persia, the beginning of spring.
3. Breathes. "Moses" and "Jesus": plants named in honor of prophets who came before Mohammed. The Persians believed that the healing power of Jesus was in his breath.
4. "A royal Garden now sunk somewhere in the Sands of Arabia" [FitzGerald's note].
5. Legendary king.
6. The classical language of Persia.

Red Wine!"—the Nightingale cries to the Rose
That sallow cheek of hers to incarnadine.

7

Come, fill the Cup, and in the fire of Spring   25
Your Winter-garment of Repentance fling;
　　The Bird of Time has but a little way
To flutter—and the Bird is on the Wing.

8

Whether at Naishápur or Babylon,
Whether the Cup with sweet or bitter run,   30
　　The Wine of Life keeps oozing drop by drop,
The Leaves of Life keep falling one by one.

9

Each Morn a thousand Roses brings, you say;
Yes, but where leaves the Rose of Yesterday?
　　And this first Summer month that brings the Rose   35
Shall take Jamshyd and Kaikobád[7] away.

10

Well, let it take them! What have we to do
With Kaikobád the Great, or Kaikhosrú?
　　Let Zál and Rustum bluster as they will,[8]
Or Hátim[9] call to Supper—heed not you.   40

11

With me along the strip of Herbage strown
That just divides the desert from the sown,
　　Where name of Slave and Sultán is forgot—
And Peace to Mahmúd[1] on his golden Throne!

12

A Book of Verses underneath the Bough,   45
A Jug of Wine, a Loaf of Bread—and Thou
　　Beside me singing in the Wilderness—
Oh, Wilderness were Paradise enow!

13

Some for the Glories of This World; and some
Sigh for the Prophet's[2] Paradise to come;   50
　　Ah, take the Cash, and let the Credit go,
Nor heed the rumble of a distant Drum!

14

Look to the blowing Rose about us—"Lo,
Laughing," she says, "into the world I blow,
　　At once the silken tassel of my Purse   55
Tear, and its Treasure on the Garden throw."

15

And those who husbanded the Golden Grain,
And those who flung it to the winds like Rain,
　　Alike to no such aureate Earth are turned
As, buried once, Men want dug up again.   60

---

7. Founder of a line of Persian kings.   9. A generous host.
8. Kaikhosrú: a king; Zál and Rustum: 1. A sultan who conquered India.
son and father who were warriors.   2. Mohammed's.

16

The Worldly Hope men set their Hearts upon
Turns Ashes—or it prospers; and anon,
   Like Snow upon the Desert's dusty Face,
Lighting a little hour or two—is gone.

17

Think, in this battered Caravanserai[3]   65
Whose Portals are alternate Night and Day,
   How Sultán after Sultán with his Pomp
Abode his destined Hour, and went his way.

18

They say the Lion and the Lizard keep
The Courts where Jamshyd gloried and drank deep;   70
   And Bahrám,[4] that great Hunter—the Wild Ass
Stamps o'er his Head, but cannot break his Sleep.

19

I sometimes think that never blows so red
The Rose as where some buried Caesar bled;
   That every Hyacinth[5] the Garden wears   75
Dropped in her Lap from some once lovely Head.

20

And this reviving Herb whose tender Green
Fledges the River-Lip on which we lean—
   Ah, lean upon it lightly! for who knows
From what once lovely Lip it springs unseen!   80

21

Ah, my Belovéd, fill the Cup that clears
TODAY of past Regrets and future Fears:
   Tomorrow!—Why, Tomorrow I may be
Myself with Yesterday's Sev'n thousand Years.

22

For some we loved, the loveliest and the best   85
That from his Vintage rolling Time hath pressed,
   Have drunk their Cup a Round or two before,
And one by one crept silently to rest.

23

And we, that now make merry in the Room
They left, and Summer dresses in new bloom,
   Ourselves must we beneath the Couch of Earth   90
Descend—ourselves to make a Couch—for whom?

24

Ah, make the most of what we yet may spend,
Before we too into the Dust descend;
   Dust into Dust, and under Dust to lie,   95
Sans Wine, sans Song, sans Singer, and—sans End!

3. Inn.
4. A king who was lost while hunting a wild ass.
5. In classical myth, the hyacinth had associations of sadness because the plant was supposed to have sprung from the blood of Hyacinthus, a beautiful youth who was killed in an accident. Its petals were marked AI, meaning "alas." FitzGerald, however, seems to be referring more particularly to the shape of the flower, as in Homer's *Odyssey* VI.231, where locks of hair are likened to hyacinth clusters.

25

Alike for those who for TODAY prepare,
And those that after some TOMORROW stare,
    A Muezzín[6] from the Tower of Darkness cries,
"Fools, your Reward is neither Here nor There." 100

26

Why, all the Saints and Sages who discussed
Of the Two Worlds so wisely—they are thrust
    Like foolish Prophets forth; their Words to Scorn
Are scattered, and their Mouths are stopped with Dust.

27

Myself when young did eagerly frequent 105
Doctor and Saint, and heard great argument
    About it and about; but evermore
Came out by the same door where in I went.

28

With them the seed of Wisdom did I sow,
And with mine own hand wrought to make it grow; 110
    And this was all the Harvest that I reaped—
"I came like Water, and like Wind I go."

29

Into this Universe, and *Why* not knowing
Nor *Whence*, like Water willy-nilly flowing;
    And out of it, as Wind along the Waste, 115
I know not *Whither*, willy-nilly blowing.

30

What, without asking, hither hurried *Whence?*
And, without asking, *Whither* hurried hence!
    Oh, many a Cup of this forbidden Wine[7]
Must drown the memory of that insolence! 120

31

Up from the Earth's Center through the Seventh Gate
I rose, and on the Throne of Saturn[8] sate,
    And many a Knot unraveled by the Road;
But not the Master-knot of Human Fate.

32

There was the Door to which I found no Key; 125
There was the Veil through which I might not see;
    Some little talk awhile of ME and THEE
There was—and then no more of THEE and ME.

33

Earth could not answer; nor the Seas that mourn
In flowing Purple, of their Lord forlorn; 130
    Nor rolling Heaven, with all his Signs[9] revealed
And hidden by the sleeve of Night and Morn.

34

Then of the THEE IN ME who works behind
The Veil, I lifted up my hands to find

6. One who calls the hour of prayer from the tower of a mosque.
7. Alcohol is forbidden to strict Moslems.
8. The seat of knowledge. According to a note by FitzGerald, Saturn was lord of the seventh heaven.
9. I.e., of the zodiac.

A lamp amid the Darkness; and I heard,
As from Without—"THE ME WITHIN THEE BLIND!"

35
Then to the Lip of this poor earthen Urn
I leaned, the Secret of my Life to learn;
   And Lip to Lip it murmured—"While you live,
Drink!—for, once dead, you never shall return."

36
I think the Vessel, that with fugitive
Articulation answered, once did live,
   And drink; and Ah! the passive Lip I kissed,
How many Kisses might it take—and give!

37
For I remember stopping by the way
To watch a Potter thumping his wet Clay;
   And with its all-obliterated Tongue
It murmured—"Gently, Brother, gently, pray!"

38
And has not such a Story from of Old
Down Man's successive generations rolled
   Of such a clod of saturated Earth
Cast by the Maker into Human mold?

39
And not a drop that from our Cups we throw
For Earth to drink of,[1] but may steal below
   To quench the fire of Anguish in some Eye
There hidden—far beneath, and long ago.

40
As then the Tulip, for her morning sup
Of Heav'nly Vintage, from the soil looks up,
   Do you devoutly do the like, till Heav'n
To Earth invert you—like an empty Cup.

41
Perplexed no more with Human or Divine,
Tomorrow's tangle to the winds resign,
   And lose your fingers in the tresses of
The Cypress-slender Minister of Wine.[2]

42
And if the Wine you drink, the Lip you press,
End in what All begins and ends in—Yes;
   Think then you are TODAY what YESTERDAY
You were—TOMORROW you shall not be less.

43
So when that Angel of the darker Drink
At last shall find you by the river brink,
   And offering his Cup, invite your Soul
Forth to your Lips to quaff—you shall not shrink.

44
Why, if the Soul can fling the Dust aside,

---

1. A reference to the custom of pouring some wine on the ground before drinking in order to refresh some dead and buried wine-drinker.
2. Maiden who serves the wine.

And naked on the Air of Heaven ride,
    Were 't not a Shame—were 't not a Shame for him   175
In this clay carcass crippled to abide?

45

'Tis but a Tent where takes his one day's rest
A Sultán to the realm of Death addressed;
    The Sultán rises, and the dark Ferrásh[3]
Strikes, and prepares it for another Guest.   180

46

And fear not lest Existence closing your
Account, and mine, should know the like no more;
    The Eternal Sákí[4] from that Bowl has poured
Millions of Bubbles like us, and will pour.

47

When You and I behind the Veil are past,   185
Oh, but the long, long while the World shall last,
    Which of our Coming and Departure heeds
As the Sea's self should heed a pebble-cast.

48

A Moment's Halt—a momentary taste
Of BEING from the Well amid the Waste—   190
    And Lo!—the phantom Caravan has reached
The NOTHING it set out from—Oh, make haste!

49

Would you that spangle of Existence spend
About THE SECRET—quick about it, Friend!
    A Hair perhaps divides the False and True—   195
And upon what, prithee, may life depend?

50

A Hair perhaps divides the False and True—
Yes; and a single Alif[5] were the clue—
    Could you but find it—to the Treasure-house,
And peradventure to THE MASTER too;   200

51

Whose secret Presence, through Creation's veins
Running Quicksilver-like, eludes your pains;
    Taking all shapes from Máh to Máhi;[6] and
They change and perish all—but He remains;

52

A moment guessed—then back behind the Fold   205
Immersed of Darkness round the Drama rolled
    Which, for the Pastime of Eternity,
He doth Himself contrive, enact, behold.

53

But if in vain, down on the stubborn floor
Of Earth, and up to Heav'n's unopening Door,   210
    You gaze TODAY, while You are You—how then
TOMORROW, when You shall be You no more?

---

3. Servant who takes down ("strikes") a tent.
4. Servant who passes the wine.
5. The first letter of the Arabic alphabet, represented by a single vertical line.
6. I.e., from lowest to highest.

54

Waste not your Hour, nor in the vain pursuit
Of This and That endeavor and dispute;
 Better be jocund with the fruitful Grape
Than sadden after none, or bitter, Fruit.

55

You know, my Friends, with what a brave Carouse
I made a Second Marriage in my house;
 Divorced old barren Reason from my Bed,
And took the Daughter of the Vine to Spouse.

56

For "Is" and "Is-NOT" though with Rule and Line,
And "UP-AND-DOWN" by Logic, I define,
 Of all that one should care to fathom, I
Was never deep in anything but—Wine.

57

Ah, but my Computations, People say,
Reduced the Year to better reckoning?[7]—Nay,
 'Twas only striking from the Calendar
Unborn Tomorrow, and dead Yesterday.

58

And lately, by the Tavern Door agape,
Came shining through the Dusk an Angel Shape
 Bearing a Vessel on his Shoulder; and
He bid me taste of it; and 'twas—the Grape!

59

The Grape that can with Logic absolute
The Two-and-Seventy jarring Sects[8] confute;
 The sovereign Alchemist that in a trice
Life's leaden metal into Gold transmute;

60

The mighty Mahmúd, Allah-breathing Lord,
That all the misbelieving and black Horde[9]
 Of Fears and Sorrows that infest the Soul
Scatters before him with his whirlwind Sword.

61

Why, be this Juice the growth of God, who dare
Blaspheme the twisted tendril as a Snare?
 A Blessing, we should use it, should we not?
And if a Curse—why, then, Who set it there?

62

I must abjure the Balm of Life, I must,
Scared by some After-reckoning ta'en on trust
 Or lured with Hope of some Diviner Drink,
To fill the Cup—when crumbled into Dust!

---

7. As a mathematician, Omar had devised an improved calendar.
8. "The 72 religions supposed to divide the world" [FitzGerald's note].
9. "Alluding to Sultan Mahmúd's Conquest of India and its dark people" [FitzGerald's note].

63

Oh threats of Hell and Hopes of Paradise!
One thing at least is certain—*This* Life flies;
   One thing is certain and the rest is Lies—
The Flower that once has blown forever dies.   250

64

Strange, is it not? that of the myriads who
Before us passed the door of Darkness through,
   Not one returns to tell us of the Road,   255
Which to discover we must travel too.

65

The Revelations of Devout and Learn'd
Who rose before us, and as Prophets burned,[1]
   Are all but Stories, which, awoke from Sleep,
They told their comrades, and to Sleep returned.   260

66

I sent my Soul through the Invisible,
Some letter of that After-life to spell;
   And by and by my Soul returned to me,
And answered, "I Myself am Heav'n and Hell"—

67

Heaven but the Vision of fulfilled Desire,   265
And Hell the Shadow from a Soul on fire
   Cast on the Darkness into which Ourselves,
So late emerged from, shall so soon expire.

68

We are no other than a moving row
Of Magic Shadow-shapes that come and go   270
   Round with the Sun-illumined Lantern held
In Midnight by the Master of the Show;

69

But helpless Pieces of the Game He plays
Upon this Checkerboard of Nights and Days;
   Hither and thither moves, and checks, and slays,   275
And one by one back in the Closet lays.

70

The Ball no question makes of Ayes and Noes,
But Here or There as strikes the Player[2] goes;
   And He that tossed you down into the Field,
He knows about it all—HE knows—HE knows!   280

71

The Moving Finger writes, and, having writ,
Moves on; nor all your Piety nor Wit
   Shall lure it back to cancel half a Line,
Nor all your Tears wash out a Word of it.

72

And that inverted Bowl they call the Sky,   285
Whereunder crawling cooped we live and die,

---

1. Inspired by burning zeal to spread their prophecies.   2. Polo player.

Lift not your hands to *It* for help—for It
As impotently moves as you or I.

73

With Earth's first Clay They did the Last Man knead,
And there of the Last Harvest sowed the Seed;
   And the first Morning of Creation wrote
What the Last Dawn of Reckoning shall read.

74

YESTERDAY *This* Day's Madness did prepare;
TOMORROW'S Silence, Triumph, or Despair.
   Drink! for you know not whence you came, nor why;
Drink, for you know not why you go, nor where.

75

I tell you this—When, started from the Goal,
Over the flaming shoulders of the Foal
   Of Heav'n Parwín and Mushtarí they flung,
In my predestined Plot of Dust and Soul[3]

76

The Vine had struck a fiber; which about
If clings my Being—let the Dervish[4] flout;
   Of my Base metal may be filed a Key,
That shall unlock the Door he howls without.

77

And this I know: whether the one True Light
Kindle to Love, or Wrath—consume me quite,
   One Flash of It within the Tavern caught
Better than in the Temple lost outright.

78

What! out of senseless Nothing to provoke
A conscious Something to resent the yoke
   Of unpermitted Pleasure, under pain
Of Everlasting Penalties, if broke!

79

What! from his helpless Creature be repaid
Pure Gold for what he lent him dross-allayed—
   Sue for a Debt he never did contract,
And cannot answer—Oh, the sorry trade!

80

O Thou, who didst with pitfall and with gin[5]
Beset the Road I was to wander in,
   Thou wilt not with Predestined Evil round
Enmesh, and then impute my Fall to Sin!

290

295

300

305

310

315

320

3. The speaker asserts that his fate was predestined in accordance with the relationship of the stars and planets at the moment of his birth when he "started from the Goal." In his horoscope, the particular relationship involved the Pleiades ("Parwín") and the planet Jupiter ("Mushtarí") which were "flung" by the gods into a special position in relation to the place in the sky of the constellation Equuleus ("the Foal" or Colt).
4. Ascetic, who would despise ("flout") wine as a means of discovering truth.
5. Trap.

81

O Thou, who Man of Baser Earth didst make,
And ev'n with Paradise devise the Snake,
    For all the Sin wherewith the Face of Man
Is blackened—Man's forgiveness give—and take!

82

As under cover of departing Day   325
Slunk hunger-stricken Ramazán[6] away,
    Once more within the Potter's house alone
I stood, surrounded by the Shapes of Clay—

83

Shapes of all Sorts and Sizes, great and small,
That stood along the floor and by the wall;   330
    And some loquacious Vessels were; and some
Listened perhaps, but never talked at all.

84

Said one among them—"Surely not in vain
My substance of the common Earth was ta'en
    And to this Figure molded, to be broke,   335
Or trampled back to shapeless Earth again."

85

Then said a Second—"Ne'er a peevish Boy
Would break the Bowl from which he drank in joy;
    And He that with his hand the Vessel made
Will surely not in after Wrath destroy."   340

86

After a momentary silence spake
Some Vessel of a more ungainly Make:
    "They sneer at me for leaning all awry;
What! did the Hand, then, of the Potter shake?"

87

Whereat someone of the loquacious Lot—   345
I think a Súfi[7] pipkin—waxing hot—
    "All this of Pot and Potter—Tell me then,
Who is the Potter, pray, and who the Pot?"

88

"Why," said another, "Some there are who tell
Of one who threatens he will toss to Hell   350
    The luckless Pots he marred in making—Pish!
He's a Good Fellow, and 'twill all be well."

89

"Well," murmured one, "Let whoso make or buy,
My Clay with long Oblivion is gone dry;
    But fill me with the old familiar Juice,   355
Methinks I might recover by and by."

6. The month of fasting—during which   7. Mystic.
no food is eaten from sunrise to sunset.

90

So while the Vessels one by one were speaking
The little Moon looked in that all were seeking;[8]
    And then they jogged each other, "Brother! Brother!
Now for the Porter's shoulder-knot[9] a-creaking!"   360

91

Ah, with the Grape my fading Life provide,
And wash the Body whence the Life has died,
    And lay me, shrouded in the living Leaf,
By some not unfrequented Garden-side—

92

That ev'n my buried Ashes such a snare   365
Of Vintage shall fling up into the Air
    As not a True-believer passing by
But shall be overtaken unaware.

93

Indeed the Idols I have loved so long
Have done my credit in this World much wrong,   370
    Have drowned my Glory in a shallow Cup,
And sold my Reputation for a Song.

94

Indeed, indeed, Repentance oft before
I swore—but was I sober when I swore?
    And then and then came Spring, and Rose-in-hand   375
My threadbare Penitence apieces tore.

95

And much as Wine has played the Infidel,
And robbed me of my Robe of Honor—Well,
    I wonder often what the Vintners buy
One-half so precious as the stuff they sell.   380

96

Yet Ah, that Spring should vanish with the Rose!
That Youth's sweet-scented manuscript should close!
    The Nightingale that in the branches sang,
Ah whence, and whither flown again, who knows!

97

Would but the Desert of the Fountain yield   385
One glimpse—if dimly, yet indeed, revealed,
    To which the fainting Traveler might spring,
As springs the trampled herbage of the field.

98

Would but some wingéd Angel ere too late
Arrest the yet unfolded Roll of Fate,   390
    And make the stern Recorder otherwise
Enregister, or quite obliterate!

8. "At the close of the Fasting Month, Ramazán * * * the first Glimpse of the New Moon * * * is looked for with the utmost Anxiety and hailed with all Acclamation" [FitzGerald's note].

9. The rope or strap on which were hung the wine jars carried by the porter.

99

Ah, Love! could you and I with Him conspire
To grasp this sorry Scheme of Things entire,
 Would not we shatter it to bits—and then   395
Remold it nearer to the Heart's Desire!

100

Yon rising Moon that looks for us again—
How oft hereafter will she wax and wane;
 How oft hereafter rising look for us
Through this same Garden—and for *one* in vain!   400

101

And when like her, O Sákí, you shall pass
Among the Guests Star-scattered on the Grass,
 And in your joyous errand reach the spot
Where I made One—turn down an empty Glass!

TAMÁM[1]

1857   1859, 1889

1. "It is ended."

ARTHUR HUGH CLOUGH
(1819–1861)

The writings of Clough (whose name is pronounced so as to rhyme with *rough*) are usually treated as a kind of footnote to those of his friend Matthew Arnold. Read in this way they can indeed add to our understanding of Arnold's early poems written during the phase of religious stress shared by both young men. Some of Clough's admirers argue, however, that such a reading is to be deplored because Clough, despite his frequent clumsiness in versification, is a poet of considerable stature in his own right. What is beyond dispute is that he provides exceptional insights into the intellectual history of his century.

Like many Victorians, Clough was permanently influenced by his mother's pious religious convictions, her influence being reinforced by his years at Rugby School, where he was the prize pupil of Dr. Thomas Arnold. Later, at Oxford, his earnest preoccupation with religious duty was undermined by a number of different intellectual developments. He was forced to think through questions of High Church authoritarianism and traditionalism—provoked by Cardinal Newman's presence at Oxford—and to confront the evidence of scientific critics who challenged the authority and authenticity of the Scriptures. Clough emerged as a skeptic in the real sense of the word. In a letter to his sister in 1847, speaking of the Atonement as an article of Christian faith, he remarks: "I think others are more right who say boldly. We don't understand it, and therefore we *won't* fall down and worship it. Though there is no occasion for adding—'there *is* noth-

ing in it—' I should say, Until I know, I will wait: and if I am not born
with the power to discover, I will do what I can * * * and neither pretend to know, nor without knowing, pretend to embrace: nor yet oppose
those who by whatever means are increasing or trying to increase knowledge." A year later, reflections of this kind led Clough to resign his fellowship at Oxford where he was expected to subscribe to the doctrines of the
Church of England. For the rest of his life he held various educational
posts and also traveled extensively—to the United States, where his early
childhood had been spent, and in Italy, a country which served as the
setting of several of his poems.

Much of Clough's poetry was published posthumously. His first volume, *The Bothie of Tober-na-Vuolich* (1848), is a delightful novel in
verse, an undergraduate love story exhibiting aspects of his character
omitted in Arnold's picture of him in *Thyrsis*. For despite his painful
exposure to religious uncertainties, Clough had a strain of high spirits
and fun that gives flavor to his best poems. In his later poems, including
Dipsychus (1850), the strains of earnestness, uncertainty, and humor are
blended into an ironic point of view different from Matthew Arnold's and,
in fact, different from the characteristic tone of most of his contemporaries.
Perhaps one of the reasons that Clough's poetry has been inadequately
appreciated is that this distinctive tone of his is most evident in his full-
length poems rather than in the short hymnlike verses by which he is
usually represented in anthologies.

Epi-strauss-ium[1]

Matthew and Mark and Luke and holy John
Evanished all and gone!
Yea, he[2] that erst, his dusky curtains quitting,
    Through Eastern pictured panes his level beams transmitting,
    With gorgeous portraits blent,   5
On them his glories intercepted spent,
Southwestering now, through windows plainly glassed,
On the inside face his radiance keen hath cast,
And in the luster lost, invisible, and gone,
Are, say you, Matthew, Mark, and Luke and holy John?   10
Lost, is it? lost, to be recovered never?
However,
The place of worship the meantime with light
Is, if less richly, more sincerely bright,
And in blue skies the Orb is manifest to sight.   15

1847   1869

1. The title is a play on *epi-thalamium*,
which means "concerning the bridal
chamber." The word usually refers to a
song in honor of a bride and bridegroom (as in Spenser's poem). Clough's
title means "concerning Strauss-ism," a
reference to D. F. Strauss, a German
Biblical scholar whose *Life of Jesus*

was translated into English by George
Eliot in 1846. The "light" of Strauss's
analysis reputedly showed up the historical inaccuracy of parts of the Gospels in the Bible.
2. The sun. Cf. lines 13–16 of *Say Not
the Struggle*, below.

The Latest Decalogue

Thou shalt have one God only; who
Would be at the expense of two?
No graven images may be
Worshiped, except the currency.
Swear not at all; for, for thy curse   5
Thine enemy is none the worse.
At church on Sunday to attend
Will serve to keep the world thy friend.
Honor thy parents; that is, all
From whom advancement may befall.   10
Thou shalt not kill; but need'st not strive
Officiously to keep alive.
Do not adultery commit;
Advantage rarely comes of it.
Thou shalt not steal; an empty feat,   15
When it's so lucrative to cheat.
Bear not false witness; let the lie
Have time on its own wings to fly.
Thou shalt not covet, but tradition
Approves all forms of competition.   20

The sum of all is, thou shalt love,
If anybody, God above:
At any rate shall never labor
More than thyself to love thy neighbor.[3]

1862

Say Not the Struggle Nought Availeth

Say not the struggle nought availeth,
   The labor and the wounds are vain,
The enemy faints not, nor faileth,
   And as things have been they remain.

If hopes were dupes, fears may be liars;   5
   It may be, in yon smoke concealed,
Your comrades chase e'en now the fliers,
   And, but for you, possess the field.

For while the tired waves, vainly breaking,
   Seem here no painful inch to gain,   10
Far back, through creeks and inlets making,
   Comes silent, flooding in, the main.

3. Lines 21–24 were discovered in one
of Clough's manuscripts and were not
originally included in published versions
of the poem.

And not by eastern windows only,
    When daylight comes, comes in the light,
In front, the sun climbs slow, how slowly,
    But westward, look, the land is bright.   15

1849   1862

From Dipsychus
I Dreamt a Dream[4]

I dreamt a dream; till morning light
A bell rang in my head all night,
Tinkling and tinkling first, and then
Tolling; and tinkling; tolling again.
So brisk and gay, and then so slow!   5
O joy, and terror! mirth, and woe!
Ting, ting, there is no God; ting, ting—
Dong, there is no God; dong,
There is no God; dong, dong!

Ting, ting, there is no God; ting, ting;   10
Come dance and play, and merrily sing—
Ting, ting a ding; ting, ting a ding!
O pretty girl who trippest along,
Come to my bed—it isn't wrong.
Uncork the bottle, sing the song!   15
Ting, ting a ding: dong, dong.
Wine has dregs; the song an end;
A silly girl is a poor friend
And age and weakness who shall mend?
Dong, there is no God; Dong!   20

Ting, ting a ding! Come dance and sing!
Staid Englishmen, who toil and slave
From your first breeching[5] to your grave,
And seldom spend and always save,
And do your duty all your life   25
By your young family and wife;
Come, be 't not said you ne'er had known
What earth can furnish you alone.
The Italian, Frenchman, German even,
Have given up all thoughts of heaven;   30
And you still linger—oh, you fool!
Because of what you learnt at school.
You should have gone at least to college,

---

4. Dipsychus, the Faust-like hero of Clough's long poem, is in Venice, a city of many bells, where he reports observations and reflections to a companion. The hero's name means "two-souled," a reference to the split between his worldliness and his idealism. This selection is from Scene V, lines 7–92 and 120–29.
5. First wearing of trousers or breeches by a boy.

And got a little ampler knowledge.
Ah well, and yet—dong, dong, dong: 35
Do, if you like, as now you do;
If work's a cheat, so's pleasure too;
And nothing's new and nothing's true;
Dong, there is no God; dong!

O Rosalie, my precious maid,   40
I think thou thinkest love is true;
And on thy fragrant bosom laid
I almost could believe it too.
O in our nook, unknown, unseen,
We'll hold our fancy like a screen,   45
Us and the dreadful fact between.
And it shall yet be long, aye, long,
The quiet notes of our low song
Shall keep us from that sad dong, dong.
Hark, hark, hark! O voice of fear![6]   50
It reaches us here, even here!
Dong, there is no God; dong!

Ring ding, ring ding, tara, tara,
To battle, to battle—haste, haste—
To battle, to battle—aha, aha!   55
On, on, to the conqueror's feast.
From east and west, and south and north,
Ye men of valor and of worth,
Ye mighty men of arms, come forth,
And work your will, for that is just;   60
And in your impulse put your trust,
Beneath your feet the fools are dust.
Alas, alas! O grief and wrong,
The good are weak, the wicked strong;
And O my God, how long, how long?   65
Dong, there is no God; dong!

Ring, ting; to bow before the strong,
There is a rapture too in this;
Speak, outraged maiden, in thy wrong
Did terror bring no secret bliss?   70
Were boys' shy lips worth half a song
Compared to the hot soldier's kiss?
Work for thy master, work, thou slave
He is not merciful, but brave.
Be 't joy to serve, who free and proud   75
Scorns thee and all the ignoble crowd;
Take that, 'tis all thou art allowed,
Except the snaky hope that they
May sometime serve, who rule today,
When, by hell-demons, shan't they pay?   80

6. Cf. *Love's Labour's Lost* (V.ii.911–12): " 'Cuckoo, cuckoo!' O word of fear, / Unpleasing to a married ear!"

O wickedness, O shame and grief,
And heavy load, and no relief!
O God, O God! and which is worst,
To be the curser or the cursed,
The victim or the murderer? Dong   85
Dong, there is no God; dong!

* * *

I had a dream, from eve to light
A bell went sounding all the night.
Gay mirth, black woe, thin joys, huge pain:
I tried to stop it, but in vain.   90
It ran right on, and never broke;
Only when day began to stream
Through the white curtains to my bed,
And like an angel at my head
Light stood and touched me—I awoke,   95
And looked, and said, "It is a dream."

"There Is No God," the Wicked Saith[7]

"There is no God," the wicked saith,
　"And truly it's a blessing,
For what he might have done with us
　It's better only guessing."

"There is no God," a youngster thinks,   5
　"Or really, if there may be,
He surely didn't mean a man
　Always to be a baby."

"There is no God, or if there is,"
　The tradesman thinks, " 'twere funny   10
If he should take it ill in me
　To make a little money."

"Whether there be," the rich man says,
　"It matters very little,
For I and mine, thank somebody,   15
　Are not in want of victual."

Some others, also, to themselves
　Who scarce so much as doubt it,
Think there is none, when they are well,
　And do not think about it.   20

But country folks who live beneath
　The shadow of the steeple;
The parson and the parson's wife,
　And mostly married people;

Youths green and happy in first love,   25
　So thankful for illusion;

7. From *Dipsychus* V.152 ff.

And men caught out in what the world
  Calls guilt, in first confusion;

And almost everyone when age,
  Disease, or sorrows strike him,   30
Inclines to think there is a God,
  Or something very like Him.

1850   1865

ALGERNON CHARLES SWINBURNE

(1837–1909)

Swinburne's writings are of interest in their own right and also as evidence
of the breakdown of conventional Victorian standards during the latter part
of the 19th century. Like the fat boy in *Pickwick Papers* who terrified the
old lady by announcing: "I wants to make your flesh creep," Swinburne set
about shocking his elders by a variety of rebellious gestures. In religion he
appeared to be a pagan; in politics, a liberal republican dedicated to the
overthrow of established governments. And on the subject of love he was
often preoccupied with the pleasures of the lover who inflicts pain or
accepts pain, pleasures of which he had read in the writings of the Marquis
de Sade. As Arnold Bennett said of *Anactoria*, Swinburne played "a rare
trick" on England by "enshrining in the topmost heights of its literature a
lovely poem that cannot be discussed."

To a more limited extent Swinburne also expressed his rebellion against
established codes by his personal behavior. He came from a distinguished
family and attended Eton and Oxford, but sought the company of the
bohemians of Paris and of London where he became temporarily associated
with D. G. Rossetti and other Pre-Raphaelites. By 1879 his dissipations had
profoundly affected his frail physique, and he was obliged to put himself
into the protective custody of a friend, Theodore Watts-Dunton, who
removed him to the countryside and kept him alive although sobered and
tamed.

Swinburne continued to write voluminously, but most of his best poetry
is in his early publications. His early play, *Atalanta in Calydon* (1865), was
described by Swinburne himself as "pure Greek," and his command of
classical allusions here, as well as in other poems, is indeed impressive. Yet
the kind of spirit which he found in Greek literature was not the traditional quality of classic serenity admired by Matthew Arnold. Like Shelley
(the poet he most closely resembles), Swinburne loved Greece as a land of
liberty in which men had expressed themselves with the most complete
unrestraint. To call such an ardently romantic poet "classical" requires a
series of qualifying clauses that make the term meaningless.

In his play and in the volume which followed it, *Poems and Ballads*
(1866), Swinburne demonstrated a metrical virtuosity which dazzled his
early readers and is still dazzling. Those who demand that poetry should
make sense, first and foremost, may find that much of his poetry is not to

their taste. What he offers, instead, are heady rhythmical patterns in which words are relished primarily for sound rather than for sense.

> There lived a singer in France of old
> By the tideless dolorous midland sea.
> In a land of sand and ruin and gold
> There shone one woman, and none but she.

These lines from *The Triumph of Time* have often been cited to illustrate Swinburne's qualities. Like some of the poems of the later French Symbolists, such passages defy traditional kinds of critical analysis and oblige us to reconsider the variety of ways in which poetry may achieve its effects.

Another noteworthy aspect of these poems is their recurring preoccupation with death, as in the memorable recreations of the underworld garden of Proserpine, frozen in timelessness. And as the critic Jerome McGann notes: "No English poet has composed more elegies than Swinburne." The death of any prominent figure, such as Browning, almost always prompted Swinburne to compose a poem for the occasion. Some of these are merely competent editorials in verse; others, especially his moving *Ave Atque Vale* in honor of Charles Baudelaire, are of a different dimension. Swinburne modestly hoped that *Ave Atque Vale* might find its niche as a fourth in line among the major elegies in English, following Milton's *Lycidas*, Shelley's *Adonais*, and Arnold's *Thyrsis*. McGann argues that the "elusive beauty and enigmatic greatness" of Swinburne's elegy make his poem clearly superior to *Thyrsis* and assure *Ave Atque Vale* the third place (at least) in this distinguished quartet.

Choruses from Atalanta in Calydon

When the Hounds of Spring[1]

When the hounds of spring are on winter's traces,
   The mother of months in meadow or plain
Fills the shadows and windy places
   With lisp of leaves and ripple of rain;
And the brown bright nightingale[2] amorous   5
Is half assuaged for Itylus,
For the Thracian ships and the foreign faces,
   The tongueless vigil and all the pain.

Come with bows bent and with emptying of quivers,
   Maiden most perfect, lady of light,   10
With a noise of winds and many rivers,
   With a clamor of waters, and with might;
Bind on thy sandals, O thou most fleet,

1. This choral hymn, with which Swinburne's tragedy opens, is addressed to Artemis (or Diana), virgin goddess and huntress. Artemis was also goddess of the moon and hence, as affecting the seasons, the "mother of months" (line 2).

2. Philomela, after being raped by her brother-in-law and having her tongue cut out, was changed into a nightingale. To obtain revenge, her sister, Procne, killed her own son, Itylus, and fed the child's body to her husband, Tereus, a Thracian king.

Over the splendor and speed of thy feet;
For the faint east quickens, the wan west shivers,   15
   Round the feet of the day and the feet of the night.

Where shall we find her, how shall we sing to her,
   Fold our hands round her knees, and cling?
O that man's heart were as fire and could spring to her,
   Fire, or the strength of the streams that spring!   20
For the stars and the winds are unto her
As raiment, as songs of the harp player;
For the risen stars and the fallen cling to her,
   And the southwest wind and the west wind sing.

For winter's rains and ruins are over,   25
   And all the season of snows and sins;
The days dividing lover and lover,
   The light that loses, the night that wins;
And time remembered is grief forgotten,
And frosts are slain and flowers begotten,   30
And in green underwood and cover
   Blossom by blossom the spring begins.

The full streams feed on flower of rushes,
   Ripe grasses trammel a traveling foot,
The faint fresh flame of the young year flushes   35
   From leaf to flower and flower to fruit;
And fruit and leaf are as gold and fire,
And the oat[3] is heard above the lyre,
And the hooféd heel of a satyr crushes
   The chestnut husk at the chestnut root.   40

And Pan by noon and Bacchus by night,
   Fleeter of foot than the fleet-foot kid,
Follows with dancing and fills with delight
   The Maenad and the Bassarid;[4]
And soft as lips that laugh and hide,   45
The laughing leaves of the trees divide,
And screen from seeing and leave in sight
   The god pursuing, the maiden hid.

The ivy falls with the Bacchanal's hair
   Over her eyebrows hiding her eyes;
The wild vine slipping down leaves bare   50
   Her bright breast shortening into sighs;
The wild vine slips with the weight of its leaves,
But the berried ivy catches and cleaves
To the limbs that glitter, the feet that scare   55
   The wolf that follows, the fawn that flies.

---

3. Musical pipe made from an oaten straw.
4. Participants in the spring festival honoring Dionysus (or Bacchus). Such festivals sometimes developed into frenzied sexual orgies.

Before the Beginning of Years

Before the begining of years
   There came to the making of man
Time, with a gift of tears;
   Grief, with a glass that ran;
Pleasure, with pain for leaven;   5
   Summer, with flowers that fell;
Remembrance fallen from heaven,
   And madness risen from hell;
Strength without hands to smite;
   Love that endures for a breath;   10
Night, the shadow of light,
   And life, the shadow of death.

And the high gods took in hand
   Fire, and the falling of tears,
And a measure of sliding sand   15
   From under the feet of the years;
And froth and drift of the sea;
   And dust of the laboring earth;
And bodies of things to be
   In the houses of death and of birth;   20
And wrought with weeping and laughter,
   And fashioned with loathing and love,
With life before and after
   And death beneath and above,
For a day and a night and a morrow,   25
   That his strength might endure for a span
With travail and heavy sorrow,
   The holy spirit of man.

From the winds of the north and the south
   They gathered as unto strife;   30
They breathed upon his mouth,
   They filled his body with life;
Eyesight and speech they wrought
   For the veils of the soul therein,
A time for labor and thought,   35
   A time to serve and to sin;
They gave him light in his ways,
   And love, and a space for delight,
And beauty and length of days,
   And night, and sleep in the night.   40
His speech is a burning fire;
   With his lips he travaileth;
In his heart is a blind desire,
   In his eyes foreknowledge of death;
He weaves, and is clothed with derision;   45
   Sows, and he shall not reap;
His life is a watch or a vision
   Between a sleep and a sleep.

1865

In the Orchard

(*Provençal Burden*)[1]

Leave go my hands, let me catch breath and see,
Let the dew-fall drench either side of me;
  Clear apple leaves are soft upon that moon
Seen sidelong like a blossom in the tree;
  Ah God, ah God, that day should be so soon.   5

The grass is thick and cool, it lets us lie.
Kissed upon either cheek and either eye,
  I turn to thee as some green afternoon
Turns toward sunset, and is loth to die;
  Ah God, ah God, that day should be so soon.   10

Lie closer, lean your face upon my side,
Feel where the dew fell that has hardly dried,
  Hear how the blood beats that went nigh to swoon;
The pleasure lives there when the sense has died;
  Ah God, ah God, that day should be so soon.   15

O my fair lord, I charge you leave me this:
Is it not sweeter than a foolish kiss?
  Nay take it then, my flower, my first in June,
My rose, so like a tender mouth it is:
  Ah God, ah God, that day should be so soon.   20

Love, till dawn sunder night from day with fire,
Dividing my delight and my desire,
  The crescent life and love the plenilune,[2]
Love me though dusk begin and dark retire;
  Ah God, ah God, that day should be so soon.   25

Ah, my heart fails, my blood draws back; I know,
When life runs over, life is near to go;
  And with the slain of love love's ways are strewn,
And with their blood, if love will have it so;
  Ah God, ah God, that day should be so soon.   30

Ah, do thy will now; slay me if thou wilt;
There is no building now the walls are built,
  No quarrying now the cornerstone is hewn,
No drinking now the vine's whole blood is spilt;
  Ah God, ah God, that day should be so soon.   35

Nay, slay me now; nay, for I will be slain;
Pluck thy red pleasure from the teeth of pain,
  Break down thy vine ere yet grape-gatherers prune,
Slay me ere day can slay desire again;
  Ah God, ah God, that day should be so soon.   40

1. The refrain in the final line of each stanza (termed a *burden*) is used here in the manner of poets of southeastern France (Provence) during the medieval period.
2. Full moon.

Yea, with thy sweet lips, with thy sweet sword; yea,
Take life and all, for I will die, I say;
    Love, I gave love, is life a better boon?
For sweet night's sake I will not live till day;
    Ah God, ah God, that day should be so soon.   45

Nay, I will sleep then only; nay, but go.
Ah sweet, too sweet to me, my sweet, I know
    Love, sleep, and death go to the sweet same tune;
Hold my hair fast, and kiss me through it so.
    Ah God, ah God, that day should be so soon.   50

                                    1865

From The Triumph of Time
I Will Go Back to the Great Sweet Mother

33
I will go back to the great sweet mother,
    Mother and lover of men, the sea.
I will go down to her, I and none other,
    Close with her, kiss her, and mix her with me;
Cling to her, strive with her, hold her fast.   5
O fair white mother, in days long past
Born without sister, born without brother,
    Set free my soul as thy soul is free.

34
O fair green-girdled mother of mine,
    Sea, that art clothed with the sun and the rain,   10
Thy sweet hard kisses are strong like wine,
    Thy large embraces are keen like pain.
Save me and hide me with all thy waves,
Find me one grave of thy thousand graves,
Those pure cold populous graves of thine   15
    Wrought without hand in a world without stain.

35
I shall sleep, and move with the moving ships,
    Change as the winds change, veer in the tide;
My lips will feast on the foam of thy lips,
    I shall rise with thy rising, with thee subside;   20
Sleep, and not know if she[1] be, if she were,
Filled full with life to the eyes and hair,
As a rose is fulfilled to the roseleaf tips
    With splendid summer and perfume and pride.

36
This woven raiment of nights and days,   25
    Were it once cast off and unwound from me,
Naked and glad would I walk in thy ways,
    Alive and aware of thy ways and thee;
Clear of the whole world, hidden at home,

---

1. The woman to whom the poem is addressed. She had deserted the speaker
for another man.

Clothed with the green and crowned with the foam,   30
A pulse of the life of thy straits and bays,
  A vein in the heart of the streams of the sea.

37

Fair mother, fed with the lives of men,
  Thou art subtle and cruel of heart, men say.
Thou hast taken, and shalt not render again;   35
  Thou art full of thy dead, and cold as they.
But death is the worst that comes of thee;
Thou art fed with our dead, O mother, O sea,
But when hast thou fed on our hearts? or when,
  Having given us love, hast thou taken away?   40

38

O tender-hearted, O perfect lover,
  Thy lips are bitter, and sweet thine heart.
The hopes that hurt and the dreams that hover,
  Shall they not vanish away and apart?
But thou, thou art sure, thou art older than earth;   45
Thou art strong for death and fruitful of birth;
Thy depths conceal and thy gulfs discover;
  From the first thou wert; in the end thou art.

1862–66   1866

Hymn to Proserpine

(AFTER THE PROCLAMATION IN ROME OF THE CHRISTIAN FAITH)

Vicisti, Galilaee [1]

I have lived long enough, having seen one thing, that love hath an
    end;
Goddess and maiden and queen, be near me now and befriend.
Thou art more than the day or the morrow, the seasons that laugh
    or that weep;
For these give joy and sorrow; but thou, Proserpina, sleep.
Sweet is the treading of wine, and sweet the feet of the dove;   5
But a goodlier gift is thine than foam of the grapes or love.
Yea, is not even Apollo, with hair and harpstring of gold,
A bitter god to follow, a beautiful god to behold?
I am sick of singing; the bays[2] burn deep and chafe. I am fain
To rest a little from praise and grievous pleasure and pain.   10

1. "Thou hast conquered, O Galilean" —words supposedly addressed to Christ by the Roman emperor, Julian the Apostate, on his deathbed in 363. Julian had tried to revive paganism and to discourage Christianity, which, after a proclamation of 313, had been tolerated in Rome. His efforts, however, were unsuccessful. The speaker of the poem, a Roman patrician and also a poet (line 9), is like the Emperor Julian: he prefers the old order of pagan gods. His hymn is addressed to the goddess Proserpine, who was carried off by Hades (or Pluto) to be queen of the lower world. In this role she is addressed in the poem as goddess of death and of sleep. The speaker also associates her with the earth itself (line 93) because she was the daughter of Demeter (or Ceres), goddess of agriculture, whose name means "earth-mother." Swinburne may have derived some details here from the 4th-century Latin poet Claudian, whose long narrative *The Rape of Proserpine* provides helpful background for this hymn.
2. Laurel leaves of a poet's crown.

For the gods we know not of, who give us our daily breath,
We know they are cruel as love or life, and lovely as death.

O gods dethroned and deceased, cast forth, wiped out in a day!
From your wrath is the world released, redeemed from your chains,
     men say.
New gods are crowned in the city; their flowers have broken your
     rods;
                                                                    15
They are merciful, clothed with pity, the young compassionate gods.
But for me their new device is barren, the days are bare;
Things long past over suffice, and men forgotten that were.
Time and the gods are at strife; ye dwell in the midst thereof,
Draining a little life from the barren breasts of love.   20
I say to you, cease, take rest; yea, I say to you all, be at peace,
Till the bitter milk of her breast and the barren bosom shall cease.

Wilt thou yet take all, Galilean? But these thou shalt not take—
The laurel, the palms, and the paean, the breasts of the nymphs in
     the brake,
Breasts more soft than a dove's, that tremble with tenderer breath;
And all the wings of the Loves, and all the joy before death;   26
All the feet of the hours that sound as a single lyre,
Dropped and deep in the flowers, with strings that flicker like fire.
More than these wilt thou give, things fairer than all these things?
Nay, for a little we live, and life hath mutable wings.   30
A little while and we die; shall life not thrive as it may?
For no man under the sky lives twice, outliving his day.
And grief is a grievous thing, and a man hath enough of his tears;
Why should he labor, and bring fresh grief to blacken his years?

Thou hast conquered, O pale Galilean; the world has grown gray
     from thy breath;
                                                                    35
We have drunken of things Lethean,[3] and fed on the fullness of
     death.
Laurel is green for a season, and love is sweet for a day;
But love grows bitter with treason, and laurel outlives not May.
Sleep, shall we sleep after all? for the world is not sweet in the end;
For the old faiths loosen and fall, the new years ruin and rend.   40
Fate is a sea without shore, and the soul is a rock that abides;
But her ears are vexed with the roar and her face with the foam of
     the tides.
O lips that the live blood faints in, the leavings of racks and rods!
O ghastly glories of saints, dead limbs of gibbeted gods!
Though all men abase them before you in spirit, and all knees bend,
I kneel not, neither adore you, but standing look to the end.   46

All delicate days and pleasant, all spirits and sorrows are cast
Far out with the foam of the present that sweeps to the surf of the
     past;

---

3. I.e., of Lethe, a river in the lower world. By drinking its waters the dead forgot
the past.

Where beyond the extreme sea wall, and between the remote sea
    gates,
Waste water washes, and tall ships founder, and deep death waits;
Where, mighty with deepening sides, clad about with the seas as
    with wings,   51
And impelled of invisible tides, and fulfilled of unspeakable things,
White-eyed and poisonous-finned, shark-toothed and serpentine-
    curled,
Rolls, under the whitening wind of the future, the wave of the
    world.
The depths stand naked in sunder behind it, the storms flee away;
In the hollow before it the thunder is taken and snared as a prey; 56
In its sides is the north wind bound; and its salt is of all men's tears,
With light of ruin, and sound of changes, and pulse of years;
With travail of day after day, and with trouble of hour upon hour.
And bitter as blood is the spray; and the crests are as fangs that de-
    vour;   60
And its vapor and storm of its steam as the sighing of spirits to be;
And its noise as the noise in a dream; and its depths as the roots of
    the sea;
And the height of its heads as the height of the utmost stars of the
    air;
And the ends of the earth at the might thereof tremble, and time
    is made bare.
Will ye bridle the deep sea with reins, will ye chasten the high sea
    with rods?   65
Will ye take her to chain her with chains, who is older than all ye
    gods?
All ye as a wind shall go by, as a fire shall ye pass and be past;
Ye are gods, and behold, ye shall die, and the waves be upon you
    at last.
In the darkness of time, in the deeps of the years, in the changes
    of things,
Ye shall sleep as a slain man sleeps, and the world shall forget you
    for kings.   70
Though the feet of thine high priests tread where thy lords and our
    forefathers trod,
Though these that were gods are dead, and thou being dead art a
    god,
Though before thee the throned Cytherean[4] be .fallen, and hidden
    her head,
Yet thy kingdom shall pass, Galilean, thy dead shall go down to
    thee dead.

Of the maiden thy mother men sing as a goddess with grace clad
    around;   75
Thou art throned where another was king; where another was queen
    she is crowned.
Yea, once we had sight of another; but now she is queen, say these.

---

4. Aphrodite (or Venus), who was born from the waves near the island of
Cythera.

Not as thine, not as thine was our mother, a blossom of flowering
    seas,
Clothed round with the world's desire as with raiment, and fair as
    the foam,
And fleeter than kindled fire, and a goddess, and mother of Rome.[5]
For thine came pale and a maiden, and sister to sorrow; but ours,   81
Her deep hair heavily laden with odor and color of flowers,
White rose of the rose-white water, a silver splendor, a flame,
Bent down unto us that besought her, and earth grew sweet with
    her name.
For thine came weeping, a slave among slaves, and rejected; but she
Came flushed from the full-flushed wave, and imperial, her foot on
    the sea.   86
And the wonderful waters knew her, the winds and the viewless
    ways,
And the roses grew rosier, and bluer the sea-blue stream of the bays.

Ye are fallen, our lords, by what token? we wist that ye should not
    fall.
Ye were all so fair that are broken; and one more fair than ye all.   90
But I turn to her[6] still, having seen she shall surely abide in the end;
Goddess and maiden and queen, be near me now and befriend.
O daughter of earth, of my mother, her crown and blossom of birth,
I am also, I also, thy brother; I go as I came unto earth.
In the night where thine eyes are as moons are in heaven, the night
    where thou art,   95
Where the silence is more than all tunes, where sleep overflows
    from the heart,
Where the poppies are sweet as the rose in our world, and the red
    rose is white,
And the wind falls faint as it blows with the fume of the flowers of
    the night,
And the murmur of spirits that sleep in the shadow of gods from
    afar
Grows dim in thine ears and deep as the deep dim soul of a star,   100
In the sweet low light of thy face, under heavens untrod by the sun,
Let my soul with their souls find place, and forget what is done and
    undone.
Thou art more than the gods who number the days of our temporal
    breath;
For these give labor and slumber; but thou, Proserpina, death.
Therefore now at thy feet I abide for a season in silence. I know   105
I shall die as my fathers died, and sleep as they sleep; even so.
For the glass of the years is brittle wherein we gaze for a span.
A little soul for a little bears up this corpse which is man.
So long I endure, no longer; and laugh not again, neither weep.   109
For there is no god found stronger than death; and death is a sleep.

                                                    1866

---

5. **Aeneas, the founder of Rome, was** said to have been the son of Aphrodite.
6. **Proserpine.**

The Garden of Proserpine[1]

Here, where the world is quiet;
　　Here, where all trouble seems
Dead winds' and spent waves' riot
　　In doubtful dreams of dreams;
I watch the green field growing 　　　　　　5
For reaping folk and sowing,
For harvest time and mowing,
　　A sleepy world of streams.

I am tired of tears and laughter,
　　And men that laugh and weep; 　　　　10
Of what may come hereafter
　　For men that sow to reap;
I am weary of days and hours,
Blown buds of barren flowers,
Desires and dreams and powers 　　　　　15
　　And everything but sleep.

Here life has death for neighbor,
　　And far from eye or ear
Wan waves and wet winds labor,
　　Weak ships and spirits steer; 　　　　20
They drive adrift, and whither
They wot not who make thither;
But no such winds blow hither,
　　And no such things grow here.

No growth of moor or coppice, 　　　　　25
　　No heather flower or vine,
But bloomless buds of poppies,
　　Green grapes of Proserpine,
Pale beds of blowing rushes,
Where no leaf blooms or blushes 　　　　30
Save this whereout she crushes
　　For dead men deadly wine.

Pale, without name or number,
　　In fruitless fields of corn,[2]
They bow themselves and slumber 　　　35
　　All night till light is born;
And like a soul belated,
In hell and heaven unmated,
By cloud and mist abated
　　Comes out of darkness morn. 　　　　40

1. Or Proserpina, the goddess who was carried off by Hades (or Pluto) to be queen of the lower world. According to some accounts, she had there a garden of ever-blooming flowers. The Greek and Roman festivals honoring her and her mother, Ceres, emphasized Proserpine's return to the upper world in spring. In Swinburne's poems, however, the emphasis is on her role as goddess of death and eternal sleep. Swinburne also associates her with the sea, which he usually represents as eternally unchanging despite its surface changefulness.
2. Wheat or grain.

Though one were strong as seven,
    He too with death shall dwell,
Nor wake with wings in heaven,
    Nor weep for pains in hell;
Though one were fair as roses,   45
His beauty clouds and closes;
And well though love reposes,
    In the end it is not well.

Pale, beyond porch and portal,
    Crowned with calm leaves, she stands   50
Who gathers all things mortal
    With cold immortal hands;
Her languid lips are sweeter
Than love's who fears to greet her
To men that mix and meet her   55
    From many times and lands.

She waits for each and other,
    She waits for all men born;
Forgets the earth her mother,
    The life of fruits and corn;   60
And spring and seed and swallow
Take wing for her and follow
Where summer song rings hollow
    And flowers are put to scorn.

There go the loves that wither,   65
    The old loves with wearier wings;
And all dead years draw thither,
    And all disastrous things;
Dead dreams of days forsaken,
Blind buds that snows have shaken,   70
Wild leaves that winds have taken,
    Red strays of ruined springs.

We are not sure of sorrow,
    And joy was never sure;
Today will die tomorrow;   75
    Time stoops to no man's lure;
And love, grown faint and fretful,
With lips but half regretful
Sighs, and with eyes forgetful
    Weeps that no loves endure.   80

From too much love of living,
    From hope and fear set free,
We thank with brief thanksgiving
    Whatever gods may be
That no life lives forever;   85
That dead men rise up never;
That even the weariest river
    Winds somewhere safe to sea.

Then star nor sun shall waken,
  Nor any change of light:
Nor sound of waters shaken,   90
  Nor any sound or sight:
Nor wintry leaves nor vernal,
Nor days nor things diurnal;
Only the sleep eternal   95
  In an eternal night.

1866

Ave Atque Vale[1]

In Memory of Charles Baudelaire

Nous devrions pourtant lui porter quelques fleurs;
Les morts, les pauvres morts, ont de grandes douleurs,
Et quand Octobre souffle, émondeur des vieux arbres,
Son vent mélancolique à l'entour de leurs marbres,
Certe, ils doivent trouver les vivants bien ingrats.
                    —"*Les Fleurs du Mal.*"

Shall I strew on thee rose or rue or laurel,[2]
  Brother, on this that was the veil[3] of thee?
  Or quiet sea-flower molded by the sea,
Or simplest growth of meadow-sweet or sorrel,
  Such as the summer-sleepy Dryads[4] weave,   5
  Waked up by snow-soft sudden rains at eve?
Or wilt thou rather, as on earth before,
  Half-faded fiery blossoms, pale with heat
  And full of bitter summer, but more sweet
To thee than gleanings of a northern shore   10
  Trod by no tropic feet?[5]

1. "Hail and farewell"—a line from an elegy by Catullus occasioned by a farewell visit to the grave of his brother to whom he brought gifts, a situation closely echoed in Swinburne's final stanza. Swinburne's elegy likewise begins with a visit to the grave of a man whom the poet regards as a brother but had never met. Charles Baudelaire (1821–1867) had impressed Swinburne as one of the "most perfect poets of the century." In 1861, in an essay on the second edition of Baudelaire's collection *Les Fleurs du Mal* ("Flowers of Evil," 1857), Swinburne had commented on the French poet's preoccupation with "sad and strange things"—"the sharp and cruel enjoyments of pain, the acrid relish of suffering felt or inflicted"; "it has the languid, lurid beauty of close and threatening weather—a heavy, heated temperature, with dangerous hothouse scents in it." These qualities are also celebrated in Swinburne's elegy into which are woven many allusions to Baudelaire's poems, especially his *Litanies de Satan*, which Swinburne regarded as the "keynote" poem of *Les Fleurs du Mal*. The epigraph, from *La servante au grand coeur* ("The great-hearted servant") may be translated: "We must nevertheless bring some flowers to her [or him]. The dead, the poor dead, have great sadnesses. And when October, the pruner of old trees, blows its melancholy wind in the vicinity of their marble tombs, then indeed they must find the living highly ungrateful."
2. Symbols of love, mourning, and poetic fame.
3. I.e., the body as a veil for the soul.
4. Wood-nymphs.
5. A voyage to the tropics in Baudelaire's youth made a lasting impact on his poetry.

II

For always thee the fervid languid glories
 Allured of heavier suns in mightier skies;
 Thine ears knew all the wandering watery sighs
Where the sea sobs round Lesbian promontories,   15
 The barren kiss of piteous wave to wave
 That knows not where is that Leucadian grave[6]
Which hides too deep the supreme head of song.
 Ah, salt and sterile as her kisses were,
 The wild sea winds her and the green gulfs bear   20
Hither and thither, and vex and work her wrong,
 Blind gods that cannot spare.

III

Thou sawest, in thine old singing season, brother,
 Secrets and sorrows unbeheld of us:
 Fierce loves, and lovely leaf-buds poisonous,   25
Bare to thy subtler eye, but for none other
 Blowing by night in some unbreathed-in clime;
 The hidden harvest of luxurious time,
Sin without shape, and pleasure without speech;
 And where strange dreams in a tumultuous sleep   30
 Make the shut eyes of stricken spirits weep;
And with each face thou sawest the shadow on each,
 Seeing as men sow men reap.[7]

IV

O sleepless heart and somber soul unsleeping,
 That were athirst for sleep and no more life   35
 And no more love, for peace and no more strife!
Now the dim gods of death have in their keeping
 Spirit and body and all the springs of song,
 Is it well now where love can do no wrong,
Where stingless pleasure has no foam or fang   40
 Behind the unopening closure of her lips?
 Is it not well where soul from body slips
And flesh from bone divides without a pang
 As dew from flower-bell drips?

V

It is enough; the end and the beginning   45
 Are one thing to thee, who art past the end.
 O hand unclasped of unbeholden friend,
For thee no fruits to pluck, no palms for winning,
 No triumph and no labor and no lust,
 Only dead yew-leaves and a little dust.   50
O quiet eyes wherein the light saith naught,
 Whereto the day is dumb, nor any night

---

6. According to legend the poetess Sappho, who was born on the island of Lesbos, destroyed herself by leaping from the rock of Leucas into the Ionian Sea.

In this section Swinburne makes allusions to Baudelaire's *Lesbos*.
7. See Galatians vi.7, "Whatsoever a man soweth, that shall he also reap."

With obscure finger silences your sight,
Nor in your speech the sudden soul speaks thought,
Sleep, and have sleep for light.   55

VI

Now all strange hours and all strange loves are over,
    Dreams and desires and somber songs and sweet,
    Hast thou found place at the great knees and feet
Of some pale Titan-woman like a lover,
    Such as thy vision here solicited,[8]   60
    Under the shadow of her fair vast head,
The deep division of prodigious breasts,
    The solemn slope of mighty limbs asleep,
    The weight of awful tresses that still keep
The savor and shade of old-world pine forests   65
    Where the wet hill-winds weep?

VII

Hast thou found any likeness for thy vision?
    O gardener of strange flowers, what bud, what bloom,
    Hast thou found sown, what gathered in the gloom?
What of despair, of rapture, of derision,   70
    What of life is there, what of ill or good?
    Are the fruits gray like dust or bright like blood?
Does the dim ground grow any seed of ours,
    The faint fields quicken any terrene root,
    In low lands where the sun and moon are mute   75
And all the stars keep silence? Are there flowers
    At all, or any fruit?

VIII

Alas, but though my flying song flies after,
    O sweet strange elder singer, thy more fleet
    Singing, and footprints of thy fleeter feet,   80
Some dim derision of mysterious laughter
    From the blind tongueless warders of the dead,
    Some gainless glimpse of Proserpine's[9] veiled head,
Some little sound of unregarded tears
    Wept by effaced unprofitable eyes,   85
And from pale mouths some cadence of dead sighs—
    These only, these the hearkening spirit hears,
    Sees only such things rise.

IX

Thou art far too far for wings of words to follow,
    Far too far off for thought or any prayer.   90
    What ails us with thee, who art wind and air?
What ails us gazing where all seen is hollow?
    Yet with some fancy, yet with some desire,
    Dreams pursue death as winds a flying fire,

---

8. An allusion to Baudelaire's *Le Géante*   9. Queen of the underworld.
("The Giantess").

Our dreams pursue our dead and do not find.   95
    Still, and more swift than they, the thin flame flies,
    The low light fails us in elusive skies,
Still the foiled earnest ear is deaf, and blind
    Are still the eluded eyes.

X

Not thee, O never thee, in all time's changes,   100
    Not thee, but this the sound of thy sad soul,
    The shadow of thy swift spirit, this shut scroll
I lay my hand on, and not death estranges
    My spirit from communion of thy song—
    These memories and these melodies that throng   105
Veiled porches of a Muse funereal—[1]
    These I salute, these touch, these clasp and fold
    As though a hand were in my hand to hold,
Or through mine ears a mourning musical
    Of many mourners rolled.   110

XI

I among these, I also, in such station
    As when the pyre was charred, and piled the sods,
    And offering to the dead made, and their gods,
The old mourners had, standing to make libation,
    I stand, and to the gods and to the dead   115
    Do reverence without prayer or praise, and shed
Offering to these unknown, the gods of gloom,
    And what of honey and spice my seedlands bear,
    And what I may of fruits in this chilled air,
And lay, Orestes-like, across the tomb   120
    A curl of severed hair.[2]

XII

But by no hand nor any treason stricken,
    Not like the low-lying head of Him, the King,
    The flame that made of Troy a ruinous thing,
Thou liest, and on this dust no tears could quicken   125
    There fall no tears like theirs[3] that all men hear
    Fall tear by sweet imperishable tear
Down the opening leaves of holy poets' pages.
    Thee not Orestes, not Electra mourns;
    But bending us-ward with memorial urns   130
The most high Muses that fulfill all ages
    Weep, and our God's heart yearns.

---

1. According to Jerome McGann, Swinburne associates Baudelaire's distinctive kind of poetry with a tenth muse, one who inspires songs of lamentation ("funereal"). What is meant by this muse's "veiled porches" seems tantalizingly obscure.
2. For lines 120–29, see Aeschylus' *Choëphoroe*, 4–8. King Agamemnon, after returning from Troy, had been treacherously slain, an event that made "a ruinous thing" of the Greek victory. His son, Orestes, visits Agamemnon's grave and dedicates on it a lock of his own hair which is later discovered by his sister, Electra, who mournfully visits her father's grave to offer libations.
3. Referring to the muses and holy poets, not to Orestes and Electra (noted by Jerome McGann).

XIII

For, sparing of his sacred strength, not often
    Among us darkling here the lord of light[4]
    Makes manifest his music and his might   135
In hearts that open and in lips that soften
    With the soft flame and heat of songs that shine.
    Thy lips indeed he touched with bitter wine,
And nourished them indeed with bitter bread;
    Yet surely from his hand thy soul's food came;   140
    The fire that scarred thy spirit at his flame
Was lighted, and thine hungering heart he fed
    Who feeds our hearts with fame.

XIV

Therefore he too now at thy soul's sunsetting,
    God of all suns and songs he too bends down   145
    To mix his laurel with thy cypress crown,[5]
And save thy dust from blame and from forgetting.
    Therefore he too, seeing all thou wert and art,
    Compassionate, with sad and sacred heart,
Mourns thee of many his children the last dead,   150
    And hallows with strange tears and alien sighs
    Thine unmelodious mouth and sunless eyes,
And over thine irrevocable head
    Sheds light from the under skies.[6]

XV

And one weeps with him in the ways Lethean,[7]   155
    And stains with tears her changing bosom chill;
    That obscure Venus of the hollow hill,
That thing transformed which was the Cytherean,
    With lips that lost their Grecian laugh divine
    Long since, and face no more called Erycine;[8]   160
A ghost, a bitter and luxurious god.
    Thee also with fair flesh and singing spell
    Did she, a sad and second prey,[9] compel
Into the footless places once more trod,
    And shadows hot from hell.   165

XVI

And now no sacred staff shall break in blossom,[1]
    No choral salutation lure to light
    A spirit sick with perfume and sweet night

4. Apollo, god of light and poetry.
5. "Laurel": the crown of Apollo, a wreath honoring poets; "Cypress": associated with mourning.
6. Flickering flaming light of the underworld.
7. Lethe was the river of oblivion in Hades.
8. The Venus of medieval legends held her court inside a mountain in Germany (the Hörselberg). This later Venus is a transformed version of the joyous foam-born goddess associated wih the island of Cythera and also worshiped in Sicily at a shrine on Mt. Eryx (hence *Erycine*). Horace described her as "blithe goddess of Eryx, about whom hover mirth and desire" (*Odes*, I, ii, 33–34).
9. The first "prey" of Venus had been Tannhäuser, whom she had lured into the "footless places" of her cave; Baudelaire is her "second prey." Swinburne, after reading Baudelaire's pamphlet on Wagner's *Tannhäuser*, described this Venus as "the queen of evil, the lady of lust."
1. After Tannhäuser's pilgrimage to Rome to seek absolution for having lived in sin with Venus, a miraculous event occurred: the Pope's staff burst into blossom:

And love's tired eyes and hands and barren bosom.
    There is no help for these things; none to mend   170
    And none to mar; not all our songs, O friend,
Will make death clear or make life durable.
    Howbeit with rose and ivy and wild vine
    And with wild notes about this dust of thine
At least I fill the place where white dreams dwell[2]   175
    And wreathe an unseen shrine.

XVII

Sleep; and if life was bitter to thee, pardon,
    If sweet, give thanks; thou hast no more to live;
    And to give thanks is good, and to forgive.
Out of the mystic and the mournful garden   180
    Where all day through thine hands in barren braid
    Wove the sick flowers of secrecy and shade,
Green buds of sorrow and sin, and remnants grey,
    Sweet-smelling, pale with poison, sanguine-hearted,
    Passions that sprang from sleep and thoughts that started, 185
Shall death not bring us all as thee one day
    Among the days departed?

XVIII

For thee, O now a silent soul, my brother,
    Take at my hands this garland, and farewell.
    Thin is the leaf, and chill the wintry smell,   190
And chill the solemn earth, a fatal mother,
    With sadder than the Niobean womb,[3]
    And in the hollow of her breasts a tomb.
Content thee, howsoe'er, whose days are done;
    There lies not any troublous thing before,   195
    Nor sight nor sound to war against thee more,
For whom all winds are quiet as the sun,
    All waters as the shore.

1866-67   1868

---

2. Presumably the abode of the ghosts of the dead.

3. Niobe's fourteen children were slain by Apollo and Artemis.

FRANCIS THOMPSON
(1859–1907)

Francis Thompson's career seems like a tale from one of the novels of Graham Greene. The son of Roman Catholic converts, he was anxious to enter the priesthood but was not considered to be an eligible candidate. Later, after an unsuccessful attempt to complete medical school, he moved to London. Here he lived for several years as a tramp, suffering painfully not only from poverty but from an addiction to opium: when in his poems Thompson speaks of being an outcast, he speaks with the authority of experience. In 1888 he was rescued by a magazine editor, Wilfred Meynell, who recognized his literary talents and encouraged him to publish his poems. Owing to shattered health and also to a marked streak of indolence, Thompson's output in poetry was not extensive, but in his few best poems his achievement is impressive and distinctive. As his friend Coventry Patmore noted, *The Hound of Heaven* is one of the finest odes in English literature. In its fast-paced passages it may remind us of the odes of Shelley, about whom Thompson wrote an appreciative essay. An even more important influence than Shelley upon Thompson was that of the 17th-century metaphysical poets, and his poetry is therefore, like Browning's, a bridge to much of the poetry of the 20th century. Thompson was especially attracted by the 17th-century Roman Catholic poet Richard Crashaw. The Crashaw-like blending of religious fervor and striking conceits (such as "traitorous trueness"), evident in the very title of *The Hound of Heaven*, seemed merely fantastic to some of Thompson's readers in the 1890's. To later readers, accustomed to the metaphysical devices of much 20th-century poetry, it has seemed less bizarre. Interesting comparisons may also be made between Thompson and Gerard Manley Hopkins, another Roman Catholic writer who likewise demonstrated, as the 19th century drew to its close, the exceptional variety of achievements in the poetry of the Victorian age.

The Hound of Heaven

I fled Him,[1] down the nights and down the days;
    I fled Him, down the arches of the years;
I fled Him, down the labyrinthine ways
    Of my own mind; and in the mist of tears
I hid from Him, and under running laughter.   5
        Up vistaed hopes I sped;
        And shot, precipitated,
Adown Titanic glooms of chasmed fears,
    From those strong Feet that followed, followed after.
        But with unhurrying chase,   10
        And unperturbéd pace,
    Deliberate speed, majestic instancy,[2]
        They beat—and a Voice beat
        More instant than the Feet—
    "All things betray thee, who betrayest Me."   15

        I pleaded, outlaw-wise,
By many a hearted casement, curtained red,
    Trellised with intertwining charities
(For, though I knew His love Who followed,
        Yet was I sore adread   20
Lest, having Him, I must have nought beside);[3]
But, if one little casement parted wide,
    The gust of His approach would clash it to.

1. Cf. St. Augustine, *Confessions* IV.iv. 7: "And lo, Thou wert close on the heels of those fleeing from Thee, God of vengeance and fountain of mercies, both at the same time, who turnest us to Thyself by most wonderful means."
2. Urgency.

3. The speaker, afraid that love of God will exclude other kinds of love, is seeking shelter in one of the warm dwellings associated with human love. But his pursuer cuts off his escape, forcing him to remain outside, an outcast (lines 22–23).

Fear wist not to evade, as Love wist to pursue.[4]
Across the margent[5] of the world I fled,   25
  And troubled the gold gateways of the stars,
  Smiting for shelter on their clangèd bars;
       Fretted to dulcet jars
And silvern chatter the pale ports o' the moon.[6]
I said to dawn, Be sudden; to eve, Be soon;   30
  With thy young skyey blossoms heap me over
      From this tremendous Lover!
Float thy vague veil about me, lest He see!
  I tempted all His servitors, but to find
My own betrayal in their constancy,   35
In faith to Him their fickleness to me,
  Their traitorous trueness, and their loyal deceit.
To all swift things for swiftness did I sue;
  Clung to the whistling mane of every wind.
      But whether they swept, smoothly fleet,   40
      The long savannahs[7] of the blue;
       Or whether, Thunder-driven,
      They clanged his chariot 'thwart a heaven
Plashy with flying lightnings round the spurn o' their feet—
  Fear wist not to evade as Love wist to pursue.   45
      Still with unhurrying chase,
      And unperturbèd pace,
    Deliberate speed, majestic instancy,
      Came on the following Feet,
      And a Voice above their beat—   50
    "Nought shelters thee, who wilt not shelter Me."

I sought no more that after which I strayed
      In face of man or maid;
But still within the little children's eyes
      Seems something, something that replies;   55
They at least are for me, surely for me!
I turned me to them very wistfully;
But, just as their young eyes grew sudden fair
      With dawning answers there,
Their angel plucked them from me by the hair.   60
"Come then, ye other children, Nature's—share
With me" (said I) "your delicate fellowship;
      Let me greet you lip to lip,
      Let me twine with you caresses,
       Wantoning   65
      With our Lady-Mother's[8] vagrant tresses,
       Banqueting
      With her in her wind-walled palace,
      Underneath her azured daïs,[9]
      Quaffing, as your taintless way is,   70

4. This line apparently means that Fear did not know how to escape so effectively as Love knew how to pursue.
5. Boundary.
6. I.e., shook the gates of the moon until they gave forth soft and silvery sounds.
7. Plains.
8. Mother Nature's.
9. Blue canopy of the sky.

From a chalice
Lucent-weeping out of the dayspring."[1]
So it was done;
I in their delicate fellowship was one—
Drew the bolt of Nature's secrecies.   75
I knew all the swift importings[2]
On the willful face of skies;
I knew how the clouds arise
Spuméd of the wild sea-snortings;
All that's born or dies   80
Rose and drooped with—made them shapers
Of mine own moods, or wailful or divine—
With them joyed and was bereaven.
I was heavy with the even,
When she lit her glimmering tapers   85
Round the day's dead sanctities.
I laughed in the morning's eyes.
I triumphed and I saddened with all weather,
Heaven and I wept together,
And its sweet tears were salt with mortal mine;   90
Against the red throb of its sunset-heart
I laid my own to beat,
And share commingling heat;
But not by that, by that, was eased my human smart.
In vain my tears were wet on Heaven's gray cheek.   95
For ah! we know not what each other says,
These things and I; in sound *I* speak—
Their sound is but their stir, they speak by silences.
Nature, poor stepdame, cannot slake my drouth;
Let her, if she would owe[3] me,   100
Drop yon blue bosom-veil of sky, and show me
The breasts o' her tenderness;
Never did any milk of hers once bless
My thirsting mouth.
Nigh and nigh draws the chase,   105
With unperturbéd pace,
Deliberate speed, majestic instancy;
And past those noiséd Feet
A voice comes yet more fleet—
"Lo nought contents thee, who content'st not Me."   110

Naked I wait Thy love's uplifted stroke!
My harness[4] piece by piece Thou hast hewn from me,
And smitten me to my knee;
I am defenseless utterly.
I slept, methinks, and woke,   115
And, slowly gazing, find me stripped in sleep.
In the rash lustihead of my young powers,
I shook the pillaring hours
And pulled my life upon me;[5] grimed with smears,

1. Overflowing with shining light from
the sun (i.e., the children of Nature
drink the sunshine).
2. Meanings.

3. Own.
4. Armor.
5. Like Samson when he shook the
pillars of the temple of Dagon and

I stand amid the dust o' the mounded years— 120
My mangled youth lies dead beneath the heap.
My days have crackled and gone up in smoke,
Have puffed and burst as sun-starts[6] on a stream.
       Yea, faileth now even dream
The dreamer, and the lute the lutanist; 125
Even the linked fantasies, in whose blossomy twist
I swung the earth a trinket at my wrist,
Are yielding;[7] cords of all too weak account
For earth with heavy griefs so overplussed.
       Ah! is Thy love indeed 130
A weed, albeit an amaranthine[8] weed,
Suffering no flowers except its own to mount?
       Ah! must—
       Designer infinite!—
Ah! must Thou char the wood ere Thou canst limn[9] with it? 135
My freshness spent its wavering shower i' the dust;
And now my heart is as a broken fount,
Wherein tear-drippings stagnate, spilt down ever
       From the dank thoughts that shiver
Upon the sightful branches of my mind. 140
       Such is; what is to be?
The pulp so bitter, how shall taste the rind?
I dimly guess what Time in mists confounds;
Yet ever and anon a trumpet sounds
From the hid battlements of Eternity; 145
Those shaken mists a space unsettle, then
Round the half-glimpséd turrets slowly wash again.
       But not ere him who summoneth
       I first have seen, enwound
With glooming robes purpureal, cypress-crowned; 150
His name I know, and what his trumpet saith.
Whether man's heart or life it be which yields
       Thee harvest, must Thy harvest fields
       Be dunged with rotten death?

         Now of that long pursuit 155
         Comes on at hand the bruit;[1]
       That Voice is round me like a bursting sea:
         "And is thy earth so marred,
         Shattered in shard[2] on shard?
       Lo, all things fly thee, for thou fliest Me! 160
         Strange, piteous, futile thing,
Wherefore should any set thee love apart?
Seeing none but I makes much of nought" (He said)
"And human love needs human meriting,
       How hast thou merited— 165
Of all man's clotted clay the dingiest clot?
       Alack, thou knowest not

---

pulled down the roof on his head (Judges xvi).
6. Bubbles.
7. I.e., even his power of creating an imaginary world by poetry and song ("linked fantasies") is now inadequate.
8. Unfading and immortal.
9. Draw, as with charcoal.
1. Noise.
2. Fragment, as of broken pottery.

How little worthy of any love thou art!
Whom wilt thou find to love ignoble thee
　　　　　Save Me, save only Me?　　　　　170
All which I took from thee I did but take,
　　　　　Not for thy harms,
But just that thou might'st seek it in My arms.
　　　　　All which thy child's mistake
Fancies as lost, I have stored for thee at home;　　175
　　　　　Rise, clasp My hand, and come!"

　　Halts by me that footfall;
　　Is my gloom, after all,
Shade of His hand, outstretched caressingly?
　　"Ah, fondest,[3] blindest, weakest,　　　　180
　　I am He Whom thou seekest!
Thou dravest love from thee, who dravest Me."

1890–92　　　　　　　　　　　　　　　　　　1893

The Kingdom of God[4]

"IN NO STRANGE LAND"

O world invisible, we view thee,
O world intangible, we touch thee,
O world unknowable, we know thee,
Inapprehensible, we clutch thee!

Does the fish soar to find the ocean,　　　　5
The eagle plunge to find the air—
That we ask of the stars in motion
If they have rumor of thee there?

Not where the wheeling systems darken,
And our benumbed conceiving soars!—　　　10
The drift of pinions, would we hearken,
Beats at our own clay-shuttered doors.

The angels keep their ancient places—
Turn but a stone and start a wing!
'Tis ye, 'tis your estrangéd faces,　　　　15
That miss the many-splendored thing.

But (when so sad thou canst not sadder)
Cry—and upon thy so sore loss
Shall shine the traffic of Jacob's ladder
Pitched betwixt Heaven and Charing Cross.[5]　　20

Yea, in the night, my Soul, my daughter,
Cry—clinging Heaven by the hems;
And lo, Christ walking on the water,
Not of Genesareth,[6] but Thames!

1908

---

3. Most foolish (archaic meaning).
4. Cf. Luke xvii.21: "The Kingdom of God is within you." See also Exodus ii.22, and Psalms cxxxvii.4.
5. An intersection in London.
6. The Sea of Galilee (cf. Matthew xiv.25–33).

Nonsense Verse

Despite its later reputation as an age of gloom, the Victorian age featured a remarkable outburst of humorous prose and verse from the time of Dickens' *Pickwick Papers* at the beginning of the period to the Gilbert and Sullivan operas near the end. The following selections are restricted to one kind of humor—a Victorian specialty—nonsense-writing. Shakespeare had exploited nonsense on occasion, and so have James Joyce and James Thurber, but the Victorians were more adept in this genre than any other generation has been. Freudian explanations can be devised to account for its appearance during this particular period, and indeed if nonsense-writing does originate in a writer's repressions we may have a clue to the undertone of melancholy that some readers detect in the verses of Edward Lear and Lewis Carroll. The best nonsense-writing, however, raises its own less solemn problems. Lear and Carroll created a zany upside-down world full of puzzles: the attempt to solve such puzzles, even when they cannot be solved, is in itself a perennial satisfaction.

EDWARD LEAR
(1812–1888)

Edward Lear was a landscape painter who spent much of his life in Mediterranean countries. In 1846 he published his first *Book of Nonsense*, a collection of limericks for children. The form of the limerick was not invented by Lear, but his use of it served to establish its popularity. In later volumes of the *Book of Nonsense* he used other forms of verse, some of them modeled on rhythms which had been developed by his close friend Tennyson. All of his own poems were characteristically classified by Lear as "nonsense pure and absolute," yet it is as the author of *The Owl and the Pussy-Cat*, *The Jumblies*, and other poems that Lear is remembered. Evidently pure and absolute nonsense is a rare art.

How Pleasant to Know Mr. Lear

"How pleasant to know Mr. Lear!"
Who has written such volumes of stuff!
Some think him ill-tempered and queer,
But a few think him pleasant enough.

His mind is concrete and fastidious,   5
    His nose is remarkably big;
His visage is more or less hideous,
    His beard it resembles a wig.

He has ears, and two eyes, and ten fingers,
    Leastways if you reckon two thumbs;   10
Long ago he was one of the singers,
    But now he is one of the dumbs.

He sits in a beautiful parlor,
    With hundreds of books on the wall;
He drinks a great deal of Marsala,   15
    But never gets tipsy at all.

He has many friends, lay men and clerical,
    Old Foss is the name of his cat;
His body is perfectly spherical,
    He weareth a runcible[1] hat.   20

When he walks in waterproof white,
    The children run after him so!
Calling out, "He's come out in his night-
    Gown, that crazy old Englishman, oh!"

He weeps by the side of the ocean,   25
    He weeps on the top of the hill;
He purchases pancakes and lotion,
    And chocolate shrimps from the mill.

He reads, but he cannot speak, Spanish,
    He cannot abide ginger beer: 30
Ere the days of his pilgrimage vanish,
    How pleasant to know Mr. Lear!

                                    1871

Limerick

There was a young man in Iowa
Who exclaimed, "Where on earth shall I stow her!"
Of his sister he spoke, who was felled by an Oak
        Which abound in the plains of Iowa.

                                    1933

The Jumblies

They went to sea in a sieve, they did;
    In a sieve they went to sea;

1. A runcible spoon is a spoon-shaped fork with a cutting edge.

In spite of all their friends could say,
On a winter's morn, on a stormy day,
   In a sieve they went to sea.   5
And when the sieve turned round and round,
And everyone cried, "You'll be drowned!"
They called aloud, "Our sieve ain't big,
But we don't care a button; we don't care a fig—
   In a sieve we'll go to sea!"   10
     Far and few, far and few,
       Are the lands where the Jumblies live.
       Their heads are green, and their hands are blue;
       And they went to sea in a sieve.

They sailed away in a sieve, they did,   15
   In a sieve they sailed so fast,
With only a beautiful pea-green veil
Tied with a ribbon, by way of a sail,
   To a small tobacco-pipe mast.
And everyone said who saw them go,   20
"Oh! won't they be soon upset, you know,
For the sky is dark, and the voyage is long;
And, happen what may, it's extremely wrong
   In a sieve to sail so fast."

The water it soon came in, it did;   25
   The water it soon came in.
So, to keep them dry, they wrapped their feet
In a pinky paper all folded neat;
   And they fastened it down with a pin.
And they passed the night in a crockery-jar;   30
And each of them said, "How wise we are!
Though the sky be dark, and the voyage be long,
Yet we never can think we were rash or wrong,
   While round in our sieve we spin."

And all night long they sailed away;   35
   And, when the sun went down,
They whistled and warbled a moony song
To the echoing sound of a coppery gong,
   In the shade of the mountains brown,
"O Timballoo! how happy we are   40
When we live in a sieve and a crockery-jar!
And all night long, in the moonlight pale,
We sail away with a pea-green sail
   In the shade of the mountains brown."

They sailed to the Western Sea, they did—   45
   To a land all covered with trees;
And they bought an owl, and a useful cart,
And a pound of rice, and a cranberry tart,
   And a hive of silvery bees;
And they bought a pig, and some green jackdaws,   50

And a lovely monkey with lollipop paws,
And seventeen bags of edelweiss tea,
And forty bottles of ring-bo-ree,
    And no end of Stilton cheese.

And in twenty years they all came back—   55
    In twenty years or more;
And everyone said, "How tall they've grown!
For they've been to the Lakes, and the Torrible Zone,
    And the hills of the Chankly Bore."
And they drank their health, and gave them a feast   60
Of dumplings made of beautiful yeast;
And everyone said, "If we only live,
We, too, will go to sea in a sieve,
    To the hills of the Chankly Bore."
        Far and few, far and few,   65
        Are the lands where the Jumblies live.
    Their heads are green, and their hands are blue;
        And they went to sea in a sieve.

                                                           1871

Cold Are the Crabs

Cold are the crabs that crawl on yonder hills,
Colder the cucumbers that grow beneath,
And colder still the brazen chops that wreathe
    The tedious gloom of philosophic pills!
For when the tardy film of nectar fills   5
The ample bowls of demons and of men,
There lurks the feeble mouse, the homely hen,
    And there the porcupine with all her quills.
Yet much remains—to weave a solemn strain
That lingering sadly—slowly dies away,   10
Daily departing with departing day.
A pea-green gamut on a distant plain
When wily walruses in congress meet—
    Such such is life—

                                                           1953

LEWIS CARROLL
(1832–1898)

Charles Lutwidge Dodgson was a deacon in the Anglican Church and a
lecturer in mathematics at Oxford. Most of his publications were mathematical treatises, but his fame rests on the strange pair of books he wrote

for children: *Alice in Wonderland* (1865) and *Through the Looking-Glass* (1871), both published under the pseudonym Lewis Carroll. Like *Gulliver's Travels* these narratives have long been enjoyed, at different levels, by both children and adults. The various songs scattered through the stories are sometimes parodies, as, for example, *The Aged, Aged Man,* but more often they are classic examples of nonsense verse. Poems such as *Jabberwocky* exhibit a mathematician's fondness for puzzles combined with a literary man's fondness for word games. At this level *Jabberwocky* can be enjoyed as a small-scale *Finnegans Wake*.

Carroll learned something of his art from Edward Lear, also an eccentric Victorian bachelor, but Carroll's nonsense, hovering often on the brink of satire, has more edge to it.

Jabberwocky[1]

'Twas brillig, and the slithy toves
    Did gyre and gimble in the wabe;
All mimsy were the borogoves,
    And the mome raths outgrabe.

"Beware the Jabberwock, my son!   5
    The jaws that bite, the claws that catch!
Beware the Jubjub bird, and shun
    The frumious Bandersnatch!"

He took his vorpal sword in hand;
    Long time the manxome foe he sought—   10
So rested he by the Tumtum tree,
    And stood awhile in thought.

And, as in uffish thought he stood,
    The Jabberwock, with eyes of flame,
Came whiffling through the tulgey wood,   15
    And burbled as it came!

One, two! One, two! And through and through
    The vorpal blade went snicker-snack!
He left it dead, and with its head
    He went galumphing back.   20

"And hast thou slain the Jabberwock?
    Come to my arms, my beamish boy!
O frabjous day! Callooh! Callay!"
    He chortled in his joy.

'Twas brillig, and the slithy toves   25
    Did gyre and gimble in the wabe;

1. From *Through the Looking-Glass,* Chapter I.

>All mimsy were the borogoves,
>   And the mome raths outgrabe.

1855   1871

[*Humpty Dumpty's Explication of* Jabberwocky][2]

"You seem very clever at explaining words, Sir," said Alice. "Would you kindly tell me the meaning of the poem *Jabberwocky?*"

"Let's hear it," said Humpty Dumpty. "I can explain all the poems that ever were invented—and a good many that haven't been invented just yet."

This sounded very hopeful, so Alice repeated the first verse:

>" 'Twas brillig, and the slithy toves
>   Did gyre and gimble in the wabe;
>All mimsy were the borogoves,
>   And the mome raths outgrabe."

"That's enough to begin with," Humpty Dumpty interrupted: "there are plenty of hard words there. 'Brillig' means four o'clock in the afternoon—the time when you begin *broiling* things for dinner."

"That'll do very well," said Alice: "and 'slithy'?"[3]

"Well, 'slithy' means 'lithe and slimy.' 'Lithe' is the same as 'active.' You see it's like a portmanteau—there are two meanings packed up into one word."

"I see it now," Alice remarked thoughtfully: "and what are 'toves'?"

"Well, 'toves' are something like badgers—they're something like lizards—and they're something like corkscrews."

"They must be very curious creatures."

"They are that," said Humpty Dumpty: "also they make their nests under sundials—also they live on cheese."

"And what's to 'gyre' and to 'gimble'?"

"To 'gyre' is to go round and round like a gyroscope. To 'gimble' is to make holes like a gimlet."

"And the 'wabe' is the grass plot round a sundial, I suppose?" said Alice, surprised at her own ingenuity.

"Of course it is. It's called 'wabe,' you know, because it goes a long way before it, and a long way behind it——"

"And a long way beyond it on each side," Alice added.

"Exactly so. Well then, 'mimsy' is 'flimsy and miserable' (there's another portmanteau for you). And a 'borogove' is a thin shabby-looking bird with its feathers sticking out all round—something like a live mop."

2. From *Through the Looking-Glass,* Chapter VI.

3. Concerning the pronunciation of these words, Carroll later said: "The 'i' in 'slithy' is long, as in 'writhe'; and 'toves' is pronounced so as to rhyme with 'groves.' Again, the first 'o' in 'borogroves' is pronounced like the 'o' in 'borrow.' I have heard people try to give it the sound of the 'o' in 'worry.' Such is Human Perversity."

"And then 'mome raths'?" said Alice. "If I'm not giving you too much trouble."

"Well, a 'rath' is a sort of green pig: but 'mome' I'm not certain about. I think it's short for 'from home'—meaning that they'd lost their way, you know."

"And what does 'outgrabe' mean?"

"Well, 'outgribing' is something between bellowing and whistling, with a kind of sneeze in the middle: however, you'll hear it done, maybe—down in the wood yonder—and when you've once heard it you'll be *quite* content. Who's been repeating all that hard stuff to you?"

"I read it in a book," said Alice.

1871

The White Knight's Song[4]

I'll tell thee everything I can;
    There's little to relate.
I saw an aged, aged man,
    A-sitting on a gate.
"Who are you, aged man?" I said.   5
    "And how is it you live?"
And his answer trickled through my head
    Like water through a sieve.

He said "I look for butterflies
    That sleep among the wheat;   10
I make them into mutton-pies,
    And sell them in the street.
I sell them unto men," he said,
    "Who sail on stormy seas;
And that's the way I get my bread—   15
    A trifle, if you please."

But I was thinking of a plan
    To dye one's whiskers green,
And always use so large a fan
    That they could not be seen.   20
So, having no reply to give
    To what the old man said,
I cried, "Come, tell me how you live!"
    And thumped him on the head.

His accents mild took up the tale;   25
    He said, "I go my ways,
And when I find a mountain-rill,

4. From Chapter VIII of *Through the Looking-Glass.* Cf. Wordsworth's poem concerning the aged leech-gatherer: *Resolution and Independence.*

I set it in a blaze;
And thence they make a stuff they call
    Rowland's Macassar Oil—   30
Yet twopence-halfpenny is all
    They give me for my toil."

But I was thinking of a way
    To feed oneself on batter,
And so go on from day to day   35
    Getting a little fatter.
I shook him well from side to side,
    Until his face was blue;
"Come, tell me how you live," I cried
    "And what it is you do!"   40

He said, "I hunt for haddocks' eyes
    Among the heather bright,
And work them into waistcoat-buttons
    In the silent night.
And these I do not sell for gold   45
    Or coin of silvery shine,
But for a copper halfpenny,
    And that will purchase nine.

"I sometimes dig for buttered rolls,
    Or set limed twigs for crabs;   50
I sometimes search the grassy knolls
    For wheels of hansom-cabs.
And that's the way" (he gave a wink)
    "By which I get my wealth—
And very gladly will I drink   55
    Your Honor's noble health."

I heard him then, for I had just
    Completed my design
To keep the Menai bridge[5] from rust
    By boiling it in wine.   60
I thanked him much for telling me
    The way he got his wealth,
But chiefly for his wish that he
    Might drink my noble health.

And now, if e'er by chance I put   65
    My fingers into glue,
Or madly squeeze a right-hand foot
    Into a left-hand shoe,
Or if I drop upon my toe
    A very heavy weight,   70
I weep, for it reminds me so
Of that old man I used to know—
Whose look was mild, whose speech was slow,

5. Railway bridge in Wales (completed in 1850).

Whose hair was whiter than the snow,
Whose face was very like a crow,   75
With eyes, like cinders, all aglow,
Who seemed distracted with his woe.
Who rocked his body to and fro,
And muttered mumblingly and low,
As if his mouth were full of dough,   80
Who snorted like a buffalo—
That summer evening long ago
   A-sitting on a gate.

1856   1871

The Walrus and the Carpenter[6]

The sun was shining on the sea,
   Shining with all his might;
He did his very best to make
   The billows smooth and bright—
And this was odd, because it was   5
   The middle of the night.

The moon was shining sulkily,
   Because she thought the sun
Had got no business to be there
   After the day was done—   10
"It's very rude of him," she said,
   "To come and spoil the fun!"

The sea was wet as wet could be,
   The sands were dry as dry.
You could not see a cloud, because   15
   No cloud was in the sky;
No birds were flying overhead—
   There were no birds to fly.

The Walrus and the Carpenter
   Were walking close at hand;   20
They wept like anything to see
   Such quantities of sand.
"If this were only cleared away,"
   They said, "it *would* be grand!"

"If seven maids with seven mops   25
   Swept it for half a year,
Do you suppose," the Walrus said,
   "That they could get it clear?"
"I doubt it," said the Carpenter,
   And shed a bitter tear.   30

6. Recited by Tweedledee in Chapter IV of *Through the Looking-Glass*.

"O Oysters, come and walk with us!"
  The Walrus did beseech.
"A pleasant walk, a pleasant talk,
  Along the briny beach;
We cannot do with more than four,
  To give a hand to each."   35

The eldest Oyster looked at him,
  But never a word he said;
The eldest Oyster winked his eye,
  And shook his heavy head—
Meaning to say he did not choose   40
  To leave the oyster-bed.

But four young Oysters hurried up,
  All eager for the treat;
Their coats were brushed, their faces washed,   45
  Their shoes were clean and neat—
And this was odd, because, you know,
  They hadn't any feet.

Four other Oysters followed them,
  And yet another four;   50
And thick and fast they came at last,
  And more, and more, and more—
All hopping through the frothy waves,
  And scrambling to the shore.

The Walrus and the Carpenter   55
  Walked on a mile or so,
And then they rested on a rock
  Conveniently low;
And all the little Oysters stood
  And waited in a row.   60

"The time has come," the Walrus said,
  "To talk of many things:
Of shoes—and ships—and sealing-wax—
  Of cabbages—and kings—
And why the sea is boiling hot—   65
  And whether pigs have wings."

"But wait a bit," the Oysters cried,
  "Before we have our chat;
For some of us are out of breath,
  And all of us are fat!"   70
"No hurry!" said the Carpenter.
  They thanked him much for that.

"A loaf of bread," the Walrus said,
  "Is what we chiefly need;
Pepper and vinegar besides   75
  Are very good indeed—

Now, if you're ready, Oysters dear,
  We can begin to feed."

"But not on us!" the Oysters cried,
  Turning a little blue.   80
"After such kindness, that would be
  A dismal thing to do!"
"The night is fine," the Walrus said,
  "Do you admire the view?

"It was so kind of you to come!   85
  And you are very nice!"
The Carpenter said nothing but
  "Cut us another slice.
I wish you were not quite so deaf—
  I've had to ask you twice!"   90

"It seems a shame," the Walrus said,
  "To play them such a trick,
After we've brought them out so far,
  And made them trot so quick!"
The Carpenter said nothing but   95
  "The butter's spread too thick!"

"I weep for you," the Walrus said;
  "I deeply sympathize."
With sobs and tears he sorted out
  Those of the largest size,   100
Holding his pocket-handkerchief
  Before his streaming eyes.

"O Oysters," said the Carpenter,
  "You've had a pleasant run!
Shall we be trotting home again?"   105
  But answer came there none—
And this was scarcely odd, because
  They'd eaten every one.

1871

From The Hunting of the Snark
The Baker's Tale

They roused him[7] with muffins—they roused him with ice—
  They roused him with mustard and cress—
They roused him with jam and judicious advice—
  They set him conundrums to guess.

7. I.e., the Baker, a member of the Snark-hunting expedition. He had fainted when the leader of the crew, the Bellman, had mentioned that one species of Snark is called Boojum. The nameless Baker's fear of Boojums turns out later to have been well founded: at the end of the poem he encounters a Boojum and is never seen again.

When at length he sat up and was able to speak,   5
  His sad story he offered to tell;
And the Bellman cried, "Silence! Not even a shriek!"
  And excitedly tingled his bell.

There was silence supreme! Not a shriek, not a scream,
  Scarcely even a howl or a groan,   10
As the man they called "Ho!" told his story of woe
  In an antediluvian tone.

"My father and mother were honest though poor—"
  "Skip all that!" cried the Bellman in haste.
"If it once becomes dark, there's no chance of a Snark— 15
  We have hardly a minute to waste!"

"I skip forty years," said the Baker, in tears,
  "And proceed without further remark
To the day when you took me aboard of your ship
  To help you in hunting the Snark.   20

"A dear uncle of mine (after whom I was named)
  Remarked, when I bade him farewell—"
"Oh, skip your dear uncle!" the Bellman exclaimed,
  As he angrily tingled his bell.

"He remarked to me then," said that mildest of men, 25
  " 'If your Snark be a Snark, that is right;
Fetch it home by all means—you may serve it with greens,
  And it's handy for striking a light.

" 'You may seek it with thimbles—and seek it with care;
  You may hunt it with forks and hope;   30
You may threaten its life with a railway-share;
  You may charm it with smiles and soap—' "

("That's exactly the method," the Bellman bold
  In a hasty parenthesis cried,
"That's exactly the way I have always been told   35
  That the capture of Snarks should be tried!")

" 'But oh, beamish[8] nephew, beware of the day,
  If your Snark be a Boojum! For then
You will softly and suddenly vanish away,
  And never be met with again!'   40

"It is this, it is this that oppresses my soul,
  When I think of my uncle's last words;
And my heart is like nothing so much as a bowl
  Brimming over with quivering curds!

"It is this, it is this—" "We have had that before!" 45
  The Bellman indignantly said.
And the Baker replied, "Let me say it once more.
  It is this, it is this that I dread!

---

8. See *Jabberwocky*, line 22.

"I engage with the Snark—every night after dark—
   In a dreamy, delirious fight;   50
I serve it with greens in those shadowy scenes,
   And I use it for striking a light;

"But if ever I meet with a Boojum, that day,
   In a moment (of this I am sure),
I shall softly and suddenly vanish away—   55
   And the notion I cannot endure!"

1874–76   1876

Critical and Controversial Prose

In his essay on *Style* (1889), Walter Pater argued that prose was "the special and opportune art of the modern world." His contention was not that prose is superior to verse but that it more readily conveys the "chaotic variety and complexity" of modern life, the "incalculable" intellectual diversity of the "master currents of the present time." Whether prose is a more appropriate medium than verse to communicate the "chaotic variety" of an age remains a matter of dispute, but what Pater says of the age itself would be much more generally agreed upon. Toward this condition of their age the Victorian writers of nonfictional prose responded in a variety of ways and in a variety of styles. Each sought in his distinctive manner to create some sort of order out of the chaos. Pater himself, coming to maturity late in the century, differs from the others in his distaste for controversy. By writing critical essays celebrating a beautifully ordered world of art and literature, Pater sought to rise above the flux and chaos which he saw as characteristic of his century. His four predecessors (featured in the following selections) were more engaged in shaping and reconstructing the social order. John Henry Newman, John Stuart Mill, John Ruskin, and T. H. Huxley use prose primarily as an instrument of persuasion and argument. Mill generally relies most upon logical argument, Ruskin upon a thunderous rhetoric, Huxley upon what seems to be common sense, and Newman upon a variety of persuasive devices, but however different their tools of argument, the writings of all four men can be appropriately grouped under the heading of "controversial prose."

The essays and treatises of each of these writers can be independently enjoyed in their own right. Even more effectively, however, each can be profitably related to the others and also to Carlyle and Arnold, two masters of nonfictional prose who are represented at length in the present anthology. Such a comparative study reduces our sense of chaotic diversity by making us aware that the Victorian prose writers were linked by a common concern for the fate of man in an industrial, democratic, and increasingly secularized society. Of their interlocking debates on education, leadership, and the role of science and religion, C. F. Harrold aptly says: "What they wrote constitutes a fascinating chapter in the history of the English mind, and also provides a perspective for viewing much that continues to perplex the world. Above all, a survey of their beliefs and assumptions will illuminate the richness of their prose, a prose which is often highly allusive, sometimes deceptively simple, and always susceptible to fresh and profitable interpretation as the symbol of their thought and the eloquent expression of their convictions."

JOHN HENRY CARDINAL NEWMAN
(1801–1890)

Newman's writings may be appropriately classified under the heading of "controversial prose," for at several points in his long lifetime he found himself at the center of some of the most intense disputes that stirred Victorian England, disputes in which he himself emerged as a controversialist of great skill—engagingly persuasive in defense of his position and devastatingly effective in disposing of opponents. Thomas Hardy, whose position was at the opposite extreme from Newman's, paid him a high compliment when he noted in his diary: "Worked at J. H. Newman's *Apologia* which we have all been talking about lately. * * * Style charming and his logic really human, being based not on syllogisms but on converging probabilities. Only—and here comes the fatal catastrophe—there is no first link to his excellent chain of reasoning, and down you come headlong."

Newman was born in London, the son (like Browning) of a banker. In his spiritual autobiography, *Apologia Pro Vita Sua* (in effect, his vindication of his life), he traces the principal stages of his religious development from the strongly Protestant period of his youth to his conversion to Roman Catholicism in 1845. Along the way, after being elected to a fellowship at Oriel College in Oxford and becoming an Anglican clergyman, he was attracted briefly into the orbit of religious liberalism. Gradually coming to realize, however, that liberalism, with its reliance upon human reason, would be powerless to defend traditional religion from attack, Newman shifted over into the new High Church wing of the Anglican Church and soon was recognized as the leading figure of the Oxford Movement. During the 1830's he attracted a large and influential following by his sermons at Oxford and his writing of tracts. His efforts to demonstrate the dogmatic and authoritative tradition of Anglicanism finally provoked so much opposition that he was reduced to silence. After much reflection he took the final step. At the age of 44 he entered the Roman Catholic priesthood and moved to Birmingham where he spent the rest of his life. In 1879 he was created Cardinal.

Despite his mastery of prose style, Newman found the act of composition to be even more painfully difficult than most of us do. During his years at Birmingham he was nevertheless prompted to write several books including works of religious poetry and fiction. Most celebrated is the series of articles, published as his *Apologia* in 1864, in which he replied to an attack upon his intellectual honesty made by Charles Kingsley. Although parts of the *Apologia*, being devoted to fine points of theological doctrine and church history, are difficult for the ordinary reader to follow, the main argument is clearly and persuasively developed. The dignity and candor with which Newman reviewed the stages of his religious development, the repeated appeals to his fellow countrymen's sense of honesty and fair play, the unobtrusively beautiful prose style, gained for his masterpiece a sympathetic audience even among those who had been least disposed to listen to his side of the dispute with Kingsley.

Seemingly less controversial than the *Apologia* are Newman's lectures on the aims of education which were delivered in Dublin at the newly-founded Catholic University of Ireland, a university of which he was for a few years the rector. These lectures, published in 1852 and later entitled *The Idea of a University*, are a classic statement of the value of "the disciplined intellect" which can be developed by a liberal education rather than by a technical training. The lectures may be compared with the later lectures of Matthew Arnold and T. H. Huxley.

It should be noted that Newman's view of a liberal education is largely independent of his religious position. Such an education, he said, could form the minds of profligates and anticlericals as well as of saints and priests of the church. In considerable measure his view reflects his admiration for the kind of intellectual enlargement he had himself enjoyed as an undergraduate at Trinity College, Oxford. One of the most touching passages in the *Apologia* is Newman's account of his farewell to an Oxford friend, in February, 1846, as he was preparing his final departure from the precincts of the university he loved:

In him I took leave of my first College, Trinity, which was so dear to me. * * * There used to be much snapdragon growing on the walls opposite my freshman's rooms there, and I had taken it as the emblem of my perpetual residence even unto death in my University.

On the morning of the 23rd I left the Observatory. I have never seen Oxford since, excepting its spires, as they are seen from the railway.

From The Idea of a University
From *Discourse* V. *Knowledge Its Own End*

6

Now bear with me, Gentlemen, if what I am about to say has at first sight a fanciful appearance. Philosophy, then, or Science, is related to Knowledge in this way: Knowledge is called by the name of Science or Philosophy, when it is acted upon, informed, or if I may use a strong figure, impregnated by Reason. Reason is the principle of that intrinsic fecundity of Knowledge, which, to those who possess it, is its especial value, and which dispenses with the necessity of their looking abroad for any end to rest upon external to itself. Knowledge, indeed, when thus exalted into a scientific form, is also power; not only is it excellent in itself, but whatever such excellence may be, it is something more, it has a result beyond itself. Doubtless; but that is a further consideration, with which I am not concerned. I only say that, prior to its being a power, it is a good; that it is, not only an instrument, but an end. I know well it may resolve itself into an art, and terminate in a mechanical process, and in tangible fruit; but it also may fall back upon that Reason which informs it, and resolve itself into Philosophy. In one case it is called Useful Knowledge, in the other Liberal. The same person may cultivate it in both ways at once; but this again is a matter foreign to my subject; here I do but say that there are two ways of using Knowledge, and in matter of fact those who use it in one way are not likely to use it in the other, or at least in a very limited measure. You see, then, here are two methods of Education; the end of the one is to be philosophical, of the other to be mechanical; the one rises towards general ideas, the other is exhausted upon what is particular and external. Let me not be thought to deny the necessity, or to decry the benefit, of such attention to what is particular and practical, as belongs to the useful or mechanical arts; life could not go on without them; we owe our daily welfare to them; their exercise is the duty of the many, and we owe to the many a debt of gratitude for fulfilling that duty. I only say that Knowledge, in proportion as it tends more and more to be particular, ceases to be Knowledge. It is a question whether Knowledge can in any proper sense be predicated of the brute creation; without pretending to metaphysical exactness of phraseology, which would be unsuitable to an occasion like this, I say, it seems to me improper to call that passive sensation, or perception of things, which brutes seem to possess, by the name of Knowledge. When I speak of Knowledge, I mean something intellectual, something which grasps what it perceives through the senses; something which takes a view of things; which sees more than the senses convey; which reasons upon what it sees, and while it sees; which invests it with an idea. It expresses itself, not in a mere enunciation, but by an enthymeme:[1] it is of the nature of science from the first, and in this consists its dignity. The principle of real dignity in Knowledge, its worth, its desirableness, considered irrespectively of its results, is this germ within it of a scientific or a philosophical process. This is how it comes to be an end in itself; this is why it admits of being called Liberal. Not to know the relative disposition of things is the state of slaves or children; to have mapped out the Universe is the boast, or at least the ambition, of Philosophy.

Moreover, such knowledge is not a mere extrinsic or accidental advantage, which is ours today and another's tomorrow, which may be got up from a book, and easily forgotten again, which we can command or communicate at our pleasure, which we can borrow for the occasion, carry about in our hand, and take into the market; it is an acquired illumination, it is a habit, a personal possession, and an inward endowment. And this is the reason why it is more correct, as well as more usual, to speak of a University as a place of education than of instruction, though, when knowledge is concerned, instruction would at first sight have seemed the more appropriate word. We are instructed, for instance, in manual exercises,

1. A syllogism in which one of the premises is understood but not stated.

in the fine and useful arts, in trades, and in ways of business; for these are methods, which have little or no effect upon the mind itself, are contained in rules committed to memory, to tradition, or to use, and bear upon an end external to themselves. But education is a higher word; it implies an action upon our mental nature, and the formation of a character; it is something individual and permanent, and is commonly spoken of in connection with religion and virtue. When, then, we speak of the communication of Knowledge as being Education, we thereby really imply that that Knowledge is a state or condition of mind; and since cultivation of mind is surely worth seeking for its own sake, we are thus brought once more to the conclusion, which the word "Liberal" and the word "Philosophy" have already suggested, that there is a Knowledge, which is desirable, though nothing come of it, as being of itself a treasure, and a sufficient remuneration of years of labor. * * *

From *Discourse VII. Knowledge Viewed in Relation to Professional Skill*

1

I have been insisting, in my two preceding Discourses, first, on the cultivation of the intellect, as an end which may reasonably be pursued for its own sake; and next, on the nature of that cultivation, or what that cultivation consists in. Truth of whatever kind is the proper object of the intellect; its cultivation then lies in fitting it to apprehend and contemplate truth. Now the intellect in its present state, with exceptions which need not here be specified, does not discern truth intuitively, or as a whole. We know, not by a direct and simple vision, not at a glance, but, as it were, by piece-meal and accumulation, by a mental process, by going round an object, by the comparison, the combination, the mutual correction, the continual adaptation, of many partial notions, by the employment, concentration, and joint action of many faculties and exercises of mind. Such a union and concert of the intellectual powers, such an enlargement and development, such a comprehensiveness, is necessarily a matter of training. And again, such a training is a matter of rule; it is not mere application, however exemplary, which introduces the mind to truth, nor the reading many books, nor the getting up many subjects, nor the witnessing many experiments, nor the attending many lectures. All this is short of enough; a man may have done it all, yet be lingering in the vestibule of knowledge: he may not realize what his mouth utters; he may not see with his mental eye what confronts him; he may have no grasp of things as they are; or at least he may have no power at all of advancing one step forward of himself, in consequence of what he has already acquired, no power of discriminating between truth and falsehood, of sifting out the grains of truth from the mass, of arranging things according to their real value, and, if I may use the phrase, of building up ideas. Such a power is the result of a scientific formation of mind; it is an acquired faculty of judgment, of clearsightedness, of sagacity, of wisdom, of philosophical reach of mind, and of intellectual self-possession and repose—qualities which do not come of mere acquirement. The bodily eye, the organ for apprehending material objects, is provided by nature; the eye of the mind, of which the object is truth, is the work of discipline and habit.

This process of training, by which the intellect, instead of being formed or sacrificed to some particular or accidental purpose, some specific trade or profession, or study or science, is disciplined for its own sake, for the perception of its own proper object, and for its own highest culture, is called Liberal Education; and though there is no one in whom it is carried as far as is conceivable, or whose intellect would be a pattern of what intellects should be made, yet there is scarcely anyone but may gain an idea of what real training is, and at least look towards it, and make its true scope and result, not something else, his standard of excellence; and numbers there are who may submit themselves to it, and secure it to themselves in good measure. And to set forth the right standard, and to train according to it, and to help forward all students toward it according to their various capacities, this I conceive to be the business of a University.

2

Now this is what some great men are very slow to allow; they insist that Education should be confined to some particular and narrow end, and should issue in some definite work, which can be weighed and measured. They argue as if every thing, as well as every person, had its price; and that where there has been a great outlay, they have a right to expect a return in kind. This they call making Education and Instruction "useful," and "Utility" becomes their watchword. With a fundamental principle of this nature, they very naturally go on to ask what there is to show for the expense of a University; what is the real worth in the market of the article called "a Liberal Education," on the supposition that it does not teach us definitely how to advance our manufactures, or to improve our lands, or to better our civil economy; or again, if it does not at once make this man a lawyer, that an engineer, and that a surgeon; or at least if it does not lead to discoveries in chemistry, astronomy, geology, magnetism, and science of every kind. * * *

5

* * * This is the obvious answer which may be made to those who urge upon us the claims of Utility in our plans of Education;[2]

2. The Utilitarians argued that a useful education would be one which trained the mind in the "habit of pushing things up to their first principles."

Newman had earlier pointed out that a liberal education does exactly that and is hence useful.

but I am not going to leave the subject here: I mean to take a wider view of it. Let us take "useful," as Locke[3] takes it, in its proper and popular sense, and then we enter upon a large field of thought, to which I cannot do justice in one Discourse, though today's is all the space that I can give to it. I say, let us take "useful" to mean, not what is simply good, but what *tends* to good, or is the *instrument* of good; and in this sense also, Gentlemen, I will show you how a liberal education is truly and fully a useful, though it be not a professional, education. "Good" indeed means one thing, and "useful" means another; but I lay it down as a principle, which will save us a great deal of anxiety, that, though the useful is not always good, the good is always useful. Good is not only good, but reproductive of good; this is one of its attributes; nothing is excellent, beautiful, perfect, desirable for its own sake, but it overflows, and spreads the likeness of itself all around it. Good is prolific; it is not only good to the eye, but to the taste; it not only attracts us, but it communicates itself; it excites first our admiration and love, then our desire and our gratitude, and that, in proportion to its intenseness and fullness in particular instances. A great good will impart great good. If then the intellect is so excellent a portion of us, and its cultivation so excellent, it is not only beautiful, perfect, admirable, and noble in itself, but in a true and high sense it must be useful to the possessor and to all around him; not useful in any low, mechanical, mercantile sense, but as diffusing good, or as a blessing, or a gift, or power, or a treasure, first to the owner, then through him to the world. I say then, if a liberal education be good, it must necessarily be useful too.

6

You will see what I mean by the parallel of bodily health. Health is a good in itself, though nothing came of it, and is especially worth seeking and cherishing; yet, after all, the blessings which attend its presence are so great, while they are so close to it and so redound back upon it and encircle it, that we never think of it except as useful as well as good, and praise and prize it for what it does, as well as for what it is, though at the same time we cannot point out any definite and distinct work or production which it can be said to effect. And so as regards intellectual culture, I am far from denying utility in this large sense as the end of Education, when I lay it down that the culture of the intellect is a good in itself and its own end; I do not exclude from the idea of intellectual culture what it cannot but be, from the very nature of things; I only deny that we must be able to point out, before we have any right to call it useful, some art, or business, or profession, or trade, or work, as resulting from it, and as its real and complete end. The parallel is

---

3. John Locke (1632–1704), whose treatise *Of Education* advocated a utilitarian concept of education.

exact: As the body may be sacrificed to some manual or other toil, whether moderate or oppressive, so may the intellect be devoted to some specific profession; and I do not call *this* the culture of the intellect. Again, as some member or organ of the body may be inordinately used and developed, so may memory, or imagination, or the reasoning faculty; and *this* again is not intellectual culture. On the other hand, as the body may be tended, cherished, and exercised with a simple view to its general health, so may the intellect also be generally exercised in order to its perfect state; and this *is* its cultivation.

Again, as health ought to precede labor of the body, and as a man in health can do what an unhealthy man cannot do, and as of this health the properties are strength, energy, agility, graceful carriage and action, manual dexterity, and endurance of fatigue, so in like manner general culture of mind is the best aid to professional and scientific study, and educated men can do what illiterate cannot; and the man who has learned to think and to reason and to compare and to discriminate and to analyze, who has refined his taste, and formed his judgment, and sharpened his mental vision, will not indeed at once be a lawyer, or a pleader, or an orator, or a statesman, or a physician, or a good landlord, or a man of business, or a soldier, or an engineer, or a chemist, or a geologist, or an antiquarian, but he will be placed in that state of intellect in which he can take up any one of the sciences or callings I have referred to, or any other for which he has a taste or special talent, with an ease, a grace, a versatility, and a success, to which another is a stranger. In this sense then, and as yet I have said but a very few words on a large subject, mental culture is emphatically *useful*.

If then I am arguing, and shall argue, against Professional or Scientific knowledge as the sufficient end of a University Education, let me not be supposed, Gentlemen, to be disrespectful towards particular studies, or arts, or vocations, and those who are engaged in them. In saying that Law or Medicine is not the end of a University course, I do not mean to imply that the University does not teach Law or Medicine. What indeed can it teach at all, if it does not teach something particular? It teaches *all* knowledge by teaching all *branches* of knowledge, and in no other way. I do but say that there will be this distinction as regards a Professor of Law, or of Medicine, or of Geology, or of Political Economy, in a University and out of it, that out of a University he is in danger of being absorbed and narrowed by his pursuit, and of giving Lectures which are the Lectures of nothing more than a lawyer, physician, geologist, or political economist; whereas in a University he will just know where he and his science stand, he has come to it, as it were, from a height, he has taken a survey of all knowledge, he is kept from extravagance by the very rivalry of other studies, he has gained from them a special illumination and largeness of mind and freedom and self-possession, and he treats his own in consequence with a philosophy and a resource, which belongs not to the study itself, but to his liberal education.

This then is how I should solve the fallacy, for so I must call it, by which Locke and his disciples would frighten us from cultivating the intellect, under the notion that no education is useful which does not teach us some temporal calling, or some mechanical art, or some physical secret. I say that a cultivated intellect, because it is a good in itself, brings with it a power and a grace to every work and occupation which it undertakes, and enables us to be more useful, and to a greater number. There is a duty we owe to human society as such, to the state to which we belong, to the sphere in which we move, to the individuals towards whom we are variously related, and whom we successively encounter in life; and that philosophical or liberal education, as I have called it, which is the proper function of a University, if it refuses the foremost place to professional interests, does but postpone them to the formation of the citizen, and, while it subserves the larger interests of philanthropy, prepares also for the successful prosecution of those merely personal objects which at first sight it seems to disparage. * * *

10

But I must bring these extracts[4] to an end. Today I have confined myself to saying that that training of the intellect, which is best for the individual himself, best enables him to discharge his duties to society. The Philosopher, indeed, and the man of the world differ in their very notion, but the methods, by which they are respectively formed, are pretty much the same. The Philosopher has the same command of matters of thought, which the true citizen and gentleman has of matters of business and conduct. If then a practical end must be assigned to a University course, I say it is that of training good members of society. Its art is the art of social life, and its end is fitness for the world. It neither confines its views to particular professions on the one hand, nor creates heroes or inspires genius on the other. Works indeed of genius fall under no art; heroic minds come under no rule; a University is not a birthplace of poets or of immortal authors, of founders of schools, leaders of colonies, or conquerors of nations. It does not promise a generation of Aristotles or Newtons, of Napoleons or Washingtons, or Raphaels or Shakespeares, though such miracles of nature it has before now contained within its precincts. Nor is it content on the other hand with forming the critic or the experimentalist, the economist or the engineer, though such too it includes within its scope. But a University training is the great ordinary means to a great but ordinary

4. Quotations cited from other authorities on education.

end; it aims at raising the intellectual tone of society, at cultivating the public mind, at purifying the national taste, at supplying true principles to popular enthusiasm and fixed aims to popular aspiration, at giving enlargement and sobriety to the ideas of the age, at facilitating the exercise of political power, and refining the intercourse of private life. It is the education which gives a man a clear conscious view of his own opinions and judgments, a truth in developing them, an eloquence in expressing them, and a force in urging them. It teaches him to see things as they are, to go right to the point, to disentangle a skein of thought, to detect what is sophistical, and to discard what is irrelevant. It prepares him to fill any post with credit, and to master any subject with facility. It shows him how to accommodate himself to others, how to throw himself into their state of mind, how to bring before them his own, how to influence them, how to come to an understanding with them, how to bear with them. He is at home in any society, he has common ground with every class; he knows when to speak and when to be silent; he is able to converse, he is able to listen; he can ask a question pertinently, and gain a lesson seasonably, when he has nothing to impart himself; he is ever ready, yet never in the way; he is a pleasant companion, and a comrade you can depend upon; he knows when to be serious and when to trifle, and he has a sure tact which enables him to trifle with gracefulness and to be serious with effect. He has the repose of a mind which lives in itself, while it lives in the world, and which has resources for its happiness at home when it cannot go abroad. He has a gift which serves him in public, and supports him in retirement,[5] without which good fortune is but vulgar, and with which failure and disappointment have a charm. The art which tends to make a man all this is in the object which it pursues as useful as the art of wealth or the art of health, though it is less susceptible of method, and less tangible, less certain, less complete in its result.

1852, 1873

5. In one of his later works, *The Grammar of Assent* (1870), Newman enlarges upon this aspect of his subject in a passage describing the impact that classical literature may have on us at different ages of our lives, a passage admired by James Joyce. "Let us consider, too, how differently young and old are affected by the words of some classic author, such as Homer or Horace. Passages, which to a boy are but rhetorical commonplaces, neither better nor worse than a hundred others which any clever writer might supply, which he gets by heart and thinks very fine, and imitates, as he thinks, successfully, in his own flowing versification, at length come home to him, when long years have passed, and he has had experience of life, and pierce him, as if he had never before known them, with their sad earnestness and vivid exactness. Then he comes to understand how it is that lines, the birth of some chance morning or evening at an Ionian festival, or among the Sabine hills, have lasted generation after generation, for thousands of years, with a power over the mind, and a charm, which the current literature of his own day, with all its obvious advantages, is utterly unable to rival. Perhaps this is the reason of the medieval opinion about Virgil, as if a prophet or magician; his single words and phrases, his pathetic half lines, giving utterance, as the voice of Nature herself, to that pain and weariness, yet hope of better things, which is the experience of her children in every time."

From Apologia Pro Vita Sua

From *Chapter III. History of My Religious Opinions from 1839 to 1841*

And now that I am about to trace, as far as I can, the course of that great revolution of mind, which led me to leave my own home, to which I was bound by so many strong and tender ties, I feel overcome with the difficulty of satisfying myself in my account of it, and have recoiled from the attempt, till the near approach of the day, on which these lines must be given to the world, forces me to set about the task. For who can know himself, and the multitude of subtle influences which act upon him? And who can recollect, at the distance of twenty-five years, all that he once knew about his thoughts and his deeds, and that, during a portion of his life, when, even at the time, his observation, whether of himself or of the external world, was less than before or after, by very reason of the perplexity and dismay which weighed upon him, when, in spite of the light given to him according to his need amid his darkness, yet a darkness it emphatically was? And who can suddenly gird himself to a new and anxious undertaking, which he might be able indeed to perform well, were full and calm leisure allowed him to look through every thing that he had written, whether in published works or private letters? yet again, granting that calm contemplation of the past, in itself so desirable, who could afford to be leisurely and deliberate, while he practices on himself a cruel operation, the ripping up of old griefs, and the venturing again upon the *infandum dolorem* [1] of years, in which the stars of this lower heaven were one by one going out? I could not in cool blood, nor except upon the imperious call of duty, attempt what I have set myself to do. It is both to head and heart an extreme trial, thus to analyze what has so long gone by, and to bring out the results of that examination. I have done various bold things in my life; this is the boldest, and, were I not sure I should after all succeed in my object, it would be madness to set about it.

In the spring of 1839 my position in the Anglican Church was at its height. I had supreme confidence in my controversial *status*, and I had a great and still growing success, in recommending it to others. I had in the foregoing autumn been somewhat sore at the Bishop's Charge,[2] but I have a letter which shows that all annoyance had passed from my mind. In January, if I recollect aright, in order to meet the popular clamor against myself and others, and to satisfy the Bishop, I had collected into one all the strong things

---

1. "Grief beyond words" (*Aeneid* II.3).
2. In 1838 Newman had been hurt when his Bishop, Richard Bagot of Oxford (whom he admired), criticized some of the Tracts published by the Anglo-Catholic group.

which they, and especially I, had said against the Church of Rome, in order to their insertion among the advertisements appended to our publications.[3] Conscious as I was that my opinions in religion were not gained, as the world said, from Roman sources, but were, on the contrary, the birth of my own mind and of the circumstances in which I had been placed, I had a scorn of the imputations which were heaped upon me. It was true that I held a large bold system of religion, very unlike the Protestantism of the day, but it was the concentration and adjustment of the statements of great Anglican authorities, and I had as much right to hold it, as the Evangelical, and more right than the Liberal party could show, for asserting their own respective doctrines. As I declared on occasion of Tract 90,[4] I claimed, in behalf of who would in the Anglican Church, the right of holding with Bramhall a comprecation with the Saints, and the Mass all but Transubstantiation with Andrewes, or with Hooker that Transubstantiation itself is not a point for Churches to part communion upon, or with Hammond that a General Council, truly such, never did, never shall err in a matter of faith, or with Bull that man had in paradise and lost on the fall, a supernatural habit of grace, or with Thorndike that penance is a propitiation for post-baptismal sin, or with Pearson [5] that the all-powerful name of Jesus is no otherwise given than in the Catholic Church. "Two can play at that," was often in my mouth, when men of Protestant sentiments appealed to the Articles, Homilies, or Reformers; in the sense that, if they had a right to speak loud, I had the liberty to speak out as well as they, and had the means, by the same or parallel appeals, of giving them tit for tat. I thought that the Anglican Church was tyrannized over by a mere party, and I aimed at bringing into effect the promise contained in the motto to the *Lyra,* "They shall know the difference now." [6] I only asked to be allowed to show them the difference.

What will best describe my state of mind at the early part of 1839 is an Article in the *British Critic* for that April. I have looked over it now, for the first time since it was published; and have been struck by it for this reason: it contains the last words which I ever spoke as an Anglican to Anglicans. It may now be

3. Tracts and articles written by High Church Anglican clergymen who made up the Tractarian Anglo-Catholic party or Oxford Movement. Their opponents, the Evangelicals and also the Broad Church liberals, accused them of favoring Roman Catholic doctrines.
4. An interpretation of Anglicanism by Newman, published in 1841, which provoked an acrimonious controversy.
5. All the names here are those of Anglican clergymen of the 16th and 17th centuries. Newman and his Anglo-Catholic party frequently reinforced their theological arguments by drawing from the writings of these earlier divines, especially from Richard Hooker's *The Laws of Ecclesiastical Polity* (1593), a defense of the Anglican position as a *via media* (middle way) between Roman Catholicism and Protestantism. See Vol. 1 of the present anthology.
6. On returning to battle the Trojans Achilles had boasted: "You shall know the difference now that I am back again." (*Iliad* XXVIII.125). His words served as the motto for *Lyra Apostolica,* a series of Anglo-Catholic articles published in the *British Magazine* of which Newman served as editor.

read as my parting address and valediction, made to my friends. I little knew it at the time. It reviews the actual state of things, and it ends by looking toward the future. It is not altogether mine; for my memory goes to this, that I had asked a friend to do the work; that then, the thought came on me, that I would do it myself; and that he was good enough to put into my hands what he had with great appositeness written, and that I embodied it in my Article. Every one, I think, will recognize the greater part of it as mine. It was published two years before the affair of Tract 90, and was entitled "The State of Religious Parties."

In this Article, I begin by bringing together testimonies from our enemies to the remarkable success of our exertions. One writer said: "Opinions and views of a theology of a very marked and peculiar kind have been extensively adopted and strenuously upheld, and are daily gaining ground among a considerable and influential portion of the members, as well as ministers of the Established Church." * * *

After thus stating the phenomenon of the time, as it presented itself to those who did not sympathize in it, the Article proceeds to account for it; and this it does by considering it as a reaction from the dry and superficial character of the religious teaching and the literature of the last generation, or century, and as a result of the need which was felt both by the hearts and the intellects of the nation for a deeper philosophy, and as the evidence and as the partial fulfillment of that need, to which even the chief authors of the then generation had borne witness. First, I mentioned the literary influence of Walter Scott, who turned men's minds in the direction of the middle ages. "The general need," I said, "of something deeper and more attractive, than what had offered itself elsewhere, may be considered to have led to his popularity; and by means of his popularity he reacted on his readers, stimulating their mental thirst, feeding their hopes, setting before them visions, which, when once seen, are not easily forgotten, and silently indoctrinating them with nobler ideas, which might afterwards be appealed to as first principles."

Then I spoke of Coleridge, thus: "While history in prose and verse was thus made the instrument of Church feelings and opinions, a philosophical basis for the same was laid in England by a very original thinker, who, while he indulged a liberty of speculation, which no Christian can tolerate, and advocated conclusions which were often heathen rather than Christian, yet after all installed a higher philosophy into inquiring minds, than they had hitherto been accustomed to accept. In this way he made trial of his age, and succeeded in interesting its genius in the cause of Catholic truth."

Then come Southey and Wordsworth, "two living poets, one of

whom in the department of fantastic fiction, the other in that of philosophical meditation, have addressed themselves to the same high principles and feelings, and carried forward their readers in the same direction."

* * *

These being the circumstances under which the Movement began and progressed, it was absurd to refer it to the act of two or three individuals. It was not so much a movement as a "spirit afloat"; it was within us, "rising up in hearts where it was least suspected, and working itself, though not in secret, yet so subtly and impalpably, as hardly to admit of precaution or encounter on any ordinary human rules of opposition. It is," I continued, "an adversary in the air, a something one and entire, a whole wherever it is, unapproachable and incapable of being grasped, as being the result of causes far deeper than political or other visible agencies, the spiritual awakening of spiritual wants."

* * *

Lastly, I proceeded to the question of that future of the Anglican Church, which was to be a new birth of the Ancient Religion. And I did not venture to pronounce upon it. "About the future, we have no prospect before our minds whatever, good or bad. Ever since that great luminary, Augustine, proved to be the last bishop of Hippo, Christians have had a lesson against attempting to foretell, *how* Providence will prosper and" [or?] "bring to an end, what it begins." Perhaps the lately revived principles would prevail in the Anglican Church; perhaps they would be lost in some miserable schism, or some more miserable compromise; but there was nothing rash in venturing to predict that "neither Puritanism nor Liberalism had any permanent inheritance within her."

Then I went on: "As to Liberalism, we think the formularies of the Church will ever, with the aid of a good Providence, keep it from making any serious inroads upon the clergy. Besides, it is too cold a principle to prevail with the multitude." But as regarded what was called Evangelical Religion or Puritanism, there was more to cause alarm. I observed upon its organization; but on the other hand it had no intellectual basis; no internal idea, no principle of unity, no theology. "Its adherents," I said, "are already separating from each other; they will melt away like a snowdrift. It has no straightforward view on any one point, on which it professes to teach, and to hide its poverty, it has dressed itself out in a maze of words. We have no dread of it at all; we only fear what it may lead to. It does not stand on intrenched ground, or make any pretense to a position; it does but occupy the space between contending powers, Catholic Truth and Rationalism. Then indeed will be the stern encounter, when two real and living principles, simple, entire, and consistent, one in the Church, the other out of it, at length rush upon each other, contending not for names and words, or half-views, but for elementary notions and distinctive moral characters."

Whether the ideas of the coming age upon religion were true or false, at least they would be real. "In the present day," I said, "mistiness is the mother of wisdom. A man who can set down a half-a-dozen general propositions, which escape from destroying one another only by being diluted into truisms, who can hold the balance between opposites so skillfully as to do without fulcrum or beam, who never enunciates a truth without guarding himself against being supposed to exclude the contradictory—who holds that Scripture is the only authority, yet that the Church is to be deferred to, that faith only justifies, yet that it does not justify without works, that grace does not depend on the sacraments, yet is not given without them, that bishops are a divine ordinance, yet those who have them not are in the same religious condition as those who have—this is your safe man and the hope of the Church; this is what the Church is said to want, not party men, but sensible, temperate, sober, well-judging persons, to guide it through the channel of no-meaning, between the Scylla and Charybdis of Aye and No."

This state of things, however, I said, could not last, if men were to read and think. They "will not keep in that very attitude which you call sound Church-of-Englandism or orthodox Protestantism. They cannot go on forever standing on one leg, or sitting without a chair, or walking with their feet tied, or like Tityrus's stags grazing in the air.[7] They will take one view or another, but it will be a consistent view. It may be Liberalism, or Erastianism, or Popery, or Catholicity; but it will be real."

I concluded the Article by saying, that all who did not wish to be "democratic, or pantheistic, or popish," must "look out for *some* Via Media which will perserve us from what threatens, though it cannot restore the dead. The spirit of Luther is dead; but Hildebrand and Loyola are alive.[8] Is it sensible, sober, judicious, to be so very angry with those writers of the day, who point to the fact, that our divines of the seventeenth century have occupied a ground which is the true and intelligible mean between extremes? Is it wise to quarrel with this ground, because it is not exactly what we should choose, had we the power of choice? Is it true moderation, instead of trying to fortify a middle doctrine, to fling stones at those who do? . . . Would you rather have your sons and daughters members of the Church of England or of the Church of Rome?"

And thus I left the matter. But, while I was thus speaking of the future of the Movement, I was in truth winding up my accounts

---

7. Virgil, *Eclogues* I.59.
8. Hildebrand (Pope Gregory VII) and St. Ignatius of Loyola, representing medieval and modern Catholicism.

with it, little dreaming that it was so to be; while I was still, in some way or other, feeling about for an available *Via Media*, I was soon to receive a shock which was to cast out of my imagination all middle courses and compromises forever.[9] As I have said, this Article appeared in the April number of the *British Critic*; in the July number, I cannot tell why, there is no Article of mine; before the number for October, the event had happened to which I have alluded.

But before I proceed to describe what happened to me in the summer of 1839, I must detain the reader for a while, in order to describe the *issue* of the controversy between Rome and the Anglican Church, as I viewed it. This will involve some dry discussion; but it is as necessary for my narrative, as plans of buildings and homesteads are at times needed in the proceedings of our law courts.

* * *

From *Chapter V. Position of My Mind Since 1845*

Starting then with the being of a God (which, as I have said, is as certain to me as the certainty of my own existence, though when I try to put the grounds of that certainty into logical shape I find a difficulty in doing so in mood and figure to my satisfaction), I look out of myself into the world of men, and there I see a sight which fills me with unspeakable distress. The world seems simply to give the lie to that great truth, of which my whole being is so full; and the effect upon me is, in consequence, as a matter of necessity, as confusing as if it denied that I am in existence myself. If I looked into a mirror, and did not see my face, I should have the sort of feeling which actually comes upon me, when I look into this living busy world, and see no reflection of its Creator. This is, to me, one of the great difficulties of this absolute primary truth, to which I referred just now. Were it not for this voice, speaking so clearly in my conscience and my heart, I should be an atheist, or a pantheist, or a polytheist when I looked into the world. I am speaking for myself only; and I am far from denying the real force of the arguments in proof of a God, drawn from the general facts of human society, but these do not warm me or enlighten me; they do not take away the winter of my desolation, or make the buds unfold and the leaves grow within me, and my moral being rejoice. The sight of the world is nothing else than the prophet's scroll, full of "lamentations, and mourning, and woe."[2]

To consider the world in its length and breadth, its various history, the many races of man, their starts, their fortunes, their

9. The "shock" was prompted by his discovery in 1839, in the course of studying
church history, that the Anglican position
seemed to be identical with that of a
heretical movement of the 5th century.
2. Ezekiel ii.9–10.

mutual alienation, their conflicts; and then their ways, habits, governments, forms of worship; their enterprises, their aimless courses, their random achievements and acquirements, the impotent conclusion of long-standing facts, the tokens so faint and broken, of a superintending design, the blind evolution of what turn out to be great powers or truth, the progress of things, as if from unreasoning elements, not towards final causes, the greatness and littleness of man, his far-reaching aims, his short duration, the curtain hung over his futurity, the disappoinments of life, the defeat of good, the success of evil, physical pain, mental anguish, the prevalence and intensity of sin, the pervading idolatries, the corruptions, the dreary hopeless irreligion, that condition of the whole race, so fearfully yet exactly described in the Apostle's words, "having no hope and without God in the world"[3]—all this is a vision to dizzy and appall; and inflicts upon the mind the sense of a profound mystery which is absolutely beyond human solution.

What shall be said to this heart-piercing, reason-bewildering fact? I can only answer that either there is no Creator, or this living society of men is in a true sense discarded from His presence. Did I see a boy of good make and mind, with the tokens on him of a refined nature, cast upon the world without provision, unable to say whence he came, his birthplace or his family connections, I should conclude that there was some mystery connected with his history, and that he was one, of whom, from one cause or other, his parents were ashamed. Thus only should I be able to account for the contrast between the promise and condition of his being. And so I argue about the world—*if* there be a God, *since* there is a God, the human race is implicated in some terrible aboriginal calamity. It is out of joint with the purposes of its Creator. This is a fact, a fact as true as the fact of its existence; and thus the doctrine of what is theologically called original sin becomes to me almost as certain as that the world exists, and as the existence of God.

And now, supposing it were the blessed and loving will of the Creator to interfere in this anarchical condition of things, what are we to suppose would be the methods which might be necessarily or naturally involved in His object of mercy? Since the world is in so abnormal a state, surely it would be no surprise to me if the interposition were of necessity equally extraordinary—or what is called miraculous. But that subject does not directly come into the scope of my present remarks. Miracles as evidence involve an argument; and of course I am thinking of some means which does not immediately run into argument. I am rather asking what must be the face-to-face antagonist, by which to withstand and baffle the fierce energy of passion and the all-corroding, all-dissolving skepticism of the intellect in religious inquiries? I have no intention at

3. Ephesians ii.12.

all to deny that truth is the real object of our reason, and that, if it does not attain to truth, either the premise or the process is in fault; but I am not speaking of right reason, but of reason as it acts in fact and concretely in fallen man. I know that even the unaided reason, when correctly exercised, leads to a belief in God, in the immortality of the soul, and in a future retribution; but I am considering it actually and historically; and in this point of view, I do not think I am wrong in saying that its tendency is towards a simple unbelief in matters of religion. No truth, however sacred, can stand against it, in the long run; and hence it is that in the pagan world, when our Lord came, the last traces of the religious knowledge of former times were all but disappearing from those portions of the world in which the intellect had been active and had had a career.

And in these latter days, in like manner, outside the Catholic Church things are tending, with far greater rapidity than in that old time from the circumstance of the age, to atheism in one shape or other. What a scene, what a prospect, does the whole of Europe present at this day! and not only Europe, but every government and every civilization through the world, which is under the influence of the European mind! Especially, for it most concerns us, how sorrowful, in the view of religion, even taken in its most elementary, most attenuated form, is the spectacle presented to us by the educated intellect of England, France, and Germany! Lovers of their country and of their race, religious men, external to the Catholic Church, have attempted various expedients to arrest fierce willful human nature in its onward course, and to bring it into subjection. The necessity of some form of religion for the interests of humanity has been generally acknowledged: but where was the concrete representative of things invisible, which would have the force and the toughness necessary to be a breakwater against the deluge? Three centuries ago the establishment of religion, material, legal, and social was generally adopted as the best expedient for the purpose, in those countries which separated from the Catholic Church; and for a long time it was successful; but now the crevices of those establishments are admitting the enemy. Thirty years ago, education was relied upon: ten years ago there was a hope that wars would cease forever, under the influence of commercial enterprise and the reign of the useful and fine arts;[4] but will anyone venture to say that there is anything anywhere on this earth, which will afford a fulcrum for us, whereby to keep the earth from moving onwards?

The judgment, which experience passes on establishments or

---

4. A reference to the optimism generated at the time of the Great Exhibition of 1851, a mood which was sobered by the sufferings endured during the Crimean War (1854–56).

education, as a means of maintaining religious truth in this anarchical world, must be extended even to Scripture, though Scripture be divine. Experience proves surely that the Bible does not answer a purpose, for which it was never intended. It may be accidentally the means of the conversion of individuals; but a book, after all, cannot make a stand against the wild living intellect of man, and in this day it begins to testify, as regards its own structure and contents, to the power of that universal solvent,[5] which is so successfully acting upon religious establishments.

Supposing then it to be the Will of the Creator to interfere in human affairs, and to make provisions for retaining in the world a knowledge of Himself, so definite and distinct as to be proof against the energy of human skepticism, in such a case—I am far from saying that there was no other way—but there is nothing to surprise the mind, if He should think fit to introduce a power into the world, invested with the prerogative of infallibility in religious matters. Such a provision would be a direct, immediate, active, and prompt means of withstanding the difficulty; it would be an instrument suited to the need; and, when I find that this is the very claim of the Catholic Church, not only do I feel no difficulty in admitting the idea, but there is a fitness in it, which recommends it to my mind. And thus I am brought to speak of the Church's infallibility, as a provision, adapted by the mercy of the Creator, to preserve religion in the world, and to restrain that freedom of thought, which of course in itself is one of the greatest of our natural gifts, and to rescue it from its own suicidal excesses. And let it be observed that, neither here nor in what follows, shall I have occasion to speak directly of the revealed body of truths, but only as they bear upon the defense of natural religion. I say that a power, possessed of infallibility in religious teaching, is happily adapted to be a working instrument, in the course of human affairs, for smiting hard and throwing back the immense energy of the aggressive intellect—and in saying this, as in the other things that I have to say, it must still be recollected that I am all along bearing in mind my main purpose, which is a defense of myself.

I am defending myself here from a plausible charge brought against Catholics, as will be seen better as I proceed. The charge is this: that I, as a Catholic, not only make profession to hold doctrines which I cannot possibly believe in my heart, but that I also believe in the existence of a power on earth, which at its own will imposes upon men any new set of *credenda*,[6] when it pleases, by a claim to infallibility; in consequence, that my own thoughts are not my own property; that I cannot tell that tomorrow I may not have to give up what I hold today, and that the necessary effect of

5. Allusion to the Higher Criticism, a method of analyzing the Bible as history.

6. Beliefs.

such a condition of mind must be a degrading bondage, or a bitter inward rebellion relieving itself in secret infidelity, or the necessity of ignoring the whole subject of religion in a sort of disgust, and of mechanically saying everything that the Church says, and leaving to others the defense of it. As then I have above spoken of the relation of my mind towards the Catholic Creed, so now I shall speak of the attitude which it takes up in the view of the Church's infallibility.

And first, the initial doctrine of the infallible teacher must be an emphatic protest against the existing state of mankind. Man had rebelled against his Maker. It was this that caused the divine interposition: and the first act of the divinely accredited messenger must be to proclaim it. The Church must denounce rebellion as of all possible evils the greatest. She must have no terms with it; if she would be true to her Master, she must ban and anathematize it. This is the meaning of a statement which has furnished matter for one of those special accusations to which I am at present replying: I have, however, no fault at all to confess in regard to it; I have nothing to withdraw, and in consequence I here deliberately repeat it. I said, "The Catholic Church holds it better for the sun and moon to drop from heaven, for the earth to fail, and for all the many millions on it to die of starvation in extremest agony, as far as temporal affliction goes, than that one soul, I will not say, should be lost, but should commit one single venial sin, should tell one willful untruth, or should steal one poor farthing without excuse." I think the principle here enunciated to be the mere preamble in the formal credentials of the Catholic Church, as an Act of Parliament might begin with a "*Whereas.*" It is because of the intensity of the evil which has possession of mankind that a suitable antagonist has been provided against it; and the initial act of that divinely-commissioned power is of course to deliver her challenge and to defy the enemy. Such a preamble then gives a meaning to her position in the world, and an interpretation to her whole course of teaching and action.

From *Liberalism*

I have been asked to explain more fully what it is I mean by "Liberalism," because merely to call it the Antidogmatic Principle is to tell very little about it. * * * Now by Liberalism I mean false liberty of thought, or the exercise of thought upon matters, in which, from the constitution of the human mind, thought cannot be brought to any successful issue, and therefore is out of place. Among such matters are first principles of whatever kind; and of these the most sacred and momentous are especially to be reckoned the truths of Revelation. Liberalism then is the mistake of subjecting to human judgment those revealed doctrines which are in their nature beyond and independent of it, and of claiming to determine on intrinsic grounds the truth and value of propositions which rest for their reception simply on the external authority of the Divine Word. * * *

I conclude this notice of Liberalism in Oxford, and the party which was antagonistic to it,[7] with some propositions in detail, which, as a member of the latter, and together with the High Church, I earnestly denounced and abjured.

1. No religious tenet is important, unless reason shows it to be so.

Therefore, e.g., the doctrine of the Athanasian Creed[8] is not to be insisted on, unless it tends to convert the soul; and the doctrine of the Atonement is to be insisted on, if it does convert the soul.

2. No one can believe what he does not understand.

Therefore, e.g., there are no mysteries in true religion.

3. No theological doctrine is anything more than an opinion which happens to be held by bodies of men.

Therefore, e.g., no creed, as such, is necessary for salvation.

4. It is dishonest in a man to make an act of faith in what he has not had brought home to him by actual proof.

Therefore, e.g., the mass of men ought not absolutely to believe in the divine authority of the Bible.

5. It is immoral in a man to believe more than he can spontaneously receive as being congenial to his moral and mental nature.

Therefore, e.g., a given individual is not bound to believe in eternal punishment.

6. No revealed doctrines or precepts may reasonably stand in the way of scientific conclusions.

Therefore, e.g., Political Economy may reverse our Lord's declarations about poverty and riches, or a system of Ethics may teach that the highest condition of body is ordinarily essential to the highest state of mind.

7. Christianity is necessarily modified by the growth of civilization, and the exigencies of times.

Therefore, e.g., the Catholic priesthood, though necessary in the Middle Ages, may be superseded now.

8. There is a system of religion more simply true than Christianity as it has ever been received.

Therefore, e.g., we may advance that Christianity is the "corn of wheat" which has been dead for 1800 years, but at length will bear fruit; and that Mahometanism is the manly religion, and existing Christianity the womanish.

9. There is a right of Private Judgment: that is, there is no existing authority on earth competent to interfere with the liberty of individuals in reasoning and judging for themselves about the Bible

7. The Tractarians or Party of the Oxford Movement.   8. Belief in the Trinity.

and its contents, as they severally please.

Therefore, e.g., religious establishments requiring subscription are Antichristian.

10. There are rights of conscience such that everyone may lawfully advance a claim to profess and teach what is false and wrong in matters, religious, social, and moral, provided that to his private conscience it seems absolutely true and right.

Therefore, e.g., individuals have a right to preach and practice fornication and polygamy.

11. There is no such thing as a national or state conscience.

Therefore, e.g., no judgments can fall upon a sinful or infidel nation.

12. The civil power has no positive duty, in a normal state of things, to maintain religious truth.

Therefore, e.g., blasphemy and sabbath-breaking are not rightly punishable by law.

13. Utility and expedience are the measure of political duty.

Therefore, e.g., no punishment may be enacted, on the ground that God commands it: e.g., on the text, "Whoso sheddeth man's blood, by man shall his blood be shed." [9]

14. The Civil Power may dispose of Church property without sacrilege.

Therefore, e.g., Henry VIII committed no sin in his spoliations.[1]

15. The Civil Power has the right of ecclesiastical jurisdiction and administration.

Therefore, e.g., Parliament may impose articles of faith on the Church or suppress Dioceses.[2]

16. It is lawful to rise in arms against legitimate princes.

Therefore, e.g., the Puritans in the seventeenth century, and the French in the eighteenth, were justified in their Rebellion and Revolution respectively.

17. The people are the legitimate source of power.

Therefore, e.g., Universal Suffrage is among the natural rights of man.

18. Virtue is the child of knowledge, and vice of ignorance.

Therefore, e.g., education, periodical literature, railroad traveling, ventilation, drainage, and the arts of life, when fully carried out, serve to make a population moral and happy.

All of these propositions, and many others too, were familiar to me thirty years ago, as in the number of the tenets of Liberalism, and, while I gave in to none of them except No. 12, and perhaps No. 11, and partly No. 1, before I began to publish, so afterwards

9. Genesis ix.6.
1. The dissolution of the monasteries by Henry VIII.
2. Allusion to the abolishing of ten Irish bishoprics by liberal reformers in Parliament in 1833. This instance of interference by the state in affairs of the church had prompted Newman and his associates into organizing a "party of opposition": the Oxford Movement.

I wrote against most of them in some part or other of my Anglican works. * * *

I need hardly say that the above Note is mainly historical. How far the Liberal party of 1830–40 really held the above eighteen Theses, which I attributed to them, and how far and in what sense I should oppose those Theses now, could scarcely be explained without a separate Dissertation.

1864–65

JOHN RUSKIN

(1819–1900)

1843:   Publication of first volume of *Modern Painters*.
1851–53: *The Stones of Venice*.
1860:   *Unto This Last*.

John Ruskin was both the leading Victorian critic of art and an important critic of society. These two roles can be traced back to two important influences of his childhood. His father, a wealthy wine merchant, was fond of travel, and on tours of the Continent he introduced his son to landscape, architecture, and art. From this exposure John Ruskin acquired a zest for beauty that animates even the most theoretical of his discussions of aesthetics. In his autobiography he describes his first view of the Swiss Alps at sunset: "the seen walls of lost Eden could not have been more beautiful" (he was 14 at the time):

> It is not possible to imagine, in any time of the world, a more blessed entrance into life, for a child of such a temperament as mine. True, the temperament belonged to the age: a very few years,—within the hundred,—before that, no child could have been born to care for mountains, or for the men that lived among them, in that way. Till Rousseau's time, there had been no "sentimental" love of nature; and till Scott's, no such apprehensive love of "all sorts and conditions of men," not in the soul merely, but in the flesh. * * * I went down that evening from the garden-terrace of Schaffhausen with my destiny fixed in all of it that was to be sacred and useful.

Ruskin's choice of phrase in evoking this dedication scene reflects the second influence in his life, often at variance with the first: his daily Bible-readings under the direction of his mother. From this Biblical indoctrination, Ruskin derived some elements of his lush and highly rhythmical prose style, but more especially his sense of prophecy and mission as a critic of modern society.

Ruskin's life was spent in traveling, lecturing, and writing. His prodigious literary output can be roughly divided into three phases. At first he was preoccupied with problems of art. *Modern Painters*, which he began writing at the age of 23 after his graduation from Oxford, was a defense of the English landscape painter J. M. W. Turner (1775–1851). This defense (which was to extend to five volumes) involved Ruskin in problems of truth in art (as in his chapter on the "Pathetic Fallacy") and in the ulti-mate importance of imagination (as in his discussion of Turner's painting, "The Slave Ship").

During the 1850's Ruskin's principal interest shifted from art to architec-ture, especially to the problem of determining what kind of society is ca-pable of producing great buildings. His enthusiasm for Gothic architecture was infectious, and he has sometimes been blamed for the prevalence of Gothic buildings on college campuses in America. A study of *The Stones of Venice* (1851–53), however (especially the chapter included below), will show that merely to revive the Gothic style was not his concern. What he wanted to revive was the kind of society that had produced such architec-ture, a society in which the individual workman could express himself and enjoy what Ruskin's disciple, William Morris, called "work-pleasure." A mechanized production-line society, such as Ruskin's or our own, could not produce Gothic architecture but only imitations of its mannerisms. Ruskin's concern was to change industrial society, not to decorate concrete towers with gargoyles.

This interest in the stultifying effects of industrialism led Ruskin grad-ually into economics. After 1860 the critic of art became (like his master, Carlyle) an outspoken critic of laissez-faire economics. His conception of the responsibilities of employers towards their workmen, as expounded in *Unto this Last* (1860), was dismissed by his contemporaries as an absurd-ity. What he was laboring to show was that self-seeking business relation-ships might be made over on the principle of dedicated service, taking as a model the learned professions and also the military. The soldier, however crude, is more highly regarded by society than the capitalist, Ruskin said, "for the soldier's trade * * * is not slaying, but being slain." Although his position was essentially conservative in the proper sense of the word (he styled himself "a violent Tory of the old school;—Walter Scott's school"), he was regarded as a radical eccentric. It was many years before his social criticism gained a following among writers as diverse as William Morris, George Bernard Shaw, and D. H. Lawrence; and in particular among the founders of the British Labour Party his influence was to be profound and lasting.

Ruskin's realization, after 1860, that despite his fame he was becoming isolated and that the world was continuing to move in directions opposite from those to which he pointed may have contributed to the recurrent mental breakdowns from which he suffered between 1870 and 1900. Also contributory may have been his unhappiness in his relations with women. His marriage to Effie Gray in 1848 was a disaster. After six years of living together an annulment was arranged on the grounds that the marriage had not been consummated. Ruskin testified that he had not found his wife's person physically attractive, although by others she was considered a great beauty. One of these admirers was the Pre-Raphaelite painter John Millais, who fell in love with her at a time when he was painting her husband's portrait; shortly after the annulment he married her. In later years Ruskin fell pathetically in love with a young Irish girl, Rose La Touche, whom he first met when he was nearly forty and she was a child of nine. They were divided not only by the gap of age but by religious differences. She was an intensely pious believer, and for several years after Ruskin proposed marriage to her, when she was 18, she tried unsuccessfully to persuade him to return to the Evangelical faith that he had abandoned. In 1875, after herself suffering attacks of mental illness, Rose La Touche died at the age of 25. In his autobiography Ruskin commented: "I wonder mightily what sort of creature I should have turned out, if instead of the distracting and useless pain, I had had the joy of approved love, and the untellable, incalculable motive of its sympathy and praise. It seems to me such things are not allowed in the world. The men capable of the highest imaginative passion are always tossed on fiery waves by it." During the last thirty years of his life, in spite of his despair following Rose's death and recurring attacks of mental illness, Ruskin remained active and productive. His publications during this period include six volumes of his lectures on art which he had delivered as Slade Professor of Fine Arts at Oxford, as well as his letters to workmen, *Fors Clavigera* (1871–84), and his delightful autobiography, *Praeterita* (1885–89). One topic that becomes especially prominent in these later writings is pollution of air and water—an ideal subject for Ruskin's eloquence. In discussing it he combines his lifelong love for beautiful landscape and landscape-painting with his later acquired conviction that modern industrial leadership was woefully irresponsible. A letter of A. E. Housman, who was an undergraduate at Oxford in 1877, provides a vivid record of how effective Ruskin could be:

This afternoon Ruskin gave us a great outburst against modern times. He had got a picture of Turner's, framed and glassed, representing Leicester and the Abbey in the distance at sunset, over a river. He read the account of Wolsey's death out of *Henry VIII*. Then he pointed to the picture as representing Leicester when Turner had drawn it. Then he said, "You, if you like, may go to Leicester to see what it is like now. I never shall. But I can make a pretty good guess." Then he caught up a paintbrush. "These stepping-stones of course have been done away with, and are replaced by a be-au-ti-ful iron bridge." Then he dashed in the iron bridge on the glass of the picture. "The colour of the stream is supplied on one side by the indigo factory." Forthwith one side of the stream became indigo. "On the other side by the soap factory." Soap dashed in. "They mix in the middle—like curds," he said, working them together with a sort of malicious deliberation. "This field, over which you see the sun setting behind the abbey, is now occupied in a *proper* manner." Then there went a flame of scarlet across the picture, which developed itself into windows and roofs and red brick, and rushed up into a chimney. "The atmosphere is supplied—thus!" A puff and cloud of smoke all over Turner's sky: and then the brush thrown down, and Ruskin confronting modern civilization amidst a tempest of applause, which he always elicits now, as he has this term become immensely popular, his lectures being crowded, whereas of old he used to prophesy to empty benches.

From Modern Painters
["*The Slave Ship*"][1]

But I think the noblest sea that Turner has ever painted, and, if so, the noblest certainly ever painted by man, is that of "The Slave Ship," the chief Academy picture of the exhibition of 1840.[2] It is a sunset on the Atlantic after prolonged storm; but the storm is partially lulled, and the torn and streaming rain clouds are moving in scarlet lines to lose themselves in the hollow of the night. The whole surface of sea included in the picture is divided into two ridges of enormous swell, not high, nor local, but a low, broad heaving of the whole ocean, like the lifting of its bosom by deep-drawn breath after the torture of the storm. Between these two ridges the fire of the sunset falls along the trough of the sea, dyeing it with an awful but glorious light, the intense and lurid splendor which burns like gold and bathes like blood. Along this fiery path and valley the tossing waves by which the swell of the sea is restlessly divided lift themselves in dark, indefinite, fantastic forms, each casting a faint and ghastly shadow behind it along the illumined foam. They do not rise everywhere, but three or four together in wild groups, fitfully and furiously, as the under-strength of the swell compels or permits them; leaving between them treacherous spaces of level and whirling water, now lighted with green and lamplike fire, now flashing back the gold of the declining sun, now fearfully shed from above with the indistinguishable images of the burning clouds, which fall upon them in flakes of crimson and scarlet and give to the reckless waves the added motion of their own fiery being. Purple and blue, the lurid shadows of the hollow breakers are cast upon the mist of night, which gathers cold and low, advancing like the shadow of death upon the guilty ship as it labors amidst the lightning of the sea, its thin masts written upon the sky in lines of blood, girded with condemnation in that fearful hue which signs the sky with horror, and mixes its flaming flood with the sunlight, and, cast far along the desolate heave of the sepulchral waves, incarnadines the multitudinous sea.[3]

I believe, if I were reduced to rest Turner's immortality upon any single work, I should choose this. Its daring conception—ideal in

---

1. From Volume I, Part II, Section v, Chapter 3.
2. The painting is of a ship in which slaves are being transported. Victims who have died during the passage are being thrown overboard at sunset: as Ruskin noted, "the near sea is encumbered with corpses." The "Academy" is the Royal Academy of Arts, founded in London in 1768.
3. See *Macbeth* II.ii.62.

the highest sense of the word—is based on the purest truth, and wrought out with the concentrated knowledge of a life; its color is absolutely perfect, not one false or morbid hue in any part or line, and so modulated that every square inch of canvas is a perfect composition; its drawing as accurate as fearless; the ship buoyant, bending, and full of motion; its tones as true as they are wonderful; and the whole picture dedicated to the most sublime of subjects and impressions—completing thus the perfect system of all truth which we have shown to be formed by Turner's works—the power, majesty, and deathfulness of the open, deep, illimitable Sea.

1843

From *Of the Pathetic Fallacy*[4]

* * * Now, therefore, putting these tiresome and absurd words[5] quite out of our way, we may go on at our ease to examine the point in question—namely, the difference between the ordinary, proper, and true appearances of things to us; and the extraordinary, or false appearances, when we are under the influence of emotion, or contemplative fancy; false appearances, I say, as being entirely unconnected with any real power of character in the object, and only imputed to it by us.

For instance—

> The spendthrift crocus, bursting through the mold
> Naked and shivering, with his cup of gold.[6]

This is very beautiful, and yet very untrue. The crocus is not a spendthrift, but a hardy plant; its yellow is not gold, but saffron. How is it that we enjoy so much the having it put into our heads that it is anything else than a plain crocus?

It is an important question. For, throughout our past reasonings about art, we have always found that nothing could be good or useful, or ultimately pleasurable, which was untrue. But here is something pleasurable in written poetry, which is nevertheless *un*-true. And what is more, if we think over our favorite poetry, we

---

4. From Volume III, Part IV, Chapter 12. In this celebrated chapter Ruskin shifts from discussing problems of truth and realism in art to the same problems in literature. The term *pathetic* refers not to something feebly ineffective but to the emotion (pathos) with which a writer invests his descriptions of objects, and of the distortion (fallacy) that may result. Poets such as Tennyson protested that Ruskin was being unfairly rigorous

in pointing up the fallacy, and it may be noted that Ruskin himself falls into it often. See, e.g., his reference to the "guilty ship" in his discussion of Turner above.
5. The metaphysical terms "objective" and "subjective" as applied to kinds of truth.
6. From a poem by Oliver Wendell Holmes.

shall find it full of this kind of fallacy, and that we like it all the more for being so.

It will appear also, on consideration of the matter, that this fallacy is of two principal kinds. Either, as in this case of the crocus, it is the fallacy of willful fancy, which involves no real expectation that it will be believed; or else it is a fallacy caused by an excited state of the feelings, making us, for the time, more or less irrational. Of the cheating of the fancy we shall have to speak presently; but, in this chapter, I want to examine the nature of the other error, that which the mind admits when affected strongly by emotion. Thus, for instance, in *Alton Locke*—

> They rowed her in across the rolling foam—
> The cruel, crawling foam.[7]

The foam is not cruel, neither does it crawl. The state of mind which attributes to it these characters of a living creature is one in which the reason is unhinged by grief. All violent feelings have the same effect. They produce in us a falseness in all our impressions of external things, which I would generally characterize as the "pathetic fallacy."

Now we are in the habit of considering this fallacy as eminently a character of poetical description, and the temper of mind in which we allow it, as one eminently poetical, because passionate. But, I believe, if we look well into the matter, that we shall find the greatest poets do not often admit this kind of falseness—that it is only the second order of poets who much delight in it.

Thus, when Dante describes the spirits falling from the bank of Acheron "as dead leaves flutter from a bough," [8] he gives the most perfect image possible of their utter lightness, feebleness, passiveness, and scattering agony of despair, without, however, for an instant losing his own clear perception that *these* are souls, and *those* are leaves: he makes no confusion of one with the other. But when Coleridge speaks of

> The one red leaf, the last of its clan,
> That dances as often as dance it can,[9]

he has a morbid, that is to say, a so far false, idea about the leaf: he fancies a life in it, and will, which there are not; confuses its powerlessness with choice, its fading death with merriment, and the wind that shakes it with music. Here, however, there is some beauty, even in the morbid passage; but take an instance in Homer and Pope. Without the knowledge of Ulysses, Elpenor, his young-

---

7. From Charles Kingsley's novel *Alton Locke* (1850). 8. Dante, *Inferno* III.112.
9. *Christabel*, lines 49–50.

est follower, has fallen from an upper chamber in the Circean palace, and has been left dead, unmissed by his leader or companions, in the haste of their departure. They cross the sea to the Cimmerian land; and Ulysses summons the shades from Tartarus. The first which appears is that of the lost Elpenor. Ulysses, amazed, and in exactly the spirit of bitter and terrified lightness which is seen in Hamlet, addresses the spirit with the simple, startled words: "Elpenor! How camest thou under the shadowy darkness? Hast thou come faster on foot than I in my black ship?"[1] Which Pope renders thus:

> O, say, what angry power Elpenor led
> To glide in shades, and wander with the dead?
> How could thy soul, by realms and seas disjoined,
> Outfly the nimble sail, and leave the lagging wind?

I sincerely hope the reader finds no pleasure here, either in the nimbleness of the sail, or the laziness of the wind! And yet how is it that these conceits are so painful now, when they have been pleasant to us in the other instances?

For a very simple reason. They are not a *pathetic* fallacy at all, for they are put into the mouth of the wrong passion—a passion which never could possibly have spoken them—agonized curiosity. Ulysses wants to know the facts of the matter; and the very last thing his mind could do at the moment would be to pause, or suggest in anywise what was *not* a fact. The delay in the first three lines, and conceit in the last, jar upon us instantly, like the most frightful discord in music. No poet of true imaginative power could possibly have written the passage.

Therefore, we see that the spirit of truth must guide us in some sort, even in our enjoyment of fallacy. Coleridge's fallacy has no discord in it, but Pope's has set our teeth on edge. * * *

1856

From The Stones of Venice
[*The Savageness of Gothic Architecture*][2]

* * * I am not sure when the word "Gothic" was first generically applied to the architecture of the North; but I presume that, whatever the date of its original usage, it was intended to imply reproach, and express the barbaric character of the nations among whom that architecture arose. It never implied that they were literally of Gothic lineage, far less that their architecture had been originally invented by the Goths themselves; but it did imply that

1. *Odyssey* XI.57.   2. From Volume II, Chapter 6.

they and their buildings together exhibited a degree of sternness and rudeness, which, in contradistinction to the character of Southern and Eastern nations, appeared like a perpetual reflection of the contrast between the Goth and the Roman in their first encounter. And when that fallen Roman, in the utmost impotence of his luxury, and insolence of his guilt, became the model for the imitation of civilized Europe,[3] at the close of the so-called Dark Ages, the word Gothic became a term of unmitigated contempt, not unmixed with aversion. From that contempt, by the exertion of the antiquaries and architects of this century, Gothic architecture has been sufficiently vindicated; and perhaps some among us, in our admiration of the magnificent science of its structure, and sacredness of its expression, might desire that the term of ancient reproach should be withdrawn, and some other, of more apparent honorableness, adopted in its place. There is no chance, as there is no need, of such a substitution. As far as the epithet was used scornfully, it was used falsely; but there is no reproach in the word, rightly understood; on the contrary, there is a profound truth, which the instinct of mankind almost unconsciously recognizes. It is true, greatly and deeply true, that the architecture of the North is rude and wild; but it is not true that, for this reason, we are to condemn it, or despise. Far otherwise: I believe it is in this very character that it deserves our profoundest reverence.

The charts of the world which have been drawn up by modern science have thrown into a narrow space the expression of a vast amount of knowledge, but I have never yet seen any one pictorial enough to enable the spectator to imagine the kind of contrast in physical character which exists between Northern and Southern countries. We know the differences in detail, but we have not that broad glance and grasp which would enable us to feel them in their fullness. We know that gentians grow on the Alps, and olives on the Apennines; but we do not enough conceive for ourselves that variegated mosaic of the world's surface which a bird sees in its migration, that difference between the district of the gentian and of the olive which the stork and the swallow see far off, as they lean upon the sirocco wind.[4] Let us, for a moment, try to raise ourselves even above the level of their flight, and imagine the Mediterranean lying beneath us like an irregular lake, and all its ancient promontories sleeping in the sun: here and there an angry spot of thunder, a gray stain of storm, moving upon the burning field; and here and

3. Renaissance architecture, based on imitating classical buildings, was distasteful to Ruskin. He later stated that his aim in *The Stones of Venice* had been "to show that the Gothic architecture of Venice had risen out of * * * a state of pure national faith and domestic virtue; and that its Renaissance architecture had arisen out of * * * a state of concealed national infidelity and domestic corruption."

4. Hot wind from the southern Mediterranean.

there a fixed wreath of white volcano smoke, surrounded by its circle of ashes; but for the most part a great peacefulness of light, Syria and Greece, Italy and Spain, laid like pieces of a golden pavement into the sea-blue, chased, as we stoop nearer to them, with bossy beaten work of mountain chains, and glowing softly with terraced gardens, and flowers heavy with frankincense, mixed among masses of laurel, and orange, and plumy palm, that abate with their gray-green shadows the burning of the marble rocks, and of the ledges of porphyry sloping under lucent sand. Then let us pass farther towards the north, until we see the orient colors change gradually into a vast belt of rainy green, where the pastures of Switzerland, and poplar valleys of France, and dark forests of the Danube and Carpathians stretch from the mouths of the Loire to those of the Volga, seen through clefts in gray swirls of rain cloud and flaky veils of the mist of the brooks, spreading low along the pasture lands: and then, farther north still, to see the earth heave into mighty masses of leaden rock and heathy moor, bordering with a broad waste of gloomy purple that belt of field and wood, and splintering into irregular and grisly islands amidst the northern seas, beaten by storm, and chilled by ice drift, and tormented by furious pulses of contending tide, until the roots of the last forests fail from among the hill ravines, and the hunger of the north wind bites their peaks into barrenness; and, at last, the wall of ice, durable like iron, sets, deathlike, its white teeth against us out of the polar twilight. And, having once traversed in thought this gradation of the zoned iris of the earth in all its material vastness, let us go down nearer to it, and watch the parallel change in the belt of animal life: the multitudes of swift and brilliant creatures that glance in the air and sea, or tread the sands of the southern zone; striped zebras and spotted leopards, glistening serpents, and birds arrayed in purple and scarlet. Let us contrast their delicacy and brilliancy of color, and swiftness of motion, with the frost-cramped strength, and shaggy covering, and dusky plumage of the northern tribes; contrast the Arabian horse with the Shetland, the tiger and leopard with the wolf and bear, the antelope with the elk, the bird of paradise with the osprey: and then, submissively acknowledging the great laws by which the earth and all that it bears are ruled throughout their being, let us not condemn, but rejoice in the expression by man of his own rest in the statutes of the lands that gave him birth. Let us watch him with reverence as he sets side by side the burning gems, and smooths with soft sculpture the jasper pillars, that are to reflect a ceaseless sunshine, and rise into a cloudless sky: but not with less reverence let us stand by him, when, with rough strength and hurried stroke, he smites an uncouth animation out of the rocks which he has torn from among the moss of the moorland, and heaves into the darkened air the pile of iron buttress and rugged wall, instinct with work of an imagination as wild and wayward as the northern sea; creations of ungainly shape and rigid limb, but full of wolfish life; fierce as the winds that beat, and changeful as the clouds that shade them.

There is, I repeat, no degradation, no reproach in this, but all dignity and honorableness: and we should err grievously in refusing either to recognize as an essential character of the existing architecture of the North, or to admit as a desirable character in that which it yet may be, this wildness of thought, and roughness of work; this look of mountain brotherhood between the cathedral and the Alp; this magnificence of sturdy power, put forth only the more energetically because the fine finger-touch was chilled away by the frosty wind, and the eye dimmed by the moor mist, or blinded by the hail; this outspeaking of the strong spirit of men who may not gather redundant fruitage from the earth, nor bask in dreamy benignity of sunshine, but must break the rock for bread, and cleave the forest for fire, and show, even in what they did for their delight, some of the hard habits of the arm and heart that grew on them as they swung the ax or pressed the plow.

If, however, the savageness of Gothic architecture, merely as an expression of its origin among Northern nations, may be considered, in some sort, a noble character, it possesses a higher nobility still, when considered as an index, not of climate, but of religious principle.

In the 13th and 14th paragraphs of Chapter XXI of the first volume of this work, it was noticed that the systems of architectural ornament, properly so called, might be divided into three: (1) Servile ornament, in which the execution or power of the inferior workman is entirely subjected to the intellect of the higher; (2) Constitutional ornament, in which the executive inferior power is, to a certain point, emancipated and independent, having a will of its own, yet confessing its inferiority and rendering obedience to higher powers; and (3) Revolutionary ornament, in which no executive inferiority is admitted at all. I must here explain the nature of these divisions at somewhat greater length.

Of Servile ornament, the principal schools are the Greek, Ninevite, and Egyptian; but their servility is of different kinds. The Greek master-workman was far advanced in knowledge and power above the Assyrian or Egyptian. Neither he nor those for whom he worked could endure the appearance of imperfection in anything; and, therefore, what ornament he appointed to be done by those beneath him was composed of mere geometrical forms—balls, ridges, and perfectly symmetrical foliage—which could be executed with absolute precision by line and rule, and were as perfect in their way, when completed, as his own figure sculpture. The Assyrian and Egyptian, on the contrary, less cognizant of accurate form in anything, were content to allow their figure sculpture to be executed by inferior workmen, but lowered the method of its treatment to a standard which every workman could reach, and then trained him by discipline so rigid that there was no chance of his falling beneath the standard appointed. The Greek gave to the lower workman no subject which he could not perfectly execute. The Assyrian gave him subjects which he could only execute imperfectly, but fixed a legal standard for his imperfection. The workman was, in both systems, a slave.

But in the medieval, or especially Christian, system of ornament, this slavery is done away with altogether; Christianity having recognized, in small things as well as great, the individual value of every soul. But it not only recognizes its value; it confesses its imperfection, in only bestowing dignity upon the acknowledgment of unworthiness. That admission of lost power and fallen nature, which the Greek or Ninevite felt to be intensely painful, and, as far as might be, altogether refused, the Christian makes daily and hourly, contemplating the fact of it without fear, as tending, in the end, to God's greater glory. Therefore, to every spirit which Christianity summons to her service, her exhortation is: Do what you can, and confess frankly what you are unable to do; neither let your effort be shortened for fear of failure, nor your confession silenced for fear of shame. And it is, perhaps, the principal admirableness of the Gothic schools of architecture, that they thus receive the results of the labor of inferior minds; and out of fragments full of imperfection, and betraying that imperfection in every touch, indulgently raise up a stately and unaccusable whole.

But the modern English mind has this much in common with that of the Greek, that it intensely desires, in all things, the utmost completion or perfection compatible with their nature. This is a noble character in the abstract, but becomes ignoble when it causes us to forget the relative dignities of that nature itself, and to prefer the perfectness of the lower nature to the imperfection of the higher; not considering that as, judged by such a rule, all the brute animals would be preferable to man, because more perfect in their functions and kind, and yet are always held inferior to him, so also in the works of man, those which are more perfect in their kind are always inferior to those which are, in their nature, liable to more faults and shortcomings. For the finer the nature, the more flaws it will show through the clearness of it; and it is a law of this universe that the best things shall be seldomest seen in their best form. The wild grass grows well and strongly, one year with another; but the wheat is, according to the greater nobleness of its nature, liable to the bitterer blight. And therefore, while in all things that we see, or do, we are to desire perfection, and strive for it, we are nevertheless not to set the meaner thing, in its narrow accomplishment, above the nobler thing, in its mighty progress; not to esteem smooth minuteness above shattered majesty; not to prefer mean victory to honorable defeat; not to lower the level of our aim, that we may the more surely enjoy the complacency of success. But above all, in our dealings with the souls of other men, we are to take care how we check, by severe requirement or narrow caution, efforts which might otherwise lead to a noble issue; and, still more, how we withhold our admiration from great excellencies, because they are mingled with rough faults. Now, in the make and nature of every man, however rude or simple, whom we employ in manual labor, there are some powers for better things: some tardy imagination, torpid capacity of emotion, tottering steps of thought, there are, even at the worst; and in most cases it is all our own fault that they *are* tardy or torpid. But they cannot be strengthened, unless we are content to take them in their feebleness, and unless we prize and honor them in their imperfection above the best and most perfect manual skill. And this is what we have to do with all our laborers; to look for the *thoughtful* part of them, and get that out of them, whatever we lose for it, whatever faults and errors we are obliged to take with it. For the best that is in them cannot manifest itself, but in company with much error. Understand this clearly: You can teach a man to draw a straight line, and to cut one; to strike a curved line, and to carve it; and to copy and carve any number of given lines or forms, with admirable speed and perfect precision; and you find his work perfect of its kind: but if you ask him to think about any of those forms, to consider if he cannot find any better in his own head, he stops; his execution becomes hesitating; he thinks, and ten to one he thinks wrong; ten to one he makes a mistake in the first touch he gives to his work as a thinking being. But you have made a man of him for all that. He was only a machine before, an animated tool.

And observe, you are put to stern choice in this matter. You must either make a tool of the creature, or a man of him. You cannot make both. Men were not intended to work with the accuracy of tools, to be precise and perfect in all their actions. If you will have that precision out of them, and make their fingers measure degrees like cogwheels, and their arms strike curves like compasses, you must unhumanize them. All the energy of their spirits must be given to make cogs and compasses of themselves. All their attention and strength must go to the accomplishment of the mean act. The eye of the soul must be bent upon the finger point, and the soul's force must fill all the invisible nerves that guide it, ten hours a day, that it may not err from its steely precision, and so soul and sight be worn away, and the whole human being be lost at last—a heap of sawdust, so far as its intellectual work in this world is concerned; saved only by its Heart, which cannot go into the form of cogs and compasses, but expands, after the ten hours are over, into fireside humanity. On the other hand, if you will make a man of the working creature, you cannot make a tool. Let him but begin to imagine, to think, to try to do anything worth doing; and the engine-turned precision is lost at once. Out come all his roughness, all his dullness, all his incapability; shame upon shame, failure upon failure, pause after pause: but out comes the whole majesty of him also; and we know the height of it only, when we see the clouds settling upon him. And, whether the clouds be bright or dark, there will be transfiguration behind and within them.

And now, reader, look round this English room of yours, about which you have been proud so often, because the work of it was so good and strong, and the ornaments of it so finished. Examine again all those accurate moldings, and perfect polishings, and unerring adjustments of the seasoned wood and tempered steel. Many a time you have exulted over them, and thought how great England was, because her slightest work was done so thoroughly. Alas! if read rightly, these perfectnesses are signs of a slavery in our England a thousand times more bitter and more degrading than that of the scourged African, or helot[5] Greek. Men may be beaten, chained, tormented, yoked like cattle, slaughtered like summer flies, and yet remain in one sense, and the best sense, free. But to smother their souls within them, to blight and hew into rotting pollards[6] the suckling branches of their human intelligence, to make the flesh and skin which, after the worm's work on it, is to see God, into leathern thongs to yoke machinery with—this is to be slave-masters indeed; and there might be more freedom in England, though her feudal lords' lightest words were worth men's lives, and though the blood of the vexed husbandman dropped in the furrows of her fields, than there is while the animation of her multitudes is sent like fuel to feed the factory smoke, and the strength of them is given daily to be wasted into the fineness of a web, or racked into the exactness of a line.

And, on the other hand, go forth again to gaze upon the old cathedral front, where you have smiled so often at the fantastic ignorance of the old sculptors: examine once more those ugly goblins, and formless monsters, and stern statues, anatomiless and rigid; but do not mock at them, for they are signs of the life and liberty of every workman who struck the stone; a freedom of thought, and rank in scale of being, such as no laws, no charters, no charities can secure; but which it must be the first aim of all Europe at this day to regain for her children.

Let me not be thought to speak wildly or extravagantly. It is verily this degradation of the operative into a machine, which, more

5. A class of serfs in Sparta.   6. Trees with top branches cut back to the trunk.

than any other evil of the times, is leading the mass of the nations everywhere into vain, incoherent, destructive struggling for a freedom of which they cannot explain the nature to themselves. Their universal outcry against wealth, and against nobility, is not forced from them either by the pressure of famine, or the sting of mortified pride. These do much, and have done much in all ages; but the foundations of society were never yet shaken as they are at this day. It is not that men are ill fed, but that they have no pleasure in the work by which they make their bread, and therefore look to wealth as the only means of pleasure. It is not that men are pained by the scorn of the upper classes, but they cannot endure their own; for they feel that the kind of labor to which they are condemned is verily a degrading one, and makes them less than men. Never had the upper classes so much sympathy with the lower, or charity for them, as they have at this day, and yet never were they so much hated by them: for, of old, the separation between the noble and the poor was merely a wall built by law; now it is a veritable difference in level of standing, a precipice between upper and lower grounds in the field of humanity, and there is pestilential air at the bottom of it. I know not if a day is ever to come when the nature of right freedom will be understood, and when men will see that to obey another man, to labor for him, yield reverence to him or to his place, is not slavery. It is often the best kind of liberty—liberty from care. The man who says to one, Go, and he goeth, and to another, Come, and he cometh, has, in most cases, more sense of restraint and difficulty than the man who obeys him. The movements of the one are hindered by the burden on his shoulder; of the other, by the bridle on his lips: there is no way by which the burden may be lightened; but we need not suffer from the bridle if we do not champ at it. To yield reverence to another, to hold ourselves and our lives at his disposal, is not slavery; often, it is the noblest state in which a man can live in this world. There is, indeed, a reverence which is servile, that is to say irrational or selfish: but there is also noble reverence, that is to say, reasonable and loving; and a man is never so noble as when he is reverent in this kind; nay, even if the feeling pass the bounds of mere reason, so that it be loving, a man is raised by it. Which had, in reality, most of the serf nature in him—the Irish peasant who was lying in wait yesterday for his landlord, with his musket muzzle thrust through the ragged hedge; or that old mountain servant, who, 200 years ago, at Inverkeithing, gave up his own life and the lives of his seven sons for his chief?[7]—as each fell, calling forth his brother to the death, "Another for Hector!" And therefore, in all ages and all countries, reverence has been paid and sacrifice made by men to each other, not only without com-

---

7. An incident described in the Preface to Walter Scott's novel *The Fair Maid of Perth.*

plaint, but rejoicingly; and famine, and peril, and sword, and all evil, and all shame, have been borne willingly in the causes of masters and kings; for all these gifts of the heart ennobled the men who gave not less than the men who received them, and nature prompted, and God rewarded the sacrifice. But to feel their souls withering within them, unthanked, to find their whole being sunk into an unrecognized abyss, to be counted off into a heap of mechanism, numbered with its wheels, and weighed with its hammer strokes—this nature bade not—this God blesses not—this humanity for no long time is able to endure.

We have much studied and much perfected, of late, the great civilized invention of the division of labor; only we give it a false name. It is not, truly speaking, the labor that is divided; but the men: Divided into mere segments of men—broken into small fragments and crumbs of life; so that all the little piece of intelligence that is left in a man is not enough to make a pin, or a nail, but exhausts itself in making the point of a pin, or the head of a nail. Now it is a good and desirable thing, truly, to make many pins in a day; but if we could only see with what crystal sand their points were polished—sand of human soul, much to be magnified before it can be discerned for what it is—we should think there might be some loss in it also. And the great cry that rises from all our manufacturing cities, louder than their furnace blast, is all in very deed for this—that we manufacture everything there except men; we blanch cotton, and strengthen steel, and refine sugar, and shape pottery; but to brighten, to strengthen, to refine, or to form a single living spirit, never enters into our estimate of advantages. And all the evil to which that cry is urging our myriads can be met only in one way: not by teaching nor preaching, for to teach them is but to show them their misery, and to preach to them, if we do nothing more than preach, is to mock at it. It can be met only by a right understanding, on the part of all classes, of what kinds of labor are good for men, raising them, and making them happy; by a determined sacrifice of such convenience, or beauty, or cheapness as is to be got only by the degradation of the workman; and by equally determined demand for the products and results of healthy and ennobling labor.

And how, it will be asked, are these products to be recognized, and this demand to be regulated? Easily: by the observance of three broad and simple rules:

1. Never encourage the manufacture of any article not absolutely necessary, in the production of which *Invention* has no share.

2. Never demand an exact finish for its own sake, but only for some practical or noble end.

3. Never encourage imitation or copying of any kind, except for the sake of preserving record of great works.

The second of these principles is the only one which directly rises out of the consideration of our immediate subject; but I shall briefly explain the meaning and extent of the first also, reserving the enforcement of the third for another place.

1. Never encourage the manufacture of anything not necessary, in the production of which invention has no share.

For instance. Glass beads are utterly unnecessary, and there is no design or thought employed in their manufacture. They are formed by first drawing out the glass into rods; these rods are chopped up into fragments of the size of beads by the human hand, and the fragments are then rounded in the furnace. The men who chop up the rods sit at their work all day, their hands vibrating with a perpetual and exquisitely timed palsy, and the beads dropping beneath their vibration like hail. Neither they, nor the men who draw out the rods or fuse the fragments, have the smallest occasion for the use of any single human faculty; and every young lady, therefore, who buys glass beads is engaged in the slave trade, and in a much more cruel one than that which we have so long been endeavoring to put down.

But glass cups and vessels may become the subjects of exquisite invention; and if in buying these we pay for the invention, that is to say for the beautiful form, or color, or engraving, and not for mere finish of execution, we are doing good to humanity.

So, again, the cutting of precious stones, in all ordinary cases, requires little exertion of any mental faculty; some tact and judgment in avoiding flaws, and so on, but nothing to bring out the whole mind. Every person who wears cut jewels merely for the sake of their value is, therefore, a slave driver.

But the working of the goldsmith, and the various designing of grouped jewelry and enamel-work, may become the subject of the most noble human intelligence. Therefore, money spent in the purchase of well-designed plate, of precious engraved vases, cameos, or enamels, does good to humanity; and, in work of this kind, jewels may be employed to heighten its splendor; and their cutting is then a price paid for the attainment of a noble end, and thus perfectly allowable.

I shall perhaps press this law farther elsewhere, but our immediate concern is chiefly with the second, namely, never to demand an exact finish, when it does not lead to a noble end. For observe, I have only dwelt upon the rudeness of Gothic, or any other kind of imperfectness, as admirable, where it was impossible to get design or thought without it. If you are to have the thought of a rough and untaught man, you must have it in a rough and untaught way; but from an educated man, who can without effort express his thoughts in an educated way, take the graceful expression, and be thankful. Only *get* the thought, and do not silence the peasant because he cannot speak good grammar, or until you have taught him his grammar. Grammar and refinement are good things, both, only be sure of the better thing first. And thus in art, delicate finish is desirable from the greatest masters, and is always given by them. In some places Michael Angelo, Leonardo, Phidias, Perugino, Turner all finished with the most exquisite care; and the finish they give always leads to the fuller accomplishment of their noble purposes. But lower men than these cannot finish, for it requires consummate knowledge to finish consummately, and then we must take their thoughts as they are able to give them. So the rule is simple: Always look for invention first, and after that, for such execution as will help the invention, and as the inventor is capable of without painful effort, and *no more*. Above all, demand no refinement of execution where there is no thought, for that is slaves' work, unredeemed. Rather choose rough work than smooth work, so only that the practical purpose be answered, and never imagine there is reason to be proud of anything that may be accomplished by patience and sandpaper.

I shall only give one example, which however will show the reader what I mean, from the manufacture already alluded to, that of glass. Our modern glass is exquisitely clear in its substance, true in its form, accurate in its cutting. We are proud of this. We ought to be ashamed of it. The old Venice glass was muddy, inaccurate in all its forms, and clumsily cut, if at all. And the old Venetian was justly proud of it. For there is this difference between the English and Venetian workman, that the former thinks only of accurately matching his patterns, and getting his curves perfectly true and his edges perfectly sharp, and becomes a mere machine for rounding curves and sharpening edges, while the old Venetian cared not a whit whether his edges were sharp or not, but he invented a new design for every glass that he made, and never molded a handle or a lip without a new fancy in it. And therefore, though some Venetian glass is ugly and clumsy enough, when made by clumsy and uninventive workmen, other Venetian glass is so lovely in its forms that no price is too great for it; and we never see the same form in it twice. Now you cannot have the finish and the varied form too. If the workman is thinking about his edges, he cannot be thinking of his design; if of his design, he cannot think of his edges. Choose whether you will pay for the lovely form or the perfect finish, and choose at the same moment whether you will make the worker a man or a grindstone.

Nay, but the reader interrupts me—"If the workman can design beautifully, I would not have him kept at the furnace. Let him be taken away and made a gentleman, and have a studio, and design his glass there, and I will have it blown and cut for him by common workmen, and so I will have my design and my finish too."

All ideas of this kind are founded upon two mistaken suppositions: the first, that one man's thoughts can be, or ought to be, executed by another man's hands; the second, that manual labor is a degradation, when it is governed by intellect.

On a large scale, and in work determinable by line and rule, it is indeed both possible and necessary that the thoughts of one man should be carried out by the labor of others; in this sense I have already defined the best architecture to be the expression of the mind of manhood by the hands of childhood. But on a smaller scale, and in a design which cannot be mathematically defined, one man's thoughts can never be expressed by another: and the difference between the spirit of touch of the man who is inventing, and of the man who is obeying directions, is often all the difference between a great and a common work of art. How wide the separation is between original and secondhand execution, I shall endeavor to show elsewhere; it is not so much to our purpose here as to mark the other and more fatal error of despising manual labor when governed by intellect; for it is no less fatal an error to despise it when thus regulated by intellect, than to value it for its own sake. We are always in these days endeavoring to separate the two; we want one man to be always thinking, and another to be always working, and we call one a gentleman, and the other an operative; whereas the workman ought often to be thinking, and the thinker often to be working, and both should be gentlemen, in the best sense. As it is, we make both ungentle, the one envying, the other despising, his brother; and the mass of society is made up of morbid thinkers, and miserable workers. Now it is only by labor that thought can be made healthy, and only by thought that labor can be made happy, and the two cannot be separated with impunity. It would be well if all of us were good handicraftsmen in some kind, and the dishonor of manual labor done away with altogether; so that though there should still be a trenchant distinction of race between nobles and commoners, there should not, among the latter, be a trenchant distinction of employment, as between idle and working men, or between men of liberal and illiberal professions. All professions should be liberal, and there should be less pride felt in peculiarity of employment, and more in excellence of achievement. And yet more, in each several profession, no master should be too proud to do its hardest work. The painter should grind his own colors; the architect work in the mason's yard with his men; the master manufacturer be himself a more skillful operative than any man in his mills; and the distinction between one man and another be only in experience and skill, and the authority and wealth which these must naturally and justly obtain.

I should be led far from the matter in hand, if I were to pursue this interesting subject. Enough, I trust, has been said to show the reader that the rudeness or imperfection which at first rendered the term "Gothic" one of reproach is indeed, when rightly understood, one of the most noble characters of Christian architecture, and not only a noble but an *essential* one. It seems a fantastic paradox, but it is nevertheless a most important truth, that no architecture can be truly noble which is *not* imperfect. And this is easily demonstrable. For since the architect, whom we will suppose capable of doing all in perfection, cannot execute the whole with his own hands, he must either make slaves of his workmen in the old Greek, and present English fashion, and level his work to a slave's capacities, which is to degrade it; or else he must take his workmen as he finds them, and let them show their weaknesses together with their strength, which will involve the Gothic imperfection, but render the whole work as noble as the intellect of the age can make it.

But the principle may be stated more broadly still. I have confined the illustration of it to architecture, but I must not leave it as if true of architecture only. Hitherto I have used the words imperfect and perfect merely to distinguish between work grossly unskillful, and work executed with average precision and science; and I have been pleading that any degree of unskillfulness should be admitted, so only that the laborer's mind had room for expression. But, accurately speaking, no good work whatever can be perfect, and *the demand for perfection is always a sign of a misunderstanding of the ends of art.*

This for two reasons, both based on everlasting laws. The first, that no great man ever stops working till he has reached his point of failure; that is to say, his mind is always far in advance of his powers of execution, and the latter will now and then give way in trying to follow it; besides that he will always give to the inferior portions of his work only such inferior attention as they require; and according to his greatness he becomes so accustomed to the feeling of dissatisfaction with the best he can do, that in moments of lassitude or anger with himself he will not care though the beholder be dissatisfied also. I believe there has only been one man who would not acknowledge this necessity, and strove always to reach perfection, Leonardo; the end of his vain effort being merely that he would take ten years to a picture, and leave it unfinished. And therefore, if we are to have great men working at all, or less men doing their best, the work will be imperfect, however beautiful. Of human work none but what is bad can be perfect, in its own bad way.[8]

8. "The Elgin marbles are supposed by many persons to be 'perfect.' In the most important portions they indeed approach perfection, but only there. The draperies are unfinished, the hair and wool of the animals are unfinished, and the entire bas-reliefs of the frieze are roughtly cut" [Ruskin's note]. Ruskin is referring to the collection of statues brought from Athens to England by Lord Elgin, statues which were considered models of perfect realism.

The second reason is that imperfection is in some sort essential to all that we know of life. It is the sign of life in a mortal body, that is to say, of a state of progress and change. Nothing that lives is, or can be, rigidly perfect; part of it is decaying, part nascent. The foxglove blossom—a third part bud, a third part past, a third part in full bloom—is a type of the life of this world. And in all things that live there are certain irregularities and deficiencies which are not only signs of life, but sources of beauty. No human face is exactly the same in its lines on each side, no leaf perfect in its lobes, no branch in its symmetry. All admit irregularity as they imply change; and to banish imperfection is to destroy expression, to check exertion, to paralyze vitality. All things are literally better, lovelier, and more beloved for the imperfections which have been divinely appointed, that the law of human life may be Effort, and the law of human judgment, Mercy.

Accept this then for a universal law, that neither architecture nor any other noble work of man can be good unless it be imperfect; and let us be prepared for the otherwise strange fact, which we shall discern clearly as we approach the period of the Renaissance, that the first cause of the fall of the arts of Europe was a relentless requirement of perfection, incapable alike either of being silenced by veneration for greatness, or softened into forgiveness of simplicity.

Thus far then of the Rudeness or Savageness, which is the first mental element of Gothic architecture. It is an element in many other healthy architectures also, as in Byzantine and Romanesque; but true Gothic cannot exist without it. * * *

1851–53

The Storm-Cloud of the Nineteenth Century

Lecture I[1]

Let me first assure my audience that I have no *arrière pensée*[2] in the title chosen for this lecture. I might, indeed, have meant, and it

1. Delivered February 4, 1884, at the London Institution. Some newspapers complained that the lecture seemed merely to blame air pollution on the Devil; however, what Ruskin was blaming was the devil of industrialism, the source of the "Manchester devil's darkness" and of the "dense manufacturing mist." As E. T. Cook noted: "industrial statistics fully bear out the date which Ruskin fixes for the growth of the phenomena in question: the storm-cloud thickened just when the consumption of coal went up by leaps and bounds, both in this country [England] and in the industrialized parts of central Europe." Much of the evidence cited in the lecture derives from diaries and sketchbooks in which, over a period of 50 years, Ruskin had recorded observations of sunsets and storms, a record that enabled him to point up the changes. As he stated in his second lecture: "Had the weather when I was young been such as it is now, no book such as *Modern Painters* ever would or *could* have been written; for every argument, and every sentiment in that book, was founded on the personal experience of the beauty and blessing of nature, all spring and summer long; and on the then demonstrable fact that over a great portion of the world's surface the air and the earth were fitted to the education of the spirit of man as closely as a schoolboy's primer is to his labor, and as gloriously as a lover's mistress is to his eyes.

"That harmony is now broken, and broken the world round. * * *"
2. Afterthought or hidden meaning.

would have been only too like me to mean, any number of things
by such a title;—but, tonight, I mean simply what I have said, and
propose to bring to your notice a series of cloud phenomena, which,
so far as I can weigh existing evidence, are peculiar to our own
times; yet which have not hitherto received any special notice or
description from meteorologists.

So far as the existing evidence, I say, of former literature can be
interpreted, the storm-cloud—or more accurately plague-cloud, for
it is not always stormy—which I am about to describe to you, never
was seen but by now living, or *lately* living eyes. It is not yet twenty
years that this—I may well call it, wonderful—cloud has been, in
its essence, recognizable. There is no description of it, so far as I
have read, or by any ancient observer. Neither Homer nor Virgil,
neither Aristophanes nor Horace, acknowledge any such clouds
among those compelled by Jove. Chaucer has no word of them, nor
Dante; Milton none, nor Thomson. In modern times, Scott,
Wordsworth, and Byron are alike unconscious of them; and the
most observant and descriptive of scientific men, De Saussure,[3] is
utterly silent concerning them. Taking up the traditions of air from
the year before Scott's death, I am able, by my own constant and
close observation, to certify you that in the forty following years
(1831 to 1871 approximately—for the phenomena in question
came on gradually)—no such clouds as these are, and are now often
for months without intermission, were ever seen in the skies of England, France, or Italy.

In those old days, when weather was fine, it was luxuriously fine;
when it was bad—it was often abominably bad, but it had its fit of
temper and was done with it—it didn't sulk for three months without letting you see the sun,—nor send you one cyclone inside out,
every Saturday afternoon, and another outside in, every Monday
morning.

In fine weather the sky was either blue or clear in its light; the
clouds, either white or golden, adding to, not abating, the luster of
the sky. In wet weather, there were two different species of clouds,
—those of beneficent rain, which for distinction's sake I will call
the non-electric rain-cloud, and those of storm, usually charged
highly with electricity. The beneficent rain-cloud was indeed often
extremely dull and gray for days together, but gracious nevertheless,
felt to be doing good, and often to be delightful after drought; capable also of the most exquisite coloring, under certain conditions;
and continually traversed in clearing by the rainbow:—and, secondly, the storm-cloud, always majestic, often dazzlingly beautiful,
and felt also to be beneficent in its own way, affecting the mass of

3. Horace Bénédict de Saussure (1740–99), Swiss geologist and alpinist.

the air with vital agitation, and purging it from the impurity of all morbific elements.

In the entire system of the Firmament, thus seen and understood, there appeared to be, to all the thinkers of those ages, the incontrovertible and unmistakable evidence of a Divine Power in creation, which had fitted, as the air for human breath, so the clouds for human sight and nourishment;—the Father who was in heaven feeding day by day the souls of His children with marvels, and satisfying them with bread, and so filling their hearts with food and gladness.[4]

* * *

Thus far then of clouds that were once familiar; now at last, entering on my immediate subject, I shall best introduce it to you by reading an entry in my diary which gives progressive description of the most gentle aspect of the modern plague-cloud.

> Bolton Abbey, 4th July, 1875.
> Half-past eight, morning; the first bright morning for the last fortnight.
> At half-past five it was entirely clear, and entirely calm; the moorlands glowing, and the Wharfe[5] glittering in sacred light, and even the thin-stemmed field-flowers quiet as stars, in the peace in which—
>
> > All trees and simples, great and small,
> > That balmy leaf do bear,
> > Than they were painted on a wall,
> > No more do move, nor steir.[6]
>
> But, an hour ago, the leaves at my window first shook slightly. They are now trembling *continuously*, as those of all the trees, under a gradually rising wind, of which the tremulous action sacrcely permits the direction to be defined,—but which falls and returns in fits of varying force, like those which precede a thunderstorm—never wholly ceasing: the direction of its upper current is shown by a few ragged white clouds, moving fast from the north, which rose, at the time of the first leaf-shaking, behind the edge of the moors in the east.
> This wind is the plague-wind of the eighth decade of years in the nineteenth century; a period which will assuredly be recognized in future meteorological history as one of phenomena hitherto unrecorded in the courses of nature, and characterized preeminently by the almost ceaseless action of this calamitous wind. While I have been writing these sentences, the white clouds above specified have increased to twice the size they had when I

---

4. Acts xiv.17.
5. River near Bolton Abbey in Yorkshire.
6. Stir. From a hymn by a Scottish clergyman, Alexander Herne (1560–1609).

began to write; and in about two hours from this time—say by eleven o'clock, if the wind continue,—the whole sky will be dark with them, as it was yesterday, and has been through prolonged periods during the last five years. I first noticed the definite character of this wind, and of the clouds it brings with it, in the year 1871, describing it then in the July number of *Fors Clavigera*; but little, at that time, apprehending either its universality, or any probability of its annual continuance. I am able now to state positively that its range of power extends from the North of England to Sicily; and that it blows more or less during the whole of the year, except the early autumn. This autumnal abdication is, I hope, beginning: it blew but feebly yesterday, though without intermission, from the north, making every shady place cold, while the sun was burning; its effect on the sky being only to dim the blue of it between masses of ragged cumulus. Today it has entirely fallen; and there seems hope of bright weather, the first for me since the end of May, when I had two fine days at Aylesbury; the third, May 28th, being black again from morning to evening. There seems to be some reference to the blackness caused by the prevalence of this wind in the old French name of Bise, "*grey* wind"; and, indeed, one of the darkest and bitterest days of it I ever saw was at Vevay in 1872.

The first time I recognized the clouds brought by the plague-wind as distinct in character was in walking back from Oxford, after a hard day's work, to Abingdon, in the early spring of 1871: it would take too long to give you any account this evening of the particulars which drew my attention to them; but during the following months I had too frequent opportunities of verifying my first thoughts of them, and on the first of July in that year wrote the description of them which begins the *Fors Clavigera* of August, thus:—

It is the first of July, and I sit down to write by the dismalest light that ever yet I wrote by; namely, the light of this midsummer morning, in mid-England (Matlock, Derbyshire), in the year 1871.

For the sky is covered with gray cloud;—not rain-cloud, but a dry black veil, which no ray of sunshine can pierce; partly diffused in mist, feeble mist, enough to make distant objects unintelligible, yet without any substance, or wreathing, or color of its own. And everywhere the leaves of the trees are shaking fitfully, as they do before a thunderstorm; only not violently, but enough to show the passing to and fro of a strange, bitter, blighting wind. Dismal enough, had it been the first morning of its kind that summer had sent. But during all this spring, in London, and at Oxford, through meager March, through changelessly sullen

April, through despondent May, and darkened June, morning after morning has come gray-shrouded thus.

And it is a new thing to me, and a very dreadful one. I am fifty years old, and more; and since I was five, have gleaned the best hours of my life in the sun of spring and summer mornings; and I never saw such as these, till now.

And the scientific men are busy as ants, examining the sun and the moon, and the seven stars, and can tell me all about *them*, I believe, by this time; and how they move, and what they are made of.

And I do not care, for my part, two copper spangles how they move, nor what they are made of. I can't move them any other way than they go, nor make them of anything else, better than they are made. But I would care much and give much, if I could be told where this bitter wind comes from, and what *it* is made of.

For, perhaps, with forethought, and fine laboratory science, one might make it of something else.

It looks partly as if it were made of poisonous smoke; very possibly it may be: there are at least two hundred furnace chimneys in a square of two miles on every side of me. But mere smoke would not blow to and fro in that wild way. It looks more to me as if it were made of dead men's souls—such of them as are not gone yet where they have to go, and may be flitting hither and thither, doubting, themselves, of the fittest place for them.

You know, if there *are* such things as souls, and if ever any of them haunt places where they have been hurt, there must be many above us, just now, displeased enough!

The last sentence refers of course to the battles of the Franco-German campaign, which was especially horrible to me, in its digging, as the Germans should have known, a moat flooded with waters of death between the two nations for a century to come.

Since that Midsummer day, my attention, however otherwise occupied, has never relaxed in its record of the phenomena characteristic of the plague-wind; and I now define for you, as briefly as possible, the essential signs of it.

(1.) It is a wind of darkness,—all the former conditions of tormenting winds, whether from the north or east, were more or less capable of co-existing with sunlight, and often with steady and bright sunlight; but whenever, and wherever the plague-wind blows, be it but for ten minutes, the sky is darkened instantly.

(2.) It is a malignant *quality* of wind, unconnected with any one quarter of the compass; it blows indifferently from all, attaching its own bitterness and malice to the worst characters of the proper winds of each quarter. It will blow either with drenching rain, or dry rage, from the south,—with ruinous blasts from the west,—with bitterest chills from the north,—and with venomous blight from the east.

Its own favorite quarter, however, is the southwest, so that it is distinguished in its malignity equally from the Bise of Provence, which is a north wind always, and from our own old friend, the east.

(3.) It always blows *tremulously*, making the leaves of the trees shudder as if they were all aspens, but with a peculiar fitfulness which gives them—and I watch them this moment as I write—an expression of anger as well as of fear and distress. You may see the kind of quivering, and hear the ominous whimpering, in the gusts that precede a great thunderstorm; but plague-wind is more panic-struck, and feverish; and its sound is a hiss instead of a wail.

When I was last at Avallon, in South France, I went to see *Faust*[7] played at the little country theater: it was done with scarcely any means of pictorial effect, except a few old curtains, and a blue light or two. But the night on the Brocken was nevertheless extremely appalling to me,—a strange ghastliness being obtained in some of the witch scenes merely by fine management of gesture and drapery; and in the phantom scenes, by the half-palsied, half-furious, faltering or fluttering past of phantoms stumbling as into graves; as if of not only soulless, but senseless, Dead, moving with the very action, the rage, the decrepitude, and the trembling of the plague-wind.

(4.) Not only tremulous at every moment, it is also *intermittent* with a rapidity quite unexampled in former weather. There are, indeed, days—and weeks, on which it blows without cessation, and is as inevitable as the Gulf Stream; but also there are days when it is contending with healthy weather, and on such days it will remit for half an hour, and the sun will begin to show itself, and then the wind will come back and cover the whole sky with clouds in ten minutes; and so on, every half-hour, through the whole day; so that it is often impossible to go on with any kind of drawing in color, the light being never for two seconds the same from morning till evening.

(5.) It degrades, while it intensifies, ordinary storm; but before I read you any description of its efforts in this kind, I must correct an impression which has got abroad through the papers, that I speak as if the plague-wind blew now always, and there were no more any natural weather. On the contrary, the winter of 1787–9 was one of the most healthy and lovely I ever saw ice in;—Coniston lake[8]

7. Goethe's drama, which Ruskin saw in 1882.
8. In the Lake District of North Lanca-shire where Ruskin's house, Brantwood, was located.

shone under the calm clear frost in one marble field, as strong as the floor of Milan Cathedral, half a mile across and four miles down; and the first entries in my diary which I read you shall be from the 22nd to 26th June, 1876, of perfectly lovely and natural weather:—

Sunday, 25th June, 1876

Yesterday, an entirely glorious sunset, unmatched in beauty since that at Abbeville,[9]—deep scarlet, and purest rose, on purple gray, in bars; and stationary, plumy, sweeping filaments above in upper sky, like *"using up the brush,"* said Joanie; remaining in glory, every moment best, changing from one good into another, (but only in color or light—*form steady,*) for half an hour full, and the clouds afterwards fading into the gray against amber twilight, *stationary in the same form for about two hours,* at least. The darkening rose tint remained till half-past ten, the grand time being at nine.

The day had been fine,—exquisite green light on afternoon hills.

Monday, 26th June, 1876.

Yesterday an entirely perfect summer light on the Old Man;[1] Lancaster Bay all clear; Ingleborough and the great Pennine fault as on a map. Divine beauty of western color on thyme and rose, —then twilight of clearest *warm* amber far into night, of *pale* amber all night long; hills dark-clear against it.

And so it continued, only growing more intense in blue and sunlight, all day. After breakfast, I came in from the well under strawberry bed, to say I had never seen anything like it, so pure or intense, in Italy; and so it went glowing on, cloudless, with soft north wind, all day.

16th July.

The sunset almost too bright *through the blinds* for me to read Humboldt at tea by,—finally, new moon like a lime-light, reflected on breeze-struck water; traces, across dark calm, of reflected hills.

These extracts are, I hope, enough to guard you against the absurdity of supposing that it all only means that I am myself soured, or doting, in my old age, and always in an ill humor. Depend upon it, when old men are worth anything, they are better-humored than young ones; and have learned to see what good there is, and pleasantness, in the world they are likely so soon to have orders to quit.

Now then—take the following sequences of accurate description of thunderstorm, *with* plague-wind.

9. Ruskin had made a sketch of this sunset, in October 1868, and described it as "a beautiful example of what * * * a sunset could then be, in the districts of Kent and Picardy unaffected by smoke." 1. Mountain near Ruskin's home.

22nd June, 1876.

Thunderstorm; pitch dark, with no *blackness*,—but deep, high, *filthiness* of lurid, yet not sublimely lurid, smoke-cloud; dense manufacturing mist; fearful squalls of shivery wind, making Mr. Severn's sails[2] quiver like a man in a fever fit—all about four, afternoon—but only two or three claps of thunder, and feeble, though near, flashes. I never saw such a dirty, weak, foul storm. It cleared suddenly after raining all afternoon, at half-past eight to nine, into pure, natural weather,—low rain-clouds on quite clear, green, wet hills.

Brantwood, 13th August, 1879.

The most terrific and horrible thunderstorm, this morning, I ever remember. It waked me at six, or a little before—then rolling incessantly, like railway luggage trains, quite ghastly in its mockery of them—the air one loathsome mass of sultry and foul fog, like smoke; scarcely raining at all, but increasing to heavier rollings, with flashes quivering vaguely through all the air, and at last terrific double streams of reddish-violet fire, not forked or zigzag, but rippled rivulets—two at the same instant some twenty to thirty degrees apart, and lasting on the eye at least half a second, with grand artillery-peals following; not rattling crashes, or irregular cracklings, but delivered volleys. It lasted an hour, then passed off, clearing a little, without rain to speak of,—not a glimpse of blue,—and now, half-past seven, seems settling down again into Manchester devil's darkness.

Quarter to eight, morning.—Thunder returned, all the air collapsed into one black fog, the hills invisible, and scarcely visible the opposite shore; heavy rain in short fits, and frequent, though less formidable, flashes, and shorter thunder. While I have written this sentence the cloud has again dissolved itself, like a nasty solution in a bottle, with miraculous and unnatural rapidity, and the hills are in sight again; a double-forked flash—rippled, I mean, like the others—starts into its frightful ladder of light between me and Wetherlam, as I raise my eyes. All black above, a rugged spray cloud on the Eaglet. The "Eaglet" is my own name for the bold and elevated crag to the west of the little lake above Coniston mines. It had no name among the country people, and is one of the most conspicuous features of the mountain chain, as seen from Brantwood.)

Half-past eight.—Three times light and three times dark since last I wrote, and the darkness seeming each time as it settles more loathsome, at last stopping my reading in mere blindness. One lurid gleam of white cumulus in upper lead-blue sky, seen for half a minute through the sulphurous chimney-pot vomit of blackguardly cloud beneath, where its rags were thinnest.

---

2. A neighbor's sailboat on Coniston Lake.

Thursday, 22nd Feb. 1883.

Yesterday a fearfully dark mist all afternoon, with steady, south plague-wind of the bitterest, nastiest, poisonous blight, and fretful flutter. I could scarcely stay in the wood for the horror of it. Today, really rather bright blue, and bright semi-cumuli, with the frantic Old Man blowing sheaves of lancets and chisels across the lake—not in strength enough, or whirl enough, to raise it in spray, but tracing every squall's outline in black on the silver grey waves, and whistling meanly, and as if on a flute made of a file.

Sunday, 17th August, 1879.

Raining in foul drizzle, slow and steady; sky pitch-dark, and I just get a little light by sitting in the bow-window; diabolic clouds over everything: and looking over my kitchen garden yesterday, I found it one miserable mass of weeds gone to seed, the roses in the higher garden putrefied into brown sponges, feeling like dead snails; and the half-ripe strawberries all rotten at the stalks.

And now I come to the most important sign of the plague-wind and the plague-cloud: that in bringing on their peculiar darkness, they *blanch* the sun instead of reddening it. And here I must note briefly to you the uselessness of observation by instruments, or machines, instead of eyes. In the first year when I had begun to notice the specialty of the plague-wind, I went of course to the Oxford observatory to consult its registrars. They have their anemometer always on the twirl, and can tell you the force, or at least the pace, of a gale, by day or night. But the anemometer can only record for you how often it has been driven round, not at all whether it went round *steadily*, or went round *trembling*. And on that point depends the entire question whether it is a plague breeze or a healthy one: and what's the use of telling you whether the wind's strong or not, when it can't tell you whether it's a strong medicine, or a strong poison?

But again—you have your *sun*-measure, and can tell exactly at any moment how strong, or how weak, or how wanting, the sun is. But the sun-measurer can't tell you whether the rays are stopped by a dense *shallow* cloud, or a thin *deep* one. In healthy weather, the sun is hidden behind a cloud, as it is behind a tree; and, when the cloud is past, it comes out again, as bright as before. But in plague-wind, the sun is choked out of the whole heaven, all day long, by a cloud which may be a thousand miles square and five miles deep.

And yet observe: that thin, scraggy, filthy, mangy, miserable cloud, for all the depth of it, can't turn the sun red, as a good, business-like fog does with a hundred feet or so of itself. By the plague-wind every breath of air you draw is polluted, half round the world;

in a London fog the air itself is pure, though you choose to mix up dirt with it, and choke yourself with your own nastiness.

Now I'm going to show you a diagram of a sunset in entirely pure weather, above London smoke.[3] I saw it and sketched it from my old post of observation—the top garret of my father's house at Herne Hill. There, when the wind is south, we are outside of the smoke and above it; and this diagram, admirably enlarged from my own drawing by my, now in all things best aide-de-camp, Mr. Collingwood, shows you an old-fashioned sunset—the sort of thing Turner and I used to have to look at,—(nobody else ever would) constantly. Every sunset and every dawn, in fine weather, had something of the sort to show us. This is one of the last pure sunsets I ever saw, about the year 1876,—and the point I want you to note in it is, that the air being pure, the smoke on the horizon, though at last it hides the sun, yet hides it through gold and vermilion. Now, don't go away fancying there's any exaggeration in that study. The *prismatic* colors, I told you, were simply impossible to paint; these, which are transmitted colors, can indeed be suggested, but no more. The brightest pigment we have would look dim beside the truth.

I should have liked to have blotted down for you a bit of plague-cloud to put beside this; but Heaven knows, you can see enough of it nowadays without any trouble of mine; and if you want, in a hurry, to see what the sun looks like through it, you've only to throw a bad half-crown into a basin of soap and water.

Blanched Sun,—blighted grass,—blinded man.—If, in conclusion, you ask me for any conceivable cause or meaning of these things—I can tell you none, according to your modern beliefs; but I can tell you what meaning it would have borne to the men of old time. Remember, for the last twenty years, England, and all foreign nations, either tempting her, or following her, have blasphemed[4] the name of God deliberately and openly; and have done iniquity by proclamation, every man doing as much injustice to his brother as it is in his power to do. Of states in such moral gloom every seer of old predicted the physical gloom, saying, "The light shall be darkened in the heavens thereof, and the stars shall withdraw their shining."[5] All Greek, all Christian, all Jewish prophecy insists on

---

3. The illustration shown at the lecture was entitled "An Old-Fashioned Sunset, 1876."
4. Ruskin, in a note, defined blasphemy as " 'harmful speaking'–not against God only, but against man, and against all the good works and purposes of Nature. The word is accurately opposed to 'Eu-

phemy,' the right or well-speaking of God and His world. * * * And the universal instinct of blasphemy in the modern scientific mind is above all manifested in its love of what is ugly, and natural enthrallment by the abominable."
5. Joel ii.10.

the same truth through a thousand myths; but of all the chief, to former thought, was the fable of the Jewish warrior and prophet, for whom the sun hasted not to go down,[6] with which I leave you to compare at leisure the physical result of your own wars and prophecies, as declared by your own elect journal not fourteen days ago,—that the Empire of England, on which formerly the sun never set, has become one on which he never rises.[7]

What is best to be done, do you ask me? The answer is plain. Whether you can affect the signs of the sky or not, you *can* the signs of the times. Whether you can bring the *sun* back or not, you can assuredly bring back your own cheerfulness, and your own honesty. You may not be able to say to the winds, "Peace; be still,"[8] but you can cease from the insolence of your own lips, and the troubling of your own passions. And all *that* it would be extremely well to do, even though the day *were* coming when the sun should be as darkness, and the moon as blood.[9] But, the paths of rectitude and piety once regained, who shall say that the promise of old time would not be found to hold for us also?—"Bring ye all the tithes into my storehouse, and prove me now herewith, saith the Lord God, if I will not open you the windows of heaven, and pour you out a blessing, that there shall not be room enough to receive it."[1]

1884

6. On Joshua's commanding the sun to stand still, see Joshua x.13.
7. In January, 1884, after weeks of sunless weather, the *Pall Mall Gazette* had made joking references to the popular boast about the sun never setting on the British dominions, for the good reason that it never rises.
8. Mark iv.39.
9. Cf. the prophecy in Revelation vi.12: "the sun became black as sackcloth of hair, and the moon became as blood."
1. Malachi iii.10.

THOMAS HENRY HUXLEY
(1825–1895)

In Victorian controversies over religion and education, one of the most distinctive participants was Thomas Henry Huxley, a scientist who wrote clear, readable, and very persuasive English prose. Huxley's literary skill was responsible for his being lured out of his laboratory onto the platforms of public debate where his role was to champion, as he said, "the application of scientific methods of investigation to all the problems of life."

Huxley, a schoolmaster's son, was born in a London suburb. Until beginning the study of medicine, at 17, he had had little formal education, having taught himself classical and modern languages as well as the rudiments of scientific theory. In 1846, after receiving his degree in medicine, he embarked on a long voyage to the South Seas during which he studied the marine life of the tropical oceans and established a considerable reputation as a zoologist. Later he made investigations in geology and physiology, completing a total of 250 research papers during his lifetime. He also held teaching positions and served on public committees, but it was as a popularizer of science that he made his real mark. His popularizing was of two kinds. The first was to make the results of scientific investigations intelligible to a large audience. Such lectures as *On a Piece of Chalk* (too long to include here) are models of clear, vivid exposition that can be studied with profit by anyone interested in the art of teaching. His second kind of popularizing consisted of expounding the values of scientific education or of the application of scientific thinking to problems in religion. Here Huxley excels not so much as a teacher as a debater. In 1860 he demonstrated his argumentative skill when, as Darwin's defender or "Bulldog," he demolished Bishop Wilberforce in a battle over *The Origin of Species*. In the 1870's, in such lectures as *Science and Culture*, he engaged in more genial fencing with Matthew Arnold concerning the relative importance of the study of science or the humanities in education. And in the 1880's he debated with Gladstone on the topic of interpreting the Bible. His essay *Agnosticism and Christianity* indicates his premises in this controversy.

Summing up his own career in his *Autobiography*, Huxley noted that he had subordinated his ambition for scientific fame to other ends: "to the popularization of science; to the development and organization of scientific education; to the endless series of battles and skirmishes over evolution; and to untiring opposition to that ecclesiastical spirit, that clericalism, which * * * to whatever denomination it may belong, is the deadly enemy of science." In fighting these "battles" Huxley operated from different bases. Most of the time he wrote as a biologist engaged in assessing all assumptions by the tests of laboratory science. In this role he argued that man is merely an animal and that traditional religion is a tissue of superstitions and lies. At other times, however, Huxley wrote as a humanist and even as a follower of Carlyle. As he stated in a letter: "*Sartor Resartus* led me to know that a deep sense of religion was compatible with the entire absence of theology." In this second role he argued that man is a very special kind of animal whose great distinction is that he is endowed with a moral sense and with freedom of the will, a creature who is admirable not for following nature but for departing from nature. The humanistic streak muddies the seemingly clear current of Huxley's thinking yet makes him a more interesting figure than he might otherwise have been. It is noteworthy that in the writings of his grandsons, Julian Huxley, the biologist, and Aldous Huxley, the novelist, a similar division of mind can once more be detected.

Even in his dying, T. H. Huxley continued his role as controversialist. The words he asked to be engraved on his tomb are typical of his view of life and typical, also, in the effect they had on his contemporaries, some of whom found the epitaph to be shocking:

> Be not afraid, ye waiting hearts that weep
> For still he giveth His beloved sleep,
> And if an endless sleep He wills, so best.

From A Liberal Education[1]

[A *Game of Chess*]

Suppose it were perfectly certain that the life and fortune of every one of us would, one day or other, depend upon his winning or losing a game of chess. Don't you think that we should all consider it to be a primary duty to learn at least the names and the moves of the pieces; to have a notion of a gambit,[2] and a keen eye for all the means of giving and getting out of check? Do you not think that we should look with a disapprobation amounting to scorn, upon the father who allowed his son, or the state which allowed its members, to grow up without knowing a pawn from a knight?

Yet it is a very plain and elementary truth that the life, the fortune, and the happiness of every one of us, and, more or less, of those who are connected with us, do depend upon our knowing something of the rules of a game infinitely more difficult and complicated than chess. It is a game which has been played for untold ages, every man and woman of us being one of the two players in a game of his or her own. The chessboard is the world, the pieces are the phenomena of the universe, the rules of the game are what we call the laws of Nature. The player on the other side is hidden from us. We know that his play is always fair, just, and patient. But also we know, to our cost, that he never overlooks a mistake, or makes the smallest allowance for ignorance. To the man who plays well, the highest stakes are paid, with that sort of overflowing generosity with which the strong shows delight in strength. And one who plays ill is checkmated—without haste, but without remorse.

My metaphor will remind some of you of the famous picture in which Retzsch[3] has depicted Satan playing at chess with man for his soul. Substitute for the mocking fiend in that picture a calm, strong angel who is playing for love, as we say, and would rather lose than win—and I should accept it as an image of human life.

Well, what I mean by Education is learning the rules of this mighty game. In other words, education is the instruction of the intellect in the laws of Nature, under which name I include not merely things and their forces, but men and their ways; and the fashioning of the affections and of the will into an earnest and loving desire to move in harmony with those laws. For me, education means neither more nor less than this. Anything which professes to call itself education must be tried by this standard, and if it

---

1. Originally an address, delivered at the South London Working Men's College in 1868.

2. Opening move in chess.

3. Friedrich A. M. Retzsch (1779–1857), German painter.

fails to stand the test, I will not call it education, whatever may be the force of authority, or of numbers, upon the other side.

It is important to remember that, in strictness, there is no such thing as an uneducated man. Take an extreme case. Suppose that an adult man, in the full vigor of his faculties, could be suddenly placed in the world, as Adam is said to have been, and then left to do as he best might. How long would he be left uneducated? Not five minutes. Nature would begin to teach him, through the eye, the ear, the touch, the properties of objects. Pain and pleasure would be at his elbow telling him to do this and avoid that; and by slow degrees the man would receive an education which, if narrow, would be thorough, real, and adequate to his circumstances, though there would be no extras and very few accomplishments.

And if to this solitary man entered a second Adam or, better still, an Eve, a new and greater world, that of social and moral phenomena, would be revealed. Joys and woes, compared with which all others might seem but faint shadows, would spring from the new relations. Happiness and sorrow would take the place of the coarser monitors, pleasure and pain; but conduct would still be shaped by the observation of the natural consequences of actions; or, in other words, by the laws of the nature of man.

To every one of us the world was once as fresh and new as to Adam. And then, long before we were susceptible of any other mode of instruction, Nature took us in hand, and every minute of waking life brought its educational influence, shaping our actions into rough accordance with Nature's laws, so that we might not be ended untimely by too gross disobedience. Nor should I speak of this process of education as past for anyone, be he as old as he may. For every man the world is as fresh as it was at the first day, and as full of untold novelties for him who has the eyes to see them. And Nature is still continuing her patient education of us in that great university, the universe, of which we are all members—Nature having no Test Acts.[4]

Those who take honors in Nature's university, who learn the laws which govern men and things and obey them, are the really great and successful men in this world. The great mass of mankind are the "Poll," [5] who pick up just enough to get through without much discredit. Those who won't learn at all are plucked;[6] and then you can't come up again. Nature's pluck means extermination.

Thus the question of compulsory education is settled so far as Nature is concerned. Her bill on that question was framed and passed long ago. But, like all compulsory legislation, that of Nature

---

4. Legislation (repealed in 1854) which excluded from Oxford and Cambridge any student who would not profess faith in the 39 Articles of the Church of England.

5. English slang term describing the mass of students who get through college with very low (but passing) grades.
6. Failed.

is harsh and wasteful in its operation. Ignorance is visited as sharply as willful disobedience—incapacity meets with the same punishment as crime. Nature's discipline is not even a word and a blow, and the blow first; but the blow without the word. It is left to you to find out why your ears are boxed.

The object of what we commonly call education—that education in which man intervenes and which I shall distinguish as artificial education—is to make good these defects in Nature's methods; to prepare the child to receive Nature's education, neither incapably nor ignorantly, nor with willful disobedience; and to understand the preliminary symptoms of her pleasure, without waiting for the box on the ear. In short, all artificial education ought to be an anticipation of natural education. And a liberal education is an artificial education which has not only prepared a man to escape the great evils of disobedience to natural laws, but has trained him to appreciate and to seize upon the rewards which Nature scatters with as free a hand as her penalties.

That man, I think, has had a liberal education who has been so trained in youth that his body is the ready servant of his will, and does with ease and pleasure all the work that, as a mechanism, it is capable of; whose intellect is a clear, cold, logic engine, with all its parts of equal strength, and in smooth working order; ready, like a steam engine, to be turned to any kind of work, and spin the gossamers as well as forge the anchors of the mind; whose mind is stored with a knowledge of the great and fundamental truths of Nature and of the laws of her operations; one who, no stunted ascetic, is full of life and fire, but whose passions are trained to come to heel by a vigorous will, the servant of a tender conscience; who has learned to love all beauty, whether of Nature or of art, to hate all vileness, and to respect others as himself.

Such a one and no other, I conceive, has had a liberal education; for he is, as completely as a man can be, in harmony with Nature. He will make the best of her, and she of him. They will get on together rarely; she as his ever beneficent mother; he as her mouthpiece, her conscious self, her minister and interpreter. * * *

1868, 1870

From An Address on University Education[1]
[*The Function of a Professor*]

Up to this point I have considered only the teaching aspect of your great foundation, that function of the university in virtue of

1. During a visit to the United States in 1876 Huxley delivered an address in Baltimore on the occasion of the founding of the Johns Hopkins University, a newly endowed institution which encouraged research.

which it plays the part of a reservoir of ascertained truth, so far as our symbols can ever interpret nature. All can learn; all can drink of this lake. It is given to few to add to the store of knowledge, to strike new springs of thought, or to shape new forms of beauty. But so sure as it is that men live not by bread, but by ideas, so sure is it that the future of the world lies in the hands of those who are able to carry the interpretation of nature a step further than their predecessors; so certain is it that the highest function of a university is to seek out those men, cherish them, and give their ability to serve their kind full play.

I rejoice to observe that the encouragement of research occupies so prominent a place in your official documents, and in the wise and liberal inaugural address of your president. This subject of the encouragement, or, as it is sometimes called, the endowment of research, has of late years greatly exercised the minds of men in England. It was one of the main topics of discussion by the members of the Royal Commission of whom I was one, and who not long since issued their report, after five years' labor. Many seem to think that this question is mainly one of money; that you can go into the market and buy research, and that supply will follow demand, as in the ordinary course of commerce. This view does not commend itself to my mind. I know of no more difficult practical problem than the discovery of a method of encouraging and supporting the original investigator without opening the door to nepotism and jobbery. My own conviction is admirably summed up in the passage of your president's address, "that the best investigators are usually those who have also the responsibilities of instruction, gaining thus the incitement of colleagues, the encouragement of pupils, and the observation of the public." * * *

It appears to me that what I have ventured to lay down as the principles which should govern the relations of a university to education in general, are entirely in accordance with the measures you have adopted. You have set no restrictions upon access to the instruction you propose to give; you have provided that such instruction, either as given by the university or by associated institutions, should cover the field of human intellectual activity. You have recognized the importance of encouraging research. You propose to provide means by which young men, who may be full of zeal for a literary or for a scientific career, but who also may have mistaken aspiration for inspiration, may bring their capacities to a test, and give their powers a fair trial. If such a one fail, his endowment terminates and there is no harm done. If he succeed, you may give power of flight to the genius of a Davy or a Faraday,[2] a Carlyle or a Locke, whose influence on the future of his fellow

2. Sir Humphry Davy (1778–1829), English chemist and inventor; Michael Faraday (1791–1867), at one time Davy's laboratory assistant, who became famous for his discovery of the induction of electric currents.

men shall be absolutely incalculable.

You have enunciated the principle that "the glory of the university should rest upon the character of the teachers and scholars, and not upon their numbers of buildings constructed for their use." And I look upon it as an essential and most important feature of your plan that the income of the professors and teachers shall be independent of the number of students whom they can attract. In this way you provide against the danger, patent elsewhere, of finding attempts at improvement obstructed by vested interests; and, in the department of medical education especially, you are free of the temptation to set loose upon the world men utterly incompetent to perform the serious and responsible duties of their profession.

1876–77

From Science and Culture[1]

From the time that the first suggestion to introduce physical science into ordinary education was timidly whispered, until now, the advocates of scientific education have met with opposition of two kinds. On the one hand, they have been pooh-poohed by the men of business who pride themselves on being the representatives of practicality; while, on the other hand, they have been excommunicated by the classical scholars, in their capacity of Levites in charge of the ark of culture[2] and monopolists of liberal education.

The practical men believed that the idol whom they worship—rule of thumb—has been the source of the past prosperity, and will suffice for the future welfare of the arts and manufactures. They are of opinion that science is speculative rubbish; that theory and practice have nothing to do with one another; and that the scientific habit of mind is an impediment, rather than an aid, in the conduct of ordinary affairs.

I have used the past tense in speaking of the practical men—for although they were very formidable thirty years ago, I am not sure that the pure species has not been extirpated. In fact, so far as mere argument goes, they have been subjected to such a *feu d'enfer*[3] that it is a miracle if any have escaped. But I have remarked that your typical practical man has an unexpected resemblance to one of Milton's angels. His spiritual wounds, such as are inflicted by logical weapons, may be as deep as a well and as wide as a church

---

1. This essay was first delivered as an address in 1880. The occasion had been the opening of a new Scientific College at Birmingham which had been endowed by Sir Josiah Mason (1795–1881), a self-made businessman. For Matthew Arnold's reply to Huxley's argument see his essay *Literature and Science*.

2. In the Old Testament, the Levites were the priests preoccupied with traditional ritual observances (see Joshua vi).

3. Hell-fire.

door, but beyond shedding a few drops of ichor,[4] celestial or otherwise, he is no whit the worse. So, if any of these opponents be left, I will not waste time in vain repetition of the demonstrative evidence of the practical value of science; but knowing that a parable will sometimes penetrate where syllogisms fail to effect an entrance, I will offer a story for their consideration.

Once upon a time, a boy, with nothing to depend upon but his own vigorous nature, was thrown into the thick of the struggle for existence in the midst of a great manufacturing population. He seems to have had a hard fight, inasmuch as, by the time he was thirty years of age, his total disposable funds amounted to twenty pounds. Nevertheless, middle life found him giving proof of his comprehension of the practical problems he had been roughly called upon to solve, by a career of remarkable prosperity.

Finally, having reached old age with its well-earned surroundings of "honor, troops of friends,"[5] the hero of my story bethought himself of those who were making a like start in life, and how he could stretch out a helping hand to them.

After long and anxious reflection this successful practical man of business could devise nothing better than to provide them with the means of obtaining "sound, extensive, and practical scientific knowledge." And he devoted a large part of his wealth and five years of incessant work to this end.

I need not point the moral of a tale which, as the solid and spacious fabric of the Scientific College assures us, is no fable, nor can anything which I could say intensify the force of this practical answer to practical objections.

We may take it for granted then, that, in the opinion of those best qualified to judge, the diffusion of thorough scientific education is an absolutely essential condition of industrial progress; and that the College which has been opened today will confer an inestimable boon upon those whose livelihood is to be gained by the practice of the arts and manufactures of the district.

The only question worth discussion is whether the conditions under which the work of the College is to be carried out are such as to give it the best possible chance of achieving permanent success.

Sir Josiah Mason, without doubt most wisely, has left very large freedom of action to the trustees, to whom he proposes ultimately to commit the administration of the College, so that they may be able to adjust its arrangements in accordance with the changing conditions of the future. But, with respect to three points, he has laid most explicit injunctions upon both administrators and teachers.

4. Ethereal fluid which supposedly flows through the veins of the gods.   5. Cf. *Macbeth* V.iii.25.

Party politics are forbidden to enter into the minds of either, so far as the work of the College is concerned; theology is as sternly banished from its precincts; and finally, it is especially declared that the College shall make no provision for "mere literary instruction and education."

It does not concern me at present to dwell upon the first two injunctions any longer than may be needful to express my full conviction of their wisdom. But the third prohibition brings us face to face with those other opponents of scientific education, who are by no means in the moribund condition of the practical man, but alive, alert, and formidable.

It is not impossible that we shall hear this express exclusion of "literary instruction and education" from a College which, nevertheless, professes to give a high and efficient education, sharply criticized. Certainly the time was that the Levites of culture would have sounded their trumpets against its walls as against an educational Jericho.[6]

How often have we not been told that the study of physical science is incompetent to confer culture; that it touches none of the higher problems of life; and, what is worse, that the continual devotion to scientific studies tends to generate a narrow and bigoted belief in the applicability of scientific methods to the search after truth of all kinds? How frequently one has reason to observe that no reply to a troublesome argument tells so well as calling its author a "mere scientific specialist." And, as I am afraid it is not permissible to speak of this form of opposition to scientific education in the past tense; may we not expect to be told that this, not only omission, but prohibition, of "mere literary instruction and education" is a patent example of scientific narrow-mindedness?

I am not acquainted with Sir Josiah Mason's reasons for the action which he has taken; but if, as I apprehend is the case, he refers to the ordinary classical course of our schools and universities by the name of "mere literary instruction and education," I venture to offer sundry reasons of my own in support of that action.

For I hold very strongly by two convictions: The first is that neither the discipline nor the subject matter of classical education is of such direct value to the student of physical science as to justify the expenditure of valuable time upon either; and the second is that for the purpose of attaining real culture, an exclusively scientific education is at least as effectual as an exclusively literary education.

I need hardly point out to you that these opinions, especially the latter, are diametrically opposed to those of the great majority of educated Englishmen, influenced as they are by school and university traditions. In their belief, culture is obtainable only by a

6. See Joshua vi.

liberal education; and a liberal education is synonymous, not merely with education and instruction in literature, but in one particular form of literature, namely, that of Greek and Roman antiquity. They hold that the man who has learned Latin and Greek, however little, is educated; while he who is versed in other branches of knowledge, however deeply, is a more or less respectable specialist, not admissible into the cultured caste. The stamp of the educated man, the University degree, is not for him.

I am too well acquainted with the generous catholicity of spirit, the true sympathy with scientific thought, which pervades the writings of our chief apostle of culture[7] to identify him with these opinions; and yet one may cull from one and another of those epistles to the Philistines, which so much delight all who do not answer to that name, sentences which lend them some support.

Mr. Arnold tells us that the meaning of culture is "to know the best that has been thought and said in the world." It is the criticism of life contained in literature. That criticism regards "Europe as being, for intellectual and spiritual purposes, one great confederation, bound to a joint action and working to a common result; and whose members have, for their common outfit, a knowledge of Greek, Roman, and Eastern antiquity, and of one another. Special, local, and temporary advantages being put out of account, that modern nation will in the intellectual and spiritual sphere make most progress, which most thoroughly carries out this program. And what is that but saying that we too, all of us, as individuals, the more thoroughly we carry it out, shall make the more progress?"[8]

We have here to deal with two distinct propositions. The first, that a criticism of life is the essence of culture; the second, that literature contains the materials which suffice for the construction of such criticism.

I think that we must all assent to the first proposition. For culture certainly means something quite different from learning or technical skill. It implies the possession of an ideal, and the habit of critically estimating the value of things by comparison with a theoretic standard. Perfect culture should supply a complete theory of life, based upon a clear knowledge alike of its possibilities and of its limitations.

But we may agree to all this, and yet strongly dissent from the assumption that literature alone is competent to supply this knowledge. After having learnt all that Greek, Roman, and Eastern antiquity have thought and said, and all that modern literature have to tell us, it is not self-evident that we have laid a sufficiently broad and deep foundation for that criticism of life which constitutes culture.

7. I.e., Matthew Arnold. For his discussion of the Philistines, see *Culture and Anarchy*.

8. From Arnold's *Function of Criticism*, fourth paragraph from the end.

Indeed, to anyone acquainted with the scope of physical science, it is not at all evident. Considering progress only in the "intellectual and spiritual sphere," I find myself wholly unable to admit that either nations or individuals will really advance, if their common outfit draws nothing from the stores of physical science. I should say that an army, without weapons of precision and with no particular base of operations, might more hopefully enter upon a campaign on the Rhine than a man, devoid of a knowledge of what physical science has done in the last century, upon a criticism of life.

When a biologist meets with an anomaly, he instinctively turns to the study of development to clear it up. The rationale of contradictory opinions may with equal confidence be sought in history.

It is, happily, no new thing that Englishmen should employ their wealth in building and endowing institutions for educational purposes. But, five or six hundred years ago, deeds of foundation expressed or implied conditions as nearly as possible contrary to those which have been thought expedient by Sir Josiah Mason. That is to say, physical science was practically ignored, while a certain literary training was enjoined as a means to the acquirement of knowledge which was essentially theological.

The reason of this singular contradiction between the actions of men alike animated by a strong and disinterested desire to promote the welfare of their fellows, is easily discovered.

At that time, in fact, if anyone desired knowledge beyond such as could be obtained by his own observation, or by common conversation, his first necessity was to learn the Latin language, inasmuch as all the higher knowledge of the western world was contained in works written in that language. Hence, Latin grammar, with logic and rhetoric, studied through Latin, were the fundamentals of education. With respect to the substance of the knowledge imparted through this channel, the Jewish and Christian Scriptures, as interpreted and supplemented by the Romish Church, were held to contain a complete and infallibly true body of information.

Theological dicta were, to the thinkers of those days, that which the axioms and definitions of Euclid are to the geometers of these. The business of the philosophers of the Middle Ages was to deduce from the data furnished by the theologians, conclusions in accordance with ecclesiastical decrees. They were allowed the high privilege of showing, by logical process, how and why that which the Church said was true, must be true. And if their demonstrations fell short of or exceeded this limit, the Church was maternally ready to check their aberrations; if need were, by the help of the secular arm.

Between the two, our ancestors were furnished with a compact and complete criticism of life. They were told how the world began and how it would end; they learned that all material existence was but a base and insignificant blot upon the fair face of the spiritual world, and that nature was, to all intents and purposes, the playground of the devil; they learned that the earth is the center of the visible universe, and that man is the cynosure of things terrestrial, and more especially was it inculcated that the course of nature had no fixed order, but that it could be, and constantly was, altered by the agency of innumerable spiritual beings, good and bad, according as they were moved by the deeds and prayers of men. The sum and substance of the whole doctrine was to produce the conviction that the only thing really worth knowing in this world was how to secure that place in a better which, under certain conditions, the Church promised.

Our ancestors had a living belief in this theory of life, and acted upon it in their dealings with education, as in all other matters. Culture meant saintliness—after the fashion of the saints of those days; the education that led to it was, of necessity, theological; and the way to theology lay through Latin.

That the study of nature—further than was requisite for the satisfaction of everyday wants—should have any bearing on human life was far from the thoughts of men thus trained. Indeed, as nature had been cursed for man's sake, it was an obvious conclusion that those who meddled with nature were likely to come into pretty close contact with Satan. And, if any born scientific investigator followed his instincts, he might safely reckon upon earning the reputation, and probably upon suffering the fate, of a sorcerer.

Had the western world been left to itself in Chinese isolation, there is no saying how long this state of things might have endured. But, happily, it was not left to itself. Even earlier than the thirteenth century, the development of Moorish civilization in Spain and the great movement of the Crusades had introduced the leaven which, from that day to this, has never ceased to work. At first, through the intermediation of Arabic translations, afterwards by the study of the originals, the western nations of Europe became acquainted with the writings of the ancient philosophers and poets, and, in time, with the whole of the vast literature of antiquity.

Whatever there was of high intellectual aspiration or dominant capacity in Italy, France, Germany, and England, spent itself for centuries in taking possession of the rich inheritance left by the dead civilizations of Greece and Rome. Marvelously aided by the invention of printing,[9] classical learning spread and flourished. Those who possessed it prided themselves on having attained the

9. In the mid-15th century.

highest culture then within the reach of mankind.

And justly. For, saving Dante on his solitary pinnacle, there was no figure in modern literature at the time of the Renaissance to compare with the men of antiquity; there was no art to compete with their sculpture; there was no physical science but that which Greece had created. Above all, there was no other example of perfect intellectual freedom—of the unhesitating acceptance of reason as the sole guide to truth and the supreme arbiter of conduct.

The new learning necessarily soon exerted a profound influence upon education. The language of the monks and schoolmen[1] seemed little better than gibberish to scholars fresh from Virgil and Cicero, and the study of Latin was placed upon a new foundation. Moreover, Latin itself ceased to afford the sole key to knowledge. The student who sought the highest thought of antiquity found only a secondhand reflection of it in Roman literature, and turned his face to the full light of the Greeks. And after a battle, not altogether dissimilar to that which is at present being fought over the teaching of physical science, the study of Greek was recognized as an essential element of all higher education.

Then the Humanists, as they were called, won the day; and the great reform which they effected was of incalculable service to mankind. But the nemesis of all reformers is finality; and the reformers of education, like those of religion, fell into the profound, however common, error of mistaking the beginning for the end of the work of reformation.

The representatives of the Humanists, in the nineteenth century, take their stand upon classical education as the sole avenue to culture as firmly as if we were still in the age of Renaissance. Yet, surely, the present intellectual relations of the modern and the ancient worlds are profoundly different from those which obtained three centuries ago. Leaving aside the existence of a great and characteristically modern literature, of modern painting, and, especially, of modern music, there is one feature of the present state of the civilized world which separates it more widely from the Renaissance than the Renaissance was separated from the Middle Ages.

This distinctive character of our own times lies in the vast and constantly increasing part which is played by natural knowledge. Not only is our daily life shaped by it; not only does the prosperity of millions of men depend upon it, but our whole theory of life has long been influenced, consciously or unconsciously, by the general conceptions of the universe which have been forced upon us by physical science.

In fact, the most elementary acquaintance with the results of scientific investigation shows us that they offer a broad and striking

---

1. **Exponents of the theology, philosophy, and logic of the medieval period in Europe.**

contradiction to the opinion so implicitly credited and taught in the Middle Ages.

The notions of the beginning and the end of the world entertained by our forefathers are no longer credible. It is very certain that the earth is not the chief body in the material universe, and that the world is not subordinated to man's use. It is even more certain that nature is the expression of a definite order with which nothing interferes, and that the chief business of mankind is to learn that order and govern themselves accordingly. Moreover this scientific "criticism of life" presents itself to us with different credentials from any other. It appeals not to authority, nor to what anybody may have thought or said, but to nature. It admits that all our interpretations of natural fact are more or less imperfect and symbolic, and bids the learner seek for truth not among words but among things. It warns us that the assertion which outstrips evidence is not only a blunder but a crime.

The purely classical education advocated by the representatives of the Humanists in our day gives no inkling of all this. A man may be a better scholar than Erasmus,[2] and know no more of the chief causes of the present intellectual fermentation than Erasmus did. Scholarly and pious persons, worthy of all respect, favor us with allocutions upon the sadness of the antagonism of science to their medieval way of thinking, which betray an ignorance of the first principles of scientific investigation, an incapacity for understanding what a man of science means by veracity, and an unconsciousness of the weight of established scientific truths, which is almost comical. * * *

Thus I venture to think that the pretensions of our modern Humanists to the possession of the monopoly of culture and to the exclusive inheritance of the spirit of antiquity must be abated, if not abandoned. But I should be very sorry that anything I have said should be taken to imply a desire on my part to depreciate the value of classical education, as it might be and as it sometimes is. The native capacities of mankind vary no less than their opportunities; and while culture is one, the road by which one man may best reach it is widely different from that which is most advantageous to another. Again, while scientific education is yet inchoate and tentative, classical education is thoroughly well organized upon the practical experience of generations of teachers. So that, given ample time for learning and estimation for ordinary life, or for a literary career, I do not think that a young Englishman in search of culture can do better than follow the course usually marked out for him, supplementing its deficiencies by his own efforts.

But for those who mean to make science their serious occupation; or who intend to follow the profession of medicine; or who have to

2. Eminent Dutch humanist and scholar (1466–1536).

enter early upon the business of life; for all these, in my opinion, classical education is a mistake; and it is for this reason that I am glad to see "mere literary education and instruction" shut out from the curriculum of Sir Josiah Mason's College, seeing that its inclusion would probably lead to the introduction of the ordinary smattering of Latin and Greek.

Nevertheless, I am the last person to question the importance of genuine literary education, or to suppose that intellectual culture can be complete without it. An exclusively scientific training will bring about a mental twist as surely as an exclusively literary training. The value of the cargo does not compensate for a ship's being out of trim; and I should be very sorry to think that the Scientific College would turn out none but lopsided men.

There is no need, however, that such a catastrophe should happen. Instruction in English, French, and German is provided, and thus the three greatest literatures of the modern world are made accessible to the student.

French and German, and especially the latter language, are absolutely indispensable to those who desire full knowledge in any department of science. But even supposing that the knowledge of these languages acquired is not more than sufficient for purely scientific purposes, every Englishman has, in his native tongue, an almost perfect instrument of literary expression; and, in his own literature, models of every kind of literary excellence. If an Englishman cannot get literary culture out of his Bible, his Shakespeare, his Milton, neither, in my belief, will the profoundest study of Homer and Sophocles, Virgil and Horace, give it to him.

Thus, since the constitution of the College makes sufficient provision for literary as well as for scientific education, and since artistic instruction is also contemplated, it seems to me that a fairly complete culture is offered to all who are willing to take advantage of it. * * *

1880, 1881

From Agnosticism and Christianity[1]

Nemo ergo ex me scire quaerat, quod me nescire scio, nisi forte ut nescire discat.
—AUGUSTINUS, *De Civ. Dei*, XII.7.[2]

The present discussion has arisen out of the use, which has become general in the last few years, of the terms "Agnostic" and

1. This essay appeared in a magazine in 1889 as a reply to critics who had argued that agnostics were simply infidels under a new name. It was later included in Huxley's volume, *Essays on Some Controverted Questions*

(1892).
2. "No one, therefore, should seek to learn knowledge from me, for I know that I do not know—unless indeed he wishes to learn that he does not know." St. Augustine, *City of God* XII.7.

"Agnosticism."[3]

The people who call themselves "Agnostics" have been charged with doing so because they have not the courage to declare themselves "Infidels." It has been insinuated that they have adopted a new name in order to escape the unpleasantness which attaches to their proper denomination. To this wholly erroneous imputation I have replied by showing that the term "Agnostic" did, as a matter of fact, arise in a manner which negatives it; and my statement has not been, and cannot be, refuted. Moreover, speaking for myself, and without impugning the right of any other person to use the term in another sense, I further say that Agnosticism is not properly described as a "negative" creed, nor indeed as a creed of any kind, except in so far as it expresses absolute faith in the validity of a principle, which is as much ethical as intellectual. This principle may be stated in various ways, but they all amount to this: that it is wrong for a man to say that he is certain of the objective truth of any proposition unless he can produce evidence which logically justifies that certainty. This is what Agnosticism asserts; and, in my opinion, it is all that is essential to Agnosticism. That which Agnostics deny and repudiate, as immoral, is the contrary doctrine, that there are propositions which men ought to believe, without logically satisfactory evidence; and that reprobation ought to attach to the profession of disbelief in such inadequately supported propositions. The justification of the Agnostic principle lies in the success which follows upon its application, whether in the field of natural, or in that of civil, history; and in the fact that, so far as these topics are concerned, no sane man thinks of denying its validity.

Still speaking for myself, I add that though Agnosticism is not, and cannot be, a creed, except in so far as its general principle is concerned; yet that the application of that principle results in the denial of, or the suspension of judgment concerning, a number of propositions respecting which our contemporary ecclesiastical "gnostics" profess entire certainty. And, in so far as these ecclesiastical persons can be justified in their old-established custom (which many nowadays think more honored in the breach than the observance) of using opprobrious names to those who differ from them, I fully admit their right to call me and those who think with me "Infidels"; all I have ventured to urge is that they must not expect us to speak of ourselves by that title.

The extent of the region of the uncertain, the number of the problems the investigation of which ends in a verdict of not proven, will vary according to the knowledge and the intellectual habits of the individual Agnostic. I do not very much care to speak of anything as "unknowable." What I am sure about is that there are many topics about which I know nothing; and which, so far as I

---

3. The term "agnostic" was coined by Huxley.

can see, are out of reach of my faculties. But whether these things are knowable by anyone else is exactly one of those matters which is beyond my knowledge, though I may have a tolerably strong opinion as to the probabilities of the case. Relatively to myself, I am quite sure that the region of uncertainty—the nebulous country in which words play the part of realities—is far more extensive than I could wish. Materialism and Idealism; Theism and Atheism; the doctrine of the soul and its mortality or immortality—appear in the history of philosophy like the shades of Scandinavian heroes, eternally slaying one another and eternally coming to life again in a metaphysical "Nifelheim."[4] It is getting on for twenty-five centuries, at least, since mankind began seriously to give their minds to these topics. Generation after generation, philosophy has been doomed to roll the stone uphill; and, just as all the world swore it was at the top, down it has rolled to the bottom again.[5] All this is written in innumerable books; and he who will toil through them will discover that the stone is just where it was when the work began. Hume saw this; Kant saw it; since their time, more and more eyes have been cleansed of the films which prevented them from seeing it; until now the weight and number of those who refuse to be the prey of verbal mystifications has begun to tell in practical life.

It was inevitable that a conflict should arise between Agnosticism and Theology; or rather, I ought to say, between Agnosticism and Ecclesiasticism. For Theology, the science, is one thing; and Ecclesiasticism, the championship of a foregone conclusion[6] as to the truth of a particular form of Theology, is another. With scientific Theology, Agnosticism has no quarrel. On the contrary, the Agnostic, knowing too well the influence of prejudice and idiosyncrasy, even on those who desire most earnestly to be impartial, can wish for nothing more urgently than that the scientific theologian should not only be at perfect liberty to thresh out the matter in his own fashion; but that he should, if he can, find flaws in the Agnostic position; and, even if demonstration is not to be had, that he should put, in their full force, the grounds of the conclusions he thinks probable. The scientific theologian admits the Agnostic principle, however widely his results may differ from those reached by the majority of Agnostics.

But, as between Agnosticism and Ecclesiasticism, or, as our neighbors across the Channel call it, Clericalism, there can be neither peace nor truce. The Cleric asserts that it is morally wrong not to believe certain propositions, whatever the results of a strict

4. Realms of cold and darkness in Norse mythology.
5. Cf. the Greek story of Sisyphus in Hades, who was condemned to keep rolling a stone uphill which always rolled downhill again before it reached the summit.
6. "Let us maintain, before we have proved. This seeming paradox is the secret of happiness. (Dr. Newman, *Tract 85*)" [Huxley's note].

scientific investigation of the evidence of these propositions. He tells us "that religious error is, in itself, of an immoral nature."[7] He declares that he has prejudged certain conclusions, and looks upon those who show cause for arrest of judgment as emissaries of Satan. It necessarily follows that, for him, the attainment of faith, not the ascertainment of truth, is the highest aim of mental life. And, on careful analysis of the nature of this faith, it will too often be found to be, not the mystic process of unity with the Divine, understood by the religious enthusiast; but that which the candid simplicity of a Sunday scholar once defined it to be. "Faith," said this unconscious plagiarist of Tertullian,[8] "is the power of saying you believe things which are incredible."

Now I, and many other Agnostics, believe that faith, in this sense, is an abomination; and though we do not indulge in the luxury of self-righteousness so far as to call those who are not of our way of thinking hard names, we do feel that the disagreement between ourselves and those who hold this doctrine is even more moral than intellectual. It is desirable there should be an end of any mistakes on this topic. If our clerical opponents were clearly aware of the real state of the case, there would be an end of the curious delusion, which often appears between the lines of their writings, that those whom they are so fond of calling "Infidels" are people who not only ought to be, but in their hearts are, ashamed of themselves. It would be discourteous to do more than hint the antipodal opposition of this pleasant dream of theirs to facts.

The clerics and their lay allies commonly tell us that if we refuse to admit that there is good ground for expressing definite convictions about certain topics, the bonds of human society will dissolve and mankind lapse into savagery. There are several answers to this assertion. One is that the bonds of human society were formed without the aid of their theology; and, in the opinion of not a few competent judges, have been weakened rather than strengthened by a good deal of it. Greek science, Greek art, the ethics of old Israel, the social organization of old Rome, contrived to come into being, without the help of anyone who believed in a single distinctive article of the simplest of the Christian creeds. The science, the art, the jurisprudence, the chief political and social theories, of the modern world have grown out of those of Greece and Rome—not by favor of, but in the teeth of, the fundamental teachings of early Christianity, to which science, art, and any serious occupation with the things of this world, were alike despicable.

Again, all that is best in the ethics of the modern world, in so far as it has not grown out of Greek thought, or Barbarian manhood, is the direct development of the ethics of old Israel. There

7. "Dr Newman, *Essay on Development*" [Huxley's note]. 8. Roman author and Church Father (ca. 155–ca. 222).

is no code of legislation, ancient or modern, at once so just and so merciful, so tender to the weak and poor, as the Jewish law; and, if the Gospels are to be trusted, Jesus of Nazareth himself declared that he taught nothing but that which lay implicitly, or explicitly, in the religious and ethical system of his people.

"And the scribe said unto him, Of a truth, Teacher, thou hast well said that he is one; and there is none other but he and to love him with all the heart, and with all the understanding, and with all the strength, and to love his neighbour as himself, is much more than all whole burnt offerings and sacrifices." (Mark xii.32–33)

Here is the briefest of summaries of the teaching of the prophets of Israel of the eighth century; does the Teacher, whose doctrine is thus set forth in his presence, repudiate the exposition? Nay; we are told, on the contrary, that Jesus saw that he "answered discreetly," and replied, "Thou art not far from the kingdom of God."

So that I think that even if the creeds,[9] from the so-called "Apostles'" to the so-called "Athanasian," were swept into oblivion; and even if the human race should arrive at the conclusion that, whether a bishop washes a cup or leaves it unwashed, is not a matter of the least consequence, it will get on very well. The causes which have led to the development of morality in mankind, which have guided or impelled us all the way from the savage to the civilized state, will not cease to operate because a number of ecclesiastical hypotheses turn out to be baseless. And, even if the absurd notion that morality is more the child of speculation than of practical necessity and inherited instinct, had any foundation; if all the world is going to thieve, murder, and otherwise misconduct itself as soon as it discovers that certain portions of ancient history are mythical; what is the relevance of such arguments to any one who holds by the Agnostic principle?

Surely, the attempt to cast out Beelzebub by the aid of Beelzebub is a hopeful procedure as compared to that of preserving morality by the aid of immorality. For I suppose it is admitted that an Agnostic may be perfectly sincere, may be competent, and may have studied the question at issue with as much care as his clerical opponents. But, if the Agnostic really believes what he says, the "dreadful consequence" argufier (consistently, I admit, with his own principles) virtually asks him to abstain from telling the truth, or to say what he believes to be untrue, because of the supposed injurious consequences to morality. "Beloved brethren, that we may be spotlessly moral, before all things let us lie," is the sum total of many an exhortation addressed to the "Infidel." Now, as I have already pointed out, we cannot oblige our exhorters. We leave the practical application of the convenient doctrines of "Reserve" and

9. Summaries of Christian doctrine.

"Non-natural interpretation" to those who invented them.

I trust that I have now made amends for any ambiguity, or want of fullness, in my previous exposition of that which I hold to be the essence of the Agnostic doctrine. Henceforward, I might hope to hear no more of the assertion that we are necessarily Materialists, Idealists, Atheists, Theists, or any other ists, if experience had led me to think that the proved falsity of a statement was any guarantee against its repetition. And those who appreciate the nature of our position will see, at once, that when Ecclesiasticism declares that we ought to believe this, that, and the other, and are very wicked if we don't, it is impossible for us to give any answer but this: We have not the slightest objection to believe anything you like, if you will give us good grounds for belief; but, if you cannot, we must respectfully refuse, even if that refusal should wreck morality and insure our own damnation several times over. We are quite content to leave that to the decision of the future. The course of the past has impressed us with the firm conviction that no good ever comes of falsehood, and we feel warranted in refusing even to experiment in that direction. * * *

1889, 1892

WALTER PATER
(1839–1894)

Studies in the History of the Renaissance, a collection of essays published in 1873, was the first of several volumes which established Walter Pater as the most important critical writer of the late Victorian period. A shy bachelor who spent his life as a tutor of classics at Oxford, Pater was surprised and even alarmed by the impact made by his books on young readers of the 1870's and 1880's. Some of his younger followers such as Oscar Wilde and George Moore may have misread him. It can be demonstrated that Pater's writings (especially his historical novel *Marius the Epicurean*, 1885) have much in common with his earnest-minded mid-Victorian predecessors, but his disciples overlooked these similarities. To them, his work seemed strikingly different and, in its quiet way, more subversive than the head-on attacks against traditional Victorianism made by Swinburne or Samuel Butler. Instead of recommending a continuation of the painful quest for Truth that had dominated Oxford in the days of Newman, Pater assured his readers that the quest was pointless. Truth, he said, is relative. And instead of echoing Carlyle's call to duty and social responsibilities, Pater reminded his readers that life passes quickly and that our only responsibility is to enjoy fully "this short day of frost and sun," to relish its sensations, especially those sensations provoked by works of art.

This epicurean gospel was conveyed in a highly-wrought prose style that baffles anyone who likes to read quickly. Pater believed that prose was as difficult an art as poetry, and he expected his own elaborate sentences to be savored. Like Flaubert, the French novelist whom he admired, Pater painstakingly revised his sentences with special attention to their rhythms and seeking always the right word, *le mot juste*, as Flaubert had called it. What Pater said of Dante is an apt description of his own polished style: "He is one of those artists whose general effect largely depends on vocabulary, on the minute particles of which his work is wrought, on the color and outline of single words and phrases."

Aside from his interest as a key figure in the transition from mid-Victorianism to the decadence of the 1890's, Pater's essays also command our attention as examples of impressionistic criticism at its best. In each of his essays he seeks to communicate what he called the "special unique impression of pleasure" made upon him by the works of some artist or writer. His range of subjects included the dialogues of Plato, the paintings of Leonardo da Vinci, the plays of Shakespeare, and the writings of the French Romantic school of the 19th century. Of particular value to students of English literature are his discriminating studies of Wordsworth, Coleridge, Lamb, and Sir Thomas Browne in his volume of *Appreciations* (1889).

The final sentences of his *Appreciations* volume are a revealing indication of Pater's critical position. After having attempted to show the differences between the classical and romantic schools of art, he concludes that most great artists combine the qualities of both. "To discriminate schools, of art, of literature," he writes, "is, of course, part of the obvious business of literary criticism: but, in the work of literary production, it is easy to be overmuch occupied concerning them. For, in truth, the legitimate contention is, not of one age or school of literary art against another, but of all successive schools alike, against the stupidity which is dead to the substance, and the vulgarity which is dead to form."

From The Renaissance
Preface

Many attempts have been made by writers on art and poetry to define beauty in the abstract, to express it in the most general terms, to find some universal formula for it. The value of these attempts has most often been in the suggestive and penetrating things said by the way. Such discussions help us very little to enjoy what has been well done in art or poetry, to discriminate between what is more and what is less excellent in them, or to use words like beauty, excellence, art, poetry, with a more precise meaning than they would otherwise have. Beauty, like all other qualities presented to human experience, is relative; and the definition of it becomes unmeaning and useless in proportion to its abstractness. To define beauty, not in the most abstract but in the most concrete terms possible, to find not its universal formula, but the formula which expresses most adequately this or that special manifestation of it, is the aim of the true student of aesthetics.

"To see the object as in itself it really is,"[1] has been justly said to be the aim of all true criticism whatever; and in aesthetic criticism the first step towards seeing one's object as it really is, is to know one's own impression as it really is, to discriminate it, to realize it distinctly. The objects with which aesthetic criticism deals —music, poetry, artistic and accomplished forms of human life— are indeed receptacles of so many powers or forces: they possess, like the products of nature, so many virtues or qualities. What is this song or picture, this engaging personality presented in life or in a book, to *me*? What effect does it really produce on me? Does it give me pleasure? and if so, what sort or degree of pleasure? How is my nature modified by its presence, and under its influence? The answers to these questions are the original facts with which the aesthetic critic has to do; and, as in the study of light, of morals, of number, one must realize such primary data for one's self, or not at all. And he who experiences these impressions strongly, and drives directly at the discrimination and analysis of them, has no need to trouble himself with the abstract question what beauty is in itself, or what its exact relation to truth or experience—metaphysical questions, as unprofitable as metaphysical questions elsewhere. He may pass them all by as being, answerable or not, of no interest to him.

The aesthetic critic, then, regards all the objects with which he has to do, all works of art, and the fairer forms of nature and human life, as powers or forces producing pleasurable sensations, each of a more or less peculiar or unique kind. This influence he feels, and wishes to explain, by analyzing and reducing it to its elements. To him, the picture, the landscape, the engaging personality in life or in a book, "La Gioconda," the hills of Carrara, Pico of Mirandola,[2] are valuable for their virtues, as we say, in speaking of a herb, a wine, a gem; for the property each has of affecting one with a special, a unique, impression of pleasure. Our education becomes complete in proportion as our susceptibility to these impressions increases in depth and variety. And the function of the aesthetic critic is to distinguish, to analyze, and separate from its adjuncts, the virtue by which a picture, a landscape, a fair personality in life or in a book, produces this special impression of beauty or pleasure, to indicate what the source of that impression is, and under what conditions it is experienced. His end is reached when he has disengaged that virtue, and noted it, as a chemist notes some natural element, for himself and others; and the rule for those who

1. See Matthew Arnold, *The Function of Criticism*, opening paragraph.
2. "La Gioconda" is Leonardo da Vinci's famous painting, the "Mona Lisa"; "the hills of Carrara" are marble quarries in Italy; Pico of Mi- randola (or Pico della Mirandola) was an Italian philosopher and classical scholar (1463–94), subject of an essay by Pater which was included in *The Renaissance*.

would reach this end is stated with great exactness in the words of a recent critic of Sainte-Beuve: *De se borner à connaître de près les belles choses, et à s'en nourrir en exquis amateurs, en humanistes accomplis.*[3]

What is important, then, is not that the critic should possess a correct abstract definition of beauty for the intellect, but a certain kind of temperament, the power of being deeply moved by the presence of beautiful objects. He will remember always that beauty exists in many forms. To him all periods, types, schools of taste, are in themselves equal. In all ages there have been some excellent workmen, and some excellent work done. The question he asks is always: In whom did the stir, the genius, the sentiment of the period find itself? where was the receptacle of its refinement, its elevation, its taste? "The ages are all equal," says William Blake, "but genius is always above its age."

Often it will require great nicety to disengage this virtue from the commoner elements with which it may be found in combination. Few artists, not Goethe or Byron even, work quite cleanly, casting off all debris, and leaving us only what the heat of their imagination has wholly fused and transformed. Take, for instance, the writings of Wordsworth. The heat of his genius, entering into the substance of his work, has crystallized a part, but only a part, of it; and in that great mass of verse there is much which might well be forgotten. But scattered up and down it, sometimes fusing and transforming entire compositions, like the stanzas on *Resolution and Independence*, or the *Ode on the Recollections of Childhood*,[4] sometimes, as if at random, depositing a fine crystal here or there, in a matter it does not wholly search through and transmute, we trace the action of his unique, incommunicable faculty, that strange, mystical sense of a life in natural things, and of man's life as a part of nature, drawing strength and color and character from local influences, from the hills and streams, and from natural sights and sounds. Well! that is the *virtue*, the active principle in Wordsworth's poetry; and then the function of the critic of Wordsworth is to follow up that active principle, to disengage it, to mark the degree in which it penetrates his verse.

The subjects of the following studies are taken from the history of the *Renaissance*, and touch what I think the chief points in that complex, many-sided movement. I have explained in the first of them what I understand by the word, giving it a much wider scope than was intended by those who originally used it to denote that revival of classical antiquity in the fifteenth century which was only one of many results of a general excitement and enlightening of the

3. "To confine themselves to knowing beautiful things intimately, and to sustain themselves by these, as sensitive amateurs and accomplished humanists do."

4. Wordsworth's *Ode* was entitled *Intimations of Immortality from Recollections of Early Childhood*.

human mind, but of which the great aim and achievements of what,
as Christian art, is often falsely opposed to the Renaissance, were
another result. This outbreak of the human spirit may be traced far
into the Middle Age itself, with its motives already clearly pronounced, the care for physical beauty, the worship of the body, the
breaking down of those limits which the religious system of the
Middle Age imposed on the heart and the imagination. I have taken
as an example of this movement, this earlier Renaissance within the
Middle Age itself, and as an expression of its qualities, two little
compositions in early French; not because they constitute the best
possible expression of them, but because they help the unity of my
series, inasmuch as the Renaissance ends also in France, in French
poetry, in a phase of which the writings of Joachim du Bellay[5] are
in many ways the most perfect illustration. The Renaissance, in
truth, put forth in France an aftermath, a wonderful later growth,
the products of which have to the full that subtle and delicate
sweetness which belongs to a refined and comely decadence, just
as its earliest phases have the freshness which belongs to all periods
of growth in art, the charm of *ascêsis*,[6] of the austere and serious
girding of the loins in youth.

But it is in Italy, in the fifteenth century, that the interest of the
Renaissance mainly lies—in that solemn fifteenth century which
can hardly be studied too much, not merely for its positive results
in the things of the intellect and the imagination, its concrete works
of art, its special and prominent personalities, with their profound
aesthetic charm, but for its general spirit and character, for the
ethical qualities of which it is a consummate type.

The various forms of intellectual activity which together make up
the culture of an age, move for the most part from different starting
points, and by unconnected roads. As products of the same generation they partake indeed of a common character, and unconsciously
illustrate each other; but of the producers themselves, each group is
solitary, gaining what advantage or disadvantage there may be in
intellectual isolation. Art and poetry, philosophy and the religious
life, and that other life of refined pleasure and action in the conspicuous places of the world, are each of them confined to its own
circle of ideas, and those who prosecute either of them are generally
little curious of the thoughts of others. There come, however, from
time to time, eras of more favorable conditions, in which the
thoughts of men draw nearer together than is their wont, and the
many interests of the intellectual world combine in one complete
type of general culture. The fifteenth century in Italy is one of these
happier eras, and what is sometimes said of the age of Pericles is
true of that of Lorenzo: it is an age productive in personalities,

5. French poet and critic (1524–60), subject of another essay in *The Ren-* *aissance.*
6. Asceticism.

many-sided, centralized, complete. Here, artists and philosophers and those whom the action of the world has elevated and made keen, do not live in isolation, but breathe a common air, and catch light and heat from each other's thoughts. There is a spirit of general elevation and enlightenment in which all alike communicate. The unity of this spirit gives unity to all the various products of the Renaissance; and it is to this intimate alliance with mind, this participation in the best thoughts which that age produced, that the art of Italy in the fifteenth century owes much of its grave dignity and influence.

I have added an essay on Winckelmann,[7] as not incongruous with the studies which precede it, because Winckelmann, coming in the eighteenth century, really belongs in spirit to an earlier age. By his enthusiasm for the things of the intellect and the imagination for their own sake, by his Hellenism, his lifelong struggle to attain to the Greek spirit, he is in sympathy with the humanists of a previous century. He is the last fruit of the Renaissance, and explains in a striking way its motive and tendencies.

[*"La Gioconda"*][8]

"La Gioconda" is, in the truest sense, Leonardo's masterpiece, the revealing instance of his mode of thought and work. In suggestiveness, only the "Melancholia" of Dürer[9] is comparable to it; and no crude symbolism disturbs the effect of its subdued and graceful mystery. We all know the face and hands of the figure, set in its marble chair, in that circle of fantastic rocks, as in some faint light under sea. Perhaps of all ancient pictures time has chilled it least. As often happens with works in which invention seems to reach its limit, there is an element in it given to, not invented by, the master. In that inestimable folio of drawings, once in the possession of Vasari, were certain designs by Verrocchio,[1] faces of such impressive beauty that Leonardo in his boyhood copied them many times. It is hard not to connect with these designs of the elder, by-past master, as with its germinal principle, the unfathomable smile, always with a touch of something sinister in it, which plays over all Leonardo's work. Besides, the picture is a portrait. From childhood we see this image defining itself on the fabric of his dreams, and but for express historical testimony, we might fancy

---

7. Johann Joachim Winckelmann (1717–68), German classicist.
8. "La Gioconda" or "Mona Lisa," famous painting by Leonardo da Vinci which now hangs in the Louvre in Paris. The sitter for the portrait may have been Lisa, the third wife of the Florentine Francesco del Giocondo (to whom Pater refers as "Il Giocondo") —hence her title, La Gioconda. *Mona* (more correctly *Monna*) *Lisa* means "Madonna Lisa" or "My Lady Lisa."

This selection is drawn from the essay on Leonardo da Vinci.
9. Albrecht Dürer (1471–1528), German artist whose picture of the spirit of Melancholy is full of details which may stimulate reflection in the spectator.
1. Andrea del Verrocchio (1435–88), Florentine painter and sculptor. Giorgio Vasari, author of *Lives of the Most Excellent Italian Painters* (1550).

that this was but his ideal lady, embodied and beheld at last. What was the relationship of a living Florentine to this creature of his thought? By what strange affinities had the dream and the person grown up thus apart, and yet so closely together? Present from the first incorporeally in Leonardo's brain, dimly traced in the designs of Verrocchio, she is found present at last in Il Giocondo's house. That there is much of mere portraiture in the picture is attested by the legend that by artificial means, the presence of mimes[2] and flute-players, that subtle expression was protracted on the face. Again, was it in four years and by renewed labor never really completed, or in four months and as by stroke of magic, that the image was projected?

The presence that rose thus so strangely beside the waters, is expressive of what in the ways of a thousand years men had come to desire. Hers is the head upon which all "the ends of the world are come,"[3] and the eyelids are a little weary. It is a beauty wrought out from within upon the flesh, the deposit, little cell by cell, of strange thoughts and fantastic reveries and exquisite passions. Set it for a moment beside one of those white Greek goddesses or beautiful women of antiquity, and how would they be troubled by this beauty, into which the soul with all its maladies has passed! All the thoughts and experience of the world have etched and molded there, in that which they have of power to refine and make expressive the outward form, the animalism of Greece, the lust of Rome, the mysticism of the Middle Age with its spiritual ambition and imaginative loves, the return of the Pagan world, the sins of the Borgias.[4] She is older than the rocks among which she sits; like the vampire,[5] she has been dead many times, and learned the secrets of the grave; and has been a diver in deep seas, and keeps their fallen day about her; and trafficked for strange webs with Eastern merchants, and, as Leda, was the mother of Helen of Troy,[6] and, as Saint Anne, the mother of Mary; and all this has been to her but as the sound of lyres and flutes, and lives only in the delicacy with which it has molded the changing lineaments, and tinged the eyelids and the hands. The fancy of a perpetual life, sweeping together ten thousand experiences, is an old one; and modern philosophy has conceived the idea of humanity as wrought upon by, and summing up in itself, all modes of thought and life. Certainly Lady Lisa might stand as the embodiment of the old fancy, the symbol of the modern idea.

2. Mimics or clowns.
3. I Corinthians x.11.
4. The Borgias were an Italian family during the Renaissance whose reputation for scandalous conduct was notorious.

5. A dead body which, according to widespread legends, returns from the grave to prey upon the living.
6. Leda's union with Zeus (who approached her in the form of a swan) produced Helen of Troy.

Conclusion[7]

Λέγει που Ἡράκλειτος ὅτι πάντα χωρεῖ καὶ οὐδὲν μένει[8]

To regard all things and principles of things as inconstant modes or fashions has more and more become the tendency of modern thought. Let us begin with that which is without—our physical life. Fix upon it in one of its more exquisite intervals, the moment, for instance, of delicious recoil from the flood of water in summer heat. What is the whole physical life in that moment but a combination of natural elements to which science gives their names? But those elements, phosphorus and lime and delicate fibers, are present not in the human body alone: we detect them in places most remote from it. Our physical life is a perpetual motion of them—the passage of the blood, the waste and repairing of the lenses of the eye, the modification of the tissues of the brain under every ray of light and sound—processes which science reduces to simpler and more elementary forces. Like the elements of which we are composed, the action of these forces extends beyond us: it rusts iron and ripens corn. Far out on every side of us those elements are broadcast, driven in many currents; and birth and gesture and death and the springing of violets from the grave are but a few out of ten thousand resultant combinations. That clear, perpetual outline of face and limb is but an image of ours, under which we group them— a design in a web, the actual threads of which pass out beyond it. This at least of flamelike our life has, that it is but the concurrence, renewed from moment to moment, of forces parting sooner or later on their ways.

Or, if we begin with the inward world of thought and feeling, the whirlpool is still more rapid, the flame more eager and devouring. There it is no longer the gradual darkening of the eye, the gradual fading of color from the wall—movements of the shore-side, where the water flows down indeed, though in apparent rest—but the race of the midstream, a drift of momentary acts of sight and passion and thought. At first sight experience seems to bury us under a flood of external objects, pressing upon us with a sharp and importunate reality, calling us out of ourselves in a thousand forms of action. But when reflection begins to play upon those objects they are dissipated under its influence; the cohesive force seems suspended like some trick of magic; each object is loosed into a group of impressions—color, odor, texture—in the mind of the observer.

7. "This brief 'Conclusion' was omitted in the second edition of this book, as I conceived it might possibly mislead some of those young men into whose hands it might fall. On the whole, I have thought it best to reprint it here, with some slight changes which bring it closer to my original meaning. I have dealt more fully in *Marius the Epicurean* with the thoughts suggested by it" [Pater's note to the third edition, 1888].

8. "Heraclitus says, 'All things give way; nothing remaineth'" [Pater's translation].

And if we continue to dwell in thought on this world, not of objects in the solidity with which language invests them, but of impressions, unstable, flickering, inconsistent, which burn and are extinguished with our consciousness of them, it contracts still further: the whole scope of observation is dwarfed into the narrow chamber of the individual mind. Experience, already reduced to a group of impressions, is ringed round for each one of us by that thick wall of personality through which no real voice has ever pierced on its way to us, or from us to that which we can only conjecture to be without. Every one of those impressions is the impression of the individual in his isolation, each mind keeping as a solitary prisoner its own dream of a world. Analysis goes a step farther still, and assures us that those impressions of the individual mind to which, for each one of us, experience dwindles down, are in perpetual flight; that each of them is limited by time, and that as time is infinitely divisible, each of them is infinitely divisible also; all that is actual in it being a single moment, gone while we try to apprehend it, of which it may ever be more truly said that it has ceased to be than that it is. To such a tremulous wisp constantly reforming itself on the stream, to a single sharp impression, with a sense in it, a relic more or less fleeting, of such moments gone by, what is real in our life fines itself down. It is with this movement, with the passage and dissolution of impressions, images, sensations, that analysis leaves off—that continual vanishing away, that strange, perpetual weaving and unweaving of ourselves.

Philosophiren, says Novalis, *ist dephlegmatisiren, vivificiren.*[9] The service of philosophy, of speculative culture, towards the human spirit is to rouse, to startle it to a life of constant and eager observation. Every moment some form grows perfect in hand or face; some tone on the hills or the sea is choicer than the rest; some mood of passion or insight or intellectual excitement is irresistibly real and attractive to us—for that moment only. Not the fruit of experience, but experience itself, is the end. A counted number of pulses only is given to us of a variegated, dramatic life. How may we see in them all that is to be seen in them by the finest senses? How shall we pass most swiftly from point to point, and be present always at the focus where the greatest number of vital forces unite in their purest energy?

To burn always with this hard, gemlike flame, to maintain this ecstasy, is success in life. In a sense it might even be said that our failure is to form habits: for, after all, habit is relative to a stereotyped world, and meantime it is only the roughness of the eye that makes any two persons, things, situations, seem alike. While all

---

9. "To philosophize is to cast off inertia, to make oneself alive." "Novalis" was the pseudonym of Friedrich von Hardenberg (1772–1801), German Romantic writer.

melts under our feet, we may well grasp at any exquisite passion, or any contribution to knowledge that seems by a lifted horizon to set the spirit free for a moment, or any stirring of the senses, strange dyes, strange colors, and curious odors, or work of the artist's hands, or the face of one's friend. Not to discriminate every moment some passionate attitude in those about us, and in the very brilliancy of their gifts some tragic dividing of forces on their ways, is, on this short day of frost and sun, to sleep before evening. With this sense of the splendor of our experience and of its awful brevity, gathering all we are into one desperate effort to see and touch, we shall hardly have time to make theories about the things we see and touch. What we have to do is to be forever curiously testing new opinions and courting new impressions, never acquiescing in a facile orthodoxy of Comte, or of Hegel,[1] or of our own. Philosophical theories or ideas, as points of view, instruments of criticism, may help us to gather up what might otherwise pass unregarded by us. "Philosophy is the microscope of thought." The theory or idea or system which requires of us the sacrifice of any part of this experience, in consideration of some interest into which we cannot enter, or some abstract theory we have not identified with ourselves, or of what is only conventional, has no real claim upon us.

One of the most beautiful passages of Rousseau is that in the sixth book of the *Confessions*, where he describes the awakening in him of the literary sense. An undefinable taint of death had clung always about him, and now in early manhood he believed himself smitten by mortal disease. He asked himself how he might make as much as possible of the interval that remained; and he was not biased by anything in his previous life when he decided that it must be by intellectual excitement, which he found just then in the clear, fresh writings of Voltaire. Well! we are all *condamnés* as Victor Hugo says: we are all under sentence of death but with a sort of indefinite reprieve—*les hommes sont tous condamnés à mort avec des sursis indéfinis*: we have an interval, and then our place knows us no more. Some spend this interval in listlessness, some in high passions, the wisest, at least among "the children of this world," in art and song. For our one chance lies in expanding that interval, in getting as many pulsations as possible into the given time Great passions may give us this quickened sense of life, ecstasy and sorrow of love, the various forms of enthusiastic activity, disinterested or otherwise, which come naturally to many of us. Only be sure it is passion—that it does yield you this fruit of a quickened, multiplied consciousness. Of such wisdom, the poetic passion, the desire of beauty, the love of art for its own sake, has most. For art comes to you proposing frankly to give nothing but the highest

1. Auguste Comte (1798–1857), French founder of positivism; Georg W. F. Hegel (1770–1831), German idealistic philosopher.

quality to your moments as they pass, and simply for those moments' sake.

1868   1873

From Appreciations
From *Style*

Since all progress of mind consists for the most part in differentiation, in the resolution of an obscure and complex object into its component aspects, it is surely the stupidest of losses to confuse things which right reason has put asunder, to lose the sense of achieved distinctions, the distinction between poetry and prose, for instance, or, to speak more exactly, between the laws and characteristic excellences of verse and prose composition. On the other hand, those who have dwelt most emphatically on the distinction between prose and verse, prose and poetry, may sometimes have been tempted to limit the proper functions of prose too narrowly; and this again is at least false economy, as being, in effect, the renunciation of a certain means or faculty, in a world where after all we must needs make the most of things. Critical efforts to limit art *a priori*,[1] by anticipations regarding the natural incapacity of the material with which this or that artist works, as the sculptor with solid form, or the prose-writer with the ordinary language of men, are always liable to be discredited by the facts of artistic production; and while prose is actually found to be a colored thing with Bacon, picturesque with Livy and Carlyle, musical with Cicero and Newman, mystical and intimate with Plato and Michelet[2] and Sir Thomas Browne, exalted or florid, it may be, with Milton and Taylor,[3] it will be useless to protest that it can be nothing at all, except something very tamely and narrowly confined to mainly practical ends—a kind of "good round hand"; as useless as the protest that poetry might not touch prosaic subjects as with Wordsworth, or an abstruse matter as with Browning, or treat contemporary life nobly as with Tennyson. In subordination to one essential beauty in all good literary style, in all literature as a fine art, as there are many beauties of poetry so the beauties of prose are many, and it is the business of criticism to estimate them as such; as it is good in the criticism of verse to look for those hard, logical, and quasi-prosaic excellences which that too has, or needs. To find in the poem, amid the flowers, the allusions, the mixed perspectives, of *Lycidas* for instance, the thought, the logical structure: how wholesome! how delightful! as to identify in prose what we call the poetry,

1. Prior to experience.
2. Jules Michelet (1798–1874), French historian.

3. Jeremy Taylor (1613–67), famous for the elaborate style of his sermons.

the imaginative power, not treating it as out of place and a kind of vagrant intruder, but by way of an estimate of its rights, that is, of its achieved powers, there.

Dryden, with the characteristic instinct of his age, loved to emphasize the distinction between poetry and prose, the protest against their confusion with each other, coming with somewhat diminished effect from one whose poetry was so prosaic. In truth, his sense of prosaic excellence affected his verse rather than his prose, which is not only fervid, richly figured, poetic, as we say, but vitiated, all unconsciously, by many a scanning line. Setting up correctness, that humble merit of prose, as the central literary excellence, he is really a less correct writer than he may seem, still with an imperfect mastery of the relative pronoun. It might have been foreseen that, in the rotations of mind, the province of poetry in prose would find its assertor; and, a century after Dryden, amid very different intellectual needs, and with the need therefore of great modifications in literary form, the range of the poetic force in literature was effectively enlarged by Wordsworth. The true distinction between prose and poetry he regarded as the almost technical or accidental one of the absence or presence of metrical beauty, or, say! metrical restraint; and for him the opposition came to be between verse and prose of course; but, as the essential dichotomy in this matter, between imaginative and unimaginative writing, parallel to De Quincey's distinction between "the literature of power and the literature of knowledge,"[4] in the former of which the composer gives us not fact, but his peculiar sense of fact, whether past or present.

Dismissing then, under sanction of Wordsworth, that harsher opposition of poetry to prose, as savoring in fact of the arbitrary psychology of the last century, and with it the prejudice that there can be but one only beauty of prose style, I propose here to point out certain qualities of all literature as a fine art, which, if they apply to the literature of fact, apply still more to the literature of the imaginative sense of fact, while they apply indifferently to verse and prose, so far as either is really imaginative—certain conditions of true art in both alike, which conditions may also contain in them the secret of the proper discrimination and guardianship of the peculiar excellences of either.

The line between fact and something quite different from external fact is, indeed, hard to draw. In Pascal,[5] for instance, in the persuasive writers generally, how difficult to define the point where, from time to time, argument which, if it is to be worth anything at all, must consist of facts or groups of facts, becomes a pleading—a theorem no longer, but essentially an appeal to the reader to catch the writer's spirit, to think with him, if one can or will—an expres-

---

4. De Quincey's essay on this topic appeared in 1848. 5. Blaise Pascal (1623–62), French scientist, philosopher, and theologian.

sion no longer of fact but of his sense of it, his peculiar intuition of a world, prospective, or discerned below the faulty conditions of the present, in either case changed somewhat from the actual world. In science, on the other hand, in history so far as it conforms to scientific rule, we have a literary domain where the imagination may be thought to be always an intruder. And as, in all science, the functions of literature reduce themselves eventually to the transcribing of fact, so all the excellences of literary form in regard to science are reducible to various kinds of painstaking; this good quality being involved in all "skilled work" whatever, in the drafting of an act of parliament, as in sewing. Yet here again, the writer's sense of fact, in history especially, and in all those complex subjects which do but lie on the borders of science, will still take the place of fact, in various degrees. Your historian, for instance, with absolutely truthful intention, amid the multitude of facts presented to him must needs select, and in selecting assert something of his own humor, something that comes not of the world without but of a vision within. So Gibbon molds his unwieldy material to a preconceived view. Livy, Tacitus, Michelet, moving full of poignant sensibility amid the records of the past, each, after his own sense, modifies—who can tell where and to what degree?—and becomes something else than a transcriber; each, as he thus modifies, passing into the domain of art proper. For just in proportion as the writer's aim, consciously or unconsciously, comes to be the transcribing, not of the world, not of mere fact, but of his sense of it, he becomes an artist, his work *fine* art; and good art (as I hope ultimately to show) in proportion to the truth of his presentment of that sense; as in those humbler or plainer functions of literature also, truth—truth to bare fact, there—is the essence of such artistic quality as they may have. Truth! there can be no merit, no craft at all, without that. And further, all beauty is in the long run only *fineness* of truth, or what we call expression, the finer accommodation of speech to that vision within.

—The transcript of his sense of fact rather than the fact, as being preferable, pleasanter, more beautiful to the writer himself. In literature, as in every other product of human skill, in the molding of a bell or a platter for instance, wherever this sense asserts itself, wherever the producer so modifies his work as, over and above its primary use or intention, to make it pleasing (to himself, of course, in the first instance) there, "fine" as opposed to merely serviceable art, exists. Literary art, that is, like all art which is in any way imitative or reproductive of fact—form, or color, or incident—is the representation of such fact as connected with soul, of a specific personality, in its preferences, its volition and power.

Such is the matter of imaginative or artistic literature—this transcript, not of mere fact, but of fact in its infinite variety, as modified by human preference in all its infinitely varied forms. It will be good literary art not because it is brilliant or sober, or rich, or impulsive, or severe, but just in proportion as its representation of that sense, that soul-fact, is true, verse being only one department of such literature, and imaginative prose, it may be thought, being the special art of the modern world. That imaginative prose should be the special and opportune art of the modern world results from two important facts about the latter: first, the chaotic variety and complexity of its interests, making the intellectual issue, the really master currents of the present time incalculable—a condition of mind little susceptible of the restraint proper to verse form, so that the most characteristic verse of the nineteenth century has been lawless verse; and secondly, an all-pervading naturalism, a curiosity about everything whatever as it really is, involving a certain humility of attitude, cognate to what must, after all, be the less ambitious form of literature. And prose thus asserting itself as the special and privileged artistic faculty of the present day, will be, however critics may try to narrow its scope, as varied in its excellence as humanity itself reflecting on the facts of its latest experience—an instrument of many stops, meditative, observant, descriptive, eloquent, analytic, plaintive, fervid. Its beauties will be not exclusively "pedestrian": it will exert, in due measure, all the varied charms of poetry, down to the rhythm which, as in Cicero, or Michelet, or Newman, at their best, gives its musical value to every syllable. * * *

If the style be the man, in all the color and intensity of a veritable apprehension, it will be in a real sense "impersonal."

I said, thinking of books like Victor Hugo's *Les Misérables*, that prose literature was the characteristic art of the nineteenth century, as others, thinking of its triumphs since the youth of Bach, have assigned that place to music. Music and prose literature are, in one sense, the opposite terms of art; the art of literature presenting to the imagination, through the intelligence, a range of interests, as free and various as those which music presents to it through sense. And certainly the tendency of what has been here said is to bring literature too under those conditions, by conformity to which music takes rank as the typically perfect art. If music be the ideal of all art whatever, precisely because in music it is impossible to distinguish the form from the substance or matter, the subject from the expression, then, literature, by finding its specific excellence in the absolute correspondence of the term to its import, will be but fulfilling the condition of all artistic quality in things everywhere, of all good art.

Good art, but not necessarily great art; the distinction between great art and good art depending immediately, as regards literature at all events, not on its form, but on the matter. Thackeray's *Esmond*, surely, is greater art than *Vanity Fair*, by the greater dignity of its interests. It is on the quality of the matter it informs or controls, its compass, its variety, its alliance to great ends, or the depth of the note of revolt, or the largeness of hope in it, that the greatness of literary art depends, as *The Divine Comedy, Paradise Lost, Les Misérables,* the English Bible, are great art. Given the conditions I have tried to explain as constituting good art—then, if it be devoted further to the increase of men's happiness, to the redemption of the oppressed, or the enlargement of our sympathies with each other, or to such presentment of new or old truth about ourselves and our relation to the world as may ennoble and fortify us in our sojourn here, or immediately, as with Dante, to the glory of God, it will be also great art; if, over and above those qualities I summed up as mind and soul—that color and mystic perfume, and that reasonable structure, it has something of the soul of humanity in it, and finds its logical, architectural place, in the great structure of human life.

1889

Topics in Victorian Literature

EVOLUTION

One of the most dramatic controversies in the Victorian age concerned theories of evolution. This controversy exploded into prominence in 1859 when Charles Darwin's *Origin of Species* was published, but it had been rumbling for many years previously. Sir Charles Lyell's *Principles of Geology* (1830) and Robert Chambers' popular book, *Vestiges of Creation* (1843–46), had already raised issues which Tennyson aired in his *In Memoriam* (1850). It was Darwin, however, with his monumental marshaling of evidence to establish his theory of natural selection, who finally brought the topic fully into the open, and the public, as well as the experts, took sides.

The opposition aroused by Darwin's treatise came from two different quarters. The first consisted of some of his fellow scientists who affirmed that his theory was unsound. The second consisted of religious leaders who attacked his theory because it seemed to contradict a literal interpretation of the Bible. Sometimes the two kinds of opposition combined forces as in 1860 when his scientific opponents selected Bishop Wilberforce to be their spokesman in spearheading their attack on *The Origin of Species*. In replying to such attacks, Darwin had the good fortune to be supported by two of the ablest popularizers of science in his day, T. H. Huxley and John Tyndall. Moreover, although shy by temperament, Darwin was himself (as Tyndall affirms and the following selections will illustrate) an exceptionally effective expositor of his own theories.

CHARLES DARWIN: *From* The Descent of Man
[*Natural Selection and Sexual Selection*][1]

A brief summary will here be sufficient to recall to the reader's mind the more salient points in this work. Many of the views which

1. Charles Darwin (1809–82) developed an interest in geology and biology at Cambridge where he was studying to become a clergyman. Aided by a private income, he resolved to devote the rest of his life to scientific research.

The observations he made during a long voyage to the South Seas on H.M.S. *Beagle* (on which he served as a naturalist) led Darwin to construct hypotheses about evolution. In 1858, more than twenty years after his re-have been advanced are highly speculative, and some no doubt will prove erroneous; but I have in every case given the reasons which have led me to one view rather than to another. It seemed worth while to try how far the principle of evolution would throw light on some of the more complex problems in the natural history of man. False facts are highly injurious to the progress of science, for they often long endure; but false views, if supported by some evidence, do little harm, as everyone takes a salutary pleasure in proving their falseness; and when this is done, one path towards error is closed and the road to truth is often at the same time opened.

The main conclusion arrived at in this work, and now held by many naturalists who are well competent to form a sound judgment, is that man is descended from some less highly organized form. The grounds upon which this conclusion rests will never be shaken, for the close similarity between man and the lower animals in embryonic development, as well as in innumerable points of structure and constitution, both of high and of the most trifling importance—the rudiments which he retains, and the abnormal reversions to which he is occasionally liable—are facts which cannot be disputed. They have long been known, but until recently they told us nothing with respect to the origin of man. Now when viewed by the light of our knowledge of the whole organic world, their meaning is unmistakable. The great principle of evolution stands up clear and firm, when these groups of facts are considered in connection with others, such as the mutual affinities of the members of the same group, their geographical distribution in past and present times, and their geological succession. It is incredible that all these facts should speak falsely. He who is not content to look, like a savage, at the phenomena of nature as disconnected cannot any longer believe that man is the work of a separate act of creation. He will be forced to admit that the close resemblance of the embryo of man to that, for instance, of a dog—the construction of his skull, limbs, and whole frame, independently of the uses to which the parts may be put, on the same plan with that of other mammals— the occasional reappearance of various structures, for instance of several distinct muscles, which man does not normally possess, but which are common to the Quadrumana[2]—and a crowd of analogous facts—all point in the plainest manner to the conclusion that man is the codescendant with other mammals of a common pro-

turn to England from his voyage, he ventured to submit a paper developing his theory of the origin of species. A year later, when his theory appeared in book form, Darwin emerged as a famous and controversial figure. During the remainder of his life he published several treatises, some of which develop and clarify the theory of *The Origin of Species*. One of these works, *The Descent of Man* (1871) was espe-cially provocative in its stress on the similarities between men and animals and in its naturalistic explanations of the beautiful colorings of birds, insects, and flowers. The present selection is from Chapter XXI of *The Descent of Man*.

2. Animals such as monkeys whose hind feet and forefeet can be used as hands—hence "four-handed."

genitor. * * *

By considering the embryological structure of man—the homologies which he presents with the lower animals, the rudiments which he retains, and the reversions to which he is liable—we can partly recall in imagination the former condition of our early progenitors; and can approximately place them in their proper position in the zoological series. We thus learn that man is descended from a hairy quadruped, furnished with a tail and pointed ears, probably arboreal in its habits, and an inhabitant of the Old World. This creature, if its whole structure had been examined by a naturalist, would have been classed amongst the Quadrumana, as surely as would the common and still more ancient progenitor of the Old and New World monkeys. The Quadrumana and all the higher mammals are probably derived from an ancient marsupial animal, and this through a long line of diversified forms, either from some reptile-like or some amphibianlike creature, and this again from some fishlike animal. In the dim obscurity of the past we can see that the early progenitor of all the Vertebrata must have been an aquatic animal, provided with branchae, with the two sexes united in the same individual, and with the most important organs of the body (such as the brain and heart) imperfectly developed. This animal seems to have been more like the larvae of our existing marine ascidians[3] than any other known form. * * *

Sexual selection has been treated at great length in these volumes; for, as I have attempted to show, it has played an important part in the history of the organic world. * * *

The belief in the power of sexual selection rests chiefly on the following considerations. The characters which we have the best reason for supposing to have been thus acquired are confined to one sex; and this alone renders it probable that they are in some way connected with the act of reproduction. These characters in innumerable instances are fully developed only at maturity; and often during only a part of the year, which is always the breeding season. The males (passing over a few exceptional cases) are the most active in courtship; they are the best armed, and are rendered the most attractive in various ways. It is to be especially observed that the males display their attractions with elaborate care in the presence of the females; and that they rarely or never display them excepting during the season of love. It is incredible that all this display should be purposeless. Lastly we have distinct evidence with some quadrupeds and birds that the individuals of the one sex are capable of feeling a strong antipathy or preference for certain individuals of the opposite sex.

Bearing these facts in mind, and not forgetting the marked re-

3. Part of a group of marine animals called Tunicata, or popularly "sea squirts," sometimes assumed to be ancestors of the vertebrate animals.

sults of man's unconscious selection, it seems to me almost certain that if the individuals of one sex were during a long series of generations to prefer pairing with certain individuals of the other sex, characterized in some peculiar manner, the offspring would slowly but surely become modified in this same manner. I have not attempted to conceal that, excepting when the males are more numerous than the females, or when polygamy prevails, it is doubtful how the more attractive males succeed in leaving a larger number of offspring to inherit their superiority in ornaments or other charms than the less attractive males; but I have shown that this would probably follow from the females—especially the more vigorous females which would be the first to breed, preferring not only the more attractive but at the same time the more vigorous and victorious males.

Although we have some positive evidence that birds appreciate bright and beautiful objects, as with the bowerbirds of Australia, and although they certainly appreciate the power of song, yet I fully admit that it is an astonishing fact that the females of many birds and some mammals should be endowed with sufficient taste for what has apparently been effected through sexual selection; and this is even more astonishing in the case of reptiles, fish, and insects. But we really know very little about the minds of the lower animals. It cannot be supposed that male birds of paradise or peacocks, for instance, should take so much pains in erecting, spreading, and vibrating their beautiful plumes before the females for no purpose. We should remember the fact given on excellent authority in a former chapter, namely that several peahens, when debarred from an admired male, remained widows during a whole season rather than pair with another bird.

Nevertheless I know of no fact in natural history more wonderful than that the female argus pheasant should be able to appreciate the exquisite shading of the ball-and-socket ornaments and the elegant patterns on the wing feathers of the male. He who thinks that the male was created as he now exists must admit that the great plumes, which prevent the wings from being used for flight, and which, as well as the primary feathers, are displayed in a manner quite peculiar to this one species during the act of courtship, and at no other time, were given to him as an ornament. If so, he must likewise admit that the female was created and endowed with the capacity of appreciating such ornaments. I differ only in the conviction that the male argus pheasant acquired his beauty gradually, through the females having preferred during many generations the more highly ornamented males; the aesthetic capacity of the females having been advanced through exercise or habit in the same manner as our own taste is gradually improved. In the male, through the fortunate chance of a few feathers not having been modified, we can distinctly see how simple spots with a little fulvous[4] shading on one side might have been developed by small and graduated steps into the wonderful ball-and-socket ornaments; and it is probable that they were actually thus developed. * * *

He who admits the principle of sexual selection will be led to the remarkable conclusion that the cerebral system not only regulates most of the existing functions of the body, but has indirectly influenced the progressive development of various bodily structures and of certain mental qualities. Courage, pugnacity, perseverance, strength and size of body, weapons of all kinds, musical organs, both vocal and instrumental, bright colors, stripes and marks, and ornamental appendages have all been indirectly gained by the one sex or the other, through the influence of love and jealousy, through the appreciation of the beautiful in sound, color or form, and through the exertion of a choice; and these powers of the mind manifestly depend on the development of the cerebral system. * * *

The main conclusion arrived at in this work, namely that man is descended from some lowly-organized form, will, I regret to think, be highly distasteful to many persons. But there can hardly be a doubt that we are descended from barbarians. The astonishment which I felt on first seeing a party of Fuegians[5] on a wild and broken shore will never be forgotten by me, for the reflection at once rushed into my mind—such were our ancestors. These men were absolutely naked and bedaubed with paint, their long hair was tangled, their mouths frothed with excitement, and their expression was wild, startled, and distrustful. They possessed hardly any arts, and like wild animals lived on what they could catch; they had no government, and were merciless to everyone not of their own small tribe. He who has seen a savage in his native land will not feel much shame, if forced to acknowledge that the blood of some more humble creature flows in his veins. For my own part I would as soon be descended from that heroic little monkey, who braved his dreaded enemy in order to save the life of his keeper; or from that old baboon, who, descending from the mountains, carried away in triumph his young comrade from a crowd of astonished dogs[6]— as from a savage who delights to torture his enemies, offers up bloody sacrifices, practices infanticide without remorse, treats his wives like slaves, knows no decency, and is haunted by the grossest superstitions.

Man may be excused for feeling some pride at having risen, though not through his own exertions, to the very summit of the

4. Dull yellow.
5. Savages inhabiting the islands off the southern tip of South America, Tierra del Fuego, which Darwin had visited in 1832. See his *Voyage of the Beagle*, Chapter X.
6. Incidents described in Chapter IV of *The Descent of Man* to demonstrate that animals may be endowed with a moral sense.

organic scale; and the fact of his having thus risen, instead of having been aboriginally placed there, may give him hopes for a still higher destiny in the distant future. But we are not here concerned with hopes or fears, only with the truth as far as our reason allows us to discover it. I have given the evidence to the best of my ability; and we must acknowledge, as it seems to me, that man with all his noble qualities, with sympathy which feels for the most debased, with benevolence which extends not only to other men but to the humblest living creature, with his godlike intellect which has penetrated into the movements and constitution of the solar system—with all these exalted powers—Man still bears in his bodily frame the indelible stamp of his lowly origin.

JOHN TYNDALL: *From* The Belfast Address
[*Darwin's Method of Argument*][7]

Mr. Darwin shirks no difficulty; and, saturated as the subject was with his own thought, he must have known, better than his critics, the weakness as well as the strength of his theory. This of course would be of little avail were his object a temporary dialectic victory, instead of the establishment of a truth which he means to be everlasting. But he takes no pains to disguise the weakness he has discerned; nay, he takes every pains to bring it into the strongest light. His vast resources enable him to cope with objections started by himself and others, so as to leave the final impression upon the reader's mind that, if they be not completely answered, they certainly are not fatal. Their negative force being thus destroyed, you are free to be influenced by the vast positive mass of evidence he is able to bring before you. This largeness of knowledge, and readiness of resource, render Mr. Darwin the most terrible of antagonists. Accomplished naturalists have leveled heavy and sustained criticisms against him—not always with the view of fairly weighing his theory, but with the express intention of exposing its weak points only. This does not irritate him. He treats every objection with a soberness and thoroughness which even Bishop Butler [8] might be proud to imitate, surrounding each fact with its appropriate detail, placing it in its proper relations, and usually giving it a significance which, as long as it was kept isolated, failed to appear. This is done without a trace of ill temper. He moves over the subject with the passionless strength of a glacier; and the

---

7. John Tyndall (1820–93) was a physicist and popularizer of science. In 1874 he delivered an address on religion and science entitled *The Belfast Address,* later published in his collection of essays, *Fragments of Sci-* *ence* (1899).
8. Joseph Butler (1692–1752), Bishop of Durham. In his book *The Analogy of Religion* (1736), objections to religious faith are aired calmly and fully before being answered by the author.

grinding of the rocks is not always without a counterpart in the logical pulverization of the objector. But though in handling this mighty theme all passion has been stilled, there is an emotion of the intellect, incident to the discernment of new truth, which often colors and warms the pages of Mr. Darwin. His success has been great; and this implies not only the solidity of his work, but the preparedness of the public mind for such a revelation. On this head, a remark of Agassiz[9] impressed me more than anything else. Sprung from a race of theologians, this celebrated man combated to the last the theory of natural selection. One of the many times I had the pleasure of meeting him in the United States was at Mr. Winthrop's beautiful residence at Brookline, near Boston. Rising from luncheon, we all halted as if by common consent, in front of a window, and continued there a discussion which had been started at table. The maple was in its autumn glory, and the exquisite beauty of the scene outside seemed, in my case, to interpenetrate without disturbance the intellectual action. Earnestly, almost sadly, Agassiz turned, and said to the gentlemen standing round, "I confess that I was not prepared to see this theory received as it has been by the best intellects of our time. Its success is greater than I could have thought possible."

1874, 1899

LEONARD HUXLEY: *From* The Life and Letters of Thomas Henry Huxley
[*The Huxley-Wilberforce Debate at Oxford*][1]

The famous Oxford Meeting of 1860 was of no small importance in Huxley's career. It was not merely that he helped to save a great cause from being stifled under misrepresentation and ridicule—that he helped to extort for it a fair hearing; it was now that he first made himself known in popular estimation as a dangerous adversary in debate—a personal force in the world of science which

9. Louis Agassiz (1807–73), Swiss naturalist who became professor of zoology and geology at Harvard. He refused to accept the concept of evolution.
1. At meetings of the British Association for the Advancement of Science, the reading of a paper is followed by a discussion. In 1860, at Oxford, this discussion developed into a debate between Thomas Henry Huxley, a defender of Darwin's theories, and Bishop Samuel Wilberforce (1805–73). Although he had majored in mathematics as an undergraduate, Wilberforce could hardly lay claim to be a scientist. He was willing, nevertheless, to serve as a spokesman for those scientists who dis-

agreed with *The Origin of Species*, and he reportedly came to the meeting ready to "smash Darwin." The bishop's principal qualifications for this role were his great powers as a smoothly persuasive orator (he was commonly known by his detractors as "Soapy Sam"), but he met more than his match in Huxley.
Because no complete transcript of this celebrated debate was made at the time, Huxley's son Leonard, in writing his father's biography, had to reconstruct the scene by combining quotations from reports made by magazine writers and other witnesses. The account given here is from Chapter XIV.

could not be neglected. From this moment he entered the front fighting line in the most exposed quarter of the field. * * *

It was the merest chance, as I have already said, that Huxley attended the meeting of the section that morning. Dr. Draper of New York was to read a paper on the *Intellectual Development of Europe considered with reference to the views of Mr. Darwin*. "I can still hear," writes one who was present, "the American accents of Dr. Draper's opening address when he asked 'Air we a fortuitous concourse of atoms?' " However, it was not to hear him, but the eloquence of the Bishop, that the members of the Association crowded in such numbers into the Lecture Room of the Museum, that this, the appointed meeting place of the section, had to be abandoned for the long west room, since cut in two by a partition for the purposes of the library. It was not term time, nor were the general public admitted; nevertheless the room was crowded to suffocation long before the protagonists appeared on the scene, 700 persons or more managing to find places. The very windows by which the room was lighted down the length of its west side were packed with ladies, whose white handkerchiefs, waving and fluttering in the air at the end of the Bishop's speech, were an unforgettable factor in the acclamation of the crowd.

On the east side between the two doors was the platform. Professor Henslow, the President of the section, took his seat in the center; upon his right was the Bishop, and beyond him again Dr. Draper; on his extreme left was Mr. Dingle, a clergyman from Lanchester, near Durham, with Sir J. Hooker and Sir J. Lubbock in front of him, and nearer the center, Professor Beale of King's College, London, and Huxley.

The clergy, who shouted lustily for the Bishop, were massed in the middle of the room; behind them in the northwest corner a knot of undergraduates (one of these was T. H. Green, who listened but took no part in the cheering) had gathered together beside Professor Brodie, ready to lift their voices, poor minority though they were, for the opposite party. Close to them stood one of the few men among the audience already in Holy orders, who joined in—and indeed led—the cheers for the Darwinians.

So "Dr. Draper droned out his paper, turning first to the right hand and then to the left, of course bringing in a reference to the *Origin of Species* which set the ball rolling."

An hour or more that paper lasted, and then discussion began. The President "wisely announced *in limine*[2] that none who had not valid arguments to bring forward on one side or the other would be allowed to address the meeting; a caution that proved necessary, for no fewer than four combatants had their utterances burked by him, because of their indulgence in vague declamation."

2. As a starting point.

"First spoke" (writes Professor Farrar) "a layman from Brompton, who gave his name as being one of the Committee of the (newly formed) Economic section of the Association. He, in a stentorian voice, let off his theological venom. Then jumped up Richard Greswell with a thin voice, saying much the same, but speaking as a scholar; but we did not merely want any theological discussion, so we shouted them down. Then a Mr. Dingle got up and tried to show that Darwin would have done much better if he had taken him into consultation. He used the blackboard and began a mathematical demonstration on the question—'Let this point A be man, and let that point B be the mawnkey.' He got no further; he was shouted down with cries of 'mawnkey.' None of these had spoken more than three minutes. It was when these were shouted down that Henslow said he must demand that the discussion should rest on *scientific* grounds only.

"Then there were calls for the Bishop, but he rose and said he understood his friend Professor Beale had something to say first. Beale, who was an excellent histologist,[3] spoke to the effect that the new theory ought to meet with fair discussion, but added, with great modesty, that he himself had not sufficient knowledge to discuss the subject adequately. Then the Bishop spoke the speech that you know, and the question about his mother being an ape, or his grandmother."

From the scientific point of view, the speech was of small value. It was evident from his mode of handling the subject that he had been "crammed up to the throat," and knew nothing at first hand; he used no argument beyond those to be found in his *Quarterly* article, which appeared a few days later, and is now admitted to have been inspired by Owen.[4] "He ridiculed Darwin badly and Huxley savagely; but," confesses one of his strongest opponents, "all in such dulcet tones, so persuasive a manner, and in such well turned periods, that I who had been inclined to blame the President for allowing a discussion that could serve no scientific purpose, now forgave him from the bottom of my heart."

The Bishop spoke thus "for full half an hour with inimitable spirit, emptiness and unfairness." "In a light, scoffing tone, florid and fluent, he assured us there was nothing in the idea of evolution; rock pigeons were what rock pigeons had always been. Then, turning to his antagonist with a smiling insolence, he begged to know, was it through his grandfather or his grandmother that he claimed his descent from a monkey?"

This was the fatal mistake of his speech. Huxley instantly grasped the tactical advantage which the descent to personalities gave him. He turned to Sir Benjamin Brodie, who was sitting beside him, and emphatically striking his hand upon his knee, exclaimed, "The

---

3. Biologist specializing in the study of the minute structure of the tissues of plants and animals.

4. Sir Richard Owen (1804–92), a leading zoologist and paleontologist, was opposed to Darwin's theories.

Lord hath delivered him into mine hands." The bearing of the exclamation did not dawn upon Sir Benjamin until after Huxley had completed his "forcible and eloquent" answer to the scientific part of the Bishop's argument, and proceeded to make his famous retort.

"On this" (continues the writer in *Macmillan's Magazine*) "Mr. Huxley slowly and deliberately arose. A slight tall figure, stern and pale, very quiet and very grave, he stood before us and spoke those tremendous words—words which no one seems sure of now, nor, I think, could remember just after they were spoken, for their meaning took away our breath, though it left us in no doubt as to what it was. He was not ashamed to have a monkey for his ancestor; but he would be ashamed to be connected with a man who used great gifts to obscure the truth. No one doubted his meaning, and the effect was tremendous. One lady fainted and had to be carried out; I, for one, jumped out of my seat."

The fullest and probably most accurate account of these concluding words is the following, from a letter of the late John Richard Green, then an undergraduate, to his friend, afterwards Professor Boyd Dawkins:

"I asserted—and I repeat—that a man has no reason to be ashamed of having an ape for his grandfather. If there were an ancestor whom I should feel shame in recalling it would rather be a man—a man of restless and versatile intellect—who, not content with an equivocal success in his own sphere of activity, plunges into scientific questions with which he has no real acquaintance, only to obscure them by an aimless rhetoric, and distract the attention of his hearers from the real point at issue by eloquent digressions and skilled appeals to religious prejudice."

The result of this encounter, though a check to the other side, cannot, of course, be represented as an immediate and complete triumph for evolutionary doctrine. This was precluded by the character and temper of the audience, most of whom were less capable of being convinced by the arguments than shocked by the boldness of the retort, although, being gentlefolk, as Professor Farrar remarks, they were disposed to admit on reflection that the Bishop had erred on the score of taste and good manners. Nevertheless, it was a noticeable feature of the occasion, Sir M. Foster tells me, that when Huxley rose he was received coldly, just a cheer of encouragement from his friends, the audience as a whole not joining in it. But as he made his points the applause grew and widened, until, when he sat down, the cheering was not very much less than that given to the Bishop. To that extent he carried an unwilling audience with him by the force of his speech. The debate on the ape question, however, was continued elsewhere during the next two years, and the evidence was completed by the unanswerable demonstrations of Sir W. H. Flower at the Cambridge meeting of the Association in 1862.

The importance of the Oxford meeting lay in the open resistance that was made to authority, at a moment when even a drawn battle was hardly less effectual than acknowledged victory. Instead of being crushed under ridicule, the new theories secured a hearing, all the wider, indeed, for the startling nature of their defense.

1901

SIR EDMUND GOSSE: *From* Father and Son[5]
[*The Dilemma of the Fundamentalist and Scientist*]

So, through my Father's brain, in that year of scientific crisis, 1857, there rushed two kinds of thought, each absorbing, each convincing, yet totally irreconcilable. There is a peculiar agony in the paradox that truth has two forms, each of them indisputable, yet each antagonistic to the other. It was this discovery, that there were two theories of physical life, each of which was true, but the truth of each incompatible with the truth of the other, which shook the spirit of my Father with perturbation. It was not, really, a paradox, it was a fallacy, if he could only have known it, but he allowed the turbid volume of superstition to drown the delicate stream of reason. He took one step in the service of truth, and then he drew back in an agony, and accepted the servitude of error.

This was the great moment in the history of thought when the theory of the mutability of species was preparing to throw a flood of light upon all departments of human speculation and action. It was becoming necessary to stand emphatically in one army or the other. Lyell was surrounding himself with disciples, who were making strides in the direction of discovery. Darwin had long been collecting facts with regard to the variation of animals and plants. Hooker and Wallace, Asa Gray and even Agassiz, each in his own sphere, were coming closer and closer to a perception of that secret which was first to reveal itself clearly to the patient and humble genius of Darwin. In the year before, in 1856, Darwin, under pressure from Lyell, had begun that modest statement of the new revelation, that "abstract of an essay," which developed so mightily into *The Origin of Species*. Wollaston's *Variation of Species* had just appeared, and had been a nine days' wonder in the wilderness.

5. Philip Henry Gosse (1810–88) was a zoologist of some repute and also an ardent adherent of a strict Protestant sect, the Plymouth Brethren. To reconcile his scientific knowledge with his fundamentalist position in religion, Gosse published a book called *Omphalos* which pleased no one. His dilemma is described by his son, the literary critic Sir Edmund Gosse (1849–1928), in an autobiography published in 1907. The present selection is from Chapter V.

On the other side, the reactionaries, although never dreaming of the fate which hung over them, had not been idle. In 1857 the astounding question had for the first time been propounded with contumely, "What, then, did we come from orangoutang?" The famous *Vestiges of Creation* had been supplying a sugar-and-water panacea for those who could not escape from the trend of evidence, and who yet clung to revelation. Owen was encouraging reaction by resisting, with all the strength of his prestige, the theory of the mutability of species.

In this period of intellectual ferment, as when a great political revolution is being planned, many possible adherents were confidentially tested with hints and encouraged to reveal their bias in a whisper. It was the notion of Lyell, himself a great mover of men, that, before the doctrine of natural selection was given to a world which would be sure to lift up at it a howl of execration, a certain bodyguard of sound and experienced naturalists, expert in the description of species, should be privately made aware of its tenor. Among those who were thus initiated, or approached with a view towards possible illumination, was my Father. He was spoken to by Hooker, and later on by Darwin, after meetings of the Royal Society in the summer of 1857.

My Father's attitude towards the theory of natural selection was critical in his career, and oddly enough, it exercised an immense influence on my own experience as a child. Let it be admitted at once, mournful as the admission is, that every instinct in his intelligence went out at first to greet the new light. It had hardly done so, when a recollection of the opening chapter of Genesis checked it at the outset. He consulted with Carpenter, a great investigator, but one who was fully as incapable as himself of remodeling his ideas with regard to the old, accepted hypotheses. They both determined, on various grounds, to have nothing to do with the terrible theory, but to hold steadily to the law of the fixity of species. * * *

My Father had never admired Sir Charles Lyell. I think that the famous Lord Chancellor manner of the geologist intimidated him, and we undervalue the intelligence of those whose conversation puts us at a disadvantage. For Darwin and Hooker, on the other hand, he had a profound esteem, and I know not whether this had anything to do with the fact that he chose, for his impetuous experiment in reaction, the field of geology, rather than that of zoology or botany. Lyell had been threatening to publish a book on the geological history of Man, which was to be a bombshell flung into the camp of the catastrophists. My Father, after long reflection, prepared a theory of his own, which, as he fondly hoped, would take the wind out of Lyell's sails, and justify geology to godly readers of Genesis. It was, very briefly, that there had been no gradual modification of the surface of the earth, or slow development of organic forms, but that when the catastrophic act of creation took place, the world presented, instantly, the structural appearance of a planet on which life had long existed.

The theory, coarsely enough, and to my Father's great indignation, was defined by a hasty press as being this—that God hid the fossils in the rocks in order to tempt geologists into infidelity. In truth, it was the logical and inevitable conclusion of accepting, literally, the doctrine of a sudden act of creation; it emphasized the fact that any breach in the circular course of nature could be conceived only on the supposition that the object created bore false witness to past processes, which had never taken place.

Never was a book cast upon the waters with greater anticipations of success than was this curious, this obstinate, this fanatical volume. My Father lived in a fever of suspense, waiting for the tremendous issue. This *Omphalos* of his, he thought, was to bring all the turmoil of scientific speculation to a close, fling geology into the arms of Scripture, and make the lion eat grass with the lamb. It was not surprising, he admitted, that there had been experienced an ever-increasing discord between the facts which geology brings to light and the direct statements of the early chapters of Genesis. Nobody was to blame for that. My Father, and my Father alone, possessed the secret of the enigma; he alone held the key which could smoothly open the lock of geological mystery. He offered it, with a glowing gesture, to atheists and Christians alike. This was to be the universal panacea; this the system of intellectual therapeutics which could not but heal all the maladies of the age. But, alas! atheists and Christians alike looked at it, and laughed, and threw it away.

In the course of that dismal winter, as the post began to bring in private letters, few and chilly, and public reviews, many and scornful, my Father looked in vain for the approval of the churches, and in vain for the acquiescence of the scientific societies, and in vain for the gratitude of those "thousands of thinking persons," which he had rashly assured himself of receiving. As his reconciliation of Scripture statements and geological deductions was welcomed nowhere; as Darwin continued silent, and the youthful Huxley was scornful, and even Charles Kingsley,[6] from whom my Father had expected the most instant appreciation, wrote that he could not "give up the painful and slow conclusion of five and twenty years' study of geology, and believe that God has written on the rocks one enormous and superfluous lie"—as all this happened or failed to happen, a gloom, cold and dismal, descended upon our morning teacups. * * *

1907

6. Charles Kingsley (1819–75), clergyman and novelist.

INDUSTRIALISM: PROGRESS OR DECLINE?

Was the machine age a blessing or a curse? Was the middle-class economic system making mankind happier or more wretched? Was human progress probable, and how, in fact, is progress to be defined? In confronting these questions, Victorian writers were generally divided into two camps. The changes brought about by industrialism impressed one group of writers as an appalling retrogression. They pointed to the dreadful living and working conditions of the industrial classes, and they deplored the disappearance of what Karl Marx called the "feudal, patriarchal, idyllic relations" between employer and employee which, they believed, had existed in earlier economies. These critics are represented by essayists such as Carlyle, Ruskin, and Morris, and by novelists such as Charles Kingsley and Charles Dickens, whose *Hard Times* was praised by Ruskin as the greatest of his novels and one that "should be studied with close and earnest care by persons interested in social questions." Related to this essentially conservative group, although working from assumptions and to conclusions altogether different from theirs, are Karl Marx and Friedrich Engels, whose interest in the English industrial experiment was keen. Engels spent 20 months observing industrial conditions in Manchester, and his book *The Condition of the Working Class in England* (1845) prepared the ground for his collaborating with Marx in writing *The Communist Manifesto* of 1848, both works being exposures of what seemed to him to be the inadequacies and inequities of middle-class industrial society. In the opposite camp from Carlyle or Engels were writers who found the new society an unqualified improvement over societies of earlier ages. The historian Thomas Babington Macaulay was the most effective Victorian spokesman for this view. A masterful debater and a memorable prose stylist, Macaulay sought to show up the absurdity of anyone who did not share his satisfaction in the accomplishments of his own century. The popularity of his writings suggests that his position was shared by many of his contemporaries. One of these was the sociologist Herbert Spencer, an extreme example of a writer whose faith in the advantage of the new system was unbounded. The "advancement" of mankind toward a state of "perfection" was, according to Spencer, a "certainty." Basing his observations on the industrial development of England, Spencer argued that future human advancement would be accelerated by individual enterprise, whereas government control was almost invariably an obstacle to progress.

THOMAS BABINGTON MACAULAY: *From* A Review
of Southey's *Colloquies*[1]
[*Evidence of Progress*]

   * * * Perhaps we could not select a better instance of the spirit which pervades the whole book than the passages in which Mr.

1. Published in the *Edinburgh Review* (1830). In a book entitled *Colloquies on the Progress and Prospects of So-* *ciety* (1829), the poet and man of letters Robert Southey (1774–1843) had sought to expose the evils of indus-

Southey gives his opinion of the manufacturing system. There is nothing which he hates so bitterly. It is, according to him, a system more tyrannical than that of the feudal ages, a system of actual servitude, a system which destroys the bodies and degrades the minds of those who are engaged in it. He expresses a hope that the competition of other nations may drive us out of the field; that our foreign trade may decline; and that we may thus enjoy a restoration of national sanity and strength. But he seems to think that the extermination of the whole manufacturing population would be a blessing, if the evil could be removed in no other way.

Mr. Southey does not bring forward a single fact in support of these views; and, as it seems to us, there are facts which lead to a very different conclusion. In the first place, the poor rate[2] is very decidedly lower in the manufacturing than in the agricultural districts. If Mr. Southey will look over the Parliamentary returns on this subject, he will find that the amount of parochial relief required by the laborers in the different counties of England is almost exactly in inverse proportion to the degree in which the manufacturing system has been introduced into those counties. The returns for the years ending in March, 1825, and in March, 1828, are now before us. In the former year we find the poor rate highest in Sussex,[3] about twenty shillings to every inhabitant. Then come Buckinghamshire, Essex, Suffolk, Bedfordshire, Huntingdonshire, Kent, and Norfolk. In all these the rate is above fifteen shillings a head. We will not go through the whole. Even in Westmoreland and the North Riding of Yorkshire, the rate is at more than eight shillings. In Cumberland and Monmouthshire, the most fortunate of all the agricultural districts, it is at six shillings. But in the West Riding of Yorkshire,[4] it is as low as five shillings: and when we come to Lancashire, we find it at four shillings, one-fifth of what it is in Sussex. The returns of the year ending in March, 1828, are a little, and but a little, more unfavorable to the manufacturing districts. Lancashire, even in that season of distress, required a smaller poor rate than any other district, and little more than one-fourth of the poor rate raised in Sussex. Cumberland alone, of the agricultural districts, was as well off as the West Riding of Yorkshire. These facts seem to indicate that the manufacturer is both in a more comfortable and in a less dependent situation than the agricultural laborer.

As to the effect of the manufacturing system on the bodily health,

trialism and to assert the superiority of the traditional feudal and agricultural way of life of England's past. His romantic Toryism provoked Macaulay (1800–59) to review the book in a long and characteristic essay. As in his popular *History of England* (1849–61), Macaulay seeks here to demolish his opponent with a bombardment of facts and figures demonstrating that industrialism and middle-class government have resulted in progress and increased comforts for mankind.

2. Taxes on property, to provide food and lodging for the unemployed or unemployable. The amount or rate of such taxes varied from district to district in England, depending upon local conditions of unemployment.

3. A predominantly agricultural district.

4. A manufacturing district.

we must beg leave to estimate it by a standard far too low and vulgar for a mind so imaginative as that of Mr. Southey, the proportion of births and deaths. We know that, during the growth of this atrocious system, this new misery, to use the phrases of Mr. Southey, this new enormity, this birth of a portentous age, this pest which no man can approve whose heart is not seared or whose understanding has not been darkened, there has been a great diminution of mortality, and that this diminution has been greater in the manufacturing towns than anywhere else. The mortality still is, as it always was, greater in towns than in the country. But the difference has diminished in an extraordinary degree. There is the best reason to believe that the annual mortality of Manchester, about the middle of the last century, was one in twenty-eight. It is now reckoned at one in forty-five. In Glasgow and Leeds a similar improvement has taken place. Nay, the rate of mortality in those three great capitals of the manufacturing districts is now considerably less than it was, fifty years ago, over England and Wales, taken together, open country and all. We might with some plausibility maintain that the people live longer because they are better fed, better lodged, better clothed, and better attended in sickness, and that these improvements are owing to that increase of national wealth which the manufacturing system has produced.

Much more might be said on this subject. But to what end? It is not from bills of mortality and statistical tables that Mr. Southey has learned his political creed. He cannot stoop to study the history of the system which he abuses, to strike the balance between the good and evil which it has produced, to compare district with district, or generation with generation. We will give his own reason for his opinion, the only reason which he gives for it, in his own words:

"We remained a while in silence looking upon the assemblage of dwellings below. Here, and in the adjoining hamlet of Millbeck, the effects of manufactures and of agriculture may be seen and compared. The old cottages are such as the poet and the painter equally delight in beholding. Substantially built of the native stone without mortar, dirtied with no white lime, and their long low roofs covered with slate, if they had been raised by the magic of some indigenous Amphion's[5] music, the materials could not have adjusted themselves more beautifully in accord with the surrounding scene; and time has still further harmonized them with weather stains, lichens, and moss, short grasses, and short fern, and stone-plants of various kinds. The ornamented chimneys, round or square, less adorned than those which, like little turrets, crest the houses of the Portuguese peasantry, and yet not less happily suited to their place; the hedge of clipped box beneath the windows, the rose bushes beside the door, the little patch of flower ground, with its

---

5. According to Greek mythology, Amphion's magical skill as a harp player caused the walls of Thebes to be erected without human aid.

tall hollyhocks in front; the garden beside, the beehives, and the orchard with its bank of daffodils and snowdrops, the earliest and the profusest in these parts, indicate in the owners some portion of ease and leisure, some regard to neatness and comfort, some sense of natural, and innocent, and healthful enjoyment. The new cottages of the manufacturers are upon the manufacturing pattern —naked, and in a row.

" 'How is it,' said I, 'that everything which is connected with manufactures presents such features of unqualified deformity? From the largest of Mammon's temples down to the poorest hovel in which his helotry are stalled, these edifices have all one character. Time will not mellow them; nature will neither clothe nor conceal them; and they will remain always as offensive to the eye as to the mind.' "

Here is wisdom. Here are the principles on which nations are to be governed. Rosebushes and poor rates, rather than steam engines and independence. Mortality and cottages with weather stains, rather than health and long life with edifices which time cannot mellow. We are told that our age has invented atrocities beyond the imagination of our fathers; that society has been brought into a state compared with which extermination would be a blessing; and all because the dwellings of cotton-spinners are naked and rectangular. Mr. Southey has found out a way, he tells us, in which the effects of manufactures and agriculture may be compared. And what is this way? To stand on a hill, to look at a cottage and a factory, and to see which is the prettier. Does Mr. Southey think that the body of the English peasantry live, or ever lived, in substantial or ornamented cottages, with boxhedges, flower gardens, beehives, and orchards? If not, what is his parallel worth? We despise those mock philosophers,[6] who think that they serve the cause of science by depreciating literature and the fine arts. But if anything could excuse their narrowness of mind, it would be such a book as this. It is not strange that, when one enthuisast makes the picturesque the test of political good, another should feel inclined to proscribe altogether the pleasures of taste and imagination. * * *

It is not strange that, differing so widely from Mr. Southey as to the past progress of society, we should differ from him also as to its probable destiny. He thinks, that to all outward appearance, the country is hastening to destruction; but he relies firmly on the goodness of God. We do not see either the piety or the rationality of thus confidently expecting that the Supreme Being will interfere to disturb the common succession of causes and effects. We, too, rely on his goodness, on his goodness as manifested, not in extraordinary interpositions, but in those general laws which it has pleased

6. Presumably such Utilitarian philosophers as Jeremy Bentham, who had equated poetry with pushpin, a trifling game. It should be noted, however, that although Macaulay often attacked the Utilitarians for their narrow preoccupation with theory, his own position has much in common with theirs.

him to establish in the physical and in the moral world. We rely on the natural tendency of the human intellect to truth, and on the natural tendency of society to improvement. We know no well-authenticated instance of a people which has decidedly retrograded in civilization and prosperity, except from the influence of violent and terrible calamities, such as those which laid the Roman Empire in ruins, or those which, about the beginning of the sixteenth century, desolated Italy. We know of no country which, at the end of fifty years of peace and tolerably good government, has been less prosperous than at the beginning of that period. The political importance of a state may decline, as the balance of power is disturbed by the introduction of new forces. Thus the influence of Holland and of Spain is much diminished. But are Holland and Spain poorer than formerly? We doubt it. Other countries have outrun them. But we suspect that they have been positively, though not relatively, advancing. We suspect that Holland is richer than when she sent her navies up the Thames,[7] that Spain is richer than when a French king was brought captive to the footstool of Charles the Fifth.[8]

History is full of the signs of this natural progress of society. We see in almost every part of the annals of mankind how the industry of individuals, struggling up against wars, taxes, famines, conflagrations, mischievous prohibitions, and more mischievous protections, creates faster than governments can squander, and repairs whatever invaders can destroy. We see the wealth of nations increasing, and all the arts of life approaching nearer and nearer to perfection, in spite of the grossest corruption and the wildest profusion on the part of rulers.

The present moment is one of great distress. But how small will that distress appear when we think over the history of the last forty years; a war,[9] compared with which all other wars sink into insignificance; taxation, such as the most heavily taxed people of former times could not have conceived; a debt larger than all the public debts that ever existed in the world added together; the food of the people studiously rendered dear; the currency imprudently debased, and imprudently restored. Yet is the country poorer than in 1790? We firmly believe that, in spite of all the misgovernment of her rulers, she has been almost constantly becoming richer and richer. Now and then there has been a stoppage, now and then a short retrogression; but as to the general tendency there can be no doubt. A single breaker may recede; but the tide is evidently coming in.

If we were to prophesy that in the year 1930 a population of

---

7. In 1667 a Dutch fleet displayed its power by sailing up the river Thames without being challenged by the English navy.
8. The Spanish king, Charles V, captured the king of France, Francis I, in the battle of Pavia (1525).
9. The wars against France and Napoleon, extending, with some interruptions, from 1792 to 1815.

fifty millions, better fed, clad, and lodged than the English of our
time, will cover these islands, that Sussex and Huntingdonshire will
be wealthier than the wealthiest parts of the West Riding of Yorkshire now are, that cultivation, rich as that of a flower garden, will
be carried up to the very tops of Ben Nevis and Helvellyn,[1] that
machines constructed on principles yet undiscovered will be in every
house, that there will be no highways but railroads, no traveling
but by steam, that our debt, vast as it seems to us, will appear to
our great-grandchildren a trifling encumbrance, which might easily
be paid off in a year or two, many people would think us insane.
We prophesy nothing; but this we say: If any person had told the
Parliament which met in perplexity and terror after the crash in
1720 that in 1830 the wealth of England would surpass all their
wildest dreams, that the annual revenue would equal the principal
of that debt which they considered as an intolerable burden, that
for one man of ten thousand pounds then living there would be
five men of fifty thousand pounds, that London would be twice as
large and twice as populous, and that nevertheless the rate of mortality would have diminished to one-half of what it then was, that
the post office would bring more into the exchequer than the excise
and customs had brought in together under Charles the Second,
that stage coaches would run from London to York in twenty-four
hours, that men would be in the habit of sailing without wind, and
would be beginning to ride without horses, our ancestors would
have given as much credit to the prediction as they gave to *Gulliver's
Travels*. Yet the prediction would have been true; and they would
have perceived that it was not altogether absurd, if they had considered that the country was then raising every year a sum which
would have purchased the fee-simple[2] of the revenue of the Plantag-
enets, ten times what supported the Government of Elizabeth, three
times what, in the time of Cromwell, had been thought intolerably
oppressive. To almost all men the state of things under which
they have been used to live seems to be the necessary state of
things. We have heard it said that five per cent is the natural interest
of money, that twelve is the natural number of a jury, that forty
shillings is the natural qualification of a county voter. Hence it is
that, though in every age everybody knows that up to his own time
progressive improvement has been taking place, nobody seems to
reckon on any improvement during the next generation. We cannot absolutely prove that those are in error who tell us that society
has reached a turning point, that we have seen our best days. But
so said all who came before us, and with just as much apparent
reason. "A million a year will beggar us," said the patriots of 1640.
"Two millions a year will grind the country to powder," was the

---

1. Mountains, in Scotland and in the
English Lake District, respectively.
2. Absolute ownership of their estates.

The Plantagenet family provided the
monarchs of England from 1145 to 1485.

cry in 1660. "Six millions a year, and a debt of fifty millions!" exclaimed Swift, "the high allies have been the ruin of us." "A hundred and forty millions of debt!" said Junius;[3] "well may we say that we owe Lord Chatham more than we shall ever pay, if we owe him such a load as this." "Two hundred and forty millions of debt!" cried all the statesmen of 1783 in chorus; "what abilities, or what economy on the part of a minister, can save a country so burdened?" We know that if, since 1783, no fresh debt had been incurred, the increased resources of the country would have enabled us to defray that debt at which Pitt, Fox, and Burke stood aghast, nay, to defray it over and over again, and that with much lighter taxation than what we have actually borne. On what principle is it that, when we see nothing but improvement behind us, we are to expect nothing but deterioration before us?

It is not by the intermeddling of Mr. Southey's idol, the omniscient and omnipotent State, but by the prudence and energy of the people, that England has hitherto been carried forward in civilization; and it is to the same prudence and the same energy that we now look with comfort and good hope. Our rulers will best promote the improvement of the nation by strictly confining themselves to their own legitimate duties, by leaving capital to find its most lucrative course, commodities their fair price, industry and intelligence their natural reward, idleness and folly their natural punishment, by maintaining peace, by defending property, by diminishing the price of law, and by observing strict economy in every department of the State. Let the Government do this: the People will assuredly do the rest.

1830

FRIEDRICH ENGELS: The Great Towns[4]

Industry and commerce attain their highest stage of development in the big towns, so that it is here that the effects of industrialization on the wage earners can be most clearly seen. It is in these big towns that the concentration of property has reached its highest point. Here the manners and customs of the good old days have been most effectively destroyed. Here the very name of "Merry

---

3. Pseudonym of a political commentator whose letters (1769–72) usually praised William Pitt, Earl of Chatham. Pitt, as leader of the war against France, which gained Canada for England, could have been blamed for running his country into debt.
4. From Chapter 3 of *The Condition of the Working Class in England* (1845)

translated from the German by W. O. Henderson and W. H. Chaloner (1958). The first two paragraphs are the conclusion of Chapter 2: "The Industrial Proletariat." These eyewitness accounts describe conditions of 1844 when Engels (1820–1895) had been living in England, chiefly in Manchester. The book was first translated into English in 1892.

England" has long since been forgotten, because the inhabitants of the great manufacturing centers have never even heard from their grandparents what life was like in those days. In these towns there are only rich and poor, because the lower middle classes are fast disappearing. At one time this section of the middle classes was the most stable social group, but now it has become the least stable. It is represented in the big factory towns today partly by a few survivors from a bygone age and partly by a group of people who are anxious to get rich as quickly as possible. Of these shady speculators and dubious traders one becomes rich while ninety-nine go bankrupt. Indeed, for more than half of those who have failed, bankruptcy has become a habit.

The vast majority of the inhabitants of these towns are the workers. We propose to discuss their condition and to discover how they have been influenced by life and work in the great factory towns.

* * *

London is unique, because it is a city in which one can roam for hours without leaving the built-up area and without seeing the slightest sign of the approach of open country. This enormous agglomeration of population on a single spot has multiplied a hundred-fold the economic strength of the two and a half million inhabitants concentrated there. This great population has made London the commercial capital of the world and has created the gigantic docks in which are assembled the thousands of ships which always cover the River Thames. I know nothing more imposing than the view one obtains of the river when sailing from the sea up to London Bridge. Especially above Woolwich the houses and docks are packed tightly together on both banks of the river. The further one goes up the river the thicker becomes the concentration of ships lying at anchor, so that eventually only a narrow shipping lane is left free in midstream. Here hundreds of steamships dart rapidly to and fro. All this is so magnificent and impressive that one is lost in admiration. The traveler has good reason to marvel at England's greatness even before he steps on English soil.

It is only later that the traveler appreciates the human suffering which has made all this possible. He can only realize the price that has been paid for all this magnificence after he has tramped the pavements of the main streets of London for some days and has tired himself out by jostling his way through the crowds and dodging the endless stream of coaches and carts which fills the streets. It is only when he has visited the slums of this great city that it dawns upon him that the inhabitants of modern London have had to sacrifice so much that is best in human nature in order to create those wonders of civilization with which their city teems. The vast majority of Londoners have had to let so many of their potential creative faculties lie dormant, stunted and unused in order that a small, closely-knit group of their fellow citizens could develop to the full the qualtities with which nature has endowed them. The restless and noisy activity of the crowded streets is highly distasteful, and it is surely abhorrent to human nature itself. Hundreds of thousands of men and women drawn from all classes and ranks of society pack the streets of London. Are they not all human beings with the same innate characteristics and potentialities? Are they not all equally interested in the pursuit of happiness? And do they not all aim at happiness by following similar methods? Yet they rush past each other as if they had nothing in common. They are tactily agreed on one thing only—that everyone should keep to the right of the pavement so as not to collide with the stream of people moving in the opposite direction. No one even thinks of sparing a glance for his neighbor in the streets. The more that Londoners are packed into a tiny space, the more repulsive and disgraceful becomes the brutal indifference with which they ignore their neighbors and selfishly concentrate upon their private affairs. We know well enough that this isolation of the individual—this narrow-minded egotism—is everywhere the fundamental principle of modern society. But nowhere is this selfish egotism so blatantly evident as in the frantic bustle of the great city. The disintegration of society into individuals, each guided by his private principles and each pursuing his own aims has been pushed to its furthest limits in London. Here indeed human society has been split into its component atoms.

From this it follows that the social conflict—the war of all against all—is fought in the open. * * * Here men regard their fellows not as human beings, but as pawns in the struggle for existence. Everyone exploits his neighbor with the result that the stronger tramples the weaker under foot. The strongest of all, a tiny group of capitalists, monopolize everything, while the weakest, who are in the vast majority, succumb to the most abject poverty.

What is true of London is true also of all the great towns, such as Manchester, Birmingham, and Leeds. Everywhere one finds on the one hand the most barbarous indifference and selfish egotism and on the other the most distressing scenes of misery and poverty. Signs of social conflict are to be found everywhere. Everyone turns his house into a fortress to defend himself—under the protection of the law—from the depredations of his neighbors. Class warfare is so open and shameless that it has to be seen to be believed. The observer of such an appalling state of affairs must shudder at the consequences of such feverish activity and can only marvel that so crazy a social and economic structure should survive at all. * * *

Every great town has one or more slum areas into which the working classes are packed. Sometimes, of course, poverty is to be found hidden away in alleys close to the stately homes of the wealthy. Generally, however, the workers are segregated in separate districts where they struggle through life as best they can out of sight of the more fortunate classes of society. The slums of the English towns have much in common—the worst houses in a town being found in the worst districts. They are generally unplanned wildernesses of one- or two-storied terrace houses built of brick. Wherever possible these have cellars which are also used as dwellings. These little houses of three or four rooms and a kitchen are called cottages, and throughout England, except for some parts of London, are where the working classes normally live. These streets themselves are usually unpaved and full of holes. They are filthy and strewn with animal and vegetable refuse. Since they have neither gutters nor drains the refuse accumulates in stagnant, stinking puddles. Ventilation in the slums is inadequate owing to the hopelessly unplanned nature of these areas. A great many people live huddled together in a very small area, and so it is easy to imagine the nature of the air in these workers' quarters. However, in fine weather the streets are used for the drying of washing, and clothes lines are stretched across the streets from house to house and wet garments are hung out on them.

We propose to describe some of these slums in detail. * * *

If we cross Blackstone Edge on foot or take the train we reach Manchester, the regional capital of South Lancashire, and enter the classic home of English industry. This is the masterpiece of the Industrial Revolution and at the same time the mainspring of all the workers' movements. Once more we are in a beautiful hilly countryside. The land slopes gently down toward the Irish Sea, intersected by the charming green valleys of the Ribble, the Irwell, the Mersey, and their tributaries. A hundred years ago this region was to a great extent thinly populated marshland. Now it is covered with towns and villages and is the most densely populated part of England. In Lancashire—particularly in Manchester—is to be found not only the origin but the heart of the industry of the United Kingdom. Manchester Exchange is the thermometer which records all the fluctuations of industrial and commercial activity. The evolution of the modern system of manufacture has reached its climax in Manchester. It was in the South Lancashire cotton industry that water and steam power first replaced hand machines. It was here that such machines as the power-loom and the self-acting mule replaced the old hand-loom and spinning wheel. It is here that the division of labor has been pushed to its furthest limits. These three factors are the essence of modern industry. In all three of them the cotton industry was the pioneer and remains ahead in all branches of industry. In the circumstances it is to be expected that it is in this region that the inevitable consequences of industrialization in so far as they affect the working classes are most strikingly evident. Nowhere else can the life and conditions of the industrial proletariat be studied in all their aspects as in South Lancashire. Here can be seen most clearly the degradation into which the worker sinks owing to the introduction of steam power, machinery, and the division of labor. Here, too, can be seen most the strenuous efforts of the proletariat to raise themselves from their degraded situation. I propose to examine conditions in Manchester in greater detail for two reasons. In the first place, Manchester is the classic type of modern industrial town. Secondly, I know Manchester as well as I know my native town and I know more about it than most of its inhabitants. * * *

Owing to the curious lay-out of the town it is quite possible for someone to live for years in Manchester and to travel daily to and from his work without ever seeing a working-class quarter or coming into contact with an artisan. He who visits Manchester simply on business or for pleasure need never see the slums, mainly because the working-class districts and the middle-class districts are quite distinct. This division is due partly to deliberate policy and partly to instinctive and tacit agreement between the two social groups. In those areas where the two social groups happen to come into contact with each other the middle classes sanctimoniously ignore the existence of their less fortunate neighbors. In the center of Manchester there is a fairly large commercial district, which is about half a mile long and half a mile broad. This district is almost entirely given over to offices and warehouses. Nearly the whole of this district has no permanent residents and is deserted at night, when only policemen patrol its dark, narrow thoroughfares with their bull's-eye lanterns. This district is intersected by certain main streets which carry an enormous volume of traffic. The lower floors of the buildings are occupied by shops of dazzling splendor. A few of the upper stories on these premises are used as dwellings and the streets present a relatively busy appearance until late in the evening. Around this commercial quarter there is a belt of built-up areas on the average one and a half miles in width, which is occupied entirely by working-class dwellings. This area of workers' houses includes all Manchester proper, except the center, all Salford and Hulme, an important part of Pendleton and Chorlton, two-thirds of Ardwick, and certain small areas of Cheetham Hill and Broughton. Beyond this belt of working-class houses or dwellings lie the districts inhabited by the middle classes and the upper classes. The former are to be found in regularly laid out streets near the working-class districts —in Chorlton and in the remoter parts of Cheetham Hill. The villas of the upper classes are surrounded by gardens and lie in the higher and remoter parts of Chorlton and Ardwick or on the breezy heights of Cheetham Hill, Broughton, and Pendleton. The upper class enjoy healthy country air and live in luxurious and comfortable dwellings which are linked to the center of Manchester by omnibuses which run every fifteen or thirty minutes. To such an extent has the convenience of the rich been considered in the planning of Manchester that these plutocrats can travel from their houses to their places of business in the center of the town by the shortest routes, which run entirely through working-class districts, without even realizing how close they are to the misery and filth which lie on both sides of the road. * * *

I will now give a description of the working-class districts of Manchester. The first of them is the Old Town, which lies between the northern limit of the commercial quarter and the River Irk. Here even the better streets, such Todd Street, Long Millgate, Withy Grove, and Shudehill are narrow and tortuous. The houses are dirty, old, and tumble-down. The sidestreets have been built in a disgraceful fashion. If one enters the district near the "Old Church" and goes down Long Millgate, one sees immediately on the right hand side a row of antiquated houses where not a single front wall is standing upright. This is a remnant of the old Manchester of the days before the town became industrialized. The original inhabitants and their children have left for better houses in other districts, while the houses in Long Millgate, which no longer satisfied them, were left to a tribe of workers containing a strong Irish element. Here one is really and truly in a district which is quite obviously given over entirely to the working classes, because even the shopkeepers and the publicans of Long Millgate make no effort to give their establishments a semblance of cleanliness. The condition of this street may be deplorable, but it is by no means as bad as the alleys and courts which lie behind it, and which can be approached only by covered passages so narrow that two people cannot pass. Anyone who has never visited these courts and alleys can have no idea of the fantastic way in which the houses have been packed together in disorderly confusion in impudent defiance of all reasonable principles of town planning. And the fault lies not merely in the survival of old property from earlier periods in Manchester's history. Only in quite modern times has the policy of cramming as many houses as possible on to such space as was not utilized in earlier periods reached its climax. The result is that today not an inch of space remains between the houses and any further building is now physically impossible. To prove my point I reproduce a small section of a plan of Manchester.[5] It is by no means the

5. Not reproduced in the present version.

worst slum in Manchester and it does not cover one-tenth of the area of Manchester.

This sketch will be sufficient to illustrate the crazy layout of the whole district lying near the River Irk. There is a very sharp drop of some 15 to 30 feet down to the south bank of the Irk at this point. As many as three rows of houses have generally been squeezed onto this precipitous slope. The lowest row of houses stands directly on the bank of the river while the front walls of the highest row stand on the crest of the ridge in Long Millgate. Moreover, factory buildings are also to be found on the banks of the river. In short the layout of the upper part of Long Millgate at the top of the rise is just as disorderly and congested as the lower part of the street. To the right and left a number of covered passages from Long Millgate give access to several courts. On reaching them one meets with a degree of dirt and revolting filth the like of which is not to be found elsewhere. The worst courts are those leading down to the Irk, which contain unquestionably the most dreadful dwellings I have ever seen. In one of these courts, just at the entrance where the covered passage ends, there is a privy without a door. This privy is so dirty that the inhabitants of the court can only enter or leave the court if they are prepared to wade through puddles of stale urine and excrement. Anyone who wishes to confirm this description should go to the first court on the bank of the Irk above Ducie Bridge. Several tanneries are situated on the bank of the river and they fill the neighborhood with the stench of animal putrefaction. The only way of getting to the courts below Ducie Bridge is by going down flights of narrow dirty steps and one can only reach the houses by treading over heaps of dirt and filth. The first court below Ducie Bridge is called Allen's Court. At the time of the cholera [1832] this court was in such a disgraceful state that the sanitary inspectors [of the local Board of Health] evacuated the inhabitants. The court was then swept and fumigated with chlorine. In his pamphlet Dr. Kay gives a horrifying description of conditions in this court at that time. Since Kay wrote this pamphlet, this court appears to have been at any rate partly demolished and rebuilt. If one looks down the river from Ducie Bridge one does at least see several ruined walls and high piles of rubble, side by side with some recently built houses. The view from this bridge, which is mercifully concealed by a high parapet from all but the tallest mortals, is quite characteristic of the whole district. At the bottom the Irk flows, or rather, stagnates. It is a narrow, coal-black, stinking river full of filth and rubbish which it deposits on the more low-lying right bank. In dry weather this bank presents the spectacle of a series of the most revolting blackish-green puddles of slime from the depths of which bubbles of miasmatic gases constantly rise and create a stench which is unbearable even to those standing on the bridge forty or fifty feet above the level of the water. Moreover, the flow of the river is continually interrupted by numerous high weirs, behind which large quantities of slime and refuse collect and putrefy. Above Ducie Bridge there are some tall tannery buildings, and further up there are dye-works, bone mills, and gasworks. All the filth, both liquid and solid, discharged by these works finds its way into the River Irk, which also receives the contents of the adjacent sewers and privies. The nature of the filth deposited by this river may well be imagined. If one looks at the heaps of garbage below Ducie Bridge one can gauge the extent to which accumulated dirt, filth, and decay permeate the courts on the steep left bank of the river. The houses are packed very closely together and since the bank of the river is very steep it is possible to see a part of every house. All of them have been blackened by soot, all of them are crumbling with age and all have broken window panes and window frames. In the background there are old factory buildings which look like barracks. On the opposite, low-lying bank of the river, one sees a long row of houses and factories. The second house is a roof-less ruin, filled with refuse, and the third is built in such a low situation that the ground floor is uninhabitable and has neither doors nor windows. In the background one sees the paupers' cemetery, and the stations of the railways to Liverpool and Leeds. Behind these buildings is situated the workhouse, Manchester's "Poor Law Bastille."[6] The workhouse is built on a hill and from behind its high walls and battlements seems to threaten the whole adjacent working-class quarter like a fortress.

Above Ducie Bridge the left bank of the Irk becomes flatter and the right bank of the Irk becomes steeper and so the condition of the houses on both sides of the river becomes worse rather than better. Turning left from the main street which is still Long Mill-gate, the visitor can easily lose his way. He wanders aimlessly from one court to another. He turns one corner after another through innumerable narrow dirty alleyways and passages, and in only a few minutes he has lost all sense of direction and does not know which way to turn. The area is full of ruined or half-ruined buildings. Some of them are actually uninhabited and that means a great deal in this quarter of the town. In the houses one seldom sees a wooden or a stone floor, while the doors and windows are nearly always broken and badly fitting. And as for the dirt! Everywhere one sees

6. The workhouses established by the Poor Laws of the 1830's, because of the strict regimens enforced on inmates, were commonly likened to prisons such as the Bastille in Paris.

heaps of refuse, garbage, and filth. There are stagnant pools instead of gutters and the stench alone is so overpowering that no human being, even partially civilized, would find it bearable to live in such a district.[7] The recently constructed extension of the Leeds railway which crosses the Irk at this point has swept away some of these courts and alleys, but it has thrown open to public gaze some of the others. So it comes about that there is to be found immediately under the railway bridge a court which is even filthier and more revolting than all the others. This is simply because it was formerly so hidden and secluded that it could only be reached with considerable difficulty, [but is now exposed to the human eye]. I thought I knew this district well, but even I would never have found it had not the railway viaduct made a breach in the slums at this point. One walks along a very rough path on the river bank, in between clothes-posts and washing lines to reach a chaotic group of little, one-storied, one-roomed cabins. Most of them have earth floors, and working, living, and sleeping all take place in the one room. In such a hole, barely six feet long and five feet wide, I saw two beds—and what beds and bedding!—which filled the room, except for the fireplace and the doorstep. Several of these huts, as far as I could see, were completely empty, although the door was open and the inhabitants were leaning against the door posts. In front of the doors filth and garbage abounded. I could not see the pavement, but from time to time, I felt it was there because my feet scraped it. This whole collection of cattle sheds for human beings was surrounded on two sides by houses and a factory and on a third side by the river. [It was possible to get to this slum by only two routes]. One was the narrow path along the river bank, while the other was a narrow gateway which led to another human rabbit warren which was nearly as badly built and was nearly in such a bad condition as the one I have just described.

Enough of this! All along the Irk slums of this type abound. There is an unplanned and chaotic conglomeration of houses, most

---

7. Cf. another account of Manchester slums of the same decade in Elizabeth Gaskell's novel *Mary Barton* (1848), Chapter 6: "Women from their doors tossed household slops of *every* description into the gutter; they ran into the next pool, which overflowed and stagnated. Heaps of ashes were stepping-stones, on which the passer-by, who cared in the least for cleanliness, took care not to put his foot. Our friends [two factory workers] were not dainty, but even they picked their way, till they got to some steps leading down . . . into the cellar in which a family of human beings lived. . . . After the account I have given of the state of the street, no one can be surprised that on going into the cellar inhabited by Davenport, the smell was so foetid as almost to knock the two men down. Quickly recovering themselves, as those inured to such things do, they began to penetrate the thick darkness of the place, and to see three or four children rolling on the damp, nay wet brick floor, through which the stagnant, filthy moisture of the street oozed up; the fireplace was empty and black; the wife sat on her husband's lair [couch], and cried in the dank loneliness."

of which are more or less unhabitable. The dirtiness of the interiors of these premises is fully in keeping with the filth that surrounds them. How can people dwelling in such places keep clean! There are not even adequate facilities for satisfying the most natural daily needs. There are so few privies that they are either filled up every day or are too far away for those who need to use them. How can these people wash when all that is available is the dirty water of the Irk? Pumps and piped water are to be found only in the better-class districts of the town. Indeed no one can blame these helots of modern civilization if their homes are no cleaner than the occasional pigsties which are a feature of these slums. There are actually some property owners who are not ashamed to let dwellings such as those which are to be found below Scotland Bridge. Here on the quayside a mere six feet from the water's edge is to be found a row of six or seven cellars, the bottoms of which are at least two feet beneath the low-water level of the Irk. [What can one say of the owner of] the corner house—situated on the opposite bank of the river above Scotland Bridge—who actually lets the upper floor although the premises downstairs are quite·uninhabitable, and no attempt has been made to·board up the gaps left by the disappearance of doors and windows? This sort of thing is by no means uncommon in this part of Manchester, where, owing to the lack of conveniences, such deserted ground floors are often used by the whole neighborhood as privies.

1845

CHARLES KINGSLEY: *From* Alton Locke[8]
[A London Slum]

It was a foul, chilly, foggy Saturday night. From the butchers' and greengrocers' shops the gaslights flared and flickered, wild and ghastly, over haggard groups of slipshod dirty women, bargaining for scraps of stale meat and frostbitten vegetables, wrangling about short weight and bad quality. Fish stalls and fruit stalls lined the edge of the greasy pavement, sending up odors as foul as the language of sellers and buyers. Blood and sewer water crawled from under doors and out of spouts, and reeked down the gutters among offal, animal and vegetable, in every stage of putrefaction. Foul vapors rose from cow sheds and slaughterhouses, and the doorways of undrained alleys, where the inhabitants carried the filth out on

8. From Chapter VIII of *Alton Locke*, a novel by Charles Kingsley (1819–75). Under the influence of Carlyle's writings and also as a result of his own observations, Kingsley, a clergyman, became deeply concerned with the sufferings of the working classes. The speaker here is a young tailor who is accompanied by an elderly Scottish bookseller, Sandy Mackaye.

their shoes from the backyard into the court, and from the court up into the main street; while above, hanging like cliffs over the streets—those narrow, brawling torrents of filth, and poverty, and sin—the houses with their teeming load of life were piled up into the dingy, choking night. A ghastly, deafening, sickening sight it was. Go, scented Belgravian![9] and see what London is! and then go to the library which God has given thee—one often fears in vain— and see what science says this London might be! * * *

We went on through a back street or two, and then into a huge, miserable house, which, a hundred years ago, perhaps, had witnessed the luxury, and rung to the laughter of some one great fashionable family, alone there in their glory. Now every room of it held its family, or its group of families—a phalanstery[1] of all the fiends—its grand staircase, with the carved balustrades rotting and crumbling away piecemeal, converted into a common sewer for all its inmates. Up stair after stair we went, while wails of children, and curses of men, steamed out upon the hot stifling rush of air from every doorway, till, at the topmost story, we knocked at a garret door. We entered. Bare it was of furniture, comfortless, and freezing cold; but, with the exception of the plaster dropping from the roof, and the broken windows, patched with rags and paper, there was a scrupulous neatness about the whole, which contrasted strangely with the filth and slovenliness outside. There was no bed in the room—no table. On a broken chair by the chimney sat a miserable old woman, fancying that she was warming her hands over embers which had long been cold, shaking her head, and muttering to herself, with palsied lips, about the guardians and the workhouse; while upon a few rags on the floor lay a girl, ugly, small-pox-marked, hollow-eyed, emaciated, her only bedclothes the skirt of a large handsome new riding habit, at which two other girls, wan and tawdry, were stitching busily, as they sat right and left of her on the floor. The old woman took no notice of us as we entered; but one of the girls looked up, and, with a pleased gesture of recognition, put her finger up to her lips, and whispered, "Ellen's asleep."

"I'm not asleep, dears," answered a faint unearthly voice; "I was only praying. Is that Mr. Mackaye?"

"Aye, my lassies; but ha' ye gotten na fire the nicht?"

"No," said one of them, bitterly, "we've earned no fire tonight, by fair trade or foul either."

1850

---

9. Inhabitant of Belgravia, a wealthy residential district of London.
1. A kind of model housing develop-ment proposed by the French socialist François Fourier (1772–1830).

HERBERT SPENCER: *From* Social Statics[1]
[*Progress Through Individual Enterprise*]

* * * Under the natural order of things, the unfolding of an intelligent, self-helping character, must keep pace with the amelioration of physical circumstances—the advance of the one with the exertions put forth to achieve the other; so that in establishing arrangements conducive to robustness of body, robustness of mind must be insensibly acquired. Contrariwise, to whatever extent activity of thought and firmness of purpose are made less needful by an artificial performance of their work, to that same extent must their increase, and the dependent social improvements be retarded.

Should proof of this be asked for, it may be found in the contrast between English energy and Continental helplessness. English engineers (Manby, Wilson, and Co.) established the first gasworks in Paris, after the failure of a French company;[2] and many of the gasworks throughout Europe have been constructed by Englishmen. An English engineer (Miller) introduced steam navigation on the Rhône; another English engineer (Pritchard) succeeded in ascending the Danube by steam, after the French and Germans had failed. The first steamboats on the Loire were built by Englishmen (Fawcett and Preston); the great suspension bridge at Pesth[3] has been built by an Englishman (Tierney Clarke); and an Englishman (Vignolles) is now building a still greater suspension bridge over the Dnieper; many continental railways have had Englishmen as consulting engineers; and in spite of the celebrated Mining College at Freyburg, several of the mineral fields along the Rhine have been opened up by English capital employing English skill. Now why is this? Why were our coaches so superior to the diligences and eilwagen[4] of our neighbours? Why did our railway system develop so much faster? Why are our towns better drained, better paved, and better supplied with water? There was originally no greater mechanical aptitude, and no greater desire to progress in us than in the connate nations of northern Europe. If anything, we were comparatively deficient in these respects. Early improvements in the arts of life were imported. The germs of our silk and woolen

1. From Chapter XXVIII. Herbert Spencer (1820–1903) was a philosopher and sociologist.
2. A demonstration of the commercial possibilities of gas for lighting was first made by a Frenchman, Philippe Lebon (1767–1804), but it was in England that his discoveries were first exploited successfully. By 1812 a gas company was chartered in London, and miles of pipes were soon laid down. English companies thereafter were frequently employed to install gas lines and fixtures in Europe and in America.
3. In Hungary.
4. Stage coaches.

manufactures came from abroad. The first waterworks in London were erected by a Dutchman. How happens it, then, that we have now reversed the relationship? How happens it, that instead of being dependent on continental skill and enterprise, our skill and enterprise are at a premuim on the Continent? Manifestly the change is due to difference of discipline. Having been left in a greater degree than others to manage their own affairs, the English people have become self-helping, and have acquired great practical ability. Whilst conversely that comparative helplessness of the paternally-governed nations of Europe, illustrated in the above facts, and commented upon by Laing, in his *Notes of a Traveler,* and by other observers, is a natural result of the state-superintendence policy—is the reaction attendant on the action of official mechanisms —is the atrophy corresponding to some artificial hypertrophy.

1850

The Twentieth Century

(1890 to the Present)

1914–18: World War I.
1918: Gerard Manley Hopkins' poetry published.
1922: T. S. Eliot's *The Waste Land*.
1922: James Joyce's *Ulysses*.
1928: W. B. Yeats's *The Tower*.
1930: Period of depression and unemployment begins.
1939–45: World War II.

THE END OF VICTORIANISM

Cultural movements do not proceed neatly by centuries, and this section, which for convenience we call "the twentieth century," begins really with the late 19th, when the sense of the passing of a major phase of English history was already in the air. Queen Victoria's Jubilee in 1887 and, even more, her Diamond Jubilee in 1897 were felt even by contemporaries to mark the end of an era. As the 19th century drew to a close there were many manifestations of a weakening of traditional stabilities. The aesthetic movement, with its insistence on "art for art's sake," assaulted the assumptions about the nature and function of art held by ordinary middle-class readers, deliberately, provocatively. It helped to widen the breach between artists and writers on the one hand and the "Philistine" public on the other —a breach whose earlier symptom was Matthew Arnold's war on the Philistines in *Culture and Anarchy* and which was later to result in the "alienation of the artist" that is now a commonplace of criticism. This was more than a purely English matter. From France came the tradition of the bohemian life that scorned the limits imposed by conventional ideas of respectability, together with other notions of the artist as rejecting and rejected by ordinary society, which in different ways fostered the view of the alienated artist. The life and work of the French Symbolist poets in France, the early novels of Thomas Mann in Germany (especially *Buddenbrooks*, 1901), and Joyce's *Portrait of the Artist as a Young Man* (1916) show some of the very different ways in which this attitude revealed itself in literature all over Europe. In England, the growth of popular education as a result of the Education Act of 1870, which finally made elementary education compulsory and universal, led to the rapid emergence of a large, unsophisticated literary public at whom new kinds of journalism, in particular the cheap "yellow press," were directed. A public that was literate but not in any real sense educated increased steadily throughout the 19th century, and one result of this was the splitting up of the audience for literature into "highbrows," "lowbrows," and "middlebrows." Although in earlier periods there had been different kinds of audience for different kinds of writing, the split now developed with unprecedented speed and to an unprecedented degree because of the mass production of "popular" literature for the semiliterate. The fragmentation of the reading public now merged with the artist's war on the Philistine (and indeed was one of the causes of that war in the first place) to widen the gap between popular art and art esteemed only by the sophisticated and the expert. This is part of the background of modern literature all over the Western world.

Another manifestation—or at least accompaniment—of the end of the Victorian age was the rise of various kinds of pessimism and stoicism. The novels and poetry of Thomas Hardy show one kind of pessimism (and it *was* pessimism, even if Hardy himself repudiated the term), and the poems of A. E. Housman show another variety, while a real or affected stoicism is to be found not only in these writers but also in many minor writers of the last decade of the 19th century and the first decade of the 20th. Examples of this stoicism—the determination to stand for human dignity by enduring bravely, with a "stiff upper lip," whatever fate may bring—range from Robert Louis Stevenson's essays and the rhetorically assertive poems of the editor and journalist W. E. Henley, to Rudyard Kipling's *Jungle Books* and many of his short stories, the last stanza of Housman's *The Chestnut Casts His Flambeaux* ("Bear them we can, and if we can we must") and Yeats's "They know that Hamlet and Lear are gay."

Although the high tide of anti-Victorianism was marked by the publication in 1918 of that classic of ironic debunking, *Eminent Victorians* by Lytton Strachey (1880–1932), the criticism of the normal attitudes and preconceptions of the Victorian middle classes first became really violent in the last two decades of the 19th century. No one could have been more savage in his attacks on the Victorian conceptions of the family, education, and religion than Samuel Butler, whose novel *The Way of All Flesh* (completed in 1884, posthumously published in 1903) is still the bitterest indictment in English literature of the Victorian way of life. The chorus of questioning of Victorian assumptions grew ever louder as the century drew to an end; sounding prominently in it was the voice of the young Bernard Shaw, one of Butler's greatest admirers. The position of women, too, was rapidly changing during this period. The Married Woman's Property Act of 1882, which allowed married women to own property in their own right; the admission of women to the universities at different times during the latter part of the century; the fight for women's suffrage, which was not won until 1918 (and not fully won until 1928)—these events marked a change in the attitude to women and in the part they played in the national life as well as in the relation between the sexes, which is reflected in a variety of ways in the literature of the period.

The Boer War (1899–1902), fought by the British to establish political and economic control over the Boer republics of South Africa, marked both the high point of and the reaction against British imperialism. It was a war against which many British intellectuals protested and one which the British in the end were slightly ashamed of having won. The development

of the British Empire into the British Commonwealth (i.e., into an association of self-governing countries) continued in fits and starts throughout
the first half of the 20th century, with imperialist and anti-imperialist
sentiment often meeting head on; writers as far apart as Kipling and E. M.
Forster occupied themselves with the problem. The Irish question also
caused a great deal of excitement from the beginning of the period until
well into the 1920's. A steadily rising Irish nationalism protested with increasing violence against the political subordination of Ireland to the
British Crown and government. In World War I some Irish nationalists
sought German help in rebelling against Britain, and this exacerbated feeling on both sides. No one can fully understand William Butler Yeats or
James Joyce without some awareness of the Irish struggle for independence,
the feelings of Anglo-Irish men of letters on this burning topic, and the
way in which the Irish Literary Revival of the late 19th and early 20th
centuries (with which Yeats was much concerned) reflected a determination
to achieve a vigorous national life culturally even if the road seemed
blocked politically.

THE IMPACT OF WORLD WAR I

Edwardian England (1901–10) was very conscious of being no longer
Victorian. Edward VII stamped his character on the decade in which
he reigned. It was a vulgar age of conspicuous enjoyment by those who
could afford it, and writers and artists kept well away from implication in
high society (though there were some conspicuous exceptions): in general,
there was no equivalent in this period of Queen Victoria's interest in Tennyson. The alienation of artists and intellectuals was proceeding apace. From
1910 (when George V came to the throne) until war broke out in August,
1914, Britain achieved a temporary equilibrium between Victorian earnestness and Edwardian flashiness; in retrospect that "Georgian" period seems
peculiarly golden, the last phase of assurance and stability before the old
order throughout Europe broke up in violence with results that are still
with us. Yet even then, under the surface, there was restlessness and experimentation. If this was the age of Rupert Brooke, it was also the age of
T. S. Eliot's first experiments in a disturbingly new kind of poetry.

"Edwardian" as a term applied to English cultural history suggests a
period in which the social and economic stabilities of the Victorian age—
country houses with numerous servants, a flourishing and confident middle
class, a strict hierarchy of social classes—remained unimpaired, though on
the level of ideas there was a sense of change and liberation. "Georgian"
refers largely to the lull before the storm of World War I.

The quiet traditionalism of much of the verse that appeared in the volumes of *Georgian Poetry* edited by Edward Marsh between 1911 and 1920
represented an attempt to wall in the garden of English poetry against the
disruptive forces of modern civilization. Cultured meditations on the
English countryside ("I love the mossy quietness / That grows upon the
great stone flags") alternated with self-conscious exercises in the exotic
("When I was but thirteen or so / I went into a golden land, / Chim-
borazo, Cotopaxi, / Took me by the hand"). Sometimes the magical note
was authentic, as in many of Walter de la Mare's poems, and sometimes
the meditative strain was original and impressive, as in the poetry of Edward Thomas. But as World War I went on, with more and more poets

killed and the survivors increasingly disillusioned, the whole world on which the Georgian imagination rested came to appear unreal. A patriotic poem such as Rupert Brooke's *The Soldier* became a ridiculous anachronism in the face of modern trench warfare, and the even more blatantly patriotic note sounded by other Georgian poets (as in John Freeman's *Happy Is England Now*, which claimed that "there's not a nobleness of heart, hand, brain / But shines the purer; happiest is England now / In those that fight") came to seem positively obscene. The savage ironies of Siegfried Sassoon's war poems and the combination of pity and irony in those of Wilfred Owen portrayed a world undreamed of in the golden years from 1910 to 1914. Over four years of tremendous slaughter under appalling conditions (the battle casualties were many times greater than those in World War II), the wiping out of virtually a whole generation of young men, the shattering of so many illusions and ideals made World War I a watershed in European civilization. No one had been prepared for what actually happened in that war—in contrast to World War II, so long anticipated and predicted by a generation brought up on the grim war books of World War I. The experience was traumatic. It left throughout all Europe a sense that the bases of civilization had been destroyed, that all traditional values had been wiped out, and we see this reflected in different ways in *The Waste Land* of Eliot and the early novels and stories of Aldous Huxley.

THE POETIC REVOLUTION

A technical revolution in poetry was going on side by side with shifts in attitude. The Imagist movement, influenced by T. E. Hulme's insistence on hard, clear, precise images and encouraged by Ezra Pound when he lived in London just before World War I, fought against romantic fuzziness and facile emotionalism in poetry. The movement developed simultaneously on both sides of the Atlantic, and its early members included Amy Lowell, Richard Aldington, Hilda Doolittle, John Gould Fletcher, and F. S. Flint. As Flint explained in an article in March, 1913, Imagists insisted on "direct treatment of the 'thing,' whether subjective or objective," on the avoidance of all words "that did not contribute to the presentation," and on a freer metrical movement than a strict adherence to "the sequence of a metronome" could allow. All this encouraged precision in imagery and freedom of rhythmic movement, but more was required for the production of poetry of any real scope and interest. Imagism went in for the short, sharply etched, descriptive lyric, but it had no technique for the production of longer and more complex poems. Other new ideas about poetry helped to provide this technique. Sir Herbert Grierson's great edition of the poems of John Donne in 1912 both reflected and helped to encourage a new enthusiasm for 17th-century metaphysical poetry. The revival of interest in metaphysical wit brought with it a desire on the part of some pioneering poets to introduce into their poetry a much higher degree of intellectual complexity than had been found among the Victorians or the Georgians. The full subtlety of French Symbolist poetry also now came to be appreciated; it had been admired in the 90's, but for its dreamy suggestiveness rather than for its imagistic precision and complexity. At the same time a need was felt to bring poetic language and rhythms closer to those of conversation, or at least to spice the formalities of poetic utterance with echoes of the colloquial and even the slangy. Irony, which made possible several levels of discourse simultaneously, and wit, with the use of puns (banished from serious poetry for over 200 years), helped to achieve that union of thought and passion which T. S. Eliot, in his review of Grierson's anthology of metaphysical poetry (1921), saw as characteristic of the metaphysicals and wished to bring back into modern poetry. A new critical and a new creative movement in poetry went hand in hand, with Eliot the high priest of both. It was Eliot who extended the scope of Imagism by bringing the English metaphysicals and the French Symbolists (as well as the English Jacobean dramatists) to the rescue, thus adding new criteria of complexity and allusiveness to the criteria of concreteness and precision stressed by the Imagists. It was Eliot, too, who introduced into modern English and American poetry the kind of irony achieved by shifting suddenly from the formal to the colloquial or by oblique allusions to objects or ideas that contrasted sharply with those carried by the surface meaning of the poem. Thus between, say, 1911 (the first year of the Georgian poets) and 1922 (the year of the publication of *The Waste Land*) a major revolution occurred in English—and for that matter American—poetic theory and practice—a revolution which determined the way in which most serious poets and critics now think about their art. If one compares the poems in Palgrave's *Golden Treasury*, a Victorian anthology which was still used as a basic school text in Britain in the 1930's, with those in a number of academic anthologies of the mid-20th century, the change in poetic taste will become startlingly apparent. In the critical discussion, if not always in the allotment of space, Donne rather than Spenser becomes the great poet of the 16th- and 17th-century period; Gerard Manley Hopkins replaces Tennyson as the great 19th-century poet; and in general what one might call the metaphysical-Symbolist tradition predominates over both the cultivated self-pity of the Romantic-Victorian tradition and the Platonic-meditative strain of both the Elizabethans and (in his own way) Wordsworth.

The posthumous publication by Robert Bridges in 1918 of the poetry of Gerard Manley Hopkins encouraged further experimentation in language and rhythms. Hopkins combined absolute precision of the individual image with a complex ordering of images and a new kind of metrical patterning. The young poets of the early 1930's—W. H. Auden, Stephen Spender, C. Day Lewis—were much influenced by Hopkins as well as by Eliot (now the presiding genius of modern English and American poetry) and by a variety of other poets from the 16th-century John Skelton to Wilfred Owen. And even when the almost flamboyant new tones of Dylan Thomas were first sounded in the late 1930's, the influence of Hopkins could still be heard. It is only since World War II that a new generation of young English poets (including Donald Davie, Elizabeth Jennings, and Philip Larkin), searching for what has been called "purity of diction," have turned away from both the 17th century and the poetry of Hopkins and Eliot to seek a poetry which avoids all kinds of verbal excess in its desire for quiet luminosity and unpretentious truth.

Meanwhile the remarkable career of W. B. Yeats, stretching across the whole modern period, showed how a truly great poet can at the same time reflect the varying developments of his age and maintain an unmistakably individual accent. Beginning among the aesthetes of the 90's, turning later to a more tough and spare ironic language without losing his characteristic verbal magic, working out his own notions of symbolism and bringing them in different ways into his poetry, developing in his full maturity a rich symbolic and metaphysical poetry with its own curiously haunting cadences and its imagery both shockingly realistic and movingly suggestive, Yeats's work is itself a history of English poetry between 1890 and 1939. Yet he is always Yeats, unique and inimitable—without doubt the greatest English-speaking poet of his age.

Two important 20th-century poets stand somewhat apart from the main map of English poetry in the first half of the century. They are Robert Graves and Edwin Muir. Each has a highly individual voice and, the latter especially, a limited range. But they both show that there were strengths in the English poetic tradition untapped by Eliot and his followers. Graves, with a strong sense of tradition combined with a highly idiosyncratic poetic personality, has played a part in English poetry comparable to that played by Robert Frost in American. Muir's more quietist and mystical temperament was nourished by the unusual circumstances of his life, and his childhood in Orkney. In him, awareness of his native Scotland and a response to the heroic stories of ancient Greece were linked. Both poets were much concerned with time and the human response to time, and both had a deep sense of history.

BETWEEN THE WARS

The postwar disillusion of the 1920's was, it might be said, a spiritual matter, just as Eliot's Waste Land was a spiritual and not a literal wasteland. Depression and unemployment in the early 1930's, followed by the rise of Hitler and the cruel shadow of Fascism and Nazism over Europe, with its threat of another war, represented another sort of wasteland which produced another sort of effect on poets and novelists. The impotence of capitalist governments in the face of Hitlerism combined with economic dislocation to turn the majority of young intellectuals (and not only intellectuals) in the 1930's to the political Left. The 1930's were the Red decade, because only the Left seemed to offer any solution. The early poetry of W. H. Auden and his contemporaries cried out for "the death of the old gang" (in Auden's phrase) and a clean sweep politically and economically, while the Franco rebellion against the republican government in Spain, which started in the summer of 1936 and soon led to full-scale civil war, was regarded as a rehearsal for an inevitable second world war and thus further emphasized the inadequacy of politicians. Yet though all this is reflected passionately in the literature of the period, particularly in the poetry, it was not accompanied by any interesting developments in technique; many younger writers were more anxious to express their attitudes than to construct new kinds of works of art. The outbreak of World War II in September, 1939, following very shortly on Hitler's pact with Russia, which shocked and disillusioned so many of the young Left-wing writers, marked the sudden end of the Red decade; the concern of writers in Britain now was to maintain their integrity and indeed their existence in what was from the beginning expected to be a long and destructive war. This they did surprisingly well, but nevertheless this second war brought inevitable exhaustion: English literature has never quite recovered the vitality and interest in technical experimentation that marked the twenty years after about 1912.

These years—roughly 1912 to 1930—were the Heroic Age of the modern English novel. Joseph Conrad, James Joyce, and D. H. Lawrence are the giants, with Virginia Woolf and E. M. Forster brilliant minor figures— to name only the most outstanding writers. An important novelist of this period who stands rather apart from any of the movements discussed here is Ford Madox Ford (1873–1939), whose four novels about Christopher Tietjens published in the 1920's (and republished in a single volume as *Parade's End* in 1950) show meticulous craftsmanship and a deep sense of the changes wrought by the war on English life and character. The poet Robert Graves is similarly independent of movements and fashions in 20th-century literature: he developed and subtilized the Georgian tradition instead of adopting that of Eliot.

NEW METHODS IN FICTION

One can trace three major influences on the changes in attitude and technique in the modern novel. The first is the novelist's realization that the general background of belief which united him with his public in a common sense of what was significant in experience had disappeared. The public values of the Victorian novel, in which major crises of plot could be shown through changes in the social or financial or marital status of the chief characters, gave way to more personally conceived notions of value, dependent on the novelist's intuitions and sensibilities rather than on public agreement. "To believe that your impressions hold good for others," Virginia Woolf once wrote (discussing Jane Austen), "is to be released from the cramp and confinement of personality." The modern novelist could no longer believe this: he had to fall back on personality, drawing his criterion of significance in human affairs (and thus his principle of selection) from his own intuitions, so that he needed to find ways of convincing the reader that his own private sense of what was significant in experience was truly valid. A new technical burden was thus imposed on the novelist's prose, for it had now to build up a world of values instead of drawing on an existing world of values. Virginia Woolf tried to solve the problem by using some of the devices of poetry in order to suggest the novelist's own sense of value and vision of the world. Joyce, on the other hand, made no attempt to convey a single personal attitude, but reacted to the breakdown of public values by employing a kind of writing so multiple in its implications that it conveyed numerous points of view simultaneously, the author being totally objective and committed to none of them—a mode which required remarkable technical virtuosity.

The second influence on the changes in attitude and technique in the modern novel was a new view of time; time was not a series of chronological moments to be presented by the novelist in sequence with an occasional deliberate retrospect ("this reminded him of," "he recalled that"), but as a continuous flow in the consciousness of the individual, with the "already" continuously merging into the "not yet" and retrospect merging into anticipation. This influence is closely bound up with a third: the new notions of the nature of consciousness, which derived in a general way from Sigmund Freud and Carl Jung but were also part of the spirit of the age and discernible even in those novelists who had not read either psychologist. Consciousness is multiple; the past is always present in it at some level and is continually coloring one's present reaction. Marcel Proust in France, in his great novel sequence *Remembrance of Things Past* (1913–28), had explored the ways in which the past impinges on the present and consciousness is determined by memory. The view that a man *is* his memories, that his present is the sum of his past, that if we dig into a man's consciousness we can tell the whole truth about him without waiting for a chronological sequence of time to take him through a series of testing circumstances, inevitably led to a technical revolution in the novel. For now, by exploring in depth into consciousness and memory rather than proceeding lengthwise along the dimension of time, a novelist could write a novel concerned ostensibly with only one day of the hero's life (Joyce's *Ulysses* and Virginia Woolf's *Mrs. Dalloway*). This view of multiple levels of consciousness existing simultaneously, coupled with the view of time as a constant flow rather than a series of separate moments, meant that a novelist preferred to plunge into the consciousness of his characters in order to tell his story rather than to provide an external framework of chronological narrative. The "stream-of-consciousness" technique, where the author tries to render directly the very fabric of his character's consciousness without reporting it in formal, quoted remarks, was developed in the 1920's as an important new technique of the English novel. It made for more difficult reading, at least for those accustomed only to the methods of the older English novel. No "porch" was constructed at the front of the novel to put the reader in possession of necessary preliminary information: such information emerged, as the novel progressed, from the consciousness of each character as it responded to the present with echoes of its past. No conventional signposts were put up to tell the reader where he was, for that was felt to interfere with the immediacy of the impression. But once the reader learns how to find his way in this unsignposted territory, he is rewarded by new delicacies of perception and new subtleties of presentation.

Concentration on the "stream of consciousness" and on the association of ideas within the individual consciousness led inevitably to stress on the essential loneliness of the individual. For all consciousnesses are unique and isolated, and if this unique, private world is the real world in which men live, if the public values to which they must pay lip service in the social world in which they move are not the real values which give meaning to their personality, then each man is condemned to live in the prison of his own incommunicable consciousness. How is true communication possible in such a world? The public gestures imposed upon us by society never correspond to our real inward needs. They are conventional in the bad sense, mechanical, imposing a crude standardization on the infinite subtlety of experience. If we do try to give out a sign from our real selves, that sign is bound to be misunderstood when read by some other self in the light of that self's quite other personality. The theme of such modern fiction is thus the possibility of love, the establishment of emotional communication, in a community of private consciousnesses. This, is, in different ways, the theme of Joyce, of Lawrence, of Virginia Woolf, and of Forster, and (on a rather different scale and not always so directly) of Conrad. The search for communion and the inevitable isolation of Leopold Bloom in *Ulysses* is symbolic of the human condition as seen by the modern novelist. Similar investigations of this basic condition are Forster's explorations of the conventions which seem to be helps to living but which in fact prevent true human contacts, and Virginia Woolf's delicate projections of the relation between the self's need for privacy and the self's need for genuine communication. The theme of all Lawrence's novels is human relationships, the ideal of which he restlessly explored with shifting emphasis throughout his career; such relationships can be all too easily distorted by the mechanical conventions of society, by notions of respectability or propriety, by all the shams and frauds of middle-class life, by the demands of power or money or success. One might almost say that the greatest modern novels are about the difficulty, and at the same time the inevitability, of being human. The dilemma of the human condition is never really solved in these novelists; but knowledge that the dilemma is shared—a knowledge so brilliantly conveyed in *Ulysses* and so wryly proffered by Forster—can both illuminate and comfort.

Not all the novelists of the period, of course, were concerned with these themes or employed the new techniques appropriate to them. The "documentary" novelists, such as Arnold Bennett and John Galsworthy (and, in some at least of his novels, H. G. Wells), presented, often with great skill, the changing social scene, showing considerable insight and sympathy in recording aspects of it through the behavior of their imagined characters. Virginia Woolf called these writers "materialists," maintaining that they were content to deal with externals and did not go on to explore those aspects of consciousness, of the true inward life of men, in which human reality resides. She was perhaps judging unfairly, by standards that were not applicable to their sort of fiction; but modern criticism has on the whole agreed with her.

The short story in this period benefited from the new techniques of exploration in depth. A greater consciousness of the symbolic uses to which objects and incidents can be put and a greater subtlety in the ways in which patterns of suggestiveness are built up below the quietly realistic surface can be found in the short stories of writers so different from each other as Joyce, Katherine Mansfield, Lawrence, and Forster. Katherine Mansfield learned from the Russian short-story writer Anton Chekhov how to use the casual-seeming incidents of ordinary life in such a way as to set up haunting overtones of meaning. The apparently inconsequential surface masking the carefully organized substructure is found in much modern fiction (perhaps most of all in *Ulysses*): it is one of the results of the coming together, in the novel and the short story, of realism and symbolism, of contemporary probability and timeless significance. These things of course come together in great fiction of all ages; but the modern writer contrives their coexistence with greater self-consciousness than his predecessors.

THE DRAMA

Modern drama begins in a sense with the witty drawing-room comedies of Oscar Wilde; yet Wilde founded no dramatic school. His wit was personal and irresponsible, unlike the wit of Restoration comedy, which reflected an attitude to the relation between the sexes which was part of a view of society held by a whole (if a small) social class. Bernard Shaw brought still another kind of wit into drama—not Wilde's exhibitionist sparkle nor yet the assured sophistication of the Restoration dramatists, but the provocative paradox that was meant to tease and disturb, to challenge the complacency of the audience. Shaw's discussion plays were given dramatic life through the mastery of theatrical techniques which he learned during his years as a dramatic critic. In his general attitudes Shaw represents the anti-Victorianism of the late Victorians; his long life should not obscure the fact that his first—and some of his best—plays belong to the 90's. Other attempts by 20th-century dramatists to debate social questions on the stage—by Galsworthy, for example—deserve respect for their humanity and intelligence and sometimes for their theatrical craftsmanship, but they lack Shaw's verbal and intellectual brilliance and his superb capacity to entertain. We must turn to Ireland to find another really impressive variety of dramatic activity. The Irish Literary Theatre was founded in 1899, with Yeats's early play *The Countess Cathleen* as its first production. The founders—Yeats, Lady Gregory, George Moore, and Edward Martyn—wanted to make a contribution to an Irish literary revival, but they were influenced also by the Independent Theatre in London, founded in 1891 by J. T. Grein in order to encourage new developments in the drama. In 1902 the Irish Literary Theatre was able to maintain a permanent all-Irish company and changed its name to the Irish National Theatre, which moved in 1904 to the Abbey Theatre, by which name it has since been known. Many of the plays produced at the Abbey Theatre were only of local and ephemeral interest, but J. M. Synge's use of the speech and imagination of Irish country people, Yeats's powerful symbolic use of themes from old Irish legend, and Sean O'Casey's use of the Irish civil war as a background for plays combining tragic melodrama, humor of character, and irony of circumstance, brought new kinds of vitality to the theater. T. S. Eliot attempted with considerable success to revive a ritual poetic drama in England with his *Murder in the Cathedral* (1935). His later attempts to combine religious symbolism with the box-office appeal of amusing society comedy (as in *The Cocktail Party*, 1950), though impressive technical achievements, were not wholly successful: the combination of contemporary social chatter with profound religious symbolism produces an unevenness of tone and disturbing shifts in levels of realism. Elsewhere in modern drama the conflict between realism and symbolism (first clearly seen in Ibsen) is acted out in a variety of ways.

In spite of the achievements of Shaw, Yeats, and Eliot, it cannot be said of the drama as it can of poetry and fiction in this period that a technical revolution occurred which changed the whole course of literary history with respect to that particular literary form. The reformers of the 1890's invoked the name of the great Norwegian playwright Henrik Ibsen: like Shaw they saw him as essentially a critic of middle-class society rather than (as critics tend to see him today) as an essentially poetic dramatist experimenting with symbolic modes of expression. This may be the reason why the influence of Ibsen soon petered out in run-of-the-mill plays of humanitarian social concern. Harley Granville-Barker, actor, director, and Shakespeare scholar and critic as well as playwright, wrote four interesting and thoughtful plays in 1909 and 1910, but for all their intelligence they never really come alive theatrically. The staple of the London West End theater remained social comedy stiffened by occasional irony and sweetened by sentimentality (Noel Coward is one of the best purveyors of this sort of fare). The cleverly contrived sentimentalities of J. M. Barrie (1860–1937) were highly popular in their day; Barrie's plays showed a high theatrical skill and a determined cunning in the exploitation of the audience's reaction. That audience consisted for the most part of tired Philistines, and it was they who determined what was to be a box-office success. An original Scottish dramatist, who at one time appeared to be achieving singlehanded a new awakening in the Scottish theater but who in the end failed to do so, was James Bridie (pseudonym of Dr. O. H. Mavor, 1885–1951), whose witty and inventive plays show an intellectual liveliness sometimes reminiscent of Shaw.

The energy which the Irish movement gave to English drama has not lasted. Sean O'Casey's later plays, where he is influenced by expressionist techniques suggested by German dramatists as well as by Eugene O'Neill, have neither the vitality nor the vivid humor of those earlier plays in which he was able to give tragic meaning to the realities of contemporary Dublin life without denying its comic elements. Another Irish playwright, William Denis Johnston, has also experimented with expressionist techniques and has achieved in some of his plays a remarkable combination of the grotesque and the ironic. But vitality has not been coming into the English theater in the 1950's and early 1960's from this direction.

In the late 1940's and early 1950's it seemed that the verse plays of Christopher Fry were about to bring a new kind of poetic life into English drama. But Fry's exuberantly witty use of metaphor soon lost its appeal, and by the late 1950's a very different kind of drama brought vitality to the British theater. John Osborne's *Look Back in Anger* was produced at the Royal Court Theatre in 1956. Angrily, violently, and in an unadorned and sometimes brutally colloquial dialogue, it thrust upon the audience the revelation of psychological and social problems left unresolved, or even exacerbated, by the welfare state. *The Entertainer* (1957) was similar in its brash virtuosity; Osborne's third play, *Luther* (1960), shows him moving out of a preoccupation with a restricted part of the contemporary social scene to wider concerns and a freer use of imagination. Arnold Wesker was another Royal Court discovery. In a trilogy that began with *Chicken Soup with Barley* (1958), he explored, though less stridently than Osborne, related social and psychological problems. Joan Littlewood's Theatre Workshop introduced another kind of vigorous new theatricalism, with an impromptu-seeming kind of play made up of numerous small scenes; distinctive examples are Brendan Behan's *The Quare Fellow* (1956) and Shelagh Delaney's *A Taste of Honey* (1958). A third significant influence on recent English drama has been the director Peter Hall, who commissioned a number of important plays for his Aldwych productions, including Robert Bolt's *A Man for All Seasons* (1960) and John Arden's *Live Like Pigs* (1958). The man, however, who is emerging as the most important and individual dramatist is Harold Pinter, whose plays, including *The Birthday Party* (1958), *The Caretaker* (1960), and *The Homecoming*

(1966), project disturbing symbolic meanings in a quietly colloquial language. These playwrights have the advantage of working with lively and innovative talent in the practical theater. In addition there is a constant and fruitful interaction between drama on the stage and drama in the film, the playwright himself usually working in both media. It is too early to say how much this dramatic revival will endure as literature, but clearly the drama and the theater is the place in contemporary Britain where the artistic action is.

LITERARY CRITICISM

Criticism occupies a much larger place on the map of modern literary culture than it has ever occupied before. New psychological and anthropological ideas have stimulated new kinds of critical activity; tools of critical analysis have been sharpened by the impact of linguistic philosophy; the increased difficulty of much modern writing, itself the result of the fragmentation of the audience for literature and the consequent withdrawal of serious writers into coteries using a more or less private symbolism, has increased the demand for critical interpretation. This is the great critical age, and criticism and creation have marched together (in Eliot's work, for example) to an unusual degree, although modern America has placed more emphasis on criticism than has modern Britain.

From one point of view, it could be maintained that Matthew Arnold is the father of modern literary criticism. Arnold thought literature was bound to replace religion as a source of inspiration and spiritual refreshment, and as a result insisted that we must have "the best" literature. If literature, rather than religion, is central to a civilization, and not a mere relaxation or optional pleasure, discrimination between good and bad literature is of the first importance, and critics become in a sense the equivalent of priests. F. R. Leavis, who edited the influential critical review *Scrutiny* from its foundation in 1932 until its demise in 1953, inherited from Arnold this view of the need to discover and proclaim "the best." His and his contributors' essays in *Scrutiny* were devoted to what they called "discrimination," to a determined winnowing of the little wheat from the abundant chaff by a careful technique of practical criticism which at first owed a great deal to I. A. Richards' methods in his Cambridge lectures. Leavis also inherited from Arnold his war against the Philistines and the view that the quality of literature which is produced and esteemed by a generation is bound up with the whole quality of its culture, of the way in which people live and work as well as think. *Culture and Environment*, by Leavis and Denys Thompson (1933), is similar in more than title to Arnold's *Culture and Anarchy*: it is an examination of the way in which the conditions of living imposed by some elements in modern civilization inhibit proper discrimination in literature as in other spheres. But Leavis repudiates any such simple ethical criterion as Arnold's "high seriousness," and sees the true moral vision of a writer embodied much more subtly and often indirectly in his work than Arnold did. In this view he has been influenced by Eliot's repudiation (in *Tradition and the Individual Talent*) of "any semi-ethical criterion of 'sublimity.'"

In general there has been in the last forty years or so—but again not to the same degree as in America—a repudiation of the older view of criticism as gentlemanly chat about books, the "hours in a library" sort of thing, in favor of a criticism much more rigorous and analytic. The revolution in taste proclaimed in the antiromantic essays of T. E. Hulme and developed in the influential essays of Eliot inevitably demanded a more strenuous kind of criticism. If poetic imagery was to be hard, dry, and precise and at the same time impregnated with metaphysical wit and irony, and if a new degree of intellectual complexity was to be demanded of poetry, then the critic had to provide himself with tools for the careful analysis of meaning and structure in order to demonstrate these qualities or the lack of them. Similarly, critics who agreed with Eliot that "the poet has, not a 'personality' to express, but a particular medium," became suspicious alike of autobiographical and exclamatory responses to literature and of the biographical approach which tended to assess literary quality in terms of the degree to which the writer genuinely expressed himself.

Thus the Arnoldian insistence on discrimination combined with the Hulme-Eliot tradition of precision and complexity to demand a more searchingly analytic kind of critical description and evaluation. At the same time I. A. Richards, interested in problems of communication and the different ways in which words work to communicate different sorts of meaning, developed his own technique of analysis of poetic imagery and structure, which had considerable influence on practical (i.e., applied) criticism. Richards turned to psychology for aid in his investigation of meaning and also for the construction of a theory of literary value. Psychology came into modern criticism in many other ways. Although the old-fashioned kind of biographical approach was now out of favor, the examination of the psychology of poetic creation became a respectable branch of criticism, sometimes used to reinforce an analytic account of how imagery works in a poem. On the whole, however, what might be called "genetic" criticism—explanation of the origins and development of a work, rather than of its present nature and value—went on apart from analytic and evaluative criticism. "Genetic" criticism could use psychology, with all the new resources brought in by Freud and Jung, or it could use sociology, studying the social factors that helped to condition particular writers and their works.

Psychology came into criticism in other ways also. Together with anthropology it helped to investigate the ways in which myth and symbol work in literature. Eliot had confessedly drawn on anthropological works in *The Waste Land*, thus virtually asking the critics to use such aids in examining the poem. They were not slow to take him up. Here Jung rather than Freud was the major influence, for Jung's view of racial memory (akin to Yeats's view of the "Great Memory," which preserved the meaning of symbols) was obviously relevant to any investigation of the way in which the mythical element in literature operates. Maud Bodkin's *Archetypal Patterns in Poetry* (1934) was a pioneer work in this field; it stimulated a host of further studies of myth and symbol on both sides of the Atlantic.

At the same time techniques of the analysis of meaning developed by Richards in his practical criticism were being developed to greater and sometimes provocative lengths by his onetime pupil, William Empson. Semantics was now an established tool of the analytic critic, used in many different ways. So the pattern is this: first, the necessity for discrimination (because we must have "the best") through rigorous critical analysis; further emphasis on critical rigor by the Hulme-Eliot tradition of precision, impersonality, and complexity; new tools for critical analysis through the study of semantics and linguistic philosophy; an interest in archetypal images through the psychological and anthropological incitements to the study of myth and symbol; side by side with all this, and sometimes interacting with it, psychological and sociological investigation of the way the creative process operates in given instances. All these elements are present in what has for many years now been called in America the "new criticism," for American critics, more than British critics, have taken up and developed, sometimes with great originality and persuasiveness, all of these critical strains.

In recent years the pattern of critical thought and practice has become less easily definable. New kinds of interests, social or linguistic and sometimes both, have emerged and interacted in varying ways with the procedures developed by Richards, Leavis, and others. The application of linguistics to the study of different styles—a branch of criticism now called stylistics—though not widely popular in Britain, is nevertheless being undertaken by some younger critics and points toward a new kind of sophistication in the analysis of literary language which may well give a new direction to the Empsonian tradition of analysis of ambiguity. Similarly, the anthropological study of myth, which has influenced the myth critics and the seekers of archetypes since the middle 1930's, has been given a new depth and complexity by the influences of the French social anthropologist Claude Lévi-Strauss. Strauss's theory of Structuralism is concerned with the way the human mind interprets and orders the phenomena perceived by the senses, and this helps to explain the symbols men use, the social structure they build, the myths they construct, and the language they employ. Thus new links between anthropology, sociology, psychology, linguistics, and literature are being forged which may well change radically the shape of literary criticism.

The Nineties

The last decade of the 19th century saw the culmination of a movement toward a self-conscious aestheticism that was partly a revolt against the moral earnestness of such Victorian prophets as Carlyle and Ruskin and partly a development of ideas implicit in the writings of Walter Pater (see, for example, the conclusion to *The Renaissance*). Ruskin, too, had insisted on beauty, but he had linked it with morality, and the Pre-Raphaelites had turned to medieval art and religion to find beauty and controlled ecstasy in clarity of detail and precision of sensation. The aesthetes of the 90's, while learning from Ruskin and the Pre-Raphaelites, preached and practiced a more self-indulgent doctrine. Art for them represented not only the embodiment of beauty but also the search for new kinds of sensation and of emotional experience. The doctrine of "art for art's sake," so often preached during this period, really meant art for the sake of the sensations and experiences it could induce, with no reference to any standard of morality or utility. The artist was in rebellion against the Victorian middle-class way of life and of thought and took a peculiar pleasure in shocking middle-class opinion.

The writers who took part in this movement were very much aware of living at the end of a great century and often cultivated a deliberately *fin-de-siècle* ("end-of-century") pose. A studied languor, a weary sophistication, a search for new ways of titillating jaded palates can be found in both the poetry and the prose of the period. *The Yellow Book*, a periodical devoted entirely to art and letters which ran from 1894 to 1897, is generally taken to represent the aestheticism of the 90's. The startling black-and-white drawings and designs of its art editor, Aubrey Beardsley (1872–98), the prose of George Moore and Max Beerbohm, and the poetry of Ernest Dowson illustrate different aspects of the movement. But *The Yellow Book* also printed Lionel Johnson and the young W. B. Yeats, naturalistic stories of contemporary life by Arnold Bennett and others, as well as essays by respectable academic critics such as George Saintsbury and Sir Edmund Gosse. It was thus not entirely the organ of the aesthetic movement, but appealed to a variety of kinds of sophistication, from the latest in aestheticism to the latest in realism.

The poets of the aesthetic movement were in a sense the last heirs of the Romantics; the appeal to sensation in their imagery goes back through Rossetti and Tennyson to Keats. They developed this sensationalism, however, much more histrionically than their predecessors, seeking compensation for the drabness of ordinary life in melancholy suggestiveness, antibourgeois sensationalism, heady ritualism, histrionic world-weariness, or mere emotional debauchery. At their best they have considerable emotional power and a certain incantatory persuasiveness. At their worst, the sensationalism of their imagery becomes merely ludicrous. Even Dowson's *To One in Bedlam*, an adroit and moving poem in its way, is spoiled by "thy moon-kissed roses" and "star-crowned solitude"—images which come out of the property-room of the 90's.

What makes the 90's important as a period of English literary history is not, however, its writers' sensationalism and desire to shock. It is their strongly held belief in the independence of art, their view that a work of art has its own unique kind of value—that, in T. S. Eliot's phrase, poetry must be judged "as poetry and not another thing"—which has most strongly influenced later generations. Not only did the aesthetic movement nurse the young Yeats and provide him with his lifelong belief in poetry as poetry rather than as a means to some moral or other end; it also provided modern criticism with its basic assumptions. "Art for art's sake" was in the 90's a provocative slogan; today it is a commonplace, and there are few significant critics who would not accept some version of it. The whole modern movement in criticism, as well as the new poetic techniques associated with it, has been largely concerned with demonstrating the uniqueness of the literary use of language and with training us to see works of literary art as possessing their special kind of form, their special kind of meaning, and hence their special kind of value. In this it is the heir of the 90's, however much it may have modified or enriched the legacy. It was the poets of the 90's, too, who first absorbed the influence of the French *symbolistes* poets, an influence which has proved pervasive in the 20th century and is especially strong (though in different ways) in the poetry of Yeats and of Eliot.

OSCAR WILDE
(1854–1900)

Oscar Fingall O'Flahertie Wills Wilde was born in Dublin; his father was a distinguished eye and ear surgeon who had been knighted for his work, his mother a minor poetess who ran a well-known literary salon. He was educated at Trinity College, Dublin, where his success in classical studies enabled him to win a scholarship to Magdalen College, Oxford. At Oxford he soon won a reputation for his brilliant conversation and studied eccentricities in dress and manner of living. He was much influenced by Walter Pater, particularly by *The Renaissance*, "that book which has had such strange influence over my life," as he later recalled, and he read, too, Rossetti and Swinburne and the work of the French poet Charles Baudelaire. He left Oxford in 1878 already known as a champion of the aesthetic movement and of the creed of "art for art's sake," and settled in London, where he published stories and poems in periodicals and continued his exhibitionist behavior. Gilbert and Sullivan's opera *Patience* (1881) satirized Wilde in the character of the poet Bunthorne, and though this satire tended to run together the earlier Pre-Raphaelite movement with the aesthetic movement of the following decades, it represented the popular view of Wilde and his activities:

Though the Philistines may jostle, you will rank as an apostle in the high
     aesthetic band,
If you walk down Piccadilly with a poppy or a lily in your medieval hand.
               And everyone will say,
               As you walk your flowery way,
"If he's content with a vegetable love which would certainly not suit *me*,
Why, what a most particularly pure young man this pure young man must
     be!"

Wilde did in fact walk in London wearing velvet knee breeches, silk stockings, and a velveteen coat with an exotic flower in the buttonhole.

   Wilde continued his writing for periodicals while his rapidly growing
reputation as a brilliant wit made him the most sought-after dinner guest
in London. He edited *The Woman's World* (1887–89), and in 1888
brought out a volume of fairy tales, *The Happy Prince and Other Tales*,
a curiously stylized cross-breeding of Hans Andersen and Pater. The following year *The Decay of Lying* appeared in *The Nineteenth Century*;
here he presented with glittering paradoxes his view of the autonomy of the
artistic imagination:

Many a young man starts in life with a natural gift for exaggeration which,
if nurtured in congenial and sympathetic surroundings, or by the imitation
of the best models, might grow into something really great and wonderful.
But, as a rule, he comes to nothing. * * * He either falls into careless
habits of accuracy, or takes to frequenting the society of the aged and the
well-informed. Both things are equally fatal to his imagination, as indeed
they would be fatal to the imagination of anybody, and in a short time he
develops a morbid and unhealthy faculty of truth-telling, begins to verify all
statements made in his presence, * * * and often ends by writing novels
which are so lifelike that no one can possibly believe in their probability.

Wilde insisted that imitation was not the function of art. "Art finds her
own perfection within, and not outside of, herself. She is not to be judged
by any external standard of resemblance." He argued, too, that Nature imitates Art, rather than the other way round. "Things are because we see
them, and what we see, and how we see it, depends on the Arts that have
influenced us."

   Wilde's first published book of *Poems* (1881) showed the influence of
Elizabethan, Romantic, Pre-Raphaelite, and 19th-century French poets,
and he continued to write for periodicals poems exploring the momentary
sensation or emotion or impression. But his most important work was in
his critical and dramatic prose and his curiously mannered prose fable,
The Picture of Dorian Gray (1891). This is the story of a young man
who, in his desire to carry out Pater's advice to savor every kind of beauty
in experience, is led into a great variety of vice with no visible sign of age
or degeneration, while his portrait gradually changes to show the corruption of his soul. The equation of the pursuit of beauty with involvement in
vice was curiously Philistine; it revealed a contradiction in Wilde's attitude, since for him art and beauty ought logically to have had no relation
to morality one way or the other. *Intentions*, published in the same year,
contained a number of dialogues in which Wilde's aesthetic philosophy was
given its most eloquent expression: *The Critic as Artist*, which first appeared in this volume, maintains that the critic's "sole aim is to chronicle

his own impressions," and not to give an objective account or estimate of the work criticized.

Wilde's greatest successes were his plays—*Lady Windermere's Fan* (1892), *A Woman of No Importance* (1893), *An Ideal Husband* (1895), and, best and most brilliant, *The Importance of Being Earnest*, written in 1894 and produced in 1895. It was while these last two plays were running simultaneously and enjoying phenomenal success—they were artificial social comedies whose verbal wit and shocking paradoxes still astonish and delight—that Wilde's spectacular fall took place. The Marquis of Queensberry had accused Wilde of homosexuality; Wilde rashly brought a libel suit against the Marquis, and lost, since it was proved that the Marquis had spoken the truth. Wilde now found himself accused of what (under a law of 1885) was a crime punishable by imprisonment. He could have left the country after the Queensberry case, but, fascinated by the melodrama of his own fate, he stayed to face the charge, defending himself with wit and confidence. The result was, however, a foregone conclusion: Wilde lost and was sentenced to two years imprisonment with hard labor. The revulsion of feeling against him in England was tremendous; his name became a bad word, and the aesthetic movement which he had championed fell—at least so far as its externals went—into immediate oblivion. Literary men and others did everything to demonstrate their healthy normality, and the public turned to the more virile writings of men like W. E. Henley and Rudyard Kipling. Wilde wrote the melodramatic but genuinely powerful *Ballad of Reading Gaol* and the searchingly autobiographical *De Profundis* as a result of his experience in prison, and after his release he lived in France under an assumed name, a ruined man, until his death three years later.

The gods had given me almost everything. I had a genius, a distinguished name, high social position, brilliancy, intellectual daring * * * I treated art as the supreme reality and life as a mere mode of fiction. * * * But I let myself be lured into long spells of senseless and sensual ease. * * * Tired of being on the heights, I deliberately went to the depths in the search for new sensation. What the paradox was to me in the sphere of thought, perversity became to me in the sphere of passion. * * * I ended in horrible disgrace. There is only one thing for me now, absolute humility.

So Wilde wrote in *De Profundis*, when he was still in prison. "Oscar Wilde's greatest play was his own life," remarked Frank Harris. "It was a five-act tragedy with Greek implications and he was its most ardent spectator."

Impression du Matin[1]

The Thames nocturne of blue and gold
   Changed to a harmony in gray;
   A barge with ocher-colored hay
Dropped from the wharf:[2] and chill and cold

The yellow fog came creeping down   5
   The bridges, till the houses' walls

1. "Impression of the Morning."
2. Left the wharf and went down river with the ebb tide.

Seemed changed to shadows, and St. Paul's
Loomed like a bubble o'er the town.

Then suddenly arose the clang
    Of waking life; the streets were stirred
    With country wagons; and a bird
Flew to the glistening roofs and sang.

But one pale woman all alone,
    The daylight kissing her wan hair,
    Loitered beneath the gas lamps' flare,
With lips of flame and heart of stone.

1881

Hélas[3]

To drift with every passion till my soul
Is a stringed lute on which all winds can play,
Is it for this that I have given away
Mine ancient wisdom, and austere control?
Methinks my life is a twice-written scroll
Scrawled over on some boyish holiday
With idle songs for pipe and virelay,[4]
Which do but mar the secret of the whole.
Surely there was a time I might have trod
The sunlit heights, and from life's dissonance
Struck one clear chord to reach the ears of God:
Is that time dead? lo! with a little rod
I did but touch the honey of romance—
And must I lose a soul's inheritance?

1881

E Tenebris[1]

Come down, O Christ, and help me! reach thy hand,
    For I am drowning in a stormier sea
    Than Simon on thy lake of Galilee:[2]
The wine of life is spilt upon the sand,
My heart is as some famine-murdered land
    Whence all good things have perished utterly,
    And well I know my soul in Hell must lie
If I this night before God's throne should stand.
"He sleeps perchance, or rideth to the chase,
    Like Baal, when his prophets howled that name

---

3. "Alas!"
4. A song or short lyric in stanzas.
1. "Out of Darkness."
2. Simon, surnamed Peter, one of the twelve apostles, was a fisherman on Lake Galilee when found there by Jesus.

From morn to noon on Carmel's smitten height."[3]
Nay, peace, I shall behold, before the night,
The feet of brass,[4] the robe more white than flame,
The wounded hands, the weary human face.

1881

The Harlot's House

We caught the tread of dancing feet,
We loitered down the moonlit street,
And stopped beneath the harlot's house.

Inside, above the din and fray,
We heard the loud musicians play
The "Treues Liebes Herz" of Strauss.[5]   5

Like strange mechanical grotesques,
Making fantastic arabesques,
The shadows raced across the blind.

We watched the ghostly dancers spin   10
To sound of horn and violin,
Like black leaves wheeling in the wind.

Like wire-pulled automatons,
Slim silhouetted skeletons
Went sidling through the slow quadrille.[6]   15

They took each other by the hand,
And danced a stately saraband;[7]
Their laughter echoed thin and shrill.

Sometimes a clockwork puppet pressed
A phantom lover to her breast,   20
Sometimes they seemed to try to sing.

Sometimes a horrible marionette
Came out, and smoked its cigarette
Upon the steps like a live thing.

Then, turning to my love, I said,   25
"The dead are dancing with the dead,
The dust is whirling with the dust."

But she—she heard the violin,
And left my side, and entered in:
Love passed into the house of lust.   30

3. The poet imagines an ironic voice discouraging him; it uses the language of Elijah when he mocked the priests of Baal for their god's impotence by suggesting that perhaps Baal was on a journey or asleep (see I Kings xviii.19–40).
4. Cf. Revelation i ff., where the "Son of man" is seen in a vision, "his feet like unto fine brass, as if they burned in a furnace."
5. "Heart of True Love," a waltz by the Austrian composer and "Waltz King," Johann Strauss (1825–99).
6. A square dance.
7. A slow and stately dance, originating in Spain.

Then suddenly the tune went false,
The dancers wearied of the waltz,
The shadows ceased to wheel and whirl.

And down the long and silent street,
The dawn, with silver-sandaled feet, 35
Crept like a frightened girl.

1885, 1908

From The Critic as Artist[1]
[*Criticism Itself an Art*]

ERNEST. Gilbert, you sound too harsh a note. Let us go back to the more gracious fields of literature. What was it you said? That it was more difficult to talk about a thing than to do it?

GILBERT. [*after a pause*] Yes: I believe I ventured upon that simple truth. Surely you see now that I am right? When man acts he is a puppet. When he describes he is a poet. The whole secret lies in that. It was easy enough on the sandy plains by windy Ilion[2] to send the notched arrow from the painted bow, or to hurl against the shield of hide and flamelike brass the long ash-handled spear. It was easy for the adulterous queen[3] to spread the Tyrian carpets for her lord, and then, as he lay couched in the marble bath, to throw over his head the purple net, and call to her smooth-faced lover to stab through the meshes at the heart that should have broken at Aulis.[4] For Antigone[5] even, with Death waiting for her as her bridegroom, it was easy to pass through the tainted air at noon, and climb the hill, and strew with kindly earth the wretched naked corse that had no tomb. But what of those who wrote about these things? What of those who gave them reality, and made them live forever? Are they not greater than the men and women they sing of? "Hector that sweet knight is dead."[6] and Lucian[7] tells us

1. In "the library of a house in Piccadilly" Gilbert and Ernest, two sophisticated young men, are talking about the use and function of criticism. Earlier in the dialogue, Ernest had complained that criticism is officious and useless: "Why should the artist be troubled by the shrill clamor of criticism? Why should those who cannot create take upon themselves to estimate the value of creative work?" Gilbert, in his reply, argues that criticism is creative in its own right. He digresses to compare the life of action unfavorably to the life of art: actions are dangerous and their results unpredictable; "if we lived long enough to see the results of our actions it may be that those who call themselves good would be sickened by a dull remorse, and those whom the world calls evil stirred by a noble joy." The excerpt printed here begins immediately following this digression.
2. Troy. Gilbert is referring to Homer's *Iliad*.
3. Clytemnestra, whose murder of her husband Agamemnon provides the plot for Aeschylus' tragedy of that name.
4. Where Agamemnon sacrificed his daughter Iphigenia, thus incurring Clytemnestra's wrath.
5. Antigone defied Creon, king of Thebes, by burying the body of her brother, an act which Creon had forbidden, and was punished by death; see Sophocles' play *Antigone*.
6. Cf. Shakespeare's *Love's Labor's Lost* V.ii.666: "The sweet war-man [Hector] is dead and rotten."
7. Late Greek satirical writer, influenced by the earlier Greek seriocomic writer Menippus.

how in the dim underworld Menippus saw the bleaching skull of
Helen, and marveled that it was for so grim a favor that all those
horned ships were launched, those beautiful mailed men laid low,
those towered cities brought to dust. Yet, every day the swanlike
daughter of Leda comes out on the battlements, and looks down
at the tide of war. The graybeards wonder at her loveliness, and
she stands by the side of the king.[8] In his chamber of stained ivory
lies her leman.[9] He is polishing his dainty armor, and combing the
scarlet plume. With squire and page, her husband passes from tent
to tent. She can see his bright hair, and hears, or fancies that she
hears, that clear cold voice. In the courtyard below, the son of
Priam is buckling on his brazen cuirass. The white arms of An-
dromache[1] are around his neck. He sets his helmet on the ground,
lest their babe should be frightened. Behind the embroidered curtains of his pavilion sits Achilles,[2] in perfumed raiment, while in
harness of gilt and silver the friend of his soul[3] arrays himself to go
forth to the fight. From a curiously carven chest that his mother
Thetis had brought to his shipside, the Lord of the Myrmidons
takes out that mystic chalice that the lip of man had never touched,
and cleanses it with brimstone, and with fresh water cools it, and,
having washed his hands, fills with black wine its burnished hollow,
and spills the thick grape-blood upon the ground in honor of Him
whom at Dodona[4] barefooted prophets worshiped, and prays to
Him, and knows not that he prays in vain, and that by the hands
of two knights from Troy, Panthous' son, Euphorbus, whose love-
locks were looped with gold, and the Priamid,[5] the lion-hearted,
Patroclus, the comrade of comrades, must meet his doom. Phantoms, are they? Heroes of mist and mountain? Shadows in a song?
No: they are real. Action! What is action? It dies at the moment of
its energy. It is a base concession to fact. The world is made by the
singer for the dreamer.

ERNEST. While you talk it seems to me to be so.

GILBERT. It is so in truth. On the moldering citadel of Troy lies
the lizard like a thing of green bronze. The owl has built her nest
in the palace of Priam. Over the empty plain wander shepherd and
goatherd with their flocks, and where, on the wine-surfaced, oily
sea, οἶνοψ πόντος,[6] as Homer calls it, copper-prowed and streaked
with vermilion, the great galleys of the Danaoi[7] came in their

---

8. Priam. Homer in the *Iliad* describes the old men of Troy admiring
the beauty of Helen, "swanlike daughter of Leda" and of Zeus (Zeus came
to Leda in the form of a swan).
9. Lover (i.e., Paris).
1. Wife of Hector, one of the sons of
Priam.
2. Achilles, son of Peleus and of the
sea nymph Thetis, was the Greek hero,
opposite number of Hector, the Trojan
hero, in the Trojan War. The scene set

here is a tissue of recollections from
the *Iliad*.
3. I.e., Patroclus.
4. Seat of a very ancient oracle of
Zeus.
5. "Son of Priam," i.e., Hector. With
the help of Euphorbus, one of the
bravest of the Trojans, he slew Patroclus and was in turn slain by
Achilles.
6. "Wine-dark sea."
7. Greeks.

gleaming crescent, the lonely tunny-fisher sits in his little boat and watches the bobbing corks of his net. Yet, every morning the doors of the city are thrown open, and on foot, or in horse-drawn chariot, the warriors go forth to battle, and mock their enemies from behind their iron masks. All day long the fight rages, and when night comes the torches gleam by the tents, and the cresset[8] burns in the hall. Those who live in marble or on painted panel know of life but a single exquisite instant, eternal indeed in its beauty, but limited to one note of passion or one mood of calm. Those whom the poet makes live have their myriad emotions of joy and terror, of courage and despair, of pleasure and of suffering. The seasons come and go in glad or saddening pageant, and with winged or leaden feet the years pass by before them. They have their youth and their manhood, they are children, and they grow old. It is always dawn for St. Helena, as Veronese saw her at the window.[9] Through the still morning air the angels bring her the symbol of God's pain. The cool breezes of the morning lift the gilt threads from her brow. On that little hill by the city of Florence, where the lovers of Giorgione[1] are lying, it is always the solstice of noon, made so languorous by summer suns that hardly can the slim naked girl dip into the marble tank the round bubble of clear glass, and the long fingers of the lute player rest idly upon the chords. It is twilight always for the dancing nymphs whom Corot[2] set free among the silver poplars of France. In eternal twilight they move, those frail diaphanous figures, whose tremulous white feet seem not to touch the dew-drenched grass they tread on. But those who walk in epos,[3] drama, or romance, see through the laboring months the young moons wax and wane, and watch the night from evening unto morning star, and from sunrise unto sunsetting can note the shifting day with all its gold and shadow. For them, as for us, the flowers bloom and wither, and the Earth, that Green-tressed Goddess as Coleridge calls her, alters her raiment for their pleasure. The statue is concentrated to one moment of perfection. The image stained upon the canvas possesses no spiritual element of growth or change. If they know nothing of death, it is because they know little of life, for the secrets of life and death belong to those, and those only, whom the sequence of time affects, and who possess not merely the present but the future, and can rise or fall from a past of glory or of shame. Movement, that problem of the visible arts, can be truly realized by Literature alone. It is Literature that shows us the body in its swiftness and the soul in its unrest.

ERNEST. Yes; I see now what you mean. But, surely, the higher

8. Metal basket holding fuel burned for illumination, often hung from the ceiling.
9. One of the best-known paintings of the 16th-century Italian Paolo Veronese is "Helena's Vision."

1. Italian painter (ca. 1477–1511), the most brilliant colorist of his time.
2. Jean Baptiste Camille Corot, 19th-century French painter, best-known for his shimmering trees.
3. Epic poetry.

you place the creative artist, the lower must the critic rank.

GILBERT. Why so?

ERNEST. Because the best that he can give us will be but an echo of rich music, a dim shadow of clear-outlined form. It may, indeed, be that life is chaos, as you tell me that it is; that its martyrdoms are mean and its heroisms ignoble; and that it is the function of Literature to create, from the rough material of actual existence, a new world that will be more marvelous, more enduring, and more true than the world that common eyes look upon, and through which common natures seek to realize their perfection. But surely, if this new world has been made by the spirit and touch of a great artist, it will be a thing so complete and perfect that there will be nothing left for the critic to do. I quite understand now, and indeed admit most readily, that it is far more difficult to talk about a thing than to do it. But it seems to me that this sound and sensible maxim, which is really extremely soothing to one's feelings, and should be adopted as its motto by every Academy of Literature all over the world, applies only to the relations that exist between Art and Life, and not to any relations that there may be between Art and Criticism.

GILBERT. But, surely, Criticism is itself an art. And just as artistic creation implies the working of the critical faculty, and, indeed, without it cannot be said to exist at all, so Criticism is really creative in the highest sense of the word. Criticism is, in fact, both creative and independent.

ERNEST. Independent?

GILBERT. Yes; independent. Criticism is no more to be judged by any low standard of imitation or resemblance than is the work of poet or sculptor. The critic occupies the same relation to the work of art that he criticizes as the artist does to the visible world of form and color, or the unseen world of passion and of thought. He does not even require for the perfection of his art the finest materials. Anything will serve his purpose. And just as out of the sordid and sentimental amours of the silly wife of a small country doctor in the squalid village of Yonville-l'Abbaye, near Rouen, Gustave Flaubert[4] was able to create a classic, and make a masterpiece of style, so, from subjects of little or of no importance, such as the pictures in this year's Royal Academy, or in any year's Royal Academy for that matter, Mr. Lewis Morris's poems, M. Ohnet's novels, or the plays of Mr. Henry Arthur Jones,[5] the true critic can, if it be his pleasure so to direct or waste his faculty of contemplation, produce work that will be flawless in beauty and instinct with

4. French novelist; the reference is to his novel, *Madame Bovary* (1857).
5. Wilde is mischievously suggesting his low opinion of the contemporary writers just named: Lewis Morris was a Welsh poet and essayist often ridi-culed by the critics; Georges Ohnet was a French novelist and dramatist; Henry Arthur Jones was one of the leading English playwrights of his time.

intellectual subtlety. Why not? Dullness is always an irresistible temptation for brilliancy, and stupidity is the permanent *Bestia Trionfans*[6] that calls wisdom from its cave. To an artist so creative as the critic, what does subject matter signify? No more and no less than it does to the novelist and the painter. Like them, he can find his motives everywhere. Treatment is the test. There is nothing that has not in it suggestion or challenge.

ERNEST. But is Criticism really a creative art?

GILBERT. Why should it not be? It works with materials, and puts them into a form that is at once new and delightful. What more can one say of poetry? Indeed, I would call criticism a creation within a creation. For just as the great artists, from Homer and Aeschylus, down to Shakespeare and Keats, did not go directly to life for their subject matter, but sought for it in myth, and legend, and ancient tale, so the critic deals with materials that others have, as it were, purified for him, and to which imaginative form and color have been already added. Nay, more, I would say that the highest Criticism, being the purest form of personal impression, is in its way more creative than creation, as it has least reference to any standard external to itself, and is, in fact, its own reason for existing, and, as the Greeks would put it, in itself, and to itself, an end. Certainly, it is never trammeled by any shackles of verisimilitude. No ignoble considerations of probability, that cowardly concession to the tedious repetitions of domestic or public life, affect it ever. One may appeal from fiction unto fact. But from the soul there is no appeal.

ERNEST. From the soul?

GILBERT. Yes, from the soul. That is what the highest criticism really is, the record of one's own soul. It is more fascinating than history, as it is concerned simply with oneself. It is more delightful than philosophy, as its subject is concrete and not abstract, real and not vague. It is the only civilized form of autobiography, as it deals not with the events, but with the thoughts of one's life, not with life's physical accidents of deed or circumstance, but with the spiritual moods and imaginative passions of the mind. I am always amused by the silly vanity of those writers and artists of our day who seem to imagine that the primary function of the critic is to chatter about their second-rate work. The best that one can say of most modern creative art is that it is just a little less vulgar than reality, and so the critic, with his fine sense of distinction and sure instinct of delicate refinement, will prefer to look into the silver mirror or through the woven veil, and will turn his eyes away from the chaos and clamor of actual existence, though the mirror be tarnished and the veil be torn. His sole aim is to chronicle his

6. "Triumphant Beast." A reference to *Spaccio della Bestia Trionfante* ("Expulsion of the Triumphant Beast," 1584), a philosophical allegory by the Italian philosopher Giordano Bruno.

own impressions. It is for him that pictures are painted, books written, and marble hewn into form.

ERNEST. I seem to have heard another theory of Criticism.

GILBERT. Yes: it has been said by one who gracious memory we all revere, and the music of whose pipe once lured Proserpina from her Sicilian fields, and made those white feet stir, and not in vain, the Cumnor cowslips, that the proper aim of Criticism is to see the object as in itself it really is.[7] But this is a very serious error, and takes no cognizance of Criticism's most perfect form, which is in its essence purely subjective, and seeks to reveal its own secret and not the secret of another. For the highest Criticism deals with art not as expressive but as impressive purely.

ERNEST. But is that really so?

GILBERT. Of course it is. Who cares whether Mr. Ruskin's views on Turner are sound or not?[8] What does it matter? That mighty and majestic prose of his, so fervid and so fiery-colored in its noble eloquence, so rich in its elaborate symphonic music, so sure and certain, at its best, in subtle choice of word and epithet, is at least as great a work of art as any of those wonderful sunsets that bleach or rot on their corrupted canvases in England's Gallery; greater indeed, one is apt to think at times, not merely because its equal beauty is more enduring, but on account of the fuller variety of its appeal, soul speaking to soul in those long-cadenced lines, not through form and color alone, though through these, indeed, completely and without loss, but with intellectual and emotional utterance, with lofty passion and with loftier thought, with imaginative insight, and with poetic aim; greater, I always think, even as Literature is the greater art. Who, again, cares whether Mr. Pater has put into the portrait of Mona Lisa something that Leonardo never dreamed of? The painter may have been merely the slave of an archaic smile, as some have fancied, but whenever I pass into the cool galleries of the Palace of the Louvre, and stand before that strange figure "set in its marble chair in that cirque of fantastic rocks, as in some faint light under sea," I murmur to myself, "She is older than the rocks among which she sits; like the vampire, she has been dead many times, and learned the secrets of the grave; and has been a diver in deep seas, and keeps their fallen day about her; and trafficked for strange webs with Eastern merchants; and, as Leda, was the mother of Helen of Troy, and, as St. Anne, the

---

7. The "one whose gracious memory we all revere" is Matthew Arnold; the references are (a) to his poem *Empedocles on Etna*, set in Sicily, where the god of the underworld carried off Proserpine; (b) to his two poems *The Scholar Gypsy* and *Thyrsis*, set in the Cumnor (or Cumnor) hills, the district westward across the Thames from Oxford; (c) to his critical essay *The Function of Criticism at the Present Time*, in which he noted with approval of French and German literature that it showed "the endeavor * * * to see the object as in itself it really is"— an endeavor which Arnold continually advocated as the true aim of literary criticism.
8. The English landscape painter J. M. W. Turner (1775–1851) was passionately defended by Ruskin, especially in his *Modern Painters*.

mother of Mary; and all this has been to her but as the sound of lyres and flutes, and lives only in the delicacy with which it has molded the changing lineaments, and tinged the eyelids and the hands." And I say to my friend, "The presence that thus so strangely rose beside the waters is expressive of what in the ways of a thousand years man had come to desire"; and he answers me, "Hers is the head upon which all 'the ends of the world are come,' and the eyelids are a little weary."[9]

And so the picture becomes more wonderful to us than it really is, and reveals to us a secret of which, in truth, it knows nothing, and the music of the mystical prose is as sweet in our ears as was that flute-player's music that lent to the lips of La Gioconda[1] those subtle and poisonous curves. Do you ask me what Leonardo would have said had any one told him of this picture that "all the thoughts and experience of the world had etched and molded therein that which they had of power to refine and make expressive the outward form, the animalism of Greece, the lust of Rome, the reverie of the Middle Age with its spiritual ambition and imaginative loves, the return of the Pagan world, the sins of the Borgias?" He would probably have answered that he had contemplated none of these things, but had concerned himself simply with certain arrangements of lines and masses, and with new and curious color-harmonies of blue and green. And it is for this very reason that the criticism which I have quoted is criticism of the highest kind. It treats the work of art simply as a starting point for a new creation. It does not confine itself—let us at least suppose so for the moment—to discovering the real intention of the artist and accepting that as final. And in this it is right, for the meaning of any beautiful created thing is, at least, as much in the soul of him who looks at it, as it was in his soul who wrought it. Nay, it is rather the beholder who lends to the beautiful thing its myriad meanings, and makes it marvelous for us, and sets it in some new relation to the age, so that it becomes a vital portion of our lives, and symbol of what we pray for, or perhaps of what, having prayed for, we fear that we may receive. The longer I study, Ernest, the more clearly I see that the beauty of the visible arts is, as the beauty of music, impressive[2] primarily, and that it may be marred, and indeed often is so, by any excess of intellectual intention on the part of the artist. For when the work is finished it has, as it were, an independent life of its own, and may deliver a message far other than that which was put into its lips to say. Sometimes, when I listen to the overture to *Tannhäuser*,[3] I seem indeed to see that comely knight treading

---

9. Wilde is quoting from Pater's *The Renaissance*.
1. I.e., the "Mona Lisa" (she was the wife of Francesco del Gioconda—hence "La Gioconda").
2. I.e., designed to create an impression on the senses.
3. Opera by Richard Wagner (1845) based on the legend of a 14th-century German poet who fell under the spell of Lady Venus and lived with her in the Venusberg.

delicately on the flower-strewn grass, and to hear the voice of Venus calling to him from the caverned hill. But at other times it speaks to me of a thousand different things, of myself, it may be, and my own life, or of the lives of others whom one has loved and grown weary of loving, or of the passions that man has known, or of the passions that man has not known, and so has sought for. To-night it may fill one with that ΕΡΩΣ ΤΩΝ ΑΔΥΝΑΤΩΝ, that *amour de l'impossible*,[4] which falls like a madness on many who think they live securely and out of reach of harm, so that they sicken suddenly with the poison of unlimited desire, and, in the infinite pursuit of what they may not obtain, grow faint and swoon or stumble. Tomorrow, like the music of which Aristotle and Plato tell us, the noble Dorian music of the Greek, it may perform the office of a physician, and give us an anodyne against pain, and heal the spirit that is wounded, and "bring the soul into harmony with all right things." And what is true about music is true about all the arts. Beauty has as many meanings as man has moods. Beauty is the symbol of symbols. Beauty reveals everything, because it expresses nothing. When it shows us itself, it shows us the whole fiery-colored world.

ERNEST. But is such work as you have talked about really criticism?

GILBERT. It is the highest Criticism, for it criticizes not merely the individual work of art, but Beauty itself, and fills with wonder a form which the artist may have left void, or not understood, or understood incompletely.

ERNEST. The highest Criticism, then, is more creative than creation, and the primary aim of the critic is to see the object as in itself it really is not; that is your theory, I believe?

GILBERT. Yes, that is my theory. To the critic the work of art is simply a suggestion for a new work of his own, that need not necessarily bear any obvious resemblance to the thing it criticizes. The one characteristic of a beautiful form is that one can put into it whatever one wishes, and see in it whatever one chooses to see; and the Beauty, that gives to creation its universal and aesthetic element, makes the critic a creator in his turn, and whispers of a thousand different things which were not present in the mind of him who carved the statue or painted the panel or graved the gem.

It is sometimes said by those who understand neither the nature of the highest Criticism nor the charm of the highest Art, that the pictures that the critic loves most to write about are those that belong to the anecdotage of painting, and that deal with scenes taken out of literature or history. But this is not so. Indeed, pictures of this kind are far too intelligible. As a class, they rank with illustrations,

---

4. The Greek (in capital letters, perhaps to give the effect of an inscrip-tion) means the same as the French phrase: "love of the impossible."

and even considered from this point of view are failures, as they do not stir the imagination, but set definite bounds to it. For the domain of the painter is, as I suggested before, widely different from that of the poet. To the latter belongs life in its full and absolute entirety; not merely the beauty that men look at, but the beauty that men listen to also; not merely the momentary grace of form or the transient gladness of color, but the whole sphere of feeling, the perfect cycle of thought. The painter is so far limited that it is only through the mask of the body that he can show us the mystery of the soul; only through conventional images that he can handle ideas; only through its physical equivalents that he can deal with psychology. And how inadequately does he do it then, asking us to accept the torn turban of the Moor for the noble rage of Othello, or a dotard in a storm for the wild madness of Lear! Yet it seems as if nothing could stop him. Most of our elderly English painters spend their wicked and wasted lives in poaching upon the domain of the poets, marring their motives by clumsy treatment, and striving to render, by visible form or color, the marvel of what is invisible, the splendor of what is not seen. Their pictures are, as a natural consequence, insufferably tedious. They have degraded the invisible arts into the obvious arts, and the one thing not worth looking at is the obvious. I do not say that poet and painter may not treat of the same subject. They have always done so, and will always do so. But while the poet can be pictorial or not, as he chooses, the painter must be pictorial always. For a painter is limited, not to what he sees in nature, but to what upon canvas may be seen.

And so, my dear Ernest, pictures of this kind will not really fascinate the critic. He will turn from them to such works as make him brood and dream and fancy, to works that possess the subtle quality of suggestion, and seem to tell one that even from them there is an escape into a wider world. It is sometimes said that the tragedy of an artist's life is that he cannot realize his ideal. But the true tragedy that dogs the steps of most artists is that they realize their ideal too absolutely. For, when the ideal is realized, it is robbed of its wonder and its mystery, and becomes simply a new starting point for an ideal that is other than itself. This is the reason why music is the perfect type of art. Music can never reveal its ultimate secret. This, also, is the explanation of the value of limitations in art. The sculptor gladly surrenders imitative color, and the painter the actual dimensions of form, because by such renunciations they are able to avoid too definite a presentation of the Real, which would be mere imitation, and too definite a realization of the Ideal, which would be too purely intellectual. It is through its very incompleteness that Art becomes complete in beauty, and so addresses itself, not to the faculty of recognition nor to the faculty of reason, but to the aesthetic sense alone, which, while accepting both reason and recognition as stages of apprehension, subordinates them both to a pure synthetic impression of the work of art as a whole, and, taking whatever alien emotional elements the work may possess, uses their very complexity as a means by which a richer unity may be added to the ultimate impression itself. You see, then, how it is that the aesthetic critic rejects these obvious modes of art that have but one message to deliver, and having delivered it become dumb and sterile, and seeks rather for such modes as suggest reverie and mood, and by their imaginative beauty make all interpretations true, and no interpretation final. Some resemblance, no doubt, the creative work of the critic will have to the work that has stirred him to creation, but it will be such resemblance as exists, not between Nature and the mirror that the painter of landscape or figure may be supposed to hold up to her, but between Nature and the work of the decorative artist. Just as on the flowerless carpets of Persia, tulip and rose blossom indeed and are lovely to look on, though they are not reproduced in visible shape or line; just as the pearl and purple of the sea shell is echoed in the church of St. Mark at Venice; just as the vaulted ceiling of the wondrous chapel at Ravenna is made gorgeous by the gold and green and sapphire of the peacock's tail, though the birds of Juno fly not across it; so the critic reproduces the work that he criticizes in a mode that is never imitative, and part of whose charm may really consist in the rejection of resemblance, and shows us in this way not merely the meaning but also the mystery of Beauty, and, by transforming each art into literature, solves once for all the problem of Art's unity.

But I see it is time for supper. After we have discussed some Chambertin [5] and a few ortolans, we will pass on to the question of the critic considered in the light of the interpreter.

ERNEST. Ah! you admit, then, that the critic may occasionally be allowed to see the object as in itself it really is.

GILBERT. I am not quite sure. Perhaps I may admit it after supper. There is a subtle influence in supper.

1890, 1891

Preface to *The Picture of Dorian Gray*

The artist is the creator of beautiful things.
To reveal art and conceal the artist is art's aim.
The critic is he who can translate into another manner or a new material his impression of beautiful things.

5. One of the finest wines of Burgundy; "ortolans" are birds esteemed by epicures for their delicate flavor.

The highest, as the lowest, form of criticism is a mode of autobiography.

Those who find ugly meaning in beautiful things are corrupt without being charming. This is a fault.

Those who find beautiful meanings in beautiful things are the cultivated. For these there is hope.

They are the elect to whom beautiful things mean only Beauty.

There is no such thing as a moral or an immoral book.

Books are well written, or badly written. That is all.

The nineteenth-century dislike of Realism is the rage of Caliban[1] seeing his own face in a glass.

The nineteenth-century dislike of Romanticism is the rage of Caliban not seeing his own face in a glass.

The moral life of man forms part of the subject matter of the artist, but the morality of art consists in the perfect use of an imperfect medium. No artist desires to prove anything. Even things that are true can be proved.

No artist has ethical sympathies. An ethical sympathy in an artist is an unpardonable mannerism of style.

No artist is ever morbid. The artist can express everything.

Thought and language are to the artist instruments of an art.

Vice and virtue are to the artist materials for an art.

From the point of view of form, the type of all the arts is the art of the musician. From the point of view of feeling, the actor's craft is the type.

All art is at once surface and symbol.

Those who go beneath the surface do so at their peril.

Those who read the symbol do so at their peril.

It is the spectator, and not life, that art really mirrors.

Diversity of opinion about a work of art shows that the work is new, complex, and vital.

When critics disagree the artist is in accord with himself.

We can forgive a man for making a useful thing as long as he does not admire it. The only excuse for making a useless thing is that one admires it intensely.

All art is quite useless.

1891

1. This character in Shakespeare's *Tempest* is half-man, half-monster.

ERNEST DOWSON
(1867–1900)

Ernest Christopher Dowson spent much of his childhood traveling with his father on the Continent, mostly in France. His education was thus irregular and informal, but he acquired a thorough knowledge of French and of his favorite French writers Gustave Flaubert, Honoré de Balzac, and Paul Verlaine, and a good knowledge of Latin poetry, especially Catullus, Propertius, and Horace. Dowson went to Oxford in 1886, but he did not take to regular academic instruction and left after a year. Though nominally assisting his father to manage a dock in the London district of Limehouse, Dowson spent most of his time writing poetry, stories, and essays, and talking with Lionel Johnson, W. B. Yeats, and other members of the Rhymers' Club, in which he played a prominent part. Between 1890 and 1894 Dowson, though leading the irregular life of so many of the 90's poets, produced his best work, and his volume of *Verses* came out in 1896. Late nights and excessive drinking impaired a constitution already threatened by tuberculosis. He moved to France in 1894, making a living by translating from the French for an English publisher, but growing steadily worse in health. After his return to England he was discovered in a dying condition by a friend, who took him to his home and nursed him until his death six weeks later.

Dowson was a member of what Yeats called "the tragic generation" of poets in the 90's who seemed to be driven by their own restless energies to dissipation and premature death. As a poet he was considerably influenced by Swinburne (whose feverish emotional tone he often captures very skillfully), but he learned also from Latin lyric poetry and from contemporary French poetry. He experimented with a variety of meters, and in *Cynara* used the alexandrine as the normal line of a six-line stanza in a manner more common in French than in English poetry. He shared with his fellow members of the Rhymers' Club a belief in the pursuit of beauty, verbal sensation, the haunting cadence, the cultivated languor. He was also interested in the work of the French Symbolist poets and in their theories of verbal suggestiveness and of poetry as incantation: he believed (as he once wrote in a letter) that a finer poetry could sometimes be achieved by "mere sound and music, with just a suggestion of sense."

[Cynara]

Non sum qualis eram bonae sub regno Cynarae[1]

Last night, ah, yesternight, betwixt her lips and mine
There fell thy shadow, Cynara! thy breath was shed

---

1. "I am not as I was under the reign of the good Cynara." This is the third and part of the fourth line of an ode of Horace (IV.1) in which the poet

Upon my soul between the kisses and the wine;
And I was desolate and sick of an old passion,
　　Yea, I was desolate and bowed my head:　　　　　　5
I have been faithful to thee, Cynara! in my fashion.

All night upon mine heart I felt her warm heart beat,
Night-long within mine arms in love and sleep she lay;
Surely the kisses of her bought red mouth were sweet;
But I was desolate and sick of an old passion,　　　　10
　　When I awoke and found the dawn was gray:
I have been faithful to thee, Cynara! in my fashion.

I have forgot much, Cynara! gone with the wind,
Flung roses, roses riotously with the throng,
Dancing, to put thy pale, lost lilies out of mind;　　　15
But I was desolate and sick of an old passion,
　　Yea, all the time, because the dance was long:
I have been faithful to thee, Cynara! in my fashion.

I cried for madder music and for stronger wine,
But when the feast is finished and the lamps expire,　20
Then falls thy shadow, Cynara! the night is thine;
And I am desolate and sick of an old passion,
　　Yea, hungry for the lips of my desire:
I have been faithful to thee, Cynara! in my fashion.

1891, 1896

Flos Lunae[1]

FOR YVANHOÉ RAMBOSSON[2]

I would not alter thy cold eyes,
Nor trouble the calm fount of speech
With aught of passion or surprise.
The heart of thee I cannot reach:
I would not alter thy cold eyes!　　　　　　　　　5

I would not alter thy cold eyes;
Nor have thee smile, nor make thee weep:
Though all my life droops down and dies,
Desiring thee, desiring sleep,
I would not alter thy cold eyes.　　　　　　　　10

pleads with Venus to stop tormenting him with love since he is growing old and is no longer what he was when under the sway of Cynara (*Sin-ah-rah*), the girl he used to love. Of Dowson's "Cynara" Yeats later wrote: "Dowson, who seemed to drink so little and had so much dignity and reserve, was breaking his heart for the daughter of the keeper of an Italian eating house, in dissipation and drink * * * " Dowson's "Cynara" was, in fact, a Polish girl by the name of Adelaide Foltinowicz.

1. "Flower of the moon."
2. This name sounds too good to be true, and perhaps is. Desmond Flower's annotated edition of Dowson's poetical works identifies the other characters to whom Dowson dedicated poems but is silent on this one.

I would not alter thy cold eyes;
I would not change thee if I might,
To whom my prayers for incense rise,
Daughter of dreams! my moon of night!
I would not alter thy cold eyes.   15

I would not alter thy cold eyes,
With trouble of the human heart:
Within their glance my spirit lies,
A frozen thing, alone, apart;
I would not alter thy cold eyes.   20

1891, 1896

To One in Bedlam[1]

FOR HENRY DAVRAY[2]

With delicate, mad hands, behind his sordid bars,
Surely he hath his posies, which they tear and twine;
Those scentless wisps of straw, that miserably line
His strait, caged universe, whereat the dull world stares,

Pedant and pitiful. O, how his rapt gaze wars   5
With their stupidity! Know they what dreams divine
Lift his long, laughing reveries like enchanted wine,
And make his melancholy germane to the stars'?

O lamentable brother! if those pity thee,
Am I not fain of all thy lone eyes promise me;   10
Half a fool's kingdom, far from men who sow and reap,
All their days, vanity?[3] Better than mortal flowers,
Thy moon-kissed roses seem: better than love or sleep,
The star-crowned solitude of thine oblivious hours!

1892, 1896

A Last Word

Let us go hence: the night is now at hand;
The day is overworn, the birds all flown;

1. Insane asylum (specifically, an ancient madhouse in London).
2. Henry Davray was a French critic and great friend of Dowson's; he reviewed English books for the *Mercure de France*. The habit of dedicating individual poems to particular friends Dowson and Lionel Johnson picked up from the French poet Paul Verlaine (1844–96), who entitled one of his volumes of poetry *Dédicaces* ("Dedications"), and explained in the introduction that "these ballads and sonnets are all intimate and are directed only to certain friends and good companions of the author who *dedicates* the poems to them exclusively, without any other intention than of pleasing them."
3. The sense of lines 10–12 is: "Would I not be glad to have all that your eyes promise me—namely, half a fool's kingdom—far from men who are engaged in ordinary mundane activities and who thus pass their days in vanity?" The "fool's kingdom" is the lunatic's world of imagination; the lunatic's eyes promise to share that kingdom with the poet.

And we have reaped the crops the gods have sown;
Despair and death; deep darkness o'er the land,
Broods like an owl; we cannot understand   5
Laughter or tears, for we have only known
Surpassing vanity: vain things alone
Have driven our perverse and aimless band.
Let us go hence, somewhither strange and cold,
To Hollow Lands where just men and unjust   10
Find end of labor, where's rest for the old,
Freedom to all from love and fear and lust.
Twine our torn hands! O pray the earth enfold
Our life-sick hearts and turn them into dust.

                                    1896, 1899

Spleen

FOR ARTHUR SYMONS[1]

I was not sorrowful, I could not weep,
And all my memories were put to sleep.

I watched the river grow more white and strange,
All day till evening I watched it change.

All day till evening I watched the rain   5
Beat wearily upon the window pane.

I was not sorrowful, but only tired
Of everything that ever I desired.

Her lips, her eyes, all day became to me
The shadow of a shadow utterly.   10

All day mine hunger for her heart became
Oblivion, until the evening came,

And left me sorrowful, inclined to weep,
With all my memories that could not sleep.

                                    1896

Dregs

The fire is out, and spent the warmth thereof,
(This is the end of every song man sings!)
The golden wine is drunk, the dregs remain,
Bitter as wormwood and as salt as pain;
   And health and hope have gone the way of love   5

1. 1865–1945. English poet and critic   England of the French symbolist poets.
influential in spreading knowledge in

Into the drear oblivion of lost things.
Ghosts go along with us until the end;
This was a mistress, this, perhaps, a friend.
With pale, indifferent eyes, we sit and wait
For the dropped curtain and the closing gate: 10
This is the end of all the songs man sings.

1899

Exchanges

All that I had I brought.
  Little enough I know;
A poor rhyme roughly wrought,
  A rose to match thy snow:
All that I had I brought.   5

Little enough I sought:
  But a word compassionate,
A passing glance, or thought,
  For me outside the gate:
Little enough I sought.   10

Little enough I found:
  All that you had, perchance!
With the dead leaves on the ground,
  I dance the devil's dance.
All that you had I found.   15

1899

THOMAS HARDY
(1840–1928)

1872–96: Career as novelist, ending with *Jude the Obscure*.
1898:   *Wessex Poems*, first collection of poetry.

Thomas Hardy was born near Dorchester, in that area of southwest England that he was to make the "Wessex" of his novels. He attended local schools until the age of 15, when he was articled to a Dorchester architect with whom he worked for six years. In 1861 he went to London to continue his studies and to practice as an architect. Meanwhile he was completing his general education informally through his own erratic reading, and becoming more and more interested in both fiction and poetry. After some early attempts at writing both short stories and poems, he decided to concentrate on fiction. His first novel was rejected by the publishers in 1868 on the advice of George Meredith, who nevertheless advised Hardy to write another. The result was *Desperate Remedies*, published anonymously in 1871, followed the next year by his first real success (also published anonymously), *Under the Greenwood Tree*. Hardy's career as a novelist was now well launched; he gave up his architectural work and produced a series of novels that ended with *Jude the Obscure* in 1896. The hostile reception of this novel sent him back to poetry. His remarkable epic-drama of the Napoleonic Wars, *The Dynasts*, came out in three parts between 1903 and 1908; after this he wrote mostly lyric poetry.

Hardy's novels, set in a predominantly rural "Wessex," show the forces of nature outside and inside man combining to shape human destiny. Against a background of immemorial agricultural labor, with ancient monuments such as Stonehenge or an old Roman amphitheater reminding us of the human past, he presents characters at the mercy of their own passions or finding temporary salvation in the age-old rhythms of rural work or rural recreation. Men in Hardy's fiction are not masters of their fates; they are at the mercy of the indifferent forces which manipulate their behavior and their relations with others; but they can achieve dignity through endurance, and heroism through simple strength of character. The characteristic Victorian novelist—e.g., Dickens and Thackeray—was concerned with the behavior and problems of men in a given social milieu, which he described in detail; Hardy preferred to go directly for the elemental in human behavior with a minimum of contemporary social detail. Most of Hardy's novels are tragic, though *Under the Greenwood Tree* has an idyllic character possessed by no other of his novels. But even here the happy ending is achieved only by ending the story with the marriage of the hero and heroine and refusing to go further; the texture of the narrative, for all its moments of gaiety and charm, has already suggested the bitter ironies of which life is capable. His later work explores those ironies with sometimes an almost malevolent staging of coincidence in order to emphasize the disparity between human desire and ambition on the one hand and what fate has in store for the characters on the other. But fate is not a wholly external force. Men are driven by the demands of their own nature as much as by anything from outside them. *Tess of the D'Urbervilles* (1891) is the story of an intelligent and sensitive girl, daughter of a poor family, driven to murder and so to death by hanging, by a concatenation of events and circumstances so bitterly ironic that many readers find it the darkest of Hardy's novels, while others would award that distinction to *Jude the Obscure*, the disturbingly powerful account of an ambitious rustic trapped between his intellect and his sensuality and as a result delivered to destruction.

Hardy himself denied that he was a pessimist, calling himself a "meliorist," i.e., one who believes that the world may be made better by human effort. But there is little sign of "meliorism" in either his most important novels or his lyric poetry. In his poems—which alone are represented here because no extract could do justice to Hardy's power as a novelist—many of his characteristic attitudes and ideas and many of his favorite situations can be found. A number of his poems are verse anecdotes illustrating the perversity of fate, the disastrous or ironic coincidence. But his best poems go beyond this mood to present with quiet gravity and a carefully controlled elegiac feeling some aspect of human sorrow or loss or frustration or regret, always projected through a particular, fully realized situation. *Hap* shows Hardy in the characteristic mood of complaining about the irony of human destiny in a universe ruled by chance; but a poem such as *The Walk* (one of a group of poems written after the death of his first wife in 1912) gives, with remarkable power, concrete embodiment to a sense of loss. That power—we see it also in *A Broken Appointment* and *She Hears the Storm*—is achieved through a kind of verbal as well as an emotional integrity. Hardy's poetry, like his prose, often has a self-taught air about it; both can be odd or pretentious or awkward or clumsy. But at their best both his poetry and his prose have an air of persuasive authenticity. The association of a given emotion with particular visual memories in *Neutral Tones*, for example, is impressive because it carries such extraordinary conviction; and it carries that conviction because the rhythms and rhymes are handled so as to suggest the kind of utterance actually wrung from the poet (consider, e.g., the curious dead fall of "They had fallen from an ash, and were gray"). At the same time, Hardy will use an antique or a poetic word or phrase ("thereby," "a-wing") if it fits in with the movement of the poem and keeps him from having to stop and search for something more deft: the result is an effect not of artificiality but of spontaneity. Hardy's use of ballad rhythms often helps to give an elemental quality to his poetry, suggesting that this incident or situation, carefully particularized though it is, nevertheless stands for some profound and recurring themes in human experience.

Sometimes in Hardy's poetry the quiet lilt of the verse and the fall of the rhymes convey a deep but controlled emotion, as in *Drummer Hodge*, where the sense of a simple English soldier buried in a far distant land and mingling with an earth that will produce vegetation so different from anything known in England is poignantly expressed. *In Time of "The Breaking of Nations"* conveys with stark clarity the same awareness of the processes of nature continuing in spite of cataclysms caused by human folly in the novels. The sadness in Hardy—his inability to believe in the government of the world by a benevolent God, his sense of the waste and frustration involved in human life, his insistent irony when faced with moral or metaphysical questions—is part of the late Victorian mood. We can see something like it in A. E. Housman, and there is an earlier version of Victorian pessimism in Edward FitzGerald's *Rubáiyát of Omar Khayyám*, published when Hardy was 19. Yet Hardy's characteristic themes and attitudes cannot be related simply to the reaction to new scientific and philosophical ideas (Darwin's theory of evolution, for example) that we see in so many forms in late 19th-century literature. The favorite poetic mood of both Tennyson and Arnold was also an elegiac one (e.g., in Tennyson's *Break, Break, Break* and Arnold's *Dover Beach*), but this is not Hardy's mood. The sad-sweet cadences of Victorian self-pity are not to be found in Hardy's poetry, which is sterner, as though braced by a long look at the worst. It is this sternness—sometimes amounting to ruggedness—together with his verbal and emotional integrity, his refusal ever to surrender to mere poetic fashion, his quietly searching individual accent, that has helped to bring about the steady rise in Hardy's poetic reputation in recent years, so that today he is regarded not only as a distinguished novelist but also as a great English poet.

Hap[1]

If but some vengeful god would call to me
From up the sky, and laugh: "Thou suffering thing,
Know that thy sorrow is my ecstasy,
That thy love's loss is my hate's profiting!"

Then would I bear it, clench myself, and die,   5
Steeled by the sense of ire unmerited;
Half-eased in that a Powerfuller than I
Had willed and meted me the tears I shed.

But not so. How arrives it joy lies slain,
And why unblooms the best hope ever sown?   10
—Crass Casualty obstructs the sun and rain,
And dicing Time for gladness casts a moan. . . .
These purblind Doomsters[2] had as readily strown
Blisses about my pilgrimage as pain.

1866   1898

The Impercipient

(AT A CATHEDRAL SERVICE)

That with this bright believing band
    I have no claim to be,
That faiths by which my comrades stand
    Seem fantasies to me,

---

1. I.e., chance (as also "Casualty," line 11).
2. Half-blind judges.

And mirage-mists their Shining Land,   5
    Is a strange destiny.

Why thus my soul should be consigned
    To infelicity,
Why always I must feel as blind
    To sights my brethren see,   10
Why joys they've found I cannot find,
    Abides a mystery.

Since heart of mine knows not that ease
    Which they know; since it be
That He who breathes All's Well to these   15
    Breathes no All's-Well to me,
My lack might move their sympathies
    And Christian charity!

I am like a gazer who should mark
    An inland company   20
Standing upfingered, with, "Hark! hark!
    The glorious distant sea!"
And feel, "Alas, 'tis but yon dark
    And wind-swept pine to me!"

Yet I would bear my shortcomings   25
    With meet tranquillity,
But for the charge that blessed things
    I'd liefer not have be.
O, doth a bird deprived of wings
    Go earth-bound willfully!   30

    .   .   .   .   .

Enough. As yet disquiet clings
    About us. Rest shall we.

                                          1898

Neutral Tones

We stood by a pond that winter day,
And the sun was white, as though chidden of God,
And a few leaves lay on the starving sod;
    —They had fallen from an ash, and were gray.

Your eyes on me were as eyes that rove   5
Over tedious riddles of years ago;
And some words played between us to and fro
    On which lost the more by our love.

The smile on your mouth was the deadest thing
Alive enough to have strength to die;   10

And a grin of bitterness swept thereby
    Like an ominous bird a-wing. . . .
Since then, keen lessons that love deceives,
And wrings with wrong, have shaped to me
Your face, and the God-cursed sun, and a tree,   15
    And a pond edged with grayish leaves.

1867   1898

I Look into My Glass

I look into my glass,
And view my wasting skin,
And say, "Would God it came to pass
My heart had shrunk as thin!"

For then, I, undistressed   5
By hearts grown cold to me,
Could lonely wait my endless rest
With equanimity.

But Time, to make me grieve,
Part steals, lets part abide;   10
And shakes this fragile frame at eve
With throbbings of noontide.

1898

A Broken Appointment

    You did not come,
And marching Time drew on, and wore me numb.—
Yet less for loss of your dear presence there
Than that I thus found lacking in your make
That high compassion which can overbear   5
Reluctance for pure loving-kindness' sake
Grieved I, when, as the hope-hour stroked its sum,
    You did not come.

    You love not me,
And love alone can lend you loyalty;   10
—I know and knew it. But, unto the store
Of human deeds divine in all but name,
Was it not worth a little hour or more
To add yet this: Once you, a woman, came
To soothe a time-torn man; even though it be   15
    You love not me?

1902

Drummer Hodge

1

They throw in Drummer Hodge, to rest
　　Uncoffined—just as found:
His landmark is a kopje-crest[1]
　　That breaks the veldt around;
And foreign constellations west[2]　　　　　　　　　5
　　Each night above his mound.

2

Young Hodge the Drummer never knew—
　　Fresh from his Wessex home—
The meaning of the broad Karoo,[3]
　　The Bush, the dusty loam,　　　　　　　　　10
And why uprose to nightly view
　　Strange stars amid the gloam.

3

Yet portion of that unknown plain
　　Will Hodge forever be;
His homely Northern breast and brain　　　　　　15
　　Grow to some Southern tree,
And strange-eyed constellations reign
　　His stars eternally.

　　　　　　　　　　　　　　　　　　　　　　1902

Lausanne[4]

IN GIBBON'S OLD GARDEN: 11–12 P.M.
JUNE 27, 1897

(The 110th anniversary of the completion of the Decline and Fall *at the same
hour and place)*

　　　A spirit seems to pass,
Formal in pose, but grave withal and grand:
He contemplates a volume in his hand,
And far lamps fleck him through the thin acacias.

1. South African Dutch (Afrikaans) word for a small hill. "Veldt": Afrikaans for a plain or prairie. The poem is a lament for an English soldier killed in the Boer War (1899–1902).
2. Set. The "foreign constellations" are those visible only in the southern hemisphere.
3. A dry table-land region in South Africa (usually spelled "Karroo"). "The Bush": British Colonial word for an uncleared area of land.
4. Edward Gibbon finished his monumental *History of the Decline and Fall of the Roman Empire* (6 vols., 1776–88) in Lausanne, Switzerland, where he lived from 1783 until his death. Gibbon records in his *Memoirs of My Life and Writings* that "It was on the day, or rather night, of the 27th of June, 1787, that I wrote the last lines of the last page, in a summer-house in my garden," and goes on to describe his emotions on having completed his life's work. Gibbon, a skeptic, saw himself fighting for truth against prejudice and superstition.

Anon the book is closed,   5
With "It is finished!" And at the alley's end
He turns, and when on me his glances bend
As from the Past comes speech—small, muted, yet composed.

"How fares the Truth now?—Ill?
—Do pens but slily further her advance?   10
May one not speed her but in phrase askance?⁵
Do scribes aver the Comic to be Reverend still?⁶

"Still rule those minds on earth
At whom sage Milton's wormwood words were hurled:
'Truth like a bastard comes into the world   15
Never without ill fame to him who gives her birth'?"⁷
1897   1902

The Darkling¹ Thrush

I leant upon a coppice gate²
    When Frost was specter-gray,
And Winter's dregs made desolate
    The weakening eye of day.
The tangled bine-stems³ scored the sky   5
    Like strings of broken lyres,
And all mankind that haunted nigh
    Had sought their household fires.

The land's sharp features seemed to be
    The Century's corpse⁴ outleant,   10
His crypt the cloudy canopy,
    The wind his death-lament.
The ancient pulse of germ and birth
    Was shrunken hard and dry,
And every spirit upon earth   15
    Seemed fervorless as I.

At once a voice arose among
    The bleak twigs overhead
In a fullhearted evensong
    Of joy illimited;   20
An aged thrush, frail, gaunt, and small,
    In blast-beruffled plume,
Had chosen thus to fling his soul
    Upon the growing gloom.

5. Oblique.
6. I.e., do theological writers still claim respect for what is ridiculous on the grounds that it is ancient and venerable?
7. From Milton's *Areopagitica* (1644), defending liberty of the press.

1. In the dark.
2. Gate leading to a small wood or thicket.
3. Twining stems of shrubs.
4. This poem was written on December 31, 1900, the last day of the 19th century.

So little cause for carolings 25
    Of such ecstatic sound
Was written on terrestrial things
    Afar or nigh around,
That I could think there trembled through
    His happy good-night air 30
Some blessed Hope, whereof he knew
    And I was unaware.

1900   1902

A Trampwoman's Tragedy

(182–)

1

From Wynyard's Gap [1] the livelong day,
    The livelong day,
We beat afoot the northward way
    We had traveled times before.
The sun-blaze burning on our backs, 5
Our shoulders sticking to our packs,
By fosseway,[2] fields, and turnpike tracks
    We skirted sad Sedge-Moor.

2

Full twenty miles we jaunted on,
    We jaunted on— 10
My fancy-man, and jeering John,
    And Mother Lee, and I.
And, as the sun drew down to west,
We climbed the toilsome Poldon [3] crest,
And saw, of landskip sights the best, 15
    The inn that beamed thereby.

3

For months we had padded side by side,
    Ay, side by side
Through the Great Forest, Blackmoor wide,
    And where the Parret ran. 20
We'd faced the gusts on Mendip ridge,
Had crossed the Yeo unhelped by bridge,
Been stung by every Marshwood midge,
    I and my fancy-man.

1. The places here named are in Somerset, in southwest England on the northern edge of the area which Hardy called "Wessex" and of which his native Dorset, the county south and southwest of Somerset, reaching to the English Channel, was the major part.
2. Path running along a ditch. See note 4 below.
3. Sad (line 8) because of the Battle of Sedgemoor (1685) when the rebellion of the Duke of Monmouth against James II was crushed with excessive cruelty. "This plain [Sedgemoor], intersected by ditches known as *rhines*, * * * is broken by isolated hills and lower ridges, of which the most conspicuous are Brent Knoll near Burnham, the Isle of Avalon, rising with Glastonbury Tor as its highest point, and the long low ridge of Polden ending to the west in a steep bluff." *Encyclopaedia Britannica*, 11th edition, 1911.

4

Lone inns we loved, my man and I,   25
    My man and I;
"King's Stag," "Windwhistle" [4] high and dry,
    "The Horse" on Hintock Green.
The cosy house at Wynyard's Gap,
"The Hut" renowned on Bredy Knap,   30
And many another wayside tap
    Where folk might sit unseen.

5

Now as we trudged—O deadly day,
    O deadly day!—
I teased my fancy-man in play   35
    And wanton idleness.
I walked alongside jeering John,
I laid his hand my waist upon;
I would not bend my glances on
    My lover's dark distress.   40

6

Thus Poldon top at last we won,
    At last we won,
And gained the inn at sink of sun
    Far-famed as "Marshal's Elm."[5]
Beneath us figured tor and lea,   45
From Mendip to the western sea—
I doubt if finer sight there be
    Within this royal realm.

7

Inside the settle all a-row—
    All four a-row   50
We sat, I next to John, to show
    That he had wooed and won.
And then he took me on his knee,
And swore it was his turn to be
My favored mate, and Mother Lee   55
    Passed to my former one.

8

Then in a voice I had never heard,
    I had never heard,
My only Love to me: "One word,
    My lady, if you please!   60
Whose is the child you are like to bear?—
His? After all my months o' care?"
God knows 'twas not! But, O despair!
    I nodded—still to tease.

4. "The highness and dryness of Windwhistle Inn was impressed upon the writer two or three years ago, when, after climbing on a hot afternoon to the beautiful spot near which it stands and entering the inn for tea, he was informed by the landlady that none could be had, unless he would fetch water from a valley half a mile off, the house containing not a drop, owing to its situation. However, a tantalizing row of full barrels behind her back testified to a wetness of a certain sort, which was not at that time desired" [Hardy's note].

5. "'Marshal's Elm,' so picturesquely situated, is no longer an inn, though the house, or part of it, still remains. It used to exhibit a fine old swinging sign" [Hardy's note].

9

Then up he sprung, and with his knife—   65
    And with his knife
He let out jeering Johnny's life,
    Yes; there, at set of sun.
The slant ray through the window nigh
Gilded John's blood and glazing eye,   70
Ere scarcely Mother Lee and I
    Knew that the deed was done.

10

The taverns tell the gloomy tale,
    The gloomy tale,
How that at Ivel-chester jail   75
    My Love, my sweetheart swung;
Though stained till now by no misdeed
Save one horse ta'en in time o' need;
(Blue Jimmy stole right many a steed
    Ere his last fling he flung).[6]   80

11

Thereaft I walked the world alone,
    Alone, alone!
On his death-day I gave my groan
    And dropt his dead-born child.
'Twas nigh the jail, beneath a tree,   85
None tending me; for Mother Lee
Had died at Glaston, leaving me
    Unfriended on the wild.

12

And in the night as I lay weak,
    As I lay weak,   90
The leaves a-falling on my cheek,
    The red moon low declined—
The ghost of him I'd die to kiss
Rose up and said: "Ah, tell me this!
Was the child mine, or was it his?   95
    Speak, that I rest may find!"

13

O doubt not but I told him then,
    I told him then,
That I had kept me from all men
    Since we joined lips and swore.   100
Whereat he smiled, and thinned away
As the wind stirred to call up day . . .
    —'Tis past! And here alone I stray
    Haunting the Western Moor.

April, 1902   1909

6. "'Blue Jimmy' was a notorious horse stealer of Wessex in those days, who appropriated more than a hundred horses before he was caught, among others one belonging to a neighbor of the writer's grandfather. He was hanged at the now demolished Ivel-chester or Ilchester jail above mentioned—that building formerly of so many sinister associations in the minds of the local peasantry, and the continual haunt of fever, which at last led to its condemnation. Its site is now an innocent-looking green meadow" [Hardy's note].

Let Me Enjoy

(MINOR KEY)

1

Let me enjoy the earth no less
Because the all-enacting Might
That fashioned forth its loveliness
Had other aims than my delight.

2

About my path there flits a Fair,   5
Who throws me not a word or sign;
I'll charm me with her ignoring air,
And laud the lips not meant for mine.

3

From manuscripts of moving song
Inspired by scenes and dreams unknown   10
I'll pour out raptures that belong
To others, as they were my own.

4

And some day hence, towards Paradise
And all its blest—if such should be—
I will lift glad, afar-off eyes,   15
Though it contain no place for me.

1909

The Rash Bride

AN EXPERIENCE OF THE MELLSTOCK QUIRE[1]

1

We Christmas-caroled down the Vale, and up the Vale, and
   round the Vale,
We played and sang that night as we were yearly wont to do—
A carol in a minor key, a carol in the major D,
Then at each house: "Good wishes: many Christmas joys to you!"

2

Next, to the widow's John and I and all the rest drew on.
   And I   5
Discerned that John could hardly hold the tongue of him for joy.
The widow was a sweet young thing whom John was bent on
   marrying,
And quiring at her casement seemed romantic to the boy.

3

"She'll make reply, I trust," said he, "to our salute? She must!"
   said he,
"And then I will accost her gently—much to her surprise!—   10
For knowing not I am with you here, when I speak up and call
   her dear
A tenderness will fill her voice, a bashfulness her eyes."

4

So, by her window-square we stood; ay, with our lanterns there
   we stood,

1. Choir.

And he along with us—not singing, waiting for a sign;
And when we'd quired her carols three a light was lit and out
    looked she,   15
A shawl about her bedgown, and her color red as wine.

5

And sweetly then she bowed her thanks, and smiled, and
    spoke aloud her thanks;
When lo, behind her back there, in the room, a man appeared.
I knew him—one from Woolcomb way—Giles Swetman—
    honest as the day,
But eager, hasty; and I felt that some strange trouble neared.   20

6

"How comes he there? . . . Suppose," said we, "she's wed of
    late! Who knows?" said we.
—"She married yestermorning—only mother yet has known
The secret o't!" shrilled one small boy. "But now I've told,
    let's wish 'em joy!"
A heavy fall aroused us: John had gone down like a stone.

7

We rushed to him and caught him round, and lifted him, and
    brought him round,   25
When, hearing something wrong had happened, oped the
    window she:
"Has one of you fallen ill?" she asked, "by these night
    labors overtasked?"
None answered. That she'd done poor John a cruel turn felt we.

8

Till up spoke Michael: "Fie, young dame! You've broke your
    promise, sly young dame,
By forming this new tie, young dame, and jilting John so true, 30
Who trudged tonight to sing to 'ee because he thought he'd
    bring to 'ee
Good wishes as your coming spouse. May ye such trifling rue!"

9

Her man had said no word at all; but being behind had heard
    it all,
And now cried: "Neighbors, on my soul I knew not 'twas
    like this!"
And then to her: "If I had known you'd had in tow not me
    alone,   35
No wife should you have been of mine. It is a dear bought bliss!"

10

She changed death-white, and heaved a cry: we'd never heard
    so grieved a cry
As came from her at this from him: heartbroken quite seemed
    she;
And suddenly, as we looked on, she turned, and rushed; and
    she was gone,
Whither, her husband, following after, knew not; nor knew we. 40

11

We searched till dawn about the house; within the house,
    without the house,

We searched among the laurel boughs that grew beneath the
    wall,
And then among the crocks and things, and stores for winter
    junketings,
In linhay,[2] loft, and dairy; but we found her not at all.

12

Then John rushed in: "O friends," he said, "hear this, this,
    this!" and bends his head: 45
"I've—searched round by the—*well*, and find the cover open
    wide!
I am fearful that—I can't say what . . . Bring lanterns, and
    some cords to knot."
We did so, and we went and stood the deep dark hole beside.

13

And then they, ropes in hand, and I—ay, John, and all the
    band, and I
Let down a lantern to the depths—some hundred feet and
    more;   50
It glimmered like a fog-dimmed star; and there, beside its light,
    afar,
White drapery floated, and we knew the meaning that it bore.

14

The rest is naught. . . . We buried her o' Sunday. Neighbors
    carried her;
And Swetman—he who'd married her—now miserablest
    of men,
Walked mourning first; and then walked John; just quivering,
    but composed anon;   55
And we the quire formed round the grave, as was the custom
    then.

15

Our old bass player, as I recall—his white hair blown—but why
    recall!—
His viol upstrapped, bent figure—doomed to follow her full
    soon—
Stood bowing, pale and tremulous; and next to him the rest
    of us. . . .
We sang the Ninetieth Psalm [3] to her—set to Saint Stephen's
    tune.   60

1909

One We Knew

(M. H.[4] 1772–1857)

She told how they used to form for the country dances—
    "The Triumph," "The New-rigged Ship"—
To the light of the guttering wax in the paneled manses
    And in cots to the blink of a dip.[5]

2. Shed.
3. A favorite psalm at funerals, contrasting God's eternity with the brevity of human life.

4. Hardy's grandmother.
5. I.e., in cottages by the light of a candle.

She spoke of the wild "poussetting" and "allemanding" [6]   5
  On carpet, on oak, and on sod;
And the two long rows of ladies and gentlemen standing,
  And the figures the couples trod.

She showed us the spot where the maypole was yearly planted,
  And where the bandsmen stood   10
While breeched and kerchiefed partners whirled, and panted
  To choose each other for good.

She told of that far-back day when they learnt astounded
  Of the death of the King of France:
Of the Terror; and then of Bonaparte's unbounded   15
  Ambition and arrogance.

Of how his threats woke warlike preparations
  Along the southern strand,
And how each night brought tremors and trepidations
  Lest morning should see him land.   20

She said she had often heard the gibbet creaking
  As it swayed in the lightning flash,
Had caught from the neighboring town a small child's shrieking
  At the cart tail under the lash. . . .

With cap-framed face and long gaze into the embers—   25
  We seated around her knees—
She would dwell on such dead themes, not as one who remembers,
  But rather as one who sees.

She seemed one left behind of a band gone distant
  So far that no tongue could hail: 30
Past things retold were to her as things existent,
    Things present but as a tale.
May 20, 1902   1909

She Hears the Storm

There was a time in former years—
    While my rooftree was his—
When I should have been distressed by fears
    At such a night as this!

I should have murmured anxiously,   5
    "The pricking rain strikes cold;
His road is bare of hedge or tree,
    And he is getting old."

But now the fitful chimney-roar,
    The drone of Thorncombe trees,   10

---

6. To pousette is to dance round with hands joined; allemande is the name of a dance originating in Germany.

The Froom in flood upon the moor,
    The mud of Mellstock Leaze,[7]

The candle slanting sooty wicked,
    The thuds upon the thatch,
The eaves-drops on the window flicked,   15
    The clacking garden-hatch,[8]

And what they mean to wayfarers,
    I scarcely heed or mind;
He has won that storm-tight roof of hers
    Which Earth grants all her kind.   20

                       1909

Channel Firing[1]

That night your great guns, unawares,
Shook all our coffins as we lay,
And broke the chancel window-squares,
We thought it was the Judgment Day
And sat upright. While drearisome   5
Arose the howl of wakened hounds:
The mouse let fall the altar-crumb,
The worms drew back into the mounds,

The glebe cow[2] drooled. Till God called, "No;
It's gunnery practice out at sea   10
Just as before you went below;
The world is as it used to be:

"All nations striving strong to make
Red war yet redder. Mad as hatters
They do no more for Christés[3] sake   15
Than you who are helpless in such matters.

"That this is not the judgment hour
For some of them's a blessed thing,
For if it were they'd have to scour
Hell's floor for so much threatening. . . .   20

"Ha, ha. It will be warmer when
I blow the trumpet (if indeed
I ever do; for you are men,
And rest eternal sorely need)."

---

7. The place names in Hardy's fictional "Wessex" were often invented ("Thorncombe," "Mellstock Leaze"), but he also used the names of real locations, as in "A Trampwoman's Tragedy." The standard edition of Hardy's novels has a map of "Wessex" showing the locale of both the real and the invented names. "The Froom" is presumably the river Frome, flowing through Dorsetshire and Somerset.
8. Gate.

1. Written in April, 1914, when Anglo-German naval rivalry was growing steadily more acute; the title refers to gunnery practice in the English Channel. Four months later (August 4) World War I broke out.
2. I.e., cow on a small plot of land belonging to a cottage (a "glebe" is a small field).
3. The archaic spelling and pronunciation suggest a ballad note of doom.

So down we lay again. "I wonder,   25
Will the world ever saner be,"
Said one, "than when He sent us under
In our indifferent century!"

And many a skeleton shook his head.
"Instead of preaching forty year,"   30
My neighbor Parson Thirdly said,
"I wish I had stuck to pipes and beer."

Again the guns disturbed the hour,
Roaring their readiness to avenge,
As far inland as Stourton Tower,   35
And Camelot, and starlit Stonehenge.[4]

1914   1914

The Convergence of the Twain

(LINES ON THE LOSS OF THE "TITANIC")[1]

1

In a solitude of the sea
Deep from human vanity,
And the Pride of Life that planned her, stilly couches she.

2

Steel chambers, late the pyres
Of her salamandrine fires,[2]   5
Cold currents thrid, and turn to rhythmic tidal lyres.

3

Over the mirrors meant
To glass the opulent
The sea worm crawls—grotesque, slimed, dumb, indifferent.

4

Jewels in joy designed   10
To ravish the sensuous mind
Lie lightless, all their sparkles bleared and black and blind.

5

Dim moon-eyed fishes near
Gaze at the gilded gear
And query: "What does this vaingloriousness down here?" . . . 15

---

4. Again the "Wessex" place names from various sources: Stonehenge is the famous prehistoric stone circle on Salisbury Plain; Camelot was the legendary location of King Arthur's court and the Round Table. There is a real river Stour in Dorset, and a town called Stour Head, which Hardy calls "Stourton."
1. The *Titanic* was the largest and most luxurious ocean liner of her day. Considered unsinkable, she sank with great loss of life on April 15, 1912, on her maiden voyage from Southampton to America, after colliding with an iceberg.
2. Probably "fires in which nothing could survive" (although, since the salamander is a lizardlike animal supposed to be able to live in fire, "salamandrine" usually means "able to resist or to live in fire"). In the next line, "thrid" is the archaic past tense of the verb "thread."

6

Well: while was fashioning
    This creature of cleaving wing,
The Immanent Will[3] that stirs and urges everything

7

Prepared a sinister mate
    For her—so gaily great—   20
A Shape of Ice, for the time far and dissociate.

8

And as the smart ship grew
    In stature, grace, and hue,
In shadowy silent distance grew the Iceberg too.

9

Alien they seemed to be: 25
    No mortal eye could see
The intimate welding of their later history,

10

Or sign that they were bent
    By paths coincident
On being anon twin halves of one august event,   30

11

Till the Spinner of the Years
    Said "Now!" And each one hears,
And consummation comes, and jars two hemispheres.
1912   1912, 1914

Ah, Are You Digging on My Grave?

"Ah, are you digging on my grave,
    My loved one?—planting rue?"[1]
—"No: yesterday he went to wed
One of the brightest wealth has bred.
'It cannot hurt her now,' he said,   5
    'That I should not be true.' "

"Then who is digging on my grave?
    My nearest dearest kin?"
—"Ah, no: they sit and think, 'What use!
What good will planting flowers produce?   10
No tendance of her mound can loose
    Her spirit from Death's gin.' "[2]

"But someone digs upon my grave?
    My enemy?—prodding sly?"
—"Nay: when she heard you had passed the Gate   15
That shuts on all flesh soon or late,
She thought you no more worth her hate,
    And cares not where you lie."

3. The force (blind, but slowly gaining consciousness throughout history) which drives the world, according to Hardy's philosophy.

1. A yellow-flowered herb, traditionally an emblem of sorrow ("rue" is also an archaic word for "sorrow").
2. Trap.

"Then, who is digging on my grave?
    Say—since I have not guessed!"   20
—"O it is I, my mistress dear,
Your little dog, who still lives near,
And much I hope my movements here
    Have not disturbed your rest?"

"Ah yes! *You* dig upon my grave . . .   25
    Why flashed it not on me
That one true heart was left behind!
What feeling do we ever find
To equal among human kind
    A dog's fidelity!"   30

"Mistress, I dug upon your grave
    To bury a bone, in case
I should be hungry near this spot
When passing on my daily trot.
I am sorry, but I quite forgot   35
    It was your resting place."

1914

Under the Waterfall

"Whenever I plunge my arm, like this,
In a basin of water, I never miss
The sweet sharp sense of a fugitive day
Fetched back from its thickening shroud of gray.
    Hence the only prime   5
    And real love-rhyme
    That I know by heart,
    And that leaves no smart,
Is the purl of a little valley fall
About three spans wide and two spans tall   10
Over a table of solid rock,
And into a scoop of the self-same block;
The purl of a runlet that never ceases
In stir of kingdoms, in wars, in peaces;
With a hollow boiling voice it speaks   15
And has spoken since hills were turfless peaks."

"And why gives this the only prime
Idea to you of a real love rhyme?
And why does plunging your arm in a bowl
Full of spring water, bring throbs to your soul?"   20

"Well, under the fall, in a crease of the stone,
Though where precisely none ever has known,
Jammed darkly, nothing to show how prized,
And by now with its smoothness opalized,

Is a drinking glass: 25
For, down that pass
My lover and I
Walked under a sky
Of blue with a leaf-wove awning of green,
In the burn of August, to paint the scene, 30
And we placed our basket of fruit and wine
By the runlet's rim, where we sat to dine;
And when we had drunk from the glass together,
Arched by the oak-copse from the weather,
I held the vessel to rinse in the fall, 35
Where it slipped, and sank, and was past recall,
Though we stooped and plumbed the little abyss
With long bared arms. There the glass still is.
And, as said, if I thrust my arm below
Cold water in basin or bowl, a throe 40
From the past awakens a sense of that time,
And the glass we used, and the cascade's rhyme.
The basin seems the pool, and its edge
The hard smooth face of the brookside ledge,
And the leafy pattern of chinaware 45
The hanging plants that were bathing there.

"By night, by day, when it shines or lours,
There lies intact that chalice of ours,
And its presence adds to the rhyme of love
Persistently sung by the fall above. 50
No lip has touched it since his and mine
In turns therefrom sipped lovers' wine."

1914

The Walk

You did not walk with me
Of late to the hilltop tree
By the gated ways,
As in earlier days;
You were weak and lame, 5
So you never came,
And I went alone, and I did not mind,
Not thinking of you as left behind.

I walked up there today
Just in the former way; 10
Surveyed around
The familiar ground
By myself again:
What difference, then?
Only that underlying sense 15
Of the look of a room on returning thence.

1914

During Wind and Rain

They sing their dearest songs—
He, she, all of them—yea,
Treble and tenor and bass,
    And one to play;
With the candles mooning each face. . . .   5
    Ah, no; the years O!
How the sick leaves reel down in throngs!

They clear the creeping moss—
Elders and juniors—aye,
Making the pathways neat   10
    And the garden gay;
And they build a shady seat. . . .
    Ah, no; the years, the years;
See, the white stormbirds wing across!

They are blithely breakfasting all—   15
Men and maidens—yea,
Under the summer tree,
    With a glimpse of the bay,
While pet fowl come to the knee. . . .
    Ah, no; the years O!   20
And the rotten rose is ripped from the wall.

They change to a high new house,
He, she, all of them—aye,
Clocks and carpets and chairs
    On the lawn all day,
And brightest things that are theirs. . . .   25
    Ah, no; the years, the years;
Down their carved names the raindrop plows.

                                              1917

In Time of "The Breaking of Nations"[1]

1
Only a man harrowing clods
    In a slow silent walk
With an old horse that stumbles and nods
    Half asleep as they stalk.

2
Only thin smoke without flame   5
    From the heaps of couch-grass;
Yet this will go onward the same
    Though Dynasties pass.

3
Yonder a maid and her wight
    Come whispering by;   10
War's annals will cloud into night
    Ere their story die.

1915   1916

1. Cf. "Thou art my battle ax and weapons of war: for with thee will I break in pieces the nations" (Jeremiah li.20). The poem was written during World War I.

He Never Expected Much

[OR]

A CONSIDERATION
[A *reflection*] ON MY EIGHTY-SIXTH BIRTHDAY

Well, World, you have kept faith with me,
　　Kept faith with me;
Upon the whole you have proved to be
　　Much as you said you were.
Since as a child I used to lie　　　　　　　　　5
Upon the leaze[2] and watch the sky,
Never, I own, expected I
　　That life would all be fair.

'Twas then you said, and since have said,
　　Times since have said,　　　　　　　　　10
In that mysterious voice you shed
　　From clouds and hills around:
"Many have loved me desperately,
Many with smooth serenity,
While some have shown contempt of me　　15
　　Till they dropped underground.

"I do not promise overmuch,
　　Child; overmuch;
Just neutral-tinted haps and such,"
　　You said to minds like mine.　　　　　　20
Wise warning for your credit's sake!
Which I for one failed not to take,
And hence could stem such strain and ache
　　As each year might assign.

1928

2. Pasture.

GERARD MANLEY HOPKINS
(1844–1889)

1866: Joins the Roman Catholic Church.
1877: Ordained.
1918: Posthumous publication of his poems by Bridges.

Gerard Manley Hopkins was educated at Highgate School, London, and at Balliol College, Oxford, where he studied classics and was influenced by the Oxford Movement, that revival of the ritualistic and dogmatic side of Christianity which began as a movement within the Church of England but which ended by taking many of its adherents, including the leading figure in the movement, John Henry Newman, to the Roman Catholic Church. After a period of spiritual turmoil Hopkins joined the Roman Catholic Church in 1866, sponsored by Newman, and two years later entered the Society of Jesus. He was ordained in 1877, and after serving as priest in a number of parishes, including one in a working-class area of Liverpool where the squalor disturbed him deeply, he was in 1884 appointed Professor of Classics at University College, Dublin.

A devoted Jesuit performing faithfully the duties assigned to him by his superiors, Hopkins was also a sensitive poet fascinated by language and rhythm and a passionately keen observer of the color and form and detail of the world of nature. The claims of religion and the duties of his religious profession were paramount, but his aesthetic interests (which included an interest in painting and music) asserted themselves with sometimes painful force, and it was not always easy for him to reconcile his religious vocation with his poetic genius. Before entering the Society of Jesus he burned his finished poems (though working copies survive) and did not write poetry again until late in 1875 or early in 1876. Hopkins went through periods of deep depression, of a listless sense of failure, and of that deep spiritual emptiness which mystics know as "the dark night of the soul" and see as one of the necessary stages on the road to spiritual fulfillment. This mood of spiritual desolation is expressed in the so-called "terrible sonnets," written between 1885 and 1889. But Hopkins also enjoyed moods of intense pleasure in the natural world, linked with a profound sense of natural beauty as a reflection of divine reality, and it is this combination of the most passionate and particularized apprehension of the sounds, shapes, and colors of the English countryside with the religious awareness of God as revealed through these sounds, shapes and colors, that is the theme of much of his poetry.

Hopkins' poems were never published in his lifetime. In spite of his eager interest in poetry and in technical problems of writing verse—an interest which is reflected in all its variety and intensity in the letters he wrote to his friends Robert Bridges (later poet laureate) and R. W. Dixon—Hopkins subordinated his poetry to his duties as a Jesuit and never sought any public fame as a poet. He resisted the suggestion made by Bridges and others in 1879 that he publish some of his poems, as he felt that his religious superiors would not approve. It is doubtful in any case whether his poetry would have been appreciated or even understood in the 19th century, for it flouted most of the contemporary expectations of what poetry should be. One of his aims was to rejuvenate the language of poetry, and he did so in a variety of ways. Sometimes he placed a familiar and much-used word in a new and startling context to bring out a lost aspect of its original meaning (e.g., addressing God as "sir" in *Thou Art Indeed Just, Lord*); sometimes he revived older words or used dialect words or phrases (such as "all road ever" in *Felix Randal*); sometimes he coined new words on the analogy of existing ones (e.g., "leafmeal" in *Spring and Fall*). He also employed devices found in other poetic modes, such as Anglo-Saxon and Welsh, to find new ways of giving exact and arresting expression to an impression or an idea or a combination of both; and he used unusual combinations of words and unusual word order to achieve the exact curve of the meaning. His study of the medieval philosopher Duns Scotus had encouraged this interest in "individuation" or "this-ness" (*haecceitas*) as a clue to the nature of reality. The essential inward pattern of the expression, what he called "inscape," was his primary concern. "No doubt," he wrote to Bridges, "my poetry errs on the side of oddness * * * but as air, melody, is what strikes me most of all in music and design in painting, so design, pattern, or what I am in the habit of calling 'inscape' is what I above all aim at in poetry. Now it is the virtue of design, pattern, or inscape to be distinctive and it is the vice of distinctiveness to become queer. This vice I cannot have escaped." Bridges, though recognizing his friend's genius, was often more aware of the oddness than of the distinctiveness; a later generation, reacting against the mellifluous poeticizings of an attenuated Romantic tradition, saw in the power and originality of Hopkins' expression not only something tremendously impressive in itself but also an invitation to experiment in new uses of language and new poetic rhythms.

Hopkins' interest in rhythms was as great as his interest in words. In his letters he developed a theory of "sprung rhythm" which broke away from the standard conception of poetic rhythms as consisting of a number of metrical feet, each having a fixed number of syllables, some stressed and some unstressed, with a limited number of possible variations and substitutions. Intead, he saw rhythm in poetry as much more flexible, much more like time and tempo in music, where the rhythmic effects are controlled by the number of beats in the measure (rather than the number of notes) and the general pattern of rising or falling movement. He also experimented with various ways of running lines into each other and of manipulating groups of "slack" or unaccented syllables within the line. He often used accent marks, which draw the reader's attention to the way the stresses fall in the line. All these devices help to produce his characteristic "sprung rhythm," which gives his poetry a different sound from that of other Victorian verse, a sound in many respects more like that of English and American poetry since Eliot.

The remarkable swinging movement of the opening of *The Windhover* is a characteristic triumph of Hopkins' rhythmic effects. He called the rhythm here "falling," meaning that the stress comes first in each foot. (The first word, "I," is conceived of as an introductory light beat outside the main movement of the line.) Hopkins himself scanned the first four lines in this way:

> I caught this morning morning's minion, king-
>
>   dom of daylight's dauphin, dapple-dawn-drawn Falcon, in his riding
>
> Of the rolling level underneath him steady air, and striding
>
> High there, how he rung upon the rein of a wimpling wing * * *

The stressed syllables are marked /, while the curved line underneath a syllable marks what he called "hangers" or "outriders," which he defined as "one, two, or three slack syllables added to a foot and not counted in the nominal scanning." He remarked elsewhere that "the strong syllable in an outriding foot has always a great stress and after the outrider follows a short pause." Thus the first syllable in "dauphin" and in "Falcon" is marked with a double stress-mark. The curious plunging effect which this rhythm achieves—reproducing so effectively the movement of the bird which is being described—is heightened by the sense of urgent forward movement achieved by splitting "kingdom" between two lines and rhyming the first syllable ("king-") with the unstressed syllable "ing" of "riding" in the next line as well as, more obviously, with "wing" in line 4. The hyphenating of groups of words, as in "dapple-dawn-drawn," is another common device of Hopkins: it can achieve a variety of effects, with each word in the hyphenated group modifying and coloring the other to achieve a simultaneous blend of meaning both more immediate and more subtle in its impact on the reader than the same words could produce if linked more conventionally by conjunctions. Hopkins always tried to squeeze all water out of his language, to avoid all unnecessary words that are required only as grammatical signs and so are liable to dissipate the meaning. To concentrate meaning (so that when the poem is finally made out its meaning "explodes," as he once put it) rather than to dissipate it was always Hopkins' aim.

Other devices used by Hopkins include patterns of alliteration (e.g., *God's Grandeur*, line 3: "It gathers to a greatness, like the ooze of oil"); internal rhymes (line 6: "And all is *seared* with trade; *bleared, smeared* with toil"); varieties of assonance (lines 11–14: "West," "went," "breast"); and different kinds of sound patterns which he adapted from the traditions of Welsh poetry.

In its kind of imagery, too, and in the way in which the imagery works, Hopkins' poetry differs sharply from that of, say, Tennyson or Rossetti. In such a poem as *The Starlight Night* we are struck not only by the arresting imperatives with which it opens and the echoes of Anglo-Saxon poetic devices in "fire-folk" and "circle-citadel" but also by the remarkable way in which excitement at an aspect of the natural world moves into a religious affirmation. This is achieved partly by a punning use of language unknown in serious English poetry since the 17th century. In line 13, for example, the harvested sheaves ("shocks") are to be safely housed in the barn. But "shocks" also suggests the other and more familiar sense of the word—"the thousand natural shocks that flesh is heir to" (*Hamlet*). By buying the beauty of nature with prayer (lines 8 ff.), we learn to see God in nature and to possess both nature and God. Thus by "owning" nature we have a home for it—and for ourselves, protecting both the "shocks" of corn and ourselves from the shocks of life. At the conclusion Christ and his saints are brought into this communion of the sheltered and protected: it becomes now the communion of saints and that, we now learn, is what "the fire-folk sitting in the air" really suggested. And what other 19th-century poet would have used the language of the auction room in talking of the beauty of nature and its relation to religious practices? ("Buy then! bid then!—What?—Prayer, patience, alms, vows.")

This combination of the startlingly colloquial and the strikingly unusual is an important feature of Hopkins' poetry. *The Lantern Out of Doors* begins with a simple, colloquial use of English ("And who goes there? / I think * * * "). The surface thought is also simple: we meet people in daily life who interest us momentarily, but our paths cross briefly and they disappear and we forget about them, because "out of sight is out of mind" (and notice the way Hopkins introduces a homely proverb here). Christ, on the other hand, never forgets people; He is always interested in them; He is their ransom, their rescue, and their eternal friend. There is, however, much more than this in the poem. The word "interests" in line 2 is not a normal poetic word; it arrests us by its very ordinariness. As the

poem develops, it comes to suggest not only its obvious, primary meaning but its financial meaning (as in "to lend at interest"). The thought
is: people whose character makes them valuable pass by but soon disappear
when they are bought by death or distance. Although death or distance
buys or consumes them, so that they are lost to sight, Christ continues to
"mind" them—in the sense (still common in Scotland) of "remember"
them as well as "look after" them, as a man minds his property. Christ's
interest is their *ransom*: the implication is that Christ gives the interest
on his property to ransom man—but of course the word "interest" is also
used in its more obvious meaning. Or consider lines 5 and following. The
sense is that men beautiful in "mould" (shape) disappear in the "mould"
(the earth of the grave): their very beauty suggests their mortality. Or we
could follow out the double meaning of "kind" in the phrase "foot follows kind." This combination of the colloquial and the formal, the building up of complex patterns of meaning through the multiple suggestiveness given to words in their poetic context, is what so excited 20th-century
poets when they discovered Hopkins.

This discovery was made in 1918, long after Hopkins' death, when
Bridges first brought out an edition of Hopkins' poems. By the time the
second edition appeared, with an introduction by Charles Williams, in
1930, Hopkins' position was established; the younger poets, such as W. H.
Auden and later Dylan Thomas, turned to him enthusiastically as one
of their masters. Hopkins is thus in a sense a 20-century poet born out
of his time who had to wait until the present century for posthumous appreciation and influence.

The text of the selections given here follows that of the third edition
of Hopkins' poems (1948), edited by W. H. Gardner, which is now the
standard text.

God's Grandeur

The world is charged with the grandeur of God.
　It will flame out, like shining from shook foil;[1]
　It gathers to a greatness, like the ooze of oil
Crushed.[2] Why do men then now not reck his rod?
Generations have trod, have trod, have trod;　　　　　　　　　　5
　And all is seared with trade; bleared, smeared with toil;
　And wears man's smudge and shares man's smell: the soil
Is bare now, nor can foot feel, being shod.

And for all this, nature is never spent;
　There lives the dearest freshness deep down things;　　　　10
And though the last lights off the black West went
　Oh, morning, at the brown brink eastward, springs—
Because the Holy Ghost over the bent
　World broods with warm breast and with ah! bright wings.

1877　　　　　　　　　　　　　　　　　　　　　　　　1918

---

1. "I mean foil in the sense of leaf or
tinsel * * * Shaken goldfoil gives off
broad glares like sheet lightning and
also, and this is true of nothing else,
owing to its zigzag dints and creasings
and network of small many cornered
facets, a sort of fork lightning too"
(Hopkins, *Letters*).
2. From olives.

The Starlight Night

Look at the stars! look, look up at the skies!
 O look at all the fire-folk sitting in the air!
 The bright boroughs, the circle-citadels there!
Down in dim woods the diamond delves! the elves'-eyes!
The grey lawns cold where gold,[3] where quickgold lies!   5
 Wind-beat whitebeam! airy abeles [4] set on a flare!
 Flake-doves sent floating forth at a farmyard scare!—
Ah well! it is all a purchase, all is a prize.

Buy then! bid then!—What?—Prayer, patience, alms, vows.
Look, look: a May-mess,[5] like on orchard boughs!   10
Look! March-bloom, like on mealed-with-yellow[6] sallows!
These are indeed the barn; withindoors house
 The shocks.[7] This piece-bright paling[8] shuts the spouse
 Christ home, Christ and his mother and all his hallows.[9]

1877   1918

Spring

Nothing is so beautiful as spring—
 When weeds, in wheels, shoot long and lovely and lush;
 Thrush's eggs look little low heavens, and thrush
Through the echoing timber does so rinse and wring
The ear, it strikes like lightnings to hear him sing;   5
 The glassy peartree leaves and blooms, they brush
 The descending blue; that blue is all in a rush
With richness; the racing lambs too have fair their fling.

What is all this juice and all this joy?
 A strain of the earth's sweet being in the beginning   10
In Eden garden.—Have, get, before it cloy,
 Before it cloud, Christ, lord, and sour with sinning,
Innocent mind and Mayday in girl and boy,
 Most, O maid's[1] child, thy choice and worthy the winning. .

1877   1918

3. Dewdrops, referred to also as "quickgold" (a word coined by analogy with "quicksilver" and thus suggesting the gleaming and volatile nature of dewdrops).
4. White poplars.
5. A profusion of May—i.e., suggesting a mass of May blossoms, such as pear blossoms ("like on orchard boughs"). "May" is also another name for the white hawthorn. There may be religious overtones, with "May" suggesting "Mary" (the Virgin) and "mess" suggesting "Mass" (the Catholic rite).
6. Yellow-spotted. "Sallows" are a variety of willow tree.
7. Sheaves of corn: see discussion of this poem in the Hopkins introduction.
8. Fencing. It is "piece-bright," i.e., bright as a gold or silver coin. "Piece" in this sense suggests the thirty pieces of silver for which Judas betrayed Christ: but line 9 implies that we can buy both Christ and the beauty of nature with a very different kind of coin.
9. Saints.
1. The Virgin Mary's. May is a popular form of the word "Mary," so "Mayday" in line 13 also suggests "Mary's day," day of innocence and purity. Cf. note 3 to *The Starlight Night*.

The Lantern Out of Doors

Sometimes a lantern moves along the night,
   That interests our eyes. And who goes there?
   I think; where from and bound, I wonder, where,
With, all down darkness wide, his wading light?

Men go by me whom either beauty bright   5
   In mould or mind or what not else makes rare:
   They rain against our much-thick and marsh air
Rich beams, till death or distance buys them quite.

Death or distance soon consumes them: wind
   What most I may eye after,[2] be in at the end   10
I cannot, and out of sight is out of mind.

Christ minds; Christ's interest, what to avow or amend
   There, éyes them, heart wánts, care haúnts, foot fóllows kínd,
  Their ránsom, théir rescue, ánd first, fást, last friénd.[3]

1877   1918

The Windhover[1]

TO CHRIST OUR LORD

I caught this morning morning's minion,[2] king-
   dom of daylight's dauphin,[3] dapple-dawn-drawn Falcon, in
     his riding
Of the rolling level underneath him steady air, and striding
High there, how he rung upon the rein[4] of a wimpling wing
In his ecstasy! then off, off forth on swing,
   As a skate's heel sweeps smooth on a bow-bend: the hurl
     and gliding   5

2. **W. H. Gardner** notes that the entire verb in this passage is "wind eye after." "I mean that the eye winds only in the sense that its focus or point of sight winds and that coincides with a point of the object and winds with that. For the object, a lantern passing further and further away and bearing now east now west of one right line, is truly and properly described as winding" (Hopkins, *Letters*).

3. For a discussion of the language in this poem, see the Hopkins introduction.

1. Kestrel, called "windhover" because it hovers in the air, head to wind. This poem, which Hopkins considered "the best thing I ever wrote" (*Letters*), has been variously explicated. The main thought seems to be that the ecstatic flying of the bird stirs the poet's heart ("in hiding," for the poet is a priest, with his heart hidden away from earthly things in the service of God). In the combination of beauty, strength, and glory which the poet sees in the bird, he sees an emblem of the beauty, strength, and glory of Christ, whom he addresses as "my chevalier" (line 11). It is "dangerous" to see these qualities in Christ, for we look to Christ for lessons in humility and the enduring of suffering. But it is "no wonder" (lines 12–14) that Christ's humility and suffering are bound up with His glory and pride; many things include their opposites; "sheer plod" can make the ploughshare shine, as it cuts its furrow, and a black coal in a fire can fall over and break and reveal its red-hot interior, its "gold-vermilion" gashes suggesting *both* beauty and pride *and* Christ's wounds and suffering.

2. Darling.

3. Heir (literally, the title of the eldest son of the king of France); the word carries overtones of chivalry and splendor.

4. There is an implied comparison to a horse circling around its trainer at the end of a long rein. "Wimpling": rippling.

Rebuffed the big wind. My heart in hiding
Stirred for a bird,—the achieve of, the mastery of the thing!

Brute beauty and valour and act, oh, air, pride, plume, here
  Buckle![5] AND[6] the fire that breaks from thee then, a billion   10
Times told lovelier, more dangerous, O my chevalier!

No wonder of it: shéer plód makes plough down sillion[7]
Shine, and blue-bleak embers, ah my dear,
  Fall, gall themselves, and gash gold-vermilion.

1877   1918

Pied Beauty

Glory be to God for dappled things—
  For skies of couple-colour as a brinded[1] cow;
    For rose-moles all in stipple[2] upon trout that swim;
Fresh-firecoal chestnut-falls;[3] finches' wings;
  Landscape plotted and pieced[4]—fold, fallow, and plough; 5
  And áll trádes, their gear and tackle and trim.[5]

All things counter,[6] original, spare, strange;
  Whatever is fickle, freckled (who knows how?)
    With swift, slow; sweet, sour; adazzle, dim;
He fathers-forth whose beauty is past change: 10
           Praise him.

1877   1918

Hurrahing in Harvest

Summer ends now; now, barbarous in beauty, the stocks[7] arise
  Around; up above, what wind-walks! what lovely
    behaviour
Of silk-sack clouds! has wilder, wilful-wavier
Meal-drift moulded ever and melted across skies?

I walk, I lift up, I lift up heart, eyes,   5
  Down all that glory in the heavens to glean our Saviour;
    And, éyes, heárt, what looks, what lips yet gave you a
Rapturous love's greeting of realer, of rounder replies?

5. The obvious sense here is "join," though some critics have understood it as "bend" or "break" and some have taken it as an imperative in that sense. But see note 1. Hopkins is celebrating the point at which animal beauty, strength, bearing, and fine display all join.

6. Hopkins emphasizes the "AND" to draw attention from the admiration of the bird to the sense of Christ behind it which that admiration brings. A movement from appreciation of the life of nature to a religious sense of the God reflected in nature is found in very many of Hopkins' poems.

7. The ridge between two furrows of a plowed field. Hopkins uses this archaic word perhaps to suggest an over-tone from "silica" (the mineral which in the form of gleaming particles of quartz often makes dull rocks shine).

1. Brindled, streaked.
2. Dots or small spots.
3. Chestnuts stripped of their husks after being roasted in "fresh-firecoal."
4. Divided into rectangles of different colors, as the English landscape appears. "Fold": enclosure for animals; "fallow": a field plowed but left unsown for a season.
5. Equipment.
6. Contrary, i.e., in contrasted patterns or colors. "Spare": rare.
7. Stooks (or shocks: see "The Starlight Night") are sheaves of corn placed upright, supporting each other at an angle, for drying.

And the azurous hung hills are his world-wielding shoulder
    Majestic—as a stallion stalwart, very-violet-sweet!—   10
These things, these things were here and but the beholder
    Wanting; which two when they once meet,
The heart rears wings bold and bolder
    And hurls for him, O half hurls earth for him off under
        his feet.

1877   1918

Binsey Poplars

FELLED 1879

My aspens dear, whose airy cages quelled,
Quelled or quenched in leaves the leaping sun,
All felled, felled, are all felled;
    Of a fresh and following folded rank[1]
        Not spared, not one   5
          That dandled a sandalled
        Shadow that swam or sank
On meadow and river and wind-wandering weed-winding bank.
    O if we but knew what we do
        When we delve[2] or hew—   10
      Hack and rack[3] the growing green!
        Since country is so tender
        To touch, her being só slender,
      That, like this sleek and seeing ball[4]
      But a prick will make no eye at all,   15
    Where we, even where we mean
          To mend her we end her,
        When we hew or delve:
After-comers cannot guess the beauty been.
    Ten or twelve, only ten or twelve   20
      Strokes of havoc únselve[5]
        The sweet especial scene,
      Rural scene, a rural scene,
      Sweet especial rural scene.

1879   1918

Duns Scotus's Oxford[6]

Towery city and branchy between towers;
Cuckoo-echoing, bell-swarmèd, lark-charmèd, rook-racked, river-
    rounded;

1. Row of trees with alternate trees set off at an angle, making the row "folded."
2. Dig.
3. Torture.
4. The eye.
5. Rob it of its "self" or individuality.
6. Duns Scotus, the 13th-century Scholastic philosopher, is supposed to have taught at Oxford ca. 1301. Hopkins admired him greatly; when he came upon two of Scotus's commentaries in 1872 he was "flush with a new stroke of enthusiasm. * * * When I took in any inscape of the sky or sea I thought of Scotus" (*Note-books*). In this poem he builds up an impression of medieval Oxford, then links this to Scotus through himself ("this air I gather and I release / He lived on") to end with a tribute to him.

The dapple-eared lily below thee; that country and town did
Once encounter in, here coped[7] and poisèd powers;

Thou hast a base and brickish skirt[8] there, sours 5
That neighbour-nature thy grey beauty is grounded
Best in; graceless growth, thou hast confounded
Rural rural keeping[9]—folk, flocks, and flowers.

Yet ah! this air I gather and I release
He lived on; these weeds and waters, these walls are what 10
He haunted who of all men most sways my spirits to peace;

Of realty[1] the rarest-veinèd unraveller; a not
Rivalled insight, be rival Italy or Greece;
Who fired France for Mary without spot.[2]
1879   1918

Felix Randal

Felix Randal the farrier,[1] O he is dead then? my duty all ended,
Who have watched his mould of man, big-boned and hardy-hand-
        some
Pining, pining, till time when reason rambled in it and some
Fatal four disorders, fleshed there, all contended?

Sickness broke him. Impatient he cursed at first, but mended 5
Being anointed and all; though a heavenlier heart began some
Months earlier, since I had our sweet reprieve and ransom
Tendered to him.[2] Ah well, God rest him all road ever[3] he offended!

This seeing the sick endears them to us, us too it endears.
My tongue had taught thee comfort, touch had quenched thy
        tears,   10
Thy tears that touched my heart, child, Felix, poor Felix Randal;

How far from then forethought of, all thy more boisterous years,
When thou at the random[4] grim forge, powerful amidst peers,
Didst fettle[5] for the great grey drayhorse his bright and battering
        sandal!
1880   1918

Spring and Fall

TO A YOUNG CHILD

Márgarét, are you grieving
Over Goldengrove unleaving?

7. Set off one against the other.
8. Refers to the appearance of 19th-century brick houses in north Oxford. Note the characteristic omission of the relative pronoun before "sours."
9. I.e., you have spoiled the effect of a rural city presiding over its rural environment.
1. Reality.
2. Reference to Scotus's work in spreading the cult of the Virgin Mary in France.
1. Blacksmith.
2. Had heard his confession and given him absolution.
3. In whatever way.
4. Built with stones of irregular shapes and sizes.
5. Prepare.

Leáves, líke the things of man, you
With your fresh thoughts care for, can you?
Áh! ás the heart grows older   5
It will come to such sights colder
By and by, nor spare a sigh
Though worlds of wanwood leafmeal[6] lie;
And yet you wíll weep and know why.
Now no matter, child, the name: 10
Sórrow's spríngs áre the same.
Nor mouth had, no nor mind, expressed
What heart heard of, ghost guessed: [7]
It ís the blight man was born for,
It is Margaret you mourn for.   15

1880   1918

Inversnaid [8]

This darksome burn,[9] horseback brown,
His rollrock highroad roaring down,
In coop and in comb [1] the fleece of his foam
Flutes and low to the lake falls home.

A windpuff-bonnet of fáwn-fróth   5
Turns and twindles [2] over the broth
Of a pool so pitchblack, féll-frówning,
It rounds and rounds Despair to drowning.

Degged [3] with dew, dappled with dew
Are the groins of the braes [4] that the brook treads through, 10
Wiry heathpacks, flitches [5] of fern,
And the beadbonny ash that sits over the burn.

What would the world be, once bereft
Of wet and of wildness? Let them be left,
O let them be left, wildness and wet;   15
Long live the weeds and the wilderness yet.

1881   1918

---

6. "I take *wanwood* to be a noun (the meaning 'bloodless' being combined with the older meaning 'dark,' 'livid' —O.E. *wann*). *Leafmeal* I take for an adverb, made 'by substitution' from *piecemeal* on the analogy of Shakespeare's *inch-meal* and *limb-meal:* hence it suggests the leaves falling one by one, then rotting to form pale, mealy fragments" [W. H. Gardner's note].

7. "*Ghost*, spirit (of the living), with a proleptic suggestion of 'phantom'— the living spirit foreknowing, through sensory experience, its own state after death. Lines 8 and 14 connect the Fall of the Leaf with the Fall of Man: 'and unto dust shalt thou return' (Genesis iii.18)" [W. H. Gardner's note].

8. On Loch Lomondside, Scotland, famous for its rushing stream and waterfall.

9. Stream.

1. "Coop": hollow; "comb": crest.

2. Apparently Hopkins' coinage: twists and dwindles.

3. Sprinkled.

4. Hills.

5. Tufts, clumps.

[Carrion Comfort] [6]

Not, I'll not, carrion comfort, Despair, not feast on thee;
Not untwist—slack they may be—these last strands of man
In me ór, most weary, cry *I can no more*. I can;
Can something, hope, wish day come, not choose not to be.
But ah, but O thou terrible, why wouldst thou rude on me   5
Thy wring-world right foot rock? [7] lay a lionlimb against me? scan
With darksome devouring eyes my bruisèd bones? and fan,
O in turns of tempest, me heaped there; me frantic to avoid thee
    and flee?

  Why? That my chaff might fly; my grain lie, sheer and clear.
Nay in all that toil, that coil, [8] since (seems) I kissed the rod,   10
Hand rather, my heart lo! lapped strength, stole joy, would laugh,
    chéer.
Cheer whom though? the hero whose heaven-handling flung me,
    fóot tród
Me? or me that fought him? O which one? is it each one? That
    night, that year
Of now done darkness I wretch lay wrestling with (my God!) my
    God.

1885   1918

[No Worst, There Is None] [9]

No worst, there is none. Pitched past pitch of grief,
More pangs will, schooled at forepangs, wilder wring.
Comforter, where, where is your comforting?
Mary, mother of us, where is your relief?
My cries heave, herds-long, [1] huddle in a main, a chief   5
Woe, world-sorrow; on an age-old anvil wince and sing—
Then lull, then leave off. Fury had shrieked "No ling-
ering! Let me be fell: [2] force I must be brief."

  O the mind, mind has mountains; cliffs of fall
Frightful, sheer, no-man-fathomed. Hold them cheap   10
May who ne'er hung there. Nor does long our small
Durance [3] deal with that steep or deep. Here! creep,
Wretch, under a comfort serves in a whirlwind: all
Life death does end and each day dies with sleep.

1885   1918

<hr>

6. Title supplied by Bridges in the 1918 edition. This is one of the "terrible sonnets," as are the two poems that follow.
7. Why wouldst thou turn roughly against me with thy right foot that wrings the world?
8. Disturbance.
9. Untitled by Hopkins. Cf. the description of "desolation" in the *Spiritual Exercises* of St. Ignatius Loyola, founder of the Jesuit order: "a darkening of the soul, trouble of mind, movement to base and earthly things,

restlessness of various agitations and temptations, moving to distrust, loss of hope, loss of love; when the soul feels herself thoroughly apathetic, sad, and as it were separated from her Creator and Lord."
1. Coming in large numbers and in a long series, like herds of cattle following each other. "Main" (like "chief") is an adjective, qualifying "woe."
2. Fierce. "Force" means here "perforce."
3. Endurance.

[Thou Art Indeed Just, Lord]

Justus quidem tu es, Domine, si disputem tecum: verumtamen
justa loquar ad te: Quare via impiorum prosperatur? etc.[4]

Thou art indeed just, Lord, if I contend
With thee; but, sir, so what I plead is just.
Why do sinners' ways prosper? and why must
Disappointment all I endeavour end?
   Wert thou my enemy, O thou my friend,   5
How wouldst thou worse, I wonder, than thou dost
Defeat, thwart me? Oh, the sots and thralls of lust
Do in spare hours more thrive than I that spend,
Sir, life upon thy cause. See, banks and brakes[5]
Now, leavèd how thick! lacèd they are again   10
With fretty[6] chervil, look, and fresh wind shakes
Them; birds build—but not I build; no, but strain,
Time's eunuch, and not breed one work that wakes.
Mine,[7] O thou lord of life, send my roots rain.

1889   1918

4. The Latin is the Vulgate version of Jeremiah xii.1, which reads in the King James version: "Righteous art thou, O Lord, when I plead with thee: yet let me talk with thee of thy judgments: Wherefore doth the way of the wicked prosper? * * * " This Latin quotation was Hopkins' title.

5. Clumps of fern.

6. Fretted, with interlacing pattern. "Chervil" is a member of the parsley family.

7. "Mine" may refer to "roots," emphasizing that the poet wants God to send "*my* roots rain" since every other creature is flourishing, or it may mean "my God."

GEORGE BERNARD SHAW
(1856–1950)

1876: Settles in London.
1892: *Widowers' Houses* produced.
1898: Publication of *Plays Pleasant and Unpleasant*.
1923: *Saint Joan*.

Bernard Shaw was born in Dublin of English stock, one of the galaxy of Anglo-Irishmen (they include Swift, Sheridan, Edmund Burke, and Yeats) who have contributed so brilliantly to English literature. He left school at the age of 14 and worked for five years (1871–76) in a land agent's office. He went to London in 1876, his mother having settled there in order to improve her prospects as a music teacher, and began his literary career as a writer of unsuccessful novels. He soon became interested in social reform: in 1884 he was one of the founders of the Fabian Society, an organization dedicated to the promotion of socialism by gradual stages. Although he was friendly with the most important socialist thinkers in England in the late 19th century, including Sidney and Beatrice Webb and William Morris, Shaw was never a conventional socialist. His social and political attitude was affected by his belief in an active and individually *willed* kind of evolution, urged on by what he called the Life Force, and by his admiration of vitality and power. He inherited from his gifted mother a love of music and learned from her to know and admire Mozartian opera; he also became a great champion of Richard Wagner, and in his regular music criticism, first for the London *Star* and then for the *World*, not only displayed his enthusiasms with lively wit but also introduced a new standard in judging both performers and composers, often mocking conventional taste and fashionable preferences. In 1895 he became dramatic critic for the *Saturday Review* (a London periodical): his deliberately provocative reviews stirred up contemporary English ideas about plays and acting and enlarged the intellectual horizons of his readers. He championed Henrik Ibsen as well as Wagner, and published in 1891 a study of Ibsen entitled *The Quintessence of Ibsenism* which presented the Norwegian dramatist as a realistic and reforming playwright who addressed himself to the problems of modern life and introduced genuine *discussion* in his dialogue. The more profound and symbolic Ibsen whom we admire today was not Shaw's Ibsen, and it is significant that for him the great plays were those which attacked middle-class conventionality and hypocrisy rather than those which probed more subtly and poetically into deeper aspects of experience.

His training in music and dramatic criticism, his interest in social reform, his admiration for Wagner and Ibsen, the influence of Samuel Butler (author of *Erewhon* and *The Way of All Flesh* and the great satirist of Victorian life and thought) helped to make Shaw a playwright who on the one hand knew all the conventional tricks of the theater and on the other was determined to use the drama as he conceived Ibsen to have used it—as a means of shaking theater audiences out of their complacencies, hypocrisies, and thoughtless acquiescence in all kinds of social evil.

Reviewing new plays over a period of years had given Shaw an expert knowledge of the structural devices employed by the authors of the "well-made play" (adroitly plotted theatrical entertainment) of the late 19th century; and when he came to write his own plays he was able to use conventional dramatic structure and even conventional themes for highly unconventional purposes. From the beginning his aim as a dramatist was to shock his audiences into taking a new view of their society and the moral problems that arose out of it. "I must warn my readers," he wrote, "that my attacks are directed against themselves, not against my stage figures." Not only did he delight in standing the popular view on its head, but he went further: beginning by persuading his audience by means of dramatic action and dialogue that the conventional hero was the villain and the conventional villain was the hero, he would swing everything around again to show that the conventional hero was the hero after all, but in a very different sense from that which the audience had originally thought. He followed this pattern in *Man and Superman*, *Major Barbara*, and *Arms and the Man*. He used paradox, both in the action and even more in the dialogue, to dazzle and even bewilder his audiences—only to demonstate that their absurd conventional views and unconscious hypocrisies were responsible for their bewilderment. Having thus destroyed the audience's self-confidence he would organize the dialogue (or sometimes a monologue) in order to allow one of his splendidly vital (but never conventionally heroic) heroes to put across the Shavian vision of society or politics or religion or whatever was the main theme of the play. And all the time he entertained and fascinated by his wit as well as by his sheer sense of fun. Sometimes this sense of fun led him to conclude a serious critical comedy in sheer farce—as in *You Never Can Tell* (1900)—but on the whole Shaw combined entertainment and intellectual provocation to bring a new kind of critical wit into English drama. The wit of Oscar Wilde's comedies had no specific critical implications; it drew on the conventions of society not in order to expose them but in order to get the maximum number of epigrams out of their delightful inconsistencies and absurdities. Shaw's wit was put at the service of a genuine passion for reform, and even if he sometimes assumed the posture of a licensed clown—a posture which members of the public were all too ready to accept as his natural one, for it enabled them to laugh off the disturbing paradoxes he thrust at them—he remained to the end a crusader as well as an entertainer.

Shaw's first play, *Widowers' Houses* (produced in 1892), dealt in a characteristically provocative manner with the problem of slum landlordism: even here, with a subject easily compartmentalized into moral blacks and whites, Shaw's techniques of reversal and inversion keep revealing new aspects of the problem, so that, instead of merely condemning the landlord, the audience is forced to comprehend the entire complex of social and economic conditions that produced the problem. *Mrs. Warren's Profession*, written in 1893, was for a long time banned from the public theater because of its concern with the tabooed subject of prostitution; it is not, however, simply about prostitution, but about well-meaning brothel-keepers and the laws of supply and demand, which it explores with boldness and wit, again substituting the revelation of causes and consequences for simple moral indignation. In 1898 Shaw published *Plays Pleasant and Unpleasant*, with long provocative prefaces attacking a great variety of things, including theatrical censorship; the plays included *Arms and the Man*, *Candida*, *The Man of Destiny*, and (among the "unpleasant") *Widowers' Houses* and *Mrs. Warren's Profession*. Among his later plays, *John Bull's Other Island* (1904) is a characteristic contribution to the discussion of Ireland's grievances against the English; *Man and Superman* (1904) is an ambitious attempt to project through comedy his views of how the Life Force works in ordinary life and contains some brilliant scenes, though the play as a whole is rather too long and too talkative; *The Doctor's Dilemma* (1906) exposes both doctors and artists while exploring some of the moral problems in which they can become involved; *Major Barbara* (1907) shows Shaw's characteristic admiration of success and energy and his contempt for those evangelists who attempt to promote religion by giving soup to the poor instead of trying to convert the strong and successful; *Pygmalion* (1912) is a brilliant exploration of the relation between social class and accent in England, which has since been made into the extraordinarily popular musical comedy, *My Fair Lady*. *Heartbreak House* (1917), subtitled "a fantasia in the Russian manner on English themes," suggests the Russian dramatist Chekhov in its depiction of the imminent collapse of a civilization, but it is essentially Shavian, and the finest example of what Eric Bentley has called the "disquisitory" Shavian play, based on the interplay of ideas in dialogue. *The Apple Cart* (1929) is a paradoxical treatment of the problems of monarchy and democracy done with a mischievous desire to shock equally both Left- and Right-wing thinkers and again shows that admiration of the strong man which is Shaw's personal heresy and goes oddly with his socialism.

Back to Methuselah (1921) was Shaw's most ambitious work, and the one which he considered his masterpiece. But it is in fact the dullest of his plays. Shaw's picture of the Life Force eventually enabling men to improve the human species to the point where they can live long enough to become little more than disembodied intellects reveals a curious coldness and abstraction at the heart of his thought. *Saint Joan* (1923), his one tragedy and often regarded as his finest play, is brilliant in its way, but it is really a comedy containing one tragic scene rather than a tragedy. Shaw had no historical imagination. He makes the past interesting by analogizing it to the present and gets his comic effects by interpreting historical characters as though they were the kind of characters who would be doing the same sort of thing today. The result is often very amusing, but it yields no real insight. Saint Joan as a girl with inspired common sense is a refreshing, funny, and, up to a point, a persuasive portrait—but this portrait is not compatible with the image of Joan as religious martyr, which Shaw does not know how to paint. Similarly, in that most entertaining play *Caesar and Cleopatra* (which is, incidentally, most brilliant theatrically) Shaw's wit takes the form of interpreting the main characters as though they lived in the 19th century. Caesar becomes a 19th-century liberal and his secretary Britannicus is a Victorian Philistine: this gives a kind of reality to the past, but at the cost of losing a dimension.

Shaw's fondness for provoking his audience with paradoxes sometimes led him to introduce elements into his plays that interfere with the clarity of his social message. In *Major Barbara*, for example, he makes abundantly clear his moral disapproval of poverty and his belief in its bad effects on human character—a point of view he found in Samuel Butler and which he developed in political discourses as well as in plays with a very Butleresque kind of wit. He also shows his admiration for energy and success, which he saw as illustrative of the working of the Life Force, which makes for the ultimate improvement of the human species. But he cannot resist making his energetic and successful millionaire also a munitions manufacturer who proudly and belligerently defends his making of destructive weapons of war and his selling them to any group who will buy them, no matter what monstrous slaughter results. The model village that Mr. Undershaft has built for his well-paid workmen shows wealth being put to a good social use, but the paradox of that wealth coming from exultantly manufactured and sold instruments of death remains simply a paradox and is not related to the total pattern of meaning in the play. True, Shaw makes a perfunctory attempt to relate it, but it is not convincing, and the reader or playgoer is struck more with the contrast between the consequences of the production of munitions and the enlightened, liberal, prosperous, contented society which actually produces them than with the logic of choosing a merchant of death as a representative of the Life Force. The fact is that Shaw admired power as such—at different times he professed admiration for Mussolini and Stalin on the grounds that they got things done, and in a broadcast prepared for the BBC but never actually given he professed his admiration for Hitler, except for the matter of his anti-Semitism—and side by side with his hatred of poverty and of everything that weakened and degraded people we also find a positively ruthless contempt for mental and physical inadequacy and a belief, expressed more than once, that those who are inadequate in this way should be painlessly eliminated. (In a letter to the London *Times* of December 5, 1947, Shaw asserted that criminals "should be liquidated humanely, not because they are wicked, but because they are mischievous or dangerous." "A man who lives by promising to marry women and deserting them as soon as he has spent all their money is a social weed to be uprooted no less than if he drowned them in their bath. Dangerous insanity, instead of exempting from liquidation, should be one of the strongest grounds for it.") One cannot help suspecting that in glorifying Andrew Undershaft as a manufacturer of munitions, Shaw is giving rein to this side of his character rather than developing his dramatic argument about the criminality of poverty and the nature of human self-respect. But the dramatic argument is there, impressively and entertainingly deployed, and it is backed up by the Preface he wrote in 1906 for the play's first publication in book form the following year. (It was first performed in 1905.)

Shaw revised the text in 1944 for a screen version, and at the same time he also made some slight alterations to the Preface. The text here printed is the original text of 1907.

Shaw was an ardent believer in spelling reform, and, while awaiting a reformed alphabet and phonetic spelling, introduced some minor simplifications in his own spelling which he insisted on his publishers retaining. These simplifications (omission of the apostrophe in a number of contractions, and the use of widely spaced letters rather than italics to indicate emphasis, for example) are retained in the text here printed.

From Preface to *Major Barbara*

* * * In the millionaire Undershaft I have represented a man who has become intellectually and spiritually as well as practically conscious of the irresistible natural truth which we all abhor and repudiate: to wit, that the greatest of our evils, and the worst of our crimes is poverty, and that our first duty, to which every other consideration should be sacrified, is not to be poor. "Poor but honest," "the respectable poor," and such phrases are as intolerable and as immoral as "drunken but amiable," "fraudulent but a good after-dinner speaker," "splendidly criminal," or the like. Security, the chief pretence of civilization, cannot exist where the worst of dangers, the danger of poverty, hangs over everyone's head, and where the alleged protection of our persons from violence is only an accidental result of the existence of a police force whose real business is to force the poor man to see his children starve whilst idle people overfeed pet dogs with the money that might feed and clothe them.

* * *

But the thoughtless wickedness with which we scatter sentences of imprisonment, torture in the solitary cell and on the plank bed, and flogging, on moral invalids and energetic rebels, is as nothing compared to the silly levity with which we tolerate poverty as if it were either a wholesome tonic for lazy people or else a virtue to be embraced as St Francis embraced it. If a man is indolent, let him be poor. If he is drunken, let him be poor. If he is not a gentleman, let him be poor. If he is addicted to the fine arts or to pure science instead of to trade and finance, let him be poor. If he chooses to spend his urban eighteen shillings a week or his agricultural thirteen shillings a week on his beer and his family instead of saving it up for his old age, let him be poor. Let nothing be done for "the undeserving": let him be poor. Serve him right! Also—somewhat inconsistently—blessed are the poor!

Now what does this Let Him Be Poor mean? It means let him be weak. Let him be ignorant. Let him become a nucleus of disease. Let him be a standing exhibition and example of ugliness and dirt. Let him have rickety children. Let him be cheap and let him drag his fellows down to his own price by selling himself to do their work. Let his habitations turn our cities into poisonous congeries of slums. Let his daughters infect our young men with the diseases of the streets, and his sons revenge him by turning the nation's manhood into scrofula, cowardice, cruelty, hypocrisy, political imbecility, and all the other fruits of oppression and malnutrition. Let the undeserving become still less deserving; and let the deserving lay up for himself, not treasures in heaven, but horrors in hell upon earth. This being so, is it really wise to let him be poor? Would he not do ten times less harm as a prosperous burglar, incendiary, ravisher or murderer, to the utmost limits of humanity's comparatively negligible impulses in these directions? Suppose we were to abolish all penalties for such activities, and decide that poverty is the one thing we will not tolerate—that every adult with less than, say, £365[1] a year, shall be painlessly but inexorably killed, and every hungry half naked child forcibly fattened and clothed, would not that be an enormous improvement on our existing system, which has already destroyed so many civilizations, and is visibly destroying ours in the same way?

* * *

Undershaft, the hero of Major Barbara, is simply a man who, having grasped the fact that poverty is a crime, knows that when society offered him the alternative of poverty or a lucrative trade in death and destruction, it offered him, not a choice between opulent villainy and humble virtue, but between energetic enterprise and cowardly infamy. His conduct stands the Kantian test, which Peter Shirley's does not. Peter Shirley is what we call the honest poor man. Undershaft is what we call the wicked rich one: Shirley is

---

1. A modest but competent income in 1906; in his revised edition of 1944 Shaw changed the figure to £1,000, then worth about $4,000.

Lazarus, Undershaft Dives. Well, the misery of the world is due to the fact that the great mass of men act and believe as Peter Shirley acts and believes. If they acted and believed as Undershaft acts and believes, the immediate result would be a revolution of incalculable beneficence. To be wealthy, says Undershaft, is with me a point of honor for which I am prepared to kill at the risk of my own life. This preparedness is, as he says, the final test of sincerity. * * *

When Major Barbara was produced in London, the second act was reported in an important northern newspaper as a withering attack on the Salvation Army, and the despairing ejaculation of Barbara deplored by a London daily as a tasteless blasphemy. * * * Even the handful of mentally competent critics got into difficulties over my demonstration of the economic deadlock in which the Salvation Army finds itself. Some of them thought that the Army would not have taken money from a distiller and a cannon founder: others thought it should not have taken it: all assumed more or less definitely that it reduced itself to absurdity or hypocrisy by taking it. On the first point the reply of the Army itself was prompt and conclusive. As one of its officers said, they would take money from the devil himself and be only too glad to get it out of his hands and into God's. They gratefully acknowledged that publicans not only give them money but allow them to collect it in the bar—sometimes even when there is a Salvation meeting outside preaching teetotalism. In fact, they questioned the verisimilitude of the play, not because Mrs Baines took the money, but because Barbara refused it.

On the point that the Army ought not to take such money, its justification is obvious. It must take the money because it cannot exist without money, and there is no other money to be had. Practically all the spare money in the country consists of a mass of rent, interest, and profit, every penny of which is bound up with crime, drink, prostitution, disease, and all the evil fruits of poverty, as inextricably as with enterprise, wealth, commercial probity, and national prosperity. The notion that you can earmark certain coins as tainted is an unpractical individualist superstition. None the less the fact that all our money is tainted gives a very severe shock to earnest young souls when some dramatic instance of the taint first makes them conscious of it. When an enthusiastic young clergyman of the Established Church first realizes that the Ecclesiastical Commissioners receive the rents of sporting public houses, brothels, and sweating dens; or that the most generous contributor at his last charity sermon was an employer trading in female labor cheapened by prostitution as unscrupulously as a hotel keeper trades in waiters' labor cheapened by tips, or commissionaries' labor cheapened by pensions; or that the only patron who can afford to rebuild his church or his schools or gives his boys' brigade a gymnasium or a library is the son-in-law of a Chicago meat King, that young clergyman has, like Barbara, a very bad quarter hour. But he cannot help himself by refusing to accept money from anybody except sweet old ladies with independent incomes and lovely ways of life. He has only to follow up the income of the sweet ladies to its industrial source, and there he will find Mrs Warren's profession and the poisonous canned meat and all the rest of it. His own stipend has the same root. He must either share the world's guilt or go to another planet. He must save the world's honor if he is to save his own. This is what all the Churches find just as the Salvation Army and Barbara find it in the play. Her discovery that she is her father's accomplice; that the Salvation Army is the accomplice of the distiller and the dynamite maker; that they can no more escape one another than they can escape the air they breathe; that there is no salvation for them through personal righteousness, but only through the redemption of the whole nation from its vicious, lazy, competitive anarchy. * * *

Let us now return to Bill Walker and his case of conscience against the Salvation Army. Major Barbara, not being a modern Tetzel,[2] or the treasurer of a hospital, refuses to sell absolution to Bill for a sovereign. Unfortunately, what the Army can afford to refuse in the case of Bill Walker, it cannot refuse in the case of Bodger. Bodger is master of the situation because he holds the purse strings. "Strive as you will," says Bodger, in effect: "me you cannot do without. You cannot save Bill Walker without my money." And the Army answers, quite rightly under the circumstances, "We will take money from the devil himself sooner than abandon the work of Salvation." So Bodger pays his conscience-money and gets the absolution that is refused to Bill. In real life Bill would perhaps never know this. But I, the dramatist whose business it is to shew the connexion between things that seem apart and unrelated in the haphazard order of events in real life, have contrived to make it known to Bill, with the result that the Salvation Army loses its hold of him at once.

But Bill may not be lost, for all that. He is still in the grip of the facts and of his own conscience, and may find his taste of blackguardism permanently spoiled. Still, I cannot guarantee that happy ending. Walk through the poorer quarters of our cities on Sunday when the men are not working, but resting and chewing the cud of their reflections. You will find one expression common to every mature face: the expression of cynicism. The discovery made by Bill Walker about the Salvation Army has been made by everyone there. They have found that every man has his price; and they have been

2. Johann Tetzel, ca. 1465–1519. Dominican monk and inquisitor who preached that punishment could be avoided by the purchase of indulgences and brought in much money as a result.

foolishly or corruptly taught to mistrust and despise him for that necessary and salutary condition of social existence. * * *

If a man cannot look evil in the face without illusion, he will never know what it really is, or combat it effectually. The few men who have been able (relatively) to do this have been called cynics, and have sometimes had an abnormal share of evil in themselves, corresponding to the abnormal strength of their minds; but they have never done mischief unless they intended to do it. That is why great scoundrels have been beneficent rulers whilst amiable and privately harmless monarchs have ruined their countries by trusting to the hocus-pocus of innocence and guilt, reward and punishment, virtuous indignation and pardon, instead of standing up to the facts without either malice or mercy. Major Barbara stands up to Bill Walker in that way, with the result that the ruffian who cannot get hated, has to hate himself. To relieve this agony he tries to get punished; but the Salvationist whom he tries to provoke is as merciless as Barbara, and only prays for him. Then he tries to pay, but can get nobody to take his money. His doom is the doom of Cain,[3] who, failing to find either a savior, a policeman, or an almoner to help him to pretend that his brother's blood no longer cried from the ground, had to live and die a murderer. Cain took care not to commit another murder, unlike our railway shareholders (I am one) who kill and maim shunters by hundreds to save the cost of automatic couplings, and make atonement by annual subscriptions to deserving charities. Had Cain been allowed to pay off his score, he might possibly have killed Adam and Eve for the mere sake of a second luxurious reconciliation with God afterwards. Bodger, you may depend on it, will go on to the end of his life poisoning people with bad whisky, because he can always depend on the Salvation Army or the Church of England to negotiate a redemption for him in consideration of a trifling percentage of his profits.

There is a third condition too, which must be fulfilled before the great teachers of the world will cease to scoff at its religions. Creeds must become intellectually honest. At present there is not a single credible established religion in the world. That is perhaps the most stupendous fact in the whole world-situation. This play of mine, Major Barbara, is, I hope, both true and inspired; but whoever says that it all happened, and that faith in it and understanding of it consist in believing that it is a record of an actual occurrence, is, to speak according to Scripture, a fool and a liar, and is hereby solemnly denounced and cursed as such by me, the author, to all posterity.

London, June 1906.

3. See Genesis iv.10–15.

Major Barbara

Act I

It is after dinner in January 1906, in the library in Lady Britomart Undershaft's house in Wilton Crescent.[1] *A large and comfortable settee is in the middle of the room, upholstered in dark leather. A person sitting on it (it is vacant at present) would have, on his right, Lady Britomart's writing-table, with the lady herself busy at it; a smaller writing-table behind him on his left; the door behind him on Lady Britomart's side; and a window with a window-seat directly on his left. Near the window is an armchair.*

Lady Britomart is a woman of fifty or thereabouts, well dressed and yet careless of her dress, well bred and quite reckless of her breeding, well mannered and yet appallingly outspoken and indifferent to the opinion of her interlocutors, amiable and yet peremptory, arbitrary, and high-tempered to the last bearable degree, and withal a very typical managing matron of the upper class, treated as a naughty child until she grew into a scolding mother, and finally settling down with plenty of practical ability and worldly experience, limited in the oddest way with domestic and class limitations, conceiving the universe exactly as if it were a large house in Wilton Crescent, though handling her corner of it very effectively on that assumption, and being quite enlightened and liberal as to the books in the library, the pictures on the walls, the music in the portfolios, and the articles in the papers.

Her son, Stephen, comes in. He is a gravely correct young man under 25, taking himself very seriously, but still in some awe of his mother, from childish habit and bachelor shyness rather than from any weakness of character.

STEPHEN. Whats the matter?

LADY BRITOMART. Presently,[2] Stephen.

Stephen submissively walks to the settee and sits down. He takes up a Liberal weekly called The Speaker.

LADY BRITOMART. Dont begin to read, Stephen. I shall require all your attention.

STEPHEN. It was only while I was waiting—

LADY BRITOMART. Dont makes excuses, Stephen. [*He puts down The Speaker*]. Now! [*She finishes her writing; rises; and comes to the settee*]. I have not kept you waiting v e r y long, I think.

STEPHEN. Not at all, mother.

LADY BRITOMART. Bring me my cushion. [*He takes the cushion from the chair at the desk and arranges it for her as she sits down on the settee*]. Sit down. [*He sits down and fingers his tie nervously*]. Dont fiddle with your tie, Stephen: there is nothing the matter with it.

1. A street in the fashionable residential district of Belgravia, in southwest London.
2. Shortly, in a few minutes. This is still the normal British sense of the word, rather than the meaning "at present," regarded in Britain as an Americanism.

STEPHEN. I beg your pardon. [*He fiddles with his watch chain instead*].

LADY BRITOMART. Now are you attending to me, Stephen?

STEPHEN. Of course, mother.

LADY BRITOMART. No: it's n o t of course. I want something much more than your everyday matter-of-course attention. I am going to speak to you very seriously, Stephen. I wish you would let that chain alone.

STEPHEN. [*hastily relinquishing the chain*] Have I done anything to annoy you, mother? If so, it was quite unintentional.

LADY BRITOMART. [*astonished*] Nonsense! [*With some remorse*] My poor boy, did you think I was angry with you?

STEPHEN. What is it, then, mother? You are making me very uneasy.

LADY BRITOMART. [*squaring herself at him rather aggressively*] Stephen: may I ask how soon you intend to realize that you are a grown-up man, and that I am only a woman?

STEPHEN. [*amazed*] Only a—

LADY BRITOMART. Dont repeat my words, please: it is a most aggravating habit. You must learn to face life seriously, Stephen. I really cannot bear the whole burden of our family affairs any longer. You must advise me: you must assume the responsibility.

STEPHEN. I!

LADY BRITOMART. Yes, you, of course. You were 24 last June. Youve been at Harrow[3] and Cambridge. Youve been to India and Japan. You must know a lot of things, now; unless you have wasted your time most scandalously. Well, a d v i s e me.

STEPHEN. [*much perplexed*] You know I have never interfered in the household—

LADY BRITOMART. No: I should think not. I dont want you to order the dinner.

STEPHEN. I mean in our family affairs.

LADY BRITOMART. Well, you must interfere now; for they are getting quite beyond me.

STEPHEN. [*troubled*] I have thought sometimes that perhaps I ought; but really, mother, I know so little about them; and what I do know is so painful—it is so impossible to mention some things to you—[*He stops, ashamed*].

LADY BRITOMART. I suppose you mean your father.

STEPHEN. [*almost inaudibly*] Yes.

LADY BRITOMART. My dear: we cant go on all our lives not mentioning him. Of course you were quite right not to open the subject until I asked you to; but you are old enough now to be taken into my confidence, and to help me to deal with him about the girls.

STEPHEN. But the girls are all right. They are engaged.

LADY BRITOMART. [*complacently*] Yes: I have made a very good match for Sarah. Charles Lomax will be a millionaire at 35. But

---

3. Famous English "public" (i.e., private) school, generally bracketed with Eton as the two most socially desirable of such schools in England.

that is ten years ahead; and in the meantime his trustees cannot under the terms of his father's will allow him more than £800[4] a year.

STEPHEN. But the will says also that if he increases his income by his own exertions, they may double the increase.

LADY BRITOMART. Charles Lomax's exertions are much more likely to decrease his income than to increase it. Sarah will have to find at least another £800 a year for the next ten years; and even then they will be as poor as church mice. And what about Barbara? I thought Barbara was going to make the most brilliant career of all of you. And what does she do? Joins the Salvation Army;[5] discharges her maid; lives on a pound a week; and walks in one evening with a professor of Greek whom she has picked up in the street, and who pretends to be a Salvationist, and actually plays the big drum for her in public because he has fallen head over ears in love with her.

STEPHEN. I was certainly rather taken aback when I heard they were engaged. Cusins is a very nice fellow, certainly: nobody would ever guess that he was born in Australia; but—

LADY BRITOMART. Oh, Adolphus Cusins will make a very good husband. After all, nobody can say a word against Greek: it stamps a man at once as an educated gentleman. And my family, thank Heaven, is not a pig-headed Tory one. We are Whigs, and believe in liberty. Let snobbish people say what they please: Barbara shall marry, not the man they like, but the man *I* like.

STEPHEN. Of course I was thinking only of his income. However, he is not likely to be extravagant.

LADY BRITOMART. Don't be too sure of that, Stephen. I know your quiet, simple, refined, poetic people like Adolphus—quite content with the best of everything! They cost more than your extravagant people, who are always as mean as they are second rate. No: Barbara will need at least £2000 a year. You see it means two additional households. Besides, my dear, y o u must marry soon. I dont approve of the present fashion of philandering bachelors and late marriages; and I am trying to arrange something for you.

STEPHEN. It's very good of you, mother; but perhaps I had better arrange that for myself.

LADY BRITOMART. Nonsense! you are much too young to begin matchmaking: you would be taken in by some pretty little nobody. Of course I dont mean that you are not to be consulted: you know that as well as I do. [STEPHEN *closes his lips and is silent*]. Now don't sulk, Stephen.

4. This was a good middle-class income at the time the play was written; the fact that Lady Britomart considers it hopelessly inadequate is an indication of her assumptions about living standards.
5. Religious and philanthropical organization founded by William Booth in 1880, organized on a quasi-military basis, with Booth as general and field officers under him. Funds were raised by voluntary offerings from local societies which were known as "corps," from open-air collections at meetings, from friends interested in evangelical and charitable work, and from the profits on publications and general trading. The Salvation Army was active (as it still is) among the poor and distressed, and, especially in times of economic depression, provided much necessary assistance in food and shelter to the down-and-out.

STEPHEN. I am not sulking, mother. What has all this got to do with—with—with my father?

LADY BRITOMART. My dear Stephen: where is the money to come from? It is easy enough for you and the other children to live on my income as long as we are in the same house; but I cant keep four families in four separate houses. You know how poor my father is: he has barely seven thousand a year now; and really, if he were not the Earl of Stevenage, he would have to give up society. He can do nothing for us. He says, naturally enough, that it is absurd that he should be asked to provide for the children of a man who is rolling in money. You see, Stephen, your father must be fabulously wealthy, because there is always a war going on somewhere.

STEPHEN. You need not remind me of that, mother. I have hardly ever opened a newspaper in my life without seeing our name in it. The Undershaft torpedo! The Undershaft quick firers! The Undershaft ten inch! The Undershaft disappearing rampart gun! The Undershaft submarine! and now the Undershaft aerial battleship! At Harrow they called me the Woolwich[6] Infant. At Cambridge it was the same. A little brute at King's[7] who was always trying to get up revivals, spoilt my Bible—your first birthday present to me—by writing under my name, "Son and heir to Undershaft and Lazarus, Death and Destruction Dealers: address, Christendom and Judea." But that was not so bad as the way I was kowtowed to everywhere because my father was making millions by selling cannons.

LADY BRITOMART. It is not only the cannons, but the war loans that Lazarus arranges under cover of giving credit for the cannons. You know, Stephen, it's perfectly scandalous. Those two men, Andrew Undershaft and Lazarus, positively have Europe under their thumbs. That is why your father is able to behave as he does. He is above the law. Do you think Bismarck or Gladstone or Disraeli[8] could have openly defied every social and moral obligation all their lives as your father has? They simply wouldnt have dared. I asked Gladstone to take it up. I asked The Times to take it up. I asked the Lord Chamberlain to take it up. But it was just like asking them to declare war on the Sultan. They w o u l d n t. They said they couldnt touch him. I believe they were afraid.

STEPHEN. What could they do? He does not actually break the law.

LADY BRITOMART. Not break the law! He is always breaking the law. He broke the law when he was born: his parents were not married.

STEPHEN. Mother! Is that true?

6. Borough in southeast London noted for its arsenal and royal military academy for engineering and artillery.
7. One of the colleges at Cambridge University.
8. Otto Eduard Leopold von Bismarck (1815–98), the "Iron Chancellor," Prussian statesman, creator and first chancellor of the German Empire. William Ewart Gladstone (1809–98), the great statesman of the Liberal Party, opponent and rival of Benjamin Disraeli (1804–81), great Tory statesman and founder of the modern British Conservative Party.

LADY BRITOMART. Of course it's true: that was why we separated.

STEPHEN. He married without letting you know this!

LADY BRITOMART. [*rather taken aback by this inference*] Oh no. To do Andrew justice, that was not the sort of thing he did. Besides, you know the Undershaft motto: Unashamed. Everybody knew.

STEPHEN. But you said that was why you separated.

LADY BRITOMART. Yes, because he was not content with being a foundling himself: he wanted to disinherit you for another foundling. That was what I couldnt stand.

STEPHEN. [*ashamed*] Do you mean for—for—for—

LADY BRITOMART. Dont stammer, Stephen. Speak distinctly.

STEPHEN. But this so frightful to me, mother. To have to speak to you about such things!

LADY BRITOMART. It's not pleasant for me, either, especially if you are still so childish that you must make it worse by a display of embarrassment. It is only in the middle classes, Stephen, that people get into a state of dumb helpless horror when they find that there are wicked people in the world. In our class, we have to decide what is to be done with wicked people; and nothing should disturb our self-possession. Now ask your question properly.

STEPHEN. Mother: you have no consideration for me. For Heaven's sake either treat me as a child, as you always do, and tell me nothing at all; or tell me everything and let me take it as best I can.

LADY BRITOMART. Treat you as a child! What do you mean? It is most unkind and ungrateful of you to say such a thing. You know I have never treated any of you as children. I have always made you my companions and friends, and allowed you perfect freedom to do and say whatever you liked, so long as you liked what I could approve of.

STEPHEN. [*desperately*] I daresay we have been the very imperfect children of a very perfect mother; but I do beg you to let me alone for once, and tell me about this horrible business of my father wanting to set me aside for another son.

LADY BRITOMART. [*amazed*] Another son! I never said anything of the kind. I never dreamt of such a thing. This is what comes of interrupting me.

STEPHEN. But you said—

LADY BRITOMART. [*cutting him short*] Now be a good boy, Stephen, and listen to me patiently. The Undershafts are descended from a foundling in the parish of St Andrew Undershaft in the city. That was long ago, in the reign of James the First.[9] Well, this foundling was adopted by an armorer and gun-maker. In the course of time the foundling succeeded to the business; and from some notion of gratitude, or some vow or something, he adopted another foundling, and left the business to him. And that foundling did the same. Ever since that, the cannon business has

9. James I of England reigned from 1603 until his death in 1625.

always been left to an adopted foundling named Andrew Undershaft.

STEPHEN. But did they never marry? Were there no legitimate sons?

LADY BRITOMART. Oh yes: they married just as your father did; and
they were rich enough to buy land for their own children and
leave them well provided for. But they always adopted and
trained some foundling to succeed them in the business; and of
course they always quarrelled with their wives furiously over it.
Your father was adopted in that way; and he pretends to consider
himself bound to keep up the tradition and adopt somebody to
leave the business to. Of course I was not going to stand that.
There may have been some reason for it when the Undershafts
could only marry women in their own class, whose sons were
not fit to govern great estates. But there could be no excuse for
passing over m y son.

STEPHEN. [*dubiously*] I am afraid I should make a poor hand of
managing a cannon foundry.

LADY BRITOMART. Nonsense! you could easily get a manager and pay
him a salary.

STEPHEN. My father evidently had no great opinion of my capacity.

LADY BRITOMART. Stuff, child! you were only a baby: it had nothing
to do with your capacity. Andrew did it on principle, just as he
did every perverse and wicked thing on principle. When my
father remonstrated, Andrew actually told him to his face that
history tells us of only two successful institutions: one the Undershaft firm, and the other the Roman Empire under the
Antonines.[1] That was because the Antonine emperors all adopted
their successors. Such rubbish! The Stevenages are as good as the
Antonines, I hope; and you are a Stevenage. But that was
Andrew all over. There you have the man! Always clever and
unanswerable when he was defending nonsense and wickedness:
always awkward and sullen when he had to behave sensibly and
decently!

STEPHEN. Then it was on my account that your home life was
broken up, mother. I am sorry.

LADY BRITOMART. Well, dear, there were other differences. I really
cannot bear an immoral man. I am not a Pharisee, I hope; and I
should not have minded his merely d o i n g wrong things: we are
none of us perfect. But your father didnt exactly d o wrong
things: he said them and thought them: that was what was so
dreadful. He really had a sort of religion of wrongness. Just as
one doesnt mind men practising immorality so long as they own
that they are in the wrong by preaching morality; so I couldnt
forgive Andrew for preaching immorality while he practised
morality. You would all have grown up without principles, without any knowledge of right and wrong, if he had been in the

1. The period of the Antonines, one of
the most stable periods of the Roman
Empire, lasted during the reigns of An-
tonius Pius (138–161 A.D.) and his
nephew (whom he adopted as his heir)
Marcus Aurelius, surnamed Antoninus
(161–180 A.D.).

house. You know, my dear, your father was a very attractive man in some ways. Children did not dislike him; and he took advantage of it to put the wickedest ideas into their heads, and make them quite unmanageable. I did not dislike him myself: very far from it; but nothing can bridge over moral disagreement.

STEPHEN. All this simply bewilders me, mother. People may differ about matters of opinion, or even about religion; but how can they differ about right and wrong? Right is right; and wrong is wrong; and if a man cannot distinguish them properly, he is either a fool or a rascal: thats all.

LADY BRITOMART. [*touched*] Thats my own boy [*She pats his cheek*]! Your father never could answer that: he used to laugh and get out of it under cover of some affectionate nonsense. And now that you understand the situation, what do you advise me to do?

STEPHEN. Well, what c a n you do?

LADY BRITOMART. I must get the money somehow.

STEPHEN. We cannot take money from him. I had rather go and live in some cheap place like Bedford Square[2] or even Hampstead[3] than take a farthing of his money.

LADY BRITOMART. But after all, Stephen, our present income comes from Andrew.

STEPHEN. [*shocked*] I never knew that.

LADY BRITOMART. Well, you surely didnt suppose your grandfather had anything to give me. The Stevenages could not do everything for you. We gave you social position. Andrew had to contribute s o m e t h i n g. He had a very good bargain, I think.

STEPHEN. [*bitterly*] We are utterly dependent on him and his cannons, then?

LADY BRITOMART. Certainly not: the money is settled. But he provided it. So you see it is not a question of taking money from him or not: it is simply a question of how much. I dont want any more for myself.

STEPHEN. Nor do I.

LADY BRITOMART. But Sarah does; and Barbara does. That is, Charles Lomax and Adolphus Cusins will cost them more. So I must put my pride in my pocket and ask for it, I suppose. That is your advice, Stephen, is it not?

STEPHEN. No.

LADY BRITOMART. [*sharply*] Stephen!

STEPHEN. Of course if you are determined—

LADY BRITOMART. I am not determined: I ask your advice; and I am waiting for it. I will not have all the responsibility thrown on my shoulders.

STEPHEN. [*obstinately*] I would die sooner than ask him for another penny.

---

2. In the Bloomsbury district of London, not fashionable though soon to be made famous by the "Bloomsbury Group." It is near the British Museum.
3. Hampstead, in northwest London, was at this time a middle-class residential area, associated with respectability and honest worth rather than with aristocracy or pretensions to high fashion.

LADY BRITOMART. [*resignedly*] You mean that *I* must ask him. Very well, Stephen: it shall be as you wish. You will be glad to know that your grandfather concurs. But he thinks I ought to ask Andrew to come here and see the girls. After all, he must have some natural affection for them.

STEPHEN. Ask him here!!!

LADY BRITOMART. Do n o t repeat my words, Stephen. Where else can I ask him?

STEPHEN. I never expected you to ask him at all.

LADY BRITOMART. Now dont tease, Stephen. Come! you see that it is necessary that he should pay us a visit, dont you?

STEPHEN. [*reluctantly*] I suppose so, if the girls cannot do without his money.

LADY BRITOMART. Thank you, Stephen: I knew you would give me the right advice when it was properly explained to you. I have asked your father to come this evening. [STEPHEN *bounds from his seat*]. Dont jump, Stephen: it fidgets me.

STEPHEN. [*in utter consternation*] Do you mean to say that my father is coming here to-night—that he may be here at any moment?

LADY BRITOMART. [*looking at her watch*] I said nine. [*He gasps. She rises*]. Ring the bell, please. [STEPHEN *goes to the smaller writing table; presses a button on it; and sits at it with his elbows on the table and his head in his hands, outwitted and over-whelmed*]. It is ten minutes to nine yet; and I have to prepare the girls. I asked Charles Lomax and Adolphus to dinner on purpose that they might be here. Andrew had better see them in case he should cherish any delusions as to their being capable of supporting their wives. [*The butler enters:* LADY BRITOMART *goes behind the settee to speak to him*]. Morrison: go up to the drawing-room and tell everybody to come down here at once. [MORRISON *withdraws.* LADY BRITOMART *turns to* STEPHEN]. Now remember, Stephen: I shall need all your countenance and authority. [*He rises and tries to recover some vestige of these attributes*]. Give me a chair, dear. [*He pushes a chair forward from the wall to where she stands, near the smaller writing table. She sits down; and he goes to the arm-chair, into which he throws himself*]. I dont know how Barbara will take it. Ever since they made her a major in the Salvation Army she has developed a propensity to have her own way and order people about which quite cows me sometimes. It's not ladylike: I'm sure I dont know where she picked it up. Anyhow, Barbara shant bully m e; but still it's just as well that your father should be here before she has time to refuse to meet him or make a fuss. Dont look nervous, Stephen: it will only encourage Barbara to make difficulties. I am nervous enough, goodness knows; but I dont shew it.

Sarah and Barbara come in with their respective young men, Charles Lomax and Adolphus Cusins. Sarah is slender, bored, and mundane. Barbara is robuster, jollier, much more energetic. Sarah is fashionably dressed: Barbara is in Salvation Army uniform. Lomax, a young man about town, is like many other young men about town. He is afflicted with a frivolous sense of humor which plunges him at the most inopportune moments into paroxysms of imperfectly suppressed laughter. Cusins is a spectacled student, slight, thin haired. and sweet voiced, with a more complex form of Lomax's complaint. His sense of humor is intellectual and subtle, and is complicated by an appalling temper. The life-long struggle of a benevolent temperament and a high conscience against impulses of inhuman ridicule and fierce impatience has set up a chronic strain which has visibly wrecked his constitution. He is a most implacable, determined, tenacious, intolerant person who by mere force of character presents himself as—and indeed actually is—considerate, gentle, explanatory, even mild and apologetic, capable possibly of murder, but not of cruelty or coarseness. By the operation of some instinct which is not merciful enough to blind him with the illusions of love, he is obstinately bent on marrying Barbara. Lomax likes Sarah and thinks it will be rather a lark to marry her. Consequently he has not attempted to resist Lady Britomart's arrangements to that end.

All four look as if they had been having a good deal of fun in the drawing room. The girls enter first, leaving the swains outside. Sarah comes to the settee. Barbara comes in after her and stops at the door.

BARBARA. Are Cholly and Dolly to come in?

LADY BRITOMART. [*forcibly*] Barbara: I will not have Charles called Cholly: the vulgarity of it postively makes me ill.

BARBARA. It's all right, mother: Cholly is quite correct nowadays. Are they to come in?

LADY BRITOMART. Yes, if they will behave themselves.

BARBARA. [*through the door*] Come in, Dolly; and behave yourself.

Barbara comes to her mother's writing table. Cusins enters smiling, and wanders towards Lady Britomart.

SARAH. [*calling*] Come in, Cholly. [LOMAX *enters, controlling his features very imperfectly, and places himself vaguely between* SARAH *and* BARBARA].

LADY BRITOMART. [*peremptorily*] Sit down, all of you. [*They sit.* CUSINS *crosses to the window and seats himself there.* LOMAX *takes a chair.* BARBARA *sits at the writing table and* SARAH *on the settee*]. I dont in the least know what you are laughing at, Adolphus. I am surprised at you, though I expected nothing better from Charles Lomax.

CUSINS. [*in a remarkably gentle voice*] Barbara has been trying to teach me the West Ham[4] Salvation March.

LADY BRITOMART. I see nothing to laugh at in that; nor should you if you are really converted.

4. A working-class district in the East End of London.

CUSINS. [*sweetly*] You were not present. It was really funny, I believe.

LOMAX. Ripping.

LADY BRITOMART. Be quiet, Charles. Now listen to me, children. Your father is coming here this evening.

General stupefaction. Lomax, Sarah and Barbara rise: Sarah scared, and Barbara amused and expectant.

LOMAX. [*remonstrating*] Oh I say!

LADY BRITOMART. You are not called on to say anything, Charles.

SARAH. Are you serious, mother?

LADY BRITOMART. Of course I am serious. It is on your account, Sarah, and also on Charles's. [*Silence.* SARAH *sits, with a shrug.* CHARLES *looks painfully unworthy*]. I hope you are not going to object, Barbara.

BARBARA. I! why should I? My father has a soul to be saved like anybody else. He's quite welcome as far as I am concerned. [*She sits on the table, and softly whistles 'Onward, Christian Soldiers'*].

LOMAX. [*still remonstrant*] But really, dont you know! Oh I say!

LADY BRITOMART. [*frigidly*] What do you wish to convey, Charles?

LOMAX. Well, you must admit that this is a bit thick.

LADY BRITOMART. [*turning with ominous suavity to* CUSINS] Adolphus: you are a professor of Greek. Can you translate Charles Lomax's remarks into reputable English for us?

CUSINS. [*cautiously*] If I may say so, Lady Brit, I think Charles has rather happily expressed what we all feel. Homer, speaking of Autolycus, uses the same phrase. πυκινὸν δόμον ἐλθεῖν [5] means a bit thick.

LOMAX. [*handsomely*] Not that I mind, you know, if Sarah dont. [*He sits*].

LADY BRITOMART. [*crushingly*] Thank you. Have I y o u r permission, Adolphus, to invite my own husband to my own house?

CUSINS. [*gallantly*] You have my unhesitating support in everything you do.

LADY BRITOMART. Tush! Sarah: have you nothing to say?

SARAH. Do you mean that he is coming regularly to live here?

LADY BRITOMART. Certainly not. The spare room is ready for him if he likes to stay for a day or two and see a little more of you; but there are limits.

SARAH. Well, he cant eat us, I suppose. *I* dont mind.

LOMAX. [*chuckling*] I wonder how the old man will take it.

LADY BRITOMART. Much as the old woman will, no doubt, Charles.

LOMAX. [*abashed*] I didnt mean—at least—

---

5. This hardly means "a bit thick," as Cusins maintains. The word here rendered as "thick" (*pukinon*) refers to *domon*, "house," and in context means "stoutly built." The reference is to *Iliad* X.267 (not accurately quoted), where Homer refers to the cap stolen by Auto- lycus "when he had broken into the well-built house of Amyntor." Cusins uses the Greek word *elthein* ("to come or go") instead of Homer's *antitoresas* ("having broken into"), which makes nonsense of the phrase (which would literally mean "to come a thick house").

LADY BRITOMART. You didnt t h i n k, Charles. You never do; and
the result is, you never mean anything. And now please attend to
me, children. Your father will be quite a stranger to us.

LOMAX. I suppose he hasnt seen Sarah since she was a little kid.

LADY BRITOMART. Not since she was a little kid, Charles, as you
express it with that elegance of diction and refinement of thought
that seem never to desert you. Accordingly—er— [*Impatiently*]
Now I have forgotten what I was going to say. That comes of
your provoking me to be sarcastic, Charles. Adolphus: will you
kindly tell me where I was.

CUSINS. [*sweetly*] You were saying that as Mr Undershaft has not
seen his children since they were babies, he will form his opinion
of the way you have brought them up from their behavior tonight, and that therefore you wish us all to be particularly careful
to conduct ourselves well, especially Charles.

LADY BRITOMART. [*with emphatic approval*] Precisely.

LOMAX. Look here, Dolly: Lady Brit didnt say that.

LADY BRITOMART. [*vehemently*] I did, Charles. Adolphus's recollection is perfectly correct. It is most important that you should
be good; and I do beg you for once not to pair off into opposite
corners and giggle and whisper while I am speaking to your
father.

BARBARA. All right, mother. We'll do you credit. [*She comes off
the table, and sits in her chair with ladylike elegance*].

LADY BRITOMART. Remember, Charles, that Sarah will want to feel
proud of you instead of ashamed of you.

LOMAX. Oh I say! theres nothing to be exactly proud of, dont you
know.

LADY BRITOMART. Well, try and look as if there was.

*Morrison, pale and dismayed, breaks into the room in uncon-
cealed disorder,*

MORRISON. Might I speak a word to you, my lady?

LADY BRITOMART. Nonsense! Shew him up.

MORRISON. Yes, my lady. [*He goes*].

LOMAX. Does Morrison know who it is?

LADY BRITOMART. Of course. Morrison has always been with us.

LOMAX. It must be a regular corker for him, dont you know.

LADY BRITOMART. Is this a moment to get on my nerves, Charles,
with your outrageous expressions?

LOMAX. But this is something out of the ordinary, really—

MORRISON. [*at the door*] The—er—Mr Undershaft. [*He retreats
in confusion*].

*Andrew Undershaft comes in. All rise. Lady Britomart meets him
in the middle of the room behind the settee.*

*Andrew is, on the surface, a stoutish, easygoing elderly man, with
kindly patient manners, and an engaging simplicity of character.
But he has a watchful, deliberate, waiting, listening face, and formidable reserves of power, both bodily and mental, in his capacious
chest and long head. His gentleness is partly that of a strong man*

who has learnt by experience that his natural grip hurts ordinary people unless he handles them very carefully, and partly the mellowness of age and success. He is also a little shy in his present very delicate situation.

LADY BRITOMART. Good evening, Andrew.

UNDERSHAFT. How d'ye do, my dear.

LADY BRITOMART. You look a good deal older.

UNDERSHAFT. [*apologetically*] I a m somewhat older. [*Taking her hand with a touch of courtship*] Time has stood still with you.

LADY BRITOMART. [*throwing away his hand*] Rubbish! This is your family.

UNDERSHAFT. [*surprised*] Is it so large? I am sorry to say my memory is failing very badly in some things. [*He offers his hand with paternal kindness to* LOMAX].

LOMAX. [*jerkily shaking his hand*] Ahdedoo.

UNDERSHAFT. I can see you are my eldest. I am very glad to meet you again, my boy.

LOMAX. [*remonstrating*] No, but look here dont you know—[*Overcome*] Oh I say!

LADY BRITOMART. [*recovering from momentary speechlessness*] Andrew: do you mean to say that you dont remember how many children you have?

UNDERSHAFT. Well, I am afraid I—. They have grown so much—er. Am I making any ridiculous mistake? I may as well confess: I recollect only one son. But so many things have happened since, of course—er—er

LADY BRITOMART. [*decisively*] Andrew: you are talking nonsense. Of course you have only one son.

UNDERSHAFT. Perhaps you will be good enough to introduce me, my dear.

LADY BRITOMART. That is Charles Lomax, who is engaged to Sarah.

UNDERSHAFT. My dear sir, I beg your pardon.

LOMAX. Notatall. Delighted, I assure you.

LADY BRITOMART. This is Stephen.

UNDERSHAFT. [*bowing*] Happy to make your acquaintance, Mr Stephen. Then [*going to* CUSINS] y o u must be my son. [*Taking* CUSINS' *hands in his*] How are you, my young friend? [*To* LADY BRITOMART] He is very like you, my love.

CUSINS. You flatter me, Mr Undershaft. My name is Cusins: engaged to Barbara. [*Very explicitly*] That is Major Barbara Undershaft, of the Salvation Army. That is Sarah, your second daughter. This is Stephen Undershaft, your son.

UNDERSHAFT. My dear Stephen, I b e g your pardon.

STEPHEN. Not at all.

UNDERSHAFT. Mr Cusins: I am much indebted to you for explaining so precisely. [*Turning to* SARAH] Barbara, my dear—

SARAH. [*prompting him*] Sarah.

UNDERSHAFT. Sarah, of course. [*They shake hands. He goes over to* BARBARA]. Barbara—I am right this time, I hope.

BARBARA. Quite right. [*They shake hands*].

LADY BRITOMART. [*resuming command*] Sit down, all of you. Sit down, Andrew. [*She comes forward and sits on the settee.* CUSINS *also brings his chair forward on her left.* BARBARA *and* STEPHEN *resume their seats.* LOMAX *gives his chair to* SARAH *and goes for another*].

UNDERSHAFT. Thank you, my love.

LOMAX. [*conversationally, as he brings a chair forward between the writing table and the settee, and offers it to* UNDERSHAFT] Takes you some time to find exactly where you are, dont it?

UNDERSHAFT. [*accepting the chair, but remaining standing*] That is not what embarrasses me, Mr Lomax. My difficulty is that if I play the part of a father, I shall produce the effect of an intrusive stranger; and if I play the part of a discreet stranger, I may appear a callous father.

LADY BRITOMART. There is no need for you to play any part at all, Andrew. You had much better be sincere and natural.

UNDERSHAFT. [*submissively*] Yes, my dear: I daresay that will be best. [*He sits down comfortably*]. Well, here I am. Now what can I do for you all?

LADY BRITOMART. You need not do anything, Andrew. You are one of the family. You can sit with us and enjoy yourself.

A painfully conscious pause. BARBARA *makes a face at* LOMAX, *whose too long suppressed mirth immediately explodes in agonized neighings.*

LADY BRITOMART. [*outraged*] Charles Lomax: if you can behave yourself, behave yourself. If not, leave the room.

LOMAX. I'm awfully sorry, Lady Brit; but really, you know, upon my soul! [*He sits on the settee between* LADY BRITOMART *and* UNDERSHAFT, *quite overcome*].

BARBARA. Why dont you laugh if you want to, Cholly? It's good for your inside.

LADY BRITOMART. Barbara: you have had the education of a lady. Please let your father see that; and dont talk like a street girl.

UNDERSHAFT. Never mind me, my dear. As you know, I am not a gentleman; and I was never educated.

LOMAX. [*encouragingly*] Nobody'd know it, I assure you. You look all right, you know.

CUSINS. Let me advise you to study Greek, Mr Undershaft. Greek scholars are privileged men. Few of them know Greek; and none of them know anything else; but their position is unchallengeable. Other languages are the qualifications of waiters and commercial travellers: Greek is to a man of position what the hallmark is to silver.

BARBARA. Dolly: dont be insincere. Cholly: fetch your concertina and play something for us.

LOMAX. [*jumps up eagerly, but checks himself to remark doubtfully to* UNDERSHAFT] Perhaps that sort of thing isnt in your line, eh?

UNDERSHAFT. I am particularly fond of music.

LOMAX. [*delighted*] Are you? Then I'll get it. [*He goes upstairs for the instrument*].

UNDERSHAFT. Do you play, Barbara?

BARBARA. Only the tambourine. But Cholly's teaching me the concertina.

UNDERSHAFT. Is Cholly also a member of the Salvation Army?

BARBARA. No: he says it's bad form to be a dissenter.[6] But I dont despair of Cholly. I made him come yesterday to a meeting at the dock gates, and take the collection in his hat.

UNDERSHAFT. [*looks whimsically at his wife*]!!

LADY BRITOMART. It is not my doing, Andrew. Barbara is old enough to take her own way. She has no father to advise her.

BARBARA. Oh yes she has. There are no orphans in the Salvation Army.

UNDERSHAFT. Your father there has a great many children and plenty of experience, eh?

BARBARA. [*looking at him with quick interest and nodding*] Just so. How did y o u come to understand that? [LOMAX *is heard at the door trying the concertina*].

LADY BRITOMART. Come in, Charles. Play us something at once.

LOMAX. Righto! [*He sits down in his former place, and preludes*].

UNDERSHAFT. One moment, Mr Lomax. I am rather interested in the Salvation Army. Its motto might be my own: Blood and Fire.

LOMAX. [*shocked*] But not your sort of blood and fire, you know.

UNDERSHAFT. My sort of blood cleanses: my sort of fire purifies.

BARBARA. So do ours. Come down to-morrow to my shelter—the West Ham shelter—and see what we're doing. We're going to march to a great meeting in the Assembly Hall at Mile End.[7] Come and see the shelter and then march with us: it will do you a lot of good. Can you play anything?

UNDERSHAFT. In my youth I earned pennies, and even shillings occasionally, in the streets and in public house parlors by my natural talent for stepdancing. Later on, I became a member of the Undershaft orchestral society, and performed passably on the tenor trombone.

LOMAX. [*scandalized—putting down the concertina*] Oh I say!

BARBARA. Many a sinner has played himself into heaven on the trombone, thanks to the Army.

LOMAX. [*to* BARBARA, *still rather shocked*] Yes; but what about the cannon business, dont you know? [*To* UNDERSHAFT] Getting into heaven is not exactly in your line, is it?

LADY BRITOMART. Charles!!!

LOMAX. Well; but it stands to reason, dont it? The cannon business may be necessary and all that: we cant get on without cannons; but it isnt right, you know. On the other hand, there may be a certain amount of tosh about the Salvation Army—I belong to the Established Church myself—but still you cant deny that it's

---

6. A Protestant who worships outside the established Anglican Church.

7. In the East End of London, a poor working-class quarter.

religion; and you cant go against religion, can you? At least unless youre downright immoral, dont you know.

UNDERSHAFT. You hardly appreciate my position, Mr Lomax—

LOMAX. [*hastily*] I'm not saying anything against you personally—

UNDERSHAFT. Quite so, quite so. But consider for a moment. Here I am, a profiteer in mutilation and murder. I find myself in a specially amiable humor just now because, this morning, down at the foundry, we blew twenty seven dummy soldiers into fragments with a gun which formerly destroyed only thirteen.

LOMAX. [*leniently*] Well, the more destructive war becomes, the sooner it will be abolished, eh?

UNDERSHAFT. Not at all. The more destructive war becomes the more fascinating we find it. No, Mr Lomax: I am obliged to you for making the usual excuse for my trade; but I am not ashamed of it. I am not one of those men who keep their morals and their business in watertight compartments. All the spare money and trade rivals spend on hospitals, cathedrals, and other receptacles for conscience money, I devote to experiments and researches in improved methods of destroying life and property. I have always done so; and I always shall. Therefore your Christmas card moralities of peace on earth and goodwill among men are of no use to me. Your Christianity, which enjoins you to resist not evil, and to turn the other cheek, would make me a bankrupt. M y morality —m y religion—must have a place for cannons and torpedoes in it.

STEPHEN. [*coldly—almost sullenly*] You speak as if there were half a dozen moralities and religions to choose from, instead of one true morality and one true religion.

UNDERSHAFT. For me there is only one true morality; but it might not fit you, as you do not manufacture aerial battleships. There is only one true morality for every man; but every man has not the same true morality.

LOMAX. [*overtaxed*] Would you mind saying that again? I didnt quite follow it.

CUSINS. It's quite simple. As Euripides says, one man's meat is another man's poison morally as well as physically.

UNDERSHAFT. Precisely.

LOMAX. Oh, t h a t. Yes, yes, yes. True. True.

STEPHEN. In other words, some men are honest and some are scoundrels.

BARBARA. Bosh. There are no scoundrels.

UNDERSHAFT. Indeed? Are there any good men?

BARBARA. No. Not one. There are neither good men nor scoundrels: there are just children of one Father; and the sooner they stop calling one another names the better. You neednt talk to me: I know them. Ive had scores of them through my hands: scoundrels, criminals, infidels, philanthropists, missionaries, county councillors, all sorts. Theyre all just the same sort of sinner; and theres the same salvation ready for them all.

UNDERSHAFT. May I ask have you ever saved a maker of cannons?

BARBARA. No. Will you let me try?

UNDERSHAFT. Well, I will make a bargain with you. If I go to see you to-morrow in your Salvation Shelter, will you come the day after to see me in my cannon works?

BARBARA. Take care. It may end in your giving up the cannons for the sake of the Salvation Army.

UNDERSHAFT. Are you sure it will not end in your giving up the Salvation Army for the sake of the cannons?

BARBARA. I will take my chance of that.

UNDERSHAFT. And I will take my chance of the other. [*They shake hands on it*]. Where is your shelter?

BARBARA. In West Ham. At the sign of the cross. Ask anybody in Canning Town.[8] Where are your works?

UNDERSHAFT. In Perivale St Andrews.[9] At the sign of the sword. Ask anybody in Europe.

LOMAX. Hadnt I better play something?

BARBARA. Yes. Give us Onward, Christian Soldiers.

LOMAX. Well, thats rather a strong order to begin with, dont you know. Suppose I sing Thou'rt passing hence, my brother. It's much the same tune.

BARBARA. It's too melancholy. You get saved, Cholly; and youll pass hence, my brother, without making such a fuss about it.

LADY BRITOMART. Really, Barbara, you go on as if religion were a pleasant subject. Do have some sense of propriety.

UNDERSHAFT. I do not find it an unpleasant subject, my dear. It is the only one that capable people really care for.

LADY BRITOMART. [*looking at her watch*] Well, if you are determined to have it, I insist on having it in a proper and respectable way. Charles: ring for prayers. [*General amazement.* STEPHEN *rises in dismay*].

LOMAX. [*rising*] Oh I say!

UNDERSHAFT. [*rising*] I am afraid I must be going.

LADY BRITOMART. You cannot go now, Andrew: it would be most improper. Sit down. What will the servants think?

UNDERSHAFT. My dear: I have conscientious scruples. May I suggest a compromise? If Barbara will conduct a little service in the drawing room, with Mr Lomax as organist, I will attend it willingly. I will even take part, if a trombone can be procured.

LADY BRITOMART. Dont mock, Andrew.

UNDERSHAFT. [*shocked—to* BARBARA] You dont think I am mocking, my love, I hope.

BARBARA. No, of course not; and it wouldnt matter if you were: half the Army came to their first meeting for a lark. [*Rising*] Come along. [*She throws her arm round her father and sweeps him*

---

8. South of West Ham, near London's dockland.

9. Perivale, Middlesex, is now part of Greater London, in the W. 13 district.

Shaw invented the "St. Andrews." He himself settled in the Hertfordshire village of Ayot Saint Lawrence.

out, calling to the others from the threshold]. Come, Dolly. Come, Cholly.

Cusins rises.

LADY BRITOMART. I will not be disobeyed by everybody. Adolphus: sit down. [*He does not*]. Charles: you may go. You are not fit for prayers: you cannot keep your countenance.

LOMAX. Oh I say! [*He goes out*].

LADY BRITOMART. [*continuing*] But you, Adolphus, can behave yourself if you choose to. I insist on your staying.

CUSINS. My dear Lady Brit: there are things in the family prayer book that I couldnt bear to hear you say.

LADY BRITOMART. What things, pray?

CUSINS. Well, you would have to say before all the servants that we have done things we ought not to have done, and left undone things we ought to have done, and that there is no health in us. I cannot bear to hear you doing yourself such an injustice, and Barbara such an injustice. As for myself, I flatly deny it: I have done my best. I shouldnt dare to marry Barbara—I couldnt look you in the face—if it were true. So I must go to the drawing room.

LADY BRITOMART. [*offended*] Well, go. [*He starts for the door*]. And remember this, Adolphus [*he turns to listen*]: I have a very strong suspicion that you went to the Salvation Army to worship Barbara and nothing else. And I quite appreciate the very clever way in which you systematically humbug me. I have found you out. Take care Barbara doesnt. Thats all.

CUSINS. [*with unruffled sweetness*] Dont tell on me. [*He steals out*].

LADY BRITOMART. Sarah: if you want to go, go. Anything's better than to sit there as if you wished you were a thousand miles away.

SARAH. [*languidly*] Very well, mamma. [*She goes*].

Lady Britomart, with a sudden flounce, gives way to a little gust of tears.

STEPHEN. [*going to her*] Mother: whats the matter?

LADY BRITOMART. [*swishing away her tears with her handkerchief*] Nothing. Foolishness. You can go with him, too, if you like, and leave me with the servants.

STEPHEN. Oh, you mustnt think that, mother. I—I dont like him.

LADY BRITOMART. The others do. That is the injustice of a woman's lot. A woman has to bring up her children; and that means to restrain them, to deny them things they want, to set them tasks, to punish them when they do wrong, to do all the unpleasant things. And then the father, who has nothing to do but pet them and spoil them, comes in when all her work is done and steals their affection from her.

STEPHEN. He has not stolen our affection from you. It is only curiosity.

LADY BRITOMART. [*violently*] I wont be consoled, Stephen. There is nothing the matter with me. [*She rises and goes towards the door*].

STEPHEN. Where are you going, mother?

LADY BRITOMART. To the drawing room, of course. [*She goes out. Onward Christian Soldiers, on the concertina, with tambourine accompaniment, is heard when the door opens*]. Are you coming, Stephen?

STEPHEN. No. Certainly not. [*She goes. He sits down on the settee, with compressed lips and an expression of strong dislike*].

Act II

The yard of the West Ham shelter of the Salvation Army is a cold place on a January morning. The building itself, an old warehouse, is newly white-washed. Its gabled end projects into the yard in the middle, with a door on the ground floor, and another in the loft above it without any balcony or ladder, but with a pulley rigged over it for hoisting sacks. Those who come from this central gable end into the yard have the gateway leading to the street on their left, with a stone horse-trough just beyond it, and, on the right, a penthouse shielding a table from the weather. There are forms at the table; and on them are seated a man and a woman, both much down on their luck, finishing a meal of bread (one thick slice each, with margarine and golden syrup) and diluted milk.

The man, a workman out of employment, is young, agile, a talker, a poser, sharp enough to be capable of anything in reason except honesty or altruistic considerations of any kind. The woman is a commonplace old bundle of poverty and hard-worn humanity. She looks sixty and probably is forty-five. If they were rich people, gloved and muffed and well wrapped up in furs and overcoats, they would be numbed and miserable; for it is a grindingly cold, raw, January day; and a glance at the background of grimy warehouses and leaden sky visible over the whitewashed walls of the yard would drive any idle rich person straight to the Mediterranean. But these two, being no more troubled with visions of the Mediterranean than of the moon, and being compelled to keep more of their clothes in the pawnshop, and less on their persons, in winter than in summer, are not depressed by the cold: rather are they stung into vivacity, to which their meal has just now given an almost jolly turn. The man takes a pull at his mug, and then gets up and moves about the yard with his hands deep in his pockets, occasionally breaking into a stepdance.

THE WOMAN. Feel better arter your meal, sir?

THE MAN. No. Call that a meal! Good enough for you, praps; but wot is it to me, an intelligent workin man.

THE WOMAN. Workin man! Wot are you?

THE MAN. Painter.

THE WOMAN. [*sceptically*] Yus, I dessay.

THE MAN. Yus, you dessay! I know. Every loafer that cant do nothink calls isself a painter. Well, I'm a real painter: grainer,[1] finisher, thirty-eight bob a week when I can get it.

1. A craftsman who paints an imitation of the grain of wood or the streaks of marble on inferior materials.

THE WOMAN. Then why dont you go and get it?

THE MAN. I'll tell you why. Fust: I'm intelligent—fffft! it's rotten cold here [*he dances a step or two*]—yes: intelligent beyond the station o life into which it has pleased the capitalists to call me; and they dont like a man that sees through em. Second, an intelligent bein needs a doo share of appiness; so I drink something cruel when I get the chawnce. Third, I stand by my class and do as little as I can so's to leave arf the job for me fellow workers. Fourth, I'm fly[2] enough to know wots inside the law and wots outside it; and inside it I do as the capitalists do: pinch wot I can lay me ands on. In a proper state of society I am sober, industrious and honest: in Rome, so to speak, I do as the Romans do. Wots the consequence? When trade is bad—and it's rotten bad just now—and the employers az to sack arf their men, they generally start on me.

THE WOMAN. Whats your name?

THE MAN. Price. Bronterre O'Brien Price. Usually called Snobby Price, for short.

THE WOMAN. Snobby's a carpenter, aint it? You said you was a painter.

PRICE. Not that kind of snob, but the genteel sort. I'm too uppish, owing to my intelligence, and my father being a Chartist[3] and a reading, thinking man: a stationer, too. I'm none of your common hewers of wood and drawers of water; and dont you forget it. [*He returns to his seat at the table, and takes up his mug*]. Wots y o u r name?

THE WOMAN. Rummy Mitchens, sir.

PRICE. [*quaffing the remains of his milk to her*] Your elth, Miss Mitchens.

RUMMY. [*correcting him*] Missis Mitchens.

PRICE. Wot! Oh Rummy, Rummy! Respectable married woman, Rummy, gittin rescued by the Salvation Army by pretendin to be a bad un. Same old game!

RUMMY. What am I to do? I cant starve. Them Salvation lasses is dear good girls; but the better you are, the worse they likes to think you were before they rescued you. Why shouldnt they av a bit o credit, poor loves? theyre worn to rags by their work. And where would they get the money to rescue us if we was to let on we're no worse than other people? You know what ladies and gentlemen are.

PRICE. Thievin swine! Wish I ad their job, Rummy, all the same. Wot does Rummy stand for? Pet name praps?

RUMMY. Short for Romola.

PRICE. For wot!?

RUMMY. Romola. It was out of a new book.[4] Somebody me mother wanted me to grow up like.

2. Smart.
3. Chartism was a movement concerned with electoral reform and improvement of social conditions in England. It began in 1837 and continued until 1848.
4. George Eliot's historical novel *Romola* (1863).

PRICE. We're companions in misfortune, Rummy. Both on us got names that nobody cawnt pronounce. Consequently I'm Snobby and youre Rummy because Bill and Sally wasnt good enough for our parents. Such is life!

RUMMY. Who saved you, Mr Price? Was it Major Barbara?

PRICE. No: I come here on my own. I'm goin to be Bronterre O'Brien Price, the converted painter. I know wot they like. I'll tell em how I blasphemed and gambled and wopped my poor old mother—

RUMMY. [*shocked*] Used you to beat your mother?

PRICE. Not likely. She used to beat me. No matter: you come and listen to the converted painter, and youll hear how she was a pious woman that taught me me prayers at er knee, an how I used to come home drunk and drag her out o bed be er snow white airs, an lam into er with the poker.

RUMMY. Thats whats so unfair to us women. Your confessions is just as big lies as ours: you dont tell what you really done no more than us; but you men can tell your lies right out at the meetins and be made much of for it; while the sort o confessions we az to make az to be whispered to one lady at a time. It aint right, spite of all their piety.

PRICE. Right! Do you spose the Army 'd be allowed if it went and did right? Not much. It combs our air and makes us good little blokes to be robbed and put upon. But I'll play the game as good as any of em. I'll see somebody struck by lightnin, or hear a voice sayin "Snobby Price: where will you spend eternity?" I'll ave a time of it, I tell you.

RUMMY. You wont be let drink, though.

PRICE. I'll take it out in gorspellin, then. I dont want to drink if I can get fun enough any other way.

Jenny Hill, a pale, overwrought, pretty Salvation lass of 18, comes in through the yard gate, leading Peter Shirley, a half hardened, half worn-out elderly man, weak with hunger.

JENNY. [*supporting him*] Come! pluck up. I'll get you something to eat. Youll be all right then.

PRICE. [*rising and hurrying officiously to take the old man off* JENNY's *hands*] Poor old man! Cheer up, brother: youll find rest and peace and appiness ere. Hurry up with the food, miss: e's fair done. [JENNY *hurries into the shelter*]. Ere, buck up, daddy! shes fetchin y'a thick slice o breadn treacle, an a mug o skyblue.[5] [*He seats him at the corner of the table*].

RUMMY. [*gaily*] Keep up your old art! Never say die!

SHIRLEY. I'm not an old man. I'm only 46. I'm as good as ever I was. The grey patch come in my hair before I was thirty. All it wants is three pennorth o hair dye: am I to be turned on the streets to starve for it? Holy God! Ive worked ten to twelve hours a day since I was thirteen, and paid my way all through; and now am I to be thrown into the gutter and my job given to a young

---

5. "Treacle" is molasses. "Skyblue": watery milk.

man that can do it no better than me because I've black hair that goes white at the first change?

PRICE. [*cheerfully*] No good jawrin about it. Youre ony a jumped-up, jerked-off, orspittle-turned-out incurable of an ole workin man: who cares about you? Eh? Make the thievin swine give you a meal: theyve stole many a one from you. Get a bit o your own back. [JENNY *returns with the usual meal*]. There you are, brother. Awsk a blessin an tuck that into you.

SHIRLEY. [*looking at it ravenously but not touching it, and crying like a child*] I never took anything before.

JENNY. [*petting him*] Come, come! the Lord sends it to you; he wasnt above taking bread from his friends; and why should you be? Besides, when we find you a job you can pay us for it if you like.

SHIRLEY. [*eagerly*] Yes, yes: thats true. I can pay you back: its only a loan. [*Shivering*] Oh Lord! oh Lord! [*He turns to the table and attacks the meal ravenously*].

JENNY. Well, Rummy, are you more comfortable now?

RUMMY. God bless you, lovey! youve fed by body and saved my soul, havent you? [JENNY, *touched, kisses her*].

JENNY. Ive been going hard since morning. But theres more work than we can do. I mustnt stop.

RUMMY. Try a prayer for just two minutes. Youll work all the better after.

JENNY. [*her eyes lighting up*] Oh isnt it wonderful how a few minutes prayer revives you! I was quite lightheaded at twelve o'clock, I was so tired; but Major Barbara just sent me to pray for five minutes; and I was able to go on as if I had only just begun. [*To* PRICE] Did you have a piece of bread?

PRICE. [*with unction*] Yes, miss; but Ive got the piece that I value more; and thats the peace that passeth hall hannerstennin.

RUMMY. [*fervently*] Glory Hallelujah!

Bill Walker, a rough customer of about 25, appears at the yard gate and looks malevolently at Jenny.

JENNY. That makes me so happy. When you say that, I feel wicked for loitering here. I must get to work again.

She is hurrying to the shelter, when the new-comer moves quickly up to the door and intercepts her. His manner is so threatening that she retreats as he comes at her truculently, driving her down the yard.

BILL. Aw knaow you. Youre the one that took awy maw girl. Youre the one that set er agen me. Well, I'm gowin to ev er aht. Not that Aw care a carse for er or you: see? Bat Aw'll let er knaow; and Aw'll let y o u knaow. Aw'm gowing to give her a doin thatll teach er to cat awy from me. Nah in wiv you and tell er to cam aht afore Aw cam in and kick er aht. Tell er Bill Walker wants er. She'll knaow wot thet means; and if she keeps me witin itll be worse. You stop to jawr beck at me; and Aw'll stawt on you: d'ye eah? Theres your wy. In you gow. [*He takes her by the arm and* slings her towards the door of the shelter. She falls on her hand and knee. RUMMY *helps her up again.*]

PRICE. [*rising, and venturing irresolutely towards* BILL] Easy there, mate. She aint doing you no arm.

BILL. Oo are you callin mite? [*Standing over him threateningly*] Youre gowin to stend ap for er, aw yer? Put ap your ends.

RUMMY. [*running indignantly to him to scold him*] Oh, you great brute— [*He instantly swings his left hand back against her face. She screams and reels back to the trough, where she sits down, covering her bruised face with her hands and rocking herself and moaning with pain*].

JENNY. [*going to her*] Oh, God forgive you! How could you strike an old woman like that?

BILL. [*seizing her by the hair so violently that she also screams, and tearing her away from the old woman*] You Gawd forgimme again and Aw'll Gawd forgive you one on the jawr thetll stop you pryin for a week. [*Holding her and turning fiercely on* PRICE] Ev you ennything to sy agen it?

PRICE. [*intimidated*] No, matey: she aint anything to do with me.

BILL. Good job for you! Aw'd pat two meals into you and fawt you with one finger arter, you stawved cur. [*To* JENNY] Nah are you gowin to fetch aht Mog Ebbijem; or em Aw to knock your fice off you and fetch her meself?

JENNY. [*writhing in his grasp*] Oh please someone go in and tell Major Barbara—[*She screams again as he wrenches her head down; and* PRICE *and* RUMMY *flee into the shelter*].

BILL. You want to gow in and tell your Mijor of me, do you?

JENNY. Oh please dont drag my hair. Let me go.

BILL. Do you or downt you? [*She stifles a scream*]. Yus or nao?

JENNY. God give me strength—

BILL. [*striking her with his fist in the face*] Gow an shaow her thet, and tell her if she wants one lawk it to cam and interfere with me. [JENNY, *crying with pain, goes into the shed. He goes to the form and addresses the old man*]. Eah: finish your mess; and git aht o maw wy.

SHIRLEY. [*springing up and facing him fiercely, with the mug in his hand*] You take a liberty with me, and I'll smash you over the face with the mug and cut your eye out. Aint you satisfied— young whelps like you—with takin the bread out o the mouths of your elders that have brought you up and slaved for you, but you must come shovin and cheekin and bullyin in here, where the bread o charity is sickenin in our stummicks?

BILL. [*contemptuously, but backing a little*] Wot good are you, you aold palsy mag?[6] Wot good are you?

SHIRLEY. As good as you and better. I'll do a day's work agen you or any fat young soaker of your age. Go and take my job at Hor-rockses, where I worked for ten year. They want young men

6. A palsied old chatterer (magpie).

there: they cant afford to keep men over forty-five. Theyre very sorry—give you a character and happy to help you to get anything suited to your years—sure a steady man wont be long out of a job. Well, let em try y o u. Theyll find the differ. What do y o u know? Not as much as how to beeyave yourself—layin your dirty fist across the mouth of a respectable woman!

BILL. Downt provowk me to ly it acrost yours: d'ye eah?

SHIRLEY. [*with blighting contempt*] Yes: you like an old man to hit, dont you, when youve finished with the women. I aint seen you hit a young one yet.

BILL. [*stung*] You loy, you aold soupkitchener, you. There was a yang menn eah. Did Aw offer to itt him or did Aw not?

SHIRLEY. Was he starvin or was he not? Was he a man or only a crosseyed thief an a loafer? Would you hit my son-in-law's brother?

BILL. Oo's ee?

SHIRLEY. Todger Fairmile o Balls Pond. Him that won £20 off the Japanese wrastler at the music hall by standing out 17 minutes, 4 seconds agen him.

BILL. [*sullenly*] Aw'm nao music awl wrastler. Ken he box?

SHIRLEY. Yes: an you cant.

BILL. Wot! Aw cawnt, cawnt Aw? Wots thet you sy [*threatening him*]?

SHIRLEY. [*not budging an inch*] Will you box Todger Fairmile if I put him on to you? Say the word.

BILL. [*subsiding with a slouch*] Aw'll stend ap to enny menn alawv, if he was ten Todger Fairmawls. But Aw dont set ap to be a perfeshnal.

SHIRLEY. [*looking down on him with unfathomable disdain*] Y o u box! Slap an old woman with the back o your hand! You hadnt even the sense to hit her where a magistrate couldnt see the mark of it, you silly young lump of conceit and ignorance. Hit a girl in the jaw and ony make her cry! If Todger Fairmile'd done it, she wouldnt a got up inside o ten minutes, no more than you would if he got on to you. Yah! I'd set about you myself if I had a week's feedin in me instead o two months' starvation. [*He turns his back on him and sits down moodily at the table*].

BILL. [*following him and stooping over him to drive the taunt in*] You loy! youve the bread and treacle in you that you cam eah to beg.

SHIRLEY. [*bursting into tears*] Oh God! it's true: I'm only an old pauper on the scrap heap. [*Furiously*] But youll come to it yourself; and then youll know. Youll come to it sooner than a teetotaller like me, fillin yourself with gin at this hour o the mornin!

BILL. Aw'm nao gin drinker, you oald lawr; bat wen Aw want to give my girl a bloomin good awdin Aw lawk to ev a bit o devil in me: see? An eah Aw emm, talking to a rotten aold blawter like you sted o given er wot for. [*Working himself into a rage*] Aw'm gowin in there to fetch her aht. [*He makes vengefully for the shelter door*].

SHIRLEY. Youre going to the station on a stretcher, more likely; and theyll take the gin and the devil out of you there when they get you inside. You mind what youre about: the major here is the Earl o Stevenage's granddaughter.

BILL. [*checked*] Garn!⁷

SHIRLEY. Youll see.

BILL. [*his resolution oozing*] Well, Aw aint dan nathin to er.

SHIRLEY. Spose she said you did! who'd believe you?

BILL. [*very uneasy, skulking back to the corner of the penthouse*]. Gawd! theres no jastice in this cantry. To think wot them people can do! Aw'm as good as er.

SHIRLEY. Tell her so. Its just what a fool like you would do.

Barbara, brisk and businesslike, comes from the shelter with a note book, and addresses herself to Shirley. Bill, cowed, sits down in the corner on a form, and turns his back on them.

BARBARA. Good morning.

SHIRLEY. [*standing up and taking off his hat*] Good morning, miss.

BARBARA. Sit down: make yourself at home. [*He hesitates; but she puts a friendly hand on his shoulder and makes him obey*]. Now then! since youve made friends with us, we want to know all about you. Names and addresses and trades.

SHIRLEY. Peter Shirley. Fitter. Chucked out two months ago because I was too old.

BARBARA. [*not at all surprised*] Youd pass still. Why didnt you dye your hair?

SHIRLEY. I did. Me age come out at a coroner's inquest on me daughter.

BARBARA. Steady?

SHIRLEY. Teetotaller. Never out of a job before. Good worker. And sent to the knackers⁸ like an old horse!

BARBARA. No matter: if you did your part God will do his.

SHIRLEY. [*suddenly stubborn*] My religion's no concern of anybody but myself.

BARBARA. [*guessing*] I know. Secularist?⁹

SHIRLEY. [*hotly*] Did I offer to deny it?

BARBARA. Why should you? My own father's a Secularist, I think. Our Father—yours and mine—fulfils himself in many ways; and I daresay he knew what he was about when he made a Secularist of you. So buck up, Peter! we can always find a job for a steady man like you. [SHIRLEY, *disarmed and a little bewildered, touches his hat. She turns from him to* BILL.] Whats y o u r name?

---

7. Get away with you!
8. A "knacker" bought old or diseased horses and slaughtered them for their hides, hooves, and meat.
9. Secularism taught that life should be interpreted in terms of this world without recourse to a belief in God or the afterlife. The Secularist movement arose about 1850 from the teachings of G. J. Holyoake.

BILL. [*insolently*] Wots thet to you?

BARBARA. [*calmly making a note*] Afraid to give his name. Any trade?

BILL. Oo's afride to give is nime? [*Doggedly, with a sense of heroically defying the House of Lords in the person of Lord Stevenage*] If you want to bring a chawge agen me, bring it. [*She waits, unruffled*]. Moy nime's Bill Walker.

BARBARA. [*as if the name were familiar: trying to remember how*] Bill Walker? [*Recollecting*] Oh, I know: youre the man that Jenny Hill was praying for inside just now. [*She enters his name in her note book*].

BILL. Oo's Jenny Ill? And wot call as she to pry for me?

BARBARA. I dont know. Perhaps it was you that cut her lip.

BILL. [*defiantly*] Yus, it w a s me that cat her lip. Aw aint afride o y o u.

BARBARA. How could you be, since youre not afraid of God? Youre a brave man, Mr Walker. It takes some pluck to do o u r work here; but none of us dare lift our hand against a girl like that, for fear of her father in heaven.

BILL. [*sullenly*] I want nan o your kentin[1] jawr. I spowse you think Aw cam eah to beg from you, like this demmiged lot eah. Not me. Aw downt want your bread and scripe[2] and ketlep. Aw dont blieve in your Gawd, no more than you do yourself.

BARBARA. [*sunnily apologetic and ladylike, as on a new footing with him*] Oh, I beg your pardon for putting your name down, Mr Walker. I didn't understand. I'll strike it out.

BILL. [*taking this as a slight, and deeply wounded by it*] Eah! you let maw nime alown. Aint it good enaff to be in your book?

BARBARA. [*considering*] Well, you see, theres no use putting down your name unless I can do something for you, is there? Whats your trade?

BILL. [*still smarting*] Thets nao concern o yours.

BARBARA. Just so. [*Very businesslike*] I'll put you down as [*writing*] the man—struck—poor little Jenny Hill—in the mouth.

BILL. [*rising threateningly*] See eah. Awve ed enaff o this.

BARBARA. [*quite sunny and fearless*] What did you come to us for?

BILL. Aw cam for maw gel, see? Aw cam to tike her aht o this and to brike er jawr for er.

BARBARA. [*complacently*] You see I was right about your trade. [BILL, *on the point of retorting furiously, finds himself, to his great shame and terror, in danger of crying instead. He sits down again suddenly*]. Whats her name?

BILL. [*dogged*] Er nime's Mog Ebbijem: thets wot her nime is.

BARBARA. Mog Habbijam! Oh, she's gone to Canning Town, to our barracks there.

BILL. [*fortified by his resentment of Mog's perfidy*] Is she?

---

1. Canting, hypocritical.
2. Scrape: a thin coating of butter. "Ket-lep" (cat-lap): tea or any other weak drink fit only for a cat to lap up.

[*Vindictively*] Then Aw'm gowin to Kennintahn arter her.
[*He crosses to the gate; hesitates; finally comes back at* BAR-
BARA]. Are you loyin to me to git shat o me?

BARBARA. I dont want to get shut of you. I want to keep you here
and save your soul. Youd better stay: youre going to have a bad
time today, Bill.

BILL. Oo's gowin to give it to me? Y o u, preps?

BARBARA. Someone you dont believe in. But youll be glad afterwards.

BILL. [*slinking off*] Aw'll gow to Kennintahn to be aht o reach o
your tangue. [*Suddenly turning on her with intense malice*]
And if Aw downt fawnd Mog there, Aw'll cam beck and do two
years for you, selp me Gawd if Aw downt!

BARBARA. [*a shade kindlier, if possible*] It's no use, Bill. She's got
another bloke.

BILL. Wot!

BARBARA. One of her own converts. He fell in love with her when
he saw her with her soul saved, and her face clean, and her hair
washed.

BILL. [*surprised*] Wottud she wash it for, the carroty slat? It's red.

BARBARA. It's quite lovely now, because she wears a new look in her
eyes with it. It's a pity youre too late. The new bloke has put
your nose out of joint, Bill.

BILL. Aw'll put his nowse aht o joint for him. Not that Aw care a
carse for er, mawnd thet. But Aw'll teach her to drop me as if
Aw was dirt. And Aw'll teach him to meddle with maw judy.[3]
Wots iz bleedin níme?

BARBARA. Sergeant Todger Fairmile.

SHIRLEY. [*rising with grim joy*] I'll go with him, miss. I want to
see them two meet. I'll take him to the infirmary when it's over.

BILL. [*to* SHIRLEY, *with undissembled misgiving*] Is thet im you
was speaking on?

SHIRLEY. Thats him.

BILL. Im that wrastled in the music awl?

SHIRLEY. The competitions at the National Sportin Club was worth
nigh a hundred a year to him. He's gev em up now for religion;
so he's a bit fresh for want of the exercise he was accustomed to.
He'll be glad to see you. Come along.

BILL. Wots is wight?

SHIRLEY. Thirteen four.[4] [BILL's *last hope expires*].

BARBARA. Go and talk to him, Bill. He'll convert you.

SHIRLEY. He'll convert your head into a mashed potato.

BILL. [*sullenly*] Aw aint afride of im. Aw aint afride of ennybody.
Bat e can lick me. She's dan me. [*He sits down moodily on the
edge of the horse trough*].

SHIRLEY. You aint goin. I thought not. [*He resumes his seat*].

BARBARA. [*calling*] Jenny!

3. Girl.
4. That is, 13 stone, 4 pounds. (A stone   is a unit of weight equal to 14 pounds.)
The sergeant weighs 186 pounds.

JENNY. [*appearing at the shelter door with a plaster on the corner of her mouth*] Yes, Major.

BARBARA. Send Rummy Mitchens out to clear away here.

JENNY. I think she's afraid.

BARBARA. [*her resemblance to her mother flashing out for a moment*] Nonsense! she must do as she's told.

JENNY. [*calling into the shelter*] Rummy: the Major says you must come.

Jenny comes to Barbara, purposely keeping on the side next Bill, lest he should suppose that she shrank from him or bore malice.

BARBARA. Poor little Jenny! Are you tired? [*Looking at the wounded cheek*] Does it hurt?

JENNY. No: it's all right now. It was nothing.

BARBARA. [*critically*] It was as hard as he could hit, I expect. Poor Bill! You dont feel angry with him, do you?

JENNY. Oh no, no, no: indeed I dont, Major, bless his poor heart! [BARBARA *kisses her; and she runs away merrily into the shelter.* BILL *writhes with an agonizing return of his new and alarming symptoms, but says nothing.* RUMMY MITCHENS *comes from the shelter*].

BARBARA. [*going to meet* RUMMY] Now Rummy, bustle. Take in those mugs and plates to be washed; and throw the crumbs about for the birds.

Rummy takes the three plates and mugs; but Shirley takes back his mug from her, as there is still some milk left in it.

RUMMY. There aint any crumbs. This aint a time to waste good bread on birds.

PRICE. [*appearing at the shelter door*] Gentleman come to see the shelter, Major. Says he's your father.

BARBARA. All right. Coming. [SNOBBY *goes back into the shelter, followed by* BARBARA].

RUMMY. [*stealing across to* BILL *and addressing him in a subdued voice, but with intense conviction*] I'd av the lor of you, you flat eared pignosed potwalloper,[5] if she'd let me. Youre no gentleman, to hit a lady in the face. [BILL, *with greater things moving in him, takes no notice*].

SHIRLEY. [*following her*] Here! in with you and dont get yourself into more trouble by talking.

RUMMY. [*with hauteur*] I aint ad the pleasure o being hintroduced to you, as I can remember. [*She goes into the shelter with the plates*].

SHIRLEY. Thats the—

BILL. [*savagely*] Downt you talk to me, d'ye eah? You lea me alown, or Aw'll do you a mischief. Aw'm not dirt under y o u r feet, ennywy.

SHIRLEY. [*calmly*] Dont you be afeerd. You aint such prime company that you need expect to be sought after. [*He is about to go into the shelter when* BARBARA *comes out, with* UNDERSHAFT *on her right*].

---

5. A pot-washer; a menial servant.

BARBARA. Oh, there you are, Mr Shirley! [*Between them*] This is my father: I told you he was a Secularist, didnt I? Perhaps youll be able to comfort one another.

UNDERSHAFT. [*startled*] A Secularist! Not the least in the world: on the contrary, a confirmed mystic.

BARBARA. Sorry, I'm sure. By the way, papa, what i s your religion? in case I have to introduce you again.

UNDERSHAFT. My religion? Well, my dear, I am a Millionaire. That is my religion.

BARBARA. Then I'm afraid you and Mr Shirley wont be able to comfort one another after all. Youre not a Millionaire, are you, Peter?

SHIRLEY. No; and proud of it.

UNDERSHAFT. [*gravely*] Poverty, my friend, is not a thing to be proud of.

SHIRLEY. [*angrily*] Who made your millions for you? Me and my like. Whats kep us poor? Keepin you rich. I wouldnt have your conscience, not for all your income.

UNDERSHAFT. I wouldnt have your income, not for all your conscience, Mr Shirley. [*He goes to the penthouse and sits down on a form*].

BARBARA. [*stopping* SHIRLEY *adroitly as he is about to retort*] You wouldnt think he was my father, would you, Peter? Will you go into the shelter and lend the lasses a hand for a while: we're worked off our feet.

SHIRLEY. [*bitterly*] Yes: I'm in their debt for a meal, aint I?

BARBARA. Oh, not because youre in their debt, but for love of them, Peter, for love of them. [*He cannot understand, and is rather scandalized*]. There! dont stare at me. In with you; and give that conscience of yours a holiday. [*Bustling him into the shelter*].

SHIRLEY. [*as he goes in*] Ah! it's a pity you never was trained to use your reason, miss. Youd have been a very taking lecturer on Secularism.

Barbara turns to her father.

UNDERSHAFT. Never mind me, my dear. Go about your work; and let me watch it for a while.

BARBARA. All right.

UNDERSHAFT. For instance, whats the matter with that out-patient over there?

BARBARA. [*looking at* BILL, *whose attitude has never changed, and whose expression of brooding wrath has deepened*] Oh, we shall cure him in no time. Just watch. [*She goes over to* BILL *and waits. He glances up at her and casts his eyes down again, uneasy, but grimmer than ever*]. It w o u l d be nice to just stamp on Mog Habbijam's face, wouldnt it, Bill?

BILL. [*starting up from the trough in consternation*] It's a loy: Aw never said so. [*She shakes her head*]. Oo taold you wot was in moy mawnd?

BARBARA. Only your new friend.

BILL. Wot new friend?

BARBARA. The devil, Bill. When he gets round people they get miserable, just like you.

BILL. [*with a heartbreaking attempt at devil-may-care cheerfulness*] Aw aint miserable. [*He sits down again, and stretches his legs in an attempt to seem indifferent*].

BARBARA. Well, if youre happy, why dont you look happy, as we do?

BILL. [*his legs curling back in spite of him*] Aw'm eppy enaff, Aw tell you. Woy cawnt you lea me alown? Wot ev I dan to you? Aw aint smashed y o u r fice, ev Aw?

BARBARA. [*softly: wooing his soul*] It's not me thats getting at you, Bill.

BILL. Oo else is it?

BARBARA. Somebody that doesnt intend you to smash women's faces, I suppose. Somebody or something that wants to make a man of you.

BILL. [*blustering*] Mike a menn o m e! Aint Aw a menn? eh? Oo sez Aw'm not a menn?

BARBARA. Theres a man in you somewhere, I suppose. But why did he let you hit poor little Jenny Hill? That wasnt very manly of him, was it?

BILL. [*tormented*] Ev dan wiv it, Aw tell you. Chack it. Aw'm sick o your Jenny Ill and er silly little fice.

BARBARA. Then why do you keep thinking about it? Why does it keep coming up against you in your mind? Youre not getting converted, are you?

BILL. [*with conviction*] Not ME. Not lawkly.

BARBARA. Thats right, Bill. Hold out against it. Put out your strength. Dont lets get you cheap. Todger Fairmile said he wrestled for three nights against his salvation harder than he ever wrestled with the Jap at the music hall. He gave in to the Jap when his arm was going to break. But he didnt give in to his salvation until his heart was going to break. Perhaps youll escape that. You havnt any heart, have you?

BILL. Wot d'ye mean? Woy aint Aw got a awt the sime as ennybody else?

BARBARA. A man with a heart wouldnt have bashed poor little Jenny's face, would he?

BILL. [*almost crying*] Ow, w i l l you lea me alown? Ev Aw ever offered to meddle with y o u, that you cam neggin and provowkin me lawk this? [*He writhes convulsively from his eyes to his toes*].

BARBARA. [*with a steady soothing hand on his arm and a gentle voice that never lets him go*] It's your soul thats hurting you, Bill, and not me. Weve been through it all ourselves. Come with us, Bill. [*He looks wildly round.*] To brave manhood on earth and eternal glory in heaven. [*He is on the point of breaking down.*] Come. [*A drum is heard in the shelter; and* BILL, *with a gasp, escapes from the spell as* BARBARA *turns quickly.* ADOLPHUS *enters from the shelter with a big drum*]. Oh! There you are, Dolly. Let me introduce a new friend of mine, Mr Bill Walker. This is my bloke, Bill; Mr Cusins. [CUSINS *salutes with his drumstick*].

BILL. Gowin to merry im?

BARBARA. Yes.

BILL. [*fervently*] Gawd elp im! Gaw-aw-aw-awd elp im!

BARBARA. Why? Do you think he wont be happy with me?

BILL. Awve aony ed to stend it for a mawnin: e'll ev to stend it for a lawftawm.

CUSINS. That is a frightful reflection, Mr Walker. But I cant tear myself away from her.

BILL. Well, Aw ken. [*To* BARBARA] Eah! do you knaow where Aw'm gowin to, and wot Aw'm gowin to do?

BARBARA. Yes: youre going to heaven; and youre coming back here before the week's out to tell me so.

BILL. You loy. Aw'm gowin to Kennintahn, to spit in Todger Fairmawl's eye. Aw beshed Jenny Ill's fice; an nar Aw'll git me aown fice beshed and cam beck and shaow it to er. Ee'll itt me ardern Aw itt er. Thatll mike us square. [*To* ADOLPHUS] Is thet fair or is it not? Youre a genlmn: you oughter knaow.

BARBARA. Two black eyes wont make one white one, Bill.

BILL. Aw didnt awst y o u. Cawnt you never keep your mahth shat? Oy awst the genlmn.

CUSINS. [*reflectively*] Yes: I think youre right, Mr Walker. Yes: I should do it. It's curious: it's exactly what an ancient Greek would have done.

BARBARA. But what good will it do?

CUSINS. Well, it will give Mr Fairmile some exercise; and it will satisfy Mr Walker's soul.

BILL. Rot! there aint nao sach a thing as a saoul. Ah kin you tell wevver Awve a saoul or not? You never seen it.

BARBARA. Ive seen it hurting you when you went against it.

BILL. [*with compressed aggravation*] If you was maw gel and took the word aht o me mahth lawk thet, Aw'd give you sathink youd feel urtin, Aw would. [*To* ADOLPHUS] You tike maw tip, mite. Stop er jawr; or youll doy afoah your tawm. [*With intense expression*] Wore aht: thets wot youll be: wore aht. [*He goes away through the gate*].

CUSINS. [*looking after him*] I wonder!

BARBARA. Dolly! [*Indignant, in her mother's manner*].

CUSINS. Yes, my dear, it's very wearing to be in love with you. If it lasts, I quite think I shall die young.

BARBARA. Should you mind?

CUSINS. Not at all. [*He is suddenly softened, and kisses her over the drum, evidently not for the first time, as people cannot kiss over a big drum without practice.* UNDERSHAFT *coughs*].

BARBARA. It's all right, papa, weve not forgotten you. Dolly: explain the place to papa: I havnt time. [*She goes busily into the shelter*].

Undershaft and Adolphus now have the yard to themselves. Undershaft, seated on a form, and still keenly attentive, looks hard at Adolphus. Adolphus looks hard at him.

UNDERSHAFT. I fancy you guess something of what is in my mind,

Mr Cusins. [CUSINS *flourishes his drumsticks as if in the act of beating a lively rataplan, but makes no sound.*] Exactly so. But suppose Barbara finds you out!

CUSINS. You know, I do not admit that I am imposing on Barbara. I am quite genuinely interested in the views of the Salvation Army. The fact is, I am a sort of collector of religions; and the curious thing is that I find I can believe them all. By the way, have you any religion?

UNDERSHAFT. Yes.

CUSINS. Anything out of the common?

UNDERSHAFT. Only that there are two things necessary to Salvation.

CUSINS. [*disappointed, but polite*] Ah, the Church Catechism. Charles Lomax also belongs to the Established Church.

UNDERSHAFT. The two things are—

CUSINS. Baptism and—

UNDERSHAFT. No. Money and gunpowder.

CUSINS. [*surprised, but interested*] That is the general opinion of our governing classes. The novelty is in hearing any man confess it.

UNDERSHAFT. Just so.

CUSINS. Excuse me: is there any place in your religion for honor, justice, truth, love, mercy and so forth?

UNDERSHAFT. Yes: they are the graces and luxuries of a rich, strong, and safe life.

CUSINS. Suppose one is forced to choose between them and money or gunpowder?

UNDERSHAFT. Choose money a n d gunpowder; for without enough of both you cannot afford the others.

CUSINS. That is your religion?

UNDERSHAFT. Yes.

The cadence of this reply makes a full close in the conversation. Cusins twists his face dubiously and contemplates Undershaft. Undershaft contemplates him.

CUSINS. Barbara wont stand that. You will have to choose between your religion and Barbara.

UNDERSHAFT. So will you, my friend. She will find out that that drum of yours is hollow.

CUSINS. Father Undershaft: you are misaken: I am a sincere Salvationist. You do not understand the Salvation Army. It is the army of joy, of love, of courage: it has banished the fear and remorse and despair of the old hell-ridden evangelical sects: it marches to fight the devil with trumpet and drum, with music and dancing, with banner and palm, as becomes a sally from heaven by its happy garrison. It picks the waster out of the public house and makes a man of him: it finds a worm wriggling in a back kitchen, and lo! a woman! Men and women of rank too, sons and daughters of the Highest. It takes the poor professor of Greek, the most artificial and self-suppressed of human creatures, from his meal of roots, and lets loose the rhapsodist in him;

reveals the true worship of Dionysos[6] to him; sends him down the public street drumming dithyrambs [*he plays a thundering flourish on the drum*].

UNDERSHAFT. You will alarm the shelter.

CUSINS. Oh, they are accustomed to these sudden ecstasies of piety. However, if the drum worries you— [*He pockets the drumsticks; unhooks the drum; and stands it on the ground opposite the gateway*].

UNDERSHAFT. Thank you.

CUSINS. You remember what Euripides says about your money and gunpowder?

UNDERSHAFT. No.

CUSINS. [*declaiming*]

> One and another
> In money and guns may outpass his brother;
> And men in their millions float and flow
> And seethe with a million hopes as leaven;
> And they win their will; or they miss their will;
> And their hopes are dead or are pined for still;
> But whoe'er can know
> As the long days go
> That to live is happy, has found h i s heaven.[7]

My translation: what do you think of it?

UNDERSHAFT. I think, my friend, that if you wish to know, as the long days go, that to live is happy, you must first acquire money enough for a decent life, and power enough to be your own master.

CUSINS. You are damnably discouraging. [*He resumes his declamation*].

> Is it so hard a thing to see
> That the spirit of God—whate'er it be—
> The law that abides and changes not, ages long,
> The Eternal and Nature-born: t h e s e things be strong?
> What else is Wisdom? What of Man's endeavor,
> Or God's high grace so lovely and so great?
> To stand from fear set free? to breathe and wait?
> To hold a hand uplifted over Fate?
> And shall not Barbara be loved for ever?

UNDERSHAFT. Euripides mentions Barbara, does he?

CUSINS. It is a fair translation. The word means Loveliness.

UNDERSHAFT. May I ask—as Barbara's father—how much a year she is to be loved for ever on?

6. Greek god of a highly emotional religion, frequently restricted in function to being simply the god of wine. His other name was Bacchus. "Dithyrambs" are songs in praise of Dionysos.

7. The verse translations from Euripides, as Shaw informed his readers in a note, come from Gilbert Murray's translation of *The Bacchae*. Shaw greatly admired Murray, who was professor of Greek at Oxford, and thought highly of his verse translations from the Greek dramatists, which are now considered inappropriately Swinburnian and over-rhetorical in style; there is more than a suggestion of Murray in Professor Higgins of *Pygmalion* as well as in Cusins.

CUSINS. As Barbara's father, that is more your affair than mine. I can feed her by teaching Greek: that is about all.

UNDERSHAFT. Do you consider it a good match for her?

CUSINS. [*with polite obstinacy*] Mr Undershaft: I am in many ways a weak, timid, ineffectual person; and my health is far from satisfactory. But whenever I feel that I must have anything, I get it, sooner or later. I feel that way about Barbara. I dont like marriage: I feel intensely afraid of it; and I dont know what I shall do with Barbara or what she will do with me. But I feel that I and nobody else must marry her. Please regard that as settled.— Not that I wish to be arbitrary; but why should I waste your time in discussing what is inevitable?

UNDERSHAFT. You mean that you will stick at nothing: not even the conversion of the Salvation Army to the worship of Dionysos.

CUSINS. The business of the Salvation Army is to save, not to wrangle about the name of the pathfinder. Dionysos or another: what does it matter?

UNDERSHAFT. [*rising and approaching him*] Professor Cusins: you are a young man after my own heart.

CUSINS. Mr Undershaft: you are, as far as I am able to gather, a most infernal old rascal; but you appeal very strongly to my sense of ironic humor.

Undershaft mutely offers his hand. They shake.

UNDERSHAFT. [*suddenly concentrating himself*] And now to business.

CUSINS. Pardon me. We were discussing religion. Why go back to such an uninteresting and unimportant subject as business?

UNDERSHAFT. Religion is our business at present, because it is through religion alone that we can win Barbara.

CUSINS. Have you, too, fallen in love with Barbara?

UNDERSHAFT. Yes, with a father's love.

CUSINS. A father's love for a grown-up daughter is the most dangerous of all infatuations. I apologize for mentioning my own pale, coy, mistrustful fancy in the same breath with it.

UNDERSHAFT. Keep to the point. We have to win her; and we are neither of us Methodists.

CUSINS. That doesnt matter. The power Barbara wields here—the power that wields Barbara herself—is not Calvinism, not Presbyterianism, not Methodism—

UNDERSHAFT. Not Greek Paganism either, eh?

CUSINS. I admit that. Barbara is quite original in her religion.

UNDERSHAFT. [*triumphantly*] Aha! Barbara Undershaft would be. Her inspiration comes from within herself.

CUSINS. How do you suppose it got there?

UNDERSHAFT. [*in towering excitement*] It is the Undershaft inheritance. I shall hand on my torch to my daughter. She shall make my converts and preach my gospel—

CUSINS. What! Money and gunpowder!

UNDERSHAFT. Yes, money and gunpowder; freedom and power; command of life and command of death.

CUSINS. [*urbanely: trying to bring him down to earth*] This is extremely interesting, Mr Undershaft. Of course you know that you are mad.

UNDERSHAFT. [*with redoubled force*] And you?

CUSINS. Oh, mad as a hatter. You are welcome to my secret since I have discovered yours. But I am astonished. Can a madman make cannons?

UNDERSHAFT. Would anyone else than a madman make them? And now [*With surging energy*] question for question. Can a sane man translate Euripides?

CUSINS. No.

UNDERSHAFT. [*seizing him by the shoulder*] Can a sane woman make a man of a waster or a woman of a worm?

CUSINS. [*reeling before the storm*] Father Colossus—Mammoth Millionaire—

UNDERSHAFT. [*pressing him.*] Are there two mad people or three in this Salvation shelter to-day?

CUSINS. You mean Barbara is as mad as we are?

UNDERSHAFT. [*pushing him lightly off and resuming his equanimity suddenly and completely*] Pooh, Professor! let us call things by their proper names. I am a millionaire; you are a poet; Barbara is a savior of souls. What have we three to do with the common mob of slaves and idolaters? [*He sits down again with a shrug of contempt for the mob*].

CUSINS. Take care! Barbara is in love with the common people. So am I. Have you never felt the romance of that love?

UNDERSHAFT. [*cold and sardonic*] Have you ever been in love with Poverty, like St. Francis? Have you ever been in love with Dirt, like St. Simeon? Have you ever been in love with disease and suffering, like our nurses and philanthropists? Such passions are not virtues, but the most unnatural of all the vices. This love of the common people may please an earl's granddaughter and a university professor; but I have been a common man and a poor man; and it has no romance for me. Leave it to the poor to pretend that poverty is a blessing: leave it to the coward to make a religion of his cowardice by preaching humility: we know better than that. We three must stand together above the common people: how else can we help their children to climb up beside us? Barbara must belong to us, not to the Salvation Army.

CUSINS. Well, I can only say that if you think you will get her away from the Salvation Army by talking to her as you have been talking to me, you dont know Barbara.

UNDERSHAFT. My friend: I never ask for what I can buy.

CUSINS. [*in a white fury*] Do I understand you to imply that you can buy Barbara?

UNDERSHAFT. No; but I can buy the Salvation Army.

CUSINS. Quite impossible.

UNDERSHAFT. You shall see. All religious organizations exist by selling themselves to the rich.

CUSINS. Not the Army. That is the Church of the poor.

UNDERSHAFT. All the more reason for buying it.

CUSINS. I dont think you quite know what the Army does for the poor.

UNDERSHAFT. Oh yes I do. It draws their teeth: that is enough for me—as a man of business—

CUSINS. Nonsense! It makes them sober—

UNDERSHAFT. I prefer sober workmen. The profits are larger.

CUSINS. —honest—

UNDERSHAFT. Honest workmen are the most economical.

CUSINS. —attached to their homes—

UNDERSHAFT. So much the better: they will put up with anything sooner than change their shop.

CUSINS. —happy—

UNDERSHAFT. An invaluable safeguard against revolution.

CUSINS. —unselfish—

UNDERSHAFT. Indifferent to their own interests, which suits me exactly.

CUSINS. —with their thoughts on heavenly things—

UNDERSHAFT. [*rising*] And not on Trade Unionism nor Socialism. Excellent.

CUSINS. [*revolted*] You really are an infernal old rascal.

UNDERSHAFT. [*indicating* PETER SHIRLEY, *who has just come from the shelter and strolled dejectedly down the yard between them*] And this is an honest man!

SHIRLEY. Yes; and what av I got by it? [*He passes on bitterly and sits on the form, in the corner of the penthouse*].

Snobby Price, beaming sanctimoniously, and Jenny Hill, with a tambourine full of coppers, come from the shelter and go to the drum, on which Jenny begins to count the money.

UNDERSHAFT. [*replying to* SHIRLEY] Oh, your employers must have got a good deal by it from first to last. [*He sits on the table, with one foot on the side form,* CUSINS, *overwhelmed, sits down on the same form nearer the shelter.* BARBARA *comes from the shelter to the middle of the yard. She is excited and a little over-wrought*].

BARBARA. Weve just had a splendid experience meeting at the other gate in Cripps's lane. Ive hardly ever seen them so much moved as they were by your confession, Mr Price.

PRICE. I could almost be glad of my past wickedness if I could believe that it would elp to keep hathers stright.

BARBARA. So it will, Snobby. How much, Jenny?

JENNY. Four and tenpence, Major.

BARBARA. Oh Snobby, if you had given your poor mother just one more kick, we should have got the whole five shillings!

PRICE. If she heard you say that, miss, she'd be sorry I didnt. But I'm glad. Oh what a joy it will be to her when she hears I'm saved!

UNDERSHAFT. Shall I contribute the odd twopence, Barbara? The millionaire's mite, eh? [*He takes a couple of pennies from his pocket*].

BARBARA. How did you make that twopence?

UNDERSHAFT. As usual. By selling cannons, torpedoes, submarines, and my new patent Grand Duke hand grenade.

BARBARA. Put it back in your pocket. You cant buy your Salvation here for twopence: you must work it out.

UNDERSHAFT. Is twopence not enough? I can afford a little more, if you press me.

BARBARA. Two million millions would not be enough. There is bad blood on your hands; and nothing but good blood can cleanse them. Money is no use. Take it away. [*She turns to* CUSINS]. Dolly: you must write another letter for me to the papers. [*He makes a wry face*]. Yes: I know you dont like it; but it must be done. The starvation this winter is beating us: everybody is unemployed. The General says we must close this shelter if we cant get more money. I force the collections at the meetings until I am ashamed: dont I, Snobby?

PRICE. It's a fair treat to see you work it, Miss. The way you got them up from three-and-six to four-and-ten with that hymn, penny by penny and verse by verse, was a caution. Not a Cheap Jack[8] on Mile End Waste could touch you at it.

BARBARA. Yes; but I wish we could do without it. I am getting at last to think more of the collection than of the people's souls. And what are those hatfuls of pence and halfpence? We want thousands! tens of thousands! hundreds of thousands! I want to convert people, not to be always begging for the Army in a way I'd die sooner than beg for myself.

UNDERSHAFT. [*in profound irony*] Genuine unselfishness is capable of anything, my dear.

BARBARA. [*unsuspectingly, as she turns away to take the money from the drum and put it in a cash bag she carries*] Yes, isnt it? [UNDERSHAFT *looks sardonically at* CUSINS].

CUSINS. [*aside to* UNDERSHAFT.] Mephistopheles! Machiavelli!

BARBARA. [*tears coming into her eyes as she ties the bag and pockets it*] How are we to feed them? I cant talk religion to a man with bodily hunger in his eyes. [*Almost breaking down*] It's frightful.

JENNY. [*running to her*] Major, dear—

BARBARA. [*rebounding*] No: dont comfort me. It will be all right. We shall get the money.

UNDERSHAFT. How?

JENNY. By praying for it, of course. Mrs Baines says she prayed for it last night; and she has never prayed for it in vain: never once. [*She goes to the gate and looks out into the street*].

BARBARA. [*who has dried her eyes and regained her composure*] By the way, dad, Mrs Baines has come to march with us to our big meeting this afternoon; and she is very anxious to meet you, for some reason or other. Perhaps she'll convert you.

---

8. A street peddler who overprices his wares and then pretends to be offering a bargain by lowering the price. Mile End Waste was the scene of many fairs and gatherings.

UNDERSHAFT. I shall be delighted, my dear.

JENNY. [*at the gate: excitedly*] Major! Major! heres that man back again.

BARBARA. What man?

JENNY. The man that hit me. Oh, I hope he's coming back to join us.

Bill Walker. with frost on his jacket, comes through the gate, his hands deep in his pockets and his chin sunk between his shoulders, like a cleaned-out gambler. He halts between Barbara and the drum.

BARBARA. Hullo, Bill! Back already!

BILL. [*nagging at her*] Bin talkin ever sence, ev you?

BARBARA. Pretty nearly. Well, has Todger paid you out for poor Jenny's jaw?

BILL. Nao e aint.

BARBARA. I thought your jacket looked a bit snowy.

BILL. Sao it is snaowy. You want to knaow where the snaow cam from, downt you?

BARBARA. Yes.

BILL. Well, it cam from orf the grahnd in Pawkinses Corner in Kennintahn. It got rabbed orf be maw shaoulders: see?

BARBARA. Pity you didnt rub some off with your knees, Bill! That would have done you a lot of good.

BILL. [*with sour mirthless humor*] Aw was sivin anather menn's knees at the tawm. E was kneelin on moy ed, e was.

JENNY. Who was kneeling on your head?

BILL. Todger was. E was pryin for me: pryin camfortable wiv me as a cawpet. Sow was Mog. Sao was the aol bloomin meetin. Mog she sez "Ow Lawd brike is stabborn sperrit; bat downt urt is dear art." Thet was wot she said. "Downt urt is dear art"! An er blowk—thirteen stun four!—kneelin wiv all is wight on me. Fanny, aint it?

JENNY. Oh no. We're so sorry, Mr Walker.

BARBARA. [*enjoying it frankly*] Nonsense! of course it's funny. Served you right, Bill! You must have done something to him first.

BILL. [doggedly] Aw did wot Aw said Aw'd do. Aw spit in is eye. E looks ap at the skoy and sez, "Ow that Aw should be fahnd worthy to be spit upon for the gospel's sike!" e sez; an Mog sez "Glaory Allelloolier!"; an then e called me Braddher, an dahned me as if Aw was a kid and e was me mather worshin me a Setterda nawt. Aw ednt jast nao shaow wiv im at all. Arf the street pryed; an the tather arf larfed fit to split theirselves. [TO BARBARA] There! are you settisfawd nah?

BARBARA. [*her eyes dancing*] Wish I'd been there, Bill.

BILL. Yus: youd a got in a hextra bit o talk on me, wouldnt you?

JENNY. I'm so sorry, Mr Walker.

BILL. [*fiercely*] Downt you gow bein sorry for me: youve no call. Listen eah. Aw browk your jawr.

JENNY. No, it didnt hurt me: indeed it didnt, except for a moment. It was only that I was frightened.

BILL. Aw downt want to be forgive be you, or be ennybody. Wot Aw did Aw'll py for. Aw trawd to gat me aown jawr browk to settisfaw you—

JENNY. [*distressed*] Oh no—

BILL. [*impatiently*] Tell y' Aw did: cawnt you listen to wots bein taold you? All Aw got be it was bein mide a sawt of in the pablic street for me pines. Well, if Aw cawnt settisfaw you one wy, Aw ken anather. Listen eah! Aw ed two quid sived agen the frost; an Awve a pahnd of it left. A mite o mawn last week ed words with the judy e's gowin to merry. E give er wot-for; an e's bin fawnd fifteen bob. E ed a rawt to itt er cause they was gowin to be merrid; but Aw ednt nao rawt to itt you; sao put anather fawv bob on an call it a pahnd's worth. [*He produces a sovereign*].⁹ Eahs the manney. Tike it; and lets ev no more o your forgivin an pryin and your Mijor jawrin me. Let wot Aw dan be dan an pide for; and let there be an end of it.

JENNY. Oh, I couldnt take it, Mr Walker. But if you would give a shilling or two to poor Rummy Mitchens! you really did hurt her; and she's old.

BILL. [*contemptuously*] Not lawkly. Aw'd give her anather as soon as look at er. Let her ev the lawr o me as she threatened! S h e aint forgiven me: not mach. Wot Aw dan to er is not on me mawnd—wot she [*indicating* BARBARA] mawt call on me conscience—no more than stickin a pig. It's this Christian gime o yours that Aw wownt ev plyed agen me: this bloomin forgivin an neggin an jawrin that mikes a menn thet sore that iz lawf's a burden to im. Aw wownt ev it, Aw tell you; sao tike your manney and stop thraowin your silly beshed fice hap agen me.

JENNY. Major: may I take a little of it for the Army?

BARBARA. No: the Army is not to be bought. We want your soul, Bill; and we'll take nothing less.

BILL. [*bitterly*] Aw knaow. Me an maw few shillins is not good enaff for you. Youre a earl's grendorter, you are. Nathink less than a andred pahnd for you.

UNDERSHAFT. Come, Barbara! you could do a great deal of good with a hundred pounds. If you will set this gentleman's mind at ease by taking his pound, I will give the other ninety-nine.

Bill, dazed by such opulence, instinctively touches his cap.

BARBARA. Oh, youre too extravagant, papa. Bill offers twenty pieces of silver. All you need offer is the other ten. That will make the standard price to buy anybody who's for sale.¹ I'm not; and the Army's not. [*To* BILL] Youll never have another quiet moment, Bill, until you come round to us. You cant stand out against your salvation.

BILL. [*sullenly*] Aw cawnt stend aht agen music awl wrastlers and awtful tangued women. Awve offered to py. Aw can do no more. Tike it or leave it. There it is. [*He throws the sovereign on the*

---

9. "Quid": pound note; "bob": shilling; "sovereign": a gold coin worth one pound.

1. Bill's sovereign is worth 20 shillings. Judas betrayed Jesus for 30 pieces of silver.

drum, and sits down on the horse-trough. The coin fascinates SNOBBY PRICE, *who takes an early opportunity of dropping his cap on it*].

Mrs Baines comes from the shelter. She is dressed as a Salvation Army Commissioner. She is an earnest looking woman of about 40, with a caressing urgent voice, and an appealing manner.

BARBARA. This is my father, Mrs. Baines. [UNDERSHAFT *comes from the table, taking his hat off with marked civility*]. Try what you can do with him. He wont listen to me, because he remembers what a fool I was when I was a baby. [*She leaves them together and chats with* JENNY].

MRS BAINES. Have you been shewn over the shelter, Mr Undershaft? You know the work we're doing, of course.

UNDERSHAFT. [*very civilly*] The whole nation knows it, Mrs Baines.

MRS BAINES. No, sir: the whole nation does not know it, or we should not be crippled as we are for want of money to carry our work through the length and breadth of the land. Let me tell you that there would have been rioting this winter in London but for us.

UNDERSHAFT. You really think so?

MRS BAINES. I know it. I remember 1886, when you rich gentlemen hardened your hearts against the cry of the poor. They broke the windows of your clubs in Pall Mall.

UNDERSHAFT. [*gleaming with approval of their method*] And the Mansion House Fund went up next day from thirty thousand pounds to seventy-nine thousand! I remember quite well.

MRS BAINES. Well, wont you help me to get at the people? They wont break windows then. Come here, Price. Let me shew you to this gentleman. [PRICE *comes to be inspected*]. Do you remember the window breaking?

PRICE. My ole father thought it was the revolution, maam.

MRS BAINES. Would you break windows now?

PRICE. Oh no maam. The windows of eaven av bin opened to me. I know now that the rich man is a sinner like myself.

RUMMY. [*appearing above at the loft door*] Snobby Price!

SNOBBY. Wot is it?

RUMMY. Your mother's askin for you at the other gate in Crippses Lane. She's heard about your confession. [PRICE *turns pale*].

MRS BAINES. Go, Mr Price; and pray with her.

JENNY. You can go through the shelter, Snobby.

PRICE. [*to* MRS BAINES] I couldnt face her now, maam, with all the weight of my sins fresh on me. Tell her she'll find her son at ome, waitin for her in prayer. [*He skulks off through the gate, incidentally stealing the sovereign on his way out by picking up his cap from the drum*].

MRS BAINES. [*with swimming eyes*] You see how we take the anger and the bitterness against you out of their hearts, Mr Undershaft.

UNDERSHAFT. It is certainly most convenient and gratifying to all large employers of labor, Mrs Baines.

MRS BAINES. Barbara: Jenny: I have good news: most wonderful news. [JENNY *runs to her*]. My prayers have been answered. I told you they would, Jenny, didnt I?

JENNY. Yes, yes.

BARBARA. [*moving nearer to the drum*] Have we got money enough to keep the shelter open?

MRS BAINES. I hope we shall have enough to keep all the shelters open. Lord Saxmundham has promised us five thousand pounds—

BARBARA. Hooray!

JENNY. Glory!

MRS BAINES. —if—

BARBARA. "If!" If what?

MRS BAINES. —if five other gentlemen will give a thousand each to make it up to ten thousand.

BARBARA. Who is Lord Saxmundham? I never heard of him.

UNDERSHAFT. [*who has pricked up his ears at the peer's name, and is now watching* BARBARA *curiously*] A new creation, my dear. You have heard of Sir Horace Bodger?

BARBARA. Bodger! Do you mean the distiller? Bodger's whisky!

UNDERSHAFT. That is the man. He is one of the greatest of our public benefactors. He restored the cathedral at Hakington. They made him a baronet for that. He gave half a million to the funds of his party: they made him a baron for that.

SHIRLEY. What will they give him for the five thousand?

UNDERSHAFT. There is nothing left to give him. So the five thousand, I should think, is to save his soul.

MRS BAINES. Heaven grant it may! Oh Mr Undershaft, you have some very rich friends. Cant you help us towards the other five thousand? We are going to hold a great meeting this afternoon at the Assembly Hall in the Mile End Road. If I could only announce that one gentleman had come forward to support Lord Saxmundham, others would follow. Dont you know somebody? couldnt you? wouldnt you? [*her eyes fill with tears*] oh, think of those poor people, Mr Undershaft: think of how much it means to them, and how little to a great man like you.

UNDERSHAFT. [*sardonically gallant*] Mrs Baines: you are irresistible. I cant disappoint you; and I cant deny myself the satisfaction of making Bodger pay up. You shall have your five thousand pounds.

MRS BAINES. Thank God!

UNDERSHAFT. You dont thank m e?

MRS BAINES. Oh sir, dont try to be cynical: dont be ashamed of being a good man. The Lord will bless you abundantly; and our prayers will be like a strong fortification round you all the days of your life. [*With a touch of caution*] You will let me have the cheque to shew at the meeting, wont you? Jenny: go in and fetch a pen and ink. [JENNY *runs to the shelter door*].

UNDERSHAFT. Do not disturb Miss Hill: I have a fountain pen. [JENNY *halts. He sits at the table and writes the cheque.* CUSINS *rises to make room for him. They all watch him silently*].

BILL. [*cynically, aside to* BARBARA, *his voice and accent horribly debased*] Wot prawce Selvytion nah?

BARBARA. Stop. [UNDERSHAFT *stops writing: they all turn to her in surprise*]. Mrs Baines: are you really going to take this money?

MRS BAINES. [*astonished*] Why not, dear?

BARBARA. Why not! Do you know what my father is? Have you forgotten that Lord Saxmundham is Bodger the whisky man? Do you remember how we implored the County Council to stop him from writing Bodger's Whisky in letters of fire against the sky; so that the poor drink-ruined creatures on the Embankment could not wake up from their snatches of sleep without being reminded of their deadly thirst by that wicked sky sign? Do you know that the worst thing I have had to fight here is not the devil, but Bodger, Bodger, Bodger, with his whisky, his distilleries, and his tied houses?[2] Are you going to make our shelter another tied house for him, and ask me to keep it?

BILL. Rotten dranken whisky it is too.

MRS BAINES. Dear Barbara: Lord Saxmundham has a soul to be saved like any of us. If heaven has found the way to make a good use of his money, are we to set ourselves up against the answer to our prayers?

BARBARA. I know he has a soul to be saved. Let him come down here; and I'll do my best to help him to his salvation. But he wants to send his cheque down to buy us, and go on being as wicked as ever.

UNDERSHAFT. [*with a reasonableness which* CUSINS *alone perceives to be ironical*] My dear Barbara: alcohol is a very necessary article. It heals the sick—

BARBARA. It does nothing of the sort.

UNDERSHAFT. Well, it assists the doctor: that is perhaps a less questionable way of putting it. It makes life bearable to millions of people who could not endure their existence if they were quite sober. It enables Parliament to do things at eleven at night that no sane person would do at eleven in the morning. Is it Bodger's fault that this inestimable gift is deplorably abused by less than one per cent of the poor? [*He turns again to the table; signs the cheque; and crosses it*].

MRS BAINES. Barbara: will there be less drinking or more if all those poor souls we are saving come tomorrow and find the doors of our shelters shut in their faces? Lord Saxmundham gives us the money to stop drinking—to take his own business from him.

CUSINS. [*impishly*] Pure self-sacrifice on Bodger's part, clearly! Bless dear Bodger! [BARBARA *almost breaks down as* ADOLPHUS, *too, fails her*].

UNDERSHAFT. [*tearing out the cheque and pocketing the book as he rises and goes past* CUSINS *to* MRS BAINES] I also, Mrs Baines, may claim a little disinterestedness. Think of my business! think of the widows and orphans! the men and lads torn to pieces with

---

2. Taverns owned by distilling or brewing firms and required to serve only their liquor.

shrapnel and poisoned with lyddite[3] [MRS BAINES *shrinks; but he goes on remorsely*]! the oceans of blood, not one drop of which is shed in a really just cause! the ravaged crops! the peaceful peasants forced, women and men, to till their fields under the fire of opposing armies on pain of starvation! the bad blood of the fierce little cowards at home who egg on others to fight for the gratification of their national vanity! All this makes money for me: I am never richer, never busier than when the papers are full of it. Well, it is your work to preach peace on earth and goodwill to men. [MRS BAINES's *face lights up again*]. Every convert you make is a vote against war. [*Her lips move in prayer*]. Yet I give you this money to help you to hasten my own commercial ruin. [*He gives her the cheque*].

CUSINS. [*mounting the form in an ecstasy of mischief*] The millennium will be inaugurated by the unselfishness of Undershaft and Bodger. Oh be joyful! [*He takes the drum-sticks frrom his pocket and flourishes them*].

MRS BAINES [*taking the cheque*] The longer I live the more proof I see that there is an Infinite Goodness that turns everything to the work of salvation sooner or later. Who would have thought that any good could have come out of war and drink? And yet their profits are brought today to the feet of salvation to do its blessed work. [*She is affected to tears*].

JENNY. [*running to* MRS BAINES *and throwing her arms round her*] Oh dear! how blessed, how glorious it all is!

CUSINS. [*in a convulsion of irony*] Let us seize this unspeakable moment. Let us march to the great meeting at once. Excuse me just an instant. [*He rushes into the shelter.* JENNY *takes her tambourine from the drum head*].

MRS BAINES. Mr Undershaft: have you ever seen a thousand people fall on their knees with one impulse and pray? Come with us to the meeting. Barbara shall tell them that the Army is saved, and saved through you.

CUSINS. [*returning impetuously from the shelter with a flag and a trombone, and coming between* MRS BAINES *and* UNDERSHAFT] You shall carry the flag down the first street, Mrs Baines. [*He gives her the flag*]. Mr Undershaft is a gifted trombonist: he shall intone an Olympian diapason[4] to the West Ham Salvation March. [*Aside to* UNDERSHAFT, *as he forces the trombone on him*]. Blow, Machiavelli, blow.

UNDERSHAFT. [*aside to him, as he takes the trombone*] The trumpet in Zion! [CUSINS *rushes to the drum, which he takes up and puts on.* UNDERSHAFT *continues, aloud*] I will do my best. I could vamp a bass if I knew the tune.

CUSINS. It is a wedding chorus from one of Donizetti's operas;[5] but we have converted it. We convert everything to good here,

---

3. A high explosive composed chiefly of picric acid.
4. The interval of the octave in Greek music.

5. Specifically, *Lucia di Lammermoor*, by Gaetano Donizetti (1797–1848), Italian composer of some 65 operas.

including Bodger. You remember the chorus. "For thee immense rejoicing—immenso giubilo—immenso giubilo." [*With drum obbligato*] Rum tum ti tum tum, tum tum ti ta—

BARBARA. Dolly: you are breaking my heart.

CUSINS. What is a broken heart more or less here? Dionysos Undershaft has descended. I am possessed.

MRS BAINES. Come, Barbara: I must have my dear Major to carry the flag with me.

JENNY. Yes, yes, Major darling.

Cusins snatches the tambourine out of Jenny's hand and mutely offers it to Barbara.

BARBARA. [*coming forward a little as she puts the offer behind her with a shudder, whilst* CUSINS *recklessly tosses the tambourine back to* JENNY *and goes to the gate*] I cant come.

JENNY. Not come!

MRS BAINES. [*with tears in her eyes*] Barbara: do you think I am wrong to take the money?

BARBARA. [*impulsively going to her and kissing her*] No, no: God help you, dear, you must: you are saving the Army. Go; and may you have a great meeting!

JENNY. But arnt you coming?

BARBARA. No. [*She begins taking off the silver S brooch from her collar*].

MRS BAINES. Barbara: what are you doing?

JENNY. Why are you taking your badge off? You cant be going to leave us, Major.

BARBARA. [*quietly*] Father: come here.

UNDERSHAFT. [*coming to her*] My dear! [*Seeing that she is going to pin the badge on his collar, he retreats to the penthouse in some alarm*].

BARBARA. [*following him*] Dont be frightened. [*She pins the badge on and steps back towards the table, shewing him to the others*]. There! It's not much for £5000, is it?

MRS BAINES. Barbara: if you wont come and pray w i t h us, promise me you will pray f o r us.

BARBARA. I cant pray now. Perhaps I shall never pray again.

MRS BAINES. Barbara!

JENNY. Major!

BARBARA. [*almost delirious*] I cant bear any more. Quick march!

CUSINS. [*calling to the procession in the street outside*] Off we go. Play up, there! I m m e n s o g i u b i l o. [*He gives the time with his drum; and the band strikes up the march, which rapidly becomes more distant as the procession moves briskly away.*]

MRS BAINES. I must go, dear. Youre overworked: you will be all right tomorrow. We'll never lose you. Now Jenny: step out with the old flag. Blood and Fire! [*She marches out through the gate with her flag*].

JENNY. Glory Hallelujah! [*Flourishing her tambourine and marching*].

UNDERSHAFT. [*to* CUSINS, *as he marches out past him easing the slide of his trombone*] "My ducats and my daughter"![6]

CUSINS. [*following him out*] Money and gunpowder!

BARBARA. Drunkenness and Murder! My God: why hast thou forsaken me?

She sinks on the form with her face buried in her hands. The march passes away into silence. Bill Walker steals across to her.

BILL. [*taunting*] Wot prawce selvytion nah?

SHIRLEY. Dont you hit her when she's down.

BILL. She itt me wen aw wiz dahn. Waw shouldnt Aw git a bit o me aown beck?

BARBARA. [*raising her head*] I didnt take y o u r money, Bill. [*She crosses the yard to the gate and turns her back on the two men to hide her face from them*].

BILL. [*sneering after her*] Naow, it warnt enaff for you. [*Turning to the drum, he misses the money*] Ellow! If you aint took it sammun else ez. Weres it gorn? Bly me if Jenny Ill didn't tike it arter all!

RUMMY. [*screaming at him from the loft*] You lie, you dirty blackguard! Snobby Price pinched it off the drum when he took up his cap. I was up here all the time an see im do it.

BILL. Wot! Stowl maw manney! Waw didn't you call thief on him, you silly aold macker you?

RUMMY. To serve you aht for ittin me across the fice. It's cost y'pahnd, that az. [*Raising a paean of squalid triumph*] I done you. I'm even with you. Ive ad it aht o y— [BILL *snatches up* SHIRLEY's *mug and hurls it at her. She slams the loft door and vanishes. The mug smashes against the door and falls in fragments*].

BILL. [*beginning to chuckle*] Tell us, aol menn, wot o'clock this mawnin was it wen im as they call Snobby Prawce was sived?

BARBARA. [*turning to him more composedly, and with unspoiled sweetness*] About half past twelve, Bill. And he pinched your pound at a quarter to two. *I* know. Well, you cant afford to lose it. I'll send it to you.

BILL. [*his voice and accent suddenly improving*] Not if Aw wiz to stawve for it. Aw aint to be bought.

SHIRLEY. Aint you? Youd sell yourself to the devil for a pint o beer; only there aint no devil to make the offer.

BILL. [*unshamed*] Sao Aw would, mite, and often ev, cheerful. But she cawnt baw me. [*Approaching* BARBARA] You wanted maw saoul, did you? Well, you aint got it.

BARBARA. I nearly got it, Bill. But weve sold it back to you for ten thousand pounds.

SHIRLEY. And dear at the money!

BARBARA. No, Peter: it was worth more than money.

---

6. Shylock's exclamation on discovering the simultaneous loss of his daughter and his money (*The Merchant of Venice* II.viii).

BILL. [*salvationproof*] It's nao good: you cawnt get rahnd me nah. Aw downt blieve in it; and Awve seen tody that Aw was rawt. [*Going*] Sao long, aol soupkitchener! Ta, ta, Mijor Earl's Grendorter! [*Turning at the gate*] Wot prawce selvytion nah? Snobby Prawce! Ha! ha!

BARBARA. [*Offering her hand*] Goodbye, Bill.

BILL. [*taken aback, half plucks his cap off; then shoves it on again defiantly*] Git aht. [BARBARA *drops her hand, discouraged. He has a twinge of remorse*]. But thets aw rawt, you knaow. Nathink pasnl. Naow mellice. Sao long, Judy. [*He goes*].

BARBARA. No malice. So long, Bill.

SHIRLEY. [*shaking his head*] You make too much of him, miss, in your innocence.

BARBARA. [*going to him*] Peter: I'm like you now. Cleaned out, and lost my job.

SHIRLEY. Youve youth an hope. Thats two better than me.

BARBARA. I'll get you a job, Peter. Thats hope for you: the youth will have to be enough for me. [*She counts her money*]. I have just enough left for two teas at Lockharts, a Rowton doss[7] for you, and my tram and bus home. [*He frowns and rises with offended pride. She takes his arm*]. Dont be proud, Peter: it's sharing between friends. And promise me youll talk to me and not let me cry. [*She draws him towards the gate*].

SHIRLEY. Well, I'm not accustomed to talk to the like of you—

BARBARA. [*urgently*] Yes, yes: you must talk to me. Tell me about Tom Paine's books and Bradlaugh's[8] lectures. Come along.

SHIRLEY. Ah, if you would only read Tom Paine in the proper spirit, miss! [*They go out through the gate together*].

Act III

Next day after lunch Lady Britomart is writing in the library in Wilton Crescent. Sarah is reading in the armchair near the window. Barbara, in ordinary fashionable dress, pale and brooding, is on the settee. Charles Lomax enters. He starts on seeing Barbara fashionably attired and in low spirits.

LOMAX. Youve left off your uniform!

Barbara says nothing; but an expression of pain passes over her face.

LADY BRITOMART. [*warning him in low tones to be careful*] Charles!

LOMAX. [*much concerned, coming behind the settee and bending sympathetically over* BARBARA] I'm awfully sorry, Barbara. You know I helped you all I could with the concertina and so forth. [*Momentously*] Still, I have never shut my eyes to the fact that

---

7. A cheap lodginghouse.

8. Tom Paine (1737–1809) was not only a champion of American independence but also a rational deist whose book *The Age of Reason* (1794–95), while affirming the existence of God, bitterly attacked the Bible and the churches ("human inventions set up to terrify and enslave mankind, and monopolize power and profit"). Charles Bradlaugh (1833–91) was a militant atheist who caused a sensation on election to Parliament in 1880 by refusing to take the parliamentary oath on the Bible.

there is a certain amount of tosh[9] about the Salvation Army. Now the claims of the Church of England—

LADY BRITOMART. Thats enough, Charles. Speak of something suited to your mental capacity.

LOMAX. But surely the Church of England is suited to all our capacities.

BARBARA. [*pressing his hand*] Thank you for your sympathy, Cholly. Now go and spoon with Sarah.

LOMAX. [*dragging a chair from the writing table and seating himself affectionately by* SARAH's *side*] How is my ownest today?

SARAH. I wish you wouldnt tell Cholly to do things, Barbara. He always comes straight and does them. Cholly: we're going to the works this afternoon.

LOMAX. What works?

SARAH. The cannon works.

LOMAX. What? your governor's shop!

SARAH. Yes.

LOMAX. Oh I say!

Cusins enters in poor condition. He also starts visibly when he sees Barbara without her uniform.

BARBARA. I expected you this morning, Dolly. Didnt you guess that?

CUSINS. [*sitting down beside her*] I'm sorry. I have only just breakfasted.

SARAH. But weve just finished lunch.

BARBARA. Have you had one of your bad nights?

CUSINS. No: I had rather a good night: in fact, one of the most remarkable nights I have ever passed.

BARBARA. The meeting?

CUSINS. No: after the meeting.

LADY BRITOMART. You should have gone to bed after the meeting. What were you doing?

CUSINS. Drinking.

LADY BRITOMART. Adolphus!
SARAH. Dolly!
BARBARA. Dolly!
LOMAX. Oh I say!

LADY BRITOMART. What were you drinking, may I ask?

CUSINS. A most devilish kind of Spanish burgundy, warranted free from added alcohol: a Temperance burgundy in fact. Its richness in natural alcohol made any addition superfluous.

BARBARA. Are you joking, Dolly?

CUSINS. [*patiently*] No. I have been making a night of it with the nominal head of this household: that is all.

LADY BRITOMART. Andrew made you drunk!

CUSINS. No: he only provided the wine. I think it was Dionysos who made me drunk. [*To* BARBARA] I told you I was possessed.

LADY BRITOMART. Youre not sober yet. Go home to bed at once.

9. Nonsense.

CUSINS. I have never before ventured to reproach you, Lady Brit; but how could you marry the Prince of Darkness?

LADY BRITOMART. It was much more excusable to marry him than to get drunk with him. That is a new accomplishment of Andrew's, by the way. He usent to drink.

CUSINS. He doesnt now. He only sat there and completed the wreck of my moral basis, the rout of my convictions, the purchase of my soul. He cares for you, Barbara. That is what makes him so dangerous to me.

BARBARA. That has nothing to do with it, Dolly. There are larger loves and diviner dreams than the fireside ones. You know that, dont you?

CUSINS. Yes: that is our understanding. I know it. I hold to it. Unless he can win me on that holier ground he may amuse me for a while; but he can get no deeper hold, strong as he is.

BARBARA. Keep to that; and the end will be right. Now tell me what happened at the meeting?

CUSINS. It was an amazing meeting. Mrs Baines almost died of emotion. Jenny Hill simply gibbered with hysteria. The Prince of Darkness played his trombone like a madman: its brazen roarings were like the laughter of the damned. 117 conversions took place then and there. They prayed with the most touching sincerity and gratitude for Bodger, and for the anonymous donor of the £5000. Your father would not let his name be given.

LOMAX. That was rather fine of the old man, you know. Most chaps would have wanted the advertisement.

CUSINS. He said all the charitable institutions would be down on him like kites on a battlefield if he gave his name.

LADY BRITOMART. Thats Andrew all over. He never does a proper thing without giving an improper reason for it.

CUSINS. He convinced me that I have all my life been doing improper things for proper reasons.

LADY BRITOMART. Adolphus: now that Barbara has left the Salvation Army, you had better leave it too. I will not have you playing that drum in the streets.

CUSINS. Your orders are already obeyed, Lady Brit.

BARBARA. Dolly: were you ever really in earnest about it? Would you have joined if you had never seen me?

CUSINS. [*disingenuously*] Well—er—well, possibly, as a collector of religions—

LOMAX. [*cunningly*] Not as a drummer, though, you know. You are a very clearheaded brainy chap, Dolly; and it must have been apparent to you that there is a certain amount of tosh about—

LADY BRITOMART. Charles: if you must drivel, drivel like a grown-up man and not like a schoolboy.

LOMAX. [*out of countenance*] Well, drivel is drivel, dont you know, whatever a man's age.

LADY BRITOMART. In good society in England, Charles, men drivel at all ages by repeating silly formulas with an air of wisdom. Schoolboys make their own formulas out of slang, like you.

When they reach your age, and get political private secretaryships and things of that sort, they drop slang and get their formulas out of The Spectator or The Times. Y o u had better confine yourself to The Times. You will find that there is a certain amount of tosh about The Times; but at least its language is reputable.

LOMAX. [*overwhelmed*] You are so awfully strong-minded, Lady Brit—

LADY BRITOMART. Rubbish! [MORRISON *comes in*]. What is it?

MORRISON. If you please, my lady, Mr Undershaft has just drove up to the door.

LADY BRITOMART. Well, let him in. [MORRISON *hesitates*]. Whats the matter with you?

MORRISON. Shall I announce him, my lady; or is he at home here, so to speak, my lady?

LADY BRITOMART. Announce him.

MORRISON. Thank you, my lady. You wont mind my asking, I hope. The occasion is in a manner of speaking new to me.

LADY BRITOMART. Quite right. Go and let him in.

MORRISON. Thank you, my lady. [*He withdraws*].

LADY BRITOMART. Children: go and get ready. [SARAH *and* BARBARA *go upstairs for their out-of-door wraps*]. Charles: go and tell Stephen to come down here in five minutes: you will find him in the drawing room. [CHARLES *goes*]. Adolphus: tell them to send round the carriage in about fifteen minutes. [ADOLPHUS *goes*].

MORRISON. [*at the door*] Mr Undershaft.

Undershaft comes in. Morrison goes out.

UNDERSHAFT. Alone! How fortunate!

LADY BRITOMART. [*rising*] Dont be sentimental, Andrew. Sit down. [*She sits on the settee: he sits beside her, on her left. She comes to the point before he has time to breathe*]. Sarah must have £800 a year until Charles Lomax comes into his property. Barbara will need more, and need it permanently, because Adolphus hasnt any property.

UNDERSHAFT. [*resignedly*] Yes, my dear: I will see to it. Anything else? for yourself, for instance?

LADY BRITOMART. I want to talk to you about Stephen.

UNDERSHAFT. [*rather wearily*] Dont, my dear. Stephen doesnt interest me.

LADY BRITOMART. He does interest me. He is our son.

UNDERSHAFT. Do you really think so? He has induced us to bring him into the world; but he chose his parents very incongruously, I think. I see nothing of myself in him, and less of you.

LADY BRITOMART. Andrew: Stephen is an excellent son, and a most steady, capable, highminded young man. You are simply trying to find an excuse for disinheriting him.

UNDERSHAFT. My dear Biddy: the Undershaft tradition disinherits him. It would be dishonest of me to leave the cannon foundry to my son.

LADY BRITOMART. It would be most unnatural and improper of you to leave it to anyone else, Andrew. Do you suppose this wicked and immoral tradition can be kept up forever? Do you pretend that Stephen could not carry on the foundry just as well as all the other sons of the big business houses?

UNDERSHAFT. Yes: he could learn the office routine without understanding the business, like all the other sons; and the firm would go on by its own momentum until the real Undershaft—probably an Italian or a German—would invent a new method and cut him out.

LADY BRITOMART. There is nothing that any Italian or German could do that Stephen could not do. And Stephen at least has breeding.

UNDERSHAFT. The son of a foundling! Nonsense!

LADY BRITOMART. My son, Andrew! And even you may have good blood in your veins for all you know.

UNDERSHAFT. True. Probably I have. That is another argument in favor of a foundling.

LADY BRITOMART. Andrew: dont be aggravating. And dont be wicked. At present you are both.

UNDERSHAFT. This conversation is part of the Undershaft tradition, Biddy. Every Undershaft's wife has treated him to it ever since the house was founded. It is mere waste of breath. If the tradition be ever broken it will be for an abler man than Stephen.

LADY BRITOMART. [*pouting*] Then go away.

UNDERSHAFT. [*deprecatory*] Go away!

LADY BRITOMART. Yes: go away. If you will do nothing for Stephen, you are not wanted here. Go to your foundling, whoever he is; and look after h i m.

UNDERSHAFT. The fact is, Biddy—

LADY BRITOMART. Dont call me Biddy. I dont call you Andy.

UNDERSHAFT. I will not call my wife Britomart: it is not good sense. Seriously, my love, the Undershaft tradition has landed me in a difficulty. I am getting on in years; and my partner Lazarus has at last made a stand and insisted that the succession must be settled one way or the other; and of course he is quite right. You see, I havnt found a fit successor yet.

LADY BRITOMART. [*obstinately*] There is Stephen.

UNDERSHAFT. Thats just it: all the foundlings I can find are exactly like Stephen.

LADY BRITOMART. Andrew!!

UNDERSHAFT. I want a man with no relations and no schooling: that is, a man who would be out of the running altogether if he were not a strong man. And I cant find him. Every blessed foundling nowadays is snapped up in his infancy by Barnardo[1] homes, or School Board officers, or Boards of Guardians; and if he shews the least ability, he is fastened on by schoolmasters; trained to win scholarships like a race horse; crammed with sec-

---

1. Dr. Thomas John Barnardo (1845–1905) worked all his life to help destitute children and founded "Dr. Bernardo's Homes" for destitute children, which still flourish. Their official name is "The National Institution for the Reformation of Destitute Waif Children."

ond hand ideas; drilled and disciplined in docility and what they call good taste; and lamed for life so that he is fit for nothing but teaching. If you want the keep the foundry in the family, you had better find an eligible foundling and marry him to Barbara.

LADY BRITOMART. Ah! Barbara! Your pet! You would sacrifice Stephen to Barbara.

UNDERSHAFT. Cheerfully. And you, my dear, would boil Barbara to make soup for Stephen.

LADY BRITOMART. Andrew: this is not a question of our likings and dislikings: it is a question of duty. It is your duty to make Stephen your successor.

UNDERSHAFT. Just as much as it is your duty to submit to your husband. Come, Biddy! these tricks of the governing class are of no use with me. I am one of the governing class myself; and it is waste of time giving tracts to a missionary. I have the power in this matter; and I am not to be humbugged into using it for your purposes.

LADY BRITOMART. Andrew: you can talk my head off; but you cant change wrong into right. And your tie is all on one side. Put it straight.

UNDERSHAFT. [*disconcerted*] It wont stay unless it's pinned—[*He fumbles at it with childish grimaces*].
Stephen comes in.

STEPHEN. [*at the door*] I beg your pardon. [*About to retire*].

LADY BRITOMART. No: come in, Stephen. [STEPHEN *comes forward to his mother's writing table*].

UNDERSHAFT. [*not very cordially*] Good afternoon.

STEPHEN. [*coldly*] Good afternoon.

UNDERSHAFT. [*to* LADY BRITOMART] He knows all about the tradition, I suppose?

LADY BRITOMART. Yes. [*To* STEPHEN]. It is what I told you last night, Stephen.

UNDERSHAFT. [*sulkily*] I understand you want to come into the cannon business.

STEPHEN. *I* go into trade! Certainly not.

UNDERSHAFT. [*opening his eyes, greatly eased in mind and manner*] Oh! in that case—

LADY BRITOMART. Cannons are not trade, Stephen. They are enterprise.

STEPHEN. I have no intention of becoming a man of business in any sense. I have no capacity for business and no taste for it. I intend to devote myself to politics.

UNDERSHAFT. [*rising*] My dear boy: this is an immense relief to me. And I trust it may prove an equally good thing for the country. I was afraid you would consider yourself disparaged and slighted. [*He moves towards* STEPHEN *as if to shake hands with him*].

LADY BRITOMART. [*rising and interposing*] Stephen: I cannot allow you to throw away an enormous property like this.

STEPHEN. [*stiffly*] Mother: there must be an end of treating me as a child, if you please. [LADY BRITOMART recoils, *deeply wounded by his tone*]. Until last night I did not take your attitude seriously, because I did not think you meant it seriously. But I find now that you left me in the dark as to matters which you should have explained to me years ago. I am extremely hurt and offended. Any further discussion of my intentions had better take place with my father, as between one man and another.

LADY BRITOMART. Stephen! [*She sits down again, her eyes filling with tears*].

UNDERSHAFT. [*with grave compassion*] You see, my dear, it is only the big men who can be treated as children.

STEPHEN. I am sorry, mother, that you have forced me—

UNDERSHAFT. [*stopping him*] Yes, yes, yes, yes: thats all right, Stephen. She wont interfere with you any more: your independence is achieved: you have won your latch-key. Dont rub it in; and above all, dont apologize. [*He resumes his seat*]. Now what about your future, as between one man and another—I beg your pardon, Biddy: as between two men and a woman.

LADY BRITOMART. [*who has pulled herself together strongly*] I quite understand, Stephen. By all means go your own way if you feel strong enough. [STEPHEN *sits down magisterially in the chair at the writing table with an air of affirming his majority*].

UNDERSHAFT. It is settled that you do not ask for the succession to the cannon business.

STEPHEN. I hope it is settled that I repudiate the cannon business.

UNDERSHAFT. Come, come! dont be so devilishly sulky: it's boyish. Freedom should be generous. Besides, I owe you a fair start in life in exchange for disinheriting you. You cant become prime minister all at once. Havnt you a turn for something? What about literature, art and so forth?

STEPHEN. I have nothing of the artist about me, either in faculty or character, thank Heaven!

UNDERSHAFT. A philosopher, perhaps? Eh?

STEPHEN. I make no such ridiculous pretension.

UNDERSHAFT. Just so. Well, there is the army, the navy, the Church, the Bar. The Bar requires some ability. What about the Bar?

STEPHEN. I have not studied law. And I am afraid I have not the necessary push—I believe that is the name barristers give to their vulgarity—for success in pleading.

UNDERSHAFT. Rather a difficult case, Stephen. Hardly anything left but the stage, is there? [STEPHEN *makes an impatient movement*]. Well, come! is there a n y t h i n g you know or care for?

STEPHEN. [*rising and looking at him steadily*] I know the difference between right and wrong.

UNDERSHAFT. [*hugely tickled*] You dont say so! What! no capacity for business, no knowledge of law, no sympathy with art, no pretension to philosophy; only a simple knowledge of the secret that has puzzled all the philosophers, baffled all the lawyers, muddled all the men of business, and ruined most of the artists: the secret of right and wrong. Why, man, youre a genius, a master of masters, a god! At twenty-four, too!

STEPHEN. [*keeping his temper with difficulty*] You are pleased to be facetious. I pretend to nothing more than any honorable English gentleman claims as his birthright. [*He sits down angrily*].

UNDERSHAFT. Oh, thats everybody's birthright. Look at poor little Jenny Hill, the Salvation lassie! she would think you were laughing at her if you asked her to stand up in the street and teach grammar or geography or mathematics or even drawing room dancing; but it never occurs to her to doubt that she can teach morals and religion. You are all alike, you respectable people. You cant tell me the bursting strain of a ten-inch gun, which is a very simple matter; but you all think you can tell me the bursting strain of a man under temptation. You darent handle high explosives; but youre all ready to handle honesty and truth and justice and the whole duty of man, and kill one another at that game. What a country! What a world!

LADY BRITOMART. [*uneasily*] What do you think he had better do, Andrew?

UNDERSHAFT. Oh, just what he wants to do. He knows nothing and he thinks he knows everything. That points clearly to a political career. Get him a private secretaryship to someone who can get him an Under Secretaryship; and then leave him alone. He will find his natural and proper place in the end on the Treasury Bench.

STEPHEN. [*springing up again*] I am sorry, sir, that you force me to forget the respect due to you as my father. I am an Englishman and I will not hear the Government of my country insulted. [*He thrusts his hands in his pockets, and walks angrily across to the window*].

UNDERSHAFT. [*with a touch of brutality*] The government of your country! I am the government of your country: I, and Lazarus. Do you suppose that you and half a dozen amateurs like you, sitting in a row in that foolish gabble shop, can govern Undershaft and Lazarus? No, my friend: you will do what pays u s. You will make war when it suits us, and keep peace when it doesnt. You will find out that trade requires certain measures when we have decided on those measures. When I want anything to keep my dividends up, you will discover that my want is a national need. When other people want something to keep my dividends down, you will call out the police and military. And in return you shall have the support and applause of my newspapers, and the delight of imagining that you are a great statesman. Government of your country! Be off with you, my boy, and play with your caucuses and leading articles and historic parties and great leaders and burning questions and the rest of your toys. I am going back to my counting house to pay the piper and call the tune.

STEPHEN. [*actually smiling, and putting his hand on his father's shoulder with indulgent patronage*] Really, my dear father, it is impossible to be angry with you. You don't know how absurd all this sounds to m e. You are very properly proud of having been industrious enough to make money; and it is greatly to your credit that you have made so much of it. But it has kept you in circles where you are valued for your money and deferred to for it, instead of in the doubtless very old-fashioned and behind-the-times public school and university where I formed my habits of mind. It is natural for you to think that money governs England; but you must allow me to think I know better.

UNDERSHAFT. And what d o e s govern England, pray?

STEPHEN. Character, father, character.

UNDERSHAFT. Whose character? Yours or mine?

STEPHEN. Neither yours nor mine, father, but the best elements in the English national character.

UNDERSHAFT. Stephen: Ive found your profession for you. Youre a born journalist. I'll start you with a high-toned weekly review. There!

Before Stephen can reply Sarah, Barbara, Lomax, and Cusins come in ready for walking. Barbara crosses the room to the window and looks out. Cusins drifts amiably to the armchair. Lomax remains near the door, whilst Sarah comes to her mother.

Stephen goes to the smaller writing table and busies himself with his letters.

SARAH. Go and get ready, mamma: the carriage is waiting. [LADY BRITOMART *leaves the room*].

UNDERSHAFT. [*to* SARAH] Good day, my dear. Good afternoon, Mr Lomax.

LOMAX. [*vaguely*] Ahdedoo.

UNDERSHAFT. [*to* CUSINS] Quite well after last night, Euripides, eh?

CUSINS. As well as can be expected.

UNDERSHAFT. Thats right. [*To* BARBARA]. So you are coming to see my death and devastation factory, Barbara?

BARBARA. [*at the window*] You came yesterday to see my salvation factory. I promised you a return visit.

LOMAX. [*coming forward between* SARAH *and* UNDERSHAFT] Youll find it awfully interesting. Ive been through the Woolwich Arsenal; and it gives you a ripping feeling of security, you know, to think of the lot of beggars we could kill if it came to fighting. [*To* UNDERSHAFT, *with sudden solemnity*]. Still, it must be rather an awful reflection for you, from the religious point of view as it were. Youre getting on, you know, and all that.

SARAH. You dont mind Cholly's imbecility, papa, do you?

LOMAX. [*much taken aback*] Oh I say!

UNDERSHAFT. Mr Lomax looks at the matter in a very proper spirit, my dear.

LOMAX. Just so. Thats all I meant, I assure you.

SARAH. Are you coming, Stephen?

STEPHEN. Well, I am rather busy—er—[*Magnanimously*] Oh well, yes: I'll come. That is, if there is room for me.

UNDERSHAFT. I can take two with me in a little motor I am experimenting with for field use. You wont mind its being rather unfashionable. It's not painted yet; but it's bullet proof.

LOMAX. [*appalled at the prospect of confronting Wilton Crescent in an unpainted motor*] Oh I s a y!

SARAH. The carriage for me, thank you. Barbara doesnt mind what shes seen in.

LOMAX. I say, Dolly old chap: do you really mind the car being a guy?[2] Because of course if you do I'll go in it. Still—

CUSINS. I prefer it.

LOMAX. Thanks awfully, old man. Come, my ownest. [*He hurries out to secure his seat in the carriage.* SARAH *follows him*].

CUSINS. [*moodily walking across to* LADY BRITOMART's *writing table*] Why are we two coming to this Works Department of Hell? that is what I ask myself.

BARBARA. I have always thought of it as a sort of pit where lost creatures with blackened faces stirred up smoky fires and were driven and tormented by my father. Is it like that, dad?

UNDERSHAFT. [*scandalized*] My dear! It is a spotlessly clean and beautiful hillside town.

CUSINS. With a Methodist chapel? Oh d o say theres a Methodist chapel.

UNDERSHAFT. There are two: a Primitive one and a sophisticated one. There is even an Ethical Society;[3] but it is not much patronized, as my men are all strongly religious. In the High Explosives Sheds they object to the presence of Agnostics as unsafe.

CUSINS. And yet they dont object to you!

BARBARA. Do they obey all your orders?

UNDERSHAFT. I never give them any orders. When I speak to one of them it is "Well, Jones, is the baby doing well? and has Mrs Jones made a good recovery?" "Nicely, thank you, sir." And thats all.

CUSINS. But Jones has to be kept in order. How do you maintain discipline among your men?

UNDERSHAFT. I dont. They do. You see, the one thing Jones wont stand is any rebellion from the man under him, or any assertion of social equality between the wife of the man with 4 shillings a week less than himself, and Mrs Jones! Of course they all rebel against me, theoretically. Practically, every man of them keeps the man just below him in his place. I never meddle with them. I never bully them. I dont even bully Lazarus. I say that certain things are to be done; but I dont order anybody to do them. I dont say, mind you, that there is no ordering about and snubbing

---

2. An object of ridicule.
3. The Primitive Methodists emphasized "camp-meetings": open-air services that lasted all day. The Society for Ethical Culture taught that morality is the basis of religion.

and even bullying. The men snub the boys and order them about; the carmen snub the sweepers; the artisans snub the unskilled laborers; the foremen drive and bully both the laborers and artisans; the assistant engineers find fault with the foremen; the chief engineers drop on the assistants; the departmental managers worry the chiefs; and the clerks have tall hats and hymnbooks and keep up the social tone by refusing to associate on equal terms with anybody. The result is a colossal profit, which comes to me.

CUSINS. [*revolted*] You really are a—well, what I was saying yesterday.

BARBARA. What was he saying yesterday?

UNDERSHAFT. Never mind, my dear. He thinks I have made you unhappy. Have I?

BARBARA. Do you think I can be happy in this vulgar silly dress? I! who have worn the uniform. Do you understand what you have done to me? Yesterday I had a man's soul in my hand. I set him in the way of life with his face to salvation. But when we took your money he turned back to drunkenness and derision. [*With intense conviction*] I will never forgive you that. If I had a child, and you destroyed its body with your explosives—if you murdered Dolly with your horrible guns—I could forgive you if my forgiveness would open the gates of heaven to you. But to take a human soul from me, and turn it into the soul of a wolf! that is worse than any murder.

UNDERSHAFT. Does my daughter despair so easily? Can you strike a man to the heart and leave no mark on him?

BARBARA. [*her face lighting up*] Oh, you are right: he can never be lost now: where was my faith?

CUSINS. Oh, clever clever devil!

BARBARA. You may be a devil; but God speaks through you sometimes. [*She takes her father's hands and kisses them*]. You have given me back my happiness: I feel it deep down now, though my spirit is troubled.

UNDERSHAFT. You have learnt something. That always feels at first as if you had lost something.

BARBARA. Well, take me to the factory of death; and let me learn something more. There must be some truth or other behind all this frightful irony. Come, Dolly. [*She goes out*].

CUSINS. My guardian angel! [*To* UNDERSHAFT] Avaunt! [*He follows* BARBARA].

STEPHEN. [*quietly, at the writing table*] You must not mind Cusins, father. He is a very amiable good fellow; but he is a Greek scholar and naturally a little eccentric.

UNDERSHAFT. Ah, quite so. Thank you, Stephen. Thank you. [*He goes out*].

Stephen smiles patronizingly; buttons his coat responsibly; and crosses the room to the door. Lady Britomart, dressed for out-of-doors, opens it before he reaches it. She looks round for the others; looks at Stephen; and turns to go without a word.

STEPHEN. [*embarrassed*] Mother—

LADY BRITOMART. Dont be apologetic, Stephen. And dont forget that you have outgrown your mother. [*She goes out.*]

Perivale St Andrews lies between two Middlesex hills, half climbing the northern one. It is an almost smokeless town of white walls, roofs of narrow green slates or red tiles, tall trees, domes, campaniles, and slender chimney shafts, beautifully situated and beautiful in itself. The best view of it is obtained from the crest of a slope about half a mile to the east, where the high explosives are dealt with. The foundry lies hidden in the depths between, the tops of its chimneys sprouting like huge skittles into the middle distance. Across the crest runs an emplacement of concrete, with a firestep, and a parapet which suggests a fortification, because there is a huge cannon of the obsolete Woolwich Infant pattern peering across it at the town. The cannon is mounted on an experimental gun carriage: possibly the original model of the Undershaft disappearing rampart gun alluded to by Stephen. The firestep, being a convenient place to sit, is furnished here and there with straw disc cushions; and at one place there is the additional luxury of a fur rug.

Barbara is standing on the firestep, looking over the parapet towards the town. On her right is the cannon; on her left the end of a shed raised on piles, with a ladder of three or four steps up to the door, which opens outwards and has a little wooden landing at the threshold, with a fire bucket in the corner of the landing. Several dummy soldiers more or less mutilated, with straw protruding from their gashes, have been shoved out of the way under the landing. A few others are nearly upright against the shed; and one has fallen forward and lies, like a grotesque corpse, on the emplacement. The parapet stops short of the shed, leaving a gap which is the beginning of the path down the hill through the foundry to the town. The rug is on the firestep near this gap. Down on the emplacement behind the cannon is a trolley carrying a huge conical bombshell with a red band painted on it. Further to the right is the door of an office, which, like the sheds, is of the lightest possible construction.

Cusins arrives by the path from the town.

BARBARA. Well?

CUSINS. Not a ray of hope. Everything perfect! wonderful! real! It only needs a cathedral to be a heavenly city instead of a hellish one.

BARBARA. Have you found out whether they have done anything for old Peter Shirley?

CUSINS. They have found him a job as gatekeeper and timekeeper. He's frightfully miserable. He calls the timekeeping brainwork, and says he isnt used to it; and the gate lodge is so splendid that hes ashamed to use the rooms, and skulks in the scullery.

BARBARA. Poor Peter!

Stephen arrives from the town. He carries a field-glass.

STEPHEN. [*enthusiastically*] Have you two seen the place? Why did you leave us?

CUSINS. I wanted to see everything I was not intended to see; and Barbara wanted to make the men talk.

STEPHEN. Have you found anything discreditable?

CUSINS. No. They call him Dandy Andy and are proud of his being a cunning old rascal; but it's all horribly, frightfully, immorally, unanswerably perfect.

Sarah arrives.

SARAH. Heavens! what a place! [*She crosses to the trolley*]. Did you see the nursing home!? [*She sits down on the shell*].

STEPHEN. Did you see the libraries and schools?

SARAH. Did you see the ball room and the banqueting chamber in the Town Hall!?

STEPHEN. Have you gone into the insurance fund, the pension fund, the building society, the various applications of co-operation!?

Undershaft comes from the office, with a sheaf of telegrams in his hand.

UNDERSHAFT. Well, have you seen everything? I'm sorry I was called away. [*Indicating the telegrams*] Good news from Manchuria.

STEPHEN. Another Japanese victory?[4]

UNDERSHAFT. Oh, I dont know. Which side wins does not concern us here. No: the good news is that the aerial battleship is a tremendous success. At the first trial it has wiped out a fort with three hundred soldiers in it.

CUSINS. [*from the platform*] Dummy soldiers?

UNDERSHAFT. [*striding across to* STEPHEN *and kicking the prostrate dummy brutally out of his way*] No: the real thing.

Cusins and Barbara exchange glances. Then Cusins sits on the step and buries his face in his hands. Barbara gravely lays her hand on his shoulder. He looks up at her in whimsical desperation.

UNDERSHAFT. Well, Stephen, what do you think of the place?

STEPHEN. Oh, magnificent. A perfect triumph of modern industry. Frankly, my dear father, I have been a fool: I had no idea of what it all meant: of the wonderful forethought, the power of organization, the administrative capacity, the financial genius, the colossal capital it represents. I have been repeating to myself as I came through your streets "Peace hath her victories no less renowned than War."[5] I have only one misgiving about it all.

UNDERSHAFT. Out with it.

STEPHEN. Well, I cannot help thinking that all this provision for every want of your workmen may sap their independence and weaken their sense of responsibility. And greatly as we enjoyed our tea at that splendid restaurant—how they gave us all that luxury and cake and jam and cream for threepence I really cannot imagine!—still you must remember that restaurants break up home life. Look at the continent, for instance! Are you sure so much pampering is really good for the men's characters?

4. The Russo-Japanese War (1904–5) was being waged when Shaw was writing this play in 1905.   5. From John Milton's sonnet "To the Lord General Cromwell, May 1652."

UNDERSHAFT. Well you see, my dear boy, when you are organizing civilization you have to make up your mind whether trouble and anxiety are good things or not. If you decide that they are, then, I take it, you simply dont organize civilization; and there you are, with trouble and anxiety enough to make us all angels! But if you decide the other way, you may as well go through with it. However, Stephen, our characters are safe here. A sufficient dose of anxiety is always provided by the fact that we may be blown to smithereens at any moment.

SARAH. By the way, papa, where do you make the explosives?

UNDERSHAFT. In separate little sheds, like that one. When one of them blows up, it costs very little; and only the people quite close to it are killed.

Stephen, who is quite close to it, looks at it rather scaredly, and moves away quickly to the cannon. At the same moment the door of the shed is thrown abruptly open; and a foreman in overalls and list slippers[6] *comes out on the little landing and holds the door for Lomax, who appears in the doorway.*

LOMAX. [*with studied coolness*] My good fellow: you neednt get into a state of nerves. Nothing's going to happen to you; and I suppose it wouldnt be the end of the world if anything did. A little bit of British pluck is what y o u want, old chap. [*He descends and strolls across to* SARAH].

UNDERSHAFT. [*to the foreman*] Anything wrong, Bilton?

BILTON. [*with ironic calm*] Gentleman walked into the high explosives shed and lit a cigaret, sir: thats all.

UNDERSHAFT. Ah, quite so. [*Going over to* LOMAX] Do you happen to remember what you did with the match?

LOMAX. Oh come! I'm not a fool. I took jolly good care to blow it out before I chucked it away.

BILTON. The top of it was red hot inside, sir.

LOMAX. Well, suppose it was! I didnt chuck it into any of y o u r messes.

UNDERSHAFT. Think no more of it, Mr Lomax. By the way, would you mind lending me your matches?

LOMAX. [*offering his box*] Certainly.

UNDERSHAFT. Thanks. [*He pockets the matches*].

LOMAX. [*lecturing to the company generally*] You know, these high explosives dont go off like gunpowder, except when theyre in a gun. When theyre spread loose, you can put a match to them without the least risk: they just burn quietly like a bit of paper. [*Warming to the scientific interest of the subject*] Did you know that, Undershaft? Have you ever tried?

UNDERSHAFT. Not on a large scale, Mr Lomax. Bilton will give you a sample of gun cotton when you are leaving if you ask him. You can experiment with it at home. [BILTON *looks puzzled*].

SARAH. Bilton will do nothing of the sort, papa. I suppose it's your business to blow up the Russians and Japs; but you might really

6. Cloth overshoes.

stop short of blowing up poor Cholly. [BILTON *gives it up and retires into the shed*].

LOMAX. My ownest, there is no danger. [*He sits beside her on the shell*].

Lady Britomart arrives from the town with a bouquet.

LADY BRITOMART. [*impetuously*] Andrew: you shouldnt have let me see this place.

UNDERSHAFT. Why, my dear?

LADY BRITOMART. Never mind why: you shouldnt have: thats all. To think of all that [*indicating the town*] being yours! and that you have kept it to yourself all these years!

UNDERSHAFT. It does not belong to me. I belong to it. It is the Undershaft inheritance.

LADY BRITOMART. It is not. Your ridiculous cannons and that noisy banging foundry may be the Undershaft inheritance; but all that plate and linen, all that furniture and those houses and orchards and gardens belong to us. They belong to m e: they are not a man's business. I wont give them up. You must be out of your senses to throw them all away; and if you persist in such folly, I will call in a doctor.

UNDERSHAFT. [*stooping to smell the bouquet*] Where did you get the flowers, my dear?

LADY BRITOMART. Your men presented them to me in your William Morris Labor Church.[7]

CUSINS. Oh! It needed only that. A Labor Church! [*He mounts the firestep distractedly, and leans with his elbows on the parapet, turning his back to them*].

LADY BRITOMART. Yes, with Morris's words in mosaic letters ten feet high round the dome. NO MAN IS GOOD ENOUGH TO BE ANOTHER MAN'S MASTER. The cynicism of it!

UNDERSHAFT. It shocked the men at first, I am afraid. But now they take no more notice of it than of the ten commandments in church.

LADY BRITOMART. Andrew: you are trying to put me off the subject of the inheritance by profane jokes. Well, you shant. I dont ask it any longer for Stephen: he has inherited far too much of your perversity to be fit for it. But Barbara has rights as well as Stephen. Why should not Adolphus succeed to the inheritance? I could manage the town for him; and he can look after the cannons, if they are really necessary.

UNDERSHAFT. I should ask nothing better if Adolphus were a foundling. He is exactly the sort of new blood that is wanted in English business. But he's not a foundling; and theres an end of it. [*He makes for the office door*].

CUSINS. [*turning to them*] Not quite. [*They all turn and stare at him*]. I think—Mind! I am not committing myself in any way

---

7. William Morris (1834–96), English poet and artist, founded the Socialist League. The first Labor Church was founded in 1891 by John Trevor, a Unitarian minister and socialist, to provide a religious movement for the working classes. The movement had nearly died out by the time the play was written.

as to my future course—but I t h i n k the foundling difficulty can be got over. [*He jumps down to the emplacement*].

UNDERSHAFT. [*coming back to him*] What do you mean?

CUSINS. Well, I have something to say which is in the nature of a confession.

SARAH.

LADY BRITOMART. } Confession!

BARBARA.

STEPHEN.

LOMAX. Oh I say!

CUSINS. Yes, a confession. Listen, all. Until I met Barbara I thought myself in the main an honorable, truthful man, because I wanted the approval of my conscience more than I wanted anything else. But the moment I saw Barbara, I wanted her far more than the approval of my conscience.

LADY BRITOMART. Adolphus!

CUSINS. It is true. You accused me yourself, Lady Brit, of joining the Army to worship Barbara; and so I did. She bought my soul like a flower at a street corner; but she bought it for herself.

UNDERSHAFT. What! Not for Dionysos or another?

CUSINS. Dionysos and all the others are in herself. I adored what was divine in her, and was therefore a true worshipper. But I was romantic about her too. I thought she was a woman of the people, and that a marriage with a professor of Greek would be far beyond the wildest social ambitions of her rank.

LADY BRITOMART. Adolphus!!

LOMAX. Oh I s a y!!!

CUSINS. When I learnt the horrible truth—

LADY BRITOMART. What do you mean by the horrible truth, pray?

CUSINS. That she was enormously rich; that her grandfather was an earl; that her father was the Prince of Darkness—

UNDERSHAFT. Chut!

CUSINS. —and that I was only an adventurer trying to catch a rich wife, then I stooped to deceive her about my birth.

BARBARA. [*rising*] Dolly!

LADY BRITOMART. Your birth! Now Adolphus, dont dare to make up a wicked story for the sake of these wretched cannons. Remember: I have seen photographs of your parents; and the Agent General for South Western Australia knows them personally and has assured me that they are most respectable married people.

CUSINS. So they are in Australia; but here they are outcasts. Their marriage is legal in Australia, but not in England. My mother is my father's deceased wife's sister; and in this island I am consequently a foundling.[8] [*Sensation*].

BARBARA. Silly! [*She climbs to the cannon, and leans, listening, in the angle it makes with the parapet*].

CUSINS. Is the subterfuge good enough, Machiavelli?

8. Marriage between a widower and his late wife's sister was illegal in Great Britain until 1907.

UNDERSHAFT. [*thoughtfully*] Biddy: this may be a way out of the difficulty.

LADY BRITOMART. Stuff! A man cant make cannons any the better for being his own cousin instead of his proper self. [*She sits down on the rug with a bounce that expresses her downright contempt for their casuistry*].

UNDERSHAFT. [*to* CUSINS] You are an educated man. That is against the tradition.

CUSINS. Once in ten thousand times it happens that the schoolboy is a born master of what they try to teach him. Greek has not destroyed my mind: it has nourished it. Besides, I did not learn it at an English public school.

UNDERSHAFT. Hm! Well, I cannot afford to be too particular: you have cornered the foundling market. Let it pass. You are eligible, Euripides: you are eligible.

BARBARA. Dolly: yesterday morning, when Stephen told us all about the tradition, you became very silent; and you have been strange and excited ever since. Were you thinking of your birth then?

CUSINS. When the finger of Destiny suddenly points at a man in the middle of his breakfast, it makes him thoughtful.

UNDERSHAFT. Aha! You have had your eye on the business, my young friend, have you?

CUSINS. Take care! There is an abyss of moral horror between me and your accursed aerial battleships.

UNDERSHAFT. Never mind the abyss for the present. Let us settle the practical details and leave your final decision open. You know that you will have to change your name. Do you object to that?

CUSINS. Would any man named Adolphus—any man called Dolly! —object to be called something else?

UNDERSHAFT. Good. Now, as to money! I propose to treat you handsomely from the beginning. You shall start at a thousand a year.

CUSINS. [*with sudden heat, his spectacles twinkling with mischief*] A thousand! You dare offer a miserable thousand to the son-in-law of a millionaire! No, by Heavens, Machiavelli! you shall not cheat m e. You cannot do without me; and I can do without you. I must have two thousand five hundred a year for two years. At the end of that time, if I am a failure, I go. But if I am a success, and stay on, you must give me the other five thousand.

UNDERSHAFT. What other five thousand?

CUSINS. To make the two years up to five thousand a year. The two thousand five hundred is only half pay in case I should turn out a failure. The third year I must have ten per cent on the profits.

UNDERSHAFT. [*taken aback*] Ten per cent! Why, man, do you know what my profits are?

CUSINS. Enormous, I hope: otherwise I shall require twentyfive per cent.

UNDERSHAFT. But, Mr Cusins, this is a serious matter of business. You are not bringing any capital into the concern.

CUSINS. What! no capital! Is my mastery of Greek no capital? Is my access to the subtlest thought, the loftiest poetry yet attained by humanity, no capital? My character! my intellect! my life! my career! what Barbara calls my soul! are these no capital? Say another word; and I double my salary.

UNDERSHAFT. Be reasonable—

CUSINS. [*peremptorily*] Mr Undershaft: you have my terms. Take them or leave them.

UNDERSHAFT. [*recovering himself*] Very well. I note your terms; and I offer you half.

CUSINS. [*disgusted*] Half!

UNDERSHAFT. [*firmly*] Half.

CUSINS. You call yourself a gentleman; and you offer me half!!

UNDERSHAFT. I do not call myself a gentleman; but I offer you half.

CUSINS. This to your future partner! your successor! your son-in-law!

BARBARA. You are selling your own soul, Dolly, not mine. Leave me out of the bargain, please.

UNDERSHAFT. Come! I will go a step further for Barbara's sake. I will give you three fifths; but that is my last word.

CUSINS. Done!

LOMAX. Done in the eye! Why, *I* get only eight hundred, you know.

CUSINS. By the way, Mac, I am a classical scholar, not an arithmetical one. Is three fifths more than half or less?

UNDERSHAFT. More, of course.

CUSINS. I would have taken two hundred and fifty. How you can succeed in business when you are willing to pay all that money to a University don who is obviously not worth a junior clerk's wages!—well! What will Lazarus say?

UNDERSHAFT. Lazarus is a gentle romantic Jew who cares for nothing but string quartets and stalls at fashionable theatres. He will be blamed for your rapacity in money matters, poor fellow! as he has hitherto been blamed for mine. You are a shark of the first order, Euripides. So much the better for the firm!

BARBARA. Is the bargain closed, Dolly? Does your soul belong to him now?

CUSINS. No: the price is settled: that is all. The real tug of war is still to come. What about the moral question?

LADY BRITOMART. There is no moral question in the matter at all, Adolphus. You must simply sell cannons and weapons to people whose cause is right and just, and refuse them to foreigners and criminals.

UNDERSHAFT. [*determinedly*] No: none of that. You must keep the true faith of an Armorer, or you dont come in here.

CUSINS. What on earth is the true faith of an Armorer?

UNDERSHAFT. To give arms to all men who offer an honest price for them, without respect of persons or principles: to aristocrat and republican, to Nihilist and Tsar, to Capitalist and Socialist, to Protestant and Catholic, to burglar and policeman, to black man, white man and yellow man, to all sorts and conditions, all nationalities, all faiths, all follies, all causes and all crimes. The first Undershaft wrote up in his shop IF GOD GAVE THE HAND, LET NOT MAN WITHHOLD THE SWORD. The second wrote up ALL HAVE THE RIGHT TO FIGHT: NONE HAVE THE RIGHT TO JUDGE. The third wrote up TO MAN THE WEAPON: TO HEAVEN THE VICTORY. The fourth had no literary turn; so he did not write up anything; but he sold cannons to Napoleon under the nose of George the Third. The fifth wrote up PEACE SHALL NOT PREVAIL SAVE WITH A SWORD IN HER HAND. The sixth, my master, was the best of all. He wrote up NOTHING IS EVER DONE IN THIS WORLD UNTIL MEN ARE PREPARED TO KILL ONE ANOTHER IF IT IS NOT DONE. After that, there was nothing left for the seventh to say. So he wrote up, simply, UNASHAMED.

CUSINS. My good Machiavelli, I shall certainly write something up on the wall; only, as I shall write it in Greek, you wont be able to read it. But as to your Armorer's faith, if I take my neck out of the noose of my own morality I am not going to put it into the noose of yours. I shall sell cannons to whom I please and refuse them to whom I please. So there!

UNDERSHAFT. From the moment when you become Andrew Undershaft, you will never do as you please again. Dont come here lusting for power, young man.

CUSINS. If power were my aim I should not come here for it. Y o u have no power.

UNDERSHAFT. None of my own, certainly.

CUSINS. I have more power than you, more will. You do not drive this place: it drives you. And what drives the place?

UNDERSHAFT. [*enigmatically*] A will of which I am a part.

BARBARA. [*startled*] Father! Do you know what you are saying; or are you laying a snare for my soul?

CUSINS. Dont listen to his metaphysics, Barbara. The place is driven by the most rascally part of society, the money hunters, the pleasure hunters, the military promotion hunters; and he is their slave.

UNDERSHAFT. Not necessarily. Remember the Armorer's Faith. I will take an order from a good man as cheerfully as from a bad one. If you good people prefer preaching and shirking to buying my weapons and fighting the rascals, dont blame me. I can make cannons: I cannot make courage and conviction. Bah! you tire me, Euripides, with your morality mongering. Ask Barbara; s h e understands. [*He suddenly reaches up and takes* BARBABA'S *hands, looking powerfully into her eyes*]. Tell him, my love, what power really means.

BARBARA. [*hypnotized*] Before I joined the Salvation Army, I was in my own power; and the consequence was that I never knew what to do with myself. When I joined it, I had not time enough for all the things I had to do.

UNDERSHAFT. [*approvingly*] Just so. And why was that, do you suppose?

BARBARA. Yesterday I should have said, because I was in the power of God. [*She resumes her self-possession, withdrawing her hands from his with a power equal to his own*]. But you came and shewed me that I was in the power of Bodger and Undershaft. Today I feel—oh! how can I put it into words? Sarah: do you remember the earthquake at Cannes,[9] when we were little children?—how little the surprise of the first shock mattered compared to the dread and horror of waiting for the second? That is how I feel in this place today. I stood on the rock I thought eternal; and without a word of warning it reeled and crumbled under me. I was safe with an infinite wisdom watching me, an army marching to Salvation with me; and in a moment, at a stroke of your pen in a cheque book, I stood alone; and the heavens were empty. That was the first shock of the earthquake: I am waiting for the second.

UNDERSHAFT. Come, come, my daughter! dont make too much of your little tinpot tragedy. What do we do here when we spend years of work and thought and thousands of pounds of solid cash on a new gun or an aerial battleship that turns out just a hairsbreadth wrong after all? Scrap it. Scrap it without wasting another hour or another pound on it. Well, you have made for yourself something that you call a morality or a religion or what not. It doesnt fit the facts. Well, scrap it. Scrap it and get one that does fit. That is what is wrong with the world at present. It scraps its obsolete steam engines and dynamos; but it wont scrap its old prejudices and its old moralities and its old religions and its old political constitutions. Whats the result? In machinery it does very well; but in morals and religion and politics it is working at a loss that brings it nearer bankruptcy every year. Dont persist in that folly. If your old religion broke down yesterday, get a newer and a better one for tomorrow.

BARBARA. Oh how gladly I would take a better one to my soul! But you offer me a worse one. [*Turning on him with sudden vehemence*] Justify yourself: shew me some light through the darkness of this dreadful place, with its beautifully clean workshops, and respectable workmen, and model homes.

UNDERSHAFT. Cleanliness and respectability do not need justification, Barbara: they justify themselves. I see no darkness here, no dreadfulness. In your Salvation shelter I saw poverty, misery, cold and hunger. You gave them bread and treacle and dreams of heaven. I give from thirty shillings a week to twelve thousand a year. They find their own dreams; but I look after the drainage.

BARBARA. And their souls?

UNDERSHAFT. I save their souls just as I saved yours.

BARBARA. [*revolted*] Y o u saved my soul! What do you mean?

UNDERSHAFT. I fed you and clothed you and housed you. I took care that you should have money enough to live handsomely—

---

9. A fashionable winter resort in the south of France. There was a major earthquake there in 1887.

more than enough; so that you could be wasteful, careless, generous. That saved your soul from the seven deadly sins.

BARBARA. [*bewildered*] The seven deadly sins!

UNDERSHAFT. Yes, the deadly seven. [*Counting on his fingers*] Food, clothing, firing,[1] rent, taxes, respectability and children. Nothing can lift those seven millstones from Man's neck but money; and the spirit cannot soar until the millstones are lifted. I lifted them from your spirit. I enabled Barbara to become Major Barbara; and I saved her from the crime of poverty.

CUSINS. Do you call poverty a crime?

UNDERSHAFT. The worst of crimes. All the other crimes are virtues beside it: all the other dishonors are chivalry itself by comparison. Poverty blights whole cities; spreads horrible pestilences; strikes dead the very souls of all who come within sight, sound or smell of it. What y o u call crime is nothing: a murder here and a theft there, a blow now and a curse then: what do they matter? they are only the accidents and illnesses of life: there are not fifty genuine professional criminals in London. But there are millions of poor people, abject people, dirty people, ill fed, ill clothed people. They poison us morally and physically: they kill the happiness of society: they force us to do away with our own liberties and to organize unnatural cruelties for fear they should rise against us and drag us down into their abyss. Only fools fear crime: we all fear poverty. Pah! [*turning on* BARBARA] you talk of your half-saved ruffian in West Ham: you accuse me of dragging his soul back to perdition. Well, bring him to me here; and I will drag his soul back again to salvation for you. Not by words and dreams; but by thirtyeight shillings a week, a sound house in a handsome street, and a permanent job. In three weeks he will have a fancy waistcoat; in three months a tall hat and a chapel sitting; before the end of the year he will shake hands with a duchess at a Primrose League[2] meeting, and join the Conservative Party.

BARBARA. And will he be the better for that?

UNDERSHAFT. You know he will. Dont be a hypocrite, Barbara. He will be better fed, better housed, better clothed, better behaved; and his children will be pounds heavier and bigger. That will be better than an American cloth mattress in a shelter, chopping firewood, eating bread and treacle, and being forced to kneel down from time to time to thank heaven for it: knee drill, I think you call it. It is cheap work converting starving men with a Bible in one hand and a slice of bread in the other. I will undertake to convert West Ham to Mahometanism[3] on the same terms. Try your hand on m y men: their souls are hungry because their bodies are full.

BARBARA. And leave the east end to starve?

UNDERSHAFT. [*his energetic tone dropping into one of bitter and brooding remembrance*] I was an east ender. I moralized and

---

1. Heating.
2. Conservative society which meets annually on the anniversary of Disraeli's
death; the primrose was Disraeli's favorite flower.
3. The Moslem religion.

starved until one day I swore that I would be a full-fed free man
at all costs—that nothing should stop me except a bullet, neither
reason nor morals nor the lives of other men. I said "Thou shalt
starve ere I starve"; and with that word I became free and great.
I was a dangerous man until I had my will: now I am a useful,
beneficent, kindly person. That is the history of most self-made
millionaires, I fancy. When it is the history of every Englishman
we shall have an England worth living in.

LADY BRITOMART. Stop making speeches, Andrew. This is not the
place for them.

UNDERSHAFT. [*punctured*] My dear: I have no other means of
conveying my ideas.

LADY BRITOMART. Your ideas are nonsense. You got on because you
were selfish and unscrupulous.

UNDERSHAFT. Not at all. I had the strongest scruples about poverty
and starvation. Your moralists are quite unscrupulous about both:
they make virtues of them. I had rather be a thief than a pauper.
I had rather be a murderer than a slave. I dont want to be either;
but if you force the alternative on me, then, by Heaven, I'll
choose the braver and more moral one. I hate poverty and slavery
worse than any other crimes whatsoever. And let me tell you this.
Poverty and slavery have stood up for centuries to your sermons
and leading articles: they will not stand up to my machine guns.
Dont preach at them: dont reason with them. Kill them.

BARBARA. Killing. Is that your remedy for everything?

UNDERSHAFT. It is the final test of conviction, the only lever strong
enough to overturn a social system, the only way of saying Must.
Let six hundred and seventy fools loose in the street; and three
policemen can scatter them. But huddle them together in a certain house in Westminster; and let them go through certain ceremonies and call themselves certain names until at last they get
the courage to kill; and your six hundred and seventy fools
become a government. Your pious mob fills up ballot papers and
imagines it is governing its masters; but the ballot paper that
really governs is the paper that has a bullet wrapped up in it.

CUSINS. That is perhaps why, like most intelligent people, I never
vote.

UNDERSHAFT. Vote! Bah! When you vote, you only change the
names of the cabinet. When you shoot, you pull down governments, inaugurate new epochs, abolish old orders and set up new.
Is that historically true, Mr Learned Man, or is it not?

CUSINS. It is historically true. I loathe having to admit it. I repudiate your sentiments. I abhor your nature. I defy you in every
possible way. Still, it is true. But it ought not to be true.

UNDERSHAFT. Ought! ought! ought! ought! ought! Are you going to
spend your life saying ought, like the rest of our moralists? Turn
your oughts into shalls, man. Come and make explosives with
me. Whatever can blow men up can blow society up. The history
of the world is the history of those who had courage enough to
embrace this truth. Have you the courage to embrace it, Barbara?

LADY BRITOMART. Barbara, I positively forbid you to listen to your father's abominable wickedness. And you, Adolphus, ought to know better than to go about saying that wrong things are true. What does it matter whether they are true if they are wrong?

UNDERSHAFT. What does it matter whether they are wrong if they are true?

LADY BRITOMART. [*rising*] Children: come home instantly. Andrew: I am exceedingly sorry I allowed you to call on us. You are wickeder than ever. Come at once.

BARBARA. [*shaking her head*] It's no use running away from wicked people, mamma.

LADY BRITOMART. It is every use. It shews your disapprobation of them.

BARBARA. It does not save them.

LADY BRITOMART. I can see that you are going to disobey me. Sarah: are you coming home or are you not?

SARAH. I daresay it's very wicked of papa to make cannons; but I dont think I shall cut him on that account.

LOMAX. [*pouring oil on the troubled waters*] The fact is, you know, there is a certain amount of tosh about this notion of wickedness. It doesnt work. You must look at facts. Not that I would say a word in favor of anything wrong; but then, you see, all sorts of chaps are always doing all sorts of things; and we have to fit them in somehow, dont you know. What I mean is that you cant go cutting everybody; and thats about what it comes to. [*Their rapt attention to his eloquence makes him nervous*]. Perhaps I dont make myself clear.

LADY BRITOMART. You are lucidity itself, Charles. Because Andrew is successful and has plenty of money to give to Sarah, you will flatter him and encourage him in his wickedness.

LOMAX. [*unruffled*] Well, where the carcase is, there will the eagles be gathered, dont you know. [*To* UNDERSHAFT] Eh? What?

UNDERSHAFT. Precisely. By the way, m a y I call you Charles?

LOMAX. Delighted. Cholly is the usual ticket.

UNDERSHAFT. [*to* LADY BRITOMART] Biddy—

LADY BRITOMART. [*violently*] Dont dare call me Biddy. Charles Lomax: you are a fool. Adolphus Cusins: you are a Jesuit. Stephen: you are a prig. Barbara: you are a lunatic. Andrew: you are a vulgar tradesman. Now you all know my opinion; and m y conscience is clear, at all events. [*She sits down with a vehemence that the rug fortunately softens*].

UNDERSHAFT. My dear: you are the incarnation of morality. [*She snorts*]. Your conscience is clear and your duty done when you have called everybody names. Come, Euripides! it is getting late; and we all want to go home. Make up your mind.

CUSINS. Understand this, you old demon—

LADY BRITOMART. Adolphus!

UNDERSHAFT. Let him alone, Biddy. Proceed, Euripides.

CUSINS. You have me in a horrible dilemma. I want Barbara.

UNDERSHAFT. Like all young men, you greatly exaggerate the difference between one young woman and another.

BARBARA. Quite true, Dolly.

CUSINS. I also want to avoid being a rascal.

UNDERSHAFT. [*with biting contempt*] You lust for personal right-eousness, for self-approval, for what you call a good conscience, for what Barbara calls salvation, for what I call patronizing people who are not so lucky as yourself.

CUSINS. I do not: all the poet in me recoils from being a good man. But there are things in me that I must reckon with. Pity—

UNDERSHAFT. Pity! The scavenger of misery.

CUSINS. Well, love.

UNDERSHAFT. I know. You love the needy and the outcast: you love the oppressed races, the negro, the Indian ryot,[4] the underdog everywhere. Do you love the Japanese? Do you love the French? Do you love the English?

CUSINS. No. Every true Englishman detests the English. We are the wickedest nation on earth; and our success is a moral horror.

UNDERSHAFT. That is what comes of your gospel of love, is it?

CUSINS. May I not love even my father-in-law?

UNDERSHAFT. Who wants your love, man? By what right do you take the liberty of offering it to me? I will have your due heed and respect, or I will kill you. But your love! Damn your imperti-nence!

CUSINS. [*grinning*] I may not be able to control my affections, Mac.

UNDERSHAFT. You are fencing, Euripides. You are weakening: your grip is slipping. Come! try your last weapon. Pity and love have broken in your hand: forgiveness is still left.

CUSINS. No: forgiveness is a beggar's refuge. I am with you there: we must pay our debts.

UNDERSHAFT. Well said. Come! you will suit me. Remember the words of Plato.

CUSINS. [*starting*] Plato! Y o u dare quote Plato to me!

UNDERSHAFT. Plato says, my friend, that society cannot be saved until either the Professors of Greek take to making gunpowder, or else the makers of gunpowder become Professors of Greek.

CUSINS. Oh, tempter, cunning tempter!

UNDERSHAFT. Come! choose, man, choose.

CUSINS. But perhaps Barbara will not marry me if I make the wrong choice.

BARBARA. Perhaps not.

CUSINS. [*desperately perplexed*] You hear!

BARBARA. Father: do you love nobody?

UNDERSHAFT. I love my best friend.

LADY BRITOMART. And who is that, pray?

UNDERSHAFT. My bravest enemy. That is the man who keeps me up to the mark.

CUSINS. You know, the creature is really a sort of poet in his way. Suppose he is a great man, after all!

UNDERSHAFT. Suppose you stop talking and make up your mind, my young friend.

4. Peasant.

CUSINS. But you are driving me against my nature. I hate war.

UNDERSHAFT. Hatred is the coward's revenge for being intimidated. Dare you make war on war? Here are the means: my friend Mr Lomax is sitting on them.

LOMAX. [*springing up*] Oh I say! You dont mean that this thing is loaded, do you? My ownest: come off it.

SARAH. [*sitting placidly on the shell*] If I am to be blown up, the more thoroughly it is done the better. Dont fuss, Cholly.

LOMAX. [*to* UNDERSHAFT, *strongly remonstrant*] Your own daughter, you know.

UNDERSHAFT. So I see. [*To* CUSINS] Well, my friend, may we expect you here at six tomorrow morning?

CUSINS. [*firmly*] Not on any account. I will see the whole establishment blown up with its own dynamite before I will get up at five. My hours are healthy, rational hours: eleven to five.

UNDERSHAFT. Come when you please: before a week you will come at six and stay until I turn you out for the sake of your health. [*Calling*] Bilton! [*He turns to* LADY BRITOMART, *who rises*]. My dear: let us leave these two young people to themselves for a moment. [BILTON *comes from the shed*]. I am going to take you through the gun cotton shed.

BILTON. [*barring the way*] You cant take anything explosive in here, sir.

LADY BRITOMART. What do you mean? Are you alluding to me?

BILTON. [*unmoved*] No, maam. Mr Undershaft has the other gentleman's matches in his pocket.

LADY BRITOMART. [*abruptly*] Oh! I beg your pardon. [*She goes into the shed*].

UNDERSHAFT. Quite right, Bilton, quite right: here you are. [*He gives* BILTON *the box of matches*]. Come, Stephen. Come, Charles. Bring Sarah. [*He passes into the shed*].

Bilton opens the box and deliberately drops the matches into the fire-bucket.

LOMAX. Oh I say! [BILTON *stolidly hands him the empty box*]. Infernal nonsense! Pure scientific ignorance! [*He goes in*].

SARAH. Am I all right, Bilton?

BILTON. Youll have to put on list slippers, miss: thats all. Weve got em inside. [*She goes in*].

STEPHEN. [*very seriously to* CUSINS] Dolly, old fellow, think. Think before you decide. Do you feel that you are a sufficiently practical man? It is a huge undertaking, an enormous responsibility. All this mass of business will be Greek to you.

CUSINS. Oh, I think it will be much less difficult than Greek.

STEPHEN. Well, I just want to say this before I leave you to yourselves. Dont let anything I have said about right and wrong prejudice you against this great chance in life. I have satisfied myself that the business is one of the highest character and a credit to our company. [*Emotionally*] I am very proud of my father. I— [*Unable to proceed, he presses* CUSINS' *hand and goes hastily into the shed, followed by* BILTON].

Barbara and Cusins, left alone together, look at one another silently.

CUSINS. Barbara: I am going to accept this offer.

BARBARA. I thought you would.

CUSINS. You understand, dont you, that I had to decide without consulting you. If I had thrown the burden of the choice on you, you would sooner or later have despised me for it.

BARBARA. Yes: I did not want you to sell your soul for me any more than for this inheritance.

CUSINS. It is not the sale of my soul that troubles me: I have sold it too often to care about that. I have sold it for a professorship. I have sold it for an income. I have sold it to escape being imprisoned for refusing to pay taxes for hangmen's ropes and unjust wars and things that I abhor. What is all human conduct but the daily and hourly sale of our souls for trifles? What I am now selling it for is neither money nor position nor comfort, but for reality and for power.

BARBARA. You know that you will have no power, and that he has none.

CUSINS. I know. It is not for myself alone. I want to make power for the world.

BARBARA. I want to make power for the world too; but it must be spiritual power.

CUSINS. I think all power is spiritual: these cannons will not go off by themselves. I have tried to make spiritual power by teaching Greek. But the world can never be really touched by a dead language and a dead civilization. The people must have power; and the people cannot have Greek. Now the power that is made here can be wielded by all men.

BARBARA. Power to burn women's houses down and kill their sons and tear their husbands to pieces.

CUSINS. You cannot have power for good without having power for evil too. Even mother's milk nourishes murderers as well as heroes. This power which only tears men's bodies to pieces has never been so horribly abused as the intellectual power, the imaginative power, the poetic, religious power that can enslave men's souls. As a teacher of Greek I gave the intellectual man weapons against the common man. I now want to give the common man weapons against the intellectual man. I love the common people. I want to arm them against the lawyers, the doctors, the priests, the literary men, the professors, the artists, and the politicians, who, once in authority, are more disastrous and tyrannical than all the fools, rascals, and impostors. I want a power simple enough for common men to use, yet strong enough to force the intellectual oligarchy to use its genius for the general good.

BARBARA. Is there no higher power than that [*pointing to the shell*]?

CUSINS. Yes; but that power can destroy the higher powers just as a tiger can destroy a man: therefore Man must master that power first. I admitted this when the Turks and Greeks were last at war.

My best pupil went out to fight for Hellas.[5] My parting gift to him was not a copy of Plato's Republic, but a revolver and a hundred Undershaft cartridges. The blood of every Turk he shot —if he shot any—is on my head as well as on Undershaft's. That act committed me to this place for ever. Your father's challenge has beaten me. Dare I make war on war? I dare. I must. I will. And now, is it all over between us?

BARBARA. [*touched by his evident dread of her answer*] Silly baby Dolly! How could it be!

CUSINS. [*overjoyed*] Then you—you—you— Oh for my drum! [*He flourishes imaginary drumsticks*].

BARBARA. [*angered by his levity*] Take care, Dolly, take care. Oh, if only I could get away from you and from father and from it all! if I could have the wings of a dove and fly away to heaven!

CUSINS. And leave m e!

BARBARA. Yes, you, and all the other naughty mischievous children of men. But I cant. I was happy in the Salvation Army for a moment. I escaped from the world into a paradise of enthusiasm and prayer and soul saving; but the moment our money ran short, it all came back to Bodger: it was he who saved our people: he, and the Prince of Darkness, my papa. Undershaft and Bodger: their hands stretch everywhere: when we feed a starving fellow creature, it is with their bread, because there is no other bread; when we tend the sick, it is in the hospitals they endow; if we turn from the churches they build, we must kneel on the stones of the streets they pave. As long as that lasts, there is no getting away from them. Turning our backs on Bodger and Undershaft is turning our backs on life.

CUSINS. I thought you were determined to turn your back on the wicked side of life.

BARBARA. There is no wicked side: life is all one. And I never wanted to shirk my share in whatever evil must be endured, whether it be sin or suffering. I wish I could cure you of middle-class ideas, Dolly.

CUSINS. [*gasping*] Middle cl—! A snub! A social snub to m e! from the daughter of a foundling!

BARBARA. That is why I have no class, Dolly: I come straight out of the heart of the whole people. If I were middle-class I should turn my back on my father's business; and we should both live in an artistic drawing room, with you reading the reviews in one corner, and I in the other at the piano, playing Schumann: both very superior persons, and neither of us a bit of use. Sooner than that, I would sweep out the gun cotton shed, or be one of Bodger's barmaids. Do you know what would have happened if you had refused papa's offer?

CUSINS. I wonder!

BARBARA. I should have given you up and married the man who accepted it. After all, my dear old mother has more sense than any of you. I felt like her when I saw this place—felt that I must have it—that never, never, never could I let it go; only she

5. Greece. The reference is to the Greco-Turkish war of 1896–97.

thought it was the houses and the kitchen ranges and the linen and china, when it was really all the human souls to be saved: not weak souls in starved bodies, sobbing with gratitude for a scrap of bread and treacle, but fullfed, quarrelsome, snobbish, uppish creatures, all standing on their little rights and dignities, and thinking that my father ought to be greatly obliged to them for making so much money for him—and so he ought. That is where salvation is really wanted. My father shall never throw it in my teeth again that my converts were bribed with bread. [*She is transfigured*]. I have got rid of the bribe of bread. I have got rid of the bribe of heaven. Let God's work be done for its own sake: the work he had to create us to do because it cannot be done except by living men and women. When I die, let him be in my debt, not I in his; and let me forgive him as becomes a woman of my rank.

CUSINS. Then the way of life lies through the factory of death?

BARBARA. Yes, through the raising of hell to heaven and of man to God, through the unveiling of an eternal light in the Valley of The Shadow. [*Seizing him with both hands*] Oh, did you think my courage would never come back? did you believe that I was a deserter? that I, who have stood in the streets, and taken my people to my heart, and talked of the holiest and greatest things with them, could ever turn back and chatter foolishly to fashionable people about nothing in a drawing room? Never, never, never, never: Major Barbara will die with the colors. Oh! and I have my dear little Dolly boy still; and he has found me my place and my work. Glory Hallelujah! [*She kisses him*].

CUSINS. My dearest: consider my delicate health. I cannot stand as much happiness as you can.

BARBARA. Yes: it is not easy work being in love with me, is it? But it's good for you. [*She runs to the shed, and calls, childlike*] Mamma! Mamma! [BILTON *comes out of the shed, followed by* UNDERSHAFT]. I want Mamma.

UNDERSHAFT. She is taking off her list slippers, dear. [*He passes on to* CUSINS]. Well? What does she say?

CUSINS. She has gone right up into the skies.

LADY BRITOMART. [*coming from the shed and stopping on the steps, obstructing* SARAH, *who follows with* LOMAX. BARBARA *clutches like a baby at her mother's skirt*] Barbara: when will you learn to be independent and to act and think for yourself? I know as well as possible what that cry of "Mamma, Mamma," means. Always running to me!

SARAH. [*touching* LADY BRITOMART's *ribs with her finger tips and imitating a bicycle horn*] Pip! pip!

LADY BRITOMART. [*highly indignant*] How dare you say Pip! pip! to me, Sarah? You are both very naughty children. What do you want, Barbara?

BARBARA. I want a house in the village to live in with Dolly. [*Dragging at the skirt*] Come and tell me which one to take.

UNDERSHAFT. [*to* CUSINS] Six o'clock tomorrow morning, Euripides.

JOSEPH CONRAD
(1857–1924)

1875–94: Career as a seaman.
1895:   *Almayer's Folly.*
1904:   *Nostromo.*

Joseph Conrad was born Jozef Teodor Konrad Nalecz Korzeniowski in Poland (then under Russian rule), son of a Polish patriot who suffered exile in Russia for his Polish nationalist activities and died in 1869, leaving Conrad to be brought up by a maternal uncle. At the age of 15 he amazed everybody by announcing his passionate desire to go to sea; he was eventually allowed to go to Marseilles in 1874, and from there he made a number of voyages on French merchant ships to Martinique and the West Indies. In 1878 he signed on an English ship which brought him to the east coast English port of Lowestoft, where (still as an ordinary seaman) he joined the crew of a small coasting vessel plying between Lowestoft and Newcastle. In six voyages between these two ports he learned English. Thus launched on a career in the British merchant service, Conrad sailed on a variety of British ships to the Orient and elsewhere and eventually gained his master's certificate in 1886, the year when he became a naturalized British subject. He received his first command in 1888, and in 1890 took a steamboat up the Congo River in nightmarish circumstances (described in *Heart of Darkness*) which produced severe illness and permanently haunted his imagination. In the early 1890's he was already thinking of turning some of his Malayan experiences into English fiction, and in 1892–93, when serving as first mate on the *Torrens* sailing from London to Adelaide, he revealed to a sympathetic passenger that he had begun a novel (*Almayer's Folly*), while on the return journey he impressed John Galsworthy, who was a passenger, with his conversation. Though possessed of a master's certificate, Conrad found it difficult to get the kind of job as master that he wished, and occasionally he had to serve in lesser capacities. His difficulty in obtaining a command, together with the interest aroused by *Almayer's Folly* when it was published in 1895, helped to turn him away from the sea to a career as a writer. He settled in London and in 1896 married an English girl; this son of a Polish patriot turned merchant seaman turned writer was henceforth an English novelist.

Conrad was for a long time regarded as a sea writer whose exotic descriptions of eastern landscapes and exploitation of the romantic atmosphere of Malaya and other unfamiliar regions gave his work a special kind of richness and splendor. But this is only one, and not in the last analysis the most important, aspect of his work. More and more Conrad used the sea and the circumstances of life on shipboard or in remote eastern settlements as means of exploring certain profound moral ambiguities in human experience. In *The Nigger of the "Narcissus"* (1897) he shows how a dying Negro seaman corrupts the morale of a ship's crew by the very fact that his plight produces sympathy, thus symbolically presenting one of his commonest themes—the necessity and at the same time the dangers of human contact. In *Lord Jim* (1900), using the device of an intermediate narrator, he probes the meaning of a gross failure of duty on the part of a romantic and idealistic young sailor, and by presenting the hero's history from a series of different points of view keeps the moral questioning continuing to the end. The use of intermediate narrators and multiple points of view is common in Conrad; it is his favorite way of suggesting the complexity of experience and the difficulty of judging human actions. In *Heart of Darkness* he draws on his Congo River experience to create an atmosphere of darkness and horror in the midst of which the hero recognizes a deep inner kinship with the corrupt villain, the Belgian trader who has lost all his earlier ideals to succumb to the worst elements in the native life he had hoped to improve.

This notion of the difficulty of true communion, coupled with the idea that communion can be unexpectedly forced on us—sometimes with someone who may be on the surface our moral opposite, so that we can at times be compelled into a mysterious recognition of our opposite as our true self—is found in many of Conrad's works; it provides one of the underlying themes of *The Secret Sharer* (1912). This story can be enjoyed for the clarity and power with which Conrad renders the atmosphere of the Gulf of Siam as felt by a young sea captain on taking on his first command, but it also uses situation and incident symbolically in order to suggest some of the paradoxes of identity and sympathy.

Other stories and novels explore the ways in which the codes we live by are tested in moments of crisis, revealing either their inadequacy or our own. Imagination can corrupt (as with Lord Jim), or save (as in *The Shadow Line*, 1917); and there are times when total lack of it can see a man through (Captain M'Whirr in *Typhoon*, 1902), though a similar lack in other circumstances can render a man comically ridiculous (Captain Mitchell in *Nostromo*, 1904).

Nostromo, a profound and subtle study of the corrupting effects of politics and "material interests" on personal relationships (set in an imaginary South American republic), is now generally regarded as Conrad's greatest work. His two other political novels—*The Secret Agent* (1906) and *Under Western Eyes* (1910)—have also recently come into their own. The latter is the story of a Russian student who becomes involuntarily associated with antigovernment violence in Czarist Russia and is irresistibly maneuvered by circumstances into a position where, although a government spy, he has to pretend to be a revolutionary among revolutionaries. This is the ultimate in human loneliness and incommunicability—when you must consistently pretend to be the opposite of what you are. It is a story of Dostoievskian power, and shows a very different Conrad from the picturesque sea-dreamer pictured by the earlier critics. Conrad was as much a pessimist as Hardy, but he projected his pessimism in subtler ways. He was also a great master of English prose, an astonishing fact when we realize that he was 21 before he learned any English, and that to the end of his life he spoke English with a thick foreign accent.

Heart of Darkness

This story is derived from Conrad's personal experience in the Congo in 1890. Like Marlow, the narrator of the story, Conrad had as a child determined one day to visit the heart of Africa. "It was in 1868, when nine years old or thereabouts, that while looking at a map of Africa at the time and putting my finger on the blank space then representing the unsolved mystery of that continent, I said to myself with absolute assurance and an amazing audacity which are no longer in my character now: 'When I grow up I shall go *there*'" (*A Personal Record*, 1912).

Conrad was promised a job as a Congo River pilot through the influence of his distant cousin Marguerite Poradowska, who lived in Brussels and knew important officials of the Belgian company which exploited the Congo. At this time the Congo, though nominally an independent state, the Congo Free State (État Indépendent du Congo), was virtually the personal property of Leopold II, king of the Belgians, who made a fortune out of it. Later, the appalling abuses involved in the naked colonial exploitation which went on in the Congo were exposed to public view and international criticism compelled the setting up of a committee of inquiry in 1904. What Conrad saw in 1890 shocked him profoundly and shook his view of the moral basis of all exploring and trading in newly discovered countries and indeed of civilization in general. (See Marlow's remarks about the Roman invasion of Britain, the reference to Elizabethan explorers, and the concluding picture of the Thames seeming "to lead into an immense darkness.") "*Heart of Darkness* is experience, too," Conrad wrote in his 1917 "Author's Note," "but it is experience pushed a little (and only very little) beyond the actual facts of the case for the perfectly legitimate, I believe, purpose of bringing it home to the minds and bosoms of the readers." And later he told Edward Garnett: "Before the Congo I was just a mere animal."

Conrad arrived in Africa in May 1890 and made his way up the Congo River very much as described in *Heart of Darkness*. At Kinshasa (which Conrad spells Kinchassa) on Stanley Pool, which he reached after an exhausting 200-mile trek from Matadi, near the mouth of the river, Conrad was much taken aback to learn that the steamer of which he was to be captain had been damaged and was undergoing repairs. He was sent as supernumerary on another steamer to learn the river. This other steamer was sent to Stanley Falls to collect and bring back to Kinshasa one Georges Antoine Klein, an agent of the company who had fallen gravely ill and who in fact died on board. Klein was the original of Kurtz. Conrad himself then fell seriously ill, and eventually returned to London in January 1891 without ever having actually served as a Congo River pilot, the job for which he went out to Africa. The Congo experience permanently impaired his health: it also permanently haunted his imagination. The nightmare atmosphere of *Heart of Darkness* is an accurate reflection of Conrad's own response to this traumatic experience.

The theme of the story is partly the "choice of nightmares" facing the white man in the Congo—either to become like the wholly commercially-minded manager, who sees Africa, its people, and its resources solely as instruments of financial gain, or to become like Kurtz, the self-tortured and corrupted idealist. The manager is a "hollow man" (T. S. Eliot quoted from this story in his poem of that title); his only objections to Kurtz are commercial, not moral; Kurtz's methods are "unsound" and would therefore lose the company money. Kurtz finally recognizes the moral horror of his having succumbed to the dark temptations which African life posed for the white man. "He had summed up—he had judged." But the story also has other levels of meaning, and the counterpointing of Western civilization in Europe with what that civilization has done in Africa (see the concluding interview between Marlow and Kurtz's "intended"—based on a real interview between Conrad and the dead Klein's fiancée) throws up several of these.

Heart of Darkness

I

The *Nellie*, a cruising yawl, swung to her anchor without a flutter of the sails, and was at rest. The flood had made, the wind was nearly calm, and being bound down the river, the only thing for it was to come to and wait for the turn of the tide.

The sea-reach of the Thames stretched before us like the beginning of an interminable waterway. In the offing the sea and the sky were welded together without a joint, and in the luminous space the tanned sails of the barges drifting up with the tide seemed to stand still in red clusters of canvas sharply peaked, with gleams of varnished sprits. A haze rested on the low shores that ran out to sea in vanishing flatness. The air was dark above Gravesend,[1] and farther back still seemed condensed into a mournful gloom, brooding motionless over the biggest, and the greatest, town on earth.

The Director of Companies was our captain and our host. We four affectionately watched his back as he stood in the bows looking to seaward. On the whole river there was nothing that looked half so nautical. He resembled a pilot, which to a seaman is trustworthiness personified. It was difficult to realize his work was not out there in the luminous estuary, but behind him, within the brooding gloom.

Between us there was, as I have already said somewhere, the bond of the sea. Besides holding our hearts together through long periods of separation, it had the effect of making us tolerant of each other's yarns—and even convictions. The Lawyer—the best of old fellows—had, because of his many years and many virtues, the only cushion on deck, and was lying on the only rug. The Accountant had brought out already a box of dominoes, and was toying architecturally with the bones. Marlow sat cross-legged right aft, leaning against the mizzen-mast. He had sunken cheeks, a yellow complex-

---

1. River port on the south bank of the Thames some 24 miles east (downriver) of London.

ion, a straight back, an ascetic aspect, and, with his arms dropped, the palms of hands outwards, resembled an idol. The Director, satisfied the anchor had good hold, made his way aft and sat down amongst us. We exchanged a few words lazily. Afterwards there was silence on board the yacht. For some reason or other we did not begin that game of dominoes. We felt meditative, and fit for nothing but placid staring. The day was ending in a serenity of still and exquisite brilliance. The water shone pacifically; the sky, without a speck, was a benign immensity of unstained light; the very mist on the Essex marshes was like a gauzy and radiant fabric, hung from the wooded rises inland, and draping the low shores in diaphanous folds. Only the gloom to the west, brooding over the upper reaches, became more somber every minute, as if angered by the approach of the sun.

And at last, in its curved and imperceptible fall, the sun sank low, and from glowing white changed to a dull red without rays and without heat, as if about to go out suddenly, stricken to death by the touch of that gloom brooding over a crowd of men.

Forthwith a change came over the waters, and the serenity became less brilliant but more profound. The old river in its broad reach rested unruffled at the decline of day, after ages of good service done to the race that peopled its banks, spread out in the tranquil dignity of a waterway leading to the uttermost ends of the earth. We looked at the venerable stream not in the vivid flush of a short day that comes and departs for ever, but in the august light of abiding memories. And indeed nothing is easier for a man who has, as the phrase goes, "followed the sea" with reverence and affection, than to evoke the great spirit of the past upon the lower reaches of the Thames. The tidal current runs to and fro in its unceasing service, crowded with memories of men and ships it has borne to the rest of home or to the battles of the sea. It had known and served all the men of whom the nation is proud, from Sir Francis Drake to Sir John Franklin,[2] knights all, titled and untitled—the great knights-errant of the sea. It had borne all the ships whose names are like jewels flashing in the night of time, from the *Golden Hind* returning with her round flanks full of treasure, to be visited by the Queen's Highness and thus pass out of the gigantic tale, to the *Erebus* and *Terror*, bound on other conquests—and that never returned. It had known the ships and the men. They had sailed from Deptford, from Greenwich, from Erith—the adventurers and the settlers; kings' ships and the ships of men on 'Change; captains,

---

2. Sir Francis Drake (ca. 1540–96), Elizabethan naval hero and explorer, sailed round the world in his ship *The Golden Hind*. Queen Elizabeth knighted Drake on board his ship, loaded with captured Spanish treasure, on his return. Sir John Franklin (1786–1847), Arctic explorer, in 1845 commanded an expedition consisting of the ships *Erebus* and *Terror* in search of the Northwest passage. The ships never returned.

admirals, the dark "interlopers" of the Eastern trade, and the commissioned "generals" of East India fleets.[3] Hunters for gold or pursuers of fame, they all had gone out on that stream, bearing the sword, and often the torch, messengers of the night within the land, bearers of a spark from the sacred fire. What greatness had not floated on the ebb of that river into the mystery of an unknown earth! . . . The dreams of men, the seed of commonwealths, the germs of empires.

The sun set; the dusk fell on the stream, and lights began to appear along the shore. The Chapman lighthouse, a three-legged thing erect on a mud-flat, shone strongly. Lights of ships moved in the fairway[4]—a great stir of lights going up and going down. And farther west on the upper reaches the place of the monstrous town was still marked ominously on the sky, a brooding gloom in sunshine, a lurid glare under the stars.

"And this also," said Marlow suddenly, "has been one of the dark places of the earth."

He was the only man of us who still "followed the sea." The worst that could be said of him was that he did not represent his class. He was a seaman, but he was a wanderer too, while most seamen lead, if one may so express it, a sedentary life. Their minds are of the stay-at-home order, and their home is always with them—the ship; and so is their country—the sea. One ship is very much like another, and the sea is always the same. In the immutability of their surroundings the foreign shores, the foreign faces, the changing immensity of life, glide past, veiled not by a sense of mystery but by a slightly disdainful ignorance; for there is nothing mysterious to a seaman unless it be the sea itself, which is the mistress of his existence and as inscrutable as Destiny. For the rest, after his hours of work, a casual stroll or a casual spree on shore suffices to unfold for him the secret of a whole continent, and generally he finds the secret not worth knowing. The yarns of seamen have a direct simplicity, the whole meaning of which lies within the shell of a cracked nut. But Marlow was not typical (if his propensity to spin yarns be excepted), and to him the meaning of an episode was not inside like a kernel but outside, enveloping the tale which brought it out only as a glow brings out a haze, in the likeness of one of these misty halos that sometimes are made visible by the spectral illumination of moonshine.

His remark did not seem at all surprising. It was just like Marlow.

---

3. Deptford, on the south bank of the Thames, on the eastern edge of London, once (but no longer) an important dockyard. Greenwich is on the south bank of the Thames immediately east of Deptford. Erith is some 8 miles further east. "Change" is the Stock Exchange. "Interlopers" were private ships muscling in on the monopoly of the East India Company, which was founded in 1600, lost its trading monopoly in 1813, and transferred its governmental functions to the Crown in 1858.

4. Navigable part of a river, through which ships enter and depart.

It was accepted in silence. No one took the trouble to grunt even; and presently he said, very slow:

"I was thinking of very old times, when the Romans first came here, nineteen hundred years ago—the other day. . . . Light came out of this river since—you say Knights? Yes; but it is like a running blaze on a plain, like a flash of lightning in the clouds. We live in the flicker—may it last as long as the old earth keeps rolling! But darkness was here yesterday. Imagine the feelings of a commander of a fine—what d'ye call 'em?—trireme[5] in the Mediterranean, ordered suddenly to the north; run overland across the Gauls in a hurry; put in charge of one of these craft the legionaries—a wonderful lot of handy men they must have been too—used to build, apparently by the hundred, in a month or two, if we may believe what we read. Imagine him here—the very end of the world, a sea the color of lead, a sky the color of smoke, a kind of ship about as rigid as a concertina—and going up this river with stores, or orders, or what you like. Sandbanks, marshes, forests, savages—precious little to eat fit for a civilized man, nothing but Thames water to drink. No Falernian wine here, no going ashore. Here and there a military camp lost in a wilderness, like a needle in a bundle of hay—cold, fog, tempests, disease, exile, and death—death skulking in the air, in the water, in the bush. They must have been dying like flies here. Oh yes—he did it. Did it very well, too, no doubt, and without thinking much about it either, except afterwards to brag of what he had gone through in his time, perhaps. They were men enough to face the darkness. And perhaps he was cheered by keeping his eye on a chance of promotion to the fleet at Ravenna[6] by and by, if he had good friends in Rome and survived the awful climate. Or think of a decent young citizen in a toga—perhaps too much dice, you know—coming out here in the train of some prefect, or tax-gatherer, or trader, even, to mend his fortunes. Land in a swamp, march through the woods, and in some inland post feel the savagery, the utter savagery, had closed round him—all that mysterious life of the wilderness that stirs in the forest, in the jungles, in the hearts of wild men. There's no initiation either into such mysteries. He has to live in the midst of the incomprehensible, which is also detestable. And it has a fascination, too, that goes to work upon him. The fascination of the abomination—you know. Imagine the growing regrets, the longing to escape, the powerless disgust, the surrender, the hate."

He paused.

---

5. Ancient Greek and Roman galley with three ranks of oars.
6. City in Northern Italy once directly on the Adriatic Sea and an important naval station in Roman times. Now about 6 miles from the sea, connected with it by a canal.

"Mind," he began again, lifting one arm from the elbow, the palm of the hand outwards, so that, with his legs folded before him, he had the pose of a Buddha preaching in European clothes and without a lotus-flower—"Mind, none of us would feel exactly like this. What saves us is efficiency—the devotion to efficiency. But these chaps were not much account, really. They were no colonists; their administration was merely a squeeze, and nothing more, I suspect. They were conquerors, and for that you want only brute force —nothing to boast of, when you have it, since your strength is just an accident arising from the weakness of others. They grabbed what they could get for the sake of what was to be got. It was just robbery with violence, aggravated murder on a great scale, and men going at it blind—as is very proper for those who tackle a darkness. The conquest of the earth, which mostly means the taking it away from those who have a different complexion or slightly flatter noses than ourselves, is not a pretty thing when you look into it too much. What redeems it is the idea only. An idea at the back of it; not a sentimental pretense but an idea; and an unselfish belief in the idea—something you can set up, and bow down before, and offer a sacrifice to. . . ."

He broke off. Flames glided in the river, small green flames, red flames, white flames, pursuing, overtaking, joining, crossing each other—then separating slowly or hastily. The traffic of the great city went on in the deepening night upon the sleepless river. We looked on, waiting patiently—there was nothing else to do till the end of the flood; but it was only after a long silence, when he said, in a hesitating voice, "I suppose you fellows remember I did once turn fresh-water sailor for a bit," that we knew we were fated, before the ebb began to run, to hear about one of Marlow's inconclusive experiences.

"I don't want to bother you much with what happened to me personally," he began, showing in this remark the weakness of many tellers of tales who seem so often unaware of what their audience would best like to hear; "yet to understand the effect of it on me you ought to know how I got out there, what I saw, how I went up that river to the place where I first met the poor chap. It was the farthest point of navigation and the culminating point of my experience. It seemed somehow to throw a kind of light on everything about me—and into my thoughts. It was somber enough too—and pitiful—not extraordinary in any way—not very clear either. No, not very clear. And yet it seemed to throw a kind of light.

"I had then, as you remember, just returned to London after a lot of Indian Ocean, Pacific, China Seas—a regular dose of the East —six years or so, and I was loafing about, hindering you fellows in your work and invading your homes, just as though I had got a heavenly mission to civilize you. It was very fine for a time, but after a bit I did get tired of resting. Then I began to look for a ship —I should think the hardest work on earth. But the ships wouldn't even look at me. And I got tired of that game too.

"Now when I was a little chap I had a passion for maps. I would look for hours at South America, or Africa, or Australia, and lose myself in all the glories of exploration. At that time there were many blank spaces on the earth, and when I saw one that looked particularly inviting on a map (but they all look that) I would put my finger on it and say, When I grow up I will go there. The North Pole was one of these places, I remember. Well, I haven't been there yet, and shall not try now. The glamour's off. Other places were scattered about the Equator, and in every sort of latitude all over the two hemispheres. I have been in some of them, and . . . well, we won't talk about that. But there was one yet—the biggest, the most blank, so to speak—that I had a hankering after.

"True, by this time it was not a blank space any more. It had got filled since my boyhood with rivers and lakes and names. It had ceased to be a blank space of delightful mystery—a white patch for a boy to dream gloriously over. It had become a place of darkness. But there was in it one river especially, a mighty big river, that you could see on the map, resembling an immense snake uncoiled, with its head in the sea, its body at rest curving afar over a vast country, and its tail lost in the depths of the land. And as I looked at the map of it in a shop-window, it fascinated me as a snake would a bird—a silly little bird. Then I remembered there was a big concern, a Company for trade on that river. Dash it all! I thought to myself, they can't trade without using some kind of craft on that lot of fresh water—steamboats! Why shouldn't I try to get charge of one? I went on along Fleet Street, but could not shake off the idea. The snake had charmed me.

"You understand it was a Continental concern, that Trading Society; but I have a lot of relations living on the Continent, because it's cheap and not so nasty as it looks, they say.

"I am sorry to own I began to worry them. This was already a fresh departure for me. I was not used to get things that way, you know. I always went my own road and on my own legs where I had a mind to go. I wouldn't have believed it of myself; but, then—you see—I felt somehow I must get there by hook or by crook. So I worried them. The men said, 'My dear fellow,' and did nothing. Then—would you believe it?—I tried the women. I, Charlie Marlow, set the women to work—to get a job. Heavens! Well, you see, the notion drove me. I had an aunt, a dear enthusiastic soul. She wrote: 'It will be delightful. I am ready to do anything, anything for you. It is a glorious idea. I know the wife of a very high personage in the Administration, and also a man who has lots of influence with,' etc. etc. She was determined to make no end of fuss to get me appointed skipper of a river steamboat, if such was my fancy.

"I got my appointment—of course; and I got it very quick. It appears the Company had received news that one of their captains had been killed in a scuffle with the natives. This was my chance, and it made me the more anxious to go. It was only months and months afterwards, when I made the attempt to recover what was left of the body, that I heard the original quarrel arose from a mis-understanding about some hens. Yes, two black hens. Fresleven—that was the fellow's name, a Dane—thought himself wronged somehow in the bargain, so he went ashore and started to hammer the chief of the village with a stick. Oh, it didn't surprise me in the least to hear this, and at the same time to be told that Fresleven was the gentlest, quietest creature that ever walked on two legs. No doubt he was; but he had been a couple of years already out there engaged in the noble cause, you know, and he probably felt the need at last of asserting his self-respect in some way. Therefore he whacked the old nigger mercilessly, while a big crowd of his people watched him, thunderstruck, till some man—I was told the chief's son—in desperation at hearing the old chap yell, made a tentative jab with a spear at the white man—and of course it went quite easy between the shoulder-blades. Then the whole population cleared into the forest, expecting all kinds of calamities to happen, while, on the other hand, the steamer Fresleven commanded left also in a bad panic, in charge of the engineer, I believe. Afterwards nobody seemed to trouble much about Fresleven's remains, till I got out and stepped into his shoes. I couldn't let it rest, though; but when an opportunity offered at last to meet my predecessor, the grass growing through his ribs was tall enough to hide his bones. They were all there. The supernatural being had not been touched after he fell. And the village was deserted, the huts gaped black, rotting, all askew within the fallen enclosures. A calamity had come to it, sure enough. The people had vanished. Mad terror had scattered them, men, women, and children, through the bush, and they had never returned. What became of the hens I don't know either. I should think the cause of progress got them, anyhow. However, through this glorious affair I got my appointment, before I had fairly begun to hope for it.

"I flew around like mad to get ready, and before forty-eight hours I was crossing the Channel to show myself to my employers, and sign the contract. In a very few hours I arrived in a city that always makes me think of a whited sepulcher. Prejudice no doubt. I had no difficulty in finding the Company's offices. It was the biggest thing in the town, and everybody I met was full of it. They were going to run an oversea empire, and make no end of coin by trade.

"A narrow and deserted street in deep shadow, high houses, innumerable windows and venetian blinds, a dead silence, grass sprouting between the stones, imposing carriage archways right and left, immense double doors standing ponderously ajar. I slipped through one of these cracks, went up a swept and ungarnished staircase, as arid as a desert, and opened the first door I came to. Two women, one fat and the other slim, sat on straw-bottomed chairs, knitting black wool. The slim one got up and walked straight at me—still knitting with downcast eyes—and only just as I began to think of getting out of her way, as you would for a somnambulist, stood still, and looked up. Her dress was as plain as an umbrella-cover, and she turned round without a word and preceded me into a waiting-room. I gave my name, and looked about. Deal table in the middle, plain chairs all round the walls, on one end a large shining map, marked with all the colors of a rainbow. There was a vast amount of red— good to see at any time, because one knows that some real work is done in there, a deuce of a lot of blue, a little green, smears of orange, and, on the East Coast, a purple patch, to show where the jolly pioneers of progress drink the jolly lager-beer. However, I wasn't going into any of these. I was going into the yellow. Dead in the center. And the river was there—fascinating—deadly—like a snake. Ough! A door opened, a white-haired secretarial head, but wearing a compassionate expression, appeared, and a skinny forefinger beckoned me into the sanctuary. Its light was dim, and a heavy writing-desk squatted in the middle. From behind that structure came out an impression of pale plumpness in a frock-coat. The great man himself. He was five feet six, I should judge, and had his grip on the handle-end of ever so many millions. He shook hands, I fancy, murmured vaguely, was satisfied with my French. *Bon voyage*.

"In about forty-five seconds I found myself again in the waiting-room with the compassionate secretary, who, full of desolation and sympathy, made me sign some document. I believe I undertook amongst other things not to disclose any trade secrets. Well, I am not going to.

"I began to feel slightly uneasy. You know I am not used to such ceremonies, and there was something ominous in the atmosphere. It was just as though I had been let into some conspiracy—I don't know—something not quite right; and I was glad to get out. In the outer room the two women knitted black wool feverishly. People were arriving, and the younger one was walking back and forth introducing them. The old one sat on her chair. Her flat cloth slippers were propped up on a foot-warmer, and a cat reposed on her lap. She wore a starched white affair on her head, had a wart on one cheek, and silver-rimmed spectacles hung on the tip of her nose. She glanced at me above the glasses. The swift and indifferent placidity of that look troubled me. Two youths with foolish and cheery countenances were being piloted over, and she threw at them the same quick glance of unconcerned wisdom. She seemed to know all about them and about me too. An eerie feeling came over me. She seemed uncanny and fateful. Often far away there I thought of these two, guarding the door of Darkness, knitting black wool as for a warm pall, one introducing, introducing continuously to the unknown, the other scrutinizing the cheery and foolish faces with unconcerned old eyes. *Ave!* Old knitter of black wool. *Morituri te salutant.*[7] Not many of those she looked at ever saw her again—not half, by a long way.

"There was yet a visit to the doctor. 'A simple formality,' assured me the secretary, with an air of taking an immense part in all my sorrows. Accordingly a young chap wearing his hat over the left eyebrow, some clerk I suppose—there must have been clerks in the business, though the house was as still as a house in a city of the dead—came from somewhere upstairs, and led me forth. He was shabby and careless, with ink-stains on the sleeves of his jacket, and his cravat was large and billowy, under a chin shaped like the toe of an old boot. It was a little too early for the doctor, so I proposed a drink, and thereupon he developed a vein of joviality. As we sat over our vermuths he glorified the Company's business, and by and by I expressed casually my surprise at him not going out there. He became very cool and collected all at once. 'I am not such a fool as I look, quoth Plato to his disciples,' he said sententiously, emptied his glass with great resolution, and we rose.

"The old doctor felt my pulse, evidently thinking of something else the while. 'Good, good for there,' he mumbled, and then with a certain eagerness asked me whether I would let him measure my head. Rather surprised, I said Yes, when he produced a thing like callipers and got the dimensions back and front and every way, taking notes carefully. He was an unshaven little man in a threadbare coat like a gaberdine, with his feet in slippers, and I thought him a harmless fool. 'I always ask leave, in the interests of science, to measure the crania of those going out there,' he said. 'And when they come back too?' I asked. 'Oh, I never see them,' he remarked; 'and, moreover, the changes take place inside, you know.' He smiled, as if at some quiet joke. 'So you are going out there. Famous. Interesting too.' He gave me a searching glance, and made another note. 'Ever any madness in your family?' he asked, in a

7. "Hail! . . . Those who are about to   salute to the Emperor on entering the
die salute you." The Roman gladiators'   arena.

matter-of-fact tone. I felt very annoyed. 'Is that question in the
interests of science too?' 'It would be,' he said, without taking
notice of my irritation, 'interesting for science to watch the mental
changes of individuals, on the spot, but . . .' 'Are you an alienist?'[8]
I interrupted. 'Every doctor should be—a little,' answered that original imperturbably. 'I have a little theory which you Messieurs who
go out there must help me to prove. This is my share in the advantages my country shall reap from the possession of such a magnificent dependency. The mere wealth I leave to others. Pardon my
questions, but you are the first Englishman coming under my observation . . .' I hastened to assure him I was not in the least typical.
'If I were,' said I, 'I wouldn't be talking like this with you.' 'What
you say is rather profound, and probably erroneous,' he said, with a
laugh. 'Avoid irritation more than exposure to the sun. Adieu. How
do you English say, eh? Good-bye. Ah! Good-bye. Adieu. In the
tropics one must before everything keep calm.' . . . He lifted a warning forefinger. . . . '*Du calme, du calme. Adieu.*'

"One thing more remained to do—say good-bye to my excellent
aunt. I found her triumphant. I had a cup of tea—the last decent
cup of tea for many days—and in a room that most soothingly
looked just as you would expect a lady's drawing-room to look, we
had a long quiet chat by the fireside. In the course of these confidences it became quite plain to me I had been represented to the
wife of the high dignitary, and goodness knows to how many more
people besides, as an exceptional and gifted creature—a piece of
good fortune for the Company—a man you don't get hold of every
day. Good Heavens! and I was going to take charge of a two-penny-
half-penny river-steamboat with a penny whistle attached! It
appeared, however, I was also one of the Workers, with a capital—
you know. Something like an emissary of light, something like a
lower sort of apostle. There had been a lot of such rot let loose in
print and talk just about that time, and the excellent woman, living
right in the rush of all that humbug, got carried off her feet. She
talked about 'weaning those ignorant millions from their horrid
ways,' till, upon my word, she made me quite uncomfortable. I ventured to hint that the Company was run for profit.

" 'You forget, dear Charlie, that the laborer is worthy of his hire,'
she said brightly. It's queer how out of touch with truth women are.
They live in a world of their own, and there had never been anything like it, and never can be. It is too beautiful altogether, and if
they were to set it up it would go to pieces before the first sunset.
Some confounded fact we men have been living contentedly with
ever since the day of creation would start up and knock the whole
thing over.

8. Doctor who treats mental diseases. (The term has now been replaced by "psychiatrist.")

"After this I got embraced, told to wear flannel, be sure to write often, and so on—and I left. In the street—I don't know why—a queer feeling came to me that I was an impostor. Odd thing that I, who used to clear out for any part of the world at twenty-four hours' notice, with less thought than most men give to the crossing of a street, had a moment—I won't say of hesitation, but of startled pause, before this commonplace affair. The best way I can explain it to you is by saying that, for a second or two, I felt as though, instead of going to the center of a continent, I were about to set off for the center of the earth.

"I left in a French steamer, and she called in every blamed port they have out there, for, as far as I could see, the sole purpose of landing soldiers and custom-house officers. I watched the coast. Watching a coast as it slips by the ship is like thinking about an enigma. There it is before you—smiling, frowning, inviting, grand, mean, insipid, or savage, and always mute with an air of whispering, Come and find out. This one was almost featureless, as if still in the making, with an aspect of monotonous grimness. The edge of a colossal jungle, so dark green as to be almost black, fringed with white surf, ran straight, like a ruled line, far, far away along a blue sea whose glitter was blurred by a creeping mist. The sun was fierce, the land seemed to glisten and drip with steam. Here and there grayish-whitish specks showed up clustered inside the white surf, with a flag flying above them perhaps—settlements some centuries old, and still no bigger than pinheads on the untouched expanse of their background. We pounded along, stopped, landed soldiers; went on, landed custom-house clerks to levy toll in what looked like a God-forsaken wilderness, with a tin shed and a flagpole lost in it; landed more soldiers—to take care of the custom-house clerks presumably. Some, I heard, got drowned in the surf; but whether they did or not, nobody seemed particularly to care. They were just flung out there, and on we went. Every day the coast looked the same, as though we had not moved; but we passed various places—trading places—with names like Gran' Bassam, Little Popo; names that seemed to belong to some sordid farce acted in front of a sinister back-cloth. The idleness of a passenger, my isolation amongst all these men with whom I had no point of contact, the oily and languid sea, the uniform somberness of the coast, seemed to keep me away from the truth of things, within the toil of a mournful and senseless delusion. The voice of the surf heard now and then was a positive pleasure, like the speech of a brother. It was something natural, that had its reason, that had a meaning. Now and then a boat from the shore gave one a momentary contact with reality. It was paddled by black fellows. You could see from afar the white of their eyeballs glistening. They shouted, sang; their bodies streamed with perspiration; they had faces like grotesque masks—these chaps; but they had bone, muscle, a wild vitality, an intense energy of movement, that was as natural and true as the surf along their coast. They wanted no excuse for being there. They were a great comfort to look at. For a time I would feel I belonged still to a world of straight-forward facts; but the feeling would not last long. Something would turn up to scare it away. Once, I remember, we came upon a man-of-war anchored off the coast. There wasn't even a shed there, and she was shelling the bush. It appears the French had one of their wars going on thereabouts. Her ensign dropped limp like a rag; the muzzles of long six-inch guns stuck out all over the low hull; the greasy, slimy swell swung her up lazily and let her down, swaying her thin masts. In the empty immensity of earth, sky, and water, there she was, incomprehensible, firing into a continent. Pop, would go one of the six-inch guns; a small flame would dart and vanish, a little white smoke would disappear, a tiny projectile would give a feeble screech—and nothing happened. Nothing could happen. There was a touch of insanity in the proceeding, a sense of lugubrious drollery in the sight; and it was not dissipated by somebody on board assuring me earnestly there was a camp of natives—he called them enemies!—hidden out of sight somewhere.

"We gave her her letters (I heard the men in that lonely ship were dying of fever at the rate of three a day) and went on. We called at some more places with farcical names, where the merry dance of death and trade goes on in a still and earthy atmosphere as of an overheated catacomb; all along the formless coast bordered by dangerous surf, as if Nature herself had tried to ward off intruders; in and out of rivers, streams of death in life, whose banks were rotting into mud, whose waters, thickened into slime, invaded the contorted mangroves, that seemed to writhe at us in the extremity of an impotent despair. Nowhere did we stop long enough to get a particularized impression, but the general sense of vague and oppressive wonder grew upon me. It was like a weary pilgrimage amongst hints for nightmares.

"It was upward of thirty days before I saw the mouth of the big river. We anchored off the seat of the government. But my work would not begin till some two hundred miles farther on. So as soon as I could I made a start for a place thirty miles higher up.

"I had my passage on a little sea-going steamer. Her captain was a Swede, and knowing me for a seaman, invited me on the bridge. He was a young man, lean, fair, and morose, with lanky hair and a shuffling gait. As we left the miserable little wharf, he tossed his head contemptuously at the shore. 'Been living there?' he asked. I said, 'Yes.' 'Fine lot these government chaps—are they not?' he went on, speaking English with great precision and considerable bitterness. 'It is funny what some people will do for a few francs a month. I wonder what becomes of that kind when it goes up country?' I said to him I expected to see that soon. 'So-o-o!' he exclaimed. He shuffled athwart, keeping one eye ahead vigilantly. 'Don't be too sure,' he continued. 'The other day I took up a man who hanged himself on the road. He was a Swede, too.' 'Hanged himself! Why, in God's name?' I cried. He kept on looking out watchfully. 'Who knows? The sun too much for him, or the country perhaps.'

"At last we opened a reach. A rocky cliff appeared, mounds of turned-up earth by the shore, houses on a hill, others with iron roofs, amongst a waste of excavations, or hanging to the declivity. A continuous noise of the rapids above hovered over this scene of inhabited devastation. A lot of people, mostly black and naked, moved about like ants. A jetty projected into the river. A blinding sunlight drowned all this at times in a sudden recrudescence of glare. 'There's your Company's station,' said the Swede, pointing to three wooden barrack-like structures on the rocky slope. 'I will send your things up. Four boxes did you say? So. Farewell.'

"I came upon a boiler wallowing in the grass, then found a path leading up the hill. It turned aside for the boulders, and also for an undersized railway truck lying there on its back with its wheels in the air. One was off. The thing looked as dead as the carcass of some animal. I came upon more pieces of decaying machinery, a stack of rusty rails. To the left a clump of trees made a shady spot, where dark things seemed to stir feebly. I blinked, the path was steep. A horn tooted to the right, and I saw the black people run. A heavy and dull detonation shook the ground, a puff of smoke came out of the cliff, and that was all. No change appeared on the face of the rock. They were building a railway. The cliff was not in the way or anything; but this objectless blasting was all the work going on.

"A slight clinking behind me made me turn my head. Six black men advanced in a file, toiling up the path. They walked erect and slow, balancing small baskets full of earth on their heads, and the clink kept time with their footsteps. Black rags were wound round their loins, and the short ends behind waggled to and fro like tails. I could see every rib, the joints of their limbs were like knots in a rope, each had an iron collar on his neck, and all were connected together with a chain whose bights swung between them, rhythmically clinking. Another report from the cliff made me think suddenly of that ship of war I had seen firing into a continent. It was the same kind of ominous voice; but these men could by no stretch of imagination be called enemies. They were called criminals, and the outraged law, like the bursting shells, had come to them, an insoluble mystery from the sea. All their meager breasts panted together, the violently dilated nostrils quivered, the eyes stared stonily uphill. They passed me within six inches, without a glance, with that complete, death-like indifference of unhappy savages. Behind this raw matter one of the reclaimed, the product of the new forces at work, strolled despondently, carrying a rifle by its middle. He had a uniform jacket with one button off, and seeing a white man on the path, hoisted his weapon to his shoulder with alacrity. This was simple prudence, white men being so much alike at a distance that he could not tell who I might be. He was speedily reassured, and with a large, white, rascally grin, and a glance at his charge, seemed to take me into partnership in his exalted trust. After all, I also was a part of the great cause of these high and just proceedings.

"Instead of going up, I turned and descended to the left. My idea was to let that chain-gang get out of sight before I climbed the hill. You know I am not particularly tender; I've had to strike and to fend off. I've had to resist and to attack sometimes—that's only one way of resisting—without counting the exact cost, according to the demands of such sort of life as I had blundered into. I've seen the devil of violence, and the devil of greed, and the devil of hot desire; but, by all the stars! these were strong, lusty, red-eyed devils, that swayed and drove men—men, I tell you. But as I stood on this hillside, I foresaw that in the blinding sunshine of that land I would become acquainted with a flabby, pretending, weak-eyed devil of a rapacious and pitiless folly. How insidious he could be, too, I was only to find out several months later and a thousand miles farther. For a moment I stood appalled, as though by a warning. Finally I descended the hill, obliquely, towards the trees I had seen.

"I avoided a vast artificial hole somebody had been digging on the slope, the purpose of which I found it impossible to divine. It wasn't a quarry or a sandpit, anyhow. It was just a hole. It might have been connected with the philanthropic desire of giving the criminals something to do. I don't know. Then I nearly fell into a very narrow ravine, almost no more than a scar in the hillside. I discovered that a lot of imported drainage-pipes for the settlement had been tumbled in there. There wasn't one that was not broken. It was a wanton smash-up. At last I got under the trees. My purpose was to stroll into the shade for a moment; but no sooner within than it seemed to me I had stepped into the gloomy circle of some Inferno. The rapids were near, and an uninterrupted, uniform, headlong, rushing noise filled the mournful stillness of the grove, where not a breath stirred, not a leaf moved, with a mysterious sound—as though the tearing pace of the launched earth had suddenly become audible.

"Black shapes crouched, lay, sat between the trees, leaning against the trunks, clinging to the earth, half coming out, half effaced within the dim light, in all the attitudes of pain, abandonment, and despair. Another mine on the cliff went off, followed by a slight shudder of the soil under my feet. The work was going on. The work! And this was the place where some of the helpers had withdrawn to die.

"They were dying slowly—it was very clear. They were not enemies, they were not criminals, they were nothing earthly now—nothing but black shadows of disease and starvation, lying confusedly in the greenish gloom. Brought from all the recesses of the coast in all the legality of time contracts, lost in uncongenial surroundings, fed on unfamiliar food, they sickened, became inefficient, and were then allowed to crawl away and rest. These moribund shapes were free as air—and nearly as thin. I began to distinguish the gleam of the eyes under the trees. Then, glancing down, I saw a face near my hand. The black bones reclined at full length with one shoulder against the tree, and slowly the eyelids rose and the sunken eyes looked up at me, enormous and vacant, a kind of blind, white flicker in the depths of the orbs, which died out slowly. The man seemed young—almost a boy—but you know with them it's hard to tell. I found nothing else to do but to offer him one of my good Swede's ship's biscuits I had in my pocket. The fingers closed slowly on it and held—there was no other movement and no other glance. He had tied a bit of white worsted round his neck—Why? Where did he get it? Was it a badge—an ornament—a charm—a propitiatory act? Was there any idea at all connected with it? It looked startling round his black neck, this bit of white thread from beyond the seas.

"Near the same tree two more bundles of acute angles sat with their legs drawn up. One, with his chin propped on his knees, stared at nothing, in an intolerable and appalling manner: his brother phantom rested its forehead, as if overcome with a great weariness; and all about others were scattered in every pose of contorted collapse, as in some picture of a massacre or a pestilence. While I stood horror-struck, one of these creatures rose to his hands and knees, and went off on all-fours towards the river to drink. He lapped out of his hand, then sat up in the sunlight, crossing his shins in front of him, and after a time let his woolly head fall on his breastbone.

"I didn't want any more loitering in the shade, and I made haste towards the station. When near the buildings I met a white man, in such an unexpected elegance of get-up that in the first moment I took him for a sort of vision. I saw a high starched collar, white cuffs, a light alpaca jacket, snowy trousers, a clear necktie, and varnished boots. No hat. Hair parted, brushed, oiled, under a green-lined parasol held in a big white hand. He was amazing, and had a pen-holder behind his ear.

"I shook hands with this miracle, and I learned he was the Company's chief accountant, and that all the bookkeeping was done at this station. He had come out for a moment, he said, 'to get a breath of fresh air.' The expression sounded wonderfully odd, with its suggestion of sedentary desk-life. I wouldn't have mentioned the fellow to you at all, only it was from his lips that I first heard the name of the man who is so indissolubly connected with the memories of that time. Moreover, I respected the fellow. Yes; I respected his collars, his vast cuffs, his brushed hair. His appearance was certainly that of a hairdresser's dummy; but in the great demoralization of the land he kept up his appearance. That's backbone. His starched collars and got-up shirt-fronts were achievements of character. He had been out nearly three years; and, later, I could not help asking him how he managed to sport such linen. He had just the faintest blush, and said modestly, 'I've been teaching one of the native women about the station. It was difficult. She had a distaste for the work.' Thus this man had verily accomplished something. And he was devoted to his books, which were in apple-pie order.

"Everything else in the station was in a muddle,—heads, things, buildings. Strings of dusty niggers with splay feet arrived and departed; a stream of manufactured goods, rubbishy cottons, beads, and brass-wire set into the depths of darkness, and in return came a precious trickle of ivory.

"I had to wait in the station for ten days—an eternity. I lived in a hut in the yard, but to be out of the chaos I would sometimes get into the accountant's office. It was built of horizontal planks, and so badly put together that, as he bent over his high desk, he was barred from neck to heels with narrow strips of sunlight. There was no need to open the big shutter to see. It was hot there too; big flies buzzed fiendishly, and did not sting, but stabbed. I sat generally on the floor, while, of faultless appearance (and even slightly scented), perching on a high stool, he wrote, he wrote. Sometimes he stood up for exercise. When a truckle-bed with a sick man (some invalided agent from up-country) was put in there, he exhibited a gentle annoyance. 'The groans of this sick person,' he said, 'distract my attention. And without that it is extremely difficult to guard against clerical errors in this climate.'

"One day he remarked, without lifting his head, 'In the interior you will no doubt meet Mr. Kurtz.' On my asking who Mr. Kurtz was, he said he was a first-class agent; and seeing my disappointment at this information, he added slowly, laying down his pen, 'He is a very remarkable person.' Further questions elicited from him that Mr. Kurtz was at present in charge of a trading-post, a very important one, in the true ivory-country, at 'the very bottom of there. Sends in as much ivory as all the others put together . . .' He began to write again. The sick man was too ill to groan. The flies buzzed in a great peace.

"Suddenly there was a growing murmur of voices and a great tramping of feet. A caravan had come in. A violent babble of uncouth sounds burst out on the other side of the planks. All the carriers were speaking together, and in the midst of the uproar the lamentable voice of the chief agent was heard 'giving it up' tearfully for the twentieth time that day. . . . He rose slowly. 'What a frightful row,' he said. He crossed the room gently to look at the sick man, and returning, said to me, 'He does not hear.' 'What! Dead.' I asked, startled. 'No, not yet,' he answered, with great composure. Then, alluding with a toss of the head to the tumult in the station-yard, 'When one has got to make correct entries, one comes to hate those savages—hate them to the death.' He remained thoughtful for a moment. 'When you see Mr. Kurtz,' he went on, 'tell him from me that everything here'—he glanced at the desk—'is very satisfactory. I don't like to write to him—with those messengers of ours you never know who may get hold of your letter—at that Central Station.' He stared at me for a moment with his mild, bulging eyes. 'Oh, he will go far, very far,' he began again. 'He will be a somebody in the Administration before long. They, above—the Council in Europe, you know—mean him to be.'

"He turned to his work. The noise outside had ceased, and presently in going out I stopped at the door. In the steady buzz of flies the homeward-bound agent was lying flushed and insensible; the other, bent over his books, was making correct entries of perfectly correct transactions; and fifty feet below the doorstep I could see the still tree-tops of the grove of death.

"Next day I left that station at last, with a caravan of sixty men, for a two-hundred-mile tramp.

"No use telling you much about that. Paths, paths, everywhere; a stamped-in network of paths spreading over the empty land, through long grass, through burnt grass, through thickets, down and up chilly ravines, up and down stony hills ablaze with heat; and a solitude, a solitude, nobody, not a hut. The population had cleared out a long time ago. Well, if a lot of mysterious niggers armed with all kinds of fearful weapons suddenly took to traveling on the road between Deal and Gravesend, catching the yokels right and left to carry heavy loads for them, I fancy every farm and cottage thereabouts would get empty very soon. Only here the dwellings were gone too. Still, I passed through several abandoned villages. There's something pathetically childish in the ruins of grass walls. Day after day, with the stamp and shuffle of sixty pair of bare feet behind me, each pair under a 60-lb. load. Camp, cook, sleep; strike camp, march. Now and then a carrier dead in harness, at rest in the long grass near the path, with an empty water-gourd and his long staff lying by his side. A great silence around and above. Perhaps on some quiet night the tremor of far-out drums, sinking, swelling, a

tremor vast, faint; a sound weird, appealing, suggestive, and wild—
and perhaps with as profound a meaning as the sound of bells in a
Christian country. Once a white man in an unbuttoned uniform,
camping on the path with an armed escort of lank Zanzibaris,[9] very
hospitable and festive—not to say drunk. Was looking after the
upkeep of the road, he declared. Can't say I saw any road or any
upkeep, unless the body of a middle-aged negro, with a bullet-hole
in the forehead, upon which I absolutely stumbled three miles farther on, may be considered as a permanent improvement. I had a
white companion too, not a bad chap, but rather too fleshy and
with the exasperating habit of fainting on the hot hillsides, miles
away from the least bit of shade and water. Annoying, you know, to
hold your own coat like a parasol over a man's head while he is
coming to. I couldn't help asking him once what he meant by
coming there at all. 'To make money, of course. What do you
think?' he said scornfully. Then he got fever, and had to be carried
in a hammock slung under a pole. As he weighed sixteen stone[1] I
had no end of rows with the carriers. They jibbed, ran away,
sneaked off with their loads in the night—quite a mutiny. So, one
evening, I made a speech in English with gestures, not one of which
was lost to the sixty pairs of eyes before me, and the next morning I
started the hammock off in front all right. An hour afterwards I
came upon the whole concern wrecked in a bush—man, hammock,
groans, blankets, horrors. The heavy pole had skinned his poor nose.
He was very anxious for me to kill somebody, but there wasn't the
shadow of a carrier near. I remembered the old doctor—'It would
be interesting for science to watch the mental changes of individuals, on the spot.' I felt I was becoming scientifically interesting.
However, all that is to no purpose. On the fifteenth day I came in
sight of the big river again, and hobbled into the Central Station. It
was on a backwater surrounded by scrub and forest, with a pretty
border of smelly mud on one side, and on the three others enclosed
by a crazy fence of rushes. A neglected gap was all the gate it had,
and the first glance at the place was enough to let you see the
flabby devil was running that show. White men with long staves in
their hands appeared languidly from amongst the buildings, strolling up to take a look at me, and then retired out of sight somewhere. One of them, a stout, excitable chap with black moustaches,
informed me with great volubility and many digressions, as soon as
I told him who I was, that my steamer was at the bottom of the
river. I was thunderstruck. What, how, why? Oh, it was 'all right.'

9. Natives of Zanzibar, an island off the
east coast of Africa, once part of the
sultanate of Zanzibar and a British pro-
tectorate, now part of the independent
state of Tanzania (made up of Zanzibar
and Tanganyika). Natives of Zanzibar
were used as mercenaries throughout Africa.
1. One stone equals 14 pounds. The man
weighed 224 pounds.

The 'manager himself' was there. All quite correct. 'Everybody had behaved splendidly! splendidly!'—'You must,' he said in agitation, 'go and see the general manager at once. He is waiting.'

"I did not see the real significance of that wreck at once. I fancy I see it now, but I am not sure—not at all. Certainly the affair was too stupid—when I think of it—to be altogether natural. Still . . . But at the moment it presented itself simply as a confounded nuisance. The steamer was sunk. They had started two days before in a sudden hurry up the river with the manager on board, in charge of some volunteer skipper, and before they had been out three hours they tore the bottom out of her on stones, and she sank near the south bank. I asked myself what I was to do there, now my boat was lost. As a matter of fact, I had plenty to do in fishing my command out of the river. I had to set about it the very next day. That, and the repairs when I brought the pieces to the station, took some months.

"My first interview with the manager was curious. He did not ask me to sit down after my twenty-mile walk that morning. He was commonplace in complexion, in feature, in manners, and in voice. He was of middle size and of ordinary build. His eyes, of the usual blue, were perhaps remarkably cold, and he certainly could make his glance fall on one as trenchant and heavy as an axe. But even at these times the rest of his person seemed to disclaim the intention. Otherwise there was only an indefinable, faint expression of his lips, something stealthy—a smile—not a smile—I remember it, but I can't explain. It was unconscious, this smile was, though just after he had said something it got intensified for an instant. It came at the end of his speeches like a seal applied on the words to make the meaning of the commonest phrase appear absolutely inscrutable. He was a common trader, from his youth up employed in these parts—nothing more. He was obeyed, yet he inspired neither love nor fear, nor even respect. He inspired uneasiness. That was it! Uneasiness. Not a definite mistrust—just uneasiness—nothing more. You have no idea how effective such a . . . a . . . faculty can be. He had no genius for organizing, for initiative, or for order even. That was evident in such things as the deplorable state of the station. He had no learning, and no intelligence. His position had come to him—why? Perhaps because he was never ill. . . . He had served three terms of three years out there. . . . Because triumphant health in the general rout of constitutions is a kind of power in itself. When he went home on leave he rioted on a large scale—pompously. Jack ashore—with a difference—in externals only. This one could gather from his casual talk. He originated nothing, he could keep the routine going—that's all. But he was great. He was great by this little thing that it was impossible to tell what could control such a man. He never gave that secret away. Perhaps there was nothing within him. Such a suspicion made one pause—for out there there were no external checks. Once when various tropical diseases had laid low almost every 'agent' in the station, he was heard to say, 'Men who come out here should have no entrails.' He sealed the utterance with that smile of his, as though it had been a door opening into a darkness he had in his keeping. You fancied you had seen things—but the seal was on. When annoyed at meal-times by the constant quarrels of the white men about precedence, he ordered an immense round table to be made, for which a special house had to be built. This was the station's mess-room. Where he sat was the first place—the rest were nowhere. One felt this to be his unalterable conviction. He was neither civil or uncivil. He was quiet. He allowed his 'boy'—an overfed young negro from the coast —to treat the white men, under his very eyes, with provoking insolence.

"He began to speak as soon as he saw me. I had been very long on the road. He could not wait. Had to start without me. The upriver stations had to be relieved. There had been so many delays already that he did not know who was dead and who was alive, and how they got on—and so on, and so on. He paid no attention to my explanations, and, playing with a stick of sealing-wax, repeated several times that the situation was 'very grave, very grave.' There were rumors that a very important station was in jeopardy, and its chief, Mr. Kurtz, was ill. Hoped it was not true. Mr. Kurtz was . . . I felt weary and irritable. Hang Kurtz, I thought. I interrupted him by saying I had heard of Mr. Kurtz on the coast. 'Ah! So they talk of him down there,' he murmured to himself. Then he began again, assuring me Mr. Kurtz was the best agent he had, an exceptional man, of the greatest importance to the Company; therefore I could understand his anxiety. He was, he said, 'very, very uneasy.' Certainly he fidgeted on his chair a good deal, exclaimed, 'Ah, Mr. Kurtz!' broke the stick of sealing-wax and seemed dumbfounded by the accident. Next thing he wanted to know 'how long it would take to' . . . I interrupted him again. Being hungry, you know, and kept on my feet too, I was getting savage. 'How can I tell?' I said. 'I haven't even seen the wreck yet—some months, no doubt.' All this talk seemed to me so futile. 'Some months,' he said. 'Well, let us say three months before we can make a start. Yes. That ought to do the affair.' I flung out of his hut (he lived all alone in a clay hut with a sort of verandah) muttering to myself my opinion of him. He was a chattering idiot. Afterwards I took it back when it was borne in upon me startlingly with what extreme nicety he had estimated the time requisite for the 'affair.'

"I went to work the next day, turning, so to speak, my back on that station. In that way only it seemed to me I could keep my hold on the redeeming facts of life. Still, one must look about some-times; and then I saw this station, these men strolling aimlessly about in the sunshine of the yard. I asked myself sometimes what it all meant. They wandered here and there with their absurd long staves in their hands, like a lot of faithless pilgrims bewitched inside a rotten fence. The word 'ivory' rang in the air, was whispered, was sighed. You would think they were praying to it. A taint of imbecile rapacity blew through it all, like a whiff from some corpse. By Jove! I've never seen anything so unreal in my life. And outside, the silent wilderness surrounding this cleared speck on the earth struck me as something great and invincible, like evil or truth, waiting patiently for the passing away of this fantastic invasion.

"Oh, these months! Well, never mind. Various things happened. One evening a grass shed full of calico, cotton prints, beads, and I don't know what else, burst into a blaze so suddenly that you would have thought the earth had opened to let an avenging fire consume all that trash. I was smoking my pipe quietly by my dismantled steamer, and saw them all cutting capers in the light, with their arms lifted high, when the stout man with moustaches came tearing down to the river, a tin pail in his hand, assured me that everybody was 'behaving splendidly, splendidly,' dipped about a quart of water and tore back again. I noticed there was a hole in the bottom of his pail.

"I strolled up. There was no hurry. You see the thing had gone off like a box of matches. It had been hopeless from the very first. The flame had leaped high, driven everybody back, lighted up every-thing—and collapsed. The shed was already a heap of embers glow-ing fiercely. A nigger was being beaten near by. They said he had caused the fire in some way; be that as it may, he was screeching most horribly. I saw him, later, for several days, sitting in a bit of shade looking very sick and trying to recover himself: afterwards he arose and went out—and the wilderness without a sound took him into its bosom again. As I approached the glow from the dark I found myself at the back of two men, talking. I heard the name of Kurtz pronounced, then the words, 'take advantage of this unfortu-nate accident.' One of the men was the manager. I wished him a good evening. 'Did you see anything like it—eh? it is incredible,' he said, and walked off. The other man remained. He was a first-class agent, young, gentlemanly, a bit reserved with a forked little beard and a hooked nose. He was stand-offish with the other agents, and they on their side said he was the manager's spy upon them. As to me, I had hardly ever spoken to him before. We got into talk, and by and by we strolled away from the hissing ruins. Then he asked me to his room, which was in the main building of the station. He struck a match, and I perceived that this young aristocrat had not only a silver-mounted dressing-case but also a whole candle all to himself. Just at that time the manager was the only man supposed to have any right to candles. Native mats covered the clay walls; a collection of spears, assegais,[2] shields, knives, was hung up in trophies. The business entrusted to this fellow was the making of bricks—so I had been informed; but there wasn't a fragment of a brick anywhere in the station, and he had been there more than a year—waiting. It seems he could not make bricks without something, I don't know what—straw maybe. Anyway, it could not be found there, and as it was not likely to be sent from Europe, it did not appear clear to me what he was waiting for. An act of special creation perhaps. However, they were all waiting—all the sixteen or twenty pilgrims of them—for something; and upon my word it did not seem an uncongenial occupation, from the way they took it, though the only thing that ever came to them was disease—as far as I could see. They beguiled the time by backbiting and intriguing against each other in a foolish kind of way. There was an air of plotting about that station, but nothing came of it, of course. It was as unreal as everything else—as the philanthropic pretense of the whole concern, as their talk, as their government, as their show of work. The only real feeling was a desire to get appointed to a trading-post where ivory was to be had, so that they could earn percentages. They intrigued and slandered and hated each other only on that account—but as to effectually lifting a little finger—oh no. By Heavens! there is something after all in the world allowing one man to steal a horse while another must not look at a halter. Steal a horse straight out. Very well. He has done it. Perhaps he can ride. But there is a way of looking at a halter that would provoke the most charitable of saints into a kick.

"I had no idea why he wanted to be sociable, but as we chatted in there it suddenly occurred to me the fellow was trying to get at something—in fact, pumping me. He alluded constantly to Europe, to the people I was supposed to know there—putting leading questions as to my acquaintances in the sepulchral city, and so on. His little eyes glittered like mica discs—with curiosity—though he tried to keep up a bit of superciliousness. At first I was astonished, but very soon I became awfully curious to see what he would find out from me. I couldn't possibly imagine what I had in me to make it worth his while. It was very pretty to see how he baffled himself, for in truth my body was full only of chills, and my head had nothing in it but that wretched steamboat business. It was evident he took me for a perfectly shameless prevaricator. At last he got angry, and

2. Slender iron-tipped spears.

to conceal a movement of furious annoyance, he yawned. I rose. Then I noticed a small sketch in oils, on a panel, representing a woman, draped and blindfolded, carrying a lighted torch. The background was somber—almost black. The movement of the woman was stately, and the effect of the torchlight on the face was sinister.

"It arrested me, and he stood by civilly, holding an empty half-pint champagne bottle (medical comforts) with the candle stuck in it. To my question he said Mr. Kurtz had painted this—in this very station more than a year ago—while waiting for means to go to his trading-post. 'Tell me, pray,' said I, 'who is this Mr. Kurtz?'

" 'The chief of the Inner Station,' he answered in a short tone, looking away. 'Much obliged,' I said, laughing. 'And you are the brickmaker of the Central Station. Every one knows that.' He was silent for a while. 'He is a prodigy,' he said at last. 'He is an emissary of pity, and science, and progress, and devil knows what else. We want,' he began to declaim suddenly, 'for the guidance of the cause entrusted to us by Europe, so to speak, higher intelligence, wide sympathies, a singleness of purpose.' 'Who says that?' I asked. 'Lots of them,' he replied. 'Some even write that; and so *he* comes here, a special being, as you ought to know?' 'Why ought I to know?' I interrupted, really surprised. He paid no attention. 'Yes. Today he is chief of the best station, next year, he will be assistant-manager, two years more and . . . but I daresay you know what he will be in two years' time. You are of the new gang—the gang of virtue. The same people who sent him specially also recommended you. Oh, don't say no. I've my own eyes to trust.' Light dawned upon me. My dear aunt's influential acquaintances were producing an unexpected effect upon that young man. I nearly burst into a laugh. 'Do you read the Company's confidential correspondence?' I asked. He hadn't a word to say. It was great fun. 'When Mr. Kurtz,' I continued severely, 'is General Manager, you won't have the opportunity.'

"He blew the candle out suddenly, and we went outside. The moon had risen. Black figures strolled about listlessly, pouring water on the glow, whence proceeded a sound of hissing; steam ascended in the moonlight; the beaten nigger groaned somewhere. 'What a row the brute makes!' said the indefatigable man with the moustaches, appearing near us. 'Serve him right. Transgression—punishment—bang! Pitiless, pitiless. That's the only way. This will prevent all conflagrations for the future. I was just telling the manager . . .' He noticed my companion, and became crestfallen all at once. 'Not in bed yet,' he said, with a kind of servile heartiness; 'it's so natural. Ha! Danger—agitation.' He vanished I went on to the riverside, and the other followed me. I heard a scathing murmur at my ear, 'Heaps of muffs—go to.' The pilgrims could be seen in knots gesticulating, discussing. Several had still their staves in their hands.

I verily believe they took these sticks to bed with them. Beyond the fence the forest stood up spectrally in the moonlight, and through the dim stir, through the faint sounds of that lamentable courtyard, the silence of the land went home to one's very heart—its mystery, its greatness, the amazing reality of its concealed life. The hurt nigger moaned feebly somewhere near by, and then fetched a deep sigh that made me mend my pace away from there. I felt a hand introducing itself under my arm. 'My dear sir,' said the fellow, 'I don't want to be misunderstood, and especially by you, who will see Mr. Kurtz long before I can have that pleasure. I wouldn't like him to get a false idea of my disposition. . . .'

"I let him run on, this papier-mâché Mephistopheles, and it seemed to me that if I tried I could poke my forefinger through him, and would find nothing inside but a little loose dirt, maybe. He, don't you see, had been planning to be assistant-manager by and by under the present man, and I could see that the coming of that Kurtz had upset them both not a little. He talked precipitately, and I did not try to stop him. I had my shoulders against the wreck of my steamer, hauled up on the slope like a carcass of some big river animal. The smell of mud, of primeval mud, by Jove! was in my nostrils, the high stillness of primeval forest was before my eyes; there were shiny patches on the black creek. The moon had spread over everything a thin layer of silver—over the rank grass, over the mud, upon the wall of matted vegetation standing higher than the wall of a temple, over the great river I could see through a somber gap glittering, glittering, as it flowed broadly by without a murmur. All this was great, expectant, mute, while the man jabbered about himself. I wondered whether the stillness on the face of the immensity looking at us two were meant as an appeal or as a menace. What were we who had strayed in here? Could we handle that dumb thing, or would it handle us? I felt how big, how confoundedly big, was that thing that couldn't talk and perhaps was deaf as well. What was in there? I could see a little ivory coming out from there, and I had heard Mr. Kurtz was in there. I had heard enough about it too—God knows! Yet somehow it didn't bring any image with it—no more than if I had been told an angel or a fiend was in there. I believed it in the same way one of you might believe there are inhabitants in the planet Mars. I knew once a Scotch sailmaker who was certain, dead sure, there were people in Mars. If you asked him for some idea how they looked and behaved, he would get shy and mutter something about 'walking on all-fours.' If you as much as smiled, he would—though a man of sixty—offer to fight you. I would not have gone so far as to fight for Kurtz, but I went for him near enough to a lie. You know I hate, detest, and can't bear a lie, not because I am straighter than the rest of us, but simply because it appalls me. There is a taint of death, a flavor of mortality in lies—which is exactly what I hate and detest in the world—what I want to forget. It makes me miserable and sick, like biting something rotten would do. Temperament, I suppose. Well, I went near enough to it by letting the young fool there believe anything he liked to imagine as to my influence in Europe. I became in an instant as much of a pretense as the rest of the bewitched pilgrims. This simply because I had a notion it somehow would be of help to that Kurtz whom at the time I did not see—you understand. He was just a word for me. I did not see the man in the name any more than you do. Do you see him? Do you see the story? Do you see anything? It seems to me I am trying to tell you a dream—making a vain attempt, because no relation of a dream can convey the dream-sensation, that commingling of absurdity, surprise, and bewilderment in a tremor of struggling revolt, that notion of being captured by the incredible which is of the very essence of dreams. . . ."

He was silent for a while.

". . . No, it is impossible; it is impossible to convey the life-sensation of any given epoch of one's existence—that which makes its truth, its meaning—its subtle and penetrating essence. It is impossible. We live, as we dream—alone. . . ."

He paused again as if reflecting, then added:

"Of course in this you fellows see more than I could then. You see me, whom you know. . . ."

It had become so pitch dark that we listeners could hardly see one another. For a long time already he, sitting apart, had been no more to us than a voice. There was not a word from anybody. The others might have been asleep, but I was awake. I listened, I listened on the watch for the sentence, for the word, that would give me the clue to the faint uneasiness inspired by this narrative that seemed to shape itself without human lips in the heavy night-air of the river.

". . . Yes—I let him run on," Marlow began again, "and think what he pleased about the powers that were behind me. I did! And there was nothing behind me! There was nothing but that wretched, old, mangled steamboat I was leaning against, while he talked fluently about 'the necessity for every man to get on.' 'And when one comes out here, you conceive, it is not to gaze at the moon.' Mr. Kurtz was a 'universal genius,' but even a genius would find it easier to work with 'adequate tools—intelligent men.' He did not make bricks—why, there was a physical impossibility in the way —as I was well aware; and if he did secretarial work for the manager, it was because 'no sensible man rejects wantonly the confidence of his superiors.' Did I see it? I saw it. What more did I want? What I really wanted was rivets, by Heaven! Rivets. To get on with the work—to stop the hole. Rivets I wanted. There were cases of them down at the coast—cases—piled up—burst—split! You kicked a loose rivet at every second step in that station yard on the hillside. Rivets had rolled into the grove of death. You could fill your pockets with rivets for the trouble of stooping down—and there wasn't one rivet to be found where it was wanted. We had plates that would do, but nothing to fasten them with. And every week the messenger, a lone negro, letter-bag on shoulder and staff in hand, left our station for the coast. And several times a week a coast caravan came in with trade goods—ghastly glazed calico that made you shudder only to look at it, glass beads value about a penny a quart, confounded spotted cotton handkerchiefs. And no rivets. Three carriers could have brought all that was wanted to set that steamboat afloat.

"He was becoming confidential now, but I fancy my unresponsive attitude must have exasperated him at last, for he judged it necessary to inform me he feared neither God nor devil, let alone any mere man. I said I could see that very well, but what I wanted was a certain quantity of rivets—and rivets were what really Mr. Kurtz wanted, if he had only known it. Now letters went to the coast every week. . . . 'My dear sir,' he cried, 'I write from dictation.' I demanded rivets. There was a way—for an intelligent man. He changed his manner; became very cold, and suddenly began to talk about a hippopotamus; wondered whether sleeping on board the steamer (I stuck to my salvage night and day) I wasn't disturbed. There was an old hippo that had the bad habit of getting out on the bank and roaming at night over the station grounds. The pilgrims used to turn out in a body and empty every rifle they could lay hands on at him. Some even had sat up o' nights for him. All this energy was wasted, though. 'That animal has a charmed life,' he said; 'but you can say this only of brutes in this country. No man—you apprehend me?—no man here bears a charmed life.' He stood there for a moment in the moonlight with his delicate hooked nose set a little askew, and his mica eyes glittering without a wink, then, with a curt Good-night, he strode off. I could see he was disturbed and considerably puzzled, which made me feel more hopeful than I had been for days. It was a great comfort to turn from that chap to my influential friend, the battered, twisted, ruined, tin-pot steamboat. I clambered on board. She rang under my feet like an empty Huntley & Palmer biscuit-tin kicked along a gutter; she was nothing so solid in make, and rather less pretty in shape, but I had expended enough hard work on her to make me love her. No influential friend would have served me better. She had given me a chance to come out a bit—to find out what I could do. No, I don't like work. I had rather laze about and think of all the fine things that can be done. I don't like work—no man does—but I like what is in the work—the chance to find yourself. Your own reality—for yourself, not for others—what no other man can ever know. They can only see the mere show, and never can tell what it really means.

"I was not surprised to see somebody sitting aft, on the deck, with his legs dangling over the mud. You see I rather chummed with the few mechanics there were in that station, whom the other pilgrims naturally despised—on account of their imperfect manners, I suppose. This was the foreman—a boiler-maker by trade—a good worker. He was a lank, bony, yellow-faced man, with big intense eyes. His aspect was worried, and his head was as bald as the palm of my hand; but his hair in falling seemed to have stuck to his chin, and had prospered in the new locality, for his beard hung down to his waist. He was a widower with six young children (he had left them in charge of a sister of his to come out there), and the passion of his life was pigeon-flying. He was an enthusiast and a connoisseur. He would rave about pigeons. After work hours he used sometimes to come over from his hut for a talk about his children and his pigeons; at work, when he had to crawl in the mud under the bottom of the steamboat, he would tie up that beard of his in a kind of white serviette[3] he brought for the purpose. It had loops to go over his ears. In the evening he could be seen squatted on the bank rinsing that wrapper in the creek with great care, then spreading it solemnly on a bush to dry.

"I slapped him on the back and shouted 'We shall have rivets!' He scrambled to his feet exclaiming 'No! Rivets!' as though he couldn't believe his ears. Then in a low voice, 'You . . . eh?' I don't know why we behaved like lunatics. I put my finger to the side of my nose and nodded mysteriously. 'Good for you!' he cried, snapped his fingers above his head, lifting one foot. I tried a jig. We capered on the iron deck. A frightful clatter came out of that hulk, and the virgin forest on the other bank of the creek sent it back in a thundering roll upon the sleeping station. It must have made some of the pilgrims sit up in their hovels. A dark figure obscured the lighted doorway of the manager's hut, vanished, then, a second or so after, the doorway itself vanished too. We stopped, and the silence driven away by the stamping of our feet flowed back again from the recesses of the land. The great wall of vegetation, an exuberant and entangled mass of trunks, branches, leaves, boughs, festoons, motionless in the moonlight, was like a rioting invasion of soundless life, a rolling wave of plants, piled up, crested, ready to topple over the creek, to sweep every little man of us out of his

3. **Table-napkin.**

little existence. And it moved not. A deadened burst of mighty splashes and snorts reached us from afar, as though an ichthyosaurus had been taking a bath of glitter in the great river. 'After all,' said the boiler-maker in a reasonable tone, 'why shouldn't we get the rivets?' Why not, indeed! I did not know of any reason why we shouldn't. 'They'll come in three weeks,' I said confidently.

"But they didn't. Instead of rivets there came an invasion, an infliction, a visitation. It came in sections during the next three weeks, each section headed by a donkey carrying a white man in new clothes and tan shoes, bowing from that elevation right and left to the impressed pilgrims. A quarrelsome band of footsore sulky niggers trod on the heels of the donkey; a lot of tents, camp-stools, tin boxes, white cases, brown bales would be shot down in the courtyard, and the air of mystery would deepen a little over the muddle of the station. Five such installments came, with their absurd air of disorderly flight with the loot of innumerable outfit shops and provision stores, that, one would think, they were lugging, after a raid, into the wilderness for equitable division. It was an inextricable mess of things decent in themselves but that human folly made look like the spoils of thieving.

"This devoted band called itself the Eldorado Exploring Expedition, and I believe they were sworn to secrecy. Their talk, however, was the talk of sordid buccaneers: it was reckless without hardihood, greedy without audacity, and cruel without courage; there was not an atom of foresight or of serious intention in the whole batch of them, and they did not seem aware these things are wanted for the work of the world. To tear treasure out of the bowels of the land was their desire, with no more moral purpose at the back of it than there is in burglars breaking into a safe. Who paid the expenses of the noble enterprise I don't know; but the uncle of our manager was leader of that lot.

"In exterior he resembled a butcher in a poor neighborhood, and his eyes had a look of sleepy cunning. He carried his fat paunch with ostentation on his short legs, and during the time his gang infested the station spoke to no one but his nephew. You could see these two roaming about all day long with their heads close together in an everlasting confab.

"I had given up worrying myself about the rivets. One's capacity for that kind of folly is more limited than you would suppose. I said Hang!—and let things slide. I had plenty of time for meditation, and now and then I would give some thought to Kurtz. I wasn't very interested in him. No. Still, I was curious to see whether this man, who had come out equipped with moral ideas of some sort, would climb to the top after all, and how he would set about his work when there."

II

"One evening as I was lying flat on the deck of my steamboat, I heard voices approaching—and there were the nephew and the uncle strolling along the bank. I laid my head on my arm again, and had nearly lost myself in a doze, when somebody said in my ear, as it were: 'I am as harmless as a little child, but I don't like to be dictated to. Am I the manager—or am I not? I was ordered to send him there. It's incredible.' . . . I became aware that the two were standing on the shore alongside the forepart of the steamboat, just below my head. I did not move; it did not occur to me to move: I was sleepy. 'It *is* unpleasant,' grunted the uncle. 'He has asked the Administration to be sent there,' said the other, 'with the idea of showing what he could do; and I was instructed accordingly. Look at the influence that man must have. Is it not frightful?' They both agreed it was frightful, then made several bizarre remarks: 'Make rain and fine weather—one man—the Council—by the nose' —bits of absurd sentences that got the better of my drowsiness, so that I had pretty near the whole of my wits about me when the uncle said, 'The climate may do away with this difficulty for you. Is he alone there?' 'Yes,' answered the manager; 'he sent his assistant down the river with a note to me in these terms: "Clear this poor devil out of the country, and don't bother sending more of that sort. I had rather be alone than have the kind of men you can dispose of with me." It was more than a year ago. Can you imagine such impudence?' 'Anything since then?' asked the other hoarsely. 'Ivory,' jerked the nephew; 'lots of it—prime sort—lots—most annoying, from him.' 'And with that?' questioned the heavy rumble. 'Invoice,' was the reply fired out, so to speak. Then silence. They had been talking about Kurtz.

"I was broad awake by this time, but, lying perfectly at ease, remained still, having no inducement to change my position. 'How did that ivory come all this way?' growled the elder man, who seemed very vexed. The other explained that it had come with a fleet of canoes in charge of an English half-caste clerk Kurtz had with him; that Kurtz had apparently intended to return himself, the station being by that time bare of goods and stores, but after coming three hundred miles, had suddenly decided to go back, which he started to do alone in a small dugout with four paddlers, leaving the half-caste to continue down the river with the ivory. The two fellows there seemed astounded at anybody attempting such a thing. They were at a loss for an adequate motive. As to me,[4] I seemed to see Kurtz for the first time. It was a distinct glimpse: the dugout, four paddling savages, and the lone white man

4. Conrad, who wrote and spoke French perfectly, sometimes slipped into a French usage when writing English. This is one of his Gallicisms, a literal rendering of *quant à moi*.

turning his back suddenly on the headquarters, on relief, on thoughts of home—perhaps; setting his face towards the depths of the wilderness, towards his empty and desolate station. I did not know the motive. Perhaps he was just simply a fine fellow who stuck to his work for its own sake. His name, you understand, had not been pronounced once. He was 'that man.' The half-caste, who, as far as I could see, had conducted a difficult trip with great prudence and pluck, was invariably alluded to as 'that scoundrel.' The 'scoundrel' had reported that the 'man' had been very ill—had recovered imperfectly. . . . The two below me moved away then a few paces, and strolled back and forth at some little distance. I heard: 'Military post—doctor—two hundred miles—quite alone now—unavoidable delays—nine months—no news—strange rumors.' They approached again, just as the manager was saying, 'No one, as far as I know, unless a species of wandering trader—a pestilential fellow, snapping ivory from the natives.' Who was it they were talking about now? I gathered in snatches that this was some man supposed to be in Kurtz's district, and of whom the manager did not approve. 'We will not be free from unfair competition till one of these fellows is hanged for an example,' he said. 'Certainly,' grunted the other; 'get him hanged! Why not? Anything—anything can be done in this country. That's what I say; nobody here, you understand, *here*, can endanger your position. And why? You stand the climate—you outlast them all. The danger is in Europe; but there before I left I took care to—' They moved off and whispered, then their voices rose again. 'The extraordinary series of delays is not my fault. I did my possible.'[5] The fat man sighed, 'Very sad.' 'And the pestiferous absurdity of his talk,' continued the other; 'he bothered me enough when he was here. "Each station should be like a beacon on the road towards better things, a center for trade of course, but also for humanizing, improving, instructing." Conceive you—that ass! And he wants to be manager! No, it's——' Here he got choked by excessive indignation, and I lifted my head the least bit. I was surprised to see how near they were—right under me. I could have spat upon their hats. They were looking on the ground, absorbed in thought. The manager was switching his leg with a slender twig: his sagacious relative lifted his head. 'You have been well since you came out this time?' he asked. The other gave a start. 'Who? I? Oh! Like a charm—like a charm. But the rest—oh, my goodness! All sick. They die so quick, too, that I haven't the time to send them out of the country—it's incredible!' 'H'm. Just so,' grunted the uncle. 'Ah! my boy, trust to this —I say, trust to this.' I saw him extend his short flipper of an arm

---

5. Another of Conrad's Gallicisms, literally translating *J'ai fait mon possible*.

for a gesture that took in the forest, the creek, the mud, the river—seemed to beckon with a dishonoring flourish before the sunlit face of the land a treacherous appeal to the lurking death, to the hidden evil, to the profound darkness of its heart. It was so startling that I leaped to my feet and looked back at the edge of the forest, as though I had expected an answer of some sort to that black display of confidence. You know the foolish notions that come to one sometimes. The high stillness confronted these two figures with its ominous patience, waiting for the passing away of a fantastic invasion.

"They swore aloud together—out of sheer fright, I believe—then, pretending not to know anything of my existence, turned back to the station. The sun was low; and leaning forward side by side, they seemed to be tugging painfully uphill their two ridiculous shadows of unequal length, that trailed behind them slowly over the tall grass without bending a single blade.

"In a few days the Eldorado Expedition went into the patient wilderness, that closed upon it as the sea closes over a diver. Long afterwards the news came that all the donkeys were dead. I know nothing as to the fate of the less valuable animals. They, no doubt, like the rest of us, found what they deserved. I did not inquire. I was then rather excited at the prospect of meeting Kurtz very soon. When I say very soon I mean it comparatively. It was just two months from the day we left the creek when we came to the bank below Kurtz's station.

"Going up that river was like traveling back to the earliest beginnings of the world, when vegetation rioted on the earth and the big trees were kings. An empty stream, a great silence, an impenetrable forest. The air was warm, thick, heavy, sluggish. There was no joy in the brilliance of sunshine. The long stretches of the waterway ran on, deserted, into the gloom of overshadowed distances. On silvery sandbanks hippos and alligators sunned themselves side by side. The broadening waters flowed through a mob of wooded islands; you lost your way on that river as you would in a desert, and butted all day long against shoals, trying to find the channel, till you thought yourself bewitched and cut off for ever from everything you had known once—somewhere—far away—in another existence perhaps. There were moments when one's past came back to one, as it will sometimes when you have not a moment to spare to yourself; but it came in the shape of an unrestful and noisy dream, remembered with wonder amongst the overwhelming realities of this strange world of plants, and water, and silence. And this stillness of life did not in the least resemble a peace. It was the stillness of an implacable force brooding over an inscrutable intention. It looked at you with a vengeful aspect. I got used to it afterwards; I did not see it any more; I had no time. I had to keep guessing at the channel; I had to discern, mostly by inspiration, the signs of hidden banks; I watched for sunken stones; I was learning to clap my teeth smartly before my heart flew out, when I shaved by a fluke some infernal sly old snag that would have ripped the life out of the tin-pot steamboat and drowned all the pilgrims; I had to keep a lookout for the signs of dead wood we could cut up in the night for next day's steaming. When you have to attend to things of that sort, to the mere incidents of the surface, the reality—the reality, I tell you—fades. The inner truth is hidden—luckily, luckily. But I felt it all the same; I felt often its mysterious stillness watching me at my monkey tricks, just as it watches you fellows performing on your respective tightropes for—what is it? half a crown a tumble——"

"Try to be civil, Marlow," growled a voice, and I knew there was at least one listener awake besides myself.

"I beg your pardon, I forgot the heartache which makes up the rest of the price. And indeed what does the price matter, if the trick be well done? You do your tricks very well. And I didn't do badly either, since I managed not to sink that steamboat on my first trip. It's a wonder to me yet. Imagine a blindfolded man set to drive a van over a bad road. I sweated and shivered over that business considerably, I can tell you. After all, for a seaman, to scrape the bottom of the thing that's supposed to float all the time under his care is the unpardonable sin. No one may know of it, but you never forget the thump—eh? A blow on the very heart. You remember it, you dream of it, you wake up at night and think of it—years after—and go hot and cold all over. I don't pretend to say that steamboat floated all the time. More than once she had to wade for a bit, with twenty cannibals splashing around and pushing. We had enlisted some of these chaps on the way for a crew. Fine fellows—cannibals—in their place. They were men one could work with, and I am grateful to them. And, after all, they did not eat each other before my face: they had brought along a provision of hippo-meat which went rotten, and made the mystery of the wilderness stink in my nostrils. Phoo! I can sniff it now. I had the manager on board and three or four pilgrims with their staves—all complete. Sometimes we came upon a station close by the bank, clinging to the skirts of the unknown, and the white men rushing out of a tumble-down hovel, with great gestures of joy and surprise and welcome, seemed very strange—had the appearance of being held there captive by a spell. The word 'ivory' would ring in the air for a while—and on we went again into the silence, along empty reaches, round the still bends, between the high walls of our winding way, reverberating in hollow claps the poderous beat of the stern-wheel. Trees,

trees, millions of trees, massive, immense, running up high; and at their foot, hugging the bank against the stream, crept the little begrimed steamboat, like a sluggish beetle crawling on the floor of a lofty portico. It made you feel very small, very lost, and yet it was not altogether depressing, that feeling. After all, if you were small, the grimy beetle crawled on—which was just what you wanted it to do. Where the pilgrims imagined it crawled to I don't know. To some place where they expected to get something, I bet! For me it crawled towards Kurtz—exclusively; but when the steam-pipes started leaking we crawled very slow. The reaches opened before us and closed behind, as if the forest had stepped leisurely across the water to bar the way for our return. We penetrated deeper and deeper into the heart of darkness. It was very quiet there. At night sometimes the roll of drums behind the curtain of trees would run up the river and remain sustained faintly, as if hovering in the air high over our heads, till the first break of day. Whether it meant war, peace, or prayer we could not tell. The dawns were heralded by the descent of a chill stillness; the woodcutters slept, their fires burned low; the snapping of a twig would make you start. We were wanderers on a prehistoric earth, on an earth that wore the aspect of an unknown planet. We could have fancied ourselves the first of men taking possession of an accursed inheritance, to be subdued at the cost of profound anguish and of excessive toil. But suddenly, as we struggled round a bend, there would be a glimpse of rush walls, of peaked grass-roofs, a burst of yells, a whirl of black limbs, a mass of hands clapping, of feet stamping, of bodies swaying, of eyes roll-ing, under the droop of heavy and motionless foliage. The steamer toiled along slowly on the edge of a black and incomprehensible frenzy. The prehistoric man was cursing us, praying to us, welcom-ing us—who could tell? We were cut off from the comprehension of our surroundings; we glided past like phantoms, wondering and secretly appalled, as sane men would be before an enthusiastic out-break in a madhouse. We could not understand because we were too far and could not remember, because we were traveling in the night of first ages, of those ages that are gone, leaving hardly a sign —and no memories.

"The earth seemed unearthly. We are accustomed to look upon the shackled form of a conquered monster, but there—there you could look at a thing monstrous and free. It was unearthly, and the men were—— No, they were not inhuman. Well, you know, that was the worst of it—this suspicion of their not being inhuman. It would come slowly to one. They howled and leaped, and spun, and made horrid faces; but what thrilled you was just the thought of their humanity—like yours—the thought of your remote kinship with this wild and passionate uproar. Ugly. Yes, it was ugly enough;

but if you were man enough you would admit to yourself that there was in you just the faintest trace of a response to the terrible frankness of that noise, a dim suspicion of there being a meaning in it which you—you so remote from the night of first ages—could comprehend. And why not? The mind of man is capable of anything— because everything is in it, all the past as well as all the future. What was there after all? Joy, fear, sorrow, devotion, valor, rage— who can tell?—but truth—truth stripped of its cloak of time. Let the fool gape and shudder—the man knows, and can look on without a wink. But he must at least be as much of a man as these on the shore. He must meet that truth with his own true stuff—with his own inborn strength. Principles? Principles won't do. Acquisitions, clothes, pretty rags—rags that would fly off at the first good shake. No; you want a deliberate belief. An appeal to me in this fiendish row—is there? Very well; I hear; I admit, but I have a voice too, and for good or evil mine is the speech that cannot be silenced. Of course, a fool, what with sheer fright and fine sentiments, is always safe. Who's that grunting? You wonder I didn't go ashore for a howl and a dance? Well, no—I didn't. Fine sentiments, you say? Fine sentiments be hanged! I had no time. I had to mess about with white-lead and strips of woolen blanket helping to put bandages on those leaky steam-pipes—I tell you. I had to watch the steering, and circumvent those snags, and get the tin-pot along by hook or by crook. There was surface-truth enough in these things to save a wiser man. And between whiles I had to look after the savage who was fireman. He was an improved specimen; he could fire up a vertical boiler. He was there below me, and, upon my word, to look at him was as edifying as seeing a dog in a parody of breeches and a feather hat, walking on his hind legs. A few months of training had done for that really fine chap. He squinted at the steam-gauge and at the water-gauge with an evident effort of intrepidity—and he had filed teeth too, the poor devil, and the wool of his pate shaved into queer patterns, and three ornamental scars on each of his cheeks. He ought to have been clapping his hands and stamping his feet on the bank, instead of which he was hard at work, a thrall to strange witchcraft, full of improving knowledge. He was useful because he had been instructed; and what he knew was this—that should the water in that transparent thing disappear, the evil spirit inside the boiler would get angry through the greatness of his thirst, and take a terrible vengeance. So he sweated and fired up and watched the glass fearfully (with an impromptu charm, made of rags, tied to his arm, and a piece of polished bone, as big as a watch, stuck flatways through his lower lip), while the wooded banks slipped past us slowly, the short noise was left behind, the interminable miles of silence—and we crept on, towards Kurtz. But the snags were thick, the water was treacherous and shallow, the boiler seemed indeed to have a sulky devil in it, and thus neither that fireman nor I had any time to peer into our creepy thoughts.

"Some fifty miles below the Inner Station we came upon a hut of reeds, an inclined and melancholy pole, with the unrecognizable tatters of what had been a flag of some sort flying from it, and a neatly stacked wood-pile. This was unexpected. We came to the bank, and on the stack of firewood found a flat piece of board with some faded pencil-writing on it. When deciphered it said: 'Wood for you. Hurry up. Approach cautiously.' There was a signature, but it was illegible—not Kurtz—a much longer word. 'Hurry up.' Where? Up the river? 'Approach cautiously.' We had not done so. But the warning could not have been meant for the place where it could be only found after approach. Something was wrong above. But what —and how much? That was the question. We commented adversely upon the imbecility of that telegraphic style. The bush around said nothing, and would not let us look very far, either. A torn curtain of red twill hung in the doorway of the hut, and flapped sadly in our faces. The dwelling was dismantled; but we could see a white man had lived there not very long ago. There remained a rude table—a plank on two posts; a heap of rubbish reposed in a dark corner, and by the door I picked up a book. It had lost its covers, and the pages had been thumbed into a state of extremely dirty softness; but the back had been lovingly stitched afresh with white cotton thread, which looked clean yet. It was an extraordinary find. Its title was, *An Inquiry into Some Points of Seamanship*, by a man Towser, Towson—some such name—Master in His Majesty's Navy. The matter looked dreary reading enough, with illustrative diagrams and repulsive tables of figures, and the copy was sixty years old. I handled this amazing antiquity with the greatest possible tenderness, lest it should dissolve in my hands. Within, Towson or Towser was inquiring earnestly into the breaking strain of ships' chains and tackle, and other such matters. Not a very enthralling book; but at the first glance you could see there a singleness of intention, an honest concern for the right way of going to work, which made these humble pages, thought out so many years ago, luminous with another than a professional light. The simple old sailor, with his talk of chains and purchases, made me forget the jungle and the pilgrims in a delicious sensation of having come upon something unmistakably real. Such a book being there was wonderful enough; but still more astounding were the notes penciled in the margin, and plainly referring to the text. I couldn't believe my eyes! They were in cipher! Yes, it looked like cipher. Fancy a man lugging with him a book of that description into this nowhere and studying it—and making notes—in cipher at that! It was an extravagant mystery.

"I had been dimly aware for some time of a worrying noise, and when I lifted my eyes I saw the wood-pile was gone, and the manager, aided by all the pilgrims, was shouting at me from the riverside. I slipped the book into my pocket. I assure you to leave off reading was like tearing myself away from the shelter of an old and solid friendship.

"I started the lame engine ahead. 'It must be this miserable trader—this intruder,' exclaimed the manager, looking back malevolently at the place we had left. 'He must be English,' I said. 'It will not save him from getting into trouble if he is not careful,' muttered the manager darkly. I observed with assumed innocence that no man was safe from trouble in this world.

"The current was more rapid now, the steamer seemed at her last gasp, the stern-wheel flopped languidly, and I caught myself listening on tiptoe for the next beat of the float,[6] for in sober truth I expected the wretched thing to give up every moment. It was like watching the last flickers of a life. But still we crawled. Sometimes I would pick out a tree a little way ahead to measure our progress towards Kurtz by, but I lost it invariably before we got abreast. To keep the eyes so long on one thing was too much for human patience. The manager displayed a beautiful resignation. I fretted and fumed and took to arguing with myself whether or no I would talk openly with Kurtz; but before I could come to any conclusion it occurred to me that my speech or my silence, indeed any action of mine, would be a mere futility. What did it matter what any one knew or ignored? What did it matter who was manager? One gets sometimes such a flash of insight. The essentials of this affair lay deep under the surface, beyond my reach, and beyond my power of meddling.

"Towards the evening of the second day we judged ourselves about eight miles from Kurtz's station. I wanted to push on; but the manager looked grave, and told me the navigation up there was so dangerous that it would be advisable, the sun being very low already, to wait where we were till next morning. Moreover, he pointed out that if the warning to approach cautiously were to be followed, we must approach in daylight—not at dusk, or in the dark. This was sensible enough. Eight miles meant nearly three hours' steaming for us, and I could also see suspicious ripples at the upper end of the reach. Nevertheless, I was annoyed beyond expression at the delay, and most unreasonably too, since one night more could not matter much after so many months. As we had plenty of wood, and caution was the word, I brought up in the middle of the stream. The reach was narrow, straight, with high sides like a railway cutting. The dusk came gliding into it long before the sun had

---

6. Automatic water-level regulator opening and closing a water-supply valve.

set. The current ran smooth and swift, but a dumb immobility sat on the banks. The living trees, lashed together by the creepers and every living bush of the undergrowth, might have been changed into stone, even to the slenderest twig, to the lightest leaf. It was not sleep—it seemed unnatural, like a state of trance. Not the faintest sound of any kind could be heard. You looked on amazed, and began to suspect yourself of being deaf—then the night came suddenly, and struck you blind as well. About three in the morning some large fish leaped, and the loud splash made me jump as though a gun had been fired. When the sun rose there was a white fog, very warm and clammy, and more blinding than the night. It did not shift or drive; it was just there, standing all round you like something solid. At eight or nine, perhaps, it lifted as a shutter lifts. We had a glimpse of the towering multitude of trees, of the immense matted jungle, with the blazing little ball of the sun hanging over it—all perfectly still—and then the white shutter came down again, smoothly, as if sliding in greased grooves. I ordered the chain, which we had begun to heave in, to be paid out again. Before it stopped running with a muffled rattle, a cry, a very loud cry, as of infinite desolation, soared slowly in the opaque air. It ceased. A complaining clamor, modulated in savage discords, filled our ears. The sheer unexpectedness of it made my hair stir under my cap. I don't know how it struck the others: to me it seemed as though the mist itself had screamed, so suddenly, and apparently from all sides at once, did this tumultuous and mournful uproar arise. It culminated in a hurried outbreak of almost intolerably excessive shrieking, which stopped short, leaving us stiffened in a variety of silly attitudes, and obstinately listening to the nearly as appalling and excessive silence. 'Good God! What is the meaning——?' stammered at my elbow one of the pilgrims—a little fat man, with sandy hair and red whiskers, who wore side-spring boots, and pink pyjamas tucked into his socks. Two others remained open-mouthed a whole minute, then dashed into the little cabin, to rush out incontinently and stand darting scared glances, with Winchesters at 'ready' in their hands. What we could see was just the steamer we were on, her outlines blurred as though she had been on the point of dissolving, and a misty strip of water, perhaps two feet broad, around her—and that was all. The rest of the world was nowhere, as far as our eyes and ears were concerned. Just nowhere. Gone, disappeared; swept off without leaving a whisper or a shadow behind.

"I went forward, and ordered the chain to be hauled in short, so as to be ready to trip the anchor and move the steamboat at once if necessary. 'Will they attack?' whispered an awed voice. 'We will be all butchered in this fog,' murmured another. The faces twitched with the strain, the hands trembled slightly, the eyes forgot to wink. It was very curious to see the contrast of expressions of the white men and of the black fellows of our crew, who were as much strangers to that part of the river as we, though their homes were only eight hundred miles away. The whites, of course greatly discomposed, had besides a curious look of being painfully shocked by such an outrageous row. The others had an alert, naturally interested expression; but their faces were essentially quiet, even those of the one or two who grinned as they hauled at the chain. Several exchanged short, grunting phrases, which seemed to settle the matter to their satisfaction. Their head-man, a young, broad-chested black, severely draped in dark-blue fringed cloths, with fierce nostrils and his hair all done up artfully in oily ringlets, stood near me. 'Aha!' I said, just for good fellowship's sake. 'Catch 'im,' he snapped, with a bloodshot widening of his eyes and a flash of sharp teeth—'catch 'im. Give 'im to us.' 'To you, eh?' I asked; 'what would you do with them?' 'Eat 'im!' he said curtly, and, leaning his elbow on the rail, looked out into the fog in a dignified and profoundly pensive attitude. I would no doubt have been properly horrified, had it not occurred to me that he and his chaps must be very hungry: that they must have been growing increasingly hungry for at least this month past. They had been engaged for six months (I don't think a single one of them had any clear idea of time, as we at the end of countless ages have. They still belonged to the beginnings of time—had no inherited experience to teach them, as it were), and of course, as long as there was a piece of paper written over in accordance with some farcical law or other made down the river, it didn't enter anybody's head to trouble how they would live. Certainly they had brought with them some rotten hippo-meat, which couldn't have lasted very long, anyway, even if the pilgrims hadn't, in the midst of a shocking hullabaloo, thrown a considerable quantity of it overboard. It looked like a high-handed proceeding; but it was really a case of legitimate self-defense. You can't breathe dead hippo waking, sleeping, and eating, and at the same time keep your precarious grip on existence. Besides that, they had given them every week three pieces of brass wire, each about nine inches long; and the theory was they were to buy their provisions with that currency in riverside villages. You can see how *that* worked. There were either no villages, or the people were hostile, or the director, who like the rest of us fed out of tins, with an occasional old he-goat thrown in, didn't want to stop the steamer for some more or less recondite reason. So, unless they swallowed the wire itself, or made loops of it to snare the fishes with, I don't see what good their extravagant salary could be to them. I must say it was paid with a regularity worthy of a large and honorable trading company. For the rest, the only thing to eat—though it didn't look eatable in the least—I saw in their possession was a few lumps of some stuff like half-cooked dough, of a dirty lavender color, they kept wrapped in leaves, and now and then swallowed a piece of, but so small that it seemed done more for the looks of the thing than for any serious purpose of sustenance. Why in the name of all the gnawing devils of hunger they didn't go for us—they were thirty to five—and have a good tuck-in for once, amazes me now when I think of it. They were big powerful men, with not much capacity to weigh the consequences, with courage, with strength, even yet, though their skins were no longer glossy and their muscles no longer hard. And I saw that something restraining, one of those human secrets that baffle probability, had come into play there. I looked at them with a swift quickening of interest—not because it occurred to me I might be eaten by them before very long, though I own to you that just then I perceived—in a new light, as it were—how unwholesome the pilgrims looked, and I hoped, yes, I positively hoped, that my aspect was not so—what shall I say?—so—unappetizing: a touch of fantastic vanity which fitted well with the dream-sensation that pervaded all my days at that time. Perhaps I had a little fever too. One can't live with one's finger everlastingly on one's pulse. I had often 'a little fever,' or a little touch of other things—the playful paw-strokes of the wilderness, the preliminary trifling before the more serious onslaught which came in due course. Yes; I looked at them as you would on any human being, with a curiosity of their impulses, motives, capacities, weaknesses, when brought to the test of an inexorable physical necessity. Restraint! What possible restraint? Was it superstition, disgust, patience, fear—or some kind of primitive honor? No fear can stand up to hunger, no patience can wear it out, disgust simply does not exist where hunger is; and as to superstition, beliefs, and what you may call principles, they are less than chaff in a breeze. Don't you know the devilry of lingering starvation, its exasperating torment, its black thoughts, its somber and brooding ferocity? Well, I do. It takes a man all his inborn strength to fight hunger properly. It's really easier to face bereavement, dishonor, and the perdition of one's soul—than this kind of prolonged hunger. Sad, but true. And these chaps too had no earthly reason for any kind of scruple. Restraint! I would just as soon have expected restraint from a hyena prowling amongst the corpses of a battlefield. But there was the fact facing me—the fact dazzling, to be seen, like the foam on the depths of the sea, like a ripple on an unfathomable enigma, a mystery greater—when I thought of it—than the curious, inexplicable note of desperate grief in this savage clamor that had swept by us on the riverbank, behind the blind whiteness of the fog.

"Two pilgrims were quarreling in hurried whispers as to which bank. 'Left.' 'No, no; how can you? Right, right, of course.' 'It is very serious,' said the manager's voice behind me; 'I would be desolated if anything should happen to Mr. Kurtz before we came up.' I looked at him, and had not the slightest doubt he was sincere. He was just the kind of man who would wish to preserve appearances. That was his restraint. But when he muttered something about going on at once, I did not even take the trouble to answer him. I knew, and he knew, that it was impossible. Were we to let go our hold of the bottom, we would be absolutely in the air—in space. We wouldn't be able to tell where we were going to—whether up or down stream, or across—till we fetched against one bank or the other—and then we wouldn't know at first which it was. Of course I made no move. I had no mind for a smash-up. You couldn't imagine a more deadly place for a shipwreck. Whether drowned at once or not, we were sure to perish speedily in one way or another. 'I authorize you to take all the risks,' he said, after a short silence. 'I refuse to take any,' I said shortly; which was just the answer he expected, though its tone might have surprised him. 'Well, I must defer to your judgment. You are captain,' he said, with marked civility. I turned my shoulder to him in sign of my appreciation, and looked into the fog. How long would it last? It was the most hopeless lookout. The approach to this Kurtz grubbing for ivory in the wretched bush was beset by as many dangers as though he had been an enchanted princess sleeping in a fabulous castle. 'Will they attack, do you think?' asked the manager, in a confidential tone.

"I did not think they would attack, for several obvious reasons. The thick fog was one. If they left the bank in their canoes they would get lost in it, as we would be if we attempted to move. Still, I had also judged the jungle of both banks quite impenetrable—and yet eyes were in it, eyes that had seen us. The riverside bushes were certainly very thick; but the undergrowth behind was evidently penetrable. However, during the short lift I had seen no canoes anywhere in the reach—certainly not abreast of the steamer. But what made the idea of attack inconceivable to me was the nature of the noise—of the cries we had heard. They had not the fierce character boding of immediate hostile intention. Unexpected, wild, and violent as they had been, they had given me an irresistible impression of sorrow. The glimpse of the steamboat had for some reason filled those savages with unrestrained grief. The danger, if any, I expounded, was from our proximity to a great human passion let loose. Even extreme grief may ultimately vent itself in violence—but more generally takes the form of apathy. . . .

"You should have seen the pilgrims stare! They had no heart to grin, or even to revile me; but I believe they thought me gone mad—with fright, maybe. I delivered a regular lecture. My dear boys, it was no good bothering. Keep a look-out? Well, you may guess I watched the fog for the signs of lifting as a cat watches a mouse; but for anything else our eyes were of no more use to us than if we had been buried miles deep in a heap of cotton-wool. It felt like it too—choking, warm, stifling. Besides, all I said, though it sounded extravagant, was absolutely true to fact. What we afterwards alluded to as an attack was really an attempt at repulse. The action was very far from being aggressive—it was not even defensive, in the usual sense: it was undertaken under the stress of desperation, and in its essence was purely protective.

"It developed itself, I should say, two hours after the fog lifted, and its commencement was at a spot, roughly speaking, about a mile and half below Kurtz's station. We had just floundered and flopped round a bend, when I saw an islet, a mere grassy hummock of bright green, in the middle of the stream. It was the only thing of the kind; but as we opened the reach more, I perceived it was the head of a long sandbank, or rather of a chain of shallow patches stretching down the middle of the river. They were discolored, just awash, and the whole lot was seen just under the water, exactly as a man's backbone is seen running down the middle of his back under the skin. Now, as far as I did see, I could go to the right or to the left of this. I didn't know either channel, of course. The banks looked pretty well alike, the depth appeared the same; but as I had been informed the station was on the west side, I naturally headed for the western passage.

"No sooner had we fairly entered it than I became aware it was much narrower than I had supposed. To the left of us there was the long uninterrupted shoal, and to the right a high steep bank heavily overgrown with bushes. Above the bush the trees stood in serried ranks. The twigs overhung the current thickly, and from distance to distance a large limb of some tree projected rigidly over the stream. It was then well on in the afternoon, the face of the forest was gloomy, and a broad strip of shadow had already fallen on the water. In this shadow we steamed up—very slowly, as you may imagine. I sheered her well inshore—the water being deepest near the bank, as the sounding-pole informed me.

"One of my hungry and forbearing friends was sounding in the bows just below me. This steamboat was exactly like a decked scow. On the deck there were two little teak-wood houses, with doors and windows. The boiler was in the fore-end, and the machinery right astern. Over the whole there was a light roof, supported on stanchions. The funnel projected through that roof, and in front of the funnel a small cabin built of light planks served for a pilot-house. It contained a couch, two camp-stools, a loaded Martini-Henry[7] leaning in one corner, a tiny table, and the steering-wheel. It had a wide

7. Rifle combining the seven-grooved barrel of the Scottish gun-maker A. Henry with the block-action breech mechanism introduced by the Swiss inventor F. Martini.

door in front and a broad shutter at each side. All these were always thrown open, of course. I spent my days perched up there on the extreme fore-end of that roof, before the door. At night I slept, or tried to, on the couch. An athletic black belonging to some coast tribe, and educated by my poor predecessor, was the helmsman. He sported a pair of brass earrings, wore a blue cloth wrapper from the waist to the ankles, and thought all the world of himself. He was the most unstable kind of fool I had ever seen. He steered with no end of a swagger while you were by; but if he lost sight of you, he became instantly the prey of an abject funk, and would let that cripple of a steamboat get the upper hand of him in a minute.

"I was looking down at the sounding-pole, and feeling much annoyed to see at each try a little more of it stick out of that river, when I saw my poleman give up the business suddenly, and stretch himself flat on the deck, without even taking the trouble to haul his pole in. He kept hold of it though, and it trailed in the water. At the same time the fireman, whom I could also see below me, sat down abruptly before his furnace and ducked his head. I was amazed. Then I had to look at the river mighty quick, because there was a snag in the fairway. Sticks, little sticks, were flying about—thick: they were whizzing before my nose, dropping below me, striking behind me against my pilot-house. All this time the river, the shore, the woods, were very quiet—perfectly quiet. I could only hear the heavy splashing thump of the stern-wheel and the patter of these things. We cleared the snag clumsily. Arrows, by Jove! We were being shot at! I stepped in quickly to close the shutter on the land-side. That fool-helmsman, his hands on the spokes, was lifting his knees high, stamping his feet, champing his mouth, like a reined-in horse. Confound him! And we were staggering within ten feet of the bank. I had to lean right out to swing the heavy shutter, and I saw a face amongst the leaves on the level with my own, looking at me very fierce and steady; and then suddenly, as though a veil had been removed from my eyes, I made out, deep in the tangled gloom, naked breasts, arms, legs, glaring eyes—the bush was swarming with human limbs in movement, glistening, of bronze color. The twigs shook, swayed, and rustled, the arrows flew out of them, and then the shutter came to. 'Steer her straight,' I said to the helmsman. He held his head rigid, face forward; but his eyes rolled, he kept on lifting and setting down his feet gently, his mouth foamed a little. 'Keep quiet!' I said in a fury. I might just as well have ordered a tree not to sway in the wind. I darted out. Below me there was a great scuffle of feet on the iron deck; confused exclamations; a voice screamed, 'Can you turn back?' I caught sight of a V-shaped ripple on the water ahead. What? Another snag? A fusillade burst out under my feet. The pilgrims had opened with their Winchesters, and were simply squirting lead into that

bush. A deuce of a lot of smoke came up and drove slowly forward.
I swore at it. Now I couldn't see the ripple or the snag either. I
stood in the doorway, peering, and the arrows came in swarms.
They might have been poisoned, but they looked as though they
wouldn't kill a cat. The bush began to howl. Our wood-cutters
raised a war-like whoop; the report of a rifle just at my back deafened me. I glanced over my shoulder, and the pilot-house was yet
full of noise and smoke when I made a dash at the wheel. The
fool-nigger had dropped everything, to throw the shutter open and
let off that Martini-Henry. He stood before the wide opening, glaring, and I yelled at him to come back, while I straightened the
sudden twist out of that steamboat. There was no room to turn
even if I had wanted to, the snag was somewhere very near ahead in
that confounded smoke, there was no time to lose, so I just crowded
her into the bank—right into the bank, where I knew the water was
deep.

"We tore slowly along the overhanging bushes in a whirl of
broken twigs and flying leaves. The fusillade below stopped short, as
I had foreseen it would when the squirts got empty. I threw my
head back to a glinting whiz that traversed the pilot-house, in at
one shutter-hole and out at the other. Looking past that mad
helmsman, who was shaking the empty rifle and yelling at the
shore, I saw vague forms of men running bent double, leaping, gliding, distinct, incomplete, evanescent. Something big appeared in
the air before the shutter, the rifle went overboard, and the man
stepped back swiftly, looked at me over his shoulder in an extraordinary, profound, familiar manner, and fell upon my feet. The side of
his head hit the wheel twice, and the end of what appeared a long
cane clattered round and knocked over a little camp-stool. It looked
as though after wrenching that thing from somebody ashore he had
lost his balance in the effort. The thin smoke had blown away, we
were clear of the snag, and looking ahead I could see that in
another hundred yards or so I would be free to sheer off, away from
the bank; but my feet felt so very warm and wet that I had to look
down. The man had rolled on his back and stared straight up at
me; both his hands clutched that cane. It was the shaft of a spear
that, either thrown or lunged through the opening, had caught him
in the side just below the ribs; the blade had gone in out of sight,
after making a frightful gash; my shoes were full; a pool of blood
lay very still, gleaming dark-red under the wheel; his eyes shone
with an amazing luster. The fusillade burst out again. He looked at
me anxiously, gripping the spear like something precious, with an
air of being afraid I would try to take it away from him. I had to
make an effort to free my eyes from his gaze and attend to the
steering. With one hand I felt above my head for the line of the
steam whistle, and jerked out screech after screech hurriedly. The

tumult of angry and war-like yells was checked instantly, and then
from the depths of the woods went out such a tremulous and prolonged wail of mournful fear and utter despair as may be imagined
to follow the flight of the last hope from the earth. There was a
great commotion in the bush; the shower of arrows stopped, a few
dropping shots rang out sharply—then silence, in which the languid
beat of the stern-wheel came plainly to my ears. I put the helm hard
a-starboard at the moment when the pilgrim in pink pyjamas, very
hot and agitated, appeared in the doorway. 'The manager sends me
—' he began in an official tone, and stopped short. 'Good God!' he
said, glaring at the wounded man.

"We two whites stood over him, and his lustrous and inquiring
glance enveloped us both. I declare it looked as though he would
presently put to us some question in an understandable language;
but he died without uttering a sound, without moving a limb, without twitching a muscle. Only in the very last moment, as though in
response to some sign we could not see, to some whisper we could
not hear, he frowned heavily, and that frown gave to his black
death-mask an inconceivably somber, brooding, and menacing
expression. The luster of inquiring glance faded swiftly into vacant
glassiness. 'Can you steer?' I asked the agent eagerly. He looked
very dubious; but I made a grab at his arm, and he understood at
once I meant him to steer whether or no. To tell you the truth, I
was morbidly anxious to change my shoes and socks. 'He is dead,'
murmured the fellow, immensely impressed. 'No doubt about it,'
said I, tugging like mad at the shoelaces. 'And by the way, I suppose Mr. Kurtz is dead as well by this time.'

"For the moment that was the dominant thought. There was a
sense of extreme disappointment, as though I had found out I had
been striving after something altogether without a substance. I
couldn't have been more disgusted if I had traveled all this way for
the sole purpose of talking with Mr. Kurtz. Talking with . . . I flung
one shoe overboard, and became aware that that was exactly what I
had been looking forward to—a talk with Kurtz. I made the strange
discovery that I had never imagined him as doing, you know, but as
discoursing. I didn't say to myself, 'Now I will never see him,' or
'Now I will never shake him by the hand,' but, 'Now I will never
hear him.' The man presented himself as a voice. Not of course that
I did not connect him with some sort of action. Hadn't I been told
in all the tones of jealousy and admiration that he had collected,
bartered, swindled, or stolen more ivory than all the other agents
together? That was not the point. The point was in his being a
gifted creature, and that of all his gifts the one that stood out pre-
eminently, that carried with it a sense of real presence, was his ability to talk, his words—the gift of expression, the bewildering, the

illuminating, the most exalted and the most contemptible, the pulsating stream of light, or the deceitful flow from the heart of an impenetrable darkness.

"The other shoe went flying unto the devil-god of that river. I thought, By Jove! it's all over. We are too late; he has vanished—the gift has vanished, by means of some spear, arrow, or club. I will never hear that chap speak after all—and my sorrow had a startling extravagance of emotion, even such as I had noticed in the howling sorrow of these savages in the bush. I couldn't have felt more of lonely desolation somehow, had I been robbed of a belief or had missed my destiny in life. . . . Why do you sigh in this beastly way, somebody? Absurd? Well, absurd. Good Lord! mustn't a man ever ——Here, give me some tobacco." . . .

There was a pause of profound stillness, then a match flared, and Marlow's lean face appeared, worn, hollow, with downward folds and dropped eyelids, with an aspect of concentrated attention; and as he took vigorous draws at his pipe, it seemed to retreat and advance out of the night in the regular flicker of the tiny flame. The match went out.

"Absurd!" he cried. "This is the worst of trying to tell . . . Here you all are, each moored with two good addresses, like a hulk with two anchors, a butcher round one corner, a policeman round another, excellent appetites, and temperature normal—you hear—normal from year's end to year's end. And you say, Absurd! Absurd be—exploded! Absurd! My dear boys, what can you expect from a man who out of sheer nervousness had just flung overboard a pair of new shoes? Now I think of it, it is amazing I did not shed tears. I am, upon the whole, proud of my fortitude. I was cut to the quick at the idea of having lost the inestimable privilege of listening to the gifted Kurtz. Of course I was wrong. The privilege was waiting for me. Oh yes, I heard more than enough. And I was right, too. A voice. He was very little more than a voice. And I heard—him—it —this voice—other voices—all of them were so little more than voices—and the memory of that time itself lingers around me, impalpable, like a dying vibration of one immense jabber, silly, atrocious, sordid, savage, or simply mean, without any kind of sense. Voices, voices—even the girl herself—now—"

He was silent for a long time.

"I laid the ghost of his gifts at last with a lie," he began suddenly. "Girl! What? Did I mention a girl? Oh, she is out of it—completely. They—the women I mean—are out of it—should be out of it. We must help them to stay in that beautiful world of their own, lest ours gets worse. Oh, she had to be out of it. You should have heard the disinterred body of Mr. Kurtz saying, 'My Intended.' You would have perceived directly then how completely she was out of it. And the lofty frontal bone of Mr. Kurtz! They say the hair goes on growing sometimes, but this—ah—specimen was impressively bald. The wilderness had patted him on the head, and, behold, it was like a ball—an ivory ball; it had caressed him, and—lo!—he had withered; it had taken him, loved him, embraced him, got into his veins, consumed his flesh, and sealed his soul to its own by the inconceivable ceremonies of some devilish initiation. He was its spoiled and pampered favorite. Ivory? I should think so. Heaps of it, stacks of it. The old mud shanty was bursting with it. You would think there was not a single tusk left either above or below the ground in the whole country. 'Mostly fossil,' the manager had remarked disparagingly. It was no more fossil than I am; but they call it fossil when it is dug up. It appears these niggers do bury the tusks sometimes—but evidently they couldn't bury this parcel deep enough to save the gifted Mr. Kurtz from his fate. We filled the steamboat with it, and had to pile a lot on the deck. Thus he could see and enjoy as long as he could see, because the appreciation of this favor had remained with him to the last. You should have heard him say, 'My ivory.' Oh yes, I heard him. 'My Intended, my ivory, my station, my river, my—' everything belonged to him. It made me hold my breath in expectation of hearing the wilderness burst into a prodigious peal of laughter that would shake the fixed stars in their places. Everything belonged to him—but that was a trifle. The thing was to know what he belonged to, how many powers of darkness claimed him for their own. That was the reflection that made you creepy all over. It was impossible—it was not good for one either—trying to imagine. He had taken a high seat amongst the devils of the land—I mean literally. You can't understand. How could you?—with solid pavement under your feet, surrounded by kind neighbors ready to cheer you or to fall on you, stepping delicately between the butcher and the policeman, in the holy terror of scandal and gallows and lunatic asylums—how can you imagine what particular region of the first ages a man's untrammeled feet may take him into by the way of solitude—utter solitude without a policeman—by the way of silence—utter silence, where no warning voice of a kind neighbor can be heard whispering of public opinion? These little things make all the great difference. When they are gone you must fall back upon your own innate strength, upon your own capacity for faithfulness. Of course you may be too much of a fool to go wrong—too dull even to know you are being assaulted by the powers of darkness. I take it, no fool ever made a bargain for his soul with the devil: the fool is too much of a fool, or the devil too much of a devil—I don't know which. Or you may be such a thunderingly exalted creature as to be altogether deaf and blind to anything but heavenly sights and sounds. Then the earth for you is only a standing place—and whether to be like this is your loss or your gain I won't pretend to say. But most of us are neither one nor the other. The earth for us is a place to live in, where we must put up with sights, with sounds, with smells, too, by Jove!—breathe dead hippo, so to speak, and not be contaminated. And there, don't you see? your strength comes in, the faith in your ability for the digging of unostentatious holes to bury the stuff in—your power of devotion, not to yourself, but to an obscure, back-breaking business. And that's difficult enough. Mind, I am not trying to excuse or even explain—I am trying to account to myself for—for—Mr. Kurtz—for the shade of Mr. Kurtz. This initiated wraith from the back of Nowhere honored me with its amazing confidence before it vanished altogether. This was because it could speak English to me. The original Kurtz had been educated partly in England, and—as he was good enough to say himself—his sympathies were in the right place. His mother was half-English, his father was half-French. All Europe contributed to the making of Kurtz; and by and by I learned that, most appropriately, the International Society for the Suppression of Savage Customs had entrusted him with the making of a report, for its future guidance. And he had written it too. I've seen it. I've read it. It was eloquent, vibrating with eloquence, but too high-strung, I think. Seventeen pages of close writing he had found time for! But this must have been before his—let us say—nerves went wrong, and caused him to preside at certain midnight dances ending with unspeakable rites, which—as far as I reluctantly gathered from what I heard at various times—were offered up to him—do you understand?—to Mr. Kurtz himself. But it was a beautiful piece of writing. The opening paragraph, however, in the light of later information, strikes me now as ominous. He began with the argument, that we whites, from the point of development we had arrived at, 'must necessarily appear to them [savages] in the nature of supernatural beings—we approach them with the might as of a diety,' and so on, and so on. 'By the simple exercise of our will we can exert a power for good practically unbounded,' etc. etc. From that point he soared and took me with him. The peroration was magnificent, though difficult to remember, you know. It gave me the notion of an exotic Immensity ruled by an august Benevolence. It made me tingle with enthusiasm. This was the unbounded power of eloquence—of words—of burning noble words. There were no practical hints to interrupt the magic current of phrases, unless a kind of note at the foot of the last page, scrawled evidently much later, in an unsteady hand, may be regarded as the exposition of a method. It was very simple, and at the end of that moving appeal to every altruistic sentiment it blazed at you, luminous and terrifying, like a flash of lightning in a serene sky: 'Exterminate all the brutes!' The curious part was that he had apparently forgotten all about that valuable postscriptum, because, later on, when he in a sense came to himself, he repeatedly entreated me to take good care of 'my pamphlet' (he called it), as it was sure to have in the future a good influence upon his career. I had full information about all these things, and, besides, as it turned out, I was to have the care of his memory. I've done enough for it to give me the indisputable right to lay it, if I choose, for an everlasting rest in the dust-bin of progress, amongst all the sweepings and, figuratively speaking, all the dead cats of civilization. But then, you see, I can't choose. He won't be forgotten. Whatever he was, he was not common. He had the power to charm or frighten rudimentary souls into an aggravated witch-dance in his honor; he could also fill the small souls of the pilgrims with bitter misgivings: he had one devoted friend at least, and he had conquered one soul in the world that was neither rudimentary nor tainted with self-seeking. No; I can't forget him, though I am not prepared to affirm the fellow was exactly worth the life we lost in getting to him. I missed my late helmsman awfully—I missed him even while his body was still lying in the pilot-house. Perhaps you will think it passing strange this regret for a savage who was no more account than a grain of sand in a black Sahara. Well, don't you see, he had done something, he had steered; for months I had him at my back —a help—an instrument. It was a kind of partnership. He steered for me—I had to look after him, I worried about his deficiencies, and thus a subtle bond had been created, of which I only became aware when it was suddenly broken. And the intimate profundity of that look he gave me when he received his hurt remains to this day in my memory—like a claim of distant kinship affirmed in a supreme moment.

"Poor fool! If he had only left that shutter alone. He had no restraint, no restraint—just like Kurtz—a tree swayed by the wind. As soon as I had put on a dry pair of slippers, I dragged him out, after first jerking the spear out of his side, which operation I confess I performed with my eyes shut tight. His heels leaped together over the little door-step; his shoulders were pressed to my breast; I hugged him from behind desperately. Oh! he was heavy, heavy; heavier than any man on earth, I should imagine. Then without more ado I tipped him overboard. The current snatched him as though he had been a wisp of grass, and I saw the body roll over twice before I lost sight of it forever. All the pilgrims and the manager were then congregated on the awning-deck about the pilot-house, chattering at each other like a flock of excited magpies, and there was a scandalized murmur at my heartless promptitude. What they wanted to keep that body hanging about for I can't guess.

Embalm it, maybe. But I had also heard another, and a very ominous, murmur on the deck below. My friends the wood-cutters were likewise scandalized, and with a better show of reason—though I admit that the reason itself was quite inadmissible. Oh, quite! I had made up my mind that if my late helmsman was to be eaten, the fishes alone should have him. He had been a very second-rate helmsman while alive, but now he was dead he might have become a first-class temptation, and possibly cause some startling trouble. Besides, I was anxious to take the wheel, the man in pink pyjamas showing himself a hopeless duffer at the business.

"This I did directly the simple funeral was over. We were going half-speed, keeping right in the middle of the stream, and I listened to the talk about me. They had given up Kurtz, they had given up the station; Kurtz was dead, and the station had been burnt—and so on, and so on. The red-haired pilgrim was beside himself with the thought that at least this poor Kurtz had been properly revenged. 'Say! We must have made a glorious slaughter of them in the bush. Eh? What do you think? Say?' He positively danced, the bloodthirsty little gingery beggar.[8] And he had nearly fainted when he saw the wounded man! I could not help saying, 'You made a glorious lot of smoke, anyhow.' I had seen, from the way the tops of the bushes rustled and flew, that almost all the shots had gone too high. You can't hit anything unless you take aim and fire from the shoulder; but these chaps fired from the hip with their eyes shut. The retreat, I maintained—and I was right—was caused by the screeching of the steam-whistle. Upon this they forgot Kurtz, and began to howl at me with indignant protests.

"The manager stood by the wheel murmuring confidentially about the necessity of getting well away down the river before dark at all events, when I saw in the distance a clearing on the river-side and the outlines of some sort of building. 'What's this?' I asked. He clapped his hands in wonder. 'The station!' he cried. I edged in at once, still going half-speed.

"Through my glasses I saw the slope of a hill interspersed with rare trees and perfectly free from undergrowth. A long decaying building on the summit was half buried in the high grass; the large holes in the peaked roof gaped black from afar; the jungle and the woods made a background. There was no enclosure or fence of any kind; but there had been one apparently, for near the house half a dozen slim posts remained in a row, roughly trimmed, and with their upper ends ornamented with round carved balls. The rails, or whatever there had been between, had disappeared. Of course the forest surrounded all that. The river-bank was clear, and on the

8. "Red-headed rascal."

water side I saw a white man under a hat like a cart-wheel beckoning persistently with his whole arm. Examining the edge of the forest above and below, I was almost certain I could see movements —human forms gliding here and there. I steamed past prudently, then stopped the engines and let her drift down. The man on the shore began to shout, urging us to land. 'We have been attacked,' screamed the manager. 'I know—I know. It's all right,' yelled back the other, as cheerful as you please. 'Come along. It's all right. I am glad.'

"His aspect reminded me of something I had seen—something funny I had seen somewhere. As I maneuvered to get alongside, I was asking myself, 'What does this fellow look like?' Suddenly I got it. He looked like a harlequin. His clothes had been made of some stuff that was brown holland probably, but it was covered with patches all over, with bright patches, blue, red, and yellow—patches on the back, patches on the front, patches on elbows, on knees; colored binding round his jacket, scarlet edging at the bottom of his trousers; and the sunshine made him look extremely gay and wonderfully neat withal, because you could see how beautifully all this patching had been done. A beardless, boyish face, very fair, no features to speak of, nose peeling, little blue eyes, smiles and frowns chasing each other over the open countenance like sunshine and shadow on a wind-swept plain. 'Look out, captain!' he cried; 'there's a snag lodged in here last night.' What! Another snag? I confess I swore shamefully. I had nearly holed my cripple, to finish off that charming trip. The harlequin on the bank turned his little pug-nose up to me. 'You English?' he asked, all smiles. 'Are you?' I shouted from the wheel. The smiles vanished, and he shook his head as if sorry for my disappointment. Then he brightened up. 'Never mind!' he cried encouragingly. 'Are we in time?' I asked. 'He is up there,' he replied, with a toss of the head up the hill, and becoming gloomy all of a sudden. His face was like the autumn sky, overcast one moment and bright the next.

"When the manager, escorted by the pilgrims, all of them armed to the teeth, had gone to the house, this chap came on board. 'I say, I don't like this. These natives are in the bush,' I said. He assured me earnestly it was all right. 'They are simple people,' he added; 'well, I am glad you came. It took me all my time to keep them off.' 'But you said it was all right,' I cried. 'Oh, they meant no harm,' he said; and as I stared he corrected himself, 'not exactly.' Then vivaciously, 'My faith, your pilot-house wants a clean-up!' In the next breath he advised me to keep enough steam on the boiler to blow the whistle in case of any trouble. 'One good screech will do more for you than all your rifles. They are simple people,' he repeated. He rattled away at such a rate he quite overwhelmed me.

He seemed to be trying to make up for lots of silence, and actually hinted, laughing, that such was the case. 'Don't you talk with Mr. Kurtz?' I said. 'You don't talk with that man—you listen to him,' he exclaimed with severe exaltation. 'But now——' He waved his arm, and in the twinkling of an eye was in the uttermost depths of despondency. In a moment he came up again with a jump, possessed himself of both my hands, shook them continuously, while he gabbled: 'Brother sailor . . . honor . . . pleasure . . . delight . . . introduce myself . . . Russian . . . son of an arch-priest . . . Government of Tambov . . . What? Tobacco! English tobacco; the excellent English tobacco! Now, that's brotherly. Smoke? Where's a sailor that does not smoke?'

"The pipe soothed him, and gradually I made out he had run away from school, had gone to sea in a Russian ship; ran away again; served some time in English ships; was now reconciled with the arch-priest. He made a point of that. 'But when one is young one must see things, gather experience, ideas; enlarge the mind.' 'Here!' I interrupted. 'You can never tell! Here I met Mr. Kurtz,' he said, youthfully solemn and reproachful. I held my tongue after that. It appears he had persuaded a Dutch trading-house on the coast to fit him out with stores and goods, and had started for the interior with a light heart, and no more idea of what would happen to him than a baby. He had been wandering about that river for nearly two years alone, cut off from everybody and everything. 'I am not so young as I look. I am twenty-five,' he said. 'At first old Van Shuyten would tell me to go to the devil,' he narrated with keen enjoyment; 'but I stuck to him, and talked and talked, till at last he got afraid I would talk the hind-leg off his favorite dog, so he gave me some cheap things and a few guns, and told me he hoped he would never see my face again. Good old Dutchman, Van Shuyten. I sent him one small lot of ivory a year ago, so that he can't call me a little thief when I get back. I hope he got it. And for the rest, I don't care. I had some wood stacked for you. That was my old house. Did you see?'

"I gave him Towson's book. He made as though he would kiss me, but restrained himself. 'The only book I had left, and I thought I had lost it,' he said, looking at it ecstatically. 'So many accidents happen to a man going about alone, you know. Canoes get upset sometimes—and sometimes you've got to clear out so quick when the people get angry.' He thumbed the pages. 'You made notes in Russian?' I asked. He nodded. 'I thought they were written in cipher,' I said. He laughed, then became serious. 'I had lots of trouble to keep these people off,' he said. 'Did they want to kill you?' I asked. 'Oh no!' he cried, and checked himself. 'Why did they attack us?' I pursued. He hesitated, then said shamefacedly,

'They don't want him to go.' 'Don't they?' I said curiously. He nodded a nod full of mystery and wisdom. 'I tell you,' he cried, 'this man has enlarged my mind.' He opened his arms wide, staring at me with his little blue eyes that were perfectly round."

III

"I looked at him, lost in astonishment. There he was before me, in motley, as though he had absconded from a troupe of mimes, enthusiastic, famulous. His very existence was improbable, inexplicable, and altogether bewildering. He was an insoluble problem. It was inconceivable how he had existed, how he had succeeded in getting so far, how he had managed to remain—why he did not instantly disappear. 'I went a little farther,' he said, 'then still a little farther—till I had gone so far that I don't know how I'll ever get back. Never mind. Plenty time. I can manage. You take Kurtz away quick—quick—I tell you.' The glamor of youth enveloped his parti-colored rags, his destitution, his loneliness, the essential desolation of his futile wanderings. For months—for years—his life hadn't been worth a day's purchase; and there he was gallantly, thoughtlessly alive, to all appearance indestructible solely by the virtue of his few years and of his unreflecting audacity. I was seduced into something like admiration—like envy. Glamor urged him on, glamor kept him unscathed. He surely wanted nothing from the wilderness but space to breathe in and to push on through. His need was to exist, and to move onwards at the greatest possible risk, and with a maximum of privation. If the absolutely pure, uncalculating, unpractical spirit of adventure had ever ruled a human being, it ruled this be-patched youth. I almost envied him the possession of this modest and clear flame. It seemed to have consumed all thought of self so completely, that, even while he was talking to you, you forgot that it was he—the man before your eyes —who had gone through these things. I did not envy him his devotion to Kurtz, though. He had not meditated over it. It came to him, and he accepted it with a sort of eager fatalism. I must say that to me it appeared about the most dangerous thing in every way he had come upon so far.

"They had come together unavoidably, like two ships becalmed near each other, and lay rubbing sides at last. I suppose Kurtz wanted an audience, because on a certain occasion, when encamped in the forest, they had talked all night, or more probably Kurtz had talked. 'We talked of everything,' he said, quite transported at the recollection. 'I forgot there was such a thing as sleep. The night did not seem to last an hour. Everything! Everything! . . . Of love too.' 'Ah, he talked to you of love!' I said, much amused. 'It isn't what you think,' he cried, almost passionately. 'It was in general. He made me see things—things.'

"He threw his arms up. We were on deck at the time, and the head-man of my wood-cutters, lounging near by, turned upon him his heavy and glittering eyes. I looked around, and I don't know why, but I assure you that never, never before, did this land, this river, this jungle, the very arch of this blazing sky, appear to me so hopeless and so dark, so impenetrable to human thought, so pitiless to human weakness. 'And, ever since, you have been with him, of course?' I said.

"On the contrary. It appears their intercourse had been very much broken by various causes. He had, as he informed me proudly, managed to nurse Kurtz through two illnesses (he alluded to it as you would to some risky feat), but as a rule Kurtz wandered alone, far in the depths of the forest. 'Very often coming to this station, I had to wait days and days before he would turn up,' he said. 'Ah, it was worth waiting for!—sometimes.' 'What was he doing? exploring or what?' I asked. 'Oh yes, of course'; he had discovered lots of villages, a lake too—he did not know exactly in what direction; it was dangerous to inquire too much—but mostly his expeditions had been for ivory. 'But he had no goods to trade with by that time,' I objected. 'There's a good lot of cartridges left even yet,' he answered, looking away. 'To speak plainly, he raided the country,' I said. He nodded. 'Not alone, surely!' He muttered something about the villages round that lake. 'Kurtz got the tribe to follow him, did he?' I suggested. He fidgeted a little. 'They adored him,' he said. The tone of these words was so extraordinary that I looked at him searchingly. It was curious to see his mingled eagerness and reluctance to speak of Kurtz. The man filled his life, occupied his thoughts, swayed his emotions. 'What can you expect?' he burst out; 'he came to them with thunder and lightning, you know—and they had never seen anything like it—and very terrible. He could be very terrible. You can't judge Mr. Kurtz as you would an ordinary man. No, no, no! Now—just to give you an idea—I don't mind telling you, he wanted to shoot me too one day—but I don't judge him.' 'Shoot you!' I cried. 'What for?' 'Well, I had a small lot of ivory the chief of that village near my house gave me. You see I used to shoot game for them. Well, he wanted it, and wouldn't hear reason. He declared he would shoot me unless I gave him the ivory and then cleared out of the country, because he could do so, and had a fancy for it, and there was nothing on earth to prevent him killing whom he jolly well pleased. And it was true too. I gave him the ivory. What did I care! But I didn't clear out. No, no. I couldn't leave him. I had to be careful, of course, till we got friendly again for a time. He had his second illness then. Afterwards I had to keep out of the way; but I didn't mind. He was living for the most part in those villages on the lake. When he came down to the river, sometimes he would take to me, and sometimes it was better for me to be careful. This man suffered too much. He hated all this, and somehow he couldn't get away. When I had a chance I begged him to try and leave while there was time; I offered to go back with him. And he would say yes, and then he would remain; go off on another ivory hunt; disappear for weeks; forget himself amongst these people —forget himself—you know.' 'Why! he's mad,' I said. He protested indignantly. Mr. Kurtz couldn't be mad. If I had heard him talk, only two days ago, I wouldn't dare hint at such a thing. . . . I had taken up my binoculars while we talked, and was looking at the shore, sweeping the limit of the forest at each side and at the back of the house. The consciousness of there being people in that bush, so silent, so quiet—as silent and quiet as the ruined house on the hill—made me uneasy. There was no sign on the face of nature of this amazing tale that was not so much told as suggested to me in desolate exclamations, completed by shrugs, in interrupted phrases, in hints ending in deep sighs. The woods were unmoved, like a mask—heavy, like the closed door of a prison—they looked with their air of hidden knowledge, of patient expectation, of unapproachable silence. The Russian was explaining to me that it was only lately that Mr. Kurtz had come down to the river, bringing along with him all the fighting men of that lake tribe. He had been absent for several months—getting himself adored, I suppose—and had come down unexpectedly, with the intention to all appearance of making a raid either across the river or downstream. Evidently the appetite for more ivory had got the better of the—what shall I say?—less material aspirations. However, he had got much worse suddenly. 'I heard he was lying helpless, and so I came up—took my chance,' said the Russian. 'Oh, he is bad, very bad.' I directed my glass to the house. There were no signs of life, but there was the ruined roof, the long mud wall peeping above the grass, with three little square window holes, no two of the same size; all this brought within reach of my hand, as it were. And then I made a brusque movement, and one of the remaining posts of that vanished fence leaped up in the field of my glass. You remember I told you I had been struck at the distance by certain attempts at ornamentation, rather remarkable in the ruinous aspect of the place. Now I had suddenly a nearer view, and its first result was to make me throw my head back as if before a blow. Then I went carefully from post to post with my glass, and I saw my mistake. These round knobs were not ornamental but symbolic; they were expressive and puzzling, striking and disturbing—food for thought and also for vultures if there had been any looking down from the sky; but at all events for such ants as were industrious enough to ascend the pole. They would have been even more impressive, those heads on the stakes, if their faces had not been turned to the house. Only one, the first I had made out, was facing my way. I was not so shocked as you may think. The start back I had given was really nothing but a movement of surprise. I had expected to see a knob of wood there, you know. I returned deliberately to the first I had seen—and there it was, black, dried, sunken, with closed eyelids—a head that seemed to sleep at the top of that pole, and, with the shrunken dry lips showing a narrow white line of the teeth, was smiling too, smiling continuously at some endless and jocose dream of that eternal slumber.

"I am not disclosing any trade secrets. In fact the manager said afterwards that Mr. Kurtz's methods had ruined the district. I have no opinion on that point, but I want you clearly to understand that there was nothing exactly profitable in these heads being there. They only showed that Mr. Kurtz lacked restraint in the gratification of his various lusts, that there was something wanting in him —some small matter which, when the pressing need arose, could not be found under his magnificent eloquence. Whether he knew of this deficiency himself I can't say. I think the knowledge came to him at last—only at the very last. But the wilderness had found him out early, and had taken on him a terrible vengeance for the fantastic invasion. I think it had whispered to him things about himself which he did not know, things of which he had no conception till he took counsel with this great solitude—and the whisper had proved irresistibly fascinating. It echoed loudly within him because he was hollow at the core. . . . I put down the glass, and the head that had appeared near enough to be spoken to seemed at once to have leaped away from me into inaccessible distance.

"The admirer of Mr. Kurtz was a bit crestfallen. In a hurried, indistinct voice he began to assure me he had not dared to take these—say, symbols—down. He was not afraid of the natives; they would not stir till Mr. Kurtz gave the word. His ascendancy was extraordinary. The camps of these people surrounded the place, and the chiefs came every day to see him. They would crawl . . . 'I don't want to know anything of the ceremonies used when approaching Mr. Kurtz,' I shouted. Curious, this feeling that came over me that such details would be more intolerable than those heads drying on the stakes under Mr. Kurtz's windows. After all, that was only a savage sight, while I seemed at one bound to have been transported into some lightless region of subtle horrors, where pure, uncomplicated savagery was a positive relief, being something that had a right to exist—obviously—in the sunshine. The young man looked at me with surprise. I suppose it did not occur to him that Mr. Kurtz was no idol of mine. He forgot I hadn't heard any of these splendid monologues on, what was it? on love, justice, conduct of life—or what not. If it had come to crawling before Mr. Kurtz, he crawled as much as the veriest savage of them all. I had no idea of the conditions, he said: these heads were the heads of rebels. I shocked him excessively by laughing. Rebels! What would be the next definition I was to hear? There had been enemies, criminals, workers—and these were rebels. Those rebellious heads looked very subdued to me on their sticks. 'You don't know how such a life tries a man like Kurtz,' cried Kurtz's last disciple. 'Well, and you? I said. 'I! I! I am a simple man. I have no great thoughts. I want nothing from anybody. How can you compare me to . . . ?' His feelings were too much for speech, and suddenly he broke down. 'I don't understand.' he groaned. 'I've been doing my best to keep him alive, and that's enough. I had no hand in all this. I have no abilities. There hasn't been a drop of medicine or a mouthful of invalid food for months here. He was shamefully abandoned. A man like this, with such ideas. Shamefully! Shamefully! I—I— haven't slept for the last ten nights. . .'

"His voice lost itself in the calm of the evening. The long shadows of the forest had slipped downhill while we talked, had gone far beyond the ruined hovel, beyond the symbolic row of stakes. All this was in the gloom, while we down there were yet in the sunshine, and the stretch of the river abreast of the clearing glittered in a still and dazzling splendor, with a murky and over-shadowed bend above and below. Not a living soul was seen on the shore. The bushes did not rustle.

"Suddenly round the corner of the house a group of men appeared, as though they had come up from the ground. They waded waist-deep in the grass, in a compact body, bearing an improvised stretcher in their midst. Instantly, in the emptiness of the landscape, a cry arose whose shrillness pierced the still air like a sharp arrow flying straight to the very heart of the land; and, as if by enchantment, streams of human beings—of naked human beings —with spears in their hands, with bows, with shields, with wild glances and savage movements, were poured into the clearing by the dark-faced and pensive forest. The bushes shook, the grass swayed for a time, and then everything stood still in attentive immobility.

" 'Now, if he does not say the right thing to them we are all done for,' said the Russian at my elbow. The knot of men with the stretcher had stopped too, halfway to the steamer, as if petrified. I saw the man on the stretcher sit up, lank and with an uplifted arm, above the shoulders of the bearers. 'Let us hope that the man who can talk so well of love in general will find some particular reason to spare us this time,' I said. I resented bitterly the absurd danger of our situation, as if to be at the mercy of that atrocious phantom had been a dishonoring necessity. I could not hear a sound, but through my glasses I saw the thin arm extended commandingly, the lower jaw moving, the eyes of that apparition shining darkly far in its bony head that nodded with grotesque jerks. Kurtz—Kurtz—that means 'short' in German—don't it? Well, the name was as true as everything else in his life—and death. He looked at least seven feet long. His covering had fallen off, and his body emerged from it pitiful and appalling as from a winding-sheet. I could see the cage of his ribs all astir, the bones of his arm waving. It was as though an animated image of death carved out of old ivory had been shaking its hand with menaces at a motionless crowd of men made of dark and glittering bronze. I saw him open his mouth wide —it gave him a weirdly voracious aspect, as though he had wanted to swallow all the air, all the earth, all the men before him. A deep voice reached me faintly. He must have been shouting. He fell back suddenly. The stretcher shook as the bearers staggered forward again, and almost at the same time I noticed that the crowd of savages was vanishing without any perceptible movement of retreat, as if the forest that had ejected these beings so suddenly had drawn them in again as the breath is drawn in a long aspiration.

"Some of the pilgrims behind the stretcher carried his arms—two shotguns, a heavy rifle, and a light revolver-carbine—the thunderbolts of that pitiful Jupiter. The manager bent over him murmuring as he walked beside his head. They laid him down in one of the little cabins—just a room for a bed-place and a camp-stool or two, you know. We had brought his belated correspondence, and a lot of torn envelopes and open letters littered his bed. His hand roamed feebly amongst these papers. I was struck by the fire of his eyes and the composed languor of his expression. It was not so much the exhaustion of disease. He did not seem in pain. This shadow looked satiated and calm, as though for the moment it had had its fill of all the emotions.

"He rustled one of the letters, and looking straight in my face said, 'I am glad.' Somebody had been writing to him about me. These special recommendations were turning up again. The volume of tone he emitted without effort, almost without the trouble of moving his lips, amazed me. A voice! a voice! It was grave, profound, vibrating, while the man did not seem capable of a whisper. However, he had enough strength in him—factitious no doubt—to very nearly make an end of us, as you shall hear directly.

"The manager appeared silently in the doorway; I stepped out at once and he drew the curtain after me. The Russian, eyed curiously by the pilgrims, was staring at the shore. I followed the direction of his glance.

"Dark human shapes could be made out in the distance, flitting indistinctly against the gloomy border of the forest, and near the river two bronze figures, leaning on tall spears, stood in the sunlight

under fantastic headdresses of spotted skins, war-like and still in statuesque repose. And from right to left along the lighted shore moved
a wild and gorgeous apparition of a woman.

"She walked with measured steps, draped in striped and fringed
cloths, treading the earth proudly, with a slight jingle and flash of
barbarous ornaments. She carried her head high; her hair was done
in the shape of a helmet; she had brass leggings to the knees, brass
wire gauntlets to the elbow, a crimson spot on her tawny cheek,
innumerable necklaces of glass beads on her neck; bizarre things,
charms, gifts of witch-men, that hung about her, glittered and trembled at every step. She must have had the value of several elephant
tusks upon her. She was savage and superb, wild-eyed and magnificent; there was something ominous and stately in her deliberate
progress. And in the hush that had fallen suddenly upon the whole
sorrowful land, the immense wilderness, the colossal body of the
fecund and mysterious life seemed to look at her, pensive, as though
it had been looking at the image of its own tenebrous and passionate soul.

"She came abreast of the steamer, stood still, and faced us. Her
long shadow fell to the water's edge. Her face had a tragic and
fierce aspect of wild sorrow and of dumb pain mingled with the fear
of some struggling, half-shaped resolve. She stood looking at us
without a stir, and like the wilderness itself, with an air of brooding
over an inscrutable purpose. A whole minute passed, and then she
made a step forward. There was a low jingle, a glint of yellow
metal, a sway of fringed draperies, and she stopped as if her heart
had failed her. The young fellow by my side growled. The pilgrims
murmured at my back. She looked at us all as if her life had
depended upon the unswerving steadiness of her glance. Suddenly
she opened her bared arms and threw them up rigid above her
head, as though in an uncontrollable desire to touch the sky, and at
the same time the swift shadows darted out on the earth, swept
around on the river, gathering the steamer in a shadowy embrace. A
formidable silence hung over the scene.

"She turned away slowly, walked on, following the bank, and
passed into the bushes to the left. Once only her eyes gleamed back
at us in the dusk of the thickets before she disappeared.

" 'If she had offered to come aboard I really think I would have
tried to shoot her,' said the man of patches nervously. 'I had been
risking my life every day for the last fortnight to keep her out of the
house. She got in one day and kicked up a row about those miserable rags I picked up in the storeroom to mend my clothes with. I
wasn't decent. At least it must have been that, for she talked like a
fury to Kurtz for an hour, pointing at me now and then. I don't
understand the dialect of this tribe. Luckily for me, I fancy Kurtz

felt too ill that day to care, or there would have been mischief. I don't understand. . . . No—it's too much for me. Ah, well, it's all over now.'

"At this moment I heard Kurtz's deep voice behind the curtain: 'Save me!—save the ivory, you mean. Don't tell me. Save *me*! Why, I've had to save you. You are interrupting my plans now. Sick! Sick! Not so sick as you would like to believe. Never mind. I'll carry my ideas out yet—I will return. I'll show you what can be done. You with your little peddling notions—you are interfering with me. I will return. I . . .'

"The manager came out. He did me the honor to take me under the arm and lead me aside. 'He is very low, very low,' he said. He considered it necessary to sigh, but neglected to be consistently sorrowful. 'We have done all we could for him—haven't we? But there is no disguising the fact, Mr. Kurtz has done more harm than good to the Company. He did not see the time was not ripe for vigorous action. Cautiously, cautiously—that's my principle. We must be cautious yet. The district is closed to us for a time. Deplorable! Upon the whole, the trade will suffer. I don't deny there is a remarkable quantity of ivory—mostly fossil. We must save it, at all events—but look how precarious the position is—and why? Because the method is unsound.' 'Do you,' said I, looking at the shore, 'call it "unsound method"?' 'Without doubt,' he exclaimed hotly. 'Don't you?' . . . 'No method at all,' I murmured after a while. 'Exactly,' he exulted. 'I anticipated this. Shows a complete want of judgment. It is my duty to point it out in the proper quarter.' 'Oh,' said I, 'that fellow—what's his name?—the brickmaker, will make a readable report for you.' He appeared confounded for a moment. It seemed to me I had never breathed an atmosphere so vile, and I turned mentally to Kurtz for relief—positively for relief. 'Nevertheless, I think Mr. Kurtz is a remarkable man,' I said with emphasis. He started, dropped on me a cold heavy glance, said very quietly. 'He *was*,' and turned his back on me. My hour of favor was over; I found myself lumped along with Kurtz as a partisan of methods for which the time was not ripe: I was unsound! Ah! but it was something to have at least a choice of nightmares.

"I had turned to the wilderness really, not to Mr. Kurtz, who, I was ready to admit, was as good as buried. And for a moment it seemed to me as if I also were buried in a vast grave full of unspeakable secrets. I felt an intolerable weight oppressing my breast, the smell of the damp earth, the unseen presence of victorious corruption, the darkness of an impenetrable night. . . . The Russian tapped me on the shoulder. I heard him mumbling and stammering something about 'brother seaman—couldn't conceal—knowledge of matters that would affect Mr. Kurtz's reputation.' I waited. For him evidently Mr. Kurtz was not in his grave; I suspect that for him Mr. Kurtz was one of the immortals. 'Well!' said I at last, 'speak out. As it happens, I am Mr. Kurtz's friend—in a way.'

"He stated with a good deal of formality that had we not been 'of the same profession,' he would have kept the matter to himself without regard to consequences. He suspected 'there was an active ill-will towards him on the part of these white men that—' 'You are right,' I said, remembering a certain conversation I had overheard. 'The manager thinks you ought to be hanged.' He showed a concern at this intelligence which amused me at first. 'I had better get out of the way quietly,' he said earnestly. 'I can do no more for Kurtz now, and they would soon find some excuse. What's to stop them? There's a military post three hundred miles from here.' 'Well, upon my word,' said I, 'perhaps you had better go if you have any friends amongst the savages near by.' 'Plenty,' he said. 'They are simple people—and I want nothing, you know.' He stood biting his lip, then: 'I don't want any harm to happen to these whites here, but of course I was thinking of Mr. Kurtz's reputation —but you are a brother seaman and——' 'All right,' said I, after a time. 'Mr. Kurtz's reputation is safe with me.' I did not know how truly I spoke.

"He informed me, lowering his voice, that it was Kurtz who had ordered the attack to be made on the steamer. 'He hated sometimes the idea of being taken away—and then again . . . But I don't understand these matters. I am a simple man. He thought it would scare you away—that you would give it up, thinking him dead. I could not stop him. Oh, I had an awful time of it this last month.' 'Very well.' I said. 'He is all right now.' 'Ye-e-es,' he muttered, not very convinced apparently. 'Thanks,' said I; 'I shall keep my eyes open.' 'But quiet—eh?' he urged anxiously. 'It would be awful for his reputation if anybody here——' I promised a complete discretion with great gravity. 'I have a canoe and three black fellows waiting not very far. I am off. Could you give me a few Martini-Henry cartridges?' I could, and did, with proper secrecy. He helped himself, with a wink at me, to a handful of my tobacco. 'Between sailors, you know—good English tobacco.' At the door of the pilot-house he turned round—'I say, haven't you a pair of shoes you could spare?' He raised one leg. 'Look.' The soles were tied with knotted strings sandal-wise under his bare feet. I rooted out an old pair, at which he looked with admiration before tucking it under his left arm. One of his pockets (bright red) was bulging with cartridges, from the other (dark blue) peeped 'Towson's Inquiry,' etc. etc. He seemed to think himself excellently well equipped for a renewed encounter with the wilderness. 'Ah! I'll never, never meet such a man again. You ought to have heard him recite poetry—his own too it was, he told me. Poetry!' He rolled his eyes at the recollection of these delights. 'Oh, he enlarged my mind!' 'Good-bye,' said I. He shook hands and vanished in the night. Sometimes I ask myself whether I had ever really seen him—whether it was possible to meet such a phenomenon! . . .

"When I woke up shortly after midnight his warning came to my mind with its hint of danger that seemed, in the starred darkness, real enough to make me get up for the purpose of having a look round. On the hill a big fire burned, illuminating fitfully a crooked corner of the station-house. One of the agents with a picket of a few of our blacks, armed for the purpose, was keeping guard over the ivory; but deep within the forest, red gleams that wavered, that seemed to sink and rise from the ground amongst confused columnar shapes of intense blackness, showed the exact position of the camp where Mr. Kurtz's adorers were keeping their uneasy vigil. The monotonous beating of a big drum filled the air with muffled shocks and a lingering vibration. A steady droning sound of many men chanting each to himself some weird incantation came out from the black, flat wall of the woods as the humming of bees comes out of a hive, and had a strange narcotic effect upon my half-awake senses. I believe I dozed off leaning over the rail, till an abrupt burst of yells, an overwhelming outbreak of a pent-up and mysterious frenzy, woke me up in a bewildered wonder. It was cut short all at once, and the low droning went on with an effect of audible and soothing silence. I glanced casually into the little cabin. A light was burning within, but Mr. Kurtz was not there.

"I think I would have raised an outcry if I had believed my eyes. But I didn't believe them at first—the thing seemed so impossible. The fact is, I was completely unnerved by a sheer blank fright, pure abstract terror, unconnected with any distinct shape of physical danger. What made this emotion so overpowering was—how shall I define it?—the moral shock I received, as if something altogether monstrous, intolerable to thought and odious to the soul, had been thrust upon me unexpectedly. This lasted of course the merest fraction of a second, and then the usual sense of commonplace, deadly danger, the possibility of a sudden onslaught and massacre, or something of the kind, which I saw impending, was positively welcome and composing. It pacified me, in fact, so much, that I did not raise an alarm.

"There was an agent buttoned up inside an ulster and sleeping on a chair on deck within three feet of me. The yells had not awakened him; he snored very slightly; I left him to his slumbers and leaped ashore. I did not betray Mr. Kurtz—it was ordered I should never betray him—it was written I should be loyal to the nightmare of my choice. I was anxious to deal with this shadow by myself alone—and to this day I don't know why I was so jealous of sharing with any one the peculiar blackness of that experience.

"As soon as I got on the bank I saw a trail—a broad trail through the grass. I remember the exultation with which I said to myself,

'He can't walk—he is crawling on all-fours—I've got him.' The grass was wet with dew. I strode rapidly with clenched fists. I fancy I had some vague notion of falling upon him and giving him a drubbing. I don't know. I had some imbecile thoughts. The knitting old woman with the cat obtruded herself upon my memory as a most improper person to be sitting at the other end of such an affair. I saw a row of pilgrims squirting lead in the air out of Winchesters held to the hip. I thought I would never get back to the steamer, and imagined myself living alone and unarmed in the woods to an advanced age. Such silly things—you know. And I remember I confounded the beat of the drum with the beating of my heart, and was pleased at its calm regularity.

"I kept to the track though—then stopped to listen. The night was very clear; a dark blue space, sparkling with dew and starlight, in which black things stood very still. I thought I could see a kind of motion ahead of me. I was strangely cocksure of everything that night. I actually left the track and ran in a wide semicircle (I verily believe chuckling to myself) so as to get in front of that stir, of that motion I had seen—if indeed I had seen anything. I was circumventing Kurtz as though it had been a boyish game.

"I came upon him, and, if he had not heard me coming, I would have fallen over him too, but he got up in time. He rose, unsteady, long, pale, indistinct, like a vapor exhaled by the earth, and swayed slightly, misty and silent before me; while at my back the fires loomed between the trees, and the murmur of many voices issued from the forest. I had cut him off cleverly; but when actually confronting him I seemed to come to my senses, I saw the danger in its right proportion. It was by no means over yet. Suppose he began to shout? Though he could hardly stand, there was still plenty of vigor in his voice. 'Go away—hide yourself,' he said, in that profound tone. It was very awful. I glanced back. We were within thirty yards of the nearest fire. A black figure stood up, strode on long black legs, waving long black arms, across the glow. It had horns—antelope horns, I think—on its head. Some sorcerer, some witchman, no doubt: it looked fiend-like enough. 'Do you know what you are doing?' I whispered. 'Perfectly,' he answered, raising his voice for that single word: it sounded to me far off and yet loud, like a hail through a speaking-trumpet. If he makes a row we are lost, I thought to myself. This clearly was not a case for fisticuffs, even apart from the very natural aversion I had to beat that Shadow—this wandering and tormented thing. 'You will be lost,' I said—'utterly lost.' One gets sometimes such a flash of inspiration, you know. I did say the right thing, though indeed he could not have been more irretrievably lost than he was at this very moment, when the foundations of our intimacy were being laid—to endure—to endure—even to the end—even beyond.

" 'I had immense plans,' he muttered irresolutely. 'Yes,' said I; 'but if you try to shout I'll smash your head with——' There was not a stick or a stone near. 'I will throttle you for good,' I corrected myself. 'I was on the threshold of great things,' he pleaded, in a voice of longing, with a wistfulness of tone that made my blood run cold. 'And now for this stupid scoundrel—' 'Your success in Europe is assured in any case,' I affirmed steadily. I did not want to have the throttling of him, you understand—and indeed it would have been very little use for any practical purpose. I tried to break the spell—the heavy, mute spell of the wilderness—that seemed to draw him to its pitiless breast by the awakening of forgotten and brutal instincts, by the memory of gratified and monstrous passions. This alone, I was convinced, had driven him out to the edge of the forest, to the bush, towards the gleam of fires, the throb of drums, the drone of weird incantations; this alone had beguiled his unlawful soul beyond the bounds of permitted aspirations. And, don't you see, the terror of the position was not in being knocked on the head—though I had a very lively sense of that danger too—but in this, that I had to deal with a being to whom I could not appeal in the name of anything high or low. I had, even like the niggers, to invoke him—himself—his own exalted and incredible degradation. There was nothing either above or below him, and I knew it. He had kicked himself loose of the earth. Confound the man! he had kicked the very earth to pieces. He was alone, and I before him did not know whether I stood on the ground or floated in the air. I've been telling you what we said—repeating the phrases we pronounced—but what's the good? They were common everyday words—the familiar, vague sounds exchanged on every waking day of life. But what of that? They had behind them, to my mind, the terrific suggestiveness of words heard in dreams, of phrases spoken in nightmares. Soul! If anybody had ever struggled with a soul, I am the man. And I wasn't arguing with a lunatic either. Believe me or not, his intelligence was perfectly clear—concentrated, it is true, upon himself with horrible intensity, yet clear; and therein was my only chance—barring, of course, the killing him there and then, which wasn't so good, on account of unavoidable noise. But his soul was mad. Being alone in the wilderness, it had looked within itself, and, by Heavens! I tell you, it had gone mad. I had—for my sins, I suppose, to go through the ordeal of looking into it myself. No eloquence could have been so withering to one's belief in mankind as his final burst of sincerity. He struggled with himself too. I saw it—I heard it. I saw the inconceivable mystery of a soul that knew no restraint, no faith, and no fear, yet struggling blindly with itself. I kept my head pretty well; but when I had him at last stretched on the couch, I wiped my forehead, while my legs shook under me as though I had carried half a ton on my back down that hill. And yet I had only supported him, his bony arm clasped round my neck—and he was not much heavier than a child.

"When next day we left at noon, the crowd, of whose presence behind the curtain of trees I had been acutely conscious all the time, flowed out of the woods again, filled the clearing, covered the slope with a mass of naked, breathing, quivering, bronze bodies. I steamed up a bit, then swung downstream, and two thousand eyes followed the evolutions of the splashing, thumping, fierce river-demon beating the water with its terrible tail and breathing black smoke into the air. In front of the first rank, along the river, three men, plastered with bright red earth from head to foot, strutted to and fro restlessly. When we came abreast again, they faced the river, stamped their feet, nodded their horned heads, swayed their scarlet bodies; they shook towards the fierce river-demon a bunch of black feathers, a mangy skin with a pendent tail—something that looked like a dried gourd; they shouted periodically together strings of amazing words that resembled no sounds of human language; and the deep murmurs of the crowd, interrupted suddenly, were like the responses of some satanic litany.

"We had carried Kurtz into the pilot-house: there was more air there. Lying on the couch, he stared through the open shutter. There was an eddy in the mass of human bodies, and the woman with helmeted head and tawny cheeks rushed out to the very brink of the stream. She put out her hands, shouted something, and all that wild mob took up the shout in a roaring chorus of articulated, rapid, breathless utterance.

" 'Do you understand this?' I asked.

"He kept on looking out past me with fiery, longing eyes, with a mingled expression of wistfulness and hate. He made no answer, but I saw a smile, a smile of indefinable meaning, appear on his colorless lips that a moment after twitched convulsively. 'Do I not?' he said slowly, gasping, as if the words had been torn out of him by a supernatural power.

"I pulled the string of the whistle, and I did this because I saw the pilgrims on deck getting out their rifles with an air of anticipating a jolly lark. At the sudden screech there was a movement of abject terror through that wedged mass of bodies. 'Don't! don't you frighten them away,' cried some one on deck disconsolately. I pulled the string time after time. They broke and ran, they leaped, they crouched, they swerved, they dodged the flying terror of the sound. The three red chaps had fallen flat, face down on the shore, as though they had been shot dead. Only the barbarous and superb woman did not so much as flinch, and stretched tragically her bare arms after us over the somber and glittering river.

"And then that imbecile crowd down on the deck started their little fun, and I could see nothing more for smoke.

"The brown current ran swiftly out of the heart of darkness, bearing us down towards the sea with twice the speed of our upward progress; and Kurtz's life was running swiftly too, ebbing, ebbing out of his heart into the sea of inexorable time. The manager was very placid, he had no vital anxieties now, he took us both in with a comprehensive and satisfied glance: the 'affair' had come off as well as could be wished. I saw the time approaching when I would be left alone of the party of 'unsound method.' The pilgrims looked upon me with disfavor. I was so to speak, numbered with the dead. It is strange how I accepted this unforeseen partnership, this choice of nightmares forced upon me in the tenebrous land invaded by these mean and greedy phantoms.

"Kurtz discoursed. A voice! a voice! It rang deep to the very last. It survived his strength to hide in the magnificent folds of eloquence the barren darkness of his heart. Oh, he struggled! he struggled! The wastes of his weary brain were haunted by shadowy images now—images of wealth and fame revolving obsequiously round his unextinguishable gift of noble and lofty expression. My Intended, my station, my career, my ideas—these were the subjects for the occasional utterances of elevated sentiments. The shade of the original Kurtz frequented the bedside of the hollow sham, whose fate it was to be buried presently in the mold of primeval earth. But both the diabolic love and the unearthly hate of the mysteries it had penetrated fought for the possession of that soul satiated with primitive emotions, avid of lying fame, of sham distinction, of all the appearances of success and power.

"Sometimes he was contemptibly childish. He desired to have kings meet him at railway stations on his return from some ghastly Nowhere, where he intended to accomplish great things. 'You show them you have in you something that is really profitable, and then there will be no limits to the recognition of your ability,' he would say. 'Of course you must take care of the motives—right motives—always.' The long reaches that were like one and the same reach, monotonous bends that were exactly alike, slipped past the steamer with their multitude of secular[9] trees looking patiently after this grimy fragment of another world, the forerunner of change, of conquest, of trade, of massacres, of blessings. I looked ahead—piloting. 'Close the shutter,' said Kurtz suddenly one day; 'I can't bear to look at this.' I did so. There was a silence. 'Oh, but I will wring your heart yet!' he cried at the invisible wilderness.

"We broke down—as I had expected—and had to lie up for repairs at the head of an island. This delay was the first thing that shook Kurtz's confidence. One morning he gave me a packet of papers and a photograph—the lot tied together with a shoe-string. 'Keep this for me,' he said. 'This noxious fool' (meaning the manager) 'is capable of prying into my boxes when I am not looking.' In the afternoon I saw him. He was lying on his back with closed eyes, and I withdrew quietly, but I heard him mutter, 'Live rightly,

9. "Centuries old."

die, die . . .' I listened. There was nothing more. Was he rehearsing some speech in his sleep, or was it a fragment of a phrase from some newspaper article? He had been writing for the papers and meant to do so again, 'for the furthering of my ideas. It's a duty.'

"His was an impenetrable darkness. I looked at him as you peer down at a man who is lying at the bottom of a precipice where the sun never shines. But I had not much time to give him, because I was helping the engine-driver to take to pieces the leaky cylinders, to straighten a bent connecting-rod, and in other such matters. I lived in an infernal mess of rust, filings, nuts, bolts, spanners, hammers, ratchet-drills—things I abominate, because I don't get on with them. I tended the little forge we fortunately had aboard; I toiled wearily in a wretched scrap-heap—unless I had the shakes too bad to stand.

"One evening coming in with a candle I was startled to hear him say a little tremulously, 'I am lying here in the dark waiting for death.' The light was within a foot of his eyes. I forced myself to murmur, 'Oh nonsense!' and stood over him as if transfixed.

"Anything approaching the change that came over his features I have never seen before, and hope never to see again. Oh, I wasn't touched. I was fascinated. It was as though a veil had been rent. I saw on that ivory face the expression of somber pride, of ruthless power, of craven terror—of an intense and hopeless despair. Did he live his life again in every detail of desire, temptation, and surrender during that supreme moment of complete knowledge? He cried in a whisper at some image, at some vision—he cried out twice, a cry that was no more than a breath:

" 'The horror! The horror!'

"I blew the candle out and left the cabin. The pilgrims were dining in the mess-room, and I took my place opposite the manager, who lifted his eyes to give me a questioning glance, which I successfully ignored. He leaned back, serene, with that peculiar smile of his sealing the unexpressed depths of his meanness. A continuous shower of small flies streamed upon the lamp, upon the cloth, upon our hands and faces. Suddenly the manager's boy put his insolent black head in the doorway, and said in a tone of scathing contempt:

" 'Mistah Kurtz—he dead.'

"All the pilgrims rushed out to see. I remained, and went on with my dinner. I believe I was considered brutally callous. However, I did not eat much. There was a lamp in there—light, don't you know—and outside it was so beastly, beastly dark. I went no more near the remarkable man who had pronounced a judgment upon the adventures of his soul on this earth. The voice was gone. What else had been there? But I am of course aware that next day the pilgrims buried something in a muddy hole.

"And then they very nearly buried me.

"However, as you see, I did not go to join Kurtz there and then. I did not. I remained to dream the nightmare out to the end, and to show my loyalty to Kurtz once more. Destiny. My destiny! Droll thing life is—that mysterious arrangement of merciless logic for a futile purpose. The most you can hope from it is some knowledge of yourself—that comes too late—a crop of unextinguishable regrets. I have wrestled with death. It is the most unexciting contest you can imagine. It takes place in an impalpable grayness, with nothing underfoot, with nothing around, without spectators, without clamor, without glory, without the great desire of victory, without the great fear of defeat, in a sickly atmosphere of tepid scepticism, without much belief in your own right, and still less in that of your adversary. If such is the form of ultimate wisdom, then life is a greater riddle than some of us think it to be. I was within a hair's-breadth of the last opportunity for pronouncement, and I found with humiliation that probably I would have nothing to say. This is the reason why I affirm that Kurtz was a remarkable man. He had something to say. He said it. Since I had peeped over the edge myself, I understand better the meaning of his stare, that could not see the flame of the candle, but was wide enough to embrace the whole universe, piercing enough to penetrate all the hearts that beat in the darkness. He had summed up—he had judged. 'The horror!' He was a remarkable man. After all, this was the expression of some sort of belief; it had candor, it had conviction, it had a vibrating note of revolt in its whisper, it had the appalling face of a glimpsed truth—the strange commingling of desire and hate. And it is not my own extremity I remember best—a vision of grayness without form filled with physical pain, and a careless contempt for the evanescence of all things—even of this pain itself. No! It is his extremity that I seem to have lived through. True, he had made that last stride, he had stepped over the edge, while I had been permitted to draw back my hesitating foot. And perhaps in this is the whole difference; perhaps all the wisdom, and all truth, and all sincerity, are just compressed into that inappreciable moment of time in which we step over the threshold of the invisible. Perhaps! I like to think my summing-up would not have been a word of careless contempt. Better his cry—much better. It was an affirmation, a moral victory paid for by innumerable defeats, by abominable terrors, by abominable satisfactions. But it was a victory! That is why I have remained loyal to Kurtz to the last, and even beyond, when a long time after I heard once more, not his own voice, but the echo of his magnificent eloquence thrown to me from a soul as translucently pure as a cliff of crystal.

"No, they did not bury me, though there is a period of time which I remember mistily, with a shuddering wonder, like a passage through some inconceivable world that had no hope in it and no desire. I found myself back in the sepulchral city resenting the sight of people hurrying through the streets to filch a little money from each other, to devour their infamous cookery, to gulp their unwholesome beer, to dream their insignificant and silly dreams. They trespassed upon my thoughts. They were intruders whose knowledge of life was to me an irritating pretence, because I felt so sure they could not possibly know the things I knew. Their bearing, which was simply the bearing of commonplace individuals going about their business in the assurance of perfect safety, was offensive to me like the outrageous flauntings of folly in the face of a danger it is unable to comprehend. I had no particular desire to enlighten them, but I had some difficulty in restraining myself from laughing in their faces, so full of stupid importance. I daresay I was not very well at that time. I tottered about the streets—there were various affairs to settle—grinning bitterly at perfectly respectable persons. I admit my behavior was inexcusable, but then my temperature was seldom normal in these days. My dear aunt's endeavors to 'nurse up my strength' seemed altogether beside the mark. It was not my strength that wanted nursing, it was my imagination that wanted soothing. I kept the bundle of papers given me by Kurtz, not knowing exactly what to do with it. His mother had died lately, watched over, as I was told, by his Intended. A clean-shaven man, with an official manner and wearing gold-rimmed spectacles, called on me one day and made inquiries, at first circuitous, afterwards suavely pressing, about what he was pleased to denominate certain 'documents.' I was not surprised, because I had had two rows with the manager on the subject out there. I had refused to give up the smallest scrap out of that package, and I took the same attitude with the spectacled man. He became darkly menacing at last, and with much heat argued that the Company had the right to every bit of information about its 'territories.' And, said he, 'Mr. Kurtz's knowledge of unexplored regions must have been necessarily extensive and peculiar—owing to his great abilities and to the deplorable circumstances in which he had been placed: therefore——' I assured him Mr. Kurtz's knowledge, however extensive, did not bear upon the problems of commerce or administration. He invoked then the name of science. 'It would be an incalculable loss if,' etc. etc. I offered him the report on the 'Suppression of Savage Customs,' with the postscriptum torn off. He took it up eagerly, but ended by sniffing at it with an air of contempt. 'This is not what we had a right to expect,' he remarked. 'Expect nothing else,' I said. 'There are only private letters.' He withdrew upon some threat of legal proceedings, and I saw him no more; but another fellow, calling himself Kurtz's cousin, appeared two days later, and was anxious to hear all the details about his dear relative's last moments. Incidentally he gave me to understand that Kurtz had been essentially a great musician. 'There was the making of an immense success,' said the man, who was an organist, I believe, with lank gray hair flowing over a greasy coat-collar. I had no reason to doubt his statement; and to this day I am unable to say what was Kurtz's profession, whether he ever had any—which was the greatest of his talents. I had taken him for a painter who wrote for the papers, or else for a journalist who could paint—but even the cousin (who took snuff during the interview) could not tell me what he had been—exactly. He was a universal genius—on that point I agreed with the old chap, who thereupon blew his nose noisily into a large cotton handkerchief and withdrew in senile agitation, bearing off some family letters and memoranda without importance. Ultimately a journalist anxious to know something of the fate of his 'dear colleague' turned up. This visitor informed me Kurtz's proper sphere ought to have been politics 'on the popular side.' He had furry straight eyebrows, bristly hair cropped short, an eyeglass on a broad ribbon, and, becoming expansive, confessed his opinion that Kurtz really couldn't write a bit—'but Heavens! how that man could talk! He electrified large meetings. He had faith—don't you see?—he had the faith. He could get himself to believe anything—anything. He would have been a splendid leader of an extreme party.' 'What party?' I asked. 'Any party,' answered the other. 'He was an—an—extremist.' Did I not think so? I assented. Did I know, he asked, with a sudden flash of curiosity, 'what it was that had induced him to go out there?' 'Yes,' said I, and forthwith handed him the famous Report for publication, if he thought fit. He glanced through it hurriedly, mumbling all the time, judged 'it would do,' and took himself off with this plunder.

"Thus I was left at last with a slim packet of letters and the girl's portrait. She struck me as beautiful—I mean she had a beautiful expression. I know that the sunlight can be made to lie too, yet one felt that no manipulation of light and pose could have conveyed the delicate shade of truthfulness upon those features. She seemed ready to listen without mental reservation, without suspicion, without a thought for herself. I concluded I would go and give her back her portrait and those letters myself. Curiosity? Yes; and also some other feeling perhaps. All that had been Kurtz's had passed out of my hands: his soul, his body, his station, his plans, his ivory, his career. There remained only his memory and his Intended—and I wanted to give that up too to the past, in a way—to surrender personally all that remained of him with me to that oblivion which is the last word of our common fate. I don't defend myself. I had no clear perception of what it was I really wanted. Perhaps it was an impulse of unconscious loyalty, or the fulfillment of one of those ironic necessities that lurk in the facts of human existence. I don't know. I can't tell. But I went.

"I thought his memory was like the other memories of the dead that accumulate in every man's life—a vague impress on the brain of shadows that had fallen on it in their swift and final passage; but before the high and ponderous door, between the tall houses of a street as still and decorous as a well-kept alley in a cemetery, I had a vision of him on the stretcher, opening his mouth voraciously, as if to devour all the earth with all its mankind. He lived then before me; he lived as much as he had ever lived—a shadow insatiable of splendid appearances, of frightful realities; a shadow darker than the shadow of the night, and draped nobly in the folds of a gorgeous eloquence. The vision seemed to enter the house with me—the stretcher, the phantom-bearers, the wild crowd of obedient worshippers, the gloom of the forests, the glitter of the reach between the murky bends, the beat of the drum, regular and muffled like the beating of a heart—the heart of a conquering darkness. It was a moment of triumph for the wilderness, an invading and vengeful rush which, it seemed to me, I would have to keep back alone for the salvation of another soul. And the memory of what I had heard him say afar there, with the horned shapes stirring at my back, in the glow of fires, within the patient woods, those broken phrases came back to me, were heard again in their ominous and terrifying simplicity. I remembered his abject pleading, his abject threats, the colossal scale of his vile desires, the meanness, the torment, the tempestuous anguish of his soul. And later on I seemed to see his collected languid manner, when he said one day, 'This lot of ivory now is really mine. The Company did not pay for it. I collected it myself at a very great personal risk. I am afraid they will try to claim it as theirs though. H'm. It is a difficult case. What do you think I ought to do—resist? Eh? I want no more than justice.' . . . He wanted no more than justice—no more than justice. I rang the bell before a mahogany door on the first floor, and while I waited he seemed to stare at me out of the glassy panel—stare with that wide and immense stare embracing, condemning, loathing all the universe. I seemed to hear the whispered cry, 'The horror! The horror!'

"The dusk was falling. I had to wait in a lofty drawing-room with three long windows from floor to ceiling that were like three luminous and bedraped columns. The bent gilt legs and backs of the furniture shone in indistinct curves. The tall marble fireplace had a cold and monumental whiteness. A grand piano stood massively in a corner; with dark gleams on the flat surfaces like a sombre and polished sarcophagus. A high door opened—closed. I rose.

"She came forward, all in black, with a pale head, floating towards me in the dusk. She was in mourning. It was more than a year since his death, more than a year since the news came; she seemed as though she would remember and mourn for ever. She took both my hands in hers and murmured, 'I had heard you were coming.' I noticed she was not very young—I mean not girlish. She had a mature capacity for fidelity, for belief, for suffering. The room seemed to have grown darker, as if all the sad light of the cloudy evening had taken refuge on her forehead. This fair hair, this pale visage, this pure brow, seemed surrounded by an ashy halo from which the dark eyes looked out at me. Their glance was guileless, profound, confident, and trustful. She carried her sorrowful head as though she were proud of that sorrow, as though she would say, I —I alone know how to mourn for him as he deserves. But while we were still shaking hands, such a look of awful desolation came upon her face that I perceived she was one of those creatures that are not the playthings of Time. For her he had died only yesterday. And, by Jove! the impression was so powerful that for me too he seemed to have died only yesterday—nay, this very minute. I saw her and him in the same instant of time—his death and her sorrow—I saw her sorrow in the very moment of his death. Do you understand? I saw them together—I heard them together. She had said, with a deep catch of the breath, 'I have survived'; while my strained ears seemed to hear distinctly, mingled with her tone of despairing regret, the summing-up whisper of his eternal condemnation. I asked myself what I was doing there, with a sensation of panic in my heart as though I had blundered into a place of cruel and absurd mysteries not fit for a human being to behold. She motioned me to a chair. We sat down. I laid the packet gently on the little table, and she put her hand over it. . . . 'You knew him well,' she murmured, after a moment of mourning silence.

"'Intimacy grows quickly out there,' I said. 'I knew him as well as it is possible for one man to know another.'

"'And you admired him,' she said. 'It was impossible to know him and not to admire him. Was it?'

"'He was a remarkable man,' I said unsteadily. Then before the appealing fixity of her gaze, that seemed to watch for more words on my lips, I went on, 'It was impossible not to——'

"'Love him,' she finished eagerly, silencing me into an appalled dumbness. 'How true! how true! But when you think that no one knew him so well as I! I had all his noble confidence. I knew him best.'

"'You knew him best,' I repeated. And perhaps she did. But with every word spoken the room was growing darker, and only her forehead, smooth and white, remained illumined by the unextinguishable light of belief and love.

"'You were his friend,' she went on. 'His friend,' she repeated, a little louder. 'You must have been, if he had given you this, and sent you to me. I feel I can speak to you—and oh! I must speak. I want you—you who have heard his last words—to know I have been worthy of him. . . . It is not pride. . . . Yes! I am proud to know I understood him better than any one on earth—he told me so himself. And since his mother died I have had no one—no one —to—to——'

"I listened. The darkness deepened. I was not even sure whether he had given me the right bundle. I rather suspect he wanted me to take care of another batch of his papers which, after his death, I saw the manager examining under the lamp. And the girl talked, easing her pain in the certitude of my sympathy; she talked as thirsty men drink. I had heard that her engagement with Kurtz had been disapproved by her people. He wasn't rich enough or some-thing. And indeed I don't know whether he had not been a pauper all his life. He had given me some reason to infer that it was his impatience of comparative poverty that drove him out there.

" '. . . Who was not his friend who had heard him speak once?' she was saying. 'He drew men towards him by what was best in them.' She looked at me with intensity. 'It is the gift of the great,' she went on, and the sound of her low voice seemed to have the accompaniment of all the other sounds, full of mystery, desolation, and sorrow, I had ever heard—the ripple of the river, the soughing of the trees swayed by the wind, the murmurs of the crowd, the faint ring of incomprehensible words cried from afar, the whisper of a voice speaking from beyond the threshold of an eternal darkness. 'But you have heard him! You know!' she cried.

" 'Yes, I know,' I said with something like despair in my heart, but bowing my head before the faith that was in her, before that great and saving illusion that shone with an unearthly glow in the darkness, in the triumphant darkness from which I could not have defended her—from which I could not even defend myself.

" 'What a loss to me—to us!'—she corrected herself with beauti-ful generosity; then added in a murmur, 'To the world.' By the last gleams of twilight I could see the glitter of her eyes, full of tears—of tears that would not fall.

" 'I have been very happy—very fortunate—very proud,' she went on. 'Too fortunate. Too happy for a little while. And now I am unhappy for—for life.'

"She stood up; her fair hair seemed to catch all the remaining light in a glimmer of gold. I rose too.

" 'And of all this,' she went on mournfully, 'of all his promise, and of all his greatness, of his generous mind, of his noble heart, nothing remains—nothing but a memory. You and I—'

" 'We shall always remember him,' I said hastily.

" 'No!' she cried. 'It is impossible that all this should be lost— that such a life should be sacrificed to leave nothing—but sorrow. You know what vast plans he had. I knew of them too—I could not perhaps understand—but others knew of them. Something must remain. His words, at least, have not died.'

" 'His words will remain,' I said.

" 'And his example,' she whispered to herself. 'Men looked up to him—his goodness shone in every act. His example——'

" 'True,' I said; 'his example too. Yes, his example. I forgot that.'

" 'But I do not. I cannot—I cannot believe—not yet. I cannot believe that I shall never see him again, that nobody will see him again, never, never, never.'

"She put out her arms as if after a retreating figure, stretching them back and with clasped pale hands across the fading and narrow sheen of the window. Never see him! I saw him clearly enough then. I shall see this eloquent phantom as long as I live, and I shall see her too, a tragic and familiar Shade, resembling in this gesture another one, tragic also, and bedecked with powerless charms, stretching bare brown arms over the glitter of the infernal stream, the stream of darkness. She said suddenly very low, 'He died as he lived.'

" 'His end,' said I, with dull anger stirring in me, 'was in every way worthy of his life.'

" 'And I was not with him,' she murmured. My anger subsided before a feeling of infinite pity.

" 'Everything that could be done——' I mumbled.

" 'Ah, but I believed in him more than any one on earth—more than his own mother, more than—himself. He needed me! Me! I would have treasured every sigh, every word, every sign, every glance.'

"I felt like a chill grip on my chest. 'Don't' I said, in a muffled voice.

" 'Forgive me. I—I—have mourned so long in silence—in silence. . . . You were with him—to the last? I think of his loneliness. Nobody near to understand him as I would have understood. Perhaps no one to hear . . .'

" 'To the very end.' I said shakily. 'I heard his very last words. . . .' I stopped in a fright.

" 'Repeat them,' she murmured in a heart-broken tone. 'I want —I want—something—something—to—to live with.'

"I was on the point of crying at her. 'Don't you hear them?' The dusk was repeating them in a persistent whisper all around us, in a whisper that seemed to swell menacingly like the first whisper of a rising wind. 'The horror! The horror!'

" 'His last word—to live with,' she insisted. 'Don't you understand I loved him—I loved him—I loved him!'

"I pulled myself together and spoke slowly.

" 'The last word he pronounced was—your name.'

"I heard a light sigh and then my heart stood still, stopped dead short by an exulting and terrible cry, by the cry of inconceivable triumph and of unspeakable pain. 'I knew it—I was sure! . . . She knew. She was sure. I heard her weeping; she had hidden her face in her hands. It seemed to me that the house would collapse before I could escape, that the heavens would fall upon my head. But nothing happened. The heavens do not fall for such a trifle. Would they have fallen, I wonder, if I had rendered Kurtz that justice which was his due? Hadn't he said he wanted only justice? But I couldn't. I could not tell her. It would have been too dark—too dark altogether. . . ."[1]

Marlow ceased, and sat apart, indistinct and silent, in the pose of a meditating Buddha. Nobody moved for a time. "We have lost the first of the ebb," said the Director suddenly. I raised my head. The offing was barred by a black bank of clouds, and the tranquil waterway leading to the uttermost ends of the earth flowed somber under an overcast sky—seemed to lead into the heart of an immense darkness.

1899   1902

1. Writing to William Blackwood (editor of *Blackwood's Magazine*, where the story first appeared) in May 1902, Conrad referred to "the last pages of Heart of Darkness where the interview of the man and the girl locks in—as it were—the whole 30,000 words of narrative description into one suggestive view of a whole phase of life, and makes of that story something quite on another plane than an anecdote of a man who went mad in the Centre of Africa" (Joseph Conrad, *Letters to William Blackwood and David S. Meldrum*, ed. William Blackburn, 1958).

WILLIAM BUTLER YEATS
(1865–1939)

1891: Organization of the Rhymers' Club.
1899: Launching of the Irish National Theatre.
1914: *Responsibilities*.
1923: Nobel Prize.
1928: *The Tower*.

William Butler Yeats was born in Sandymount, Dublin. His father's family, of English stock, had been in Ireland for at least 200 years; his mother's, the Pollexfens, hailing originally from Devon, had been for some generations in Sligo, in the west of Ireland. J. B. Yeats, his father, had abandoned the law to take up painting, at which he made a somewhat precarious living. The Yeatses were in London from 1874 until 1883, when they returned to Ireland—to Howth, a few miles from Dublin. On leaving high school in Dublin in 1883 Yeats decided to be an artist, with poetry as his avocation, and attended art school; but he soon left, to concentrate on poetry. His first published poems appeared in the *Dublin University Review* in 1885.

Yeats's father was a religious skeptic, but he believed in the "religion of art." Yeats himself, religious by temperament but unable to believe in Christian orthodoxy, sought all his life for traditions of esoteric thought that would compensate for a lost religion. This search led him to various kinds of mysticism, to folklore, theosophy, spiritualism, and Neo-Platonism—not in any strict chronological order, for he kept returning to and reworking earlier aspects of his thought. In middle life he elaborated a symbolic system of his own, based on a variety of sources, which enabled him to strengthen the pattern and coherence of his poetic imagery. The student of Yeats is constantly coming up against this willful and sometimes baffling esotericism which he cultivated sometimes playfully, sometimes earnestly, sometimes treating it as though it were a body of truths and sometimes as though it were a convenient language of symbols. Modern scholarship has traced most of Yeats's mystical and quasi-mystical ideas to sources that were common to Blake and Shelley and which sometimes go far back into pre-Platonic beliefs and traditions. But his greatness as a poet lies in his ability to communicate the power and significance of his symbols, by the way he expresses and organizes them, even to readers who know nothing of his system.

Yeats's childhood and young manhood were spent between Dublin, London, and Sligo, and each of these places contributed something to his poetic development. In London in the 1890's he met the important poets of the day, and in 1891 was one of the founders of the Rhymers' Club, whose members included Lionel Johnson, Ernest Dowson, and many other characteristic figures of the 90's. Here he acquired ideas of poetry which were vaguely Pre-Raphaelite: he believed, in this early stage of his career, that a poet's language should be dreamy, evocative, and ethereal. From the countryside around Sligo he got something much more vigorous and earthy—a knowledge of the life of the peasantry and of their folklore. In Dublin he was influenced by the currents of Irish nationalism and, while often in disagreement with those who wished to use literature for crude political ends, he nevertheless learned to see his poetry as a contribution to a rejuvenated Irish culture. The three influences of Dublin, London, and Sligo did not develop in chronological order—he was going to and fro between these places throughout his early life—and we sometimes find a poem based on Sligo folklore in the midst of a group of dreamy poems written under the influence of the Rhymers' Club or an echo of Irish nationalist feeling in a lyric otherwise wholly Pre-Raphaelite in tone.

We can distinguish quite clearly, however, the main periods into which Yeats's poetic career falls. He began in the tradition of self-conscious romanticism which he learned from the London poets of the 90's. Spenser and Shelley, and a little later Blake, were also important influences. One of his early verse plays ends with a song:

> The woods of Arcady are dead
> And over is their antique joy;
> Of old the world on dreaming fed;
> Gray Truth is now her painted toy.

About the same time he was writing poems (e.g., *The Stolen Child*) deriving from his Sligo experience, with a quiet precision of natural imagery, country place names, and themes from folklore. A little later—i.e., in the latter part of his first period—Dublin literary circles sent him to Standish O'Grady's *History of Ireland: Heroic Period*, where he found the great stories of the heroic age of Irish history, and to George Sigerson's and Douglas Hyde's translations of Gaelic poetry into "that dialect which gets from Gaelic its syntax and keeps its still partly Tudor vocabulary." Even when he plays with Neo-Platonic ideas, as in *The Rose of the World* (also the product of the latter part of his early period), he can link them with Irish heroic themes and so give a dignity and a *style* to his imagery not normally associated with this sort of poetic dreaminess. Thus the heroic legends of old Ireland and the folk traditions of the modern Irish countryside provided Yeats with a stiffening for his early dreamlike imagery, which is why even his first, "90's" phase is productive of interesting poems. *The Lake Isle of Innisfree*, spoiled for some by overanthologizing, is nevertheless a fine poem of its kind: it is the clarity and control shown in the handling of the imagery which keeps all romantic fuzziness out of it and gives it its haunting quality. In *The Man Who Dreamed of Faeryland* he makes something peculiarly effective out of the contrast between human activities and the strangeness of nature. In *The Madness of King Goll* the disturbing sense of the *otherness* of the natural world drives the king mad. (Such contrasts are common in the early Yeats; in his later poetry he tries to resolve what he called these "antinomies" in inclusive symbols. See, for example, *Crazy Jane Talks to the Bishop*.)

It is important to realize that Yeats had a habit of revising his earlier poems in later printings, tightening up the language and getting rid of the more self-indulgent romantic imagery. The revised versions are found in his *Collected Poems*, which therefore present a somewhat muted picture of his poetic development. For the complete picture one should consult the Variorum Edition edited by Peter Allt and Russell K. Alspach, 1957.

It was Irish nationalism that first sent Yeats in search of a consistently simpler and more popular style. He tells in one of his autobiographical essays how he sought for a style in which to express the elemental facts about Irish life and aspirations. This led him to the concrete image, as did Hyde's translations from Gaelic folk songs, in which "nothing * * * was abstract, nothing worn-out." But other forces were also working on him. He began to feel more and more that his earlier poetic styles could not speak for the whole self. Looking back in 1906, he found that he had mistaken the poetic ideal. "Without knowing it, I had come to care for nothing but impersonal beauty. * * * We should ascend out of common interests, the thoughts of the newspapers, of the market place, but only so far as we can carry the normal, passionate, reasoning self, the personality as a whole." The result of the abandonment of "impersonal beauty," and of the desire to "carry the normal, passionate, reasoning self" into his poetry, is seen in the volumes of collected poems, *In the Seven Woods* (1903) and *The Green Helmet and Other Poems* (1910). *The Folly of Being Comforted*, *Adam's Curse*, and *The Old Men Admiring Themselves* are from the former of these, and one can see immediately how Yeats here combines the colloquial with the formal. This is characteristic of his "second period."

By this time Yeats had met the beautiful actress and violent Irish nationalist Maud Gonne, with whom he was desperately in love for many years, but who persistently refused to marry him. This affair is reflected in many of the poems of his second period, notably *No Second Troy*, published in *The Green Helmet*. He had also met Lady Gregory, Irish writer and promoter of Irish literature, in 1896 and she invited him to spend the following summer at her country house, Coole Park, in Galway. Yeats spent many holidays with Lady Gregory and discovered the attractiveness of the "country house ideal," seeing in an aristocratic life of elegance and leisure in a great house a method of imposing order on chaos and a symbol of the Neo-Platonic dance of life. He expresses this view many times in his poetry—e.g., at the end of *A Prayer for My Daughter*—and it became an important part of Yeats's complex of attitudes. The middle classes, with their Philistine money-grubbing, he detested, and for his ideal characters he looked either below them, to peasants and beggars, or above them, to the aristocracy, for each of these had their own traditions and lived according to them.

It was under Lady Gregory's influence that Yeats became involved in the founding of the Irish National Theatre in 1899. This led to his active participation in problems of play production, which included political problems of censorship, economic problems of paying carpenters and actors, and other aspects of "theater business, management of men." All this had an effect on his style. The reactions of Dublin audiences did not encourage Yeats's trust in popular judgment, and his bitterness with the "Paudeens," middle-class shopkeepers—who seemed to him to be without any dignity, or understanding, or nobility of spirit—produced some of the most effective poems (e.g., *September 1913* and *To a Shade*) of his third or middle period. This period is best represented by the volume *Responsibilities* (1914), whose title is significant of the change in Yeats's view of the poetic function. Yeats was now becoming more and more of a public figure. In 1922 he was appointed a senator of the recently established Irish Free State and served until 1928, playing an active part not only in promoting the arts but also in general political affairs, in which he supported the views of the Protestant landed class.

Meanwhile Yeats was responding in his own way to the change in poetic taste represented in the poetry and criticism of Ezra Pound and T. S. Eliot immediately before World War I. A gift for epigram had already begun to emerge in his poetry: in the volume entitled *The Wild Swans at Coole* (1919) he has a poem citing Walter Savage Landor (the 19th-century poet who wrote some fine lapidary verse) and John Donne as masters. To the precision, and the combination of colloquial and formal, which he had achieved early in the century, he now added a "metaphysical" as well as an epigrammatic element, and this is seen in the later poems of his third period. He also continued his experiments with different kinds of rhythm. At the same time he was continuing his search for a language of symbols and pursuing his esoteric studies. Yeats married in 1917, and his wife proved so sympathetic to his imaginative needs that the automatic writing which she produced (believed by Yeats to have been dictated by spirits, but apparently faked by Mrs. Yeats to help her husband) gave him the elements of a symbolic system which he later worked out in his book *A Vision* (1925, 1937) and which he used in all sorts of ways in much of his later poetry. The system was both a theory of the movements of history and a theory of the different types of personality, each movement and type being related in various complicated ways to a different phase of the moon. Some of Yeats's poetry is unintelligible without a knowledge of *A Vision;* but the better poems, such as the two on Byzantium, can be appreciated without such knowledge by the experienced reader who responds sensitively to the patterning of the imagery reinforced by the incantatory effect of the rhythms. Some recent criticism decries attempts by those who are not experts in the background of Yeats's esoteric thought to discuss his poetry and insists that only a detailed knowledge of Yeats's sources can yield his poetic meaning; but while it is true that some particular images do not yield all their significance to whose who are ignorant of the background, it is also true that too literal a paraphase of the symbolism in the light of the sources robs the poems of their power by reducing them to mere exercises in the use of a code.

The Tower (1928) and *The Winding Stair* (1933), from which the poems from *Sailing to Byzantium* through *After Long Silence* have been here selected, represent the mature Yeats at his very best—a realist-symbolist-metaphysical poet with an uncanny power over words. These volumes represent his fourth and greatest period. Here, in his poems of the 1920's and 1930's, winding stairs, spinning tops, "gyres," spirals of all kinds, are important symbols; not only are they connected with Yeats's philosophy of history and of personality, but they also serve as a means of resolving some of those contraries that had arrested him from the beginning. Life is a journey up a spiral staircase; as we grow older we cover the ground we have covered before, only higher up; as we look down the winding stair below us we measure our progress by the number of places where we were but no longer are. The journey is both repetitious and progressive; we go both round and upward Through symbolic images of this kind Yeats explores the paradoxes of time and change, of growth and identity, of love and age, of life and art, of madness and wisdom.

The Byzantium poems show Yeats trying to escape from the turbulence of life to the calm eternity of art. But in his fifth and final period he returned to the turbulence after (if only partly as a result of) undergoing the Steinach glandular operations in 1934, and his last poems have a controlled yet startling wildness. Yeats's return to life, to "the foul rag-and-bone shop of the heart," is one of the most impressive final phases of any poet's career. "I shall be a sinful man to the end, and think upon my deathbed of all the nights I wasted in my youth," he wrote in old age to a correspondent, and in his very last letter he wrote: "When I try to put all into a phrase I say, 'Man can embody truth but he cannot know it.' * * * The abstract is not life and everywhere draws out its contradictions. You can refute Hegel but not the Saint or the Song of Sixpence." When he died in January, 1939, he left a body of verse which, in variety and power, makes him beyond question the greatest 20th-century poet of the English language.

The Madness of King Goll[1]

I sat on cushioned otter skin:
My word was law from Ith to Emain,
And shook at Inver Amergin [2]
The hearts of the world-troubling seamen,
And drove tumult and war away   5
From girl and boy and man and beast;
The fields grew fatter day by day,
The wild fowl of the air increased;
And every ancient Ollave [3] said,
While he bent down his fading head,   10
"He drives away the Northern cold."
They will not hush, the leaves a-flutter round me, the
    beech leaves old.

I sat and mused and drank sweet wine;
A herdsman came from inland valleys,
Crying, the pirates drove his swine   15
To fill their dark-beaked hollow galleys.
I called my battle-breaking men
And my loud brazen battle cars
From rolling vale and rivery glen;
And under the blinking of the stars   20
Fell on the pirates by the deep,
And hurled them in the gulph of sleep:
These hands won many a torque of gold.
They will not hush, the leaves a-flutter round me, the
    beech leaves old.

But slowly, as I shouting slew   25
And trampled in the bubbling mire,
In my most secret spirit grew
A whirling and a wandering fire:
I stood: keen stars above me shone,
Around me shone keen eyes of men: 30
I laughed aloud and hurried on
By rocky shore and rushy fen;
I laughed because birds fluttered by,
And starlight gleamed, and clouds flew high,
And rushes waved and waters rolled.   35
They will not hush, the leaves a-flutter round me, the
    beech leaves old.

1. Yeats's first poem to be published in England (in *The Leisure Hour*, September, 1887). Its original title was *King Goll, An Irish Legend*. Like most of Yeats's early poems, the text was later much revised, and it is the revised version that is printed here. (In all cases of revision, we print the version revised by Yeats for his *Collected Poems*.) The legend tells of an ancient Irish king, who went mad and hid himself in a valley near Cork, where all the madmen of Ireland were believed to wish to gather if they were free. Yeats's father painted his son (in the latter's words) "as King Goll, tearing the strings out of a harp, being insane with youth."
2. The ancient Irish place names evoke the old heroic legends of Ireland. Emain, said to have been founded by Queen Macha of the Golden Hair (3rd or 4th century B.C.), was in County Armagh (Armagh-Ard-macha, hill of Macha); it is now Navan Rath.
3. Learned man.

And now I wander in the woods
When summer gluts the golden bees,
Or in autumnal solitudes
Arise the leopard-colored trees;
Or when along the wintry strands   40
The cormorants shiver on their rocks;
I wander on, and wave my hands,
And sing, and shake my heavy locks.
The gray wolf knows me; by one ear
I lead along the woodland deer;   45
The hares run by me growing bold.
They will not hush, the leaves a-flutter round me, the
  beech leaves old.

I came upon a little town
That slumbered in the harvest moon,
And passed a-tiptoe up and down,   50
Murmuring, to a fitful tune,
How I have followed, night and day,
A tramping of tremendous feet,
And saw where this old tympan lay   55
Deserted on a doorway seat,
And bore it to the woods with me;
Of some inhuman misery
Our married voices wildly trolled.
They will not hush, the leaves a-flutter round me, the
  beech leaves old.   60

I sang how, when day's toil is done,
Orchil shakes out her long dark hair
That hides away the dying sun
And sheds faint odors through the air:
When my hand passed from wire to wire   65
It quenched, with sound like falling dew,
The whirling and the wandering fire;
But lift a mournful ulalu,
For the kind wires are torn and still,
And I must wander wood and hill   70
Through summer's heat and winter's cold.
They will not hush, the leaves a-flutter round me, the
  beech leaves old.

1887, 1888

The Stolen Child

Where dips the rocky highland
Of Sleuth Wood [4] in the lake,
There lies a leafy island

4. This and other places mentioned in
the poem are in County Sligo, in northwestern Ireland, where Yeats spent much
of his childhood.

Where flapping herons wake
The drowsy water rats;
There we've hid our faery vats,
Full of berries
And of reddest stolen cherries.
Come away, O human child!
To the waters and the wild
With a faery, hand in hand,
For the world's more full of weeping than you can understand.

Where the wave of moonlight glosses
The dim gray sands with light,
Far off by furthest Rosses
We foot it all the night,
Weaving olden dances
Mingling hands and mingling glances
Till the moon has taken flight;
To and fro we leap
And chase the frothy bubbles,
While the world is full of troubles
And is anxious in its sleep.
Come away, O human child!
To the waters and the wild
With a faery, hand in hand,
For the world's more full of weeping than you can understand.

Where the wandering water gushes
From the hills above Glen-Car,
In pools among the rushes
That scarce could bathe a star,
We seek for slumbering trout
And whispering in their ears
Give them unquiet dreams;
Leaning softly out
From ferns that drop their tears
Over the young streams.
Come away, O human child!
To the waters and the wild
With a faery, hand in hand,
For the world's more full of weeping than you can understand.

Away with us he's going,
The solemn-eyed:
He'll hear no more the lowing
Of the calves on the warm hillside
Or the kettle on the hob
Sing peace into his breast,
Or see the brown mice bob
Round and round the oatmeal chest.
For he comes, the human child,
To the waters and the wild

5

10

15

20

25

30

35

40

45

50

With a faery, hand in hand,
From a world more full of weeping than he can understand.

1886, 1889

Down by the Salley Gardens[5]

Down by the salley gardens my love and I did meet;
She passed the salley gardens with little snow-white feet.
She bid me take love easy, as the leaves grow on the tree;
But I, being young and foolish, with her would not agree.

In a field by the river my love and I did stand,   5
And on my leaning shoulder she laid her snow-white hand.
She bid me take life easy, as the grass grows on the weirs;
But I was young and foolish, and now am full of tears.

1889

The Rose of the World[1]

Who dreamed that beauty passes like a dream?
For these red lips, with all their mournful pride,
Mournful that no new wonder may betide,
Troy passed away in one high funeral gleam,
And Usna's children died.[2]   5

We and the laboring world are passing by:
Amid men's souls, that waver and give place
Like the pale waters in their wintry race,
Under the passing stars, foam of the sky,
Lives on this lonely face.   10

Bow down, archangels, in your dim abode:
Before you were, or any hearts to beat,
Weary and kind one lingered by His seat;
He made the world to be a grassy road
Before her wandering feet.   15

1892

5. Originally entitled *An Old Song Re-sung*, with Yeats's footnote: "This is an attempt to reconstruct an old song from three lines imperfectly remembered by an old peasant woman in the village of Ballysodare, Sligo, who often sings them to herself." "Salley" is a variant of "sallow," a species of willow tree.
1. The Platonic Idea of eternal Beauty. "I notice upon reading these poems for the first time for several years that the quality symbolized as The Rose differs from the Intellectual Beauty of Shelley and of Spenser in that I have imagined it as suffering with man and not as something pursued and seen from afar" (Yeats, in 1925).
2. In Old Irish legend, the Ulster warrior Naoise, son of Usna or Usnach (pronounced *Úshna*), carried off the beautiful Deirdre, whom King Conchubar of Ulster had intended to marry, and with his two brothers took her to Scotland. Eventually Conchubar lured the four of them back to Ireland and killed the three brothers.

The Lake Isle of Innisfree[3]

I will arise and go now, and go to Innisfree,
And a small cabin build there, of clay and wattles[4] made:
Nine bean-rows will I have there, a hive for the honeybee,
And live alone in the bee-loud glade.

And I shall have some peace there, for peace comes dropping slow,   5
Dropping from the veils of the morning to where the cricket sings;
There midnight's all a glimmer, and noon a purple glow,
And evening full of the linnet's wings.

I will arise and go now, for always night and day
I hear lake water lapping with low sounds by the shore;   10
While I stand on the roadway, or on the pavements gray,
I hear it in the deep heart's core.

                                                    1890, 1892

The Sorrow of Love

The brawling of a sparrow in the eaves,
The brilliant moon and all the milky sky,
And all that famous harmony of leaves,
Had blotted out man's image and his cry.

A girl arose that had red mournful lips   5
And seemed the greatness of the world in tears,
Doomed like Odysseus and the laboring ships
And proud as Priam murdered with his peers;[5]

Arose, and on the instant clamorous eaves,
A climbing moon upon an empty sky,   10
And all that lamentation of the leaves,
Could but compose man's image and his cry.

                                                    1892

When You Are Old[6]

When you are old and gray and full of sleep,
And nodding by the fire, take down this book,

---

3. Island in Lough Gill, County Sligo. "My father had read to me some passage out of [Thoreau's] *Walden*, and I planned to live some day in a cottage on a little island called Innisfree * * * "
4. Stakes interwoven with twigs or branches.
5. Odysseus (whom the Romans called Ulysses), hero of Homer's *Odyssey* which describes how, after having fought in the siege of Troy, he wandered for ten years before reaching his home, the Greek island of Ithaca. Priam was king of Troy at the time of the siege and was killed when the Greeks captured the city.
6. A poem suggested by a sonnet of the 16th-century French poet Pierre de Ronsard; it begins *"Quand vous serez bien vieille, au soir, à la chandelle"* ("When you are old, sitting at evening by candle light"), but ends very differently from Yeats's poem.

And slowly read, and dream of the soft look
Your eyes had once, and of their shadows deep;

How many loved your moments of glad grace,   5
And loved your beauty with love false or true,
But one man loved the pilgrim soul in you,
And loved the sorrows of your changing face;

And bending down beside the glowing bars,
Murmur, a little sadly, how Love fled   10
And paced upon the mountains overhead
And hid his face amid a crowd of stars.

                                        1892

Who Goes with Fergus?[7]

Who will go drive with Fergus now,
And pierce the deep wood's woven shade,
And dance upon the level shore?
Young man, lift up your russet brow,
And lift your tender eyelids, maid,   5
And brood on hopes and fear no more.

And no more turn aside and brood
Upon love's bitter mystery;
For Fergus rules the brazen cars,
And rules the shadows of the wood,   10
And the white breast of the dim sea
And all disheveled wandering stars.

                                        1893

The Man Who Dreamed of Faeryland

He stood among a crowd at Dromahair;[8]
His heart hung all upon a silken dress,
And he had known at last some tenderness,
Before earth took him to her stony care;
But when a man poured fish into a pile,   5
It seemed they raised their little silver heads,
And sang what gold morning or evening sheds
Upon a woven world-forgotten isle
Where people love beside the raveled[9] seas;

7. In a late version of this Irish heroic legend, Fergus, "king of the proud Red Branch Kings," gave up his throne voluntarily to Conchubar to learn by dreaming and meditating the bitter wisdom of the poet and philosopher. This poem is quoted by Buck Mulligan in *Ulysses*, and a line of it also comes into Stephen Dedalus' mind.
8. This and other place names in the poem refer to places in County Sligo.
9. Tangled; hence here "turbulent."

That Time can never mar a lover's vows   10
Under that woven changeless roof of boughs:
The singing shook him out of his new ease.

He wandered by the sands of Lissadell;
His mind ran all on money cares and fears,
And he had known at last some prudent years   15
Before they heaped his grave under the hill;
But while he passed before a plashy place,
A lugworm with its gray and muddy mouth
Sang that somewhere to north or west or south
There dwelt a gay, exulting, gentle race   20
Under the golden or the silver skies;
That if a dancer stayed his hungry foot
It seemed the sun and moon were in the fruit:
And at that singing he was no more wise.

He mused beside the well of Scanavin,   25
He mused upon his mockers: without fail
His sudden vengeance were a country tale,
When earthy night had drunk his body in;
But one small knotgrass growing by the pool
Sang where—unnecessary cruel voice—   30
Old silence bids its chosen race rejoice,
Whatever raveled waters rise and fall
Or stormy silver fret the gold of day,
And midnight there enfold them like a fleece
And lover there by lover be at peace.   35
The tale drove his fine angry mood away.

He slept under the hill of Lugnagall;
And might have known at last unhaunted sleep
Under that cold and vapor-turbaned steep,
Now that the earth had taken man and all: 40
Did not the worms that spired about his bones
Proclaim with that unwearied, reedy cry
That God has laid his fingers on the sky,
That from those fingers glittering summer runs
Upon the dancer by the dreamless wave.   45
Why should those lovers that no lovers miss
Dream, until God burn Nature with a kiss?
The man has found no comfort in the grave.

1891, 1892

The Secret Rose[1]

Far-off, most secret, and inviolate Rose,
Enfold me in my hour of hours; where those

---

1. **The Rose is a symbol of beauty** (see "The Rose of the World," below), and in this poem "this spiritual beauty was seen as part of Yeats's own belief that there would be a revelation due to the creation of Celtic mysteries (and a complete understanding between Yeats and Maud Gonne)" [A. N. Jeffares]. Yeats

Who sought thee in the Holy Sepulcher,
Or in the wine-vat, dwell beyond the stir
And tumult of defeated dreams; and deep   5
Among pale eyelids, heavy with the sleep
Men have named beauty. Thy great leaves enfold
The ancient beards, the helms of ruby and gold
Of the crowned Magi;[2] and the king whose eyes
Saw the Pierced Hands and Rood of elder rise   10
In Druid vapor and make the torches dim;
Till vain frenzy awoke and he died;[3] and him
Who met Fand walking among flaming dew
By a gray shore where the wind never blew,
And lost the world and Emer for a kiss;[4]   15
And him who drove the gods out of their liss,[5]
And till a hundred morns had flowered red
Feasted, and wept the barrows of his dead;
And the proud dreaming king who flung the crown
And sorrow away, and calling bard and clown   20
Dwelt among wine-stained wanderers in deep woods;[6]
And him who sold tillage, and house, and goods,
And sought through lands and islands numberless years,
Until he found, with laughter and with tears,
A woman of so shining loveliness   25
That men threshed corn at midnight by a tress,
A little stolen tress.[7] I, too, await

reveals how he used his sources in an interesting note: "I find that I have unintentionally changed the old story of Conchubar's death. He did not see the Crucifixion in a vision but was told of it * * * I have imagined Cuchulain meeting Fand 'walking among the flaming dew,' because, I think, of something in Mr. Standish O'Grady's books. [See above, p. 1563.] I have founded the man 'who drove the gods out of their liss,' or fort, upon something I have read about Caoilte after the battle of Gabhra, when almost all his companions were killed, driving the gods out of their liss, * * * I have founded 'the proud dreaming king' upon Fergus, the son of Rogh, but when I wrote my poem here, and in the song in my early book, 'Who will drive with Fergus now?' I only knew him in Mr. Standish O'Grady. * * * I have founded 'him who sold tillage, and house, and goods,' upon something in 'The Red Pony,' a folktale in Mr. Larminie's *West Irish Folk Tales*. A young man 'saw a light before him on the high-road. When he came as far, there was an open box on the road, and a light coming up out of it. He took up the box. There was a lock of hair in it. Presently he had to go to become the servant of a king for his living. There were eleven boys. When they were going out into the stable at ten o'clock, each of them took a light but he. He took no candle at all with

him. Each of them went into his own stable. When he went into his stable he opened the box. He left it in a hole in the wall. The light was great. It was twice as much as in the other stables.' The king hears of it, and makes him show him the box. The king says, 'You must go and bring me the woman to whom the hair belongs.' In the end the young man, and not the king, marries the woman."

2. The Magi are of course the "wise men" from the East who came to do homage to the infant Jesus. Mrs. Yeats told T. R. Henn that the image in lines 7–9 was "perhaps based on Botticelli's 'Adoration of the Magi,' with a Pre-Raphaelite overlay."

3. King Conchubar, in early Christian legend, is said to have died on the day of Christ's crucifixion in a fit of rage at hearing the news. Yeats, as his note explains, makes Conchubar see the crucifixion in a vision raised by the magic of the ancient Celtic priests, or Druids. The "Pierced Hands" are, of course, Christ's, and the "Rood" is the Cross.

4. The ancient Irish hero Cuchulain was seduced by Fand away from his wife Emer.

5. Fort. This is Caoilte, legendary Irish hero and companion of Oisin, son of Finn, poet and warrior.

6. The "proud dreaming king" is Fergus. See Yeats's note.

7. Yeats describes this tale in his note.

The hour of thy great wind of love and hate.
When shall the stars be blown about the sky,
Like the sparks blown out of a smithy, and die?   30
Surely thine hour has come, thy great wind blows,
Far-off, most secret, and inviolate Rose?

                                        1896, 1897

The Folly of Being Comforted

One that is ever kind said yesterday:
"Your well-beloved's hair has threads of gray,
And little shadows come about her eyes;
Time can but make it easier to be wise
Though now it seem impossible, and so   5
All that you need is patience."

                              Heart cries, "No,
I have not a crumb of comfort, not a grain.
Time can but make her beauty over again:
Because of that great nobleness of hers
The fire that stirs about her, when she stirs,   10
Burns but more clearly. O she had not these ways
When all the wild summer was in her gaze."

O heart! O heart! if she'd but turn her head,
You'd know the folly of being comforted.

                                        1902, 1903

Adam's Curse[1]

We sat together at one summer's end,
That beautiful mild woman, your close friend,
And you and I, and talked of poetry.
I said: "A line will take us hours maybe;
Yet if it does not seem a moment's thought,   5
Our stitching and unstitching has been naught.
Better go down upon your marrowbones
And scrub a kitchen pavement, or break stones
Like an old pauper, in all kinds of weather;
For to articulate sweet sounds together   10
Is to work harder than all these, and yet
Be thought an idler by the noisy set
Of bankers, schoolmasters, and clergymen
The martyrs call the world."

1. To work for a living was the curse imposed by God upon Adam after the Fall (see Genesis iii.17–19). The poem reflects an incident in Yeats's passionate but hopeless love for the beautiful actress Maud Gonne (see A. N. Jeffares, *W. B. Yeats: Man and Poet*, 1949, pp. 128–29).

And thereupon   15
That beautiful mild woman for whose sake
There's many a one shall find out all heartache
On finding that her voice is sweet and low
Replied: "To be born woman is to know—
Although they do not talk of it at school—   20
That we must labor to be beautiful."

I said: "It's certain there is no fine thing
Since Adam's fall but needs much laboring.
There have been lovers who thought love should be
So much compounded of high courtesy   25
That they would sigh and quote with learned looks
Precedents out of beautiful old books;
Yet now it seems an idle trade enough."

We sat grown quiet at the name of love;
We saw the last embers of daylight die,
And in the trembling blue-green of the sky   30
A moon, worn as if it had been a shell
Washed by time's waters as they rose and fell
About the stars and broke in days and years.

I had a thought for no one's but your ears: 35
That you were beautiful, and that I strove
To love you in the old high way of love;
That it had all seemed happy, and yet we'd grown
As weary-hearted as that hollow moon.

                                    1902, 1903

The Old Men Admiring Themselves in the Water

I heard the old, old men say,
"Everything alters,
And one by one we drop away."
They had hands like claws, and their knees
Were twisted like the old thorn trees   5
By the waters.
I heard the old, old men say,
"All that's beautiful drifts away
Like the waters."

                                    1903

No Second Troy[1]

Why should I blame her that she filled my days
With misery, or that she would of late
Have taught to ignorant men most violent ways,
Or hurled the little streets upon the great,
Had they but courage equal to desire?   5

1. Another poem about Maud Gonne, who was a passionate Irish nationalist, preaching violence to achieve Irish independence (see lines 3–5).

What could have made her peaceful with a mind
That nobleness made simple as a fire,
With beauty like a tightened bow, a kind
That is not natural in an age like this,
Being high and solitary and most stern?   10
Why, what could she have done, being what she is?
Was there another Troy for her to burn?[2]

           1910

The Fascination of What's Difficult[3]

The fascination of what's difficult
Has dried the sap out of my veins, and rent
Spontaneous joy and natural content
Out of my heart. There's something ails our colt
That must, as if it had not holy blood   5
Nor on Olympus leaped from cloud to cloud,
Shiver under the lash, strain, sweat and jolt
As though it dragged road-metal. My curse on plays
That have to be set up in fifty ways,
On the day's war with every knave and dolt,   10
Theater business, management of men.
I swear before the dawn comes round again
I'll find the stable and pull out the bolt.

           1910

September 1913[4]

What need you, being come to sense,
But fumble in a greasy till
And add the halfpence to the pence
And prayer to shivering prayer, until
You have dried the marrow from the bone?   5
For men were born to pray and save:
Romantic Ireland's dead and gone,
It's with O'Leary[5] in the grave.

Yet they were of a different kind,
The names that stilled your childish play,   10
They have gone about the world like wind,
But little time had they to pray

2. Helen of Troy was, of course, the cause of the destruction of the "first" Troy. The mixture of admiration and bitterness reflected here is characteristic of many of Yeats's poems about Maud Gonne.
3. Written when Yeats was director-manager of the Abbey Theatre. "Subject. To complain of the fascination of what's difficult. It spoils spontaneity and pleasure, and wastes time. Repeat the line ending difficult three times and rhyme on bolt, exalt, colt, jolt" (Yeats's diary for September, 1909).
4. The poem reflects Yeats's disillusion with the state of the Irish national movement (for independence from Great Britain). Contrast *Easter 1916*, where the heroism of the Easter Rebellion, 1916, has led him to withdraw his criticism.
5. John O'Leary, Irish nationalist of great spirit and integrity who died in 1907.

For whom the hangman's rope was spun,
And what, God help us, could they save?
Romantic Ireland's dead and gone,   15
It's with O'Leary in the grave.

Was it for this the wild geese spread
The gray wing upon every tide;
For this that all that blood was shed,
For this Edward Fitzgerald[6] died,   20
And Robert Emmet and Wolfe Tone,
All that delirium of the brave?
Romantic Ireland's dead and gone,
It's with O'Leary in the grave.

Yet could we turn the years again,   25
And call those exiles as they were
In all their loneliness and pain,
You'd cry, "Some woman's yellow hair
Has maddened every mother's son":
They weighed so lightly what they gave.   30
But let them be, they're dead and gone,
They're with O'Leary in the grave.

                                            1913

To a Shade[1]

If you have revisited the town, thin Shade,
Whether to look upon your monument
(I wonder if the builder has been paid)
Or happier-thoughted when the day is spent
To drink of that salt breath out of the sea   5
When gray gulls flit about instead of men,
And the gaunt houses put on majesty:
Let these content you and be gone again;
For they are at their old tricks yet.

                                    A man
Of your own passionate serving kind who had brought 10
In his full hands what, had they only known,
Had given their children's children loftier thought,
Sweeter emotion, working in their veins
Like gentle blood, has been driven from the place,
And insult heaped upon him for his pains,   15

6. Lord Edward Fitzgerald (1763–98), a British officer who, after being dismissed from the army for disloyal activities, joined the United Irishmen (an Irish nationalist organization), was arrested, and died in prison. Robert Emmet (1778–1803) was also an Irish patriot, executed for treason after a heroic career. Theobald Wolfe Tone (1763–98), one of the chief founders of the United Irishmen, committed suicide in prison in Dublin.
1. I.e., the spirit of the great Irish nationalist leader, Charles Stewart Parnell (1846–91). Yeats is here expressing his disgust at the grubby materialism and Philistinism of the Dublin middle classes.

And for his openhandedness, disgrace;[2]
Your enemy, an old foul mouth, had set
The pack upon him.
                    Go, unquiet wanderer,
And gather the Glasnevin[3] coverlet
About your head till the dust stops your ear,   20
The time for you to taste of that salt breath
And listen at the corners has not come;
You had enough of sorrow before death—
Away, away! You are safer in the tomb.

1913   1913

The Cold Heaven[4]

Suddenly I saw the cold and rook-delighting heaven
That seemed as though ice burned and was but the more ice,
And thereupon imagination and heart were driven
So wild that every casual thought of that and this
Vanished, and left but memories, that should be out of season   5
With the hot blood of youth, of love crossed long ago;
And I took all the blame out of all sense and reason,
Until I cried and trembled and rocked to and fro,
Riddled with light. Ah! when the ghost begins to quicken,[5]
Confusion of the deathbed over, is it sent   10
Out naked on the roads, as the books say, and stricken
By the injustice of the skies for punishment?

                                                                 1912

The Wild Swans at Coole[1]

The trees are in their autumn beauty,
The woodland paths are dry,
Under the October twilight the water
Mirrors a still sky;
Upon the brimming water among the stones   5
Are nine-and-fifty swans.

2. Sir Hugh Lane, Lady Gregory's nephew, had collected a number of important modern French paintings which he wished to give to the city of Dublin, provided they were permanently housed in a suitable building. Fierce abuse of the paintings and of the proposed design of the gallery in the Dublin nationalist press caused Lane to send the pictures to the London National Gallery. (Lane was drowned on the *Lusitania* in 1915; after years of bitter court dispute over an unwitnessed codicil to his will bequeathing the paintings to Dublin, an arrangement was reached in 1959 for the pictures to hang first in Dublin and then in London, for five years at a time.)

3. The cemetery where Parnell is buried.

4. Yeats told Maud Gonne, in answer to her inquiry, that this poem "was an attempt to describe the feelings aroused in him by the cold and detachedly beautiful winter sky. He felt alone and responsible in that loneliness for all the past mistakes that tortured his peace of mind. It was a momentary intensity of dreamlike perception, where physical surroundings remained fixed clear in the mind, to accentuate the years of thought and reality that passed in review in an instantaneous and yet eternal suspension of time" (A. N. Jeffares).

5. Come alive.

1. I.e., Coole Park, Lady Gregory's country estate, where Yeats was a frequent guest.

The nineteenth autumn has come upon me
Since I first made my count;[2]
I saw, before I had well finished,
All suddenly mount   10
And scatter wheeling in great broken rings
Upon their clamorous wings.

I have looked upon those brilliant creatures,
And now my heart is sore.
All's changed since I, hearing at twilight,   15
The first time on this shore,
The bell-beat of their wings above my head,
Trod with a lighter tread.

Unwearied still, lover by lover,
They paddle in the cold   20
Companionable streams or climb the air;
Their hearts have not grown old;
Passion or conquest, wander where they will,
Attend upon them still.

But now they drift on the still water,   25
Mysterious, beautiful;
Among what rushes will they build,
By what lake's edge or pool
Delight men's eyes when I awake some day
To find they have flown away?

1916   1917

Easter 1916[1]

I have met them at close of day
Coming with vivid faces
From counter or desk among gray
Eighteenth-century houses.
I have passed with a nod of the head   5
Or polite meaningless words,
Or have lingered awhile and said
Polite meaningless words,
And thought before I had done
Of a mocking tale or a gibe   10
To please a companion
Around the fire at the club,
Being certain that they and I
But lived where motley is worn:

2. His first visit had been in 1897 (nineteen years earlier).

1. On Easter Sunday of 1916, Irish nationalists launched a heroic but unsuccessful revolt against the British government; the week of street fighting that followed is known as the Easter Rebellion. As a result, a number of the nationalists were executed: Britain, at war with Germany, was in no mood to tolerate Irish agitation for independence —which was supported, for obvious reasons, by Germany. Yeats knew the chief rebels personally.

All changed, changed utterly: 15
A terrible beauty is born.

That woman's days were spent
In ignorant good will,
Her nights in argument
Until her voice grew shrill.   20
What voice more sweet than hers
When, young and beautiful,
She rode to harriers?[2]
This man had kept a school
And rode our wingéd horse;[3]   25
This other his helper and friend
Was coming into his force;
He might have won fame in the end,
So sensitive his nature seemed,
So daring and sweet his thought.   30
This other man I had dreamed
A drunken, vainglorious lout.[4]
He had done most bitter wrong
To some who are near my heart,
Yet I number him in the song;   35
He, too, has resigned his part
In the casual comedy;
He, too, has been changed in his turn,
Transformed utterly:
A terrible beauty is born.   40

Hearts with one purpose alone
Through summer and winter seem
Enchanted to a stone
To trouble the living stream.
The horse that comes from the road,   45
The rider, the birds that range
From cloud to tumbling cloud,
Minute by minute they change;
A shadow of cloud on the stream
Changes minute by minute;   50
A horse-hoof slides on the brim,
And a horse plashes within it;
The long-legged moorhens dive,
And hens to moorcocks call;
Minute by minute they live: 55
The stone's in the midst of all.

Too long a sacrifice
Can make a stone of the heart.
O when may it suffice?

---

2. Constance Gore-Booth (afterwards Countess Markiewicz), a member of the Sligo county aristocracy. A gay and beautiful girl, she had annoyed Yeats by becoming an embittered nationalist.
3. Patrick Pearse, who was a schoolmaster, a leader in the movement to restore the Gaelic language in Ireland, and a poet (hence the reference to "our wingéd horse"—Pegasus, the horse of the Muses). "His helper and friend" was Thomas MacDonagh.
4. Major John MacBride. Maud Gonne, to Yeats's great disgust, had married MacBride in 1903, only to be separated from him after two years.

That is Heaven's part, our part   60
To murmur name upon name,
As a mother names her child
When sleep at last has come
On limbs that had run wild.
What is it but nightfall?   65
No, no, not night but death;
Was it needless death after all?
For England may keep faith
For all that is done and said.
We know their dream; enough   70
To know they dreamed and are dead;
And what if excess of love
Bewildered them till they died?
I write it out in a verse—
MacDonagh and MacBride   75
And Connolly[5] and Pearse
Now and in time to be,
Wherever green is worn,
Are changed, changed utterly:
A terrible beauty is born.   80

                                          1916, 1920

On a Political Prisoner[1]

She that but little patience knew,
From childhood on, had now so much
A gray gull lost its fear and flew
Down to her cell and there alit,
And there endured her fingers' touch   5
And from her fingers ate its bit.

Did she in touching that lone wing
Recall the years before her mind
Became a bitter, an abstract thing,
Her thought some popular enmity: 10
Blind and leader of the blind
Drinking the foul ditch where they lie?

When long ago I saw her ride
Under Ben Bulben[2] to the meet,
The beauty of her countryside   15
With all youth's lonely wildness stirred,
She seemed to have grown clean and sweet
Like any rock-bred, sea-borne bird:

Sea-borne, or balanced on the air
When first it sprang out of the nest   20

5. James Connolly, Pearse's partner in leading the insurrection. Like the other rebels named here, he was executed by shooting.
1. Constance Gore-Booth Markiewicz, who was imprisoned after the Easter Rebellion. She also figures in *Easter 1916*.
2. Mountain in County Sligo. The Gore-Booths lived at Lissadell, not far from Ben Bulben.

Upon some lofty rock to stare
Upon the cloudy canopy,
While under its storm-beaten breast
Cried out the hollows of the sea.

1920, 1921

The Second Coming[1]

Turning and turning in the widening gyre
The falcon cannot hear the falconer;
Things fall apart; the center cannot hold;
Mere anarchy is loosed upon the world,
The blood-dimmed tide is loosed, and everywhere   5
The ceremony of innocence is drowned;
The best lack all conviction, while the worst
Are full of passionate intensity.[2]

Surely some revelation is at hand;   10
Surely the Second Coming is at hand.
The Second Coming! Hardly are those words out
When a vast image out of *Spiritus Mundi*[3]
Troubles my sight: somewhere in sands of the desert
A shape with lion body and the head of a man,
A gaze blank and pitiless as the sun,   15
Is moving its slow thighs, while all about it
Reel shadows of the indignant desert birds.
The darkness drops again; but now I know
That twenty centuries of stony sleep
Were vexed to nightmare by a rocking cradle,[4]   20

1. This poem expresses Yeats's sense of the dissolution of the civilization of his time, the end of one cycle of history and the approach of another. He called each cycle of history a "gyre" (line 1) —literally a circular or spiral turn (Yeats pronounced it with a hard *g*). He imagines a falcon losing control of the falcon which sweeps in ever widening circles around him until it breaks away altogether, and sees this as a symbol of the end of the present gyre of civilization—what he once described as "all our scientific democratic fact-finding heterogeneous civilization." The birth of Christ brought to an end the cycle that had lasted from what Yeats called the "Babylonian mathematical starlight" (2000 B.C.) to the dissolution of Greco-Roman culture. "What if the irrational return?" Yeats asked in his prose work *A Vision*. "What if the circle begin again?" He speculates that "we may be about to accept the most implacable authority the world has known." The new Nativity ("the rough

beast" of lines 21–22) is deliberately mysterious, both terrible and regenerative.
2. Lines 4–8 refer to the Russian Revolution of 1917, seen as a portent, but later Yeats accepted the poem as an unconscious prophecy of the rise of Fascism also. Speaking in 1924, Yeats declared: "It is impossible not to ask oneself to what great task of the nations we have been summoned in this transformed world where there is so much that is obscure and terrible." "The ceremony of innocence" suggests Yeats's view of ritual as the basis of civilized living. Cf. the last stanza of *A Prayer for My Daughter.*
3. The Spirit or Soul of the Universe, with which all individual souls are connected through the "Great Memory," which Yeats held to be a universal subconscious in which the human race preserves its past memories. It is thus a source of symbolic images for the poet.
4. I.e., the cradle of the infant Christ.

And what rough beast, its hour come round at last,
Slouches towards Bethlehem to be born?

1920, 1921

A Prayer for My Daughter[1]

Once more the storm is howling, and half hid
Under this cradle-hood and coverlid
My child sleeps on. There is no obstacle
But Gregory's wood[2] and one bare hill
Whereby the haystack- and roof-leveling wind,   5
Bred on the Atlantic, can be stayed;
And for an hour I have walked and prayed
Because of the great gloom that is in my mind.

I have walked and prayed for this young child an hour
And heard the sea-wind scream upon the tower,   10
And under the arches of the bridge, and scream
In the elms above the flooded stream;
Imagining in excited reverie
That the future years had come,
Dancing to a frenzied drum,
Out of the murderous innocence of the sea.[3]   15

May she be granted beauty and yet not
Beauty to make a stranger's eye distraught,
Or hers before a looking glass, for such,
Being made beautiful overmuch,   20
Consider beauty a sufficient end,
Lose natural kindness and maybe
The heart-revealing intimacy
That chooses right, and never find a friend.

Helen being chosen found life flat and dull   25
And later had much trouble from a fool,[4]
While that great Queen, that rose out of the spray,[5]
Being fatherless could have her way
Yet chose a bandy-legged smith for man.
It's certain that fine women eat   30
A crazy salad with their meat
Whereby the Horn of Plenty[6] is undone.

1. Yeats's daughter, christened Anne Butler, was born on February 26, 1919, in the refitted Norman tower of Thoor Ballylee (Ballylee Castle) in Galway, where Yeats lived: it is not far from Coole Park. The wind from the Atlantic roared in constantly (lines 1, 5–6).
2. Originally part of the Gregory estate, which had once also included Thoor Ballylee.
3. A reference to Yeats's visions of the future (cf. *The Second Coming*).

4. Presumably Paris, who carried Helen off from her husband.
5. Venus, wife (in the *Odyssey* and later accounts) of Vulcan, "bandy-legged" god of fire and forge (line 29).
6. The traditional image of the "Horn of Plenty" is generally associated by Yeats not only with abundance of the good things of the earth but also with the good life, conceived to be based on order and elegance (see concluding lines).

In courtesy I'd have her chiefly learned;
Hearts are not had as a gift but hearts are earned
By those that are not entirely beautiful;   35
Yet many, that have played the fool
For beauty's very self, has charm made wise,
And many a poor man that has roved,
Loved and thought himself beloved,
From a glad kindness cannot take his eyes.   40

May she become a flourishing hidden tree
That all her thoughts may like the linnet[7] be,
And have no business but dispensing round
Their magnanimities of sound,
Nor but in merriment begin a chase,   45
Nor but in merriment a quarrel.
O may she live like some green laurel
Rooted in one dear perpetual place.

My mind, because the minds that I have loved,
The sort of beauty that I have approved,   50
Prosper but little, has dried up of late,
Yet knows that to be choked with hate
May well be of all evil chances chief.
If there's no hatred in a mind
Assault and battery of the wind   55
Can never tear the linnet from the leaf.

An intellectual hatred is the worst,
So let her think opinions are accursed.
Have I not seen the loveliest woman born[8]
Out of the mouth of Plenty's horn,   60
Because of her opinionated mind
Barter that horn and every good
By quiet natures understood
For an old bellows full of angry wind?

Considering that, all hatred driven hence,   65
The soul recovers radical innocence
And learns at last that it is self-delighting,
Self-appeasing, self-affrighting,
And that its own sweet will is Heaven's will;
She can, though every face should scowl   70
And every windy quarter howl
Or every bellows burst, be happy still.

And may her bridegroom bring her to a house
Where all's accustomed, ceremonious;
For arrogance and hatred are the wares   75
Peddled in the thoroughfares.
How but in custom and in ceremony
Are innocence and beauty born?

7. A small European songbird.   8. Maud Gonne.

Ceremony's a name for the rich horn,
And custom for the spreading laurel tree.   80
June, 1919   1919, 1921

Sailing to Byzantium[1]

1

That is no country for old men. The young
In one another's arms, birds in the trees
—Those dying generations—at their song,
The salmon-falls, the mackerel-crowded seas,
Fish, flesh, or fowl, commend all summer long   5
Whatever is begotten, born, and dies.
Caught in that sensual music all neglect
Monuments of unaging intellect.

2

An aged man is but a paltry thing,
A tattered coat upon a stick, unless   10
Soul clap its hands and sing, and louder sing
For every tatter in its mortal dress,
Nor is there singing school but studying
Monuments of its own magnificence;
And therefore I have sailed the seas and come   15
To the holy city of Byzantium.

3

O sages standing in God's holy fire
As in the gold mosaic of a wall,[2]
Come from the holy fire, perne in a gyre,[3]
And be the singing-masters of my soul.
Consume my heart away; sick with desire   20

1. This poem should be read together with *Byzantium*. Byzantium had become for Yeats the symbol of art or artifice as opposed to the natural world of biological activity, and as he grew older he turned away from the sensual world of growth and change to the timeless world of art (though he returned to the sensual world later on). He wrote in *A Vision:* "I think that if I could be given a month of antiquity and leave to spend it where I chose, I would spend it in Byzantium [modern Istanbul] a little before Justinian opened St. Sophia and closed the Academy of Plato [i.e., ca. A.D. 535]. * * * I think that in early Byzantium, maybe never before or since in recorded history, religious, aesthetic, and practical life were one, that architects and artificers * * * spoke to the multitude in gold and silver. The painter, the mosaic worker, the worker in gold and silver, the illuminator of sacred books were almost impersonal, almost perhaps without the consciousness of individual design, absorbed in their subject matter and that the vision of a whole people." In his old age, the poet repudiates the world of biological change (of birth, growth, and death), putting behind him images of breeding and sensuality to turn to "monuments of unaging intellect," in a world of art and artifice outside of time. The theme of this poem, though not the treatment, is similar to that of Keats's *Ode on a Grecian Urn.* Note that the stanza form is *ottava rima,* used with great originality in the placing of pauses.
2. Like the mosaic figures on the walls of the Church of Hagia Sophia ("Holy Wisdom") in Byzantium.
3. I.e., whirl round in a spiral motion. "Perne" (or "pirn") is literally a bobbin, reel, or spool, on which something is wound. It became a favorite word of Yeats's, used as a verb meaning "to spin round"; he associated the spinning with the spinning of fate. Here he asks the saints on the wall to descend in this symbolic spinning motion and help him to enter into their state.

And fastened to a dying animal
It knows not what it is; and gather me
Into the artifice of eternity.

4

Once out of nature I shall never take   25
My bodily form from any natural thing,
But such a form as Grecian goldsmiths make
Of hammered gold and gold enameling
To keep a drowsy Emperor awake;[4]
Or set upon a golden bough to sing   30
To lords and ladies of Byzantium
Of what is past, or passing, or to come.

1927   1927

Leda and the Swan[1]

A sudden blow: the great wings beating still
Above the staggering girl, her thighs caressed
By the dark webs, her nape caught in his bill,
He holds her helpless breast upon his breast.

How can those terrified vague fingers push   5
The feathered glory from her loosening thighs?
And how can body, laid in that white rush,
But feel the strange heart beating where it lies?

A shudder in the loins engenders there
The broken wall, the burning roof and tower[2]   10
And Agamemnon dead.
                              Being so caught up,
So mastered by the brute blood of the air,
Did she put on his knowledge with his power
Before the indifferent beak could let her drop?

1923   1924, 1928

4. "I have read somewhere," Yeats wrote, "that in the Emperor's palace at Byzantium was a tree made of gold and silver, and artificial birds that sang." Cf. also Hans Christian Andersen's *Emperor's Nightingale*, which may have been in Yeats's mind at the time. 1. In Greek mythology Zeus visited Leda in the form of a swan. As a result of the union Leda gave birth to Helen and to Clytemnestra (wife of Agamemnon). Yeats saw Zeus's visit to Leda as an "annunciation," marking the beginning of Greek civilization: "I imagine the annunciation that founded Greece as made to Leda, remembering that they showed in a Spartan temple, strung up to the roof as a holy relic, an unhatched egg of hers, and that from one of her eggs came love and from the other war" (*A Vision*). In the original Cuala Press edition Yeats noted: "I wrote *Leda and the Swan* because the editor of a political review asked me for a poem. I thought, 'After the individualist, demagogic movement, founded by Hobbes and popularized by the Encyclopedists and the French Revolution, we have a soil so exhausted that it cannot grow that crop again for centuries.' Then I thought, 'Nothing is now possible but some movement from above preceded by some violent annunciation.' My fancy began to play with Leda and the Swan for metaphor, and I began this poem; but as I wrote, bird and lady took such possession of the scene that all politics went out of it, and my friend tells me that his 'conservative readers would misunderstand the poem.'" Note that this poem is in sonnet form; the placing of the pauses gives it a rhetorical pattern not normally associated with the sonnet.
2. I.e., the destruction of Troy, caused by Helen's elopement with the Trojan Paris. Agamemnon was murdered by his wife Clytemnestra, the other daughter of Leda and the Swan.

Among School Children

1

I walk through the long schoolroom questioning;
A kind old nun in a white hood replies;
The children learn to cipher and to sing,
To study reading-books and history,
To cut and sew, be neat in everything 5
In the best modern way—the children's eyes
In momentary wonder stare upon
A sixty-year-old smiling public man.

2

I dream of a Ledaean body,[1] bent
Above a sinking fire, a tale that she 10
Told of a harsh reproof, or trivial event
That changed some childish day to tragedy—
Told, and it seemed that our two natures blent
Into a sphere from youthful sympathy,
Or else, to alter Plato's parable, 15
Into the yolk and white of the one shell.[2]

3

And thinking of that fit of grief or rage
I look upon one child or t'other there
And wonder if she stood so at that age—
For even daughters of the swan can share 20
Something of every paddler's heritage—
And had that color upon cheek or hair,
And thereupon my heart is driven wild:
She stands before me as a living child.

4

Her present image floats into the mind— 25
Did Quattrocento[3] finger fashion it
Hollow of cheek as though it drank the wind
And took a mess of shadows for its meat?
And I though never of Ledaean kind
Had pretty plumage once—enough of that, 30
Better to smile on all that smile, and show
There is a comfortable kind of old scarecrow.

5

What youthful mother, a shape upon her lap
Honey of generation had betrayed,

1. "Ledaean": adjective from "Leda," meaning "like Helen of Troy" (Leda's daughter). The reference is to Maud Gonne (as also in lines 19–28).
2. In Plato's *Symposium* Aristophanes explains Love by supposing that "the primeval man was round and had four hands and four feet, back and sides forming a circle, one head with two faces," and was subsequently divided into two. "After the division, the two parts of man, each desiring his other half, came together, and threw their arms about one another eager to grow into one." The fact that Helen was born from an egg (as the daughter of Leda and the Swan) suggests Yeats's image for such a union.
3. 15th-century; a reference to Italian painters of the period, especially Botticelli (ca. 1444–1510).

And that must sleep, shriek, struggle to escape   35
As recollection or the drug decide,[4]
Would think her son, did she but see that shape
With sixty or more winters on its head,
A compensation for the pang of his birth,
Or the uncertainty of his setting forth?   40

6

Plato thought nature but a spume that plays
Upon a ghostly paradigm of things;
Solider Aristotle played the taws
Upon the bottom of a king of kings;[5]
World-famous golden-thighed Pythagoras[6]   45
Fingered upon a fiddle-stick or strings
What a star sang and careless Muses heard:
Old clothes upon old sticks to scare a bird.[7]

7

Both nuns and mothers worship images,[8]
But those the candles light are not as those   50
That animate a mother's reveries,
But keep a marble or a bronze repose.
And yet they too break hearts—O Presences
That passion, piety, or affection knows,
And that all heavenly glory symbolize—   55
O self-born mockers of man's enterprise;

8

Labor is blossoming or dancing where
The body is not bruised to pleasure soul,
Nor beauty born out of its own despair,
Nor blear-eyed wisdom out of midnight oil.   60
O chestnut tree, great-rooted blossomer,
Are you the leaf, the blossom, or the bole?
O body swayed to music, O brightening glance,
How can we know the dancer from the dance?[9]

1927

4. "I have taken the 'honey of generation' from Porphyry's essay on 'The Cave of the Nymphs,' but find no warrant in Porphyry for considering it the 'drug' that destroys the 'recollection' of prenatal freedom" [Yeats's note]. Porphyry was a Neo-Platonic philosopher of the 3rd century A.D. "Honey of generation," by blotting out the memory of prenatal happiness, "betrays" an infant to be born into this world. The infant will either "sleep" or "struggle to escape" (from this world) depending on whether the drug works or the recollection of blissful prenatal life overcomes the oblivion caused by the drug.
5. Plato thought nature was a mere appearance ("spume") veiling the ultimate spiritual and mathematical reality ("ghostly paradigm"); Aristotle was "solider" in that he believed that form really inhered in the matter of nature, and thus that nature itself had reality.

Aristotle was tutor to Alexander the Great, and disciplined him by applying the "taws" or strap.
6. Greek philosopher (early 6th century B.C.), interested in mathematics and the mathematical study of acoustics and music; his disciples, the Pythagoreans, developed a mystical philosophy of numerical relations and united the notions of astronomical and mathematical relations in the theory of the music of the spheres. Pythagoreans regarded their master with veneration as a god with a golden thigh.
7. A contemptuous description of the philosophies of Plato, Aristotle, and Pythagoras.
8. Nuns worship images of Christ or the Virgin; mothers worship their own inward images of their children.
9. Yeats's view of life as a cosmic dance, in which every human faculty joins harmoniously. The individual be-

A Dialogue of Self and Soul[1]

1

MY SOUL. I summon to the winding ancient stair;
    Set all your mind upon the steep ascent,
    Upon the broken, crumbling battlement,
    Upon the breathless starlit air,
    Upon the star that marks the hidden pole;   5
    Fix every wandering thought upon
    That quarter where all thought is done:
    Who can distinguish darkness from the soul?

MY SELF. The consecrated blade upon my knees
    Is Sato's ancient blade,[2] still as it was,   10
    Still razor-keen, still like a looking glass
    Unspotted by the centuries;
    That flowering, silken, old embroidery, torn
    From some court lady's dress and round
    The wooden scabbard bound and wound,   15
    Can, tattered, still protect, faded adorn.

MY SOUL. Why should the imagination of a man
    Long past his prime remember things that are
    Emblematical of love and war?
    Think of ancestral night that can,   20
    If but imagination scorn the earth
    And intellect its wandering
    To this and that and t'other thing,
    Deliver from the crime of death and birth.

MY SELF. Montashigi, third of his family, fashioned it   25
    Five hundred years ago, about it lie
    Flowers from I know not what embroidery—
    Heart's purple—and all these I set
    For emblems of the day against the tower
    Emblematical of the night,   30
    And claim as by a soldier's right
    A charter to commit the crime once more.

---

comes involved in the process, as the dancer becomes part of the dance. Yeats relates the idea of the cosmic dance to his views of ritual, elegance, and order (cf. "the ceremony of innocence" in *The Second Coming* and the end of *Prayer for my Daughter*), and sees it as a means of reconciling the conflicting opposites of ordinary life.

1. Yeats here debates two opposing claims: the soul's summons to wisdom, resignation from an active life, the spiritual ascent—symbolized by the winding stair, a symbol similar to that of Byzantium—against the summons to the life of action and passion, symbolized by the sword of the second stanza and championed by the "Self."

2. A Japanese called Sato had given Yeats a sword, telling him that it was a symbol of life and that its silk-embroidered sheath was a symbol of beauty. Thus the sword in its scabbard is "emblematical of love and war" (line 19) and represents the "day," as opposed to the "night" represented by the tower and the winding stair (lines 29–30).

MY SOUL. Such fullness in that quarter overflows
   And falls into the basin of the mind
   That man is stricken deaf and dumb and blind,   35
   For intellect no longer knows
   Is from the *Ought*, or *Knower* from the *Known*—
   That is to say, ascends to Heaven;
   Only the dead can be forgiven;
   But when I think of that my tongue's a stone.   40

2

MY SELF. A living man is blind and drinks his drop.
   What matter if the ditches are impure?
   What matter if I live it all once more?
   Endure that toil of growing up;
   The ignominy of boyhood; the distress   45
   Of boyhood changing into man;
   The unfinished man and his pain
   Brought face to face with his own clumsiness;

   The finished man among his enemies?—
   How in the name of Heaven can he escape   50
   That defiling and disfigured shape
   The mirror of malicious eyes
   Casts upon his eyes until at last
   He thinks that shape must be his shape?
   And what's the good of an escape   55
   If honor find him in the wintry blast?

   I am content to live it all again
   And yet again, if it be life to pitch
   Into the frog-spawn of a blind man's ditch,
   A blind man battering blind men;   60
   Or into that most fecund ditch of all,
   The folly that man does
   Or must suffer, if he woos
   A proud woman not kindred of his soul.

   I am content to follow to its source   65
   Every event in action or in thought;
   Measure the lot; forgive myself the lot!
   When such as I cast out remorse
   So great a sweetness flows into the breast
   We must laugh and we must sing,   70
   We are blest by everything,
   Everything we look upon is blest.

        1929

For Anne Gregory

   "Never shall a young man,
   Thrown into despair
   By those great honey-colored

Ramparts at your ear,
Love you for yourself alone
And not your yellow hair."   5

"But I can get a hair-dye
And set such color there,
Brown, or black, or carrot,
That young men in despair
May love me for myself alone   10
And not my yellow hair."

"I heard an old religious man
But yesternight declare
That he had found a text to prove
That only God, my dear,   15
Could love you for yourself alone
And not your yellow hair."

1931, 1932

Byzantium[1]

The unpurged images of day recede;
The Emperor's drunken soldiery are abed;
Night resonance recedes, night-walkers' song
After great cathedral gong;
A starlit or a moonlit dome[2] disdains   5

1. The world of artifice and eternity to which Yeats journeyed in *Sailing to Byzantium* is now seen also as the world of death and spiritual purification from the "mire or blood" of life. As the poem opens, the "unpurged images of day" and then "night resonance" recede after the sounding of the gong at midnight (symbolic of the summons to death)—i.e., images of both the conscious (day) mind and the subconscious (night) mind depart, leaving the self in the hushed starlight or moonlight, purged of the "mere complexities" of flesh-and-blood life. This purified self "disdains" the confusion and murkiness of the unpurified self. In the second stanza the soul, released from what Yeats once called "the strain one upon another of opposites" of ordinary life, sees his spirit-guide leading him to the world of changelessness and purity. He hails this guide (a mediating figure between man, image, and shade) because he is now far enough beyond life to be able to do so. The third stanza shows the poet in the midst of the death-world of artifice and eternity, admiring the golden artifacts which, "in glory of changeless metal" (line 22), scorn the "complexities" and impurities of earthly creatures. In the next stanza the poet sees purgatorial fires burning away the "complexities" of bodily life; yet, unlike earthly flame which consumes as it burns, this flame "cannot singe a sleeve" (line 32). Finally, the poet finds himself no longer clearly in the world of pure spirit: he is pulled back by the tug of human emotion. He sees the smithies of the metalworkers buttressing the city against the dark tides of impurity and lust, while the dance of eternal life on the cold marble floor similarly helps to stem the flood (these are Platonic and Neo-Platonic images). But art and artifice cannot succeed in repelling the sensual life that beats against the city walls: in the end, human images break through and "beget" yet further images (cf. *Sailing to Byzantium,* in which he wanted to escape from "whatever is begotten, born, and dies"). The poem concludes on a note of human passion, "that dolphin-torn, that gong-tormented sea." In this instance, the gong is calling the poet back to life, not from life to death. He has discovered that art is nourished by life and in the end leads back to it. Yeats himself said that this poem was written "to warm myself back to life" after a serious illness.

2. "Starlit" and "moonlit" had a special symbolic significance for Yeats, as part of his theory of history and personality

All that man is,
All mere complexities,
The fury and the mire of human veins.

Before me floats an image, man or shade,
Shade more than man, more image than a shade;   10
For Hades' bobbin bound in mummy-cloth
May unwind the winding path;[3]
A mouth that has no moisture and no breath
Breathless mouths may summon;
I hail the superhuman;   15
I call it death-in-life and life-in-death.

Miracle, bird or golden handiwork,
More miracle than bird or handiwork,
Planted on the starlit golden bough,[4]
Can like the cocks of Hades crow,   20
Or, by the moon embittered, scorn aloud
In glory of changeless metal
Common bird or petal
And all complexities of mire or blood.

At midnight on the Emperor's pavement flit   25
Flames that no faggot feeds, nor steel has lit,
Nor storm disturbs, flames begotten of flame,
Where blood-begotten spirits come
And all complexities of fury leave,
Dying into a dance,   30
An agony of trance,
An agony of flame[5] that cannot singe a sleeve.

Astraddle on the dolphin's mire and blood,[6]
Spirit after spirit! The smithies break the flood,

in terms of the phases of the moon (in *A Vision*). The first phase—that of the dark of the moon, when only the stars shine—is the phase when "body is completely absorbed in its supernatural environment." The fifteenth phase—the full moon—is the phase of complete subjectivity, where the mind is "completely absorbed by being." Thus both phases are states of *being*: they reject the complexities of the world of *becoming* and change.

In the Cuala Press edition of 1932, "disdains" is printed as "distains" (i.e., discolors, pollutes); all subsequent printings, however, read "disdains." It has been argued that the first reading must be correct, but it makes less sense, and Yeats never corrected the "disdains" in later printings.

3. The spool of man's fate, which spins his destiny and which is symbolized by the wrappings around a mummy, may lead man, as it unwinds, to the realm of pure spirit (or up the winding stair, in another of Yeats's favorite images).

4. The "starlit golden bough" is part of the death-world of artifice and eter-nity; it is opposed to a real, living bough, which would be lighted by the sun or the moon (cf. note 2). The bough is also associated with the mystical tree of the esoteric Hebrew doctrine of the cabala, in whose branches "the birds lodge and build their nests; that is, the souls or angels have their place." The "cocks of Hades" are the birds standing outside time whose crowing proclaims the cycles of rebirth to mortal beings: the golden birds of art, who live in the same tree, are similarly eternal.

5. The "agony of flame" was suggested to Yeats by a Japanese *Nō* play, *Motomezulka*, wherein a young girl suffers from perpetual burning, which is a sense of her own guilt. A priest tells her that the flames will cease if she no longer believes in their reality; she finds herself incapable of disbelief, however, and the play ends in "the dance of her agony."

6. The dolphin, in ancient art, was a symbol of the soul in transit from one state to another. Mounted on its back, the poet here is able to ride over the

The golden smithies of the Emperor!   35
Marbles of the dancing floor
Break bitter furies of complexity,
Those images that yet
Fresh images beget,
That dolphin-torn, that gong-tormented sea.   40

1930   1932

Crazy Jane Talks with the Bishop[1]

I met the Bishop on the road
And much said he and I.
"Those breasts are flat and fallen now,
Those veins must soon be dry;
Live in a heavenly mansion,   5
Not in some foul sty."

"Fair and foul are near of kin,
And fair needs foul," I cried.
"My friends are gone, but that's a truth
Nor grave nor bed denied,   10
Learned in bodily lowliness
And in the heart's pride.

"A woman can be proud and stiff
When on love intent;
But Love has pitched his mansion in   15
The place of excrement;
For nothing can be sole or whole
That has not been rent."

                                                                       1932

After Long Silence

Speech after long silence; it is right,
All other lovers being estranged or dead,
Unfriendly lamplight hid under its shade,
The curtains drawn upon unfriendly night,
That we descant and yet again descant   5
Upon the supreme theme of Art and Song:
Bodily decrepitude is wisdom; young
We loved each other and were ignorant.

                                                                       1932

sea of human passions—except that the
dolphin itself is made of "mire or
blood."
1. One of a series of poems dealing
with the paradox that wisdom may reside with fools and beggars (such as
Jane) rather than with the respectable
representatives of orthodoxy (such as
the Bishop). This poem also deals with
a favorite Yeatsian theme, the resolution of opposites, of what he called
elsewhere "all those antinomies / Of
day and night."

Lapis Lazuli[1]

(FOR HARRY CLIFTON)

I have heard that hysterical women say
They are sick of the palette and fiddle bow,
Of poets that are always gay,
For everybody knows or else should know
That if nothing drastic is done   5
Aeroplane and Zeppelin will come out,
Pitch like King Billy[2] bomb-balls in
Until the town lie beaten flat.

All perform their tragic play,
There struts Hamlet, there is Lear,   10
That's Ophelia, that Cordelia;
Yet they, should the last scene be there,
The great stage curtain about to drop,
If worthy their prominent part in the play,
Do not break up their lines to weep.   15
They know that Hamlet and Lear are gay;
Gaiety transfiguring all that dread.
All men have aimed at, found and lost;
Black out; Heaven blazing into the head:
Tragedy wrought to its uttermost.   20
Though Hamlet rambles and Lear rages,
And all the drop-scenes drop at once
Upon a hundred thousand stages,
It cannot grow by an inch or an ounce.

On their own feet they came, or on shipboard,   25
Camel-back, horse-back, ass-back, mule-back,
Old civilizations put to the sword.
Then they and their wisdom went to rack:
No handiwork of Callimachus,[3]
Who handled marble as if it were bronze,   30

1. A deep blue stone. "I notice that you have much lapis lazuli; someone has sent me a present of a great piece carved by some Chinese sculptor into the semblance of a mountain with temple, trees, paths, and an ascetic and pupil about to climb the mountain. Ascetic, pupil, hard stone, eternal theme of the sensual east. The heroic cry in the midst of despair. But no, I am wrong, the east has its solutions always and therefore knows nothing of tragedy. It is we, not the east, that must raise the heroic cry" (Yeats to Dorothy Wellesley, July 6, 1935).
2. King William III (William of Orange), who defeated the army of King James II at the Battle of the Boyne in 1690.
3. Greek sculptor (5th century B.C.), supposedly the originator of the Corinthian column and of the use of the running drill to imitate folds in drapery in statues. Yeats wrote of him: "With Callimachus pure Ionic revives again * * * and upon the only example of his work known to us, a marble chair, a Persian is represented, and may one not discover a Persian symbol in that bronze lamp, shaped like a palm * * * ? But he was an archaistic workman, and those who set him to work brought back public life to an older form" (*A Vision*).

Made draperies that seemed to rise
When sea wind swept the corner, stands;
His long lamp chimney shaped like the stem
Of a slender palm, stood but a day;
All things fall and are built again,   35
And those that build them again are gay.

Two Chinamen, behind them a third,
Are carved in lapis lazuli,
Over them flies a long-legged bird,
A symbol of longevity;   40
The third, doubtless a servingman,
Carries a musical instrument.

Every discoloration of the stone,
Every accidental crack or dent,
Seems a watercourse or an avalanche,   45
Or lofty slope where it still snows
Though doubtless plum or cherry branch
Sweetens the little halfway house
Those Chinamen climb towards, and I
Delight to imagine them seated there;   50
There, on the mountain and the sky,
On all the tragic scene they stare.
One asks for mournful melodies;
Accomplished fingers begin to play.
Their eyes mid many wrinkles, their eyes,   55
Their ancient, glittering eyes, are gay.

                                                      1938

Long-legged Fly[1]

That civilization may not sink,
Its great battle lost,
Quiet the dog, tether the pony
To a distant post;
Our master Caesar is in the tent   5
Where the maps are spread,
His eyes fixed upon nothing,
A hand under his head.
Like a long-legged fly upon the stream
His mind moves upon silence.   10

1. The first stanza shows Caesar planning one of his history-making campaigns: any disturbing noise now will alter the course of civilization. In the next stanza Helen of Troy as a child practices a part: the future of Troy and of the ancient world depends on her being allowed to train herself to be a woman. Finally, Michelangelo works in the Sistine Chapel in Rome: he must be undisturbed if his art is to be unspoiled, so that it can give to future generations of "girls at puberty" their first disturbing thoughts of men.

That the topless towers[2] be burnt
And men recall that face,
Move most gently if move you must
In this lonely place.
She thinks, part woman, three parts a child,   15
That nobody looks; her feet
Practice a tinker shuffle
Picked up on a street.
Like a long-legged fly upon the stream
Her mind moves upon silence.   20

That girls at puberty may find
The first Adam in their thought,
Shut the door of the Pope's chapel,
Keep those children out.
There on that scaffolding reclines   25
Michael Angelo.
With no more sound than the mice make
His hand moves to and fro.
Like a long-legged fly upon the stream
His mind moves upon silence.   30

                                                                1939

The Circus Animals' Desertion[1]

1

I sought a theme and sought for it in vain,
I sought it daily for six weeks or so.
Maybe at last, being but a broken man,
I must be satisfied with my heart, although
Winter and summer till old age began   5
My circus animals were all on show,
Those stilted boys, that burnished chariot,
Lion and woman[2] and the Lord knows what.

2

What can I but enumerate old themes?
First that sea-rider Oisin[3] led by the nose   10
Through three enchanted islands, allegorical dreams,
Vain gaiety, vain battle, vain repose,
Themes of the embittered heart, or so it seems,
That might adorn old songs or courtly shows;

2. Of Troy. Cf. "Was this the face that launched a thousand ships / And burnt the topless towers of Ilium?" (Marlowe, *Dr. Faustus*).
1. Yeats in old age looks back on some of the main themes of his poems and plays as circus animals that have now deserted him, leaving him with only the refuse of his human passions.
2. Cf. "On the gray rock of Cashel I suddenly saw / A Sphinx with woman breast and lion paw * * *" (Yeats, *The Double Vision of Michael Robartes*).
3. Pronounced *Ushéen*. Hero of an Old Irish legend, he was beguiled by a fairy woman to the fairy world and returned 150 years later to find his friends dead and Ireland Christian. Subject of an early long poem by Yeats (1889).

But what cared I that set him on to ride,   15
I, starved for the bosom of his faery bride?

And then a counter-truth filled out its play,
The Countess Cathleen was the name I gave it;
She, pity-crazed, had given her soul away,
But masterful Heaven had intervened to save it.[4]   20
I thought my dear must her own soul destroy,
So did fanaticism and hate enslave it,
And this brought forth a dream and soon enough
This dream itself had all my thought and love.

And when the Fool and Blind Man stole the bread   25
Cuchulain fought the ungovernable sea;[5]
Heart-mysteries there, and yet when all is said
It was the dream itself enchanted me:
Character isolated by a deed
To engross the present and dominate memory.   30
Players and painted stage took all my love,
And not those things that they were emblems of.

3

Those masterful images because complete
Grew in pure mind, but out of what began?
A mound of refuse or the sweepings of a street,   35
Old kettles, old bottles, and a broken can,
Old iron, old bones, old rags, that raving slut
Who keeps the till. Now that my ladder's gone,
I must lie down where all the ladders start,
In the foul rag-and-bone shop of the heart.   40

                                                          1939

Under Ben Bulben[1]

1

Swear by what the sages spoke
Round the Mareotic Lake[2]

4. Title of an early Yeats play (1892) about an Irish countess who, although she sold her soul to the devil to get food for the starving people, goes to Heaven anyway, for God looks "on the motive, not the deed."
5. In Yeats's play *On Baile's Strand* (1904), where he probes for symbolic meanings in an old Irish legend.
1. One of Yeats's last poems, ending with the epitaph he wrote for himself. He wished to be buried in the churchyard of the village of Drumcliff, which lies "under Ben Bulben," mountain in County Sligo. Although he died on the French Riviera, his body was later brought back and buried at Drumcliff.

2. Lake Mareotis, bordering the city of Alexandria where a school of Neo-Pythagorean philosophers flourished in the 1st century A.D. By Lake Mareotis also flourished (3rd century A.D.) the Christian Neo-Platonists, in whom Yeats was much interested. The lake is mentioned in Shelley's poem *The Witch of Atlas*, a poem which Yeats admired and interpreted in his own way, seeing the Witch as a symbol of timeless, absolute beauty; hence what she "knew" and "spoke" and what "set the cocks a-crow" can be related to the "miracle" that "can like the cocks of Hades crow" in *Byzantium*.

That the Witch of Atlas knew,
Spoke and set the cocks a-crow.

Swear by those horsemen, by those women   5
Complexion and form prove superhuman,[3]
That pale, long-visaged company
That air in immortality
Completeness of their passions won;
Now they ride the wintry dawn   10
Where Ben Bulben sets the scene.

Here's the gist of what they mean.

2

Many times man lives and dies
Between his two eternities,
That of race and that of soul,   15
And ancient Ireland knew it all.
Whether man die in his bed
Or the rifle knocks him dead,
A brief parting from those dear
Is the worst man has to fear.   20
Though gravediggers' toil is long,
Sharp their spades, their muscles strong,
They but thrust their buried men
Back in the human mind again.

3

You that Mitchel's prayer have heard,   25
"Send war in our time, O Lord!"[4]
Know that when all words are said
And a man is fighting mad,
Something drops from eyes long blind,
He completes his partial mind,   30
For an instant stands at ease,
Laughs aloud, his heart at peace.
Even the wisest man grows tense
With some sort of violence
Before he can accomplish fate,   35
Know his work or choose his mate.

4

Poet and sculptor, do the work,
Nor let the modish painter shirk
What his great forefathers did,
Bring the soul of man to God,   40
Make him fill the cradles right.

Measurement began our might:
Forms a stark Egyptian thought,

---

3. The *sidhe* or fairy folk, who were believed to ride through the countryside near Ben Bulben. The gist of Yeats's thought here is: "Swear by those who speak superhuman, eternal truths." These truths are summed up in the second section of the poem: man has an afterlife both in the future of his individual soul and in the memory he leaves behind on earth.
4. John Mitchel, an Irish patriot imprisoned for his activities, wrote in his *Jail Journal:* "Give us war in our time, O Lord!"

Forms that gentler Phidias wrought.[5]
Michael Angelo left a proof
On the Sistine Chapel roof,   45
Where but half-awakened Adam
Can disturb globe-trotting Madam
Till her bowels are in heat,[6]
Proof that there's a purpose set   50
Before the secret working mind:
Profane perfection of mankind.

Quattrocento[7] put in paint
On backgrounds for a God or Saint
Gardens where a soul's at ease;   55
Where everything that meets the eye,
Flowers and grass and cloudless sky,
Resemble forms that are or seem
When sleepers wake and yet still dream,
And when it's vanished still declare,   60
With only bed and bedstead there,
That heavens had opened.
                              Gyres run on;
When that greater dream had gone
Calvert and Wilson, Blake and Claude,[8]
Prepared a rest for the people of God,   65
Palmer's phrase, but after that
Confusion fell upon our thought.

5

Irish poets, learn your trade,
Sing whatever is well made,
Scorn the sort now growing up   70
All out of shape from toe to top,
Their unremembering hearts and heads
Base-born products of base beds.
Sing the peasantry, and then
Hard-riding country gentlemen,   75
The holiness of monks, and after
Porter-drinkers' randy laughter;
Sing the lords and ladies gay
That were beaten into the clay
Through seven heroic centuries;   80

5. Greek sculptor (5th century B.C.), generally thought to have raised the classical ideal in art to its highest culmination. Yeats here itemizes steps in his history of knowledge and the arts, beginning with Babylonian mathematics ("measurement"), through "stark Egyptian thought," to the Renaissance of Michelangelo. Each of these steps is related to Yeats's cyclical theory of history.
6. Cf. *Long-Legged Fly*, stanza 3.
7. 15th-century Italian art.
8. Works by the five artists mentioned in lines 64–66 all provided images for Yeats's poetry: Edward Calvert, 19th-century wood-engraver; Richard Wilson, 18th-century landscape painter; William Blake, "one of the great mythmakers and mask-makers"; Claude Lorrain, 17th-century landscape painter; and (in line 66) Samuel Palmer, 19th-century landscape painter and etcher, one of whose works was "The Lonely Tower." Calvert, Blake, and Palmer knew each other and shared a view of the holiness of art. (See T. R. Henn, *The Lonely Tower*, 1950.)

Cast your mind on other days
That we in coming days may be
Still the indomitable Irishry.
                    6
Under bare Ben Bulben's head
In Drumcliff churchyard Yeats is laid.   85
An ancestor was rector there
Long years ago, a church stands near,
By the road an ancient cross.
No marble, no conventional phrase;
On limestone quarried near the spot   90
By his command these words are cut:
            Cast a cold eye
            On life, on death.
            Horseman, pass by!

September 4, 1938   1939

From Memoirs[1]

From *Autobiography*[2]

I began to read Ruskin's *Unto This Last,*[3] and this when added
to my interest in psychical research and mysticism, enraged my
father, who was a disciple of John Stuart Mill's. One night a quarrel
over Ruskin came to such a height that in putting me out of the
room he broke the glass in a picture with the back of my head.
Another night when we had been in argument over Ruskin or mysticism, I cannot now remember what theme, he followed me
upstairs to the room I shared with my brother. He squared up at
me, and wanted to box, and when I said I could not fight my own
father replied, "I don't see why you should not." My brother, who
had been in bed for some time, started up in a violent passion
because we had awaked him. My father fled without speaking, and

1. In 1915, Yeats published his first autobiographical volume, *Reveries over
Childhood and Youth* (1915). He had,
however, been keeping a journal since
1908, and in 1917 completed the first
draft of an autobiography; neither of
these was published until 1972, when
Denis Donoghue edited them under the
title *Memoirs*. In later autobiographical
publications (including The *Trembling of
the Veil,* 1922, and *Autobiography,*
1938), he included materials from this
first draft, but, as Donoghue says, "he
excluded much for tact or privacy." We
reprint here selections from the draft
Autobiography that show some of
Yeats's sexual, mystical, and political explorations; we reprint from the *Journal*
passages that show him at work on the
poem *The Fascination of What's Difficult.*
2. "On the envelope containing the manuscript, Yeats wrote: 'Private. A First
rough draft of Memoirs made in 1916–17
and containing much that is not for publication now if ever. Memoirs come
down to 1896 or thereabouts. W.B.Y.
March 1921.' John Butler Yeats (1839–
1922) and his family moved from Dublin to London (58 Eardley Crescent,
Earls Court) in the spring of 1887"
[Donoghue's note].
3. A book, published in 1860, on the responsibilities of employers toward their
workmen.

my brother turned to me with, "Mind, not a word till he apologizes." Though my father and I are very talkative, a couple of days passed before I spoke or he apologized.

* * *

In what year did I first meet Oscar Wilde?[4] I remember that he seemed to think that I was alone in London, for he asked me to eat my Christmas dinner at his house. I was delighted by his pretty wife and children, and his beautiful house designed by Godwin.[5] He had a white dining-room, the first I had seen, chairs, walls, cushions all white, but in the middle of the table a red cloth table-center with a red terracotta statue and above it a red hanging lamp. I have never and shall never meet conversation that could match with his. Perplexed by my own shapelessness, my lack of self-possession and of easy courtesy, I was astonished by this scholar who as a man of the world was so perfect. He had not yet written a successful play and was still a poor man, and I saw nothing of the insolence that perhaps grew upon him later. "Ah, Yeats," he said that Christmas day—he had been reading to me from the proof sheets of his unpublished *Decay of Lying*—"we Irish are too poetical to be poets; we are a nation of brilliant failures."

Neither then nor later did I care greatly for anything in his writings but the wit—it was the man I admired, who was to show so much courage and who was so loyal to the intellect. "He is one of our eighteenth-century duelists born in the wrong century," I would say of him to some young men of letters who decried him, as the fashion was among us; "he would be a good leader in a cavalry charge." Or then I would say, "He is like Benvenuto Cellini, who, because he found it impossible to equal Michelangelo, turned bravo out of the pride of his art. Wilde is cowed by Swinburne and Browning." Yet like us all it was from Pater that he had learned, but in him the cadence became over-elaborate and swelling, the diction a little lacked in exactness. In that witty fantasy he had read me, he had derived the pessimism of German philosophy from Hamlet, and when he came to the sentence, "The world has grown sad because a puppet was once melancholy," I said, "Why have you varied the word; are not sadness and melancholy the same?" And all he could say was that he wanted a full sound for the close of the sentence.[6]

He spoke with a deliberate slowness, in drawling speech copied from Walter Pater's speech, somebody told me, and this had become an artistic convention that gave him greater freedom of lan-

4. "September, 1888" [Donoghue's note].
5. Edward William Godwin was a Victorian architect and stage designer.
6. " 'Schopenhauer has analyzed the pessimism that characterizes modern thought, but Hamlet invented it. The world has become sad because a puppet was once melancholy.' 'The Decay of Lying,' *Intentions* (London, Methuen, 1913), pp. 32–33. First published in 1891" [Donoghue's note].

guage. He could be elaborate when it pleased him, without seeming affectation. "I do not like *King Lear*, give me *The Winter's Tale*— 'Daffodils, that come before the swallow dares.' What is *King Lear* but poor life staggering in the fog?" The next moment would come a swift retort, some eddy of spontaneous wit. "I never travel anywhere without Pater's essay on the Renaissance, that is my golden book, but the last trumpet should have sounded the moment it was written—it is the very flower of the Decadence." "But," said somebody, "would you not have given us time, Mr. Wilde, to read it?" "Oh no, plenty of time afterwards in either world."

I was much among the Theosophists, having drifted there from the Dublin Hermetic Society.[7] Like the Socialists, they thought little of those who did not share their belief, and talked much of what they called Materialism. All good work, whether practical or in the arts, had been done, they held, with the conscious aim of improving mankind, and they were very conscious themselves of possessing that aim. I would say that so much in life had no aim but itself, and there would be an evening of argument. I began to see everything in an argumentative form and became alarmed for my poetical faculty.

I was a member of their Esoteric Section, an inner ring of the more devout students, which met weekly to study tables of oriental symbolism. Every organ of the body had its correspondence in the heavens, and the seven principles[8] which made the human soul and body corresponded to the seven colors and the planets and the notes of the musical scale. We lived in perpetual discussion. Among the symbols of one[9] of the seven principles was indigo, extracted from the plant in some particular way. I got with some trouble a bottle of this indigo and got various members to try experiments, fixing their minds upon the bottle and then [allowing them] to drift. They got impressions of mountainous country, and I began to divide up the different qualities of landscape according to the principles, that I might escape from the astral when I thought of them.

* * *

I was introduced to the kabalist MacGregor Mathers,[1] not yet married to the sister of the philosopher Bergson, in some Fitzroy Street studio, and accepted his invitation to join an Order of Chris-

7. The Dublin Hermetic Society was founded by Yeats and some of his friends in 1885 in order to study magic and Eastern religions. Theosophy, founded in 1875 by Madame Elena Blavatsky, is an occult movement offering a "synthesis of science, religion, and philosophy."
8. "Saturn, Jupiter, Mars, Sun, Venus, Mercury, Moon" [Donoghue's note].
9. "Venus" [Donoghue's note].

1. "1887" [Donoghue's note]. The Kabbala is a collection of ancient Hebrew writings of interest to students of the occult. Samuel Liddell ("MacGregor") Mathers was an important figure in late 19th-century occult circles; his powers as a magician impressed Yeats. Mathers was a founder of the Order of the Golden Dawn, which Yeats joined in 1890 (Mathers was later expelled from the Order).

tian kabalists, "the Hermetic Students." I am still a member and, though I attend but little, value a ritual full of the symbolism of the Middle Ages and the Renaissance, with many later additions. One passes from degree to degree, and if the wisdom one had once hoped for is still far off there [is] no exhortation to alarm one's dignity, no abstraction to deaden the nerves of the soul. "We only give you symbols," MacGregor Mathers had said to me, "because we respect your liberty." And now I made a curious discovery. After I had been moved by ritual, I formed plans for deeds of all kinds I wished to return to Ireland to find there some public work; whereas when I had returned from meetings of the Esoteric Section I had no desire but for more thought, more discussion.

Now too I learned a practice, a form of meditation that has perhaps been the intellectual chief influence on my life up to perhaps my fortieth year. MacGregor was now married and the curator of a private museum a little out of London. A friend, a member of the Order, returned from a visit to him with a most wonderful tale. He had made her fix her attention on a certain symbol, and by a process she could not describe a seashore and a flight of seagulls had risen before her. Then my turn came for a visit, and I was made to look at a colored geometric form and then, closing my eyes, see it again in the mind's eye. I was then shown how to allow my reveries to drift, following the suggestion of the symbol. I saw a desert, and a gigantic Negro raising up his head and shoulders among great stones. There was nothing in the symbol, as far as I could judge, to have called up the result—if it was association of ideas, they were subtle and subconscious. As I watched the kabalist I discovered that his geometrical symbols were a series which I could classify according to the four elements and what the ancients called the fifth element, and the subdivisions of these.

* * *

I was twenty-three years old when the troubling of my life began. I had heard from time to time in letters from Miss O'Leary, John O'Leary's old sister, of a beautiful girl who had left the society of the Viceregal Court for Dublin nationalism. In after years I persuaded myself that I felt premonitory excitement at the first reading of her name. Presently she drove up to our house in Bedford Park with an introduction from John O'Leary to my father.[2] I had never thought to see in a living woman so great beauty. It belonged to famous pictures, to poetry, to some legendary past. A complexion like the blossom of apples, and yet face and body had the beauty of lineaments which Blake calls the highest beauty because it changes least from youth to age, and a stature so great that she seemed of a divine race. Her movements were worthy of her form, and I under-

2. "30 January 1889. O'Leary (1830–1907), the Fenian leader, had returned to Ireland in 1885 after five years' im- prisonment and fifteen years' exile" [Donoghue's note]. The "beautiful girl" is Maud Gonne.

stood at last why the poet of antiquity, where we would but speak of face and form, sings, loving some lady, that she paces like a goddess. I remember nothing of her speech that day except that she vexed my father by praise of war, for she too was of the Romantic movement and found those uncontrovertible Victorian reasons, that seemed to announce so prosperous a future, a little gray. As I look backward, it seems to me that she brought into my life in those days—for as yet I saw only what lay upon the surface—the middle of the tint, a sound as of a Burmese gong, an overpowering tumult that had yet many pleasant secondary notes.

She asked [me] to dine with her that evening in her rooms in Ebury Street, and I think that I dined with her all but every day during her stay in London of perhaps nine days, and there was something so exuberant in her ways that it seemed natural she should give her hours in overflowing abundance. She had heard of me from O'Leary; he had praised me, and it was natural that she should give and take without stint. She lived surrounded by cages of innumerable singing birds and with these she always traveled, it seemed, taking them even upon short journeys, and they and she were now returning to Paris where their home was.

* * *

She, like myself, had received the political tradition of Davis with an added touch of hardness and heroism from the hand of O'Leary, and when she spoke of William O'Brien,[3] [who] was in jail making a prolonged struggle against putting on the prison clothes, she said, "There was a time when men sacrificed their lives for their country, but now they sacrifice their dignity." But mixed with this feeling for what is permanent in human life there was something declamatory, Latin in a bad sense, and perhaps even unscrupulous. She spoke of her desire for power, apparently for its own sake, and when we talked of politics spoke much of mere effectiveness, or the mere winning of this or that election. Her two and twenty years had taken some color, I thought, from French Boulangist[4] adventurers and journalist *arrivistes* of whom she had seen too much, and [she] already had made some political journey into Russia in their interest. I was full of that thought of the "Animula Vagula" chapter, I had heard it at the feet of a young Brahmin[5] in Dublin, "Only the means can justify the end." She meant her ends to be unselfish, but she thought almost any means justified in their success. We were

3. "Thomas Davis (1814–55), leader of the young Ireland movement, and one of the founders of the *Nation* in 1842. William O'Brien (1852–1928), journalist, Nationalist member of Parliament, founder of the agrarian and Nationalist paper, *United Ireland*, in 1881" [Donoghue's notes].
4. The Boulangists were followers of General Ernest Jean Marie Boulanger, then a popular anti-Republican demagogue in France; the Boulangists included Bonapartists and the party demanding revenge on Germany for the Franco-Prussian war.
5. Mohini Chatterjee, an Indian sage, whom Yeats and his associates invited to Dublin in 1885 or 1886. The "Animula Vagula" chapter is in Walter Pater's *Marius the Epicurean*.

seeking different things: she, some memorable action for final consecration of her youth, and I, after all, but to discover and communicate a state of being. Perhaps even in politics it would in the end be enough to have lived and thought passionately and have, like O'Leary, a head worthy of a Roman coin.

* * *

I was tortured by sexual desire and had been for many years. I have often said to myself that some day I would put it all down in a book that some young man of talent might not think as I did that my shame was mine alone. It began when I was fifteen years old. I had been bathing, and lay down in the sun on the sand on the Third Rosses[6] and covered my body with sand. Presently the weight of the sand began to affect the organ of sex, though at first I did not know what the strange, growing sensation was. It was only at the orgasm that I knew, remembering some body's description or the description in my grandfather's encyclopedia. It was many days before I discovered how to renew that wonderful sensation. From that on it was a continual struggle against an experience that almost invariably left me with exhausted nerves. Normal sexual intercourse does not affect me more than other men, but that, though never frequent, was plain ruin. It filled me with loathing of myself; and yet at first pride and perhaps, a little, lack of obvious opportunity, and now love kept me in unctuous celibacy. When I returned to London in my twenty-seventh year I think my love seemed almost hopeless, and I knew that my friends had all mistresses of one kind or another and that most, at need, went home with harlots. Henley, indeed, mocked at any other life. I had never since childhood kissed a woman's lips. At Hammersmith I saw a woman of the town walking up and down in the empty railway station. I thought of offering myself to her, but the old thought came back, "No, I love the most beautiful woman in the world."

* * *

I found I had the reputation of a magician; there was a story among the country people of my being carried five miles in the winking of an eye, and of my sending my cousin from her house at the First Rosses to the rocks of the Third in a like eye-wink—I had indeed sent her there in vision. I do not remember if it was now or at some later visit that a servant at her house gave notice after a water evocation of mine, begun long after she was in her bed. She had seen mermaids in the night who soaked her in sea water. I remember hearing as I went upstairs after an evening of evocation my uncle's old, second-sighted servant moaning in the midst of some terrifying dream. Certainly our thoughts, and we were not yet

6. Rosses Point, County Sligo—where Yeats grew up.

sure if it was more than this, affected all neighboring sensitive minds.

* * *

I had received while at Sligo many letters from Diana Vernon,[7] kind letters that gave me a sense of half-conscious excitement. I remember after one such letter asking some country woman to throw the tea leaves for me and my disappointment at the vagueness of the oracle. (I think Mary Battle, my uncle's second-sighted servant, was again ill and away.) She was to tell me later on that my letters were unconscious love-letters, and I was taken by surprise at the description. I do not know how long after my return the conversation that was to decide so much in my life took place. I had found the Rhymer who had introduced me under the influence of drink,[8] speaking vaguely and with vague movements, and while we were speaking this recent memory came back. She[9] spoke of her pagan life in a way that made me believe that she had had many lovers and loathed her life. I thought of that young man so nearly related. Here is the same weakness, I thought; two souls so distinguished and contemplative that the common world seems empty. What is there left but sanctity, or some satisfying affection, or mere dissipation?—"Folly the comforter," some Elizabethan had called it. Her beauty, dark and still, had the nobility of defeated things, and how could it help but wring my heart? I took a fortnight to decide what I should do.

I was poor and it would be a hard struggle if I asked her [to] come away, and perhaps after all I would but add my tragedy to hers, for she might return to that evil life. But, after all, if I could not get the woman I loved, it would be a comfort even but for a little while to devote myself to another. No doubt my excited senses had their share in the argument, but it was an unconscious one. At the end of the fortnight I asked her to leave home with me. She became very gay and joyous and a few days later praised me [for] what she thought my beautiful tact in giving at the moment but a brother's kiss. Doubtless at the moment I was exalted above the senses, and yet I do not [think] I knew any better way of kissing, for when on our first railway journey together—we were to spend the day at Kew—she gave me the long passionate kiss of love I was startled and a little shocked.

Presently I told something of my thoughts during that fortnight, and she [was] perplexed and ashamed that I should have had such

---

7. Mrs. Olivia Shakespear. "In this book," Yeats writes in an earlier section, "I cannot give her her real name—Diana Vernon sounds pleasantly in my ears and will suit her as well as any other."

8. " 'drugs' deleted" [Donoghue's note]. "Rhymer": a member of the Rhymers' Club.

9. "Diana Vernon" [Donoghue's note].

imagination of her. Her wickedness had never gone further than her own mind; I would be her first lover. We decided that we should be but friends till she could leave her home for mine, but agreed to wait until her mother, a very old woman, had died. We decided to consult each a woman friend that we might be kept to these resolutions, as sponsors of our adventure, and for nearly a year met in railway carriages and at picture galleries and occasionally at her house. At Dulwich Gallery she taught me to care for Watteau—she too was of Pater's school—and at the National Gallery for the painter who pleased her best of all, Mantegna. I wrote her several poems, all curiously elaborate in style, "The Shadowy Horses," and ―――― and―――――,[1] and thought I was once more in love. I noticed that she was like the mild heroines of my plays. She seemed a part of myself.

I noticed that she did not talk so well as when I had at first known her, her mind seemed more burdened, but she would show in her movements an unforeseen youth; she seemed to have gone back to her twentieth year. For a short time, a few months I think, I shared a flat with Arthur Symons in the Temple.[2] Symons knew I had such a friend and plan, but did [not] know her name. He indeed met my friend somewhere in society and asked if he might call, and came back with her praises. At last she and her sponsor were to come to tea. I do not think I had asked Symons, for I went myself to buy the cake. As I came home with the parcel I began to think of Maud Gonne till my thought was interrupted by my finding the door locked. I had forgotten the key and I went off in a great fuss to find a locksmith and found instead a man who climbed along the roof and in at an attic window.

That night at twelve o'clock I said to Symons, who had just come in, "Did I ever tell you about Maud Gonne?" and till two or three in the morning I spoke of my love for her. Of all the men I have known he was the best listener; he could listen as a woman listens, never meeting one's thought as a man does with a rival thought, but taking up what one said and changing [it], giving it as it were flesh and bone. A couple of days later I got a wild letter from Maud Gonne, who was in Dublin. "Was I ill? Had some accident happened?" On a day that was, I found, the day I had had those guests and lost the key, I had walked into the room in her hotel where she was sitting with friends. At first she thought I was really there, but presently on finding that no one else saw me knew that it was my ghost. She told me to return at twelve that night and I vanished. At twelve I had stood, dressed in some strange, priest-like costume, at

1. *He Bids His Beloved Be at Peace; He Gives His Beloved Certain Rhymes; A Poet to His Beloved* (noted by Donoghue).
2. Arthur Symons (1865–1945), poet and critic, author of *The Symbolist Move-* ment *in Literature* (1899); this book, dedicated to Yeats, was an important early influence on the modernist tradition. Donoghue notes that Symons and Yeats shared rooms in the autumn of 1895.

her bedside and brought her soul away, and we had wandered round the cliffs [of] Howth where we had been together years before. I remember one phrase very clearly, "It was very sad, and all the sea-gulls were asleep." All my old love had returned and began to struggle with the new.[3]

Presently I was asked to call and see my friend's sponsor. She condemned our idea of going away from home. There were various arguments that I cannot recall without perhaps, against my will, revealing Diana Vernon's true name. My sponsor came to see me and used the same arguments, and both, people of the world, advised us to live together without more ado. Then Diana Vernon tried to get a separation from the husband who had for her, she believed, aversion or indifference. "He ceased to pay court to me from the day of our marriage," she had said. He was deeply distressed and became ill, and she gave up the project and said to me, "It will be kinder to deceive him." Our senses were engaged now, and though we spoke of parting it was but to declare it impossible. I took my present rooms at Woburn Buildings and furnished them very meagerly with such cheap furniture as I could throw away without regret as I grew more prosperous. She came with me to make every purchase, and I remember an embarrassed conversation in the presence of some Tottenham Court [Road] shop man upon the width of the bed—every inch increased the expense.

At last she came to me in I think January of my thirtieth year, and I was impotent from nervous excitement. The next day we met at the British Museum—we were studying together—and I wondered that there seemed no change in me or in her. A week later she came to me again, and my nervous excitement was so painful that it seemed best but to sit over our tea and talk. I do not think we kissed each other except at the moment of her leaving. She understood instead of, as another would, changing liking for dislike —was only troubled by my trouble. My nervousness did not return again and we had many days of happiness. It will always be a grief to me that I could not give the love that was her beauty's right, but she was too near my soul, too salutary and wholesome to my inmost being. All our lives long, as da Vinci says,[4] we long, thinking it is

---

3. " 'All my old love had now come back to me. Years afterwards she told me that she had wished, during those days, to take me for her husband.' deleted" [Donoghue's note].

4. " 'Behold now the hope and desire of going back to one's own country or returning to primal chaos, like that of the moth to the light, of the man who with perpetual longing always looks forward with joy to each new spring and each new summer, and to the new months and the new years, deeming that the things he longs for are too slow in com-ing; and who does not perceive that he is longing for his own destruction. But this longing is in its quintessence the spirit of the elements, which finding itself imprisoned within the life of the human body desires continually to return to its source.

'And I would have you to know that this same longing is in its quintessence inherent in nature, and that man is a type of the world.' *The Notebooks of Leonardo da Vinci*, trans. Edward MacCurdy (London, Cape 1938), vol. 1, pp. 80-1 " [Donoghue's note].

but the moon that we long [for], for our destruction, and how, when we meet [it] in the shape of a most fair woman, can we do less than leave all others for her? Do we not seek our dissolution upon her lips?

My liaison lasted but a year, interrupted by one journey to Italy upon her part and by one of mine also to Paris. I had a struggle to earn my living, and that made it harder for me, I was so often preoccupied when she came. Then Maud Gonne wrote to me; she was in London and would I come to dine? I dined with her and my trouble increased—she certainly had no thought of the mischief she was doing. And at last one morning instead of reading much love poetry, as my way was to bring the right mood round, I wrote letters. My friend found my mood did not answer hers and burst into tears. "There is someone else in your heart," she said. It was the breaking between us for many years.

* * *

Dowson[5] came in from time to time, but was for the most part at Dieppe or in some Normandy village near; he was writing poems for the *Savoy* and translations for Smithers,[6] and received with two or three others, who had, it was half-understood, no duties but to associate with Smithers—a task nobody liked—two pounds a week. Dowson, vague and drifting, gave me always [a] sense of that weakness that seems to go with certain high virtues of sweetness and of courtesy. I cannot imagine the world where he would have succeeded. At best, if best it should be called, he might have escaped that unlucky passion for the restaurant-keeper's daughter and the drink and dissipation that were soon to bring him to his death, and lived a harmless, sheltered, and probably inarticulate life. As it was he was burning to the socket, in exquisite songs celebrating in words full of subtle refinement all those whom he named with himself "us the bitter and gay."[7] While I was at Fountain Court, Symons, who had sent him proofs of his too-candid essay,[8] received a letter of remonstrance. "I am living an industrious and innocent

5. Ernest Dowson (1867–1900), poet and member of the Rhymers' Club.
6. Leonard Smithers (1861–1907), publisher and founder of the *Savoy* magazine, which Arthur Symons edited for him.
7. "'Villanelle of the Poets' Road': Dowson, *Poetical Works*, ed. Desmond Flower (London, Cassell and John Lane, The Bodley Head, 1934), p. 74" [Donoghue's note].
8. "Arthur Symons, 'A Literary Causerie: On a Book of Verses,' *Savoy*, no. 4, August 1896, pp. 91-93. Symons does not name Dowson, but the reference is clear: 'a young poet whom I have the privilege to know somewhat intimately . . . a look and manner of pathetic charm, a sort of Keats-like face, the face of demoralized Keats . . . a gradual slipping into deeper and steadier waters of oblivion . . . the swift, disastrous, and suicidal energy of genius . . . I liked to see him occasionally, for a change, drinking nothing stronger than coffee or tea. At Oxford, I believe, his favorite form of intoxication has been hashish; afterwards he gave up his somewhat elaborate experiment in visionary sensations for readier means of oblivion; but he returned to it, I remember, for at least one afternoon, in a company of which I had been the gatherer, and of which I was the host. The experiment was not a successful one . . .'" [Donoghue's note].

life in a small Norman village," the letter said.[9] But before the
letter, though it had been dispatched later, came a telegram. "Sell
my ring and send money: arrested." There was a ring he had left
with Symons for such an occasion. He had got drunk and fought
the village baker. His money proved unnecessary, for the French
magistrate on being told by some sympathetic villager that he had
"an illustrious English poet" before him had said, "Quite right, I
will imprison the baker."

When he was sober, Symons would say, for I have no intimate
knowledge of Dowson but through him—I avoided the haunts
where he could be best known—he would not look at a woman; did
he not belong to the restaurant-keeper's daughter? But, drunk, any
woman, dirty or clean, served his purpose. Living as often as not in
some common lodging-house, where he paid perhaps threepence for
his bed, less from poverty than indifference, he was content with
coarse fare. Could not a glass of wine, absinthe perhaps, transfigure
all? "Symons," he had cried, taking Symons by the coat as he had
passed in some Dieppe restaurant, and pointing to the harlot he was
drinking with, "she writes poetry. It is like Browning and Mrs.
Browning." Just before I had come to stay at Fountain Court he
had arrived one evening with a woman, perhaps the woman Symons
called "Penny plain and twopence coloured"[1] or, for short, "Penny
plain." One or two other young men of letters had dropped in and
sat round the fire, and presently the harlot, having taken off all her
clothes to enjoy the better the pleasant blaze of the fire, began to
tell her life history: her first perception of sex—she had tried to rub
away the first hair from her body—her seduction, and then
accounts of this or that man, especially of one old man who got his
sexual excitement by watching her wring the necks of two pigeons,
which he always brought in a basket. Two or three times she interrupted her story to go into the bedroom with one or other of the
men of letters, Symons alone, who prided himself on his fastidious-
ness, scorning her. That scene comes into my memory very constantly in connection with my memory of Dowson never choosing,
taking whatever life brought in his vague hands. Under the pressure
of wayward emotions, he produced a music with no rhetoric, no
emphasis, no egotism of any kind—a pure music.

* * *

That evening there was a meeting of our council in the City
Hall,[2] and when we came out after it the crowds were waiting for

9. "Dowson did not remonstrate: the letter merely suggested that Symons might
consider toning down a few phrases
which would 'give an erroneous & too
lurid account of me.' Otherwise, Dowson
was content that Symons's text should
stand. *The Letters of Ernest Dowson*,
edited by Desmond Flower and Henry
Mass (London, Cassell, 1967), letter
dated 5 July 1896, p. 371" [Donoghue's
note].
1. I.e., plain and fancy.
2. In Dublin, where Yeats, Maud
Gonne, and others had been attending
political meetings. It was June, 1897—
Queen Victoria's Jubilee.

us all round the Hall. We were going to the National Club in Rutland Square, and they came too. Outside the National Club a magic
lantern was to show on a white screen statistics of evictions, deaths
from starvation, etc., during Victoria's reign. Somewhere in front of
us was a mock funeral Maud Gonne devised, a coffin with "The
British Empire" printed upon it, and black flags with the names of
all those who had been hanged for treason during Queen Victoria's
reign. Presently they began breaking windows where there were decorations. Maud Gonne was walking with a joyous face; she had
taken all those people into her heart. I knew she would not interfere. I knew her principle. If a crowd does anything illegal and you
try to stop it, you may succeed, but you are certain to seem to have
done it to keep from danger yourself. I tried to speak and could only
whisper. I had spoken too much through a disorderly debate at the
council, and my voice had gone. Then I too resigned myself and
felt the excitement of the moment, that joyous irresponsibility and
sense of power.

At the National Club she and I were given tea, and I settled
down to a long table, as I believed, on which I had been writing all
day upon some subject in no way connected with politics. Thereupon a man more excited than I have ever seen anybody or ever shall
see anybody ran in calling out, "Oh, it is awful; it is awful. Police
are batoning the people outside. It is awful," and so on. Maud
Gonne got [up] and said she was going out and somebody else said
she would be hurt. I told them to lock the door and keep her in.
My brain was not working quickly; I remember regretting my tea,
which was getting cold. She was perhaps right to be angry when I
refused to let her out unless she explained what she meant to do.
"How do I know till I get out?" she said. I offered to go out myself
if she would not try to get out when the door was opened, though
what I could have done with my whisper I do not know, but she
would make no promise. Later on she told me that I had made her
do the only cowardly thing of her life. That night I went to all the
newspaper offices and took responsibility for my action.[3] My
memory is that two hundred people were taken to hospital and that
one old woman was killed.

* * *

I joined Maud Gonne from time to time, once at Belfast, where
she [had] gone on some political mission, sometimes at Paris, often
in Dublin. In Dublin I never went to the same hotel, fearing to
compromise her, though she often laughed at my scruple. Once she
complained that she saw too much of me. "I do not say," she said,
"that the crowds are in love with me, but they would hate anybody

---

3. " 'and asked the editors not to attack
the police. I had an idea that the police
could be won over.' deleted" Donoghue's note].

who was." But I never failed to get my letter saying when we could meet. One morning I woke in my hotel somewhere near Rutland Square with the fading vision of her face bending over mine and the knowledge that she had just kissed me. I joined her after breakfast in the Nassau Hotel. We were to spend the day together and visit in the afternoon the old Fenian leader, James Stephens. She said, "Had you a strange dream last night?" I said, "I dreamed this morning for the first time in my life that you kissed me." She made no answer, but late that night when dinner was over and I was about to return home she said, "I will tell you now what happened. When I fell asleep last night I saw standing at my bedside a great spirit. He took me to a great throng of spirits, and you were among them. My hand was put into yours and I was told that we were married. After that I remember nothing." Then and there for the first time with the bodily mouth, she kissed me.

The next day I found her sitting very gloomily over the fire. "I should not have spoken to you in that way," she said, "for I can never be your wife in reality." I said, "Do you love anyone else?" and she said "No" but added that there was somebody else, and that she had to be a moral nature for two. Then bit by bit came out the story of her life, things I had heard all twisted awry by scandal, and disbelieved.

She had met in the South of France the French Boulangist deputy, Millevoye,[4] while staying with a relative in her nineteenth year, and had at once and without any urging on his part fallen in love with him. She then returned to Dublin where her father had a military command. She had sat one night over the fire thinking over her future life. She longed to have control over her own life, and chance discovery of some book on magic among her father's books had made her believe that the Devil, if she prayed to him, might help her. He was rather a real personage to her, for in her earlier girlhood she had wanted to join a convent. She asked the Devil to give her control of her own life and offered in return her soul. At that moment the clock struck twelve, and she felt of a sudden that the prayer had been heard and answered. Within a fortnight her father died suddenly, and she was stricken with remorse.

She had control of her life now, and when she was of age settled in Paris, and after some months became Millevoye's mistress. She was often away from him, for sexual love soon began to repel her, but was for all that very much in love. Then he failed her in various ways. But [she] gave me no coherent account and when I asked some questions clenched her hands together and said it was not well to speak of such things. He had, I discovered, at one time urged her

4. "Lucien Millevoye, French political journalist, editor of *La Patrie*" [Donoghue's note].

to become the mistress of one man to help his political projects, and that she had refused. Then a little boy was born, the adopted child I had been told of—she thought that sexual love was only justified by children. If the boy had not died, she would have broken with Millevoye altogether and lived in Ireland. As it was, after its death she had thought of breaking with him, and had engaged herself for a week to someone else—I thought, I may have had that poor betrothal for my reward—but had broken it off. The idea came to her that the lost child might be reborn, and she had gone back to Millevoye, in the vault under the memorial chapel. A girl child was born, now two years old. Since the child's birth, I understood her to say amid so much broken speech, she and Millevoye had lived apart.

But she was necessary to him, "She did not know what would happen to him if her influence was not there." I wonder as I write these words if I rightly understood, if she had not [in] mind some service he might fall from, to a political ideal. I thought at the time that [she] was appeasing a troubled conscience by performing to the last tittle every duty, and Lady Gregory confirmed me later in this thought. And in all that followed I was careful to touch [her] as one might a sister. If she was to come to me, it must be from no temporary passionate impulse, but with the approval of her conscience. Many a time since then, as I lay awake at night, have I accused myself of acting, not as I thought from a high scruple, but from a dread of moral responsibility, and my thoughts have gone round and round, as do miserable thoughts, coming to no solution.

A little later, how many days I do not remember, we were sitting together when she said, "I hear a voice saying, 'You are about to receive the initiation of the spear.'" We became silent; a double vision unfolded itself, neither speaking till all was finished. She thought herself a great stone statue through which passed flame, and I felt myself becoming flame and mounting up through and looking out of the eyes of a great stone Minerva. Were the beings which stand behind human life trying to unite us, or had we brought it by our own dreams? She was now always very emotional, and would kiss me very tenderly, but when I spoke of marriage on the eve of her leaving said, "No, it seems to me impossible." And then, with clenched hands, "I have a horror and terror of physical love." Lady Gregory was in Venice, but had come home at once on receiving from me an incoherent letter. She offered me money to travel, and told me not to leave Maud Gonne till I had her promise of marriage, but I said, "No, I am too exhausted; I can do no more."

From *Journal*

185

September [1909]. Subject: To complain of the fascination of what's difficult. It spoils spontaneity and pleasure and it wastes time. Repeat the line ending "difficult" three times, and rhyme on bolt, exult, colt, jolt. One could use the thought of the wild-winged and unbroken colt must drag a cart of stones out of pride because it's difficult, and end by denouncing drama, accounts, public contests—all that's merely difficult.

* * *

209

March [1910]

The fascination of what's difficult
Has dried the sap out of my veins and rent
Spontaneous joy and natural content
Out of my heart. What is it/There is something ails our colt
That must, as if it had not holy blood
Nor on Olympus leaped from cloud to cloud
Endure/Shiver at the lash, and strain and sweat and jolt
As though it dragged road metal. My curse on plays
That have to be set up in fifty ways
On the day's war with every fool/knave and dolt
On the day's letters/Theatre business/On correspondence,
    management of men.
I swear before the dawn comes round again
I'll find the stable and pull out the bolt.

———————

Life is memory of what has never happened and hope for what never will happen.

———————

         on[5]
 ✕ On the day with every fool and dolt
 ✕ Content to
 ✕ Arranging this/and that
 ✕ Arranging this
 ✕ On plans
   Arranging this/that, to call the tune
   I swear this night, if but there is no moon
   To find etc.

5. "The rest of this entry is written on the opposite page" [Donoghue's note]. In his transcriptions of Yeats's early drafts, Donoghue uses an X to indicate that a line is completely canceled.

or
Arranging that, and setting this thing/to right
× I'll swear I'll
I swear it that if/if but there is no moon tonight
I'll/To find the stable and pull out the bolt.
× On settling/planning, or setting that thing straight

210

When Adam named the beasts, there was one beast that he forgot to name, or else, taking it for some common horse, named wrongly; and so as time went on men came to have much knowledge of what lives and moves, but of the creature whose name they did not know they had no knowledge, for they could not call it and, having looked at it, speak to one another. That creature permits us to call it Pegasus, but it does not answer to that or any name.

1972

JAMES JOYCE
(1882–1941)

1915: *Dubliners.*
1916: *A Portrait of the Artist as a Young Man.*
1922: *Ulysses.*
1939: *Finnegans Wake.*

James Joyce was born in Dublin, son of a talented but feckless father who is accurately described by Stephen Dedalus in *A Portrait of the Artist as a Young Man* as a man who had in his time been "a medical student, an oarsman, a tenor, an amateur actor, a shouting politician, a small landlord, a small investor, a drinker, a good fellow, a storyteller, somebody's secretary, something in a distillery, a tax-gatherer, a bankrupt, and at present a praiser of his own past." The elder Joyce drifted steadily down the financial and social scale, his family moving from house to house, each one less genteel and more shabby than the previous. James Joyce's whole education was Catholic, from the age of 6 to the age of 9 at Clongowes Wood College, and from 11 to 16 at Belvedere College, Dublin. Both were Jesuit institutions, and were normal roads to the priesthood. He then studied modern languages at University College, Dublin.

From a comparatively early age Joyce regarded himself as a rebel against the shabbiness and Philistinism of Dublin. In his early youth he was very religious, but in his last year at Belvedere he began to reject his Catholic faith in favor of a literary mission which he saw as involving rebellion and exile. He refused to play any part in the nationalist or other popular activities of his fellow students, and created some stir by his outspoken articles, one of which, on the Norwegian playwright Henrik Ibsen, appeared in the *Fortnightly Review* for April, 1900. He taught himself Norwegian to be able to read Ibsen and to write to him. When an article by Joyce, significantly entitled *The Day of the Rabblement*, was refused, on instructions of the faculty adviser, by the student magazine that had commissioned it, he had it printed privately. By 1902, when he received his B.A. degree, he was already committed to a career as exile and writer. For Joyce, as for his character Stephen Dedalus, the latter implied the former. To preserve his integrity, to avoid involvement in popular sentimentalities and dishonesties, and above all to be able to re-create with both total understanding and total objectivity the Dublin life he knew so well, he felt that he had to go abroad.

Joyce went to Paris after graduation, was recalled to Dublin by his mother's fatal illness, had a short spell there as a schoolteacher, then returned to the Continent in 1904 to teach English at Trieste and then at Zurich. He took with him Nora Barnacle, an uneducated Galway girl with no interest in literature; her native vivacity and peasant wit charmed Joyce, and the two lived in devoted companionship until Joyce's death, though they were not married until 1931. In 1920 Joyce settled in Paris, where he lived until December, 1940, when the war forced him to take refuge in Switzerland; he died in Zurich a few weeks later.

Proud, obstinate, absolutely convinced of his genius, given to fits of sudden gaiety and of sudden silence, Joyce was not always an easy person to get on with, yet he never lacked friends and throughout his 36 years on the Continent was always the center of a literary circle. Life was hard at first. At Trieste he had very little money, and he did not improve matters by drinking heavily, a habit checked somewhat by his brother Stanislaus who came out from Dublin to act (as Stanislaus put it much later) as his "brother's keeper." His financial position was much improved by the patronage of Mrs. Harold McCormick (Edith Rockefeller), who provided him with a monthly stipend from March, 1917, until September, 1919, when they quarreled, apparently because Joyce refused to submit to psychoanalysis by Carl Jung, who had been heavily endowed by Mrs. McCormick. The New York lawyer and art patron John Quinn, steered in Joyce's direction by Ezra Pound, also helped Joyce financially in 1917. A more permanent benefactor was the English feminist and editor Harriet Shaw Weaver, who not only subsidized Joyce generously from 1917 to the end of his life, but occupied herself indefatigably with arrangements for publishing his work.

Joyce's almost life-long exile from his native Ireland has something paradoxical about it. No writer has ever been more soaked in Dublin, its atmosphere, its history, its topography; in spite of doing most of his writing in Trieste, Zurich, and Paris, he wrote only and always about Dublin. He devised ways of expanding his accounts of Dublin, however, so that they became microcosms, small-scale models, of all human life, of all history and all geography. Indeed that was his life's work: to write about Dublin in such a way that he was writing about all of human experience.

Joyce began his career by writing a series of stories etching with extraordinary clarity aspects of Dublin life. But these stories—published as *Dubliners* in 1915—are more than sharp realistic sketches. In each, the detail is so chosen and organized that carefully interacting symbolic meanings are set up, and as a result *Dubliners* is a book about man's fate as well as a series of sketches of Dublin. (*Araby*, for example, is meticulously accurate in every physical detail, yet it is also a symbolic story about the relation between dreams and reality.) Further, the stories are presented in a particular order so that new meanings arise from the relation between them.

This was Joyce's first phase: he had to come directly to terms with the life he had rejected, to see it for what it was and for what it meant. Next, he had to come to terms with the meaning of his own development as a man dedicated to writing. He did this by weaving his autobiography into a novel so finely chiseled and carefully organized, so stripped of everything superfluous, that each word contributes to the presentation of the theme: the parallel movement toward art and toward exile. A part of Joyce's first draft has been posthumously published under the original title of *Stephen Hero* (1944): a comparison between it and the final version which Joyce gave to the world, *A Portrait of the Artist as a Young Man* (1916), will show how carefully Joyce reworked and compressed his material for maximum effect. The *Portrait* is not literally true as autobiography, though it has many autobiographical elements; but it is representatively true not only of Joyce but of the relation between the artist and society in the modern world.

In the *Portrait* Stephen worked out a theory of art which considers that art moves from the lyrical form—which is the simplest, the personal expression of an instant of emotion—through the narrative form—no longer purely personal—to the dramatic—the highest and most perfect form, where "the artist, like the God of creation, remains within or behind or beyond or above his handiwork, invisible, refined out of existence, indifferent, paring his fingernails." This view of art, which involves the objectivity, even the exile, of the artist (even though the artist uses only the materials provided for him by his own life) is related to that held by the poets of the 90's. More widely, it is related to the rejection by the artist of the ordinary world of middleclass values and activities which we see equally, though in different ways, in Matthew Arnold's war against the Philistines and in the concept (very un-Arnoldian) of the artist as bohemian. Joyce's career belongs to that long chapter in the history of the arts in Western civilization which begins with the artist's declaring his independence and ends with his feeling his inevitable "alienation." But if Joyce was alienated, as in certain ways he clearly was, he made his alienation serve his art: the kinds of writing represented by *Ulysses* and *Finnegans Wake* represent the most consummate craftsmanship put at the service of a humanely comic vision of all life. Some (though surprisingly few) of Joyce's innovations in organization and style have been imitated by other writers, but these books are, and will probably remain, unique in our literature. They are not freaks or historical oddities, but serious and exciting works.

From the beginning Joyce had trouble with the Philistines. Publication of *Dubliners* was held up for many years while he fought with both English and Irish publishers about certain words and phrases which they wished to eliminate. (It was the former who finally published the book.) His masterpiece *Ulysses* was banned in both Britain and America on its first appearance in 1922, its earlier serialization in the *Little Review* (March 1918–December 1920) having had to stop abruptly when the U.S. Post Office brought a charge of obscenity against it. Fortunately, Judge Woolsey's history-making decision in favor of *Ulysses* in the United States District Court on December 6, 1933, resulted in the lifting of the ban and the free circulation of the work first in America and soon afterwards in Britain.

ULYSSES

Ulysses is an account of one day in the lives of citizens of Dublin in the year 1904: it is thus the description of a limited number of events involving a limited number of people in a limited environment. Yet Joyce's ambition—which took him seven years to realize—is to make his action into a microcosm of all human experience. The events are not therefore told on a single level; the story is presented in such a manner that depth and implication are given to them and they become symbolic of the activity of Man in the World. The most obvious of the devices which Joyce employs in order to make clear the microcosmic aspect of his story is the parallel with Homer's *Odyssey*: every episode in *Ulysses* corresponds in some way to an episode in the *Odyssey*. Joyce regarded Homer's Ulysses as the most "complete" man in literature, a man who is shown in all his aspects—both coward and hero, cautious and reckless, weak and strong, husband and lover, father and son, sublime and ridiculous; so he makes his hero, Leopold Bloom, an Irish Jew, into a modern Ulysses, and by so doing helps to make him Everyman and to make Dublin the world.

The book opens at eight o'clock on the morning of June 16, 1904. Stephen Dedalus (the same character we saw in the *Portrait*, but this is two years after our last glimpse of him there) had been summoned back to Dublin by his mother's fatal illness and now lives in an old military tower on the shore with Buck Mulligan, a rollicking medical student, and an Englishman called Haines. In the first three episodes of *Ulysses*, which concentrate on Stephen, he is built up as an aloof, uncompromising artist, rejecting all advances by representatives of the normal world, the incomplete man, to be contrasted later with the complete Leopold Bloom, who is much more "normal" and conciliatory. After tracing Stephen through his early-morning activities and learning the main currents of his mind, we go, in the fourth episode, to the home of Bloom. We follow closely his every activity: attending a funeral, transacting his business, eating his lunch, walking through the Dublin streets, worrying about his wife's infidelity with Blazes Boylan—and at each point the contents of his mind, including retrospect and anticipation, are presented to the reader, until all his past history is revealed. Finally, Bloom and Stephen, who have just been missing each other all day, get together. By this time it is late, and Stephen, who has been drinking with some medical students, is the worse for liquor. Bloom, moved by a paternal feeling towards Stephen (his own son had died in infancy and in a symbolic way Stephen takes his place), follows him during subsequent adventures in the role of protector. The climax of the book comes when Stephen, far gone in drink, and Bloom, worn out with fatigue, succumb to a series of hallucinations where their subconscious and unconscious come to the surface in dramatic form and their whole personalities are revealed with a completeness and a frankness unique in literature. Then Bloom takes the unresponsive Stephen home and gives him a meal. After Stephen's departure Bloom retires to bed—it is now 2 A.M. on June 17—while his wife Molly, representing the principles of sex and reproduction on which all human life is based, closes the book with a long monologue in which her experiences as woman are remembered.

On the level of realistic description, *Ulysses* pulses with life and can be enjoyed for its evocation of early 20th-century Dublin. On the level of psychological exploration, it gives a profound and moving presentation of the personality and consciousness of Leopold Bloom and (to a lesser extent) Stephen Dedalus. On the level of style, it exhibits the most fascinating linguistic virtuosity. On a deeper symbolic level, the novel explores the paradoxes of human loneliness and sociability (for Bloom is both Jew and Dubliner, both exile and citizen, just as all men are in a sense both exiles and citizens), and it explores the problems posed by the relations between parent and child, between the generations, and between the sexes. At the same time, through its use of themes from Homer, Dante, and Shakespeare, from literature, philosophy, and history, the book weaves a subtle pattern of allusion and suggestion which illuminates many aspects of human experience. The more one reads *Ulysses* the more one finds in it, but at the same time one does not need to probe into the symbolic meaning in order to relish both its literary artistry and its human feeling. At the forefront stands Leopold Bloom, from one point of view a frustrated and confused outsider in the society in which he moves, from another a champion of kindness and justice whose humane curiosity about his fellows redeems him from mere vulgarity and gives the book its positive human foundation.

Readers who come to *Ulysses* with expectations about the way the story is to be presented derived from their reading of Victorian novels or even of such 20th-century novelists as Conrad and Lawrence will find much that is at first puzzling. Joyce presents the consciousness of his characters directly, without any explanatory comment which tells the reader whose consciousness is being rendered (this is the "stream-of-consciousness" method). He may move, in the same paragraph and without any sign that he is making such a transition, from a description of a character's action—e.g., Stephen walking along the shore or Bloom entering a restaurant —to an evocation of the character's mental response to this action. That response is always multiple: it derives partly from the character's immediate situation and partly from the whole complex of attitudes which his past history has created in him. To suggest this multiplicity, Joyce may vary his style, from the flippant to the serious or from a realistic description to a suggestive set of images which indicate what might be called the general tone of the character's consciousness. Past and present mingle in the texture of the prose because they mingle in the texture of consciousness; and this mingling can be indicated by puns, by sudden breaks into a new kind of style or a new kind of subject matter, or by some other device for keeping the reader constantly in sight of the shifting, kaleidoscopic nature of human awareness. With a little experience, the reader learns to follow the implications of Joyce's shifts in manner and content—even to follow that at first sight bewildering passage in the "Proteus" episode where Stephen does not go to visit his uncle and aunt but, passing the road that leads to their house, imagines the kind of conversation that would take place in his home *if* he had gone to visit his uncle and had then returned home and reported that he had done so. *Ulysses* must not be approached as though it were a novel written in a traditional manner; all preconceptions must be set aside and we must follow wherever the author leads us and let the language tell us what it has to say without our troubling whether language is being used "properly" or not.

FINNEGANS WAKE

Joyce's last work, *Finnegans Wake*, was published in 1939; it took more than fourteen years to write, and Joyce considered it his masterpiece. In *Ulysses* he had made the symbolic aspect of the novel at least as important as the realistic aspect, but in *Finnegans Wake* he gave up realism altogether. This vast story of a symbolic Irishman's cosmic dream develops by enormous reverberating puns a continuous expansion of meaning, the elements in the puns deriving from every conceivable source in history, literature, mythology, and Joyce's personal experience. The whole book being (on one level at least) a dream, Joyce invents his own dream language in which words are combined, distorted, created by fitting together bits of other words, used with several different meanings at once, often drawn from several different languages at once, and fused in all sorts of ways to achieve whole clusters of meaning simultaneously. In fact, so many echoing suggestions can be found in every word or phrase that a full annotation of even a few pages would require a large book. It has taken the co-operative work of a number of devoted readers to make clear the complex interactions of the multiple puns and pun-clusters through which the ideas are projected, and every rereading reveals new meanings. It is true that many readers find the efforts of explication demanded by *Finnegans Wake* too arduous; some, indeed, feel that the law of diminishing returns has now begun to operate, and that the effort of both author and reader is disproportionate. Nevertheless, the book has great beauty and fascination even for the casual reader. Students are advised to read aloud— or to listen to the record of Joyce reading aloud—the extract printed in this anthology, in order to appreciate the degree to which the rhythms of the prose assist in conveying the meaning.

To an even greater extent than *Ulysses, Finnegans Wake* aims at embracing all of human history. The title is from an Irish-American ballad about Tom Finnegan, a hod carrier who falls off a ladder when drunk and is apparently killed, but who revives when during the "wake" (the watch by the dead body) someone spills whiskey on him. The theme of death and resurrection, of cycles of change coming round in the course of history, is central to *Finnegans Wake*, which derives one of its main principles of organization from the cyclical theory of history put forward in 1725 by the Italian philosopher Giambattista Vico. Vico held that history passes through four phases: the divine or theocratic, when people are governed by their awe of the supernatural; the aristocratic (the "heroic age" reflected in Homer and in *Beowulf*); the democratic and individualistic; and the final stage of chaos, a fall into confusion which startles man back into supernatural reverence and starts the process once again. Joyce, like Yeats, saw his own generation as in the final stage awaiting the shock that will bring man back to the first.

A mere account of the narrative line of *Finnegans Wake* cannot, of course, give any idea of the content of the work. If one explains that it opens with Finnegan's fall, then introduces his successor Humphrey Chimpden Earwicker, who is Everyman, and whose dream constitutes the novel; that he is presented as having guilt feelings about an indecency he committed (or may have committed) in Phoenix Park, Dublin; that his wife Anna Livia Plurabelle or ALP (who is also Eve, Iseult, Ireland, the River Liffey) changes her role just as he does; that he has two sons Shem and Shaun (or Jerry and Kevin), who represent introvert and extrovert, artist and practical man, creator and popularizer, and symbolize this basic dichotomy in human nature by all kinds of metamorphoses; and if one adds that, in the four books into which *Finnegans Wake* is divided (after Vico's pattern), actions comic or grotesque or sad or tender or desperate or passionate or terribly ordinary (and very often several of these things at the same time) take place with all the shifting meanings of a dream, so that characters change into others or into inanimate objects and the setting keeps shifting—if we explain all this, we still have said very little about what makes *Finnegans Wake* what it is. The dreamer, whose initials HCE indicate his universality ("Here Comes Everybody"), is at the same time a particular person, who keeps a pub in Chapelizod, a Dublin suburb on the River Liffey near Phoenix Park. His mysterious misdemeanor in Phoenix Park is in a sense Original Sin: Earwicker is Adam as well as a primeval giant, the Hill of Howth, the Great Parent ("Haveth Childers Everywhere" is another expansion of HCE), and Man in History. Other characters who flit and change through the book, such as the Twelve Customers (who are also twelve jurymen and public opinion) and the Four Old Men (who are also judges, the authors of the four Gospels, and the four elements), help to weave the texture of multiple significance so characteristic of the work. But always it is the punning language, extending significance downwards—rather than the plot, developing it lengthwise—that bears the main load of meaning.

Araby[1]

North Richmond Street, being blind, was a quiet street except at the hour when the Christian Brothers' School set the boys free.[2]

[1]. The third of the fifteen stories in *Dubliners*. This tale of the frustrated quest for beauty in the midst of drabness is both meticulously realistic in its handling of details of Dublin life and the Dublin scene and highly symbolic in that almost every image and incident suggests some particular aspect of the theme (e.g., the suggestion of the Holy Grail in the image of the chalice, mentioned in the fifth paragraph). Joyce was drawing on his own childhood

An uninhabited house of two storeys stood at the blind end, detached from its neighbours in a square ground. The other houses of the street, conscious of decent lives within them, gazed at one another with brown imperturbable faces.

The former tenant of our house, a priest, had died in the back drawing-room. Air, musty from having been long enclosed, hung in all the rooms, and the waste room behind the kitchen was littered with old useless papers. Among these I found a few paper-covered books, the pages of which were curled and damp: *The Abbot*, by Walter Scott, *The Devout Communicant* and *The Memoirs of Vidocq*.[3] I liked the last best because its leaves were yellow. The wild garden behind the house contained a central apple-tree and a few straggling bushes under one of which I found the late tenant's rusty bicycle-pump. He had been a very charitable priest; in his will he had left all his money to institutions and the furniture of his house to his sister.

When the short days of winter came dusk fell before we had well eaten our dinners. When we met in the street the houses had grown sombre. The space of sky above us was the colour of ever-changing violet and towards it the lamps of the street lifted their feeble lanterns. The cold air stung us and we played till our bodies glowed. Our shouts echoed in the silent street. The career of our play brought us through the dark muddy lanes behind the houses where we ran the gauntlet of the rough tribes from the cottages, to the back doors of the dark dripping gardens where odours arose from the ashpits, to the dark odorous stables where a coachman smoothed and combed the horse or shook music from the buckled harness. When we returned to the street light from the kitchen windows had filled the areas. If my uncle was seen turning the corner we hid in the shadow until we had seen him safely housed. Or if Mangan's sister came out on the doorstep to call her brother in to his tea we watched her from our shadow peer up and down the street. We waited to see whether she would remain or go in and, if she remained, we left our shadow and walked up to Mangan's steps resignedly. She was waiting for us, her figure defined by the light from the half-opened door. Her brother always teased her before he obeyed and I stood by the railings looking at

recollections, and the uncle in the story is a reminiscence of Joyce's father. But in all the stories in *Dubliners* dealing with childhood, the child lives not with his parents but with an uncle and aunt —a symbol of that isolation and lack of proper relation between "consubstantial" ("in the flesh") parents and children which is a major theme in Joyce's work.
2. The Joyce family moved to 17 North Richmond Street, Dublin, in 1894, and Joyce had earlier briefly attended the Christian Brothers' school a few doors away (The Christian Brothers are a Catholic religious community). The details of the house described here correspond exactly to those of No. 17.
3. François Eugène Vidocq (1775–1857) had an extraordinary career as soldier, thief, chief of the French detective force, and private detective. *The Abbot* is a historical novel dealing with Mary Queen of Scots, *The Devout Communicant* a Catholic religious manual.

her. Her dress swung as she moved her body and the soft rope of her hair tossed from side to side.

Every morning I lay on the floor in the front parlour watching her door. The blind was pulled down to within an inch of the sash so that I could not be seen. When she came out on the doorstep my heart leaped. I ran to the hall, seized my books and followed her. I kept her brown figure always in my eye and, when we came near the point at which our ways diverged, I quickened my pace and passed her. This happened morning after morning. I had never spoken to her, except for a few casual words, and yet her name was like a summons to all my foolish blood.

Her image accompanied me even in places the most hostile to romance. On Saturday evenings when my aunt went marketing I had to go to carry some of the parcels. We walked through the flaring streets, jostled by drunken men and bargaining women, amid the curses of labourers, the shrill litanies of shop-boys who stood on guard by the barrels of pigs' cheeks, the nasal chanting of street-singers, who sang a *come-all-you*[4] about O'Donovan Rossa, or a ballad about the troubles in our native land. These noises converged in a single sensation of life for me: I imagined that I bore my chalice safely through a throng of foes. Her name sprang to my lips at moments in strange prayers and praises which I myself did not understand. My eyes were often full of tears (I could not tell why) and at times a flood from my heart seemed to pour itself out into my bosom. I thought little of the future. I did not know whether I would ever speak to her or not or, if I spoke to her, how I could tell her of my confused adoration. But my body was like a harp and her words and gestures were like fingers running upon the wires.

One evening I went into the back drawing-room in which the priest had died. It was a dark rainy evening and there was no sound in the house. Through one of the broken panes I heard the rain impinge upon the earth, the fine incessant needles of water playing in the sodden beds. Some distant lamp or lighted window gleamed below me. I was thankful that I could see so little. All my senses seemed to desire to veil themselves and, feeling that I was about to slip from them, I pressed the palms of my hands together until they trembled, murmuring: "O love! O love!" many times.

At last she spoke to me. When she addressed the first words to me I was so confused that I did not know what to answer. She asked me was I going to *Araby*.[5] I forgot whether I answered yes

---

4. Street ballad, so called from its opening words. This one was about the 19th-century Irish nationalist Jeremiah Donovan, popularly known as O'Donovan Rossa.

5. The bazaar, described by its "official catalogue" as a "Grand Oriental Fête," was actually held in Dublin on May 14–19, 1894.

or no. It would be a splendid bazaar, she said she would love to go.

"And why can't you?" I asked.

While she spoke she turned a silver bracelet round and round her wrist. She could not go, she said, because there would be a retreat[6] that week in her convent. Her brother and two other boys were fighting for their caps and I was alone at the railings. She held one of the spikes, bowing her head towards me. The light from the lamp opposite our door caught the white curve of her neck, lit up her hair that rested there and, falling, lit up the hand upon the railing. It fell over one side of her dress and caught the white border of a petticoat, just visible as she stood at ease.

"It's well for you," she said.

"If I go," I said, "I will bring you something."

What innumerable follies laid waste my waking and sleeping thoughts after that evening! I wished to annihilate the tedious intervening days. I chafed against the work of school. At night in my bedroom and by day in the classroom her image came between me and the page I strove to read. The syllables of the word *Araby* were called to me through the silence in which my soul luxuriated and cast an Eastern enchantment over me. I asked for leave to go to the bazaar on Saturday night. My aunt was surprised and hoped it was not some Freemason affair.[7] I answered few questions in class. I watched my master's face pass from amiability to sternness; he hoped I was not beginning to idle. I could not call my wandering thoughts together. I had hardly any patience with the serious work of life which, now that it stood between me and my desire, seemed to me child's play, ugly monotonous child's play.

On Saturday morning I reminded my uncle that I wished to go to the bazaar in the evening. He was fussing at the hallstand, looking for the hat-brush, and answered me curtly:

"Yes, boy, I know."

As he was in the hall I could not go into the front parlour and lie at the window. I left the house in bad humour and walked slowly towards the school. The air was pitilessly raw and already my heart misgave me.

When I came home to dinner my uncle had not yet been home. Still it was early. I sat staring at the clock for some time and, when its ticking began to irritate me, I left the room. I mounted the staircase and gained the upper part of the house. The high cold empty gloomy rooms liberated me and I went from room to room singing. From the front window I saw my companions playing below in the street. Their cries reached me weakened and indistinct and, leaning my forehead against the cool glass, I looked over at the

6. Period of seclusion from ordinary activities devoted to religious exercises; "her convent" is, of course, her convent school.

7. His aunt shares her church's distrust of the Freemasons, an old European secret society, reputedly anti-Catholic.

dark house where she lived. I may have stood there for an hour, seeing nothing but the brown-clad figure cast by my imagination, touched discreetly by the lamplight at the curved neck, at the hand upon the railings and at the border below the dress.

When I came downstairs again I found Mrs. Mercer sitting at the fire. She was an old garrulous woman, a pawnbroker's widow, who collected used stamps for some pious purpose. I had to endure the gossip of the tea-table. The meal was prolonged beyond an hour and still my uncle did not come. Mrs. Mercer stood up to go: she was sorry she couldn't wait any longer, but it was after eight o'clock and she did not like to be out late, as the night air was bad for her. When she had gone I began to walk up and down the room, clenching my fists. My aunt said:

"I'm afraid you may put off your bazaar for this night of Our Lord."

At nine o'clock I heard my uncle's latchkey in the halldoor. I heard him talking to himself and heard the hallstand rocking when it had received the weight of his overcoat. I could interpret these signs. When he was midway through his dinner I asked him to give me the money to go to the bazaar. He had forgotten.

"The people are in bed and after their first sleep now," he said.

I did not smile. My aunt said to him energetically:

"Can't you give him the money and let him go? You've kept him late enough as it is."

My uncle said he was very sorry he had forgotten. He said he believed in the old saying: "All work and no play makes Jack a dull boy." He asked me where I was going and, when I had told him a second time he asked me did I know *The Arab's Farewell to his Steed*.[8] When I left the kitchen he was about to recite the opening lines of the piece to my aunt.

I held a florin tightly in my hand as I strode down Buckingham Street towards the station. The sight of the streets thronged with buyers and glaring with gas recalled to me the purpose of my journey. I took my seat in a third-class carriage of a deserted train. After an intolerable delay the train moved out of the station slowly. It crept onward among ruinous houses and over the twinkling river. At Westland Row Station a crowd of people pressed to the carriage doors; but the porters moved them back, saying that it was a special train for the bazaar. I remained alone in the bare carriage. In a few minutes the train drew up beside an improvised wooden platform. I passed out on to the road and saw by the lighted dial of a clock that it was ten minutes to ten. In front of me was a large building which displayed the magical name.

I could not find any sixpenny entrance and, fearing that the bazaar would be closed, I passed in quickly through a turnstile,

8. Once-popular sentimental poem by Caroline Norton.

handing a shilling to a weary-looking man. I found myself in a big hall girdled at half its height by a gallery. Nearly all the stalls were closed and the greater part of the hall was in darkness. I recognised a silence like that which pervades a church after a service. I walked into the centre of the bazaar timidly. A few people were gathered about the stalls which were still open. Before a curtain, over which the words *Café Chantant*[9] were written in coloured lamps, two men were counting money on a salver. I listened to the fall of the coins.

Remembering with difficulty why I had come I went over to one of the stalls and examined porcelain vases and flowered tea-sets. At the door of the stall a young lady was talking and laughing with two young gentlemen. I remarked their English accents and listened vaguely to their conversation.

"O, I never said such a thing!"

"O, but you did!"

"O, but I didn't!"

"Didn't she say that?"

"Yes. I heard her."

"O, there's a . . . fib!"

Observing me the young lady came over and asked me did I wish to buy anything. The tone of her voice was not encouraging; she seemed to have spoken to me out of a sense of duty. I looked humbly at the great jars that stood like eastern guards at either side of the dark entrance to the stall and murmured:

"No, thank you."

The young lady changed the position of one of the vases and went back to the two young men. They began to talk of the same subject. Once or twice the young lady glanced at me over her shoulder.

I lingered before her stall, though I knew my stay was useless, to make my interest in her wares seem the more real. Then I turned away slowly and walked down the middle of the bazaar. I allowed the two pennies to fall against the sixpence in my pocket. I heard a voice call from one end of the gallery that the light was out. The upper part of the hall was now completely dark.

Gazing up into the darkness I saw myself as a creature driven and derided by vanity; and my eyes burned with anguish and anger.

1905   1914

9. Literally "singing café" (café providing musical entertainment, popular early in this century).

Clay[1]

The matron had given her leave to go out as soon as the women's tea was over and Maria looked forward to her evening out. The kitchen was spick and span: the cook said you could see yourself in the big copper boilers. The fire was nice and bright and on one of the side-tables were four very big barmbracks. These barmbracks seemed uncut; but if you went closer you would see that they had been cut into long thick even slices and were ready to be handed round at tea. Maria had cut them herself.

Maria was a very, very small person indeed but she had a very long nose and a very long chin. She talked a little through her nose, always soothingly: "Yes, my dear," and "No, my dear." She was always sent for when the women quarreled over their tubs and always succeeded in making peace. One day the matron had said to her:

"Maria, you are a veritable peacemaker!"

And the sub-matron and two of the Board ladies had heard the compliment. And Ginger Mooney was always saying what she wouldn't do to the dummy who had charge of the irons if it wasn't for Maria. Everyone was so fond of Maria.

The women would have their tea at six o'clock and she would be able to get away before seven. From Ballsbridge to the Pillar, twenty minutes; from the Pillar to Drumcondra, twenty minutes; and twenty minutes to buy the things. She would be there before eight. She took out her purse with the silver clasps and read again the words *A Present from Belfast.* She was very fond of that purse because Joe had brought it to her five years before when he and Alphy had gone to Belfast on a Whit-Monday trip. In the purse were two half-crowns and some coppers. She would have five shillings clear after paying tram fare. What a nice evening they would have, all the children singing! Only she hoped that Joe wouldn't come in drunk. He was so different when he took any drink.

Often he had wanted her to go and live with them; but she would have felt herself in the way (though Joe's wife was ever so nice with her) and she had become accustomed to the life of the laundry. Joe was a good fellow. She had nursed him and Alphy too; and Joe used often say:

---

1. Originally entitled *Hallow Eve.* For an interesting discussion of the significance of Joyce's change of title, and of the symbolic patterns underlying the apparently simple realistic sketch, see *Joyce, the Man, the Work, the Reputation,* by Marvin Magalaner and Richard M. Kain, pp. 84–90. Hallow Eve is Halloween, the evening of October 31, preceding All Saints Day. It is an evening on which a variety of traditional ceremonies and customs are observed. In this story the custom of having blindfolded players choose from a group of traditional objects in order to foretell their future provides a critical point in the action. The children have jokingly included a dish of clay, into which the blindfolded Maria puts her finger. Maria gets neither the prayer book (symbolizing life in a convent) nor the ring (symbolizing marriage), but the unexpected clay, symbol of death.

"Mamma is mamma but Maria is my proper mother."

After the break-up at home the boys had got her that position in the *Dublin by Lamplight* laundry, and she liked it. She used to have such a bad opinion of Protestants but now she thought they were very nice people, a little quiet and serious, but still very nice people to live with. Then she had her plants in the conservatory and she liked looking after them. She had lovely ferns and wax-plants and, whenever anyone came to visit her, she always gave the visitor one or two slips from her conservatory. There was one thing she didn't like and that was the tracts on the walls; but the matron was such a nice person to deal with, so genteel.

When the cook told her everything was ready she went into the women's room and began to pull the big bell. In a few minutes the women began to come in by twos and threes, wiping their steaming hands in their petticoats and pulling down the sleeves of their blouses over their red steaming arms. They settled down before their huge mugs which the cook and the dummy filled up with hot tea, already mixed with milk and sugar in huge tin cans. Maria superintended the distribution of the barmbrack and saw that every woman got her four slices. There was a great deal of laughing and joking during the meal. Lizzie Fleming said Maria was sure to get the ring and, though Fleming had said that for so many Hallow Eves, Maria had to laugh and say she didn't wany any ring or man either; and when she laughed her gray-green eyes sparkled with disappointed shyness and the tip of her nose nearly met the tip of her chin. Then Ginger Mooney lifted up her mug of tea and proposed Maria's health while all the other women clattered with their mugs on the table, and said she was sorry she hadn't a sup of porter to drink it in. And Maria laughed again till the tip of her nose nearly met the tip of her chin and till her minute body nearly shook itself asunder because she knew that Mooney meant well though, of course, she had the notions of a common woman.

But wasn't Maria glad when the women had finished their tea and the cook and the dummy had begun to clear away the tea-things! She went into her little bedroom and, remembering that the next morning was a mass morning, changed the hand of the alarm from seven to six. Then she took off her working skirt and her house-boots and laid her best skirt out on the bed and her tiny dress-boots beside the foot of the bed. She changed her blouse too and, as she stood before the mirror, she thought of how she used to dress for mass on Sunday morning when she was a young girl; and she looked with quaint affection at the diminutive body which she had so often adorned. In spite of its years she found it a nice tidy little body.

When she got outside the streets were shining with rain and she was glad of her old brown waterproof. The tram was full and she had to sit on the little stool at the end of the car, facing all the people, with her toes barely touching the floor. She arranged in her mind all she was going to do and thought how much better it was to be independent and to have your own money in your pocket. She hoped they would have a nice evening. She was sure they would but she could not help thinking what a pity it was Alphy and Joe were not speaking. They were always falling out now but when they were boys together they used to be the best of friends: but such was life.

She got out of her tram at the Pillar and ferreted her way quickly among the crowds. She went into Downes's cake-shop but the shop was so full of people that it was a long time before she could get herself attended to. She bought a dozen of mixed penny cakes, and at last came out of the shop laden with a big bag. Then she thought what else would she buy: she wanted to buy something really nice. They would be sure to have plenty of apples and nuts. It was hard to know what to buy and all she could think of was cake. She decided to buy some plumcake but Downes's plumcake had not enough almond icing on top of it so she went over to a shop in Henry Street. Here she was a long time in suiting herself and the stylish young lady behind the counter, who was evidently a little annoyed by her, asked her was it wedding cake she wanted to buy. That made Maria blush and smile at the young lady; but the young lady took it all very seriously and finally cut a thick slice of plumcake, parceled it up and said:

"Two-and-four, please."

She thought she would have to stand in the Drumcondra tram because none of the young men seemed to notice her but an elderly gentleman made room for her. He was a stout gentleman and he wore a brown hard hat; he had a square red face and a grayish moustache. Maria thought he was a colonel-looking gentleman and she reflected how much more polite he was than the young men who simply stared straight before them. The gentleman began to chat with her about Hallow Eve and the rainy weather. He supposed the bag was full of good things for the little ones and said it was only right that the youngsters should enjoy themselves while they were young. Maria agreed with him and favored him with demure nods and hems. He was very nice with her, and when she was getting out at the Canal Bridge she thanked him and bowed, and he bowed to her and raised his hat and smiled agreeably; and while she was going up along the terrace, bending her tiny head under the rain, she thought how easy it was to know a gentleman even when he has a drop taken.

Everybody said: "O, *here's Maria!*" when she came to Joe's house. Joe was there, having come home from business, and all the children had their Sunday dresses on. There were two big girls in from next door and games were going on. Maria gave the bag of cakes to the eldest boy, Alphy, to divide and Mrs. Donnelly said it was too good of her to bring such a big bag of cakes and made all the children say:

"Thanks, Maria."

But Maria said she had brought something special for papa and mamma, something they would be sure to like, and began to look for her plumcake. She tried in Downe's bag and then in the pockets of her water-proof and then on the hallstand but nowhere could she find it. Then she asked all the children had any of them eaten it—by mistake, of course—but the children all said no and looked as if they did not like to eat cakes if they were to be accused of stealing. Everybody had a solution for the mystery and Mrs. Donnelly said it was plain that Maria had left it behind her in the tram. Maria, remembering how confused the gentleman with the grayish moustache had made her, colored with shame and vexation and disappointment. At the thought of the failure of her little surprise and of the two and fourpence she had thrown away for nothing she nearly cried outright.

But Joe said it didn't matter and made her sit down by the fire. He was very nice with her. He told her all that went on in his office, repeating for her a smart answer which he had made to the manager. Maria did not understand why Joe laughed so much over the answer he had made but she said that the manager must have been a very overbearing person to deal with. Joe said he wasn't so bad when you knew how to take him, that he was a decent sort so long as you didn't rub him the wrong way. Mrs. Donnelly played the piano for the children and they danced and sang. Then the two next-door girls handed round the nuts. Nobody could find the nutcrackers and Joe was nearly getting cross over it and asked how did they expect Maria to crack nuts without a nutcracker. But Maria said she didn't like nuts and that they weren't to bother about her. Then Joe asked would she take a bottle of stout and Mrs. Donnelly said there was port wine too in the house if she would prefer that. Maria said she would rather they didn't ask her to take anything; but Joe insisted.

So Maria let him have his way and they sat by the fire talking over old times and Maria thought she would put in a good word for Alphy. But Joe cried that God might strike him stone dead if ever he spoke a word to his brother again and Maria said she was sorry she had mentioned the matter. Mrs. Donnelly told her husband it was a great shame for him to speak that way of his own flesh and blood but Joe said that Alphy was no brother of his and there was nearly being a row on the head of it. But Joe said he would not lose his temper on account of the night it was and asked his wife to open some more stout. The two next-door girls had arranged some

Hallow Eve games and soon everything was merry again. Maria was delighted to see the children so merry and Joe and his wife in such good spirits. The next-door girls put some saucers on the table and then led the children up to the table, blindfold. One got the prayer-book and the other three got the water; and when one of the next-door girls got the ring Mrs. Donnelly shook her finger at the blushing girl as much as to say: O, I know all about it! They insisted then on blindfolding Maria and leading her up to the table to see what she would get; and, while they were putting on the bandage, Maria laughed and laughed again till the tip of her nose nearly met the tip of her chin.

They led her up to the table amid laughing and joking and she put her hand out in the air as she was told to do. She moved her hand about here and there in the air and descended on one of the saucers. She felt a soft wet substance with her fingers and was surprised that nobody spoke or took off her bandage. There was a pause for a few seconds; and then a great deal of scuffling and whispering. Somebody said something about the garden, and at last Mrs. Donnelly said something very cross to one of the next-door girls and told her to throw it out at once: that was no play. Maria understood that it was wrong that time and so she had to do it over again: and this time she got the prayer-book.

After that Mrs. Donnelly played Miss McCloud's Reel for the children and Joe made Maria take a glass of wine. Soon they were all quite merry again and Mrs. Donnelly said Maria would enter a convent before the year was out because she had got the prayer-book. Maria had never seen Joe so nice to her as he was that night, so full of pleasant talk and reminiscences. She said they were all very good to her.

At last the children grew tired and sleepy and Joe asked Maria would she not sing some little song before she went, one of the old songs. Mrs. Donnelly said "Do, please, Maria!" and so Maria had to get up and stand beside the piano. Mrs. Donnelly bade the children be quiet and listen to Maria's song. Then she played the prelude and said "Now, Maria!" and Maria, blushing very much, began to sing in a tiny quavering voice. She sang I Dreamt that I Dwelt,[2] and when she came to the second verse she sang again:

> I dreamt that I dwelt in marble halls
>> With vassals and serfs at my side,
> And of all who assembled within those walls
>> That I was the hope and the pride.

2. A well-known song from the opera *The Bohemian Girl* by the Dublin-born operatic composer Michael William Balfe (1808–1870). The words are by Alfred Bunn (d. 1860).

I had riches too great to count; could boast
Of a high ancestral name,
But I also dreamt, which pleased me most,
That you loved me still the same.

But no one tried to show her her mistake; and when she had ended her song Joe was very much moved. He said that there was no time like the long ago and no music for him like poor old Balfe, whatever other people might say; and his eyes filled up so much with tears that he could not find what he was looking for and in the end he had to ask his wife to tell him where the corkscrew was.

1915

From A Portrait of the Artist as a Young Man[1]
[*The Interview with the Director*]

The director stood in the embrasure of the window, his back to the light, leaning an elbow on the brown crossblind, and, as he spoke and smiled, slowly dangling and looping the cord of the other blind, Stephen stood before him, following for a moment with his eyes the waning of the long summer daylight above the roofs or

1. *A Portrait of the Artist as a Young Man* is the story of the development of Stephen Dedalus from earliest childhood until his full realization of his destiny as artist and of the implications of that destiny. There is a considerable amount of autobiography in the book, but it is far from straight autobiography. Everything is organized to show the parallel development of artist and exile: for Joyce, the writer can only achieve the objectivity proper to an artist by totally withdrawing from all implication in the life of the community from which he is to draw his material. In the novel Stephen rejects one by one his home, his religion, his country, growing ever more aloof and independent, exclaiming *"Non serviam"* ("I will not serve") to all the representatives of orthodoxy and convention, and even to the claims of friendship and personal affection. Stephen the artist comes into being at the moment when he has successfully resisted the temptation to enter the Jesuit order: he suddenly realizes that he is born to dwell apart, to look objectively on the world of men and record their doings with the artist's disinterested craftsmanship. He might well have become a priest, but the choice lay only between priest and artist, between "the power of the keys, the power to bind and loose from sin," and the artist's godlike power to re-create the world with the word. That is why Stephen's rejection of the call to join the Jesuit order preludes the climax of the *Portrait* (which comes at the end of the second extract here printed). The first extract shows Stephen's response to that call, and the second shows him shortly afterwards experiencing his first true aesthetic vision as he looks at the girl standing with kilted skirts in the water and sees her without the desire either to possess or to convert but with the artist's joy in the presence of her reality.

As so often, Joyce in this book combines meticulous realism of detail with a persistent symbolism. The hero's name, for example, is itself symbolic. Stephen was the first Christian martyr, and in Greek mythology Daedalus was the first craftsman (or artist: the Greeks had one word for both), who made the labyrinth for King Minos at Crete; later, when Minos turned against him, he made himself wings and escaped by flying across the sea—symbol for Joyce of the artist's flight into necessary exile. The name "Daedalus" means "cunning craftsman": the artist for Joyce was both martyr and pioneer craftsman.

the slow deft movements of the priestly fingers. The priest's face was in total shadow, but the waning daylight from behind him touched the deeply grooved temples and the curves of the skull. Stephen followed also with his ears the accents and intervals of the priest's voice as he spoke gravely and cordially of indifferent themes, the vacation which had just ended, the colleges of the order abroad, the transference of masters. The grave and cordial voice went on easily with its tale, and in the pauses Stephen felt bound to set it on again with respectful questions. He knew that the tale was a prelude and his mind waited for the sequel. Ever since the message of summons had come for him from the director his mind had struggled to find the meaning of the message; and during the long restless time he had sat in the college parlour waiting for the director to come in his eyes had wandered from one sober picture to another around the walls and his mind wandered from one guess to another until the meaning of the summons had almost become clear. Then, just as he was wishing that some unforeseen cause might prevent the director from coming, he had heard the handle of the door turning and the swish of a soutane.[2]

The director had begun to speak of the Dominican and Franciscan orders and of the friendship between Saint Thomas and Saint Bonaventure.[3] The Capuchin dress, he thought, was rather too . . .

Stephen's face gave back the priest's indulgent smile and, not being anxious to give an opinion, he made a slight dubitative movement with his lips.

—I believe, continued the director, that there is some talk now among the Capuchins themselves of doing away with it and following the example of the other Franciscans.

—I suppose they would retain it in the cloisters? said Stephen.

—O, certainly, said the director. For the cloister it is all right, but for the street I really think it would be better to do away with, don't you?

—It must be troublesome, I imagine?

—Of course it is, of course. Just imagine when I was in Belgium I used to see them out cycling in all kinds of weather with this thing up about their knees! It was really ridiculous. *Les jupes*,[4] they call them in Belgium.

The vowel was so modified as to be indistinct.

—What do they call them?

—*Les jupes.*

2. Cassock.
3. St. Bonaventure, Italian Scholastic philosopher (known as "the seraphic doctor"), became general of the Franciscan order in 1256; his contemporary, St. Thomas Aquinas (*doctor angelicus*, or "the angelic doctor"), leading Scholastic philosopher, was a member of the Dominican order. The Capuchins were a special order of Franciscans, so called from the long pointed "capuche," or hood, which they wore.
4. Skirts.

—O!

Stephen smiled again in answer to the smile which he could not see on the priest's shadowed face, its image or spectre only passing rapidly across his mind as the low discreet accent fell upon his ear. He gazed calmly before him at the waning sky, glad of the cool of the evening and the faint yellow glow which hid the tiny flame kindling upon his cheek.

The names of articles of dress worn by women or of certain soft and delicate stuffs used in their making brought always to his mind a delicate and sinful perfume. As a boy he had imagined the reins by which horses are driven as slender silken bands and it shocked him to feel at Stradbrooke the greasy leather of harness. It had shocked him, too, when he had felt for the first time beneath his tremulous fingers the brittle texture of a woman's stocking for, retaining nothing of all he read save that which seemed to him an echo or a prophecy of his own state, it was only amid softworded phrases or within rosesoft stuffs that he dared to conceive of the soul or body of a woman moving with tender life.

But the phrase on the priest's lips was disingenuous for he knew that a priest should not speak lightly on that theme. The phrase had been spoken lightly with design and he felt that his face was being searched by the eyes in the shadow. Whatever he had heard or read of the craft of jesuits he had put aside frankly as not borne out by his own experience. His masters, even when they had not attracted him, had seemed to him always intelligent and serious priests, athletic and highspirited prefects. He thought of them as men who washed their bodies briskly with cold water and wore clean cold linen. During all the years he had lived among them in Clongowes[5] and in Belvedere he had received only two pandies[6] and, though these had been dealt him in the wrong, he knew that he had often escaped punishment. During all those years he had never heard from any of his masters a flippant word: it was they who had taught him christian doctrine and urged him to live a good life and, when he had fallen into grievous sin, it was they who had led him back to grace. Their presence had made him diffident of himself when he was a muff in Clongowes and it had made him diffident of himself also while he had held his equivocal position in Belvedere. A constant sense of this had remained with him up to the last year of his school life. He had never once disobeyed or allowed turbulent companions to seduce him from his habit of quiet obedience: and, even when he doubted some statement of a master, he had never presumed to doubt openly. Lately some of their judgments had sounded a little childish in his ears

5. The Jesuit school which Stephen (and the young Joyce) attended before going to Belvedere College.

6. Hard blows on the palm of the hand (for punishment).

and had made him feel a regret and pity as thought he were slowly passing out of an accustomed world and were hearing its language for the last time. One day when some boys had gathered round a priest under the shed near the chapel, he heard the priest say:

—I believe that Lord Macaulay was a man who probably never committed a mortal sin in his life, that is to say, a deliberate mortal sin.[7]

Some of the boys had then asked the priest if Victor Hugo were not the greatest French writer. The priest had answered that Victor Hugo had never written half so well when he had turned against the church as he had written when he was a catholic.

—But there are many eminent French critics, said the priest, who consider that even Victor Hugo, great as he certainly was, had not so pure a French style as Louis Veuillot.[8]

The tiny flame which the priest's allusion had kindled upon Stephen's cheek had sunk down again and his eyes were still fixed calmly on the colourless sky. But an unresting doubt flew hither and thither before his mind. Masked memories passed quickly before him: he recognised scenes and persons yet he was conscious that he had failed to perceive some vital circumstance in them. He saw himself walking about the grounds watching the sports in Clongowes and eating slim jim out of his cricket-cap. Some jesuits were walking round the cycletrack in the company of ladies. The echoes of certain expressions used in Clongowes sounded in remote caves of his mind.

His ears were listening to these distant echoes amid the silence of the parlour when he became aware that the priest was addressing him in a different voice.

—I sent for you today, Stephen, because I wished to speak to you on a very important subject.

—Yes, sir.

—Have you ever felt that you had a vocation?

Stephen parted his lips to answer yes and then withheld the word suddenly. The priest waited for the answer and added:

—I mean have you ever felt within yourself, in your soul, a desire to join the order. Think.

—I have sometimes thought of it, said Stephen.

The priest let the blindcord fall to one side and, uniting his hands, leaned his chin gravely upon them, communing with himself.

—In a college like this, he said at length, there is one boy or perhaps two or three boys whom God calls to the religious life.

---

7. The life of the Whig historian Thomas Babington Macaulay (1800–59) was noted for its purity.
8. A 19th-century French journalist and leader of the French "Ultramontanes" (who supported the Pope's claim to be spiritual head of the church everywhere).

Such a boy is marked off from his companions by his piety, by the good example he shows to others. He is looked up to by them; he is chosen perhaps as prefect by his fellow sodalists. And you, Stephen, have been such a boy in this college, prefect of Our Blessed Lady's sodality.[9] Perhaps you are the boy in this college whom God designs to call to Himself.

A strong note of pride reinforcing the gravity of the priest's voice made Stephen's heart quicken in response. —To receive that call, Stephen, said the priest, is the greatest honour that the Almighty God can bestow upon a man. No king or emperor on this earth has the power of the priest of God. No angel or archangel in heaven, no saint, not even the Blessed Virgin herself has the power of a priest of God: the power of the keys, the power to bind and to loose from sin, the power of exorcism, the power to cast out from the creatures of God the evil spirits that have power over them, the power, the authority, to make the great God of Heaven come down upon the altar and take the form of bread and wine. What an awful power, Stephen!

A flame began to flutter again on Stephen's cheek as he heard in this proud address an echo of his own proud musings. How often had he seen himself as a priest wielding calmly and humbly the awful power of which angels and saints stood in reverence! His soul had loved to muse in secret on this desire. He had seen himself, a young and silentmannered priest, entering a confessional swiftly, ascending the altarsteps, incensing, genuflecting, accomplishing the vague acts of the priesthood which pleased him by reason of their semblance of reality and of their distance from it. In that dim life which he had lived through in his musings he had assumed the voices and gestures which he had noted with various priests. He had bent his knee sideways like such a one, he had shaken the thurible[1] only slightly like such a one, his chasuble[2] had swung open like that of such another as he turned to the altar again after having blessed the people. And above all it had pleased him to fill the second place in those dim scenes of his imagining. He shrank from the dignity of celebrant because it displeased him to imagine that all the vague pomp should end in his own person or that the ritual should assign to him so clear and final an office. He longed for the minor sacred offices, to be vested with the tunicle of subdeacon at high mass, to stand aloof from the altar, forgotten by the people, his shoulders covered with a humeral veil,[3] holding the paten within its folds or, when the sacrifice had been accomplished, to stand as

---

9. A religious fellowship.
1. Censer (container in which incense is burned).
2. Sleeveless outer garment worn by celebrant at Mass.

3. Veil covering the shoulders. "Paten": plate on which bread is placed in celebration of the Eucharist (Holy Communion).

deacon in a dalmatic of cloth of gold on the step below the celebrant, his hands joined and his face towards the people, and sing the chant, *Ite missa est*.[4] If ever he had seen himself celebrant it was as in the pictures of the mass in his child's massbook, in a church without worshippers, save for the angel of the sacrifice, at a bare altar and served by an acolyte scarcely more boyish than himself. In vague sacrificial or sacramental acts alone his will seemed drawn to go forth to encounter reality: and it was partly the absence of an appointed rite which had always constrained him to inaction whether he had allowed silence to cover his anger or pride or had suffered only an embrace he longed to give.

He listened in reverent silence now to the priest's appeal and through the words he heard even more distinctly a voice bidding him approach, offering him secret knowledge and secret power. He would know then what was the sin of Simon Magus[5] and what the sin against the Holy Ghost for which there was no forgiveness. He would know obscure things, hidden from others, from those who were conceived and born children of wrath. He would know the sins, the sinful longings and sinful thoughts and sinful acts, of others, hearing them murmured into his ears in the confessional under the shame of a darkened chapel by the lips of women and of girls: but rendered immune mysteriously at his ordination by the imposition of hands his soul would pass again uncontaminated to the white peace of the altar. No touch of sin would linger upon the hands with which he would elevate and break the host; no touch of sin would linger on his lips in prayer to make him eat and drink damnation to himself not discerning the body of the Lord. He would hold his secret knowledge and secret power, being as sinless as the innocent: and he would be a priest for ever according to the order of Melchisedec.[6]

—I will offer up my mass tomorrow morning, said the director, that Almighty God may reveal to you His holy will. And let you, Stephen, make a novena[7] to your holy patron saint, the first martyr who is very powerful with God, that God may enlighten your mind. But you must be quite sure, Stephen, that you have a vocation because it would be terrible if you found afterwards that you had none. Once a priest always a priest, remember. Your catechism tells you that the sacrament of Holy Orders is one of those which can be received only once because it imprints on the soul an indelible

4. "Go; it is sent forth." The traditional formula of dismissal at the end of the Mass.
5. The Simon who offered money in order to be given the power of laying on of hands possessed by the apostles (see Acts viii.18–19).
6. "Thou art a priest forever after the order of Melchisedec" (Hebrews v.6). Cf. Genesis xiv.18: "And Melchizedek king of Salem brought forth bread and wine: and he was the priest of the most high God."
7. Devotion consisting of prayers on nine consecutive days.

spiritual mark which can never be effaced. It is before you must weigh well, not after. It is a solemn question, Stephen, because on it may depend the salvation of your eternal soul. But we will pray to God together.

He held open the heavy hall door and gave his hand as if already to a companion in the spiritual life. Stephen passed out on to the wide platform above the steps and was conscious of the caress of mild evening air. Towards Findlater's church a quartette of young men were striding along with linked arms, swaying their heads and stepping to the agile melody of their leader's concertina. The music passed in an instant, as the first bars of sudden music always did, over the fantastic fabrics of his mind, dissolving them painlessly and noiselessly as a sudden wave dissolves the sandbuilt turrets of children. Smiling at the trivial air he raised his eyes to the priest's face and, seeing in it a mirthless reflection of the sunken day, detached his hand slowly which had acquiesced faintly in that companionship.

As he descended the steps the impression which effaced his troubled selfcommunion was that of a mirthless mask reflecting a sunken day from the threshold of the college. The shadow, then, of the life of the college passed gravely over his consciousness. It was a grave and ordered and passionless life that awaited him, a life without material cares. He wondered how he would pass the first night in the novitiate and with what dismay he would wake the first morning in the dormitory. The troubling odour of the long corridors of Clongowes came back to him and he heard the discreet murmur of the burning gasflames. At once from every part of his being unrest began to irradiate. A feverish quickening of his pulses followed and a din of meaningless words drove his reasoned thoughts hither and thither confusedly. His lungs dilated and sank as if he were inhaling a warm moist unsustaining air, and he smelt again the moist warm air which hung in the bath in Clongowes above the sluggish turfcoloured water.

Some instinct, waking at these memories, stronger than education or piety quickened within him at every near approach to that life, an instinct subtle and hostile, and armed him against acquiescence. The chill and order of the life repelled him. He saw himself rising in the cold of the morning and filing down with the others to early mass and trying vainly to struggle with his prayers against the fainting sickness of his stomach. He saw himself sitting at dinner with the community of a college. What, then, had become of that deeprooted shyness of his which had made him loth to eat or drink under a strange roof? What had come of the pride of his spirit which had always made him conceive himself as a being apart in every order?

The Reverend Stephen Dedalus, S. J.[8]

His name in that new life leaped into characters before his eyes and to it there followed a mental sensation of an undefined face or colour of a face. The colour faded and became strong like a changing glow of pallid brick red. Was it the raw reddish glow he had so often seen on wintry mornings on the shaven gills of the priests? The face was eyeless and sourfavoured and devout, shot with pink tinges of suffocated anger. Was it not a mental spectre of the face of one of the jesuits whom some of the boys called Lantern Jaws and others Foxy Campbell?

He was passing at that moment before the jesuit house in Gardiner Street, and wondered vaguely which window would be his if he ever joined the order. Then he wondered at the vagueness of his wonder, at the remoteness of his soul from what he had hitherto imagined her sanctuary, at the frail hold which so many years of order and obedience had of him when once a definite and irrevocable act of his threatened to end for ever, in time and in eternity, his freedom. The voice of the director urging upon him the proud claims of the church and the mystery and power of the priestly office repeated itself idly in his memory. His soul was not there to hear and greet it and he knew now that the exhortation he had listened to had already fallen into an idle formal tale. He would never swing the thurible before the tabernacle as priest. His destiny was to be elusive of social or religious orders. The wisdom of the priest's appeal did not touch him to the quick. He was destined to learn his own wisdom apart from others or to learn the wisdom of others himself wandering among the snares of the world.

The snares of the world were its ways of sin. He would fall. He had not yet fallen but he would fall silently, in an instant. Not to fall was too hard, too hard: and he felt the silent lapse of his soul, as it would be at some instant to come, falling, falling, but not yet fallen, still unfallen, but about to fall.

[*The Walk on the Shore*]

He could wait no longer.

From the door of Byron's publichouse to the gate of Clontarf Chapel, from the gate of Clontarf Chapel to the door of Byron's publichouse, and then back again to the chapel and then back again to the publichouse he had paced slowly at first, planting his steps scrupulously in the spaces of the patchwork of the footpath, then timing their fall to the fall of verses. A full hour had passed since his father had gone in with Dan Crosby, the tutor, to find out for him something about the university. For a full hour he had paced up and down, waiting: but he could wait no longer.

8. Society of Jesus (the Jesuit order).

He set off abruptly for the Bull,[9] walking rapidly lest his father's shrill whistle might call him back; and in a few moments he had rounded the curve at the police barrack and was safe.

Yes, his mother was hostile to the idea, as he had read from her listless silence. Yet her mistrust pricked him more keenly than his father's pride and he thought coldly how he had watched the faith which was fading down in his soul aging and strengthening in her eyes. A dim antagonism gathered force within him and darkened his mind as a cloud against her disloyalty: and when it passed, cloudlike, leaving his mind serene and dutiful towards her again, he was made aware dimly and without regret of a first noiseless sundering of their lives.

The university! So he had passed beyond the challenge of the sentries who had stood as guardians of his boyhood and had sought to keep him among them that he might be subject to them and serve their ends. Pride after satisfaction uplifted him like long slow waves. The end he had been born to serve yet did not see had led him to escape by an unseen path: and now it beckoned to him once more and a new adventure was about to be opened to him. It seemed to him that he heard notes of fitful music leaping upwards a tone and downwards a diminished fourth, upwards a tone and downwards a major third, like triple-branching flames leaping fitfully, flame after flame, out of a midnight wood. It was an elfin prelude, endless and formless; and, as it grew wilder and faster, the flames leaping out of time, he seemed to hear from under the boughs and grasses wild creatures racing, their feet pattering like rain upon the leaves. Their feet passed in pattering tumult over his mind, the feet of hares and rabbits, the feet of harts and hinds and antelopes, until he heard them no more and remembered only a proud cadence from Newman:[1]—

—Whose feet are as the feet of harts and underneath the everlasting arms.

The pride of that dim image brought back to his mind the dignity of the office he had refused. All through his boyhood he had mused upon that which he had so often thought to be his destiny and when the moment had come for him to obey the call he had turned aside, obeying a wayward instinct. Now time lay between: the oils of ordination would never anoint his body. He had refused. Why?

He turned seaward from the road at Dollymount and as he passed on to the thin wooden bridge he felt the planks shaking with the tramp of heavily shod feet. A squad of Christian Brothers was on its way back from the Bull and had begun to pass, two by two,

9. The places and buildings referred to in this extract are all in Dublin. The Bull is a long tongue of land by the sea, fortified to form a protecting sea wall.
1. John Henry Cardinal Newman.

across the bridge. Soon the whole bridge was trembling and resounding. The uncouth faces passed him two by two, stained yellow or red or livid by the sea, and as he strove to look at them with ease and indifference, a faint stain of personal shame and commiseration rose to his own face. Angry with himself he tried to hide his face from their eyes by gazing down sideways into the shallow swirling water under the bridge but he still saw a reflection therein of their topheavy silk hats, and humble tapelike collars and loosely hanging clerical clothes.

—Brother Hickey.

Brother Quaid.

Brother MacArdle.

Brother Keogh.

Their piety would be like their names, like their faces, like their clothes; and it was idle for him to tell himself that their humble and contrite hearts,[2] it might be, paid a far richer tribute of devotion than his had ever been, a gift tenfold more acceptable than his elaborate adoration. It was idle for him to move himself to be generous towards them, to tell himself that if he ever came to their gates, stripped of his pride, beaten and in beggar's weeds, that they would be generous towards him, loving him as themselves. Idle and embittering, finally, to argue, against his own dispassionate certitude, that the commandment of love bade us not to love our neighbour as ourselves with the same amount and intensity of love but to love him as ourselves with the same kind of love.

He drew forth a phrase from his treasure and spoke it softly to himself:

—A day of dappled seaborne clouds.—

The phrase and the day and the scene harmonised in a chord. Words. Was it their colours? He allowed them to glow and fade, hue after hue: sunrise gold, the russet and green of apple orchards, azure of waves, the greyfringed fleece of clouds. No, it was not their colours: it was the poise and balance of the period itself. Did he then love the rhythmic rise and fall of words better than their associations of legend and colour? Or was it that, being as weak of sight as he was shy of mind, he drew less pleasure from the reflection of the glowing sensible world through the prism of a language manycoloured and richly storied than from the contemplation of an inner world of individual emotions mirrored perfectly in a lucid supple periodic prose?

He passed from the trembling bridge on to firm land again. At that instant, as it seemed to him, the air was chilled; and looking

---

2. "The sacrifices of God are a broken spirit: a broken and a contrite heart, O God, thou wilt not despise" (Psalms li.17).

askance towards the water he saw a flying squall darkening and crisping suddenly the tide. A faint click at his heart, a faint throb in his throat told him once more of how his flesh dreaded the cold infra-human odour of the sea: yet he did not strike across the downs on his left but held straight on along the spine of rocks that pointed against the river's mouth.

A veiled sunlight lit up faintly the grey sheet of water where the river was embayed. In the distance along the course of the slow-flowing Liffey slender masts flecked the sky and, more distant still, the dim fabric of the city lay prone in haze. Like a scene on some vague arras, old as man's weariness, the image of the seventh city of Christendom was visible to him across the timeless air, no older nor more weary nor less patient of subjection than in the days of the thingmote.[3]

Disheartened, he raised his eyes towards the slowdrifting clouds, dappled and seaborne. They were voyaging across the deserts of the sky, a host of nomads on the march, voyaging high over Ireland, westward bound. The Europe they had come from lay out there beyond the Irish Sea, Europe of strange tongues and valleyed and woodbegirt and citadelled and of entrenched and marshalled races. He heard a confused music within him as of memories and names which he was almost conscious of but could not capture even for an instant; then the music seemed to recede, to recede, to recede: and from each receding trail of nebulous music there fell always one long-drawn calling note, piercing like a star the dusk of silence. Again! Again! Again! A voice from beyond the world was calling.

—Hello, Stephanos!

—Here comes The Dedalus!

—Ao! . . . Eh, give it over, Dwyer, I'm telling you or I'll give you a stuff in the kisser for yourself. . . . Ao!

—Good man, Towser! Duck him!

—Come along, Dedalus! Bous Stephanoumenos![4] Bous Stephane-foros!

—Duck him! Guzzle him now, Towser!

—Help! Help! . . . Ao!

He recognised their speech collectively before he distinguished their faces. The mere sight of that medley of wet nakedness chilled him to the bone. Their bodies, corpsewhite or suffused with a pallid golden light or rawly tanned by the suns, gleamed with the wet of the sea. Their divingstone, poised on its rude supports and rocking

3. Ancient Scandinavian public assembly; Dublin, "the seventh city of Christendom," was settled and ruled by the Danes in the 9th and 10th centuries.
4. Greek, "garlanded ox." "Stephanos" is the Greek for "crown," and sacrificial animals were crowned with garlands. "Bous Stephaneforos" means similarly "crown-bearing (or garland-bearing) ox."

under their plunges, and the rough-hewn stones of the sloping breakwater over which they scrambled in their horseplay, gleamed with cold wet lustre. The towels with which they smacked their bodies were heavy with cold seawater: and drenched with cold brine was their matted hair.

He stood still in deference to their calls and parried their banter with easy words. How characterless they looked: Shuley without his deep unbuttoned collar, Ennis without his scarlet belt with the snaky clasp, and Connolly without his Norfolk coat with the flapless sidepockets! It was a pain to see them and a sword-like pain to see the signs of adolescence that made repellent their pitiable nakedness. Perhaps they had taken refuge in number and noise from the secret dread in their souls. But he, apart from them and in silence, remembered in what dread he stood of the mystery of his own body.

—Stephanos Dedalos! Bous Stephanoumenos! Bous Stephaneforos!

Their banter was not new to him and now it flattered his mild proud sovereignty. Now, as never before, his strange name seemed to him a prophecy. So timeless seemed the grey warm air, so fluid and impersonal his own mood, that all ages were as one to him. A moment before the ghost of the ancient kingdom of the Danes had looked forth through the vesture of the hazewrapped city. Now, at the name of the fabulous artificer,[5] he seemed to hear the noise of dim waves and to see a winged form flying above the waves and slowly climbing the air. What did it mean? Was it a quaint device opening a page of some medieval book of prophecies and symbols, a hawklike man flying sunward above the sea, a prophecy of the end he had been born to serve and had been following through the mists of childhood and boyhood, a symbol of the artist forging anew in his workshop out of the sluggish matter of the earth a new soaring impalpable imperishable being?

His heart trembled; his breath came faster and a wild spirit passed over his limbs as though he were soaring sunward. His heart trembled in an ecstasy of fear and his soul was in flight. His soul was soaring in an air beyond the world and the body he knew was purified in a breath and delivered of incertitude and made radiant and commingled with the element of the spirit. An ecstasy of flight made radiant his eyes and wild his breath and tremulous and wild and radiant his windswept limbs.

—One! Two! . . . Look out!

—O, Cripes, I'm drownded!

—One! Two! Three and away!

—The next! The next!

5. The Greek craftsman Daedalus: see introductory note to *A Portrait*.

—One! . . . Uk!

—Stephaneforos!

His throat ached with a desire to cry aloud, the cry of a hawk or eagle on high, to cry piercingly of his deliverance to the winds. This was the call of life to his soul not the dull gross voice of the world of duties and despair, not the inhuman voice that had called him to the pale service of the altar. An instant of wild flight had delivered him and the cry of triumph which his lips withheld cleft his brain.

—Stephaneforos!

What were they now but the cerements shaken from the body of death—the fear he had walked in night and day, the incertitude that had ringed him round, the shame that had abased him within and without—cerements, the linens of the grave?

His soul had arisen from the grave of boyhood, spurning her graveclothes. Yes! Yes! Yes! He would create proudly out of the freedom and power of his soul, as the great artificer whose name he bore, a living thing, new and soaring and beautiful, impalpable, imperishable.

He started up nervously from the stoneblock for he could no longer quench the flame in his blood. He felt his cheeks aflame and his throat throbbing with song. There was a lust of wandering in his feet that burned to set out for the ends of the earth. On! On! his heart seemed to cry. Evening would deepen above the sea, night fall upon the plains, dawn glimmer before the wanderer and show him strange fields and hills and faces. Where?

He looked northward towards Howth. The sea had fallen below the line of seawrack on the shallow side of the breakwater and already the tide was running out fast along the foreshore. Already one long oval bank of sand lay warm and dry amid the wavelets. Here and there warm isles of sand gleamed above the shallow tides and about the isles and around the long bank and amid the shallow currents of the beach were lightclad figures, wading and delving.

In a few moments he was barefoot, his stockings folded in his pockets, and his canvas shoes dangling by their knotted laces over his shoulders and, picking a pointed salteaten stick out of the jetsam among the rocks, he clambered down the slope of the breakwater.

There was a long rivulet in the strand and, as he waded slowly up its course, he wondered at the endless drift of seaweed. Emerald and black and russet and olive, it moved beneath the current, swaying and turning. The water of the rivulet was dark with endless drift and mirrored the highdrifting clouds. The clouds were drifting above him silently and silently the seatangle was drifting below him; and the grey warm air was still: and a new wild life was singing in his veins.

Where was his boyhood now? Where was the soul that had hung

back from her destiny, to brood alone upon the shame of her wounds and in her house of squalor and subterfuge to queen it in faded cerements and in wreaths that withered at the touch? Or where was he?

He was alone. He was unheeded, happy, and near to the wild heart of life. He was alone and young and wilful and wildhearted, alone amid a waste of wild air and brackish waters and the sea-harvest of shells and tangle and veiled grey sunlight and gayclad lightclad figures of children and girls and voices childish and girlish in the air.

A girl stood before him in midstream, alone and still, gazing out to sea. She seemed like one whom magic had changed into the likeness of a strange and beautiful seabird. Her long slender bare legs were delicate as a crane's and pure save where an emerald trail of seaweed had fashioned itself as a sign upon the flesh. Her thighs, fuller and softhued as ivory, were bared almost to the hips where the white fringes of her drawers were like feathering of soft white down. Her slateblue skirts were kilted boldly about her waist and dovetailed behind her. Her bosom was as a bird's, soft and slight, slight and soft as the breast of some darkplumaged dove. But her long fair hair was girlish: and girlish, and touched with the wonder of mortal beauty, her face.

She was alone and still, gazing out to sea; and when she felt his presence and the worship of his eyes her eyes turned to him in quiet sufferance of his gaze, without shame or wantonness. Long, long she suffered his gaze and then quietly withdrew her eyes from his and bent them towards the stream, gently stirring the water with **her foot hither and thither. The first faint noise of gently moving water broke the silence, low and faint and whispering, faint as the bells of sleep; hither and thither, hither and thither: and a faint flame trembled on her cheek.**

—Heavenly God! cried Stephen's soul, in an outburst of profane joy.

He turned away from her suddenly and set off across the strand. His cheeks were aflame; his body was aglow; his limbs were trembling. On and on and on and on he strode, far out over the sands, singing wildly to the sea, crying to greet the advent of the life that had cried to him.

Her image had passed into his soul for ever and no word had broken the holy silence of his ecstasy. Her eyes had called him and his soul had leaped at the call. To live, to err, to fall, to triumph, to recreate life out of life! A wild angel had appeared to him, the angel of mortal youth and beauty, an envoy from the fair courts of life, to throw open before him in an instant of ecstasy the gates of all the ways of error and glory. On and on and on and on!

He halted suddenly and heard his heart in the silence. How far had he walked? What hour was it?

There was no human figure near him nor any sound borne to him over the air. But the tide was near the turn and already the day was on the wane. He turned landward and ran towards the shore and, running up the sloping beach, reckless of the sharp shingle, found a sandy nook amid a ring of tufted sandknolls and lay down there that the peace and silence of the evening might still the riot of his blood.

He felt above him the vast indifferent dome and the calm processes of the heavenly bodies; and the earth beneath him, the earth that had borne him, had taken him to her breast.

He closed his eyes in the languor of sleep. His eyelids trembled as if they felt the vast cyclic movement of the earth and her watchers, trembled as if they felt the strange light of some new world. His soul was swooning into some new world, fantastic, dim, uncertain as under sea, traversed by cloudy shapes and beings. A world, a glimmer, or a flower? Glimmering and trembling, trembling and unfolding, a breaking light, an opening flower, it spread in endless succession to itself, breaking in full crimson and unfolding and fading to palest rose, leaf by leaf and wave of light by wave of light, flooding all the heavens with its soft flushes, every flush deeper than other.

Evening had fallen when he woke and the sand and arid grasses of his bed glowed no longer. He rose slowly and, recalling the rapture of his sleep, sighed at its joy.

He climbed to the crest of the sandhill and gazed about him. Evening had fallen. A rim of the young moon cleft the pale waste of sky like the rim of a silver hoop embedded in grey sand; and the tide was flowing in fast to the land with a low whisper of her waves, islanding a few last figures in distant pools.

1904–14   1916

From Ulysses

[*Proteus*][1]

Ineluctable modality of the visible: at least that if no more, thought through my eyes.[2] Signatures of all things I am here to read, seaspawn and seawrack, the nearing tide, that rusty boot. Snotgreen, bluesilver, rust: coloured signs. Limits of the diaphane.[3] But he adds: in bodies. Then he was aware of them bodies before of them coloured. How? By knocking his sconce against them, sure. Go easy. Bald he was and a millionaire, *maestro di color che sanno.*[4] Limit of the diaphane in. Why in? Diaphane, adiaphane.[5] If you can put your five fingers through it, it is a gate, if not a door. Shut your eyes and see.

Stephen closed his eyes to hear his boots crush crackling wrack

1. "Proteus" is so titled because of the deliberate analogies that exist between it and the description of Proteus in *Odyssey* IV. (Joyce did not title any of the episodes in *Ulysses*, but the names are his; he used them in correspondence and in talk with friends.)

In Homer's *Odyssey*, Proteus is the changing sea god who continually alters his shape: when Telemachus, the son of Ulysses, asks Menelaus for help in finding his father, Menelaus tells that he encountered Proteus by the seashore on the island of Pharos "in front of Egypt," and that, by holding on to him while he changed from one shape to another, he was able to force him to tell what had happened to Ulysses and the other Greek heroes of the Trojan war. In Joyce's narrative, Stephen Dedalus (who, like Homer's Telemachus, is looking for a father, but not in the literal "consubstantial" sense) is walking by the Dublin shore alone, "along Sandymount strand," speculating on the shifting shapes of things and the possibility of knowing truth by mere appearances.

First Stephen meditates on the "modality of the visible" and on the mystical notion that God writes his signature on all His works; then on the "modality of the audible," closing his eyes and trying to know reality simply through the sense of hearing. As he continues his walk, the people and objects he sees mingle in his thoughts with memories of his past relations with his family, of his schooldays, his residence in Paris whence he was recalled by his mother's fatal illness, his feeling of guilt about his mother's death (he had refused to kneel down and pray at her bedside, since he considered it would be a betrayal of his integrity as an unbeliever), and a variety of speculations about life and reality often derived from mystical works he had read "in the stagnant bay of Marsh's library" (in Dublin). This episode gives the reader a profound awareness of the nature of Stephen's sensibility and the contents of his conscious and subconscious mind and also sets going themes to be developed later in other episodes of *Ulysses*. The highly theoretical, inquiring, musing, speculating mind of Stephen is in sharp contrast to the practical, humane, sensual, concrete imagination of the book's real hero, Leopold Bloom, but there are also significant parallels between the streams of consciousness of the two. Some of the more important themes which emerge in Stephen's reverie are pointed out in footnotes.

The text given here has been collated with the Odyssey Press edition of *Ulysses* (1932), which is accepted as the "definitive standard edition."

2. I.e., the sense of sight provides an unavoidable way ("ineluctable modality") of knowing reality, the knowledge thus provided being a kind of "thought through [the] eyes." The phrase "signature of all things" comes from the German mystic Jakob Böhme, (1575–1624).

3. Transparency. Stephen is speculating on Aristotle's view of perception as developed in his *De Anima*.

4. There was a tradition that Aristotle was bald, with thin legs, small eyes, and a lisp. Aristotle is also traditionally supposed to have inherited considerable wealth and to have been presented with a fortune by his former pupil Alexander the Great. The Italian phrase is Dante's description of Aristotle in the *Inferno*, and means "the master of them that know."

5. What is not transparent (opposite of "diaphane").

and shells. You are walking through it howsomever. I am, a stride at a time. A very short space of time through very short times of space. Five, six: the *nacheinander*.[6] Exactly: and that is the ineluctable modality of the audible. Open your eyes. No. Jesus! If I fell over a cliff that beetles o'er his base,[7] fell through the *nebeneinander* ineluctably. I am getting on nicely in the dark. My ash sword hangs at my side. Tap with it: they do.[8] My two feet in his boots are at the end of my legs, *nebeneinander*. Sounds solid: made by the mallet of *Los Demiurgos*.[9] Am I walking into eternity along Sandymount strand? Crush, crack, crik, crick. Wild sea money. Dominie[1] Deasy kens them a'.

> *Won't you come to Sandymount,*
> *Madeline the mare?*

Rhythm begins, you see. I hear. A catalectic tetrameter[2] of iambs marching. No, agallop: *deline the mare*.

Open your eyes now. I will. One moment. Has all vanished since? If I open and am for ever in the black adiaphane. *Basta!*[3] I will see if I can see.

See now. There all the time without you: and ever shall be, world without end.

They came down the steps from Leahy's terrace prudently, *Frauenzimmer:*[4] and down the shelving shore flabbily their splayed feet sinking in the silted sand. Like me, like Algy,[5] coming down to our mighty mother. Number one swung lourdily[6] her midwife's

---

6. "After one another." Stephen, with eyes shut, is now sensing reality through the sense of sound only: unlike sight, sound falls on the sense of hearing in chronological sequence, one sound after another.

7. "What if it tempt you toward the flood,' my lord, / Or to the dreadful summit of the cliff / That beetles o'er his base into the sea * * * " (*Hamlet* I.iv.69–71). "*Nebeneinander*': beside one another.

8. Stephen is still walking with his eyes shut, tapping with his "ash sword" (the walking stick of ash wood he always carried), as "they" (i.e., blind people) do. "His boots": Buck Mulligan's. Stephen, lacking boots of his own, had borrowed a castoff pair of Mulligan's.

9. The Demiurge, supernatural being who made the world in subordination to God. The mystical notion of the Demiurge who created the world haunts Stephen's mind; it is the Demiurge who writes his signature on created objects and whose mallet fashioned them. The world, sensed by the ear only, "sounds solid," as though made by the Demiurge's hammer.

1. Schoolmaster. Mr. Deasy was the headmaster of the school where Stephen taught (the previous episode has shown Stephen teaching). "Kens them a''": knows them all; Stephen is putting Deasy into a mock-Scottish folk song.

2. The first of the two lines of popular verse which have come into Stephen's head consists metrically of four iambic feet ("tetrameter") with the unstressed syllable of the first iamb missing ("catalectic").

3. Italian, "Enough!"

4. "Midwives"; Stephen sees them coming from Leahy's Terrace, which runs by the beach.

5. Algernon Charles Swinburne, who wrote: "I will go back to the great sweet mother, / Mother and lover of men, the sea. I will go down to her, I and none other * * * " (*The Triumph of Time*).

6. Heavily (coined by Stephen from the French *lourd*). Stephen, like Joyce, had studied modern languages at University College, Dublin, and his preoccupation with words and languages is part of his character as potential literary artist. "Gamp": umbrella; and perhaps reference to Mrs. Gamp, the nurse in Dickens' *Martin Chuzzlewit*.

bag, the other's gamp poked in the beach. From the liberties, out for the day. Mrs. Florence MacCabe,[7] relict of the late Patk Mac-Cabe, deeply lamented, of Bride Street. One of her sisterhood lugged me squealing into life. Creation from nothing. What has she in the bag? A misbirth with a trailing navelcord, hushed in ruddy wool. The cords of all link back, strandentwining cable of all flesh. That is why mystic monks. Will you be as gods? Gaze in your omphalos. Hello. Kinch here. Put me on to Edenville. Aleph, alpha: nought, nought, one.[8]

Spouse and helpmate of Adam Kadmon:[9] Heva, naked Eve. She had no navel. Gaze. Belly without blemish, bulging big, a buckler of taut vellum, no, whiteheaped corn, orient and immortal, standing from everlasting to everlasting.[1] Womb of sin.

Wombed in sin darkness I was too, made not begotten. By them, the man with my voice and my eyes and a ghostwoman with ashes on her breath.[2] They clasped and sundered, did the coupler's will. From before the ages He willed me and now may not will me away or ever. A *lex eterna*[3] stays about Him. Is that then the divine substance wherein Father and Son are consubstantial? Where is poor dear Arius[4] to try conclusions? Warring his life long on the contransmagnificandjewbangtantiality.[5] Illstarred heresiarch.[6] In a Greek

7. Stephen imagines the first midwife is called Mrs. MacCabe. "Relict": widow.

8. Stephen is speculating on the mystical significance of the navel cord, seeing it as linking the generations, the combined navel cords stretching back to Adam and Eve. A mystic gazed in his *omphalos* (navel) to make contact with the first man. Stephen thinks of himself ("Kinch," his nickname) calling up Adam in "Edenville" through his navel, using the line of linked navel cords as a telephone line. Adam's telephone number, "Aleph, alpha: nought, nought, one," begins with the first letters of the Hebrew and of the Greek alphabet to suggest the great primeval number.

9. "Adam the Beginner," so called in Hebrew cabalistic literature of the Middle Ages; "Heva" is Hebrew for Eve. Because she was not born in the regular way, but created from Adam's rib, she had no navel.

1. Stephen is led, through reflection on Eve's navel-less "belly without blemish," to a recollection of the description of the original Eden (Paradise) by Thomas Traherne (ca. 1637–74), from whose prose *Centuries of Meditation* he quotes: "The corn was orient and immortal wheat, which should never be reaped, nor was ever sown. I thought it had stood from everlasting to everlasting. * * * " But immediately afterwards Stephen reflects that such language is inappropriate to Eve's body, as hers was the "womb of sin"—i.e., she first ate the fatal apple and brought

forth sin.

2. Stephen is haunted by thoughts of his mother in this guise.

3. Eternal law. God's eternal law, Stephen reflects, willed his birth from the beginning. He then goes on to speculate on the nature of the divine substance and whether God the Father and God the Son are of the same substance ("consubstantial").

4. 3rd-century theologian who "tried conclusions" on this matter, maintaining that Christ was less divine than God (Arius' views were condemned as heretical by the Council of Nicaea in 325).

5. Ironic "portmanteau word" made up of terms connected with the Arian controversy—"consubstantial," "transubstantial" (of a substance that changes into another)—and with the facts of Christ's nature (e.g., "Jew"; Jesus was a Jew, as Leopold Bloom in a later episode reminds an anti-Semitic Irishman).

6. Arch-heretic. Arius died suddenly in Constantinople in 336. He was never a bishop, and Stephen's image of him at the moment of death in full episcopal attire seems to combine recollections of other early "heresiarchs." In an earlier reverie Stephen had conjured up in his mind "a horde of heresies fleeing with mitres awry." These heretics are connected in Stephen's mind with argument about the relation between God the Father and God the Son and so with the problem of the true nature of paternity, which haunts him constantly.

watercloset he breathed his last: euthanasia. With beaded mitre and with crozier, stalled upon his throne, widower of a widowed see, with upstiffed omophorion, with clotted hinderparts.

Airs romped around him, nipping and eager airs. They are coming, waves. The whitemaned seahorses, champing, brightwindbridled, the steeds of Mananaan.[7]

I mustn't forget his letter for the press. And after? The Ship, half twelve. By the way go easy with that money like a good young imbecile. Yes, I must.[8]

His pace slackened. Here. Am I going to Aunt Sara's or not? My consubstantial father's voice. Did you see anything of your artist brother Stephen lately? No? Sure he's not down in Strasburg terrace with his aunt Sally? Couldn't he fly a bit higher than that, eh? And and and and tell us Stephen, how is uncle Si? O weeping God, the things I married into. De boys up in de hayloft. The drunken little costdrawer and his brother, the cornet player. Highly respectable gondoliers. And skeweyed Walter sirring his father, no less. Sir. Yes, sir. No, sir. Jesus wept: and no wonder, by Christ.[9]

I pull the wheezy bell of their shuttered cottage: and wait. They take me for a dun, peer out from a coign of vantage.[1]

—It's Stephen, sir.

—Let him in. Let Stephen in.

A bolt drawn back and Walter welcomes me.

—We thought you were someone else.

In his broad bed nuncle Richie, pillowed and blanketed, extends over the hillock of his knees a sturdy forearm. Clean chested. He has washed the upper moiety.

—Morrow, nephew.

He lays aside the lapboard whereon he drafts his bills of costs for the eyes of Master Goff and Master Shapland Tandy, filing consents and common searches and a writ of *Duces Tecum*.[2] A bogoak frame over his bald head: Wilde's *Requiescat*.[3] The drone of his misleading whistle brings Walter back.

—Yes, sir?

—Malt[4] for Richie and Stephen, tell mother. Where is she?

---

7. Mananaan MacLir, Celtic sea god; his steeds are the "white horses" (still the name in Britain for the white foam on top of waves).

8. Mr. Deasy had given Stephen a letter to the press to be taken to the newspaper office. After that he has an appointment with Mulligan at The Ship, a tavern. "That money" is Mr. Deasy's last payment to him.

9. Stephen has been wondering whether to call on his uncle and aunt, Richie and Sara Goulding. He imagines his father interrogating him about the visit as if he had gone, and then pictures his cousins asking after his father, Simon Dedalus (his cousins' "uncle Si"). Simon Dedalus is contemptuous of his wife's relations (Sara Goulding is his wife's sister). Stephen knows that any mention of them will bring on the familiar abuse of "the things I married into"—at best "highly respectable gondoliers" (from Gilbert and Sullivan's opera *The Gondoliers*). The scene that follows is also Stephen's purely imaginary picture of what the visit would be like.

1. Favorable corner.

2. "You shall take with you": opening words of search warrant. Goulding was a law clerk with Messrs. Goff and Tandy.

3. Poem by Oscar Wilde.

4. Whisky.

—Bathing Crissie, sir.

Papa's little bedpal. Lump of love.

—No, uncle Richie. . .

—Call me Richie. Damn your lithia water. It lowers. Whusky!

—Uncle Richie, really. . .

—Sit down or by the law Harry I'll knock you down.

Walter squints vainly for a chair.

—He has nothing to sit down on, sir.

—He has nowhere to put it, you mug. Bring in our Chippendale chair. Would you like a bite of something? None of your damned lawdeedaw air here; the rich of a rasher fried with a herring? Sure? So much the better. We have nothing in the house but backache pills.

All'erta![5]

He drones bars of Ferrando's *aria di sortita*. The grandest number, Stephen, in the whole opera. Listen.

His tuneful whistle sounds again, finely shaded, with rushes of the air, his fists bigdrumming on his padded knees.

This wind is sweeter.

Houses of decay, mine, his and all. You told the Clongowes gentry you had an uncle a judge and an uncle a general in the army.[6] Come out of them, Stephen. Beauty is not there. Nor in the stagnant bay of Marsh's library where you read the fading prophecies of Joachim Abbas.[7] For whom? The hundredheaded rabble of the cathedral close.[8] A hater of his kind ran from them to the wood of madness, his mane foaming in the moon, his eyeballs stars. Houyhnhnm, horsenostrilled.[9] The oval equine faces, Temple, Buck Mulligan, Foxy Campbell. Lantern jaws. Abbas father,[1] furious dean, what offence laid fire to their brains? Paff! *Descende, calve, ut ne nimium decalveris.*[2] A garland of grey hair

5. "Look out!" The first words of the *aria di sortita* (aria of a singer's entrance) sung by Ferrando, captain of the guard, in Verdi's opera *Il Trovatore*.
6. Stephen, reflecting on the steady social decline of his family, is remembering that, while at school at Clongowes Wood College, he had pretended to have important relations.
7. Abbot Joachim of Floris (the monastery of San Giovanni in Fiore, Italy), 12th-century mystic and theologian, whose prophetic work *Expositio in Apocalypsin* Stephen (i.e., Joyce) had read in Marsh's Library.
8. I.e., the precinct of a cathedral (Marsh's Library is in the close of St. Patrick's Cathedral).
9. St. Patrick's Close has recalled Jonathan Swift (who was Dean of St. Patrick's). Stephen remembers Swift's misanthropy (he was "a hater of his kind") and his creation of the Houyhnhnms (noble horses) in Book IV of *Gulliver's Travels*. Then he thinks of people he knew who have horse-faces.
1. "Abbas" means literally "father."
2. "Go down, bald-head, lest you become even balder." This sentence, from Joachim's *Concordia* of the Old and New Testaments, is based on the mocking cry of the children to the prophet Elisha (II Kings ii.23: "Go up, thou bald head"); Joachim saw Elisha as a forerunner of St. Benedict—both had shaven or baldish heads. Stephen imagines the "comminated" (i.e., threatened) head of Joachim descending, clutching a "monstrance" (receptacle in which the consecrated host is exposed for adoration), in the midst of a nightmare church service.

on his comminated head see him me clambering down to the foot-
pace (*descende*), clutching a monstrance, basiliskeyed. Get down,
bald poll! A choir gives back menace and echo, assisting about the
altar's horns, the snorted Latin of jackpriests moving burly in their
albs, tonsured and oiled and gelded, fat with the fat of kidneys of
wheat.

And at the same instant perhaps a priest round the corner is
elevating it. Dringdring! And two streets off another locking it into
a pyx.[3] Dringadring! And in a ladychapel another taking housel
all to his own cheek. Dringdring! Down, up, forward, back. Dan
Occam[4] thought of that, invincible doctor. A misty English morning the imp hypostasis tickled his brain. Bringing his host down
and kneeling he heard twine with his second bell the first bell in
the transept (he is lifting his) and, rising, heard (now I am lifting) their two bells (he is kneeling) twang in diphthong.

Cousin Stephen, you will never be a saint.[5] Isle of saints.[6] You
were awfully holy, weren't you? You prayed to the Blessed Virgin
that you might not have a red nose. You prayed to the devil in
Serpentine avenue that the fubsy widow in front might lift her
clothes still more from the wet street. *O si, certo!*[7] Sell your soul
for that, do, dyed rags pinned round a squaw. More tell me, more
still! On the top of the Howth tram alone crying to the rain: *naked
women!* What about that, eh?

What about what? What else were they invented for?

Reading two pages apiece of seven books every night, eh? I was
young. You bowed to yourself in the mirror, stepping forward to
applause earnestly, striking face. Hurray for the Goddamned idiot!
Hray! No-one saw: tell no-one. Books you were going to write with
letters for titles. Have you read his F? O yes, but I prefer Q. Yes,
but W is wonderful. O yes, W. Remember your epiphanies[8] on
green oval leaves, deeply deep, copies to be sent if you died to all
the great libraries of the world, including Alexandria? Someone
was to read them there after a few thousand years, a mahamanvan-

3. Vessel in which the Host (consecrated bread or wafer) is kept. Stephen
is imagining such a service, with himself officiating (he almost became a
priest).
4. William of Occam or Ockham
("Dan" means "master"), 14th-cen-
tury English theologian, who held that
the individual thing is the reality and
its name, the universal, an abstraction;
he was concerned with "hypostasis"—
the essential part of a thing as distinct
from its attributes.
5. A parody of the words of Dryden
to his distant relative Swift: "Cousin,
you will never make a poet."
6. Ireland was called *"insula sanc-*

torum," ("isle of saints") in the Middle Ages.
7. "Oh yes, certainly!"
8. Joyce's own term for the prose
poems he wrote as a young man. An
epiphany, he said, was the sudden
"revelation of the whatness of a thing"
—of a gesture, a phrase, or a thought
which he had experienced; he attempted
to express, in the writing, the moment
at which "the soul of the commonest
object * * * seems to us radiant."
Stephen's recollection of early and
exotic literary ambitions is drawn directly from Joyce's own ambitions at
the same age.

tara.[9] Pico della Mirandola like. Ay, very like a whale.[1] When one reads these strange pages of one long gone one feels that one is at one with one who once. . .

The grainy sand had gone from under his feet. His boots trod again a damp crackling mast, razorshells, squeaking pebbles, that on the unnumbered pebbles beats, wood sieved by the shipworm, lost Armáda. Unwholesome sandflats waited to suck his treading soles, breathing upward sewage breath. He coasted them, walking warily. A porterbottle stood up, stogged to its waist, in the cakey sand dough. A sentinel: isle of dreadful thirst.[2] Broken hoops on the shore; at the land a maze of dark cunning nets; farther away chalkscrawled backdoors and on the higher beach a dryingline with two crucified shirts. Ringsend: wigwams of brown steersmen and master mariners. Human shells.

He halted. I have passed the way to aunt Sara's. Am I not going there? Seems not. No-one about. He turned northeast and crossed the firmer sand towards the Pigeonhouse.[3]

—*Qui vous a mis dans cette fichue position?*

—*C'est le pigeon, Joseph.*

Patrice, home on furlough, lapped warm milk with me in the bar MacMahon. Son of the wild goose, Kevin Egan of Paris. My father's a bird, he lapped the sweet *lait chaud* with pink young tongue, plump bunny's face. Lap, *lapin*. He hopes to win in the *gros lots*. About the nature of women he read in Michelet. But he must send me *La Vie de Jésus* by M. Léo Taxil. Lent it to his friend.[4]

9. Cycle of change and recurrence, in Indian mystical thought. It is connected in Stephen's mind with the constant ebb and flow of the sea by which he is walking. Pico della Mirandola was a 15th-century mystical philosopher; his *Heptaplus* is a mystical account of the creation, much influenced by Jewish cabalistic thought.
1. Polonius to Hamlet (*Hamlet* III.ii.399) with reference to the changing shape of a cloud. The Protean theme of constant change, of ebb and flow, and of metempsychosis (i.e., transmigration of souls: a major theme in *Ulysses*), is working in Stephen's mind. The following sentence is a parody of an elegant, condescending modern essay on Pico or some other early mystic.
2. The atmosphere of the sandflats reminds Stephen of a desert island where men die of thirst. (The island of Pharos, where Menelaus found Proteus, was an "island of dreadful hunger.")
3. The Pigeon house in Ringsend, an old structure built on a breakwater in Dublin Bay and which in the course of time has served a great variety of purposes, suggests to Stephen the Dove which is the symbol of the Holy Spirit, and this in turn suggests an irreverent dialogue (supposedly between Joseph and Mary when Mary is found to be pregnant: "Who has got you into this wretched condition?" "It was the pigeon" [i.e., the Holy Dove], Joseph"). This he had picked up in Paris from the blasphemous M. Léo Taxil, whose book *La Vie de Jésus* ("The Life of Jesus") is mentioned in the next paragraph.
4. Stephen had first met Léo Taxil through Patrice, the son of "Kevin Egan of Paris," who in real life was the exiled nationalist Joseph Casey. The phrase "my father's a bird" comes from *The Song of the Cheerful Jesus*, a blasphemous poem by Buck Mulligan (actually Oliver Gogarty, who really wrote the poem); Stephen recalls Patrice reciting it as he drank warm milk ("*lait chaud*"), lapping it like a "*lapin*" ("rabbit"), and expressing the hope that he would win something substantial in the French national lottery (*gros lot*: "first prize"). Jules Michelet (1798–1874) was a French historian.

—*C'est tordant, vous savez. Moi je suis socialiste. Je ne crois pas en l'existence de Dieu. Faut pas le dire à mon père.*

—*Il croit?*

—*Mon père, oui.*

Schluss. He laps.[5]

My Latin quarter hat. God, we simply must dress the character. I want puce gloves. You were a student, weren't you? Of what in the other devil's name? Paysayenn. P. C. N., you know: *physiques, chimiques et naturelles.*[6] Aha. Eating your groatsworth of *mou en civet*, fleshpots of Egypt, elbowed by belching cabmen. Just say in the most natural tone: when I was in Paris, *boul' Mich',*[7] I used to. Yes, used to carry punched tickets to prove an alibi if they arrested you for murder somewhere. Justice. On the night of the seventeenth of February 1904 the prisoner was seen by two witnesses. Other fellow did it: other me. Hat, tie, overcoat, nose. *Lui, c'est moi.*[8] You seem to have enjoyed yourself.

Proudly walking. Whom were you trying to walk like? Forget: a dispossessed. With mother's money order, eight shillings, the banging door of the post office slammed in your face by the usher. Hunger toothache. *Encore deux minutes.* Look clock. Must get. *Fermé.* Hired dog! Shoot him to bloody bits with a bang shotgun, bits man spattered walls all brass buttons. Bits all khrrrrklak in place clack back. Not hurt? O, that's all right. Shake hands. See what I meant, see? O, that's all right. Shake a shake. O, that's all only all right.[9]

You were going to do wonders, what? Missionary to Europe after fiery Columbanus.[1] Fiacre and Scotus on their creepystools in heaven spilt from their pintpots, loudlatinlaughing: *Euge! Euge!*[2] Pretending to speak broken English as you dragged your valise, porter threepence, across the slimy pier at Newhaven. *Comment?* Rich booty you brought back; *Le tutu,* five tattered numbers of

5. Conversation between Stephen and Patrice: "It's screamingly funny, you know. I'm a socialist myself. I don't believe in the existence of God. Mustn't tell my father." "He is a believer?" "My father, yes." *"Schluss":* end.

6. I.e., the faculty of physics, chemistry, and biology at the École de Médecine in Paris, where Stephen, like Joyce, took a premedical course for a short time. The faculty was popularly known as "P. C. N." (pronounced "Paysayenn"). *"Mou en civet":* stew.

7. Popular Parisian abbreviation for the Boulevard Saint Michel.

8. "He is me"—a parody of Louis XIV's remark, *"L'état c'est moi"* ("I am the state").

9. A recollection of the occasion when, desperate for money, Stephen had received a money order for eight shillings from his mother. Afflicted with both hunger and toothache, he had gone to cash it at the post office—which was closed, even though, as he expostulated with the man at the door, there were still two minutes (*"encore deux minutes"*) until the official closing time. In his retrospective rage he imagines himself shooting the "hired dog" to bits, and then in a revulsion of feeling has a mental reconciliation with him.

1. 6th-century Irish missionary on the Continent. Fiacre was a 6th-century Irish saint. Duns Scotus (ca. 1265–1308): Scholastic theologian and philosopher. "Creepystools": low stools.

2. "Well done!"

Pantalon Blanc et Culotte Rouge,[3] a blue French telegram, curiosity to show:
—Mother dying come home father.[4]
The aunt thinks you killed your mother. That's why she won't.[5]

> *Then here's a health to Mulligan's aunt*
> *And I'll tell you the reason why.*
> *She always kept things decent in*
> *The Hannigan famileye.*

His feet marched in sudden proud rhythm over the sand furrows, along by the boulders of the south wall. He stared at them proudly, piled stone mammoth skulls. Gold light on sea, on sand, on boulders. The sun is there, the slender trees, the lemon houses.

Paris rawly waking, crude sunlight on her lemon streets. Moist pith of farls[6] of bread, the froggreen wormwood, her matin incense, court the air. Belluomo rises from the bed of his wife's lover's wife, the kerchiefed housewife is astir, a saucer of acetic acid in her hands. In Rodot's Yvonne and Madeleine newmake their tumbled beauties, shattering with gold teeth *chaussons* of pastry, their mouths yellowed with the *pus* of *flan breton*.[7] Faces of Paris men go by, their wellpleased pleasers, curled conquistadores.[8]

Noon slumbers. Kevin Egan rolls gunpowder cigarettes through fingers smeared with printer's ink,[9] sipping his green fairy as Patrice his white. About us gobblers fork spiced beans down their gullets. *Un demi setier!*[1] A jet of coffee steam from the burnished caldron. She serves me at his beck. *Il est irlandais. Hollandais? Non fromage. Deux irlandais, nous, Irlande, vous savez? Ah oui!*[2] She thought you wanted a cheese *hollandais*. Your postprandial, do you know that word? Postprandial. There was a fellow I knew once in Barcelona, queer fellow, used to call it his postprandial. Well: *slainte!*[3] Around the slabbed tables the tangle of wined breaths and grumbling gorges. His breath hangs over our saucestained plates, the green fairy's fang thrusting between his lips. Of Ireland, the Dalcassions, of hopes, conspiracies, of Arthur Griffith now.[4] To yoke me

3. Like the preceding name, name of French popular periodical.
4. This telegram was actually received by Joyce in Paris.
5. Stephen recalls Buck Mulligan's telling him that his (Mulligan's) aunt disapproved of Stephen because, by refusing to pray at his dying mother's bedside, he had hastened her death. Stephen then tries to laugh away his feeling of guilt by quoting mentally a (slightly parodied) verse of a popular song.
6. Thin circular cakes.
7. Memories of a restaurant in Paris: *"chaussons"* are pastry turnovers; *"flan breton"* is a pastry filled with custard.
8. Conquerors (Spanish).
9. Egan (i.e., Joseph Casey) became a typesetter for the Parisian edition of the *New York Herald*.
1. Abusive Parisian slang for a liquid measure (about one fourth of a liter) —here, presumably, of wine or beer.
2. "He is Irish. Dutch? Not cheese. We are two Irishmen, Ireland, you understand? Oh, yes!"
3. Gaelic, "Your health!"
4. Two extremes of Irish history: from the Dalcassian line came the early kings of Munster (from A.D. 300 on); Arthur Griffith (1872–1922) was an Irish revolutionary leader, founder of the Sinn Fein ("We Ourselves") movement.

as his yokefellow, our crimes our common cause. You're your father's son. I know the voice. His fustian shirt, sanguineflowered, trembles its Spanish tassels at his secrets. M. Drumont,[5] famous journalist, Drumont, know what he called queen Victoria? Old hag with the yellow teeth. *Vieille ogresse* with the *dents jaunes.* Maud Gonne, beautiful woman, *La Patrie*, M. Millevoye, Félix Faure,[6] know how he died? Licentious men. The froeken, *bonne à tout faire*,[7] who rubs male nakedness in the bath at Upsala. *Moi faire*, she said. *Tous les messieurs.*[8] Not this *Monsieur*, I said. Most licentious custom. Bath a most private thing. I wouldn't let my brother, not even my own brother, most lascivious thing. Green eyes, I see you. Fang, I feel. Lascivious people.

The blue fuse burns deadly between hands and burns clear. Loose tobacco shreds catch fire: a flame and acrid smoke light our corner. Raw facebones under his peep of day boy's hat. How the head centre got away, authentic version. Got up as a young bride, man, veil, orangeblossoms, drove out the road to Malahide. Did, faith. Of lost leaders, the betrayed, wild escapes. Disguises, clutched at, gone, not here.[9]

Spurned lover. I was a strapping young gossoon[1] at that time, I tell you, I'll show you my likeness one day. I was, faith. Lover, for her love he prowled with colonel Richard Burke, tanist[2] of his sept, under the walls of Clerkenwell[3] and, crouching, saw a flame of vengeance hurl them upward in the fog. Shattered glass and toppling masonry. In gay Paree he hides, Egan of Paris, unsought by any save by me. Making his day's stations, the dingy printing-case, his three taverns, the Montmartre lair he sleeps short night in, rue de la Goutte-d'Or, damascened with flyblown faces of the gone. Loveless, landless, wifeless. She is quite nicey comfy without her outcast man,[4] madame, in rue Gît-le-Coeur, canary and two buck lodgers. Peachy cheeks, a zebra skirt, frisky as a young thing's. Spurned and undespairing. Tell Pat[5] you saw me, won't you? I wanted to get poor Pat a job one time. *Mon fils*, soldier of France. I taught him to sing. *The boys of Kilkenny are stout roaring blades.*

5. Édouard Drumont (1844–1917), French politician and bitter anti-Semite.
6. Maud Gonne, the beautiful actress and violent Irish nationalist whom Yeats loved; *"La Patrie"*: journal edited by Lucien Millevoye, French Nationalist Deputy and Maud Gonne's lover; Félix Faure, 19th century French statesman.
7. Maid-of-all-work (French, translating the preceding Swedish word).
8. "I do all the gentlemen" (in broken French).
9. Another Protean theme of change. Egan had told Stephen of his cousin James Stephens' escape from prison disguised as a bride (Stephens was really the cousin of Casey, the original of Egan in this episode).
1. Boy.
2. Successor-apparent to a Celtic chief. "Sept": clan.
3. District in east central London. Stephen is recalling Egan's conversation about the Fenian violence in London which necessitated his fleeing to France.
4. I.e., Egan's wife, who is "quite nicey comfy" in the metaphorical "rue Gît-le-Cœur" (i.e., the street where the heart lies dead) back home in Ireland.
5. Patrice, Egan's son.

Know that old lay? I taught Patrice that. Old Kilkenny:[6] saint Canice, Strongbow's castle on the Nore. Goes like this. O, O. He takes me, Napper Tandy,[7] by the hand.

> O, O the boys of
> Kilkenny. . .

Weak wasting hand on mine. They have forgotten Kevin Egan, not he them. Remembering thee, O Sion.[8]

He had come nearer the edge of the sea and wet sand slapped his boots. The new air greeted him, harping in wild nerves, wind of wild air of seeds of brightness. Here, I am not walking out to the Kish lightship, am I? He stood suddenly, his feet beginning to sink slowly in the quaking soil. Turn back.

Turning, he scanned the shore south, his feet sinking again slowly in new sockets. The cold domed room of the tower[9] waits. Through the barbicans[1] the shafts of light are moving ever, slowly ever as my feet are sinking, creeping duskward over the dial floor. Blue dusk, nightfall, deep blue night. In the darkness of the dome they wait, their pushedback chairs, my obelisk valise, around a board of abandoned platters. Who to clear it? He has the key.[2] I will not sleep there when this night comes. A shut door of a silent tower entombing their blind bodies, the panthersahib and his pointer.[3] Call: no answer. He lifted his feet up from the suck and turned back by the mole of boulders. Take all, keep all. My soul walks with me, form of forms. So in the moon's midwatches I pace the path above the rocks, in sable silvered, hearing Elsinore's tempting flood.[4]

The flood is following me. I can watch it flow past from here. Get back then by the Poolbeg road to the strand there. He climbed over the sedge and eely oarweeds and sat on a stool of rock, resting his ashplant in a grike.

A bloated carcass of a dog lay lolled on bladderwrack. Before him the gunwale of a boat, sunk in sand. *Un coche ensablé.*[5] Louis Veuil-

---

6. Kilkenny is called after the Irish St. Canice (its Irish name is Cill Chainnigh), on the river Nore, where Strongbow (the second Earl of Pembroke, who invaded Ireland in the 12th century), had his stronghold.

7. James Napper Tandy (1740–1803), Irish revolutionary, hero of the song *The Wearing of the Green.*

8. Cf. Psalm cxxxvii.1 (in the King James Bible): "we wept, when we remembered Zion." But "Zion" in the Douay (Roman Catholic) Bible, is spelled "Sion," and the Book of Common Prayer has "When we remembered thee, O Sion."

9. Where Stephen lived with Buck Mulligan.

1. Outworks of a castle.

2. In the preceding episode, Mulligan asked for and got the key of the tower from Stephen.

3. I.e., Mulligan and the Englishman Haines, who live with Stephen in the tower. Stephen thinks of them as calling for him in vain, since he has decided not to return.

4. Cf. *Hamlet* I.ii.242, where the ghost of Hamlet's murdered father is described as having a beard of "sable silver'd." Allusions to *Hamlet* occur often in *Ulysses;* in a later episode Stephen expounds the theory that Shakespeare is to be identified, not with Hamlet himself, but with his betrayed father.

5. "A coach embedded in the sand." Louis Veuillot was a 19th-century French journalist; Théophile Gautier, a 19th-century French poet, novelist, and critic.

lot called Gautier's prose. These heavy sands are language tide and wind have silted here. And there, the stoneheaps of dead builders, a warren of weasel rats. Hide gold there. Try it. You have some. Sands and stones. Heavy of the past. Sir Lout's toys. Mind you don't get one bang on the ear. I'm the bloody well gigant rolls all them bloody well boulders, bones for my steppingstones. Feefaw-fum. I zmells de bloodz oldz an Iridzman.[6]

A point, live dog, grew into sight running across the sweep of sand. Lord, is he going to attack me? Respect his liberty. You will not be master of others or their slave. I have my stick. Sit tight. From farther away, walking shoreward across from the crested tide, figures, two. The two maries. They have tucked it safe among the bulrushes. Peekaboo. I see you. No, the dog. He is running back to them. Who?

Galleys of the Lochlanns[7] ran here to beach, in quest of prey, their bloodbeaked prows riding low on a molten pewter surf. Dane vikings, torcs of tomahawks aglitter on their breasts when Malachi wore the collar of gold. A school of turlehide whales stranded in hot noon, spouting, hobbling in the shallows. Then from the starving cagework city a horde of jerkined dwarfs, my people, with flayers' knives, running, scaling, hacking in green blubbery whalemeat. Famine, plague and slaughters. Their blood is in me, their lusts my waves. I moved among them on the frozen Liffey, that I, a changeling, among the spluttering resin fires. I spoke to no-one: none to me.

The dog's bark ran towards him, stopped, ran back.[8] Dog of my enemy. I just simply stood pale, silent, bayed about. *Terribilia meditans.*[9] A primrose doublet, fortune's knave, smiled on my fear. For that are you pining, the bark of their applause? Pretenders: live their lives. The Bruce's brother, Thomas Fitzgerald, silken knight, Perkin Warbeck, York's false scion, in breeches of silk of whiterose ivory, wonder of a day, and Lambert Simnel, with a tail of nans and sutlers, a scullion crowned.[1] All kings' sons. Paradise of pretenders then and now. He saved men from drowning[2] and you shake at a cur's yelping. But the courtiers who mocked Guido in Or san Michele were in their own house. House of . . . We don't want any of your medieval abstrusiosities. Would you do what

6. Stephen is thinking of the boulders on the shore as the work of a large but clumsy giant ("Sir Lout"). "They [Sir Lout and his family] were giants right enough * * * My Sir Lout has rocks in his mouth instead of teeth. He articulates badly" (Joyce to Frank Budgen, reported in Budgen's *James Joyce and the Making of Ulysses*, 1934).
7. Scandinavians (Gaelic). Stephen is meditating on the Vikings who settled Dublin; it was here that they came ashore, he thinks.

8. The dog in this and subsequent paragraphs keeps changing in appearance; he "is the mummer among beasts—the Protean animal" (Joyce to Budgen). Joyce himself was afraid of dogs.
9. "Meditating terrible things."
1. Stephen is meditating on pretenders (i.e., false claimants): the names here are those of pretenders who have figured in English history. This is the Proteus theme again—disguises and changes.
2. Mulligan had saved a man from drowning.

he did? A boat would be near, a lifebuoy. *Natürlich*,[3] put there for you. Would you or would you not? The man that was drowned nine days ago off Maiden's rock. They are waiting for him now. The truth, spit it out. I would want to. I would try. I am not a strong swimmer. Water cold soft. When I put my face into it in the basin at Clongowes. Can't see! Who's behind me? Out quickly, quickly! Do you see the tide flowing quickly in on all sides, sheeting the lows of sands quickly, shellcocoacoloured? If I had land under my feet. I want his life still to be his, mine to be mine. A drowning man. His human eyes scream to me out of horror of his death. I. . . With him together down . . . I could not save her.[4] Waters: bitter death: lost.

A woman and a man. I see her skirties. Pinned up, I bet.

Their dog ambled about a bank of dwindling sand, trotting, sniffing on all sides. Looking for something lost in a past life. Suddenly he made off like a bounding hare, ears flung back, chasing the shadow of a lowskimming gull. The man's shrieked whistle struck his limp ears. He turned, bounded back, came nearer, trotted on twinkling shanks. On a field tenney a buck, trippant, proper, unattired.[5] At the lacefringe of the tide he halted with stiff forehoofs, seawardpointed ears. His snout lifted barked at the wavenoise, herds of seamorse. They serpented towards his feet, curling, unfurling many crests, every ninth, breaking, plashing, from far, from farther out, waves and waves.

Cocklepickers.[6] They waded a little way in the water and, stooping, soused their bags, and, lifting them again, waded out. The dog yelped running to them, reared up and pawed them, dropping on all fours, again reared up at them with mute bearish fawning. Unheeded he kept by them as they came towards the drier sand, a rag of wolf's tongue redpanting from his jaws. His speckled body ambled ahead of them and then loped off at a calf's gallop. The carcass lay on his path. He stopped, sniffed, stalked round it, brother, nosing closer, went round it, sniffling rapidly like a dog all over the dead dog's bedraggled fell. Dogskull, dogsniff, eyes on the ground, moves to one great goal. Ah, poor dogsbody. Here lies poor dogsbody's body.

—Tatters! Out of that, you mongrel.

The cry brought him skulking back to his master and a blunt

3. Of course.

4. A man had been drowned off the coast, and his body had not yet been recovered. As Stephen thinks of the horror of drowning he recalls once again his mother's death.

5. At this point in its constantly changing appearance the dog looks like a heraldic animal and is described in the language of heraldry; the sentence "On a field * * * unattired" means: "On an orange-brown (tawny) background, a buck, tripping, in natural colors, without horns."

6. Stephen recognizes the man and woman on the beach as gypsy cocklepickers (cockles are edible shellfish, like mussels).

bootless kick sent him unscathed across a spit of sand, crouched in flight. He slunk back in a curve. Doesn't see me. Along by the edge of the mole he lolloped, dawdled, smelt a rock and from under a cocked hindleg pissed against it. He trotted forward and, lifting his hindleg, pissed quick short at an unsmelt rock. The simple pleasures of the poor. His hindpaws then scattered sand: then his forepaws dabbled and delved. Something he buried there, his grandmother.[7] He rooted in the sand, dabbling, delving and stopped to listen to the air, scraped up the sand again with a fury of his claws, soon ceasing, a pard,[8] a panther, got in spousebreach,[9] vulturing the dead.

After he woke me up last night same dream or was it? Wait. Open hallway. Street of harlots. Remember. Haroun al Raschid.[1] I am almosting it. That man led me, spoke. I was not afraid. The melon he had he held against my face. Smiled: creamfruit smell. That was the rule, said. In. Come. Red carpet spread. You will see who.

Shouldering their bags they trudged, the red Egyptians.[2] His blued feet out of turnedup trousers slapped the clammy sand, a dull brick muffler strangling his unshaven neck. With woman steps she followed: the ruffian and his strolling mort.[3] Spoils slung at her back. Loose sand and shellgrit crusted her bare feet. About her windraw face her hair trailed. Behind her lord his helpmate, bing awast, to Romeville.[4] When night hides her body's flaws calling under her brown shawl from an archway where dogs have mired. Her fancyman is treating two Royal Dublins in O'Loughlin's of Blackpitts. Buss her, wap in rogue's rum lingo, for, O, my dimber wapping dell.[5] A shefiend's whiteness under her rancid rags. Fumbally's lane that night: the tanyard smells.

> *White thy fambles, red thy gan*
> *And thy quarrons dainty is.*

7. Reference to a joke Stephen had made to his pupils in school that morning about "the fox burying his grandmother under a hollybush." This has many symbolic reverberations throughout *Ulysses.* The buried grandmother suggests Stephen's mother, the Church, and Ireland (the "Poor Old Woman"), while the hollybush, evergreen tree of life, represents resurrection in which, in spite of his religious disbelief, Stephen is much interested and about which (as about metempsychosis) he is continually brooding.
8. Leopard or panther.
9. I.e., begotten in adultery.
1. Stephen's dream of the famous Caliph of Baghdad, of the "street of harlots," and of his meeting a man with a melon, foreshadows his meeting later in the day with Leopold Bloom and his visit to the brothel area of Dublin.
2. I.e., gypsies. As Stephen watches the gypsy cockle-pickers with their dog he imagines their vagabond life and recalls fragments of gypsy speech and of thieves' slang.
3. Gypsies' "freewoman" (i.e., a harlot). "Spoils": the association gypsy-Egyptian reminds Stephen of the Israelites "spoiling the Egyptians" in Exodus xii.36.
4. Go away to London.
5. 17th-century thieves' slang—"buss": kiss; "wap": copulate with; "rum": good; "dimber": pretty; "wapping dell": whore.

> *Couch a hogshead with me then.*
> *In the darkmans clip and kiss.*[6]

Morose delectation Aquinas tunbelly calls this, *frate porcospino.*[7] Unfallen Adam rode and not rutted. Call away let him:[8] *thy quarrons dainty is.* Language no whit worse than his. Monkwords, marybeads jabber on their girdles: roguewords, tough nuggets patter in their pockets.

Passing now.

A side-eye at my Hamlet hat. If I were suddenly naked here as I sit? I am not. Across the sands of all the world, followed by the sun's flaming sword, to the west, trekking to evening lands. She trudges, schlepps, trains, drags, trascines her load.[9] A tide westering, moondrawn, in her wake. Tides, myriadislanded, within her, blood not mine, *oinopa ponton,*[1] a winedark sea. Behold the handmaid of the moon. In sleep the wet sign calls her hour, bids her rise. Bridebed, childbed, bed of death, ghostcandled.[2] *Omnis caro ad te veniet.* He comes, pale vampire, through storm his eyes, his bat sails bloodying the sea, mouth to her mouth's kiss.[3]

Here. Put a pin in that chap, will you? My tablets.[4] Mouth to her kiss. No. Must be two of em. Glue 'em well. Mouth to her mouth's kiss.

His lips lipped and mouthed fleshless lips of air: mouth to her womb. Oomb, allwombing tomb.[5] His mouth moulded issuing breath, unspeeched: ooeeehah: roar of cataractic planets, globed, blazing, roaring wayawayawayawayawayaway. Paper. The banknotes, blast them. Old Deasy's letter. Here. Thanking you for hospitality tear the blank end off. Turning his back to the sun he bent over far to a table of rock and scribbled words.[6] That's twice I forgot to take slips from the library counter.

His shadow lay over the rocks as he bent, ending. Why not endless till the farthest star? Darkly they are there behind this light,

6. More thieves' slang: "fambles": hands; "gan": mouth; "quarrons": body; "couch a hogshead": come to bed; "darkmans": night; "clip": kiss. These four lines and some of the phrases in the preceding paragraph are quoted from a song of the period, *The Rogue's Delight in Praise of His Strolling Mort* (cf. note 3).

7. "Brother porcupine" (Italian), a reference to the fat ("tunbelly") but prickly philosopher, St. Thomas Aquinas.

8. The gypsy is calling his dog.

9. All words suggesting moving or dragging. " 'I like that crescendo of verbs,' he [Joyce] said. 'The irresistible tug of the tides' " (Budgen).

1. "Winedark sea" (Homer).

2. He is thinking of his mother again. The Latin (from the burial service)

means: "All flesh will come to thee."

3. Death comes like the Flying Dutchman in a phantom ship to give the fatal kiss.

4. Cf. Hamlet I.v.107: "My tables!"

5. Stephen's consciousness here can be illuminated with reference to Blake's poem *The Gates of Paradise,* which concludes: "The door of death I open found / And the worm weaving in the ground: / Thou'rt my mother from the womb, / Wife, sister, daughter, to the tomb * * * " Cf. also "the earth that's nature's mother is her tomb. / What is her burying ground that is her womb * * * " (*Romeo and Juliet*, II.iii.9–10).

6. Stephen tears off the blank end of Mr. Deasy's letter to the press and writes a poem that will be quoted later in the novel.

darkness shining in the brightness, delta of Cassiopeia, worlds. Me sits there with his augur's rod of ash, in borrowed sandals, by day beside a livid sea, unbeheld, in violet night walking beneath a reign of uncouth stars.[7] I throw this ended shadow from me, manshape ineluctable, call it back. Endless, would it be mine, form of my form? Who watches me here? Who ever anywhere will read these written words? Signs on a white field. Somewhere to someone in your flutiest voice. The good bishop of Cloyne[8] took the veil of the temple out of his shovel hat: veil of space with coloured emblems hatched on its field. Hold hard. Coloured on a flat: yes, that's right. Flat I see, then think distance, near, far, flat I see, east, back. Ah, see now. Falls back suddenly, frozen in stereoscope. Click does the trick. You find my words dark. Darkness is in our souls, do you not think? Flutier. Our souls, shamewounded by our sins, cling to us yet more, a woman to her lover clinging, the more the more.

She trusts me, her hand gentle, the longlashed eyes. Now where the blue hell am I bringing her beyond the veil?[9] Into the ineluctable modality of the ineluctable visuality. She, she, she. What she? The virgin at Hodges Figgis' window on Monday looking in for one of the alphabet books you were going to write. Keen glance you gave her. Wrist through the braided jess of her sunshade. She lives in Leeson park, with a grief and kickshaws, a lady of letters. Talk that to some else, Stevie: a pickmeup. Bet she wears those curse of God stays suspenders and yellow stockings, darned with lumpy wool. Talk about apple dumplings, *piuttosto*.[1] Where are your wits?

Touch me. Soft eyes. Soft soft soft hand. I am lonely here. O, touch me soon, now. What is that word known to all men? I am quiet here alone. Sad too. Touch, touch me.

He lay back at full stretch over the sharp rocks, cramming the scribbled note and pencil into a pocket, his hat tilted down on his eyes. That is Kevin Egan's movement I made nodding for his nap, sabbath sleep. *Et vidit Deus. Et erant valde bona.*[2] Alo! *Bonjour,* welcome as the flowers in May. Under its leaf he watched through peacocktwittering lashes the southing sun. I am caught in this burn-

---

7. He imagines himself as the constellation Cassiopeia, supposed to represent the wife of Cepheus (an Ethiopian king) seated in a chair and holding up her arms. His ash walking stick he thinks of as an "augur's [Roman soothsayer's] rod of ash."
8. George Berkeley, Bishop of Cloyne (in Ireland), 1685-1753, who argued that the external world has no objective reality but exists only in the mind of the perceiver. Stephen (as at the opening of this episode) is experiment-

ing again with ways of sensing reality.
9. "She" is Psyche, the soul, whom he is bringing from "beyond the veil." But from metaphysical speculations on reality and the soul Stephen is led (by the Psyche association) to think of "the virgin at Hodges Figgis' window."
1. Rather, sooner.
2. Connecting two phrases from the Vulgate: "And God saw" (Genesis i.4) and "And they were very good" (Genesis i.31).

ing scene. Pan's hour, the faunal noon. Among gumheavy serpent-plants, milkoozing fruits, where on the tawny waters leaves lie wide. Pain is far.

And no more turn aside and brood.[3]

His gaze brooded on his broadtoed boots, a buck's castoffs *nebeneinander.* He counted the creases of rucked leather wherein another's foot had nested warm. The foot that beat the ground in tripudium, foot I dislove. But you were delighted when Esther Osvalt's shoe went on you: girl I knew in Paris. *Tiens, quel petit pied!*[4] Staunch friend, a brother soul: Wilde's love that dare not speak its name. He now will leave me. And the blame? As I am. As I am. All or not at all.

In long lassoes from the Cock lake the water flowed full, covering greengoldenly lagoons of sand, rising, flowing. My ashplant will float away. I shall wait. No, they will pass on, passing chafing against the low rocks, swirling, passing. Better get this job over quick. Listen: a fourworded wavespeech: seesoo, hrss, rsseeiss ooos. Vehement breath of waters amid seasnakes, rearing horses, rocks. In cups of rocks it slops: flop, slop, slap: bounded in barrels. And, spent, its speech ceases. It flows purling, widely flowing, floating foampool, flower unfurling.

Under the upswelling tide he saw the writhing weeds lift languidly and sway reluctant arms, hising up their petticoats,[5] in whispering water swaying and upturning coy silver fronds. Day by day: night by night: lifted, flooded and let fall. Lord, they are weary: and, whispered to, they sigh. Saint Ambrose heard it, sigh of leaves and waves, waiting, awaiting the fullness of their times, *diebus ac noctibus iniurias patiens ingemiscit.*[6] To no end gathered: vainly then released, forth flowing, wending back: loom of the moon. Weary too in sight of lovers, lascivious men, a naked woman shining in her courts, she draws a toil of waters.

Five fathoms out there. Full fathom five thy father lies.[7] At one he said. Found drowned. High water at Dublin bar. Driving before it a loose drift of rubble, fanshoals of fishes, silly shells. A corpse rising saltwhite from the undertow, bobbing landward, a pace a pace a porpoise. There he is. Hook it quick. Sunk though he be beneath the watery floor. We have him. Easy now.

---

3. The first line of the second (and last) stanza of Yeats's poem *Who Goes with Fergus,* which is often in Stephen's mind. The line expresses for him the mood of noontide stillness and of lotoseating in a lush oriental scene which overcomes him momentarily when he realizes that it is 12 o'clock, the hour of the Greek nature god Pan, "faunal noon." This oriental lotos-eating theme, which is associated also with Bloom, is important in the *Ulysses.*
4. "Look, what a little foot!"
5. A phrase from a vulgar song sung by Mulligan earlier that morning.
6. "Night and day he patiently groaned forth his wrongs" (St. Ambrose).
7. The theme of the drowned man is important in this episode (cf. the drowned sailor in Eliot's *Waste Land*). This line is from Ariel's song in *The Tempest* (I.ii.396).

Bag of corpsegas sopping in foul brine. A quiver of minnows, fat of a spongy titbit, flash though the slits of his buttoned trouserfly. God becomes man becomes fish becomes barnacle goose becomes featherbed mountain. Dead breaths I living breathe, tread dead dust, devour a urinous offal from all dead. Hauled stark over the gunwale he breathes upward the stench of his green grave, his leprous nosehole snoring to the sun.

A seachange this, brown eyes saltblue. Seadeath, mildest of all deaths known to man. Old Father Ocean. *Prix de Paris:*[8] beware of imitations. Just you give it a fair trial. We enjoyed ourselves immensely.

Come. I thirst. Clouding over. No black clouds anywhere, are there?[9] Thunderstorm. Allbright he falls, proud lightning of the intellect, *Lucifer, dico, qui nescit occasum.*[1] No. My cockle hat and staff and his my sandal shoon.[2] Where? To evening lands. Evening will find itself.

He took the hilt of his ashplant, lunging with it softly, dallying still. Yes, evening will find itself in me, without me. All days make their end. By the way next when is it? Tuesday will be the longest day. Of all the glad new year, mother,[3] the rum tum tiddledy tum. Lawn Tennyson, gentleman poet. *Già.*[4] For the old hag with the yellow teeth. And Monsieur Drumont, gentleman journalist. *Già.* My teeth are very bad. Why, I wonder? Feel. That one is going too. Shells. Ought I go to a dentist, I wonder, with what money? That one. Toothless Kinch, the superman. Why is that, I wonder, or does it mean something perhaps?

My handkerchief. He threw it. I remember. Did I not take it up?

His hand groped vainly in his pockets. No, I didn't. Better buy one.

He laid the dry snot picked from his nostril on a ledge of rock, carefully. For the rest let look who will.

Behind. Perhaps there is someone.

He turned his face over a shoulder, rere regardant.[5] Moving

8. "Prize of Paris"; the reference is probably to the Paris Exposition of 1889, where prizes were awarded in various categories of food, etc.: the prize-winning commodities bear the seal of the prize on the label (hence, "beware of imitations"). Stephen mentally awards the prize to death by drowning. "Seachange" is from Ariel's song, once more.

9. Stephen is looking up to make sure the sky does not threaten a thunderstorm; like Joyce, he hates thunder.

1. Thunder and lightning recall the Fall of Lucifer, "Lucifer, I say, who knows not his fall."

2. From Ophelia's mad song (*Hamlet*, IV.v.23–26): "How should I your true-love know / From another one? / By his cockle hat and staff, / And his sandal shoon." Ophelia, too, was drowned.

3. "You must wake and call me early, call me early, mother dear; / Tomorrow 'ill be the happiest time of all the glad New Year * * * " From *The May Queen* by Alfred, Lord Tennyson ("Lawn Tennyson").

4. Of course!

5. Looking behind him (heraldic terminology). Stephen, as we leave him sitting by the shore, is described in a highly stylized, heraldic language, as though he had himself become a work of art.

through the air high spars of a threemaster, her sails brailed up on the crosstrees,[6] homing, upstream, silently moving, a silent ship.

[*Lestrygonians*][1]

Pineapple rock, lemon platt, butter scotch. A sugarsticky girl shovelling scoopfuls of creams for a christian brother. Some school treat. Bad for their tummies. Lozenge and comfit manufacturer to His Majesty the King. God. Save. Our. Sitting on his throne, sucking red jujubes white.

A sombre Y. M. C. A. young man, watchful among the warm sweet fumes of Graham Lemon's, placed a throwaway in a hand of Mr Bloom.

Heart to heart talks.

Bloo . . . Me? No.

Blood of the Lamb.[2]

His slow feet walked him riverward, reading. Are you saved? All are washed in the blood of the lamb. God wants blood victim. Birth, hymen, martyr, war, foundation of a building, sacrifice, kidney burntoffering, druid's altars. Elijah is coming. Dr John Alex-

---

6. When Budgen pointed out to Joyce that "crosstrees" was not the proper nautical term for the spars to which the sails are bent, Joyce thanked him but added: "But the word 'crosstrees' is essential. It comes in later on and I can't change it. After all, a yard is also a crosstree for the onlooking landlubber." Joyce later uses "crosstree" in a reference to the crucifixion of Christ, so that the suggestion here is of Stephen as both artist and martyr (as his name implies). But the ship is also a real ship, which actually arrived in Dublin on June 16, 1904.

1. It is lunch time in Dublin and Leopold Bloom, as he walks through the city in no great hurry (for he likes to linger and watch what goes on around him), thinks of food. The Lestrygonians in Book X of the *Odyssey* are cannibals, and throughout this episode there are suggestions of the slaughter of living creatures for food, or of food as something disgusting, which make somewhat tenuous contact with Homer's description of the cannibals spearing Ulysses' men for food; the parallel is not, however, profound or very important. What is most important about this episode is that it shows us Bloom's consciousness responding to the sights and sounds of Dublin. His humane curiosity, his desire to learn and to improve the human lot, his sympathetic concern for Mrs. Breen and Mrs. Purefoy, his feeding the gulls, his recollections of a happier time when his daughter was a baby and his relations with his wife Molly were thoroughly satisfactory, his interest in opera, his continuous shying away from thoughts of his wife's rendezvous with the dashing Blazes Boylan—all this helps to build up his character in depth and to differentiate him sharply from Stephen. Unlike Stephen, Bloom's interest in language is confined to simple puns and translations, his interest in poetry is obvious and sentimental; his interest in the nature of reality takes the form of half-forgotten fragments of science remaining in his mind from schooldays. Everything about him is concrete, practical, sensual, and middlebrow or lowbrow, as distinct from the abstract, theoretical, esoteric speculations of Stephen in the "Proteus" episode. For example, when Stephen saw seagulls, he speculated on Daedalus and on flying as a symbol of the artist going into exile; when Bloom sees them, he thinks they must be hungry and buys a bun to feed them. There are parallels between their two streams of consciousness. Bloom's thoughts, in a sense, include Stephen's, but in a popularized and even vulgarized form.

The text of this selection has also been collated with the Odyssey Press edition of 1932.

2. Bloom has been handed a religious leaflet ("throwaway") containing the phrase "Blood of the Lamb." He at first mistakes "Blood" for "Bloom."

ander Dowie, restorer of the church in Zion, is coming.[3]

> *Is coming! Is coming!! Is coming!!!*
> *All heartily welcome.*

Paying game. Torry and Alexander last year. Polygamy. His wife will put the stopper on that. Where was that ad some Birmingham firm the luminous crucifix? Our Saviour. Wake up in the dead of night and see him on the wall, hanging. Pepper's ghost idea. Iron nails ran in.

Phosphorous it must be done with. If you leave a bit of codfish for instance. I could see the bluey silver over it. Night I went down to the pantry in the kitchen. Don't like all the smells in it waiting to rush out. What was it she wanted?[4] The Malaga raisins. Thinking of Spain. Before Rudy[5] was born. The phosphorescence, that bluey greeny. Very good for the brain.

From Butler's monument house corner he glanced along Bachelor's walk. Dedalus' daughter there still outside Dillon's auctionrooms. Must be selling off some old furniture. Knew her eyes at once from the father. Lobbing about waiting for him. Home always breaks up when the mother goes. Fifteen children he had. Birth every year almost. That's in their theology or the priest won't give the poor woman the confession, the absolution. Increase and multiply. Did you ever hear such an idea? Eat you out of house and home. No families themselves to feed. Living on the fat of the land. Their butteries and larders. I'd like to see them do the black fast Yom Kippur.[6] Crossbuns. One meal and a collation for fear he'd collapse on the altar. A housekeeper of one of those fellows if you could pick it out of her. Never pick it out of her. Like getting L s. d.[7] out of him. Does himself well. No guests. All for number one. Watching his water. Bring your own bread and butter. His reverence. Mum's the word.

Good Lord, that poor child's dress is in flitters. Underfed she looks too. Potatoes and marge, marge and potatoes. It's after they feel it. Proof of the pudding. Undermines the constitution.

As he set foot on O'Connell bridge a puffball of smoke plumed up from the parapet. Brewery barge with export stout. England. Sea air sours it, I heard. Be interesting some day get a pass through Hancock to see the brewery. Regular world in itself. Vats of porter, wonderful. Rats get in too. Drink themselves bloated as big as a collie floating. Dead drunk on the porter. Drink till they puke again

---

3. Dowie was a Scottish-American evangelist who established the "Christian Catholic Apostolic Church in Zion" (i.e., Zion City, Illinois) in 1901.
4. "She" is Bloom's wife Molly, born in Gibraltar.

5. Their son, who had died in infancy eleven years before.
6. Jewish Day of Atonement.
7. I.e., cash: £, s., d. are the abbreviations, respectively, for pounds, shillings, and pence.

like christians. Imagine drinking that! Rats: vats. Well of course if we knew all the things.

Looking down he saw flapping strongly, wheeling between the gaunt quay walls, gulls. Rough weather outside. If I threw myself down? Reuben J's son must have swallowed a good bellyful of that sewage.[8] One and eightpence too much. Hhhhm. It's the droll way he comes out with the things. Knows how to tell a story too.

They wheeled lower. Looking for grub. Wait.

He threw down among them a crumpled paper ball. Elijah thirtytwo feet per sec is com.[9] Not a bit. The ball bobbed unheeded on the wake of swells, floated under by the bridge piers. Not such damn fools. Also the day I threw that stale cake out of the Erin's King picked it up in the wake fifty yards astern. Live by their wits. They wheeled, flapping.

> *The hungry famished gull*
> *Flaps o'er the waters dull.*

That is how poets write, the similar sounds. But then Shakespeare has no rhymes: blank verse. The flow of the language it is. The thoughts. Solemn.

> *Hamlet, I am thy father's spirit*
> *Doomed for a certain time to walk the earth.*[1]

—Two apples a penny! Two for a penny!

His gaze passed over the glazed apples serried on her stand. Australians they must be this time of year. Shiny peels: polishes them up with a rag or a handkerchief.

Wait. Those poor birds.

He halted again and bought from the old applewoman two Banbury cakes for a penny and broke the brittle paste and threw its fragments down into the Liffey. See that? The gulls swooped silently two, then all, from their heights, pouncing on prey. Gone. Every morsel.

Aware of their greed and cunning he shook the powdery crumb from his hands. They never expected that. Manna.[2] Live on fishy flesh they have to, all sea birds, gulls, seagoose. Swans from Anna

---

8. Reuben J. Dodd, Dublin solicitor (lawyer), whose son had been rescued from the Liffey River by a man to whom Reuben J. had given two shillings as a reward—"one and eightpence too much," as Simon Dedalus had remarked to Bloom earlier that morning when they were discussing the incident. It is Dedalus' comment that Bloom is thinking of in the following sentences.

9. I.e., Elijah is coming, accelerating at the rate of 32 feet per second per second, the acceleration rate of falling bodies. ("Elijah is coming" is the legend on the handbill Bloom is tossing away).
1. *Hamlet* I.v.9–10 (slightly misquoted).
2. The divine food (small, round, and white) which the children of Israel ate in the wilderness (Exodus xvi.14–15).

Liffey[3] swim down here sometimes to preen themselves. No accounting for tastes. Wonder what kind is swanmeat. Robinson Crusoe had to live on them.

They wheeled, flapping weakly. I'm not going to throw any more. Penny quite enough. Lot of thanks I get. Not even a caw. They spread foot and mouth disease too. If you cram a turkey, say, on chestnut meal it tastes like that. Eat pig like pig. But then why is it that saltwater fish are not salty? How is that?

His eyes sought answer from the river and saw a rowboat rock at anchor on the treacly swells lazily its plastered board.

Kino's

11/–

Trousers.[4]

Good idea that. Wonder if he pays rent to the corporation. How can you own water really? It's always flowing in a stream, never the same, which in the stream of life we trace. Because life is a stream. All kinds of places are good for ads. That quack doctor for the clap used to be stuck up in all the greenhouses. Never see it now. Strictly confidential. Dr Hy Franks. Didn't cost him a red like Maginni the dancing master self advertisement. Got fellows to stick them up or stick them up himself for that matter on the q. t. running in to loosen a button. Fly by night. Just the place too. POST NO BILLS. POST NO PILLS. Some chap with a dose burning him.

If he. . .

O!

Eh?

No . . . No.

No, no. I don't believe it. He wouldn't surely?

No, no.[5]

Mr Bloom moved forward raising his troubled eyes. Think no more about that. After one. Timeball on the ballast office is down. Dunsink time. Fascinating little book that is of Sir Robert Ball's.[6] Parallax. I never exactly understood. There's a priest. Could ask

---

3. The Liffey flows from the Wicklow Mountains northeast and east to Dublin Bay.

4. I.e., eleven shillings ("11/–") for Kino's Trousers. Bloom is a canvasser for advertisements: he receives commissions from newspapers for getting tradesmen to place advertisements with them.

5. Blazes Boylan, flashy philanderer, is due to call on Molly Bloom that afternoon, to discuss the program of a concert which he is managing for her (Molly is a singer). Bloom knows that Boylan and his wife will commit adultery together. Here it suddenly occurs to him that Boylan might give Molly

a "dose" of venereal disease, but he puts the thought from him as incredible.

6. The "timeball on the ballastoffice" registers the official time of the observatory at Dunsink. Noticing that the timeball is down, which means that it is after 1 o'clock, Bloom is reminded of the observatory, then of the Irish astronomer Sir Robert Ball's popular book on astronomy, *The Story of the Heavens* (1886), and of the astronomical term "parallax" he found in the book but which he "never exactly understood."

him. Par it's Greek: parallel, parallax. Met him pikehoses[7] she called it till I told her about the transmigration. O rocks!

Mr Bloom smiled O rocks at two windows of the ballast office. She's right after all. Only big words for ordinary things on account of the sound. She's not exactly witty. Can be rude too. Blurt out what I was thinking. Still I don't know. She used to say Ben Dollard had a base barreltone voice. He has legs like barrels and you'd think he was singing into a barrel. Now, isn't that wit? They used to call him big Ben. Not half as witty as calling him base barreltone. Appetite like an albatross. Get outside of a baron of beef. Powerful man he was at storing away number one Bass.[8] Barrel of Bass. See? It all works out.

A procession of whitesmocked men marched slowly towards him along the gutter, scarlet sashes across their boards. Bargains. Like that priest they are this morning: we have sinned: we have suffered. He read the scarlet letters on their five tall white hats: H. E. L. Y. S. Wisdom Hely's. Y lagging behind drew a chunk of bread from under his foreboard, crammed it into his mouth and munched as he walked. Our staple food. Three bob a day, walking along the gutters, street after street. Just keep skin and bone together, bread and skilly. They are not Boyl: no: M'Glade's men. Doesn't bring in any business either. I suggested to him about a transparent show cart with two smart girls sitting inside writing letters, copybooks, envelopes, blotting paper. I bet that would have caught on. Smart girls writing something catch the eye at once. Everyone dying to know what she's writing. Get twenty of them round you if you stare at nothing. Have a finger in the pie. Women too. Curiosity. Pillar of salt. Wouldn't have it of course because he didn't think of it himself first. Or the inkbottle I suggested with a false stain of black celluloid. His ideas for ads like Plumtree's potted under the obituaries, cold meat department. You can't lick 'em. What? Our envelopes. Hello! Jones, where are you going? Can't stop, Robinson, I am hastening to purchase the only reliable inkeraser *Kansell*, sold by Hely's Ltd, 85 Dame Street. Well out of that ruck I am. Devil of a job it was collecting accounts of those convents. Tranquilla convent. That was a nice nun there, really sweet face. Wimple suited her small head. Sister? Sister? I am sure she was crossed in love by her eyes. Very hard to bargain with that sort of woman. I disturbed her at her devotions that morning. But glad to communicate with the outside world. Our great day, she said.

---

7. Molly's way of pronouncing "metempsychosis." When Bloom had explained metempsychosis to her that morning, she had exclaimed "O rocks" at the pretentious term. He now mentally repeats "O rocks!" at the thought of the word "parallax."

8. A popular British beer.

Feast of Our Lady of Mount Carmel. Sweet name too: caramel. She knew, I think she knew by the way she. If she had married she would have changed. I suppose they really were short of money. Fried everything in the best butter all the same. No lard for them. My heart's broke eating dripping. They like buttering themselves in an out. Molly tasting it, her veil up. Sister? Pat Claffey, the pawnbroker's daughter. It was a nun they say invented barbed wire.

He crossed Westmoreland street when apostrophe S had plodded by. Rover cycleshop. Those races are on today. How long ago is that? Year Phil Gilligan died. We were in Lombard street west. Wait, was in Thom's. Got the job in Wisdom Hely's year we married. Six years. Ten years ago: ninetyfour he died, yes that's right, the big fire at Arnott's. Val Dillon was lord mayor. The Glencree dinner. Alderman Robert O'Reilly emptying the port into his soup before the flag fell, Bobbob lapping it for the inner alderman. Couldn't hear what the band played. For what we have already received may the Lord make us. Milly[9] was a kiddy then. Molly had that elephantgrey dress with the braided frogs. Mantailored with selfcovered buttons. She didn't like it because I sprained my ankle first day she wore choir picnic at the Sugarloaf. As if that. Old Goodwin's tall hat done up with some sticky stuff. Flies' picnic too. Never put a dress on her back like it. Fitted her like a glove, shoulder and hips. Just beginning to plump it out well. Rabbit pie we had that day. People looking after her.

Happy. Happier then. Snug little room that was with the red wallpaper, Dockrell's, one and ninepence a dozen. Milly's tubbing night. American soap I bought: elderflower. Cosy smell of her bathwater. Funny she looked soaped all over. Shapely too. Now photography.[1] Poor papa's daguerreotype atelier he told me of. Hereditary taste.

He walked along the curbstone.

Stream of life. What was the name of that priestlylooking chap was always squinting in when he passed? Weak eyes, woman. Stopped in Citron's saint Kevin's parade. Pen something. Pendennis? My memory is getting. Pen . . . ? of course it's years ago. Noise of the trams probably. Well, if he couldn't remember the dayfather's name that he sees every day.

Bartell d'Arcy was the tenor, just coming out then. Seeing her home after practice. Conceited fellow with his waxedup moustache. Gave her that song *Winds that blow from the south.*

Windy night that was I went to fetch her there was that lodge meeting on about those lottery tickets after Goodwin's concert in the supper room or oakroom of the mansion house. He and I be-

9. Bloom's 15-year-old daughter.   1. Milly is working at a photographer's.

hind. Sheet of her music blew out of my hand against the high
school railings. Lucky it didn't. Thing like that spoils the effect
of a night for her. Professor Goodwin linking her in front. Shaky
on his pins, poor old sot. His farewell concerts. Positively last appearance on any stage. May be for months and may be for never.
Remember her laughing at the wind, her blizzard collar up. Corner
of Harcourt road remember that gust? Brrfoo! Blew up all her skirts
and her boa nearly smothered old Goodwin. She did get flushed
in the wind. Remember when we got home raking up the fire and
frying up those pieces of lap of mutton for her supper with the
Chutney sauce she liked. And the mulled rum. Could see her in the
bedroom from the hearth unclamping the busk of her stays. White.

Swish and soft flop her stays made on the bed. Always warm
from her. Always liked to let herself out. Sitting there after till near
two, taking out her hairpins. Milly tucked up in beddyhouse. Happy.
Happy. That was the night. . .

—O, Mr Bloom, how do you do?

—O, how do you do, Mrs Breen?[2]

—No use complaining. How is Molly those times? Haven't seen
her for ages.

—In the pink, Mr Bloom said gaily, Milly has a position down
in Mullingar, you know.

—Go away! Isn't that grand for her?

—Yes, in a photographer's there. Getting on like a house on fire.
How are all your charges?

—All on the baker's list, Mrs Breen said.

How many has she? No other in sight.

—You're in black I see. You have no. . .

—No, Mr Bloom said. I have just come from a funeral.

Going to crop up all day, I foresee. Who's dead, when and what
did he die of? Turn up like a bad penny.

—O dear me, Mrs Breen said, I hope it wasn't any near relation.

May as well get her sympathy.

—Dignam, Mr Bloom said. An old friend of mine. He died quite
suddenly, poor fellow. Heart trouble, I believe. Funeral was this
morning.

> *Your funeral's tomorrow*
> *While you're coming through the rye.*
> *Diddlediddle dumdum*
> *Diddlediddle. . .*

—Sad to lose the old friends, Mrs Breen's woman eyes said mel-
ancholily.

Now that's quite enough about that. Just quietly: husband.

2. Mrs. Breen had been an old sweetheart of Bloom's.

—And your lord and master?

Mrs Breen turned up her two large eyes. Hasn't lost them anyhow.

—O, don't be talking, she said. He's a caution to rattlesnakes. He's in there now with his lawbooks finding out the law of libel. He has me heartscalded. Wait till I show you.

Hot mockturtle vapour and steam of newbaked jampuffs rolypoly poured out from Harrison's. The heavy noonreek tickled the top of Mr Bloom's gullet. Want to make good pastry, butter, best flour, Demerara sugar, or they'd taste it with the hot tea. Or is it from her? A barefoot arab stood over the grating, breathing in the fumes. Deaden the gnaw of hunger that way. Pleasure or pain is it? Penny dinner. Knife and fork chained to the table.

Opening her handbag, chipped leather, hatpin: ought to have a guard on those things. Stick it in a chap's eye in the tram. Rummaging. Open. Money. Please take one. Devils if they lose sixpence. Raise Cain. Husband barging. Where's the ten shillings I gave you on Monday? Are you feeding your little brother's family? Soiled handkerchief: medicinebottle. Pastille that was fell. What is she? . . .

—There must be a new moon out, she said. He's always bad then.[3] Do you know what he did last night?

Her hand ceased to rummage. Her eyes fixed themselves on him, wide in alarm, yet smiling.

—What? Mr Bloom asked.

Let her speak. Look straight in her eyes. I believe you. Trust me.

—Woke me up in the night, she said. Dream he had, a nightmare.

Indiges.

—Said the ace of spades[4] was walking up the stairs.

—The ace of spades! Mr Bloom said.

She took a folded postcard from her handbag.

—Read that, she said. He got it this morning.

—What is it? Mr Bloom asked, taking the card. U. P.?

—U. P.: up, she said. Someone taking a rise out of him. It's a great shame for them whoever he is.

—Indeed it is, Mr Bloom said.

She took back the card, sighing.

—And now he's going round to Mr Menton's office. He's going to take an action for ten thousand pounds, he says.

She folded the card into her untidy bag and snapped the catch.

Same blue serge dress she had two years ago, the nap bleaching. Seen its best days. Wispish hair over her ears. And that dowdy

---

3. Mr. Breen is mentally disturbed.   4. Symbol of death.

toque, three old grapes to take the harm out of it. Shabby genteel. She used to be a tasty dresser. Lines round her mouth. Only a year or so older than Molly.

See the eye that woman gave her, passing. Cruel. The unfair sex.

He looked still at her, holding back behind his look his discontent. Pungent mockturtle oxtail mulligatawny. I'm hungry too. Flakes of pastry on the gusset of her dress: daub of sugary flour stuck to her cheek. Rhubarb tart with liberal fillings, rich fruit interior. Josie Powell that was. In Luke Doyle's long ago, Dolphin's Barn, the charades. U. P.: up.

Change the subject.

—Do you ever see anything of Mrs Beaufoy, Mr Bloom asked.

—Mina Purefoy? she said.

Philip Beaufoy I was thinking. Playgoer's club.[5] Matcham often thinks of the masterstroke. Did I pull the chain? Yes. The last act.

—Yes.

—I just called to ask on the way in is she over it. She's in the lying-in hospital in Holles street. Dr Horne got her in. She's three days bad now.

—O, Mr Bloom said. I'm sorry to hear that.

—Yes, Mrs Breen said. And a houseful of kids at home. It's a very stiff birth, the nurse told me.

—O, Mr Bloom said.

His heavy pitying gaze absorbed her news. His tongue clacked in compassion. Dth! Dth!

—I'm sorry to hear that, he said. Poor thing! Three days! That's terrible for her.

Mrs Breen nodded.

—She was taken bad on the Tuesday. . .

Mr Bloom touched her funnybone gently, warning her.

—Mind! Let this man pass.

A bony form strode along the curbstone from the river, staring with a rapt gaze into the sunlight through a heavy stringed glass. Tight as a skullpiece a tiny hat gripped his head. From his arm a folded dustcoat, a stick and an umbrella dangled to his stride.

—Watch him, Mr Bloom said. He always walks outside the lampposts. Watch!

—Who is he if it's a fair question, Mrs. Breen asked. Is he dotty?

—His name is Cashel Boyle O'Connor Fitzmaurice Tisdall Farrell, Mr Bloom said, smiling. Watch!

---

5. Bloom is thinking of the story *Matcham's Masterstroke*, by "Mr. Philip Beaufoy, Playgoers' club, London," which he had read in the toilet that morning. He then mentally quotes the opening sentence.

—He has enough of them, she said. Denis will be like that one of these days.

She broke off suddenly.

—There he is, she said. I must go after him. Goodbye. Remember me to Molly, won't you?

—I will, Mr Bloom said.

He watched her dodge through passers towards the shopfronts. Denis Breen in skimpy frockcoat and blue canvas shoes shuffled out of Harrison's hugging two heavy tomes to his ribs. Blown in from the bay. Like old times. He suffered her to overtake him without surprise and thrust his dull grey beard towards her, his loose jaw wagging as he spoke earnestly.

Meshuggah.[6] Off his chump.

Mr Bloom walked on again easily, seeing ahead of him in sunlight the tight skullpiece, the dangling stick, umbrella, dustcoat. Going the two days. Watch him! Out he goes again. One way of getting on in the world. And that other old mosey lunatic in those duds. Hard time she must have with him.

U. P.: up. I'll take my oath that's Alf Bergan or Richie Goulding. Wrote it for a lark in the Scotch house, I bet anything. Round to Menton's office. His oyster eyes staring at the postcard. Be a feast for the gods.

He passed the *Irish Times*. There might be other answers lying there. Like to answer them all. Good system for criminals. Code. At their lunch now. Clerk with the glasses there doesn't know me. O, leave them there to simmer. Enough bother wading through fortyfour of them. Wanted smart lady typist to aid gentleman in literary work. I called you naughty darling because I do not like that other world. Please tell me what is the meaning. Please tell me what perfume does your wife.[7] Tell me who made the world. The way they spring those questions on you. And the other one Lizzie Twigg. My literary efforts have had the good fortune to meet with the approval of the eminent poet A. E. (Mr Geo Russell).[7a] No time to do her hair drinking sloppy tea with a book of poetry.

Best paper by long chalks for a small ad. Got the provinces now. Cook and general, exc cuisine, housemaid kept. Wanted live man for spirit counter. Resp girl (R. C.) wishes to hear of post in fruit or pork shop. James Carlisle made that. Six and a half per cent

---

6. Yiddish, "mad."

7. Bloom is mentally quoting a letter written to him by the typist Martha Clifford, with whom he is carrying on a purely epistolary love affair (she had misspelled "word" as "world": "I do not like that other *world*"). Lizzie Twigg was one of the other typists who had answered his advertisement for a secretary "to aid gentleman in literary work" (Bloom's pretext for beginning such an affair).

7a. A. E. (George Russell, 1867–1935), the Irish poet mentioned as a reference by Lizzie Twigg when she answered Bloom's advertisement, is later encountered by Bloom with a woman who Bloom speculates might be Lizzie.

dividend. Made a big deal on Coates's shares. Ca'canny. Cunning old Scotch hunks. All the toady news. Our gracious and popular vicereine.[8] Bought the *Irish Field* now. Lady Mountcashel has quite recovered after her confinement and rode out with the Ward Union staghounds at the enlargement yesterday at Rathoath. Uneatable fox. Pothunters too. Fear injects juices make it tender enough for them. Riding astride. Sit her horse like a man. Weightcarrying huntress. No sidesaddle or pillion for her, not for Joe. First to the meet and in at the death. Strong as a brood mare some of those horsey women. Swagger around livery stables. Toss off a glass of brandy neat while you'd say knife. That one at the Grosvenor this morning. Up with her on the car: wishwish. Stonewall or fivebarred gate put her mount to it. Think that pugnosed driver did it out of spite. Who is this she was like? O yes! Mrs Miriam Dandrade that sold me her old wraps and black underclothes in the Shelbourne hotel. Divorced Spanish American. Didn't take a feather out of her my handling them. As if I was her clotheshorse. Saw her in the viceregal party when Stubbs the park ranger got me in with Whelan of the *Express*. Scavenging what the quality left. High tea. Mayonnaise I poured on the plums thinking it was custard. Her ears ought to have tingled for a few weeks after. Want to be a bull for her. Born courtesan. No nursery work for her, thanks.

Poor Mrs Purefoy! Methodist husband. Method in his madness. Saffron bun and milk and soda lunch in the educational dairy. Eating with a stopwatch, thirtytwo chews to the minute. Still his muttonchop whiskers grew. Supposed to be well connected. Theodore's cousin in Dublin Castle. One tony relative in every family. Hardy annuals he presents her with. Saw him out at the Three Jolly Topers marching along bareheaded and his eldest boy carrying one in a marketnet. The squallers. Poor thing! Then having to give the breast year after year all hours of the night. Selfish those t.t's are. Dog in the manger. Only one lump of sugar in my tea, if you please.

He stood at Fleet street crossing. Luncheon interval a six penny at Rowe's? Must look up that ad in the national library.[9] An eightpenny in the Burton. Better. On my way.

He walked on past Bolton's Westmoreland house. Tea. Tea. Tea. I forgot to tap Tom Kernan.[1]

Sss. Dth, dth, dth! Three days imagine groaning on a bed with a vinegared handkerchief round her forehead, her belly swollen out!

8. Wife of the Viceroy, who represented the British Crown in Ireland; Bloom is thinking of the society column in the *Irish Times*.
9. Bloom's goal, on his walk through Dublin, is the National Library, where he wants to look up an advertisement in a back number of the *Kilkenny People*.
1. A Dublin tea merchant and friend of Bloom's, whom Bloom had earlier intended to ask ("tap") for some tea.

Phew! Dreadful simply! Child's head too big: forceps. Doubled up inside her trying to butt its way out blindly, groping for the way out. Kill me that would. Lucky Molly got over hers lightly. They ought to invent something to stop that. Life with hard labour. Twilight-sleep idea: queen Victoria was given that. Nine she had. A good layer. Old woman that lived in a shoe she had so many children. Suppose he was consumptive. Time someone thought about it instead of gassing about the what was it the pensive bosom of the silver effulgence. Flapdoodle to feed fools on. They could easily have big establishments. Whole thing quite painless out of all the taxes give every child born five quid at compound interest up to twentyone, five per cent is a hundred shillings and five tiresome pounds, multiply by twenty decimal system, encourage people to put by money save hundred and ten and a bit twentyone years want to work it out on paper come to a tidy sum, more than you think.

Not stillborn of course. They are not even registered. Trouble for nothing.

Funny sight two of them together, their bellies out. Molly and Mrs Moisel. Mothers' meeting. Phthisis retires for the time being, then returns. How flat they look after all of a sudden! Peaceful eyes. Weight off their minds. Old Mrs Thornton was a jolly old soul. All my babies, she said. The spoon of pap in her mouth before she fed them. O, that's nyumyum. Got her hand crushed by old Tom Wall's son. His first bow to the public. Head like a prize pumpkin. Snuffy Dr Murren. People knocking them up at all hours. For God's sake doctor. Wife in her throes. Then keep them waiting months for their fee. To attendance on your wife. No gratitude in people. Humane doctors, most of them.

Before the huge high door of the Irish house of parliament a flock of pigeons flew. Their little frolic after meals. Who will we do it on? I pick the fellow in black. Here goes. Here's good luck. Must be thrilling from the air. Apjohn, myself and Owen Goldberg up in the trees near Goose green playing the monkeys. Mackerel they called me.

A squad of constables debouched from College street, marching in Indian file. Goose step. Foodheated faces, sweating helmets, patting their truncheons. After their feed with a good load of fat soup under their belts. Policeman's lot is oft a happy one. They split up into groups and scattered, saluting towards their beats. Let out to graze. Best moment to attack one in pudding time. A punch in his dinner. A squad of others, marching irregularly, rounded Trinity railings, making for the station. Bound for their troughs. Prepare to receive cavalry. Prepare to receive soup.

He crossed under Tommy Moore's roguish finger. They did right to put him up over a urinal: meeting of the waters.[2] Ought to be places for women. Running into cakeshops. Settle my hat straight. *There is not in this wide world a vallee.* Great song of Julia Morkan's. Kept her voice up to the very last. Pupil of Michael Balfe's wasn't she?

He gazed after the last broad tunic. Nasty customers to tackle. Jack Power could a tale unfold: father a G man. If a fellow gave them trouble being lagged they let him have it hot and heavy in the bridewell.[3] Can't blame them after all with the job they have especially the young hornies. That horse policeman the day Joe Chamberlain was given his degree in Trinity he got a run for his money.[4] My word he did! His horse's hoofs clattering after us down Abbey street. Luck I had the presence of mind to dive into Manning's or I was souped. He did come a wallop, by George. Must have cracked his skull on the cobblestones. I oughtn't to have got myself swept along with those medicals. And the Trinity jibs[5] in their mortarboards. Looking for trouble. Still I got to know that young Dixon who dressed that sting for me in the Mater and now he's in Holles street where Mrs Purefoy. Wheels within wheels. Police whistle in my ears still. All skedaddled. Why he fixed on me. Give me in charge. Right here it began.

—Up the Boers!

—Three cheers for De Wet![6]

—We'll hang Joe Chamberlain on a sourapple tree.

Silly billies: mob of young cubs yelling their guts out. Vinegar hill. The Butter exchange band. Few years time half of them magistrates and civil servants. War comes on: into the army helterskelter: same fellows used to whether on the scaffold high.

Never know who you're talking to. Corney Kelleher he has Harvey Duff in his eye. Like that Peter or Denis or James Carey that blew the gaff on the invincibles. Member of the corporation too. Egging raw youths on to get in the know. All the time drawing secret service pay from the castle.[7] Drop him like a hot potato. Why those plain clothes men are always courting slaveys. Easily twig a man used to uniform. Squarepushing up against a backdoor. Maul her a bit. Then the next thing on the menu. And who is the gentleman does be visiting there? Was the young master saying anything? Peeping Tom through the keyhole. Decoy duck. Hotblooded young student fooling round her fat arms ironing.

---

2. *The Meeting of the Waters* was a famous poem by the much-loved Irish poet Thomas Moore (1779–1852) whose statue Bloom now passes.
3. Prison.
4. When Joseph Chamberlain, the British Colonial Secretary, came to Dublin to receive an honorary degree from Trinity College, a group of medical students rioted against him and against the Boer War.
5. Trinity College students.
6. Boer general.
7. I.e., from the British government, whose representative lived at Dublin Castle.

—Are those yours, Mary?

—I don't wear such things. . . Stop or I'll tell the missus on you. Out half the night.

—There are great times coming, Mary. Wait till you see.

—Ah, get along with your great times coming.

Barmaids too. Tobacco shopgirls.

James Stephens'[8] idea was the best. He knew them. Circles of ten so that a fellow couldn't round on more than his own ring. Sinn Fein.[9] Back out you get the knife. Hidden hand. Stay in. The firing squad. Turnkey's daughter got him out of Richmond, off from Lusk. Putting up in the Buckingham Palace hotel under their very noses. Garibaldi.[1]

You must have a certain fascination: Parnell.[2] Arthur Griffith is a squareheaded fellow but he has no go in him for the mob. Want to gas about our lovely land. Gammon and spinach. Dublin Bakery Company's tearoom. Debating societies. That republicanism is the best form of government. That the language question should take precedence of the economic question. Have your daughters inveigling them to your house. Stuff them up with meat and drink. Michaelmas goose. Here's a good lump of thyme seasoning under the apron for you. Have another quart of goosegrease before it gets too cold. Halffed enthusiastists. Penny roll and a walk with the band. No grace for the carver. The thought that the other chap pays best sauce in the world. Make themselves thoroughly at home. Shove us over those apricots, meaning peaches. The not far distant day. Home Rule sun rising up in the northwest.[3]

His smile faded as he walked, a heavy cloud hiding the sun slowly, shadowing Trinity's surly front. Trams passed one another, ingoing, outgoing, clanging. Useless words. Things go on same; day after day: squads of police marching out, back: trams in, out. Those two loonies mooching about. Dignam carted off. Mina Purefoy swollen belly on a bed groaning to have a child tugged out of her. One born every second somewhere. Other dying every second. Since I fed the birds five minutes. Three hundred kicked the bucket. Other three hundred born, washing the blood off, all are washed in the blood of the lamb, bawling maaaaaa.

Cityful passing away, other cityful coming, passing away too: other coming on, passing on. Houses, lines of houses, streets, miles

8. Irish nationalist revolutionary.
9. Irish revolutionary movement; the Gaelic words mean "We Ourselves."
1. Bloom is thinking of a variety of nationalist conspirators who escaped from danger, among them the 19th-century Italian patriot and general Giuseppe Garibaldi.

2. Charles Stewart Parnell (1846–91), Irish nationalist political leader. Arthur Griffith was founder of the Sinn Fein.
3. Reference to Arthur Griffith's comment on the *Freeman* masthead, which showed the sun rising in the northwest from behind the bank of Ireland. Bloom has a *Freeman* in his pocket.

of pavements, piledup bricks, stones. Changing hands. This owner, that. Landlord never dies they say. Other steps into his shoes when he gets his notice to quit. They buy the place up with gold and still they have all the gold. Swindle in it somewhere. Piled up in cities, worn away age after age. Pyramids in sand. Built on bread and onions. Slaves Chinese wall. Babylon. Big stones left. Round towers. Rest rubble, sprawling suburbs, jerrybuilt, Kerwan's mushroom houses, built of breeze. Shelter for the night.

No one is anything.

This is the very worst hour of the day. Vitality. Dull, gloomy: hate this hour. Feel as if I had been eaten and spewed.

Provost's house. The reverend Dr Salmon: tinned salmon. Well tinned in there. Wouldn't live in it if they paid me. Hope they have liver and bacon today. Nature abhors a vacuum.

The sun freed itself slowly and lit glints of light among the silver ware in Walter Sexton's window opposite by which John Howard Parnell[4] passed, unseeing.

There he is: the brother. Image of him. Haunting face. Now that's a coincidence. Course hundreds of times you think of a person and don't meet him. Like a man walking in his sleep. No-one knows him. Must be a corporation meeting today. They say he never put on the city marshal's uniform since he got the job. Charley Boulger used to come out on his high horse, cocked hat, puffed, powdered and shaved. Look at the woebegone walk of him. Eaten a bad egg. Poached eyes on ghost. I have a pain. Great man's brother: his brother's brother. He'd look nice on the city charger. Drop into the D. B. C. probably for his coffee, play chess there. His brother used men as pawns. Let them all go to pot. Afraid to pass a remark on him. Freeze them up with that eye of his. That's the fascination: the name. All a bit touched. Mad Fanny and his other sister Mrs Dickinson driving about with scarlet harness. Bolt upright like surgeon M'Ardle. Still David Sheehy beat him for south Meath. Apply for the Chiltern Hundreds and retire into public life. The patriot's banquet. Eating orangepeels in the park. Simon Dedalus said when they put him in parliament that Parnell would come back from the grave and lead him out of the House of Commons by the arm.

—Of the twoheaded octopus, one of whose heads is the head upon which the ends of the world have forgotten to come while the other speaks with a Scotch accent. The tentacles. . .

They passed from behind Mr Bloom along the curbstone. Beard and bicycle. Young woman.

And there he is too. Now that's really a coincidence: secondtime. Coming events cast their shadows before. With the approval of the

4. C. S. Parnell's brother.

eminent poet Mr Geo Russell.[5] That might be Lizzie Twigg with him. A. E.: what does that mean? Initials perhaps. Albert Edward, Arthur Edmund, Alphonsus Eb Ed El Esquire. What was he saying? The ends of the world with a Scotch accent. Tentacles: octopus. Something occult: symbolism. Holding forth. She's taking it all in. Not saying a word. To aid gentleman in literary work.

His eyes followed the high figure in homespun, beard and bicycle, a listening woman at his side. Coming from the vegetarian. Only weggebobbles and fruit. Don't eat a beefsteak. If you do the eyes of that cow will pursue you through all eternity. They say it's healthier. Wind and watery though. Tried it. Keep you on the run all day. Bad as a bloater. Dreams all night. Why do they call that thing they gave me nutsteak? Nutarians. Fruitarians. To give you the idea you are eating rumpsteak. Absurd. Salty too. They cook in soda. Keep you sitting by the tap all night.

Her stockings are loose over her ankles. I detest that: so tasteless. Those literary ethereal people they are all. Dreamy, cloudy, symbolistic. Esthetes they are. I wouldn't be surprised if it was that kind of food you see produces the like waves of the brain the poetical. For example one of those policemen sweating Irish stew into their shirts; you couldn't squeeze a line of poetry out of him. Don't know what poetry is even. Must be in a certain mood.

> *The dreamy cloudy gull*
> *Waves o'er the waters dull.*

He crossed at Nassau street corner and stood before the window of Yeates and Son, pricing the field glasses. Or will I drop into old Harris's and have a chat with young Sinclair? Wellmannered fellow. Probably at his lunch. Must get those old glasses of mine set right. Gœrz lenses, six guineas. Germans making their way everywhere. Sell on easy terms to capture trade. Undercutting. Might chance on a pair in the railway lost property office. Astonishing the things people leave behind them in trains and cloak rooms. What do they be thinking about? Women too. Incredible. Last year travelling to Ennis had to pick up that farmer's daughter's bag and hand it to her at Limerick junction. Unclaimed money too. There's a little watch up there on the roof of the bank to test those glasses by.

His lids came down on the lower rims of his irides. Can't see it. If you imagine it's there you can almost see it. Can't see it.

He faced about and, standing between the awnings, held out his right hand at arm's length towards the sun. Wanted to try that often. Yes: completely. The tip of his little finger blotted out the

5. Bloom wonders whether the woman with A.E. might be Lizzie Twigg and then goes on to speculate on the meaning of "A.E." and on Russell's mystical ideas.

sun's disk. Must be the focus where the rays cross. If I had black glasses. Interesting. There was a lot of talk about those sunspots when we were in Lombard street west. Terrific explosions they are. There will be a total eclipse this year: autumn some time.

Now that I come to think of it, that ball falls at Greenwich time. It's the clock is worked by an electric wire from Dunsink. Must go out there some first Saturday of the month. If I could get an introduction to professor Joly or learn up something about his family. That would do to: man always feels complimented. Flattery where least expected. Nobleman proud to be descended from some king's mistress. His foremother. Lay it on with a trowel. Cap in hand goes through the land. Not go in and blurt out what you know you're not to: what's parallax? Show this gentleman the door.

Ah.

His hand fell again to his side.

Never know anything about it. Waste of time. Gasballs spinning about, crossing each other, passing. Same old dingdong always. Gas, then solid, then world, then cold, then dead shell drifting around, frozen rock like that pineapple rock. The moon. Must be a new moon out, she said. I believe there is.

He went on by la Maison Claire.

Wait. The full moon was the night we were Sunday fortnight exactly there is a new moon. Walking down by the Tolka. Not bad for a Fairview moon. She was humming: The young May moon she's beaming, love. He other side of her. Elbow, arm. He. Glow-worm's la-amp is gleaming, love. Touch. Fingers. Asking. Answer. Yes.

Stop. Stop. If it was it was.[6] Must.

Mr Bloom, quick breathing, slowlier walking, passed Adam court.

With a deep quiet relief, his eyes took note: this is street here middle of the day Bob Doran's bottle shoulders. On his annual bend, M'Coy said. They drink in order to say or do something or *cherchez la femme.*[7] Up in the Coombe with chummies and street-walkers and then the rest of the year as sober as a judge.

Yes. Thought so. Sloping into the Empire. Gone. Plain soda would do him good. Where Pat Kinsella had his Harp theater before Whitbread ran the Queen's.[8] Broth of a boy. Dion Boucicault business with his harvestmoon face in a poky bonnet. Three Purty Maids from School. How time flies eh? Showing long red pantaloons under his skirts. Drinkers, drinking, laughed spluttering, their drink against their breath. More power, Pat. Coarse red: fun for drunkards: guffaw and smoke. Take off that white hat. His parboiled eyes. Where is he now? Beggar somewhere. The harp that

---

6. Bloom is thinking again of his wife's infidelities.
7. "Look for the woman" (in the case).
8. The Queen's Theatre. Dion Boucicault was an Irish-born American dramatist, manager, and actor.

once did starve us all.[9]

I was happier then. Or was that I? Or am I now I? Twentyeight I was. She twentythree when we left Lombard street west something changed. Could never like it again after Rudy. Can't bring back time. Like holding water in your hand. Would you go back to then? Just beginning then. Would you? Are you not happy in your home, you poor little naughty boy? Wants to sew on buttons for me. I must answer. Write it in the library.

Grafton street gay with housed awnings lured his senses. Muslin prints silk, dames and dowagers, jingle of harnesses, hoofthuds low-ringing in the baking causeway. Thick feet that woman has in the white stockings. Hope the rain mucks them up on her. Country bred chawbacon. All the beef to the heels were in. Always gives a woman clumsy feet. Molly looks out of plumb.

He passed, dallying, the windows of Brown Thomas, silk mercers. Cascades of ribbons. Flimsy China silks. A tilted urn poured from its mouth a flood of bloodhued poplin: lustrous blood. The hugue-nots brought that here. *La causa è santa!*[1] Tara tara. Great chorus that. Tara. Must be washed in rainwater. Meyerbeer. Tara: bom bom bom.

Pincushions. I'm a long time threatening to buy one. Stick them all over the place. Needles in window curtains.

He bared slightly his left forearm. Scrape: nearly gone. Not to-day anyhow. Must go back for that lotion. For her birthday per-haps. Junejuly augseptember eighth. Nearly three months off. Then she mightn't like it. Women won't pick up pins. Say it cuts lo.

Gleaming silks, petticoats on slim brass rails, rays of flat silk stockings.

Useless to go back. Had to be. Tell me all.

High voices. Sunwarm silk. Jingling harnesses. All for a woman, home and houses, silk webs, silver, rich fruits, spicy from Jaffa. Agendath Netaim.[2] Wealth of the world.

A warm human plumpness settled down on his brain. His brain yielded. Perfume of embraces all him assailed. With hungered flesh obscurely, he mutely craved to adore.

Duke street. Here we are. Must eat. The Burton. Feel better then.

He turned Combridge's corner, still pursued. Jingling hoofthuds. Perfumed bodies, warm, full. All kissed, yielded: in deep summer fields, tangled pressed grass, in trickling hallways of tenements, along sofas, creaking beds.

9. A reference to the lack of financial success of the Harp Theatre through a punning reworking (almost worthy of Stephen Dedalus) of Tom Moore's famous *Harp That Once Through Tara's Halls*.

1. "The cause is sacred," chorus from Meyerbeer's opera *Les Huguenots*, which Bloom is recalling. The Huguenots were 16th- and 17th-century French Protes-tants, many of whom fled to Britain to escape persecution.

2. "Planters' Company" (Hebrew). Bloom recalls a leaflet advertising an early Zionist settlement which he had seen that morning and is still carrying in his pocket.

—Jack, love!
—Darling!
—Kiss me, Reggy!
—My boy!
—Love![3]

His heart astir he pushed in the door of the Burton restaurant. Stink gripped his trembling breath: pungent meatjuice, slop of greens. See the animals feed.

Men, men, men.

Perched on high stools by the bar, hats shoved back, at the tables calling for more bread no charge, swilling, wolfing gobfuls of sloppy food, their eyes bulging, wiping wetted moustaches. A pallid suetfaced young man polished his tumbler knife fork and spoon with his napkin. New set of microbes. A man with an infant's saucestained napkin tucked round him shovelled gurgling soup down his gullet. A man spitting back on his plate: halfmasticated gristle: no teeth to chewchewchew it. Chump chop from the grill. Bolting to get it over. Sad booser's eyes. Bitten off more than he can chew. Am I like that? See ourselves as others see us. Hungry man is an angry man. Working tooth and jaw. Don't! O! A bone! That last pagan king of Ireland Cormac in the schoolpoem choked himself at Sletty southward of the Boyne.[4] Wonder what he was eating. Something galoptious. Saint Patrick converted him to Christianity. Couldn't swallow it all however.

—Roast beef and cabbage.
—One stew.

Smells of men. His gorge rose. Spaton sawdust, sweetish warmish cigarette smoke, reek of plug, spilt beer, men's beery piss, the stale of ferment.

Couldn't eat a morsel here. Fellow sharpening knife and fork, to eat all before him, old chap picking his tootles. Slight spasm, full, chewing the cud. Before and after. Grace after meals. Look on this picture then on that. Scoffing up stewgravy with sopping sippets of bread. Lick it off the plate, man! Get out of this.

He gazed round the stooled and tabled eaters, tightening the wings of his nose.

—Two stouts here.
—One corned and cabbage.

That fellow ramming a knifeful of cabbage down as if his life depended on it. Good stroke. Give me the fidgets to look. Safer to eat from his three hands. Tear it limb from limb. Second nature to

3. Sensual images are leading Bloom to imagine love scenes from a sentimental novel. The cannibal Lestrygonians had used "the handsome daughter of Lestrygonian Antiphates" as a decoy to lure Ulysses' men to her father, and Bloom is drawn by his sensual and sexual im-agination to enter Burton's restaurant—only to be disgusted by the grossness of the atmosphere.

4. Bloom is recalling a "schoolpoem" about a legendary incident in Irish history.

him. Born with a silver knife in his mouth. That's witty, I think.
Or no. Silver means born rich. Born with a knife. But then the
allusion is lost.

An illgirt server gathered sticky clattering plates. Rock, the bailiff,
standing at the bar blew the foamy crown from his tankard. Well
up: it splashed yellow near his boot. A diner, knife and fork upright,
elbows on table, ready for a second helping stared towards the food-
lift across his stained square of newspaper. Other chap telling him
something with his mouth full. Sympathetic listener. Table talk.
I munched hum un thu Unchster Bunk un Munchday. Ha? Did
you, faith?

Mr Bloom raised two fingers doubtfully to his lips. His eyes said.

—Not here. Don't see him.[5]

Out. I hate dirty eaters.

He backed towards the door. Get a light snack in Davy Byrne's.
Stopgap. Keep me going. Had a good breakfast.

—Roast and mashed here.

—Pint of stout.

Every fellow for his own, tooth and nail. Gulp. Grub. Gulp.
Gobstuff.

He came out into clearer air and turned back towards Grafton
street. Eat or be eaten. Kill! Kill!

Suppose that communal kitchen years to come perhaps. All
trotting down with porringers and tommycans to be filled. Devour
contents in the street. John Howard Parnell example the provost
of Trinity every mother's son don't talk of your provosts and provost
of Trinity women and children, cabmen, priests, parsons, field-
marshals, archbishops. From Ailesbury road, Clyde road, artisan's
dwellings north Dublin union, lord mayor in his gingerbread coach,
old queen in a bathchair. My plate's empty. After you with our incorporated drinkingcup. Like sir Philip Crampton's fountain. Rub
off the microbes with your handkerchief. Next chap rubs on a new
batch with his. Father O'Flynn would make hares of them all. Have
rows all the same. All for number one. Children fighting for the
scrapings of the pot. Want a soup pot as big as the Phoenix Park.
Harpooning flitches and hindquarters out of it. Hate people all
around you. City Arms hotel *table d'hôte* she called it. Soup, joint
and sweet. Never know whose thoughts you're chewing. Then who'd
wash up all the plates and forks? Might be all feeding on tabloids
that time. Teeth getting worse and worse.

After all there's a lot in that vegetarian fine flavour of things
from the earth garlic, of course, it stinks Italian organgrinders crisp
of onions, mushrooms truffles. Pain to animal too. Pluck and draw
fowl. Wretched brutes there at the cattlemarket waiting for the

5. He pretends he is looking for someone he cannot see, so that he has an excuse
to leave without eating.

poleaxe to split their skulls open. Moo. Poor trembling calves. Meh. Staggering bob. Bubble and squeak. Butchers' buckets wobble lights. Give us that brisket off the hook. Plup. Rawhead and bloody bones. Flayed glasseyed sheep hung from their haunches, sheep-snouts bloodypapered sniveling nosejam on sawdust. Top and lashers going out. Don't maul them pieces, young one.

Hot fresh blood they prescribe for decline. Blood always needed. Insidious. Lick it up, smoking hot, thick sugary. Famished ghosts.

Ah, I'm hungry.

He entered Davy Byrne's. Moral pub. He doesn't chat. Stands a drink now and then. But in leapyear once in four. Cashed a cheque for me once.

What will I take now? He drew his watch. Let me see now. Shandygaff?

—Hello, Bloom! Nosey Flynn said from his nook.

—Hello, Flynn.

—How's things?

—Tiptop . . . Let me see. I'll take a glass of burgundy and . . . let me see.

Sardines on the shelves. Almost taste them by looking. Sandwich? Ham and his descendants mustered and bred there. Potted meats. What is home without Plumtree's potted meat? Incomplete. What a stupid ad! Under the obituary notices they stuck it. All up a plumtree. Dignam's potted meat. Cannibals would with lemon and rice. White missionary too salty. Like pickled pork. Except the chief consumes the parts of honour. Ought to be tough from exercise. His wives in a row to watch the effect. *There was a right royal old nigger. Who ate or something the somethings of the reverend Mr MacTrigger.* With it an abode of bliss. Lord knows what concoction. Cauls mouldy tripes windpipes faked and minced up. Puzzle find the meat. Kosher. No meat and milk together. Hygiene that was what they call now. Yom kippur fast spring cleaning of inside. Peace and war depend on some fellow's digestion. Religions. Christmas turkeys and geese. Slaughter of innocents. Eat, drink and be merry. Then casual wards full after. Heads bandaged. Cheese digests all but itself. Mighty cheese.

—Have you a cheese sandwich?

—Yes, sir.

Like a few olives too if they had them. Italian I prefer. Good glass of burgundy; take away that. Lubricate. A nice salad, cool as a cucumber. Tom Kernan can dress. Puts gusto into it. Pure olive oil. Milly served me that cutlet with a sprig of parsley. Take one Spanish onion. God made food, the devil the cooks. Devilled crab.

—Wife well?

—Quite well, thanks . . . A cheese sandwich, then. Gorgonzola, have you?

—Yes, sir.

Nosey Flynn sipped his grog.

—Doing any singing those times?

Look at his mouth. Could whistle in his own ear. Flap ears to match. Music. Knows as much about it as my coachman. Still better tell him. Does no harm. Free ad.

—She's engaged for a big tour end of this month. You may have heard perhaps.

—No. O, that's the style. Who's getting it up?

The curate[6] served.

—How much is that?

—Seven d., sir . . . Thank you, sir.

Mr Bloom cut his sandwich into slender strips. *Mr MacTrigger. Easier than the dreamy creamy stuff. His five hundred wives. Had the time of their lives.*

—Mustard, sir?

—Thank you.

He studded under each lifted strip yellow blobs. *Their lives.* I have it. *It grew bigger and bigger and bigger.*

—Getting it up? he said. Well, it's like a company idea, you see. Part shares and part profits.

—Ay, now I remember, Nosey Flynn said, putting his hand in his pocket to scratch his groin. Who is this was telling me? Isn't Blazes Boylan mixed up in it?

A warm shock of air heat of mustard haunched on Mr Bloom's heart. He raised his eyes and met the stare of a bilious clock. Two. Pub clock five minutes fast. Time going on. Hands moving. Two. Not yet.[7]

His midriff yearned then upward, sank within him, yearned more longly, longingly.

Wine.

He smellsipped the cordial juice and, bidding his throat strongly to speed it, set his wineglass delicately down.

—Yes, he said. He's the organiser in point of fact.

No fear. No brains.

Nosey Flynn snuffed and scratched. Flea having a good square meal.

—He had a good slice of luck, Jack Mooney was telling me, over that boxing match Myler Keogh won again that soldier in the Portobello barracks. By God, he had the little kipper down in the county Carlow he was telling me. . . .

Hope that dewdrop doesn't come down into his glass. No, snuffled it up.

—For near a month, man, before it came off. Sucking duck eggs

---

6. Bartender.

7. I.e., not yet time for Boylan to visit Molly.

by God till further orders. Keep him off the boose, see? O, by God, Blazes is a hairy chap.

Davy Byrne came forward from the hindbar in tuckstitched shirt-sleeves, cleaning his lips with two wipes of his napkin. Herring's blush. Whose smile upon each feature plays with such and such replete. Too much fat on the parsnips.

—And here's himself and pepper on him, Nosey Flynn said. Can you give us a good one for the Gold cup?

—I'm off that, Mr Flynn, Davy Byrne answered. I never put anything on a horse.

—You're right there, Nosey Flynn said.

Mr Bloom ate his strips of sandwich, fresh clean bread, with relish of disgust, pungent mustard, the feety savour of green cheese. Sips of his wine soothed his palate. Not logwood that. Tastes fuller this weather with the chill off.

Nice quiet bar. Nice piece of wood in that counter. Nicely planed. Like the way it curves there.

—I wouldn't do anything at all in that line, Davy Byrne said. It ruined many a man the same horses.

Vintners' sweepstake. Licensed for the sale of beer, wine and spirits for consumption on the premises. Heads I win tails you lose.

—True for you, Nosey Flynn said. Unless you're in the know. There's no straight sport going now. Lenehan gets some good ones. He's giving Sceptre today. Zinfandel's the favourite, lord Howard de Walden's, won at Epsom. Morny Cannon is riding him. I could have got seven to one against Saint Amant a fortnight before.

—That so? Davy Byrne said.

He went towards the window and, taking up the pettycash book, scanned its pages.

—I could, faith, Nosey Flynn said, snuffling. That was a rare bit of horseflesh. Saint Frusquin was her sire. She won in a thunderstorm, Rothschild's filly, with wadding in her ears. Blue jacket and yellow cap. Bad luck to big Ben Dollard and his John O'Gaunt. He put me off it. Ay.

He drank resignedly from his tumbler, running his fingers down the flutes.

—Ay, he said, sighing.

Mr Bloom, champing, standing, looked upon his sigh. Nosey numbskull. Will I tell him that horse Lenehan?[8] He knows already. Better let him forget. Go and lose more. Fool and his money. Dewdrop coming down again. Cold nose he'd have kissing a woman. Still they might like. Prickly beards they like. Dogs' cold noses. Old Mrs Riordan with the rumbling stomach's Skye terrier in the City Arms hotel. Molly fondling him in her lap. O

---

8. Bloom is wondering whether to pass on a tip from Lenehan, who wrote for the racing paper *Sport*.

wowsywowsy!

Wine soaked and softened rolled pith of bread mustard a moment mawkish cheese. Nice wine it is. Taste it better because I'm not thirsty. Bath of course does that. Just a bite or two. Then about six o'clock I can. Six, six. Time will be gone then. She. . .

Mild fire of wine kindled his veins. I wanted that badly. Felt so off colour. His eyes unhungrily saw shelves of tins, sardines, gaudy lobster's claws. All the odd things people pick up for food. Out of shells, periwinkles with a pin, off trees, snails out of the ground the French eat, out of the sea with bait on a hook. Silly fish learn nothing in a thousand years. If you didn't know risky putting anything into your mouth. Poisonous berries. Johnny Magories. Roundness you think good. Gaudy colour warns you off. One fellow told another and so on. Try it on the dog first. Led on by the smell or the look. Tempting fruit. Ice cones. Cream. Instinct. Orangegroves for instance. Need artificial irrigation. Bleibtreustrasse.[9] Yes but what about oysters. Unsightly like a clot of phlegm. Filthy shells. Devil to open them too. Who found them out? Garbage, sewage they feed on. Fizz and Red bank oysters. Effect on the sexual. Aphrodis. He was in the Red bank this morning. Was he oyster old fish at table. Perhaps he young flesh in bed. No. June has no ar no oysters. But there are people like tainted game. Jugged hare. First catch your hare. Chinese eating eggs fifty years old, blue and green again. Dinner of thirty courses. Each dish harmless might mix inside. Idea for a poison mystery. That archduke Leopold was it. No. Yes, or was it Otto one of those Habsburgs? Or who was it used to eat the scruff off his own head? Cheapest lunch in town. Of course, aristocrats. Then the others copy to be in the fashion. Milly too rock oil and flour. Raw pastry I like myself. Half the catch of oysters they throw back in the sea to keep up the price. Cheap. No one would buy. Caviare. Do the grand. Hock in green glasses. Swell blowout. Lady this. Powdered bosom pearls. The *élite. Crème de la crème*.[1] They want special dishes to pretend they're. Hermit with a platter of pulse keep down the stings of the flesh. Know me come eat with me. Royal sturgeon. High sheriff, Coffey, the butcher, right to venisons of the forest from his ex.[2] Send him back the half of a cow. Spread I saw down in the Master of the Rolls' kitchen area. Whitehatted *chef* like a rabbi. Combustible duck. Curly cabbage *à la duchesse de Parme*. Just as well to write it on the bill of fare so you can know what you've eaten too many drugs spoil the broth. I know it myself. Dosing it with Edward's desiccated soup. Geese stuffed silly for them. Lobsters boiled alive. Do ptake some

9. The Berlin street which contained the offices of the "Planters' Company."
1. "Cream of the cream" (i.e., the very best, socially).
2. All sturgeon caught in or off Britain were the property of the king, according to the ancient traditional rights to certain kinds of fish or game. Bloom goes on to imagine a Dublin butcher having a "right to venisons of the forest from his ex[cellency]"—i.e., the Viceroy.

ptarmigan. Wouldn't mind being a waiter in a swell hotel. Tips, evening dress, halfnaked ladies. May I tempt you to a little more filleted lemon sole, miss Dubedat? Yes, do bedad. And she did bedad. Huguenot name I expect that. A miss Dubedat lived in Killiney I remember. *Du, de la*, French. Still it's the same fish, perhaps old Micky Hanlon of Moore street ripped the guts out of making money, hand over fist, finger in fishes' gills, can't write his name on a cheque, think he was painting the landscape with his mouth twisted. Moooikill A Aitcha Ha. Ignorant as a kish of brogues,[3] worth fifty thousand pounds.

Stuck on the pane two flies buzzed, stuck.

Glowing wine on his palate lingered swallowed. Crushing in the winepress grapes of Burgundy. Sun's heat it is. Seems to a secret touch telling me memory. Touched his sense moistened remembered. Hidden under wild ferns on Howth. Below us bay sleeping sky. No sound. The sky. The bay purple by the Lion's head. Green by Drumleck. Yellowgreen towards Sutton. Fields of undersea, the lines faint brown in grass, buried cities. Pillowed on my coat she had her hair, earwigs in the heather scrub my hand under her nape, you'll toss me all. O wonder! Coolsoft with ointments her hand touched me, caressed: her eyes upon me did not turn away. Ravished over her I lay, full lips full open, kissed her mouth. Yum. Softly she gave me in my mouth the seedcake warm and chewed. Mawkish pulp her mouth had mumbled sweet and sour with spittle. Joy: I ate it: joy. Young life, her lips that gave me pouting. Soft, warm, sticky gumjelly lips. Flowers her eyes were, take me, willing eyes. Pebbles fell. She lay still. A goat. No-one. High on Ben Howth rhododendrons a nannygoat walking surefooted, dropping currants. Screened under ferns she laughed warmfolded. Wildly I lay on her, kissed her; eyes, her lips, her stretched neck, beating, woman's breasts full in her blouse of nun's veiling, fat nipples upright. Hot I tongued her. She kissed me. I was kissed. All yielding she tossed my hair. Kissed, she kissed me.[4]

Me. And me now.

Stuck, the flies buzzed.

His downcast eyes followed the silent veining of the oaken slab. Beauty: it curves: curves are beauty. Shapely goddesses, Venus, Juno: curves the world admires. Can see them library museum standing in the round hall, naked goddesses. Aids to digestion. They don't care what man looks. All to see. Never speaking, I mean to

---

3. A basket of shoes.
4. Bloom is remembering when he first proposed to Molly, on the Hill of Howth, near Dublin. Molly also recalls this in the final "Penelope" episode, which is her soliloquy: " * * * we were lying on the rhododendrons on Howth head in the grey tweed suit and his straw hat the day I got him to propose to me yes * * * my God after that long kiss I near lost my breath * * * I saw he understood or felt what a woman is and I knew I could always get round him and I gave him all the pleasure I could leading him on * * * "

say to fellows like Flynn. Suppose she did Pygmalion and Galatea[5] what would she say first? Mortal! Put you in your proper place. Quaffing nectar at mess with gods, golden dishes, all ambrosial. Not like a tanner lunch we have, boiled mutton, carrots and turnips, bottle of Allsop. Nectar, imagine it drinking electricity: god's food. Lovely forms of woman sculped Junonian. Immortal lovely. And we stuffing food in one hole and out behind: food, chyle, blood, dung, earth, food: have to feed it like stoking an engine. They have no. Never looked. I'll look today. Keeper won't see. Bend down let something fall see if she.

Dribbling a quiet message from his bladder came to go to do not to do there to do. A man and ready he drained his glass to the lees and walked, to men too they gave themselves, manly conscious, lay with men lovers, a youth enjoyed her, to the yard.

When the sound of his boots had ceased Davy Byrne said from his book:

—What is this he is? Isn't he in the insurance line?

—He's out of that long ago, Nosey Flynn said. He does canvassing for the *Freeman*.

—I know him well to see, Davy Byrne said. Is he in trouble?

—Trouble? Nosey Flynn said. Not that I heard of. Why?

—I noticed he was in mourning.

—Was he? Nosey Flynn said. So he was, faith. I asked him how was all at home. You're right, by God. So he was.

—I never broach the subject, Davy Byrne said humanely, if I see a gentleman is in trouble that way. It only brings it up fresh in their minds.

—It's not the wife anyhow, Nosey Flynn said. I met him the day before yesterday and he coming out of that Irish farm dairy John Wyse Nolan's wife has in Henry street with a jar of cream in his hand taking it home to his better half. She's well nourished, I tell you. Plovers on toast.

—And is he doing for the *Freeman?* Davy Byrne said.

Nosey Flynn pursed his lips.

—He doesn't buy cream on the ads he picks up. You can make bacon of that.

—How so? Davy Byrne asked, coming from his book.

Nosey Flynn made swift passes in the air with juggling fingers. He winked.

—He's in the craft,[6] he said.

—Do you tell me so? Davy Byrne said.

—Very much so, Nosey Flynn said. Ancient free and accepted

5. Pygmalion was the sculptor whose statue of Galatea came alive.
6. I.e., in the "free and accepted order" of Freemasons, one of the oldest European secret societies; it was not in good repute in predominantly Roman Catholic countries like Ireland.

order. Light, life and love, by God. They give him a leg up. I was told that by a, well, I won't say who.

—Is that a fact?

—O, it's a fine order, Nosey Flynn said. They stick to you when you're down. I know a fellow was trying to get into it, but they're as close as damn it. By God they did right to keep the women out of it.

Davy Byrne smiledyawnednodded all in one:

—Iiiiiichaaaaaaach!

—There was one woman, Nosey Flynn said, hid herself in a clock to find out what they do be doing. But be damned but they smelt her out and swore her in on the spot a master mason. That was one of the Saint Legers of Doneraile.

Davy Byrne, sated after his yawn, said with tearwashed eyes:

—And is that a fact? Decent quiet man he is. I often saw him in here and I never once saw him, you know, over the line.

—God Almighty couldn't make him drunk, Nosey Flynn said firmly. Slips off when the fun gets too hot. Didn't you see him look at his watch? Ah, you weren't there. If you ask him to have a drink first thing he does he outs with the watch to see what he ought to imbibe. Declare to God he does.

—There are some like that, Davy Byrne said. He's a safe man, I'd say.

—He's not too bad, Nosey Flynn said, snuffling it up. He has been known to put his hand down too to help a fellow. Give the devil his due. O, Bloom has his good points. But there's one thing he'll never do.

His hand scrawled a dry pen signature beside his grog.

—I know, Davy Byrne said.

—Nothing in black and white, Nosey Flynn said.

Paddy Leonard and Bantam Lyons came in. Tom Rochford followed, a plaining hand on his claret waistcoat.

—Day, Mr. Byrne.

—Day, gentlemen.

They paused at the counter.

—Who's standing? Paddy Leonard asked.

—I'm sitting anyhow, Nosey Flynn answered.

—Well, what'll it be? Paddy Leonard asked.

—I'll take a stone ginger, Bantam Lyons said.

—How much? Paddy Leonard cried. Since when, for God's sake? What's yours, Tom?

—How is the main drainage? Nosey Flynn asked, sipping.

For answer Tom Rochford pressed his hand to his breastbone and hiccupped.

—Would I trouble you for a glass of fresh water, Mr Byrne? he said.

—Certainly, sir.

Paddy Leonard eyed his alemates.

—Lord love a duck, he said, look at what I'm standing drinks to! Cold water and gingerpop! Two fellows that would suck whisky off a sore leg. He has some bloody horse up his sleeve for the Gold cup. A dead snip.

—Zinfandel is it? Nosey Flynn asked.

Tom Rochford spilt powder from a twisted paper into the water set before him.

—That cursed dyspepsia, he said before drinking.

—Breadsoda is very good, Davy Byrne said.

Tom Rochford nodded and drank.

—Is it Zinfandel?

—Say nothing, Bantam Lyons winked. I'm going to plunge five bob on my own.

—Tell us if you're worth your salt and be damned to you, Paddy Leonard said. Who gave it to you?

Mr Bloom on his way out raised three fingers in greeting.

—So long, Nosey Flynn said.

The others turned.

—That's the man now that gave it to me, Bantam Lyons whispered.

—Prrwht! Paddy Leonard said with scorn. Mr Byrne, sir, we'll take two of your small Jamesons after that and a. . .

—Stone ginger, Davy Byrne added civilly.

—Ay, Paddy Leonard said. A suckingbottle for the baby.

Mr Bloom walked towards Dawson street, his tongue brushing his teeth smooth. Something green it would have to be: spinach say. Then with those Röntgen rays searchlight you could.

At Duke lane a ravenous terrier choked up a sick knuckly cud on the cobble stones and lapped it with new zest. Surfeit. Returned with thanks having fully digested the contents. First sweet then savoury. Mr Bloom coasted warily. Ruminants. His second course. Their upper jaw they move. Wonder if Tom Rochford will do anything with that invention of his. Wasting time explaining it to Flynn's mouth. Lean people long mouths. Ought to be a hall or a place where inventors could go in and invent free. Course then you'd have all the cranks pestering.

He hummed, prolonging in solemn echo, the closes of the bars:

> *Don Giovanni, a cenar teco*
> *M'invitasti.*[8]

8. Since Molly is a singer, Bloom is familiar with opera. Here he recalls the song sung by the Commendatore's statue in Mozart's *Don Giovanni*, and translates accurately the Italian words he quotes, except for *"teco"* ("with you"). This opera supplies some of the key themes in *Ulysses*, and the famous duet between Don Giovanni and Zerlina, *"Là ci darèm la mano"* ("There we will join hands"), haunts Bloom's mind continually throughout the day. It is on the program of Molly's concert which she is discussing with Boylan that after-

Feel better. Burgundy. Good pick me up. Who distilled first? Some chap in the blues. Dutch courage. That *Kilkenny People* in the national library now I must.

Bare clean closestools, waiting, in the window of William Miller, plumber, turned back his thoughts. They could: and watch it all the way down, swallow a pin sometimes come out of the ribs years after, tour round the body, changing biliary duct, spleen squirting liver, gastric juice coils of intestines like pipes. But the poor buffer would have to stand all the time with his insides entrails on show. Science.

—*A cenar teco.*

What does that *teco* mean? Tonight perhaps.

> *Don Giovanni, thou hast me invited*
> *To come to supper tonight,*
> *The rum the rumdum.*

Doesn't go properly.

Keyes: two months if I get Nannetti[9] to. That'll be two pounds ten, about two pounds eight. Three Hynes owes me. Two eleven. Presscott's ad. Two fifteen. Five guineas about. On the pig's back.

Could buy one of those silk petticoats for Molly, colour of her new garters.

Today. Today. Not think.[1]

Tour the south then. What about English watering places? Brighton, Margate. Piers by moonlight. Her voice floating out. Those lovely sideside girls. Against John Long's a drowsing loafer lounged in heavy thought, gnawing a crusted knuckle. Handy man wants job. Small wages. Will eat anything.

Mr Bloom turned at Gray's confectioner's window of unbought tarts and passed the reverend Thomas Connellan's bookstore. *Why I left the church of Rome? Bird's Nest.* Women run him. They say they used to give pauper children soup to change to protestants in the time of the potato blight. Society over the way papa went to for the conversion of poor jews. Same bait. Why we left the church of Rome?

A blind stripling stood tapping the curbstone with his slender cane. No tram in sight. Wants to cross.

—Do you want to cross? Mr Bloom asked.

The blind stripling did not answer. His wall face frowned weakly. He moved his head uncertainly.

—You're in Dawson street, Mr Bloom said. Molesworth street is opposite. Do you want to cross? There's nothing in the way.

noon, and Bloom associates it with her adultery with Boylan.

9. Proofreader and business manager of the *Freeman's Journal*, and in charge of the advertising Bloom is trying to get for the paper. If he will add a

complimentary reference to Keyes, a grocer, in a gossip column, Keyes promises to renew his advertisement, which means a commission for Bloom.

1. I.e., of Molly and Boylan.

The cane moved out trembling to the left. Mr Bloom's eye followed its line and saw again the dyeworks' van drawn up before Drago's. Where I saw his brilliantined hair just when I was. Horse drooping. Driver in John Long's. Slaking his drouth.

—There's a van there, Mr Bloom said, but it's not moving. I'll see you across. Do you want to go to Molesworth street?

—Yes, the stripling answered. South Frederick street.

—Come, Mr Bloom said.

He touched the thin elbow gently: then took the limp seeing hand to guide it forward.

Say something to him. Better not do the condescending. They mistrust what you tell them. Pass a common remark.

—The rain kept off.

No answer.

Stains on his coat. Slobbers his food, I suppose. Tastes all different for him. Have to be spoonfed first. Like a child's hand his hand. Like Milly's was. Sensitive. Sizing me up I daresay from my hand. Wonder if he has a name. Van. Keep his cane clear of the horse's legs tired drudge get his doze. That's right. Clear. Behind a bull: in front of a horse.

—Thanks, sir.

Knows I'm a man. Voice.

—Right now? First turn to the left.

The blind stripling tapped the curbstone and went on his way, drawing his cane back, feeling again.

Mr Bloom walked behind the eyeless feet, a flatcut suit of herringbone tweed. Poor young fellow! How on earth did he know that van was there? Must have felt it. See things in their foreheads perhaps. Kind of sense of volume. Weight would he feel it if something was removed. Feel a gap. Queer idea of Dublin he must have, tapping his way round by the stones. Could he walk in a beeline if he hadn't that cane? Bloodless pious face like a fellow going in to be a priest.

Penrose! That was that chap's name.

Look at all the things they can learn to do. Read with their fingers. Tune pianos. Or we are surprised they have any brains. Why we think a deformed person or a hunchback clever if he says something we might say. Of course the other senses are more. Embroider. Plait baskets. People ought to help. Work basket I could buy Molly's birthday. Hates sewing. Might take an objection. Dark men they call them.

Sense of smell must be stronger too. Smells on all sides bunched together. Each person too. Then the spring, the summer: smells. Tastes. They say you can't taste wines with your eyes shut or a cold in the head. Also smoke in the dark they say get no pleasure.

And with a woman, for instance. More shameless not seeing.

That girl passing the Stewart institution, head in the air. Look at me. I have them all on. Must be strange not to see her. Kind of a form in his mind's eye. The voice temperature when he touches her with fingers must almost see the lines, the curves. His hands on her hair, for instance. Say it was black for instance. Good. We call it black. Then passing over her white skin. Different feel perhaps. Feeling of white.

Postoffice. Must answer.[2] Fag today. Send her a postal order two shillings half a crown. Accept my little present. Stationer's just here too. Wait. Think over it.

With a gentle finger he felt ever so slowly the hair combed back above his ears. Again. Fibres of fine fine straw. Then gently his finger felt the skin of his right cheek. Downy hair there too. Not smooth enough. The belly is the smoothest. No-one about. There he goes into Frederick street. Perhaps to Levenston's dancing academy piano. Might be settling my braces.

Walking by Doran's public house he slid his hand between waistcoat and trousers and, pulling aside his shirt gently, felt a slack fold of his belly. But I know it's whiteyellow. Want to try in the dark to see.

He withdrew his hand and pulled his dress to.

Poor fellow! Quite a boy. Terrible. Really terrible. What dreams would he have, not seeing. Life a dream for him. Where is the justice being born that way. All those women and children excursion beanfeast burned and drowned in New York.[3] Holocaust. Karma they call that transmigration for sins you did in a past life the reincarnation met him pikehoses.[4] Dear, dear, dear. Pity of course: but somehow you can't cotton on to them someway.

Sir Frederick Falkiner going into the freemasons' hall. Solemn as Troy. After his good lunch in Earlsfort terrace. Old legal cronies cracking a magnum. Tales of the bench and assizes and annals of the bluecoat school.[5] I sentenced him to ten years. I suppose he'd turn up his nose at that stuff I drank. Vintage wine for them, the year marked on a dusty bottle. Has his own ideas of justice in the recorder's court. Wellmeaning old man. Police chargesheets crammed with cases get their percentage manufacturing crime. Sends them to the rightabout. The devil on moneylenders. Gave Reuben J. a great strawcalling. Now he's really what they call a dirty jew. Power those judges have. Crusty old topers in wigs. Bear with a sore paw. And may the Lord have mercy on your soul.

Hello, placard. Mirus bazaar. His excellency the lord lieuten-

2. Martha Clifford's letter.
3. This terrible disaster on an excursion steamer on the Hudson took place on June 15, 1904, and was reported in the Dublin papers on June 16.
4. I.e., metempsychosis: Bloom is remembering again their morning conversation on this subject, when Molly exclaimed "O rocks!"
5. Sir Frederick Falkiner wrote the history of the "bluecoat school" in Oxmantown, Dublin. The Dublin "bluecoat school" was founded by Charles II for poor children.

ant. Sixteenth today it is. In aid of funds for Mercer's hospital. *The Messiah* was first given for that. Yes. Handel. What about going out there. Ballsbridge. Drop in on Keyes. No use sticking to him like a leech. Wear out my welcome. Sure to know someone on the gate.

Mr Bloom came to Kildare street. First I must. Library.

Straw hat in sunlight. Tan shoes. Turnedup trousers. It is. It is.[6]

His heart quopped softly. To the right. Museum. Goddesses. He swerved to the right.

Is it? Almost certain. Won't look. Wine in my face. Why did I? Too heady. Yes, it is. The walk. Not see. Not see. Get on.

Making for the museum gate with long windy strides he lifted his eyes. Handsome building. Sir Thomas Deane designed. Not following me?

Didn't see me perhaps. Light in his eyes.

The flutter of his breath came forth in short sighs. Quick. Cold statues: quiet there. Safe in a minute.

No, didn't see me. After two. Just at the gate.

My heart!

His eyes beating looked steadfastly at cream curves of stone. Sir Thomas Deane was the Greek architecture.

Look for something I.

His hasty hand went quick into a pocket, took out, read unfolded Agendath Netaim. Where did I?

Busy looking for.

He thrust back quickly Agendath.

Afternoon she said.

I am looking for that. Yes, that. Try all pockets. Handker. *Freeman*. Where did I? Ah, yes. Trousers. Purse. Potato. Where did I?

Hurry. Walk quietly. Moment more. My heart.

His hand looking for the where did I put found in his hip pocket soap lotion have to call tepid paper stuck. Ah, soap there! Yes. Gate.[7]

Safe!

1914–21   1922

6. Bloom catches a glimpse of Boylan and tries to avoid an encounter.
7. Anxious to avoid Boylan, Bloom pretends to admire the architecture of the Museum and National Library building, and then pretends to be looking for something in his pockets, where he finds the "Agendath Netaim" leaflet. He continues to search desperately in his pockets to avoid looking up and seeing Boylan, discovers the potato he carries as a remedy against rheumatism and a cake of soap he had bought that morning (the soap reminds him that he must call at the chemist's to collect a face lotion he had ordered for Molly). At last he goes through the National Library gate and feels safe.

From Finnegans Wake[1]

From *Anna Livia Plurabelle*

* * * Well, you know or don't you kennet[2] or haven't I told
you every telling has a taling and that's the he and the she of it.
Look, look, the dusk is growing! My branches lofty are taking root.
And my cold cher's[3] gone ashley. Fieluhr?[4] Filou! What age is at? It
saon[5] is late. 'Tis endless now senne[6] eye or erewone[7] last saw
Waterhouse's clogh.[8] They took it asunder, I hurd thum sigh.
When will they reassemble it? O, my back, my back, my bach![9]
I'd want to go to Aches-les-Pains.[10] Pingpong! There's the Belle
for·Sexaloitez![11] And Concepta de Send-us-pray! Pang! Wring out
the clothes! Wring in the dew![12] Godavari,[13] vert the showers! And

1. Because the meanings in *Finnegans
Wake* are developed not by action but
by language—a great network of multiple puns that echo themes back and
forth throughout the book—the careful
reading of a single passage, even out
of context, will convey more than any
summary of the "plot" (some discussion of the general plan of the work is
given in the Joyce introduction). The
particular passage selected here was one
of Joyce's favorites, and there exists a
phonograph recording of it made by
himself. It consists of the closing pages
of the eighth chapter of Book I; the
chapter was published separately as
Anna Livia Plurabelle in 1928 and
1930, although the finished book omits
this title.
   The entire chapter is a dialogue, and
the scene is the river Liffey: two washerwomen are washing in public the dirty
linen of HCE and ALP (the "hero"
and "heroine"; see the Joyce introduction), and gossiping as they work. As
this excerpt opens, it is growing dark;
things become gradually less and less
distinct, so that the washerwomen cannot be sure what the objects seen in the
dusk really are. As it grows darker, the
river becomes wider (we get nearer its
mouth) and the wind rises, so that the
women have more and more difficulty
hearing each other. At last, as night
falls, they become part of the landscape, an elm tree and a stone on the
river bank. Toward the end of the
dialogue they ask to hear a tale of
Shem and Shaun (HCE's two sons),
and this question points the way to
Book II, which opens with the two
boys (metamorphosed for the moment
into Glugg and Chuff) playing in front
of the tavern in the evening.
   A complete annotation of even this
brief passage is, of course, a physical
impossibility in this anthology. The
notes that are provided are intended to
indicate the nature of what Joyce does
with language and to enable the reader

to see what is going on. But there are
all sorts of suggestions built up in the
language that are not referred to in the
notes: each reader will find some for
himself.
2. Ken it ("know it") + Kennet (river
in England). Rivers in *Finnegans Wake*
symbolize the flow of life, and thousands
of river names are suggested throughout the book in allusive pun-combina-
tions, as here.
3. Cold cheer (i.e., cold comfort) +
cold chair + (perhaps) culture. "Gone
ashley": gone to ashes. Going to ashes
suggests the fiery death and rebirth of
the mythical phoenix: from the ashes
of the dead phoenix rises a new one.
Modern culture, which can provide only
cold cheer, is in the state of decay, the
"going to ashes," which precedes the
stage of rebirth into a new cultural
cycle (according to Giambattista Vico's
cyclical theory of history, which is important to *Finnegans Wake*). "Gone
ashley" also means "turned into an ash
tree" (i.e., it is so cold that the speaker
feels herself turning into a tree).
4. *Viel Uhr?* (German, "What's the
time?") "Filou": pickpocket, thief
(French). The question echoes so as to
suggest that time is a thief.
5. Soon + Saône (river in France).
6. Since + Senne (river in Belgium).
7. E'er a one + *Erewhon* (novel by
Samuel Butler—"Nowhere" spelled
backwards).
8. Clock or bell (Irish) + the name of
an Irish river.
9. Brook (German) + dear (Welsh).
10. Cf. Aix-les-Bains, France.
11. *Sex* (Latin, "six") + *laüten* (German, "to ring [the bells]"). The Angelus bell is rung every six hours.
12. Cf. "Ring out the old, ring in the
new" (Tennyson, *In Memoriam*).
13. God of Eire; also the name of a
river in India. "Vert": *avert* + *vert*
(French, "green"), for "the showers"
make grass green.

grant thaya grace! Aman. Will we spread them here now? Ay, we will. Flip! Spread on your bank and I'll spread mine on mine. Flep! It's what I'm doing. Spread! It's churning chill. Der went[14] is rising. I'll lay a few stones on the hostel sheets. A man and his bride embraced between them. Else I'd have sprinkled and folded them only. And I'll tie my butcher's apron here. It's suety yet. The strollers will pass it by. Six shifts, ten kerchiefs, nine to hold to the fire and this for the code,[15] the convent napkins, twelve, one baby's shawl. Good mother Jossiph[16] knows, she said. Whose head? Mutter snores? Deataceas![17] Wharnow are alle her childer, say? In kingdome gone or power to come or gloria be to them farther? Allalivial, allalluvial![18] Some here, more no more, more again lost alla stranger.[19] I've heard tell that same brooch of the Shannons[20] was married into a family in Spain. And all the Dunders de Dunnes[21] in Markland's[22] Vineland beyond Brendan's herring pool[23] takes number nine in yangsee's[24] hats. And one of Biddy's[25] beads went bobbing till she rounded up lost histereve[26] with a marigold and a cobbler's candle in a side strain of a main drain of a manzinahurries[27] off Bachelor's Walk. But all that's left to the last of the Meaghers[28] in the loup of the years prefixed and between is one kneebuckle and two hooks in the front. Do you tell me that now? I do in troth. Orara por Orbe and poor Las Animas![29]

14. *Der Wind* (German, "the wind") + Derwent (river in England).
15. Cold + code (i.e., the code in which the book is written). The numbers in this sentence have special meanings indicated in other episodes.
16. Joseph + *joss* (pidgin English, "God") + gossip (which derives from *god-sib*, Middle English, "godparent").
17. Latin, "Goddess, may you be silent!" Dea Tacita, in Roman mythology, is the name sometimes given to Acca Laurentia, mistress of Hercules and foster-mother of Romulus and Remus.
18. Multiple punning—Anna Livia + all alive + *la lluvia* (Spanish, "rain") + alluvial—suggesting the mother-river-fertility associations of ALP. At least two other meanings are also present: All alive O! (street cry of shellfish vendors) + Alleluia (Vulgate Latin form of "Hallelujah").
19. Cf. *à l'étranger* (French, "abroad").
20. Ornament and branch of the Shannons (family and river).
21. The form of the name suggests an aristocratic Anglo-Norman family. "Dunder" suggests thunder; *dun* is an Irish word meaning "hill," "fort on a hill."
22. Borderland + land of the mark (i.e., land of money, or America; "Vineland" or Vinland was the Norse name for America). Both King Mark of Cornwall (a character in the Tristan and

Iseult story) and Mark of the Gospels are primary symbolic characters in *Finnegans Wake.*
23. The Atlantic Ocean; St. Brendan was an Irish monk who sailed out into the Atlantic to find the terrestrial paradise.
24. Yankees' + Yangtze (river in China). The de Dunnes have swollen heads now that they have emigrated to America.
25. Diminutive form of the name Bridget; St. Brigid (or Bridget) is a patron saint of Ireland. "Biddy" is also a term for an Irish maidservant.
26. Yester eve (last night) + eve of history. The sentence may be paraphrased: "Irish history got lost when she went off in a side branch of the main Roman Catholic Church, and Biddy (i.e., Ireland) landed herself in the dirt." There are also Freudian implications here.
27. Man's in a hurry + Manzanares (river in Spain).
28. Thomas Francis Meagher, Irish patriot and revolutionary, who was transported to Van Diemen's Land in 1849 and escaped to America in 1852. "Loup": loop + *loup* (French, "wolf" and also "solitary man"). Cf. Wolfe Tone, the ill-fated Irish revolutionist.
29. *Ora pro nobis* (Latin, "pray for us") + Orara (river in New South Wales) + *pro orbe* (Latin, "for the world") + Orbe (river in France). "Las Animas": souls (Spanish); also

Ussa, Ulla, we're umbas[30] all! Mezha, didn't you hear it a deluge
of times, ufer[31] and ufer, respund to spond?[32] You deed, you deed!
I need, I need! It's that irrawaddyng[33] I've stoke in my aars. It all
but husheth the lethest zswound. Oronoko![34] What's your trouble?
Is that the great Finnleader[35] himself in his joakimono on his statue
riding the high horse there forehengist?[36] Father of Otters,[37] it is
himself! Yonne there! Isset that? On Fallareen Common? You're
thinking of Astley's Amphitheayter where the bobby restrained you
making sugarstuck pouts to the ghostwhite horse of the Peppers.[38]
Throw the cobwebs from your eyes, woman, and spread your washing proper! It's well I know your sort of slop. Flap! Ireland sober
is Ireland stiff. Lord help you, Maria, full of grease, the load is
with me! Your prayers. I sonht zo![39] Madammangut! Were you
lifting your elbow, tell us, glazy cheeks, in Conway's Carrigacurra
canteen? Was I what, hobbledyhips?[40] Flop! Your rere gait's creak-
orheuman bitts your butts disagrees.[41] Amn't I up since the damp
dawn, marthared mary allacook, with Corrigan's pulse and varicoarse
veins, my pramaxle smashed, Alice Jane in decline and my oneeyed
mongrel twice run over, soaking and bleaching boiler rags, and
sweating cold, a widow like me, for to deck my tennis champion
son, the laundryman with the lavandier flannels? You won your
limpopo[42] limp fron the husky[43] hussars when Collars and Cuffs
was heir to the town and your slur gave the stink to Carlow.[44] Holy
Scamander,[45] I sar it again! Near the golden falls. Icis on us! Seints
of light! Zezere![46] Subdue your noise, you hamble creature! What

the name of a river in Colorado. The
entire sentence may be read: "Pray for
us and for all souls."
30. *Umbra* (Latin, "shade") + Umba
(river in Africa). "Ussa," "Ulla," and
"Mezha" are also river names; each
contains a number of other meanings.
31. Bank (of river).
32. *Spund* (German, "bung").
33. A multiple pun: Irrawady (river in
Burma) + irritating + wadding. This
and the following sentence may be
paraphrased: "It's that wadding I've
stuck in my ears. It hushes the least
sound."
34. *Oroonoko* (novel by Mrs. Aphra
Behn about a "noble savage," published
ca. 1678).
35. Fionn mac Cumhail (Finn Mac-
Cool), legendary hero of ancient Ireland. "Joakimono": i.e., comic kimono;
joki is the Finnish word for river; the
name Joachim is perhaps also implied.
36. Hengist was the Jute invader of
England (with Horsa), ca. 449; he
founded the kingdom of Kent.
37. Father of Waters (i.e., the Mis-
sissippi) + Father of Orders (i.e., Saint
Patrick).
38. Philip Astley's Royal Amphithea-
tre was a famous late 18th-century English circus, specializing in trained

horses; "Pepper's Ghost" was a popular circus act. One of the washerwomen
has been reproving the other, who
thought she saw the great Finn himself riding his high horse, by telling her
that once before she had to be restrained by a policeman for making
"sugarstuck pouts" at a circus horse.
39. I thought so + Izontzo (river in
Italy).
40. Hobbledehoy + wobbly hips.
41. The sentence is a punning discussion of her hard work and ailments.
The first four words may also be read:
"Your rear gait (i.e., your last child) is
Greek or Roman."
42. Name of a river in south Africa.
43. Cf. *uisge* (Gaelic, "whisky," but
literally, "water [of life]").
44. I.e., "You got a slur on your reputation carrying on with soldiers in the
Age of Elegance, and the scandal was
all over Ireland" (ALP is being addressed, and some of her many lovers
are mentioned). "Carlow" is a county
in Ireland.
45. River near Troy, famous in classical legend. "I sar": I saw + Isar (river
in Germany).
46. See there + Zezere (river in Portugal).

is it but a blackburry growth or the dwyergray ass them four old codgers[47] owns. Are you meanam[48] Tarpey and Lyons and Gregory? I meyne now, thank all, the four of them, and the roar of them, that draves[49] that stray in the mist and old Johnny MacDougal along with them. Is that the Poolbeg flasher beyant,[50] pharphar, or a fireboat coasting nyar[51] the Kishtna or a glow I behold within a hedge or my Garry come back from the Indes? Wait till the honeying of the lune,[52] love! Die eve, little eve, die![53] We see that wonder in your eye. We'll meet again, we'll part once more. The spot I'll seek if the hour you'll find. My chart shines high where the blue milk's upset. Forgivemequick, I'm going! Bubye! And you, pluck your watch, forgetmenot. Your evenlode.[54] So save to jurna's[55] end! My sights are swimming thicker on me by the shadows to this place. I sow[56] home slowly now by own way, moyvalley way. Towy[57] I too, rathmine.

Ah, but she was the queer old skeowsha anyhow, Anna Livia, trinkettoes! And sure he was the quare old buntz too, Dear Dirty Dumpling,[58] foostherfather of fingalls[59] and dotthergills. Gammer and gaffer we're all their gangsters. Hadn't he seven dams to wive him? And every dam had her seven crutches. And every crutch had its seven hues.[60] And each hue had a differing cry. Sudds[61] for me and supper for you and the doctor's bill for Joe John. Befor! Bifur![62] He married his markets, cheap by foul, I know, like any Etrurian

---

47. The Four Old Men, who represent, among other things, the authors of the Gospels and the four elements.
48. Meaning + Menam (river in Thailand). The precise connotations of the three proper names that follow escape the present annotator.
49. Drives + Drave (river in Hungary).
50. I.e., the Poolbeg Lighthouse beyond (this lighthouse is in Dublin Bay); "pharphar": far far + Pharphar (river in Damascus) + *pharos* (Greek, "lighthouse").
51. Near + Nyar (river in India). "Kishtna": Kish (city in ancient Mesopotamia, traditionally the ruling city after the Flood) + Krishna (Hindu god of joy) + Kistna (river in India) + the Kish lightship (in Dublin Bay).
52. Loon (Scottish, "boy") + *luna* (Latin, "moon"). "Honeying of the lune": honeymoon, etc.
53. This sentence suggests traditional lovers' prayers for the day to die and night to come, and it also recalls the death of "little Eva" in *Uncle Tom's Cabin*. The sentences that follow are echoes of popular songs.
54. Evening load + Evenlode (river in England).
55. Journey + Jurna (river in Brazil).
56. Sow (river in England).
57. Name of a river in Wales. Moy is

the name of an Irish river, and Moyvalley and Rathmine are names of Dublin suburbs.
58. "Dumpling" suggests Humpty Dumpty, whose fall is one of the many involved in the vastly symbolic fall of Finnegan. The phrase "Dear Dirty Dublin" occurs in *Ulysses*.
59. A pun-cluster: Fine Gael (the United Ireland Party) + fine Gaels + Fingal (river in Tasmania) + *Fingal* (the poem by James Macpherson, supposedly a translation from the Gaelic original of Ossian, an ancient Gaelic poet and son of Fingal—who is the same as Fionn mac Cumhail or Finn MacCool).
60. Colors of the rainbow (suggested a few lines later by "pinky limony creamy" and "turkiss indienne mauves"). In these sentences Joyce is punningly parodying the nursery rhyme, "As I was going to St. Ives / I met a man with seven wives * * * "
61. Suds (slang term for beer) + soapsuds + sudd (the floating vegetable matter which often obstructs navigation on the White Nile).
62. Bifurcated creature! This image of man as a forked being suggests HCE (cf. "*Etrurian Catholic Heathen*"). HCE's marital history, in his role as the Great Parent or generator, is one of the themes in this passage.

Catholic Heathen, in their pinky limony creamy birnies[63] and their turkiss indienne mauves. But at milkidmass[64] who was the spouse? Then all that was was fair. Tys Elvenland![65] Teems of times and happy returns. The seim anew.[66] Ordovico[67] or viricordo. Anna was, Livia is, Plurabelle's to be. Northmen's thing made southfolk's place but howmulty plurators made eachone in person?[68] Latin me that, my trinity scholard, out of eure sanscreed into oure eryan![69] *Hircus Civis Eblanensis!*[70] He had buckgoat paps on him, soft ones for orphans. Ho,[71] Lord! Twins of his bosom. Lord save us! And ho! Hey? What all men. Hot? His tittering daughters of. Whawk?

Can't hear with the waters of. The chittering waters of. Flittering bats, fieldmice bawk talk. Ho! Are you not gone ahome? What Thom Malone? Can't hear with bawk of bats, all thim liffeying waters of. Ho, talk save us! My foos won't moos.[72] I feel as old as yonder elm. A tale told of Shaun or Shem? All Livia's daughter-sons. Dark hawks hear us. Night! Night! My ho head halls. I feel as heavy as yonder stone. Tell me of John or Shaun? Who were Shem and Shaun the living sons or daughters of? Night now! Tell me, tell me, tell me, elm! Night night! Telmetale of stem or stone.[73] Beside the rivering waters of, hitherandthithering waters of. Night!

1923–38   1939

63. Coats of mail.
64. Milking time + Michaelmas (September 29).
65. 'Tis the land of Elves + Tys Elv (Norway).
66. The same again + Seim (river in Ireland).
67. The Ordovices were an ancient British tribe in northern Wales, and Ordovician is a term for a geological period. "Ordovico" is also a pun on Vico and his order of historical phases. Joyce is here suggesting the cyclical nature of things: the marital history of HCE is the history of ever-renewing life ("the seim anew"), and HCE's bride is Everywoman, past, present, and future ("Anna was, Livia is, Plurabelle's to be"). "Viricordo" is another verbal twist to Vico and his cycles, suggesting his *ricorso* ("recurrence," i.e., the 4th stage of the cycle which brings back the 1st), as well as overtones from the Latin *vir* (man) and *cor* (heart): the heart of man beats on, through all phases of civilization.
68. This sentence may be paraphrased: "The assembly of the Norsemen made the South-folk's place (i.e., as the Vikings settled Dublin), but how many marital pluralists (the word 'plurators'

suggests men who had many wives or mistresses) went into the making of each of us?" The question is another link with the theme of HCE as the Great Parent.
69. I.e., out of your Sanskrit into your Aryan. "Sanscreed" has further punning meanings: *sans* screed (without script) + *sans* creed (without faith). Thus the phrase can read: "out of your illiteracy or faithlessness into Irish" (Eire-an). The greatest skeptic must pause in reverence before the endless flow of life, represented by Irish history.
70. Latin, "The Goat-Citizen of Dublin!" The goat is the symbol of lust and so of fecundity; *"Eblanensis"* is the adjective form of Eblana, the name given by the 3rd-century Alexandrian geographer Ptolemy to what may have been the site of the modern Dublin.
71. Chinese, "river."
72. Move + *Moos* (German, "moss"). Her foot ("foos") won't move; it is also turning to moss.
73. Stone and elm tree are important symbols in *Finnegans Wake*. Signifying permanence and change, time and space, mercy and justice, they undergo many changes of symbolic meaning throughout the book.

D. H. LAWRENCE
(1885–1930)

> 1912: Gives up school teaching for literature.
> 1915: *The Rainbow*, first of the "new" novels.

David Herbert Lawrence was born in the Midland mining village of East-wood, Nottinghamshire. His father was a miner; his mother, better educated than her husband and self-consciously genteel, fought all her married life to lift her children out of the working class. Lawrence was aware from an early age of the struggle between his parents; he was very much on his mother's side during his childhood, resenting his father's coarse and sometimes drunken behavior and allying himself with his mother's delicacy and refinement. After the death of an elder brother he became the center of his mother's emotional life and played in his own relation to her a loving and protective role. His mother's claims on him kept frustrating his relationships with girls, and the personal problems and conflicts that resulted are presented in his first really distinguished novel, *Sons and Lovers* (1913), where, against a background of paternal coarseness and vitality conflicting with maternal refinement and gentility, he sets the theme of the demanding mother who has given up the prospect of achieving a true emotional life with her husband and turns to her sons with a stultifying and possessive love. Many years later Lawrence came to feel that he had misjudged his father, whose coarseness represented after all a genuine vitality and some wholeness of personality, even if these qualities were impoverished and distorted by the civilization in which he lived.

Spurred on by his mother, Lawrence escaped through education from the mining world of his father. He won a scholarship to Nottingham high school and later, after working first as a clerk and then as an elementary school teacher (1902–6), studied for two years at Nottingham University College, where he obtained his teacher's certificate in 1908. Meanwhile he was reading on his own a great deal of literature and some philosophy and was working on his first novel, encouraged (as he was in all his early writing) by Jessie Chambers, the "Miriam" of *Sons and Lovers*. His first published work was a group of poems which appeared in the *English Review* for November, 1909. The following February the same periodical published his first short story. He was now regarded in London literary circles as a promising young writer; his first novel, *The White Peacock* (1910), was received with respect. From 1908 to 1912 he taught school in Croydon, a southern suburb of London, but he gave this up after falling in love with Frieda von Richthofen, the German wife of a Professor of French at Nottingham. They went to Germany together and married in 1914, after Frieda had been divorced by her first husband.

Abroad with Frieda, Lawrence finished *Sons and Lovers*, the autobiographical novel at which he had been working off and on for years. The war brought them back to England, where Frieda's German origins and Lawrence's fierce objection to the war gave him trouble with the authorities. More and more—especially after the banning of his next novel, *The Rainbow*, in 1915—Lawrence came to feel that the forces of modern civilization were arrayed against him. As soon as he could leave England after the war he sought refuge in Italy, Australia, Mexico, then again in Italy, and finally in the south of France, often desperately ill, restlessly searching for an ideal, or at least a tolerable, community in which to live. He died of tuberculosis in the south of France on the 2nd of March, 1930, at the early age of 44.

Shortly before his death he had written:

> Give me the moon at my feet
> Put my feet upon the crescent, like a Lord!
> O let my ankles be bathed in moonlight, that I may go
> sure and moon-shod, cool and bright-footed
> towards my goal.
>
> For the sun is hostile, now
> his face is like the red lion . . .

In these elemental images he invoked his end, a gesture at once heroic and desperate. It was typical of him to symbolize his passing with reference to the sun and moon, for Lawrence was at home with such cosmic images as no other English writer except Blake has ever been; he was at home, one might say, with the universe, with all that is deep-rooted and elemental in man and nature, and at constant war with the mechanical and artificial, with the constraints and hypocrisies that civilization imposes on man's fundamental self. His most characteristic writings are essentially a record in symbolic terms of his explorations of human individuality and of all that hindered it and all that might fulfill it, whether in the natural world or in the world of other individuals.

This is not what the English novel is generally supposed to do, and Lawrence, with new things to say and a new way of using the novel form, was not easily or quickly appreciated. His early novels, *The White Peacock*, *The Trespasser*, and even the original and impressive *Sons and Lovers*, were more conventional in style and treatment; they aroused contemporary interest and even acclaim, and it appeared that he might be on his way to becoming one of the acknowledged and popular Georgian novelists. But with the publication of *The Rainbow* in 1915 the true, original Lawrence first emerged clearly, and the critics turned away in bewilderment and condemnation. *The Rainbow* was suppressed as indecent a month after its publication, and the war between Lawrence and the world of timid convention was on. The rest of his life, during which he produced about a dozen more novels and many poems, short stories, sketches, and miscellaneous articles, was, in his own words, "a savage enough pilgrimage," marked by incessant struggle and by moments of frustration and despair. Lawrence was one of those artists who had to create the taste by which he could be appreciated. He had no gift for explaining his attitude and literary technique in simple expository prose. He could explain himself only by performing, by operating in his own way as an artist, letting the work of art speak with its own voice and pulse with its own life. When he tried to talk *about* his ideas, instead of projecting them symbolically in art, he was often irritatingly and vaguely rhetorical. "Sense of truth," "supreme impulse" are phrases characteristic of Lawrence's belief in intuition, in the dark forces of the inner self, that must not be allowed to be swamped by the rational faculties but must be brought into a harmonious relation with them. It was a point of view—or rather, a perception, a passionate insight—which could not be convincingly expressed in argument, but demanded direct projection in art.

The genteel culture of Lawrence's mother came more and more to represent death for Lawrence. In much of his later work, and especially in some of his short stories, he sets the deadening restrictiveness of middle-class conventional living against the forces of liberation that are often represented by an outsider—a peasant, a gypsy, a working man, a primitive of some kind, someone free by circumstance or personal effort. The recurring theme of his short stories—which contain some of his best work—is the distortion of love by possessiveness or gentility or a false romanticism or a false conception of the life of the artists, and the achievement of a living relation between a man and a woman against the pressure of class-feeling or tradition or habit or prejudice.

His two masterpieces, *The Rainbow* and *Women in Love* (both of which developed out of what was originally conceived as a single novel to be called *The Sisters*), are to be read as symbolic and dramatic poems in prose. In these novels Lawrence probes with both subtlety and power into various aspects of relationship—the relationship between man and his environment, the relationship between the generations, the relationship between man and woman, the relationship between instinct and intellect, and above all the proper basis for the marriage relationship as he conceived it. He is concerned too with the impact of modern industrial civilization on human sensibility, and finds many ways, at once realistic and symbolic, of projecting this. At the very opening of *The Rainbow*, where Lawrence is dealing with the family history of the Brangwens, whose annals he is about to tell, he makes clear even by the rhythms of his prose, as well as by his tone and imagery, that this is not to be a chronicle family novel like Galsworthy's *Forsyte Saga*.

The Rainbow is built on sets of human relationships, both horizontal and vertical. Thus we first see the marriage of Tom Brangwen with the Polish widow Lydia Lensky; then Tom's relationship with his step-daughter Anna; then Anna's relationship with her husband Will; then Will's relationship with his daughters Ursula and Gudrun; and so on. The truth of emotional detail in the presentation of these developing relationships is rendered with extraordinary force and subtlety. A fine example is in the extract below, which shows Tom Brangwen comforting his little step-daughter Anna.

In the relationship of Anna and Will in marriage we begin to find the true Laurentian doctrine that marriage is a fight and at the same time, if properly realized, a means of mystic knowledge through the awareness by one partner (in ultimate intimacy) of the essential *otherness* of the other. After the amorous luxury and mutual discovery of the first few days of marriage, Anna suddenly turns into the brisk housewife and sends the bewildered Will out of doors while she sets about her housework. Lawrence's view of marriage as a struggle derived from his own relationship with his strong-minded German-born wife Frieda. There are more and bitterer lovers' quarrels in Lawrence's novels than anywhere else in English literature. Lawrence's "crockery-throwing" view of love could become tedious, except that, as he presents it, it is bound up with the deepest rhythms and most profound instincts of the man-woman relationship. It is even more strong in *Women in Love*, which deals with Ursula and Gudrun Brangwen and their search for an adequate love relationship. The novel is, however, very much more than the traditional love quest, the developing relationships of Ursula and Rupert Birkin on the one hand and Gudrun and Gerald Crich on the other.

In Rupert there is more than a little of Lawrence himself, yet Lawrence is still able occasionally to laugh at him. Gerald, coldly handsome son of a powerful Midland mineowner, accumulates for himself, as the novel progresses, all the deadening and distorting effects of modern industrial civilization. Lawrence does not simply make Gerald's behavior inadequate or offensive; he is able to invent for his characters actions which while wholly realistic on the surface, or social level, are at the same time profoundly symbolic. This symbolism does not always come off, but when it does the effect is remarkable, as in a scene where Gerald forces his terrified mare to stand by the railway line while a shunting train hisses and clanks back and forth. The novel reveals a deep sense of English provincial life, in which—in spite of all Lawrence's wanderings abroad and of the foreign setting of many of his novels—his sensibility was really deeply rooted, much as George Eliot's was. His intimacy with the English scene, especially with provincial middle-class and working-class patterns of thought and feeling and the relation between them, is revealed again and again in the short stories, notably in "Fanny and Annie," "Daughters of the Vicar," "The Fox," "The Christening," and "Tickets Please."

In *The Rainbow* and *Women in Love*, then, Lawrence is developing a radically new kind of novel in which he explores kinds of human relationships with a combination of uncanny psychological precision and intense poetic feeling. They have an acute surface realism, a sharp sense of time and place, and brilliant topographical detail, and at the same time their high poetic symbolism, both of the total pattern of action and of incidents and objects within it, establishes a rhythm of meaning that is missed by those who read the novels with the conventional categories of "plot" and "characters" in mind. His next novel, *Aaron's Rod* (1922), is more uneven; in it Lawrence, employing many of his own experiences, explores problems of human relations under the question of moral and political leadership, which for a time obsessed him. He was concerned with the struggle for leadership in marriage as well as in politics. Two other novels on the theme of leadership, *Kangaroo* (1923), set in Australia, and *The Plumed Serpent* (1926), set in Mexico, similarly uneven, show him trying to give symbolic fictional form to his own problems and preoccupations. But *Kangaroo* in particular has its moments of uncanny perceptiveness, and it is extraordinary how Lawrence, drawing on his experiences during a short stay in Australia, was able to get beneath the skin of the country and evoke so much of the essential reality of both place and people.

It is hard to think of another English novelist whose best and most characteristic work makes such a disquieting assault on our normal patterns of thought and feeling. It is not simply that Lawrence is a rebel against convention—many writers have been that—or that his views are startling, though they sometimes are. It is rather that the whole response to life, and in particular to the problems posed by human relationships, that emerges from his novels and stories seems to come so profoundly from the deepest recesses of his being and therefore assault the deepest recesses of *our* being, that the challenge seems to go beyond that which is normally asserted by a work of art. It is difficult to escape the challenge; to make any attempt to respond fully to what he is saying is to be drawn into his world, forced to share his vision.

Although there are complex critical reasons for the posthumous triumph of this writer who was so much reviled in his lifetime, there is also a simple and striking reason that must not be forgotten. Lawrence had vision; he had a poetic sense of life; he had a keen ear and a piercing eye for every kind of vitality and color and sound in the world, for landscape—be it of England or Italy or New Mexico—for the individuality and concreteness of things in nature, and for the individuality and concreteness of people. His travel sketches are as impressive in their way as his novels; he seizes both on the symbolic incident and on the concrete reality, and each is interpreted in terms of the other. He looked at the world freshly, with his own eyes, avoiding formulas and clichés; and he forged for himself a kind of utterance which, at his best, was able to convey powerfully and vividly what his fresh, original vision showed him. This kind of originality has its drawbacks; he was sometimes shrill, sometimes repetitive, sometimes almost hysterical; some scenes in his novels are murky with unachieved symbolism or splutter with unresolved passion. But the great Lawrence remains.

This restless pilgrim with his uncanny perceptions into the depths of physical things, with his uncompromising honesty and originality in his view of men and the world, cannot be dismissed as merely a great eccentric. Nor is he a great prophet. He is essentially an artist; it is his *rendering* of life in his art, not his preaching about life's meaning, that matters.

Odor of Chrysanthemums

I

The small locomotive engine, Number 4, came clanking, stumbling down from Selston with seven full wagons. It appeared round the corner with loud threats of speed, but the colt that it startled from among the gorse,[1] which still flickered indistinctly in the raw afternoon, out-distanced it at a canter. A woman, walking up the railway line to Underwood, drew back into the hedge, held her basket aside, and watched the footplate of the engine advancing. The trucks[2] thumped heavily past, one by one, with slow inevitable movement, as she stood insignificantly trapped between the jolting black wagons and the hedge; then they curved away towards the coppice[3] where the withered oak leaves dropped noiselessly, while the birds, pulling at the scarlet hips beside the track, made off into the dusk that had already crept into the spinney.[4] In the open, the smoke from the engine sank and cleaved to the rough grass. The fields were dreary and forsaken, and in the marshy strip that led to the whimsey,[5] a reedy pit pond, the fowls had already abandoned their run among the alders, to roost in the tarred fowl house. The pit bank loomed up beyond the pond, flames like red sores licking its ashy sides, in the afternoon's stagnant light. Just beyond rose the tapering chimneys and the clumsy black headstocks of Brinsley Colliery.[6] The two wheels were spinning fast up against the sky, and the winding engine rapped out its little spasms. The miners were being turned up.

The engine whistled as it came into the wide bay of railway lines beside the colliery, where rows of trucks stood in harbor.

Miners, single, trailing, and in groups, passed like shadows diverging home. At the edge of the ribbed level of sidings squat a low cottage, three steps down from the cinder track. A large bony vine clutched at the house, as if to claw down the tiled roof. Round the bricked yard grew a few wintry primroses. Beyond, the long garden sloped down to a bush-covered brook course. There were some twiggy apple trees, winter-crack trees, and ragged cabbages. Beside the path hung disheveled pink chrysanthemums, like pink cloths hung on bushes. A woman came stooping out of the felt-covered fowl house, halfway down the garden. She closed and

---

1. Also known as furze or whin, a prickly bush with yellow flowers common on heaths, moors, and hillsides all over Britain.
2. Open freight cars.
3. A wood of small trees or shrubs.

4. Copse, thicket.
5. Machine for raising ore or water from a mine.
6. Coal mine; "headstocks" support revolving parts of a machine.

padlocked the door, then drew herself erect, having brushed some bits from her white apron.

She was a tall woman of imperious mien, handsome, with definite black eyebrows. Her smooth black hair was parted exactly. For a few moments she stood steadily watching the miners as they passed along the railway: then she turned towards the brook course. Her face was calm and set, her mouth was closed with disillusionment. After a moment she called:

"John!" There was no answer. She waited, and then said distinctly:

"Where are you?"

"Here!" replied a child's sulky voice from among the bushes. The woman looked piercingly through the dusk.

"Are you at that brook?" she asked sternly.

For answer the child showed himself before the raspberry canes that rose like whips. He was a small, sturdy boy of five. He stood quite still, defiantly.

"Oh!" said the mother, conciliated. "I thought you were down at that wet brook—and you remember what I told you——"

The boy did not move or answer.

"Come, come on in," she said more gently, "it's getting dark. There's your grandfather's engine coming down the line!"

The lad advanced slowly, with resentful, taciturn movement. He was dressed in trousers and waistcoat of cloth that was too thick and hard for the size of the garments. They were evidently cut down from a man's clothes.

As they went slowly towards the house he tore at the ragged wisps of chrysanthemums and dropped the petals in handfuls among the path.

"Don't do that—it does look nasty," said his mother. He refrained, and she, suddenly pitiful, broke off a twig with three or four wan flowers and held them against her face. When mother and son reached the yard her hand hesitated, and instead of laying the flower aside, she pushed it in her apron-band. The mother and son stood at the foot of the three steps looking across the bay of lines at the passing home of the miners. The trundle of the small train was imminent. Suddenly the engine loomed past the house and came to a stop opposite the gate.

The engine-driver, a short man with round gray beard, leaned out of the cab high above the woman.

"Have you got a cup of tea?" he said in a cheery, hearty fashion.

It was her father. She went in, saying she would mash.[7] Directly,

---

7. Infuse the tea, i.e., let it stand after pouring boiling water over the tea leaves in order to gain strength.

she returned.

"I didn't come to see you on Sunday," began the little gray-bearded man.

"I didn't expect you," said his daughter.

The engine driver winced; then, reassuming his cheery, airy manner, he said:

"Oh, have you heard then? Well, and what do you think——?"

"I think it is soon enough," she replied.

At her brief censure the little man made an impatient gesture, and said coaxingly, yet with dangerous coldness:

"Well, what's a man to do? It's no sort of life for a man of my years, to sit at my own hearth like a stranger. And if I'm going to marry again it may as well be soon as late—what does it matter to anybody?"

The woman did not reply, but turned and went into the house. The man in the engine-cab stood assertive, till she returned with a cup of tea and a piece of bread and butter on a plate. She went up the steps and stood near the footplate of the hissing engine.

"You needn't 'a' brought me bread an' butter," said her father. "But a cup of tea"—he sipped appreciatively—"it's very nice." He sipped for a moment or two, then: "I hear as Walter's got another bout on," he said.

"When hasn't he?" said the woman bitterly.

"I heerd tell of him in the Lord Nelson braggin' as he was going to spend that b—— afore he went: half a sovereign that was."

"When?" asked the woman.

"A' Sat'day night—I know that's true."

"Very likely," she laughed bitterly. "He gives me twenty-three shillings."

"Aye, it's a nice thing, when a man can do nothing with his money but make a beast of himself!" said the gray-whiskered man. The woman turned her head away. Her father swallowed the last of his tea and handed her the cup.

"Aye," he sighed, wiping his mouth. "It's a settler,[8] it is——"

He put his hand on the lever. The little engine strained and groaned, and the train rumbled towards the crossing. The woman again looked across the metals. Darkness was settling over the spaces of the railway and trucks: the miners, in gray somber groups, were still passing home. The winding engine pulsed hurriedly, with brief pauses. Elizabeth Bates looked at the dreary flow of men, then she went indoors. Her husband did not come.

The kitchen was small and full of firelight; red coals piled glowing up the chimney mouth. All the life of the room seemed in the

8. Crushing (or final) blow.

white, warm hearth and the steel fender reflecting the red fire. The cloth was laid for tea; cups glinted in the shadows. At the back, where the lowest stairs protruded into the room, the boy sat struggling with a knife and a piece of white wood. He was almost hidden in the shadow. It was half-past four. They had but to await the father's coming to begin tea. As the mother watched her son's sullen little struggle with the wood, she saw herself in his silence and pertinacity; she saw the father in her child's indifference to all but himself. She seemed to be occupied by her husband. He had probably gone past his home, slunk past his own door, to drink before he came in, while his dinner spoiled and wasted in waiting. She glanced at the clock, then took the potatoes to strain them in the yard. The garden and fields beyond the brook were closed in uncertain darkness. When she rose with the saucepan, leaving the drain steaming into the night behind her, she saw the yellow lamps were lit along the high road that went up the hill away beyond the space of the railway lines and the field.

Then again she watched the men trooping home, fewer now and fewer.

Indoors the fire was sinking and the room was dark red. The woman put her saucepan on the hob, and set a batter pudding near the mouth of the oven. Then she stood unmoving. Directly, gratefully, came quick young steps to the door. Someone hung on the latch a moment, then a little girl entered and began pulling off her outdoor things, dragging a mass of curls, just ripening from gold to brown, over her eyes with her hat.

Her mother chid her for coming late from school, and said she would have to keep her at home the dark winter days.

"Why, mother, it's hardly a bit dark yet. The lamp's not lighted, and my father's not home."

"No, he isn't. But it's a quarter to five! Did you see anything of him?"

The child became serious. She looked at her mother with large, wistful blue eyes.

"No, mother, I've never seen him. Why? Has he come up an' gone past, to Old Brinsley? He hasn't, mother, 'cos I never saw him."

"He'd watch that," said the mother bitterly, "he'd take care as you didn't see him. But you may depend upon it, he's seated in the Prince o' Wales. He wouldn't be this late."

The girl looked at her mother piteously.

"Let's have our teas, mother, should we?" said she.

The mother called John to table. She opened the door once more and looked out across the darkness of the lines. All was deserted:

she could not hear the winding-engines.

"Perhaps," she said to herself, "he's stopped to get some ripping⁹ done."

They sat down to tea. John, at the end of the table near the door, was almost lost in the darkness. Their faces were hidden from each other. The girl crouched against the fender slowly moving a thick piece of bread before the fire. The lad, his face a dusky mark on the shadow, sat watching her who was transfigured in the red glow.

"I do think it's beautiful to look in the fire," said the child.

"Do you?" said her mother. "Why?"

"It's so red, and full of little caves—and it feels so nice, and you can fair smell it."

"It'll want mending directly," replied her mother, "and then if your father comes he'll carry on and say there never is a fire when a man comes home sweating from the pit. A public house is always warm enough."

There was silence till the boy said complainingly: "Make haste, our Annie."

"Well, I am doing! I can't make the fire do it no faster, can I?"

"She keeps wafflin' it about so's to make 'er slow," grumbled the boy.

"Don't have such an evil imagination, child," replied the mother.

Soon the room was busy in the darkness with the crisp sound of crunching. The mother ate very little. She drank her tea determinedly, and sat thinking. When she rose her anger was evident in the stern unbending of her head. She looked at the pudding in the fender, and broke out:

"It is a scandalous thing as a man can't even come home to his dinner! If it's crozzled up to a cinder I don't see why I should care. Past his very door he goes to get to a public house, and here I sit with his dinner waiting for him——"

She went out. As she dropped piece after piece of coal on the red fire, the shadows fell on the walls, till the room was almost in total darkness.

"I canna see," grumbled the invisible John. In spite of herself, the mother laughed.

"You know the way to your mouth," she said. She set the dustpan outside the door. When she came again like a shadow on the hearth, the lad repeated, complaining sulkily:

"I canna see."

"Good gracious!" cried the mother irritably, "you're as bad as your father if it's a bit dusk!"

9. Taking out or cutting away coal or stone (a mining and quarrying term).

Nevertheless, she took a paper spill from a sheaf on the mantelpiece and proceeded to light the lamp that hung from the ceiling in the middle of the room. As she reached up, her figure displayed itself just rounding with maternity.

"Oh, mother——!" exclaimed the girl.

"What?" said the woman, suspended in the act of putting the lamp glass over the flame. The copper reflector shone handsomely on her, as she stood with uplifted arm, turning to face her daughter.

"You've got a flower in your apron!" said the child, in a little rapture at this unusual event.

"Goodness me!" exclaimed the woman, relieved. "One would think the house was afire." She replaced the glass and waited a moment before turning up the wick. A pale shadow was seen floating vaguely on the floor.

"Let me smell!" said the child, still rapturously, coming forward and putting her face to her mother's waist.

"Go along, silly!" said the mother, turning up the lamp. The light revealed their suspense so that the woman felt it almost unbearable. Annie was still bending at her waist. Irritably, the mother took the flowers out from her apron band.

"Oh, mother—don't take them out!" Annie cried, catching her hand and trying to replace the sprig.

"Such nonsense!" said the mother, turning away. The child put the pale chrysanthemums to her lips, murmuring:

"Don't they smell beautiful!"

Her mother gave a short laugh.

"No," she said, "not to me. It was chrysanthemums when I married him, and chrysanthemums when you were born, and the first time they ever brought him home drunk, he'd got brown chrysanthemums in his buttonhole."

She looked at the children. Their eyes and their parted lips were wondering. The mother sat rocking in silence for some time. Then she looked at the clock.

"Twenty minutes to six!" In a tone of fine bitter carelessness she continued: "Eh, he'll not come now till they bring him. There he'll stick! But he needn't come rolling in here in his pit dirt, for I won't wash him. He can lie on the floor——Eh, what a fool I've been, what a fool! And this is what I came here for, to this dirty hole, rats and all, for him to slink past his very door. Twice last week—he's begun now——"

She silenced herself, and rose to clear the table.

While for an hour or more the children played, subduedly intent, fertile of imagination, united in fear of the mother's wrath, and in dread of their father's home-coming, Mrs. Bates sat in her rocking chair making a "singlet" of thick cream-colored flannel, which gave a dull wounded sound as she tore off the gray edge. She worked at her sewing with energy, listening to the children, and her anger wearied itself, lay down to rest, opening its eyes from time to time and steadily watching, its ears raised to listen. Sometimes even her anger quailed and shrank, and the mother suspended her sewing, tracing the footsteps that thudded along the sleepers outside; she would lift her head sharply to bid the children "hush," but she recovered herself in time, and the footsteps went past the gate, and the children were not flung out of their play-world.

But at last Annie sighed, and gave in. She glanced at her wagon of slippers, and loathed the game. She turned plaintively to her mother.

"Mother!"—but she was inarticulate.

John crept out like a frog from under the sofa. His mother glanced up.

"Yes," she said, "just look at those shirt-sleeves!"

The boy held them out to survey them, saying nothing. Then somebody called in a hoarse voice away down the line, and suspense bristled in the room, till two people had gone by outside, talking.

"It is time for bed," said the mother.

"My father hasn't come," wailed Annie plaintively. But her mother was primed with courage.

"Never mind. They'll bring him when he does come—like a log." She meant there would be no scene. "And he may sleep on the floor till he wakes himself. I know he'll not go to work tomorrow after this!"

The children had their hands and faces wiped with a flannel. They were very quiet. When they had put on their nightdresses, they said their prayers, the boy mumbling. The mother looked down at them, at the brown silken bush of intertwining curls in the nape of the girl's neck, at the little black head of the lad, and her heart burst with anger at their father, who caused all three such distress. The children hid their faces in her skirts for comfort.

When Mrs. Bates came down, the room was strangely empty, with a tension of expectancy. She took up her sewing and stitched for some time without raising her head. Meantime her anger was tinged with fear.

II

The clock struck eight and she rose suddenly, dropping her sewing on her chair. She went to the stair-foot door, opened it, listening. Then she went out, locking the door behind her.

Something scuffled in the yard, and she started, though she knew it was only the rats with which the place was over-run. The night was very dark. In the great bay of railway lines, bulked with trucks, there was no trace of light, only away back she could see a few yellow lamps at the pit top, and the red smear of the burning pit bank on the night. She hurried along the edge of the track, then, crossing the converging lines, came to the stile by the white gates, whence she emerged on the road. Then the fear which had led her shrank. People were walking up to New Brinsley; she saw the lights in the houses; twenty yards farther on were the broad windows of the Prince of Wales, very warm and bright, and the loud voices of men could be heard distinctly. What a fool she had been to imagine that anything had happened to him! He was merely drinking over there at the Prince of Wales. She faltered. She had never yet been to fetch him, and she never would go. So she continued her walk towards the long straggling line of houses, standing back on the highway. She entered a passage between the dwellings.

"Mr. Rigley?—Yes! Did you want him? No, he's not in at this minute."

The raw-boned woman leaned forward from her dark scullery and peered at the other, upon whom fell a dim light through the blind of the kitchen window.

"Is it Mrs. Bates?" she asked in a tone tinged with respect.

"Yes. I wondered if your Master was at home. Mine hasn't come yet."

" 'Asn't 'e! Oh, Jack's been 'ome an' 'ad 'is dinner an' gone out. 'E's just gone for 'alf an hour afore bedtime. Did you call at the Prince of Wales?"

"No——"

"No, you didn't like——! It's not very nice." The other woman was indulgent. There was an awkward pause. "Jack never said nothink about—about your Master," she said.

"No!—I expect he's stuck in there!"

Elizabeth Bates said this bitterly, and with recklessness. She knew that the woman across the yard was standing at her door listening, but she did not care. As she turned:

"Stop a minute! I'll just go an' ask Jack if 'e knows anythink," said Mrs. Rigley.

"Oh no—I wouldn't like to put——!"

"Yes, I will, if you'll just step inside an' see as th' childer doesn't come downstairs and set theirselves afire."

Elizabeth Bates, murmuring a remonstrance, stepped inside. The other woman apologized for the state of the room.

The kitchen needed apology. There were little frocks and trousers and childish undergarments on the squab and on the floor, and a litter of playthings everywhere. On the black American cloth [1] of the table were pieces of bread and cake, crusts, slops, and a teapot with cold tea.

"Eh, ours is just as bad," said Elizabeth Bates, looking at the woman, not at the house. Mrs. Rigley put a shawl over her head and hurried out, saying:

"I shanna be a minute."

The other sat, noting with faint disapproval the general untidiness of the room. Then she fell to counting the shoes of various sizes scattered over the floor. There were twelve. She sighed and said to herself: "No wonder!"—glancing at the litter. There came the scratching of two pairs of feet on the yard, and the Rigleys entered. Elizabeth Bates rose. Rigley was a big man, with very large bones. His head looked particularly bony. Across his temple was a blue scar, caused by a wound got in the pit, a wound in which the coal dust remained blue like tattooing.

" 'Asna 'e come whoam yit?" asked the man, without any form of greeting, but with deference and sympathy. "I couldna say wheer he is—'e's non ower theer!"—he jerked his head to signify the Prince of Wales.

" 'E's 'appen gone up to th' Yew," said Mrs. Rigley.

There was another pause. Rigley had evidently something to get off his mind:

"Ah left 'im finishin' a stint," he began. "Loose-all [2] 'ad bin gone about ten minutes when we com'n away, an' I shouted: 'Are ter comin', Walt?' an' 'e said: 'Go on, Ah shanna be but a'ef a minnit,' so we com'n ter th' bottom, me an' Bowers, thinkin' as 'e wor just behint, an' 'ud come up i' th' next bantle [3]——"

He stood perplexed, as if answering a charge of deserting his mate. Elizabeth Bates, now again certain of disaster, hastened to reassure him:

"I expect 'e's gone up to th' Yew Tree, as you say. It's not the first time. I've fretted myself into a fever before now. He'll come home when they carry him."

"Ay, isn't it too bad!" deplored the other woman.

"I'll just step up to Dick's an' see if 'e is theer," offered the man, afraid of appearing alarmed, afraid of taking liberties.

"Oh, I wouldn't think of bothering you that far," said Elizabeth Bates, with emphasis, but he knew she was glad of his offer.

As they stumbled up the entry, Elizabeth Bates heard Rigley's wife run across the yard and open her neighbor's door. At this, suddenly all the blood in her body seemed to switch away from her

1. Oilcloth.
2. Signal for end of work.
3. Group.

heart.

"Mind!" warned Rigley. "Ah've said many a time as Ah'd fill up them ruts in this entry, sumb'dy 'll be breakin' their legs yit."

She recovered herself and walked quickly along with the miner.

"I don't like leaving the children in bed, and nobody in the house," she said.

"No, you dunna!" he replied courteously. They were soon at the gate of the cottage.

"Well, I shanna be many minnits. Dunna you be frettin' now, 'e'll be all right," said the butty.[4]

"Thank you very much, Mr. Rigley," she replied.

"You're welcome!" he stammered, moving away. "I shanna be many minnits."

The house was quiet. Elizabeth Bates took off her hat and shawl, and rolled back the rug. When she had finished, she sat down. It was a few minutes past nine. She was startled by the rapid chuff of the winding engine at the pit, and the sharp whirr of the brakes on the rope as it descended. Again she felt the painful sweep of her blood, and she put her hand to her side, saying aloud: "Good gracious!—it's only the nine o'clock deputy[5] going down," rebuking herself.

She sat still, listening. Half an hour of this, and she was wearied out.

"What am I working myself up like this for?" she said pitiably to herself, "I s'll only be doing myself some damage."

She took out her sewing again.

At a quarter to ten there were footsteps. One person! She watched for the door to open. It was an elderly woman, in a black bonnet and a black woolen shawl—his mother. She was about sixty years old, pale, with blue eyes, and her face all wrinkled and lamentable. She shut the door and turned to her daughter-in-law peevishly.

"Eh, Lizzie, whatever shall we do, whatever shall we do!" she cried.

Elizabeth drew back a little, sharply.

"What is it, mother?" she said.

The elder woman seated herself on the sofa.

"I don't know, child, I can't tell you!"—she shook her head slowly. Elizabeth sat watching her, anxious and vexed.

"I don't know," replied the grandmother, sighing very deeply. "There's no end to my troubles, there isn't. The things I've gone through, I'm sure it's enough——!" She wept without wiping her

4. Workmate (cf. "buddy"). Among English coal-miners it has the special meaning of "a supervisor intermediary between the employers and the men."
5. Minor coal-mine official.

eyes, the tears running.

"But, mother," interrupted Elizabeth, "what do you mean? What is it?"

The grandmother slowly wiped her eyes. The fountains of her tears were stopped by Elizabeth's directness. She wiped her eyes slowly.

"Poor child! Eh, you poor thing!" she moaned. "I don't know what we're going to do, I don't—and you as you are—it's a thing, it is indeed!"

Elizabeth waited.

"Is he dead?" she asked, and at the words her heart swung violently, though she felt a slight flush of shame at the ultimate extravagance of the question. Her words sufficiently frightened the old lady, almost brought her to herself.

"Don't say so, Elizabeth! We'll hope it's not as bad as that; no, may the Lord spare us that, Elizabeth. Jack Rigley came just as I was sittin' down to a glass afore going to bed, an' 'e said: ' 'Appen you'll go down th' line, Mrs. Bates. Walt's had an accident. 'Appen you'll go an' sit wi' 'er till we can get him home.' I hadn't time to ask him a word afore he was gone. An' I put my bonnet on an' come straight down, Lizzie. I thought to myself: 'Eh, that poor blessed child, if anybody should come an' tell her of a sudden, there's no knowin' what'll 'appen to 'er.' You mustn't let it upset you, Lizzie —or you know what to expect. How long is it, six months—or is it five, Lizzie? Ay!"—the old woman shook her head—"time slips on, it slips on! Ay!"

Elizabeth's thoughts were busy elsewhere. If he was killed— would she be able to manage on the little pension and what she could earn?—she counted up rapidly. If he was hurt—they wouldn't take him to the hospital—how tiresome he would be to nurse!—but perhaps she'd be able to get him away from the drink and his hateful ways. She would—while he was ill. The tears offered to come to her eyes at the picture. But what sentimental luxury was this she was beginning? She turned to consider the children. At any rate she was absolutely necessary for them. They were her business.

"Ay!" repeated the old woman, "it seems but a week or two since he brought me his first wages. Ay—he was a good lad, Elizabeth, he was, in his way. I don't know why he got to be such a trouble, I don't. He was a happy lad at home, only full of spirits. But there's no mistake he's been a handful of trouble, he has! I hope the Lord'll spare him to mend his ways. I hope so, I hope so. You've had a sight o' trouble with him, Elizabeth, you have indeed. But he was a jolly enough lad wi' me, he was, I can assure you. I don't know how it is. . . ."

The old woman continued to muse aloud, a monotonous irritating sound, while Elizabeth thought concentratedly, startled once, when she heard the winding engine chuff quickly, and the brakes skirr with a shriek. Then she heard the engine more slowly, and the brakes made no sound. The old woman did not notice. Elizabeth waited in suspense. The mother-in-law talked, with lapses into silence.

"But he wasn't your son, Lizzie, an' it makes a difference. Whatever he was, I remember him when he was little, an' I learned to understand him and to make allowances. You've got to make allowances for them——"

It was half-past ten, and the old woman was saying: "But it's trouble from beginning to end; you're never too old for trouble, never too old for that——" when the gate banged back, and there were heavy feet on the steps.

"I'll go, Lizzie, let me go," cried the old woman, rising. But Elizabeth was at the door. It was a man in pit clothes.

"They're bringin' 'im, Missis," he said. Elizabeth's heart halted a moment. Then it surged on again, almost suffocating her.

"Is he—is it bad?" she asked.

The man turned away, looking at the darkness:

"The doctor says 'e'd been dead hours. 'E saw 'im i' th' lamp-cabin."

The old woman, who stood just behind Elizabeth, dropped into a chair, and folded her hands, crying: "Oh, my boy, my boy!"

"Hush!" said Elizabeth, with a sharp twitch of a frown. "Be still, mother, don't waken th' children: I wouldn't have them down for anything!"

The old woman moaned softly, rocking herself. The man was drawing away. Elizabeth took a step forward.

"How was it?" she asked.

"Well, I couldn't say for sure," the man replied, very ill at ease. "'E wor finishin' a stint an' th' butties 'ad gone, an' a lot o' stuff come down atop 'n 'im."

"And crushed him?" cried the widow, with a shudder.

"No," said the man, "it fell at th' back of 'im. 'E wor under th' face an' it niver touched 'im. It shut 'im in. It seems 'e wor smothered."

Elizabeth shrank back. She heard the old woman behind her cry:

"What?—what did 'e say it was?"

The man replied, more loudly: "'E wor smothered!"

Then the old woman wailed aloud, and this relieved Elizabeth.

"Oh, mother," she said, putting her hand on the old woman, "don't waken th' children, don't waken th' children."

She wept a little, unknowing, while the old mother rocked herself and moaned. Elizabeth remembered that they were bringing him home, and she must be ready. "They'll lay him in the parlor," she said to herself, standing a moment pale and perplexed.

Then she lighted a candle and went into the tiny room. The air was cold and damp, but she could not make a fire, there was no fireplace. She set down the candle and looked round. The candlelight glittered on the luster-glasses, on the two vases that held some of the pink chrysanthemums, and on the dark mahogany. There was a cold, deathly smell of chrysanthemums in the room. Elizabeth stood looking at the flowers. She turned away, and calculated whether there would be room to lay him on the floor, between the couch and the chiffonier. She pushed the chairs aside. There would be room to lay him down and to step round him. Then she fetched the old red tablecloth, and another old cloth, spreading them down to save her bit of carpet. She shivered on leaving the parlor; so, from the dresser drawer she took a clean shirt and put it at the fire to air. All the time her mother-in-law was rocking herself in the chair and moaning.

"You'll have to move from there, mother," said Elizabeth. "They'll be bringing him in. Come in the rocker."

The old mother rose mechanically, and seated herself by the fire, continuing to lament. Elizabeth went into the pantry for another candle, and there, in the little penthouse under the naked tiles, she heard them coming. She stood still in the pantry doorway, listening. She heard them pass the end of the house, and come awkwardly down the three steps, a jumble of shuffling footsteps and muttering voices. The old woman was silent. The men were in the yard.

Then Elizabeth heard Matthews, the manager of the pit, say: "You go in first, Jim. Mind!"

The door came open, and the two women saw a collier backing into the room, holding one end of a stretcher, on which they could see the nailed pit boots of the dead man. The two carriers halted, the man at the head stooping to the lintel of the door.

"Wheer will you have him?" asked the manager, a short, white-bearded man.

Elizabeth roused herself and came from the pantry carrying the unlighted candle.

"In the parlor," she said.

"In there, Jim!" pointed the manager, and the carriers backed round into the tiny room. The coat with which they had covered the body fell off as they awkwardly turned through the two door-ways, and the women saw their man, naked to the waist, lying stripped for work. The old woman began to moan in a low voice of horror.

"Lay th' stretcher at th' side," snapped the manager, "an' put 'im on th' cloths. Mind now, mind! Look you now——!"

One of the men had knocked off a vase of chrysanthemums. He stared awkwardly, then they set down the stretcher. Elizabeth did not look at her husband. As soon as she could get in the room, she went and picked up the broken vase and the flowers.

"Wait a minute!" she said.

The three men waited in silence while she mopped up the water with a duster.

"Eh, what a job, what a job, to be sure!" the manager was saying, rubbing his brow with trouble and perplexity. "Never knew such a thing in my life, never! He'd no business to ha' been left. I never knew such a thing in my life! Fell over him clean as a whistle, an' shut him in. Not four foot of space, there wasn't—yet it scarce bruised him."

He looked down at the dead man, lying prone, half naked, all grimed with coal dust.

"'Sphyxiated', the doctor said. It *is* the most terrible job I've ever known. Seems as if it was done o' purpose. Clean over him, an' shut 'im in, like a mouse-trap"—he made a sharp, descending gesture with his hand.

The colliers standing by jerked aside their heads in hopeless comment.

The horror of the thing bristled upon them all.

Then they heard the girl's voice upstairs calling shrilly: "Mother, mother—who is it? Mother, who is it?"

Elizabeth hurried to the foot of the stairs and opened the door:

"Go to sleep!" she commanded sharply. "What are you shouting about? Go to sleep at once—there's nothing——"

Then she began to mount the stairs. They could hear her on the boards, and on the plaster floor of the little bedroom. They could hear her distinctly:

"What's the matter now?—what's the matter with you, silly thing?"—her voice was much agitated, with an unreal gentleness.

"I thought it was some men come," said the plaintive voice of the child. "Has he come?"

"Yes, they've brought him. There's nothing to make a fuss about. Go to sleep now, like a good child."

They could hear her voice in the bedroom, they waited whilst she covered the children under the bedclothes.

"Is he drunk?" asked the girl, timidly, faintly.

"No! No—he's not! He—he's asleep."

"Is he asleep downstairs?"

"Yes—and don't make a noise."

There was silence for a moment, then the men heard the frightened child again:

"What's that noise?"

"It's nothing, I tell you, what are you bothering for?"

The noise was the grandmother moaning. She was oblivious of everything, sitting on her chair rocking and moaning. The manager put his hand on her arm and bade her "Sh—sh! !"

The old woman opened her eyes and looked at him. She was shocked by this interruption, and seemed to wonder.

"What time is it?" the plaintive thin voice of the child, sinking back unhappily into sleep, asked this last question.

"Ten o'clock," answered the mother more softly. Then she must have bent down and kissed the children.

Matthews beckoned to the men to come away. They put on their caps and took up the stretcher. Stepping over the body, they tiptoed out of the house. None of them spoke till they were far from the wakeful children.

When Elizabeth came down she found her mother alone on the parlor floor, leaning over the dead man, the tears dropping on him.

"We must lay him out," the wife said. She put on the kettle, then returning knelt at the feet, and began to unfasten the knotted leather laces. The room was clammy and dim with only one candle, so that she had to bend her face almost to the floor. At last she got off the heavy boots and put them away.

"You must help me now," she whispered to the old woman. Together they stripped the man.

When they arose, saw him lying in the naïve dignity of death, the woman stood arrested in fear and respect. For a few moments they remained still, looking down, the old mother whimpering. Elizabeth felt countermanded. She saw him, how utterly inviolable he lay in himself. She had nothing to do with him. She could not accept it. Stooping, she laid her hand on him, in claim. He was still warm, for the mine was hot where he had died. His mother had his face between her hands, and was murmuring incoherently. The old tears fell in succession as drops from wet leaves; the mother was not weeping, merely her tears flowed. Elizabeth embraced the body of her husband, with cheek and lips. She seemed to be listening, inquiring, trying to get some connection. But she could not. She was driven away. He was impregnable.

She rose, went into the kitchen, where she poured warm water into a bowl, brought soap and flannel and a soft towel. "I must wash him," she said.

Then the old mother rose stiffly, and watched Elizabeth as she carefully washed his face, carefully brushing his big blond moustache from his mouth with the flannel. She was afraid with a bottomless fear, so she ministered to him. The old woman, jealous, said:

"Let me wipe him!"—and she kneeled on the other side drying slowly as Elizabeth washed, her big black bonnet sometimes brushing the dark head of her daughter-in-law. They worked thus in silence for a long time. They never forgot it was death, and the touch of the man's dead body gave them strange emotions, different in each of the women; a great dread possessed them both, the mother felt the lie was given to her womb, she was denied; the wife felt the utter isolation of the human soul, the child within her was a weight apart from her.

At last it was finished. He was a man of handsome body, and his face showed no traces of drink. He was blond, full fleshed, with fine limbs. But he was dead.

"Bless him," whispered his mother, looking always at his face, and speaking out of sheer terror. "Dear lad—bless him!" She spoke in a faint, sibilant ecstasy of fear and mother love.

Elizabeth sank down again to the floor, and put her face against his neck, and trembled and shuddered. But she had to draw away again. He was dead, and her living flesh had no place against his. A great dread and weariness held her: she was so unavailing. Her life was gone like this.

"White as milk he is, clear as a twelve-month baby, bless him, the darling!" the old mother murmured to herself. "Not a mark on him, clear and clean and white, beautiful as ever a child was made," she murmured with pride. Elizabeth kept her face hidden.

"He went peaceful, Lizzie—peaceful as sleep. Isn't he beautiful, the lamb? Ay—he must ha' made his peace, Lizzie. 'Appen he made it all right, Lizzie, shut in there. He'd have time. He wouldn't look like this if he hadn't made his peace. The lamb, the dear lamb. Eh, but he had a hearty laugh. I loved to hear it. He had the heartiest laugh, Lizzie, as a lad———"

Elizabeth looked up. The man's mouth was fallen back, slightly open under the cover of the moustache. The eyes, half shut, did not show glazed in the obscurity. Life with its smoky burning gone from him, had left him apart and utterly alien to her. And she knew what a stranger he was to her. In her womb was ice of fear, because of this separate stranger with whom she had been living as one flesh. Was this what it all meant—utter, intact separateness, obscured by heat of living? In dread she turned her face away. The fact was too deadly. There had been nothing between them, and yet they had come together, exchanging their nakedness repeatedly. Each time he had taken her, they had been two isolated beings, far apart as now. He was no more responsible than she. The child was like ice in her womb. For as she looked at the dead man, her mind, cold and detached, said clearly: "Who am I? What have I been doing? I have been fighting a husband who did not exist. *He* existed all the time. What wrong have I done? What was that I have been living with? There lies the reality, this man." And her soul died in her for fear: she knew she had never seen him, he had never seen her, they had met in the dark and had fought in the dark, not knowing whom they met or whom they fought. And now she saw, and turned silent in seeing. For she had been wrong. She had said he was something he was not; she had felt familiar with him. Whereas he was apart all the while, living as she never lived, feeling as she never felt.

In fear and shame she looked at his naked body, that she had known falsely. And he was the father of her children. Her soul was torn from her body and stood apart. She looked at his naked body and was ashamed, as if she had denied it. After all, it was itself. It seemed awful to her. She looked at his face, and she turned her own face to the wall. For his look was other than hers, his way was not her way. She had denied him what he was—she saw it now. She had refused him as himself. And this had been her life, and his life. She was grateful to death, which restored the truth. And she knew she was not dead.

And all the while her heart was bursting with grief and pity for him. What had he suffered? What stretch of horror for this helpless man! She was rigid with agony. She had not been able to help him. He had been cruelly injured, this naked man, this other being, and she could make no reparation. There were the children—but the children belonged to life. This dead man had nothing to do with them. He and she were only channels through which life had flowed to issue in the children. She was a mother—but how awful she knew it now to have been a wife. And he, dead now, how awful he must have felt it to be a husband. She felt that in the next world he would be a stranger to her. If they met there, in the beyond, they would only be ashamed of what had been before. The children had come, for some mysterious reason, out of both of them. But the children did not unite them. Now he was dead, she knew how eternally he was apart from her, how eternally he had nothing more to do with her. She saw this episode of her life closed. They had denied each other in life. Now he had withdrawn. An anguish came over her. It was finished then: it had become hopeless between them long before he died. Yet he had been her husband. But how little!

"Have you got his shirt, 'Lizabeth?"

Elizabeth turned without answering, though she strove to weep and behave as her mother-in-law expected. But she could not, she was silenced. She went into the kitchen and returned with the garment.

"It is aired," she said, grasping the cotton shirt here and there to try. She was almost ashamed to handle him; what right had she or anyone to lay hands on him; but her touch was humble on his body. It was hard work to clothe him. He was so heavy and inert. A terrible dread gripped her all the while: that he could be so heavy and utterly inert, unresponsive, apart. The horror of the distance between them was almost too much for her—it was so infinite a gap she must look across.

At last it was finished. They covered him with a sheet and left him lying, with his face bound. And she fastened the door of the little parlor, lest the children should see what was lying there. Then, with peace sunk heavy on her heart, she went about making tidy the kitchen. She knew she submitted to life, which was her immediate master. But from death, her ultimate master, she winced with fear and shame.

1911, 1914

From The Rainbow

From *Chapter II. They Live at the Marsh* [1]

One afternoon, the pains began, Mrs. Brangwen was put to bed, the midwife came. Night fell, the shutters were closed, Brangwen came in to tea, to the loaf and the pewter teapot, the child, silent and quivering, playing with glass beads, the house, empty, it seemed, or exposed to the winter night, as if it had no walls.

Sometimes there sounded, long and remote in the house, vibrating through everything, the moaning cry of a woman in labor. Brangwen, sitting downstairs, was divided. His lower, deeper self

1. Tom Brangwen, a Nottinghamshire farmer, married Lydia Lensky, widow of a Polish émigré doctor. Anna is Lydia's child by her first marriage. The scene is Marsh Farm, a few miles south of East-wood, where Lawrence was born, and just across the Nottinghamshire-Derbyshire border from the town of Ilkeston where Lawrence trained as a teacher. Lydia is about to have her first child by Tom.

was with her, bound to her, suffering. But the big shell of his body remembered the sound of owls that used to fly round the farmstead when he was a boy. He was back in his youth, a boy, haunted by the sound of the owls, waking up his brother to speak to him. And his mind drifted away to the birds, their solemn, dignified faces, their flight so soft and broad-winged. And then to the birds his brother had shot, fluffy, dust-colored, dead heaps of softness with faces absurdly asleep. It was a queer thing, a dead owl.

He lifted his cup to his lips, he watched the child with the beads. But his mind was occupied with owls, and the atmosphere of his boyhood, with his brothers and sisters. Elsewhere, fundamental, he was with his wife in labor, the child was being brought forth out of their one flesh. He and she, one flesh, out of which life must be put forth. The rent was not in his body, but it was of his body. On her the blows fell, but the quiver ran ran through to him, to his last fiber. She must be torn asunder for life to come forth, yet still they were one flesh, and still, from further back, the life came out of him to her, and still he was the unbroken that has the broken rock in its arms, their flesh was one rock from which the life gushed, out of her who was smitten and rent, from him who quivered and yielded.

He went upstairs to her. As he came to the bedside she spoke to him in Polish.

"Is it very bad?" he asked.

She looked at him, and oh, the weariness to her, of the effort to understand another language, the weariness of hearing him, attending to him, making out who he was, as he stood there fair-bearded and alien, looking at her. She knew something of him, of his eyes. But she could not grasp him. She closed her eyes.

He turned away, white to the gills.

"It's not so very bad," said the midwife.

He knew he was a strain on his wife. He went downstairs.

The child glanced up at him, frightened.

"I want my mother," she quavered.

"Ay, but she's badly," he said mildly, unheeding.

She looked at him with lost, frightened eyes.

"Has she got a headache?"

"No—she's going to have a baby."

The child looked round. He was unaware of her. She was alone again in terror.

"I want my mother," came the cry of panic.

"Let Tilly undress you," he said. "You're tired."

There was another silence. Again came the cry of labor.

"I want my mother," rang automatically from the wincing, panic-stricken child, that felt cut off and lost in a horror of desolation.

Tilly came forward, her heart wrung.

"Come an' let me undress her then, pet lamb," she crooned. "You s'll have your mother in th' mornin', don't you fret, my duckie; never mind, angel."

But Anna stood upon the sofa, her back to the wall.

"I want my mother," she cried, her little face quivering, and the great tears of childish, utter anguish falling.

"She's poorly, my lamb, she's poorly tonight, but she'll be better by mornin'. Oh, don't cry, don't cry, love, she doesn't want you to cry, precious little heart, no, she doesn't."

Tilly took gently hold of the child's skirts. Anna snatched back her dress, and cried, in a little hysteria:

"No, you're not to undress me—I want my mother,"—and her child's face was running with grief and tears, her body shaken.

"Oh, but let Tilly undress you. Let Tilly undress you, who loves you, don't be wilful tonight. Mother's poorly, she doesn't want you to cry."

The child sobbed distractedly, she could not hear.

"I want my mother," she wept.

"When you're undressed, you s'll go up to see your mother— when you're undressed, pet, when you've let Tilly undress you, when you're a little jewel in your nightie, love. Oh, don't you cry, don't you——"

Brangwen sat stiff in his chair. He felt his brain going tighter. He crossed over the room, aware only of the maddening sobbing.

"Don't make a noise," he said.

And a new fear shook the child from the sound of his voice. She cried mechanically, her eyes looking watchful through her tears, in terror, alert to what might happen.

"I want—my—mother," quavered the sobbing, blind voice.

A shiver of irritation went over the man's limbs. It was the utter, persistent unreason, the maddening blindness of the voice and the crying.

"You must come and be undressed," he said, in a quiet voice that was thin with anger.

And he reached his hand and grasped her. He felt her body catch in a convulsive sob. But he too was blind, and intent, irritated into mechanical action. He began to unfasten her little apron. She would have shrunk from him, but could not. So her small body remained in his grasp, while he fumbled at the little buttons and tapes, unthinking, intent, unaware of anything but the irritation of her. Her body was held taut and resistant, he pushed off the little dress and the petticoats, revealing the white arms. She kept stiff, overpowered, violated, he went on with his task. And all the while she sobbed, choking:

"I want my mother."

He was unheedingly silent, his face stiff. The child was now incapable of understanding, she had become a little, mechanical thing of fixed will. She wept, her body convulsed, her voice repeating the same cry.

"Eh, dear o' me!" cried Tilly, becoming distracted herself. Brangwen, slow, clumsy, blind, intent, got off all the little garments, and stood the child naked in its shift upon the sofa.

"Where's her nightie?" he asked.

Tilly brought it, and he put it on her. Anna did not move her limbs to his desire. He had to push them into place. She stood, with fixed, blind will, resistant, a small, convulsed, unchangeable thing weeping ever and repeating the same phrase. He lifted one foot after the other, pulled off slippers and socks. She was ready.

"Do you want a drink?" he asked.

She did not change. Unheeding, uncaring, she stood on the sofa, standing back, alone, her hands shut and half lifted, her face, all tears, raised and blind. And through the sobbing and choking came the broken:

"I—want—my—mother."

"Do you want a drink?" he said again.

There was no answer. He lifted the stiff, denying body between his hands. Its stiff blindness made a flash of rage go through him. He would like to break it.

He set the child on his knee, and sat again in his chair beside the fire, the wet, sobbing, inarticulate noise going on near his ear, the child sitting stiff, not yielding to him or anything, not aware.

A new degree of anger came over him. What did it all matter? What did it matter if the mother talked Polish and cried in labor, if this child were stiff with resistance, and crying? Why take it to heart? Let the mother cry in labor, let the child cry in resistance, since they would do so. Why should he fight against it, why resist? Let it be, if it were so. Let them be as they were, if they insisted.

And in a daze he sat, offering no fight. The child cried on, the minutes ticked away, a sort of torpor was on him.

It was some little time before he came to, and turned to attend to the child. He was shocked by her little wet, blinded face. A bit dazed, he pushed back the wet hair. Like a living statue of grief, her blind face cried on.

"Nay," he said, "not as bad as that. It's not as bad as that, Anna, my child. Come, what are you crying for so much? Come, stop now, it'll make you sick. I wipe you dry, don't wet your face any more. Don't cry any more wet tears, don't, it's better not to. Don't cry—it's not so bad as all that. Hush now, hush—let it be enough."

His voice was queer and distant and calm. He looked at the child.

She was beside herself now. He wanted her to stop, he wanted it all to stop, to become natural.

"Come," he said, rising to turn away, "we'll go an' supper-up the beast."

He took a big shawl, folded her round, and went out into the kitchen for a lantern.

"You're never taking the child out, of a night like this," said Tilly.

"Ay, it'll quieten her," he answered.

It was raining. The child was suddenly still, shocked, finding the rain on its face, the darkness.

"We'll just give the cows their something-to-eat, afore they go to bed," Brangwen was saying to her, holding her close and sure.

There was a trickling of water into the butt, a burst of raindrops sputtering on to her shawl, and the light of the lantern swinging, flashing on a wet pavement and the base of a wet wall. Otherwise it was black darkness: one breathed darkness.

He opened the doors, upper and lower, and they entered into the high, dry barn, that smelled warm even if it were not warm. He hung the lantern on the nail and shut the door. They were in another world now. The light shed softly on the timbered barn, on the whitewashed walls, and the great heap of hay; instruments cast their shadows largely, a ladder rose to the dark arch of a loft. Outside there was the driving rain, inside, the softly illuminated stillness and calmness of the barn.

Holding the child on one arm, he set about preparing the food for the cows, filling a pan with chopped hay and brewer's grains and a little meal. The child, all wonder, watched what he did. A new being was created in her for the new conditions. Sometimes, a little spasm, eddying from the bygone storm of sobbing, shook her small body. Her eyes were wide and wondering, pathetic. She was silent, quite still.

In a sort of dream, his heart sunk to the bottom, leaving the surface of him still, quite still, he rose with the panful of food, carefully balancing the child on one arm, the pan in the other hand. The silky fringe of the shawl swayed softly, grains and hay trickled to the floor; he went along a dimly lit passage behind the mangers, where the horns of the cows pricked out of the obscurity. The child shrank, he balanced stiffly, rested the pan on the manger wall, and tipped out the food, half to this cow, half to the next. There was a noise of chains running, as the cows lifted or dropped their heads sharply; then a contented, soothing sound, a long snuffing as the beasts ate in silence.

The journey had to be performed several times. There was the rhythmic sound of the shovel in the barn, then the man returned walking stiffly between the two weights, the face of the child peering out from the shawl. Then the next time, as he stooped, she freed her arm and put it round his neck, clinging soft and warm, making all easier.

The beasts fed, he dropped the pan and sat down on a box, to arrange the child.

"Will the cows go to sleep now?" she said, catching her breath as she spoke.

"Yes."

"Will they eat all their stuff up first?"

"Yes. Hark at them."

And the two sat still listening to the snuffing and breathing of cows feeding in the sheds communicating with this small barn. The lantern shed a soft, steady light from one wall. All outside was still in the rain. He looked down at the silky folds of the paisley shawl. It reminded him of his mother. She used to go to church in it. He was back again in the old irresponsibility and security, a boy at home.

The two sat very quiet. His mind, in a sort of trance, seemed to become more and more vague. He held the child close to him. A quivering little shudder, re-echoing from her sobbing, went down her limbs. He held her closer. Gradually she relaxed, the eyelids began to sink over her dark, watchful eyes. As she sank to sleep, his mind became blank.

When he came to, as if from sleep, he seemed to be sitting in a timeless stillness. What was he listening for? He seemed to be listening for some sound a long way off, from beyond life. He remembered his wife. He must go back to her. The child was asleep, the eyelids not quite shut, showing a slight film of black pupil between. Why did she not shut her eyes? Her mouth was also a little open.

He rose quickly and went back to the house.

"Is she asleep?" whispered Tilly.

He nodded. The servant woman came to look at the child who slept in the shawl, with cheeks flushed hot and red, and a whiteness, a wanness round the eyes.

"God-a-mercy!" whispered Tilly, shaking her head.

He pushed off his boots and went upstairs with the child. He became aware of the anxiety grasped tight at his heart, because of his wife. But he remained still. The house was silent save for the wind outside, and the noisy trickling and splattering of water in the water butts. There was a slit of light under his wife's door.

He put the child into bed wrapped as she was in the shawl, for the sheets would be cold. Then he was afraid that she might not be able to move her arms, so he loosened her. The black eyes opened, rested on him vacantly, sank shut again. He covered her up. The last little quiver from the sobbing shook her breathing.

This was his room, the room he had had before he married. It was familiar. He remembered what it was to be a young man, untouched.

He remained suspended. The child slept, pushing her small fists from the shawl. He could tell the woman her child was asleep. But he must go to the other landing. He started. There was the sound of the owls—the moaning of the woman. What an uncanny sound! It was not human—at least to a man.

He went down to her room, entering softly. She was lying still, with eyes shut, pale, tired. His heart leapt, fearing she was dead. Yet he knew perfectly well she was not. He saw the way her hair went loose over her temples, her mouth was shut with suffering in a sort of grin. She was beautiful to him—but it was not human. He had a dread of her as she lay there. What had she to do with him? She was other than himself.

Something made him go and touch her fingers that were still grasped on the sheet. Her brown-gray eyes opened and looked at him. She did not know him as himself. But she knew him as the man. She looked at him as a woman in childbirth looks at the man who begot the child in her: an impersonal look, in the extreme hour, female to male. Her eyes closed again. A great, scalding peace went over him, burning his heart and his entrails, passing off into the infinite.

When her pains began afresh, tearing her, he turned aside, and could not look. But his heart in torture was at peace, his bowels were glad. He went downstairs, and to the door, outside, lifted his face to the rain, and felt the darkness striking unseen and steadily upon him.

The swift, unseen threshing of the night upon him silenced him and he was overcome. He turned away indoors, humbly. There was the infinite world, eternal, unchanging, as well as the world of life.

1912–14   1915

The Horse Dealer's Daughter

"Well, Mabel, and what are you going to do with yourself?" asked Joe, with foolish flippancy. He felt quite safe himself. Without listening for an answer, he turned aside, worked a grain of tobacco to the tip of his tongue, and spat it out. He did not care about anything, since he felt safe himself.

The three brothers and the sister sat round the desolate breakfast-table, attempting some sort of desultory consultation. The morning's post had given the final tap to the family fortunes, and all was over. The dreary dining-room itself, with its heavy mahogany furniture, looked as if it were waiting to be done away with.

But the consultation amounted to nothing. There was a strange air of ineffectuality about the three men, as they sprawled at table, smoking and reflecting vaguely on their own condition. The girl was alone, a rather short, sullen-looking young woman of twenty-seven. She did not share the same life as her brothers. She would have been good-looking, save for the impressive fixity of her face, "bull-dog," as her brothers called it.

There was a confused tramping of horses' feet outside. The three men all sprawled round in their chairs to watch. Beyond the dark holly bushes that separated the strip of lawn from the highroad, they could see a cavalcade of shire horses swinging out of their own yard, being taken for exercise. This was the last time. These were the last horses that would go through their hands. The young men watched with critical, callous look. They were all frightened at the collapse of their lives, and the sense of disaster in which they were involved left them no inner freedom.

Yet they were three fine, well-set fellows enough. Joe, the eldest, was a man of thirty-three, broad and handsome in a hot, flushed way. His face was red, he twisted his black moustache over a thick finger, his eyes were shallow and restless. He had a sensual way of uncovering his teeth when he laughed, and his bearing was stupid. Now he watched the horses with a glazed look of helplessness in his eyes, a certain stupor of downfall.

The great draught horses swung past. They were tied head to tail, four of them, and they heaved along to where a lane branched off from the highroad, planting their great hoofs floutingly in the fine black mud, swinging their great rounded haunches sumptuously, and trotting a few sudden steps as they were led into the lane, round the corner. Every movement showed a massive, slumbrous strength, and a stupidity which held them in subjection. The groom at the head looked back, jerking the leading rope. And the cavalcade moved out of sight up the lane, the tail of the last horse, bobbed up tight and stiff, held out taut from the swinging great haunches as they rocked behind the hedges in a motion-like sleep.

Joe watched with glazed hopeless eyes. The horses were almost like his own body to him. He felt he was done for now. Luckily he was engaged to a woman as old as himself, and therefore her father, who was steward of a neighboring estate, would provide him with a job. He would marry and go into harness. His life was over, he would be a subject animal now.

He turned uneasily aside, the retreating steps of the horses echoing in his ears. Then, with foolish restlessness, he reached for the scraps of bacon rind from the plates, and making a faint whistling sound, flung them to the terrier that lay against the fender. He watched the dog swallow them, and waited till the creature looked into his eyes. Then a faint grin came on his face, and in a high, foolish voice he said:

"You won't get much more bacon, shall you, you little b——?"

The dog faintly and dismally wagged its tail, then lowered its haunches, circled round, and lay down again.

There was another helpless silence at the table. Joe sprawled uneasily in his seat, not willing to go till the family conclave was dissolved. Fred Henry, the second brother, was erect, clean-limbed, alert. He had watched the passing of the horses with more *sang froid*. If he was an animal, like Joe, he was an animal which controls, not one which is controlled. He was master of any horse, and he carried himself with a well-tempered air of mastery. But he was not master of the situations of life. He pushed his coarse brown moustache upwards, off his lip, and glanced irritably at his sister, who sat impassive and inscrutable.

"You'll go and stop with Lucy for a bit, shan't you?" he asked. The girl did not answer.

"I don't see what else you can do," persisted Fred Henry.

"Go as a skivvy," [1] Joe interpolated laconically.

The girl did not move a muscle.

"If I was her, I should go in for training for a nurse," said Malcolm, the youngest of them all. He was the baby of the family, a young man of twenty-two, with a fresh, jaunty *museau*.[2]

But Mabel did not take any notice of him. They had talked at her and round her for so many years, that she hardly heard them at all.

The marble clock on the mantelpiece softly chimed the half-hour, the dog rose uneasily from the hearth-rug and looked at the party at the breakfast-table. But still they sat on an ineffectual conclave.

"Oh, all right," said Joe suddenly, apropos of nothing. "I'll get a move on."

He pushed back his chair, straddled his knees with a downward jerk, to get them free, in horsey fashion, and went to the fire. Still he did not go out of the room; he was curious to know what the

1. Servant girl.   2. Face (French slang).

others would do or say. He began to charge his pipe, looking down at the dog and saying in a high, affected voice:

"Going wi' me? Going wi' me are ter? Tha'rt goin' further than tha counts on just now, dost hear?"

The dog faintly wagged his tail, the man stuck out his jaw and covered his pipe with his hands, and puffed intently, losing himself in the tobacco, looking down all the while at the dog with an absent brown eye. The dog looked up at him in mournful distrust. Joe stood with his knees stuck out, in real horsey fashion.

"Have you had a letter from Lucy?" Fred Henry asked of his sister.

"Last week," came the neutral reply.

"And what does she say?"

There was no answer.

"Does she *ask* you to go and stop there?" persisted Fred Henry.

"She says I can if I like."

"Well, then, you'd better. Tell her you'll come on Monday."

This was received in silence.

"That's what you'll do then, is it?" said Fred Henry, in some exasperation.

But she made no answer. There was a silence of futility and irritation in the room. Malcolm grinned fatuously.

"You'll have to make up your mind between now and next Wednesday," said Joe loudly, "or else find yourself lodgings on the curbstone."

The face of the young woman darkened, but she sat on immutable.

"Here's Jack Ferguson!" exclaimed Malcolm, who was looking aimlessly out of the window.

"Where?" exclaimed Joe loudly.

"Just gone past."

"Coming in?"

Malcolm craned his neck to see the gate.

"Yes," he said.

There was a silence. Mabel sat on like one condemned, at the head of the table. Then a whistle was heard from the kitchen. The dog got up and barked sharply. Joe opened the door and shouted:

"Come on."

After a moment a young man entered. He was muffled up in overcoat and a purple woolen scarf, and his tweed cap, which he did not remove, was pulled down on his head. He was of medium height, his face was rather long and pale, his eyes looked tired.

"Hello, Jack! Well, Jack!" exclaimed Malcolm and Joe. Fred Henry merely said: "Jack."

"What's doing?" asked the newcomer, evidently addressing Fred Henry.

"Same. We've got to be out by Wednesday. Got a cold?"

"I have—got it bad, too."

"Why don't you stop in?"

"*Me* stop in? When I can't stand on my legs, perhaps I shall have a chance." The young man spoke huskily. He had a slight Scotch accent.

"It's a knockout, isn't it," said Joe, boisterously, "if a doctor goes round croaking with a cold. Looks bad for the patients, doesn't it?"

The young doctor looked at him slowly.

"Anything the matter with *you*, then?" he asked sarcastically.

"Not as I know of. Damn your eyes, I hope not. Why?"

"I thought you were very concerned about the patients, wondered if you might be one yourself."

"Damn it, no, I've never been patient to no flaming doctor, and hope I never shall be," returned Joe.

At this point Mabel rose from the table, and they all seemed to become aware of her existence. She began putting the dishes together. The young doctor looked at her, but did not address her. He had not greeted her. She went out of the room with the tray, her face impassive and unchanged.

"When are you off then, all of you?" asked the doctor.

"I'm catching the eleven-forty," replied Malcolm. "Are you goin' down wi' th' trap, Joe?"

"Yes, I've told you I'm going down wi' th' trap, haven't I?"

"We'd better be getting her in then. So long, Jack, if I don't see you before I go," said Malcolm, shaking hands.

He went out, followed by Joe, who seemed to have his tail between his legs.

"Well, this is the devil's own," exclaimed the doctor, when he was left alone with Fred Henry. "Going before Wednesday, are you?"

"That's the orders," replied the other.

"Where, to Northampton?"

"That's it."

"The devil!" exclaimed Ferguson, with quiet chagrin.

And there was silence between the two.

"All settled up, are you?" asked Ferguson.

"About."

There was another pause.

"Well, I shall miss yer, Freddy, boy," said the young doctor.

"And I shall miss thee, Jack," returned the other.

"Miss you like hell," mused the doctor.

Fred Henry turned aside. There was nothing to say. Mabel

came in again, to finish clearing the table.

"What are *you* going to do, then, Miss Pervin?" asked Ferguson. "Going to your sister's, are you?"

Mabel looked at him with her steady, dangerous eyes, that always made him uncomfortable, unsettling his superficial ease.

"No," she said.

"Well, what in the name of fortune *are* you going to do? Say what you mean to do," cried Fred Henry, with futile intensity.

But she only averted her head, and continued her work. She folded the white table cloth, and put on the chenille cloth.

"The sulkiest bitch that ever trod!" muttered her brother.

But she finished her task with perfectly impassive face, the young doctor watching her interestedly all the while. Then she went out.

Fred Henry stared after her, clenching his lips, his blue eyes fixing in sharp antagonism, as he made a grimace of sour exasperation.

"You could bray her into bits, and that's all you'd get out of her," he said, in a small, narrowed tone.

The doctor smiled faintly.

"What's she *going* to do, then?" he asked.

"Strike me if *I* know!" returned the other.

There was a pause. Then the doctor stirred.

"I'll be seeing you tonight, shall I?" he said to his friend.

"Ay—where's it to be? Are we going over to Jessdale?"

"I don't know. I've got such a cold on me. I'll come round to the Moon and Stars, anyway."

"Let Lizzie and May miss their night for once, eh?"

"That's it—if I feel as I do now."

"All's one————"

The two young men went through the passage and down to the back door together. The house was large, but it was servantless now, and desolate. At the back was a small bricked house yard and beyond that a big square, graveled fine and red, and having stables on two sides. Sloping, dank, winter-dark fields stretched away on the open sides.

But the stables were empty. Joseph Pervin, the father of the family, had been a man of no education, who had become a fairly large horse dealer. The stables had been full of horses, there was a great turmoil and come-and-go of horses and of dealers and grooms. Then the kitchen was full of servants. But of late things had declined. The old man had married a second time, to retrieve his fortunes. Now he was dead and everything was gone to the dogs, there was nothing but debt and threatening.

For months, Mabel had been servantless in the big house, keeping the home together in penury for her ineffectual brothers.

She had kept house for ten years. But previously it was with unstinted means. Then, however brutal and coarse everything was, the sense of money had kept her proud, confident. The men might be foul-mouthed, the women in the kitchen might have had reputations, her brothers might have illegitimate children. But so long as there was money, the girl felt herself established, and brutally proud, reserved.

No company came to the house, save dealers and coarse men. Mabel had no associates of her own sex, after her sister went away. But she did not mind. She went regularly to church, she attended to her father. And she lived in the memory of her mother, who had died when she was fourteen, and whom she had loved. She had loved her father, too, in a different way, depending upon him, and feeling secure in him, until at the age of fifty-four, he married again. And then she had set hard against him. Now he had died and left them all hopelessly in debt.

She had suffered badly during the period of poverty. Nothing, however, could shake the curious, sullen, animal pride that dominated each member of the family. Now, for Mabel, the end had come. Still she would not cast about her. She would follow her own way just the same. She would always hold the keys of her own situation. Mindless and persistent, she endured from day to day. Why should she think? Why should she answer anybody? It was enough that this was the end, and there was no way out. She need not pass any more darkly along the main street of the small town, avoiding every eye. She need not demean herself any more, going into the shops and buying the cheapest food. This was at an end. She thought of nobody, not even of herself. Mindless and persistent, she seemed in a sort of ecstasy to be coming nearer to her fulfilment, her own glorification, approaching her dead mother, who was glorified.

In the afternoon, she took a little bag, with shears and sponge and a small scrubbing-brush, and went out. It was a gray, wintry day, with saddened, dark green fields and an atmosphere blackened by the smoke of foundries not far off. She went quickly, darkly along the causeway, heeding nobody, through the town to the churchyard.

There she always felt secure, as if no one could see her, although as a matter of fact she was exposed to the stare of everyone who passed along under the churchyard wall. Nevertheless, once under the shadow of the great looming church, among the graves, she felt immune from the world, reserved within the thick churchyard wall as in another country.

Carefully she clipped the grass from the grave, and arranged the pinky-white, small chrysanthemums in the tin cross. When this was done, she took an empty jar from a neighboring grave, brought water, and carefully, most scrupulously sponged the marble head-stone and the coping-stone.

It gave her sincere satisfaction to do this. She felt in immediate contact with the world of her mother. She took minute pains, went through the park in a state bordering on pure happiness, as if in performing this task she came into a subtle, intimate con-nection with her mother. For the life she followed here in the world was far less real than the world of death she inherited from her mother.

The doctor's house was just by the church. Ferguson, being a mere hired assistant, was slave to the countryside. As he hurried now to attend to the out-patients in the surgery, glancing across the graveyard with his quick eye, he saw the girl at her task at the grave. She seemed so intent and remote, it was like looking into another world. Some mystical element was touched in him. He slowed down as he walked, watching her as if spellbound.

She lifted her eyes, feeling him looking. Their eyes met. And each looked again at once, each feeling, in some way, found out by the other. He lifted his cap and passed on down the road. There remained distinct in his consciousness, like a vision, the memory of her face, lifted from the tombstone in the churchyard, and looking at him with slow, large, portentous eyes. It *was* por-tentous, her face. It seemed to mesmerize him. There was a heavy power in her eyes which laid hold of his whole being, as if he had drunk some powerful drug. He had been feeling weak and done before. Now the life came back into him, he felt delivered from his own fretted, daily self.

He finished his duties at the surgery as quickly as might be, hastily filling up the bottles of the waiting people with cheap drugs. Then, in perpetual haste, he set off again to visit several cases in another part of his round, before tea-time. At all times he preferred to walk if he could, but particularly when he was not well. He fancied the motion restored him.

The afternoon was falling. It was gray, deadened, and wintry, with a slow, moist, heavy coldness sinking in and deadening all the faculties. But why should he think or notice? He hastily climbed the hill and turned across the dark green fields, following the black cinder-track. In the distance, across a shallow dip in the country, the small town was clustered like smouldering ash, a tower, a spire, a heap of low, raw, extinct houses. And on the nearest fringe of the town, sloping into the dip, was Oldmeadow, the Pervins' house. He could see the stables and the outbuildings distinctly, as they lay towards him on the slope. Well, he would not go there many more times! Another resource would be lost to him, another place gone: the only company he cared for in the alien, ugly little town he was losing. Nothing but work, drudgery, constant hastening from dwelling to dwelling among the colliers and the iron-workers. It wore him out, but at the same time he had a craving for it. It was a stimulant to him to be in the homes of the working people, moving, as it were, through the innermost body of their life. His nerves were excited and gratified. He could come so near, into the very lives of the rough, inarticulate, powerfully emotional men and women. He grumbled, he said he hated the hellish hole. But as a matter of fact it excited him, the contact with the rough, strongly-feeling people was a stimulant applied direct to his nerves.

Below Oldmeadow, in the green, shallow, soddened hollow of fields, lay a square, deep pond. Roving across the landscape, the doctor's quick eye detected a figure in black passing through the gate of the field, down towards the pond. He looked again. It would be Mabel Pervin. His mind suddenly became alive and attentive.

Why was she going down there? He pulled up on the path on the slope above, and stood staring. He could just make sure of the small black figure moving in the hollow of the failing day. He seemed to see her in the midst of such obscurity, that he was like a clairvoyant, seeing rather with the mind's eye than with ordinary sight. Yet he could see her positively enough, whilst he kept his eye attentive. He felt, if he looked away from her, in the thick, ugly falling dusk, he would lose her altogether.

He followed her minutely as she moved, direct and intent, like something transmitted rather than stirring in voluntary activity, straight down the field towards the pond. There she stood on the bank for a moment. She never raised her head. Then she waded slowly into the water.

He stood motionless as the small black figure walked slowly and deliberately towards the center of the pond, very slowly, gradually moving deeper into the motionless water, and still moving forward as the water got up to her breast. Then he could see her no more in the dusk of the dead afternoon.

"There!" he exclaimed. "Would you believe it?"

And he hastened straight down, running over the wet, soddened fields, pushing through the hedges, down into the depression of callous wintry obscurity. It took him several minutes to come to the pond. He stood on the bank, breathing heavily. He could see nothing. His eyes seemed to penetrate the dead water. Yes, perhaps that was the dark shadow of her black clothing beneath the surface of the water.

He slowly ventured into the pond. The bottom was deep, soft clay, he sank in, and the water clasped dead cold round his legs.

As he stirred he could smell the cold, rotten clay that fouled up into the water. It was objectionable in his lungs. Still, repelled and yet not heeding, he moved deeper into the pond. The cold water rose over his thighs, over his loins, upon his abdomen. The lower part of his body was all sunk in the hideous cold element. And the bottom was so deeply soft and uncertain, he was afraid of pitching with his mouth underneath. He could not swim, and was afraid.

He crouched a little, spreading his hands under the water and moving them round, trying to feel for her. The dead cold pond swayed upon his chest. He moved again, a little deeper, and again, with his hands underneath, he felt all around under the water. And he touched her clothing. But it evaded his fingers. He made a desperate effort to grasp it.

And so doing he lost his balance and went under, horribly, suffocating in the foul earthy water, struggling madly for a few moments. At last, after what seemed an eternity, he got his footing, rose again into the air and looked around. He gasped, and knew he was in the world. Then he looked at the water. She had risen near him. He grasped her clothing, and drawing her nearer, turned to take his way to land again.

He went very slowly, carefully, absorbed in the slow progress. He rose higher, climbing out of the pond. The water was now only about his legs; he was thankful, full of relief to be out of the clutches of the pond. He lifted her and staggered on to the bank, out of the horror of wet, gray clay.

He laid her down on the bank. She was quite unconscious and running with water. He made the water come from her mouth, he worked to restore her. He did not have to work very long before he could feel the breathing begin again in her; she was breathing naturally. He worked a little longer. He could feel her live beneath his hands; she was coming back. He wiped her face, wrapped her in his overcoat, looked round into the dim, dark gray world, then lifted her and staggered down the bank and across the fields.

It seemed an unthinkably long way, and his burden so heavy he felt he would never get to the house. But at last he was in the stable yard, and then in the house yard. He opened the door and went into the house. In the kitchen he laid her down on the hearthrug and called. The house was empty. But the fire was burning in the grate.

Then again he kneeled to attend to her. She was breathing regularly, her eyes were wide open and as if conscious, but there seemed something missing in her look. She was conscious in herself, but unconscious of her surroundings.

He ran upstairs, took blankets from a bed, and put them before the fire to warm. Then he removed her saturated, earthy-smelling clothing, rubbed her dry with a towel, and wrapped her naked in the blankets. Then he went into the dining room, to look for spirits. There was a little whisky. He drank a gulp himself, and put some into her mouth.

The effect was instantaneous. She looked full into his face, as if she had been seeing him for some time, and yet had only just become conscious of him.

"Dr. Ferguson?" she said.

"What?" he answered.

He was divesting himself of his coat, intending to find some dry clothing upstairs. He could not bear the smell of the dead, clayey water, and he was mortally afraid for his own health.

"What did I do?" she asked.

"Walked into the pond," he replied. He had begun to shudder like one sick, and could hardly attend to her. Her eyes remained full on him, he seemed to be going dark in his mind, looking back at her helplessly. The shuddering became quieter in him, his life came back to him, dark and unknowing, but strong again.

"Was I out of my mind?" she asked, while her eyes were fixed on him all the time.

"Maybe, for the moment," he replied. He felt quiet, because his strength had come back. The strange fretful strain had left him.

"Am I out of my mind now?" she asked.

"Are you?" he reflected a moment. "No," he answered truthfully. "I don't see that you are." He turned his face aside. He was afraid now, because he felt dazed, and felt dimly that her power was stronger than his, in this issue. And she continued to look at him fixedly all the time. "Can you tell me where I shall find some dry things to put on?" he asked.

"Did you dive into the pond for me?" she asked.

"No," he answered. "I walked in. But I went in overhead as well."

There was silence for a moment. He hesitated. He very much wanted to go upstairs to get into dry clothing. But there was another desire in him. And she seemed to hold him. His will seemed to have gone to sleep, and left him, standing there slack before her. But he felt warm inside himself. He did not shudder at all, though his clothes were sodden on him.

"Why did you?" she asked.

"Because I didn't want you to do such a foolish thing," he said.

"It wasn't foolish," she said, still gazing at him as she lay on the floor, with a sofa cushion under her head. "It was the right thing to do. *I* knew best, then."

"I'll go and shift these wet things," he said. But still he had not the power to move out of her presence, until she sent him. It was as if she had the life of his body in her hands, and he could not extricate himself. Or perhaps he did not want to.

Suddenly she sat up. Then she became aware of her own immediate condition. She felt the blankets about her, she knew her own limbs. For a moment it seemed as if her reason were going. She looked round, with wild eye, as if seeking something. He stood still with fear. She saw her clothing lying scattered.

"Who undressed me?" she asked, her eyes resting full and inevitable on his face.

"I did," he replied, "to bring you round."

For some moments she sat and gazed at him awfully, her lips parted.

"Do you love me, then?" she asked.

He only stood and stared at her, fascinated. His soul seemed to melt.

She shuffled forward on her knees, and put her arms round him, round his legs, as he stood there, pressing her breasts against his knees and thighs, clutching him with strange, convulsive certainty, pressing his thighs against her, drawing him to her face, her throat, as she looked up at him with flaring, humble eyes of transfiguration, triumphant in first possession.

"You love me," she murmured, in strange transport, yearning and triumphant and confident. "You love me. I know you love me, I know."

And she was passionately kissing his knees, through the wet clothing, passionately and indiscriminately kissing his knees, his legs, as if unaware of everything.

He looked down at the tangled wet hair, the wild, bare, animal shoulders. He was amazed, bewildered, and afraid. He had never thought of loving her. He had never wanted to love her. When he rescued her and restored her, he was a doctor, and she was a patient. He had had no single personal thought of her. Nay, this introduction of the personal element was very distasteful to him, a violation of his professional honor. It was horrible to have her there embracing his knees. It was horrible. He revolted from it, violently. And yet—and yet—he had not the power to break away.

She looked at him again, with the same supplication of powerful love, and that same transcendent, frightening light of triumph. In view of the delicate flame which seemed to come from her face like a light, he was powerless. And yet he had never intended to love her. He had never intended. And something stubborn in him could not give way.

"You love me," she repeated, in a murmur of deep, rhapsodic assurance. "You love me."

Her hands were drawing him, drawing him down to her. He was afraid, even a little horrified. For he had, really, no intention of loving her. Yet her hands were drawing him towards her. He put out his hand quickly to steady himself, and grasped her bare shoulder. A flame seemed to burn the hand that grasped her soft shoulder. He had no intention of loving her: his whole will was against his yielding. It was horrible. And yet wonderful was the touch of her shoulders, beautiful the shining of her face. Was she perhaps mad? He had a horror of yielding to her. Yet something in him ached also.

He had been staring away at the door, away from her. But his hand remained on her shoulder. She had gone suddenly very still. He looked down at her. Her eyes were now wide with fear, with doubt, the light was dying from her face, a shadow of terrible grayness was returning. He could not bear the touch of her eyes' question upon him, and the look of death behind the question.

With an inward groan he gave way, and let his heart yield towards her. A sudden gentle smile came on his face. And her eyes, which never left his face, slowly, slowly filled with tears. He watched the strange water rise in her eyes, like some slow fountain coming up. And his heart seemed to burn and melt away in his breast.

He could not bear to look at her any more. He dropped on his knees and caught her head with his arms and pressed her face against his throat. She was very still. His heart, which seemed to have broken, was burning with a kind of agony in his breast. And he felt her slow, hot tears wetting his throat. But he could not move.

He felt the hot tears wet his neck and the hollows of his neck, and he remained motionless, suspended through one of man's eternities. Only now it had become indispensable to him to have her face pressed close to him; he could never let her go again. He could never let her head go away from the close clutch of his arm. He wanted to remain like that for ever, with his heart hurting him in a pain that was also life to him. Without knowing, he was looking down on her damp, soft brown hair.

Then, as it were suddenly, he smelt the horrid stagnant smell of that water. And at the same moment she drew away from him and looked at him. Her eyes were wistful and unfathomable. He was afraid of them, and he fell to kissing her, not knowing what he was doing. He wanted her eyes not to have that terrible, wistful, unfathomable look.

When she turned her face to him again, a faint delicate flush was glowing, and there was again dawning that terrible shining of joy in her eyes, which really terrified him, and yet which he now wanted to see, because he feared the look of doubt still more.

"You love me?" she said, rather faltering.

"Yes." The word cost him a painful effort. Not because it wasn't true. But because it was too newly true, the *saying* seemed to tear open again his newly torn heart. And he hardly wanted it to be true, even now.

She lifted her face to him, and he bent forward and kissed her on the mouth, gently, with the one kiss that is an eternal pledge. And as he kissed her his heart strained again in his breast. He never intended to love her. But now it was over. He had crossed over the gulf to her, and all that he had left behind had shriveled and become void.

After the kiss, her eyes again slowly filled with tears. She sat still, away from him, with her face drooped aside, and her hands folded in her lap. The tears fell very slowly. There was complete silence. He too sat there motionless and silent on the hearth rug. The strange pain of his heart that was broken seemed to consume him. That he should love her? That this was love! That he should be ripped open in this way! Him, a doctor! How they would all jeer if they knew! It was agony to him to think they might know.

In the curious naked pain of the thought he looked again to her. She was sitting there drooped into a muse. He saw a tear fall, and his heart flared hot. He saw for the first time that one of her shoulders was quite uncovered, one arm bare, he could see one of her small breasts; dimly, because it had become almost dark in the room.

"Why are you crying?" he asked, in an altered voice.

She looked up at him, and behind her tears the consciousness of her situation for the first time brought a dark look of shame to her eyes.

"I'm not crying, really," she said, watching him, half frightened.

He reached his hand, and softly closed it on her bare arm.

"I love you! I love you!" he said in a soft, low vibrating voice, unlike himself.

She shrank, and dropped her head. The soft, penetrating grip of his hand on her arm distressed her. She looked up at him.

"I want to go," she said. "I want to go and get you some dry things."

"Why?" he said. "I'm all right."

"But I want to go," she said. "And I want you to change your things."

He released her arm, and she wrapped herself in the blanket, looking at him, rather frightened. And still she did not rise.

"Kiss me," she said wistfully.

He kissed her, but briefly, half in anger.

Then, after a second, she rose nervously, all mixed up in the blanket. He watched her in her confusion as she tried to extricate herself and wrap herself up so that she could walk. He watched her relentlessly, as she knew. And as she went, the blanket trailing, and as he saw a glimpse of her feet and her white leg, he tried to remember her as she was when he had wrapped her in the blanket. But then he didn't want to remember, because she had been nothing to him then, and his nature revolted from remembering her as she was when she was nothing to him.

A tumbling muffled noise from within the dark house startled him. Then he heard her voice: "There are clothes." He rose and went to the foot of the stairs, and gathered up the garments she had thrown down. Then he came back to the fire, to rub himself down and dress. He grinned at his own appearance when he had finished.

The fire was sinking, so he put on coal. The house was now quite dark, save for the light of a street-lamp that shone in faintly from beyond the holly trees. He lit the gas with matches he found on the mantelpiece. Then he emptied the pockets of his own clothes, and threw all his wet things in a heap into the scullery. After which he gathered up her sodden clothes, gently, and put them in a separate heap on the copper-top in the scullery.

It was six o'clock on the clock. His own watch had stopped. He ought to go back to the surgery. He waited, and still she did not come down. So he went to the foot of the stairs and called: "I shall have to go."

Almost immediately he heard her coming down. She had on her best dress of black voile, and her hair was tidy, but still damp. She looked at him—and in spite of herself, smiled.

"I don't like you in those clothes," she said.

"Do I look a sight?" he answered.

They were shy of one another.

"I'll make you some tea," she said.

"No, I must go."

"Must you?" And she looked at him again with the wide, strained, doubtful eyes. And again, from the pain of his breast, he knew how he loved her. He went and bent to kiss her, gently, passionately, with his heart's painful kiss.

"And my hair smells so horrible," she murmured in distraction. "And I'm so awful, I'm so awful! Oh no, I'm too awful." And she broke into bitter, heart-broken sobbing. "You can't want to love me, I'm horrible."

"Don't be silly, don't be silly," he said, trying to comfort her, kissing her, holding her in his arms. "I want you, I want to marry you, we're going to be married, quickly, quickly—tomorrow if I can."

But she only sobbed terribly, and cried:

"I feel awful. I feel awful. I feel I'm horrible to you."

"No, I want you, I want you," was all he answered, blindly, with that terrible intonation which frightened her almost more than her horror lest he should *not* want her.

1922

The Fox

The two girls were usually known by their surnames, Banford and March. They had taken the farm together, intending to work it all by themselves: that is, they were going to rear chickens, make a living by poultry, and add to this by keeping a cow, and raising one or two young beasts. Unfortunately, things did not turn out well.

Banford was a small, thin, delicate thing with spectacles. She, however, was the principal investor, for March had little or no money. Banford's father, who was a tradesman in Islington, gave his daughter the start, for her health's sake, and because he loved her, and because it did not look as if she would marry. March was more robust. She had learned carpentry and joinery at the evening classes in Islington. She would be the man about the place. They had, moreover, Banford's old grandfather living with them at the start. He had been a farmer. But unfortunately the old man died after he had been at Bailey Farm for a year. Then the two girls were left alone.

They were neither of them young: that is, they were near thirty. But they certainly were not old. They set out quite gallantly with their enterprise. They had numbers of chickens, black Leghorns and white Leghorns, Plymouths and Wyandottes; also some ducks; also two heifers in the fields. One heifer, unfortunately, refused absolutely to stay in the Bailey Farm closes. No matter how March made up the fences, the heifer was out, wild in the woods, or trespassing on the neighboring pasture, and March and Banford were away, flying after her, with more haste than success. So this heifer they sold in despair. Then, just before the other beast was expecting her first calf, the old man died, and the girls, afraid of the coming event, sold her in a panic, and limited their attentions to fowls and ducks.

In spite of a little chagrin, it was a relief to have no more cattle on hand. Life was not made merely to be slaved away. Both girls agreed in this. The fowls were quite enough trouble. March had set up her carpenter's bench at the end of the open shed. Here she worked, making coops and doors and other appurtenances. The fowls were housed in the bigger building, which had served as barn and cow-shed in old days. They had a beautiful home, and should have been perfectly content. Indeed, they looked well enough. But the girls were disgusted at their tendency to strange illnesses, at their exacting way of life, and at their refusal, obstinate refusal to lay eggs.

March did most of the outdoor work. When she was out and about, in her puttees[1] and breeches, her belted coat and her loose cap, she looked almost like some graceful, loose-balanced young man, for her shoulders were straight, and her movements easy and confident, even tinged with a little indifference or irony. But her face was not a man's face, ever. The wisps of her crisp dark hair blew about her as she stooped, her eyes were big and wide and dark, when she looked up again, strange, startled, shy and sardonic at once. Her mouth, too, was almost pinched as if in pain and irony. There was something odd and unexplained about her. She would stand balanced on one hip, looking at the fowls pattering about in the obnoxious fine mud of the sloping yard, and calling to her favorite white hen, which came in answer to her name. But there was an almost satirical flicker in March's big, dark eyes as she looked at her three-toed flock pottering about under her gaze, and the same slight dangerous satire in her voice as she spoke to the favored Patty, who pecked at March's boot by way of friendly demonstration.

Fowls did not flourish at Bailey Farm, in spite of all that March did for them. When she provided hot food for them in the morning, according to rule, she noticed that it made them heavy and dozy for hours. She expected to see them lean against the pillars of the shed in their languid processes of digestion. And she knew quite well that they ought to be busily scratching and foraging about, if they were to come to any good. So she decided to give them their hot food at night, and let them sleep on it. Which she did. But it made no difference.

War conditions,[2] again, were very unfavorable to poultry-keeping. Food was scarce and bad. And when the Daylight Saving Bill was passed, the fowls obstinately refused to go to bed as usual, about nine o'clock in the summertime. That was late enough, indeed, for there was no peace till they were shut up and asleep. Now they cheerfully walked around, without so much as glancing at the barn, until ten o'clock or later. Both Banford and March disbelieved in living for work alone. They wanted to read or take a cycle-ride in the evening, or perhaps March wished to paint curvilinear swans on porcelain, with green background, or else make a marvelous fire-

1. Leather or heavy cloth covering extending from the ankle to the knee.   2. I.e., World War I.

screen by processes of elaborate cabinet work. For she was a creature of odd whims and unsatisfied tendencies. But from all these things she was prevented by the stupid fowls.

One evil there was greater than any other. Bailey Farm was a little homestead, with ancient wooden barn and low-gabled farmhouse, lying just one field removed from the edge of the wood. Since the war the fox was a demon. He carried off the hens under the very noses of March and Banford. Banford would start and stare through her big spectacles with all her eyes, as another squawk and flutter took place at her heels. Too late! Another white Leghorn gone. It was disheartening.

They did what they could to remedy it. When it became permitted to shoot foxes, they stood sentinel with their guns, the two of them, at the favored hours. But it was no good. The fox was too quick for them. So another year passed, and another, and they were living on their losses, as Banford said. They let their farmhouse one summer, and retired to live in a railway-carriage that was deposited as a sort of outhouse in a corner of the field. This amused them, and helped their finances. None the less, things looked dark.

Although they were usually the best of friends, because Banford, though nervous and delicate, was a warm, generous soul, and March, though so odd and absent in herself, had a strange magnanimity, yet, in the long solitude, they were apt to become a little irritable with one another, tired of one another. March had four-fifths of the work to do, and though she did not mind, there seemed no relief, and it made her eyes flash curiously sometimes. Then Banford, feeling more nerve-worn than ever, would become despondent, and March would speak sharply to her. They seemed to be losing ground, somehow, losing hope as the months went by. There alone in the fields by the wood, with the wide country stretching hollow and dim to the round hills of the White Horse, in the far distance, they seemed to have to live too much off themselves. There was nothing to keep them up—and no hope.

The fox really exasperated them both. As soon as they had let the fowls out, in the early summer mornings, they had to take their guns and keep guard: and then again as soon as evening began to mellow, they must go once more. And he was so sly. He slid along in the deep grass; he was difficult as a serpent to see. And he seemed to circumvent the girls deliberately. Once or twice March had caught sight of the white tip of his brush, or the ruddy shadow of him in the deep grass, and she had let fire at him. But he made no account of this.

One evening March was standing with her back to the sunset, her gun under her arm, her hair pushed under her cap. She was half watching, half musing. It was her constant state. Her eyes were keen and observant, but her inner mind took no notice of what she saw. She was always lapsing into this odd rapt state, her mouth rather screwed up. It was a question whether she was there, actually consciously present, or not.

The trees on the wood-edge were a darkish, brownish green in the full light—for it was the end of August. Beyond, the naked, copper-like shafts and limbs of the pine trees shone in the air. Nearer the rough grass, with its long, brownish stalks all agleam, was full of light. The fowls were round about—the ducks were still swimming on the pond under the pine trees. March looked at it all, saw it all, and did not see it. She heard Banford speaking to the fowls in the distance—and she did not hear. What was she thinking about? Heaven knows. Her consciousness was, as it were, held back.

She lowered her eyes, and suddenly saw the fox. He was looking up at her. His chin was pressed down, and his eyes were looking up. They met her eyes. And he knew her. She was spellbound—she knew he knew her. So he looked into her eyes, and her soul failed her. He knew her, he was not daunted.

She struggled, confusedly she came to herself, and saw him making off, with slow leaps over some fallen boughs, slow, impudent jumps. Then he glanced over his shoulder, and ran smoothly away. She saw his brush held smooth like a feather, she saw his white buttocks twinkle. And he was gone, softly, soft as the wind.

She put her gun to her shoulder, but even then pursed her mouth, knowing it was nonsense to pretend to fire. So she began to walk slowly after him, in the direction he had gone, slowly, pertinaciously. She expected to find him. In her heart she was determined to find him. What she would do when she saw him again she did not consider. But she was determined to find him. So she walked abstractedly about on the edge of the wood, with wide, vivid dark eyes, and a faint flush in her cheeks. She did not think. In strange mindlessness she walked hither and thither.

At last she became aware that Banford was calling her. She made an effort of attention, turned, and gave some sort of screaming call in answer. Then again she was striding off towards the homestead. The red sun was setting, the fowls were retiring towards their roost. She watched them, white creatures, black creatures, gathering to the barn. She watched them spellbound, without seeing them. But her automatic intelligence told her when it was time to shut the door.

She went indoors to supper, which Banford had set on the table. Banford chatted easily. March seemed to listen, in her distant, manly way. She answered a brief word now and then. But all the time she was as if spellbound. And as soon as supper was over, she rose again to go out, without saying why.

She took her gun again and went to look for the fox. For he had lifted his eyes upon her, and his knowing look seemed to have entered her brain. She did not so much think of him: she was possessed by him. She saw his dark, shrewd, unabashed eye looking into her, knowing her. She felt him invisibly master her spirit. She knew the way he lowered his chin as he looked up, she knew his muzzle, the golden brown, and the grayish white. And again she saw him glance over his shoulder at her, half inviting, half contemptuous and cunning. So she went, with her great startled eyes glowing, her gun under her arm, along the wood edge. Meanwhile the night fell, and a great moon rose above the pine trees. And again Banford was calling.

So she went indoors. She was silent and busy. She examined her gun, and cleaned it, musing abstractedly by the lamp-light. Then she went out again, under the great moon, to see if everything was right. When she saw the dark crests of the pine trees against the blood-red sky, again her heart beat to the fox, the fox. She wanted to follow him, with her gun.

It was some days before she mentioned the affair to Banford. Then suddenly one evening she said:

"The fox was right at my feet on Saturday night."

"Where?" said Banford, her eyes opening behind her spectacles.

"When I stood just above the pond."

"Did you fire?" cried Banford.

"No, I didn't."

"Why not?"

"Why, I was too much surprised, I suppose."

It was the same old, slow, laconic way of speech March always had. Banford stared at her friend for a few moments.

"You saw him?" she cried.

"Oh yes! He was looking up at me, cool as anything."

"I tell you," cried Banford—"the cheek! They're not afraid of us, Nellie."

"Oh no," said March.

"Pity you didn't get a shot at him," said Banford.

"Isn't it a pity! I've been looking for him ever since. But I don't suppose he'll come so near again."

"I don't suppose he will," said Banford.

And she proceeded to forget about it, except that she was more indignant than ever at the impudence of the beggar. March also was not conscious that she thought of the fox. But whenever she fell into her half-musing, when she was half rapt and half intelligently aware of what passed under her vision, then it was the fox which somehow dominated her unconsciousness, possessed the blank half of her musing. And so it was for weeks, and months. No matter whether she had been climbing the trees for the apples, or beating down the last of the damsons, or whether she had been digging out the ditch from the duck-pond, or clearing out the barn, when she had finished, or when she straightened herself, and pushed the wisps of hair away again from her forehead, and pursed up her mouth again in an odd, screwed fashion, much too old for her years, there was sure to come over her mind the old spell of the fox, as it came when he was looking at her. It was as if she could smell him at these times. And it always recurred, at unexpected moments, just as she was going to sleep at night, or just as she was pouring the water into the teapot to make tea—it was the fox, it came over her like a spell.

So the months passed. She still looked for him unconsciously when she went towards the wood. He had become a settled effect in her spirit, a state permanently established, not continuous, but always recurring. She did not know what she felt or thought: only the state came over her, as when he looked at her.

The months passed, the dark evenings came, heavy, dark November, when March went about in high boots, ankle deep in mud, when the night began to fall at four o'clock, and the day never properly dawned. Both girls dreaded these times. They dreaded the almost continuous darkness that enveloped them on their desolate little farm near the wood. Banford was physically afraid. She was afraid of tramps, afraid lest someone should come prowling around. March was not so much afraid as uncomfortable, and disturbed. She felt discomfort and gloom in all her physique.

Usually the two girls had tea in the sitting-room. March lighted a fire at dusk, and put on the wood she had chopped and sawed during the day. Then the long evening was in front, dark, sodden, black outside, lonely and rather oppressive inside, a little dismal. March was content not to talk, but Banford could not keep still. Merely listening to the wind in the pines outside, or the drip of water, was too much for her.

One evening the girls had washed up the teacups in the kitchen, and March had put on her house-shoes, and taken up a roll of crochet-work, which she worked at slowly from time to time. So she lapsed into silence. Banford stared at the red fire, which, being of wood, needed constant attention. She was afraid to begin to read too early, because her eyes would not bear any strain. So she sat staring at the fire, listening to the distant sounds, sound of cattle lowing, of a dull, heavy moist wind, of the rattle of the evening train on the little railway not far off. She was almost fascinated by the red glow of the fire.

Suddenly both girls started, and lifted their heads. They heard a footstep—distinctly a footstep. Banford recoiled in fear. March stood listening. Then rapidly she approached the door that led into the kitchen. At the same time they heard the footsteps approach the back door. They waited a second. The back door opened softly. Banford gave a loud cry. A man's voice said softly:

"Hello!"

March recoiled, and took a gun from a corner.

"What do you want?" she cried, in a sharp voice.

Again the soft, softly-vibrating man's voice said:

"Hello! What's wrong?"

"I shall shoot!" cried March. "What do you want?"

"Why, what's wrong? What's wrong?" came the soft, wondering, rather scared voice: and a young soldier, with his heavy kit on his back, advanced into the dim light.

"Why," he said, "who lives here then?"

"We live here," said March. "What do you want?"

"Oh!" came the long, melodious, wonder-note from the young soldier. "Doesn't William Grenfel live here then?"

"No—you know he doesn't."

"Do I? Do I? I don't, you see. He *did* live here, because he was my grandfather, and I lived here myself five years ago. What's become of him then?"

The young man—or youth, for he would not be more than twenty—now advanced and stood in the inner doorway. March, already under the influence of his strange, soft, modulated voice, stared at him spellbound. He had a ruddy, roundish face, with fairish hair, rather long, flattened to his forehead with sweat. His eyes were blue, and very bright and sharp. On his cheeks, on the fresh ruddy skin were fine, fair hairs, like a down, but sharper. It gave him a slightly glistening look. Having his heavy sack on his shoulders, he stooped, thrusting his head forward. His hat was loose in one hand. He stared brightly, very keenly from girl to girl, particularly at March, who stood pale, with great dilated eyes, in her belted coat and puttees, her hair knotted in a big crisp knot behind. She still had the gun in her hand. Behind her, Banford, clinging to the sofa-arm, was shrinking away, with half-averted head.

"I thought my grandfather still lived here? I wonder if he's dead."

"We've been here for three years," said Banford, who was beginning to recover her wits, seeing something boyish in the round head with its rather long, sweaty hair.

"Three years! You don't say so! And you don't know who was here before you?"

"I know it was an old man, who lived by himself."

"Ay! Yes, that's him! And what became of him then?"

"He died. I know he died."

"Ay! He's dead then!"

The youth stared at them without changing color or expression.

If he had any expression, besides a slight baffled look of wonder, it was one of sharp curiosity concerning the two girls; sharp, impersonal curiosity, the curiosity of that round young head.

But to March he was the fox. Whether it was the thrusting forward of his head, or the glisten of fine whitish hairs on the ruddy cheekbones, or the bright, keen eyes, that can never be said: but the boy was to her the fox, and she could not see him otherwise.

"How is it you didn't know if your grandfather was alive or dead?" asked Banford, recovering her natural sharpness.

"Ay, that's it," replied the softly-breathing youth. "You see, I joined up in Canada, and I hadn't heard for three or four years. I ran away to Canada."

"And now have you just come from France?"

"Well—from Salonika really."

There was a pause, nobody knowing quite what to say.

"So you've nowhere to go now?" said Banford rather lamely.

"Oh, I know some people in the village. Anyhow, I can go to the 'Swan.'"

"You came on the train, I suppose. Would you like to sit down a bit?"

"Well—I don't mind."

He gave an odd little groan as he swung off his kit. Banford looked at March.

"Put the gun down," she said. "We'll make a cup of tea."

"Ay," said the youth. "We've seen enough of rifles."

He sat down rather tired on the sofa, leaning forward.

March recovered her presence of mind, and went into the kitchen. There she heard the soft young voice musing:

"Well, to think I should come back and find it like this!" He did not seem sad, not at all—only rather interestedly surprised.

"And what a difference in the place, eh?" he continued, looking round the room.

"You see a difference, do you?" said Banford.

"Yes—don't I!"

His eyes were unnaturally clear and bright, though it was the brightness of abundant health.

March was busy in the kitchen preparing another meal. It was about seven o'clock. All the time, while she was active, she was attending to the youth in the sitting-room, not so much listening to what he said as feeling the soft run of his voice. She primmed up her mouth tighter and tighter, puckering it as if it were sewed, in her effort to keep her will uppermost. Yet her large eyes dilated and glowed in spite of her; she lost herself. Rapidly and carelessly she prepared the meal, cutting large chunks of bread and margarine—for there was no butter. She racked her brain to think of something

2096 · D. H. Lawrence

else to put on the tray—she had only bread, margarine, and jam, and the larder was bare. Unable to conjure anything up, she went into the sitting-room with her tray.

She did not want to be noticed. Above all, she did not want him to look at her. But when she came in, and was busy setting the table just behind him, he pulled himself up from his sprawling, and turned and looked over his shoulder. She became pale and wan.

The youth watched her as she bent over the table, looked at her slim, well-shapen legs, at the belted coat dropping around her thighs, at the knot of dark hair, and his curiosity, vivid and widely alert, was again arrested by her.

The lamp was shaded with a dark-green shade, so that the light was thrown downwards and the upper half of the room was dim. His face moved bright under the light, but March loomed shadowy in the distance.

She turned round, but kept her eyes sideways, dropping and lifting her dark lashes. Her mouth unpuckered as she said to Banford:

"Will you pour out?"

Then she went into the kitchen again.

"Have your tea where you are, will you?" said Banford to the youth—"unless you'd rather come to the table."

"Well," said he, "I'm nice and comfortable here, aren't I? I will have it here, if you don't mind."

"There's nothing but bread and jam," she said. And she put his plate on a stool by him. She was very happy now, waiting on him. For she loved company. And now she was no more afraid of him than if he were her own younger brother. He was such a boy.

"Nellie," she called. "I've poured you a cup out."

March appeared in the doorway, took her cup, and sat down in a corner, as far from the light as possible. She was very sensitive in her knees. Having no skirts to cover them, and being forced to sit with them boldly exposed, she suffered. She shrank and shrank, trying not to be seen. And the youth, sprawling low on the couch, glanced up at her, with long, steady, penetrating looks, till she was almost ready to disappear. Yet she held her cup balanced, she drank her tea, screwed up her mouth and held her head averted. Her desire to be invisible was so strong that it quite baffled the youth. He felt he could not see her distinctly. She seemed like a shadow within the shadow. And ever his eyes came back to her, searching, unremitting, with unconscious fixed attention.

Meanwhile he was talking softly and smoothly to Banford, who loved nothing so much as gossip, and who was full of perky interest, like a bird. Also he ate largely and quickly and voraciously, so that March had to cut more chunks of bread and margarine, for the roughness of which Banford apologized.

"Oh, well," said March, suddenly speaking, "if there's no butter to put on it, it's no good trying to make dainty pieces."

Again the youth watched her, and he laughed, with a sudden, quick laugh, showing his teeth and wrinkling his nose.

"It isn't, is it," he answered in his soft, near voice.

It appeared he was Cornish by birth and upbringing. When he was twelve years old he had come to Bailey Farm with his grandfather, with whom he had never agreed very well. So he had run away to Canada, and worked far away in the West. Now he was here—and that was the end of it.

He was very curious about the girls, to find out exactly what they were doing. His questions were those of a farm youth; acute, practical, a little mocking. He was very much amused by their attitude to their losses: for they were amusing on the score of heifers and fowls.

"Oh, well," broke in March, "we don't believe in living for nothing but work."

"Don't you?" he answered. And again the quick young laugh came over his face. He kept his eyes steadily on the obscure woman in the corner.

"But what will you do when you've used up all your capital?" he said.

"Oh, I don't know," answered March laconically. "Hire ourselves out for land-workers, I suppose."

"Yes, but there won't be any demand for women land-workers now the war's over," said the youth.

"Oh, we'll see. We shall hold on a bit longer yet," said March, with a plangent, half-sad, half-ironical indifference.

"There wants a man about the place," said the youth softly.

Banford burst out laughing.

"Take care what you say," she interrupted. "We consider ourselves quite efficient."

"Oh," came March's slow plangent voice, "it isn't a case of efficiency, I'm afraid. If you're going to do farming you must be at it from morning till night, and you might as well be a beast yourself."

"Yes, that's it," said the youth. "You aren't willing to put yourselves into it."

"We aren't," said March, "and we know it."

"We want some of our time for ourselves," said Banford.

The youth threw himself back on the sofa, his face tight with laughter, and laughed silently but thoroughly. The calm scorn of the girls tickled him tremendously.

"Yes," he said, "but why did you begin then?"

"Oh," said March, "we had a better opinion of the nature of fowls then than we have now."

"Of Nature altogether, I'm afraid," said Banford. "Don't talk to me about Nature."

Again the face of the youth tightened with delighted laughter.

"You haven't a very high opinion of fowls and cattle, have you?" he said.

"Oh no—quite a low one," said March.

He laughed out.

"Neither fowls nor heifers," said Banford, "nor goats nor the weather."

The youth broke into a sharp yap of laughter, delighted. The girls began to laugh too, March turning aside her face and wrinkling her mouth in amusement.

"Oh, well," said Banford, "we don't mind, do we, Nellie?"

"No," said March, "we don't mind."

The youth was very pleased. He had eaten and drunk his fill. Banford began to question him. His name was Henry Grenfel—no, he was not called Harry, always Henry. He continued to answer with courteous simplicity, grave and charming. March, who was not included, cast long, slow glances at him from her recess, as he sat there on the sofa, his hands clasping his knees, his face under the lamp bright and alert, turned to Banford. She became almost peaceful at last. He was identified with the fox—and he was here in full presence. She need not go after him any more. There in the shadow of her corner she gave herself up to a warm, relaxed peace, almost like sleep, accepting the spell that was on her. But she wished to remain hidden. She was only fully at peace whilst he forgot her, talking to Banford. Hidden in the shadow of the corner, she need not any more be divided in herself, trying to keep up two planes of consciousness. She could at last lapse into the odor of the fox.

For the youth, sitting before the fire in his uniform, sent a faint but distinct odor into the room, indefinable, but something like a wild creature. March no longer tried to reserve herself from it. She was still and soft in her corner like a passive creature in its cave.

At last the talk dwindled. The youth relaxed his clasp of his knees, pulled himself together a little, and looked round. Again he became aware of the silent, half-invisible woman in the corner.

"Well," he said unwillingly, "I suppose I'd better be going, or they'll be in bed at the 'Swan.'"

"I'm afraid they're in bed, anyhow," said Banford. "They've all got this influenza."

"Have they!" he exclaimed. And he pondered. "Well," he continued, "I shall find a place somewhere."

"I'd say you could stay here, only——" Banford began.

He turned and watched her, holding his head forward.

"What?" he asked.

"Oh, well," she said, "propriety, I suppose." She was rather confused.

"It wouldn't be improper, would it?" he said, gently surprised.

"Not as far as we're concerned," said Banford.

"And not as far as *I'm* concerned," he said, with grave naiveté. "After all, it's my own home, in a way."

Banford smiled at this.

"It's what the village will have to say," she said.

There was a moment's blank pause.

"What do you say, Nellie?" asked Banford.

"I don't mind, said March, in her distinct tone. "The village doesn't matter to me, anyhow."

"No," said the youth, quick and soft. "Why should it? I mean, what should they say?"

"Oh, well," came March's plangent, laconic voice, "they'll easily find something to say. But it makes no difference what they say. We can look after ourselves."

"Of course you can," said the youth.

"Well then, stop *if* you like," said Banford. "The spare room is quite ready."

His face shone with pleasure.

"If you're quite sure it isn't troubling you too much," he said, with that soft courtesy which distinguished him.

"Oh, it's no trouble," they both said.

He looked, smiling with delight, from one to another.

"It's awfully nice not to have to turn out again, isn't it?" he said gratefully.

"I suppose it is," said Banford.

March disappeared to attend to the room. Banford was as pleased and thoughtful as if she had her own young brother home from France. It gave her just the same kind of gratification to attend on him, to get out the bath for him, and everything. Her natural warmth and kindliness had now an outlet. And the youth luxuriated in her sisterly attention. But it puzzled him slightly to know that March was silently working for him too. She was so curiously silent and obliterated. It seemed to him he had not really seen her. He felt he should not know her if he met her in the road.

That night March dreamed vividly. She dreamed she heard a singing outside which she could not understand, a singing that roamed round the house, in the fields, and in the darkness. It moved her so that she felt she must weep. She went out and suddenly she knew it was the fox singing. He was very yellow and bright, like corn. She went nearer to him, but he ran away and ceased singing. He seemed near, and she wanted to touch him. She stretched out her hand, but suddenly he bit her wrist, and at the same instant, as she drew back, the fox, turning round to bound away, whisked his brush across her face, and it seemed his brush was on fire, for it seared and burned her mouth with a great pain. She awoke with the pain of it, and lay trembling as if she were really seared.

In the morning, however, she only remembered it as a distant memory. She arose and was busy preparing the house and attending to the fowls. Banford flew into the village on her bicycle to try and buy food. She was a hospitable soul. But alas, in the year 1918 there was not much food to buy.

The youth came downstairs in his shirt-sleeves. He was young and fresh, but he walked with his head thrust forward, so that his shoulders seemed raised and rounded, as if he had a slight curvature of the spine. It must have been only a manner of bearing himself, for he was young and vigorous. He washed himself and went outside, whilst the women were preparing breakfast.

He saw everything, and examined everything. His curiosity was quick and insatiable. He compared the state of things with that which he remembered before, and cast over in his mind the effect of the changes. He watched the fowls and the ducks, to see their condition; he noticed the flight of wood-pigeons overhead: they were very numerous; he saw the few apples high up, which March had not been able to reach; he remarked that they had borrowed a draw-pump, presumably to empty the big soft-water cistern which was on the north side of the house.

"It's a funny, dilapidated old place," he said to the girls, as he sat at breakfast.

His eyes were wise and childish, with thinking about things. He did not say much, but ate largely. March kept her face averted. She, too, in the early morning could not be aware of him, though something about the glint of his khaki reminded her of the brilliance of her dream-fox.

During the day the girls went about their business. In the morning he attended to the guns, shot a rabbit and a wild duck that was flying high towards the woods. That was a great addition to the empty larder. The girls felt that already he had earned his keep. He said nothing about leaving, however. In the afternoon he went to the village. He came back at tea-time. He had the same alert, forward-reaching look on his roundish face. He hung his hat on a peg with a little swinging gesture. He was thinking about something.

"Well," he said the girls, as he sat at table. "What am I going to do?"

"How do you mean—what are you going to do?" said Banford.

"Where am I going to find a place in the village to stay?" he said.

"I don't know," said Banford. "Where do you think of staying?"

"Well"—he hesitated—"at the 'Swan' they've got this 'flu, and at the 'Plough and Harrow' they've got the soldiers who are collecting the hay for the army: besides, in the private houses, there's ten men and a corporal altogether billeted in the village, they tell me. I'm not sure where I could get a bed."

He left the matter to them. He was rather calm about it. March sat with her elbows on the table, her two hands supporting her chin, looking at him unconsciously. Suddenly he lifted his clouded blue eyes, and unthinking looked straight into March's eyes. He was startled as well as she. He, too, recoiled a little. March felt the same sly, taunting, knowing spark leap out of his eyes, as he turned his head aside, and fall into her soul, as had fallen from the dark eyes of the fox. She pursed her mouth as if in pain, as if asleep too.

"Well, I don't know," Banford was saying. She seemed reluctant, as if she were afraid of being imposed upon. She looked at March. But, with her weak, troubled sight, she only saw the usual semi-abstraction on her friend's face. "Why don't you speak, Nellie?" she said.

But March was wide-eyed and silent, and the youth, as if fascinated, was watching her without moving his eyes.

"Go on—answer something," said Banford. And March turned her head slightly aside, as if coming to consciousness, or trying to come to consciousness.

"What do you expect me to say?" she asked automatically.

"Say what you think," said Banford.

"It's all the same to me," said March.

And again there was silence. A pointed light seemed to be on the boy's eyes, penetrating like a needle.

"So it is to me," said Banford. "You can stop on here if you like."

A smile like a cunning little flame came over his face, suddenly and involuntarily. He dropped his head quickly to hide it, and remained with his head dropped, his face hidden.

"You can stop on here if you like. You can please yourself, Henry," Banford concluded.

Still he did not reply, but remained with his head dropped. Then he lifted his face. It was bright with a curious light, as if exultant, and his eyes were strangely clear as he watched March. She turned her face aside, her mouth suffering as if wounded, and her consciousness dim.

Banford became a little puzzled. She watched the steady, pellucid gaze of the youth's eyes as he looked at March, with the invisible smile gleaming on his face. She did not know how he was smiling, for no feature moved. It seemed only in the gleam, almost the glitter of the fine hairs on his cheeks. Then he looked with quite a changed look at Banford.

"I'm sure," he said in his soft, courteous voice, "you're awfully good. You're too good. You don't want to be bothered with me, I'm sure."

"Cut a bit of bread, Nellie," said Banford uneasily, adding: "It's no bother, if you like to stay. It's like having my own brother here for a few days. He's a boy like you are."

"That's awfully kind of you," the lad repeated. "I should like to stay ever so much, if you're sure I'm not a trouble to you."

"No, of course you're no trouble. I tell you, it's a pleasure to have somebody in the house besides ourselves," said warm-hearted Banford.

"But Miss March?" he said in his soft voice, looking at her.

"Oh, it's quite all right as far as I'm concerned," said March vaguely.

His face beamed, and he almost rubbed his hands with pleasure.

"Well then," he said, "I should love it, if you'd let me pay my board and help with the work."

"You've no need to talk about board," said Banford.

One or two days went by, and the youth stayed on at the farm. Banford was quite charmed by him. He was so soft and courteous in speech, not wanting to say much himself, preferring to hear what she had to say, and to laugh in his quick, half-mocking way. He helped readily with the work—but not too much. He loved to be out alone with the gun in his hands, to watch, to see. For his sharp-eyed, impersonal curiosity was insatiable, and he was most free when he was quite alone, half-hidden, watching.

Particularly he watched March. She was a strange character to him. Her figure, like a graceful young man's, piqued him. Her dark eyes made something rise in his soul, with a curious elate excitement, when he looked into them, an excitement he was afraid to let be seen, it was so keen and secret. And then her odd, shrewd speech made him laugh outright. He felt he must go further, he was inevitably impelled. But he put away the thought of her and went off towards the wood's edge with the gun.

The dusk was falling as he came home, and with the dusk, a fine, late November rain. He saw the firelight leaping in the window of the sitting-room, a leaping light in the little cluster of the dark buildings. And he thought to himself it would be a good thing to have this place for his own. And then the thought entered him shrewdly: Why not marry March? He stood still in the middle of the field for some moments, the dead rabbit hanging still in his hand, arrested by this thought. His mind waited in amazement—it seemed to calculate—and then he smiled curiously to himself in acquiescence. Why not? Why not indeed? It was a good idea. What if it was rather ridiculous? What did it matter? What if she was older than he? It didn't matter. When he thought of her dark, startled, vulnerable eyes he smiled subtly to himself. He was older than she, really. He was master of her.

He scarcely admitted his intention even to himself. He kept it as a secret even from himself. It was all too uncertain as yet. He would have to see how things went. Yes, he would have to see how things went. If he wasn't careful, she would just simply mock at the idea. He knew, sly and subtle as he was, that if he went to her plainly and said: "Miss March, I love you and want you to marry me," her inevitable answer would be: "Get out. I don't want any of that tomfoolery." This was her attitude to men and their "tomfoolery." If he was not careful, she would turn round on him with her savage, sardonic ridicule, and dismiss him from the farm and from her own mind forever. He would have to go gently. He would have to catch her as you catch a deer or a woodcock when you go out shooting. It's no good walking out into the forest and saying to the deer: "Please fall to my gun." No, it is a slow, subtle battle. When you really go out to get a deer, you gather yourself together, you coil yourself inside yourself, and you advance secretly, before dawn, into the mountains. It is not so much what you *do*, when you go out hunting, as how you feel. You have to be subtle and cunning and absolutely fatally ready. It becomes like a fate. Your own fate overtakes and determines the fate of the deer you are hunting. First of all, even before you come in sight of your quarry, there is a strange battle, like mesmerism. Your own soul, as a hunter, has gone out to fasten on the soul of the deer, even before you see any deer. And the soul of the deer fights to escape. Even before the deer has any wind of you, it is so. It is a subtle, profound battle of wills which takes place in the invisible. And it is a battle never finished till your bullet goes home. When you are *really* worked up to the true pitch, and you come at last into range, you don't then aim as you do when you are firing at a bottle. It is your own *will* which carries the bullet into the heart of your quarry. The bullet's flight home is a sheer projection of your own fate into the fate of the deer. It happens like a supreme wish, a supreme act of volition, not as a dodge of cleverness.

He was a huntsman in spirit, not a farmer, and not a soldier stuck in a regiment. And it was as a young hunter that he wanted to bring down March as his quarry, to make her his wife. So he gathered himself subtly together, seemed to withdraw into a kind of invisibility. He was not quite sure how he would go on. And March was suspicious as a hare. So he remained in appearance just the nice, odd stranger-youth, staying for a fortnight on the place.

He had been sawing logs for the fire in the afternoon. Darkness came very early. It was still a cold, raw mist. It was getting almost too dark to see. A pile of short sawed logs lay beside the trestle. March came to carry them indoors, or into the shed, as he was busy sawing the last log. He was working in his shirt-sleeves, and did not notice her approach; she came unwillingly, as if shy. He saw her stooping to the bright-ended logs, and he stopped sawing. A fire like lightning flew down his legs in the nerves.

"March?" he said in his quiet, young voice.

She looked up from the logs she was piling.

"Yes!" she said.

He looked down on her in the dusk. He could see her not too distinctly.

"I wanted to ask you something," he said.

"Did you? What was it?" she said. Already the fright was in her voice. But she was too much mistress of herself.

"Why"—his voice seemed to draw out soft and subtle, it penetrated her nerves—"why, what do you think it is?"

She stood up, placed her hands on her hips, and stood looking at him transfixed, without answering. Again he burned with a sudden power.

"Well," he said, and his voice was so soft it seemed rather like a subtle touch, like the merest touch of a cat's paw, a feeling rather than a sound. "Well—I wanted to ask you to marry me."

March felt rather than heard him. She was trying in vain to turn aside her face. A great relaxation seemed to have come over her. She stood silent, her head slightly on one side. He seemed to be bending towards her, invisibly smiling. It seemed to her fine sparks came out of him.

Then very suddenly she said:

"Don't try any of your tomfoolery on me."

A quiver went over his nerves. He had missed. He waited a moment to collect himself again. Then he said, putting all the strange softness into his voice, as if he were imperceptibly stroking her:

"Why, it's not tomfoolery. It's not tomfoolery. I mean it. I mean it. What makes you disbelieve me?"

He sounded hurt. And his voice had such a curious power over her; making her feel loose and relaxed. She struggled somewhere for her own power. She felt for a moment that she was lost—lost—lost. The word seemed to rock in her as if she were dying. Suddenly again she spoke.

"You don't know what you are talking about," she said, in a brief and transient stroke of scorn. "What nonsense! I'm old enough to be your mother."

"Yes, I do know what I'm talking about. Yes, I do," he persisted softly, as if he were producing his voice in her blood. "I know quite well what I'm talking about. You're not old enough to be my mother. That isn't true. And what does it matter even if it was? You can marry me whatever age we are. What is age to me? And what is age to you! Age is nothing."

A swoon went over her as he concluded. He spoke rapidly—in the rapid Cornish fashion—and his voice seemed to sound in her somewhere where she was helpless against it. "Age is nothing!" The soft, heavy insistence of it made her sway dimly out there in the darkness. She could not answer.

A great exultance leaped like fire over his limbs. He felt he had won.

"I want to marry you, you see. Why shouldn't I?" he proceeded, soft and rapid. He waited for her to answer. In the dusk he saw her almost phosphorescent. Her eyelids were dropped, her face half-averted and unconscious. She seemed to be in his power. But he waited, watchful. He dared not yet touch her.

"Say then," he said, "say then you'll marry me. Say—say!" He was softly insistent.

"What?" she asked, faint, from a distance, like one in pain. His voice was now unthinkably near and soft. He drew very near to her. "Say yes."

"Oh, I can't," she wailed helplessly, half-articulate, as if semi-conscious, and as if in pain, like one who dies. "How can I?"

"You can," he said softly, laying his hand gently on her shoulder as she stood with her head averted and dropped, dazed. "You can. Yes, you can. What makes you say you can't? You can. You can." And with awful softness he bent forward and just touched her neck with his mouth and his chin.

"Don't!" she cried, with a faint mad cry like hysteria, starting away and facing round on him. "What do you mean?" But she had no breath to speak with. It was as if she was killed.

"I mean what I say," he persisted softly and cruelly. "I want you to marry me. I want you to marry me. You know that, now, don't you? You know that, now? Don't you? Don't you?"

"What?" she said.

"Know," he replied.

"Yes," she said. "I know you say so."

"And you know I mean it, don't you?"

"I know you say so."

"You believe me?" he said.

She was silent for some time. Then she pursed her lips.

"I don't know what I believe," she said.

"Are you out there?" came Banford's voice, calling from the house.

"Yes, we're bringing in the logs," he answered.

"I thought you'd gone lost," said Banford disconsolately. "Hurry up, do, and come and let's have tea. The kettle's boiling."

He stooped at once to take an armful of little logs and carry them into the kitchen, where they were piled in a corner. March also helped, filling her arms and carrying the logs on her breast as if they were some heavy child. The night had fallen cold.

When the logs were all in, the two cleaned their boots noisily on the scraper outside, then rubbed them on the mat. March shut the door and took off her old felt hat—her farm-girl hat. Her thick, crisp, black hair was loose, her face was pale and strained. She pushed back her hair vaguely and washed her hands. Banford came hurrying into the dimly-lighted kitchen, to take from the oven the scones she was keeping hot.

"Whatever have you been doing all this time?" she asked fretfully. "I thought you were never coming in. And it's ages since you stopped sawing. What were you doing out there?"

"Well," said Henry, "we had to stop that hole in the barn to keep the rats out."

"Why, I could see you standing there in the shed. I could see your shirt-sleeves," challenged Banford.

"Yes, I was just putting the saw away."

They went in to tea. March was quite mute. Her face was pale and strained and vague. The youth, who always had the same ruddy, self-contained look on his face, as though he were keeping himself to himself, had come to tea in his shirt-sleeves as if he were at home. He bent over his plate as he ate his food.

"Aren't you cold?" said Banford spitefully. "In your shirt-sleeves."

He looked up at her, with his chin near his plate, and his eyes very clear, pellucid, and unwavering as he watched her.

"No, I'm not cold," he said with his usual soft courtesy. "It's much warmer in here than it is outside, you see."

"I hope it is," said Banford, feeling nettled by him. He had a strange, suave assurance and a wide-eyed bright look that got on her nerves this evening.

"But perhaps," he said softly and courteously, "you don't like me coming to tea without my coat. I forgot that."

"Oh, I don't mind," said Banford: although she *did*.

"I'll go and get it, shall I?" he said.

March's dark eyes turned slowly down to him.

"No, don't you bother," she said in her queer, twanging tone. "If you feel all right as you are, stop as you are." She spoke with a crude authority.

"Yes," said he, "I *feel* all right, if I'm not rude."

"It's usually considered rude," said Banford. "But we don't mind."

"Go along, 'considered rude,'" ejaculated March. "Who considers it rude?"

"Why, you do, Nellie, in anybody else," said Banford, bridling a little behind her spectacles, and feeling her food stick in her throat.

But March had again gone vague and unheeding, chewing her food as if she did not know she was eating at all. And the youth looked from one to another, with bright, watching eyes.

Banford was offended. For all his suave courtesy and soft voice, the youth seemed to her impudent. She did not like to look at him. She did not like to meet his clear, watchful eyes, she did not like to see the strange glow in his face, his cheeks with their delicate fine hair, and his ruddy skin that was quite dull and yet which seemed to burn with a curious heat of life. It made her feel a little ill to look at him: the quality of his physical presence was too penetrating, too hot.

After tea the evening was very quiet. The youth rarely went into the village. As a rule, he read: he was a great reader, in his own hours. That is, when he did begin, he read absorbedly. But he was not very eager to begin. Often he walked about the fields and along the hedges alone in the dark at night, prowling with a queer instinct for the night, and listening to the wild sounds.

To-night, however, he took a Captain Mayne Reid[3] book from Banford's shelf and sat down with knees wide apart and immersed himself in his story. His brownish fair hair was long, and lay on his head like a thick cap, combed sideways. He was still in his shirt-sleeves, and bending forward under the lamplight, with his knees stuck wide apart and the book in his hand and his whole figure absorbed in the rather strenuous business of reading, he gave Banford's sitting-room the look of a lumber-camp. She resented this. For on her sitting-room floor she had a red Turkey rug and dark stain round, the fireplace had fashionable green tiles, the piano stood open with the latest dance music: she played quite well: and on the walls were March's hand-painted swans and water-lilies. Moreover, with the logs nicely, tremulously burning in the grate, the thick curtains drawn, the doors all shut, and the pine trees hissing and shuddering in the wind outside, it was cozy, it was refined and nice. She resented the big, raw, long-legged youth sticking his khaki knees out and sitting there with his soldier's shirt-cuffs buttoned on his thick red wrists. From time to time he turned a page, and from time to time he gave a sharp look at the fire, settling the logs. Then he immersed himself again in the intense and isolated business of reading.

March, on the far side of the table, was spasmodically crocheting.

3. Irish-born (1818–83) writer of adventure novels. He went to Mexico as a young man and served in the Mexican War, then lived for some time in Philadelphia before returning to Britain.

Her mouth was pursed in an odd way, as when she had dreamed the fox's brush burned it, her beautiful, crisp black hair strayed in wisps. But her whole figure was absorbed in its bearing, as if she herself was miles away. In a sort of semi-dream she seemed to be hearing the fox singing round the house in the wind, singing wildly and sweetly and like a madness. With red but well-shaped hands she slowly crocheted the white cotton, very slowly, awkwardly.

Banford was also trying to read, sitting in her low chair. But between those two she felt fidgety. She kept moving and looking round and listening to the wind, and glancing secretly from one to the other of her companions. March, seated on a straight chair, with her knees in their close breeches crossed, and slowly, laboriously crocheting, was also a trial.

"Oh dear!" said Banford. "My eyes are bad tonight." And she pressed her fingers on her eyes.

The youth looked up at her with his clear, bright look, but did not speak.

"Are they, Jill?" said March absently.

Then the youth began to read again, and Banford perforce returned to her book. But she could not keep still. After a while she looked up at March, and a queer, almost malignant little smile was on her thin face.

"A penny for them, Nell," she said suddenly.

March looked round with big, startled black eyes, and went pale as if with terror. She had been listening to the fox singing so tenderly, so tenderly, as he wandered round the house.

"What?" she said vaguely.

"A penny for them," said Banford sarcastically. "Or twopence, if they're as deep as all that."

The youth was watching with bright, clear eyes from beneath the lamp.

"Why," came March's vague voice, "what do you want to waste your money for?"

"I thought it would be well spent," said Banford.

"I wasn't thinking of anything except the way the wind was blowing," said March.

"Oh dear," replied Banford, "I could have had as original thoughts as that myself. I'm afraid I *have* wasted my money this time."

"Well, you needn't pay," said March.

The youth suddenly laughed. Both women looked at him: March rather surprised-looking, as if she had hardly known he was there.

"Why, do you ever pay up on these occasions?" he asked.

"Oh yes," said Banford. "We always do. I've sometimes had to pass a shilling a week to Nellie, in the wintertime. It costs much less in summer."

"What, paying for each other's thoughts?" he laughed.

"Yes, when we've absolutely come to the end of everything else."

He laughed quickly, wrinkling his nose sharply like a puppy and laughing with quick pleasure, his eyes shining.

"It's the first time I ever heard of that," he said.

"I guess you'd hear of it often enough if you stayed a winter on Bailey Farm," said Banford lamentably.

"Do you get so tired, then?" he asked.

"So bored," said Banford.

"Oh!" he said gravely. "But why should you be bored?"

"Who wouldn't be bored?" said Banford.

"I'm sorry to hear that," he said gravely.

"You must be, if you were hoping to have a lively time here," said Banford.

He looked at her long and gravely.

"Well," he said, with his odd, young seriousness, "it's quite lively enough for me."

"I'm glad to hear it," said Banford.

And she returned to her book. In her thin, frail hair were already many threads of grey, though she was not yet thirty. The boy did not look down, but turned his eyes to March, who was sitting with pursed mouth laboriously crocheting, her eyes wide and absent. She had a warm, pale, fine skin and a delicate nose. Her pursed mouth looked shrewish. But the shrewish look was contradicted by the curious lifted arch of her dark brows, and the wideness of her eyes; a look of startled wonder and vagueness. She was listening again for the fox, who seemed to have wandered farther off into the night.

From under the edge of the lamplight the boy sat with his face looking up, watching her silently, his eyes round and very clear and intent. Banford, biting her fingers irritably, was glancing at him under her hair. He sat there perfectly still, his ruddy face tilted up from the low level under the light, on the edge of the dimness, and watching with perfect abstract intentness. March suddenly lifted her great, dark eyes from her crocheting and saw him. She started, giving a little exclamation.

"There he is!" she cried involuntarily, as if terribly startled.

Banford looked around in amazement, sitting up straight.

"Whatever has got you, Nellie?" she cried.

But March, her face flushed a delicate rose color, was looking away to the door.

"Nothing! Nothing!" she said crossly. "Can't one speak?"

"Yes, if you speak sensibly," said Banford. "Whatever did you mean?"

"I don't know what I meant," cried March testily.

"Oh, Nellie, I hope you aren't going jumpy and nervy. I feel I can't stand another *thing*! Whoever did you mean? Did you mean

Henry?" cried poor, frightened Banford.

"Yes. I suppose so," said March laconically. She would never confess to the fox.

"Oh dear, my nerves are all gone for tonight," wailed Banford.

At nine o'clock March brought in a tray with bread and cheese and tea—Henry had confessed that he liked a cup of tea. Banford drank a glass of milk and ate a little bread. And soon she said:

"I'm going to bed, Nellie. I'm all nerves to-night. Are you coming?"

"Yes, I'm coming the minute I've taken the tray away," said March.

"Don't be long then," said Banford fretfully. "Good-night, Henry. You'll see the fire is safe, if you come up last, won't you?"

"Yes, Miss Banford, I'll see it's safe," he replied in his reassuring way.

March was lighting the candle to go to the kitchen. Banford took her candle and went upstairs. When March came back to the fire, she said to him:

"I suppose we can trust you to put out the fire and everything?" She stood there with her hand on her hip, and one knee loose, her head averted shyly, as if she could not look at him. He had his face lifted, watching her.

"Come and sit down a minute," he said softly.

"No, I'll be going. Jill will be waiting, and she'll get upset, if I don't come."

"What made you jump like that this evening?" he asked.

"When did I jump?" she retorted, looking at him.

"Why, just now you did," he said. "When you cried out."

"Oh!" she said. "Then!—Why, I thought you were the fox!" And her face screwed into a queer smile, half-ironic.

"The fox! Why the fox?" he asked softly.

"Why, one evening last summer when I was out with the gun I saw the fox in the grass nearly at my feet, looking straight up at me. I don't know—I suppose he made an impression on me." She turned aside her head again and let one foot stray loose, self-consciously.

"And did you shoot him?" asked the boy.

"No, he gave me such a start, staring straight at me as he did, and then stopping to look back at me over his shoulder with a laugh on his face."

"A laugh on his face!" repeated Henry, also laughing. "He frightened you, did he?"

"No, he didn't frighten me. He made an impression on me, that's all."

"And you thought I was the fox, did you?" he laughed, with the same queer, quick little laugh, like a puppy wrinkling his nose.

"Yes, I did, for the moment," she said. "Perhaps he'd been in my mind without my knowing."

"Perhaps you think I've come to steal your chickens or something," he said, with the same young laugh.

But she only looked at him with a wide, dark, vacant eye.

"It's the first time," he said, "that I've ever been taken for a fox. Won't you sit down for a minute?" His voice was very soft and cajoling.

"No," she said. "Jill will be waiting." But still she did not go, but stood with one foot loose and her face turned aside, just outside the circle of light.

"But won't you answer my question?" he said, lowering his voice still more.

"I don't know what question you mean."

"Yes, you do. Of course you do. I mean the question of you marrying me."

"No, I shan't answer that question," she said flatly.

"Won't you?" The queer, young laugh came on his nose again. "Is it because I'm like the fox? Is that why?" And still he laughed.

She turned and looked at him with a long, slow look.

"I wouldn't let that put you against me," he said. "Let me turn the lamp low, and come and sit down a minute."

He put his red hand under the glow of the lamp and suddenly made the light very dim. March stood there in the dimness quite shadowy, but unmoving. He rose silently to his feet, on his long legs. And now his voice was extraordinarily soft and suggestive, hardly audible.

"You'll stay a moment," he said. "Just a moment." And he put his hand on her shoulder. She turned her face from him. "I'm sure you don't really think I'm like the fox," he said, with the same softness and with a suggestion of laughter in his tone, a subtle mockery. "Do you now?" And he drew her gently towards him and kissed her neck, softly. She winced and trembled and hung away. But his strong, young arm held her, and he kissed her softly again, still on the neck, for her face was averted.

"Won't you answer my question? Won't you now?" came his soft, lingering voice. He was trying to draw her near to kiss her face. And he kissed her cheek softly, near the ear.

At that moment Banford's voice was heard calling fretfully, crossly from upstairs.

"There's Jill!" cried March, starting and drawing erect.

And as she did so, quick as lightning he kissed her on the mouth, with a quick, brushing kiss. It seemed to burn through her every fiber. She gave a queer little cry.

"You will, won't you? You will?" he insisted softly.

"Nellie! *Nellie!* Whatever are you so long for?" came Banford's faint cry from the outer darkness.

But he held her fast, and was murmuring with that intolerable softness and insistency:

"You will, won't you? Say yes! Say yes!"

March, who felt as if the fire had gone through her and scathed her, and as if she could do no more, murmured:

"Yes! Yes! Anything you like! Anything you like! Only let me go! Only let me go! Jill's calling."

"You know you've promised," he said insidiously.

"Yes! Yes! I do!" Her voice suddenly rose into a shrill cry. "All right, Jill, I'm coming."

Startled, he let her go, and she went straight upstairs.

In the morning at breakfast, after he had looked round the place and attended to the stock and thought to himself that one could live easily enough here, he said to Banford:

"Do you know what, Miss Banford?"

"Well, what?" said the good-natured, nervy Banford.

He looked at March, who was spreading jam on her bread.

"Shall I tell?" he said to her.

She looked up at him, and a deep pink color flushed over her face.

"Yes, if you mean Jill," she said. "I hope you won't go talking all over the village, that's all." And she swallowed her dry bread with difficulty.

"Whatever's coming?" said Banford, looking up with wide, tired, slightly reddened eyes. She was a thin, frail little thing, and her hair, which was delicate and thin, was bobbed, so it hung softly by her worn face in its faded brown and grey.

"Why, what do you think?" he said, smiling like one who has a secret.

"How do I know!" said Banford.

"Can't you guess?" he said, making bright eyes and smiling, pleased with himself.

"I'm sure I can't. What's more, I'm not going to try."

"Nellie and I are going to be married."

Banford put down her knife out of her thin, delicate fingers, as if she would never take it up to eat any more. She stared with blank, reddened eyes.

"You what?" she exclaimed.

"We're going to get married. Aren't we, Nellie?" and he turned to March.

"You say so, anyway," said March, laconically. But again she flushed with an agonized flush. She, too, could swallow no more.

Banford looked at her like a bird that has been shot: a poor, little sick bird. She gazed at her with all her wounded soul in her face, at the deep-flushed March.

"Never!" she exclaimed, helpless.

"It's quite right," said the bright and gloating youth.

Banford turned aside her face, as if the sight of the food on the table made her sick. She sat like this for some moments, as if she were sick. Then, with one hand on the edge of the table, she rose to her feet.

"I'll *never* believe it, Nellie," she cried. "It's absolutely impossible!"

Her plaintive, fretful voice had a thread of hot anger and despair.

"Why? Why shouldn't you believe it?" asked the youth, with all his soft, velvety impertinence in his voice.

Banford looked at him from her wide, vague eyes, as if he were some creature in a museum.

"Oh," she said languidly, "because she can never be such a fool. She can't lose her self-respect to such an extent." Her voice was cold and plaintive, drifting.

"In what way will she lose her self-respect?" asked the boy.

Banford looked at him with vague fixity from behind her spectacles.

"If she hasn't lost it already," she said.

He became very red, vermilion, under the slow, vague stare from behind the spectacles.

"I don't see it at all," he said.

"Probably you don't. I shouldn't expect you would," said Banford, with that straying mild tone of remoteness which made her words even more insulting.

He sat stiff in his chair, staring with hot, blue eyes from his scarlet face. An ugly look had come on his brow.

"My word, she doesn't know what she's letting herself in for," said Banford, in her plaintive, drifting, insulting voice.

"What has it got to do with you, anyway?" said the youth, in a temper.

"More than it has to do with you, probably," she replied, plaintive and venomous.

"Oh, has it! I don't see that at all," he jerked out.

"No, you wouldn't," she answered, drifting.

"Anyhow," said March, pushing back her hair and rising uncouthly. "It's no good arguing about it." And she seized the bread and the teapot and strode away to the kitchen.

Banford let her fingers stray across her brow and along her hair, like one bemused. Then she turned and went away upstairs.

Henry sat stiff and sulky in his chair, with his face and his eyes on fire. March came and went, clearing the table. But Henry sat on, stiff with temper. He took no notice of her. She had regained her composure and her soft, even, creamy complexion. But her mouth was pursed up. She glanced at him each time as she came to take things from the table, glanced from her large, curious eyes, more in curiosity than anything. Such a long, red-faced, sulky boy! That was all he was. He seemed as remote from her as if his red face were a red chimney-pot on a cottage across the fields, and she looked at him just as objectively, as remotely.

At length he got up and stalked out into the fields with the gun. He came in only at dinnertime, with the devil still in his face, but his manners quite polite. Nobody said anything particular; they sat each one at the sharp corner of a triangle, in obstinate remoteness. In the afternoon he went out again at once with the gun. He came in at nightfall with a rabbit and a pigeon. He stayed in all the evening, but hardly opened his mouth. He was in the devil of a temper, feeling he had been insulted.

Banford's eyes were red, she had evidently been crying. But her manner was more remote and supercilious than ever; the way she turned her head if he spoke at all, as if he were some tramp or inferior intruder of that sort, made his blue eyes go almost black with rage. His face looked sulkier. But he never forgot his polite intonation, if he opened his mouth to speak.

March seemed to flourish in this atmosphere. She seemed to sit between the two antagonists with a little wicked smile on her face, enjoying herself. There was even a sort of complacency in the way she laboriously crocheted this evening.

When he was in bed, the youth could hear the two women talking and arguing in their room. He sat up in bed and strained his ears to hear what they said. But he could hear nothing, it was too far off. Yet he could hear the soft, plaintive drip of Banford's voice, and March's deeper note.

The night was quiet, frosty. Big stars were snapping outside, beyond the ridge-tops of the pine trees. He listened and listened. In the distance he heard a fox yelping: and the dogs from the farms barking in answer. But it was not that he wanted to hear. It was what the two women were saying.

He got stealthily out of bed and stood by his door. He could hear no more than before. Very, very carefully he began to lift the door latch. After quite a time he had his door open. Then he stepped stealthily out into the passage. The old oak planks were cold under his feet, and they creaked preposterously. He crept very, very gently up the one step, and along by the wall, till he stood outside their door. And there he held his breath and listened. Banford's voice:

"No, I simply couldn't stand it. I should be dead in a month.

Which is just what he would be aiming at, of course. That would just be his game, to see me in the churchyard. No, Nellie, if you were to do such a thing as to marry him, you could never stop here. I couldn't, I couldn't live in the same house with him. Oh!—h! I feel quite sick with the smell of his clothes. And his red face simply turns me over. I can't eat my food when he's at the table. What a fool I was ever to let him stop. One ought *never* to try to do a kind action. It always flies back in your face like a boomerang."

"Well, he's only got two more days," said March.

"Yes, thank heaven. And when he's gone he'll never come in this house again. I feel so bad while he's here. And I know, I know he's only counting what he can get out of you. I *know* that's all it is. He's just a good-for-nothing, who doesn't want to work, and who thinks he'll live on us. But he won't live on me. If you're such a fool, then it's your own lookout. Mrs. Burgess knew him all the time he was here. And the old man could never get him to do any steady work. He was off with the gun on every occasion, just as he is now. Nothing but the gun! Oh, I do hate it. You don't know what you're doing, Nellie, you don't. If you marry him he'll just make a fool of you. He'll go off and leave you stranded. I know he will, if he can't get Bailey Farm out of us—and he's not going to, while I live. While I live he's never going to set foot here. I know what it would be. He'd soon think he was master of both of us, as he thinks he's master of you already."

"But he isn't," said Nellie.

"He thinks he is, anyway. And that's what he wants: to come and be master here. Yes, imagine it! That's what we've got the place together for, is it, to be bossed and bullied by a hateful, red-faced boy, a beastly laborer. Oh, we *did* make a mistake when we let him stop. We ought never to have lowered ourselves. And I've had such a fight with all the people here, not to be pulled down to their level. No, he's not coming here. And then you see—if he can't have the place, he'll run off to Canada or somewhere again, as if he'd never known you. And here you'll be, absolutely ruined and made a fool of. I know I shall never have any peace of mind again."

"We'll tell him he can't come here. We'll tell him that," said March.

"Oh, don't you bother; I'm going to tell him that, and other things as well, before he goes. He's not going to have all his own way while I've got the strength left to speak. Oh, Nellie, he'll despise you, he'll despise you, like the awful little beast he is, if you give way to him. I'd no more trust him than I'd trust a cat not to steal. He's deep, he's deep, and he's bossy, and he's selfish through and through, as cold as ice. All he wants is to make use of you. And when you're no more use to him, then I pity you."

"I don't think he's as bad as all that," said March.

"No, because he's been playing up to you. But you'll find out, if you see much of him. Oh, Nellie, I can't bear to think of it."

"Well, it won't hurt you, Jill, darling."

"Won't it! Won't it! I shall never know a moment's peace again while I live, nor a moment's happiness. No, Nellie——" and Banford began to weep bitterly.

The boy outside could hear the stifled sound of the woman's sobbing, and could hear March's soft, deep, tender voice comforting, with wonderful gentleness and tenderness, the weeping woman.

His eyes were so round and wide that he seemed to see the whole night, and his ears were almost jumping off his head. He was frozen stiff. He crept back to bed, but felt as if the top of his head were coming off. He could not sleep. He could not keep still. He rose, quietly dressed himself, and crept out on to the landing once more. The women were silent. He went softly downstairs and out to the kitchen.

Then he put on his boots and his overcoat and took the gun. He did not think to go away from the farm. No, he only took the gun. As softly as possible he unfastened the door and went out into the frosty December night. The air was still, the stars bright, the pine trees seemed to bristle audibly in the sky. He went stealthily away down a fence-side, looking for something to shoot. At the same time he remembered that he ought not to shoot and frighten the women.

So he prowled round the edge of the gorse[4] cover, and through the grove of tall old hollies, to the woodside. There he skirted the fence, peering through the darkness with dilated eyes that seemed to be able to grow black and full of sight in the dark, like a cat's. An owl was slowly and mournfully whooing round a great oak tree. He stepped stealthily with his gun, listening, listening, watching.

As he stood under the oaks of the wood-edge he heard the dogs from the neighboring cottage up the hill yelling suddenly and startlingly, and the wakened dogs from the farms around barking answer. And suddenly it seemed to him England was little and tight, he felt the landscape was constricted even in the dark, and that there were too many dogs in the night, making a noise like a fence of sound, like the network of English hedges netting the view. He felt the fox didn't have a chance. For it must be the fox that had started all this hullabaloo.

Why not watch for him, anyhow! He would, no doubt, be coming sniffing round. The lad walked downhill to where the farmstead with its few pine trees crouched blackly. In the angle of the long shed, in the black dark, he crouched down. He knew the fox

4. A spiny, thickset shrub with yellow flowers.

would be coming. It seemed to him it would be the last of the foxes in this loudly-barking, thick-voiced England, tight with innumerable little houses.

He sat a long time with his eyes fixed unchanging upon the open gateway, where a little light seemed to fall from the stars or from the horizon, who knows. He was sitting on a log in a dark corner with the gun across his knees. The pine trees snapped. Once a chicken fell off its perch in the barn with a loud crawk and cackle and commotion that startled him, and he stood up, watching with all his eyes, thinking it might be a rat. But he *felt* it was nothing. So he sat down again with the gun on his knees and his hands tucked in to keep them warm, and his eyes fixed unblinking on the pale reach of the open gateway. He felt he could smell the hot, sickly, rich smell of live chickens on the cold air.

And then—a shadow. A sliding shadow in the gateway. He gathered all his vision into a concentrated spark, and saw the shadow of the fox, the fox creeping on his belly through the gate. There he went, on his belly like a snake. The boy smiled to himself and brought the gun to his shoulder. He knew quite well what would happen. He knew the fox would go to where the fowl door was boarded up and sniff there. He knew he would lie there for a minute, sniffing the fowls within. And then he would start again prowling under the edge of the old barn, waiting to get in.

The fowl door was at the top of a slight incline. Soft, soft as a shadow the fox slid up this incline, and crouched with his nose to the boards. And at the same moment there was the awful crash of a gun reverberating between the old buildings, as if all the night had gone smash. But the boy watched keenly. He saw even the white belly of the fox as the beast beat his paws in death. So he went forward.

There was a commotion everywhere. The fowls were scuffling and crawking, the ducks were quark-quarking, the pony had stamped wildly to his feet. But the fox was on his side, struggling in his last tremors. The boy bent over him and smelt his foxy smell.

There was a sound of a window opening upstairs, then March's voice calling:

"Who is it?"

"It's me," said Henry; "I've shot the fox."

"Oh, goodness! You nearly frightened us to death."

"Did I? I'm awfully sorry."

"Whatever made you get up?"

"I heard him about."

"And have you shot him?"

"Yes, he's here," and the boy stood in the yard holding up the warm, dead brute. "You can't see, can you? Wait a minute." And he took his flashlight from his pocket and flashed it on to the dead animal. He was holding it by the brush. March saw, in the middle of the darkness, just the reddish fleece and the white belly and the white underneath of the pointed chin, and the queer, dangling paws. She did not know what to say.

"He's a beauty," he said. "He will make you a lovely fur."

"You don't catch me wearing a fox fur," she replied.

"Oh!" he said. And he switched off the light.

"Well, I should think you'll come in and go to bed again now," she said.

"Probably I shall. What time is it?"

"What time is it, Jill?" called March's voice. It was a quarter to one.

That night March had another dream. She dreamed that Banford was dead, and that she, March, was sobbing her heart out. Then she had to put Banford into her coffin. And the coffin was the rough wood-box in which the bits of chopped wood were kept in the kitchen, by the fire. This was the coffin, and there was no other, and March was in agony and dazed bewilderment, looking for something to line the box with, something to make it soft with, something to cover up the poor, dead darling. Because she couldn't lay her in there just in her white, thin nightdress, in the horrible wood-box. So she hunted and hunted, and picked up thing after thing, and threw it aside in the agony of dream-frustration. And in her dream-despair all she could find that would do was a fox-skin. She knew that it wasn't right, that this was not what she should have. But it was all she could find. And so she folded the brush of the fox, and laid her darling Jill's head on this, and she brought round the skin of the fox and laid it on the top of the body, so that it seemed to make a whole ruddy, fiery coverlet, and she cried and cried, and woke to find the tears streaming down her face.

The first thing that both she and Banford did in the morning was to go out to see the fox. Henry had hung it up by the heels in the shed, with its poor brush falling backwards. It was a lovely dog-fox in its prime, with a handsome, thick, winter coat: a lovely golden-red color, with gray as it passed to the belly, and belly all white, and a great full brush with a delicate black and gray and pure white tip.

"Poor brute!" said Banford. "If it wasn't such a thieving wretch, you'd feel sorry for it."

March said nothing, but stood with her foot trailing aside, one hip out; her face was pale and her eyes big and black, watching the dead animal that was suspended upside down. White and soft as snow his belly: white and soft as snow. She passed her hand softly down it. And his wonderful black-glinted brush was full and frictional, wonderful. She passed her hand down this also, and quivered. Time after time she took the full fur of that thick tail between her fingers, and passed her hand slowly downwards. Wonderful, sharp, thick, splendor of a tail. And he was dead! She pursed her lips, and her eyes went black and vacant. Then she took the head in her hand.

Henry was sauntering up, so Banford walked rather pointedly away. March stood there bemused, with the head of the fox in her hand. She was wondering, wondering, wondering over his long, fine muzzle. For some reason it reminded her of a spoon or a spatula. She felt she could not understand it. The beast was a strange beast to her, incomprehensible, out of her range. Wonderful silver whiskers he had, like ice-threads. And pricked ears with hair inside. But that long, long, slender spoon of a nose!—and the marvellous white teeth beneath! It was to thrust forward and bite with, deep, deep, deep into the living prey, to bite and bite the blood.

"He's a beauty, isn't he?" said Henry, standing by.

"Oh yes, he's a fine big fox. I wonder how many chickens he's responsible for," she replied.

"A good many. Do you think he's the same one you saw in the summer?"

"I should think very likely he is," she replied.

He watched her, but he could make nothing of her. Partly she was so shy and virgin, and partly she was so grim, matter-of-fact, shrewish. What she said seemed to him so different from the look of her big, queer, dark eyes.

"Are you going to skin him?" she asked.

"Yes, when I've had breakfast, and got a board to peg him on."

"My word, what a strong smell he's got! Poo! It'll take some washing off one's hands. I don't know why I was so silly as to handle him." And she looked at her right hand, that had passed down his belly and along his tail, and had even got a tiny streak of blood from one dark place in his fur.

"Have you seen the chickens when they smell him, how frightened they are?" he said.

"Yes, aren't they!"

"You must mind you don't get some of his fleas."

"Oh, fleas!" she replied, nonchalant.

Later in the day she saw the fox's skin nailed flat on a board, as if crucified. It gave her an uneasy feeling.

The boy was angry. He went about with his mouth shut, as if he had swallowed part of his chin. But in behavior he was polite and affable. He did not say anything about his intention. And he left March alone.

That evening they sat in the dining-room. Banford wouldn't have him in her sitting-room any more. There was a very big log on the fire. And everybody was busy. Banford had letters to write, March was sewing a dress, and he was mending some little contrivance.

Banford stopped her letter-writing from time to time to look round and rest her eyes. The boy had his head down, his face hidden over his job.

"Let's see," said Banford. "What train do you go by, Henry?"

He looked up straight at her.

"The morning train. In the morning," he said.

"What, the eight-ten or the eleven-twenty?"

"The eleven-twenty, I suppose," he said.

"That is the day after to-morrow?" said Banford.

"Yes, the day after to-morrow."

"Mm!" murmured Banford, and she returned to her writing. But as she was licking her envelope, she asked:

"And what plans have you made for the future, if I may ask?"

"Plans?" he said, his face very bright and angry.

"I mean about you and Nellie, if you are going on with this business. When do you expect the wedding to come off?" She spoke in a jeering tone.

"Oh, the wedding!" he replied. "I don't know."

"Don't you know anything?" said Banford. "Are you going to clear out on Friday and leave things no more settled than they are?"

"Well, why shouldn't I? We can always write letters."

"Yes, of course you can. But I wanted to know because of this place. If Nellie is going to get married all of a sudden, I shall have to be looking round for a new partner."

"Couldn't she stay on here if she were married?" he said. He knew quite well what was coming.

"Oh," said Banford, "this is no place for a married couple. There's not enough work to keep a man going, for one thing. And there's no money to be made. It's quite useless your thinking of staying on here if you marry. Absolutely!"

"Yes, but I wasn't thinking of staying on here," he said.

"Well, that's what I want to know. And what about Nellie, then? How long is *she* going to be here with me, in that case?"

The two antagonists looked at one another.

"That I can't say," he answered.

"Oh, go along," she cried petulantly. "You must have some idea what you are going to do, if you ask a woman to marry you. Unless it's all a hoax."

"Why should it be a hoax? I am going back to Canada."

"And taking her with you?"

"Yes, certainly."

"You hear that, Nellie?" said Banford.

March, who had had her head bent over her sewing, now looked up with a sharp, pink blush on her face, and a queer, sardonic laugh in her eyes and on her twisted mouth.

"That's the first time I've heard that I was going to Canada," she said.

"Well, you have to hear it for the first time, haven't you?" said the boy.

"Yes, I suppose I have," she said nonchalantly. And she went back to her sewing.

"You're quite ready, are you, to go to Canada? Are you, Nellie?" asked Banford.

March looked up again. She let her shoulders go slack, and let her hand that held the needle lie loose in her lap.

"It depends on *how* I'm going," she said. "I don't think I want to go jammed up in the steerage, as a soldier's wife. I'm afraid I'm not used to that way."

The boy watched her with bright eyes.

"Would you rather stay over here while I go first?" he asked.

"I would, if that's the only alternative," she replied.

"That's much the wisest. Don't make it any fixed engagement," said Banford. "Leave yourself free to go or not after he's got back and found you a place, Nellie. Anything else is madness, madness."

"Don't you think," said the youth, "we ought to get married before I go—and then go together, or separate, according to how it happens?"

"I think it's a terrible idea," cried Banford.

But the boy was watching March.

"What do you think?" he asked her.

She let her eyes stray vaguely into space.

"Well, I don't know," she said. "I shall have to think about it."

"Why?" he asked pertinently.

"Why?" She repeated his question in a mocking way and looked at him laughing, though her face was pink again. "I should think there's plenty of reasons why."

He watched her in silence. She seemed to have escaped him. She had got into league with Banford against him. There was again the queer, sardonic look about her; she would mock stoically at everything he said or which life offered.

"Of course," he said, "I don't want to press you to do anything you don't wish to do."

"I should think not, indeed," cried Banford indignantly.

At bedtime Banford said plaintively to March:

"You take my hot-bottle up for me, Nellie, will you?"

"Yes, I'll do it," said March, with the kind of willing unwillingness she so often showed towards her beloved but uncertain Jill.

The two women went upstairs. After a time March called from the top of the stairs: "Good-night, Henry. I shan't be coming down. You'll see to the lamp and fire, won't you?"

The next day Henry went about with the cloud on his brow and his young cub's face shut up tight. He was cogitating all the time. He had wanted March to marry him and go back to Canada with him. And he had been sure she would do it. Why he wanted her he didn't know. But he did want her. He had set his mind on her. And he was convulsed with a youth's fury at being thwarted. To be thwarted, to be thwarted! It made him so furious inside that he did not know what to do with himself. But he kept himself in hand. Because even now things might turn out differently. She might come over to him. Of course she might. It was her business to do so.

Things drew to a tension again towards evening. He and Banford had avoided each other all day. In fact, Banford went in to the little town by the 11:20 train. It was market day. She arrived back on the 4:25. Just as the night was falling Henry saw her little figure in a dark-blue coat and a dark-blue tam-o'-shanter hat crossing the first meadow from the station. He stood under one of the wild pear trees, with the old dead leaves round his feet. And he watched the little blue figure advancing persistently over the rough winter-ragged meadow. She had her arms full of parcels, and advanced slowly, frail thing she was, but with that devilish little certainty which he so detested in her. He stood invisible under the pear tree, watching her every step. And if looks could have affected her, she would have felt a log of iron on each of her ankles as she made her way forward. "You're a nasty little thing, you are," he was saying softly, across the distance. "You're a nasty little thing. I hope you'll be paid back for all the harm you've done me for nothing. I hope you will—you nasty little thing. I hope you'll have to pay for it. You will, if wishes are anything. You nasty little creature that you are."

She was toiling slowly up the slope. But if she had been slipping back at every step towards the Bottomless Pit, he would not have gone to help her with her parcels. Aha, there went March, striding with her long, land stride in her breeches and her short tunic! Striding downhill at a great pace, and even running a few steps now and then, in her great solicitude and desire to come to the rescue of the little Banford. The boy watched her with rage in his heart. See her leap a ditch, and run, run as if a house was on fire, just to get to that creeping, dark little object down there! So, the Banford just stood still and waited. And March strode up and took *all* the parcels except a bunch of yellow chrysanthemums. These the Banford still carried—yellow chrysanthemums!

"Yes, you look well, don't you?" he said softly into the dusk air.

"You look well, pottering up there with a bunch of flowers, you do. I'd make you eat them for your tea if you hug them so tight. And I'd give them you for breakfast again, I would. I'd give you flowers, Nothing but flowers."

He watched the progress of the two women. He could hear their voices: March always outspoken and rather scolding in her tenderness, Banford murmuring rather vaguely. They were evidently good friends. He could not hear what they said till they came to the fence of the home meadow, which they must climb. Then he saw March manfully climbing over the bars with all her packages in her arms, and on the still air he heard Banford's fretful:

"Why don't you let me help you with the parcels?" She had a queer, plaintive hitch in her voice. Then came March's robust and reckless:

"Oh, I can manage. Don't you bother about me. You've all you can do to get yourself over."

"Yes, that's all very well," said Banford fretfully. "You say, *Don't you bother about me*, and then all the while you feel injured because nobody thinks of you."

"When do I feel injured?" said March.

"Always. You always feel injured. Now you're feeling injured because I won't have that boy to come and live on the farm."

"I'm not feeling injured at all," said March.

"I know you are. When he's gone you'll sulk over it. I know you will."

"Shall I?" said March. "We'll see."

"Yes, we *shall* see, unfortunately. I can't think how you can make yourself so cheap. I can't *imagine* how you can lower yourself like it."

"I haven't lowered myself," said March.

"I don't know what you call it, then. Letting a boy like that come so cheeky and impudent and make a mug of you. I don't know what you think of yourself. How much respect do you think he's going to have for you afterwards? My word, I wouldn't be in your shoes, if you married him."

"Of course you wouldn't. My boots are a good bit too big for you, and not half dainty enough," said March, with rather a misfire sarcasm.

"I thought you had too much pride, really I did. A woman's got to hold herself high, especially with a youth like that. Why, he's impudent. Even the way he forced himself on us at the start."

"We asked him to stay," said March.

"Not till he'd almost forced us to. And then he's so cocky and self-assured. My word, he puts my back up. I simply can't imagine how you can let him treat you so cheaply."

"I don't let him treat me cheaply," said March. "Don't you worry yourself, nobody's going to treat me cheaply. And even you aren't, either." She had a tender defiance and a certain fire in her voice.

"Yes, it's sure to come back to me," said Banford bitterly. "That's always the end of it. I believe you only do it to spite me."

They went now in silence up the steep, grassy slope and over the brow, through the gorse bushes. On the other side of the hedge the boy followed in the dusk, at some little distance. Now and then, through the huge ancient hedge of hawthorn, risen into trees, he saw the two dark figures creeping up the hill. As he came to the top of the slope he saw the homestead dark in the twilight, with a huge old pear tree leaning from the near gable, and a little yellow light twinkling in the small side windows of the kitchen. He heard the clink of the latch and saw the kitchen door open into light as the two women went indoors. So they were at home.

And so!—this was what they thought of him. It was rather in his nature to be a listener, so he was not at all surprised whatever he heard. The things people said about him always missed him personally. He was only rather surprised at the women's way with one another. And he disliked the Banford with an acid dislike. And he felt drawn to the March again. He felt again irresistibly drawn to her. He felt there was a secret bond, a secret thread between him and her, something very exclusive, which shut out everybody else and made him and her possess each other in secret.

He hoped again that she would have him. He hoped with his blood suddenly firing up that she would agree to marry him quite quickly: at Christmas, very likely. Christmas was not far off. He wanted, whatever else happened, to snatch her into a hasty marriage and a consummation with him. Then for the future, they could arrange later. But he hoped it would happen as he wanted it. He hoped that tonight she would stay a little while with him, after Banford had gone upstairs. He hoped he could touch her soft, creamy cheek, her strange, frightened face. He hoped he could look into her dilated, frightened dark eyes, quite near. He hoped he might even put his hand on her bosom and feel her soft breasts under her tunic. His heart beat deep and powerful as he thought of that. He wanted very much to do so. He wanted to make sure of her soft woman's breasts under her tunic. She always kept the brown linen coat buttoned so close up to her throat. It seemed to him like some perilous secret, that her soft woman's breasts must be buttoned up in that uniform. It seemed to him, moreover, that they were so much softer, tenderer, more lovely and lovable, shut up in that tunic, than were the Banford's breasts, under her soft blouses and chiffon dresses. The Banford would have little iron breasts, he said to himself. For all her frailty and fretfulness and delicacy, she would have tiny iron breasts. But March, under her crude, fast, workman's tunic, would have soft, white breasts, white and unseen. So he told himself, and his blood burned.

When he went in to tea, he had a surprise. He appeared at the inner door, his face very ruddy and vivid and his blue eyes shining, dropping his head forward as he came in, in his usual way, and hesitating in the doorway to watch the inside of the room, keenly and cautiously, before he entered. He was wearing a long-sleeved waistcoat. His face seemed extraordinarily like a piece of the out-of-doors come indoors: as holly-berries do. In his second of pause in the doorway he took in the two women sitting at table, at opposite ends, saw them sharply. And to his amazement March was dressed in a dress of dull, green silk crape. His mouth came open in surprise. If she had suddenly grown a moustache he could not have been more surprised.

"Why," he said, "do you wear a dress, then?"

She looked up, flushing a deep rose color, and twisting her mouth with a smile, said:

"Of course I do. What else do you expect me to wear but a dress?"

"A land girl's uniform, of course," said he.

"Oh," she cried, nonchalant, "that's only for this dirty, mucky work about here."

"Isn't it your proper dress, then?" he said.

"No, not indoors it isn't." she said. But she was blushing all the time as she poured out his tea. He sat down in his chair at table, unable to take his eyes off her. Her dress was a perfectly simple slip of bluey-green crape, with a line of gold stitching round the top and round the sleeves, which came to the elbow. It was cut just plain and round at the top, and showed her white, soft throat. Her arms he knew, strong and firm muscled, for he had often seen her with her sleeves rolled up. But he looked her up and down, up and down.

Banford, at the other end of the table, said not a word, but piggled with the sardine on her plate. He had forgotten her existence. He just simply stared at March while he ate his bread and margarine in huge mouthfuls, forgetting even his tea.

"Well, I never knew anything make such a difference!" he murmured, across his mouthfuls.

"Oh, goodness!" cried March, blushing still more. "I might be a pink monkey!"

And she rose quickly to her feet and took the teapot to the fire, to the kettle. And as she crouched on the hearth with her green slip about her, the boy stared more wide-eyed than ever. Through the crape her woman's form seemed soft and womanly. And when she stood up and walked he saw her legs move soft within her modernly short skirt. She had on black silk stockings, and small patent shoes with little gold buckles.

No, she was another being. She was something quite different. Seeing her always in the hard-cloth breeches, wide on the hips, buttoned on the knee, strong as armor, and in the brown puttees and thick boots, it had never occurred to him that she had a woman's legs and feet. Now it came upon him. She had a woman's soft, skirted legs, and she was accessible. He blushed to the roots of his hair, shoved his nose in his teacup and drank his tea with a little noise that made Banford simply squirm: and strangely, suddenly he felt a man, no longer a youth. He felt a man, with all a man's grave weight of responsibility. A curious quietness and gravity came over his soul. He felt a man, quiet, with a little of the heaviness of male destiny upon him.

She was soft and accessible in her dress. The thought went home in him like an everlasting responsibility.

"Oh, for goodness' sake, say something, somebody," cried Banford fretfully. "It might be a funeral." The boy looked at her, and she could not bear his face.

"A funeral!" said March, with a twisted smile. "Why, that breaks my dream."

Suddenly she had thought of Banford in the wood-box for a coffin.

"What, have you been dreaming of a wedding?" said Banford sarcastically.

"Must have been," said March.

"Whose wedding?" asked the boy.

"I can't remember," said March.

She was shy and rather awkward that evening, in spite of the fact that, wearing a dress, her bearing was much more subdued than in her uniform. She felt unpeeled and rather exposed. She felt almost improper.

They talked desultorily about Henry's departure next morning, and made the trivial arrangement. But of the matter on their minds, none of them spoke. They were rather quiet and friendly this evening; Banford had practically nothing to say. But inside herself she seemed still, perhaps kindly.

At nine o'clock March brought in the tray with the everlasting tea and a little cold meat which Banford had managed to procure. It was the last supper, so Banford did not want to be disagreeable. She felt a bit sorry for the boy, and felt she must be as nice as she could.

He wanted her to go bed. She was usually the first. But she sat on in her chair under the lamp, glancing at her book now and then, and staring into the fire. A deep silence had come into the room. It was broken by March asking, in a rather small tone:

"What time is it, Jill?"

"Five past ten," said Banford, looking at her wrist.

And then not a sound. The boy had looked up from the book he was holding between his knees. His rather wide, cat-shaped face had its obstinate look, his eyes were watchful.

"What about bed?" said March at last.

"I'm ready when you are," said Banford.

"Oh, very well," said March. "I'll fill your bottle."

She was as good as her word. When the hot-water bottle was ready, she lit a candle and went upstairs with it. Banford remained in her chair, listening acutely. March came downstairs again.

"There you are, then," she said. "Are you going up?"

"Yes, in a minute," said Banford. But the minute passed, and she sat on in her chair under the lamp.

Henry, whose eyes were shining like a cat's as he watched from under his brows, and whose face seemed wider, more chubbed and cat-like with unalterable obstinacy, now rose to his feet to try his throw.

"I think I'll go and look if I can see the she-fox," he said. "She may be creeping round. Won't you come as well for a minute, Nellie, and see if we see anything?"

"Me!" cried March, looking up with her startled, wondering face.

"Yes. Come on," he said. It was wonderful how soft and warm and coaxing his voice could be, how near. The very sound of it made Banford's blood boil. "Come on for a minute," he said, looking down into her uplifted, unsure face.

And she rose to her feet as if drawn up by his young, ruddy face that was looking down on her.

"I should think you're never going out at this time of night, Nellie!" cried Banford.

"Yes, just for a minute," said the boy, looking round on her, and speaking with an odd, sharp yelp in his voice.

March looked from one to the other, as if confused, vague. Banford rose to her feet for battle.

"Why, it's ridiculous. It's bitter cold. You'll catch your death in that thin frock. And in those slippers. You're not going to do any such thing."

There was a moment's pause. Banford turtled up like a little fighting cock, facing March and the boy.

"Oh, I don't think you need worry yourself," he replied. "A moment under the stars won't do anybody any damage. I'll get the rug off the sofa in the dining-room. You're coming, Nellie."

His voice had so much anger and contempt and fury in it as he spoke to Banford: and so much tenderness and proud authority as he spoke to March, that the latter answered:

"Yes, I'm coming."

And she turned with him to the door.

Banford, standing there in the middle of the room, suddenly burst into a long wail and a spasm of sobs. She covered her face with her poor, thin hands, and her thin shoulders shook in an agony of weeping. March looked back from the door.

"Jill!" she cried in a frantic tone, like someone just coming awake. And she seemed to start towards her darling.

But the boy had March's arm in his grip, and she could not move. She did not know why she could not move. It was as in a dream when the heart strains and the body cannot stir.

"Never mind," said the boy softly. "Let her cry. Let her cry. She will have to cry sooner or later. And the tears will relieve her feelings. They will do her good."

So he drew March slowly through the doorway. But her last look was back to the poor little figure which stood in the middle of the room with covered face and thin shoulders shaken with bitter weeping.

In the dining-room he picked up the rug and said:

"Wrap yourself up in this."

She obeyed—and they reached the kitchen door, he holding her soft and firm by the arm, though she did not know it. When she saw the night outside she started back.

"I must go back to Jill," she said. "I must! Oh yes, I must."

Her tone sounded final. The boy let go of her and she turned indoors. But he seized her again and arrested her.

"Wait a minute," he said. "Wait a minute. Even if you go, you're not going yet."

"Leave go! Leave go!" she cried. "My place is at Jill's side. Poor little thing, she's sobbing her heart out."

"Yes," said the boy bitterly. "And your heart too, and mine as well."

"Your heart?" said March. He still gripped her and detained her.

"Isn't it as good as her heart?" he said. "Or do you think it's not?"

"Your heart?" she said again, incredulous.

"Yes, mine! Mine! Do you think I haven't got a heart?" And with his hot grasp he took her hand and pressed it under his left breast. "There's my heart," he said, "if you don't believe in it."

It was wonder which made her attend. And then she felt the deep, heavy, powerful stroke of his heart, terrible, like something from beyond. It was like something from beyond, something awful from outside, signaling to her. And the signal paralyzed her. It beat upon her very soul, and made her helpless. She forgot Jill. She could not think of Jill any more. She could not think of her. That terrible signaling from outside!

The boy put his arm round her waist.

"Come with me," he said gently. "Come and let us say what we've got to say."

And he drew her outside, closed the door. And she went with him darkly down the garden path. That he should have a beating heart! And that he should have his arm around her, outside the blanket! She was too confused to think who he was or what he was.

He took her to a dark corner of the shed, where there was a tool-box with a lid, long and low.

"We'll sit here a minute," he said.

And obediently she sat down by his side.

"Give me your hand," he said.

She gave him both her hands, and he held them between his own. He was young, and it made him tremble.

"You'll marry me. You'll marry me before I go back, won't you?" he pleaded.

"Why, aren't we both a pair of fools?" she said.

He had put her in the corner, so that she should not look out and see the lighted window of the house across the dark garden. He tried to keep her all there inside the shed with him.

"In what way a pair of fools?" he said. "If you go back to Canada with me, I've got a job and a good wage waiting for me, and it's a nice place, near the mountains. Why shouldn't you marry me? Why shouldn't we marry? I should like to have you there with me. I should like to feel I'd got somebody there, at the back of me, all my life."

"You'd easily find somebody else who'd suit you better." she said.

"Yes, I might easily find another girl. I know I could. But not one I really wanted. I've never met one I really wanted for good. You see, I'm thinking of all my life. If I marry, I want to feel it's for all my life. Other girls: well, they're just girls, nice enough to go a walk with now and then. Nice enough for a bit of play. But when I think of my life, then I should be very sorry to have to marry one of them, I should indeed."

"You mean they wouldn't make you a good wife."

"Yes, I mean that. But I don't mean they wouldn't do their duty to me. I mean—I don't know what I mean. Only when I think of my life, and of you, then the two things go together."

"And what if they didn't?" she said, with her odd, sardonic touch.

"Well, I think they would."

They sat for some time silent. He held her hands in his, but he did not make love to her. Since he had realized that she was a woman, and vulnerable, accessible, a certain heaviness had possessed his soul. He did not want to make love to her. He shrank from any such performance, almost with fear. She was a woman, and vulnerable, accessible to him finally, and he held back from that which was ahead, almost with dread. It was a kind of darkness he knew he would enter finally, but of which he did not want as yet even to think. She was the woman, and he was responsible for the strange vulnerability he had suddenly realized in her.

"No," she said at last. "I'm a fool. I know I'm a fool."

"What for?" he asked.

"To go on with this business."

"Do you mean me?" he asked.

"No, I mean myself. I'm making a fool of myself, and a big one."

"Why, because you don't want to marry me, really?"

"Oh, I don't know whether I'm against it, as a matter of fact. That's just it. I don't know."

He looked at her in the darkness, puzzled. He did not in the least know what she meant.

"And don't you know whether you like to sit here with me this minute or not?" he asked.

"No, I don't really. I don't know whether I wish I was somewhere else, or whether I like being here. I don't know, really."

"Do you wish you were with Miss Banford? Do you wish you'd gone to bed with her?" he asked, as a challenge.

She waited a long time before she answered.

"No," she said at last. "I don't wish that."

"And do you think you would spend all your life with her—when your hair goes white, and you are old?" he said.

"No," she said, without much hesitation. "I don't see Jill and me two old women together."

"And don't you think, when I'm an old man and you're an old woman, we might be together still, as we are now?" he said.

"Well, not as we are now," she replied. "But I could imagine— no, I can't. I can't imagine you an old man. Besides, it's dreadful!"

"What, to be an old man?"

"Yes, of course."

"Not when the times comes," he said. "But it hasn't come. Only it will. And when it does, I should like to think you'd be there as well."

"Sort of old age pensions," she said dryly.

Her kind of witless humor always startled him. He never knew what she meant. Probably she didn't quite know herself.

"No," he said, hurt.

"I don't know why you harp on old age," she said. "I'm not ninety."

"Did anybody ever say you were?" he asked, offended.

They were silent for some time, pulling different ways in the silence.

"I don't want you to make fun of me," he said.

"Don't you?" she replied, enigmatic.

"No, because just this minute I'm serious. And when I'm serious, I believe in not making fun of it."

"You mean nobody else must make fun of you," she replied.

"Yes, I mean that. And I mean I don't believe in making fun of it myself. When it comes over me so that I'm serious, then—there it is, I don't want it to be laughed at."

She was silent for some time. Then she said, in a vague, almost pained voice:

"No, I'm not laughing at you."

A hot wave rose in his heart.

"You believe me, do you?" he asked.

"Yes, I believe you," she replied, with a twang of her old, tired nonchalance, as if she gave in because she was tired. But he didn't care. His heart was hot and clamorous.

"So you agree to marry me before I go?—perhaps at Christmas?"

"Yes, I agree."

"There!" he exclaimed. "That's settled it."

And he sat silent, unconscious, with all the blood burning in all his veins, like fire in all the branches and twigs of him. He only pressed her two hands to his chest, without knowing. When the curious passion began to die down, he seemed to come awake to the world.

"We'll go in, shall we?" he said: as if he realized it was cold.

She rose without answering.

"Kiss me before we go, now you've said it," he said.

And he kissed her gently on the mouth, with a young, frightened kiss. It made her feel so young, too, and frightened, and wondering: and tired, tired, as if she were going to sleep.

They went indoors. And in the sitting-room, there, crouched by the fire like a queer little witch, was Banford. She looked round with reddened eyes as they entered, but did not rise. He thought she looked frightening, unnatural, crouching there and looking round at them. Evil he thought her look was, and he crossed his fingers.

Banford saw the ruddy, elate face on the youth: he seemed strangely tall and bright and looming. And March had a delicate look on her face; she wanted to hide her face, to screen it, to let it not be seen.

"You've come at last," said Banford uglily.

"Yes, we've come," said he.

"You've been long enough for anything," she said.

"Yes, we have. We've settled it. We shall marry as soon as possible," he replied.

"Oh, you've settled it, have you! Well, I hope you won't live to repent it," said Banford.

"I hope so too," he replied.

"Are you going to bed *now*, Nellie?" said Banford.

"Yes, I'm going now."

"Then for goodness' sake come along."

March looked at the boy. He was glancing with his very bright eyes at her and at Banford. March looked at him wistfully. She wished she could stay with him. She wished she had married him already, and it was all over. For oh, she felt suddenly so safe with him. She felt so strangely safe and peaceful in his presence. If only she could sleep in his shelter, and not with Jill. She felt afraid of Jill. In her dim, tender state, it was agony to have to go with Jill and sleep with her. She wanted the boy to save her. She looked again at him.

And he, watching with bright eyes, divined something of what she felt. It puzzled and distressed him that she must go with Jill.

"I shan't forget what you've promised," he said, looking clear into her eyes, right into her eyes, so that he seemed to occupy all herself with his queer, bright look.

She smiled to him faintly, gently. She felt safe again—safe with him.

But in spite of all the boy's precautions, he had a setback. The morning he was leaving the farm he got March to accompany him to the market-town, about six miles away, where they went to the registrar and had their names stuck up as two people who were going to marry. He was to come at Christmas, and the wedding was to take place then. He hoped in the spring to be able to take March back to Canada with him, now the war was really over. Though he was so young, he had saved some money.

"You never have to be without *some* money at the back of you, if you can help it," he said.

So she saw him off in the train that was going West: his camp was on Salisbury Plain. And with big, dark eyes she watched him go, and it seemed as if everything real in life was retreating as the train retreated with his queer, chubby, ruddy face, that seemed so broad across the cheeks, and which never seemed to change its expression, save when a cloud of sulky anger hung on the brow, or the bright eyes fixed themselves in their stare. This was what happened now. He leaned there out of the carriage window as the train drew off, saying good-bye and staring back at her, but his face quite

With this one fixed idea in his mind, he went to ask for twenty-four hours' leave of absence. He knew it was not due to him. His consciousness was supernaturally keen. He knew where he must go—he must go to the captain. But how could he get at the captain? In that great camp of wooden huts and tents he had no idea where his captain was.

But he went to the officers' canteen. There was his captain standing talking with three other officers. Henry stood in the doorway at attention.

"May I speak to Captain Berryman?" The captain was Cornish like himself.

"What do you want?" called the captain.

"May I speak to you, Captain?"

"What do you want?" replied the captain, not stirring from among his group of fellow officers.

Henry watched his superior for a minute without speaking.

"You won't refuse me, sir, will you?" he asked gravely.

"It depends what it is."

"Can I have twenty-four hours' leave?"

"No, you've no business to ask."

"I know I haven't. But I must ask you."

"You've had your answer."

"Don't send me away, Captain."

There was something strange about the boy as he stood there so everlasting in the doorway. The Cornish captain felt the strangeness at once, and eyed him shrewdly.

"Why, what's afoot?" he said, curious.

"I'm in trouble about something. I must go to Blewbury," said the boy.

"Blewbury, eh? After the girls?"

"Yes, it is a woman, Captain." And the boy, as he stood there with his head reaching forward a little, went suddenly terribly pale, or yellow, and his lips seemed to give off pain. The captain saw and paled a little also. He turned aside.

"Go on, then," he said. "But for God's sake don't cause any trouble of any sort."

"I won't, Captain, thank you."

He was gone. The captain, upset, took a gin and bitters. Henry managed to hire a bicycle. It was twelve o'clock when he left the camp. He had sixty miles of wet and muddy crossroads to ride. But he was in the saddle and down the road without a thought of food.

At the farm, March was busy with a work she had had some time in hand. A bunch of Scotch fir trees stood at the end of the open shed, on a little bank where ran the fence between two of the gorse-shaggy meadows. The farthest of these trees was dead—it had died in the summer, and stood with all its needles brown and sere in the air. It was not a very big tree. And it was absolutely dead. So March determined to have it, although they were not allowed to cut any of the timber. But it would make such splendid firing, in these days of scarce fuel.

She had been giving a few stealthy chops at the trunk for a week or more, every now and then hacking away for five minutes, low down, near the ground, so no one should notice. She had not tried the saw, it was such hard work, alone. Now the tree stood with a great yawning gap in his base, perched, as it were, on one sinew, and ready to fall. But he did not fall.

It was late in the damp December afternoon, with cold mists creeping out of the woods and up the hollows, and darkness waiting to sink in from above. There was a bit of yellowness where the sun was fading away beyond the low woods of the distance. March took her axe and went to the tree. The small thud-thud of her blows resounded rather ineffectual about the wintry homestead. Banford came out wearing her thick coat, but with no hat on her head, so that her thin, bobbed hair blew on the uneasy wind that sounded in the pines and in the wood.

"What I'm afraid of," said Banford, "is that it will fall on the shed and we sh'll have another job repairing that."

"Oh, I don't think so," said March, straightening herself and wiping her arm over her hot brow. She was flushed red, her eyes were very wide open and queer, her upper lip lifted away from her two white, front teeth with a curious, almost rabbit look.

A little stout man in a black overcoat and a bowler hat came pottering across the yard. He had a pink face and a white beard and smallish, pale-blue eyes. He was not very old, but nervy, and he walked with little short steps.

"What do you think, father?" said Banford. "Don't you think it might hit the shed in falling?"

"Shed, no!" said the old man. "Can't hit the shed. Might as well say the fence."

"The fence doesn't matter," said March, in her high voice.

"Wrong as usual, am I!" said Banford, wiping her straying hair from her eyes.

The tree stood as it were on one spelch of itself, leaning, and creaking in the wind. It grew on the bank of a little dry ditch between the two meadows. On the top of the bank straggled one fence, running to the bushes uphill. Several trees clustered there in the corner of the field near the shed and near the gate which led into the yard. Towards this gate, horizontal across the weary meadows, came the grassy, rutted approach from the high road. There trailed another rickety fence, long split poles joining the short, thick, wide-apart uprights. The three people stood at the back of the tree, in the corner of the shed meadow, just above the yard gate. The house, with its two gables and its porch, stood tidy in a little grassed garden across the yard. A little, stout, rosy-faced woman in a little red woolen shoulder shawl had come and taken her stand in the porch.

"Isn't it down yet?" she cried, in a high little voice.

"Just thinking about it," called her husband. His tone towards the two girls was always rather mocking and satirical. March did not want to go on with her hitting while he was there. As for him, he wouldn't lift a stick from the ground if he could help it, complaining, like his daughter, of rheumatics in his shoulder. So the three stood there a moment silent in the cold afternoon, in the bottom corner near the yard.

They heard the far-off taps of a gate, and craned to look. Away across, on the green horizontal approach, a figure was just swinging on to a bicycle again, and lurching up and down over the grass, approaching.

"Why, it's one of our boys—it's Jack," said the old man.

"Can't be," said Banford.

March craned her head to look. She alone recognized the khaki figure. She flushed, but said nothing.

"No, it isn't Jack, I don't think," said the old man, staring with little round blue eyes under his white lashes.

In another moment the bicycle lurched into sight, and the rider dropped off at the gate. It was Henry, his face wet and red and spotted with mud. He was altogether a muddy sight.

"O!" cried Banford, as if afraid. "Why, it's Henry!"

"What!" muttered the old man. He had a thick, rapid, muttering way of speaking, and was slightly deaf. "What? What? Who is it? Who is it, do you say? That young fellow? That young fellow of Nellie's? Oh! Oh!" And the satiric smile came on his pink face and white eyelashes.

Henry, pushing the wet hair off his steaming brow, had caught sight of them and heard what the old man said. His hot, young face seemed to flame in the cold light.

"Oh, are you all there!" he said, giving his sudden, puppy's little laugh. He was so hot and dazed with cycling he hardly know where he was. He leaned the bicycle against the fence and climbed over into the corner on to the bank, without going into the yard.

"Well, I must say, we weren't expecting *you*," said Banford laconically.

"No, I suppose not," said he, looking at March.

She stood aside, slack, with one knee drooped and the axe resting its head loosely on the ground. Her eyes were wide and vacant, and her upper lip lifted from her teeth in that helpless, fascinated rabbit look. The moment she saw his glowing, red face it was all over with her. She was as helpless as if she had been bound. The moment she saw the way his head seemed to reach forward.

"Well, who is it? Who is it, anyway?" asked the smiling, satiric old man in his muttering voice.

"Why, Mr. Grenfel, whom you've heard us tell about, father," said Banford coldly.

"Heard you tell about, I should think so. Heard of nothing else practically," muttered the elderly man, with his queer little jeering smile on his face. "How do you do," he added, suddenly reaching out his hand to Henry.

The boy shook hands just as startled. Then the two men fell apart.

"Cycled over from Salisbury Plain, have you?" asked the old man.

"Yes."

"Hm! Longish ride. How long d'it take you, eh? Some time, eh? Several hours, I suppose."

"About four."

"Eh? Four! Yes, I should have thought so. When are you going back, then?"

"I've got till tomorrow evening."

"Till tomorrow evening, eh? Yes. Hm! Girls weren't expecting you, were they?"

And the old man turned his pale-blue, round little eyes under their white lashes mockingly towards the girls. Henry also looked round. He had become a little awkward. He looked at March, who was still staring away into the distance as if to see where the cattle were. Her hand was on the pommel of the axe, whose head rested loosely on the ground.

"What were you doing there?" he asked in his soft, courteous voice. "Cutting a tree down?"

March seemed not to hear, as if in a trance.

"Yes," said Banford. "We've been at it for over a week."

"Oh! And have you done it all by yourselves then?"

"Nellie's done it all, I've done nothing," said Banford.

"Really! You must have worked quite hard," he said, addressing himself in a curious gentle tone direct to March. She did not answer, but remained half averted staring away towards the woods above as if in a trance.

"*Nellie!*" cried Banford sharply. "Can't you answer?"

"What—me?" cried March, starting round and looking from one to the other. "Did anyone speak to me?"

"Dreaming!" muttered the old man, turning aside to smile. "Must be in love, eh, dreaming in the daytime!"

"Did you say anything to me?" said March, looking at the boy as from a strange distance, her eyes wide and doubtful, her face delicately flushed.

"I said you must have worked hard at the tree," he replied courteously.

"Oh, that! Bit by bit. I thought it would have come down by now."

"I'm thankful it hasn't come down in the night, to frighten us to death," said Banford.

"Let me just finish it for you, shall I?" said the boy.

March slanted the axe-shaft in his direction.

"Would you like to?" she said.

"Yes, if you wish it," he said.

"Oh, I'm thankful when the thing's down, that's all," she replied, nonchalant.

"Which way is it going to fall?" said Banford. "Will it hit the shed?"

"No, it won't hit the shed," he said. "I should think it will fall there—quite clear. Though it might give a twist and catch the fence."

"Catch the fence!" cried the old man. "What, catch the fence! When it's leaning at that angle? Why, it's farther off than the shed. It won't catch the fence."

"No," said Henry, "I don't suppose it will. It has plenty of room to fall quite clear, and I suppose it will fall clear."

"Won't tumble backwards on top of *us*, will it?" asked the old man, sarcastic.

"No, it won't do that," said Henry, taking off his short overcoat and his tunic. "Ducks! Ducks! Go back!"

A line of four brown-speckled ducks led by a brown-and-green drake were stemming away downhill from the upper meadow, coming like boats running on a ruffled sea, cockling their way top speed downwards towards the fence and towards the little group of people, and cackling as excitedly as if they brought news of the Spanish Armada.

"Silly things! Silly things!" cried Banford, going forward to turn them off. But they came eagerly towards her, opening their yellow-green beaks and quacking as if they were so excited to say something.

"There's no food. There's nothing here. You must wait a bit," said Banford to them. "Go away. Go away. Go round to the yard."

They didn't go, so she climbed the fence to swerve them round under the gate and into the yard. So off they waggled in an excited string once more, wagging their rumps like the stems of little gondolas, ducking under the bar of the gate. Banford stood on the top of the bank, just over the fence, looking down on the other three.

Henry looked up at her, and met her queer, round-pupiled, weak eyes staring behind her spectacles. He was perfectly still. He looked away, up at the weak, leaning tree. And as he looked into the sky, like a huntsman who is watching a flying bird, he thought to himself: "If the tree falls in just such a way, and spins just so much as it falls, then the branch there will strike her exactly as she stands on top of that bank."

He looked at her again. She was wiping the hair from her brow again, with that perpetual gesture. In his heart he had decided her death. A terrible still force seemed in him, and a power that was just his. If he turned even a hair's breadth in the wrong direction, he would lose the power.

"Mind yourself, Miss Banford," he said. And his heart held perfectly still, in the terrible pure will that she should not move.

"Who, me, mind myself?" she cried, her father's jeering tone in her voice. "Why, do you think you might hit me with the axe?"

"No, it's just possible the tree might, though," he answered soberly. But the tone of his voice seemed to her to imply that he was only being falsely solicitous, and trying to make her move because it was his will to move her.

"Absolutely impossible," she said.

He heard her. But he held himself icy still, lest he should lose his power.

"No, it's just possible. You'd better come down this way."

"Oh, all right. Let us see some crack Canadian tree-felling," she retorted.

"Ready, then," he said, taking the axe, looking round to see he was clear.

There was a moment of pure, motionless suspense, when the world seemed to stand still. Then suddenly his form seemed to flash up enormously tall and fearful, he gave two swift, flashing blows, in immediate succession, the tree was severed, turning slowly, spinning strangely in the air and coming down like a sudden darkness on the earth. No one saw what was happening except himself. No one heard the strange little cry which the Banford gave as the dark end of the bough swooped down, down on her. No one saw her crouch a little and receive the blow on the back of the neck. No one saw her flung outwards and laid, a little twitching heap, at the foot of the fence. No one except the boy. And he watched with intense bright eyes, as he would watch a wild goose he had shot. Was it winged or dead? Dead!

Immediately he gave a loud cry. Immediately March gave a wild shriek that went far, far down the afternoon. And the father started a strange bellowing sound.

The boy leapt the fence and ran to the fringe. The back of the neck and head was a mass of blood, of horror. He turned it over.

The body was quivering with little convulsions. But she was dead really. He knew it, that it was so. He knew it in his soul and his blood. The inner necessity of his life was fulfilling itself, it was he who was to live. The thorn was drawn out of his bowels. So he put her down gently. She was dead.

He stood up. March was standing there petrified and absolutely motionless. Her face was dead white, her eyes big black pools. The old man was scrambling horribly over the fence.

"I'm afraid it's killed her," said the boy.

The old man was making curious, blubbering noises as he huddled over the fence. "What!" cried March, starting electric.

"Yes, I'm afraid," repeated the boy.

March was coming forward. The boy was over the fence before she reached it.

"What do you say, killed her?" she asked in a sharp voice.

"I'm afraid so," he answered softly.

She went still whiter, fearful. The two stood facing one another. Her black eyes gazed on him with the last look of resistance. And then in a last agonized failure she began to grizzle, to cry in a shivery little fashion of a child that doesn't want to cry, but which is beaten from within, and gives that little first shudder of sobbing which is not yet weeping, dry and fearful.

He had won. She stood there absolutely helpless, shuddering her dry sobs and her mouth trembling rapidly. And then, as in a child, with a little crash came the tears and the blind agony of sightless weeping. She sank down on the grass, and sat there with her hands on her breast and her face lifted in sightless, convulsed weeping. He stood above her, looking down on her, mute, pale, and everlasting seeming. He never moved, but looked down on her. And among all the torture of the scene, the torture of his own heart and bowels, he was glad, he had won.

After a long time he stooped to her and took her hands.

"Don't cry," he said softly. "Don't cry."

She looked up at him with tears running from her eyes, a senseless look of helplessness and submission. So she gazed on him as if sightless, yet looking up to him. She would never leave him again. He had won her. And he knew it and was glad, because he wanted her for his life. His life must have her. And now he had won her. It was what his life must have.

But if he had won her, he had not yet got her. They were married at Christmas as he had planned, and he got again ten days' leave. They went to Cornwall, to his own village, on the sea. He realized that it was awful for her to be at the farm any more.

But though she belonged to him, though she lived in his shadow, as if she could not be away from him, she was not happy. She did not want to leave him: and yet she did not feel free with him. Everything round her seemed to watch her, seemed to press on her. He had won her, he had her with him, she was his wife. And she— she belonged to him, she knew it. But she was not glad. And he was still foiled. He realized that though he was married to her and possessed her in every possible way, apparently, and though she wanted him to possess her, she wanted it, she wanted nothing else, now, still he did not quite succeed.

Something was missing. Instead of her soul swaying with new life, it seemed to droop, to bleed, as if it were wounded. She would sit for a long time with her hand in his, looking away at the sea. And in her dark, vacant eyes was a sort of wound, and her face looked a little peaked. If he spoke to her, she would turn to him with a faint new smile, the strange, quivering little smile of a woman who has died in the old way of love, and can't quite rise to the new way. She still felt she ought to *do* something, to strain herself in some direction. And there was nothing to do, and no direction in which to strain herself. And she could not quite accept the submergence which his new love put upon her. If she was in love, she ought to *exert* herself, in some way, loving. She felt the weary need of our day to *exert* herself in love. But she knew that in fact she must no more exert herself in love. He would not have the love which exerted itself towards him. It made his brow go black. No, he wouldn't let her exert her love towards him. No, she had to be passive, to acquiesce, and to be submerged under the surface of love. She had to be like the seaweeds she saw as she peered down from the boat, swaying forever delicately under water, with all their delicate fibrils put tenderly out upon the flood, sensitive, utterly sensitive and receptive within the shadowy sea, and never, never rising and looking forth above water while they lived. Never. Never looking forth from the water until they died, only then washing, corpses, upon the surface. But while they lived, always submerged, always beneath the wave. Beneath the wave they might have powerful roots, stronger than iron; they might be tenacious and dangerous in their soft waving within the flood. Beneath the water they might be stronger, more indestructible than resistant oak trees are on land. But it was always underwater, always underwater. And she, being a woman, must be like that.

And she had been so used to the very opposite. She had had to take all the thought for love and for life, and all the responsibility. Day after day she had been responsible for the coming day, for the coming year: for her dear Jill's health and happiness and well-being. Verily, in her own small way, she had felt herself responsible for the well-being of the world. And this had been her great stimulant, this grand feeling that, in her own small sphere, she was responsible for the well-being of the world.

And she had failed. She knew that, even in her small way, she had failed. She had failed to satisfy her own feeling of responsibility. It was so difficult. It seemed so grand and easy at first. And the more you tried, the more difficult it became. It had seemed so easy to make one beloved creature happy. And the more you tried, the worse the failure. It was terrible. She had been all her life reaching, reaching, and what she reached for seemed so near, until she had stretched to her utmost limit. And then it was always beyond her.

Always beyond her, vaguely, unrealizably beyond her, and she was left with nothingness at last. The life she reached for, the happiness she reached for, the well-being she reached for all slipped back, became unreal, the farther she stretched her hand. She wanted some goal, some finality—and there was none. Always this ghastly reaching, reaching, striving for something that might be just beyond. Even to make Jill happy. She was glad Jill was dead. For she had realized that she could never make her happy. Jill would always be fretting herself thinner and thinner, weaker and weaker. Her pains grew worse instead of less. It would be so for ever. She was glad she was dead.

And if Jill had married a man it would have been just the same. The woman striving, striving to make the man happy, striving within her own limits for the well-being of her world. And always achieving failure. Little, foolish successes in money or in ambition. But at the very point where she most wanted success, in the anguished effort to make some one beloved human being happy and perfect, there the failure was almost catastrophic. You wanted to make your beloved happy, and his happiness seemed always achievable. If only you did just this, that and the other. And you did this, that, and the other, in all good faith, and every time the failure became a little more ghastly. You could love yourself to ribbons and strive and strain yourself to the bone, and things would go from bad to worse, bad to worse, as far as happiness went. The awful mistake of happiness.

Poor March, in her good-will and her responsibility, she had strained herself till it seemed to her that the whole of life and everything was only a horrible abyss of nothingness. The more you reach after the fatal flower of happiness, which trembles so blue and lovely in a crevice just beyond your grasp, the more fearfully you become aware of the ghastly and awful gulf of the precipice below you, into which you will inevitably plunge, as into the bottomless pit, if you reach any farther. You pluck flower after flower—it is never *the* flower. The flower itself—its calyx[5] is a horrible gulf, it is the bottomless pit.

That is the whole history of the search for happiness, whether it

5. The outer covering of a flower while in the bud.

be your own or somebody else's that you want to win. It ends, and it always ends, in the ghastly sense of the bottomless nothingness into which you will inevitably fall if you strain any farther.

And women?—what goal can any woman conceive, except happiness? Just happiness for herself and the whole world. That, and nothing else. And so, she assumes the responsibility and sets off towards her goal. She can see it there, at the foot of the rainbow. Or she can see it a little way beyond, in the blue distance. Not far, not far.

But the end of the rainbow is a bottomless gulf down which you can fall forever without arriving, and the blue distance is a void pit which can swallow you and all your efforts into its emptiness, and still be no emptier. You and all your efforts. So, the illusion of attainable happiness!

Poor March, she had set off so wonderfully towards the blue goal. And the farther and farther she had gone, the more fearful had become the realization of emptiness. An agony, an insanity at last.

She was glad it was over. She was glad to sit on the shore and look westwards over the sea, and know the great strain had ended. She would never strain for love and happiness any more. And Jill was safely dead. Poor Jill, poor Jill. It must be sweet to be dead.

For her own part, death was not her destiny. She would have to leave her destiny to the boy. But then, the boy. He wanted more than that. He wanted her to give herself without defenses, to sink and become submerged in him. And she—she wanted to sit still, like a woman on the last milestone, and watch. She wanted to see, to know, to understand. She wanted to be alone: with him at her side.

And he! He did not want her to watch any more, to see any more, to understand any more. He wanted to veil her woman's spirit, as Orientals veil the woman's face. He wanted her to commit herself to him, and to put her independent spirit to sleep. He wanted to take away from her all her effort, all that seemed her very *raison d'être*. He wanted to make her submit, yield, blindly pass away out of all her strenuous consciousness. He wanted to take away her consciousness, and make her just his woman. Just his woman.

And she was so tired, so tired, like a child that wants to go to sleep, but which fights against sleep as if sleep were death. She seemed to stretch her eyes wider in the obstinate effort and tension of keeping awake. She *would* keep awake. She *would* know. She *would* consider and judge and decide. She *would* have the reins of her own life between her own hands. She *would* be an independent woman to the last. But she was so tired, so tired of everything. And sleep seemed near. And there was such rest in the boy.

Yet, there, sitting in a niche of the high, wild cliffs of West Cornwall, looking over the westward sea, she stretched her eyes wider and wider. Away to the West, Canada, America. She *would* know and she *would* see what was ahead. And the boy, sitting beside her, staring down at the gulls, had a cloud between his brows and the strain of discontent in his eyes. He wanted her asleep, at peace in him. He wanted her at peace, asleep in him. And *there* she was, dying with the strain of her own wakefulness. Yet she would not sleep: no, never. Sometimes he thought bitterly that he ought to have left her. He ought never to have killed Banford. He should have left Banford and March to kill one another.

But that was only impatience: and he knew it. He was waiting, waiting to go West. He was aching almost in torment to leave England, to go West, to take March away. To leave this shore! He believed that as they crossed the seas, as they left this England which he so hated, because in some way it seemed to have stung him with poison, she would go to sleep. She would close her eyes at last and give in to him.

And then he would have her, and he would have his own life at last. He chafed, feeling he hadn't got his own life. He would never have it till she yielded and slept in him. Then he would have all his own life as a young man and a male, and she would have all her own life as a woman and a female. There would be no more of this awful straining. She would not be a man any more, an independent woman with a man's responsibility. Nay, even the responsibility for her own soul she would have to commit to him. He knew it was so, and obstinately held out against her, waiting for the surrender.

"You'll feel better when once we get over the seas to Canada over there," he said to her as they sat among the rocks on the cliff.

She looked away to the sea's horizon, as if it were not real. Then she looked round at him, with the strained, strange look of a child that is struggling against sleep.

"Shall I?" she said.

"Yes," he answered quietly.

And her eyelids dropped with the slow motion, sleep weighing them unconscious. But she pulled them open again to say:

"Yes, I may. I can't tell. I can't tell what it will be like over there."

"If only we could go soon!" he said, with pain in his voice.

1923

Why the Novel Matters

We have curious ideas of ourselves. We think of ourselves as a body with a spirit in it, or a body with a soul in it, or a body with a mind in it. *Mens sana in corpore sano.* The years drink up the wine, and at last throw the bottle away, the body, of course, being the bottle.

It is a funny sort of superstition. Why should I look at my hand, as it so cleverly writes these words, and decide that it is a mere nothing compared to the mind that directs it? Is there really any huge difference between my hand and my brain? Or my mind? My hand is alive, it flickers with a life of its own. It meets all the strange universe in touch, and learns a vast number of things, and knows a vast number of things. My hand, as it writes these words, slips gaily along, jumps like a grasshopper to dot an *i*, feels the table rather cold, gets a little bored if I write too long, has its own rudiments of thought, and is just as much *me* as is my brain, my mind, or my soul. Why should I imagine that there is a *me* which is more *me* than my hand is? Since my hand is absolutely alive, me alive.

Whereas, of course, as far as I am concerned, my pen isn't alive at all. My pen *isn't me* alive. Me alive ends at my finger tips.

Whatever is me alive is me. Every tiny bit of my hands is alive, every little freckle and hair and fold of skin. And whatever is me alive is me. Only my fingernails, those ten little weapons between me and an inanimate universe, they cross the mysterious Rubicon [1] between me alive and things like my pen, which are not alive, in my own sense.

So, seeing my hand is all alive, and me alive, wherein is it just a bottle, or a jug, or a tin can, or a vessel of clay, or any of the rest of that nonsense? True, if I cut it it will bleed, like a can of cherries. But then the skin that is cut, and the veins that bleed, and the bones that should never be seen, they are all just as alive as the blood that flows. So the tin can business, or vessel of clay, is just bunk.

And that's what you learn, when you're a novelist. And that's what you are very liable *not* to know, if you're a parson, or a philosopher, or a scientist, or a stupid person. If you're a parson, you talk about souls in heaven. If you're a novelist, you know that paradise is in the palm of your hand, and on the end of your nose, because both are alive; and alive, and man alive, which is more than you can say,

---

1. When Julius Caesar crossed the River Rubicon (near Rimini, Italy) in 49 B.C., in defiance of the Senate's orders, this indicated his intention of advancing against Pompey and thus involving the country in civil war. Hence to "cross the Rubicon" means to take an important and irrevocable decision.

for certain, of paradise. Paradise is after life, and I for one am not keen on anything that is *after* life. If you are a philosopher, you talk about infinity, and the pure spirit which knows all things. But if you pick up a novel, you realize immediately that infinity is just a handle to this self-same jug of a body of mine; while as for knowing, if I find my finger in the fire, I know that fire burns, with a knowledge so emphatic and vital, it leaves Nirvana merely a conjecture. Oh, yes, my body, me alive, *knows*, and knows intensely. And as for the sum of all knowledge, it can't be anything more than an accumulation of all the things I know in the body, and you, dear reader, know in the body.

These damned philosophers, they talk as if they suddenly went off in steam, and were then much more important than they are when they're in their shirts. It is nonsense. Every man, philosopher included, ends in his own finger tips. That's the end of his man alive. As for the words and thoughts and sighs and aspirations that fly from him, they are so many tremulations in the ether, and not alive at all. But if the tremulations reach another man alive, he may receive them into his life, and his life may take on a new color, like a chameleon creeping from a brown rock on to a green leaf. All very well and good. It still doesn't alter the fact that the so-called spirit, the message or teaching of the philosopher or the saint, isn't alive at all, but just a tremulation upon the ether, like a radio message. All this spirit stuff is just tremulations upon the ether. If you, as man alive, quiver from the tremulation of the ether into new life, that is because you are man alive, and you take sustenance and stimulation into your alive man in a myriad ways. But to say that the message, or the spirit which is communicated to you, is more important than your living body, is nonsense. You might as well say that the potato at dinner was more important.

Nothing is important but life. And for myself, I can absolutely see life nowhere but in the living. Life with a capital L is only man alive. Even a cabbage in the rain is cabbage alive. All things that are alive are amazing. And all things that are dead are subsidiary to the living. Better a live dog than a dead lion. But better a live lion than a live dog. *C'est la vie!*

It seems impossible to get a saint, or a philosopher, or a scientist, to stick to this simple truth. They are all, in a sense, renegades. The saint wishes to offer himself up as spiritual food for the multitude. Even Francis of Assisi turns himself into a sort of angel-cake, of which anyone may take a slice. But an angel-cake is rather less than man alive. And poor St. Francis might well apologize to his body, when he is dying: "Oh, pardon me, my body, the wrong I did you through the years!" It was no wafer, for others to eat.

The philosopher, on the other hand, because he can think, decides that nothing but thoughts matter. It is as if a rabbit, because he can make little pills, should decide that nothing but little pills matter. As for the scientist, he has absolutely no use for me so long as I am man alive. To the scientist, I am dead. He puts under the microscope a bit of dead me, and calls it me. He takes me to pieces, and says first one piece, and then another piece, is me. My heart, my liver, my stomach have all been scientifically me, according to the scientist; and nowadays I am either a brain, or nerves, or glands, or something more up-to-date in the tissue line.

Now I absolutely flatly deny that I am a soul, or a body, or a mind, or an intelligence, or a brain, or a nervous system, or a bunch of glands, or any of the rest of these bits of me. The whole is greater than the part. And therefore, I, who am man alive, am greater than my soul, or spirit, or body, or mind, or consciousness, or anything else that is merely a part of me. I am a man, and alive. I am man alive, and as long as I can, I intend to go on being man alive.

For this reason I am a novelist. And being a novelist, I consider myself superior to the saint, the scientist, the philosopher, and the poet, who are all great masters of different bits of man alive, but never get the whole hog.

The novel is the one bright book of life. Books are not life. They are only tremulations on the ether. But the novel as a tremulation can make the whole man alive tremble. Which is more than poetry, philosophy, science, or any other book-tremulation can do.

The novel is the book of life. In this sense, the Bible is a great confused novel. You may say, it is about God. But it is really about man alive. Adam, Eve, Sarai, Abraham, Isaac, Jacob, Samuel, David, Bath-Sheba, Ruth, Esther, Solomon, Job, Isaiah, Jesus, Mark, Judas, Paul, Peter: what is it but man alive, from start to finish? Man alive, not mere bits. Even the Lord is another man alive, in a burning bush, throwing the tablets of stone at Moses's head.

I do hope you begin to get my idea, why the novel is supremely important, as a tremulation on the ether. Plato makes the perfect ideal being tremble in me. But that's only a bit of me. Perfection is only a bit, in the strange make-up of man alive. The Sermon on the Mount makes the selfless spirit of me quiver. But that, too, is only a bit of me. The Ten Commandments set the old Adam shivering in me, warning me that I am a thief and a murderer, unless I watch it. But even the old Adam is only a bit of me.

I very much like all these bits of me to be set trembling with life and the wisdom of life. But I do ask that the whole of me shall tremble in its wholeness, some time or other.

And this, of course, must happen in me, living.

But as far as it can happen from a communication, it can only happen when a whole novel communicates itself to me. The Bible —but *all* the Bible—and Homer, and Shakespeare: these are the supreme old novels. These are all things to all men. Which means that in their wholeness they affect the whole man alive, which is the man himself, beyond any part of him. They set the whole tree trembling with a new access of life, they do not just stimulate growth in one direction.

I don't want to grow in any one direction any more. And, if I can help it, I don't want to stimulate anybody else into some particular direction. A particular direction ends in a *cul-de-sac*. We're in a *cul-de-sac* at present.

I don't believe in any dazzling revelation, or in any supreme Word. "The grass withereth, the flower fadeth, but the Word of the Lord shall stand for ever." That's the kind of stuff we've drugged ourselves with. As a matter of fact, the grass withereth, but comes up all the greener for that reason, after the rains. The flower fadeth, and therefore the bud opens. But the Word of the Lord, being man-uttered and a mere vibration on the ether, becomes staler and staler, more and more boring, till at last we turn a deaf ear and it ceases to exist, far more finally than any withered grass. It is grass that renews its youth like the eagle, not any Word.

We should ask for no absolutes, or absolute. Once and for all and for ever, let us have done with the ugly imperialism of any absolute. There is no absolute good, there is nothing absolutely right. All things flow and change, and even change is not absolute. The whole is a strange assembly of apparently incongruous parts, slipping past one another.

Me, man alive, I am a very curious assembly of incongruous parts. My yea! of today is oddly different from my yea! of yesterday. My tears of tomorrow will have nothing to do with my tears of a year ago. If the one I love remains unchanged and unchanging, I shall cease to love her. It is only because she changes and startles me into change and defies my inertia, and is herself staggered in her inertia by my changing, that I can continue to love her. If she stayed put, I might as well love the pepper pot.

In all this change, I maintain a certain integrity. But woe betide me if I try to put my finger on it. If I say of myself, I am this, I am that!—then, if I stick to it, I turn into a stupid fixed thing like a lamp-post. I shall never know wherein lies my integrity, my individuality, my me. I *can* never know it. It is useless to talk about my ego. That only means that I have made up an *idea* of myself, and that I am trying to cut myself out to pattern. Which is no good. You can cut your cloth to fit your coat, but you can't clip bits off your living body, to trim it down to your idea. True, you can put yourself into ideal corsets. But even in ideal corsets, fashions change.

Let us learn from the novel. In the novel, the characters can do nothing but *live*. If they keep on being good, according to pattern, or bad, according to pattern, or even volatile, according to pattern, they cease to live, and the novel falls dead. A character in a novel has got to live, or it is nothing.

We, likewise, in life have got to live, or we are nothing.

What we mean by living is, of course, just as indescribable as what we mean by *being*. Men get ideas into their heads, of what they mean by Life, and they proceed to cut life out to pattern. Sometimes they go into the desert to seek God, sometimes they go into the desert to seek cash, sometimes it is wine, woman, and song, and again it is water, political reform, and votes. You never know what it will be next: from killing your neighbor with hideous bombs and gas that tears the lungs, to supporting a Foundlings Home and preaching infinite Love, and being co-respondent in a divorce.

In all this wild welter, we need some sort of guide. It's no good inventing Thou Shalt Nots!

What then? Turn truly, honorably to the novel, and see wherein you are man alive, and wherein you are dead man in life. You may love a woman as man alive, and you may be making love to a woman as sheer dead man in life. You may eat your dinner as man alive, or as a mere masticating corpse. As man alive you may have shot at your enemy. But as a ghastly simulacrum of life you may be firing bombs into men who are neither your enemies nor your friends, but just things you are dead to. Which is criminal, when the things happen to be alive.

To be alive, to be man alive, to be whole man alive: that is the point. And at its best, the novel, and the novel supremely, can help you. It can help you not to be dead man in life. So much of a man walks about dead and a carcass in the street and house, today: so much of women is merely dead. Like a pianoforte with half the notes mute.

But the novel you can see, plainly, when the man goes dead, the woman goes inert. You can develop an instinct for life, if you will, instead of a theory of right and wrong, good and bad.

In life, there is right and wrong, good and bad, all the time. But what is right in one case is wrong in another. And in the novel you see one man becoming a corpse, because of his so-called goodness, another going dead because of his so-called wickedness. Right and wrong is an instinct: but an instinct of the whole consciousness in a man, bodily, mental, spiritual at once. And only in the novel are *all* things given full play, or at least, they may be given full play, when we realize that life itself, and not inert safety, is the reason for living. For out of the full play of all things emerges the only thing that is anything, the wholeness of a man, the wholeness of a woman, man alive, and live woman.

1936

Love on the Farm[1]

What large, dark hands are those at the window
Grasping in the golden light
Which weaves its way through the evening wind
    At my heart's delight?

Ah, only the leaves! But in the west   5
I see a redness suddenly come
Into the evening's anxious breast—
    'Tis the wound of love goes home!

The woodbine creeps abroad
Calling low to her lover: 10
   The sunlit flirt who all the day
   Has poised above her lips in play
   And stolen kisses, shallow and gay
   Of pollen, now has gone away—
   She woos the moth with her sweet, low word;   15
And when above her his moth-wings hover
Then her bright breast she will uncover
And yield her honey-drop to her lover.

Into the yellow, evening glow
Saunters a man from the farm below;   20
Leans, and looks in at the low-built shed
Where the swallow has hung her marriage bed.
   The bird lies warm against the wall.
   She glances quick her startled eyes
   Towards him, then she turns away   25
   Her small head, making warm display
   Of red upon the throat. Her terrors sway
   Her out of the nest's warm, busy ball,
   Whose plaintive cry is heard as she flies
   In one blue stoop from out the sties   30
   Into the twilight's empty hall.
Oh, water-hen, beside the rushes
Hide your quaintly scarlet blushes,
Still your quick tail, lie still as dead,
Till the distance folds over his ominous tread!   35

The rabbit presses back her ears,
Turns back her liquid, anguished eyes
And crouches low; then with wild spring
Spurts from the terror of *his* oncoming;
To be choked back, the wire ring   40
Her frantic effort throttling:

---

1. Called *Cruelty and Love* when first
published in 1913, and *Love on the Farm*
when it appeared in *Collected Poems*
(1928).

Piteous brown ball of quivering fears!
Ah, soon in his large, hard hands she dies,
And swings all loose from the swing of his walk!
Yet calm and kindly are his eyes   45
And ready to open in brown surprise
Should I not answer to his talk
Or should he my tears surmise.

I hear his hand on the latch, and rise from my chair
Watching the door open; he flashes bare   50
His strong teeth in a smile, and flashes his eyes
In a smile like triumph upon me; then careless-wise
He flings the rabbit soft on the table board
And comes towards me: ah! the uplifted sword
Of his hand against my bosom! and oh, the broad   55
Blade of his glance that asks me to applaud
His coming! With his hand he turns my face to him
And caresses me with his fingers that still smell grim
Of the rabbit's fur! God, I am caught in a snare!
I know not what fine wire is round my throat;   60
I only know I let him finger there
My pulse of life, and let him nose like a stoat
Who sniffs with joy before he drinks the blood.

And down his mouth comes to my mouth! and down
His bright dark eyes come over me, like a hood   65
Upon my mind! his lips meet mine, and a flood
Of sweet fire sweeps across me, so I drown
Against him, die, and find death good.

                                                            1913, 1928

The Bride[1]

My love looks like a girl tonight,
    But she is old.
The plaits that lie along her pillow
    Are not gold,
But threaded with filigree silver,   5
    And uncanny cold.

She looks like a young maiden, since her brow
    Is smooth and fair;
Her cheeks are very smooth, her eyes are closed,
    She sleeps a rare,   10
Still, winsome sleep, so still, and so composed.

---

1. Called *The Dead Mother* when post-   pers in *Young Lorenzo* (1932).
humously printed from Lawrence's pa-

Nay, but she sleeps like a bride, and dreams her dreams
   Of perfect things.
She lies at last, the darling, in the shape of her dream,
   And her dead mouth sings
By its shape, like thrushes in clear evenings.   15

1916

A Young Wife

The pain of loving you
Is almost more than I can bear.

I walk in fear of you.   The darkness starts up where
You stand, and the night comes through
Your eyes when you look at me.   5

Ah never before did I see
The shadows that live in the sun!

Now every tall glad tree
Turns round its back to the sun
And looks down on the ground, to see   10
The shadow it used to shun.

At the foot of each glowing thing
A night lies looking up.
Oh, and I want to sing
And dance, but I can't lift up   15
My eyes from the shadows: dark
They lie spilt round the cup.

What is it?—Hark
The faint fine seethe in the air!

Like the seething sound in a shell!   20
It is death still seething where
The wild-flower shakes its bell
And the skylark twinkles blue—

The pain of loving you
Is almost more than I can bear.   25

1917

Piano

Softly, in the dusk, a woman is singing to me;
Taking me back down the vista of years, till I see
A child sitting under the piano, in the boom of the tingling
   strings

And pressing the small, poised feet of a mother who smiles
    as she sings.

In spite of myself, the insidious mastery of song   5
Betrays me back, till the heart of me weeps to belong
To the old Sunday evenings at home, with winter outside
And hymns in the cozy parlor, the tinkling piano our guide.

So now it is vain for the singer to burst into clamor
With the great black piano appassionato. The glamor   10
Of childish days is upon me, my manhood is cast
Down in the flood of remembrance, I weep like a child for the
    past.

                                                1918

Bavarian Gentians

Not every man has gentians in his house
in Soft September, at slow, Sad Michaelmas.

Bavarian gentians, big and dark, only dark
darkening the daytime torchlike with the smoking blueness of
    Pluto's gloom,[1]
ribbed and torchlike, with their blaze of darkness spread blue   5
down flattening into points, flattened under the sweep of white day
torch-flower of the blue-smoking darkness, Pluto's dark-blue daze,
black lamps from the halls of Dis, burning dark blue,
giving off darkness, blue darkness, as Demeter's pale lamps give off
    light,
lead me then, lead me the way.   10

Reach me a gentian, give me a torch
let me guide myself with the blue, forked torch of this flower
down the darker and darker stairs, where blue is darkened on blue-
    ness.
even where Persephone[2] goes, just now, from the frosted September
to the sightless realm where darkness was awake upon the dark   15
and Persephone herself is but a voice
or a darkness invisible enfolded in the deeper dark
of the arms Plutonic, and pierced with the passion of dense gloom,
among the splendor of torches of darkness, shedding darkness on
    the lost bride and her groom.

                                            1923

1. Pluto was god of the underworld in classical mythology; he was also called "Dis" (line 8).
2. Bride of Pluto, who abducted her from the earth, and daughter of Demeter, goddess of the fruits of the earth (line 14). She was allowed to return to earth every spring but had to descend again to Hades in the autumn, "the frosted September." Demeter and Persephone were central figures in ancient fertility myths, where Persephone's annual descent and return were linked with the death and rebirth of vegetation.

Snake

A snake came to my water trough
On a hot, hot day, and I in pajamas for the heat,
To drink there.

In the deep, strange-scented shade of the great dark carob tree
I came down the steps with my pitcher 5
And must wait, must stand and wait, for there he was at the trough
    before me.

He reached down from a fissure in the earth-wall in the gloom
And trailed his yellow-brown slackness soft-bellied down, over the
    edge of the stone trough
And rested his throat upon the stone bottom,
And where the water had dripped from the tap, in a small clear-
    ness, 10
He sipped with his straight mouth,
Softly drank through his straight gums, into his slack long body,
Silently.

Someone was before me at my water trough,
And I, like a second-comer, waiting. 15

He lifted his head from his drinking, as cattle do,
And looked at me vaguely, as drinking cattle do,
And flickered his two-forked tongue from his lips, and mused a
    moment,
And stooped and drank a little more,
Being earth-brown, earth-golden from the burning bowels of the
    earth 20
On the day of Sicilian July, with Etna smoking.

The voice of my education said to me
He must be killed,
For in Sicily the black, black snakes are innocent, the gold are veno-
    mous.

And voices in me said, If you were a man 25
You would take a stick and break him now, and finish him off.

But must I confess how I liked him,
How glad I was he had come like a guest in quiet, to drink at my
    water trough
And depart peaceful, pacified, and thankless
Into the burning bowels of this earth? 30

Was it cowardice, that I dared not kill him?
Was it perversity, that I longed to talk to him?
Was it humility, to feel so honored?
I felt so honored.

And yet those voices:
If you were not afraid, you would kill him! 35

And truly I was afraid, I was most afraid,
But even so, honored still more
That he should seek my hospitality
From out the dark door of the secret earth.   40

He drank enough
And lifted his head, dreamily, as one who has drunken,
And flickered his tongue like a forked night on the air, so black,
Seeming to lick his lips,
And looked around like a god, unseeing, into the air,   45
And slowly turned his head,
And slowly, very slowly, as if thrice adream
Proceeded to draw his slow length curving round
And climb the broken bank of my wall-face.

And as he put his head into that dreadful hole,   50
And as he slowly drew up, snake-easing his shoulders, and entered
    further,
A sort of horror, a sort of protest against his withdrawing into that
    horrid black hole,
Deliberately going into the blackness, and slowly drawing himself
    after,
Overcame me now his back was turned.

I looked round, I put down my pitcher,   55
I picked up a clumsy log
And threw it at the water trough with a clatter.

I think it did not hit him;
But suddenly that part of him that was left behind convulsed in un-
    dignified haste,
Writhed like lightning, and was gone   60
Into the black hole, the earth-lipped fissure in the wall-front
At which, in the intense still noon, I stared with fascination.

And immediately I regretted it.
I thought how paltry, how vulgar, what a mean act!
I despised myself and the voices of my accursed human education.   65

And I thought of the albatross,[1]
And I wished he would come back, my snake.

For he seemed to me again like a king,
Like a king in exile, uncrowned in the underworld,   70
Now due to be crowned again.

And so, I missed my chance with one of the lords
Of life.
And I have something to expiate:
A pettiness.   1923

---

1. Coleridge's *Ancient Mariner*.

The Ship of Death

1

Now it is autumn and the falling fruit
and the long journey towards oblivion.

The apples falling like great drops of dew
to bruise themselves an exit from themselves.

And it is time to go, to bid farewell   5
to one's own self, and find an exit
from the fallen self.

2

Have you built your ship of death, O have you?
O build your ship of death, for you will need it.

The grim frost is at hand, when the apples will fall   10
thick, almost thundrous, on the hardened earth.

And death is on the air like a smell of ashes!
Ah! can't you smell it?

And in the bruised body, the frightened soul
finds itself shrinking, wincing from the cold   15
that blows upon it through the orifices.

3

And can a man his own quietus make
with a bare bodkin?

With daggers, bodkins, bullets, man can make
a bruise or break of exit for his life;
but is that a quietus, O tell me, is it quietus?   20

Surely not so! for how could murder, even self-murder
ever a quietus make?

4

O let us talk of quiet that we know,
that we can know, the deep and lovely quiet
of a strong heart at peace!   25

How can we this, our own quietus, make?

5

Build then the ship of death, for you must take
the longest journey, to oblivion.

And die the death, the long and painful death   30
that lies between the old self and the new.

Already our bodies are fallen, bruised, badly bruised,
already our souls are oozing through the exit
of the cruel bruise.

Already the dark and endless ocean of the end   35
is washing in through the breaches of our wounds,
already the flood is upon us.

Oh build your ship of death, your little ark
and furnish it with food, with little cakes, and wine
for the dark flight down oblivion.   40

6

Piecemeal the body dies, and the timid soul
has her footing washed away, as the dark flood rises.

We are dying, we are dying, we are all of us dying
and nothing will stay the death-flood rising within us
and soon it will rise on the world, on the outside world.   45

We are dying, we are dying, piecemeal our bodies are
        dying
and our strength leaves us,
and our soul cowers naked in the dark rain over the flood,
cowering in the last branches of the tree of our life.

7

We are dying, we are dying, so all we can do   50
is now to be willing to die, and to build the ship
of death to carry the soul on the longest journey.

A little ship, with oars and food
and little dishes, and all accoutrements
fitting and ready for the departing soul.   55

Now launch the small ship, now as the body dies
and life departs, launch out, the fragile soul
in the fragile ship of courage, the ark of faith
with its store of food and little ccoking pans
and change of clothes,   60
upon the flood's back waste
upon the waters of the end
upon the sea of death, where still we sail
darkly, for we cannot steer, and have no port.

There is no port, there is nowhere to go   65
only the deepening blackness darkening still
blacker upon the soundless, ungurgling flood
darkness at one with darkness, up and down
and sideways utterly dark, so there is no direction any
        more
and the little ship is there; yet she is gone.   70
She is not seen, for there is nothing to see her by.
She is gone! gone! and yet
somewhere she is there.
Nowhere!

8

And everything is gone, the body is gone   75
completely under, gone, entirely gone.
The upper darkness is heavy as the lower,
between them the little ship
is gone
It is the end, it is oblivion.

9

And yet out of eternity a thread   80
separates itself on the blackness,
a horizontal thread
that fumes a little with pallor upon the dark.

Is it illusion? or does the pallor fume
A little higher?
Ah wait, wait, for there's the dawn,   85
the cruel dawn of coming back to life
out of oblivion

Wait, wait, the little ship
drifting, beneath the deathly ashy gray
of a flood-dawn.   90

Wait, wait! even so, a flush of yellow
and strangely, O chilled wan soul, a flush of rose.

A flush of rose, and the whole thing starts again.

10

The flood subsides, and the body, like a worn sea-shell
emerges strange and lovely.   95
And the little ship wings home, faltering and lapsing
on the pink flood,
and the frail soul steps out, into her house again
filling the heart with peace.

Swings the heart renewed with peace   100
even of oblivion.

Oh build your ship of death, oh build it!
for you will need it.
For the voyage of oblivion awaits you.

1929–30   1933

T. S. ELIOT

(1888–1965)

1915: Settles in London.
1917: *Prufrock and Other Observations.*
1922: *The Waste Land.*
1927: Becomes British subject; confirmed in Anglican Church.
1944: *Four Quartets.*

Thomas Stearns Eliot was born in St. Louis, Missouri, of New England stock. He entered Harvard in 1906, and was influenced there by the anti-romanticism of Irving Babbitt and the philosophical and critical interests of George Santayana, as well as by the enthusiasm that prevailed in certain Harvard circles for Elizabethan and Jacobean literature, the Italian Renaissance, and Indian mystical philosophy. His philosophical studies included intensive work on the English idealist philosopher F. H. Bradley, on whom he eventually wrote his Harvard dissertation. (Bradley's emphasis on the private nature of individual experience, "a circle enclosed on the outside," had considerable influence on the private imagery of Eliot's poetry and on the view of the relation between the individual and other individuals reflected in much of his poetry.) Later Eliot studied literature and philosophy in France and Germany, before going to England shortly after the outbreak of World War I in 1914. He studied Greek philosophy at Oxford, taught school in London, and then obtained a position with Lloyd's Bank which he held until 1925, when he joined the London publishing firm of Faber and Gwyer, becoming a director when the firm became Faber and Faber in 1929.

Eliot started writing literary and philosophical reviews soon after settling in London. He wrote for the *Athenaeum* and the *Times Literary Supplement*, among other periodicals, and was assistant editor of the *Egoist* from 1917 to 1919. In 1922 he founded the influential quarterly, the *Criterion*, which he edited until it ceased publication in 1939. His poetry first appeared in 1915, when *The Love Song of J. Alfred Prufrock* was printed in *Poetry* magazine (Chicago) and a few other short poems were published in the short-lived periodical, *Blast*. His first published collection of poems was *Prufrock and Other Observations*, 1917; two other small collections followed in 1919 and 1920; in 1922 *The Waste Land* appeared, first in the *Criterion* in October, then in the *Dial* (in America) in November, and finally in book form. *Poems 1909–25* (1925) collected these earlier poems. Meanwhile he was also publishing collections of his critical essays, notably *The Sacred Wood* in 1920 and *Homage to John Dryden* in 1924. *For Lancelot Andrewes* followed in 1928 and in 1932 he included most of these earlier essays with some new ones in *Selected Essays*. Eliot became a British subject and joined the Church of England in 1927.

"Our civilization comprehends great variety and complexity, and this variety and complexity, playing upon a refined sensibility, must produce various and complex results. The poet must become more and more comprehensive, more allusive, more indirect, in order to force, to dislocate if necessary, language into his meaning." This remark, from Eliot's essay on *The Metaphysical Poets* (1921), gives one clue to his poetic method from *Prufrock* through *The Waste Land*. In the attenuated romantic tradition of the Georgian poets who were active when he settled in London, in their quietly meditative pastoralism, faded exoticism, or self-consciously realistic descriptions of urban life, he saw an exhausted poetic mode being employed, with no verbal excitement or original craftsmanship. He sought to make poetry more subtle, more suggestive, and at the same time more precise. He had learned from the Imagists the necessity of clear and precise images, and he learned, too, from T. E. Hulme and from his early supporter and adviser Ezra Pound to fear romantic softness and to regard the poetic medium rather than the poet's personality as the important factor. At the same time, the "hard dry" images advocated by Hulme were not enough for him; he wanted wit, allusiveness, irony. He saw in the metaphysical poets how wit and passion could be combined, and he saw in the French Symbolists how an image could be both absolutely precise in what it referred to physically and at the same time endlessly suggestive in the meanings it set up because of its relationship to other images. The combination of precision, symbolic suggestion, and ironic mockery in the poetry of the late 19th-century French poet Jules Laforgue attracted and influenced him, and he was influenced too by other 19th-century French poets: by Théophile Gautier's artful carving of impersonal shapes of meaning; by Charles Baudelaire's strangely evocative explorations of the symbolic suggestions of objects and images; by the Symbolist poets Paul Verlaine, Arthur Rimbaud, and Stéphane Mallarmé. He also found in the Jacobean dramatists a flexible blank verse with overtones of colloquial movement: Middleton, Tourneur, Webster, and others, taught him as much—in the way of verse movement, imagery, the counterpointing of the accent of conversation and the note of terror—as either the metaphysicals or the French Symbolists.

Hulme's protests against the romantic concept of poetry fitted in well enough with what Eliot had learned from Irving Babbitt at Harvard; yet for all his severity with such poets as Shelley, for all his conscious cultivation of a classical viewpoint and his insistence on order and discipline rather than on mere self-expression in art, one side of Eliot's poetic genius is, in one sense of the word, romantic. The Symbolist influence on his imagery, his interest in the evocative and the suggestive, such lines as "And fiddled whisper music on those strings / And bats with baby faces in the violet light / Whistled, and beat their wings," and such recurring images as the hyacinth girl and the rose garden, all show what could be called a romantic element in his poetry. But it is combined with a dry ironic allusiveness, a play of wit, and a colloquial element, which are not normally found in poets of the romantic tradition.

Eliot's real novelty—and the cause of much bewilderment when his poems first appeared—was his deliberate elimination of all merely connective and transitional passages, his building up of the total pattern of meaning through the immediate juxtaposition of images without overt explanation of what they are doing, together with his use of oblique references to other works of literature (some of them quite obscure to most contemporary readers). *Prufrock* presents a symbolic landscape where the meaning emerges from the mutual interaction of the images, and that meaning is enlarged by echoes, often ironic, of Hesiod and Dante and Shakespeare. *The Waste Land* is a series of scenes and images with no author's voice intervening to tell us where we are, but with the implications developed through multiple contrasts and through analogies with older literary works often referred to in a distorted quotation or half-concealed allusion. Further, the works referred to are not necessarily works which are central in the Western literary tradition: besides Dante and Shakespeare there are pre-Socratic philosophers, minor (as well as major) 17th-century poets and dramatists, works of anthropology, history, and philosophy, and other echoes of the poet's private reading. In a culture where there is no longer any assurance on the part of the poet that his public has a common cultural heritage, a common knowledge of works of the past, Eliot felt it necessary to build up his own body of references. It is this which marks the difference between Eliot's use of earlier literature and, say, Milton's. Both poets are difficult to the modern reader, who needs editorial assistance in recognizing and understanding many of the allusions—but Milton was drawing on a body of knowledge common to educated men in his day. Nevertheless, this aspect of Eliot can be exaggerated: the fact remains that the nature of his imagery together with the movement of his verse generally succeed in setting the tone he requires, in establishing the area of meaning to be developed, so that even a reader ignorant of most of the literary allusions can often get the "feel" of the poem and achieve some understanding of what it says.

Eliot's early poetry, until at least the middle 1920's, is mostly concerned in one way or another with the Waste Land, with aspects of the decay of culture in the modern Western world. After his formal acceptance of Anglican Christianity we find a penitential note in much of his verse, a note of quiet searching for spiritual peace, with considerable allusion to Biblical, liturgical, and mystical religious literature and to Dante. *Ash Wednesday* (1930), a poem in six parts, much less fiercely concentrated in style than the earlier poetry, explores with gentle insistence a mood both penitential and questioning. The so-called "Ariel" poems (the title is accidental, and has nothing to do with their form or content) present or explore aspects of religious doubt or discovery or revelation, sometimes, as in *Marina*, using a purely secular imagery and sometimes, as in *Journey of the Magi*, drawing on Biblical incident. In *Four Quartets* (of which the first, *Burnt Norton*, appeared in the *Collected Poems* of 1935, though all four were not completed until 1943, when they were published together) Eliot further explored essentially religious moods, dealing with the relation between time and eternity and the cultivation of that selfless passivity which can yield the moment of timeless revelation in the midst of time. The mocking irony, the savage humor, the deliberately startling juxtaposition of the sordid and the romantic, give way in these later poems to a quieter poetic idiom, often still complexly allusive but never deliberately shocking.

Eliot's criticism was the criticism of a practicing poet who worked out in relation to his reading of older literature what he needed to hold and to admire. He lent the growing weight of his authority to that shift in literary taste that replaced Milton by Donne as the great 17th-century English poet, and replaced Tennyson in the 19th century by Hopkins. His often-quoted description of the late 17th-century "dissociation of sensibility"— keeping wit and passion in separate compartments—which he saw as determining the course of English poetry throughout the 18th and 19th centuries, is both a contribution to the rewriting of English literary history and an explanation of what he was aiming at in his own poetry: the re-establishment of that *unified* sensibility he found in Donne and other early 17th-century poets and dramatists. His view of tradition, his dislike of the poetic exploitation of the author's own personality, his advocacy of what he called "orthodoxy," made him suspicious of what he considered eccentric geniuses such as Blake and D. H. Lawrence. On the other side, his dislike of the grandiloquent and his insistence on complexity and on the mingling of the formal with the conversational made him distrustful of the influence of Milton on English poetry. He considered himself "classicist in literature, royalist in politics, and Anglo-Catholic in religion" (*For Lancelot Andrewes*, 1928), in favor of order against chaos, tradition against eccentricity, authority against rampant individualism; yet his own poetry is in many respects untraditional and certainly highly individual in tone. His conservative and even authoritarian habit of mind has alienated some who admire—and some whose own poetry has been much influenced by—his poetry.

Eliot's plays have all been, directly or indirectly, on religious themes. *Murder in the Cathedral* (1935) deals with the murder of Archbishop Thomas à Becket in an appropriately ritual manner, with much use of a chorus and with the central speech in the form of a sermon by the archbishop in his cathedral shortly before his murder. *The Family Reunion* (1939) deals with the problem of guilt and redemption in a modern upper-class English family; it makes a deliberate attempt to combine choric devices from Greek tragedy with a poetic idiom subdued to the accents of drawing-room conversation. In his three later plays, all written in the 1950's, *The Cocktail Party, The Confidential Clerk,* and *The Elder Statesman,* he achieved popular success by casting a serious religious theme in the form of a sophisticated modern social comedy, using a verse that is so conversational in movement that when spoken in the theater it does not sound like verse at all.

Critics differ on the degree to which Eliot succeeded in his last plays in combining box-office success with dramatic effectiveness. But there is no disagreement on his importance as one of the great renovators of the English poetic dialect, whose influence on a whole generation of poets, critics, and intellectuals generally was enormous. His range as a poet is limited, and his interest in the great middle ground of human experience (as distinct from the extremes of saint and sinner) deficient: but when in 1948 he was awarded the rare honor of the Order of Merit by King George VI and also gained the Nobel Prize in literature, his positive qualities were widely and fully recognized—his poetic cunning, his fine craftsmanship, his original accent, his historical and representative importance as *the* poet of the modern Symbolist-metaphysical tradition.

The Love Song of J. Alfred Prufrock[1]

S'io credesse che mia risposta fosse
A persona che mai tornasse al mondo,
Questa fiamma staria senza piu scosse.
Ma perciocche giammai di questo fondo
Non torno vivo alcun, s'i'odo il vero,
Senza tema d'infamia ti rispondo.[2]

Let us go then, you and I,
When the evening is spread out against the sky
Like a patient etherized[3] upon a table;
Let us go, through certain half-deserted streets,
The muttering retreats   5
Of restless nights in one-night cheap hotels
And sawdust restaurants with oyster shells:
Streets that follow like a tedious argument
Of insidious intent
To lead you to an overwhelming question . . .   10
Oh, do not ask, "What is it?"
Let us go and make our visit.

In the room the women come and go
Talking of Michelangelo.

The yellow fog that rubs its back upon the windowpanes,   15
The yellow smoke that rubs its muzzle on the windowpanes
Licked its tongue into the corners of the evening,
Lingered upon the pools that stand in drains,
Let fall upon its back the soot that falls from chimneys,
Slipped by the terrace, made a sudden leap,   20

1. A dramatic monologue in which the speaker builds up a mood of social futility and inadequacy through the thoughts and images which haunt his consciousness and by means of the symbolic landscape in which he moves. The title implies an ironic contrast between the romantic suggestions of "love song" and the dully prosaic name, "J. Alfred Prufrock." The quotation from Dante's *Inferno* which stands at the head of the poem adds to this contrast a note of profound hopelessness. Prufrock himself, middle-aged and unhappy, is not really at home in the society in which he is condemned to live; he is aware of the futility of such visits as he is paying, of his own awkwardness and maladjustment, and his self-conscious response to the demands made on him. He is haunted not only by a knowledge of the pettiness and triviality of this world, but also by a sense of his own sexual inadequacy and a feeling that once, somewhere, he had had a vision of a life more real and more beautiful, but that he has long since strayed from that reality to the artificial and barren existence in which he now suffocates. The lost dream-world was paradoxically the only real world, man's true element, and out of it he drowns.
2. "If I thought that my reply would be to one who would ever return to the world, this flame would stay without further movement; but since none has ever returned alive from this depth, if what I hear is true, I answer you without fear of infamy." Dante, *Inferno* XXVII.61–66. Guido da Montefeltro, shut up in his flame (the punishment given to false counselors), tells the shame of his evil life to Dante because he believes Dante will never return to earth to report it.
3. A contrast is perhaps here implied between "ether" as the free sky or the heavens and the word's medical connotations—helplessness, disease, the elimination of consciousness and personality.

And seeing that it was a soft October night,
Curled once about the house, and fell asleep.

And indeed there will be time[4]
For the yellow smoke that slides along the street,
Rubbing its back upon the windowpanes;
There will be time, there will be time   25
To prepare a face to meet the faces that you meet;
There will be time to murder and create,
And time for all the works and days of hands[5]
That lift and drop a question on your plate;   30
Time for you and time for me,
And time yet for a hundred indecisions,
And for a hundred visions and revisions,
Before the taking of a toast and tea.

In the room the women come and go   35
Talking of Michelangelo.

And indeed there will be time
To wonder, "Do I dare?" and, "Do I dare?"
Time to turn back and descend the stair,
With a bald spot in the middle of my hair—   40
(They will say: "How his hair is growing thin!")
My morning coat, my collar mounting firmly to the chin,
My necktie rich and modest, but asserted by a simple pin—
(They will say: "But how his arms and legs are thin!")
Do I dare   45
Disturb the universe?
In a minute there is time
For decisions and revisions which a minute will reverse.

For I have known them all already, known them all—
Have known the evenings, mornings, afternoons,
I have measured out my life with coffee spoons;   50
I know the voices dying with a dying fall[6]
Beneath the music from a farther room.
    So how should I presume?

And I have known the eyes already, known them all—
The eyes that fix you in a formulated phrase,   55
And when I am formulated, sprawling on a pin,
When I am pinned and wriggling on the wall,
Then how should I begin
To spit out all the butt-ends of my days and ways?   60
    And how should I presume?

And I have known the arms already, known them all—
Arms that are braceleted and white and bare

4. Cf. Andrew Marvell's *To His Coy Mistress*: "Had we but world enough and time * * * "
5. *Works and Days* is a poem about the farming year by Hesiod, Greek poet of 8th century B.C. Eliot's contrast is between useful agricultural labor and the futile "works and days of hands" engaged in meaningless social gesturing.
6. Ironic recollection of Orsino's speech in *Twelfth Night* (I.i.4): "That strain again! It had a dying fall."

(But in the lamplight, downed with light brown hair!)
Is it perfume from a dress 65
That makes me so digress?
Arms that lie along a table, or wrap about a shawl.
And should I then presume?
And how should I begin?

. . . . .

Shall I say, I have gone at dusk through narrow streets 70
And watched the smoke that rises from the pipes
Of lonely men in shirt-sleeves, leaning out of windows? . . .

I should have been a pair of ragged claws
Scuttling across the floors of silent seas.[7]

. . . . .

And the afternoon, the evening, sleeps so peacefully! 75
Smoothed by long fingers,
Asleep . . . tired . . . or it malingers,
Stretched on the floor, here beside you and me.
Should I, after tea and cakes and ices,
Have the strength to force the moment to its crisis? 80
But though I have wept and fasted, wept and prayed,
Though I have seen my head (grown slightly bald) brought in upon
    a platter,[8]
I am no prophet—and here's no great matter;
I have seen the moment of my greatness flicker,
And I have seen the eternal Footman hold my coat, and snicker, 85
And in short, I was afraid.

And would it have been worth it, after all,
After the cups, the marmalade, the tea,
Among the porcelain, among some talk of you and me,
Would it have been worth while, 90
To have bitten off the matter with a smile,
To have squeezed the universe into a ball
To roll it toward some overwhelming question,
To say: "I am Lazarus,[9] come from the dead,
Come back to tell you all, I shall tell you all"— 95
If one, settling a pillow by her head,
    Should say: "That is not what I meant at all.
    That is not it, at all."

And would it have been worth it, after all,
Would it have been worth while, 100
After the sunsets and the dooryards and the sprinkled streets,

---

7. I.e., he would have been better as a
crab on the ocean bed. Perhaps, too, the
motion of a crab suggests futility and
growing old; cf. *Hamlet* II.ii.205–6:
"for you yourself, sir, should be old as
I am, if, like a crab, you could go backward."
8. Like that of John the Baptist. See
Mark vi.17–28 and Matthew xiv.3–11.
9. Cf. Luke xvi.19–31 and John xi.1–
44.

After the novels, after the teacups, after the skirts that trail along
    the floor—
And this, and so much more?—
It is impossible to say just what I mean!
But as if a magic lantern threw the nerves in patterns on a
    screen: 105
Would it have been worth while
If one, settling a pillow or throwing off a shawl,
And turning toward the window, should say:
  "That is not it at all,
  That is not what I meant, at all."   110

     ·   ·   ·   ·   ·

No! I am not Prince Hamlet, nor was meant to be;
Am an attendant lord, one that will do
To swell a progress,[1] start a scene or two,
Advise the prince; no doubt, an easy tool,
Deferential, glad to be of use,   115
Politic, cautious, and meticulous;
Full of high sentence,[2] but a bit obtuse;
At times, indeed, almost ridiculous—
Almost, at times, the Fool.

I grow old . . . I grow old . . .   120
I shall wear the bottoms of my trousers rolled.

Shall I part my hair behind? Do I dare to eat a peach?
I shall wear white flannel trousers, and walk upon the beach.
I have heard the mermaids singing, each to each.

I do not think that they will sing to me.   125

I have seen them riding seaward on the waves
Combing the white hair of the waves blown back
When the wind blows the water white and black.

We have lingered in the chambers of the sea
By sea-girls wreathed with seaweed red and brown   130
Till human voices wake us, and we drown.
1910–11   1915, 1917

From Landscapes[3]
Rannoch, by Glencoe[4]

  Here the crow starves, here the patient stag
  Breeds for the rifle. Between the soft moor

1. In the Elizabethan sense of a state journey made by a royal or noble person. Elizabethan plays sometimes showed such "progresses" crossing the stage.
2. In its older meanings, "opinions," "sententiousness."
3. Under this title Eliot grouped five short poems, each dealing with a specific place. The last two are reprinted here.
4. In Scotland.

And the soft sky, scarcely room
To leap or soar. Substance crumbles, in the thin air
Moon cold or moon hot. The road winds in⁣   5
Listlessness of ancient war
Languor of broken steel,
Clamor of confused wrong, apt
In silence. Memory is strong
Beyond the bone. Pride snapped,   10
Shadow of pride is long, in the long pass
No concurrence of bone.

Cape Ann[5]

O quick quick quick, quick hear the song sparrow,
Swamp sparrow, fox sparrow, vesper sparrow
At dawn and dusk. Follow the dance
Of the goldfinch at noon. Leave to chance
The Blackburnian warbler, the shy one. Hail   5
With shrill whistle the note of the quail, the bobwhite
Dodging by baybush. Follow the feet
Of the walker, the water thrush. Follow the flight
Of the dancing arrow, the purple martin. Greet
In silence the bullbat. All are delectable. Sweet sweet sweet   10
But resign this land at the end, resign it
To its true owner, the tough one, the sea gull.
The palaver is finished.

1933–34   1936

Sweeney Among the Nightingales[1]

ὤμοι, πέπληγμαι καιρίαν πληγὴν ἔσω.[2]

Apeneck Sweeney spreads his knees
Letting his arms hang down to laugh,
The zebra stripes along his jaw
Swelling to maculate[3] giraffe.

5. On the northern coast of Massachusetts, not far from the New Hampshire border; a wilderness area in the middle of the cape is inhabited by the birds Eliot here describes.

1. This poem shows Eliot's characteristic method of presenting his meaning through multiple parallels and contrasts. Lust, cruelty, and violence have always existed in the world; but in heroic periods of history they have sprung from grand passions of love or hate and have later been embodied in meaningful myths. The nightingale, in Greek myth, was the symbol of the transformation of human lust into art: Philomela, having been ravished and had her tongue cut out by her sister's husband Tereus, was turned into a nightingale and sings

eternally. The horrors of Agamemnon's murder are similarly subsumed in the search for and achievement of divine justice (cf. Aeschylus' dramatic trilogy, the *Oresteia*). But the shabby animality of Sweeney and his drunken lady friend (significantly anonymous), frolicking lewdly in a restaurant, is unrelieved by any such transmutation. In Sweeney's world violence is limited to overturning a coffee cup and tearing at grapes, and lust has become only a "gambit," easily "declined."
2. "Alas, I am struck with a mortal blow within" (Aeschylus, *Agamemnon*, line 1343). The voice of Agamemnon heard crying out from the palace as he is murdered by his wife Clytemnestra.
3. Spotted, stained.

The circles of the stormy moon   5
Slide westward toward the River Plate,[4]
Death and the Raven drift above
And Sweeney guards the hornéd gate.[5]

Gloomy Orion and the Dog
Are veiled;[6] and hushed the shrunken seas;   10
The person in the Spanish cape
Tries to sit on Sweeney's knees

Slips and pulls the tablecloth
Overturns a coffee cup,
Reorganized upon the floor   15
She yawns and draws a stocking up;

The silent man in mocha brown
Sprawls at the window sill and gapes;
The waiter brings in oranges
Bananas figs and hothouse grapes;   20

The silent vertebrate in brown
Contracts and concentrates, withdraws;
Rachel *née* Rabinovitch
Tears at the grapes with murderous paws;

She and the lady in the cape   25
Are suspect, thought to be in league;
Therefore the man with heavy eyes
Declines the gambit, shows fatigue,

Leaves the room and reappears
Outside the window, leaning in,   30
Branches of wistaria
Circumscribe a golden grin;

The host with someone indistinct
Converses at the door apart,
The nightingales are singing near   35
The Convent of the Sacred Heart,

And sang within the bloody wood
When Agamemnon cried aloud,[7]
And let their liquid siftings fall
To stain the stiff dishonored shroud.   40

1918, 1919

4. Estuary on South American coast between Argentina and Uruguay, formed by the Uruguay and Paraná rivers.
5. The gates of horn, in Hades, through which true dreams come to the upper world.
6. "Orion" and the "Dog" are the constellations. For Sweeney and his friend, the gate of vision is blocked and the great mythmaking constellations are "veiled."
7. Agamemnon was not murdered in a "bloody wood," but in his bath. Eliot is here telescoping Agamemnon's murder with the wood where Philomela was ravished and also with the "bloody wood" of Nemi, where, in ancient times, the old priest was slain by his successor (as described in the first chapter of Sir James Frazer's *Golden Bough*). The great myths of regeneration represented by this ritual slaying are meaningless for Sweeney and his friends, as are the song of the nightingales and the spiritual reality represented by the Convent of the Sacred Heart.

Whispers of Immortality[1]

Webster[2] was much possessed by death
And saw the skull beneath the skin;
And breastless creatures under ground
Leaned backward with a lipless grin.

Daffodil bulbs instead of balls   5
Stared from the sockets of the eyes!
He knew that thought clings round dead limbs
Tightening its lusts and luxuries.

Donne,[3] I suppose, was such another
Who found no substitute for sense,   10
To seize and clutch and penetrate;
Expert beyond experience,

He knew the anguish of the marrow
The ague of the skeleton;
No contact possible to flesh   15
Allayed the fever of the bone.

.   .   .   .   .   .

Grishkin is nice: her Russian eye
Is underlined for emphasis;
Uncorseted, her friendly bust
Gives promise of pneumatic bliss.   20

The couched Brazilian jaguar
Compels the scampering marmoset
With subtle effluence of cat;
Grishkin has a maisonette;

The sleek Brazilian jaguar   25
Does not in its arboreal gloom
Distil so rank a feline smell
As Grishkin in a drawing room.

And even the Abstract Entities
Circumambulate her charm;   30
But our lot crawls between dry ribs
To keep our metaphysics warm.

1918, 1919

---

1. The effects are here again achieved by contrasts and parallels. The Elizabethan and Jacobean poets and dramatists were obsessed by death and suffered the anguish of those for whom all knowledge comes through the senses but who know that the senses, doomed to decay, cannot satisfy the ultimate longings. By contrast Grishkin, high-class prostitute, is wholly committed to the flesh, like an animal; even abstract philosophy is seduced by her charms.
2. John Webster, Jacobean dramatist, author of *The Duchess of Malfi* and *The White Devil.*
3. The poet John Donne (1572–1631).

The Waste Land　is a poem about spiritual dryness, about the
kind of existence in which no regenerating belief gives significance and
value to men's daily activities, sex brings no fruitfulness, and death heralds
no resurrection. Eliot himself gives one of the main clues to the theme
and structure of the poem in a general note, in which he stated that "not
only the title, but the plan and a good deal of the symbolism of the poem
were suggested by Miss Jessie L. Weston's book on the Grail legend: *From
Ritual to Romance"* (1920). He further acknowledged a general indebted-
ness to Sir James Frazer's *Golden Bough* (12 volumes, 1890–1915), "especially the two volumes *Adonis, Attis, Osiris,*" in which Frazer deals with
ancient vegetation myths and fertility ceremonies. Miss Weston's study,
drawing on material from Frazer and other anthropologists, traced the relationship of these myths and rituals to Christianity and most especially
to the legend of the Holy Grail. She found an archetypal fertility myth
in the story of the Fisher King whose death, infirmity, or impotence (there
are many forms of the myth) brought drought and desolation to the land
and failure of the power to reproduce themselves among both men and
beasts. This symbolic Waste Land can be revived only if a "questing
knight" goes to the Chapel Perilous, situated in the heart of it, and there
asks certain ritual questions about the Grail (or Cup) and the Lance—
originally fertility symbols, female and male respectively. The proper
asking of these questions revives the king and restores fertility to the land.
The relation of this original Grail myth to fertility cults and rituals found
in many different civilizations, and represented by stories of a dying god
who is later resurrected (e.g., Tammuz, Adonis, Attis), shows their common origin in a response to the cyclical movement of the seasons, with
vegetation dying in winter to be resurrected again in the spring. Christianity, according to Miss Weston, gave its own spiritual meaning to the
myth; it "did not hesitate to utilize the already existing medium of instruction, but boldly identified the Deity of Vegetation, regarded as Life
Principle, with the God of the Christian Faith." The Fisher King is related to the use of the fish symbol in early Christianity. Miss Weston
states "with certainty that the Fish is a Life symbol of immemorial antiquity,
and that the title of Fisher has, from the earliest ages, been associated
with the Deities who were held to be specially connected with the origin
and preservation of Life." Eliot, following Miss Weston, thus uses a great
variety of mythological and religious material, both occidental and oriental,
in order to paint a symbolic picture of the modern Waste Land and the
need for regeneration. The terror of that life—its loneliness, emptiness, and
irrational apprehensions—as well as its misuse of sexuality are vividly presented, but, paradoxically, the poem ends with a benediction. Another significant general source for the poem is the composer Richard Wagner,
some of whose operas (*Götterdämmerung* ["Twilight of the Gods"], *Parsifal, Rheingold,* and *Tristan and Isolde*) are drawn on.

　The poem as published owed a great deal to the severe pruning of Ezra
Pound; recently the original manuscript, with Pound's excisions and comments, has turned up, providing fascinating information about the genesis
and development of the poem. It was reproduced in facsimile in 1971,
edited by Eliot's widow Valerie Eliot, who also supplied notes supplementing those that Eliot himself added when the poem was first published in
book form in 1922 and which are included with the present editor's footnotes to the poem.

The Waste Land

"Nam Sibyllam quidem Cumis ego ipse oculis meis vidi in ampulla pendere, et cum illi pueri dicerent: Σίβυλλα τί θέλεις; respondebat illa: ἀποθανεῖν θέλω."[1]

FOR EZRA POUND[2]

il miglior fabbro

I. The Burial of the Dead[3]

April is the cruelest month, breeding
Lilacs out of the dead land, mixing
Memory and desire, stirring
Dull roots with spring rain.
Winter kept us warm, covering   5
Earth in forgetful snow, feeding
A little life with dried tubers.
Summer surprised us, coming over the Starnbergersee[4]
With a shower of rain; we stopped in the colonnade,
And went on in sunlight, into the Hofgarten,[5]   10
And drank coffee, and talked for an hour.
Bin gar keine Russin, stamm' aus Litauen, echt deutsch.[6]
And when we were children, staying at the archduke's,

1. From the *Satyricon* of Petronius (1st century A.D.): "For once I myself saw with my own eyes the Sibyl at Cumae hanging in a cage, and when the boys said to her 'Sibyl, what do you want?' she replied, 'I want to die.'" The Cumaean Sibyl was the most famous of the Sibyls, the prophetic old women of Greek mythology: she guided Aeneas through Hades in the *Aeneid*. She had been granted immortality by Apollo, but since she forgot to ask for perpetual youth, she shrank into withered old age and her authority declined. Cf. other prophets in the poem: Madame Sosostris and Tiresias.
2. Ezra Pound (1885–), the American expatriate poet who was a key figure in the modern movement in poetry, helped Eliot with the final revisions. "*Il miglior fabbro*" (i.e., the better craftsman) was a tribute originally paid to the Provencal poet Arnaut Daniel in Dante's *Purgatorio* XXVI.117.
3. The title comes from the Anglican burial service. April is the cruelest month because it brings no true renewal but instead tortures us with vain recollections. The seasons as they are here described do not form part of a living cycle; the people whose chatter we hear in international holiday resorts do not wish a really new life, and April is thus cruel in another sense because it suggests resurrection to those who do not wish it. With a sudden shift in tone the voice becomes suggestive of the

prophet Ezekiel announcing the dryness and hopeless fragmentation of civilization; then this voice gives way to songs of romantic passion and memories of lost opportunities for love. We next see the mysteries of ancient religion transformed into fashionable fortune-telling by a fake Egyptian clairvoyante; the elemental symbols of the ancient Tarot pack of cards have degenerated into a trickster's patter (but still immensely evocative, and with each character in the pack related to themes to be developed later in the poem). Then the vision changes to a more direct picture of modern civilization: Baudelaire's Paris, modern London, Dante's Limbo, all three seen as really the same; the feverish speaker turns the great resurrection ritual into a mad and sinister question about gardening; and the author rounds on the reader to insist that he see himself in the the same situation.
4. Lake near Munich. The scene in this and the following eight lines, which evokes European decadence before World War I, seems to have been suggested by an autobiographical work by Countess Marie Larisch, *My Past* (London, 1913), but Valerie Eliot says that Eliot had never read the book and got his information from the Countess directly, in conversations with her.
5. A small public park in Munich.
6. "I am not Russian at all; I come from Lithuania, a true German."

My cousin's, he took me out on a sled,
And I was frightened. He said, Marie,
Marie, hold on tight. And down we went.   15
In the mountains, there you feel free.
I read, much of the night, and go south in the winter.

What are the roots that clutch, what branches grow
Out of this stony rubbish? Son of man,[7]   20
You cannot say, or guess, for you know only
A heap of broken images, where the sun beats,
And the dead tree gives no shelter, the cricket no relief,[8]
And the dry stone no sound of water. Only
There is shadow under this red rock,[9]   25
(Come in under the shadow of this red rock),
And I will show you something different from either
Your shadow at morning striding behind you
Or your shadow at evening rising to meet you;
I will show you fear in a handful of dust.   30
            Frisch weht der Wind
            Der Heimat zu
            Mein Irisch Kind,
            Wo weilest du?[1]
"You gave me hyacinths first a year ago;   35
They called me the hyacinth girl."
—Yet when we came back, late, from the Hyacinth garden,
Your arms full, and your hair wet, I could not
Speak, and my eyes failed, I was neither
Living nor dead, and I knew nothing,   40
Looking into the heart of light, the silence.
Oed' und leer das Meer.[2]

Madame Sosostris,[3] famous clairvoyante,
Had a bad cold, nevertheless
Is known to be the wisest woman in Europe,   45

---

7. "Cf. Ezekiel II, i" [Eliot's note]. Here God is addressing Ezekiel, "Son of man." God continues, "stand upon thy feet, and I will speak unto thee." 8. "Cf. Ecclesiastes XII, v" [Eliot's note]. The verse cited by Eliot is part of the Preacher's picture of the desolation of old age, "when they shall be afraid of that which is high, and fears shall be in the way, and the almond tree shall flourish, and the grasshopper shall be a burden, and desire shall fail * * * " 9. Cf. Isaiah xxxii.2: the "righteous king" "shall be * * * as rivers of water in a dry place, as the shadow of a great rock in a weary land." 1. "V. *Tristan und Isolde*, I, verses 5–8" [Eliot's note]. In Wagner's opera, a sailor recalls the girl he has left be-

hind: "Fresh blows the wind to the homeland; my Irish child, where are you waiting?" 2. "Id. III, verse 24" [Eliot's note]. In Act III of *Tristan und Isolde*, Tristan lies dying. He is waiting for Isolde to come to him from Cornwall, but a shepherd, appointed to watch for her sail, can only report, "Waste and empty is the sea." 3. A mock Egyptian name (suggested to Eliot by "Sesostris, the Sorceress of Ecbatana," the name assumed by a character in Aldous Huxley's novel *Crome Yellow* who dresses up as a gypsy to tell fortunes at a fair). The anticlimactic effect of "had a bad cold" is deliberate; it is intended to be ironic and debunking.

With a wicked pack of cards.[4] Here, said she,
Is your card, the drowned Phoenician Sailor,[5]
(Those are pearls that were his eyes. Look!)
Here is Belladonna, the Lady of the Rocks,[6]
The lady of situations.   50
Here is the man with three staves,[7] and here the Wheel,
And here is the one-eyed merchant,[8] and this card,
Which is blank, is something he carries on his back,
Which I am forbidden to see. I do not find
The Hanged Man.[9] Fear death by water.   55
I see crowds of people, walking round in a ring.
Thank you. If you see dear Mrs. Equitone,
Tell her I bring the horoscope myself:
One must be so careful these days.

4. I.e., the Tarot deck of cards. The four suits of the Tarot pack, discussed by Jessie Weston in *From Ritual to Romance*, are the cup, lance, sword, and dish—the life symbols found in the Grail story. Miss Weston noted that "today the Tarot has fallen somewhat into disrepute, being principally used for purposes of divination." Some of the cards mentioned in lines 46–56 are discussed by Eliot in his note to this passage: "I am not familiar with the exact constitution of the Tarot pack of cards, from which I have obviously departed to suit my own convenience. The Hanged Man, a member of the traditional pack, fits my purpose in two ways: because he is associated in my mind with the Hanged God of Frazer, and because I associate him with the hooded figure in the passage of the disciples to Emmaus in Part V. The Phoenician Sailor and the Merchant appear later; also the 'crowds of people,' and Death by Water is executed in Part IV. The Man with Three Staves (an authentic member of the Tarot pack) I associate, quite arbitrarily, with the Fisher King himself."
5. See Part IV. Phlebas the Phoenician and Mr. Eugenides, the Smyrna merchant—both of whom appear later in the poem—are different phases of the same symbolic character, here identified as the "Phoenician Sailor." Mr. Eugenides exports "currants" (line 210); the drowned Phlebas floats in the "current" (line 315). The line that follows is from Shakespeare's *Tempest* (I.ii.398). Ariel's song to the ship-wrecked Ferdinand, who was "sitting on a bank / Weeping again the King my father's wrack," when "this music crept by me on the waters." The song is about the supposed drowning of Ferdinand's father, Alonso. *The Waste Land* contains many references to *The Tempest:* the supposed drowning of Alonso and Ferdinand is regarded as their purification by water, and the

"sea change" suffered by Alonso typifies, from one point of view, suffering transmuted into art (Eliot was impressed by the ritual element in Shakespeare's last plays). Ferdinand is also associated with Phlebas and Mr. Eugenides and therefore with the "drowned Phoenician Sailor." Drowning and sea change are both, of course, the work of water. Symbol of purification, baptism, refreshment, and growth, water plays diverse roles in the poem.
6. "Belladonna": beautiful lady. The word also suggests Madonna (the Virgin Mary) and therefore the Madonna of the Rocks (as in Leonardo da Vinci's painting); the rocks symbolize the Church. But there are other rocks—the rocks of dryness, of the Waste Land (e.g., lines 331 ff.). Belladonna is also an eye-cosmetic and a poison—the "deadly" nightshade. In the next line, the woman-figure of the Virgin becomes "the lady of situations," foreshadowing the neurasthenic lady of intrigue in Part II.
7. Life-force symbol, associated by Eliot with the Fisher King. The "Wheel" is the wheel of fortune, whose turning represents the reversals of human life.
8. Mr. Eugenides, "one-eyed" because the figure is in profile on the card and also as a suggestion of evil or crookedness. The mysterious burden on his back may be the mysteries of the fertility cults which, Miss Weston emphasizes, Phoenician merchants carried throughout the Mediterranean, or simply "the burthen of the mystery," "the heavy and the weary weight / Of all this unintelligible world" in Wordsworth's *Tintern Abbey*.
9. On his card in the Tarot pack he is shown hanging from one foot from a T-shaped cross. He symbolizes the self-sacrifice of the fertility god who is killed in order that his resurrection may bring fertility once again to land and people.

Unreal City,[1]   60
Under the brown fog of a winter dawn,
A crowd flowed over London Bridge, so many,[2]
I had not thought death had undone so many.
Sighs, short and infrequent, were exhaled,[3]
And each man fixed his eyes before his feet.   65
Flowed up the hill and down King William Street,
To where Saint Mary Woolnoth kept the hours
With a dead sound on the final stroke of nine.[4]
There I saw one I knew, and stopped him, crying: "Stetson![5]
You who were with me in the ships at Mylae![6]   70
That corpse you planted last year in your garden,
Has it begun to sprout?[7] Will it bloom this year?
Or has the sudden frost disturbed its bed?
Oh keep the Dog far hence, that's friend to men,
Or with his nails he'll dig it up again![8]   75
You! hypocrite lecteur!—mon semblable—mon frère!"[9]

1. "Cf. Baudelaire: *'Fourmillante cité, cité pleine de rêves, / Où le spectre en plein jour raccroche le passant"* [Eliot's note]. The lines are quoted from *Les Sept Vieillards* ("The Seven Old Men") by Charles Baudelaire (1821–67); it is poem XCIII of *Les Fleurs du Mal* ("The Flowers of Evil"). The lines may be translated: "Swarming city, city full of dreams, / Where the specter in broad daylight accosts the passerby."
2. "Cf. Inferno III, 55–57 * * * " [Eliot's note]. The note goes on to quote Dante's lines, which may be translated: "So long a train of people, / that I should never have believed / That death had undone so many." Dante, just outside the gate of Hell, has seen "the wretched souls of those who lived without disgrace and without praise." In his essay on Baudelaire Eliot argued that in a sense it was better to be positively evil than to be neither good nor evil.
3. "Cf. Inferno IV, 25–27 * * * " [Eliot's note]. In Limbo, the first circle of Hell, Dante has found the virtuous heathen, who lived before Christianity and are therefore eternally unable to achieve their desire of seeing God. Dante's lines, cited by Eliot, mean: "Here, so far as I could tell by listening, / there was no lamentation except sighs, / which caused the eternal air to tremble."
4. "A phenomenon which I have often noticed" [Eliot's note]. St. Mary Woolnoth is a church in the "City" of London (the financial district); the crowd is flowing across London Bridge to work in the City.
5. Presumably representing the "aver-

age businessman."
6. The battle of Mylae (260 B.C.) in the First Punic War, which, like World War I, was fought for economic reasons.
7. A distortion of the ritual death of the fertility god.
8. "Cf. the Dirge in Webster's *White Devil*" [Eliot's note]. In the play by John Webster (d. 1625), the dirge, sung by Cornelia, has the lines: "But keep the wolf far thence, that's foe to men, / For with his nails he'll dig them up again." Eliot makes the "wolf" into a "Dog," which is not a "foe" but a "friend" to man. The image may be intended to suggest the ultimate degeneration of the fertility ritual, where the dying god is something buried in a suburban back garden to be dug up again by a friendly dog. There may be a reference to Sirius, the Dog Star, which is important in Egyptian mythology as heralding the fertilizing floods of the Nile (this is discussed by Miss Weston). But most important in this passage is the feverish nightmare atmosphere which it develops.
9. "V. Baudelaire, Preface to *Fleurs du Mal*" [Eliot's note]. The passage is the last line of the introductory poem *Au Lecteur* ("To the Reader") in Baudelaire's *Fleurs du Mal;* it may be translated: "Hypocrite reader!—my likeness —my brother!" *Au Lecteur* describes man as sunk in stupidity, sin, and evil; but the worst in "each man's foul menagerie of sin" is Boredom, the *"monstre délicat"*—"You know him, reader * * * " Like Baudelaire, Eliot is here shocking the reader into full participation in the poem.

II. A Game of Chess[1]

The Chair she sat in, like a burnished throne,[2]
Glowed on the marble, where the glass
Held up by standards wrought with fruited vines
From which a golden Cupidon peeped out   80
(Another hid his eyes behind his wing)
Doubled the flames of sevenbranched candelabra
Reflecting light upon the table as
The glitter of her jewels rose to meet it,
From satin cases poured in rich profusion;   85
In vials of ivory and colored glass
Unstoppered, lurked her strange synthetic perfumes,
Unguent, powdered, or liquid—troubled, confused
And drowned the sense in odors; stirred by the air
That freshened from the window, these ascended   90
In fattening the prolonged candle flames,
Flung their smoke into the laquearia,[3]
Stirring the pattern on the coffered ceiling.
Huge sea-wood fed with copper
Burned green and orange, framed by the colored stone,   95
In which sad light a carvéd dolphin swam.
Above the antique mantel was displayed
As though a window gave upon the sylvan scene[4]
The change of Philomel,[5] by the barbarous king

1. The title suggests two plays by Thomas Middleton (1580–1627): *A Game at Chess* and, more significantly, *Women Beware Women*, which has a scene in which a mother-in-law is distracted by a game of chess while her daughter-in-law is seduced: every move in the chess game represents a move in the seduction. Section II opens with a bored woman of leisure sitting before her dressing table in an atmosphere where the ornaments, the perfumes, the sheer excess of objects stifle the senses, while works of art emphasize the distinction between grandeur and futility. The neurasthenia and mounting hysteria revealed by the dialogue (or an interior monologue, or the remarks in quotation marks may be spoken by the lady and those not in quotation marks may represent her husband's unspoken answers) and the degeneration of culture through parody and jazzing up of lines from Shakespeare culminate in the meaningless yet terrifying "knock." This at once becomes the barman's knock on the counter as he calls closing time, and thus the scene changes to the lower end of the social scale, with women talking in a pub about methods of abortion—another aspect of that sterility and misuse of sex which help to make up the modern Waste Land.
2. "Cf. *Antony and Cleopatra*, II, ii, 1. 190" [Eliot's note]. In Shakespeare's play, Enobarbus' famous description of the first meeting of Antony and Cleopatra begins, "The barge she sat in, / like a burnish'd throne, / Burn'd on the water. * * * " Eliot's language in the opening lines of Part II is full of ironic distortions of Enobarbus' speech.
3. "Laquearia. V. *Aeneid*, I, 726 * * * " [Eliot's note]. *Laquearia* means "a paneled ceiling," and Eliot's note quotes the passage in the *Aeneid* which was his source for the word. The passage may be translated: "Blazing torches hang from the gold-paneled ceiling [*laquearibus aureis*], and torches conquer the night with flames." Virgil is here describing the banquet given by Dido, queen of Carthage, for Aeneas, with whom she fell in love. (Carthage is the scene of more "unholy loves" later in the poem; cf. line 307 and Eliot's note on it.)
4. "Sylvan scene. V. Milton, *Paradise Lost*, IV, 140" [Eliot's note]. The phrase is part of the first description of Eden, which we see through Satan's eyes.
5. "V. Ovid, *Metamorphoses*, VI, Philomela" [Eliot's note]. The note is a reference to Ovid's version of the Greek myth of the rape of Philomela by "the barbarous king" Tereus, husband of her sister Procne. Philomela was transformed into a nightingale. Eliot's note for line 100 refers ahead to his elaboration of the nightingale's song.

So rudely forced; yet there the nightingale   100
Filled all the desert with inviolable voice
And still she cried, and still the world pursues,
"Jug Jug"[6] to dirty ears.
And other withered stumps of time
Were told upon the walls; staring forms   105
Leaned out, leaning, hushing the room enclosed.
Footsteps shuffled on the stair.
Under the firelight, under the brush, her hair
Spread out in fiery points
Glowed into words, then would be savagely still.   110

"My nerves are bad tonight. Yes, bad. Stay with me.
Speak to me. Why do you never speak. Speak.
   What are you thinking of? What thinking? What?
I never know what you are thinking. Think."

I think we are in rats' alley[7]   115
Where the dead men lost their bones.

"What is that noise?"
          The wind under the door.[8]
"What is that noise now? What is the wind doing?"
          Nothing again nothing.   120
              "Do
You know nothing? Do you see nothing? Do you remember
Nothing?"

    I remember
Those are pearls that were his eyes.   125
"Are you alive, or not? Is there nothing in your head?"
                  But
O O O O that Shakespeherian Rag—
It's so elegant
So intelligent
"What shall I do now? What shall I do?"   130
"I shall rush out as I am, and walk the street
With my hair down, so. What shall we do tomorrow?
What shall we ever do?"
          The hot water at ten.   135
And if it rains, a closed car at four.
And we shall play a game of chess,[1]
Pressing lidless eyes and waiting for a knock upon the door.

When Lil's husband got demobbed,[2] I said—
I didn't mince my words, I said to her myself,   140

6. Conventional representation of night-ingale's song in Elizabethan poetry. The tragic myth has become degraded into a dirty story.
7. "Cf. Part III, l. 195" [Eliot's note].
8. "Cf. Webster: 'Is the wind in that door still?'" [Eliot's note]. The line cited in the note is from John Web-ster's *The Devil's Law Case* (III.ii.162).
1. "Cf. the game of chess in Middle-ton's *Women Beware Women*" [Eliot's note]. The significance of this chess game is discussed in note 1 for this section.
2. British slang for "demobilized" (dis-charged from the army).

HURRY UP PLEASE ITS TIME[3]
Now Albert's coming back, make yourself a bit smart.
He'll want to know what you done with that money he gave you
To get yourself some teeth. He did, I was there.
You have them all out, Lil, and get a nice set,   145
He said, I swear, I can't bear to look at you.
And no more can't I, I said, and think of poor Albert,
He's been in the army four years, he wants a good time,
And if you don't give it him, there's others will, I said.
Oh is there, she said. Something o' that, I said.   150
Then I'll know who to thank, she said, and give me a straight look.
HURRY UP PLEASE ITS TIME
If you don't like it you can get on with it, I said.
Others can pick and choose if you can't.
But if Albert makes off, it won't be for lack of telling.   155
You ought to be ashamed, I said, to look so antique.
(And her only thirty-one.)
I can't help it, she said, pulling a long face,
It's them pills I took, to bring it off, she said.
(She's had five already, and nearly died of young George.)   160
The chemist[4] said it would be all right, but I've never been the
      same.
You *are* a proper fool, I said.
Well, if Albert won't leave you alone, there it is, I said,
What you get married for if you don't want children?
HURRY UP PLEASE ITS TIME   165
Well, that Sunday Albert was home, they had a hot gammon,[5]
And they asked me in to dinner, to get the beauty of it hot—
HURRY UP PLEASE ITS TIME
HURRY UP PLEASE ITS TIME
Goonight Bill. Goonight Lou. Goonight May. Goonight.   170
Ta ta. Goonight. Goonight.
Good night, ladies, good night, sweet ladies, good night, good night.[6]

III. The Fire Sermon[7]

The river's tent is broken: the last fingers of leaf
Clutch and sink into the wet bank. The wind

3. The traditional call of the British bartender at closing time.
4. Druggist.
5. Ham or bacon.
6. Cf. the mad Ophelia's departing words (*Hamlet* IV.v.72). Ophelia, too, met "death by water."
7. Just as water both purifies and drowns, so fire both purges and destroys: in this part, the roles of fire are emphasized. The Fire Sermon itself was preached by the Buddha against the fires of lust and other passions which destroy men and prevent their regeneration. The section opens with an autumn scene on the Thames, which is made increasingly sinister by such devices as ironic references to or distortions of famous passages in literature and the mocking equation of noble rituals of the past with modern trivialities and obscenities. We turn briefly to Mr. Eugenides, degenerate descendant of the Syrian merchants who had once spread the fertility cults throughout the Mediterranean, and then to the deliberately horrible scene of modern lust, sex without meaning. Seductions on the Thames, old and new, with parodic echoes of Wagner, Shakespeare, and Dante, lead to a further expression of the sense of nothingness and meaninglessness that characterizes the modern Waste Land, and the section ends with the Occidental St. Augustine echoing the Oriental Buddha in a call for the renunciation of lust.

Crosses the brown land, unheard. The nymphs are departed. 175
Sweet Thames, run softly, till I end my song.[8]
The river bears no empty bottles, sandwich papers,
Silk handkerchiefs, cardboard boxes, cigarette ends
Or other testimony of summer nights. The nymphs are departed.
And their friends, the loitering heirs of city directors; 180
Departed, have left no addresses.
By the waters of Leman I sat down and wept . . .[9]
Sweet Thames, run softly till I end my song,
Sweet Thames, run softly, for I speak not loud or long.
But at my back in a cold blast I hear[1] 185
The rattle of the bones, and chuckle spread from ear to ear.
A rat crept softly through the vegetation
Dragging its slimy belly on the bank
While I was fishing[2] in the dull canal
On a winter evening round behind the gashouse 190
Musing upon the king my brother's wreck[3]
And on the king my father's death before him.
White bodies naked on the low damp ground
And bones cast in a little low dry garret,
Rattled by the rat's foot only, year to year. 195
But at my back from time to time I hear[4]
The sound of horns and motors, which shall bring
Sweeney to Mrs. Porter in the spring.[5]
O the moon shone bright on Mrs. Porter
And on her daughter 200
They wash their feet in soda water[6]
Et O ces voix d'enfants, chantant dans la coupole![7]

8. "V. Spenser, *Prothalamion*" [Eliot's note]. Eliot's line is the refrain from Spenser's marriage song, which is also set by the Thames in London—but a very different Thames from the modern littered river.
9. Cf. Psalms cxxxvii.1, in which the exiled Hebrews mourn for their homeland: "By the rivers of Babylon, there we sat down, yea, we wept, when we remembered Zion." Lake Leman is another name for Lake Geneva; Eliot wrote *The Waste Land* in Lausanne, by that lake. The common noun "leman" is an archaic word meaning, in the bad sense, an illicit sweetheart or mistress; hence "the waters of Leman" become associated with the fires of lust.
1. An ironic distortion of Andrew Marvell's famous lines from *To His Coy Mistress*: "But at my back I always hear / Time's wingèd chariot hurrying near * * * " Cf. line 196.
2. To fish is to seek eternity and salvation (cf. the Fisher King), but this activity is now degraded and dirtied.
3. "Cf. *The Tempest*, I, ii" [Eliot's note]. See line 48.
4. "Cf. Marvell, *To His Coy Mistress*" [Eliot's note].
5. "Cf. Day, *Parliament of Bees*: 'When

of the sudden, listening, you shall hear, / A noise of horns and hunting, which shall bring / Actaeon to Diana in the spring, / Where all shall see her naked skin . . .' " [Eliot's note]. Actaeon was changed to a stag and hunted to death after he saw Diana, the goddess of chastity, bathing with her nymphs. In parodying the poem by John Day (1574–ca. 1640), Eliot is implying that Actaeon's fate indicates a very different set of values from those represented by the association of Sweeney and Mrs. Porter.
6. "I do not know the origin of the ballad from which these lines are taken: it was reported to me from Sydney, Australia" [Eliot's note]. One of the less vulgar versions of the song, which was popular among Australian troops in World War I, went as follows: "O the moon shines bright on Mrs. Porter / And on the daughter / Of Mrs. Porter. / They wash their feet in soda water / And so they oughter / To keep them clean."
7. "V. Verlaine, *Parsifal*" [Eliot's note]. The line is translated, "And O those children's voices singing in the dome!" Verlaine's sonnet describes Parsifal, the questing knight, resisting all

Twit twit twit
Jug jug jug jug jug jug
So rudely forc'd.   205
Tereu[8]

Unreal City
Under the brown fog of a winter noon
Mr. Eugenides, the Smyrna[9] merchant
Unshaven, with a pocket full of currants   210
C.i.f.[1] London: documents at sight,
Asked me in demotic French[2]
To luncheon at the Cannon Street Hotel[3]
Followed by a weekend at the Metropole.

At the violet hour, when the eyes and back   215
Turn upward from the desk, when the human engine waits
Like a taxi throbbing waiting,
I Tiresias,[4] though blind, throbbing between two lives,
Old man with wrinkled female breasts, can see
At the violet hour, the evening hour that strives   220
Homeward, and brings the sailor home from sea,[5]
The typist home at teatime, clears her breakfast, lights

sensual temptations to keep himself pure for the Grail; Wagner's Parsifal had his feet washed before entering the castle of the Grail.

8. "Tereu" is a reference to Tereus, who "rudely forc'd" Philomela; it was also one of the conventional words for a nightingale's song in Elizabethan poetry. Cf. the song from John Lyly's *Alexander and Campaspe* (1564): "Oh, 'tis the ravished nightingale. / *Jug, jug, jug, jug, tereu!* she cries," and lines 100 ff.

9. Seaport in western Turkey; here associated with Carthage and the ancient Phoenician and Syrian merchants (unlike those of modern Smyrna), who spread the old mystery cults. The sort of cult spread by Mr. Eugenides is indicated by his suggestion of "a weekend at the Metropole" (a luxury hotel at Brighton).

1. "The currants were quoted at a price 'carriage and insurance free to London'; and the Bill of Lading etc. were to be handed to the buyer upon payment of the sight draft" [Eliot's note].

2. Popular, vulgar French.

3. By the station which was then chief terminus for travelers to the continent; hence, a favorite meeting place for businessmen going or coming from abroad.

4. "Tiresias, although a mere spectator and not indeed a 'character,' is yet the most important personage in the poem, uniting all the rest. Just as the one-eyed merchant, seller of currants, melts into the Phoenician Sailor, and the latter is not wholly distinct from Ferdinand Prince of Naples, so all the women are one woman, and the two

sexes meet in Tiresias. What Tiresias *sees*, in fact, is the substance of the poem. The whole passage from Ovid is of great anthropological interest * * * " [Eliot's note]. The note then quotes the Latin text of Ovid's *Metamorphoses* which tells the story of Tiresias' change of sex. The Latin may be translated: "[The story goes that once Jove, having drunk a great deal,] jested with Juno. He said, 'Your pleasure in love is really greater than that enjoyed by men.' She denied it; so they decided to seek the opinion of the wise Tiresias, for he knew both aspects of love. For once, with a blow of his staff, he had committed violence on two huge snakes as they copulated in the green forest; and—wonderful to tell—was turned from a man into a woman and thus spent seven years. In the eighth year he saw the same snakes again and said: 'If a blow struck at you is so powerful that it changes the sex of the giver, I will now strike at you again.' With these words he struck the snakes, and his former shape was restored to him and he became as he had been born. So he was appointed arbitrator in the playful quarrel, and supported Jove's statement. It is said that Saturnia [i.e., Juno] was quite disproportionately upset, and condemned the arbitrator to perpetual blindness. But the almighty father (for no god may undo what has been done by another god), in return for the sight that was taken away, gave him the power to know the future and so lightened the penalty paid by the honor."

5. "This may not appear as exact as Sappho's lines, but I had in mind the

Her stove, and lays out food in tins.
Out of the window perilously spread
Her drying combinations touched by the sun's last rays.[5a]   225
On the divan are piled (at night her bed)
Stockings, slippers, camisoles, and stays.
I Tiresias, old man with wrinkled dugs
Perceived the scene, and foretold the rest—
I too awaited the expected guest.   230
He, the young man carbuncular,[6] arrives,
A small house agent's clerk, with one bold stare,
One of the low on whom assurance sits
As a silk hat on a Bradford[7] millionaire.
The time is now propitious, as he guesses,   235
The meal is ended, she is bored and tired,
Endeavors to engage her in caresses
Which still are unreproved, if undesired.
Flushed and decided, he assaults at once;
Exploring hands encounter no defense;   240
His vanity requires no response,
And makes a welcome of indifference.
(And I Tiresias have foresuffered all
Enacted on this same divan or bed;
I who have sat by Thebes[8] below the wall   245
And walked among the lowest of the dead.)
Bestows one final patronizing kiss,
And gropes his way, finding the stairs unlit . . .

She turns and looks a moment in the glass,
Hardly aware of her departed lover;   250
Her brain allows one half-formed thought to pass;
"Well now that's done: and I'm glad it's over."
When lovely woman stoops to folly and
Paces about her room again, alone,
She smoothes her hair with automatic hand,   255
And puts a record on the gramophone.[9]

"This music crept by me upon the waters"[1]
And along the Strand, up Queen Victoria Street.

'longshore' or 'dory' fisherman, who returns at nightfall" [Eliot's note]. Sappho's poem addressed Hesperus, the evening star, as the star that brings everyone home from work to evening rest; her poem is here distorted by Eliot. There is also an echo of Robert Louis Stevenson's *Requiem* in line 221 ("Home is the sailor, home from sea").

5a. The present editor has been informed that this and the preceding line constitute a "great allusion" to Keats's lines "Charmed magic casements, opening on the foam/ Of perilous seas, in faery lands forlorn" (*Ode to a Nightingale*, lines 69–70) but he remains skeptical. It is, however, certainly a powerful anti-romantic image.

6. Pimply.

7. A Yorkshire woolen-manufacturing town, where many rapid fortunes were made in World War I.

8. Tiresias lived in Thebes for many generations, where he witnessed the tragic fates of Oedipus and Creon; he prophesied in the market place by the wall of Thebes.

9. "V. Goldsmith, the song in *The Vicar of Wakefield*" [Eliot's note]. Olivia, a character in Oliver Goldsmith's novel, sings the following song when she returns to the place where she was seduced: "When lovely woman stoops to folly / And finds too late that men betray / What charm can soothe her melancholy, / What art can wash her guilt away? / The only art her guilt to cover, / To hide her shame from every

O City city, I can sometimes hear
Beside a public bar in Lower Thames Street,   260
The pleasant whining of a mandolin
And a clatter and a chatter from within
Where fishmen lounge at noon: where the walls
Of Magnus Martyr hold
Inexplicable splendor of Ionian white and gold [2]   265

    The river sweats[3]
    Oil and tar
    The barges drift
    With the turning tide
    Red sails   270
    Wide
    To leeward, swing on the heavy spar.
    The barges wash
    Drifting logs
    Down Greenwich reach   275
    Past the Isle of Dogs.[4]
            Weialala leia
            Wallala leialala

    Elizabeth and Leicester[5]
    Beating oars   280
    The stern was formed
    A gilded shell
    Red and gold
    The brisk swell
    Rippled both shores   285
    Southwest wind
    Carried down stream
    The peal of bells

---

eye, / To give repentance to her lover / And wring his bosom—is to die."

1. "V. *The Tempest,* as above" [Eliot's note]. Cf. line 48. (The line is from Ferdinand's speech, continuing after "weeping again the King my father's wrack.")

2. "The interior of St. Magnus Martyr is to my mind one of the finest among [Sir Christopher] Wren's interiors. * * * " [Eliot's note]. In these lines, the "pleasant" music, the "fishmen" resting after labor, and the splendor of the church interior all suggest a world of true values, where work and relaxation are both real and take place in a context of religious meaning. It is but a momentary glimpse of an almost lost world.

3. "The Song of the (three) Thames-daughters begins here. From line 292 to 306 inclusive they speak in turn. V. *Götterdämmerung,* III, i: the Rhine-daughters" [Eliot's note]. The Thames-daughters, both old and new, reflect a barren world of shabbiness and lust. Eliot parallels them with the Rhine-maidens in Wagner's opera *Die Götter-*

dämmerung ("The Twilight of the Gods") who lament that, with the gold of the Nibelungs stolen, the beauty of the river is gone. The refrain in lines 277–78 is borrowed from Wagner.

4. Greenwich is a borough in London on the south side of the Thames; opposite is the Isle of Dogs (a peninsula): Eliot presumably intends a reference to the earlier theme of the Dog.

5. The fruitless love of Queen Elizabeth and the Earl of Leicester (Sir Robert Dudley) is recalled in Eliot's note: "V. [J. A.] Froude, *Elizabeth,* Vol. I, ch. iv, letter of De Quadra to Philip of Spain: 'In the afternoon we were in a barge, watching the games on the river. (The queen) was alone with Lord Robert and myself on the poop, when they began to talk nonsense, and went so far that Lord Robert at last said, as I was on the spot there was no reason why they should not be married if the queen pleased.'" Even these two great figures from the 16th century represent no past glory and no contrast to present sordidness. (Queen Elizabeth was born in the old Green-

White towers
        Weialala leia 290
        Wallala leialala

"Trams and dusty trees.
Highbury bore me. Richmond and Kew
Undid me.[6] By Richmond I raised my knees
Supine on the floor of a narrow canoe." 295

"My feet are at Moorgate,[7] and my heart
Under my feet. After the event
He wept. He promised 'a new start.'
I made no comment. What should I resent?"

"On Margate[8] Sands. 300
I can connect
Nothing with nothing.
The broken fingernails of dirty hands.
My people humble people who expect
Nothing." 305
      la la

To Carthage then I came[9]

Burning burning burning burning[1]
O Lord Thou pluckest me out[2]
O Lord Thou pluckest 310

burning

IV. Death by Water[3]

Phlebas the Phoenician, a fortnight dead,
Forgot the cry of gulls, and the deep sea swell

---

wich House, by the river, where Greenwich Hospital now stands.)
6. "Cf. *Purgatorio*, V, 133 * * * " [Eliot's note]. The *Purgatorio* lines, which Eliot here parodies, may be translated: "Remember me, who am La Pia. / Siena made me, Maremma undid me." Highbury is a residential London suburb; Richmond is a pleasant part of London westward up the Thames, with boating and riverside hotels; Kew, adjoining Richmond, has the famous Kew Gardens.
7. Slum area in east London.
8. Popular seaside resort on Thames estuary.
9. "V. St. Augustine's *Confessions*: 'to Carthage then I came, where a caldron of unholy loves sang all about mine ears' " [Eliot's note]. The passage from the *Confessions* quoted here occurs in St. Augustine's account of his youthful life of lust. Cf. line 92 and its note.
1. "The complete text of the Buddha's Fire Sermon (which corresponds in importance to the Sermon on the Mount) from which these words are taken, will be found translated in the late Henry

Clarke Warren's *Buddhism in Translation* (Harvard Oriental Series). * * * " [Eliot's note]. In the sermon, the Buddha instructs his priests that all things "are on fire. * * * The eye * * * is on fire; forms are on fire; eye-consciousness is on fire; impressions received by the eye are on fire; and whatever sensation, pleasant, unpleasant, or indifferent, originates in dependence on impressions received by the eye, that also is on fire. And with what are these on fire? With the fire of passion, say I, with the fire of hatred, with the fire of infatuation * * * " For Christ's Sermon on the Mount see Matthew v-vii.
2. "From St. Augustine's *Confessions* again. The collocation of these two representatives of eastern and western asceticism, as the culmination of this part of the poem, is not an accident" [Eliot's note]. Cf. also Zechariah iii.2, where God, rebuking Satan, speaks of Joshua the high priest as "a brand plucked out of the fire."
3. This section has been interpreted in two ways: either it signifies death by water without resurrection (water *mis-*

And the profit and loss.

A current under sea   315
Picked his bones in whispers. As he rose and fell
He passed the stages of his age and youth
Entering the whirlpool.

Gentile or Jew
O you who turn the wheel and look to windward,   320
Consider Phlebas, who was once handsome and tall as you.

V. What the Thunder Said[4]

After the torchlight red on sweaty faces
After the frosty silence in the gardens
After the agony in stony places
The shouting and the crying   325
Prison and palace and reverberation
Of thunder of spring over distant mountains
He who was living is now dead[5]
We who were living are now dying
With a little patience   330

Here is no water but only rock
Rock and no water and the sandy road
The road winding above among the mountains
Which are mountains of rock without water
If there were water we should stop and drink   335
Amongst the rock one cannot stop or think
Sweat is dry and feet are in the sand
If there were only water amongst the rock
Dead mountain mouth of carious teeth that cannot spit
Here one can neither stand nor lie nor sit   340

used), or it symbolizes the sacrificial death which precedes rebirth. It is true that Phlebas is purged of his commercial interests and vanities when he suffers a sea change, and Miss Weston tells of the annual casting into the sea at Alexandria of an effigy of the head of Adonis—to be taken out after seven days by jubilant celebrators of the cult. The majority of interpreters, however, see Phlebas' drowning as a death by water which brings no resurrection, although there is a strange sense of peace in the death. Cf. line 47 and its note.
4. "In the first part of Part V three themes are employed: the journey to Emmaus, the approach to the Chapel Perilous (see Miss Weston's book), and the present decay of eastern Europe" [Eliot's note]. The journey to Emmaus (see line 360 and its note) is a significant feature in the story of Christ, and in this section the Waste Land is more clearly related to that story. Christ is associated with the slain fertility god, but there is still no resurrection. The rocky landscape is described with a new and agonizing intensity until everything breaks down in

hallucination in which visions of the decay of the great cities of Western civilization give way to nightmare images of horror. Then the scene changes to the Chapel Perilous in the midst of the Waste Land: it seems empty and derelict and apparently the quest has been in vain. But suddenly the cock crows, the lightning flashes, and the fertilizing rain falls. The thunder peals and gives its message of salvation in terms of Oriental wisdom, the Sanskrit words for "Give, Sympathize, Control." But we are too timidly prudent to give properly, too shut in within our own individualities to be able to sympathize properly, and we can more easily respond to control than exercise it. Salvation remains problematical.
5. These lines, containing allusions to Christ's imprisonment and trial, and to Gethsemane and Golgotha, suggest the hopeless days between Good Friday and Easter, between the Crucifixion and the Resurrection—associated with the death of the Fisher King and the moment of despair in the Waste Land when regeneration seems impossible.

There is not even silence in the mountains
But dry sterile thunder without rain
There is not even solitude in the mountains
But red sullen faces sneer and snarl
From doors of mudcracked houses   345
             If there were water

   And no rock
   If there were rock
   And also water
   And water   350
   A spring
   A pool among the rock
   If there were the sound of water only
   Not the cicada[6]
   And dry grass singing   355
   But sound of water over a rock
   Where the hermit thrush[7] sings in the pine trees
   Drip drop drip drop drop drop drop
   But there is no water

Who is the third who walks always beside you?[8]   360
When I count, there are only you and I together
But when I look ahead up the white road
There is always another one walking beside you
Gliding wrapped in a brown mantle, hooded
I do not know whether a man or a woman   365
—But who is that on the other side of you?

What is that sound high in the air[9]
Murmur of maternal lamentation
Who are those hooded hordes swarming
Over endless plains, stumbling in cracked earth   370
Ringed by the flat horizon only
What is the city over the mountains
Cracks and reforms[1] and bursts in the violet air
Falling towers

6. Grasshopper. Cf. the prophecy of Ecclesiastes, "the grasshopper shall be a burden, and desire shall fail * * * " (and cf. also line 23 and its note).
7. "This is * * * the hermit thrush which I have heard in Quebec County. * * * Its 'water-dripping song' is justly celebrated" [Eliot's note].
8. "The following lines were stimulated by the account of one of the Antarctic expeditions (I forget which, but I think one of Shackleton's): it was related that the party of explorers, at the extremity of their strength, had the constant delusion that there was *one more member* than could actually be counted" [Eliot's note]. This reminiscence is associated with the journey of Christ's disciples to Emmaus given in Luke xxiv.13–16: "And it came to pass, that,

while they communed together and reasoned, Jesus himself drew near, and went with them. But their eyes were holden that they should not know him."
9. Eliot's note for lines 367–77 is: "Cf. Herman Hesse, *Blick ins Chaos* ["A Glimpse into Chaos"] * * * " The note then quotes a passage from the German text, which is translated: "Already half of Europe, already at least half of Eastern Europe, on the way to Chaos, drives drunk in sacred infatuation along the edge of the precipice, sings drunkenly, as though hymn singing, as Dmitri Karamazov [in Dostoyevski's *Brothers Karamazov*] sang. The offended bourgeois laughs at the songs; the saint and the seer hear them with tears."
1. Used ironically.

Jerusalem Athens Alexandria   375
Vienna London
Unreal

A woman drew her long black hair out tight
And fiddled whisper music on those strings
And bats with baby faces in the violet light   380
Whistled, and beat their wings
And crawled head downward down a blackened wall
And upside down in air were towers
Tolling reminiscent bells, that kept the hours
And voices singing out of empty cisterns and exhausted wells.   385

In this decayed hole among the mountains
In the faint moonlight, the grass is singing
Over the tumbled graves, about the chapel
There is the empty chapel, only the wind's home.[2]
It has no windows, and the door swings,   390
Dry bones can harm no one.
Only a cock stood on the rooftree
Co co rico co co rico[3]
In a flash of lightning. Then a damp gust
Bringing rain   395

Ganga[4] was sunken, and the limp leaves
Waited for rain, while the black clouds
Gathered far distant, over Himavant.[5]
The jungle crouched, humped in silence.
Then spoke the thunder   400
Da[6]
Datta: what have we given?
My friend, blood shaking my heart
The awful daring of a moment's surrender
Which an age of prudence can never retract   405
By this, and this only, we have existed
Which is not to be found in our obituaries
Or in memories draped by the beneficent spider[7]
Or under seals broken by the lean solicitor

2. Suggesting the moment of near despair before the Chapel Perilous, when
the questing knight sees nothing there
but decay. This illusion of nothingness
is the knight's final test.
3. The crowing of the cock signals the
departure of ghosts and evil spirits.
Cf. *Hamlet* I.i.157 ff.
4. The river Ganges.
5. I.e., snowy mountain; the name of
a peak in the Himalayas.
6. "'Datta, dayadhvam, damyata'
(Give, sympathize, control). The fable
of the meaning of the Thunder is found
in the *Brihadaranyaka—Upanishad*, 5,
1. * * * " [Eliot's note]. The Hindu
fable referred to is that of gods, men,
and demons each in turn asking of

their father Prajapati, "Speak to us,
O Lord." To each he replied with the
one syllable "*DA*," and each group interpreted it in a different way: "*Datta*,"
to give alms; "*Dayadhvam*," to have
compassion; "*Damyata*," to practice
self-control. The fable concludes, "This
is what the divine voice, the Thunder,
repeats when he says: *DA, DA, DA*:
'Control yourselves; give alms; be compassionate.' Therefore one should practice these three things: self-control,
alms-giving, and compassion."
7. "Cf. Webster, *The White Devil*, V,
vi: ' . . . they'll remarry / Ere the
worm pierce your winding-sheet, ere
the spider / Make a thin curtain for
your epitaphs'" [Eliot's note].

In our empty rooms   410
DA
Dayadhvam: I have heard the key[8]
Turn in the door once and turn once only
We think of the key, each in his prison
Thinking of the key, each confirms a prison   415
Only at nightfall, ethereal rumours
Revive for a moment a broken Coriolanus[9]
DA
Damyata: The boat responded
Gaily, to the hand expert with sail and oar   420
The sea was calm, your heart would have responded
Gaily, when invited, beating obedient
To controlling hands

                    I sat upon the shore
Fishing,[1] with the arid plain behind me   425
Shall I at least set my lands in order?[2]
London Bridge is falling down falling down falling down[3]
Poi s'ascose nel foco che gli affina[4]
Quando fiam uti chelidon[5]—O swallow swallow

8. "Cf. *Inferno*, XXXIII, 46 * * * "
[Eliot's note]. In this passage from
the *Inferno* Ugolino recalls his imprisonment in the tower with his children,
where they starved to death: "And I
heard below the door of the horrible
tower being locked up." Eliot implies
that we cannot obey the command to
sympathize because we are imprisoned
within the circle of our own egotism.
Eliot's note for this line goes on to
quote F. H. Bradley, *Appearance and
Reality*, p. 346, as follows: " 'My external sensations are no less private
to myself than are my thoughts or my
feelings. In either case my experience
falls within my own circle, a circle
closed on the outside; and, with all its
elements alike, every sphere is opaque
to the others which surround it. . . .
In brief, regarded as an existence which
appears in a soul, the whole world for
each is peculiar and private to that
soul.' "
9. Coriolanus, who acted out of pride
rather than duty, is an obvious example of a man locked in the prison of
his own self. He led the enemy against
his native city out of injured pride
(cf. Shakespeare's *Coriolanus*).
1. "V. Weston: *From Ritual to Romance;* chapter on the Fisher King"
[Eliot's note].
2. The inclusive "I," who sits in the
symbolic act of fishing (seeking salvation, regeneration, eternity) with the
Waste Land behind him, wonders how
far he can order his affairs. There is
a note of subdued hope or at least of
determination in these lines. The "at
least" suggests a reasonable minimum
of achievement.

3. One of the later lines of this nursery
rhyme is: "Take the key and lock her
up, my fair lady."
4. "V. *Purgatorio*, XXVI, 148 * * * "
[Eliot's note]. The note goes on to
quote lines 145–48 of the *Purgatorio*,
in which Arnaut Daniel, the Provençal
poet, addresses Dante: " 'Now I pray
you, by that virtue which guides you
to the summit of the stairway, be mindful in due time of my pain.' " Then
(in the line Eliot quotes here) "he
hid himself in the fire which refines
them." The purgatorial vision of refining fire—as distinct from the fires
of lust—represents one of the hopeful
fragments shored up by the seeker for
regeneration and order.
5. "V. *Pervigilium Veneris*. Cf. Philomela in Parts II and III" [Eliot's
note]. The Latin phrase in the text
means, "When shall I be as the swallow?" It comes from the *Pervigilium
Veneris* ("Vigil of Venus"), an anonymous late Latin poem combining a
hymn to Venus with a description of
spring. In the last two stanzas of the
Pervigilium occurs a recollection of the
Tereus-Procne-Philomela myth (except
that in this version the swallow is identified with Philomela); the anonymous
poet's mood changes to one of sadness,
combined with hope for renewal: "The
maid of Tereus sings under the poplar
shade, so that you would think musical
trills of love came from her mouth and
not a sister's complaint of a barbarous
husband. * * * She sings, we are silent. When will my spring come? When
shall I be as the swallow that I may
cease to be silent? I have lost the Muse
in silence, and Apollo regards me not

Le Prince d'Aquitaine à la tour abolie[6]   430
These fragments I have shored against my ruins[7]
Why then Ile fit you. Hieronymo's mad againe.[8]
Datta. Dayadhvam. Damyata.
        Shantih   shantih   shantih[9]
1921   1922

Journey of the Magi[1]

"A cold coming we had of it,
Just the worst time of the year
For a journey, and such a long journey:
The ways deep and the weather sharp,
The very dead of winter."[2]   5
And the camels galled, sore-footed, refractory,
Lying down in the melting snow.
There were times we regretted
The summer palaces on slopes, the terraces,
And the silken girls bringing sherbet.   10
Then the camel men cursing and grumbling
And running away, and wanting their liquor and women,
And the night-fires going out, and the lack of shelters,
And the cities hostile and the towns unfriendly
And the villages dirty and charging high prices: 15
A hard time we had of it.

* * * " For "O swallow swallow" cf. Swinburne's *Itylus*, which begins, "Swallow, my sister, O sister swallow, / How can thine heart be full of spring?" and Tennyson's lyric in *The Princess*: "O Swallow, Swallow, flying, flying south * * * "

6. "V. Gerard de Nerval, Sonnet *El Desdichado*" [Eliot's note]. The French line may be translated, "The Prince of Aquitaine in the ruined tower." One of the cards in the Tarot pack is "the tower struck by lightning." The ruined tower is symbolic of a decayed tradition.

7. This may refer to the whole poem —fragments assembled by the poet in the attempt to come to terms with his situation.

8. "V. Kyd's *Spanish Tragedy*" [Eliot's note]. Subtitled "Hieronymo's Mad Againe," Kyd's play (1594) is an early example of the Elizabethan tragedy of revenge. Hieronymo, driven mad by the murder of his son, has his revenge when he is asked to write a court entertainment. He replies, "Why then Ile fit you!" (i.e., accommodate you), and assigns the parts in the entertainment so that, in the course of the action, his son's murderers are killed.

9. "Shantih. Repeated as here, a formal ending to an Upanishad. 'The Peace which passeth understanding' is our equivalent to this word" [Eliot's note]. The Upanishads are poetic dialogues on Hindu metaphysics, written after the Vedas, the ancient Hindu scriptures, and in part commenting on them. The fact that the benediction is in a language so foreign to Western tradition may indicate that the solution is willed, not achieved. The fragments with which the poem ends seem like a desperate attempt at ordering chaos, but it breaks down in madness ("Hieronymo's mad againe"). We end with the threefold message repeated and the benediction uttered; but the issue remains in doubt.

1. One of the three wise men who came from the east to Jerusalem to do homage to the infant Jesus (Matthew ii.1–12) is recalling in old age the meaning of the experience.

2. Adapted from a passage in a Nativity sermon by the 17th-century divine Lancelot Andrewes: "A cold coming they had of it at this time of the year, just the worst time of the year to take a journey, and specially a long journey in. The ways deep, the weather sharp, the days short, the sun farthest off, *in solstitio brumali*, 'the very dead of winter.' "

At the end we preferred to travel all night,
Sleeping in snatches,
With the voices singing in our ears, saying
That this was all folly.   20

Then at dawn we came down to a temperate valley,
Wet, below the snow line, smelling of vegetation;
With a running stream and a water mill beating the darkness,
And three trees on the low sky,
And an old white horse galloped away in the meadow.[3]   25
Then we came to a tavern with vine-leaves over the lintel,
Six hands at an open door dicing for pieces of silver,[4]
And feet kicking the empty wineskins.
But there was no information, and so we continued
And arrived at evening, not a moment too soon   30
Finding the place; it was (you may say) satisfactory.

All this was a long time ago, I remember,
And I would do it again, but set down
This set down
This: were we led all that way for   35
Birth or Death? There was a Birth, certainly,
We had evidence and no doubt. I had seen birth and death,
But had thought they were different; this Birth was
Hard and bitter agony for us, like Death, our death.
We returned to our places, these Kingdoms,   40
But no longer at ease here, in the old dispensation,
With an alien people clutching their gods.
I should be glad of another death.

1927

Marina[1]

Quis hic locus, quae regio, quae mundi plaga?[2]

What seas what shores what gray rocks and what islands
What water lapping the bow

3. A series of images of freshness and renewal, combined with anticipations of disaster. The "three trees on the low sky" suggest the three crosses, with Christ crucified on the center one; the men dicing for pieces of silver suggest the soldiers dicing for Christ's garments and Judas' betrayal of him for thirty pieces of silver.
4. "Why, for all of us, out of all that we have heard, seen, felt, in a lifetime, do certain images recur, charged with emotion, rather than others? * * * six ruffians seen through an open window playing cards at night at a small French railway junction where there was a water mill" (Eliot, *The Use of*

Poetry and the Use of Criticism).
1. Marina is Pericles' daughter in Shakespeare's play *Pericles Prince of Tyre:* she was born at sea, lost to her father, then as a young woman found by him again. This poem evokes the mood of hushed wonder with which Pericles rediscovered his daughter, who had almost miraculously preserved her innocence and virtue through harrowing experiences. The situation is of course symbolic: a mood is established of regeneration, of escape from lust into love and from violence and confusion into peace. The symbolic boat on which the reunion takes place was originally made by the speaker, but for

And scent of pine and the woodthrush singing through the fog
What images return
O my daughter.   5

Those who sharpen the tooth of the dog, meaning
Death
Those who glitter with the glory of the hummingbird, meaning
Death
Those who sit in the sty of contentment, meaning   10
Death
Those who suffer the ecstasy of the animals, meaning
Death

Are become unsubstantial, reduced by a wind,
A breath of pine, and the woodsong fog   15
By this grace dissolved in place

What is this face, less clear and clearer
The pulse in the arm, less strong and stronger—
Given or lent? more distant than stars and nearer than the eye

Whispers and small laughter between leaves and hurrying feet   20
Under sleep, where all the waters meet.

Bowsprit cracked with ice and paint cracked with heat.
I made this, I have forgotten
And remember.
The rigging weak and the canvas rotten   25
Between one June and another September.
Made this unknowing, half conscious, unknown, my own.
The garboard strake[3] leaks, the seams need calking.
This form, this face, this life
Living to live in a world of time beyond me; let me   30
Resign my life for this life, my speech for that unspoken,
The awakened, lips parted, the hope, the new ships.

What seas what shores what granite islands towards my timbers
And woodthrush calling through the fog
My daughter.   35

1930

---

a purpose he cannot remember; it is
battered and frail; but it serves its
purpose, having led him to this moment
of grace, dedication, and new hope.
One must not be too literal in pressing a meaning on each of the images:
this is the most delicately evocative of
all Eliot's poems.
2. "What place is this, what country,
what region of the world?" Spoken by
Hercules on regaining sanity after having killed his children in his madness,
in Seneca's play *Hercules Furens* ("The

Mad Hercules"). This is a situation
contrary to the one evoked in the poem.
Eliot once wrote to a correspondent
that he wished to achieve a "crisscross"
between the scenes in the Senecan and
the Shakespearean plays. He appears to
be making that association between
birth and death which he uses so often
(as in *The Waste Land* and *Journey
of the Magi*).
3. The planking nearest to the boat's
keel—hence its most vital spot.

From FOUR QUARTETS
Little Gidding[1]

I

Midwinter spring is its own season
Sempiternal[2] though sodden towards sundown,
Suspended in time, between pole and tropic.
When the short day is brightest, with frost and fire,
The brief sun flames the ice, on pond and ditches,   5
In windless cold that is the heart's heat,
Reflecting in a watery mirror
A glare that is blindness in the early afternoon.
And glow more intense than blaze of branch, or brazier,
Stirs the dumb spirit: no wind, but pentecostal fire[3]   10
In the dark time of the year. Between melting and freezing

1. This is the fourth of Eliot's *Four Quartets,* four related poems each divided into five "movements" in a manner reminiscent of the structure of a quartet or a sonata and each dealing with some aspect of the relation of time and eternity, the meaning of history, the achievement of the moment of timeless insight. Though the *Four Quartets* constitute a unified sequence, they were each written separately and can be read as individual poems. "*Little Gidding* can be understood by itself, without reference to the preceding poems, which it yet so beautifully completes" (Helen Gardner). Each of the four is named after a place. Little Gidding is a village in Huntingdonshire where in 1625 Nicholas Ferrar established an Anglican religious community; it was broken up in 1647, toward the end of the Civil War, by the victorious Puritans; the chapel, however, was rebuilt in the 19th century and still exists. The poet recalls a midwinter visit to the chapel; he evokes the scene and uses it for a starting point for a meditation on England's past and present, on the possibility of redemption through purgation. Eliot wrote the poem in 1942, when he was a fire-watcher during World War II, and he looks back at the history and meaning of Little Gidding from his own war experience in order to project its present significance.

The first section or movement is itself in three parts of which the first sets the scene and the season, the second asserts the significance of this place at any season, and the third reminds us of the original purpose of the community and suggests what these dead can communicate to us now, to achieve "the intersection of the timeless moment." The second movement is much more lyrical in tone, and broods over change and decay. It then changes to a Dan-tesque verse form (suggesting Dante's *terza rima,* but unrhymed) in which the poet describes himself walking at dawn after an air raid and encountering a "dead master" returned temporarily from Purgatory. (The scene also recalls Dante's meeting his own dead master Brunetto Latini in Hell.) The spirit talks of the relation between past and present, their common concern with language, and the slow and difficult progress toward purgation; he disappears when the All Clear sounds. The third movement broods over the uses of memory and attitudes toward history; recalls that the combatants in that earlier war are now "folded in a single party"; concedes that one cannot revive lost causes; and suggests that in detachment and in the view of past suffering as purgation a sense of peace and of renewal might be achieved. The short lyrical fourth movement elaborates the notion of purgation (the dove of peace has become the bombing plane), sees fire as purgative as well as destructive, and emphasizes the dual nature of love and the alternative of the two kinds of fire. The final movement accepts the movements of history and sees history as "a pattern of timeless moments," so that here at this moment in Little Gidding "while the light fails / On a winter afternoon, in a secluded chapel / History is now and England." The poet now sees the rose of life and the yew tree of death interpenetrating at each moment and ends with a vision of suffering and love, the fire and the rose, as one.
2. Eternal, everlasting.
3. On the Pentecost day after the death and resurrection of Christ, there appeared to His apostles "cloven tongues like as of fire * * * And they were all filled with the Holy Ghost" (Acts ii).

The soul's sap quivers. There is no earth smell
Or smell of living thing. This is the springtime
But not in time's covenant. Now the hedgerow
Is blanched for an hour with transitory blossom   15
Of snow, a bloom more sudden
Than that of summer, neither budding nor fading,
Not in the scheme of generation.
Where is the summer, the unimaginable
Zero summer?   20

        If you came this way,
Taking the route you would be likely to take
From the place you would be likely to come from,
If you came this way in may time, you would find the hedges
White again, in May, with voluptuary sweetness.   25
It would be the same at the end of the journey,
If you came at night like a broken king,[4]
If you came by day not knowing what you came for,
It would be the same, when you leave the rough road
And turn behind the pigsty to the dull façade   30
And the tombstone. And what you thought you came for
Is only a shell, a husk of meaning
From which the purpose breaks only when it is fulfilled
If at all. Either you had no purpose
Or the purpose is beyond the end you figured   35
And is altered in fulfillment. There are other places
Which also are the world's end, some at the sea jaws,
Or over a dark lake, in a desert or a city—
But this is the nearest, in place and time,
Now and in England.   40

        If you came this way,
Taking any route, starting from anywhere,
At any time or at any season,
It would always be the same: you would have to put off
Sense and notion. You are not here to verify,   45
Instruct yourself, or inform curiosity
Or carry report. You are here to kneel
Where prayer has been valid. And prayer is more
Than an order of words, the conscious occupation
Of the praying mind, or the sound of the voice praying. 50
And what the dead had no speech for, when living,
They can tell you, being dead: the communication
Of the dead is tongued with fire beyond the language of the living.
Here, the intersection of the timeless moment
Is England and nowhere. Never and always.   55

               II

Ash on an old man's sleeve
Is all the ash the burnt roses leave.

---

4. I.e., Charles I. King Charles visited Ferrar's community more than once, and is said to have paid his last visit in secret after his final defeat in the Civil War.

Dust in the air suspended
Marks the place where a story ended.
Dust inbreathed was a house—   60
The wall, the wainscot, and the mouse.
The death of hope and despair,
        This is the death of air.[5]

There are flood and drouth
Over the eyes and in the mouth,   65
Dead water and dead sand
Contending for the upper hand.
The parched eviscerate soil
Gapes at the vanity of toil,
Laughs without mirth.   70
        This is the death of earth.

Water and fire succeed
The town, the pasture, and the weed.
Water and fire deride
The sacrifice that we denied.   75
Water and fire shall rot
The marred foundations we forgot,
Of sanctuary and choir.
        This is the death of water and fire.

In the uncertain hour before the morning   80
    Near the ending of interminable night
    At the recurrent end of the unending
After the dark dove with the flickering tongue
    Had passed below the horizon of his homing
    While the dead leaves still rattled on like tin   85
Over the asphalt where no other sound was
    Between three districts whence the smoke arose
    I met one walking, loitering and hurried
As if blown towards me like the metal leaves
    Before the urban dawn wind unresisting.   90
    And as I fixed upon the down-turned face
That pointed scrutiny with which we challenge
    The first-met stranger in the waning dusk
    I caught the sudden look of some dead master
Whom I had known, forgotten, half recalled   95
    Both one and many; in the brown baked features
    The eyes of a familiar compound ghost[6]
Both intimate and unidentifiable.

5. "The death of air," like that of "earth" and of "water and fire" in the succeeding stanzas, recalls the theory of the creative strife of the four elements propounded by Heraclitus (Greek philosopher of 4th and 5th centuries B.C.): "Fire lives in the death of air; air lives in the death of fire; water lives in the death of earth; and earth lives in the death of water." But at this point in the poem, unlike Heraclitus' theory, death is not intermingled with life.
6. Cf. Shakespeare, *Sonnet* LXXXVI, line 9: "that affable familiar ghost." W. B. Yeats is the "dead master" who is an important part of this "compound ghost."

So I assumed a double part,[7] and cried
And heard another's voice cry: "What! are *you* here?"   100
Although we were not. I was still the same,
  Knowing myself yet being someone other—
  And he a face still forming; yet the words sufficed
To compel the recognition they preceded.
  And so, compliant to the common wind,   105
  Too strange to each other for misunderstanding,
In concord at this intersection time
  Of meeting nowhere, no before and after,
  We trod the pavement in a dead patrol.
I said: "The wonder that I feel is easy,   110
  Yet ease is cause of wonder. Therefore speak:
  I may not comprehend, may not remember."
And he: "I am not eager to rehearse
  My thought and theory which you have forgotten.
  These things have served their purpose: let them be.   115
So with your own, and pray they be forgiven
  By others, as I pray you to forgive
  Both bad and good. Last season's fruit is eaten
And the fullfed beast shall kick the empty pail.
  For last year's words belong to last year's language   120
  And next year's words await another voice.
But, as the passage now presents no hindrance
  To the spirit unappeased and peregrine[8]
  Between two worlds become much like each other,
So I find words I never thought to speak   125
  In streets I never thought I should revisit
  When I left my body on a distant shore.
Since our concern was speech, and speech impelled us
  To purify the dialect of the tribe[9]
  And urge the mind to aftersight and foresight,   130
Let me disclose the gifts reserved for age
  To set a crown upon your lifetime's effort.
  First, the cold friction of expiring sense
Without enchantment, offering no promise
  But bitter tastelessness of shadow fruit   135
  As body and soul begin to fall asunder.
Second, the conscious impotence of rage
  At human folly, and the laceration
  Of laughter at what ceases to amuse.
And last, the rending pain of re-enactment   140
  Of all that you have done, and been; the shame
  Of motives late revealed, and the awareness
Of things ill done and done to others' harm

---

7. Two interpretations have been suggested: either the poet assumes the part of Dante as he accosted people in Hell or Purgatory, or else he assumes the part of his own other self.
8. Foreign, coming from abroad.
9. A rendering of the line *"Donner un sens plus pur aux mots de la tribu"* in Stéphane Mallarmé's sonnet *Le Tombeau d'Edgar Poe* ("The Tomb of Edgar Poe"). There are many less direct literary echoes in this passage, some recalling Milton, some various Jacobean dramatists, some Dante.

Which once you took for exercise of virtue.
Then fools' approval stings, and honor stains.   145
From wrong to wrong the exasperated spirit
   Proceeds, unless restored by that refining fire[1]
   Where you must move in measure, like a dancer."
The day was breaking. In the disfigured street
   He left me, with a kind of valediction,   150
   And faded on the blowing of the horn.[2]

III

There are three conditions which often look alike
Yet differ completely, flourish in the same hedgerow:
Attachment to self and to things and to persons, detachment
From self and from things and from persons; and, growing between
     them, indifference   155
Which resembles the others as death resembles life,
Being between two lives—unflowering, between
The live and the dead nettle. This is the use of memory:
For liberation—not less of love but expanding
Of love beyond desire, and so liberation   160
From the future as well as the past. Thus, love of a country
Begins as attachment to our own field of action
And comes to find that action of little importance
Though never indifferent. History may be servitude,
History may be freedom. See, now they vanish,   165
The faces and places, with the self which, as it could, loved them,
To become renewed, transfigured, in another pattern.

Sin is Behovely, but
All shall be well, and
All manner of thing shall be well.[3]   170
If I think, again, of this place,
And of people, not wholly commendable,
Of no immediate kin or kindness,
But some of peculiar genius,
All touched by a common genius,   175
United in the strife which divided them;
If I think of a king at nightfall,[4]

1. Cf. *The Waste Land*, line 428 and its note.
2. Cf. *Hamlet*, I.ii.157. "It faded on the crowing of the cock." The horn is the All Clear signal after an air raid (the dialogue has taken place between the dropping of the last bomb and the sounding of the All Clear). Eliot called the section which ends with this line "the nearest equivalent to a canto of the *Inferno* or *Purgatorio*" that he could achieve, and spoke of his intention to present "a parallel, by means of contrast, between the *Inferno* and the *Purgatorio* * * * and a hallucinated scene after an air raid."
3. A quotation from the 14th-century English mystic, Dame Juliana of Norwich: "Sin is behovabil [inevitable], but all shall be well and all shall be well and all manner of thing shall be well." It is the accent of genuine mystical experience and authority that Eliot wishes to convey in using Dame Juliana's words. The thought expressed—that in spite of sin or even through sin all shall be well—is a variation of the "fortunate fall" (*felix culpa*) idea found in Milton and elsewhere.
4. Charles I. He died "on the scaffold" in 1649, while his principal advisers, Archbishop Laud and Thomas Wentworth, Earl of Strafford, were both executed earlier by the victorious Parliamentary forces. Eliot is here meditating on the English Civil War and refusing to take sides, for history subsumes both sides. The war becomes a symbol of purgation through suffering. Cf. conclusion of this section.

Of three men, and more, on the scaffold
And a few who died forgotten
In other places, here and abroad,   180
And of one who died blind and quiet[4a]
Why should we celebrate
These dead men more than the dying?
It is not to ring the bell backward
Nor is it an incantation   185
To summon the specter of a Rose.
We cannot revive old factions
We cannot restore old policies
Or follow an antique drum.
These men, and those who opposed them   190
And those whom they opposed
Accept the constitution of silence
And are folded in a single party.
Whatever we inherit from the fortunate
We have taken from the defeated   195
What they had to leave us—a symbol:
A symbol perfected in death.
And all shall be well and
All manner of thing shall be well
By the purification of the motive   200
In the ground of our beseeching.

IV

The dove descending breaks the air
With flame of incandescent terror
Of which the tongues declare
The one discharge from sin and error.   205
The only hope, or else despair
    Lies in the choice of pyre or pyre—
    To be redeemed from fire by fire.

Who then devised the torment? Love.
Love is the unfamiliar Name   210
Behind the hands that wove
The intolerable shirt of flame[5]
Which human power cannot remove.
    We only live, only suspire
    Consumed by either fire or fire.   215

V

What we call the beginning is often the end
And to make an end is to make a beginning.
The end is where we start from. And every phrase
And sentence that is right (where every word is at home,
Taking its place to support the others,   220
The word neither diffident nor ostentatious,

4a. Milton.
5. Out of love for her husband Hercules, Deianira gave him the poisoned
shirt of Nessus. She had been told
that it would increase his love for
her, but instead it so corroded his flesh
that in his agony he mounted a funeral
pyre and burned himself to death.

An easy commerce of the old and the new,
The common word exact without vulgarity,
The formal word precise but not pedantic,
The complete consort[6] dancing together)   225
Every phrase and every sentence is an end and a beginning,
Every poem an epitaph. And any action
Is a step to the block, to the fire, down the sea's throat
Or to an illegible stone: and that is where we start.
We die with the dying: 230
See, they depart, and we go with them.
We are born with the dead:
See, they return, and bring us with them.
The moment of the rose and the moment of the yew tree
Are of equal duration. A people without history   235
Is not redeemed from time, for history is a pattern
Of timeless moments. So, while the light fails
On a winter's afternoon, in a secluded chapel
History is now and England.

With the drawing of this Love and the voice of this Calling[7]   240
We shall not cease from exploration
And the end of all our exploring
Will be to arrive where we started
And know the place for the first time.
Through the unknown, remembered gate   245
When the last of earth left to discover
Is that which was the beginning;
At the source of the longest river
The voice of the hidden waterfall
And the children in the apple tree   250
Not known, because not looked for
But heard, half-heard, in the stillness
Between two waves of the sea.[8]
Quick now, here, now, always—
A condition of complete simplicity   255
(Costing not less than everything)
And all shall be well and
All manner of thing shall be well
When the tongues of flame are in-folded
Into the crowned knot of fire   260
And the fire and the rose are one.
1942   1942, 1943

---

6. The word means both "company" and "harmony of sounds."
7. This line is from an anonymous 14th-century mystical work, the *Cloud of Unknowing.*
8. The voice of the children in the apple tree symbolizes the sudden moment of insight. Cf. the conclusion to *Burnt Norton* (the first of the *Four Quartets*), where the laughter of the children in the garden has a like meaning: "Sudden in a shaft of sunlight / Even while the dust moves / There rises the hidden laughter / Of children in the foliage / Quick now, here, now, always * * * "

Tradition and the Individual Talent[1]

I

In English writing we seldom speak of tradition, though we occasionally apply its name in deploring its absence. We cannot refer to "the tradition" or to "a tradition"; at most, we employ the adjective in saying that the poetry of So-and-so is "traditional" or even "too traditional." Seldom, perhaps, does the word appear except in a phrase of censure. If otherwise, it is vaguely approbative, with the implication, as to the work approved, of some pleasing archaeological reconstruction. You can hardly make the word agreeable to English ears without this comfortable reference to the reassuring science of archaeology.

Certainly the word is not likely to appear in our appreciations of living or dead writers. Every nation, every race, has not only its own creative, but its own critical turn of mind; and is even more oblivious of the shortcomings and limitations of its critical habits than of those of its creative genius. We know, or think we know, from the enormous mass of critical writing that has appeared in the French language the critical method or habit of the French; we only conclude (we are such unconscious people) that the French are "more critical" than we, and sometimes even plume ourselves a little with the fact, as if the French were the less spontaneous. Perhaps they are; but we might remind ourselves that criticism is as inevitable as breathing, and that we should be none the worse for articulating what passes in our minds when we read a book and feel an emotion about it, for criticizing our own minds in their work of criticism. One of the facts that might come to light in this process is our tendency to insist, when we praise a poet, upon those aspects of his work in which he least resembles anyone else. In these aspects or parts of his work we pretend to find what is individual, what is the peculiar essence of the man. We dwell with satisfaction upon the poet's difference from his predecessors, especially his immediate predecessors; we endeavor to find something that can be isolated in order to be enjoyed. Whereas if we approach a poet without this prejudice we shall often find that not only the best, but the most individual parts of his work may be those in which the dead poets, his ancestors, assert their immortality most vigorously. And I do not mean the impressionable period of adolescence, but the period of full maturity.

Yet if the only form of tradition, of handing down, consisted in

---

1. First published in the *Egoist* (1919) and later collected in *The Sacred Wood* (1920), this essay is one of Eliot's most influential pieces of criticism.

following the ways of the immediate generation before us in a blind or timid adherence to its successes, "tradition" should positively be discouraged. We have seen many such simple currents soon lost in the sand; and novelty is better than repetition. Tradition is a matter of much wider significance. It cannot be inherited, and if you want it you must obtain it by great labor. It involves, in the first place, the historical sense, which we may call nearly indispensable to any one who would continue to be a poet beyond his twenty-fifth year; and the historical sense involves a perception, not only of the pastness of the past, but of its presence; the historical sense compels a man to write not merely with his own generation in his bones, but with a feeling that the whole of the literature of Europe from Homer and within it the whole of the literature of his own country has a simultaneous existence and composes a simultaneous order. This historical sense, which is a sense of the timeless as well as of the temporal and of the timeless and of the temporal together, is what makes a writer traditional. And it is at the same time what makes a writer most acutely conscious of his place in time, of his own contemporaneity.

No poet, no artist of any art, has his complete meaning alone. His significance, his appreciation is the appreciation of his relation to the dead poets and artists. You cannot value him alone; you must set him, for contrast and comparison, among the dead. I mean this as a principle of aesthetic, not merely historical, criticism. The necessity that he shall conform, that he shall cohere, is not one-sided; what happens when a new work of art is created is something that happens simultaneously to all the works of art which preceded it. The existing monuments form an ideal order among themselves, which is modified by the introduction of the new (the really new) work of art among them. The existing order is complete before the new work arrives; for order to persist after the supervention of novelty, the *whole* existing order must be, if ever so slightly, altered; and so the relations, proportions, values of each work of art toward the whole are readjusted; and this is conformity between the old and the new. Whoever has approved this idea of order, of the form of European, of English literature will not find it preposterous that the past should be altered by the present as much as the present is directed by the past. And the poet who is aware of this will be aware of great difficulties and responsibilities.

In a peculiar sense he will be aware also that he must inevitably be judged by the standards of the past. I say judged, not amputated, by them; not judged to be as good as, or worse or better than, the dead; and certainly not judged by the canons of dead critics. It is a judgment, a comparison, in which two things are measured by each other. To conform merely would be for the new work not really to conform at all; it would not be new, and would therefore not be a work of art. And we do not quite say that the new is more valuable because it fits in; but its fitting in is a test of its value—a test, it is true, which can only be slowly and cautiously applied, for we are none of us infallible judges of conformity. We say: it appears to conform, and is perhaps individual, or it appears individual, and may conform; but we are hardly likely to find that it is one and not the other.

To proceed to a more intelligible exposition of the relation of the poet to the past: he can neither take the past as a lump, an indiscriminate bolus,[2] nor can he form himself wholly on one or two private admirations, nor can he form himself wholly upon one preferred period. The first course is inadmissible, the second is an important experience of youth, and the third is a pleasant and highly desirable supplement. The poet must be very conscious of the main current, which does not at all flow invariably through the most distinguished reputations. He must be quite aware of the obvious fact that art never improves, but that the material of art is never quite the same. He must be aware that the mind of Europe—the mind of his own country—a mind which he learns in time to be much more important than his own private mind—is a mind which changes, and that this change is a development which abandons nothing en route, which does not superannuate either Shakespeare, or Homer, or the rock drawing of the Magdalenian[3] draftsmen. That this development, refinement perhaps, complication certainly, is not, from the point of view of the artist, any improvement. Perhaps not even an improvement from the point of view of the psychologist or not to the extent which we imagine; perhaps only in the end based upon a complication in economics and machinery. But the difference between the present and the past is that the conscious present is an awareness of the past in a way and to an extent which the past's awareness of itself cannot show.

Someone said: "The dead writers are remote from us because we *know* so much more than they did." Precisely, and they are that which we know.

I am alive to a usual objection to what is clearly part of my program for the métier of poetry. The objection is that the doctrine requires a ridiculous amount of erudition (pedantry), a claim which can be rejected by appeal to the lives of poets in any pantheon. It will even be affirmed that much learning deadens or perverts poetic sensibility. While, however, we persist in believing that a poet ought to know as much as will not encroach upon his necessary receptivity and necessary laziness, it is not desirable to confine knowledge to whatever can be put into a useful shape for examinations, drawing rooms, or the still more pretentious modes of pub-

2. A round mass of anything: a large pill.
3. The most advanced culture of the European Paleolithic period (from discoveries at La Madeleine, France).

licity. Some can absorb knowledge, the more tardy must sweat for it. Shakespeare acquired more essential history from Plutarch[4] than most men could from the whole British Museum. What is to be insisted upon is that the poet must develop or procure the consciousness of the past and that he should continue to develop this consciousness throughout his career.

What happens is a continual surrender of himself as he is at the moment to something which is more valuable. The progress of an artist is a continual self-sacrifice, a continual extinction of personality.

There remains to define this process of depersonalization and its relation to the sense of tradition. It is in this depersonalization that art may be said to approach the condition of science. I, therefore, invite you to consider, as a suggestive analogy, the action which takes place when a bit of finely filiated[5] platinum is introduced into a chamber containing oxygen and sulphur dioxide.

II

Honest criticism and sensitive appreciation are directed not upon the poet but upon the poetry. If we attend to the confused cries of the newspaper critics and the *susurrus*[6] of popular repetition that follows, we shall hear the names of poets in great numbers; if we seek not Blue-book[7] knowledge but the enjoyment of poetry, and ask for a poem, we shall seldom find it. I have tried to point out the importance of the relation of the poem to other poems by other authors, and suggested the conception of poetry as a living whole of all the poetry that has ever been written. The other aspect of this Impersonal theory of poetry is the relation of the poem to its author. And I hinted, by an analogy, that the mind of the mature poet differs from that of the immature one not precisely in any valuation of "personality," not being necessarily more interesting, or having "more to say," but rather by being a more finely perfected medium in which special, or very varied, feelings are at liberty to enter into new combinations.

The analogy was that of the catalyst.[8] When the two gases previously mentioned are mixed in the presence of a filament of platinum, they form sulphurous acid. This combination takes place only if the platinum is present; nevertheless the newly formed acid contains no trace of platinum, and the platinum itself is apparently unaffected; has remained inert, neutral, and unchanged. The mind of the poet is the shred of platinum. It may partly or exclusively operate upon the experience of the man himself; but, the more perfect the artist, the more completely separate in him will be the

---

4. Greek biographer (1st century A.D.) of Greek and Roman celebrities, from whose work Shakespeare drew the plots of his Roman plays.
5. Drawn out like a thread.
6. Murmuring, buzzing.

7. British official government publication.
8. Substance that triggers a chemical change without itself being affected by the reaction.

man who suffers and the mind which creates; the more perfectly will the mind digest and transmute the passions which are its material.

The experience, you will notice, the elements which enter the presence of the transforming catalyst, are of two kinds: emotions and feelings. The effect of a work of art upon the person who enjoys it is an experience different in kind from any experience not of art. It may be formed out of one emotion, or may be a combination of several; and various feelings, inhering for the writer in particular words or phrases or images, may be added to compose the final result. Or great poetry may be made without the direct use of any emotion whatever: composed out of feelings solely. Canto XV of the *Inferno* (Brunetto Latini)[9] is a working up of the emotion evident in the situation; but the effect, though single as that of any work of art, is obtained by considerable complexity of detail. The last quatrain gives an image, a feeling attaching to an image, which "came," which did not develop simply out of what precedes, but which was probably in suspension in the poet's mind until the proper combination arrived for it to add itself to.[1] The poet's mind is in fact a receptacle for seizing and storing up numberless feelings, phrases, images, which remain there until all the particles which can unite to form a new compound are present together.

If you compare several representative passages of the greatest poetry you see how great is the variety of types of combination, and also how completely any semi-ethical criterion of "sublimity" misses the mark. For it is not the "greatness," the intensity, of the emotions, the components, but the intensity of the artistic process, the pressure, so to speak, under which the fusion takes place, that counts. The episode of Paolo and Francesca[2] employs a definite emotion, but the intensity of the poetry is something quite different from whatever intensity in the supposed experience it may give the impression of. It is no more intense, furthermore, than Canto XXVI,[3] the voyage of Ulysses, which has not the direct dependence upon an emotion. Great variety is possible in the process of transmutation of emotion: the murder of Agamemnon,[4] or the agony of Othello, gives an artistic effect apparently closer to a possible

9. Dante meets in Hell his old master Brunetto Latini, suffering eternal punishment for unnatural lust, yet still loved and admired by Dante, who addresses him with affectionate courtesy. It is one of the most moving passages in the *Inferno*.

1. Dante's strange interview with Brunetto is over, and Brunetto moves off to continue his punishment: "Then he turned round, and seemed like one of those / Who run for the green cloth [in the footrace] at Verona / In the field; and he seemed among them / Not the loser but the winner."

2. Illicit lovers whom Dante meets in the second circle of Hell (*Inferno* V) and at whose punishment and sorrows he swoons with pity.

3. Of the *Inferno*. Ulysses, suffering in Hell for "false counseling," tells Dante of his final voyage.

4. By his wife Clytemnestra; the central action of Aeschylus' play *Agamemnon*.

original than the scenes from Dante. In the *Agamemnon,* the artistic emotion approximates to the emotion of an actual spectator; in *Othello* to the emotion of the protagonist himself. But the difference between art and the event is always absolute; the combination which is the murder of Agamemnon is probably as complex as that which is the voyage of Ulysses. In either case there has been a fusion of elements. The ode of Keats contains a number of feelings which have nothing particular to do with the nightingale, but which the nightingale, partly, perhaps, because of its attractive name, and partly because of its reputation, served to bring together.

The point of view which I am struggling to attack is perhaps related to the metaphysical theory of the substantial unity of the soul: for my meaning is, that the poet has, not a "personality" to express, but a particular medium, which is only a medium and not a personality, in which impressions and experiences combine in peculiar and unexpected ways. Impressions and experiences which are important for the man may take no place in the poetry, and those which become important in the poetry may play quite a negligible part in the man, the personality.

I will quote a passage which is unfamiliar enough to be regarded with fresh attention in the light—or darkness—of these observations:

> And now methinks I could e'en chide myself
> For doting on her beauty, though her death
> Shall be revenged after no common action.
> Does the silkworm expend her yellow labors
> For thee? For thee does she undo herself?
> Are lordships sold to maintain ladyships
> For the poor benefit of a bewildering minute?
> Why does yon fellow falsify highways,
> And put his life between the judge's lips,
> To refine such a thing—keeps horse and men
> To beat their valors for her? . . .[5]

In this passage (as is evident if it is taken in its context) there is a combination of positive and negative emotions: an intensely strong attraction toward beauty and an equally intense fascination by the ugliness which is contrasted with it and which destroys it. This balance of contrasted emotion is in the dramatic situation to which the speech is pertinent, but that situation alone is inadequate to it. This is, so to speak, the structural emotion, provided by the drama. But the whole effect, the dominant tone, is due to the fact that a number of floating feelings, having an affinity to this emotion by no means superficially evident, have combined with it to give us a new art emotion.

It is not in his personal emotions, the emotions provoked by par-

5. From Cyril Tourneur's *The Revenger's Tragedy* (1607), III.iv.

ticular events in his life, that the poet is in any way remarkable or interesting. His particular emotions may be simple, or crude, or flat. The emotion in his poetry will be a very complex thing, but not with the complexity of the emotions of people who have very complex or unusual emotions in life. One error, in fact, of eccentricity in poetry is to seek for new human emotions to express; and in this search for novelty in the wrong place it discovers the perverse. The business of the poet is not to find new emotions, but to use the ordinary ones and, in working them up into poetry, to express feelings which are not in actual emotions at all. And emotions which he has never experienced will serve his turn as well as those familiar to him. Consequently, we must believe that "emotion recollected in tranquility"[6] is an inexact formula. For it is neither emotion, nor recollection, nor, without distortion of meaning, tranquility. It is a concentration, and a new thing resulting from the concentration, of a very great number of experiences which to the practical and active person would not seem to be experiences at all; it is a concentration which does not happen consciously or of deliberation. These experiences are not "recollected," and they finally unite in an atmosphere which is "tranquil" only in that it is a passive attending upon the event. Of course this is not quite the whole story. There is a great deal, in the writing of poetry, which must be conscious and deliberate. In fact, the bad poet is usually unconscious where he ought to be conscious, and conscious where he ought to be unconscious. Both errors tend to make him "personal." Poetry is not a turning loose of emotion, but an escape from emotion; it is not the expression of personality, but an escape from personality. But, of course, only those who have personality and emotions know what it means to want to escape from these things.

III

ὁ δὲ νοῦς ἴσως θειότερόν τι χαὶ ἀπαθές ἐστιν.[7]

This essay proposes to halt at the frontier of metaphysics or mysticism, and confine itself to such practical conclusions as can be applied by the responsible person interested in poetry. To divert interest from the poet to the poetry is a laudable aim: for it would conduce to a juster estimation of actual poetry, good and bad. There are many people who appreciate the expression of sincere emotion in verse, and there is a smaller number of people who can appreciate technical excellence. But very few know when there is an expression of *significant* emotion, emotion which has its life in the poem and not in the history of the poet. The emotion of art is impersonal. And the poet cannot reach this impersonality with-

6. Wordsworth, Preface to *Lyrical Ballads*, 2nd edition (1800). Wordsworth said that poetry "takes its origin from emotion recollected in tranquility."

7. "The mind is doubtless something more divine and unimpressionable." Aristotle, *De Anima* ("On the Soul"), I.4.

out surrendering himself wholly to the work to be done. And he is not likely to know what is to be done unless he lives in what is not merely the present, but the present moment of the past, unless he is conscious, not of what is dead, but of what is already living.

1919, 1920

The Metaphysical Poets

By collecting these poems[1] from the work of a generation more often named than read, and more often read than profitably studied, Professor Grierson has rendered a service of some importance. Certainly the reader will meet with many poems already preserved in other anthologies, at the same time that he discovers poems such as those of Aurelian Townshend or Lord Herbert of Cherbury here included. But the function of such an anthology as this is neither that of Professor Saintsbury's admirable edition of Caroline poets nor that of the *Oxford Book of English Verse*. Mr. Grierson's book is in itself a piece of criticism and a provocation of criticism; and we think that he was right in including so many poems of Donne, elsewhere (though not in many editions) accessible, as documents in the case of "metaphysical poetry." The phrase has long done duty as a term of abuse or as the label of a quaint and pleasant taste. The question is to what extent the so-called metaphysicals formed a school (in our own time we should say a "movement"), and how far this so-called school or movement is a digression from the main current.

Not only is it extremely difficult to define metaphysical poetry, but difficult to decide what poets practice it and in which of their verses. The poetry of Donne (to whom Marvell and Bishop King are sometimes nearer than any of the other authors) is late Elizabethan, its feeling often very close to that of Chapman. The "courtly" poetry is derivative from Jonson, who borrowed liberally from the Latin; it expires in the next century with the sentiment and witticism of Prior. There is finally the devotional verse of Herbert, Vaughan, and Crashaw (echoed long after by Christina Rossetti and Francis Thompson); Crashaw, sometimes more profound and less sectarian than the others, has a quality which returns through the Elizabethan period to the early Italians. It is difficult to find any precise use of metaphor, simile, or other conceit, which is common to all the poets and at the same time important enough as an element of style to isolate these poets as a group. Donne, and

1. *Metaphysical Lyrics and Poems of the Seventeenth Century: Donne to Butler.* Selected and edited, with an Essay, by Herbert J. C. Grierson (1921). Eliot's essay was originally a review of this book in the London *Times Literary Supplement*.

often Cowley, employ a device which is sometimes considered characteristically "metaphysical"; the elaboration (contrasted with the condensation) of a figure of speech to the farthest stage to which ingenuity can carry it. Thus Cowley develops the commonplace comparison of the world to a chessboard through long stanzas (*To Destiny*), and Donne, with more grace, in A *Valediction*,[2] the comparison of two lovers to a pair of compasses. But elsewhere we find, instead of the mere explication of the content of a comparison, a development by rapid association of thought which requires considerable agility on the part of the reader.

> On a round ball
> A workman that hath copies by, can lay
> An Europe, Afrique, and an Asia,
> And quickly make that which was nothing, all;
> So doth each tear,
> Which thee doth wear,
> A globe, yea world, by that impression grow,
> Till thy tears mixed with mine do overflow
> This world; by waters sent from thee, my heaven dissolvéd so.[3]

Here we find at least two connections which are not implicit in the first figure, but are forced upon it by the poet: from the geographer's globe to the tear, and the tear to the deluge. On the other hand, some of Donne's most successful and characteristic effects are secured by brief words and sudden contrasts:

> A bracelet of bright hair about the bone,[4]

where the most powerful effect is produced by the sudden contrast of associations of "bright hair" and of "bone." This telescoping of images and multiplied associations is characteristic of the phrase of some of the dramatists of the period which Donne knew: not to mention Shakespeare, it is frequent in Middleton, Webster, and Tourneur, and is one of the sources of the vitality of their language.

Johnson, who employed the term "metaphysical poets," apparently having Donne, Cleveland, and Cowley chiefly in mind, remarks of them that "the most heterogeneous ideas are yoked by violence together."[5] The force of this impeachment lies in the failure of the conjunction, the fact that often the ideas are yoked but not united; and if we are to judge of styles of poetry by their abuse, enough examples may be found in Cleveland to justify Johnson's condemnation. But a degree of heterogeneity of material compelled into unity by the operation of the poet's mind is omnipresent in poetry. We need not select for illustration such a line as:

2. I.e., *A Valediction: Forbidding Mourning.*
3. Donne's *A Valediction: Of Weeping,* lines 10–18.
4. *The Relique,* line 6.
5. See Samuel Johnson's *Life of Cowley.*

Notre âme est un trois-mâts cherchant son Icarie;[6]

we may find it in some of the best lines of Johnson himself (*The Vanity of Human Wishes*):

> His fate was destined to a barren strand,
> A petty fortress, and a dubious hand;
> He left a name at which the world grew pale,
> To point a moral, or adorn a tale.

where the effect is due to a contrast of ideas, different in degree but the same in principle, as that which Johnson mildly reprehended. And in one of the finest poems of the age (a poem which could not have been written in any other age), the *Exequy* of Bishop King, the extended comparison is used with perfect success: the idea and the simile become one, in the passage in which the Bishop illustrates his impatience to see his dead wife, under the figure of a journey:

> Stay for me there; I will not fail
> To meet thee in that hollow Vale.
> And think not much of my delay;
> I am already on the way,
> And follow thee with all the speed
> Desire can make, or sorrows breed.
> Each minute is a short degree,
> And ev'ry hour a step towards thee.
> At night when I betake to rest,
> Next morn I rise nearer my West
> Of life, almost by eight hours sail,
> Than when sleep breathed his drowsy gale. . . .
> But hark! My pulse, like a soft drum
> Beats my approach, tells Thee I come;
> And slow howe'er my marches be,
> I shall at last sit down by Thee.

(In the last few lines there is that effect of terror which is several times attained by one of Bishop King's admirers, Edgar Poe.) Again, we may justly take these quatrains from Lord Herbert's Ode,[7] stanzas which would, we think, be immediately pronounced to be of the metaphysical school:

> So when from hence we shall be gone,
>   And be no more, nor you, nor I,
>   As one another's mystery,
> Each shall be both, yet both but one.

6. "Our soul is a three-masted ship searching for her Icarie"; a line from Charles Baudelaire's poem, *Le Voyage* (Icarie is an imaginary utopia in *Voyage en Icarie*, 1840, a novel by the French socialist Etienne Cabet).

7. Lord Herbert of Cherbury (1583–1648), brother of George Herbert. The "Ode" is his *Ode upon a Question moved, whether Love should continue forever?*

This said, in her uplifted face,
    Her eyes, which did that beauty crown,
    Were like two stars, that having faln down,
Look up again to find their place:

While such a moveless silent peace
    Did seize on their becalméd sense,
    One would have thought some influence
Their ravished spirits did possess.

There is nothing in these lines (with the possible exception of the stars, a simile not at once grasped, but lovely and justified) which fits Johnson's general observations on the metaphysical poets in his essay on Cowley. A good deal resides in the richness of association which is at the same time borrowed from and given to the word "becalmed"; but the meaning is clear, the language simple and elegant. It is to be observed that the language of these poets is as a rule simple and pure; in the verse of George Herbert this simplicity is carried as far as it can go—a simplicity emulated without success by numerous modern poets. The *structure* of the sentences, on the other hand, is sometimes far from simple, but this is not a vice; it is a fidelity to thought and feeling. The effect, at its best, is far less artificial than that of an ode by Gray. And as this fidelity induces variety of thought and feeling, so it induces variety of music. We doubt whether, in the eighteenth century, could be found two poems in nominally the same meter, so dissimilar as Marvell's *Coy Mistress* and Crashaw's *Saint Teresa*; the one producing an effect of great speed by the use of short syllables, and the other an ecclesiastical solemnity by the use of long ones:

    Love, thou art absolute sole lord
    Of life and death.

If so shrewd and sensitive (though so limited) a critic as Johnson failed to define metaphysical poetry by its faults, it is worth while to inquire whether we may not have more success by adopting the opposite method: by assuming that the poets of the seventeenth century (up to the Revolution[8]) were the direct and normal development of the precedent age; and, without prejudicing their case by the adjective "metaphysical," consider whether their virtue was not something permanently valuable, which subsequently disappeared, but ought not to have disappeared. Johnson has hit, perhaps by accident, on one of their peculiarities, when he observes that "their attempts were always analytic"; he would not agree that, after the dissociation, they put the material together again in a new unity.

It is certain that the dramatic verse of the later Elizabethan and early Jacobean poets expresses a degree of development of sensibil-

8. Of 1688; when James II was replaced by William and Mary.

ity which is not found in any of the prose, good as it often is. If we except Marlowe, a man of prodigious intelligence, these dramatists were directly or indirectly (it is at least a tenable theory) affected by Montaigne. Even if we except also Jonson and Chapman, these two were probably erudite, and were notably men who incorporated their erudition into their sensibility: their mode of feeling was directly and freshly altered by their reading and thought. In Chapman especially there is a direct sensuous apprehension of thought, or a recreation of thought into feeling, which is exactly what we find in Donne:

> in this one thing, all the discipline
> Of manners and of manhood is contained;
> A man to join himself with th' Universe
> In his main sway, and make in all things fit
> One with that All, and go on, round as it;
> Not plucking from the whole his wretched part,
> And into straits, or into nought revert,
> Wishing the complete Universe might be
> Subject to such a rag of it as he;
> But to consider great Necessity.[9]

We compare this with some modern passage:

> No, when the fight begins within himself,
> A man's worth something. God stoops o'er his head,
> Satan looks up between his feet—both tug—
> He's left, himself, i' the middle; the soul wakes
> And grows. Prolong that battle through his life![1]

It is perhaps somewhat less fair, though very tempting (as both poets are concerned with the perpetuation of love by offspring), to compare with the stanzas already quoted from Lord Herbert's Ode the following from Tennyson:

> One walked between his wife and child,
> With measured footfall firm and mild,
> And now and then he gravely smiled.
>   The prudent partner of his blood
>   Leaned on him, faithful, gentle, good,
>   Wearing the rose of womanhood.
> And in their double love secure,
> The little maiden walked demure,
> Pacing with downward eyelids pure.
>   These three made unity so sweet,
>   My frozen heart began to beat,
>   Remembering its ancient heat.[2]

9. From *The Revenge of Bussy d'Ambois* (IV.i.137–46).
1. Robert Browning's *Bishop Blou-*
gram's Apology, lines 693–97.
2. Tennyson's *The Two Voices*, lines 412–23.

The difference is not a simple difference of degree between poets. It is something which had happened to the mind of England between the time of Donne or Lord Herbert of Cherbury and the time of Tennyson and Browning; it is the difference between the intellectual poet and the reflective poet. Tennyson and Browning are poets, and they think; but they do not feel their thought as immediately as the odor of a rose. A thought to Donne was an experience; it modified his sensibility. When a poet's mind is perfectly equipped for its work, it is constantly amalgamating disparate experience; the ordinary man's experience is chaotic, irregular, fragmentary. The latter falls in love, or reads Spinoza, and these two experiences have nothing to do with each other, or with the noise of the typewriter or the smell of cooking; in the mind of the poet these experiences are always forming new wholes.

We may express the difference by the following theory: The poets of the seventeenth century, the successors of the dramatists of the sixteenth, possessed a mechanism of sensibility which could devour any kind of experience. They are simple, artificial, difficult, or fantastic, as their predecessors were; no less nor more than Dante, Guido Cavalcanti, Guinicelli, or Cino.[3] In the seventeenth century a dissociation of sensibility set in, from which we have never recovered; and this dissociation, as is natural, was aggravated by the influence of the two most powerful poets of the century, Milton and Dryden. Each of these men performed certain poetic functions so magnificently well that the magnitude of the effect concealed the absence of others. The language went on and in some respects improved; the best verse of Collins, Gray, Johnson, and even Goldsmith satisfies some of our fastidious demands better than that of Donne or Marvell or King. But while the language became more refined, the feeling became more crude. The feeling, the sensibility, expressed in the *Country Churchyard* (to say nothing of Tennyson and Browning) is cruder than that in the *Coy Mistress*.

The second effect of the influence of Milton and Dryden followed from the first, and was therefore slow in manifestation. The sentimental age began early in the eighteenth century, and continued. The poets revolted against the ratiocinative, the descriptive; they thought and felt by fits, unbalanced; they reflected. In one or two passages of Shelley's *Triumph of Life*, in the second *Hyperion*, there are traces of a struggle toward unification of sensibility. But Keats and Shelley died, and Tennyson and Browning ruminated.

After this brief exposition of a theory—too brief, perhaps, to

---

3. These last three poets, all of whom lived in the 13th century, were members of the Tuscan school of lyric love poets (Guido Guinicelli was hailed by Dante in the *Purgatorio* as "father of Italian poets"; Cino da Pistoia was a friend of Dante and Petrarch).

carry conviction—we may ask, what would have been the fate of the "metaphysical" had the current of poetry descended in a direct line from them, as it descended in a direct line to them? They would not, certainly, be classified as metaphysical. The possible interests of a poet are unlimited; the more intelligent he is the better; the more intelligent he is the more likely that he will have interests: our only condition is that he turn them into poetry, and not merely meditate on them poetically. A philosophical theory which has entered into poetry is established, for its truth or falsity in one sense ceases to matter, and its truth in another sense is proved. The poets in question have, like other poets, various faults. But they were, at best, engaged in the task of trying to find the verbal equivalent for states of mind and feeling. And this means both that they are more mature, and that they wear better, than later poets of certainly not less literary ability.

It is not a permanent necessity that poets should be interested in philosophy, or in any other subject. We can only say that it appears likely that poets in our civilization, as it exists at present, must be *difficult*. Our civilization comprehends great variety and complexity, and this variety and complexity, playing upon a refined sensibility, must produce various and complex results. The poet must become more and more comprehensive, more allusive, more indirect, in order to force, to dislocate if necessary, language into his meaning. (A brilliant and extreme statement of this view, with which it is not requisite to associate oneself, is that of M. Jean Epstein, *La Poésie d'aujourd'hui*.[4]) Hence we get something which looks very much like the conceit—we get, in fact, a method curiously similar to that of the "metaphysical poets," similar also in its use of obscure words and of simple phrasing.

> *O géraniums diaphanes, guerroyeurs sortilèges,*
> *Sacrilèges monomanes!*
> *Emballages, dévergondages, douches! O pressoirs*
> *Des vendanges des grands soirs!*
> *Layettes aux abois,*
> *Thyrses au fond des bois!*
> *Transfusions, représailles,*
> *Relevailles, compresses et l'éternel potion,*
> *Angélus! n'en pouvoir plus*
> *De débâcles nuptiales! de débâcles nuptiales!*[5]

4. "Poetry of Today."

5. "O transparent geraniums, warrior incantations, / Monomaniac sacrileges! / Packing materials, shamelessnesses, shower baths! O wine presses / Of great evening vintages! / Hard-pressed baby linen, / Thyrsis in the depths of the woods! / Transfusions, reprisals, / Churchings, compresses, and the eternal potion, / Angelus! no longer to be borne [are] / Catastrophic marriages! catastrophic marriages!" This passage is from *Derniers vers X* ("Last Poems," 1890), by Jules Laforgue (1860–87). Eliot oddly sees a similarity between this kind of hysterical free association and the strictly ordered imagery of the metaphysicals. But it is the combination of "obscure words and simple phrasing" that strikes him in both.

The same poet could write also simply:

> *Elle est bien loin, elle pleure,*
> *Le grand vent se lamente aussi . . .*[6]

Jules Laforgue, and Tristan Corbière[7] in many of his poems, are nearer to the "school of Donne" than any modern English poet. But poets more classical than they have the same essential quality of transmuting ideas into sensations, of transforming an observation into a state of mind.

> *Pour l'enfant, amoureux de cartes et d'estampes,*
> *L'univers est égal à son vaste appétit.*
> *Ah, que le monde est grand à la clarté des lampes!*
> *Aux yeux du souvenir que le monde est petit!*[8]

In French literature the great master of the seventeenth century —Racine—and the great master of the nineteenth—Baudelaire— are in some ways more like each other than they are like any one else. The greatest two masters of diction are also the greatest two psychologists, the most curious explorers of the soul. It is interesting to speculate whether it is not a misfortune that two of the greatest masters of diction in our language, Milton and Dryden, triumph with a dazzling disregard of the soul. If we continued to produce Miltons and Drydens it might not so much matter, but as things are it is a pity that English poetry has remained so incomplete. Those who object to the "artificiality" of Milton or Dryden sometimes tell us to "look into our hearts and write." But that is not looking deep enough; Racine or Donne looked into a good deal more than the heart. One must look into the cerebral cortex, the nervous system, and the digestive tracts.

May we not conclude, then, that Donne, Crashaw, Vaughan, Herbert and Lord Herbert, Marvell, King, Cowley at his best, are in the direct current of English poetry, and that their faults should be reprimanded by this standard rather than coddled by antiquarian affection? They have been enough praised in terms which are implicit limitations because they are "metaphysical" or "witty," "quaint" or "obscure," though at their best they have not these attributes more than other serious poets. On the other hand, we must not reject the criticism of Johnson (a dangerous person to disagree with) without having mastered it, without having assimilated the Johnsonian canons of taste. In reading the celebrated passage in his essay on Cowley we must remember that by wit he clearly means something more serious than we usually mean today;

---

6. "She is far away, she weeps, / The great wind mourns also." From *Derniers vers XI, Sur une défunte* ("On a Dead Woman").
7. 1845–75; also a French Symbolist poet.

8. From Baudelaire's *Le Voyage:* "For the child, in love with maps and prints, / The universe matches his vast appetite. / Ah, how big the world is by lamplight! How small the world is to the eyes of memory!"

in his criticism of their versification we must remember in what a narrow discipline he was trained, but also how well trained; we must remember that Johnson tortures chiefly the chief offenders, Cowley and Cleveland. It would be a fruitful work, and one requiring a substantial book, to break up the classification of Johnson (for there has been none since) and exhibit these poets in all their difference of kind and of degree, from the massive music of Donne to the faint, pleasing tinkle of Aurelian Townshend—whose *Dialogue Between a Pilgrim and Time* is one of the few regrettable omissions from the excellent anthology of Professor Grierson.

1921

HUGH MacDIARMID

(1892-)

1925:   *Sangschaw.*
1926:   *A Drunk Man Looks at the Thistle.*
1933-42: Lives in Whalsay, Shetland Islands.
1955:   *In Memoriam James Joyce.*

Hugh MacDiarmid is the pen name of Christopher Murray Grieve, who was born in the Scottish Border town of Langholm, son of a rural postman. The family lived below the town library of over 12,000 books, almost all of which MacDiarmid later claimed to have read. This passion for reading independently of any academic program has stayed with him all his life, and helps to explain the air of massive self-education that pervades much of his later writing. At school he was lucky enough to have for his English teacher the Scottish composer Francis George Scott, who remained a lifelong friend and composed brilliant settings to many of his lyrics. MacDiarmid relied heavily on Scott's encouragement and criticism of his early poetry. He went from Langholm to Broughton Junior Student Centre in Edinburgh to train as a teacher, but on his father's death in 1911 he gave up this training and embarked on a career as a journalist. During World War I he served with the Royal Army Medical Corps in Salonika, Italy, and France. In 1920 he settled in Montrose, an attractive town on the east coast of Scotland, and worked for the *Montrose Review*. Shortly after, he brought out three volumes of new Scottish poetry by different hands, which he edited under the title *Northern Numbers, being Representative Selections from Certain Living Scottish Poets.* The aim of these volumes was to do for Scottish poetry what *Georgian Poetry* had done for English, though Grieve's own poetry had even at this stage little in common with anything that can be considered characteristically Georgian. It was uneven and sometimes wordy, though marked by a highly individual sense of language and a fondness for cosmological imagery. Though at this stage he was writing in standard English rather than Scots, he had already developed a deep concern for Scottish literary culture, which he saw as decayed and requiring rejuvenation by association with all that was best in new literary ideas and movements throughout Europe.

MacDiarmid lived in Montrose until 1929, becoming active as a Labour member of the Town Council and as a founding member of the Scottish Center of the international literary organization P. E. N. and of the National Party of Scotland, but his highly individual political views led to conflict with all these organizations. His most important activity was to champion a Scottish Renaissance Movement, to redeem Scottish culture from the sentimentality and pallid imitativeness which he saw as its chief faults. An unhappy period in England from 1930 to 1932, when he engaged in a variety of occupations, strengthened his passion for Scotland and forced on him a reappraisal of his own social and political views. In 1932 he called himself a Communist (though still a Scottish Nationalist) and he joined the Communist Party in 1934. He was expelled because of his Scottish Nationalism in 1938 and rejoined in 1957, but he was always a very special kind of Communist. As he once explained,

> * * * I must be a Bolshevik
> Before the Revolution, but I'll cease to be one quick
> When Communism rules the roost.

He also wrote: "As a Socialist * * * I am * * * interested only in a very subordinate way in the politics of socialism as a political theory; my real concern with Socialism is as an artist's organized approach to the interdependencies of life."

The true emergence of "Hugh MacDiarmid" came with the publication of *Sangschaw* in 1925. The adoption of this pen name served notice that he associated himself with the Celtic element in Scottish history and culture, and later he was to associate Scotland with Ireland, Wales, and Cornwall as part of a Celtic ring of peoples who could produce an alternative culture to that of Anglo-Saxondom. But more significant than this new name was the kind of poetry he was now producing. This consisted largely of short lyrics in Scots, which is not a Celtic language at all (as Scottish Gaelic is), but the language originally identical with that spoken in northern England and developed into a powerful literary medium by the great medieval poets of Scotland, notably Robert Henryson and William Dunbar. The growth of standard English as the written language of Scotland, encouraged as early as the late 16th century by the adoption of an English translation of the Bible by Scottish Protestants, accelerated by the departure of the Scottish Court, with its Court poets, for England in 1603 when James VI of Scotland inherited the throne of England, and given still greater impetus by the disappearance of Scotland as a separate political entity by the "incorporating union" between Scotland and England in 1707, drove the Scots language into the position of a spoken vernacular that was no longer a fully developed literary language, and it was largely by concentration on the folk tradition that 18th-century Scottish poets, notably Robert Burns, were able to use Scots vigorously in their poetry. But in the 19th century the Burns tradition became debased and sentimentalized. MacDiarmid's great achievement was to recognize that the Scottish poetic tradition needed to be radically reshaped and that the decadent post-Burns tradition was beyond disciplining into a poetry of any maturity or originality.

MacDiarmid therefore looked back to Scottish poetry of the 15th century and saw that it was written in a rich and assured Scottish language that grew out of a living speech yet reached far beyond it. He saw too that the poetry of the Scottish "makars" (as the medieval Scottish poets were called) was European in scope, that it combined its genuinely distinctive Scottishness with a relaxed air of being at home in the culture of Europe as a whole. In this respect he saw Scotland as less provincial, less insular in attitude than England: Scotland's long alliance with France and the long tradition of Scotsmen going to Europe to study or soldier or offer services of one kind or another gave some historical evidence for such a view, which in some degree lies behind MacDiarmid's often expressed Anglophobia.

At this stage MacDiarmid believed that a truly creative Scottish poetry had to be in some form of Scots, yet not the emasculated dialect Scots of the post-Burns tradition, and not standard English, which he did not see as able to tap the real roots of Scottish experience. He therefore ransacked the rich vocabulary of Dunbar and Henryson and used it together with modern dialect Scots and standard English. This revived Scots, or "Lallans" (i.e., Lowland Scots) as it was often called, was unashamedly synthetic, put together out of a combination of older Scots words and modern words. Some of the words were culled from dictionaries. Like Joyce, MacDiarmid had an enormous linguistic curiosity and wanted to increase the expressiveness of his poetic speech by every resource of vocabulary he could lay his hands on. In his later poetry, when he wrote in English, he ransacked the technical vocabularies of the sciences in the same spirit. His Scots lyrics have much more energy and vitality than the English poems he had hitherto written, homing in on their subject without any verbal padding or traditional "poetic" language (which can be seen in some of his earlier verse) and using Scots words, in conjunction with English, in ways that startle and shake the reader.

The lyrics of *Sangschaw* and his next volume *Penny Wheep* (1926) vindicated MacDiarmid's choice of Scots. They display a wonderful verbal delicacy which combines precise observation of natural objects with a tense mystical clarity of vision. He has a vision of the contradictions that lie deep in the heart of man and nature and of the possibility of reconciling them by tense concentration on the individual reality of separate things. This is bound up with his view that the proper *naming* of objects can in some way release their energies and place them all in their rich selfhood in the total pattern of the universe. Hence MacDiarmid can be simultaneously a passionate Scot and an internationalist who embraces with excited affection every odd little language, everything different and challenging and offbeat and *itself*. (His view of the self-ness, the individual reality of natural objects, is very like the concept of *haecceitas*, "this-ness," which Gerard Manley Hopkins got from Duns Scotus.)

MacDiarmid's early Scots lyrics are brilliant poems, but they are minia-

tures, small and finely etched pieces, which avoid large pronouncements. In
A Drunk Man Looks at the Thistle (1936), however, he builds up an epic
statement about Scotland out of a series of related lyrics and passages of
descriptive and reflective poetry. It is in a way a modern version of the
medieval dream poem, in which drunkenness plays the part that sleep plays
in the medieval tradition, being used as a means of removing the speaker's
inhibitions and getting him into that visionary predicament. Like William
Dunbar, MacDiarmid is a poet of sharply contrasting moods, and in *A
Drunk Man* he alternates between lyricism, savage satire, comic irony, philosophic reflection, and personal confession. It is MacDiarmid's masterpiece,
but it is far too long for inclusion in this anthology.

In 1933 Hugh MacDiarmid and his second wife, the Cornish Valda
Trevlyn who shares his pan-Celticism and has always supported him with
enormous loyalty, settled in a small cottage on the island of Whalsay, in
the remote Shetland Islands, and lived there with their small son, often in
acute poverty. For though MacDiarmid had now thoroughly established
himself as an explosive force in Scottish literature and as the creator of a
Scottish Renaissance, his books did not provide him with a reasonable
income and his continuous fight against the Establishment led to his condemnation by large numbers of respectable and influential people. "The
poetry I want turns its back contemptuously on all the cowardly and brain-
less staples of Anglo-Scottish literature," he wrote in his autobiographical
Lucky Poet (1943), "—the whole base business of people who do not act
but are acted upon * * * though they include every irresponsible who occupies a 'responsible position' in Scotland today, * * *" He wanted to get rid
of "the whole gang of high mucky-mucks, famous fatheads, old wives of
both sexes, stuffed shirts, hollow men with headpieces stuffed with straw,
bird-wits, lookers-under-beds, trained seals, creeping Jesuses, Scots Wha
Ha'evers, village idiots, policemen, leaders of white-mouse factions and
noted connoisseurs of bread and butter, glorified gangsters, and what 'Billy'
Phelps calls Medlar Novelists (the medlar being a fruit that becomes rotten
before it is ripe), Commercial Calvinists, makers of 'noises like a turnip,'
and all the touts, toadies and lickspittles of the English Ascendancy, and
their infernal women-folk, and all their skunkoil skulduggery." This kind of
invective, which MacDiarmid indulged in with enormous relish, is part of
the old Scottish tradition of "flyting," or mutual rhetorical abuse by two
opponents; for him, however, it was not a game, but passionately meant.

MacDiarmid remained on Whalsay until 1942, cut off from the "civilization" of the mainland and, worst of all, from new books and periodicals.
But his isolation gave him a period of retrenchment and new development.
His encounter with the stark geographical and geological realities of his
remote island increased his awareness of the strange reality of natural
objects. He became interested in rocks and stones and in the technical
vocabulary used to describe and classify them. The volume *Stony Limits
and Other Poems* reflects this interest. He was now writing more and more
in English rather than Scots, but an English with its own kind of vocabulary. His use of geological terms in the opening of *On a Raised Beach*,
the longest and finest poem in the collection, and other aspects of that poem's
individual use of language, show his interest in exploring new ways of
engaging the strange reality he was trying to come to terms with. These

attempts to reach out through language to a way of expressing the uncanny "quiddity" of natural objects and their relation to human feelings went on side by side with his political and social polemics, yet in a sense they were related, for MacDiarmid's political vision was hardly political at all, but a vision of a society redeemed from all second-handness in living, united in an intense relishing of the reality of experience. This involved a discipline that transcended all known norms and a view of life which went beyond humanism to something that can only be called trans-humanist.

In 1942 MacDiarmid was directed to a war job in a steel factory in Glasgow, and from this he moved to the Merchant Service to work on ships engaged in duties in the Clyde estuary until the end of the war. In 1951 he settled in the little cottage in Biggar, Lanarkshire, where he and his wife still live. To the disappointment of many who considered his Scots lyrics his finest achievement, he turned more and more to what he called "the poetry of fact," trying to embrace, sometimes with an almost desperate use of enormous catalogues, all the new scientific and technological knowledge that the modern world had brought into being and to relate it to human awareness. He included a great deal of this kind of poetry in *Lucky Poet*, especially in a remarkable chapter entitled "The Kind of Poetry I Want," which includes the lines:

> I dream of poems like the bread-knife
> Which cuts three slices at once;
> Of poems concerned with technical matters * * *
> Or in cut-gem clearness surpass even Huxley's
> Prose account of the endophragmal system of the crayfish
> And his Anatomy of the Vertebrata; * * *

But perhaps the most remarkable example of MacDiarmid's later style is *In Memoriam James Joyce: from A Vision of a World Language* (1955). This is a poem—and presented as part of a longer one—of over 6,000 lines, written (more or less) in English, with an enormous number of quotations from and references to other languages and literatures. It is built of verse paragraphs of varying length, unrhymed for the most part, with the lines expanding or contracting according to the flow of the thought and the meter free and flexible. The movement of the verse is essentially colloquial; the rhythms are those of conversation; but the rise and fall of the sound and the carefully controlled shifts in tempo provide enough underlying formal pattern to prevent the poem from disintegrating into mere discursiveness. Its theme might be described as the essential kinship of everything in the world that is fully realized and properly possessed of its identity. This was a favorite subject of Walt Whitman. Whitman accepted and celebrated everything in the world so long as it was true to itself and not faked or (to use one of his characteristic terms) "dandified." Whitman, like MacDiarmid, used in his poems the long catalogue; he taught himself how to give a meaning to lists of things by placing them in a context in terms of which each list became a confession of faith in all that was of value in the world. MacDiarmid's poem is a confession of faith. The world language he talks about is the ever-sought, never wholly attainable, ideal means of expression which will be able, merely by describing things, to reveal the glory of their essential quiddity. But the paradox is that in order to make a complete statement about anything you must refer, however obliquely, both by way of contrast and of comparison, to everything else. The ideal world language must thus consist of cosmic puns, in which everything is said when anything is said and which nevertheless at the same time identifies individual things with the utmost precision. Joyce went further towards the realization of such a language than any other writer has done: it is therefore appropriate that a poem in memory of Joyce should have this theme.

MacDiarmid is now generally recognized as the greatest Scottish poet since Burns (and some see him as greater than Burns), and one of a trilogy with Burns and Dunbar. He early achieved fame in France, but in later years he has achieved recognition all over Europe, and he has made many a triumphant progress in Communist countries, including China. His wide-ranging curiosity about and sympathy with other literatures is one reason for his international fame. His output has been very large, and it is not consistent in quality. Some of his later work, with its enormous catalogues, lists of names, quotations from scientific and philosophical authorities, its apparent garrulity, has defeated some critics who have the highest admiration for his lyrics. MacDiarmid was awarded a Civil List pension in 1950, and he has felt ever since very much as Dr. Johnson did when he accepted a pension from George III; he might well have used Johnson's words: "My pension is more out of the usual course of things than any instance that I have known. Here, Sir, was a man avowedly no friend to Government at the time, who got a pension without asking for it. I never courted the great; they sent for me; but I think they now give me up." Neither his pension nor the honorary doctorate of laws he received from Edinburgh University in 1957 in any way diminished his attack on governmental and university establishments. A long discursive poem in his later style published in 1957 was entitled *The Battle Continues*.

The list of books edited, written, or translated by MacDiarmid amounts to over 70. In addition to poems in his different styles, he has written critical, historical, and political essays, edited other poets (including Dunbar and Burns) and founded or edited five periodicals. He belongs with Yeats and Eliot, both of whom were friends and admirers of his, as one of the strikingly original poets of the modern world, and he belongs especially with Joyce, whom he greatly admired, as one who strove to push back the limits of literary speech. He is also the greatest example in modern history of the Poet as Rebel. He himself has said that he would like to have engraved on his tombstone simply his name and the dates of his birth and death and the words:

"A Disgrace to the community."—Mr. Justice Mugge.

The Watergaw[1]

Ae weet forenicht i' the yow-trummle[2]
I saw yon antrin thing,
A watergaw wi' its chitterin' licht
Ayont the on-ding;
An' I thocht° o' the last wild look ye gied°   *thought / gave*
Afore ye deed!°   *died*

There was nae reek i' the laverock's hoose
That nicht—an' nane i' mine;
But I hae thocht o' that foolish licht
Ever sin' syne;
An' I think that mebbe at last I ken
What your look meant then.

1922   1925

The Bonnie Broukit Bairn[1]

Mars is braw° in crammasy,°   *brave / red*
Venus in a green silk goun,°   *gown*
The auld mune[2] shak's her gowden° feathers,   *golden*
Their starry talk's a wheen o' blethers,[3]
Nane for thee a thochtie[4] sparin',
Earth, thou bonnie broukit bairn!
—*But greet,° an' in your tears ye'll droun*   *cry*
The haill clanjamfrie![5]

1925

1. "Watergaw" is a Fifeshire word meaning "the fragment of a rainbow appearing on the horizon." MacDiarmid himself, as C. M. Grieve, editor of *The Scottish Chapbook*, where this poem (his first written in Scots) originally appeared, commented on it as follows: "Doric economy of expressiveness is impressively illustrated in the first four lines of Mr. MacDiarmid's poem. Translate them into English. That is the test. You will find that the shortest possible translation runs something like this: 'One wet afternoon (or early evening) in the cold weather in July after the sheep-shearing I saw that rare thing—an indistinct rainbow, with its shivering light, above the heavily-falling rain.' " The second stanza may be rendered: "There was no smoke in the lark's house that night [meaning, MacDiarmid explains, "it was a dark and stormy night"], and none in mine ["and my heart was dark and stormy too"]. But I have thought of that foolish light ever since then; and I think that maybe at last I know what your look meant then."

2. The "yow-trummle," literally "ewe-tremble," refers to a cold snap after the summer sheep-shearing, which makes the sheared sheep tremble with cold; it is the kind of expressive Scots word that appealed to MacDiarmid.

1. The pretty, neglected child.
2. Old moon.
3. A lot of meaningless chatter.
4. Diminutive of thought.
5. The whole collection. (Jamieson's *Dictionary of the Scottish Language*, which was much used by MacDiarmid, explains "clanjamfrie" as "a term used to denote low, worthless people, or those who are viewed in this light" and cites Scott's use of the word in this sense in *Guy Mannering*.)

Moonstruck[1]

When the warl's couped soon' as a peerie
That licht-lookin' craw o' a body, the moon,
Sits on the fower cross-win's
Peerin' a' roon'.

5 She's seen me—she's seen me—an' straucht°   *straight*
Loupit° clean on the quick o' my hert.°   *leaped / heart*
The quhither o' cauld gowd's fairly
Gi'en me a stert.[2]

An' the roarin' o' oceans noo'
10 Is peerieweerie[3] to me:
Thunner's° a tinklin' bell: an' Time   *thunder's*
Whuds° like a flee.°   *flits / fly*

1925

The Eemis Stane[1]

I' the how-dumb-deid o' the cauld hairst nicht
The warl' like an eemis stane
Wags i' the lift;
An' my eerie memories fa'
5 Like a yowdendrift.

Like a yowdendrift so's I couldna read
The words cut oot i' the stane
Had the fug o' fame
An' history's hazelraw
10 No' yirdit thaim.

1925

From A Drunk Man Looks at the Thistle

1. *Farewell to Dostoevski*

The wan leafs shak, atour° us like the snaw.   *around*
Here is the cavaburd[1] in which Earth's tint.°   *lost*
There's naebody but Oblivion and us,
Puir gangrel° buddies, waunderin' hameless in't.   *wanderer*

5 The stars are larochs° o' auld cottages,   *foundations*
And a' Time's glen is fu' o' blinnin' stew.[2]
Nae freen'ly lozen° skimmers:° and the   *window / gleams /*
  wund°   *wind*
Rises and separates even me and you.

I ken nae Russian and you ken nae Scots.
10 We canna tell oor voices frae the wund.
The snaw is seekin' everywhere: oor herts
At last like roofless ingles° it has f'und.   *hearths*

And gethers there in drift on endless drift,
Oor broken herts that it can never fill;
15 And still—its leafs like snaw, its growth like wund—
The thistle[3] rises and forever will!

                                   1926

2. *Yet Ha'e I Silence Left*

Yet ha'e I Silence left, the croon° o' a'.   *crown*

No' her, wha on the hills langsyne° I saw   *long ago*
Liftin' a foreheid o' perpetual snaw.

No' her, wha in the how-dumb-deid o' nicht[1]
5 Kyths,[2] like Eternity in Time's despite.

No' her, withooten° shape, wha's name is   *without /*
  Daith,°   *Death*
No' Him, unkennable° abies° to faith   *unknowable / except*

—God whom, gin° e'er He saw a Man, 'ud be   *if*
E'en mair dumfooner'd[3] at the sicht° than he.   *sight*

10 —But Him, whom nocht° in man or Deity,   *nothing*
Or Daith or Dreid or Laneliness can touch,
Wha's deed owre often and has seen owre much.[4]

O I ha'e Silence left.

                                   1926

---

1. Dense snowstorm.
2. A storm through which it is impossible to see.
3. The thistle is the emblem of Scotland.
1. The still center of night.
2. Makes herself known, appears.
3. More dumbfounded.
4. Who has died too often and seen too much.

From To Circumjack Cencrastus

Lourd on My Hert

Lourd° on my hert as winter lies   *heavy*
The state that Scotland's in the day.
Spring to the North has aye come slow
But noo° dour¹ winter's like to stay   *now*
5   For guid,°   *good*
    And no' for guid!

O wae's me on the weary days
When it is scarce grey licht° at noon;   *light*
It maun° be a' the stupid folk   *must*
10 Diffusin' their dullness roon and roon
    Like soot
    That keeps the sunlicht oot.

Nae wonder if I think I see
A lichter° shadow than the neist°   *lighter / next*
15 I'm fain to cry: "The dawn, the dawn!
I see it brakin' in the East."
    But ah
    —It's juist mair snaw!²

                             1930

From On a Raised Beach

All is lithogenesis¹—or lochia,
Carpolite² fruit of the forbidden tree,
Stones blacker than any in the Caaba,³
Cream-colored caen-stone, chatoyant pieces,⁴

1. Hard, stern.
2. Just more snow.

1. From Greek *lithos*, stone, and *genesis*, origin. This word is apparently a coinage of MacDiarmid's, on the analogy of "lithology," the study of stones and rocks. Stones and rocks, and their relation to human experience, is the theme of this long poem, which deliberately uses a strange technical vocabulary to communicate the poet's sense of the mysterious otherness of the natural world of geology. The massing of geological and other technical words that follow illustrates MacDiarmid's joy in harnessing to his poetry specialist terms from the sciences.

2. An adjective from the Greek *karpos*, fruit (cf. "carpology," that branch of plant anatomy relating to the structure of fruit and seeds); following the em-phatic word "lithogenesis," the origin or birth of the rock structure of the earth, and the reference to "lochia," a discharge from the uterus after childbirth, the word helps to build up the suggestion of some primeval birth of the earth's crust.

3. More usually Ka'ba or Kaaba, the sacred shrine of Mohammedanism, containing the famous "black stone" in the middle of the great mosque at Mecca.

4. The Caen stone of Normandy is a well-known stone of the Bathonian series; "chatoyant": glistening, shot through with gleaming colors; "celadon" (also from the French) is a pale, soft, sea-green color; "corbeau" (literally "raven" in French) is the same as corbel, an architectural term meaning a projection from the face of a wall, supporting a weight.

5   Celadon and corbeau, bistre and beige,[5]
     Glaucous, hoar, enfouldered, cyathiform,[6]
     Making mere faculae[7] of the sun and moon,
     I study you glout° and gloss, but have   *frown*
     No cadrans[8] to adjust you with, and turn again
10   From optik to haptik[9] and like a blind man run
     My fingers over you, arris by arris, burr by burr,[1]
     Slickensides,[2] truité,° rugas,[3] foveoles,[4]   *speckled*
     Bringing my aesthesis° in vain to bear,   *perception*
     An angle-titch[5] to all your corrugations and coigns,°   *corners*
15   Hatched foraminous[6] cavo-rilieva[7] of the world,
     Diectic,[8] fiducial[9] stones. Chiliad by chiliad
     What bricole[1] piled you here, stupendous cairn?[2]
     What artist poses the Earth écorché[3] thus,
     Pillar of creation engouled[4] in me?
20   What eburnation[5] augments you with men's bones,
     Every energumen[6] an Endymion[7] yet?
     All the other stones are in this hæcceity[8] it seems,
     But where is the Christophanic[9] rock that moved?
     What Cabirian[1] song from this catasta[2] comes?

25   Deep conviction or preference can seldom
     Find direct terms in which to express itself.

5. Color words, meaning respectively dark brown, the color of natural wood, grayish-blue (or grayish-green), white (or gray).

6. The word "enfouldered" occurs once in Spenser's *Faerie Queene* ("with foul enfouldred smoake") and is thought to mean "like a thundercloud." Mac-Diarmid apparently uses it to denote a shape, for he is here moving on from color to shape; he seems to have invented "cyathiform" to mean "shaped like a cup" (Greek *kyathos + form*).

7. Bright spots or streaks on the surface of the sun.

8. A machine for cutting gems and adjusting the angles of the facets.

9. From sight to touch.

1. Rough edge or ridge. "Arris": the edge formed by the meeting of two straight or curved surfaces.

2. Surfaces of rocks that have been ground against each other.

3. Wrinkled, presumably from Latin *ruga*, a wrinkle; the normal English word derived from *ruga* and meaning wrinkled is "rugate."

4. Small depressions or pits.

5. Apparently an invented word, perhaps meaning the poet's particular tilt or angle of observation.

6. Having foramina, which are small perforations or openings.

7. A style of relief in which the highest portions of the figures are on a level with the general surface.

8. Perhaps equivalent to diecious, a term in zoology and botany indicating the separation of the sexes.

9. Probably used in the technical sense employed by astronomers, surveyors, and others, to mean a line, point, etc., used as a fixed basis of comparison. "Chiliad": a thousand years.

1. A medieval engine for throwing stones or bolts; a catapult.

2. A heap of stones.

3. Anatomical figure with the skin removed for the study of muscles.

4. In heraldry, referring to bends, crosses, etc., which enter the mouths of animals.

5. A term in pathology, meaning the act or process of becoming hard and dense like ivory.

6. Someone possessed by a devil.

7. In Greek mythology, a young man loved by Selene, the moon goddess.

8. The *haecceitas* or "this-ness," specific individuality, that so interested the medieval philosopher Duns Scotus.

9. Indicating the appearance of Christ (Christophany is the theological term for the appearance of Christ).

1. Adjective from Cabiri, a group of non-Hellenic deities (perhaps Phyrigian) about whose nature and function there is considerable mystery.

2. A block on which slaves stood for sale. The Latin word means simply a scaffold.

Today on this shingle[3] shelf
I understand this pensive reluctance so well,
This not discommendable obstinacy,
30   These contrivances of an inexpressive critical feeling,
These stones with their resolve that Creation shall not
          be
Injured by iconoclasts and quacks. Nothing has stirred
Since I lay down this morning an eternity ago
But one bird. The widest open door is the least liable to
          intrusion,
35   Ubiquitous as the sunlight, unfrequented as the sun.
The inward gates of a bird are always open.
It does not know how to shut them.
That is the secret of its song,
But whether any man's are ajar is doubtful.
40   I look at these stones and know little about them,
But I know their gates are open too,
Always open, far longer open, than any bird's can be,
That every one of them has had its gates wide open far
          longer
Than all birds put together, let alone humanity,
45   Though through them no man can see,
No man nor anything more recently born than them-
          selves
And that is everything else on the Earth.
I too lying here have dismissed all else.
Bread from stones is my sole and desperate dearth,
50   From stones, which are to the Earth as to the sunlight
Is the naked sun which is for no man's sight.
I would scorn to cry to any easier audience
Or, having cried, to lack patience to await the response.
I am no more indifferent or ill-disposed to life than
          death is;
55   I would fain accept it all completely as the soil does;
Already I feel all that can perish perishing in me
As so much has perished and all will yet perish in these
          stones.
I must begin with these stones as the world began.

Shall I come to a bird quicker than the world's course
          ran?
60   To a bird, and to myself, a man?
And what if I do, and further?
I shall only have gone a little way to go back again
And be like a fleeting deceit of development,
Iconoclasts, quacks. So these stones have dismissed
65   All but all of evolution, unmoved by it,

3. Beds of small stones on the seashore.

(Is there anything to come they will not likewise
    dismiss?)
As the essential life of mankind in the mass
Is the same as their earliest ancestors' yet.

Actual physical conflict or psychological warfare
70   Incidental to love or food
Brings out animal life's bolder and more brilliant
    patterns
    Concealed as a rule in habitude.
    There is a sudden revelation of color,
    The protrusion of a crest,
75   The expansion of an ornament,
—But no general principle can be guessed
From these flashing fragments we are seeing,
These foam-bells on the hidden currents of being.
The bodies of animals are visible substances
And must therefore have color and shape, in the first
80   place
Depending on chemical composition, physical structure,
    mode of growth,
Psychological rhythms and other factors in the case,
But their purposive function is another question.
Brilliant-hued animals hide away in the ocean deeps;
85   The mole has a rich sexual coloring in due season
Under the ground; nearly every beast keeps
Brighter colors inside it than outside.
What the seen shows is never anything to what it's
    designed to hide,
The red blood which makes the beauty of a maiden's
    cheek
90   Is as red under a gorilla's pigmented and hairy face.
Varied forms and functions though life may seem to
    have shown
They all come back soon to the likeness of stone,
So to the intervening stages we can best find a clue
In what we all came from and return to.
95   There are no twirly bits in this ground bass.

We must be humble. We are so easily baffled by appear-
    ances
And do not realize that these stones are one with the
    stars.
It makes no difference to them whether they are high
    or low,
Mountain peak or ocean floor, palace, or pigsty.
There are plenty of ruined buildings in the world but
100   no ruined stones.
No visitor comes from the stars

But is the same as they are.
—Nay, it is easy to find a spontaneity here,
An adjustment to life, an ability
105 To ride it easily, akin to "the buoyant
Prelapsarian[4] naturalness of a country girl
Laughing in the sun, not passion-rent,
But sensing in the bound of her breasts vigors to come
Powered to make her one with the stream of earth-life
round her,"
110 But not yet as my Muse is, with this ampler scope,
This more divine rhythm, wholly at one
With the earth, riding the Heavens with it, as the stones do
And all soon must.
But it is wrong to indulge in these illustrations
115 Instead of just accepting the stones.
It is a paltry business to try to drag down
The arduus furor of the stones to the futile imaginings of men,
To all that fears to grow roots into the common earth,
As it soon must, lest it be chilled to the core,
120 As it will be—and none the worse for that.
Impatience is a poor qualification for immortality.
Hot blood is of no use in dealing with eternity.
It is seldom that promises or even realizations
Can sustain a clear and searching gaze.
125 But an emotion chilled is an emotion controlled;
This is the road leading to certainty,
Reasoned planning for the time when reason can no longer avail.
It is essential to know the chill of all the objections
That come creeping into the mind, the battle between
opposing ideas
130 Which gives the victory to the strongest and most universal
Over all others, and to wage it to the end
With increasing freedom, precision, and detachment
A detachment that shocks our instincts and ridicules our desires.
All else in the world cancels out, equal, capable
135 Of being replaced by other things (even as all the ideas
That madden men now must lose their potency in a few years
And be replaced by others—even as all the religions,
All the material sacrifices and moral restraints,
That in twenty thousand years have brought us no nearer to God
140 Are irrelevant to the ordered adjustments
Out of the reach of perceptive understanding
Forever taking place on the Earth and in the unthinkable
regions around it;
This cats' cradle of life; this reality volatile yet determined;
This intense vibration in the stones
145 That makes them seem immobile to us)

4. From before the Fall of Man.

But the world cannot dispense with the stones.
They alone are not redundant. Nothing can replace them
Except a new creation of God.
* * *

All is lithogenesis—or lochia;
And I can desire nothing better,
An immense familiarity with other men's imaginings
Convinces me they cannot either
305 (If they could, it would instantly be granted
    —The present order must continue till then)
  Though, of course, I still keep an open mind,
  A mind as open as the grave.
  You may say that the truth cannot be crushed out,
310 That the weight of the whole world may be tumbled on it,
  And yet, in puny, distorted, phantasmal shapes albeit,
  It will braird° again; it will force its way up   *sprout*
  Through unexpectable fissures? look over this beach.
  What ruderal° and rupestrine° growth is here?   *stony / rocky*
315 What crop confirming any credulities?
  Conjure a fescue[5] to teach me with from this
  And I will listen to you, but until then
  Listen to me—Truth is not crushed;
  It crushes, gorgonizes[6] all else into itself.
320 The trouble is to know it when you see it?
  You will have no trouble with it when you do.
  Do not argue with me. Argue with these stones.
  Truth has no trouble in knowing itself.
  This is it. The hard fact. The inoppugnable[7] reality,
325 Here is something for you to digest.
  Eat this and we'll see what appetite you have left
  For a world hereafter.
  I pledge you in the first and last crusta,[8]
  The rocks rattling in the bead-proof seas.
* * *

1934

Second Hymn to Lenin

Ah, Lenin, you were richt.° But I'm a poet   *right*
(And you c'ud mak allowances for that!)
Aimin' at mair° than you aimed at   *more*
Tho' yours comes first, I know it.

---

5. A genus of grass.
6. Turns into stone, as in Greek mythology the Gorgon did to beholders.
7. Not to be fought against.

8. Crustacean, class of aquatic creatures (crabs, lobsters, etc.) covered with a horny shell.

5 An unexamined life is no' worth ha'in'.[1]
Yet Burke[2] was richt; owre muckle° concern   *too much*
Wi' Life's foundations is a sure
Sign o' decay; tho' Joyce in turn

Is richt, and the principal question
10 Aboot a work o' art is frae hoo° deep   *from how*
A life it springs—and syne hoo faur°   *how far*
Up frac't it has the poo'er° to leap.   *power*

And hoo muckle° it lifts up wi' it   *much*
Into the sunlicht like a saumon° there,   *salmon*
15 Universal Spring! For Morand's[3] richt—
It s'ud be like licht in the air—

Are my poems spoken in the factories and fields,
    In the streets o' the toon?
Gin they're no', then I'm failin' to dae
20   *What I ocht° to ha' dune.*   *ought*

Gin° I canna win through to the man in the street,   *if*
    The wife by the hearth.
A' the cleverness on earth'll no' mak' up
    For the damnable dearth.

25 *"Haud° on haud on; what poet's dune that?*   *hold*
    Is Shakespeare read,
Or Dante or Milton or Goethe or Burns?"
    —You heard what I said.

—A means o' world locomotion,
30 The maist perfected and aerial o' a'.
Lenin's name's gane owre° the haill° earth,   *gone over / whole*
But the names o' the ithers?—Ha!

What hidie-hole o' the vineyard d'they scart°   *scratch*
Wi' minds like the look on a hen's face,
35 Morand, Joyce, Burke, and the rest
That e'er wrote; me noo in like case?

Great poets hardly onybody kens° o'?   *knows*
Geniuses like a man talkin' t'm sel'?
Nonsense! They're nocht° o' the sort   *nothing*
40 Their character's easy to tell.

---

1. "The unexamined life is not worth living"—Socrates.
2. Edmund Burke (1729–1797), the English political writer and orator.
3. Paul Morand, b. 1888, French diplomat and writer of novels and travel books. Ironically, he later supported Vichy France and remained in Switzerland after the liberation of France in 1944.

They're nocht but romantic rebels
Strikin' dilletante poses;
Trotsky[4]—Christ, no' wi' a croon o' thorns
But a wreath o' paper roses.

45   A' that's great is free and expansive.
What ha' they expanded tae?
They've affected nocht but a fringe
O' mankind in ony way.

Barbarian saviour o' civilization
50   Hoo weel ye kent (we're owre° dull witted)   *too*
Naething is dune save as we ha'e
Means to en's transparently fitted.

Poetry like politics maun° cut   *must*
The cackle and pursue real ends,
55   Unerringly as Lenin, and to that
Its nature better tends.

Wi' Lenin's vision equal poet's gift
And what unparalleled force was there!
Nocht in a' literature wi' that
60   Begins to compare.

Nae simple rhymes for silly folk
But the haill° art, as Lenin gied   *whole*
Nae Marx-without-tears to workin' men
But the fu' course insteed.

65   Organic constructional work,
Practicality, and work by degrees;
First things first; and poetry in turn
'll be built by these.

You saw it faur° off when you thocht   *far*
70   O' mass-education yet.
Hoo lang till they rise to Pushkin?[5]
And that's but a fit!°   *foot*

Oh, it's nonsense, nonsense, nonsense,
Nonsense at this time o' day
75   *That breid-and-butter problems*
S'ud be in ony man's way.

---

4. Leon Trotsky (1879–1940), Russian revolutionary leader, banished from the U.S.S.R. by Stalin in the latter's rise to power and assassinated on Stalin's orders in Mexico City on August 20, 1940.
5. The famous Russian poet.

They s'ud be like the tails we tint°   lost
On leavin' the monkey stage;
A' maist folk fash[6] aboot's alike
80   Primaeval to oor age.

We're grown-ups that haena° yet   have not
Put bairnly° things aside   childish
—A' that's material and moral—
And oor new state descried.

85   Sport, love, and parentage,
Trade, politics, and law
S'ud be nae mair to us than braith
We hardly ken we draw.

Freein' oor poo'ers for greater things,
90   And fegs° there's plenty o' them,   certainly
Tho' wha's still trammelt in alow°   below
Canna be tenty[7] o' them—

In the meantime Montéhus[8] sangs—
But as you were ready to tine°   lose
95   The Russian Revolution to the German
Gin that ser'd better syne,[9]

Or foresaw that Russia maun° lead   must
The workers' cause, and then
Pass the lead elsewhere, and aiblins°   perhaps
100   Fa' faur° backward again,   falls far

Sae here, twixt poetry and politics,
There's nae doot in the en'.
Poetry includes that and s'ud be
The greatest poo'er amang men.

105   —It's the greatest, *in posse*° at least,   potentially
That men ha'e discovered yet
Tho' nae doot they're unconscious still
O' ithers faur° greater than it.   others far

You confined yoursel' to your work
110   —A step at a time;
But, as the loon° is in the man,   boy
That'll be ta'en up i' the rhyme,

---

6. Most people worry.
7. Careful, heedful.
8. Gaston **Montéhus**, French satirical

poet and playwright, whose work was
published between 1905 and 1920.
9. If that would have served better than.

Ta'en up like a pool in the sands
Aince° the tide rows in,   *once*
115 When life opens its hert and sings
Withoot scrupe° or sin.   *scruple*

Your knowledge in your ain° sphere   *own*
Was exact and complete
But your sphere's elementary and sune by°   *soon gone*
120 As a poet maun see't.

For a poet maun see in a'thing,
Ev'n what looks trumpery or horrid,
A subject equal to ony
—A star for the forehead!

125 A poet has nae choice left
Betwixt Beaverbrook,[1] say, and God.
Jimmy Thomas[2] or you,
A cat, carnation, or clod.

He daurna° turn awa' frae ocht°   *dare not / from anything*
130 For a single act o' neglect
And straucht° he may fa' frae grace   *straight*
And be void o' effect.

Disinterestedness,
Oor profoundest word yet,
135 *But how far yont° even that*   *beyond*
The sense o' onything's set!

The inward necessity yont
Ony laws o' cause
The intellect conceives
140 *That a'thing° has!*   *everything*

Freend, foe; past, present, future;
Success, failure; joy, fear;
Life, Death; and a'thing else,
For us, are equal here.

145 Male, female; quick or deid,
Let us fike° nae mair;   *fuss*
The deep line o'cleavage
Disna° lie there.   *doesn't*

1. William Maxwell Aitken, Lord Beaverbrook (1879–1964), Canadian-born newspaper proprietor and politician, champion of the British imperial idea, a man of enormous energy and flamboyant right-wing patriotism who publicized his views in his newspapers.
2. James Thomas (1874–1949), trade-union leader and Labour politician, considered by some to have betrayed the Labour Party by continuing in the "national" government after 1931.

> *Black in the pit the miner is,*
> 150 *The shepherd reid° on the hill,*   red
> *And I'm wi' them baith until*
> *The end of mankind, I wis.°*   I guess
>
> *Whatever their jobs a' men are ane*
> *In life, and syne° in daith*   then
> 155 *(Tho' it's sma' patience I can ha'e*
> *Wi' life's ideas o' that by the way)*
> *And he's nae poet but kens it, faith,*
> *And ony job but the hardest's ta'en.*
>
> *The sailor gangs owre° the curve o' the sea,*   goes over
> 160 *The hoosewife's thrang° in the wash-tub,*   busy
> *And whatna° rhyme can I find but hub,*   whatever
> *And what else can poetry be?*
>
> *The core o' a' activity,*
> *Changin't in accordance wi'*
> 165 *Its inward necessity*
> *And mede o' integrity.*
>
> *Unremittin', relentless,*
> *Organized to the last degree,*
> *Ah, Lenin, politics is bairns° play*   children's
> 170 *To what this maun° be!*   must
> 1932   1935

From In Memoriam James Joyce

We Must Look at the Harebell[1]

We must look at the harebell as if
We had never seen it before.
Remembrance gives an accumulation of satisfaction
Yet the desire for change is very strong in us
And change is in itself a recreation.   5
To those who take any pleasure
In flowers, plants, birds, and the rest
An ecological change is recreative.
(Come. Climb with me. Even the sheep are different
And of new importance.   10
The coarse-fleeced, hardy Herdwick,
The Hampshire Down, artificially fed almost from birth,

---

1. The Scottish bluebell, a blue flower with a bell-shaped blossom.

And butcher-fat from the day it is weaned,
The Lincoln-Longwool, the biggest breed in England,
With the longest fleece, and the Southdown　　　　　15
Almost the smallest—and between them thirty other breeds,
Some whitefaced, some black,
Some with horns and some without,
Some long-wooled, some short-wooled,
In England where the men, and women too,　　　　　20
Are almost as interesting as the sheep.)
Everything is different, everything changes,
Except for the white bedstraw which climbs all the way
Up from the valleys to the tops of the high passes
The flowers are all different and more precious　　　　　25
Demanding more search and particularity of vision.
Look! Here and there a pinguicula[2] eloquent of the Alps
Still keeps a purple-blue flower
On the top of its straight and slender stem.
Bog-asphodel, deep-gold, and comely in form,　　　　　30
The queer, almost diabolical, sundew,
And when you leave the bog for the stag moors and the rocks
The parsley fern—a lovelier plant
Than even the proud Osmunda Regalis[3]—
Flourishes in abundance　　　　　35
Showing off oddly contrasted fronds
From the cracks of the lichened stones.
It is pleasant to find the books
Describing it as "very local."
Here is a change indeed!
The universal *is* the particular.　　　　　40

　　　　　　　　　　　　　　　　　　　　1955

2. The butterwort, a genus of small herbs whose leaves secrete a sticky substance in which small insects are caught.

3. The "flowering fern" or "royal fern," a plant with large fronds.

SAMUEL BECKETT

(1906–)

1937: Moved to Paris.
1952: *Waiting for Godot.*
1969: Nobel Prize.

Samuel Beckett, born near Dublin, took a degree at Trinity College (Dublin's Protestant university), but went to Paris from 1928 to 1930, where he met James Joyce and breathed the larger air of the Continent. He returned to Ireland briefly, spent a couple of wretched years in London, and finally settled in Paris in 1937. He has lived in France ever since, teaching in

French *lycées*, serving for a while as Joyce's secretary, and writing—generally in French as a first tongue, but then translating his own works into eloquent, Irish-tinged English. In a cosmopolitan age, when a major American novelist is named Vladimir Vladimirovich Nabokov, when a major English poet (T. S. Eliot) hailed from Saint Louis, Missouri, and when a major British poet (W. H. Auden), who was an American citizen, spent most of his time in Austria, Beckett has every right to be considered an Irishman in exile, and to take his place in the English literary tradition.

Though now recognized as a major achievement, the novels which Beckett published in the late forties and early fifties won little acclaim. Public recognition came with his first play, *Waiting for Godot* (1952 in French, 1954 in English), followed by *Endgame* (1957 in French, 1958 in English). Each of these agonizing, tragic vaudevilles was hailed as a theatrical masterpiece; each was also declared to be inevitably the author's "last word." They are, indeed, dramas about the last things. The title of *Endgame*, for instance, refers to the closing moves in a game of chess, where most of the pieces have been eliminated, and the contest reduces itself to a few stylized moves, the end of which is clearly foreseen. Of the four characters appearing on stage, three are paralyzed. The old folk, Nagg and Nell (whose names perhaps suggest, in degraded form, Agammenon and Helen), have been discarded to garbage cans, literally as well as symbolically. Hamm, whose name is that of Noah's accursed son, as well as that of a corny actor, plays out his game on a lonely throne from which, blind and despairing, he controls the last pawn remaining to him, his adopted son Clov. Little flurries of intermittent life are stirred up by the senile erotic memories of Nagg and Nell, by a possible flea in Clov's pants, by a possible rat in the kitchen, by a toy dog with three legs, and by Hamm's yearning for his pain-killer. But the attempt to fill time with words or actions fails again and again; the game against time is lost from the beginning. "If I don't kill that rat," Clov says earnestly at one point, "he'll die." Thought bound by its own helpless contradictions could not be more concisely illustrated. No exterior force confines the characters to the repetition of their ghastly routines in the icy, mist-bound room; they are like Sartre's characters in *Huis-Clos*, punishers of themselves in a do-it-yourself hell. Yet the play is also lit by a mocking and derisive humor; it is continually undercutting itself by turning its irony in upon itself and juxtaposing, for grotesque effect, burlesque and vaudeville routines with moans of metaphysical anguish.

Beckett is unique among contemporary writers in a number of respects, but particularly in his fundamental premises. He is a deeply protestant man deprived of his faith—a quester, a pilgrim, a man who seeks to purify the truth down to its last bitter, almost unbearably pure negation. He is also a philosopher, building with extraordinary rigor on the work of the 17th-century French thinker Descartes. From Descartes and his successors Beckett took over those premises regarding the separation of body and mind which led him to represent, throughout much of his work, mind in an almost perfect state of abstraction. Fastened to a dying animal, as Yeats said, the mind as Beckett represents it seeks constantly to reassure itself of its own existence by developing its own brilliant, futile dialectic. It says something, unsays it, looks into itself, looks away from itself, then patters frantically on, lest it fall into silence and non-being, the death it knows is inevitable and imminent. The fullest working out of this tragic monodrama is in a trilogy of novels titled *Molloy, Malone Dies,* and *The Unnamable,* first published in French (1951, 1951, 1953) and later translated into English (1955, 1956, and 1958), the first one by Patrick Bowles in collaboration with the author, the second and third by the author alone. All the novels deal with old men in an advanced stage of decrepitude. During the course of the narration they inevitably deteriorate still further. Molloy starts off to his mother's house, not only ambulatory but capable of riding a bicycle; his legs stiffen up on him, one of them shrinks, he takes to crutches, loses the crutches, and is last seen rolling compulsively forward toward what he merely surmises is his destination. Moran sets out to seek Molloy in obedience to mysterious commands; he too makes use of a bicycle and crutches before returning home in badly battered condition. Malone appears before us from the first as a bedridden cripple in a madhouse or hospital for the incurable. All these old men, and several other Beckett heroes as well, from outside the trilogy, have names beginning with *M,* perhaps to suggest that they represent the condition—or, rather, the problem—of Man. In the last novel of the series, the *Unnamable* (who feels he may be or perhaps once was Mahood, but who often refers to himself as Worm), has shed not only all the appendages of mobility like bicycles and crutches, but arms and legs and sex, ears and nose as well, and is simply a brain and a mouth, compulsively talking as if to persuade himself that there is still truth in the famous argument of Descartes "*Cogito ergo sum*"—I think, therefore I am.

Of these terrifying novels (characterized in a brilliant student coinage as "crucifictions") we reprint here chiefly the first. *Molloy* consists of two long monologues, the first by Molloy, the second by Moran. The relation between these two characters is perhaps intimated by a capsule episode which Molloy prefixes, by way of overture, to his story. It is the story of two men, A and C, who leave the same spot at different times, but meet face to face when the first turns back along a road already traversed and encounters the second. Whether A represents Moran and C Molloy, or vice versa, is left in doubt; but the fact of the encounter is evidently of great importance in both men's lives. Applying this tiny story to the larger one, we find in Molloy and his counterpart Moran two radically different human types. Molloy, penniless, battered, and physically revolting though he is, evidently touches on some element of the sacred; he is in touch with inner voices, he enacts, in the vaudeville of his absurd theater, the agony of all mankind. Moran is given to us as a very different type: he is an official, a functionary, a householder, a taxpayer, a churchgoer, strict with his son and his servant, strict also with himself. His search for Molloy is one of those burlesque, directionless quests of which a magnificent model is found in Lewis Carroll's comic epic *The Hunting of the Snark.* The climax of this search is his encounter, in the depths of a dark forest, with two figures, one of whom may be Molloy, the other of whom is probably some version of himself or at least of his official self. In some way of which we cannot be sure, perhaps simply as a result of hefting the stick which Molloy seems to carry, Moran is imbued with some of his inner strength; he beats his former self to death, and returns home after a long, bitter journey, evidently a sadder and a wiser man than when he set out. But in a longer perspective, it may be felt that the end of his journey is not reformation or reconstruction at all. It is the glimpse, within him or before him, of a pale, suffering, neutral face which may be that of the final moribund in Beckett's series, the *Unnamable* who is all the old men reduced to their lowest common multiple, a brain and a mouth.

Beckett's writing is characterized by aseptic economy of word and gesture, extreme simplicity of style, and a rigor of metaphysical thought most exceptional among English writers. His work has exercised wide influence on the literature of many different cultures, and has accumulated, within only a couple of decades, bewildering quantities of commentary and explanation.

In 1969 Beckett received the Nobel Prize for Literature.

From Endgame

[*The End*]

HAMM. Is it not time for my pain-killer?

CLOV. Yes.

HAMM. Ah! At last! Give it to me! Quick!

(*Pause.*)

CLOV. There's no more pain-killer.

(*Pause.*)

HAMM (*appalled*). Good. . . !

(*Pause.*)

No more pain-killer!

CLOV. No more pain-killer. You'll never get any more pain-killer.

(*Pause.*)

HAMM. But the little round box. It was full!

CLOV. Yes. But now it's empty.

(*Pause. Clov starts to move about the room. He is looking for a place to put down the alarm-clock.*)

HAMM (*soft*). What'll I do?

(*Pause. In a scream.*)

What'll I do?

(*Clov sees the picture, takes it down, stands it on the floor with its face to the wall, hangs up the alarm-clock in its place.*)

What are you doing?

CLOV. Winding up.

HAMM. Look at the earth.

CLOV. Again!

HAMM. Since it's calling to you.

CLOV. Is your throat sore?
  (*Pause.*)
  Would you like a lozenge?
  (*Pause.*)
  No.
  (*Pause.*)
  Pity.
  (*Clov goes, humming, towards window right, halts before it, looks up at it.*)
HAMM. Don't sing.
CLOV (*turning towards Hamm*). One hasn't the right to sing any more?
HAMM. No.
CLOV. Then how can it end?
HAMM. You want it to end?
CLOV. I want to sing.
HAMM. I can't prevent you.
  (*Pause. Clov turns towards window right.*)
CLOV. What did I do with that steps?
  (*He looks around for ladder.*)
  You didn't see that steps?
  (*He sees it.*)
  Ah, about time.
  (*He goes towards window left.*)
  Sometimes I wonder if I'm in my right mind. Then it passes over and I'm as lucid as before.
  (*He gets up on ladder, looks out of window.*)
  Christ, she's under water!
  (*He looks.*)
  How can that be?
  (*He pokes forward his head, his hand above his eyes.*)
  It hasn't rained.
  (*He wipes the pane, looks. Pause.*)
  Ah what a fool I am! I'm on the wrong side!
  (*He gets down, takes a few steps towards window right.*)
  Under water!
  (*He goes back for ladder.*)
  What a fool I am!
  (*He carries ladder towards window right.*)
  Sometimes I wonder if I'm in my right senses. Then it passes off and I'm as intelligent as ever.
  (*He sets down ladder under window right, gets up on it, looks out of window. He turns towards Hamm.*)
  Any particular sector you fancy? Or merely the whole thing?
HAMM. Whole thing.
CLOV. The general effect? Just a moment.
  (*He looks out of window. Pause.*)
HAMM. Clov.
CLOV. (*absorbed*). Mmm.

HAMM. Do you know what it is?

CLOV. (*as before*). Mmm.

HAMM. I was never there.

(*Pause.*)

Clov!

CLOV (*turning towards Hamm, exasperated*). What is it?

HAMM. I was never there.

CLOV. Lucky for you.

(*He looks out of window.*)

HAMM. Absent, always. It all happened without me. I don't know what's happened.

(*Pause.*)

Do you know what's happened?

(*Pause.*)

Clov!

CLOV (*turning towards Hamm, exasperated*). Do you want me to look at this muckheap, yes or no?

HAMM. Answer me first.

CLOV. What?

HAMM. Do you know what's happened?

CLOV. When? Where?

HAMM (*violently*). When! What's happened? Use your head, can't you! What has happened?

CLOV. What for Christ's sake does it matter?

(*He looks out of window.*)

HAMM. I don't know.

(*Pause. Clov turns towards Hamm.*)

CLOV. (*harshly*). When old Mother Pegg asked you for oil for her lamp and you told her to get out to hell, you knew what was happening then, no?

(*Pause.*)

You know what she died of, Mother Pegg? Of darkness.

HAMM (*feebly*). I hadn't any.

CLOV (*as before*). Yes, you had.

(*Pause.*)

HAMM. Have you the glass?

CLOV. No, it's clear enough as it is.

HAMM. Go and get it.

(*Pause. Clov casts up his eyes, brandishes his fists. He loses balance, clutches on to the ladder. He starts to get down, halts.*)

CLOV. There's one thing I'll never understand.

(*He gets down.*)

Why I always obey you. Can you explain that to me?

HAMM. No. . . . Perhaps it's compassion.

(*Pause.*)

A kind of great compassion.

(*Pause.*)

Oh you won't find it easy, you won't find it easy.

(*Pause. Clov begins to move about the room in search of the telescope.*)

CLOV. I'm tired of our goings on, very tired.
(He searches.)
You're not sitting on it?
(He moves the chair, looks at the place where it stood, resumes his search.)
HAMM *(anguished)*. Don't leave me there!
(Angrily Clov restores the chair to its place.)
Am I right in the center?
CLOV. You'd need a microscope to find this—
(He sees the telescope.)
Ah, about time.
(He picks up the telescope, gets up on the ladder, turns the telescope on the without.)
HAMM. Give me the dog.
CLOV *(looking)*. Quiet!
HAMM *(angrily)*. Give me the dog!
(Clove drops the telescope, clasps his hands to his head. Pause. He gets down precipitately, looks for the dog, sees it, picks it up, hastens towards Hamm and strikes him violently on the head with the dog.)
CLOV. There's your dog for you!
(The dog falls to the ground. Pause.)
HAMM. He hit me!
CLOV. You drive me mad, I'm mad!
HAMM. If you must hit me, hit me with the axe.
(Pause.)
Or with the gaff, hit me with the gaff. Not with the dog. With the gaff. Or with the axe.
(Clov picks up the dog and gives it to Hamm who takes it in his arms.)
CLOV. *(imploringly)*. Let's stop playing!
HAMM. Never!
(Pause.)
Put me in my coffin.
CLOV. There are no more coffins.
HAMM. Then let it end!
(Clov goes towards ladder.)
With a bang!
(Clov gets up on ladder, gets down again, looks for telescope, sees it, picks it up, gets up ladder, raises telescope.)
Of darkness! And me? Did anyone ever have pity on me?
CLOV *(lowering the telescope, turning towards Hamm)*. What?
(Pause.)
Is it me you're referring to?
HAMM *(angrily)*. An aside, ape! Did you never hear an aside before?
(Pause.)
I'm warming up for my last soliloquy.
CLOV. I warn you. I'm going to look at this filth since it's an order. But it's the last time.

(*He turns the telescope on the without.*)
Let's see.
(*He moves the telescope.*)
Nothing . . . nothing . . . good . . . good . . . nothing . . . goo—
(*He starts, lowers the telescope, examines it, turns it again on the without. Pause.*)
Bad luck to it!

HAMM. More complications!
(*Clov gets down.*)
Not an underplot, I trust.
(*Clov moves ladder nearer window, gets up on it, turns telescope on the without.*)

CLOV (*dismayed*). Looks like a small boy!

HAMM (*sarcastic*). A small . . . boy!

CLOV. I'll go and see.
(*He gets down, drops the telescope, goes towards door, turns.*)
I'll take the gaff.
(*He looks for the gaff, sees it, picks it up, hastens towards door.*)

HAMM. No!
(*Clov halts.*)

CLOV. No? A potential procreator?

HAMM. If he exists he'll die there or he'll come here. And if he doesn't . . .
(*Pause.*)

CLOV. You don't believe me? You think I'm inventing?
(*Pause.*)

HAMM. It's the end, Clov, we've come to the end. I don't need you any more.
(*Pause.*)

CLOV. Lucky for you.
(*He goes towards door.*)

HAMM. Leave me the gaff.
(*Clov gives him the gaff, goes towards door, halts, looks at alarm-clock, takes it down, looks round for a better place to put it, goes to bins, puts it on lid of Nagg's bin. Pause.*)

CLOV. I'll leave you.
(*He goes towards door.*)

HAMM. Before you go . . .
(*Clov halts near door.*)
. . . say something.

CLOV. There is nothing to say.

HAMM. A few words . . . to ponder . . . in my heart.

CLOV. Your heart!

HAMM. Yes.
(*Pause. Forcibly.*)
Yes!
(*Pause.*)
With the rest, in the end, the shadows, the murmurs, all the trouble, to end up with.
(*Pause.*)

CLOV. . . . He never spoke to me. Then, in the end, before he went, without my having asked him, he spoke to me. He said . . .

CLOV (*despairingly*). Ah. . . !

HAMM. Something . . . from your heart.

CLOV. My heart!

HAMM. A few words . . . from your heart.

(*Pause.*)

CLOV (*fixed gaze, tonelessly, towards auditorium*). They said to me, That's love, yes, yes, not a doubt, now you see how—

HAMM. Articulate!

CLOV (*as before*). How easy it is. They said to me, That's friendship, yes, yes, no question, you've found it. They said to me, Here's the place, stop, raise your head and look at all that beauty. That order! They said to me, Come now, you're not a brute beast, think upon these things and you'll see how all becomes clear. And simple! They said to me, What skilled attention they get, all these dying of their wounds.

HAMM. Enough!

CLOV (*as before*). I say to myself—sometimes, Clov, you must learn to suffer better than that if you want them to weary of punishing you—one day. I say to myself—sometimes, Clov, you must be there better than that if you want them to let you go—one day. But I feel too old, and too far, to form new habits. Good, it'll never end, I'll never go.

(*Pause.*)

Then one day, suddenly, it ends, it changes, I don't understand, it dies, or it's me, I don't understand, that either. I ask the words that remain—sleeping, waking, morning, evening. They have nothing to say.

(*Pause.*)

I open the door of the cell and go. I am so bowed I only see my feet, if I open my eyes, and between my legs a little trail of black dust. I say to myself that the earth is extinguished, though I never saw it lit.

(*Pause.*)

It's easy going.

(*Pause.*)

When I fall I'll weep for happiness.

(*Pause. He goes towards door.*)

HAMM. Clov!

(*Clove halts, without turning.*)

Nothing.

(*Clov moves on.*)

Clov!

(*Clov halts, without turning.*)

CLOV. This is what we call making an exit.

HAMM. I'm obliged to you, Clov. For your services.

CLOV (*turning, sharply*). Ah pardon, it's I am obliged to you.

HAMM. It's we are obliged to each other.

(*Pause. Clov goes towards door.*)

One thing more.
(*Clov halts.*)
A last favor.
(*Exit Clov.*)
Cover me with the sheet.
(*Long pause.*)
No? Good.
(*Pause.*)
Me to play.
(*Pause. Wearily.*)
Old endgame lost of old, play and lose and have done with losing.
(*Pause. More animated.*)
Let me see.
(*Pause.*)
Ah yes!
(*He tries to move the chair, using the gaff as before. Enter Clov, dressed for the road. Panama hat, tweed coat, raincoat over his arm, umbrella, bag. He halts by the door and stands there, impassive and motionless, his eyes fixed on Hamm, till the end. Hamm gives up.*)
Good.
(*Pause.*)
Discard.
(*He throws away the gaff, makes to throw away the dog, thinks better of it.*)
Take it easy.
(*Pause.*)
And now?
(*Pause.*)
Raise hat.
(*He raises his toque.*)
Peace to our . . . arses.
(*Pause.*)
And put on again.
(*He puts on his toque.*)
Deuce.
(*Pause. He takes off his glasses.*)
Wipe.
(*He takes out his handkerchief and, without unfolding it, wipes his glasses.*)
And put on again.
(*He puts on his glasses, puts back the handkerchief in his pocket.*)
We're coming. A few more squirms like that and I'll call.
(*Pause.*)
A little poetry.
(*Pause.*)
You prayed—
(*Pause. He corrects himself.*)
You CRIED for night; it comes—

(Pause. He corrects himself.)
It FALLS: now cry in darkness.
(He repeats, chanting.)
You cried for night; it falls: now cry in darkness.
(Pause.)
Nicely put, that.
(Pause.)
And now?
(Pause.)
Moments for nothing, now as always, time was never and time is over, reckoning closed and story ended.
(Pause. Narrative tone.)
If he could have his child with him. . . .
(Pause.)
It was the moment I was waiting for.
(Pause.)
You don't want to abandon him? You want him to bloom while you are withering? Be there to solace your last million last moments?
(Pause.)
He doesn't realize, all he knows is hunger, and cold, and death to crown it all. But you! You ought to know what the earth is like, nowadays. Oh I put him before his responsibilities!
(Pause. Normal tone.)
Well, there we are, there I am, that's enough.
(He raises the whistle to his lips, hesitates, drops it. Pause.)
Yes, truly!
(He whistles. Pause. Louder. Pause.)
Good.
(Pause.)
Father!
(Pause. Louder.)
Father!
(Pause.)
Good.
(Pause.)
We're coming.
(Pause.)
And to end up with?
(Pause.)
Discard.
(He throws away the dog. He tears the whistle from his neck.)
With my compliments.
(He throws whistle towards auditorium. Pause. He sniffs. Soft.)
Clov!
(Long pause.)
No? Good.
(He takes out the handkerchief.)

Since that's the way we're playing it . . .
(*he unfolds handkerchief*)
. . . let's play it that way . . .
(*he unfolds*)
. . . and speak no more about it . . .
(*he finishes unfolding*)
. . . speak no more.
(*He holds handkerchief spread out before him.*)
Old stancher!
(*Pause.*)
You . . . remain.
(*Pause. He covers his face with handkerchief, lowers his arms to armrests, remains motionless.*)
(*Brief tableau.*)

1958

CURTAIN

From Molloy

[*Overture: A and C*]

* * * People pass too, hard to distinguish from yourself. That is discouraging. So I saw A and C[1] going slowly towards each other, unconscious of what they were doing. It was on a road remarkably bare, I mean without hedges or ditches or any kind of edge, in the country, for cows were chewing in enormous fields, lying and stand- ing, in the evening silence. Perhaps I'm inventing a little, perhaps embellishing, but on the whole that's the way it was. They chew, swallow, then after a short pause effortlessly bring up the next mouthful. A neck muscle stirs and the jaws begin to grind again. But perhaps I'm remembering things. The road, hard and white, seared the tender pastures, rose and fell at the whim of hills and hollows. The town was not far. It was two men, unmistakably, one small and one tall. They had left the town, first one, then the other, and then the first, weary or remembering a duty, had retraced his steps. The air was sharp for they wore greatcoats. They looked alike, but no more than others do. At first a wide space lay between them. They couldn't have seen each other, even had they raised their heads and looked about, because of this wide space, and then because of the undulating land, which caused the road to be in waves, not high, but high enough, high enough. But the moment

---

1. In the French text, A and C are re- ferred to as A and B; Beckett may be playing with English puns on "being" and "seeing."

came when together they went down into the same trough and in this trough finally met. To say they knew each other, no, nothing warrants it. But perhaps at the sound of their steps, or warned by some obscure instinct, they raised their heads and observed each other, for a good fifteen paces, before they stopped, breast to breast. Yes, they did not pass each other by, but halted, face to face, as in the country, of an evening, on a deserted road, two wayfaring strangers will, without there being anything extraordinary about it. But they knew each other perhaps. Now in any case they do, now I think they will know each other, greet each other, even in the depths of the town. They turned towards the sea, which, far in the east, beyond the fields, loomed high[2] in the waning sky, and exchanged a few words. Then each went on his way. Each went on his way, A back towards the town, C on byways he seemed hardly to know, or not at all, for he went with uncertain step and often stopped to look about him, like someone trying to fix landmarks in his mind, for one day perhaps he may have to retrace his steps, you never know. The treacherous hills where fearfully he ventured were no doubt only known to him from afar, seen perhaps from his bed- room window or from the summit of a monument which, one black day, having nothing in particular to do and turning to height for solace, he had paid his few coppers to climb, slower and slower, up the winding stones. From there he must have seen it all, the plain, the sea, and then these self-same hills, that some call mountains, indigo in places in the evening light, their serried ranges crowding to the skyline, cloven with hidden valleys that the eye divines from sudden shifts of color and then from other signs for which there are no words, nor even thoughts. But all are not divined, even from that height, and often where only one escarpment is discerned, and one crest, in reality there are two, two escarpments, two crests, riven by a valley. But now he knows these hills, that is to say he knows them better, and if ever again he sees them from afar it will be I think with other eyes, and not only that but the within, all that inner space one never sees, the brain and heart and other caverns where thought and feeling dance their sabbath, all that too quite differently disposed. He looks old and it is a sorry sight to see him solitary after so many years, so many days and nights unthinkingly given to that rumor rising at birth and even earlier, What shall I do? What shall I do? now low, a murmur, now precise as the head- waiter's And to follow?[3] and often rising to a scream. And in the end, or almost, to be abroad alone, by unknown ways, in the gather-

---

2. That the sea looms high in the wan- ing sky may excite wonder, but the translation from French, where no puns are to be found, is literally accurate.

3. French waiters are more likely to ask "What will you have to drink with your meal?" and in the original of this pas- sage that's what is said: *"Et à boire?"*

ing night, with a stick. It was a stout stick, he used it to thrust himself onward, or as a defense, when the time came, against dogs and marauders. Yes, night was gathering, but the man was innocent, greatly innocent, he had nothing to fear, though he went in fear, he had nothing to fear, there was nothing they could do to him, or very little. But he can't have known it. I wouldn't know myself, if I thought about it. Yes, he saw himself threatened, his body threatened, his reason threatened, and perhaps he was, perhaps they were, in spite of his innocence. What business has innocence here? What relation to the innumerable spirits of darkness? It's not clear. It seemed to me he wore a cocked hat. I remember being struck by it, as I wouldn't have been for example by a cap or by a bowler.[4] I watched him recede, overtaken (myself) by his anxiety, at least by an anxiety which was not necessarily his, but of which as it were he partook. Who knows if it wasn't my own anxiety overtaking him. He hadn't seen me. I was perched higher than the road's highest point and flattened what is more against a rock the same color as myself, that is gray. The rock he probably saw. He gazed around as if to engrave the landmarks on his memory and must have seen the rock in the shadow of which I crouched like Belaqua, or Sordello,[5] I forget. But a man, a fortiori myself, isn't exactly a landmark, because I mean if by some strange chance he were to pass that way again, after a long lapse of time, vanquished, or to look for some lost thing, or to destroy something, his eyes would search out the rock, not the haphazard in its shadow of that unstable fugitive thing, still living flesh. No, he certainly didn't see me, for the reasons I've given and then because he was in no humor for that, that evening, no humor for the living, but rather for all that doesn't stir, or stirs so slowly that a child would scorn it, let alone an old man. However that may be, I mean whether he saw me or whether he didn't, I repeat I watched him recede, at grips (myself) with the temptation to get up and follow him, perhaps even to catch up with him one day, so as to know him better, be myself less lonely. But in spite of my soul's leap out to him, at the end of its elastic, I saw him only darkly, because of the dark and then because of the terrain, in the folds of which he disappeared from time to time, to reemerge further on, but most of all I think because of other things calling me and towards which too one after the other my soul was straining, wildly. I mean of course the fields, whitening under the dew, and the animals, ceasing from wandering and settling for the night, and the sea, of which nothing,[6] and the sharpening line of

---

4. Derby.
5. Belaqua and Sordello, rather different characters encountered by Dante on the slopes of Mount Purgatory (Cantos II and IV); Belaqua symbolizes spiritual sloth, a vice of which Beckett often ac-

cuses himself; Sordello was a visionary and prophetic poet. "a fortiori": particularly, especially.
6. The French is specific: "of which I will say nothing."

crests, and the sky where without seeing them I felt the first stars tremble, and my hand on my knee and above all the other wayfarer, A or C, I don't remember, going resignedly home. Yes, towards my hand also, which my knee felt tremble and of which my eyes saw the wrist only, the heavily veined back, the pallid rows of knuckles. But that is not, I mean my hand, what I wish to speak of now, everything in due course, but A or C returning to the town he had just left. But after all what was there particularly urban in his aspect? He was bare-headed, wore sand-shoes,[7] smoked a cigar. He moved with a kind of loitering indolence which rightly or wrongly seemed to me expressive. But all that proved nothing, refuted nothing. Perhaps he had come from afar, from the other end of the island even, and was approaching the town for the first time or returning to it after a long absence. A little dog followed him, a pomeranian I think, but I don't think so. I wasn't sure at the time and I'm still not sure, though I've hardly thought about it. The little dog followed wretchedly, after the fashion of pomeranians, stopping, turning in slow circles, giving up and then, a little further on, beginning all over again. Constipation is a sign of good health in pomeranians. At a given moment, pre-established if you like, I don't much mind, the gentleman turned back, took the little creature in his arms, drew the cigar from his lips and buried his face in the orange fleece, for it was a gentleman, that was obvious. Yes, it was an orange pomeranian, the less I think of it the more certain I am. And yet. But would he have come from afar, bare-headed, in sand-shoes, smoking a cigar, followed by a pomeranian? Did he not seem rather to have issued from the ramparts, after a good dinner, to take his dog and himself for a walk, like so many citizens, dreaming and farting, when the weather is fine? But was not perhaps in reality the cigar a cutty,[8] and were not the sand-shoes boots, hobnailed, dust-whitened, and what prevented the dog from being one of those stray dogs that you pick up and take in your arms, from compassion or because you have long been straying with no other company than the endless roads, sands, shingle, bogs and heather, than this nature answerable to another court, than at long intervals the fellow-convict you long to stop, embrace, suck, suckle and whom you pass by, with hostile eyes, for fear of his familiarities? Until the day when, your endurance gone, in this world for you without arms, you catch up in yours the first mangy cur you meet, carry it the time needed for it to love you and you it, then throw it away. Perhaps he had come to that, in spite of appearances. He disappeared, his head on his chest, the smoking object in his hand.
* * *

---

7. Espadrilles, rope-soled canvas shoes.
8. A *brule-gueule*, "burn-the-gob"; we might call it a stinker, or El Ropo.

[*Molloy and His Sucking-Stones*]

* * * I took advantage of being at the seaside to lay in a store of sucking-stones. They were pebbles but I call them stones. Yes, on this occasion I laid in a considerable store. I distributed them equally among my four pockets, and sucked them turn and turn about. This raised a problem which I first solved in the following way. I had say sixteen stones, four in each of my four pockets these being the two pockets of my trousers and the two pockets of my greatcoat. Taking a stone from the right pocket of my greatcoat, and putting it in my mouth, I replaced it in the right pocket of my greatcoat by a stone from the right pocket of my trousers, which I replaced by a stone from the left pocket of my trousers, which I replaced by a stone from the left pocket of my greatcoat, which I replaced by the stone which was in my mouth, as soon as I had finished sucking it. Thus there were still[9] four stones in each of my four pockets, but not quite the same stones. And when the desire to suck took hold of me again, I drew again on the right pocket of my greatcoat, certain of not taking the same stone as the last time. And while I sucked it I rearranged the other stones in the way I have just described. And so on. But this solution did not satisfy me fully. For it did not escape me that, by an extraordinary hazard, the four stones circulating thus might always be the same four. In which case, far from sucking the sixteen stones turn and turn about, I was really only sucking four, always the same, turn and turn about. But I shuffled them well in my pockets, before I began to suck, and again, while I sucked, before transferring them, in the hope of obtaining a more general circulation of the stones from pocket to pocket. But this was only a makeshift that could not long content a man like me. So I began to look for something else. And the first thing I hit upon was that I might do better to transfer the stones four by four, instead of one by one, that is to say, during the sucking, to take the three stones remaining in the right pocket of my greatcoat and replace them by the four in the right pocket of my trousers, and these by the four in the left pocket of my trousers, and these by the four in the left pocket of my greatcoat, and finally these by the three from the right pocket of my greatcoat, plus the one, as soon as I had finished sucking it, which was in my mouth. Yes, it seemed to me at first that by so doing I would arrive at a better result. But on further reflection I had to change my mind and confess that the circulation of the stones four by four came to exactly the same thing as their circulation one by one. For if I was certain of finding each time, in the right pocket of my greatcoat,

9. Always.

four stones totally different from their immediate predecessors, the possibility nevertheless remained of my always chancing on the same stone, within each group of four, and consequently of my sucking, not the sixteen turn and turn about as I wished, but in fact four only, always the same, turn and turn about. So I had to seek elsewhere than in the mode of circulation. For no matter how I caused the stones to circulate, I always ran the same risk. It was obvious that by increasing the number of my pockets I was bound to increase my chances of enjoying my stones in the way I planned, that is to say one after the other until their number was exhausted. Had I had eight pockets, for example, instead of the four I did have, then even the most diabolical hazard could not have prevented me from sucking at least eight of my sixteen stones, turn and turn about. The truth is I should have needed sixteen pockets in order to be quite easy in my mind. And for a long time I could see no other conclusion than this, that short of having sixteen pockets, each with its stone, I could never reach the goal I had set myself, short of an extraordinary hazard. And if at a pitch I could double the number of my pockets, were it only by dividing each pocket in two, with the help of a few safety-pins let us say, to quadruple them seemed to be more than I could manage. And I did not feel inclined to take all that trouble for a half-measure. For I was beginning to lose all sense of measure, after all this wrestling and wrangling, and to say, All or nothing. And if I was tempted for an instant to establish a more equitable proportion between my stones and my pockets, by reducing the former to the number of the latter, it was only for an instant. For it would have been an admission of defeat. And sitting on the shore, before the sea, the sixteen stones spread out before my eyes, I gazed at them in anger and perplexity. For just as I had difficulty in sitting on a chair, or in an arm-chair, because of my stiff leg you understand, so I had none in sitting on the ground, because of my stiff leg,[1] for it was about this time that my good leg, good in the sense that it was not stiff, began to stiffen. I needed a prop under the ham you understand, and even under the whole length of the leg, the prop of the earth. And while I gazed thus at my stones, revolving interminable martingales[2] all equally defective, and crushing handfuls of sand, so that the sand ran through my fingers and fell back on the strand, yes, while thus I lulled my mind and part of my body, one day suddenly it dawned on the former, dimly, that I might perhaps achieve my purpose without increasing the number of my pockets, or reducing the number of my stones, but simply by sacrificing the principle of

1. In the French, "stiff and stiffening leg."   2. A doubling of bets, in the hope of regaining what has already been lost.

trim. The meaning of this illumination, which suddenly began to sing within me, like a verse of Isaiah, or of Jeremiah,[3] I did not penetrate at once, and notably the word trim, which I had never met with, in this sense, long remained obscure. Finally I seemed to grasp that this word trim could not here mean anything else, anything better, than the distribution of the sixteen stones in four groups of four, one group in each pocket, and that it was my refusal to consider any distribution other than this that had vitiated my calculations until then and rendered the problem literally insoluble. And it was on the basis of this interpretation, whether right or wrong, that I finally reached a solution, inelegant assuredly, but sound, sound. Now I am willing to believe, indeed I firmly believe, that other solutions to this problem might have been found, and indeed may still be found, no less sound, but much more elegant, than the one I shall now describe, if I can. And I believe too that had I been a little more insistent, a little more resistant, I could have found them myself. But I was tired, but I was tired, and I contented myself ingloriously with the first solution that was a solution, to this problem. But not to go over the heartbreaking stages through which I passed before I came to it, here it is, in all its hideousness. All (all!) that was necessary was to put for example, to begin with, six stones in the right pocket of my greatcoat, or supply-pocket, five in the right pocket of my trousers, and five in the left pocket of my trousers, that makes the lot, twice five ten plus six sixteen, and none, for none remained, in the left pocket of my greatcoat, which for the time being remained empty, empty of stones that is, for its usual contents remained, as well as occasional objects. For where do you think I hid my vegetable knife, my silver, my horn and the other things that I have not yet named, perhaps shall never name? Good. Now I can begin to suck. Watch me closely. I take a stone from the right pocket of my greatcoat, suck it, stop sucking it, put it in the left pocket of my greatcoat, the one empty (of stones). I take a second stone from the right pocket of my greatcoat, suck it, put it in the left pocket of my greatcoat. And so on until the right pocket of my greatcoat is empty (apart from its usual and casual contents) and the six stones I have just sucked, one after the other, are all in the left pocket of my greatcoat. Pausing then, and concentrating, so as not to make a balls of it, I transfer to the right pocket of my greatcoat, in which there are no stones left, the five stones in the right pocket of my trousers, which I replace by the five stones in the left pocket of my trousers, which I replace by the six stones in the left pocket of my greatcoat. At this stage then the left pocket of my greatcoat is again empty of stones,

---

3. Notably gloomy but exalted prophets of the Old Testament.

while the right pocket of my greatcoat is again supplied, and in the right way, that is to say with other stones than those I have just sucked. These other stones I then begin to suck, one after the other, and to transfer as I go along to the left pocket of my greatcoat, being absolutely certain, as far as one can be in an affair of this kind, that I am not sucking the same stones as a moment before, but others. And when the right pocket of my greatcoat is again empty (of stones), and the five I have just sucked are all without exception in the left pocket of my greatcoat, then I proceed to the same redistribution as a moment before, or a similar redistribution, that is to say I transfer to the right pocket of my greatcoat, now again available, the five stones in the right pocket of my trousers, which I replace by the six stones in the left pocket of my trousers, which I replace by the five stones in the left pocket of my greatcoat. And there I am ready to begin again. Do I have to go on? No, for it is clear that after the next series, of sucks and transfers, I shall be back where I started, that is to say with the first six stones back in the supply-pocket, the next five in the right pocket of my stinking old trousers and finally the last five in left pocket of same, and my sixteen stones will have been sucked once at least in impeccable succession, not one sucked twice, not one left unsucked. It is true that the next time I could scarcely hope to suck my stones in the same order as the first time and that the first, seventh and twelfth for example of the first cycle might very well be the sixth, eleventh and sixteenth respectively of the second, if the worst came to the worst. But that was a drawback I could not avoid. And if in the cycles taken together utter confusion was bound to reign, at least within each cycle taken separately I could be easy in my mind, at least as easy as one can be, in a proceeding of this kind. For in order for each cycle to be identical, as to the succession of stones in my mouth, and God knows I had set my heart on it, the only means were numbered stones or sixteen pockets. And rather than make twelve more pockets or number my stones, I preferred to make the best of the comparative peace of mind I enjoyed within each cycle taken separately. For it was not enough to number the stones, but I would have had to remember, every time I put a stone in my mouth, the number I needed and look for it in my pocket. Which would have put me off stone for ever, in a very short time. For I would never have been sure of not making a mistake, unless of course I had kept a kind of register, in which to tick off the stones one by one, as I sucked them. And of this I believed myself incapable. No, the only perfect solution would have been the sixteen pockets, symmetrically disposed, each one with its stone. Then I would have needed neither to number nor to think, but merely, as I sucked a given stone, to move on the fifteen others, each to the next pocket, a delicate business admittedly, but within my power, and to call always on the same pocket when I felt like a suck. This would have freed me from all anxiety, not only within each cycle taken separately, but also for the sum of all cycles, though they went on forever. But however imperfect my own solution was, I was pleased at having found it all alone, yes, quite pleased. And if it was perhaps less sound than I had thought in the first flush of discovery, its inelegance never diminished. And it was above all inelegant in this, to my mind, that the uneven distribution was painful to me, bodily. It is true that a kind of equilibrium was reached, at a given moment, in the early stages of each cycle, namely after the third suck and before the fourth, but it did not last long, and the rest of the time I felt the weight of the stones dragging me now to one side, now to the other. So it was something more than a principle I abandoned, when I abandoned the equal distribution, it was a bodily need. But to suck the stones in the way I have described, not haphazard, but with method, was also I think a bodily need. Here then were two incompatible bodily needs, at loggerheads. Such things happen. But deep down I didn't give a tinker's curse about being off my balance, dragged to the right hand and the left, backwards and forwards. And deep down it was all the same to me whether I sucked a different stone each time or always the same stone, until the end of time. For they all tasted exactly the same. And if I had collected sixteen, it was not in order to ballast myself in such and such a way, or to suck them turn about, but simply to have a little store, so as never to be without. But deep down I didn't give a fiddler's curse about being without, when they were all gone they would be all gone, I wouldn't be any the worse off, or hardly any. And the solution to which I rallied in the end was to throw[4] away all the stones but one, which I kept now in one pocket, now in another, and which of course I soon lost, or threw away, or gave away, or swallowed. * * *

[Moran in Service]

It is midnight. The rain is beating on the windows. I am calm. All is sleeping. Nevertheless I get up and go to my desk. I can't sleep. My lamp sheds a soft and steady light. I have trimmed it. It will last till morning. I hear the eagle-owl. What a terrible battle-cry! Once I listened to it unmoved.[5] My son is sleeping. Let him sleep. The night will come when he too, unable to sleep, will get up and go to his desk. I shall be forgotten.

---

4. In the French, *foutre*, literally "screw off," but more forceful in its disgust than any English equivalent.

5. "Once," i.e., at the point when the story begins; it is being told after its completion.

My report will be long. Perhaps I shall not finish it. My name is Moran, Jacques. That is the name I am known by. I am done for. My son too. All unsuspecting. He must think he's on the threshold of life, of real life. He's right there. His name is Jacques, like mine. This cannot lead to confusion.

I remember the day I received the order to see about Molloy. It was a Sunday in summer. I was sitting in my little garden, in a wicker chair, a black book[6] closed on my knees. It must have been about eleven o'clock, still too early to go to church. I was savoring the day of rest, while deploring the importance attached to it, in certain parishes. To work, even to play on Sunday, was not of necessity reprehensible, in my opinion. It all depended on the state of mind of him who worked, or played, and on the nature of his work, of his play, in my opinion. I was reflecting with satisfaction on this, that this slightly libertarian view[7] was gaining ground, even among the clergy, more and more disposed to admit that the sabbath, so long as you go to mass and contribute to the collection, may be considered a day like any other, in certain respects. This did not affect me personally, I've always loved doing nothing. And I would gladly have rested on weekdays too, if I could have afforded it. Not that I was positively lazy. It was something else. Seeing something done which I could have done better myself, if I had wished, and which I did do better whenever I put my mind to it, I had the impression of discharging a function to which no form of activity could have exalted me. But this was a joy in which, during the week, I could seldom indulge.

The weather was fine. I watched absently the coming and going of my bees. I heard on the gravel the scampering steps of my son, caught up in I know not what fantasy of flight and pursuit. I called to him not to dirty himself. He did not answer.

All was still. Not a breath. From my neighbors' chimneys the smoke rose straight and blue. None but tranquil sounds, the clicking of mallet and ball, a rake of pebbles, a distant lawn-mower, the bell of my beloved church. And birds of course, blackbird and thrush, their song sadly dying, vanquished by the heat, and leaving dawn's high boughs for the bushes' gloom. Contentedly I inhaled the scent of my lemon-verbena.

In such surroundings slipped away my last moments of peace and happiness.

A man came into the garden and walked swiftly towards me. I knew him well. Now I have no insuperable objection to a neighbor's dropping in, on a Sunday to pay his respects, if he feels the

6. Allusively, the Bible.
7. Actually, Moran's "liberalism" about the exterior forms of worship seems to be a means of insisting with special rigor on the contents.

need, though I much prefer to see nobody. But this man was not a neighbor. Our dealings were strictly of a business nature and he had journeyed from afar, on purpose to disturb me. So I was disposed to receive him frostily enough, all the more so as he had the impertinence to come straight to where I was sitting, under my Beauty of Bath.[8] With people who took this liberty I had no patience. If they wished to speak to me they had only to ring at the door of my house. Martha had her instructions. I thought I was hidden from anybody coming into my grounds and following the short path which led from the garden-gate to the front door, and in fact I must have been. But at the noise of the gate being slammed I turned angrily and saw, blurred by the leaves, this high mass bearing down on me, across the lawn. I neither got up nor invited him to sit down. He stopped in front of me and we stared at each other in silence. He was dressed in his heavy, somber Sunday best, and at this my displeasure knew no bounds. This gross external observance, while the soul exults in its rags, has always appeared to me an abomination. I watched the enormous feet crushing my daisies. I would gladly have driven him away, with a knout.[9] Unfortunately it was not he who mattered. Sit down, I said, mollified by the reflection that after all he was only acting his part of go-between. Yes, suddenly I had pity on him, pity on myself. He sat down and mopped his forehead. I caught a glimpse of my son spying on us from behind a bush. My son was thirteen or fourteen at the time. He was big and strong for his age. His intelligence seemed at times little short of average. My son, in fact. I called him and ordered him to go and fetch some beer. Peeping and prying were part of my profession. My son imitated me instinctively. He returned after a remarkably short interval with two glasses and a quart bottle of beer. He uncorked the bottle and served us. He was very fond of uncorking bottles. I told him to go and wash himself, to straighten his clothes, in a word to get ready to appear in public, for it would soon be time for mass. He can stay, said Gaber.[1] I don't wish him to stay, I said. And turning to my son I told him again to go and get ready. If there was one thing displeased me, at that time, it was being late for the last mass. Please yourself, said Gaber. Jacques went away grumbling with his finger in his mouth, a detestable and unhygienic habit, but preferable all things considered to that of the finger in the nose, in my opinion. If putting his finger in his mouth prevented my son from putting it in his nose, or elsewhere, he was right to do it, in a sense.

Here are your instructions, said Gaber. He took a notebook from

---

8. In the French it is a simple *pommier*, "apple-tree." Martha, below, is Moran's cook: the family is without a mother or even the implication of one.
9. Whip.
1. I.e., Gabriel?

his pocket and began to read. Every now and then he closed the notebook, taking care to leave his finger as a marker, and indulged in comments and observations of which I had no need, for I knew my business. When at last he had finished I told him the job did not interest me and that the chief[2] would do better to call on another agent. He wants it to be you, God knows why, said Gaber. I presume he told you why, I said, scenting flattery for which I had a weakness. He said, replied Gaber, that no one could do it but you. This was more or less what I wanted to hear. And yet, I said, the affair seems childishly simple. Gaber began bitterly to inveigh against our employer, who had made him get up in the middle of the night, just as he was getting into position to make love to his wife. For this kind of nonsense, he added. And he said he had confidence in no one but me? I said. He doesn't know what he says, said Gaber. He added, Nor what he does. He wiped the lining of his bowler, peering inside as if in search of something. In that case it's hard for me to refuse, I said, knowing perfectly well that in any case it was impossible for me to refuse. Refuse! But we agents often amused ourselves with grumbling among ourselves and giving ourselves the airs of free men. You leave today, said Gaber. Today! I cried, but he's out of his mind! Your son goes with you, said Gaber. I said no more. Gaber buttoned his notebook and put it back in his pocket, which he also buttoned. He stood up, rubbing his hands over his chest. I could do with another beer, he said. Go to the kitchen, I said, the maid will serve you. Goodbye, Moran, he said.

It was too late for mass. I did not need to consult my watch to know, I could feel mass had begun without me. I who never missed mass, to have missed it on that Sunday of all Sundays! When I so needed it! To buck me up. I decided to ask for a private communion, in the course of the afternoon. I would go without lunch. Father Ambrose was always very kind and accommodating.

I called Jacques. Without result. I said, Seeing me still in conference he has gone to mass alone. This explanation turned out subsequently to be the correct one. But I added, He might have come and seen me, before leaving. I liked thinking in monologue and then my lips moved visibly. But no doubt he was afraid of disturbing me and of being reprimanded. For I was sometimes inclined to go too far when I reprimanded my son, who was consequently a little afraid of me. I myself had never been sufficiently chastened. Oh I had not been spoiled either, merely neglected. Whence bad habits ingrained beyond remedy and of which even the most meticulous piety has never been able to break me. I hoped to spare my

---

2. The chief, as we shall learn later, is named "Youdi," i.e., Jehovah or Ye-hudi, with overtones from "You die." / "God knows why" may thus have to be taken perfectly seriously.

son this misfortune, by giving him a good clout from time to time, together with my reasons for doing so. Then I said, Is he barefaced enough to tell me, on his return, that he has been to mass if he has not, if for example he has merely run off to join his little friends, behind the slaughterhouse? And I determined to get the truth out of Father Ambrose, on this subject. For it was imperative my son should not imagine he was capable of lying to me with impunity. And if Father Ambrose could not enlighten me, I would apply to the verger, whose vigilance it was inconceivable that the presence of my son at twelve o'clock mass had escaped. For I knew for a fact that the verger had a list of the faithful and that, from his place beside the font, he ticked us off when it came to the absolution. It is only fair to say that Father Ambrose knew nothing of these maneuvers, yes, anything in the nature of surveillance was hateful to the good Father Ambrose. And he would have sent the verger flying about his business if he had suspected him of such a work of supererogation. It must have been for his own edification that the verger kept this register, with such assiduity. Admittedly I knew only what went on at the last mass, having no experience personally of the other offices, for the good reason that I never went within a mile of them. But I had heard it said that they were the occasion of exactly the same supervision, at the hands either of the verger himself or, when his duties called him elsewhere, of one of his sons. A strange parish whose flock knew more than its pastor of a circumstance which seemed rather in his province than in theirs.

Such were my thoughts as I waited for my son to come back and Gaber, whom I had not yet heard leave, to go. And tonight I find it strange I could have thought of such things, I mean my son, my lack of breeding, Father Ambrose, Verger Joly with his register, at such a time. Had I not something better to do, after what I had just heard? The fact is I had not yet begun to take the matter seriously. And I am all the more surprised as such light-mindedness was not like me. Or was it in order to win a few more moments of peace that I instinctively avoided giving my mind to it? Even if, as set forth in Gaber's report, the affair had seemed unworthy of me, the chief's insistence on having me, me Moran, rather than anybody else, ought to have warned me that it was no ordinary one. And instead of bringing to bear upon it without delay all the resources of my mind and of my experience, I sat dreaming of my breed's infirmities and the singularities of those about me. And yet the poison was already acting on me, the poison I had just been given. I stirred restlessly in my armchair, ran my hands over my face, crossed and uncrossed my legs, and so on. The color and weight of the world were changing already, soon I would have to admit I was anxious.

I remembered with annoyance the lager I had just absorbed. Would I be granted the body of Christ after a pint of Wallenstein? And if I said nothing? Have you come fasting, my son? He would not ask. But God would know, sooner or later. Perhaps he would pardon me. But would the eucharist produce the same effect, taken on top of beer, however light? I could always try. What was the teaching of the Church on the matter? What if I were about to commit sacrilege? I decided to suck a few peppermints on the way to the presbytery.

I got up and went to the kitchen. I asked if Jacques was back. I haven't seen him, said Martha. She seemed in bad humor. And the man? I said. What man? she said. The man who came for a glass of beer, I said. No one came for anything, said Martha. By the way, I said, unperturbed apparently, I shall not eat lunch today. She asked if I were ill. For I was naturally a rather heavy eater. And my Sunday midday meal especially I always liked extremely copious. It smelt good in the kitchen. I shall lunch a little later today, that's all, I said. Martha looked at me furiously. Say four o'clock, I said. In that wizened, gray skull what raging and rampaging then, I knew. You will not go out today, I said coldly, I regret. She flung herself at her pots and pans, dumb with anger. You will keep all that hot for me, I said, as best you can. And knowing her capable of poisoning me I added, You can have the whole day off tomorrow, if that is any good to you.

I left her and went out on the road. So Gaber had gone without his beer. And yet he had wanted it badly. It was a good brand, Wallenstein. I stood there on the watch for Jacques. Coming from church he would appear on my right, on my left if he came from the slaughterhouse. A neighbor passed. A freethinker. Well well, he said, no worship today? He knew my habits, my Sunday habits I mean. Everyone knew them and the chief perhaps better than any, in spite of his remoteness. You look as if you had seen a ghost, said the neighbor. Worse than that, I said, you. I went in, at my back the dutifully hideous smile. I could see him running to his concubine with the news. You know that poor bastard Moran, you should have heard me, I had him leppin![3] Couldn't speak! Took to his heels!

Jacques came back soon afterwards. No trace of frolic. He said he had been to church alone. I asked him a few pertinent questions concerning the march[4] of the ceremony. His answers were plausible. I told him to wash his hands and sit down to his lunch. I went back to the kitchen. I did nothing but go to and fro. You may dish up, I said. She had wept. I peered into the pots. Irish stew. A nourishing

---

3. Jumping.   4. Form.

and economical dish, if a little indigestible. All honor to the land it has brought before the world. I shall sit down at four o'clock, I said. I did not need to add sharp. I liked punctuality, all those whom my roof sheltered had to like it too. I went up to my room. And there, stretched on my bed, the curtains drawn, I made my first attempt to grasp the Molloy affair.

[Two Encounters]

The day seemed very long. I missed my son! I busied myself as best I could. I ate several times. I took advantage of being alone at last, with no other witness than God, to masturbate. My son must have had the same idea, he must have stopped on the way to masturbate. I hope he enjoyed it more than I did. I circled the shelter several times, thinking the exercise would benefit my knee. I moved at quite a good speed and without much pain, but I soon tired. After ten or eleven steps a great weariness seized hold of my leg, a heaviness rather, and I had to stop. It went away at once and I was able to go on. I took a little morphine. I asked myself certain questions. Why had I not told my son to bring me back something for my leg? Why had I hidden my condition[5] from him? Was I secretly glad that this had happened to me, perhaps even to the point of not wanting to get well? I surrendered myself to the beauties of the scene, gazed at the trees, the fields, the sky, the birds, and I listened attentively to the sounds, faint and clear, borne to me on the air. For an instant I fancied I heard the silence mentioned, if I am not mistaken, above. Stretched out in the shelter, I brooded on the undertaking in which I was embarked. I tried again to remember what I was to do with Molloy, when I found him. I dragged myself down to the stream. I lay down and looked at my reflection, then I washed my face and hands. I waited for my image to come back, I watched it as it trembled towards an ever increasing likeness. Now and then a drop, falling from my face, shattered it again. I did not see a soul all day. But towards evening I heard a prowling about the shelter. I did not move, and the footsteps died away. But a little later, having left the shelter for some reason or other, I saw a man a few paces off, standing motionless. He had his back to me. He wore a coat much too heavy for the time of the year and was leaning on a stick so massive, and so much thicker at the bottom than at the top, that it seemed more like a club. He turned and we looked at each other for some time in silence. That is to say I looked him full in the face, as I always do, to make people think I am not afraid, whereas he merely threw me a rapid

5. More specifically in the French, "that I was sick."

glance from time to time, then lowered his eyes, less from timidity apparently than in order quietly to think over what he had just seen, before adding to it. There was a coldness in his stare, and a thrust, the like of which I never saw. His face was pale and noble, I could have done with it. I was thinking he could not be much over fifty-five when he took off his hat, held it for a moment in his hand, then put it back on his head. No resemblance to what is called raising one's hat. But I thought it advisable to nod. The hat was quite extraordinary, in shape and color. I shall not attempt to describe it, it was like none I had ever seen.[6] He had a huge shock of dirty snow-white hair. I had time, before he squeezed it in back under his hat, to see the way it swelled up on his skull. His face was dirty and hairy, yes, pale, noble,[7] dirty and hairy. He made a curious movement, like a hen that puffs up its feathers and slowly dwindles till it is smaller than before. I thought he was going to depart without a word to me. But suddenly he asked me to give him a piece of bread. He accompanied this humiliating request with a fiery look. His accent was that of a foreigner or of one who had lost the habit of speech. But had I not said already, with relief, at the mere sight of his back, He's a foreigner. Would you like a tin of sardines? I said. He asked for bread and I offered him fish. That is me all over. Bread, he said. I went into the shelter and took the piece of bread I was keeping for my son, who would probably be hungry when he came back. I gave it to him. I expected him to devour it there and then. But he broke it in two and put the pieces in his coat-pockets. Do you mind if I look at your stick, I said. I stretched out my hand. He did not move. I put my hand on the stick, just under his. I could feel his fingers gradually letting go. Now it was I who held the stick. Its lightness astounded me. I put it back in his hand. He threw me a last look and went. It was almost dark. He walked with swift uncertain step, often changing his course, dragging the stick like a hindrance. I wished I could have stood there looking after him, and time at a standstill. I wished I could have been in the middle of a desert, under the midday sun, to look after him till he was only a dot, on the edge of the horizon. I stayed out in the air for a long time. Every now and then I listened. But my son did not come. Beginning to feel cold I went back into the shelter and lay down, under my son's raincoat. But beginning to feel sleepy I went out again and lit a big wood-fire, to guide my son towards me. When the fire had kindled I said, Why of course, now I can warm myself! I warmed myself, rubbing my hands together after having held them to the flame and before holding them to it again, and

6. In French "Fitted into none of the categories I had ever known." Moran is losing his many logical but irrational rigidities.

7. French *beau* equals "beautiful," but is rightly translated here as "noble."

turning my back to the flame and lifting the tail of my coat, and turning as on a spit. And in the end, overcome with heat and weariness, I lay down on the ground near the fire and fell asleep, saying, Perhaps a spark will set fire to my clothes and I wake a living torch. And saying many other things besides, belonging to separate and apparently unconnected trains of thought. But when I woke it was day again and the fire was out. But the embers were still warm. My leg was no better, but it was no worse either. That is to say it was perhaps a little worse; without my being in a condition to realize it, for the simple reason that this leg was becoming a habit, mercifully. But I think not. For at the same time as I listened to my knee, and then submitted it to various tests, I was on my guard against the effects of this habit and tried to discount them. And it was not so much Moran as another, in the secret of Moran's sensations exclusively, who said, No change, Moran, no change. This may seem impossible. I went into the copse to cut myself a stick. But having finally found a suitable branch, I remembered I had no knife. I went back to the shelter, hoping to find my son's knife among the things he had laid on the ground and neglected to pick up. It was not among them. To make up for this I came across my umbrella and said, Why cut myself a stick when I have my umbrella? And I practiced walking with the help of my umbrella. And though in this way I moved no faster and no less painfully, at least I did not tire so quickly. And instead of having to stop every ten steps, to rest, I easily managed fifteen, before having to stop. And even while I rested my umbrella was a help. For I found that when I leaned upon it the heaviness in my leg, due probably to a defect in the bloodstream, disappeared even more quickly than when I stood supported only by my muscles and the tree of life. And thus equipped I no longer confined myself to circling about the shelter, as I had done the previous day, but I radiated from it in every direction. And I even gained a little knoll from which I had a better view of the expanse where my son might suddenly rise into view, at any moment. And in my mind's eye from time to time I saw him, bent over the handlebars or standing on the pedals, drawing near, and I heard him panting and saw written on the chubby face his joy at being back at last. But at the same time I kept my eye on the shelter, which drew me with an extraordinary pull, so that to cut across from the terminus of one sally[8] to the terminus of the next, and so on, which would have been convenient, was out of the question. But each time I had to retrace my steps, the way I had come, to the shelter, and make sure all was in order, before I sallied forth again.

---

8. Moran thinks of his shelter as the axle of a wheel, of his various "sallies" from that center as spokes; he cannot pass from the outer tip of one spoke to that of the next without returning to the center.

And I consumed the greater part of this second day in these vain comings and goings, these vigils and imaginings, but not all of it. For I also lay down from time to time in the shelter, which I was beginning to think of as my little house, to ruminate in peace on certain things and notably on my provisions of food which were rapidly running out, so that after a meal devoured at five o'clock I was left with only two tins of sardines, a handful of biscuits and a few apples. But I also tried to remember what I was to do with Molloy, once I had found him. And on myself too I pored, on me so changed from what I was. And I seemed to see myself aging as swiftly as a day-fly. But the idea of aging was not exactly the one which offered itself to me. And what I saw was more like a crumbling, a frenzied collapsing of all that had always protected me from all I was always condemned to be. Or it was like a kind of clawing towards a light and countenance I could not name, that I had once known and long denied. But what words can describe this sensation at first all darkness and bulk, with a noise like the grinding of stones, then suddenly as soft as water flowing. And then I saw a little globe swaying up slowly from the depths, through the quiet water, smooth at first, and scarcely paler than its escorting ripples, then little by little a face, with holes for the eyes and mouth and other wounds,[9] and nothing to show if it was a man's face or a woman's face, a young face or an old face, or if its calm too was not an effect of the water trembling between it and the light. But I confess I attended but absently to these poor figures, in which I suppose my sense of disaster sought to contain myself. And that I did not labor at them more diligently was a further index of the great changes I had suffered and of my growing resignation to being dispossessed of self.[1] And doubtless I should have gone from discovery to discovery, concerning myself, if I had persisted. But at the first faint light, I mean in these wild shadows gathering about me, dispensed by a vision or by an effort of thought, at the first light I fled to other cares. And all had been for nothing. And he who acted thus was a stranger to me too.[2] For it was not my nature, I mean it was not my custom, to conduct my calculations simultaneously, but separately and turn about, pushing each one as far as it would go before turning in desperation to another. Similarly the missing instructions concerning Molloy, when I felt them stirring in the depths of my memory, I turned from them in haste towards other unknowns. And I who a fortnight before would joyfully have reckoned how long I could survive on the provisions that remained, probably with reference to the question of calories and vitamins,

9. In French, "stigmates."
1. Literally, in the French, "it became indifferent to me to possess myself."

2. Literally, in the French, "And in this manner of behaving, I had trouble recognizing myself."

and established in my head a series of menus asymptotically[3] approaching nutritional zero, was now content to note feebly that I should soon be dead of inanition, if I did not succeed in renewing my provisions. So much for the second day. But one incident remains to be noted, before I go on to the third.

It was evening, I had lit my fire and was watching it take when I heard myself hailed. The voice, already so near that I started violently, was that of a man. But after this one violent start I collected myself and continued to busy myself with my fire as if nothing had happened, poking it with a branch I had torn from its tree for the purpose a little earlier and stripped of its twigs and leaves and even part of its bark, with my bare nails. I have always loved skinning branches and laying bare the pretty white glossy shaft of sapwood. But obscure feelings of love and pity for the tree held me back most of the time. And I numbered among my familiars the dragon-tree of Tenerife[4] that perished at the age of five thousand years, struck by lightning. It was an example of longevity. The branch was thick and full of sap and did not burn when I stuck it in the fire. I held it by the thin end. The crackling of the fire, of the writhing brands rather, for fire triumphant does not crackle, but makes an altogether different noise, had permitted the man to come right up to me, without my knowledge. If there is one thing infuriates me it is being taken myself by surprise. I continued then, in spite of my spasm of fright, hoping it had passed unnoticed, to poke the fire as if I were alone. But at the thump of his hand on my shoulder I had no choice but to do what anyone else would have done in my place, and this I achieved by suddenly spinning round in what I trust was a good imitation of fear and anger. There I was face to face with a dim man, dim of face and dim of body, because of the dark. Put it there,[5] he said. But little by little I formed an idea of the type of individual it was. And indeed there reigned between his various parts great harmony and concord, and it could be truly said that his face was worthy of his body, and vice versa. And if I could have seen his arse, I do not doubt I should have found it on a par with the whole. What are you doing in this God-forsaken place, he said, you unexpected pleasure. And moving aside from the fire which was now burning merrily, so that its light fell full on the intruder, I could see he was precisely the kind of pest I had thought he was, without being sure, because of the dark. Can you tell me, he said. I shall have to describe him briefly, though such a thing is contrary to

---

3. A line which continually approaches a curve, but will not meet it within a finite distance, is an asymptote.

4. A tree famous for its antiquity, on the mountain of Tenerife, in the Canary Islands.

5. In French, *Salut l'ami*, more closely

"Hi, pal." The entire conversation between Moran and the dim, familiar stranger consists of colloquial stereotypes, for which, in the different languages, only approximate equivalents can be found.

my principles. He was on the small side, but thick-set. He wore a thick navy-blue suit (double-breasted) of hideous cut and a pair of outrageously wide black shoes, with the toe-caps higher than the uppers. This dreadful shape seems only to occur in black shoes. Do you happen to know, he said. The fringed extremities of a dark muffler, seven feet long at least, wound several times round his neck, hung down his back. He had a narrow-brimmed dark blue felt hat on his head, with a fish-hook and an artificial fly stuck in the band, which produced a highly sporting effect. Do you hear me? he said. But all this was nothing compared to the face which I regret to say vaguely resembled my own, less the refinement of course, same little abortive moustache, same little ferrety eyes, same paraphimosis[6] of the nose, and a thin red mouth that looked as if it was raw from trying to shit its tongue. Hey you! he said. I turned back to my fire. It was doing nicely. I threw more wood on it. Do you hear me talking to you? he said. I went towards the shelter, he barred my way, emboldened by my limp. Have you a tongue in your head? he said. I don't know you, I said. I laughed. I had not intended to be witty. Would you care to see my card? he said. It would mean nothing to me, I said. He came closer to me. Get out of my way, I said. It was his turn to laugh. You refuse to answer? he said. I made a great effort. What do you want to know? I said. He must have thought I was weakening. That's more like it, he said. I called to my aid the image of my son who might arrive at any moment. I've already told you, he said. I was trembling all over. Have the goodness to tell me again, I said. To cut a long story short he wanted to know if I had seen an old man with a stick pass by. He described him. Badly. The voice seemed to come to me from afar. No, I said. What do you mean no? he said. I have seen no one. I said. And yet he passed this way, he said. I said nothing. How long have you been here? he said. His body too grew dim, as if coming asunder. What is your business here? he said. Are you on night patrol? I said. He thrust his hand at me. I have an idea I told him once again to get out of my way. I can still see the hand coming towards me, pallid, opening and closing. As if self-propelled. I do not know what happened then. But a little later, perhaps a long time later, I found him stretched on the ground, his head in a pulp. I am sorry I cannot indicate more clearly how this result was obtained, it would have been something worth reading. But it is not at this late stage of my relation that I intend to give way to literature. I myself was unscathed, except for a few scratches I did not discover till the following day. I bent over him. As I did so I realized my leg was bending normally.[7] He no

---

6. Permanent retraction of the foreskin.
7. A great many important things have been happening to Moran in the collapse of everything that had always protected

him from his new self; the unstiffening of his previously rigid leg seems to stand for many of them.

longer resembled me. I took him by the ankles and dragged him backwards into the shelter. * * *

[Moran Back from Service]

Now I may make an end.

I skirted the graveyard. It was night. Midnight perhaps. The lane is steep, I labored. A little wind was chasing the clouds over the faint sky. It is a great thing to own a plot in perpetuity,[8] a very great thing indeed. If only that were the only perpetuity. I came to the wicket. It was locked. Very properly. But I could not open it. The key went into the hole, but would not turn. Long disuse? A new lock? I burst it open. I drew back to the other side of the lane and hurled myself at it. I had come home, as Youdi had commanded me. In the end I got to my feet. What smelt so sweet? The lilacs? The primroses perhaps. I went towards my hives. They were there, as I feared. I lifted the top off one and laid it on the ground. It was a little roof, with a sharp ridge, and steep overhanging slopes. I put my hand in the hive, moved it among the empty trays, felt along the bottom. It encountered, in a corner, a dry light ball. It crumbled under my fingers. They had clustered together for a little warmth, to try and sleep. I took out a handful. It was too dark to see, I put it in my pocket. It weighed nothing. They had been left out all winter, their honey taken away, without sugar. Yes, now I may make an end. I did not go to the hen-house. My hens were dead too. I knew they were dead. They had not been killed in the same way, except the gray one perhaps, that was the only difference. My bees, my hens, I had deserted them. I went towards the house. It was in darkness. The door was locked. I burst it open. Perhaps I could have opened it, with one of my keys. I turned the switch. No light. I went to the kitchen, to Martha's room. No one. There is nothing more to tell. The house was empty. The company had cut off the light. They have offered to let me have it back. But I told them they could keep it. That is the kind of man I have become. I went back to the garden. The next day I looked at my handful of bees. A little dust of annulets and wings. I found some letters, at the foot of the stairs, in the box. A letter from Savory.[9] My son was well. He would be. Let us hear no more about him. He has come back. He is sleeping. A letter from Youdi, in the third person, asking for a report. He will get his report. It is summer again. This time a year ago I was setting out. I am clearing out.

---

8. In the British Isles, where land (including cemetery plots) is often held on leasehold, though with very long leases, to hold "in perpetuity" is more remarkable than it is in America.

9. Evidently a neighbor, but not previously mentioned.

One day I received a visit from Gaber. He wanted the report. That's funny, I thought I was done with people and talk. Call back, I said. One day I received a visit from Father Ambrose. Is it possible! he said when he saw me. I think he really liked me, in his own way. I told him not to count on me any more. He began to talk. He was right. Who is not right? I left him. I am clearing out. Perhaps I shall meet Molloy. My knee is no better. It is no worse either. I have crutches now. I shall go faster, all will go faster. They will be happy days. I shall learn. All there was to sell I have sold. But I had heavy debts. I have been a man long enough, I shall not put up with it any more, I shall not try any more. I shall never light this lamp again. I am going to blow it out and go into the garden. I think of the long May days, June days, when I lived in the garden. One day I talked to Hanna. She gave me news of Zulu, of the Elsner sisters.[1] She knew who I was, she was not afraid of me. She never went out, she disliked going out. She talked to me from her window. The news was bad, but might have been worse. There was a bright side. They were lovely days. The winter had been exceptionally rigorous, everybody said so. We had therefore a right to this superb summer. I do not know if we had a right to it. My birds had not been killed. They were wild birds. And yet quite trusting. I recognized them and they seemed to recognize me. But one never knows. Some were missing and some were new. I tried to understand their language better. Without having recourse to mine. They were the longest, loveliest days of all the year. I lived in the garden. I have spoken of a voice telling me things. I was getting to know it better now, to understand what it wanted. It did not use the words that Moran had been taught when he was little and that he in his turn had taught to his little one.[2] So that at first I did not know what it wanted. But in the end I understood this language. I understood it, I understood it, all wrong perhaps. That is not what matters. It told me to write the report. Does this mean I am freer now than I was? I do not know. I shall learn. Then I went back into the house and wrote, It is midnight. The rain is beating on the windows. It was not midnight. It was not raining.

1951, French; 1955, English

1. The Elsner sisters are neighbors, Hannah their servant, Zulu their dog.
2. In speaking of himself in the third person, Moran formalizes his separation of new self from old.

From The Unnamable

[*Into the Silence*]

* * * The silence, speak of the silence before going into it, was I
there already, I don't know, at every instant I'm there, listen to me
speaking of it, I knew it would come, I emerge from it to speak of
it, I stay in it to speak of it, if it's I who speak, and it's not, I act as
if it were, sometimes I act as if it were,[1] but at length, was I ever
there at length, a long stay, I understand nothing about duration, I
can't speak of it, oh I know I speak of it, I say never and ever, I
speak of the four seasons and the different parts of the day and
night, the night has no parts, that's because you are asleep, the seasons must be very similar, perhaps it's springtime now, that's all
words they taught me, without making their meaning clear to me,
that's how I learnt to reason, I use them all, all the words they
showed me, there were columns of them, oh the strange glow all of
a sudden, they were on lists, with images opposite, I must have forgotten them, I must have mixed them up, these nameless images I
have, these imageless names, these windows I should perhaps rather
call doors, at least by some other name, and this word man[2] which
is perhaps not the right one for the thing I see when I hear it, but
an instant, an hour, and so on, how can they be represented, a life,
how could that be made clear to me, here, in the dark, I call that
the dark, perhaps it's azure, blank words, but I use them, they keep
coming back, all those they showed me, all those I remember, I
need them all, to be able to go on, it's a lie, a score would be
plenty,[3] tried and trusty, unforgettable, nicely varied, that would be
palette enough, I'd mix them, I'd vary them, that would be gamut
enough, all the things I'd do if I could, if I wished, if I could wish,
no need to wish, that's how it will end, in heart-rending cries, inarticulate murmurs, to be invented, as I go along, improvised, as I
groan along, I'll laugh, that's how it will end, in a chuckle, chuck
chuck, ow, ha, pa, I'll practice, nyum, hoo, plop, psss, nothing but
emotion, bing bang, that's blows, ugh, pooh, what else, oooh, aaah,
that's love, enough, it's tiring, hee hee, that's the Abderite,[4] no, the
other, in the end, it's the end, the ending end, it's the silence, a few
gurgles on the silence, the real silence, not the one where I macer-

---

1. Literally in the French, "as if it were
I, as if it were I"; if the voice is not
"I," perhaps the silence from which it
arose and to which it will return may
be.
2. The problematic of "man," hung halfway between a curtain of silence and a
voice strangely independent of individual

volition, is the basic theme of the passage.
3. Literally, "twenty would suffice."
Beckett does indeed manage with remarkably few and plain words.
4. Democritus of Abdera, "the laughing
philosopher"; "the other" is therefore
Heraclitus of Ephesus, "the weeping philosopher."

ate up to the mouth, up to the ear, that covers me, uncovers me, breathes with me, like a cat with a mouse, that of the drowned, I've drowned more than once, it wasn't I, suffocated, set fire to me, thumped on my head with wood and iron,[5] it wasn't I, there was no head, no wood, no iron, I didn't do anything to me, I didn't do anything to anyone, no one did anything to me, there is no one, I've looked, no one but me, no, not me either, I've looked everywhere, there must be someone, the voice[6] must belong to someone, I've no objection, what it wants I want, I am it, I've said so, it says so, from time to time it says so, then it says not, I've no objection, I want it to go silent, it wants to go silent, it can't, it does for a second, then it starts again, that's not the real silence, it says that's not the real silence, what can be said of the real silence, I don't know, that I don't know what it is, that there is no such thing, that perhaps there is such a thing, yes, that perhaps there is, somewhere, I'll never know. But when it falters and when it stops, but it falters every instant, it stops every instant, yes, but when it stops for a good few moments, a good few moments, what are a good few moments, what then, murmurs, then it must be murmurs, and listening, someone listening, no need of an ear, no need of a mouth, the voice listens, as when it speaks, listens to its silence, that makes a murmur, that makes a voice, a small voice, the same voice only small, it sticks in the throat, there's the throat again, there's the mouth again, it fills the ear, there's the ear again, then I vomit, someone vomits, someone starts vomiting again, that must be how it happens, I have no explanations to offer, none to demand, the comma will come where I'll drown for good, then the silence, I believe it this evening, still this evening, how it drags on, I've no objection, perhaps it's springtime, violets, no, that's autumn, there's a time for everything, for the things that pass, the things that end, they could never get me to understand that, the things that stir, depart, return, a light changing, they could never get me to see that, and death into the bargain, a voice dying, that's a good one, silence at last, not a murmur, no air, no one listening, not for the likes of me, amen, on we go. Enormous prison, like a hundred thousand cathedrals, never anything else any more, from this time forth, and in it, somewhere, perhaps, riveted, tiny, the prisoner, how can he be found, how false this space is, what falseness instantly, to want to draw that round you, to want to put a being there, a cell

---

5. Running through *The Unnamable* is a recurrent covert identification of Beckett himself with a sign which hung over a tavern opposite his house in Paris. The tavern was called "Ali Baba," and the sign showed Ali Baba peeping over the edge of a barrel—a man immobilized in a cask or jar. This is a recurrent theme in Beckett.

6. The voice is perhaps the language, which wants to make use of the person's mouth to prolong speech and therefore a sort of consciousness—or consciousness and therefore a sort of speech.

2268 · *Samuel Beckett*

would be plenty, if I gave up, if only I could give up, before beginning, before beginning again, what breathlessness, that's right, ejac-
ulations, that helps you on, that puts off the fatal hour, no, the
reverse, I don't know, start again, in this immensity, this obscurity,
go through the motions of starting again, you who can't stir, you
who never started, you the who, go through the motions, what
motions, you can't stir, you launch your voice, it dies away in the
vault, it calls that a vault,[7] perhaps it's the abyss, those are words, it
speaks of a prison, I've no objection, vast enough for a whole
people, for me alone, or waiting for me, I'll go there now, I'll try
and go there now, I can't stir, I'm there already, I must be there
already, perhaps I'm not alone, perhaps a whole people is here, and
the voice its voice, coming to me fitfully, we would have lived, been
free a moment, now we talk about it, each one to himself, each one
out loud for himself, and we listen, a whole people, talking and listening, all together, that would ex,[8] no, I'm alone, perhaps the first,
or perhaps the last, talking alone, listening alone, alone alone, the
others are gone, they have been stilled, their voices stilled, their listening stilled, one by one, at each new-coming, another will come, I
won't be the last, I'll be with the others, I'll be as gone, in the
silence, it won't be I, it's not I, I'm not there yet, I'll go there now,
I'll try and go there now, no use trying, I wait for my turn, my turn
to go there, my turn to talk there, my turn to listen there, my turn
to wait there for my turn to go, to be as gone, it's unending, it will
be unending, gone where, where do you go from there, you must go
somewhere else, wait somewhere else, for your turn to go again, and
so on, a whole people, or I alone, and come back, and begin again,
no, go on, go on again, it's a circuit, a long circuit, I know it well, I
must know it well, it's a lie, I can't stir, I haven't stirred, I launch
the voice, I hear a voice, there is nowhere but here, there are not
two places, there are not two prisons, it's my parlor, it's a parlor,
where I wait for nothing, I don't know where it is, I don't know
what it's like, that's no business of mine, I don't know if it's big, or
if it's small, or if it's closed, or if it's open, that's right, reiterate,
that helps you on, open on what, there is nothing else, only it, open
on the void, open on the nothing, I've no objection, those are
words, open on the silence, looking out on the silence, straight out,
why not, all this time on the brink of silence, I knew it, on a rock,
lashed to a rock, in the midst of silence, its great swell rears towards
me, I'm streaming with it, it's an image, those are words, it's a
body, it's not I, I knew it wouldn't be I, I'm not outside, I'm
inside, I'm in something, I'm shut up, the silence is outside, out-

---

7. In the French, "perhaps it's the firmament, perhaps it's the abyss."
8. I.e., that would explain.

side, inside, there is nothing but here, and the silence outside, nothing but this voice and the silence all round, no need of walls, yes, we must have walls, I need walls, good and thick, I need a prison, I was right, for me alone, I'll go there now, I'll put me in it, I'm there already, I'll start looking for me now, I'm there somewhere, it won't be I, no matter, I'll say it's I, perhaps it will be I, perhaps that's all they're waiting for, there they are again, to give me quittance, waiting for me to say I'm someone, to say I'm somewhere, to put me out, into the silence, I see nothing, it's because there is nothing, or it's because I have no eyes, or both, that makes three possibilities, to choose from, but do I really see nothing, it's not the moment to tell a lie, but how can you not tell a lie, what an idea, a voice like this, who can check it, it tries everything, it's blind, it seeks me blindly, in the dark, it seeks a mouth, to enter into, who can query it, there is no other, you'd need a head, you'd need things, I don't know, I look too often as if I knew, it's the voice does that, it goes all knowing, to make me think I know, to make me think it's mine, it has no interest in eyes, it says I have none, or that they are no use to me, then it speaks of tears, then it speaks of gleams, it is truly at a loss, gleams, yes, far, or near, distances, you know, measurements, enough said, gleams, as at dawn, then dying, as at evening, or flaring up, they do that too, blaze up more dazzling than snow, for a second, that's short, then fizzle out, that's true enough, if you like, one forgets, I forget, I say I see nothing, or I say it's all in my head, as if I felt a head on me, that's all hypotheses, lies, these gleams too, they were to save me, they were to devour me, that came to nothing, I see nothing, either because of this or else on account of that, and these images at which they watered me, like a camel, before the desert, I don't know, more lies, just for the fun of it, fun, what fun we've had, what fun of it, all lies, that's soon said, you must say soon, it's the regulations. The place, I'll make it all the same, I'll make it in my head, I'll draw it out of my memory, I'll gather it all about me, I'll make myself a head, I'll make myself a memory, I have only to listen, the voice will tell me everything, tell it to me again, everything I need, in dribs and drabs, breathless, it's like a confession, a last confession, you think it's finished, then it starts off again, there were so many sins, the memory is so bad, the words don't come, the words fail, the breath fails, no it's something else, it's an indictment, a dying voice[9] accusing, accusing me, you must accuse someone, a culprit is indispensable, it speaks of my sins, it speaks of my head, it says it's mine, it says that I repent, that I want to be punished, better than

---

9. In the original, *une mourante*—a dying thing, a dying voice, a dying memory, a dying person.

I am, that I want to go, give myself up, a victim is essential, I have only to listen, it will show me my hiding place, what it's like, where the door is, if there's a door, and whereabouts I am in it, and what lies between us, how the land lies, what kind of country, whether it's sea, or whether it's mountain, and the way to take, so that I may go, make my escape, give myself up, come to the place where the axe falls, without further ceremony, on all who come from here, I'm not the first, I won't be the first, it will best me in the end, it has bested better than me, it will tell me what to do, in order to rise, move, act like a body endowed with despair, that's how I reason, that's how I hear myself reasoning, all lies, it's not me they're calling, not me they're talking about, it's not yet my turn, it's someone else's turn, that's why I can't stir, that's why I don't feel a body on me, I'm not suffering enough yet, it's not yet my turn, not suffering enough to be able to stir, to have a body, complete with head, to be able to understand, to have eyes to light the way, I merely hear, without understanding, without being able to profit by it, by what I hear, to do what, to rise and go and be done with hearing, I don't hear everything, that must be it, the important things escape me, it's not my turn, the topographical and anatomical information in particular is lost on me, no, I hear everything, what difference does it make, the moment it's not my turn, my turn to understand, my turn to live, my turn of the lifescrew, it calls that living, the space of the way from here to the door, it's all there, in what I hear, somewhere, if all has been said, all this long time, all must have been said, but it's not my turn to know what, to know what I am, where I am, and what I should do to stop being it, to stop being there, that's coherent, so as to be another, no, the same, I don't know, depart into life, travel the road, find the door, find the axe, perhaps it's a cord, for the neck, for the throat, for the cords, or fingers, I'll have eyes, I'll see fingers, it will be the silence, perhaps it's a drop, find the door, open the door, drop, into the silence, it won't be I, I'll stay here, or there, more likely there, it will never be I, that's all I know, it's all been done already, said and said again, the departure, the body that rises, the way, in color, the arrival, the door that opens, closes again, it was never I, I've never stirred, I've listened, I must have spoken, why deny it, why not admit it, after all, I deny nothing, I admit nothing, I say what I hear, I hear what I say, I don't know, one or the other, or both, that makes three possibilities, pick your fancy, all these stories about travelers, these stories about paralytics, all are mine, I must be extremely old, or it's memory playing tricks, if only I knew if I've lived, if I live, if I'll live, that would simplify everything, impossible to find out, that's where you're buggered, I haven't stirred, that's all I know, no, I know something else, it's not I, I always forget that,

I resume, you must resume, never stirred from here, never stopped telling stories, to myself, hardly hearing them, hearing something else, listening for something else, wondering now and then where I got them from, was I in the land of the living, were they in mine, and where, where do I store them, in my head, I don't feel a head on me, and what do I tell them with, with my mouth, same remark, and what do I hear them with, and so on, the old rigmarole, it can't be I, or it's because I pay no heed, it's such an old habit, I do it without heeding, or as if I were somewhere else, there I am far again, there I am the absentee again, it's his turn again now, he who neither speaks nor listens, who has neither body nor soul, it's something else he has, he must have something, he must be somewhere, he is made of silence, there's a pretty analysis, he's in the silence, he's the one to be sought, the one to be, the one to be spoken of, the one to speak, but he can't speak, then I could stop, I'd be he, I'd be the silence, I'd be back in the silence, we'd be reunited, his story the story to be told, but he has no story, he hasn't been in story, it's not certain, he's in his own story, unimaginable, unspeakable, that doesn't matter, the attempt must be made, in the old stories incomprehensibly mine, to find his, it must be there somewhere, it must have been mine, before being his, I'll recognize it, in the end I'll recognize it, the story of the silence that he never left, that I should never have left, that I may never find again, that I may find again, then it will be he, it will be I, it will be the place, the silence, the end, the beginning, the beginning again, how can I say it, that's all words, they're all I have, and not many of them, the words fail, the voice fails, so be it, I know that well, it will be the silence, full of murmurs, distant cries, the usual silence, spent listening, spent waiting, waiting for the voice, the cries abate, like all cries, that is to say they stop, the murmurs cease, they give up, the voice begins again, it begins trying again, quick now before there is none left, no voice left, nothing left but the core of murmurs, distant cries, quick now and try again, with the words that remain, try what, I don't know, I've forgotten, it doesn't matter, I never knew, to have them carry me into my story, the words that remain, my old story, which I've forgotten, far from here, through the noise, through the door, into the silence, that must be it, it's too late, perhaps it's too late, perhaps they have, how would I know, in the silence you don't know, perhaps it's the door, perhaps I'm at the door, that would surprise me, perhaps it's I, perhaps somewhere or other it was I, I can depart, all this time I've journeyed without knowing it, it's I now at the door, what door, what's a door doing here, it's the last words, the true last, or it's the murmurs, the murmurs are coming, I know that well, no, not even that, you talk of murmurs, distant cries, as long as you can talk, you talk of them before and you talk of them after, more lies, it will be the silence, the one that doesn't last, spent listening, spent waiting, for it to be broken, for the voice to break it, perhaps there's no other, I don't know, it's not worth having, that's all I know, it's not I, that's all I know, it's not mine, it's the only one I ever had, that's a lie, I must have had the other, the one that lasts, but it didn't last, I don't understand, that is to say it did, it still lasts, I'm still in it, I left myself behind in it, I'm waiting for me there, no, there you don't wait, you don't listen, I don't know, perhaps it's a dream, all a dream, that would surprise me, I'll wake, in the silence, and never sleep again, it will be I, or dream, dream again, dream of a silence, a dream silence, full of murmurs, I don't know, that's all words, never wake, all words, there's nothing else, you must go on, that's all I know, they're going to stop, I know that well, I can feel it, they're going to abandon me, it will be the silence, for a moment, a good few moments, or it will be mine, the lasting one, that didn't last, that still lasts, it will be I, you must go on, I can't go on, you must go on, I'll go on, you must say words, as long as there are any, until they find me, until they say me, strange pain, strange sin, you must go on, perhaps it's done already, perhaps they have said me already, perhaps they have carried me to the threshold of my story, before the door that opens on my story, that would surprise me, if it opens, it will be I, it will be the silence, where I am, I don't know, I'll never know, in the silence you don't know, you must go on, I can't go on, I'll go on.

1953, French; 1958, English

Distinctive Voices in Poetry and Fiction

A. E. HOUSMAN
(1859–1936)

Alfred Edward Housman was born in Fockbury, Worcestershire (close to the Shropshire border). After attending school at the nearby town of Bromsgrove he proceeded to Oxford where he studied classics and philosophy and in 1881 shocked his friends and teachers by failing his final examinations (he was at the time in a state of psychological turmoil resulting from his suppressed homosexual love for a fellow student). He obtained a civil service job and pursued his classical studies alone, gradually building up a reputation as a great textual critic of Latin literature by his contributions to learned periodicals. In 1892 he was appointed to the Chair of Latin at University College, London, and from 1911 until his death he was professor of Latin at Cambridge.

It was characteristic of Housman that his classical studies consisted of meticulous, impersonal textual investigations; there was something reserved and solitary about his life as there was about his scholarship, in which he allowed no trace of his feeling for literature to appear. That feeling nevertheless ran strong and deep, and in his lecture *The Name and Nature of Poetry* (1933) he expressed the view that poetry cannot be explained or analyzed, but is recognized by its almost physical effects on the reader as he reads. His own poetry was limited both in quantity and in range. Two "slim volumes"—*A Shropshire Lad* (1896) and *Last Poems* (1922) —were all that appeared during his lifetime, and after his death his brother Laurence Housman, playwright and poet, brought out another small book of *More Poems* (1936), on the whole inferior in quality to the first two.

Housman's writings on classical subjects consisted of articles and reviews marked by bitterly sarcastic exposure of the work of inferior editors punctuated by gloomy remarks about life. He was a very great textual critic of Latin poetry, but his remarks on the folly and incompetence of other textual critics go far beyond anything normally expected of superior scholarship talking of inferior. "If a man will comprehend the richness and variety of the universe, and inspire his mind with a due measure of wonder and of awe, he must contemplate the human intellect not only on its heights of genius but in its abysses of ineptitude. * * * Elias Stoeber['s] reprint * * * saw the light in 1767 at Strasburg, a city still famous for its geese. * * * Stoeber's mind, though that is no name to call it by, was one which turned as unswervingly to the false, the meaningless, the unmetrical, and the ungrammatical, as the needle to the pole" (Preface to *Manilius*, 1903).

Housman's aim as a poet was not to expand or develop the resources of English poetry but by limitation and concentration to achieve an utterance both compact and moving. He was influenced by Greek and Latin lyric poetry, by the traditional ballad, and by the lyrics of the early 19th-century German poet Heinrich Heine. His favorite theme is that of the doomed youth acting out the tragedy of his brief life in a context of agricultural activity and against a specific English background containing visual reminders of man's long history there. Nature is beautiful but indifferent and is to be enjoyed while we are still able to enjoy it. Love, friendship, and conviviality cannot last and may well result in betrayal or death, but are likewise to be relished while there is time. The wryly ironic tone sometimes degenerates into melodrama, and the stoicism seems at time histrionic, but at his best Housman's control of cadence enabled him to sound the note of resigned wisdom with quiet poignancy. Housman avoids self-pity by projecting the emotion through an imagined character, notably the "Shropshire lad," so that even the first-person poems seem to be distanced in some degree. At the same time the poems are distinguished sharply from the "gather ye rosebuds" tradition by the undertones of fatalism and even of doom.

Loveliest of Trees

Loveliest of trees, the cherry now
Is hung with bloom along the bough,
And stands about the woodland ride
Wearing white for Eastertide.

Now, of my threescore years and ten,   5
Twenty will not come again,
And take from seventy springs a score,
It only leaves me fifty more.

And since to look at things in bloom
Fifty springs are little room,   10
About the woodlands I will go
To see the cherry hung with snow.

1896

When I Was One-and-Twenty

When I was one-and-twenty
   I heard a wise man say,
"Give crowns and pounds and guineas
   But not your heart away;
Give pearls away and rubies   5
   But keep your fancy free."
But I was one-and-twenty,
   No use to talk to me.

When I was one-and-twenty
   I heard him say again,   10

"The heart out of the bosom
Was never given in vain;
And with sighs a plenty
And for endless rue."

...and-twenty,
..., 'tis true.   15

1896

...Athlet... Young

The time you won your town...
We chaired you through the mark...
...and boy stood cheering by,
Today the ... runners come,
Shoulder-high we bring you shoulder-high.
And set you at your threshold down,
Townsman of a stiller town.

Smart lad, to slip betimes away
From fields where glory does not stay
And early though the laurel grows
It withers quicker than the rose.   5

Eyes the shady night has shut
Cannot see the record cut,
And silence sounds no worse than cheers
After earth has stopped the ears: 10

Now you will not swell the rout
Of lads that wore their honors out,
Runners whom renown outran   15
Now hold to the low-lintelled head
The still-defended ... curls
...strengthless dead   25

1896

Bredon[1] Hill

In summertime on Bredon
The bells they sound so clear;

1896

1. "Pronounced Breedon" [Housman's note]. The hill is in Worcestershire, adjacent to Shropshire.

Round both the shires they ring them
  In steeples far and near,
  A happy noise to hear.   5

Here of a Sunday morning
  My love and I would lie,
And see the colored coun...   15
  And hear the larks...
  About us in the...

The bells would ... good people;
  In valley... come and pray."   20
  "Come... my love would stay.
...ower,
...nd I would turn and...
  Among the springing thyme,
"O, peal upon our wed... chime,
  And come to church in time."

But when the snows at Christmas   25
  On Bredon top were strown,
My love rose up so early
  And stole out unbeknown
  And went to church alone.

They tolled the one bell only,   30
  Groom there was none to see,
The mourners followed after,
  And so to church went she,
  And would not wait for me.

The bells they sound on Bredon,
  And still the church, good people"—
"Come all to church, good people"—
  ...
  I hear you, I will come.

'Tis spring; the hilly brakes[1]... ally
  The hilly bra... ily
For under thorn and groun...
  About the hollow groun... found.
  The primroses are found.

And there's the windflower[2] chilly
  With all the winds at play,

1. Clumps of bushes.

2. Anemone.

Round both the shires they ring them
  In steeples far and near,
  A happy noise to hear.   5

Here of a Sunday morning
  My love and I would lie,
And see the colored counties,
  And hear the larks so high
  About us in the sky.   10

The bells would ring to call her
  In valleys miles away:
"Come all to church, good people;
  Good people, come and pray."
  But here my love would stay.   15

And I would turn and answer
  Among the springing thyme,
"O, peal upon our wedding,
  And we will hear the chime,
  And come to church in time."   20

But when the snows at Christmas
  On Bredon top were strown,
My love rose up so early
  And stole out unbeknown
  And went to church alone.   25

They tolled the one bell only,
  Groom there was none to see,
The mourners followed after,
  And so to church went she,
  And would not wait for me.   30

The bells they sound on Bredon,
  And still the steeples hum,
"Come all to church, good people"—
  Oh, noisy bells, be dumb;
  I hear you, I will come.   35

1896

The Lent Lily

'Tis spring; come out to ramble
  The hilly brakes[1] around,
For under thorn and bramble
  About the hollow ground
  The primroses are found.   5

And there's the windflower[2] chilly
  With all the winds at play,

---

1. Clumps of bushes.   2. Anemone.

"The heart out of the bosom
    Was never given in vain;
'Tis paid with sighs a plenty
    And sold for endless rue."
And I am two-and-twenty,   15
    And oh, 'tis true, 'tis true.

                                 1896

To an Athlete Dying Young

The time you won your town the race
We chaired you through the market place;
Man and boy stood cheering by,
And home we brought you shoulder-high.

Today, the road all runners come,   5
Shoulder-high we bring you home,
And set you at your threshold down,
Townsman of a stiller town.

Smart lad, to slip betimes away
From fields where glory does not stay
And early though the laurel grows   10
It withers quicker than the rose.

Eyes the shady night has shut
Cannot see the record cut,
And silence sounds no worse than cheers   15
After earth has stopped the ears:

Now you will not swell the rout
Of lads that wore their honors out,
Runners whom renown outran
And the name died before the man.   20

So set, before its echoes fade,
The fleet foot on the sill of shade,
And hold to the low lintel up
The still defended challenge cup.

And round that early laureled head   25
Will flock to gaze the strengthless dead
And find unwithered on its curls
The garland briefer than a girl's.

                                 1896

Bredon[1] Hill

In summertime on Bredon
    The bells they sound so clear;

---

1. "Pronounced Breedon" [Housman's note]. The hill is in Worcestershire, adjacent to Shropshire.

And there's the Lenten lily
   That has not long to stay
And dies on Easter day.   10

And since till girls go maying
   You find the primrose still,
And find the windflower playing
   With every wind at will,
   But not the daffodil,   15

Bring baskets now, and sally
   Upon the spring's array,
And bear from hill and valley
   The daffodil away
   That dies on Easter day.   20

1896

On Wenlock Edge[3]

On Wenlock Edge the wood's in trouble;
   His forest fleece the Wrekin[4] heaves;
The gale, it plies the saplings double,
   And thick on Severn[5] snow the leaves.

'Twould blow like this through holt[6] and hanger   5
   When Uricon[7] the city stood:
'Tis the old wind in the old anger,
   But then it threshed another wood.

Then, 'twas before my time, the Roman
   At yonder heaving hill would stare: 10
The blood that warms an English yeoman,
   The thoughts that hurt him, they were there.

There, like the wind through woods in riot,
   Through him the gale of life blew high;
The tree of man was never quiet: 15
   Then 'twas the Roman, now 'tis I.

The gale, it plies the saplings double,
   It blows so hard, 'twill soon be gone:
Today the Roman and his trouble
   Are ashes under Uricon.   20

1896

3. A sharp ridge, twenty miles long, in southeastern Shropshire.
4. A sugar-loaf hill at the northeast end of the Caradoc Hills in Shropshire.
5. The Severn River flows through Shropshire past the Wrekin into Wales.
6. Wooded hill; "hanger": wood on the side of a steep hill.
7. The Roman city of Uriconium (whose site is near Shrewsbury, the county seat of Shropshire).

With Rue My Heart Is Laden

With rue my heart is laden
    For golden friends I had,
For many a rose-lipped maiden
    And many a lightfoot lad.

By brooks too broad for leaping   5
    The lightfoot boys are laid;
The rose-lipped girls are sleeping
    In fields where roses fade.

1896

Terence,[1] This Is Stupid Stuff

"Terence, this is stupid stuff:
You eat your victuals fast enough;
There can't be much amiss, 'tis clear,
To see the rate you drink your beer.
But oh, good Lord, the verse you make,   5
It gives a chap the bellyache.
The cow, the old cow, she is dead;
It sleeps well, the hornéd head:
We poor lads, 'tis our turn now
To hear such tunes as killed the cow.   10
Pretty friendship 'tis to rhyme
Your friends to death before their time
Moping melancholy mad:
Come, pipe a tune to dance to, lad."

    Why, if 'tis dancing you would be,   15
There's brisker pipes than poetry.
Say, for what were hopyards meant,
Or why was Burton built on Trent?[2]
Oh many a peer of England brews
Livelier liquor than the Muse,   20
And malt does more than Milton can
To justify God's ways to man.
Ale, man, ale's the stuff to drink
For fellows whom it hurts to think:
Look into the pewter pot   25
To see the world as the world's not.
And faith, 'tis pleasant till 'tis past:

1. *The Poems of Terence Hearsay* was Housman's intended title for *The Shropshire Lad.*
2. Burton-on-Trent is the most famous of all English brewing towns; "many a peer" refers to the "beer barons," brewery magnates raised to the peerage.

The mischief is that 'twill not last.
Oh I have been to Ludlow[3] fair
And left my necktie God knows where,   30
And carried halfway home, or near,
Pints and quarts of Ludlow beer:
Then the world seemed none so bad,
And I myself a sterling lad;
And down in lovely muck I've lain,   35
Happy till I woke again.
Then I saw the morning sky.
Heigho, the tale was all a lie;
The world, it was the old world yet,
I was I, my things were wet,   40
And nothing now remained to do
But begin the game anew.

Therefore, since the world has still
Much good, but much less good than ill,
And while the sun and moon endure   45
Luck's a chance, but trouble's sure,
I'd face it as a wise man would,
And train for ill and not for good.
'Tis true the stuff I bring for sale
Is not so brisk a brew as ale: 50
Out of a stem that scored[4] the hand
I wrung it in a weary land.
But take it: if the smack is sour,
The better for the embittered hour;
It should do good to heart and head   55
When your soul is in my soul's stead;
And I will friend you, if I may,
In the dark and cloudy day.

There was a king reigned in the East:
There, when kings will sit to feast,   60
They get their fill before they think
With poisoned meat and poisoned drink.
He gathered all that springs to birth
From the many-venomed earth;
First a little, thence to more,   65
He sampled all her killing store;
And easy, smiling, seasoned sound,
Sate the king when healths went round.
They put arsenic in his meat
And stared aghast to watch him eat;   70
They poured strychnine in his cup
And shook to see him drink it up:
They shook, they stared as white's their shirt.
Them it was their poison hurt.

3. A market town in Shropshire.   4. Cut.

—I tell the tale that I heard told.
Mithridates, he died old.[5]   75

1896

The Chestnut Casts His Flambeaux[1]

The chestnut casts his flambeaux, and the flowers
    Stream from the hawthorn on the wind away,
The doors clap to, the pane is blind with showers.
    Pass me the can, lad; there's an end of May.

There's one spoilt spring to scant our mortal lot,   5
    One season ruined of our little store.
May will be fine next year as like as not:
    Oh ay, but then we shall be twenty-four.

We for a certainty are not the first
    Have sat in taverns while the tempest hurled   10
Their hopeful plans to emptiness, and cursed
    Whatever brute and blackguard made the world.

It is in truth iniquity on high
    To cheat our sentenced souls of aught they crave,
And mar the merriment as you and I   15
    Fare on our long fool's-errand to the grave.

Iniquity it is; but pass the can.
    My lad, no pair of kings our mothers bore;
Our only portion is the estate of man:
    We want the moon, but we shall get no more.   20

If here today the cloud of thunder lours
    Tomorrow it will hie on far behests;
The flesh will grieve on other bones than ours
    Soon, and the soul will mourn in other breasts.

The troubles of our proud and angry dust   25
    Are from eternity, and shall not fail.
Bear them we can, and if we can we must.
    Shoulder the sky, my lad, and drink your ale.

1922

Could Man Be Drunk Forever

Could man be drunk forever
    With liquor, love, or fights,

---

5. The story of Mithridates, king of
Pontus, who made himself immune to
poison by taking small doses daily, is
told in Pliny's *Natural History*.

1. Literally, torches. Housman is here
referring to the erect flower-clusters
(white, dashed with red and yellow)
of the horse-chestnut tree.

Lief should I rouse at morning
And lief lie down of nights.

But men at whiles are sober   5
And think by fits and starts,
And if they think, they fasten
Their hands upon their hearts.

1896   1922

Epitaph on an Army of Mercenaries

These, in the day when heaven was falling,
    The hour when earth's foundations fled,
Followed their mercenary calling
    And took their wages and are dead.

Their shoulders held the sky suspended;   5
    They stood, and earth's foundations stay;
What God abandoned, these defended,
    And saved the sum of things for pay.

1922

RUDYARD KIPLING
(1865–1936)

Kipling was born in Bombay, India; his father was the curator of the
Lahore Museum and a well-known illustrator. He went to school in Eng-
land, and returned to India as a journalist in 1882, coming back again to
England in 1889 to achieve rapid fame as a poet and short-story writer.
He married an American in 1892 and lived in Vermont until driven out
in 1897 by a violent quarrel with his brother-in-law; he spent the rest of
his life in England. He was the first Englishman to receive the Nobel
Prize for Literature (1907).

Kipling's poetry owed much to the strong rhythms of the Methodist
hymns he heard in his childhood. He had a real gift for communal poetic
utterance, creating what might be called a public emotion by swinging
movement carefully varied in accordance with the demands of the particular theme. He is often thought of as the poet of British imperialism,
but in fact he looked at the British Empire from the point of view of the
ordinary "tommy" (private soldier) doing his duty in a distant outpost
without any awareness of the policies or problems which determined it,
and thus gave a new vividness and reality to the subject. This approach,
together with his rhythmic skill, won an immediate audience for his *Bar-
rack-Room Ballads* (1890, 1892). At the same time he was gaining a
reputation as a gifted story-teller whose tales of military life in India again

stressed the unconscious heroism of the "tommy" and explored some of the psychological and moral problems of a white community living in the midst of a subject people. Gradually Kipling built up a code of honor and duty which combined something from the English public school, something from the English code of fair play in sport, something from biological notions of the survival of the fittest, and something from the idea of "the white man's burden." *Plain Tales from the Hills* (1888) are stories of India; later he extended his scope and wrote a great variety of stories and novels in which he applied his ethical code to many different kinds of modern societies and situations. At his best, his stories possess vividness, strength, and real narrative cunning; at his worst, the code becomes intrusive and (to modern minds) offensive. The two *Jungle Books* (1894, 1895) apply the code with real brilliance to the animals of the Indian jungle; *Captains Courageous* (1897) applies it to life at sea and the education, through such a life, of a spoiled millionaire's son. *Stalky and Co.* (1899), which draws on his own schooldays, applies the code to boys' boarding-school life, and *Puck of Pook's Hill* (1906) applies it with unusual subtlety and a fine historical imagination to Roman and Anglo-Saxon Britain. *Kim* (1901), set in India, transcends the bounds of the normal Kipling formula. It presents the interrelations of two vocations, the active and imperialist (British) and the contemplative and religious (Indian); each is treated with equal sympathy, and the result is the most complex of Kipling's novels and his masterpiece.

Kipling's poetry is far removed from the poetry of the modern movement associated with the name of T. S. Eliot. His vigorous rhythms, relatively simple moral and psychological diagnosis, and simplicity of verbal texture account for the natural reaction against him in the 1920's and 1930's. It is true that some of his verse is both jingling and jingoist; but much, too, shows a power to handle elemental themes, such as loyalty or endurance or loss or fear, with remarkable power. He is now recognized as a considerable craftsman in verse; a selection of his poetry has, in fact, been edited by Eliot himself.

Danny Deever

"What are the bugles blowin' for?" said Files-on-Parade.[1]
"To turn you out, to turn you out," the Color-Sergeant said.
"What makes you look so white, so white?" said Files-on-Parade.
"I'm dreadin' what I've got to watch," the Color-Sergeant said.
    For they're hangin' Danny Deever, you can hear the Dead
       March play,   5
    The regiment's in 'ollow square—they're hangin' him today;
    They've taken of his buttons off an' cut his stripes away,
    An they're hangin' Danny Deever in the mornin'.

"What makes the rear rank breathe so 'ard?" said Files-on-Parade.
"It's bitter cold, it's bitter cold," the Color-Sergeant said.   10
"What makes that front-rank man fall down?" said Files-on-Parade.

1. Private soldier.

"A touch o' sun, a touch o' sun," the Color-Sergeant said.
  They are hangin' Danny Deever, they are marchin' of 'im round,
  They 'ave 'alted Danny Deever by 'is coffin on the ground;
  An' 'e'll swing in 'arf a minute for a sneakin' shootin' hound— 15
  O they're hangin' Danny Deever in the mornin'!

" 'Is cot was right-'and cot to mine," said Files-on-Parade.
" 'E's sleepin' out an' far tonight," the Color-Sergeant said.
"I've drunk 'is beer a score o' times," said Files-on-Parade.
" 'E's drinkin' bitter beer[2] alone," the Color-Sergeant said. 20
  They are hangin' Danny Deever, you must mark 'im to 'is place,
  For 'e shot a comrade sleepin'—you must look 'im in the face;
  Nine 'undred of 'is county an' the Regiment's disgrace,
  While they're hangin' Danny Deever in the mornin'.

"What's that so black agin the sun?" said Files-on-Parade. 25
"It's Danny fightin' 'ard for life," the Color-Sergeant said.
"What's that that whimpers over'ead?" said Files-on-Parade.
"It's Danny's soul that's passin' now," the Color-Sergeant said.
  For they're done with Danny Deever, you can 'ear the quickstep
    play,
  The regiment's in column, an' they're marchin' us away; 30
  Ho! the young recruits are shakin', an' they'll want their beer
    today,
  After hangin' Danny Deever in the mornin'.

1890

Recessional[3]

1897

God of our fathers, known of old—
  Lord of our far-flung battle-line—
Beneath whose awful Hand we hold
  Dominion over palm and pine—
Lord God of Hosts, be with us yet 5
Lest we forget—lest we forget!

The tumult and the shouting dies—
  The Captains and the Kings depart—
Still stands Thine ancient Sacrifice,
  An humble and a contrite heart.[4] 10

2. "Bitter beer" or simply "bitter" is one of the favorite varieties of draught beer drunk in English pubs; the word "bitter" thus becomes a grim pun.
3. A hymn for Queen Victoria's Diamond Jubilee, first published near the close of the celebrations. It has a simple gravity of utterance appropriate to such an occasion, and in reversing the coin of imperial self-congratulation strikes a note peculiarly fitting in a "recessional" (technically a hymn sung at the end of a church service, as the clergy and choir leave the church in procession).
4. "The sacrifices of God are a broken spirit: a broken and a contrite heart, O God, thou wilt not despise" (Psalms li.17).

Lord God of Hosts, be with us yet,
  Lest we forget—lest we forget!

Far-called, our navies melt away—
  On dune and headland sinks the fire—
Lo, all our pomp of yesterday 15
  Is one with Nineveh and Tyre![5]
Judge of the Nations, spare us yet,
  Lest we forget—lest we forget!

If, drunk with sight of power, we loose
  Wild tongues that have not Thee in awe— 20
Such boasting as the Gentiles use
  Or lesser breeds without the Law[6]—
Lord God of Hosts, be with us yet,
  Lest we forget—lest we forget!

For heathen heart that puts her trust 25
  In reeking tube and iron shard—
All valiant dust that builds on dust,
  And guarding calls not Thee to guard—
For frantic boast and foolish word,
  Thy mercy on Thy People, Lord! 30

1897   1897, 1899

Edgehill Fight[1]

(CIVIL WARS, 1642)

Naked and gray the Cotswolds[2] stand
  Beneath the summer sun,
And the stubble fields on either hand
  Where Stour and Avon[3] run.
There is no change in the patient land 5
  That has bred us every one.

She should have passed in cloud and fire
  And saved us from this sin
Of war—red war—'twixt child and sire,
  Household and kith and kin, 10
In the heart of a sleepy Midland shire,
  With the harvest scarcely in.

5. Once-great cities of Assyria and Phoenicia, respectively; Nineveh is now buried in the desert; Tyre is a small Lebanese town.

6. "For when the Gentiles, which have not the law, do by nature the things contained in the law, these, having not the law, are a law unto themselves" (Romans ii.14).

1. Edgehill was the first battle in the English Civil War, between the Royalists under Charles I and the Parliamentarians under the Earl of Essex. The result was indecisive. Edgehill itself is a ridge in the western English county of Warwickshire.

2. The Cotswold Hills lie south of Edgehill, in Gloucestershire.

3. Rivers that flow through this part of England (Shakespeare's Stratford is on the Avon).

But there is no change as we meet at last
  On the brow-head or the plain,
And the raw astonished ranks stand fast   15
  To slay or to be slain
By the men they knew in the kindly past
  That shall never come again—

By the men they met at dance or chase,
  In the tavern or the hall,   20
At the justice bench and the market place,
  At the cudgel play or brawl—
Of their own blood and speech and race,
  Comrades or neighbors all!

More bitter than death this day must prove   25
  Whichever way it go,
For the brothers of the maids we love
  Make ready to lay low
Their sisters' sweethearts, as we move
  Against our dearest foe.   30

Thank Heaven! At last the trumpets peal
  Before our strength gives way.
For King or for the Commonweal—
  No matter which they say,
The first dry rattle of new-drawn steel   35
  Changes the world today!

                                        1903

The Runes on Weland's Sword[1]

A Smith makes me
To betray my Man
In my first fight.

To gather Gold
At the world's end   5
I am sent.

The Gold I gather
Comes into England
Out of deep Water.

Like a shining Fish   10
Then it descends
Into deep Water.

1. This poem appears in *Puck of Pook's Hill* (1906), a collection of tales about adventures into England's past. Weland, once blacksmith to the old English gods, forges a magic sword for Hugh of Dallington, protagonist of the stories; the runes, or magic songs, prophesy an adventure in quest of African gold.

It is not given
For goods or gear,
But for The Thing.   15

The Gold I gather
A King covets
For an ill use.

The Gold I gather
Is drawn up   20
Out of deep Water.

Like a shining Fish
Then it descends
Into deep Water.

It is not given   25
For goods or gear,
But for the Thing.

1906

RUPERT BROOKE
(1887–1915)

Rupert Brooke was educated at Rugby School and at King's College, Cambridge. Thereafter he traveled extensively in Europe, America, Canada, and the South Seas, writing poems and essays. In 1914, when World War I broke out, he saw service in Belgium; the next year he was dead of a fever on the Greek island of Skyros.

Brooke is often, and with considerable justice, taken as representative of the golden world of liberal culture immediately before World War I. His early death was symbolic of the death of a whole generation of dedicated English youth—brilliant and beautiful youth as they seemed in retrospect, for Brooke was noted for his physical beauty as well as for his talents. The irony of his poem *Heaven* is much more genial and contentedly civilized than anything in Eliot, while *The Soldier*, traditional both in its sonnet form and its idealistic patriotic mood, represents the last significant expression of an attitude that could not survive the horrors of trench warfare. The war poets who followed Brooke expressed extreme bitterness and showed a much more savage irony, manifesting the disillusion, the sense of a whole world of values having disappeared, that influenced every aspect of serious English literature in the immediate postwar period.

Brooke is the one poet represented here to whom the term "Georgian" can be applied without qualification. George V succeeded Edward VII in 1910 and "Georgian" refers to the early years of his reign, up to the 1914–18 World War. This term was first used of poets when Edward Marsh brought out in 1912 the first of a series of volumes, *Georgian Poetry*. For the most part, the poets represented in these anthologies were not interested in major changes in poetic technique and attitude; their subject matter was often the English countryside or else the exotic and the magical; their craftsmanship was on the whole traditional; their mood tended to be quietly meditative. Yet, though essentially conservative in his poetic tastes, Marsh was reasonably catholic in his choices: some of D. H. Lawrence's poems appeared first in *Georgian Poetry* (though Lawrence called Marsh a "bit of a policeman in poetry"). Brooke, however, was more at home in Marsh's poetic environment. Both the poems printed below first appeared in *Georgian Poetry 1913–15* (1915).

Heaven

Fish (fly-replete, in depth of June,
Dawdling away their wat'ry noon)
Ponder deep wisdom, dark or clear,
Each secret fishy hope or fear.
Fish say, they have their Stream and Pond;   5
But is there anything Beyond?
This life cannot be All, they swear,
For how unpleasant, if it were!
One may not doubt that, somehow, Good
Shall come of Water and of Mud;   10
And, sure, the reverent eye must see
A Purpose in Liquidity.
We darkly know, by Faith we cry,
The future is not Wholly Dry.
Mud unto mud!—Death eddies near—   15
Not here the appointed End, not here!
But somewhere, beyond Space and Time,
Is wetter water, slimier slime!
And there (they trust) there swimmeth One
Who swam ere rivers were begun,   20
Immense, of fishy form and mind,
Squamous,[1] omnipotent, and kind;
And under that Almighty Fin,
The littlest fish may enter in.
Oh! never fly conceals a hook,   25
Fish say, in the Eternal Brook,
But more than mundane weeds are there,
And mud, celestially fair;

___

1. Scaly.

Fat caterpillars drift around,
And Paradisal grubs are found;   30
Unfading moths, immortal flies,
And the worm that never dies.
And in that Heaven of all their wish,
There shall be no more land, say fish.

1913   1915

The Soldier²

If I should die, think only this of me,
    That there's some corner of a foreign field
That is forever England. There shall be
    In that rich earth a richer dust concealed,
A dust whom England bore, shaped, made aware,   5
    Gave, once, her flowers to love, her ways to roam,
A body of England's, breathing English air,
    Washed by the rivers, blest by suns of home.

And think, this heart, all evil shed away,
    A pulse in the Eternal mind, no less   10
    Gives somewhere back the thoughts by England given,
Her sights and sounds; dreams happy as her day;
    And laughter, learnt of friends; and gentleness,
    In hearts at peace, under an English heaven.

1914   1915

2. The text given here follows Brooke's MS. in the British Museum.

EDWARD THOMAS
(1878–1917)

Edward Thomas was one of many English poets whose lives were cut short by World War I. He began his literary career as a writer for the *Manchester Guardian*, but turned to serious poetry under the influence of his close friend Robert Frost, with whose work his poems have some affinity. He was able to bring out two books of poems (1916, 1917) before his death in France. *Last Poems* was published posthumously in 1918.

Thomas's poetry manages to distill an extraordinary intensity of meaning and atmosphere out of quite ordinary experiences by a quiet precision of imagery, a careful placing of words and phrases where they will take on an intriguing light from their context, and a combination of simplicity of surface meaning with an echoing suggestiveness. Thomas is one "Georgian" poet who, while never moving beyond the accepted limits of Georgian poetry in either subject or technique, enjoys a reputation today as a minor poet of distinction.

Tears

It seems I have no tears left. They should have fallen—
Their ghosts, if tears have ghosts, did fall—that day
When twenty hounds streamed by me, not yet combed out
But still all equals in their rage of gladness
Upon the scent, made one, like a great dragon   5
In Blooming Meadow that bends towards the sun
And once bore hops: and on that other day
When I stepped out from the double-shadowed Tower
Into an April morning, stirring and sweet
And warm. Strange solitude was there and silence.   10
A mightier charm than any in the Tower
Possessed the courtyard. They were changing guard,
Soldiers in line, young English countrymen,
Fair-haired and ruddy, in white tunics. Drums
And fifes were playing "The British Grenadiers."   15
The men, the music piercing that solitude
And silence, told me truths I had not dreamed,
And have forgotten since their beauty passed.

                                                       1917

The Owl

Downhill I came, hungry, and yet not starved;
Cold, yet had heat within me that was proof
Against the north wind; tired, yet so that rest
Had seemed the sweetest thing under a roof.

Then at the inn I had food, fire, and rest,   5
Knowing how hungry, cold, and tired was I.
All of the night was quite barred out except
An owl's cry, a most melancholy cry

Shaken out long and clear upon the hill,
No merry note, nor cause of merriment,   10
But one telling me plain what I escaped
And others could not, that night, as in I went.

And salted was my food, and my repose,
Salted and sobered, too, by the bird's voice
Speaking for all who lay under the stars,   15
Soldiers and poor, unable to rejoice.

                                                       1917

The Path

Running along a bank, a parapet
That saves from the precipitous wood below

The level road, there is a path. It serves
Children for looking down the long smooth steep,
Between the legs of beech and yew, to where   5
A fallen tree checks the sight: while men and women
Content themselves with the road and what they see
Over the bank, and what the children tell.
The path, winding like silver, trickles on,
Bordered and even invaded by thinnest moss   10
That tries to cover roots and crumbling chalk
With gold, olive, and emerald, but in vain.
The children wear it. They have flattened the bank
On top, and silvered it between the moss
With the current of their feet, year after year.   15
But the road is houseless, and leads not to school.
To see a child is rare there, and the eye
Has but the road, the wood that overhangs
And underyawns it, and the path that looks
As if it led on to some legendary   20
Or fancied place where men have wished to go
And stay; till, sudden, it ends where the wood ends.

1917

Adlestrop[1]

Yes. I remember Adlestrop—
The name, because one afternoon
Of heat the express train drew up there
Unwontedly. It was late June.
The steam hissed. Someone cleared his throat.   5
No one left and no one came
On the bare platform. What I saw
Was Adlestrop—only the name.

And willows, willow herb, and grass,
And meadowsweet, and haycocks dry,   10
No whit less still and lonely fair
Than the high cloudlets in the sky.

And for that minute a blackbird sang
Close by, and round him, mistier,
Farther and farther, all the birds   15
Of Oxfordshire and Gloucestershire.

1917

The Gallows

There was a weasel lived in the sun
With all his family,
Till a keeper shot him with his gun
And hung him up on a tree,

1. A small town in Gloucestershire.

Where he swings in the wind and rain,　　　　5
In the sun and in the snow,
Without pleasure, without pain,
On the dead oak tree bough.

There was a crow who was no sleeper,
But a thief and a murderer　　　　　　　　10
Till a very late hour; and this keeper
Made him one of the things that were,
To hang and flap in rain and wind,
In the sun and in the snow.
There are no more sins to be sinned　　　　15
On the dead oak tree bough.

There was a magpie, too,
Had a long tongue and a long tail;
He could both talk and do—
But what did that avail?　　　　　　　　20
He, too, flaps in the wind and rain
Alongside weasel and crow,
Without pleasure, without pain,
On the dead oak tree bough.

And many other beasts　　　　　　　　　25
And birds, skin, bone, and feather,
Have been taken from their feasts
And hung up there together,
To swing and have endless leisure
In the sun and in the snow,　　　　　　　30
Without pain, without pleasure,
On the dead oak tree bough.

　　　　　　　　　　　　　　　　1917

Ambition

Unless it was that day I never knew
Ambition. After a night of frost, before
The March sun brightened and the Southwest blew,
Jackdaws began to shout and float and soar
Already, and one was racing straight and high　　5
Alone, shouting like a black warrior
Challenges and menaces to the wide sky.
With loud long laughter then a woodpecker
Ridiculed the sadness of the owl's last cry.
And through the valley where all the folk astir　　10
Made only plumes of pearly smoke to tower
Over dark trees and white meadows happier
Than was Elysium in that happy hour,
A train that roared along raised after it

And carried with it a motionless white bower 15
Of purest cloud, from end to end close-knit,
So fair it touched the roar with silence. Time
Was powerless while that lasted. I could sit
And think I had made the loveliness of prime,
Breathed its life into it and were its lord, 20
And no mind lived save this 'twixt clouds and rime.[1]
Omnipotent I was, nor even deplored
That I did nothing. But the end fell like a bell:
The bower was scattered; far off the train roared.
But if this was ambition I cannot tell. 25
What 'twas ambition for I know not well.

1918

1. Hoarfrost.

WILFRED OWEN
(1893–1918)

Wilfred Owen was the most brilliantly promising of all the English poets who were killed in World War I. In his early poems he had experimented with new varieties of Keatsian sensuousness, but, under the influence of his war experiences, he matured rapidly and remarkably. His powerful and concentrated poems transcend bitterness to evoke what he called "the pity of war" and to suggest the human waste and confusions involved in modern warfare.

Owen was also concerned to expand the resources of English poetic expression, but in a different way from Eliot and those influenced by Eliot. His "pararhymes"—imperfect or half rhymes—and his flexible stanza forms show him adapting rather than abandoning traditional techniques, while his attitude, combining irony, compassion, and a sense of personal involvement in all human suffering, differs from characteristic Victorian poetic attitudes without showing the studied objectivity of the early Eliot. Had he lived, English poetry would almost certainly have been less dependent upon the Eliot school; indeed, there might have developed an alternative and equally valuable new tradition in postwar English poetry.

Owen's poems were collected and published posthumously (1920) by his friend Siegfried Sassoon.

Greater Love

Red lips are not so red
    As the stained stones kissed by the English dead.
Kindness of wooed and wooer
Seems shame to their love pure.
O Love, your eyes lose lure 5
    When I behold eyes blinded in my stead!

Your slender attitude
  Trembles not exquisite like limbs knife skewed,
Rolling and rolling there
Where God seems not to care; 10
Till the fierce love they bear
  Cramps them in death's extreme decrepitude.

Your voice sings not so soft—
  Though even as wind murmuring through raftered loft—
Your dear voice is not dear, 15
Gentle, and evening clear,
As theirs whom none now hear,
  Now earth has stopped their piteous mouths that coughed.

Heart, you were never hot
  Nor large, nor full like hearts made great with shot; 20
And though your hand be pale,
Paler are all which trail
Your cross through flame and hail:
  Weep, you may weep, for you may touch them not.

1920

Futility

     Move him into the sun—
     Gently its touch awoke him once,
     At home, whispering of fields unsown.
     Always it woke him, even in France,
     Until this morning and this snow.
     If anything might rouse him now 5
     The kind old sun will know.

     Think how it wakes the seeds—
     Woke, once, the clays of a cold star.
     Are limbs, so dear-achieved, are sides,
     Full-nerved—still warm—too hard to stir? 10
     Was it for this the clay grew tall?
     —O what made fatuous sunbeams toil
     To break earth's sleep at all?

1920

Sonnet

On Seeing a Piece of Our Artillery Brought Into Action

  Be slowly lifted up, thou long black arm,
  Great gun towering towards Heaven, about to curse;
  Sway steep against them, and for years rehearse
  Huge imprecations like a blasting charm!
  Reach at that Arrogance which needs thy harm, 5
  And beat it down before its sins grow worse;

Spend our resentment, cannon—yea, disburse
Our gold in shapes of flame, our breaths in storm.

Yet, for men's sakes whom thy vast malison [1]   10
Must wither innocent of enmity,
Be not withdrawn, dark arm, thy spoilure done,
Safe to the bosom of our prosperity.
But when thy spell be cast complete and whole,
May God curse thee, and cut thee from our soul!   15

1920

Anthem for Doomed Youth

What passing-bells for these who die as cattle?
Only the monstrous anger of the guns.
Only the stuttering rifles' rapid rattle
Can patter out their hasty orisons.
No mockeries for them from prayers or bells,   5
Nor any voice of mourning save the choirs—
The shrill, demented choirs of wailing shells;
And bugles calling for them from sad shires.

What candles may be held to speed them all?
Not in the hands of boys, but in their eyes   10
Shall shine the holy glimmers of good-byes.
The pallor of girls' brows shall be their pall;
Their flowers the tenderness of patient minds,
And each slow dusk a drawing-down of blinds.

1920

Apologia Pro Poemate Meo[2]

I, too, saw God through mud—
    The mud that cracked on cheeks when wretches smiled.
    War brought more glory to their eyes than blood,
    And gave their laughs more glee than shakes a child.

Merry it was to laugh there—   5
    Where death becomes absurd and life absurder.
    For power was on us as we slashed bones bare
    Not to feel sickness or remorse of murder.

I, too, have dropped off fear—
    Behind the barrage, dead as my platoon,   10
    And sailed my spirit surging light and clear
    Past the entanglement where hopes lay strewn;

1. Curse, malediction.   2. "Apology for My Poem."

And witnessed exultation—
  Faces that used to curse me, scowl for scowl,
  Shine and lift up with passion of oblation,
  Seraphic for an hour; though they were foul.   15

I have made fellowships—
  Untold of happy lovers in old song.
  For love is not the binding of fair lips
  With the soft silk of eyes that look and long,   20

By Joy, whose ribbon slips,
  But wound with war's hard wire whose stakes are strong;
  Bound with the bandage of the arm that drips;
  Knit in the webbing of the rifle thong.

I have perceived much beauty   25
  In the hoarse oaths that kept our courage straight;
  Heard music in the silentness of duty;
  Found peace where shell-storms spouted reddest spate.

Nevertheless, except you share
  With them in hell the sorrowful dark of hell,
  Whose world is but the trembling of a flare,   30
  And heaven but as the highway for a shell,

You shall not hear their mirth:
  You shall not come to think them well content
  By any jest of mine. These men are worth
  Your tears. You are not worth their merriment.   35

November, 1917   1920

Strange Meeting[1]

It seemed that out of battle I escaped
Down some profound dull tunnel, long since scooped
Through granites which titanic wars had groined.
Yet also there encumbered sleepers groaned,
Too fast in thought or death to be bestirred.   5
Then, as I probed them, one sprang up, and stared
With piteous recognition in fixed eyes,
Lifting distressful hands as if to bless.
And by his smile, I knew that sullen hall;
By his dead smile I knew we stood in Hell.   10

---

1. This poem, one of the last that Owen wrote, is unfinished. It shows his use of "pararhyme" (e.g., "groined," "groaned"; "hall," "Hell"), one of his technical experiments which have influenced later poets. The poem is "peculiarly a poem of the Western Front; it is a dream only a stage further on than the actuality of the tunneled dugouts with their muffled security, their smoky dimness, their rows of soldiers painfully sleeping, their officers and sergeants and corporals attempting to awaken those for duty, and the sense presently of 'going up' the ugly stairway to do someone in the uglier mud above a good turn. Out of these and similar materials Owen's transforming spirit has readily created his wonderful phantasma" (Edmund Blunden).

With a thousand pains that vision's face was grained;
Yet no blood reached there from the upper ground,
And no guns thumped, or down the flues made moan.
"Strange friend," I said, "here is no cause to mourn."
"None," said the other, "save the undone years,   15
The hopelessness. Whatever hope is yours,
Was my life also; I went hunting wild
After the wildest beauty in the world,
Which lies not calm in eyes, or braided hair,
But mocks the steady running of the hour,   20
And if it grieves, grieves richlier than here.
For by my glee might many men have laughed,
And of my weeping something had been left,
Which must die now. I mean the truth untold,
The pity of war, the pity war distilled.   25
Now men will go content with what we spoiled,
Or, discontent, boil bloody, and be spilled.
They will be swift with swiftness of the tigress,
None will break ranks, though nations trek from progress.
Courage was mine, and I had mystery,   30
Wisdom was mine, and I had mastery;
To miss the march of this retreating world
Into vain citadels that are not walled.
Then when much blood had clogged their chariot wheels
I would go up and wash them from sweet wells,   35
Even with truths that lie too deep for taint.
I would have poured my spirit without stint
But not through wounds; not on the cess[2] of war.
Foreheads of men have bled where no wounds were.
I am the enemy you killed, my friend.   40
I knew you in this dark; for so you frowned
Yesterday through me as you jabbed and killed.
I parried; but my hands were loath and cold.
Let us sleep now. . . ."

1918   1920

2. A somewhat archaic Anglo-Irish word meaning either "tax, levy" or (more probably, here) "luck"—as used in the phrase "bad cess to you" (may evil befall you).

E. M. FORSTER

(1879–1970)

Edward Morgan Forster was born in London; his father was an architect of Welsh extraction and his mother a member of a family distinguished during several generations for its evangelical religion and its philanthropic activities. He was educated at Tonbridge School (the "Sawston" of *The Longest Journey*), where he suffered the tribulations of a day boy at a boarding school, and King's College, Cambridge. The friends he made and the intellectual companionship he found at Cambridge have influenced his entire life. He visited Greece and spent some time in Italy in 1901, and this experience also had a permanent influence on him; throughout his life he has tended to set Greek and Italian peasant life in symbolic contrast to the stuffy and repressed life of middle-class England. Both Greek mythology and Italian Renaissance art opened up to him a world of what Matthew Arnold called "spontaneity of consciousness," and most of his work is concerned with ways of discovering such a quality in personal relationships amid the complexities and distortions of modern life. He began writing as a contributor to the newly founded liberal *Independent Review* in 1903, and in 1905 published his first novel, *Where Angels Fear to Tread*, a tragicomic projection of conflicts between refined English gentility and coarse Italian vitality.

English tutoring in Germany; an extended visit to India in 1912 and a shorter one in 1922; continuous intellectual companionship with members of the "Bloomsbury group" and others; and in 1946 an honorary fellowship at King's College, Cambridge, where he has mostly lived since, though with a good deal of traveling abroad—all this adds up to a civilized and humane existence, and (as Forster himself insists) an unusually happy one. His main interest has always been in personal relations, the "little society" we make for ourselves with our friends. But he has also cast a critical and reforming eye on the abuses of the world, his point of view being always that of the independent liberal, suspicious of all political slogans and catchwords.

Forster's second novel, *The Longest Journey* (1907), explores the differences between living and dead relationships with much incidental satire of English public-school education and English notions of respectability. A *Room with a View* (1908) explores the nature of love with a great deal of subtlety, using (as with his first novel) Italy as a liberating agent. *Howards End* (1910) probes the relation between inward feeling and outward action, between the kinds of reality in which people get involved in living. "Only connect!" exclaims one of the characters. "Only connect the prose and the passion, and both will be exalted, and human love will soon be at its height." But no one knew better than Forster that this is more easily said than done, and that false or premature connections, connections made by rule and not achieved through total realization of the personality, can destroy and corrupt. The halfway house to salvation is often grimmer than the starting point. In his last novel (for Forster has written no more fiction), *A Passage to India* (1924), he takes the relations between the English and the Indians in India in the early 1920's as a background against which to erect the most searching and complex of all his explorations of the possibilities and the limitations, the promises and the pitfalls, of human relationships. This remains his best-known novel, as well as his best.

Forster's short stories are as a rule much simpler in theme and treatment than his novels; many of them draw on Greek mythology to project the moment of escape or illumination for a character struggling against the meshes of convention. *The Road from Colonus* draws on themes from Greek tragedy to present a modern ironic picture of the moment of escape seen but not seized, with the inevitable consequence of loss and degeneration. There is a conscious use of symbolism here (for example, in the running water that so enchants Mr. Lucas in the magical spot in Greece, and his horror of the noise of running tap water at the end of the story) which is more successful than in most of his other short stories. Forster has also written critical, autobiographical and descriptive prose, notably *Aspects of the Novel* (1927), which, as a discussion of the techniques of fiction by a practicing novelist, has become a minor classic of criticism.

The Road from Colonus[1]

I

For no very intelligible reason, Mr. Lucas had hurried ahead of his party. He was perhaps reaching the age at which independence becomes valuable, because it is so soon to be lost. Tired of attention and consideration, he liked breaking away from the younger members, to ride by himself, and to dismount unassisted. Perhaps he also relished that more subtle pleasure of being kept waiting for lunch, and of telling the others on their arrival that it was of no consequence.

So, with childish impatience, he battered the animal's sides with his heels, and made the muleteer bang it with a thick stick and prick it with a sharp one, and jolted down the hillsides through clumps of flowering shrubs and stretches of anemones and asphodel, till he heard the sound of running water, and came in sight of the group of plane trees where they were to have their meal.

Even in England those trees would have been remarkable, so huge were they, so interlaced, so magnificently clothed in quivering green. And here in Greece they were unique, the one cool spot in that hard brilliant landscape, already scorched by the heat of an April sun. In their midst was hidden a tiny Khan or country inn, a frail and mud building with a broad wooden balcony in which sat an old woman spinning, while a small brown pig, eating orange peel, stood beside her. On the wet earth below squatted two children, playing some primeval game with their fingers; and their mother, none too clean either, was messing with some rice inside. As Mrs. Forman would have said, it was all very Greek, and the fastidious Mr. Lucas felt thankful that they were bringing their own food with them, and should eat it in the open air.

Still, he was glad to be there—the muleteer had helped him

1. Having been banished from Thebes on the discovery that he had unwittingly killed his father and married his mother, Oedipus wandered until he came to Colonus, and there with his daughter Antigone he rested on a rock within the sacred grove of the Furies. A passing native bade him depart, but, knowing that he had reached the last resting place appointed for him, he refused, and was eventually allowed to stay by Theseus, king of Athens. Shortly afterward he met his death mysteriously, having been taken by the gods in some unknown way to final rest. See Sophocles' play, *Oedipus at Colonus*.

off—and glad that Mrs. Forman was not there to forestall his opinions—glad even that he should not see Ethel for quite half an hour. Ethel was his youngest daughter, still unmarried. She was unselfish and affectionate, and it was generally understood that she was to devote her life to her father, and be the comfort of his old age. Mrs. Forman always referred to her as Antigone, and Mr. Lucas tried to settle down to the role of Oedipus, which seemed the only one that public opinion allowed him.

He had this in common with Oedipus, that he was growing old. Even to himself it had become obvious. He had lost interest in other people's affairs, and seldom attended when they spoke to him. He was fond of talking himself but often forgot what he was going to say, and even when he succeeded, it seldom seemed worth the effort. His phrases and gestures had become stiff and set, his anecdotes, once so successful, fell flat, his silence was as meaningless as his speech. Yet he had led a healthy, active life, had worked steadily, made money, educated his children. There was nothing and no one to blame: he was simply growing old.

At the present moment, here he was in Greece, and one of the dreams of his life was realized. Forty years ago he had caught the fever of Hellenism, and all his life he had felt that could he but visit that land, he would not have lived in vain. But Athens had been dusty, Delphi wet, Thermopylae flat, and he had listened with amazement and cynicism to the rapturous exclamations of his companions. Greece was like England: it was a man who was growing old, and it made no difference whether that man looked at the Thames or the Eurotas.[2] It was his last hope of contradicting that logic of experience, and it was failing.

Yet Greece had done something for him, though he did not know it. It had made him discontented, and there are stirrings of life in discontent. He knew that he was not the victim of continual ill-luck. Something great was wrong, and he was pitted against no mediocre or accidental enemy. For the last month a strange desire had possessed him to die fighting.

"Greece is the land for young people," he said to himself as he stood under the plane trees, "but I will enter into it, I will possess it. Leaves shall be green again, water shall be sweet, the sky shall be blue. They were so forty years ago; and I will win them back. I do mind being old, and I will pretend no longer."

He took two steps forward, and immediately cold waters were gurgling over his ankle.

"Where does the water come from?" he asked himself. "I do not even know that." He remembered that all the hillsides were dry; yet here the road was suddenly covered with flowing streams.

2. In ancient times, the river on which Sparta stood, in southern Greece (now the Iri or Iris).

He stopped still in amazement, saying: "Water out of a tree—out of a hollow tree? I never saw nor thought of that before."

For the enormous plane that leant towards the Khan was hollow—it had been burnt out for charcoal—and from its living trunk there gushed an impetuous spring, coating the bark with fern and moss, and flowing over the mule track to create fertile meadows beyond. The simple country folk had paid to beauty and mystery such tribute as they could, for in the rind of the tree a shrine was cut, holding a lamp and a little picture of the Virgin, inheritor of the Naiad's[3] and Dryad's joint abode.

"I never saw anything so marvelous before," said Mr. Lucas. "I could even step inside the trunk and see where the water comes from."

For a moment he hesitated to violate the shrine. Then he remembered with a smile his own thought—"the place shall be mine; I will enter it and possess it"—and leapt almost aggressively onto a stone within.

The water pressed up steadily and noiselessly from the hollow roots and hidden crevices of the plane, forming a wonderful amber pool ere it spilt over the lip of bark on to the earth outside. Mr. Lucas tasted it and it was sweet, and when he looked up the black funnel of the trunk he saw sky which was blue, and some leaves which were green; and he remembered, without smiling, another of his thoughts.

Others had been before him—indeed he had a curious sense of companionship. Little votive offerings to the presiding Power were fastened on to the bark—tiny arms and legs and eyes in tin, grotesque models of the brain or the heart—all tokens of some recovery of strength or wisdom or love. There was no such thing as the solitude of nature, for the sorrows and joys of humanity had pressed even into the bosom of a tree. He spread out his arms and steadied himself against the soft charred wood, and then slowly leant back, till his body was resting on the trunk behind. His eyes closed, and he had the strange feeling of one who is moving, yet at peace—the feeling of the swimmer, who, after long struggling with chopping seas, finds that after all the tide will sweep him to his goal.

So he lay motionless, conscious only of the stream below his feet, and that all things were a stream, in which he was moving.

He was aroused at last by a shock—the shock of an arrival perhaps, for when he opened his eyes, something unimagined, indefinable, had passed over all things, and made them intelligible and good.

There was meaning in the stoop of the old woman over her work, and in the quick motions of the little pig, and in her diminishing globe of wool. A young man came singing over the streams on a

3. Water nymph. "Dryad": wood nymph.

mule, and there was beauty in his pose and sincerity in his greeting. The sun made no accidental patterns upon the spreading roots of the trees, and there was intention in the nodding clumps of asphodel, and in the music of the water. To Mr. Lucas, who, in a brief space of time, had discovered not only Greece, but England and all the world and life, there seemed nothing ludicrous in the desire to hang within the tree another votive offering—a little model of an entire man.

"Why, here's papa, playing at being Merlin."

All unnoticed they had arrived—Ethel, Mrs. Forman, Mr. Graham, and the English-speaking dragoman.[4] Mr. Lucas peered out at them suspiciously. They had suddenly become unfamiliar, and all that they did seemed strained and coarse.

"Allow me to give you a hand," said Mr. Graham, a young man who was always polite to his elders.

Mr. Lucas felt annoyed. "Thank you, I can manage perfectly well by myself," he replied. His foot slipped as he stepped out of the tree, and went into the spring.

"Oh papa, my papa!" said Ethel, "what are you doing? Thank goodness I have got a change for you on the mule."

She tended him carefully, giving him clean socks and dry boots, and then sat him down on the rug beside the lunch basket, while she went with the others to explore the grove.

They came back in ecstasies, in which Mr. Lucas tried to join. But he found them intolerable. Their enthusiasm was superficial, commonplace, and spasmodic. They had no perception of the coherent beauty that was flowering around them. He tried at least to explain his feelings, and what he said was:

"I am altogether pleased with the appearance of this place. It impresses me very favorably. The trees are fine, remarkably fine for Greece, and there is something very poetic in the spring of clear running water. The people too seem kindly and civil. It is decidedly an attractive place."

Mrs. Forman upbraided him for his tepid praise.

"Oh, it is a place in a thousand!" she cried, "I could live and die here! I really would stop if I had not to be back at Athens! It reminds me of the Colonus of Sophocles."

"Well, *I* must stop," said Ethel. "I positively must."

"Yes, do! You and your father! Antigone and Oedipus. Of course you must stop at Colonus!"

Mr. Lucas was almost breathless with excitement. When he stood within the tree, he had believed that his happiness would be independent of locality. But these few minutes' conversation had undeceived him. He no longer trusted himself to journey through the world, for old thoughts, old wearinesses might be waiting to rejoin

4. Interpreter.

him as soon as he left the shade of the planes, and the music of the virgin water. To sleep in the Khan with the gracious, kind-eyed country people, to watch the bats flit about within the globe of shade, and see the moon turn the golden patterns into silver—one such night would place him beyond relapse, and confirm him forever in the kingdom he had regained. But all his lips could say was: "I should be willing to put in a night here."

"You mean a week, papa! It would be sacrilege to put in less."

"A week then, a week," said his lips, irritated at being corrected, while his heart was leaping with joy. All through lunch he spoke to them no more, but watched the place he should know so well, and the people who would so soon be his companions and friends. The inmates of the Khan only consisted of an old woman, a middle-aged woman, a young man and two children, and to none of them had he spoken, yet he loved them as he loved everything that moved or breathed or existed beneath the benedictory shade of the planes.

"En route!" said the shrill voice of Mrs. Forman. "Ethel! Mr. Graham! The best of things must end."

"Tonight," thought Mr. Lucas, "they will light the little lamp by the shrine. And when we all sit together on the balcony, perhaps they will tell me which offerings they put up."

"I beg your pardon, Mr. Lucas," said Graham, "but they want to fold up the rug you are sitting on."

Mr. Lucas got up, saying to himself: "Ethel shall go to bed first, and then I will try to tell them about my offering too—for it is a thing I must do. I think they will understand if I am left with them alone."

Ethel touched him on the cheek. "Papa! I've called you three times. All the mules are here."

"Mules? What mules?"

"Our mules. We're all waiting. Oh, Mr. Graham, do help my father on."

"I don't know what you're talking about, Ethel."

"My dearest papa, we must start. You know we have to get to Olympia tonight."

Mr. Lucas in pompous, confident tones replied: "I always did wish, Ethel, that you had a better head for plans. You know perfectly well that we are putting in a week here. It is your own suggestion."

Ethel was startled into impoliteness. "What a perfectly ridiculous idea. You must have known I was joking. Of course I meant I wished we could."

"Ah! if we could only do what we wished!" sighed Mrs. Forman, already seated on her mule.

"Surely," Ethel continued in calmer tones, "you didn't think I meant it."

"Most certainly I did. I have made all my plans on the supposition that we are stopping here, and it will be extremely inconvenient, indeed, impossible for me to start."

He delivered this remark with an air of great conviction, and Mrs. Forman and Mr. Graham had to turn away to hide their smiles.

"I am sorry I spoke so carelessly; it was wrong of me. But, you know, we can't break up our party, and even one night here would make us miss the boat at Patras."

Mrs. Forman, in an aside, called Mr. Graham's attention to the excellent way in which Ethel managed her father.

"I don't mind about the Patras boat. You said that we should stop here, and we are stopping."

It seemed as if the inhabitants of the Khan had divined in some mysterious way that the altercation touched them. The old woman stopped her spinning, while the young man and the two children stood behind Mr. Lucas, as if supporting him.

Neither arguments nor entreaties moved him. He said little, but he was absolutely determined, because for the first time he saw his daily life aright. What need had he to return to England? Who would miss him? His friends were dead or cold. Ethel loved him in a way, but, as was right, she had other interests. His other children he seldom saw. He had only one other relative, his sister Julia, whom he both feared and hated. It was no effort to struggle. He would be a fool as well as a coward if he stirred from the place which brought him happiness and peace.

At last Ethel, to humor him, and not disinclined to air her modern Greek, went into the Khan with the astonished dragoman to look at the rooms. The woman inside received them with loud welcomes, and the young man, when no one was looking, began to lead Mr. Lucas' mule to the stable.

"Drop it, you brigand!" shouted Graham, who always declared that foreigners could understand English if they chose. He was right, for the man obeyed, and they all stood waiting for Ethel's return.

She emerged at last, with close-gathered skirts, followed by the dragoman bearing the little pig, which he had bought at a bargain.

"My dear papa, I will do all I can for you, but stop in that Khan—no."

"Are there—fleas?" asked Mrs. Forman.

Ethel intimated that "fleas" was not the word.

"Well, I am afraid that settles it," said Mrs. Forman, "I know how particular Mr. Lucas is."

"It does not settle it," said Mr. Lucas. "Ethel, you go on. I do not want you. I don't know why I ever consulted you. I shall stop here alone."

"That is absolute nonsense," said Ethel, losing her temper. "How can you be left alone at your age? How would you get your meals or your bath? All your letters are waiting for you at Patras. You'll miss the boat. That means missing the London operas, and upsetting all your engagements for the month. And as if you could travel by yourself!"

"They might knife you," was Mr. Graham's contribution.

The Greeks said nothing; but whenever Mr. Lucas looked their way, they beckoned him towards the Khan. The children would even have drawn him by the coat, and the old woman on the balcony stopped her almost completed spinning, and fixed him with mysterious appealing eyes. As he fought, the issue assumed gigantic proportions, and he believed that he was not merely stopping because he had regained youth or seen beauty or found happiness, but because in that place and with those people a supreme event was awaiting him which would transfigure the face of the world. The moment was so tremendous that he abandoned words and arguments as useless, and rested on the strength of his mighty unrevealed allies: silent men, murmuring water, and whispering trees. For the whole place called with one voice, articulate to him, and his garrulous opponents became every minute more meaningless and absurd. Soon they would be tired and go chattering away into the sun, leaving him to the cool grove and the moonlight and the destiny he foresaw.

Mrs. Forman and the dragoman had indeed already started, amid the piercing screams of the little pig, and the struggle might have gone on indefinitely if Ethel had not called in Mr. Graham.

"Can you help me?" she whispered. "He is absolutely unmanageable."

"I'm no good at arguing—but if I could help you in any other way—" and he looked down complacently at his well-made figure.

Ethel hesitated. Then she said: "Help me in any way you can. After all, it is for his good that we do it."

"Then have his mule led up behind him."

So when Mr. Lucas thought he had gained the day, he suddenly felt himself lifted off the ground, and set sideways on the saddle, and at the same time the mule started off at a trot. He said nothing, for he had nothing to say, and even his face showed little emotion as he felt the shade pass and heard the sound of the water cease. Mr. Graham was running at his side, hat in hand, apologizing.

"I know I had no business to do it, and I do beg your pardon awfully. But I do hope that some day you too will feel that I was— damn!"

A stone had caught him in the middle of the back. It was thrown by the little boy, who was pursuing them along the mule track. He was followed by his sister, also throwing stones.

Ethel screamed to the dragoman, who was some way ahead with Mrs. Forman, but before he could rejoin them, another adversary appeared. It was the young Greek, who had cut them off in front, and now dashed down at Mr. Lucas' bridle. Fortunately Graham was an expert boxer, and it did not take him a moment to beat down the youth's feeble defense, and to send him sprawling with a bleeding mouth into the asphodel. By this time the dragoman had arrived, the children, alarmed at the fate of their brother, had desisted, and the rescue party, if such it is to be considered, retired in disorder to the trees.

"Little devils!" said Graham, laughing with triumph. "That's the modern Greek all over. Your father meant money if he stopped, and they consider we were taking it out of their pocket."

"Oh, they are terrible—simple savages! I don't know how I shall ever thank you. You've saved my father."

"I only hope you didn't think me brutal."

"No," replied Ethel with a little sigh. "I admire strength."

Meanwhile the cavalcade reformed, and Mr. Lucas, who, as Mrs. Forman said, bore his disappointment wonderfully well, was put comfortably on to his mule. They hurried up the opposite hillside, fearful of another attack, and it was not until they had left the eventful place far behind that Ethel found an opportunity to speak to her father and ask his pardon for the way she had treated him.

"You seemed so different, dear father, and you quite frightened me. Now I feel that you are your old self again."

He did not answer, and she concluded that he was not unnaturally offended at her behavior.

By one of those curious tricks of mountain scenery, the place they had left an hour before suddenly reappeared far below them. The Khan was hidden under the green dome, but in the open there still stood three figures, and through the pure air rose up a faint cry of defiance or farewell.

Mr. Lucas stopped irresolutely, and let the reins fall from his hand.

"Come, father dear," said Ethel gently.

He obeyed, and in another moment a spur of the hill hid the dangerous scene forever.

II

It was breakfast time, but the gas was alight, owing to the fog. Mr. Lucas was in the middle of an account of a bad night he had spent. Ethel, who was to be married in a few weeks, had her arms on the table, listening.

"First the door bell rang, then you came back from the theater. Then the dog started, and after the dog the cat. And at three in the morning a young hooligan passed by singing. Oh yes: then there was the water gurgling in the pipe above my head."

"I think that was only the bath water running away," said Ethel, looking rather worn.

"Well, there's nothing I dislike more than running water. It's perfectly impossible to sleep in the house. I shall give it up. I shall give notice next quarter. I shall tell the landlord plainly, 'The reason I am giving up the house is this: it is perfectly impossible to sleep in it.' If he says—says—well, what has he got to say?"

"Some more toast, father?"

"Thank you, my dear." He took it, and there was an interval of peace.

But he soon recommenced. "I'm not going to submit to the practicing next door as tamely as they think. I wrote and told them so—didn't I?"

"Yes," said Ethel, who had taken care that the letter should not reach. "I have seen the governess, and she has promised to arrange it differently. And Aunt Julia hates noise. It will be sure to be all right."

Her aunt, being the only unattached member of the family, was coming to keep house for her father when she left him. The reference was not a happy one, and Mr. Lucas commenced a series of half articulate sighs, which was only stopped by the arrival of the post.

"Oh, what a parcel!" cried Ethel. "For me! What can it be! Greek stamps. This is most exciting!"

It proved to be some asphodel bulbs, sent by Mrs. Forman from Athens for planting in the conservatory.

"Doesn't it bring it all back! You remember the asphodels, father. And all wrapped up in Greek newspapers. I wonder if I can read them still. I used to be able to, you know."

She rattled on, hoping to conceal the laughter of the children next door—a favorite source of querulousness at breakfast time.

"Listen to me! 'A rural disaster.' Oh, I've hit on something sad. But never mind. 'Last Tuesday at Plataniste, in the province of Messenia, a shocking tragedy occurred. A large tree'—aren't I getting on well?—'blew down in the night and'—wait a minute—oh, dear! 'crushed to death the five occupants of the little Khan there, who had apparently been sitting in the balcony. The bodies of Maria Rhomaides, the aged proprietress, and of her daughter, aged forty-six, were easily recognizable, whereas that of her grandson'—oh, the rest is really too horrid; I wish I had never tried it, and what's more I feel to have heard the name Plataniste before. We didn't stop there, did we, in the spring?"

"We had lunch," said Mr. Lucas, with a faint expression of trouble on his vacant face. "Perhaps it was where the dragoman bought the pig."

"Of course," said Ethel in a nervous voice. "Where the dragoman bought the little pig. How terrible!"

"Very terrible!" said her father, whose attention was wandering to the noisy children next door. Ethel suddenly started to her feet with genuine interest.

"Good gracious!" she exclaimed. "This is an old paper. It happened not lately but in April—the night of Tuesday the eighteenth —and we—we must have been there in the afternoon."

"So we were," said Mr. Lucas. She put her hand to her heart, scarcely able to speak.

"Father, dear father, I must say it: you wanted to stop there. All those people, those poor half savage people, tried to keep you, they're dead. The whole place, it says, is in ruins, and even the stream has changed its course. Father, dear, if it had not been for me, and if Arthur had not helped me, you must have been killed."

Mr. Lucas waved his hand irritably. "It is not a bit of good speaking to the governess, I shall write to the landlord and say, 'The reason I am giving up the house is this: the dog barks, the children next door are intolerable, and I cannot stand the noise of running water.'"

Ethel did not check his babbling. She was aghast at the narrowness of the escape, and for a long time kept silence. At last she said: "Such a marvelous deliverance does make one believe in Providence."

Mr. Lucas, who was still composing his letter to the landlord, did not reply.

1911

VIRGINIA WOOLF
(1882–1941)

Virginia Woolf was born in London, daughter of Leslie Stephen, the late Victorian critic, philosopher, biographer, and scholar. She grew up as a member of a large and talented family, educating herself in her father's magnificent library, meeting in childhood many eminent Victorians, learning Greek from Walter Pater's sister. After her father's death in 1904 she settled with her sister and two brothers in Bloomsbury, that district of London which later was to become associated with her and the group among whom she moved. The "Bloomsbury group" included Lytton Strachey, the biographer; J. M. Keynes, the eminent economist; Roger Fry, an art critic; and E. M. Forster. When her sister Vanessa married Clive Bell, an art critic, in 1907, Virginia and her brother took together another house in Bloomsbury, and there they entertained their literary and artistic friends at evening gatherings where the conversation sparkled. In 1912 she married Leonard Woolf, journalist, essayist, and political thinker; together they founded the Hogarth Press in 1917—a press which has published some of the most interesting literature of our time, including an early volume of Eliot's poems (1919) and his *Homage to John Dryden* (1924) as well as her own novels. Virginia Woolf's suicide in March, 1941, resulting from the fear that she was about to lose her mind and become a burden on her husband, first revealed to the public that she had been subject to periods of nervous depression, particularly after finishing a book, and that underneath the liveliness and wit so well known among the Bloomsbury group lay disturbing psychological tensions.

Virginia Woolf came naturally into the profession of writing. Moving among writers and artists, her world was from the beginning the cultured world of the middle-class and upper-middle-class London intelligentsia. She was comfortably off, she had leisure to cultivate her sensibility, she wrote because she wanted to. She rebelled against what she called the "materialism" of such novelists as Arnold Bennett and John Galsworthy, and sought a more delicate rendering of those aspects of consciousness in which she felt that the truth of human experience really lay. After two novels cast rather cumbersomely in traditional form, she developed her own subtle style, which handled the "stream of consciousness" with a carefully modulated poetic flow and brought into prose fiction something of the rhythms and the imagery of lyric poetry. The sketches in which she explored the possibilities of moving between action and contemplation, between specific external events in time and delicate tracings of the flow of consciousness where the mind moves between retrospect and anticipation, were collected in *Monday or Tuesday* (1921), from which *The Mark on the Wall* is printed below. These were technical experiments, and they made possible those later novels where her characteristic method is fully developed—*Jacob's Room* (1922); *Mrs. Dalloway* (1925), the first completely successful novel in her "new" style; *To the Lighthouse* (1927); *The Waves* (1931), the most stylized of her novels; and *Between the Acts* (1941), published after her death. Virginia Woolf was a skilled exponent of the "stream of consciousness" technique in her novels, exploring with great subtlety problems of personal identity and personal relationships as well as the significance of time, change, and memory for human personality. The delicate, lyrical prose of her finest novels was a remarkable technical achievement. Virginia Woolf also wrote a great many reviews and critical essays, collected in *The Common Reader* (1925) and *The Second Common Reader* (1932); informal and personal in tone, her criticism is suggestive rather than authoritative and has an engaging air of spontaneity.

The Mark on the Wall

Perhaps it was the middle of January in the present year that I first looked up and saw the mark on the wall. In order to fix a date it is necessary to remember what one saw. So now I think of the fire; the steady film of yellow light upon the page of my book; the three chrysanthemums in the round glass bowl on the mantelpiece. Yes, it must have been the wintertime, and we had just finished our tea, for I remember that I was smoking a cigarette when I looked up and saw the mark on the wall for the first time. I looked up through the smoke of my cigarette and my eye lodged for a moment upon the burning coals, and that old fancy of the crimson flag flapping from the castle tower came into my mind, and I thought of the cavalcade of red knights riding up the side of the black rock. Rather to my relief the sight of the mark interrupted the fancy, for it is an old fancy, an automatic fancy, made as a child perhaps. The mark was a small round mark, black upon the white wall, about six or seven inches above the mantelpiece.

How readily our thoughts swarm upon a new object, lifting it a little way, as ants carry a blade of straw so feverishly, and then leave it. . . . If that mark was made by a nail, it can't have been for a picture, it must have been for a miniature—the miniature of a lady with white powdered curls, powder-dusted cheeks, and lips like red carnations. A fraud of course, for the people who had this house before us would have chosen pictures in that way—an old picture for an old room. That is the sort of people they were—very interesting people, and I think of them so often, in such queer places, because one will never see them again, never know what happened next. They wanted to leave this house because they wanted to change their style of furniture, so he said, and he was in process of saying that in his opinion art should have ideas behind it when we were torn asunder, as one is torn from the old lady about to pour out tea and the young man about to hit the tennis ball in the back garden of the suburban villa as one rushes past in the train.

But for that mark, I'm not sure about it; I don't believe it was made by a nail after all; it's too big, too round, for that. I might get up, but if I got up and looked at it, ten to one I shouldn't be able to say for certain; because once a thing's done, no one ever knows how it happened. Oh! dear me, the mystery of life; the inaccuracy of thought! The ignorance of humanity! To show how very little control of our possessions we have—what an accidental affair this living is after all our civilization—let me just count over a few of the things lost in one lifetime, beginning, for that seems always the most mysterious of losses—what cat would gnaw, what rat would nibble—three pale blue canisters of bookbinding tools? Then there were the bird cages, the iron hoops, the steel skates, the Queen Anne coal scuttle, the bagatelle board, the hand organ—all gone, and jewels, too. Opals and emeralds, they lie about the roots of turnips. What a scraping paring affair it is to be sure! The wonder is that I've any clothes on my back, that I sit surrounded by solid furniture at this moment. Why, if one wants to compare life to anything, one must liken it to being blown through the Tube[1] at fifty miles an hour—landing at the other end without a single hairpin in one's hair! Shot out at the feet of God entirely naked! Tumbling head over heels in the asphodel meadows[2] like brown paper parcels pitched down a shoot in the post office! With one's hair flying back like the tail of a race horse. Yes, that seems to express the rapidity of life, the perpetual waste and repair; all so casual, all so haphazard. . . .

But after life. The slow pulling down of thick green stalks so that the cup of the flower, as it turns over, deluges one with purple and red light. Why, after all, should one not be born there as one is born here, helpless, speechless, unable to focus one's eyesight, groping at the roots of the grass, at the toes of the Giants? As for saying which are trees, and which are men and women, or whether there are such things, that one won't be in a condition to do for fifty years or so. There will be nothing but spaces of light and dark, intersected by thick stalks, and rather higher up perhaps, rose-shaped blots of an indistinct color—dim pinks and blues— which will, as time goes on, become more definite, become—I don't know what. . . .

And yet that mark on the wall is not a hole at all. It may even be caused by some round black substance, such as a small rose leaf, left over from the summer, and I, not being a very vigilant housekeeper—look at the dust on the mantelpiece, for example, the dust which, so they say, buried Troy three times over, only fragments of pots utterly refusing annihilation, as one can believe.

The tree outside the window taps very gently on the pane. . . . I want to think quietly, calmly, spaciously, never to be interrupted, never to have to rise from my chair, to slip easily from one thing to another, without any sense of hostility, or obstacle. I want to sink deeper and deeper, away from the surface, with its hard separate facts. To steady myself, let me catch hold of the first idea that passes . . . Shakespeare. . . . Well, he will do as well as another. A man who sat himself solidly in an armchair, and looked into the fire, so— A shower of ideas fell perpetually from some very high Heaven down through his mind. He leant his forehead on his hand, and people, looking in through the open door—for this scene is supposed to take place on a summer's evening— But how dull this is, this historical fiction! It doesn't interest me at all. I wish I could hit upon a pleasant track of thought, a track indirectly reflecting credit upon myself, for those are the pleasantest thoughts, and very frequent even in the minds of modest mouse-colored people, who believe genuinely that they dislike to hear their own praises. They are not thoughts directly praising oneself; that is the beauty of them; they are thoughts like this:

"And then I came into the room. They were discussing botany.

1. London underground railway.
2. I.e., heaven, the next world (in Greek mythology, asphodel flowers grow in the Elysian fields).

I said how I'd seen a flower growing on a dust heap on the site of an old house in Kingsway.[3] The seed, I said, must have been sown in the reign of Charles the First. What flowers grew in the reign of Charles the First?" I asked— (But I don't remember the answer.) Tall flowers with purple tassels to them perhaps. And so it goes on. All the time I'm dressing up the figure of myself in my own mind, lovingly, stealthily, not openly adoring it, for if I did that, I should catch myself out, and stretch my hand at once for a book in self-protection. Indeed, it is curious how instinctively one protects the image of oneself from idolatry or any other handling that could make it ridiculous, or too unlike the original to be believed in any longer. Or is it not so very curious after all? It is a matter of great importance. Suppose the looking glass smashes, the image disappears, and the romantic figure with the green of forest depths all about it is there no longer, but only that shell of a person which is seen by other people—what an airless, shallow, bald, prominent world it becomes! A world not to be lived in. As we face each other in omnibuses and underground railways we are looking into the mirror; that accounts for the vagueness, the gleam of glassiness, in our eyes. And the novelists in future will realize more and more the importance of these reflections, for of course there is not one reflection but an almost infinite number; those are the depths they will explore, those the phantoms they will pursue, leaving the description of reality more and more out of their stories, taking a knowledge of it for granted, as the Greeks did and Shakespeare perhaps—but these generalizations are very worthless. The military sound of the word is enough. It recalls leading articles, cabinet ministers—a whole class of things indeed which, as a child, one thought the thing itself, the standard thing, the real thing, from which one could not depart save at the risk of nameless damnation. Generalizations bring back somehow Sunday in London, Sunday afternoon walks, Sunday luncheons, and also ways of speaking of the dead, clothes, and habits—like the habit of sitting all together in one room until a certain hour, although nobody liked it. There was a rule for everything. The rule for tablecloths at that particular period was that they should be made of tapestry with little yellow compartments marked upon them, such as you may see in photographs of the carpets in the corridors of the royal palaces. Tablecloths of a different kind were not real tablecloths. How shocking, and yet how wonderful it was to discover that these real things, Sunday luncheons, Sunday walks, country houses, and tablecloths were not entirely real, were indeed half phantoms, and the damnation which visited the disbeliever in them was only a sense of illegitimate freedom. What now takes the place of those things I wonder, those real standard things?

3. Street in London.

Men perhaps, should you be a woman; the masculine point of view which governs our lives, which sets the standard, which establishes Whitaker's Table of Precedency,[4] which has become, I suppose, since the war, half a phantom to many men and women, which soon, one may hope, will be laughed into the dustbin where the phantoms go, the mahogany sideboards and the Landseer[5] prints, Gods and Devils, Hell and so forth, leaving us all with an intoxicating sense of illegitimate freedom—if freedom exists. . . .

In certain lights that mark on the wall seems actually to project from the wall. Nor is it entirely circular. I cannot be sure, but it seems to cast a perceptible shadow, suggesting that if I ran my finger down that strip of the wall it would, at a certain point, mount and descend a small tumulus, a smooth tumulus like those barrows[6] on the South Downs which are, they say, either tombs or camps. Of the two I should prefer them to be tombs, desiring melancholy like most English people, and finding it natural at the end of a walk to think of the bones stretched beneath the turf. . . . There must be some book about it. Some antiquary must have dug up those bones and given them a name. . . . What sort of a man is an antiquary, I wonder? Retired Colonels for the most part, I daresay, leading parties of aged laborers to the top here, examining clods of earth and stone, and getting into correspondence with the neighboring clergy, which, being opened at breakfast time, gives them a feeling of importance, and the comparison of arrowheads necessitates cross-country journeys to the county towns, an agreeable necessity both to them and to their elderly wives, who wish to make plum jam or to clean out the study, and have every reason for keeping that great question of the camp or the tomb in perpetual suspension, while the Colonel himself feels agreeably philosophic in accumulating evidence on both sides of the question. It is true that he does finally incline to believe in the camp; and, being opposed, indites a pamphlet which he is about to read at the quarterly meeting of the local society when a stroke lays him low, and his last conscious thoughts are not of wife or child, but of the camp and that arrowhead there, which is now in the case at the local museum, together with the foot of a Chinese murderess, a handful of Elizabethan nails, a great many Tudor clay pipes, a piece of Roman pottery, and the wineglass that Nelson drank out of—proving I really don't know what.

---

4. Whitaker's Almanack, an annual compendium of information, prints a "Table of Precedency," which shows the order in which the various ranks in public life and society proceed on formal occasions.
5. Edwin Henry Landseer, 19th-century animal painter, reproductions of whose "Stag at Bay," "Monarch of the Glen," and similar paintings were often found in Victorian homes.
6. Mounds of earth or stones erected by prehistoric peoples, usually as burial places; the South Downs are a range of low hills in southeastern England.

No, no, nothing is proved, nothing is known. And if I were to get up at this very moment and ascertain that the mark on the wall is really—what shall we say?—the head of a gigantic old nail, driven in two hundred years ago, which has now, owing to the patient attrition of many generations of housemaids, revealed its head above the coat of paint, and is taking its first view of modern life in the sight of a white-walled firelit room, what should I gain? —Knowledge? Matter for further speculation? I can think sitting still as well as standing up. And what is knowledge? What are our learned men save the descendants of witches and hermits who crouched in caves and in woods brewing herbs, interrogating shrewmice and writing down the language of the stars? And the less we honor them as our superstitions dwindle and our respect for beauty and health of mind increases. . . . Yes, one could imagine a very pleasant world. A quiet, spacious world, with the flowers so red and blue in the open fields. A world without professors or specialists or housekeepers with the profiles of policemen, a world which one could slice with one's thought as a fish slices the water with his fin, grazing the stems of the water lilies, hanging suspended over nests of white sea eggs. . . . How peaceful it is down here, rooted in the center of the world and gazing up through the gray waters, with their sudden gleams of light, and their reflections—if it were not for Whitaker's Almanack—if it were not for the Table of Precedency!

I must jump up and see for myself what that mark on the wall really is—a nail, a rose leaf, a crack in the wood?

Here is nature once more at her old game of self-preservation. This train of thought, she perceives, is threatening mere waste of energy, even some collision with reality, for who will ever be able to lift a finger against Whitaker's Table of Precedency? The Archbishop of Canterbury is followed by the Lord High Chancellor; the Lord High Chancellor is followed by the Archbishop of York. Everybody follows somebody, such is the philosophy of Whitaker; and the great thing is to know who follows whom. Whitaker knows, and let that, so Nature counsels, comfort you, instead of enraging you; and if you can't be comforted, if you must shatter this hour of peace, think of the mark on the wall.

I understand Nature's game—her prompting to take action as a way of ending any thought that threatens to excite or to pain. Hence, I suppose, comes our slight contempt for men of action— men, we assume, who don't think. Still, there's no harm in putting a full stop to one's disagreeable thoughts by looking at a mark on the wall.

Indeed, now that I have fixed my eyes upon it, I feel that I have grasped a plank in the sea; I feel a satisfying sense of reality which at once turns the two Archbishops and the Lord High Chancellor to the shadows of shades. Here is something definite, something real. Thus, waking from a midnight dream of horror, one hastily turns on the light and lies quiescent, worshiping the chest of drawers, worshiping solidity, worshiping reality, worshiping the impersonal world which is a proof of some existence other than ours. That is what one wants to be sure of. . . . Wood is a pleasant thing to think about. It comes from a tree; and trees grow, and we don't know how they grow. For years and years they grow, without paying any attention to us, in meadows, in forests, and by the side of rivers —all things one likes to think about. The cows swish their tails beneath them on hot afternoons; they paint rivers so green that when a moorhen dives one expects to see its feathers all green when it comes up again. I like to think of the fish balanced against the stream like flags blown out; and of water beetles slowly raising domes of mud upon the bed of the river. I like to think of the tree itself: first of the close dry sensation of being wood; then the grinding of the storm; then the slow, delicious ooze of sap; I like to think of it, too, on winter's nights standing in the empty field with all leaves close-furled, nothing tender exposed to the iron bullets of the moon, a naked mast upon an earth that goes tumbling, tumbling, all night long. The song of birds must sound very loud and strange in June; and how cold the feet of insects must feel upon it, as they make laborious progresses up the creases of the bark, or sun themselves upon the thin green awning of the leaves, and look straight in front of them with diamond-cut red eyes. . . . One by one the fibers snap beneath the immense cold pressure of the earth, than the last storm comes and, falling, the highest branches drive deep into the ground again. Even so, life isn't done with; there are a million patient, watchful lives still for a tree, all over the world, in bedrooms, in ships, on the pavement, living rooms, where men and women sit after tea, smoking cigaretts. It is full of peaceful thoughts, happy thoughts, this tree. I should like to take each one separately—but something is getting in the way. . . . Where was I? What has it all been about? A tree? A river? The Downs? Whitaker's Almanack? The fields of asphodel? I can't remember a thing. Everything's moving, falling, slipping, vanishing. . . . There is a vast upheaval of matter. Someone is standing over me and saying:

"I'm going out to buy a newspaper."

"Yes?"

"Though it's no good buying newspapers. . . . Nothing ever happens. Curse this war; God damn this war! . . . All the same, I don't see why we should have a snail on our wall."

Ah, the mark on the wall! It was a snail.

1919, 1921

EDWIN MUIR
(1887–1959)

Edwin Muir was born on a farm in the Orkney Islands, Scotland, but moved with his family to Glasgow at the age of 14. This move from a simple farming community with deep roots in the past to a large, dirty, industrial city represented a change that haunted his imagination for the rest of his life and which he described vividly in his autobiography, *The Story and the Fable*, 1940. His life in Glasgow was for some years wretched and poverty-stricken. Father, mother, and two brothers died in rapid succession. Muir worked at a variety of jobs in the city—officeboy in a law office, then with an engineering firm, then with a publishing firm, clerk in the office of a beer-bottling factory—before getting a job in a bone factory in Fairport where "except for making a return of the weight of the bones and enduring their stench during the various stages they passed through, I had nothing to do with the stuff out of which the firm ground its profits." Meanwhile he was reading widely and educating himself in both literature and politics. In 1919 he married the novelist and critic Willa Anderson and moved to London. He was by now making his living as a literary journalist on the staff of the periodical *The New Age*. The Muirs lived on the continent for a while, then settled in St. Andrews, still making a precarious living by writing. After World War II Muir was head of the British Council in Prague until the Communists took over Czechoslovakia; he then became Warden of Newbattle Abbey, near Edinburgh. The last few years of his life he spent in a small village near Cambridge.

Muir published his first volume of poems in 1925, and thereafter his poems were to be found regularly (though never in any great number) in periodicals and in nine further slim volumes. He also published several books of criticism, notably *The Structure of the Novel* (1928) and *Scott and Scotland* (1936). He also, with his wife, translated Kafka's novels from the German. It was only on the publication of his last book of poems, *One Foot in Eden* (1956), that more than a small minority of perceptive critics came to recognize his poetic stature. With the posthumous publication of his *Collected Poems* in 1960 his reputation as one of the most original poets of the 20th century was assured.

Muir's range is limited: he was always fascinated by time, by links between generations, by the modern meaning of ancient myths, by the question of identity and change. These interests provide the themes of almost all his poetry. Yet if he had but few themes, the grave precision of his language, the translucent quality of his imagery, the supple, unforced rhythms, and the delicacy of observation and of sensibility that underlies all this, combine to make poetry of remarkable individuality and power. Writing in his autobiography of his first few years in Glasgow, Muir described them as "so stupidly wretched, such a meaningless waste of inherited virtue, that I cannot write of them even now without confused grief and anger." "Inherited virtue" meant much to him, and its waste was to him always a tragedy. For all the sophistication and the knowledge of modern psychology and political theory that Muir acquired, he never ceased to be aware that his roots had been torn from the primitive traditions of Orkney, and he sought to replant these with new ways. He was far from being a rustic escapist or an idealizer of the country life. His poetry is often grim and sometimes nightmarish. But the integrity of feeling, the delicacy and precision of awareness, and the quiet, seemingly effortless, mastery of a supple language that we find in his poetry produce in the end a reassurance. Muir belonged to no modern school and followed no contemporary fashion. Like Graves, but in a very different manner, he found his own way of relating traditional myth to the tensions of modern life.

Troy[1]

He all that time among the sewers of Troy
Scouring for scraps. A man so venerable
He might have been Priam's self, but Priam was dead,
Troy taken. His arms grew meager as a boy's,
And all that flourished in that hollow famine   5
Was his long, white, round beard. Oh, sturdily
He swung his staff and sent the bold rats skipping
Across the scurfy hills and worm-wet valleys,
Crying: "Achilles, Ajax, turn and fight!
Stop cowards!" Till his cries, dazed and confounded,   10
Flew back at him with: "Coward, turn and fight!"
And the wild Greeks yelled round him.
Yet he withstood them, a brave, mad old man,
And fought the rats for Troy. The light was rat-gray,
The hills and dells, the common drain, his Simois,   15
Rat-gray. Mysterious shadows fell
Affrighting him whenever a cloud offended
The sun up in the other world. The rat-hordes,
Moving, were gray dust shifting in gray dust.
Proud history has such sackends. He was taken   20
At last by some chance robber seeking treasure
Under Troy's riven roots. Dragged to the surface.
And there he saw Troy like a burial ground
With tumbled walls for tombs, the smooth sward wrinkled
As Time's last wave had long since passed that way,   25
The sky, the sea, Mount Ida and the islands,
No sail from edge to edge, the Greeks clean gone.
They stretched him on a rock and wrenched his limbs,
Asking: "Where is the treasure?" till he died.

1937

---

1. Priam was king of Troy at the time it was besieged and finally captured and destroyed by the Greeks. He himself was killed by the victorious Greek army. Achilles (hero of Homer's *Iliad*) and Ajax were Greek heroes in the Trojan War. Simois (line 15) was the river that flowed across the Trojan plain.

The Return

I see myself sometimes, an old old man
Who has walked so long with time as time's true servant,
That he's grown strange to me—who was once myself—
Almost as strange as time, and yet familiar
With old man's staff and legendary cloak,   5
For see, it is I, it is I. And I return
So altered, so adopted, to the house
Of my own life. There all the doors stand open
Perpetually, and the rooms ring with sweet voices,
And there my long life's seasons sound their changes,   10
Childhood and youth and manhood all together,
And welcome waits, and not a room but is
My own, beloved and longed for. And the voices,
Sweeter than any sound dreamt of or known,
Call me, recall me. I draw near at last,   15
An old old man, and scan the ancient walls
Rounded and softened by the compassionate years,
The old and heavy and long-leaved trees that watch
This my inheritance in friendly darkness.
And yet I cannot enter, for all within   20
Rises before me there, rises against me,
A sweet and terrible labyrinth of longing,
So that I turn aside and take the road
That always, early or late, runs on before.

                                      1947, 1949

The Animals

    They do not live in the world,
    Are not in time and space.
    From birth to death hurled
    No word do they have, not one
    To plant a foot upon,   5
    Were never in any place.

    For with names the world was called
    Out of the empty air,
    With names was built and walled,
    Line and circle and square,   10
    Dust and emerald;
    Snatched from deceiving death
    By the articulate breath.

    But these have never trod
    Twice the familiar track,   15
    Never never turned back
    Into the memoried day.
    All is new and near

In the unchanging Here
Of the fifth great day of God,[2]   20
That shall remain the same,
Never shall pass away.

On the sixth day we came.

                                                                1949, 1952

Adam's Dream

They say the first dream Adam our father had
After his agelong daydream in the Garden [3]
When heaven and sun woke in his wakening mind,
The earth with all its hills and woods and waters,
The friendly tribes of trees and animals,   5
And earth's last wonder Eve (the first great dream
Which is the ground of every dream since then)—
They say he dreamt lying on the naked ground,
The gates shut fast behind him as he lay
Fallen in Eve's fallen arms, his terror drowned   10
In her engulfing terror, in the abyss
Whence there's no further fall, and comfort is—
That he was standing on a rocky ledge
High on the mountainside, bare crag behind,
In front a plain as far as eye could reach,   15
And on the plain a few small figures running
That were like men and women, yet were so far away
He could not see their faces. On they ran,
And fell, and rose again, and ran, and fell,
And rising were the same yet not the same,   20
Identical or interchangeable,
Different in indifference. As he looked
Still there were more of them, the plain was filling
As by an alien arithmetical magic
Unknown in Eden, a mechanical   25
Addition without meaning, joining only
Number to number in no mode or order,
Weaving no pattern. For these creatures moved
Towards no fixed mark even when in growing bands
They clashed against each other and clashing fell   30
In mounds of bodies. For they rose again,
Identical or interchangeable,
And went their way that was not like a way;

2. God created fish and fowl on the fifth day; then he created the land animals on the sixth day, and after that (still on the sixth day) created man (Genesis i). Muir seems to have put the animals together with the birds and fishes in the fifth day.

3. I.e., after the Fall. After they had eaten of the forbidden Tree of the Knowledge of Good and Evil, Adam and Eve were expelled from the Garden of Eden: Muir here imagines Adam's first dream after the expulsion.

Some back and forward, back and forward, some
In a closed circle, wide or narrow, others   35
In zigzags on the sand. Yet all were busy,
And tense with purpose as they cut the air
Which seemed to press them back. Sometimes they paused
While one stopped one—fortuitous assignations
In the disorder, whereafter two by two   40
They ran awhile,
Then parted and again were single. Some
Ran straight against the frontier of the plain
Till the horizon drove them back. A few
Stood still and never moved. Then Adam cried   45
Out of his dream, "What are you doing there?"
And the crag answered "Are you doing there?"
"What are you doing there?"—"you doing there?"
The animals had withdrawn and from the caves
And woods stared out in fear or condemnation,   50
Like outlaws or like judges. All at once
Dreaming or half-remembering, "This is time,"
Thought Adam in his dream, and time was strange
To one lately in Eden. "I must see,"
He cried, "the faces. Where are the faces? Who   55
Are you all out there?" Then in his changing dream
He was a little nearer, and he saw
They were about some business strange to him
That had a form and sequence past their knowledge;
And that was why they ran so frenziedly.   60
Yet all, it seemed, made up a story, illustrated
By these the living, the unknowing, cast
Each singly for his part. But Adam longed
For more, not this mere moving pattern, not
This illustrated storybook of mankind   65
Always a-making, improvised on nothing.
At that he was among them, and saw each face
Was like his face, so that he would have hailed them
As sons of God but that something restrained him.
And he remembered all, Eden, the Fall,   70
The Promise, and his place, and took their hands
That were his hands, his and his children's hands,
Cried out and was at peace, and turned again
In love and grief in Eve's encircling arms.

1950, 1952

The Horses

Barely a twelvemonth after
The seven days war that put the world to sleep,
Late in the evening the strange horses came.
By then we had made our covenant with silence,

But in the first few days it was so still   5
We listened to our breathing and were afraid.
On the second day
The radios failed; we turned the knobs; no answer.
On the third day a warship passed us, heading north,
Dead bodies piled on the deck. On the sixth day   10
A plane plunged over us into the sea. Thereafter
Nothing. The radios dumb;
And still they stand in corners of our kitchens,
And stand, perhaps, turned on, in a million rooms
All over the world. But now if they should speak,   15
If on a sudden they should speak again,
If on the stroke of noon a voice should speak,
We would not listen, we would not let it bring
That old bad world that swallowed its children quick[4]
At one great gulp. We would not have it again.   20
Sometimes we think of the nations lying asleep,
Curled blindly in impenetrable sorrow,
And then the thought confounds us with its strangeness.
The tractors lie about our fields; at evening
They look like dank sea-monsters couched and waiting.   25
We leave them where they are and let them rust:
"They'll molder away and be like other loam."
We make our oxen drag our rusty plows,
Long laid aside. We have gone back
Far past our fathers' land.
                                    And then, that evening   30
Late in the summer the strange horses came.
We heard a distant tapping on the road,
A deepening drumming; it stopped, went on again
And at the corner changed to hollow thunder.
We saw the heads   35
Like a wild wave charging and were afraid.
We had sold our horses in our fathers' time
To buy new tractors. Now they were strange to us
As fabulous steeds set on an ancient shield
Or illustrations in a book of knights.   40
We did not dare go near them. Yet they waited,
Stubborn and shy, as if they had been sent
By an old command to find our whereabouts
And that long-lost archaic companionship.
In the first moment we had never a thought   45
That they were creatures to be owned and used.
Among them were some half a dozen colts
Dropped in some wilderness of the broken world,
Yet new as if they had come from their own Eden.
Since then they have pulled our plows and borne our loads,   50
But that free servitude still can pierce our hearts.
Our life is changed; their coming our beginning.

                                                                          1956

4. Alive.

DAVID JONES

(1895–)

David Jones was born in Brockley, Kent, son of a Welsh father and an
English mother, and studied at the Camberwell School of Art before joining the army in January, 1915, to serve as a private soldier until the end of
World War I. It is his experiences during the earlier part of this service
that provided the material for his modern epic of war, *In Parenthesis*. He
attended Westminster Art School after the war, and subsequently made a
name for himself as an illustrator, engraver, and water colorist. In 1924 he
worked with Eric Gill, the stone-carver and engraver whose strong Roman
Catholic feeling and belief are reflected in his work, and under Gill's influence Jones also joined the Roman Catholic Church. Jones's joint Welsh
and English origins, his visual sensitivity as an artist, and his interest in
Catholic liturgy and ritual are all reflected in his literary work, which
includes the obscure but powerful long religious poem *The Anathémata*
(1952) and *The Sleeping Lord and Other Fragments* (1973), as well as *In
Parenthesis*, which combines prose and poetry with remarkable effect.

In Parenthesis, Jones's first literary work, was published in 1937 and won
the Hawthornden Prize. It is an evocation in 40,000 words of the activities
of members of a British infantry unit from its period of training in England
to its participation in the murderous Somme offensive of July, 1916. The
book is epic in scope and tone, echoing in carefully patterned moments
themes from English and Welsh history and literature—especially the 6th-
century heroic Welsh poem by Aneirin, *Y Gododdin*, which tells of an
expedition of 300 Celtic warriors from Dineidyn (Edinburgh) against a
vastly superior force of Saxons at Catraeth (Catterick) to perish except for
three survivors, among them the bard himself. *In Parenthesis* avoids the traditional heroic poet's concentration on high-ranking heroes to build the narrative around very ordinary characters, both English and Welsh, who are
presented in vivid silhouettes and sudden stabs of personal memory or
reflections of them in the eyes of their fellow soldiers—Mr. Jenkins, Sergeant Snell, Corporal Quilter, Lance-Corporal Lewis, and (in a sense the
central figure, suggesting the poet himself, the sole if wounded survivor of
his unit at the end of the work) Private John Ball. Other characters flit in
and out, some real, some legendary, some both. Here, for example, in a passage from Part 4, is a list of John Ball's companions (pp. 69–70):

> From where John Ball sat and did his brother-keeping, mirror-
> gazing, in the corner of the fire-bay, he could easily observe
> the dispositions of his companions, and the nature of the place
> the fully-come day had now exposed, and robbed of mystery.
> Bill Crower,
> Jack Float,
> Tom Thomas,
> Siôn Evans,
> Jones, rations,
> Jones Mitchell-Troy, with
> Lizzie Tallboy, with
> Dai de la Cote male taille,

Watcyn, Wastebottom, and the rest,
his friends.

In a note to "Dai de la Cote male taille" Jones refers us to Malory, Book
9, Chapter 1, where we find the story of the knight called La Cote Male
Tayle, which Malory renders as "The Evyll-Shapyn Cote." "Dai" is the
familiar Welsh form of David; the addition of heroic echoes from Malory
gives this Welsh soldier of World War I another dimension, which the
author exploits some pages further on in putting into his mouth an epic
boast which is derived from both early Welsh and Anglo-Saxon poetry. He
is the same character as Dai Great-coat whom we see among the dead in
the concluding section, below.

In Parenthesis is in seven parts, beginning with a battalion parade in
England before embarkation for France and moving in later sections ever
nearer to the front lines, with a great number of incidental episodes and
widenings of reference, until (after a break in time from Christmas Day,
1915, to June, 1916) we reach the preparations for the offensive, with the
battalion moving up ready to attack, the terrible moments before zero hour,
and the final action in which John Ball's platoon is destroyed and he himself crawls wounded away from the action. Yet though the work has a
chronological sequence it is far from being a straightforward narrative; there
are multiple identifications of present characters with historical or mythological figures; echoes of Christian liturgy and ritual, suggesting that the soldiers are in some way acting out a ritual sacrifice, which contrast with or at
least are modified by echoes of Old English and Welsh epic poetry suggesting that the suffering is to some extent redeemed by willed heroic action.

This war poem (if poem it can be called) could not have been written
during the actual period of World War I, the time when Wilfred Owen
and Siegfried Sassoon wrote their war poems. For Jones is writing after
Joyce's *Ulysses* and Eliot's *Waste Land* and is able to profit by the ways in
which Joyce and Eliot brought mythology and ritual into narrative to give
it a new kind of depth and scope. Eliot himself, in an introduction to a
new edition of the work (New York, 1961), pointed this out. Jones has
brought together the committed pity and irony of the serving soldier that
we see in Owen with the distanced, more elaborately illustrated, less immediately personal, more complexly textured style of Eliot's long poem, and
like Eliot he introduces notes to help the reader in following the mythological and literary references. Another significant difference between Jones and
Owen is that Jones's is essentially a religious work. There is a meaning in
all this suffering and killing, and in spite of ironies, comic or sardonic reference to popular soldier's songs, follies and vices and vanities and every kind
of trivial behavior that goes to make up the texture of experience for a
group of men serving in an army (and here again we can see parallels with
similar aspects of *The Waste Land*), the notes of ritual and mystery on the
one hand and of history and heroic myth on the other combine to suggest
that, though the experience of war was "in parenthesis," bracketed outside
normal living, it had its own secret meaning.

The extracts printed here are, first, from Jones's Preface, in which he
explains his intention and method, and, secondly, from Part 7, describing
events immediately before, during, and after the attack. At the beginning of

the last section quoted, Private John Ball, wounded, is crawling painfully toward the rear through the mingled bodies of British and German soldiers: in his fevered imagination he sees the Queen of the Woods distributing flowers to the dead. He then wonders whether he is able to continue carrying his rifle. (At the end of the *Chanson de Roland* the dying Roland tries in vain to shatter his sword Durendal to prevent it from being taken as a trophy by the Saracens; he finally puts it under his body. John Ball finally leaves his rifle under an oak tree.) In the end he lies still under the oak beside a dead German and a dead Englishman, hearing the reserves coming forward to continue the battle.

From In Parenthesis

From *Preface*

This writing has to do with some things I saw, felt, & was part of. The period covered begins early in December 1915 and ends early in July 1916. The first date corresponds to my going to France. The latter roughly marks a change in the character of our lives in the Infantry on the West Front. From then onward things hardened into a more relentless, mechanical affair, took on a more sinister aspect. The wholesale slaughter of the later years, the conscripted levies filling the gaps in every file of four, knocked the bottom out of the intimate, continuing, domestic life of small contingents of men, within whose structure Roland could find, and, for a reasonable while, enjoy, his Oliver. In the earlier months there was a certain attractive amateurishness, and elbow-room for idiosyncrasy that connected one with a less exacting past. The period of the individual rifle-man, of the "old sweat" of the Boer campaign, the "Bairns-father"[1] war, seemed to terminate with the Somme battle. There were, of course, glimpses of it long after—all through in fact—but it seemed never quite the same. * * *

My companions in the war were mostly Londoners with an admixture of Welshmen, so that the mind and folk-life of those two differing racial groups are an essential ingredient to my theme. Nothing could be more representative. These came from London. Those from Wales. Together they bore in their bodies the genuine tradition of the Island of Britain, from Bendigeid Vran to Jingle and Marie Lloyd. These were the children of Doll Tearsheet. Those are before Caractacus[2] was. Both speak in parables, the wit of both

1. Bruce Bairnsfather, English cartoonist and journalist, best known for his sketches of life in the trenches during World War I.
2. Bendigeid Van, hero in Welsh heroic legend. Alfred Jingle, character in Dickens' *Pickwick Papers*. Marie Lloyd (real name Matilda Alice Victoria Wood), English music-hall comedian. Doll Tear-sheet, prostitute in Shakespeare's *II Henry IV*. Caractacus or Caradoc, king of the Silures in the west of Britain during the reign of the Roman Emperor Claudius. He was taken to Rome as a prisoner in A.D. 51 but was pardoned by Claudius, who was impressed by his nobility of spirit.

is quick, both are natural poets; yet no two groups could well be more dissimilar. It was curious to know them harnessed together, and together caught in the toils of "good order and military discipline"; to see them shape together to the remains of an antique regimental tradition, to see them react to the few things that united us—the same jargon, the same prejudice against "other arms" and against the Staff, the same discomforts, the same grievances, the same maims, the same deep fears, the same pathetic jokes; to watch them, oneself part of them, respond to the war landscape; for I think the day by day in the Waste Land, the sudden violences and the long stillnesses, the sharp contours and unformed voids of that mysterious existence, profoundly affected the imaginations of those who suffered it. It was a place of enchantment. It is perhaps best described in Malory,[3] book iv, chapter 15—that landscape spoke "with a grimly voice."

I suppose at no time did one so much live with a consciousness of the past, the very remote, and the more immediate and trivial past, both superficially and more subtly. No one, I suppose, however much not given to association, could see infantry in tin-hats, with ground-sheets over their shoulders, with sharpened pine-stakes in their hands, and not recall

> . . . or may we cram,
> Within this wooden O . . .[4]

But there were deeper complexities of sight and sound to make ever present

> the pibble pabble in Pompey's camp.[5]

Every man's speech and habit of mind were a perpetual showing: now of Napier's expedition, now of the Legions at the Wall, now of "train-band captain," now of Jack Cade, of John Ball, of the commons in arms. Now of *High Germany*, of *Dolly Gray*, of Bullcalf, Wart and Poins; of Jingo largenesses, of things as small as the Kingdom of Elmet; of Wellington's raw shire recruits, of ancient border antipathies, of our contemporary, less intimate, larger unities, of *John Barleycorn*, of "sweet Sally Frampton." Now of Coel Hên—of the Celtic cycle that lies, a subterranean influence as a deep water troubling, under every tump[6] in this Island, like Merlin[7] complaining under his big rock.[8] * * *

---

3. Sir Thomas Malory, author of *Morte Darthur*.
4. Shakespeare's *Henry V*, prologue. The "wooden O" is the stage of the theater.
5. *Ibid.*, IV.i.
6. Mound or tumulus.

7. Merlin is the powerful enchanter of the Arthurian legends.
8. The mass of references here provide a wide area of historical and literary association, beginning with *Henry V* and going on to refer to Sir William Napier,

We who are of the same world of sense with hairy ass and furry wolf and who presume to other and more radiant affinities, are finding it difficult, as yet, to recognize these creatures of chemicals as true extensions of ourselves, that we may feel for them a native affection, which alone can make them magical for us. It would be interesting to know how we shall ennoble our new media as we have already ennobled and made significant our old—candle-light, fire-light, Cups, Wands and Swords, to choose at random.

Some of us ask ourselves if Mr. X adjusting his box-respirator can be equated with what the poet envisaged, in

I saw young Harry with his beaver on.[9]

We are in no doubt at all but what Bardolph's marching kiss for Pistol's "quondam Quickly" is[1] an experience substantially the same as you and I suffered on Victoria[2] platform. For the old authors there appears to have been no such dilemma—for them the embrace of battle seemed one with the embrace of lovers. For us it is different. There is no need to labour the point, nor enquire into the causes here. I only wish to record that for me such a dilemma exists, and that I have been particularly conscious of it during the making of this writing.

* * *

This writing is called *In Parenthesis* because I have written it in a kind of space between—I don't know between quite what—but as you turn aside to do something; and because for us amateur soldiers (and especially for the writer, who was not only amateur, but grotesquely incompetent, a knocker-over of piles, a parade's despair) the war itself was a parenthesis—how glad we thought we were to step outside its brackets at the end of '18—and also because our curious type of existence here is altogether in parenthesis.

D.J.

who fought in the Peninsular War and later wrote a famous history of that campaign; to the Roman legions who manned the Great Wall built by the Romans in Britain; to Jack Cade, who led an unsuccessful popular revolt against the misrule of Henry VI in 1450 and John Ball, a leader of the Peasants' Revolt of 1381; to a number of English ballads and popular songs and to characters in Shakespeare's *Henry IV*; to the ancient British kingdom of Elmet in southwest Yorkshire, overthrown by Anglo-Saxon invaders early in the 7th cen-tury; to Wellington's "raw shire recruits" who helped to win the Battle of Waterloo; and concluding with a reference to the old Celtic British myths that lie beneath everything.

9. Sir Richard Vernon's admiring description of the reformed Prince Hal ready for battle, *I Henry IV*, IV.i.104.

1. All are characters from *Henry IV*.

2. Victoria Station, London station for trains going to the south coast and hence the station for the Continent; troops for France left from Victoria.

2326 · David Jones

From Part 7: The Five Unmistakeable Marks[1]

Gododdin I demand thy support.
It is our duty to sing: a meeting
place has been found.[2]

* * *

They shook out into a single line and each inclined his body to
the slope to wait.   21
And this is the manner of their waiting:
Those happy who had borne the yoke
who kept their peace
and these other in a like condemnation   25
to the place of a skull.

Immediately behind where Private 25201 Ball pressed his body to
the earth and the white chalk womb to mother him,
          Colonel Dell presumed to welcome
some other, come out of the brumous morning
at leisure and well-dressed and all at ease   30
as thriving on the nitrous air.
Well Dell!
          and into it they slide . . . of the admirable salads of Mrs. Cur-
tis-Smythe: they fall for her in Poona,[3] and its worth one's while
—but the comrade close next you screamed so after the last salvo
that it was impossible to catch any more the burthen of this white-
man talk.

And the place of their waiting a long burrow,
in the chalk a cutting, and steep clift—   35
but all but too shallow against his violence.
Like in long-ship, where you flattened face to kelson[4] for the shock-
breaking on brittle pavissed free-board, and the gunnel stove, and
no care to jettison the dead.

No one to care there for Aneirin Lewis spilled there
who worshipped his ancestors like a Chink
who sleeps in Arthur's lap   40
who saw Olwen-trefoils some moonlighted night
on precarious slats at Festubert,
on narrow foothold on le Plantin marsh—

1. "Carroll's *Hunting of the Snark*, Fit
the 2nd verse 15" [Jones's note]. Lewis
Carroll's mock-heroic nonsense poem
concerns the hunting of the elusive animal Snark, which may be known by
"five unmistakable marks."
2. "From *Y Gododdin*, early Welsh epi-
cal poem attributed to Aneirin (6th century); commemorates raid of 300 Welsh
of Gododdin (the territory of the Otad-
ini located near the Firth of Forth) into
English kingdom of Deira. Describes the
ruin of this 300 in battle at Catraeth

(perhaps Catterick in Yorkshire). Three
men alone escaped death, including the
poet, who laments his friends" [Jones's
note].
3. City in India, formerly headquarters
of the 6th division of the British southern army in India and a residence of the
governor of Bombay during the rainy
season; thus a symbol of the social life
of British India in the early part of this
century.
4. Inner keel fitted over the floor timbers
of a ship.

more shaved he is to the bare bone than
Yspaddadan Penkawr.   45
    Properly organized chemists can let make more riving power
than ever Twrch Trwyth;
more blistered he is than painted Troy Towers
and unwholer, limb from limb, than any of them fallen at Catraeth
or on the seaboard-down, by Salisbury,[5]
and no maker to contrive his funerary song.   50
    And the little Jew lies next him
cries out for Deborah his bride
and offers for stretcher-bearers
        gifts for their pains
and walnut suites in his delirium
        from Grays Inn Road.[6]   55

But they already look at their watches and it is zero minus seven
minutes.
Seven minutes to go . . . and seventy times seven times to the
minute⁄
this drumming of the diaphragm.
From deeply inward thumping all through you beating   60
no peace to be still in
and no one is there not anyone to stop
can't anyone—someone turn off the tap
or won't any one before it snaps.

Racked out to another turn of the screw   65
the acceleration heightens;
the sensibility of these instruments to register,
fails;
needle dithers disorientate.
The responsive mercury plays laggard to such fevers—you simply
can't take any more in.   70
And the surfeit of fear steadies to dumb incognition, so that when
they give the order to move upward to align with "A," hugged already just under the lip of the acclivity inches below where his traversing machine-guns perforate to powder white—
white creature of chalk pounded
and the world crumbled away
and get ready to advance

5. "Arthur's lap. Cf. *Henry V*, Act II,
Sc. iii. [This is a comic mistake by the
hostess for "Abraham's bosom." To
sleep in Abraham's bosom is to be at
peace after death (cf. Luke xvi.22), and
the hostess is saying that Falstaff is at
peace after death. But when Jones takes
over the substitution of Arthur for Abraham, it is not a comic mistake but a deliberate introduction of the British Celtic
hero Arthur.]   Olwen-trefoils.   Cf.
Kulhwch ac Olwen [ancient Welsh
poem]: 'Four white trefoils sprang up
wherever she trod.' Yspaddaden Penkawr. The Giant task-setter in the
Kulhwch. "And Kaw of North Britain
came and shaved his beard, skin, and
flesh, clean to the very bone from ear to
ear. "Art shaved, man?" said Kulhwch.
"I am shaved," answered he.' Twrch
Trwyth. The mysterious destroying beast
which is the subject of much of the
Kulhwch story. Seaboard-down, by Salisbury. Refers to the Battle of Camlann.
Malory, book xxi, ch. 3" [Jones's note].
6. In London.

you have not capacity for added fear only the limbs are leaden to
negotiate the slope and rifles all out of balance, clumsied with long
auxiliary steel   75
seem five times the regulation weight—
it bitches the aim as well;
                and we ourselves as those small
cherubs, who trail awkwardly the weapons of the God in
                                Fine Art works.   80

The returning sun climbed over the hill, to lessen the shadows of
small and great things; and registered the minutes to zero hour.
Their saucer hats made dial for his passage: long thin line of them,
vivid domes of them,
cut elliptical with light
as cupola on Byzantine wall,
stout turrets to take the shock
and helmets of salvation.   85
Long side by side lie like friends lie
on daisy-down on warm days
cuddled close down kindly close with the mole
in down and silky rodent,
and if you look more intimately all manner of small creatures,   90
created-dear things creep about quite comfortably
yet who travail until now
beneath your tin-hat shade.
                He bawls at ear-hole:
Two minutes to go.   95
                Minutes to excuse me to make excuse.
Responde mihi?[7]
                for surely I must needs try them
so many, much undone
and lose on roundabouts as well and vari-colored polygram   100
to love and know
                and we have a little sister[8]
whose breasts will be as towers
and the gilly-flowers will blow next month
below the pound
with Fred Karno billed for *The Holloway*.[9]   105

He's getting it now more accurately and each salvo brackets more
narrowly and a couple right in, just as "D" and "C" are forming for
the second wave.

---

7. ["Answer me."] "Cf. Dominican Little Office of the Blessed Virgin Mary.
Office of the Dead, 2nd Nocturn, Lesson
IV (Job xiii. 22 to end of chapter)"
[Jones's note].
8. Cf. Song of Solomon viii. 8. "We
have a little sister, and she hath no
breasts."
9. The Holloway Empire Music Hall.
Fred Karno was a popular comedian
who performed there.

Wastebottom married a wife on his Draft-leave but the whinnying
splinter razored diagonal and mess-tin fragments drove inward and
toxined underwear.

    He maintained correct alignment with the others, face down,
and you never would have guessed.

                   *   *   *

The gentle slopes are green to remind you   281
of South English places, only far wider and flatter spread and
grooved and harrowed criss-cross whitely and the disturbed subsoil
heaped up albescent.[1]

Across upon this undulated board of verdure chequered bright
when you look to left and right
small, drab, bundled pawns severally make effort   285
moved in tenuous line
and if you looked behind—the next wave came slowly, as successive
surfs creep in to dissipate on flat shore;
and to your front, stretched long laterally,
and receded deeply,
the dark wood.   290

And now the gradient runs more flatly toward the separate scarred
saplings, where they make fringe for the interior thicket and you take
notice.

    There between the thinning uprights
at the margin
straggle tangled oak and flayed sheeny beech-bole, and fragile birch
    whose silver queenery is draggled and ungraced   295
and June shoots lopt
and fresh stalks bled
            runs the Jerry[2] trench.
And cork-screw stapled trip-wire
to snare among the briars   300
and iron warp with bramble weft
with meadow-sweet and lady-smock
for a fair camouflage.

Mr. Jenkins half inclined his head to them—he walked just barely
in advance of his platoon and immediately to the left of Private Ball.

    He makes the conventional sign   305
and there is the deeply inward effort of spent men who would make
response for him,
and take it at the double.
He sinks on one knee

---

1. Becoming white.
2. British army slang for "German" in both World Wars.

and now on the other,
his upper body tilts in rigid inclination   310
this way and back;
weighted lanyard runs out to full tether,
                swings like a pendulum
                and the clock run down.
Lurched over, jerked iron saucer over tilted brow,   315
clampt unkindly over lip and chin
nor no ventaille to this darkening
                and masked face lifts to grope the air
and so disconsolate;
enfeebled fingering at a paltry strap—   320
buckle holds,
holds him blind against the morning.
      Then stretch still where weeds pattern the chalk predella—
where it rises to his wire[3]—and Sergeant T. Quilter takes over.
                            * * *

It's difficult with the weight of the rifle.   636
Leave it—under the oak.
Leave it for a salvage-bloke
let it lie bruised for a monument
dispense the authenticated fragments to the faithful.   640
It's the thunder-besom for us
it's the bright bough borne
it's the tensioned yew for a Genoese jammed arbalest and a scarlet
square for a mounted *mareschal*,[4] it's that county-mob back to back.[5]
Majuba mountain and Mons Cherubim[6] and spreaded mats for
Sydney Street East,[7] and come to Bisley for a Silver Dish.[8] It's
R.S.M. O'Grady[9] says, it's the soldier's best friend if you care for
the working parts and let us be 'aving those springs released smartly
in Company billets on wet forenoons and clickerty-click and one up
the spout and you men must really cultivate the habit of treating

3. "The approach to the German trenches here rose slightly, in low chalk ridges" [Jones's note]; "predella": a platform or shelf (strictly, below or behind an altar).
4. "Mareschal": marshal (French); "arbalest": a powerful medieval crossbow.
5. "The Gloucestershire Regiment, during an action near Alexandria, in 1801, about-turned their rear rank and engaged the enemy back to back" [Jones's note].
6. The British were defeated by the Boers on Majuba Hill on Feb. 27, 1881. The "Angels of Mons" were angels (varying in number from two to a platoon) widely believed to have assisted the British to repel an attack at Mons by superior German forces on August 23, 1914.
7. In what became known as the Siege or Battle of Sydney Street, Winston Churchill, when he was Home Secretary in 1911, directed military operations in London against a group of anarchists. "It is said that in 'The Battle of Sydney Street' under Mr. Churchill's Home Secretaryship mats were spread on the pavement for troops firing from the prone position" [Jones's note].
8. At ,Bisley, marksmen compete annually in rifle-shooting for such trophies as "a Silver Dish."
9. "R.S.M.": Regimental Sergeant-Major. "R.S.M. O'Grady," according to Jones's note, "refers to mythological personage figuring in Army exercises, the precise describing of which would be tedious. Anyway these exercises were supposed to foster alertness in dull minds—and were a curious blend of the parlor game and military drill."

this weapon with the very greatest care and there should be a healthy rivalry among you—it should be a matter of very proper pride and

Marry it man! Marry it! **645**
Cherish her, she's your very own.

Coax it man coax it—it's delicately and ingeniously made—it's an instrument of precision—it costs us tax-payers, money—I want you men to remember that.

Fondle it like a granny—talk to it—consider it as you would a friend—and when you ground these arms she's not a rooky's gas-pipe for greenhorns to tarnish.[1]

You've known her hot and cold.
You would choose her from among many.
You know her by her bias, and by her exact error at 300, and by the deep scar at the small, by the fair flaw in the grain, above the lower sling-swivel—
but leave it under the oak. **650**

* * *

The secret princes between the leaning trees have diadems given them. **663**
Life the leveller hugs her impudent equality—she may proceed at once to less discriminating zones.

The Queen of the Woods has cut bright boughs of various flowering.
These knew her influential eyes. Her awarding hands can pluck for each their fragile prize.

She speaks to them according to precedence. She knows what's due to this elect society. She can choose twelve gentle-men. She knows who is most lord between the high trees and on the open down.

Some she gives white berries
    some she gives brown
Emil has a curious crown it's **670**
    made of golden saxifrage.
Fatty wears sweet-briar,
he will reign with her for a thousand years.
For Balder she reaches high to fetch his.
Ulrich smiles for his myrtle wand. **675**
That swine Lillywhite has daisies to his chain—you'd hardly credit it.

She plaits torques of equal splendour for Mr. Jenkins and Billy Crower.

Hansel with Gronwy share dog-violets for a palm, where they lie in serious embrace beneath the twisted tripod.

Siôn gets St. John's Wort—that's fair enough.

Dai Great-coat,[2] she can't find him anywhere—she calls both

---

1. "I have employed here only such ideas as were common to the form of speech affected by Instructors in Musketry" [Jones's note].
2. See reference in introduction.

high and low, she had a very special one for him.   680
    Among this July noblesse she is mindful of December wood—
when the trees of the forest beat against each other because of him.
    She carries to Aneirin-in-the-nullah a rowan sprig,[3] for the
glory of Guenedota.[4] You couldn't hear what she said to him, because
she was careful for the Disciplines of the Wars.

At the gate of the wood you try a last adjustment, but slung so, it's
an impediment, it's of detriment to your hopes, you had best be rid
of it—the sagging webbing and all and what's left of your two fifty—
but it were wise to hold on to your mask.

You're clumsy in your feebleness, you implicate your tin-hat rim
with the slack sling of it.
    Let it lie for the dews to rust it, or ought you to decently cover
the working parts.   685
    Its dark barrel, where you leave it under the oak, reflects the
solemn star that rises urgently from Cliff Trench.
    It's a beautiful doll for us
it's the Last Reputable Arm.
    But leave it—under the oak.
leave it for a Cook's tourist to the Devastated Areas and crawl as far
    as you can and wait for the bearers.[5]   690

Mrs. Willy Hartington has learned to draw sheets and so has Miss
Melpomené; and on the south lawns,
men walk in red white and blue
under the cedars
and by every green tree   695
and beside comfortable waters.
But why dont the bastards come—
Bearers!—stret-cher bear-errs!
or do they divide the spoils at the Aid-Post.[6]

3. "Nullah": a river, stream, or riv-
erbed. The rowan, or mountain ash, is a
tree with magical properties in Celtic
folklore.
4. The northwest parts of Wales. The
last king of Wales, Llywelyn, was killed
there in 1282. Jones refers to his death
in another note on this part of Wales.
He adds: "His [Llywelyn's] contemporary, Gruffydd ap yr Ynad Côch, sang
of his death: 'The voice of lamentation
is heard in every place . . . the course of
nature is changed . . . the trees of the
forest furiously rush against each other.' "
5. "This may appear to be an anachronism, but I remember in 1917 discussing
with a friend the possibilities of tourist
activity if peace ever came. I remember

we went into details and wondered if the
unexploded projectile lying near us
would go up under a holiday-maker, and
how people would stand up to be photographed on our parapets. I recall feeling
very angry about this, as you do if you
think of strangers ever occupying a
house you live in, and which has, for
you, particular associations" [Jones's
note].
6. "The R.A.M.C." [Royal Army Medical Corps] was suspected by disgruntled
men of the fighting units of purloining
articles from the kit of the wounded and
the dead. Their regimental initials were
commonly interpreted: 'Rob All My
Comrades' " [Jones's note].

But how many men do you suppose could bear away a third of us:
drag just a little further—he yet may counter-attack.   700

Lie still under the oak
next to the Jerry
and Sergeant Jerry Coke.
The feet of the reserves going up tread level with your forehead; and no word for you; they whisper one with another;
pass on, inward;   705
these latest succours:
green Kimmerii[7] to bear up the war.

Oeth and Annoeth's hosts they were
who in that night grew
younger men   710
younger striplings.[8]

The geste says this and the man who was on the field . . . and who
wrote the book . . . the man who does not know this has not understood anything.[9]

                                                                    1937

7. Kimmerioi or Cimmerians, in Homer a fabulous people "on whom the sun never looks." They were, however, a real historical people who broke the power of Phrygia, overran Lydia, and invaded cities on the west coast of Greece.
8. "*Oeth and Annoeth's hosts . . . strip-lings*. Cf. Englyn 30 of the *Englynion y Beddeu*, 'The Stanzas of the Graves.' See Rhys, *Origin of the Englyn, Y Cymmro-dor*, vol. xviii. Oeth and Annoeth's hosts occur in Welsh tradition as a mysterious body of troops that seem to have some affinity with the Legions. They were said to 'fight as well in the covert as in the open.' Cf. *The Iolo MSS*" [Jones's note].
9. "*The Geste says . . . anything*. Cf. *Chanson de Roland*, lines 2095—8:
'Co dit la geste e cil qui el camp fut,
[Li ber Gilie por qui Deus fait vertuz]
E fist la chartre [el muster de Loüm].
Ki tant ne set, ne l'ad prod entendut.'
    I have used Mr. René Hague's transla-tion" [Jones's note].

ROBERT GRAVES
(1895–)

Robert Ranke Graves was born in London of partly Anglo-Irish and partly German descent—his great-uncle was the distinguished German historian Leopold von Ranke—but his voice is peculiarly English. He left Charterhouse School to go immediately into the army, serving in World War I until he was invalided out in 1917. After the war he went to Oxford, took a B.Litt. degree and in 1926 began a brief period as Professor of English at the Egyptian University in Cairo. In 1929 he published *Goodbye to All That,* an account of his experiences in the war, which, as he himself put it, "paid my debts and enabled me to set up in Majorca as a writer." He returned to Majorca after World War II and has made his home there ever since.

Graves began as a Georgian poet, but from an early stage it was clear that he was a Georgian with a difference. The mingling of the colloquial and the visionary in his vocabulary, the accent of conversation underlying the regular rhythms of his stanzas, the tension between a romantic indulgence in emotion and a cool appraisal of its significance—these are qualities found even in his early poetry, though it is only in his later work that we find them more consistently employed and effectively disciplined. His best work combines the ironic and the visionary in a highly individual manner, and he is also capable of a down-to-earth poetry, often ironical and mocking in tone and dealing with simple domestic facts or the more annoying of personal relationships, which nevertheless is seen on further reading to reach out to ever wider and deeper implications. He himself has said: "I write poems for poets, and satires or grotesques for wits. For people in general I write prose, and am content that they should be unaware that I do anything else. To write poems for other than poets is wasteful" (Foreword to *Poems 1938–45*). But this is mischievous exaggeration. "What Mr. Graves means," Lionel Trilling has observed, "is that, in our day, only poets can be counted on not to be misled by the lightness and clarity of his verse, by the irony and the humor; that only poets will be sufficiently aware of the tradition in which he writes, and of hearing the truth that lies not only in the doctrinal statements that the poem makes but also in the justice of its diction, in the pitch and tone of its voice * * * " (*A Gathering of Fugitives,* p. 23).

Graves has long made his living by his prose, which is extensive and varied and includes, in addition to *Goodbye to All That,* a number of historical novels in which characters and events from the classical or Biblical past are reconstructed in a lively modern idiom: the most notable of his historical novels are *I, Claudius* (1934), *Claudius the God* (1934), and *King Jesus* (1946). Graves is a good classical and Biblical scholar, though an eccentric one. His interest in classical and Biblical myth is closely related to his theory of poetry and of poetic inspiration, which he expressed in *The White Goddess* (1948), a study of mythology drawn from a great variety of sources but essentially original in its main emphases and interpretations. The book begins as a history of myth, develops into an attack on fashionable kinds of poetry, and ends with his own view of poetry. It preserves the secret wisdom of a people and derives from the great female inspirational principle which he called the White Goddess. Only a return to goddess-worship and an abandonment of patriarchal in favor of matriarchal society can help modern poetry to recover its lost force, clarity, and mythic wisdom. There is often a note of willful exaggeration or mocking mischief in Graves' criticism: he loves to flutter the academic dovecotes, and in the lectures he gave as Clark Lecturer at Cambridge in 1954–55

(*The Crowning Privilege*, 1955) and as Professor of Poetry at Oxford (the professorship of poetry at Oxford is not a regular academic appointment but a visiting lectureship chosen by the vote of all Oxford M.A.'s) in 1964–65 (*Poetic Craft and Principle*, 1967) he deliberately provoked the local academics by contemptuously dismissing most of the accepted great figures of English poetry.

Among the early influences on Graves' poetry were the late 15th- and early 16th-century poet John Skelton, the ballads, Welsh and Irish heroic and popular poetry, and Thomas Hardy (one of the few poets surviving into his own lifetime whom he admired). From 1925 to 1939 the American poet Laura Riding was in Europe and Graves worked closely with and was much influenced by her: they collaborated in the influential critical work, *A Survey of Modernist Poetry* (1927). But for Graves modernism was not represented by the later Yeats or by Pound or Eliot; it had more in common with the work of the American poets John Crowe Ransom, E. E. Cummings, and William Carlos Williams. In his own later poetry Graves becomes more and more the poet of personal relationships, especially of love between the sexes.

In successive editions of his poems Graves has ruthlessly pruned away what he has come to dislike or believes to represent a phase of his poetic career that he has outgrown. He has published over 15 volumes of poetry, of which *Collected Poems 1959* represents most of what he wants to preserve. He has continued to publish slim volumes of new poetry (*New Poems 1961*; *New Poems 1962*), but the 1959 volume well represents the range and quality of his genius. Its publication was the sign for clear critical affirmation, on both sides of the Atlantic, that Graves is a major English poet of our time. He won the Russell Loines Award for Poetry in 1958 and the Gold Medal of the National Poetry Society of America in 1960.

Flying Crooked

The butterfly, a cabbage-white,
(His honest idiocy of flight)
Will never now, it is too late,
Master the art of flying straight,
Yet has—who knows so well as I?—   5
A just sense of how not to fly:
He lurches here and here by guess
And God and hope and hopelessness.
Even the aerobatic swift [1]
Has not his flying-crooked gift.   10

1931

1. A bird outwardly resembling the swallow, conspicuous for rushing through the air with vigorous wheeling; it is constantly in flight and is only accidentally on the ground.

Down, Wanton, Down!

Down, wanton, down! Have you no shame
That at the whisper of Love's name,
Or Beauty's, presto! up you raise
Your angry head and stand at gaze?

Poor bombard-captain, sworn to reach   5
The ravelin and effect a breach—
Indifferent what you storm or why,
So be that in the breach you die!

Love may be blind, but Love at least
Knows what is man and what mere beast;   10
Or Beauty wayward, but requires
More delicacy from her squires.

Tell me, my witless, whose one boast
Could be your staunchness at the post,
When were you made a man of parts   15
To think fine and profess the arts?

Will many-gifted Beauty come
Bowing to your bald rule of thumb,
Or Love swear loyalty to your crown?
Be gone, have done! Down, wanton, down!   20

1933

The Reader Over My Shoulder

You, reading over my shoulder, peering beneath
My writing arm—I suddenly feel your breath
   Hot on my hand or on my nape,
So interrupt my theme, scratching these few
Words on the margin for you, namely you,   5
   Too-human shape fixed in that shape:—

All the saying of things against myself
And for myself I have well done myself.
   What now, old enemy, shall you do
But quote and underline, thrusting yourself   10
Against me, as ambassador of myself,
   In damned confusion of myself and you?

For you in strutting, you in sycophancy,
Have played too long this other self of me,
   Doubling the part of judge and patron   15
With that of creaking grind-stone to my wit.
Know me, have done: I am a proud spirit
   And you forever clay. Have done.

1938

The Devil's Advice to Story-tellers

Lest men suspect your tale to be untrue,
Keep probability—some say—in view.
But my advice to story-tellers is:
Weigh out no gross of probabilities,
Nor yet make diligent transcriptions of   5
Known instances of virtue, crime or love.
To forge a picture that will pass for true,
Do conscientiously what liars do—
Born liars, not the lesser sort that raid
The mouths of others for their stock-in-trade: 10
Assemble, first, all casual bits and scraps
That may shake down into a world perhaps;
People this world, by chance created so,
With random persons whom you do not know—
The teashop sort, or travelers in a train   15
Seen once, guessed idly at, not seen again;
Let the erratic course they steer surprise
Their own and your own and your readers' eyes;
Sigh then, or frown, but leave (as in despair)
Motive and end and moral in the air;   20
Nice contradiction between fact and fact
Will make the whole read human and exact.

1938

A Civil Servant

While in this cavernous place emploved
   Not once was I aware
Of my officious other-self
   Poised high above me there,

My self reversed, my rage-less part,   5
   A slimy yellowish cone—
Drip, drip; drip, drip—so down the vears
   I stalagmized in stone.

Now pilgrims to the cave, who come
   To chip off what they can,
Prod me with child-like merriment: 10
   "Look, look! It's like a man!"

1948

Gulls and Men

The naturalists of the Bass Rock [2]
   On this vexatious point agree:

2. A small, roughly circular, rocky island in the Firth of Forth, Scotland, on which there are a lighthouse and huge numbers of sea birds.

That sea-birds of all sorts that flock
  About the Bass, repeatedly
    Collide in mid-flight,   5

And neither by design, in play,
  Nor by design, in shrewd assault,
But (as these patient watchers say,
  Eyes that are seldom proved at fault)
    By lack of foresight.   10

Stupidity, which poor and rich
  Hold the recognizance of man,
Precious stupidity, of which
  Let him denude himself who can
    And stand at God's height—   15

Stupidity that brings to birth
  More, always more, than to the grave,
The burden of all songs on earth,
  And by which men are brave
    And women contrite—   20

This jewel bandied from a cliff
  By gulls and razor-bills and such!
Where is man's vindication if
  Perfectibility's as much
    Bird-right as man-right?   25

                                                1947, 1948

The White Goddess[3]

All saints revile her, and all sober men
Ruled by the God Apollo's golden mean—
In scorn of which we sailed to find her
In distant regions likeliest to hold her
Whom we desired above all things to know,   5
Sister of the mirage and echo.

It was a virtue not to stay,
To go our headstrong and heroic way
Seeking her out at the volcano's head,
Among pack ice, or where the track had faded   10
Beyond the cavern of the seven sleepers:[4]
Whose broad high brow was white as any leper's,
Whose eyes were blue, with rowan-berry lips,
With hair curled honey-colored to white hips.

Green sap of Spring in the young wood astir   15
Will celebrate the Mountain Mother,
And every song-bird shout awhile for her;

---

3. The significance of the White Goddess for Graves is explained in the introductory headnote.

4. Cf. Donne, *The Good-Morrow*—"Or snorted we in the seven sleepers' den."

But we are gifted, even in November
Rawest of seasons, with so huge a sense
Of her nakedly worn magnificence   20
We forget cruelty and past betrayal,
Heedless of where the next bright bolt may fall.

1953

The Straw

Peace, the wild valley streaked with torrents,
A hoopoe [5] perched on his warm rock. Then why
This tremor of the straw between my fingers?

What should I fear? Have I not testimony
In her own hand, signed with her own name   5
That my love fell as lightning on her heart?

These questions, bird, are not rhetorical.
Watch how the straw twitches and leaps
As though the earth quaked at a distance.

Requited love; but better unrequited   10
If this chance instrument gives warning
Of cataclysmic anguish far away.

Were she at ease, warmed by the thought of me,
Would not my hand stay steady as this rock?
Have I undone her by my vehemence?   15

1951, 1953

Dialogue on the Headland

SHE: You'll not forget these rocks and what I told you?
HE: How could I? Never: whatever happens.
SHE: What do you think might happen?
       Might you fall out of love?—did you mean that?
HE: Never, never! "Whatever" was a sop   5
       For jealous listeners in the shadows.
SHE: You haven't answered me. I asked:
       "What do you think might happen?"
HE: Whatever happens: though the skies should fall
       Raining their larks and vultures in our laps—   10
SHE: "Though the seas turn to slime"—say that—
       "Though water-snakes be hatched with six heads."
HE: Though the seas turn to slime, or tower
       In an arching wave above us, three miles high—
SHE: "Though she should break with you," —dare you say that?— 15
       "Though she deny her words on oath."

5. Bird with pinkish-cinnamon mantle   and barred black-and-white wings and
and breast, prominent black-tipped crest,   tail.

HE: I had that in my mind to say, or nearly;
   It hurt so much I choked it back.
SHE: How many other days can't you forget?
   How many other loves and landscapes?   20
HE: You are jealous?
SHE: Damnably.
HE: The past is past.
SHE: And this?
HE: Whatever happens, this goes on. 25
SHE: Without a future? Sweetheart, tell me now:
   What do you want of me? I must know that.
HE: Nothing that isn't freely mine already.
SHE: Say what is freely yours and you shall have it.
HE: Nothing that, loving you, I could dare take. 30
SHE: O, for an answer with no "nothing" in it!
HE: Then give me everything that's left.
SHE: Left after what?
HE: After whatever happens:
   Skies have already fallen, seas are slime, 35
   Water-snakes poke and peer six-headedly—
SHE: And I lie snugly in the Devil's arms.
HE: I said: "Whatever happens." Are you crying?
SHE: You'll not forget me—ever, ever, ever?

                1952, 1953

The Blue-fly

Five summer days, five summer nights,
The ignorant, loutish, giddy blue-fly
Hung without motion on the cling peach,
Humming occasionally: "O my love, my fair one!"
  As in the Canticles.[6]   5

Magnified one thousand times, the insect
Looks farcically human; laugh if you will!
Bald head, stage-fairy wings, blear eyes,
A caved-in chest, hairy black mandibles,
  Long spindly thighs.   10

The crime was detected on the sixth day.
What then could be said or done? By anyone?
It would have been vindictive, mean and what-not
To swat that fly for being a blue-fly,
  For debauch of a peach.   15

Is it fair, either, to bring a microscope
To bear on the case, even in search of truth?

6. The Biblical Song of Songs, or Song of Solomon.

Nature, doubtless, has some compelling cause
To glut the carriers of her epidemics—
    Nor did the peach complain.   20

1952, 1953

A Plea to Boys and Girls

You learned Lear's *Nonsense Rhymes* by heart, not rote;
    You learned Pope's *Iliad* by rote, not heart;
These terms should be distinguished if you quote
    My verses, children—keep them poles apart—
And call the man a liar who says I wrote   5
    All that I wrote in love, for love of art.

1956, 1958

Friday Night

Love, the sole Goddess fit for swearing by,
Concedes us graciously the little lie:
The white lie, the half-lie, the lie corrective
Without which love's exchange might prove defective,
Confirming hazardous relationships   5
By kindly *maquillage* [7] of Truth's pale lips.
This little lie was first told, so they say,
On the sixth day (Love's planetary day)
When, meeting her full-bosomed and half dressed,
Jove roared out suddenly: "Hell take the rest!   10
Six hard days of Creation are enough"—
And clasped her to him, meeting no rebuff.

Next day he rested, and she rested too.
The busy little lie between them flew:
"If this be not perfection," Love would sigh,
"Perfection is a great, black, thumping lie . . ."   15
Endearments, kisses, grunts, and whispered oaths;
But were her thoughts on breakfast, or on clothes?

1957, 1958

The Naked and the Nude

    For me, the naked and the nude
    (By lexicographers construed
    As synonyms that should express
    The same deficiency of dress
    Or shelter) stand as wide apart   5
    As love from lies, or truth from art.

7. Make-up (French).

Lovers without reproach will gaze
On bodies naked and ablaze;
The Hippocratic [8] eye will see
In nakedness, anatomy;   10
And naked shines the Goddess when
She mounts her lion among men.

The nude are bold, the nude are sly
To hold each treasonable eye.
While draping by a showman's trick   15
Their dishabille in rhetoric,
They grin a mock-religious grin
Of scorn at those of naked skin.

The naked, therefore, who compete
Against the nude may know defeat;   20
Yet when they both together tread
The briary pastures of the dead,
By Gorgons [9] with long whips pursued,
How naked go the sometime nude!

1957, 1958

A Slice of Wedding Cake

Why have such scores of lovely, gifted girls
  Married impossible men?
Simple self-sacrifice may be ruled out,
  And missionary endeavor, nine times out of ten.

Repeat "impossible men": not merely rustic,   5
  Foul-tempered or depraved
(Dramatic foils chosen to show the world
  How well women behave, and always have behaved).

Impossible men: idle, illiterate,
  Self-pitying, dirty, sly,   10
For whose appearance even in City parks
  Excuses must be made to casual passers-by.

Has God's supply of tolerable husbands
  Fallen, in fact, so low?
Or do I always over-value woman   15
  At the expense of man?
              Do I?
                  It might be so.

1959

8. Medical: Hippocrates, the "Father   9. Monsters in Greek mythology: three
of Medicine," was a Greek physician,   horrible sisters with hair composed of
5th–4th century B.C.   snakes, brazen claws, and staring eyes.

W. H. AUDEN

(1907–1973)

Wystan Hugh Auden was born in York and educated at Gresham's School, Holt, Cheshire, and Christ Church, Oxford. After leaving Oxford he taught school from 1930 to 1935 and later worked for a government film unit. His sympathies in the 1930's were with the Left, like those of most intellectuals of his age, and he spent a short time as an ambulance driver on the republican side in the Spanish Civil War. He traveled in Iceland and China before coming to America in 1939; in 1946 he became an American citizen. He has taught at a number of American colleges, and was elected Professor of Poetry at Oxford for the 1956–60 tenure (the position requires the giving of only a few lectures a year).

Auden was the most active of the group of young English poets who, in the late 1920's and early 1930's, saw themselves bringing new techniques and attitudes to English poetry. Stephen Spender and Cecil Day Lewis were at the time the most prominent of the other members of the new school, which soon afterward fell apart, each poet going his own separate way. Like all his generation, Auden learned poetic wit and irony from Eliot, and he also learned metrical and verbal techniques from Hopkins and from Wilfred Owen. His English studies at Oxford familiarized him with the rhythms and long alliterative line of Anglo-Saxon poetry as well as with the rapid and rollicking short lines (a sort of inspired doggerel) of the early 16th-century poet John Skelton: both influenced his own versification. He learned, too, from the songs of the English music hall and, later, from American blues singers.

The depression which upset America in 1929 hit England soon afterwards, and Auden and his contemporaries looked out at an England of industrial stagnation and mass unemployment, seeing not the metaphorical Waste Land of Eliot but a more literal Waste Land of poverty and "depressed areas." His early poetry is much concerned with a diagnosis of the ills of his country. This diagnosis, conducted in a verse which combined deliberate irreverence and sometimes even clowning with a cunning verbal craftsmanship, drew on both Freud and Marx to show England now as a nation of neurotic invalids who must learn to "throw away their rugs," and now as the victim of an antiquated economic system. The liveliness and nervous force of this early poetry of Auden's made a great impression, even though an uncertainty about his audience led him to introduce purely private symbols, intelligible only to a few friends, in some of his poems.

Gradually, Auden learned to clarify his imagery and control his desire to shock, and he produced, in the years around 1940, some poems (such as, in this anthology, *Lullaby*) of finely disciplined movement, pellucid clarity, and deep yet unsentimental feeling. At the same time he was developing a more complex view of the world, moving from his earlier diagnosis of modern ills in terms of Freud and Marx to a more religious view of personal responsibility and traditional value without, however, abandoning the ideas and terms he had learned from modern psychology. But he never lost his ear for popular speech or his ability to combine elements from popular art with an extreme technical formality. He was always the experimenter, particularly in ways of bringing together high artifice and a colloquial tone.

Some of Auden's most exciting work is found in his early volumes, *Poems* (1930) and *On This Island* (1937). *Another Time* (1940) shows greater control and less violence. Of his later volumes, *Nones* (1951) shows most clearly his characteristic ways of combining or alternating the grave and the flippant. For the first part of his career—the English and the early American phase—Auden was very much the poet of his times, first of the Depression and then of the Age of the Refugee. In the poems of this period he preferred to confront modern problems directly rather than to filter them, as Eliot did, through symbolic situations. The poems of the last phase of his career, notably those in *About the House* (1967) and *City without Walls* (1970), are increasingly personal in tone and combine an apparent air of offhand informality with remarkable technical skill in versification. Auden grew increasingly hostile to the modern world and skeptical of all remedies offered for modern ills: he took refuge in friendship, grounded in an ever deepening but rarely obtrusive religious feeling. In the last year of his life he returned to England to live in Oxford, feeling the need to be part of a university community as a protection against loneliness. An uneven poet, a poet who in the opinion of some critics never quite fulfilled the enormous promise of his early work, Auden is nevertheless now generally recognized as one of the masters of 20th-century English poetry, a thoughtful, seriously playful (if one may put it in this paradoxical way) poet whom more than one critic has compared to Dryden in his combination of lively intelligence and immense craftsmanship.

This Lunar Beauty[1]

This lunar beauty
Has no history
Is complete and early;
If beauty later
Bear any feature   5
It had a lover
And is another.

This like a dream
Keeps other time
And daytime is   10
The loss of this;
For time is inches
And the heart's changes
Where ghost has haunted
Lost and wanted.   15

1. The poem contrasts "lunar beauty," which is complete, changeless, and impersonal, to the beauty of daylight, which is involved in time and changing human passion.

But this was never
A ghost's endeavor
Nor finished this,
Was ghost at ease;
And till it pass   20
Love shall not near
The sweetness here
Nor sorrow take
His endless look.

1930

Petition

Sir, no man's enemy, forgiving all
But will its negative inversion, be prodigal:
Send to us power and light, a sovereign touch[1]
Curing the intolerable neural itch,
The exhaustion of weaning, the liar's quinsy,[2]   5
And the distortions of ingrown virginity.
Prohibit sharply the rehearsed response
And gradually correct the coward's stance;
Cover in time with beams those in retreat
That, spotted, they turn though the reverse were great;   10
Publish each healer that in city lives
Or country houses at the end of drives;
Harrow the house of the dead; look shining at
New styles of architecture, a change of heart.

1930

On This Island

Look, stranger, on this island now
The leaping light for your delight discovers,
Stand stable here
And silent be,
That through the channels of the ear   5
May wander like a river
The swaying sound of the sea.

Here at the small field's ending pause
When the chalk wall falls to the foam, and its tall ledges
Oppose the pluck
And knock of the tide,   10
And the shingle scrambles after the suck-
-ing surf, and the gull lodges
A moment on its sheer side.

1. The "king's touch" was often re-   meaning "the best").
garded as a miraculous cure for dis-   2. Tonsillitis.
ease (cf. "sovereign" as an adjective,

Far off like floating seeds the ships   15
Diverge on urgent voluntary errands;
And the full view
Indeed may enter
And move in memory as now these clouds do,
That pass the harbor mirror   20
And all the summer through the water saunter.

1936

Spain 1937[1]

Yesterday all the past. The language of size
Spreading to China along the trade routes; the diffusion
          Of the counting-frame and the cromlech;[2]
Yesterday the shadow-reckoning in the sunny climates.

Yesterday the assessment of insurance by cards,   5
The divination of water; yesterday the invention
          Of cart wheels and clocks, the taming of
Horses; yesterday the bustling world of the navigators.

Yesterday the abolition of fairies and giants;
The fortress like a motionless eagle eyeing the valley, 10
          The chapel built in the forest;
Yesterday the carving of angels and of frightening gargoyles.

The trial of heretics among the columns of stone;
Yesterday the theological feuds in the taverns
          And the miraculous cure at the fountain;   15
Yesterday the Sabbath of Witches. But today the struggle.

Yesterday the installation of dynamos and turbines;
The construction of railways in the colonial desert;
          Yesterday the classic lecture
On the origin of Mankind. But today the struggle.   20

Yesterday the belief in the absolute value of Greek;
The fall of the curtain upon the death of a hero;
          Yesterday the prayer to the sunset,
And the adoration of madmen. But today the struggle.

As the poet whispers, startled among the pines   25
Or, where the loose waterfall sings, compact, or upright
          On the crag by the leaning tower:
"O my vision. O send me the luck of the sailor."

---

1. Written when the Spanish Civil War was raging. The rebellion by General Franco's Right-wing army against the Left-wing Spanish government, which broke out in 1936 and provoked full-scale civil war, was viewed by British liberal intellectuals at the time as a testing struggle between fascism and democracy. The poem first appeared separately in 1937, the proceeds of its sale going to "Medical Aid for Spain." This is Auden's revised version of 1940. 2. Ancient stone circle (archaeological term).

And the investigator peers through his instruments
At the inhuman provinces, the virile bacillus   30
        Or enormous Jupiter finished:
"But the lives of my friends. I inquire, I inquire."

And the poor in their fireless lodgings dropping the sheets
Of the evening paper: "Our day is our loss. O show us
        History the operator, the   35
Organizer, Time the refreshing river."

And the nations combine each cry, invoking the life
That shapes the individual belly and orders
        The private nocturnal terror:
"Did you not found once the city-state of the sponge,   40

"Raise the vast military empires of the shark
And the tiger, establish the robin's plucky canton?[3]
        Intervene. O descend as a dove or
A furious papa or a mild engineer: but descend."

And the life, if it answers at all, replies from the heart   45
And the eyes and the lungs, from the shops and squares of the city:
        "O no, I am not the Mover,
Not today, not to you. To you I'm the
"Yes-man, the bar-companion, the easily-duped:
I am whatever you do; I am your vow to be   50
        Good, your humorous story;
I am your business voice; I am your marriage.

"What's your proposal? To build the Just City? I will.
I agree. Or is it the suicide pact, the romantic
        Death? Very well, I accept, for   55
I am your choice, your decision: yes, I am Spain."

Many have heard it on remote peninsulas,
On sleepy plains, in the aberrant fishermen's islands,
        In the corrupt heart of the city;
Have heard and migrated like gulls or the seeds of a flower.   60

They clung like burrs to the long expresses that lurch
Through the unjust lands, through the night, through the alpine
    tunnel;
        They floated over the oceans;
They walked the passes: they came to present their lives.

On that arid square, that fragment nipped off from hot   65
Africa, soldered so crudely to inventive Europe,
        On that tableland scored by rivers,
Our fever's menacing shapes are precise and alive.

Tomorrow, perhaps, the future: the research on fatigue
And the movements of packers; the gradual exploring of all the   70
        Octaves of radiation;
Tomorrow the enlarging of consciousness by diet and breathing.

3. District.

Tomorrow the rediscovery of romantic love;
The photographing of ravens; all the fun under
            Liberty's masterful shadow;
Tomorrow the hour of the pageant-master and the musician.

Tomorrow, for the young, the poets exploding like bombs,
The walks by the lake, the winter of perfect communion;
            Tomorrow the bicycle races
Through the suburbs on summer evenings: but today the struggle

Today the inevitable increase in the chances of death;
The conscious acceptance of guilt in the fact of murder;
            Today the expending of powers
On the flat ephemeral pamphlet and the boring meeting.

Today the makeshift consolations; the shared cigarette;
The cards in the candle-lit barn and the scraping concert,
            The masculine jokes; today the
Fumbled and unsatisfactory embrace before hurting.

The stars are dead; the animals will not look:
We are left alone with our day, and the time is short and
            History to the defeated
May say Alas but cannot help or pardon.
1937   1937, 19

Musée des Beaux Arts[1]

About suffering they were never wrong,
The Old Masters: how well they understood
Its human position; how it takes place
While someone else is eating or opening a window or just walki
        dully along;
How, when the aged are reverently, passionately waiting
For the miraculous birth, there always must be
Children who did not specially want it to happen, skating
On a pond at the edge of the wood:
They never forgot
That even the dreadful martyrdom must run its course
Anyhow in a corner, some untidy spot
Where the dogs go on with their doggy life and the torturer's ho
Scratches its innocent behind on a tree.

In Brueghel's *Icarus*,[2] for instance: how everything turns away
Quite leisurely from the disaster; the plowman may

1. "Museum of Fine Arts." The reference is to the Museum of Fine Arts in Brussels, which contains Brueghel's *Icarus*.
2. Icarus was the son of Daedalus, the cunning craftsman of ancient legend. Together they flew on artificial wings fastened to their shoulders with wax, but Icarus ventured too near the s which melted the wax, and so he and perished. The painting of the of Icarus is by the Flemish pain Pieter Brueghel (ca. 1520–69): Ica legs are disappearing into the sea one corner of the picture, the rest which has nothing to do with him.

Have heard the splash, the forsaken cry,
But for him it was not an important failure; the sun shone
As it had to on the white legs disappearing into the green
Water; and the expensive delicate ship that must have seen
Something amazing, a boy falling out of the sky,   20
Had somewhere to get to and sailed calmly on.

1940

Lullaby

Lay your sleeping head, my love,
Human on my faithless arm;
Time and fevers burn away
Individual beauty from
Thoughtful children, and the grave   5
Proves the child ephemeral:
But in my arms till break of day
Let the living creature lie,
Mortal, guilty, but to me
The entirely beautiful.   10

Soul and body have no bounds:
To lovers as they lie upon
Her tolerant enchanted slope
In their ordinary swoon,
Grave the vision Venus sends   15
Of supernatural sympathy,
Universal love and hope;
While an abstract insight wakes
Among the glaciers and the rocks
The hermit's sensual ecstasy.   20

Certainty, fidelity
On the stroke of midnight pass
Like vibrations of a bell,
And fashionable madmen raise
Their pedantic boring cry: 25
Every farthing of the cost,
All the dreaded cards foretell,
Shall be paid, but from this night
Not a whisper, not a thought,
Not a kiss nor look be lost.   30

Beauty, midnight, vision dies:
Let the winds of dawn that blow
Softly round your dreaming head
Such a day of sweetness show
Eye and knocking heart may bless,   35
Find the mortal world enough;
Noons of dryness see you fed
By the involuntary powers,
Nights of insult let you pass
Watched by every human love.   40

1940

In Memory of W. B. Yeats

(D. JAN. 1939)

1

He disappeared in the dead of winter:
The brooks were frozen, the airports almost deserted,
And snow disfigured the public statues;
The mercury sank in the mouth of the dying day.
O all the instruments agree   5
The day of his death was a dark cold day.

Far from his illness
The wolves ran on through the evergreen forests,
The peasant river was untempted by the fashionable quays;
By mourning tongues   10
The death of the poet was kept from his poems.

But for him it was his last afternoon as himself,
An afternoon of nurses and rumors;
The provinces of his body revolted,
The squares of his mind were empty,   15
Silence invaded the suburbs,
The current of his feeling failed: he became his admirers.

Now he is scattered among a hundred cities
And wholly given over to unfamiliar affections;
To find his happiness in another kind of wood   20
And be punished under a foreign code of conscience.
The words of a dead man
Are modified in the guts of the living.

But in the importance and noise of tomorrow
When the brokers are roaring like beasts on the floor of the
     Bourse,[1]   25
And the poor have the sufferings to which they are fairly
     accustomed,
And each in the cell of himself is almost convinced of his freedom;
A few thousand will think of this day
As one thinks of a day when one did something slightly unusual.
O all the instruments agree   30
The day of his death was a dark cold day.

2

You were silly like us: your gift survived it all;
The parish of rich women, physical decay,
Yourself; mad Ireland hurt you into poetry.
Now Ireland has her madness and her weather still,   35
For poetry makes nothing happen: it survives
In the valley of its saying where executives
Would never want to tamper; it flows south

1. Stock exchange.

From ranches of isolation and the busy griefs,
Raw towns that we believe and die in; it survives,   40
A way of happening, a mouth.

3

Earth, receive an honored guest;
William Yeats is laid to rest:
Let the Irish vessel lie
Emptied of its poetry.   45

Time that is intolerant
Of the brave and innocent,
And indifferent in a week
To a beautiful physique,

Worships language and forgives   50
Everyone by whom it lives;
Pardons cowardice, conceit,
Lays its honours at their feet.

Time that with this strange excuse
Pardoned Kipling and his views,   55
And will pardon Paul Claudel,
Pardons him for writing well.[4]

In the nightmare of the dark
All the dogs of Europe bark,
And the living nations wait,   60
Each sequestered in its hate;

Intellectual disgrace
Stares from every human face,
And the seas of pity lie
Locked and frozen in each eye.   65

Follow, poet, follow right
To the bottom of the night,
With your unconstraining voice
Still persuade us to rejoice;

With the farming of a verse   70
Make a vineyard of the curse,
Sing of human unsuccess
In a rapture of distress;

In the deserts of the heart
Let the healing fountain start,   75
In the prison of his days
Teach the free man how to praise.

1940

4. Kipling's "views" were imperialistic and jingoistic; Paul Claudel (1868–1955), French poet, dramatist, and diplomat, was an extreme Right-winger in his political ideas. Yeats's own politics were at times antidemocratic and appeared to favor dictatorship.

Their Lonely Betters

As I listened from a beach-chair in the shade
To all the noises that my garden made,
It seemed to me only proper that words
Should be withheld from vegetables and birds.

A robin with no Christian name ran through   5
The Robin-Anthem which was all it knew,
And rustling flowers for some third party waited
To say which pairs, if any, should get mated.

No one of them was capable of lying,
There was not one which knew that it was dying   10
Or could have with a rhythm or a rhyme
Assumed responsibility for time.

Let them leave language to their lonely betters
Who count some days and long for certain letters;
We, too, make noises when we laugh or weep,   15
Words are for those with promises to keep.

1951

In Praise of Limestone

If it form the one landscape that we the inconstant ones
    Are consistently homesick for, this is chiefly
Because it dissolves in water. Mark these rounded slopes
    With their surface fragrance of thyme and beneath
A secret system of caves and conduits; hear these springs   5
    That spurt out everywhere with a chuckle
Each filling a private pool for its fish and carving
    Its own little ravine whose cliffs entertain
The butterfly and the lizard; examine this region
    Of short distances and definite places: 10
What could be more like Mother or a fitter background
    For her son, for the nude young male who lounges
Against a rock displaying his dildo, never doubting
    That for all his faults he is loved, whose works are but
Extensions of his power to charm? From weathered outcrop   15
    To hill-top temple, from appearing waters to
Conspicuous fountains, from a wild to a formal vineyard,
    Are ingenious but short steps that a child's wish
To receive more attention than his brothers, whether
    By pleasing or teasing, can easily take.   20

Watch, then, the band of rivals as they climb up and down
    Their steep stone gennels [1] in twos and threes, sometimes

1. A "gennel," in the dialect of Auden's native Yorkshire and other northern counties, is a long narrow passage between houses. Here it is a passage between rocks.

Arm in arm, but never, thank God, in step; or engaged
    On the shady side of a square at midday in
Voluble discourse, knowing each other too well to think   25
    There are any important secrets, unable
To conceive a god whose temper-tantrums are moral
    And not to be pacified by a clever line
Or a good lay: for, accustomed to a stone that responds,
    They have never had to veil their faces in awe   30
Of a crater whose blazing fury could not be fixed;
    Adjusted to the local needs of valleys
Where everything can be touched or reached by walking,
    Their eyes have never looked into infinite space
Through the lattice-work of a nomad's comb;[2] born lucky,   35
    Their legs have never encountered the fungi
And insects of the jungle, the monstrous forms and lives
    With which we have nothing, we like to hope, in common.
So, when one of them goes to the bad, the way his mind works
    Remains comprehensible: to become a pimp   40
Or deal in fake jewelry or ruin a fine tenor voice
    For effects that bring down the house could happen to all
But the best and the worst of us . . .
                         That is why, I suppose,
    The best and worst never stayed here long but sought   45
Immoderate soils where the beauty was not so external,
    The light less public and the meaning of life
Something more than a mad camp. "Come!" cried the granite wastes,
    "How evasive is your humor, how accidental
Your kindest kiss, how permanent is death." (Saints-to-be
    Slipped away sighing.) "Come!" purred the clays and gravels.   50
"On our plains there is room for armies to drill; rivers
    Wait to be tamed and slaves to construct you a tomb
In the grand manner: soft as the earth is mankind and both
    Need to be altered." (Intendant Caesars rose and
Left, slamming the door.) But the really reckless were fetched   55
    By an older colder voice, the oceanic whisper:
"I am the solitude that asks and promises nothing;
    That is how I shall set you free. There is no love;
There are only the various envies, all of them sad."

They were right, my dear, all those voices were right   60
And still are; this land is not the sweet home that it looks,
    Nor its peace the historical calm of a site
Where something was settled once and for all: A backward
    And delapidated province, connected
To the big busy world by a tunnel, with a certain   65
    Seedy appeal, is that all it is now? Not quite:
It has a worldly duty which in spite of itself

---

2. The context suggests that this might be a popular name for a plant or tree (cf. "traveler's joy" and "traveler's palm"), but Auden is probably using the phrase quite literally to suggest that these people have never led a nomad's (wanderer's) life. The "nomad's comb" might be the fringe of unkempt hair through which the nomad peers at wild landscapes.

It does not neglect, but calls into question
All the Great Powers assumed; it disturbs our rights. The poet,
    Admired for his earnest habit of calling   70
The sun the sun, his mind Puzzle, is made uneasy
    By these solid statues which so obviously doubt
His antimythological myth; and these gamins,
    Pursuing the scientist down the tiled colonnade
With such lively offers,[3] rebuke his concern for Nature's   75
    Remotest aspects: I, too, am reproached, for what
And how much you know. Not to lose time, not to get caught,
    Not to be left behind, not, please! to resemble
The beasts who repeat themselves, or a thing like water
    Or stone whose conduct can be predicted, these   80
Are our Common Prayer, whose greatest comfort is music
    Which can be made anywhere, is invisible,
And does not smell. In so far as we have to look forward
    To death as a fact, no doubt we are right: But if
Sins can be forgiven, if bodies rise from the dead,   85
    These modifications of matter into
Innocent athletes and gesticulating fountains,
    Made solely for pleasure, make a further point:
The blessed will not care what angle they are regarded from,
    Having nothing to hide. Dear, I know nothing of   90
Either, but when I try to imagine a faultless love
    Or the life to come, what I hear is the murmur
Of underground streams, what I see is a limestone landscape.

                                  1948, 1951

3. These are not to be taken as literal statues of gamins (urchins) or man-made colonnades; they suggest rather that limestone is easily worked (by nature as well as by art) into shapes that remind us of familiar objects in the customary human world, unlike the "granite wastes" (line 47) and other sterner landscapes with which the limestone landscape is contrasted. The scientist, concerned with "Nature's remotest aspects," is "rebuked" by the familiar limestone shapes which suggest that man and his ordinary needs are more important. A basic theme of the poem is that easily weathered and easily worked limestone joins the natural to the human world, so that there is an easy transition "From weathered outcrop / To hilltop temple, from appearing waters to / Conspicuous fountains, from a wild to a formal vineyard" (lines 15–18). Saints, would-be world conquerors, and solitary mystics prefer less comfortable landscapes; and even the limestone landscape is not as reassuring as it may seem ("this land is not the sweet home that it looks," line 61). But it asserts the primacy of the ordinary human, and as an ordinary man, not a saint, the poet finds in it the only satisfactory symbol of the good life. The landscape of this poem derives from Auden's native Yorkshire. Cf. "New Year Letter": "I see the nature of my kind / As a locality I love / Those limestone moors that stretch from Brough / To Hexham on the Roman Wall / That is my symbol of us all."

LOUIS MacNEICE
(1907–1963)

Louis MacNeice was born in Belfast, Northern Ireland, and educated at
Marlborough and at Merton College, Oxford, where he studied classics.

For the next ten years he lectured in classics—at the University of Birmingham from 1930 to 1936, and at Bedford College for Women, London, from 1936 to 1940. He was feature-writer and producer for the British Broadcasting Corporation from 1941 to 1949, and after that became director of the British Institute in Athens.

MacNeice uses the modern tradition of irony in his own way. His dry, precise style has none of Auden's verbal brilliance, but it can be highly effective through its very restraint. He has never joined any of the movements in modern English poetry. A carefully controlled melancholy underlies much of his poetry; he has a somber sense of modern life, of its tragicomedies and futilities, and above all of the sadness that underlies all modern attempts to recapture, in memories of youth or by sudden emotion when listening to a street singer or watching a landscape, a sense of significance in daily living. His best poetry has always been fairly low-pressured, sardonic in a subdued manner, but with an occasional burst of wild Celtic irony. There is an integrity of feeling and a consistently high level of craftsmanship in his work that give his poems their special air of full realization: one never finds on a second reading that one had been taken in by an initial showiness. MacNeice is coming to be regarded more and more in England as second only to Auden among poets of his generation.

Sunday Morning

Down the road someone is practicing scales,
The notes like little fishes vanish with a wink of tails,
Man's heart expands to tinker with his car
For this is Sunday morning, Fate's great bazaar,
Regard these means as ends, concentrate on this Now,   5
And you may grow to music or drive beyond Hindhead[1] anyhow,
Take corners on two wheels until you go so fast
That you can clutch a fringe or two of the windy past,
That you can abstract this day and make it to the week of time
A small eternity, a sonnet self-contained in rhyme.   10

But listen, up the road, something gulps, the church spire
Opens its eight bells out, skulls' mouths which will not tire
To tell how there is no music or movement which secures
Escape from the weekday time. Which deadens and endures.

1935

The Sunlight on the Garden

The sunlight on the garden
Hardens and grows cold,

1. This upland district in Surrey is a usual place to stop on the typical Sunday outing.

We cannot cage the minute
Within its nets of gold;
When all is told   5
We cannot beg for pardon.

Our freedom as free lances
Advances towards its end;
The earth compels, upon it
Sonnets and birds descend;   10
And soon, my friend,
We shall have no time for dances.

The sky was good for flying
Defying the church bells
And every evil iron   15
Siren and what it tells:
The earth compels,
We are dying, Egypt, dying[2]

And not expecting pardon,
Hardened in heart anew,   20
But glad to have sat under
Thunder and rain with you,
And grateful too
For sunlight on the garden.

1937   1938

Bagpipe Music

It's no go the merrygoround, it's no go the rickshaw,
All we want is a limousine and a ticket for the peepshow.
Their knickers are made of crepe-de-chine, their shoes are made of
    python,
Their halls are lined with tiger rugs and their walls with heads of
    bison.

John MacDonald found a corpse, put it under the sofa,   5
Waited till it came to life and hit it with a poker,
Sold its eyes for souvenirs, sold its blood for whisky,
Kept its bones for dumbbells to use when he was fifty.

It's no go the Yogi-Man, it's no go Blavatsky,[3]
All we want is a bank balance and a bit of skirt in a taxi.   10

Annie MacDougall went to milk, caught her foot in the heather,
Woke to hear a dance record playing of Old Vienna.
It's no go your maidenheads, it's no go your culture,
All we want is a Dunlop tire and the devil mend the puncture.

2. Cf. Antony's speech in *Antony and Cleopatra:* "I am dying, Egypt, dying" (IV.xv.41).
3. **Madame Blavatsky** (1831–91), the famous theosophist whose ideas were popular in some quarters in Britain in the 1930's.

The Laird o' Phelps spent Hogmanay[4] declaring he was sober,   15
Counted his feet to prove the fact and found he had one foot over.
Mrs. Carmichael had her fifth, looked at the job with repulsion,
Said to the midwife, "Take it away; I'm through with overproduc-
    tion."

It's no go the gossip column, it's no go the Ceilidh,[5]
All we want is a mother's help and a sugar-stick for the baby.   20

Willie Murray cut his thumb, couldn't count the damage,
Took the hide of an Ayrshire cow and used it for a bandage.
His brother caught three hundred cran[6] when the seas were lavish,
Threw the bleeders back in the sea and went upon the parish.[7]

It's no go the Herring Board, it's no go the Bible,
All we want is a packet of fags[8] when our hands are idle.

It's no go the picture palace, it's no go the stadium,
It's no go the country cot with a pot of pink geraniums.
It's no go the Government grants, it's no go the elections,
Sit on your arse for fifty years and hang your hat on a pension.   30

It's no go my honey love, it's no go my poppet;
Work your hands from day to day, the winds will blow the profit.
The glass is falling hour by hour, the glass will fall forever,
But if you break the bloody glass you won't hold up the weather.

           1938

Mahabalipuram[9]

All alone from his dark sanctum the lingam[1] fronts, affronts the
    sea,
The world's dead weight of breakers against sapling, bull and candle
       Where worship comes no more,
Yet how should these cowherds and gods continue to dance in the
    rock
All the long night along ocean in this lost border between   5
That thronging gonging mirage of paddy and toddy[2] and dung
       And this uninhabited shore?
Silent except for the squadrons of water, the dark grim chargers
    launched from Australia,
Dark except for their manes of phosphorus, silent in spite of the
    rockhewn windmill

---

4. New Year's Eve.
5. Pronounced *kaley:* a Scottish Gaelic word meaning a social evening spent in singing and story-telling.
6. A measure of fresh herrings, about 750 fish. The Scottish herring industry failed in the 1930's; the Herring Board (line 25) was a government attempt to provide helpful direction.
7. I.e., "went on the county" (on relief).

8. Cigarettes.
9. Mahabalipuram, a fishing village south of Madras on the eastern coast of India, is near an enclave of ruined ancient Hindu temples.
1. Phallus; here an emblem of Shiva, the Hindu god of generative energy but also primarily of destruction.
2. In India, palm wine.

That brandishes axe and knife[3]—   10
The many-handed virgin facing, abasing the Oaf, the Demon;
Dark in spite of the rockhewn radiance of Vishnu[4] and Shiva and
      silent
In spite of the mooing of Krishna's herds;[5] yet in spite of this dark-
      ness and silence
      Behold what a joy of life—

Which goes with an awe and a horror; the innocence which sur-
      mounted the guilt   15
Thirteen centuries back when an artist eyeing this litter of granite
      Saw it for waste and took
A header[6] below the rockface, found there already like a ballet of
      fishes
Passing, repassing each other, these shapes of gopi and goblin,
Of elephant, serpent and antelope, saw them and grasped his mallet
      And cried with a clear stroke: Look!   21
And now we look, we to whom mantra and mudra[7] mean little,
And who find in this Hindu world a zone that is ultra-violet
      Balanced by an infra-red,
Austerity and orgy alike being phrased, it seems, in a strange dead
      language   25
But now that we look without trying to learn and only look in the
      act of leaping
After the sculptor into the rockface, now we can see, if not hear,
      those phrases
      To be neither strange nor dead.

Not strange for all their ingrown iconography, not so strange as our
      own dreams
Because better ordered, these are the dreams we have needed   30
      Since we forgot how to dance;
This god asleep on the snake[8] is the archetype of the sleep that we
      lost
When we were born, and these wingless figures that fly
Merely by bending the knee are the earnest of what we aspire to
      Apart from science and chance.   35

And the largest of all these reliefs, forty foot high by a hundred,
Is large in more senses than one, including both heaven and the
      animal kingdom
      And a grain of salt as well
For the saint stands always above on one leg fasting

---

3. Kali, the four-armed goddess of death
and destruction, who was the wife of
Shiva.
4. The god of preservation.
5. Krishna was said to have been an incarnation of Vishnu. Raised as a cow-
herd, he was notorious for his dalliance
with milkmaids (or Gopis).
6. That is, a head-first dive.

7. A mantra is a mystical incantation;
mudras, in Hindu temple dancing, are
stylized positions of the hands by which
the dancer conveys states of mind.
8. Between the cycles of creation, each
of which was attended by an incarnation
of Vishnu, the god slept on a coiled
snake resting on the waters of the cosmos.

Acquiring power while the smug hypocritical cat beneath him   40
Stands on his hindlegs too admired by the mice
    Whom the sculptor did not tell.

Nor did he tell the simple and beautiful rustics
Who saved from their doom by Krishna are once more busy and
    happy
    Absorbed in themselves and Him,   45
That trapped in this way in the rock their idyl would live to excite
And at once annul the lust and the envy of tourists
Taking them out of themselves and to find themselves in a world
    That has neither rift nor rim:

A monochrome world that has all the indulgence of color,   50
A still world whose every harmonic is audible,
    Largesse of spirit and stone;
Created things for once and for all featured in full while for once
    and never
The creator who is destroyer stands at the last point of land
Featureless; in a dark cell, a phallus of granite, as abstract   55
    As the North Pole; as alone.

But the visitor must move on and the waves assault the temple,
Living granite against dead water, and time with its weathering
    action
    Make phrase and feature blurred;
Still from today we know what an avatar[9] is, we have seen   60
God take shape and dwell among shapes, we have felt
Our aging limbs respond to those ageless limbs in the rock
    Reliefs. Relief is the word.

                          1948

Good Dream

He woke in his usual room, decided
Feeling completely awake to switch
The reading lamp on and read—but where
Is the switch? No switch no light. No light
No chapter nor verse. Competely awake   5
   He gropes for the switch and finds the book
He left in the dark but what is a book
Left in the dark? He feels the book
Suddenly gently taken away
By someone's hand and warm voice   10
   Begins, beginneth, aloud in the dark:

9. The incarnation of a Hindu deity, such as Krishna.

Here beginneth the first chapter—
But it wasn't the first, he was half way through.
No, says the voice, *the first chapter*
At the first verse in the first voice,
Which is mine, none other's: Here beginneth—   15
But I tell you, he says, I was half way through,
I am completely awake, I can prove it;
Where is the switch? I will show you the place
Half way through.
     There is no switch,   20
The voice replies; *in the beginning*
Is darkness upon the face of the earth
In which you must wait for me till I
Show you the place not half way through
But just begun, the place you never   25
Knew was here.
     But I know this place,
It is my usual room, except
The switch has gone.
     The switch was never
There to start with; which is why
You refuse to wake.
     But I am completely   30
Awake, I told you.
     You will tell me
Once you are. Here beginneth—
I tell you this is my usual room;
I can put my hand from the bed and feel the . . .
Yes?
  The wall—but I can't. Where   35
Has the wall gone? My bed was against it.
What was against it?
     Why is your voice
Moving away? Why do I hear
Water over it?
     There is water
Between us, I am here on the bank,   40
You will have to row.
     Row?
     What
Is a boat for? I am here on the bank
But I need light to row.
     No.
No light until you reach this bank.
Feel for your oars.
     Here are my oars.   45
Then loose that rope. Are you ready? Row.
Here beginneth. . . .
     He dips his oars
And knows the walls receding, hears

The ripples round the chair legs, hears
Larksong high in the chimney, hears   50

Rustling leaves in the wardrobe, smells
All the smells of a river, and yet
Feeling, smelling, hearing, knowing,
Still cannot see. This boat has no
Switch. No switch no light.
                       No light?   55
Pull on your oars. I am here.
                           He pulls.
Splutter of water, crackle and grinding
Of reeds and twigs; then bump. The hand
That stole the book that was left in the dark
Comes out of the dark, the hand that is hers,   60
Hers, none other's, and seizes his
To help him on to the bank.
                        "And God
Said Let there be light"[1]

                       His usual room
Has lost its usual walls and found
Four walls of sky, incredible blue   65
Enclosing incredible green enclosing
Her, none other.
                      Completely awake.

1. Genesis i.3. "And God said, let there be light: and there was light."

                                         1961

DYLAN THOMAS
(1914–1953)

Dylan Thomas was born in Swansea, Wales, and educated at Swansea
Grammar School. After working for a time as a newspaper reporter, he
was "discovered" as a poet in 1933 through a poetry contest in a popular
newspaper. The following year his *Eighteen Poems* caused considerable
excitement because of the strange violence of their imagery and their
powerfully suggestive obscurity. It looked as though a new kind of strength
and romantic picturesqueness had been restored to English poetry after
the deliberately muted tones of Eliot and his followers. Thomas did not,
however, turn out to be the founder of a neo-romantic movement, though
some early critics took him to be so. As his poetry became better known,
and after he had clarified the somewhat clotted imagery of his early style
in his later volumes—*The Map of Love* (1939), *Deaths and Entrances*
(1946), *Collected Poems* (1953)—it became clear that Thomas was an
extremely craftsmanlike poet, and not the shouting rhapsodist that some

had taken him to be. His images were most carefully ordered in a patterned sequence, and his major theme was the unity of all life, the continuing *process* of life and death and new life which linked the generations to each other. Thomas saw the workings of biology as a magical transformation producing unity out of diversity, and again and again in his poetry he sought a poetic ritual to celebrate this unity ("The force that through the green fuse drives the flower / Drives my green age"). He saw man locked in a round of identities—with the beginning of growth also the first movement toward death, the beginning of love leading to procreation, new growth, and so in turn to death again and to life again, and because of this view he comforted himself with the unity of man and nature, of past and present, of life and death, and so "refused to mourn the death of a child." In his best poems the closely woven imagery (deriving from the Bible, Welsh folklore and preaching, and Freud) is organized to present aspects of this theme. His more open-worked poems of reminiscence and autobiographical emotion, such as *Poem in October*, communicate more immediately to the reader through their fine lyrical feeling and compelling use of simple natural images. His autobiographical work *Portrait of the Artist as a Young Dog* and his radio play *Under Milk Wood* reveal a vividness of observation and a combination of violence and tenderness in expression that shows he could handle prose as excitingly as verse.

Thomas was a brilliant talker (when he felt like it), a considerable drinker, a reckless and impulsive man whose short life was packed with emotional ups and downs. His poetry readings in America between 1950 and 1953 were enormous successes, in spite of his sometimes reckless antics and his deliberately offensive behavior to academic stuffed shirts or those he imagined to be such. He died suddenly in New York, on his third American trip, in November 1953. He acted the bohemian poet as that role had not been played since the 90's; some thought this behavior wonderful, though others deplored it. He was a brilliant reader of his own and others' poems, and many people who do not normally read poetry were drawn to Thomas's by the magic of his own reading. After his premature death a reaction set in: some critics declared that he had been overrated as a poet because of the sensational role he had played in life. But a balanced view is now possible; it is clear that at his best he was an original poet of great power and beauty.

The Force That Through the Green Fuse Drives the Flower

The force that through the green fuse drives the flower
Drives my green age; that blasts the roots of trees
Is my destroyer.
And I am dumb to tell the crooked rose
My youth is bent by the same wintry fever.   5

The force that drives the water through the rocks
Drives my red blood; that dries the mouthing streams
Turns mine to wax.
And I am dumb to mouth unto my veins
How at the mountain spring the same mouth sucks.   10

The hand that whirls the water in the pool
Stirs the quicksand; that ropes the blowing wind
Hauls my shroud sail.
And I am dumb to tell the hanging man
How of my clay is made the hangman's lime.   15

The lips of time leech to the fountain head;
Love drips and gathers, but the fallen blood
Shall calm her sores.
And I am dumb to tell a weather's wind
How time has ticked a heaven round the stars.   20

And I am dumb to tell the lover's tomb
How at my sheet goes the same crooked worm.

                                                    1933

This Bread I Break

This bread I break was once the oat,
This wine upon a foreign tree
Plunged in its fruit;
Man in the day or wind at night
Laid the crops low, broke the grape's joy.   5

Once in this wine the summer blood
Knocked in the flesh that decked the vine,
Once in this bread
The oat was merry in the wind;
Man broke the sun, pulled the wind down.   10

This flesh you break, this blood you let
Make desolation in the vein,
Were oat and grape
Born of the sensual root and sap;
My wine you drink, my bread you snap.   15

                                                    1936

After the Funeral[1]

(IN MEMORY OF ANN JONES)

After the funeral, mule praises, brays,
Windshake of sailshaped ears, muffle-toed tap
Tap happily of one peg in the thick
Grave's foot, blinds down the lids, the teeth in black,
The spittled eyes, the salt ponds in the sleeves,   5
Morning smack of the spade that wakes up sleep,
Shakes a desolate boy who slits his throat
In the dark of the coffin and sheds dry leaves,
That breaks one bone to light with a judgment clout,
After the feast of tear-stuffed time and thistles   10
In a room with a stuffed fox and a stale fern,
I stand, for this memorial's sake, alone
In the sniveling hours with dead, humped Ann
Whose hooded, fountain heart once fell in puddles
Round the parched worlds of Wales and drowned each sun   15
(Though this for her is a monstrous image blindly
Magnified out of praise; her death was a still drop;
She would not have me sinking in the holy
Flood of her heart's fame; she would lie dumb and deep
And need no druid[2] of her broken body).   20
But I, Ann's bard on a raised hearth, call all
The seas to service that her wood-tongued virtue
Babble like a bellbuoy over the hymning heads,
Bow down the walls of the ferned and foxy woods
That her love sing and swing through a brown chapel,   25
Bless her bent spirit with four, crossing birds.
Her flesh was meek as milk, but this skyward statue
With the wild breast and blessed and giant skull
Is carved from her in a room with a wet window
In a fiercely mourning house in a crooked year.   30
I know her scrubbed and sour humble hands
Lie with religion in their cramp, her threadbare
Whisper in a damp word, her wits drilled hollow,
Her fist of a face died clenched on a round pain;
And sculptured Ann is seventy years of stone.   35
These cloud-sopped, marble hands, this monumental
Argument of the hewn voice, gesture and psalm,
Storm me forever over her grave until
The stuffed lung of the fox twitch and cry Love
And the strutting fern lay seeds on the black sill.   40

1938, 1939

1. Ann Jones was Thomas's aunt; she lived in a farmhouse in the Welsh landscape described in *Poem in October*. The opening lines of the poem describe, in deliberately mixed metaphors and "transferred epithets," the insincerity of the behavior at the funeral in contrast to the genuine grief of the "desolate boy" who in imagination is already dead (lines 7 ff.).
2. Priest of the ancient Celtic pagans (forefathers of the modern Welsh).

There Was a Saviour

There was a saviour
Rarer than radium,
Commoner than water, crueller than truth;
Children kept from the sun
Assembled at his tongue   5
To hear the golden note turn in a groove,
Prisoners of wishes locked in their eyes
In the jails and studies of his keyless smiles.

The voice of children says
From a lost wilderness   10
There was calm to be done in his safe unrest,
When hindering man hurt
Man, animal, or bird
We hid our fears in that murdering breath,
Silence, silence to do, when earth grew loud,   15
In lairs and asylums of the tremendous shout.

There was glory to hear
In the churches of his tears,
Under his downy arm you sighed as he struck,
O you who could not cry   20
On to the ground when a man died
Put a tear for joy in the unearthly flood
And laid your cheek against a cloud-formed shell:
Now in the dark there is only yourself and myself.

Two proud, blacked brothers cry,   25
Winter-locked side by side,
To this inhospitable hollow year,
O we who could not stir
One lean sigh when we heard
Greed on man beating near and fire neighbor   30
But wailed and nested in the sky-blue wall
Now break a giant tear for the little known fall,

For the drooping of homes
That did not nurse our bones,
Brave deaths of only ones but never found,   35
Now see, alone in us,
Our own true strangers' dust
Ride through the doors of our unentered house.
Exiled in us we arouse the soft,
Unclenched, armless, silk and rough love that breaks all rocks. 40

1940

The Hunchback in the Park

The hunchback in the park
A solitary mister
Propped between trees and water
From the opening of the garden lock
That lets the trees and water enter   5
Until the Sunday somber bell at dark

Eating bread from a newspaper
Drinking water from the chained cup
That the children filled with gravel
In the fountain basin where I sailed my ship   10
Slept at night in a dog kennel
But nobody chained him up.

Like the park birds he came early
Like the water he sat down
And Mister they called Hey mister   15
The truant boys from the town
Running when he had heard them clearly
On out of sound

Past lake and rockery
Laughing when he shook his paper   20
Hunchbacked in mockery
Through the loud zoo of the willow groves
Dodging the park keeper
With his stick that picked up leaves.

And the old dog sleeper   25
Alone between nurses and swans
While the boys among willows
Made the tigers jump out of their eyes
To roar on the rockery stones
And the groves were blue with sailors   30

Made all day until bell time
A woman figure without fault
Straight as a young elm
Straight and tall from his crooked bones
That she might stand in the night   35
After the locks and chains

All night in the unmade park
After the railings and shrubberies
The birds the grass the trees the lake
And the wild boys innocent as strawberries   40
Had followed the hunchback
To his kennel in the dark.

1941

Poem in October

It was my thirtieth year to heaven
Woke to my hearing from harbor and neighbor wood
 And the mussel pooled and the heron
   Priested shore
  The morning beckon   5
With water praying and call of seagull and rook
And the knock of sailing boats on the net webbed wall
  Myself to set foot
   That second
In the still sleeping town and set forth.   10

 My birthday began with the water-
Birds and the birds of the winged trees flying my name
 Above the farms and the white horses
   And I rose
  In rainy autumn   15
And walked abroad in a shower of all my days.
High tide and the heron dived when I took the road
  Over the border
   And the gates
Of the town closed as the town awoke.   20

 A springful of larks in a rolling
Cloud and the roadside bushes brimming with whistling
 Black birds and the sun of October
   Summery
  On the hill's shoulder,   25
Here were fond climates and sweet singers suddenly
Come in the morning where I wandered and listened
  To the rain wringing
   Wind blow cold
In the wood faraway under me.   30

 Pale rain over the dwindling harbor
And over the sea wet church the size of a snail
 With its horns through mist and the castle
   Brown as owls
  But all the gardens   35
Of spring and summer were blooming in the tall tales
Beyond the border and under the lark full cloud.
  There could I marvel
   My birthday
Away but the weather turned around.   40

 It turned away from the blithe country
And down the other air and the blue altered sky
 Streamed again a wonder of summer
   With apples
  Pears and red currants   45
And I saw in the turning so clearly a child's
Forgotten mornings when he walked with his mother

Through the parables
Of sun light
And the legends of the green chapels   50

And the twice told fields of infancy
That his tears burned my cheeks and his heart moved in mine.
These were the woods the river and sea
Where a boy
In the listening   55
Summertime of the dead whispered the truth of his joy
To the trees and the stones and the fish in the tide.
And the mystery
Sang alive
Still in the water and singingbirds.   60

And there could I marvel my birthday
Away but the weather turned around. And the true
Joy of the long dead child sang burning
In the sun.
It was my thirtieth   65
Year to heaven stood there then in the summer noon
Though the town below lay leaved with October blood.
O may my heart's truth
Still be sung
On this high hill in a year's turning.   70

                                                                1945, 1946

Do Not Go Gentle into That Good Night

Do not go gentle into that good night,
Old age should burn and rave at close of day;
Rage, rage against the dying of the light.

Though wise men at their end know dark is right,
Because their words had forked no lightning they   5
Do not go gentle into that good night.

Good men, the last wave by, crying how bright
Their frail deeds might have danced in a green bay,
Rage, rage against the dying of the light.

Wild men who caught and sang the sun in flight,   10
And learn, too late, they grieved it on its way,
Do not go gentle into that good night.

Grave men, near death, who see with blinding sight
Blind eyes could blaze like meteors and be gay,
Rage, rage against the dying of the light.   15

And you, my father, there on the sad height,
Curse, bless, me now with your fierce tears, I pray.
Do not go gentle into that good night.
Rage, rage against the dying of the light.

1951, 1952

DORIS LESSING

(1919–)

Born in Persia of British parents, Doris Lessing (née Tayler) lived on a
Southern Rhodesian farm from 1924 to 1949 before settling in England.
Her novel tetralogy with the general title *Children of Violence* (beginning
with *Martha Quest*, 1952) combines elements of psychological autobiography with powerful exploration of the relationship between black and white
in Africa. Her combination of psychological introspection, political analysis,
social documentary, and feminism gives a characteristic tone to her novels
and short stories. These elements are powerfully combined in her novel *The
Golden Notebook* (1962), which explores the sexual problems of an independent woman in a man's world with unexhibitionist frankness while at
the same time probing the political conscience of an ex-communist and the
needs and dilemmas of a creative writer. Some of her short stories, which
deal with racial and social dilemmas as well as with loneliness, the claims of
politics, the problems of aging (especially for women), the conflict between
the generations, and a whole spectrum of problems of alienation and isolation, have a pungency and force lacking in her more discursive novels. Mrs.
Lessing (she uses the name of her second husband, though both her marriages have been dissolved) is very much a writer of her time, deeply
involved with the changing patterns of thought, feeling, and culture during
the last quarter century. One feels that there is an absolute continuity
between her life and her work. The story below is taken from her volume
of short stories, *A Man and Two Women*.

To Room Nineteen

This is a story, I suppose, about a failure in intelligence: the
Rawlings' marriage was grounded in intelligence.

They were older when they married than most of their married friends: in their well-seasoned late twenties. Both had had a number of affairs, sweet rather than bitter; and when they fell in love—for they did fall in love—had known each other for some time. They joked that they had saved each other "for the real thing." That they had waited so long (but not too long) for this real thing was to them a proof of their sensible discrimination. A good many of their friends had married young, and now (they felt) probably regretted lost opportunities; while others, still unmarried, seemed to them arid, self-doubting, and likely to make desperate or romantic marriages.

Not only they, but others, felt they were well matched: their friends' delight was an additional proof of their happiness. They had played the same roles, male and female, in this group or set, if such a wide, loosely connected, constantly changing constellation of people could be called a set. They had both become, by virtue of their moderation, their humor, and their abstinence from painful experience people to whom others came for advice. They could be, and were, relied on. It was one of those cases of a man and a woman linking themselves whom no one else had ever thought of linking, probably because of their similarities. But then everyone exclaimed: Of course! How right! How was it we never thought of it before!

And so they married amid general rejoicing, and because of their foresight and their sense for what was probable, nothing was a surprise to them.

Both had well-paid jobs. Matthew was a subeditor on a large London newspaper, and Susan worked in an advertising firm. He was not the stuff of which editors or publicized journalists are made, but he was much more than "a subeditor," being one of the essential background people who in fact steady, inspire and make possible the people in the limelight. He was content with this position. Susan had a talent for commercial drawing. She was humorous about the advertisements she was responsible for, but she did not feel strongly about them one way or the other.

Both, before they married, had had pleasant flats, but they felt it unwise to base a marriage on either flat, because it might seem like a submission of personality on the part of the one whose flat it was not. They moved into a new flat in South Kensington on the clear understanding that when their marriage had settled down (a process they knew would not take long, and was in fact more a humorous concession to popular wisdom than what was due to themselves) they would buy a house and start a family.

And this is what happened. They lived in their charming flat for two years, giving parties and going to them, being a popular young

married couple, and then Susan became pregnant, she gave up her job, and they bought a house in Richmond. It was typical of this couple that they had a son first, then a daughter, then twins, son and daughter. Everything right, appropriate, and what everyone would wish for, if they could choose. But people did feel these two had chosen; this balanced and sensible family was no more than what was due to them because of their infallible sense for *choosing* right.

And so they lived with their four children in their gardened house in Richmond and were happy. They had everything they had wanted and had planned for.

And yet . . .

Well, even this was expected, that there must be a certain flatness. . . .

Yes, yes, of course, it was natural they sometimes felt like this. Like what?

Their life seemed to be like a snake biting its tail. Matthew's job for the sake of Susan, children, house, and garden—which caravanserai needed a well-paid job to maintain it. And Susan's practical intelligence for the sake of Matthew, the children, the house and the garden—which unit would have collapsed in a week without her.

But there was no point about which either could say: "For the sake of *this* is all the rest." Children? But children can't be a center of life and a reason for being. They can be a thousand things that are delightful, interesting, satisfying, but they can't be a wellspring to live from. Or they shouldn't be. Susan and Matthew knew that well enough.

Matthew's job? Ridiculous. It was an interesting job, but scarcely a reason for living. Matthew took pride in doing it well; but he could hardly be expected to be proud of the newspaper: the newspaper he read, *his* newspaper, was not the one he worked for.

Their love for each other? Well, that was nearest it. If this wasn't a center, what was? Yes, it was around this point, their love, that the whole extraordinary structure revolved. For extraordinary it certainly was. Both Susan and Matthew had moments of thinking so, of looking in secret disbelief at this thing they had created: marriage, four children, big house, garden, charwomen, friends, cars . . . and this *thing*, this entity, all of it had come into existence, been blown into being out of nowhere, because Susan loved Matthew and Matthew loved Susan. Extraordinary. So that was the central point, the wellspring.

And if one felt that it simply was not strong enough, important enough, to support it all, well whose fault was that? Certainly nei-

ther Susan's nor Matthew's. It was in the nature of things. And they sensibly blamed neither themselves nor each other.

On the contrary, they used their intelligence to preserve what they had created from a painful and explosive world: they looked around them, and took lessons. All around them, marriages collapsing, or breaking, or rubbing along (even worse, they felt). They must not make the same mistakes, they must not.

They had avoided the pitfall so many of their friends had fallen into—of buying a house in the country *for the sake of the children*; so that the husband became a weekend husband, a weekend father, and the wife always careful not to ask what went on in the town flat which they called (in joke) a bachelor flat. No, Matthew was a full-time husband, a full-time father, and at nights, in the big married bed in the big married bedroom (which had an attractive view of the river) they lay beside each other talking and he told her about his day, and what he had done, and whom he had met; and she told him about her day (not as interesting, but that was not her fault) for both knew of the hidden resentments and deprivations of the woman who has lived her own life—and above all, has earned her own living—and is now dependent on a husband for outside interests and money.

Nor did Susan make the mistake of taking a job for the sake of her independence, which she might very well have done, since her old firm, missing her qualities of humor, balance, and sense, invited her often to go back. Children needed their mother to a certain age, that both parents knew and agreed on; and when these four healthy wisely brought-up children were of the right age, Susan would work again, because she knew, and so did he, what happened to women of fifty at the height of their energy and ability, with grown-up children who no longer needed their full devotion.

So here was this couple, testing their marriage, looking after it, treating it like a small boat full of helpless people in a very stormy sea. Well, of course, so it was. . . . The storms of the world were bad, but not too close—which is not to say they were selfishly felt: Susan and Matthew were both well-informed and responsible people. And the inner storms and quicksands were understood and charted. So everything was all right. Everything was in order. Yes, things were under control.

So what did it matter if they felt dry, flat? People like themselves, fed on a hundred books (psychological, anthropological, sociological) could scarcely be unprepared for the dry, controlled wistfulness which is the distinguishing mark of the intelligent marriage. Two people, endowed with education, with discrimination, with judgment, linked together voluntarily from their will to be happy together and to be of use to others—one sees them every-

where, one knows them, one even is that thing oneself: sadness because so much is after all so little. These two, unsurprised, turned toward each other with even more courtesy and gentle love: this was life, that two people, no matter how carefully chosen, could not be everything to each other. In fact, even to say so, to think in such a way, was banal, they were ashamed to do it.

It was banal, too, when one night Matthew came home late and confessed he had been to a party, taken a girl home and slept with her. Susan forgave him, of course. Except that forgiveness is hardly the word. Understanding, yes. But if you understand something, you don't forgive it, you are the thing itself: forgiveness is for what you *don't* understand. Nor had he *confessed*—what sort of word is that?

The whole thing was not important. After all, years ago they had joked: Of course I'm not going to be faithful to you, no one can be faithful to one other person for a whole lifetime. (And there was the word *faithful*—stupid, all these words, stupid, belonging to a savage old world.) But the incident left both of them irritable. Strange, but they were both bad-tempered, annoyed. There was something unassimilable about it.

Making love splendidly after he had come home that night, both had felt that the idea that Myra Jenkins, a pretty girl met at a party, could be even relevant was ridiculous. They had loved each other for over a decade, would love each other for years more. Who, then, was Myra Jenkins?

Except, thought Susan, unaccountably bad-tempered, she was (is?) the first. In ten years. So either the ten years' fidelity was not important, or she isn't. (No, no, there is something wrong with this way of thinking, there must be.) But if she isn't important, presumably it wasn't important either when Matthew and I first went to bed with each other that afternoon whose delight even now (like a very long shadow at sundown) lays a long, wand-like finger over us. (Why did I say sundown?) Well, if what we felt that afternoon was not important, nothing is important, because if it hadn't been for what we felt, we wouldn't be Mr. and Mrs. Rawlings with four children, etc., etc. The whole thing is *absurd*—for him to have come home and told me was absurd. For him not to have told me was absurd. For me to care, or for that matter not to care, is absurd . . . and who is Myra Jenkins? Why, no one at all.

There was only one thing to do, and of course these sensible people did it: they put the thing behind them, and consciously, knowing what they were doing, moved forward into a different phase of their marriage, giving thanks for past good fortune as they did so.

For it was inevitable that the handsome, blond, attractive, manly

man, Matthew Rawlings, should be at times tempted (oh, what a word!) by the attractive girls at parties she could not attend because of the four children; and that sometimes he would succumb (a word even more repulsive, if possible) and that she, a good-looking woman in the big well-tended garden at Richmond, would sometimes be pierced as by an arrow from the sky with bitterness. Except that bitterness was not in order, it was out of court. Did the casual girls touch the marriage? They did not. Rather it was they who knew defeat because of the handsome Matthew Rawlings' marriage body and soul to Susan Rawlings.

In that case why did Susan feel (though luckily not for longer than a few seconds at a time) as if life had become a desert, and that nothing mattered, and that her children were not her own?

Meanwhile her intelligence continued to assert that all was well. What if her Matthew did have an occasional sweet afternoon, the odd affair? For she knew quite well, except in her moments of aridity, that they were very happy, that the affairs were not important.

Perhaps that was the trouble? It was in the nature of things that the adventures and delights could no longer be hers, because of the four children and the big house that needed so much attention. But perhaps she was secretly wishing, and even knowing that she did, that the wildness and the beauty could be his. But he was married to her. She was married to him. They were married inextricably. And therefore the gods could not strike him with the real magic, not really. Well, was it Susan's fault that after he came home from an adventure he looked harassed rather than fulfilled? (In fact, that was how she knew he had been *unfaithful*, because of his sullen air, and his glances at her, similar to hers at him: What is it that I share with this person that shields all delight from me?) But none of it by anybody's fault. (But what did they feel ought to be somebody's fault?) Nobody's fault, nothing to be at fault, no one to blame, no one to offer or to take it . . . and nothing wrong, either, except that Matthew never was really struck, as he wanted to be, by joy; and that Susan was more and more often threatened by emptiness. (It was usually in the garden that she was invaded by this feeling: she was coming to avoid the garden, unless the children or Matthew were with her.) There was no need to use the dramatic words, unfaithful, forgive, and the rest: intelligence forbade them. Intelligence barred, too, quarreling, sulking, anger, silences of withdrawal, accusations and tears. Above all, intelligence forbids tears.

A high price has to be paid for the happy marriage with the four healthy children in the large white gardened house.

And they were paying it, willingly, knowing what they were doing. When they lay side by side or breast to breast in the big civilized bedroom overlooking the wild sullied river, they laughed, often, for no particular reason; but they knew it was really because

of these two small people, Susan and Matthew, supporting such an edifice on their intelligent love. The laugh comforted them; it saved them both, though from what, they did not know.

They were now both fortyish. The older children, boy and girl, were ten and eight, at school. The twins, six, were still at home. Susan did not have nurses or girls to help her: childhood is short; and she did not regret the hard work. Often enough she was bored, since small children can be boring; she was often very tired; but she regretted nothing. In another decade, she would turn herself back into being a woman with a life of her own.

Soon the twins would go to school, and they would be away from home from nine until four. These hours, so Susan saw it, would be the preparation for her own slow emancipation away from the role of hub-of-the-family into woman-with-her-own life. She was already planning for the hours of freedom when all the children would be "off her hands." That was the phrase used by Matthew and by Susan and by their friends, for the moment when the youngest child went off to school. "They'll be off your hands, darling Susan, and you'll have time to yourself." So said Matthew, the intelligent husband, who had often enough commended and consoled Susan, standing by her in spirit during the years when her soul was not her own, as she said, but her children's.

What it amounted to was that Susan saw herself as she had been at twenty-eight, unmarried; and then again somewhere about fifty, blossoming from the root of what she had been twenty years before. As if the essential Susan were in abeyance, as if she were in cold storage. Matthew said something like this to Susan one night: and she agreed that it was true—she did feel something like that. What, then, was this essential Susan? She did not know. Put like that it sounded ridiculous, and she did not really feel it. Anyway, they had a long discussion about the whole thing before going off to sleep in each other's arms.

So the twins went off to their school, two bright affectionate children who had no problems about it, since their older brother and sister had trodden this path so successfully before them. And now Susan was going to be alone in the big house, every day of the school term, except for the daily woman who came in to clean.

It was now, for the first time in this marriage, that something happened which neither of them had foreseen.

This is what happened. She returned, at nine-thirty, from taking the twins to the school by car, looking forward to seven blissful hours of freedom. On the first morning she was simply restless, worrying about the twins "naturally enough" since this was their first day away at school. She was hardly able to contain herself until they came back. Which they did happily, excited by the world of school, looking forward to the next day. And the next day Susan

took them, dropped them, came back, and found herself reluctant to enter her big and beautiful home because it was as if something was waiting for her there that she did not wish to confront. Sensibly, however, she parked the car in the garage, entered the house, spoke to Mrs. Parkes the daily woman about her duties, and went up to her bedroom. She was possessed by a fever which drove her out again, downstairs, into the kitchen, where Mrs. Parkes was making cake and did not need her, and into the garden. There she sat on a bench and tried to calm herself, looking at trees, at a brown glimpse of the river. But she was filled with tension, like a panic: as if an enemy was in the garden with her. She spoke to herself severely, thus: All this is quite natural. First, I spent twelve years of my adult life working, *living my own life*. Then I married, and from the moment I became pregnant for the first time I signed myself over, so to speak, to other people. To the children. Not for one moment in twelve years have I been alone, had time to myself. So now I have to learn to be myself again. That's all.

And she went indoors to help Mrs. Parkes cook and clean, and found some sewing to do for the children. She kept herself occupied every day. At the end of the first term she understood she felt two contrary emotions. First: secret astonishment and dismay that during those weeks when the house was empty of children she had in fact been more occupied (had been careful to keep herself occupied) than ever she had been when the children were around her needing her continual attention. Second: that now she knew the house would be full of them, and for five weeks, she resented the fact she would never be alone. She was already looking back at those hours of sewing, cooking (but by herself), as at a lost freedom which would not be hers for five long weeks. And the two months of term which would succeed the five weeks stretched alluringly open to her—freedom. But what freedom—when in fact she had been so careful *not* to be free of small duties during the last weeks? She looked at herself, Susan Rawlings, sitting in a big chair by the window in the bedroom, sewing shirts or dresses, which she might just as well have bought. She saw herself making cakes for hours at a time in the big family kitchen: yet usually she bought cakes. What she saw was a woman alone, that was true, but she had not felt alone. For instance, Mrs. Parkes was always somewhere in the house. And she did not like being in the garden at all, because of the closeness there of the enemy—irritation, restlessness, emptiness, whatever it was, which keeping her hands occupied made less dangerous for some reason.

Susan did not tell Matthew of these thoughts. They were not sensible. She did not recognize herself in them. What should she say to her dear friend and husband Matthew? "When I go into the garden, that is, if the children are not there, I feel as if there is an

enemy there waiting to invade me." "What enemy, Susan darling?" "Well I don't know, really. ..." "Perhaps you should see a doctor?"

No, clearly this conversation should not take place. The holidays began and Susan welcomed them. Four children, lively, energetic, intelligent, demanding: she was never, not for a moment of her day, alone. If she was in a room, they would be in the next room, or waiting for her to do something for them; or it would soon be time for lunch or tea, or to take one of them to the dentist. Something to do: five weeks of it, thank goodness.

On the fourth day of these so welcome holidays, she found she was storming with anger at the twins, two shrinking beautiful children who (and this is what checked her) stood hand in hand looking at her with sheer dismayed disbelief. This was their calm mother, shouting at them. And for what? They had come to her with some game, some bit of nonsense. They looked at each other, moved closer for support, and went off hand in hand, leaving Susan holding on to the windowsill of the living room, breathing deep, feeling sick. She went to lie down, telling the older children she had a headache. She heard the boy Harry telling the little ones: "It's all right, Mother's got a headache." She heard that *It's all right* with pain.

That night she said to her husband: "Today I shouted at the twins, quite unfairly." She sounded miserable, and he said gently: "Well, what of it?"

"It's more of an adjustment than I thought, their going to school."

"But Susie, Susie darling. ..." For she was crouched weeping on the bed. He comforted her: "Susan, what is all this about? You shouted at them? What of it? If you shouted at them fifty times a day it wouldn't be more than the little devils deserve." But she wouldn't laugh. She wept. Soon he comforted her with his body. She became calm. Calm, she wondered what was wrong with her, and why she should mind so much that she might, just once, have behaved unjustly with the children. What did it matter? They had forgotten it all long ago: Mother had a headache and everything was all right.

It was a long time later that Susan understood that that night, when she had wept and Matthew had driven the misery out of her with his big solid body, was the last time, ever in their married life, that they had been—to use their mutual language—with each other. And even that was a lie, because she had not told him of her real fears at all.

The five weeks passed, and Susan was in control of herself, and good and kind, and she looked forward to the holidays with a mixture of fear and longing. She did not know what to expect. She

took the twins off to school (the elder children took themselves to school) and she returned to the house determined to face the enemy wherever he was, in the house, or the garden or—where?

She was again restless, she was possessed by restlessness. She cooked and sewed and worked as before, day after day, while Mrs. Parkes remonstrated: "Mrs. Rawlings, what's the need for it? I can do that, it's what you pay me for."

And it was so irrational that she checked herself. She would put the car into the garage, go up to her bedroom, and sit, hands in her lap, forcing herself to be quiet. She listened to Mrs. Parkes moving around the house. She looked out into the garden and saw the branches shake the trees. She sat defeating the enemy, restlessness. Emptiness. She ought to be thinking about her life, about herself. But she did not. Or perhaps she could not. As soon as she forced her mind to think about Susan (for what else did she want to be alone for?) it skipped off to thoughts of butter or school clothes. Or it thought of Mrs. Parkes. She realized that she sat listening for the movements of the cleaning woman, following her every turn, bend, thought. She followed her in her mind from kitchen to bathroom, from table to oven, and it was as if the duster, the cleaning cloth, the saucepan, were in her own hand. She would hear herself saying: No, not like that, don't put that there. . . . Yet she did not give a damn what Mrs. Parkes did, or if she did it at all. Yet she could not prevent herself from being conscious of her, every minute. Yes, this was what was wrong with her: she needed, when she was alone, to be really alone, with no one near. She could not endure the knowledge that in ten minutes or in half an hour Mrs. Parkes would call up the stairs: "Mrs. Rawlings, there's no silver polish. Madam, we're out of flour."

So she left the house and went to sit in the garden where she was screened from the house by trees. She waited for the demon to appear and claim her, but he did not.

She was keeping him off, because she had not, after all, come to an end of arranging herself.

She was planning how to be somewhere where Mrs. Parkes would not come after her with a cup of tea, or a demand to be allowed to telephone (always irritating since Susan did not care who she telephoned or how often), or just a nice talk about something. Yes, she needed a place, or a state of affairs, where it would not be necessary to keep reminding herself: In ten minutes I must telephone Matthew about . . . and at half past three I must leave early for the children because the car needs cleaning. And at ten o'clock tomorrow I must remember. . . . She was possessed with resentment that the seven hours of freedom in every day (during weekdays in the school term) were not free, that never, not for one second, ever, was she free from the pressure of time, from having to remember this or

that. She could never forget herself; never really let herself go into forgetfulness.

Resentment. It was poisoning her. (She looked at this emotion and thought it was absurd. Yet she felt it.) She was a prisoner. (She looked at this thought too, and it was no good telling herself it was a ridiculous one.) She must tell Matthew—but what? She was filled with emotions that were utterly ridiculous, that she despised, yet that nevertheless she was feeling so strongly she could not shake them off.

The school holidays came round, and this time they were for nearly two months, and she behaved with a conscious controlled decency that nearly drove her crazy. She would lock herself in the bathroom, and sit on the edge of the bath, breathing deep, trying to let go into some kind of calm. Or she went up into the spare room, usually empty, where no one would expect her to be. She heard the children calling "Mother, Mother," and kept silent, feeling guilty. Or she went to the very end of the garden, by herself, and looked at the slow-moving brown river; she looked at the river and closed her eyes and breathed slow and deep, taking it into her being, into her veins.

Then she returned to the family, wife and mother, smiling and responsible, feeling as if the pressure of these people—four lively children and her husband—were a painful pressure on the surface of her skin, a hand pressing on her brain. She did not once break down into irritation during these holidays, but it was like living out a prison sentence, and when the children went back to school, she sat on a white stone seat near the flowing river, and she thought: It is not even a year since the twins went to school, since *they were off my hands* (What on earth did I think I meant when I used that stupid phrase?) and yet I'm a different person. I'm simply not myself. I don't understand it.

Yet she had to understand it. For she knew that this structure— big white house, on which the mortgage still cost four hundred a year, a husband, so good and kind and insightful, four children, all doing so nicely, and the garden where she sat, and Mrs. Parkes the cleaning woman—all this depended on her, and yet she could not understand why, or even what it was she contributed to it.

She said to Matthew in their bedroom: "I think there must be something wrong with me."

And he said: "Surely not, Susan? You look marvelous—you're as lovely as ever."

She looked at the handsome blond man, with his clear, intelligent, blue-eyed face, and thought: Why is it I can't tell him? Why not? And she said: "I need to be alone more than I am."

At which he swung his slow blue gaze at her, and she saw what she had been dreading: Incredulity. Disbelief. And fear. An incredu-

lous blue stare from a stranger who was her husband, as close to her as her own breath.

He said: "But the children are at school and off your hands."

She said to herself: I've got to force myself to say: Yes, but do you realize that I never feel free? There's never a moment I can say to myself: There's nothing I have to remind myself about, nothing I have to do in half an hour, or an hour, or two hours. . . .

But she said: "I don't feel well."

He said: "Perhaps you need a holiday."

She said, appalled: "But not without you, surely?" For she could not imagine herself going off without him. Yet that was what he meant. Seeing her face, he laughed, and opened his arms, and she went into them, thinking: Yes, yes, but why can't I say it? And what is it I have to say?

She tried to tell him, about never being free. And he listened and said: "But Susan, what sort of freedom can you possibly want—short of being dead! Am I ever free? I go to the office, and I have to be there at ten—all right, half past ten, sometimes. And I have to do this or that, don't I? Then I've got to come home at a certain time—I don't mean it, you know I don't—but if I'm not going to be back home at six I telephone you. When can I ever say to myself: I have nothing to be responsible for in the next six hours?"

Susan, hearing this, was remorseful. Because it was true. The good marriage, the house, the children, depended just as much on his voluntary bondage as it did on hers. But why did he not feel bound? Why didn't he chafe and become restless? No, there was something really wrong with her and this proved it.

And that word *bondage*—why had she used it? She had never felt marriage, or the children, as bondage. Neither had he, or surely they wouldn't be together lying in each other's arms content after twelve years of marriage.

No, her state (whatever it was) was irrelevant, nothing to do with her real good life with her family. She had to accept the fact that after all, she was an irrational person and to live with it. Some people had to live with crippled arms, or stammers, or being deaf. She would have to live knowing she was subject to a state of mind she could not own.

Nevertheless, as a result of this conversation with her husband, there was a new regime next holidays.

The spare room at the top of the house now had a cardboard sign saying: PRIVATE! DO NOT DISTURB! on it. (This sign had been drawn in coloured chalks by the children, after a discussion between the parents in which it was decided this was psychologically the right thing.) The family and Mrs. Parkes knew this was "Mother's Room" and that she was entitled to her privacy. Many serious conversations took place between Matthew and the children about not

taking Mother for granted. Susan overheard the first, between father and Harry, the older boy, and was surprised at her irritation over it. Surely she could have a room somewhere in that big house and retire into it without such a fuss being made? Without it being so solemnly discussed? Why couldn't she simply have announced: "I'm going to fit out the little top room for myself, and when I'm in it I'm not to be disturbed for anything short of fire"? Just that, and finished; instead of long earnest discussions. When she heard Harry and Matthew explaining it to the twins with Mrs. Parkes coming in—"Yes, well, a family sometimes gets on top of a woman"—she had to go right away to the bottom of the garden until the devils of exasperation had finished their dance in her blood.

But now there was a room, and she could go there when she liked, she used it seldom: she felt even more caged there than in her bedroom. One day she had gone up there after a lunch for ten children she had cooked and served because Mrs. Parkes was not there, and had sat alone for a while looking into the garden. She saw the children stream out from the kitchen and stand looking up at the window where she sat behind the curtains. They were all— her children and her friends—discussing Mother's Room. A few minutes later, the chase of children in some game came pounding up the stairs, but ended as abruptly as if they had fallen over a ravine, so sudden was the silence. They had remembered she was there, and had gone silent in a great gale of "Hush! Shhhhhh! Quiet, you'll disturb her. . . ." And they went tiptoeing downstairs like criminal conspirators. When she came down to make tea for them, they all apologized. The twins put their arms around her, from front and back, making a human cage of loving limbs, and promised it would never occur again. "We forgot, Mummy, we forgot all about it!"

What it amounted to was that Mother's Room, and her need for privacy, had become a valuable lesson in respect for other people's rights. Quite soon Susan was going up to the room only because it was a lesson it was a pity to drop. Then she took sewing up there, and the children and Mrs. Parkes came in and out: it had become another family room.

She sighed, and smiled, and resigned herself—she made jokes at her own expense with Matthew over the room. That is, she did from the self she liked, she respected. But at the same time, something inside her howled with impatience, with rage. . . . And she was frightened. One day she found herself kneeling by her bed and praying: "Dear God, keep it away from me, keep him away from me." She meant the devil, for she now thought of it, not caring if she were irrational, as some sort of demon. She imagined him, or it, as a youngish man, or perhaps a middle-aged man pretending to be young. Or a man young-looking from immaturity? At any rate, she

saw the young-looking face which, when she drew closer, had dry lines about mouth and eyes. He was thinnish, meager in build. And he had a reddish complexion, and ginger hair. That was he—a gingery, energetic man, and he wore a reddish hairy jacket, unpleasant to the touch.

Well, one day she saw him. She was standing at the bottom of the garden, watching the river ebb past, when she raised her eyes and saw this person, or being, sitting on the white stone bench. He was looking at her, and grinning. In his hand was a long crooked stick, which he had picked off the ground, or broken off the tree above him. He was absent-mindedly, out of an absent-minded or freakish impulse of spite, using the stick to stir around in the coils of a blindworm or a grass snake (or some kind of snakelike creature: it was whitish and unhealthy to look at, unpleasant). The snake was twisting about, flinging its coils from side to side in a kind of dance of protest against the teasing prodding stick.

Susan looked at him thinking: Who is the stranger? What is he doing in our garden? Then she recognized the man around whom her terrors had crystalized. As she did so, he vanished. She made herself walk over to the bench. A shadow from a branch lay across thin emerald grass, moving jerkily over its roughness, and she could see why she had taken it for a snake, lashing and twisting. She went back to the house thinking: Right, then, so I've seen him with my own eyes, so I'm not crazy after all—there *is* a danger because I've seen him. He is lurking in the garden and sometimes even in the house, and he wants *to get into me and to take me over*.

She dreamed of having a room or a place, anywhere, where she could go and sit, by herself, no one knowing where she was.

Once, near Victoria, she found herself outside a news agent that had Rooms to Let advertised. She decided to rent a room, telling no one. Sometimes she could take the train in to Richmond and sit alone in it for an hour or two. Yet how could she? A room would cost three or four pounds a week, and she earned no money, and how could she explain to Matthew that she needed such a sum? What for? It did not occur to her that she was taking it for granted she wasn't going to tell him about the room.

Well, it was out of the question, having a room; yet she knew she must.

One day, when a school term was well established, and none of the children had measles or other ailments, and everything seemed in order, she did the shopping early, explained to Mrs. Parkes she was meeting an old school friend, took the train to Victoria, searched until she found a small quiet hotel, and asked for a room for the day. They did not let rooms by the day, the manageress said, looking doubtful, since Susan so obviously was not the kind of woman who needed a room for unrespectable reasons. Susan made a

long explanation about not being well, being unable to shop without frequent rests for lying down. At last she was allowed to rent
the room provided she paid a full night's price for it. She was taken
up by the manageress and a maid, both concerned over the state of
her health ... which must be pretty bad if, living at Richmond
(she had signed her name and address in the register), she needed a
shelter at Victoria.

The room was ordinary and anonymous, and was just what Susan
needed. She put a shilling in the gas fire, and sat, eyes shut, in a
dingy armchair with her back to a dingy window. She was alone.
She was alone. She could feel pressures lifting off her. First the
sounds of traffic came very loud; then they seemed to vanish; she
might even have slept a little. A knock on the door: it was Miss
Townsend the manageress, bringing her a cup of tea with her own
hands, so concerned was she over Susan's long silence and possible
illness.

Miss Townsend was a lonely woman of fifty, running this hotel
with all the rectitude expected of her, and she sensed in Susan the
possibility of understanding companionship. She stayed to talk.
Susan found herself in the middle of a fantastic story about her illness, which got more and more improbable as she tried to make it
tally with the large house at Richmond, well-off husband, and four
children. Suppose she said instead: Miss Townsend, I'm here in
your hotel because I need to be alone for a few hours, above all
alone and with no one knowing where I am. She said it mentally,
and saw, mentally, the look that would inevitably come on Miss
Townsend's elderly maiden's face. "Miss Townsend, my four children and my husband are driving me insane, do you understand
that? Yes, I can see from the gleam of hysteria in your eyes that
comes from loneliness controlled but only just contained that I've
got everything in the world you've ever longed for. Well, Miss
Townsend, I don't want any of it. You can have it, Miss Townsend.
I wish I was absolutely alone in the world, like you. Miss Townsend, I'm besieged by seven devils, Miss Townsend, Miss Townsend, let me stay here in your hotel where the devils can't get me.
. . ." Instead of saying all this, she described her anemia, agreed to
try Miss Townsend's remedy for it, which was raw liver, minced,
between whole-meal bread, and said yes, perhaps it would be better
if she stayed at home and let a friend do shopping for her. She paid
her bill and left the hotel, defeated.

At home Mrs. Parkes said she didn't really like it, no, not really,
when Mrs. Rawlings was away from nine in the morning until five.
The teacher had telephoned from school to say Joan's teeth were
paining her, and she hadn't known what to say; and what was she
to make for the children's tea, Mrs. Rawlings hadn't said.

All this was nonsense, of course. Mrs. Parkes's complaint was that

Susan had withdrawn herself spiritually, leaving the burden of the big house on her.

Susan looked back at her day of "freedom" which had resulted in her becoming a friend to the lonely Miss Townsend, and in Mrs. Parkes's remonstrances. Yet she remembered the short blissful hour of being alone, really alone. She was determined to arrange her life, no matter what it cost, so that she could have that solitude more often. An absolute solitude, where no one knew her or cared about her.

But how? She thought of saying to her old employer: I want to back you up in a story with Matthew that I am doing part-time work for you. The truth is that . . . but she would have to tell him a lie too, and which lie? She could not say: I want to sit by myself three or four times a week in a rented room. And besides, he knew Matthew, and she could not really ask him to tell lies on her behalf, apart from his being bound to think it meant a lover.

Suppose she really took a part-time job, which she could get through fast and efficiently, leaving time for herself. What job? Addressing envelopes? Canvassing?

And there was Mrs. Parkes, working widow, who knew exactly what she was prepared to give to the house, who knew by instinct when her mistress withdrew in spirit from her responsibilities. Mrs. Parkes was one of the servants of this world, but she needed someone to serve. She had to have Mrs. Rawlings, her madam, at the top of the house or in the garden, so that she could come and get support from her: "Yes, the bread's not what it was when I was a girl. . . . Yes, Harry's got a wonderful appetite, I wonder where he puts it all. . . . Yes, it's lucky the twins are so much of a size, they can wear each other's shoes, that's a saving in these hard times. . . . Yes, the cherry jam from Switzerland is not a patch on the jam from Poland, and three times the price. . . ." And so on. That sort of talk Mrs. Parkes must have, every day, or she would leave, not knowing herself why she left.

Susan Rawlings, thinking these thoughts, found that she was prowling through the great thicketed garden like a wild cat: she was walking up the stairs, down the stairs, through the rooms, into the garden, along the brown running river, back, up through the house, down again. . . . It was a wonder Mrs. Parkes did not think it strange. But on the contrary, Mrs. Rawlings could do what she liked, she could stand on her head if she wanted, provided she was *there*. Susan Rawlings prowled and muttered through her house, hating Mrs. Parkes, hating poor Miss Townsend, dreaming of her hour of solitude in the dingy respectability of Miss Townsend's hotel bedroom, and she knew quite well she was mad. Yes, she was mad.

She said to Matthew that she must have a holiday. Matthew

agreed with her. This was not as things had been once—how they had talked in each other's arms in the marriage bed. He had, she knew, diagnosed her finally as *unreasonable*. She had become some-one outside himself that he had to manage. They were living side by side in this house like two tolerably friendly strangers.

Having told Mrs. Parkes, or rather, asked for her permission, she went off on a walking holiday in Wales. She chose the remotest place she knew of. Every morning the children telephoned her before they went off to school, to encourage and support her, just as they had over Mother's Room. Every evening she telephoned them, spoke to each child in turn, and then to Matthew. Mrs. Parkes, given permission to telephone for instructions or advice, did so every day at lunchtime. When, as happened three times, Mrs. Rawlings was out on the mountainside, Mrs. Parkes asked that she should ring back at such and such a time, for she would not be happy in what she was doing without Mrs. Rawlings' blessing.

Susan prowled over wild country with the telephone wire holding her to her duty like a leash. The next time she must telephone, or wait to be telephoned, nailed her to her cross. The mountains themselves seemed trammeled by her unfreedom. Everywhere on the mountains, where she met no one at all, from breakfast time to dusk, excepting sheep, or a shepherd, she came face to face with her own craziness which might attack her in the broadest valleys, so that they seemed too small; or on a mountaintop from which she could see a hundred other mountains and valleys, so that they seemed too low, too small, with the sky pressing down too close. She would stand gazing at a hillside brilliant with ferns and bracken, jeweled with running water, and see nothing but her devil, who lifted inhuman eyes at her from where he leaned negligently on a rock, switching at his ugly yellow boots with a leafy twig.

She returned to her home and family, with the Welsh emptiness at the back of her mind like a promise of freedom.

She told her husband she wanted to have an *au pair* girl.

They were in their bedroom, it was late at night, the children slept. He sat, shirted and slippered, in a chair by the window, look-ing out. She sat brushing her hair and watching him in the mirror. A time-hallowed scene in the connubial bedroom. He said nothing, while she heard the arguments coming in to his mind, only to be rejected because every one was *reasonable*.

"It seems strange to get one now, after all, the children are in school most of the day. Surely the time for you to have help was when you were stuck with them day and night. Why don't you ask Mrs. Parkes to cook for you? She's even offered to—I can under-stand if you are tired of cooking for six people. But you know that an *au pair* girl means all kinds of problems, it's not like having an ordinary char in during the day. . . ."

Finally he said carefully: "Are you thinking of going back to work?"

"No," she said, "no, not really." She made herself sound vague, rather stupid. She went on brushing her black hair and peering at herself so as to be oblivious of the short uneasy glances her Matthew kept giving her. "Do you think we can't afford it?" she went on vaguely, not at all the old efficient Susan who knew exactly what they could afford.

"It's not that," he said, looking out of the window at dark trees, so as not to look at her. Meanwhile she examined a round, candid, pleasant face with clear dark brows and clear grey eyes. A sensible face. She brushed thick healthy black hair and thought: Yet that's the reflection of a madwoman. How very strange! Much more to the point if what looked back at me was the gingery green-eyed demon with his dry meager smile. . . . Why wasn't Matthew agreeing? After all, what else could he do? She was breaking her part of the bargain and there was no way of forcing her to keep it: that her spirit, her soul, should live in this house, so that the people in it could grow like plants in water, and Mrs. Parkes remain content in their service. In return for this, he would be a good loving husband, and responsible towards the children. Well, nothing like this had been true of either of them for a long time. He did his duty, perfunctorily; she did not even pretend to do hers. And he had become like other husbands, with his real life in his work and the people he met there, and very likely a serious affair. All this was her fault.

At last he drew heavy curtains, blotting out the trees, and turned to force her attention: "Susan, are you really sure we need a girl?" But she would not meet his appeal at all: She was running the brush over her hair again and again, lifting fine black clouds in a small hiss of electricity. She was peering in and smiling as if she were amused at the clinging hissing hair that followed the brush.

"Yes, I think it would be a good idea on the whole," she said, with the cunning of a madwoman evading the real point.

In the mirror she could see her Matthew lying on his back, his hands behind his head, staring upwards, his face sad and hard. She felt her heart (the old heart of Susan Rawlings) soften and call out to him. But she set it to be indifferent.

He said: "Susan, the children?" It was an appeal that *almost* reached her. He opened his arms, lifting them from where they had lain by his sides, palms up, empty. She had only to run across and fling herself into them, onto his hard, warm chest, and melt into herself, into Susan. But she could not. She would not see his lifted arms. She said vaguely: "Well, surely it'll be even better for them? We'll get a French or a German girl and they'll learn the language."

In the dark she lay beside him, feeling frozen, a stranger. She felt as if Susan had been spirited away. She disliked very much this woman who lay here, cold and indifferent beside a suffering man, but she could not change her.

Next morning she set about getting a girl, and very soon came Sophie Traub from Hamburg, a girl of twenty, laughing, healthy, blue-eyed, intending to learn English. Indeed, she already spoke a good deal. In return for a room—"Mother's Room"—and her food, she undertook to do some light cooking, and to be with the children when Mrs. Rawlings asked. She was an intelligent girl and understood perfectly what was needed. Susan said: "I go off sometimes, for the morning or for the day—well, sometimes the children run home from school, or they ring up, or a teacher rings up. I should be here, really. And there's the daily woman. . . ." And Sophie laughed her deep fruity *Fräulein's* laugh, showed her fine white teeth and her dimples, and said: "You want some person to play mistress of the house sometimes, not so?"

"Yes, that is just so," said Susan, a bit dry, despite herself, thinking in secret fear how easy it was, how much nearer to the end she was than she thought. Healthy Fräulein Traub's instant understanding of their position proved this to be true.

The *au pair* girl, because of her own common sense, or (as Susan said to herself with her new inward shudder) because she had been *chosen* so well by Susan, was a success with everyone, the children liking her, Mrs. Parkes forgetting almost at once that she was German, and Matthew finding her "nice to have around the house." For he was now taking things as they came, from the surface of life, withdrawn both as a husband and a father from the household.

One day Susan saw how Sophie and Mrs. Parkes were talking and laughing in the kitchen, and she announced that she would be away until teatime. She knew exactly where to go and what she must look for. She took the District Line to South Kensington, changed to the Circle, got off at Paddington, and walked around looking at the smaller hotels until she was satisfied with one which had FRED'S HOTEL painted on windowpanes that needed cleaning. The façade was a faded shiny yellow, like unhealthy skin. A door at the end of a passage said she must knock; she did, and Fred appeared. He was not at all attractive, not in any way, being fattish, and run-down, and wearing a tasteless striped suit. He had small sharp eyes in a white creased face, and was quite prepared to let Mrs. Jones (she chose the farcical name deliberately, staring him out) have a room three days a week from ten until six. Provided of course that she paid in advance each time she came? Susan produced fifteen shillings (no price had been set by him) and held it out, still fixing him with a bold unblinking challenge she had not known until then she

could use at will. Looking at her still, he took up a ten-shilling note from her palm between thumb and forefinger, fingered it; then shuffled up two half crowns, held out his own palm with these bits of money displayed thereon, and let his gaze lower broodingly at them. They were standing in the passage, a red-shaded light above, bare boards beneath, and a strong smell of floor polish rising about them. He shot his gaze up at her over the still-extended palm, and smiled as if to say: What do you take me for? "I shan't," said Susan, "be using this room for the purposes of making money." He still waited. She added another five shillings, at which he nodded and said: "You pay, and I ask no questions." "Good," said Susan. He now went past her to the stairs, and there waited a moment: the light from the street door being in her eyes, she lost sight of him momentarily. Then she saw a sober-suited, white-faced, white-balding little man trotting up the stairs like a waiter, and she went after him. They proceeded in utter silence up the stairs of this house where no questions were asked—Fred's Hotel, which could afford the freedom for its visitors that poor Miss Townsend's hotel could not. The room was hideous. It had a single window, with thin green brocade curtains, a three-quarter bed that had a cheap green satin bedspread on it, a fireplace with a gas fire and a shillling meter by it, a chest of drawers, and a green wicker armchair.

"Thank you," said Susan, knowing that Fred (if this was Fred, and not George, or Herbert or Charlie) was looking at her, not so much with curiosity, an emotion he would not own to, for professional reasons, but with a philosophical sense of what was appropriate. Having taken her money and shown her up and agreed to everything, he was clearly disapproving of her for coming here. She did not belong here at all, so his look said. (But she knew, already, how very much she did belong: the room had been waiting for her to join it.) "Would you have me called at five o'clock, please?" and he nodded and went downstairs.

It was twelve in the morning. She was free. She sat in the armchair, she simply sat, she closed her eyes and sat and let herself be alone. She was alone and no one knew where she was. When a knock came on the door she was annoyed, and prepared to show it: but it was Fred himself, it was five o'clock and he was calling her as ordered. He flicked his sharp little eyes over the room—bed, first. It was undisturbed. She might never have been in the room at all. She thanked him, said she would be returning the day after tomorrow, and left. She was back home in time to cook supper, to put the children to bed, to cook a second supper for her husband and herself later. And to welcome Sophie back from the pictures where she had gone with a friend. All these things she did cheerfully, willingly. But she was thinking all the time of the hotel room, she was longing for it with her whole being.

Three times a week. She arrived promptly at ten, looked Fred in the eyes, gave him twenty shillings, followed him up the stairs, went into the room, and shut the door on him with gentle firmness. For Fred, disapproving of her being here at all, was quite ready to let friendship, or at least acquaintanceship, follow his disapproval, if only she would let him. But he was content to go off on her dismissing nod, with the twenty shillings in his hand.

She sat in the armchair and shut her eyes.

What did she *do* in the room? Why, nothing at all. From the chair, when it had rested her, she went to the window, stretching her arms, smiling, treasuring her anonymity, to look out. She was no longer Susan Rawlings, mother of four, wife of Matthew, employer of Mrs. Parkes and of Sophie Traub, with these and those relations with friends, schoolteachers, tradesmen. She no longer was mistress of the big white house and garden, owning clothes suitable for this and that activity or occasion. She was Mrs. Jones, and she was alone, and she had no past and no future. Here I am, she thought, after all these years of being married and having children and playing those roles of responsibility—and I'm just the same. Yet there have been times I thought that nothing existed of me except the roles that went with being Mrs. Matthew Rawlings. Yes, here I am, and if I never saw any of my family again, here I would still be . . . how very strange that is! And she leaned on the sill, and looked into the street, loving the men and women who passed, because she did not know them. She looked at the downtrodden buildings over the street, and at the sky, wet and dingy, or sometimes blue, and she felt she had never seen buildings or sky before. And then she went back to the chair, empty, her mind a blank. Sometimes she talked aloud, saying nothing—an exclamation, meaningless, followed by a comment about the floral pattern on the thin rug, or a stain on the green satin coverlet. For the most part, she wool-gathered—what word is there for it?—brooded, wandered, simply went dark, feeling emptiness run deliciously through her veins like the movement of her blood.

This room had become more her own than the house she lived in. One morning she found Fred taking her a flight higher than usual. She stopped, refusing to go up, and demanded her usual room, Number 19. "Well, you'll have to wait half an hour then." he said. Willingly she descended to the dark disinfectant-smelling hall, and sat waiting until the two, man and woman, came down the stairs, giving her swift indifferent glances before they hurried out into the street, separating at the door. She went up to the room, *her* room, which they had just vacated. It was no less hers, though the windows were set wide open, and a maid was straightening the bed as she came in.

After these days of solitude, it was both easy to play her part as

mother and wife, and difficult—because it was so easy: she felt an imposter. She felt as if her shell moved here, with her family, answering to Mummy, Mother, Susan, Mrs. Rawlings. She was surprised no one saw through her, that she wasn't turned out of doors, as a fake. On the contrary, it seemed the children loved her more; Matthew and she "got on" pleasantly, and Mrs. Parkes was happy in her work under (for the most part, it must be confessed) Sophie Traub. At night she lay beside her husband, and they made love again, apparently just as they used to, when they were really married. But she, Susan, or the being who answered so readily and improbably to the name of Susan, was not there: she was in Fred's Hotel, in Paddington, waiting for the easing hours of solitude to begin.

Soon she made a new arrangement with Fred and with Sophie. It was for five days a week. As for the money, five pounds, she simply asked Matthew for it. She saw that she was not even frightened he might ask what for: he would give it to her, she knew that, and yet it was terrifying it could be so, for this close couple, these partners, had once known the destination of every shilling they must spend. He agreed to give her five pounds a week. She asked for just so much, not a penny more. He sounded indifferent about it. It was as if he were paying her, she thought: *paying her off*—yes, that was it. Terror came back for a moment, when she understood this, but she stilled it: things had gone too far for that. Now, every week, on Sunday nights, he gave her five pounds, turning away from her before their eyes could meet on the transaction. As for Sophie Traub, she was to be somewhere in or near the house until six at night, after which she was free. She was not to cook, or to clean, she was simply to be there. So she gardened or sewed, and asked friends in, being a person who was bound to have a lot of friends. If the children were sick, she nursed them. If teachers telephoned, she answered them sensibly. For the five daytimes in the school week, she was altogether the mistress of the house.

One night in the bedroom, Matthew asked: "Susan, I don't want to interfere—don't think that, please—but are you sure you are well?"

She was brushing her hair at the mirror. She made two more strokes on either side of her head, before she replied: "Yes, dear, I am sure I am well."

He was again lying on his back, his big blond head on his hands, his elbows angled up and part-concealing his face. He said: "Then Susan, I have to ask you this question, though you must understand, I'm not putting any sort of pressure on you." (Susan heard the word pressure with dismay, because this was inevitable, of course she could not go on like this.) "Are things going to go on like this?"

"Well," she said, going vague and bright and idiotic again, so as

to escape: "Well, I don't see why not."

He was jerking his elbows up and down, in annoyance or in pain, and, looking at him, she saw he had got thin, even gaunt; and restless angry movements were not what she remembered of him. He said: "Do you want a divorce, is that it?"

At this, Susan only with the greatest difficulty stopped herself from laughing: she could hear the bright bubbling laughter she *would* have emitted, had she let herself. He could only mean one thing: she had a lover, and that was why she spent her days in London, as lost to him as if she had vanished to another continent.

Then the small panic set in again: she understood that he hoped she did have a lover, he was begging her to say so, because otherwise it would be too terrifying.

She thought this out, as she brushed her hair, watching the fine black stuff fly up to make its little clouds of electricity, hiss, hiss, hiss. Behind her head, across the room, was a blue wall. She realized she was absorbed in watching the black hair making shapes against the blue. She would be answering him. "Do *you* want a divorce, Matthew?"

He said: "That surely isn't the point, is it?"

"You brought it up, I didn't," she said, brightly, suppressing meaningless tinkling laughter.

Next day she asked Fred: "Have inquiries been made for me?"

He hesitated, and she said: "I've been coming here a year now. I've made no trouble, and you've been paid every day. I have a right to be told."

"As a matter of fact, Mrs. Jones, a man did come asking."

"A man from a detective agency?"

"Well, he could have been, couldn't he?"

"I was asking you . . . well, what did you tell him?"

"I told him a Mrs. Jones came every weekday from ten until five or six and stayed in Number Nineteen by herself."

"Describing me?"

"Well Mrs. Jones, I had no alternative. Put yourself in my place."

"By rights I should deduct what that man gave you for the information."

He raised shocked eyes: she was not the sort of person to make jokes like this! Then he chose to laugh: a pinkish wet slit appeared across his white crinkled face: his eyes positively begged her to laugh, otherwise he might lose some money. She remained grave, looking at him.

He stopped laughing and said: "You want to go up now?"—returning to the familiarity, the comradeship, of the country where no questions are asked, on which (and he knew it) she depended completely.

She went up to sit in her wicker chair. But it was not the same.

Her husband had searched her out. (The world had searched her out.) The pressures were on her. She was here with his connivance. He might walk in at any moment, here, into Room 19. She imagined the report from the detective agency: "A woman calling herself Mrs. Jones, fitting the description of your wife (etc., etc., etc.), stays alone all day in Room No. 19. She insists on this room, waits for it if it is engaged. As far as the proprietor knows, she receives no visitors there, male or female." A report something on these lines, Matthew must have received.

Well of course he was right: things couldn't go on like this. He had to put an end to it all simply by sending the detective after her.

She tried to shrink herself back into the shelter of the room, a snail perked out of its shell and trying to squirm back. But the peace of the room had gone. She was trying consciously to revive it, trying to let go into the dark creative trance (or whatever it was) that she had found there. It was no use, yet she craved for it, she was as ill as a suddenly deprived addict.

Several times she returned to the room, to look for herself there, but instead she found the unnamed spirit of restlessness, a prickling fevered hunger for movement, an irritable self-consciousness that made her brain feel as if it had colored lights going on and off inside it. Instead of the soft dark that had been the room's air, were now waiting for her demons that made her dash blindly about, muttering words of hate; she was impelling herself from point to point like a moth dashing itself against a windowpane, sliding to the bottom, fluttering off on broken wings, then crashing into the invisible barrier again. And again and again. Soon she was exhausted, and she told Fred that for a while she would not be needing the room, she was going on holiday. Home she went, to the big white house by the river. The middle of a weekday, and she felt guilty at returning to her own home when not expected. She stood unseen, looking in at the kitchen window. Mrs. Parkes, wearing a discarded floral overall of Susan's, was stooping to slide something into the oven. Sophie, arms folded, was leaning her back against a cupboard and laughing at some joke made by a girl not seen before by Susan—a dark foreign girl, Sophie's visitor. In an armchair Molly, one of the twins, lay curled, sucking her thumb and watching the grownups. She must have some sickness, to be kept from school. The child's listless face, the dark circles under her eyes, hurt Susan: Molly was looking at the three grownups working and talking in exactly the same way Susan looked at the four through the kitchen window: she was remote, shut off from them.

But then, just as Susan imagined herself going in, picking up the little girl, and sitting in an armchair with her, stroking her probably heated forehead, Sophie did just that: she had been standing on one leg, the other knee flexed, its foot set against the wall. Now she

let her foot in its ribbon-tied red shoe slide down the wall, stood solid on two feet, clapping her hands before and behind her, and sang a couple of lines in German, so that the child lifted her heavy eyes at her and began to smile. Then she walked, or rather skipped, over to the child, swung her up, and let her fall into her lap at the same moment she sat herself. She said "Hopla! Hopla! Molly . . ." and began stroking the dark untidy young head that Molly laid on her shoulder for comfort.

Well. . . . Susan blinked the tears of farewell out of her eyes, and went quietly up the house to her bedroom. There she sat looking at the river through the trees. She felt at peace, but in a way that was new to her. She had no desire to move, to talk, to do anything at all. The devils that had haunted the house, the garden, were not there; but she knew it was because her soul was in Room 19 in Fred's Hotel; she was not really here at all. It was a sensation that should have been frightening: to sit at her own bedroom window, listening to Sophie's rich young voice sing German nursery songs to her child, listening to Mrs. Parkes clatter and move below, and to know that all this had nothing to do with her: she was already out of it.

Later, she made herself go down and say she was home: it was unfair to be here unannounced. She took lunch with Mrs. Parkes, Sophie, Sophie's Italian friend Maria, and her daughter Molly, and felt like a visitor.

A few days later, at bedtime, Matthew said: "Here's your five pounds," and pushed them over at her. Yet he must have known she had not been leaving the house at all.

She shook her head, gave it back to him, and said, in explanation, not in accusation: "As soon as you knew where I was, there was no point."

He nodded, not looking at her. He was turned away from her: thinking, she knew, how best to handle this wife who terrified him.

He said: "I wasn't trying to . . . it's just that I was worried."

"Yes, I know."

"I must confess that I was beginning to wonder . . ."

"You thought I had a lover?"

"Yes, I am afraid I did."

She knew that he wished she had. She sat wondering how to say: "For a year now I've been spending all my days in a very sordid hotel room. It's the place where I'm happy. In fact, without it I don't exist." She heard herself saying this, and understood how terrified he was that she might. So instead she said: "Well, perhaps you're not far wrong."

Probably Matthew would think the hotel proprietor lied: he would want to think so.

"Well," he said, and she could hear his voice spring up, so to

speak, with relief: "in that case I must confess I've got a bit of an affair on myself."

She said, detached and interested: "Really? Who is she?" and saw Matthew's startled look because of this reaction.

"It's Phil. Phil Hunt."

She had known Phil Hunt well in the old unmarried days. She was thinking: No, she won't do, she's too neurotic and difficult. She's never been happy yet. Sophie's much better: Well Matthew will see that himself, as sensible as he is.

This line of thought went on in silence, while she said aloud: "It's no point telling you about mine, because you don't know him."

Quick, quick, invent, she thought. Remember how you invented all that nonsense for Miss Townsend.

She began slowly, careful not to contradict herself: "His name is Michael"—(*Michael What?*)—"Michael Plant." (What a silly name!) "He's rather like you—in looks, I mean." And indeed, she could imagine herself being touched by no one but Matthew himself. "He's a publisher." (Really? Why?) "He's got a wife already and two children."

She brought out this fantasy, proud of herself.

Matthew said: "Are you two thinking of marrying?"

She said, before she could stop herself: "Good God, *no!*"

She realized, if Matthew wanted to marry Phil Hunt, that this was too emphatic, but apparently it was all right, for his voice sounded relieved as he said: "It is a bit impossible to imagine oneself married to anyone else, isn't it?" With which he pulled her to him, so that her head lay on his shoulder. She turned her face into the dark of his flesh, and listened to the blood pounding through her ears saying: I am alone, I am alone, I am alone.

In the morning Susan lay in bed while he dressed.

He had been thinking things out in the night, because now he said: "Susan, why don't we make a foursome?"

Of course, she said to herself, of course he would be bound to say that. If one is sensible, if one is reasonable, if one never allows oneself a base thought or an envious emotion, naturally one says: Let's make a foursome!

"Why not?" she said.

"We could all meet for lunch. I mean, it's ridiculous, you sneaking off to filthy hotels, and me staying late at the office, and all the lies everyone has to tell."

What on earth did I say his name was?—she panicked, then said: "I think it's a good idea, but Michael is away at the moment. When he comes back though—and I'm sure you two would like each other."

"He's away, is he? So that's why you've been . . ." Her husband

put his hand to the knot of his tie in a gesture of male coquetry she would not before have associated with him; and he bent to kiss her cheek with the expression that goes with the words: Oh you naughty little puss! And she felt its answering look, naughty and coy, come onto her face.

Inside she was dissolving in horror at them both, at how far they had both sunk from honesty of emotion.

So now she was saddled with a lover, and he had a mistress! How ordinary, how reassuring, how jolly! And now they would make a foursome of it, and go about to theaters and restaurants. After all, the Rawlings could well afford that sort of thing, and presumably the publisher Michael Plant could afford to do himself and his mistress quite well. No, there was nothing to stop the four of them developing the most intricate relationship of civilized tolerance, all enveloped in a charming afterglow of autumnal passion. Perhaps they would all go off on holidays together? She had known people who did. Or perhaps Matthew would draw the line there? Why should he, though, if he was capable of talking about "foursomes" at all?

She lay in the empty bedroom, listening to the car drive off with Matthew in it, off to work. Then she heard the children clattering off to school to the accompaniment of Sophie's cheerfully ringing voice. She slid down into the hollow of the bed, for shelter against her own irrelevance. And she stretched out her hand to the hollow where her husband's body had lain, but found no comfort there: he was not her husband. She curled herself up in a small tight ball under the clothes: she could stay here all day, all week, indeed, all her life.

But in a few days she must produce Michael Plant, and—but how? She must presumably find some agreeable man prepared to impersonate a publisher called Michael Plant. And in return for which she would—what? Well, for one thing they would make love. The idea made her want to cry with sheer exhaustion. Oh no, she had finished with all that—the proof of it was that the words "make love," or even imagining it, trying hard to revive no more than the pleasures of sensuality, let alone affection, or love, made her want to run away and hide from the sheer effort of the thing. . . . Good Lord, why make love at all? Why make love with anyone? Or if you are going to make love, what does it matter who with? Why shouldn't she simply walk into the street, pick up a man and have a roaring sexual affair with him? Why not? Or even with Fred? What difference did it make?

But she had let herself in for it—an interminable stretch of time with a lover, called Michael, as part of a gallant civilized foursome. Well, she could not, and she would not.

She got up, dressed, went down to find Mrs. Parkes, and asked

her for the loan of a pound, since Matthew, she said, had forgotten to leave her money. She exchanged with Mrs. Parkes variations on the theme that husbands are all the same, they don't think, and without saying a word to Sophie, whose voice could be heard upstairs from the telephone, walked to the underground, traveled to South Kensington, changed to the Inner Circle, got out at Paddington, and walked to Fred's Hotel. There she told Fred that she wasn't going on holiday after all, she needed the room. She would have to wait an hour, Fred said. She went to a busy tearoom-cum-restaurant around the corner, and sat watching the people flow in and out the door that kept swinging open and shut, watched them mingle and merge and separate, felt her being flow into them, into their movement. When the hour was up she left a half crown for her pot of tea, and left the place without looking back at it, just as she had left her house, the big, beautiful white house, without another look, but silently dedicating it to Sophie. She returned to Fred, received the key of No. 19, now free, and ascended the grimy stairs slowly, letting floor after floor fall away below her, keeping her eyes lifted, so that floor after floor descended jerkily to her level of vision, and fell away out of sight.

No. 19 was the same. She saw everything with an acute, narrow, checking glance: the cheap shine of the satin spread, which had been replaced carelessly after the two bodies had finished their convulsions under it; a trace of powder on the glass that topped the chest of drawers; an intense green shade in a fold of the curtain. She stood at the window, looking down, watching people pass and pass and pass until her mind went dark from the constant movement. Then she sat in the wicker chair, letting herself go slack. But she had to be careful, because she did not want, today, to be surprised by Fred's knock at five o'clock.

The demons were not here. They had gone forever, because she was buying her freedom from them. She was slipping already into the dark fructifying dream that seemed to caress her inwardly, like the movement of her blood . . . but she had to think about Matthew first. Should she write a letter for the coroner? But what should she say? She would like to leave him with the look on his face she had seen this morning—banal, admittedly, but at least confidently healthy. Well, that was impossible, one did not look like that with a wife dead from suicide. But how to leave him believing she was dying because of a man—because of the fascinating publisher Michael Plant? Oh, how ridiculous! How absurd! How humiliating! But she decided not to trouble about it, simply not to think about the living. If he wanted to believe she had a lover, he would believe it. And he *did* want to believe it. Even when he had found out that there was no publisher in London called Michael Plant, he would think: Oh poor Susan, she was afraid to give me his real name.

And what did it matter whether he married Phil Hunt or Sophie? Though it ought to be Sophie, who was already the mother of those children . . . and what hypocrisy to sit here worrying about the children, when she was going to leave them because she had not got the energy to stay.

She had about four hours. She spent them delightfully, darkly, sweetly, letting herself slide gently, gently, to the edge of the river. Then, with hardly a break in her consciousness, she got up, pushed the thin rug against the door, made sure the windows were tight shut, put two shillings in the meter, and turned on the gas. For the first time since she had been in the room she lay on the hard bed that smelled stale, that smelled of sweat and sex.

She lay on her back on the green satin cover, but her legs were chilly. She got up, found a blanket folded in the bottom of the chest of drawers, and carefully covered her legs with it. She was quite content lying there, listening to the faint soft hiss of the gas that poured into the room, into her lungs, into her brain, as she drifted off into the dark river.

1963

The Critical Revolt Against Romanticism and Impressionism

T. E. HULME

(1883–1917)

Thomas Ernest Hulme was born in Endon, North Staffordshire, and attended St. John's College, Cambridge. He was expelled from college for brawling in 1904 and spent some years of independent study in London and Brussels (where he taught English and learned French and German). His interests turned more and more to philosophy, and he met and impressed the French philosopher Henri Bergson through whose influence he was readmitted to Cambridge, though he did not stay long. He spent some time in Berlin before settling in London. He translated Bergson's *Introduction to Metaphysics* (1913) and George Sorel's *Réflections sur la violence* (*Reflections on Violence*, 1916). In the years immediately preceding World War I, he was a friend of Ezra Pound and other avant-garde writers, artists, and critics then in London. He was a frequent contributor to the political and literary weekly *The New Age*, edited by the influential A. R. Orage. His most important work was done in articles for this periodical. His insistence on hard, clear, precise images and on the avoidance of any kind of emotional self-indulgence or sloppiness in poetry lay behind the Imagist movement, which Pound supported. Five of his own poems, under the title "Complete Poetical Works of T. E. Hulme," appeared as an appendix to Ezra Pound's *Ripostes* (1915). Hulme enlisted in the army after the outbreak of the war and was killed in France in September 1917.

From Romanticism and Classicism

I want to maintain that after a hundred years of romanticism, we are in for a classical revival, and that the particular weapon of this new classical spirit, when it works in verse, will be fancy.[1] And in this I imply the superiority of fancy—not superior generally or

1. Hulme is here deliberately reversing Coleridge's "romantic" elevation of imagination over fancy in his *Biographia Literaria*.

absolutely, for that would be obvious nonsense, but superior in the sense that we use the word good in empirical ethics—good for something, superior for something. I shall have to prove then two things, first that a classical revival is coming, and, secondly, for its particular purposes, fancy will be superior to imagination. * * *

What I mean by classical in verse, then, is this. That even in the most imaginative flights there is always a holding back, a reservation. The classical poet never forgets this finiteness, this limit of man. He remembers always that he is mixed up with earth. He may jump, but he always returns back; he never flies away into the circumambient gas.

You might say if you wished that the whole of the romantic attitude seems to crystallize in verse round metaphors of flight. Hugo[2] is always flying, flying over abysses, flying up into the eternal gases. The word infinite in every other line.

In the classical attitude you never seem to swing right along to the infinite nothing. If you say an extravagant thing which does exceed the limits inside which you know man to be fastened, yet there is always conveyed in some way at the end an impression of yourself standing outside it, and not quite believing it, or consciously putting it forward as a flourish. You never go blindly into an atmosphere more than the truth, an atmosphere too rarefied for man to breathe for long. You are always faithful to the conception of a limit. It is a question of pitch; in romantic verse you move at a certain pitch of rhetoric which you know, man being what he is, to be a little highfalutin. The kind of thing you get in Hugo or Swinburne. In the coming classical reaction that will feel just wrong. For an example of the opposite thing, a verse written in the proper classical spirit, I can take the song from *Cymbeline* beginning with "Fear no more the heat of the sun." I am just using this as a parable. I don't quite mean what I say here. Take the last two lines:

> Golden lads and girls all must,
> Like chimney sweepers come to dust.

Now, no romantic would have ever written that. Indeed, so ingrained is romanticism, so objectionable is this to it, that people have asserted that these were not part of the original song.

Apart from the pun, the thing that I think quite classical is the word lad. Your modern romantic could never write that. He would have to write golden youth, and take up the thing at least a couple of notes in pitch.

I want now to give the reasons which make me think that we are nearing the end of the romantic movement.

2. Victor Hugo (1802–85), the French poet and novelist.

The first lies in the nature of any convention or tradition in art. A particular convention or attitude in art has a strict analogy to the phenomena of organic life. It grows old and decays. It has a definite period of life and must die. All the possible tunes get played on it and then it is exhausted; moreover its best period is its youngest. Take the case of the extraordinary efflorescence of verse in the Elizabethan period. All kinds of reasons have been given for this —the discovery of the new world and all the rest of it. There is a much simpler one. A new medium had been given them to play with—namely, blank verse. It was new and so it was easy to play new tunes on it.

The same law holds in other arts. All the masters of painting are born into the world at a time when the particular tradition from which they start is imperfect. The Florentine tradition was just short of full ripeness when Raphael came to Florence, the Bellinesque[3] was still young when Titian was born in Venice. Landscape was still a toy or an appanage of figure-painting when Turner and Constable[4] arose to reveal its independent power. When Turner and Constable had done with landscape they left little or nothing for their successors to do on the same lines. Each field of artistic activity is exhausted by the first great artist who gathers a full harvest from it.

This period of exhaustion seems to me to have been reached in romanticism. We shall not get any new efflorescence of verse until we get a new technique, a new convention, to turn ourselves loose in. * * *

I object even to the best of the romantics. I object still more to the receptive attitude. I object to the sloppiness which doesn't consider that a poem is a poem unless it is moaning or whining about something or other. I always think in this connection of the last line of a poem of John Webster's which ends with a request I cordially endorse:

End your moan and come away.[5]

The thing has got so bad now that a poem which is all dry and hard, a properly classical poem, would not be considered poetry at all. How many people now can lay their hands on their hearts and say they like either Horace or Pope? They feel a kind of chill when they read them.

The dry hardness which you get in the classics is absolutely repugnant to them. Poetry that isn't damp isn't poetry at all. They

---

3. Jacopo Bellini, Venetian painter, died in 1470; his two sons continued the Bellinesque tradition into the 16th century. Titian was born ca. 1477.
4. J. M. Turner (1775–1851) and John Constable (1776–1837), British landscape painters.
5. From a song in *The Duchess of Malfi* (IV.ii). The line is misquoted: Hulme substituted "moan" for the original "groan."

cannot see that accurate description is a legitimate object of verse. Verse to them always means a bringing in of some of the emotions that are grouped round the word infinite.

The essence of poetry to most people is that it must lead them to a beyond of some kind. Verse strictly confined to the earthly and the definite (Keats is full of it) might seem to them to be excellent writing, excellent craftsmanship, but not poetry. So much has romanticism debauched us, that, without some form of vagueness, we deny the highest.

In the classic it is always the light of ordinary day, never the light that never was on land or sea. It is always perfectly human and never exaggerated: man is always man and never a god.

But the awful result of romanticism is that, accustomed to this strange light, you can never live without it. Its effect on you is that of a drug.

There is a general tendency to think that verse means little else than the expression of unsatisfied emotion. People say: "But how can you have verse without sentiment?" You see what it is: the prospect alarms them. A classical revival to them would mean the prospect of an arid desert and the death of poetry as they understand it, and could only come to fill the gap caused by that death. Exactly why this dry classical spirit should have a positive and legitimate necessity to express itself in poetry is utterly inconceivable to them. What this positive need is, I shall show later. It follows from the fact that there is another quality, not the emotion produced, which is at the root of excellence in verse. Before I get to this I am concerned with a negative thing, a theoretical point, a prejudice that stands in the way and is really at the bottom of this reluctance to understand classical verse.

It is an objection which ultimately I believe comes from a bad metaphysic of art. You are unable to admit the existence of beauty without the infinite being in some way or another dragged in. * * * It is essential to prove that beauty may be in small, dry things.

The great aim is accurate, precise and definite description. The first thing is to recognize how extraordinarily difficult this is. It is no mere matter of carefulness; you have to use language, and language is by its very nature a communal thing; that is, it expresses never the exact thing but a compromise—that which is common to you, me and everybody. But each man sees a little differently, and to get out clearly and exactly what he does see, he must have a terrific struggle with language, whether it be with words or the technique of other arts. Language has its own special nature, its own conventions and communal ideas. It is only by a concentrated effort of the mind that you can hold it fixed to your own purpose. * * *

This is the point I aim at, then, in my argument. I prophesy

that a period of dry, hard, classical verse is coming. I have met the preliminary objection founded on the bad romantic aesthetic that in such verse, from which the infinite is excluded, you cannot have the essence of poetry at all. * * *

1913   1924

I. A. RICHARDS

(1893–)

Ivor Armstrong Richards was born at Sandbach, Cheshire, and attended Magdalene College, Cambridge, where he became a college lecturer in English and Moral Sciences (philosophy) in 1922 and a Fellow in 1926. He taught at Tsing Hua University, Peking, in 1929–30 and from 1939 to 1944 he was director of the Harvard Commission in English Language Studies, in which capacity he continued work he had started as director of the Orthological Institute of China, notably the development of Basic English, an English vocabulary of 850 words for the use of non-native speakers. In 1923 he published, with C. K. Ogden, his pioneer work in semantics, *The Meaning of Meaning*, and this was followed in 1925 by his immensely influential *Principles of Literary Criticism* in which he tried to ground evaluative criticism in a scientific psychology. *Practical Criticism* appeared in 1929 and set the tone for generations of practical criticism among students at Cambridge University and elsewhere. His later work includes psychological, philosophical, linguistic, and educational studies, and original poetry. He became professor at Harvard in 1944 and is now University Professor Emeritus of that university.

From Practical Criticism

From *Part I. Introductory*

* * * Whenever we hear or read any not too nonsensical opinion, a tendency so strong and so automatic that it must have been formed along with our earliest speech-habits leads us to consider *what seems to be said* rather than the *mental operations* of the person who said it. If the speaker is a recognized and obvious liar this tendency is, of course, arrested. We do then neglect what he has said and turn our attention instead to the motives or mechanisms that have caused him to say it. But ordinarily we at once try to consider the objects his words seem to stand for and not the mental goings-on that led him to use the words. We say that we "follow his thought" and mean, not that we have traced what

happened in his mind, but merely that we have gone through a train of thinking that seems to end where he ended. We are in fact so anxious to discover whether we agree or not with what is being said that we overlook the mind that says it, unless some very special circumstance calls us back.

Compare now the attitude to speech of the alienist attempting to "follow" the ravings of mania or the dream maunderings of a neurotic. I do not suggest that we should treat one another altogether as "mental cases" but merely that for some subject matters and some types of discussion the alienist's attitude, his direction of attention, his order or plan of interpretation, is far more fruitful, and would lead to better understanding on both sides of the discussion, than the usual method that our language habits force upon us. For normal minds are easier to "follow" than diseased minds, and even more can be learned by adopting the psychologist's attitude to ordinary speech-situations than by studying aberrations.

It is very strange that we have no simple verbal means by which to describe these two different kinds of "meaning." Some device as unmistakable as the "up" or "down" of a railway signal ought to be available. But there is none. Clumsy and pedantic looking psychological periphrases have to be employed instead. I shall, however, try to use one piece of shorthand consistently. In handling the piles of material supplied by the protocols[1] I shall keep the term "statement" for those utterances whose "meaning" in the sense of what they *say*, or purport to say, is the prime object of interest. I shall reserve the term "expression" for those utterances where it is the mental operations of the writers which are to be considered.

When the full range of this distinction is realized the study of criticism takes on a new significance. But the distinction is not easy to observe. Even the firmest resolution will be constantly broken down, so strong are our native language habits. When views that seem to conflict with our own prepossessions are set before us, the impulse to refute, to combat, or to reconstruct them, rather than to investigate them, is all but overwhelming. So the history of criticism,[2] like the history of all the middle subjects alluded to above, is a history of dogmatism and argumentation rather than a history of research. And like all such histories the chief lesson to be learnt from it is the futility of all argumentation that precedes understanding. We cannot profitably attack any opinion until we have discovered what it expresses as well as what it states; and our present technique for investigating opinions must be ad-

1. Richards' term for the critiques written by his students on the unidentified poems which he asked them to comment on. The opinions expressed in the protocols are discussed and quoted extensively in *Practical Criticism;* they are the data upon which Richards bases his critical conclusions.

2. "We shall meet in the protocols plenty of living instances of famous critical doctrines that are often thought to be now merely curiosities of opinion long since extinct" [Richards' note].

mitted, for all these middle subjects, to be woefully inadequate.

Therefore, the second aim of this book is to improve this technique. We shall have before us several hundreds of opinions upon particular aspects of poetry, and the poems themselves to help us to examine them. We shall have the great advantage of being able to compare numbers of extremely different opinions upon the same point. We shall be able to study what may be called the same opinion in different stages of development as it comes from different minds. And further, we shall be able in many instances to see what happens to a given opinion, when it is applied to a different detail or a different poem.

The effect of all this is remarkable. When the first dizzy bewilderment has worn off, as it very soon does, it is as though we were strolling through and about a building that hitherto we were only able to see from one or two distant standpoints. We gain a much more intimate understanding both of the poem and of the opinions it provokes.[3] Something like a plan of the most usual approaches can be sketched and we learn what to expect when a new object, a new poem, comes up for discussion.

It is as a step towards another training and technique in discussion that I would best like this book to be regarded. If we are to begin to understand half the opinions which appear in the protocols we shall need no little mental plasticity. And in the course of our comparisons, interpretations, and extrapolations something like a plan of the ways in which the likely ambiguities of any given term or opinion-formula may radiate will make itself apparent. For the hope of a new technique in discussion lies in this: that the study of the ambiguities of one term assists in the elucidation of another. To trace the meanings of "sentimentality," "truth," "sincerity," or "meaning" itself, as these terms are used in criticism, can help us with other words used in other topics. Ambiguity in fact is systematic; the separate senses that a word may have are related to one another, if not as strictly as the various aspects of a building, at least to a remarkable extent. Something comparable to a "perspective" which will include and enable us to control and "place" the rival meanings that bewilder us in discussion and hide our minds from one another can be worked out. Perhaps every intelligence that has ever reflected upon this matter will agree that this may be so. Everyone agrees but no one does any research into the matter, although this is an affair in which even the slightest step forward affects the whole frontier line of human thought and discussion.

3. "A strange light, incidentally, is thrown upon the sources of popularity for poetry. Indeed I am not without fears that my efforts may prove of assistance to young poets (and others) desiring to increase their sales. A set of formulae for 'nation-wide appeal' seems to be a just possible outcome" [Richards' note].

The indispensable instrument for this inquiry is psychology. I am anxious to meet as far as may be the objection that may be brought by some psychologists, and these the best, that the protocols do not supply enough evidence for us really to be able to make out the motives of the writers and that therefore the whole investigation is superficial. But the *beginning* of every research ought to be superficial, and to find something to investigate that is accessible and detachable is one of the chief difficulties of psychology. I believe the chief merit of the experiment here made is that it gives us this. Had I wished to plumb the depths of these writers' Unconscious, where I am quite willing to agree the real motives of their likings and dislikings would be found, I should have devised something like a branch of psychoanalytic technique for the purpose. But it was clear that little progress would be made if we attempted to drag too deep a plow. However, even as it is, enough strange material is turned up.

After these explanations the reader will be prepared to find little argumentation in these pages, but much analysis, much rather strenuous exercise in changing our ground, and a good deal of rather intricate navigation. Navigation, in fact—the art of knowing where we are wherever, as mental travelers, we may go—is the main subject of the book. To discuss poetry and the ways in which it may be approached, appreciated and judged is, of course, its prime purpose. But poetry itself is a mode of communication. What it communicates and how it does so and the worth of what is communicated form the subject matter of criticism. It follows that criticism itself is very largely, though not wholly, an exercise in navigation. It is all the more surprising then that no treatise on the art and science of intellectual and emotional navigation has yet been written; for logic, which might appear to cover part of this field, in actuality hardly touches it.

That the one and only goal of all critical endeavors, of all interpretation, appreciation, exhortation, praise, or abuse, is improvement in communication may seem an exaggeration. But in practice it is so. The whole apparatus of critical rules and principles is a means to the attainment of finer, more precise, more discriminating communication. There is, it is true, a valuation side to criticism. When we have solved, completely, the communication problem, when we have got, perfectly, the experience, *the mental condition* relevant to the poem, we have still to judge it, still to decide upon its worth. But the later question nearly always settles itself; or rather, our own inmost nature and the nature of the world in which we live decide it for us. Our prime endeavor must be to get the relevant mental condition and then see what happens. If we cannot then decide whether it is good or bad, it is doubtful whether any principles, however refined and subtle, can help us

much. Without the capacity to get the experience they cannot help us at all. This is still clearer if we consider the use of critical maxims in teaching. Value cannot be demonstrated except through the communication of what is valuable.

Critical principles, in fact, need wary handling. They can never be a substitute for discernment though they may assist us to avoid unnecessary blunders. There has hardly ever been a critical rule, principle, or maxim which has not been for wise men a helpful guide but for fools a will-o'-the-wisp. All the great watchwords of criticism, from Aristotle's "Poetry is an imitation" down to the doctrine that "Poetry is expression," are ambiguous pointers that different people follow to very different destinations. Even the most sagacious critical principles may, as we shall see, become merely a cover for critical ineptitude; and the most trivial or baseless generalization may really mask good and discerning judgment. Everything turns upon how the principles are applied. It is to be feared that critical formulas, even the best, are responsible for more bad judgment than good, because it is far easier to forget their subtle sense and apply them crudely than to remember it and apply them finely.

The astonishing variety of human responses makes irksome any too systematic scheme for arranging these extracts. I wish to present a sufficient selection to bring the situation concretely before the reader, reserving to the chapters of Part III any serious attempt to clear up the various difficulties with which the protocol-writers have been struggling. I shall proceed poem by poem, allowing the internal drama latent in every clash of opinion, of taste or temperament to guide the arrangement. Not all the poems, needless to say, raise the same problems in equal measure. In most, some one outstanding difficulty, some special occasion for a division of minds, takes precedence.

It is convenient therefore to place here a somewhat arbitrary list of the principal difficulties that may be encountered by one reader or another in the presence of almost any poem. This list is suggested by a study of the protocols themselves, and drawn up in an order which proceeds from the simplest, infant's, obstacle to successful reading up to the most insidious, intangible and bewildering of critical problems.

If some of these difficulties seem so simple as to be hardly worth discussion, I would beg my reader who feels a temptation to despise them not to leap lightly to his decision. Part of my purpose is *documentation* and I am confident of showing that the simple difficulties are those that most need attention as they are those that in fact receive least.

We soon advance, however, to points on which more doubt may be felt—where controversy, more and less enlightened, still con-

tinues—and we finish face to face with questions which no one will pretend are yet settled and with some which will not be settled till the Day of Judgment. In the memorable words of Benjamin Paul Blood,[4] "What is concluded that we should conclude anything about it?"

The following seem to be the chief difficulties of criticism or, at least, those which we shall have most occasion to consider here:

A. First must come the difficulty of *making out the plain sense* of poetry. The most disturbing and impressive fact brought out by this experiment is that a large proportion of average-to-good (and in some cases, certainly, devoted) readers of poetry frequently and repeatedly *fail to understand it,* both as a statement and as an expression. They fail to make out its prose sense, its plain, overt meaning, as a set of ordinary, intelligible, English sentences, taken quite apart from any further poetic significance. And equally, they misapprehend its feeling, its tone, and its intention. They would travesty it in a paraphrase. They fail to construe it just as a school-boy fails to construe a piece of Caesar. How serious in its effects in different instances this failure may be, we shall have to consider with care. It is not confined to one class of readers; not only those whom we would suspect fall victims. Nor is it only the most abstruse poetry which so betrays us. In fact, to set down, for once, the brutal truth, no immunity is possessed on any occasion, not by the most reputable scholar, from this or any other of these critical dangers.

B. Parallel to, and not unconnected with, these difficulties of interpreting the meaning are the difficulties of *sensuous apprehension.* Words in sequence have a form to the mind's ear and the mind's tongue and larynx, even when silently read. They have a movement and may have a rhythm. The gulf is wide between a reader who naturally and immediately perceives this form and movement (by a conjunction of sensory, intellectual, and emotional sagacity) and another reader, who either ignores it or has to build it up laboriously with finger-counting, table-tapping and the rest; and this difference has most far-reaching effects.

C. Next may come those difficulties that are connected with the place of *imagery,* principally visual imagery, in poetic reading. They arise in part from the incurable fact that we differ immensely in our capacity to visualize, and to produce imagery of the other senses. Also the importance of our imagery as a whole, as well as of some pet particular type of image, in our mental lives varies surprisingly. Some minds can do nothing and get nowhere without images; others seem to be able to do everything and get anywhere, reach any and every state of thought and feeling without making use of

4. 1832–1919; American poet and philosopher.

them. Poets on the whole (though by no means all poets always) may be suspected of exceptional imaging capacity, and some readers are constitutionally prone to stress the place of imagery in reading, to pay great attention to it, and even to judge the value of the poetry by the images it excites in them. But images are erratic things; lively images aroused in one mind need have no similarity to the equally lively images stirred by the same line of poetry in another, and neither set need have anything to do with any images which may have existed in the poet's mind. Here is a troublesome source of critical deviations.

D. Thirdly, more obviously, we have to note the powerful very pervasive influence of *mnemonic irrelevances*. These are misleading effects of the reader's being reminded of some personal scene or adventure, erratic associations, the interference of emotional reverberations from a past which may have nothing to do with the poem. Relevance is not an easy notion to define or to apply, though some instances of irrelevant instrusions are among the simplest of all accidents to diagnose.

E. More puzzling and more interesting are the critical traps that surround what may be called *stock responses*. These have their opportunity whenever a poem seems to, or does, involve views and emotions already fully prepared in the reader's mind, so that what happens appears to be more of the reader's doing than the poet's. The button is pressed, and then the author's work is done, for immediately the record starts playing in quasi- (or total) independence of the poem which is supposed to be its origin or instrument.

Whenever this lamentable redistribution of the poet's and reader's share in the labor of poetry occurs, or is in danger of occurring, we require to be especially on our guard. Every kind of injustice may be committed as well by those who just escape as by those who are caught.

F. *Sentimentality* is a peril that needs less comment here. It is a question of the due measure of response. This overfacility in certain emotional directions is the Scylla[5] whose Charybdis is—

G. *Inhibition*. This, as much as Sentimentality, is a positive phenomenon, though less studied until recent years and somewhat masked under the title of Hardness of Heart. But neither can well be considered in isolation.

H. *Doctrinal adhesions* present another troublesome problem. Very much poetry—religious poetry may be instanced—seems to contain or imply views and beliefs, true or false, about the world. If this be so, what bearing has the truth-value of the views upon

5. Scylla and Charybdis were two rocks between Italy and Sicily. In classical legend, the first one contained the cave of a six-headed man-eating monster; in the other lived a monster who thrice daily swallowed and regurgitated the waters of the sea. It was extremely difficult to navigate between them.

the worth of the poetry? Even if it be not so, if the beliefs are not really contained or implied, but only seem so to a nonpoetical reading, what should be the bearing of the reader's conviction, if any, upon his estimate of the poetry? Has poetry anything to say; if not, why not, and if so, how? Difficulties at this point are a fertile source of confusion and erratic judgment.

I. Passing now to a different order of difficulties, the effects of *technical presuppositions* have to be noted. When something has once been well done in a certain fashion we tend to expect similar things to be done in the future in the same fashion, and are disappointed or do not recognize them if they are done differently. Conversely, a technique which has shown its ineptitude for one purpose tends to become discredited for all. Both are cases of mistaking means for ends. Whenever we attempt to judge poetry from outside by technical details we are putting means before ends, and—such is our ignorance of cause and effect in poetry—we shall be lucky if we do not make even worse blunders. We have to try to avoid judging pianists by their hair.

J. Finally, *general critical preconceptions* (prior demands made upon poetry as a result of theories—conscious or unconscious—about its nature and value), intervene endlessly, as the history of criticism shows only too well, between the reader and the poem. Like an unlucky dietetic formula they may cut him off from what he is starving for, even when it is at his very lips.

These difficulties, as will have been observed, are not unconnected with one another and indeed overlap. They might have been collected under more heads or fewer. Yet, if we set aside certain extreme twists or trends of the personality (for example, blinding narcissism or groveling self-abasement—aberrations, temporary or permanent, of the self-regarding sentiment) together with undue accumulations or depletions of energy, I believe that most of the principal obstacles and causes of failure in the reading and judgment of poetry may without much straining be brought under these ten heads. But they are too roughly sketched here for this to be judged. * * *

1929

F. R. LEAVIS

(1895–)

Frank Raymond Leavis was born at Cambridge and educated there at the Perse School and Emmanuel College. In 1936 he became Fellow of Downing College, Cambridge, where he directed English studies and rapidly

made the college a distinctive English school within the university. His insistence on rigorous evaluative criticism, his championship of T. S. Eliot and D. H. Lawrence before either was academically respectable, his scorn for the genteel academic tradition with its catholicity of taste and gentlemanly tone, and his contemptuous dismissal of all literature except the small amount of genuinely realized work which represented the "great tradition" made him an isolated and embattled figure, but an immensely influential one. He was one of the founders of the periodical *Scrutiny* (1932–53) through which his influence was exercised. On his retirement from Cambridge teaching in 1962 he was for some years professor at the new English University of York.

From Revaluation[1]

From *Chapter 6. Shelley*

* * * It will be well to start, in fact, by examining the working of Shelley's poetry—his characteristic modes of expression—as exemplified in one of his best poems.[2]

> Thou on whose stream, mid the steep sky's commotion
> Loose clouds like earth's decaying leaves are shed,
> Shook from the tangled boughs of Heaven and Ocean,
>
> Angels of rain and lightning: there are spread
> On the blue surface of thine aëry surge,
> Like the bright hair uplifted from the head
>
> Of some fierce Maenad,[3] even from the dim verge
> Of the horizon to the zenith's height,
> The locks of the approaching storm.

The sweeping movement of the verse, with the accompanying plangency, is so potent that, as many can testify, it is possible to have been for years familiar with the *Ode*—to know it by heart—without asking the obvious questions. In what respects are the "loose clouds" like "decaying leaves"? The correspondence is certainly not in shape, color, or way of moving. It is only the vague general sense of windy tumult that associates the clouds and the leaves; and, accordingly, the appropriateness of the metaphor "stream" in the first line is not that it suggests a surface on which, like leaves, the clouds might be "shed," but that it contributes to the general "streaming" effect in which the inappropriateness of "shed" passes unnoticed. What again, are those "tangled boughs

---

1. Leavis's complete title is *Revaluation: Tradition and Development in English Poetry*. The text is that of the 1949 edition.
2. Shelley's *Ode to the West Wind*, lines 15–23.
3. Frenzied woman (specifically, attendant on and celebrator of the wine god Bacchus).

of Heaven and Ocean"? They stand for nothing that Shelley could have pointed to in the scene before him; the "boughs," it is plain, have grown out of the "leaves" in the previous line, and we are not to ask what the tree is. Nor are we to scrutinize closely the "stream" metaphor as developed: that "blue surface" must be the concave of the sky, an oddly smooth surface for a "surge"—if we consider a moment. But in this poetic surge, while we let ourselves be swept along, there is no considering, the image doesn't challenge any inconvenient degree of realization, and the oddness is lost. Then again, in what ways does the approach of a storm ("loose clouds like earth's decaying leaves," "like ghosts from an enchanter fleeing") suggest streaming hair? The appropriateness of the Maenad, clearly, lies in the pervasive suggestion of frenzied onset, and we are not to ask whether her bright hair is to be seen as streaming out in front of her (as, there is no need to assure ourselves, it might be doing if she were running before a still swifter gale: in the kind of reading that got so far as proposing to itself this particular reassurance no general satisfaction could be exacted from Shelley's imagery).

Here, clearly, in these peculiarities of imagery and sense, peculiarities analyzable locally in the mode of expression, we have the manifestation of essential characteristics—the Shelleyan characteristics as envisaged by the criticism that works on a philosophical plane and makes judgments of a moral order. In the growth of those "tangled boughs" out of the leaves, exemplifying as it does a general tendency of the images to forget the status of the metaphor or simile that introduced them and to assume an autonomy and a right to propagate, so that we lose in confused generations and perspectives the perception or thought that was the ostensible *raison d'être* of imagery, we have a recognized essential trait of Shelley's: his weak grasp upon the actual. This weakness, of course, commonly has more or less creditable accounts given of it—idealism, Platonism, and so on; and even as unsentimental a judge as Mr. Santayana[4] correlates Shelley's inability to learn from experience with his having been born a "nature preformed," a "spokesman of the *a priori*," "a dogmatic, inspired, perfect and incorrigible creature."[5] It seems to me that Mr. Santayana's essay, admirable as it is, rates the poetry too high. But for the moment it will be enough to recall limitations that are hardly disputed: Shelley was not gifted for drama or narrative. Having said this, I realize that I had forgotten the conventional standing of *The Cenci*;[6] but controversy may be postponed: it is at any rate universally agreed that (to shift tactfully to positive terms) Shelley's genius was "essentially lyrical."

This predicate would, in common use, imply a special emotional

4. George Santayana (1863–1952), Spanish-born American critic and philosopher.
5. "See the essay on Shelley in *Winds of Doctrine*" [Leavis's note].
6. Poetic drama by Shelley.

intensity—a vague gloss, but it is difficult to go further without slipping into terms that are immediately privative and limiting. Thus there is certainly a sense in which Shelley's poetry is peculiarly emotional, and when we try to define this sense we find ourselves invoking an absence of something. The point may be best made, perhaps, by recalling the observation noted above, that one may have been long familiar with the *Ode to the West Wind* without ever having asked the obvious questions; questions that propose themselves at the first critical inspection. This poetry induces—depends for its success on inducing—a kind of attention that doesn't bring the critical intelligence into play: the imagery feels right, the associations work appropriately, if (as it takes conscious resistance not to do) one accepts the immediate feeling and doesn't slow down to think.

Shelley himself can hardly have asked the questions. Not that he didn't expend a great deal of critical labor upon his verse. "He composed rapidly and attained to perfection by intensive correction. He would sometimes write down a phrase with alterations and rejections time after time until it came within a measure of satisfying him. Words are frequently substituted for others and lines interpolated." The *Ode to the West Wind* itself, as is shown in the repository of fragments[7] the preface to which supplies these observations, profited by the process described, which must be allowed to have been in some sense critical. But the critical part of Shelley's creative labor was a matter of getting the verse to feel right, and feeling, for Shelley as a poet, had—as the insistent concern for "rightness," the typical final product being what it is, serves to emphasize—little to do with thinking (though Shelley was in some ways a very intelligent man). * * *

The transition from the lighter concerns of literary criticism to the diagnosis of radical disabilities and perversions, such as call for moral comment, may be conveniently illustrated from a favorite anthology piece, *When the Lamp Is Shattered*:

> When the lamp is shattered
> The light in the dust lies dead—
> When the cloud is scattered
> The rainbow's glory is shed.
> When the lute is broken,
> Sweet tones are remembered not;
> When the lips have spoken,
> Loved accents are soon forgot.
>
> As music and splendor
> Survive not the lamp and the lute,

---

7. *"Verse and Prose from the Manuscripts of Percy Bysshe Shelley.* Edited by Sir John C. E. Shelley-Rolls, Bart., and Roger Ingpen" [Leavis's note].

The heart's echoes render
No song when the spirit is mute—
　No song but sad dirges,
Like the wind through a ruined cell;
　Or the mournful surges
That ring the dead seaman's knell.

When hearts have once mingled
Love first leaves the well-built nest;
　The weak one is singled
To endure what it once possessed.
　O Love! who bewailest
The frailty of all things here,
　Why choose you the frailest
For your cradle, your home, and your bier?

Its passions will rock thee
As the storms rock the ravens on high;
　Bright reason will mock thee,
Like the sun from a wintry sky.

From thy nest every rafter
Will rot, and thine eagle home
　Leave thee naked to laughter,
When leaves fall and cold winds come.

The first two stanzas call for no very close attention—to say so, indeed, is to make the main criticism, seeing that they offer a show of insistent argument. However, reading with an unsolicited closeness, one may stop at the second line and ask whether the effect got with "lies dead" is legitimate. Certainly, the emotional purpose of the poem is served, but the emotional purpose that went on being served in that way would be suspect. Leaving the question in suspense, perhaps, one passes to "shed"; "shed" as tears, petals, and coats are shed, or as light is shed? The latter would be a rather more respectable use of the word in connection with a rainbow's glory, but the context indicates the former. Only in the vaguest and slackest state of mind—if imagination and thought—could one so describe the fading of a rainbow; but for the right reader "shed" sounds right, the alliteration with "shattered" combining with the verse-movement to produce a kind of inevitability. And, of course, suggesting tears and the last rose of summer, it suits with the general emotional effect. The nature of this is by now so unmistakable that the complete nullity of the clinching "so," when it arrives—of the two lines that justify the ten preparatory lines of analogy—seems hardly worth stopping to note:

The heart's echoes render
No song when the spirit is mute.

Nor is it surprising that there should turn out to be a song after all, and a pretty powerful one—for those who like that sort of thing; the "sad dirges," the "ruined cell," the "mournful surges," and the "dead seamen's knell" being immediately recognizable as currency values. Those who take pleasure in recognizing and accepting them are not at the same time exacting about sense.

The critical interest up to this point has been to see Shelley, himself (when inspired) so unexacting about sense, giving himself so completely to sentimental banalities. With the next stanza it is much the same, though the emotional clichés take on a grosser unction and the required abeyance of thought (and imagination) becomes more remarkable. In what form are we to imagine Love leaving the well-built nest? For readers who get so far asking, there can be no acceptable answer. It would be unpoetically literal to suggest that, since the weak one is singled, the truant must be the mate, and, besides, it would raise unnecessary difficulties. Perhaps the mate, the strong one, is what the weak one, deserted by Love, whose alliance made possession once possible, now has to endure? But the suggestion is frivolous; the sense is plain enough—enough, that is, for those who respond to the sentiment. Sufficient recognition of the sense depends neither on thinking, nor on realization of the metaphors, but on response to the sentimental commonplaces: it is only when intelligence and imagination insist on intruding that difficulties arise. So plain is this that there would be no point in contemplating the metaphorical complexity that would develop if we could take the tropes seriously and tried to realize Love making of the weak one, whom it (if we evade the problem of sex) leaves behind in the well-built nest, a cradle, a home, and a bier.

The last stanza brings a notable change; it alone in the poem has any distinction, and its personal quality, characteristically Shelleyan, stands out against the sentimental conventionality of the rest. The result is to compel a more radical judgment on the poem than has yet been made. In "its passions will rock thee" the "passions" must be those of Love, so that it can no longer be Love that is being apostrophized. Who, then, is "thee"? The "frailest"—the "weak one"—it would appear. But any notion one may have had that the "weak one," as the conventional sentiments imply, is the woman must be abandoned: the "eagle home," to which the "well-built nest" so incongruously turns, is the Poet's. The familiar timbre, the desolate intensity (note particularly the use of "bright" in "bright reason"), puts it beyond doubt that Shelley is, characteristically, addressing himself—the "pardlike Spirit beautiful and swift," the "Love in desolation masked," the "Power girt round with weakness."

Characteristically: that is, Shelley's characteristic pathos is self-regarding, directed upon an idealized self in the way suggested by

the tags just quoted. This is patently so in some of his best poetry; for instance, in the *Ode to the West Wind*. Even there, perhaps, one may find something too like an element of luxury in the poignancy (at any rate, one's limiting criticism of the *Ode* would move towards such a judgment); and that in general there must be dangers and weakness attending upon such a habit will hardly be denied. The poem just examined shows how gross may be, in Shelley, the corruptions that are incident. He can make self-pity a luxury at such a level that the conventional pathos of album poeticizing, not excluding the banalities about (it is plainly so in the third stanza) the sad lot of woman, can come in to gratify the appetite.

The abeyance of thought exhibited by the first three stanzas now takes on a more sinister aspect. The switching-off of intelligence that is necessary if the sentiments of the third stanza are to be accepted has now to be invoked in explanation of a graver matter— Shelley's ability to accept the grosser, the truly corrupt, gratifications that have just been indicated. The antipathy of his sensibility to any play of the critical mind, the uncongeniality of intelligence to inspiration, these clearly go in Shelley, not merely with a capacity for momentary self-deceptions and insincerities, but with a radical lack of self-knowledge. He could say of Wordsworth, implying the opposite of himself, that

> he never could
> Fancy another situation
> From which to dart his contemplation
> Than that wherein he stood.

But, for all his altruistic fervors and his fancied capacity for projecting his sympathies, Shelley is habitually—it is no new observation—his own hero: Alastor, Laon, The Sensitive Plant

> (It loves, even like Love, its deep heart is full,
> It desires what it has not, the Beautiful),

and Prometheus. It is characteristic that he should say to the West Wind,

> A heavy weight of hours has chained and bowed
> One too like thee: tameless, and swift, and proud,

and conclude:

> Be thou, Spirit fierce,
> My spirit! Be thou me, impetuous one!

1936

WILLIAM EMPSON

(1906–)

William Empson was born in Yorkshire and educated at Winchester College and at Cambridge, where he was taught by I. A. Richards. His first book, originally written as an essay for Richards, was *Seven Types of Ambiguity* (1930), which had great influence on the techniques of analytic criticism and the search for complexities and tensions in great poetry that was characteristic of the "New Criticism." *Some Versions of Pastoral* (1935) and *The Structure of Complex Words* (1951) developed his interest in ambiguities and semantic complexities in a variety of ways. Empson was professor of English literature at Tokyo, 1931–34, at Peking, 1937–39, and at Sheffield University, 1953–71. His knowledge of China and of Chinese has had an interesting effect on his attitude to language. Empson has also written poetry, "metaphysical" in tone and characterized by delicate verbal complexities.

From Seven Types of Ambiguity[1]
[*Wordsworth*]

* * * Wordsworth was not an ambiguous poet, for reasons that I have discussed; the cult of simplicity moved its complexity back into the subconscious, poisoned only the sources of thought, in the high bogs of the mountains, and stated as simply as possible the fundamental disorders of the mind. But he sometimes uses what may be called philosophical ambiguities when he is not sure how far this process can tolerably be pushed. In the third type we were among the uses of ambiguity for jokes; the fourth type includes its electoral applications. Thus the degree of pantheism implied by some of Wordsworth's most famous passages depends very much on the taste of the reader, who can impose grammar without difficulty to uphold his own views.

> For I have learnt
> To look on nature, not as in the hour
> Of thoughtless youth, but hearing oftentimes
> The still, sad music of humanity,
> Not harsh nor grating, but of ample power
> To chasten and subdue. And I have felt
> A presence that disturbs me with the joy

1. The selection here reprinted is from the first edition of 1930, Chapter 4.

> Of elevated thoughts; a sense sublime
> Of something far more deeply interfused,
> Whose dwelling is the light of setting suns,
> And the round ocean, and the living air,
> And the blue sky, and in the mind of man,
> A motion and a spirit, that impels
> All thinking things, all objects of all thought,
> And rolls through all things.[2]

It is not sufficient to say that these lines convey with great beauty the mood intended; Wordsworth seems to have believed in his own doctrines and wanted his readers to know what they were. It is reasonable, then, to try to extract from this passage definite opinions on the relations of God, man, and nature, and on the means by which such relations can be known.

There are several points of difficulty in the grammar when one tries to do this. It is not certain what is *more deeply interfused* than what. It is not certain whether the *music of humanity* is the same as the *presence*; they are separated by the word *and* and a full stop. We may notice, too, that the word *in* seems to distinguish, though but faintly, the *mind of man* from the *light*, the *ocean*, the *air* and the *sky*; this tends to separate the *motion* and the *spirit* form from the *presence* and the *something*; but they may, again, all be identical with the *music*. Wordsworth may then have *felt a something far more deeply interfused* than the *presence* that *disturbed* him; we seem here to have God revealing himself in particular to the mystic, but being in a more fundamental sense immanent in his whole creation.[3] Or the *something* may be in apposition to the *presence* (the *sense* equal to the *joy*); so that both are *more deeply interfused* than the *music of humanity*, but apparently in the same way. This version only conceives God as immanent in his creation, and as affecting the poet in the same way as he affects everything else; or as only imagined by the poet as immanent in creation, in the same way as the *music of humanity* is imagined as immanent. Thus, the first version is Christian, the second in part pantheistic, in part agnostic. Again, the *something* may possibly dwell only in the natural objects mentioned, ending at *sky*; the *motion* and the *spirit* are then not thought of at all as *interfused* into nature, like the *something*; they are things active *in the mind of man*. At the same time they are similar to the *something*; thus Wordsworth either *feels* them or *feels a sense* of them. With this reading the voice would rise in some triumph at the words *mind of man*; man has a spirit immanent in nature in the same way as in the spirit of God, and is decently independent from him. Or the *something* may

---

2. Wordworth's *Tintern Abbey*, lines 88–102.
3. "Or one may stand for paganism (the local deity of a bit of lake scenery, say) and the other for the more puzzling doctrine (far more deeply interfused) on which Wordsworth would support it" [Empson's note, added to 2nd edition].

also *dwell in the mind of man*, and have the *motion* and the spirit in apposition to it; under this less fortunate arrangement a God who is himself nature subjects us at once to determinism and predestination.

So far I have been examining grammatical ambiguities, but the last three lines also admit of doubt, as to the purpose of what seems an irrelevant distinction. Whether man or some form of God is subject here, he distinguishes between *things* which are objects or subjects of *thought*, these he *impels*, and *things* which are neither objects nor subjects of *thought*, through these he merely *rolls*. (I am not sure what is the logical status of the *things* not the objects of *thought* about which Wordsworth is *thinking* here; after all, he is not thinking very hard, so it may be all right.) The only advantage I can see in this distinction is that it makes the *spirit* at once intelligent and without intelligence; at once God and nature; allows us to think of him as the second, without compromising his position as the first.[4]

And, indeed, whether or not a great deal of wisdom is enshrined in these lines, lines just as muddled, superficially speaking, may convey a mode of using their antinomies,[5] and so act as creeds. The reason why one grudges Wordsworth this source of strength is that he talks as if he owned a creed by which his half-statements might be reconciled, whereas, in so far as his creed was definite, he found these half-statements necessary to keep it at bay. There is something rather shuffling about this attempt to be uplifting yet nondenominational, to put across as much pantheism as would not shock his readers. I must protest again that I enjoy the lines very much, and find, like everybody else, that I remember them; probably it was necessary for Wordsworth to shuffle, if he was to maintain his peculiar poetical attitude. And, of course, by considering the example in this chapter, I have shown that I regard the shuffling as a deeply-rooted necessity, not conscious at the time when it was achieved. But, perhaps, this last example may serve as a sort of applied ambiguity, may show how these methods may be used to convict a poet of holding muddled opinions rather than to praise the complexity of the order of his mind. * * *

1930

4. "Critics have disliked the meanness and fussiness of this passage, and I wish that I had something wise and reconciling to say after all these years. Miss M. C. Bradbrook wrote that the nouns after the full stop are all obviously in apposition, because the theme is the transcendence of the subject-object relationship. It is, I suppose, almost certain that Wordsworth meant the grammar to run on like this. But surely, even if clauses are in apposition, they must be supposed to be somehow distinguishable, or why do they have to be said one after the other? One could give a much more sympathetic account of the philosophic background of Wordsworth, and no doubt if I. A. Richards' *Coleridge on Imagination* had been already published I would have written differently. But the more seriously one takes the doctrine, it seems to me, the more this expression of it seems loose rhetoric" [Empson's note, added to 2nd edition].
5. Contradictions.

Poetry after Mid-Century

In sharp contrast to the literature of anti-culture and alienation represented by some of the most interesting English drama of the 1950's, there
emerged about the same time less divided figures, of more modest dimensions, more clearly devoted to revivifying inherited artistic forms and the
humanist tradition of Western cultural values. This group of young poets
and critics has been known generically since the middle 1950's as "the
Movement." These are not by any means the hardshelled traditionalists of
the traditional Anglican-royalist-and-classical persuasion; they reject the rig-
idity of the T. S. Eliot formulations as earnestly as the near-nihilism of the
extreme existentialists, and have tried to carve out a middle course of their
own. Perhaps the most significant critical champion of the Movement is
the poet, critic, and scholar Donald Davie, whose revealingly entitled book,
Purity of Diction in English Verse (1952), sets out to demonstrate the
eighteenth-century virtues of plainness, clarity, economy of metaphor, and
urbanity of statement in which the Augustan poets excelled and the romantic poets were often deficient. His second critical work, *Articulate Energy:
An Inquiry into the Syntax of English Poetry* (1955) urges the advantages
of retaining prose syntax in poetry and concludes with a frontal attack on
Northrop Frye's view as expressed in the following quotation: "Language in
a human mind is not a list of words with their customary meanings
attached, but a single interlocking structure, one's total power of expressing
oneself. Literature is the objective counterpart of this, a total form of verbal
expression which is re-created in miniature whenever a new poem is written." Not so, argues Davie:

The appeal of theories such as Mr. Frye's is manifest in the loaded words
that their promoters use, in recommending them. A poetry in which the
syntax articulates only "the world of the poem" is said to be "pure,"
"absolute," "sheer," "self-sufficient." Wordsworth's poems are "impure"
because they have about them the smell of soil and soiled flesh, the reek of
humanity. Their syntax is not "pure" syntax because it refers to, it mimes,
something outside itself and outside the world of its poem, something that
smells of the human, of generation and hence of corruption. It is my case
against the symbolist theorists that, in trying to remove the human smell
from poetry, they are only doing harm. For poetry to be great, it must reek
of the human as Wordsworth's poetry does. This is not a novel contention; but perhaps it is one of those things that cannot be said too often.

The miniature anthology of English poetry of the fifties, sixties, and seventies presented below begins with some examples of Movement poets and
then presents work by poets who, in one direction or another, break out of
the chastened humanism of the Movement. For new forces kept coming in
during the sixties and seventies. British poetry today is more diverse than
any critical schematization would suggest, ranging from various kinds of pop
poetry associated with jazz and intended for performance at large gatherings
—this is often a poetry containing much facile rhetoric and devices which
strike the ear impressively but which fail to yield anything further to reading and reflection—to delicate, sophisticated verse in which the meaning is

set off and enhanced by reticence. Between these two extremes are a great variety of poets with a great variety of talents. Since the end of the 1950's a new element of both rhetoric and myth (or at least legend) has been coming into English poetry. At the same time, there remains an important difference betwen some of the most interesting and significant recent English poetry and recent American poetry. The English poets do not risk everything in what M. L. Rosenthal has called a "bitter grappling with the gross, the anti-human, the inarticulable," but prefer to face modern experience in the light of coherent knowledge of how the world has grown to be what it is, and how the language they use can be accommodated to express modern experience without sacrificing lucidity to power or control to anguish.

The charge sometimes brought against modern English poetry is that it is too reticent, too genteel, and at the same time too fond of a "humane articulateness" (in Rosenthal's phrase). We can recognize in this charge some of the characteristics of the Movement poets. It is perhaps true that English poets of today have a greater sense of responsibility toward the language they use, a greater desire not to force on it meanings or emotions greater than it can semantically bear, than modern American poets. But they have their own strengths. The young English poet Alan Brownjohn, writing on English poetry in the 1970's, has stressed these strengths and pleaded for a proper awareness of them: "We move daily deeper into a complex and alarming kind of technical, late capitalist civilization where the surfaces get smoother and the realities ever more violent, irrational, and ruthless. One's first, instinctive response is to resort to the counter-irrationality of a counter-culture. But the only effective response, in the long term, will come from a rational, skeptical temperament which will calmly and wisely dismantle the machinery of horror and organize the commonwealth of decency."

Not all recent English poets would agree with this, but in general it can be said that they feel the importance of not losing control, of using their art to combat rather than to embody disorder. In the largest sense this is a classical position.

DONALD DAVIE

(1922–)

Donald Davie was born at Barnsley and attended St. Catherine's College, Cambridge. He has pursued an academic career and has held teaching posts at Trinity College, Dublin, Cambridge University, and the University of Essex before taking up his present position as professor of English at Stanford University. He is the most influential critic among the English poets of his generation, and although now living in America he participates frequently in critical debates going on in England. He has published seven volumes of poetry and *Collected Poems* in 1972.

A Voice from the Garden

We have a lawn of moss.
The next house is called The Beeches.
A towering squirrel-haunted

Trellis of trees, across
Our matt and trefoil, reaches
Shade where our guests have sauntered.   5

Cars snap by in the road.
In a famous photographed village
The High Street is our address.
Our guests write from abroad   10
Delighted to envisage
Rose-arbor and wilderness.

They get them, and the lilacs.
Some frenzy in us discards
Lilacs and all, and will harden,   15
However England stacks
Her dear discolored cards
Against us, us to her garden.

Anglophobia rises
In Brooklyn to hysteria   20
At some British verses.
British, one sympathizes.
Diesel-fumes cling to wistaria.
One conceives of worse reverses.

The sough of the power-brake   25
Makes every man an island;
But we are the island race.
We must be mad to take
Offense at our poisoned land
And the gardens that pock her face.   30
1963

Across the Bay

A queer thing about those waters: there are no
Birds there, or hardly any.
I did not miss them, I do not remember
Missing them, or thinking it uncanny.

The beach so-called was a blinding splinter of limestone,   5
A quarry outraged by hulls.
We took pleasure in that: the emptiness, the hardness
Of the light, the silence, and the water's stillness.

But this was the setting for one of our murderous scenes.
This hurt, and goes on hurting: 10
The venomous soft jelly, the undersides.
We could stand the world if it were hard all over.

1964

PHILIP LARKIN

(1922–)

Philip Larkin was born in Coventry and studied at Oxford, after which he worked as a university librarian in a number of universities; he is now librarian of the University of Hull. He is perhaps the most quietly English of all the Movement poets. He has produced three volumes of poems and a novel, and edited the controversial *Oxford Book of Twentieth Century English Verse* (1973).

Lines on a Young Lady's Photograph Album

At last you yielded up the album, which,
Once open, sent me distracted. All your ages
Matt and glossy on the thick black pages!
Too much confectionery, too rich:
I choke on such nutritious images.   5

My swivel eye hungers from pose to pose—
In pigtails, clutching a reluctant cat;
Or furred yourself, a sweet girl-graduate;
Or lifting a heavy-headed rose
Beneath a trellis, or in a trilby hat   10

(Faintly disturbing, that, in several ways)—
From every side you strike at my control,
Not least through these disquieting chaps who loll
At ease about your earlier days:
Not quite your class, I'd say, dear, on the whole.   15

But O, photography! as no art is,
Faithful and disappointing! that records
Dull days as dull, and hold-it smiles as frauds,
And will not censor blemishes
Like washing-lines, and Hall's-Distemper boards,   20

But shows the cat as disinclined, and shades
A chin as doubled when it is, what grace
Your candor thus confers upon her face!
How overwhelmingly persuades
That this is a real girl in a real place,   25

In every sense empirically true!
Or is it just *the past*? Those flowers, that gate,
These misty parks and motors, lacerate
Simply by being over; you
Contract my heart by looking out of date.   30

Yes, true; but in the end, surely, we cry
Not only at exclusion, but because
It leaves us free to cry. We know *what was*
Won't call on us to justify
Our grief, however hard we yowl across   35

The gap from eye to page. So I am left
To mourn (without a chance of consequence)
You, balanced on a bike against a fence;
To wonder if you'd spot the theft
Of this one of you bathing; to condense,   40

In short, a past that no one now can share,
No matter whose your future; calm and dry,
It holds you like a heaven, and you lie
Unvariably lovely there,
Smaller and clearer as the years go by.   45

                                        1956

Faith Healing

Slowly the women file to where he stands
Upright in rimless glasses, silver hair,
Dark suit, white collar. Stewards tirelessly
Persuade them onwards to his voice and hands,
Within whose warm spring rain of loving care   5
Each dwells some twenty seconds. *Now, dear child,*
What's wrong, the deep American voice demands,
And, scarcely pausing, goes into a prayer
Directing God about this eye, that knee.
Their heads are clasped abruptly; then, exiled   10

Like losing thoughts, they go in silence; some
Sheepishly stray, not back into their lives
Just yet; but some stay stiff, twitching and loud
With deep hoarse tears, as if a kind of dumb
And idiot child within them still survives   15
To reawake at kindness, thinking a voice
At last calls them alone, that hands have come
To lift and lighten; and such joy arrives
Their thick tongues blort, their eyes squeeze grief, a crowd
Of huge unheard answers jam and rejoice—   20

What's wrong! Moustached in flowered frocks they shake:
By now, all's wrong. In everyone there sleeps
A sense of life lived according to love.
To some it means the difference they could make
By loving others, but across most it sweeps   25

As all they might have done had they been loved.
That nothing cures. An immense slackening ache,
As when, thawing, the rigid landscape weeps,
Spreads slowly through them—that, and the voice above
Saying *Dear child*, and all time has disproved.   30

1964

Ambulances

Closed like confessionals, they thread
Loud noons of cities, giving back
None of the glances they absorb.
Light glossy gray, arms on a plaque,
They come to rest at any curb: 5
All streets in time are visited.

Then children strewn on steps or road,
Or women coming from the shops
Past smells of different dinners, see
A wild white face that overtops   10
Red stretcher-blankets momently
As it is carried in and stowed,

And sense the solving emptiness
That lies just under all we do,
And for a second get it whole,   15
So permanent and blank and true.
The fastened doors recede. *Poor soul*,
They whisper at their own distress;

For borne away in deadened air
May go the sudden shut of loss   20
Round something nearly at an end,
And what cohered in it across
The years, the unique random blend
Of families and fashions, there

At last begin to loosen. Far   25
From the exchange of love to lie
Unreachable inside a room
The traffic parts to let go by
Brings closer what is left to come,
And dulls to distance all we are.   30

1964

ELIZABETH JENNINGS

(1926–)

The daughter of a doctor, Elizabeth Jennings took a degree in English at Oxford before working in the Oxford public library and then embarking on a career in publishing and journalism in London. A visit to Italy made possible by her winning a Somerset Maugham Award in 1955 for her second volume of poems has had a permanent influence on her language and feeling. She was the only woman among the original Movement poets and the only one, too, whose feeling is deeply religious (she is a Roman Catholic).

An English Summer

An English summer—and a sense of form
Rides the five senses that dispute their claims.
Lawns leveled against nature, airs which warm
Each plant, perpetuate the hours and names.
We cannot see beyond the blue; no storm   5
Vies with the children ardent at their games.

Childhood returns with summer. It is strange
That such a season brings one's memories back.
Springs have their homesickness, autumns arrange
The sweet nostalgias that we long to lack.   10
But summer is itself; it's we who change
And lay our childhoods on the golden stack.

My fingers rest and eyes concern their sight
Simply with what would live were I not here.
It is the concentration of the light   15
That shows the other side of pain and fear.
I watch, incredulous of such delight,
Wanting the meaning not the landscape clear.

Was it for this the breath once breathed upon
The waters that we rose from? I can see   20
Only a summer with its shadows gone,
Skies that refuse an alien dignity.
But gardens, gardens echo. What sun shone
To make this truce with pain and ecstasy?

1963

In Memory of Anyone Unknown to Me

At this particular time I have no one
Particular person to grieve for, though there must
Be many, many unknown ones going to dust

Slowly, not remembered for what they have done
Or left undone. For these, then, I will grieve   5
Being impartial, unable to deceive.

How they lived or died is quite unknown,
And, by that fact gives my grief purity—
An important person quite apart from me
Or one obscure who drifted down alone.   10
Both or all I remember, have a place.
For these I never encountered face to face.

Sentiment will creep in. I cast it out
Wishing to give these classical repose,
No epitaph, no poppy and no rose   15
From me, and certainly no wish to learn about
The way they lived or died. In earth or fire
They are gone. Simply because they were human, I admire.

                                                   1972

CHARLES TOMLINSON

(1927–)

"I knew a little girl who left her garden noisily, and then came back stealthily 'to see how it looked when she wasn't there.'" Tomlinson quotes this from Jean-Paul Sartre as an epigraph to one of his most recent poems, and it sums up a great deal about his attitude to the physical world. Does the external world of nature have a real self apart from the observer, or does the artist-observer give it meaning by the framework of ideas and feelings within which he views it? Some of his early poems suggest that the poet must cultivate a disciplined passiveness in order to discover and capture in language the truly objective reality of a natural scene. He can describe the physical world with an intense opulence of imagery—reminding us of the American poet Wallace Stevens, who was an important early influence on him— in order to try and project its absolute self (the opposite, in a sense, of Wordsworth, for whom Nature was a means to the discovery of his own moral self). Yet Tomlinson is also present in his poetry, reflecting, categorizing, constructing systems, and most of all *caring* about what he sees. His later poetry is more reflective, more "metaphysical" even, yet he preserves the disciplined lucidity of line and movement that has always characterized his verse technique. Tomlinson has published six volumes of poetry up to 1972, of which the most important are *Seeing is Believing* (1958), *A Peopled Landscape* (1963), and *Written on Water* (1972).

Reflections

Like liquid shadows. The ice is thin
        Whose mirror smears them as it intercepts

Withdrawing colors; and where the crust,
   As if a skin livid with tautening scars,
Whitens, cracks, it steals from these deformations   5
   A style too tenuous for the image. A mirror lies, and
Flawed like this, may even lie with art,
   With reticence: "I exaggerate nothing,
For the reflections—scarcely half you see—
   Tell nothing of what you feel." Nature is blind   10
Like habit. Distrust them. We, since no mirrors,
   Are free both to question this deployment
And to arrange it—what we reflect
   Being what we choose. Though without deference,
We are grateful. When we perceive, as keen   15
   As the bridge itself, a bridge inlaying the darkness
Of smooth water, our delight acknowledges our debt—
   To nature, from whom we choose;
And, fencing that fullness back, to habit,
   The unsheathed image piercing our winter sleep.   20

                                         1958

A Meditation on John Constable[1]

"Painting is a science, and should be pursued as an inquiry into the laws of nature. Why, then, may not landscape painting be considered as a branch of natural philosophy, of which pictures are but the experiments?"

              JOHN CONSTABLE, *The History of Landscape Painting*

He replied to his own question, and with the unmannered
   Exactness of art; enriched his premises
By confirming his practice: the labor of observation
   In face of meteorological fact. Clouds
Followed by others, temper the sun in passing   5
   Over and off it. Massed darks
Blotting it back, scattered and mellowed shafts
   Break damply out of them, until the source
Unmasks, floods its retreating bank
   With raw fire. One perceives (though scarcely)   10
The remnant clouds trailing across it
   In rags, and thinned to a gauze.
But the next will dam it. They loom past
   And narrow its blaze. It shrinks to a crescent
Crushed out, a still lengthening ooze   15
   As the mass thickens, though cannot exclude
Its silvered-yellow. The eclipse is sudden,
   Seen first on the darkening grass, then complete
In a covered sky.
               Facts. And what are they?
He admired accidents, because governed by laws,   20

1. English landscape painter, 1776–1837.

Representing them (since the illusion was not his end)
As governed by feeling. The end is our approval
  Freely accorded, the illusion persuading us
That it exists as a human image. Caught
  By a wavering sun, or under a wind   25
Which moistening among the outlines of banked foliage
  Prepares to dissolve them, it must grow constant;
Though there, ruffling and parted, the disturbed
  Trees let through the distance, like white fog
Into their broken ranks. It must persuade   30
  And with a constancy, not to be swept back
To reveal what it half-conceals. Art is itself
  Once we accept it. The day veers. He would have judged
Exactly in such a light, that strides down
  Over the quick stains of cloud-shadows   35
Expunged now, by its conflagration of color.
  A descriptive painter? If delight
Describes, which wrings from the brush
  The errors of a mind, so tempered,
It can forego all pathos; for what he saw   40
  Discovered what he was, and the hand—unswayed
By the dictation of a single sense—
  Bodied the accurate and total knowledge
In a calligraphy of present pleasure. Art
  Is complete when it is human. It is human   45
Once the looped pigments, the pinheads of light
  Securing space under their deft restrictions
Convince, as the index of a possible passion,
  As the adequate gauge, both of the passion
And its object. The artist lies   50
  For the improvement of truth. Believe him.

1960

Hawks

Hawks hovering, calling to each other
  Across the air, seem swung
Too high on the risen wind
  For the earth-clung contact of our world:
And yet we share with them that sense   5
  The season is bringing in, of all
The lengthening light is promising to exact
  From the obduracy of March. The pair
After their kind are lovers and their cries
  Such as lovers alone exchange, and we   10
Though we cannot tell what it is they say,
  Caught up into their calling, are in their sway,
And ride where we cannot climb the steep
  And altering air, breathing the sweetness
Of our own excess, till we are kinned   15

By space we never thought to enter
On capable wings to such reaches of desire.

1972

Autumn Piece

Baffled
by the choreography of the season
the eye could not
with certainty see
whether it was wind　　　　　　　　　　　　5
stripping the leaves or
the leaves were struggling to be free:

They came at you
in decaying spirals
plucked flung and regathered by the same　　10
force that was twisting
the scarves of the vapor trails
dragging all certainties out of course:

As the car resisted it
you felt it in either hand　　　　　　　　　15
commanding car, tree, sky,
master of chances,
and at a curve was a red
board said "Danger":
I thought it said dancer.　　　　　　　　　20

1972

THOM GUNN

(1929–)

Son of a London journalist, Thom Gunn was educated at University College School, London and at Trinity College, Cambridge. His poems (*The Sense of Movement*, 1957, *My Sad Captains*, 1961, *Touch*, 1967, *Moly*, 1971) show that insistence on exactness of image and movement can produce something more than agreeable verse craftsmanship. Reminiscent sometimes of Graves, sometimes of Muir, sometimes of the American poet Yvor Winters (with whom Gunn studied in California), Gunn's poems have a special kind of modest and honest individuality which makes them, if not continually exciting, at least always engaging. His long stay in America has turned him into what one critic has called "a mid-Atlantic or Anglo-American poet," and he is one of the few English poets who has on occasion adopted the method of composition by syllable count (rather than stress patterns) which has been so significant in modern American poetry.

Considering the Snail

The snail pushes through a green
night, for the grass is heavy
with water and meets over
the bright path he makes, where rain
has darkened the earth's dark. He   5
moves in a wood of desire,

pale antlers barely stirring
as he hunts. I cannot tell
what power is at work, drenched there
with purpose, knowing nothing.   10
What is a snail's fury? All
I think is that if later

I parted the blades above
the tunnel and saw the thin
trail of broken white across   15
litter, I would never have
imagined the slow passion
to that deliberate progress.

                                        1956

Human Condition

Now it is fog, I walk
Contained within my coat;
No castle more cut off
By reason of its moat:
Only the sentry's cough,   5
The mercenaries' talk.

The street lamps, visible,
Drop no light on the ground,
But press beams painfully
In a yard of fog around.   10
I am condemned to be
An individual.

In the established border
There balances a mere
Pinpoint of consciousness.   15
I stay, or start from, here:
No fog makes more or less
The neighboring disorder.

Particular, I must
Find out the limitation   20
Of mind and universe,

To pick thought and sensation
And turn to my own use
Disordered hate or lust.

I seek, to break, my span.   25
I am my one touchstone.
This is a test more hard
Than any ever known.
And thus I keep my guard
On that which makes me man.   30

Much is unknowable.
No problem shall be faced
Until the problem is;
I, born to fog, to waste,
Walk through hypothesis,
An individual.   35

1957

Moly[1]

Nightmare of beasthood, snorting, how to wake.
I woke. What beasthood skin she made me take?

Leathery toad that ruts for days on end,
Or cringing dribbling dog, man's servile friend,

Or cat that prettily pounces on its meat,   5
Tortures it hours, then does not care to eat:

Parrot, moth, shark, wolf, crocodile, ass, flea.
What germs, what jostling mobs there were in me.

These seem like bristles, and the hide is tough.
No claw or web here: each foot ends in hoof.   10

Into what bulk has method disappeared?
Like ham, streaked. I am gross—gray, gross, flap-eared.

The pale-lashed eyes my only human feature.
My teeth tear, tear. I am the snouted creature

That bites through anything, root, wire, or can.   15
If I was not afraid I'd eat a man.

Oh a man's flesh already is in mine.
Hand and foot poised for risk. Buried in swine.

1. A magic herb of Greek mythology. The enchantress Circe transformed Odysseus' shipmates into swine; Odysseus, protected by the herb moly which he had been given by the gods' messenger Hermes, compelled her to restore them to human shape.

I root and root, you think that it is greed,
It is, but I seek out a plant I need.   20

Direct me gods, whose changes are all holy,
To where it flickers deep in grass, the moly:

Cool flesh of magic in each leaf and shoot,
From milk flower to the black forked root.

From this fat dungeon I could rise to skin   25
And human title, putting pig within.

I push my big gray wet snout through the green,
Dreaming the flower I have never seen.

1971

TED HUGHES

(1930–)

Ted Hughes was born in Yorkshire, brought up in the West Country, and educated at Cambridge. His wife was the intense and anguished American poet Sylvia Plath, who committed suicide at 31. His poetry from the beginning showed a greater urgency of both imagery and feeling than is found in the Movement poets. He was early influenced by Hopkins and by the later Yeats, but his anthropological sense of history and of nature is very much his own. He shares, however, with some other contemporary poets an ambivalent attitude to nature—seen as both startlingly apart from human sensitivities and simultaneously parallel to and symbolic of the human situation. His poems show an inventiveness, a joy in the exercise of his art, that exists side by side with a curiosity which is sometimes compassionate, sometimes simply fierce. He has published seven volumes of poetry, including *The Hawk in the Rain* (1957), *Lupercal* (1960) and *Crow: From the Life and Songs of the Crow* (1970), from which the poems below are taken. The English critic A. Alvarez wrote on *Crow*'s publication that "Hughes . . . now joins the select band of survivor-poets whose work is adequate to the destructive reality we inhabit," adding that he believes that "he is the only British poet to have done so." Many of these poems are flamboyant, exhibitionist, and could be accused of self-indulgence, a vice that most British poets today do all they can to avoid. But no one can deny their power. The Crow is a symbolic figure who in these poems acts out human history as a creature capable of anything so long as it ensures survival.

Wind

This house has been far out at sea all night,
The woods crashing through darkness, the booming hills,

Winds stampeding the fields under the window
Floundering black astride and blinding wet

Till day rose; then under an orange sky   5
The hills had new places, and wind wielded
Blade-light, luminous and emerald,
Flexing like the lens of a mad eye.

At noon I scaled along the house-side as far as
The coal-house door. I dared once to look up—   10
Through the brunt wind that dented the balls of my eyes
The tent of the hills drummed and strained its guyrope,

The fields quivering, the skyline a grimace,
At any second to bang and vanish with a flap:
The wind flung a magpie away and a black-   15
Back gull bent like an iron bar slowly. The house

Rang like some fine green goblet in the note
That any second would shatter it. Now deep
In chairs, in front of the great fire, we grip
Our hearts and cannot entertain book, thought,   20

Or each other. We watch the fire blazing,
And feel the roots of the house move, but sit on,
Seeing the window tremble to come in,
Hearing the stones cry out under the horizons.

                                                                            1957

A Dream of Horses

We were born grooms, in stable-straw we sleep still,
All our wealth horse-dung and the combings of horses,
And all we can talk about it what horses ail.

Out of the night that gulfed beyond the palace-gate
There shook hooves and hooves and hooves of horses: 5
Our horses battered their stalls; their eyes jerked white.

And we ran out, mice in our pockets and straw in our hair,
Into darkness that was avalanching to horses
And a quake of hooves. Our lantern's little orange flare

Made a round mask of our each sleep-dazed face,   10
Bodiless, or else bodied by horses
That whinnied and bit and cannoned the world from its place.

The tall palace was so white, the moon was so round,
Everything else this plunging of horses
To the rim of our eyes that strove for the shapes of the sound.   15

We crouched at our lantern, our bodies drank the din,
And we longed for a death trampled by such horses
As every grain of the earth had hooves and mane.

We must have fallen like drunkards into a dream
Of listening, lulled by the thunder of the horses.   20
We awoke stiff; broad day had come.

Out through the gate the unprinted desert stretched
To stone and scorpion; our stable-horses
Lay in their straw, in a hag-sweat, listless and wretched.

Now let us, tied, be quartered by these poor horses,   25
If but doomsday's flames be great horses,
   he forever itself a circling of the hooves of horses.

                                             1960

Relic

I found this jawbone at the sea's edge:
There crabs, dogfish, broken by the breakers or tossed
To flap for half an hour and turn to a crust
Continue the beginning. The deeps are cold:
In that darkness camaraderie does not hold: 5
Nothing touches but, clutching, devours. And the jaws,
Before they are satisfied or their stretched purpose
Slacken, go down jaws; go gnawn bare. Jaws
Eat and are finished and the jawbone comes to the beach:
This is the sea's achievement; with shells,   10
Vertebrae, claws, carapaces, skulls.

Time in the sea eats its tail, thrives, casts these
Indigestibles, the spars of purposes
That failed far from the surface. None grow rich
In the sea. This curved jawbone did not laugh   15
But gripped, gripped and is now a cenotaph.

                                             1960

Examination at the Womb-Door

Who owns these scrawny little feet? *Death.*
Who owns this bristly scorched-looking face? *Death.*
Who owns these still-working lungs? *Death.*
Who owns this utility coat of muscles? *Death.*
Who owns these unspeakable guts? *Death.*   5
Who owns these questionable brains? *Death.*
All this messy blood? *Death.*
These minimum-efficiency eyes? *Death.*
This wicked little tongue? *Death.*
This occasional wakefulness? *Death.*   10

Given, stolen, or held pending trial?
Held.

Who owns the whole rainy, stony earth? *Death.*
Who owns all of space? *Death.*

Who is stronger than hope? *Death.*   15
Who is stronger than the will? *Death.*
Stronger than love? *Death.*
Stronger than life? *Death.*

But who is stronger than death?
                  Me, evidently.

Pass, Crow.   20
            1970

A Disaster

There came news of a word.
Crow saw it killing men. He ate well.
He saw it bulldozing

Whole cities to rubble. Again he ate well.
He saw its excreta poisoning seas.   5
He became watchful.
He saw its breath burning whole lands
To dusty char.
He flew clear and peered.

The word oozed its way, all mouth,   10
Earless, eyeless.
He saw it sucking the cities
Like the nipples of a sow
Drinking out all the people
Till there were none left,   15
All digested inside the word.

Ravenous, the word tried its great lips
On the earth's bulge, like a giant lamprey—
There it started to suck.

But its effort weakened.   20
It could digest nothing but people.
So there it shrank, wrinkling weaker,
Puddling
Like a collapsing mushroom.
Finally, a drying salty lake.   25
Its era was over.

All that remained of it a brittle desert
Dazzling with the bones of earth's people

Where Crow walked and mused.

1970

PETER PORTER

(1930–)

Peter Porter, an Australian by birth, began as a satirical poet using a powerful imagery drawn from physical objects ("the stewing meat / smells savory
past the pruned back roses / and wafts on the street's spindly limits") to
convey his sense of the limitations and frustrations of ordinary life, where
"Death is a relation / waiting to get in touch." Though fiercely modern in
his response to experience, Porter does not hesitate to use references to the
classical world, especially in his more recent poetry, which has a distinct
historical dimension, looking back and forth in time; his later manner has
also become more allusive and personal. The poems by Porter here selected
are from the third volume, *A Porter Folio* (1969), of the four he has so far
published.

Seahorses

When we were children
We would cheer to find a seahorse
Among the wrack the breakers lifted
On to the beach. Sometimes two or three were together,
A team to pull a chariot of cuttle,   5
Or like a suicide wreathed in fine
Sea ivy and bleached sea roses
One stiff but apologetic in its trance.
Seahorses were vikings;
Somewhere they impassively   10
Launched on garrulous currents
Seeking a far grave: wherever
That was, they set their stallion
Noses to it, ready to be garnered
In the sea's time at the sea's pleasure.   15
If we wondered why we loved them
We might have thought
They were the only creatures which had to die
Before we could see them—
In this early rule of death we'd recognize   20
The armorial pride of head, the unbending
Seriousness of small creatures,
Credit them with the sea's rare love

Which threw them to us in their beauty,
Unlike the vast and pitiable whale   25
Which must be quickly buried for its smell.

                                                                    1969

Five Generations[1]

A common name for five of us
tap-rooted to the world's work;
we are the unknown bearers,
the weavers of fatty uniforms.

But only five? Where I'm writing   5
men of one name have lived in one place
for three hundred years. Our family's modern,
moving out of historic darkness
in a diaspora of the undistinguished.

Christopher Porter starts from the dark—   10
I wouldn't pay to trace him farther back,
I simply put him down as something in the town,
the town a sprawling somewhere stealing
a march upon the pelting countryside.
In the blackening days of Captain Swing   15
for some unmentioned tic of change
he sailed for New South Wales. I see him
walking the deck to escape his wife,

donating a spit to Liverpool in his wake:
too cold a man to care what lies ahead   20
he takes an unimportant step from England's shadow.

Robert, his son, is different. An enema'd Victorian,
Master Builder of a pushing city,
he went up spires of speculation
breathing port and senna, was prig enough   25
to put his money into banking: the brewery
he wouldn't back is worth a million now.
Family legend says he entertained
Trollope[2] but never saw a kangaroo—
pride did what cupidity could not   30
and he lost his money—unbending
in late madness, he fulminated
through maidenhair, berated crotons,[3]
killed ants by matchlight in his bush house.
He built Brisbane's jail and deep water pier   35

1. I.e., of Australians. Porter comes
from Australia.
2. Anthony Trollope (1815–1882), the
novelist.
3. Genus of herbs and shrubs of a family known as spurge.

and was hated by a little boy, my father.
When Robert cried the flood of '93 began;
the little boy whistling at his birds
lived with a mad god. Thereinafter
he broke his traps and read   40
the small print on council bye-laws.

Frederick, my grandfather, filled his house
with pictures of "the *Thermopylae* doing eight knots
in a breeze that wouldn't blow a candle out."
He looked like Bernard Shaw and sat   45
stiff as a row of Georgette Heyers
navigating on green baize. He sailed
in his emptiness like a cloud, yet once
rode the Queensland customs boundary
never out of plumb upon his horse.   50
Over a steaming saddle of mutton his face
was a plastic monument to severity—
while he partitioned meat
the Congress of Vienna would have paused.
For love of him his daughter used herself,   55
a dowry of cancer being bait
no girl of fifty should lay out.
I remember the tepid lump of eucalyptus sugar
moving in his meccano fingers;
he became a place of work   60
and laboratory of a Yankee quack.

William's the good man of them all.
It hurts to think of that sandy shore
he loves, that bitumen and mangrove
bird house he must raise his voice in.   65
He's given eighty years of disenchanted
love to it: when he dies, they should
trawl him over river sand to Avalon[4]
out of the choppy, bitching bay.

Peter from necessity cannot speak.   70
This crop of bones might tumble on his coffin
claiming its own. Death's a relation
waiting to get in touch. Born to that sad
reversal of light, he'll know
when to pull the blinds down and go home.   75
                                                             1969

4. The earthly paradise of the western seas in Arthurian legend.

JON SILKIN

(1930–)

Jon Silkin was born in London, and before winning a Gregory Poetry Fellowship at Leeds University spent some years working as a manual laborer. He took a degree in English at Leeds and then did research on the poets of World War I, which bore fruit in his book *Out of Battle: The Poetry of the Great War* (1972). He has been editor of the important "little magazine" *Stand* since 1952. He has published seven volumes of poetry, including *Nature with Man* (1965) and *Amana Grass* (1971), from which the poems below are taken. Silkin's early poetry is characterized by a direct and violent imagery that conveys a sense of moral yearning, an awareness of the built-in obstacles to peace and fulfillment that exist in both man and nature. His later poetry manages to give a new dimension to an imagery still often elemental, exploring the complex relations between man and nature and linking this exploration to an awareness of social and psychological problems. Silkin has visited America several times, and some of his poems have American themes.

Nature with Man

The lank summer grass
As it is, bent and wailing;
A scorching wind
Scours a whole plain of it.
Dust still oppresses. Then   5
As if the earth received
A bruise a pool of brown
Slime erupts slowly
From among the stems. Summer mud . . .
Hot and stagnant. The grass stalks   10
Stand pricked without root
In the rimless mud . . . in what eye.
On some field of gray stone
A white sud of saliva,
So fine it seems a mildew,   15
Agonizes over the crop.

But are the humans here? Nature
Had a human head. The mouth
Turned on its long neck, biting through
Scale, sinew; and the blood   20
Carried through the flesh
Beyond the ends of veins
As the severed head
Rolled into the bulrushes.

This limp and useless   25
Going off among tall weeds
Has soured the earth, whose body
Decays and perishes.
As for the pain
That suds onto the stone;   30
That, simply, is pain.

How much else is there?
There is only one head.
But it has several minds
Which still give out   35
Great reticulations
Of ideas, nets willful and sharp
Over it; binding it
In pride and thought that cut
The smiling face of pleasure.   40

"O pity, pity, pity"?
But the weedy soul is shrinking.
Nor can it see how
To join itself unto
The membered flesh. The whole   45
Of nature is turning slowly
Into an eye that searches
For its most developed
And treacherous creature, man.
Monstrous and huge eye: 50
The entire process
Of nature perverted
Into the search for him.

                                              1965

A Bluebell[1]

Most of them in the first tryings
Of nature, hang at angles,
Like lamps. These though
Look round, like young birds,
Poised on their stems. Closer,   5
In all their sweetness, malevolent. For there is
In the closed, blue flower, gas-colored,

1. *A Bluebell* is one of a series of "Flower Poems" of which Silkin has written: "The method is to take one particular species of flower, and to look at the flower quite closely. I also try to characterize the life and process of the flower and, in making all three substantial, to suggest certain correspondences with human types and situations. Yet although the poems are not only, and not simply, about flowers, they are not only or simply about human beings and their predicaments. They hover tentatively between the two, although whatever object or situation they temporarily absent themselves to they never lose sight of the flower. . . ."

A seed-like dark green eye.
Carroway, grained, supple,
And watching; it is always there,   10
Fibrous, alerted,
Coarse grained enough to print
Out all your false delight
In "sweet nature." This is struggle.
The beetle exudes rot: the bee   15
Grapples the reluctant nectar
Coy, suppurating, and unresigned.
Buds print the human passion
Pure now not still immersed
In fighting wire worms.   20

                                                   1965

Creatures

Shells are now found
Of creatures not still subsisting,
Chipped from the hardened mud under
Which oil lurks.

Men came with their chipped diamonds   5
And a pole with these smelted onto it
To bore rock. Oil broke out
Into the clear American air.

Barely noticed at the time
Among the soil screwed from   10
Above the crude useful oil,
Shells, about half an inch.
They were whorled, and chipped from
What they had been hardening in,
Falling through the glistening mud   15
They filled with the spiral
Wriggling creature gone from them.
It is a spiral horn, silent;
And shaped like an inert
Clammy-skinned spring.   20

They grew property:
An amnion,[1] a house;
Their grave no more special,
No more particular than
A pattern, a repetition of curving   25
Continuous shape, for survival.

                                                   1971

---

1. Membrane enclosing the fetus before birth.

GEOFFREY HILL

(1932–)

Geoffrey Hill, born at Bromsgrove, Worcestershire and educated at Broms-grove County High School and Keble College, Oxford, is a university teacher of English with a highly sophisticated critical mind which can be seen at work in his poetry. His precise and subtle use of imagery is com-bined with a disciplined irony and a fine sense of form. He has published three volumes of poetry, *For the Unfallen* (1959), *King Log* (1968) and *Mercian Hymns* (1971). The poems selected here are from *King Log*. *September Song* is of course about the gassing of Jews in German concentra-tion camps (Zyklon was the gas they used). His fellow poet Jon Silkin has drawn attention to the kind of wit involved in the subtitle of this poem, "where the natural event is placed, simply, beside the human and murder-ous 'deported' as if the latter were of the same order and inevitability for the victim"; he discusses, too, "the irony of conjuncted meanings between 'undesirable' (touching on both sexual desire and racism) and 'untoucha-ble,' which exploits a similar ambiguity but reverses the emphases," and is "unusually dense *and* simple." The other two poems are from a sequence of 8 poems suggested by certain episodes in the 15th-century English civil war known as the War of the Roses. "In this sequence I was attempting a florid grim music broken by grunts and shrieks," the poet has written. He explains that there is no "overt narrative or dramatic structure" in the sequence: "the whole inference, though, has value if it gives a key to the ornate and heartless music punctuated by mutterings, blasphemies, and cries for help."

September Song

born 19.6.32—deported 24.9.42

Undesirable you may have been, untouchable
you were not. Not forgotten
or passed over at the proper time.

As estimated, you died. Things marched,
sufficient, to that end.   5
Just so much Zyklon and leather, patented
terror, so many routine cries.

(I have made
an elegy for myself it
is true)   10

September fattens on vines. Roses
flake from the wall. The smoke
of harmless fires drifts to my eyes.

This is plenty. This is more than enough.

1968

From Funeral Music

3

They bespoke doomsday and they meant it by
God, their curved metal rimming the low ridge.
But few appearances are like this. Once
Every five hundred years a comet's
Over-riding stillness might reveal men   5
In such array, livid and featureless,
With England crouched beastwise beneath it all.
"Oh, that old northern business . . ." A field
After battle utters its own sound
Which is like nothing on earth, but is earth.   10
Blindly the questing snail, vulnerable
Mole emerge, blindly we lie down, blindly
Among carnage the most delicate souls
Tup in their marriage-blood, gasping "Jesus."

7

"Prowess, vanity, mutual regard,
It seemed I stared at them, they at me.
That was the gorgon's[1] true and mortal gaze:
Averted conscience turned against itself."
A hawk and a hawk-shadow. "At noon,   5
As the armies met, each mirrored the other;
Neither was outshone. So they flashed and vanished
And all that survived them was the stark ground
Of this pain. I made no sound, but once
I stiffened as though a remote cry   10
Had heralded my name. It was nothing . . ."
Reddish ice tinged the reeds; dislodged, a few
Feathers drifted across; carrion birds
Strutted upon the armor of the dead.

                                                        1968

---

1. Greek mythological snake-haired woman whose terrible aspect turned the viewer to stone.

SEAMUS HEANEY

(1939–)

Seamus Heaney was born in Northern Ireland and brought up on a farm in County Derry. He attended Queen's University, Belfast, and at Belfast became friendly with Henry Chambers, editor of *Phoenix*, originally a liter-

ary-cum-political magazine founded in 1959 and professing "a faith in words and all that reflects ordinary human activity." Though the magazine had now given up its direct political interests, it still encouraged poets who showed a humanist directness in their work (this phrase covers a wide range, from Hardyesque tragic lyrics to biting social and cultural satire). Heaney, who had already published two "slim volumes" of poetry, appeared in *Phoenix* in 1967, and his work has some of the qualities associated with that magazine. There is no cultural posturing or calculated incoherence in Heaney's quietly human poems, which project their subject with an objectivity of mood and imagery that sets off rather than conceals the underlying sympathy with daily rhythms of ordinary experience. Some of Heaney's poems seem at first sight to possess the sort of realism we associate with Flemish painting; they are subtler than they at first appear and show considerable formal skill and delicacy. The two poems of his selected here are from his volume *Death of a Naturalist* (1966). Other volumes by Heaney are A *Lough Neath Sequence* (1969) and *Door into Dark* (1969).

Churning Day

A thick crust, coarse-grained as limestone rough-cast,
hardened gradually on top of the four crocks
that stood, large pottery bombs, in the small pantry.
After the hot brewery of gland, cud and udder
cool porous earthenware fermented the buttermilk   5
for churning day, when the hooped churn was scoured
with plumping kettles and the busy scrubber
echoed daintily on the seasoned wood.
It stood then, purified, on the flagged kitchen floor.

Out came the four crocks, spilled their heavy lip   10
of cream, their white insides, into the sterile churn.
The staff, like a great whisky muddler fashioned
in deal wood, was plunged in, the lid fitted.
My mother took first turn, set up rhythms
that slugged and thumped for hours. Arms ached.   15
Hands blistered. Cheeks and clothes were spattered
with flabby milk.

               Where finally gold flecks
began to dance. They poured hot water then,
sterilized a birchwood-bowl   20
and little corrugated butter-spades.
Their short stroke quickened, suddenly
a yellow curd was weighting the churned up white,
heavy and rich, coagulated sunlight
that they fished, dripping, in a wide tin strainer,   25
heaped up like gilded gravel in the bowl.

The house would stink long after churning day,
acrid as a sulfur mine. The empty crocks

were ranged along the wall again, the butter
in soft printed slabs was piled on pantry shelves.   30
And in the house we moved with gravid ease,
our brains turned crystals full of clean deal churns,
the plash and gurgle of the sour-breathed milk,
the pat and slap of small spades on wet lumps.

1966

Poor Women in a City Church

The small wax candles melt to light,
Flicker in marble, reflect bright
Asterisks on brass candlesticks:
At the Virgin's altar on the right
Blue flames are jerking on wicks.   5

Old dough-faced women with black shawls
Drawn down tight kneel in the stalls.
Cold yellow candle-tongues, blue flame
Mince and caper as whispered calls
Take wing up to the Holy Name.   10

Thus each day in the sacred place
They kneel. Golden shrines, altar lace,
Marble columns and cool shadows
Still them. In the gloom you cannot trace
A wrinkle on their beeswax brows.   15

1966

Selected Bibliographies

The symbol ‡ following a title indicates that the volume is available in a paperbound edition.

SUGGESTED GENERAL READINGS

Histories of England and of English Literature

George Macaulay Trevelyan's *History of England*,‡ rev., 1945, is an excellent survey in one volume; for detailed studies of single periods, see *The Oxford History of England*, 15 vols., 1934 ff., by a variety of historians. The projected 12-volume *Oxford History of English Literature*, edited by F. P. Wilson and Bonamy Dobrée, 1945–, is nearing completion; see the listings below. *A Guide to English Literature*, ed. Boris Ford (1954–61), is available in 6 paperback volumes. Up-to-date one-volume histories are Albert C. Baugh and others, *A Literary History of England*,‡ rev., 1967; Hardin Craig and others, *A History of English Literature*, 1950; and (less densely factual, and more a running literary appreciation) David Daiches, *A Critical History of English Literature*, 2 vols., 1961.

Drama

Allardyce Nicoll, *British Drama*, rev., 1962, and *A History of English Drama, 1660–1900*, 6 vols., rev., 1952–59.

The Novel

The most detailed, although somewhat pedestrian, history is Ernest A. Baker's *History of the English Novel*, 10 vols., 1924–39. Among the short histories are Walter A. Raleigh, *The English Novel*, rev., 1911, which stops at Walter Scott; and, more up-to-date, Arnold Kettle, *An Introduction to the English Novel*,‡ 2 vols., 1951–53; Walter Allen, *The English Novel*,‡ 1954; Ian Watt, *The Rise of the Novel*,‡ 1957; and Lionel Stevenson, *The English Novel*,‡ 1960.

Poetry

W. J. Courthope, *A History of English Poetry*, 6 vols., 1895–1910, and H. J. C. Grierson and J. C. Smith, *A Critical History of English Poetry*, rev., 1947. In addition, Douglas Bush's two books, *Mythology and the Renaissance Tradition in English Poetry*,‡ 1932, 1957, and *Mythology and the Romantic Tradition in English Poetry*,‡ 1937, 1957, constitute an excellent running account, from their special perspective, of English poetry from the 16th century through T. S. Eliot. Another book which ranges widely in English poetry from the Middle Ages through the 18th century is E. M. W. Tillyard, *The English Epic and Its Background*,‡ 1954.

Literary Criticism

George Saintsbury, *A History of English Criticism*, 1911, is still referred to. More recent histories of English criticism are M. H. Abrams, *The Mirror and the Lamp: Romantic Theory and the Critical Tradition*,‡ 1953; W. K. Wimsatt, Jr., and Cleanth Brooks, *Literary Criticism: A Short History*,‡ 1957; George Watson, *The Literary Critics*, 1962; and René Wellek, *A History of Modern Criticism: 1750–1950*, 1955–, of which four of the projected five volumes have been published.

Reference Works

The Cambridge Bibliography of English Literature, edited by F. W. Bateson, 4 vols., 1941, with a supplementary vol. 5, edited by George Watson, 1957, lists all the books of the major and many minor British authors, together with a large selection from biographical, scholarly, and critical works written about these authors. A revision, *The New Cambridge Bibliography*, is nearing completion. Literary biographies and critical books published since that time can be found in the "Annual Bibliography" *PMLA*; for separate periods,

see the listings below. *Poetry Explication*,‡ rev. by Joseph M. Kuntz, 1962, lists close analyses of English poems, old and recent, and I. F. Bell and Donald Baird, *The English Novel, 1578–1956*,‡ 1958, provides a useful list of 20th-century criticisms of fiction. Further bibliographical aids are described in Richard D. Altick and Andrew Wright, *Selective Bibliography for the Study of English and American Literature*,‡ 1971, and Arthur G. Kennedy, *A Concise Bibliography for Students of English*, rev., 1972.

For compact biographies of English authors see the multi-volumed *Dictionary of National Biography*, edited by Leslie Stephen and Sidney Lee in 1885–1900, with supplements that carry the work to persons who died up to 1950; condensed biographies will be found in the *Concise Dictionary of National Biography*, Part I (1953) and Part II (1961). Handy reference books on authors, works, and various literary terms and allusions are *The Oxford Companion to English Literature*, edited by Paul Harvey, rev., 1967; *The Oxford Companion to the Theater*, edited by Phyllis Hartnoll, rev., 1967; *Dictionary of World Literature*,† edited by Joseph T. Shipley, rev., 1953; and *Encyclopedia of Poetry and Poetics*, ed. Alex Preminger and others, 1965. Low-priced handbooks which define and illustrate literary concepts and terms are: M. H. Abrams, *A Glossary of Literary Terms*, rev., 1971; W. F. Thrall and Addison Hibbard, *A Handbook to Literature*,‡ revised by G. Hugh Holman, 1960; and Lee T. Lemon, *A Glossary for the Study of English*,‡ 1971.

Albert C. Baugh, *A History of the English Language*, rev., 1957, will be found helpful, as will various treatments of English meters and stanza forms, such as: R. M. Alden, *English Verse*, 1903; Karl Shapiro and Robert Beum, *A Prosody Handbook*, 1965; Paul Fussell, Jr., *Poetic Meter and Poetic Form*,‡ 1966; and *The Structure of Verse: Modern Essays in Prosody*,‡ ed. Harvey Gross, 1966.

Intellectual History and Criticism

Students interested in intellectual history as a background for reading English literature will profit from Arthur T. Lovejoy, *The Great Chain of Being*,‡ 1936, and *Essays in the History of Ideas*,‡ 1948; Marjorie Nicolson, *The Breaking of the Circle*,‡ 1950, *Science and Imagination*,‡ 1956, and *Mountain Gloom and Mountain Glory*,‡ 1959; John Herman Randall, Jr., *The Making of the Modern Mind*, rev., 1940; Basil Willey, *The Seventeenth Century Background*, 1934, *The Eighteenth Century Background*, 1940, and *Nineteenth Century Studies*, 1949; and M. H. Abrams, *Natural Supernaturalism: Tradition and Revolution in Romantic Literature*,‡ 1971. In addition, the following is a selection from those books in literary history and criticism which have been notably influential in shaping modern approaches to English literature and literary forms: Erich Auerbach, *Mimesis: The Representation of Reality in Western Literature*,‡ 1953; Maud Bodkin, *Archetypal Patterns in Poetry*,‡ 1934; Cleanth Brooks, *The Well Wrought Urn*,‡ 1947; Ronald Crane, *The Languages of Criticism and the Structure of Poetry*,‡ 1953, *The Idea of the Humanities*, 2 vols., 1967; and, as editor, *Critics and Criticism, Ancient and Modern*,‡ 1952; T. S. Eliot, *Selected Essays*,‡ 3rd edition, 1951, and *On Poetry and Poets*,‡ 1957; William Empson, *Seven Types of Ambiguity*,‡ 3rd edition, 1953; Francis Fergusson, *The Idea of a Theater*,† 1949; Northrop Frye, *Anatomy of Criticism*, 1957; Henry James, *The Art of the Novel: Critical Prefaces*,‡ 1934; F. R. Leavis, *Revaluation*,‡ 1936, and *The Great Tradition*‡ (i.e., in the novel), 1948; C. S. Lewis, *The Allegory of Love*,‡ rev., 1938; John Livingston Lowes, *The Road to Xanadu*,‡ rev., 1930; Percy Lubbock, *The Craft of Fiction*,‡ 1926; I. A. Richards, *Principles of Literary Criticism*,‡ 5th edition, 1934, and *Practical Criticism*,‡ 1930; Caroline Spurgeon, *Shakespeare's Imagery*,‡ 1935; Lionel Trilling, *The Liberal Imagination*,‡ 1950, and *The Opposing Self*,‡ 1955; Edmund Wilson, *Axel's Castle: A Study in the Imaginaitve Literature of 1870–1930*,‡ 1936, and *The Wound and the Bow*,‡ 1941; and Wayne C. Booth, *The Rhetoric of Fiction*,‡ 1961.

THE ROMANTIC PERIOD

Succinct and reliable treatments of the political and social events in this period are the relevant chapters of G. M. Trevelyan's *British History of the Nineteenth Century*,‡ 2nd edition, 1937, and *English Social History*, 1942. More detailed histories are Elie Halévy, *England in 1815*,‡ rev., 1949, and *The Liberal Awakening*, 1815–1830, rev. ed., 1949, and J. Steven Watson, *The Reign of George III, 1760–1815*, 1960. Gilbert Slater, *The*

Growth of Modern England, 1932, deals especially with the industrial revolution. For English literary relations to the French Revolution, see Edward Dowden, *The French Revolution and English Literature*, 1897, and A. E. Hancock, *The French Revolution and the English Poets*, 1899. Illuminating analyses of important intellectual movements will be found in A. O. Lovejoy's *The Great Chain of Being*,‡ 1936, Chapters IX and X, and *Essays in the History of Ideas*,‡ 1948. Other particularly useful works on intellectual history are Basil Willey, *Nineteenth-Century Studies: Coleridge to Matthew Arnold*,‡ 1949; Joseph Warren Beach, *The Concept of Nature in Nineteenth-Century English Poetry*, 1936; Hoxie Neale Fairchild, *Religious Trends in English Poetry*, of which vol. III (1949) deals with 1780–1830; H. W. Piper, *The Active Universe: Pantheism and the Concept of Imagination in the English Romantic Poets*, 1962, and Carl Woodring's excellent survey of *Politics in English Romantic Poetry*, 1970. On Romantic literature in its social matrix, see the relevant chapters in Raymond Williams, *Culture and Society, 1780–1950*, 1960. In *Romanticism: Points of View*, rev., 1970, Robert F. Gleckner and Gerald E. Enscoe reprint major essays on the defining features of "Romanticism"; see also the essays in *Romanticism Reconsidered*, ed. Northrop Frye, 1963.

Among the histories of Romantic literature are: Oliver Elton, *A Survey of English Literature, 1780–1830*, 2 vols., 1928; W. L. Renwick's rather inadequate *English Literature, 1789–1815*, 1963; and Ian Jack's *English Literature, 1815–1832*, 1963. Mario Praz's *The Romantic Agony*,‡ 2nd ed. 1951, treats Satanism, sadism, vampirism, and others of the more exotic literary interests of the time; and Peter Thorslev's *The Byronic Hero*, 1962, discusses the solitary or alienated hero in other writers, as well as Byron. Douglas Bush's *Mythology and the Romantic Tradition in English Poetry*,‡ 1937, is so broad in its range that it constitutes an excellent survey of Romantic poetry in general. The older negative appraisals of the Romantic achievement by the neohumanist, Irving Babbitt, in *Rousseau and Romanticism*,‡ 1919, and *On Being Creative and Other Essays*, 1932, have been taken up and expanded by Edward E. Bostetter in *The Romantic Ventriloquists*, 1963. G. Wilson Knight, *The Starlit Dome*, 1941, reprinted 1960, is an influential early example of the approach to Romantic poets by the analysis of characteristic patterns of imagery. Harold

Bloom, *The Visionary Company*, rev., 1971, which relates these poets to the prophetic tradition of Spenser and Milton, includes brief and stimulating commentaries on each of the important poems; Bloom's *The Ringers of the Tower*, 1971, consists of influential essays on both nineteenth and twentieth-century "Romantic" writers. David Perkins treated *The Quest for Permanence* in Wordsworth, Shelley, and Keats, 1959; and Northrop Frye presents an archetypal overview in *A Study of English Romanticism*, 1968. In *Natural Supernaturalism: Tradition and Revolution in Romantic Literature*, 1971, M. H. Abrams deals with persistent themes, concepts, and designs in English and German Romantic literature, and stresses their relation both to the biblical tradition and the intellectual ambiance of a revolutionary age. *English Romantic Poets: Modern Essays in Criticism*, ed. M. H. Abrams, 1960, is a collection of broadly representative essays by major contemporary critics; *Romanticism and Consciousness: Essays in Criticism*, edited by Harold Bloom, 1970, focuses on some leading topics in Romantic literature.

Following are studies of various forms of Romantic literature. On literary criticism: M. H. Abrams, *The Mirror and the Lamp: Romantic Theory and the Critical Tradition*,‡ 1953; René Wellek, *A History of Modern Criticism: 1750–1950*, Vol. II, *The Romantic Age*, 1955. On narrative poetry: Karl Kroeber, *Romantic Narrative Art*,‡ 1960, and Brian Wilkie, *Romantic Poets and Epic Tradition*, 1965. On the novel: Ernest A. Baker, *The History of the English Novel*, Vol. VI, 1961; Montague Summers, *The Gothic Quest: A History of the Gothic Novel*, 1938. On drama: Allardyce Nicoll, *History of Early Nineteenth-Century Drama, 1800–50*, 2 vols., rev. ed. 1955. On the essay: William F. Bryan and Ronald S. Crane, Introduction, *The English Familiar Essay*, 1916; Marie H. Law, *The English Familiar Essay in the Early Nineteenth Century*, 1934.

Donald A. Reiman reprints the early reviews of all the major romantic poets, as well as some of the lesser poets and some of the prose essayists, in *The Romantics Reviewed: Contemporary Reviews of British Romantic Writers*, 9 vols., 1972. For further references on Romantic literature consult Frank Jordan and other editors, *The English Romantic Poets, A Review of Research and Criticism*, rev., 1972, on Wordsworth, Coleridge, Byron, Shelley, and Keats; and Carolyn W. Houtchens and Lawrence H. Houtchens, *The English Romantic*

Poets and Essayists, rev., 1966, on Blake, the lesser poets, and the major essayists. A short bibliography, designed for students, is *Romantic Poets and Prose Writers*, compiled by R. H. Fogle, 1967. Annual bibliographies of publications about these writers are to be found in *ELH*, 1937–49; *Philological Quarterly*, 1950–64; and *English Language Notes*, 1965–.

Robert Burns

The standard reference for Burns's poems is the three-volume Clarendon Press edition, edited by James Kinsley, 1968. A good one-volume edition is that by Charles S. Dougall, *Robert Burns, The Poems*, 1927; and a useful selection has been edited by John DeLancey Ferguson, *Selected Poems of Robert Burns*, 1926. Ferguson has also given us a reliable edition of *The Letters of Robert Burns*, 2 vols., 1931, and a brilliant portrait of Burns, *Pride and Passion*, 1939. A detailed and thoroughly documented biography is by Franklyn Bliss Snyder, *The Life of Robert Burns*, 1932. James C. Dick has written an excellent study of the texts and music of *The Songs of Robert Burns*, 1903. David Daiches' *Robert Burns*, 1950, provides a critical analysis of all the major poems, while Thomas Crawford's *Burns: A Study of the Poems and Songs*,‡ 1960, is a detailed and comprehensive commentary. See also James Kinsley, ed., *Scottish Poetry, A Critical Survey*, 1955.

William Blake

The beautifully printed *The Complete Writings of William Blake*, edited by Geoffrey Keynes, 1957, has now been replaced as the scholar's edition by *The Poetry and Prose of William Blake*, edited by David Erdman and Harold Bloom, 1965, which includes painstaking textual notes and brief commentaries on many of the poems. There is a *Life of William Blake* by Mona Wilson, 1927, rev., 1948, and Raymond Lister's *William Blake: An Introduction to the Man and His Work*, 1968; but the first full account, Alexander Gilchrist's *The Life of William Blake*, which appeared in 1863, is a charming work which has been a source-book for all later biographers, and is available (expertly edited and supplemented by Ruthven Todd) in Everyman's Library, 1945.

The modern era of the scholarly explication of Blake symbolism was begun by S. Foster Damon's *William Blake: His Philosophy and Symbols*, 1924; the same scholar has also published a very helpful *Blake Dictionary: The Ideas and Symbols of William Blake*, 1965. Of more recent books perhaps the most useful are: Northrop Frye's classic analysis of Blake's moral allegory, *Fearful Symmetry*,‡ 1947; Mark Schorer's study emphasizing Blake's characteristic union of political, moral, and religious radicalism, *William Blake: The Politics of Vision*,‡ 1946; David V. Erdman's detailed investigation of the relation of Blake's poetry to the historical events of his time, *Blake: Prophet Against Empire*, 1954; Peter Fisher's incisive exposition of Blake's thought, *The Valley of Vision*, 1961; and Harold Bloom's commentaries on the individual poems, *Blake's Apocalypse: A Study in Poetic Argument*,‡ 1963. Modern critical essays are collected in *Blake*,‡ edited by Northrop Frye, 1966, and in *Blake's Visionary Forms Dramatic*, edited by D. V. Erdman and J. E. Grant, 1970. H. M. Margoliouth's *William Blake*, 1951, is a concise introduction to the man and his work. Studies emphasizing the shorter poems are: Hazard Adams, *William Blake: A Reading of the Shorter Poems*, 1963; Robert F. Gleckner, *The Piper and the Bard*, 1959; and E. D. Hirsch, Jr., *Innocence and Experience: An Introduction to Blake*,‡ 1964. *A Concordance to the Writings of William Blake*, edited by David Erdman, 1967, is an important aid in elucidating his symbolism. Finally, there is a large and growing list of books which reproduce (some of them in color) Blake's etched poems, drawings, and engravings. The excellent *Blake Bibliography*, edited by G. E. Bentley, Jr., and Martin K. Nurmi, 1964, includes an annotated list of all works by and about Blake, as well as Blake's illustrations for the work of others, published reproductions of his drawings, paintings, and engravings, and other Blakeana.

William Wordsworth

Ernest de Selincourt, the great Wordsworth scholar, has edited *The Poetical Works* (with Helen Darbishire), 5 vols., 1940–49; the variorum edition of *The Prelude*, with the texts of 1805 and 1850 on facing pages (revised by Helen Darbishire, 1959); and *The Letters of William and Dorothy Wordsworth*, 6 vols. 1935–39 (now being revised by C. L. Shaver and others, 1967–). The 1805 and 1850 *Preludes*, on facing pages, are also available in an edition by J. C. Maxwell, 1971, and (together with the "Two-Part *Prelude*" of 1799 and modern critical essays) in an edition by Jonathan Wordsworth, Stephen

Gill, and M. H. Abrams (in preparation). Wordsworth's poems in one volume were edited for Oxford Standard Authors by Thomas Hutchinson and revised by Ernest de Selincourt,‡ 1950; a convenient collection of Wordsworth's critical essays, edited by Paul Zall, is *The Literary Criticism of William Wordsworth*, 1966. Until recently, the standard biography was George McLean Harper, *William Wordsworth: His Life, Works, and Influence*, 2 vols., 1916, rev., 1929; Mary Moorman's *William Wordsworth*, vol. I, rev. 1968, and vol. II, 1965, takes advantage of the greatly expanded scholarship of the last three decades. Edith Batho, *The Later Wordsworth*, 1933, and W. L. Sperry, *Wordsworth's Anti-Climax*, 1935, are studies of the poet after 1805. H. M. Margoliouth deals briefly with the relations between two great poets in *Wordsworth and Coleridge, 1795–1835*, 1953.

Walter Raleigh's *Wordsworth*, 1903, Helen Darbishire's *The Poet' Wordsworth*,‡ 1950, and Carl Woodring's, *Wordsworth*,‡ 1965, are useful introductions to Wordsworth's poetry. Stephen M. Parrish, *Art of the Lyrical Ballads*, 1973, is an illuminating examination of Wordsworth's early poems. *The Mind of a Poet*, by Raymond D. Havens, 2 vols., 1941, is a detailed study of *The Prelude*; Herbert Lindenberger, *On Wordsworth's Prelude*,‡ 1963, is a more recent and lively exploration; and Richard J. Onorato, *The Character of the Poet: Wordsworth in "The Prelude,"* 1971, applies psychoanalytic concepts to the poem. Various aspects of Wordsworth's thought are discussed in Basil Willey, *The Eighteenth Century Background*,‡ 1940; N. P. Stallknecht, *Strange Seas of Thought*, 2nd ed., 1958, and Geoffrey Durrant, *Wordsworth and the Great System*, 1970. Prominent among the books which attest the growing interest in Wordsworth are John Jones, *The Egotistical Sublime*, 1954, David Ferry, *The Limits of Mortality*, 1959; David Perkins, *Wordsworth and the Poetry of Sincerity*, 1964; and Geoffrey Hartman's impressive study of *Wordsworth's Poetry, 1787–1814*, 1964. The range and diversity of recent critical studies is represented in *Wordsworth: A Collection of Critical Essays*, edited by M. H. Abrams, 1972.

Dorothy Wordsworth

The biography is by Ernest de Selincourt, *Dorothy Wordsworth*, 1933. Her letters are collected with those of her brother in *The Letters of William and Dorothy Wordsworth*, 6 vols., 1935–39, now in the process of revision by C. L. Shaver and others, 1967–. *The Journals of Dorothy Wordsworth* were edited by Ernest de Selincourt in 2 vols., 1941; a more accurate version of the early Alfoxden and Grasmere Journals (1798–1803) is now available, *Journals of Dorothy Wordsworth*, ed. Mary Moorman, 1971. See also Catherine Macdonald Maclean, *Dorothy Wordsworth, the Early Years*, 1932.

Samuel Taylor Coleridge

The *Complete Works*, ed. W. G. T. Shedd, 7 vols., 1853, 1884, though far from complete, is the most inclusive collection of Coleridge's works; it will be superseded by the edition of Coleridge's writings now in process under the general editorship of Kathleen Coburn, 1969–. The standard edition of the *Complete Poetical Works* is by E. H. Coleridge, 2 vols., 1912; a one-volume edition of the *Poetical Works* by the same editor is available in Oxford Standard Authors. The most fully annotated edition of *Biographia Literaria* is by John Shawcross, 2 vols., 1907; a good reprint of the critical classic was edited by George Watson, rev. 1965. Thomas Middleton Raysor has edited the fragmentary remains of *Coleridge's Shakespearean Criticism*, 2 vols., 1930, and *Coleridge's Miscellaneous Criticism*, 1936. The definitive edition of Coleridge's *Collected Letters* is edited by E. L. Griggs, 6 vols., 1956–62. The first three volumes of Coleridge's extraordinary *Notebooks* are available, meticulously edited by Kathleen Coburn, 1957–71.

E. K. Chambers, *Samuel Taylor Coleridge*, 1938, gives a condensed and unsympathetic factual account of Coleridge's life. Lawrence Hanson, *The Life of S. T. Coleridge: The Early Years*, 1938, is an extensive study of the poet's life and writings to 1800; there is a good short study of the life and works by Walter J. Bate, *Coleridge*, 1968, and, with emphasis on the philosophical and religious writings, by Basil Willey, *Samuel Taylor Coleridge*, 1972. H. M. Margoliouth has described the most fruitful literary association on record in his *Wordsworth and Coleridge, 1795–1834*, 1953. The best inclusive critique of Coleridge as poet is by Humphry House, *Coleridge*, 1953; for a more modern analysis, see *The Poetic Voices of Coleridge*, by Max F. Schulz, 1963. *The Road to Xanadu*, 1927, rev.,‡ 1930, by J. L. Lowes, which investigates the sources and composition of *The Ancient Mariner* and *Kubla Khan*, has achieved the status of a critical classic. Recent discussion of Coleridge as critic will be

found in M. H. Abrams, *The Mirror and the Lamp*,‡ 1953, René Wellek, *A History of Modern Criticism 1750–1950*, Vol. II, 1955, Richard Harter Fogle, *The Idea of Coleridge's Criticism*, 1962, and J. A. Appleyard, *Coleridge's Philosophy of Literature*, 1965. Norman Fruman, *Coleridge, The Damaged Archangel*, 1971, collects all the charges and evidence concerning Coleridge's "plagiarism." Among the excellent recent studies of Coleridge's philosophical and theological interests and achievements are: Richard Haven, *Patterns of Consciousness*, 1969; Thomas McFarland, *Coleridge and the Pantheist Tradition*, 1969; and Owen Barfield, *What Coleridge Thought*, 1971. On opium and Coleridge's poetry, see M. H. Abrams, *The Milk of Paradise*, new edition, 1970; Elisabeth Schneider, *Coleridge, Opium and Kubla Khan*, 1953; and Alethea Hayter, *Opium and the Romantic Imagination*, 1968. Modern essays in criticism have been collected by Kathleen Coburn, *Coleridge*, 1967.

George Gordon, Lord Byron

The Works of Lord Byron, 1898–1904, contains seven volumes of *Poetry*, edited by Ernest Hartley Coleridge, and six volumes of *Letters and Journals*, edited by Rowland E. Prothero; the latter have been supplemented by *Lord Byron's Correspondence*, 2 vols., 1922, edited by Sir John Murray. There are numerous editions of the collected poems; a well-chosen and annotated selection has been published in two volumes in the Odyssey Press Series: *Don Juan and Other Satiric Poems*, edited by Louis I. Bredvold, 1935, and *Childe Harold's Pilgrimage and Other Romantic Poems*, edited by Samuel C. Chew, 1936. Selections from the letters have been prepared by V. H. Collins, *Lord Byron in His Letters*, 1927, and by R. G. Howarth, *Letters of Lord Byron*, 1933. *His Very Self and Voice*, by Ernest J. Lovell, Jr., 1954, is a compilation of Byron's conversations, and *Byron: A Self-Portrait*, edited by Peter Quennell, 2 vols., 1950, reprints selected letters and the text of his diaries.

The standard biography, a circumstantial and objective narrative, is Leslie A. Marchand's *Byron: A Biography*, 3 vols., 1957; a one-volume condensation is *Byron, a Portrait*, 1970. A very readable short life is Peter Quennell, *Byron*, 1934. Among the many recent books on Byron as poet are: G. Wilson Knight's symbolic interpretations and praises of Byron, *The Burning Oracle*, 1939, and *Lord Byron: Christian Virtues*,

1954; E. J. Lovell, Jr., *Byron: The Record of a Quest*, 1950; Paul West, *Byron and the Spoiler's Art*, 1960; Andrew Rutherford, *Byron*, 1961; L. A. Marchand, *Byron's Poetry: A Critical Introduction*,‡ 1965; and Jerome L. McGann, *Fiery Dust: Byron's Poetic Development*, 1968. *Byron*,‡ 1963, edited by Paul West, is a collection of 20th-century essays in criticism.

An edition of *Don Juan* which incorporates the changes Byron made in his manuscripts is *Byron's Don Juan*, edited by T. G. Steffan and W. W. Pratt, 4 vols., 1957; the first volume, by Steffan, is a full commentary on his poem. Other discussions of Byron's masterpiece are: P. G. Trueblood, *The Flowering of Byron's Genius: Studies in Byron's Don Juan*, 1945; E. F. Boyd, *Byron's Don Juan: A Critical Study*, 1945; George M. Ridenour, *The Style of "Don Juan,"* 1960; and E. E. Bostetter's collection of *Twentieth-Century Interpretations of "Don Juan,"* 1969.

Percy Bysshe Shelley

The standard collection of Shelley's writings is *The Complete Works*, edited in 10 vols. by Roger Ingpen and Walter E. Peck, 1926–30. The most useful single volume of the poems is in the Oxford Standard Authors, edited by Thomas Hutchinson and revised by G. M. Matthews, 1970. *Shelley's Prose* was collected by David Lee Clark in 1954; and *The Letters* were edited by Frederick L. Jones in 2 vols., 1964. Because of the erratic way in which Shelley's poems and essays were published, all the collected editions are faulty; Shelley's writings are now in the process of being revised and reprinted by a number of editors.

The classic life is Newman Ivey White's *Shelley*, 2 vols., 1940, which is also available in a condensed single volume, *Portrait of Shelley*, 1945. A graceful short biography and appreciation is Edmund Blunden's *Shelley: A Life Story*,‡ 1946; the latest life is J. O. Fuller, *Shelley*, 1968. Kenneth Neill Cameron, in *The Young Shelley*,‡ 1950, emphasizes the development of Shelley's radical social and political thinking. C. E. Pulos, *The Deep Truth: A Study of Shelley's Scepticism*,‡ 1954, a valuable corrective of standard views of Shelley, emphasizes the philosophic scepticism at the center of his idealism.

Shelley's Major Poetry,‡ by Carlos Baker, 1948, provides useful analyses of the longer poems which stress their ideational content; Carl H. Grabo, in *A Newton Among Poets*, 1930, and Desmond King-Hele, in *Shelley: His*

Thought and Work, 1960, deal with Shelley's conversion of scientific knowledge into poetic imagery. *The Imagery of Keats and Shelley*, 1949, by Richard H. Fogle, is an analysis of the stylistic qualities of Shelley's poetry.

As early as 1900, W. B. Yeats, in "The Philosophy of Shelley's Poetry" (reprinted in *Essays*, 1924) dealt with Shelley as one of the great symbolist poets; the essay reveals the paradoxical position of modern critics who revere Yeats but condemn Shelley, one of Yeats's most important poetic models. Recent treatments of Shelley's symbolic imagery are Peter Butter, *Shelley's Idols of the Cave*, 1954, and Harold Bloom's innovative study, *Shelley's Mythmaking*, 1959, which puts Shelley in the line of the visionary poets whose imaginative processes were instinctively mythopeic. Earl Wasserman's *Shelley: A Critical Reading*, 1971, replaces his earlier treatments of Shelley; it is a massive and illuminating series of close readings of Shelley's most important poems and essays. Other recent critiques are Milton Wilson, *Shelley's Later Poetry*, 1959; R. G. Woodman, *The Apocalyptic Tradition in the Poetry of Shelley*, 1964; and Donald Reiman, *Percy Bysshe Shelley*, 1969. *Shelley,‡* ed. George M. Ridenour, 1965, is an anthology of modern critical essays.

John Keats

The two best editions of Keats's poems are H. W. Garrod's *Poetical Works,‡* 2nd edition, 1958, and the annotated edition by Miriam Allott, *The Poems of John Keats*, 1970. Hyder E. Rollins's *The Letters of John Keats*, 2 vols., 1958, is an exact reprint from the manuscripts.

The best biography is W. J. Bate's notable study of the poet's life, writings, and place in the English poetic tradition, *John Keats,‡* 1963. Shorter critical biographies are Aileen Ward, *John Keats: The Making of a Poet,‡* 1963, Douglas Bush, *John Keats*, 1966, and Robert Gittings, *John Keats*, 1968. Among the many critical writings on the poet, the following are especially useful: C. D. Thorpe, *The Mind of John Keats*, 1926 (on Keats's thought); M. R. Ridley, *Keats's Craftsmanship,‡* 1933 (based on the revisions in Keats's manuscripts); R. H. Fogle, *The Imagery of Keats and Shelley*, 1949 (a study of Keats's characteristic diction and figurative language); Earl Wasserman, *The Finer Tone*, 1953 (a close and sometimes oversubtle analysis of the major poems); E. C. Pettet, *On the Poetry of Keats*, 1957; Morris Dick-

stein, *Keats and His Poetry*, 1971; and Stuart Sperry, *Keats the Poet*, 1973. *Keats,‡* edited by W. J. Bate, 1964, reprints a number of recent critical essays.

William Lisle Bowles

The Poetical Works, ed. G. Gilfillan, 1855. G. Greeve, *A Wiltshire Parson and His Friends: The Correspondence of W. L. Bowles*, 1926.

Sir Walter Scott

Scott's novels have been often reprinted, both collectively and individually, and most of the best ones are available in cheap editions. A useful collection of the *Poetical Works* is that in the Oxford Standard Authors, edited in 1904 by J. L. Robertson. The letters have been edited by H. J. C. Grierson in 12 vols., 1932–37, and the *Journal* has been edited by J. G. Tait in 3 vols., 1939–46. The official *Memoirs of the Life of Sir Walter Scott* by Scott's son-in-law, J. G. Lockhart, 7 vols., 1837–38, is an English classic; its facts and evaluations are supplemented by H. J. C. Grierson's *Sir Walter Scott, Bart.*, 1938. There is also a lively and engaging life, *Sir Walter Scott*, by the novelist John Buchan, 1932. See also James T. Hillhouse, *The Waverly Novels and their Critics*, 1936, and the many treatments of Scott as poet and novelist listed in Chapter IV of *The English Romantic Poets and Essayists*, edited by Carolyn W. and Lawrence H. Houtchens, rev., 1966.

Robert Southey

The *Poetical Works*, edited by Southey himself, are in 10 vols., 1837–38, reprinted, 1860; the best one-volume selection is *Poems*, edited by M. H. Fitzgerald, 1909. The prose works have not been collected. There is a *Life and Correspondence*, edited in 6 vols. by C. C. Southey in 1849–50, and a selection of the *Letters*, edited by M. H. Fitzgerald for World's Classics, 1912. For biography see Edward Dowden's *Southey*, 1874; William Haller's *The Early Life*, 1917; Jack Simmons' *Southey*, 1945; and Robert Carnall's *Robert Southey and His Age*, 1960.

Walter Savage Landor

The Complete Works have been edited by T. E. Welby and Stephen Wheeler, 16 vols., 1927–36, and the poems alone by Stephen Wheeler in 3 vols., 1937. A more reliable edition of the prose writings is by C. G. Crump, 2 vols., 1891–93. There is a volume of selected *Poetry and Prose*, edited

by E. K. Chambers, 1946. The official biography is *Walter Savage Landor*, by his friend, John Forster, 2 vols., 1869, but it is long and dull; a recent, full, and readable biography is R. H. Super's *Landor: A Biography*, 1954. For criticism, see also Malcolm Elwin, *Landor: A Replevin*, 1958, Chapter VII in Douglas Bush, *Mythology and the Romantic Tradition*,‡ 1937, and Robert Pinsky, *Landor's Poetry*, 1968.

Thomas Moore

Poetical Works, edited by A. D. Godley, 1910; a selection of *Lyrics and Satires*, edited by Sean O'Faolain, 1929; *Memoirs, Journals, and Correspondence*, edited by Lord John Russell, 8 vols., 1853–56. A selection from the memoirs was published as *Tom Moore's Diary*, edited by J. B. Priestley, 1925. The best biography is Howard M. Jones's lively *The Harp That Once—A Chronicle of the Life of Thomas Moore*, 1937.

Leigh Hunt

Hunt's complete journalistic output (it is estimated that it would take up between 50 and 60 volumes) has never been collected. Following are the best editions and useful selections of various types of his writing: *Poetical Works*, edited by H. S. Milford, Oxford Standard Authors, 1923; *Leigh Hunt's Literary Criticism*, edited by Carolyn W. and Lawrence H. Houtchens, 1956 (it includes a general appreciation of Hunt as a man of letters by C. D. Thorpe), and by the same editors, *Leigh Hunt's Dramatic Criticism, 1808–1831*, 1949; *Selected Essays*, edited by J. B. Priestley, 1929. Hunt's *Autobiography* is available in The World's Classics. The best English biography is Edmund Blunden's *Leigh Hunt: A Biography*, 1930, but the fullest and most scholarly is in French, the first volume of Louis Landré's monumental *Leigh Hunt* (1935–36); the second volume of this treatise constitutes the best critical survey of all of Hunt's writings.

Thomas Love Peacock

The Works have been edited by H. F. B. Brett-Smith and C. E. Jones in 10 vols., 1924–34, and the poems alone by R. B. Johnson, 1906. The novels have been often reprinted, singly and collectively. There are good lives of Peacock by Carl Van Doren, 1911, and by J. B. Priestley, 1927. For a critical analysis of his writings, see Carl Dawson, *His Fine Wit: A Study of T. L. Peacock*, 1970.

John Clare

The fullest selection from Clare's published poems and from the great mass of his unpublished remains is *The Poems of John Clare*, edited by J. W. Tibble, 2 vols., 1935. The same scholar, with Anne Tibble, has written *Clare: His Life and Poetry*, 1956, and has edited *The Prose*, 1951, and *The Letters*, 1951. Shorter selections, edited independently from the manuscripts, are Geoffrey Grigson's editions of *Poems of John Clare's Madness*, 1949, and *Selected Poems*, 1950; and *Selected Poems and Prose*, edited by Eric Robinson and Geoffrey Summerfield, 1967. The essays on Clare by J. M. Murry, collected in his *John Clare and Other Studies*, 1959, will indicate the sudden leap forward of Clare's reputation when he was "rediscovered" in the 1920's. See also the section on Clare in J. Heath-Stubbs, *The Darkling Plain*, 1950.

George Darley

Complete Poetical Works, edited by Ramsay Colles, 1908; C. C. Abbott, *The Life and Letters of George Darley*, 1928. See the section on Darley in J. Heath-Stubbs, *The Darkling Plain*, 1950.

Thomas Lovell Beddoes

The standard edition of Beddoes' writings, including his manuscript remains, is the *Works*, edited by H. W. Donner, 1935. The same scholar has edited a good selection of the *Plays and Poems*, 1950, and has written the best biography. *Thomas Lovell Beddoes: The Making of a Poet*, 1935. See also R. H. Snow, *Thomas Lovell Beddoes*, 1928.

Charles Lamb

We are indebted to E. V. Lucas for the standard *Works of Charles and Mary Lamb*, 7 vols., 1903–5; for the standard edition of their *Letters*, 3 vols., 1935; and for the standard *Life of Charles Lamb*, 2 vols., rev., 1921. The shorter work, *Charles Lamb*, written by Alfred Ainger for the English Men of Letters series in 1882, is still a useful critical biography. The influential essay on Lamb by Walter Pater in his *Appreciations* set the tone for much of the standard commentary on the essayist; Edmund Blunden's *Charles Lamb and His Contemporaries*, 1933, is an appreciation by a more recent devotee; Denys Thompson's "Our Debt to Lamb," in *Determinations*, ed. F. R. Leavis, 1934, offers a contrary view. A selection from his critical writings, *Lamb's Criticism*, 1923, was edited by E. M. W. Tillyard, and includes an intro-

ductory essay on "Lamb as a Literary Critic." On the criticism see also René Wellek, *History of Modern Criticism*, Vol. II, 1955.

William Hazlitt

The Complete Works of William Hazlitt, 21 vols., 1930–34, has been well edited by P. P. Howe; the final volume includes a full general index, as well as an index of Hazlitt's quotations. Useful selections of Hazlitt's writings are *Selected Essays*, edited by Geoffrey Keynes, 1930, and *Hazlitt on English Literature*, edited by Jacob Zeitlin, 1926. P. P. Howe's largely• factual *Life of William Hazlitt*, revised ed., 1947, has been superseded by Catherine M. Maclean's *Born Under Saturn*, 1944, and by Herschel Baker's comprehensive study of his thought and writings, *William Hazlitt*, 1962. Stewart C. Wilcox described *Hazlitt in the Workshop*, 1943. The chapter on Hazlitt in Oliver Elton's *A Survey of English Literature 1780–1830*, 2 vols., 1912, remains a useful comment on Hazlitt as essayist and prose stylist. Virginia Woolf includes an appreciation of Hazlitt in *The Second Common Reader*,‡ 1932. On Hazlitt as a critic of literature and the arts, see the Introduction in Jacob Zeitlin's anthology, *Hazlitt on English Literature*, 1913; Elizabeth Schneider, *The Aesthetics of William Hazlitt*, 1933; W. J. Bate's comments in *Criticism: The Major Texts*, 1952; and René Wellek, *A History of Modern Criticism 1750–1950*, Vol. II, 1955.

Thomas De Quincey

The Collected Writings, edited by David Masson, 14 vols., 1889–90, although incomplete, is still the standard edition of De Quincey's writings; other essays will be found in *Uncol-lected Writings*, ed. James Hogg, 2 vols., 1890, and *Posthumous Writings*, ed. A. H. Japp, 2 vols. 1891–93. There are numerous books of selections from De Quincey, and *The Confessions of an English Opium-Eater*,‡ has been frequently reprinted. Horace Ainsworth Eaton's *Thomas De Quincey: A Biography*, 1936, is a detailed and reliable biography; Edward Sackville-West's *A Flame in Sunlight*, 1936, offers a speculative depth-analysis of De Quincey's temperament. Good short biographies and critiques are Malcolm Elwin's *De Quincey*, 1935, and J. C. Metcalf's *De Quincey: A Portrait*, 1940; see also John E. Jordan, *DeQuincey to Wordsworth: A Biography of a Relationship*, 1962. For the effect of opium-addiction on his writings, see M. H. Abrams, *The Milk of Paradise*, rev. 1970, and Alethea Hayter, *Opium and the Romantic Imagination*, 1968. On his criticism see John E. Jordan, *Thomas DeQuincey, Literary Critic*, 1952, and on his thought, the section in J. Hillis Miller, *The Disappearance of God: Five Nineteenth-Century Writers*,‡ 1963.

The Satanic and Byronic Hero

Mario Praz, *The Romantic Agony*, rev. 1951; Peter Thorslev, *The Byronic Hero*, 1962; Joseph A. Wittreich, ed., *The Romantics on Milton*, 1970.

Romantic Poems in Process

Students interested in the process of composition, as this is discussed by poets and demonstrated in their manuscripts, may refer to: Charles D. Abbott, ed., *Poets at Work*, 1948; Phyllis Bartlett, *Poems in Process*, 1951; A. F. Scott, *The Poet's Craft*,‡ 1957.

THE VICTORIAN AGE

Studies of the Victorian age and its point of view include Asa Briggs, *The Age of Improvement*, 1962; W. L. Burn, *The Age of Equipoise: A Study of the Mid-Victorian Generation*,‡ 1964; Jerome Buckley, *The Victorian Temper*,‡ 1951; Walter E. Houghton, *The Victorian Frame of Mind, 1830–1870*, 1957; G. Kitson Clark, *The Making of Victorian England*, 1962; J. B. Schneewind, *Backgrounds of English Victorian Literature*, 1970, and G. M. Young, *Victorian England: Portrait of an Age*,‡ 1936. Young's essay is a brilliant synthesis, but it can be incomprehensible to readers who are not yet adequately familiar with the his-tory of the age. Such readers should consult David Thomson's *England in the Nineteenth Century*,‡ 1950, or Derek Beales, *From Castlereagh to Gladstone: 1815–1885*, 1970. Also useful historically is the readable biography of Queen Victoria by Elizabeth Longford, *Victoria R. I.*, 1964. Studies of special aspects of the age include Richard Altick, *The English Common Reader*,‡ 1957; Jerome Buckley, *The Triumph of Time*, 1966; E. P. Thompson, *The Making of the English Working Class*, 1963; Steven Marcus, *The Other Victorians: A Study of Sexuality and Pornography in Mid-Nineteenth-Century England*, 1964; Herbert Sussman, *Victorians*

and the Machine, 1968; Martha Vicinus, ed., *Suffer and Be Still: Women in the Victorian Age*, 1972, and *The Victorian City*, edited by H. J. Dyos and Michael Wolff, 2 vols., 1973. For pictures and paintings of the Victorian scene, see Jeremy Maas, *Victorian Painters*, 1969, and J. B. Priestley, *Victorian Heyday* (with 200 pictures), 1971. Also revealing are the illustrations for Henry Mayhew's *London Labour and London Poor*, originally published 1851, reprinted 1967, and Gustav Doré's *London: A Pilgrimage*, originally published 1872 and reprinted 1970.

Studies of Victorian literature include Douglas Bush, *Mythology and the Romantic Tradition*,‡ 1937; Oliver Elton, *A Survey of English Literature*, 1920, vols. 3 and 4; George Ford, *Keats and the Victorians* 1944–70; Graham Hough, *The Last Romantics*,‡ 1949; E. D. H. Johnson, *The Alien Vision of Victorian Poetry*, 1952; F. L. Lucas, *Ten Victorian Poets*, 1940; Robert Langbaum, *The Poetry of Experience*, 1957, and *The Modern Spirit: Essays on the Continuity of . . . Literature*, 1970; J. Hillis Miller, *The Disappearance of God: Five Nineteenth-Century Writers*,‡ 1963; Morse Peckham, *Beyond the Tragic Vision*, 1962; René Wellek, *A History of Modern Criticism*, Vol. 4, 1965, and Harold Bloom, *The Ringers in the Tower*, 1971. Helpful collections of critical essays have been compiled by Robert Preyer in his *Victorian Literature: Selected Essays*,‡ 1965; Robert Langbaum, *The Victorian Age*, 1967; Richard Levine in his *Backgrounds to Victorian Literature*, 1967, and by Isabel Armstrong, *The Major Victorian Poets: Reconsiderations*, 1969. Especially noteworthy is *The Art of Victorian Prose*, edited by George Levine and William Madden, 1968.

For classified or annotated lists of other books and articles, see *The Victorian Poets: A Guide to Research*, edited by F. E. Faverty (rev., 1968); *Victorian Fiction: A Guide to Research*, edited by Lionel Stevenson, 1964 (revised version projected for 1974); *Victorian Prose: A Guide to Research*, edited by David J. DeLaura, 1973.

For developments in prose fiction during the period see Walter Allen, *The English Novel*,‡ 1954; Lionel Stevenson, *The English Novel: A Panorama*,‡ 1960, and Kathleen Tillotson, *The Novel of the Eighteen-Forties*,‡ 1956. For special critical issues, see J. Hillis Miller, *The Form of Victorian Fiction*, 1968.

Thomas Carlyle

The *Works* have been edited by H. D. Traill, 30 vols., 1898–1901. Four volumes of the *Collected Letters*, projected to extend to 30 volumes, were published in 1971 (ed. C. R. Sanders and others). C. F. Harrold's edition of *Sartor Resartus*, 1937, is helpful concerning Carlyle's debt to German literature, as is Louis Cazamian's *Carlyle*, translated in 1932, concerning his religious background. J. A. Froude's *Thomas Carlyle*, 1882–84, remains, despite its inaccuracies, the standard biography. Emery Neff's *Carlyle and Mill*, 1926, and Eric Bentley's *A Century of Hero-Worship*,‡ 1944, are recommended as studies of Carlyle's thought. That he has affinities with 20th-century "myth-makers" such as D. H. Lawrence is argued by Albert J. LaValley in *Carlyle and the Idea of the Modern*, 1968. John Holloway's *The Victorian Sage*, 1953, includes a chapter analyzing Carlyle's rhetoric. George B. Tennyson's *Sartor Called Resartus*, 1965, is an important critical study. See also George Levine's *The Boundaries of Fiction*, 1968, on Carlyle, Macaulay, and Newman.

John Stuart Mill

Since 1963 several of the projected 20 volumes of the *Collected Works*, edited by F. E. L. Priestley and John M. Robson, have been published (Robson is also the author of a study of Mill's thought, *The Improvement of Mankind*, 1968). Four volumes of the *Letters* were edited by Frances Mineka and Dwight Lindley, 1963–73. Studies include A. W. Benn, *The History of English Rationalism in the Nineteenth Century*, 2 vols., 1906; Karl Britton, *John Stuart Mill*, 1953; Emery Neff, *Carlyle and Mill*, 1926; M. St. J. Packe, *The Life of J. S. Mill*, 1954.

Alfred, Lord Tennyson

Tennyson's *Works* were edited by his son Hallam, Lord Tennyson, in 9 vols., 1907–8. The *Poems*, in one volume, were edited by Christopher Ricks, 1969. Hallam Tennyson's *Alfred Lord Tennyson: A Memoir*, 2 vols., 1897, is a mine of scattered anecdotes and valuable information. The best biography is Sir Charles Tennyson's *Alfred Tennyson*, 1949. Sir Harold Nicolson's *Tennyson*, 1923, a critical study more than a biography, gives a lively but distorted assessment of Tennyson's achievement. A judicious corrective is supplied by Jerome H. Buckley's *Tenny-*

son: The Growth of a Poet,‡ 1961; Valerie Pitt's *Tennyson Laureate,* 1962, and Christopher Ricks' *Tennyson,* 1972.

Some of the most interesting discussions are in introductory essays to Tennyson's poems by T. S. Eliot, 1936; W. H. Auden, 1944; H. Marshall McLuhan, 1956; Jerome Buckley, 1958, and George MacBeth, 1971. Also useful are *A Commentary on Tennyson's "In Memoriam,"* by A. C. Bradley, 1901; *The Formation of Tennyson's Style,* by J. F. A. Pyre, 1921; *The Alien Vision of Victorian Poetry,* by E. D. H. Johnson, 1952; and *Critical Essays on the Poetry of Tennyson,* edited by John Kilham, 1960. Book-length studies of the *Idylls* have been published by Clyde de L. Ryals (1967) and John R. Reed (1969). A collection of critical essays on *In Memoriam* was edited by John Dixon Hunt, 1970.

Robert Browning

In 1969 was published the first of 13 projected volumes of a variorum edition of Browning's *Complete Works* (edited by Roma A. King, Jr., and others). A standard edition has been that edited by F. G. Kenyon, 10 vols., 1912; a one-volume collection was edited by Ian Jack, 1971. W. Hall Griffin and H. C. Minchin's *The Life of Robert Browning,* 1910, rev., 1938, is the standard biography. It may be compared with Betty Miller's *Robert Browning: A Portrait,* 1952, a lively psychoanalytical study, and also with Maisie Ward's enthusiastic *Robert Browning,* 2 vols., 1968–70. W. C. DeVane's *A Browning Handbook,* rev., 1955, is a model compilation of factual data concerning each of Browning's poems: sources, composition, and reputation.

The critical assessments in G. K. Chesterton's *Robert Browning,* 1903, are colorfully expressed and often shrewd. Roma A. King, Jr.'s *The Bow and the Lyre,*‡ 1957, and *The Focusing Artifice,* 1969, contain detailed discussions of some of the principal monologues. Robert Langbaum's *The Poetry of Experience*‡ is an admirable attempt to relate Browning's monologues to some of the main developments in modern literature. For an understanding of Browning's ideas, W. O. Raymond's *The Infinite Moment,*‡ 1965, is suggestive. Many of the best discussions of Browning's achievement, especially discussions of individual poems, have been conveniently assembled in two collections that rarely overlap each other: *Robert Browning: A Collection of Criti-*

cal Essays, edited by Philip Drew,‡ 1966, and *The Browning Critics,*‡ edited by Boyd Litzinger and K. L. Knickerbocker, 1965. The latter collection also includes an extensive bibliography. Litzinger has also edited (with Donald Smalley) *Browning: The Critical Heritage,* 1970.

Charles Dickens

A comprehensive survey of writings about Dickens has been provided by Ada Nisbet in *Victorian Fiction: A Guide to Research,* ed. Lionel Stevens, 1964, pp. 44–153. A revised and expanded version is projected for publication in 1974. The two most important biographies are John Forster's *Charles Dickens,* originally published 1872–74, and Edgar Johnson's *Charles Dickens: His Tragedy and Triumph,* 1952. Also containing much biography and background is Angus Wilson's lavishly illustrated *The World of Charles Dickens,* 1970. Three volumes of Dickens' letters have been published in the Pilgrim Edition, edited by Madeline House and Graham Storey, 1965–73, and 8 or 9 more are projected. Also informative is *The Speeches of Charles Dickens,* edited by K. J. Fielding, 1960.

The quantity of critical studies of Dickens is prodigious, and selection is difficult. A collection of criticism which includes selections from earlier critics such as G. K. Chesterton and G. B. Shaw as well as later critics is *The Dickens Critics,* ed. George H. Ford and Lauriat Lane, Jr., 1961. On a smaller scale is Martin Price's *Dickens: A Collection of Critical Essays,* 1967. Concerning his status among Victorian reviewers, see *Dickens: The Critical Heritage,* ed. Philip Collins, 1971; and for a review of his status among readers (including other novelists) see George H. Ford's *Dickens and his Readers,* 1955/65. In 1970–71, in honor of the centenary of Dickens' death, appeared several collections of essays such as those edited by Michael Slater, Robert B. Partlow, Jr., and Ada Nisbet with Blake Nevius.

Book length studies include Humphry House, *The Dickens World,* 1941; Sylvère Monod, *Dickens the Novelist,* 1953/68; J. Hillis Miller, *Charles Dickens: The World of his Novels,* 1958; Robert Garis, *The Dickens Theatre,* 1965, and H. M. Daleski, *Dickens and the Art of Analogy,* 1970.

George Eliot

George Eliot's Life as Related in

Her Letters and Journals, 1885, by her husband, J. W. Cross, provides the official account of her life, but this book has been in many ways superseded by Gordon Haight's biography, 1968, a work based on the monumental 7-volume collection of her letters which Haight had edited and published in 1954–55. Haight has also compiled a useful collection of critical essays, *A Century of George Eliot Criticism*, 1965, which includes some lively reviews of Eliot by Henry James, and also chapters of critical discussions from books such as F. R. Leavis' *The Great Tradition*, 1948, and Barbara Hardy's *The Novels of George Eliot*, 1959. Other critical works are W. J. Harvey, *The Art of George Eliot*, 1961, and U. C. Knoepflmacher, *George Eliot's Early Novels*, 1968, which includes an extensive analysis of *The Mill on the Floss* that is stimulating even when it provokes disagreement, as it often does.

Studies of her philosophy and its backgrounds include P. Bourl'honne's *George Eliot* (in French, 1933), and Bernard J. Paris, *George Eliot's Quest for Values*, 1965. Highly recommended is George Levine's article: "Determinism and Responsibility in the Works of George Eliot," *PMLA*, 1962.

Matthew Arnold

The Works, 1903, is an incomplete collection of Arnold's writings; it must be supplemented by later editions such as *The Poetical Works*, edited by C. B. Tinker and H. F. Lowry, 1950, and the elaborately annotated *Poems of Arnold*, edited by Kenneth Allott, 1965; the *Note-Books*, edited by H. F. Lowry, Karl Young, and W. H. Dunn, 1952; and *The Letters of Arnold to * * * Clough*, edited by H. F. Lowry, 1932. Since 1960 9 of the projected 10 volumes of Arnold's *Complete Prose Works*, edited by R. H. Super, have been published (Super is also the author of *The Time Spirit of Matthew Arnold*, 1970). For a study of these prose works see William Robbins' *The Ethical Idealism of Matthew Arnold*, 1959.

Lionel Trilling's excellent *Matthew Arnold‡* (1949) remains a standard critical and biographical study but see also W. Stacy Johnson's *The Voices of Matthew Arnold*, 1961; Dwight Culler's *Imaginative Reason*, 1966; G. Robert Stange's *The Poet as Humanist*, 1967, and Douglas Bush's *Matthew Arnold*, 1972. Two useful investigations of Arnold's literary and intellectual background are Leon Gottfried's *Matthew Arnold and the Ro-*

mantics, 1963, and Edward Alexander's *Arnold and John Stuart Mill*, 1965. One of the best shorter essays is E. K. Brown's Introduction to *Representative Essays of Arnold*, 1936, and see also Geoffrey and Kathleen Tillotson, *Mid-Victorian Studies*, 1965, pp. 152–238.

Elizabeth Barrett Browning

The standard *Complete Works* were edited by Charlotte Porter and Helen Clarke, 6 vols, 1900. A reasonable biography is Gardner B. Taplin's *The Life of Elizabeth Barrett Browning*, 1957. See also Alethea Hayter, *Elizabeth Barrett Browning*, 1965.

Emily Brontë

The Complete Poems were edited by C. W. Hatfield in 1941. Information about the Gondal narrative is supplied by Fannie R. Ratchford's *The Brontës' Web of Childhood*, 1941, and *Gondal's Queen, A Novel in Verse,‡* 1955. The most satisfactory biography is Winifred Gerin's *Emily Brontë*, 1971.

Dante Gabriel Rossetti

Rossetti's *Works* were edited by W. M. Rossetti, 1911; *The House of Life* was edited by P. F. Baum, 1928, and *The Letters* by Oswald Doughty and J. R. Wahl, 4 vols., 1965–7 (an incomplete collection). See Oswald Doughty's *D. G. Rossetti: A Victorian Romantic*, 1960, and Lionel Stevenson, *The Pre-Raphaelite Poets*, 1973. Jerome McGann's "Rossetti's Significant Details," *Victorian Poetry* (Spring, 1969) is also recommended.

Christina Rossetti

The standard edition of the *Poetical Works of Christian Rossetti* was edited by W. M. Rossetti in 1904. Virginia Woolf's *The Second Common Reader,‡* 1932, contains an essay on the poetess. Also useful are Marya Zaturenska, *Christina Rossetti: A Portrait*, 1949; H. N. Fairchild, *Religious Trends in English Poetry*, 1957, Vol. IV, Chapter 10, and Lona M. Packer, *Christina Rossetti*, 1963.

George Meredith

The Poetical Works were edited by G. M. Trevelyan in 1928. See Lionel Stevenson, *The Ordeal of George Meredith*, 1953, and C. Day Lewis, Introduction to *Modern Love*, 1948, and Norman Kelvin, *A Troubled Eden*, 1961.

William Morris

Collected Works, 24 vols., 1910–15; J. W. Mackail, *The Life of Wil-*

liam Morris, 2 vols., 1899; George Bernard Shaw, *William Morris, As I Knew Him*, 1936; Graham Hough, *The Last Romantics*,‡ 1949; Peter Faulkner, *William Morris and William Butler Yeats*, 1962, and Peter Faulkner, ed., *William Morris: The Critical Heritage*, 1973.

Edward FitzGerald

George Bentham edited *The Variorum Edition of the * * * Writings of Edward FitzGerald*, 7 vols., 1902. A. McKinley Terhune, *The Life of Edward Fitzgerald*, 1947; A. J. Arberry, *The Romance of the Rubáiyát*, 1959.

Arthur Hugh Clough

The Poems have been edited by H. F. Lowry, A. L. F. Norrington, and F. L. Mulhauser, 1951; *The Correspondence* by F. L. Mulhauser, 1957. *A. H. Clough: The Uncommitted Mind*, by Katherine Chorley, 1962, is a lively but frequently misleading study. *The Poetry of Clough* by Walter Houghton, 1963, contends that Clough is a major satirical poet. On Clough's religious and intellectual background see Paul Veyriras, *A. H. Clough*, 1965 (in French).

Algernon Charles Swinburne

Complete Works, edited by E. W. Gosse and T. J. Wise, 20 vols., 1925–27; *The Swinburne Letters*, edited by Cecil Y. Lang, 6 vols., 1959–62 (reviewed by Edmund Wilson in *The Bit Between My Teeth*, 1965); G. Lafourcade, *Swinburne: A Literary Biography*, 1932. For an attack on Swinburne's shortcomings as a poet, see A. E. Housman's essay of 1910, first published in *American Scholar* (Winter 1969–70). For more sympathetic readings see the special Swinburne issue of *Victorian Poetry* (Spring-Summer 1971) and also see the exceptionally fine study by Jerome J. McGann: *Swinburne: An Experiment in Criticism*, 1972.

Francis Thompson

Complete Poetical Works were edited by Wilfred Meynell, 3 vols., 1913. Biographies are Paul van K. Thomson, *Francis Thompson*, 1961, and John Walsh, *Strange Harp ... the Life of Francis Thompson*, 1967.

Edward Lear

The Complete Nonsense,‡ edited by Holbrook Jackson, 1947. Angus Davidson, *Edward Lear: Landscape Painter and Nonsense Poet*, 1938; Elizabeth Sewell, *The Field of Nonsense*, 1952.

Lewis Carroll

The Complete Writings of Lewis Carroll, 1939. A highly recommended selection is *Alice in Wonderland*,‡ ed. Donald J. Gray, 1971. See also Derek Hudson, *Lewis Carroll*, 1954; William Empson, *Some Versions of Pastoral*,‡ 1935; Martin Gardner, *The Annotated Snark*, 1962; and Virginia Woolf, *The Moment and Other Essays*, 1948.

John Henry Cardinal Newman

The 41 volumes of Newman's works were published over a period of years, but no standard edition has as yet appeared. Several of the projected 30 volumes of the *Letters and Diaries*, edited by C. S. Dessain, have been published since 1961. Meriol Trevor's *New Man*, 2 vols., 1962, is a comprehensive biography. For Newman's religious background and development, two of the most helpful studies are R. W. Church's *The Oxford Movement*, 1891, and Charles F. Harold's *John Henry Newman*, 1945. His literary skill is analyzed in John Holloway's *The Victorian Sage*,‡ 1953, Chapter VI; Walter E. Houghton's *The Art of Newman's "Apologia,"* 1945; and Martin J. Svaglic's "The Structure of Newman's *Apologia*," *PMLA*, LXVI (1951), 138–48. Especially recommended is Dwight Culler's *The Imperial Intellect*,‡ 1955. William Robbins' *The Newman Brothers*, 1966, develops an interesting contrast between Newman and his free-thinking brother, Francis Newman.

John Ruskin

The *Works* were edited by E. T. Cook and Alexander Wedderburn, 39 vols., 1903–12. Ruskin's biography is being at present rewritten, but meanwhile E. T. Cook's *The Life of Ruskin*, 2 vols., 1911, is informative. His *Diaries*, edited by Joan Evans and J. H. Whitehouse, were published in 1956. An interesting digest of his aesthetic theories was compiled by Joan Evans in *The Lamp of Beauty: Writings on Art by John Ruskin*, 1958. Also recommended are R. H. Wilenski, *John Ruskin*, 1933; John D. Rosenberg, *The Darkening Glass*, 1961, and George P. Landow, *The Aesthetic and Critical Theories of John Ruskin*, 1971.

Thomas Henry Huxley

The *Life and Letters of Thomas Henry Huxley* was edited by Leonard Huxley, 2 vols., 1900. William Irvine, *Apes, Angels, and Victorians*,‡ 1955, is lively and informative. See also

1859: Entering an Age of Crisis, edited by P. Appleman, W. A. Madden, and M. Wolff, 1959, and A. O. J. Cockshut, *Unbelievers: English Agnostic Thought, 1840–90*, 1964.

Walter Pater

Works, 10 vols., 1910. Thomas Wright, *The Life of Walter Pater*, 2 vols., 1907; Germain d'Hangest, *Walter Pater: l'homme et l'oeuvre*, 2 vols., 1962. Critical essays include T. S. Eliot's "Arnold and Pater" in *Selected Essays 1917–32*, 1932; Graham Hough, *The Last Romantics*,‡ 1949, Chapter IV; Ruth Z. Temple, "The Ivory Tower as Lighthouse" in *Edwardians and Late Victorians*, edited by Richard Ellman, 1960; U. C. Knoepflmacher, *Religious Humanism and the Victorian Novel*, 1965, and David J. DeLaura, *Hebrew and Hellene in Victorian England: Newman, Arnold, and Pater*, 1969.

THE TWENTIETH CENTURY

The following critical works deal with some general aspects of modern English literature: *New Bearings in English Poetry*,‡ by F. R. Leavis, 2nd edition, 1950; *Forces in Modern British Literature*,‡ by William Y. Tindall, 1947, 1956; *The Modern Writer and His World*,‡ by G. S. Fraser, 1953; *The Present Age in British Literature*, by David Daiches, 1958; *The Novel and the Modern World*,‡ by David Daiches, 2nd edition, 1960; *The Modern Poets, A Critical Introduction*,‡ by M. L. Rosenthal, 1960; *Twentieth Century British Literature: A Reference Guide and Bibliography*, by Ruth Z. Temple, 1968. *Eight Modern Writers*, by J. I. M. Stewart (*Oxford History of English Literature* vol. XII), 1963, includes valuable chapters on Hardy, Shaw, Conrad, Kipling, Yeats, Joyce, and Lawrence, and a comprehensive bibliography. *The Modern Age*,‡ vol. 7 of *The Pelican Guide to English Literature*, 1961, edited by B. Ford, contains some helpful critical essays and a bibliography. *Contemporary British Literature*, by Fred B. Millett, 1935, contains bibliographies of modern British writers up to that date. Bibliographies also appear in the periodical *20th-Century Literature*. The first three chapters of *Image and Experience: Studies in a Literary Revolution*,‡ by Graham Hough, 1960, attempt to put the whole modern movement in perspective.

The Long Week-End: a Social History of Great Britain 1918–1939,‡ by Robert Graves and Alan Hodge, 1940; *The Thirties*, by Julian Symons, 1960; and *The Baldwin Age*, edited by John Raymond, 1960, give helpful social and political background.

Volume 4 of *The New Cambridge Bibliography of English Literature*, edited by I. R. Willison, 1972, deals with the period 1900–1950 and gives a full list of critical and scholarly works about the authors of the period produced up to 1970.

The Nineties

Some helpful books on the period are: *The Last Romantics*,‡ by Graham Hough, 1947; *The Eighteen Nineties*,‡ by Holbrook Jackson, 1913; *The Beardsley Period*, by Osbert Burdett, 1925; *John Lane and the Nineties*, by J. L. May, 1936. Two useful anthologies of the poetry of the period are *An Anthology of "Nineties" Verse*, by A. J. A. Symons, 1928, and *British Poetry of the Eighteen-Nineties*, edited by Donald Davidson, 1937.

Oscar Wilde

There are many modern editions of selections of Wilde's work, and a convenient one-volume edition of *The Works of Oscar Wilde*, edited by G. F. Maine, 1948, new ed. 1966. Maine's edition is virtually complete; it includes "everything written by Wilde that can be published at present" (for legal reasons) and everything of his that ever has been published. Wilde's *Letters* were edited by R. Hart-Davis, 1962. *Oscar Wilde and the Yellow Nineties*, by Frances Winwar, 1940, gives a picture of Wilde in his setting, and *The Life of Oscar Wilde, His Life and Wit* by Hesketh Pearson, 1946, is a lively biography. *Oscar Wilde*, by Edouard Roditi, 1947, is a critical study. Frank Harris's somewhat sensational biography,‡ first published in 1916, has been reprinted in 1960, together with G. B. Shaw's *Memories of Oscar Wilde* and Robert Ross's account of Wilde's last days. *Oscar Wilde, a Pictorial Biography*, 1960, by Vyvyan Holland, Oscar Wilde's son, has some splendid photographs of Wilde and his contemporaries and also provides a vivid narrative.

Ernest Dowson

The standard modern edition of Dowson's poems is *The Poetical Works of Ernest Christopher Dow-*

son, edited with an introduction by Desmond Flower, 3rd ed., 1967. Much lively and illuminating comment on Dowson will be found in W. B. Yeats's *Autobiography*, 1955. *Ernest Dowson*, by J. M. Longaker, 1944, and *Ernest Dowson*, by T. B. Swann, 1965, are critical biographies; *Letters of Ernest Dowson*, edited by Desmond Flower and Henry Maas, was published in 1967.

Thomas Hardy

Hardy published about a dozen volumes of poetry in his lifetime; of these, the most important are *Wessex Poems and Other Verses*, 1898; *Poems of the Past and Present*, 1902; *Time's Laughingstocks*, 1909; *Satires of Circumstance*, 1914. The *Collected Poems* were issued in one volume in 1932 and have several times been reprinted. There are several collected editions of Hardy's works, notably the Wessex Edition, 21 vols., 1912–14, and the Mellstock Edition, 37 vols., 1919–20.

Hardy of Wessex, by Carl J. Weber, 1940, is the best general account of Hardy's life and work. The two biographical volumes by his wife —*The Early Life of Thomas Hardy*, 1928, and *The Later Years of Thomas Hardy*, 1930—are packed with information, much of it dictated by Hardy himself. *Thomas Hardy*, by Douglas Brown, 1954, is an excellent critical study. "The Shorter Poems of Hardy," by R. P. Blackmur, to be found in Blackmur's *Language as Gesture*, 1952, is one of the finest critical discussions of Hardy's poetry. *Hardy: A Collection of Critical Essays*,‡ edited by A. J. Guerard, 1963, is a useful collection. Other critical studies are *Thomas Hardy*, by Irving Howe, 1967; *The Major Novels of Hardy*, by B. Sankey, 1965; and *Thomas Hardy and British Poetry*, by Donald Davie, 1973.

Gerard Manley Hopkins

Robert Bridges edited the first (posthumous) edition of Hopkins' poems in 1918; a second edition, with "An Appendix of Additional Poems," appeared with a critical introduction by Charles Williams in 1930; the third edition, adding some further unpublished poems, was edited by W. H. Gardner in 1948 with additional notes and a biographical introduction. This is now the standard edition.

In addition to the poems, Hopkins' letters and parts of his notebooks have been published, and these are of great interest to students of Hopkins' mind and of his poetic techniques: *The Letters of Gerard Manley Hopkins to Robert Bridges* and *The Correspondence of G. M. Hopkins and Richard Watson Dixon*, edited by C. C. Abbot, 2 vols., 1935; *Further Letters of Gerard Manley Hopkins*, edited by C. C. Abbott, 1937, rev., 1956; and *Notebooks and Papers of Gerard Manley Hopkins*, edited by Humphry House, 1937. House has also edited *Journals and Papers*, 1959; the edition was completed by Graham Storey. This, together with *Sermons and Devotional Writings*, edited by Christopher Devlin, 1959, constitutes a revised edition of the *Notebooks and Papers*. A useful selection of Hopkins' poetry and prose is *A Hopkins Reader*,‡ edited by John Pick, 1953.

The most elaborate study of Hopkins is *G. M. Hopkins: A Study of Poetic Idiosyncrasy in Relation to Poetic Tradition*, by W. H. Gardner, 2 vols., 1944, 1949. *Gerard Manley Hopkins*, by the Kenyon Critics, 1945, contains some helpful critical essays, and *The Shaping Vision of Gerard Manley Hopkins*, by Alan Heuser, 1958, is a careful study of the relation of certain of Hopkins' dominating ideas to his poetic theory and practice. *Gerard Manley Hopkins*, by G. F. Lahey, 1930, is a biography, as is *Gerard Manley Hopkins, Priest and Poet*,‡ by J. Pick, 2nd ed., 1966.

George Bernard Shaw

The Collected Works of Bernard Shaw, in the Ayot St. Lawrence Edition, 30 vols., appeared in 1930 ff. Selections of drama are *Nine Plays*, 1931; *Seven Plays*, 1951; and *Selected Plays*, 4 vols. (containing 27 plays), 1948–57. Many of the plays are also available in inexpensive reprints. Selections of his prose include *Bernard Shaw, Selected Prose*, edited by Diarmuid Russell, 1952; *Plays and Players* (drama criticism), edited by A. C. Ward, 1952; and *Shaw on Music*,‡ edited by Eric Bentley, 1955.

Of the many books on Shaw, the best critical study is Eric Bentley's *Bernard Shaw: A Reconsideration*,‡ 1947. Hesketh Pearson's biography, *Shaw: A Full-length Portrait*, was first published in 1942; Pearson added in 1950 *G.B.S.: A Postscript*. The two books are now available in a single volume. Edmund Wilson's essay, "Shaw at Eighty," in *The Triple Thinkers*,‡ 1938, 1952, is a stimulating discussion of Shaw as thinker and playwright. *G.B.S. 90: Aspects of Shaw's Life and Works*, edited by S. Winsten, 1946, contains essays by a variety of writers. *G. B. Shaw, A Collection of Critical Essays*,‡ edited by R. J. Kaufmann, 1965. *Shaw: "The Chucker Out": A Biographical Exposition and Critique*, by Alan Chappelow, 1969, prints a wide range of articles, letters, comments, and observations by Shaw which vividly illustrate his thought on politics, economics, society, and literature.

Joseph Conrad

Standard is *The Uniform Edition of the Works of Joseph Conrad*, 22 vols., 1923–28, reprinted in 1946 ff, as *The Collected Edition of the Works of Joseph Conrad*. Other collections are the Concord Edition, 22 vols., 1923–28, and the Memorial Edition, 21 vols., 1925.

Two perceptive studies of Conrad are *Conrad the Novelist*,‡ by Albert J. Guerard, 1958, and *Joseph Conrad, Achievement and Decline*, by Thomas Mosher, 1957. *The Portable Conrad*,‡ edited by Morton D. Zabel, 1947, contains a good selection with a helpful introduction (Zabel has also edited *Tales of the East and West*, 1958; *Lord Jim*,‡ *Youth*, and *The Shadow-Line*, all 1959; and, in one volume, *The Shadow-Line, Typhoon*, and *The Secret Sharer*, under the title *The Shadow-Line and Two Other Tales*,‡ 1959). *The Conrad Companion*, 1948 (originally published as *The Conrad Reader*, 1946), edited by A. J. Hoppé, contains a large selection from the stories and other writings with a biographical introduction. The discussion of Conrad in *The Great Tradition*,‡ by F. R. Leavis, 1949, is valuable. There is a chapter on Conrad in *The Novel and the Modern World*,‡ by D. Daiches, 2nd edition, 1960, which deals at length with *The Nigger of the "Narcissus," Lord Jim*, and *Nostromo. Joseph Conrad, Life and Letters*, edited by G. Jean-Aubry, 2 vols., 1927; *The Sea Dreamer*, by G. Jean-Aubry, 1957; and *Joseph Conrad*,‡ by Jocelyn Baines, 1960, are biographies. The last is now the standard biography.

William Butler Yeats

In addition to poems and verse plays, Yeats published essays, short stories, and autobiographical writings, and produced editions of William Blake (with Edwin Ellis) and of some poems of Spenser. He also edited the *Oxford Book of Modern Verse. Collected Poems*, Definitive Edition, 1956, and *Collected Plays*, 2nd edition, 1952, collect Yeats's main work into two convenient volumes, while his letters are collected in *The Letters of W. B. Yeats*, edited by Allan Wade, 1954. Yeats's mystical work *A Vision* was first published in 1925; a new, much revised edition appeared in 1937. *Mythologies* was published in 1959. Yeats's autobiographical writings are combined in *The Autobiography of W. B. Yeats*,‡ 1938 ff. Neither the first draft of Yeats's *Autobiography* nor his *Journals* were published until 1972, when Denis Donoghue edited them under the title *Memoirs*. Peter Alt and Russell K. Alspach edited a variorum edition of the *Poems* in 1957.

Three helpful books on Yeats as both man and poet are: *Yeats, the Man and the Masks*,‡ by Richard Ellmann, 1948; *W. B. Yeats, Man and Poet*,‡ by Norman Jeffares, 1949; *The Lonely Tower: Studies in the Poetry of W. B. Yeats*, by T. R. Henn, 1950. *W. B. Yeats*,‡ by Joseph Hone, 1942, 2nd ed., 1962, is a biography. *The Permanence of Yeats*,‡ edited by James Hall and Martin Steinmann, 1950, *Yeats: A Collection of Critical Essays*,‡ edited by John Unterecker, 1963, and *In Excited Reverie*, edited by A. N. Jeffares and K. G. W. Cross, 1965, are three of several useful collections of critical essays on the poet. The most helpful commentary on the whole of the poems, poem by poem, is *A Commentary on the Collected Poems of W. B. Yeats*, by A. N. Jeffares, 1968.

James Joyce

Dubliners‡ is available in various editions. A critical edition of *A Portrait of the Artist as a Young Man*,‡ based on the autograph manuscript, was published in 1964. *Ulysses*‡ was first published in the United States in 1934; a greatly superior text was published in 1961. *Finnegans Wake*‡ was published in 1939, and a revised text, incorporating the author's corrections, in 1958. There are three volumes of Joyce's *Letters*, the first edited by Stuart Gilbert, 1957, and the second and third by Richard Ellmann, 1966.

Good general accounts of Joyce's work will be found in *James Joyce*,‡ by Harry Levin, 1941, and *James Joyce*,‡ by William Y. Tindall, 1950. *James Joyce's Ulysses*,‡ by Stuart Gilbert, 1930, rev., 1952, and *James Joyce and the Making of Ulysses*,‡ by Frank Budgen, 1934, 1937, are almost necessary works for the reader of *Ulysses*, as are *A Skeleton Key to Finnegans Wake*,‡ by J. Campbell and H. M. Robinson, 1944, and *The Books at the Wake*, by J. S. Atherton, 1959, for the reader of *Finnegans Wake*. Four chapters in *The Novel and the Modern World*,‡ by David Daiches, 2nd ed., 1960, give a general critical account of Joyce's work. *James Joyce: Two Decades of Criticism*, edited by Seon Givens, 1948, is a useful anthology of criticism. *James Joyce*,‡ by Richard Ellmann, 1959, is the standard biography; also highly recommended is Ellmann's *Ulysses on the Liffey*, 1973. *Surface and Symbol*,‡ by Robert M. Adams, 1963, studies the raw material of actual Dublin life in *Ulysses*. Two useful critical works on *Dubliners* are *Twentieth Century Interpretations of Dubliners: A Collection of Critical Essays*, ed. P. K. Garrett, 1968, and *James Joyce's Dubliners: Critical Essays*, ed. C. Hart, 1969. *James Joyce* by A. Goldman (Profiles in Literature series) is a helpful critical survey of all the works.

D. H. Lawrence

The standard edition of the collected works is the Phoenix Edition, 1955. *Collected Poems* appeared in 1928 and 1932, *Selected Poems* (selected by Richard Aldington) in 1934, and *Complete Poems*, 3 vols., in 1964. *Studies in Classical American Literature*,‡ was published in 1923.

Lawrence was a highly controversial figure long before his death, and soon after it a spate of books about him by friends, enemies, and acquaintances began to pour from the press. Most of these are one-sided, but his wife's memoir, *Not I, But the Wind . . .* by Frieda Lawrence, 1934, is an important and moving book. Two critical studies neatly supplement each other, *D. H. Lawrence: Novelist*, by F. R. Leavis, 1955, which is an impassioned argument for Lawrence's supreme greatness, and the much cooler, less "committed," but not unsympathetic *The Dark Sun*, by Graham Hough, 1956, which has a helpful chapter on Lawrence's poetry. *Double Measure*, by George Ford, 1965, is an excellent study of *Women in Love* and *The Rainbow,* and various short stories that illustrate the same themes. The best biography is *The Intelligent Heart*,‡ by Harry T. Moore, 1954; but Lawrence's own *Letters*, ed. by Aldous Huxley, 1932, and much more fully but still incompletely by Harry T. Moore in 1962, provide the best introduction to his life. *The Deed of Life: The Novels and Tales of D. H. Lawrence* by J. Moynahan, 1966, is a helpful critical study of the novels and stories, while *D. H. Lawrence: Sons and Lovers* by Gamini Salgado, is a critical essay on this one novel. Salgado has also edited *Sons and Lovers: A Casebook*, 1969. Another work on this novel is *D. H. Lawrence and "Sons and Lovers": Sources and Criticism*, by E. W. Tedlock, 1965.

T. S. Eliot

The fullest one-volume collections of Eliot's poetry are *Collected Poems, 1909–1963*, 1963, and *The Complete Poems and Plays* (including the plays through *The Cocktail Party*), 1952. Some critical essays are in *Selected Essays*, 1932, and *On Poetry and Poets*,‡ 1957. T. S. Eliot, *The Waste Land: a Facsimile and Transcript of the Original Drafts including the Annotations of Ezra Pound*, edited by Valerie Eliot, 1971, is an indispensable tool for study of *The Waste Land*. T. S. Eliot, *The Waste Land*, by Helen Williams (2nd rev. ed., 1973) is a critical study of the poem taking full account of the new material made available in Valerie Eliot's edition. *T. S. Eliot, Poems in the Making*, by Gertrude Patterson, 1971, also makes use of the rediscovered Eliot manuscripts of *The Waste Land* but ranges widely throughout Eliot's work.

Among the many books on Eliot, *The Achievement of T. S. Eliot*,‡ by F. O. Matthiessen, rev., 1947, has the enthusiasm of a pioneer work; *T. S. Eliot: A Study of His Writings by Various Hands*, edited by B. Rajan, 1947, and *T. S. Eliot, a Selected Critique*,‡ edited by Leonard Unger, 1948, bring together a variety of critical essays including some helpful explications of *The Waste Land* and *Four Quartets; The Art of T. S. Eliot*,‡ by Helen Gardner, is a perceptive critical study of his poetry; *T. S. Eliot, the Design of his Poetry*,‡ by Elizabeth Drew, 1950, is a systematic chronological survey and explanation; *A Reader's Guide to T. S. Eliot*,‡ by George Williamson, 1953, is thorough and informative in its explanation of obscurities and references; and *T. S. Eliot's Poetry and Plays*,‡ by Grover Smith, Jr., 1956, goes through the poems and plays in an exhaustive and even exhausting manner. The best short critical book on Eliot is *T. S. Eliot*, by Northrop Frye, 1963. An important study by a fellow poet is *T. S. Eliot: The Man and His Work* by Allen Tate, 1967. *A Student's Guide to the Selected Poems of T. S. Eliot*, by B. C. Southam, 1968, is a thoroughly helpful commentary.

Hugh MacDiarmid

Collected Poems of Hugh MacDiarmid, revised edition with enlarged glossary prepared by John C. Weston, 1967, is the most conveninet volume for American readers of MacDiarmid's poetry, but, though it contains a great deal, it is far from complete and, in spite of Weston's corrections of errors in the first edition, it still contains too many mistakes. And it prints *A Drunk Man Looks at the Thistle* as a series of separate poems with individual titles, thus obscuring the structure and unity of the work. However, Weston's admirable edition of *A Drunk Man* with critical and explanatory notes, published by the University of Massachusetts Press in 1971, provides a first-rate text for American readers. MacDiarmid was first introduced to American readers in a volume of selected lyrics, *Speaking for Scotland*, 1946. His principal volumes, in addition to those mentioned in the headnote, are *First Hymn to Lenin, and Other Poems*, 1931; *Second Hymn to Lenin*, 1932; *Scots Unbound, and Other Poems*, 1932; *At the Sign of the Thistle: a Collection of Essays*, 1934; *The Golden Treasury of Scottish Poetry* (ed.), 1940; *Cornish Heroic Song for Valda Trevlyn*, 1943; *A Kist of Whistles: New Poems*, 1947; *The Company I've Kept* (autobiographical), 1966.

Two useful selections of MacDiarmid's prose are: *The Uncanny Scot: A Selection of Prose by Hugh MacDiarmid*, edited with an introduction by Kenneth Buthlay, 1968, and *Selected Essays of Hugh MacDiarmid*, edited with an introduction by Duncan Glen, 1969.

The best general account of MacDiarmid and his poetry is *Hugh MacDiarmid*, by Kenneth Buthlay, 1964. A good account of the Scottish cultural background, and of MacDiarmid's part in Scottish literary movements is *Hugh MacDiarmid and the Scottish Renaissance*, by Duncan Glen, 1964. *Hugh MacDiarmid, A Festschrift*, edited by K . D. Duval and Sydney Goodsir Smith, published in 1962 on the occasion of the poet's seventieth birthday, contains fifteen essays by different hands on aspects of his life and work and is the most important single critical book on MacDiarmid. *Hugh MacDiarmid: A Critical Survey*, edited by Duncan Glen, 1972, also contains fifteen essays by different critics, together with a comprehensive bibliography.

Samuel Beckett

The volume of Beckett criticism is already formidable. One valuable and hardheaded book is David T. Hesla's *The Shape of Chaos*, 1972; another is by Hugh Kenner, *Samuel Beckett, a critical study*, 1961. Of the several collections of critical essays, the most available are those edited by Martin Esslin, 1965, and M. J. Friedman, 1970. A useful little volume dedicated specifically to discussion of the *Molloy-Malone-Unnamable* trilogy is ed-

ited by J. D. O'Hara for the "Twentieth Century Interpretations" series, 1970. Raymond Federman and John Fletcher in *Samuel Beckett His Works and His Critics* open a wide gate to much further study.

A. E. Housman

Housman's three volumes of poetry —*A Shropshire Lad*, 1896; *Last Poems*, 1922; and the posthumous *More Poems*, 1936—were brought together in *Collected Poems*, 1939, 1953; the fourteenth (revised) impression is the most accurate text. A *Complete Poems*, edited by Basil Davenport, with a history of the text by Tom Burns Haber, was published in 1959. *Selected Prose*,‡ ed. John Carter, 1961, includes some of the notorious prefaces.

There is an interesting critical essay on Houseman by Edmund Wilson in *The Triple Thinkers*,‡ 1952. "Housman: A Controversy," in *The Condemned Playground*, by Cyril Connolly, 1946, is a lively discussion of the case for and against Housman as poet. There is a critical essay on Housman in *Collected Essays*, by John P. Bishop, 1948. *A. E. Housman: A Divided Life*, by George L. Watson, 1957, is a biography.

Rudyard Kipling

The Sussex Edition of the complete works, 35 vols., 1937–39, is the standard complete edition. *Rudyard Kipling's Verse, 1885–1936* (Definitive Edition), 1940, contains all the poetry. T. S. Eliot has edited, with an appreciative and discerning introduction, *A Choice of Kipling's Verse*,‡ 1941 (the introduction contains a valuable analysis of *Danny Deever*). Edmund Wilson's essay on Kipling in *The Wound and the Bow*,‡ 1941, is stimulating and illuminating; so, in a very different way, is George Orwell's essay on Kipling in his *Critical Essays*, 1946. Lionel Trilling's essay on Kipling in *The Liberal Imagination*,‡ 1950, is the third in an important trilogy of modern estimates. *Kipling's Mind and Art*,‡ ed. A. Rutherford, 1964, is an important collection of critical essays. *Rudyard Kipling, Realist and Fabulist* by Bonamy Dobrée, 1967, is the fullest critical study. *Rudyard Kipling* by Charles E. Carrington, 1955, is the official biography. *The Wheel of Empire*, by Alan Sandison, 1967, is an important revaluation of the man and his work.

Rupert Brooke

The Collected Poems of Rupert Brooke,‡ 1932, and *The Poetical Works*, edited by G. Keynes, 1946,

1960. Walter de la Mare wrote an essay on "Rupert Brooke and the Intellectual Imagination," which is collected in his *Pleasures and Speculations*, 1940. *Rupert Brooke*, by Christopher Hassall, 1964, is a biography.

Edward Thomas

Collected Poems, with a foreword by Walter de la Mare, 1928, 1936. *Edward Thomas,* by Henry Coombes, 1956, is a critical study of the man, the poet, and the prose writer. See also *Edward Thomas,* by R. George Thomas, 1972.

Wilfred Owen

The Collected Poems,‡ edited by C. Day Lewis, 1963, is the definitive edition. *The Poetry of Wilfred Owen* has been edited with a memoir by Edmund Blunden, 1931, 1933, 1949. D. S. R. Welland's *Wilfred Owen,* 1960, is a critical study. William Harold Owen, Wilfred's brother, has published two volumes of a projected trilogy on his brother's life—*Journey from Obscurity: Wilfred Owen 1893–1918* (vol. 1, 1963; vol. 2, 1965). The *Collected Letters,* edited by Harold Owen and John Bell, was published in 1967. *Wilfred Owen,* by Gertrude White, 1969, is a critical study.

E. M. Forster

The Collected Tales of E. M. Forster appeared in 1947. Forster has also collected some eighty of his essays and articles in *Abinger Harvest,*‡ 1936. His study of fictional technique, *Aspects of the Novel,*‡ appeared in 1927, and other essays are included in *Two Cheers for Democracy,*‡ 1951. His novels are available in various editions. Two important critical studies are *E. M. Forster*‡ by Lionel Trilling, 2nd rev. ed., 1965, and *The Cave and the Mountain: A Study of E. M. Forster,* by Wilfred Stone, 1966. The posthumous publication in 1971 of Forster's novel *Maurice* dealing openly with a homosexual hero, while of interest to students of Forster's psychology, added nothing to his reputation as a novelist. *The Life to Come and Other Stories,* edited by Oliver Stallybrass, 1972, is a posthumous collection of mostly unpublished stories with an illuminating introduction.

Virginia Woolf

Extracts from Virginia Woolf's fascinating journal were published by her husband, Leonard Woolf, after her death in 1953, under the title *A Writer's Diary. Virginia Woolf,* by E. M. Forster, 1942, is a brief personal account. *Virginia Woolf,*‡ by David Daiches, 1942; *Virginia Woolf: Her Art as a Novelist,*‡ by Joan Bennett, 1945; and *Virginia Woolf: A Commentary,* by Bernard Blackstone, 1949, are critical studies. *Virginia Woolf and her Works,* by Jean Guiget (trans. Jean Stewart), 1965, is the most detailed critical study of her works. *Critics on Virginia Woolf,* edited by Jacqueline Latham, 1970, is a collection of critical essays by over 20 different critics, with a helpful bibliography. The standard (and only) biography is *Virginia Woolf,* by Quentin Bell (her nephew). 2 vols., 1972. Of interest also are Leonard Woolf's four volumes of autobiography, *Sowing,* 1960, *Growing,* 1961, *Beginning Again,* 1964, and *Downhill all the Way,* 1967. See also J. K. Johnstone, *The Bloomsbury Group,*‡ 1954, and *Bloomsbury,* by Quentin Bell, 1968.

Edwin Muir

Collected Poems 1921–1958, 1960, is the standard complete edition of the poems. Muir's important autobiography, *The Story and the Fable,* 1940, was reissued in a revised and enlarged form in 1954 entitled simply *An Autobiography.* In addition to the works mentioned in the headnote, Muir has written *John Knox: Portrait of a Calvinist,* 1929, and two collections of critical essays, *Transition,* 1926, and *Essays on Literature and Society,* 1949. Peter Butter's *Edwin Muir,* 1962, is a critical study; Butter has also written a biography, *Edwin Muir, Man and Poet,* 1966.

David Jones

Among important studies of Jones and his work are David Blamires, *David Jones, Artist and Writer,* 1971; John H. Johnston, *English Poetry of the First World War,* 1964, chapter VIII; Jon Silkin, *Out of Battle, The Poetry of the Great War,* 1972, chapter 11; E. R. Swank, *Jones: In Parenthesis,* Carnegie Institute of Technology Lectures on Modern Novelists, 1963.

Robert Graves

Collected Poems 1959, 1959, is the fullest of Graves's volumes, but he has published further slim volumes since. *Robert Graves: Poems Chosen by Himself,* 1957, provides an admirable introduction to his poetry. *The White Goddess*‡ was first published in 1948, but the 1952 edition is amended and enlarged. *Robert Graves,* by J. M. Cohen, 1960, and *Swifter than Reason, The Poetry and Criticism of Robert Graves,* by Douglas Day, 1963, are critical studies. "A Ramble on Graves" by Lionel Trilling (in *A Gathering of Fugitives,*‡ 1956) is a highly agreeable critical essay.

W. H. Auden

The Collected Poetry of W. H. Auden, 1945, includes everything the poet wished to preserve up to that date; a more recent volume, edited by Auden on the same principle, is *Collected Shorter Poems 1927–1957,* 1966. Volumes published in the interim included *The Shield of Achilles,* 1935; *The Age of Anxiety,* 1947; *Nones,* 1951; *Homage to Clio,* 1960; *About the House,* 1965; *City Without Walls,* 1969; *Academic Graffiti,* 1971; *Epistle to a Godson,* 1973. He edited a number of anthologies, including (with Norman Pearson) *Poets of the English Language,*‡ 5 vols., 1950, and (with Noah Greenberg and Charles Kallman) *An Elizabethan Songbook,*‡ 1955. *Auden: An Introductory Essay,* by Richard Hoggart, 1951; *The Making of the Auden Canon,* by J. W. Beach, 1957; *The Poetry of W. H. Auden,* by M. K. Spears, 1963; *Auden,* by Barbara Everett, 1964; *The Poetic Art of W. H. Auden,*‡ by J. G. Blair, 1965; and *Auden's Poetry,* by Justin Replogle, 1969, are critical studies. *A Reader's Guide to W. H. Auden,* by John Fuller, 1970, provides a commentary on Auden's poetry and drama in chronological order.

Louis MacNeice

All of MacNeice's poetry has now been collected in one volume, *Collected Poems,* 1967. *The Strings Are False,* 1966, is a posthumously published unfinished autobiography. *Varieties of Parable,* 1965, are lectures on poetry given at Cambridge. MacNeice made verse translations of Aeschylus' *Agamemnon,* 1937, and, with E. L. Stahl, of Goethe's *Faust* (an abridged version of parts I and II), 1951. *Apollo's Blended Dream: A Study of the Poetry of Louis MacNeice,* by William T. McKinnon, 1971, is the fullest critical study.

Dylan Thomas

The Poems of Dylan Thomas, 1973, is the fullest collection of Thomas's poetry. In addition to his poetry Thomas wrote the autobiographical prose *Portrait of the Artist as a Young Dog,*‡ 1940, and *Adventures in the Skin Trade,*‡ 1955, as well as a radio play *Under Milk Wood,*‡ 1954, which has proved a great popular success. *Quite Early One Morning,*‡ 1954, is a colleciton of stories, essays, and minor pieces.
The Poetry of Dylan Thomas,‡ by Elder Olsen, 1954, is a helpful if somewhat over-systematized discussion of his poetry; *Dylan Thomas,* by Henry Treece, rev., 1956, is an account by a British fellow poet; *Dylan Thomas in America,*‡ by John M. Brinnin, 1955, is a moving if indiscreet account of Thomas's last years. In 1957 Vernon Watkins edited Thomas's *Letters to Vernon Watkins.* "The Poetry of Dylan Thomas," in *Literary Essays,* by D. Daiches, 1956, is an appraisal of Thomas's poetic achievement, which includes an analysis and evaluation of *A Refusal to Mourn.* See also *The Craft and Art of Dylan Thomas,* by William T. Moynihan, 1966, and *Dylan Thomas: A Journey from Darkness to Light,* by A. M. Reddington, 1968.

Doris Lessing

Among Doris Lessing's books are *The Grass Is Singing,* 1950; *This Was the Old Chief's Country,* 1951; *Five* (five short novels), 1953; *Children of Violence* (Martha Quest, 1952; *A Proper Marriage,* 1954; *A Ripple from the Storm,* 1958; *Landlocked,* 1965); *Retreat to Innocence,* 1956; *Going Home* (an account of a return visit to Rhodesia), 1957, *The Habit of Loving* (short stories), 1957; *In Pursuit of the English* (social observation), 1960; *The Golden Notebook,* 1962; *A Man and Two Women* (short stories), 1963; *African Stories,* 1964; *The Four-Gated City,* 1969; *Briefing for a Descent into Hell,* 1972. *Doris Lessing,* by Dorothy Brewster, 1965, is a critical study.

T. E. Hulme

Hulme's essays have been gathered and edited by Herbert Read under the title *Speculations,*‡ 1924; 2nd edition, 1936. A volume of *Further Speculations*‡ appeared in 1955, edited by S. Hynes. A biography is *The Life and Opinions of T. E. Hulme,* by Alun R. Jones, 1960.

I. A. Richards

Richards collaborated with C. K. Ogden on *The Foundations of Aesthetics.* 1921 (2nd edition, 1948, with James Wood), and *The Meaning of Meaning,*‡ 1922, much reprinted since. Later books include *Principles of Literary Criticism,*‡ 1925; *Science and Poetry,* 1926, rev., 1970 as *Poetries and Sciences*; *Practical Criticism,*‡ 1929; *Mencius on the Mind,* 1932; *Coleridge on Imagination,*‡ 1935, 1950; and *Speculative Instruments,* 1955. A book of poems, *Goodbye, Earth,* was published in 1958; *The Screens and Other Poems,* 1960, is another book of verse.

F. R. Leavis

Among Leavis' important books are *Revaluation*,‡ 1936, 1950; *New Bearings in English Poetry*,‡ 1932; *For Continuity*, 1933; *The Great Tradition*,‡ 1948; *The Common Pursuit*,‡ 1952; *Anna Karenina and Other Essays*, 1967; *Lectures in America*, 1969 (with Q. D. Leavis). Leavis edited the critical periodical *Scrutiny* from 1932 to 1953.

William Empson

Among Empson's books are *Seven Types of Ambiguity*,‡ 1930, 1953; *Some Versions of Pastoral*,‡ 1935; and *The Structure of Complex Words*,‡ 1951. He published his *Collected Poems*‡ in 1955. See *William Empson*, by J. H. Willis, 1969.

Poetry after Midcentury

Critical materials may be found in John Press, *Rule and Energy: Trends in British Poetry since the Second World War*, 1963; M. L. Rosenthal, *The New Poets*,‡ 1967; F. Grubb, *A Vision of Reality*, 1965; M. Schmidt and G. Lindop, eds., *British Poetry since 1960: A Critical Survey*, 1972 (this contains, in an appendix, a list of nearly 250 living British poets and their works and a list of 42 anthologies of modern British poetry). Donald Davie's *Collected Poems* were published in 1972. Philip Larkin's books include *The North Ship*, 1945, rev. 1966, *The Less Deceived*, 1955, and *The Whitsun Weddings*,‡ 1964. Elizabeth Jennings' volumes of poetry include *A Sense of the World*, 1958; *Song for a Birth or a Death*, 1961; *Recoveries*, 1964; *Collected Poems*, 1967. Thom Gunn has published *Fighting Terms*, 1954, rev. 1962, *The Sense of Movement*,‡ 1957; *My Sad Captains*,‡ 1961; *Touch*,‡ 1967; *Poems 1950–1966*, 1969; *Moly*,‡ 1971. Bibliographies of Tomlinson, Hughes, Porter, Silkin, Hill, and Heaney are given in the headnotes. Davie, Jennings, Larkin, Gunn, and others were first significantly anthologized in Robert Conquest's *New Lines*, 1957, and *New Lines 2*, 1963. Other anthologies of recent British poetry are: *British Poetry since 1945*,‡ ed. E. Lucie-Smith, 1970; *The New Poetry*, ed. A. Alvarez, 1962; and *The Young British Poets*, ed. Jeremy Robson, 1971 (which includes a younger generation of poets than those represented here).

Poetic Forms and Literary Terminology

Verse is generally distinguished from prose as a more compressed and more regularly rhythmic form of statement. This approximate truth underlines the importance of **meter** in poetry, as the means by which rhythm is measured and described.

In the classical languages, meter was established on a **quantitative** basis, by the regular alternation of long and short syllables (that is, syllables classified according to the time taken to pronounce them). Outside of a few experiments (and the songs of Thomas Campion), this system has never proved congenial to English, which distinguishes, instead, between **stressed** and **unstressed,** or accented and unaccented syllables. Two varieties of accented stress may be distinguished. On the one hand, there is the natural stress pattern of words themselves; *sýllable* is accented on the first syllable, *deplórable* on the second, and so on. Then there is the sort of stress which indicates rhetorical emphasis. If the sentence "You went to Greece?" is given a pronounced accent on the last word, it implies "Greece (of all places)?" If the accent falls on the first word, it implies "you (of all people)?" The meter of poetry—that is, its rhythm—is ordinarily built up out of a regular recurrence of accents, whether established as **word accents** or **rhetorical accents**; once started in the reader's mind, it has (like all rhythm) a persistent effect of its own.

The unit which is repeated to give steady rhythm to a poem is called a **poetic foot**; in English it usually consists of accented and unaccented syllables in one of five fairly simple patterns:

The **iambic foot** (or **iamb**) consists of an unstressed followed by a stressed syllable, as in *uníte, repeát,* or *insíst.* Most English verse falls naturally into the iambic pattern.

The **trochaic foot** (**trochee**) inverts this order; it is a stressed followed by an unstressed syllable—for example, *únit, réaper,* or *ínstant.*

The **anapestic foot** (**anapest**) consists of two unstressed syllables followed by a stressed syllable, as in *intercéde, disarránge,* or *Cameróon.*

The **dactylic foot** (**dactyl**) consists of a stressed syllable followed by two unstressed syllables, as in *Wáshington, Écuador,* or *ápplejack.*

The **spondaic foot** (**spondee**) consists of two successive stressed syllables, as in *heartbreak, headline,* or *Kashmir.*

In all the examples above, word accent and the quality of the metrical foot coincide exactly. But the metrical foot may well consist of several words, or, on the other hand, one word may well consist of several metrical feet. *Phótolithógraphy* consists of two excellent dactyls in a single word; *dárk and with spóts on it,* though it consists of six words rather than one, is also two dactyls—not quite such good ones. When we read a piece of poetry with the intention of discovering its underlying metrical pattern, we are said to **scan** it—that is, we go through it line by line, indicating by conventional signs which are the accented and which the unaccented syllables within the feet (the ictus ´ generally designates accented, the mora ˘ unaccented syllables). We also count the number of feet in each line, or, more properly, **verse**—since a single poetic line is generally called a "verse." Verse lengths are conventionally described in terms derived from the Greek:

Monometer: one foot (of rare occurrence)
Dimeter: two feet (also rare)
Trimeter: three feet
Tetrameter: four feet
Pentameter: five feet
Hexameter: six feet (six iambic feet make an **Alexandrine**)
Heptameter: seven feet (also rare)

Doctor Johnson's little parody of simpleminded poets would thus be scanned this way:

> Ĭ pút mय़ hắt ŭpón mय़ heád
> Aňd wálked ínto thĕ Stránd,
> Aňd thére Ĭ mét ănóthĕr mán
> Whŏse hắt wăs ín hĭs hánd.

The poem is iambic in rhythm, alternating tetrameter and trimeter in verse length. The fact that it scans so nicely is, however, no proof that it is good poetry. Quite the contrary. Many of poetry's most subtle effects are achieved by establishing an underlying rhythm and then varying it by means of a whole series of devices, some dramatic and expressive, others designed simply to lend variety and interest to the verse. A well-known sonnet of Shakespeare's (CXVI) begins,

> Let me not to the marriage of true minds
> Admit impediments. Love is not love
> Which alters when it alteration finds,
> Or bends with the remover to remove.

It is perfectly possible, if one crushes all one's sensitivities, to read the first line of this poem as mechanical iambic pentameter:

> Lĕt mé nŏt tó thĕ márriăge óf trúe mínds.

But of course nobody ever reads it that way, except to make a point; read with normal English accent and some sense of what it is saying, the line would probably form a pattern something like this:

> Lét mĕ nŏt tŏ thĕ márriăge óf trúe mínds,

which is neither pentameter nor in any way iambic. The second line is a little more iambic, but, read for expression, falls just as far short of pentameter:

$$\breve{A}dmít\ impédĭménts.\ Lóve\ ĭs\ nŏt\ lóve.$$

Only in the third and fourth lines of the sonnet do we get verses which read as well as scan like five iambic feet.

The fact is that perfectly regular metrical verse is easy to write and dull to read. Among the devices in common use for varying too regular a pattern are, for instance, the insertion of a trochaic foot among iambics, especially at the opening of a line, where the soft first syllable of the iambic foot often needs stiffening (see line 1 above); the more or less free addition of extra unaccented syllables; and the use of **caesura,** or strong grammatical pause within a line (conventionally indicated, in scanning, by the sign ||). The second line of the sonnet above is a good example of caesura:

$$Admit\ impediments.\ ||\ Love\ is\ not\ love.$$

The strength of the caesura, and its placing in the line, may be varied to produce striking variations of effect. More broadly, the whole relation between the poem's sound- and rhythm-patterns and its pattern as a sequence of assertions (phrases, clauses, sentences) may be manipulated by the poet. Sometimes his statements fit neatly within the lines, so that each line ends with a strong mark of punctuation; they are then known as **end-stopped lines.** Sometimes the sense flows over the ends of the lines, creating **run-on lines;** this process is also known, from the French, as **enjambment** (literally, "straddling").

End-stopped lines (Marlowe, *Hero and Leander*, First Sestiad, lines 45–48):

> So lovely fair was Hero, Venus' nun,
> As Nature wept, thinking she was undone,
> Because she took more from her than she left,
> And of such wondrous beauty her bereft.

Run-on lines (Keats, *Endymion* I.89–93):

> Full in the middle of this pleasantness
> There stood a marble altar, with a tress
> Of flowers budded newly; and the dew
> Had taken fairy fantasies to strew
> Daisies upon the sacred sward, * * *

Following the example of such poets as Blake, Rimbaud, and Whitman, many poets of the 20th century have undertaken to write what is called **free verse**—that is, verse which has neither a fixed metrical foot, nor (consequently) a fixed number of feet in its lines, but which depends for its rhythm on a pattern of cadences, or the rise and fall of the voice in utterance. All freedom in art is of course relative; free verse, with its special aptitude for metrical variety and nervous, colloquial phrasing—its total responsiveness, in other words, to its subject matter—has so successfully established itself that it is now widely recognized as a new and rather demanding form of artistic discipline.

SENSE AND SOUND

The very words of which poetic lines—whether free or traditional—are composed cause them to have different sounds and produce different effects. Polysyllables, being pronounced fast, often cause a line to move swiftly; monosyllables, especially when heavy and requiring distinct accents, may cause it to move heavily, as in Milton's famous line (*Paradise Lost* II.621):

> Rocks, caves, lakes, fens, bogs, dens, and shades of death.

Poetic assertions are often dramatized and reinforced by means of **alliteration**—that is, the use of several nearby words or stressed syllables beginning with the same consonant. When Shakespeare writes (*Sonnet LXIV*),

> Ruin hath taught me thus to ruminate
> That Time will come and take my love away,

the rich, round, vague echoes of the first line contrast most effectively with the sharp anxiety and directness of the alliterative *t*'s in the second. When Dryden starts *Absalom and Achitophel* with that wicked couplet,

> In pious times, ere priestcraft did begin,
> Before polygamy was made a sin,

the satiric undercutting is strongly reinforced by the triple alliteration which links "*p*ious" with "*p*riestcraft" and "*p*olygamy."

Assonance, or repetition of the same or similar vowel sounds within a passage (usually in accented syllables), also serves to enrich it, as in two lines from Keats's *Ode on Melancholy*:

> For shade to shade will come too drowsily,
> And drown the wakeful anguish of the soul.

It is clear that the round, hollow tones of "drowsily," repeated in "drown" and darkening to the full *o*-sound of "soul," have much to do with the effect of the passage. A related device is **consonance,** or the repetition of a pattern of consonants with changes in the intervening vowels—for example: *linger, longer, languor; rider, reader, raider, ruder.*

Direct verbal imitation of natural sounds (known as **onomatopoeia**) has has been much attempted, from Virgil's galloping horse—

> *Quadrupedante putrem sonitu quatit ungula campum—*

to Tennyson's account, in *The Princess*, of

> The moan of doves in immemorial elms
> And murmuring of innumerable bees.

Often ingeniously exploited as a side effect, onomatopoeia is essentially a trick, with about the same value in poetry as it has in music.

RHYME AND STANZA

Rhyme consists of a repetition of accented sounds in words, usually those falling at the end of verse lines. If the rhyme sound is the very last syllable of the line (*rebound, sound*), the rhyme is called **masculine;** if the accented syllable is followed by an unaccented syllable (*hounding, bounding*), the rhyme is called **feminine.** Rhymes amounting to three or more syllables, like forced rhymes, generally have a comic effect in English, and have been freely used for this purpose, e.g., by Ogden Nash (*opportunity, impunity; failure, azalea*). Rhymes occurring within a single line are called **internal;** for instance, the Mother-Goose rhyme, "Mary, Mary, quite contrary," or Coleridge's *Ancient Mariner* ("We were the first that ever burst / Into that silent sea"). **Eye rhymes** are words used as rhymes which look alike but actually sound different (for example, *alone, lone; remove, love*); **off rhymes** (sometimes called **partial, imperfect,** or **slant rhymes**) are occasionally the result of pressing exigencies or lack of skill, but are also, at times, used deliberately by modern poets for special effects. For instance, a sonnet by Dylan Thomas contains such "rhymes" as *knees, toes; Eve, grave; van, bone;* and *winter, ladder* (*Holy Sonnet* 3). Pairings like the last two are sometimes loosely described as consonance, rather than rhyme.

Blank verse is unrhymed iambic pentameter; until the recent advent of free verse, it was the only unrhymed measure to achieve general popularity in English. First used by the Earl of Surrey, blank verse was during the 16th century largely dramatic in character. *Paradise Lost* was one of the first nondramatic poems in English to use blank verse. But Milton's authority and his success were so great that during the 18th and 19th centuries blank verse came to be used for a great variety of discursive, descriptive, and philosophical poems—besides remaining the standard metrical form for epics. Thomson's *Seasons*, Cowper's *Task*, Wordsworth's *Prelude*, and Tennyson's *Idylls of the King* were all written in blank verse.

A **stanza** is a recurring unit of a poem, consisting of a number of verses. Certain poetic forms (as a notable example, Pindaric odes) have stanzas comprising a variable number of verses, of varying lengths. Others are more regular, hence easier to describe.

The simplest form of stanza is the **couplet;** it is simply two lines rhyming together. When a single couplet is considered in isolation, it is sometimes called a **distich;** when it includes a complete unified thought, ending with a terminal mark of punctuation, it is called a **closed couplet.** The iambic pentameter couplet seems to work best when it is strict and regular, but to regularize it was a work of considerable time and practice. Even as skillful a versifier as Ben Jonson, though he writes iambic pentameter couplets in a poem like *To Penshurst*, has not yet mastered what we call the **heroic couplet.** This is a strictly iambic pentameter couplet, strongly end-stopped, and with the couplets prevailingly closed. Heroic couplets generally are varied by means of a decided caesura, and limited to precisely ten syllables per line. The heroic couplet is the principal form of English neoclassical style. A model of its swift, keen, yet weighty wit is the opening of Dryden's *Absalom and Achitophel*. Occasionally, as in this poem, heroic couplets are varied by the introduction of a third rhyme, to make a **tercet** (usually enclosed by a marginal brace); and a striking terminal effect is sometimes achieved by the introduction of an Alexandrine (a line of iambic hexameter) as the third line of the tercet.

Another customary and challenging form of couplet is the **tetrameter,** or **four-beat couplet.** The more closely rhymes recur, the harder couplets are to manage; in addition, a four-beat line is hard to divide by caesura

without splitting it into two tick-tock dimeters. For this reason, tetramete
couplets have posed a perpetual challenge to poets, and still provide a
admirable finger-exercise for aspiring versifiers. A model of tetramete
couplets managed with marvelous variety, complexity, and expressivenes
is Marvell's *To His Coy Mistress:*

> Thou by the Indian Ganges' side
> Shouldst rubies find; I by the tide
> Of Humber would complain. I would
> Love you ten years before the flood,
> And you should, if you please, refuse
> Till the conversion of the Jews.

English has not done much with rhymes grouped in threes, but ha
borrowed from Italian the form known as **terza rima,** in which Dant
composed his *Divine Comedy.* This form consists of linked groups of thre
rhymes according to the following pattern: *aba bcb cdc ded,* etc. Shelley
Ode to the West Wind is composed in stanzas of terza rima, the poem
as a whole ending with a couplet.

   Quatrains are stanzas of four lines; the lines usually rhyme alternately
abab, or in the second and fourth lines, *abcb.* When they alternate tetra
meter and trimeter lines, as in Johnson's little poem about men in hat
(above), or as in *Sir Patrick Spens,* they are called **ballad stanza.** Dry
den's *Annus Mirabilis* and Gray's *Elegy Written in a Country Church
yard* are in heroic quatrains; these rhyme alternately, and employ five-stres
iambic verse throughout. Tennyson used for *In Memoriam* a tetramete
quatrain rhymed *abba,* and FitzGerald translated *The Rubáiyát of Oma
Khayyám* into a pentameter rhymed *aaba;* but these forms have not bee
very generally adopted.

   Chaucer's *Troilus and Criseyde* is an early example in English of **rim
royal,** a seven-line iambic pentameter stanza consisting essentially of
quatrain dovetailed onto two couplets, according to the rhyme schem
ababbcc (the fourth line serves both as the final line of the quatrain an
the first line of the first couplet). Closely akin to rime royal, but differ
entiated by an extra *a*-rhyme between the two *b*-rhymes, is **ottava rima
that is, an eight-line stanza rhyming *abababcc.* As its name suggests, ottav
rima is of Italian origin; it was first used in English by Wyatt. Its fina
couplet, being less prepared for than in rime royal, and usually set off a
a separate verbal unit, has a special witty snap to it, for which Byron foun
good use in *Don Juan.*

   The longest and most intricate stanza generally used for narrative pur
poses in English is that devised by Edmund Spenser for *The Faerie Queene
The **Spenserian stanza** has nine lines rhyming *ababbcbcc;* the first eigh
lines are pentameter, the last line an Alexandrine. Slow-moving, intricat
of pattern, and demanding in its rhyme scheme (the *b*-sound recurs fou
times, the *c*-sound three), the Spenserian stanza has nonetheless appeale
widely to poets seeking a rich and complicated metrical form. Keats's *Ev
of St. Agnes* and Shelley's *Adonais* are brilliantly successful 19th-centur
examples of its use.

   The **sonnet,** originally a stanza of Italian origin which has develope into an independent lyric form, is usually defined as fourteen lines of iambic pentameter. None of the elements in this definition is absolute. The first sonnet of Sidney's *Astrophel and Stella* is in hexameters, and Milton has one sonnet of twenty lines (*On the New Forcers of Conscience*), while Meredith wrote a whole series of sixteen-line sonnets (*Modern Love*). Most sonnets, however, conform to the definition. Sonnets generally follow one of two conventional rhyme schemes. The **Petrarchan** or **Italian sonnet** is divided into sections of eight lines (**octave**) and six lines (**sestet**), rhyming *abba abba* and *cdecde*. (There are many variations of the rhyme scheme in the sestet; that described is the most frequent.) Under this arrangement, the poet tends to use his octave to state the problem and his sestet to resolve it. The **English** or **Shakespearean** sonnet takes the form of three quatrains and a final couplet, rhyming *abab cdcd efef gg*. The couplet is ideally suited for producing a summary statement or witty twist after the problem has been turned about in the three quatrains. Both these forms represent ideal models, not absolute prescriptions. Many sonnets approximate these patterns without following them precisely; indeed, the term "sonnet" was slow in acquiring any meaning more specific than that of "short lyric poem." Among Donne's *Songs and Sonnets* there is just one sonnet in the more modern sense, *The Token*, and it has eighteen lines.

In the Elizabethan period, the sonnet underwent its most intensive cultivation in connection with themes of courtly love. Perhaps in revulsion, Donne used the sonnet mostly to express religious devotion (*Holy Sonnets, La Corona*), while Milton employed it on satiric, social, or political themes. In Wordsworth, it expanded in the direction of moral reflection and commentary, while G. M. Hopkins loaded it with a rich philosophical and rhetorical complexity which sometimes threatened to swamp the form altogether. But the applications of the sonnet are truly limitless, for it is a form just long and complex enough to provide compressed yet dignified statement of almost any major theme.

In blank verse or irregularly rhymed verse, where stanzaic divisions do not exist or are indistinct, the poetry sometimes falls into **verse paragraphs,** which are in effect divisions of sense like prose paragraphs. This division can be clearly seen in Milton's *Lycidas* or Spenser's *Epithalamion*. In the latter poem, it is reinforced by a **refrain,** which is simply a line repeated at the end of each stanza. Ballads also customarily have refrains; for example, the refrain of *Lord Randall* is

> mother, make my bed soon,
> For I'm weary wi' hunting, and fain wad lie down.

FIGURATIVE LANGUAGE

The act of bringing words together into rich and vigorous poetic lines is complex and demanding, chiefly because so many variables require control. There is the "thought" of the lines, their verbal texture, their emotional resonance, the developing perspective of the reader—all these to be managed at once. One of the poet's chief resources toward this end is figurative language. Here, as in matters of meter, one may distinguish a great variety of devices, some of which we use in everyday speech without special awareness of their names and natures. When we say someone eats "like a horse" or "like a bird," we are using a **simile**, that is, a comparison marked out by a specific word of likening—"like" or "as." When we omit the word of comparison but imply a likeness—as in the sentence, "That hog has guzzled all the champagne"—we are making use of **metaphor.** The **epic simile**, frequent in epic poetry, is an extended simile in which the thing compared is described as an object in its own right, beyond its point of likeness with the main subject. Milton starts to compare Satan to Leviathan, but concludes his simile with the story of a sailor who moored his ship by mistake, one night, to a whale (*Paradise Lost* I.200–208). Metaphors and similes have been complexly but usefully distinguished according to their special effects; they may be, for instance, violent, comic, degrading, decorative.

When we speak of "forty head of cattle" or ask someone to "lend a hand" with a job, we are using **synecdoche**, a figure which substitutes the part for the whole. When we speak of a statement "coming from the White House," or a man much interested in "the turf," we are using **metonymy**, or the substitution of one term for another with which it is closely associated. **Antithesis** is a device for placing opposing ideas in grammatical parallel, as, for example, in the following passage from Pope's *Rape of the Lock* (V.25–30), where there are more examples of antithesis than there are lines:

> But since, alas! frail beauty must decay,
> Curled or uncurled, since locks will turn to gray;
> Since painted, or not painted, all shall fade,
> And she who scorns a man, must die a maid;
> What then remains but well our power to use,
> And keep good humor still whate'er we lose?

Irony is a verbal device which implies an attitude quite different from (and often opposite to) that which is literally expressed. When Job answers his comforters, saying "No doubt but ye are the people, and wisdom shall die with you" (Job xii.2), he is using irony thick to the point of sarcasm. When Eliot writes, in *Whispers of Immortality*, that "Grishkin is nice," the adjective is carefully chosen to let an ironic grimace of distaste appear. And when Donne "proves," in *The Canonization*, that he and his mistress are going to found a new religion of love, he seems to be inviting us to take a subtly ironic attitude toward religion as well as love.

Because it is easy to see through, **hyperbole**, or willful exaggeration, is a favorite device of irony—which is not to say that it may not be "serious" as well. When she hears that a young man is "dying for love" of her, a sensible girl does not accept this statement literally, but it may convey a serious meaning to her nonetheless. The **pun**, or play on words (known to the learned, sometimes, as **paronomasia**), may also be serious or comic in intent; witness, for example, the famous series of puns in Donne's *Hymn to God the Father*. **Oxymoron** is a figure of flat contradiction—for instance, Milton's famous description of hell as containing "darkness visible" (*Paradise Lost* I.63). A **paradox** is a statement which seems absurd but turns out to have rational meaning after all, usually in some unexpected sense; Donne speaks of fear being great courage and high valor (*Satire III*, line 16), and turns out to mean that fear of God is greater courage than any earthly bravery. The **Petrarchan conceit** was an ingenious, complimentary comparison or turn of thought; Wyatt compares the state of a lover to a ship tossed in a storm, and a hundred different sonneteers explored the possibility of describing their ladies' anatomy in conventional Petrarchan conceits—her teeth like pearls, lips like rubies, hair like finespun gold, etc. On the other hand, the **metaphysical conceit** was a more ingenious many-leveled comparison, worked out in some detail and giving a strong sense of the poet's ingenuity in overcoming obstacles—for instance, Donne's comparison of separated lovers to the legs of a compass (*A Valediction: Forbidding Mourning*) or Herbert's comparison of devotion to a pulley (*The Pulley*).

Images are often described as "mental pictures"; it is more accurate to say that they are verbal representations of something capable of being visualized: some readers have such mental pictures, some do not. Images not only convey what things look like, but direct us, by their pattern of associated and involved feelings, in our reactions to what is being represented. Indeed, there may be such a weight of meaning or feeling behind the image that the verbal picture itself becomes transparent and its "meaning" becomes primary. Abstract ideas can get attached to specific images—water, snake, bird, sun, worm, lion, whatever—in a multitude of ways, of which the reader need sometimes only be reminded. Of course the poet can also be arbitrary about it, letting his reader know simply that Red Cross "stands for" Holiness and Archimago "stands for" Hypocrisy. If that's as far as it goes, we have a primitive variety of **allegory.** But the relation between the tenor of the image (its abstract meaning) and the vehicle (the concrete picture) can be much more indefinite and insubstantial. If the poet mentions a peacock, he may or may not intend his reader to think of immortality, because the unfolding of the peacock's tail and the opening of its "eyes" has traditionally suggested the rebirth of the soul after death. If that is the way the image works, then it is a **symbol.** Or again, if the poet mentions a fish, he may well intend the reader to think of Christ. This isn't because of any similarity between the fish and Christ; the identification depends on a mildly esoteric bit of information, that the Greek word for fish, *ichthys*, forms an anagram of the Greek words for "Jesus Christ, Son of God, Savior." When the connection between tenor and vehicle is arbitrary, or involves the elements of a puzzle, the image may be referred to as an **emblem.** In the 16th and 17th centuries, emblems often took the form of puzzling little drawings, the meaning of which was explained in appended verses: for an example see the emblem prefixed to Crashaw's poem *To the Countess of Denbigh.*

Personification is the attribution of human qualities to an inanimate object (for example, the Sea) or an abstract concept (Freedom); a special variety of it is called (in a term of John Ruskin's invention) the **pathetic fallacy.** When we speak of leaves "dancing" or a lake "smiling," we attribute human traits to nonhuman objects. Ruskin thought this was false and therefore "morbid"; modern criticism tends to view the practice as artistically and morally neutral. A more formal and abstract variety of personification is **allegory,** in which a narrative (such as *Pilgrim's Progress*) is constructed by representing general concepts (Faithfulness, Sin, Despair) as persons. A **fable** (like the Nun's Priest's Tale) represents beasts behaving like humans; a **parable** is a brief story, or simply an observation, with strong moral application; and an **exemplum** is a story told to illustrate a point in a sermon. A special series of devices, nearly obsolete today, used to be available to poets who could count on readers trained in the classics. These were the devices of **classical epithet** and **allusion.** In their simplest form, the classic myths used to provide a repertoire of agreeable stage properties, and a convenient shorthand for expressing emotional attitudes. Picturesque creatures like centaurs, satyrs, and sphinxes, heroes and heroines like Hector and Helen, and the whole pantheon of Olympic deities could be used to make ready reference to a great many aspects of human nature. One does not have to explain the problems of a man who is "cleaning the Augean stables"; if he is afflicted with an "Achilles' heel," or is assailing "Hydra-headed difficulties," his state is clear. These epithets, or descriptive phrases, making reference to mythological stories, suggest in a phrase situations which would normally require cumbersome explanations. Conceivably other mythologies might have served the same end in analogous ways. But because they could be taken for granted as the common possession of all educated readers, the classic myths entered into English literature as early as Chaucer, and are only now passing away as a viable system of allusions. In poets like Spenser and Milton, classical allusion becomes a kind of enormously learned game, in which the poet seeks to make his points as indirectly as possible. For instance, Spenser writes in the *Epithalamion*, lines 328–29:

> Lyke as when Jove with fayre Alcmena lay,
> When he begot the great Tirynthian groom.

The mere mention of Alcmena in the first line suggests, to the knowing reader, Hercules; Spenser's problem in the second line is to find a way of referring to him which is neither redundant nor heavy-handed. "Tirynthian" reminds us of his long connection with the city of Tiryns, stretching our minds (as it were) across his whole career; and "groom" compresses references to a man-child, a servant, and a bridegroom, all of which apply to different aspects of Hercules' history. Thus, far from simply avoiding redundancy, Spencer has enriched the whole texture of his verse, thought, and feeling by his gift for precise classical epithet.

PERIODS

Dividing English literature into manageable, more or less homogeneous periods is bound to be an arbitrary, an inexact, and in the end an inconsistent procedure. But a few handy dates are worth memorizing as a frame on which to hang details. Chaucer died in 1400; he was the literary high point of the English **Middle Ages,** a millennium reaching from 500 to 1500. Though no thousand-year period of existence can be compressed to a phrase, we may say that the Christian church structured and came close to dominating the imaginative life of this period. The first flowering of the English **Renaissance** took place around 1500; it has often been called the **Age of Humanism.** Less a formal philosophy than an attitude of interest in the full potentialities of the human mind, Humanism took on many colorings; most English writers, as **Christian Humanists,** tried to reconcile or combine the values of Greece and Rome with those of Christianity, while granting the former an independent authenticity that the Middle Ages had never conceded. The precise end of the Renaissance, with its tumultuous sense of human potential and delight in verbal invention, is hard to fix; but the death of Dryden in 1700 is a handy date for marking the onset of the **Age of Reason,** also called the **Enlightenment** or the **Neo-Classical Age.** Frequently, this age is expanded to include also the **Restoration** (1660–1700). The new era, emphasizing correctness, sought to discipline the individual consciousness to a generalized definition of rational human nature, one pattern for which was sought in the classics. To this vision of general human nature the age tended to subordinate any particular religious dispensation or creed, any social custom peculiar to a single time or place. The publication of *Lyrical Ballads* in 1798 opens the English **Age of Romanticism,** in which many writers undertook to explore the individual human mind independent of Christian dogma, and also as transcending experience—as an agent with active characteristics and initiatives of its own.

After 1798, the periods of English literature get shorter and less distinct. (From a longer perspective than we can easily assume, the whole era from 1798 to the present may someday be known as the age of Romanticism.) For the last half of the 19th century we have no real name but that of the ruling monarch: it is the **Age of Victorianism.** Some writers have tried to follow through with **Edwardian** for the period 1901–1910, and **Georgian** for the period after 1910. But George V ruled till 1936, and the postwar generation did not at all think of themselves as Georgians. Besides, somewhere in here we have to find room to start the **Modern Period,** whatever that is—if only so that we will have space to inaugurate our own time, for which there exist as yet only makeshift titles like the **Post-Modern Age.** Concerning all these periods, it is idle to dispute exact boundaries and precise characteristics. They don't have or need any, for the simple reason that their only function is to help the memory make a few gross distinctions and groupings within an otherwise uncontrollable sea of particulars.

SCHOOLS

Within the broad periods it is customary to group in **schools** writers who show common stylistic traits or thematic concerns. Whether they considered themselves a group doesn't much matter. None of the **Romantic poets** knew they were being romantic, although Hazlitt, Shelley, and other writers of the time recognized shared features that they called "the spirit of the age." The followers of Spenser are known as **Spenserians;** they knew they liked Spenser, but didn't realize that made them a group. **Cavalier** poets are set decisively apart from **metaphysical** poets, though pretty surely none of the two dozen men involved knew that was what they were. And so with the **Gothic novelists,** and the so-called **Graveyard School** at the end of the 18th century, so with the modern surrealists. These schools are generally grouped, defined, and named by scholars and critics after the event. Use of a common form or subject matter constitutes a more superficial similarity than use of a common style, common techniques, or common philosophical backgrounds. But literary history, being nothing if not pragmatic, makes use of all sorts of common denominators.

Intellectual affinities have led some writers to be classified under the names of the philosophical schools of Greece and Rome. These are chiefly the **Epicureans,** who specify that the aim of life and the source of value is pleasure; the **Stoics,** who emphasize the avoidance of pain and the dignified endurance of what cannot be avoided; and the **Skeptics,** who doubt that anything can be known for sure. These categories are useful as capsule descriptions, but they aren't very tidy, as they overlap one another and cut across other categories. Dryden is an author strongly tinged with **skepticism,** but many of his poems suggest an unabashed **epicureanism.** *The Vanity of Human Wishes,* by Doctor Johnson, is the classic poem in English of **stoic** philosophy, but it also expresses a particularly strong coloring of **Christian humanism.**

Plato and **Aristotle,** as they summarized contrasting attitudes toward existence, are often used to define the outlook of writers. Both were prolific writers of enormous range and complexity, but in literary contexts their names most often define attitudes toward reality. Aristotle tended to find reality, not exclusively but primarily, in concrete and particular substances, which he brilliantly categorized and generalized. Plato tended to place reality in abstract ideal forms, of which the concrete things we experience in daily life are but partial and shadowy manifestations. During the Middle Ages, the Dominican friars (St. Thomas Aquinas was one) were **Aristotelians;** the Franciscans (St. Bonaventura was one) were **Platonists.** During the Renaissance Spenser, and during the Romantic period Shelley, were **Platonists** or **Neo-Platonists.** (A neo-Platonist is a Platonist diluted with other world-views—perhaps Pythagorean mysticism, perhaps Christian theology, perhaps Aristotelian thought itself. In a narrower sense, the term is applied to philosophers writing in the tradition of Plotinus (3rd century A.D.), who held that all things in the world, spiritual and material, "emanate," or flow out, from the "Absolute," or the "One"—the single source of all truth, goodness, and beauty. **Aristotelianism,** as it is more commonsensical, had faded by Spenser's time to the common teaching of the schools, and by Shelley's time to the practical, pragmatic materialism of everyday life.

SECTS

Religious distinctions and denominations are important in British social history, hence deeply woven into the nation's literature. The numerous (over 300) British churches and sects divide along a scale from high to low, depending on the amount of authority they give to the church or the amount of liberty they concede to the individual conscience. At one end of the scale is the **Roman Catholic Church,** asserting papal infallibility, universal jurisdiction, and the supreme importance of hierarchy as guide and intercessor. For political and social reasons, Catholicism struck deep roots in Ireland but was the object of prolonged, bitter hatred on the part of Protestants from the Reformation through the 19th century. The **Established English (Anglican) Episcopal Church** has been the official national church since the 16th century; it enjoys the support (once direct and exclusive, now indirect and peripheral) of the national government. Its creed is defined by Thirty-Nine Articles, but these are intentionally vague, so there are numerous ways of adhering to the Church of England. Roughly and intermittently, the chief classes of Anglicans have been known as **High Church** (with its highest portion calling itself **Anglo-Catholic**); **Broad Church** or **Latitudinarian** (when they get so broad that they admit anyone believing in God, they may be known as **Deists,** or some may leave the church altogether and be known as **Unitarians**); and **Low Church,** whose adherents may stay in the English church and yet come close to shaking hands with **Presbyterians** or **Methodists**. These various groups may be arranged, from the High down to the Low Church, in direct relation to the amount of ritual each prefers and in the degree of authority conceded to the upper clergy—and in inverse relation to the importance ascribed to a saving faith directly infused by God into an individual conscience.

All Protestants who decline to subscribe to the English established church are classed as **Dissenters** or **Nonconformists**; for a time in the 16th and 17th centuries, they were also known as **Puritans.** The **Presbyterians** model their church government on that established by John Calvin in the Swiss city of Geneva. It has no bishops, and therefore is more democratic for the clergy; but it gains energy by associating lay elders with clergymen in matters of social discipline, and tends to be strict with the ungodly. From its first reformation the Scottish Kirk was fixed on the Presbyterian model. During the civil wars of the 17th century, a great many sects sprang up on the left wing of the Presbyterians, most of them touched by Calvinism but some rebelling against it; a few of these still survive. The **Independents** became our modern **Congregationalists**; the **Quakers** are still Quakers, as **Baptists** are still Baptists, though multiply divided. But many of the sects flourished and perished within the space of a few years. Among these now-vanished groups were the Shakers (though a few groups still exist in America), the Seekers, the Ranters, the Anabaptists, the Muggletonians, the Fifth Monarchy Men, the Family of Love, the Sweet Singers of Israel, and many others, forgotten by all except scholars. During the 18th and 19th centuries, new sects arose, supplanting old ones; the **Methodists**, under John and Charles Wesley, became numerous and important, taking root particularly in Wales. (The three "subject" nationalities, Ireland, Scotland, and Wales, thus turned three different ways to avoid the Anglican church.) With the passage of time a small number of Swedenborgians sprang up, followers of the Swedish mystic Emmanuel Swedenborg—to be followed by the Plymouth Brethren, Christian Scientists, Jehovah's Witnesses, and countless other 19th-century groups. All these sects constantly grow, shrink, split, and occasionally disappear as they succeed or fail in attracting new converts.

Within the various churches and sects, independent of them all but amazingly persistent, there has always survived a stream of **esoteric** or **hermetic** thought—a belief in occult powers, and sometimes in magic as well, exemplified by the pseudo-sciences of astrology and alchemy but taking many other forms. From the mythical Egyptian seer Hermes Trismegistus through Paracelsus, Cornelius Agrippa, Giordano Bruno, Jakob Boehme, the society of Rosicrucians, and a hundred other shadowy figures, the line can be traced to William Blake and William Butler Yeats, who both in their different ways brought hermetic protestantism close to its ultimate goal, a mystic church of one single man, poised within his own mind-elaborated cosmos.

TERMS OF ART

The following section groups together various sets of frequently used and closely related literary terms in an effort to discriminate and define them.

Allegory, Symbolism. They are both extended metaphors, distinguished chiefly by the fact that the figures in an **allegory** are more tightly and unequivocally related to their underlying meanings than in a work of symbolism. Though he has other significances as well, Spenser's Red Cross Knight stands squarely for Holiness. In a work of **symbolism**, the meaning of the individual symbol grows out of its configuration with other symbols—it is an indirect and multiplex, not a one-for-one relation, as in Blake's poem *The Sick Rose*.

Baroque and **Mannerist** are terms imported into literary study from the history of art, and applied by analogy. Michelangelo is a **baroque** artist; he holds great masses in powerful dynamic tension, his style is heavily ornamented and restless. In these respects he is sometimes compared to Milton. El Greco is a **mannerist,** whose gaunt and distorted figures often seem to be laboring under great spiritual stress, whose light seems to be focused in spots against a dark background. He has been compared to Donne. Analogies of this sort are occasionally suggestive, but they must be carefully handled to avoid degenerating into parallels which are forced and nominal rather than substantial.

Burlesque and **Mock Heroic** differ in that the former makes its subject ludicrous by inflating it. In Pope's mock-heroic **Dunciad,** the figure of Dulness (Colley Cibber) is given inappropriately heroic dimensions; in Butler's burlesque **Hudibras,** the knightly hero is characterized by low and vulgar attributes, and persistently engages in inappropriately low adventures.

Genre, Decorum. A **genre** is an established literary form, such as a stage comedy, the picaresque novel, the epic, the sonnet. Being of a certain genre predisposes a work to represent certain characters and events and to seek certain effects. Its success in achieving these effects and avoiding incongruous ones can thus be judged; and this is one sort of **decorum** (fittingness), the decorum of genre. Satire was once considered a low, popular form, for which only low, popular speech was decorous (fitting). There are also decorums of character, of occasion, of rhetorical mode, etc.

Gothic and **Classic** distinguish styles and tendencies in art and literature. **Gothic** implies vital, primitive, and deeply energetic work, with the qualities of Northern barbarism. **Classic** implies lucid, rational, and idealized work, as in the Southern sunlit civilizations of Greece and Rome. For the 18th century, the classics, which had proved their universality by maintaining their popularity for so many centuries, were the school of all civilized thinking; "Gothic" was a term connoting barbarity, wild and disorganized details, and a lack of artistic decorum and control. For a man like Ruskin, deeply imbued with the ideal of organic unity, "Gothic" was a term of ultimate approval; partly under his influence, Victorian Gothic (often called the "Gothic Revival") became a widely popular style. Currently, the term "Gothic" refers mainly to the artistic (and primarily architectural) style prevalent in Western Europe from the 12th to about the end of the 15th century.

Humors and **Temperaments** are psychological terms used by Renaissance writers. The four basic humors of every constitution were the **choleric** (bile), the **sanguine** (blood), the **phlegmatic** (phlegm), and the **melancholy** (black bile). A man's **temperament** was determined by the mix ture of these humors, the way in which they were "tempered." When a particular humor predominated, it pushed the character in that direction: choler = anger; sanguine = geniality; phlegm = cold torpor; and melancholy = gloomy self-absorption.

Imitation and **Parody** are devices by which a literary work assumes an attitude toward its own predecessor. **Imitation** involves not simply copying, but transposing the different features of the earlier work into modern particulars, while retaining the same pattern and the same approximate tonal level. **Parody** generally lowers the level of its original; it is a device of ridicule, though sometimes of self-ridicule. When Joyce parodies ancient Irish legend (as in the "Cyclops" chapter of *Ulysses*), there is no separating ridicule of the past from contempt for the present.

Irony, Sarcasm, Satire. **Irony** and **Sarcasm** are distinct, though both are ways of saying one thing and meaning another. Sarcasm is broader and more deliberate in its reversal of meanings; irony may be, and in literature generally is, very fine. It often conveys an attitude of detachment. In **dramatic irony,** a character says something which has one meaning for him but quite another for the privileged audience. **Satire** includes all of the many literary ways for diminishing a subject by making it ridiculous.

Myth and **Legend** are stories which incorporate themselves into men's instinctual thinking. **Myths** are narratives which purport to account, in supernatural terms, for why the world is as it is, why men act as they do. Myths often spring up to explain rituals, the original meanings of which have been forgotten; or they may be folk tales based on popular nightmares or fantasies. An ordinary or even inferior tale may take on mythic dimensions—witness Mrs. Shelley's *Frankenstein* or the wooden volumes of Horatio Alger, Jr. A **legend** is any old and popularly repeated story; the word usually implies, in addition, that the story is false. But a proper myth hardly pretends to be historically true—it is a flowering of the mind into narrative. Three great bodies of mythical material are the Celtic, the Norse or Germanic, and the classical fables. A body of associated myths is a **mythology;** a student and collector of myths is a **mythographer.**

Ode, Elegy, Lyric. **Lyric** poetry gets its name from once having been set to music and chanted to the accompaniment of a lyre; but that's ancient history. Now any short poem directly expressing the poet's thought or feeling will be classed as a lyric; and within this general class, **odes** and **elegies** are two specific varieties. The former implies a dignified occasion and a formal effort to praise or judge its subject. **Pindaric odes,** following the example of the Theban Pindar, are enthusiastic, irregular, and sublime; **Horatian odes,** after the Roman Horace, are cool, judicious, and regular. **Elegies** were originally poems written in elegiac meter, alternating hexameters and pentameters. This limping meter, which has never done as well in English as in the classical tongues, was thought appropriate to the expression of serious, even mournful sentiments. In the narrow sense, then, an elegy is a poem of mourning for the dead. But it can also be any pensive poem on a meditative theme; and a man like Donne, who enjoyed overstepping boundaries, wrote some elegies which are jocose, even bawdy.

Realism and **Naturalism** are both terms used to describe fiction which aims at minute fidelity to actual existence. **Realism** connotes an attempt to give the illusion of ordinary life, in which unexceptional people undergo everyday experiences. **Naturalism** is associated with the example of Emile Zola and the thesis that a novel should present a "slice of life," a cross-section of actual existence; the emphasis is usually on man's instinctual nature, especially the sexual and acquisitive instincts. This type flourished during the late 19th and early 20th centuries. Harold Biffen, a character in George Gissing's novel *New Grub Street*, is devoting his life to a work of "absolute realism in the sphere of the ignobly decent"—and this can epitomize realism. A work of naturalism, on the other hand, might be said to devote itself to the ignobly indecent.

Romance, Novel. Medieval romances are narratives of adventure, following a hero through the successive episodes of a quest toward his chosen or appointed goal. Novels are more or less realistic studies of social relationships, more tightly structured than romances, less given to the fabulous, and dealing generally with the middle strata of society. But these distinctions were far from airtight to begin with, and with the years have grown steadily vaguer. Is Kafka's *The Castle* a novel or a romance? It is always called the former, it looks much more like the latter, and it is actually more like an extended parable.

Style in a minimal sense is the way anyone uses language; thus each of us possesses (for better or worse) his own style. In the better sense, of language endowed with point and force, language of special distinction which accomplishes its ends swiftly and clearly, it has been described by Swift as "proper words in proper places"—a definition on which there is no improving.

Wit is one of those words which are too useful ever to be defined. As employed during the 17th and 18th centuries, it may mean general intelligence or the ability to say something funny, wisdom or ability, prudence, fancy, vivacity of speech, quickness of repartee, spiritual insight, and a plethora of other qualities.

Contents of Volume 1

The Sixteenth Century (1485–1603)   47□

The Restoration and the Eighteenth Century (1660–1798)

Contents of Volume 1 · 2501

Index

DATE

GAYLORD   PRINTED IN U.S.A.